American Literature

The Makers and the Making

VOLUME II

American Literature

The Makers and the Making

VOLUME II

Cleanth Brooks R. W. B. Lewis Robert Penn Warren

St. Martin's Press   New York

iv

1965, 1969 by Elizabeth Bishop, copyright renewed 1968 by Elizabeth Bishop. ("Travelling in the Family" is a translation from the Portuguese of a poem by Carlos de Andrade.)

"Old Red" from *Old Red and Other Stories* by Caroline Gordon (published 1971 by Cooper Square Publishers Inc.), copyright © 1963 by Caroline Gordon.

"90 North," "The Death of the Ball Turret Gunner," "Losses," and "Eighth Air Force" from *The Complete Poems* by Randall Jarrell, copyright © 1941, 1947, 1948, 1969 by Mrs. Randall Jarrell, copyright renewed 1968, 1973 by Mrs. Randall Jarrell. Copyright 1945 by Randall Jarrell.

"Skunk Hour," "To Delmore Schwartz," "For the Union Dead," "The Old Flame," and "Hawthorne" from *For the Union Dead* by Robert Lowell, copyright © 1960, 1962, 1964 by Robert Lowell; and from *Life Studies* by Robert Lowell, copyright © 1958 by Robert Lowell.

"The First Seven Years" from *The Magic Barrel* by Bernard Malamud, copyright © 1950, 1958 by Bernard Malamud.

"Novelists of the Post-War South: Albion W. Tourgée" from *Patriotic Gore* by Edmund Wilson, published by Oxford University Press, copyright © 1962 by Edmund Wilson.

BARTHOLD FLES, LITERARY AGENCY: "Ballad of Jesse James," "The Old Chisholm Trail," "Frankie and Johnnie (Albert)," and "Git Along, Little Dogies" from *Singing Cowboy*, ed. by M. Larkin. By permission of Barthold Fles, Literary Agency.

GORDIAN PRESS: "Chickamauga" from *The Collected Works of Ambrose Bierce*, 12 volumes, published by Gordian Press. Reprinted by permission of Gordian Press.

GROSSMAN PUBLISHERS: "Easy Rider Blues" by Blind Lemon Jefferson from *Blues Lines*, published by Grossman Publishers.

GROVE PRESS, INC.: Excerpt from *Tropic of Cancer* by Henry Miller. Reprinted by permission of Grove Press, Inc. Copyright © 1961 by Anais Nin.

HAFNER PUBLISHING COMPANY, INC.: "What Pragmatism Means" by William James from *Pragmatism*. Reprinted by permission of Hafner Publishing Company, Inc.

HARCOURT BRACE JOVANOVICH, INC.: All of the following selections are reprinted by permission of Harcourt Brace Jovanovich, Inc. Excerpt from "Emily Dickinson: Notes on Prejudice and Fact" by R. P. Blackmur. Copyright, 1940, by Richard P. Blackmur; renewed, 1968, by the First National Bank of Princeton. Reprinted from *Language as Gesture* by R. P. Blackmur.

"o sweet spontaneous," "in Just," "the Cambridge ladies," "Tumbling-hair," and "i was considering how" by E. E. Cummings, Copyright, 1923, 1951, by E. E. Cummings. "come, gaze" and "since feeling is first" by E. E. Cummings, Copyright, 1926, by Horace Liveright, copyright, 1954, by E. E. Cummings. "the first president" and "somewhere i have never travelled" by E. E. Cummings, Copyright, 1931, 1959, by E. E. Cummings. "my father moved through dooms of love" by E. E. Cummings, Copyright, 1940, by E. E. Cummings, copyright, 1968 by Marion Morehouse Cummings. "plato told" by E. E. Cummings, Copyright, 1944, by E. E. Cummings; copyright, 1972, by Nancy Andrews. "nine birds" by E. E. Cummings, Copyright, 1950, by E. E. Cummings. All reprinted from his volume *Complete Poems 1913–1962*.

"The Metaphysical Poets" and "Tradition and the Individual Talent" by T. S. Eliot. From *Selected Essays*, New Edition, by T. S. Eliot, copyright, 1932, 1936, 1950, by Harcourt Brace Jovanovich, Inc.; copyright, 1960, 1964, by T. S. Eliot. "The Love Song of J. Alfred Prufrock," "Sweeney Among the Nightingales," "Whispers of Immortality," "Gerontion," "The Waste Land," and "Little Gidding" by T. S. Eliot. From *Collected Poems 1909–1962* by T. S. Eliot, copyright, 1936, by Harcourt Brace Jovanovich, Inc.; copyright, © 1943, 1963, 1964, by T. S. Eliot.

Excerpt from *Babbitt* by Sinclair Lewis, copyright, 1922, by Harcourt Brace Jovanovich, Inc.; copyright, 1950, by Sinclair Lewis.

"Mr. Edwards and the Spider" and "The Quaker Graveyard in Nantucket" by Robert Lowell. From *Lord Weary's Castle*, copyright, 1944, 1946, by Robert Lowell.

"A Good Man Is Hard to Find" by Flannery O'Connor. Copyright, 1953, by Flannery O'Connor. Reprinted from her volume, *A Good Man Is Hard to Find and Other Stories*.

"Old Mortality" by Katherine Anne Porter. From *Pale Horse, Pale Rider*, copyright, 1937, 1965 by Katherine Anne Porter.

"Chicago" and "I Am the People, the Mob" by Carl Sandburg. From *Chicago Poems* by Carl Sandburg, copyright, 1916, by Holt, Rinehart and Winston, Inc.; renewed, 1944, by Carl Sandburg. "Psalm of Those Who Go Forth Before Daylight" by Carl Sandburg. From *Cornhuskers* by Carl Sandburg, copyright, 1918, by Holt, Rinehart and Winston, Inc.; renewed, 1946, by Carl Sandburg.

Excerpt from *The Making of Americans* by Gertrude Stein, copyright, 1934, by Harcourt Brace Jovanovich, Inc.; renewed, 1962, by Alice B. Toklas.

"Why I Live at the P.O." by Eudora Welty. Copyright, 1941, 1969, by Eudora Welty. Reprinted from her volume *A Curtain of Green and Other Stories*.

"The Death of a Toad" and "Still, Citizen Sparrow" by Richard Wilbur, from *Ceremony and Other Poems*, copyright, 1948, 1949, 1950, by Richard Wilbur. "Folk Tune" by Richard Wilbur, from *The Beautiful Changes*, copyright, 1947, by Richard Wilbur. "Juggler" by Richard Wilbur, Copyright, 1949, by Richard Wilbur, reprinted from his volume *Ceremony and Other Poems;* first published in *The New Yorker*.

HARPER & ROW, PUBLISHERS, INC.: All of the following selections are reprinted by permission of Harper & Row, Publishers, Inc. "O Youth and Beauty!" in *The Housebreaker of Shady Hill and Other Stories* by John Cheever. Copyright, 1953 by John Cheever.

From *On These I Stand* by Countee Cullen: "From the Dark Tower," Copyright 1927 by Harper & Row Publishers, Inc., renewed 1955 by Ida M. Cullen; "Heritage," Copyright 1925 by Harper & Row Publishers, Inc., renewed 1953 by Ida M. Cullen.

Excerpt from *Mules and Men* by Zora Neale Hurston. Copyright 1935 by Zora Neale Hurston.

From *Ariel* by Sylvia Plath: "The Applicant," "Daddy," and "Lady Lazarus," Copyright © 1963 by Ted Hughes.

"The Celebrated Jumping Frog of Calaveras County" from *The Celebrated Jumping Frog of Calaveras County and Other Sketches* by Mark Twain (Harper & Row); "Fenimore Cooper's Literary Offenses" from *In Defense of Harriet Shelley and Other Essays* by Mark Twain (Harper & Row); "How to Tell a Story" from *How to Tell a Story and Other Essays* by Mark Twain (Harper & Row); Chapter 34 in *The Innocents Abroad* by Mark Twain (Harper & Row); Chapters 4, 54, 8 in *Life on the Mississippi* by Mark Twain (Harper & Row); "The Man That Corrupted Hadleyburg" from *The Man That Corrupted Hadleyburg and Other Stories and Essays* by Mark Twain (Harper & Row); "To the Person Sitting in Darkness" from *Europe and Elsewhere* by Mark Twain (Harper & Row).

(Play) "The Skin of Our Teeth" in *Three Plays* by Thornton Wilder. Copyright 1942, 1970 by Thornton Wilder. *Caution!* "The Skin of Our Teeth" is the sole property of the author and is fully protected by copyright. It may not be acted by professionals or amateurs without formal permission and the payment of a royalty. All rights, including professional, amateur, stock, radio and television, broadcasting, motion picture, recitation, lecturing, public reading, and the rights of translation into foreign languages are reserved. All professional inquiries should be addressed to the author's agent: Harold Freedman, Brandt & Brandt Dramatic Department, Inc., 101 Park Avenue, New York, N.Y. 10017. All requests for amateur rights should be addressed to Samuel French, 25 West 45th Street, New York, N.Y. 10019.

Excerpt from pp. 34–36, 57–60, 68–72, 174–181 in *Black Boy* by Richard Wright. Copyright, 1937, 1942, 1944, 1945 by Richard Wright.

HARVARD LAW REVIEW: "Natural Law" by Oliver Wendell Holmes, Jr., from 32, *Harvard Law Review*, 40 (1918). Copyright 1918 by The Harvard Law Review Association. Reprinted by permission of the Harvard Law Review and the Estate of Oliver Wendell Holmes, Jr.

HARVARD UNIVERSITY PRESS: Poems 448, 290, 326, 1129, 315, 441, 1035, 585, 333, 1672, 214, 1333, 401, 754, 249, 303, 745, 348, 536, 280, 341, 553, 764, 812, 1068, 258, 1575, 986, 412, 465, 389, 712, 528, 721, and 501 by Emily Dickinson. Reprinted by permission of the publishers and the Trustees of Amherst College from Thomas H. Johnson, Editor, *The Poems of Emily Dickinson*, Cambridge, Mass.: The Belknap Press of Harvard University Press, Copyright, 1951, 1955, by The President and Fellows of Harvard College.

HILL AND WANG: Excerpt reprinted with the permission of Hill and Wang, a division of Farrar, Straus & Giroux, Inc., from *Conversations with Nelson Algren* by H. E. F. Donohue, copyright © 1963, 1964 by H. E. F. Donohue and Nelson Algren.

Excerpts reprinted with the permission of Hill and Wang, a division of Farrar, Straus & Giroux, Inc., from the following titles by Langston Hughes: *The Best of Simple*, copyright © 1961 by Langston Hughes, and *The Big Sea*, copyright 1940 by Langston Hughes.

HOLIDAY HOUSE: "The Whistling River" from *Ol' Paul, The Mighty Logger* by Glen Rounds. Reprinted by permission of Holiday House.

HOLT, RINEHART AND WINSTON, INC.: All of the following selections are reprinted by permission of Holt, Rinehart and Winston, Inc. Excerpt from "Irradiations" from *Selected Poems* by John Gould Fletcher, Copyright 1938 by John Gould Fletcher, Copyright © 1966 by Charlie May Fletcher. "The Skaters" by John Gould Fletcher, from *Selected Poems* (1938), reprinted by permission of Mrs. John Gould Fletcher.
  "After Apple-Picking," "Acquainted with the Night," "Away," "Come In," "The Death of the Hired Man," "Desert Places," "Design," "Fire and Ice," "The Most of It," "The Need of Being Versed in Country Things," "Neither Out Far Nor In Deep," "Once by the Pacific," "The Onset," "The Oven Bird," "The Pasture," "Provide, Provide," "Stopping by Woods on a Snowy Evening," and "Two Tramps in Mud Time" from *The Poetry of Robert Frost* edited by Edward Connery Lathem. Copyright 1916, 1923, 1928, 1930, 1939, 1947, © 1967, 1969 by Holt, Rinehart and Winston, Inc. Copyright 1936, 1942, 1944, 1951, © 1956, 1958, 1962 by Robert Frost. Copyright © 1964, 1967, 1970 by Lesley Frost Ballantine.

HOUGHTON MIFFLIN COMPANY: All of the following selections are reprinted by permission of Houghton Mifflin Company. Excerpts from *The Education of Henry Adams* by Henry Adams, Copyright © by the Massachusetts Historical Society, Copyright © 1946 by Charles F. Adams; excerpt from *Mont-St.-Michel and Chartres* by Henry Adams, Copyright © 1905 by Henry Adams, Copyright © 1933 by Charles F. Adams.
  Excerpts from *Democracy and Leadership* by Irving Babbitt, Copyright © 1924 by Irving Babbitt, Copyright © 1952 by Esther Babbitt Howe.
  Excerpts from *A Diary from Dixie* by Mary Boykin Chesnut, ed. by Ben Ames Williams, Copyright © 1905 by D. Appleton & Co., Copyright © 1945 by Houghton Mifflin Company.
  "That Heathen Chinee" and "Tennessee's Partner" by Bret Harte from *The Writings of Bret Harte*.
  "A Decade," "A Lady," "Lilacs," "Meeting-House Hill," and "Night Clouds" by Amy Lowell from *Complete Poetical Works*, Copyright © 1955 by Harvey H. Bundy and G. d'Andelot Belin, Jr., Trustees of the Estate of Amy Lowell.
  Excerpts from *The Member of the Wedding* by Carson McCullers, Copyright © 1946 by Carson McCullers.
  "Ars Poetica," "Memorial Rain," "Ezry," "You, Andrew Marvell," excerpts from "Frescoes for Mr. Rockefeller's City," and excerpts from "Conquistador" by Archibald MacLeish from *Collected Poems*, Copyright © 1962 by Archibald MacLeish.
  Excerpts from "Eride," "Fragments," and "Mnemosyne" by Trumbull Stickney from *The Poems of Trumbull Stickney*.

OLWYN HUGHES LITERARY AGENT: "The Applicant," "Daddy," and "Lady Lazarus" by Sylvia Plath from *Ariel*. Copyright Ted Hughes, 1965, and published by Faber & Faber, London. Reprinted by permission of Olwyn Hughes, literary agent representing the Estate of Sylvia Plath.

INDIANA UNIVERSITY PRESS: "Devil's Dream," "Homage," and "No Credit" by Kenneth Fearing from *New and Selected Poems*. Reprinted by permission of the Indiana University Press.

THE JOHNS HOPKINS UNIVERSITY PRESS: "Corn" and "The Marshes of Glynn" by Sidney Lanier from the *Centennial Edition of the Works of Sidney Lanier*, edited by Charles Anderson. Reprinted by permission of The Johns Hopkins University Press.

ALFRED A. KNOPF, INC.: All of the following selections are reprinted by permission of Alfred A. Knopf, Inc. "Neighbour Rosicky" by Willa Cather. Copyright 1930 by Willa Cather and renewed 1958 by the Executors of the Estate of Willa Cather. From *Obscure Destinies*, by Willa Cather.
  "November Night," "Triad," and "The Warning" from *Verse*, by Adelaide Crapsey. Copyright 1922 by Algernon S. Crapsey, renewed 1950 by The Adelaide Crapsey Foundation.
  Excerpt from *Hiroshima*, by John Hersey. Copyright 1946 by John Hersey. Originally appeared in *The New Yorker*.
  "Early Evening Quarrel," "Me and the Mule," and "Stony Lonesome," Copyright 1942 by Alfred A. Knopf, Inc.; "Mama and Daughter," "Midnight Raffle," "Notes on Commercial Theatre," and "Puzzled," Copyright 1948 by Alfred A. Knopf, Inc.; "The Negro Speaks of Rivers," Copyright 1926 by Alfred A. Knopf, Inc. and renewed 1954 by Langston Hughes; "Young Gal's Blues," Copyright 1927 by Alfred A. Knopf, Inc. and renewed 1955 by Langston Hughes; "Sylvester's Dying Bed," Copyright © 1959 by Langston Hughes; "Border Line," Copyright 1947 by Langston Hughes; "When Sue Wears Red," Copyright 1926 by Alfred A. Knopf, Inc. and renewed 1954 by Langston Hughes. All from *Selected Poems*, by Langston Hughes.
  Excerpt from *Autobiography of an Ex-Colored Man*, by James Weldon Johnson. Copyright 1927 by Alfred A. Knopf, Inc., renewed 1955 by Carl Van Vechten.
  Excerpt from "The National Letters," Copyright 1920 by Alfred A. Knopf, Inc., renewed 1948 by H. L. Mencken. From *The Vintage Mencken*, by H. L. Mencken, and edited by Alistair Cooke.
  "Hydraulics" and "Winter Verse for His Sister" from *Earth Walk: New and Selected Poems*, by William Meredith. Copyright © 1970 by William Meredith.
  "Antique Harvesters," "The Equilibrists," "Janet Waking," "Persistent Explorer," "Two in August," "Morning," "Vision by Sweetwater," and an excerpt from "A Man Without a Sense of Direction," Copyright 1927 by Alfred A. Knopf, Inc., renewed 1955 by John Crowe Ransom; "Bells for John Whiteside's Daughter," "Captain Carpenter," "Judith of Bethulia," and "Spiel of Three Montebanks," Copyright 1924 by Alfred A. Knopf, Inc., renewed 1952 by John Crowe Ransom; "Agitato ma non troppo," Copyright 1924 by Alfred A. Knopf, Inc., renewed 1952 by John Crowe Ransom; "Painted Head," Copyright 1934 by Alfred A. Knopf, Inc. and renewed 1962 by John Crowe Ransom. All from *Selected Poems*, Third Edition, Revised and Enlarged, by John Crowe Ransom.
  "Anecdote of the Jar," "Bantams in Pine-Woods," "Disillusionment of Ten O'Clock," "Peter Quince at the Clavier," "The Snow Man," and "Sunday Morning," Copyright 1923, renewed 1951 by Wallace Stevens; "Asides on the Oboe" and "Of Modern Poetry," Copyright 1942 by Wallace Stevens; "Evening Without Angels" and "The Idea of Order at Key West," Copyright 1936 by Wallace Stevens and renewed 1964 by Holly Stevens; "To an Old Philosopher in Rome" and "The World as Meditation," Copyright 1952 by Wallace Stevens, "No Possum, No Sop, No Taters," Copyright 1947 by Wallace Stevens. All from *The Collected Poems of Wallace Stevens*, by Wallace Stevens.

LEEDS MUSIC CORPORATION: "Yonder Comes the Blues" by Ma Rainey. Words and music by Ma Rainey. Copyright 1926 by Northern Music Company, a division of MCA Entertainment Inc. Used by permission. All rights reserved.

J. B. LIPPINCOTT COMPANY: Excerpt from the book *Dust Tracks on a Road* by Zora Neale Hurston. Copyright 1942 by Zora Neale Hurston. Renewal © 1970 by John C. Hurston. Reprinted by permission of J. B. Lippincott Company.

LITTLE, BROWN AND COMPANY, PUBLISHERS: "The People's Choice" by Erskine Caldwell from *The Complete Stories of Erskine Caldwell*. Copyright 1932, by Erskine Caldwell. Copyright © renewed 1960 by Erskine Caldwell. Reprinted by permission of Little, Brown and Co.
  Poems #448, #326, #1672, #1333 by Emily Dickinson. Copyright 1914, 1942 by Martha Dickinson Bianchi. #745, #754, #721 by Emily Dickinson. Copyright 1929, © 1957 by Mary L. Hampson. From *The Complete Poems of Emily Dickinson*, edited by Thomas H. Johnson, by permission of Little, Brown and Co.
  "Around Pastor Bonhoeffer," "River Road," and "The Testing Tree" by Stanley Kunitz from *The Testing Tree: Poems*. Copyright © 1966, 1968, 1970 by Stanley Kunitz. Reprinted by permission of Atlantic-Little, Brown and Co.

LIVERIGHT PUBLISHING CORPORATION: "The Broken Tower," "To Brooklyn Bridge," excerpt from "Cape Hatteras," "At Melville's Tomb," "Praise for an Urn," "Repose of Rivers," excerpt from "The River," excerpt from "The Tunnel," and "Voyages II and VI" by Hart Crane from *The Collected Poems and Selected Letters and Prose of Hart Crane* by Hart Crane. Copyright © 1933, 1958, 1966 by Liveright Publishing Corp. Reprinted by permission of the publisher.
  "Fern," "Georgia Dusk," "November Cotton Flower," and "Portrait in Georgia" from *Cane* by Jean Toomer. Copyright © 1951 by Jean Toomer. Reprinted by permission of Liveright, Publishers, New York.

LOUISIANA STATE UNIVERSITY PRESS: Excerpt from "Still Rebels, Still Yankees" by Donald Davidson in *Still Rebels, Still Yankees and Other Essays*. Reprinted by permission of Louisiana State University Press.

ANDREW LYTLE: "Jericho, Jericho, Jericho" by Andrew Lytle from *A Novel, a Novella and Four Stories*. © 1958 by Andrew Lytle. Reprinted with the permission of the author.

MCA MUSIC: "Joe Hill," words by Alfred Hayes, music by Earl Robinson. © Copyright 1938 by *MCA Music*, A Division of MCA, Inc., Copyright renewed 1965 and assigned to *MCA Music*, A Division of MCA, Inc. © Copyright 1970 by *MCA Music*, A Division of MCA, Inc., 445 Park Ave., New York, N.Y. 10022, Used by Permission, All Rights Reserved.

THE MACMILLAN COMPANY: All of the following selections are reprinted with permission of The Macmillan Company. "The Bird of Night" from *The Bat-Poet* by Randall Jarrell, Copyright © The Macmillan Company 1963, 1964; "In Montecito" from *Lost World* by Randall Jarrell, Copyright © Randall Jarrell 1963, 1965, originally appeared in *The New Yorker* Magazine.
Excerpt from "Bryan, Bryan, Bryan, Bryan," Copyright 1920 by The Macmillan Company, renewed 1948 by Elizabeth C. Lindsay; excerpt from "The Congo," Copyright 1914 by The Macmillan Company, renewed 1942 by Elizabeth C. Lindsay; excerpt from "General William Booth Enters into Heaven," Copyright 1913 by The Macmillan Company. All from *Collected Poems* of Vachel Lindsay.
"The Frigate Pelican," "No Swan so Fine," "Poetry," and "Silence," Copyright 1935 by Marianne Moore, renewed 1963 by Marianne Moore and T. S. Eliot; "Bird-Witted" and "The Paper Nautilus," Copyright 1941 and renewed 1969 by Marianne Moore; "The Steeple-Jack," Copyright 1951 by Marianne Moore. All from *Collected Poems* by Marianne Moore.
"Eros Turannos," "Old Trails," "The Poor Relation" and "Veteran Sirens," Copyright 1916 by Edwin Arlington Robinson, renewed 1944 by Ruth Nivison; "The Mill," Copyright 1920 by Edwin Arlington Robinson, renewed 1948 by Ruth Nivison; "Mr. Flood's Party," Copyright 1921 by Edwin Arlington Robinson, renewed 1949 by Ruth Nivison. All from *Collected Poems* by Edwin Arlington Robinson.

EDGAR LEE MASTERS: "Knowlt Hoheimer," "Rutherford McDowell," "Lucinda Matlock," "Petit, the Poet," and "Anne Rutledge" by Edgar Lee Masters. Reprinted by permission of Weissberger & Frosch, attorneys for Mrs. Edgar Lee Masters.

SCOTT MEREDITH LITERARY AGENCY, INC.: Excerpts from *The Armies of the Night* by Norman Mailer. Reprinted by permission of the author and his agents, Scott Meredith Literary Agency, Inc., 580 Fifth Avenue, New York, N.Y. 10036.

GEORGE MILBURN: "Pie in the Sky" (The Preacher and the Slave) from *Hobo's Hornbook*, collected and annotated by George Milburn. Copyright 1930 and published by Ives Washburn, Inc.

NEW DIRECTIONS PUBLISHING CORP.: All of the following selections are reprinted by permission of New Directions Publishing Corporation. "The Crack-Up" and excerpts from "The Notebooks" by F. Scott Fitzgerald, *The Crack-Up.* Copyright 1936 by Esquire, Inc. Copyright 1945 by New Directions Publishing Corporation.
"The Garden," "Hugh Selwyn Mauberley," "The Jewel Stairs' Grievance," "Portrait d'une Femme," "The River-Merchant's Wife: a Letter," "The Seafarer," and "In a Station of the Metro" by Ezra Pound, *Personae.* Copyright 1926 by Ezra Pound. "Canto I," "Canto II," "Canto IV," "Canto VII," "Canto XVII," "Canto XLV," "Canto LXXXI," and "Canto LXXXIII" by Ezra Pound, *The Cantos.* Copyright 1934, 1948 by Ezra Pound.
Excerpt from Nathanael West's *Miss Lonelyhearts and the Day of the Locust.* Copyright 1939 by the Estate of Nathanael West, © 1966 by Laura Perelman.
"Flowers by the Sea," "Nantucket," "The Red Wheelbarrow," and "Spring and All (By the road . . .)" by William Carlos Williams, *Collected Earlier Poems,* Copyright 1938 by New Directions Publishing Corporation; "The Dance," "Paterson: The Falls," and "A Sort of a Song" by William Carlos Williams, *Collected Later Poems,* Copyright 1944 by William Carlos Williams; "Asphodel, That Greeny Flower" and "Song" by William Carlos Williams, *Pictures from Brueghel and Other Poems,* Copyright 1955, © 1959 by William Carlos Williams.

HAROLD OBER ASSOCIATES, INC.: All of the following selections are reprinted by permission of Harold Ober Associates Incorporated. "Death in the Woods" by Sherwood Anderson, Copyright 1926 by The American Mercury, Inc., Copyright renewed 1953 by Eleanor Copenhaver Anderson; "I Want to Know Why" by Sherwood Anderson, Copyright 1921 by B. W. Huebsch, Copyright renewed 1948 by Eleanor Copenhaver Anderson.
"A Summer Tragedy" by Arna Bontemps from *The Best Short Stories by Negro Writers,* edited by Langston Hughes. Copyright 1933 by Arna Bontemps. Copyright renewed.

"Dream Boogie" by Langston Hughes from *Montage of a Dream Deferred.* Copyright 1951 by Langston Hughes.

OXFORD UNIVERSITY PRESS: Excerpts from "The Crystal," from "A Letter from Li Po," from "Preludes for Memnon," and from "Time in the Rock" by Conrad Aiken from *Collected Poems,* Second Edition, by Conrad Aiken. Copyright © 1970 by Conrad Aiken. Reprinted by permission of Oxford University Press.
"The Fury of Aerial Bombardment," "The Goal of Intellectual Man," "The Groundhog," "In a Hard Intellectual Light," "I Walked Out to the Graveyard to See the Dead," "The Ides of March," "If I Could Only Live at the Pitch That Is Near Madness," "In Prisons of Established Craze," and "Where Are Those High and Haunting Skies," from *Collected Poems, 1930–1960,* by Richard Eberhart, © 1960 by Richard Eberhart. Reprinted by permission of Oxford University Press.

NORMAN HOLMES PEARSON: "Heat," "Lais," "Orchard," "Oread," "Pear Tree," and "Sea Rose" by Hilda Doolittle (H.D.). Reprinted by permission of Norman Holmes Pearson, owner of the copyright.

RANDOM HOUSE, INC.: All of the following selections are reprinted by permission of Random House, Inc. Excerpt from *Invisible Man,* by Ralph Ellison. Copyright 1947 by Ralph Ellison.
Excerpts from *Light in August,* by William Faulkner, Copyright 1932, renewed 1960 by William Faulkner. "An Odor of Verbena," Copyright 1938, renewed 1966 by Estelle Faulkner and Jill Faulkner Summers, from *The Unvanquished,* by William Faulkner. "A Rose for Emily," Copyright 1930, renewed 1958 by William Faulkner; and "That Evening Sun," Copyright 1931, renewed 1959 by William Faulkner. Both from *Collected Stories of William Faulkner,* by William Faulkner. "Spotted Horses," Copyright 1931, renewed 1959 by William Faulkner. An expanded version of this story appears as part of *The Hamlet.*
"The Bonfire" by John O'Hara. Copyright © 1964 by John O'Hara. From *The O'Hara Generation,* by John O'Hara.
"Desire Under the Elms," Copyright 1924, renewed 1952 by Eugene O'Neill. From *Selected Plays of Eugene O'Neill,* by Eugene O'Neill.
"Auto Wreck" and "Hollywood," Copyright 1942 and renewed 1970 by Karl Shapiro; "The Leg," Copyright 1944 by Karl Shapiro. All from *Selected Poems,* by Karl Shapiro.
"Melanctha" from *Three Lives,* by Gertrude Stein. Copyright 1909 and renewed 1937 by Gertrude Stein.
Excerpt from *The Confessions of Nat Turner,* by William Styron. Copyright © 1966, 1967 by William Styron.
Audubon: A Vision, by Robert Penn Warren. Copyright © 1969 by Robert Penn Warren.
Condensation of *Homage to Theodore Dreiser,* by Robert Penn Warren. Copyright © 1971 by Robert Penn Warren.

RUSSELL & RUSSELL, PUBLISHERS: Selected remarks by William James from *Collected Essays and Reviews,* Edited by Ralph Barton Perry (1920) New York: Russell & Russell, 1969. Reprinted by permission of Russell & Russell, Publishers.

CHARLES SCRIBNER'S SONS: All of the following selections are reprinted by permission of Charles Scribner's Sons. "The Rich Boy" (Copyright 1925, 1926 Consolidated Magazines Corporation; renewal copyright 1953, 1954 Frances Scott Fitzgerald Lanahan) is reprinted from *All the Sad Young Men* by F. Scott Fitzgerald.
Excerpts from the Introduction by Robert Penn Warren to *A Farewell to Arms* by Ernest Hemingway, Copyright 1929 Charles Scribner's Sons; renewal copyright © 1957 Ernest Hemingway; Copyright 1949 Charles Scribner's Sons. "The Snows of Kilimanjaro" (Copyright 1936 Ernest Hemingway; renewal copyright © 1964 Mary Hemingway) is reprinted from *The Short Stories of Ernest Hemingway.*
Notice: Quotations from the works of Ernest Hemingway and F. Scott Fitzgerald are fully protected by United States and International Copyright. Used by permission of Charles Scribner's Sons.
"The Beast in the Jungle" and "The Jolly Corner" by Henry James are reprinted from Volume XVII, *The Novels and Tales of Henry James* (New York Edition), Copyright 1909 Charles Scribner's Sons; renewal copyright 1937 Henry James. "The Pupil" by Henry James is reprinted from Volume XI, *The Novel and Tales of Henry James* (New York Edition), Copyright 1908 Charles Scribner's Sons; renewal copyright 1936 Henry James. "Joseph" by Henry James from *Notes on Novelists and Other Notes,* Copyright 1914 Charles Scribner's Sons; renewal

copyright 1942 Henry James. "New York Revisited" by Henry James from *The American Scene*, Copyright 1907 Charles Scribner's Sons; renewal copyright 1934 Henry James.

"Poetry: A Note in Ontology" is reprinted from *The World's Body* by John Crowe Ransom, Copyright 1934 Bookman Publishing Company; renewal copyright © 1962 John Crowe Ransom.

Edwin Arlington Robinson's "Luke Havergal," "The Clerks," "Reuben Bright," and "The Pity of the Leaves" are reprinted from *The Children of the Night* (1897). "Miniver Cheevy" (copyright 1907 Charles Scribner's Sons; renewal copyright 1935 Ruth Nivison) and "For a Dead Lady" (copyright 1910 Charles Scribner's Sons; renewal copyright 1938 Ruth Nivison) are reprinted from *The Town Down the River*.

The Genteel Tradition in American Philosophy by George Santayana, Copyright 1931 Charles Scribner's Sons. "Poetry of Barbarism" and "Emerson" by George Santayana are reprinted from *Interpretations of Poetry and Religion*. "In My Deep Heart" by George Santayana is reprinted from *Poems*, Copyright 1923 Charles Scribner's Sons.

Excerpts from *A Backward Glance* by Edith Wharton, Copyright 1933, 1934 William R. Tyler; renewal copyright © 1961, 1962. "The Eyes" by Edith Wharton (Copyright 1910 Charles Scribner's Sons; renewal copyright 1938 William R. Tyler) is reprinted from *The Collected Short Stories of Edith Wharton*.

Excerpts from *Look Homeward Angel* by Thomas Wolfe, Copyright 1929 Charles Scribner's Sons; renewal copyright © 1957 Edward C. Aswell, Administrator C.T.A. and/or Fred W. Wolfe.

SOUTHERN ILLINOIS UNIVERSITY PRESS: Excerpts from "What the Revolutionary Movement Can Do for a Writer" by Malcolm Cowley from *Think Back on Us*, © 1967 by Southern Illinois University Press. Reprinted by permission of Malcolm Cowley and the Southern Illinois University Press.

JESSE STUART: "Uncle Casper" by Jesse Stuart from *Head o'W-Hollow*, published by E. P. Dutton and Co. Reprinted by permission of the author.

THE SWALLOW PRESS INCORPORATED: Allen Tate: "Last Days of Alice," "The Meaning of Death: An After-Dinner Speech," "The Meaning of Life: A Monologue," "The Mediterranean," "Mother and Son," "The Oath," "Ode to the Confederate Dead," "Seasons of the Soul," and "The Swimmers," reprinted from *The Swimmers and Other Selected Poems* © 1970, by permission of The Swallow Press, Chicago. "A Southern Mode of the Imagination" by Allen Tate, reprinted from *Essays of Four Decades*, by permission of The Swallow Press, Chicago.

TEMPLE UNIVERSITY PRESS: From *Paul Bunyan: Last of the Frontier Demigods* by Daniel Hoffman. Copyright 1952 Temple University. First published 1952 by the University of Pennsylvania Press for Temple University publications. Reissued 1966 by Columbia University Press for Temple University Publications. Reprinted by permission of the author and publisher.

JEAN TOOMER: "Blue Meridian" from *Cane* by Jean Toomer. Reprinted by permission of Marjorie Content Toomer.

TRO: THE RICHMOND ORGANIZATION: All of the following selections are used by permission of TRO: The Richmond Organization. "On the Banks of the Wabash," new words and new music arrangement by Joseph Sherman. TRO–© Copyright 1956 *Hampshire House Publishing Corp.*, New York, N.Y.

"Careless Love," words & music by Huddie Ledbetter. Collected and adapted by John A. Lomax & Alan Lomax. TRO–© Copyright 1936 and renewed 1964 *Folkways Music Publishers, Inc.*, New York, N.Y.

"Casey Jones," collected, adapted and arranged by John A. Lomax & Alan Lomax. TRO–© Copyright 1934 and renewed 1962 *Ludlow Music, Inc.*, New York, N.Y.

"The Cowboy's Lament," collected, adapted and arranged by John A. Lomax & Alan Lomax. TRO–© Copyright 1938 and renewed 1966 *Ludlow Music, Inc.*, New York, N.Y.

"De Ballit of De Boll Weevil," words & music by Huddie Ledbetter. Collected, adapted and arranged by John A. Lomax & Alan Lomax. TRO–© Copyright 1936 and renewed 1964 *Folkways Music Publishers, Inc.*, New York, N.Y.

"Drill, Ye Tarriers, Drill!" new words and new music adaptation by Jessie Cavanaugh & Albert Stanton. TRO–© Copyright 1960 *Hollis Music, Inc.*, New York, N.Y.

"Hallelujah, Bum Again," collected, adapted and arranged by John A. Lomax & Alan Lomax. TRO–© Copyright 1941 and renewed 1969 *Ludlow Music, Inc.*, New York, N.Y.

"John Henry," collected, adapted and arranged by John A. Lomax & Alan Lomax. TRO–© Copyright 1934 and renewed 1962 *Ludlow Music, Inc.*, New York, N.Y.

"Keep Your Hands on That Plow," collected, adapted and arranged by John A. Lomax & Alan Lomax. TRO–© Copyright 1941 and renewed 1969 *Ludlow Music, Inc.*, New York, N.Y.

"The Midnight Special," words & music by Huddie Ledbetter. Collected & adapted by John A. Lomax & Alan Lomax. TRO–© Copyright 1936 and renewed 1964 *Folkways Music Publishers, Inc.*, New York, N.Y.

"Pastures of Plenty," words & music by Woody Guthrie. TRO–© Copyright 1960 & 1963 *Ludlow Music, Inc.*, New York, N.Y.

"The Range of the Buffalo" (The Buffalo Skinners), collected, adapted and arranged by John A. Lomax & Alan Lomax. TRO–© Copyright 1938 and renewed 1966 *Ludlow Music, Inc.*, New York, N.Y.

TWAYNE PUBLISHERS, INC.: "If We Must Die" and "The Tropics in New York" by Claude McKay from *Selected Poems of Claude McKay*, copyright 1953 by Bookman Associates. Reprinted by permission of Twayne Publishers, Inc.

UNIVERSITY OF CALIFORNIA PRESS: "Motives and Motifs in the Poetry of Marianne Moore" by Kenneth Burke from *A Grammar of Motives*. Originally published by the University of California Press; reprinted by permission of The Regents of the University of California and the author.

UNIVERSITY OF ILLINOIS PRESS: "Marginal Notes on Civilization in the United States" by George Santayana from *George Santayana's America*, edited by James Ballowe, 1967. Reprinted by permission of the University of Illinois Press.

UNIVERSITY OF MINNESOTA PRESS: "Joe Clisby's Song" by Donald Davidson from *Poems 1922–1961*. University of Minnesota Press, Minneapolis, © 1924, 1927, 1934, 1935, 1938, 1952, 1961, 1966 Donald Davidson. Reprinted by permission.

UNIVERSITY OF NORTH CAROLINA PRESS: "Little Black Train Is A'Comin'" from *The Negro Sings a New Heaven*, by M. A. Grimmon. Reprinted by permission of the University of North Carolina Press.

VANGUARD PRESS, INC.: Excerpt from *The Young Manhood of Studs Lonigan* by James T. Farrell. Copyright 1934, by The Vanguard Press, Inc. Reprinted by permission of The Publisher, The Vanguard Press, Inc.

THE VIKING PRESS, INC.: All of the following selections are reprinted by permission of The Viking Press, Inc. "Queer" from *Winesburg, Ohio* by Sherwood Anderson. Copyright 1919 by B. W. Huebsch, Inc., renewed 1947 by Eleanor Copenhaver Anderson.

Excerpt from *Mr. Sammler's Planet* by Saul Bellow. Copyright © 1969, 1970 by Saul Bellow. All rights reserved.

Excerpt from *Exiles Return* by Malcolm Cowley. Copyright 1934, © 1962 by Malcolm Cowley. All rights reserved.

"The Crucifixion" from *God's Trombones* by James Weldon Johnson. Copyright 1927 by The Viking Press, Inc., renewed 1955 by Grace Nail Johnson. "O Black and Unknown Bards" from *St. Peter Relates an Incident* by James Weldon Johnson. Copyright 1917 by James Weldon Johnson. All rights reserved.

"To a Chameleon" from *Complete Poems* by Marianne Moore. All rights reserved.

Excerpt from *The Grapes of Wrath* by John Steinbeck. Copyright 1939, © 1967 by John Steinbeck. All rights reserved.

From "Freud and Literature" from *The Liberal Imagination* by Lionel Trilling. Copyright 1940, 1947 by Lionel Trilling. All rights reserved.

WESLEYAN UNIVERSITY PRESS: "Cherrylog Road" and "Gamecock," Copyright © 1963, 1965 by James Dickey. Reprinted from *Poems 1957–1967*, by James Dickey, by permission of Wesleyan University Press. "Cherrylog Road" was first published in *The New Yorker*.

THE WORLD PUBLISHING COMPANY: "The Man Who Was Almost a Man," reprinted by permission of The World Publishing Company from *Eight Men* by Richard Wright. Copyright © 1961, 1940 by Richard Wright.

Letter to the Reader

number of years ago the three of us, friends of long standing, came together to plan a textbook on American literature. We set out to read the body of our literature, no small part of it by some of us for the first time, and to try to divest ourselves of preconceptions about it. As we read and reread it and discussed it among ourselves, we constantly discovered new ranges of meaning, new relationships, and new dimensions of interest. In fact, as we worked and talked, our notion of the book kept changing and expanding, and what the book now is we could not have remotely envisaged in our early discussions.

How we began work on this book

We were aware that we represented divergent personalities, interests, and degrees of specialization, but we hoped to make a virtue of these very differences. Different perspectives on an author might produce a portrait more nearly in the round. Somewhat contradictory judgments might not result in mere anemic compromises but might, in fact, stimulate further explorations and new insights. At the very least, our divergences could be mutually corrective: we could hope to eliminate the more obvious errors and the more shallow oversimplifications. But allowing for differences, it was plain that we shared a community of interests within which our occasional disagreements could be contained and might even prove to have positive value.

How shall we describe that community of interests? In the first place, we were not concerned to perpetuate any previously established pattern—nor to set up a new orthodoxy. Our method was inductive, and our mode of working was social; that is, we read and we talked. There was a certain liberation in realizing that we could discover the nature and scale of our book only in the open-ended process of our own explorations.

*What we chose
and why*

From the beginning we had to ask ourselves, in what way was material to justify itself to us for inclusion and discussion? Literary quality would obviously be the primary consideration, but early on we agreed that our book was not to be simply a treasury of masterpieces. It would also concern itself with the origin and development of masterpieces and with the circumstances that might account for the failure, or partial failure, of other works. Thus on occasion we might include a work that we thought was, by absolute literary standards, second or third rate, provided it told us something about the background of some first-rate achievement or about the taste of a period, or had proved politically significant, or illustrated a temptation to which this or that author was peculiarly susceptible.

In addition to the distinction between good and bad work, or significant and insignificant, we were forced, in choosing our materials, to recognize a more radical distinction—the distinction between what one may call "primary" and "secondary" literature. By primary literature we mean writing that was printed and transmitted as formal literary art—in this book mainly fiction and poetry, though we do include three plays. By secondary literature we mean writing that, however "artful," was regarded by the author as an instrument for achieving some extrinsic and nonliterary purpose—works such as essays, letters, travel writing, nature writing, diaries, philosophy, and history; or compositions that have basically survived by oral transmission or at least by reason of something like "folk consciousness."

Though it does seem sensible in a book on American literature to put stress on works that make the formal claim to be literature, we have included a large amount of secondary literature as well, and perhaps we ought to say something about what may strike some readers as an unusual hospitality toward such work. In the first place, it is not always easy to draw a hard and fast line between primary and secondary literature. Works written to serve a nonliterary purpose may also have genuine literary qualities and may even embody a powerful imaginative vision. Jonathan Edwards' "terror sermon" at Enfield, in 1740, was presumably delivered with the aim of bringing his listeners to religious conversion, but present-day readers—whether Christians or not—recognize it as a magnificent artistic creation: and in this book, in fact, we regard it chiefly, though not exclusively, at this level. There are, however, other types of composition, folk materials especially, which, though clearly secondary by reason of origin and transmission, spring basically or in considerable part from the artistic impulse and, as in the case of Appalachian ballads or Negro spirituals and the blues, may achieve great charm or power.

But there is a reason beyond intrinsic value for drawing heavily on sec-

ondary literature. It can often throw light on the creation of primary literature and may, in fact, have inspired or nourished it. For example, the
muckraking literature of the 1890's can illuminate aspects of Stephen Crane's
Maggie: A Girl of the Streets; Theodore Dreiser's autobiography can tell us
much about the impulse behind his fiction and the personal experiences that
he incorporated into it; and behind Mark Twain lies a vast body of folk
creation. Secondary literature often represents the raw experience on which
the artist worked.

Literature, clearly, does not exist in a vacuum. It feeds on life and life
feeds on it. Without a deep awareness of the complex relationship between
the two, the reader cannot understand nor, in the full sense, appreciate literature—even literature rigorously contemplated as art. The keenest enjoyment of literature—and the most fruitful study of it—derives from a sense
of the continuing dialectic between the formal aspects of art and the raw,
undefined, and finally perhaps undefinable reality that is the stuff of art. By
"dialectic" we here mean the interplay between the artist's drive toward his
special conception of form and meaning and the resistance set up by the
qualities, and even by the competing "meanings," of his materials. In one
sense, the interplay is a contest between two sets of forces. Even the truly
great artist never, perhaps, wins absolutely—or if he does win a particular
battle, he never wins the war. The conflict, fought next year and on fresh
terrain, will go on and on, for reality is in some sense incorrigible, perhaps
never to be fully conquered—fully encompassed and understood. Yet a
Moby-Dick or *Scarlet Letter* is an individual victory. In our selections of
primary literature we have meant to take account of such victories, great
and small; but we have also tried to keep alive in the reader's mind—through
our selections of secondary literature and through our own critical commentaries, many of which have to do with the writer's background and problems—a sense of the stubborn, cross-grained, and ultimately mysterious reality
with which the artist is forced to wrestle.

As we have said, this book has come to be very different from our original   *How we came*
notion of it. Though we began by thinking of an anthology with relatively   *to see our*
brief introductions and headnotes, we found, as the work proceeded, that   *book as a*
this plan would not accommodate a discussion of the urgent issues that kept   *"history"*
arising. Eventually we found that we were being driven to write a history,
though a history of a very special kind. To begin with, we always remembered that a work of literature is written by an individual, marked by his
special personality and personal past, and that the literary work represents
in a deep way the writer's attempt to confront and find meaning in his
experience. But the individual writer, we also wanted to emphasize, exists
in a certain milieu—the political and economic context, the social institu-

tions, the emotional and intellectual climate; and literature, as we have suggested, represents a continuing dialectic between the individual and his world. Thus, in one perspective at least, our book developed into a history of the American sensibility. But it remains peculiarly a *literary* history in that it characteristically takes into account aesthetic considerations and theories, the growth of literary modes, techniques, and forms, and the changes in literary tastes and fashions. Nor could such a history fail to recall, if only occasionally and sparingly, literary and intellectual currents emanating from Great Britain and Europe.

Yet our concern remained focused, naturally, on the American scene, and we became more and more urgently aware of what may be called thematic continuities in American history, which, in turn, become the basic and recurring themes of American literature. Here is a very informal list: America vs. Europe, relation of the past and the future to the present; East vs. West; the American "mission," the American Eden, and millennialism; apocalypse—the coming horror; the self vs. society, secession vs. unity, private intuition vs. collective wisdom; materialism vs. idealism; technology vs. nature (including human nature); poetry vs. science.

All of this sounds very ambitious and pretentious—even, perhaps, schematic and abstract. But our history is in fact informal and essayistic. It reflects the inductive process of reading, discussing, and working outward from the individual works of literature. Our historical commentary is constantly interrupted by a contemplation of particular poems and pieces of fiction. The reader is thus forced to return again and again, as we were, to the concrete literary documents. These are never merely "illustrations" of historical generalizations. If a literary work has any artistic value it will always reveal itself to be in excess of the historical comment, speaking to the reader in its own mode and living its own life. Though we trust that our commentaries will throw some light on the literature presented here, we are never allowed to forget that the literature presented is also lighting up history—is even changing history. In dealing with literature we have sought, above all, to give a sense of the "thingness" rather than the "aboutness"— we want the sense of "aboutness" in the end to return the reader to a richer experience of the literature itself.

Some critical approaches

In this book we have engaged in several kinds of literary criticism, and they can be best distinguished by referring to the "three R's" of criticism— the writer, the writing, and the reader. In a certain sense, a piece of writing can, indeed, be said to exist in itself, and can be examined more or less in its own terms. But it also exists in a shifting complex of relationships, each of which contributes in a subtle and sometimes mysterious way to the actuality—even the aesthetic actuality—of the work. A work, of course, is created by an individual in his particular evolving world, but it is responded to variously, by readers of widely different backgrounds, and over successive generations. It has, too, its own literary ancestry, but it may, in its turn, exert influence on later work and, even, on general attitudes toward life.

We feel such relationships to be complex rather than simple, dynamic rather than static. As with the biographer's help we learn more about Hemingway's personal life, and with the historian's help more about the epoch he lived through, we may find ourselves perceiving more artistry and more richness of experience in, say, *A Farewell to Arms*. Melville was a good deal ahead of his time, imaginatively and as a literary technician; today *Moby-Dick* is understood so much more fully than it was a century ago that in some real sense it has become a different book. When Emily Dickinson's poems were first published in the 1890's, critical theory and literary taste were simply not ready to cope with them; but developments in criticism in the twenties and thirties of this century, the resulting return to favor of seventeenth-century English metaphysical verse, and a clearer grasp of the American romantic tradition prepared a generation of readers for whom it could almost be said that Dickinson's poetry had at last been born.

To such aspects as these we have tried to do some justice, but they do not exhaust the critical possibilities. There is, for instance, what is known as genre criticism, a mode much in fashion today and in certain quarters brilliantly practiced. In some respects, this approach develops out of formal criticism (which stresses the work, the writing), but genre criticism aims to identify and to define the literary work as a member of a special class rather than to evaluate it for itself. With genre study as a self-enclosed system we ourselves have here little to do; but some discrimination among literary forms has, of course, been an indispensable part of our job. We have pursued the distinction, somewhat anxiously debated in the early nineteenth century, between the "novel" and the "romance"; later, we have traced the ascendancy of romance fiction in the work of Hawthorne and Melville; and we have had a good deal to say about the realistic novel in its various states from Howells through Stephen Crane to Dreiser and beyond. In poetry, "imagism" and "symbolism" demanded discussion, and long ambitious poems, like Eliot's *The Waste Land*, Hart Crane's *The Bridge*, and Archibald MacLeish's *Conquistador*, required some reflection on the traditional epic and its availability as a genre to poets in our time.

As an example of the flexibility of critical treatment we have tried to maintain, take the case of Henry James's "The Jolly Corner." It is a kind of ghost story of 1909 in which a man (after half a lifetime's absence) returns to this country to inspect his property on a "jolly corner" in New York City, and, as he wanders through the house at night, finds that he is stalking a phantom figure who oddly and menacingly seems to resemble him. Immediately preceding the story is an editorial headnote that very briefly combines three different critical perspectives: first, with James's help it identifies the genre of the story—a ghost story of the kind James liked as being akin to the fairy tale; second, it relates the work to James's visit to the United States in 1904–5, his first view of his native country in more than two decades; and third, it offers a few analytic remarks and raises a question or two about the inner movement of the tale.

But the headnote, especially under the second and third topics, simply brings to focus certain issues treated in more detail elsewhere in the section on James. For the second topic, there is considerable biographical material in the general introduction to James, material that will allow the student to locate the story in the larger frame of James's life. He will find there a discussion of James's slowly worked out and fateful decision to expatriate himself and to pursue the life of art in England and on the Continent—an act whose consequences reverberated through the writing of "The Jolly Corner" and beyond it. The biographical account can also help the student to perceive the story as one moment in the unending process by which James sought to understand his own nature. One of the creative motives behind the story is, we suggest, James's deep suspicion that had he remained in America instead of becoming an expatriate he might have succumbed, in some degree at least, to the demoralizing materialism by which, as he saw it, the country was being consumed; and, as the headnote to "The Jolly Corner" indicates, we have provided, in a selection from *The American Scene*, a glimpse of the New York that the returning James found under the spell of rampant and disorderly greed. Furthermore, we have given a broader context to the world of New York by a discussion, in the preliminary note to the period 1861–1914, of the dominant values in America during the Gilded Age and the decades following.

James was an extraordinarily fascinating individual, and the relation of his work to his period is fascinating and complex; and in our space we have been able to do little more than suggest the biographical and social origins of "The Jolly Corner"; even so we have had to push on beyond those concerns, for, after all, the story itself is central to our interest. So we have tried to offer in the introduction a sufficient amount of analysis and commentary on style to allow the student to grasp the rich implications of the story and to arrive at some estimate of James as a literary craftsman.

We do not mean to suggest by this anatomy of the critical context of "The Jolly Corner" that there is a set pattern which we have followed in every case. There is, obviously, considerable difference in the scale of various treatments, in procedure and emphasis. In one case, we may have felt that the most useful thing we can say about a work in the headnote is to mention the historical event that inspired it; in another—say, a poem by Emily Dickinson—it might have seemed appropriate to limit comment to analysis of her unusual manner of punctuation or to point out the alternative verbal possibilities she can be shown to have contemplated; in still a third, the point worth making may be the work's place in some particularly American literary tradition.

The introductions to authors vary in much the same way as do those to individual works. Whittier, for instance, requires us to look more closely at the politics of his time (in particular, the antislavery movement) than does Edwin Arlington Robinson or Hart Crane. Henry James was, in his own phrase, "that obstinate finality," an artist: the growth of his art and of James himself as a personage in the world of letters occupies much of the James section. William Faulkner has clearly emerged as one of the towering figures in American literary history and would undoubtedly warrant the elaborate separate treatment accorded to Hawthorne, Melville, Mark Twain, and Dreiser; yet, in our view, Faulkner can best be understood and appreciated within the long and mixed tradition of southern writing, and he appears accordingly as the climax of two related sections, the first of which goes back as early as 1861. By the time we come to his work in the second of these sections, so much has been said about "the southern imagination" and southern culture and society that relatively few words are needed to introduce Faulkner himself, before getting on into the riches of his fiction.

How to handle the novel was one of our most vexing problems, and one for which, at various times, we considered different solutions. Of the American novels written before the Second World War, there are, we decided, nine necessary to a basic knowledge of American literature—though this is not to say that all nine can always be read in a single course. The novels are: *A special topic: the novel*

The Scarlet Letter, by Hawthorne
Moby-Dick, by Melville
One of the several masterpieces by Henry James (*Portrait of a Lady*, *The Ambassadors*, *The Wings of the Dove*, *The Golden Bowl*)
The Adventures of Huckleberry Finn, by Twain
The Red Badge of Courage, by Crane
An American Tragedy, by Dreiser
The Great Gatsby, by Fitzgerald
The Sun Also Rises or *A Farewell to Arms*, by Hemingway
One of the several masterpieces by Faulkner (*The Sound and the Fury*, *Light in August, Absalom, Absalom!*)

The nine basic novels could not, of course, be accommodated in this work; they would run to more than 1,500,000 words—that is, to three-quarters of the available space in our volumes. In addition to these nine items, there are also other novels with which, for a variety of reasons, we think the student should have more than a passing acquaintance:

The Leatherstocking cycle, by Cooper
Uncle Tom's Cabin, by Stowe
The Rise of Silas Lapham or *A Hazard of New Fortunes*, by Howells
Main Street or *Babbitt*, by Lewis
Look Homeward, Angel or *Of Time and the River*, by Wolfe
U.S.A., by Dos Passos
Miss Lonelyhearts or *The Day of the Locust*, by West
Studs Lonigan, by Farrell
The Grapes of Wrath, by Steinbeck
Native Son, by Wright

We realize, of course, that America has no more persuasive claim to literary eminence than its novelists. Yet to include even three or four novels (but which three or four?) would have severely restricted our use of other material that we felt to be of the utmost importance and that was readily adapted for our use and not always readily available elsewhere. So for complete texts of novels we are depending on the many available soft-cover editions, from among which the teacher can make his own selections. We have, however, provided here elaborate discussions and analyses of the nine novels we have named as basic, and somewhat more limited treatments of the novels on our second list, plus a few others besides.

In spite of the fact that a part of a novel cannot stand for the whole, we have sometimes, nevertheless, printed particular sections of a number of novels. We have done so for special reasons, trying to consider each case on its own merits. For instance, the Leatherstocking cycle is, we think, basic; but, clearly, the whole cycle could not be used in a course, nor does any one novel suggest the impact of the whole. So we have used key parts of each of the items in the cycle to give a sense of the structure and meaning of the whole. A teacher may wish, of course, to use one complete novel (and that, if time permits, would be highly desirable), but even so, he could scarcely expect one novel to stand for the cycle.

To take another kind of example, we have used a sequence from *An American Tragedy* that we regard not only as central to an understanding of that novel and of Dreiser's method, but as central to Dreiser's work in general. Even if a teacher should agree with us that *An American Tragedy* is basic, he might not, because of its length, want to require that his students read it; in which case, our selection, in conjunction with the critical discussion, would give the student some feeling at least for Dreiser's characteristic qualities.

*Some ways
to use
this book*

Just as we have varied our methods and emphases in our critical treatment of different authors, the teacher, we assume, will want to do the same. In fact, in all our discussions, we three have always envisaged a fourth editor: the teacher. He will have his own methods, opinions, and interpretations and may sometimes find ours downright wrong-headed. We expect this. We have had our own critical disputes. What we do hope, however, is that we have stated our views clearly enough, have developed them cogently enough, and have drawn issues sharply enough to enable the teacher or student more positively and dramatically to frame and present his own convictions.

Since this book is, among other things, a history, it is only natural that its organization should be, in the main, chronological. But it is not strictly so; other considerations inevitably cross-hatch pure chronology. We have mentioned the two sections on southern writing, which overlap periods treated elsewhere. Similarly, the two sections on black literature together span many decades, for like Faulkner and other white southern writers, black writers in America, whether of the North or the South, have worked in terms of a special tradition and cultural context. Again, as another example, we have a broad section on "Literature of the Nonliterary World," with such subsections as "Political Writing" and "Tale and Character." Any one of these subsections may overlap periods covered earlier or later in the book. One teacher may choose to follow our arrangement only partially and, having covered the writers in the "main stream" of, say, Volume Two, may then, preferring to treat southern literature as an entity in itself, cut back in time to the Reconstruction period by taking up the first of the two southern sections and follow that immediately with the second. A similar procedure could be followed by the teacher who wished to pursue, without a break in the continuity, the development of black literature from 1861 to 1945.

Or the teacher may prefer to devise other groupings. For instance, for that period between the Civil War and the Second World War he might make a chronological study of a category such as "realism," including poetry and fiction written by black and by white writers. Having done this, he might then return to the Civil War period and follow through with another category of his choice and devising—for instance, the literature of the expatriates. Either of these procedures would afford special values and insights. Again, a teacher might find it useful to follow poetry, fiction, or the literature of ideas through, as independent units. Or one can imagine a course organized around recurrent themes of American literature—or at least with them as a basis for continuing discussion.

To return to the crucial matter of critical judgments: Are they ever to be settled once and for all? The vitality of a literary work is attested to by the fact that it continues to provoke new explorations and new assessments, to provide new perspectives of meaning and invite new insights. This is not to say that anything goes, that pure impressionism or pure relativism is to be accepted, but it is to say that one should be wary of dogmatism; and that, even while driving as hard as possible to make distinctions, perform analyses, and clarify formulations, one should realize that absolute and total "truth" is certainly not possible in such matters and, if it were, perhaps not wholly desirable. We do not delude ourselves that our book is in any sense "definitive." Nor do we offer a precise prescription for its use. There are many ways to cut the cake. We have baked it; the teacher must cut it to suit himself. What we hope for is that what we have written will be regarded as a serious, thoughtful, and reasonably well-informed effort to make sense of a rich and various body of literature.

Cleanth Brooks
R. W. B. Lewis
Robert Penn Warren

New Haven, Connecticut
January 15, 1973

Acknowledgments

We are deeply and obviously indebted to many critics and scholars in the field of American literature, but there are a few individuals to whom we wish to make more particular acknowledgment: Daniel Aaron, June Guicharnaud, Daniel Hoffman, Mary Pitlick, Louis Popp, David Rosen, and C. Vann Woodward. We would also like to thank Sylvia Newman, who edited the manuscript. And special gratitude is owed to David Milch for long, devoted, and invaluable assistance.

C. B.
R. W. B. L.
R. P. W.

Contents

5 The Moderns: Founders and Beyond (1914–1945) 1803

6 Experiments and Continuities: Some Instances in Our Time (1945 to the Present)   2859

4

The New Consciousness
1861–1914

In William Dean Howells' novel *A Traveler from Altruria*, a character, when asked who is the typical American hero, winds up his account of the shifting ideals of heroism from the Revolution on by saying: "That period [ending with the Civil War] passed and the great era of national prosperity set in. The big fortunes began to tower up, and heroes of another sort [than the military] began to appeal to our imagination. I don't think there is any doubt but the millionaire is now the American ideal."

When the Civil War began there were fewer than one hundred million-aires in the country. Fifteen years later, at the time of the Great Centennial of the Declaration of Independence, there were more than a thousand. The "ideal" could, it seemed, become real. Already in the period of Jackson, the American, as Tocqueville observed, was losing the European idea that busi-ness was degrading and not a worthy occupation for a man of birth, breed-ing, high intelligence, or ambition. By 1876, business was the main source in the country of prestige and power and was producing the "great" men. A decade earlier, in 1865, at the Harvard commemoration celebrating those who had died for the Union and freedom, Emerson said: "We shall not again disparage America, now that we have seen what men it will bear." He should have said, "what men it has borne." But he did not have the slightest notion of the breed of men that were soon to dominate America: Commodore Vanderbilt, Diamond Jim Brady, Jim Fisk, Dan'l Drew *et al.*

The literature we are about to consider belongs to the world in which, only a few years after Appomattox, President Grant, a hero who felt already outmoded, was ready to abase himself, in spite of his high office, before almost any stray millionaire and could wish no grander destiny for his son than that of a businessman. How was this new world different from the old that had ended when the first cannon ball hurtled toward Fort Sumter?

By 1866, when *Battle-Pieces* appeared, Melville, a good Unionist and an emancipationist who felt that the war had been waged for freedom, would ask, in the poem called "The Conflict of Convictions," what new forces the struggle would release and could say that history is a wind that sometimes "spins against the way it drives"; and he added that, with victory,

> Power unanointed may come—
> Dominion (unsought by the free)
>   And the Iron Dome [of the Capitol],
> Stronger for stress and strain,
> Fling her huge shadow athwart the main;
> But the Founder's dream shall flee.

In other words, Melville, with preternatural prescience, saw that the old order, with the democratic mystique for which it sought fulfillment in the war for the Union and emancipation, might well be destroyed by victory in the field.

The Union was, indeed, saved; and possessed incidentally the greatest supply of raw materials held by any nation in the world, and a vast market of some 3,500,000 square miles—almost the size of Europe—with a population, by 1900, of 76,000,000. The slaves were freed and then relegated defenselessly to the mercies of their erstwhile masters, who, in turn—along with a great many nonsoutherners, including middle-class farmers in the Middle West and the hordes of immigrants from Europe—were relegated, with almost equal defenselessness, to the mercies, and blessings, of the new order of big industry and finance capitalism. Appomattox, that is, had ushered in the great period of the development of the continent, and what that amounted to, in one perspective at least, was what we may call domestic imperialism, a process of extracting minerals and raw materials from the West, Middle West, and South and funneling the profits into the northeast corner of the continent, with as little as possible allowed to splash over, in the form of wages or social benefits, to the "colonial" regions.

The objective achievements of the new order, however, staggered the imagination. They exceeded, even, the dreams of the architects of that order. To begin with, the West was occupied and exploited. In 1861, once the refractory southern members were, by secession, out of Congress, the systematic development of the continent began—the transcontinental telegraph in 1861; the Homestead Act of 1862, which threw open the vast national holdings of land; in the same year, the definitive choice of the route for the first transcontinental railroad; and, in 1862, the beginning of a systematic military pressure on the western Indians—as though a war against the holders of black slaves weren't a full-time occupation. War or no war, population (including the young man who was to become Mark Twain) was unpatriotically pushing westward in such numbers that it is hard to imagine how the ranks of federal armies were kept filled—until one remembers that Europe was a vast reservoir of manpower, that the federal government paid attractive bounties for enlistment abroad, and that enough foreigners to constitute whole armies responded, with more than one hundred thousand coming from Ireland alone.

During the war, Kansas, West Virginia, and Nevada were admitted as states, and the territories of Dakota, Colorado, Arizona, Montana, and Idaho were organized; and, as mining boom after boom occurred, gold poured eastward during the war at an average of some fifty million dollars a year. By 1866, with the new know-how and organizational skills bred by the war and with, as the saying went, a dead Irishman (or Chinese on the western slope of the Rockies) for every crosstie, the actual construction of the first transcontinental railroad was under way at a spanking pace. By May 16, 1869, at Promontory Point, Utah, the last spike was driven home to connect the lines being pushed from east and west, and the impact of the sledge hammer was carried by telegraph wire to every important city in the country—which was now being welded into a new nation as much by that hammer blow as it had been, four years earlier, by the event at Appomattox. But even as other transcontinental railroads were in the making, the United States was expanding beyond old boundaries. In 1867, William H. Seward, Secretary of State, looking forward to the time when the Pacific might be an American lake, had bought Alaska from Russia, for the price of two cents an acre.

The West was won. By 1867, the "pacification" of the Indians, begun, as we have said, five years earlier, was being pushed with new energy under General Sheridan, of Civil War fame, who held that the only good Indian was a dead one; and with this the philosophy of the commander in the field (and of most of the civilian population), it scarcely mattered that, in a strange burst of candor not ordinarily found in official utterances, President Rutherford B. Hayes declared, in his message to Congress of 1877: "Many, if not most of our Indian wars have had their origin in broken promises and acts of injustice on our part." In 1889, at the battle (or massacre) of Wounded Knee, some 450 regulars, assisted by Indian scouts, broke the Sioux for good and all. Already the fabulous herds of buffalo, that self-renewing commissary of the Plains Indians, were gone, and the great herds of cattle on free range were soon to follow the buffalo, along with the cattle barons and cowboys; all disappeared before the advance of the barbed wire of sheep-raisers and farmers.

The Old West survived only in the dime novel and the Wild West shows, the most famous being that of Buffalo Bill—William Frederick Cody —with an entourage including Wild Bill Hickok, Annie Oakley (the fastest female gun on the plains), and Sitting Bull (the victor over Custer at the Little Big Horn). Geronimo, the wily and ferocious leader of the Apaches in their last uprising, after having been an attraction at the St. Louis World's Fair of 1894, was now an old man vegetating at Fort Sill, soon to become a Christian and join the Dutch Reformed Church. In 1912, the last of the western states, New Mexico and Arizona, were admitted to the Union. The population of the Old West, not including Texas and the states bordering on the Mississippi, was now eleven million.

The romance of the West was, however, surpassed by that of the East— the "romance of business," as it was called in the new world in which the Horatio Alger books promised every lad that by energy, honesty, faithful attention to duty, and a little luck with his pluck, he would someday be rich too. Meanwhile, by 1900, the United States, which in 1861 had enjoyed a merely provincial comfort, was rich, now outstripping the national wealth of the United Kingdom with something upward of seventy billion dollars— and could, as Carnegie put it, "buy up the Russians, Austrians, and Spaniards"; or after purchasing wealthy France would have pocket money to acquire Denmark, Norway, Switzerland, and Greece. It was a world in which a great new structure of corporations and financial organizations had sprung up. By the turn of the century, with the Spanish-American War, and with the gospel of William Seward, Rudyard Kipling, and Admiral Mahan (the author of *The Influence of Sea Power upon History*) ringing in its ears, the United States had entered the arena of international power, and in 1906 the victorious fleet of new dreadnaughts showed the flag in the great ports of the world. By now, too, the United States, which had been a debtor nation (the expansion after the Civil War having been largely financed by foreign capital), was entering upon its own credit operations, J. P. Morgan having floated, in 1901, a loan of fifty million dollars for Great Britain to support the imperialistic venture of the Boer War; and shortly afterward the Japanese were to come to New York for money to support their war with Russia. The straws were in the wind.

Meanwhile, the physical face of the country had changed almost unrecognizably (though not as unrecognizably as had the spiritual geography). In 1861 America had been a land of farms, plantations, and villages, with only a few cities. By 1900 less than 40 percent of the population was on farms. New York City, with some six hundred thousand inhabitants in 1861, now had upward of three million. Chicago, with only some thirty thousand inhabitants in 1861, had spectacularly passed the mark of one million. And there were the great new industrial cities like Pittsburgh and Cleveland. The nature of the population, too, had changed. The English and Scots names were becoming rare in many places. In the Middle West, as Willa Cather would show in her Nebraska tales, there were masses of Germans, Scandinavians, and Irish, but the eastern cities and industrial centers were full of Irish, Poles, Italians, Greeks, and Jews from Eastern Europe. On the West Coast there were the Chinese and the Japanese. It was the time of the great unrestricted immigration, with almost twenty-three million foreigners pouring into the United States between 1860 and 1910.

There was, in short, a vast new technology, a vast new social and industrial system, a vast new wealth, and a vast new population. It was a land in which a vast drama, involving profound and often secret forces, was working itself out, and the literature to which we shall shortly turn is both the record and the fruit of that age.

The new order, of course, had roots in the old. From the start, the Americans had been, perforce, "tinkerers" and inventors, and if they were not themselves notable scientists, they quickly recognized the profit that science could make possible. By 1861 the mills and manufacturing techniques that were to supply the Union armies were already available. The McCormick reaper was already on the flat wheatlands of the Middle West, ready to feed those armies. Already the railroads were unifying the country and were to do as much as any other single factor to save the Union—for instance, most dramatically by guaranteeing the victory at Gettysburg, where General Haupt threw, overnight, his rails up to the battle line to supply the federal batteries that were blazing away, not missing a beat, while the Confederate guns were silent from lack of ammunition. Already there had been a systematic and scientific exploration, by federal and state governments, of deposits of iron, coal, and other minerals. And already the great thrust westward, to occupy the lands seized from Mexico, was in full swing.

The war, of course, did provide a terrific stimulus to inventiveness, to the expansion of industrial plants, and to the exploiting of resources; but perhaps even more importantly, it created a great school for organization and management. When Charles Francis Adams, the wartime ambassador to England, came back home, he remarked on the "greatly enlarged grasp of enterprise and increased facility for combination." And he added: "The great operations of war, the handling of large masses of men, the influence of discipline, the lavish expenditure of unprecedented sums of money, the immense financial operations, the possibilities of effective cooperation were lessons not likely to be lost on men quick to receive and to apply new ideas." The lessons were, indeed, not lost, and as Howells was later to put it, the "war for freedom" was quickly replaced by the "war for the dollar."

The most obvious nexus between the old and the new orders was a sense of expansive optimism, which expressed itself generally in the hopeful restlessness and rootlessness of a population now brimming westward over a rich continent: politically in the old, but newly flourishing, doctrine of manifest destiny (to instruct the world in democratic virtue and to occupy, use, and, incidentally, redeem such parts of the world as seemed desirable); and theologically, after the first rigors of Puritanism were overpassed, in the notion that evil did not exist or, existing, could be disposed of with new techniques, that evil was—as Emerson, according to Henry James, had held— "merely the mumps and measles of the soul, belonging to the childhood of the race." In this expansive optimism, most Americans were inclined to agree with what the historian George Bancroft had earlier said, that "Every thing is in motion, and for the better." The law of life—at least for America—was progress. Organically connected with this optimism was, of course, the individualism inculcated from the first by the American world and by American thought.

There were more particular relations between the new age and the old theology. Long since, Cotton Mather had said that a man must have twin callings, "to serve Jesus Christ" and to pursue his "certain *Particular Employment*," and that the two callings are like the two oars of a boat—a man must pull both oars to reach the "Shoar of Eternal Blessedness." In short, work was not next to Godliness; it was equal to Godliness in the progress toward "blessedness." But long before Mather Protestantism, as certain historians hold, had inculcated the virtues that make for the acquisition of wealth. In the heyday of the new prosperity after the Civil War, the president of Yale, Noah Porter, along with President James McCosh of Princeton, President Mark Hopkins of Williams, and battalions of lesser clergymen, philosophers, and other intellectual yes men, would hymn the Godliness of gainful pursuits, and the "Gospel of Wealth"—as Andrew Carnegie was to call it. "Even a selfish getting of prosperity" was to be preferred over "selfish indolence," as Hopkins said, and by the end of the century Bishop Lawrence of Massachusetts, paraphrasing Emerson in a new context (see p. 347), summed up everything: "Godliness is in league with riches. . . . Material prosperity is helping to make the national character sweeter, more joyous, more unselfish, more Christlike." In fact, the bishop, like many other Americans, held the good Calvinist view that "Godliness" was not only "in league with riches," but that riches were the evidence of Godliness: "In the long run, it is only to the man of morality that wealth comes." So if God, in his wisdom and justice, decreed wealth for Jim Fisk, familiarly known as the "Skunk of Wall Street," it was impiety for anyone—the government included —to try to tamper with that wealth. In fact, the God-assigned role of government was to protect wealth.

Furthermore, there emerged a very important corollary to the notion that wealth was the result of God's decree and was a mark of the "man of morality": poverty was, by the same line of reasoning, also the result of God's decree and was very likely to be the mark of the man of immorality—whom one might think twice before helping, or at least helping too much. There was, of course, such a thing as Christian charity, and this contradictory notion did complicate matters, as did the notion that God might, after all, have given the wealth merely to be used for His glory and the good of mankind: that, in other words, the wealthy man was responsible for his stewardship—an idea that, without the theological underpinnings, had been held by Benjamin Franklin, as well as by Cooper. (See p. 284.) But the contradiction between the idea that poverty is the mark of immorality and the dictates of Christian charity was usually resolved in a practical American fashion. In the process of getting, God clearly intended you to go the limit; in the process of spending, you might act for the social good—so long as you didn't, of course, alter society in such a way as to make future getting impossible, or even too difficult.

Education, in one form or another, was the primary object of philanthropy, for education gave the young man of talent, energy, and, of course, morality a chance to get ahead—to justify the system by his success. So with Carnegie we see, on the one hand, the bloody July 6 of the Homestead strike[1] and, on the other, a Carnegie library in almost every city. Or with Rockefeller, on the one hand, the grim history of Standard Oil and, on the other, the University of Chicago, the monument to Rockefeller's munificence, to whose first graduating class the great philanthropist stated: "The

---

[1] The American Federation of Labor, through its affiliate the Amalgamated Iron, Steel, and Tin Workers Union, struck the Homestead mill of the Carnegie Steel Company in Pittsburgh in 1892. The strike was intended both to obtain higher wages for the workers and to demonstrate the new union's power. (It had been organized in 1890.) There was armed conflict between the strikers and Pinkerton detectives and guards hired by the company to protect the mill, and the strike was broken when troops from the Pennsylvania National Guard came in on the side of management. The labor union was virtually destroyed, and Henry C. Frick, the plant manager, cabled Andrew Carnegie in Europe: "Our victory is now complete. . . . Do not think we will ever have any serious labor trouble again."

good Lord gave me the money, and how could I withhold it from the University of Chicago?"

Another force, quite antithetical to religion as such, coalesced with Protestant theology and morality to confirm the new order. Scientific thought more and more shifted emphasis from the qualitative to the quantitative, to what could be objectively measured: the proof of the pudding now was conceived to be, not in the eating of the pudding, but in the weighing of it. Since morality naturally involves qualitative judgment, the new line of thought clearly implied that the world was to be accepted as amoral, that is, quantitative. Furthermore, the idea of scientific determinism also tended to bleach the world of moral value. If the world was proceeding by certain natural laws in an immutable course, how could life, including economic and social events, be otherwise than it was at any given moment? And so the idea of natural law and that of God's will amounted to the same justification of wealth and of the means of its acquisition, with the corollary that government was to defend rather than tamper with wealth. Hence, in the new order, Thomas Jefferson, with his notion of nature as happily self-regulating and of man in nature so basically good that the least government was the best (see pp. 115–16), would find himself with some embarrassing company.

Another idea justified even more specifically the status quo—that offered by Herbert Spencer, the enormously influential English philosopher of the "survival of the fittest": "The poverty of the incapable, the distresses that come upon the imprudent, the starvation of the idle, and those shoulderings aside of the weak by the strong, which leave so many 'in shallows and in miseries,' are the decrees of a large, far-seeing benevolence." Society must purge itself of "its unhealthy, imbecile, slow, vacillating, faithless members" and must suppress all impulse toward sentimental pity and self-indulgent charity.

Spencer's "far-seeing benevolence" was in itself too abstract to carry the authority of a wealth-distributing God, but Spencer's key idea of the survival of the fittest was to receive, several years after its formulation, a sudden authority that even God could no longer match. In 1859 Charles Darwin's *The Origin of Species* appeared, to be followed in 1871 by *The Descent of Man*; so the speculations of the philosopher were given, presumably, the factual validation of the scientist, with even a monitory note on the destructive consequences of sympathy and charity in the civilized world that might work, as Darwin himself suggested, against the law of nature.

If the law of nature gives victory to the strong and disposes of the weak, on what basis could the fact be criticized? If Darwin, a decent man, might turn an appalled gaze on the ice-blooded Dan'l Drew or the full-fleshed and concupiscent Jim Fisk, those worthies might reply that they, in an amorality as innocent as that of a hungry wolf, were only exercising their creative freedom as creatures of nature—that, in fact, they were his own devoted disciples. But what primarily emerges here, we must emphasize, is not an irony at the expense of Darwin; we find, rather, that the situation is merely an example of the great overarching problem of that age—and of our own— the problem of how to establish values on a naturalistic basis.[2]

So to the scientific emphasis on quantity and to the notion of natural determinism Darwin added the specific picture of a merciless and amoral struggle, in which the victor needed no justification beyond the fact of victory. And if the spoils belonged to the victor, it was really superfluous to say anything about his having them in stewardship from God; the spoils were, simply, his, with no strings attached. The doctrine was succinctly put by President McCosh of Princeton, a student of philosophy in his scholarly role: "Under the same head [that of theft] may be placed all purposes [of government] to deprive us of the right to earn property or use it as we see fit."

What we observe here is that both the old religion (what there was left of it) and the new science were used to justify the doctrine of laissez-faire— which meant the franchise of the new breed to do exactly what they liked. As Frank Algernon Cowperwood, the hero of Dreiser's novels about business, *The Financier* and *The Titan*, says: "I satisfy myself." In 1879, one of the new breed, William H. Vanderbilt (son of the old commodore), said of his own kind:

> You can't keep such men down. . . . I don't believe that by any legislative enactment or anything else, through any of the States or all of the States, you can keep such men down. You can't do it!

And nothing did keep them down. They were, as Matthew Josephson has called them, the Robber Barons. They raped a continent and often left an irremediable natural ruin behind them. They mounted monstrous swindles and indulged in stock-jobbery that, over and over, left millions of people bankrupt. They suborned public officials, they infected the White House, they bought Congressmen like sacks of potatoes (with the able help of Sam Ward, "King of the Lobby" and brother of Julia Ward Howe, the

---

[2] Melville's *Billy Budd*, begun in 1885, and which we have discussed at length elsewhere, provides, in the dilemma faced by Vere, a dramatic illustration of the problem we have posed hypothetically for Darwin. But Melville characteristically heightens the ambiguities (and ironies) of the problem by offering as the figure to be judged not a Drew, or a Fisk, or a Claggart, but Billy, whose amorality is not that of the wolf but of the lamb.

author of "The Battle Hymn of the Republic"), stole public lands and embezzled public funds, ruthlessly attempted to suppress the aspirations of labor, made the very idea of democracy a matter of obscene mirth, and brought the rule of law into general contempt. Before the Civil War was over, Lincoln had had forebodings of what big combinations of business would bring about, and as early as 1871 Walt Whitman could write: "The depravity of the business classes of our country is not less than has been supposed, but infinitely greater"; and he declared that around him in America he saw a "dry and flat Sahara," relieved only by "cities, crowded with petty grotesques, malformations, phantoms, playing meaningless antics."

The Robber Barons, who had created and ruled this Sahara envisioned by Whitman, were, in fact, the final flower of the individualism that had been demanded from the first for survival in the American world. Emerson's essay "Self-Reliance" had been the glittering rhetorical spume flung up by this tumultuous, streaming actuality of that world, and now in the new world it provided another ideal justification for what the strong man was going to do anyhow, willy-nilly. And the gentle Emerson, who had grandly declared, "Let man stand erect, go forth and possess the universe," lived on into the time when Diamond Jim Brady and Jim Fisk took his advice quite literally and exhibited the success of his doctrine to a pitch appallingly beyond his wildest dreams. Emerson found himself a little like the poor woman in the fairy tale whose wishes come distortedly and disastrously true.

There seems to have been an exhaustion of moral energy after the Civil War, a tendency among northern men of good will, liberal instincts, and high ideals to take their ease in the Zion of the Emancipation Proclamation and the Fourteenth Amendment and to make little protest even when, in 1877, a political deal between the Republicans and Democrats made Rutherford B. Hayes President in payment for the federal abandonment of the black freedom in the South.[3] A certain number of men of good will even learned to accept some of the concrete benefits of the new order.

[3] The end of Reconstruction, signaled by the Compromise of 1877 and the withdrawal of federal troops from the South, was not an isolated event prompted by political considerations. In spite of Confederate piety or bitterness and of the perennial waving of the "Bloody Shirt" up North, a strong sentiment for reconciliation was arising. Even with the Reconstruction, the attitude of Lee must have had some effect in the South, and more and more northerners desired to rebuild a nation rather than occupy a conquered province, and by 1900, in the first roll call for the newly established Hall of Fame, Lee was chosen by the board of one hundred distinguished electors—but received only sixty-eight votes against Daniel Webster's ninety-six (a total also exceeding Jefferson's). By 1907 Charles Francis Adams, whose father had been the United States minister to the Court of St. James and who himself had commanded

But the exhaustion of moral energy was not universal. We have already seen in Whittier, in spite of his inability to grasp the social and economic issues of the new age, a real sense of the need, expressed in *Snow-Bound*, to find some human continuity with the past and to maintain a human community, and in Melville's *Clarel* an awareness of the inner contradictions and complications of the age. In the same year as the publication of *Clarel*, the year of the Centennial Celebration of the birth of the United States, Brooks Adams (a son of the elder Charles Francis and a brother of Henry) made a Fourth of July address at Taunton, Massachusetts, in which he demanded: "Can we look over the United States and honestly tell ourselves that all things are well with us?" And he answered his question: "We cannot conceal from ourselves that all things are not well." And the same year Lowell, in the "Ode" he wrote for the Centennial, reported on the national scene:

> Show your new bleaching process, cheap and brief,
> To wit; a jury chosen by the thief,
> Show your State Legislatures; show your Rings,
> And challenge Europe to produce such things
> As high officials sitting half in sight
> To share the plunder and to fix things right.

As Kenneth Stampp, the author of a corrosive interpretation of slavery, says:

The Yankees went to war animated by the highest ideals of the nineteenth-century middle classes. . . . But what the Yankees achieved—for their generation at least—was a triumph not of middle-class ideals but of middle-class vices. The most striking products of their crusade were the shoddy aristocracy

---

a black regiment in the war, delivered the Lee Centennial Address at Washington and Lee University and declared, in effect, that the reconciliation of the North and South had been consummated, that if Lee were to be classed as a traitor, then names such as Washington and Jefferson would have to be similarly classified.

Various motives besides the mere desire for re-union had entered into the reconciliation. Disgust with the Reconstruction had made a number of northerners wonder if the freeing of the slaves had been worth the expense of blood and treasure. Disgust, too, with the moral temper of the world that the war had brought forth made a man like Ambrose Bierce (see pp. 1626–29) feel like taking the hand of a dead Confederate and apologizing, or made other writers such as Melville (in *Clarel*), Henry James (in *The Bostonians*), and Henry Adams (in *Democracy*) put the ex-Confederate into their work—in much the same spirit that Cooper had put Chingachgook in the Leatherstocking tales—in a heroic role to give a contrast to the sleaziness of contemporary life (see pp. 286–89). With the war safely won, there was, too, a sentimental relish for tales of the Old South and the plantation myth (see pp. 1687–88). In the end, the black freedman got pretty well forgotten.

of the North and the ragged children of the South. Among the masses of Americans there were no victors, only the vanquished.

And in *The Oxford History of the United States*, Samuel Eliot Morison has written of his native region, New England: "In the generation to come after the Civil War, that region would no longer furnish the nation teachers and men of letters, but with a mongrel breed of politicians, sired by abolition out of profiteering."

Brooks Adams, like his father and brother, suffered deep moral offense from what he saw around him, but the distaste of men like Lowell and the Adamses carried also another kind of revulsion; they were appalled by the ignorance, the grossness of manner, the ostentation, the lack of respect for intellect, and the simple and glaring defects in taste among men of what Charles Eliot Norton, of Harvard, termed "barbaric wealth." Of such men Charles Francis Adams, the younger, could later say: "I have known, and known tolerably well, a good many 'successful' men—'big' financially—men famous during the last half-century; and a less interesting crowd I do not care to encounter."

Some of the "successful" men might, indeed, be cultured, or like Carnegie might respect culture and seek out such acquaintances as Herbert Spencer, Matthew Arnold, and Mark Twain. Others might at least regard intellect as a social ornament, as did even Commodore Vanderbilt, who confessed: "I've been to England, and seen them lords, and other fellows, and knew that I had twice as much brains as they had maybe, and yet I had to keep still, and couldn't say anything through fear of exposing myself." But the men of "barbaric wealth" were, by and large, barbarians, and the thin blue-blooded line of American aristocracy tended to be too thin-blooded to overawe and civilize its plutocracy, as the ruling class in England had more or less managed to do.

The difference, as Henry Adams was to find out (see pp. 1474–78), was that the American aristocracy was *not* the ruling class. It had pride without place, and wealth without power, for what wealth it had was merely genteel comfort in comparison to the towering wealth of the new men. So the aristocrat's personal standards of intellect or morality could scarcely impress a financial titan like Drew, who, as he put it, "never took" to "schooling," and blandly added: "I always got spelled down the very first time around. But I never minded that very much."

The northern aristocracy (the southern was too poor to count) tended to withdraw into the citadels of culture—that is, those among them who cultivated the life of the mind—and cut themselves off from their place and time, and took solace in the Middle Ages, as did Henry Adams and Charles

Eliot Norton, or in Catholicism, or in the elegant if sometimes vapid poetry of a Trumbull Stickney or George Cabot Lodge. At the same time, there was the exception in Henry James,[4] who, though flinching from much of American life—and indeed from much of life in general—and though taking refuge in Europe and in class isolation, yet had the energy to revolutionize the art of the novel.

Disgust with the new order was not confined, however, to certain members of the old aristocracy. As we have seen, the very prophet of democracy, Walt Whitman, was appalled by the moral collapse of America. Melville wrote *Clarel*, and Mark Twain, who in one half of his nature dearly loved a multimillionaire and tried to be a Robber Baron himself, was to write, with Charles Dudley Warner, the novel called *The Gilded Age*, which gave the period its name and, in the course of the story, presented a fictional (but all too painfully true) newspaper item:

> We are reminded of a note which we received from the notorious burglar Murphy, in which he finds fault with a statement of ours to the effect that he has served one term in the penitentiary and also one in the U.S. Senate. He says, "The latter statement is untrue and does me great injustice."

Coupled with moral disgust there was, too, the fear of the practical consequences of an order in which chicanery, manipulation of law, and unrestrained rapacity were dominant. The poverty and degradation of the slums and the oppression of labor began to be recognized generally. William Dean Howells experienced something like a religious conversion when he read Tolstoi's tract *What to Do*—an account of how, in Moscow, his eyes had been opened to the hideous injustice of modern industrial society; and thereafter the temper of Howells' own work drastically changed. Edward Bellamy wrote, in 1888, a novel, *Looking Backward: 2000–1887*, which with its utopian depiction of a rational world offered a shocking contrast to the "inferno of poverty beneath our civilization" and by that contrast gave new stimulation to the impulse to reform that had already been inflamed by Henry George, with his program of the single tax. *Looking Backward* became, in fact, a sort of latter-day version of *Uncle Tom's Cabin*, directed not at the evil of chattel slavery but of the general economic and social enslavement.

It was the middle class that had its conscience aroused by writers like Bellamy and the reports of the muckrakers (see pp. 1213–14) of their findings in the slums and mines; but the middle class had more than generosity of spirit to stimulate its interest in reform. It was caught between the "tower-

---

[4] James, actually, was not of the old aristocracy.

ing fortunes" on one hand and by what it took to be the revolutionary turbulence of labor on the other. William Graham Sumner, one of the founders of modern sociology and a staunch exponent of social Darwinism, called the ordinary middle-class citizen the "Forgotten Man"—the phrase later and somewhat differently used in the Depression, by Franklin Delano Roosevelt. The middle-class virtues of thrift and rectitude were of no avail in a society where the economic system was at the mercy of irresponsible buccaneers.

All urban industrial workers, in a way never known before, were more or less defenseless against the anonymous power of the great corporations. The misery of labor moved many hearts that were higher in the social scale, but a critical factor in change was labor's own will to organize and resist. In the 1870's began the Noble Order of the Knights of Labor, intended to draw all workingmen, of all categories and origins, into one powerful fraternal organization for mutual betterment. The educational role of the Knights was enormous, but it was badly led, and it was the American Federation of Labor, the result of the secession of skilled workers led by Samuel Gompers, that gave the cutting edge to the labor movement.

The strike and the doctrine of the closed shop were the practical weapons, but Gompers aimed at practical gains as well as at the restoration of the sense of freedom and dignity that had belonged to the old America. And this involved another old idea, that men must assume responsibility for their own fate: "Doing for people what they can and ought to do for themselves is a dangerous experiment," Gompers maintained, and the union was the weapon by which the powerless individual facing the great combinations of wealth could achieve manhood. What is important to observe here is that Gompers' theory was based on the idea of competition—fair competition, of course, as guaranteed by the government—and not on any idea of subsidy. Basically, it was a transference of the old doctrine of individualism into the context of the new industrial organization; but Gompers, by advocating the closed shop, did challenge the absolutism of ownership, and thus flew directly in the face of President McCosh and others who, validating individualism by divine fiat, held that the wealthy man's right to control and dispose of his wealth was inalienable.

The rise of labor was slow and bloody, marked notably by the famous Haymarket riot of 1886, the railroad strikes of 1877, the Homestead steel strike of 1892, and the Pullman strike of 1894. Such events entered folklore, but the spectacular events were not as important in the end as the slow overall process by which labor gained its status and the strike became an accepted feature of American life; for example, before the end of the century there was an average of more than five thousand strikes a year, big and little. By that time, the relation of labor and capital had become a standard subject in American literature.

The situation of the farmer was, in this period, somewhat more complex than that of any other class. The farmer—not the sharecropper or farm laborer—was traditionally an independent entrepreneur, in his small or large way, with his small or large mortgage. He was a capitalist, even if a peculiarly vulnerable one. He had been, too, the ideal citizen in Jefferson's conception of society, but now, in the age of the great urban expansion, the status of that ideal citizen sank precipitately in the social scale, and the erstwhile hero of Jefferson became the "hick," the "rube," the simpleton at whom any guttersnipe would feel obligated to sneer. The change did not reflect merely an economic shift, but a profound and complex psychological shift; after all, the guttersnipe, however penniless, would sneer at a rich farmer[5] (such as Daniel Webster, Henry Clay, or Andrew Jackson had been) as readily as at a poor one like Jeeter Lester (see pp. 2480–81), and only in parts of New England and the South did the old association of land and status (with various sectional differences) continue. In the Gilded Age a farmer, no matter how well off, began to feel himself declassed; but he also began to know himself poor, by and large, and getting poorer. In 1867, a year after Whittier's *Snow-Bound* had celebrated the old agrarian virtues and blisses, farmers found it necessary to found the society of the Patrons of Husbandry —the Grange—and to salve the wounded ego by singing

> The farmer's the chief of the nation,
> The oldest of nobles is he.

But the Grange was almost as powerless against the economic system as against the weather. Increasing miseries led to the more direct political action known as Populism, a general revolt against not only the most obvious enemy, the railroads, but against the "monopolies," the "trusts," the "interests," Wall Street, and the gold standard: "We have witnessed," the Populists declared, "for more than a quarter of a century the struggles of two great political parties for power and plunder." But by 1896, with William Jennings Bryan[6] as candidate for President, Populism and the Democratic party merged.

---

[5] The rancher, because of the romance of the Far West, was for a long time spared the city man's contempt. But the western farmer of the late nineteenth century was not spared. In reviewing Hamlin Garland's *Main-Travelled Roads* (1891), William Dean Howells could write: "The stories are full of those gaunt, grim, sordid, pathetic, ferocious figures, whom our satirists find so easy to caricature as Hayseeds and whose blind gropings for fairer conditions is so grotesque to the newspapers. . . ."

[6] See Vachel Lindsay's poem on Bryan (pp. 1853–55) as an indication of the enormous emotional appeal that he exercised as the hero of Populism and reform.

The whole of American society was suffering the strains, dislocations, and injustices of the explosive development of an industrial order; but perhaps an even more fundamental strain, a psychological and even physiological strain, in adapting to the age of the machine, in particular, and to the shocking effects of the age of science, in general. Historians, notably Brooks Adams in *The Law of Civilization and Decay* of 1895 (and Karl Marx, more notably), were thinking in terms of irreversible processes at work in society. Writing of Europe, Adams saw that process as one in which the dispersed agricultural population is drawn into the constantly growing cities to become the victims of usurious wealth, mercilessly exploited, this stage being followed by social and moral decay and collapse. Even for those who did not accept an iron law of history, the situation described by Brooks Adams (and accepted by his brother Henry) seemed painfully close to what was actually happening in the United States.

Among thinking men there was growing alarm and among the unthinking there was, more and more often, a blank misery. As early as 1877, Peter Cooper, who had built the first American locomotive, invented a washing machine, and made a fortune in industry, and now (anomalously for a capitalist) was running for President on the Greenback ticket,[7] warned his victorious Republican adversary Rutherford B. Hayes: "Millions of men and women, in this hitherto rich and prosperous country, have been thrown out of employment or living on precarious and inadequate wages, have felt embittered with a lot, in which neither economy nor industry, nor a cheerful willingness to work hard, can bring any alleviation." As distresses grew more acute, labor unions and Populism were only two of the many manifestations of the will to reform; there were all sorts of ideas afoot, socialism (in a spectrum from Marxist to Christian), single tax-ism (as we have already mentioned in connection with Henry George), anarchism, Greenback-ism, free silver-ism, and numberless minor prescriptions for utopia. In spite of the variety of these prescriptions, there was one underlying idea in all, that of the natural right of the individual man. That idea had to be restressed, for the nation had gone astray and forgotten the basic meaning of the Declaration of Independence.

It was not until 1901, when, by the assassination of the conservative William McKinley, the Vice President Theodore Roosevelt entered the White House, that the impulse to reform was "legitimized." Roosevelt was an aris-

---

[7] The Greenback party, sometimes called the National party, urged the payment of the national debt in greenbacks (the treasury notes issued during the Civil War not supported by specie), as a means of relieving the disastrous situation of those who had contracted debts in greenbacks during the war and were now compelled to pay in hard money.

tocrat by blood and education, an adventurer by temperament, and a Progressive Republican in politics—that is, a Republican who had absorbed some of the tenets of the reformers. Roosevelt was, indeed, an acute embarrassment to some of the stalwarts of his party; later, with the election of Woodrow Wilson, the tradition of reform passed into the sometimes unenthusiastic stewardship of the Democrats.

Before the Civil War the relation between the historical background and the literature of America was rather general and simple. There was variety, certainly; Hawthorne and Cooper are not concerned with the same things in their background, nor do they look at their particular concerns in the same way; and Emerson, repudiating the past, looked not to a "background" but to a "foreground"—literally, in the future. But even with the intensification of the issue of slavery, and with the Mexican War, the relation between literature and the background remained simple—we may even say oversimplified—partly because of the tendency to treat issues merely at a moral level, abstracted from contexts, but primarily because the world was simple, or at least was seen as simple.

After the Civil War, however, all was changed. There was a new complexity of economic organization, new social classes, more intricate tensions, new ethnic complexities, and all the moral and philosophical tensions and ironies introduced by the rise of science. And most of the issues came to focus on the new national hero, the businessman; it was only natural that he should be a center, and sometimes a storm center, of literature.

Most obviously the businessman and his role came in for treatment in the literature of history, politics, and polemics. Under the great pressure of events, the twin ideas of business as the salvation of society and business as the new form of romance or art were gravely modified; and by such works as *Progress and Poverty*, by Henry George (1879), *Wealth Against Commonwealth*, by Henry Demarest Lloyd (1894),[8] *History of the Great American Fortunes*, by Gustavus Myers (1910), *How the Other Half Lives*, by Jacob A. Riis (1890), *The Shame of the Cities*, by Lincoln Steffens (1904), and the general contributions of the "muckrakers" to such magazines as *Cosmopolitan, Munsey's*, and *McClure's*.

But fiction grew out of the same general social situation. We have already mentioned Mark Twain's *The Gilded Age*, but in a sense *A Connecticut Yankee in King Arthur's Court* is, as we shall see, even more important.

---

[8] As early as 1881, in the *Atlantic*, under the editorship of Howells, Lloyd's article "The Story of a Great Monopoly" (Standard Oil) had been the first major assault on the methods of the great new corporations. It made a tremendous sensation.

And there were almost numberless other works, including *Sevenoaks* (1875), by Josiah Gilbert Holland, a story based on the career of Jim Fisk; *McTeague* (1899), *The Octopus* (1901), and *The Pit* (1903), by Frank Norris; *The Rise of Silas Lapham* (1885) and *A Hazard of New Fortunes* (1890), by William Dean Howells; *Looking Backward* (1888), by Edward Bellamy; *Maggie: A Girl of the Streets* (1893), by Stephen Crane; *The American* (1876), by Henry James; *The Iron Heel* (1907), by Jack London; *The Jungle* (1906), by Upton Sinclair; *The Financier* (1912) and *The Titan* (1914), by Theodore Dreiser; and *The Custom of the Country* (1913), by Edith Wharton.

The literature of analysis or protest, or fiction that takes the businessman or economic conditions as its focus, was simply the work most obviously treating the period. But when we come to William James and his philosophy of pragmatism or to his successor John Dewey, we find a way of thinking that reflects the new scientists' skepticism about large general ideas and the scientific respect for fact; that yet on the other hand has been associated with the practical bias of American life and is sometimes said to be the only indigenously developed school of philosophy.

Not as a result of this philosophy, but as an associated development, we find the rise of realism in fiction—and later in poetry. Realism, as concerning literature, may be taken in two senses, in relation to technique and in relation to content. As a technique, it refers simply to the means of giving a work the impression of "reality." Even in a most fantastic story, for example, the details of houses, of clothing, of landscape, of human faces, may be rendered with great fidelity to nature—that is, "realistically." In reference to content, realism implies a preference for the here and now, instead of the far away and long ago, for material drawn from common life, for ordinary people facing ordinary problems. Realistic literature may be very powerful and may evoke deep feeling, even tragic intensity, but it does so by presenting the natural, the commonplace. It thrives on fidelity to fact—the physical fact, the social fact, and the psychological fact.

As an aside, but as one necessary to the understanding of realism, it should be remarked that realism is not instinctive and primary and that it does not characteristically emerge early in human history. Early literature tends to deal with the marvelous, the terrible, the mysterious, the miraculous, the sense of powers beyond human pitch and is not, generally, concerned with the commonplace. To look at the matter in another way, the settlers who came to America were not a primitive people, and the literature

—to take the English—they left behind, that of the Elizabethan age, had strong realistic elements; but for a variety of reasons, and in spite of the hard-driven and hard-driving practicality of much American life, realism as a literary mode emerged later here than in England or France: Balzac died in France in 1850, a year before Hawthorne published *The Scarlet Letter*, and Flaubert, another great French realistic novelist, published *Madame Bovary* in 1858, before *The Marble Faun* appeared. When realism did officially appear in America, with the work of William Dean Howells, it was of a rather timid order. It was not until the 1890's, when the movement in France and England had run its course, that realism here, with Stephen Crane, Frank Norris, and Theodore Dreiser, was finally established, and even then there was great popular resistance to it.

Since realism represents a respect for fact as fact rather than a concern for the imaginative and symbolic, close observation, logicality, impersonality, and precision rank high among the virtues of the realistic writer. It is easy to see how such a literature would thrive in a period of grim social struggle, with issues of poverty and political abuses, and to see how it would blend into the reportage of the muckraking journalist. In fact, Crane and Dreiser were both journalists exploring the life of the slum long before they were novelists; they drew their fictional impulse from the world of fact. The novelist Henry B. Fuller (*The Cliff-Dwellers*, 1892, and *With the Procession*, 1895) even declared that to be in the spirit of the age writers should give up fiction altogether and create a literature of "fact," preferably biography. (See pp. 1356–57.)

The big underlying development behind realism was, of course, the rise of science. Indeed, in the specialized development of realism called naturalism, science was avowedly taken as the model for the novelist. The French novelist Emile Zola, the theorist if not the founder of naturalism, says in his essay "The Experimental Novel" (1893) that the "naturalistic evolution which marks this [the nineteenth] century, drives little by little all the manifestations of human intelligence into the same scientific path." He argues that the "experimental novelist is one who accepts proven facts, who points out in man and in society the mechanism of the phenomena over which science is mistress, and also does not interpose his personal sentiments, except in the phenomena whose determinism is not yet settled . . . by observation or experiment."

Zola's own practice, no more than that of other naturalistic novelists (notably Norris and Dreiser in the United States), carried out his prescription, and in spite of his elaborate technical researches for background, his novels were often highly charged with "personal sentiment" and tended toward the method of symbolism. But this did not mean that work in the naturalistic mode was not original and strong; the naturalists did open up new subject matter, especially in the lower reaches of society, did take a more analytical view of the social structure and broadened the base of sympathy, did explore new psychological dimensions—as we find in Dreiser's work—and did shift the center of gravity of style further from the strictly literary tradition toward common speech.

Simultaneously with the rise of realism (and naturalism), another impulse of great importance was emerging in American fiction—the concern with the novel as an art form. The impulse had its first manifestation, both in practice and related theory, in France, with Flaubert as the master of the school, and it was under French influence that it made its way into American literature, by way of Henry James.

Of course, any novel that hangs together at all, that has a more or less coherent action and makes a point, has a form; without a form it would be neither comprehensible nor interesting. But there is an obvious difference between, say, one of the Leatherstocking novels by Cooper and a novel by Henry James. In Cooper there is a rather direct, straight-line narrative interest, with the relations among characters simply stated, without subtlety of shading or development, and with style regarded primarily as a medium of factual communication. In a novel by James there are, characteristically, very subtle balancings of proportion among the elements of plot, very complicated interrelations among characters, with the point of the narrative often residing in a reordering of relationships, with the awareness of a character often the determinant of the angle from which narrative is given, and with the style itself regarded as expressive and as a device for the control of the feelings of the reader.

It is true, of course, that some writers of earlier periods, notably Hawthorne in American literature, exhibited a fine sense of novelistic form well before the rise of Flaubert and James; but such writers were exceptional and certainly did not embody a tradition.

What we have said should not be taken to imply that there was a necessary split between the realists and the writers working in the tradition of the art novel. If the elegant world of which James wrote and his highly developed, and sometimes mannered, style seem to set him off from the realists, it is yet true that he was a master of psychological realism; and if Hemingway wrote of low life, he was a devotee of the gospel of style who regarded formal discipline as having a moral significance. Between the realistic impulse and that of the art novel, we should see not so much a split as the relationship between the opposing terms of a dialectic, and that dialectic contributes much to the vitality of our literature of the last hundred years.

Another literary development of the period is the paradoxical rise of both the idea of the "Great American Novel" and that of local color. After 1865, the United States was a nation in a new sense, as much from the new up-rootings, the new mobility, and the growth of big organization as from the political conception affirmed by the northern victory; and it was only natural that out of the epic military struggle and the epic of taming the continental distances the New American would expect an *Aeneid* for his new Rome.[9] The word "epic" grew common on literary lips. Frank Norris, in projecting his novel *The Pit*, wrote: "I think a big Epic *could* be made out of such a subject that at the same time would be modern and distinctly American." The idea was current and commanding not only among novelists, but among historians, from Theodore Roosevelt's *The Winning of the West* (1889–96) to Frederick Jackson Turner's "The Significance of the Frontier in American History" (1893).

The "Great American Novel" never got written, though the dream persisted into the 1920's, and even into the 1930's, with *An American Tragedy*, by Dreiser, *U.S.A.*, by John Dos Passos, and the work of Thomas Wolfe. Dreiser's book may be, in fact, the nearest thing to the "Great American Novel," simply because he avoided the trap of quantitative thinking—the notion of the "big," the inclusive, the "epic"—and tried to write the drama of a characteristic and pervasive value in American life, as we shall later see. But even though no single book can qualify as the great epic fiction of America, there was a new kind of writer. As Norris (in the essay "An American School of Fiction?") said of Howells, he was "at once a New Englander and a New Yorker, an Easterner and—in the Eastern sense—a Westerner," and his range of scene was as various, even reaching to Italy. But Howells himself pointed to the even more symbolic figure of his friend and idol Mark Twain, whom he called the "Lincoln of our literature"—southerner, westerner, easterner, world traveler, beloved by the world, the distinct "American" incarnate.

---

[9] The *Aeneid*, as the model epic of the founding of a great civilization, has appeared in the American consciousness in at least four periods. William Bradford and Cotton Mather, with the vision of heroic fugitives from the Old World crossing the waters to found a home in a New World, explicitly echoed it (see pp. 17–24; 29–31). After the Revolution, Joel Barlow wrote *The Columbiad* (see pp. 197–99) in direct imitation of Virgil, and George Bancroft, in his romantic *History of the United States*, envisaged America in the same terms (see p. 1126). As for the fourth period, the poet Hart Crane, in the midst of writing his "epic" of the American consciousness *The Bridge*, in a letter to his patron Otto Kahn, compared his enterprise to Virgil's.

At the same time that the new nationalism appeared, there was a rediscovery, with the school of local color, of the individual regions—which could be seen in a new light simply because of the new sense of bigness and unity. When Hawthorne said, in reference to the war for the Union, that New England was as big a country as he was able to embrace, he was not speaking as a local colorist: New England was, simply, what he happened to know. But another meaning creeps in, as we shall see, when we reach the work of Rose Terry Cooke, Mary E. Wilkins Freeman, and Sarah Orne Jewett, and their pictures of New England life. By that time, in the reader, if not necessarily in the writer, a condescension enters, a concern with the quaint, the cute, the antique, the primitive. But local color was found outside of New England—in the West, with Bret Harte as the most eminent practitioner, along with Mark Twain in *Roughing It*; in the Middle West, with Edward Eggleston (*The Hoosier Schoolmaster*, 1871), E. W. Howe (*The Story of a Country Town*, 1883), and Hamlin Garland (*Prairie Folk*, 1892, and *Main-Travelled Roads*, 1891); in the South, with George Washington Cable (*The Grandissimes*, 1880), Thomas Nelson Page (*In Ole Virginia*, 1887), and Joel Chandler Harris (*Uncle Remus: His Songs and His Sayings*, 1880, and *Nights with Uncle Remus*, 1883).

It is not to be understood that all writers using local color necessarily adopted the same attitude toward their material. Howe, in *The Story of a Country Town*, gives a grimly realistic account of the blighted hopes of men who had immigrated to the Middle West to work the rich land. In contrast to this, for instance, we find the romantic sentimentality of Bret Harte in the tales of mining camps in early California, and the humor of Harris's Uncle Remus, and the improbable daydreams of Thomas Nelson Page.

In the local-color fiction of the South (which became very popular in the post–Civil War North), and with the simultaneous criticism of southern society by southern writers (George Washington Cable, for instance), we find emerging the polarity of the southern literature that developed later as the voice of a clearly marked subculture, eventuating in the epic scheme of Faulkner's Yoknapatawpha County fictions. At the same time, with Paul Laurence Dunbar, Charles W. Chesnutt, and W. E. B. Du Bois, there is the beginning of the literature of another strongly marked subculture, that of black America, with a rich folk tradition and a formal literature that is now in the full tide of development.

There is one more aspect of the pluralism of American life. A folk literature of occupation—of railroading, of lumbering, of mining, of ranching— had entered very fruitfully into our formal literature, and has strongly tinged the American sensibility.

As a kind of footnote, we must remind ourselves that it is all too easy to be moralistic about history. The record of human events is, by and large, one of injustice, distress, suffering, oppression, and degradation—but the record is illuminated by flashes of courage, fortitude, generosity, and hope. We may detest some of the values, deeds, and consequences of the post–Civil War period in America, but, in the blundering and often tragic way that gains are made in history, it was a period of enormous energy, inventiveness, and achievement. We must ask ourselves how, given the context of the American world and of human nature in general, the process could have been different—and this question will throw us back upon the first principles of our philosophy, whatever that may be. We must remember that, within limits, the abuses of the age generated their own antidotes. There are, as William James said, no total solutions in history; as urgencies mount—as steam pressure builds up in the pot, to use his metaphor—the lid gets lifted a little, some steam escapes, and then the process starts over again; in the dialectic of historical events, any equilibrium is bound to be temporary. Each age has its special focus of both energy and moral urgency.

It is worth reminding ourselves, too, that many of the most violent critics of the values of the period—muckrakers like Ida Tarbell and Lincoln Steffens —had more than a sneaking admiration for the villains of the story. And Richard Hofstadter, in *The Progressive Historians*, writes of the divided mind of the historian Charles A. Beard:

> On one side there was Beard the reformer, the moralist, the rebel against authority, the young Beard of Oxford, the Beard who all his days loved the gadfly's role. . . . On the other side was the Beard of Knightstown [Beard's birthplace, in Indiana, where his father from penniless beginnings had made a small fortune], reared in solid Republicanism, himself strongly driven to achievement, a man who admired mastery and control.

Furthermore, both Mark Twain and Theodore Dreiser, who in literature have best rendered the drama of the age, were divided men, both highly ambivalent toward the age. If Mark Twain is the author of *The Gilded Age* and of the nostalgia and lyricism of *Huckleberry Finn*, he also yearned to be a great financial and industrial success and dearly loved the society of Robber Barons. *A Connecticut Yankee in King Arthur's Court* is, at the very core, a document of his ambivalence. Dreiser's life and work exhibit the same doubleness. In the final sense, that doubleness *is* the great drama of the age.

EMILY DICKINSON (1830–1886)

No one could seem more remote from the social turbulence and the crowding historical developments we have just surveyed than Emily Dickinson, the recluse poet of Amherst, Massachusetts. Yet as we shall see, her poetry took account of some of those matters on both superficial and deeper levels, and in certain important ways she was, intellectually, ahead of her time. To put it differently: though Emily Dickinson, who was born in 1830, was only eleven years younger than Whitman, and though she took to herself much of Emerson's theory of poetry and the imagination, in many respects she belongs—as a poet—to a later age, perhaps to our own.

She was much more innovative than Whitman. She experimented tirelessly with language: resurrecting old words, coining new ones, employing familiar terms in sometimes startlingly unfamiliar contexts. Conventional grammar and syntax, no less than conventional rhyming, gave way before the exigencies of her imagination. She shared in good part the Romantic admiration of the poet as hero and the Romantic concern with the relation between consciousness and nature. But her verse—with its sharp intellectual wit, its capacity to pack several different kinds of meaning into individual metaphors, its interplay of diverse vocabularies, and its profusion of paradox, ambiguity, and irony—has strong affinities with seventeenth-century English metaphysical poetry. It was, indeed, only in the course of the revival of interest in that body of poetry some fifty years ago that Emily Dickinson's work began to come into its own.

Her poetry reflects the modern and contemporary involvement with the shifting psychic state, and with the theme of identity—especially (as in "I felt a Funeral in my Brain") the fear of the loss of identity. And she is modern, or modernist, as well in her determination to leave open the available options—for example, between the grip of religious faith and the bite of skepticism. Add to that the literal fact, as we shall explain, that for a number of reasons her work became generally accessible only in quite recent years, and we are confronted, in Emily Dickinson, with a poet very much of our time.

But she was also, of course, a poet and a person very much of *her* own time. It was not only that Whitman, too, was absorbed by the vicissitudes of his inner being, or that Thoreau on occasion could display a talent for witty inversion and paradox ("What devil possessed me that I behaved so well?"), or that Emerson led the way in directing American literary attention back behind the Augustans to the writers of the seventeenth century (in his case, particularly the prose of Sir Thomas Browne), or that Melville was simultaneously immersing himself in Elizabethan and Jacobean dramatic verse. It was much more that her imagination, as here variously defined, worked on the cultural tradition into which she was born: New England Calvinist Christianity, at the moment when it was beginning to shred. In a poem called "The Robin's my Criterion for Tune," she explained that she sang of the American robin rather than of the English cuckoo "because I see— New Englandly"; and so she did. She saw with eyes trained by the world around her: by family and friends; by the town of Amherst, Massachusetts; by advances in science and technology (the laboratory, the railroad train); by the literary achievements and enthusiasms of the period; and most of all, to repeat, by her peculiar sensitivity (who can explain it?) to the fragmenting vision of Protestant orthodoxy. In a certain perspective, Emily Dickinson brought together in her poetry the past, the present, and the future of her country and its culture.

To Thomas Wentworth Higginson, her well-disposed but myopic literary mentor, Emily Dickinson remarked in 1870 that "I find ecstasy in living—the mere sense of living is joy enough." And Allen Tate, one of the first critics able to discern Emily Dickinson's genius, wrote in 1932 that "All pity for Miss Dickinson's 'starved life' is misdirected. Her life was one of the richest and deepest ever lived on this continent." These several remarks have to do with the sometimes unbearable intensity of the poet's interior life, but they were made out of an awareness that the facts of her external life were, at first glance, so meager as to arouse both pity and bewilderment.

In order to grasp that inner richness, the meager externals can be reduced to a few sentences. Emily Dickinson was born in Amherst, Massachusetts, and spent her entire life in the Dickinson family home there (two different homes, to be precise). She attended Amherst Academy for six years and the nearby Mount Holyoke Female Seminary for one year. She went occasionally to Springfield, a distance of about twenty-five miles, and a couple of times to Boston; in 1854 she spent three weeks in Washington and two more in Philadelphia. She died in 1886.

But Emily Dickinson, in her life as in her poetry, followed the injunctions of Emerson and Whitman (and to an extent the doctrine of Jonathan Edwards): she perceived and experienced the greatest richness, beauty, and terror in the familiar and the near-at-hand. She found miracles of meaning, exalted or anguished, in a bobolink, a bat, a hummingbird, a cricket; in a sermon, a shadow on the grass, the slanting light of a winter afternoon; in a buzzing fly, a traveling circus, the look on a dying man's face. She made out whole ranges of expressive human nature in the members of her closely knit family, in the small circle of friends and correspondents, in a valued acquaintance she never saw face to face but talked with around the corner of the upstairs hall, in a clergyman she seems not to have encountered more than three times in twenty-five years. The very pots and pans and aprons in the Dickinson kitchen were objects not only to be used, but to be experienced.

If a whaling ship, making its way through a series of extraordinary adventures across the far Pacific, had been (as he said) Melville's Harvard and his Yale, it might almost be said that Mount Holyoke Seminary and the town of Amherst were Emily Dickinson's whaling ship.

At the nationally known seminary, founded and run by the brilliant and redoubtable Miss Mary Lyon, Emily met girls from Canada and the American South, and from as far west as Iowa and Wisconsin. She became a great favorite with students and headmistress as well and excelled in the study of Latin and literature, as well as training in voice and piano. It was at the seminary, as we shall see, that she faced what was perhaps the most important religious crisis of her life; but it was here also that she was often seen surrounded by a group of classmates who gathered to hear her make up a series of very funny stories, as she could always do on the spot. Amherst, too, provided her with sources both of deepest meditation and of liveliest amusement, the latter sometimes tightening into piercing irony.

In 1851, an aurora borealis caused great excitement in the village, and Emily's father, one of the first to observe it, hurried over to the church and rang the bell violently to draw attention to the phenomenon. "The sky was a beautiful red, bordering on a crimson," Emily wrote her brother, "and rays of a gold pink color were constantly shooting off from a kind of sun in the center. . . . The exhibition lasted for nearly 15 minutes, and the streets were full of people wondering and admiring." Ten years later the memory of that spectacle became the basis of a stunning lyric poem, "Of Bronze—and Blaze," on the intricately meditated theme of visionary transcendence. At other times, Emily Dickinson took stock of the villagers. "There is that which is called an 'awakening' in the church," she informed a cousin in 1873, "and I know of no choicer ecstasy than to see Mrs. Sweetser roll out in crepe every morning. I suppose to intimidate antichrist; at least it would have that effect upon me. It reminds me of Don Quixote demanding the surrender of the wind-mill." And there is the merciless analysis of the pious gentlewomen of Amherst, with their dim horror of the carnal:

What Soft—Cherubic Creatures—
These Gentlewomen are—
One would as soon assault a Plush—
Or violate a Star—

"Father and mother sit in state in the sitting-room, perusing such papers, only, as they are well assured, have nothing carnal in them." The remark, made to her brother Austin in the early 1850's, is evidence enough that her family was not spared the wit Emily Dickinson visited upon outsiders. But in the case of her father, the wit was mixed with abiding affection and a sense of awe. Edward Dickinson came from many generations of Dickinsons in the Connecticut Valley (*his* father, Samuel Fowler Dickinson, had helped found both Amherst Academy and, in 1821, Amherst College). While he was at Yale, he met Emily Norcross, who was in a New Haven finishing school; and after he was admitted to the bar in 1826, they married. Edward Dickinson became one of Amherst's most distinguished and admired citizens. He was treasurer of Amherst College for almost four decades; served three terms in the Massachusetts legislature; was in the state senate, on the governor's council, and in 1852 a delegate to the Baltimore convention that attempted unsuccessfully to nominate Daniel Webster. He was a stern man, an eighteenth-century rationalist in the line rather of Edwards than of Franklin, and a person altogether committed to his duty to God, his family, and his community. To his daughter, Edward Dickinson was an immensely imposing figure, more than any other in her life. If she did not precisely see him as Godlike, she seems at least to have seen God as fatherlike: as in the several poems where she addresses God as a stern but watchful parent.

"Father steps like Cromwell when he gets the kindlings," Emily said; but she was fully aware of the gentleness that was hidden in his awesome nature, and the strength of his love for his children. "Father is as uneasy when you are gone away," she reported to her brother, "as if you catch a trout and put him in Sahara." After his death in 1874, she recalled that there had been severe snowstorms the winter before, "and the birds were so frightened and cold they sat by the kitchen door. Father went to the barn in his slippers and came back with a breakfast of grain for each, and hid himself while he scattered it, lest it embarrass them."

"My father only reads on Sunday," Emily said to Higginson. "He reads *lonely* and *rigorous* books." But about Mrs. Dickinson, she commented only that "My mother does not care for thought," adding that "I never had a mother. I suppose a mother is one to whom you hurry when you are troubled. I always ran home to Awe when a child, if anything befell me." [1] If Emily Norcross Dickinson's negative, housewifely personality counted for nothing in her daughter's larger education, young Emily's brother and sister, Austin and Lavinia Dickinson, and Sue Gilbert, who became Austin's wife, supplied Emily with an instructive wealth of human association for many years.

With Lavinia, Emily was on terms of happy intimacy all her life. Their bond, she wrote, was "early, earnest, indissoluble." "Vinnie," like Emily, learned to be content with her spinster's role. In the late 1840's, she had a rather passionate affair with Joseph Lyman, a schoolmate and friend of Austin; for a period, Lyman and Vinnie planned to marry, but for various reasons—including his removal to New Orleans and his growing proslavery sentiments—the relationship was broken off. While it lasted, it gave Emily (who liked Lyman and hoped for the marriage and was greatly admired by him) her most immediate view of erotic passion.[2] Vinnie, though she became somewhat severe in her later years, had a vital nature and a pungent

---

[1] In a recent study—*After Great Pain: The Inner Life of Emily Dickinson* (1971)—John Cody argues implausibly that the tensions in Emily Dickinson's relation to her mother, and their damaging effect upon her psyche, were the making of her as a poet. The tensions were largely nonexistent, and in fact during her mother's long period of invalidism Emily grew rather closer to her.

[2] "I was very happy once in Vinnie's arms—very happy," Lyman wrote, in 1858, to the young lady he eventually did marry and to whom he provocatively confided the entire course of the affair. "She sat in my lap and pulled the pins from her long soft chestnut hair and tied the long silken mass around my neck and kissed me again and again. . . . Her arms were fat & white and I was very, very happy with her. But that was all. Vinnie hasn't brains at all superior." See Richard B. Sewall's delightful study (based on completely new evidence), *The Lyman Letters: New Light on Emily Dickinson and Her Family* (1965).

wit; she was out and about much more than her sister and paid more and longer visits to friends. She could convert these modest events into high and often comical adventure. Her only flaw, from Emily's point of view, was her love of cats. For Emily, who loved birds and had a favorite dog named Carlo, cats were the natural enemy, and after reporting one Christmas that "Vinnie had four Pussies for Christmas gifts," she added, "finding Assassins for them, is my stealthy aim." Vinnie, increasingly, was her sister's protectress against the invading world; and after Emily Dickinson's death, it was Lavinia who discovered the nearly eighteen hundred poems that Emily had written and tucked away in bureau drawers and who was the principal agent in the publication of the first volume of Emily's verses.

William Austin Dickinson (1829–1895) was perhaps the first citizen of Amherst during his long maturity. He could have been more than that if he had clung to his decision to move to some middle western city, where there were opportunities for civic leadership equal to his talents; but he yielded to his father's wish and entered Edward Dickinson's law office, thereafter busying himself with community matters, the college, the town meeting, the Village Improvement Association, the bank, the church, the construction of new buildings. Emily adored him in her early years and admired his quickness of wit and skill at repartee (she enjoyed nothing more than watching Austin and her father engaged in verbal fisticuffs). But she recognized something unfulfilled in him, a slackening of energy over the years; in 1875, after Austin had been staying with her for four weeks, she remarked that "It seemed peculiar—pathetic —and Antediluvian. We missed him while he was with us and we missed him when he was gone." Apart from the diminishing effect of his father's shadow, the chief source of Austin's failure—failure, that is, of that larger achievement of which he was capable—seems to have been his marriage to Susan Gilbert.

Sue Dickinson was in some ways the most interesting, and certainly the most contradictory, of Emily's younger associates. She was the daughter of the proprietor of the Mansion House in Amherst, and she was beautiful, worldly, a dazzling social figure, and a brilliant conversationalist. She had a cultivated mind and shared with Emily a good many literary excitements. In the first years, Sue and Emily Dickinson were in each other's homes almost daily (the Austin Dickinsons lived next door), and messages were sent back and forth between visits. To Sue, Emily Dickinson showed several hundred of her poems, more than any other relative or friend was even aware of. But Sue Dickinson's worldly charm also contained a vein of dishonesty, or at least a lack of regard for truth in her scintillating narratives, and a decided streak of cruelty. Her words could, perhaps without her knowing it, cut and wound. "She dealt her pretty words like Blades," Emily wrote in 1862:

> How glittering they shone—
> And every One unbared a Nerve—
> Or wantoned with a Bone—

When in 1866 Sue so far betrayed her sister-in-law's confidence as to have one of Emily Dickinson's poems printed in the Springfield *Republican* ("A narrow Fellow in the Grass"), Emily remarked flatly that "it was robbed me," and felt the more bitter since, as so often was to happen to her later, several lines were botched by the editor. By 1881 Emily was referring to Sue Dickinson as her "pseudo-sister." At almost the same time she sent Sue a note saying: "With the exception of Shakespeare, you have told me of more knowledge than any one living. To say that sincerely is strange praise." Strange indeed, if some of the knowledge imparted was of those darker corners of the heart that Melville especially admired in Shakespeare. To anyone who opened Emily Dickinson's eyes to any strange aspect of human nature, one must be extremely grateful. But meanwhile, the effect of this charming and difficult, this vivacious and untrustworthy woman upon her gentle-spirited and much less complex husband was increasingly unfortunate. He became estranged from his wife and isolated from his children; to his watchful sister, as we have seen, his very personality seemed to diminish.

Beyond the family circle, there were a series of individuals of great if varying importance to Emily Dickinson. They were not many, and with none of them were the actual encounters frequent. As she grew older, Emily Dickinson found it ever more painful to be in the presence of anyone except a member of her family. Her occasional visitors found the experience of an hour with her not much less unsettling. A cousin, asked by his children what Emily Dickinson had been like, could only say, "She was different. Emily Dick had more charm than anyone I ever knew." But it was a charm that exhausted. After his first call on her, one summer afternoon in 1870, Thomas Higginson wrote his wife: "I never was with any one who drained my nerve power so much. Without touching her she drew from me. I am glad not to live near her." She held her friends, she told Higginson in turn, "in a brittle love—of more alarm than peace"—alarm lest the friendship suddenly end, through estrangement, or physical separation, or death. Such a communicated sense of alarm can hardly have made intercourse with her very peaceful, or something to be regularly attempted.

"My friends are my 'estate,'" Emily Dickinson told Samuel Bowles. They seem to form an almost chronological procession, as though Emily's alarmed, brittle love could only concentrate on one beloved friend at a time. This is not strictly true, of course, though she seems to have said so in one of her most occultly telling poems:

The Soul selects her own Society—
Then—shuts the Door—
To her divine Majority—
Presents no more—

. . .

I've known her—from an ample nation—
Choose One—
Then—close the Valves of her attention—
Like Stone—

After the friends of her school days and her youth (Abiah Root, Jane Humphrey, the short-lived and much cherished "tutor," Ben Newton), Emily's first mature friendship was with Samuel Bowles, who inherited the editorship of the Springfield *Republican* from his father and who turned it into one of the most admired journals in the country. What Bowles could offer was both human and (to a more limited extent) literary understanding, a kind of warm and highly good-humored kinship of spirit. Emily rejoiced in the swift mobility of his mind, as it raced ahead of others in conversation, but even Bowles, welcome as he was in the Dickinson home, did not have unlimited access to her. "I have the errand from my heart," she wrote him in 1862, when he was abroad; "would you please come home?" But when he did, and came at once to call, Emily stayed upstairs in her room, sending down a note (it is almost a poem) which read: "Dear Friend,—I cannot see you. . . . That you return to us alive is better than any summer, and more to hear your voice below than news of any bird." Bowles teased her a little in a note of reply, and Emily wrote back a stammering, touching letter seeking to explain herself. When she absented herself on still another occasion, Bowles called up to her: "Emily, you damned rascal! No more of this nonsense! Come down at once." Surprisingly enough, she did so, and talked brilliantly all evening. She signed a subsequent letter to him "Your 'Rascal,'" observing that she had "washed the Adjective."

Emily Dickinson's friendships, it is apparent, were few and intense; and these qualities have led her biographers to choose one or another of the few as the key friendship, indeed the crucial love affair, of her mysterious and fascinating life—as though each biographer, perhaps taking the poem just quoted too literally, has felt called upon to select that one person who must have constituted the whole of the society of Emily Dickinson's soul. Samuel Bowles, for example, has been singled out as the chosen one, in a recent book-length argument; so, with more reason, has Judge Otis

Lord, to whom we shall be coming shortly. The matter is intricate, not only because of the lack of anything like sufficient evidence, but because one is not always clear about the nature of the question. Is one asking about a centrally important and reciprocal love affair, with distinct stages and with some mode or other of consummation? Or is one inquiring into the sources of Emily Dickinson's most passionate love *poetry*? As to the former, no such affair ever existed: at different times, and with differing degrees of intensity, Emily Dickinson no doubt felt love for several different men, but in no case, even using the word with all decorousness, could it have been called an "affair" (like Lavinia's with Joseph Lyman). As to the latter, if one individual rather than another is to be named as helping release her greatest flood of imaginative energy and her most clearly erotic verse, it is fairly well established that the person was the Reverend Charles Wadsworth, pastor of the Arch Street Presbyterian Church in Philadelphia from 1850 to 1862. The latter date is especially important.

On their visit to Philadelphia in 1854, Emily and Lavinia Dickinson evidently went to hear Wadsworth preach. Wadsworth was an uncommonly compelling preacher, with a reputation second only to that of Henry Ward Beecher; his style, however, had none of Beecher's histrionic devices, but was direct, intense, charged with the enormous force of a moral and spiritual personality. Emily was enthralled, in almost the literal meaning of that word. In the years that followed, they exchanged letters, perhaps frequently. There is no doubt that, in the late fifties, Emily was not only in love with Wadsworth, but that she felt a powerful physical as well as spiritual passion for him—the poem "Wild Nights—Wild Nights!" among others, seems clear testimony to that. There is equally no doubt that, although probably much taken with his young disciple, Wadsworth in no way reciprocated her passion and may scarcely have been aware of it. He was sixteen years older than Emily, much closer to her father's generation than to hers; he was the de-

voted husband of a most beautiful and gracious woman, and the father of several children. Emily spoke of him, after his death in 1882, as her "dearest earthly friend," her "beloved clergyman," her "shepherd." She also described him as a "Man of Sorrows," and retrospectively built up an image of him as a gloomy, introspective man, "a dusk gem, born of troubled waters." This may be due to the fact that on his first visit to her, in 1860, he was in mourning for the death of his mother; he appears in fact to have been a rather gay and amusing person in private. In any event, the crucial moment came in the spring of 1862, when Wadsworth left Philadelphia to accept a call to Calvary Church in San Francisco.

Emily Dickinson was utterly stricken. She had had a dear friend who taught her much, she wrote Higginson in April of that year; "but he was not contented I be his scholar—so he left the land." Wadsworth, with his family, had in all actuality left the land; he might as well have been heading for another planet, for in 1862 one could travel from the east coast to California only by a long sea voyage. Emily Dickinson's response was an unprecedented outburst of poetry, a phenomenon she herself recognized as having its origin in Wadsworth's departure. She said to Higginson that "I had a terror—since September [when Wadsworth evidently forewarned her of his impending decision] I could tell to none—and so I sing, as the Boy does by the Burying Ground—because I was afraid."

She told her sister Lavinia about it and may well have made to her a full confession of her feelings. To Samuel Bowles, her only other confidant in the matter, she followed her own principle about telling the truth—she told it "slant," indirectly and even enigmatically, by means of poetry. In April she sent Bowles the following poem, with a message which read: "*Here's*—what I had to 'tell you'— You will tell no other? Honor—is its own pawn."

Title divine—is mine!
The Wife—without the Sign!

Acute Degree—conferred on me—
Empress of Calvary!
Royal—all but the Crown!
Betrothed—without the swoon
God sends us Women—
When you—hold—Garnet to Garnet—
Gold—to Gold—
Born—Bridalled—Shrouded—   10
In a Day—
Tri Victory
"My Husband"—women say—
Stroking the Melody—
Is *this*—the way?[3]

Bowles seems to have intuited something of the state of things from this oblique and exclamatory poem—namely, that she had been denied the overwhelming experience of earthly marriage and that she was undergoing an emotional crucifixion which, however, might lead eventually to a heavenly bridal.

The reverberations within Emily Dickinson's lacerated imagination of Wadsworth's removal may be suggested by the fact that, after writing about 80 poems in 1861 and 65 the year before that, she composed no less than 366 in the course of 1862, 150 in 1863, and more than 100 in 1864. There is no reason to modify the succinct statement of her biographer Thomas H. Johnson that "Wadsworth as muse made her a poet"—except perhaps to repeat that it was Wadsworth's absence, not his presence, that produced the poetic eruption; that it was a devastating sense of loss which, working like a catalyst upon her other strong emotions, brought about the flood tide of 1862. Wadsworth was the muse of the poetry of fear, loss, renunciation, exquisite despair; of poems like "I got so I could take his name," "I dreaded

[3] Note the phrase "Empress of Calvary" in the fourth line and recall that Wadsworth had gone to San Francisco to become rector of Calvary Church in that city. "Calvary" was one of the words Emily Dickinson used to indicate excruciating torment; yet in this poem of torment, loss, and renunciation, she may also be deploying the word to affirm, secretly, her right to be seated beside the man she loved. Emily Dickinson's best poetry, we may observe, is always moving in more than one direction.

that first Robin, so," "I envy Seas, whereon He rides," "After great pain, a formal feeling comes," "It will be Summer—eventually." Some of those are among the great lyrics in English. While writing them, she told Higginson that "I made no verse, but one or two, until this winter." Even if we take the phrase "this winter" to be metaphorical and to mean the start of the season of her anguish (the previous September), she had before that in fact written about 250 poems, and they include "I taste a liquor never brewed," "Success is counted sweetest," and "I never lost as much but twice." Still, Emily Dickinson was telling a profoundly serious truth in her slant-wise manner. It was the onset of winter in her soul that fully and finally confirmed her genius.

It was no coincidence that the beginning of Emily Dickinson's long correspondence with Thomas Wentworth Higginson occurred within days of Charles Wadsworth's departure. It was not only that she needed another person near at hand with whom to communicate. It was even more that, as she felt the enormous creative energy welling up within her—she was composing at the rate of a poem a day—she felt the need in particular of a *literary* confidant. Higginson had written an interesting article in the *Atlantic Monthly* about the country's literary needs and expectations; and on April 16, 1862, Emily Dickinson sent him four poems and a short letter in which she asked: "Are you too deeply occupied to say if my verse is alive? . . . Should you think it breathed, and had you the leisure to tell me, I should feel quick gratitude." To the day of his death, Higginson would not make up his mind whether Emily Dickinson's poems did or did not live and breathe.

It is easy to be scornful of Higginson's kindly obtuseness, his worried bafflement, his feeling that the poems Emily Dickinson continued to send him were not really poems at all, that they were fatally defective in language, syntax, meter, and rhyme. But even today an intelligent critic who by some accident had never known Emily Dickinson's poems might be slow to recognize at once that the following, which she enclosed with a letter to Higginson, is a superior lyric on the theme of death and eternity:

Safe in their Alabaster Chambers—
Untouched by Morning—
And untouched by Noon—
Lie the meek members of the Resurrection—
Rafter of Satin—and Roof of Stone!

Grand go the Years—in the Crescent—above
    them—
Worlds scoop their Arcs—
And Firmaments—row—
Diadems—drop—and Doges—surrender—
Soundless as dots—on a Disc of Snow.   10

Remarkable, though odd, Higginson decided; but formless, imperfectly rhymed, and with a "spasmodic" beat; certainly not fit for publication.

Emily Dickinson's relationship with Higginson might have been yet another source of anguish. For despite her disclaimers, in prose and verse, she did very much hope at this time that her poetry might be published. By the middle of June, Higginson had convinced her otherwise; and except for a few random poems that saw the light almost by accident, her verse would not be printed in her lifetime. She was convinced exactly and paradoxically because of the inept and usually irrelevant nature of Higginson's criticism. *He* represented as high a literary standard as one could find within the literary establishment in the early 1860's, and he was quite obviously intrigued by both the poetry and the poetess. If Higginson, whose good intentions could not be doubted, remained so obdurately blind to the quality of her writing, there was no point in turning elsewhere. Emily Dickinson had to renounce any thought of fame, and there was a special poignancy in her plea, having done so, "But will you be my Preceptor, Mr. Higginson?" The truth is that Emily Dickinson at this stage needed no preceptor, nor any literary mentor or guide. She accepted his judgment as to publication, for it was the judgment of the contemporary literary world. But his strictures had no effect upon her whatever: she

began to play with them, as in a game. "You think my gait 'spasmodic'—I am in danger—Sir. You think me 'uncontrolled'—I have no Tribunal." She had of course the finest tribunal she could want: her own powerfully developed and almost perfectly controlled sense of poetic fitness. What she needed, and what in Higginson she found, was not a preceptor, but a correspondent.

All things considered, she could not have made a happier choice than Higginson—"my safest friend," as she called him. He was much associated with Harvard, where his father was bursar and where he attended both the college and, after a schoolteaching interval, the divinity school. He became pastor of a Unitarian church in Newburyport in 1847; but he was more and more caught up in the abolitionist cause, speaking vehemently about it on public platforms and engaging in various violent undertakings on behalf of fugitive slaves. He resigned his Unitarian pulpit, to the relief of his parishioners, and though he was vaguely connected with the "Free Church" in Worcester, his energies were directed mainly to antislavery and related liberal crusades. During the Civil War he organized and commanded the first Negro regiment (his experiences are described in his book of 1870, *Army Life in a Black Regiment*).[4] Emily Dickinson addressed a letter to him at his camp in South Carolina:

I should have liked to see you before you became improbable. War feels to me an oblique place. Should there be other summers, would you perhaps come?

I found you were gone, by accident, as I find systems are, or seasons of the year, and obtain no cause, but suppose it a treason of progress that dissolves as it goes. . . .

Should you, before this reaches you, experience Immortality, who will inform me of the exchange? Could you, with honor, avoid death, I entreat you, sir, It would bereave

YOUR GNOME

---

[4] For more on Higginson in the Civil War, see also Edmund Wilson's *Patriotic Gore*.

Higginson was, in fact, wounded but recovered and returned safely from the oblique place to continue his correspondence with his "partially cracked poetess of Amherst," as he referred to her in a sort of defensive, mystified admiration. He still cautioned her about her poetic irregularities, but he gradually realized that she was quite immune to his critical suggestions and that what she held with regard to him—it was his most acute perception—was the "hope, always rather baffled, that I should afford some aid in solving her abstruse problem of life." He was capable of understanding, as he told her in the late sixties, that her withdrawn life was intelligible—"It isolates one anywhere to think beyond a certain point, or have flashes as come to you"; but he was also capable of urging her to come to Boston to attend a Woman's Club meeting and to read the poetry of another woman writer (much like her, he implied), Harriet Prescott Spofford. In 1890 and 1891, he collaborated with Mabel Loomis Todd in bringing out the first two volumes of Emily Dickinson's verse. But even while performing this honorable feat, he could not bring himself to let the poems stand as written. When, for example, it came to a sprightly poem expressing envy of the grass for having little to do except enjoy itself and ending with the lines:

And then, in Sovereign Barns to dwell—
And dream the Days away,
The Grass so little has to do
I wish I were a Hay—

Higginson exclaimed agitatedly to his coeditor, "It cannot go in so. Don't you see? Everybody would say that *hay* is a collective noun requiring the definite article; nobody would, even in fun, call it *a* hay." Nobody except Emily Dickinson. So *the* hay it became, and the poem was quietly ruined.

In the late seventies, as she approached her fiftieth year, Emily Dickinson fell in love with Otis Phillips Lord, a graduate of Amherst, a distinguished lawyer and member of the Massachusetts legislature, and, since 1875, associate justice of the Massachusetts Supreme Court.

Lord, born in 1812, was a close friend of Emily Dickinson's father, perhaps his best friend, and Emily had known him for many years before Lord's wife died in 1877. This love was outspoken and apparently it was reciprocated; Lord seems to have offered marriage, over the objection of his several nieces. A passage from one of Emily's letters to him is thought to refer to this, and to her inability to accept:

It is Anguish I long conceal from you to let you leave me hungry, but you ask the divine Crust and that would doom the Bread. . . . I was reading a little Book—because it broke my Heart I want it to break your's. Will you think that fair? I often have read it, but not before since loving you. I find that makes a difference—it makes a difference with all. . . . The withdrawal of the Fuel of Rapture does not withdraw the Rapture itself.

Lord died in 1884. If, as is generally believed, Emily's emotional involvement with him dates only from about 1877, it had no important effect upon her poetry or her poetic career. Emily herself lived on only until 1886, partially invalided, continuing to send her messages to the outside world, a steady flow of letters, and poems as pungent and disconcerting as this, written only a year or two before her death:

Apparently with no surprise
To any happy Flower
The Frost beheads it at its play—
In accidental power—
The blonde Assassin passes on—
The Sun proceeds unmoved
To measure off another Day
For an Approving God.

She became an epigrammatic recluse, clad exclusively in the white gown she adopted as what might be called her stage costume at the moment Charles Wadsworth sailed for San Francisco in May, 1862. But the process of withdrawal was gradual. After a visit to Boston in 1864, to have her eye trouble looked into (no greater physical affliction for Emily Dickinson can be imagined than even partial blindness, but she was entirely cured), she did not again go beyond the town of Amherst. By 1868, she could write Higginson, in a line that sounds like the beginning of a poem, "I do not cross my father's ground for any house or town." Not long after that she ceased venturing outside the Dickinson house. She enjoyed the company and support of Lavinia and their Irish maid and gladly distributed cookies to such small children as might wander by. But she retreated upstairs before most visitors, as we have seen her do when Samuel Bowles came to call at her own request. When the recently married Mabel Loomis Todd came by with her husband in 1881 and played charmingly upon the piano, Emily lurked on the upper landing, calling down little breathless exclamations of pleasure. Mrs. Todd edited five volumes of Emily Dickinson's poems and a selection of her letters, but never actually laid eyes on her.

This withdrawal, this hovering behind the scenes, may well have been, as Thomas Johnson has suggested, a way of dramatizing life, of shrinking conspicuously from encounters that would have too much excited her, as well as avoiding those that held no interest for her. It was also a way of solving what Higginson called her abstruse problem of life. It was a retreat into intensity, as though only from a distance, only from a position of invisibility, could the intensity be truly experienced, controlled—and converted into poetry. Richard Wilbur, who has the fine poet's intuition of the imaginative strategies of other poets, has said that Emily Dickinson created and lived in "a huge world of delectable distances." That is not the only thing to say about her; she also extracted delectable meanings from the near at hand; but it is one very important thing to say about her. "It was the Distance—Was Savory," she remarked at the close of a poem in 1862:

Undue Significance a starving man attaches
To Food—
Far off—He sighs—and therefore—Hopeless—
And therefore—Good—

Partaken—it relieves—indeed—
But proves us
That Spices fly

In the Receipt—It was the Distance—
Was Savory—

"Far off . . . And therefore—Good."

Renunciation, which she called a "piercing virtue," was, she came to believe, the only real source of fulfillment for her. Renouncing the pleasure of talking with Samuel Bowles, she could experience the keener pleasure of hearing him talk with Austin and Lavinia and the pleasure of *their* pleasure. Renouncing contact with friends, she could shower them with letters, though they lived next door or only down the street. Renouncing membership in the church, she could allow her profoundly religious imagination to play over a much larger range of things spiritual than the formalities and doctrines of orthodoxy. Renouncing the possibility of publication and of fame, she could exercise the varieties of technical freedom and experimentation her creative genius fed upon. Renouncing the very thought of marriage, she could retain intact the rapture of the beloved image and live on in the hope of a different marriage in the domain of immortality. It is impossible not to conclude that her role of recluse was not only not eccentric, it was precisely and logically the one role by which living and writing were possible for her.

One imagines her in the upstairs room in the house on Main Street, sometimes listening to the conversation below, perhaps joining in occasionally from afar; more often, writing and rewriting, experimenting with this word and that, before tucking the poem carefully away in a drawer; at other times, reading. As to the latter, she told Higginson that her father "buys me many books, but begs me not to read them, because he fears they joggle the mind." In answer to Higginson's inquiry about her reading, she said, "For poets, I have Keats, and Mr. and Mrs. Browning.[5] For prose, Mr. Ruskin, Sir

[5] In another recent book about Emily Dickinson—*The Hidden Life of Emily Dickinson* (1971)—John Evangelist Walsh argues, not very persuasively, that "Aurora Leigh," Mrs. Browning's long blank verse narrative poem, was not only the source of untold numbers of Emily Dickinson's images, but also "taught her at a

Thomas Browne, and the *Revelations.*" For both media, she could have added the name of Emerson. As early as 1850, she received a handsome copy of "Ralph Emerson's poems" from Ben Newton, and she is known to have steeped herself in the essays. She may even have met Emerson, who visited Amherst several times and spent a night in Austin Dickinson's house. In any case, the coincidence of theme, attitude, and language between Emerson and Emily Dickinson is often striking, though it will also be necessary to show distinctions between them. Whitman, whose poetic innovations Higginson seems rather helplessly to have suggested her studying, remained unknown to her, or so she said. "You speak of Mr. Whitman. I never read his book, but was told it was disgraceful."

In addition to Emerson, there were of course a good many other writers whose books joggled Emily Dickinson's mind. She moved among books as among much loved familiars and equals; they were, she said, her "enthralling friends." Supremely, there was Shakespeare, every one of whose plays she read and reread closely. For her, Shakespeare was *the* poet; and her several poems about "the poet" (for example, "This was a Poet—It is That") refer to Shakespeare rather than anyone else. Charles Anderson, in *Emily Dickinson's Poetry*, has a valuable discussion of the rhetorical devices Emily Dickinson could find to her use in Shakespeare: the substitution of concrete terms for abstract ones, the bringing together of words taken from different contexts (for example, physical nature and scientific experiment), the conversion of noun into adjective. But she could also study in Shakespeare those crises of the

soul for which the rhetorical innovations were employed; the "knowledge" she spoke of as having learned from Shakespeare (when she said her sister-in-law had "told" her a good deal of similar knowledge) had to do with these *agons* of spirit, these intense internal dramas.

Emily Dickinson was not a compulsive reader like Melville, and the range of her reading did not, like Melville's, take in Greek tragedy, gnostic philosophy, the Spanish epic. Of classical and continental European literature, she knew little. Apart from Sir Thomas Browne, and for all her affinity with the metaphysical poets, she seems not to have explored very widely in seventeenth-century writing; she was, fortunately in her own case, not interested in the Augustan age. She knew Wordsworth and Byron as well as Keats; but she makes no mention of Blake or Shelley, though her poetry suggests some absorption at least of Blake. She admired George Eliot and reveled all her life in Dickens; her word for Emily Bronte (the poet rather than the novelist) was "gigantic." She faithfully read and duly honored the American fireside poets— Longfellow, Lowell, Holmes; Hawthorne stung her imagination much more sharply—"Hawthorne appals—entices," she remarked; but before the fiction of Howells and the early Henry James, she said that "one hesitates." Of Poe, she told Higginson, "I know too little to think."

Emily Dickinson's poetic career cannot, like Whitman's, be convincingly divided into a series of successive "stages." As early as 1858, she could write a poem such as "I never lost as much but twice," and as late as 1884 "Apparently with no surprise." During the intervening quarter of a century, the poems might be superior or inferior to the lyrics just cited, but one hears in all of them the same voice, one observes the same wit, the same capacity to startle, the same mixture of skepticism and ardor, the same strange devices of punctuation and syntax (though the irregularity in this latter regard only became regular, so to speak, about 1860 or 1861). A partial exception should perhaps be made for the critical year 1862 and the trans-

---

stroke" the true nature of poetry. "Aurora Leigh" was not published until 1856, and Emily Dickinson may not have come upon it for a year or two after that—by which time, according to the best scholarship, she had already written poems such as "I never lost as much but twice," "The Gentian weaves her fringes," and "Heart! We will forget him!" But the inner tensions, the wit, the slantwise perceptions, the unique way with words that characterize Emily Dickinson's poetry make it as far removed as can be from Mrs. Browning's verse and her now almost wholly forgotten "Aurora Leigh."

ferral of Charles Wadsworth from east coast to west coast. The moment initiated, as we have seen, what was, quantitatively, Emily Dickinson's most productive phase. It also marked, if not a decided shift in tone, at least something of a shift in emotional balance. There is, in that major phase, less of the ecstasy of previous years, and of unimpeded joy in the phenomena of nature. She had experienced and had movingly expressed the emotion of grief before; but now grief becomes a house of pain, to be explored in its every nook and cranny—grief deepening into anguish, into despair, into psychic numbness. "After great pain, a formal feeling comes."

Yet, however one might chart Emily Dickinson's emotional career, what gives unmistakable unity to her entire poetic career is not only a continuity of devices and resources, but a sustained and fertile ambiguity in her religious attitude. She was first and foremost a religious poet. But one has scarcely phrased that formula before one plunges into modifications, emendations, paradoxes. Emily Dickinson was not, to begin with, a member of the church; in the hard language of her day and her region, she never became a Christian. Amherst, when Emily was growing up there, was still undergoing those periodic religious "awakenings" first stimulated in the valley by Solomon Stoddard and energetically spurred on, as it will be recalled, by his son-in-law Jonathan Edwards. At Mount Holyoke Seminary, the girls were frequently examined as to their religious condition: some had been converted, some "had hope" of eventual conversion, some were "without hope." Emily Dickinson came to realize that she was one of the latter, that it was certain she would never have the experience of conversion. It was no joyful discovery.

"Christ is calling every one here," she wrote her friend Jane Humphrey in April, 1848; "all my companions have answered, even my darling Vinnie believes she loves, and trusts him, and I am standing alone in rebellion and growing very careless." And to Abiah Root: "It is not now too late, so my friends tell me, so my offended conscience whispers, but it is hard for me to give up the world." "*I* am one of the lingering bad ones," she said to the same correspondent a little later, "and so do I slink away, and pause and ponder, and ponder and pause, and do work without knowing why, not surely, for this brief world, and more sure it is not for heaven." Within a decade she had found out what her work was for: the embodiment of her own unique religious and poetic vision, a vision quickened and troubled by a sense of guilt, a consciousness of what she called her "freckled bosom," her unredeemed yet perhaps not unredeemable soul.

By the late fifties, she stopped attending church service at all. "Some keep the Sabbath going to Church," she wrote in a poem of 1860:

> I keep it, staying at Home—
> With a Bobolink for a Chorister—
> And an Orchard, for a Dome—

The common rituals of the church became important ingredients in her poetry—sermons, marriages, funerals; but in their new environment they are transformed into metaphors of spiritual experience ("I felt a funeral in my *brain*"). At the same time, the stanzaic and metrical structures of her poems are brilliantly modified and varied versions of the Protestant hymn structures she studied in two collections by Isaac Watts, *Christian Psalmody* and *The Psalms, Hymns and Spiritual Songs,* both volumes to be found in her father's library. We shall have more to say about Emily Dickinson's experiments and her extraordinary successes in fresh metrical arrangements (as about her rhyming and other technical inventions); here a single example can suffice:

> I never lost as much but twice,
> And that was in the sod.
> Twice have I stood a beggar
> Before the door of God!
>
> Angels—twice descending
> Reimbursed my store—
> Burglar! Banker—Father!
> I am poor once more!

The first stanza of this uncannily intricate little lyric is in what is known in hymnology as iambic common meter: alternating eight and six syllable lines (with an adroit variation, for emphasis, in the third line). The adjective "common" indicates accurately that this is the most frequently encountered meter in the familiar old hymns; but any hymn which began with common meter would hold to it throughout. Emily Dickinson, however, shifts boldly in the second stanza to another familiar hymn meter, the so-called trochaic sixes and fives, lending stress and urgency to the poetic statement—"*Burglar! Banker—Father!*" The point is that the conventions of hymn writing have been appropriated and put, modified, to the service of poetry. It was by no means an irreverent undertaking, for poetry was Emily Dickinson's mode of prayer. To a cousin who, like the speaker in the poem just quoted, had lost someone dear to her, Emily Dickinson wrote: "Let Emily sing for you, because she cannot pray."

Her intellectual relation to the Puritan heritage, still very strong but slowly breaking up in the Connecticut Valley of her adolescence, may be seen as paralleling in some wise these acts of metaphoric and technical expropriation. In his invaluable essay, Allen Tate has remarked that "Poetry does not dispense with tradition; it probes the deficiencies of a tradition. But it must have a tradition to probe." And he goes on to say that Emily Dickinson found herself in "the perfect literary situation"—a devout skeptic confronting a once powerful and massively articulated theological tradition which was yet giving way, losing its ability to compel the alert soul, no longer able to account for the whole of experience by its now stiffening vocabulary. The grand considerations for Emily Dickinson were supplied her by that vocabulary: God, heaven, hell, sin, redemption, immortality; but they did not drag with them the weight of established doctrine; they impinged on her imagination as things to be experienced, puzzled over, yearned toward, doubted. Mulling over the thought of a world beyond this earthly world ("This World is not Conclusion"), she describes "Faith" as

slipping and rallying and observes that, for all the Hallelujahs that might be shouted,

> Narcotics cannot still the Tooth
> That nibbles at the soul—

" 'Faith' is a fine invention," she suggested in an early poem, "When Gentlemen can *see*,"

> But *Microscopes* are prudent
> In an Emergency.

Nothing more impudent, in this four-line meditation on contrasting instruments of understanding, than the sly conversion of religious faith into a human invention like the laboratory microscope. Nothing, that is, except a whole series of poems addressed to God. An undated eight-line poem that begins with a description of the stars coming out and the moon rising—in language that at first seems delicately beautiful but is in fact a gentle parody of lushness—concludes abruptly:

> Father, I observed to Heaven,
> You are punctual.

"God is a distant—stately Lover," she says elsewhere, who woos mankind vicariously through His son, as Miles Standish wooed Priscilla through his envoy John Alden. The doctrine of original sin tantalized her and made her wittily resentful:

> "Heavenly Father"—take to thee
> The supreme iniquity
> Fashioned by thy candid Hand
> In a moment contraband—
> Though to trust us—seem to us
> More respectful—"We are Dust"—
> We apologize to thee
> For thine own Duplicity—

This is a perfect example of Emily Dickinson's manner of conducting a dialogue with orthodox Christianity. The quoted phrases are standard ones of Christian language; the rest is the play of Emily Dickinson's sensibility around their implications. It is a daring poem, and considering the circumstances of her culture and the strong religious bent of her family ("They are religious, except me," she told Higginson), Emily Dickinson is as daring a poet as this country has produced.

"It is hard for me to give up the world," we recall her saying to Abiah Root in 1848. A disdain for this world, for human life on earth as against the expectations of the life hereafter, was a staple of Protestant doctrine in Emily Dickinson's religious culture; the voice of Jonathan Edwards still rang menacingly in the valley. But it was just the things of this world that Emily Dickinson could not forswear. By 1860, when she had discovered once and for all her purpose and her profession, her genius and the ranges of which it was capable, she understood why. The poet is bound to the things of this world. She might indeed, like Emerson, explore those things to detect the miraculous within them; but they must be allowed their own integrity. Both her temperament and her poetic genius strenuously resisted the temptation toward transcendence: such is the burden of one of her greatest poems, "Of Bronze—and Blaze," in which, after describing how the aurora borealis had "infected" her with the desire to imitate its transcendent grandeur—

> Till I take vaster attitudes—
> And strut upon my stem—
> Disdaining Men, and Oxygen,
> For Arrogance of them—

she nonetheless almost literally came down to earth, back within the oxygen belt, and acknowledges that her "splendors are Menagerie," no more than a traveling circus in comparison with the remote wonders of the sky. It is not only that her poems cannot compete with the heavenly spectacle. It is that *as a poet* she is committed to avoiding that competition. Hers is by definition a "Competeless Show."

In an important sense, Emily Dickinson is the youngest—that is, the most recently arrived—of major American poets. During her lifetime only eight of her poems were published. Of these, two were early finger exercises; one ("A narrow Fellow in the Grass") was printed without

Emily Dickinson's consent; and most were damaged by clumsy editing. The first stanza of "Success is counted sweetest," for example, originally ran as follows:

> Success is counted sweetest
> By those who ne'er succeed.
> To comprehend a nectar
> Requires sorest need.

But when it appeared in a volume called *A Masque of Poets* in 1878, it read like this:

> Success is counted sweetest
> By those that ne'er succeed.
> To comprehend the nectar
> Requires the sorest need.

Editorial violations of this kind (by which, in the present case, an astringent insight is reduced to a cliché) were among the reasons why Emily Dickinson withdrew her poems as resolutely as her person from the inquiring world. In 1890, four years after her death, the first collection of her poems was brought out by Mabel Loomis Todd and Thomas Wentworth Higginson. Two more volumes followed in 1891 and 1896, random and disorderly selections, many of them edited right out of existence. In 1924, there was *The Complete Poems of Emily Dickinson*, but that title was belied by *Further Poems* in 1929 and several more gatherings over the succeeding twelve years.

Finally, in 1955, Thomas H. Johnson published *The Poems of Emily Dickinson* in three volumes, "including variant readings critically compared with all known manuscripts." Now at last almost (though not quite) every line of verse Emily Dickinson ever wrote—1775 poems in all—was in print; but this magnificent variorum edition was really accessible and useful only to scholars and unusually well-informed critics. In 1960, Mr. Johnson issued the complete poems in a single volume, without the variants and comparisons. This was still a little out of the range of most students and "average readers," and it was not until 1961 when the same editor published *Final Harvest*, a reasonably priced paperback containing almost six hundred of Emily Dickinson's poems and almost all of the best of them, that her poetry could be said to be available to everybody. That final date, 1961, can therefore not inaccurately be said to be the moment when Emily Dickinson truly arrived on the literary scene.

Several other considerations add to the uniqueness of the challenge so rewardingly posed by Emily Dickinson's poetry. One, of course, is her visual and verbal oddity. Comment on this is better reserved for headnotes to particular poems; but it can be said here that even after several decades of every kind of experimentation (one poet, briefly fashionable some years back, attempted the device of placing a comma after every word in his poems), there is still something arresting, and provocative, about Emily Dickinson's system of dashes, her capitalizations, her interchangings of the parts of speech, her sheer inventions.

Much more important, however, is the fact that so many of her poems must be regarded as incomplete. Charles Anderson puts the matter more strongly: "Because of her ambiguous character of being a poet yet not a publishing poet, one must simply accept the fact that Emily Dickinson did not leave any of her poems in final form, strictly speaking, nor indicate her preferences absolutely." She left behind her a mass of jottings, scribbled drafts on odd scraps of paper, semifinal drafts, and sometimes as many as three quite different "fair copies" of individual poems. Thomas Johnson performed an enormous feat in sorting much of this out; but his choices—of alternative words, lines, stanzas—have been widely questioned, as they could not help but be. Charles Anderson is frank to say that "I have felt free to choose any version and adopt any variant that struck me as best," and the interested reader is invited to do the same thing. To do so, needless to say, he must consult the variorum edition; but, as with Melville's *Billy Budd*, yet on a far vaster scale, he has the opportunity to engage in the creative as well as the critical act, and to merge his imagination and ingenuity with those of Emily Dickinson. It is a heady experience, unlike anything else that American literary history provides.

The critical act remains. To see the scope and challenge of it, we can compare the case of Emily Dickinson with that of Melville and of Henry James. Except for *Billy Budd*, all of Melville's fiction saw print almost immediately after it was written. *Moby-Dick* was there for all to examine from 1851 onward; but though it was never entirely neglected (Edith Wharton, for example, spoke deprecatingly but knowingly about it in 1911), it was not until the 1940's, almost a full century after publication, that it became generally recognized as one of the world's masterpieces. Henry James's stories and novels followed one another to press for more than forty years; a nearly complete edition was published between 1904 and 1909. But his once large following dwindled to an exceedingly small if passionate group of cultists; for years he was, for the most part, simply unread; and only after the end of the Second World War was he firmly established as one of the supreme craftsmen in the art of fiction and one of the greatest novelists in English. Consider, then, Emily Dickinson, whose poetry has been truly available to the common reader for only a few years.

Thus the critical act has a magnitude and novelty to match that of creative collaboration. No one now seriously doubts that Emily Dickinson is a poet of the very highest order. But what *kind* of a poet was she? What were her essential and revealing themes, what her characteristic strategy? How do her poems *work*? Which are the best, and which the less or the least successful? One need only read through the splendid collection of critical essays edited by Richard B. Sewall (in 1963) to discover the range, one almost says the anarchy, of critical disagreement. One critic identifies her as a mystic, another as a viewer of beauties from afar, another as a supreme artist in the handling of delicate description. Yvor Winters calls her poem "I like to see it lap the Miles" "abominable" and speaks, rather in the manner of Thomas Wentworth Higginson, of "the desert of her crudities"; R. P. Blackmur, more winningly but no less severely, says, "It sometimes seems as if in her work a cat came at us speaking English . . . without the pressure of all other structures we are accustomed to attend," and finds her on occasion willful, arbitrary, and immature.

Both these eminent critics hold Emily Dickinson's poetry, ultimately, in considerable esteem; but younger or later critics, in Sewall's volume, not only rank her more highly, but also discover in the alleged crudity and waywardness often superbly worked out creative efforts, a valid and utterly significant originality at the service of the most profoundly serious poetic intention. Winters estimates that no more than a hundred of Emily Dickinson's poems will endure (Charles Anderson agrees); that would be a very large achievement; but others, to judge from the tone of their criticism, would tend to double the number. Richard Sewall's volume makes it clear that we are still in the early stages of the evaluation and interpretation of Emily Dickinson's poetry. It is a far more epochal moment in American criticism than was the exciting discovery, in 1937, of the poems of Edward Taylor (a poetic ancestor of Emily Dickinson, could she have known it). It is as though the whole body of John Donne's work were suddenly thrust at us, or all the lyrics of Andrew Marvell.

The poems selected have been grouped thematically, not chronologically. Emily Dickinson's poems, as has been said, do not fall conveniently into a series of life stages, as do those of Whitman; in any case several of the better poems are still undated, while other dates are only proximate.

The groupings are necessarily tentative. Emily Dickinson's work used to be divided into such categories as "Nature," "Love," and "Death"; but if terms like those are unsatisfactory, it is not because they are irrelevant, but because they are misleadingly flat. A poem like "I dreaded that first Robin, so" is about love *and* nature: more precisely, about the death of love and the rebirth of nature. Other poems may be important less for their ostensible subject than for the play of wit in them.

We follow the styling of Thomas H. Johnson. The number and date preceding each poem are those assigned by Johnson.

BIOGRAPHICAL CHART

1830 Born, December 10, in Amherst, Massachusetts
1840 Enters Amherst Academy (graduated 1847)
1844 Visits relatives in Boston, Cambridge, Worcester in May and June
1847–48 Attends Mount Holyoke Female Seminary, South Hadley, Massachusetts
1850 Valentine to George Gould, "Awake ye muses nine, sing me a strain divine," published, Amherst College *Indicator*, in February
1851 Visits her brother Austin in Boston, Massachusetts
1853 Visits in Springfield, Massachusetts
1855 (?) Visits Washington, D.C., and Philadelphia
1857 Emerson lectures in Amherst, on December 16, and visits the Austin Dickinsons
1861 Visits Middletown, Connecticut
1862 First writes to Thomas Wentworth Higginson asking for literary advice
1864 Travels to Boston, for eye treatment
1870 Higginson visits Emily Dickinson in Amherst, August 17

1873 Higginson makes a second and final visit, December 3
1874 Father, Edward Dickinson, dies in Boston
1876 Helen Hunt Jackson asks Emily Dickinson to contribute to *A Masque of Poets*
1878 Article in Springfield *Daily Republican* suggests Emily Dickinson as collaborator on the "Saxe Holm" stories with Helen Hunt Jackson
1882 Mother dies
1883 Thomas Niles asks Emily Dickinson to submit a volume of poems for publication
1886 Dies, May 15, in Amherst
1890 *Poems by Emily Dickinson*, First Series, edited by Mabel Loomis Todd and T. W. Higginson
1891 *Poems by Emily Dickinson*, Second Series, edited by T. W. Higginson and Mabel Loomis Todd
1894 *Letters of Emily Dickinson*, edited by Mabel Loomis Todd
1896 *Poems by Emily Dickinson*, Third Series, edited by Mabel Loomis Todd

FURTHER READINGS

R. B. Sewall is presently working on a biography of Emily Dickinson, which will be published in 1973.

Thomas H. Johnson, ed., *Final Harvest: Emily Dickinson's Poems* (1961)
———, *The Poems of Emily Dickinson* (1955; 3 vols.)
——— and Theodora Ward, eds., *The Letters of Emily Dickinson* (1958; 3 vols.)

Charles R. Anderson, *Emily Dickinson's Poetry: Stairway of Surprise* (1960)
Millicent Todd Bingham, *Ancestors' Brocades: The Literary Debut of Emily Dickinson* (1945)
———, *Emily Dickinson: A Revelation* (1954)
———, *Emily Dickinson's Home* (1955)

R. P. Blackmur, "Emily Dickinson's Notation," *Kenyon Review* (Spring, 1956)
———, *Language as Gesture* (1952)
Richard Chase, *Emily Dickinson* (1951)
Jay Leyda, *The Years and Hours of Emily Dickinson* (1960)
John Crowe Ransom, "Emily Dickinson: A Poet Restored," *Perspectives USA* (Spring, 1956)
Allen Tate, *Collected Essays* (1959)
Theodora Ward, *The Capsule of the Mind: Chapters in the Life of Emily Dickinson* (1961)
Austin Warren, "Emily Dickinson," *Sewanee Review* (Autumn, 1957)
George F. Whicher, *This Was a Poet: A Critical Biography of Emily Dickinson* (1938)

(448) This Was a Poet—It Is That (c. 1862)

To say of any nineteenth-century New England poet that his or her poetry plays a fresh sensibility against the vestiges of Puritan culture is to say that, in some degree or other, such a poet is a Romantic. It is also to say that such a poet will be much concerned with the nature of poetry itself—as the medium in which new awarenesses of the human condition can best be expressed; with the reaches *and* the limits of poetic vision; with the figure of the poet; and with the power of poetry to compel and transform. The first seven poems selected are meditations within and around those themes.

The following poem attributes to the poet the capacity (which Emerson declared to be the mark of wisdom) of perceiving the miraculous in the common—in Emily Dickinson's idiom, of distilling an amazing "attar" from the familiar roses that fade and die at one's front door.

This was a Poet—It is That
Distills amazing sense
From ordinary Meanings—
And Attar so immense

From the familiar species
That perished by the Door—
We wonder it was not Ourselves
Arrested it—before—

Of Pictures, the Discloser—
The Poet—it is He—   10
Entitles Us—by Contrast—
To ceaseless Poverty—

Of Portion—so unconscious—
The Robbing—could not harm—
Himself—to Him—a Fortune—
Exterior—to Time—

(290) Of Bronze—and Blaze (c. 1861)

Here Emily Dickinson makes immediate her memory of the aurora borealis observed in Amherst a decade earlier. "Of Bronze—and Blaze" pairs to some extent with "This was a Poet," for in contrasting her own limited splendors with the spectacular display of the skies, Emily Dickinson shows a becoming modesty about just

how "amazing" a purely human poetic vision can be.

As so often, it is a poem in which every word counts and every important word brushes against every other, forcing new insights and attitudes into being. When the poem appeared in 1892, the eighth and ninth lines had been changed to:

paints my simple spirit
with tints of majesty—

which not only missed but quite reversed Emily Dickinson's point: that the aurora borealis had afflicted her with a feverish ambition to go beyond mortal possibility. To say that her "splendors, are Menagerie" is an uncommonly succinct way of both asserting and denying that her poetry contains splendor by bringing it together with the glitter and triviality of a traveling circus.

If every word counts, so does every bit of punctuation. To see the impact of Emily Dickinson's recurring dashes, one need only rewrite and then reread the opening lines as follows:

> Of bronze and blaze
> The north tonight,
> So adequate it forms,
> So preconcerted with itself,
> So distant to alarms

As written by Emily Dickinson, each successive key word seems wrenched out of an imagination that is watching and reflecting with the greatest intensity, straining every nerve to bring forth the exact word, the exact perception; as rewritten it is a mere singsong, in which no word counts for much of anything on a surface over which the mind slides unnoticing.

Of Bronze—and Blaze—
The North—Tonight—
So adequate—it forms—
So preconcerted with itself—
So distant—to alarms—
An Unconcern so sovereign
To Universe, or me—
Infects my simple spirit
With Taints of Majesty—
Till I take vaster attitudes—   10
And strut upon my stem—
Disdaining Men, and Oxygen,
For Arrogance of them—

My Splendors, are Menagerie—
But their Competeless Show
Will entertain the Centuries
When I, am long ago,
An Island in dishonored Grass—
Whom none but Beetles—know.

(326) I Cannot Dance upon My Toes (c. 1862)

Emily Dickinson, in this poem, seems again to be belittling her poetic capabilities. But she was never wittier, or more cunning, than here. It was included in a letter to Higginson, in which she asked—responding to Higginson's complaint about her irregularities—"Are these more orderly?" The techniques of classical ballet, which provide the encompassing metaphor of the poem, stand for the techniques of Victorian poetry. In saying that she cannot perform as a ballerina and in then displaying a thorough knowledge of all the moves, leaps, and gestures of ballet, Emily Dickinson is saying that she does not know how to perform poetically like Longfellow, and then proceeds to outdistance him at his own game.

I cannot dance upon my Toes—
No Man instructed me—

But oftentimes, among my mind,
A Glee possesseth me,

That had I Ballet knowledge—
Would put itself abroad
In Pirouette to blanch a Troupe—
Or lay a Prima, mad,

And though I had no Gown of Gauze—
No Ringlet, to my Hair,   10
Nor hopped to Audiences—like Birds,
One Claw upon the Air,

Nor tossed my shape in Eider Balls,
Nor rolled on wheels of snow
Till I was out of sight, in sound,
The House encore me so—

Nor any know I know the Art
I mention—easy—Here—
Nor any Placard boast me—
It's full as Opera—   20

(1129) Tell All the Truth but Tell It Slant (c. 1868)

These eight lines contain the fundamental principle of Emily Dickinson's poetry, perhaps of all great lyric poetry.

Tell all the Truth but tell it slant—
Success in Circuit lies

Too bright for our infirm Delight
The Truth's superb surprise
As Lightning to the Children eased
With explanation kind
The Truth must dazzle gradually
Or every man be blind—

(315) He Fumbles at Your Soul (c. 1862)

The "He" of this poem may well be a great preacher, and the poem may record the impact upon Emily Dickinson of the sermon she heard Charles Wadsworth preach in 1854. But the preacher, if that is who he is, is likened first to a piano player tuning up, then to a carpenter with a hammer, then to an Olympian figure hurling thunderbolts, and finally to an Indian warrior scalping a white man. Amid these clustering images, "he" seems to enlarge into the God of Jonathan Edwards (the kind of devastating force, swooping down all-powerfully upon the human spirit, that was envisaged in several early poems by Robert Lowell). But it was of poetry and its capacity to stun that Emily Dickinson spoke in language closest to that of this poem. To Higginson, when he visited her in Amherst in 1879, she remarked (Higginson called it "a crowning extravaganza"): "If I read a book and it makes my whole body so

cold no fire can ever warm me, I know that is poetry. If I feel physically as if the top of my head were taken off, I know that is poetry. These are the only ways I know it. Is there any other way?"

He fumbles at your Soul
As Players at the Keys
Before they drop full Music on—
He stuns you by degrees—
Prepares your brittle Nature
For the Ethereal Blow
By fainter Hammers—further heard—
Then nearer—Then so slow
Your Breath has time to straighten—
Your Brain—to bubble Cool—   10
Deals—One—imperial—Thunderbolt—
That scalps your naked Soul—

When Winds take Forests in their Paws—
The Universe—is still—

(441) This Is My Letter to the World (c. 1862)

The last poem in this sequence reflects Emily Dickinson's characteristically contradictory attitude toward publication and fame.

This is my letter to the World
That never wrote to Me—

The simple News that Nature told—
With tender Majesty

Her Message is committed
To Hands I cannot see—
For love of Her—Sweet—countrymen—
Judge tenderly—of Me

(1035) Bee! I'm Expecting You! (c. 1865)

Wit is perhaps the first striking feature of Emily Dickinson's poetry: the unexpected word or turn of phrase which reveals the unexpected

twist of mind or spirit; the unlikely combination of terms; the startling and meaningful juxtaposition of disparate elements. If such elements are not, in these poems, yoked by violence together, as in the most famous definition of the figures of speech in metaphysical poetry, they are at least very adroitly wedded. Even Emily Dickinson's most somber poems are witty in the fundamental sense of the adjective; but a number are witty in the more familiar sense of joining delight to verbal and intellectual surprise. Sometimes, she simply enjoyed herself in poetry; she had fun. Here are seven poems that illustrate Emily Dickinson's sportive and satiric side.

She was at her greatest ease socially with children. At school, she had diverted her classmates by making up funny stories; in her mature years she entertained the neighboring young by inventing verses for them—of which the following is an example. It reminds us that, along with the hymn book, nursery rhymes were a main source of Emily Dickinson's poems, especially rhymes—like "Who Killed Cock Robin"—which tell of the strange transactions and the mysterious dialogues of the animal kingdom.

Bee! I'm expecting you!
Was saying Yesterday
To Somebody you know
That you were due—

The Frogs got Home last Week—
Are settled, and at work—
Birds, mostly back—
The Clover warm and thick—

You'll get my Letter by
The seventeenth; Reply
Or better, be with me—
Yours, Fly.

10

(585) I Like to See It Lap the Miles (c. 1862)

The Amherst and Belchertown railway was opened in 1853, thanks in part to the civic efforts of Edward Dickinson. At the opening ceremony, Emily wrote her brother, "Father was, as usual, chief marshal, and went marching around . . . like some old Roman general upon a triumph day." Nine years later, the event provided the basis for the following poem.

Yvor Winters, who thought it "abominable," dismissed the poem as "silly playfulness." Others have rejoiced in it. The basic device—to speak of what used to be called "the iron horse" as though it really were a horse—may seem obvious enough. But it is no slight feat to sustain a seventeen-line poem with a string of infinitives controlled by a single verbal phrase ("I like"); and as always there are some attractions and some puzzles.

I like to see it lap the Miles—
And lick the Valleys up—

And stop to feed itself at Tanks—
And then—prodigious step

Around a Pile of Mountains—
And supercilious peer
In Shanties—by the sides of Roads—
And then a Quarry pare

To fit its Ribs
And crawl between
Complaining all the while
In horrid—hooting stanza—
Then chase itself down Hill—

10

And neigh like Boanerges[1]—
Then—punctual as a Star
Stop—docile and omnipotent
At its own stable door—

[1] The name Christ gave to the disciples James and John—hence, a vociferous preacher or orator.

(333) The Grass So Little Has to Do (c. 1862)

This is the poem whose last two words so shook Higginson's grammatical soul.

The Grass so little has to do—

A Sphere of simple Green—
With only Butterflies to brood
And Bees to entertain—

And stir all day to pretty Tunes
The Breezes fetch along—
And hold the Sunshine in its lap
And bow to everything—

And thread the Dews, all night, like Pearls—
And make itself so fine   10
A Duchess were too common
For such a noticing—

And even when it dies—to pass
In Odors so divine—
Like Lowly spices, lain to sleep—
Or Spikenards, perishing—

And then, in Sovereign Barns to dwell—
And dream the Days away,
The Grass so little has to do
I wish I were a Hay—   20

(1672) Lightly Stepped a Yellow Star (?)

Here, as in the previous poem, the ending is almost everything. The final two lines throw a sudden new light back upon both the imagery and the very poetic style of what had preceded them. In fact, Emily Dickinson very rarely used inversions like "Lightly stepped" or "Loosed the Moon"—they were, precisely, the staple of the conventional verse (with its striving to be "poetic") that she is here satirizing.

Lightly stepped a yellow star
To its lofty place—
Loosed the Moon her silver hat
From her lustral Face—
All of Evening softly lit
As an Astral Hall—
Father, I observed to Heaven,
You are punctual.

(214) I Taste a Liquor Never Brewed (c. 1860)

Several critics have suggested that this poem contains a parody of Emerson's "Bacchus," with Emily Dickinson announcing her preference for strong beer as against the Dionysiac wine of inspiration called for by Emerson. But if so, the poem swoops beyond parody to evoke an all-possessing glee, an intoxication of spirit in the midst of physical nature that has the angels in heaven cheering and the saints hurrying to the window to watch.

In the *Atlantic Monthly*, in January, 1892, Thomas Bailey Aldrich declared the poem might pass muster if the first stanza were revised and proposed his own version:

> I taste a liquor never brewed
> In vats upon the Rhine;
> No tankard ever held a draught
> Of alcohol like mine.

I taste a liquor never brewed—
From Tankards scooped in Pearl—
Not all the Vats upon the Rhine
Yield such an Alcohol!

Inebriate of Air—am I—
And Debauchee of Dew—
Reeling—thro endless summer days—
From inns of Molten Blue—

When "Landlords" turn the drunken Bee
Out of the Foxglove's door—   10
When Butterflies—renounce their "drams"—
I shall but drink the more!

Till Seraphs swing their snowy Hats—
And Saints—to windows run—
To see the little Tippler
Leaning against the—Sun—

(1333) A Little Madness in the Spring (c. 1875)

We have spoken of the "incomplete" quality of most of Emily Dickinson's poems, and here is a good place to elaborate on it. The worksheet of this poem lists a number of alternative adjectives and nouns for the next-to-last line and looks something like this:

But God be with the clown
Who ponders this tremendous scene
This sudden legacy of green
As if it were his own.

                          gay bright
quick whole — swift — fleet — sweet
fair Apocalypse — (green) whole
This whole apocalypse
of green
experience — Astonishment —
periphery — Experiment
wild experiment

There are many different combinations suggested there: gay apocalypse, swift experiment, sweet astonishment, and so on. Emily Dickinson's own fair copy selects "whole experiment" for the key phrase; Charles Anderson concurs; and this indeed is the way the poem reads in Johnson's editions.

Yet it is also a fact that the fair copy by no means necessarily indicates what would have been Emily Dickinson's final choice had the poem been sent out for publication. The reader is invited to try his hand at the stimulating game of completing the poem. What is involved, of course, is an interpretation of the preceding lines and then a decision as to which combination of adjective and noun best brings the poem out where it seems to want to go.

The chief alternative nouns seem to be "apocalypse" and "experiment," those being the two underlined by Emily Dickinson. But the difference between those two is enormous and brings into question, as it were, Emily Dickinson's entire theory of culture. "Apocalypse" was, for her, a theological word, carrying with it a vast range of implication; "experiment" comes from the vocabulary of science. "Apocalypse" announces an absolute finality (an ultimate revelation); "experiment" is, precisely, tentative, provisional. To choose one or the other is, for the moment, to identify the fundamental nature of Emily Dickinson's imagination.

A little Madness in the Spring
Is wholesome even for the King,
But God be with the Clown—
Who ponders this tremendous scene—
This whole Experiment of Green—
As if it were his own!

(401) What Soft—Cherubic Creatures (c. 1862)

The genteel ladies of Amherst here provoke Emily Dickinson to a kind of erotic hilarity: one would as soon commit sexual assault upon a plush chair as upon them, or attempt to rape a remote star. They have a horror of human nature as it actually is: "freckled," tainted, prone to sin. Similarly, they feel that "redemption" should be reserved for the few, like the A.B. degree at Amherst College; they are ashamed that it is available even to fishermen (such as St. Peter). The poem concludes with an unexpectedly severe irony: redemption and the Redeemer will be ashamed of *them*. "Whosoever shall be ashamed of me, of him also shall the Son of Man be ashamed when he cometh in the glory of the father" (Mark 8:38).

What Soft—Cherubic Creatures—
These Gentlewomen are—
One would as soon assault a Plush—
Or violate a Star—

Such Dimity Convictions—
A Horror so refined
Of freckled Human Nature—
Of Deity—ashamed—

It's such a common—Glory—
A Fisherman's—Degree—
Redemption—Brittle Lady—
Be so—ashamed of Thee—

10

(754) My Life Had Stood—a Loaded Gun (c. 1863)

Emily Dickinson wrote a great many love poems, but the most emotionally charged among them are not always the most successful. Especially when she was pouring out her anguish at the moment of Charles Wadsworth's departure for California, the circumstances of her situation sometimes defeated her talent. But there are major exceptions, several of them included in the half dozen poems in this group. If one were to choose a title for this sequence, it might be the phrase "Calvaries of Love," which concludes "There came a Day at Summer's full" (a poem not included here). Love, for Emily Dickinson, often led to a kind of crucifixion of the heart and was associated with thoughts of evanescence and loss.

The central figure in the following poem is remarkable, even shocking: the female lover as a loaded hunting rifle galvanized into life by its huntsman owner. It is an unconscious defiance of the Freudian theory of symbolism, according to which a rifle is *always* a phallic symbol. But the poem gains much of its strange force from Emily Dickinson's tact in sometimes exploiting the implications of her symbol (as in the "yellow eye" of the gun barrel) and sometimes suppressing them.

The poem is a ballad of sorts and conveys the same sense of immediacy and remoteness as did the old English ballad, which, with the hymn book and the nursery rhyme, was still another source for the shape and tone of Emily Dickinson's poems. It may be noticed, too, that the speaker was not only taken hold of by her master, she was "identified"—given identity. For Emily Dickinson, love was an identifying emotion; before love a person is not even a "he" or a "she," but merely a neutral "it." Congratulating a friend upon her engagement, Emily once wrote: "Til it has loved—no man or woman can become itself."

My Life had stood—a Loaded Gun—
In Corners—till a Day
The Owner passed—identified—
And carried Me away—

And now We roam in Sovereign Woods—
And now We hunt the Doe—
And every time I speak for Him—
The Mountains straight reply—

And do I smile, such cordial light
Upon the Valley glow—   10
It is as a Vesuvian face
Had let its pleasure through—

And when at Night—Our good Day done—
I guard My Master's Head—
'Tis better than the Eider-Duck's
Deep Pillow—to have shared—

To foe of His—I'm deadly foe—
None stir the second time—
On whom I lay a Yellow Eye—
Or an emphatic Thumb—   20

Though I than He—may longer live
He longer must—than I—
For I have but the power to kill,
Without—the power to die—

(249) Wild Nights—Wild Nights! (c. 1861)

This is perhaps the most candidly erotic of Emily Dickinson's poems (as against the no less intense but usually more covert eroticism one finds elsewhere). It expresses an almost violent physical passion for what she calls "luxury," no doubt recalling from her Latin studies that one of the meanings of *luxuria* is lust. Freudian symbolism is again violated by the image of the male figure as the sea, in which the female symbolically "moors" herself. One may keep in mind Emily Dickinson's statement to Higginson: "When I state myself, as the representative of the verse, it does not mean me, but a supposed person"; and in "A narrow Fellow in the

Grass," she explicitly supposes herself to be a boy. The speaker in the love poems, however, is invariably a woman.

Wild Nights—Wild Nights!
Were I with thee
Wild Nights should be
Our luxury!

Futile—the Winds—
To a Heart in port—
Done with the Compass—
Done with the Chart!

Rowing in Eden—
Ah, the Sea!
Might I but moor—Tonight—
In Thee!

10

(303) The Soul Selects Her Own Society (c. 1862)

The introduction offers some remarks about this poem and the "one" specially chosen by Emily Dickinson as her "society."

The Soul selects her own Society—
Then—shuts the Door—
To her divine Majority—
Present no more—

Unmoved—she notes the Chariots—pausing—
At her low Gate—
Unmoved—an Emperor be kneeling
Upon her Mat—

I've known her—from an ample nation—
Choose One—
Then—close the Valves of her attention—
Like Stone—

10

(745) Renunciation—Is a Piercing Virtue (c. 1863)

In the following poem we hear Emily Dickinson meditating aloud, groping slowly for the precise image, the painfully articulated series of images by which the act of renunciation can be identified and made tolerable. Renunciation is a virtue, but it is a virtue that wounds and must be explained to the soul bereft. How can renunciation—the choosing against one's inmost desire, the acceptance of "the covered vision"—be made to seem the supreme human gesture?

Words like "expectation" (perhaps of a life hereafter) and "justify" (as in "justification by faith") suggest that Emily Dickinson may to some extent be drawing upon the Protestant doctrine of renunciation, the turning away from the beguiling things of this world. That same doctrine haunted the Puritan-descended imaginations of Hawthorne and, perhaps even more, of Henry James; renunciation is one of the major themes of nineteenth-century American literature. But like both Hawthorne and James, Emily Dickinson dramatizes and personalizes the theme: for all its abstraction, this is a

tremblingly personal poem. For a visionary poet like Emily Dickinson, no more personally excruciating image could be devised than that of putting out one's eyes just as the sun was rising on a new day.

Renunciation—is a piercing Virtue—
The letting go
A Presence—for an Expectation—
Not now—
The putting out of Eyes—
Just Sunrise—
Lest Day—
Day's Great Progenitor—
Outvie
Renunciation—is the Choosing
Against itself—
Itself to justify
Unto itself—
When larger function—
Make that appear—
Smaller—that Covered Vision—Here—

10

(348) I Dreaded That First Robin, So (c. 1862)

This poem can be placed alongside Whitman's "When Lilacs Last in the Dooryard Bloom'd," as juxtaposing the sense of profoundest loss with the rebirth of nature in the spring. As with Whitman's poem, the source of loss is not identified; nor should it be, for if it was initially Charles Wadsworth, it has deepened into more general pain: she grieves for what happens to life. Where Whitman, however, moves characteristically toward a total fusing and reconciliation of the conflicting elements (lilac and star and bird and poet), Emily Dickinson no less characteristically faces up to the cruel indifference of nature, the fundamental irreconcilability and lack of communication between the poet and the natural environment.

The nightmare fears of the central stanzas—that the bird songs in the woods would mangle her in her raw emotional state, and the very charm of the daffodils would pierce her—are subdued by the opening and closing verses, where it is made clear that that is what she desperately *feared* would happen but which did not—quite. "He hurts a little, though."

The third line—"I'm some accustomed to Him grown"—shows Emily Dickinson adapting, as she often did, a laconic New England colloquialism to moving poetic expression. In "The Robin's my Criterion for Tune," she remarked: "I see—New Englandly."

I dreaded that first Robin, so,
But He is mastered, now,
I'm some accustomed to Him grown,
He hurts a little, though—

I thought if I could only live
Till that first Shout got by—
Not all Pianos in the Woods
Had power to mangle me—

I dared not meet the Daffodils—
For fear their Yellow Gown   10
Would pierce me with a fashion
So foreign to my own—

I wished the Grass would hurry—
So—when 'twas time to see—
He'd be too tall, the tallest one
Could stretch—to look at me—

I could not bear the Bees should come,
I wished they'd stay away
In those dim countries where they go,
What word had they, for me?   20

They're here, though; not a creature failed—
No Blossom stayed away
In gentle deference to me—
The Queen of Calvary—

Each one salutes me, as he goes,
And I, my childish Plumes,
Lift, in bereaved acknowledgment
Of their unthinking Drums—

(536) The Heart Asks Pleasure—First (c. 1862)

If the preceding poems seem to spring from a specific and devastating experience of loss, the next four explore the experience of extreme *pain* —the severest kind of suffering, by which the psyche can be consumed, and which leads to the extinction of consciousness.

The first of them traces a progression of psychological states, connected by the phrase "and then," which suggests the inevitability and universality of the psychic career. Denied pleasure, the heart asks at least to be "excused" from pain, like a child being excused from an unpleasant ordeal. Denied that, the heart asks for drugs to deaden the suffering. God—now the soul's Grand Inquisitor, applying various tortures as punishment for sin—is finally begged to permit the soul to be obliterated.

The Heart asks Pleasure—first—
And then—Excuse from Pain—
And then—those little Anodynes
That deaden suffering—

And then—to go to sleep—
And then—if it should be
The will of its Inquisitor
The privilege to die—

(280) I Felt a Funeral, in My Brain (c. 1861)

Here is Emily Dickinson's most brilliant and in its way most appalling use of the Protestant funeral service to dramatize the slow death of personality, of mind and reason, senses and spirit. It is connected directly with those dramas of the soul, those relentless metaphorical journeys through the corrupted "heart" that Puritan writers rendered with such force and that, in Emily Dickinson's lifetime, Hawthorne and Henry James continued to represent with every kind of subtlety.

The soul—or "brain"—is the setting of its own terrible drama: it is the little church where the "Mourners" (mournful, grief-stricken thoughts) mill about and where the service is then held; and the path to the cemetery across which the coffin is carried. But under the persistent, intolerable throbbing of pain, the soul gradually shreds and dissociates, is reduced to an ear hearing nothing but the booming deathknell of its being, is wrecked, stranded, isolated—until, as in the dramatic figure the coffin is lowered into the grave, reason collapses utterly, and the soul plunges down ravines of unconsciousness, striking world after world of nothingness.

I felt a Funeral, in my Brain,
And Mourners to and fro
Kept treading—treading—till it seemed
That Sense was breaking through—

And when they all were seated,
A Service, like a Drum—
Kept beating—beating—till I thought
My Mind was going numb—

And then I heard them lift a Box
And creak across my Soul   10
With those same Boots of Lead, again,
Then Space—began to toll,

As all the Heavens were a Bell,
And Being, but an Ear,
And I, and Silence, some strange Race
Wrecked, solitary, here—

And then a Plank in Reason, broke,
And I dropped down, and down—
And hit a World, at every plunge,
And Finished knowing—then—   20

(341) After Great Pain, a Formal Feeling Comes (c. 1862)

The funeral service is again exploited to enact the ravaging of the spirit by pain—or rather, in this more muted drama, the exhaustion of spirit in the wake of pain. There is a loss of identity (if love *gives* identity, as Emily Dickinson believed, intense suffering destroys it), and of any sense of time and place. Everything is foreshortened or disconnected, even in the very texture of this poem: verbs without predicates ("bore"), phrases unrelated syntactically ("Of Ground, or Air, or Ought—"), a sort of rhythmic shrinking and dragging, a verbal drift into oblivion.

After great pain, a formal feeling comes—
The Nerves sit ceremonious, like Tombs—
The stiff Heart questions was it He, that bore,
And Yesterday, or Centuries before?

The Feet, mechanical, go round—
Of Ground, or Air, or Ought—
A Wooden way
Regardless grown,
A Quartz contentment, like a stone—

This is the Hour of Lead—   10
Remembered, if outlived,
As Freezing persons, recollect the Snow—
First—Chill—then Stupor—then the letting go—

(553) One Crucifixion Is Recorded—Only (c. 1862)

Here is a fine instance of Emily Dickinson's capacity to bend the Biblical vocabulary to an account of her own psychic condition, with "Gethsemane" as a province at the center of being.

One Crucifixion is recorded—only—
How many be
Is not affirmed of Mathematics—
Or History—

One Calvary—exhibited to Stranger—
As many be
As persons—or Peninsulas—
Gethsemane—

Is but a Province—in the Being's Centre—
Judea—   10
For Journey—or Crusade's Achieving—
Too near—

Our Lord—indeed—made Compound Witness—
And yet—
There's newer—nearer Crucifixion
Than That—

(764) Presentiment—Is That Long Shadow—on the Lawn (c. 1863)

What used to be called Emily Dickinson's "nature poems" are more often than not poems wherein the observation of some natural phenomenon stirs into being some feeling or reflection on the poet's part, to the point where a revelation seems to hover on the rim of consciousness. It is at this point that Emily Dickinson departs most clearly from Jonathan Edwards on the one hand and Emerson on the other. Natural phenomena did not for her, as they did for Edwards, comprise a system of "types" through which one could read the divine scheme; nor did she have the confidence expressed by Emerson in *Nature* that the objects close around us were perfectly understandable symbols of the world of the moral law. Emily Dickinson was closer to Hawthorne in her delicate sense of the ambiguity of natural things, yet she did not share Hawthorne's frustration over nature's resistance to the inquiring eye.

The next six poems are variously representative of Emily Dickinson's imaginative negotiations with nature.

Presentiment—is that long Shadow—on the Lawn—
Indicative that Suns go down—

The Notice to the startled Grass
That Darkness—is about to pass—

(812) A Light Exists in Spring (c. 1864)

Emily Dickinson was peculiarly skillful in suggesting the tantalizing brevity of revelation, and even more the revelation that does not quite take place. The following is a poem of "scarcely" and "almost": a poem about something that science and reason are unable to define, but that human nature can distinctly feel.

A Light exists in Spring
Not present on the Year
At any other period—
When March is scarcely here

A Color stands abroad
On Solitary Fields

That Science cannot overtake
But Human Nature feels.

It waits upon the Lawn,
It shows the furthest Tree   10
Upon the furthest Slope you know
It almost speaks to you.

Then as Horizons step
Or Noons report away
Without the Formula of sound
It passes and we stay—

A quality of loss
Affecting our Content
As Trade had suddenly encroached
Upon a Sacrament.   20

(1068) Further in Summer Than the Birds (c. 1866)

This poem is a mingling of potent rituals: natural, Christian, and pagan; and its cluster of meanings (for it clearly cannot be reduced to a single meaning) must be looked for within the ritual pattern. The cricket's song bespeaks the passing of summer at the very height of summer; he is "further in summer than the birds" in the sense that he is aware of autumn's coming, he is further along in time, in his own consciousness, than the birds are—because he is further into the secret of the natural cycle. The language of Christian liturgy suggests that if nature will die with the year's end, it will later be reborn. But the pagan element tends rather to separate the human onlooker from the natural process and invests him with a feeling of loneliness and isolation.

Further in Summer than the Birds
Pathetic from the Grass
A minor Nation celebrates
Its unobtrusive Mass.

No Ordinance be seen
So gradual the Grace
A pensive Custom it becomes
Enlarging Loneliness.

Antiquest felt at Noon
When August burning low   10
Arise this spectral Canticle
Repose to typify

Remit as yet no Grace
No Furrow on the Glow
Yet a Druidic Difference
Enhances Nature now

(258) There's a Certain Slant of Light (c. 1861)

This poem concludes the little cycle that began with "A Light exists in Spring" and that continued through those that reflect on the height of summer, late summer and early fall, and now winter.

Yet to borrow a phrase from Robert Frost, this is "contrary stuff." The poem is a bundle of interacting contraries. To take a single example: the slant of light observed (particularly in New England) on winter afternoons oppresses the soul "like the heft/Of Cathedral Tunes." When the poem was first published, in 1890, the editors polished up the author's crudity by substituting "weight" for "heft"—thus committing several kinds of blunders. The colloquial "heft" is more pungent than "weight"; more important, heft means not only a heavy weight but also the straining effort to lift such a weight (to *heave* it upward: "heave" and "heavy" come from the same root). The slant of light at once oppresses and bestirs one to shake off the depression; even as the music of the cathedral bells is at once doleful and tuneful. Emily Dickinson, as we said in the introduction, always left her spiritual and psychological options open.

There's a certain Slant of light,
Winter Afternoons—
That oppresses, like the Heft
Of Cathedral Tunes—

Heavenly Hurt, it gives us—
We can find no scar,
But internal difference,
Where the Meanings, are—

None may teach it—Any—
'Tis the Seal Despair—   10
An imperial affliction
Sent us of the Air—

When it comes, the Landscape listens—
Shadows—hold their breath—
When it goes, 'tis like the Distance
On the look of Death—

(1575) The Bat Is Dun, with Wrinkled Wings (c. 1876)

The Bat is dun, with wrinkled Wings—
Like fallow Article—
And not a song pervade his Lips—
Or none perceptible.

His small Umbrella quaintly halved
Describing in the Air
An Arc alike inscrutable
Elate Philosopher.

Deputed from what Firmament—
Of what Astute Abode—   10
Empowered with what Malignity
Auspiciously withheld—

To his adroit Creator
Ascribe no less the praise—
Beneficent, believe me,
His Eccentricities—

(986) A Narrow Fellow in the Grass (c. 1865)

Emily Dickinson was on friendly terms with a
number of animals, as she says here, but the
snake never failed to make her feel (it is one of
her most exact metaphors) "a zero at the bone."

A narrow Fellow in the Grass
Occasionally rides—
You may have met Him—did you not
His notice sudden is—

The Grass divides as with a Comb—
A spotted shaft is seen—
And then it closes at your feet
And opens further on—

He likes a Boggy Acre

A Floor too cool for Corn—   10
Yet when a Boy, and Barefoot—
I more than once at Noon

Have passed, I thought, a Whip lash
Unbraiding in the Sun
When stooping to secure it
It wrinkled, and was gone—

Several of Nature's People
I know, and they know me—
I feel for them a transport
Of cordiality—   20

But never met this Fellow
Attended, or alone
Without a tighter breathing
And Zero at the Bone—

(412) I Read My Sentence—Steadily (c. 1862)

In *Democratic Vistas*, Walt Whitman argued
that what American literature needed above all
else was poets who could write great poems of
death. He himself had, of course, already written
several such, including "Out of the Cradle Endlessly Rocking" and "When Lilacs Last in the
Dooryard Bloom'd." But it was a penetrating
observation to make in the midst of the chaotic
bustle of the Gilded Age, when death was the
phenomenon the American imagination was
least inclined to meditate.

If in Emily Dickinson's case death was a
reality constantly impinging on the scene of
mortal aspiration, nevertheless it was countered

by the recurring hope of immortality. These final
seven poems display some of the twists and turns
Emily Dickinson's imagination so brilliantly
took as it moved among the enormous ultimates.

Emily Dickinson—rather like Albert Camus
in some of his philosophical writings—here declares that man is mortal by identifying him as
a being *condemned* to death. The "sentence"
being read and reviewed in the first lines is the
death sentence. The poem then expands on
that notion in a deft employment of legal and
courtroom language—a somber parody, as it
were, of the legalistic vocabulary of Calvinist
doctrine.

I read my sentence—steadily—
Reviewed it with my eyes,
To see that I made no mistake
In its extremest clause—
The Date, and manner, of the shame—
And then the Pious Form
That "God have mercy" on the Soul

The Jury voted Him—
I made my soul familiar—with her extremity—
That at the last, it should not be a novel Agony—   10
But she, and Death, acquainted—
Meet tranquilly, as friends—
Salute, and pass, without a Hint—
And there, the Matter ends—

(465) I Heard a Fly Buzz—When I Died (c. 1862)

"Tell all the truth, but tell it slant." This poem tells a disconcerting truth: that one's death may be a most trivial event, hedged about with ir-relevancies, and leading to no afterlife. But it tells that truth circuitously: undermining the pieties of Protestant theology by references to the last parceling out of small possessions, the uncertain and irrelevant buzzing of a blue fly, the slow loss of physical vision. No grand final words or gestures; no heavenly music or angels descending; no vision of God's eternity.

In the version published in 1896, the editors so misread the poem as to substitute "in his power" for "in the Room." The pieties that Emily Dickinson was undermining evidently long survived her.

I heard a Fly buzz—when I died—
The Stillness in the Room
Was like the Stillness in the Air—
Between the Heaves of Storm—

The Eyes around—had wrung them dry—
And Breaths were gathering firm
For that last Onset—when the King
Be witnessed—in the Room—

I willed my Keepsakes—Signed away
What portion of me be   10
Assignable—and then it was
There interposed a Fly—

With Blue—uncertain stumbling Buzz—
Between the light—and me—
And then the Windows failed—and then
I could not see to see—

(389) There's Been a Death, in the Opposite House (c. 1862)

On the level of sheer description—of the death of someone in a nearby house in a small town—this is a matchless poem. The images follow one another with gravely witty precision: the house's numb look, the window opening like a pod, a mattress thrown from the window, the arrival of the self-important minister, the children's speculations, the coming of the undertaker (the "man of the appalling trade"), the funeral pro-cession. But by implication the poem conveys a good deal more than that—about what is lack-ing in this scurry of activities, about death being busily robbed of dignity and significance.

There's been a Death, in the Opposite House,
As lately as Today—

I know it, by the numb look
Such Houses have—alway—

The Neighbors rustle in and out—
The Doctor—drives away—
A Window opens like a Pod—
Abrupt—mechanically—

Somebody flings a Mattress out—
The Children hurry by—   10
They wonder if it died—on that—
I used to—when a Boy—

The Minister—goes stiffly in—
As if the House were His—
And He owned all the Mourners—now—
And little Boys—besides—

And then the Milliner—and the Man
Of the Appalling Trade—

To take the measure of the House—
There'll be that Dark Parade—   20

Of Tassels—and of Coaches—soon—

It's easy as a Sign—
The Intuition of the News—
In just a Country Town—

(712) Because I Could Not Stop for Death (c. 1863)

There is no reason to dispute Allen Tate's pronouncement that this is "one of the perfect poems in English. . . . If the word 'great' means anything in poetry, this poem is one of the greatest in the English language." Tate's further remarks can be taken as our gloss:

> The rhythm charges with movement the pattern of suspended action back of the poem. Every image is precise and, moreover, not merely beautiful, but fused with the central idea. Every image extends and intensifies every other. The third stanza especially shows Miss Dickinson's power to fuse, into a single order of perception, a heterogeneous series. . . . She has presented a typical Christian theme in its final irresolution, without making any final statement about it. . . . We are not told what to think; we are told to look at the situation.

Because I could not stop for Death—
He kindly stopped for me—

The Carriage held but just Ourselves—
And Immortality.

We slowly drove—He knew no haste
And I had put away
My labor and my leisure too,
For His Civility—

We passed the School, where Children strove
At Recess—in the Ring—   10
We passed the Fields of Gazing Grain—
We passed the Setting Sun—

Or rather—He passed Us—
The Dews drew quivering and chill—
For only Gossamer, my Gown—
My Tippet—only Tulle—

We paused before a House that seemed
A Swelling of the Ground—
The Roof was scarcely visible—
The Cornice—in the Ground—   20

Since then—'tis Centuries—and yet
Feels shorter than the Day
I first surmised the Horses' Heads
Were toward Eternity—

(528) Mine—By the Right of the White Election! (c. 1862)

If, in "I heard a Fly buzz—when I died," Emily Dickinson insinuated with bold irony that death was simply and entirely the final loss of consciousness, here, writing at another moment and out of different emotional and imaginative pressures, she expressed the absolute conviction that immortality awaited her. A comparison with two other poems will help place this small masterpiece. Its anvil-ringing exclamations may remind one of "Wild Nights—Wild Nights!" But there the theme is exclusively that of human and sensual love; here what is claimed is freedom from the grave, a soul purified ("white") and regenerate, and the life eternal ("long as

Ages steal!"). And where the legal language in "I read my sentence—steadily" serves to rivet the acknowledgment of man's mortality, here the legalisms—"right," "seal," "prison," "bars," "repeal," "charter"—work all in the other direction.

At the same time, her ecstatic vision of immortality has its effect upon her sense of the earthly life. The human world is a scarlet (sin-infested) prison, as against the white election promised her. More poignantly, she asserts: "Mine—here—in Vision—and in Veto!" Here on earth, she is granted the vision of eternal life, but she receives it at the cost of earthly desire. Immortality is the *quid pro quo* of renunciation.

Mine—by the Right of the White Election!
Mine—by the Royal Seal!
Mine—by the Sign in the Scarlet prison—

Bars—cannot conceal!

Mine—here—in Vision—and in Veto!
Mine—by the Grave's Repeal—
Titled—Confirmed—
Delirious Charter!
Mine—long as Ages steal!

(721) Behind Me—Dips Eternity (c. 1863)

Emily Dickinson again, here, confronts the enormous theme of immortality, and in the second stanza even reports not on the precise nature of Christ's princely rule in the heavenly kingdom, but on what rumor and tradition have said about it. But the force of the poem derives from the almost violent shift in the final lines from the twice repeated "miracle" to the twice repeated "midnight." For as the heavenly vision recedes, consciousness edges back to earthly experience; and seen from within, the latter seems a chaos, a maelstrom, existing between two domains that are now (from the earthly perspective) as dark as midnight.

Behind Me—dips Eternity—
Before Me—Immortality—

Myself—the Term between—
Death but the Drift of Eastern Gray,
Dissolving into Dawn away,
Before the West begin—

'Tis Kingdoms—afterward—they say—
In perfect—pauseless Monarchy—
Whose Prince—is Son of None—
Himself—His Dateless Dynasty—   10
Himself—Himself diversify—
In Duplicate divine—

'Tis Miracle before Me—then—
'Tis Miracle behind—between—
A Crescent in the Sea—
With Midnight to the North of Her—
And Midnight to the South of Her—
And Maelstrom—in the Sky—

(501) This World Is Not Conclusion (c. 1862)

Emily Dickinson could apply the invigorating quality of her wit no less to the question of life after death than to any other theme. Here, after beginning with a feigned confidence that there is a world beyond this world, the poem slips into confessed uncertainty—it is all a riddle and a puzzle. Faith is then seen, with a kind of comical desperation, attempting to convince itself. But though ministers may pound the pulpit and choirs sing Hallelujahs, the soul is constantly bitten by doubt.

This World is not Conclusion.
A Species stands beyond—
Invisible, as Music—

But positive, as Sound—
It beckons, and it baffles—
Philosophy—don't know—
And through a Riddle, at the last—
Sagacity, must go—
To guess it, puzzles scholars—
To gain it, Men have borne   10
Contempt of Generations
And Crucifixion, shown—
Faith slips—and laughs, and rallies—
Blushes, if any see—
Plucks at a twig of Evidence—
And asks a Vane, the way—
Much Gesture, from the Pulpit—
Strong Hallelujahs roll—
Narcotics cannot still the Tooth
That nibbles at the soul—   20

BRET HARTE (1836–1902) AND LOCAL COLOR

For a brief time Bret Harte was the dominant literary figure in America. But the shifting tides of taste have left many such reputations high and dry like stranded jellyfish, and Harte now offers little more than a certain historical interest, a seminal example of local color and regionalism, and a footnote to the career of Mark Twain.

Harte was an important part of Mark Twain's experience in California, especially San Francisco. He was already an established figure when, in 1864, Mark Twain arrived from the wilds of Nevada. Francis Bret Harte [1] had, in fact, arrived in California ten years before, from Albany, New York, a youth of seventeen, rather slight, good-looking, fastidious in manner and tastes, witty and agreeable. Mark Twain, on whose ample hate list Bret Harte's name came to lead all the rest, later declared, in his autobiography, that Harte had been "distinctly pretty, in spite of the fact that his face was badly pitted with smallpox," and that he exhibited "dainty self-complacencies" and a carriage of the "mincing sort." Even if we remember Mark Twain's notorious disregard for truth and discount the venomous innuendo, Harte was clearly not the sort of man to make his presence favorably felt in the bonhomie of a mining camp saloon or in the serious work of a frontier brawl. Furthermore, Harte did not uncritically accept every local prejudice; when, on his first newspaper job, in his early twenties, in a frontier town in northern California, he wrote an

unvarnished report of a massacre of Indian women and children, he was fired.

Back in San Francisco he began to make his way in literary circles (for such already existed there), was taken up by the wife of the great General Frémont, got a well-paying sinecure in the U.S. Mint (which was supposed to leave him time for writing), got married (to a woman somewhat older than he, of some musical talent, considerable ambition, and a distinct inclination to be a nag), and in a community where Union sentiment, even in the middle of the war, was far from solid, assumed the role of the literary champion of freedom. Well before 1868, when he became the first editor of the *Overland Monthly*, a new literary magazine that immediately attracted national attention, Harte had clearly become the kingpin of a group that included Ambrose Bierce, Joaquin Miller, and Mark Twain. During his San Francisco period, Twain was Harte's close friend, learned much from him about literary craftsmanship, and after the success of "The Celebrated Jumping Frog" enjoyed his public prediction of a glamorous future for the "new star rising in this western horizon." After Twain had gone East and was sending back to his San Francisco paper the letters that were to be the basis of *The Innocents Abroad* (see pp. 1298–99), Harte republished several of them in the *Overland Monthly*, criticized the manuscript of the book for his friend, and when it appeared reviewed it in glowing terms. Meanwhile, Harte had struck his own vein, for by 1870 the *Overland Monthly* had carried, unsigned, the stories that were to make him world-famous, "The Luck of Roaring Camp," "The Outcasts of Poker Flat," and "Tennessee's Partner."

Long before people knew what lay on the other side of the Appalachians, the "West" had hung on the American psychological horizon with a manifold of meanings, sometimes

[1] The name Harte came from Bernard Hart (without the *e*), secretary of the New York Stock Exchange Board and a member of the first synagogue of New York, who married Catherine Brett of a prominent family of Dutch origin. Within a year Bernard had put Catherine away, later took a proper wife, and as long as he lived kept away from his Jewish children the disgraceful secret of his first ill-considered matrimonial venture. Catherine, however, had a son by Bernard, and the son altered his mother's family name from *Brett* to *Bret* and added the *e* to *Hart*.

mutually contradictory. It stood for Edenic innocence. It was the Promised Land. It was the Virgin Land. It held out the hope of infinite wealth. It was the guarantee of perfect democracy. It was the place where men were men, and where Francis Parkman had gone in 1846 to test his young manhood on the Oregon Trail. It was, as Lord Bryce was to say, in his *American Commonwealth*, the "most distinctly American part of America."

The West, however, might be viewed in a somewhat less romantic perspective. From early times, by many cultivated easterners the "West" (whatever happened to be the "West" at any given moment) had been regarded merely as a geographical area populated for the most part by debt-dodgers, adulterers, drunkards, brawlers, fornicators, and, worst of all, illiterates, and when Twain went East in 1867, he was to encounter, in cultured circles, the suspicion that he still carried with him the aroma of those cesspools of moral depravity and intellectual degradation known as Virginia City, Nevada, and San Francisco, California.

The great secret of Bret Harte's popularity was to resolve all contradictions in the attitude toward the West. Romantic associations were there in the background to be exploited, as was the beauty and grandeur of the natural setting. In the foreground of his picture of the West were certain depraved and illiterate characters, but he treated them with a discreet touch of condescending humor, which amounted to a plea for Christian tolerance of their moral and social failings ("It's not really their fault, they never had your religious and cultural background"). Then, to clinch the matter, he showed these characters to have, after all, hearts of gold, tender sensibilities, and deep loyalties to the highest as they might know it. What we find here is a debased Wordsworthianism, with the whores, gamblers, and highwaymen taking the place, in Harte's mythology, of Wordsworth's idiot, child, and peasant. But more immediately than the spirit of Wordsworth, Harte evoked that of Dickens, who was the great master of the interfusion of humor and sentimentality. All in all, Harte's secret was to appeal to

the genteel eastern reader's curiosity about the romantic and exotic West (where there were few inhibitions), to his social and moral prurience, and to his general sense of superiority—and at the same time to disinfect the materials offered.

It was a sure-fire formula. Quite appropriately, in far-off England, Dickens, when he read "The Luck of Roaring Camp," was so touched that he invited Harte to pay him a visit. In 1871, when Harte went East (in spite of the offer from the University of California to make him "Professor of Recent Literature" at the then munificent salary of three thousand dollars a year), Harte's journey, as Twain puts it, was greeted with such excitement that one might have supposed he was "Halley's comet come again after seventy-five years of lamented absence,"[2] and even in Boston, where Mark Twain was always an outsider, Harte was received like a potentate or a visiting Englishman of reputation.[3] The owner of the *Atlantic Monthly* and *Every Saturday* offered Harte a contract for twelve pieces, poetry or prose, for ten thousand dollars—an unprecedented sum and an arrangement that, to the rage and envy of Twain, got prodigious publicity.

After the glorious dawn of Harte's reputation, his promise was never quite fulfilled. He turned playwright and collaborated with Mark Twain on a play called *Ah Sin*, after the character in his poem "That Heathen Chinee" (see below) and only succeeded in making a lifelong enemy and a tireless slanderer out of that dear old friend. In spite of his success and hard work,

---

[2] The image of the comet here has certain reverberations. Mark Twain was born in 1835, at the time of the previous appearance of the comet, and had the superstitious belief that he would die (as it came to pass, seventy-five years later) when it returned. In other words, if we interpret the latent meaning of Twain's remark, we get: the success of Bret Harte announces my (literary) death.

[3] Lowell, however, even though he was later to entertain Harte at the American Embassy in London, held off, not from superior critical acumen but, as Howells reports in *My Mark Twain*, because Harte had Jewish blood. Lowell, again according to Howells, also held off from Twain because he suspected him of having the same taint.

he was chronically in debt and compounded his difficulties by the habit of constant borrowing. He got some relief by obtaining a consular post in Germany and later lived in England, where he and his work had had a glamorous reception and where his writings continued to sell. But his great moment had passed.

When in 1899, the young Hamlin Garland, who greatly admired Harte for his leadership of the local color school (the "most vital development of our literature," as he called it), first visited England and met Harte at tea, he found an aging, white-haired man, with striped trousers, cutaway coat, assertive waistcoat, spats, and monocle, not exactly reminiscent of the world of Poker Flat. But Harte, the English dandy, was lonely for America and California, sometimes regretting, he said, that he "had ever come away." He died in 1902, of cancer of the throat, and was buried in Frimley Churchyard, near Camberley, England.

Local color and regionalism were not invented by Bret Harte. They already existed as a natural development of the American experience. In a literal sense, whenever we find concern with a more or less special geographical and social background we have local color and regionalism. We have observed, for instance, how the early emphasis on such materials preceded, and in a way led to, the notion of the "American." (See pp. 1087–90.) How could it be otherwise? Man's awareness moves outward from the local, the particular, the concrete, into widening generalizations of experience, and the notion of "America," or of the "American," was, in early days, an abstraction of very great power. During the Civil War, in "Long, Too Long, America," Whitman might sing of the banner that absorbed all and exult in the hope that the individual states would be subdued ("by the tap of the war drum if necessary") to the abstraction of that sacred symbol. He believed that democracy "en masse" would bring the necessary power to unify; but the antithetical, centrifugal force was still working. Robert E. Lee's loyalty was to Virginia; the Confederacy, hamstrung by the doctrine of states' rights, had far more unity in later myth than ever in actuality; and during the Civil War, Hawthorne (a local colorist and regionalist, in the literal sense, if ever there was one) could say that New England was as large an area as he could imagine his own affections encompassing.

The northern victory proclaimed the Union as a principle and a fact, and the wartime mobility, the new railroads, the new technology, finance-capitalism, and massive immigration, all made for the erosion of special fidelities and local memories; but at the same time, paradoxically, as we have noted earlier, the new order bred a nostalgia for the old, the literal expansiveness of life sharpened the attachments to the local and particular, and the future was often felt as more of a threat than a promise. *Snow-Bound* is a perfect example of local color and regional feeling, and it embodies, quite specifically in its theme, characters, and decor, the key elements that led to the new school of local color and regionalism. But Whittier was not unique. Lowell, with his *Biglow Papers*, Harriet Beecher Stowe, with *Oldtown Folks*, and George Washington Harris, with *Sut Lovingood*, indicate the same temper.

What differentiates poets like Whittier and Lowell from the number of self-declared local colorists and regionalists is the programmatic and more exclusive emphasis in both interest and method in that school, the self-conscious effort to set themselves up in contrast to other ideals, social, political, and literary. As for the literary ideals against which they would assert themselves, the most obvious was that of the "Great American Novel" (see p. 1217), the notion that there was a quintessential American experience and mode of expression to be embodied in fiction; but there was also the international novel, the notion that there was a typical American who might, for purposes of definition, fruitfully be brought into contact with the Old World.

As we have remarked, the work of Bret Harte is romantic—and we may call it romantic in two distinct, but related, ways. First, human nature is grossly oversimplified in terms of the heart-of-gold formula, and, second, the place of man in both nature and society is really purged, in spite of some passing references, of all its grim and grinding actualities. Even a hanging is an excuse for sweet sentiment; the real rope is forgotten. This romantic temper, however, is not necessarily found in other examples of the local color school, even in the West. A little later, as the dream of the West is more and more replaced by the struggle for a livelihood, and free land by mortgages and freight rates, the romantic bias is replaced by the realistic. Edward Eggleston, for instance, though born in Indiana, went, at the age of nineteen, to Minnesota, then in part a frontier, and there he found little romance among either the palefaces or the redskins, but often "savages" of both complexions, either in the grim villages or the boom towns striving to become cities, as in *The Mystery of Metropolisville*. In the next generation, Hamlin Garland, though a worshiper of Harte, was, for a time at least, an avowed realist of the West.

Local color and regionalism will be treated at some length in other discussions of literature since the Civil War, but for the moment we may say that two quite contradictory strains were there involved. On one side, there is an origin in such work as *Georgia Scenes*, by Augustus Baldwin Longstreet, realistic in temper and plebeian in material, or the humorous brutalities of the tall tale which, though having elements of poetic grotesquerie, is also plebeian in material and echoes a world of hard actuality. And there is, too, the folk tradition of the blacks, which appears most famously in Joel Chandler Harris and his *Uncle Remus*. On the other side, there is the romantic tradition that would glorify the past, representing an impulse that, as Mark Twain says, was disastrously nourished by Sir Walter Scott and that was present long before the Civil War, as we have found, for instance, in John Pendleton Kennedy's *Swallow Barn* and in John Esten Cooke's *Virginia Come-*

dians (1854), concerned with life in the Old Dominion before the Revolution. With the Civil War and defeat, there came, too, the need to take refuge in an idealized version of the Confederate past, and we have in half a generation after Appomattox Thomas Nelson Page and his Rebel dream taken to the sentimental bosom of the Yankee.

To return to Bret Harte: he did not, of course, invent either local color or regionalism. He was not even the master of some of the early practitioners. The sensibilities of the middle-western "westerner" Edward Eggleston and the southerner John Esten Cooke were formed before they could have seen the stories in the *Overland Monthly*. But Harte had the first great public success in that school, and thus defined it. Indeed, he defined it so narrowly in both type and temper of feeling that little remained to give his work survival value when fashion changed. He provides a perfect contrast with Twain, who had a far truer eye and ear for regional peculiarities than Harte ever had, but who managed to absorb them into larger patterns and deeper meanings. As a matter of fact, it is only on second thought and after analysis that we ever call *The Adventures of Huckleberry Finn*, for example, a work of regional or local color interest. *The Scarlet Letter* is, in one sense, strictly regional and is full of local color, and nothing could be more specifically regional and more drenched in local color than the Yoknapatawpha cycle of William Faulkner, but we never think of such works in those terms. The point seems to be that when a work engages fundamental moral or psychological issues at a deep level, the other elements are subordinated, and no matter how deeply rooted it may be in place and time, its interest no longer depends on quaintness, charm, the report of curious manners and customs, or nostalgia. Clearly, this is not to say that the good writer is rootless. It is all a question of what he can grow from his roots—what meaning he can develop from his local materials.

FURTHER READINGS

The Writings of Bret Harte (1896–1914; 20 vols.) (no editor cited)

Frederick Anderson, ed., *"Ah Sin," A Dramatic Work by Mark Twain and Bret Harte* (1961)
Geoffrey Bret Harte, ed., *Letters* (1926)

Van Wyck Brooks, *The Times of Melville and Whitman* (1947)
Guy Cardwell, *Twins of Genius* (1953)

Everett Carter, *Howells and the Age of Realism* (1950)
Bernard De Voto, ed., *Mark Twain in Eruption* (1940)
Margaret Duckett, *Mark Twain and Bret Harte* (1964)
T. Edgar Pemberton, *The Life of Bret Harte* (1903)
Josiah Royce, *California, from the Conquest in 1846 to the Second Vigilance Committee in San Francisco: A Study in American Character* (1948)
George R. Stewart, *Bret Harte, Argonaut and Exile* (1931)

That Heathen Chinee (1870)

"Plain Language from Truthful James," better known as "That Heathen Chinee," was published in the *Overland Monthly* in September, 1870, and immediately swept the country, actually contributing more to Bret Harte's immediate fame than the stories that had been appearing there. The composition is, to say the least, trivial, and the author recognized the fact, calling it "possibly the worst poem anybody ever wrote."

But the moment was ripe for the poem, for the "Chinese Question" was occupying the public mind, with fear of cheap labor compounding race prejudice; and there is comedy in the fact that the poem may have owed some of its popularity to a simple inversion of meaning that would make it anti-Chinese. What the poem offers is the simple irony that William, the friend of Truthful James, discovers, even as he is busy at cheating, that Ah Sin, his intended victim, has a few "ways that are dark"—darker, in fact, than his own.

Harte's defense of the Indians and the Chinese in California is sometimes set in contrast with Twain's rather ambiguous attitude. The long, very funny, and scurrilous account of Harte in Twain's autobiography as edited by Bernard De Voto in *Mark Twain in Eruption* would seem to indicate that by 1906 Twain was trying to tidy up his own early years. There is not much to be done, however, about his view of the Indians in *Roughing It*. (See pp. 1270–72.)

Which I wish to remark—
  And my language is plain—
That for ways that are dark
  And for tricks that are vain,
The heathen Chinee is peculiar,
  Which the same I would rise to explain.

Ah Sin was his name;
  And I shall not deny
In regard to the same
  What that name might imply,   10
But his smile it was pensive and child-like,
  As I frequently remarked to Bill Nye.

It was August the third;
  And quite soft was the skies;
Which it might be inferred
  That Ah Sin was likewise;
Yet he played it that day upon William
  And me in a way I despise.

Which we had a small game,
  And Ah Sin took a hand: 20
It was Euchre. The same
  He did not understand;
But he smiled as he sat by the table,
  With the smile that was child-like and bland.

Yet the cards they were stocked
  In a way that I grieve,
And my feelings were shocked
  At the state of Nye's sleeve:
Which was stuffed full of aces and bowers,
  And the same with intent to deceive.   30

But the hands that were played
  By that heathen Chinee,
And the points that he made
  Were quite frightful to see—
Till at last he put down a right bower,
  Which the same Nye had dealt unto me.

Then I looked up at Nye,
    And he gazed upon me;
And he rose with a sigh
    And said, "Can this be? 40
We are ruined by Chinese cheap labour"—
    And he went for that heathen Chinee.

In the scene that ensued
    I did not take a hand,
But the floor it was strewed
    Like the leaves on the strand
With the cards that Ah Sin had been hiding,
    In the game "he did not understand."

In his sleeves which were long,
    He had twenty-four jacks— 50
Which was coming it strong,
    Yet I state but the facts;
And we found on his nails, which were taper,
    What is frequent in tapers—that's wax.

Which is why I remark,
    And my language is plain,
That for ways that are dark,
    And for tricks that are vain,
The heathen Chinee is peculiar—
    Which the same I am free to maintain. 60

Tennessee's Partner (1870)

I do not think that we ever knew his real name. Our ignorance of it certainly never gave us any social inconvenience, for at Sandy Bar in 1854 most men were christened anew. Sometimes these appellatives were derived from some distinctiveness of dress, as in the case of "Dungaree Jack;" or from some peculiarity of habit, as shown in "Saleratus Dill," so called from an undue proportion of that chemical in his daily bread; or from some unlucky slip, as exhibited in "The Iron Pirate," a mild, inoffensive man, who earned that baleful title by his unfortunate mispronunciation of the term "iron pyrites." Perhaps this may have been the beginning of a rude heraldry; but I am constrained to think that it was because a man's real name in that day rested solely upon his own unsupported statements. "Call yourself Clifford, do you?" said Boston, addressing a timid new-comer with infinite scorn; "hell is full of such Cliffords!" He then introduced the unfortunate man, whose name happened to be really Clifford, as "Jay-bird Charley,"—an unhallowed inspiration of the moment, that clung to him ever after.

But to return to Tennessee's Partner, whom we never knew by any other than this relative title; that he had ever existed as a separate and distinct individuality we only learned later. It seems that in 1853 he left Poker Flat to go to San Francisco, ostensibly to procure a wife. He never got any farther than Stockton. At that place he was attracted by a young person who waited upon the table at the hotel where he took his meals. One morning he said something to her which caused her to smile not unkindly, to somewhat coquet-tishly break a plate of toast over his upturned, serious, simple face, and to retreat to the kitchen. He followed her, and emerged a few moments later, covered with more toast and victory. That day week they were married by a Justice of the Peace, and returned to Poker Flat. I am aware that something more might be made of this episode, but I prefer to tell it as it was current at Sandy Bar—in the gulches and bar rooms—where all sentiment was modified by a strong sense of humour.

Of their married felicity but little is known, perhaps for the reason that Tennessee, then living with his partner, one day took occasion to say something to the bride on his own account, at which, it is said, she smiled not unkindly and chastely retreated,—this time as far as Marysville, where Tennessee followed her, and where they went to housekeeping without the aid of a Justice of the Peace. Tennessee's Partner took the loss of his wife simply and seriously, as was his fashion. But to everybody's surprise, when Tennessee one day returned from Marysville, without his partner's wife,—she having smiled and retreated with somebody else,—Tennessee's Partner was the first man to shake his hand and greet him with affection. The boys who had gathered in the cañon to see the shooting were naturally indignant. Their indignation might have found vent in sarcasm but for a certain look in Tennessee's Partner's eye that indicated a lack of humourous appreciation. In fact, he was a grave man, with a steady application to practical detail which was unpleasant in a difficulty.

Meanwhile a popular feeling against Tennessee had grown up on the Bar. He was known to be a gambler; he was suspected to be a thief. In these suspicions Tennessee's Partner was equally compromised; his continued intimacy with Tennessee after the affair above quoted could only be accounted for on the hypothesis of a copartnership of crime. At last Tennessee's guilt became flagrant. One day he overtook a stranger on his way to Red Dog. The stranger afterward related that Tennessee beguiled the time with interesting anecdote and reminiscence, but illogically concluded the interview in the following words: "And now, young man, I'll trouble you for your knife, your pistols, and your money. You see your weppings might get you into trouble at Red Dog, and your money's a temptation to the evilly disposed. I think you said your address was San Francisco. I shall endeavor to call." It may be stated here that Tennessee had a fine flow of humour, which no business preoccupation could wholly subdue.

This exploit was his last. Red Dog and Sandy Bar made common cause against the highwayman. Tennessee was hunted in very much the same fashion as his prototype, the grizzly. As the toils closed around him, he made a desperate dash through the Bar, emptying his revolver at the crowd before the Arcade Saloon, and so on up Grizzly Cañon; but at its farther extremity he was stopped by a small man on a gray horse. The men looked at each other a moment in silence. Both were fearless, both self-possessed and independent; and both types of a civilization that in the seventeenth century would have been called heroic, but, in the nineteenth, simply "reckless." "What have you got there?—I call," said Tennessee, quietly. "Two bowers and an ace," said the stranger, as quietly, showing two revolvers and a bowie knife. "That takes me," returned Tennessee; and with this gambler's epigram, he threw away his useless pistol, and rode back with his captor.

It was a warm night. The cool breeze which usually sprang up with the going down of the sun behind the *chaparral*-crested mountain was that evening withheld from Sandy Bar. The little cañon was stifling with heated resinous odours, and the decaying drift-wood on the Bar sent forth faint, sickening exhalations. The feverishness of day, and its fierce passions, still filled the camp. Lights moved restlessly along the bank of the river, striking no answering reflection from its tawny current. Against the blackness of the pines the windows of the old loft above the express-office stood out staringly bright; and through their curtainless panes the loungers below could see the forms of those who were even then deciding the fate of Tennessee. And above all this, etched on the dark firmament, rose the Sierra, remote and passionless, crowned with remoter passionless stars.

The trial of Tennessee was conducted as fairly as was consistent with a judge and jury who felt themselves to some extent obliged to justify, in their verdict, the previous irregularities of arrest and indictment. The law of Sandy Bar was implacable, but not vengeful. The excitement and personal feeling of the chase were over; with Tennessee safe in their hands they were ready to listen patiently to any defence, which they were already satisfied was insufficient. There being no doubt in their own minds, they were willing to give the prisoner the benefit of any that might exist. Secure in the hypothesis that he ought to be hanged, on general principles, they indulged him with more latitude of defence than his reckless hardihood seemed to ask. The Judge appeared to be more anxious than the prisoner, who, otherwise unconcerned, evidently took a grim pleasure in the responsibility he had created. "I don't take any hand in this yer game," had been his invariable, but good-humoured reply to all questions. The Judge —who was also his captor—for a moment vaguely regretted that he had not shot him "on sight," that morning, but presently dismissed this human weakness as unworthy of the judicial mind. Nevertheless, when there was a tap at the door, and it was said that Tennessee's Partner was there on behalf of the prisoner, he was admitted at once without question. Perhaps the younger members of the jury, to whom the proceedings were becoming irksomely thoughtful, hailed him as a relief.

For he was not, certainly, an imposing figure. Short and stout, with a square face, sunburned into a preternatural redness, clad in a loose duck "jumper," and trousers streaked and splashed with red soil, his aspect under any circumstances would have been quaint, and was now even ridiculous. As he stooped to deposit at his feet a heavy carpet-bag he was carrying, it became obvious, from partially developed regions and inscriptions, that the material with which his trousers had been patched had been originally intended for a less ambitious covering. Yet he advanced with great gravity, and after having shaken the hand of each person in the room with laboured cordiality, he wiped his serious, perplexed face on a red bandanna handkerchief, a shade lighter than his complexion, laid his powerful hand upon the table to steady himself, and thus addressed the Judge:—

"I was passin' by," he began, by way of apology, "and I thought I'd just step in and see how things was gittin' on with Tennessee thar—my pardner. It's a hot night. I disremember any sich weather before on the Bar."

He paused a moment, but nobody volunteering any other meteorological recollection, he again had recourse to his pocket-handkerchief, and for some moments mopped his face diligently.

"Have you anything to say in behalf of the prisoner?" said the Judge, finally.

"Thet's it," said Tennessee's Partner, in a tone of relief. "I come yar as Tennessee's pardner—knowing him nigh on four year, off and on, wet and dry, in luck and out o' luck. His ways ain't allers my ways, but thar ain't any p'ints in that young man, thar ain't any liveliness as he's been up to, as I don't know. And you sez to me, sez you—confidential-like, and between man and man —sez you, 'Do you know anything in his behalf?' and I sez to you, sez I—confidential-like, as between man and man—'What should a man know of his pardner?'"

"Is this all you have to say?" asked the Judge, impatiently, feeling, perhaps, that a dangerous sympathy of humour was beginning to humanize the Court.

"Thet's so," continued Tennessee's Partner. "It ain't for me to say anything agin' him. And now what's the case? Here's Tennessee wants money, wants it bad, and doesn't like to ask it of his old pardner. Well, what does Tennessee do? He lays for a stranger, and he fetches that stranger. And you lays for *him*, and you fetches *him*; and the honours is easy. And I put it to you, bein' a far-minded man, and to you, gentlemen, all, as far-minded men, ef this isn't so."

"Prisoner," said the Judge, interrupting, "have you any questions to ask this man?"

"No! no!" continued Tennessee's Partner, hastily. "I play this yer hand alone. To come down to the bed-rock, it's just this Tennessee, thar, has played it pretty rough and expensive-like on a stranger, and on this yer camp. And now, what's the fair thing? Some would say more; some would say less. Here's seventeen hundred dollars in coarse gold and a watch,—it's about all my pile,—and call it square!" And before a hand could be raised to prevent him, he had emptied the contents of the carpet-bag upon the table.

For a moment his life was in jeopardy. One or two men sprang to their feet, several hands groped for hidden weapons, and a suggestion to "throw him from the window" was only overridden by a gesture from the Judge. Tennessee laughed. And apparently oblivious of the excitement, Tennessee's Partner improved the opportunity to mop his face again with his handkerchief.

When order was restored, and the man was made to understand, by the use of forcible figures and rhetoric, that Tennessee's offence could not be condoned by money, his face took a more serious and sanguinary hue, and those who were nearest to him noticed that his rough hand trembled slightly on the table. He hesitated a moment as he slowly returned the gold to the carpet-bag, as if he had not yet entirely caught the elevated sense of justice which swayed the tribunal, and was perplexed with the belief that he had not offered enough. Then he turned to the Judge, and saying, "This yer is a lone hand, played alone, and without my pardner," he bowed to the jury and was about to withdraw, when the Judge called him back. "If you have anything to say to Tennessee, you had better say it now." For the first time that evening the eyes of the prisoner and his strange advocate met. Tennessee smiled, showed his white teeth, and saying, "Euchred, old man!" held out his hand. Tennessee's Partner took it in his own, and saying, "I just dropped in as I was passin' to see how things was gettin' on," let the hand passively fall, and adding that "it was a warm night," again mopped his face with his handkerchief, and without another word withdrew.

The two men never again met each other alive. For the unparalleled insult of a bribe offered to Judge Lynch—who, whether bigoted, weak, or narrow, was at least incorruptible—firmly fixed in the mind of that mythical personage any wavering determination of Tennessee's fate; and at the break of day he was marched, closely guarded, to meet it at the top of Marley's Hill.

How he met it, how cool he was, how he refused to say anything, how perfect were the arrangements of the committee, were all duly reported, with the addition of a warning moral and example to all future evil-doers, in the Red Dog Clarion, by its editor, who was present, and to whose vigorous English I cheerfully refer the reader. But the beauty of that midsummer morning, the blessed amity of earth and air and sky, the awakened life of the free woods and hills, the joyous removal and promise of Nature, and above all, the infinite

Serenity that thrilled through each, was not reported, as not being a part of the social lesson.
And yet, when the weak and foolish deed was
done, and a life, with its possibilities and responsibilities, had passed out of the misshapen thing
that dangled between earth and sky, the birds sang,
the flowers bloomed, the sun shone, as cheerily as
before; and possibly the Red Dog Clarion was
right.

Tennessee's Partner was not in the group that
surrounded the ominous tree. But as they turned
to disperse, attention was drawn to the singular
appearance of a motionless donkey-cart halted at
the side of the road. As they approached, they at
once recognised the venerable "Jenny" and the
two-wheeled cart as the property of Tennessee's
Partner,—used by him in carrying dirt from his
claim; and a few paces distant the owner of the
equipage himself, sitting under a buckeye-tree, wiping the perspiration from his glowing face. In
answer to an inquiry, he said he had come for the
body of the "diseased" "if it was all the same to
the committee." He didn't wish to "hurry anything;" he could "wait." He was not working that
day; and when the gentlemen were done with the
"diseased," he would take him. "Ef thar is any
present," he added, in his simple, serious way, "as
would care to jine in the fun'l, they kin come."
Perhaps it was from a sense of humour, which I
have already intimated was a feature of Sandy Bar,
—perhaps it was from something even better than
that; but two-thirds of the loungers accepted the
invitation at once.

It was noon when the body of Tennessee was
delivered into the hands of his partner. As the cart
drew up to the fatal tree, we noticed that it contained a rough oblong box, apparently made from
a section of sluicing,—and half filled with bark and
the tassels of pine. The cart was further decorated
with slips of willow, and made fragrant with buck-
eye-blossoms. When the body was deposited in
the box, Tennessee's Partner drew over it a piece
of tarred canvas, and gravely mounting the narrow
seat in front, with his feet upon the shafts, urged
the little donkey forward. The equipage moved
slowly on, at that decorous pace which was habitual with "Jenny," even under less solemn circumstances. The men—half-curiously, half-jestingly, but
all good-humouredly—strolled along beside the cart;
some in advance, some a little in the rear of the
homely catafalque. But, whether from the narrowing of the road or some present sense of decorum,
as the cart passed on the company fell to the rear

in couples, keeping step, and otherwise assuming
the external show of a formal procession. Jack Fol-
insbee, who had at the outset played a funeral
march in dumb show upon an imaginary trombone,
desisted, from a lack of sympathy and appreciation,
—not having, perhaps, your true humourist's capacity to be content with the enjoyment of his
own fun.

The way led through Grizzly Cañon—by this
time clothed in funereal drapery and shadows.
The red-woods, burying their moccasoned feet in
the red soil, stood in Indian file along the track,
trailing an uncouth benediction from their bending boughs upon the passing bier. A hare, surprised into helpless activity, sat upright and pulsat-
ing in the ferns by the roadside as the *cortége*
went by. Squirrels hastened to gain a secure outlook from higher boughs; and the blue-jays, spreading their wings, fluttered before them like outriders, until the outskirts of Sandy Bar were reached,
and the solitary cabin of Tennessee's Partner.

Viewed under more favourable circumstances, it
would not have been a cheerful place. The unpic-
turesque site, the rude and unlovely outlines, the
unsavoury details, which distinguish the nest-build-
ing of the California miner, were all here, with the
dreariness of decay superadded. A few paces from
the cabin there was a rough enclosure, which, in
the brief days of Tennessee's Partner's matrimonial
felicity, had been used as a garden, but was now
overgrown with fern. As we approached it, we were
surprised to find that what we had taken for a
recent attempt at cultivation was the broken soil
about an open grave.

The cart was halted before the enclosure; and
rejecting the offers of assistance with the same air
of simple self-reliance he had displayed throughout,
Tennessee's Partner lifted the rough coffin on his
back, and deposited it, unaided, within the shallow
grave. He then nailed down the board which
served as a lid; and mounting the little mound of
earth beside it, took off his hat, and slowly mopped
his face with his handkerchief. This the crowd felt
was a preliminary to speech; and they disposed
themselves variously on stumps and boulders, and
sat expectant.

"When a man," began Tennessee's Partner,
slowly, "has been running free all day, what's the
natural thing for him to do? Why, to come home.
And if he ain't in a condition to go home, what
can his best friend do? Why, bring him home!
And here's Tennessee has been running free, and
we brings him home from his wandering." He

paused, and picked up a fragment of quartz, rubbed it thoughtfully on his sleeve, and went on: "It ain't the first time that I've packed him on my back, as you see'd me now. It ain't the first time that I brought him to this yer cabin when he couldn't help himself; it ain't the first time that I and 'Jenny' have waited for him on yon hill, and picked him up and so fetched him home, when he couldn't speak, and didn't know me. And now that it's the last time, why——" he paused, and rubbed the quartz gently on his sleeve—"you see it's a sort of rough on his partner. And now, gentlemen," he added, abruptly, picking up his long-handled shovel, "the fun'l's over; and my thanks, and Tennessee's thanks to you for your trouble."

Resisting any proffers of assistance, he began to fill in the grave, turning his back upon the crowd, that after a few moments' hesitation gradually withdrew. As they crossed the little ridge that hid Sandy Bar from view, some, looking back, thought they could see Tennessee's Partner, his work done, sitting upon the grave, his shovel between his knees, and his face buried in his red bandanna handkerchief. But it was argued by others that you couldn't tell his face from his handkerchief at that distance; and this point remained undecided.

In the reaction that followed the feverish excitement of that day, Tennessee's Partner was not forgotten. A secret investigation had cleared him of any complicity in Tennessee's guilt, and left only a suspicion of his general sanity. Sandy Bar made a point of calling on him, and proffering various uncouth, but well-meant kindnesses. But from that day this rude health and great strength seemed visibly to decline; and when the rainy season fairly set in, and the tiny grass-blades were beginning to peep from the rocky mound above Tennessee's grave, he took to his bed.

One night, when the pines beside the cabin were swaying in the storm, and trailing their slender fingers over the roof, and the roar and rush of the swollen river were heard below, Tennessee's Partner lifted his head from the pillow, saying, "It is time to go for Tennessee; I must put 'Jinny' in the cart;" and would have risen from his bed but for the restraint of his attendant. Struggling, he still pursued his singular fancy: "There, now, steady, 'Jinny,'—steady, old girl. How dark it is! Look out for the ruts,—and look out for him, too, old gal. Sometimes, you know, when he's blind drunk, he drops down right in the trail. Keep on straight up to the pine on the top of the hill. Thar—I told you so!—thar he is,—coming this way, too,—all by himself, sober, and his face a-shining. Tennessee! Pardner!"

And so they met.

SAMUEL CLEMENS (1835–1910)

The man who was to become Mark Twain was reared, like Hawthorne and Melville, in an atmosphere of fallen gentility, and, as with them, the early death of the father was a shocking fact that conditioned his life and work. For him, too, the past was an obsessive subject. For Hawthorne the obsession was not, overtly at least, a special concern with a personal past. It was with the historical past in which the personal past could be shrouded. Melville, similarly, while obsessed by the personal past, characteristically projected it into dramas and issues apparently unrelated to it. For Twain, however, though there is a concealed relation between the personal past and the work, there is another that is direct and simple. In this respect, he is somewhat like Whittier of *Snow-Bound*, for both men looked back to an Arcady of childhood, to a Peaceable Kingdom.

But there is another similarity between Twain and Whittier. In *Snow-Bound*, the poet, after depicting the idyllic world of old America where he was a protected child, lifts his eyes to the world of modernity and its "thronged city ways" and hopes to find some fruitful continuity, a projective strength from the past to the future. Twain's boyhood belonged, too, to the old America, but just as he settled into manhood the Civil War came to change everything, and his glittering success belonged to the new order.

In part at least, his success, like Whittier's with *Snow-Bound,* came from a re-creation of the world of the old America to flatter the nostalgic dreams of the new.

The similarity, however, merely underscores a difference. Whittier could find in his religious sense, his abiding family affections, and his deep social commitments a principle of continuity in life. Twain had no such things to find support in. The split between the past and the present was, for him, traumatic. Worse, there was in the past itself a deep split. He could dream back, at moments, on a boyhood Eden, but he could also repudiate the culture of which the Eden was a part. Then, if he took refuge in the booming present, and, as in *The Innocents Abroad* and *A Connecticut Yankee in King Arthur's Court,* became the spokesman for the values of the new America, he might suddenly find himself overwhelmed by disgust. The real split was in him, deep and mysterious. He was a divided man—and writer: and it is possible that if he had not been a divided man, he would not have been a writer at all. Every man is entitled to the theme of his work—or life.

Samuel Clemens, who was later to take the *nom de plume* that he made immortal, was of prosperous, middle-class Virginia stock, in which Quakerism and slaveholding were mixed, sometimes in the same person. His father, John Marshall Clemens, was taken, at the age of seven, when his own father died, to Kentucky. There he grew up, studied law and was admitted to practice, on coming of age inherited three slaves and a mahogany sideboard from his father's estate, and married one Jane Lampton, who was reputed to be the most beautiful woman in a state fabled for breeding beauties. She was also witty, high-spirited, and generous, and was, according to the testimony of her son —whose opinion should count for something in this department—a great teller of tales. Looking back, many years later, the son said:

> I have been abroad in the world for twenty years and knew and have listened to many of its best talkers before it at last dawned on me that in the matter of moving and pathetic eloquence none of them was the equal of that untrained and artless talker out there in the western village, that obscure little woman with the beautiful spirit and the great heart and the enchanted tongue.

Jane Lampton was a strange mate for John Marshall Clemens, a severe, humorless man, incapable of showing affection, with a rigorous puritanical conscience (but no religious faith), mysterious ailments, uncrackable dignity, and a pride that hardened more with each affront from fate. Intelligent, well-bred, educated in the law, possessed of energy and ambition, he seemed to have all the qualifications for success in that world, fluid and on the make, in which he found himself; but he was the born failure, always on the move, with only the unquenchable optimism of the westward march to sustain him. Kentucky, Tennessee, Missouri—but something always went wrong. In Sam's memory, the high point of his father's career was his holding office as a justice of the peace: "I supposed he possessed the power of life and death over all men, and could hang anybody that offended him." When that limited glory petered out, the father was an aging man stranded in the village of Hannibal, Missouri, with nothing left but the Virginia pride, the air of fallen grandeur, the threadbare dignity that somehow demanded respect, and a barony of wild land left in Tennessee that was supposed to be worth a fortune, some day.

In 1847 John Marshall Clemens died, and the precious dignity of the dead man, whose mysterious ailments had piqued the curiosity of the local doctor, was submitted to a last affront. In his own house, in the dining room, presumably laid out on the family table, the body was carved up in a postmortem, at night, by candlelight. Through a key hole, the twelve-year-old boy, who was to grow up to be the humorist, witnessed the grisly business, the butchering of the father with whom he was only "on the most distant terms . . . a sort of armed neutrality, so to speak," but who was the childhood symbol of power. The shock of the event—the guilty shock, we may hazard—was to stay with him for life.

Samuel Langhorne Clemens had been born November 30, 1835, a premature and sickly infant, in the village of Florida, Missouri, in a small cabin that the family, recently arrived from Tennessee, was renting from a certain Major Penn. Florida, like so many other things in "Judge" Clemens' life, was to prove a snare and a delusion, and when Sam was four years old, the family moved on to Hannibal, on the Mississippi. Here was the Eden place, here and over at Florida on the bounteous farmstead of John Quarles, who was married to Sam's maternal aunt. In this world was the real Jimmy Finn, a "monument of rags and dirt," who was to enter literature as Huck's drunkard father and sleep with the hogs in the tanyard; here the archetype of Colonel Sherburn gunned Boggs to death; here Sam worshiped Uncle Dan'l, a slave on the Quarles farm who became, with little or no retouching, Nigger Jim; here Sam discovered the stiffened body of a stabbed man, lying in moonlight on the floor of the office of his father, the justice of the peace; here was a real boy named Tom Blankenship who was to be rebaptized as Huck; here Widow Holliday, in her house on the hill, provided the model for Widow Douglas, and Sam's own mother that for Aunt Polly. The Quarles farm became the Grangerford plantation, Holiday Hill became Cardiff Hill, and there was a real limestone cave where real boys pretended to be a gang of robbers. And always there was the great river flowing past, with its romantic burden of life and legend. Here is the town as Twain described it:

. . . the white town drowsing in the sunshine of a summer's morning; the streets empty, or pretty nearly so; one or two clerks sitting in front of the Water Street stores, with their split-bottomed chairs tilted back against the walls; chins in breasts, hats slouched over their faces, asleep—with shingle-shavings enough around to show what broke them down; a sow and a litter of pigs loafing along the sidewalk, doing a good business in watermelon rinds and seeds; two or three lonely little freight piles scattered about the "levee"; a pile of "skids" on the slope of the stone-paved wharf, and the fragrant town drunkard asleep in the shadow of them; two or three wood flats at the head of the wharf, but nobody to listen to the peaceful lapping of the wavelets against them; the great Mississippi, the majestic, the magnificent Mississippi, rolling its mile-wide tide along, shining in the sun; the dense forest away on the other side; the "point" above the town, and the "point" below, bounding the river-glimpse and turning it into a sort of sea, and withal a very still and brilliant and lonely one.

Sam Clemens grew up in this world, and as the years closed in on him it sometimes seemed the only world worth the having. "I should greatly like to relive my youth," he wrote long after to the widow of one of his boyhood companions, ". . . and be as we were, and make holiday until fifteen, then all drown together."

But the holiday ended and he did not get drowned. Instead he went out into the world beyond Hannibal, his head chock-full of memories, his ears ringing with the language of that village, his heart torn with a tumult of conflicting feelings and loyalties. This was his only patrimony. It was to turn out to be more valuable, even in hard cash, than anything his father, even if his wildest dreams had materialized, could have left him.

Mark Twain's first biographer, Albert Bigelow Paine, says that after Judge Clemens' death, the young son stood by the coffin, overwhelmed with grief for the father with whom he had had at best only an "armed neutrality," and promised his mother that he would be "a better boy." Another biographer, Van Wyck Brooks, in one of his early books, *The Ordeal of Mark Twain*, takes this episode to be crucial in the process that led, according to his theory, to the maiming of the artist's creative powers by the pressures of the conventionality of American life. In any case, with the death of the failed father and the increasing pinch of poverty, Sam Clemens' boyhood was over. An older brother, Orion, was working as a printer in St. Louis, and soon Sam himself was apprenticed locally to the same trade, for his board (which was thin and grudgingly given) and two suits of clothes a year (unredeemed hand-me-downs)—a "little sandy-haired boy" as a contemporary recalled long after, with a big cigar stuck in his mouth (although once already in his short life he had joined the Cadets of Temperance and sworn off tobacco).

In 1851 Orion came back to Hannibal to run a paper called the *Western Union*. Now Sam worked for his brother, who was as much a born failure as Judge Clemens had ever been. It was soon Sam who was actually keeping the paper together, finding time, too, to write humorous sketches based on current journalistic models. His first, "The Dandy Frightening the Squatter," was published in the *Carpet Bag*, a weekly in far-off Boston, and a career was begun.

Sam was eighteen now, and Hannibal was getting too small; so he packed his bag, laid his hand on the Bible and swore to his mother he would not "throw a card or drink a drop of liquor," and was gone—a penniless vagabond with his eyes and ears open and his memory a vast repository of all sorts of odds and ends and unconsidered trifles of American life. He was in New York, Philadelphia, Washington, and Cincinnati and wrote humorous travel sketches back to local papers. By 1857 he had read a book on the exploration of the Amazon, and with this new version of the old frontier fever in his blood and thirty dollars in his pocket, he left Cincinnati by steamboat for New Orleans, headed for the Amazon.

He was going down the river that for Hannibal had been the point of contact with the great world. As a boy he had heard the torpor of a hot afternoon stabbed by the cry "Steamboat a-coming!" and had seen one of the floating palaces of gimcrackery and glory, whiteness laced over with red paint and gilt, heading majestically in, meek as a lamb under the will of that demigod of the river who, high in his house on the texas deck, laid hand to the wheel. Now, in the pilot house of the *Paul Jones* was the great Horace E. Bixby, and Sam forgot the Amazon and signed on as Bixby's apprentice. After the apprentice period of seventeen months, he had scribbled down in a memorandum book all the utterances of his mentor and had memorized

every sand bar and spit, bluff, point, island, reach, and blasted tree of the great river, by sunlight and moonlight; on September 9, 1858, he received his license. He was good enough at his trade, later libels to the contrary, for his mentor Bixby to take him on as a partner—even though Bixby was to say that Sam, in spite of his knowledge and skill, "lacked confidence." In any case, Sam had achieved "the official rank and dignity of a pilot" and was himself a demigod now, familiar with both high and low life afloat and in New Orleans. "When I find a well-drawn character in fiction or biography," he was later to say, "I generally take a warm personal interest in him, for the reason that I have known him before—met him on the river."

The Civil War fell across the glory of the texas deck. Though Orion was an abolitionist, Sam decided to go with his state and joined an irregular command called the "Marion Rangers," an organization not too unlike Tom Sawyer's band of pirates, with experiences which, with some embroidery, he was to report in "The Private History of a Campaign That Failed." Discomfort, boils, and a sprained ankle somewhat ingloriously achieved were all that Lieutenant Clemens suffered in his military career, and when the Rangers, never having fired a shot in anger, simply disintegrated, Sam joined Orion, who, thanks to the friendship of one Edmund Bates, who had a friend in Lincoln's cabinet, was now setting out for Nevada as territorial secretary.

Thus Sam cut himself off from his southern heritage—resigned, in a sense, from history, which indifferently he left in the hands of Rebel and Yankee heroes—and went West, where the future was all. Later he was to regard Walter Scott and the dream of chivalry as the southern disease whose contagion he thus fled, and he was, in *A Connecticut Yankee*, to equate chivalry with the barbarous irrationality that the rational Yankee tries to redeem. It is tempting to see this antipathy for self-delusion and highfalutin daydreams as a revulsion against Judge Clemens' pride in high lineage, high manners, the aura of glory about the mahogany sideboard brought from Kentucky, and the romantically bad judgment in money matters. As for Sam, he had a hard streak of realism in his nature and knew the value of money to a point just this side of idolatry.

Though the young Sam Clemens did repudiate the historical past, he did not repudiate his personal past, and for Mark Twain, the telling, directly or indirectly, of the story of that past became his chief stock-in-trade. But what is equally significant is the complex feeling that went into the telling of the tale.

On the one hand, Twain was capable of mordant realism, as in a letter written, in 1876, to one of the erstwhile boys of Hannibal, whom he chides for nostalgic yearnings:

As to the past, there is but one good thing about it, . . . that it *is* past. . . . I can see by your manner of speech, that for more than twenty years you have stood dead still in the midst of the dreaminess, the melancholy, the romance, the heroics, of sweet but happy sixteen. Man, do you know that this is simply mental and moral masturbation? It belongs eminently to the period usually devoted to *physical* masturbation, and should be left there and outgrown.

That is, Twain knew the hard facts of his world. He knew that Hannibal had its full quota of degradation and despair. He knew that the glittering majesty of the steamboat was not much more than a cross between a floating brothel richly afflicted with venereal disease and a gambling hell full of stacked decks and loaded dice. In the main part of *The Adventures of Huckleberry Finn*, both Hannibal and the South in general get their realistic due, and the author, in cold print elsewhere, scorned both the myth of the Middle Ages and that of the Old South. Nevertheless, when Twain turned to his boyhood in Hannibal or to the hours on the texas deck with stars reflected in the mysterious river, his memory could edit out all details that did not fulfill his deep need to believe that the past had been a time of freedom and peace. So he described *The Adventures of Tom Sawyer* as "simply a hymn, put into prose to give it a worldly air" and longed for the later freedom from civilized restraints (even those of his truly beloved wife), remembering the glory of the pilot—"the only unfettered and entirely independent human being that lived upon the earth."

While the Civil War dragged bloodily on, Sam was making his way in the new world of boom and bust, gold-panning and gun-play, crooked legislatures and drunken reporters, tall tale and lynch law, living in a world that was totally of the ballyhoo present and the beckoning future, with no past at all. He tried his hand at mining but soon learned that, for him at least, the pen was mightier than the pick or placer pan. His gift for humor, which had had good training from the conversation of Hannibal and the bars of New Orleans, received refining instruction by campfires and in newspaper offices. He met Artemus Ward when that most popular humorist visited California, studied his lecture style, and was encouraged by him to try the eastern market; and so "Those Blasted Children" appeared, in 1864, in the *Mercury* of New York. He got himself sent as a journalist to the Sandwich Islands and, once back in San Francisco, was launched as a humorous lecturer.

In the world of the oral tale, where such masters as Augustus Baldwin Longstreet, Davy Crockett, and Abraham Lincoln had learned their craft, Sam had already learned not only the nature of the tale but how to tell it. Apparently he had perfect pace and timing, and his Missouri drawl could be a marvelous asset to his virtuoso performance on the platform. One reviewer described him:

The aggrieved way in which he gazes with tilted chin over the convulsed faces of his audience, as much as to say, "Why are you laughing?" is irresistible in the extreme. . . . His face is immovable while his hearers laugh, and as he waits for the merriment to subside, his right hand plays with his chin. . . . These characteristics agree so well with his description of himself in his books—Innocence victimized by the world, flesh, and Devil—that one cannot fail to establish the resemblance and laugh at the grotesque image.

He was, in sum, an actor, and he had found his starring role. In the days as a reporter in Nevada, when his articles began to be quoted up and down the coast, he had sought a device to tie them together, to give them a distinct flavor and personality; and so, following the fashion of the day, he finally, after much reflection, selected a *nom de plume*, Mark Twain. The term, which he remembered from his steamboat days, meant two fathoms of water, twelve feet, a clear passage.

When Sam Clemens, the actor, played the role of Mark Twain, he was simply doing what many other writers have done, some quite consciously. What we think of as the personality of a writer is often different from that of the man who happens to be the writer. The Robert Frost of the poems and the lecture platform, for instance, was very different from the man of the same name.[1] The personality the writer takes—his mask—simply clarifies and brings to focus the elements that may be diffused, confused, and obscured in his literal self, and the role of Mark Twain gave Samuel Clemens such a clarification and focus. Especially in the days in the West when Sam was deeply involved in the polemics of politics and was developing a native gift for vituperation and insult, the split between the two identities, Mark Twain and Samuel Clemens, was great; Samuel Clemens, in fact, seems to have felt little responsibility for what his alter ego said. There was in even deeper ways a split in the nature of Sam, and the theme of the "double," the twin, runs throughout his work. The relation of the man and his role indicated by the *nom de plume* is merely one manifestation of a central fact of his existence.

By 1866 Mark Twain had tasted life in the West to the full, had lived low and lived high,

had slept by campfires in the Washoe country and in the beds of the best hotels in San Francisco, had drunk champagne in gilded salons and spent a night in jail, had sometimes gone hairy and unwashed and had somtimes sported varnished boots and shirts glittering with starch. He had been described in print, not with entire accuracy, as a jailbird, deadbeat, and alcoholic, and with more accuracy as a "Bohemian from the sagebrush," but he was also famous on the coast as a lecturer, humorist, and journalist. He even enjoyed a certain fame back East, for his tale "The Celebrated Jumping Frog of Calaveras County" had been published there. He was now ready to push his fortune, and so East he went.

Among the letters of introduction that Mark Twain had brought East was one to Henry Ward Beecher, the brother of Harriet Beecher Stowe and the most famous preacher of his time, whose fame was to be extended in 1875, when, under indictment for adultery, he was cast in the starring role in the gaudiest trial of the century. Now the sagebrush Bohemian dined at the Beecher house, got advice on his career from that expert platform artist, and, as an indirect result of his acquaintance, came to write his first book. Under the auspices of Beecher, as a flowering of the Civil War boom and the social and intellectual ambition of the new middle class, a great pilgrimage, half religious and half cultural, had been arranged to Europe and the Holy Land, on board the *Quaker City*. Instinctively, Mark Twain recognized in this project a subject made for his brand of humor. He got the *Alta California*, a newspaper back in San Francisco, to buy him a ticket.

The trip was, for the sagebrush Bohemian, penitential: "Solemnity, decorum, dinner, dominoes, prayers, slander"—that was the way he put it. There were too many people aboard who reminded him of the "way God looks when he has just had a successful season." But he had two cases of champagne in his cabin, and there were a few men aboard who shared some tastes with the Bohemian. As for the non-Bohemian part of Mark Twain, he found a lady who would advise him on moral and social matters and to whom he could play the role of wayward and charm-

---

[1] See p. 1860. In classic times the actor spoke through a mask that declared the role he was playing. The Latin word for mask is "persona," and from this, in fact, we have our word "personality."

ing boy, and who would mother him. He called her "Mother" Fairbanks, and for years was to keep her in that role.

Twain was now seeing *en masse* the rising new middle class of America. He loathed them for their Puritanism, hypocrisy, stupidity, and pretensions, and the boredom they visited upon him; but he also felt a sympathy for them, could find a rapport with them. These were not the kind of people who had roared at his jokes with adoring laughter back in Virginia City or in San Francisco, but they were the class who would buy his as yet unwritten books—even the book he was very shortly to write about them and this voyage—and who would take him to their hearts and make him very rich. They were the class into which he himself would penetrate, for on the voyage was a young man named Charles Langdon, whose family had a new fortune from coal, and who showed Mark Twain a miniature of his very pretty sister.

After the voyage, one Elisha Bliss, of the American Publishing Company, suggested that Mark Twain turn his journalistic letters into a book. Bliss and his company were at the lower end of the spectrum of literary respectability, for they specialized in subscription books sold from door to door by high-pressure artists. Bliss, himself an artist of ballyhoo, was the heaven-sent publisher for Mark Twain; the author, haunted by his father's failures and the poverty of his boyhood, saw eye to eye with his publisher concerning the primacy of hard cash. Furthermore, Twain, however much he may have nurtured secret yearnings for literary fame, had a very clear notion of the human target at which he aimed. Enunciating a half truth, but one important for one half of his divided nature, he was to say, at the height of his career: "I never cared what became of the cultured classes; they could go to the theater and the opera, they had no use for me and the melodeon." And he added: "Yes, you see, I have always catered for the Belly and the Members."

Though appropriate, the union of Twain and Bliss was stormy. There were delays in publication, and Twain was already paranoidally suspicious of publishers (and of most other people to boot). But *The Innocents Abroad* finally appeared, in 1869, in a small tempest of promotion, in which Bliss was ably seconded by the author, himself no mean practitioner of the art of self-advertisement and log-rolling. It reached a gratifying number of the Belly-and-Members set, but even Dr. Oliver Wendell Holmes praised the book—in a letter with the cautious injunction to keep the praise decorously private and unspotted of the world of commercial exploitation. The Delphic *Atlantic Monthly*, though it took proper pride in its catering to the mind and soul, was not a private newsletter. It hailed this catering to the Belly and Members as "literature," after all.

The Innocents Abroad was a double success, financial and literary, and the secret of the success lay in the author's discovery of his true vein in the doubleness of his own nature and experience, a tension that creates both his humor and the haunting undertone of the darker possibilities of life. The first and most obvious doubleness, however, lies in the objective fact that the work is a hybrid creation. Here, for the first time, Twain brings together the platform artist and the writer. To this material of foreign travel in a sophisticated world, the platform artist brings the method—and with the method certain elemental echoes—of the form of narration from which he had developed his craft.

That original form of narration was the frontier tale. As Bernard De Voto points out in *Mark Twain's America*, and as Mark Twain had put it in "How to Tell a Story" (see below), the form of frontier humor was the oral anecdote, casual, apparently improvised, full of turns and booby traps, rich in tonal variations; and the account of this misbegotten pilgrimage as experienced by a certain character called Mark Twain gave a perfect frame and continuity for a series of such anecdotes. Mark Twain once said that his characteristic lecture was like a plank with a line of square holes into which he could put the plugs appropriate for a particular audience. The voyage of the *Quaker City* provided the plank into which the plugs of anecdote, with all their variety, could be set; and this very method implied a contrast between the frontier world from which it derived and the sophisticated world into which the Innocents were adventuring.

The nature of the book was, also, double. It was, as it has been shrewdly called, both a travel book and a burlesque of the travel book. For instance, in the episode of the moonlight visit to the Parthenon, in which Twain and three friends take a boat and illegally slip ashore, we find this description of the view from the Acropolis:

The full moon was riding high in the cloudless heavens, now. We sauntered carelessly and unthinkingly to the edge of the lofty battlements of the citadel, and looked down—a vision! And such a vision! Athens by moonlight! The prophet that thought the splendors of the New Jerusalem were revealed to him, surely saw this instead! It lay in the level plain right under our feet—all spread abroad like a picture—and we looked down upon it as we might have looked from a balloon. We saw no semblance of a street, but every house, every window, every clinging vine, every projection, was as distinct and sharply marked as if the time were noonday; and yet there was no glare, no glitter, nothing harsh or repulsive—the noiseless city was flooded with the mellow light that ever streamed from the moon, and seemed like some living creature wrapped in peaceful slumber. . . .

This passage, except for its effectiveness, might have been found in any standard travel book of the period, but in *The Innocents Abroad* the lyric mood is played against other effects, and this reverential interlude is immediately followed by a boisterous episode of grape-stealing on the way down from the Acropolis. Again, in the section on the Holy Land (Chap. 48), Twain presents two lyric passages from earlier travel writers and then gives himself great sport in setting their effusions against the grim actualities of the scene they claim to be describing. The Sea of Galilee is nothing, he declares, beside Lake Tahoe, which is his standard for lakes. Not only Lake Tahoe but "home" in general, with its

flattering superiorities and its safe familiarity, is always in the background, and a characteristic effect is the transliteration of the exotic into the domestic commonplace. For instance, in chummily describing Venice:

We see visiting young ladies stand on the stoop, and laugh, and kiss goodbye, and flirt their fans and say "Come soon—now do—you've been just as mean as ever you can be—mother's dying to see you—and we've moved into the new house, O such a love of a place! —so convenient to the post office and the church, and the Young Men's Christian Association; and we do have such fishing, and such carrying on, and *such* swimming-matches in the back yard—Oh, you *must* come—no distance at all, and if you go down through by St. Mark's and the Bridge of Sighs, and cut through the alley." . . .

This chumminess stems, of course, from one pole of Twain's ambivalent attitude toward his fellow pilgrims. He finds them hard to bear, but he is, in the deepest sense, one of them. He will not run the danger of being taken for a snob or a schoolmarm—certainly not for a toady who accepts foreign parts as culturally, aesthetically, or socially superior to the good old U.S.A. The tone of disparagement—from faint to boisterous—is common. For instance: "St. Mark died at Alexandria, in Egypt. He was martyred, I think." The writer cannot be accused of pretending really to *know* that St. Mark was martyred—and certainly not of giving a damn, particularly since Mark was a foreigner and seems to have had some relation to Catholicism, being a saint. But the effect here is subtle compared to that of some episodes—for instance, the Turkish bath in Constantinople or the baiting of the guide in Genoa.

Some of the humor of *The Innocents Abroad*, subtle or broad, has survived its time and social context. For one reason, the fact that it is grounded on a doubleness—an ambivalence in response to Europe—still touches a nerve in the American psyche. There is the appeal, too, of the sometimes feckless character created in Mark Twain, who is puzzled or appalled by the complexities and irrationalities of the world into which he has stumbled, a victim, as the reviewer of his lectures said, of the "world, the flesh, and the Devil." Underlying such appeals, there is, however, the infectious energy of the telling, the verve, the élan, the simple will to command the reader. These qualities are associated, too, with Twain's effort to develop a natural, colloquial style, a style based on the rhythms of speech. In spite of all the lapses from such a style here, a style not fully developed until *Huckleberry Finn*, the sense of life does come through.

The success of *The Innocents Abroad* helped the author set up housekeeping. Not long after the return from the pilgrimage Mark Twain had visited, in Elmira, New York, the young Langdon, whom he had known on shipboard, and now met his sister Olivia, the lady whose miniature he had admired. The Langdons were the very substance of the new American middle class, rich out of the war boom, and equally devout before God, their pastor Thomas Beecher (brother to Henry Ward Beecher), and the higher idols of respectability. The sagebrush Bohemian, only recently out of the cesspools of iniquity of the Far West, with a livelihood from only a most speculative business, was scarcely the son-in-law whom old Jervis Langdon would have chosen. Furthermore, Livy was the apple of her father's eye, with his paternal passion accentuated by the fact that she was a semi-invalid, perhaps not prepared for marriage at all, and certainly not for a union with this highly inappropriate adventurer. Jervis Langdon wrote letters of inquiry back to California about the habits and reputation of the aspirant to Livy's hand, and the responses were unflattering. Meanwhile, the suitor, with the cunning of the serpent, had made an asset of his liabilities. He cast Livy in the role he had used for "Mother" Fairbanks and again played the wayward, charming boy. If he was socially uncouth and had certain bad habits, he was eager to reform, and clearly Livy was the angelic being who would stoop to lift him from his fallen condition. She accepted the role, but only, she insisted, in a sisterly spirit. In the end her sisterliness broke down, and Jervis Langdon developed pity for the young man whose friends in California were so busy maligning him.

The lovers were married, at Elmira, on February 2, 1870, in all the pomp that the Langdon money, piety, and respectability could muster, with two ministers in the parlor to divide the duties of the occasion and a private railroad car —that nineteenth-century symbol of conspicuous success—waiting to take them off to Buffalo, where the groom had bought an interest in a newspaper.

In Buffalo, to his surprise, the groom found himself and his bride conducted not to the superior boarding house where he had engaged rooms, but to a mansion, which he discovered was his very own, a wedding present from Jervis Langdon, along with horses, carriage, groom, cook, housemaid, and a bank account for maintenance. So Sam Clemens, the son of the penniless failure, old Judge Clemens of Hannibal, had entered the world of which his father had only dreamed. He discovered the taste of ease and money and liked it.

He now discovered something else, too. The past of boyhood, and Hannibal, came flooding over him. As he put it in a letter to one of the companions of that lost boyhood, written in the first days of marriage:

> The old life has swept before me like a panorama; the old days have trooped by in their old glory again; the old faces have looked out of the mists of the past; old footsteps have sounded in my listening ears; old hands have clasped mine, and the songs I loved ages and ages ago have come wailing down the centuries.

In all the new splendor and in the bliss of mutual love, he discovered not only certain benefits in the old life, but also certain restrictions in the new. He had to go to church now. Liquor was scowled upon, and his father-in-law tried to bribe him with ten thousand dollars and a trip to Europe to quit smoking. He declined the offer. He had to cling to something.

Things began to go wrong. Livy bore a sickly child. She was ill a long time. Twain had begun a book based on his adventures in the West, but he sank into depression and could not write. His old friend of San Francisco and enemy-to-be, Bret Harte, had become the literary idol of the moment, and, tortured by envy, Twain felt himself outdistanced in the race for fame. The stock of mysterious guilt and self-loathing that had always been in him found focus in his feeling that as a humorous lecturer he had demeaned himself past redemption; nevertheless he felt compelled to go on tour. He badly needed a success to restore his self-esteem. At least people still laughed at his jokes.

Roughing It, which appeared in 1872, though well received, was not the kind of success he craved, but it did mark a gain in both understanding and literary craftsmanship. By intention, it was a companion piece to *The Innocents Abroad* (and in England was published under the title *The Innocents at Home*); the two books deal, as Henry Nash Smith has pointed out in *Mark Twain: The Development of a Writer*, with the "two poles of nineteenth-century American culture: the Europe from which the first colonists came, and the beckoning West." But *Roughing It* has a psychological and philosophical interest far more complex than that of the earlier book. Here the core of interest is what happens to the narrator; he goes to the West a tenderfoot, innocent and full of romantic dreams, and in the end he has entered the world of reality.[2] The story is one of initiation, of growing up, and the inner drama of the work is the contrast between the "simple self that was" (the "I" that is told about) and the mature self (the "I" that does the telling). This, like Hemingway's *A Farewell to Arms*, in which Frederick Henry tells how he came to wisdom through experience, is an example of what may be termed the "narrative of retrospective evaluation," and as such it provides both depth and resonance not possible in the two-dimensional

treatment of *The Innocents Abroad*. Moreover, the narrator-Twain is definitely further than before from Clemens—is becoming, that is, a "fictional character."

This movement toward fiction, as has been suggested by Kenneth S. Lynn, in *Mark Twain and Southwestern Humor*, may have been prompted by a need to define and control the humor that was Twain's stock-in-trade. If the "I" who goes West seems more innocent and feckless than Sam Clemens, it is because that "I" is the butt of humor as his illusions are subjected to the ruthless enlightenment of experience. Humor—specifically self-humor—is the way to conquer the suffering entailed in the confrontation with reality, and here we see that the humor entailed in facing the death of one's romantic illusions (about the world *and* the self) is parallel to the humor derived from watching the illusions of others blasted by the breath of the hard facts of the world. In *The Innocents Abroad*, we have the humor of watching the illusions of others set against reality, and in *Roughing It* we can see the same sort of contrast between Twain's realistic view of the West and the sentimentality of the stories of Bret Harte, who, as we have already seen, invented the literary "West" of rough exteriors and hearts of gold. And here we should not forget that while *Roughing It* was in progress Mark Twain was suffering the anguish of envy at Harte's incredible success.

The redemptive public success that Twain needed to purge his envy and that *Roughing It* did not give came when he went to England, was greeted with a tremendous public reception, and privately dined with dukes. He had gone to England to gather material for a satirical book on that country but was now rapturously defanged. No praise was, suddenly, too high for England. And it began to appear, by some Twainian law of compensation, that no dispraise was too low for America.

America did deserve some dispraise, and Twain was filled with loathing for what he saw—the corruption of democracy, the social scramble, the greed—the age when men were determined to get rich, "dishonestly if we can, honestly if

---

[2] The theme of what we may call the "education in the West" became common in literature and in life. For instance, see the great and subtle story of Stephen Crane, "The Blue Hotel," and Owen Wister's *The Virginian*, and the actual life stories of Theodore Roosevelt and Francis Biddle.

we must." After one of Commodore Vanderbilt's more heinous performances, Twain savaged that worthy in a public letter: "All I wish to urge you now, is that you crush out your native instincts and do something worthy of praise. . . . Go boldly, proudly, nobly, and give four dollars to some worthy charity." Meanwhile, Twain fancied that he himself was immune to the lust of the age, "not much fired with a mania for money getting," and could look back on the simpler time before the Civil War when that "mania" had not yet possessed men's souls; but he was also a child of that age, passionately concerned with business operations, dreaming of inventions (Twain did invent and market at considerable profit a self-gumming album), speculating, loving the company of nabobs, and even while at work on *The Gilded Age* building a mansion worthy of a nabob and enjoying a style of life that would finally do its part in bankrupting him. Now at Hartford, Connecticut, where he had moved after a brief stay in Buffalo, he was in a little colony of intimates whose wealth and fame depended on the new class represented by the "Innocents" of the *Quaker City*, and who, though they felt themselves to reside in a little enclave of intellect, idealism, and aristocratic taste, led a life marked by the new ostentation and self-indulgence.[3]

So, out of loathing and complicity came *The Gilded Age*—which gave the period its name. For the novel Twain had a collaborator, Charles Dudley Warner, a writer who, like Harriet Beecher Stowe and Twain himself, had found the new mass market and who was handily resident in Nook Farm. Twain had never written a novel, and the collaborator was supposed to bring novelistic skill to the project. But the

[3] Among the denizens of Nook Farm, as this de luxe real-estate development was known, were Harriet Beecher Stowe and her husband Calvin, a theologian as wildly unbalanced as she was coming to be, and two other sisters of Henry Ward Beecher, Mary Perkins and Isabella Hooker, the latter a great snob and queen bee of the domain. She once sneered at Twain's taste as represented in a lamp; he replied that when an established house said a thing was good and charged a good price for it, that was all he cared for. Mere wit or mere truth?

work suffered from all the hazards of collaboration. It lacked unity of purpose and of execution, being, in fact, little more than a huddle of improvisations; but it is interesting on two counts. First, it is full of scarcely disguised topical matters, both events and persons, and is an index to Mark Twain's feelings about the times. Second, it presents Twain's first full-scale fictional character, Colonel Beriah Sellers, modeled on his cousin James Lampton. From the pages of the disastrously bad novel Colonel Sellers walked out abidingly alive—"*the* American character," as William Dean Howells called him, a combination of promoter and buncombe-artist, dreamer and con man, idealist and cynic, ballyhoo expert, vote-broker, and, in the Reconstruction world, an expert at bribery, the old Confederate learning the ways of the new Yankeedom and collaborating with a good Unionist to get rich at the public expense while ostensibly trying to elevate the black freedman: "Yes, sir! make his soul immortal but don't touch the nigger as he is."

The Gilded Age, bad book that it is, prepared the way for Mark Twain's greatness. Beyond presenting the Colonel, it pictures for the first time the towns and villages of back-country America, and if it does so with a grim realism, that very realism (which was to reappear in later works) was also the matrix for Twain's ideal vision of that world. For another thing, in *The Gilded Age* he explored the world of luxury, self-deception, hypocrisy, and greed, the contempt for which was to force him back to his dream of the morning world of Hannibal. What the bliss of marriage and financial ease had done to turn his thoughts back to boyhood was now compounded by disgust at the ways of the world of success into which he had penetrated.

In *Roughing It*, Twain had taken a step into his personal past. In 1874, as the result of an invitation from Howells to do something for the *Atlantic Monthly*, he took another step and did a series of pieces about his life as a Mississippi pilot entitled "Old Times on the Mississippi." Later, after a journey on the river to refresh his memories and set them in contrast with the new times, he wrote a book called *Life on the Mississippi*, which, developed from the articles, appeared in 1883. But "Old Times" was, too, a preparation for that greatest achievement, *Huckleberry Finn*, for with it Twain entered the world of Hannibal and the river.[4]

"Old Times" is not only a preparation for the future, but a development of the past, in that it repeats the theme that already informs *Roughing It*, that of initiation. As the tenderfoot learns the West, so the landlubber learns the great river. As one romantic illusion is corrected by the reality of the West, so another is corrected on the river. This particular illusion is explicit only in its aesthetic form; to the uninitiated observer the river is a beautiful spectacle, but to old Bixby, the pilot who is Mark Twain's mentor, it was a "wonderful book." This book was a "dead language to the uneducated passenger [who] . . . saw nothing but all manner of pretty pictures . . . whereas to the trained eye these were not pictures at all, but the grimmest and most dead-earnest of reading matter." Twain is, in fact, dealing with an image of one of the oldest of human questions—that of innocence and experience. The question, in one form or another, haunted him all his days.

Both "Old Times" and *Roughing It* have another important aspect in common. Though he began to write before the Civil War, Whitman was the first poet to affirm the new national experience, but Mark Twain, who repudiated the war and went West, was the first prose writer—of imaginative prose, that is, to take a term more inclusive than fiction—to affirm that national experience, and it was in "Old Times" and *Roughing It* that he found this role. As a writer, he was like Melville, Stephen Crane, Dreiser, and Hemingway in that he lacked a boldly projective imagination; his imagination had to work on the literal personal experience. Mark Twain had to have the board, to use his simile, before he could put the pegs in, and the board was what he got

from direct, and massively varied, experience. He was a wanderer on the face of the land, and he knew many regions, many occupations, many social levels and manifestations; an exemplar of the American as migrant. He was specifically the modern American in other ways, too. He was the apostle of progress, change, prosperity, technology, the dollar, and the new nationalism, repudiating the past and all provincialisms except that of Nook Farm. But he also enacted the old American dream of the search for Eden; his journey West was toward a redemptive simplicity, and the joy of the pilot's life was in the independence of spirit not possible in organized society. The tenderfoot going West, the apprentice pilot, and Huck on his raft—they all dream the same dream.

The dream of boyhood freedom first seized Mark Twain, as we have seen, in the earliest days of his happy marriage to Livy, and not much later he began the first literary expressions of that nostalgia, a sketch that led to *Tom Sawyer*.[5] Bit by bit, over four years, he tinkered

---

[4] For a detailed discussion of the relationship between "Old Times" and *Huckleberry Finn* see *Mark Twain and Huck Finn* (1960), by Walter Blair.

[5] The sketch, known as the "Boy's Manuscript," is a story of courtship made into a burlesque by having it enacted by children—as it is later enacted in Tom Sawyer's courtship of Becky Thatcher. Whatever the reason that adults are pleased by the parody of sexuality by children, as in the old-fashioned "Children Troupes" on the stage, or similarly in such things as the street carnival wedding of the midget to the Fat Lady, something prurient, obscene, and debasing is involved; and it is very strange that in the rosy glow of the honeymoon Mark Twain should have indulged in this particular subject treated in this particular way. It would seem to have a relation to his ambivalence toward sex. He was, for instance, an ardent collector of dirty jokes and was the author of such famous but not very amusing obscenities as "Some Thoughts on the Science of Onanism" and "1601"; but at the same time he could find certain admired paintings of the female nude disgusting and was constantly appalled by what he regarded as the immorality of France: the "two great branches of French thought," he said in one of his broader-minded and less hysterical moments, were "science and adultery." He loved Germany, for its lack of sensuality. In spite of his years as a pilot and in the mining camps and San Francisco, the Langdons' fears that their prospective son-in-law was of impure morals may have been groundless, for there is some evidence that, at the age of thirty-four, when he took their Livy to the marriage bed, he was as spotless as she. To a friend Mark Twain boasted that he was about to marry the "purest" woman

with the story, now and then laying it aside to wait, as he put it, for the "tank" to refill with memories. By July, 1875, he had finished what he called "simply a hymn, put into prose to give it a worldy air." *Tom Sawyer* was a hymn, not to the literal Hannibal or to Twain's literal boyhood, but to those things translated by some alchemy of the heart. It was an illusion that, even though he knew it as illusion, Twain had to have.

With whatever differences, Twain's illusion was enough like the illusion of many Americans to make the book a success. And here the historical moment is of importance. As Whittier's *Snow-Bound* expressed the nostalgia for the simpler world before the Civil War and the rise of the new industrial order and urban complexities, so the world of Hannibal, as transmuted into the St. Petersburg of *Tom Sawyer*, stirred the same yearnings for Eden. *Snow-Bound*, though the most famous example, was not alone in exploiting this nostalgia. For instance, there are Harriet Beecher Stowe's *Old-town Folks* (1869) and Edward Eggleston's *The Hoosier Schoolmaster* (1871), and later the Confederate version in Thomas Nelson Page's *In Ole Virginia* or the Creole version in the work of George Washington Cable. The element of nostalgia is deeply associated with the rise of local color fiction and regionalism in general, though the local colorist or regionalist could sometimes be ambivalent toward the past. But with ambivalence or no, the nostalgia for

the past (or for the simplicities of a frontier, as expressed in Bret Harte) evoked Edenic yearnings that are connected with the American dream.

Tom Sawyer has significances other than that of a record of Mark Twain's boyhood or a document in American social history. It is a novel, the first completely by Twain, and the first book that is, in a deeper sense, really his, that comes out of his primary world of feeling. But it also comes from the popular literature of the period, reaching as far back as Longstreet's *Georgia Scenes*, and even for certain episodes levying upon Dickens' *A Tale of Two Cities* or Poe's "The Gold Bug."

Behind it, too, lies the cult of childhood. In a sense, it can be said that only after the Civil War was the child discovered as a literary subject, as an association, on the one hand, with the nostalgia for lost innocence and, on the other, as a result of the new evolutionary psychology, that saw in the development of the human being a recapitulation of the history of the race.[6] There came a flood of books about children, including such staples as Louisa May Alcott's *Little Women* (1868) and *Little Men* (1871), Thomas Bailey Aldrich's *Story of a Bad Boy* (1870), and Charles Dudley Warner's *Being a Boy* (1879). The flood continued for generations, through Booth Tarkington's *Penrod and Sam*, and merged with the guff of the women's magazines, such as the *Delineator* under the editorship of Theodore Dreiser, and with social and psychological developments to create the child-oriented society and the regime of Dr. Spock. In the beginning of the cult of the child there had been Victorian pietistic sentimentality, which carried some last echo of the medieval tales of child saints, and it was a reaction from the stories of goody-good children that set the stage for Tom Sawyer and Huck Finn.

As a novel, *Tom Sawyer* forced the author to face a new problem. Here "Mark Twain" could

---

that ever lived, and when he gave her *Gulliver's Travels* to read, he carefully expurgated it.

Nothing just said is to be taken to imply, however, that the marriage of Mark Twain and Livy was not a happy one. From London, several years after the honeymoon, he could write her: "If I'm not homesick to see you, no other lover ever *was* homesick to see his sweetheart.—And when I get there, remember, 'Expedition's the word!' " And a few weeks later: "I love to write about arriving—it seems as if it were to be tomorrow. And I love to picture myself ringing the bell at midnight —then a pause of a second or two—then the turning of the bolt, and 'Who is it?'—then ever so many kisses— then you and I in the bath-room, I drinking my cock-tail and undressing, and you standing by—then to bed, and— everything happy and jolly as it should be." This scarcely suggests frigidity or Victorian prudery.

[6] For a discussion of the relation of the new psychology and literature see *Harvests of Change* (1967), by Jay Martin; also, *The Innocent Eye* (1961), by Albert E. Stone.

not be the persona for him, and the humor of Twain's personal role was no longer available; the story demanded to be told objectively and this meant that the presence of the narrator could not serve to give unity and control. In fact, a defect of the book is that the author never seems quite sure whether he is writing a book for boys (which is what, on the authority of Howells, Mark Twain finally decided it was) or a book about boys for the adult reader. There is, as a result, an uncertainty about style, about the way of the telling. For instance, take the following passage:

Saturday morning was come, and all the summer world was come, and all the summer world was bright and fresh, and brimming with life. There was a song in every heart; and if the heart was young the music issued at the lips. There was cheer in every face and a spring in every step. The locust trees were in bloom and the fragrance of the blossoms filled the air. Cardiff Hill, beyond the village and above it, was green with vegetation, and it lay just far enough away to seem a Delectable Land, dreamy, reposeful, and inviting.

This is the background for the terrible ordeal of Tom's being sent to whitewash the fence, and his subsequent triumph of psychological cunning. But the fancy "literary" style does not give a sense of the way Tom would feel at the moment. It is an appeal to the reader, with a nudge to him to appreciate the condescending humor in the highfalutin paraphrase of Tom's own feelings.

At another moment, however, there can be a clear, vigorous, colloquial style which conforms to the nature of a subject:

After breakfast they went whooping and prancing out on the bar, and chased each other round and round, shedding clothes as they went, until they were naked, and then continued the frolic far away up the shoal water of the bar, against the stiff current, which later tripped their legs down under them from time to time and greatly increased the fun. And now and then they stooped in a group and splashed water in each other's faces with their palms, gradually approaching each other, with averted faces to avoid the strangling sprays, and finally gripping and struggling till the best man ducked his neighbor, and then they all went under in a tangle of white legs and arms, and came up blowing, sputtering, laughing, and gasping for breath at one and the same time.

In 1876, at the very moment when he was reading proofs on *Tom Sawyer*, Twain began *Huckleberry Finn*, which, with the subtitle "Tom Sawyer's Comrade," he regarded as a companion volume. But the new book did not get finished for seven years. Mark Twain had got only as far as the ramming of the raft by a steamboat before he laid it aside. Over the years he added to it, but before he picked it up for the finish he had written, among other things, *The Prince and the Pauper, Life on the Mississippi*, and *A Tramp Abroad*. The book was finally published in February, 1885, by the Charles Webster Company, which was really a stalking horse for Twain himself—for publishing was one of his business ventures and a way to give Samuel Clemens two levels of profit and the full benefit of being a close connection of Mark Twain. The results were very gratifying, even to the double-barreled avarice of the author-publisher.

Reviewers, however, were inclined to find the book crude, irreverent, and even vicious. This is the same book that Mencken was to call "Himalayan," that Hemingway would regard as the fountainhead of our modern fiction, that T. S. Eliot would name "great," and that would make Faulkner, with peculiar stylistic contortion, say, "Twain was all our grandfather." Perhaps some ten million copies have now been printed.

Let us rehearse the simple facts of the story. With the treasure that he now shares with Tom, as a result of the earlier adventures, Huck has been adopted into the respectable world of St. Petersburg, and begins to accept the new regime of spelling, soap, and prayers. Pap then reappears to claim Huck, but when, in one of his drunken rages, he threatens his life, Huck, after making it seem that he has been murdered by a robber, escapes to the island. Here he is joined by Nigger Jim, the slave of Miss Watson, who, in spite of her piety, is being tempted to sell him down river. Huck, disguised as a girl, makes a scouting expedition to shore and finds that the island is not safe from slave-catchers, and they take to the river. Huck is troubled in his conscience at thus depriving Miss Watson of her property, but follows his natural instinct. The plan to escape to freedom in a northern state fails when they miss Cairo, Illinois, in a fog. When the raft is sunk by a steamboat, the two, barely escaping with their lives, are separated.

Huck is taken in by the Grangerford family, aristocratic planters, and enjoys their hospitality until a slaughterous outbreak of the bloody feud with the Shepherdsons puts him again on his own. He manages to rejoin Jim, and the growth of his human understanding of Jim constitutes the psychological action, which concludes when Huck decides that though saving Jim may get him damned, he'll just have to go to hell.

Meanwhile, the pair pass through various adventures that exhibit the irrationalities of society and the cruelties possible to human nature. The life on the river comes to an end when the vagabond "King" and "Duke," the rogues whom they have befriended, betray Jim for a share in a presumptive reward and Jim is held captive on the down-river plantation of the Phelps family, kin of Tom Sawyer. When Huck goes to the plantation with the idea of rescuing Jim, he is taken for Tom, who is expected on a visit. To save Jim, he accepts the role, and when the real Tom appears, Tom accepts the role of Sid, another boy in the family connection. Tom institutes one of his elaborate adventures to rescue Jim, with Huck participating in the nonsense to placate Tom. After the rescue of Jim, during which Tom gets shot in the leg, Jim stays with him and is recaptured; but all comes out happily, for, as is now explained, Miss Watson, on her deathbed, had long since freed Jim, and Tom had withheld this information merely to enjoy a romantic adventure.

Huck is now taken in by the Phelps family to be civilized but is thinking of escape to the Indian country.

The story, or rather Twain's treatment of the story, has provoked a vast body of criticism and various interpretations. The most simple view is to regard *Huckleberry Finn* as merely a companion piece to *Tom Sawyer*—more of the same tale of what it was like to be a boy in mythical Hannibal. As far as it goes, this view is valid. But it does not accommodate certain features of the book that are undeniably there.

The book is, indeed, a series of boyish adventures, but these adventures take place in an adult world, and the journey on the raft is, as Bernard De Voto has put it, a "faring forth with inexhaustible delight through the variety of America." The "faring forth" gives, "objectively and inwardly, a panorama of American life, comic and serious, or with the comic and serious intertwined, all levels, all types of that life."

We must remember, however, that here we refer to the objective world of the novel and to the "inwardness" of that world. But what of the "inwardness" of the observers of that adult world? With this question we engage the central issue of the novel, for whenever the boyish world of Huck and Jim touches the adult world —the "shore" world—something significantly impinges upon the "river" idyll. If the basic fact of the novel is that it is a journey, we must think, not only of the things seen on the journey, but also of who sees them and the effect of the seeing. The journey, in fact, has begun with inward motives of great urgency. Both Huck and Jim are more than footloose wanderers; they are escaping from their respective forms of bondage, forms imposed by society. To flee they give themselves to the river; and it is not illogical to agree with the poet T. S. Eliot and the critic Lionel Trilling that the river may be taken to have a central role. As Eliot implies when he says that the river has no clear point of beginning and fades out into its delta toward the sea, the river seems to be an image of a timeless life force different from the fixed order of the dry land, an image of freedom and regeneration; or as Trilling puts it, the river is a god to which Huck can turn for renewal.

In any case, the river provides not only a principle of structural continuity, but also a principle of thematic continuity. The experience on the river, with its special tone of being, is set against that on land. Huck says: "It was kind of solemn, drifting down the big, still river—looking up at the stars, and we didn't ever feel like talking loud, and it warn't often we laughed." Not only does the river teach a feeling of awe before the universe, but also a kind of human relationship at odds with the vanity, selfishness, competitiveness, and hypocrisy of society: "What you want, above all things, on a raft is for everybody to be satisfied, and feel right and kind toward the others."

But society—in which people are not "satisfied"—pursues the fugitives even on the river; the steamboat, as we have seen, runs down the raft. When Huck and Jim escape by diving deep into the bosom of the river, beneath the murderous paddle wheels, this event is a baptism that frees them—fully, it now seems—into the new life.[7]

If we are to understand the significance of the land-river contrast, and of Huck's baptism, we must understand Huck himself, for Huck is the carrier of the meaning of the novel, and however unrelated the adventures of the picaresque tale may seem, they come to focus in what the adventurer makes of them. The focal significance of Huck is emphasized by the fact that as early as 1875, Twain, in considering a sequel to *Tom Sawyer*, said to Howells, who had urged him to make Tom grow up in another book, that Tom "would not be a good character for it." He was, he said, considering a novel that would take a boy of twelve "through life" and added that the tale would have to be told "auto-

biographically—like *Gil Blas*." If the wanderings of the new picaro are to be "through life," we expect the wanderer to learn something about life, and if, as Twain declared, the tale must be told as autobiography (it would be "fatal" otherwise, he said to Howells), the reason must be that the personality of the learner is crucially important.

In other words, Twain needed a hero sensitive enough to ask the right questions of his adventures in growing up, and intelligent enough to demand the right answers. Furthermore, if Twain was to make the process of learning dramatically central to the tale, he could not well trust it to a third-person narrator, as in *Tom Sawyer*. The hero would have to tell his own tale, with all its inwardness, and in his own telling, in the language itself, exhibit both his own nature and the meaning of experience.

In Huck's language—"a magnificent expression," as Bernard De Voto has put it, "of the folk mind"—Twain found a miraculous solution. It is not less miraculous for springing from a well-defined tradition, or, rather, from two traditions. The first was that of the frontier humorists from Augustus Baldwin Longstreet, Davy Crockett, and the anonymous writers of the Crockett almanacs on to George Washington Harris and his *Sut Lovingood*, a tradition that had fed the humor of lecturers and journalists like Artemus Ward and the early Mark Twain; the second was that of the early writers of the local color school, such as James Russell Lowell, Harriet Beecher Stowe, and Bret Harte. But the use of dialect by such writers had become more and more cumbersome and mechanical; it set up a screen between the language and the meaning. Furthermore, the dialect itself was a mark of condescension. (See p. 607.) The writer and reader, proud of superior literacy, looked down on the dialect, and the speaker.

What Twain needed was a language based on colloquial usage, and carrying that flavor, but flexible and natural, with none of the mechanical burden of dialect writing. At the same time, even if the speaker was of inferior literacy, his language had to be expressive enough to re-

---

[7] The episode may be fruitfully placed beside the "baptism" in *A Farewell to Arms*, when Frederick Henry dives into the Tagliamento River to escape the Fascist battle police and the insanity of the world of institutions. See p. 2264.

port subtleties of feeling and thought. In achieving this, Twain established a new relation between American experience as *content* and language as a direct *expression*—not merely a *medium of expression*—of that experience. The language, furthermore, implied a certain kind of fiction, a fiction that claimed a certain relation to the experience it treated. That Mark Twain was aware of this situation is indicated at the very beginning of the novel: "You didn't know about me without you have read a book by the name of *The Adventures of Tom Sawyer*; but that ain't no matter. The book was made by Mr. Mark Twain, and he told the truth, mainly." Here Huck asserts himself as the literal subject about which Mr. Mark Twain had written in *Tom Sawyer*; but now he himself is to tell his own tale. He is, then, free-standing, in his natural habitat outside of both "Mr. Mark Twain's" book and his own, insisting on a special veracity about experience. Actually, Huck Finn is only another fictional dramatization, but a dramatization validated by the language that springs directly from the world treated. The invention of this language, with all its implications, gave a new dimension to our literature.

Huck's language *is* Huck. On the one hand, it reaches back into the origins of Huck as the son of whisky-sodden Pap, sleeping it off with the hogs; it was a language Pap could speak. It is indicative of the world of common, or even debased, life from which Huck moves to his awakening, but, as we have said, it is a language capable of poetry, as in this famous description of dawn on the river:

Not a sound anywhere—perfectly still—just like the whole world was asleep, only sometimes the bull-frogs a-cluttering, maybe. The first thing to see, looking away over the water, was a kind of dull line—that was the woods on t'other side—you couldn't make nothing else out; then a pale place in the sky; then more paleness, spreading around; then the river softened up, away off, and warn't black any more, but gray; you could see little dark spots drifting along, ever so far away—trading scows and such things; and long black streaks —rafts; sometimes you could hear a sweep screaking; or jumbled up voices, it was so still, and sounds come so far; and by-and-by you could see a streak on the water which you know by the look of the streak that there's a snag there in a swift current which breaks on it and makes that streak look that way; and you see the mist curl up off of the water, and the east reddens up, and the river, and you make out a log cabin in the edge of the woods, away on the bank on t'other side of the river, being a wood-yard, likely, and piled by them cheats so you can throw a dog through it anywheres; then the nice breeze springs up, and comes fanning you from over there, so cool and fresh, and sweet to smell, on account of the woods and the flowers; but sometimes not that way, because they've left dead fish laying around, gars, and such, and they do get pretty rank; and next you've got the full day, and everything smiling in the sun, and the song-birds just going it!

The style that Twain developed for Huck is of such importance that we must interrupt the discussion of the novel to try to place it in its general context. To begin with, it has effects far beyond its magnificent immediate function as a dramatization of the personality of the speaker. It constitutes, in fact, a watershed in Twain's own style. This is best seen in connection with the general revolution in prose style after the Civil War, a revolution that Twain himself remarked in *Life on the Mississippi*. There he blames the sluggish, inflated style generally current on Walter Scott: "If one takes up a Northern or Southern literary periodical of forty or fifty years ago, he will find it filled with wordy, windy, flowery 'eloquence,' romanticism, sentimentality—all imitated from Sir Walter, and sufficiently badly done, too—innocent travesties of his style and methods, in fact." But Scott was not the only cause. The social structure of the eastern seaboard and much of the South encouraged an ostentation of learning: the writer had to show his wares as a mark of his status, and flowers of style, quite unrelated to whatever business was in hand, attested to his intellectual and social superiority. Even in a great writer like Hawthorne, the style has a life quite separate from the life of the subject. The writer was taken to be more of a performer than a creator. Political oratory shared this disability, sometimes even more disastrously, for in it figures of style and Ciceronian pirouettes were often more in evidence than cogency of argument, astute analysis of fact, or direct appeal to feeling. Into the muggy weather of this world, Lincoln's Gettysburg Address came like a bolt of lightning. (The sermon had sometimes avoided the vices of the period, however, because of theological rigor or the need to make an assault on the heart.)

The essence of the new style arising after the Civil War lies in the will to fuse form and function. Various factors are involved here. The open-ended society of the Middle West and West gave a background for the use of language, with the declarative sentence the core of style and the presentation of hard fact its characteristic function. If the tall tale did have its own kind of poetry, that poetry, even in its wildest grotesquerie, was aimed at expression, not decoration. The Civil War, too, had its effect on the new style, and not a few writers who contributed to it, for instance, Ambrose Bierce and Oliver Wendell Holmes, were graduates of that tough school; it was a school that emphasized the terse and precise, not the flowery—a West Point style, quite literally for some of its practitioners, which, as with Grant in his *Memoirs*, might achieve a dynamic purity of effect. To the West and the war, we may add the influence of the new journalism, especially the reporting of the war: news was urgent, and the facts mattered. And of course, overarching all and absorbing all, there was the pragmatic spirit.

Twain, as we have seen, early turned toward a realistic base for his style, as in *The Innocents Abroad*, but we have also seen that as late as *Tom Sawyer* the split might persist between form and function. In Huck's style that split is healed, and Twain, later writing as himself and not as Huck, could assimilate the principle there stumbled upon. He had, indeed, begun

to move toward his later style in "Old Times," where feeling and fact were intertwined in his review of old scenes, but this new sense of style is much more marked in *Life on the Mississippi*, which comes after Huck had already begun to speak his vulgar, and divine, tongue. With *A Connecticut Yankee*, now far away from Hannibal and the river, we see the new style with a new grounding and a new application. Howells called Mark Twain the Lincoln of our literature. We may interpret this by observing that Lincoln freed the slave, and Mark Twain freed the writer.

What does Huck's style signify about him? When we find a language capable of poetic force, we must remember that it is spoken by a speaker, and a speaker capable of poetic thought and feeling. The language derives from Pap's world, but it indicates a most un-Paplike sensibility, and this sensibility, even in its simplest poetic utterances, prepares us for Huck's moral awakening as, bit by bit, he becomes aware of the way the world really wags. The language of Huck is, then, an index to the nature of his personal story—his growing up.

Tom Sawyer, it is true, is also the story of growing up, but there is a crucial difference between the two versions. Huck's growing up is by the process of a radical criticism of society, while Tom's is by a process of achieving acceptance in society. Tom's career is really a triumph of conventionality, and though Tom is shown as the "bad" boy, we know that he is not "really bad." He is simply a good healthy boy making the normal experiments with life, and we know, from our height of indulgent condescension, that in the end all will be well. And all is well. Tom is accepted into the world of civilized and rational St. Petersburg. Even Huck, as an adjunct to Tom, is also accepted as worthy to be "civilized," and this, in the light of his deplorable beginnings and generally unwashed condition, is a good American success story, cheering to parents and comforting to patriots.

Huckleberry Finn is a companion piece, but a companion piece in reverse, a mirror image; it is the American un-success story, the story that has been embodied in Leatherstocking, proclaimed by Thoreau, and again embodied in Ike McCaslin of Faulkner's *The Bear*, the drama of the innocent outside of society. Tom's story ends once he has been reclaimed by society, but Huck's real story does not even begin until he has successfully penetrated the world of respectability and, in the well-meaning clutches of the Widow and Miss Watson, begins to chafe under their ministrations. Here Twain indicates the thematic complexity of Huck's rebellion. It is not the mere tyranny of prayers, spelling, manners, and soap that drives Huck forth; Tom and Pap also play significant roles in this story.

Tom, in a sense, dominates not only his gang but Huck, too. He is an organizer and has a flair for leadership, but the secret of his power is his imagination: medieval chivalry, piracy, treasure hunts, and wild adventures drawn from his reading fill his head and must be enacted, with Tom, of course, in the major role. Against this world of fantasy and exaggeration, which Huck calls "stretchers" or else plain lies, Huck brings the criticism of fact, and when he can't keep his mouth shut, Tom calls him a "numbskull." Huck rejects this "dream" escape from civilization:

So then I judged that all that stuff was only just one of Tom Sawyer's lies. I reckoned he believed in the A-rabs and the elephants, but as for me, I think different. It had all the marks of a Sunday-school.

In repudiating romantic adventure and criticizing the romantic view of life, Huck is simply doing what Twain had done in *Roughing It*, and was to do in *Life on the Mississippi* with its criticism of his own nostalgic memories and the southern legend, and more specifically in *A Connecticut Yankee in King Arthur's Court*. It is not merely that the romantic lies offend Huck's realistic sense. They offend his moral sense, too; for it is behind the facade of such lies, rationalized and justified by them, that society operates, and we notice that he concludes the remark on Tom's fantasy by saying, "It had all the marks of a Sunday-school"—

Sunday school, and religion in general, being the most effective facade behind which society may carry on its secular operations. The equation of Tom's romantic lies with the lies of Sunday school tells us that Tom, in his romantic fantasies, is merely using his "stretchers" to escape from society's "stretchers"—lies as a cure for lies. And the point is this: the repudiation of Tom's lies prepares us for the bitter unmasking of society's lies that is to occur on the journey down river.

We have said that Huck has sensitivity and a poetic sense; so, we must ask how this squares with his repudiation of Tom's imagination. Tom's brand of imagination is basically self-indulgent, even self-aggrandizing—in its social dimension, for instance, it makes Tom the leader, and more broadly considered, justifies the injustices of society. But Huck's imagination, as we learn on the journey, has two distinct differences from this brand. First, it is a way of dealing with natural fact, of relating to fact, as in the night scene on the raft or the description of dawn; the poetry here derives from a scrupulously accurate rendering of natural fact. Second, it is a way of discovering and dealing with moral fact, a poetry that is concerned with the human condition, and as such is the root of his growth; and this distinction comes clear in the end when Tom, on the Phelps plantation, is willing to put Jim through the rigamarole of the rescue, just to satisfy his romantic imagination, when he could easily free him by reporting the facts of Miss Watson's deathbed manumission.[8] To sum up, the repudiation of Tom's imagination is of deeper significance than the flight from the Widow's soap and Miss Watson's "pecking."

Pap's role is more complex than Tom's. When

[8] The English critic V. S. Pritchett, in an essay in the *New Statesman and Nation* (August 2, 1941), says that "Huck never imagines anything except fear" and contrasts him with Tom, who might grow up "to build a civilization" because "he is imaginative." Huck, he continues, "is low-down plain ornery, because of the way he was brought up with 'Pap.'" That is, he is a natural "bum." It would seem that the critic is, simply, wrong. If his view is correct, what of the series of moral criticisms that Huck brings to bear on society?

he reappears, he seems at first a means of escape from prayers, spelling, manners, and soap into the freedom of nature. Certainly Pap has little contact with civilization at this level, and for one moment he seems to be the free "outsider." But he is an "outsider" only insofar as he is *rejected*; he is the offal of civilization, a superfluous and peculiarly filthy part and parcel of civilization. His outsideness means no regeneration, for in his own filthiness he carries all the filth of civilization, as is clearly illustrated by his railing against the free Negro and his talk about the government and his vote. Pap is an outsider only by vice and misfortune—in contrast to the outsider by philosophy, which is what Huck is in the process of becoming. Pap, Tom, and the Widow, that apparently ill-assorted crew, all represent aspects of bondage and aspects of civilization from which Huck flees.

Huck, moreover, is fleeing from Pap to save his quite literal life, for whether or not Pap is the "natural" man, he is a most unnatural father bent on carving up his son with a clasp knife. This literal fact symbolically underscores the significance of the journey. The escape from Pap is symbolically, as Kenneth S. Lynn puts it in *Mark Twain and Southwestern Humor*, a murder. Literally, Huck has had a gun on Pap all night, clearly prepared to pull the trigger if he goes on another rampage; and when, later, to fool Pap about his flight, he kills a pig and sprinkles the blood around the shack, the pig is a surrogate for Pap, who sleeps with the pigs. But the blood is to indicate that Huck himself has been murdered, and so we have, symbolically, not only a murder but a suicide; Huck "murders" the piglike past and himself "dies" into a new life—a theme restated by the baptism in the river.

This episode has, in fact, another dimension; to grow up implies the effort of seeking individuation from society and from the father—that is, from the bond of the group and from the bond of blood. So now Huck, free from both society and the father, goes forth to find the terms on which his own life may be possible. *So we have here a journey undertaken, at the conscious level, as a flight, but signifying, at the unconscious level, a quest*; and this doubleness is precisely what we find in the pattern of adolescence.

To speak of the journey as a quest, the stages in the movement toward freedom, we refer to the fact that Huck, episode by episode, is divesting himself of illusions. Illusion, in other words, means bondage: Tom's lies, the lies of Sunday school, all the lies that society tells to justify its values and extenuate its conduct, are the bonds. For Huck, the discovery of reality, as opposed to illusion, will mean freedom. And here we may note that the pattern of the movement from illusion to reality follows that of *Roughing It* and of *Life on the Mississippi*. The main action of *Huckleberry Finn*, in fact, may—and this should be emphasized—be taken as the movement toward reality after the Edenic illusion of *Tom Sawyer*—that is, Twain's revision of his own idyllic dream of boyhood and Hannibal after his return to that world preparatory to writing *Life on the Mississippi*. And the contrast between illusion and reality is, of course, central to Twain's work in its most serious manifestations; it is, as well, at the root of his humor.

To return to the theme of the quest, Huck's voyage toward spiritual freedom is counterpointed structurally by Jim's search for quite literal freedom. This contrapuntal relationship is complex, but the most obvious element is that many of the lies of society have to do with the enslavement of Jim. Miss Watson, though a praying woman, will sell him down river. The woman who receives Huck in his disguise as Sarah Mary Williams will be kind to him and protect him, but when it comes to catching Jim for the reward, she innocently asks, "Does three hundred dollars lay round every day for people to pick up?" And in Pap's drunken tirade about the "free nigger" with his fine clothes and gold watch and chain, we see a deeper motivation than greed, the need of even the lowest to feel superior to some one.

Not that all of the evils of society have to do directly with Jim. There are the men on the river who would let a raft with a dying man drift on because they are afraid of smallpox. There are the Grangerfords with their bloody code of honor, and Colonel Sherburn's cold-blooded gunning of Boggs. There is the mob that under the guise of administering justice would gratify its sadism and envy by lynching Sherburn, but will turn coward before him, and then, right afterward, go to the circus; and the mob that, justly, takes care of the rascally King and Duke, but in doing so becomes, for Huck, the image of human cruelty. Even so, all the lies, as we have observed, are forms of bondage, and the dynamic image for this theme is the slave; and this dominant image implies the idea that all lies are one lie, that all evil springs from the same secret root.

This idea of the fusion of evil with evil leads to a fundamental lesson that Huck learns in his continuing scrutiny of society: good and evil rarely appear in isolable form. Society is a mixture, and the human being is, too. The woman who would catch Jim for three hundred dollars is a kind woman. The men on the river, who are in fact chasing runaway slaves, do have a human conscience, at least enough of one to make them pay two twenty-dollar gold pieces as conscience money. The Grangerfords, even with their blood-drenched honor, are kind, hospitable, dignified, totally courageous, and even chivalric in their admiration of the courage of the Shepherdsons. Sherburn, too, is a man of intelligence and courage.[9]

The discovery of the interfusion of evil with good marks a step toward Huck's growing up, but he has reached another stage when he learns that the locus of the problem of evil is his own soul. And here the relationship with Jim is crucial; for it is this relationship that provides a specific focus for all the general questions raised by the scrutiny of society. Coming down the river, Huck has more and more freed himself from the definition of Jim that society would prescribe: an inferior creature justly regarded as property. Huck even comes to "humble" himself before a "nigger" and apologize to him. The climax of this process comes in the famous Chapter 31 when Huck's "conscience" dictates that he write to Miss Watson and turn Jim over to her. Having written the letter, he feels cleansed, "reformed," saved from the danger of hell fire. But the human reality of Jim on the raft, of Jim's affection for him, undoes all Huck's good intentions, and in a moment of magnificently unconscious irony, he bursts out, "All right, then, I'll go to hell," and tears up the letter.

Conscience, in short, is merely the voice of the particular society in which a person has been bred.[10] Against this "conscience" Huck would

---

[9] The treatment of Colonel Sherburn and, especially, the Grangerfords illustrates how Twain, the artist, lifts himself above the specific views and prejudices of Clemens, the man. Clemens, shall we say, abhors Sir Walter Scott and the Scott-infected South with its chivalric pretensions, but Twain, in spite of the brutal gunning of Boggs, recognizes the basic courage in Sherburn when he stands off the mob. As for the Grangerfords, Huck is enchanted by them, even by the "Battle of Prague" played on the tinny little piano by the Grangerford girls. Here it must be remembered that Huck is the index of response for the novel, and even if a little fun is being had at Huck's innocence, we cannot basically discount his response. The Grangerfords are indeed full of absurdity—even bloody absurdity—but they play out their drama with generosity, warmth, courage, and flair. They are, to say the least, outside the "genteel tradition," from which Huck—and Twain the artist— flee. Another aspect of the Grangerford interlude, the love passage between the Shepherdson Romeo and the

Grangerford Juliet, is very important: a little later we have the absurdity of the balcony scene of Shakespeare's play presented by the King and the Duke, and this counterpoints the absurd, but real—and in the end tragic—parody of Shakespeare already given. The relation between the absurd and the serious is very complex: irony within irony. By the way, it is of some significance that Huck is drawn into the Shepherdson-Grangerford love story, and this counterpoints, with differences, the way he is drawn into the romantic charades of Tom Sawyer.

[10] In his *Notebook* (edited by Albert Bigelow Paine) Mark Twain describes his conscience: "My conscience is a part of *me*. It is a mere machine, like my heart—but moral, not physical. . . . It is merely a *thing*; the creature of *training*; it is whatever one's mother and Bible and comrades and laws and system of government and habitat and heredities have made it." The question of the nature of conscience was an obsessive concern for Mark Twain, with his morbid sense of guilt and pathological need to assume the responsibility for all evil and misfortune around him. If conscience could be regarded as merely a "thing," merely a "machine," then his anguish might be alleviated. This issue is connected, of

set what we may call a "consciousness" forged by the unillusioned inspection of experience. Huck wants to look at the world directly, with his own eyes, and this desire, and talent, is the reward for being outside society, having no stake in it. When, on the Phelps plantation, in the plot with Tom to rescue Jim, Huck objects to some of Tom's romantic irrelevancies, Tom says: "Huck, you don't ever seem to want to do anything regular; you want to be starting something fresh all the time." Huck is a moral pragmatist; he wants to derive his values "fresh," from experience, to create his own moral consciousness.[11] For only in such a consciousness may a man be free.

With Huck we have, too, another version of the story of antinomianism in America, which we have referred to in our discussions of Whittier and Garrison. There are, however, some significant differences. Huck's free consciousness comes not from revelation or "higher law," but from a long and humble scrutiny of experience; humility, not arrogance, is the mark of Huck's mind. If Huck recognizes anything, it is that "conscience" is conditioned, and once this fact is recognized, there is the corollary that more things than society may do the conditioning; the response to "conscience," to the "higher law," or to revelation from on High may simply be a response to the antinomian's own deep psychic needs, not necessarily holy. Huck is an antinomian of the educable "consciousness," not of the absolute "conscience." He is an anti-

nomian far closer to William James (see pp. 1519–28) than to Theodore Parker (see pp. 345–46). And if his consciousness has been educated to freedom, the process has also been an education in humility, not in dogmatic arrogance; Huck has had to learn to recognize and accept the love of a creature for whom he had had a contempt, however amiable, and whose company he had originally accepted only because of an animal loneliness.

The forging of Huck's free consciousness has, indeed, other aspects. With the flight from society, with the symbolic patricide, the symbolic suicide, and the symbolic baptism, Huck has lost the old self. He must seek the new self. And so we see emerging the psychological pattern in which, with every new venture back to the shore—that is, to society—Huck takes on a new role, has a new personal history to tell, a new "self" to try on for size. There is, of course, always a good practical reason for this role-playing, but beyond such a reason, the act represents a seeking for identity, such an identity as will, presumably, allow him to achieve freedom even in contact with society. For Huck is not, in other words, seeking to exist outside of society—to be merely an outcast, like Pap. When he is alone at the beginning of the journey he suffers loneliness;[12] what he seeks is simply a new kind of society, a kind prefigured by the harmony and mutual respect necessary on a raft. He is also seeking a new kind of father, and here is where Jim assumes another significance; Jim is the "father" who can give love, even when the son, Huck, is undeserving and ungrateful. This role finds its clearest definition in Chapter 31, when Huck thinks back upon the relationship, but it has a subsidiary confirmation in the fact that Jim on the raft is the father deprived of his blood children (whose freedom he intends to buy once he has his own) and

course, with Twain's concern with the problem of free will and determinism, and if he could regard man as "merely a machine, moved wholly by outside influences," then he was guiltless. In Huck, Twain is exploring another possibility of the alleviation of his constant and intolerable sense of guilt—by developing what we may call a "free consciousness."

11 Here we find a more profound connection of Hemingway with Mark Twain than in the matter of style and perception. The emphasis on the concrete—the "names of villages and the numbers of regiment"—and the style tied to the dramatic act of perception are an index of Hemingway's own attempt to forge a "consciousness" to take the place of, to undercut, the traditional values that had brought the world to the debacle of 1914–18. See pp. 2257–58. But see also Henry James, p. 1373.

12 Jim comes to Huck in this moment of loneliness, and he is originally accepted primarily in terms of it; it is significant, too, that when Huck goes to seek Jim after his reported capture, the description of the Phelps plantation is focused on loneliness; ". . . then I knowed for certain I wished I was dead—for that [the distant wail and hum of a spinning wheel] is the lonesomest sound in the whole world."

now needs to find a "son" to spend his love on.[13]

To sum up: though on the negative side the novel recounts the discovery of the "lies" in society and even in the "conscience," it recounts, on the positive side, the discovery of a redemptive vision both for society and for the individual. This is a vision of freedom to be achieved by fidelity to experience, humility, love, and pity for suffering, even for the suffering of those who, like the King and the Duke, are justly punished. This is not to say that such a vision is explicitly stated. It is implied, bit by bit, as Huck drifts down the river; it is, we might say, the great lesson inculcated by the symbolic river—the lesson that men can never learn on shore.

But what is the relation between this vision and the world of reality on shore?

In the last section of the novel, Huck does come back to shore, and the crucial nature of the return is signaled by the question that Mrs. Phelps asks him when he tells his lie about the blowing up of a cylinder head on the steamboat that never existed:

> "Good gracious! anybody hurt?"
> "No'm. Killed a nigger."

So with his answer Huck has fallen back into society and society's view that a "nigger" is not human, is not "anybody"—this in the very moment when he has come ashore to rescue Jim.

This moment signals, too, the issue that has provoked the most searching critical debate about the novel. According to one side of the debate, the last section undercuts all the meaning developed in the main body of the novel,

[13] The need of Huck for paternal love may well be related to Twain's own experience with an unloving father, but this does not acount for the episode. In the South, both before and after the Civil War, the more or less intimate relation between a boy and an aging Negro man was a common situation, as in Twain's relation to Uncle Dan'l; both the boy and the Negro were outsiders to the official society of white adults, and both lived in an underground world.

and the working out of the end is, as Hemingway puts it, "just cheating."

Here we see the repetition of the old situation in which Huck had been reared, the "good" people, now Silas Phelps and Aunt Sally, holding Jim for a reward, but this fact, which earlier, on the raft, would have been recognized as one of the "lies" of society, is now quite casually accepted. Even the rescuing of Jim is presented to the reader, not in terms of Huck's values as earned on the river—even though he is still the narrator—but in terms of Tom's, as a comic game. Huck's role now is simply to underscore the comic point of this game, by giving the same realistic criticisms of Tom's romantic fancies that we have known from long back.

These "land-changes" that the novel undergoes imply other, more important ones. Huck is no longer the central character, the focus of action and meaning, but now merely the narrator; and indeed he has regressed to the stage of limited awareness exhibited in *Tom Sawyer*. Associated with this regression is a change in the role of Jim: Huck no longer recognizes him as the surrogate father (whose love had been the crucial factor in his own redemptive awakening), and now simply regards him as a thing (a chattel slave is, legally, a "thing"), and so the reader is presumed to accept him as that, a counter to be manipulated in the plot, and a minstrel show comic.

All of the changes that we have enumerated are associated with a basic change of tone. We are back in the world of *Tom Sawyer*, with a condescending and amused interest in the pranks and fancies of boyhood, and even the rescue of Jim becomes merely a lark not to be taken seriously, for at the end we learn that Jim was free all the time, and presumably we are to accept as a charming stunt the fact that Tom has withheld this information in order to have his "adventure."

The third section simply does not hang together, and our first impulse is to ask what brought Twain to this pass. Clearly, during the process of writing the book, he was feeling his way into it, "discovering" it, and when he got to the end of the second section, he did not know where to go. Henry Nash Smith, in "Sound Heart and a Deformed Conscience," a chapter in his *Mark Twain: The Development of a Writer*, holds that Twain finally took refuge in the tradition of backwoods humor. It is true that the novel had been, from the start, a "hybrid"—"a comic story in which the protagonists have acquired something like a tragic depth"—and so there was a certain logic in choosing the comic resolution, which would establish, by returning to the tone of the beginning, a structural symmetry, and which would solve the main plot problem by getting Jim legally freed. In one sense, the trouble was that Twain, in the river journey, had wrought better than he knew and differently from his original intention, and the "tragic depths" he had opened up were not now to be easily papered over. Twain was, apparently, aware that he hadn't been quite able to paper things over, and so at the end does try to fuse the serious elements of the novel with the comic. First, he gives a flicker of the old role of Jim, in having him stay with the wounded Tom (significantly Tom, not Huck), in that act reconverting him from "thing" to man and echoing Jim's old role in relation to Huck. Second, Twain tacks on the last few sentences—to which we must return.

From the foregoing account, it would seem that the last section is, indeed, "cheating." But, on the other side of the debate, we find, for example, Lionel Trilling and T. S. Eliot. Trilling follows much the same line of thought as Smith's in commenting on the "formal aptness" that returns us at the end to the world of Tom Sawyer, but he finds this grounding of the arch much more satisfying than does Smith, seeming to feel that the problem of the "tragic depths" is thus exorcised. T. S. Eliot goes further, and in addition to recognizing a formal aptness in that the "mood of the end should bring us back to that of the beginning," argues that, since the river, with its symbolic function of a life force, has "no beginning and no end," it is "impossible for Huck as for the River to have a beginning or end—a *career*." The novel, that is, can have no form more significant than the mere closure on tonal repetition. If this is not the

right end, what, Eliot asks, "would have been right?" And he adds that no book ever written "ends more certainly with the right words"—the statement of Huck that he can't stand to be adopted and "sivilized" as Aunt Sally now threatens to do: "I been there before." He is now about ready to cut out for the "territory."

Let us explore what might be involved in a "right" ending for the novel. Clearly, such an ending would have to take into account the main impulse of meaning up through the second section; it would, in other words, have to accommodate the new Huck. This does not imply that the story should have a happy ending—that is, Huck in a society embodying the values of the vision on the river. Such an ideal society never existed, nor is ever likely to exist; as Bertrand Russell has remarked, the essence of an ideal is that it is *not* real. But there are different degrees in which a society may vary from the ideal; there are more acceptable and less acceptable compromises, and the new vision gained by Huck would certainly preclude the easy acceptance of the old values exemplified on the Phelps plantation and by the whole action of the third section. The compromise here simply isn't good enough. We want *both* the "formal satisfaction" of returning the arch of narrative to the firm grounding in the original world of Tom Sawyer (that is, in the "real" world), and a "thematic satisfaction."

Here we must emphasize the fact that the novel is not, ultimately, about a literal Huck (though he is literal enough, God knows) and the possibility of a final perfection in the literal world. Imagine, for example, an ending in which land society, like that on the raft, would become a utopia, with all tensions resolved between man and man, man and society, and man and nature. Such an ending would be totally irrelevant to the novel we now have. What the present novel is about is, rather, the *eternal dialectic between the real and the ideal*. It is, more specifically, about the never-ending need in life to define the values of self-perfection in freedom. But, if the distinction made earlier between "conscience" and "consciousness" be followed to its logical conclusion, the freedom would be one in which man, even in repudiating the "lies" of society, would not deny the necessity of the human community and would assume that the "dream" of such a freedom would somehow work to mitigate the "slavery" of the real world.

Or should the novel be taken to deny the necessity of community? Does it suggest that the human community is not only beyond redemption in the ideal, but beyond hope in the slow grinding amelioration perhaps possible in the real process of history, and that, therefore, the only integrity to be found is in the absolute antinomianism of "flight"—literal or symbolic —to the "territory"? But even if Huck must take flight from society, is the flight negative or positive in its motivation? Does Huck—or will Huck—flee merely in protest against the real world, or in the expectation that in the "territory" he will find the ideal community? The original flight from Pap and Miss Watson was, of course, negative—simply "flight from." What about the possibility now envisaged in the end? Even if one professes to be uncertain about Huck's expectations, there can be no uncertainty about Twain's. He knew all too well what Huck, however far west he went, would find—a land soon to be swept by buffalo-skinners, railroad-builders, blue-coated cavalry, Robber Barons, cold-deck artists, miners, whores, schoolteachers, cowhands, bankers, sheep-raisers, "bar-critters," and a million blood brothers of old Pap and blood sisters of Miss Watson. Or, to treat the flight west as symbolic rather than literal, Twain knew that there is no escaping the real world—not even by dreaming of Hannibal or the Mississippi in moonlight, viewed from the texas deck.

Considering all this, we may take Huck as the embodiment of the incorrigible idealism of man's nature, pathetic in its hopeful self-deception and admirable in its eternal gallantry, forever young, a kind of Peter Pan in patched britches, with a corncob pipe stuck in the side of his mouth, a penchant for philosophical speculation, a streak of poetry in his nature, and no capacity for growing up.

But thus far we have been scanting one very important element that bears on interpretation —the function of Jim. His reduction, in the third section, from the role of father seems to be more than what we have been taking it to be —merely one of the sad aspects of the land world. To go back, we remember that he had assumed that role after the symbolic patricide performed by Huck and that the role was central to the development of Huck on the journey down river. But once he and Huck are ashore, the relationship ends; Huck loses the symbolic father. But—and we must emphasize this—he also loses the literal father, for now Jim tells him that old Pap is, literally, dead. So, to translate, Huck is now "grown up." He has entered the world; he must face life without a father, symbolic or literal, the "good" father of the dream on the river or the "bad" father of the reality on shore.

Huck must now go it alone, and in doing so face the grim necessity of reliving and relearning, over and over, all the old lessons. The world has not changed, but Huck may have changed enough to deal with the world—and with himself. Or has he changed enough? If he lights out for the territory will that mean that he has grown up? Or that he has not? Is the intent of that famous last sentence so clear, after all? It often seems clear—but.[14]

There are, indeed, incoherences in *Huckleberry Finn*, but the book survives everything. It survives not merely because it is a seminal invention of a language for American fiction, nor because Huck's search for a freedom of "consciousness" dramatizes the new philosophical spirit which was to find formulation with William James, nor because it is a veracious and compelling picture of life in a time and place, nor because Huck is vividly alive as of that time and

[14] There is an enlightening parallel here with Hawthorne's "My Kinsman, Major Molineux." We remember that "My Kinsman" is open-ended. Robin is given an option—to go home and escape the complexity of life, or to stay in the city and be a man. The end of *Huckleberry Finn* is very close, also, to that of Katherine Anne Porter's "Old Mortality," in which the young girl determines that she will find the "truth" missed by her elders, making this "promise" to herself, but "in her hopefulness, her ignorance."

place, nor because, in the shadow of the Civil War and the bitter aftermath, it embodies a deep skepticism about the millennial dream of America, nor because it hymns youthful hope and gallantry in the face of the old desperate odds of the world. All these things, and more, are there, but the book survives, ultimately, because all is absorbed into a powerful, mythic image.

That mythic image, like all great myths, is full of internal tensions and paradoxes, and it involves various dimensions—the relation of the real and the ideal, the nature of maturity, the fate of the lone individual in society. In its fullness the myth is not absorbed formally into the novel. It bursts out of the novel, stands behind the novel, overshadows the novel, undercuts the novel. Perhaps what coherence we can expect is not to be sought in the novel itself, in formal structure, plot, theme, and so on. Perhaps it resides in the attitude of the author who, as novelist facing the myth he has evoked, finally throws up his hands and takes refuge, cynically if you will, in the tradition of backwoods humor, repudiating all sophisticated demands and norms. He throws up his hands, however, not merely because he cannot solve a novelistic problem (which is true), but because the nature of the "truth" in the myth cannot be confronted except by irony—perhaps an irony bordering upon desperation—an irony that finds a desperately appropriate expression in the refuge in a reductive, primitive form that makes a kind of virtue of the inability to control the great, dark, and towering genii long since and unwittingly released from the bottle.

And so we may find in the ending of *Huckleberry Finn* a strange parallel to Twain's manner on the lecture platform as reported by the reviewer whom we have previously quoted. According to that report, Twain would gaze out over "the convulsed faces of his audience, as much as to say, 'Why are you laughing?'" Now, having released the dark genii from the bottle, he turns his "immovable" face on us, his audience, and pretends there is no genii towering above us, and goes on with his avowed business of being the "funny man." And mean-while, with this very act, he has taken another step toward the dire time when he will be "never quite sane in the night."

The Prince and the Pauper (1881), a children's book laid in Tudor England, was nothing more than a piece of sentimental junk devised to captivate Twain's own children, "Mother" Fairbanks, clergymen of literary inclinations, nervous parents, and genteel reviewers. But it broke ground for *A Connecticut Yankee*, which was on the direct line of Twain's inspiration and was connected with the grinding issues of his nature. Laid in the sixth century, in Arthurian England, it put the new American mind in contrast with feudal Europe, the remains of which the "Innocents" of the *Quaker City*, and their chronicler, had had to face on their tour. But *A Connecticut Yankee* also harks back to the contrast between the "feudal" South and the "modern" North that looms so large in *Life on the Mississippi*; it not only embodies the spirit of social criticism found in *Huckleberry Finn*, but something of Huck's pragmatic mind that always wanted to start things "fresh"; and in a paradoxical way, after it celebrates the new Yankee order of industry, big business, and finance-capitalism, it also returns to the Edenic vision of Hannibal and the river found in *Tom Sawyer* and *Huckleberry Finn*.

Most deeply, however, *A Connecticut Yankee* draws on the social and personal contexts of the moment in which it was composed. At this time Twain was totally bemused by one James W. Paige, the inventor of a typesetting machine which Twain was trying to organize a company to manufacture, and by which he dreamed of becoming a financial titan. Behind Hank Morgan, the Yankee, stands Paige. And, we may add, stands Twain himself, for if Hank (a superintendent in the Colt Arms Company) is an inventor (he claims that he can "invent, contrive, create" anything), he quickly becomes the "Boss"—a titan of business such as Twain dreamed of becoming. And so the daydream of Twain prefigures the daydream that Theodore Dreiser was to project in *The Financier* and *The Titan*.

The medieval values that Hank confronts were not confined to Arthurian Britain. For one thing, there was also present-day England, for whatever remnants had survived of Twain's old anglophilia were now totally annihilated by Matthew Arnold, who, after a visit to America, had declared, in "Civilization in the United States," that the idea of "distinction" in this country could not survive the "glorification of the 'average man,' and the addiction to the 'funny man.'" In his outraged patriotism and outraged *amour-propre*, Twain, a "funny man," tended to merge the England of Arthur and that of Victoria.

For a second thing, the Romantic movement had discovered—or created—the Middle Ages and made them current in nineteenth-century thought and art. Tennyson's *Idylls of the King* ranked in the esteem of the pious only a little lower than the New Testament, and James Russell Lowell's *The Vision of Sir Launfal* was a close contender for the popularity prize with the Book of Common Prayer. The poetry of William Morris and the painting of the Pre-Raphaelites, with Ruskin's Gothic aestheticism and the related social theories that pitted medieval spirituality and happy craftsmanship against the age of the machine, had great vogue in the United States, a vogue that found its finest bloom in Charles Eliot Norton, who wistfully pointed out to his students at Harvard that there were in America no French cathedrals, and in Henry Adams' *Mont-Saint-Michel and Chartres*.

This cult of medievalism had a strongly marked class element; usually it was cultivated by persons of aristocratic background or pretensions, often with an overlay of sentimental Catholicism. It was also associated with wealth, but with inherited wealth as contrasted with that, usually greater, of the new kind of capitalist; for inherited wealth, untainted by immediate contact with the crude world of business, was "genteel."[15] It was only natural, then, that a poem like Sidney Lanier's "Symphony" and the

early novels attacking business should use the aristocratic feudal virtues as the thongs with which to scourge the businessman. So when Hank, with his six-shooters, guns down Malory's knights in armor, he is also gunning down Tennyson, Ruskin, Lowell, Lanier *et al*. A *Connecticut Yankee* is, in fact, the first fictional glorification of the businessman.

But Hank is arrayed not only against Sir Sagramor le Desirious and Alfred, Lord Tennyson and their ilk, but also against the spectral legions of Lee, abetted by the ghost of Sir Walter Scott. It was highly appropriate that Twain should have given a first public reading of A *Connecticut Yankee* (an early version) to an audience in which sat General William Tecumseh Sherman; for if anybody was equipped to understand Hank's kind of warfare, it was the gentleman who, as first president of the Louisiana State University, had remarked to a southern friend that "In all history no nation of mere agriculturalists had ever made successful war against a nation of mechanics," and who, a little later, was to lift the last gauzy film of chivalric nonsense to expose the stark nakedness of war.[16]

If the anachronistically slaveholding society of Britain is an image of the Old South, and if Hank's military masterpiece, the Battle of the Sand Belt, in which, after the explosion of Hank's mines, the air is filled with the ghastly drizzle of the atomized remains of men and horses, is an image of the Civil War (the first "modern" war), then Hank's program for Britain is a fable of the Reconstruction of the South and the pacification of that undeveloped country. Furthermore, in being a fable of that colonial project, this is also a fable of colonialism in general and of the great modern period of colonialism in particular, which was now well under way from the Ganges to the Congo; thus to Hank, Britain is simply something to develop in economic terms—with, of course, the by-product, as a paternalistic benefit for the natives, of a rational modern society. In this context A

---

[15] See the discussion of Santayana's "The Genteel Tradition in American Philosophy," which appears in our text.

[16] See the last stanza of "A Utilitarian View of the Monitor's Fight," by Melville, and "Chiefly About War Matters," by Hawthorne (pp. 921 and 529–34).

Connecticut Yankee is to be set alongside Conrad's *Nostromo* and *Heart of Darkness* and the works of Kipling.

There is, however, another and more inclusive context in which to regard *A Connecticut Yankee*. More and more in our century we have seen a special variety of "millennialism" (see pp. 1822–26)—the variety in which bliss (in the form of a "rational" society) is distributed at gunpoint or inculcated in concentration camps. So in this context, *A Connecticut Yankee* is to be set alongside historical accounts of Fascist Italy, Nazi Germany, or Communist Russia. The novel was prophetic.

The germ of *A Connecticut Yankee* was, however, much more simple than may have just been suggested. An entry in 1884 in Mark Twain's notebook reads:

> Dream of being a knight errant in armor in the middle ages. Have the notions and habits of thought of the present day mixed with the necessities of that. No pockets in the armor. No way to manage certain requirements of nature. Can't scratch. Cold in the head—can't blow—can't get a handkerchief, can't use iron sleeve. Iron gets red hot in the sun—leaks in the rain, gets white with frost and freezes me solid in winter. Suffer from lice and fleas. Make disagreeable clatter when I enter church. Can't dress or undress myself. Always getting struck by lightning. Fall down, can't get up. See Morte d'Arthur.

What Twain began with was burlesque, merely the torpedoing of highfalutin pretensions. But within a year after the first entry, there is a note for a battle scene "between a modern army with gatling guns (automatic) 600 shots a minute . . . torpedos, balloons, 100-ton cannon, iron-clad fleet & Prince de Joinville's Middle Age Crusaders." Thus we have what we may take as the poles of Twain's inspiration for the book, on the one hand the satirical burlesque and on the other the sadistic and massive violence motivated by a mysterious hatred of the past.

The body of the work has to do with Hank's operations from the moment when he decides that he is "just another Robinson Crusoe" and has to "invent, contrive, create, reorganize things." The narrative proceeds in a two-edged fashion: there is the satirical exposure of the inhuman and stultifying life in Arthur's kingdom, with the mission for modernization and humanitarian improvement, but there is also the development of Hank's scheme for his economic and political aggrandizement, his way of becoming the "Boss." By and large, it seems that the humanitarian and selfish interests coincide; what is good for Hank is good for the people of Britain, and this would imply a simple fable of progress, with the reading that technology in a laissez-faire order automatically confers the good life on all. There is no hint, certainly, that Twain is writing in a period of titanic struggle between labor and capital, a struggle consequent upon the advent of big technology. In the new order in Britain there are no labor problems. The boys whom Hank had secretly recruited and instructed in technology are completely loyal to him, and as his Janizaries will fight for him in the great Armageddon to come, enraptured by their own godlike proficiency; if they represent "labor" they have no parallel in the nineteenth-century America of the Homestead strike and the Haymarket riot.

In the fable there are, indeed, many lags and incoherences that, upon the slightest analysis, are visible. Twain had not systematically thought through the issues in his world, or his own attitudes, and he did not grasp, or did not wish to grasp, the implications of his own tale. During the course of composition he had written to "Mother" Fairbanks—in a letter of either cynical deception or confusion of mind—that he had no intention of degrading any of the "great and beautiful characters" found in Malory, and that Arthur would keep his "sweetness and purity," but this scarcely squares with the finished product. Again, though the narrative, once finished, shows no hint of the tensions in the world of the new capitalism, Twain most inconsistently could, when the socialist Dan Beard illustrated the first edition and made the fable apply to contemporary persons and abuses,[17] enthusiastically exclaim, "What luck it was to find you!" And though Twain, now reading Carlyle's *French Revolution*, could proclaim himself a "sans-culotte," he was, at the same time, dreaming of his elevation to the angelic choir of Vanderbilt, Rockefeller, and other bosses. And most telling of all, though *A Connecticut Yankee* was rapturously received, even by such a discerning reader as Howells, as a great document of the democratic faith, and though Twain himself, sometimes at least, took it as such, Hank, in many of his manipulations, is not ethically superior to Jay Gould or Diamond Jim Brady. What Hank turns out to be is merely the "Boss," more of a Boss than even Boss Tweed ever was, something like a cross between a Carnegie and a commissar.

There are various other logical confusions in *A Connecticut Yankee*, but one is fundamental. If the original idea of the book had been a celebration of nineteenth-century technology, something happened to that happy inspiration, and in the end progress appears a delusion, Hank's modernization winds up in a bloody farce, and Hank himself can think of the people whom he had undertaken to liberate as merely "human muck." In the end Hank hates life, and all he can do is to look nostalgically back on the beauty of premodern Britain as what he calls his "Lost World," and on the love of his lost wife Sandy, just as Twain could look back on his vision of boyhood Hannibal.

What emerges here is not only the deep tension in Twain, but that in the period. Some men had hoped to achieve happiness in a natural world—as had Jefferson; but some had hoped to achieve it by the conquest of nature. The tension, in its objective terms, was, then, between an agrarian and an industrial order; but the tension existed in subjective terms as well, and in a deep, complex way it conditioned the

American sensibility, from *Snow-Bound* through *A Connecticut Yankee* and Henry Adams' idea of the Virgin versus the dynamo (see pp. 1487–94), on through the poetry of T. S. Eliot and John Crowe Ransom to the debased Rousseauism of a hippie commune.

The notion of the Edenic vision reminds us of *Huckleberry Finn*, for thematically *A Connecticut Yankee* is a development of that work—and the parallel in the very names of the heroes suggests the relation: *Huck-Hank*. Huck journeys through the barbarous South, Hank through barbarous Britain, both mythic journeys into a land where mania and brutality are masked by pretensions of chivalry, humanity, and Christianity. After each encounter with a shocking fact of the land world, Huck returns to his private Eden on the river and in the end contemplates flight to an Edenic West. In other words, Huck belongs to the world of Jefferson's dream, in which man finds harmony with man in an overarching harmony of man in nature. Hank, however, is of sterner stuff. When he encounters a shocking fact he undertakes to change it—to conquer, at any cost, both nature and human nature in order to create a rational society.

But both Huck and Hank come to a desperate collision with reality, Huck on the Phelps farm and Hank at the battle of the Sand Belt; but the end of the project of regeneration through technology and know-how is more blankly horrible than life on the Phelps farm, with not even a facade of humor, only the manic glee of the victors exalted by their expertise of destruction. The "human muck" has refused the rule of reason—but the prophet of reason has done little more than provide magnificently lethal instruments by which man may vent his mania.

When the book was finished, Twain wrote to Howells: "Well, my book is written—let it go. But if it were only to write over again there wouldn't be so many things left out. They burn in me. . . . They would require a library—and a pen warmed up in hell." But the pen had already been warm enough to declare that dark forces were afoot in history and in the human soul to betray all aspiration, and with this we

---

[17] For instance, one illustration shows two examples of the standard allegorical female figure of Justice blindfolded, one for the sixth century and one for the nineteenth, the former holding up scales in which a hammer tagged "Labor" is outweighed by a crown tagged "Title," and the latter with scales in which a hammer is outweighed by a fat bag tagged "$1,000,000."

find, at the visceral level of fable, the same view of history later to be learnedly, abstractly, and pitilessly proclaimed by Henry Adams and to be embodied, redeemed—perhaps—by pity, in the works of Theodore Dreiser.

As for Twain himself the shadows were soon to gather. The metaphysical despair of *A Connecticut Yankee* was shortly to be compounded by personal disasters, bankruptcy (from which, with an irony worthy of his own invention, he was to be rescued by one H. H. Rogers, of the Standard Oil trust, one of the Barons), the death of Livy (with grief compounded by his sense of guilt for having robbed her of the Christian faith), the deaths of the adored Suzy and of a second daughter, Jean, the deaths of friends, and what seems to have been a struggle against madness. His fame continued; he walked up and down Fifth Avenue in his eye-catching white suit that advertised his identity; he consorted with the rich and great, and once Andrew Carnegie even addressed him in a letter as "Saint Mark"; he played billiards to the point of exhaustion; he received an honorary degree from Oxford, which mollified the anglophobia that had been enshrined in *A Connecticut Yankee*; he railed at the degeneracy of the age and the abuses of wealth and power and at American imperialism in the Philippines and at Belgian imperialism in the Congo, and greeted Gorky, on his visit to the United States, as an apostle of Russian democracy. But nothing really helped much, and he was "never quite sane in the night."

Nothing helped much, that is, except writing. He kept on wielding his pen "warmed up in hell," with flashes of genius, as in *Pudd'nhead Wilson* (1894), "The Man That Corrupted Hadleyburg" (1899), and *The Mysterious Stranger* (published posthumously), in work that obsessively rehearsed, in various disguises, his own story and his own anguish. He took refuge in a massive autobiography, in which chronology is replaced by association as a principle of continuity and as a method for mastering his own experience and plumbing his own nature; he was trying to achieve truth by thus recording a voice to speak from the grave.

But perhaps there was no truth ever to be achieved. Perhaps there was only illusion, after all, as he put it in the unfinished story called "The Great Dark" and in a letter to Sue Crane, his sister-in-law:

> I dreamed that I was born and grew up and was a pilot on the Mississippi and a miner and a journalist in Nevada and a pilgrim in the *Quaker City*, and had a wife and children and went to live in a villa at Florence—and this dream goes on and on and sometimes seems so real that I almost believe it is real. But there is no way to tell, for if one applied tests they would be part of the dream, too, and so would simply aid the deceit. I wish I knew whether it is a dream or real.

But in the late fiction, well before this, he had introduced into our literature the theme of illusion, which was to loom so large in the next century.

Mark Twain died on April 12, 1910, surfeited with fame, nursing hatreds to the last, without hope in the nature or fate of man, having found what comfort he could in the thought that all life might be only a dream. In his last coma, out of an old obsession and a self-knowledge that, however, had never proved deep enough to become redemptive, he spoke of a dual personality and of Dr. Jekyll and Mr. Hyde.

BIOGRAPHICAL CHART

1835   Born, November 30, in Florida, Missouri, son of John Marshall Clemens and Jane Lampton
1838   Clemenses move to Hannibal, Missouri
1847   Father dies
1848–53 Apprenticed to brother Orion, printer in Hannibal

1852   First appears in print: "The Dandy Frightening the Squatter" in the *Boston Carpet Bag*, May 1
1853   Leaves Hannibal; works as printer in St. Louis, New York, Philadelphia, Muscatine and Keokuk (in Iowa), and Cincinnati
1857   Trains as pilot on Mississippi

1861   Leaves piloting and joins Confederate "irregulars"; leaves Missouri for Nevada, with brother Orion
1861–62   Prospects in Nevada
1862–64   Reports for Virginia City *Territorial Enterprise*
1864–66   Reporter and free-lance writer in San Francisco
1865   "Jim Smiley and His Jumping Frog" in New York *Saturday Press*, in November
1866   Correspondent for Sacramento *Union* in Sandwich Islands; success as lecturer
1866–67   Correspondent in New York for *Alta California* of San Francisco
1867   Makes pilgrimage on the *Quaker City* to Europe and the Holy Land (June to November)
1868–69   Lectures and writes for newspapers
1869   *The Innocents Abroad*
1870   Marries Olivia Langdon; edits the *Express* in Buffalo, N.Y.
1871   Moves to Hartford, to Nook Farm
1872   *Roughing It*; lecture tour in England
1873   *The Gilded Age*, in collaboration with Charles Dudley Warner

1876   *The Adventures of Tom Sawyer*
1880   *A Tramp Abroad*, the result of European tour of the two previous years
1882   *The Prince and the Pauper*, first historical fiction
1883   *Life on the Mississippi*
1885   *The Adventures of Huckleberry Finn* and the *Memoirs* of General Grant, both published by the Webster Company, owned by Mark Twain
1889   *A Connecticut Yankee in King Arthur's Court*
1891–95   Resides in Europe, except for business trips to America
1894   Paige typesetter a failure; *Pudd'nhead Wilson*
1896   *Personal Recollections of Joan of Arc*; favorite daughter, Susy, dies
1897–1900   Resides in Vienna and London
1900   *The Man That Corrupted Hadleyburg and Other Stories and Essays*; works in anti-imperialism campaign in New York
1901   Honorary Litt.D. from Yale
1904   Wife dies
1907   Litt.D. from Oxford
1909   Daughter Jean dies
1910   Dies, April 21, at Stormfield, house near Redding, Connecticut; buried in Elmira, New York

FURTHER READINGS

The University of California Press is in the process of publishing editions of the papers and works of Mark Twain. These will become the standard (CEAA) editions.

The Writings of Mark Twain (1899–1910) (no editor cited)
Bernard De Voto, ed., *Mark Twain in Eruption* (1940)
Albert Bigelow Paine, ed., *Mark Twain's Autobiography* (1925)
———, ed., *Mark Twain's Letters* (1917)
———, *Mark Twain's Notebook* (1935)
Dixon Wecter, ed., *Love Letters of Mark Twain* (1946)
Sculley Bradley, Richmond Croom Beatty, and W. Hudson Long, eds., *The Adventures of Huckleberry Finn* (1961)

Gladys Carmen Bellamy, *Mark Twain as a Literary Artist* (1950)
Walter Blair, *Mark Twain and Huck Finn* (1960)
Van Wyck Brooks, *The Ordeal of Mark Twain* (1920)
Clara Clemens, *My Father: Mark Twain* (1931)
James M. Cox, *Mark Twain: The Fate of Humor* (1966)
Bernard De Voto, *Mark Twain at Work* (1942)
———, *Mark Twain's America* (1932)
Margaret Duckett, *Mark Twain and Bret Harte* (1964)
T. S. Eliot, "Introduction," *The Adventures of Huckleberry Finn* (1950)

DeLancey Ferguson, *Mark Twain: Man and Legend* (1943)
Leslie A. Fiedler, *Love and Death in the American Novel* (1966)
Philip S. Foner, *Mark Twain: Social Critic* (1958)
Maxwell Geismar, *Mark Twain: An American Prophet* (1970)
Daniel G. Hoffman, *Form and Fable in American Fiction* (1961)
William Dean Howells, *My Mark Twain* (1910)
Justin Kaplan, *Mr. Clemens and Mark Twain* (1966)
———, ed., *Mark Twain: A Profile* (1967)
Lewis Leary, ed., *Mark Twain's Wound* (1962)
Kenneth S. Lynn, *Mark Twain and Southwestern Humor* (1959)
Jay Martin, *Harvests of Change* (1967)
Leo Marx, "Mr. Eliot, Mr. Trilling, and Huckleberry Finn," *American Scholar* (Fall, 1935)
———, "The Pilot and the Passenger: Landscape Conventions and the Style of Huckleberry Finn," *American Literature* (May, 1956)
Edgar Lee Masters, *Mark Twain: A Portrait* (1938)
Albert Bigelow Paine, *Mark Twain: A Biography* (1935)
Constance Rourke, *American Humor: A Study of the National Character* (1931)
Roger B. Salomon, *Twain and the Image of History* (1961)
Henry Nash Smith, *Mark Twain: The Development of a Writer* (1962)
———, *Mark Twain's Fable of Progress* (1964)

———, ed., *Mark Twain: A Collection of Critical Essays* (1963)

Claude Simpson, ed., *The Adventures of Huckleberry Finn: A Collection of Critical Essays* (1968)

Albert E. Stone, *The Innocent Eye* (1961)

Lionel Trilling, "Introduction," *The Adventures of Huckleberry Finn* (1948)

Edward Wagenknecht, *Mark Twain: The Man and His Work* (1935)

Dixon Wecter, *Sam Clemens of Hannibal* (1952)

Philip Young, *Three Bags Full: Essays in American Fiction* (1971)

How to Tell a Story (1895)

I do not claim that I can tell a story as it ought to be told. I only claim to know how a story ought to be told, for I have been almost daily in the company of the most expert story-tellers for many years.

There are several kinds of stories, but only one difficult kind—the humorous. I will talk mainly about that one. The humorous story is American, the comic story is English, the witty story is French. The humorous story depends for its effect upon the *manner* of the telling; the comic story and the witty story upon the *matter*.

The humorous story may be spun out to great length, and may wander around as much as it pleases, and arrive nowhere in particular; but the comic and witty stories must be brief and end with a point. The humorous story bubbles gently along, the others burst.

The humorous story is strictly a work of art—high and delicate art—and only an artist can tell it; but no art is necessary in telling the comic and witty story; anybody can do it. The art of telling a humorous story—understand, I mean by word of mouth, not print—was created in America, and has remained at home.

The humorous story is told gravely; the teller does his best to conceal the fact that he even dimly suspects that there is anything funny about it; but the teller of the comic story tells you beforehand that it is one of the funniest things he has ever heard, then tells it with eager delight, and is the first person to laugh when he gets through. And sometimes, if he has good success, he is so glad and happy that he will repeat the "nub" of it and glance around from face to face, collecting applause, and then repeat it again. It is a pathetic thing to see.

Very often, of course, the rambling and disjointed humorous story finishes with a nub, point, snapper, or whatever you like to call it. Then the listener must be alert, for in many cases the teller will divert attention from that nub by dropping it in a carefully casual and indifferent way, with the pretense that he does not know it is a nub.

Artemus Ward used that trick a good deal; then when the belated audience presently caught the joke he would look up with innocent surprise, as if wondering what they had found to laugh at. Dan Setchell used it before him, Nye and Riley and others use it to-day.

But the teller of the comic story does not slur the nub; he shouts it at you—every time. And when he prints it, in England, France, Germany, and Italy, he italicizes it, puts some whooping exclamation-points after it, and sometimes explains it in a parenthesis. All of which is very depressing, and makes one want to renounce joking and lead a better life.

Let me set down an instance of the comic method, using an anecdote which has been popular all over the world for twelve or fifteen hundred years. The teller tells it in this way:

THE WOUNDED SOLDIER

In the course of a certain battle a soldier whose leg had been shot off appealed to another soldier who was hurrying by to carry him to the rear, informing him at the same time of the loss which he had sustained; whereupon the generous son of Mars, shouldering the unfortunate, proceeded to carry out his desire. The bullets and cannonballs were flying in all directions, and presently one of the latter took the wounded man's head off—without, however, his deliverer being aware of it. In no long time he was hailed by an officer, who said:

"Where are you going with that carcass?"

"To the rear, sir—he's lost his leg!"

"His leg, forsooth?" responded the astonished officer; "you mean his head, you booby."

Whereupon the soldier dispossessed himself of his burden, and stood looking down upon it in great perplexity. At length he said:

"It is true, sir, just as you have said." Then after a pause he added, "*But he* TOLD *me* IT WAS HIS LEG!!!!!"

Here the narrator bursts into explosion after explosion of thunderous horse-laughter, repeating that nub from time to time through his gaspings and shriekings and suffocatings.

It takes only a minute and a half to tell that in its comic-story form; and isn't worth the telling, after all. Put into the humorous-story form it takes ten minutes, and is about the funniest thing I have ever listened to—as James Whitcomb Riley tells it.

He tells it in the character of a dull-witted old farmer who has just heard it for the first time, thinks it is unspeakably funny, and is trying to repeat it to a neighbor. But he can't remember it; so he gets all mixed up and wanders helplessly round and round, putting in tedious details that don't belong in the tale and only retard it; taking them out conscientiously and putting in others that are just as useless; making minor mistakes now and then and stopping to correct them and explain how he came to make them; remembering things which he forgot to put in in their proper place and going back to put them in there; stopping his narrative a good while in order to try to recall the name of the soldier that was hurt, and finally remembering that the soldier's name was not mentioned, and remarking placidly that the name is of no real importance, anyway—better, of course, if one knew it, but not essential, after all—and so on, and so on, and so on.

The teller is innocent and happy and pleased with himself, and has to stop every little while to hold himself in and keep from laughing outright; and does hold in, but his body quakes in a jelly-like way with interior chuckles; and at the end of the ten minutes the audience have laughed until they are exhausted, and the tears are running down their faces.

The simplicity and innocence and sincerity and unconsciousness of the old farmer are perfectly simulated, and the result is a performance which is thoroughly charming and delicious. This is art—and fine and beautiful, and only a master can compass it; but a machine could tell the other story.

To string incongruities and absurdities together in a wandering and sometimes purposeless way, and seem innocently unaware that they are absurdities, is the basis of the American art, if my position is correct. Another feature is the slurring of the point. A third is the dropping of a studied remark apparently without knowing it, as if one were thinking aloud. The fourth and last is the pause.

Artemus Ward dealt in numbers three and four a good deal. He would begin to tell with great animation something which he seemed to think was wonderful; then lose confidence, and after an apparently absent-minded pause add an incongruous remark in a soliloquizing way; and that was the remark intended to explode the mine—and it did.

For instance, he would say eagerly, excitedly, "I once knew a man in New Zealand who hadn't a tooth in his head"—here his animation would die out; a silent, reflective pause would follow, then he would say dreamily, and as if to himself, "and yet that man could beat a drum better than any man I ever saw."

The pause is an exceedingly important feature in any kind of story, and a frequently recurring feature, too. It is a dainty thing, and delicate, and also uncertain and treacherous; for it must be exactly the right length—no more and no less—or it fails of its purpose and makes trouble. If the pause is too short the impressive point is passed, and the audience have had time to divine that a surprise is intended—and then you can't surprise them, of course.

On the platform I used to tell a negro ghost story that had a pause in front of the snapper on the end, and that pause was the most important thing in the whole story. If I got it the right length precisely, I could spring the finishing ejaculation with effect enough to make some impressible girl deliver a startled little yelp and jump out of her seat—and that was what I was after. This story was called "The Golden Arm," and was told in this fashion. You can practise with it yourself—and mind you look out for the pause and get it right.

THE GOLDEN ARM

Once 'pon a time dey wuz a monsus mean man, en he live 'way out in de prairie all 'lone by hisself, 'cep'n he had a wife. En bimeby she died, en he tuck en toted her way out dah in de prairie en buried her. Well, she had a golden arm—all solid gold, fum de shoulder down. He wuz pow'ful mean—pow'ful; en dat night he couldn't sleep, caze he want dat golden arm so bad.

When it come midnight he couldn't stan' it no mo'; so he git up, he did, en tuck his lantern en shoved out thoo de storm en dug her up en got de golden arm; en he bent his head down 'gin de win', en plowed en plowed en plowed thoo de snow. Den all on a sudden he stop (make a considerable pause here, and look startled, and take a listening attitude) en say: "My *lan'*, what's dat?"

En he listen—en listen—en de win' say (set your teeth together and imitate the wailing and wheezing singsong of the wind), "Bzzz-z-zzz"—en den, way back yonder whah de grave is, he hear a *voice!* —he hear a voice all mix' up in de win'—can't hardly tell 'em 'part—"Bzzz—zzz—W-h-o—g-o-t—m-y-g-o-l-d-e-n *arm?"* (You must begin to shiver violently now.)

En he begin to shiver en shake, en say, "Oh, my! *Oh,* my lan'!" en de win' blow de lantern out, en de snow en sleet blow in his face en mos' choke him, en he start aplowin' knee-deep towards home mos' dead, he so sk'yerd—en pooty soon he hear de voice agin, en (pause) it 'us comin' *after* him! "Bzzz —zzz—zzz—W-h-o—g-o-t—m-y—g-o-l-d-e-n *arm?"*

When he git to de pasture he hear it agin— closter now, en a-*comin'!*—a-comin' back dah in de dark en de storm—(repeat the wind and the voice). When he git to de house he rush up-stairs en jump in de bed en kiver up, head and years, en lay dah shiverin' en shakin'—en den way out dah he hear it *agin!*—en a-*comin'!* En bimeby he hear

(pause—awed, listening attitude)—pat—pat—pat— *hit's a-comin' up-stairs!* Den he hear de latch, en he *know* it's in de room!

Den pooty soon he know it's a-*stannin' by de bed!* (Pause.) Den—he know it's a-*bendin' down over him*—en he cain't skasely git his breath! Den— den—he seem to feel someth'n' *c-o-l-d,* right down 'most agin his head! (Pause.)

Den de voice say, *right at his year*—"W-h-o— g-o-t—m-y-g-o-l-d-e-n *arm?"* (You must wail it out very plaintively and accusingly; then you stare steadily and impressively into the face of the far-thest-gone auditor—a girl, preferably—and let that awe-inspiring pause begin to build itself in the deep hush. When it has reached exactly the right length, jump suddenly at that girl and yell, "*You've* got it!"

If you've got the *pause* right, she'll fetch a dear little yelp and spring right out of her shoes. But you *must* get the pause right; and you will find it the most troublesome and aggravating and uncertain thing you ever undertook.

The Celebrated Jumping Frog of Calaveras County (1865)

"Jim Smiley and His Jumping Frog" was published in 1865, in the *Saturday Press* of New York, and then, in 1867, in a little book under the title *The Celebrated Jumping Frog of Calaveras County.* The book was not a popular success, and even if James Russell Lowell, the then-reigning literary pundit, called it the "finest piece of humorous writing ever produced in America," Mark Twain himself, in his disappointment at the returns on the book, and not yet sure of his own line of development, referred to it as a "villainous backwoods sketch," and didn't want Livy, whom he was then courting, to read it. But in 1869 he was in a mood to echo Lowell, saying that the book was the "best humorous sketch America has produced yet, and I must read it in public some day in order that people may know what there is in it."

One thing in it was, by implication, the in-struction as to how to read it—or rather, to tell it, for Simon Wheeler, who "reeled off the monotonous narrative," "never smiled," "never frowned," and "never betrayed the slightest suspicion of enthusiasm," or any notion of "any-

thing ridiculous or funny," was clearly one of the artists of the humorous story with whom, as Mark Twain says in "How to Tell a Story," he had had the privilege of consorting.

The story itself was not new. Probably having originated as a Negro tale in the slaveholding South, it had reappeared in the West and, in its basic form, had already been printed in news-papers. But Mark Twain encountered it in an oral version, and that moment was, apparently, a moment of revelation to him. Up to this time, he had been experimenting with all kinds of burlesque and parody and high jinks, and with the notion of an alter ego that was to find its inspired fulfillment in "Mark Twain." Now, in 1864, having developed a journalistic feud with the chief of police of San Francisco, Mark Twain took refuge in a cabin on Jackass Hill, in Tuolomne County. In that backward region he heard the tale of the fabulous frog. Later, back in San Francisco, he recounted it, pre-sumably with "high and delicate" skill, to Arte-mus Ward, who suggested that he write it. In doing so Twain found the vein of his characteristic humor—a way of adapting the oral tale of the old Southwest, or the literary tradition of that tale, to his special purposes as a writer.

For one thing, he adapted the literary frame of telling that was characteristic of earlier writers working from the oral tale, such as Augustus Baldwin Longstreet and Thomas B. Thorpe. Most such men, as Kenneth S. Lynn has pointed out in *Mark Twain and Southwestern Humor*, and as we have remarked earlier, were Whigs in politics and set themselves above the "vernacular" characters (who would represent Jacksonian democracy) that they wrote about; such a narrator might well exhibit the brutality, roguery, or stupidity of the vernacular character, but he would do it straight, without any of the condescension such as Cooper or Harriet Beecher Stowe would exhibit in trying to ennoble their plain characters, or as James Russell Lowell exhibited in the *Biglow Papers*. So Mark Twain, like the Whig observer, sets himself above Simon Wheeler, who tells the story of Jim Smiley. But with an important difference. Mark Twain, the observer, does not *seem* to appreciate the art of Wheeler. It is we, the readers, who, looking over the head of the stupid Mark Twain, do appreciate the art of Wheeler, with all its pretense of irrelevances and the richness of metaphor and dramatic effect. In Wheeler's style, for instance, we have the germ of Huck's poetry that was to come. As for the action, in its humorous involutions and reversals, we have aspects of the motif of the "biter bit," not only in the telling (as Mark Twain, the real writer and teller of tales does not appreciate the apparently guileless Wheeler), but in the content of Wheeler's narrative, for it is Smiley, the "biter," who gets "bit" by the apparent "innocent," who "out-innocences" him.

In compliance with the request of a friend of mine, who wrote me from the East, I called on good-natured, garrulous old Simon Wheeler, and inquired after my friend's friend, Leonidas W. Smiley, as requested to do, and I hereunto append the result. I have a lurking suspicion that *Leonidas W. Smiley* is a myth; that my friend never knew such a personage; and that he only conjectured

that if I asked old Wheeler about him, it would remind him of his infamous *Jim* Smiley, and he would go to work and bore me to death with some exasperating reminiscence of him as long and as tedious as it should be useless to me. If that was the design, it succeeded.

I found Simon Wheeler dozing comfortably by the bar-room stove of the dilapidated tavern in the decayed mining camp of Angel's, and I noticed that he was fat and bald-headed, and had an expression of winning gentleness and simplicity upon his tranquil countenance. He roused up, and gave me good day. I told him that a friend of mine had commissioned me to make some inquiries about a cherished companion of his boyhood named *Leonidas W. Smiley—Rev. Leonidas W.* Smiley, a young minister of the Gospel, who he had heard was at one time a resident of Angel's Camp. I added that if Mr. Wheeler could tell me anything about this Rev. Leonidas W. Smiley, I would feel under many obligations to him.

Simon Wheeler backed me into a corner and blockaded me there with his chair, and then sat down and reeled off the monotonous narrative which follows this paragraph. He never smiled, he never frowned, he never changed his voice from the gentle-flowing key to which he tuned his initial sentence, he never betrayed the slightest suspicion of enthusiasm; but all through the interminable narrative there ran a vein of impressive earnestness and sincerity, which showed me plainly that, so far from his imagining that there was anything ridiculous or funny about his story, he regarded it as a really important matter, and admired its two heroes as men of transcendent genius in *finesse*. I let him go on in his own way, and never interrupted him once.

"Rev. Leonidas W. H'm, Reverend Le—well, there was a feller here once by the name of *Jim* Smiley, in the winter of '49—or maybe it was the spring of '50—I don't recollect exactly, somehow, though what makes me think it was one or the other is because I remember the big flume warn't finished when he first come to the camp; but anyway, he was the curiousest man about always betting on anything that turned up you ever see, if he could get anybody to bet on the other side; and if he couldn't he'd change sides. Any way that suited the other man would suit *him*—any way just so's he got a bet, *he* was satisfied. But still he was lucky, uncommon lucky; he most always come out winner. He was always ready and laying for a chance; there couldn't be no solit'ry thing mentioned but that feller'd offer to bet on it, and take ary side you please, as I was just telling you. If there was a horse-race, you'd find him flush or you'd find him busted at the end of it; if there was a dog-fight, he'd bet on it; if there was a cat-fight, he'd bet on it; if there was a chicken-fight, he'd bet on it; why, if there was two birds setting on a fence, he would bet you which one would fly first; or if there was a camp-meeting, he would be there reg'lar to bet on Parson Walker, which he judged to be the best exhorter about here, and so he was too, and a good man. If he even see a straddle-bug start to go anywhere, he would bet you how long it would take him to get to—to wherever he was going to, and if you took him up, he would foller that straddle-bug to Mexico but what he would find out where he was bound for and how long he was on the road. Lots of the boys here has seen that Smiley, and can tell you about him. Why, it never made no difference to *him*—he'd bet on *any* thing—the dangdest feller. Parson Walker's wife laid very sick once, for a good while, and it seemed as if they warn't going to save her; but one morning he come in, and Smiley up and asked him how she was, and he said she was considerable better—thank the Lord for his inf'nite mercy—and coming on so smart that with the blessing of Prov'dence she'd get well yet; and Smiley, before he thought, says, 'Well, I'll resk two-and-a-half she don't anyway.'

"Thish-yer Smiley had a mare—the boys called her the fifteen-minute nag, but that was only in fun, you know, because of course she was faster than that—and he used to win money on that horse, for all she was so slow and always had the asthma, or the distemper, or the consumption, or something of that kind. They used to give her two or three hundred yards' start, and then pass her under way; but always at the fag end of the race she'd get excited and desperate like, and come cavorting and straddling up, and scattering her legs around limber, sometimes in the air, and sometimes out to one side among the fences, and kicking up m-o-r-e dust and raising m-o-r-e racket with her coughing and sneezing and blowing her nose—and *always* fetch up at the stand just about a neck ahead, as near as you could cipher it down.

"And he had a little small bull-pup, that to look at him you'd think he warn't worth a cent but to set around and look ornery and lay for a chance to steal something. But as soon as money was up on him he was a different dog; his under-jaw'd begin to stick out like the fo'castle of a steamboat, and

his teeth would uncover and shine like the furnaces. And a dog might tackle him and bully-rag him, and bite him, and throw him over his shoulder two or three times, and Andrew Jackson—which was the name of the pup—Andrew Jackson would never let on but what *he* was satisfied, and hadn't expected nothing else—and the bets being doubled and doubled on the other side all the time, till the money was all up; and then all of a sudden he would grab that other dog jest by the j'int of his hind leg and freeze to it—not chaw, you understand, but only just grip and hang on till they throwed up the sponge, if it was a year. Smiley always come out winner on that pup, till he harnessed a dog once that didn't have no hind legs, because they'd been sawed off in a circular saw, and when the thing had gone along far enough, and the money was all up, and he come to make a snatch for his pet holt, he see in a minute how he'd been imposed on, and how the other dog had him in the door, so to speak, and he 'peared surprised, and then he looked sorter discouraged-like, and didn't try no more to win the fight, and so he got shucked out bad. He give Smiley a look; as much as to say his heart was broke, and it was *his* fault, for putting up a dog that hadn't no hind legs for him to take holt of, which was his main dependence in a fight, and then he limped off a piece and laid down and died. It was a good pup, was that Andrew Jackson, and would have made a name for hisself if he'd lived, for the stuff was in him and he had genius—I know it, because he hadn't no opportunities to speak of, and it don't stand to reason that a dog could make such a fight as he could under them circumstances if he hadn't no talent. It always makes me feel sorry when I think of that last fight of his'n, and the way it turned out.

"Well, thish-yer Smiley had rat-tarriers, and chicken cocks, and tomcats and all them kind of things, till you couldn't rest, and you couldn't fetch nothing for him to bet on but he'd match you. He ketched a frog one day, and took him home, and said he cal'lated to educate him; and so he never done nothing for three months but set in his back yard and learn that frog to jump. And you bet you he *did* learn him, too. He'd give him a little punch behind, and the next minute you'd see that frog whirling in the air like a doughnut—see him turn one summerset, or maybe a couple, if he got a good start, and come down flat-footed and all right, like a cat. He got him up so in the matter of ketching flies, and kep' him in practice so constant, that he'd nail a fly every time as fur as he could see him. Smiley said all a frog wanted was education, and he could do 'most anything—and I believe him. Why, I've seen him set Dan'l Webster down here on this floor—Dan'l Webster was the name of the frog—and sing out, 'Flies, Dan'l, flies!' and quicker'n you could wink he'd spring straight up and snake a fly off'n the counter there, and flop down on the floor ag'in as solid as a gob of mud, and fall to scratching the side of his head with his hind foot as indifferent as if he hadn't no idea he'd been doin' any more'n any frog might do. You never see a frog so modest and straightfor'ard as he was, for all he was so gifted. And when it come to fair and square jumping on a dead level, he could get over more ground at one straddle than any animal of his breed you ever see. Jumping on a dead level was his strong suit, you understand; and when it come to that, Smiley would ante up money on him as long as he had a red. Smiley was monstrous proud of his frog, and well he might be, for fellers that had traveled and been everywheres all said he laid over any frog that ever *they* see.

"Well, Smiley kep' the beast in a little lattice box, and he used to fetch him down-town sometimes and lay for a bet. One day a feller—a stranger in the camp, he was—come acrost him with his box, and says:

" 'What might it be that you've got in the box?'

"And Smiley says, sorter indifferent-like, 'It might be a parrot, or it might be a canary, maybe, but it ain't—it's only just a frog.'

"And the feller took it, and looked at it careful, and turned it round this way and that, and says, 'H'm—so 'tis. Well, what's *he* good for?'

" 'Well,' Smiley says, easy and careless, 'he's good enough for *one* thing, I should judge—he can outjump any frog in Calaveras County.'

"The feller took the box again, and took another long, particular look, and give it back to Smiley, and says, very deliberate, 'Well,' he says, 'I don't see no p'ints about that frog that's any better'n any other frog.'

" 'Maybe you don't,' Smiley says. 'Maybe you understand frogs and maybe you don't understand 'em; maybe you've had experience, and maybe you ain't only a amature, as it were. Anyways, I've got *my* opinion, and I'll resk forty dollars that he can outjump any frog in Calaveras County.'

"And the feller studied a minute, and then says, kinder sadlike, 'Well, I'm only a stranger here, and I ain't got no frog; but if I had a frog, I'd bet you.'

"And then Smiley says, 'That's all right—that's all right—if you'll hold my box a minute, I'll go and get you a frog.' And so the feller took the box, and put up his forty dollars along with Smiley's, and set down to wait.

"So he set there a good while thinking and thinking to himself, and then he got the frog out and prized his mouth open and took a teaspoon and filled him full of quail-shot—filled him pretty near up to his chin—and set him on the floor. Smiley he went to the swamp and slopped around in the mud for a long time, and finally he ketched a frog, and fetched him in, and give him to this feller, and says:

" 'Now, if you're ready, set him alongside of Dan'l, with his fore paws just even with Dan'ls, and I'll give the word.' Then he says, 'One—two—three—*git!*' and him and the feller touched up the frogs from behind, and the new frog hopped off lively, but Dan'l give a heave, and hysted up his shoulders—so—like a Frenchman, but it warn't no use—he couldn't budge; he was planted as solid as a church, and he couldn't no more stir than if he was anchored out. Smiley was a good deal surprised, and he was disgusted too, but he didn't have no idea what the matter was, of course.

"The feller took the money and started away; and when he was going out at the door, he sorter jerked his thumb over his shoulder—so—at Dan'l, and says again, very deliberate, 'Well,' he says, '*I* don't see no p'ints about that frog that's any better'n any other frog.'

"Smiley he stood scratching his head looking down at Dan'l a long time, and at last he says, 'I do wonder what in the nation that frog throw'd off for—I wonder if there ain't something the matter with him—he 'pears to look mighty baggy, somehow.' And he ketched Dan'l by the nap of the neck, and hefted him, and says, 'Why blame my cats if he don't weigh five pound!' and turned him upside down and he belched out a double handful of shot. And then he see how it was, and he was the maddest man—he set the frog down and took out after that feller, but he never ketched him. And—"

[Here Simon Wheeler heard his name called from the front yard, and got up to see what was wanted.] And turning to me as he moved away, he said: "Just set where you are, stranger, and rest easy—I ain't going to be gone a second."

But, by your leave, I did not think that a continuation of the history of the enterprising vagabond *Jim* Smiley would be likely to afford me much information concerning the Rev. *Leonidas W*. Smiley, and so I started away.

At the door I met the sociable Wheeler returning, and he buttonholed me and recommenced:

"Well, thish-yer Smiley had a yaller one-eyed cow that didn't have no tail, only just a short stump like a bannanner, and—"

However, lacking both time and inclination, I did not wait to hear about the afflicted cow, but took my leave.

From The Innocents Abroad (1869)

FROM CHAPTER 34

When I think how I have been swindled by books of Oriental travel, I want a tourist for breakfast. For years and years I have dreamed of the wonders of the Turkish bath; for years and years I have promised myself that I would yet enjoy one. Many and many a time, in fancy, I have lain in the marble bath, and breathed the slumbrous fragrance of Eastern spices that filled the air; then passed through a weird and complicated system of pulling and hauling, and drenching and scrubbing, by a gang of naked savages who loomed vast and vaguely through the steaming mists, like demons; then rested for a while on a divan fit for a king; then passed through another complex ordeal, and one more fearful than the first; and, finally, swathed in soft fabrics, been conveyed to a princely saloon and laid on a bed of eider down, where eunuchs, gorgeous of costume, fanned me while I drowsed and dreamed, or contentedly gazed at the rich hangings of the apartment, the soft carpets, the sumptuous furniture, the pictures, and drank delicious coffee, smoked the soothing narghili, and dropped, at the last, into tranquil repose, lulled by sensuous odors from unseen censers, by the gentle influence of the narghili's Persian tobacco, and by the music of fountains that counterfeited the pattering of summer rain.

That was the picture, just as I got it from incendiary books of travel. It was a poor, miserable imposture. The reality is no more like it than the Five Points are like the Garden of Eden. They received me in a great court, paved with marble slabs; around it were broad galleries, one above another, carpeted with seedy matting, railed with unpainted balustrades, and furnished with huge rickety chairs, cushioned with rusty old mattresses, indented with impressions left by the forms of nine successive generations of men who had reposed upon them. The place was vast, naked, dreary; its court a barn, its galleries stalls for human horses. The cadaverous, half nude varlets that served in the establishment had nothing of poetry in their appearance, nothing of romance, nothing of Oriental splendor. They shed no entrancing odors—just the contrary. Their hungry eyes and their lank forms continually suggested one glaring, unsentimental fact—they wanted what they term in California "a square meal."

I went into one of the racks and undressed. An unclean starveling wrapped a gaudy table-cloth about his loins, and hung a white rag over my shoulders. If I had had a tub then, it would have come natural to me to take in washing. I was then conducted down stairs into the wet, slippery court, and the first things that attracted my attention were my heels. My fall excited no comment. They expected it, no doubt. It belonged in the list of softening, sensuous influences peculiar to this home of Eastern luxury. It was softening enough, but its application was not happy. They now gave me a pair of wooden clogs—benches in miniature, with leather straps over them to confine my feet (which they would have done, only I do not wear No. 13s). These things dangled uncomfortably by the straps when I lifted up my feet, and came down in awkward and unexpected places when I put them on the floor again, and sometimes turned sideways and wrenched my ankles out of joint. However, it was all Oriental luxury, and I did what I could to enjoy it.

They put me in another part of the barn and laid me on a stuffy sort of pallet, which was not made of cloth of gold, or Persian shawls, but was merely the unpretending sort of thing I have seen in the negro quarters of Arkansas. There was nothing whatever in this dim marble prison but five more of these biers. It was a very solemn place. I expected that the spiced odors of Araby were going to steal over my senses now, but they did not. A copper-colored skeleton, with a rag around him, brought me a glass decanter of water, with a lighted tobacco pipe in the top of it, and a pliant stem a yard long, with a brass mouth-piece to it.

It was the famous "narghili" of the East—the

thing the Grand Turk smokes in the pictures. This began to look like luxury. I took one blast at it, and it was sufficient; the smoke went in a great volume down into my stomach, my lungs, even into the uttermost parts of my frame. I exploded one mighty cough, and it was as if Vesuvius had let go. For the next five minutes I smoked at every pore, like a frame house that is on fire on the inside. Not any more narghili for me. The smoke had a vile taste, and the taste of a thousand infidel tongues that remained on that brass mouthpiece was viler still. I was getting discouraged. Whenever, hereafter, I see the cross-legged Grand Turk smoking his narghili, in pretended bliss, on the outside of a paper of Connecticut tobacco, I shall know him for the shameless humbug he is.

This prison was filled with hot air. When I had got warmed up sufficiently to prepare me for a still warmer temperature, they took me where it was—into a marble room, wet, slippery and steamy, and laid me out on a raised platform in the centre. It was very warm. Presently my man sat me down by a tank of hot water, drenched me well, gloved his hand with a coarse mitten, and began to polish me all over with it. I began to smell disagreeably. The more he polished the worse I smelt. It was alarming. I said to him:

"I perceive that I am pretty far gone. It is plain that I ought to be buried without any unnecessary delay. Perhaps you had better go after my friends at once, because the weather is warm, and I can not 'keep' long."

He went on scrubbing, and paid no attention. I soon saw that he was reducing my size. He bore hard on his mitten, and from under it rolled little cylinders, like maccaroni. It could not be dirt, for it was too white. He pared me down in this way for a long time. Finally I said:

"It is a tedious process. It will take hours to trim me to the size you want me; I will wait; go and borrow a jack-plane."

He paid no attention at all.

After a while he brought a basin, some soap, and something that seemed to be the tail of a horse. He made up a prodigious quantity of soap-suds, deluged me with them from head to foot, without warning me to shut my eyes, and then swabbed me viciously with the horse-tail. Then he left me there, a snowy statue of lather, and went away. When I got tired of waiting I went and hunted him up. He was propped against the wall, in another room, asleep. I woke him. He was not disconcerted. He took me back and flooded me with hot water, then turbaned by head, swathed me with dry table-cloths, and conducted me to a latticed chicken-coop in one of the galleries, and pointed to one of those Arkansas beds. I mounted it, and vaguely expected the odors of Araby again. They did not come.

The blank, unornamented coop had nothing about it of that oriental voluptuousness one reads of so much. It was more suggestive of the county hospital than any thing else. The skinny servitor brought a narghili, and I got him to take it out again without wasting any time about it. Then he brought the world-renowned Turkish coffee that poets have sung so rapturously for many generations, and I seized upon it as the last hope that was left of my old dreams of Eastern luxury. It was another fraud. Of all the unchristian beverages that ever passed my lips, Turkish coffee is the worst. The cup is small, it is smeared with grounds; the coffee is black, thick, unsavory of smell, and execrable in taste. The bottom of the cup has a muddy sediment in it half an inch deep. This goes down your throat, and portions of it lodge by the way, and produce a tickling aggravation that keeps you barking and coughing for an hour.

Here endeth my experience of the celebrated Turkish bath, and here also endeth my dream of the bliss the mortal revels in who passes through it. It is a malignant swindle. The man who enjoys it is qualified to enjoy any thing that is repulsive to sight or sense, and he that can invest it with a charm of poetry is able to do the same with any thing else in the world that is tedious, and wretched, and dismal, and nasty.

From Life on the Mississippi (1883)

CHAPTER 4, THE BOYS' AMBITION

When I was a boy, there was but one permanent ambition among my comrades in our village[1] on the west bank of the Mississippi River. That was, to be a steamboatman. We had transient ambitions of other sorts, but they were only transient. When a circus came and went, it left us all burn-

[1] Hannibal, Missouri [Twain].

ing to become clowns; the first negro minstrel show that came to our section left us all suffering to try that kind of life; now and then we had a hope that if we lived and were good, God would permit us to be pirates. These ambitions faded out, each in its turn; but the ambition to be a steamboatman always remained.

Once a day a cheap, gaudy packet arrived upward from St. Louis, and another downward from Keokuk. Before these events, the day was glorious with expectancy; after them, the day was a dead and empty thing. Not only the boys, but the whole village, felt this. After all these years I can picture that old time to myself now, just as it was then: the white town drowsing in the sunshine of a summer's morning; the streets empty, or pretty nearly so; one or two clerks sitting in front of the Water Street stores, with their splint-bottomed chairs tilted back against the wall, chins on breasts, hats slouched over their faces, asleep—with shingle-shavings enough around to show what broke them down; a sow and a litter of pigs loafing along the sidewalk, doing a good business in watermelon rinds and seeds; two or three lonely little freight piles scattered about the "levee;" a pile of "skids" on the slope of the stone-paved wharf, and the fragrant town drunkard asleep in the shadow of them; two or three wood flats at the head of the wharf, but nobody to listen to the peaceful lapping of the wavelets against them; the great Mississippi, the majestic, the magnificent Mississippi, rolling its mile-wide tide along, shining in the sun; the dense forest away on the other side; the "point" above the town, and the "point" below, bounding the river-glimpse and turning it into a sort of sea, and withal a very still and brilliant and lonely one. Presently a film of dark smoke appears above one of those remote "points;" instantly a negro drayman, famous for his quick eye and prodigious voice, lifts up the cry, "S-t-e-a-m-boat a-comin'!" and the scene changes! The town drunkard stirs, the clerks wake up, a furious clatter of drays follows, every house and store pours out a human contribution, and all in a twinkling the dead town is alive and moving. Drays, carts, men, boys, all go hurrying from many quarters to a common centre, the wharf. Assembled there, the people fasten their eyes upon the coming boat as upon a wonder they are seeing for the first time. And the boat *is* rather a handsome sight, too. She is long and sharp and trim and pretty; she has two tall, fancy-topped chimneys, with a gilded device of some kind swung between them; a fanciful pilot-house, all glass and

"gingerbread," perched on top of the "texas" deck behind them; the paddle-boxes are gorgeous with a picture or with gilded rays above the boat's name; the boiler deck, the hurricane deck, and the texas deck are fenced and ornamented with clean white railings; there is a flag gallantly flying from the jack-staff; the furnace doors are open and the fires glaring bravely; the upper decks are black with passengers; the captain stands by the big bell, calm, imposing, the envy of all; great volumes of the blackest smoke are rolling and tumbling out of the chimneys—a husbanded grandeur created with a bit of pitch pine just before arriving at a town; the crew are grouped on the forecastle; the broad stage is run far out over the port bow, and an envied deck-hand stands picturesquely on the end of it with a coil of rope in his hand; the pent steam is screaming through the gauge-cocks; the captain lifts his hand, a bell rings, the wheels stop; then they turn back, churning the water to foam, and the steamer is at rest. Then such a scramble as there is to get aboard, and to get ashore, and to take in freight and to discharge freight, all at one and the same time; and such a yelling and cursing as the mates facilitate it all with! Ten minutes later the steamer is under way again, with no flag on the jack-staff and no black smoke issuing from the chimneys. After ten more minutes the town is dead again, and the town drunkard asleep by the skids once more.

My father was a justice of the peace, and I supposed he possessed the power of life and death over all men and could hang anybody that offended him. This was distinction enough for me as a general thing; but the desire to be a steamboatman kept intruding, nevertheless. I first wanted to be a cabin-boy, so that I could come out with a white apron on and shake a table-cloth over the side, where all my old comrades could see me; later I thought I would rather be the deck-hand who stood on the end of the stage-plank with the coil of rope in his hand because he was particularly conspicuous. But these were only day-dreams, —they were too heavenly to be contemplated as real possibilities. By and by one of our boys went away. He was not heard of for a long time. At last he turned up as apprentice engineer or "striker" on a steamboat. This thing shook the bottom out of all my Sunday-school teachings. That boy had been notoriously worldly, and I just the reverse; yet he was exalted to this eminence, and I left in obscurity and misery. There was nothing generous about this fellow in his greatness. He would always manage to have a rusty bolt to scrub while his boat tarried at our town, and he would sit on the inside guard and scrub it, where we could all see him and envy him and loathe him. And whenever his boat was laid up he would come home and swell around the town in his blackest and greasiest clothes, so that nobody could help remembering that he was a steamboatman; and he used all sorts of steamboat technicalities in his talk, as if he were so used to them that he forgot common people could not understand them. He would speak of the "labboard" side of a horse in an easy, natural way that would make one wish he was dead. And he was always talking about "St. Looy" like an old citizen; he would refer casually to occasions when he "was coming down Fourth Street," or when he was "passing by the Planter's House," or when there was a fire and he took a turn on the brakes of "the old Big Missouri;" and then he would go on and lie about how many towns the size of ours were burned down there that day. Two or three of the boys had long been persons of consideration among us because they had been to St. Louis once and had a vague general knowledge of its wonders, but the day of their glory was over now. They lapsed into a humble silence, and learned to disappear when the ruthless "cub" engineer approached. This fellow had money, too, and hair oil. Also an ignorant silver watch and a showy brass watch chain. He wore a leather belt and used no suspenders. If ever a youth was cordially admired and hated by his comrades, this one was. No girl could withstand his charms. He "cut out" every boy in the village. When his boat blew up at last, it diffused a tranquil contentment among us such as we had not known for months. But when he came home the next week, alive, renowned, and appeared in church all battered up and bandaged, a shining hero, stared at and wondered over by everybody, it seemed to us that the partiality of Providence for an undeserving reptile had reached a point where it was open to criticism.

This creature's career could produce but one result, and it speedily followed. Boy after boy managed to get on the river. The minister's son became an engineer. The doctor's and the postmaster's sons became "mud clerks;" the wholesale liquor dealer's son became a bar-keeper on a boat; four sons of the chief merchant, and two sons of the county judge, became pilots. Pilot was the grandest position of all. The pilot, even in those days of trivial wages, had a princely salary—from a hundred and fifty to two hundred and fifty dollars a month, and no board to pay. Two months of his wages would pay a preacher's salary for a year. Now some of us were left disconsolate. We could not get on the river—at least our parents would not let us.

So by and by I ran away. I said I never would come home again till I was a pilot and could come in glory. But somehow I could not manage it. I went meekly aboard a few of the boats that lay packed together like sardines at the long St. Louis wharf, and very humbly inquired for the pilots, but got only a cold shoulder and short words from mates and clerks. I had to make the best of this sort of treatment for the time being, but I had comforting day-dreams of a future when I should be a great and honored pilot, with plenty of money, and could kill some of these mates and clerks and pay for them.

CHAPTER 54, PAST AND PRESENT

Being left to myself, up there, I went on picking out old houses in the distant town, and calling back their former inmates out of the mouldy past. Among them I presently recognized the house of the father of Lem Hackett (fictitious name). It carried me back more than a generation in a moment, and landed me in the midst of a time when the happenings of life were not the natural and logical results of great general laws, but of special orders, and were freighted with very precise and distinct purposes—partly punitive in intent, partly admonitory; and usually local in application.

When I was a small boy, Lem Hackett was drowned—on a Sunday. He fell out of an empty flat-boat, where he was playing. Being loaded with sin, he went to the bottom like an anvil. He was the only boy in the village who slept that night. We others all lay awake, repenting. We had not needed the information, delivered from the pulpit that evening, that Lem's was a case of special judgment—we knew that, already. There was a ferocious thunder-storm, that night, and it raged continuously until near dawn. The winds blew, the windows rattled, the rain swept along the roof in pelting sheets, and at the briefest of intervals the inky blackness of the night vanished, the houses over the way glared out white and blinding for a quivering instant, then the solid darkness shut down again and a splitting peal of thunder followed which seemed to rend everything in the neighborhood to shreds and splinters. I sat up in bed quaking and shuddering, waiting for the destruction of the world, and expecting it. To me there was nothing strange or incongruous in heaven's making such an uproar about Lem Hackett. Apparently it was the right and proper thing to do. Not a doubt entered my mind that all the angels were grouped together, discussing this boy's case and observing the awful bombardment of our beggarly little village with satisfaction and approval. There was one thing which disturbed me in the most serious way; that was the thought that this centering of the celestial interest on our village could not fail to attract the attention of the observers to people among us who might otherwise have escaped notice for years. I felt that I was not only one of those people, but the very one most likely to be discovered. That discovery could have but one result: I should be in the fire with Lem before the chill of the river had been fairly warmed out of him. I knew that this would be only just and fair. I was increasing the chances against myself all the time, by feeling a secret bitterness against Lem for having attracted this fatal attention to me, but I could not help it—this sinful thought persisted in infesting my breast in spite of me. Every time the lightning glared I caught my breath, and judged I was gone. In my terror and misery, I meanly began to suggest other boys, and mention acts of theirs which were wickeder than mine, and peculiarly needed punishment —and I tried to pretend to myself that I was simply doing this in a casual way, and without intent to divert the heavenly attention to them for the purpose of getting rid of it myself. With deep sagacity I put these mentions into the form of sorrowing recollections and left-handed sham-supplications that the sins of those boys might be allowed to pass unnoticed—"Possibly they may repent." "It is true that Jim Smith broke a window and lied about it—but maybe he did not mean any harm. And although Tom Holmes says more bad words than any other boy in the village, he probably intends to repent—though he has never said he would. And whilst it is a fact that John Jones did fish a little on Sunday, once, he didn't really catch anything but only just one small useless mud-cat; and maybe that wouldn't have been so awful if he had thrown it back—as he says he did, but he didn't. Pity but they would repent of these dreadful things—and maybe they will yet."

But while I was shamefully trying to draw attention to these poor chaps—who were doubtless di-

recting the celestial attention to me at the same moment, though I never once suspected that—I had heedlessly left my candle burning. It was not a time to neglect even trifling precautions. There was no occasion to add anything to the facilities for attracting notice to me—so I put the light out.

It was a long night to me, and perhaps the most distressful one I ever spent. I endured agonies of remorse for sins which I knew I had committed, and for others which I was not certain about, yet was sure that they had been set down against me in a book by an angel who was wiser than I and did not trust such important matters to memory. It struck me, by and by, that I had been making a most foolish and calamitous mistake, in one respect: doubtless I had not only made my own destruction sure by directing attention to those other boys, but had already accomplished theirs!—Doubtless the lightning had stretched them all dead in their beds by this time! The anguish and the fright which this thought gave me made my previous sufferings seem trifling by comparison.

Things had become truly serious. I resolved to turn over a new leaf instantly; I also resolved to connect myself with the church the next day, if I survived to see its sun appear. I resolved to cease from sin in all its forms, and to lead a high and blameless life forever after. I would be punctual at church and Sunday-school; visit the sick; carry baskets of victuals to the poor (simply to fulfil the regulation conditions, although I knew we had none among us so poor but they would smash the basket over my head for my pains); I would instruct other boys in right ways, and take the resulting trouncings meekly; I would subsist entirely on tracts; I would invade the rum shop and warn the drunkard—and finally, if I escaped the fate of those who early become too good to live, I would go for a missionary.

The storm subsided toward daybreak, and I dozed gradually to sleep with a sense of obligation to Lem Hackett for going to eternal suffering in that abrupt way, and thus preventing a far more dreadful disaster—my own loss.

But when I rose refreshed, by and by, and found that those other boys were still alive, I had a dim sense that perhaps the whole thing was a false alarm; that the entire turmoil had been on Lem's account and nobody's else. The world looked so bright and safe that there did not seem to be any real occasion to turn over a new leaf. I was a little subdued, during that day, and perhaps the next; after that, my purpose of reforming slowly dropped out of my mind, and I had a peaceful, comfortable time again, until the next storm.

That storm came about three weeks later; and it was the most unaccountable one, to me, that I had ever experienced; for on the afternoon of that day, "Dutchy" was drowned. Dutchy belonged to our Sunday-school. He was a German lad who did not know enough to come in out of the rain; but he was exasperatingly good, and had a prodigious memory. One Sunday he made himself the envy of all the youth and the talk of all the admiring village, by reciting three thousand verses of Scripture without missing a word; then he went off the very next day and got drowned.

Circumstances gave to his death a peculiar impressiveness. We were all bathing in a muddy creek which had a deep hole in it, and in this hole the coopers had sunk a pile of green hickory hoop poles to soak, some twelve feet under water. We were diving and "seeing who could stay under longest." We managed to remain down by holding on to the hoop poles. Dutchy made such a poor success of it that he was hailed with laughter and derision every time his head appeared above water. At last he seemed hurt with the taunts, and begged us to stand still on the bank and be fair with him and give him an honest count—"be friendly and kind just this once, and not miscount for the sake of having the fun of laughing at him." Treacherous winks were exchanged, and all said "All right, Dutchy—go ahead, we'll play fair."

Dutchy plunged in, but the boys, instead of beginning to count, followed the lead of one of their number and scampered to a range of blackberry bushes close by and hid behind it. They imagined Dutchy's humiliation, when he should rise after a superhuman effort and find the place silent and vacant, nobody there to applaud. They were "so full of laugh" with the idea, that they were continually exploding into muffled cackles. Time swept on, and presently one who was peeping through the briers, said, with surprise:—

"Why, he hasn't come up, yet!"

The laughing stopped.

"Boys, it's a splendid dive," said one.

"Never mind that," said another, "the joke on him is all the better for it."

There was a remark or two more, and then a pause. Talking ceased, and all began to peer through the vines. Before long, the boys' faces began to look uneasy, then anxious, then terrified. Still there was no movement of the placid water. Hearts began to beat fast, and faces to turn pale.

We all glided out, silently, and stood on the bank, our horrified eyes wandering back and forth from each other's countenances to the water.

"Somebody must go down and see!"

Yes, that was plain; but nobody wanted that grisly task.

"Draw straws!"

So we did—with hands which shook so, that we hardly knew what we were about. The lot fell to me, and I went down. The water was so muddy I could not see anything, but I felt around among the hoop poles, and presently grasped a limp wrist which gave me no response—and if it had I should not have known it, I let it go with such a frightened suddenness.

The boy had been caught among the hoop poles and entangled there, helplessly. I fled to the surface and told the awful news. Some of us knew that if the boy were dragged out at once he might possibly be resuscitated, but we never thought of that. We did not think of anything; we did not know what to do, so we did nothing—except that the smaller lads cried, piteously, and we all struggled frantically into our clothes, putting on anybody's that came handy, and getting them wrong-side-out and upside-down, as a rule. Then we scurried away and gave the alarm, but none of us went back to see the end of the tragedy. We had a more important thing to attend to: we all flew home, and lost not a moment in getting ready to lead a better life.

The night presently closed down. Then came on that tremendous and utterly unaccountable storm. I was perfectly dazed; I could not understand it. It seemed to me that there must be some mistake. The elements were turned loose, and they rattled and banged and glazed away in the most blind and frantic manner. All heart and hope went out of me, and the dismal thought kept floating through my brain, "If a boy who knows three thousand verses by heart is not satisfactory, what chance is there for anybody else?"

Of course I never questioned for a moment that the storm was on Dutchy's account, or that he or any other inconsequential animal was worthy of such a majestic demonstration from on high; the lesson of it was the only thing that troubled me; for it convinced me that if Dutchy, with all his perfections, was not a delight, it would be vain for me to turn over a new leaf, for I must infallibly fall hopelessly short of that boy, no matter how hard I might try. Nevertheless I did turn it over—a highly educated fear compelled me to do that

—but succeeding days of cheerfulness and sunshine came bothering around, and within a month I had so drifted backward that again I was as lost and comfortable as ever.

Breakfast time approached while I mused these musings and called these ancient happenings back to mind; so I got me back into the present and went down the hill.

On my way through town to the hotel, I saw the house which was my home when I was a boy. At present rates, the people who now occupy it are of no more value than I am; but in my time they would have been worth not less than five hundred dollars apiece. They are colored folk.

After breakfast, I went out alone again, intending to hunt up some of the Sunday-schools and see how this generation of pupils might compare with their progenitors who had sat with me in those places and had probably taken me as a model —though I do not remember as to that now. By the public square there had been in my day a shabby little brick church called the "Old Ship of Zion," which I had attended as a Sunday-school scholar; and I found the locality easily enough, but not the old church; it was gone, and a trig and rather hilarious new edifice was in its place. The pupils were better dressed and better looking than were those of my time; consequently they did not resemble their ancestors; and consequently there was nothing familiar to me in their faces. Still, I contemplated them with a deep interest and a yearning wistfulness, and if I had been a girl I would have cried; for they were the offspring, and represented, and occupied the places, of boys and girls some of whom I had loved to love, and some of whom I had loved to hate, but all of whom were dear to me for the one reason or the other, so many years gone by—and, Lord, where be they now!

I was mightily stirred, and would have been grateful to be allowed to remain unmolested and look my fill; but a bald-summited superintendent who had been a tow-headed Sunday-school mate of mine on that spot in the early ages, recognized me, and I talked a flutter of wild nonsense to those children to hide the thoughts which were in me, and which could not have been spoken without a betrayal of feeling that would have been recognized as out of character with me.

Making speeches without preparation is no gift of mine; and I was resolved to shirk any new opportunity, but in the next and larger Sunday-school I found myself in the rear of the assem-

blage; so I was very willing to go on the platform a moment for the sake of getting a good look at the scholars. On the spur of the moment I could not recall any of the old idiotic talks which visitors used to insult me with when I was a pupil there; and I was sorry for this, since it would have given me time and excuse to dawdle there and take a long and satisfying look at what I feel at liberty to say was an array of fresh young comeliness not matchable in another Sunday-school of the same size. As I talked merely to get a chance to inspect; and as I strung out the random rubbish solely to prolong the inspection, I judged it but decent to confess these low motives, and I did so.

If the Model Boy was in either of these Sunday-schools, I did not see him. The Model Boy of my time—we never had but the one—was perfect: perfect in manners, perfect in dress, perfect in conduct, perfect in filial piety, perfect in exterior godliness; but at bottom he was a prig; and as for the contents of his skull, they could have changed place with the contents of a pie and nobody would have been the worse off for it but the pie. This fellow's reproachlessness was a standing reproach to every lad in the village. He was the admiration of all the mothers, and the detestation of all their sons. I was told what became of him, but as it was a disappointment to me, I will not enter into details. He succeeded in life.

CHAPTER 8, PERPLEXING LESSONS

At the end of what seemed a tedious while, I had managed to pack my head full of islands, towns, bars, "points," and bends and a curiously inanimate mass of lumber it was, too. However, inasmuch as I could shut my eyes and reel off a good long string of these names without leaving out more than ten miles of river in every fifty, I began to feel that I could take a boat down to New Orleans if I could make her skip those little gaps. But of course my complacency could hardly get start enough to lift my nose a trifle into the air, before Mr. Bixby would think of something to fetch it down again. One day he turned on me suddenly with this settler:—

"What is the shape of Walnut Bend?"

He might as well have asked me my grandmother's opinion of protoplasm. I reflected respectfully, and then said I didn't know it had any particular shape. My gunpowdery chief went off with a bang, of course, and then went on loading and firing until he was out of adjectives.

I had learned long ago that he only carried just so many rounds of ammunition, and was sure to subside into a very placable and even remorseful old smooth-bore as soon as they were all gone. That word "old" is merely affectionate; he was not more than thirty-four. I waited. By and by he said,—

"My boy, you've got to know the *shape* of the river perfectly. It is all there is left to steer by on a very dark night. Everything else is blotted out and gone. But mind you, it hasn't the same shape in the night that it has in the day-time."

"How on earth am I ever going to learn it, then?"

"How do you follow a hall at home in the dark? Because you know the shape of it. You can't see it."

"Do you mean to say that I've got to know all the million trifling variations of shape in the banks of this interminable river as well as I know the shape of the front hall at home?"

"On my honor, you've got to know them *better* than any man ever did know the shapes of the halls in his own house."

"I wish I was dead!"

"Now I don't want to discourage you, but"—

"Well, pile it on me; I might as well have it now as another time."

"You see, this has got to be learned; there isn't any getting around it. A clear starlight night throws such heavy shadows that if you didn't know the shape of a shore perfectly you would claw away from every bunch of timber, because you would take the black shadow of it for a solid cape; and you see you would be getting scared to death every fifteen minutes by the watch. You would be fifty yards from shore all the time when you ought to be within fifty feet of it. You can't see a snag in one of those shadows, but you know exactly where it is, and the shape of the river tells you when you are coming to it. Then there's your pitch-dark night; the river is a very different shape on a pitch-dark night from what it is on a starlight night. All shores seem to be straight lines, then, and mighty dim ones, too; and you'd *run* them for straight lines only you know better. You boldly drive your boat right into what seems to be a solid, straight wall (you knowing very well that in reality there is a curve there), and that wall falls back and makes way for you. Then there's your gray mist. You take a night when there's one of these grisly,

drizzly, gray mists, and then there isn't *any* particular shape to a shore. A gray mist would tangle the head of the oldest man that ever lived. Well, then, different kinds of *moonlight* change the shape of the river in different ways. You see"—

"Oh, don't say any more, please! Have I got to learn the shape of the river according to all these five hundred thousand different ways? If I tried to carry all that cargo in my head it would make me stoop-shouldered."

"*No!* you only learn *the* shape of the river; and you learn it with such absolute certainty that you can always steer by the shape that's *in your head,* and never mind the one that's before your eyes."

"Very well, I'll try it; but after I have learned it can I depend on it? Will it keep the same form and not go fooling around?"

Before Mr. Bixby could answer, Mr. W—— came in to take the watch, and he said,—

"Bixby, you'll have to look out for President's Island and all that country clear away up above the Old Hen and Chickens. The banks are caving and the shape of the shores changing like everything. Why, you wouldn't know the point above 40. You can go up inside the old sycamore snag, now."[2]

So that question was answered. Here were leagues of shore changing shape. My spirits were down in the mud again. Two things seemed pretty apparent to me. One was, that in order to be a pilot a man had got to learn more than any one man ought to be allowed to know; and the other was, that he must learn it all over again in a different way every twenty-four hours.

That night we had the watch until twelve. Now it was an ancient river custom for the two pilots to chat a bit when the watch changed. While the relieving pilot put on his gloves and lit his cigar, his partner, the retiring pilot, would say something like this:—

"I judge the upper bar is making down a little at Hale's Point; had quarter twain with the lower lead and mark twain[3] with the other."

"Yes, I thought it was making down a little, last trip. Meet any boats?"

"Met one abreast the head of 21, but she was away over hugging the bar, and I couldn't make

[2] It may not be necessary, but still it can do no harm to explain that "inside" means between the snag and the shore [Twain].

[3] Two fathoms. Quarter twain is 2¼ fathoms, 13½ feet. Mark three is three fathoms [Twain].

her out entirely. I took her for the 'Sunny South' —hadn't any skylights forward of the chimneys."

And so on. And as the relieving pilot took the wheel his partner[4] would mention that we were in such-and-such a bend, and say we were abreast of such-and-such a man's wood-yard or plantation. This was courtesy; I supposed it was *necessity*. But Mr. W—— came on watch full twelve minutes late on this particular night,—a tremendous breach of etiquette; in fact, it is the unpardonable sin among pilots. So Mr. Bixby gave him no greeting whatever, but simply surrendered the wheel and marched out of the pilot-house without a word. I was appalled; it was a villainous night for blackness, we were in a particularly wide and blind part of the river, where there was no shape or substance to anything, and it seemed incredible that Mr. Bixby should have left that poor fellow to kill the boat trying to find out where he was. But I resolved that I would stand by him any way. He should find that he was not wholly friendless. So I stood around, and waited to be asked where we were. But Mr. W—— plunged on serenely through the solid firmament of black cats that stood for an atmosphere, and never opened his mouth. Here is a proud devil, thought I; here is a limb of Satan that would rather send us all to destruction than put himself under obligations to me, because I am not yet one of the salt of the earth and privileged to snub captains and lord it over everything dead and alive in a steamboat. I presently climbed up on the bench; I did not think it was safe to go to sleep while this lunatic was on watch.

However, I must have gone to sleep in the course of time, because the next thing I was aware of was the fact that day was breaking, Mr. W—— gone, and Mr. Bixby at the wheel again. So it was four o'clock and all well—but me; I felt like a skinful of dry bones and all of them trying to ache at once.

Mr. Bixby asked me what I had stayed up there for. I confessed that it was to do Mr. W—— a benevolence,—tell him where he was. It took five minutes for the entire preposterousness of the thing to filter into Mr. Bixby's system, and then I judge it filled him nearly up to the chin; because he paid me a compliment—and not much of a one either. He said,—

"Well, taking you by-and-large, you do seem to be more different kinds of an ass than any creature

[4] "Partner" is technical for "the other pilot" [Twain].

I ever saw before. What did you suppose he wanted to know for?"

I said I thought it might be a convenience to him.

"Convenience! D-nation! Didn't I tell you that a man's got to know the river in the night the same as he'd know his own front hall?"

"Well, I can follow the front hall in the dark if I know it *is* the front hall; but suppose you set me down in the middle of it in the dark and not tell me which hall it is; how am *I* to know?"

"Well, you've *got* to, on the river!"

"All right. Then I'm glad I never said anything to Mr. W——"

"I should say so. Why, he'd have slammed you through the window and utterly ruined a hundred dollars' worth of window-sash and stuff."

I was glad this damage had been saved, for it would have made me unpopular with the owners. They always hated anybody who had the name of being careless, and injuring things.

I went to work now to learn the shape of the river; and of all the eluding and ungraspable objects that ever I tried to get mind or hands on, that was the chief. I would fasten my eyes upon a sharp, wooded point that projected far into the river some miles ahead of me, and go to laboriously photographing its shape upon my brain; and just as I was beginning to succeed to my satisfaction, we would draw up toward it and the exasperating thing would begin to melt away and fold back into the bank! If there had been a conspicuous dead tree standing upon the very point of the cape, I would find that tree inconspicuously merged into the general forest, and occupying the middle of a straight shore, when I got abreast of it! No prominent hill would stick to its shape long enough for me to make up my mind what its form really was, but it was as dissolving and changeful as if it had been a mountain of butter in the hottest corner of the tropics. Nothing ever had the same shape when I was coming down-stream that it had borne when I went up. I mentioned these little difficulties to Mr. Bixby. He said,—

"That's the very main virtue of the thing. If the shapes didn't change every three seconds they wouldn't be of any use. Take this place where we are now, for instance. As long as that hill over yonder is only one hill, I can boom right along the way I'm going; but the moment it splits at the top and forms a V, I know I've got to scratch to starboard in a hurry, or I'll bang this boat's brains out against a rock; and then the moment one of the prongs of the V swings behind the other, I've got to waltz to larboard again, or I'll have a misunderstanding with a snag that would snatch the keelson out of this steamboat as neatly as if it were a sliver in your hand. If that hill didn't change its shape on bad nights there would be an awful steamboat grave-yard around here inside of a year."

It was plain that I had got to learn the shape of the river in all the different ways that could be thought of,—upside down, wrong end first, inside out, fore-and-aft, and "thort-ships,"—and then know what to do on gray nights when it hadn't any shape at all. So I set about it. In the course of time I began to get the best of this knotty lesson, and my self-complacency moved to the front once more. Mr. Bixby was all fixed, and ready to start it to the rear again. He opened on me after this fashion:—

"How much water did we have in the middle crossing at Hole-in-the-Wall, trip before last?"

I considered this an outrage. I said:—

"Every trip, down and up, the leadsmen are singing through that tangled place for three quar-

ters of an hour on a stretch. How do you reckon I can remember such a mess as that?"

"My boy, you've got to remember it. You've got to remember the exact spot and the exact marks the boat lay in when we had the shoalest water, in every one of the five hundred shoal places between St. Louis and New Orleans; and you mustn't get the shoal soundings and marks of one trip mixed up with the shoal soundings and marks of another, either, for they're not often twice alike. You must keep them separate."

When I came to myself again, I said,—

"When I get so that I can do that, I'll be able to raise the dead, and then I won't have to pilot a steamboat to make a living. I want to retire from this business. I want a slush-bucket and a brush; I'm only fit for a roustabout. I haven't got brains enough to be a pilot; and if I had I wouldn't have strength enough to carry them around, unless I went on crutches."

"Now drop that! When I say I'll learn a man the river, I mean it. And you can depend on it, I'll learn him or kill him."

The Man That Corrupted Hadleyburg (1898)

"The Man That Corrupted Hadleyburg" is clearly a fable of the vulnerability of human nature, a manifestation of the despair that more and more possessed Mark Twain in the latter part of his life. It is closely related, in fact, to "The Mysterious Stranger," which was not published until after Mark Twain's death, for in both a stranger appears and opens the seams of man and society. The difference is simply that in the former story we see a single village subjected to the moral pressure and scrutiny, and in the latter the dire revelation concerns all human history, and rage overwhelms irony.

"The Man That Corrupted Hadleyburg" is incidentally interesting from another point of view. In Obedsville of *The Gilded Age* or Brickville of *Huckleberry Finn*, as in *Life on the Mississippi*, we find a disenchanted view of the village; but Mark Twain was ambivalent on this matter, and for years, to balance Obedsville and Brickville, there was the vision of St. Petersburg and the memories of the actual Hannibal.

But by 1898, in Hadleyburg, what had seemed to be the vision of Jeffersonian and Edenic faith in America is reduced to its actuality: only human beings live here, after all.

I

It was many years ago. Hadleyburg was the most honest and upright town in all the region round about. It had kept that reputation unsmirched during three generations, and was prouder of it than of any other of its possessions. It was so proud of it, and so anxious to insure its perpetuation, that it began to teach the principles of honest dealing to its babies in the cradle, and made the like teachings the staple of their culture thenceforward through all the years devoted to their education. Also, throughout the formative years temptations were kept out of the way of the young people, so that their honesty could have every chance to harden and solidify, and become a part of their very bone. The neighbouring towns were jealous of this honourable supremacy, and affected to sneer at Hadleyburg's pride in it and call it vanity; but all the same they were obliged to acknowledge that Hadleyburg was in reality an incorruptible town; and if pressed they would also acknowledge that the mere fact that a young man hailed from Hadleyburg was all the recommendation he needed when he went forth from his natal town to seek for responsible employment.

But at last, in the drift of time, Hadleyburg had the ill luck to offend a passing stranger—possibly without knowing it, certainly without caring, for Hadleyburg was sufficient unto itself, and cared not a rap for strangers or their opinions. Still, it would have been well to make an exception in this one's case, for he was a bitter man, and revengeful. All through his wanderings during a whole year he kept his injury in mind, and gave all his leisure moments to trying to invent a compensating satisfaction for it. He contrived many plans, and all of them were good, but none of them was quite sweeping enough: the poorest of them would hurt a great many individuals, but what he wanted was a plan which would comprehend the entire town, and not let so much as one person escape unhurt. At last he had a fortunate idea, and when it fell into his brain it lit up his whole head with an evil joy. He began to form a plan at once, saying to himself 'That is the thing to do—I will corrupt the town.'

Six months later he went to Hadleyburg, and arrived in a buggy at the house of the old cashier of the bank about ten at night. He got a sack out of the buggy, shouldered it, and staggered with it through the cottage yard, and knocked at the door. A woman's voice said 'Come in,' and he entered, and set his sack behind the stove in the parlour, saying politely to the old lady who sat reading the 'Missionary Herald' by the lamp:

'Pray keep your seat, madam, I will not disturb you. There—now it is pretty well concealed; one would hardly know it was there. Can I see your husband a moment, madam?'

No, he was gone to Brixton, and might not return before morning.

'Very well, madam, it is no matter. I merely wanted to leave that sack in his care, to be delivered to the rightful owner when he shall be found. I am a stranger; he does not know me; I am merely passing through the town to-night to discharge a matter which has been long in my mind. My errand is now completed, and I go pleased and a little proud, and you will never see me again.

There is a paper attached to the sack which will explain everything. Good-night, madam.'

The old lady was afraid of the mysterious big stranger, and was glad to see him go. But her curiosity was roused, and she went straight to the sack and brought away the paper. It began as follows:

To be Published; or, the right man sought out by private inquiry—either will answer. This sack contains gold coin weighing a hundred and sixty pounds four ounces—

'Mercy on us, and the door not locked!'

Mrs. Richards flew to it all in a tremble and locked it, then pulled down the window-shades and stood frightened, worried, and wondering if there was anything else she could do toward making herself and the money more safe. She listened awhile for burglars, then surrendered to curiosity, and went back to the lamp and finished reading the paper:

I am a foreigner, and am presently going back to my own country, to remain there permanently. I am grateful to America for what I have received at her hands during my long stay under her flag, and to one of her citizens—a citizen of Hadleyburg—I am especially grateful for a great kindness done me a year or two ago. Two great kindnesses in fact. I will explain. I was a gambler. I say I was. I was a ruined gambler. I arrived in this village at night, hungry and without a penny. I asked for help—in the dark; I was ashamed to beg in the light. I begged of the right man. He gave me twenty dollars—that is to say, he gave me life, as I considered it. He also gave me fortune; for out of that money I have made myself rich at the gaming-table. And finally, a remark which he made to me has remained with me to this day, and has at last conquered me; and in conquering has saved the remnant of my morals: I shall gamble no more. Now I have no idea who that man was, but I want him found, and I want him to have this money, to give away, throw away, or keep, as he pleases. It is merely my way of testifying my gratitude to him. If I could stay, I would find him myself; but no matter, he will be found. This is an honest town, an incorruptible town, and I know I can trust it without fear. This man can be identified by the remark which he made to me; I feel persuaded that he will remember it.

And now my plan is this: If you prefer to conduct the inquiry privately, do so. Tell the contents of this present writing to any one who is likely to be the right man. If he shall answer, 'I am the man; the remark I made was so-and-so,' apply the test—to wit: open the sack, and in it you will find a sealed envelope containing that remark. If the remark mentioned by the candidate tallies with it, give him the money, and ask no further questions, for he is certainly the right man.

But if you shall prefer a public inquiry, then publish this present writing in the local paper—with these instructions added, to wit: Thirty days from now, let the candidate appear at the town-hall at eight in the evening (Friday), and hand his remark, in a sealed envelope, to the Rev. Mr. Burgess (if he will be kind enough to act); and let Mr. Burgess there and then destroy the seals of the sack, open it, and see if the remark is correct: if correct, let the money be delivered, with my sincere gratitude, to my benefactor thus identified.

Mrs. Richards sat down, gently quivering with excitement, and was soon lost in thinkings—after this pattern: 'What a strange thing it is! . . . And what a fortune for that kind man who set his bread afloat upon the waters! . . . If it had only been my husband that did it!—for we are so poor, so old and poor! . . .' Then, with a sigh—'But it was not my Edward; no, it was not he that gave a stranger twenty dollars. It is a pity too; I see it now. . . . Then, with a shudder—'But it is *gamblers*' money! the wages of sin; we couldn't take it; we couldn't touch it. I don't like to be near it; it seems a defilement.' She moved to a farther chair. . . . 'I wish Edward would come, and take it to the bank; a burglar might come at any moment; it is dreadful to be here all alone with it.'

At eleven Mr. Richards arrived, and while his wife was saying 'I am *so* glad you've come!' he was saying, 'I am so tired—tired clear out; it is dreadful to be poor, and have to make these dismal journeys at my time of life. Always at the grind, grind, grind, on a salary—another man's slave, and he sitting at home in his slippers, rich and comfortable.'

'I am so sorry for you, Edward, you know that; but be comforted; we have our livelihood; we have our good name—'

'Yes, Mary, and that is everything. Don't mind my talk—it's just a moment's irritation and doesn't mean anything. Kiss me—there, it's all gone now, and I am not complaining any more. What have you been getting? What's in the sack?'

Then his wife told him the great secret. It dazed him for a moment; then he said:

'It weighs a hundred and sixty pounds? Why, Mary, it's for-ty thou-sand dollars—think of it—a whole fortune! Not ten men in this village are worth that much. Give me the paper.'

He skimmed through it and said:

'Isn't it an adventure! Why, it's a romance; it's like the impossible things one reads about in books, and never sees in life.' He was well stirred up now; cheerful, even gleeful. He tapped his old wife on the cheek, and said humorously, 'Why, we're rich, Mary, rich; all we've got to do is to bury the money and burn the papers. If the gambler ever comes to inquire, we'll merely look coldly upon him and say: "What is this nonsense you are talking? We have never heard of you and your sack of gold before;" and then he would look foolish, and—'

'And in the meantime, while you are running on with your jokes, the money is still here, and it is fast getting along toward burglar-time.'

'True. Very well, what shall we do—make the inquiry private? No, not that; it would spoil the romance. The public method is better. Think what a noise it will make! And it will make all the other towns jealous; for no stranger would trust such a thing to any town but Hadleyburg, and they know it. It's a great card for us. I must get to the printing-office now, or I shall be too late.'

'But stop—stop—don't leave me here alone with it, Edward!'

But he was gone. For only a little while, however. Not far from his own house he met the editor-proprietor of the paper, and gave him the document, and said 'Here is a good thing for you, Cox—put it in.'

'It may be too late, Mr. Richards, but I'll see.'

At home again, he and his wife sat down to talk the charming mystery over; they were in no condition for sleep. The first question was, Who could the citizen have been who gave the stranger the twenty dollars? It seemed a simple one; both answered it in the same breath—

'Barclay Goodson.'

'Yes,' said Richards, 'he could have done it, and it would have been like him, but there's not another in the town.'

'Everybody will grant that, Edward—grant it privately, anyway. For six months, now, the village has been its own proper self once more—honest, narrow, self-righteous, and stingy.'

'It is what he always called it, to the day of his death—said it right out publicly, too.'

'Yes, and he was hated for it.'

'Oh, of course; but he didn't care. I reckon he was the best-hated man among us, except the Reverend Burgess.'

'Well, Burgess deserves it—he will never get another congregation here. Mean as the town is, it knows how to estimate *him*. Edward, doesn't it seem odd that the stranger should appoint Burgess to deliver the money?'

'Well, yes—it does. That is—that is—'

'Why so much that-*is*-ing? Would *you* select him?'

'Mary, maybe the stranger knows him better than this village does.'

'Much *that* would help Burgess!'

The husband seemed perplexed for an answer; the wife kept a steady eye upon him, and waited. Finally Richards said, with the hesitancy of one who is making a statement which is likely to encounter doubt,

'Mary, Burgess is not a bad man.'

His wife was certainly surprised.

'Nonsense!' she exclaimed.

'He is not a bad man. I know. The whole of his unpopularity had its foundation in that one thing—the thing that made so much noise.'

'That "one thing," indeed! As if that "one thing" wasn't enough, all by itself.'

'Plenty. Plenty. Only he wasn't guilty of it.'

'How you talk! Not guilty of it! Everybody knows he *was* guilty.'

'Mary, I give you my word—he was innocent.'

'I can't believe it and I don't. How do you know?'

'It is a confession. I am ashamed, but I will make it. I was the only man who knew he was innocent. I could have saved him, and—and—well, you know how the town was wrought up—I hadn't the pluck to do it. It would have turned everybody against me. I felt mean, ever so mean; but I didn't dare; I hadn't the manliness to face that.'

Mary looked troubled, and for a while was silent. Then she said stammeringly:

'I—I don't think it would have done for you to—to—One mustn't—er—public opinion—one has to be so careful—so—' It was a difficult road, and she got mired; but after a little she got started again. 'It

was a great pity, but— Why, we couldn't afford it, Edward—we couldn't indeed. Oh, I wouldn't have had you do it for anything!'

'It would have lost us the good-will of so many people, Mary; and then—and then—'

'What troubles me now is, what *he* thinks of us, Edward.'

'He? *He* doesn't suspect that I could have saved him.'

'Oh,' exclaimed the wife, in a tone of relief, 'I am glad of that. As long as he doesn't know that you could have saved him, he—he—well that makes it a great deal better. Why, I might have known he didn't know, because he is always trying to be friendly with us, as little encouragement as we give him. More than once people have twitted me with it. There's the Wilsons, and the Wilcoxes, and the Harknesses, they take a mean pleasure in saying "*Your friend* Burgess," because they know it pesters me. I wish he wouldn't persist in liking us so; I can't think why he keeps at it.'

'I can explain it. It's another confession. When the thing was new and hot, and the town made a plan to ride him on a rail, my conscience hurt me so that I couldn't stand it, and I went privately and gave him notice, and he got out of the town and stayed out till it was safe to come back.'

'Edward! If the town had found it out—'

'*Don't!* It scares me yet, to think of it. I repented of it the minute it was done; and I was even afraid to tell you lest your face might betray it to somebody. I didn't sleep any that night, for worrying. But after a few days I saw that no one was going to suspect me, and after that I got to feeling glad I did it. And I feel glad yet, Mary—glad through and through.'

'So do I, now, for it would have been a dreadful way to treat him. Yes, I'm glad; for really you did owe him that, you know. But, Edward, suppose it should come out yet, some day!'

'It won't.'

'Why?'

'Because everybody thinks it was Goodson.'

'Of course they would!'

'Certainly. And of course *he* didn't care. They persuaded poor old Sawlsberry to go and charge it on him, and he went blustering over there and did it. Goodson looked him over, like as if he was hunting for a place on him that he could despise the most; then he says, "So you are the Committee of Inquiry, are you?" Sawlsberry said that was about what he was. "H'm. Do they require particulars, or do you reckon a kind of a *general* answer will do?" "If they require particulars, I will come back, Mr. Goodson; I will take the general answer first." "Very well, then, tell them to go to hell—I reckon that's general enough. And I'll give you some advice, Sawlsberry; when you come back for the particulars, fetch a basket to carry what is left of yourself home in." '

'Just like Goodson; it's got all the marks. He had only one vanity; he thought he could give advice better than any other person.'

'It settled the business, and saved us, Mary. The subject was dropped.'

'Bless you, I'm not doubting *that*.'

Then they took up the gold-sack mystery again, with strong interest. Soon the conversation began to suffer breaks—interruptions caused by absorbed thinkings. The breaks grew more and more frequent. At last Richards lost himself wholly in thought. He sat long, gazing vacantly at the floor, and by-and-by he began to punctuate his thoughts with little nervous movements of his hands that seemed to indicate vexation. Meantime his wife too had relapsed into a thoughtful silence, and her movements were beginning to show a troubled discomfort. Finally Richards got up and strode aimlessly about the room, ploughing his hands through his hair, much as a somnambulist might do who was having a bad dream. Then he seemed to arrive at a definite purpose; and without a word he put on his hat and passed quickly out of the house. His wife sat brooding, with a drawn face, and did not seem to be aware that she was alone. Now and then she murmured, 'Lead us not into t . . . but —but—we are so poor, so poor! . . . Lead us not into . . . Ah, who would be hurt by it?—and no one would ever know . . . Lead us . . .' The voice died out in mumblings. After a little she glanced up and muttered in a half-frightened, half-glad way—

'He is gone! But, oh dear, he may be too late—too late . . . Maybe not—maybe there is still time.' She rose and stood thinking, nervously clasping and unclasping her hands. A slight shudder shook her frame, and she said, out of a dry throat, 'God forgive me—it's awful to think such things—but . . . Lord, how we are made—how strangely we are made!'

She turned the light low, and slipped stealthily over and knelt down by the sack and felt of its ridgy sides with her hands, and fondled them lovingly; and there was a gloating light in her poor old eyes. She fell into fits of absence; and came half out of them at times to mutter 'If we had only waited!—oh, if we had only waited a little, and not been in such a hurry!'

Meantime Cox had gone home from his office and told his wife all about the strange thing that had happened, and they had talked it over eagerly, and guessed that the late Goodson was the only man in the town who could have helped a suffering stranger with so noble a sum as twenty dollars. Then there was a pause, and the two became thoughtful and silent. And by-and-by nervous and fidgety. At last the wife said, as if to herself,

'Nobody knows this secret but the Richardses . . . and us . . . nobody.'

The husband came out of his thinkings with a slight start, and gazed wistfully at his wife, whose face was become very pale; then he hesitatingly rose, and glanced furtively at his hat, then at his wife—a sort of mute inquiry. Mrs. Cox swallowed once or twice, with her hand at her throat, then in place of speech she nodded her head. In a moment she was alone, and mumbling to herself.

And now Richards and Cox were hurrying through the deserted streets, from opposite directions. They met, panting, at the foot of the printing-office stairs; by the night-light there they could read each other's face. Cox whispered:

'Nobody knows about this but us?'

The whispered answer was:

'Not a soul—on honour, not a soul!'

'If it isn't too late to—'

The men were starting up-stairs; at this moment they were overtaken by a boy, and Cox asked,

'Is that you, Johnny?'

'Yes, sir.'

'You needn't ship the early mail—nor *any* mail; wait till I tell you.'

'It's already gone, sir.'

'*Gone?*' It had the sound of an unspeakable disappointment in it.

'Yes, sir. Time-table for Brixton and all the towns beyond changed to-day, sir—had to get the papers in twenty minutes earlier than common. I had to rush; if I had been two minutes later—'

The men turned and walked slowly away, not waiting to hear the rest. Neither of them spoke during ten minutes; then Cox said, in a vexed tone,

'What possessed you to be in such a hurry, I can't make out.'

The answer was humble enough:

'I see it now, but somehow I never thought, you know, until it was too late. But the next time—'

'Next time be hanged! It won't come in a thousand years.'

Then the friends separated without a good-night, and dragged themselves home with the gait of mortally stricken men. At their homes their wives sprang up with an eager 'Well?'—then saw the answer with their eyes and sank down sorrowing, without waiting for it to come in words. In both houses a discussion followed of a heated sort —a new thing; there had been discussions before, but not heated ones, not ungentle ones. The discussions to-night were a sort of seeming plagiarisms of each other. Mrs. Richards said:

'If you had only waited, Edward—if you had only stopped to think; but no, you must run straight to the printing-office and spread it all over the world.'

'It *said* publish it.'

'That is nothing; it also said do it privately, if you liked. There, now—is that true, or not?'

'Why, yes—yes, it is true; but when I thought what a stir it would make, and what a compliment it was to Hadleyburg that a stranger should trust it so—'

'Oh, certainly, I know all that; but if you had only stopped to think, you would have seen that you *couldn't* find the right man, because he is in his grave, and hasn't left chick nor child nor relation behind him; and as long as the money went to somebody that awfully needed it, and nobody would be hurt by it, and—and—'

She broke down, crying. Her husband tried to think of some comforting thing to say, and presently came out with this:

'But after all, Mary, it must be for the best—it *must* be; we know that. And we must remember that it was so ordered—'

'Ordered! Oh, everything's *ordered*, when a person has to find some way out when he has been stupid. Just the same, it was *ordered* that the money should come to us in this special way, and it was you that must take it on yourself to go meddling with the designs of Providence—and who gave you the right? It was wicked, that is what it was—just blasphemous presumption, and no more becoming to a meek and humble professor of—'

'But, Mary, you know how we have been trained all our lives long, like the whole village, till it is absolutely second nature to us to stop not a single moment to think when there's an honest thing to be done—'

'Oh, I know it, I know it—it's been one everlasting training and training and training in honesty—

honesty shielded, from the very cradle, against every possible temptation, and so it's *artificial* honesty, and weak as water when temptation comes, as we have seen this night. God knows I never had shade nor shadow of a doubt of my petrified and indestructible honesty until now—and now, under the very first big and real temptation, I—Edward, it is my belief that this town's honesty is as rotten as mine is; as rotten as yours. It is a mean town, a hard, stingy town, and hasn't a virtue in the world but this honesty it is so celebrated for and so conceited about; and so help me, I do believe that if ever the day comes that its honesty falls under great temptation, its grand reputation will go to ruin like a house of cards. There, now, I've made confession, and I feel better; I am a humbug, and I've been one all my life, without knowing it. Let no man call me honest again—I will not have it.'

'I— Well, Mary, I feel a good deal as you do: I certainly do. It seems strange, too, so strange. I never could have believed it—never.'

A long silence followed; both were sunk in thought. At last the wife looked up and said:

'I know what you are thinking, Edward.'

Richards had the embarrassed look of a person who is caught.

'I am ashamed to confess it, Mary, but—'

'It's no matter, Edward, I was thinking the same question myself.'

'I hope so. State it.'

'You were thinking, if a body could only guess out *what the remark was* that Goodson made to the stranger.'

'It's perfectly true. I feel guilty and ashamed. And you?'

'I'm past it. Let us make a pallet here; we've got to stand watch till the bank vault opens in the morning and admits the sack. . . . Oh dear, oh dear—if we hadn't made the mistake!'

The pallet was made, and Mary said:

'The open sesame—what could it have been? I do wonder what that remark could have been. But come; we will get to bed now.'

'And sleep?'

'No; think.'

'Yes; think.'

By this time the Coxes too had completed their spat and their reconciliation, and were turning in —to think, to think, and toss, and fret, and worry over what the remark could possibly have been which Goodson made to the stranded derelict; that golden remark; that remark worth forty thousand dollars, cash.

The reason that the village telegraph-office was open later than usual that night was this: The foreman of Cox's paper was the local representative of the Associated Press. One might say its honorary representative, for it wasn't four times a year that he could furnish thirty words that would be accepted. But this time it was different. His despatch stating what he had caught got an instant answer:

Send the whole thing—all the details—twelve hundred words.

A colossal order! The foreman filled the bill; and he was the proudest man in the State. By breakfast-time the next morning the name of Hadleyburg the Incorruptible was on every lip in America, from Montreal to the Gulf, from the glaciers of Alaska to the orange-groves of Florida; and millions and millions of people were discussing the stranger and his money-sack, and wondering if the right man would be found, and hoping some more news about the matter would come soon—right away.

II

Hadleyburg village woke up world-celebrated—astonished—happy—vain. Vain beyond imagination. Its nineteen principal citizens and their wives went about shaking hands with each other, and beaming, and smiling, and congratulating, and saying *this* thing adds a new word to the dictionary—*Hadleyburg*, synonym for *incorruptible*—destined to live in dictionaries for ever! And the minor and unimportant citizens and their wives went around acting in much the same way. Everybody ran to the bank to see the gold-sack; and before noon grieved and envious crowds began to flock in from Brixton and all neighbouring towns; and that afternoon and next day reporters began to arrive from everywhere to verify the sack and its history and write the whole thing up anew, and make dashing free-hand pictures of the sack, and of Richards's house, and the bank, and the Presbyterian church, and the Baptist church, and the public square, and the town-hall where the test would be applied and the money delivered; and damnable portraits of the Richardses, and Pinkerton the banker, and Cox, and the foreman, and Reverend Burgess, and the postmaster—and even of Jack Halliday, who was the loafing, good-natured, no-account, irreverent fisherman, hunter, boys' friend, stray-dogs'

friend, typical 'Sam Lawson' of the town. The little mean, smirking, oily Pinkerton showed the sack to all comers, and rubbed his sleek palms together pleasantly, and enlarged upon the town's fine old reputation for honesty and upon this wonderful endorsement of it, and hoped and believed that the example would now spread far and wide over the American world, and be epoch-making in the matter of moral regeneration. And so on, and so on.

By the end of a week things had quieted down again; the wild intoxication of pride and joy had sobered to a soft, sweet, silent delight—a sort of deep, nameless, unutterable content. All faces bore a look of peaceful, holy happiness.

Then a change came. It was a gradual change; so gradual that its beginnings were hardly noticed; maybe were not noticed at all, except by Jack Halliday, who always noticed everything; and always made fun of it, too, no matter what it was. He began to throw out chaffing remarks about people not looking quite so happy as they did a day or two ago; and next he claimed that the new aspect was deepening to positive sadness; next, that it was taking on a sick look; and finally he said that everybody was become so moody, thoughtful, and absent-minded that he could rob the meanest man in town of a cent out of the bottom of his breeches pocket and not disturb his reverie.

At this stage—or at about this stage—a saying like this was dropped at bedtime—with a sigh, usually—by the head of each of the nineteen principal households:

'Ah, what *could* have been the remark that Goodson made?'

And straightway—with a shudder—came this, from the man's wife:

'Oh, *don't*! What horrible thing are you mulling in your mind? Put it away from you, for God's sake!'

But that question was wrung from those men again the next night—and got the same retort. But weaker.

And the third night the men uttered the question yet again—with anguish, and absently. This time—and the following night—the wives fidgeted feebly, and tried to say something. But didn't.

And the night after that they found their tongues and responded—longingly:

'Oh, if we *could* only guess!'

Halliday's comments grew daily more and more sparklingly disagreeable and disparaging. He went diligently about, laughing at the town, individually and in mass. But his laugh was the only one left in the village: it fell upon a hollow and mournful vacancy and emptiness. Not even a smile was findable anywhere. Halliday carried a cigar-box around on a tripod, playing that it was a camera, and halted all passers and aimed the thing and said 'Ready!—now look pleasant, please,' but not even this capital joke could surprise the dreary faces into any softening.

So three weeks passed—one week was left. It was Saturday evening after supper. Instead of the aforetime Saturday-evening flutter and bustle and shopping and larking, the streets were empty and desolate. Richards and his old wife sat apart in their little parlour—miserable and thinking. This was become their evening habit now: the life-long habit which had preceded it, of reading, knitting, and contented chat, or receiving or paying neighbourly calls, was dead and gone and forgotten, ages ago—two or three weeks ago; nobody talked now, nobody read, nobody visited—the whole village sat at home, sighing, worrying, silent. Trying to guess out that remark.

The postman left a letter. Richards glanced listlessly at the superscription and the post-mark—unfamiliar, both—and tossed the letter on the table and resumed his might-have-beens and his hopeless dull miseries where he had left them off. Two or three hours later his wife got wearily up and was going away to bed without a good-night—custom now—but she stopped near the letter and eyed it awhile with a dead interest, then broke it open, and began to skim it over. Richards, sitting there with his chair tilted back against the wall and his chin between his knees, heard something fall. It was his wife. He sprang to her side, but she cried out:

'Leave me alone, I am too happy. Read the letter—read it!'

He did. He devoured it, his brain reeling. The letter was from a distant State, and it said:

I am a stranger to you, but no matter: I have something to tell. I have just arrived home from Mexico, and learned about that episode. Of course you do not know who made that remark, but I know, and I am the only person living who does know. It was GOODSON. I knew him well, many years ago. I passed through your village that very night, and was his guest till the midnight train came along. I overheard him make that remark to the stranger in the dark—it was in Hale Alley. He and I talked of it the rest of the way home, and while smoking in his house. He mentioned many of your villagers in the course of his talk—most of them in a very uncomplimentary way, but two or three favourably: among these latter yourself. I say "favourably"—nothing stronger. I remember his saying he did not actually LIKE any person in the town—not one; but that you—*I* THINK he said you—am almost sure—had done him a very great service once, possibly without knowing the full value of it, and he wished he had a fortune, he would leave it to you when he died, and a curse apiece for the rest of the citizens. Now, then, if it was you that did him that service, you are his legitimate heir, and entitled to the sack of gold. I know that I can trust to your honour and honesty, for in a citizen of Hadleyburg these virtues are an unfailing inheritance, and so I am going to reveal to you the remark, well satisfied that if you are not the right man you will seek and find the right one and see that poor Goodson's debt of gratitude for the service referred to is paid. This is the remark: 'YOU ARE FAR FROM BEING A BAD MAN: GO, AND REFORM.'

HOWARD L. STEPHENSON.

'Oh, Edward, the money is ours, and I am so grateful, *oh*, so grateful,—kiss me, dear, it's for ever since we kissed—and we needed it so—the money—and now you are free of Pinkerton and his bank, and nobody's slave any more; it seems to me I could fly for joy.'

It was a happy half-hour that the couple spent there on the settee caressing each other; it was the old days come again—days that had begun with their courtship and lasted without a break till the stranger brought the deadly money. By-and-by the wife said:

'Oh, Edward, how lucky it was you did him that grand service, poor Goodson! I never liked him, but I love him now. And it was fine and beautiful of you never to mention it or brag about it.' Then, with a touch of reproach, 'But you ought to have told *me*, Edward, you ought to have told your wife, you know.'

'Well, I—er—well, Mary, you see—'

'Now stop hemming and hawing, and tell me about it, Edward. I always loved you, and now I'm proud of you. Everybody believes there was only one good generous soul in this village, and now it turns out that you— Edward, why don't you tell me?'

'Well—er—er— Why, Mary, I can't!'

'You *can't*? *Why* can't you?'

'You see, he—well, he—he made me promise I wouldn't.'

The wife looked him over, and said, very slowly: 'Made—you—promise? Edward, what do you tell me that for?'

'Mary, do you think I would lie?'

She was troubled and silent for a moment, then she laid her hand within his and said:

'No . . . no. We have wandered far enough from our bearings—God spare us that! In all your life you have never uttered a lie. But now—now that the foundations of things seem to be crumbling from under us, we—we—' She lost her voice for a moment, then said, brokenly, 'Lead us not into temptation. . . . I think you made the promise, Edward. Let it rest so. Let us keep away from that ground. Now—that is all gone by; let us be happy again; it is no time for clouds.'

Edward found it something of an effort to comply, for his mind kept wandering—trying to remember what the service was that he had done Goodson.

The couple lay awake the most of the night, Mary happy and busy, Edward busy, but not so happy. Mary was planning what she would do with the money. Edward was trying to recall that service. At first his conscience was sore on account of the lie he had told Mary—if it was a lie. After much reflection—suppose it *was* a lie? What then? Was it such a great matter? Aren't we always *acting* lies? Then why not tell them? Look at Mary—look what she had done. While he was hurrying off on his honest errand, what was she doing? Lamenting because the papers hadn't been destroyed and the money kept. Is theft better than lying?

That point lost its sting—the lie dropped into the background and left comfort behind it. The next point came to the front: *had* he rendered that service? Well, here was Goodson's own evidence as reported in Stephenson's letter; there could be no better evidence than that—it was even *proof* that he had rendered it. Of course. So that point was settled. . . . No, not quite. He recalled with a wince that this unknown Mr. Stephenson was just a trifle unsure as to whether the performer of it was Richards or some other—and, oh dear, he had put Richards on his honour! He must himself decide whither that money must go—and Mr. Stephenson was not doubting that if he was the wrong man he would go honourably and find the right one. Oh, it was odious to put a man in such a situation—ah, why couldn't Stephenson

have left out that doubt? What did he want to intrude that for?

Further reflection. How did it happen that *Richards's* name remained in Stephenson's mind as indicating the right man, and not some other man's name? That looked good. Yes, that looked very good. In fact it went on looking better and better, straight along—until by-and-by it grew into positive *proof*. And then Richards put the matter at once out of his mind, for he had a private instinct that a proof once established is better left so.

He was feeling reasonably comfortable now, but there was still one other detail that kept pushing itself on his notice: of course he had done that service—that was settled; but what *was* that service? He must recall it—he would not go to sleep till he had recalled it; it would make his peace of mind perfect. And so he thought and thought. He thought of a dozen things—possible services, even probable services—but none of them seemed adequate, none of them seemed large enough, none of them seemed worth the money—worth the fortune Goodson had wished he could leave in his will. And besides, he couldn't remember having done them, anyway. Now, then—now, then—what *kind* of a service would it be that would make a man so inordinately grateful? Ah—the saving of his soul! That must be it. Yes, he could remember, now, how he once set himself the task of converting Goodson, and laboured at it as much as—he was going to say three months; but upon closer examination it shrunk to a month, then to a week, then to a day, then to nothing. Yes, he remembered now, and with unwelcome vividness, that Goodson had told him to go to thunder and mind his own business—*he* wasn't hankering to follow Hadleyburg to heaven!

So that solution was a failure—he hadn't saved Goodson's soul. Richards was discouraged. Then after a little came another idea: had he saved Goodson's property? No, that wouldn't do—he hadn't any. His life? That is it! Of course. Why, he might have thought of it before. This time he was on the right track, sure. His imagination-mill was hard at work in a minute, now.

Thereafter, during a stretch of two exhausting hours, he was busy saving Goodson's life. He saved it in all kinds of difficult and perilous ways. In every case he got it saved satisfactorily up to a certain point; then, just as he was beginning to get well persuaded that it had really happened, a troublesome detail would turn up which made the whole thing impossible. As in the matter of drowning, for instance. In that case he had swum out and tugged Goodson ashore in an unconscious state with a great crowd looking on and applauding, but when he had got it all thought out and was just beginning to remember all about it, a whole swarm of disqualifying details arrived on the ground: the town would have known of the circumstance, Mary would have known of it, it would glare like a limelight in his own memory instead of being an inconspicuous service which he had possibly rendered 'without knowing its full value.' And at this point he remembered that he couldn't swim anyway.

Ah—*there* was a point which he had been overlooking from the start: it had to be a service which he had rendered 'possibly without knowing the full value of it.' Why, really, that ought to be an easy hunt—much easier than those others. And sure enough, by-and-by he found it. Goodson, years and years ago, came near marrying a very sweet and pretty girl, named Nancy Hewitt, but in some way or other the match had been broken off; the girl died, Goodson remained a bachelor, and by-and-by became a soured one and a frank despiser of the human species. Soon after the girl's death the village found out, or thought it had found out, that she carried a spoonful of negro blood in her veins. Richards worked at these details a good while, and in the end he thought he remembered things concerning them which must have gotten mislaid in his memory through long neglect. He seemed to dimly remember that it was *he* that found out about the negro blood; that it was he that told the village; that the village told Goodson where they got it; that he thus saved Goodson from marrying the tainted girl; that he had done him this great service 'without knowing the full value of it,' in fact without knowing that he *was* doing it; but that Goodson knew the value of it, and what a narrow escape he had had, and so went to his grave grateful to his benefactor and wishing he had a fortune to leave him. It was all clear and simple, now, and the more he went over it the more luminous and certain it grew; and at last, when he nestled to sleep, satisfied and happy, he remembered the whole thing just as if it had been yesterday. In fact, he dimly remembered Goodson's *telling* him his gratitude once. Meantime Mary had spent six thousand dollars on a new house for herself and a pair of slippers for her pastor, and then had fallen peacefully to rest.

That same Saturday evening the postman had delivered a letter to each of the other principal citizens—nineteen letters in all. No two of the envelopes were alike, and no two of the superscriptions were in the same hand, but the letters inside were just like each other in every detail but one. They were exact copies of the letter received by Richards—handwriting and all—and were all signed by Stephenson, but in place of Richards's name each receiver's own name appeared.

All night long eighteen principal citizens did what their caste-brother Richards was doing at the same time—they put in their energies trying to remember what notable service it was that they had unconsciously done Barclay Goodson. In no case was it a holiday job; still they succeeded.

And while they were at this work, which was difficult, their wives put in the night spending the money, which was easy. During that one night the nineteen wives spent an average of seven thousand dollars each out of the forty thousand in the sack—a hundred and thirty-three thousand altogether.

Next day there was a surprise for Jack Halliday. He noticed that the faces of the nineteen chief citizens and their wives bore that expression of peaceful and holy happiness again. He could not understand it, neither was he able to invent any remarks about it that could damage it or disturb it. And so it was his turn to be dissatisfied with life. His private guesses at the reasons for the happiness failed in all instances, upon examination. When he met Mrs. Wilcox and noticed the placid ecstasy in her face, he said to himself, 'Her cat has had kittens'—and went and asked the cook; it was not so, the cook had detected the happiness, but did not know the cause. When Halliday found the duplicate ecstasy in the face of 'Shadbelly' Billson (village nickname), he was sure some neighbour of Billson's had broken his leg, but inquiry showed that this had not happened. The subdued ecstasy in Gregory Yate's face could mean but one thing—he was a mother-in-law short; it was another mistake. 'And Pinkerton—Pinkerton—he has collected ten cents that he thought he was going to lose.' And so on, and so on. In some cases the guesses had to remain in doubt, in the others they proved distinct errors. In the end Halliday said to himself, 'Anyway it foots up that there's nineteen Hadleyburg families temporarily in heaven: I don't know how it happened; I only know Providence is off duty to-day.'

An architect and builder from the next State had lately ventured to set up a small business in this unpromising village, and his sign had now been hanging out a week. Not a customer yet; he was a discouraged man, and sorry he had come. But his weather changed suddenly now. First one and then another chief citizen's wife said to him privately:

'Come to my house Monday week—but say nothing about it for the present. We think of building.'

He got eleven invitations that day. That night he wrote his daughter and broke off her match with her student. He said she could marry a mile higher than that.

Pinkerton the banker and two or three other well-to-do men planned country-seats—but waited. That kind don't count their chickens until they are hatched.

The Wilsons devised a grand new thing—a fancy-dress ball. They made no actual promises, but told all their acquaintanceship in confidence that they were thinking the matter over and thought they should give it—'and if we do, you will be invited, of course.' People were surprised, and said, one to another, 'Why, they are crazy, those poor Wilsons, they can't afford it.' Several among the nineteen said privately to their husbands, 'It is a good idea, we will keep still till their cheap thing is over, then *we* will give one that will make it sick.'

The days drifted along, and the bill of future squanderings rose higher and higher, wilder and wilder, more and more foolish and reckless. It began to look as if every member of the nineteen would not only spend his whole forty thousand dollars before receiving-day, but be actually in debt by the time he got the money. In some cases light-headed people did not stop with planning to spend, they really spent—on credit. They bought land, mortgages, farms, speculative stocks, fine clothes, horses, and various other things, paid down the bonus, and made themselves liable for the rest—at ten days. Presently the sober second thought came, and Halliday noticed that a ghastly anxiety was beginning to show up in a good many faces. Again he was puzzled, and didn't know what to make of it. 'The Wilcox kittens aren't dead, for they weren't born; nobody's broken a leg; there's no shrinkage in mother-in-laws; *nothing* has happened—it is an insolvable mystery.'

There was another puzzled man, too—the Rev. Mr. Burgess. For days, wherever he went, people seemed to follow him or to be watching out for him; and if he ever found himself in a retired spot, a member of the nineteen would be sure to appear, thrust an envelope privately into his hand, whisper 'To be opened at the town-hall Friday evening,' then vanish away like a guilty thing. He was expecting that there might be one claimant for the sack—doubtful, however, Goodson being dead—but it never occurred to him that all this crowd might be claimants. When the great Friday came at last, he found that he had nineteen envelopes.

III

The town-hall had never looked finer. The platform at the end of it was backed by a showy draping of flags; at intervals along the walls were festoons of flags; the gallery fronts were clothed in flags; the supporting columns were swathed in flags; all this was to impress the stranger, for he would be there in considerable force, and in a large degree he would be connected with the press. The house was full. The 412 fixed seats were occupied; also the 68 extra chairs which had been packed into the aisles; the steps of the platform were occupied; some distinguished strangers were given seats on the platform; at the horseshoe of tables which fenced the front and sides of the platform sat a strong force of special correspondents who had come from everywhere. It was the best-dressed house the town had ever produced. There were some tolerably expensive toilets there, and in several cases the ladies who wore them had the look of being unfamiliar with that kind of clothes. At least the town thought they had that look, but the notion could have arisen from the town's knowledge of the fact that these ladies had never inhabited such clothes before.

The gold-sack stood on a little table at the front of the platform where all the house could see it. The bulk of the house gazed at it with a burning interest, a mouth-watering interest, a wistful and pathetic interest; a minority of nineteen couples gazed at it tenderly, lovingly, proprietarily, and the male half of this minority kept saying over to themselves the moving little impromptu speeches of thankfulness for the audience's applause and congratulations which they were presently going to get up and deliver. Every now and then one of these got a piece of paper out of his vest pocket and privately glanced at it to refresh his memory.

Of course there was a buzz of conversation going on—there always is; but at last, when the Rev. Mr. Burgess rose and laid his hand on the sack, he could hear his microbes gnaw, the place was so still. He related the curious history of the sack, then went on to speak in warm terms of Hadleyburg's old and well-earned reputation for spotless honesty, and of the town's just pride in this reputation. He said that this reputation was a treasure of priceless value; that under Providence its value had now become inestimably enhanced, for the recent episode had spread this fame far and wide, and thus had focussed the eyes of the American world upon this village, and made its name for all time, as he hoped and believed, a synonym for commercial incorruptibility. [*Applause.*] 'And who is to be the guardian of this noble fame—the community as a whole? No! The responsibility is individual, not communal. From this day forth each and every one of you is in his own person its special guardian, and individually responsible that no harm shall come to it. Do you—does each of you—accept this great trust? [*Tumultuous assent.*] Then all is well. Transmit it to your children and to your children's children. To-day your purity is beyond reproach—see to it that it shall remain so. To-day there is not a person in your community who could be beguiled to touch a penny not his own—see to it that you abide in this grace. ['*We will! we will!*'] This is not the place to make comparisons between ourselves and other communities—some of them ungracious towards us; they have their ways, we have ours; let us be content. [*Applause.*] I am done. Under my hand, my friends, rests a stranger's eloquent recognition of what we are; through him the world will always henceforth know what we are. We do not know who he is, but in your name I utter your gratitude, and ask you to raise your voices in indorsement.'

The house rose in a body and made the walls quake with the thunders of its thankfulness for the space of a long minute. Then it sat down, and Mr. Burgess took an envelope out of his pocket. The house held its breath while he slit the envelope open and took from it a slip of paper. He read its contents—slowly and impressively—the audience listening with tranced attention to this magic document, each of whose words stood for an ingot of gold:

'"*The remark which I made to the distressed stranger was this: 'You are very far from being a bad man; go, and reform.'*"' Then he continued: 'We shall know in a moment now whether the remark here quoted corresponds with the one concealed in the sack; and if that shall prove to be so —and it undoubtedly will—this sack of gold belongs to a fellow-citizen who will henceforth stand before the nation as the symbol of the special virtue which has made our town famous throughout the land—Mr. Billson!'

The house had gotten itself all ready to burst into the proper tornado of applause; but instead of doing it, it seemed stricken with a paralysis; there was a deep hush for a moment or two, then a wave of whispered murmurs swept the place—of about this tenor: '*Billson!* oh, come, this is *too* thin! Twenty dollars to a stranger—or *anybody—Billson!* Tell it to the marines!' And now at this point the house caught its breath all of a sudden in a new access of astonishment, for it discovered that whereas in one part of the hall Deacon Billson was standing up with his head meekly bowed, in another part of it Lawyer Wilson was doing the same. There was a wondering silence now for a while. Everybody was puzzled, and nineteen couples were surprised and indignant.

Billson and Wilson turned and stared at each other. Billson asked, bitingly:

'Why do *you* rise, Mr. Wilson?'

'Because I have a right to. Perhaps you will be good enough to explain to the house why *you* rise.'

'With great pleasure. Because I wrote that paper.'

'It is an impudent falsity! I wrote it myself.'

It was Burgess's turn to be paralysed. He stood looking vacantly at first one of the men and then the other, and did not seem to know what to do. The house was stupefied. Lawyer Wilson spoke up now, and said:

'I ask the Chair to read the name signed to that paper.'

That brought the Chair to itself, and it read out the name:

' "John Wharton *Billson.*" '

'There!' shouted Billson, 'what have you got to say for yourself now? And what kind of apology are you going to make to me and to this insulted house for the imposture which you have attempted to play here?'

'No apologies are due, sir; and as for the rest of it, I publicly charge you with pilfering my note from Mr. Burgess and substituting a copy of it signed with your own name. There is no other way by which you could have gotten hold of the test-remark; I alone, of living men, possessed the secret of its wording.'

There was likely to be a scandalous state of things if this went on; everybody noticed with distress that the shorthand scribes were scribbling like mad; many people were crying 'Chair, chair!

Order! order!' Burgess rapped with his gavel, and said:

'Let us not forget the proprieties due. There has evidently been a mistake somewhere, but surely that is all. If Mr. Wilson gave me an envelope—and I remember now that he did—I still have it.'

He took one out of his pocket, opened it, glanced at it, looked surprised and worried, and stood silent a few moments. Then he waved his hand in a wandering and mechanical way, and made an effort or two to say something, then gave it up, despondently. Several voices cried out:

'Read it! read it! What is it?'

So he began, in a dazed and sleep-walker fashion:

' "*The remark which I made to the unhappy stranger was this: 'You are far from being a bad man.* [The house gazed at him marvelling.] *Go, and reform.*' " [*Murmurs:* 'Amazing! what can this mean?'] This one,' said the Chair, 'is signed Thurlow G. Wilson.'

'There!' cried Wilson, 'I reckon that settles it! I knew perfectly well my note was purloined.'

'Purloined!' retorted Billson. 'I'll let you know that neither you nor any man of your kidney must venture to—'

The Chair: 'Order, gentlemen, order! Take your seats, both of you, please.'

They obeyed, shaking their heads and grumbling angrily. The house was profoundly puzzled; it did not know what to do with this curious emergency. Presently Thompson got up. Thompson was the hatter. He would have liked to be a Nineteener; but such was not for him; his stock of hats was not considerable enough for the position. He said:

'Mr. Chairman, if I may be permitted to make a suggestion, can both of these gentlemen be right? I put it to you, sir, can both have happened to say the very same words to the stranger? It seems to me—'

The tanner got up and interrupted him. The tanner was a disgruntled man; he believed himself entitled to be a Nineteener, but he couldn't get recognition. It made him a little unpleasant in his ways and speech. Said he:

'Sho, *that's* not the point! *That* could happen —twice in a hundred years—but not the other thing. *Neither* of them gave the twenty dollars!' [*A ripple of applause.*]

Billson. 'I did!'

Wilson. 'I did!'

Then each accused the other of pilfering.

The Chair. 'Order! Sit down, if you please—

both of you. Neither of the notes has been out of my possession at any moment.'

A Voice. 'Good—that settles *that!*'

The Tanner. 'Mr. Chairman, one thing is now plain: one of these men has been eavesdropping under the other one's bed, and filching family secrets. If it is not unparliamentary to suggest it, I will remark that both are equal to it. [*The Chair.* 'Order! order!'] I withdraw the remark, sir, and will confine myself to suggesting that *if* one of them has overheard the other reveal the test-remark to his wife, we shall catch him now.'

A Voice. 'How?'

The Tanner. 'Easily. The two have not quoted the remark in exactly the same words. You would have noticed that, if there hadn't been a considerable stretch of time and an exciting quarrel inserted between the two readings.'

A Voice. 'Name the difference.'

The Tanner. 'The word *very* is in Billson's note, and not in the other.'

Many Voices. 'That's so—he's right!'

The Tanner. 'And so, if the Chair will examine the test-remark in the sack, we shall know which of these two frauds—[*The Chair.* 'Order!']—which of these two adventurers—[*The Chair.* 'Order! order!']—which of these two gentlemen—[*laughter and applause*]—is entitled to wear the belt as being the first dishonest blatherskite ever bred in this town—which he has dishonoured, and which will be a sultry place for him from now out!' [*Vigorous applause.*]

Many Voices. 'Open it!—open the sack!'

Mr. Burgess made a slit in the sack, slid his hand in, and brought out an envelope. In it were a couple of folded notes. He said:

'One of these is marked, "Not to be examined until all written communications which have been addressed to the Chair—if any—shall have been read." The other is marked "The Test." Allow me. It is worded—to wit:

' "I do not require that the first half of the remark which was made to me by my benefactor shall be quoted with exactness, for it was not striking, and could be forgotten; but its closing fifteen words are quite striking, and I think easily rememberable; unless *these* shall be accurately reproduced, let the applicant be regarded as an impostor. My benefactor began by saying he seldom gave advice to anyone, but that it always bore the hallmark of high value when he did give it. Then he said this—and it has never faded from my memory: *"You are far from being a bad man—"* '

Fifty Voices. 'That settles it—the money's Wilson's! Wilson! Wilson! Speech! Speech!'

People jumped up and crowded around Wilson, wringing his hand and congratulating fervently—meantime the Chair was hammering with the gavel and shouting:

'Order, gentlemen! Order! Order! Let me finish reading, please.' When quiet was restored, the reading was resumed—as follows:

Go, and reform—or, mark my words—some day, for your sins you will die and go to hell or Hadleyburg—TRY AND MAKE IT THE FORMER.

A ghastly silence followed. First an angry cloud began to settle darkly upon the faces of the citizenship; after a pause the cloud began to rise, and a tickled expression tried to take its place; tried so hard that it was only kept under with great and painful difficulty; the reporters, the Brixtonites, and other strangers bent their heads down and shielded their faces with their hands, and managed to hold in by main strength and heroic courtesy. At this most inopportune time burst upon the stillness the roar of a solitary voice—Jack Halliday's:

'*That's* got the hall-mark on it!'

Then the house let go, strangers and all. Even Mr. Burgess's gravity broke down presently, then the audience considered itself officially absolved from all restraint, and it made the most of its privilege. It was a good long laugh, and a tempestuously whole-hearted one, but it ceased at last—long enough for Mr. Burgess to try to resume, and for the people to get their eyes partially wiped; then it broke out again, and afterward yet again; then at last Burgess was able to get out these serious words:

'It is useless to try to disguise the fact—we find ourselves in the presence of a matter of grave import. It involves the honour of your town—it strikes at the town's good name. The difference of a single word between the test-remarks offered by Mr. Wilson and Mr. Billson was itself a serious thing, since it indicated that one or the other of these gentlemen had committed a theft—'

The two men were sitting limp, nerveless, crushed; but at these words both were electrified into movement, and started to get up.

'Sit down!' said the Chair, sharply, and they obeyed. 'That, as I have said, was a serious thing. And it was—but for only one of them. But the matter has become graver; for the honour of *both* is now in formidable peril. Shall I go even further, and say in inextricable peril? *Both* left out the crucial fifteen words.' He paused. During several moments he allowed the pervading stillness to gather and deepen its impressive effects, then added: 'There would seem to be but one way whereby this could happen. I ask these gentlemen—Was there *collusion?—agreement?*'

A low murmur sifted through the house; its import was, 'He's got them both.'

Billson was not used to emergencies; he sat in a helpless collapse. But Wilson was a lawyer. He struggled to his feet, pale and worried, and said:

'I ask the indulgence of the house while I explain this most painful matter. I am sorry to say what I am about to say, since it must inflict irreparable injury upon Mr. Billson, whom I have always esteemed and respected until now, and in whose invulnerability to temptation I entirely believed—as did you all. But for the preservation of my own honour I must speak—and with frankness. I confess with shame—and I now beseech your pardon for it—that I said to the ruined stranger all of the words contained in the test-remark, including the disparaging fifteen. [*Sensation.*] When the late publication was made I recalled them, and I resolved to claim the sack of coin, for by every right I was entitled to it. Now I will ask you to consider this point, and weigh it well; that stranger's gratitude to me that night knew no bounds; he said himself that he could find no words for it that were adequate, and that if he should ever be able he would repay me a thousandfold. Now, then, I ask you this; could I expect—could I believe—could I even remotely imagine—that, feeling as he did, he would do so ungrateful a thing as to add those quite unnecessary fifteen words to his test?—set a trap for me?—expose me as a slanderer of my own town before my own people assembled in a public hall? It was preposterous; it was impossible. His test would contain only the kindly opening clause of my remark. Of that I had no shadow of doubt. You would have thought as I did. You would not have expected a base betrayal from one whom you had befriended and against whom you had committed no offence. And so with perfect confidence, perfect trust, I wrote on a piece of paper the opening words—ending with "Go, and reform,"—and signed it. When I was about to put it in an envelope I was called into my back office, and without thinking I left the paper lying open on my desk.' He stopped, turned his head slowly toward Billson, waited a moment, then added: 'I ask you to note this; when I returned, a little later, Mr.

Billson was retiring by my street door.' [*Sensation.*]

In a moment Billson was on his feet and shouting:

'It's a lie! It's an infamous lie!'

The Chair. 'Be seated, sir! Mr. Wilson has the floor.'

Billson's friends pulled him into his seat and quieted him, and Wilson went on:

'Those are the simple facts. My note was now lying in a different place on the table from where I had left it. I noticed that, but attached no importance to it, thinking a draught had blown it there. That Mr. Billson would read a private paper was a thing which could not occur to me; he was an honourable man, and he would be above that. If you will allow me to say it, I think his extra word "*very*" stands explained: it is attributable to a defect of memory. I was the only man in the world who could furnish here any detail of the test-mark—by *honourable* means. I have finished.'

There is nothing in the world like a persuasive speech to fuddle the mental apparatus and upset the convictions and debauch the emotions of an audience not practised in the tricks and delusions of oratory. Wilson sat down victorious. The house submerged him in tides of approving applause; friends swarmed to him and shook him by the hand and congratulated him, and Billson was shouted down and not allowed to say a word. The Chair hammered and hammered with its gavel, and kept shouting:

'But let us proceed, gentlemen, let us proceed!'

At last there was a measurable degree of quiet, and the hatter said:

'But what is there to proceed with, sir, but to deliver the money!'

Voices. 'That's it! That's it! Come forward, Wilson!'

The Hatter. 'I move three cheers for Mr. Wilson, Symbol of the special virtue which—'

The cheers burst forth before he could finish; and in the midst of them—and in the midst of the clamour of the gavel also—some enthusiasts mounted Wilson on a big friend's shoulder and were going to fetch him in triumph to the platform. The Chair's voice now rose above the noise:

'Order! To your places! You forget that there is still a document to be read.' When quiet had been restored he took up the document, and was going to read it, but laid it down again saying 'I forgot; this is not to be read until all written communications received by me have first been read.' He took an envelope out of his pocket, removed its en-

closure, glanced at it—seemed astonished—held it out and gazed at it—stared at it.

Twenty or thirty voices cried out:

'What is it? Read it! read it!'

And he did—slowly, and wondering:

' "The remark which I made to the stranger— [*Voices.* 'Hello! how's this?']—was this: 'You are far from being a bad man. [*Voices.* 'Great Scott!'] Go, and reform.' " [*Voice.* 'Oh, saw my leg off!'] Signed by Mr. Pinkerton the banker.'

The pandemonium of delight which turned itself loose now was of a sort to make the judicious weep. Those whose withers were unwrung laughed till the tears ran down; the reporters, in throes of laughter, set down disordered pot-hooks which would never in the world be decipherable; and a sleeping dog jumped up scared out of its wits, and barked itself crazy at the turmoil. All manner of cries were scattered through the din: 'We're getting rich—*two* Symbols of Incorruptibility!—without counting Billson!' '*Three!*—count Shadbelly in —we can't have too many!' 'All right—Billson's elected!' 'Alas, poor Wilson! victim of *two* thieves!'

A Powerful Voice. 'Silence! The Chair's fished up something more out of its pocket.'

Voices. 'Hurrah! Is it something fresh? Read it! read! read!'

The Chair [*reading*]. ' "The remark which I made," etc. "You are far from being a bad man. Go," etc. Signed, "Gregory Yates." '

Tornado of Voices. 'Four Symbols!' ' 'Rah for Yates!' 'Fish again!'

The house was in a roaring humour now, and ready to get all the fun out of the occasion that might be in it. Several Nineteeners, looking pale and distressed, got up and began to work their way towards the aisles, but a score of shouts went up:

'The doors, the doors—close the doors; no Incorruptible shall leave this place! Sit down, everybody!'

The mandate was obeyed.

'Fish again! Read! read!'

The Chair fished again, and once more the familiar words began to fall from its lips—' "You are far from being a bad man—" '

'Name! name! What's his name?'

' "L. Ingoldsby Sargent." '

'Five elected! Pile up the Symbols! Go on, go on!'

' "You are far from being a bad—" '

'Name! name!'

' "Nicholas Whitworth." '

'Hooray! hooray! it's a symbolical day!'

Somebody wailed in, and began to sing this rhyme (leaving out 'it's') to the lovely 'Mikado' tune of 'When a man's afraid of a beautiful maid;' the audience joined in, with joy; then, just in time, somebody contributed another line—

And don't you this forget—

The house roared it out. A third line was at once furnished –

Corruptibles far from Hadleyburg are—

The house roared that one too. As the last note died, Jack Halliday's voice rose high and clear, freighted with a final line—

But the Symbols are here you bet!

That was sung, with booming enthusiasm. Then the happy house started in at the beginning and sang the four lines through twice, with immense swing and dash, and finished up with a crashing three-times-three and a tiger for 'Hadleyburg the Incorruptible and all Symbols of it which we shall find worthy to receive the hall-mark to-night.'

Then the shoutings at the Chair began again, all over the place:

'Go on! go on! Read! read some more! Read all you've got!'

'That's it—go on! We are winning eternal celebrity!'

A dozen men got up now and began to protest. They said that this farce was the work of some abandoned joker, and was an insult to the whole community. Without a doubt these signatures were all forgeries—

'Sit down! sit down! Shut up! You are confessing. We'll find *your* names in the lot.'

'Mr. Chairman, how many of those envelopes have you got?'

The Chair counted.

'Together with those that have been already examined, there are nineteen.'

A storm of derisive applause broke out.

'Perhaps they all contain the secret. I move that you open them all and read every signature that is attached to a note of that sort—and read also the first eight words of the note.'

'Second the motion!'

It was put and carried—uproariously. Then poor old Richards got up, and his wife rose and stood at his side. Her head was bent down, so that none might see that she was crying. Her husband gave her his arm, and so supporting her, he began to speak in a quavering voice:

'My friends, you have known us two—Mary and me—all our lives, and I think you have liked us and respected us—'

The Chair interrupted him:

'Allow me. It is quite true—that which you are saying, Mr. Richards; this town *does* know you two; it *does* like you; it *does* respect you; more—it honours you and *loves* you—'

Halliday's voice rang out:

'That's the hall-marked truth, too! If the Chair is right, let the house speak up and say it. Rise! Now, then—hip! hip! hip!—all together!'

The house rose in mass, faced toward the old couple eagerly, filled the air with a snow-storm of waving handkerchiefs, and delivered the cheers with all its affectionate heart.

The Chair then continued:

'What I was going to say is this: We know your good heart, Mr. Richards, but this is not a time for the exercise of charity toward offenders. [*Shouts of 'Right! right!'*] I see your generous purpose in your face, but I cannot allow you to plead for these men—'

'But I was going to—'

'Please take your seat, Mr. Richards. We must examine the rest of these notes—simple fairness to the men who have already been exposed requires this. As soon as that has been done—I give you my word for this—you shall be heard.'

Many voices. 'Right!—the Chair is right—no interruption can be permitted at this stage! Go on!—the names! the names!—according to the terms of the motion!'

The old couple sat reluctantly down, and the husband whispered to the wife, 'It is pitifully hard to have to wait; the shame will be greater than ever when they find we were only going to plead for *ourselves.*'

Straightway the jollity broke loose again with the reading of the names.

' "You are far from being a bad man—" Signature, "Robert J. Titmarsh." '

' "You are far from being a bad man—" Signature, "Eliphalet Weeks." '

' "You are far from being a bad man—" Signature, "Oscar B. Wilder." '

At this point the house lit upon the idea of taking the eight words out of the Chairman's hands. He was not unthankful for that. Thenceforward he held up each note in its turn and waited. The house droned out the eight words in a massed and measured and musical deep volume of sound (with a daringly close resemblance to a well-known church chant)—'You are f-a-r from being a b-a-a-a-d man.' Then the Chair said, 'Signature, "Archibald Wilcox."' And so on, and so on, name after name, and everybody had an increasingly and gloriously good time except the wretched Nineteen. Now and then, when a particularly shining name was called, the house made the Chair wait while it chanted the whole of the test-remark from the beginning to the closing words, 'And go to hell or Hadleyburg—try and make it the for-or-m-e-r!' and in these special cases they added a grand and agonised and imposing 'A-a-a-a-*men!*'

The list dwindled, dwindled, dwindled, poor old Richards keeping tally of the count, wincing when a name resembling his own was pronounced, and waiting in miserable suspense for the time to come when it would be his humiliating privilege to rise with Mary and finish his plea, which he was intending to word thus: '. . . for until now we have never done any wrong thing, but have gone our humble way unreproached. We are very poor, we are old, and have no chick nor child to help us; we were sorely tempted, and we fell. It was my purpose when I got up before to make confession and beg that my name might not be read out in this public place, for it seemed to us that we could not bear it; but I was prevented. It was just; it was our place to suffer with the rest. It has been hard for us. It is the first time we have ever heard our name fall from any one's lips—sullied. Be merciful —for the sake of the better days; make our shame as light to bear as in your charity you can.' At this point in his reverie Mary nudged him, perceiving that his mind was absent. The house was chanting, 'You are f-a-r,' etc.

'Be ready,' Mary whispered. 'Your name comes now; he has read eighteen.'

The chant ended.

'Next! next! next!' came volleying from all over the house.

Burgess put his hand into his pocket. The old couple, trembling, began to rise. Burgess fumbled a moment, then said:

'I find I have read them all.'

Faint with joy and surprise, the couple sank into their seats, and Mary whispered:

'Oh, bless God, we are saved!—he has lost ours —I wouldn't give this for a hundred of those sacks!'

The house burst out with its 'Mikado' travesty, and sang it three times with ever-increasing enthusi-

asm, rising to its feet when it reached for the third time the closing line—

But the Symbols are here, you bet!

and finishing up with cheers and a tiger for 'Hadleyburg purity and our eighteen immortal representatives of it.'

Then Wingate, the saddler, got up and proposed cheers 'for the cleanest man in town, the one solitary important citizen in it who didn't try to steal that money—Edward Richards.'

They were given with great and moving heartiness; then somebody proposed that 'Richards be elected sole Guardian and Symbol of the now Sacred Hadleyburg Tradition, with power and right to stand up and look the whole sarcastic world in the face.'

Passed, by acclamation; then they sang the 'Mikado' again, and ended it with—

And there's *one* Symbol left, you bet!

There was a pause; then—

A Voice. 'Now, then, who's to get the sack?'

The Tanner [*with bitter sarcasm*]. 'That's easy. The money has to be divided among the eighteen Incorruptibles. They gave the suffering stranger twenty dollars apiece—and that remark—each in his turn—it took twenty-two minutes for the procession to move past. Staked the stranger—total contribution, $360. All they want is just the loan back —and interest—forty thousand dollars altogether.'

Many Voices [*derisively*]. 'That's it! Divvy; divvy! Be kind to the poor—don't keep them waiting!'

The Chair. 'Order! I now offer the stranger's remaining document. It says: "If no claimant shall appear [*grand chorus of groans*], I desire that you open the sack and count out the money to the principal citizens of your town, they to take it in trust [*Cries of 'Oh! Oh! Oh!'*], and use it in such ways as to them shall seem best for the propagation and preservation of your community's noble reputation for incorruptible honesty [*more cries*] —a reputation to which their names and their efforts will add a new and far-reaching lustre." [*Enthusiastic outburst of sarcastic applause.*] That seems to be all. No—here is a postscript:

' "P.S.—CITIZENS OF HADLEYBURG: There *is* no test-remark—nobody made one. [*Great sensation.*] There wasn't any pauper stranger, nor any twenty-dollar contribution, nor any accompanying benediction and compliment—these are all inventions. [*General buzz and hum of astonishment and delight.*] Allow me to tell my story—it will take but a word or two. I passed through your town at a certain time, and received a deep offence which I had not earned. Any other man would have been content to kill one or two of you and call it square, but to me that would have been a trivial revenge, and inadequate; for the dead do not *suffer*. Besides, I could not kill you all—and, anyway, made as I am, even that would not have satisfied me. I wanted to damage every man in the place, and every woman—and not in their bodies or in their estate, but in their vanity—the place where feeble and foolish people are most vulnerable. So I disguised myself and came back and studied you. You were easy game. You had an old and lofty reputation for honesty, and naturally you were proud of it—it was your treasure of treasures, the very apple of your eye. As soon as I found out that you carefully and vigilantly kept yourselves and your children *out of temptation*, I knew how to proceed. Why, you simple creatures, the weakest of all weak things is a virtue which has not been tested in the fire. I laid a plan, and gathered a list of names. My project was to corrupt Hadleyburg the Incorruptible. My idea was to make liars and thieves of nearly half a hundred smirchless men and women who had never in their lives uttered a lie or stolen a penny. I was afraid of Goodson. He was neither born nor reared in Hadleyburg. I was afraid that if I started to operate my scheme by getting my letter laid before you, you would say to yourselves, 'Goodson is the only man among us who would give away twenty dollars to a poor devil'—and then you might not bite at my bait. But heaven took Goodson; then I knew I was safe, and I set my trap and baited it. It may be that I shall not catch all the men to whom I mailed the pretended test-secret, but I shall catch the most of them, if I know Hadleyburg nature. [*Voices*. 'Right—he got every last one of them.'] I believe they will even steal ostensible *gamble*-money, rather than miss, poor, tempted, and mistrained fellows. I am hoping to eternally and everlastingly squelch your vanity and give Hadleyburg a new renown—one that will *stick*—and spread far. If I have succeeded, open the sack and summon the Committee on Propagation and Preservation of the Hadleyburg Reputation." '

A Cyclone of Voices. 'Open it! Open it! The Eighteen to the front! Committee on Propagation of the Tradition! Forward—the Incorruptibles!'

The Chair ripped the sack wide, and gathered up a handful of bright, broad, yellow coins, shook them together, then examined them.

'Friends, they are only gilded disks of lead!'

There was a crashing outbreak of delight over this news, and when the noise had subsided, the tanner called out:

'By right of apparent seniority in this business, Mr. Wilson is Chairman of the Committee on Propagation of the Tradition. I suggest that he step forward on behalf of his pals, and receive in trust the money.'

A Hundred Voices. 'Wilson! Wilson! Wilson! Speech! Speech!'

Wilson [*in a voice trembling with anger*]. 'You will allow me to say, and without apologies for my language, *damn* the money!'

A Voice. 'Oh, and him a Baptist!'

A Voice. 'Seventeen Symbols left! Step up, gentlemen, and assume your trust!'

There was a pause—no response.

The Saddler. 'Mr. Chairman, we've got *one* clean man left, anyway, out of the late aristocracy; and he needs money, and deserves it. I move that you appoint Jack Halliday to get up there and auction off that sack of gilt twenty-dollar pieces, and give the result to the right man—the man whom Hadleyburg delights to honour—Edward Richards.'

This was received with great enthusiasm, the dog taking a hand again; the saddler started the bids at a dollar, the Brixton folk and Barnum's representative fought hard for it, the people cheered every jump that the bids made, the excitement climbed moment by moment higher and higher, the bidders got on their mettle and grew steadily more and more daring, more and more determined, the jumps went from a dollar up to five, then to ten, then to twenty, then fifty, then to a hundred, then—

At the beginning of the auction Richards whispered in distress to his wife: 'Oh, Mary, can we allow it? It—it—you see, it is an honour-reward, a testimonial to purity of character, and—and—can we allow it? Hadn't I better get up and—Oh, Mary, what ought we to do?—what do you think we—' [*Halliday's voice. 'Fifteen I'm bid!—fifteen for the sack!—twenty!—ah, thanks!—thirty—thanks again! Thirty, thirty, thirty!—do I hear forty?—forty it is! Keep the ball rolling, gentlemen, keep it rolling!—fifty!—thanks, noble Roman!—going at fifty, fifty, fifty!—seventy!—ninety!—splendid!—a hundred! —pile it up, pile it up!—hundred and twenty— forty!—just in time!—hundred and fifty!—*two hundred!*—superb! Do I hear two h—thanks!—two hundred and fifty!—*'*]

'It is another temptation, Edward—I'm all in a tremble—but, oh, we've escaped *one* temptation, and that ought to warn us,—['*Six did I hear?—thanks!—six fifty, six f—*SEVEN *hundred!*'] And yet, Edward, when you think—nobody susp—['*Eight hundred dollars—hurrah!—make it nine!—Mr. Parsons, did I hear you say—thanks!—nine!—this noble sack of virgin lead going at only nine hundred dollars, gilding and all—come! do I hear—a thousand!—gratefully yours!—did some one say eleven?—a sack which is going to be the most celebrated in the whole Uni—*'] Oh, Edward' (beginning to sob), 'we are so poor!—but—but—do as you think best—do as you think best.'

Edward fell—that is, he sat still; sat with a conscience which was not satisfied, but which was overpowered by circumstances.

Meantime a stranger, who looked like an amateur detective gotten up as an impossible English earl, had been watching the evening's proceedings with manifest interest, and with a contented expression in his face; and he had been privately commenting to himself. He was now soliloquising somewhat like this: 'None of the Eighteen are bidding; that is not satisfactory; I must change that—the dramatic unities require it; they must buy the sack they tried to steal; they must pay a heavy price, too—some of them are rich. And another thing, when I make a mistake in Hadleyburg nature the man that puts that error upon me is entitled to a high honorarium, and some one must pay. This poor old Richards has brought my judgment to shame; he is an honest man:—I don't understand it, but I acknowledge it. Yes, he saw my deuces-*and* with a straight flush, and by rights the pot is his. And it shall be a jack-pot, too, if I can manage it. He disappointed me, but let that pass.'

He was watching the bidding. At a thousand, the market broke: the prices tumbled swiftly. He waited—and still watched. One competitor dropped out; then another, and another. He put in a bid or two, now. When the bids had sunk to ten dollars, he added a five; some one raised him a three; he waited a moment, then flung in a fifty-dollar jump, and the sack was his—at $1,282. The house broke out in cheers—then stopped; for he was on his feet, and had lifted his hand. He began to speak.

'I desire to say a word, and ask a favour. I am a speculator in rarities, and I have dealings with persons interested in numismatics all over the world. I can make a profit on this purchase, just as it stands; but there is a way, if I can get your approval, whereby I can make every one of these leaden twenty-dollar pieces worth its face in gold, and perhaps more. Grant me that approval, and I will give part of my gains to your Mr. Richards, whose invulnerable probity you have so justly and so cordially recognised tonight; his share shall be ten thousand dollars, and I will hand him the money to-morrow. [*Great applause from the house.* But the 'invulnerable probity' made the Richardses blush prettily; however, it went for modesty, and did no harm.] If you will pass my proposition by a good majority—I would like a two-thirds vote—I will regard that as the town's consent, and that is all I ask. Rarities are always helped by any device which will rouse curiosity and compel remark. Now if I may have your permission to stamp upon the faces of each of these ostensible coins the names of the eighteen gentlemen who—'

Nine-tenths of the audience were on their feet in a moment—dog and all—and the proposition was carried with a whirlwind of approving applause and laughter.

They sat down, and all the Symbols except 'Dr.' Clay Harkness got up, violently protesting against the proposed outrage, and threatening to—

'I beg you not to threaten me,' said the stranger calmly. 'I know my legal rights, and am not accustomed to being frightened at bluster.' [*Applause.*] He sat down. 'Dr.' Harkness saw an opportunity here. He was one of the two very rich men of the place, and Pinkerton was the other. Harkness was proprieter of a mint; that is to say, a popular patent medicine. He was running for the Legislature on one ticket, and Pinkerton on the other. It was a close race and a hot one, and getting hotter every day. Both had strong appetites for money; each had bought a great tract of land, with a purpose; there was going to be a new railway, and each wanted to be in the Legislature and help locate the route to his own advantage; a single vote might make the decision, and with it two or three fortunes. The stake was large, and Harkness was a daring speculator. He was sitting close to the stranger. He leaned over while one or another of the other Symbols was entertaining the house with protests and appeals, and asked, in a whisper,

'What is your price for the sack?'

'Forty thousand dollars.'

'I'll give you twenty.'

'No.'

'Twenty-five.'

'No.'

'Say thirty.'

'The price is forty thousand dollars; not a penny

less.'

'All right. I'll give it. I will come to the hotel at ten in the morning. I don't want it known; will see you privately.'

'Very good.' Then the stranger got up and said to the house:

'I find it late. The speeches of these gentlemen are not without merit, not without interest, not without grace; yet if I may be excused I will take my leave. I thank you for the great favour which you have shown me in granting my petition. I ask the Chair to keep the sack for me until to-morrow, and to hand these three five-hundred-dollar notes to Mr. Richards.' They were passed up to the Chair.

'At nine I will call for the sack, and at eleven will deliver the rest of the ten thousand to Mr. Richards in person at his home. Good-night.'

Then he slipped out, and left the audience making a vast noise, which was composed of a mixture of cheers, the 'Mikado' song, dog-disapproval, and the chant, 'You are f-a-r from being a b-a-a-d man —a-a-a a-men!'

IV

At home the Richardses had to endure congratulations and compliments until midnight. Then they were left to themselves. They looked a little sad, and they sat silent and thinking. Finally Mary sighed and said:

'Do you think we are to blame, Edward—*much* to blame?' and her eyes wandered to the accusing triplet of big bank-notes lying on the table, where the congratulators had been gloating over them and reverently fingering them. Edward did not answer at once; then he brought out a sigh and said, hesitatingly:

'We—we couldn't help it, Mary. It—well it was ordered. *All* things are.'

Mary glanced up and looked at him steadily, but he didn't return the look. Presently she said:

'I thought congratulations and praises always tasted good. But—it seems to me, now— Edward?'

'Well?'

'Are you going to stay in the bank?'

'N-no.'

'Resign?'

'In the morning—by note.'

'It does seem best.'

Richards bowed his head in his hands and muttered:

'Before I was not afraid to let oceans of people's money pour through my hands, but— Mary, I am so tired, so tired—'

'We will go to bed.'

At nine in the morning the stranger called for the sack and took it to the hotel in a cab. At ten Harkness had a talk with him privately. The stranger asked for and got five cheques on a metropolitan bank—drawn to 'Bearer,'—four for $1,500 each, and one for $34,000. He put one of the former in his pocket-book, and the remainder, representing $38,500, he put in an envelope, and with these he added a note which he wrote after Harkness was gone. At eleven he called at the Richards' house and knocked. Mrs. Richards peeped through the shutters, then went and received the envelope, and the stranger disappeared without a word. She came back flushed and a little unsteady on her legs, and gasped out:

'I am sure I recognised him! Last night it seemed to me that maybe I had seen him somewhere before.'

'He is the man that brought the sack here?'

'I am almost sure of it.'

'Then he is the ostensible Stephenson too, and sold every important citizen in this town with his bogus secret. Now if he has sent cheques instead of money, we are sold too, after we thought we had escaped. I was beginning to feel fairly comfortable once more, after my night's rest, but the look of that envelope makes me sick. It isn't fat enough; $8,500 in even the largest bank-notes makes more bulk than that.'

'Edward, why do you object to cheques?'

'Cheques signed by Stephenson! I am resigned to take the $8,500 if it could come in bank-notes —for it does seem that it was so ordered, Mary— but I have never had much courage, and I have not the pluck to try to market a cheque signed with that disastrous name. It would be a trap. That man tried to catch me; we escaped somehow or other; and now he is trying a new way. If it is cheques—'

'Oh, Edward, it is *too* bad!' And she held up the cheques and began to cry.

'Put them in the fire! quick! we mustn't be tempted. It is a trick to make the world laugh at *us*, along with the rest, and— Give them to *me*, since you can't do it!' He snatched them and tried to hold his grip till he could get to the stove; but he was human, he was a cashier, and he stopped a moment to make sure of the signature. Then he came near to fainting.

'Fan me, Mary, fan me! They are the same as gold!'

'Oh, how lovely, Edward! Why?'

'Signed by Harkness. What can the mystery of that be, Mary?'

'Edward, do you think—'

'Look here—look at this! Fifteen—fifteen—fifteen—thirty-four. Thirty-eight thousand five hundred! Mary, the sack isn't worth twelve dollars, and Harkness—apparently—has paid about par for it.'

'And does it all come to us, do you think—instead of the ten thousand?'

'Why, it looks like it. And the cheques are made to "Bearer," too.'

'Is that good, Edward? What is it for?'

'A hint to collect them at some distant bank, I reckon. Perhaps Harkness doesn't want the matter known. What is that—a note?'

'Yes. It was with the cheques.'

It was in the 'Stephenson' handwriting, but there was no signature. It said:

I am a disappointed man. Your honesty is beyond the reach of temptation. I had a different idea about it, but I wronged you in that, and I beg pardon, and do it sincerely. I honour you —and that is sincere too. This town is not worthy to kiss the hem of your garment. Dear sir, I made a square bet with myself that there were nineteen debauchable men in your self-righteous community. I have lost. Take the whole pot, you are entitled to it.

Richards drew a deep sigh, and said:

'It seems written with fire—it burns so. Mary— I am miserable again.'

'I, too. Ah, dear, I wish—'

'To think, Mary—he *believes* in me.'

'Oh, don't, Edward—I can't bear it.'

'If those beautiful words were deserved, Mary —and God knows I believed I deserved them once —I think I could give the forty thousand dollars for them. And I would put that paper away, as representing more than gold and jewels, and keep it always. But now— We could not live in the shadow of its accusing presence, Mary.'

He put it in the fire.

A messenger arrived and delivered an envelope. Richards took from it a note and read it; it was from Burgess:

You saved me, in a difficult time. I saved you last night. It was at cost of a lie, but I made the sacrifice freely, and out of a grateful heart. None in this village knows so well as I know how brave and good and noble you are. At bottom you cannot respect me, knowing as you do

of that matter of which I am accused, and by the general voice condemned; but I beg that you will at least believe that I am a grateful man; it will help me to bear my burden.

[Signed]   BURGESS.

'Saved, once more. And on such terms!' He put the note in the fire. 'I—I wish I were dead, Mary, I wish I were out of it all!'

'Oh, these are bitter, bitter days, Edward. The stabs, through their very generosity, are so deep— and they come so fast!'

Three days before the election each of two thousand voters suddenly found himself in possession of a prized memento—one of the renowned bogus double-eagles. Around one of its faces was stamped these words: 'THE REMARK I MADE TO THE POOR STRANGER WAS—' Around the other face was stamped these: 'GO, AND REFORM. [SIGNED] PINKERTON.' Thus the entire remaining refuse of the renowned joke was emptied upon a single head, and with calamitous effect. It revived the recent vast laugh and concentrated it upon Pinkerton; and Harkness's election was a walk-over.

Within twenty-four hours after the Richardses had received their cheques their consciences were quieting down, discouraged; the old couple were learning to reconcile themselves to the sin which they had committed. But they were to learn, now, that a sin takes on new and real terrors when there seems a chance that it is going to be found out. This gives it a fresh and most substantial and important aspect. At church the morning sermon was of the usual pattern; it was the same old things said in the same old way; they had heard them a thousand times and found them innocuous, next to meaningless, and easy to sleep under; but now it was different: the sermon seemed to bristle with accusations; it seemed aimed straight and specially at people who were concealing deadly sins. After church they got away from the mob of congratulators as soon as they could, and hurried homeward, chilled to the bone at they did not know what—vague, shadowy, indefinite fears. And by chance they caught a glimpse of Mr. Burgess as he turned a corner. He paid no attention to their nod of recognition! He hadn't seen it; but they did not know that. What could his conduct mean? It might mean—it might—mean—oh, a dozen dreadful things. Was it possible that he knew that Richards could have cleared him of guilt in that bygone time, and had been silently waiting for a chance to even up accounts? At home, in their distress they got to imagining that their servant might have been in the next room listening when

Richards revealed the secret to his wife that he knew of Burgess's innocence; next Richards began to imagine that he had heard the swish of a gown in there at that time; next, he was sure he *had* heard it. They would call Sarah in, on a pretext, and watch her face; if she had been betraying them to Mr. Burgess, it would show in her manner. They asked her some questions—questions which were so random and incoherent and seemingly purposeless that the girl felt sure that the old people's minds had been affected by their sudden good fortune; the sharp and watchful gaze which they bent upon her frightened her, and that completed the business. She blushed, she became nervous and confused, and to the old people these were plain signs of guilt—guilt of some fearful sort or other—without doubt she was a spy and a traitor. When they were alone again they began to piece many unrelated things together and get horrible results out of the combination. When things had got about to the worst Richards was delivered of a sudden gasp and his wife asked:

'Oh, what is it?—what is it?'

'The note—Burgess's note! Its language was sarcastic, I see it now.' He quoted: ' "At bottom you cannot respect me, *knowing*, as you do, of *that matter* of which I am accused"—oh, it is perfectly plain, now, God help me! He knows that I know! You see the ingenuity of the phrasing. It was a trap—and like a fool, I walked into it. And Mary—!'

'Oh, it is dreadful—I know what you are going to say—he didn't return your transcript of the pretended test-remark.'

'No—kept it to destroy us with. Mary, he has exposed us to some already. I know it—I know it well. I saw it in a dozen faces after church. Ah, he wouldn't answer our nod of recognition—*he* knew what he had been doing!'

In the night the doctor was called. The news went around in the morning that the old couple were rather seriously ill—prostrated by the exhausting excitement growing out of their great windfall, the congratulations, and the late hours, the doctor said. The town was sincerely distressed; for these old people were about all it had left to be proud of, now.

Two days later the news was worse. The old couple were delirious, and were doing strange things. By witness of the nurses, Richards had exhibited cheques—for $8,500? No—for an amazing sum—$38,500! What could be the explanation of this gigantic piece of luck?

The following day the nurses had more news—and wonderful. They had concluded to hide the cheques, lest harm come to them; but when they searched they were gone from under the patient's pillow—vanished away. The patient said:

'Let the pillow alone; what do you want?'

'We thought it best that the cheques—'

'You will never see them again—they are destroyed. They came from Satan. I saw the hell-brand on them, and I knew they were sent to betray me to sin.' Then he fell to gabbling strange and dreadful things which were not clearly understandable, and which the doctor admonished them to keep to themselves.

Richards was right; the cheques were never seen again.

A nurse must have talked in her sleep, for within two days the forbidden gabblings were the property of the town; and they were of a surprising sort. They seemed to indicate that Richards had been a claimant for the sack himself, and that Burgess had concealed that fact and then maliciously betrayed it.

Burgess was taxed with this and stoutly denied it. And he said it was not fair to attach weight to the chatter of a sick old man who was out of his mind. Still, suspicion was in the air, and there was much talk.

After a day or two it was reported that Mrs. Richards's delirious deliveries were getting to be duplicates of her husband's. Suspicion flamed up into conviction, now, and the town's pride in the purity of its one undiscredited important citizen began to dim down and flicker toward extinction.

Six days passed, then came more news. The old couple were dying. Richards's mind cleared in his latest hour, and he sent for Burgess. Burgess said:

'Let the room be cleared. I think he wishes to say something in privacy.'

'No!' said Richards; 'I want witnesses. I want you all to hear my confession, so that I may die a man, and not a dog. I was clean—artificially—like the rest; and like the rest I fell when temptation came. I signed a lie, and claimed the miserable sack. Mr. Burgess remembered that I had done him a service, and in gratitude (and ignorance) he suppressed my claim and saved me. You know the thing that was charged against Burgess years ago. My testimony, and mine alone, could have cleared him, and I was a coward and left him to suffer disgrace—'

'No—no—Mr. Richards, you—'

'My servant betrayed my secret to him—'

'No one has betrayed anything to me—'

—'And then he did a natural and justifiable thing; he repented of the saving kindness which he had done me, and he *exposed* me—as I deserved—'

'Never!—I make oath—'

'Out of my heart I forgive him.'

Burgess's impassioned protestations fell upon deaf ears; the dying man passed away without knowing that once more he had done poor Burgess a wrong. The old wife died that night.

The last of the sacred Nineteen had fallen a prey to the fiendish sack; the town was stripped of the last rag of its ancient glory. Its mourning was not showy, but it was deep.

By act of the Legislature—upon prayer and petition—Hadleyburg was allowed to change its name

to (never mind what—I will not give it away), and leave one word out of the motto that for many generations had graced the town's official seal.

It is an honest town once more, and the man will have to rise early that catches it napping again.

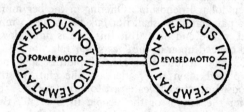

Fenimore Cooper's Literary Offenses (1894)

The Pathfinder and The Deerslayer *stand at the head of Cooper's novels as artistic creations. There are others of his works which contain parts as perfect as are to be found in these, and scenes even more thrilling. Not one can be compared with either of them as a finished whole.*

The defects in both of these tales are comparatively slight. They were pure works of art.—Prof. Lounsbury.

The five tales reveal an extraordinary fullness of invention.

. . . One of the very greatest characters in fiction, Natty Bumppo. . . .

The craft of the woodsman, the tricks of the trapper, all the delicate art of the forest, were familiar to Cooper from his youth up.—Prof. Brander Matthews.

Cooper is the greatest artist in the domain of romantic fiction yet produced by America.—Wilkie Collins.

It seems to me that it was far from right for the Professor of English Literature in Yale, the Professor of English Literature in Columbia, and Wilkie Collins to deliver opinions on Cooper's literature without having read some of it. It would have been much more decorous to keep silent and let persons talk who have read Cooper.

Cooper's art has some defects. In one place in *Deerslayer*, and in the restricted space of two-thirds of a page, Cooper has scored 114 offenses against literary art out of a possible 115. It breaks the record.

There are nineteen rules governing literary art in the domain of romantic fiction—some say twenty-

two. In *Deerslayer* Cooper violated eighteen of them. These eighteen require:

1. That a tale shall accomplish something and arrive somewhere. But the *Deerslayer* tale accomplishes nothing and arrives in the air.

2. They require that the episodes of a tale shall be necessary parts of the tale, and shall help to develop it. But as the *Deerslayer* tale is not a tale, and accomplishes nothing and arrives nowhere, the episodes have no rightful place in the work, since there was nothing for them to develop.

3. They require that the personages in a tale shall be alive, except in the case of corpses, and that always the reader shall be able to tell the corpses from the others. But this detail has often been overlooked in the *Deerslayer* tale.

4. They require that the personages in a tale, both dead and alive, shall exhibit a sufficient excuse for being there. But this detail also has been overlooked in the *Deerslayer* tale.

5. They require that when the personages of a tale deal in conversation, the talk shall sound like human talk, and be talk such as human beings would be likely to talk in the given circumstances, and have a discoverable meaning, also a discoverable purpose, and a show of relevancy, and remain in the neighborhood of the subject in hand, and be interesting to the reader, and help out the tale, and stop when the people cannot think of anything more to say. But this requirement has been ignored from the beginning of the *Deerslayer* tale to the end of it.

6. They require that when the author describes the character of a personage in his tale, the con-

duct and conversation of that personage shall justify said description. But this law gets little or no attention in the *Deerslayer* tale, as Natty Bumppo's case will amply prove.

7. They require that when a personage talks like an illustrated, gilt-edged, tree-calf, hand-tooled, seven-dollar Friendship's Offering in the beginning of a paragraph, he shall not talk like a negro minstrel in the end of it. But this rule is flung down and danced upon in the *Deerslayer* tale.

8. They require that crass stupidities shall not be played upon the reader as "the craft of the woodsman, the delicate art of the forest," by either the author or the people in the tale. But this rule is persistently violated in the *Deerslayer* tale.

9. They require that the personages of a tale shall confine themselves to possibilities and let miracles alone; or, if they venture a miracle, the author must so plausibly set it forth as to make it look possible and reasonable. But these rules are not respected in the *Deerslayer* tale.

10. They require that the author shall make the reader feel a deep interest in the personages of his tale and in their fate; and that he shall make the reader love the good people in the tale and hate the bad ones. But the reader of the *Deerslayer* tale dislikes the good people in it, is indifferent to the others, and wishes they would all get drowned together.

11. They require that the characters in a tale shall be so clearly defined that the reader can tell beforehand what each will do in a given emergency. But in the *Deerslayer* tale this rule is vacated.

In addition to these large rules there are some little ones. These require that the author shall

12. *Say* what he is proposing to say, not merely come near it.

13. Use the right word, not its second cousin.

14. Eschew surplusage.

15. Not omit necessary details.

16. Avoid slovenliness of form.

17. Use good grammar.

18. Employ a simple and straightforward style.

Even these seven are coldly and persistently violated in the *Deerslayer* tale.

Cooper's gift in the way of invention was not a rich endowment; but such as it was he liked to work it, he was pleased with the effects, and indeed he did some quite sweet things with it. In his little box of stage-properties he kept six or eight cunning devices, tricks, artifices for his savages and woodsmen to deceive and circumvent each other with, and he was never so happy as when he was working these innocent things and seeing them go. A favorite one was to make a moccasined person tread in the tracks of the moccasined enemy, and thus hide his own trail. Cooper wore out barrels and barrels of moccasins in working that trick. Another stage-property that he pulled out of his box pretty frequently was his broken twig. He prized his broken twig above all the rest of his effects, and worked it the hardest. It is a restful chapter in any book of his when somebody doesn't step on a dry twig and alarm all the reds and whites for two hundred yards around. Every time a Cooper person is in peril, and absolute silence is worth four dollars a minute, he is sure to step on a dry twig. There may be a hundred handier things to step on, but that wouldn't satisfy Cooper. Cooper requires him to turn out and find a dry twig; and if he can't do it, go and borrow one. In fact, the Leatherstocking Series ought to have been called the Broken Twig Series.

I am sorry there is not room to put in a few dozen instances of the delicate art of the forest, as practised by Natty Bumppo and some of the other Cooperian experts. Perhaps we may venture two or three samples. Cooper was a sailor—a naval officer; yet he gravely tells us how a vessel, driving toward a lee shore in a gale, is steered for a particular spot by her skipper because he knows of an *undertow* there which will hold her back against the gale and save her. For just pure woodcraft, or sailorcraft, or whatever it is, isn't that neat? For several years Cooper was daily in the society of artillery, and he ought to have noticed that when a cannon-ball strikes the ground it either buries itself or skips a hundred feet or so; skips again a hundred feet or so—and so on, till finally it gets tired and rolls. Now in one place he loses some "females"—as he always calls women—in the edge of a wood near a plain at night in a fog, on purpose to give Bumppo a chance to show off the delicate art of the forest before the reader. These mislaid people are hunting for a fort. They hear a cannon-blast, and a cannon-ball presently comes rolling into the wood and stops at their feet. To the females this suggests something. The case is very different with the admirable Bumppo. I wish I may never know peace again if he doesn't strike out promptly and *follow the track* of that cannon-ball across the plain through the dense fog and find the fort. Isn't it a daisy? If Cooper had any real knowledge of Nature's ways of doing things, he had a most delicate art in concealing the fact. For instance: one of his acute Indian experts, Chingachgook (pronounced Chicago, I think), has lost the trail of a person he is tracking through the forest. Apparently that trail is hopelessly lost. Neither you nor I could ever have guessed out the way to find it. It was very different with Chicago. Chicago was not stumped for long. He turned a running stream out of its course, and there, in the slush in its old bed, were that person's moccasin tracks. The current did not wash them away, as it would have done in all other like cases—no, even the eternal laws of Nature have to vacate when Cooper wants to put up a delicate job of wood-craft on the reader.

We must be a little wary when Brander Matthews tell us that Cooper's books "reveal an extraordinary fullness of invention." As a rule, I am quite willing to accept Brander Matthews's literary judgments and applaud his lucid and graceful phrasing of them; but that particular statement needs to be taken with a few tons of salt. Bless your heart, Cooper hadn't any more invention than a horse; and I don't mean a high-class horse, either; I mean a clothes-horse. It would be very difficult to find a really clever "situation" in Cooper's books, and still more difficult to find one of any kind which he has failed to render absurd by his handling of it. Look at the episodes of "the caves"; and at the celebrated scuffle between Maqua and those others on the table-land a few days later; and at Hurry Harry's queer water-transit from the castle to the ark; and at Deerslayer's half-hour with his first corpse; and at the quarrel between Hurry Harry and Deerslayer later; and at—but choose for yourself; you can't go amiss.

If Cooper had been an observer his inventive faculty would have worked better; not more interestingly, but more rationally, more plausibly. Cooper's proudest creations in the way of "situations" suffer noticeably from the absence of the observer's protecting gift. Cooper's eye was splendidly inaccurate. Cooper seldom saw anything correctly. He saw nearly all things as through a glass eye, darkly. Of course a man who cannot see the commonest little every-day matters accurately is working at a disadvantage when he is constructing a "situation." In the *Deerslayer* tale Cooper has a stream which is fifty feet wide where it flows out of a lake; it presently narrows to twenty as it meanders along for no given reason, and yet when a stream acts like that it ought to be required to explain itself. Fourteen pages later the width of

the brook's outlet from the lake has suddenly shrunk thirty feet, and become "the narrowest part of the stream." This shrinkage is not accounted for. The stream has bends in it, a sure indication that it has alluvial banks and cuts them; yet these bends are only thirty and fifty feet long. If Cooper had been a nice and punctilious observer he would have noticed that the bends were oftener nine hundred feet long than short of it.

Cooper made the exit of that stream fifty feet wide, in the first place, for no particular reason; in the second place, he narrowed it to less than twenty to accommodate some Indians. He bends a "sapling" to the form of an arch over this narrow passage, and conceals six Indians in its foliage. They are "laying" for a settler's scow or ark which is coming up the stream on its way to the lake; it is being hauled against the stiff current by a rope whose stationary end is anchored in the lake; its rate of progress cannot be more than a mile an hour. Cooper describes the ark, but pretty obscurely. In the matter of dimensions "it was little more than a modern canal-boat." Let us guess, then, that it was about one hundred and forty feet long. It was of "greater breadth than common." Let us guess, then, that it was about sixteen feet wide. This leviathan had been prowling down bends which were but a third as long as itself and scraping between banks where it had only two feet of space to spare on each side. We cannot too much admire this miracle. A low-roofed log dwelling occupies "two-thirds of the ark's length"—a dwelling ninety feet long and sixteen feet wide, let us say—a kind of vestibule train. The dwelling has two rooms—each forty-five feet long and sixteen feet wide, let us guess. One of them is the bedroom of the Hutter girls, Judith and Hetty; the other is the parlor in the daytime, at night it is papa's bedchamber. The ark is arriving at the stream's exit now, whose width has been reduced to less than twenty feet to accommodate the Indians—say to eighteen. There is a foot to spare on each side of the boat. Did the Indians notice that there was going to be a tight squeeze there? Did they notice that they could make money by climbing down out of that arched sapling and just stepping aboard when the ark scraped by? No, other Indians would have noticed these things, but Cooper's Indians never notice anything. Cooper thinks they are marvelous creatures for noticing, but he was almost always in error about his Indians. There was seldom a sane one among them.

The ark is one hundred and forty-feet long; the

dwelling is ninety feet long. The idea of the Indians is to drop softly and secretly from the arched sapling to the dwelling as the ark creeps along under it at the rate of a mile an hour, and butcher the family. It will take the ark a minute and a half to pass under. It will take the ninety-foot dwelling a minute to pass under. Now, then, what did the six Indians do? It would take you thirty years to guess, and even then you would have to give it up, I believe. Therefore, I will tell you what the Indians did. Their chief, a person of quite extraordinary intellect for a Cooper Indian, warily watched the canal-boat as it squeezed along under him, and when he had got his calculations fined down to exactly the right shade, as he judged, he let go and dropped. And *missed the house!* That is actually what he did. He missed the house, and landed in the stern of the scow. It was not much of a fall, yet it knocked him silly. He lay there unconscious. If the house had been ninety-seven feet long he would have made the trip. The fault was Cooper's, not his. The error lay in the construction of the house. Cooper was no architect.

There still remained in the roost five Indians. The boat has passed under and is now out of their reach. Let me explain what the five did—you would not be able to reason it out for yourself. No. 1 jumped for the boat, but fell in the water astern of it. Then No. 2 jumped for the boat, but fell in the water still farther astern of it. Then No. 3 jumped for the boat, and fell a good way astern of it. Then No. 4 jumped for the boat, and fell in the water *away* astern. Then even No. 5 made a jump for the boat—for he was a Cooper Indian. In the matter of intellect, the difference between a Cooper Indian and the Indian that stands in front of the cigar-shop is not spacious. The scow episode is really a sublime burst of invention; but it does not thrill, because the inaccuracy of the details throws a sort of air of fictitiousness and general improbability over it. This comes of Cooper's inadequacy as an observer.

The reader will find some examples of Cooper's high talent for inaccurate observation in the account of the shooting-match in *The Pathfinder*.

A common wrought nail was driven lightly into the target, its head having been first touched with paint.

The color of the paint is not stated—an important omission, but Cooper deals freely in important omissions. No, after all, it was not an important omission; for this nail-head is *a hundred yards from* the marksmen, and could not be seen by them at that distance, no matter what its color might be. How far can the best eyes see a common house-fly? A hundred yards? It is quite impossible. Very well; eyes that cannot see a house-fly that is a hundred yards away cannot see an ordinary nail-head at that distance, for the size of the two objects is the same. It takes a keen eye to see a fly or a nail-head at fifty yards—one hundred and fifty feet. Can the reader do it?

The nail was lightly driven, its head painted, and game called. Then the Cooper miracles began. The bullet of the first marksman chipped an edge of the nail-head; the next man's bullet drove the nail a little way into the target—and removed all the paint. Haven't the miracles gone far enough now? Not to suit Cooper; for the purpose of this whole scheme is to show off his prodigy, Deerslayer-Hawkeye-Long-Rifle-Leatherstocking-Pathfinder-Bumppo before the ladies.

"Be all ready to clench it, boys!" cried out Pathfinder, stepping into his friend's tracks the instant they were vacant. "Never mind a new nail; I can see that, though the paint is gone, and what I can see I can hit at a hundred yards, though it were only a mosquito's eye. Be ready to clench!"

The rifle cracked, the bullet sped its way, and the head of the nail was buried in the wood, covered by the piece of flattened lead.

There, you see, is a man who could hunt flies with a rifle, and command a ducal salary in a Wild West show to-day if we had him back with us.

The recorded feat is certainly surprising just as it stands; but it is not surprising enough for Cooper. Cooper adds a touch. He has made Pathfinder do this miracle with another man's rifle; and not only that, but Pathfinder did not have even the advantage of loading it himself. He had everything against him, and yet he made that impossible shot; and not only made it, but did it with absolute confidence, saying, "Be ready to clench." Now a person like that would have undertaken that same feat with a brickbat, and with Cooper to help he would have achieved it, too.

Pathfinder showed off handsomely that day before the ladies. His very first feat was a thing which no Wild West show can touch. He was standing with the group of marksmen, observing—

a hundred yards from the target, mind; one Jasper raised his rifle and drove the center of the bull's-eye. Then the Quartermaster fired. The target exhibited no result this time. There was a laugh. "It's a dead miss," said Major Lundie. Pathfinder waited an impressive moment or two; then said, in that calm, indifferent, know-it-all way of his, "No, Major, he has covered Jasper's bullet, as will be seen if any one will take the trouble to examine the target."

Wasn't it remarkable! How *could* he see that little pellet fly through the air and enter that distant bullet-hole? Yet that is what he did; for nothing is impossible to a Cooper person. Did any of those people have any deep-seated doubts about this thing? No; for that would imply sanity, and these were all Cooper people.

The respect for Pathfinder's skill and for his *quickness and accuracy of sight* [the italics are mine] was so profound and general, that the instant he made this declaration the spectators began to distrust their own opinions, and a dozen rushed to the target in order to ascertain the fact. There, sure enough, it was found that the Quartermaster's bullet had gone through the hole made by Jasper's, and that, too, so accurately as to require a minute examination to be certain of the circumstance, which, however, was soon clearly established by discovering one bullet over the other in the stump against which the target was placed.

They made a "minute" examination; but never mind, how could they know that there were two bullets in that hole without digging the latest one out? for neither probe nor eyesight could prove the presence of any more than one bullet. Did they dig? No; as we shall see. It is the Pathfinder's turn now; he steps out before the ladies, takes aim, and fires.

But, alas! here is a disappointment; an incredible, an unimaginable disappointment—for the target's aspect is unchanged; there is nothing there but that same old bullet-hole!

"If one dared to hint at such a thing," cried Major Duncan, "I should say that the Pathfinder has also missed the target!"

As nobody had missed it yet, the "also" was not necessary; but never mind about that, for the Pathfinder is going to speak.

"No, no, Major," said he, confidently, "that *would* be a risky declaration. I didn't load the piece, and can't say what was in it; but if it was lead, you will find the bullet driving down those of the Quartermaster and Jasper, else is not my name Pathfinder."

A shout from the target announced the truth of this assertion.

Is the miracle sufficient as it stands? Not for Cooper. The Pathfinder speaks again, as he "now slowly advances toward the stage occupied by the females":

That's not all, boys, that's not all; if you find the target touched at all, I'll own to a miss. The Quartermaster cut the wood, but you'll find no wood cut by that last messenger.

The miracle is at last complete. He knew—doubtless *saw*—at the distance of a hundred yards—that his bullet had passed into the hole without *fraying the edges*. There were now three bullets in that one hole—three bullets embedded processionally in the body of the stump back of the target. Everybody knew this—somehow or other—and yet nobody had dug any of them out to make sure. Cooper is not a close observer, but he is interesting. He is certainly always that, no matter what happens. And he is more interesting when he is not noticing what he is about than when he is. This is a considerable merit.

The conversations in the Cooper books have a curious sound in our modern ears. To believe that such talk really ever came out of people's mouths would be to believe that there was a time when time was of no value to a person who thought he had something to say; when it was the custom to spread a two-minute remark out to ten; when a man's mouth was a rolling-mill, and busied itself all day long in turning four-foot pigs of thought into thirty-foot bars of conversational railroad iron by attenuation; when subjects were seldom faithfully stuck to, but the talk wandered all around and arrived nowhere; when conversations consisted mainly of irrelevancies, with here and there a relevancy, a relevancy with an embarrassed look, as not being able to explain how it got there.

Cooper was certainly not a master in the construction of dialogue. Inaccurate observation defeated him here as it defeated him in so many other enterprises of his. He even failed to notice that the man who talks corrupt English six days in the week must and will talk it on the seventh, and can't help himself. In the *Deerslayer* story he lets Deerslayer talk the showiest kind of book-talk sometimes, and at other times the basest of base dialects. For instance, when some one asks him if he has a sweetheart, and if so, where she abides, this is his majestic answer:

> She's in the forest—hanging from the boughs of the trees, in a soft rain—in the dew on the open grass—the clouds that float about in the blue heavens—the birds that sing in the woods —the sweet springs where I slake my thirst—and in all the other glorious gifts that come from God's Providence!

And he preceded that, a little before, with this:

> It consarns me as all things that touches a fri'nd consarns a fri'nd.

And this is another of his remarks:

> If I was Injin born, now, I might tell of this, or carry in the scalp and boast of the expl'ite afore the whole tribe; or if my inimy had only been a bear—[and so on].

We cannot imagine such a thing as a veteran Scotch Commander-in-Chief comporting himself in the field like a windy melodramatic actor, but Cooper could. On one occasion Alice and Cora were being chased by the French through a fog in the neighborhood of their father's fort:

> *"Point de quartier aux coquins!"* cried an eager pursuer, who seemed to direct the operations of the enemy.
> "Stand firm and be ready my gallant 6oths!" suddenly exclaimed a voice above them; "wait to see the enemy; fire low, and sweep the glacis."
> "Father! father!" exclaimed a piercing cry from out the mist; "it is I! Alice! thy own Elsie! spare, O! save your daughters!"
> "Hold!" shouted the former speaker, in the awful tones of parental agony, the sound reaching even to the woods, and rolling back in solemn echo. "'Tis she! God has restored me my children! Throw open the sally port; to the field, 6oths, to the field! pull not a trigger, lest ye kill my lambs! Drive off these dogs of France with your steel!"

Cooper's word-sense was singularly dull. When a person has a poor ear for music he will flat and sharp right along without knowing it. He keeps near the tune, but it is *not* the tune. When a person has a poor ear for words, the result is a literary flatting and sharping; you perceive what he is intending to say, but you also perceive that he doesn't *say* it. This is Cooper. He was not a word-musician. His ear was satisfied with the *approximate* word. I will furnish some circumstantial evidence in support of this charge. My instances are gathered from half a dozen pages of the tale called *Deerslayer*. He uses "verbal" for "oral"; "precision" for "facility"; "phenomena" for "marvels"; "necessary" for "predetermined"; "unsophisticated" for "primitive"; "preparation" for "expectancy"; "rebuked" for "subdued"; "dependent on" for "resulting from"; "fact" for "condition"; "fact" for "conjecture"; "precaution" for "caution"; "explain" for "determine"; "mortified" for "disappointed"; "meretricious" for "factitious"; "materially" for "considerably"; "decreasing" for "deepening"; "increasing" for "disappearing"; "embedded" for "inclosed"; "treacherous" for "hostile"; "stood" for "stooped"; "softened" for "replaced"; "rejoined" for "remarked"; "situation" for "condition"; "different" for "differing"; "insensible" for "unsentient"; "brevity" for "celerity"; "distrusted" for "suspicious"; "mental imbecility" for "imbecility"; "eyes" for "sight"; "counteracting" for "opposing"; "funeral obsequies" for "obsequies."

There have been daring people in the world who claimed that Cooper could write English, but they are all dead now—all dead but Lounsbury. I don't remember that Lounsbury makes the claim in so many words, still he makes it, for he says that *Deerslayer* is a "pure work of art." Pure, in that connection, means faultless—faultless in all details—and language is a detail. If Mr. Lounsbury had only compared Cooper's English with the English which he writes himself—but it is plain that he didn't; and so it is likely that he imagines until this day that Cooper's is as clean and compact as his own. Now I feel sure, deep down in my heart, that Cooper wrote about the poorest English that exists in our language, and that the English of *Deerslayer* is the very worst that even Cooper ever wrote.

I may be mistaken, but it does seem to me that *Deerslayer* is not a work of art in any sense; it does seem to me that it is destitute of every detail that goes to the making of a work of art; in truth, it seems to me that *Deerslayer* is just simply a literary *delirium tremens*.

A work of art? It has no invention; it has no order, system, sequence, or result; it has no lifelikeness, no thrill, no stir, no seeming of reality;

its characters are confusedly drawn, and by their acts and words they prove that they are not the sort of people the author claims that they are; its humor is pathetic; its pathos is funny; its conversations are—oh! indescribable; its love-scenes odious; its English a crime against the language.

Counting these out, what is left is Art. I think we must all admit that.

To the Person Sitting in Darkness (1901)

In late years Mark Twain once remarked: "Money lust has always existed, but not in the history of the world was it ever a craze, a madness, until your time and mine." And the final and most vicious focus of this infection was, as he saw it, in the new imperialism of Europe and, as manifested in the Philippines, of the United States. In a late sketch called "History 1000 Years from Now," Mark Twain, looking back on the fictional history of the country, could see the annexation of the Philippines as the first stage in rescuing America "from democracy"—that is, he regarded the new imperialism of the United States as a return to the darkness of the Old World. In his historical determinism he predicted a long swing to monarchy and tyranny. Though, at first, Mark Twain had regarded the Spanish American War as a philanthropic adventure (not following the lead of his friend Howells, who said that it would inaugurate an "era of blood-bought prosperity"), he became disenchanted by the events of the war in the Far East, and grew more and more bitter in the years when the native resistance in the Philippines was being crushed.

"To the Person Sitting in Darkness" was published in the *North American Review*, in February, 1901, provoked not only by the Philippine adventure but by the consequences of the Boxer Rebellion in China and the Boer War. A storm of outrage followed from the pulpit and patriotic laymen. Teddy Roosevelt, whom Mark Twain had termed the "Tom Sawyer of the political world," said how he would like to skin Mark Twain alive. But liberals in general hailed him as a hero, and when, in the fall of 1901, he went to New Haven to accept an honorary degree, the students greeted him with an ovation.

Two other pieces of social and political polemics deserve mention: "King Leopold's Soliloquy," in reference to the notorious Belgian policy in the Congo, and "The United States of Lyncherdom," which was provoked by a peculiarly heinous lynching in Missouri.

Extending the Blessings of Civilization to our Brother who Sits in Darkness has been a good trade and has paid well, on the whole; and there is money in it yet, if carefully worked—but not enough, in my judgment, to make any considerable risk advisable. The People that Sit in Darkness are getting to be too scarce—too scarce and too shy. And such darkness as is now left is really of but an indifferent quality, and not dark enough for the game. The most of those People that Sit in Darkness have been furnished with more light than was good for them or profitable for us. We have been injudicious.

The Blessings-of-Civilization Trust, wisely and cautiously administered, is a Daisy. There is more money in it, more territory, more sovereignty and other kinds of emolument, than there is in any other game that is played. But Christendom has been playing it badly of late years, and must certainly suffer by it, in my opinion. She has been so eager to get every stake that appeared on the green cloth, that the People who Sit in Darkness have noticed it—they have noticed it, and have begun to show alarm. They have become suspicious of the Blessings of Civilization. More—they have begun to examine them. This is not well. The Blessings of Civilization are all right, and a good commercial property; there could not be a better, in a dim light. In the right kind of a light, and at a proper distance, with the goods a little out of focus, they furnish this desirable exhibit to the Gentlemen who Sit in Darkness:

LOVE,
JUSTICE,
GENTLENESS,

CHRISTIANITY,
PROTECTION
TO THE WEAK,

TEMPERANCE,	HONORABLE
LAW AND ORDER,	DEALING,
LIBERTY,	MERCY,
EQUALITY,	EDUCATION,
	—and so on.

There. Is it good? Sir, it is pie. It will bring into camp any idiot that sits in darkness anywhere. But not if we adulterate it. It is proper to be emphatic upon that point. This brand is strictly for Export—apparently. *Apparently*. Privately and confidentially, it is nothing of the kind. Privately and confidentially, it is merely an outside cover, gay and pretty and attractive, displaying the special patterns of our Civilization which we reserve for Home Consumption, while *inside* the bale is the Actual Thing that the Customer Sitting in Darkness buys with his blood and tears and land and liberty. That Actual Thing is, indeed, Civilization, but it is only for Export. Is there a difference between the two brands? In some of the details, yes.

We all know that the Business is being ruined. The reason is not far to seek. It is because our Mr. McKinley, and Mr. Chamberlain, and the Kaiser, and the Czar and the French have been exporting the Actual Thing *with the outside cover left off*. This is bad for the Game. It shows that these new players of it are not sufficiently acquainted with it.

It is a distress to look on and note the mis-moves, they are so strange and awkward. Mr. Chamberlain manufactures a war out of materials so inadequate and so fanciful that they make the boxes grieve and the gallery laugh, and he tries hard to persuade himself that it isn't purely a private raid for cash, but has a sort of dim, vague respectability about it somewhere, if he could only find the spot; and that, by and by, he can scour the flag clean again after he has finished dragging it through the mud, and make it shine and flash in the vault of heaven once more as it had shone and flashed there a thousand years in the world's respect until he laid his unfaithful hand upon it. It is bad play—bad. For it exposes the Actual Thing to Them that Sit in Darkness, and they say: "What! Christian against Christian? And only for money? Is *this* a case of magnanimity, forbearance, love, gentleness, mercy, protection of the weak—this strange and over-showy onslaught of an elephant upon a nest of field-mice, on the pretext that the mice had squeaked an insolence at him—conduct which 'no self-respecting government could allow to pass unavenged?' as Mr. Chamberlain

said. Was that a good pretext in a small case, when it had not been a good pretext in a large one?—for only recently Russia had affronted the elephant three times and survived alive and unsmitten. Is this Civilization and Progress? Is it something better than we already possess? These harryings and burnings and desert-makings in the Transvaal—is this an improvement on our darkness? Is it, perhaps, possible that there are two kinds of Civilization—one for home consumption and one for the heathen market?"

Then They that Sit in Darkness are troubled, and shake their heads; and they read this extract from a letter of a British private, recounting his exploits in one of Methuen's victories, some days before the affair of Magersfontein, and they are troubled again:

> We tore up the hill and into the intrenchments, and the Boers saw we had them; so they dropped their guns and went down on their knees and put up their hands clasped, and begged for mercy. And we gave it them—*with the long spoon.*

The long spoon is the bayonet. See *Lloyd's Weekly*, London, of those days. The same number —and the same column—contains some quite unconscious satire in the form of shocked and bitter upbraidings of the Boers for their brutalities and inhumanities!

Next to our heavy damage, the Kaiser went to playing the game without first mastering it. He lost a couple of missionaries in a riot in Shantung, and in his account he made an overcharge for them. China had to pay a hundred thousand dollars apiece for them, in money; twelve miles of territory, containing several millions of inhabitants and worth twenty million dollars, and to build a monument and also a Christian Church; whereas the people of China could have been depended upon to remember the missionaries without the help of these expensive memorials. This was all bad play. Bad, because it would not, and could not, and will not now or ever, deceive the Person Sitting in Darkness. He knows that it was an overcharge. He knows that a missionary is like any other man: he is worth merely what you can supply his place for, and no more. He is useful, but so is a doctor, so is a sheriff, so is an editor; but a just Emperor does not charge war-prices for such. A diligent, intelligent, but obscure missionary, and a diligent, intelligent country editor are worth much, and we know it; but they are not worth the earth. We esteem such an editor, and we are sorry to see him go; but, when he goes, we should consider twelve miles of territory, and a church, and a fortune, over-compensation for his loss. I mean, if he was a Chinese editor, and we had to settle for him. It is no proper figure for an editor or a missionary; one can get shop-worn kings for less. It was bad play on the Kaiser's part. It got this property, true; but it *produced the Chinese revolt*, the indignant uprising of China's traduced patriots, the Boxers. The results have been expensive to Germany, and to the other Disseminators of Progress and the Blessings of Civilization.

The Kaiser's claim was paid, yet it was bad play, for it could not fail to have an evil effect upon Persons Sitting in Darkness in China. They would muse upon the event, and be likely to say: "Civilization is gracious and beautiful, for such is its reputation; but can we afford it? There are rich Chinamen, perhaps they could afford it; but this tax is not laid upon them, it is laid upon the peasants of Shantung; it is they that must pay this mighty sum, and their wages are but four cents a day. Is this a better civilization than ours, and holier and higher and nobler? Is not this rapacity? Is not this extortion? Would Germany charge America two hundred thousand dollars for two missionaries, and shake the mailed fist in her face, and send warships, and send soldiers, and say: 'Seize twelve miles of territory, worth twenty millions of dollars, as additional pay for the missionaries; and make those peasants build a monument to the missionaries, and a costly Christian church to remember them by?' And later would Germany say to her soldiers: 'March through America and slay, *giving no quarter*; make the German face there, as has been our Hun-face here, a terror for a thousand years; march through the Great Republic and slay, slay, slay, carving a road for our offended religion through its heart and bowels?' Would Germany do like this to America, to England, to France, to Russia? Or only to China the helpless—imitating the elephant's assault upon the field-mice? Had we better invest in this Civilization—this Civilization which called Napoleon a buccaneer for carrying off Venice's bronze horses, but which steals our ancient astronomical instruments from our walls, and goes looting like common bandits—that is, all the alien soldiers except America's; and (Americans again excepted) storms frightened villages and cables the result to glad journals at home every day: 'Chinese losses, 450 killed; ours, *one officer and two men wounded*. Shall proceed against neighboring village to-morrow, where a *massacre* is reported.' Can we afford Civilization?"

And, next, Russia must go and play the game injudiciously. She affronts England once or twice —with the Person Sitting in Darkness observing and noting; by moral assistance of France and Germany, she robs Japan of her hard-earned spoil, all swimming in Chinese blood—Port Arthur—with the Person again observing and noting; then she seizes Manchuria, raids its villages, and chokes its great rivers with the swollen corpses of countless massacred peasants—that astonished Person still observing and noting. And perhaps he is saying to himself: "It is yet *another* Civilized Power, with its banner of the Prince of Peace in one hand and its loot-basket and its butcher-knife in the other. Is there no salvation for us but to adopt Civilization and lift ourselves down to its level?"

And by and by comes America, and our Master of the Game plays it badly—plays it as Mr. Chamberlain was playing it in South Africa. It was a mistake to do that; also, it was one which was quite unlooked for in a Master who was playing it so well in Cuba. In Cuba, he was playing the usual and regular *American* game, and it was winning, for there is no way to beat it. The Master, contemplating Cuba, said: "Here is an oppressed and friendless little nation which is willing to fight to be free; we go partners, and put up the strength of seventy million sympathizers, and the resources of the United States: play!" Nothing but Europe combined could call that hand: and Europe cannot combine on anything. There, in Cuba, he was following our great traditions in a way which made us very proud of him, and proud of the deep dissatisfaction which his play was provoking in Continental Europe. Moved by a high inspiration, he threw out those stirring words which proclaimed that forcible annexation would be "criminal aggression;" and in that utterance fired another "shot heard round the world." The memory of that fine saying will be outlived by the remembrance of no act of his but one—that he forgot it within the twelvemonth, and its honorable gospel along with it.

For, presently, came the Philippine temptation. It was strong; it was too strong, and he made that bad mistake: he played the European game, the Chamberlain game. It was a pity; it was a great pity, that error; that one grievous error, that irrevocable error. For it was the very place and time to play the American game again. And at no cost. Rich winnings to be gathered in, too; rich and permanent; indestructible; a fortune transmissible forever to the children of the flag. Not land, not money, not dominion—no, something worth many times more than that dross: our share, the spectacle of a nation of long harassed and persecuted slaves set free through our influence; our posterity's share, the golden memory of that fair deed. The game was in our hands. If it had been played according to the American rules, Dewey would have sailed away from Manila as soon as he had destroyed the Spanish fleet—after putting up a sign on shore guaranteeing foreign property and life against damage by the Filipinos, and warning the Powers that interference with the emancipated patriots would be regarded as an act unfriendly to the United States. The Powers cannot combine, in even a bad cause, and the sign would not have been molested.

Dewey could have gone about his affairs elsewhere, and left the competent Filipino army to starve out the little Spanish garrison and send it home, and the Filipino citizens to set up the form of government they might prefer, and deal with the friars and their doubtful acquisitions according to Filipino ideas of fairness and justice—ideas which have since been tested and found to be of as high an order as any that prevail in Europe or America.

But we played the Chamberlain game, and lost the chance to add another Cuba and another honorable deed to our good record.

The more we examine the mistake, the more clearly we perceive that it is going to be bad for the Business. The Person Sitting in Darkness is almost sure to say: "There is something curious about this—curious and unaccountable. There must be two Americas: one that sets the captive free, and one that takes a once-captive's new freedom away from him, and picks a quarrel with him with nothing to found it on; then kills him to get his land."

The truth is, the Person Sitting in Darkness *is* saying things like that; and for the sake of the Business we must persuade him to look at the Philippine matter in another and healthier way. We must arrange his opinions for him. I believe it can be done; for Mr. Chamberlain has arranged England's opinion of the South African matter, and done it most cleverly and successfully. He presented the facts—some of the facts—and showed those confiding people what the facts meant. He did it statistically, which is a good way. He used the formula: "Twice 2 are 14, and 2 from 9 leaves

35." Figures are effective; figures will convince the elect.

Now, my plan is a still bolder one than Mr. Chamberlain's, though apparently a copy of it. Let us be franker than Mr. Chamberlain; let us audaciously present the whole of the facts, shirking none, then explain them according to Mr. Chamberlain's formula. This daring truthfulness will astonish and dazzle the Person Sitting in Darkness, and he will take the Explanation down before his mental vision has had time to get back into focus. Let us say to him:

"Our case is simple. On the 1st of May, Dewey destroyed the Spanish fleet. This left the Archipelago in the hands of its proper and rightful owners, the Filipino nation. Their army numbered 30,000 men, and they were competent to whip out or starve out the little Spanish garrison; then the people could set up a government of their own devising. Our traditions required that Dewey should now set up his warning sign, and go away. But the Master of the Game happened to think of another plan—the European plan. He acted upon it. This was, to send out an army—ostensibly to help the native patriots put the finishing touch upon their long and plucky struggle for independence, but really to take their land away from them and keep it. That is, in the interest of Progress and Civilization. The plan developed, stage by stage, and quite satisfactorily. We entered into a military alliance with the trusting Filipinos, and they hemmed in Manila on the land side, and by their valuable help the place, with its garrison of 8,000 or 10,000 Spaniards, was captured—a thing which we could not have accomplished unaided at that time. We got their help by—by ingenuity. We knew they were fighting for their independence, and that they had been at it for two years. We knew they supposed that we also were fighting in their worthy cause—just as we had helped the Cubans fight for Cuban independence—and we allowed them to go on thinking so. *Until Manila was ours and we could get along without them.* Then we showed our hand. Of course, they were surprised—that was natural; surprised and disappointed; disappointed and grieved. To them it looked un-American; un-characteristic; foreign to our established traditions. And this was natural, too; for we were only playing the American Game in public—in private it was the European. It was neatly done, very neatly, and it bewildered them so they could not understand it; for we had been so friendly—so affectionate, even—with those simple-minded patriots! We, our own selves, had brought back out of exile their leader, their hero, their hope, their Washington—Aguinaldo; brought him in a warship, in high honor, under the sacred shelter and hospitality of the flag; brought him back and restored him to his people, and got their moving and eloquent gratitude for it. Yes, we had been so friendly to them, and had heartened them up in so many ways! We had lent them guns and ammunition; advised with them; exchanged pleasant courtesies with them; placed our sick and wounded in their kindly care; entrusted our Spanish prisoners to their humane and honest hands; fought shoulder to shoulder with them against "the common enemy" (our own phrase); praised their courage, praised their gallantry, praised their mercifulness, praised their fine and honorable conduct; borrowed their trenches, borrowed strong positions which they had previously captured from the Spaniards; petted them, lied to them—officially proclaiming that our land and naval forces came to give them their freedom and displace the bad Spanish Government—fooled them, used them until we needed them no longer; then derided the sucked orange and threw it away. We kept the positions which we had beguiled them of; by and by, we moved a force forward and overlapped patriot ground—a clever thought, for we needed trouble, and this would produce it. A Filipino soldier, crossing the ground, where no one had a right to forbid him, was shot by our sentry. The badgered patriots resented this with arms, without waiting to know whether Aguinaldo, who was absent, would approve or not. Aguinaldo did not approve; but that availed nothing. What we wanted, in the interest of Progress and Civilization, was the Archipelago, unencumbered by patriots struggling for independence; and the War was what we needed. We clinched our opportunity. It is Mr. Chamberlain's case over again—at least in its motive and intention; and we played the game as adroitly as he played it himself."

At this point in our frank statement of fact to the Person Sitting in Darkness, we should throw in a little trade-taffy about the Blessings of Civilization—for a change, and for the refreshment of his spirit—then go on with our tale:

"We and the patriots having captured Manila, Spain's ownership of the Archipelago and her sovereignty over it were at an end—obliterated—annihilated—not a rag or shred of either remaining

behind. It was then that we conceived the divinely humorous idea of *buying* both of these spectres from Spain! [It is quite safe to confess this to the Person Sitting in Darkness, since neither he nor any other sane person will believe it.] In buying those ghosts for twenty millions, we also contracted to take care of the friars and their accumulations. I think we also agreed to propagate leprosy and smallpox, but as to this there is doubt. But it is not important; persons afflicted with the friars do not mind the other diseases.

"With our treaty ratified, Manila subdued, and our Ghosts secured, we had no further use for Aguinaldo and the owners of the Archipelago. We forced a war, and we have been hunting America's guest and ally through the woods and swamps ever since."

At this point in the tale, it will be well to boast a little of our war-work and our heroisms in the field, so as to make our performance look as fine as England's in South Africa; but I believe it will not be best to emphasize this too much. We must be cautious. Of course, we must read the war-telegrams to the Person, in order to keep up our frankness; but we can throw an air of humorousness over them, and that will modify their grim eloquence a little, and their rather indiscreet exhibitions of gory exultation. Before reading to him the following display heads of the dispatches of November 18, 1900, it will be well to practice on them in private first, so as to get the right tang of lightness and gaiety into them:

"ADMINISTRATION WEARY OF PROTRACTED HOSTILITIES!"
"REAL WAR AHEAD FOR FILIPINO REBELS!"[1]
"WILL SHOW NO MERCY!"
"KITCHENER'S PLAN ADOPTED!"

Kitchener knows how to handle disagreeable people who are fighting for their homes and their liberties, and we must let on that we are merely imitating Kitchener, and have no national interest in the matter, further than to get ourselves admired by the Great Family of Nations, in which august company our Master of the Game has bought a place for us in the back row.

Of course, we must not venture to ignore our General MacArthur's reports—oh, why do they

[1] "Rebels!" Mumble that funny word—don't let the Person catch it distinctly [Twain].

keep on printing those embarrassing things?—we must drop them trippingly from the tongue and take the chances:

During the last ten months our losses have been 268 killed and 750 wounded: Filipino loss, *three thousand two hundred and twenty-seven killed*, and 694 wounded.

We must stand ready to grab the Person Sitting in Darkness, for he will swoon away at this confession, saying: "Good God, those 'niggers' spare their wounded, and the Americans massacre theirs!"

We must bring him to, and coax him and coddle him, and assure him that the ways of Providence are best, and that it would not become us to find fault with them; and then, to show him that we are only imitators, not originators, we must read the following passage from the letter of an American soldier-lad in the Philippines to his mother, published in *Public Opinion*, of Decorah, Iowa, describing the finish of a victorious battle:

"We NEVER LEFT ONE ALIVE. IF ONE WAS WOUNDED, WE WOULD RUN OUR BAYONETS THROUGH HIM."

Having now laid all the historical facts before the Person Sitting in Darkness, we should bring him to again, and explain them to him. We should say to him:

"They look doubtful, but in reality they are not. There have been lies; yes, but they were told in a good cause. We have been treacherous; but that was only in order that real good might come out of apparent evil. True, we have crushed a deceived and confiding people; we have turned against the weak and the friendless who trusted us; we have stamped out a just and intelligent and well-ordered republic; we have stabbed an ally in the back and slapped the face of a guest; we have bought a Shadow from an enemy that hadn't it to sell; we have robbed a trusting friend of his land and his liberty; we have invited our clean young men to shoulder a discredited musket and do bandit's work under a flag which bandits have been accustomed to fear, not to follow; we have debauched America's honor and blackened her face before the world; but each detail was for the best. We know this. The Head of every State and Sovereignty in Christendom and ninety per cent of every legislative body in Christendom, including our Congress and our fifty State Legislatures, are members not only of the church, but also of the Blessings-of-Civilization Trust. This world-girdling accumula-

tion of trained morals, high principles, and justice, cannot do an unright thing, an unfair thing, an ungenerous thing, an unclean thing. It knows what it is about. Give yourself no uneasiness; it is all right."

Now then, that will convince the Person. You will see. It will restore the Business. Also, it will elect the Master of the Game to the vacant place in the Trinity of our national gods; and there on their high thrones the Three will sit, age after age, in the people's sight, each bearing the Emblem of his service: Washington, the Sword of the Liberator; Lincoln, the Slave's Broken Chains; the Master, the Chains Repaired.

It will give the Business a splendid new start. You will see.

Everything is prosperous, now; everything is just as we should wish it. We have got the Archipelago, and we shall never give it up. Also, we have every reason to hope that we shall have an opportunity before very long to slip out of our Congressional contract with Cuba and give her something better in the place of it. It is a rich country, and many of us are already beginning to see that the contract was a sentimental mistake. But now—right now— is the best time to do some profitable rehabilitating work—work that will set us up and make us comfortable, and discourage gossip. We cannot conceal from ourselves that, privately, we are a little troubled about our uniform. It is one of our prides; it is acquainted with honor; it is familiar with great deeds and noble; we love it, we revere it; and so this errand it is on makes us uneasy. And our flag—another pride of ours, our chiefest! We have worshipped it so; and when we have seen it in far lands—glimpsing it unexpectedly in that strange sky, waving its welcome and benediction to us—we have caught our breath and uncovered our heads, and couldn't speak, for a moment, for the thought of what it was to us and the great ideals it stood for. Indeed, we *must* do something about these things; we must not have the flag out there, and the uniform. They are not needed there; we can manage in some other way. England manages, as regards the uniform, and so can we. We have to send soldiers—we can't get out of that—but we can disguise them. It is the way England does in South Africa. Even Mr. Chamberlain himself takes pride in England's honorable uniform, and makes the army down there wear an ugly and odious and appropriate disguise, of yellow stuff such as quarantine flags are made of, and which are hoisted to warn the healthy away from unclean disease and repulsive death. This cloth is called khaki. We could adopt it. It is light, comfortable, grotesque, and deceives the enemy, for he cannot conceive of a soldier being concealed in it.

And as for a flag for the Philippine Province, it is easily managed. We can have a special one—our States do it: we can have just our usual flag, with the white stripes painted black and the stars replaced by the skull and cross-bones.

And we do not need that Civil Commission out there. Having no powers, it has to invent them, and that kind of work cannot be effectively done by just anybody; an expert is required. Mr. Croker can be spared. We do not want the United States represented there, but only the Game.

By help of these suggested amendments, Progress and Civilization in the country can have a boom, and it will take in the Persons who are Sitting in Darkness, and we can resume Business at the old stand.

WILLIAM DEAN HOWELLS (1837–1920)

One important part of the ongoing story of American literature between the Civil War and about 1900 was a constant movement, on the part of writers, between New England—primarily Boston—and other sections of the country, especially the Midwest, the Southwest, and the Northwest. Some writers who had been born and raised in one of those outlying districts moved permanently to New England—like Mark Twain, who came from Missouri by way of California and New York to settle in Hartford, Connecticut. Some made a trial stay in New England and then returned for good to their native region, escaping from what Henry B. Fuller—who went from Chicago to Harvard and back again—described as the Boston sickness, a sort of cultural "anemia" with which the Boston literary society seemed to be increasingly afflicted. Others tended to commute, both literally and mentally: Hamlin Garland made his way east from Iowa, put in several years in Boston, paid a visit back home, and returned to New England to write about the western farming country from a partially eastern perspective. A number of New Englanders born and bred, sensing a growing sterility in the old environment, turned emigré: among them the minor naturalistic novelist Robert Herrick, whose family had lived in New England since the first generation of Puritans and who swapped a teaching job at Harvard for one at the University of Chicago. He remained there for thirty years, hating every minute of it, yet finding the bustling city a stimulating challenge.

Such incessant shuttling signified two quite opposite phenomena: the continuing lure of Boston and New England; and the simultaneously loosening hold on the American imagination of what had for so very long been the country's cultural center. Not the least striking aspect of the Gilded Age was the gradual giving over of artistic and intellectual leadership from New England to other regions. In the course of time, New York City was the greatest gainer, particularly since economic power had moved there; Wall Street took over from State Street, and imaginative energy followed the dollar. But the older stronghold's grip on the native mind had—say, in 1875—still a good many years to run.

The intermixture of New England and the West provides a parallel to—if it is not, indeed, a primary source for—the early development of fictional realism. The work of the first realists, as we shall see, shows an odd mingling of newly discovered phenomena freshly and closely observed (farm life in Iowa, small-town life in Indiana) with a residue of Puritan piety. And the representative par excellence of this entire chapter of literary history and achievement was William Dean Howells.

Howells grew up in Ohio, moved almost as a matter of course to Boston immediately after the end of the Civil War, presided benevolently over the literary world of New England for twenty years—and then, when he could stand it no longer (Boston, he said in the mid-eighties, had become a death-in-life), shifted down to New York City, taking with him as it were the country's literary hegemony.[1] Howells, who knew and had a pronounced influence upon every one of the other writers just named, was the chief spokesman for realism in his time and its most accomplished practitioner. To a large degree, the decades after the war were, from a literary viewpoint, the age of Howells.

When Henry Adams called the period "our Howells-and-James epoch," few readers would have gainsaid the description. But with the turn of time the association with James became a liability; James's reputation continued to grow, and he emerged as eminently superior—in most respects, though not in all—as a literary artist. Measured against his achievement, Howells' work has suffered severely. Then, too, there was Mark Twain looming more and more mountainously to divide the age with James—and with no room for a third. Howells lived on to see the world change before his eyes, and the old realist found himself becoming a symbol of the "genteel tradition" and polite timidities; and it was not long before he was being savaged by brash young men like H. L. Mencken and Sinclair Lewis. In the energetic hurly-burly of the 1920's, Howells faded into a literary period piece—a writer who once, fatally, had seemed to say that American novelists should devote themselves exclusively to "the smiling aspects of life." [2] He deserved a better fate.

Howells certainly wrote too much; he wrote

---

[1] There had of course been a certain amount of literary vitality in New York for a long time. One thinks, for example, of Whitman, Melville, Bryant, and of Duyckinck's influential periodical, the *Literary World*.

[2] In fact, that unlucky phrase occurred in a review of Dostoevski's *Crime and Punishment*, in September, 1886, and Howells' point was simply that the circumstances of life in Russia led novelists there to deal with personally experienced horrors, while the much less oppressive conditions in America induced writers to take a kindlier view. At just this time, Howells' personal life happened to be exceedingly grim, and he was soon to be appalled—one has to say radicalized—by the Haymarket riot and its aftermath. See below, pp. 1352–54.

1500 words a day almost every day of his life, wrote on trains and ships and in hotel rooms; and before he was through he had completed more than two dozen novels, thirty-one plays of various kinds, several volumes of poetry, eleven travel books, and an enormous amount of practical and theoretical criticism (not to speak of his voluminous correspondence). But among these works as many as ten or twelve novels must be ranked as superior by any standards, and three or four are better than that. Several of his travel books remain classics of their not unimportant kind. And for thirty years, from 1870 to 1900, he was the most powerful and valuable (though not always the shrewdest) literary critic in the country. It was Howells more than any other single person who created the atmosphere within which the modern American novel has flourished: an atmosphere of cordiality to new modes and varieties of fiction, and to younger writers far removed from New England; in particular, an atmosphere that encouraged realistic and down-to-earth fiction, as against the Romantic styles of earlier generations both in America and in England.

If Howells was closely tied to Henry James, he was also the best and most valuable friend Mark Twain ever had, and it was typical of Howells that he could be so honestly admiring and fond of two writers who could not abide one another. James said about Mark Twain that he was a writer fit only for primitive minds (if he had said that Twain appealed to the primitive *in* every cultivated mind, he would have been as unerringly on target as he usually was). Twain referred to James as "Henrietta Maria," and remarked that he would rather be sent to John Bunyan's heaven than be forced to read *The Bostonians*. Yet Howells understood, encouraged, and gave endless wise counsel to these giant opposites. He was no less acutely appreciative of other literary compatriots; for as one of his biographers, Van Wyck Brooks, has put it, Howells was "the one American writer who was aware of all the others." He was even aware of Herman Melville when most people had forgotten his name, insisting that in *Moby-Dick* and elsewhere Melville had shown himself to be the greatest of our romancers and responding amid the general silence and neglect to the "tender and subtle music" of *Battle-Pieces*. In 1890, he voiced warm praise for the totally unknown and, for what few readers there were, perversely strange poems of Emily Dickinson, discerning shrewdly enough "a radiant happiness in the twilight of [Miss Dickinson's] hidden, silent life." Howells was always on the alert for fresh talent, to be welcomed, analyzed, come to terms with. Against all his principles, to be sure, he seems to have disliked Dreiser's *Sister Carrie* and never mentioned it in public (its unlegitimized sexuality may have put him off); but Dreiser admired him as having been a "look-out on the watch-tower, straining for a fresh glimpse of genius." He thought to find such genius in the writers we have mentioned and in a number of others: in Stephen Crane as well as Hamlin Garland, in Frank Norris as well as Fuller, in the poems of Edwin Arlington Robinson and Robert Frost. Long before it was thought feasible to do so, Howells was looking hard for imaginative achievement in the work of New York's Jewish writers.

As editor of the *Atlantic Monthly*, Howells worked to create an awareness of American literature as a national manifestation. Not for nothing had he been connected for a number of months with the New York periodical—it was his first eastern job, in 1866—named in the very spirit of postwar America: E. L. Godkin's *Nation*.[3] It was precisely the moment for thinking along national lines (as a much later American President would put it), in literary as well as in political and economic terms. Howells thus opened the *Atlantic*—cautiously, so as not to alienate too rapidly the still dominant Brahmin group—to the midwestern stories of Edward Eggleston, the far western stories of Bret

Harte, the southwestern reminiscences of Mark Twain, the southern tales of George Washington Cable.

He also enlarged upon the national to take in the international. In the course of years, he reviewed and wrote essays on and prefaces to the works of the Russian writers—Turgenev, Pushkin, Dostoevski, Chekhov, and above all Tolstoi; of the French—Stendhal, Balzac, Zola; of Verga in Italy, Valdés in Spain, Björnson and Ibsen in Norway. Nor did this extraordinary hospitality spring from any vast vapid enthusiasm for anything that got printed. Howells could be magisterially negative, especially with the writings of the English, with whom he never hit it off (an essay by Howells in 1882, which declared that fiction had "become a finer art in our day than it was with Dickens and Thackeray" and which pointed to the American Henry James as the writer of the future, caused a storm all across the British Isles). He had a fine command of several foreign languages and read the Europeans in the original (the Russians in French and English). He was, in general, a discriminating and knowledgeable, and on the whole a courageous, critic.

As to his fiction, one can still feel as James did when he told Howells in 1882 that "I am greatly struck with the extreme *freshness* of your work. I mean that newness and directness of personal impression, of feeling as to what you write about, which is the most precious thing in literature." In *A Modern Instance*, in *The Rise of Silas Lapham*, in *A Hazard of New Fortunes*, and in a number of other books, one has just this sense of the freshly direct and personal, the steady and penetrating gaze of an uncommonly kindly and yet robust-spirited man —a man who knew, knew increasingly, that life had tragic overtones and that values were slippery and even treacherous things, but who also knew that human beings are wonderfully various and contradictory, and that there is something truly remarkable in the trivia and routines of our lives.

Howells was for the moment the chief proponent of "realism" in fiction, and for him

[3] Godkin dramatized his editorial intention by bringing out the first issue of the *Nation* on the Fourth of July, 1885. The periodical was devoted not only to healing the divisions between North and South, but to across-the-board reform; it was both antiracist and antimaterialist, and it set up high standards of artistic performance.

this meant, among many other things, drawing endlessly upon his own experiences for his novels and plays. And yet, looked at in a different perspective, those experiences comprise an oddly allegorical pattern, an allegory as it were of American literary and cultural history over six or seven decades. It is tempting to give allegorical, or at least representative, names to the distinguishable phases of his life, as though Howells (like Benjamin Franklin) had passed through a series of "types." To begin with, for example, there was the westerner: the boy who had been born in Ohio (in 1837) and who grew up in a succession of frontier Ohio villages where his father, an itinerant country editor, set up his print shop and published his little papers. The elder Howells was on friendly terms with several Congressmen, including the future President James A. Garfield. William Dean inherited his sense of ease with the politically prominent, but what the father bequeathed him in particular was the vision of a utopian society (the elder Howells was a Swedenborgian and a millennialist), and a love of poetry. William Dean had written five plays and a good deal of verse before he was thirteen, and he read everything he could lay his hands on—*Don Quixote* becoming his favorite book and remaining so, a model, for Howells, with its simplicity and freedom of design. He had almost no formal schooling at all, hardly a year of it, but in his adolescence he taught himself French, German, and Spanish, and a smattering of Latin. Meanwhile, he was absorbing the backwoods life: the deer and squirrels and free-running pigs, the covered wagons and the trappers and hunters heading for Oregon, the foghorns on the great Miami River, the tavern dances and the sleigh-rides, the thin rituals of courtship.

When he was about nineteen, Howells came to the state capital, Columbus, as a reporter attached to the state legislature. In Columbus he met Artemus Ward, the Cleveland humorist; he heard Emerson lecture and listened to speeches by Abraham Lincoln and Kossuth, the Magyar patriot. But by 1860, when he was twenty-three, the Middle West was beginning to feel too cramped, socially and intellectually.

And just as Henry James, out of a very similar feeling about New England and New York, left Boston to settle in Europe, Howells left Ohio to settle in Cambridge, Massachusetts. He entered his second phase and became a Bostonian.

The process, to be sure, was not quite that simple. In 1860, he wrote a campaign biography for Abraham Lincoln of Illinois, and out of the proceeds made his first visit to Boston. To the attractive and properly respectful young westerner (Howells then and later had what almost amounted to genius in his personal relations), the eminent men of letters in and around Boston were exceedingly cordial. Lowell, for whom Howells had an enormous regard, sent him to Hawthorne, in Concord; Hawthorne took him for a walk in the woods and asked questions (as did everyone else in the area) about that strange emerging thing, the American West. From Hawthorne, he went to Emerson, who had him to dine and spoke with gentle disparagement about Edgar Allan Poe (a "jingle man"). In Boston, he enjoyed a four-hour dinner with Lowell and Dr. Oliver Wendell Holmes, at the end of which Holmes remarked with amiable irony: "Well, James, this is something like the apostolic succession; this is the laying on of hands." Nothing could have been more prophetic; for if Holmes was the leading *causeur* of his time (in his published breakfast-table talks) and Lowell the lord among literary critics, Howells succeeded them both from 1870 onward.

Howells had hoped to find a position on the *Atlantic Monthly*, but there was nothing there for him at the time. He went to New York for a look around, and there met Walt Whitman at Pfaff's, the popular Swiss saloon; they got along very well, though Howells was at once attracted and puzzled by *Leaves of Grass*. Whitman, for whom Henry James was "only feathers," would later find Howells the one American novelist who interested him (though Howells, however moved he had been by the meeting, never quite had the nerve to publish Whitman in the *Atlantic*). But then Lincoln was elected, and in the wake of Howells' biography of him (which Lincoln had read carefully, with annotations and checkmarks opposite a dozen errors), the young writer was appointed American consul in Venice.

Howells sailed for Europe in November, 1861: that is, almost a year after South Carolina had seceded from the Union; nine months after the establishment of the Confederacy and the presidency of Jefferson Davis; and seven months after federal guns had fired on Fort Sumter, and the Civil War had begun. Yet Howells displayed little interest in these enormous events. One of the curiosities of his career is the long indifference to the political history surging around him—and another is a belated but direct involvement with that history perhaps more vigorous than any writer in his generation. He had not even bothered to interview Lincoln while preparing the biography, but simply sent a research assistant down to Springfield (a decision he would regret to his dying day). Now, arriving in Venice, he was under no illusion that he was usefully serving his country in time of tremendous stress: "I'm afraid," he admitted later, "my prime intent was to add to [my country's] literature and to my own credit." He sat out the entire war in Venice, vaguely convinced that, like a good novel, it would come to a happy ending: that is, it would bring about the end of southern slavery; for Howells had been antislavery from youth onward, though at this time he was still as ignorant and cliché-ridden about black Americans as everyone else of his class and background. Yet his case was as complex in this as it was in so many other regards. Guilt feelings about his remoteness from the conflict began to express themselves at once—in ironical allusions to the war as a "bloody farce," in proposals to dash back home and enlist, in an assortment of squirmings and denials. And Howells would look back time and again in his older age to probe the reasons why he (and others, like his close friends Henry James and Mark Twain) had somehow missed out on the greatest episode in American history.[4]

During his second year in Venice, Howells married Elinor Mead, a lively and artistically inclined girl from Vermont (her brother joined Stanford White and Charles McKim to form one of the most famous New York architectural firms of the century). They moved into an old palace on the Grand Canal; and since Howells' consular duties were light, they had much time to explore the ever-beguiling city. At the theater, they saw a number of plays by Goldoni, the eighteenth-century comic genius; it was Goldoni who helped shift Howells' own interest from writing poetry to writing prose. In contrast to any plays that Howells had written or had seen, Goldoni's plays depicted people in their ordinary reality. Such a concern with reality was reflected in the little sketches he began to write about Venice, and in which he was as observant of an old man brewing coffee in the courtyard as he was of the moon rising over the Lido; instead of guidebook monotonies, Howells concentrated on the lack of heating in winter and the chilblained feet of the fishmonger. *Venetian Life* was serialized in a Boston newspaper and published to much acclaim in 1866; by that time, Howells had written another book about Italy and, after a stint with the *Nation* in New York, had returned to Boston as assistant to James T. Fields, the editor of the *Atlantic*.[5]

He was a Bostonian for twenty-two years, and between 1871 and 1881, when he was editor-in-

---

[4] For a more detailed look at Howells and the Civil War, see Daniel Aaron's forthcoming study of American writers and the Civil War. We have also drawn elsewhere from this richly informative book. It can be em-

phasized here that a great many "northerners" took no part in the fighting. There were various devices for avoiding conscription (like the so-called bounty system), and the immense number of foreign troops could take up the slack (see the preliminary note to the period 1861–1914). The point is the long-lasting *effect* of non-participation on persons who, like Howells and James, felt a powerful if ambiguous involvement with the conditions of their American society.

[5] Howells' travel writing compares interestingly with that of Mark Twain, for example, in the latter's *Innocents Abroad*. Twain interlarded fairly direct and often eloquent physical descriptions with passages of zestful buffoonery—with the aim of establishing a complex of attitudes toward the foreign scenes and of ingratiating himself with his readers back home. Howells' method might be called compassionate realism: meticulous accuracy in his little vignettes, accompanied by a sense of the poignant or the endearing.

chief of the *Atlantic,* he might well have been called *the* Bostonian, at least within the world of letters. Soon after Howells and his wife settled in Cambridge, the James family moved into the neighborhood, and Howells at once struck up the warmest friendship with Henry James. They met every other day for long talks about art and literature and their own work; Howells published James's short stories and novellas and before long was serializing *Roderick Hudson.* (He also maintained cordial relations with Henry's brothers William and Robertson, and with Henry James, Sr., who, like Howells' father, was a Swedenborgian and a visionary.) Howells saw at once that James had genius—was an "unrivalled artist"—and offered to turn over half the magazine to his fiction. For literature it was already Indian summer in Boston, the season was a bright one and there still flourished the most vigorous intellectual and literary society the country could boast of—men who were all friends of Howells and many of them contributors to the *Atlantic:* Longfellow, Lowell, and the distinguished Dantean and Harvard professor Charles Eliot Norton; Henry Adams and Brooks Adams; Dr. Holmes; Francis Parkman; Charles Sanders Peirce, on the threshold of his career as a philosopher and logician; publisher Thomas Sergeant Perry, an editor of Lowell's *North American Review* and the person who performed the singularly important act of introducing both Howells and James to the fiction of Turgenev and Balzac.

In December, 1869, Howells took the risk of reviewing for the *Atlantic* a book called *The Innocents Abroad,* by a Californian (so Howells understood) named Mark Twain. Soon after, Twain dropped by the magazine's office to thank his anonymous supporter; and almost on the spot the two became closest friends for life. Twain induced Howells to stay up later and drink rather more Scotch than he would have liked, and he could always upset Howells by the boisterous masculinity of his language.[6] But

Howells enjoyed Twain's company immensely and took the measure of his genius as did no other contemporary critic. He labored tirelessly over Twain's manuscripts and made invaluable editorial suggestions; Twain in turn insisted to Howells that "You are really my only author. . . . I wouldn't give a damn for the rest." (It was in this letter of 1885 that Twain spoke so disparagingly about James's *The Bostonians* and confessed to having "nearly died from the overwork" of trying to read George Eliot's *Middlemarch:* "I wouldn't read another of those books for a farm.") Even when Twain, at a dinner for Whittier in 1877, woefully miscalculated his audience and made sport of Emerson, Longfellow and the honored guest, Howells, though shaken, stood firm. It may even be, as has been argued by Howells' most recent and perceptive biographer, Kenneth S. Lynn, that a part of Howells—the unregenerately midwestern and surreptitiously anti–eastern-establishment part—secretly rejoiced in the episode.

It was only slowly and tentatively that Howells himself turned to the writing of fiction. He was still trying his hand at playwriting in the late sixties and showed a talent for handling farcical situations of an everyday variety. Then, in December, 1871, there appeared *Their Wedding Journey,* a string of quasi-fictional vignettes through which the recently married Basil and Isabel March—characters based rather closely on Howells and Elinor—reenact the trip from Boston to Niagara and Montreal that the Howellses had made a little time before. The narrative is nothing, but the relationship between the newlyweds has an authentic ring to it, and in the successive glimpses of the American landscape Howells applied his considerable skill at "travel writing" to native grounds. There followed *A Chance Acquaintance* in late 1872: another travel story, this one taking place on a trip up

---

[6] When Howells wrote to suggest deleting some of "the profane words" in "Old Times on the Mississippi," then running serially in the *Atlantic* (1874), Twain

fired back a letter which read: "My dear Howells: Mrs. Clemens received the mail this morning & the next minute she lit into the study with danger in her eye & this demand on her tongue: where is the profanity Mr. Howells speaks of? Then I had to miserably confess that I had left it out when reading the mss. to her. Nothing but almost inspired lying got me out of this scrape with my scalp."

the Saguenay River, with a sprightly and ardently American young woman, Kitty Ellison, engaging in a series of debates about the values of American life with a self-consciously Europeanized Bostonian named Miles Arbuton. James admired the story a good deal, though he had some reservations; but it evidently hung about in his imagination until the two young people reappeared five years later, quickened into enduring life, as Daisy Miller and Winterbourne.

In between these first two efforts at fiction, Howells made a critical move which was, in effect, an overt endorsement of realism in fiction: a review, which Howells wrote only after some hesitation, of Edward Eggleston's *The Hoosier Schoolmaster*. Eggleston, Indiana-born, had lived for a number of years in Minnesota; by 1872, he was in Chicago; but he would soon follow the trail east—in his case to Brooklyn and New York, though at heart he was an adoptive New Englander. "I wish I was a Yankee," he had remarked in 1869. "I think I should like to be a Pilgrim Father. . . . I begin to think that Puritanism is Tip-topism." That latter phrase almost provides a metaphor for the first phase of American realistic writing, which was committed to the actual, the homely, and the slangy ("Tip-topism"), but which was still partly imbued with the moral vision of an earlier age ("Puritanism"). *The Hoosier Schoolmaster*, like most of Eggleston's other writings, reveals just that combination: the story of the young schoolteacher, Ralph Hartsook, encountering all the savagery and disorder of a hideous small Indiana town, Flat Creek—but with the story taking the mythic form of a battle between good angels and bad angels, to the point where Ralph "like the knights who could only find the Holy Grail in losing themselves . . . found the purest happiness." Howells, who knew that Lowell and the other guardians of the Brahmin culture would be offended even by an acknowledgment of Eggleston's book, took pains to stress both elements in the mix. In *The Hoosier Schoolmaster*, he wrote, "we are made acquainted with the rudeness and ugliness of the intermediate West . . . the West of horse-thief gangs and of mobs, of protracted

meetings and of extended sprees"; but, he continued, the story was, finally, one of "ignorance drawn slowly towards the desire of knowledge and decency in this world."

A concern with knowledge and decency, Howells implied, must be allowed to prevail: which was to say that for the time being concessions must still be made to the literary standards of local authorities like Lowell and Dr. Holmes. This meant that certain actualities in the American scene were not yet being truly grappled with in literature—and among these, much the most important was a major phenomenon coming into being with a rush in the wake of the Civil War: the big city. As we shall later remark, fiction did not really come to the big city until Stephen Crane's novel of 1893, *Maggie*. By that time, attention was at last being closely focused on the sometimes appalling conditions of urban life, as in the energetic if sometimes moralistic exposés by the Danish-born journalist Jacob Riis (*How the Other Half Lives*, for example, in 1890, and *The Children of the Poor*, in 1892). The age of muckraking, of journalistic revelations of corruption in high places, would by then be almost at hand; and these and other developments were about to have their crucial effect in releasing a second and very different wave of literary realism. (See, below, the discussion of "The New Realism.")

Howells himself was not a part of that second wave, though he was almost always generous toward it. But at the least he can be credited with having helped prepare for its coming. It was Howells, more than anyone else, who insisted that realism was fundamentally a matter of telling the truth— the truth about "the motives, the impulses, the principles that shape the life of actual men and women." If Howells and the realists contemporary with him tended to imbue their materials with a fund of moral piety, they did also and openly detest the sentimental falsehoods that crowded the pages of fiction in the 1860's. There was a romantic superstition, Howells would remember, that in every novel "the hero must *do* something to *win* the heroine; perform some valorous or generous act; save her from danger. . . ."

But after I began to look about me and consider, I observed that none of the loved husbands of the happy wives I knew had done anything to "win" them except pay a certain number of visits, send them flowers, dance or sit out dances with them at parties, then muster the courage to ask if they would have them.

Howells tried to get at the reality of the relation between the sexes in *Their Wedding Journey*—with complete success in the case of one notable reader (who, however, exaggerated the matter in retrospect). The book was "one fine piece of work," Theodore Dreiser was to say; "not a sentimental passage in it, quarrels from beginning to end, just the way it would be, don't you know, really beautiful and true."

It is impossible to date the beginnings of realism in America, or of any other comparable literary development; but March, 1872, may be taken as the moment when it won acceptance in high quarters. Realism, Howells once observed, was not started at one certain time by one manifest cause. It just "came"; one was abruptly aware that it had "come everywhere at once." Part of its local ancestry lay in Emerson's proclaimed interest in the immediate, the familiar, the low, as the materials of literary art. "What would we know the meaning of?" Emerson had asked: "the news from the boat, the meal in the firkin, the sound in the street." Emerson, of course, following the Puritan tradition, sought to discover the miraculous in these commonplaces, the moral law aglow amidst the here and now; and it can even be argued that Emerson's influential insistence upon the miraculous and the moral held back realism in America (for better or worse) as much as his stress upon the immediate spurred it on. It was the Emersonian side, we may say, of Henry James, which would lead him to declare the subject matter of the French novelists to be "unclean," however much he envied their freedom and admired their technique, and which prevented him (for better or worse) from confronting such subject matter himself. In any event, what is to be noted is that, while the

seeds of realism can indeed be found in the American background, realism arrived relatively late in this country—as compared with Europe, and most especially France; and that when it did arrive, it exhibited at first a certain native timidity. By 1872, Balzac had been dead for more than two decades and Flaubert had already made his mark; when James came to Paris three years later, he could rejoice in the company of Zola, the Goncourt brothers, and De Maupassant, as well as Flaubert.

These latter slowly gained recognition, by Howells and others, in America, and their example mingled with the native traditions. There were other ingredients in early realism. The Scottish philosophy of "common sense" was having an influence: the earthy view that the way we know things is simply to look at them and see them. There was the rising prestige of scientific empiricism and the theories of Darwin (what St. Paul had called the "Old Adam," Eggleston suggested, "Darwin would call the remains of the wild beast"). And as a key literary factor, there was the argument of the French critic Hippolyte Taine that a literature should above all express its own time and place. (Eggleston, again, took Taine's philosophy as his own and said as much in his preface to *The Mysteries of Metropolisville* [1873], where he announced his wish "to make my stories of value as a contribution to the history of civilization in America.")[7]

Howells had followed *Their Wedding Journey* and *A Chance Acquaintance* with five other novels during the seventies. But it was the eighties that constituted the great decade for him. He resigned from the *Atlantic* to devote himself full-time to his writing. In 1886, he signed a contract with Harper and Brothers in New York—though he was still a resident of Boston—by which Howells agreed to give Harper's all his occasional writings, one novel a year, and a monthly column ("The Easy Chair" in *Harper's* magazine), for $10,000 a year: an

[7] For this and much other information about the early realists, we are indebted to *Harvests of Change: American Literature, 1865–1914* (1967), by Jay Martin.

amount that has to be multiplied seven or eight times over to give it contemporary resonance. He was independent, affluent, honored, and endlessly productive.

Was he also contented? The image of Howells that comes down from those years is one of a short (five feet, four inches), stout, kindly, and somewhat complacent man; a smiling public person; moving almost effortlessly from success to success. In the space of nine years he wrote novels of the very high order of *A Modern Instance* (1882), *The Rise of Silas Lapham* (1885), and *A Hazard of New Fortunes* (1890) —not to mention several others which would have secured the lasting reputation of a lesser talent (*Indian Summer, April Hopes, Annie Kilburn*). But the complacent, smiling face belied the secret story. Howells lived with anxieties and tensions, some rooted deep in his nature, some provoked by the vicissitudes of his life.

As for temperament, Howells did, Kenneth Lynn argues, have a propensity for guilt feelings, particularly about things that he did *not* do. He felt guilty about not keeping up a friendship, during his childhood, with a boy his parents disapproved of; he condemned himself for not reaching his mother's bedside before her death in 1868; he found no sufficient excuse for his failure to take part in the Civil War; and most deeply of all, perhaps, he felt that he had never, since 1880, strained his creative abilities to the utmost. There were other and very real family problems. Howells' younger brother Henry was born an idiot and was looked after by his beloved sister Veronica, whom Howells helped financially as best he could; Elinor Howells suffered from chronic illness and spent the last twenty years of her life (she died in 1910) as a virtually complete invalid. Worst of all, Howells' daughter Winifred, a charming and talented girl, underwent a mysterious but almost total breakdown in the summer of 1880, when she was sixteen. She was subjected to various alleged cures (one of them had her eat eight meals a day, napping in between), recovered from time to time only to have a worse relapse than ever, and was finally placed in an asylum. Dr. S. Weir Mitchell, a famous nerve specialist, took over; but in March, 1889, Winifred quite suddenly died.

Winifred's hopeless affliction (which an autopsy showed to have been organic) thus lasted through nearly the entire decade of Howells' greatest literary achievement; and it was, one judges, among the elements that drove Howells to his most intensive efforts. The achievement began, in 1882, with *A Modern Instance*, the novel Howells found hardest to finish. He made a start on it as early as 1875, after seeing a romantic German version of the *Medea* of Euripides. He saw in the drama of ardent love turning into murderous hate something as contemporary as an "Indiana divorce case" and set himself to writing a novel on the theme. But the going proved slow, even painful (it is difficult not to suspect that the idea of divorce was nibbling at Howells' mind and was being resolutely thrust away); and he put the manuscript aside after two chapters. He returned to it in the winter of 1881 and wrote steadily for nine months—until, in November, he himself collapsed and lay bedridden and inert for seven weeks. Crawling back to life, Howells managed, drudgingly, to complete the novel in a few more months.

The book's title is a covert statement of the realist creed. The tangled story of Bartley and Marcia Hubbard is a modern instance of the tragedy of Medea and Jason exactly insofar as it suggests how a gradually estranged couple would really behave under the modern circumstances: far from engaging in ferocious deeds, they would probably end up, like the Hubbards, in a divorce court. Nor are the central characters outsize tragic figures caught in conditions of extreme tension. Bartley is a clever and attractive young man with a nice sense of humor; but he is morally tone-deaf—"deplorably smart," his college classmate Ben Halleck says of him, "and regrettably handsome . . . with no more moral nature than a base-ball." Marcia Gaylord is a country girl, from Equity, Maine, the daughter of a fanatically stern but not unintelligent father and a blank of a mother, who falls desperately in love, runs after her lover to Boston, marries him and bears him a child, tries in her ignorant way to make him a comfortable home, but never succeeds in understanding her husband or the Boston world that eventually undermines him.

The deterioration of Bartley Hubbard is handled with remarkable subtlety; it is perfectly paced and is probably Howells' masterpiece of character analysis. The same cannot be said for the plot as a whole. Howells despised what he called "the foolish joys of mere fable," no doubt because firmness of plot structure would give an unrealistic impression of life. In *A Modern Instance*, Howells allows himself coincidences (accidental and crucially important meetings, for example) that must have made Henry James wince with aesthetic pain. But the individual episodes are splendid. About one of them—in which Bartley, after a tiff with Marcia, flings out of the house and proceeds to a night on the town—Mark Twain wrote delightedly: "That's the best drunk-scene—because the truest—that I ever read. . . . How very drunk, and how recently drunk, and how altogether admirably drunk you must have been to enable you to contrive that masterpiece." No less accurate and much more difficult to create is the moral murkiness that pervades the atmosphere of the book, the whole of the novel's world—an ethical vagueness and slackness that goes far to explain Bartley's downfall and that so strikingly characterizes the Gilded Age. The quality is reflected in the last words of the book, when Atherton, a minor figure who has been deposing pompously about Marcia Hubbard and Ben Halleck, is asked impatiently by his wife what moral advice he would offer them: "Atherton . . . drew a troubled sigh. 'Ah, I don't know! I don't know!'"

Edith Wharton, who admired Howells and thought that he "was the first to feel the tragic potentialities of life in the drab American small town," nonetheless felt in him an "incurable moral timidity which . . . drew him back even from the logical conclusion of *A Modern Instance*." She would have preferred, one supposes, that Howells show Marcia and Ben living on each into a lonely, bleak, and self-punishing old age. But Howells was seeking to remain faithful to the realistic vision. He was convinced that life *was* ambiguous, and experience—perhaps unsatisfactorily—open-ended.

Hippolyte Taine was much taken with *The Rise of Silas Lapham:* "the best novel written by an American," he called it, "the most like Balzac's"; he urged that it be translated into French. In creating Lapham and his family ("for us new types," Taine said) and in juxtaposing them with the socially elegant and well-born Coreys, Howells was doing what Taine thought serious literature had always done and should do—he was giving expression to his time and place. The place was Boston, more largely the eastern United States. The time was the 1870's, more largely the postwar period when the business class came into its own. Silas Lapham, the wealthy paint manufacturer, was not a brand new type in history (he puts one somewhat in mind of Cornelius Vanderbilt), but he was relatively new to fiction. There had been, to be sure, the occasional fictional portraits of men "in trade," and in 1875 there had been *Sevenoaks*, the novel by Josiah Gilbert Holland based on the extraordinary financial depredations of the Robber Baron Jim Fisk. But *Silas Lapham* was probably the first American work of fiction which succeeded in conveying—in embodying and dramatizing—the developing new attitude to money and manufacturing, and almost (though not quite) to technology. It may well be that the fundamental narrative treatment of the business mentality in America was that of Mark Twain in *A Connecticut Yankee* (published four years after *Silas Lapham*); and certainly the most exhaustive and powerful sketch of the American man of financial affairs would be Dreiser's trilogy about "the financier," Frank Cowperwood. But here again, as in so many other significant instances, Howells demonstrably led the way.

"Money is the romance, the poetry of our age," says Bromfield Corey with a tired but accurate irony, in *Silas Lapham*. "It's the thing that chiefly strikes the imagination. The Englishmen who come here are more curious about the great new millionaires than about anyone else." This was true, and it was equally true of French intellectuals like Paul Bourget, who came to America in 1893 not so much to meet writers and artists as to observe, with Gallic eye, the manners of the men of wealth (like the enormously affluent "Jack" Gardiner of Boston). For Silas Lapham, there is something magical, almost literally enchanting, about paint and the making of it; when he names his favorite brand after his wife Persis he is half-consciously investing it with his wife's stern and simple moral nature; and when young Tom Corey says without a trace of irony that Lapham's paint is "a blessing to the world," we realize suddenly that religious motifs have been diverted into business affairs.

This story about the romance of money is at the same time the story of the social drama of the new wealth, and nobody, not even James, could render that drama with greater fidelity to the underlying significance of the historical moment. James might conceivably have drawn a character like Bromfield Corey, the witty, cultivated, effete Boston Brahmin; but he could never have set him in a relation with the vigorous crudity of Silas Lapham (it is hard indeed to think of any writer in Howells' time who could have put two such men in the same book) —and in a way to make each figure reveal himself, for better and worse, the more fully. "The whole Lapham tribe is distasteful to me," Corey says without rancor. "I ask myself, what have I done nothing for, all my life, and lived as a gentleman should upon the earnings of somebody else, in the possession of every polite taste and feeling that adorns leisure, if I'm to come at last to this? It wasn't their behavior . . . ; but their conversation was terrible." The latter contention does not, of course, hold for Penelope, Lapham's articulate, well-read, sardonic, and secretly passionate daughter; and it is characteristic of Howells' subtle pattern of character movement that while Lapham and the elder Corey are worlds apart, young Tom Corey, who goes to work for Silas, moves in the direction of Lapham and contemporary reality, and Penelope, whom he eventually marries and carries off to Mexico, shares something of the Corey style of life.

But it is, finally, the *moral* drama that gives

the novel its great distinction. Howells' supreme gift was for detecting, and finding the fictional resources for describing, the moral fogginess that the Gilded Age brought with it. (Here, it should be acknowledged, James in *The Bostonians,* published the year before *Silas Lapham,* proved himself Howells' equal.) It is not simply a matter of making manifest a deterioration in American moral values; it is rather one of showing the profoundly unsettling effect upon those values of the new lust for producing commodities and the new drive to acquire immense riches: more generally, of the bringing into being of moral dilemmas the old morality had never had to cope with.

In the course of his financial "rise," Lapham had treated his former partner, a certain Rogers, with ruthless injustice. This troubles Persis Lapham, but for a long period Silas is honestly unable to see that he had done anything wrong. But it quietly colors his relations with his family, adds to his defensiveness with the Coreys, and disturbs his sense of himself. Then, in the climactic episode, Lapham has the opportunity to save himself from financial ruin and also to be of assistance to Rogers—who has, in fact, turned out to be a shabby specimen—by performing an unmistakably unethical transaction. He struggles mightily against the temptation and overcomes it; he goes out of business; but having paid off his moral debt, he also manages to pay off all his monetary debts. His financial fall is thus his moral rise; but Howells the realist does not exaggerate the case. Lapham does not become a philosopher of ethics. The morality of life remains a puzzle; and at the end Lapham, though fairly cheerful and content, is still scratching his head and biting at his moustache in puzzlement over what he had done. He knows that, morally speaking, he had barely made it: "Seems sometimes as if it was a hole opened for me, and I crept out of it. I don't know."

We may cite a key moment in the moral drama, as indicating something about the technique of realism. During the night when Silas Lapham is fighting his way mentally toward a decision,

his wife heard him begin walking up and

down; and then the rest of the night she lay awake and listened to him walking up and down. But when the first light whitened the window, the words of the scripture came into her mind: "And there wrestled a man with him until the breaking of the day. . . . And he said, Let me go, for the day breaketh. And he said, I will not let thee go, except thou bless me."

It would be overhasty to assume that Howells has here given us the clue to his novel's "larger meanings," and that the quotation from the Old Testament story of Jacob wrestling with the angel tells us that the story of Silas Lapham is an allegory about the battle between conscience and pride. Howells only says that the Scriptural words *came into Persis Lapham's mind*. It is Lapham's wife, and she alone, who sees her husband reenacting the struggle of Jacob. The same kind of thing is true of the other "symbols" in the book, and there are many, including the extravagant house Lapham is building on Beacon Street. These objects mean *what* they mean—social advancement, cultural elevation, sexual play—purely in the minds of the characters involved. These meanings may be intense; they may also (as in the case of Irene, who wrong-headedly believes Tom Corey to be in love with her) be woefully in error. Howells, in any event, is insisting that this is the way significance realistically accumulates in the minds of actual people.

Another turning point in Howells' life, perhaps the most important of all, occurred between 1886 and 1889; and as a result of it, Howells the Bostonian became the New Yorker; Howells the realist became the critical realist; and Howells the democrat became the socialist. The crucial event was the Haymarket Square riot in 1886, and its appalling aftermath. On May 3, 1886, a meeting was held in Chicago to agitate in favor of an eight-hour work day—a demand which, needless to say, was vociferously opposed by the whole of American industry on constitutional, Biblical, and economic grounds. A fight broke out between strikers and non-

strikers, and the police fired into the crowd, killing one man and wounding several others. Next day there was a mass protest meeting; while the assembly was being harangued, a force of 125 policemen marched upon it, and at that moment, from behind the speaker's wagon, a bomb was thrown directly at them. One policeman was killed outright, and six more died as a result of wounds; perhaps as many as seventy were injured. The country, which already had the jitters over the alleged threat of anarchism, became hysterical; and Chicago, where bands of furious citizens prowled the streets hoping to track down anarchists, became, in the words of the novelist Robert Herrick, "an illuminating demonstration of what a city and its forces of law and order are capable when in the grip of fear, suspicion, and a lust for revenge." Eight anarchists were rounded up apparently at random; they were brought to trial and four of them were condemned to death. One committed suicide, and in November, 1887, the other three were hanged. Nothing that came out during the trial connected any one of them with the bomb-throwing.

Howells read the transcript of the trial with the utmost care and growing horror. He came to the conclusion not only that the verdict was a travesty of justice and the later execution (as he wrote a friend) hideous, damnable, and abominable, but that there was something seriously, perhaps radically, wrong with American society. It is as difficult to account for the sudden eruption of Howells' social conscience as it is to explain why it took him so long to perceive the deeper currents of immediate history. He is not, however, the only liberal-minded American on record who has sought to atone for a lifetime of political indolence by an abrupt flurry of involvement. In Howells' case, his imagination—in *A Modern Instance* and *Silas Lapham*—had understood what was happening to America long before his rational intellect succeeded in taking it in. And his imagination, we have suggested, had itself been stung and stretched by personal calamity. By the mid-eighties, Howells was in a condition, psychologically and otherwise, to plunge into the arena.

So he became the champion of the condemned men in Chicago, and virtually the only one in the world of letters. Between the trial and the execution, he appealed to friends for help (Whittier turned him down flatly and made rather a show of having done so), discussed matters with the defense counsel, petitioned the Governor of Illinois for mercy, and wrote an open letter to the New York *Tribune*. For all this, he was violently abused on all sides, and he had reason to fear that he would lose his position with *Harper's*.

It was at just this time that he fell, once and for all, under the influence of Tolstoi. He had admired Tolstoi for some years; now he felt that the Russian novelist's books were "worth all the other novels ever written." In them one came face to face with human nature for the first time in fiction. He imbibed Tolstoi's brand of Christian socialism (or anarchism) as laid forth in *What to Do* (the French version of which, *Que Faire*, he reviewed for *Harper's* in 1887), with its absolute rejection of violence or governmental coercion in any form; but he felt that such theories might be better conveyed in fiction than in didactic essays. He also adopted, as part of his new theoretical luggage, the anti-industrial view of the English poet and fabulist William Morris.

Howells pronounced his socialist creed, well-stocked with quotations from Tolstoi, frequently enough, but he was only intermittently an activist. He claimed to be a "theoretical socialist" but a "practical aristocrat," going to a fashionable tea in the afternoon and to a workers' meeting in the evening. He came out as strongly as William James and Mark Twain against America's involvement in the Philippines; he joined the crowds marching in favor of the vote for women; and in 1909 he took a leading part in founding the National Association for the Advancement of Colored People.[8] But Howells' socialism took the primary form of a revised view of realism.

Critical realism, he now argued, demanded that literature deal with the actual conditions of society at large, and while it should never lecture or seek to impose a morality, it should subtly stir men to try to improve those conditions. It should add its American testimony to that of Tolstoi in condemning "the system by which a few men win wealth and miserably waste it . . . and the vast mass of men are overworked and underfed." It should above all expose the inequality and move men to work for "equality, which is justice writ large."

Howells felt that, as a result of the Haymarket affair and his readings in Tolstoi and Morris, his own horizons had "infinitely widened." Boston could no longer contain him; the old intellectual society had withered, and he felt that life there had in fact become a kind of death-in-life. He wanted now to feel himself in touch with the entire United States. And so, in 1889, he moved to New York—"the one city," he had a fictional character say, "that belongs to the whole country." He thus became Howells the New Yorker, and in the allegory of his life his shift from New England to Manhattan symbolized very accurately a similar and larger shift of literary interest and activity.

Annie Kilburn (1889) was the first fictional fruit of Howells' critical realism. That novel suffers somewhat from the explicitly and not always convincingly Tolstoian sentiments of the minister Julius Peck; for, given those actualities of the American scene which Howells had committed himself to depict, it would be better and truer to life to have the Tolstoian figure occupy a lesser place. In *A Hazard of New Fortunes*, Howells kept the balance much better. He felt that this novel was his "most vital book," and it certainly presents the broadest range of human vitality of any of his writings. The sense of New York as representing the whole of America is conveyed when Ohio-born Basil March and his New England wife come to New York, there to work with Fulkerson from the Midwest, and to meet the Pennsylvania Dutch Dryfoos and his family, Angus Beaton from Syracuse, his former German teacher Lindau (who carries the burden of Tolstoi in the novel), Colonel Woodburn and his daughter from Virginia, and others still who have come

---

[8] On the origins of the NAACP, see the introduction to W. E. B. Du Bois, below.

from afar to join in the "vast, gay, shapeless" scene of the city. (We have more to say about this novel in the headnote to our selection from it.)

Howells continued to enact his role of the traveler. In 1882, he had gone back to Italy and England; he visited Switzerland and later made long tours of Germany and Spain. In 1894, he was in Paris and, calling upon the painter Whistler one evening, in the Rue du Bac, he met a friend of Henry James. Laying his hand on the young man's shoulder, he said broodingly: "Live all you can. It's a mistake not to. I'm old; it's too late. But you have time; you are young. Live!" That little speech made its way back to James, who centered an entire novel, *The Ambassadors,* around it—after hastening to assure Howells that the story had "got away from you, or anything like you, and become impersonal and independent." Howells was in fact only fifty-seven when he said the words; but his extraordinary productivity over thirty years had left him feeling tired and dissatisfied, while the observable aspects of his country gave him little to smile at.

But there was no letting up in the nineties: ten novels, including *A Hazard of New Fortunes,* and a steady stream of criticism and travel writing. Among the novels were Howells' two contributions to the explosion of utopian literature set off by Edward Bellamy's *Looking Backward: 2000–1887* ("a fairy tale of social felicity," as Bellamy called it), Julian West's dreamlike survey of a model society, against which the oppressions and injustices of the later nineteenth century stand out with intolerable sharpness.[9] Howells, who had reviewed

Looking Backward in 1888, praised Bellamy's imagination as akin to Hawthorne's (the Hawthorne, presumably, of "Dr. Heidegger's Experiment" and "The Birthmark"), and in *A Traveler from Altruria* (1894) he tried his own hand at the utopian game. The traveler in question is a Mr. Homos, who listens while a group of Americans at a summer hotel explain, defend, and even complacently praise every abuse the country was suffering from—and then politely describes his own Altruria, which is based on equality and human brotherhood, where money has been abolished, self-seeking is unknown, and every individual is a kind of artist pursuing his personal calling and taste. It is a book that makes some telling points in its rather mechanical way; and its sequel, *Through the Eye of the Needle*—letters exchanged between Mr. Homos and the American woman whom he marries and takes back to Altruria—adds further elements to the general indictment.

The last of Howells' novels that still repays attention is *The Landlord at Lion's Head* (1897), which more than one critic (Kenneth Lynn, for example) tends to regard as his best. Certainly the characterization of Jeff Durgin, the landlord of another New England summer hotel—a "bad mixture," as someone calls him, attractive to women but inconstant and given to very bad judgment—almost rivals that of Bartley Hubbard in *A Modern Instance.* Unlike Bartley, however, Jeff—who at one time is involved with three different girls—ends up in financial triumph. Working as he so often did with significant contrasts, Howells juxtaposes the energetic, unstable Durgin against the older and morally more solid Westover; and perhaps the most telling aspect of the novel is that Durgin does not altogether lose in the process of mutual measurement. In publishing *The Landlord at Lion's Head,* Howells seemed to have moved into still another stage of fiction —of which, unfortunately, that novel was to be the only memorable example.

But it was in the nineties and the decade fol-

---

[9] Bellamy's work was not, of course, the first in the socialist-visionary vein, but no other book had anything remotely like its impact. There were myriad imitations; Bellamy clubs were founded; and a political party got under way in Bellamy's name. John Dewey found in it the first statement of "the *human* meaning of democracy," and Thorstein Veblen's wife attributed much of her husband's early economic thought to the book. As Jay Martin points out in *Harvests of Change,* it was precisely because of the *literary* power of *Looking Back-*

ward that it had an impact far greater than any economic or political tract.

lowing that Howells gave so much encouragement and public support to younger writers, and the more so as he felt his own creative vitality flagging. A single episode can suggest the thickening network of Howells' literary campaigning. In 1893, Hamlin Garland, who had been a devotee of Howells since the latter got him started with praise of *Main-Travelled Roads*, sent his benefactor a cheaply published paperback novel called *Maggie*, by a totally unknown writer named Stephen Crane. Infected by Garland's excitement, Howells read the book, was much struck by it, and invited Crane to tea. Crane, who was depressed by the lack of attention *Maggie* had received, went around, hoping for some promise of a public statement about it. But Howells, after speaking kindly of Crane's abilities, spent most of the evening reading to his guests from the work of still another recent discovery—the poems of Emily Dickinson. A little later, however, Howells did declare, in a newspaper interview, that a very impressive new writer had appeared in the person of Crane.

In 1912, on his seventy-fifth birthday, Howells' publishers gave a party for him at Sherry's restaurant. President Taft was among the four hundred guests, and letters poured in from H. G. Wells, Thomas Hardy, Henry James (his arriving too late to be read at the banquet), and countless others. It was a grand occasion; but Howells was already in eclipse. He had the humiliation of having an article rejected by *Harper's*; Mencken and other young Turks were readying for the attack. Five years before, indeed, he had written James that "I am comparatively a dead cult" and spoke of "scornings and buffetings on all sides." His energy, nonetheless, never entirely deserted him; he kept at work, writing, revising, translating. He moved to an apartment on Central Park; and there, in 1920, while trying desperately to complete a long retrospective essay on James, he died.

Hamlin Garland (1860–1940)

Another way to define the first stage of American realism, and to understand Howells' place in it, is to follow the careers of two of his many protégés, Hamlin Garland and Henry B. Fuller.

Garland's father was a transplanted New Englander, who had first settled in a midwestern village with, as it were, a transplanted New England name: West Salem, Wisconsin. The family moved to Iowa in 1869 (when Hamlin was nine), and twelve years later, in the wake of successive crop failures, to what was still known as the Dakota Territory. Young Garland, who had just turned twenty-one, broke free at this time, tried an assortment of jobs, wandered through the East, and ended up in Boston living on five dollars a week and spending almost every day for three years in the public library. In the wilds of Dakota, he had already hit upon *The Hoosier Schoolmaster*, along with Hawthorne and Shakespeare, and (it is an odd symbol of the speed of cultural diffusion) the writings of Taine. Now, in Boston, he discovered Herbert Spencer and Walt Whitman, with a horde of other writers. With all this in his head, he made a return visit to Iowa and South Dakota in 1887 and was appalled. His rather happy childhood memories vanished before "the gracelessness of these homes, and the sordid quality of the mechanical daily routine of these lives."

He determined to write about that scene, but to do so truthfully (for his own brand of writing, Garland coined the awkward word "veritism"); he would present "rural life . . . from an entirely new angle" to depict "the ugliness, the endless drudgery, and the loneliness of the farmer's lot." Beginning with "Mrs. Ripley's Trip" in 1888, Garland published a series of bleak tales about farming life, which he collected, in 1891, in *Main-Travelled Roads*. Howells, now writing for *Harper's* in New York, saluted it warmly. Alluding to the wave of agrarian protest, Howells wrote:

If any one is still at a loss to account for that uprising of the farmers in the West . . . let him read *Main-Travelled Roads*, and he will begin to understand. . . . The stories are full of those gaunt, grim, sordid, pathetic, ferocious figures, whom our satirists find so easy to caricature as Hayseeds and whose blind gropings for fairer conditions are so grotesque to the newspapers and so menacing to the politicians. . . .

Howells, with his enlarging social conscience, had become so alert to the social and political implications of new fiction by 1891 that he overlooked Garland's tendency to slip from pathos into sentimentality (as in the otherwise moving little story "Mrs. Ripley's Trip," about a worndown farming woman who saves her nickels for twenty years to make a brief visit back east to her folks in "Yaark State"). Elsewhere, his figures are characterized not so much by "blind gropings" as by a fierce puritanic outrage at the selfishness and cruelty of those who hold the upper hand (for example, in "Under the Lion's Paw," the best story in the group).

In *Main-Travelled Roads,* Garland maintained a tension of sorts between realistic observation and emotionalism or moral fervor. But the mixture did not hold for long. He went on to write a number of novels, all extremely popular, which tackled contemporary social issues by means of highly romantic plots full of those "valorous or generous acts" which realism, in the person of Howells, had set itself to reject. After the appearance of *Cavanaugh, Forest Ranger* in 1910, a thriller which touches on the problem of the conservation of natural resources, Howells implored him to "revert to the temper of your first work, and give us a picture of the wild life you know so well on the lines of *Main-Travelled Roads.*" But Garland turned instead to a series of ostensibly autobiographical volumes—the *Middle Border* books, which the public ate up—designed to create an almost entirely mythical American West, a land of romance, nobility, and derring-do. In 1920, he reviewed quite unfavorably Sinclair Lewis's *Main Street,* dismissing it in terms that revealed the inherent contradiction of early realism: Lewis, he wrote, "is not quite large enough, not quite generous enough, to fuse the minute, distressing details into something noble." Like many realists contemporary with him, Garland, it seems, could not stand very much reality.

Henry B. Fuller (1857–1929)

Henry B. Fuller could stand reality only in small doses. If "reality" was represented by the physical and human American landscape, Fuller preferred to pay it only an occasional visit. His writing career began with two novels set respectively in Italy and France (*The Chevalier of Pensieri-Vani,* 1890, and *The Chatelaine de la Trinité,* 1892), where his informed affection for European habits and countrysides was well demonstrated. But he was a great admirer of Howells' *Silas Lapham*—"the great representative novel of American manners," he called it— and after Howells had urged him to "write of Chicago whether you like it or not," Fuller applied himself to *The Cliff-Dwellers* in 1892, and *With the Procession* three years later. The realists were always telling each other to stick to the subject closest at hand, just as in later years they were always debating, in a rather futile fashion, as to who, in Dreiser's words, "led the van of realism in America." For Dreiser, "that honour—if any American will admit it to be such—goes to Henry B. Fuller of Chicago," since Fuller, in *With the Procession,* had written "as sound and agreeable a piece of American realism as that decade, or any since [he was writing in 1928], has produced."

Fuller was on record as believing that the traditional novel was dead, or should be encouraged to die, and that fiction in its single-minded pursuit of fact should emulate the art of journalism and should even perhaps give way entirely to biography. Thus early was there formulated the concept of "fact fiction," which has flourished periodically in the literary culture of the United States during the present century (most recently, of course, in the work of John Hersey and Norman Mailer, for example); and thus early was journalism acknowledged to *be* an art, and one that a writer of fiction might profitably engage in.[10] Even muckraking investi-

---

[10] Among others who had come to fiction from journalism, or vice versa, or who have at least occasionally applied their creative talents to newspaper or magazine

gations of scandals in the nation's capital sprang from the same concern with getting the data straight.

Literary realism, nonetheless, could not restrict itself to a sheer accumulation of fact, however much it might feed on fact. Something had yet to be added, but Fuller would not be the one to discover what it was. In his first two Chicago novels, there was indeed little of the moralistic residue one finds in Eggleston and even the early Garland. But nature abhors a literary vacuum as much as any other kind; and Fuller replaced moral attitudes with simple melodrama—especially in *The Cliff-Dwellers,* which introduces us to embezzlement, blackmail, legal vengeance, murder, suicide, and timely death. None of this has much to do with the novel's basic intention: which is to inspect the inhabitants of a Chicago skyscraper (the Clifton, eighteen stories high) with a well-educated anthropological eye, as if they were the members of a curious and unfamiliar tribe,

reporting (in generations after Mark Twain and Stephen Crane), have been Dreiser, Willa Cather, Edith Wharton, and Ernest Hemingway.

In addition to the particular sections on these writers, see also the introduction to 1861–1914.

with strange rituals and practices. *With the Procession,* which is less histrionic and also less interesting, owes much to *Silas Lapham* in its family portrait of a narrow-visioned but essentially decent businessman, his suitably bourgeois wife, and their children, and of the family's sociologically indicative ambitions (cultural refinement, good works, social status). Unfortunately, the characters strike one as being manipulated: not by history or fate, but simply by the author.

Fuller thereafter alternated between undisguised romances, almost fantasies, set in Italy, and further explorations of the Chicago scene. Despite the genuine promise of the first Chicago stories, Fuller contributed nothing further to the development of fictional realism. It was as though he had been shut out of some creative secret—some way of rendering immediate actuality so as to give it permanence and meaning. Howells, fairly late in his life and when he felt his own creative energy ebbing, said to Fuller: "Now you will have to write my novels for me." It was perhaps a shrewder remark than Howells knew—for Fuller at his best would only have repeated Howells. For writers that went clearly beyond Howells, one must look to Stephen Crane and to Dreiser.

BIOGRAPHICAL CHART

1837 Born, March 1, in Martin's Ferry, Ohio, son of William Cooper Howells and Mary Dean

1846 Begins work as typesetter in his father's printing shop

1856–61 Writes for *Ohio State Journal* in Columbus

1860 Travels to New England; makes contact with Lowell, Emerson, Holmes, Hawthorne; publishes *Poems of Two Friends* with J. J. Piatt; wins consulate of Venice for his campaign biography of Lincoln and remains in Venice for four years

1862 Marries Elinor Gertrude Mead of Brattleboro, Vermont

1865 Briefly associated with the *Nation* before before becoming editor for the *Atlantic Monthly,* taking up residence in Boston; friendship begins with Henry James

1866 *Venetian Life*

1867 *Italian Journals*

1871 Becomes editor-in-chief of the *Atlantic*

1872 *Their Wedding Journey,* his first novel

1873 *A Chance Acquaintance*

1881 *A Fearful Responsibility; Dr. Brien's Practice;* leaves *Atlantic* and begins serializing stories in the *Century Magazine*

1882 *A Modern Instance*

1885 *The Rise of Silas Lapham*

1886 *Indian Summer*

1888 *April Hopes*

1889 Moves to New York as a member of the editorial staff of *Harper's; Annie Kilburn*

1890 *A Hazard of New Fortunes*

1894 *A Traveler from Altruria*

1897 *The Landlord at Lion's Head*

1900 *Literary Friends and Acquaintances*

1910 *My Mark Twain;* wife dies

1912 75th birthday celebrated at Sherry's, in New York City, with President Taft attending

1920 Dies, May 11

FURTHER READINGS

The Indiana University Press is now in the process of compiling a forty-one-volume edition of Howells' works to be completed shortly. This will become the standard (CEAA) edition.

George N. Bennett, *William Dean Howells: The Development of a Novelist* (1959)

Van Wyck Brooks, *Howells: His Life and World* (1959)

Edwin H. Cady, *The Road to Realism: The Early Years, 1837–1885, of William Dean Howells* (1956)

———, *The Realist at War: The Mature Years, 1885–1920, of William Dean Howells* (1958)

——— and David L. Frazier, eds., *The War of the*

Critics over William Dean Howells (1962)

Everett Carter, *Howells and the Age of Realism* (1954)

Kenneth E. Eble, ed., *Howells: A Century of Criticism* (1961)

William M. Gibson, *William Dean Howells* (1967)

Clara M. Kirk and Rudolf Kirk, *William Dean Howells* (1962)

Kenneth S. Lynn, *William Dean Howells: An American Life* (1971)

William McMurray, *The Literary Realism of William Dean Howells* (1967)

Kermit Vanderbilt, *The Achievement of William Dean Howells: A Reinterpretation* (1968)

From A Hazard of New Fortunes (1890)

A Hazard of New Fortunes was written soon after Howells and his wife moved down from Boston to New York, and it reflects some of their first experiences—for example, the rigors and the comedy of house-hunting in Manhattan —and their sense of that momentous change. It was a change, as we have said, that in retrospect has come to symbolize a general shift of energy from the old cultural domination of New England to the new concentration of talent and activity in New York.

Basil March, in the novel, is invited by his friend Fulkerson, himself originally a middle-westerner, to become editor of a new, lively, and unorthodox literary periodical called *Every Other Week*. Largely through the periodical, March meets a number of uncommonly well-characterized people. There is old Dryfoos, a Pennsylvania Dutchman, who is as crude as Silas Lapham and even richer; his wife and daughters; his son Conrad, who is something of a saint and who interests himself with quiet passion in the social conditions of the poor. There are the Leightons from New England, the impoverished mother and the daughter, who is one of Howells' intelligent and ironic young women. Colonel Woodburn, a gentleman of the Old South, who is said to have been modeled after George Fitzhugh (see our text), writes articles in favor of restoring the institution of slavery on a more workable basis; his sprightly daughter represents

the new postwar South. March encounters Lindau, his old German teacher, an immigrant who had his hand shot off fighting for the Union; Lindau is a confirmed socialist and oversees the translation of foreign essays. From Syracuse comes Angus Beaton, a gifted young artist but as devoid of moral perception as Bartley Hubbard. This gallery of characters is designed to show that, as Fulkerson puts it, New York is "the one city that belongs to the whole country."

A Hazard of New Fortunes is in a sense about "the whole country," about America as compressed into the "vast gay shapeless" scene of Manhattan. Though there is a great deal of vitality in it (Howells rightly called it "the most vital of my fictions"), the novel can hardly be said to have a plot. It is rather Howells' most successful effort to fulfill the prescription of the French critic Taine and to give narrative expression to his time and place. And beyond the individuals whom we actually meet and come to know, there are countless others glimpsed in the book: the Italians crowding about Mott Street, the Russians and French, the inhabitants of "the gay ugliness . . . of the Bowery." It is a many-sided, many-colored New York, teeming with life, as different as can be from the sedate and circumscribed "old New York" described no less effectively by Edith Wharton in *The Age of Innocence*.

Though he was a definite, if limited, innovator as regards the *stuff* of fiction, Howells was anything but innovative as to narrative *method*. In the brief section following, he draws upon the traditional and always useful device of the banquet scene to bring many of his chief characters together and to let each grow more visible by juxtaposition with the others.

In the course of the fitful dinner conversations, two motifs arise that we have touched on earlier. The first is the habit of northerners rich enough to do so to hire someone else to take their place in the Union army. Dryfoos' substitute, it will be noticed, was in fact killed, and ironically after Lee's surrender. In the "old rankling shame" that March imputes to Dryfoos "for not having gone into the war," one senses something of Howells' own lingering unease at having failed to participate in the fighting—an unease that seems more rather than less marked by March's thought that the feeling of shame "suggested a dormant nobleness" in Dryfoos.

More important, within the context of this novel, is the theme of impending and sometimes bloody conflict between "capitalists" and labor unions. At this stage, we hear the voice of the Howells who had been partially radicalized by the Haymarket riots. But if *A Hazard of New Fortunes* is the best of the novels Howells wrote as a "critical realist," it is because in the matter of the labor struggle, as in the other matters represented in the book, he does what he praised Turgenev for doing—he permits his characters to observe the conditions of society and to have their varied say entirely according to their own natures. Each is observant and each is myopic in his own way and to his own degree.

In the aftermath of the banquet, it can be added, Dryfoos demands that Lindau be fired from the magazine because of his radical opinions, and Basil March announces that if Lindau goes, he goes too. It is the most important moral crisis in the story and is resolved by Lindau resigning in outrage at receiving money for his magazine work from hands as bloodied as Dryfoos'. This may seem like what a later genera-tion would call a cop-out on Howells' part, but in fact it is a testimony to his realistic outlook. If there are few clear-cut moral victories in Howells' work, it is because he knew well and sadly enough that there are few indeed in the real world.

CHAPTER 6

So far as the Dryfoos family was concerned, the dinner might as well have been given at Frescobaldi's rooms. None of the ladies appeared. Mrs. Dryfoos was glad to escape to her own chamber, where she sat before an autumnal fire, shaking her head and talking to herself at times, with the foreboding of evil which old women like her make part of their religion. The girls stood just out of sight at the head of the stairs, and disputed which guest it was at each arrival; Mrs. Mandel had gone to her room to write letters, after beseeching them not to stand there. When Kendricks came, Christine gave Mela a little pinch, equivalent to a little mocking shriek; for, on the ground of his long talk with Mela at Mrs. Horn's, in the absence of any other admirer, they based a superstition of his interest in her; when Beaton came, Mela returned the pinch, but awkwardly, so that it hurt, and then Christine involuntarily struck her.

Frescobaldi's men were in possession everywhere: they had turned the cook out of her kitchen and the waitress out of her pantry; the reluctant Irishman at the door was supplemented by a vivid Italian, who spoke French with the guests, and said, "*Bien, Monsieur,*" and "*Toute suite,*" and "*Merci!*" to all, as he took their hats and coats, and effused a hospitality that needed no language but the gleam of his eyes and teeth and the play of his eloquent hands. From his professional dress-coat, lustrous with the grease spotted on it at former dinners and parties, they passed to the frocks of the elder and younger Dryfoos in the drawing-room, which assumed informality for the affair, but did not put their wearers wholly at their ease. The father's coat was of black broadcloth, and he wore it unbuttoned; the skirts were long, and the sleeves came down to his knuckles; he shook hands with his guests, and the same dryness seemed to be in his palm and throat, as he huskily asked each to take a chair. Conrad's coat was of modern texture and cut, and was buttoned about him as if it concealed a bad conscience within its lapels; he met March with his entreating smile, and he seemed no more capable of coping with the situation than his father. They both waited for Fulkerson, who went about and did his best to keep life in the party during the half-hour that passed before they sat down at dinner. Beaton stood gloomily aloof, as if waiting to be approached on the right basis before yielding an inch of his ground; Colonel Woodburn, awaiting the moment when he could sally out on his hobby, kept himself intrenched within the dignity of a gentleman, and examined askance the figure of old Lindau as he stared about the room, with his fine head up, and his empty sleeve dangling over his wrist. March felt obliged to him for wearing a new coat in the midst of that hostile luxury, and he was glad to see Dryfoos make up to him and begin to talk with him, as if he wished to show him particular respect, though it might have been because he was less afraid of him than of the others. He heard Lindau saying, "Boat, the name is Choarman?" and Dryfoos beginning to explain his Pennsylvania Dutch origin, and he suffered himself, with a sigh of relief, to fall into talk with Kendricks, who was always pleasant; he was willing to talk about something besides himself, and had no opinions that he was not ready to hold in abeyance for the time being out of kindness to others. In that group of impassioned individualities, March felt him a refuge and comfort—with his harmless dilettante intention of some day writing a novel, and his belief that he was meantime collecting material for it.

Fulkerson, while breaking the ice for the whole company, was mainly engaged in keeping Colonel Woodburn thawed out. He took Kendricks away from March and presented him to the colonel as a person who, like himself, was looking into social conditions; he put one hand on Kendricks's shoulder, and one on the colonel's, and made some flattering joke, apparently at the expense of the young fellow, and then left them. March heard Kendricks protest in vain, and the colonel say, gravely: "I do not wonder, sir, that these things interest you. They constitute a problem which society must solve or which will dissolve society," and he knew from that formula, which the colonel had once used with him, that he was laying out a road for the exhibition of the hobby's paces later.

Fulkerson came back to March, who had turned toward Conrad Dryfoos, and said, "If we don't get this thing going pretty soon, it'll be the death of me," and just then Frescobaldi's butler came in and announced to Dryfoos that dinner was served.

The old man looked toward Fulkerson with a troubled glance, as if he did not know what to do; he made a gesture to touch Lindau's elbow. Fulkerson called out, "Here's Colonel Woodburn, Mr. Dryfoos," as if Dryfoos were looking for him; and he set the example of what he was to do by taking Lindau's arm himself. "Mr. Lindau is going to sit at my end of the table, alongside of March. Stand not upon the order of your going, gentlemen, but fall in at once." He contrived to get Dryfoos and the colonel before him, and he let March follow with Kendricks. Conrad came last with Beaton, who had been turning over the music at the piano, and chafing inwardly at the whole affair. At the table Colonel Woodburn was placed on Dryfoos's right, and March on his left. March sat on Fulkerson's right, with Lindau next him; and the young men occupied the other seats.

"Put you next to March, Mr. Lindau," said Fulkerson, "so you can begin to put Apollinaris in his champagne-glass at the right moment; you know his little weakness of old; sorry to say it's grown on him."

March laughed with kindly acquiescence in Fulkerson's wish to start the gayety, and Lindau patted him on the shoulder. "I know hiss veakness. If he liges a class of vine, it is begause his loaf ingludes efen hiss enemy, as Shakespeare galled it."

"Ah, but Shakespeare couldn't have been thinking of champagne," said Kendricks.

"I suppose, sir," Colonel Woodburn interposed, with lofty courtesy, "champagne could hardly have been known in his day."

"I suppose not, Colonel," returned the younger man, deferentially. "He seemed to think that sack and sugar might be a fault; but he didn't mention champagne."

"Perhaps he felt there was no question about that," suggested Beaton, who then felt that he had not done himself justice in the sally.

"I wonder just when champagne did come in," said March.

"I know when it ought to come in," said Fulkerson. "Before the soup!"

They all laughed, and gave themselves the air of drinking champagne out of tumblers every day, as men like to do. Dryfoos listened uneasily; he did not quite understand the allusions, though he knew what Shakespeare was, well enough; Conrad's face expressed a gentle deprecation of joking on such a subject, but he said nothing.

The talk ran on briskly through the dinner. The young men tossed the ball back and forth; they made some wild shots, but they kept it going, and they laughed when they were hit. The wine loosed Colonel Woodburn's tongue; he became very companionable with the young fellows; with the feeling that a literary dinner ought to have a didactic scope, he praised Scott and Addison as the only authors fit to form the minds of gentlemen.

Kendricks agreed with him, but wished to add the name of Flaubert as a master of style. "Style, you know," he added, "is the man."

"Very true, sir: you are quite right, sir," the colonel assented; he wondered who Flaubert was.

Beaton praised Baudelaire and Maupassant; he said these were the masters. He recited some lurid verses from Baudelaire; Lindau pronounced them a disgrace to human nature, and gave a passage from Victor Hugo on Louis Napoleon, with his heavy German accent, and then he quoted Schiller. "Ach, boat that iss peaudifool! Not zo?" he demanded of March.

"Yes, beautiful; but, of course, you know I think there's nobody like Heine!"

Lindau threw back his great old head and laughed, showing a want of teeth under his mustache. He put his hand on March's back. "This poy—he wass a poy den—wass so gracy to pekin reading Heine that he gommence with the tictionary bevore he knows any crammar, and ve bick it out vort by vort togeder."

"He was a pretty cay poy in those days, heigh, Lindau?" asked Fulkerson, burlesquing the old man's accent, with an impudent wink that made Lindau himself laugh. "But in the dark ages, I mean, there in Indianapolis. Just how long ago did you old codgers meet there, anyway?" Fulkerson saw the restiveness in Dryfoos's eye at the purely literary course the talk had taken; he had intended it to lead up that way to business, to *Every Other Week*; but he saw that it was leaving Dryfoos too far out, and he wished to get it on the personal ground, where everybody is at home.

"Ledt me zee," mused Lindau. "Wass it in fifty-nine or zixty, Passil? Idt wass a year or dwo pefore the war proke oudt, anyway."

"Those were exciting times," said Dryfoos, making his first entry into the general talk. "I went down to Indianapolis with the first company from our place, and I saw the red-shirts pouring in everywhere. They had a song,

Oh, never mind the weather, but git over double trouble,
For we're bound for the land of Canaan.

The fellows locked arms and went singin' it up and down four or five abreast in the moonlight; crowded everybody else off the sidewalk."

"I remember, I remember," said Lindau, nodding his head slowly up and down. "A coodt many off them nefer gome pack from that landt of Ganaan, Mr. Dryfoos?"

"You're right, Mr. Lindau. But I reckon it was worth it—the country we've got now. Here, young man!" He caught the arm of the waiter who was going round with the champagne bottle. "Fill up Mr. Lindau's glass, there. I want to drink the health of those old times with him. Here's to your empty sleeve, Mr. Lindau. God bless it! No offense to *you*, Colonel Woodburn," said Dryfoos, turning to him before he drank.

"Not at all, sir, not at all," said the colonel. "I will drink with you, if you will permit me."

"We'll all drink—standing!" cried Fulkerson. "Help March to get up, somebody! Fill high the bowl with Samian Apollinaris for Coonrod! Now, then, hurrah for Lindau!"

They cheered, and hammered on the table with the butts of their knife-handles. Lindau remained seated. The tears came into his eyes; he said, "I thank you, chendlemen," and hiccoughed.

"I'd 'a' went into the war myself," said Dryfoos, "but I was raisin' a family of young children, and I didn't see how I could leave my farm. But I helped to fill up the quota at every call, and when the volunteering stopped I went round with the subscription paper myself; and we offered as good bounties as any in the State. My substitute was killed in one of the last skirmishes—in fact, after Lee's surrender—and I've took care of his family, more or less, ever since."

"By-the-way, March," said Fulkerson, "what sort of an idea would it be to have a good war story—might be a serial—in the magazine? The war has never fully panned out in fiction yet. It was used a good deal just after it was over, and then it was dropped. I think it's time to take it up again. I believe it would be a card."

It was running in March's mind that Dryfoos had an old rankling shame in his heart for not having gone into the war, and that he had often made that explanation of his course without having ever been satisfied with it. He felt sorry for him; the fact seemed pathetic; it suggested a dormant nobleness in the man.

Beaton was saying to Fulkerson: "You might get a series of sketches by substitutes; the substitutes haven't been much heard from in the war literature. How would 'The Autobiography of a Substitute' do? You might follow him up to the moment he was killed in the other man's place, and inquire whether he had any right to the feelings of a hero when he was only hired in the place of one. Might call it 'The Career of a Deputy Hero.'"

"I fancy," said March, "that there was a great deal of mixed motive in the men who went into the war as well as in those who kept out of it. We canonized all that died or suffered in it, but some of them must have been self-seeking and low-minded, like men in other vocations." He found himself saying this in Dryfoos's behalf; the old man looked at him gratefully at first, he thought, and then suspiciously.

Lindau turned his head toward him and said: "You are righdt, Passil; you are righdt. I haf zeen on the fieldt of pattle the voarst eggsipitions of human paseness—chelousy, fanity, ecodistic bridte. I haf zeen men in the face off death itself gofferned by motifes as low as—as pusiness motifes."

"Well," said Fulkerson, "it would be a grand thing for *Every Other Week* if we could get some of those ideas worked up into a series. It would make a lot of talk."

Colonel Woodburn ignored him in saying, "I think, Major Lindau—"

"High brifate; prefet gorporal," the old man interrupted, in rejection of the title.

Kendricks laughed and said, with a glance of appreciation at Lindau, "Brevet corporal is good."

Colonel Woodburn frowned a little, and passed over the joke. "I think Mr. Lindau is right. Such exhibitions were common to both sides, though if you gentlemen will pardon me for saying so, I think they were less frequent on ours. We were fighting more immediately for existence; we were fewer than you were, and we knew it; we felt more intensely that if each were not for all, then none was for any."

The colonel's words made their impression. Dryfoos said, with authority, "That is so."

"Colonel Woodburn," Fulkerson called out, "if you'll work up those ideas into a short paper—say, three thousand words—I'll engage to make March take it."

The colonel went on without replying: "But Mr. Lindau is right in characterizing some of the motives that led men to the cannon's mouth as no higher than business motives, and his comparison is the most forcible that he could have used. I was very much struck by it."

The hobby was out, the colonel was in the saddle with so firm a seat that no effort sufficed to dislodge him. The dinner went on from course to course with barbaric profusion, and from time to time Fulkerson tried to bring the talk back to *Every Other Week*. But perhaps because that was only the ostensible and not the real object of the dinner, which was to bring a number of men together under Dryfoos's roof, and make them the witnesses of his splendor, make them feel the power of his wealth, Fulkerson's attempts failed. The colonel showed how commercialism was the poison at the heart of our national life; how we began as a simple, agricultural people, who had fled to these shores with the instinct, divinely implanted, of building a state such as the sun never shone upon before; how we had conquered the wilderness and the savage; how we had flung off, in our struggle with the mother-country, the trammels of tradition and precedent, and had settled down, a free nation, to the practice of the arts of peace; how the spirit of commercialism had stolen insidiously upon us, and the infernal impulse of competition had embroiled us in a perpetual warfare of interests, developing the worst passions of our nature, and teaching us to trick and betray and destroy one another in the strife for money, till now that impulse had exhausted itself, and we found competition gone and the whole economic problem in the hands of monopolies—the Standard Oil Company, the Sugar Trust, the Rubber Trust, and what not. And now what was the next thing? Affairs could not remain as they were; it was impossible; and what was the next thing?

The company listened for the main part silently. Dryfoos tried to grasp the idea of commercialism as the colonel seemed to hold it; he conceived of it as something like the dry-goods business on a vast scale, and he knew he had never been in that. He did not like to hear competition called infernal; he had always supposed it was something sacred; but he approved of what Colonel Woodburn said of the Standard Oil Company; it was all true; the Standard Oil had squeezed Dryfoos once, and made him sell it a lot of oil-wells by putting down the price of oil so low in that region that he lost money on every barrel he pumped.

All the rest listened silently, except Lindau; at every point the colonel made against the present condition of things he said more and more fiercely, "You are righdt, you are righdt." His eyes glowed, his hand played with his knife-hilt. When the colonel demanded, "And what is the next thing?" he threw himself forward, and repeated: "Yes, sir! What is the next thing?"

"Natural gas, by thunder!" shouted Fulkerson. One of the waiters had profited by Lindau's posture to lean over him and put down in the middle of the table a structure in white sugar. It expressed Frescobaldi's conception of a derrick, and a touch of nature had been added in the flame of brandy, which burned luridly up from a small pit in the centre of the base, and represented the gas in combustion as it issued from the ground. Fulkerson burst into a roar of laughter with the words that recognized Frescobaldi's personal tribute to Dryfoos. Everybody rose and peered over at the thing, while he explained it to Frescobaldi. In the midst of his lecture he caught sight of the caterer himself, where he stood in the pantry doorway, smiling with an artist's anxiety for the effect of his masterpiece.

"Come in, come in, Frescobaldi! We want to congratulate you," Fulkerson called to him. "Here, gentlemen! Here's Frescobaldi's health."

They all drank; and Frescobaldi, smiling brilliantly and rubbing his hands as he bowed right and left, permitted himself to say to Dryfoos: "You are please; no? You like?"

"First-rate, first-rate!" said the old man; but when the Italian had bowed himself out and his guests had sunk into their seats again, he said dryly to Fulkerson, "I reckon they didn't have to torpedo that well, or the derick wouldn't look quite so nice and clean."

"Yes," Fulkerson answered, "and that ain't quite the style—that little wiggly-waggly blue flame—that the gas acts when you touch off a good vein of it. This might do for weak gas"; and he went on to explain: "They call it weak gas when they tap it two or three hundred feet down; and anybody can sink a well in his back yard and get enough gas to light and heat his house. I remember one fellow that had it blazing up from a pipe through a flower-bed, just like a jet of water from a fountain. My, my, my! You fel—you gentlemen—ought to go out and see that country, all of you. Wish we *could* torpedo this well, Mr. Dryfoos, and let 'em see how it works! Mind that one you torpedoed for me? You know, when they sink a well," he went on to the company, "they can't always most generally sometimes tell whether they're goin' to get gas or oil or salt water. Why, when they first began to bore for salt water out on the Kanawha, back about the beginning of the century, they used to get gas now and then, and then they considered it a failure; they called a gas-well a blower, and give it up in disgust; the time wasn't ripe for gas yet. Now they bore away sometimes till they get half-way to China, and don't seem to strike anything worth speaking of. Then they put a dynamite torpedo down in the well and explode it. They have a little bar of iron that they call a Go-devil, and they just drop it down on the business end of the torpedo, and then stand from under, if you please! You hear a noise, and in about half a minute you begin to *see* one, and it begins to rain oil and mud and salt water and rocks and pitchforks and adoptive citizens; and when it clears up the derrick's painted—got a coat on that'll wear in any climate. That's what our honored host meant. Generally get some visiting lady, when there's one round, to drop the Go-devil. But that day we had to put up with Conrad here. They offered to let me drop it, but I declined. I told 'em I hadn't much practice with Go-devils in the newspaper syndicate business, and I wasn't very well myself, anyway. Astonishing," Fulkerson continued, with the air of relieving his explanation by an anecdote, "how reckless they get using dynamite when they're torpedoing wells. We stopped at one place where a fellow was handling the cartridges pretty freely, and Mr. Dryfoos happened to caution him a little, and that ass came up with one of 'em in his hand, and began to pound it on the buggy-wheel to show us how safe it was. I turned green, I was so scared; but Mr. Dryfoos kept his color, and kind of coaxed the fellow till he quit. You could see he was the fool kind, that if you tried to stop him he'd keep on hammering that cartridge, just to show that it wouldn't explode, till he blew you into Kingdom Come. When we got him to go away, Mr. Dryfoos drove up to his foreman. 'Pay Sheney off, and discharge him on the spot,' says he. 'He's too safe a man to have round; he knows too much about dynamite.' I never saw anybody so cool."

Dryfoos modestly dropped his head under Fulkerson's flattery and, without lifting it, turned his eyes toward Colonel Woodburn. "I had all sorts of men to deal with in developing my property out there, but I had very little trouble with them, generally speaking."

"Ah, ah! You foundt the laboring-man reasonable—dractable—tocile?" Lindau put in.

"Yes, generally speaking," Dryfoos answered. "They mostly knew which side of their bread was buttered. I did have one little difficulty at one time. It happened to be when Mr. Fulkerson was out there. Some of the men tried to form a union—"

"No, no!" cried Fulkerson. "Let *me* tell that! I know you wouldn't do yourself justice, Mr. Dryfoos, and I want 'em to know how a strike can be managed, if you take it in time. You see, some of those fellows got a notion that there ought to be a union among the workingmen to keep up wages, and dictate to the employers, and Mr. Dryfoos's foreman was the ringleader in the business. They understood pretty well that as soon as he found it out that foreman would walk the plank, and so they watched out till they thought they had Mr. Dryfoos just where they wanted him—everything on the keen jump, and every man worth his weight in diamonds—and then they came to him, and told him to sign a promise to keep that foreman to the end of the season, or till he was through with the work on the Dryfoos and Hendry Addition, under penalty of having them all knock off. Mr. Dryfoos smelled a mouse, but he couldn't tell where the mouse was; he saw that they did have him, and he signed, of course. There wasn't anything really against the fellow, anyway; he was a first-rate man, and he did his duty every time; only he'd got some of those ideas into his head, and they turned it. Mr. Dryfoos signed, and then he laid low."

March saw Lindau listening with a mounting intensity, and heard him murmur in German, "Shameful! Shameful!"

Fulkerson went on: "Well, it wasn't long before they began to show their hand, but Mr. Dryfoos kept dark. He agreed to everything; there never was such an obliging capitalist before; there wasn't a thing they asked of him that he didn't do, with the greatest of pleasure, and all went merry as a marriage-bell till one morning a whole gang of fresh men marched into the Dryfoos and Hendry Addition, under the escort of a dozen Pinkertons with repeating rifles at half-cock, and about fifty fellows found themselves out of a job. You never saw such a mad set."

"Pretty neat," said Kendricks, who looked at the affair purely from an æsthetic point of view. "Such a *coup* as that would tell tremendously in a play."

"That was vile treason," said Lindau in German to March. "He's an infamous traitor! I cannot stay here. I must go."

He struggled to rise, while March held him by the coat, and implored him under his voice: "For Heaven's sake, don't, Lindau! You owe it to yourself not to make a scene, if you come here." Something in it all affected him comically; he could not help laughing.

The others were discussing the matter, and seemed not to have noticed Lindau, who controlled himself and sighed: "You are right. I must have patience."

Beaton was saying to Dryfoos, "Pity your Pinkertons couldn't have given them a few shots before they left."

"No, that wasn't necessary," said Dryfoos. "I succeeded in breaking up the union. I entered into an agreement with other parties not to employ any man who would not swear that he was non-union. If they had attempted violence, of course they could have been shot. But there was no fear of that. Those fellows can always be depended upon to cut one another's throats in the long run."

"But sometimes," said Colonel Woodburn, who had been watching throughout for a chance to mount his hobby again, "they make a good deal of trouble first. How was it in the great railroad strike of '77?"

"Well, I guess there was a little trouble that time, Colonel," said Fulkerson. "But the men that undertake to override the laws and paralyze the industries of a country like this generally get left in the end."

"Yes, sir, generally; and up to a certain point, always. But it's the exceptional that is apt to happen, as well as the unexpected. And a little reflection will convince any gentleman here that there is always a danger of the exceptional in your system. The fact is, those fellows have the game in their own hands already. A strike of the whole body of the Brotherhood of Engineers alone would starve out the entire Atlantic seaboard in a week; labor insurrection could make head at a dozen given points, and your government couldn't move a man over the roads without the help of the engineers."

"That is so," said Kendricks, struck by the dramatic character of the conjecture. He imagined a fiction dealing with the situation as something already accomplished.

"Why don't some fellow do the *Battle of Dorking* act with that thing?" said Fulkerson. "It would be a card."

"Exactly what I was thinking, Mr. Fulkerson," said Kendricks.

Fulkerson laughed. "Telepathy—clear case of mind-transference. Better see March, here, about it. *I'd* like to have it in *Every Other Week*. It would make talk."

"Perhaps it might set your people to thinking as well as talking," said the colonel.

"Well, sir," said Dryfoos, settling his lips so tightly together that his imperial stuck straight outward, "if I had my way, there wouldn't *be* any Brotherhood of Engineers, nor any other kind of labor union in the whole country."

"What!" shouted Lindau. "You would sobbress the unionss of the voarking-men?"

"Yes, I would."

"And what would you do with the unionss of the gabidalists—the drosts—and gompines, and boolss? Would you dake the righdt from one and gif it to the odder?"

"Yes, sir, I would," said Dryfoos, with a wicked look at him.

Lindau was about to roar back at him with some furious protest, but March put his hand on his shoulder imploringly, and Lindau turned to him to say in German: "But it is infamous—infamous! What kind of man is this? Who is he? He has the heart of a tyrant."

Colonel Woodburn cut in. "You couldn't do that, Mr. Dryfoos, under your system. And if you attempted it with your conspiracy laws, and that kind of thing, it might bring the climax sooner than you expected. Your commercialized society has built its house on the sands. It will have to go. But I should be sorry if it went before its time."

"You are righdt, sir," said Lindau. "It would be a bity. I hobe it will last till it feelss its rottenness, like Herodt. Boat, when its hour gomes, when it trops to bieces with the veight off its own gorrubtion—what then?"

"It's not to be supposed that a system of things like this can drop to pieces of its own accord, like the old Republic of Venice," said the colonel. "But when the last vestige of commercial society is gone, then we can begin to build anew; and we shall build upon the central idea, not of the false liberty you now worship, but of responsibility—responsibility. The enlightened, the moneyed, the cultivated class shall be responsible to the central authority—emperor, duke, president; the name does not matter—for the national expense and the national defence, and it shall be responsible to the working-classes of all kinds for homes and lands and implements, and the opportunity to labor at all times. The working-classes shall be responsible to the leisure class for the support of its dignity in peace, and shall be subject to its command in war. The rich shall warrant the poor against planless production and the ruin that now follows, against danger from without and famine from within, and the poor—"

"No, no, no!" shouted Lindau. "The *State* shall do that—the whole beople. The men who voark shall have and shall eat; and the men that will not voark, they shall sdarfe. But no man need sdarfe. He will go to the State, and the State will see that he haf voark, and that he haf foodt. All the roadts and mills and mines and landts shall be the beople's and be ron *by* the beople *for* the beople. There shall be no rich and no boor; and there shall not be war any more, for what bower wouldt dare to addack a beople bound togeder in a broderhood like that?"

"Lion and lamb act," said Fulkerson, not well knowing, after so much champagne, what words he was using.

No one noticed him, and Colonel Woodburn said coldly to Lindau, "You are talking paternalism, sir."

"And *you* are dalking *feutalism!*" retorted the old man.

The colonel did not reply. A silence ensued, which no one broke till Fulkerson said: "Well, now, look here. If either one of these millenniums was brought about, by force of arms, or otherwise, what would become of *Every Other Week*? Who would want March for an editor? How would Beaton sell his pictures? Who would print Mr. Kendrick's little society verses and short stories? What would become of Conrad and his good works?" Those named grinned in support of Fulkerson's diversion, but Lindau and the colonel did not speak; Dryfoos looked down at his plate, frowning. A waiter came round with cigars, and Fulkerson took one. "Ah," he said, as he bit off the end, and leaned over to the emblematic masterpiece, where the brandy was still feebly flickering, "I wonder if there's enough natural gas left to light my cigar." His effort put the flame out and knocked the derrick over; it broke in fragments on the table. Fulkerson cackled over the ruin: "I wonder if all

Moffitt will look that way after labor and capital have fought it out together. I hope this ain't ominous of anything personal, Dryfoos?"

"I'll take the risk of it," said the old man, harshly.

He rose mechanically, and Fulkerson said to Frescobaldi's man, "You can bring us the coffee in the library."

The talk did not recover itself there. Lindau would not sit down; he refused coffee, and dismissed himself with a haughty bow to the company; Colonel Woodburn shook hands elaborately all round, when he had smoked his cigar; the others followed him. It seemed to March that his own good-night from Dryfoos was dry and cold.

Review of Henry James's Hawthorne (1880)

This review does not contain one of Howells' major critical statements, but it is an interesting part of Howells' continuing conversation with his old friend about the nature of fiction. As the reader will notice, Howells accuses James of failing to distinguish between the novel (for Howells, the realistic novel) and the kind of romance which Hawthorne habitually wrote—a distinction which had been asserted on and off in American literary periodicals since the beginning of the century. One notices, too, Howells' rebuttal to James's famous list of the paraphernalia which Europe made available to the novelist and which were lacking in America: courts, aristocracy, castles, Epsom and Ascot, and so on. "We have," Howells replies, "the whole of human life remaining, and a social structure presenting the only fresh and novel opportunities left to fiction." For James, of course, those opportunities could hardly be taken hold of in the absence of the institutionalized and mannered kind of life by which the novelist (as he thought) renders experience.

But Howells also finds much to praise in James's remarkable study. The review is valuable as well in the strong sense it reflects of an established American literature with its developing relations and lengthening traditions. Howells writes as one who is at home in that firmly based and clearly known literary world. Still, he was quite accurate in predicting that James's *Hawthorne* would kick up a storm back home (the book was written for an English Men of Letters series), for its calling Hawthorne provincial. There was in fact a rather violent tempest of patriotic resentment, and James was astonished and dismayed by it.

Mr. James's book on Hawthorne, in Morley's English Men of Letters series, merits far closer examination and carefuller notice than we can give it here, alike for the interest of its subject, the peculiarity of its point of view, and the charm and distinction of its literature. An American author writing of an American author for an English public incurs risks with his fellow-countrymen which Mr. James must have faced, and is much more likely to possess the foreigner whom he addresses with a clear idea of our conditions than to please the civilization whose portrait is taken. Forty-six, fifty, sixty-four, are not dates so remote, nor are Salem and Concord societies so extinct, that the people of those periods and places can be safely described as provincial, not once, but a dozen times; and we foresee, without any very powerful prophetic lens, that Mr. James will be in some quarters attainted of high treason. For ourselves, we will be content with saying that the provinciality strikes us as somewhat over-insisted upon, and that, speaking from the point of not being at all provincial ourselves, we think the epithet is sometimes mistaken. If it is not provincial for an Englishman to be English, or a Frenchman French, then it is not so for an American to be American; and if Hawthorne was "exquisitely provincial," one had better take one's chance of universality with him than with almost any Londoner or Parisian of his time. Provinciality, we understand it, is a thing of the mind or the soul; but if it is a thing of the experiences, then that is another matter, and there is no quarrel. Hawthorne undoubtedly saw less of the world in New England than one sees in Europe, but he was no cockney, as Europeans are apt to be.

At the same time we must not be thought to deny the value and delightfulness of those chapters on Salem and Brook Farm and Concord. They are not very close in description, and the places seem deliciously divined rather than studied. But where they are used unjustly, there will doubtless be abundant defense; and if Salem or Brook Farm be mute, the welkin will probably respond to the cries of certain critics who lie in wait to make life sorrowful to any one dealing lightly with the memory of Thoreau or the presence of the poet Channing. What will happen to a writer who says of the former that he was "worse than provincial, he was parochial," and of the latter that he resembles the former in "having produced literary compositions more esteemed by the few than by the many," we wait with the patience and security of a spectator at an *auto da fé*, to see. But even an unimbattled outsider may suggest that the essential large-mindedness of Concord, as expressed in literature, is not sufficiently recognized, although it is thoroughly felt. The treatment of the culture foible and of the colorless æsthetic joys, the attribution of "a great deal of Concord five and thirty years ago" to the remark of a visitor of Hawthorne that Margaret Fuller "had risen perceptibly into a higher state of being since their last meeting," are exquisite,—too exquisite we fear, for the sense of most Englishmen, and not too fine only for the rarefied local consciousness which they may sting. Emerson is indeed devoutly and amply honored, and there is something particularly sweet and tender in the characterization of such surviving Brook Farmers as the author remembers to have met; but even in speaking of Emerson, Mr. James has the real misfortune to call his grand poem for the dedication of the monument to Concord Fight a "little hymn." It is little as Milton's sonnet on Shakespeare is little.

We think, too, that in his conscience against brag and *chauvinism* Mr. James puts too slight a value upon some of Hawthorne's work. It is not enough to say of a book so wholly unexampled and unrivaled as The Scarlet Letter that it was "the finest piece of imaginative writing put forth in" America; as if it had its parallel in any literature. When he comes to speak of the romances in detail, he repairs this defect of estimation in some degree; but here again his strictures seem somewhat mistaken. No one better than Mr. James knows the radical difference between a romance and a novel, but he speaks now of Hawthorne's novels, and now of his romances, throughout, as if the terms were convertible; whereas the romance and the novel are as distinct as the poem and the novel. Mr. James excepts to the people in The Scarlet Letter, because they are rather types than persons, rather conditions of the mind than characters; as if it were not almost precisely the business of the romance to deal with types and mental conditions. Hawthorne's fictions being always and essentially, in conception and performance, romances, and not novels, something of all Mr. James's special criticism is invalidated by the confusion which, for some reason not made clear, he permits himself. Nevertheless, his analysis of the several books and of the shorter tales is most interesting; and though we should ourselves place The Blithedale Romance before The House of Seven Gables, and should rank it much higher than Mr. James seems to do, we find ourselves consenting oftener than dissenting as we read his judgments. An admirably clear and just piece of criticism, we think, is that in which he pronounces upon the slighter and cheaper *motif* of Septimus Felton. But here there are not grounds for final sentence; it is possible, if that book had received the author's last touches, it might have been, after all, a playful and gentle piece of irony rather than a tragedy.

What gives us entire satisfaction, however, is Mr. James's characterization, or illustrations of Hawthorne's own nature. He finds him an innocent, affectionate heart, extremely domestic, a life of definite, high purposes singularly unbaffled, and an "unperplexed intellect." The black problem of evil, with which his Puritan ancestors wrestled concretely, in groans and despair, and which darkens with its portentous shadow nearly everything that Hawthorne wrote, has become his literary material; or, in Mr. James's finer and more luminous phrase, he "transmutes this heavy moral burden into the very substance of the imagination." This strikes us as beautifully reasonable and true, and we will not cloud it with comment of ours. But satisfactorily as Mr. James declares Hawthorne's personality in large, we do not find him sufficient as to minor details and facts. His defect, or his error, appears oftenest in his discussion of the note-books, where he makes plain to himself the simple, domestic, democratic qualities in Hawthorne, and yet maintains that he sets down slight and little aspects of nature because his world is small and vacant. Hawthorne noted these because he loved them, and as a great painter, however full and vast his world is, continues to jot down whatever strikes him as picturesque and characteristic. The disposition to allege this inadequate reason comes partly from that confusion of the novelist's and the romancer's work of which we have spoken, and partly from a theory, boldly propounded, that it needs a long history and "a complex social machinery to set a writer in motion." Hawthorne himself shared, or seemed to share, this illusion, and wrote The Marble Faun, so inferior, with its foreign scene, to the New England romances, to prove the absurdity of it. As a romancer, the twelve years of boyhood which he spent in the wild solitudes of Maine were probably of greater advantage to him than if they had been passed at Eton and Oxford. At least, until some other civilization has produced a romantic genius at all comparable to his, we must believe this. After leaving out all those novelistic "properties," as sovereigns, courts, aristocracy, gentry, castles, cottages, cathedrals, abbeys, universities, museums, political class, Epsoms, and Ascots, by the absence of which Mr. James suggests our poverty to the English conception, we have the whole of human life remaining, and a social structure presenting the only fresh and novel opportunities left to fiction, opportunities manifold and inexhaustible. No man would have known less what to do with that dreary and worn-out paraphernalia than Hawthorne.

We can only speak of the excellent comment upon Hawthorne's Old Home, and the skillful and manly way in which Mr. James treats of that delicate subject to his English audience. Skillful and manly the whole book is,—a miracle of tact and of self-respect, which the author need not fear to trust to the best of either of his publics. There is nothing to regret in the attitude of the book; and its literature is always a high pleasure, scarcely marred by some evidences of hurry, and such *writ-erish* passages as that in which *sin* is spoken of as "this baleful substantive with its attendant adjective."

It is a delightful and excellent essay, refined and delicate in perception, generous in feeling, and a worthy study of the unique romancer whom its closing words present with justice so subtle and expression so rich:—

"He was a beautiful, natural, original genius, and his life had been singularly exempt from worldly preoccupations and vulgar efforts. It had been as pure, as simple, as unsophisticated, as his work. He had lived primarily in his domestic affections, which were of the tenderest kind; and then —without eagerness, without pretension, but with a great deal of quiet devotion—in his charming art. His work will remain; it is too original and exquisite to pass away; among the men of imagination he will always have his niche. No one has had just that vision of life, and no one has had a literary form that more successfully expressed his vision. He was not a moralist, and he was not simply a poet. The moralists are weightier, denser, richer, in a sense; the poets are more purely inconclusive and irresponsible. He combined in a singular degree the spontaneity of the imagination with a haunting care for moral problems. Man's conscience was his theme, but he saw it in the light of a creative fancy which added, out of its own substance, an interest, and, I may almost say, an importance."

On Zola and Others (1895)

Although Howells was introduced to Turgenev and wrote about him relatively early in his career, his serious interest in the other foreign masters—in particular, Tolstoi, Zola, and Ibsen —was more or less coincident with his commitment to Christian socialism and, in literature, to critical realism in the later eighties and nineties. Speaking of writers like the ones just mentioned, Alfred Kazin, in an introduction to *Studies in European Realism* by the very powerful Hungarian critic George Lukacs, says that their realism "by its very nature is nothing if it is not critical realism." In Lukacs' view, Kazin says admiringly, the typical hero in the realistic tradition is "one who brings to dramatic focus the social forces that are embodied in himself and thus opposes them"; the heroes of Tolstoi and Balzac "make themselves forces equal to the force of the society they resist and seek to transform. For Lukacs, the hero of a literary work must in some sense be equal to the achievement of a new society."

Howells might not have put it exactly like that, but he moved toward a comparable insight when, in another essay, he said about Zola, whom he here called "the greatest poet of his day," that "Not Tolstoi, not Ibsen himself, has more profoundly and indignantly felt the injustice of civilization, or more insistently shown the falsity of its fundamental pretensions." And there is no doubt that as a critical realist, Howells sought to enlist his own work and that of his fellow realists in the cause of resisting and transforming a bad society and of achieving a new one. But Howells' own earlier brand of realism and his commitment to the ordinary and everyday kept him from making any grandiloquent statements about the heroic destiny and from seeking to embody it in fiction.

What follows is the last three sections of a five-part review of a book called *Degeneration* in which the author, Max Nordau, cited Zola, Tolstoi, and Ibsen among others as symptoms of cultural decline.

———

The world, in its thinking and feeling, was never so sound and sane before. There is a great deal of fevered and foolish thinking and feeling about thinking and feeling, as there always has been and will be, but there is no more of it than ever. It is no part of my business to defend the nineteenth century, and if I thought the noble mood of its last years merely a death-bed repentance, and not an effect of all the former events of the ages, I should not rejoice in it. Dr. Nordau himself is able to see that there really is no such thing as a *fin de siècle* spirit; but the race is in a certain mood, and the century is near its end, and so the phrase serves as well as another. The only question is whether the mood is a good one, and I have already expressed my sense of it.

I believe it is extremely well to have the underpinning of sentiment and opinion examined, from time to time, and this is what our age above all others has done. It is not a constructive or a reconstructive age, as compared with some other epochs, but it is eminently critical, and whatever is creative in it, is critically creative. It is very conscious, it not only knows, but it keenly feels, what it is about. It is not for nothing, it is not blindly or helplessly that it has tried this or that, that it has gone forward to new things or reverted to old things. It experiments perpetually, but not empirically; knowledge and greater knowledge are the cause and the effect of all that it has done in the arts as well as in the sciences.

If we stand at the end of things, we also stand at the beginning; we are the new era as well as the old. It is not at all important that certain things have fulfilled themselves and passed away; but it is very important that certain others have just begun their fulfillment, and it is these that we are to judge our time by. Our condition is that of a youth and health unknown to human thought before, and it is an excellent thing that with these we have so much courage; if it were only the courage of youth and health it would be well; but it is in fact the courage of a soul that is as old as the world.

A great many good, elderly minded people think it dreadful Ibsen should show us that the house we have lived in so long is full of vermin, that its drainage is bad, that the roof leaks and the chimney smokes abominably; but if it is true, is it not well for us to know it? It is dreadful because it is so, not because he shows it so; and the house is no better because our fathers got on in it as it is. He has not done his work without showing his weakness as well as his strength, and as I do not believe in genius in the miraculous sense, I am not at all troubled by his occasional weakness. It is really no concern of mine whether he solves his problems or not; generally, I see that he does not solve them, and I see that life does not; the longer I live the more I am persuaded that the problems of this life are to be solved elsewhere, or never. It is not by the solution of problems that the moralist teaches, but by the question that his handling of them suggests to us respecting ourselves. Artistically he is bound, Ibsen as a dramatist is bound, to give an aesthetic completeness to his works, and I do not find that he ever fails to do this; to my thinking they have a high beauty and propriety; but ethically he is bound not to be final; for if he forces himself to be final in things that do not and cannot end here, he becomes dishonest, he becomes a Nordau. What he can and must do ethically, is to make us take thought of ourselves, and look to it whether we have in us the making of this or that wrong, whether we are hypocrites, tyrants, pretenders, shams conscious or unconscious; whether our most unselfish motives are not really secret shapes of egotism; whether our convictions are not mere brute acceptations; whether we believe what we profess; whether when we force good to a logical end we are not doing evil. This is what Ibsen does; he gives us pause; and in that bitter muse he leaves us thinking not of his plays, but of our own lives; not of his fictitious people, but of ourselves. If we find ourselves all right we can go ahead with a good conscience, but never quite so cocksure afterwards.

He does in the region of motive pretty much the same work that Tolstoi does in the region of conduct. If he makes you question yourself before God, Tolstoi makes you question yourself before man. With the one you ask yourself, Am I true? With the other you ask yourself, Am I just? You cannot release yourself from them on any other terms. They will neither of them let you go away, feeling smoothly self-satisfied, patronizingly grateful, smugly delighted, quite charmed. If you want that feeling, you must go to some other shop for it, and there are shops a plenty where you can get it. Both of these great writers now and then overrun each other's province, for their provinces are not very separable, except by a feat of the fancy, though if the reader wishes a distinction between them, I have offered one. I should say, however, that Ibsen dealt with conduct in the ideal, and Tolstoi in the real. How shall I behave with regard to myself? How shall I behave with regard to my neighbor? I imagine that in either case the answer would be the same. It is only the point of view that is different.

As far as any finality is concerned, Tolstoi is no more satisfactory than Ibsen; that is to say, he is quite as honest. He does not attempt to go beyond Christ, who bade us love the neighbor, and cease to do evil; but I suppose this is what Dr. Nordau means by his mysticism, his sentimentality. In fact, Tolstoi has done nothing more than bring us back to the gospels as the fountain of righteousness. Those who denounce him cannot or will not see this, but that does not affect the fact. He asks us to be as the first Christians were, but this is difficult, and it has been so difficult ever since the times of the first Christians, that very few of the later Christians have been at all like them. Even in his most recent crusade, his crusade against the chauvinism which we miscall patriotism, he only continues that warfare against the spirit of provinciality which Christianity began. He preaches no new doctrine, he practices no new life. It is all as old as Calvary; it is the law and life of self-sacrifice. This was and always will be to the Jews a stumbling-block, and to the Greeks foolishness; but it is nothing mystical. There is nothing mystical in Tolstoi's books; as far as they are fictions they are the closest and clearest transcripts of the outer and inner life of man; as far as they are lessons in the form of allegory or essay, they are of the simplest and plainest meaning. His office in the world has been like Ibsen's, to make us look where we are standing, and see whether our feet are solidly planted or not. What is our religion, what is our society, what is our country, what is our civilization? You cannot read him without asking yourself these questions, and the result is left with you. Tolstoi's solution of the problem in his own life is not the final answer, and as things stand it is not the possible answer. We cannot all go dig in the fields, we cannot all cobble peasants' shoes. But we can all do something to lift diggers and cobblers to the same level with ourselves, to see that their work is equally rewarded, and that they share fully with the wisest and the strongest in the good of life. We can get off their backs, or try to get off, and this, after all, is what Tolstoi means us to do.

There is the same mixture of weakness in his power that qualifies the power of Ibsen, and makes his power the more admirable. There are flaws enough in his reasoning; he is not himself the best exponent of his own belief; there is no finality in his precept or his practice. On the other hand, his work has the same aesthetic perfection as Ibsen's, and as an intellect dealing imaginatively with life, he is without a rival. There is the like measure of weakness in Zola, whom Dr. Nordau chooses as the type of realist, with much the same blundering wilfulness that he chooses Ibsen as the type of egomaniac, and Tolstoi as the type of mystic. Zola never was a realist in the right sense, and no one has known this better, or has said it more frankly than Zola himself. He is always showing, as he has often owned that he came too early to be a realist; but it was he who imagined realism, in all its sublime, its impossible beauty, as Ibsen imagined truth, as Tolstoi imagined justice. One has to deal with words that hint rather than say what one means, but the meaning will be clear enough to any one capable of giving the matter thought. What Zola has done has been to set before us an ideal of realism, to recall the wandering mind of the world to that ideal, which was always in the world, and to make the reader feel it by what he has tried to do, rather than by what he has done. He has said, in effect, You must not aim in art to be less than perfectly faithful; and you must not lie about the fact any more than you can help. Go to life; see what it is like, and then tell it as honestly as possible. Above all he has shown us what rotten foundations the most of fiction rested on, and how full of malaria the whole region was. He did not escape the infection himself; he was born in that region; the fever of romanticism was in his blood; the taint is in his work. But he has written great epics, and the time will come when it will be seen that he was the greatest poet of his day, and perhaps the greatest poet that France has produced.

HENRY JAMES (1843–1916)

Henry James, by his own example, showed a new way of becoming an American writer. He arrived at his artistic maturity by virtually abandoning his native country and by exercising his talents not in Boston or New York, but in London, in Paris, in Florence. It was for the most part a carefully thought-out move, but it was not really an act of expatriation. Rather, it was a search for the vantage point from which James —given his personal and family experience, and his special sensibility—might best discern and give fictional form to the defining qualities of the American character. Such a vantage point, for James, was a European setting, in which, as it might be, a freshly arrived American (Daisy Miller, Christopher Newman, Isabel Archer) could reveal himself or herself and could be seen pursuing his or her destiny by contrast and often by collision with truly expatriated and Europeanized Americans and with members of English or French or Italian society.

In the earlier phases of his career, James found his own best fictional mode in the novel of manners, and in particular with the kind of novel that contrasts various *national* manners with each other. James cannot be credited with inventing what (following his own practice) is usually called "the international theme"—Hawthorne had contributed importantly to the mode in his romance of Americans and Italians in Rome, *The Marble Faun*, and in fact Cooper was the first American novelist to try his hand at it.[1] James, however, gave that theme its richest treatment. The novel of international manners, in any case, requires a larger amount of sheer technical skill than most other brands of fiction; and James, meeting the challenge, went on to become the model craftsman, perhaps the greatest craftsman in American literary history. The process, nonetheless, was only one phase of a considerably more significant and far-reaching process—as regards both James's personal development and the development of his narrative art.

What we make out, as we survey James's long life, with its quite clearly marked stages, and the enormous range of his writing in many genres, is something that might be called "the dialectics of personality." That phrase will not convey very much at first hearing. But put most simply, it has to do with the slow establishment of the self *as* a self, and then the effort to transcend the self in a nourishing communion with others. For James, in the course of time, that latter process became more absorbing and more important—it possessed a greater degree of universality—than anything provided by the international theme.

It should be stressed at the outset that James inherited an immense concern with the self simply by being an alert and observant member of his time and his American culture. It has been argued recently (for example, by Quentin Anderson in *The Imperial Self*; see also the preliminary note to this section) that it was at once the hallmark and the gravest defect of

[1] On Cooper, in this regard, see the introduction to his work. Needless to say, there had been and would continue to be characters of assorted nationalities in a number of English and continental novels. But the juxtaposition of an *American* figure with a transatlantic personality made possible contrasts more significant than those, say, between a Frenchman and an Italian.

the age of Emerson and Thoreau that it found man's highest fulfillment in the virtually un-limited expansion of the individual ego; and that American men of letters ever since have persistently failed to respect the needs of the social order or to perceive the necessary limita-tion of the individual self when it enters into intercourse with others. The argument is un-doubtedly true up to a point; though it is also true that Hawthorne regularly denounced un-due self-assertion (which he was likely to call *pride*), and so in a more oblique manner did Melville. And nowhere, as we shall see in a moment, was man's need to get beyond egotism more hotly discussed than in the James family. His intellectual world, in any event, provided Henry James with what would be at once his greatest challenge and his greatest theme.

He began to escape the international theme in his fiction when he began to escape his own selfhood in his personal relations. The charac-ters in James's later fiction may continue to be Americans and Englishmen and Italians mingling together; but in fact they are repre-sentatives of fundamental human nature caught up in a universal drama. That last word should be stressed: for reasons to be explained, as James's vision became more universal, his work became more overtly dramatic in conception and execution.

All this may well seem exceedingly abstract, yet the developments touched on had their origins in James's personal life, and in the actual vicissitudes of his career. To take a single ex-ample: for an American writer living and prac-ticing his craft in London, and feeling himself something of an outsider there, the question of the self will naturally loom larger than it will for an American living in his own home town, surrounded by things familiar to his child-hood. By the same token, such a transplanted person may eventually come to perceive na-tional differences melting away in an emergence of common humanity. If the person also hap-pens to be a writer of genius, he will be im-pelled to seize upon those perceptions and ex-periences and make them the stuff of art.

The founder of the James family in the New World was William James, who, at the age of eighteen in 1789, came from County Cavan in Ireland to New York City, carrying with him a "very small sum of money." He moved to Al-bany, New York, in 1793, and during the next decades became one of the city's most pros-perous and eminent citizens. He was a banker, an extensive landowner, a manufacturer of salt; a stern and active member of the Presbyterian church; a civic leader. At his death in 1832, he left an estate of three million dollars, an enormous fortune at the time. Henry James, Sr., William's fourth son by his third marriage, re-ceived an annual income of ten thousand dollars (mostly from real estate); and thereafter, Henry, Jr., would say, no member of the family over several generations would be guilty of a single stroke of business. It was even, during the novel-ist's childhood, a source of humiliation "that the head of our little family was *not* in business, and that even among our relatives on each side we couldn't so much as name proudly anyone who was." The youthful Henry's experience was limited to the leisured life, with its special pace and gathering expectations; it took in little if anything of the world of practical affairs. Busi-nessmen, in Henry James's fiction, are seen only after hours, or, like Christopher Newman in *The American,* in the wake of retirement.

Henry's older brother William—destined to be the most scintillating figure in Harvard's re-markable philosophy department, and the author of *Pragmatism* and *The Varieties of Religious Experience*—was born in 1842; Henry himself in 1843. Henry was born in Washington Place, New York City; but it was characteristic that his first memory should be of Europe—specifically of Paris, of the Rue Castiglione and the Place Vendôme. The family had come to England when the child was six months old, and the following year they spent some time in Paris. Henry was therefore less than two when he absorbed and retained ("for all my time," as he wrote) an exceedingly sen-suous impression of being pushed in his baby carriage into the Place Vendôme, waggling his feet under his long robe and staring at the "tall and glorious column" in the middle of the Place, with its celebration of the triumphs of the Emperor Napoleon.

What Henry and William would not know about for years was the appalling experience their father had undergone the previous spring, in England. Henry James, Sr., was a robust, ebullient, and vigorously optimistic man—those qualities not the slightest impaired by the loss of a leg in his fifteenth year, as the result of burns received during a fire in a stable near his Albany school. By 1844, he had grown quite accustomed to an artificial limb made of cork; he was cheerful and reasonably affluent, the happy father of two infant sons, the devoted husband of a devoted wife. One evening in May of that year, in the pleasant cottage he had rented at Windsor, sitting serenely in front of the fire (the family being elsewhere), he was suddenly seized by a hideous nightmare. An invisible shape seemed to be squatting near him in the room, "raying out its fetid personality, influences fatal to life." "To all appearances," he wrote later in an autobiographical passage, "it was a perfectly insane and abject terror, without ostensible cause"; but "the thing had not lasted ten seconds before I felt myself a wreck; that is, reduced from a state of firm, vigorous, joyful manhood to one of almost helpless infancy." He was finally able to stagger out of the room and summon his wife.

Henry, Sr., called the event a "vastation," and it became the source and basis of that range of philosophico-theological speculation referred to reverently by Mrs. James, in the family circle, as "Father's ideas." A friend at the watering place to which Henry hurriedly betook himself suggested that he might find an encouraging explanation of his experience in the writings of the Swedish mystic Emmanuel Swedenborg. From the volumes of Swedenborg that he at once acquired, the elder James took and made his own the thesis that for an individual to arrive at full human maturity he must suffer a devastation of his ego, the very destruction of his selfhood. Only then could the individual

be reborn into what James called "the divine-natural humanity," an invisible and ideal community of sovereign persons, the consciousness of each of whom was nourished by the loftier universal consciousness.

Father's ideas, as they evolved in a series of books (one of them being *The Secret of Swedenborg*, about which his son's friend Howells said that James had kept it very well), were rooted in a muscular hostility to puritanic moralism. This may have reflected a continuing reaction against the bleak piety of the first William. Henry, Sr., in any event, according to the novelist's affectionate memory, had a "prime horror" of prigs: "He only cared for virtue that was more or less ashamed of itself"; and the boys, as they grew up and listened to the family table talk, had "the amusement . . . of hearing morality, or moralism as it was more invidiously worded, made hay of in the very interest of character and conduct." The elder James associated the self with pure selfishness, the ego with lethal self-righteousness, and conscience with the desire to appropriate the sacred reality of others, to treat human beings as acquirable things. It was all of this that had to be destroyed, however harrowing the "vastation" might in fact be. But out of the death of *conscience* there might be brought into being that supreme human quality, in the Jamesian vision, *consciousness*—ultimately a social virtue, since it consisted in a deep awareness of the reality of others and a capacity for true intercourse with others.[2]

The basic elements of Henry, Sr.'s general view were indicated in the very title of his most important book, *Society the Redeemed Form of Man* (1879). Fallen man, for James, was precisely egotistic man, the individual who has shed his initial innocence and acquired his selfhood. Redemption was fundamentally a social

[2] The image both Henry, Sr., and Henry, Jr., drew of the ego-driven man resembles, of course, Hawthorne's Ethan Brand. What is more surprising is that the Jamesian elevation of "consciousness" over "conscience" and the ensuing search for a genuine society (or better, community) so markedly parallel certain tendencies in Mark Twain's thinking. See above, p. 1282. One looks in vain for any other point of similarity between Mark Twain and either Henry James.

event. "We need never fear not to be good enough," his son recalled Henry, Sr., insisting, "if we were only social enough: a splendid meaning indeed being attached to the latter term." Part of the splendor of meaning was due to the term "social"—though it referred to every form of human intercourse—being imbued with the religious sentiment. The home atmosphere, in the younger Henry's words, was permeated with the sense of "an order of goodness and power greater than any this world by itself can show." But if such a religious spirit was the primary gift of the father, it had nothing to do with specific creeds or practices: "My father's possession of this spirit . . . [was] unaccompanied with a single one of the outward or formal, the theological, devotional, ritual, or even implicitly pietistic signs by which we usually know it."[3] Henry, Jr., also attached a splendid meaning to the term "social": his very definition of experience (in the preface to *The Princess Casamassima*) was "our apprehension and measure of ourselves as social beings." It might almost be said, though the point would need elaborating, that for the son, too, society was the *redeemed* form of man. What is certain, however, is that James's fiction abounds in figures who exemplify in different ways Henry, Sr.'s concept of selfhood: Gilbert Osmond in *The Portrait of a Lady* most obviously, but many more, from Winterbourne in *Daisy Miller* to Lord Mark in *The Wings of the Dove*. And perhaps in those characteristic moments of self-confrontation in James's stories —Isabel Archer's vigil before the fire, John Marcher's dreadful vision of truth in *The Beast in the Jungle*—we may recognize versions of what the father had called a "vastation."

By July, 1845, the Jameses were back in Albany, and two years later they settled in a house on West 14th Street, in New York City. This was to be young Henry's home for the next eight years. It was here that he first began to take in bits of his father's impassioned, elusive conversation; and here, no doubt more importantly, he first began to read fiction—particularly the novels of Charles Dickens (who entered very early, as he would say, "into the blood and bone of our intelligence"). More important yet, perhaps, was the experience of the New York theaters, which the boy was attending with rapturous regularity from his ninth year. At the Broadway and Wallack's, at Burton's and Barnum's and elsewhere, Henry saw Shakespeare, popular melodramas, farces; local companies and English companies; and in November, 1853, at Barnum's, *Uncle Tom's Cabin*. James's almost fierce addiction to the actual theater thus started early and never left him. Later, he would write about the Paris and London stages for American periodicals; and after gesturing in that direction for a long time, he ventured at last into the theater on his own in 1890—to no very happy effect, as we shall see. But what evidently worked upon James's imagination from the outset, beneath the actualities of theater-going, was the sense of the dramatic: a feel for the histrionic view of life. In consequence, and in a very strict meaning of the adjective, James would become the most devotedly *dramatic* novelist in American literature.

Henry, Sr., believed in the greatest flexibility as regards the education of his children, and the latter were accordingly switched from school to school and teacher to teacher at a rate they found bewildering. In retrospect, this may have been to the good; the boys were never submitted long to the dogmas and systems of any one institution or instructor; and Henry had his first taste of what William would call "the buzz and hum of experience," a chaotic stream of impressions into which (so the novelist would feel) only the artist can introduce order and meaning. Following his principle, the elder James took the family to Europe again in 1855 —"to educate the babies in strange lingoes," as he remarked—and, except for an interlude

[3] The best account of "Father's ideas" can be found in William James's introduction to *The Literary Remains of Henry James* (1885). It can be noted here that while the elder James's theories derived in good part from Swedenborg, he was able later to detect a quite similar pattern (the passage from innocence to moralistic selfhood to participation in the human community) in the prophetic poems of William Blake. Henry James, Sr., was one of the first Americans to discover and honor Blake's poetry.

in Newport, they stayed in Europe until the fall of 1860. Most of the time was spent in London and Paris, with excursions to Switzerland and Germany; and once again, Henry was handed along through a series of tutors and schools. Once again, too, it was what he did more or less on his own that counted: reading, especially in England ("he is a devourer of libraries," his father said); and play-going, especially in Paris—from this time on, the Paris theater was the theater par excellence for Henry James.

Having registered his earliest remembered sensations in Europe, Henry thus passed the key years of his adolescence within the same surroundings. To say so is to insist—as Leon Edel, James's biographer, has aptly done—that it is beside the point to complain about James not writing more often about the American scene. He could write about New York and Boston and did so in books like *Watch and Ward*, *Washington Square*, and *The Bostonians*; but for the rest, what the aspiring novelist really *knew* was in fact the look, shape, and feel of things European to a visiting American. "Henry James could not write about prairie schooners," Edel observes, "but he could write about Americans spending the fruits of their native wealth in Europe and riding in carriages through Switzerland." As a novelist, James was peculiarly dependent upon scene or setting and very nearly the equal of Proust in his mastery of it: the scene fully visualized, utterly palpable, yet at the same time a central and symbolic component of the action. And the scenes he felt most confident about artistically, with the course of years, were London and the English countryside, Paris, Venice, Rome.

A fresh American scene was awaiting him, meanwhile, when the family returned in 1860. They came this time, not to New York or Albany, but to Newport, Rhode Island; and here they remained during most of the Civil War, later moving only as far as Boston and Cambridge. The parents and William were, indeed, residents of New England from this period until their deaths; and it was to Cambridge, or to William's summer home in New Hampshire,

that Henry—after the long process of his expatriation had been completed—would come on his occasional visits "back home."

Henry made several lifelong friends during the Newport days, chief among them John La Farge, a young man of French Catholic descent, a gifted painter and something of a genius in the medium of stained glass windows. (It was with the latter interest that La Farge infected Henry Adams, leading Adams to his fascinated study, in particular, of the cathedral at Chartres and hence to one of Adams's two most important books, *Mont-Saint-Michel and Chartres*.) La Farge had lived in Paris and was conversant with French literature; he, with another friend, T. S. Penny, was able to introduce Henry James early in the latter's career to several French writers—Prosper Mérimée and Alfred de Musset, and above all to Balzac,[4] one of the two or three novelists James would come most to revere and, in his own Jamesian way, to draw upon. But the event which overwhelmed all others at this time was, of course, the firing on Fort Sumter in what James called "the soft spring of '61," and the outbreak of the Civil War.

James would forever associate the convulsions of the war with a personal calamity he suffered in late October of the same year. This was a "horrid even if an obscure hurt"; "a single vast visitation"; an injury suffered while jammed into a corner formed by two fences in a Newport field, working a small hand-engine, with others, to put out a "shabby conflagration." Certain students of James's life have suspected some odd form of castration; but Edel, surveying the evidence in toto for the first time, has persuasively diagnosed a severe back strain, perhaps a slipped disk—something with which, unquestionably, James was afflicted on and off for the rest of his life. It must have been exceedingly painful—but what is to be noticed is the shape this "obscure hurt" assumed in James's consciousness.

The phrase "vast visitation" is, as it were, a stammering version of Henry, Sr.'s word "vastation" (Henry, Jr., in fact, never did overcome

[4] To Dreiser, too, Balzac was of seminal importance. See pp. 1879, 1900.

his own stammer); and we can venture that the incident was closely related in the son's mind to the crucial experience of his father, in the English cottage. Nor could the son have failed to meditate the remarkable parallel between his own injury-by-fire to that sustained by the elder James. There is a larger parallel that is still more remarkable. For the younger Henry's calamity led almost at once to a profound sense of community strangely similar to the father's vision of the commonalty of all humanity. It led to a feeling of "tragic fellowship" with all those of his countrymen who were caught up in the agony of war. He felt a "huge comprehensive ache"; and there were many hours, he later wrote, "at which one could scarce have told whether it came most from one's own poor organism . . . or from the enclosing social body, a body rent with a thousand wounds." [5]

That passage, to be sure, may be taken as a part of James's continuing discussion about why he, along with his friend Howells, had been what more bellicose contemporaries (like Francis Parkman) would call a "malingerer" during the Civil War. Nothing is harder to imagine than Henry James, even at the age of twenty-one, in a soldier's uniform and carrying a rifle; yet doubts and a certain amount of guilt feeling persisted. The affirmation of tragic fellowship, however, was deeply felt, and something like it would be implicit in many of James's best writings. As an artist, James would become (even more than Hemingway, who in this and other ways is clearly a literary descendant of James) the compassionate observer of the wounded life.

Before the war was over, James spent a year, surprisingly, at the Harvard Law School, faith-

fully attending lectures, but mainly taking in the Cambridge scene. By 1864, he was living in Boston, and his literary career had quietly begun. In February, the *Continental Monthly* published a twelve-page unsigned story by James called "A Tragedy of Errors," a romantic melodrama about the ironically unsuccessful effort of a married woman to have her crippled husband murdered (like other young writers, male and female, James entertained in his early days quite lethal views about the married state); a year later, William Dean Howells initiated his long friendship with James by publishing the apprentice writer's tale "The Story of a Year" in the *Atlantic Monthly*. Meanwhile, Charles Eliot Norton and James Russell Lowell paid James twelve dollars for a review of a book about the art of fiction in the journal they were hoping to revivify, the *North American Review*; other reviews followed, there and in the *Nation*, articles which appraised new fiction by Trollope or Dickens (*Our Mutual Friend*), or which reflected with youthful learnedness on the craft of George Eliot and Wilkie Collins, of Hawthorne and George Sand. [6] He had hardly turned twenty-one, but there were already very faint traces of the special stature James would eventually reach: that of the most eminent man of letters, in the fullest sense of that latter phrase, in American literary history.

James went back to Europe in 1869, to England first, where he was introduced as a promising new writer to John Ruskin and William Morris. He paid an especially memorable call upon George Eliot, the English novelist with whom, as an aspiring artist, he felt most in tune. "She is magnificently ugly—deliciously hideous," he wrote his father. He ended by falling in love "with this great horse-faced bluestocking." Her rich, soft voice, her immense feminine dignity, the "hundred conflicting shades of consciousness and simpleness" gave her, James felt, "a larger circumference than any woman I have ever seen." Later in the year, he was in Italy, carrying in his pocket Stendhal's *La Chartreuse de Parme* and reading it in a

---

[5] The pattern of physical ailment and psychic disturbance in the James family is remarkably consistent, and both Henry's sister Alice and his brother William shared in it. Alice James (an uncommonly brilliant woman, as her diary attests) was a chronic invalid, given to pitching forward in a faint and showing evidence of severe neurosis. As to William James, it can almost be said that his very career and his philosophical convictions (essentially, his theory of pragmatism) grew out of his personal psychic difficulties.

[6] Most of these articles were collected in *Notes and Reviews* in 1921.

Milan café; in Venice, carrying Ruskin's history of Venetian art; in Florence, exploring a Carthusian monastery; and, finally, in Rome, where he went "reeling and moaning thro' the streets, in a fever of enjoyment."

It was not until 1876 that James, writing to his father from England, declared that he had made his choice: he had settled in England once and for all, and it was there that he would concentrate his energies and pursue his literary career. A quarter of a century later, in a letter to Edith Wharton (before the two met) about her novel of eighteenth-century Italy, *The Valley of Decision*, James urged Mrs. Wharton with vehement sincerity to stick to "the American subject" and the American scene—and to profit by his "awful example of exile and ignorance." That was typical Jamesian hyperbole. Whatever else he may have become an example of, it was not ignorance. His experience and his wanderings may have taught him less than, say, Edith Wharton knew about the inner workings of a segment of American society. But it had taught him a good deal about the behavior of Americans in Europe; and much more than that, by sensitively observing the contrast between American and European behavior in social intercourse, James had penetrated more deeply than any writer of his time into the core of the American personality. And doing that, he had come close to grasping the human condition under modern circumstances: the motives by which men and women are really compelled, the values they live by and those they pretend to live by. He had, moreover, become privy to a broader range not only of writings but also of writers—English, French, Italian, Russian—than almost any of his compatriots.

The decision to settle in England was certainly not made lightly or in haste. James had spent most of 1870 and 1871 in Cambridge, Massachusetts, living with his family. He saw much of William Dean Howells, who, as editor of the *Atlantic Monthly*, was contributing ever more vigorously to James's literary fortunes; he strolled with Henry Adams, then teaching history at Harvard; and held long talks with young

Wendell Holmes. He was writing and publishing steadily: tales (including "The Passionate Pilgrim"), a short novel set in Boston (*Watch and Ward*), travel sketches, reviews. All the while he was mulling the problem of *where*—in Europe or in America—he might best exercise his creative powers; and he had come to perceive that to be an American was "a complex fate." But it may be that the event that most determined James's course occurred just before his return to America in the spring of 1870.

This was the death of his cousin Minnie Temple. James had loved her, not as a romantic suitor perhaps, but with a definite passion. Minnie had represented for James the rarest of all good qualities: "moral spontaneity." He felt in her an unequaled "sense for verity of character and play of life in others," and as a result "life claimed her and used her and beset her"—until she died, at the age of twenty-four, of lung hemorrhage. Minnie Temple would be a main source (even to her very initials) of Milly Theale in *The Wings of the Dove*, who has a similarly intense desire for life itself and who is similarly beset and destroyed by the life she clutches after. But there are recollections of Minnie as well in James's Daisy Miller, with her own fund of moral spontaneity, and in Isabel Archer and her ambiguous passion for personal freedom. It can be argued that the death of Minnie Temple, and James's response to it, liberated something in his imagination and made it possible for him to write those stories. James would later feel that Minnie's death was the death of his youth and, by implication, the start of his true maturity.

Through the early seventies, James had continued to study at first hand his two options: to live in Europe (during long visits to Germany, Paris, Rome, Florence) or to live in America (during 1874–75 in New York City). In Bad Homburg, James wrote "Madame de Mauves," perhaps the first of the tales to explore in some depth and with a remarkably artful duplicity one of the characteristic Jamesian "situations"—an American male observing with frustrated bafflement the dilemma of an American woman married to a European aristocrat;

and in Florence he began work on his first major novel, *Roderick Hudson*—a novel which confronts the complex fate not only of being an American and an artist, but an American artist living abroad. Back in America, James spent a restive year on East 25th Street, an uninspiring environment which would serve as the Manhattan habitat of Basil Ransom in *The Bostonians*. It was during this period that the first volume of James's tales was published.

When James sailed for Europe in the autumn of 1875, his commuting days were over to all intents and purposes. Howells, with whom he had breakfast the last morning, sensed as much: "Harry James is going abroad again," he wrote a mutual friend, "not to return, I fancy, even for visits." There would of course be occasional visits, but Howells was essentially right. James knew it too, and wrote his family upon arrival in London: "I take possession of the old world —I inhale it—I appropriate it!" For a season, it was Paris that represented the old world James was appropriating as the proper setting for his creative life; and between stretches of work at what he called his "picturesque address" (29 rue de Luxembourg), he consorted to his great benefit with the Paris-based Russian novelist Turgenev ("a beautiful genius," in James's phrase, who made James even more aware than he had been how storytelling can start with the simple image of a *personage*), and with a number of French writers: Daudet, Flaubert, the Goncourt brothers, Zola, De Maupassant. All of these between them helped establish what was the essentially tangential nature of James's relation to American literary realism—that development which was just beginning to show itself in the work of De Forest, Eggleston, Howells, and several others. Zola at once startled and intrigued James by his scientific interest in the use of obscenities by the French working class; but Flaubert in particular could confirm James's belief in the importance of *form*, and of precision of language, in narrative. James shared Howells' conviction about the novelist's need to be true to life. But he was beginning to see that he should, as it were, be truer to life than life was to itself: to attend carefully to actual experience, but, in giving an impression of it, to reveal—by means of form and diction—shapes and tendencies which remained hidden or implicit in real life.

By the time, in late 1876, that James crossed over to England and took up lodgings in Piccadilly, he had already completed a novel, *The American*, in which he exploited his new understanding of the fictional art, his sharpening skills, and the materials he was making peculiarly his own.

The title suggests what the substance of the novel confirms: that James is now ready to offer a full-scale analysis of the American personality by thrusting a prime example of it into the European social scene. Immeasurably wealthy and retired from business affairs while still young, Christopher Newman—the very type of "new man" which the New World has brought into being—determines, like James himself, to take possession of the Old World: and precisely by marrying into the French aristocracy as represented by the Bellegarde family of the Faubourg St. Germain in Paris. In no other novel does James more brilliantly and tellingly play off the contrasts between European and American habits of social conduct, moral presuppositions, senses of humor, speech, gesture. The intricacy of the dramatic pattern is peculiarly Jamesian. Eliot once remarked that the special qualities of James's novels lay in the characters' awareness of each other; and in *The American*, as in the larger masterpieces that followed, we become aware of Newman, the Marquise, her daughter Claire, her son Valentin, and others almost entirely through their growing consciousness one of another. Newman's force of personality, his ignorance, his candor, his innocence, his limitations, his blunt nobility: this amalgam of features becomes visible and acquires significance only by contrast. At the end, Claire is shut up by her family in an uncommonly bleak convent, to prevent her from marrying Newman; and Newman, after pondering revenge on the Bellegarde family, gives it up and goes back home. Howells and others had begged James to provide his readers with a happy ending, but James remained firm in his conviction that no such ending was realistically possible for representatives of worlds with as little in common as those of Newman and Claire de Cintré.

England was to be James's home country for the rest of his life, and his city London—until, in the late 1890's, he moved down to Lamb House in Rye, Sussex. By 1876, the crucial decision had been reached; the great commitment made; and stories like "Madame de Mauves" and, much more, *The American* showed what benefits could be reaped by an American writer (of genius) residing in the Old World. But in *Daisy Miller*, which James wrote only a year or so after settling in Piccadilly, one can observe James's subtle recognition of certain risks in his situation. It is of course Daisy herself who is the memorable center of this most famous of James's tales: the somewhat crude and wholly beguiling girl from Schenectady whose "moral spontaneity" earns her cruel snubs from the expatriated American social figures in Rome, and whose ill-considered visit to the Colosseum with an outré Italian escort leads to an attack of "Roman fever" and to her death. Daisy's spirit, as one critic has put it, goes marching on; and despite some grumbling on this side of the water that the portrait of Daisy was an insult to American girlhood, she quickly became established as an unmistakable type of New World female—before long, what is known as an archetype: socially inexperienced, at once audacious and pure, utterly without deceit; touching and doomed.

But if we focus for a moment on other characters in the story—the narrator Winterbourne, his aunt Mrs. Belloc, the imperious Mrs. Walker in Rome—we notice James's alertness to the danger of living too long abroad; for they too, in varying degrees, are "awful examples of exile and ignorance," an ignorance in matters of the heart (for which Daisy has a kind of perfect intuition) a good deal more unpardonable than Daisy's ignorance of sterile social discrimination. If Daisy represents the peril of exerting American instincts in Europe, the others represent the peril of permanent uprootedness. James, who as a writer and a social being was courting both

risks, knew well enough the hazardous adventure he was launched upon.

He thought of himself, in the first London years, as an "observant stranger." There was, certainly, a great deal to observe. James was writing steadily; but he was also elected to several London clubs, to his great pleasure; he was an indefatigable diner out; he was a guest at country-house parties of the wealthy and distinguished. He came to know Browning, Thackeray, Froude the historian, James Bryce, Whistler, Arnold, Leslie Stephen. But he moved among them as a man without intimates: increasingly familiar and respected, yet a stranger nonetheless. Such, anyhow, was his posture, his felt relation to the world about him. His title for the first volume of his autobiography in 1913 would be *A Small Boy and Others*, and he would describe there his youthful sense of the *otherness* of people and liken his status to that of a child peering through a window at glittering and unreachable confectionary. The maturing American artist, in England and on the continent, now in his late thirties, assumed a somewhat similar stance.

It would not endure forever. He would eventually come, as has been said, to define experience itself as "our apprehension and measure of ourselves as social beings"; and his own deeply inward and only half-conscious desire was to arrive at just that social state. He would work out the process in his greatest fiction as in his life. But for the time being, he lingered in the condition his father had called that of "selfhood." He seems to have known it. After joining the Reform Club in Pall Mall, he wrote his sister Alice that this event had "doubled my 'selfhood,' as Father would say." His thickening sense *of* himself—as a literary artist, an individual, in his own phrase a citizen of the James country—absorbed all his attention.

Having brought a series of fictive Americans to Europe to their own assorted misfortune, James, in *The Europeans* (1878), reversed the process and brought a cluster of Europeans to New England. The novel is graceful, witty, and compact; a kind of narrative gaming, or finger exercise in the fictional mode—the novel of manners—over which James was gaining mastery. It is still a delight to read, especially for its acutely knowing sketch of New England inhibitions; but it served, so one feels, as a final rehearsal of theme and flexing of talent before James began work, as he did the following year, on his first truly ambitious novel, *The Portrait of a Lady*. The latter was completed, in Venice, in 1881.

During the intervening few years, James had produced *Washington Square*, among many other novellas and short stories. He had responded with ambiguous affection to the news of his brother William's marriage and had later enjoyed a visit, in London, by William and his bride. He had spent many months in Florence, where much of *The Portrait* was written and where he struck up a rather close friendship with Constance Fenimore Woolson, a slightly deaf but oddly attractive American woman of some literary pretension and talent. The relationship, undoubtedly more ardent on the side of Fenimore, as she was called, was a sign that James's selfhood might be yielding a little but was still very strong. And *The Portrait of a Lady*, one of James's two or three greatest novels, suggested that he had mastered the truth of human intercourse, insofar as it consisted in the inability or disinclination of individuals to overcome their self-involvement. Realism, honestly pursued, could go no further; but James would finally find the terms to do so. Having already indicated the limits of realism by investing experience with significant structure, he would eventually allow his structures to expand from the shapely to the quasi-mythic, where humanity reaches and achieves beyond itself.

James and Howells once vowed to each other never to write a novel about courtship, but neither was able to avoid the subject. The heroine of *The Portrait of a Lady*, Isabel Archer, is courted by three different men and most deeply and genuinely loved by still a fourth—her cousin Ralph Touchett, who confesses his love for her only on his deathbed. In his preface to *The Portrait* in the New York edition, in 1907, James would say that the theme of the book was that of a young woman "affronting her destiny." That tautly formulated action is, to borrow a phrase from another essay, "the idea [that] permeates and penetrates" the novel; and the destiny "affronted" takes the form, seriatim, of Caspar Goodwood, an energetic and affluent American who pops up from time to time rather like a jack-in-the-box; Lord Warburton, a perhaps even wealthier English landowner, of aristocratic political leanings; and Gilbert Osmond, a superficially charming and cultivated but in fact a sterile and wholly self-absorbed American expatriate, living in Italy. Isabel makes the fatal mistake of marrying Osmond, and though at the end she has taken the full measure of his appalling "selfhood," she chooses to stay with him in order to protect the interests of his vulnerable adolescent daughter Pansy.

But as that brief outline may well show, plot summaries of James's novels rarely sound very impressive, and sometimes not even very interesting. It is what James *made* out of his often sparse and unpromising materials that constitutes his real achievement.[7] We have suggested that if Hawthorne was one of the first authentic American literary artists, it was because for Hawthorne, in any given work, the *treatment* was as important as the thing treated. (See pp. 446–54.) This was even truer for James, and he was a good deal more self-conscious about the matter, more of a theorist, than Hawthorne. During a debate with H. G. Wells in the year before James died, as we shall see, he summed up a lifetime of creative experience by maintaining that "It is art that *makes* life, makes interest,

---

[7] A relatively late tale, "The Story in It" (1903), plays ironically on this creative theme. A virile English gentleman, Colonel Voyt, is informed by his mistress that her friend Mrs. Blessingbourne is also, secretly, in love with him. The Colonel finds this hard to believe, but he finally acknowledges that Mrs. Blessingbourne's hidden feelings may amount to "a kind of shy romance." It could, however, be no more in his view than "a small starved subjective satisfaction." "Who but a duffer—he stuck to his contention—would see the shadow of a 'story' in it?" Thus James concludes a first-class story in which one of the major characters feels the dramatic situation to be totally lacking in story value.

makes importance . . . and I know of no substitute whatever for the force and beauty of its
process."

Given James's profound conviction along these
lines, the critic who turns to *The Portrait of a
Lady* is well advised to address himself to the art
that makes the life, the interest, and the importance of the novel. The difficulty for the
critic is that James's art, here, as always when he
is at his best, simultaneously manipulates all the
various resources of fiction—what is happening,
artistically, is happening everywhere at once. On
a single page, the art may reveal itself in the
treatment of incident, character, dialogue, imagery, and setting. More than that, those individual elements are constantly implicated in each
other. For example, a setting—let us say, a
garden—may have some significance in itself; it
may also be the scene of a key incident; it can
stand as a kind of symbol for one of the characters (Ralph Touchett, and all he has come to
mean to Isabel, is forever associated in her mind
with a certain garden in Florence—and that
garden with Ralph); and it can enter into the
imagery.

To do justice to the artistry of *The Portrait*
would thus require an essay of considerable
length. It has seemed better to take one central
passage in the novel as a paradigm of what James
is accomplishing at every turn over nearly six
hundred pages (in a standard edition). The passage we have chosen—it is one of the most
memorable and the most widely admired in all
of James's fiction—runs from the middle of
Chapter 40 through Chapter 42. We can approach it by rehearsing a little further the outer
trappings of the narrative.

Isabel Archer, a handsome and spirited, but
also penniless, young woman comes from Albany to England (the time is about 1870) to
visit her aunt Mrs. Touchett, and that lady's
millionaire husband. She is introduced to us as
a person who, for all her admirable qualities,
"was probably very liable to the sin of self-
esteem," and hence, more dangerously, of self-
delusion. She longs passionately, though in no
very coherent manner, for freedom—freedom,
somehow (and this too is, of course, attractive),

to perform some supremely generous act. This
intensity of her desire greatly intrigues her
seriously ailing cousin Ralph Touchett; and he
is the more intrigued when she turns down a
proposal of marriage from the eminently eligible
Lord Warburton. It is now the aim of his life,
Ralph tells Isabel, to experience "the thrill of
seeing what a young woman does who won't
marry Lord Warburton." To hasten that thrill,
Ralph in secret persuades his father to leave the
bulk of his fortune to Isabel, rather than to
himself.

Shortly, on Mr. Touchett's death, Isabel becomes an heiress, though she is quite unaware
of the provenance of her legacy. She becomes
friends with Madame Merle, an always perfectly groomed but rather mysterious acquaintance of her aunt's, and through Madame Merle
she comes to know Gilbert Osmond. To Ralph,
who sees with the eyes of disinterested love,
Osmond is plainly nothing but a "sterile dilettante." But for Isabel he resembles a once shining prince who has merely fallen on unlucky
days, and to Ralph's bitter disappointment she
marries the older man. She had always, James
tells us, been addicted to theorizing, even intel-
lectualizing (James, like Hawthorne, found this
a serious flaw in a female makeup), and her
theory now is that to give herself to Osmond
and to use her money in the creation of a life
of cultivated ease for him is the finest way she
can exercise her newfound freedom.

The narrative then moves forward three years
to an "afternoon of the autumn of 1876," and
the Palazzo Roccanera in Rome, where the Os-
monds are living with Gilbert's docile, immature
daughter Pansy. In the expanding courtship
theme, another young American, Ned Rosier,
has been pressing for Pansy's hand; but Osmond
has his eye on a bigger catch, Lord Warburton,
who has also arrived in the city. Warburton in
fact has come to Rome because of his continuing devotion to Isabel; to Osmond's vexation, he
makes no gesture toward Pansy, and when he
sees he can only harm Isabel rather than help
her, he prepares to leave.

The passage we want to discuss begins at
about this point, on a spring afternoon when

Isabel returns to the palazzo from a drive in the country with Pansy. As she is making her way to her own room, she passes the drawing room and, looking in, sees something that obscurely startles her.

Madame Merle was standing on the rug, a little way from the fire; Osmond was in a deep chair, leaning back and looking up at her. Her head was erect, as usual, but her eyes were bent upon his. What struck Isabel first was that he was sitting while Madame Merle stood; there was an anomaly in this that arrested her.

Here is as telling an instance as one could wish of the fictional use of social "manners," and in particular James's expert deployment of them. In the society James was dealing with, no gentleman ever sat while a lady stood—unless the relations between them were extremely intimate. (The disappearance of such social conventions, while it may make for greater flexibility of conduct, has robbed the novelist of one of his chief traditional resources.) Isabel realizes slowly that Madame Merle and her husband must be much more intimate—must for a long time have been more intimate—than she had suspected. As a result of that casual tableau, Isabel's entire "situation," and its hitherto unguessed-at origins, begins to clarify itself in Isabel's mind. Eventually, indeed, she learns that Madame Merle had been Osmond's mistress, that Pansy is *her* child by Osmond, and that she had engineered Isabel's marriage in order to give Pansy a mother.

The afternoon's revelation hovers behind Isabel's share in the dialogue with Osmond that evening (Chap. 41). It is here that Osmond, by word and look, fully discloses the absolute egotism of his nature. We can give only a taste of it. Osmond asks Isabel what she understands Warburton's intentions to be, and Isabel replies guardedly that she has waited for Osmond to describe them.

"That's a consideration you don't always show," Osmond answered, after a moment.
"I have determined, this time, to try and act as you would like. I have so often failed in that."

Osmond turned his head, slowly, looking at her.

"Are you trying to quarrel with me?"
"No, I am trying to live at peace."
"Nothing is more easy; you know I don't quarrel myself."
"What do you call it when you try to make me angry?" Isabel asked.
"I don't try; if I have done so, it has been the most natural thing in the world. Moreover, I am not in the least trying now."

Isabel smiled. "It doesn't matter. I have determined never to be angry again."
"That's an excellent resolve. Your temper isn't good."
"No—it's not good." She pushed away the book she had been reading, and took up the band of tapestry that Pansy had left on the table.

James's dialogues, like this one (which continues for several more pages), are customarily dynamic rather than static. They are no mere exchange of views: rather, they contribute vitally to the story's dramatic momentum and move the action steadily forward. As character is disclosed by speech, the disclosure has an immediate effect upon the other character involved; relationships change and re-form under the quiet pressure of conversation. In the present case, not only does Osmond's language manifest his talent for wounding, his cold enjoyment at inflicting psychological hurt; at the same time, by way of response, Isabel is rallying her own emotional forces and more or less openly establishing a new posture toward her husband.

In this chapter and the one following, Osmond stands forth as the very embodiment of human evil in the Jamesian secular theology. Hatred is the only emotion in this deadly person. There is not the slightest impulse to kindness in him, nor any of the sensitivity that goes with kindness: hence the occasional crudeness (notable in other passages) in this devotee of the conventional. Over all of this, and more, Isabel broods, sitting up late in front of the fire, after Osmond has gone to his room.

The narrative style in *The Portrait of a Lady* is that of the earlier James: still the nearly omniscient narrator, speaking out in his own voice ("as I say," "on the evening I speak of," and so on), and scrupulous as to fact—the precise amount of Isabel's inheritance has been given, dates are pinned down with precision. James could never be said to absent himself entirely from his narratives, for he had one of the most palpable authorial "presences" in modern fiction. But the later James, from *The Spoils of Poynton* onward, tended, as we shall see, to allow situations to develop dramatically, through objectively recorded gesture and speech. Yet even in *The Portrait* the dramatic method is beginning to emerge, especially in the alternation between what James would call the "scene" and the "interval" (see our headnote to *The Pupil*). A "scene" is a direct confrontation, with dialogue; an "interval" is a portion of narrative which—through silent meditation on some person's part, or through (as it were) reporting from a certain distance—covers a longer period of time. Isabel's vigil before the fire, following the scene with Osmond, is a masterful instance of the "interval."

James was highly pleased with it. "My young woman's extraordinary meditative vigil on the occasion that was to become for her such a landmark," he wrote in the preface to the New York edition, "is obviously the best thing in the book." What he quite impersonally admired in retrospect was that, while Isabel never stirs from her chair or speaks aloud, the episode was as thoroughly dramatic as the most sensational scene might be.

Reduced to its essence, it is but the vigil of searching criticism; but it throws the action further forward than twenty "incidents" might have done. . . . She sits up, by her dying fire, far into the night, under the spell of recognitions on which she finds the last sharpness suddenly wait. It is a representation simply of her motionlessly *seeing*, and an attempt withal to make the mere still lucidity of her act as "interesting" as the surprise of a caravan or the identification of a pirate.

It is, we may summarize, an act of consciousness on Isabel's part. And what she *sees*, "under the spell of recognitions," is the truth of her life, her marriage, her husband, and herself. To get at a part of James's accomplishment here, we may quote a crucial moment. When she had first met Osmond, Isabel reminds herself, he had had "all the appearance of a man living in the open air of the world."

But when, as the months elapsed, she followed him further and he led her into the mansion of his own habitation, then, then, she had seen where she really was. She could live it over again, the incredulous terror with which she had taken the measure of her dwelling. Between those four walls she had lived ever since; they were to surround her for the rest of her life. It was the house of darkness, the house of dumbness, the house of suffocation. Osmond's beautiful mind gave it neither light nor air; Osmond's beautiful mind, indeed, seemed to peep down from a small high window and mock at her. . . . Under all his culture, his cleverness, his amenity, under his good nature, his facility, his knowledge of life, his egotism lay hidden like a serpent in a bank of flowers.

Where, in the preceding chapter, the action had progressed chiefly through the thrust and response of dialogue, here it is carried primarily through the play of imagery. James is, in fact, concentrating a good many of the image clusters, symbols, and metaphors he had set going in the first pages of the novel, and they come together here in ever-widening vistas of Isabel's understanding. Fundamentally, *The Portrait* is a drama of freedom and entrapment—more accurately, of the desire for freedom leading *to* entrapment; and most of the images and symbols have contributed to that theme. There has been a succession of houses, for instance, each of which has slowly taken on symbolic meaning: Gardencourt, the Twitchetts' English home, which had seemed a promise of freedom; Osmond's Florentine villa, with its masklike façade; and the Palazzo Roccanera (or "black rock"), which now appears to Isabel as a "house

of darkness" and of "suffocation." There had
been a series of real and imagined lights,
lamps, and lanterns, and all now culminate in
the darkening sitting room of Isabel's vigil, and
the spiritual darkness of her dwelling.

As we have said, gardens and flowers have
played both actual and figurative roles from the
beginning, contributing now to the theme of
openness and freedom, now to that of enclosure, secrecy, imprisonment. The story starts
and concludes in the spacious garden at Gardencourt, and it was in the garden in Florence that
Ralph had spoken most passionately against
Isabel's marriage. In his first description of Isabel, James has remarked that her "nature had,
in her conceit, a certain garden-like quality";
and when Isabel is attempting to take the bearings of Madame Merle, she feels she is merely
wandering "as by the wrong side of a wall of a
private garden, round the enclosed talents, accomplishments, aptitudes of" her new friend.
There is floral imagery even in the proper names
of Pansy and Ned Rosier. This whole process
reaches its intense climax in Isabel's realization
that the egotism of Osmond—a man she had
first thought of as "living in the open air"—"lay
hidden like a serpent in a bank of flowers."

The chapter ends with Isabel recalling her
glimpse "of her husband and Madame Merle,
grouped unconsciously and familiarly," the afternoon before. Meditation then yields to further
scenes and intervals over thirteen more chapters.
But Isabel has in her hands all the elements of
the destiny she had come to Europe to "affront."
On learning that Ralph is dying, back at
Gardencourt, Isabel goes to him, despite Osmond's icy warning that to do so would be an
act of deliberate disobedience. She attends
Ralph's deathbed and hears his confession of
love. Isabel herself experiences a longing to
die: but "deep in her soul . . . was the sense
that life would be her business for a long time
to come." It will be in particular the life of
Pansy Osmond that Isabel must make it her
business to protect and nourish. She prepares
to return to her lightless Roman prison—but
James lets us believe that she has, at least, won

a measure of freedom in the tragic wisdom she
has acquired.

James made two fairly long visits "back
home," in 1881 and 1882, the first coinciding
with and the second occasioned by the death of
a parent. James's mother died in January 1882:
"the perfection of a mother," James wrote;
"the sweetest, gentlest, most beneficent human
being I have ever known." He lingered on in
Boston for some time, dwelling, in letters, on
the "beneficent memory" of Mary James, then
returned to Europe to make a carefully planned
tour of France (the basis, later, for an excellent
book about that country). But he had scarcely
been back six months when word reached him
that his father had been stricken. He took boat
hurriedly, only to learn, on his arrival in New
York in December, that Henry, Sr., had died.
Several mornings later, James walked over to
the Mt. Auburn cemetery in Cambridge, and,
over his father's grave, read aloud a letter from
William (who was spending the year abroad)—
a letter in which William lovingly acknowledged
the overwhelming importance to him of Henry,
Sr., as a man, a father, a thinker. "Good-
night, my sacred old Father," the letter ended.
"If I don't see you again—Farewell! A blessed
farewell!" Soon after this, and even as the
father's estate was being settled, Henry's young
brother Wilkinson, bankrupt and crippled, died
in Milwaukee, at the age of thirty-eight.

Along with his deep and genuine grief over
this swift succession of family deaths, James
also undoubtedly felt a strong sense of liberation.
This time, when he reestablished himself in
London, he would not return to the United
States for more than twenty years. He no longer
had an American home; London was now his
home, and the continental cities and countryside its suburbs. He began to form actual friendships: with the Edmund Gosses, the George du
Mauriers, with the painter John Singer Sargent
and the brilliant scholar of Italian cultural history Vernon Lee, with the ailing and fascinating Robert Louis Stevenson whose work James
so shrewdly admired. In Paris, he was on terms

of friendly equality with Flaubert, De Maupassant, Zola, the Goncourt brothers. Speaking of them in a letter to Howells, James declared that nothing interested him more "than the effort and experiment of this little group, with its truly infernal intelligence of art, form, manner— its intense artistic life. They do the only kind of work, today, that I respect," he went on; "and in spite of their ferocious pessimism and their handling of unclean things, they are at least serious and honest."

James, at forty, was at last his own man, living in a place of his own (in the form of a furnished flat), and—partly out of his searching admiration for the French writers—following what he knew to be his own creative line. He even felt liberated from the "international theme," on which as an American living abroad he had so long depended and which he had so impressively exploited. *The Bostonians* (1884) is set in the United States and is populated entirely by Americans; the two other major novels of the eighties, *The Princess Casamassima* (1885) and *The Tragic Muse* (1889), are equally confined to the English scene. His essay "The Art of Fiction" (1884) not only contained some of the most cogent observations ever made on that subject; it is also, on the personal level, James's remarkable declaration of freedom as an artist, along with his covert but extremely bold recognition of himself *as* an artist and (very nearly) as a man of genius.

The essay was written as a commentary upon a public lecture by the novelist Walter Besant. James applauded Besant for taking fiction seriously and insisting that it was or could be one of the fine arts; around the novel, James noted, there still hovered the old idea that it somehow represented a danger to morality and was thus acceptable only if it confessed itself to be a kind of joke. (See pp. 224–26.) Serious discussion and serious criticism of the form might now finally be possible. But James questioned Besant's attempt to lay down laws for the writing of novels. The good health of every art, he said, demanded "that it be perfectly free. It lives upon exercise, and the very meaning of

exercise is freedom." [8] As to the particular art form of the novel, James argued that it "is in its broadest definition a personal, a direct impression of life; that, to begin with, constitutes its value, which is greater or less according to the intensity of the impression. But there will be no intensity at all, and therefore no value, unless there is freedom to feel and say." Returning to this theme later in the essay, James made some astringent remarks about the inhibitions of the Anglo-American writer (as distinguished to an important extent from the French), and with regard to the difference between what he knew and talked about in conversation, and what he felt able to put down in print. Much less strenuously than Melville (in "Hawthorne and His Mosses"), but speaking out of his own special artistic dedication, James thus likewise addressed himself to the unshackled creative spirit.

James also found something vaguely limiting in Besant's requirement that a novelist write only out of personal experience.

> What kind of experience is intended, and where does it begin and end? Experience is never limited, and it is never complete; it is an immense sensibility, a kind of huge spider-web of the finest silken threads suspended in the chamber of consciousness, and catching every air-borne particle in its tissue. It is the very atmosphere of the mind; and when the mind is imaginative—much more when it happens to be that of a man of genius—it takes to itself the faintest hints of life, it converts the very pulses of the air into revelations.

One hears the echo there of the long American tradition, to which literary realism was now making its contribution, according to which it is the great task of the imagination to make visible the poetic, the significant, even the miraculous in the minute and ordinary. "Try," James was inclined to advise the novice, "—try to be one of the people on whom nothing is

---

[8] This statement should be emphasized in the light of the dogmatic interpretations that some critics have placed on James's theorizing about fiction.

lost!" And he added later that "the deepest quality of a work of art"—by all means including its moral quality—"will always be the quality of the mind of the producer."

There was much to question, James went on, in Besant's familiar and conventional distinctions between plot and character in a novel, between novels of character and novels of incident, between books that could be called novels and those that could be called romances. The only distinctions James allowed were between good novels and bad novels, those that interest us and those that do not. Every good work of fiction is a personal impression of life; and every good novel is "a living thing, all one and continuous, like any other organism." The "story" can be distinguished from the rest of the novel only in the sense that it is the starting point, the generative idea:

and since in proportion as the work is successful the idea permeates and penetrates it, informs and animates it, so that every word and every punctuation-point contribute directly to the expression, in that proportion do we lose our sense of the story being a blade which may be drawn more or less out of its sheath.

By that extraordinarily exacting standard, *The Bostonians* cannot be reckoned an altogether successful work. The two major elements in the book do not quite make a perfect fit; there is no single idea penetrating, informing, and animating the novel. On the one hand, there is the central intrigue, the struggle between the neurotic Bostonian, Olive Chancellor, and the gentleman from Mississippi, Basil Ransom, for possession of the impressionable Verena Tarrant; on the other, the portrait of reformist agitation, particularly on behalf of the status of women. The former is tightly dramatic and moves through a pattern of carefully placed and beautifully juxtaposed scenes of confrontation. The latter is broadly drawn, contains a swarm of characters, and expands into a large chapter of the social history of New England and New York in the wake of the Civil War.

The relation between the two elements is subtle and significant, nonetheless. For the historical world being defined is the influential *context* of the intrigue, and it is a fallen world, a world that has seen better days and in which phenomena are losing their outlines. Gazing out of the window in Olive Chancellor's apartment on Charles Street, in Boston, Ransom observes "an horizon indented at empty intervals with wooden spires, the masts of lonely boats, the chimneys of dirty 'works,' over a brackish expanse of anomalous character, which was too big for a river and too small for a bay." The physical confusion recorded there, in which even a body of water has lost its identity, hints at a spiritual and cultural confusion: church spires and factory chimneys blurring together. Individual characters are no less anomalous: Selah Tarrant is "a moralist without a moral sense"; Mrs. Luna, Olive's sister, is a kind of willful parody of the conservative social matron; and about Dr. Prance, the lady doctor, James remarks that "if she had been a boy she would have borne some relation to a girl, whereas Dr. Prance appeared to bear none whatever." A climax is reached in the description of Miss Birdseye, the weak-eyed and aging heroine of the reform movement, whose sad pale face "looked as if it had been soaked, blurred, and made vague by exposure to some slow dissolvent." She was "a confused, entangled, inconsequent, discursive old woman, whose charity began at home and ended nowhere"; she was "essentially formless" and "had no more outline than a bundle of hay."

The quality of that world is constantly measured against the spartan, clear-eyed, tough-minded idealism of pre–Civil War Concord. But its murkiness, meanwhile, has its effect upon the three figures in the central drama, each of whom has an incomplete or blurred identity. Olive, especially, suffers from the loss of sexual identity noted in Dr. Prance. It is probably too simple to see her as an out-and-out lesbian; she is, so to speak, not even that. In his notebook, James said that he "wished to write a very *American* tale" and asked himself "what was the most salient and peculiar point in our social life." Meditating this question in Boston, in the weeks after his father's death (and staring down from his Beacon Street window onto the anarchic and desolate scene studied by Ransom, and, in a still more detailed and suggestive passage in Chapter 20, by Verena), James concluded: "The answer was: the situation of women, the decline of the sentiment of sex, the agitation on their behalf." It seems likely that James drew upon his recent experience of the tug-of-war between his invalided sister Alice and another invalid, Louisa Loring, for the attentions of Louisa's sister Katharine—both as a model of sorts for his fictional struggle and as an example of the attraction of female to female. But more generally, he was giving an account of the same thing that would strike Henry Adams: the disappearance of womanliness in American society. If Ransom at the end wins a precarious victory over Olive, it is because he has a more clearly defined sexual nature; but James holds out little hope of a happy future for Basil and Verena.

The Bostonians was not well received. When the first chapters appeared in the *Century*, William James among others wrote Henry that, in the figure of Miss Birdseye, he had provided only a thinly disguised and intolerable satire of the zealous reformist Elizabeth Peabody (Sophia Hawthorne's older sister). James denied the charge but took pains in the later chapters to transform Miss Birdseye from an entangled and foolish old woman into something of a saint. If he initiated the change in order to assuage his New England readers, his imagination helped him justify it on human and artistic grounds—for Miss Birdseye alone in this cluster of blurred and embattled egos, this war of self-hoods, is seen as devoted to others, to humanity itself. It is indeed a mark of Verena Tarrant's human potential that she can recognize this. When she addresses the dying old woman as "our heroine . . . our saint," it is because, Verena says, "If you were to live for a thousand years, you would think only of others—you would think only of helping on humanity." James wrote *The Princess Casamassima* over about fifteen months between the summer of

1885 and the fall of 1886, a period spent almost entirely in London. He had now, as Edel remarks, become finally and fully domesticated in the English capital. He had taken a long lease on an unfurnished flat in Kensington and had furnished it himself with leisurely enjoyment. He dined out less and less; he had served his time as a stranger observing the dinner tables and the social habits of the prominent and now preferred his personal friends to visit with him in his own home. *The Princess Casamassima* is in fact James's major "London novel," and into it he poured his accumulated impressions of the city he lived in. It is also his major political novel and centers on the revolutionary aspirations of the working class in odd conjunction with the aristocracy. James's knowledge of the English workingman and revolutionist was of course largely external. But even in this area, his genius carried him to cunning and prophetic insights: for example, into the helpless dilemma of the merely liberal figure in a revolutionary situation; and into the nature of the coldly calculating, as against the romantically reckless, radical personality. The memory of his father's commitment to "the divine-natural humanity," in a transcendence of egotism, allowed James implicitly to contrast actual political maneuverings with a dimly felt humane ideal. For the rest, the gap of knowledge, such as it was, seems to be filled by the enabling presences of the novelists James most esteemed: by Dickensian melodrama (illegitimacy, murder, suicide); by Balzac's social penetration; by Zola's description of the French workers; by Flaubert's mastery of form.

As though temporarily sated with London, James went to Italy soon after the appearance of *The Princess Casamassima* and spent eight months in Venice and Florence. He saw much of Fenimore Woolson (she was, for a period, his landlady in a villa in Bellosguardo, south of Florence) and renewed his acquaintance with Vernon Lee. But the main event of this period was the writing of *The Aspern Papers*, one of the finest of James's novellas, his most memorable evocation of Venice, and a further stage in James's imaginative involvement with self-hood and the impulse to get beyond it.

The plot of *The Aspern Papers* was provided by Vernon Lee and her brother, who told James about Claire Clairmont, the former mistress of Lord Byron, who had lived on in Florence to a great age, her only companion a fifty-year-old niece. Her boarder, an American retired sea captain, was a devotee of Shelley, some of whose papers, along with letters from Byron, were in Claire Clairmont's possession. After Claire Clairmont's death in 1879, the American sought to persuade the niece to give him the Shelley papers; the niece agreed to do so, on condition of marriage; and the American fled in horror. In the novella, the scene shifts to Venice; the dead poet becomes an American, Jeffrey Aspern; the American narrator, when his designs upon the precious papers are exposed, is denounced by the decrepit Juliana Bordereau as a "publishing scoundrel"—and both the character and the physical features of Tina the niece (she has become a grandniece) are left deliberately and significantly vague. She is vague, that is, in the limited vision of the narrator, who is too obsessed with his literary longings and stratagems ever to *see* her as an individual human being. He almost does near the end of the story, when Tina suddenly seems to him transfigured, "beautified"; but the moment is shattered when Tina explains gently that she has burned all the papers ("It took a long time—there were so many"), and "the transfiguration was over . . . she had changed back to a plain dingy elderly person."

Leon Edel is undoubtedly right in suggesting that the relationship between the narrator and Tina reflects James's uneasiness about his relations with Fenimore Woolson, his feeling of having exploited her, socially, without giving her the affection she so yearned for. But on a more general level, the story also shows James exploring ways to escape the restraints of self-hood. The larger implications are carried by an atmosphere of the legendary and fabulous: of archetypal journeys across water, of magic formulas for admission to the secret palace. One senses in *The Aspern Papers*, and especially in the final scene, an ironic inversion of the medieval tale (adapted by Chaucer in "The Wife of Bath's Tale"), whereby an ugly old crone is transformed into a beautiful young woman the instant her youthful husband promises to love and be true to her all his days. The narrator almost promises that, and Tina is very nearly transformed. But it is already too late; and the narrator is left with an ambiguous sense of loss —of something, perhaps, far more important than "the precious papers."

Back in London, James continued to produce, with astonishing speed and on a remarkably high level, "A London Life," "The Liar," "The Lesson of the Master," and *The Reverberator* among other fiction, and essays on De Maupassant, the Goncourts, and Stevenson. For an inexplicable period, however, his stories, after being accepted by magazine editors, remained unpublished; and it was then that James wrote Howells that he had been "condemned to eternal silence" and that his last two novels might have ruined his reputation. He clung to the conviction that "some day all my buried prose will kick off its various tombstones again"—by which he meant that he would soon be bursting into print again. And so it was; suddenly James's tales and essays were everywhere, and Howells was writing in *Harper's* that "one turned from one masterpiece to another. . . . The language does not hold their betters for a high perfection of literary execution at all points." Howells regretted only that the "best criticism" appeared wholly unable to take the measure of James's extraordinary achievements, and at times, indeed, in its vulgarity and ignorance tended to scoff at them. But meanwhile, even William James—his brother's constantly worried and self-appointed literary mentor—was impressed. "How you can keep up such productivity and live, I don't see," he wrote from Cambridge; he marveled at "the technical ease" Henry had attained and found *The Reverberator* (a sprightly story of two young Boston ladies in Paris) "simply delicious."

"Delicious" would hardly be the word for *The Tragic Muse*, which came out in book form, after serialization, in 1890. It is a large and crowded novel—overcrowded, one feels: there are too many subjects, too many themes, too many key characters. The title refers to Miriam Rooth, a highly determined English, Jewish girl, who succeeds in becoming a genuinely great actress. Her career is juxtaposed to that of Nick Dormer, who resists the pressing wishes of his family and his bride-to-have-been that he go into politics and dedicates himself instead to the lonely life of artistic creation. Not less significant in the novel are Peter Sherringham, an able diplomat who fails to persuade Miriam to give up the stage and marry him; and the somewhat mysterious aesthete, the brilliant but unproductive Gabriel Nash. It is hard to make out the design of this often wonderfully absorbing novel; but we are again clearly confronted with what James, in an article on Ibsen, spoke of as "the lunging of ego against ego"; in short, another struggle of selfhoods. But the *direction* of James's imagination is less evident than usual, especially since James seems, if anything, to stand closest to Nick Dormer—a figure whose commitment to art exactly rules out entering into those nourishing relationships with other human beings that James, like his father, felt were a chief source of individual fulfillment. It was almost as though it were impossible to be at once an artist and a human being, if the latter involved what the Jameses called "the social."

The Tragic Muse had been written in that profound solitude—that utter and isolated communion between the artist and his muse—which Nick Dormer found to be the challenging necessity of the creative life. James had long pursued his own literary career out of a similar conviction; but now he had to face up to a different kind of necessity—a "simplifying and chastening necessity," as he told Stevenson. He simply "had to try to make somehow or other the money I don't make by literature." He lived entirely on his earnings (his paternal legacy having been turned over to his sister Alice), and his novels no longer sold enough to maintain him in his London flat, on his travels, in his private generosities. He would, he decided,

try to restore his financial situation by writing plays: in short, by moving out of his creative solitude into the world of Miriam Rooth—the world of the London theater.

James had cherished a passion for the theater since his earliest play-going days. During his young manhood, as a roving correspondent, he had written a number of exceptionally acute dispatches for a New York magazine on the Paris and London stages, on actors, actresses, and playwrights (these have been collected in a volume called *The Scenic Art*). He had already the most highly developed histrionic imagination of any novelist in American literary history, though it would develop a great deal more. Naturally enough, he had for many years dreamed (as he said in his notebook) "of doing something for the stage, for fame's sake, and art's, and fortune's." His contempt for the aesthetic debasement of the English-speaking theater had prevented him from making the effort. But in 1890 and 1891, he was, as he felt, forced to do so—not for fame or art, but for money. "My books don't sell," he continued to Stevenson, "and it looks as if my plays might. Therefore I am going with a brazen front to write half a dozen."

His first venture was a dramatization of his novel *The American*. It opened in a provincial theater in January, 1891, and was a modest success. In September of the same year it opened in London. By this time, James, retreating step by step before the demands of director and actors, had made many changes in the script and had given the play a happy ending (he was astonished and appalled to discover how little a playwright is his own man, as a novelist could insist on being). The play, which was badly miscast, received a mixed but respectful reception and ran for seventy-one nights. But for the knowingly watchful, it was already evident that James would never be a popular playwright (as Oscar Wilde, who entered the theater at the same moment with *The Importance of Being Earnest*, so instantly was); nor even, by any standards, a very good one. His devotion to the dramatic form collided with his belief that in the England of the 1890's only a bad play could succeed ("how very bad it must be," he told himself about *The American*); and his deep inclination to creative solitude warred with the bustling requirements of rehearsals, revisions, provincial openings. This way fortune would not lie.

James stuck at it, nonetheless. During the year 1892, he wrote some of his best shorter fiction, including *The Pupil*, "The Real Thing," "Greville Fane," and "Owen Wingrave." But for the next several years, his enthusiasm, if not his talent, was in the theater. He wrote two more plays, a melodrama and a comedy, which were not to be performed; he traveled restlessly in Italy; he negotiated with managers; he sketched out further dramas. Then, in early January, 1895, came the disaster of *Guy Domville*.

The play dealt with a young Englishman, in the late eighteenth century, who alternates between his desire to enter a Benedictine monastery and his sense that, as the last of his clan, he has a duty to remain in the world and perpetuate his family. After various disillusioning experiences, he chooses the monastic life. The theme (Edel makes the point) was rooted in James's personal ambivalence, at the time, about solitude and the worldly life. *Guy Domville* contains some splendid scenes, with passages of dialogue well beyond—too far beyond—anything being written for the stage in London. But the production was again miscast; on opening night there were a series of ghastly accidents; the players lost their nerve; and for the gallery, the ending was at once ludicrous and disappointing. James, who had spent the evening nervously attending a performance of Wilde's *The Ideal Husband*, returned all unsuspecting to the theater and was ushered on stage to confront a madhouse—the intelligent portion of the audience applauding vigorously, and the gallery erupting in jeers, hisses, and shouts of obscenity. It was, James said later, the most horrible hour of his life.

Several of the younger critics had praise for *Guy Domville*. Bernard Shaw challenged any of the popular dramatists "to write a scene in verse with half the beauty of Mr. James's prose" and aligned himself with "the cultivated major-ity who . . . applauded Mr. James" against "the handful of rowdies who brawled at him." H. G. Wells noted the play's weaknesses but found the conception fine and the writing beautiful. Another reviewer declared that Wilde's successful play did nothing for the dramatic art, while *Guy Domville* represented "a defeat out of which it is possible for many victories to spring." The play ran on for a month, and the remaining performances were at once more decorous and less accident prone. James rapidly recovered his outer equilibrium. But the shock to his self-esteem was deep indeed.

Two weeks after the disaster, James replied to a letter from Howells, in which the old friend had reminded James that he was, after all, primarily a writer of fiction.

> You put your finger sympathetically on the place and spoke of what I wanted you to speak of [James wrote]. I *have* felt, for a long time past, that I have fallen on evil days—every sign or symbol of one's being in the least *wanted*, anywhere or by any one, having so utterly failed. A new generation, that I know not, and mainly prize not, has taken universal possession. The sense of being utterly out of it weighed me down, and I asked myself what the future would be. All these melancholies were qualified indeed by one redeeming reflection—the sense of how little, for a good while past (for reasons very logical, but accidental and temporary), I had been producing. I *did* say to myself "Produce again—produce; produce better than ever and all will be well."

By "new generation," James meant a new generation of writers and readers who had taken possession of the magazine trade; it was the latter, James felt, who no longer wanted him. But meanwhile, James had drawn to himself a new generation of younger admirers and "acolytes" who wanted him very much and sought him out almost reverently on all occasions.

The James cult, which reached its peak in the early 1900's, began in fact during the unhappy theatrical years. As his personal fortunes were declining, his emergence as "the Master" was taking place. Against the gain of the new devotees, however, there had to be set certain losses. In 1893, Vernon Lee published a short story, "Lady Tal," which overtly and maliciously satirized Henry James; James never forgave her. More seriously, the previous year, Alice James had died in London, her stricken brother Henry beside her. Most seriously of all, there was the suicide early in 1894 of Fenimore Woolson, who had flung herself into the street from the second-story window of her bedroom in the Casa Semitecolo in Venice. "It is too horrible to me to write about," James told a friend; "—and I mention it really only to tell you that for the present I *can't* write." He was too shaken to attend the funeral; but he later made his way to Venice, darkly inspected the scene of the tragedy, brooded over the possible motives for the act and his own burden of responsibility and guilt—but did not neglect to recover the many letters he had written Fenimore over the years.

The loss of Alice and Fenimore's suicide, followed by the catastrophe of *Guy Domville,* evidently constituted a sort of middle-aged "vastation" for James (who was fifty-two in 1895). It was, all in all, not as serious as the experience which had shattered his father five decades earlier; but it was a great deal more unsettling than the "vast visitation," the wrenched back which, in the spring of 1861, had led James to a sense of tragic fellowship with all those caught up in the agony of war. The earlier episode had occurred before James was properly started on a literary career and provided him from the outset with an understanding, both in actuality and in fiction, of the life that has been hurt. The pattern of calamities in the 1890's served eventually to carry James into an entirely new realm of experience and imagination—beyond selfhood in the one, and beyond realism in the other. Henry, Sr.'s philosophical solution of the devastated self was, we recall, to seek participation in "the divine-natural humanity." Henry, Jr.'s long-range response was more concrete and tangible, and it necessarily involved new and larger creative efforts; but it amounted in the

end to a suggestive parallel to the father's theory.

There was, to begin with, the determination to turn back to fiction and to "produce better than ever." "I take up my *own* old pen again," he confided to his notebook; "—the pen of all my old unforgettable efforts and sacred struggles." The years immediately following 1895 saw James producing "The Altar of the Dead," "The Coxon Fund," "The Death of the Lion," "The Middle Years," "The Figure in the Carpet," and *The Turn of the Screw,* as well as *The Spoils of Poynton, What Maisie Knew,* and *The Awkward Age.* James was in very fact producing better than ever; those stories and novels alone would guarantee another writer a decidedly honorable place in the history of fiction in English. They were also, once again, the products of long lonely hours, the new harvest of recovered solitude.

As a matter of fact, James was finding his existence in the city of London, as it moved toward the twentieth century, by no means solitary enough. Perhaps his experience of the theater had sickened him, temporarily, with the urban life. In any case, by the summer of 1896 he was looking for a country retreat where he could exercise his energies in greater peace and quiet. He spent that summer at Playden, in Sussex, in a small house from which he could catch a glimpse of the town of Rye—"a small red-roofed town, of great antiquity, perched on its sea-rock." A year later, he signed a long-term lease for Lamb House in Rye: an inviting little place on a high point in the town, rich in atmosphere, with a pleasant terrace and garden, and a garden room with a bow window which would serve him as a study. Lamb House, for the most part, would be James's home for the rest of his life.

Leon Edel, in one of the most provocative passages in his biography, argues with considerable evidence not only that James's new home in Rye, Sussex, is the basis for the house called Blye, in Essex, in *The Turn of the Screw;* but that that last-named masterpiece on its deepest level reveals James's initial feeling that Lamb House was a kind of prison for him, a place of doom—because James at this time was obscurely driven to relive his trapped childhood. If so, Lamb House soon became "The Great Good Place" (to borrow the title of the story James wrote within a year or so of moving down from London to Rye). He now had a home of his own more securely than ever—a private dwelling, moreover, in which he increasingly felt *at* home, as he did in the village itself, where in the course of time he became one of its best-liked residents and something of a village squire. James journeyed up to London periodically (it was little more than an hour by train), but he preferred to receive visitors in Rye, where they came in a steady stream.

This was the image Lamb House acquired over the years: the home of a distinguished, severely disciplined, and hard-working novelist; and the meeting place of a small host of friends. Rural solitude and peace and beauty (in James's words), the ideal condition for work, on the one hand; and on the other, more intimate and self-giving friendships, especially with younger people: here was the combination by which James worked his way out of the shattering defeat of 1895. In the summer of 1898 alone, he was visited by such old friends as Oliver Wendell Holmes, Edmund Gosse, Paul Bourget, with Henry Adams nearby; then and later came such younger friends as Jonathan Sturgis, the invalided writer; Morton Fullerton, an American journalist based in Paris; Logan Pearsall Smith, the witty Philadelphia-born essayist, and Howard Sturgis (no relation to Jonathan), the oddly engaging effeminate expatriate who had his own hospitable home in Windsor. It hardly represented Henry James, Sr.'s "divine-natural humanity," but it did represent Henry, Jr.'s companionable human equivalent; it was a community of sorts. Lamb House was the scene of James's greatest creative effort.

It was during that effort that the so-called late James came into being: the prolix, hesitant, ever-verbally circling James; the James of evasions, of exquisite refinements of psychological analysis, sometimes of super-subtleties; the James, in short, who is most admired by those who relish mastery of craft and most scorned by those who, as James once put it, read novels as an exercise in skipping. As for the highly involuted style of these years, it was perhaps surprisingly a perfectly natural and indeed a *spoken* style. From 1897 on, when James bought a typewriter for the first time (an "admirable and expensive machine"), James dictated his stories and novels to his secretary; and what we hear in them is the elaborate organ tones of the master's voice. James really did talk like that, as a number of people have reported; and when we get the hang of it, we can read aloud from James's most intricate pages and catch the magnificent flow and rhythm of his speech.

Along with the unique style of speech, there was, on James's part, a greatly increased concern and experimentation with narrative technique. This was due in part, as Edel indicates, to James's determination to exploit the resources of drama, as he had further discovered them in his playwriting years, and for the purposes of fiction to put those years to creative profit. James had always done this to a considerable extent; more than any other American novelist, he had focused his imagination on the *action* he was allowing to unfold in his story—action in virtually the Aristotelian sense of the design of psychic movement or momentum. Now the focus became narrower and more intense. James commented overtly far less often; he provided the reader with many fewer clues to event and meaning than before; he permitted the action to reveal itself largely through dramatic gesture and dialogue, through the silent juxtaposition of encounters, through the manipulation and contrast of symbolic setting. The reader, consequently, had to work a great deal harder, but he might find that the rewards were much richer.

Beyond that, it became the mark of the characters James most honored that they shared a portion of his own histrionic imagination—they saw themselves as in a play: that is, in a life experience given form and made significant by the dramatic art. Fleda Vetch, in *The Spoils of Poynton* (1897), is perhaps the first of James's heroines to possess such a sensibility. To the watchful Fleda, the parlormaid at Ricks as she comes flying out to announce the arrival of the young master becomes "on the instant an actress in the drama." The rather intricate story turns on the efforts of Mrs. Gereth to ensure the safekeeping of her assorted treasures of art ("spoils") by having her son Owen abandon his fiancée, who is a vulgarian, and instead marry Fleda, an art-worshiper. In due course the fiancée's mother comes to Fleda to beg her to step aside. "I came, I believe, Fleda," she says in the Jamesian manner, "just, you know, to plead with you." To this, Fleda, after a moment, answers: "As if I were one of those bad women in a play?" The play in question was probably *La Dame aux camélias*, by Dumas *fils*; but the remark, James adds, was disastrous: Mrs. Brigstock is too unimaginative to see life dramatically and too priggish to discuss bad women in plays.

The Spoils of Poynton is also grounded in one of James's most important but also one of his subtlest beliefs: that is, the belief that was slowly growing in him about the histrionic sensibility on the one hand, and on the other the capacity for the genuine and intimate human relationship—the relationship that mutes or transcends the lunging of egos, the relationship that sanctifies and redeems. For the person of true histrionic sensibility is profoundly aware of the reality of others, and strives above all to be in touch with and to honor that reality. James's characters, as has been said, had always been aware of each other: but more often than not in the earlier novels, they were aware of each other as mysteries or adversaries or objects to be used. The latter attitude is what characterizes Mrs. Gereth—who was, Fleda reflects, "nothing if not practical; almost the only thing she took account of in her friend's soft secret [Fleda's love for Owen] was the excellent use she could make of it." The word "thing" in that sentence is not casual: Mrs. Gereth, it has already been said, had "a maniacal disposition to thrust in everywhere the question of 'things'" (the original title of *The Spoils of Poynton* was *The Old Things*); and for James at this stage, it was the very essence of the egotistic spirit that it treated persons as things. It made use

of them. But Fleda's self-transcending nature enables her to see persons as persons, even Mrs. Gereth, even Mona Brigstock. She insists that Owen do likewise, and that—in a phrase James gave a special twist and accent to—he *play fair* with Mona. Fleda Vetch is the first of James's later heroines who understands the full meaning of "fair play" and who thus embodies James's developing vision of beauty in action.

What Maisie Knew (1897) and *The Awkward Age* (1899) do not carry that vision much further, but they do explore in greater depths the cruelties, treacheries, and moral disorder of the world in which the sense of fair play (the histrionic imagination) was invited to operate, and which would invariably seek to thwart or defeat it. The novels represent, as well, fresh technical experiments for James: the action of the first (an assortment of adulteries and betrayals) being observed for us by a child between her fifth and ninth year; that of the second (the troubled initiation of two adolescent girls) not being observed *for* us at all, but presented directly as though literally on stage, through a succession of scenes and dialogues. Leon Edel was the first to notice that *The Awkward Age* was also the last of a series of six tales and novels, embedded in James's other fiction of the nineties, which introduce us to a series of females ranging from four years old (in *The Other House*, 1896) to eighteen (Nanda Brookenham in *The Awkward Age*). James, according to Edel, was rehearsing his own childhood, adolescence, and young manhood in these stories, and in the course of it reconstructing the self that had been fragmented by the *Guy Domville* affair. If so, the newly organized self was other and richer and more compassionate (in the profoundest meaning of that word) than the former one. By the turn of the century, James was on the verge of what—with regard both to his work and to his quality as a human being—has properly become known as his "major phase."

Two events in the spring of 1900 marked the prologue to that major phase: James shaved off the well-groomed beard he had worn for many years, and he completed his most mystifying novel, *The Sacred Fount*. The removal of the beard, according to a friend, disclosed "the special and only genuine Henry James" at last; he looked, it was said, rather like a benevolent Napoleon (among other comparisons), but the act was clearly a symbolic gesture, the conscious announcement of a new *persona*. As to the novel, it has persistently puzzled and irritated most readers, though recent critics have been thinking better of it. One reviewer called it "as brilliantly stupid a piece of work as Mr. James has ever done"; others dismissed it as a massive narrative rumination about matters of no importance whatever. The action, such as it is, takes place during a weekend at a country estate called Newmarch, where the nameless narrator seeks, by relentless probing, prying, watching, and inquiring, to discover how a certain Gilbert Long, formerly a hollow shell of a being, has mysteriously become a lively and intelligent fellow. Noticing that a Mrs. Brissenden, who had married a man younger than herself, had strangely grown younger herself while her husband had visibly aged, the narrator suspects there must also be a "secret fount" for Long's new personality and that it may well be the restive, unhappy May Seaver. Neither the novel nor the narrator arrives at any definite conclusion; nor should they. For while obviously playing with the themes of vampirism (the draining of one person's psychic energy by another) and of the phenomenon of the radically changing self, James also reverts—in the figure of the narrator—to the position from which others appear as enigmas, as objects of intellectual inquiry. But the entire atmosphere of the novel suggests that this is a deeply wrong, very nearly blasphemous, position, one that (to borrow a phrase from Hawthorne) violates the sanctity of the human heart. Negatively, *The Sacred Fount*—and the adjective in that title is crucial—is a powerful if also subtle and secretive tribute to the primacy of love, spontaneity, and self-surrender in the human relation.

James was producing at an incredible rate in the late 1890's and early 1900's; and despite the critical unpopularity of his work, he was earning a good deal of money—more than enough to fur-

nish Lamb House and, when its absent owner died, to make a down payment of about four thousand dollars on the actual purchase of it. "My whole being cries out aloud for something that I can call my own," he wrote William during the negotiations; now he was the possessor in very fact of his own home. His rate of production, it should be added, was the more astonishing since he was so constantly besieged by visitors. Among the latter was a handsome young Danish sculptor named Hendrik Anderson, toward whom James's language (in letters) was suggestively tender, even physically so. It may indeed be noticed that a number of James's unattached young male friends at this time seem to have had in varying degrees latently or actively homoerotic natures—a fact of considerably less significance than the fact that James was capable of truly loving relationships with other individuals.

Yet the output of these years was no more, after all, than prologue to the composition—at a pitch of creative energy that rivals that of Melville in the forties and fifties—of *The Ambassadors* (completed in 1901, published in 1903), *The Wings of the Dove* (1902), and *The Golden Bowl* (1904).

The germ of the first of these masterworks was an anecdote James's friend Jonathan Sturgis had told him in the fall of 1895. Sturgis had encountered William Dean Howells some time earlier, at a gathering in the garden of Whistler's house in Paris; and Howells, who had been feeling old and sad, suddenly burst out: "Oh, you are young, you are young—be glad of it: be glad of it and *live*. Live all you can: it's a mistake not to. It doesn't so much matter what you do—but live." Those at least are the words James wrote in his notebook, and in *The Ambassadors* they are addressed by middle-aged Lambert Strether to a young friend in Gloriani's garden in Paris. It is a major turning point in Strether's psychic life; for Strether has come from Woollett, Massachusetts, as the ambassador of the extremely wealthy Mrs. Newsome with the mission of disentangling her son Chad from whatever unfortunate alliance he must have contracted and of getting him back to

Woollett and the family business. But Strether has just discovered not only that Chad's alliance has changed him for the better, but that a serious love affair with a cultivated and attractive woman is one of the supreme forms of *living*.

True, Strether at first mistakenly believes Chad to be in love with the charming young Mlle. de Vionnet; only later, in one of James's great recognition scenes, does he discover that Chad is actually attached to the girl's mother. In the classic and European manner, Chad's erotic education is at the hands of a woman almost old enough to be *his* mother—and this, too, Lambert Strether, engrained New Englander that he is, is slow to understand. Strether now becomes the ambassador of love, urging Chad to remain in Paris. He is repudiated by Mrs. Newsome, who sends another and harder-headed ambassador, Chad's sister Mrs. Pocock, to replace him. Ironically, Chad, whose selfhood has been insufficiently overcome even by Mme. de Vionnet, seems inclined at the novel's end to abandon his mistress and return to Woollett. Strether's personal hopes have been shattered— had he been successful, he would probably have married Mrs. Newsome and entered into a comfortable old age of literary dilettantism. He is left with his own silent devotion to Mme. de Vionnet; but he has learned the truth about life, which is the truth about the genuine human relationship. He is, in his limited way, at last living.

James regarded *The Ambassadors* as the most perfectly constructed of his novels and talked to himself—or rather to his muse—about it in his notebook with a kind of breathless wonder. No plot summary can suggest the beautifully planned choreography of the book, the arrivals and departures, the encounters and gatherings, the multiple relationships as they shift and reform. The action takes place entirely within Strether's enlarging sensibility; for the action *is* Strether's psychic development from provincial American innocence to a certain sense of himself *as* a self, and on to his self-giving dedication to Mme. de Vionnet and the pathos of her "situation." And always there is the palpable presence of the city of Paris—glittering, enchanting, beguiling; the land of ultimate moral decision.

If *The Ambassadors* is essentially a comedy with tragic overtones, *The Wings of the Dove* is a tragedy with comic elements. The latter novel is not so handsomely composed as *The Ambassadors*: the early sections are, relatively speaking, overly long, and the final sections are unduly foreshortened. The moral dilemma in the long climax is, moreover, almost too complex to sort out. But the situation of the book's heroine, Milly Theale, has been designed to provide the supreme test of the main thematic concern of James's "major phase": for Milly is possessed of an overpowering desire to live, and she is stricken by an unnamed disease (apparently consumption) from which she is probably fated to die. The flawlessly controlled action proceeds with classical inexorability. The purpose of the American girl Milly, which is to live, runs up against the counter-purpose of the English girl Kate Croy, which is to marry *and* to achieve material comfort. The impoverished Kate is in love with and secretly committed to the equally impoverished Merton Densher, an engaging but psychologically and spiritually incomplete young English journalist. As the plot turns, it brings all the main characters from London to Milly's *palazzo* in Venice; and here Kate Croy's personal plot is rounded out. Milly has fallen shyly in love with Merton Densher—this is her form of "living"; and Kate knowing this, and knowing also of her new American friend's physical plight, proposes to Merton that he marry Milly—so that, after her death, he will inherit her measureless wealth, and he and Kate can then marry.

The true state of things, however, is revealed to poor Milly by a jealous rejected suitor of Kate named Lord Mark; Milly thereupon "turns her face to the wall" and slowly sinks into death. She bequeaths to Merton nonetheless an enormous sum of money; but Merton, appalled by his temporary acquiescence in the whole scheme and transformed by the experience, tells Kate—they are now back in his dingy rooms in London—that he will marry her without the money, or he will turn it over to Kate without marriage. The final unforgettable lines are these:

> "Her memory's your love. You *want* no other."
>
> He heard her out in stillness, watching her face, but not moving. Then he only said: "I'll marry you, mind you, in an hour."
>
> "As we were?"
>
> "As we were."
>
> But she turned to the door, and her head-shake was now the end. "We shall never again be as we were."

Although, like *The Portrait of a Lady* twenty years earlier, *The Wings of the Dove* tells of an American girl of vast inherited wealth who comes to Europe seeking life and freedom only to be caught up and defeated by a density of intrigue, the international theme is quite transcended in the later novel. It is convenient but unimportant that Milly should be American and the others English; they are all participants in a universal human drama. We can see them, indeed, across a spectrum of spiritual possibility, with Lord Mark at one extreme as the embodiment of implacable selfhood. Kate Croy occupies an ambiguous middle position: she convinces herself that she acts only out of a good conscience, but that is just the Jamesian symptom of her moral fall; imbued with conscience, she lacks what the James family really honored —consciousness. Yet James is scrupulously fair with her; and so strong do our sympathies become for Kate in her struggle to escape a sordid family background and, as her aunt puts it, go "high up and in the light" that we tend finally to feel that she may be quite the best that poor, flawed humanity has to offer.

Merton Densher is at the end, we are to understand, an example of the redeemed form of man. He so tells himself, haltingly and confusedly, as he prowls London pondering the decision he must make.

> He himself, for that matter, at moments, took in the scene again as from the page of a book. He saw a young man, far off, in a relation inconceivable, saw him hushed, passive, staying his breath, but half understanding, yet dimly conscious of something immense and holding himself, not to lose it, painfully together. The young man, at these moments, so seen, was too distant and strange for the right identity; and yet outside, afterwards, it was his own face Densher had known. . . . The essence was that something had happened to him too beautiful and too sacred to describe. He had been, to his recovered sense, forgiven, dedicated, blessed; but this he couldn't coherently express.

All the telling language is there: Densher's feeling of being in a "book"—he has been gifted by the histrionic imagination (for we may be sure that the book in question is James's kind of dramatistic novel); a young man "in a relation inconceivable," to whom something "beautiful" and "sacred" had happened. Through his experience of Milly Theale, and the extraordinary index of her forgiveness of him and abiding love for him, Merton has been put in touch with something he can give no name to— but which James's father would have called the divine-natural humanity. As to Milly Theale, the dove herself, she strikes us as perhaps more or other than human. There is pathos, and a touch of enchantment, in her; but she seems to represent a spiritual reach which the world, as constituted, must inevitably destroy, but which can yet endure in the transfigured personalities of others.

The novel has, obviously, pushed far beyond realism and has in fact arrived at the borders of the mythic. It is, among other things, an allegory—firmly anchored in the visible and concrete—of modern Western history. This is given to Merton to intuit, as a sign of his mental growth. Walking through rain-swept Venice, while Milly lies silent and dying high up in her *palazzo*, the city seems suddenly to Merton to become the scene of a radical moral betrayal. The scheme against Milly now represents something far worse than a sordid little conspiracy. Only a general debasement of spirit, a corruption at the heart of the culture, could make such a scheme conceivable; and as to Venice, "the whole place, in its huge elegance, the grace of its conception and the beauty of its detail, was more than ever like a great drawing-room, the drawing-room of Europe, profaned and bewildered by some reversal of fortune."

And that vision of historical disaster ("I have," James once told a friend, "the imagination of disaster") is contained within an elusive yet potent and as it were transhistorical religious atmosphere. Biblical names, phrases, terminology thicken that atmosphere: Mark and Luke (Sir Luke Strett is Milly's godlike London doctor); the title phrase, which comes from the Book of Psalms; words like "sacred," "blessed," "redeemed," "consecrated." In the sacrificial life and death of Milly Theale, one dimly senses a remote, secularized, modernized reenactment of the Passion of Christ. None of this is bound together by anything approaching a religious creed or doctrine; in his autobiography, James would comment whimsically on "the particular crookedness of" the James family "being so extremely religious without having, as it were, anything in the least clarified or striking to show for it." The weakening of Christianity's grip on the minds of modern men was a central part of the cultural dilemma in which James worked. But in his artist's way, he could draw upon traditional Christian elements and themes to transform the petty intrigue of a few English people and a stricken American millionairess into a drama of grand and abiding significance.[9]

Neither *The Ambassadors* nor *The Wings of the Dove* was well received. Typically, an American critic named Colby declared that any reader of those novels found himself in "darkest James," a phrase that stuck; and he said about the second of them that "there are chapters like wonderful games of solitaire, broken by no human sound save [the author's] own chuckle when he takes some mysterious trick or makes

a move that he says is 'beautiful.'" No one, except possibly his publisher, was more surprised than James when *The Golden Bowl*—which completed what has been called the "triad" of the major phase—sold out four editions in this country within a year. The reason must have been that James had unexpectedly reappeared in the American eye, in 1904, by returning literally to America after an absence of twenty years. He rapidly became a public curiosity. He was extensively interviewed; he was feted at the White House; he lectured widely and for fat fees—mainly on Balzac, and on "The Question of Our Speech." Readers hurried to buy his new novel to see what the fuss was all about. They could not but have been bewildered: *The Golden Bowl* was the least penetrable of James's major novels and has remained so.

As early as 1892 James had jotted down in his notebook an anecdote he had heard, which seemed to him an idea for a short story: about a young woman and her widowed father who, after respectively marrying and remarrying, discover that their spouses are themselves having an affair together. That was to be the essential plot of *The Golden Bowl*: the unfolding intrigue involving Maggie Verver; her immensely wealthy father Adam Verver; Prince Amerigo, whom Maggie marries; and Charlotte Stant, the prince's once and future mistress, whom Adam marries. Conceived as a short work, *The Golden Bowl* expanded into one of James's longest and most elaborately furnished novels; yet one has the impression that its great size only conceals what should have been a compact and sparsely populated novella. A case can certainly be made out (and has been, for example, by R. P. Blackmur) that the felt thinness of the air in *The Golden Bowl* is a sign that James's imagination had moved to more rarefied heights than it had reached even in *The Wings of the Dove*, levels at which breathing is difficult. One understands the brilliant suggestion of Stephen Spender that, in the figure of Maggie Verver, James had at last answered the question of "whether it is possible in the modern world to choose to live," instead of choosing to renounce, like Strether, or to die, like Milly Theale. Maggie is possessed, more

[9] For the title of *The Wings of the Dove*, two Biblical sources come to mind. In Psalms 55:6, we find: "And I said, Oh that I had wings like a dove! for then would I fly away and be at rest." And in Psalms 68:13: "Though ye have lien among the pots, yet shall ye be as the wings of a dove covered with silver, and her feathers with yellow gold." Both passages seem to apply to the novel, albeit rather ambiguously.

overtly and consciously than any other character
James ever invented, of the histrionic imagination; her perception of others, and of the intimate relations between them as well as between
herself and them, is superlative. Yet there is an
odd ruthlessness in both Maggie and her father,
an iron quality based on a kind of absolute
wealth; and although the two married couples
are reconciled at the end—Maggie and the
prince, in particular, in a scene of extraordinary power—the moral and spiritual perplexities have scarcely been resolved. There is
greatness in *The Golden Bowl;* but in it, one
feels, James has mysteriously pushed beyond (by
no means fallen back from) the overpowering
clarity about human relations that slowly reveals
itself in *The Wings of the Dove.* It is as though
he had envisaged still another meaning for
"living" and for "life," but had not found or
developed the narrative terms to convey it.

The American tour of 1904-5 was in most
respects enjoyable and successful. James revisited
New England (and his brother William), went
down to New York, Philadelphia, and Washington—staying with Henry Adams in the latter
city and dining with President Roosevelt; and
spent the winter days in the mild climate of
Richmond and Charleston, before journeying
on down to Florida. In the spring of 1905, his
lecture schedule took him to Chicago and St.
Louis and out to California. The long trip had
been made possible by *Harper's,* which had
commissioned James to write a series of impressionistic articles on the "new" United
States; but it was also, we may well assume,
another chapter in James's continuing rediscovery of himself. The book that resulted, *The
American Scene* (1907), was anything but a
cheerful portrait of James's native country. It
had much of the pungent gloom, the sense of
corruption and decay, of change for the radically
worse, that had emanated from Whitman's
Democratic Vistas in 1871.

James hardly seemed aware that much of what
he pointed out had been a subject of ironic
observation for three quarters of a century,
though rarely so wittily and abrasively articu-

lated. He spoke of the cult of impermanence
in America, its repudiation of the past, its addiction to "the expensively provisional"—something that had been underscored by Tocqueville
and Hawthorne, to name only two of the best
commentators on America before the Civil War.
(In an article about the American passion for
"the immediate," the *Literary World* had very
long since muttered that "the immediate makes
steamboats of tinder, and roasts passengers
alive.") James noted how, in the Wall Street
section of New York, the arrogantly towering
skyscrapers hemmed in and overshadowed Trinity Church, forgetting for the moment his own
artful and prophetic picture, in *The Bostonians,*
of the blurring together of church spires and factory chimneys. There was gold dust in the American air, James remarked; the country represented
"the apotheosis of the raw"—as Mark Twain,
Howells, Whitman, and other reporters on the
Gilded Age had also said earlier. What James
added to the recurring American self-indictment
was a darker consciousness of impending catastrophe. This is particularly evident in his account of the urban spectacle: the astonishing
coexistence, as he put it, of "sane Society and
pestilent City."

> The thing presents itself, in its prime unlikeli-
> hood, as a thorough good neighbouring of
> the Happy Family and the Infernal Machine
> —the machine so rooted as to continue to
> defy removal, and the family still so indiffer-
> ent, while it carries on the family business
> of buying and selling, of chattering and danc-
> ing, to the danger of being blown up.

The explosion of the cities and the horrors of
pollution are there, implicitly, just beyond the
range of James's somber prophetic vision.[10]

The most important addition to the circle
of James's younger friends in the early 1900's
was the forty-year-old novelist Edith Wharton.
From the time of their first meeting in 1903,

[10] Apprehensions about the American city and the
quality of life it tended to foster had been voiced as
early as Thomas Jefferson, in *Notes on the State of
Virginia,* and by Washington. See pp. 172-75.

the two exchanged visits at least once a year. James stayed in the Wharton house in Lenox, Massachusetts, in the fall of 1904 and the summer of 1905, during the American tour, and again in 1910 and 1911; and he spent days at a time in Mrs. Wharton's apartment in the Faubourg St. Germain, departing with her from that address (in 1907) for what Mrs. Wharton, in her book about it, called "a motor-flight through France." Mrs. Wharton's annual descent upon James at Lamb House was a regular source of hyperbolic consternation: for, while Edith Wharton progressed regally across Europe like a sort of robust Milly Theale, James liked to pretend that he cowered in abject poverty and that her visits wrought irremediable havoc with his work schedule. In fact, James enjoyed nothing more than those visits. Mrs. Wharton, in her memoir *A Backward Glance*, describes the histrionics with which she was always greeted at Lamb House.

> There *he* stood on the doorstep, the white-panelled hall with its old prints and crowded book-cases forming a background to his heavy loosely-clothed figure. Arms outstretched, lips and eyes twinkling, he came down to the car, uttering cries of mock amazement and mock humility at the undeserved honour of a visit. The arrival at Lamb House was an almost ritual performance, from those first ejaculations to the large hug and the two solemn kisses executed in the middle of the hall rug.

Nowhere else, indeed, than in *A Backward Glance* do we receive so rounded, so fully-etched, and so endearing a picture of Henry James the man—who appears always, at the same time, as Henry James the literary genius.[11]

In her letters to James, Edith Wharton normally addressed him as "Cher Maître." For her, too, James was the Master, though she drew less from him for her own literary art than has sometimes been alleged. What she did inherit was James's sense of *form* and of the exacting discipline of the craft of fiction. It undoubtedly

encouraged the aging master to see so much of him carried forward by so gifted a practitioner. But their relation on the human side was perhaps even more important. During Edith Wharton's period of personal tribulation, especially between 1907 and 1913, James demonstrated how firmly, once his affections and loyalty had been given, he could support a soul in trouble.[12]

In 1903, James had published one of his two or three greatest novellas, *The Beast in the Jungle*. This is the psychologically harrowing tale, told in the quintessential style of the major phase, of John Marcher and his lifelong apprehension that he has been singled out for some special, some absolutely unique and presumably dreadful destiny. It is this conviction that makes him hold back from marrying the devoted May Bartram: he can ask no one to share the hideous fate held somewhere in store for him. Only after May Bartram dies—when, standing by her grave, he notices another visitor to the cemetery experiencing a passion of grief—does the crushing realization come to him. His fate has been, precisely, a life given over entirely to passive waiting, a life of self-engrossed aloofness, a life without love. He had been, he now understands, the one man in the world to whom nothing was ever to happen.

James, fresh from completing *The Wings of the Dove* and well into *The Golden Bowl*, could hardly have supposed that his creatively eventful life resembled Marcher's; yet the beast lurked in his consciousness. It is the penalty, and sign, of genius to distrust itself, measuring however formidable an achievement against the ideal reaches of the imagination. "We work in the dark," James had had an aging novelist say in "The Middle Years" in 1895. "Our doubt is our passion and our passion is our task. The rest is the madness of art." It may have been a doubt of this kind that led James soon after

---

[11] An excellent study of James the man can be found in the compilation of reminiscences and anecdotes by Montgomery Hyde, *Henry James at Home* (1969).

[12] Not all the facts about Edith Wharton's troubles during this period have been yet established. Among them was her husband's "neurasthenia," as it was called —he seems to have become a manic depressive. See also the introduction to Edith Wharton.

The Beast in the Jungle to reconsider every novel and tale he had ever written. The eventual result was the twenty-four-volume edition of *The Novels and Tales of Henry James* brought out by Scribner's between 1907 and 1909. To each of the volumes, James appended a preface, dealing with the origins and the artistic intentions of the various works; and the prefaces taken together (they were later collected by R. P. Blackmur under the title of *The Art of the Novel*) comprise probably the most significant and instructive statement in English on the literary craft and on the purposes and processes of fictional composition. They are, in particular, James's testimony to the dramatic quality of fiction when it is truest to its own nature. In the course of preparing the New York edition (as it is called), James also meticulously revised a great many passages. The changes, several critics have felt, were not always for the better; but the whole gigantic task was arduous—nearly beyond the powers even of Henry James.

By 1910, James was thoroughly exhausted. He underwent the deep depression that so often follows upon grand accomplishment, and the sixty-seven-year-old novelist talked seriously with his brother William about suicide. William's death that same year might have been the final blow to a less resilient spirit: Henry's ambiguous emotional involvement with William had been one of the central elements in his life for more than six decades.[13] But his enormous talent for survival and recovery got him through once again. And once again he renewed himself by reviewing himself: this time by plunging into

what became three thick volumes of autobiography—appearing seriatim as *A Small Boy and Others* (1913), *Notes of a Son and Brother* (1914), and *The Middle Years* (posthumous and unfinished, 1917). Anyone who seeks a chronological and factual account of James's life and that of his family should look elsewhere than in these volumes of autobiography; but anyone who wishes to explore at length and in depth the atmosphere of James's mind could not do better. The reader who makes his cautious way through the autobiographies has the rare experience of watching the most dedicated of watchers watching himself.

The war which broke out in Europe in 1914 interrupted *The Middle Years*, as well as James's work on the two novels he left uncompleted at his death: *The Ivory Tower* and *The Sense of the Past* (the latter, which would become a well-made play and a fine film called *Berkeley Square*, was an elaborate ghost story about a young man who, entering a London house in the early twentieth century, finds he has stepped back into the London of a century earlier). For James, as the German bombardments began to reduce to rubble some of the greatest treasures of Europe, the war took the form of that ultimate catastrophe he had for so long, and almost unwittingly, been prophesying: in the apocalyptic vision of Merton Densher in *The Wings of the Dove*; in his own vision in *The American Scene*; in all those places where his imagination of disaster had been in command.[14] He saw now

---

[13] Leon Edel and Gay Wilson Allen, in their biographies, respectively, of Henry and of William James, have demonstrated how complicated were the emotional relations between the two brothers, and between each of them and their sister Alice. "Love-hate" is perhaps too strong, or too simple, a formula for those relations; but on Henry's side, at least, there was a shifting mixture of pride, admiration, affection, and resentment vis-à-vis William—resentment in particular of William's customary big-brother attitude and his often fussy and uncomprehending comments on Henry's fiction. But Henry's underlying devotion to William is not to be doubted, and it was never more evident than in the grief-stricken letters he wrote (among others, to Edith Wharton) after William's death.

[14] It has to be realized that although the devastation of the European continent during the Second World War was on an incomparably greater scale than that of the First World War, it actually had less impact upon most sensitive and imaginative observers than the earlier wreckage. The partial destruction of Rheims cathedral in 1915, for example, was something literally unparalleled, unprecedented, within the consciousness of a man like Henry James. There was a kind of absolute finality to such a destruction of ancient beauty that James and many others simply could not absorb. In the modern Western world, every person seems to live through a period that can seem, in retrospect, to be a major watershed; but it is improbable that this century will include another historical moment as catastrophic for onlookers and participants as the First World War. The signs of it are apparent enough in Eliot's *The*

what he had stubbornly refused to acknowledge, even while surreptitiously revealing it in his fiction. "The plunge of civilization into this abyss of blood and darkness by the wanton feat of those two infamous autocrats," he wrote Howard Sturgis, "is a thing that so gives away the whole long age during which we have supposed the world to be, with whatever abatement, gradually bettering, that to have to take it all now for what the treacherous years were all the while really making for and meaning is too tragic for words."

In July, 1915, with the United States still a professed neutral and with European civilization, as it seemed, literally crumbling about him, James signified his whole-souled dedication to the Allied cause by becoming a British citizen (the prime minister speeding the process by being one of the sponsors). Later that same year, the king of England bestowed upon James the Order of Merit. By this time, James was gravely ill, having suffered what turned out to be a fatal stroke, the last of a series of attacks which had plagued him for half a dozen years. Edmund Gosse, his friend of many years, conveyed the news of the lofty decoration, and James was able to ask that the light in his bedroom be turned off—to "spare my blushes." He lingered on till late February, 1916, alternating moments of seeming recovery with hallucinatory moments when he imagined himself to be the Emperor Napoleon and dictated to his secretary letters about the restoration of the Tuileries and about Joseph Bonaparte accepting the throne of Spain.[15] An instant before the stroke, so he had

told a visitor to his bedside, James had heard a strange voice saying: "So here it is at last, the distinguished thing!" The thing came, finally, on the evening of February 28.

The summer before, James had engaged in a singularly illuminating exchange with H. G. Wells. Wells had published a slovenly volume purporting to be the literary remains of one George Boon, and the book included a surprisingly savage attack (voiced by Boon) on the fiction of Wells's admiring old friend and benevolent patron, Henry James. "The only living human motives left in the novels of Henry James," declared Wells-Boon, "are a certain avidity and an entirely superficial curiosity." As a writer, James resembled a hippopotamus trying to pick up a pea; his narratives were "tales of nothingness," and a James novel was "like a church lit but without a congregation to distract you, with every light and line focused on the high altar. And on the altar, very reverently placed, intensely there, is a dead kitten, an eggshell, a bit of string."

Others had talked in the same vein, especially about *The Sacred Fount* (the prime case for anti-Jamesians), and no less wickedly; but coming from Wells, the assault was a shock. James said as much to Wells. He had enjoyed Wells's work, he remarked, "from far back . . . and the fact that a mind as brilliant as yours *can* resolve me into such an unmitigated mistake, can't enjoy me in anything like the degree in which I like to think I may be enjoyed, makes me want to fix myself, for as long as my nerves can stand it, with such a pair of eyes." So viewing himself, James still made out his own "measure of fullness—fullness of life and of the projection of it." Wells was in part apologetic. *Boon*, he wrote, was only wastepaper basket stuff, and he wished he had stated his views more gracefully. But there was, he felt, an issue between them: "To you literature like painting is an end, to

---

Waste Land, Hemingway's *A Farewell to Arms,* and writings by F. Scott Fitzgerald and John Dos Passos—works which have little echo in the literature that followed the Second World War.

15 The figure of Napoleon provides an oddly recurring theme in James's life. We have mentioned his earliest memory of the "column" in the Place Vendôme in Paris, with its inscribed record of Napoleon's victories. In 1900, when he shaved off his beard for the first time in more than thirty years, several friends remarked on James's resemblance to the emperor—that is, in the shape of his head and the curve of his face. Add to that James's frequent use of elaborate military metaphors, of a kind drawn rather from the time of Napoleonic war-

fare than a more recent age. All this suggests a bellicose and imperial element in James's makeup that must, one supposes, have worked surreptitiously against his psychic thrust toward the social.

me literature like architecture is a means, it has a use."

James's reply summed up a lifetime of experience—of living and of writing about it. It was the final distillation of everything he had learned. "I am bound to tell you," he began, "that I don't think your letter makes out any sort of case for the bad manners of 'Boon,' as far as your indulgence in them at the expense of your poor old H. J. is concerned—I say 'your' simply because he has *been* yours, in the most liberal, continual, sacrificial, the most admiring and abounding critical way, ever since he began to know your writings." The adjectives should be paused over: they represent James's configuration of genuine friendship, even literary friendship. He went on: "Your comparison of the book to a waste-basket strikes me as the reverse of felicitous, for what one throws into that receptacle is exactly what one doesn't commit to publicity."

James then got down to what was for him the real issue. And the real issue was what is now called *relevance*—the relevance of art to life: the fundamental value of the literary art; the whole point and purpose of writing books and of reading books. "I hold your distinction between a form that is (like) painting and a form that is (like) architecture wholly null and void. There is no sense in which architecture is aesthetically 'for us' that doesn't leave any other art whatever exactly as much so." Then James reached the climax of the statement of his credo:

So far from [the form] of literature being irrelevant to the literary report upon life, I regard it as relevant in a degree that leaves everything else behind. It is art that *makes* life, makes interest, makes importance, for our consideration and application of these things, and I know of no substitute whatever for the force and beauty of its process. If I were Boon I should say that every pretence of such a substitute is helpless and hopeless humbug; but I wouldn't be Boon for the world, and am only yours faithfully, Henry James.

It is art that "*makes* life, makes interest, makes importance." By "art," James meant primarily the literary art, and by the latter primarily the art of the novel, particularly the dramatic kind of novel James had given himself to with ever-deepening faith for twenty years. It was in that kind of novel that the very essence and meaning of life could best be disclosed. For it was there that the human attempts, the customary failures, the occasional fleeting successes—with regard to the human relationship that sanctifies and redeems—could best be enacted. James knew that life in itself, life apart from art, was too disorderly and ego-infested to manifest the subtle motions of spirit toward such nourishing relationships. So much the worse for life, James was quite willing to say. Only the force and beauty of the artistic process could give shape, and hence give meaning and value, to the disorder of actual experience. It is art, James was saying, that tells us who we are, tells us too of the perils inherent in human nature and of our noblest possibilities.

BIOGRAPHICAL CHART

1885   *The Bostonians* runs in the *Century Magazine* with *The Rise of Silas Lapham* and *The Adventures of Huckleberry Finn*

1890–95   *The Tragic Muse*; career as playwright culminates January 5, 1895, with poor reception of *Guy Domville*; first notebook entry for *The Ambassadors*

1897   *What Maisie Knew*; settles at Lamb House, Rye, England

1899–1900   *The Awkward Age*; *The Sacred Fount*

1902–4   *The Wings of the Dove*; *The Ambassadors*; *The Golden Bowl*

1904–11   Visits the United States; *The American Scene*; New York edition of selected works prepared and published

1915   Becomes British subject after outbreak of First World War

1916   Dies, February 28, in Chelsea; ashes buried in Mount Auburn Cemetery, Cambridge, Massachusetts

FURTHER READINGS

The Novels and Tales of Henry James (1907–17; 26 vols.) (no editor cited)

The Novels and Stories of Henry James (1921–23; 35 vols.) (no editor cited)

R. P. Blackmur, ed., *The Art of the Novel* (1935; critical prefaces by James)

Leon Edel, ed., *The Complete Plays of Henry James* (1949)

————, ed., *The Selected Letters of Henry James* (1956)

Henry James, *The American Scene* (1907; with introduction by W. H. Auden, 1946)

————, *Henry James: Autobiography* (1956)

F. O. Matthiessen and Kenneth B. Murdock, eds., *The Notebooks of Henry James* (1947)

Allan Wade, ed., *The Scenic Art: Notes on Acting and the Drama, 1872–1901* (1949)

Quentin Anderson, *The American Henry James* (1958)

J. W. Beach, *The Method of Henry James* (1918)

Marius Bewley, *The Complex Fate* (1952; 1954)

————, *The Eccentric Design: Form in the Classic American Novel* (1959)

R. P. Blackmur, "Henry James," in *Literary History of the United States*, R. E. Spiller et al., eds. (1948)

Van Wyck Brooks, *The Pilgrimage of Henry James* (1955)

John A. Clair, *The Ironic Dimension in the Fiction of Henry James* (1966)

Dorothea Crook, *The Ordeal of Consciousness in Henry James* (1962)

F. W. Dupee, *Henry James* (1951)

————, ed., *The Question of Henry James: A Collection of Critical Essays* (1947)

Leon Edel, *The Life of Henry James: I. The Untried Years; II. The Conquest of London; III. The Middle Years; IV. The Treacherous Years; V. The Master* (1953–72)

Ernest Ernest, *Expatriates and Patriots* (1972)

Maxwell Geismar, *Henry James and the Jacobins* (1963)

Clinton Grattan, *The Three Jameses* (1932)

H. Montgomery Hyde, *Henry James at Home* (1969)

F. O. Matthiessen, *Henry James: The Major Phase* (1944)

————, *The James Family* (1947)

Samuel Gorley Putt, *Henry James: A Reader's Guide* (1966)

S. Nowell-Smith, ed., *The Legend of the Master* (1948)

The Pupil (1892)

The Pupil is one of many stories by James about the victimization of the young, like "The Author of Beltraffio," *The Turn of the Screw*, and several others. The theme periodically compelled James's imagination: it was another way, and a peculiarly poignant way, in which to indicate the manipulation of the vulnerable personality by the selfish and self-seeking.

Nowhere does James deal with this theme to better or more moving effect than in *The Pupil*.

In "The Author of Beltraffio," the child Dolcino is merely a pawn in the lethal struggle between his moralistic mother and his pagan-spirited father. But in the present story, Morgan Moreen is at the very center of things—or rather he shares that center with his English tutor, Pemberton. There is indeed a nice ambiguity in the story's title. As between the youthful Morgan and Pemberton, which is in fact the pupil and which the tutor? What James had aimed at, as he says in the preface to Volume 11 of the New York edition, "is little Morgan's troubled vision of them" (that is, of the Moreen family) "as reflected in the vision, also troubled enough, of his devoted friend."

That preface contains James's memory of first hearing about an American family like the Moreens, and the youngest member thereof, "a small boy, acute and precocious, afflicted with a heart of weak action," who perfectly understood and took the measure of his family. It also contains James's tribute to "the classic years of the great American European legend; the years of limited communication, of monstrous and unattentuated contrast"—the years, in short, of James's own earliest recollections of being carted about Europe by *his* much-moving family. The Americans living abroad at that time were a far cry, James insists, from "the unconscious Barbarians" who were trooping about the continent in the 1890's. The Moreens belong to that earlier and more romantic epoch; and for all their pretensions and their vapid selfishness they seemed to retain a portion of James's affections.

Out of the simple portrait of such a family as given James (so he reports) by his physician friend, James drew an *action*, the outlines of a specific little drama. The preface concludes with James's most succinct statement about his "dramatic" method in narrative—the alternation, in particular, between what he calls "scene" and what he calls "interval." The scene invariably brings together two or more persons in significant and developing relationship; it covers a brief, measurable period of time; and in it the action is steadily prodded forward by gesture and response, dialogue and insinuation. The interval is, as it were, in the imperfect tense; it compresses the happenings and changes of several years. Chapters 6 and 7 provide an excellent example of this method of alternation. Studying these chapters in sequence, we do feel "with the definite alternation," as James remarks, "how the theme *is* being treated." That is, James is forced to acknowledge, we feel it if we are inclined to study such matters in the first place. "I shouldn't really go on," James concludes with a melancholy contemporary editors are sometimes apt to share, "as if this were the case with many readers."

I

The poor young man hesitated and procrastinated: it cost him such an effort to broach the subject of terms, to speak of money to a person who spoke only of feelings, as it were, of the aristocracy. Yet he was unwilling to take leave, treating his engagement as settled, without some more conventional glance in that direction than he could find an opening for in the manner of the large, affable lady who sat there drawing a pair of soiled *gants de Suède* through a fat, jewelled hand and, at once pressing and gliding, repeated over and over everything but the thing he would have liked to hear. He would have liked to hear the figure of his salary; but just as he was nervously about to sound that note the little boy came back—the little boy Mrs. Moreen had sent out of the room to fetch her fan. He came back without the fan, only with the casual observation that he couldn't find it. As he dropped this cynical confession he looked straight and hard at the candidate for the honour of taking his education in hand. This personage reflected, somewhat grimly, that the first thing he should have to teach his little charge would be to appear to address himself to his mother when he spoke to her—especially not to make her such an improper answer as that.

When Mrs. Moreen bethought herself of this pretext for getting rid of their companion, Pemberton supposed it was precisely to approach the delicate subject of his remuneration. But it had been only to say some things about her son which it was better that a boy of eleven shouldn't catch. They were extravagantly to his advantage, save when she lowered her voice to sigh, tapping her left side familiarly: "And all overclouded by *this*, you know—all at the mercy of a weakness—!" Pemberton gathered that the weakness was in the region of the heart. He had known the poor child was not robust: this was the basis on which he had been invited to treat, through an English lady, an Oxford acquaintance, then at Nice, who happened to know both his needs and those of the amiable American family looking out for something really superior in the way of a resident tutor.

The young man's impression of his prospective

pupil, who had first come into the room, as if to see for himself, as soon as Pemberton was admitted, was not quite the soft solicitation the visitor had taken for granted. Morgan Moreen was, somehow, sickly without being delicate, and that he looked intelligent (it is true Pemberton wouldn't have enjoyed his being stupid), only added to the suggestion that, as with his big mouth and big ears he really couldn't be called pretty, he might be unpleasant. Pemberton was modest—he was even timid; and the chance that his small scholar might prove cleverer than himself had quite figured, to his nervousness, among the dangers of an untried experiment. He reflected, however, that these were risks one had to run when one accepted a position, as it was called, in a private family; when as yet one's University honours had, pecuniarily speaking, remained barren. At any rate, when Mrs. Moreen got up as if to intimate that, since it was understood he would enter upon his duties within the week she would let him off now, he succeeded, in spite of the presence of the child, in squeezing out a phrase about the rate of payment. It was not the fault of the conscious smile which seemed a reference to the lady's expensive identity, if the allusion did not sound rather vulgar. This was exactly because she became still more gracious to reply: "Oh, I can assure you that all that will be quite regular."

Pemberton only wondered, while he took up his hat, what "all that" was to amount to—people had such different ideas. Mrs. Moreen's words, however, seemed to commit the family to a pledge definite enough to elicit from the child a strange little comment, in the shape of the mocking, foreign ejaculation, "Oh, là-là!"

Pemberton, in some confusion, glanced at him as he walked slowly to the window with his back turned, his hands in his pockets and the air in his elderly shoulders of a boy who didn't play. The young man wondered if he could teach him to play, though his mother had said it would never do and that this was why school was impossible. Mrs. Moreen exhibited no discomfiture; she only continued blandly: "Mr. Moreen will be delighted to meet your wishes. As I told you, he has been called to London for a week. As soon as he comes back you shall have it out with him."

This was so frank and friendly that the young man could only reply, laughing as his hostess laughed: "Oh! I don't imagine we shall have much of a battle."

"They'll give you anything you like," the boy remarked unexpectedly, returning from the window. "We don't mind what anything costs—we live awfully well."

"My darling, you're too quaint!" his mother exclaimed, putting out to caress him a practiced but ineffectual hand. He slipped out of it, but looked with intelligent, innocent eyes at Pemberton, who had already had time to notice that from one moment to the other his small satiric face seemed to change its time of life. At this moment it was infantine; yet it appeared also to be under the influence of curious intuitions and knowledges. Pemberton rather disliked precocity, and he was disappointed to find gleams of it in a disciple not yet in his teens. Nevertheless he divined on the spot that Morgan wouldn't prove a bore. He would prove on the contrary a kind of excitement. This idea held the young man, in spite of a certain repulsion.

"You pompous little person! We're not extravagant!" Mrs. Moreen gayly protested, making another unsuccessful attempt to draw the boy to her side. "You must know what to expect," she went on to Pemberton.

"The less you expect the better!" her companion interposed. "But we *are* people of fashion."

"Only so far as *you* make us so!" Mrs. Moreen mocked, tenderly. "Well, then, on Friday—don't tell me you're superstitious—and mind you don't fail us. Then you'll see us all. I'm so sorry the girls are out. I guess you'll like the girls. And, you know, I've another son, quite different from this one."

"He tries to imitate me," said Morgan to Pemberton.

"He tries? Why, he's twenty years old!" cried Mrs. Moreen.

"You're very witty," Pemberton remarked to the child—a proposition that his mother echoed with enthusiasm, declaring that Morgan's sallies were the delight of the house. The boy paid no heed to this; he only inquired abruptly of the visitor, who was surprised afterwards that he hadn't struck him as offensively forward: "Do you *want* very much to come?"

"Can you doubt it, after such a description of what I shall hear?" Pemberton replied. Yet he didn't want to come at all; he was coming because he had to go somewhere, thanks to the collapse of his fortune at the end of a year abroad, spent on the system of putting his tiny patrimony into a single full wave of experience. He had had his full wave, but he couldn't pay his hotel bill. Moreover, he had caught in the boy's eyes the glimpse of a far-off appeal.

"Well, I'll do the best I can for you," said Morgan; with which he turned away again. He passed out of one of the long windows; Pemberton saw him go and lean on the parapet of the terrace. He remained there while the young man took leave of his mother, who, on Pemberton's looking as if he expected a farewell from him, interposed with: "Leave him, leave him; he's so strange!" Pemberton suspected she was afraid of something he might say. "He's a genius—you'll love him," she added. "He's much the most interesting person in the family." And before he could invent some civility to oppose to this, she wound up with: "But we're all good, you know!"

"He's a genius—you'll love him!" were words that recurred to Pemberton before the Friday, suggesting, among other things that geniuses were not invariably lovable. However, it was all the better if there was an element that would make tutorship absorbing: he had perhaps taken too much for granted that it would be dreary. As he left the villa after his interview, he looked up at the balcony and saw the child leaning over it. "We shall have great larks!" he called up.

Morgan hesitated a moment; then he answered, laughing: "By the time you come back I shall have thought of something witty!"

This made Pemberton say to himself: "After all he's rather nice."

II

On the Friday he saw them all, as Mrs. Moreen had promised, for her husband had come back and the girls and the other son were at home. Mr. Moreen had a white moustache, a confiding manner and, in his buttonhole, the ribbon of a foreign order—bestowed, as Pemberton eventually learned, for services. For what services he never clearly ascertained: this was a point—one of a large number—that Mr. Moreen's manner never confided. What it emphatically did confide was that he was a man of the world. Ulick, the firstborn, was in visible training for the same profession—under the disadvantage as yet, however, of a buttonhole only feebly floral and a moustache with no pretensions to type. The girls had hair and figures and manners and small fat feet, but had never been out alone. As for Mrs. Moreen, Pemberton saw on a nearer view that her elegance was intermittent and

her parts didn't always match. Her husband, as she had promised, met with enthusiasm Pemberton's ideas in regard to a salary. The young man had endeavoured to make them modest, and Mr. Moreen confided to him that *he* found them positively meagre. He further assured him that he aspired to be intimate with his children, to be their best friend, and that he was always looking out for them. That was what he went off for, to London and other places—to look out; and this vigilance was the theory of life, as well as the real occupation, of the whole family. They all looked out, for they were very frank on the subject of its being necessary. They desired it to be understood that they were earnest people, and also that their fortune, though quite adequate for earnest people, required the most careful administration. Mr. Moreen, as the parent bird, sought sustenance for the nest. Ulick found sustenance mainly at the club, where Pemberton guessed that it was usually served on green cloth. The girls used to do up their hair and their frocks themselves, and our young man felt appealed to to be glad, in regard to Morgan's education, that, though it must naturally be of the best, it didn't cost too much. After a little he *was* glad, forgetting at times his own needs in the interest inspired by the child's nature and education and the pleasure of making easy terms for him.

During the first weeks of their acquaintance Morgan had been as puzzling as a page in an unknown language—altogether different from the obvious little Anglo-Saxons who had misrepresented childhood to Pemberton. Indeed the whole mystic volume in which the boy had been bound demanded some practice in translation. To-day, after a considerable interval, there is something phantasmagoric, like a prismatic reflection or a serial novel, in Pemberton's memory of the queerness of the Moreens. If it were not for a few tangible tokens—a lock of Morgan's hair, cut by his own hand, and the half-dozen letters he got from him when they were separated—the whole episode and the figures peopling it would seem too inconsequent for anything but dreamland. The queerest thing about them was their success (as it appeared to him for a while at the time), for he had never seen a family so brilliantly equipped for failure. Wasn't it success to have kept him so hatefully long? Wasn't it success to have drawn him in that first morning at *déjeuner*, the Friday he came—it was enough to *make* one superstitious—so that he utterly committed himself, and this not by calculation or a *mot d'ordre*, but by a happy instinct which made them, like a band of gipsies, work so neatly together? They amused him as much as if they had really been a band of gipsies. He was still young and had not seen much of the world—his English years had been intensely usual; therefore the reversed conventions of the Moreens (for they had their standards), struck him as topsyturvy. He had encountered nothing like them at Oxford; still less had any such note been struck to his younger American ear during the four years at Yale in which he had richly supposed himself to be reacting against Puritanism. The reaction of the Moreens, at any rate, went ever so much further. He had thought himself very clever that first day in hitting them all off in his mind with the term "cosmopolite." Later, it seemed feeble and colourless enough—confessedly, helplessly provisional.

However, when he first applied it to them he had a degree of joy—for an instructor he was still empirical—as if from the apprehension that to live with them would really be to see life. Their sociable strangeness was an intimation of that—their chatter of tongues, their gaiety and good humour, their infinite dawdling (they were always getting themselves up, but it took forever, and Pemberton had once found Mr. Moreen shaving in the drawing-room), their French, their Italian and, in the spiced fluency, their cold, tough slices of American. They lived on macaroni and coffee (they had these articles prepared in perfection), but they knew recipes for a hundred other dishes. They overflowed with music and song, were always humming and catching each other up, and had a kind of professional acquaintance with continental cities. They talked of "good places" as if they had been strolling players. They had at Nice a villa, a carriage, a piano and a banjo, and they went to official parties. They were a perfect calendar of the "days" of their friends, which Pemberton knew them, when they were indisposed, to get out of bed to go to, and which made the week larger than life when Mrs. Moreen talked of them with Paula and Amy. Their romantic initiations gave their new inmate at first an almost dazzling sense of culture. Mrs. Moreen had translated something, at some former period—an author whom it made Pemberton feel *borné* never to have heard of. They could imitate Venetian and sing Neapolitan, and when they wanted to say something very particular they communicated with each other in an ingenious dialect of their own—a sort of spoken cipher, which Pemberton at first took for Volapuk, but which he learned to understand as he would not have understood Volapuk.

"It's the family language—Ultramoreen," Morgan explained to him drolly enough; but the boy rarely condescended to use it himself, though he attempted colloquial Latin as if he had been a little prelate.

Among all the "days" with which Mrs. Moreen's memory was taxed she managed to squeeze in one of her own, which her friends sometimes forgot. But the house derived a frequented air from the number of fine people who were freely named there and from several mysterious men with foreign titles and English clothes whom Morgan called the princes and who, on sofas with the girls, talked French very loud, as if to show they were saying nothing improper. Pemberton wondered how the princes could ever propose in that tone and so publicly: he took for granted cynically that this was what was desired of them. Then he acknowledged that even for the chance of such an advantage Mrs. Moreen would never allow Paula and Amy to receive alone. These young ladies were not at all timid, but it was just the safeguards that made them so graceful. It was a houseful of Bohemians who wanted tremendously to be Philistines.

In one respect, however, certainly, they achieved no rigour—they were wonderfully amiable and ecstatic about Morgan. It was a genuine tenderness, an artless admiration, equally strong in each. They even praised his beauty, which was small, and were rather afraid of him, as if they recognised that he was of a finer clay. They called him a little angel and a little prodigy and pitied his want of health effusively. Pemberton feared at first that their extravagance would make him hate the boy, but before this happened he had become extravagant himself. Later, when he had grown rather to hate the others, it was a bribe to patience for him that they were at any rate nice about Morgan, going on tiptoe if they fancied he was showing symptoms, and even giving up somebody's "day" to procure him a pleasure. But mixed with this was the oddest wish to make him independent, as if they felt that they were not good enough for him. They passed him over to Pemberton very much as if they wished to force a constructive adoption on the obliging bachelor and shirk altogether a responsibility. They were delighted when they perceived that Morgan liked his preceptor, and could think of no higher praise for the young man. It was strange how they contrived to reconcile the

appearance, and indeed the essential fact, of adoring the child with their eagerness to wash their
hands of him. Did they want to get rid of him
before he should find them out? Pemberton was
finding them out month by month. At any rate,
the boy's relations turned their backs with exaggerated delicacy, as if to escape the charge of interfering. Seeing in time how little he had in common
with them (it was by *them* he first observed it—
they proclaimed it with complete humility), his
preceptor was moved to speculate on the mysteries
of transmission, the far jumps of heredity. Where
his detachment from most of the things they represented had come from was more than an observer could say—it certainly had burrowed under
two or three generations.

As for Pemberton's own estimate of his pupil,
it was a good while before he got the point of
view, so little had he been prepared for it by the
smug young barbarians to whom the tradition of
tutorship, as hitherto revealed to him, had been
adjusted. Morgan was scrappy and surprising, de-
ficient in many properties supposed common to
the *genus* and abounding in others that were the
portion only of the supernaturally clever. One day
Pemberton made a great stride: it cleared up the
question to perceive that Morgan *was* supernaturally clever and that, though the formula was temporarily meagre, this would be the only assumption
on which one could successfully deal with him.
He had the general quality of a child for whom life
had not been simplified by school, a kind of home-
bred sensibility which might have been bad for
himself but was charming for others, and a whole
range of refinement and perception—little musical
vibrations as taking as picked-up airs—begotten by
wandering about Europe at the tail of his migratory tribe. This might not have been an education
to recommend in advance, but its results with
Morgan were as palpable as a fine texture. At the
same time he had in his composition a sharp spice
of stoicism, doubtless the fruit of having had to
begin early to bear pain, which produced the impression of pluck and made it of less consequence
that he might have been thought at school rather
a polyglot little beast. Pemberton indeed quickly
found himself rejoicing that school was out of the
question: in any million of boys it was probably
good for all but one, and Morgan was that mil-
lionth. It would have made him comparative and
superior—it might have made him priggish. Pemberton would try to be school himself—a bigger
seminary than five hundred grazing donkeys; so

that, winning no prizes, the boy would remain unconscious and irresponsible and amusing—amusing,
because, though life was already intense in his
childish nature, freshness still made there a strong
draught for jokes. It turned out that even in the
still air of Morgan's various disabilities jokes flourished greatly. He was a pale, lean, acute, under-
developed little cosmopolite, who liked intellectual
gymnastics and who, also, as regards the behaviour
of mankind, had noticed more things than you
might suppose, but who nevertheless had his proper
playroom of superstitions, where he smashed a
dozen toys a day.

III

At Nice once, towards evening, as the pair sat
resting in the open air after a walk, looking over
the sea at the pink western lights, Morgan said
suddenly to his companion: "Do you like it—You
know, being with us all in this intimate way?"

"My dear fellow, why should I stay if I didn't?"

"How do I know you will stay? I'm almost sure
you won't, very long."

"I hope you don't mean to dismiss me," said
Pemberton.

Morgan considered a moment, looking at the
sunset. "I think if I did right I ought to."

"Well, I know I'm supposed to instruct you in
virtue; but in that case don't do right."

"You're very young—fortunately," Morgan went
on, turning to him again.

"Oh yes, compared with you!"

"Therefore, it won't matter so much if you do
lose a lot of time."

"That's the way to look at it," said Pemberton
accommodatingly.

They were silent a minute; after which the boy
asked: "Do you like my father and mother very
much?"

"Dear me, yes. They're charming people."

Morgan received this with another silence; then,
unexpectedly, familiarly, but at the same time
affectionately, he remarked: "You're a jolly old
humbug!"

For a particular reason the words made Pemberton change colour. The boy noticed in an instant
that he had turned red, whereupon he turned red
himself and the pupil and the master exchanged
a longish glance in which there was a consciousness of many more things than are usually touched
upon, even tacitly, in such a relation. It produced

for Pemberton an embarrassment; it raised, in a shadowy form, a question (this was the first glimpse of it), which was destined to play as singular and, as he imagined, owing to the altogether peculiar conditions, an unprecedented part in his intercourse with his little companion. Later, when he found himself talking with this small boy in a way in which few small boys could ever have been talked with, he thought of that clumsy moment on the bench at Nice as the dawn of an understanding that had broadened. What had added to the clumsiness then was that he thought it his duty to declare to Morgan that he might abuse him (Pemberton) as much as he liked, but must never abuse his parents. To this Morgan had the easy reply that he hadn't dreamed of abusing them; which appeared to be true: it put Pemberton in the wrong.

"Then why am I a humbug for saying I think them charming?" the young man asked, conscious of a certain rashness.

"Well—they're not *your* parents."

"They love you better than anything in the world—never forget that," said Pemberton.

"Is that why you like them so much?"

"They're very kind to me," Pemberton replied, evasively.

"*You are* a humbug!" laughed Morgan, passing an arm into his tutor's. He leaned against him, looking off at the sea again and swinging his long, thin legs.

"Don't kick my shins," said Pemberton, while he reflected: "Hang it, I can't complain of them to the child!"

"There's another reason, too," Morgan went on, keeping his legs still.

"Another reason for what?"

"Besides their not being your parents."

"I don't understand you," said Pemberton.

"Well, you will before long. All right!"

Pemberton did understand, fully, before long; but he made a fight even with himself before he confessed it. He thought it the oddest thing to have a struggle with the child about. He wondered he didn't detest the child for launching him in such a struggle. But by the time it began the resource of detesting the child was closed to him. Morgan was a special case, but to know him was to accept him on his own odd terms. Pemberton had spent his aversion to special cases before arriving at knowledge. When at last he did arrive he felt that he was in an extreme predicament. Against every interest he had attached himself. They would

have to meet things together. Before they went home that evening, at Nice, the boy had said, clinging to his arm:

"Well, at any rate you'll hang on to the last."

"To the last?"

"Till you're fairly beaten."

"*You* ought to be fairly beaten!" cried the young man, drawing him closer.

IV

A year after Pemberton had come to live with them Mr. and Mrs. Moreen suddenly gave up the villa at Nice. Pemberton had got used to suddenness, having seen it practiced on a considerable scale during two jerky little tours—one in Switzerland the first summer, and the other late in the winter, when they all ran down to Florence and then, at the end of ten days, liking it much less than they had intended, straggled back in mysterious depression. They had returned to Nice "for ever," as they said; but this didn't prevent them from squeezing, one rainy, muggy May night, into a second-class railway-carriage—you could never tell by which class they would travel—where Pemberton helped them to stow away a wonderful collection of bundles and bags. The explanation of this manœuvre was that they had determined to spend the summer "in some bracing place"; but in Paris they dropped into a small furnished apartment—a fourth floor in a third-rate avenue, where there was a smell on the staircase and the *portier* was hateful—and passed the next four months in blank indigence.

The better part of this baffled sojourn was for the preceptor and his pupil, who, visiting the Invalides and Notre Dame, the Conciergerie and all the museums, took a hundred remunerative rambles. They learned to know their Paris, which was useful, for they came back another year for a longer stay, the general character of which in Pemberton's memory to-day mixes pitiably and coinfusedly with that of the first. He sees Morgan's shabby knickerbockers—the everlasting pair that didn't match his blouse and that as he grew longer could only grow faded. He remembers the particular holes in his three or four pair of coloured stockings.

Morgan was dear to his mother, but he never was better dressed than was absolutely necessary—partly, no doubt, by his own fault, for he was as indifferent to his appearance as a German philosopher. "My dear fellow, you *are* coming to pieces,"

Pemberton would say to him in sceptical remonstrance; to which the child would reply, looking at him serenely up and down: 'My dear fellow, so are you! I don't want to cast you in the shade." Pemberton could have no rejoinder for this—the assertion so closely represented the fact. If however the deficiencies of his own wardrobe were a chapter by themselves he didn't like his little charge to look too poor. Later he used to say: "Well, if we are poor, why, after all, shouldn't we look it?" and he consoled himself with thinking there was something rather elderly and gentlemanly in Morgan's seediness—it differed from the untidiness of the urchin who plays and spoils his things. He could trace perfectly the degrees by which, in proportion as her little son confined himself to his tutor for society, Mrs. Moreen shrewdly forbore to renew his garments. She did nothing that didn't show, neglected him because he escaped notice, and then, as he illustrated this clever policy, discouraged at home his public appearances. Her position was logical enough—those members of her family who did show had to be showy.

During this period and several others Pemberton was quite aware of how he and his comrade might strike people; wandering languidly through the Jardin des Plantes as if they had nowhere to go, sitting, on the winter days, in the galleries of the Louvre, so splendidly ironical to the homeless, as if for the advantage of the *calorifère*. They joked about it sometimes: it was the sort of joke that was perfectly within the boy's compass. They figured themselves as part of the vast, vague, hand-to-mouth multitude of the enormous city and pretended they were proud of their position in it—it showed them such a lot of life and made them conscious of a sort of democratic brotherhood. If Pemberton could not feel a sympathy in destitution with his small companion (for after all Morgan's fond parents would never have let him really suffer), the boy would at least feel it with him, so it came to the same thing. He used sometimes to wonder what people would think they were—fancy they were looked askance at, as if it might be a suspected case of kidnapping. Morgan wouldn't be taken for a young patrician with a preceptor—he wasn't smart enough; though he might pass for his companion's sickly little brother. Now and then he had a five-franc piece, and except once, when they bought a couple of lovely neckties, one of which he made Pemberton accept, they laid it out scientifically in old books. It was a great day,

always spent on the quays, rummaging among the dusty boxes that garnish the parapets. These were occasions that helped them to live, for their books ran low very soon after the beginning of their acquaintance. Pemberton had a good many in England, but he was obliged to write to a friend and ask him kindly to get some fellow to give him something for them.

If the bracing climate was untasted that summer the young man had an idea that at the moment they were about to make a push the cup had been dashed from their lips by a movement of his own. It had been his first blow-out, as he called it, with his patrons; his first successful attempt (though there was little other success about it), to bring them to a consideration of his impossible position. As the ostensible eve of a costly journey the moment struck him as a good one to put in a signal protest—to present an ultimatum. Ridiculous as it sounded he had never yet been able to compass an uninterrupted private interview with the elder pair or with either of them singly. They were always flanked by their elder children, and poor Pemberton usually had his own little charge at his side. He was conscious of its being a house in which the surface of one's delicacy got rather smudged; nevertheless he had kept the bloom of his scruple against announcing to Mr. and Mrs. Moreen with publicity that he couldn't go on longer without a little money. He was still simple enough to suppose Ulick and Paula and Amy might not know that since his arrival he had only had a hundred and forty francs; and he was magnanimous enough to wish not to compromise their parents in their eyes. Mr. Moreen now listened to him, as he listened to every one and to everything, like a man of the world, and seemed to appeal to him—though not of course too grossly—to try and be a little more of one himself. Pemberton recognised the importance of the character from the advantage it gave Mr. Moreen. He was not even confused, whereas poor Pemberton was more so than there was any reason for. Neither was he surprised—at least any more than a gentleman had to be who freely confessed himself a little shocked, though not, strictly, at Pemberton.

"We must go into this, mustn't we, dear?" he said to his wife. He assured his young friend that the matter should have his very best attention; and he melted into space as elusively as if, at the door, he were taking an inevitable but deprecatory precedence. When, the next moment, Pemberton found himself alone with Mrs. Moreen it was to hear her say: "I see, I see," stroking the roundness of her chin and looking as if she were only hesitating between a dozen easy remedies. If they didn't make their push Mr. Moreen could at least disappear for several days. During his absence his wife took up the subject again spontaneously, but her contribution to it was merely that she had thought all the while they were getting on so beautifully. Pemberton's reply to this revelation was that unless they immediately handed him a substantial sum he would leave them for ever. He knew she would wonder how he would get away, and for a moment expected her to inquire. She didn't, for which he was almost grateful to her, so little was he in a position to tell.

"You won't, you know you won't—you're too interested," she said. "You *are* interested, you know you are, you dear, kind man!" She laughed, with almost condemnatory archness, as if it were a reproach (but she wouldn't insist), while she flirted a soiled pocket-handkerchief at him.

Pemberton's mind was fully made up to quit the house the following week. This would give him time to get an answer to a letter he had despatched to England. If he did nothing of the sort—that is, if he stayed another year and then went away only for three months—it was not merely because before the answer to his letter came (most unsatisfactory when it did arrive), Mr. Moreen generously presented him—again with all the precautions of a man of the world—three hundred francs. He was exasperated to find that Mrs. Moreen was right, that he couldn't bear to leave the child. This stood out clearer for the very reason that, the night of his desperate appeal to his patrons, he had seen fully for the first time where he was. Wasn't it another proof of the success with which those patrons practiced their arts that they had managed to avert for so long the illuminating flash? It descended upon Pemberton with a luridness which perhaps would have struck a spectator as comically excessive, after he had returned to his little servile room, which looked into a closed court where a bare, dirty opposite wall took, with the sound of shrill clatter, the reflection of lighted back-windows. He had simply given himself away to a band of adventurers. The idea, the word itself, had a sort of romantic horror for him—he had always lived on such safe lines. Later it assumed a more interesting, almost a soothing, sense: it pointed a moral, and Pemberton could enjoy a moral. The Moreens were adventurers not merely because they didn't pay their debts, because they lived on society, but

because their whole view of life, dim and confused and instinctive, like that of clever colour-blind animals, was speculative and rapacious and mean. Oh! they were "respectable," and that only made them more *immondes*. The young man's analysis of them put it at last very simply—they were adventurers because they were abject snobs. That was the completest account of them—it was the law of their being. Even when this truth became vivid to their ingenious inmate he remained unconscious of how much his mind had been prepared for it by the extraordinary little boy who had now become such a complication in his life. Much less could he then calculate on the information he was still to owe to the extraordinary little boy.

V

But it was during the ensuing time that the real problem came up—the problem of how far it was excusable to discuss the turpitude of parents with a child of twelve, of thirteen, of fourteen. Absolutely inexcusable and quite impossible it of course at first appeared; and indeed the question didn't press for a while after Pemberton had received his three hundred francs. They produced a sort of lull, a relief from the sharpest pressure. Pemberton frugally amended his wardrobe and even had a few francs in his pocket. He thought the Moreens looked at him as if he were almost too smart, as if they ought to take care not to spoil him. If Mr. Moreen hadn't been such a man of the world he would perhaps have said something to him about his neckties. But Mr. Moreen was always enough a man of the world to let things pass—he had certainly shown that. It was singular how Pemberton guessed that Morgan, though saying nothing about it, knew something had happened. But three hundred francs, especially when one owed money, couldn't last for ever; and when they were gone— the boy knew when they were gone—Morgan did say something. The party had returned to Nice at the beginning of the winter, but not to the charming villa. They went to an hotel, where they stayed three months, and then they went to another hotel, explaining that they had left the first because they had waited and waited and couldn't get the rooms they wanted. These apartments, the rooms they wanted, were generally very splendid; but fortunately they never *could* get them—fortunately, I mean, for Pemberton, who reflected always that if they had got them there would have been still less for educational expenses. What Morgan said at last was said suddenly, irrelevantly, when the moment came, in the middle of a lesson, and consisted of the apparently unfeeling words: "You ought to *filer*, you know—you really ought."

Pemberton stared. He had learnt enough French slang from Morgan to know that to *filer* meant to go away. "Ah, my dear fellow, don't turn me off!"

Morgan pulled a Greek lexicon toward him (he used a Greek-German), to look out a word, instead of asking it of Pemberton. "You can't go on like this, you know."

"Like what, my boy?"

"You know they don't pay you up," said Morgan, blushing and turning his leaves.

"Don't pay me?" Pemberton stared again and feigned amazement. "What on earth put that into your head?"

"It has been there a long time," the boy replied, continuing his search.

Pemberton was silent, then he went on: "I say, what are you hunting for? They pay me beautifully."

"I'm hunting for the Greek for transparent fiction," Morgan dropped.

"Find that rather for gross impertinence, and disabuse your mind. What do I want of money?"

"Oh, that's another question!"

Pemberton hesitated—he was drawn in different ways. The severely correct thing would have been to tell the boy that such a matter was none of his business and bid him go on with his lines. But they were really too intimate for that; it was not the way he was in the habit of treating him; there had been no reason it should be. On the other hand Morgan had quite lighted on the truth—he really shouldn't be able to keep it up much longer; therefore why not let him know one's real motive for forsaking him? At the same time it wasn't decent to abuse to one's pupil the family of one's pupil; it was better to misrepresent than to do that. So in reply to Morgan's last exclamation he just declared, to dismiss the subject, that he had received several payments.

"I say—I say!" the boy ejaculated, laughing.

"That's all right," Pemberton insisted. "Give me your written rendering."

Morgan pushed a copybook across the table, and his companion began to read the page, but with something running in his head that made it no sense. Looking up after a minute or two he found the child's eyes fixed on him, and he saw something strange in them. Then Morgan said: "I'm not afraid of the reality."

"I haven't yet seen the thing that you *are* afraid of—I'll do you that justice!"

This came out with a jump (it was perfectly true), and evidently gave Morgan pleasure. "I've thought of it a long time," he presently resumed.

"Well, don't think of it any more."

The child appeared to comply, and they had a comfortable and even an amusing hour. They had a theory that they were very thorough, and yet they seemed always to be in the amusing part of lessons, the intervals between the tunnels, where there were waysides and views. Yet the morning was brought to a violent end by Morgan's suddenly leaning his arms on the table, burying his head in them and bursting into tears. Pemberton would have been startled at any rate; but he was doubly startled because, as it then occurred to him, it was the first time he had ever seen the boy cry. It was rather awful.

The next day, after much thought, he took a decision and, believing it to be just, immediately acted upon it. He cornered Mr. and Mrs. Moreen again and informed them that if, on the spot, they didn't pay him all they owed him, he would not only leave their house, but would tell Morgan exactly what had brought him to it.

"Oh, you *haven't* told him?" cried Mrs. Moreen, with a pacifying hand on her well-dressed bosom.

"Without warning you? For what do you take me?"

Mr. and Mrs. Moreen looked at each other, and Pemberton could see both that they were relieved and that there was a certain alarm in their relief. "My dear fellow," Mr. Moreen demanded, "what use *can* you have, leading the quiet life we all do, for such a lot of money?"—an inquiry to which Pemberton made no answer, occupied as he was in perceiving that what passed in the mind of his patrons was something like: "Oh, then, if we've felt that the child, dear little angel, has judged us and how he regards us, and we haven't been betrayed, he must have guessed—and, in short, it's *general!*" an idea that rather stirred up Mr. and Mrs. Moreen, as Pemberton had desired that it should. At the same time, if he had thought that his threat would do something towards bringing them round, he was disappointed to find they had taken for granted (how little they appreciated his delicacy!) that he had already given them away to his pupil. There was a mystic uneasiness in their parental breasts, and that was the way they had accounted for it.

None the less his threat did touch them; for if they had escaped it was only to meet a new danger. Mr. Moreen appealed to Pemberton, as usual, as a man of the world; but his wife had recourse, for the first time since the arrival of their inmate, to a fine *hauteur*, reminding him that a devoted mother, with her child, had arts that protected her against gross misrepresentation.

"I should misrepresent you grossly if I accused you of common honesty!" the young man replied; but as he closed the door behind him sharply, thinking he had not done himself much good, while Mr. Moreen lighted another cigarette, he heard Mrs. Moreen shout after him, more touchingly:

"Oh, you do, you *do*, put the knife to one's throat!"

The next morning, very early, she came to his room. He recognised her knock, but he had no hope that she brought him money; as to which he was wrong, for she had fifty francs in her hand. She squeezed forward in her dressing-gown, and he received her in his own, between his bath-tub and his bed. He had been tolerably schooled by this time to the "foreign ways" of his hosts. Mrs. Moreen was zealous, and when she was zealous she didn't care what she did; so she now sat down on his bed, his clothes being on the chairs, and, in her preoccupation, forgot, as she glanced round, to be ashamed of giving him such a nasty room. What Mrs. Moreen was zealous about on this occasion was to persuade him that in the first place she was very good-natured to bring him fifty francs, and, in the second, if he would only see it, he was really too absurd to expect to be *paid*. Wasn't he paid enough, without perpetual money —wasn't he paid by the comfortable, luxurious home that he enjoyed with them all, without a care, an anxiety, a solitary want? Wasn't he sure of his position, and wasn't that everything to a young man like him, quite unknown, with singularly little to show, the ground of whose exorbitant pretensions it was not easy to discover? Wasn't he paid, above all, by the delightful relation he had established with Morgan—quite ideal, as from master to pupil—and by the simple privilege of knowing and living with so amazingly gifted a child, than whom really—she meant literally what she said—there was no better company in Europe? Mrs. Moreen herself took to appealing to him as a man of the world; she said "Voyons, mon cher," and "My dear sir, look here now"; and urged him to be reasonable, putting it before him that it was

really a chance for him. She spoke as if, according as he *should* be reasonable, he would prove himself worthy to be her son's tutor and of the extraordinary confidence they had placed in him.

After all, Pemberton reflected, it was only a difference of theory, and the theory didn't matter much. They had hitherto gone on that of remunerated, as now they would go on that of gratuitous, service; but why should they have so many words about it? Mrs. Moreen, however, continued to be convincing; sitting there with her fifty francs she talked and repeated, as women repeat, and bored and irritated him, while he leaned against the wall with his hands in the pockets of his wrapper, drawing it together round his legs and looking over the head of his visitor at the grey negations of his window. She wound up with saying: "You see I bring you a definite proposal."

"A definite proposal?"

"To make our relations regular, as it were—to put them on a comfortable footing."

"I see—it's a system," said Pemberton. "A kind of blackmail."

Mrs. Moreen bounded up, which was what the young man wanted.

"What do you mean by that?"

"You practice on one's fears—one's fears about the child if one should go away."

"And pray, what would happen to him in that event?" demanded Mrs. Moreen, with majesty.

"Why, he'd be alone with *you*."

"And pray, with whom *should* a child be but with those whom he loves most?"

"If you think that, why don't you dismiss me?"

"Do you pretend that he loves you more than he loves *us*?" cried Mrs. Moreen.

"I think he ought to. I make sacrifices for him. Though I've heard of those *you* make, I don't see them."

Mrs. Moreen stared a moment; then, with emotion, she grasped Pemberton's hand. "*Will* you make it—the sacrifice?"

Pemberton burst out laughing. "I'll see—I'll do what I can—I'll stay a little longer. Your calculation is just—I *do* hate intensely to give him up; I'm fond of him and he interests me deeply, in spite of the inconvenience I suffer. You know my situation perfectly; I haven't a penny in the world, and, occupied as I am with Morgan, I'm unable to earn money."

Mrs. Moreen tapped her undressed arm with her folded banknote. "Can't you write articles? Can't you translate, as *I* do?"

"I don't know about translating; it's wretchedly paid."

"I am glad to earn what I can," said Mrs. Moreen virtuously, with her head high.

"You ought to tell me who you do it for." Pemberton paused a moment, and she said nothing; so he added: "I've tried to turn off some little sketches, but the magazines won't have them—they're declined with thanks."

"You see then you're not such a phœnix—to have such pretensions," smiled his interlocutress.

"I haven't time to do things properly," Pemberton went on. Then as it came over him that he was almost abjectly good-natured to give these explanations he added: "If I stay on longer it must be on one condition—that Morgan shall know distinctly on what footing I am."

Mrs. Moreen hesitated. "Surely you don't want to show off to a child?"

"To show *you* off, do you mean?"

Again Mrs. Moreen hesitated, but this time it was to produce a still finer flower. "And *you* talk of blackmail!"

"You can easily prevent it," said Pemberton.

"And *you* talk of practicing on fears," Mrs. Moreen continued.

"Yes, there's no doubt I'm a great scoundrel."

His visitor looked at him a moment—it was evident that she was sorely bothered. Then she thrust out her money at him. "Mr. Moreen desired me to give you this on account."

"I'm much obliged to Mr. Moreen; but we have no account."

"You won't take it?"

"That leaves me more free," said Pemberton.

"To poison my darling's mind?" groaned Mrs. Moreen.

"Oh, your darling's mind!" laughed the young man.

She fixed him a moment, and he thought she was going to break out tormentedly, pleadingly. "For God's sake, tell me what *is* in it!" But she checked this impulse—another was stronger. She pocketed the money—the crudity of the alternative was comical—and swept out of the room with the desperate concession: "You may tell him any horror you like!"

VI

A couple of days after this, during which Pemberton had delayed to profit by Mrs. Moreen's permission to tell her son any horror, the two had been for a quarter of an hour walking together in silence when the boy became sociable again with the remark: "I'll tell you how I know it; I know it through Zénobie."

"Zénobie? Who in the world is *she*?"

"A nurse I used to have—ever so many years ago. A charming woman. I liked her awfully, and she liked me."

"There's no accounting for tastes. What is it you know through her?"

"Why, what their idea is. She went away because they didn't pay her. She did like me awfully, and she stayed two years. She told me all about it—that at last she could never get her wages. As soon as they saw how much she liked me they stopped giving her anything. They thought she'd stay for nothing, out of devotion. And she did stay ever so long—as long as she could. She was only a poor girl. She used to send money to her mother. At last she couldn't afford it any longer, and she went away in a fearful rage one night—I mean of course in a rage against *them*. She cried over me tremendously, she hugged me nearly to death. She told me all about it," Morgan repeated. "She told me it was their idea. So I guessed, ever so long ago, that they have had the same idea with you."

"Zénobie was very shrewd," said Pemberton. "And she made you so."

"Oh, that wasn't Zénobie; that was nature. And experience!" Morgan laughed.

"Well, Zénobie was a part of your experience."

"Certainly I was a part of hers, poor dear!" the boy exclaimed. "And I'm a part of yours."

"A very important part. But I don't see how you know that I've been treated like Zénobie."

"Do you take me for an idiot?" Morgan asked. "Haven't I been conscious of what we've been through together?"

"What we've been through?"

"Our privations—our dark days."

"Oh, our days have been bright enough."

Morgan went on in silence for a moment. Then he said: "My dear fellow, you're a hero!"

"Well, you're another!" Pemberton retorted.

"No, I'm not; but I'm not a baby. I won't stand it any longer. You must get some occupation that pays. I'm ashamed, I'm ashamed!" quavered the boy in a little passionate voice that was very touching to Pemberton.

"We ought to go off and live somewhere together," said the young man.

"I'll go like a shot if you'll take me."

"I'd get some work that would keep us both afloat," Pemberton continued.

"So would I. Why shouldn't *I* work? I ain't such a *crétin!*"

"The difficulty is that your parents wouldn't hear of it," said Pemberton. "They would never part with you; they worship the ground you tread on. Don't you see the proof of it? They don't dislike me; they wish me no harm; they're very amiable people; but they're perfectly ready to treat me badly for your sake."

The silence in which Morgan received this graceful sophistry struck Pemberton somehow as expressive. After a moment Morgan repeated: "You *are* a hero!" Then he added: "They leave me with you altogether. You've all the responsibility. They put me off on you from morning till night. Why, then, should they object to my taking up with you completely? I'd help you."

"They're not particularly keen about my being helped, and they delight in thinking of you as *theirs*. They're tremendously proud of you."

"I'm not proud of them. But you know *that*," Morgan returned.

"Except for the little matter we speak of they're charming people," said Pemberton, not taking up the imputation of lucidity, but wondering greatly at the child's own, and especially at this fresh reminder of something he had been conscious of from the first—the strangest thing in the boy's large little composition, a temper, a sensibility, even a sort of ideal, which made him privately resent the general quality of his kinsfolk. Morgan had in secret a small loftiness which begot an element of reflection, a domestic scorn not imperceptible to his companion (though they never had any talk about it), and absolutely anomalous in a juvenile nature, especially when one noted that it had not made this nature "old-fashioned," as the word is of children—quaint or wizened or offensive. It was as if he had been a little gentleman and had paid the penalty by discovering that he was the only such person in the family. This comparison didn't make him vain; but it could make him melancholy and a trifle austere. When Pemberton guessed at these young dimnesses he saw him serious and gallant, and was partly drawn on and partly checked, as if with a scruple, by the charm of attempting to sound the little cool shallows which were quickly growing deeper. When he tried to figure to himself the morning twilight of childhood, so as to deal with it safely, he perceived that it was never fixed, never arrested, that ignorance,

at the instant one touched it, was already flushing faintly into knowledge, that there was nothing that at a given moment you could say a clever child didn't know. It seemed to him that *he* both knew too much to imagine Morgan's simplicity and too little to disembroil his tangle.

The boy paid no heed to his last remark; he only went on: "I should have spoken to them about their idea, as I call it, long ago, if I hadn't been sure what they would say."

"And what would they say?"

"Just what they said about what poor Zénobie told me—that it was a horrid, dreadful story, that they had paid her every penny they owed her."

"Well, perhaps they had," said Pemberton.

"Perhaps they've paid you!"

"Let us pretend they have, and *n'en parlons plus*."

"They accused her of lying and cheating," Morgan insisted perversely. "That's why I don't want to speak to them."

"Lest they should accuse me, too?"

To this Morgan made no answer, and his companion, looking down at him (the boy turned his eyes, which had filled, away), saw that he couldn't have trusted himself to utter.

"You're right. Don't squeeze them," Pemberton pursued. "Except for that, they *are* charming people."

"Except for *their* lying and *their* cheating?"

"I say—I say!" cried Pemberton, imitating a little tone of the lad's which was itself an imitation.

"We must be frank, at the last; we *must* come to an understanding," said Morgan, with the importance of the small boy who lets himself think he is arranging great affairs—almost playing at shipwreck or at Indians. "I know all about everything," he added.

"I daresay your father has his reasons," Pemberton observed, too vaguely, as he was aware.

"For lying and cheating?"

"For saving and managing and turning his means to the best account. He has plenty to do with his money. You're an expensive family."

"Yes, I'm very expensive," Morgan rejoined, in a manner which made his preceptor burst out laughing.

"He's saving for *you*," said Pemberton. "They think of you in everything they do."

"He might save a little—" The boy paused. Pemberton waited to hear what. Then Morgan brought out oddly "A little reputation."

"Oh, there's plenty of that. That's all right!"

"Enough of it for the people they know, no doubt. The people they know are awful."

"Do you mean the princes? We mustn't abuse the princes."

"Why not? They haven't married Paula—they haven't married Amy. They only clean out Ulick."

"You *do* know everything!" Pemberton exclaimed.

"No, I don't, after all. I don't know what they live on, or how they live, or *why* they live! What have they got and how did they get it? Are they rich, are they poor, or have they a *modeste aisance*? Why are they always chiveying about—living one year like ambassadors and the next like paupers? Who are they, any way, and what are they? I've thought of all that—I've thought of a lot of things. They're so beastly worldly. That's what I hate most—oh, I've *seen* it! All they care about is to make an appearance and to pass for something or other. What do they want to pass for? What *do* they, Mr. Pemberton?"

"You pause for a reply," said Pemberton, treating the inquiry as a joke, yet wondering too, and greatly struck with the boy's intense, if imperfect, vision. "I haven't the least idea."

"And what good does it do? Haven't I seen the way people treat them—the 'nice' people, the ones they want to know? They'll take anything from them—they'll lie down and be trampled on. The nice ones hate that—they just sicken them. You're the only really nice person we know."

"Are you sure? They don't lie down for me!"

"Well, you shan't lie down for them. You've got to go—that's what you've got to do," said Morgan.

"And what will become of you?"

"Oh, I'm growing up. I shall get off before long. I'll see you later."

"You had better let me finish you," Pemberton urged, lending himself to the child's extraordinarily competent attitude.

Morgan stopped in their walk, looking up at him. He had to look up much less than a couple of years before—he had grown, in his loose leanness, so long and high. "Finish me?" he echoed.

"There are such a lot of jolly things we can do together yet. I want to turn you out—I want you to do me credit."

Morgan continued to look at him. "To give you credit—do you mean?"

"My dear fellow, you're too clever to live."

"That's just what I'm afraid you think. No, no; it isn't fair—I can't endure it. We'll part next

week. The sooner it's over the sooner to sleep."

"If I hear of anything—any other chance, I promise to go," said Pemberton.

Morgan consented to consider this. "But you'll be honest," he demanded; "you won't pretend you haven't heard?"

"I'm much more likely to pretend I have."

"But what can you hear of, this way, stuck in a hole with us? You ought to be on the spot, to go to England—you ought to go to America."

"One would think you were *my* tutor!" said Pemberton.

Morgan walked on, and after a moment he began again: "Well, now that you know that I know and that we look at the facts and keep nothing back—it's much more comfortable, isn't it?"

"My dear boy, it's so amusing, so interesting, that it surely will be quite impossible for me to forego such hours as these."

This made Morgan stop once more. "You *do* keep something back. Oh, you're not straight—I am!"

"Why am I not straight?"

"Oh, you've got your idea!"

"My idea?"

"Why, that I probably sha'n't live, and that you can stick it out till I'm removed."

"You *are* too clever to live!" Pemberton repeated.

"I call it a mean idea," Morgan pursued. "But I shall punish you by the way I hang on."

"Look out or I'll poison you!" Pemberton laughed.

"I'm stronger and better every year. Haven't you noticed that there hasn't been a doctor near me since you came?"

"*I'm* your doctor," said the young man, taking his arm and drawing him on again.

Morgan proceeded, and after a few steps he gave a sigh of mingled weariness and relief. "Ah, now that we look at the facts, it's all right!"

VII

They looked at the facts a good deal after this; and one of the first consequences of their doing so was that Pemberton stuck it out, as it were, for the purpose. Morgan made the facts so vivid and so droll, and at the same time so bald and so ugly, that there was fascination in talking them over with him, just as there would have been heartlessness in leaving him alone with them. Now that they had such a number of perceptions in common it was useless for the pair to pretend that they didn't judge such people; but the very judgment, and the exchange of perceptions, created another tie. Morgan had never been so interesting as now that he himself was made plainer by the sidelight of these confidences. What came out in it most was the soreness of his characteristic pride. He had plenty of that, Pemberton felt—so much that it was perhaps well it should have had to take some early bruises. He would have liked his people to be gallant, and he had waked up too soon to the sense that they were perpetually swallowing humble-pie. His mother would consume any amount, and his father would consume even more than his mother. He had a theory that Ulick had wriggled out of an "affair" at Nice: there had once been a flurry at home, a regular panic, after which they all went to bed and took medicine, not to be accounted for on any other supposition. Morgan had a romantic imagination, fed by poetry and history, and he would have liked those who "bore his name" (as he used to say to Pemberton with the humour that made his sensitiveness manly), to have a proper spirit. But their one idea was to get in with people who didn't want them and to take snubs as if they were honourable scars. Why people didn't want them more he didn't know—that was people's own affair; after all they were not superficially repulsive—they were a hundred times cleverer than most of the dreary grandees, the "poor swells" they rushed about Europe to catch up with. "After all, they *are* amusing—they are!" Morgan used to say, with the wisdom of the ages. To which Pemberton always replied: "Amusing—the great Moreen troupe? Why, they're altogether delightful; and if it were not for the hitch that you and I (feeble performers!) make in the *ensemble*, they would carry everything before them."

What the boy couldn't get over was that this particular blight seemed, in a tradition of self-respect, so undeserved and so arbitrary. No doubt people had a right to take the line they liked; but why should *his* people have liked the line of pushing and toadying and lying and cheating? What had their forefathers—all decent folk, so far as he knew—done to them, or what had *he* done to them? Who had poisoned their blood with the fifth-rate social ideal, the fixed idea of making smart acquaintances and getting into the *monde chic*, especially when it was foredoomed to failure

and exposure? They showed so what they were after; that was what made the people they wanted not want *them*. And never a movement of dignity, never a throb of shame at looking each other in the face, never any independence or resentment or disgust. If his father or his brother would only knock some one down once or twice a year! Clever as they were they never guessed how they appeared. They were good-natured, yes—as good-natured as Jews at the doors of clothing-shops! But was that the model one wanted one's family to follow? Morgan had dim memories of an old grandfather, the maternal, in New York, whom he had been taken across the ocean to see, at the age of five: a gentleman with a high neckcloth and a good deal of pronunciation, who wore a dress-coat in the morning, which made one wonder what he wore in the evening, and had, or was supposed to have, "property" and something to do with the Bible Society. It couldn't have been but that *he* was a good type. Pemberton himself remembered Mrs. Clancy, a widowed sister of Mr. Moreen's, who was as irritating as a moral tale and had paid a fortnight's visit to the family at Nice shortly after he came to live with them. She was "pure and refined," as Amy said, over the banjo, and had the air of not knowing what they meant and of keeping something back. Pemberton judged that what she kept back was an approval of many of their ways; therefore it was to be supposed that she too was of a good type, and that Mr. and Mrs. Moreen and Ulick and Paula and Amy might easily have been better if they would.

But that they wouldn't was more and more perceptible from day to day. They continued to "chivey," as Morgan called it, and in due time became aware of a variety of reasons for proceeding to Venice. They mentioned a great many of them—they were always strikingly frank, and had the brightest friendly chatter, at the late foreign breakfast in especial, before the ladies had made up their faces, when they leaned their arms on the table, had something to follow the *demi-tasse*, and, in the heat of familiar discussion as to what they "really ought" to do, fell inevitably into the languages in which they could *tutoyer*. Even Pemberton liked them, then; he could endure even Ulick when he heard him give his little flat voice for the "sweet sea-city." That was what made him have a sneaking kindness for them—that they were so out of the workaday world and kept him so out of it. The summer had waned when, with cries of ecstasy, they all passed out on the balcony that overhung the Grand Canal; the sunsets were splendid—the Dorringtons had arrived. The Dorringtons were the only reason they had not talked of at breakfast; but the reasons that they didn't talk of at breakfast always came out in the end. The Dorringtons, on the other hand, came out very little; or else, when they did, they stayed—as was natural —for hours, during which periods Mrs. Moreen and the girls sometimes called at their hotel (to see if they had returned) as many as three times running. The gondola was for the ladies; for in Venice too there were "days," which Mrs. Moreen knew in their order an hour after she arrived. She immediately took one herself, to which the Dorringtons never came, though on a certain occasion when Pemberton and his pupil were together at St. Mark's—where, taking the best walks they had ever had and haunting a hundred churches, they spent a great deal of time—they saw the old lord turn up with Mr. Moreen and Ulick, who showed him the dim basilica as if it belonged to them. Pemberton noted how much less, among its curiosities, Lord Dorrington carried himself as a man of the world; wondering too whether, for such services, his companions took a fee from him. The autumn, at any rate, waned, the Dorringtons departed, and Lord Verschoyle, the eldest son, had proposed neither for Amy nor for Paula.

One sad November day, while the wind roared round the old palace and the rain lashed the lagoon, Pemberton, for exercise and even somewhat for warmth (the Moreens were horribly frugal about fires—it was a cause of suffering to their inmate), walked up and down the big bare *sala* with his pupil. The scagliola floor was cold, the high battered casement shook in the storm, and the stately decay of the place was unrelieved by a particle of furniture. Pemberton's spirits were low, and it came over him that the fortune of the Moreens was now even lower. A blast of desolation, a prophecy of disaster and disgrace, seemed to draw through the comfortless hall. Mr. Moreen and Ulick were in the Piazza, looking out for something, strolling drearily, in mackintoshes, under the arcades; but still, in spite of mackintoshes unmistakable men of the world. Paula and Amy were in bed—it might have been thought they were staying there to keep warm. Pemberton looked askance at the boy at his side, to see to what extent he was conscious of these portents. But Morgan, luckily for him, was now mainly conscious of growing taller and stronger and indeed of being in his

fifteenth year. This fact was intensely interesting to him—it was the basis of a private theory (which, however, he had imparted to his tutor) that in a little while he should stand on his own feet. He considered that the situation would change—that, in short, he should be "finished," grown up, producible in the world of affairs and ready to prove himself of sterling ability. Sharply as he was capable, at times, of questioning his circumstances, there were happy hours when he was as superficial as a child; the proof of which was his fundamental assumption that he should presently go to Oxford, to Pemberton's college, and, aided and abetted by Pemberton, do the most wonderful things. It vexed Pemberton to see how little, in such a project, he took account of ways and means: on other matters he was so sceptical about them. Pemberton tried to imagine the Moreens at Oxford, and fortunately failed; yet unless they were to remove there as a family there would be no *modus vivendi* for Morgan. How could he live without an allowance, and where was the allowance to come from? He (Pemberton) might live on Morgan; but how could Morgan live on him? What was to become of him anyhow? Somehow, the fact that he was a big boy now, with better prospects of health, made the question of his future more difficult. So long as he was frail the consideration that he inspired seemed enough of an answer to it. But at the bottom of Pemberton's heart was the recognition of his probably being strong enough to live and not strong enough to thrive. He himself, at any rate, was in a period of natural, boyish rosiness about all this, so that the beating of the tempest seemed to him only the voice of life and the challenge of fate. He had on his shabby little overcoat, with the collar up, but he was enjoying his walk.

It was interrupted at last by the appearance of his mother at the end of the *sala*. She beckoned to Morgan to come to her, and while Pemberton saw him, complacent, pass down the long vista, over the damp false marble, he wondered what was in the air. Mrs. Moreen said a word to the boy and made him go into the room she had quitted. Then, having closed the door after him, she directed her steps swiftly to Pemberton. There *was* something in the air, but his wildest flight of fancy wouldn't have suggested what it proved to be. She signified that she had made a pretext to get Morgan out of the way, and then she inquired—without hesitation —if the young man could lend her sixty francs. While, before bursting into a laugh, he stared at her with surprise, she declared that she was awfully pressed for the money; she was desperate for it—it would save her life.

"Dear lady, *c'est trop fort!*" Pemberton laughed. "Where in the world do you suppose I should get sixty francs, *du train dont vous allez?*"

"I thought you worked—wrote things; don't they pay you?"

"Not a penny."

"Are you such a fool as to work for nothing?"

"You ought surely to know that."

Mrs. Moreen stared an instant, then she coloured a little. Pemberton saw she had quite forgotten the terms—if "terms" they could be called—that he had ended by accepting from herself; they had burdened her memory as little as her conscience. "Oh, yes, I see what you mean—you have been very nice about that; but why go back to it so often?" She had been perfectly urbane with him ever since the rough scene of explanation in his room, the morning he made her accept *his* "terms" —the necessity of his making his case known to Morgan. She had felt no resentment, after seeing that there was no danger of Morgan's taking the matter up with her. Indeed, attributing this immunity to the good taste of his influence with the boy, she had once said to Pemberton: "My dear fellow; it's an immense comfort you're a gentleman." She repeated this, in substance, now. "Of course you're a gentleman—that's a bother the less!" Pemberton reminded her that he had not "gone back" to anything; and she also repeated her prayer that, somewhere and somehow, he would find her sixty francs. He took the liberty of declaring that if he could find them it wouldn't be to lend them to *her*—as to which he consciously did himself injustice, knowing that if he had them he would certainly place them in her hand. He accused himself, at bottom and with some truth, of a fantastic, demoralised sympathy with her. If misery made strange bedfellows it also made strange sentiments. It was moreover a part of the demoralisation and of the general bad effect of living with such people that one had to make rough retorts, quite out of the tradition of good manners. "Morgan, Morgan, to what pass have I come for you?" he privately exclaimed, while Mrs. Moreen floated voluminously down the *sala* again, to liberate the boy; groaning, as she went, that everything was too odious.

Before the boy was liberated there came a thump at the door communicating with the staircase, followed by the apparition of a dripping youth who poked in his head. Pemberton recog-

nised him as the bearer of a telegram and recognised the telegram as addressed to himself. Morgan came back as, after glancing at the signature (that of a friend in London), he was reading the words: "Found jolly job for you—engagement to coach opulent youth on own terms. Come immediately." The answer, happily, was paid, and the messenger waited. Morgan, who had drawn near, waited too, and looked hard at Pemberton; and Pemberton, after a moment, having met his look, handed him the telegram. It was really by wise looks (they knew each other so well), that, while the telegram-boy, in his waterproof cape, made a great puddle on the floor, the thing was settled between them. Pemberton wrote the answer with a pencil against the frescoed wall, and the messenger departed. When he had gone Pemberton said to Morgan:

"I'll make a tremendous charge; I'll earn a lot of money in a short time, and we'll live on it."

"Well, I hope the opulent youth will be stupid —he probably will—" Morgan parenthesised, "and keep you a long time."

"Of course, the longer he keeps me the more we shall have for our old age."

"But suppose *they* don't pay you!" Morgan awfully suggested.

"Oh, there are not two such—!" Pemberton paused, he was on the point of using an invidious term. Instead of this he said "two such chances."

Morgan flushed—the tears came to his eyes. "*Dites toujours*, two such rascally crews!" Then, in a different tone, he added: "Happy opulent youth!"

"Not if he's stupid!"

"Oh, they're happier then. But you can't have everything, can you?" the boy smiled.

Pemberton held him, his hands on his shoulders. "What will become of *you*, what will you do?" He thought of Mrs. Moreen, desperate for sixty francs.

"I shall turn into a man." And then, as if he recognised all the bearings of Pemberton's allusion: "I shall get on with them better when you're not here."

"Ah, don't say that—it sounds as if I set you against them!"

"You do—the sight of you. It's all right; you know what I mean. I shall be beautiful. I'll take their affairs in hand; I'll marry my sisters."

"You'll marry yourself!" joked Pemberton; as high, rather tense pleasantry would evidently be the right, or the safest, tone for their separation.

It was, however, not purely in this strain that Morgan suddenly asked: "But I say—how will you get to your jolly job? You'll have to telegraph to the opulent youth for money to come on."

Pemberton bethought himself. "They won't like that, will they?"

"Oh, look out for them!"

Then Pemberton brought out his remedy. "I'll go to the American Consul; I'll borrow some money of him—just for the few days, on the strength of the telegram."

Morgan was hilarious. "Show him the telegram—then stay and keep the money!"

Pemberton entered into the joke enough to reply that, for Morgan, he was really capable of that; but the boy, growing more serious, and to prove that he hadn't meant what he said, not only hurried him off to the Consulate (since he was to start that evening, as he had wired to his friend), but insisted on going with him. They splashed through the tortuous perforations and over the hump-backed bridges, and they passed through the Piazza, where they saw Mr. Moreen and Ulick go into a jeweller's shop. The Consul proved accommodating (Pemberton said it wasn't the letter, but Morgan's grand air), and on their way back they went into St. Mark's for a hushed ten minutes. Later they took up and kept up the fun of it to the very end; and it seemed to Pemberton a part of that fun that Mrs. Moreen, who was very angry when he had announced to her his intention, should charge him, grotesquely and vulgarly, and in reference to the loan she had vainly endeavoured to effect, with bolting lest they should "get something out" of him. On the other hand he had to do Mr. Moreen and Ulick the justice to recognise that when, on coming in, *they* heard the cruel news, they took it like perfect men of the world.

VIII

When Pemberton got at work with the opulent youth, who was to be taken in hand for Balliol, he found himself unable to say whether he was really an idiot or it was only, on his own part, the long association with an intensely living little mind that made him seem so. From Morgan he heard half-a-dozen times: the boy wrote charming young letters, a patchwork of tongues, with indulgent postscripts in the family Volapuk and, in little squares and rounds and crannies of the text, the drollest illustrations—letters that he was divided between the impulse to show his present disciple,

as a kind of wasted incentive, and the sense of something in them that was profanable by publicity. The opulent youth went up, in due course, and failed to pass; but it seemed to add to the presumption that brilliancy was not expected of him all at once that his parents, condoning the lapse, which they good-naturedly treated as little as possible as if it were Pemberton's, should have sounded the rally again, begged the young coach to keep his pupil in hand another year.

The young coach was now in a position to lend Mrs. Moreen sixty francs, and he sent her a post-office order for the amount. In return for this favour he received a frantic, scribbled line from her: "Implore you to come back instantly—Morgan dreadfully ill." They were on the rebound, once more in Paris—often as Pemberton had seen them depressed he had never seen them crushed—and communication was therefore rapid. He wrote to the boy to ascertain the state of his health, but he received no answer to his letter. Accordingly he took an abrupt leave of the opulent youth and, crossing the Channel, alighted at the small hotel, in the quarter of the Champs Elysées, of which Mrs. Moreen had given him the address. A deep if dumb dissatisfaction with this lady and her companions bore him company: they couldn't be vulgarly honest, but they could live at hotels, in velvety *entresols*, amid a smell of burnt pastilles, in the most expensive city in Europe. When he had left them, in Venice, it was with an irrepressible suspicion that something was going to happen; but the only thing that had happened was that they succeeded in getting away. "How is he? where is he?" he asked of Mrs. Moreen; but before she could speak, these questions were answered by the pressure round his neck of a pair of arms, in shrunken sleeves, which were perfectly capable of an effusive young foreign squeeze.

"Dreadfully ill—I don't see it!" the young man cried. And then, to Morgan: "Why on earth didn't you relieve me? Why didn't you answer my letter?"

Mrs. Moreen declared that when she wrote he was very bad, and Pemberton learned at the same time from the boy that he had answered every letter he had received. This led to the demonstration that Pemberton's note had been intercepted. Mrs. Moreen was prepared to see the fact exposed, as Pemberton perceived, the moment he faced her, that she was prepared for a good many other things. She was prepared above all to maintain that she had acted from a sense of duty, that she was enchanted she had got him over, whatever they might say; and that it was useless of him to pretend that he didn't *know*, in all his bones, that his place at such a time was with Morgan. He had taken the boy away from them, and now he had no right to abandon him. He had created for himself the gravest responsibilities; he must at least abide by what he had done.

"Taken him away from you?" Pemberton exclaimed indignantly.

"Do it—do it, for pity's sake; that's just what I want. I can't stand *this*—and such scenes. They're treacherous!" These words broke from Morgan, who had intermitted his embrace, in a key which made Pemberton turn quickly to him, to see that he had suddenly seated himself, was breathing with evident difficulty and was very pale.

"Now do you say he's not ill—my precious pet?" shouted his mother, dropping on her knees before him with clasped hands, but touching him no more than if he had been a gilded idol. "It will pass—it's only for an instant; but don't say such dreadful things!"

"I'm all right—all right," Morgan panted to Pemberton, whom he sat looking up at with a strange smile, his hands resting on either side on the sofa.

"Now do you pretend I've been treacherous— that I've deceived?" Mrs. Moreen flashed at Pemberton as she got up.

"It isn't *he* says it, it's I!" the boy returned, apparently easier, but sinking back against the wall; while Pemberton, who had sat down beside him, taking his hand, bent over him.

"Darling child, one does what one can; there are so many things to consider," urged Mrs. Moreen. "It's his *place*—his only place. You see *you* think it is now."

"Take me away—take me away," Morgan went on, smiling to Pemberton from his white face.

"Where shall I take you, and how—oh, *how*, my boy?" the young man stammered, thinking of the rude way in which his friends in London held that, for his convenience, and without a pledge of instantaneous return, he had thrown them over; of the just resentment with which they would already have called in a successor, and of the little help as regarded finding fresh employment that resided for him in the flatness of his having failed to pass his pupil.

"Oh, we'll settle that. You used to talk about it," said Morgan. "If we can only go, all the rest's a detail."

"Talk about it as much as you like, but don't think you can attempt it. Mr. Moreen would never consent—it would be so precarious," Pemberton's hostess explained to him. Then to Morgan she explained: "It would destroy our peace, it would break our hearts. Now that he's back it will be all the same again. You'll have your life, your work and your freedom, and we'll all be happy as we used to be. You'll bloom and grow perfectly well, and we won't have any more silly experiments, will we? They're too absurd. It's Mr. Pemberton's place—every one in his place. You in yours, your papa in his, me in mine—*n'est-ce pas, chéri?* We'll all forget how foolish we've been, and we'll have lovely times."

She continued to talk and to surge vaguely about the little draped, stuffy *salon*, while Pemberton sat with the boy, whose colour gradually came back; and she mixed up her reasons, dropping that there were going to be changes, that the other children might scatter (who knew?—Paula had her ideas), and that then it might be fancied how much the poor old parent-birds would want the little nestling. Morgan looked at Pemberton, who wouldn't let him move; and Pemberton knew exactly how he felt at hearing himself called a little nestling. He admitted that he had had one or two bad days, but he protested afresh against the iniquity of his mother's having made them the ground of an appeal to poor Pemberton. Poor Pemberton could laugh now, apart from the comicality of Mrs. Moreen's producing so much philosophy for her defense (she seemed to shake it out of her agitated petticoats, which knocked over the light gilt chairs), so little did the sick boy strike him as qualified to repudiate any advantage.

He himself was in for it, at any rate. He should have Morgan on his hands again indefinitely; though indeed he saw the lad had a private theory to produce which would be intended to smooth this down. He was obliged to him for it in advance; but the suggested amendment didn't keep his heart from sinking a little, any more than it prevented him from accepting the prospect on the spot, with some confidence moreover that he would do so even better if he could have a little supper. Mrs. Moreen threw out more hints about the changes that were to be looked for, but she was such a mixture of smiles and shudders (she confessed she was very nervous), that he couldn't tell whether she were in high feather or only in hysterics. If the family were really at last going to pieces why shouldn't she recognise the necessity of pitching Morgan into some sort of lifeboat? This presumption was fostered by the fact that they were established in luxurious quarters in the capital of pleasure; that was exactly where they naturally *would* be established in view of going to pieces. Moreover didn't she mention that Mr. Moreen and the others were enjoying themselves at the opera with Mr. Granger, and wasn't *that* also precisely where one would look for them on the eve of a smash? Pemberton gathered that Mr. Granger was a rich, vacant American—a big bill with a flourishy heading and no items; so that one of Paula's "ideas" was probably that this time she had really done it, which was indeed an unprecedented blow to the general cohesion. And if the cohesion was to terminate what was to become of poor Pemberton? He felt quite enough bound up with them to figure, to his alarm, as a floating spar in case of a wreck.

It was Morgan who eventually asked if no supper had been ordered for him; sitting with him below, later, at the dim, delayed meal, in the presence of a great deal of corded green plush, a plate of ornamental biscuit and a languor marked on the part of the waiter. Mrs. Moreen had explained that they had been obliged to secure a room for the visitor out of the house; and Morgan's consolation (he offered it while Pemberton reflected on the nastiness of lukewarm sauces), proved to be, largely, that this circumstance would facilitate their escape. He talked of their escape (recurring to it often afterwards), as if they were making up a "boy's book" together. But he likewise expressed his sense that there was something in the air, that the Moreens couldn't keep it up much longer. In point of fact, as Pemberton was to see, they kept it up for five or six months. All the while, however, Morgan's contention was designed to cheer him. Mr. Moreen and Ulick, whom he had met the day after his return, accepted that return like perfect men of the world. If Paula and Amy treated it even with less formality an allowance was to be made for them, inasmuch as Mr. Granger had not come to the opera after all. He had only placed his box at their service, with a bouquet for each of the party; there was even one apiece, embittering the thought of his profusion, for Mr. Moreen and Ulick. "They're all like that," was Morgan's comment; "at the very last, just when we think we've got them fast, we're chucked!"

Morgan's comments, in these days, were more and more free; they even included a large recognition of the extraordinary tenderness with which

he had been treated while Pemberton was away. Oh, yes, they couldn't do enough to be nice to him, to show him they had him on their mind and make up for his loss. That was just what made the whole thing so sad, and him so glad, after all, of Pemberton's return—he had to keep thinking of their affection less, had less sense of obligation. Pemberton laughed out at this last reason, and Morgan blushed and said: "You know what I mean." Pemberton knew perfectly what he meant; but there were a good many things it didn't make any clearer. This episode of his second sojourn in Paris stretched itself out wearily, with their resumed readings and wanderings and maunderings, their potterings on the quays, their hauntings of the museums, their occasional lingerings in the Palais Royal, when the first sharp weather came on and there was a comfort in warm emanations, before Chevet's wonderful succulent window. Morgan wanted to hear a great deal about the opulent youth—he took an immense interest in him. Some of the details of his opulence—Pemberton could spare him none of them—evidently intensified the boy's appreciation of all his friend had given up to come back to him; but in addition to the greater reciprocity established by such a renunciation he had always his little brooding theory, in which there was a frivolous gaiety too, that their long probation was drawing to a close. Morgan's conviction that the Moreens couldn't go on much longer kept pace with the unexpended impetus with which, from month to month, they did go on. Three weeks after Pemberton had rejoined them they went on to another hotel, a dingier one than the first; but Morgan rejoiced that his tutor had at least still not sacrificed the advantage of a room outside. He clung to the romantic utility of this when the day, or rather the night, should arrive for their escape.

For the first time, in this complicated connection, Pemberton felt sore and exasperated. It was, as he had said to Mrs. Moreen in Venice, *trop fort* —everything was *trop fort*. He could neither really throw off his blighting burden nor find in it the benefit of a pacified conscience or of a rewarded affection. He had spent all the money that he had earned in England, and he felt that his youth was going and that he was getting nothing back for it. It was all very well for Morgan to seem to consider that he would make up to him for all inconveniences by settling himself upon him permanently— there was an irritating flaw in such a view. He saw what the boy had in his mind; the conception that as his friend had had the generosity to come back to him he must show his gratitude by giving him his life. But the poor friend didn't desire the gift —what could he do with Morgan's life? Of course at the same time that Pemberton was irritated he remembered the reason, which was very honourable to Morgan and which consisted simply of the fact that he was perpetually making one forget that he was after all only a child. If one dealt with him on a different basis one's misadventures were one's own fault. So Pemberton waited in a queer confusion of yearning and alarm for the catastrophe which was held to hang over the house of Moreen, of which he certainly at moments felt the symptoms brush his cheek and as to which he wondered much in what form it would come.

Perhaps it would take the form of dispersal—a frightened *sauve qui peut*, a scuttling into selfish corners. Certainly they were less elastic than of yore; they were evidently looking for something they didn't find. The Dorringtons hadn't reappeared, the princes had scattered; wasn't that the beginning of the end? Mrs. Moreen had lost her reckoning of the famous "days"; her social calendar was blurred—it had turned its face to the wall. Pemberton suspected that the great, the cruel, discomfiture had been the extraordinary behaviour of Mr. Granger, who seemed not to know what he wanted, or, what was much worse, what *they* wanted. He kept sending flowers, as if to bestrew the path of his retreat, which was never the path of return. Flowers were all very well, but— Pemberton could complete the proposition. It was now positively conspicuous that in the long run the Moreens were a failure; so that the young man was almost grateful the run had not been short. Mr. Moreen, indeed, was still occasionally able to get away on business, and, what was more surprising, he was also able to get back. Ulick had no club, but you could not have discovered it from his appearance, which was as much as ever that of a person looking at life from the window of such an institution; therefore Pemberton was doubly astonished at an answer he once heard him make to his mother, in the desperate tone of a man familiar with the worst privations. Her question Pemberton had not quite caught; it appeared to be an appeal for a suggestion as to whom they could get to take Amy. "Let the devil take her!" Ulick snapped; so that Pemberton could see that not only they had lost their amiability, but had ceased to believe in themselves. He could also see that if Mrs. Moreen was trying to get people to take her children she might be regarded as closing the hatches for the storm. But Morgan would be the last she would part with.

One winter afternoon—it was a Sunday—he and the boy walked far together in the Bois de Boulogne. The evening was so splendid, the cold lemon-coloured sunset so clear, the stream of carriages and pedestrians so amusing and the fascination of Paris so great, that they stayed out later than usual and became aware that they would have to hurry home to arrive in time for dinner. They hurried accordingly, arm-in-arm, good-humoured and hungry, agreeing that there was nothing like Paris after all and that after all, too, that had come and gone they were not yet sated with innocent pleasures. When they reached the hotel they found that, though scandalously late, they were in time for all the dinner they were likely to sit down to. Confusion reigned in the apartments of the Moreens (very shabby ones this time, but the best in the house), and before the interrupted service of the table (with objects displaced almost as if there had been a scuffle, and a great wine stain from an overturned bottle), Pemberton could not blink the fact that there had been a scene of proprietary mutiny. The storm had come—they were all seeking refuge. The hatches were down—Paula and Amy were invisible (they had never tried the most casual art upon Pemberton, but he felt that they had enough of an eye to him not to wish to meet him as young ladies whose frocks had been confiscated), and Ulick appeared to have jumped overboard. In a word, the host and his staff had ceased to "go on" at the pace of their guests, and the air of embarrassed detention, thanks to a pile of gaping trunks in the passage, was strangely commingled with the air of indignant withdrawal.

When Morgan took in all this—and he took it in very quickly—he blushed to the roots of his hair. He had walked, from his infancy, among difficulties and dangers, but he had never seen a public exposure. Pemberton noticed, in a second glance at him, that the tears had rushed into his eyes and that they were tears of bitter shame. He wondered for an instant, for the boy's sake, whether he might successfully pretend not to understand. Not successfully, he felt, as Mr. and Mrs. Moreen, dinnerless by their extinguished hearth, rose before him in their little dishonoured *salon*, considering apparently with much intensity what lively capital would be next on their list. They were not prostrate, but they were very pale, and Mrs. Moreen had evidently been crying. Pemberton quickly learned however that her grief was not for the loss of her dinner, much as she usually enjoyed it, but on account of a necessity much more tragic. She lost no time in laying this necessity bare, in telling him how the change had come, the bolt had fallen, and how they would all have to turn themselves about. Therefore cruel as it was to them to part with their darling she must look to him to carry a little further the influence he had so fortunately acquired with the boy—to induce his young charge to follow him into some modest retreat. They depended upon him, in a word, to take their delightful child temporarily under his protection—it would leave Mr. Moreen and herself so much more free to give the proper attention (too little, alas! had been given), to the readjustment of their affairs.

"We trust you—we feel that we can," said Mrs. Moreen, slowly rubbing her plump white hands and looking, with compunction, hard at Morgan, whose chin, not to take liberties, her husband stroked with a tentative paternal forefinger.

"Oh, yes; we feel that we can. We trust Mr. Pemberton fully, Morgan," Mr. Moreen conceded.

Pemberton wondered again if he might pretend not to understand; but the idea was painfully complicated by the immediate perception that Morgan had understood.

"Do you mean that he may take me to live with him—for ever and ever?" cried the boy. "Away, away, anywhere he likes?"

"For ever and ever? *Comme vous-y-allez!*" Mr. Moreen laughed indulgently. "For as long as Mr. Pemberton may be so good."

"We've struggled, we've suffered," his wife went on; "but you've made him so your own that we've already been through the worst of the sacrifice."

Morgan had turned away from his father—he stood looking at Pemberton with a light in his face. His blush had died out, but something had come that was brighter and more vivid. He had a moment of boyish joy, scarcely mitigated by the reflection that, with this unexpected consecration of his hope—too sudden and too violent; the thing was a good deal less like a boy's book—the "escape" was left on their hands. The boyish joy was there for an instant, and Pemberton was almost frightened at the revelation of gratitude and affection that shone through his humiliation. When Morgan stammered "My dear fellow, what do you say to *that?*" he felt that he should say something enthusiastic. But he was still more frightened at something else that immediately followed and that made the lad sit down quickly on the nearest chair. He had turned very white and had raised his hand to his left side. They were all three looking at him, but Mrs. Moreen was the first to bound forward. "Ah, his darling little heart!" she broke out; and this time, on her knees before him and without respect for the idol, she caught him ardently in her arms. "You walked him too far, you hurried him too fast!" she tossed over her shoulder at Pemberton. The boy made no protest, and the next instant his mother, still holding him, sprang up with her face convulsed and with the terrified cry "Help, help! he's going, he's gone!" Pemberton saw, with equal horror, by Morgan's own stricken face, that he *was* gone. He pulled him half out of his mother's hand, and for a moment, while they held him together, they looked, in their dismay, into each other's eyes. "He couldn't stand it, with his infirmity," said Pemberton—"the shock, the whole scene, the violent emotion."

"But I thought he *wanted* to go to you!" wailed Mrs. Moreen.

"I *told* you he didn't, my dear," argued Mr. Moreen. He was trembling all over, and he was, in his way, as deeply affected as his wife. But, after the first, he took his bereavement like a man of the world.

The Beast in the Jungle (1903)

A brief comment on this story will be found in the introduction. It was written soon after James completed *The Ambassadors;* and his portrait of a man who never lives—because, out of assorted fears, he has never loved—is the correlative to Strether's outburst in *The Ambassadors,* "Live all you can!"

The Beast in the Jungle is a haunting and a haunted story: James was quite right to include it with *The Altar of the Dead* and others, in Volume 17 of the New York edition, as stories of the "quasi-supernatural." Behind it, one feels, there lies Hawthorne's truncated romance "Ethan Brand." Brand travels the world searching for the Unpardonable Sin, only to discover that the search itself had been the sin—the search which has cut him off from all humanity and all humane feelings. John Marcher, waiting through the years for the unique and probably hideous fate he is sure is in store for him, discovers that that passive life-long waiting had been the fate itself.

The story contains ironies within ironies, and it is written in James's most intricate and slowly wheeling "late" style. But it is a masterly account of abject spiritual failure. And it is a triumph of technique—to reveal all so gradually through the consciousness of one man that same man's total and harrowing lack of any consciousness whatever.

I

What determined the speech that startled him in the course of their encounter scarcely matters, being probably but some words spoken by himself quite without intention—spoken as they lingered and slowly moved together after their renewal of acquaintance. He had been conveyed by friends, an hour or two before, to the house at which she was staying; the party of visitors at the other house, of whom he was one, and thanks to whom it was his theory, as always, that he was lost in the crowd, had been invited over to luncheon. There had been after luncheon much dispersal, all in the interest of the original motive, a view of Weatherend itself and the fine things, intrinsic features, pictures, heirlooms, treasures of all the arts, that made the place almost famous; and the great rooms were so numerous that guests could wander at their will, hang back from the principal group, and, in cases where they took such matters with the last seriousness, give themselves up to mysterious appreciations and measurements. There were persons to be observed, singly or in couples, bending toward objects in out-of-the-way corners with their hands on their knees and their heads nodding quite as with the emphasis of an excited sense of smell. When they were two they either mingled their sounds of ecstasy or melted into silences of even deeper import, so that there were aspects of the occasion that gave it for Marcher much the air of the "look round," previous to a sale highly advertised, that excites or quenches, as may be, the dream of acquisition. The dream of

acquisition at Weatherend would have had to be wild indeed, and John Marcher found himself, among such suggestions, disconcerted almost equally by the presence of those who knew too much and by that of those who knew nothing. The great rooms caused so much poetry and history to press upon him that he needed to wander apart to feel in a proper relation with them, though his doing so was not, as happened, like the gloating of some of his companions, to be compared to the movements of a dog sniffing a cupboard. It had an issue promptly enough in a direction that was not to have been calculated.

It led, in short, in the course of the October afternoon, to his closer meeting with May Bartram, whose face, a reminder, yet not quite a remembrance, as they sat, much separated, at a very long table, had begun merely by troubling him rather pleasantly. It affected him as the sequel of something of which he had lost the beginning. He knew it, and for the time quite welcomed it, as a continuation, but didn't know what it continued, which was an interest, or an amusement, the greater as he was also somehow aware—yet without a direct sign from her—that the young woman herself had not lost the thread. She had not lost it, but she wouldn't give it back to him, he saw, without some putting forth of his hand for it; and he not only saw that, but saw several things more, things odd enough in the light of the fact that at the moment some accident of grouping brought them face to face he was still merely fumbling with the idea that any contact between them in the past would have had no importance. If it had had no importance he scarcely knew why his actual impression of her should so seem to have so much; the answer to which, however, was that in such a life as they all appeared to be leading for the moment one could but take things as they came. He was satisfied, without in the least being able to say why, that this young lady might roughly have ranked in the house as a poor relation; satisfied also that she was not there on a brief visit, but was more or less a part of the establishment—almost a working, a remunerated part. Didn't she enjoy at periods a protection that she paid for by helping, among other services, to show the place and explain it, deal with the tiresome people, answer questions about the dates of the buildings, the styles of the furniture, the authorship of the pictures, the favourite haunts of the ghost? It wasn't that she looked as if you could have given her shillings—it was impossible to look less so. Yet when she finally drifted toward him, distinctly handsome, though ever so much older—older than when he had seen her before—it might have been as an effect of her guessing that he had, within the couple of hours, devoted more imagination to her than to all the others put together, and had thereby penetrated to a kind of truth that the others were too stupid for. She *was* there on harder terms than anyone; she was there as a consequence of things suffered, in one way and another, in the interval of years; and she remembered him very much as she was remembered—only a good deal better.

By the time they at last thus came to speech they were alone in one of the rooms—remarkable for a fine portrait over the chimney-place—out of which their friends had passed, and the charm of it was that even before they had spoken they had practically arranged with each other to stay behind for talk. The charm, happily, was in other things too; it was partly in there being scarce a spot at Weatherend without something to stay behind for. It was in the way the autumn day looked into the high windows as it waned; in the way the red light, breaking at the close from under a low, sombre sky, reached out in a long shaft and played over old wainscots, old tapestry, old gold, old colour. It was most of all perhaps in the way she came to him as if, since she had been turned on to deal with the simpler sort, he might, should he choose to keep the whole thing down, just take her mild attention for a part of her general business. As soon as he heard her voice, however, the gap was filled up and the missing link supplied; the slight irony he divined in her attitude lost its advantage. He almost jumped at it to get there before her. "I met you years and years ago in Rome. I remember all about it." She confessed to disappointment—she had been so sure he didn't; and to prove how well he did he began to pour forth the particular recollections that popped up as he called for them. Her face and her voice, all at his service now, worked the miracle—the impression operating like the torch of a lamplighter who touches into flame, one by one, a long row of gas jets. Marcher flattered himself that the illumination was brilliant, yet he was really still more pleased on her showing him, with amusement, that in his haste to make everything right he had got most things rather wrong. It hadn't been at Rome—it had been at Naples; and it hadn't been seven years before—it had been more nearly ten. She hadn't been either with her uncle and aunt,

but with her mother and her brother; in addition to which it was not with the Pembles that *he* had been, but with the Boyers, coming down in their company from Rome—a point on which she insisted, a little to his confusion, and as to which she had her evidence in hand. The Boyers she had known, but she didn't know the Pembles, though she had heard of them, and it was the people he was with who had made them acquainted. The incident of the thunderstorm that had raged round them with such violence as to drive them for refuge into an excavation—this incident had not occurred at the Palace of the Caesars, but at Pompeii, on an occasion when they had been present there at an important find.

He accepted her amendments, he enjoyed her corrections, though the moral of them was, she pointed out, that he *really* didn't remember the least thing about her; and he only felt it as a drawback that when all was made comfortable to the truth there didn't appear much of anything left. They lingered together still, she neglecting her office—for from the moment he was so clever she had no proper right to him—and both neglecting the house, just waiting as to see if a memory or two more wouldn't again breathe upon them. It had not taken them many minutes, after all, to put down on the table, like the cards of a pack, those that constituted their respective hands; only what came out was that the pack was unfortunately not perfect—that the past, invoked, invited, encouraged, could give them, naturally, no more than it had. It had made them meet—her at twenty, him at twenty-five; but nothing was so strange, they seemed to say to each other, as that, while so occupied, it hadn't done a little more for them. They looked at each other as with the feeling of an occasion missed; the present one would have been so much better if the other, in the far distance, in the foreign land, hadn't been so stupidly meagre. There weren't, apparently, all counted, more than a dozen little old things that had succeeded in coming to pass between them; trivialities of youth, simplicities of freshness, stupidities of ignorance, small possible germs, but too deeply buried—too deeply (didn't it seem?) to sprout after so many years. Marcher said to himself that he ought to have rendered her some service—saved her from a capsized boat in the Bay, or at least recovered her dressing-bag, filched from her cab, in the streets of Naples, by a lazzarone with a stiletto. Or it would have been nice if he could have been taken with fever, alone, at his hotel, and she could have come to look after him, to write to his people, to drive him out in convalescence. *Then* they would be in possession of the something or other that their actual show seemed to lack. It yet somehow presented itself, this show, as too good to be spoiled; so that they were reduced for a few minutes more to wondering a little helplessly why—since they seemed to know a certain number of the same people—their reunion had been so long averted. They didn't use that name for it, but their delay from minute to minute to join the others was a kind of confession that they didn't quite want it to be a failure. Their attempted supposition of reasons for their not having met but showed how little they knew of each other. There came in fact a moment when Marcher felt a positive pang. It was vain to pretend she was an old friend, for all the communities were wanting, in spite of which it was as an old friend that he saw she would have suited him. He had new ones enough—was surrounded with them, for instance, at that hour at the other house; as a new one he probably wouldn't have so much as noticed her. He would have liked to invent something, get her to make-believe with him that some passage of a romantic or critical kind *had* originally occurred. He was really almost reaching out in imagination—as against time—for something that would do, and saying to himself that if it didn't come this new incident would simply and rather awkwardly close. They would separate, and now for no second or for no third chance. They would have tried and not succeeded. Then it was, just at the turn, as he afterwards made it out to himself, that, everything else failing, she herself decided to take up the case and, as it were, save the situation. He felt as soon as she spoke that she had been consciously keeping back what she said and hoping to get on without it; a scruple in her that immensely touched him when, by the end of three or four minutes more, he was able to measure it. What she brought out, at any rate, quite cleared the air and supplied the link—the link it was such a mystery he should frivolously have managed to lose.

"You know you told me something that I've never forgotten and that again and again has made me think of you since; it was that tremendously hot day when we went to Sorrento, across the bay, for the breeze. What I allude to was what you said to me, on the way back, as we sat, under the awning of the boat, enjoying the cool. Have you forgotten?"

He had forgotten, and he was even more sur-prised than ashamed. But the great thing was that he saw it was no vulgar reminder of any "sweet" speech. The vanity of women had long memories, but she was making no claim on him of a compliment or a mistake. With another woman, a totally different one, he might have feared the recall of possibly even some imbecile "offer." So, in having to say that he had indeed forgotten, he was conscious rather of a loss than of a gain; he already saw an interest in the matter of her reference. "I try to think—but I give it up. Yet I remember the Sorrento day."

"I'm not very sure you do," May Bartram after a moment said; "and I'm not very sure I ought to want you to. It's dreadful to bring a person back, at any time, to what he was ten years before. If you've lived away from it," she smiled, "so much the better."

"Ah, if *you* haven't why should I?" he asked.

"Lived away, you mean, from what I myself was?"

"From what I was. I was of course an ass," Marcher went on; "but I would rather know from you just the sort of ass I was than—from the moment you have something in your mind—not know anything."

Still, however, she hesitated. "But if you've completely ceased to be that sort——?"

"Why, I can then just so all the more bear to know. Besides, perhaps I haven't."

"Perhaps. Yet if you haven't," she added, "I should suppose you would remember. Not indeed that *I* in the least connect with my impression the invidious name you use. If I had only thought you foolish," she explained, "the thing I speak of wouldn't so have remained with me. It was about yourself." She waited, as if it might come to him; but as, only meeting her eyes in wonder, he gave no sign, she burnt her ships. "Has it ever happened?"

Then it was that, while he continued to stare, a light broke for him and the blood slowly came to his face, which began to burn with recognition. "Do you mean I told you——?" But he faltered, lest what came to him shouldn't be right, lest he should only give himself away.

"It was something about yourself that it was natural one shouldn't forget—that is if one remembered you at all. That's why I ask you," she smiled, "if the thing you then spoke of has ever come to pass?"

Oh, then he saw, but he was lost in wonder and found himself embarrassed. This, he also saw, made her sorry for him, as if her allusion had been a mistake. It took him but a moment, however, to feel that it had not been, much as it had been a surprise. After the first little shock of it her knowledge on the contrary began, even if rather strangely, to taste sweet to him. She was the only other person in the world then who would have it, and she had had it all these years, while the fact of his having so breathed his secret had unaccountably faded from him. No wonder they couldn't have met as if nothing had happened. "I judge," he finally said, "that I know what you mean. Only I had strangely enough lost the consciousness of having taken you so far into my confidence."

"Is it because you've taken so many others as well?"

"I've taken nobody. Not a creature since then."

"So that I'm the only person who knows?"

"The only person in the world."

"Well," she quickly replied, "I myself have never spoken. I've never, never repeated of you what you told me." She looked at him so that he perfectly believed her. Their eyes met over it in such a way that he was without a doubt. "And I never will."

She spoke with an earnestness that, as if almost excessive, put him at ease about her possible derision. Somehow the whole question was a new luxury to him—that is, from the moment she was in possession. If she didn't take the ironic view she clearly took the sympathetic, and that was what he had had, in all the long time, from no one whomsoever. What he felt was that he couldn't at present have begun to tell her and yet could profit perhaps exquisitely by the accident of having done so of old. "Please don't then. We're just right as it is."

"Oh, I am," she laughed, "if you are!" To which she added: "Then you do still feel in the same way?"

It was impossible to him not to take to himself that she was really interested, and it all kept coming as a sort of revelation. He had thought of himself so long as abominably alone, and, lo, he wasn't alone a bit. He hadn't been, it appeared, for an hour—since those moments on the Sorrento boat. It was *she* who had been, he seemed to see as he looked at her—she who had been made so by the graceless fact of his lapse of fidelity. To tell her what he had told her—what had it been but to ask something of her? something that she had given, in her charity, without his having, by a remembrance, by a return of the spirit, failing another

encounter, so much as thanked her. What he had asked of her had been simply at first not to laugh at him. She had beautifully not done so for ten years, and she was not doing so now. So he had endless gratitude to make up. Only for that he must see just how he had figured to her. "What, exactly was the account I gave——?"

"Of the way you did feel? Well, it was very simple. You said you had had from your earliest time, as the deepest thing within you, the sense of being kept for something rare and strange, possibly prodigious and terrible, that was sooner or later to happen to you, that you had in your bones the foreboding and the conviction of, and that would perhaps overwhelm you."

"Do you call that very simple?" John Marcher asked.

She thought a moment. "It was perhaps because I seemed, as you spoke, to understand it."

"You do understand it?" he eagerly asked.

Again she kept her kind eyes on him. "You still have the belief?"

"Oh!" he exclaimed helplessly. There was too much to say.

"Whatever it is to be," she clearly made out, "it hasn't yet come."

He shook his head in complete surrender now. "It hasn't yet come. *Only*, you know, it isn't anything I'm to *do*, to achieve in the world, to be distinguished for. I'm not such an ass as *that*. It would be much better, no doubt, if I were."

"It's to be something you're merely to suffer?"

"Well, say to wait for—to have to meet, to face, to see suddenly break out in my life; possibly destroying all further consciousness, possibly annihilating me; possibly, on the other hand, only altering everything, striking at the root of all my world and leaving me to the consequences, however they shape themselves."

She took this in, but the light in her eyes continued for him not to be that of mockery. "Isn't what you describe perhaps but the expectation—or, at any rate, the sense of danger, familiar to so many people—of falling in love"

John Marcher thought. "Did you ask me that before?"

"No—I wasn't so free-and-easy then. But it's what strikes me now."

"Of course," he said after a moment, "it strikes you. Of course it strikes *me*. Of course what's in store for me may be no more than that. The only thing is," he went on, "that I think that if it had been that, I should by this time know."

"Do you mean because you've *been* in love?" And then as he but looked at her in silence: "You've been in love, and it hasn't meant such a cataclysm, hasn't proved the great affair?"

"Here I am, you see. It hasn't been overwhelming."

"Then it hasn't been love," said May Bartram.

"Well, I at least thought it was. I took it for that—I've taken it till now. It was agreeable, it was delightful, it was miserable," he explained. "But it wasn't strange. It wasn't what *my* affair's to be."

"You want something all to yourself—something that nobody else knows or *has* known?"

"It isn't a question of what I 'want'—God knows I don't want anything. It's only a question of the apprehension that haunts me—that *I* live with day by day."

He said this so lucidly and consistently that, visibly, it further imposed itself. If she had not been interested before she would have been interested now. "Is it a sense of coming violence?"

Evidently now too, again, he liked to talk of it. "I don't think of it as—when it does come—necessarily violent. I only think of it as natural and as of course, above all, unmistakable. I think of it simply as *the* thing. *The* thing will of itself appear natural."

"Then how will it appear strange?"

Marcher bethought himself. "It won't—to *me*."

"To whom then?"

"Well," he replied, smiling at last, "say to you."

"Oh then, I'm to be present?"

"Why, you *are* present—since you know."

"I see." She turned it over. "But I mean at the catastrophe."

At this, for a minute, their lightness gave way to their gravity; it was as if the long look they exchanged held them together. "It will only depend on yourself—if you'll watch with me."

"Are you afraid?" she asked.

"Don't leave me *now*," he went on.

"Are you afraid?" she repeated.

"Do you think me simply out of my mind?" he pursued instead of answering. "Do I merely strike you as a harmless lunatic?"

"No," said May Bartram. "I understand you. I believe you."

"You mean you feel how my obsession—poor old thing!—may correspond to some possible reality?"

"To some possible reality."

"Then you *will* watch with me?"

She hesitated, then for the third time put her question. "Are you afraid?"

"Did I tell you I was—at Naples?"

"No, you said nothing about it."

"Then I don't know. And I should *like* to know," said John Marcher. "You'll tell me yourself whether you think so. If you'll watch with me you'll see."

"Very well then." They had been moving by this time across the room, and at the door, before passing out, they paused as if for the full wind-up of their understanding. "I'll watch with you," said May Bartram.

II

The fact that she "knew"—knew and yet neither chaffed him nor betrayed him—had in a short time begun to constitute between them a sensible bond, which became more marked when, within the year that followed their afternoon at Weatherend, the opportunities for meeting multiplied. The event that thus promoted these occasions was the death of the ancient lady, her great-aunt, under whose wing, since losing her mother, she had to such an extent found shelter, and who, though but the widowed mother of the new successor to the property, had succeeded—thanks to a high tone and a high temper—in not forfeiting the supreme position at the great house. The deposition of this personage arrived but with her death, which, followed by many changes, made in particular a difference for the young woman in whom Marcher's expert attention had recognised from the first a dependent with a pride that might ache though it didn't bristle. Nothing for a long time had made him easier than the thought that the aching must have been much soothed by Miss Bartram's now finding herself able to set up a small home in London. She had acquired property, to an amount that made that luxury just possible, under her aunt's extremely complicated will, and when the whole matter began to be straightened out, which indeed took time, she let him know that the happy issue was at last in view. He had seen her again before that day, both because she had more than once accompanied the ancient lady to town and because he had paid another visit to the friends who so conveniently made of Weatherend one of the charms of their own hospitality. These friends had taken him back there; he had achieved there again with Miss Bartram some quiet detachment; and he had in London succeeded in persuading her to more than one brief absence from her aunt. They went together, on these latter occasions, to the National Gallery and the South Kensington Museum, where, among vivid reminders, they talked of Italy at large—not now attempting to recover, as at first, the taste of their youth and their ignorance. That recovery, the first day at Weatherend, had served its purpose well, had given them quite enough; so that they were, of Marcher's sense, no longer hovering about the head-waters of their stream, but had felt their boat pushed sharply off and down the current.

They were literally afloat together; for our gentleman this was marked, quite as marked as that the fortunate cause of it was just the buried treasure of her knowledge. He had with his own hands dug up this little hoard, brought to light—that is to within reach of the dim day constituted by their discretions and privacies—the object of value the hiding-place of which he had, after putting it into the ground himself, so strangely, so long forgotten. The exquisite luck of having again just stumbled on the spot made him indifferent to any other question; he would doubtless have devoted more time to the odd accident of his lapse of memory if he had not been moved to devote so much to the sweetness, the comfort, as he felt, for the future, that this accident itself had helped to keep fresh. It had never entered into his plan that anyone should "know," and mainly for the reason that it was not in him to tell anyone. That would have been impossible, since nothing but the amusement of a cold world would have waited on it. Since, however, a mysterious fate had opened his mouth in youth, in spite of him, he would count that a compensation and profit by it to the utmost. That the right person *should* know tempered the asperity of his secret more even than his shyness had permitted him to imagine; and May Bartram was clearly right, because—well, because there she was. Her knowledge simply settled it; he would have been sure enough by this time had she been wrong. There was that in his situation, no doubt, that disposed him too much to see her as a mere confidant, taking all her light for him from the fact—the fact only—of her interest in his predicament, from her mercy, sympathy, seriousness, her consent not to regard him as the funniest of the funny. Aware, in fine, that her price for him was just in her giving him this constant sense of his being admirably spared, he was careful to remember that she had, after all, also a life of her own, with things that might happen to *her*, things that in friendship one should likewise take account of.

Something fairly remarkable came to pass with him, for that matter, in this connection—something represented by a certain passage of his consciousness, in the suddenest way, from one extreme to the other.

He had thought himself, so long as nobody knew, the most disinterested person in the world, carrying his concentrated burden, his perpetual suspense, ever so quietly, holding his tongue about it, giving others no glimpse of it nor of its effect upon his life, asking of them no allowance and only making on his side all those that were asked. He had disturbed nobody with the queerness of having to know a haunted man, though he had had moments of rather special temptation on hearing people say that they were "unsettled." If they were as unsettled as he was—he who had never been settled for an hour in his life—they would know what it meant. Yet it wasn't, all the same, for him to make them, and he listened to them civilly enough. This was why he had such good—though possibly such rather colourless—manners; this was why, above all, he could regard himself, in a greedy world, as decently—as, in fact, perhaps even a little sublimely—unselfish. Our point is accordingly that he valued this character quite sufficiently to measure his present danger of letting it lapse, against which he promised himself to be much on his guard. He was quite ready, none the less, to be selfish just a little, since, surely no more charming occasion for it had come to him. "Just a little," in a word, was just as much as Miss Bartram, taking one day with another, would let him. He never would be in the least coercive, and he would keep well before him the lines on which consideration for her—the very highest—ought to proceed. He would thoroughly establish the heads under which her affairs, her requirements, her peculiarities—he went so far as to give them the latitude of that name—would come into their intercourse. All this naturally was a sign of how much he took the intercourse itself for granted. There was nothing more to be done about *that*. It simply existed; had sprung into being with her first penetrating question to him in the autumn light there at Weatherend. The real form it should have taken on the basis that stood out large was the form of their marrying. But the devil in this was that the very basis itself put marrying out of the question. His conviction, his apprehension, in short, was not a condition he could invite a woman to share; and that consequence of it was precisely what was the matter with him. Something or other lay in wait for him, amid the twists

and the turns of the months and the years, like a
crouching beast in the jungle. It signified little
whether the crouching beast were destined to slay
him or to be slain. The definite point was the inevitable spring of the creature; and the definite
lesson from that was that a man of feeling didn't
cause himself to be accompanied by a lady on a
tiger-hunt. Such was the image under which he
had ended by figuring his life.

They had at first, none the less, in the scattered
hours spent together, made no allusion to that
view of it; which was a sign he was handsomely
ready to give that he didn't expect, that he in fact
didn't care always to be talking about it. Such a
feature in one's outlook was really like a hump
on one's back. The difference it made every minute of the day existed quite independently of discussion. One discussed, of course, *like* a hunchback, for there was always, if nothing else, the
hunchback face. That remained, and she was watching him; but people watched best, as a general
thing, in silence, so that such would be predominantly the manner of their vigil. Yet he didn't
want, at the same time, to be solemn; solemn was
what he imagined he too much tended to be with
other people. The thing to be, with the one person
who knew, was easy and natural—to make the reference rather than be seeming to avoid it, to avoid
it rather than be seeming to make it, and to keep
it, in any case, familiar, facetious even, rather than
pedantic and portentous. Some such consideration
as the latter was doubtless in his mind, for instance,
when he wrote pleasantly to Miss Bartram that
perhaps the great thing he had so long felt as in
the lap of the gods was no more than this circumstance, which touched him so nearly, of her acquiring a house in London. It was the first allusion
they had yet again made, needing any other hitherto so little; but when she replied, after having
given him the news, that she was by no means
satisfied with such a trifle, as the climax to so special a suspense, she almost set him wondering if
she hadn't even a larger conception of singularity
for him than he had for himself. He was at all
events destined to become aware little by little, as
time went by, that she was all the while looking at
his life, judging it, measuring it, in the light of
the thing she knew, which grew to be at last, with
the consecration of the years, never mentioned between them save as "the real truth" about him.
That had always been his own form of reference
to it, but she adopted the form so quietly that,
looking back at the end of a period, he knew there

was no moment at which it was traceable that she
had, as he might say, got inside his condition, or
exchanged the attitude of beautifully indulging for
that of still more beautifully believing him.

It was always open to him to accuse her of seeing him but as the most harmless of maniacs, and
this, in the long run—since it covered so much
ground—was his easiest description of their friendship. He had a screw loose for her, but she liked
him in spite of it, and was practically, against the
rest of the world, his kind, wise keeper, unremu-
nerated, but fairly amused and, in the absence of
other near ties, not disreputably occupied. The rest
of the world of course thought him queer, but she,
she only, knew how, and above all why, queer;
which was precisely what enabled her to dispose
the concealing veil in the right folds. She took his
gaiety from him—since it had to pass with them for
gaiety—as she took everything else; but she certainly so far justified by her unerring touch his
finer sense of the degree to which he had ended
by convincing her. *She* at least never spoke of the
secret of his life except as "the real truth about
you," and she had in fact a wonderful way of making it seem, as such, the secret of her own life too.
That was in fine how he so constantly felt her as
allowing for him; he couldn't on the whole call it
anything else. He allowed for himself, but she, exactly, allowed still more; partly because, better
placed for a sight of the matter, she traced his unhappy perversion through portions of its course
into which he could scarce follow it. He knew how
he felt, but, besides knowing that, she knew how
he *looked* as well; he knew each of the things of
importance he was insidiously kept from doing,
but she could add up the amount they made, understand how much, with a lighter weight on his
spirit, he might have done, and thereby establish
how, clever as he was, he fell short. Above all she
was in the secret of the difference between the
forms he went through—those of his little office
under Government, those of caring for his modest
patrimony, for his library, for his garden in the
country, for the people in London whose invitations he accepted and repaid—and the detachment
that reigned beneath them and that made of all
behaviour, all that could in the least be called behaviour, a long act of dissimulation. What it had
come to was that he wore a mask painted with
the social simper, out of the eye-holes of which
there looked eyes of an expression not in the least
matching the other features. This the stupid world,
even after years, had never more than half discov-

ered. It was only May Bartram who had, and she achieved, by an art indescribable, the feat of at once—or perhaps it was only alternately—meeting the eyes from in front and mingling her own vision, as from over his shoulder, with their peep through the apertures.

So, while they grew older together, she did watch with him, and so she let this association give shape and colour to her own existence. Beneath *her* forms as well detachment had learned to sit, and behaviour had become for her, in the social sense, a false account of herself. There was but one account of her that would have been true all the while, and that she could give, directly, to nobody, least of all to John Marcher. Her whole attitude was a virtual statement, but the perception of that only seemed destined to take its place for him as one of the many things necessarily crowded out of his consciousness. If she had, moreover, like himself, to make sacrifices to their real truth, it was to be granted that her compensation might have affected her as more prompt and more natural. They had long periods, in this London time, during which, when they were together, a stranger might have listened to them without in the least pricking up his ears; on the other hand, the real truth was equally liable at any moment to rise to the surface, and the auditor would then have wondered indeed what they were talking about. They had from an early time made up their mind that society was, luckily, unintelligent, and the margin that this gave them had fairly become one of their commonplaces. Yet there were still moments when the situation turned almost fresh— usually under the effect of some expression drawn from herself. Her expressions doubtless repeated themselves, but her intervals were generous. "What saves us, you know, is that we answer so completely to so usual an appearance: that of the man and woman whose friendship has become such a daily habit, or almost, as to be at last indispensable." That, for instance, was a remark she had frequently enough had occasion to make, though she had given it at different times different developments. What we are especially concerned with is the turn it happened to take from her one afternoon when he had come to see her in honour of her birthday. This anniversary had fallen on a Sunday, at a season of thick fog and general outward gloom; but he had brought her his customary offering, having known her now long enough to have established a hundred little customs. It was one of his proofs to himself, the present he made

her on her birthday, that he had not sunk into real selfishness. It was mostly nothing more than a small trinket, but it was always fine of its kind, and he was regularly careful to pay for it more than he thought he could afford. "Our habit saves you, at least, don't you see? because it makes you, after all, for the vulgar, indistinguishable from other men. What's the most inveterate mark of men in general? Why, the capacity to spend endless time with dull women—to spend it, I won't say without being bored, but without minding that they are, without being driven off at a tangent by it; which comes to the same thing. I'm your dull woman, a part of the daily bread for which you pray at church. That covers your tracks more than anything."

"And what covers yours?" asked Marcher, whom his dull woman could mostly to this extent amuse. "I see of course what you mean by your saving me, in one way and another, so far as other people are concerned—I've seen it all along. Only, what is it that saves *you*? I often think, you know, of that."

She looked as if she sometimes thought of that too, but in rather a different way. "Where other people, you mean, are concerned?"

"Well, you're really so in with me, you know— as a sort of result of my being so in with yourself. I mean of my having such an immense regard for you, being so tremendously grateful for all you've done for me. I sometimes ask myself if it's quite fair. Fair I mean to have so involved and—since one may say it—interested you. I almost feel as if you hadn't really had time to do anything else."

"Anything else but be interested?" she asked. "Ah, what else does one ever want to be? If I've been 'watching' with you, as we long ago agreed that I was to do, watching is always in itself an absorption."

"Oh certainly," John Marcher said, "if you hadn't had your curiosity——! Only, doesn't it sometimes come to you, as time goes on, that your curiosity is not being particularly repaid?"

May Bartram had a pause. "Do you ask that, by any chance, because you feel at all that yours isn't? I mean because you have to wait so long."

Oh, he understood what she meant. "For the thing to happen that never does happen? For the beast to jump out? No, I'm just where I was about it. It isn't a matter as to which I can *choose*, I can decide for a change. It isn't one as to which there *can* be a change. It's in the lap of the gods. One's in the hands of one's law—there one is. As to the form the law will take, the way it will operate, that's its own affair."

"Yes," Miss Bartram replied; "of course one's fate is coming, of course it *has* come, in its own form and its own way, all the while. Only, you know, the form and the way in your case were to have been—well, something so exceptional and, as one may say, so particularly *your* own."

Something in this made him look at her with suspicion. "You say 'were to *have* been,' as if in your heart you had begun to doubt."

"Oh!" she vaguely protested.

"As if you believed," he went on, "that nothing will now take place."

She shook her head slowly, but rather inscrutably. "You're far from my thought."

He continued to look at her. "What then is the matter with you?"

"Well," she said after another wait, "the matter with me is simply that I'm more sure than ever my curiosity, as you call it, will be but too well repaid."

They were frankly grave now; he had got up from his seat, had turned once more about the little drawing-room to which, year after year, he brought his inevitable topic; in which he had, as he might have said, tasted their intimate community with every sauce, where every object was as familiar to him as the things of his own house and the very carpets were worn with his fitful walk very much as the desk in old counting-houses are worn by the elbows of generations of clerks. The generations of his nervous moods had been at work there, and the place was the written history of his whole middle life. Under the impression of what his friend had just said he knew himself, for some reason, more aware of these things, which made him, after a moment, stop again before her. "It is, possibly, that you've grown afraid?"

"Afraid?" He thought, as she repeated the word, that his question had made her, a little, change colour; so that, lest he should have touched on a truth, he explained very kindly, "You remember that that was what you asked *me* long ago—that first day at Weatherend."

"Oh yes, and you told me you didn't know—that I was to see for myself. We've said little about it since, even in so long a time."

"Precisely," Marcher interposed—"quite as if it were too delicate a matter for us to make free with. Quite as if we might find, on pressure, that I *am* afraid. For then," he said, "we shouldn't, should we? quite know what to do."

She had for the time no answer to this question. "There have been days when I thought you were. Only, of course," she added, "there have been days when we have thought almost anything."

"Everything. Oh!" Marcher softly groaned as with a gasp, half spent, at the face, more uncovered just then than it had been for a long while, of the imagination always with them. It had always had its incalculable moments of glaring out, quite as with the very eyes of the very Beast, and, used as he was to them, they could still draw from him the tribute of a sigh that rose from the depths of his being. All that they had thought, first and last, rolled over him; the past seemed to have been reduced to mere barren speculation. This in fact was what the place had just struck him as so full of—the simplification of everything but the state of suspense. That remained only by seeming to hang in the void surrounding it. Even his original fear, if fear it had been, had lost itself in the desert. "I judge, however," he continued, "that you see I'm not afraid now."

"What I see is, as I make it out, that you've achieved something almost unprecedented in the way of getting used to danger. Living with it so long and so closely, you've lost your sense of it; you know it's there, but you're indifferent, and you cease even, as of old, to have to whistle in the dark. Considering what the danger is," May Bartram wound up, "I'm bound to say that I don't think your attitude could well be surpassed."

John Marcher faintly smiled. "It's heroic?"

"Certainly—call it that."

He considered. "I *am*, then, a man of courage?"

"That's what you were to show me."

He still, however, wondered. "But doesn't the man of courage know what he's afraid of—or *not* afraid of? I don't know *that*, you see. I don't focus it. I can't name it. I only know I'm exposed."

"Yes, but exposed—how shall I say?—so directly. So intimately. That's surely enough."

"Enough to make you feel, then—at what we may call the end of our watch—that I'm not afraid?"

"You're not afraid. But it isn't," she said, "the end of our watch. That is it isn't the end of yours. You've everything still to see."

"Then why haven't *you?*" he asked. He had had, all along, today, the sense of her keeping something back, and he still had it. As this was his first impression of that, it made a kind of date. The case was the more marked as she didn't at first answer; which in turn made him go on. "You know something I don't." Then his voice, for that of a man of courage, trembled a little. "You know what's to happen." Her silence, with the face she showed, was almost a confession—it made him sure. "You know, and you're afraid to tell me. It's so bad that you're afraid I'll find out."

All this might be true, for she did look as if, unexpectedly to her, he had crossed some mystic line that she had secretly drawn round her. Yet she might, after all, not have worried; and the real upshot was that he himself, at all events, needn't. "You'll never find out."

III

It was all to have made, none the less, as I have said, a date; as came out in the fact that again and again, even after long intervals, other things that passed between them wore, in relation to this hour, but the character of recalls and results. Its immediate effect had been indeed rather to lighten insistence—almost to provoke a reaction; as if their topic had dropped by its own weight and as if moreover, for that matter, Marcher had been visited by one of his occasional warnings against egotism. He had kept up, he felt, and very decently on the whole, his consciousness of the importance of not being selfish, and it was true he had never sinned in that direction without promptly enough trying to press the scales the other way. He often repaired his fault, the season permitting, by inviting his friend to accompany him to the opera; and it not infrequently thus happened that, to show he didn't wish her to have but one sort of food for her mind, he was the cause of her appearing there with him a dozen nights in the month. It even happened that, seeing her home at such times, he occasionally went in with her to finish, as he called it, the evening, and, the better to make his point, sat down to the frugal but always careful little supper that awaited his pleasure. His point was made, he thought, by his not eternally insisting with her on himself; made for instance, at such hours, when it befell that, her piano at hand and each of them familiar with it, they went over passages of the opera together. It chanced to be on one of these occasions, however, that he reminded her of her not having answered a certain question he had put to her during the talk that had taken place between them on her last birthday. "What is it that saves *you?*"—saved her, he meant, from that appearance of variation from the usual human type. If he had practically escaped

remark, as she pretended, by doing, in the most important particular, what most men do—find the answer to life in patching up an alliance of a sort with a woman no better than himself—how had she escaped it, and how could the alliance, such as it was, since they must suppose it had been more or less noticed, have failed to make her rather positively talked about?

"I never said," May Bartram replied, "that it hadn't made me talked about."

"Ah well then, you're not 'saved.'"

"It has not been a question for me. If you've had your woman, I've had," she said, "my man."

"And you mean that makes you all right?"

She hesitated. "I don't know why it shouldn't make me—humanly, which is what we're speaking of—as right as it makes you."

"I see," Marcher returned. "'Humanly,' no doubt, as showing that you're living for something. Not, that is, just for me and my secret."

May Bartram smiled. "I don't pretend it exactly shows that I'm not living for you. It's my intimacy with you that's in question."

He laughed as he saw what she meant. "Yes, but since, as you say, I'm only, so far as people make out, ordinary, you're—aren't you?—no more than ordinary either. You help me to pass for a man like another. So if I *am*, as I understand you, you're not compromised. Is that it?"

She had another hesitation, but she spoke clearly enough. "That's it. It's all that concerns me—to help you to pass for a man like another."

He was careful to acknowledge the remark handsomely. "How kind, how beautiful, you are to me! How shall I ever repay you?"

She had her last grave pause, as if there might be a choice of ways. But she chose. "By going on as you are."

It was into this going on as he was that they relapsed, and really for so long a time that the day inevitably came for a further sounding of their depths. It was as if these depths, constantly bridged over by a structure that was firm enough in spite of its lightness and of its occasional oscillation in the somewhat vertiginous air, invited on occasion, in the interest of their nerves, a dropping of the plummet and a measurement of the abyss. A difference had been made moreover, once for all, by the fact that she had, all the while, not appeared to feel the need of rebutting his charge of an idea within her that she didn't dare to express, uttered just before one of the fullest of their later discussions ended. It had come up for him then that she "knew" something and that what she knew was bad—too bad to tell him. When he had spoken of it as visibly so bad that she was afraid he might find it out, her reply had left the matter too equivocal to be let alone and yet, for Marcher's special sensibility, almost too formidable again to touch. He circled about it at a distance that alternately narrowed and widened and that yet was not much affected by the consciousness in him that there was nothing she could "know," after all, any better than he did. She had no source of knowledge that he hadn't equally—except of course that she might have finer nerves. That was what women had where they were interested; they made out things, where people were concerned, that the people often couldn't have made out for themselves. Their nerves, their sensibility, their imagination, were conductors and revealers, and the beauty of May Bartram was in particular that she had given herself so to his case. He felt in these days what, oddly enough, he had never felt before, the growth of a dread of losing her by some catastrophe— some catastrophe that yet wouldn't at all be *the* catastrophe: partly because she had, almost of a sudden, begun to strike him as useful to him as never yet, and partly by reason of an appearance of uncertainty in her health, coincident and equally new. It was characteristic of the inner detachment he had hitherto so successfully cultivated and to which our whole account of him is a reference, it was characteristic that his complications, such as they were, had never yet seemed so as at this crisis to thicken about him, even to the point of making him ask himself if he were, by any chance, of a truth, within sight or sound, within touch or reach, within the immediate jurisdiction of the thing that waited.

When the day came, as come it had to, that his friend confessed to him her fear of a deep disorder in her blood, he felt somehow the shadow of a change and the chill of a shock. He immediately began to imagine aggravations and disasters, and above all to think of her peril as the direct menace for himself of personal privation. This indeed gave him one of those partial recoveries of equanimity that were agreeable to him—it showed him that what was still first in his mind was the loss she herself might suffer. "What if she should have to die before knowing, before seeing——?" It would have been brutal, in the early stages of her trouble, to put that question to her; but it had immediately sounded for him to his own concern, and the possibility was what most made him sorry for her. If she did "know," moreover, in the sense of her having had some—what should he think?—mystical, irresistible light, this would make the matter not better, but worse, inasmuch as her original adoption of his own curiosity had quite become the basis of her life. She had been living to see what would *be* to be seen, and it would be cruel to her to have to give up before the accomplishment of the vision. These reflections, as I say, refreshed his generosity; yet, make them as he might, he saw himself, with the lapse of the period, more and more disconcerted. It lapsed for him with a strange, steady sweep, and the oddest oddity was that it gave him, independently of the threat of much inconvenience, almost the only positive surprise his career, if career it could be called, had yet offered him. She kept the house as she had never done; he had to go to her to see her—she could meet him nowhere now, though there was scarce a corner of their loved old London in which she had not in the past, at one time or another, done so; and he found her always seated by her fire in the deep, old-fashioned chair she was less and less able to leave. He had been struck one day, after an absence exceeding his usual measure, with her suddenly looking much older to him than he had ever thought of her being; then he recognized that the suddenness was all on his side—he had just been suddenly struck. She looked older because inevitably, after so many years, she *was* old, or almost; which was of course true in still greater measure of her companion. If she was old, or almost, John Marcher assuredly was, and yet it was her showing of the lesson, not his own, that brought the truth home to him. His surprises began here; when once they had begun they multiplied; they came rather with a rush: it was as if, in the oddest way in the world, they had all been kept back, sown in a thick cluster, for the late afternoon of life, the time at which, for people in general, the unexpected has died out.

One of them was that he should have caught himself—for he *had* so done—*really* wondering if the great accident would take form now as nothing more than his being condemned to see this charming woman, this admirable friend, pass away from him. He had never so unreservedly qualified her as while confronted in thought with such a possibility; in spite of which there was small doubt for him that as an answer to his long riddle the mere effacement of even so fine a feature of his situation would be an abject anticlimax. It would represent, as connected with his past attitude, a drop of dignity under the shadow of which his existence could only become the most grotesque of failures. He had been far from holding it a failure—long as he had waited for the appearance that was to make it a success. He had waited for a quite other thing, not for such a one as that. The breath of his good faith came short, however, as he recognised how long he had waited, or how long, at least, his companion had. That she, at all events, might be recorded as having waited in vain—this affected him sharply, and all the more because of his at first having done little more than amuse himself with the idea. It grew more grave as the gravity of her condition grew, and the state of mind it produced in him, which he ended by watching, himself, as if it had been some definite disfigurement of his outer person, may pass for another of his surprises. This conjoined itself still with another, the really stupefying consciousness of a question that he would have allowed to shape itself had he dared. What did everything mean—what, that is, did *she* mean, she and her vain waiting and her probable death and the soundless admonition of it all—unless that, at this time of day, it was simply, it was overwhelmingly too late? He had never, at any stage of his queer consciousness, admitted the whisper of such a correction; he had never, till within these last few months, been so false to his conviction as not to hold that what was to come to him had time, whether *he* struck himself as having it or not. That at last, at last, he certainly hadn't it, to speak of, or had it but in the scantiest measure—such, soon enough, as things went with him, became the inference with which his old obsession had to reckon: and this it was not helped to do by the more and more confirmed appearance that the great vagueness casting the long shadow in which he had lived had, to attest itself, almost no margin left. Since it was in Time that he was to have met his fate, so it was in Time that this fate was to have acted; and as he waked up to the sense of no longer being young, which was exactly the sense of being stale, just as that, in turn, was the sense of being weak, he waked up to another matter beside. It all hung together; they were subject, he and the great vagueness, to an equal and indivisible law. When the possibilities themselves had, accordingly, turned stale, when the secret of the gods had grown faint, had perhaps even quite evaporated, that, and that only, was failure. It wouldn't have been failure to be bankrupt, dishonoured, pilloried, hanged; it was failure not to be anything. And so, in the dark valley into which his path had taken its unlooked-for twist, he wondered not a little as he groped. He didn't care what awful crash might overtake him, with what ignominy or what monstrosity he might yet be associated—since he wasn't, after all, too utterly old to suffer—if it would only be decently proportionate to the posture he had kept, all his life, in the promised presence of it. He had but one desire left—that he shouldn't have been "sold."

IV

Then it was that one afternoon, while the spring of the year was young and new, she met, all in her own way, his frankest betrayal of these alarms. He had gone in late to see her, but evening had not settled, and she was presented to him in that long, fresh light of waning April days which affects us often with a sadness sharper than the greyest hours of autumn. The week had been warm, the spring was supposed to have begun early, and May Bartram sat, for the first time in the year, without a fire, a fact that, to Marcher's sense, gave the scene of which she formed part a smooth and ultimate look, an air of knowing, in its immaculate order and its cold, meaningless cheer, that it would never see a fire again. Her own aspect—he could scarce have said why—intensified this note. Almost as white as wax, with the marks and signs in her face as numerous and as fine as if they had been etched by a needle, with soft white draperies relieved by a faded green scarf, the delicate tone of which had been consecrated by the years, she was the picture of a serene, exquisite, but impenetrable sphinx, whose head, or indeed all whose person, might have been powdered with silver. She was a sphinx, yet with her white petals and green fronds she might have been a lily too—only an artificial lily, wonderfully imitated and constantly kept, without dust or stain, though not exempt from a slight droop and a complexity of faint creases, under some clear glass bell. The perfection of household care, of high polish and finish, always reigned in her rooms, but they especially looked to Marcher at present as if everything had been wound up, tucked in, put away, so that she might sit with folded hands and with nothing more to do. She was "out of it," to his vision; her work was over; she communicated with him as across some gulf, or from some island of rest that she had already reached, and it made him feel strangely abandoned. Was it—or, rather, wasn't it—that if for so long she had been watching with him the answer to their question had swum into her ken and taken on its name, so that her occupation was verily gone? He had as much as charged her with this in saying to her, many months before, that she even then knew something she was keeping from him. It was a point he had never since ventured to press vaguely fearing, as he did, that it might become a difference, perhaps a disagreement, between them. He had in short, in this later time, turned nervous, which was what, in all the other years, he had never been; and the oddity was that his nervousness should have waited till he had begun to doubt, should have held off so long as he was sure. There was something, it seemed to him, that the wrong word would bring down on his head, something that would so at least put an end to his suspense. But he wanted not to speak the wrong word; that would make everything ugly. He wanted the knowledge he lacked to drop on him, if drop it could, by its own august weight. If she was to forsake him it was surely for her to take leave. This was why he didn't ask her again, directly, what she knew; but it was also why, approaching the matter from another side, he said to her in the course of his visit: "What do you regard as the very worst that, at this time of day, *can* happen to me?"

He had asked her that in the past often enough; they had, with the odd, irregular rhythm of their intensities and avoidances, exchanged ideas about it and then had seen the ideas washed away by cool intervals, washed like figures traced in seasand. It had ever been the mark of their talk that the oldest allusions in it required but a little dismissal and reaction to come out again, sounding for the hour as new. She could thus at present meet his inquiry quite freshly and patiently. "Oh yes, I've repeatedly thought, only it always seemed to me of old that I couldn't quite make up my mind. I thought of dreadful things, between which it was difficult to choose; and so must you have done."

"Rather! I feel now as if I had scarce done anything else. I appear to myself to have spent my life in thinking of nothing *but* dreadful things. A great many of them I've at different times named to you, but there were others I couldn't name."

"They were too, too dreadful?"

"Too, too dreadful—some of them."

She looked at him a minute, and there came to him as he met it an inconsequent sense that her

eyes, when one got their full clearness, were still as beautiful as they had been in youth, only beautiful with a strange, cold light—a light that somehow was a part of the effect, if it wasn't rather a part of the cause, of the pale, hard sweetness of the season and the hour. "And yet," she said at last, "there are horrors we have mentioned."

It deepened the strangeness to see her, as such a figure in such a picture, talk of "horrors," but she was to do, in a few minutes, something stranger yet—though even of this he was to take the full measure but afterwards—and the note of it was already in the air. It was, for the matter of that, one of the signs that her eyes were having again such a high flicker of their prime. He had to admit, however, what she said. "Oh yes, there were times when we did go far." He caught himself in the act of speaking as if it all were over. Well, he wished it were; and the consummation depended, for him, clearly, more and more on his companion.

But she had now a soft smile. "Oh, far——!"

It was oddly ironic. "Do you mean you're prepared to go further?"

She was frail and ancient and charming as she continued to look at him, yet it was rather as if she had lost the thread. "Do you consider that we went so far?"

"Why, I thought in the point you were just making—that we *had* looked most things in the face."

"Including each other?" She still smiled. "But you're quite right. We've had together great imaginations, often great fears; but some of them have been unspoken."

"Then the worst—we haven't faced that. I *could* face it, I believe, if I knew what you think it. I feel," he explained, "as if I had lost my power to conceive such things." And he wondered if he looked as blank as he sounded. "It's spent."

"Then why do you assume," she asked, "that mine isn't?"

"Because you've given me signs to the contrary. It isn't a question for you of conceiving, imagining, comparing. It isn't a question now of choosing." At last he came out with it. "You know something that I don't. You've shown me that before."

These last words affected her, he could see in a moment, remarkably, and she spoke with firmness. "I've shown you, my dear, nothing."

He shook his head. "You can't hide it."

"Oh, oh!" May Bartram murmured over what

she couldn't hide. It was almost a smothered groan.

"You admitted it months ago, when I spoke of it to you as of something you were afraid I would find out. Your answer was that I couldn't, that I wouldn't, and I don't pretend I have. But you had something therefore in mind, and I see now that it must have been, that it still is, the possibility that, of all possibilities, has settled itself for you as the worst. This," he went on, "is why I appeal to you. I'm only afraid of ignorance now—I'm not afraid of knowledge." And then as for a while she said nothing: "What makes me sure is that I see in your face and feel here, in this air and amid these appearances, that you're out of it. You've done. You've had your experience. You leave me to my fate."

Well, she listened, motionless and white in her chair, as if she had in fact a decision to make, so that her whole manner was a virtual confession, though still with a small, fine, inner stiffness, an imperfect surrender. "It *would* be the worst," she finally let herself say. "I mean the thing that I've never said."

It hushed him a moment. "More monstrous than all the monstrosities we've named?"

"More monstrous. Isn't that what you sufficiently express," she asked, "in calling it the worst?"

Marcher thought, "Assuredly—if you mean, as I do, something that includes all the loss and all the shame that are thinkable."

"It would if it *should* happen," said May Bartram. "What we're speaking of, remember, is only my idea."

"It's your belief," Marcher returned. "That's enough for me. I feel your beliefs are right. Therefore if, having this one, you give me no more light on it, you abandon me."

"No, no!" she repeated. "I'm with you—don't you see?—still." And as if to make it more vivid to him she rose from her chair—a movement she seldom made in these days—and showed herself, all draped and all soft, in her fairness and slimness. "I haven't forsaken you."

It was really, in its effort against weakness, a generous assurance; and had the success of the impulse not, happily, been great, it would have touched him to pain more than to pleasure. But the cold charm in her eyes had spread, as she hovered before him, to all the rest of her person, so that it was, for the minute, almost like a re-

covery of youth. He couldn't pity her for that; he could only take her as she showed—as capable still of helping him. It was as if, at the same time, her light might at any instant go out; wherefore he must make the most of it. There passed before him with intensity the three or four things he wanted most to know; but the question that came of itself to his lips really covered the others. "Then tell me if I shall consciously suffer."

She promptly shook her head. "Never!"

It confirmed the authority he imputed to her, and it produced on him an extraordinary effect. "Well, what's better than that? Do you call that the worst?"

"You think nothing is better?" she asked.

She seemed to mean something so special that he again sharply wondered, though still with the dawn of a prospect of relief. "Why not, if one doesn't *know?*" After which, as their eyes, over his question, met in a silence, the dawn deepened and something to his purpose came, prodigiously, out of her very face. His own, as he took it in, suddenly flushed to the forehead, and he gasped with the force of a perception to which, on the instant, everything fitted. The sound of his gasp filled the air; then he became articulate. "I see—if I don't suffer!"

In her own look, however, was doubt. "You see what?"

"Why, what you mean—what you've always meant."

She again shook her head. "What I mean isn't what I've always meant. It's different."

"It's something new?"

She hesitated. "Something new. It's not what you think. I see what you think."

His divination drew breath then; only her correction might be wrong. "It isn't that I *am* a donkey?" he asked between faintness and grimness. "It isn't that it's all a mistake?"

"A mistake?" she pityingly echoed. *That* possibility, for her, he saw, would be monstrous; and if she guaranteed him the immunity from pain it would accordingly not be what she had in mind. "Oh, no," she declared; "it's nothing of that sort. You've been right."

Yet he couldn't help asking himself if she weren't, thus pressed, speaking but to save him. It seemed to him he should be most lost if his history should prove all a platitude. "Are you telling me the truth, so that I sha'n't have been a bigger idiot than I can bear to know? I *haven't* lived with a vain imagination, in the most besotted illusion? I haven't waited but to see the door shut in my face?"

She shook her head again. "However the case stands *that* isn't the truth. Whatever the reality, it *is* a reality. The door isn't shut. The door's open," said May Bartram.

"Then something's to come?"

She waited once again, always with her cold, sweet eyes on him. "It's never too late." She had, with her gliding step, diminished the distance between them, and she stood nearer to him, close to him, a minute, as if still full of the unspoken. Her movement might have been for some finer emphasis of what she was at once hesitating and deciding to say. He had been standing by the chimney-piece, fireless and sparely adorned, a small, perfect old French clock and two morsels of rosy Dresden constituting all its furniture; and her hand grasped the shelf while she kept him waiting, grasped it a little as for support and encouragement. She only kept him waiting, however; that is he only waited. It had become suddenly, from her movement and attitude, beautiful and vivid to him that she had something more to give him; her wasted face delicately shone with it, and it glittered, almost as with the white lustre of silver, in her expression. She was right, incontestably, for what he saw in her face was the truth, and strangely, without consequence, while their talk of it as dreadful was still in the air, she appeared to present it as inordinately soft. This, prompting bewilderment, made him but gape the more gratefully for her revelation, so that they continued for some minutes silent, her face shining at him, her contact imponderably pressing, and his stare all kind, but all expectant. The end, none the less, was that what he had expected failed to sound. Something else took place instead, which seemed to consist at first in the mere closing of her eyes. She gave way at the same instant to a slow, fine shudder, and though he remained staring—though he stared, in fact, but the harder—she turned off and regained her chair. It was the end of what she had been intending, but it left him thinking only of that.

"Well, you don't say——?"

She had touched in her passage a bell near the chimney and had sunk back, strangely pale. "I'm afraid I'm too ill."

"Too ill to tell me?" It sprang up sharp to him, and almost to his lips, the fear that she would die

without giving him light. He checked himself in time from so expressing his question, but she answered as if she had heard the words.

"Don't you know—now?"

"'Now'—?" She had spoken as if something that had made a difference had come up within the moment. But her maid, quickly obedient to her bell, was already with them. "I know nothing." And he was afterwards to say to himself that he must have spoken with odious impatience, such an impatience as to show that, supremely disconcerted, he washed his hands of the whole question.

"Oh!" said May Bartram.

"Are you in pain?" he asked, as the woman went to her.

"No," said May Bartram.

Her maid, who had put an arm round her as if to take her to her room, fixed on him eyes that appealingly contradicted her; in spite of which, however, he showed once more his mystification. "What then has happened?"

She was once more, with her companion's help, on her feet, and, feeling withdrawal imposed on him, he had found, blankly, his hat and gloves and had reached the door. Yet he waited for her answer. "What *was* to," she said.

V

He came back the next day, but she was then unable to see him, and as it was literally the first time this had occurred in the long stretch of their acquaintance he turned away, defeated and sore, almost angry—or feeling at least that such a break in their custom was really the beginning of the end—and wandered alone with his thoughts, especially with one of them that he was unable to keep down. She was dying, and he would lose her; she was dying, and his life would end. He stopped in the park, into which he had passed, and stared before him at his recurrent doubt. Away from her the doubt pressed again; in her presence he had believed her, but as he felt his forlornness he threw himself into the explanation that, nearest at hand, had most of a miserable warmth for him and least of a cold torment. She had deceived him to save him—to put him off with something in which he should be able to rest. What could the thing that was to happen to him be, after all, but just this thing that had begun to happen? Her dying, her death, his consequent solitude—*that* was what he had figured as the beast in the jungle, that was what had been in the lap of the gods. He had had her word for it as he left her; for what else, on earth, could she have meant? It wasn't a thing of a monstrous order; not a fate rare and distinguished; not a stroke of fortune that overwhelmed and immortalised; it had only the stamp of the common doom. But poor Marcher, at this hour, judged the common doom sufficient. It would serve his turn, and even as the consummation of infinite waiting he would bend his pride to accept it. He sat down on a bench in the twilight. He hadn't been a fool. Something had *been*, as she had said, to come. Before he rose indeed it had quite struck him that the final fact really matched with the long avenue through which he had had to reach it. As sharing his suspense, and as giving herself all, giving her life, to bring it to an end, she had come with him every step of the way. He had lived by her aid, and to leave her behind would be cruelly, damnably to miss her. What could be more overwhelming than that?

Well, he was to know within the week, for though she kept him a while at bay, left him restless and wretched during a series of days on each of which he asked about her only again to have to turn away, she ended his trial by receiving him where she had always received him. Yet she had been brought out at some hazard into the presence of so many of the things that were, consciously, vainly, half their past, and there was scant service left in the gentleness of her mere desire, all too visible, to check his obsession and wind up his long trouble. That was clearly what she wanted; the one thing more, for her own peace, while she could still put out her hand. He was so affected by her state that, once seated by her chair, he was moved to let everything go; it was she herself therefore who brought him back, took up again, before she dismissed him, her last word of the other time. She showed how she wished to leave their affair in order. "I'm not sure you understood. You've nothing to wait for more. It *has* come."

Oh, how he looked at her! "Really?"

"Really."

"The thing that, as you said, *was* to?"

"The thing that we began in our youth to watch for."

Face to face with her once more he believed her; it was a claim to which he had so abjectly little to oppose. "You mean that it has come as a positive, definite occurrence, with a name and a date?"

"Positive. Definite. I don't know about the 'name,' but, oh, with a date!"

He found himself again too helplessly at sea. "But come in the night—come and passed me by?"

May Bartram had her strange, faint smile, "Oh no, it hasn't passed you by!"

"But if I haven't been aware of it, and it hadn't touched me——?"

"Ah, your not being aware of it," and she seemed to hesitate an instant to deal with this— "your not being aware of it is the strangeness *in* the strangeness. It's the wonder *of* the wonder." She spoke as with the softness almost of a sick child, yet now at last, at the end of all, with the perfect straightness of a sibyl. She visibly knew that she knew, and the effect on him was of something co-ordinate, in its high character, with the law that had ruled him. It was the true voice of the law; so on her lips would the law itself have sounded. "It *has* touched you," she went on. "It has done its office. It has made you all its own."

"So utterly without my knowing it?"

"So utterly without your knowing it." His hand, as he leaned to her, was on the arm of her chair, and, dimly smiling always now, she placed her own on it. "It's enough if *I* know it."

"Oh!" he confusedly sounded, as she herself of late so often had done.

"What I long ago said is true. You'll never know now, and I think you ought to be content. You've *had* it," said May Bartram.

"But had what?"

"Why, what was to have marked you out. The proof of your law. It has acted. I'm too glad," she then bravely added, "to have been able to see what it's *not*."

He continued to attach his eyes to her, and with the sense that it was all beyond him, and that *she* was too, he would still have sharply challenged her, had he not felt it an abuse of her weakness to do more than take devoutly what she gave him, take it as hushed as to a revelation. If he did speak, it was out of foreknowledge of his loneliness to come. "If you're glad of what it's 'not,' it might then have been worse?"

She turned her eyes away, she looked straight before her with which, after a moment: "Well, you know our fears."

He wondered. "It's something then we never feared?"

On this, slowly, she turned to him. "Did we ever dream, with all our dreams, that we should sit and talk of it thus?"

He tried for a little to make out if they had; but it was as if their dreams, numberless enough, were in solution in some thick, cold mist, in which thought lost itself. "It might have been that we couldn't talk?"

"Well"—she did her best for him—"not from this side. This, you see," she said, "is the *other* side."

"I think," poor Marcher returned, "that all sides are the same to me." Then, however, as she softly shook her head in correction: "We mightn't, as it were, have got across——?"

"To where we are—no. We're *here*"—she made her weak emphasis.

"And much good does it do us!" was her friend's frank comment.

"It does us the good it can. It does us the good that *it* isn't here. It's past. It's behind," said May Bartram. "Before——" but her voice dropped.

He had got up, not to tire her, but it was hard to combat his yearning. She after all told him nothing but that his light had failed—which he knew well enough without her. "Before——?" he blankly echoed.

"Before, you see, it was always to *come*. That kept it present."

"Oh, I don't care what comes now! Besides," Marcher added, "it seems to me I liked it better present, as you say, than I can like it absent with *your* absence."

"Oh, mine!"—and her pale hands made light of it.

"With the absence of everything." He had a dreadful sense of standing there before her for—so far as anything but this proved, this bottomless drop was concerned—the last time of their life. It rested on him with a weight he felt he could scarce bear, and this weight it apparently was that still pressed out what remained in him of speakable protest. "I believe you; but I can't begin to pretend I understand. *Nothing*, for me, is past; nothing *will* pass until I pass myself, which I pray my stars may be as soon as possible. Say, however," he added, "that I've eaten my cake, as you contend, to the last crumb—how can the thing I've never felt at all be the thing I was marked out to feel?"

She met him, perhaps, less directly, but she met him unperturbed. "You take your 'feelings' for granted. You were to suffer your fate. That was not necessarily to know it."

"How in the world—when what is such knowledge but suffering?"

She looked up at him a while, in silence. "No—you don't understand."

"I suffer," said John Marcher.

"Don't, don't!"

"How can I help at least *that?*"

"*Don't!*" May Bartram repeated.

She spoke it in a tone so special, in spite of her weakness, that he stared an instant—stared as if some light, hitherto hidden, had shimmered across his vision. Darkness again closed over it, but the gleam had already become for him an idea. "Because I haven't the right——?"

"Don't *know*—when you needn't," she mercifully urged. "You needn't—for we shouldn't."

"Shouldn't?" If he could but know what she meant!

"No—it's too much."

"Too much?" he still asked—but with a mystification that was the next moment, of a sudden, to give way. Her words, if they meant something, affected him in this light—the light also of her wasted face—as meaning *all*, and the sense of what knowledge had been for herself came over him with a rush which broke through into a question. "Is it of that, then, you're dying?"

She but watched him, gravely at first, as if to see, with this, where he was, and she might have seen something, or feared something, that moved her sympathy. "I would live for you still—if I could." Her eyes closed for a little, as if, withdrawn into herself, she were, for a last time, trying. "But I can't!" she said as she raised them again to take leave of him.

She couldn't indeed, as but too promptly and sharply appeared, and he had no vision of her after this that was anything but darkness and doom. They had parted forever in that strange talk; access to her chamber of pain, rigidly guarded, was almost wholly forbidden him; he was feeling now moreover, in the face of doctors, nurses, the two or three relatives attracted doubtless by the presumption of what she had to "leave," how few were the rights, as they were called in such cases, that he had to put forward, and how odd it might even seem that their intimacy shouldn't have given him more of them. The stupidest fourth cousin had more, even though she had been nothing in such a person's life. She had been a feature of features in *his*, for what else was it to have been so indispensable? Strange beyond saying were the ways of existence, baffling for him the anomaly of his lack, as he felt it to be, of producible claim. A woman might have been, as it were, everything to him, and it might yet present him in no connection that anyone appeared obliged to recognise. If this was the case in these closing weeks it was the case more sharply on the occasion of the last offices rendered, in the great grey London cemetery, to what had been mortal, to what had been precious, in his friend. The concourse at her grave was not numerous, but he saw himself treated as scarce more nearly concerned with it than if there had been a thousand others. He was in short from this moment face to face with the fact that he was to profit extraordinarily little by the interest May Bartram had taken in him. He couldn't quite have said what he expected, but he had somehow not expected this approach to a double privation. Not only had her interest failed him, but he seemed to feel himself unattended—and for a reason he couldn't sound—by the distinction, the dignity, the propriety, if nothing else, of the man markedly bereaved. It was as if, in the view of society, he had not *been markedly* bereaved, as if there still failed some sign or proof of it, and as if, none the less, his character could never be affirmed, nor the deficiency ever made up. There were moments, as the weeks went by, when he would have liked, by some almost aggressive act, to take his stand on the intimacy of his loss, in order that it *might* be questioned and his retort, to the relief of his spirit, so recorded; but the moments of an irritation more helpless followed fast on these, the moments during which, turning things over with a good conscience but with a bare horizon, he found himself wondering if he oughtn't to have begun, so to speak, further back.

He found himself wondering indeed at many things, and this last speculation had others to keep it company. What could he have done, after all, in her lifetime, without giving them both, as it were, away? He couldn't have made it known she was watching him, for that would have published the superstition of the Beast. This was what closed his mouth now—now that the Jungle had been threshed to vacancy and that the Beast had stolen away. It sounded too foolish and too flat; the difference for him in this particular, the extinction in his life of the element of suspense, was such in fact as to surprise him. He could scarce have said what the effect resembled; the abrupt cessation, the positive prohibition, of music perhaps, more than anything else, in some place all adjusted and all accustomed to sonority and to attention. If he could at any rate have conceived lifting the veil from his image at some moment of the past (what had he done, after all, if not lift it to *her*?), so to do this to-day, to talk to people at large of the jungle cleared and confide to them that he now felt it as safe, would have been not only to see them listen as to a goodwife's tale, but really to hear himself tell one. What it presently came to in truth was that poor Marcher waded through his beaten grass, where no life stirred, where no breath sounded, where no evil eye seemed to gleam from a possible lair, very much as if vaguely looking for the Beast, and still more as if missing it. He walked about in an existence that had grown strangely more spacious, and, stopping fitfully in places where the undergrowth of life struck him as closer, asked himself yearningly, wondered secretly and sorely, if it would have lurked here or there. It would have at all events *sprung*; what was at least complete was his belief in the truth itself of the assurance given him. The change from his old sense to his new was absolute and final: what was to happen *had* so absolutely and finally happened that he was as little able to know a fear for his future as to know a hope; so absent in short was any question of anything still to come. He was to live entirely with the other question, that of his unidentified past, that of his having to see his fortune impenetrably muffled and masked.

The torment of this vision became then his occupation; he couldn't perhaps have consented to live but for the possibility of guessing. She had told him, his friend, not to guess; she had forbidden him, so far as he might, to know, and she had even in a sort denied the power in him to learn: which were so many things, precisely, to deprive him of rest. It wasn't that he wanted, he argued for fairness, that anything that had happened to him should happen over again; it was only that he shouldn't, as an anticlimax, have been taken sleeping so sound as not to be able to win back by an effort of thought the lost stuff of consciousness. He declared to himself at moments that he would either win it back or have done with consciousness for ever; he made this idea his one motive, in fine, made it so much his passion that none other, to compare with it, seemed ever to have touched him. The lost stuff of consciousness became thus for him as a strayed or stolen child to an unappeasable father; he hunted it up and down very much as if he were knocking at doors and inquiring of the police. This was the spirit in which, inevitably, he set himself to travel; he started on a journey that was to be as long as he could make it; it danced before him that, as the other side of the globe couldn't possibly have less to say to him, it might, by a possibility of suggestion, have more. Before he quitted London, however, he made a pilgrimage to May Bartram's grave, took his way to it through the endless avenues of the grim suburban necropolis, sought it out in the wilderness of tombs, and, though he had come but for the renewal of the act of farewell, found himself, when he had at last stood by it, beguiled into long intensities. He stood for an hour, powerless to turn away and yet powerless to penetrate the darkness of death; fixing with his eyes her inscribed name and date, beating his forehead against the fact of the secret they kept, drawing his breath, while he waited as if, in pity of him, some sense would rise from the stones. He kneeled on the stones, however, in vain; they kept what they concealed; and if the face of the tomb did become a face for him it was because her two names were like a pair of eyes that didn't know him. He gave them a lost long look, but no palest light broke.

VI

He stayed away, after this, for a year; he visited the depths of Asia, spending himself on scenes of romantic interest, of superlative sanctity; but what was present to him everywhere was that for a man who had known what *he* had known the world was vulgar and vain. The state of mind in which he had lived for so many years shone out to him, in reflection, as a light that coloured and refined, a light beside which the glow of the East was garish, cheap and thin. The terrible truth was that he had lost—with everything else—a distinction as well; the things he saw couldn't help being common when he had become common to look at them. He was simply now one of them himself—he was in the dust, without a peg for the sense of difference; and there were hours when, before the temples of gods and the sepulchres of kings, his spirit turned, for nobleness of association, to the barely discriminated slab in the London suburb. That had become for him, and more intensely with time and distance, his one witness of a past glory. It was all that was left to him for proof or pride, yet the past glories of Pharaohs were nothing to him as he thought of it. Small wonder then that he came back to it on the morrow of his return. He was drawn there this time as irresistibly as the other, yet with a confidence, almost, that was

doubtless the effect of the many months that had elasped. He had lived, in spite of himself, into his change of feeling, and in wandering over the earth had wondered, as might be said, from the circumference to the centre of his desert. He had settled to his safety and accepted perforce his extinction; figuring to himself, with some colour, in the likeness of certain little old men he remembered to have seen, of whom, all meagre and wizened as they might look, it was related that they had in their time fought twenty duels or been loved by ten princesses. They indeed had been wondrous for others, while he was but wondrous for himself; which, however, was exactly the cause of his haste to renew the wonder by getting back, as he might put it, into his own presence. That had quickened his steps and checked his delay. If his visit was prompt it was because he had been separated so long from the part of himself that alone he now valued.

It is accordingly not false to say that he reached his goal with a certain elation and stood there again with a certain assurance. The creature beneath the sod *knew* of his rare experience, so that, strangely now, the place had lost for him its mere blankness of expression. It met him in mildness—not, as before, in mockery; it wore for him the air of conscious greeting that we find, after absence, in things that have closely belonged to us and which seem to confess of themselves to the connection. The plot of ground, the graven tablet, the tended flowers affected him so as belonging to him that he quite felt for the hour like a contented landlord reviewing a piece of property. Whatever had happened—well, had happened. He had not come back this time with the vanity of that question, his former worrying, "What, *what?*" now practically so spent. Yet he would, none the less, never again so cut himself off from the spot; he would come back to it every month, for if he did nothing else by its aid he at least held up his head. It thus grew for him, in the oddest way, a positive resource; he carried out his idea of periodical returns, which took their place at last among the most inveterate of his habits. What it all amounted to, oddly enough, was that, in his now so simplified world, this garden of death gave him the few square feet of earth on which he could still most live. It was as if, being nothing anywhere else for anyone, nothing even for himself, he were just everything here, and if not for a crowd of witnesses, or indeed for any witness but John Marcher, then by clear right of the register that he could scan like an open page. The open page was the tomb of his friend, and *there* were the facts of the past, there the truth of his life, there the backward reaches in which he could lose himself. He did this, from time to time, with such effect that he seemed to wonder through the old years with his hand in the arm of a companion who was, in the most extraordinary manner, his other, his younger self; and to wander, which was more extraordinary yet, round and round a third presence—not wandering she, but stationary, still, whose eyes, turning with his revolution, never ceased to follow him, and whose seat was his point, so to speak, of orientation. Thus in short he settled to live—feeding only on the sense that he once *had* lived, and dependent on it not only for a support but for an identity.

It sufficed him, in its way, for months, and the year elapsed; it would doubtless even have carried him further but for an accident, superficially slight, which moved him, in a quite other direction, with a force beyond any of his impressions of Egypt or of India. It was a thing of the merest chance—the turn, as he afterwards felt, of a hair, though he was indeed to live to believe that if light hadn't come to him in this particular fashion it would still have come in another. He was to live to believe this, I say, though he was not to live, I may not less definitely mention, to do much else. We allow him at any rate the benefit of the conviction, struggling up for him at the end, that, whatever might have happened or not happened, he would have come round of himself to the light. The incident of an autumn day had put the match to the train laid from of old by his misery. With the light before him he knew that even of late his ache had only been smothered. It was strangely drugged, but it throbbed; at the touch it began to bleed. And the touch, in the event, was the face of a fellow-mortal. This face, one grey afternoon when the leaves were thick in the alleys, looked into Marcher's own, at the cemetery, with an expression like the cut of a blade. He felt it, that is, so deep down that he winced at the steady thrust. The person who so mutely assaulted him was a figure he had noticed, on reaching his own goal, absorbed by a grave a short distance away, a grave apparently fresh, so that the emotion of the visitor would probably match it for frankness. This fact alone forbade further attention, though during the time he stayed he remained vaguely conscious of his neighbour, a middle-aged man apparently, in mourning, whose bowed back, among the clustered monuments and mortuary yews, was constantly presented. Marcher's theory that these were elements in contact with which he himself revived, had suffered, on this occasion, it may be granted, a sensible though inscrutable check. The autumn day was dire for him as none had recently been, and he rested with a heaviness he had not yet known on the low stone table that bore May Bartram's name. He rested without power to move, as if some spring in him, some spell vouchsafed, had suddenly been broken forever. If he could have done that moment as he wanted he would simply have stretched himself on the slab that was already to take him, treating it as a place prepared to receive his last sleep. What in all the wide world had he now to keep awake for? He stared before him with the question, and it was then that, as one of the cemetery walks passed near him, he caught the shock of the face.

His neighbour at the other grave had withdrawn, as he himself, with force in him to move, would have done by now, and was advancing along the path on his way to one of the gates. This brought him near, and his pace was slow, so that—and all the more as there was a kind of hunger in his look—the two men were for a minute directly confronted. Marcher felt him on the spot as one of the deeply stricken—a perception so sharp that nothing else in the picture lived for it, neither his dress, his age, nor his presumable character and class; nothing lived but the deep ravage of the features that he showed. He *showed* them—that was the point; he was moved, as he passed, by some impulse that was either a signal for sympathy or, more possibly, a challenge to another sorrow. He might already have been aware of our friend, might, at some previous hour, have noticed in him the smooth habit of the scene, with which the state of his own senses so scantly consorted, and might thereby have been stirred as by a kind of overt discord. What Marcher was at all events conscious of was, in the first place, that the image of scarred passion presented to him was conscious too—of something that profaned the air; and, in the second, that, roused, startled, shocked, he was yet the next moment looking after it, as it went, with envy. The most extraordinary thing that had happened to him—though he had given that name to other matters as well—took place, after his immediate vague stare, as a consequence of this impression. The stranger passed, but the raw glare of his grief remained, making our friend wonder in pity what wrong, what wound it expressed, what injury not to be healed. What had the man *had* to make him, by the loss of it, so bleed and yet live?

Something—and this reached him with a pang—that *he*, John Marcher, hadn't; the proof of which was precisely John Marcher's arid end. No passion had ever touched him, for this was what passion meant; he had survived and maundered and pined, but where had been *his* deep ravage? The extraordinary thing we speak of was the sudden rush of the result of this question. The sight that had just met his eyes named to him, as in letters of quick flame, something he had utterly, insanely missed, and what he had missed made these things a train of fire, made them mark themselves in an anguish of inward throbs. He had seen *outside* of his life, not learned it within, the way a woman was mourned when she had been loved for herself; such was the force of his conviction of the meaning of the stranger's face, which still flared for him like a smoky torch. It had not come to him, the knowledge, on the wings of experience; it had brushed him, jostled him, upset him, with the disrespect of chance, the insolence of an accident. Now that the illumination had begun, however, it blazed to the zenith, and what he presently stood there gazing at was the sounded void of his life. He gazed, he drew breath, in pain; he turned in his dismay, and, turning, he had before him in sharper incision than ever the open page of his story. The name on the table smote him as the passage of his neighbour had done, and what it said to him, full in the face, was that *she* was what he had missed. This was the awful thought, the answer to all the past, the vision at the dread clearness of which he turned as cold as the stone beneath him. Everything fell together, confessed, explained, overwhelmed; leaving him most of all stupefied at the blindness he had cherished. The fate he had been marked for he had met with a vengeance—he had emptied the cup to the lees; he had been the man of his time, *the* man, to whom nothing on earth was to have happened. That was the rare stroke—that was his visitation. So he saw it, as we say, in pale horror, while the pieces fitted and fitted. So *she* had seen it, while he didn't, and so she served at this hour to drive

the truth home. It was the truth, vivid and monstrous, that all the while he had waited the wait was itself his portion. This the companion of his vigil had at a given moment perceived, and she had then offered him the chance to baffle his doom. One's doom, however, was never baffled, and on the day she had told him that his own had come down she had seen him but stupidly stare at the escape she offered him.

The escape would have been to love her; then, *then* he would have lived. *She* had lived—who could say now with what passion?—since she had loved him for himself; whereas he had never thought of her (ah, how it hugely glared at him!) but in the chill of his egotism and the light of her use. Her spoken words came back to him, and the chain stretched and stretched. The beast had lurked indeed, and the beast, at its hour, had sprung; it had sprung in that twilight of the cold April when, pale, ill, wasted, but all beautiful, and perhaps even then recoverable, she had risen from her chair to stand before him and let him imaginably guess. It had sprung as he didn't guess; it had sprung as she hopelessly turned from him, and the mark, by the time he left her, had fallen where it *was* to fall. He had justified his fear and achieved his fate; he had failed, with the last exactitude, of all he was to fail of; and a moan now rose to his lips as he remembered she had prayed he mightn't know. This horror of waking—*this* was knowledge, knowledge under the breath of which the very tears in his eyes seemed to freeze. Through them, none the less, he tried to fix it and hold it; he kept it there before him so that he might feel the pain. That at least, belated and bitter, had something of the taste of life. But the bitterness suddenly sickened him, and it was as if, horribly, he saw, in the truth, in the cruelty of his image, what had been appointed and done. He saw the Jungle of his life and saw the lurking Beast; then, while he looked, perceived it, as by a stir of the air, rise, huge and hideous, for the leap that was to settle him. His eye darkened—it was close and, instinctively turning, in his hallucination, to avoid it, he flung himself, on his face, on the tomb.

The Jolly Corner (1909)

Along with *The Turn of the Screw*, "The Jolly Corner" is probably the best of James's ghost stories—of that genre to which James, like many another Victorian writer, was so addicted and in which (like Edith Wharton) he so excelled. James enjoyed the genre because, as he said, "the fairy-tale side of life" always tugged at his sensibility, and "the 'ghost-story' has ever been for me the most possible form of the fairy-tale."

Spencer Brydon's motive—as he returns to America after many years abroad to inspect his property on a "jolly corner" in New York—reflects James's self-inquiry when he came back to this country a few years before, for the first time in two decades. What, James asked himself, might he have become if he had remained in America and passed his long middle years amid the burgeoning skyscrapers and the (for James) ugly and degrading changes New York had undergone? Searching out the might-have-been, whatever its form, was also a way of searching out his inmost self.

The central scene, in which Brydon stalks and is stalked in turn by his ghostly alter ego, has the quality of horror in slow motion; and the confrontation, near dawn and just inside the front door of the house, is wonderfully shocking. But there is a mystery within the general ghostliness, or at least a large ambiguity, as most readers now feel also with *The Turn of the Screw*.

Are we to understand that Brydon really does perceive an apparition—something that is, as James might say, in all actuality intensely there, with its ravaged face and mutilated hand? Or has the very force of what Brydon himself calls his "morbid obsession" conjured up something that is no more than a hallucination, a projection of his most disturbed feelings about himself? We notice that, when Brydon enters the house on the fateful evening, he has the sense that it is like "some great glass bowl . . . set delicately humming by the play of a moist finger around the edge."

The concave crystal held, as it were, this mystical other world, and the indescribably fine murmur of its rim was the sigh there, the scarce audible pathetical wail to his strained ear, of all the old baffled foresworn possibilities. What he did therefore by this appeal of his hushed presence was to wake them into such measure of ghostly life as they might still enjoy.

Perhaps the testimony of the nice Alice Staverton—that she too had seen the alter ego in a dream and was prepared to like him—should persuade us that the apparition was a genuine one. Or perhaps it is the special quality of James's fairy-tale ghost stories that these "realistic" questions are quite beside the point.

For James's impression of the New York City of these years, see the selection from *The American Scene* later in this section.

I

"Every one asks me what I 'think' of everything," said Spencer Brydon; "and I make answer as I can —begging or dodging the question, putting them off with any nonsense. It wouldn't matter to any of them really," he went on, "for, even were it possible to meet in that stand-and-deliver way so silly a demand on so big a subject, my 'thoughts' would still be almost altogether about something that concerns only myself." He was talking to Miss Staverton, with whom for a couple of months now he had availed himself of every possible occasion to talk; this disposition and this resource, this comfort and support, as the situation in fact presented itself, having promptly enough taken the first place in the considerable array of rather unattenuated surprises attending his so strangely belated return to America. Everything was somehow a surprise; and that might be natural when one had so long and so consistently neglected everything, taken pains to give surprises so much margin for play. He had given them more than thirty years—thirty-three, to be exact; and they now seemed to him to have organised their performance quite on the scale of that licence. He had been twenty-three on leaving New York—he was fifty-six today: unless indeed he were to reckon as he had sometimes, since his repatriation, found himself feeling; in which case he would have lived longer than is often allotted to man. It would have taken a century, he repeatedly said to himself, and said also to Alice Staverton, it would have taken a longer absence and a more averted mind than those even of which he had been guilty, to pile up the differences, the newnesses, the queernesses, above all the bignesses, for the better or the worse, that at present assaulted his vision wherever he looked.

The great fact all the while however had been the incalculability; since he *had* supposed himself, from decade to decade, to be allowing, and in the most liberal and intelligent manner, for brilliancy of change. He actually saw that he had allowed for nothing; he missed what he would have been sure of finding, he found what he would never have imagined. Proportions and values were upside-down; the ugly things he had expected, the ugly things of his far-away youth, when he had too promptly waked up to a sense of the ugly—these uncanny phenomena placed him rather, as it happened, under the charm; whereas the "swagger" things, the modern, the monstrous, the famous things, those he had more particularly, like thousands of ingenuous enquirers every year, come over to see, were exactly his sources of dismay. They were as so many set traps for displeasure, above all for reaction, of which his restless tread was constantly pressing the spring. It was interesting, doubtless, the whole show, but it would have been too disconcerting hadn't a certain finer truth saved the situation. He had distinctly not, in this steadier light, come over *all* for the monstrosities; he had come, not only in the last analysis but quite on the face of the act, under an impulse with which they had nothing to do. He had come—putting the thing pompously—to look at his "property," which he had thus for a third of a century not been within four thousand miles of; or, expressing it less sordidly, he had yielded to the humour of seeing again his house on the jolly corner, as he usually, and quite fondly, described it—the one in which he had first seen the light, in which various members of his family had lived and had died, in which the holidays of his over-schooled boyhood had been passed and the few social flowers of his chilled adolescence gathered, and which, alienated then for so long a period, had, through the successive deaths of his two brothers and the termination of old arrangements, come wholly into his hands. He was the owner of another, not quite so "good"—the jolly corner having been, from far back, superlatively extended and consecrated; and the value of the pair represented his main capital, with an income consisting, in these later years, of their respective rents which (thanks precisely to their original excellent type) had never been depressingly low. He could live in "Europe," as he had been in the habit of living, on the product of these flourishing New York leases, and all the better since, that of the second structure, the mere number in its long row, having within a twelve-month fallen in, renovation at a high advance had proved beautifully possible.

These were items of property indeed, but he had found himself since his arrival distinguishing more than ever between them. The house within the street, two bristling blocks westward, was already in course of reconstruction as a tall mass of flats; he had acceded, some time before, to overtures for this conversion—in which, now that it was going forward, it had been not the least of his astonishments to find himself able, on the spot, and though without a previous ounce of such experience, to participate with a certain intelligence, almost with a certain authority. He had lived his life with his back so turned to such concerns and his face addressed to those of so different an order that he scarce knew what to make of this lively stir, in a compartment of his mind never yet penetrated, of a capacity for business and a sense for construction. These virtues, so common all round him now, had been dormant in his own organism—where it might be said of them perhaps that they had slept the sleep of the just. At present, in the splendid autumn weather—the autumn at least was a pure boon in the terrible place—he loafed about his "work" undeterred, secretly agitated; not in the least "minding" that the whole proposition, as they said, was vulgar and sordid, and ready to climb ladders, to walk the plank, to handle materials and look wise about them, to ask questions, in fine, and challenge explanations and really "go into" figures.

It amused, it verily quite charmed him; and, by the same stroke, it amused, and even more, Alice Staverton, though perhaps charming her perceptibly less. She wasn't however going to be better off for it, as *he* was—and so astonishingly much: nothing was now likely, he knew, ever to make her better off than she found herself, in the afternoon of life, as the delicately frugal possessor and tenant of the small house in Irving Place to which she had subtly managed to cling through her almost unbroken New York career. If he knew the way to it now better than to any other address among the dreadful multiplied numberings which seemed to him to reduce the whole place to some vast ledger-page, overgrown, fantastic, of ruled and crisscrossed lines and figures—if he had formed, for his consolation, that habit, it was really not a little because of the charm of his having encountered and recognised, in the vast wilderness of the wholesale, breaking through the mere gross generalisation of wealth and force and success, a small still scene where items and shades, all delicate things, kept the sharpness of the notes of a high voice perfectly trained, and where economy hung about like the scent of a garden. His old friend lived with one maid and herself dusted her relics and trimmed her lamps and polished her silver; she stood off, in the awful modern crush, when she could, but she sallied forth and did battle when the challenge was really to "spirit," the spirit she after all confessed to, proudly and a little shyly, as to that of the better time, that of *their* common, their quite far-away and antediluvian social period and order. She made use of the street-cars when need be, the terrible things that people scrambled for as the panic-stricken at sea scramble for the boats; she affronted, inscrutably, under stress, all the public concussions and ordeals; and yet, with that slim mystifying grace of her appearance, which defied you to say if she were a fair young woman who looked older through trouble, or a fine smooth older one who looked young through successful indifference; with her precious reference, above all, to memories and histories into which he could enter, she was as exquisite for him as some pale pressed flower (a rarity to begin with), and, failing other sweetnesses, she was a sufficient reward of his effort. They had communities of knowledge, "their" knowledge (this discriminating possessive was always on her lips) of presences of the other age, presences all over laid, in his case, by the experience of a man and the freedom of a wanderer, overlaid by pleasure, by infidelity, by passages of life that were strange and dim to her, just by "Europe" in short, but still unobscured, still exposed and cherished, under that pious visitation of the spirit from which she had never been diverted.

She had come with him one day to see how his "apartment-house" was rising; he had helped her over gaps and explained to her plans, and while they were there had happened to have, before her, a brief but lively discussion with the man in charge, the representative of the building-firm that had undertaken his work. He had found himself quite "standing-up" to this personage over a failure on the latter's part to observe some detail of one of their noted conditions, and had so lucidly urged his case that, besides ever so prettily flushing, at the time, for sympathy in his triumph, she had afterwards said to him (though to a slightly greater effect of irony) that he had clearly for too many years neglected a real gift. If he had but stayed at home he would have anticipated the inventor of the sky-scraper. If he had but stayed at home he

would have discovered his genius in time really to start some new variety of awful architectural hare and run it till it burrowed in a gold-mine. He was to remember these words, while the weeks elapsed, for the small silver ring they had sounded over the queerest and deepest of his own lately most disguised and most muffled vibrations.

It had begun to be present to him after the first fortnight, it had broken out with the oddest abruptness, this particular wanton wonderment: it had met him there—and this was the image under which he himself judged the matter, or at least, not a little, thrilled and flushed with it—very much as he might have been met by some strange figure, some unexpected occupant, at a turn of one of the dim passages of an empty house. The quaint analogy quite hauntingly remained with him, when he didn't indeed rather improve it by a still intenser form: that of his opening a door behind which he would have made sure of finding nothing, a door into a room shuttered and void, and yet so coming, with a great suppressed start, on some quite erect confronting presence, something planted in the middle of the place and facing him through the dusk. After that visit to the house in construction he walked with his companion to see the other and always so much the better one, which in the eastward direction formed one of the corners, the "jolly" one precisely, of the street now so generally dishonoured and disfigured in its westward reaches, and of the comparatively conservative Avenue. The Avenue still had pretensions, as Miss Staverton said, to decency; the old people had mostly gone, the old names were unknown, and here and there an old association seemed to stray, all vaguely, like some very aged person, out too late, whom you might meet and feel the impulse to watch or follow, in kindness, for safe restoration to shelter.

They went in together, our friends; he admitted himself with his key, as he kept no one there, he explained, preferring, for his reasons, to leave the place empty, under a simple arrangement with a good woman living in the neighbourhood and who came for a daily hour to open windows and dust and sweep. Spencer Brydon had his reasons and was growingly aware of them; they seemed to him better each time he was there, though he didn't name them all to his companion, any more than he told her as yet how often, how quite absurdly often, he himself came. He only let her see for the present, while they walked through the great blank rooms, that absolute vacancy reigned and that, from top to bottom, there was nothing but Mrs. Muldoon's broomstick, in a corner, to tempt the burglar. Mrs. Muldoon was then on the premises, and she loquaciously attended the visitors, preceding them from room to room and pushing back shutters and throwing up sashes—all to show them, as she remarked, how little there was to see. There was little indeed to see in the great gaunt shell where the main dispositions and the general apportionment of space, the style of an age of ampler allowances, had nevertheless for its master their honest pleading message, affecting him as some good old servant's, some lifelong retainer's appeal for a character, or even for a retiring-pension; yet it was also a remark of Mrs. Muldoon's that, glad as she was to oblige him by her noonday round, there was a request she greatly hoped he would never make of her. If he should wish her for any reason to come in after dark she would just tell him, if he "plased," that he must ask it of somebody else.

The fact that there was nothing to see didn't militate for the worthy woman against what one *might* see, and she put it frankly to Miss Staverton that no lady could be expected to like, could she? "craping up to thim top storeys in the ayvil hours." The gas and the electric light were off the house, and she fairly evoked a gruesome vision of her march through the great grey rooms—so many of them as there were too!—with her glimmering taper. Miss Staverton met her honest glare with a smile and the profession that she herself certainly would recoil from such an adventure. Spencer Brydon meanwhile held his peace—for the moment; the question of the "evil" hours in his old home had already become too grave for him. He had begun some time since to "crape," and he knew just why a packet of candles addressed to that pursuit had been stowed by his own hand, three weeks before, at the back of a drawer of the fine old sideboard that occupied, as a "fixture," the deep recess in the dining-room. Just now he laughed at his companions—quickly however changing the subject; for the reason that, in the first place, his laugh struck him even at that moment as starting the odd echo, the conscious human resonance (he scarce knew how to qualify it) that sounds made while he was there alone sent back to his ear or his fancy; and that, in the second, he imagined Alice Staverton for the instant on the point of asking him, with a divination, if he ever so prowled.

There were divinations he was unprepared for, and he had at all events averted enquiry by the time Mrs. Muldoon had left them, passing on to other parts.

There was happily enough to say, on so consecrated a spot, that could be said freely and fairly; so that a whole train of declarations was precipitated by his friend's having herself broken out, after a yearning look round: "But I hope you don't mean they want you to pull *this* to pieces!" His answer came, promptly, with his re-awakened wrath: it was of course exactly what they wanted, and what they were "at" him for, daily, with the iteration of people who couldn't for their life understand a man's liability to decent feelings. He had found the place, just as it stood and beyond what he could express, an interest and a joy. There were values other than the beastly rent-values, and in short, in short—! But it was thus Miss Staverton took him up. "In short you're to make so good a thing of your sky-scraper that, living in luxury on *those* ill-gotten gains, you can afford for a while to be sentimental here!" Her smile had for him, with the words, the particular mild irony with which he found half her talk suffused; an irony without bitterness and that came, exactly, from her having so much imagination—not, like the cheap sarcasms with which one heard most people, about the world of "society," bid for the reputation of cleverness, from nobody's really having any. It was agreeable to him at this very moment to be sure that when he had answered, after a brief demur, "Well yes: so precisely, you may put it!" her imagination would still do him justice. He explained that even if never a dollar were to come to him from the other house he would doubtless cherish this one; and he dwelt, further, while they lingered and wandered, on the fact of the stupefaction he was already exciting, the positive mystification he felt himself create.

He spoke of the value of all he read into it, into the mere sight of the walls, mere shapes of the rooms, mere sound of the floors, mere feel, in his hand, of the old silver-plated knobs of the several mahogany doors, which suggested the pressure of the palms of the dead; the seventy years of the past in fine that these things represented, the annals of nearly three generations, counting his grandfather's, the one that had ended there, and the impalpable ashes of his long-extinct youth, afloat in the very air like microscopic motes. She listened to everything; she was a woman who answered intimately but who utterly didn't chatter. She scattered abroad therefore no cloud of words; she could assent, she could agree, above all she could encourage, without doing that. Only at the last she went a little further than he had done himself. "And then how do you know? You may still, after all, want to live here." It rather indeed pulled him up, for it wasn't what he had been thinking, at least in her sense of the words. "You mean I may decide to stay on for the sake of it?"

"Well, *with* such a home—!" But, quite beautifully, she had too much tact to dot so monstrous an *i*, and it was precisely an illustration of the way she didn't rattle. How could any one—of any wit—insist on any one else's "wanting" to live in New York?

"Oh," he said, "I *might* have lived here (since I had my opportunity early in life); I might have put in here all these years. Then everything would have been different enough—and, I dare say, 'funny' enough. But that's another matter. And then the beauty of it—I mean of my perversity, of my refusal to agree to a 'deal'—is just in the total absence of a reason. Don't you see that if I had a reason about the matter at all it would *have* to be the other way, and would then be inevitably a reason of dollars? There are no reasons here *but* of dollars. Let us therefore have none whatever—not the ghost of one."

They were back in the hall then for departure, but from where they stood the vista was large, through an open door, into the great square main saloon, with its almost antique felicity of brave spaces between windows. Her eyes came back from that reach and met his own a moment. "Are you very sure the 'ghost' of one doesn't, much rather, serve—?"

He had a positive sense of turning pale. But it was as near as they were then to come. For he made answer, he believed, between a glare and a grin: "Oh ghosts—of course the place must swarm with them! I should be ashamed of it if it didn't. Poor Mrs. Muldoon's right, and it's why I haven't asked her to do more than look in."

Miss Staverton's gaze again lost itself, and things she didn't utter, it was clear, came and went in her mind. She might even for the minute, off there in the fine room, have imagined some element dimly gathering. Simplified like the death-mask of a handsome face, it perhaps produced for her just then an effect akin to the stir of an expression in the "set" commemorative plaster. Yet whatever her impression may have been she produced in-

stead a vague platitude. "Well, if it were only furnished and lived in—!"

She appeared to imply that in case of its being still furnished he might have been a little less opposed to the idea of a return. But she passed straight into the vestibule, as if to leave her words behind her, and the next moment he had opened the house-door and was standing with her on the steps. He closed the door and, while he re-pocketed his key, looking up and down, they took in the comparatively harsh actuality of the Avenue, which reminded him of the assault of the outer light of the Desert on the traveller emerging from an Egyptian tomb. But he risked before they stepped into the street his gathered answer to her speech. "For me it *is* lived in. For me it *is* furnished." At which it was easy for her to sigh "Ah yes—!" all vaguely and discreetly; since his parents and his favourite sister, to say nothing of other kin, in numbers, had run their course and met their end there. That represented, within the walls, ineffaceable life.

It was a few days after this that, during an hour passed with her again, he had expressed his impatience of the too flattering curiosity—among the people he met—about his appreciation of New York. He had arrived at none at all that was socially producible, and as for that matter of his "thinking" (thinking the better or the worse of anything there) he was wholly taken up with one subject of thought. It was mere vain egoism, and it was moreover, if she liked, a morbid obsession. He found all things come back to the question of what he personally might have been, how he might have led his life and "turned out," if he had not so, at the outset, given it up. And confessing for the first time to the intensity within him of this absurd speculation—which but proved also, no doubt, the habit of too selfishly thinking—he affirmed the impotence there of any other source of interest, any other native appeal. "What would it have made of me, what would it have made of me? I keep for ever wondering, all idiotically; as if I could possibly know! I see what it has made of dozens of others, those I meet, and it positively aches within me, to the point of exasperation, that it would have made something of me as well. Only I can't make out *what*, and the worry of it, the small rage of curiosity never to be satisfied, brings back what I remember to have felt, once or twice, after judging best, for reasons, to burn some important letter unopened. I've been sorry, I've hated it—I've never known what was in the letter. You may of course say it's a trifle—!"

"I don't say it's a trifle," Miss Staverton gravely interrupted.

She was seated by her fire, and before her, on his feet and restless, he turned to and fro between this intensity of his idea and a fitful and unseeing inspection, through his single eye-glass, of the dear little old objects on her chimney-piece. Her interruption made him for an instant look at her harder. "I shouldn't care if you did!" he laughed, however; "and it's only a figure, at any rate, for the way I now feel. *Not* to have followed my perverse young course—and almost in the teeth of my father's curse, as I may say; not to have kept it up, so, 'over there,' from that day to this, without a doubt or a pang; not, above all, to have liked it, to have loved it so much, loved it, no doubt, with such an abysmal conceit of my own preference: some variation from *that*, I say, must have produced some different effect for my life and for my 'form.' I should have stuck here—if it had been possible; and I was too young, at twenty-three, to judge, *pour deux sous*, whether it *were* possible. If I had waited I might have seen it was, and then I might have been, by staying here, something nearer to one of these types who have been hammered so hard and made so keen by their conditions. It isn't that I admire them so much—the question of any charm in them, or of any charm, beyond that of the rank money-passion, exerted by their conditions *for* them, has nothing to do with the matter; it's only a question of what fantastic, yet perfectly possible, development of my own nature I mayn't have missed. It comes over me that I had then a strange *alter ego* deep down somewhere within me, as the full-blown flower is in the small tight bud, and that I just took the course, I just transferred him to the climate, that blighted him for once and for ever."

"And you wonder about the flower," Miss Staverton said. "So do I, if you want to know; and so I've been wondering these several weeks. I believe in the flower," she continued, "I feel it would have been quite splendid, quite huge and monstrous."

"Monstrous above all!" her visitor echoed; "and I imagine, by the same stroke, quite hideous and offensive."

"You don't believe that," she returned; "if you did you wouldn't wonder. You'd know, and that would be enough for you. What you feel—and what I feel *for* you—is that you'd have had power."

"You'd have liked me that way?" he asked.

She barely hung fire. "How should I not have liked you?"

"I see. You'd have liked me, have preferred me, a billionaire!"

"How should I not have liked you?" she simply again asked.

He stood before her still—her question kept him motionless. He took it in, so much there was of it; and indeed his not otherwise meeting it testified to that. "I know at least what I am," he simply went on; "the other side of the medal's clear enough. I've not been edifying—I believe I'm thought in a hundred quarters to have been barely decent. I've followed strange paths and worshipped strange gods; it must have come to you again and again—in fact you've admitted to me as much—that I was leading, at any time these thirty years, a selfish frivolous scandalous life. And you see what it has made of me."

She just waited, smiling at him. "You see what it has made of *me*."

"Oh you're a person whom nothing can have altered. You were born to be what you are, anywhere, anyway: you've the perfection nothing else could have blighted. And don't you see how, without my exile, I shouldn't have been waiting till now—?" But he pulled up for the strange pang.

"The great thing to see," she presently said, "seems to me to be that it has spoiled nothing. It hasn't spoiled your being here at last. It hasn't spoiled this. It hasn't spoiled your speaking—" She also however faltered.

He wondered at everything her controlled emotion might mean. "Do you believe then—too dreadfully!—that I *am* as good as I might ever have been?"

"Oh no! Far from it!" With which she got up from her chair and was nearer to him. "But I don't care," she smiled.

"You mean I'm good enough?"

She considered a little. "Will you believe it if I say so? I mean will you let that settle your question for you?" And then as if making out in his face that he drew back from this, that he had some idea which, however absurd, he couldn't yet bargain away: "Oh you don't care either—but, very differently: you don't care for anything but yourself."

Spencer Brydon recognised it—it was in fact what he had absolutely professed. Yet he importantly qualified. "*He* isn't myself. He's the just so totally other person. But I do want to see him," he added. "And I can. And I shall."

Their eyes met for a minute while he guessed from something in hers that she divined his strange sense. But neither of them otherwise expressed it, and her apparent understanding, with no protesting shock, no easy derision, touched him more deeply than anything yet, constituting for his stifled perversity, on the spot, an element that was like breathable air. What she said however was unexpected. "Well, *I've* seen him."

"You—?"

"I've seen him in a dream."

"Oh a 'dream'—!" It let him down.

"But twice over," she continued. "I saw him as I see you now."

"You've dreamed the same dream—?"

"Twice over," she repeated. "The very same."

This did somehow a little speak to him, as it also gratified him. "You dream about me at that rate?"

"Ah about *him!*" she smiled.

His eyes again sounded her. "Then you know all about him." And as she said nothing more: "What's the wretch like?"

She hesitated, and it was as if he were pressing her so hard that, resisting for reasons of her own, she had to turn away. "I'll tell you some other time!"

II

It was after this that there was most of a virtue for him, most of a cultivated charm, most of a preposterous secret thrill, in the particular form of surrender to his obsession and of address to what he more and more believed to be his privilege. It was what in these weeks he was living for—since he really felt life to begin but after Mrs. Muldoon had retired from the scene and, visiting the ample house from attic to cellar, making sure he was alone, he knew himself in safe possession and, as he tacitly expressed it, let himself go. He sometimes came twice in the twenty-four hours; the moments he liked best were those of gathering dusk, of the short autumn twilight; this was the time of which, again and again, he found himself hoping most. Then he could, as seemed to him, most intimately wander and wait, linger and listen, feel his fine attention, never in his life before so fine, on the pulse of the great vague place: he preferred the lampless hour and only wished he might have prolonged each day the deep crepuscular spell. Later—rarely much before midnight, but then for a considerable vigil—he watched with his glimmering light; moving slowly, holding it high,

playing it far, rejoicing above all, as much as he might, in open vistas, reaches of communication between rooms and by passages; the long straight chance or show, as he would have called it, for the revelation he pretended to invite. It was practice he found he could perfectly "work" without exciting remark; no one was in the least the wiser for it; even Alice Staverton, who was moreover a well of discretion, didn't quite fully imagine.

He let himself in and let himself out with the assurance of calm proprietorship; and accident so far favoured him that, if a fat Avenue "officer" had happened on occasion to see him entering at eleven-thirty, he had never yet, to the best of his belief, been noticed as emerging at two. He walked there on the crisp November nights, arrived regularly at the evening's end; it was as easy to do this after dining out as to take his way to a club or to his hotel. When he left his club, if he hadn't been dining out, it was ostensibly to go to his hotel; and when he left his hotel, if he had spent a part of the evening there, it was ostensibly to go to his club. Everything was easy in fine; everything conspired and promoted: there was truly even in the strain of his experience something that glossed over, something that salved and simplified, all the rest of consciousness. He circulated, talked, renewed, loosely and pleasantly, old relations—met indeed, so far as he could, new expectations and seemed to make out on the whole that in spite of the career, of such different contacts, which he had spoken of to Miss Staverton as ministering so little, for those who might have watched it, to edification, he was positively rather liked than not. He was a dim secondary social success—and all with people who had truly not an idea of him. It was all mere surface sound, this murmur of their welcome, this popping of their corks—just as his gestures of response were the extravagant shadows, emphatic in proportion as they meant little, of some game of *ombres chinoises*. He projected himself all day, in thought, straight over the bristling line of hard unconscious heads and into the other, the real, the waiting life; the life that, as soon as he had heard behind him the click of his great house-door, began for him, on the jolly corner, as beguilingly as the slow opening bars of some rich music follows the tap of the conductor's wand.

He always caught the first effect of the steel point of his stick on the old marble of the hall pavement, large black-and-white squares that he remembered as the admiration of his childhood and that had then made in him, as he now saw, for the growth of an early conception of style. This effect was the dim reverberating tinkle as of some far-off bell hung who should say where?—in the depths of the house, of the past, of that mystical other world that might have flourished for him had he not, for weal or woe, abandoned it. On this impression he did ever the same thing; he put his stick noiselessly away in a corner—feeling the place once more in the likeness of some great glass bowl, all precious concave crystal, set delicately humming by the play of a moist finger round its edge. The concave crystal held, as it were, this mystical other world, and the indescribably fine murmur of its rim was the sigh there, the scarce audible pathetic wail to his strained ear, of all the old baffled forsworn possibilities. What he did therefore by this appeal of his hushed presence was to wake them into such measure of ghostly life as they might still enjoy. They were shy, all but unappeasably shy, but they weren't really sinister; at least they weren't as he had hitherto felt them—before they had taken the Form he so yearned to make them take, the Form he at moments saw himself in the light of fairly hunting on tiptoe, the points of his evening-shoes, from room to room and from storey to storey.

That was the essence of his vision—which was all rank folly, if one would, while he was out of the house and otherwise occupied, but which took on the last verisimilitude as soon as he was placed and posted. He knew what he meant and what he wanted; it was as clear as the figure on a cheque presented in demand for cash. His *alter ego* "walked"—that was the note of his image of him, while his image of his motive for his own odd pastime was the desire to waylay him and meet him. He roamed, slowly, warily, but all restlessly, he himself did—Mrs. Muldoon had been right, absolutely, with her figure of their "craping"; and the presence he watched for would roam restlessly too. But it would be as cautious and as shifty; the conviction of its probable, in fact its already quite sensible, quite audible evasion of pursuit grew for him from night to night, laying on him finally a rigour to which nothing in his life had been comparable. It had been the theory of many superficially-judging persons, he knew, that he was wasting that life in a surrender to sensations, but he had tasted of no pleasure so fine as his actual tension, had been introduced to no sport that demanded at once the patience and the nerve of this stalking of a creature more subtle, yet at bay perhaps more formidable, than any beast of the forest.

The terms, the comparisons, the very practices of the chase positively came again into play; there were even moments when passages of his occasional experience as a sportsman, stirred memories, from his younger time, of moor and mountain and desert, revived for him—and to the increase of his keenness—by the tremendous force of analogy. He found himself at moments—once he had placed his single light on some mantel-shelf or in some recess —stepping back into shelter or shade, effacing himself behind a door or in an embrasure, as he had sought of old the vantage of rock and tree; he found himself holding his breath and living in the joy of the instant, the supreme suspense created by big game alone.

He wasn't afraid (though putting himself the question as he believed gentlemen on Bengal tiger-shoots or in close quarters with the great bear of the Rockies had been known to confess to having put it); and this indeed—since here at least he might be frank!—because of the impression, so intimate and so strange, that he himself produced as yet a dread, produced certainly a strain, beyond the liveliest he was likely to feel. They fell for him into categories, they fairly became familiar, the signs, for his own perception, of the alarm his presence and his vigilance created; though leaving him always to remark, portentously, on his probably having formed a relation, his probably enjoying a consciousness, unique in the experience of man. People enough, first and last, had been in terror of apparitions, but who had ever before so turned the tables and become himself, in the apparitional world, an incalculable terror? He might have found this sublime had he quite dared to think of it; but he didn't too much insist, truly, on that side of his privilege. With habit and repetition he gained to an extraordinary degree the power to penetrate the dusk of distances and the darkness of corners, to resolve back into their innocence the treacheries of uncertain light, the evil-looking forms taken in the gloom by mere shadows, by accidents of the air, by shifting effects of perspective; putting down his dim luminary he could still wander on without it, pass into other rooms and, only knowing it was there behind him in case of need, see his way about, visually project for his purpose a comparative clearness. It made him feel, this acquired faculty, like some monstrous stealthy cat; he wondered if he would have glared at these moments with large shining yellow eyes, and what it mightn't verily be, for the poor hard-pressed *alter ego*, to be confronted with such a type.

He liked however the open shutters; he opened everywhere those Mrs. Muldoon had closed, closing them as carefully afterwards, so that she shouldn't notice: he liked—oh this he did like, and above all in the upper rooms!—the sense of the hard silver of the autumn stars through the window-panes, and scarcely less the flare of the street-lamps below, the white electric lustre which it would have taken curtains to keep out. This was human actual social; this was of the world he had lived in, and he was more at his ease certainly for the countenance, coldly general and impersonal, that all the while and in spite of his detachment it seemed to give him. He had support of course mostly in the rooms at the wide front and the prolonged side; it failed him considerably in the central shades and the parts at the back. But if he sometimes, on his rounds, was glad of his optical reach, so none the less often the rear of the house affected him as the very jungle of his prey. The place was there more subdivided; a large "extension" in particular, where small rooms for servants had been multiplied, abounded in nooks and corners, in closets and passages, in the ramifications especially of an ample back staircase over which he leaned, many a time, to look far down—not deterred from his gravity even while aware that he might, for a spectator, have figured some solemn simpleton playing at hide-and-seek. Outside in fact he might himself make that ironic *rapprochement*; but within the walls, and in spite of the clear windows, his consistency was proof against the cynical light of New York.

It had belonged to that idea of the exasperated consciousness of his victim to become a real test for him; since he had quite put it to himself from the first that, oh distinctly! he could "cultivate" his whole perception. He had felt it as above all open to cultivation—which indeed was but another name for his manner of spending his time. He was bringing it on, bringing it to perfection, by practice; in consequence of which it had grown so fine that he was now aware of impressions, attestations of his general postulate, that couldn't have broken upon him at once. This was the case more specifically with a phenomenon at last quite frequent for him in the upper rooms, the recognition —absolutely unmistakeable, and by a turn dating from a particular hour, his resumption of his campaign after a diplomatic drop, a calculated absence of three nights—of his being definitely followed, tracked at a distance carefully taken and to the express end that he should the less confidently, less arrogantly, appear to himself merely to pursue. It worried, it finally quite broke him up, for it proved, of all the conceivable impressions, the one least suited to his book. He was kept in sight while remaining himself—as regards the essence of his position—sightless, and his only recourse then was in abrupt turns, rapid recoveries of ground. He wheeled about, retracing his steps, as if he might so catch in his face at least the stirred air of some other quick revolution. It was indeed true that his fully dislocalised thought of these manœuvres recalled to him Pantaloon, at the Christmas farce, buffeted and tricked from behind by ubiquitous Harlequin; but it left intact the influence of the conditions themselves each time he was re-exposed to them, so that in fact this association, had he suffered it to become constant, would on a certain side have but ministered to his intenser gravity. He had made, as I have said, to create on the premises the baseless sense of a reprieve, his three absences; and the result of the third was to confirm the after-effect of the second.

On his return, that night—the night succeeding his last intermission—he stood in the hall and looked up the staircase with a certainty more intimate than any he had yet known. "He's *there*, at the top, and waiting—not, as in general, falling back for disappearance. He's holding his ground, and it's the first time—which is a proof, isn't it? that something has happened for him." So Brydon argued with his hand on the banister and his foot on the lowest stair; in which position he felt as never before the air chilled by his logic. He himself turned cold in it, for he seemed of a sudden to know what now was involved. "Harder pressed? —yes, he takes it in, with its thus making clear to him that I've come, as they say, 'to stay.' He finally doesn't like and can't bear it, in the sense, I mean, that his wrath, his menaced interest, now balances with his dread. I've hunted him till he has 'turned': that, up there, is what has happened—he's the fanged or the antlered animal brought at last to bay." There came to him, as I say—but determined by an influence beyond my notation!— the acuteness of this certainty; under which however the next moment he had broken into a sweat that he would as little have consented to attribute to fear as he would have dared immediately to act upon it for enterprise. It marked none the less a prodigious thrill, a thrill that represented sudden dismay, no doubt, but also represented, and with the self-same throb, the strangest, the most joyous, possibly the next minute almost the proudest, duplication of consciousness.

"He has been dodging, retreating, hiding, but now, worked up to anger, he'll fight!"—this intense impression made a single mouthful, as it were, of terror and applause. But what was wondrous was that the applause, for the felt fact, was so eager, since, if it was his other self he was running to earth, this ineffable identity was thus in the last resort not unworthy of him. It bristled there—somewhere near at hand, however unseen still—as the hunted thing, even as the trodden worm of the adage *must* at last bristle; and Brydon at this instant tasted probably of a sensation more complex than had ever before found itself consistent with sanity. It was as if it would have shamed him that a character so associated with his own should triumphantly succeed in just skulking, should to the end not risk the open, so that the drop of this danger was, on the spot, a great lift of the whole situation. Yet with another rare shift of the same subtlety he was already trying to measure by how much more he himself might now be in peril of fear; so rejoicing that he could, in another form, actively inspire that fear, and simultaneously quaking for the form in which he might passively know it.

The apprehension of knowing it must after a little have grown in him, and the strangest moment of his adventure perhaps, the most memorable or really most interesting, afterwards, of his crisis, was the lapse of certain instants of concentrated conscious *combat*, the sense of a need to hold on to something, even after the manner of a man slipping and slipping on some awful incline; the vivid impulse, above all, to move, to act, to charge, somehow and upon something—to show himself, in a word, that he wasn't afraid. The state of "holding-on" was thus the state to which he was momentarily reduced; if there had been anything, in the great vacancy, to seize, he would presently have been aware of having clutched it as he might under a shock at home have clutched the nearest chair-back. He had been surprised at any rate—of this he *was* aware—into something unprecedented since his original appropriation of the place; he had closed his eyes, held them tight, for a long minute, as with that instinct of dismay and that terror of vision. When he opened them the room, the other contiguous rooms, extraordinarily, seemed lighter—so light, almost, that at first he took the change for

day. He stood firm, however that might be, just where he had paused; his resistance had helped him—it was as if there were something he had tided over. He knew after a little what this was—it had been in the imminent danger of flight. He had stiffened his will against going; without this he would have made for the stairs, and it seemed to him that, still with his eyes closed, he would have descended them, would have known how, straight and swiftly, to the bottom.

Well, as he had held out, here he was—still at the top, among the more intricate upper rooms and with the gauntlet of the others, of all the rest of the house, still to run when it should be his time to go. He would go at his time—only at his time: didn't he go every night very much at the same hour? He took out his watch—there was light for that; it was scarcely a quarter past one, and he had never withdrawn so soon. He reached his lodgings for the most part at two—with his walk of a quarter of an hour. He would wait for the last quarter—he wouldn't stir till then; and he kept his watch there with his eyes on it, reflecting while he held it that this deliberate wait, a wait with an effort, which he recognised, would serve perfectly for the attestation he desired to make. It would prove his courage—unless indeed the latter might most be proved by his budging at last from his place. What he mainly felt now was that, since he hadn't originally scuttled, he had his dignities—which had never in his life seemed so many—all to preserve and to carry aloft. This was before him in truth as a physical image, an image almost worthy of an age of greater romance. That remark indeed glimmered for him only to glow the next instant with a finer light; since what age of romance, after all, could have matched either the state of his mind or, "objectively," as they said, the wonder of his situation? The only difference would have been that, brandishing his dignities over his head as in a parchment scroll he might then—that is in the heroic time—have proceeded downstairs with a drawn sword in his other grasp.

At present, really, the light he had set down on the mantel of the next room would have to figure his sword; which utensil, in the course of a minute, he had taken the requisite number of steps to posssess himself of. The door between the rooms was open, and from the second another door opened to a third. These rooms, as he remembered, gave all three upon a common corridor as well, but there was a fourth, beyond them, without issue save through the preceding. To have moved, to have heard his step again, was appreciably a help; though even in recognising this he lingered once more a little by the chimney-piece on which his light had rested. When he next moved, just hesitating where to turn, he found himself considering a circumstance that, after his first and comparatively vague apprehension of it, produced in him the start that often attends some pang of recollection, the violent shock of having ceased happily to forget. He had come into sight of the door in which the brief chain of communication ended and which he now surveyed from the nearer threshold, the one not directly facing it. Placed at some distance to the left of this point, it would have admitted him to the last room of the four, the room without other approach or egress, had it not, to his intimate conviction, been closed *since* his former visitation, the matter probably of a quarter of an hour before. He stared with all his eyes at the wonder of the fact, arrested again where he stood and again holding his breath while he sounded its sense. Surely it had been *subsequently* closed—that is it had been on his previous passage indubitably open!

He took it full in the face that something had happened between—that he couldn't not have noticed before (by which he meant on his original tour of all the rooms that evening) that such a barrier had exceptionally presented itself. He had indeed since that moment undergone an agitation so extraordinary that it might have muddled for him any earlier view; and he tried to convince himself that he might perhaps then have gone into the room and, inadvertently, automatically, on coming out, have drawn the door after him. The difficulty was that this exactly was what he never did; it was against his whole policy, as he might have said, the essence of which was to keep vistas clear. He had them from the first, as he was well aware, quite on the brain: the strange apparition, at the far end of one of them, of his baffled "prey" (which had become by so sharp an irony so little the term now to apply!) was the form of success his imagination had most cherished, projecting into it always a refinement of beauty. He had known fifty times the start of perception that had afterwards dropped; had fifty times gasped to himself "There!" under some fond brief hallucination. The house, as the case stood, admirably lent itself; he might wonder at the taste, the native architecture of the particular time, which could rejoice so in the multiplication of doors—the opposite extreme to the modern, the actual almost complete proscription of them, but it had fairly contributed to provoke this obsession of the presence encountered telescopically, as he might say, focussed and studied in diminishing perspective and as by a rest for the elbow.

It was with these considerations that his present attention was charged—they perfectly availed to make what he saw portentous. He *couldn't*, by any lapse, have blocked that aperture; and if he hadn't, if it was unthinkable, why what else was clear but that there had been another agent? Another agent? —he had been catching, as he felt, a moment back, the very breath of him; but when had he been so close as in this simple, this logical, this completely personal act? It was so logical, that is, that one might have *taken* it for personal; yet for what did Brydon take it, he asked himself, while, softly panting, he felt his eyes almost leave their sockets. Ah this time at last they *were*, the two, the opposed projections of him, in presence; and this time, as much as one would, the question of danger loomed. With it rose, as not before, the question of courage—for what he knew the blank face of the door to say to him was "Show us how much you have!" It stared, it glared back at him with that challenge; it put to him the two alternatives; should he just push it open or not? Oh to have this consciousness was to *think*—and to think, Brydon knew, as he stood there, was, with the lapsing moments, not to have acted! Not to have acted —that was the misery and the pang—was even still not to act; was in fact *all* to feel the thing in another, in a new and terrible way. How long did he pause and how long did he debate? There was presently nothing to measure it; for his vibration had already changed—as just by the effect of its intensity. Shut up there, at bay, defiant, and with the prodigy of the thing palpably proveably *done*, thus giving notice like some stark signboard— under that accession of accent the situation itself had turned; and Brydon at last remarkably made up his mind on what it had turned to.

It had turned altogether to a different admonition; to a supreme hint, for him, of the value of Discretion! This slowly dawned, no doubt—for it could take its time; so perfectly, on his threshold, had he been stayed, so little as yet had he either advanced or retreated. It was the strangest of all things that now when, by his taking ten steps and applying his hand to a latch, or even his shoulder and his knee, if necessary, to a panel, all the hunger of his prime need might have been met, his high curiosity crowned, his unrest assuaged—it was amazing, but it was also exquisite and rare, that insistence should have, at a touch, quite dropped from him. Discretion—he jumped at that; and yet not, verily, at such a pitch, because it saved his nerves or his skin, but because, much more valuably, it saved the situation. When I say he "jumped" at it I feel the consonance of this term with the fact that—at the end indeed of I know not how long—he did move again, he crossed straight to the door. He wouldn't touch it—it seemed now that he might *if* he would: he would only just wait there a little, to show, to prove, that he wouldn't. He had thus another station, close to the thin partition by which revelation was denied him; but with his eyes bent and his hands held off in a mere intensity of stillness. He listened as if there had been something to hear, but this attitude, while it lasted, was his own communication. "If you won't then—good: I spare you and I give up. You affect me as by the appeal positively for pity: you convince me that for reasons rigid and sublime—what do I know?—we both of us should have suffered. I respect them then, and, though moved and privileged as, I believe, it has never been given to man, I retire, I renounce—never, on my honour, to try again. So rest for ever—and let *me!*"

That, for Brydon was the deep sense of this last demonstration—solemn, measured, directed, as he felt it to be. He brought it to a close, he turned away; and now verily he knew how deeply he had been stirred. He retraced his steps, taking up his candle, burnt, he observed, well-nigh to the socket, and marking again, lighten it as he would, the distinctness of his footfall; after which, in a moment, he knew himself at the other side of the house. He did here what he had not yet done at these hours —he opened half a casement, one of those in the front, and let in the air of the night; a thing he would have taken at any time previous for a sharp rupture of his spell. His spell was broken now, and it didn't matter—broken by his concession and his surrender, which made it idle henceforth that he should ever come back. The empty street—its other life so marked even by the great lamplit vacancy— was within call, within touch; he stayed there as to be in it again, high above it though he was still perched; he watched as for some comforting common fact, some vulgar human note, the passage of a scavenger or a thief, some night-bird however base. He would have blessed that sign of life; he would have welcomed positively the slow approach of his friend the policeman, whom he had hitherto only sought to avoid, and was not sure that if the patrol had come into sight he mightn't have felt the impulse to get into relation with it, to hail it, on some pretext, from his fourth floor.

The pretext that wouldn't have been too silly or too compromising, the explanation that would have saved his dignity and kept his name, in such a case, out of the papers, was not definite to him: he was so occupied with the thought of recording his Discretion—as an effect of the vow he had just uttered to his intimate adversary—that the importance of this loomed large and something had overtaken all ironically his sense of proportion. If there had been a ladder applied to the front of the house, even one of the vertiginous perpendiculars employed by painters and roofers and sometimes left standing overnight, he would have managed somehow, astride of the window-sill, to compass by outstretched leg and arm that mode of descent. If there had been some such uncanny thing as he had found in his room at hotels, a workable fire-escape in the form of notched cable or a canvas shoot, he would have availed himself of it as a proof—well, of his present delicacy. He nursed that sentiment, as the question stood, a little in vain, and even—at the end of he scarce knew, once more, how long—found it, as by the action on his mind of the failure of response of the outer world, sinking back to vague anguish. It seemed to him he had waited an age for some stir of the great grim hush; the life of the town was itself under a spell—so unnaturally, up and down the whole prospect of known and rather ugly objects, the blankness and the silence lasted. Had they ever, he asked himself, the hard-faced houses, which had begun to look livid in the dim dawn, had they ever spoken so little to any need of his spirit? Great builded voids, great crowded stillnesses put on, often, in the heart of cities, for the small hours, a sort of sinister mask, and it was of this large collective negation that Brydon presently became conscious—all the more the break of day was, almost incredibly, now at hand, proving to him what a night he had made of it.

He looked again at his watch, saw what had become of his time-values (he had taken hours for minutes—not, as in other tense situations, minutes for hours) and the strange air of the streets was but the weak, the sullen flush of a dawn in which everything was still locked up. His choked appeal from his own open window had been the sole note of life, and he could but break off at last as for a worse despair. Yet while so deeply demoralised he was capable again of an impulse denoting—at least by his present measure—extraordinary resolution; of retracing his steps to the spot where he had turned cold with the extinction of his last pulse of doubt as to there being in the place another presence than his own. This required an effort strong enough to sicken him; but he had his reason, which over-mastered for the moment everything else. There was the whole of the rest of the house to traverse, and how should he screw himself to that if the door he had seen closed were at present open? He could hold to the idea that the closing had practically been for him an act of mercy, a chance offered him to descend, depart, get off the ground and never again profane it. This conception held together, it worked; but what it meant for him depended now clearly on the amount of forbearance his recent action, or rather his recent inaction, had engendered. The image of the "presence," whatever it was, waiting there for him to go—this image had not yet been so concrete for his nerves as when he stopped short of the point at which certainty would have come to him. For with all his resolution, or more exactly with all his dread, he did stop short—he hung back from really seeing. The risk was too great and his fear too definite: it took at this moment an awful specific form.

He knew—yes, as he had never known anything —that, *should* he see the door open, it would all too abjectly be the end of him. It would mean that the agent of his shame—for his shame was the deep abjection—was once more at large and in general possession; and what glared him thus in the face was the act that this would determine for him. It would send him straight about to the window he had left open, and by that window, be long ladder and dangling rope as absent as they would, he saw himself uncontrollably insanely fatally take his way to the street. The hideous chance of this he at least could avert; but he could only avert it by recoiling in time from assurance. He had the whole house to deal with, this fact was still there; only he now knew that uncertainty alone could start him. He stole back from where he had checked himself—merely to do so was suddenly like safety—and, making blindly for the greater staircase, left gaping rooms and sounding passages behind. Here was the top of the stairs, with a fine large dim descent and three spacious landings to mark off. His instinct was all for mildness, but his feet were harsh on the floors, and,

strangely, when he had in a couple of minutes become aware of this, it counted somehow for help. He couldn't have spoken, the tone of his voice would have scared him, and the common conceit or resource of "whistling in the dark" (whether literally or figuratively) have appeared basely vulgar; yet he liked none the less to hear himself go, and when he had reached his first landing—taking it all with no rush, but quite steadily—that stage of success drew from him a gasp of relief.

The house, withal, seemed immense, the scale of space again inordinate; the open rooms to no one of which his eyes deflected, gloomed in their shuttered state like mouths of caverns; only the high skylight that formed the crown of the deep well created for him a medium in which he could advance, but which might have been, for queerness of colour, some watery under-world. He tried to think of something noble, as that his property was really grand, a splendid possession; but this nobleness took the form too of the clear delight with which he was finally to sacrifice it. They might come in now, the builders, the destroyers— they might come as soon as they would. At the end of two flights he had dropped to another zone, and from the middle of the third, with only one more left, he recognised the influence of the lower windows, of half-drawn blinds, of the occasional gleam of street-lamps, of the glazed spaces of the vestibule. This was the bottom of the sea, which showed an illumination of its own and which he even saw paved—when at a given moment he drew up to sink a long look over the banisters—with the marble squares of his childhood. By that time indubitably he felt, as he might have said in a commoner cause, better; it had allowed him to stop and draw breath, and the ease increased with the sight of the old black-and-white slabs. But what he most felt was that now surely, with the element of impunity pulling him as by hard firm hands, the case was settled for what he might have seen above had he dared that last look. The closed door, blessedly remote now, was still closed—and he had only in short to reach that of the house.

He came down further, he crossed the passage forming the access to the last flight; and if here again he stopped an instant it was almost for the sharpness of the thrill of assured escape. It made him shut his eyes—which opened again to the straight slope of the remainder of the stairs. Here was impunity still, but impunity almost excessive; inasmuch as the side-lights and the high fan-tracery of the entrance were glimmering straight into the hall; an appearance produced, he the next instant saw, by the fact that the vestibule gaped wide, that the hinged halves of the inner door had been thrown far back. Out of that again the *question* sprang at him, making his eyes, as he felt, half-start from his head, as they had done, at the top of the house, before the sign of the other door. If he had left that one open, hadn't he left this one closed, and wasn't he now in *most* immediate presence of some inconceivable occult activity? It was as sharp, the question, as a knife in his side, but the answer hung fire still and seemed to lose itself in the vague darkness to which the thin admitted dawn, glimmering archwise over the whole outer door, made a semicircular margin, a cold silvery nimbus that seemed to play a little as he looked—to shift and expand and contract.

It was as if there had been something within it, protected by indistinctness and corresponding in extent with the opaque surface behind, the painted panels of the last barrier to his escape, of which the key was in his pocket. The indistinctness mocked him even while he stared, affected him as somehow shrouding or challenging certitude, so that after faltering an instant on his step he let himself go with the sense that here *was* at last something to meet, to touch, to take, to know—something all unnatural and dreadful, but to advance upon which was the condition for him either of liberation or of supreme defeat. The penumbra, dense and dark, was the virtual screen of a figure which stood in it as still as some image erect in a niche or as some black-vizored sentinel guarding a treasure. Brydon was to know afterwards, was to recall and make out, the particular thing he had believed during the rest of his descent. He saw, in its great grey glimmering margin, the central vagueness diminish, and he felt it to be taking the very form toward which, for so many days, the passion of his curiosity had yearned. It gloomed, it loomed, it was something, it was somebody, the prodigy of a personal presence.

Rigid and conscious, spectral yet human, a man of his own substance and stature waited there to measure himself with his power to dismay. This only could it be—this only till he recognised, with his advance, that what made the face dim was the pair of raised hands that covered it and in which, so far from being offered in defiance, it was buried as for dark deprecation. So Brydon, before him, took him in; with every fact of him now, in the higher light, hard and acute—his planted stillness, his vivid truth, his grizzled bent head and white

masking hands, his queer actuality of evening-dress, of dangling double eye-glass, of gleaming silk lappet and white linen, of pearl button and gold watch-guard and polished shoe. No portrait by a great modern master could have presented him with more intensity, thrust him out of his frame with more art, as if there had been "treatment," of the consummate sort, in his every shade and salience. The revulsion, for our friend, had become, before he knew it, immense—this drop, in the act of apprehension, to the sense of his adversary's inscrutable manœuvre. That meaning at least, while he gaped, it offered him; for he could but gape at his other self in this other anguish, gape as a proof that *he*, standing there for the achieved, the enjoyed, the triumphant life, couldn't be faced in his triumph. Wasn't the proof in the splendid covering hands, strong and completely spread?—so spread and so intentional that, in spite of a special verity that surpassed every other, the fact that one of these hands had lost two fingers, which were reduced to stumps, as if accidentally shot away, the face was effectually guarded and saved.

"Saved," though, *would* it be?—Brydon breathed his wonder till the very impunity of his attitude and the very insistence of his eyes produced, as he felt, a sudden stir which showed the next instant as a deeper portent, while the head raised itself, the betrayal of a braver purpose. The hands, as he looked, began to move, to open; then, as if deciding in a flash, dropped from the face and left it uncovered and presented. Horror, with the sight, had leaped into Brydon's throat, gasping there in a sound he couldn't utter; for the bared identity was too hideous as *his*, and his glare was the passion of his protest. The face, *that* face, Spencer Brydon's?—he searched it still, but looking away from it in dismay and denial, falling straight from his height and sublimity. It was unknown, inconceivable, awful, disconnected from any possibility—! He had been "sold," he inwardly moaned, stalking such game as this: the presence before him was a presence, the horror within him a horror; but the waste of his nights had been only grotesque and the success of his adventure an irony. Such an identity fitted his at *no* point, made its alternative monstrous. A thousand times yes, as it came upon him nearer now—the face was the face of a stranger. It came upon him nearer now, quite as one of those expanding fantastic images projected by the magic lantern of childhood; for the stranger, whoever he might be, evil, odious, blatant, vulgar, had advanced as for aggression, and he knew himself give ground. Then harder pressed still, sick with the force of his shock, and falling back as under the hot breath and the roused passion of a life larger than his own, a rage of personality before which his own collapsed, he felt the whole vision turn to darkness and his very feet give way. His head went round; he was going; he had gone.

III

What had next brought him back, clearly—though after how long?—was Mrs. Muldoon's voice, coming to him from quite near, from so near that he seemed presently to see her as kneeling on the ground before him while he lay looking up at her; himself not wholly on the ground, but half-raised and upheld—conscious, yes, of tenderness of support and, more particularly, of a head pillowed in extraordinary softness and faintly refreshing fragrance. He considered, he wondered, his wit but half at his service; then another face intervened, bending more directly over him, and he finally knew that Alice Staverton had made her lap an ample and perfect cushion to him, and that she had to this end seated herself on the lowest degree of the staircase, the rest of his long person remaining stretched on his old black-and-white slabs. They were cold, these marble squares of his youth; but *he* somehow was not, in this rich return of consciousness—the most wonderful hour, little by little, that he had ever known, leaving him, as it did, so gratefully, so abysmally passive, and yet as with a treasure of intelligence waiting all round him for quiet appropriation; dissolved, he might call it, in the air of the place and producing the golden glow of a late autumn afternoon. He had come back, yes—come back from further away than any man but himself had ever travelled; but it was strange how with this sense what he had come back *to* seemed really the great thing, and as if his prodigious journey had been all for the sake of it. Slowly but surely his consciousness grew, his vision of his state thus completing itself: he had been miraculously *carried* back—lifted and carefully borne as from where he had been picked up, the uttermost end of an interminable grey passage. Even with this he was suffered to rest, and what had now brought him to knowledge was the break in the long mild motion.

It had brought him to knowledge, to knowledge —yes, this was the beauty of his state; which came to resemble more and more that of a man who has gone to sleep on some news of a great inheritance, and then, after dreaming it away, after profaning it with matters strange to it, has waked up again to serenity of certitude and has only to lie and watch it grow. This was the drift of his patience— that he had only to let it shine on him. He must moreover, with intermissions, still have been lifted and borne; since why and how else should he have known himself, later on, with the afternoon glow intenser, no longer at the foot of his stairs—situated as these now seemed at that dark other end of his tunnel—but on a deep window-bench of his high saloon, over which had been spread, couch-fashion, a mantle of soft stuff lined with grey fur that was familiar to his eyes and that one of his hands kept fondly feeling as for its pledge of truth. Mrs. Muldoon's face had gone, but the other, the second he had recognised, hung over him in a way that showed how he was still propped and pillowed. He took it all in, and the more he took it the more it seemed to suffice: he was as much at peace as if he had had food and drink. It was the two women who had found him, on Mrs. Muldoon's having plied, at her usual hour, her latch-key—and on her having above all arrived while Miss Staverton still lingered near the house. She had been turning away, all anxiety, from worrying the vain bell-handle—her calculation having been of the hour of the good woman's visit; but the latter, blessedly, had come up while she was still there, and they had entered together. He had then lain, beyond the vestibule, very much as he was lying now—quite, that is, as he appeared to have fallen, but all so wondrously without bruise or gash; only in a depth of stupor. What he most took in, however, at present, with the steadier clearance, was that Alice Staverton had for a long unspeakable moment not doubted he was dead.

"It must have been that I *was*." He made it out as she held him. "Yes—I can only have died. You brought me literally to life. Only," he wondered, his eyes rising to her, "only, in the name of all the benedictions, how?"

It took her but an instant to bend her face and kiss him, and something in the manner of it, and in the way her hands clasped and locked his head while he felt the cool charity and virtue of her lips, something in all this beatitude somehow answered everything. "And now I keep you," she said.

"Oh keep me, keep me!" he pleaded while her

face still hung over him: in response to which it dropped again and stayed close, clingingly close. It was the seal of their situation—of which he tasted the impress for a long blissful moment in silence. But he came back. "Yet how did you know—?"

"I was uneasy. You were to have come, you remember—and you had sent no word."

"Yes, I remember—I was to have gone to you at one today." It caught on to their "old" life and relation—which were so near and so far. "I was still out there in my strange darkness—where was it, what was it? I must have stayed there so long." He could but wonder at the depth and the duration of his swoon.

"Since last night?" she asked with a shade of fear for her possible indiscretion.

"Since this morning—it must have been: the cold dim dawn of today. Where have I been," he vaguely wailed, "where have I been?" He felt her hold him close, and it was as if this helped him now to make in all security his mind moan. "What a long dark day!"

All in her tenderness she had waited a moment. "In the cold dim dawn?" she quavered.

But he had already gone on piecing together the parts of the whole prodigy. "As I didn't turn up you came straight—?"

She barely cast about. "I went first to your hotel—where they told me of your absence. You had dined out last evening and hadn't been back since. But they appeared to know you had been at your club."

"So you had the idea of this—?"

"Of what?" she asked in a moment.

"Well—of what has happened."

"I believed at least you'd have been here. I've known, all along," she said, "that you've been coming."

" 'Known' it—?"

"Well, I've believed it. I said nothing to you after that talk we had a month ago—but I felt sure. I knew you would," she declared.

"That I'd persist, you mean?"

"That you'd see him."

"Ah but I didn't!" cried Brydon with his long wail. "There's somebody—an awful beast; whom I brought, too horribly, to bay. But it's not me."

At this she bent over him again, and her eyes were in his eyes. "No—it's not you." And it was as if, while her face hovered, he might have made out in it, hadn't it been so near, some particular meaning blurred by a smile. "No, thank heaven,"

she repeated—"it's not you! Of course it wasn't to have been."

"Ah but it *was*," he gently insisted. And he stared before him now as he had been staring for so many weeks. "I was to have known myself."

"You couldn't!" she returned consolingly. And then reverting, and as if to account further for what she had herself done, "But it wasn't only *that*, that you hadn't been at home," she went on. "I waited till the hour at which we had found Mrs. Muldoon that day of my going with you; and she arrived, as I've told you, while, failing to bring any one to the door, I lingered in my despair on the steps. After a little, if she hadn't come, by such a mercy, I should have found means to hunt her up. But it wasn't," said Alice Staverton, as if once more with her fine intention—"it wasn't only that."

His eyes, as he lay, turned back to her. "What more then?"

She met it, the wonder she had stirred. "In the cold dim dawn, you say? Well, in the cold dim dawn of this morning I too saw you."

"Saw *me*—?"

"Saw *him*," said Alice Staverton. "It must have been at the same moment."

He lay an instant taking it in—as if he wished to be quite reasonable. "At the same moment?"

"Yes—in my dream again, the same one I've named to you. He came back to me. Then I knew it for a sign. He had come to you."

At this Brydon raised himself; he had to see her better. She helped him when she understood his movement, and he sat up, steadying himself beside her there on the window-bench and with his right hand grasping her left. "*He* didn't come to me."

"You came to yourself," she beautifully smiled.

"Ah I've come to myself now—thanks to you, dearest. But this brute, with his awful face—this brute's a black stranger. He's none of *me*, even as I *might* have been," Brydon sturdily declared.

But she kept the clearness that was like the breath of infallibility. "Isn't the whole point that you'd have been different?"

He almost scowled for it. "As different as *that*—?"

Her look again was more beautiful to him than the things of this world. "Haven't you exactly wanted to know *how* different? So this morning," she said, "you appeared to me."

"Like *him*?"

"A black stranger!"

"Then how did you know it was I?"

"Because, as I told you weeks ago, my mind, my

imagination, had worked so over what you might, what you mightn't have been—to show you, you see, how I've thought of you. In the midst of that you came to me—that my wonder might be answered. So I knew," she went on; "and believed that, since the question held you too so fast, as you told me that day, you too would see for yourself. And when this morning I again saw I knew it would be because you had—and also then, from the first moment, because you somehow wanted me. *He* seemed to tell me of that. So why," she strangely smiled, "shouldn't I like him?"

It brought Spencer Brydon to his feet. "You 'like' that horror—?"

"I *could* have liked him. And to me," she said, "he was no horror. I had accepted him."

"'Accepted'—?" Brydon oddly sounded.

"Before, for the interest of his difference—yes. And as *I* didn't disown him, as *I* knew him—which you at last, confronted with him in his difference, so cruelly didn't, my dear—well, he must have been, you see, less dreadful to me. And it may have pleased him that I pitied him."

She was beside him on her feet, but still holding his hand—still with her arm supporting him. But though it all brought for him thus a dim light, "You 'pitied' him?" he grudgingly, resentfully asked.

"He has been unhappy; he has been ravaged," she said.

"And haven't I been unhappy? Am not I—you've only to look at me!—ravaged?"

"Ah I don't say I like him *better*," she granted after a thought. "But he's grim, he's worn—and things have happened to him. He doesn't make shift, for sight, with your charming monocle."

"No"—it struck Brydon: "I couldn't have sported mine 'downtown.' They'd have guyed me there."

"His great convex pince-nez—I saw it, I recognised the kind—is for his poor ruined sight. And his poor right hand—!"

"Ah!" Brydon winced—whether for his proved identity or for his lost fingers. Then, "He has a million a year," he lucidly added. "But he hasn't you."

"And he isn't—no, he isn't—*you!*" she murmured as he drew her to his breast.

From The American Scene (1907)

Some remarks on this book, written during and after James's tour of America in 1904–5, have been offered in the introduction. An inveterate traveler, James was also one of the most acute and poetic of travel writers and had over the years described with great felicity the exterior and, as it were, the interior landscapes of England, France, and Italy. Now, returning to his native country after two decades, he applied his well-developed powers to the "new" United States. What impressions did America make available to the imaginative observer? What vision of life could be drawn from it?

The present brief section is taken from Chapter 2, "New York Revisited." It contains, in particular, James's ruminative picture of the Manhattan harbor and the impression that arises from it of "dauntless power . . . the power of the most extravagant of cities, rejoicing, as with the voice of morning, in its might, its fortune, its unsurpassable conditions." But lurking in this account is a formidable question, the question James invariably addressed to the scenes he inspected: to what extent was this domain of power plastic to the creative imagination? Hart Crane, looking at the same spectacle in various moments of his long poem *The Bridge* (1931), would raise the same question and would attempt to answer it positively by the very energy of his poetry. James was more skeptical.

His skepticism rested in part upon his sense of the Wall Street area of downtown New York —where the fine old buildings had been "mercilessly deprived of their visibility" by the crowding, looming skyscrapers. There was the sense, too—especially for a person with twenty years at his back of the experience of Europe—of systematic *im*permanence, of "the expensively provisional." James felt that New York, and by implication the modern American city as such, and by further implication the American character in the twentieth century, was "crowned not only with no history, but with no credible possibility of time for history, and consecrated by no uses save the commercial at any cost."

James's reflections on New York in this section can be suggestively set alongside his ghost-story enactment of his intuitions and apprehensions in "The Jolly Corner."

———

The single impression or particular vision most answering to the greatness of the subject would have been, I think, a certain hour of large circumnavigation that I found prescribed, in the fulness of the spring, as the almost immediate crown of a return from the Far West. I had arrived at one of the transpontine stations of the Pennsylvania Railroad; the question was of proceeding to Boston, for the occasion, without pushing through the terrible town—why "terrible," to my sense, in many ways, I shall presently explain—and the easy and agreeable attainment of this great advantage was to embark on one of the mightiest (as appeared to me) of train-bearing barges and, descending the western waters, pass round the bottom of the city and remount the other current to Harlem; all without "losing touch" of the Pullman that had brought me from Washington. This absence of the need of losing touch, this breadth of effect, as to the whole process, involved in the prompt floating of the huge concatenated cars not only without arrest or confusion, but as for positive prodigal beguilement of the artless traveller, had doubtless much to say to the ensuing state of mind, the happily-excited and amused view of the great face of New York. The extent, the ease, the energy, the quantity and number, all notes scattered about as if, in the whole business and in the splendid light, nature and science were joyously romping together, might have been taking on again, for their symbol, some collective presence of great circling and plunging, hovering and perching sea-birds, white-winged images of the spirit, of the restless freedom of the Bay. The Bay had always, on other opportunities, seemed to blow its immense character straight into one's face—coming "at" you, so to speak, bearing down on you, with the full force of a thousand prows of steamers seen exactly on the line of their longitudinal axis; but I had never before been so conscious of its boundless cool assurance or seemed to see its genius so grandly at play. This was presumably indeed because I had never before enjoyed the remarkable adventure of taking in so much of the vast bristling promontory from the water, of ascending the East River, in especial, to its upper diminishing expanses.

Something of the air of the occasion and of the mood of the moment caused the whole picture to speak with its largest suggestion; which suggestion is irresistible when once it is sounded clear. It is all, absolutely, an expression of things lately and currently *done*, done on a large impersonal stage and on the basis of inordinate gain—it is not an expression of any other matters whatever; and yet the sense of the scene (which had at several previous junctures, as well, put forth to my imagination its power) was commanding and thrilling, was in certain lights almost charming. So it befell, exactly, that an element of mystery and wonder entered into the impression—the interest of trying to make out, in the absence of features of the sort usually supposed indispensable, the reason of the beauty and the joy. It is indubitably a "great" bay, a great harbour, but no one item of the romantic, or even of the picturesque, as commonly understood, contributes to its effect. The shores are low and for the most part depressingly furnished and prosaically peopled; the islands, though numerous, have not a grace to exhibit, and one thinks of the other, the real flowers of geography in this order, of Naples, of Capetown, of Sydney, of Seattle, of San Francisco, of Rio, asking how if *they* justify a reputation, New York should seem to justify one. Then, after all, we remember that there are reputations and reputations; we remember above all that the imaginative response to the conditions here presented may just happen to proceed from the intellectual extravagance of the given observer. When this personage is open to corruption by almost any large view of an intensity of life, his vibrations tend to become a matter difficult even for *him* to explain. He may have to confess that the group of evident facts fails to account by itself for the complacency of his appreciation. Therefore it is that I find myself rather backward with a perceived sanction, of an at all proportionate kind, for the fine exhilaration with which, in this free wayfaring relation to them, the wide waters of New York inspire me. There is the beauty of light and air, the great scale of space, and, seen far away to the west, the open gates of the Hudson, majestic in their degree, even at a distance, and announcing still nobler things. But the real appeal, unmistakably, is in that note of vehemence in the local life of which I have spoken, for it is the appeal of a particular type of dauntless power.

The aspect the power wears then is indescribable; it is the power of the most extravagant of cities, rejoicing, as with the voice of the morning, in its might, its fortune, its unsurpassable conditions, and imparting to every object and element, to the motion and expression of every floating, hurrying, panting thing, to the throb of ferries and tugs, to the plash of waves and the play of winds and the glint of lights and the shrill of whistles and the quality and authority of breeze-borne cries —all, practically, a diffused, wasted clamour of *detonations*—something of its sharp free accent and, above all, of its sovereign sense of being "backed" and able to back. The universal *applied* passion struck me as shining unprecedentedly out of the composition; in the bigness and bravery and insolence, especially, of everything that rushed and shrieked; in the air as of a great intricate frenzied dance, half merry, half desperate, or at least half defiant, performed on the huge watery floor. This appearance of the bold lacing-together, across the waters, of the scattered members of the monstrous organism—lacing as by the ceaseless play of an enormous system of steam-shuttles or electric bobbins (I scarce know what to call them), commensurate in form with their infinite work—does perhaps more than anything else to give the pitch of the vision of energy. One has the sense that the monster grows and grows, flinging abroad its loose limbs even as some unmannered young giant at his "larks," and that the binding stitches must for ever fly further and faster and draw harder; the future complexity of the web, all under the sky and over the sea, becoming thus that of some colossal set of clockworks, some steel-souled machine-room of brandished arms and hammering fists and opening and closing jaws. The immeasurable bridges are but as the horizontal sheaths of pistons working at high pressure, day and night, and subject, one apprehends with perhaps inconsistent gloom, to certain, to fantastic, to merciless multiplication. In the light of this apprehension indeed the breezy brightness of the Bay puts on the semblance of the vast white page that awaits beyond any other perhaps the black overscoring of science.

Let me hasten to add that its present whiteness is precisely its charming note, the frankest of the signs you recognize and remember it by. That is the distinction I was just feeling my way to name as the main ground of its doing so well, for effect, without technical scenery. There are great imposing ports—Glasgow and Liverpool and London— that have already their page blackened almost

beyond redemption from any such light of the picturesque as can hope to irradiate fog and grime, and there are others, Marseilles and Constantinople say, or, for all I know to the contrary, New Orleans, that contrive to abound before everything else in colour, and so to make a rich and instant and obvious show. But memory and the actual impression keep investing New York with the tone, predominantly, of summer dawns and winter frosts, of sea-foam, of bleached sails and stretched awnings, of blanched hulls, of scoured decks, of new ropes, of polished brasses, of streamers clear in the blue air; and it is by this harmony, doubtless, that the projection of the individual character of the place, of the candour of its avidity and the freshness of its audacity, is most conveyed. The "tall buildings," which have so promptly usurped a glory that affects you as rather surprised, as yet, at itself, the multitudinous sky-scrapers standing up to the view, from the water, like extravagant pins in a cushion already overplanted, and stuck in as in the dark, anywhere and anyhow, have at least the felicity of carrying out the fairness of tone, of taking the sun and the shade in the manner of towers of marble. They are not all of marble, I believe, by any means, even if some may be, but they are impudently new and still more impudently "novel" —this in common with so many other terrible things in America—and they are triumphant payers of dividends; all of which uncontested and unabashed pride, with flash of innumerable windows and flicker of subordinate gilt attributions, is like the flare, up and down their long, narrow faces, of the lamps of some general permanent "celebration."

You see the pin-cushion in profile, so to speak, on passing between Jersey City and Twenty-third Street, but you get it broadside on, this loose nosegay of architectural flowers, if you skirt the Battery, well out, and embrace the whole plantation. Then the "American beauty," the rose of interminable stem, becomes the token of the cluster at large—to that degree that, positively, this is all that is wanted for emphasis of your final impression. Such growths, you feel, have confessedly arisen but to be "picked," in time, with a shears; nipped short off, by waiting fate, as soon as "science," applied to gain, has put upon the table, from far up its sleeve, some more winning card. Crowned not only with no history, but with no credible possibility of time for history, and consecrated by no uses save the commercial at any cost, they are simply the most piercing notes in that concert of the expensively provisional into which your supreme sense of New York resolves itself. They never begin to speak to you, in the manner of the builded majesties of the world as we have heretofore known such—towers or temples or fortresses or palaces—with the authority of things of permanence or even of things of long duration. One story is good only till another is told, and sky-scrapers are the last word of economic ingenuity only till another word be written. This shall be possibly a word of still uglier meaning, but the vocabulary of thrift at any price shows boundless resources, and the consciousness of that truth, the consciousness of the finite, the menaced, the essentially *invented* state, twinkles ever, to my perception, in the thousand glassy eyes of these giants of the mere market. Such a structure as the comparatively windowless bell-tower of Giotto, in Florence, looks supremely serene in its beauty. You don't feel it to have risen by the breath of an interested passion that, restless beyond all passions, is for ever seeking more pliable forms. Beauty has been the object of its creator's idea, and, having found beauty, it has found the form in which it splendidly rests.

Beauty indeed was the aim of the creator of the spire of Trinity Church, so cruelly overtopped and so barely distinguishable, from your train-bearing barge, as you stand off, in its abject helpless humility; and it may of course be asked how much of this superstition finds voice in the actual shrunken presence of that laudable effort. Where, for the eye, is the felicity of simplified Gothic, of noble pre-eminence, that once made of this highly-pleasing edifice the pride of the town and the feature of Broadway? The answer is, as obviously, that these charming elements are still there, just where they ever were, but that they have been mercilessly deprived of their visibility. It aches and throbs, this smothered visibility, we easily feel, in its caged and dishonoured condition, supported only by the consciousness that the dishonour is no fault of its own. We commune with it, in tenderness and pity, through the encumbered air; our eyes, made, however unwillingly, at home in strange vertiginous upper atmospheres, look down on it as on a poor ineffectual thing, an architectural object addressed, even in its prime aspiration, to the patient pedestrian sense and permitting thereby a relation of intimacy. It was to speak to me audibly enough on two or three other occasions—even through the thick of that frenzy of Broadway just where Broadway receives from Wall Street the fiercest application of the maddening lash; it was to put its tragic case there with irresistible lucidity. "Yes, the wretched figure I am making is as little as you see my fault—it is the fault of the buildings whose very first care is to deprive churches of their visibility. There are but two or three—two or three outward and visible churches—left in New York 'anyway,' as you must have noticed, and even they are hideously threatened: a fact at which no one, indeed, appears to be shocked, from which no one draws the least of the inferences that stick straight out of it, which every one seems in short to take for granted either with remarkable stupidity or with remarkable cynicism." So, at any rate, they may still effectively communicate, ruddy-brown (where not browny-black) old Trinity and any pausing, any attending survivor of the clearer age— and there is yet more of the bitterness of history to be tasted in such a tacit passage, as I shall presently show.

From The New Novel (1914)

This appraisal of Conrad's literary art formed part of a long essay called "The New Novel," originally written for the London *Times Literary Supplement* in the late winter of 1914. Though James still retained some of the flexibility and generosity of judgment expressed in *The Art of Fiction*, and though he still insisted on the freedom of the individual artist to work as he might, he here acknowledges his preference for the kind of fiction Joseph Conrad was practicing as against that of D. H. Lawrence, H. G. Wells, and Arnold Bennett.

Conrad is presented as "a votary of the way to do a thing that shall make it undergo the most doing. The way to do it that shall make it undergo least," James adds, "is the line on which we are mostly now used to see prizes carried off." James's style in this late essay is at its most evasive, circling, and self-modifying. But amid the hesitations and subordinate clauses, we make out as fine an image of Conrad's narrative method as has ever been offered—an image, that is, of the impression one gathers of the *movement* of a Conradian novel, especially when the consciousness of his frequent narrator Marlow is in control: "a prolonged hovering flight of the subjective over the outstretched ground of the case beneath."

James wrote about a great range of novelists over the years and always with remarkable, and remarkably vigorous, insight. He addressed himself to Americans like Hawthorne; to English writers—Dickens, Trollope, George Eliot; to Turgenev and Tolstoi; and above all perhaps to the French: Flaubert, Zola, Balzac, De Maupassant. The range testifies to James's basic and never-abandoned conviction—despite his own personal predilections—about the enormous variety of which fiction was capable. "Any point of view is interesting," he wrote to a symposium on the novel in 1889, "that is a direct impression of life. . . . The field is vast for freedom, for study, for observation, for satire, for truth. . . . I have only two little words for the matter remotely approaching to rule or doctrine: one is life and the other freedom." James's letter containing these remarks is appended.

JOSEPH CONRAD

If those remarks represent all the while, further, that the performances we have glanced at, with others besides, lead our attention on, we hear ourselves the more naturally asked what it is then that we expect or want, confessing as we do that we have been in a manner interested, even though, from case to case, in a varying degree, and that Thackeray, Turgenev, Balzac, Dickens, Anatole France, no matter who, can not do more than interest. Let us therefore concede to the last point that small mercies are better than none, that there are latent within the critic numberless liabilities to being "squared" (the extent to which he may on occasion betray his price!) and so great a preference for being pleased over not being, that you may again and again see him assist with avidity at the attempt of the slice of life to butter itself thick. Its explanation that it *is* a slice of life and pretends to be nothing else figures for us, say, while we watch, the jam super-added to the butter.

For since the jam, on this system, descends upon our desert, in its form of manna, from quite another heaven than the heaven of method, the mere demonstration of its agreeable presence is alone sufficient to hint at our more than one chance of being supernaturally fed. The happy-go-lucky fashion of it is indeed not then, we grant, an objection so long as we do take in refreshment: the meal may be of the last informality and yet produce in the event no small sense of repletion. The slice of life devoured, the butter and the jam duly appreciated, we are ready, no doubt, on another day, to trust ourselves afresh to the desert. We break camp, that is, and face toward a further stretch of it, all in the faith that we shall be once more provided for. We take the risk, we enjoy more or less the assistance—more or less, we put it, for the vision of a possible arrest of the miracle or failure of our supply never wholly leaves us. The phenomenon is too uncanny, the happy-go-lucky, as we know it in general, never *has* been trustable to the end; the absence of the last true touch in the preparation of its viands becomes with each renewal of the adventure a more sensible fact. By the last true touch we mean of course the touch of the hand of selection; the principle of selection having been involved at the worst or the least, one would suppose, in any approach whatever to the loaf of life with the *arrière-pensée* of a slice. There being no question of a slice upon which the further question of where and how to cut it does not wait, the office of method, the idea of choice and comparison, have occupied the ground from the first. This makes clear, to a moment's reflection, that there can be no such thing as an amorphous slice, and that any waving aside of inquiry as to the sense and value of a chunk of matter has to reckon with the simple truth of its having been *born* of naught else but measured excision. Reasons have been the fairies waiting on its cradle, the possible presence of a bad fairy in the form of a bad reason to the contrary notwithstanding. It has thus had connections at the very first stage of its detachment that are at no later stage logically to be repudiated; let it lie as lumpish as it will—for adoption, we mean, of the ideal of the lump—it has been tainted from too far back with the hard liability to form, and thus carries in its very breast the hapless contradiction of its sturdy claim to have none. This claim has the inevitable challenge at once to meet. How can a slice of life be anything but illustrational of the loaf, and how can illustration not immediately bristle with every sign of the extracted and related state? The relation is at once to what the thing comes from and to what it waits upon—which last is our act of recognition. We accordingly appreciate it in proportion as it so accounts for itself; the quantity and the intensity of its reference are the measure of our knowledge of it. This is exactly why illustration breaks down when reference, otherwise application, runs short, and why before any assemblage of figures or aspects, otherwise of samples and specimens, the question of what there are, extensively, samples and specimens *of* declines not to beset us—why, otherwise again, we look ever for the supreme reference that shall avert the bankruptcy of sense.

Let us profess all readiness to repeat that we may still have had, on the merest "life" system, or that of the starkest crudity of the slice, all the entertainment that can come from watching a wayfarer engage with assurance in an alley that we know to have no issue—and from watching for the very sake of the face that he may show us on reappearing at its mouth. The recitals of Mr. Arnold Bennett, Mr. Gilbert Cannan, Mr. D. H. Lawrence, fairly smell of the real, just as the *Fortitude* and *The Duchess* of Mr. Hugh Walpole smell of the romantic; we have sufficiently noted then that, once on the scent, we are capable of pushing ahead. How far it is at the same time from being all a matter of smell the terms in which we just above glanced at the weakness of the spell of the happy-go-lucky may here serve to indicate. There faces us all the while the fact that the act of consideration confidently knowing us to *have* sooner or later to arrive at it, may be again and again postponed, but can never hope not some time to fall due. Consideration is susceptible of many forms, some one or other of which no conscious esthetic effort fails to cry out for; and the simplest description of the cry of the novel when sincere— for have we not heard such compositions bluff us, as it were, with false cries?—is as an appeal to us when we have read it once to read it yet again. *That* is the act of consideration; no other process of considering approaches this for directness, so that anything short of it is virtually not to consider at all. The word has sometimes another sense, that of the appeal to us *not*, for the world, to go back—this being of course consideration of a sort; the sort clearly that the truly flushed production should be the last to invoke. The effect of consideration, we need scarce remark, is to light for us in a work of art the hundred questions of how and why and whither, and the effect of these questions,

once lighted, is enormously to thicken and complicate, even if toward final clarifications, what we have called the amused state produced in us by the work. The more our amusement multiplies its terms the more fond and the more rewarded consideration becomes; the fewer it leaves them, on the other hand, the less to be resisted for us is the impression of "bare ruined choirs where late the sweet birds sang." Birds that have appeared to sing, or whose silence we have not heeded, on a first perusal, prove on a second to have no note to contribute, and whether or no a second is enough to admonish us of those we miss, we mostly expect much from it in the way of emphasis of those we find. Then it is that notes of intention become more present or more absent; then it is that we take the measure of what we have already called our effective provision. The bravest providers and designers show at this point something still in store which only the second rummage was appointed to draw forth. To the variety of these ways of not letting our fondness fast is there not practically no limit?—and of the arts, the devices, the graces, the subtle secrets applicable to such an end what presumptuous critic shall pretend to draw the list? Let him for the moment content himself with saying that many of the most effective are mysteries, precisely, of method, or that even when they are not most essentially and directly so it takes method, blessed method, to extract their soul and to determine their action.

It is odd and delightful perhaps that at the very moment of our urging this truth we should happen to be regaled with a really supreme specimen of the part playable in a novel by the source of interest, the principle of provision attended to, for which we claim importance. Mr. Joseph Conrad's *Chance* is none the less a signal instance of provision the most earnest and the most copious for its leaving ever so much to be said about the particular provision effected. It is none the less an extraordinary exhibition of method by the fact that the method is, we venture to say, without a precedent in any like work. It places Mr. Conrad absolutely alone as a votary of the way to do a thing that shall make it undergo most doing. The way to do it that shall make it undergo least is the line on which we are mostly now used to see prizes carried off; so that the author of *Chance* gathers up on this showing all sorts of comparative distinction. He gathers up at least two sorts—that of bravery in absolutely reversing the process most accredited, and that, quite separate, we make out, of performing the maneuver under salvos of recognition. It is not in these days often given to a refinement of design to be recognized, but Mr. Conrad has made his achieve that miracle—save in so far indeed as the miracle has been one thing and the success another. The miracle is of the rarest, confounding all calculation and suggesting more reflections than we can begin to make place for here; but the sources of surprise surrounding it might be, were this possible, even greater and yet leave the fact itself in all independence, the fact that the whole undertaking was committed by its very first step either to be "art" exclusively or to be nothing. This is the prodigious rarity, since surely we have known for many a day no other such case of the whole clutch of eggs, and these withal of the freshest, in that one basket; to which it may be added that if we say for many a day this is not through our readiness positively to associate the sight with any very definite moment of the past. What concerns us is that the general effect of *Chance* is arrived at by a pursuance of means to the end in view contrasted with which every other current form of the chase can only affect us as cheap and futile; the carriage of the burden or amount of service required on these lines exceeding surely all other such displayed degrees of energy put together. Nothing could well interest us more than to see the exemplary value of attention, attention given by the author and asked of the reader, attested in a case in which it has had almost unspeakable difficulties to struggle with—since so we are moved to qualify the particular difficulty Mr. Conrad has "elected" to face: the claim for method in itself, method in this very sense of attention applied, would be somehow less lighted if the difficulties struck us as less consciously, or call it even less wantonly, invoked. What they consist of we should have to diverge here a little to say, and should even then probably lose ourselves in the dim question of why so special, eccentric and desperate a course, so deliberate a plunge into threatened frustration, should alone have seemed open. It has been the course, so far as three words may here serve, of his so multiplying his creators or, as we are now fond of saying, producers, as to make them almost more numerous and quite emphatically more material than the creatures and the production itself in whom and which we by the general law of fiction expect such agents to lose themselves. We take for granted by the general law of fiction a primary author, take him so much for granted that we forget him in proportion as he

works upon us, and that he works upon us most in fact by making us forget him.

Mr. Conrad's first care on the other hand is expressly to posit or set up a reciter, a definite responsible intervening first person singular, possessed of infinite sources of reference, who immediately proceeds to set up another, to the end that this other may conform again to the practice, and that even at that point the bridge over to the creature, or in other words to the situation or the subject, the thing "produced," shall, if the fancy takes it, once more and yet once more glory in a gap. It is easy to see how heroic the undertaking of an effective fusion becomes on these terms, fusion between what we are to know and that prodigy of our knowing which is ever half the very beauty of the atmosphere of authenticity; from the moment the reporters are thus multiplied from pitch to pitch the tone of each, especially as "rendered" by his precursor in the series, becomes for the prime poet of all an immense question—these circumferential tones having not only to be such individually separate notes, but to keep so clear of the others, the central, the numerous and various voices of the agents proper, those expressive of the action itself and in whom the objectivity resides. We usually escape the worst of this difficulty of a tone *about* the tone of our characters, our projected performers, by keeping it single, keeping it "down" and thereby comparatively impersonal or, as we may say, inscrutable; which is what a creative force, in its blessed fatuity, likes to be. But the omniscience, remaining indeed nameless, though constantly active, which sets Marlow's omniscience in motion from the very first page, insisting on a reciprocity with it throughout, this original omniscience invites consideration of itself only in a degree less than that in which Marlow's own invites it; and Marlow's own is a prolonged hovering flight of the subjective over the outstretched ground of the case exposed. We make out this ground but through the shadow cast by the flight, clarify it though the real author visibly reminds himself again and again that he must—all the more that, as if by some tremendous forecast of future applied science, the upper airplane causes another, as we have said, to depend from it and that one still another; these dropping shadow after shadow, to the no small menace of intrinsic color and form and whatever, upon the passive expanse. What shall we most call Mr. Conrad's method accordingly but his attempt to clarify *quand même*—ridden as he has been, we perceive at the end of fifty pages of *Chance*, by such a danger of steeping his matter in perfect eventual obscuration as we recall no other artist's consenting to with an equal grace. This grace, which presently comes over us as the sign of the whole business, is Mr. Conrad's gallantry itself, and the shorter account of the rest of the connection for our present purpose is that his gallantry is thus his success. It literally strikes us that his volume sets in motion more than anything else a drama in which his own system and his combined eccentricities of recital represent the protagonist in face of powers leagued against it, and of which the dénouement gives us the system fighting in triumph, though with its back desperately to the wall, and laying the powers piled up at its feet. This frankly has been *our* spectacle, our suspense and our thrill; with the one flaw on the roundness of it all the fact that the predicament was not imposed rather than invoked, was not the effect of a challenge from without, but that of a mystic impulse from within.

Of an exquisite refinement at all events are the critical questions opened up in the attempt, the question in particular of by what it exactly is that the experiment is crowned. Pronouncing it crowned and the case saved by sheer gallantry, as we did above, is perhaps to fall just short of the conclusion we might reach were we to push further. *Chance is* an example of objectivity, most precious of aims, not only menaced but definitely compromised; whereby we are in presence of something really of the strangest, a general and diffused lapse of authenticity which an inordinate number of common readers—since it always takes this and these to account encouragingly for "editions"— have not only condoned but have emphatically commended. They can have done this but through the bribe of some authenticity other in kind, no doubt, and seeming to them equally great if not greater, which gives back by the left hand what the right has, with however dissimulated a grace, taken away. What Mr. Conrad's left hand gives back then is simply Mr. Conrad himself. We asked above what would become, by such a form of practice, of indispensable "fusion" or, to call it by another name, of the fine process by which our impatient material, at a given moment, shakes off the humiliation of the handled, the fumbled state, puts its head in the air and, to its own beautiful illusory consciousness at least, simply runs its race. Such an amount of handling and fumbling and repointing has it, on the system of the multiplied "putter into marble," to shake off! And yet behold,

the sense of discomfort, as the show here works out, *has* been conjured away. The fusion has taken place, or at any rate *a* fusion; only it has been transferred in wondrous fashion to an unexpected, and on the whole more limited plane of operation; it has succeeded in getting effected, so to speak, not on the ground but in the air, not between our writer's idea and his machinery, but between the different parts of his genius itself. His genius is what is left over from the other, the compromised and compromising quantities—the Marlows and their determinant inventors and interlocutors, the Powells, the Franklins, the Fynes, the tell-tale little dogs, the successive members of a cue from one to the other of which the sense and the interest of the subject have to be passed on together, in the manner of the buckets of water for the improvised extinction of a fire, before reaching our apprehension: all with whatever result, to this apprehension, of a quantity to be allowed for as spilled by the way. The residuum has accordingly the form not of such and such a number of images discharged and ordered, but that rather of a wandering, circling, yearning imaginative *faculty*, encountered in its habit as it lives and diffusing itself as a presence or a tide, a noble sociability of vision. So we have as the force that fills the cup just the highwater mark of a beautiful and generous mind at play in conditions comparatively thankless— thoroughly, unweariedly, yet at the same time ever so elegantly at play, and doing more for itself than it succeeds in getting done for it. Than which nothing could be of a greater reward to critical curiosity were it not still for the wonder of wonders, a new page in the record altogether—the fact that these things are apparently what the common reader has seen and understood. Great then would seem to be after all the common reader!

We must not fail of the point, however, that we have made these remarks not at all with an eye to the question of whether *Chance* has been well or ill inspired as to its particular choice of a way of really attending to itself among all the possible alternatives, but only on the ground of its having compared, selected and held on; since any alternative that might have been preferred and that should have been effectively adopted would point our moral as well—and this even if it is of profit none the less to note the most striking of Mr. Conrad's compositional consequences. There is one of these that has had most to do with making his pages differ in texture, and to our very first glance, from that straggle of ungoverned verbiage which leads us up and down those of his fellow fabulists in general on a vain hunt for some projected mass of truth, some solidity of substance, as to which the deluge of "dialogue," the flooding report of things said, or at least of words pretendedly spoken, shall have learned the art of being merely illustrational. What first springs from any form of real attention, no matter which, we on a comparison so made quickly perceive to be a practical challenge of the preposterous pretension of this most fatuous of the luxuries of looseness to acquit itself with authority of the structural and compositional office. Infinitely valid and vivid as illustration, it altogether depends for dignity and sense upon our state of possession of its historic preliminaries, its promoting conditions, its supporting ground; that is upon our waiting occupancy of the chamber it proposes to light and which, when no other source of effect is more indicated, it doubtless quite inimitably fills with life. Then its relation to what encloses and confines and, in its sovereign interest, finely compresses it, offering it constituted aspects, surfaces, presences, faces and figures of the matter we are either generally or acutely concerned with to play over and hang upon, then this relation gives it all its value: it has flowered from the soil prepared and sheds back its richness into the field of cultivation. It is interesting, in a word, only when nothing else is equally so, carrying the vessel of the interest with least of a stumble or a sacrifice; but it is of the essence that the sounds so set in motion (it being as sound above all that they undertake to convey sense) should have something to proceed from, in their course, to address themselves to and be affected by, with all the sensibility of sounds. It is of the essence that they should

live in a medium, and in a medium only, since it takes a medium to give them an identity, the intenser the better, and that the medium should subserve them by enjoying in a like degree the luxury of an existence. We need of course scarce expressly note that the play, as distinguished from the novel, lives exclusively on the spoken word—not on the report of the thing said but, directly and audibly, on that very thing; that it thrives by its law on the exercise under which the novel hopelessly collapses when the attempt is made disproportionately to impose it. There is no danger for the play of the cart before the horse, no disaster involved in it; that form being *all* horse and the interest itself mounted and astride, and not, as that of the novel, dependent in the first instance on wheels. The order in which the drama simply says things gives it all its form, while the story told and the picture painted, as the novel at the pass we have brought it to embraces them, reports of an infinite diversity of matters, gathers together and gives out again a hundred sorts, and finds its order and its structure, its unity and its beauty, in the alternation of parts and the adjustment of differences. It is no less apparent that the novel may be fundamentally *organized*—such things as *The Egoist* and *The Awkward Age* are there to prove it; but in this case it adheres unconfusedly to that logic and has nothing to say to any other. Were it not for a second exception, one at this season rather pertinent, *Chance* then, to return to it a moment, would be as happy an example as we might just now put our hand on of the automatic working of a scheme unfavorable to that treatment of the colloquy by endless dangling strings which makes the current "story" in general so figure to us a porcupine of extravagant yet abnormally relaxed bristles.

A Letter to the Deerfield Summer School

[*Summer, 1889*]

I am afraid I can do little more than thank you for your courteous invitation to be present at the sittings of your delightfully sounding school of romance, which ought to inherit happiness and honor from such a name. I am so very far away from you that I am afraid I can't participate very intelligently in your discussions, but I can only give them the furtherance of a dimly discriminating sympathy. I am not sure that I apprehend very well your apparent premise, "the materialism of

our present tendencies," and I suspect that this would require some clearing up before I should be able (if even then) to contribute any suggestive or helpful word. To tell the truth, I can't help thinking that we already talk too much about the novel, about and around it, in proportion to the quantity of it having any importance that we produce. What I should say to the nymphs and swains who propose to converse about it under the great trees at Deerfield is: "Oh, do something from your point of view; an ounce of example is worth a ton of generalities; do something with the great art and the great form; do something with life. Any point of view is interesting that is a direct impression of life. You each have an impression colored by your individual conditions; make that into a picture, a picture framed by your own personal wisdom, your glimpse of the American world. The field is vast for freedom, for study, for observation, for satire, for truth." I don't think I really do know what you mean by "materializing tendencies" any more than I should by "spiritualizing" or "etherealizing." There are no tendencies worth anything but to see the actual or the imaginative, which is just as visible, and to paint it. I have only two little words for the matter remotely approaching to rule or doctrine; one is life and the other freedom. Tell the ladies and gentlemen, the ingenious inquirers, to consider life directly and closely, and not to be put off with mean and puerile falsities, and be conscientious about it. It is infinitely large, various and comprehensive. Every sort of mind will find what it looks for in it, whereby the novel becomes truly multifarious and illustrative. That is what I mean by liberty; give it its head and let it range. If it is in a bad way, and the English novel is, I think, nothing but absolute freedom can refresh it and restore its self-respect. Excuse these raw brevities and please convey to your companions, my dear sir, the cordial good wishes of yours and theirs,

Henry James

Intellectual History

In this section we present four men who not only are central to the intellectual history of America in this period but who possessed literary gifts of a high order.

Henry Adams, who began his career as secretary to his father when the latter was minister to the Court of St. James during the Civil War, did not die until near the end of the First World War. He knew almost everybody of consequence during his long life and his books represent a memorable struggle to interpret the inner meaning of the age. Oliver Wendell Holmes, Jr., spans generations even more spectacularly. As a senior at Harvard in 1861, he took his final examinations in uniform, fought in the Civil War, and more than seventy years later, in 1933, interrupted his reading of Plato's Greek long enough to receive Franklin Delano Roosevelt, the new President, who had come to pay his respects.

In a sense, Adams illustrates the inability of some New Englanders to come to grips in action with modernity and took a rather grim relish in playing out his role, but Holmes, of the same class and heritage, carried over his tradition into effective action in the modern world. William James, whom we come to next, though of Harvard, was not of New England, and had had an international education before setting foot there; perhaps because of his personal background, he can be said to have moved more freely into modernity and to have been a more original force in shaping it than even Holmes was.

Santayana, by far the youngest of the group and a student of James, was, for all his years in Cambridge, not an American at all and always had a distaste for American life. For these very reasons, he had a unique and invaluable perspective on our culture, and, in fact, it was his attacks on it, a few years before the First World War, that gave a rallying cry for the young men who were to repudiate the "genteel tradition" in the hope of establishing a new freedom and a new contact with reality in both life and letters.

In the broad sense of intellectual history—in the history of science, for instance—there are, of course, other names of great importance, but even within the limits of our special concern there are a few others who should be mentioned. Frederick Jackson Turner, with "The Significance of the Frontier in American History" (1893), brought to focus one of the great themes of our literature. William Graham Sumner, a famous figure in the history of sociology and anthropology, carried to its logical conclusion the idea of Darwinism in its social reference and at the same time emphasized the idea that the individual is primarily a social product, a bubble on the stream—an idea that had been formulated by others but gained special currency through him.

Thorstein Veblen and Randolph Bourne are somewhat more immediate to our concerns. Veblen, of immigrant Norwegian stock (his father could not even speak English), an economist by profession, was an eccentric, original, proud, and sensitive man, like Santayana very much the outsider, and it scarcely seems an accident that his most famous work, *The Theory of the Leisure Class* (1899), should have been an unmasking of the hidden motives of the Gilded Age, with its conspicuous consumption, invidious distinctions, and hollow pretensions. Veblen's corrosive attacks on American life, including a notable treatment of universities called *The Higher Learning*, were absorbed into the increasing dissatisfaction with the mass, industrial society of the modern world, and into the rebellious forces that were to bring forth a new culture after the First World War. Strangely enough, Veblen, the poor immigrant, is close, on the one hand, to the aristocratic Henry Adams, with all his preciosity, salon wit, and medievalism, and, on the other, to the totally indigenous Mark Twain, with his ambivalences toward society and mankind, and his sense of doom.

Randolph Bourne is important to us not for a body of work (he left very little), but for his role. The role was, in fact, achieved against tremendous odds. Hunchbacked and dwarfish, his face distorted by a birth injury, Bourne early showed keen powers of mind, but because of his family's financial reverses, he was twenty-seven years old before he graduated from Columbia.

Bourne was appalled by the economic injustices, spiritual barrenness, and cultural tepidity of American life in the years just before the First World War, echoing in his own way the import of Santayana's recent indictment in "The Genteel Tradition." He was one of the young men who prepared the creative outburst of the 1920's. He envisaged a League of Youth to redeem America from the rule of the "old": "The stupidity and cruelties of their management of the world fill youth with an intolerant rage." It is youth, he continues in an essay called "Youth," in the *Atlantic Monthly*, in 1912, that has all the "valuable experiences" and is "ever laying the foundations for the future," creating the "world ideas" that will be "orthodox gospel thirty years hence."

More specifically, Bourne, though not a systematic thinker, was a socialist, an internationalist, and a pacifist. Shortly after graduation he became a member, though a very junior one, of the staff of the liberal-to-radical *New Republic*, just established to awaken America from its self-complacent torpor. Soon, however, the great majority of the intellectuals, including the philosopher John Dewey,[1] whom Bourne had worshiped, and the editors of the *New Republic* itself, were supporting the entry of America into the First World War, and Bourne was attacking them for their "betrayal" of a generation. "War," Bourne ironically asserted, "is the health of the state," and is "almost an upper-class sport," and in his disgust he was giving preliminary utterance to the contempt for society and the nausea with war that was to inform the work of such writers of the 1920's as John Dos Passos and Ernest Hemingway. Bourne was now writing for the *Seven Arts*, which was hospitable to his protests as well as to the work of such young writers as Robert Frost, Amy Lowell, Van Wyck Brooks, Theodore Dreiser, Sherwood Anderson, and Carl Sandburg, who represented the future.

It was a future that Bourne did not live to see. He died, in the great influenza epidemic of 1918, at the age of thirty-two. He did not live to become one of the "old."

[1] The philosopher (1859–1952) whose doctrine of instrumentalism is closely related to James's pragmatism (see our selection from *Pragmatism* later in the text) and who became one of the most influential figures in American thought and in liberal politics in the first half of the twentieth century.

HENRY ADAMS (1838–1918)

If a republic could be said to have a princeling, Henry Brooks Adams was a princeling. He was of blood that had made the American Republic. Samuel Adams, a kinsman, had, as a propagandist and manipulator of mobs, fanned the flames of the Revolution. Henry's great-grandfather John, one of the committee of four who drafted the Declaration, was Vice President under Washington and the second President. Henry's grandfather John Quincy was a diplomat, the Secretary of State, then President. In a sense, the continuing Adams family was the repository of the Revolution, the keepers of the faith, for the other great makers of America, Washington, Jefferson, and Franklin, had died without legitimate male issue.

The Adamses had been strong-willed, passionate men, of rigid conscience and powerful minds, capable of subtle theorizing but targeted toward action. Charles Francis Adams, Henry's father, was a man of action, too; he was minister to the Court of St. James, and during the Civil War it might be said that he carried the fate of the northern cause in his hands, for English recognition of the Confederacy might well have proved decisive. Young Henry, a secretary to his father during this period, felt himself tempered by blood, training, and talent for action, but the blind drive of ambition was disciplined and mollified by a conscience that would make ambition virtue by directing it to the public good. The power he craved had to be sanctified.

Henry Adams, however, never managed to lay hands on power. The raw new world of post-Civil War America went roaring past him, not even contemptuous, merely oblivious, and Henry Adams, as the poet Allen Tate has put it in a poem called "Fragment of a Meditation," was left behind, "fuddled in the shade." There is a strange parallel, in fact, between Henry Adams, of New England, of the nineteenth century, and the Italian Machiavelli of the sixteenth century. Both were men thirsting for power, both failed to grasp it, and both turned to the study of history and tried to anatomize the nature of power, Machiavelli in his *History of Florence* and *The Prince* and Henry Adams in his *History of The United States of America During the Administrations of Thomas Jefferson and James Madison* and *The Education of Henry Adams*. This with one difference: Machiavelli drew, in *The Prince*, the portrait of a man (Cesare Borgia) who, by divesting himself of "conscience," could act rationally to achieve power, and Adams drew, in the *Education*, the portrait of a man (himself) who, unable to divest himself of "conscience," could not achieve power. But the similarities are greater than the differences, and the fundamental similarity is that both men sought to find a law of history that, like a law of physics, would make prediction scientifically possible.

Henry was born on February 16, 1838, to the highest privilege, to Adams blood, and to a share in the biggest fortune in Boston, brought by his mother Abigail Brooks of the great mercantile family. His father was a man remote in attitude and cold in manner, inspiring little love in any of his children and something like hate in at least one; and so it was natural that Henry, like the others, should seek sympathy and comprehension from the mother. The era of the child-centered home had not yet begun, and the boy Henry, who was later to refer to himself as a "ten-year-old priest and politician," was more likely to hear politics than fairy tales. In this family circle, though abolitionism was still not condoned in proper Boston families, much of the talk was of the evil of slavery, and when Henry was twelve a major event occurred in his education: he was taken on a visit to Washington and saw the real world of slaveholding; there, to his considerable puzzlement, he realized that certain non-Adams makers of the Revolution, like Washington and Jefferson, had been southerners, and slaveholders. A little later, at Harvard, one of his friends was Rooney Lee, the son of then Colonel Robert E. Lee. The Lees, Adams by then knew, had had a not insignificant hand in the making of America, too.

Henry went back to Boston, to school (which he always hated), to Harvard (which, he said, did not "educate" him), to Europe (to see the sights and study German), to a law office in Boston (which he found dull), and again, in the winter before the Civil War began, to Washington, as secretary to his father (now in Congress). By May 13, 1861, with war an actuality, Henry was in London, still as secretary to his father, who was now minister. As he watched his father's success in crisis after crisis, he felt, in moments at least, that an individual could really contribute to the shaping of history—that will and conscience *did* matter. He could write to his brother Charles that the "great principle of democracy is still capable of rewarding a conscientious servant." But he was reading science, too, and he could also say

> my philosophy teaches me, and I firmly believe it, that the laws which govern animated beings will be ultimately found to be at bottom the same with those which rule inanimate nature, and, as I entertain a profound

mechanistic history

conviction of the littleness of our kind, and the curious enormity of creation, I am quite ready to receive with pleasure any basis for a systematic conception at all.

Thus, by affirming the naturalistic philosophy, Henry Adams flew in the face of the comforting revelation of Emerson that there was one "law for man" and another "law for thing."

To go further, Adams saw science itself as a force outside of the human will, again writing to his brother:

Man has mounted science, and is now run away with. I firmly believe that before many centuries more, science will be the master of man. The engines he will have invented will be beyond his strength to control. Some day science may have the existence of mankind in its power, and the human race commit suicide by blowing up the world.

So we find stated early the problem that was to underlie his whole career and provide the fundamental and unifying topic of his work: in a universe where animate and inanimate matter respond to the same law, and where science itself, as a knowledge of law, leads merely to further enslavement, what can will and conscience matter? How, in fact, can they even be said to exist?

After the war was over, the young Adams, still in London, read the news from home and pondered another paradox:

It does seem to me as though everything in America has turned a back somersault. I find the pure northern Congress, just such a one as we prayed for twenty-five years ago, violating the rights of minorities more persistently than the worst pro-slavery Congress ever could do. . . . I find all our old friends in Massachusetts, those who suffered so bitterly as a minority, utterly savage, intolerant, and intolerable towards minorities now that they have themselves become a majority.[1]

[1] Back in America, John, the oldest brother, was successfully courting unpopularity by criticizing the Reconstruction policy of the Radical Republicans in Congress.

In 1868, drawn to the center of power, Adams came to Washington. He had already written his brother Charles that after the war their obligation would be to call the nation "back to its true course," by which he meant a rule of law and the Constitution, before "we lose all our landmarks and go ahead . . . with a mere blind necessity to get on." He saw himself and his friends, including Charles, as an elite of the intellect and the spirit. If the government—and the country—was wrong, he was, he felt, the man to set it right. He was brilliant, learned, experienced, with social grace, family prestige, ample means, and, even though very short, good looks—and he was soon to be known as one of the three best dancers in the city. How could he fail to make himself felt in the cause of decency?

The role he chose was that of a journalist or, rather, a critic grounding his views in moral theory and political history which would provide the cutting edge for his treatment of the events of the day. The essays that came out of this period of Grant's administration trace the corruption of government and the corruption, and corrupting influence, of business. Adams' concern was for the well-being of the whole society as opposed to the rule of Grab and the special interests, and if he was against the high tariff it was because he felt that though the tariff might increase the national wealth it would do so by a process of concentrating wealth in fewer and fewer hands. Here, in a new context, he was animated by the same impulse that had made John Quincy fight to hold the vast wealth in public lands for the benefit of the public instead of turning it over for private exploitation.

In the *Education*, Adams, looking back, says that the Civil War had "made a new system," and the country "would have to recognize the machinery in practice and theory." Even so, he never quite understood that system and pinned his faith more and more on mere constitutionality. He would write, again in the *Education*, that "Chaos often breeds life, when order breeds habit," but he, though an early disciple of Darwin and an apostle of evolution, often set the norm of evolution by a model from the past.

When he left Washington, after two years, he felt that he had failed to connect with the course of events and had certainly failed to influence them. He saw in Congress and in the country "an indifference to strict rules of right and wrong, a contempt for personal dignity, a cynical assumption of official dishonesty . . . a patient assent to the supposed necessity of corruption." Worst of all, he had found no cause to support—"something that would let itself be supported." He had crossed a decisive philosophic and emotional line: philosophically he had come, in pain and disillusionment, to question the old assumption that had sustained the Adams family (and many others of their time) in public life, the assumption that society was ✓ founded on moral law; and emotionally he had come to feel that he, personally, was out of tune with the world he was doomed to live in. So he became a professor at Harvard.

Adams became, as of 1870, Assistant Professor of Medieval History and, being ill-trained for that role, set furiously about preparing himself, often only one lecture ahead of the class; and in the process, unwittingly, he was preparing for one of his masterpieces to come, *Mont-Saint-Michel and Chartres*. More immediately, knowing that he thus turned away from the world of power, he was taking the first step toward his study of the American past, which was to eventuate in two biographies, of Albert Gallatin and John Randolph, and his multivolume *History of the United States*. But meanwhile, in 1872, he got married to Marian Hooper, —whose nickname was "Clover"—a young lady of impeccable family connections and friends (among them Henry James and Oliver Wendell Holmes), great intelligence and charm, and a solid income.

Of her Adams wrote to an English friend:

She is certainly not handsome; nor would she be quite called plain, I think. She is twenty-eight years old. She knows her own mind uncommon well. She does not talk *very* American. Her manners are quiet. She reads German—also Latin—also, I fear, a little Greek, but very little. She talks garrulously,

but on the whole pretty sensibly. She is very open to instruction. We shall improve her. She dresses badly. She decidedly has humor and will appreciate *our* wit. She has enough money to be quite independent. She rules me as only American women rule men, and I cower before her. Lord! how she would lash me if she read this description of her!

He wound up the passage by saying: "I must stop to make love."

Adams, sometimes stiff and shy among men, had always had a gift for understanding women and for evoking their confidence and confidences. "The proper study of mankind is woman," he once said, and added that "by common agreement since the time of Adam, it is the most complex and arduous." His marriage was a happy one, and when his wife was dead, in 1885, a suicide by poison, from no objectively discernible motive (but presumably from fear of madness, which was in her family), he wrote to E. L. Godkin, editor of the *Nation:* "I have had happiness enough to carry me over some years of misery."

Now, at Harvard, Adams taught and edited the *North American Review*, which he was trying to use as an organ for reform. As a teacher, he was a great success, with the talent, as one of his students was later to say, to arouse a young man's "dormant faculties." But after seven years, Adams was ready to leave. For all his success, he had failed to find a vocation. Of his fellow professors, in a tone to be echoed by George Santayana when he resigned from Harvard, Adams said: "All these brilliant men are greedy for companionship, all were famished for want of it." He was famished, too, and no companionship that they, however brilliant, could give would satisfy him. For all his scholarship, he was a man of the world, and he was ready to go back into it. To him, the world was Washington.

But in trying to understand power, he now, curiously enough, turned novelist, and even more curiously chose as a sort of alter ego a woman for his central character. The heroine of *Democracy*, the novel which Adams published in 1880, is Mrs. Lightfoot Lee, a widow with a personal tragedy, beautiful, intelligent, rich, cultivated. Bored with the society of the great cities of America and Europe, as with all other projects to fill up a mysterious void in her life, she comes to Washington "to see with her own eyes the action of primary forces; to touch with her own hand the massive machinery of society; to measure with her own mind the capacity of the motive power." She is, in short, an image of Adams' own need, not only his need now to understand power but the old need that had, in 1868, drawn the young man to Washington. She is seeking a cause to which she can give her loyalty—"eating her heart out" because she can find "no one object worth a sacrifice."

When the novel opens, a new President has just taken office, and there have begun not only all the struggles for power and preferment natural to the moment, but also a more fundamental struggle, that between the President himself and Senator Silas P. Ratcliffe, the "Prairie Giant of Peonia, the Favorite Son of Illinois," and the party boss. Soon the issue is drawn between Ratcliffe and Madeleine Lee. To her, Ratcliffe is the "high priest of American politics," charged with the "clue to political hieroglyphics," and through him "she hoped to sound the depth of statesmanship and to bring up from its oozy bed that pearl for which she was in search." As she pursues her end, Ratcliffe seeks to subdue and use her, as a screen and redemption for his political machinations; and later, falling in love, seeks to marry her. He is almost a match for her, luring her with glimpses of the clue to the hieroglyphics of power; bit by bit involving her, by studied confessions, as an accomplice in his corruption, each time justifying the means by the noble end he professes; appealing to her feminine need to give herself to a cause and seeking to make himself that cause as a last blurring out of all distinctions. He almost succeeds, for he had a "curious instinct for human weakness," and "no magnetic needle was ever truer than his finger when he touched the vulnerable spot in an opponent's mind."

Mrs. Lee is saved only by a letter, written by a man she knows to be honorable, that exposes Ratcliffe as a taker of bribes. She comes out of the shadows of moral ambiguity that Ratcliffe had cast on her, throws him over as a suitor, and contemptuously rejects his last bait, that he can put her in the White House. The final meaning of the conclusion is the same that Adams had received from his own experience in Washington: "democracy" Madeleine says, "has shaken my nerves to pieces."

And she adds: "Oh, what rest it would be to live in the Great Pyramid and look out forever at the Polar Star!" Here, too, she speaks for the author of *Democracy*. He, in his continuing historical researches and philosophical speculations, was seeking some principle of continuity with the past and some universal point of reference: Pyramid and Star. And she, too, as Adams was to do, goes back to her travels.

There are some cunning details in the cast of characters in *Democracy*. First, the master of duplicity and corruption is not from the stews of metropolitan degradation that Jefferson had feared; he is from the heartland of America, the region famed for physical vigor, moral rectitude, and homespun virtue—the Middle West; he is the "Favorite Son" of the state of Illinois, which had sent Lincoln to the White House, and physically Ratcliffe is described in terms that suggest Lincoln, with some blend, perhaps, of Daniel Webster, that apotheosis of the New England farmer. So we have here, symbolically, the final irony of the corruption of democracy masked by the Lincolnian virtues—the fated degradation of the Jeffersonian dream.

Furthermore, the heroine, who hopes to find power redeemed by good and a cause to which she can give herself, is, in blood at least, half a southerner and, to emphasize the point, bears the name of the dead husband, Lightfoot Lee—a name that evokes the full range of Virginia history, from the Revolution, with Lighthorse Harry Lee, to the Civil War, with Robert E. Lee. To underscore this point, Madeleine's distant cousin, John Carruthers, a Virginian and once a Confederate officer, now a lawyer in Washington, is presented as the soul of honor and, by the exposure of Ratcliffe, her savior.

Ironically, it is thus the defeated enemy, the southerner, who is put in favorable contrast to the new North created by the war waged for, presumably, human freedom. The defeated, as "outsiders" to the new order, can see the defects of the victorious "insiders": and they can, in their failure, at least cherish "honor"—there being, as it were, nothing else left to cherish.[2] Such a type as Carruthers would be respected, even admired (it is suggested that, in the end, Mrs. Lee will marry him and thus find the "revelation" that she has sought), for his simplicity and unity of being, even if a unity achieved by a limitation of the intellect; and so Carruthers in his "unity" prefigures a type Adams was to come to admire in the man of the thirteenth century who built the cathedrals of Mont-Saint-Michel and Chartres.

To return more specifically to *Democracy*, it was taken as a sort of *roman à clef*, not only a picture of Washington society, but in its suggested portraiture of individuals (Ratcliffe is James G. Blaine, but not quite), and Washingtonians in the know amused themselves by trying to determine the originals behind the fictional characters; and by trying to identify the author, for the book was published anonymously. But *Democracy*, however fascinating as a document of its period, is even more fascinating as a document of Adams' mind: by projecting himself and his experience into fiction, and particularly into a woman character,[3] he takes an assessing distance on the subject; and in this sense, *Democracy* is a trial run, as it were, for the *Education*.

Democracy is not a good novel. For all his powers of social and psychological observation, Adams had no shred of novelistic instinct, no capacity for letting character or feeling burst into light by a word or gesture, and no ear whatsoever for dialogue. These limitations are instructive in the light of his achievement as a writer of history. Especially in the *History of the United States*, he is admired for his ability to choose the right quotation from a character, the illuminating anecdote—in short, for the ability to give immediacy, concreteness, and humanity to the bareness of historical narrative. He could choose *imaginatively*; but his own imagination could not create. He had to deal with the literal *given* of life.

With work on the *History*, Adams had returned to the *given* of life. If he had in his experience and meditation found his country to be entering into a period of degradation, and if by consequence he felt, as Denis Brogan has put it, like an *émigré de l'intérieur*, he was impelled

[2] In an essay "A Southern Critique for the Gilded Age" (in *The Burden of Southern History*), C. Vann Woodward points out that three significant northern writers, disillusioned with the new order, use the defeated southerner in their works as an implicit criticism of the society established by the victors. These writers, besides Adams, are Melville, with the figure of Ungar in *Clarel*, and Henry James, with Basil Ransom in *The Bostonians*. This would not imply that Adams (or Melville or James) had an unqualified admiration for the South. In discussing Grant, in the *Education*, Adams compares him, in his limitations of mind, to Lee, who, he says, "betrayed the same intellectual commonplace, in a Virginian form." What this means is that neither Grant nor Lee exhibited the special dexterity of mind in handling concepts or language that Adams exhibited and prized as the mark of civilization; and certainly both Grant and Lee were as devoid of irony, a special quality of Adams' mind, as a child or a saint. Both Grant and Lee had powerful minds, but their minds fulfilled themselves in action, and action was the one thing that Adams yearned for but could never understand. In regard to Lee, Adams' view resembles that of Justice Holmes toward a certain type of southerner which Lee could be taken to represent. See pp. 1505–6. To return to Adams on Grant: We owe Adams gratitude for the anecdote that Grant remarked that Venice would be a pretty good city if only it could be drained.

[3] Strangely enough, Adams' other novel, *Esther*, less interesting than the first, has a woman also for its main character. The heroine winds up in a moment similar to that which Mrs. Lee finds in the collocation of the Great Pyramid and the Polar Star; Esther, at the end of her quest for "meaning," winds up staring at Niagara Falls, with the roar in her ears. Instead of the "religion" that she had sought, she has the overpowering symbol of a life force. Here again Adams has projected his own story, for the roar of Niagara becomes, in his own story, the law of history. It should be added that by external circumstance, there is a tragic undertone to *Esther* not found in *Democracy*; Adams had used his wife as a model for Esther herself (as he had used many real persons for other characters), and not long after the novel was finished the model for the heroine came to the end of her own quest for meaning and swallowed the potassium cyanide.

to return to its origins and try to see where and why things went wrong. He chose—and for an Adams this seems strange—the era of Jefferson and Madison as the key to the American story; strange, for the Adamses, with the shadow of Calvinism and the doctrine of Original Sin in their very blood, could have no share in Jefferson's notion of the perfectibility of man and his hope for an Edenic democracy in which man's natural good would render the need for government minimal. But the idealism of Jefferson did express the extreme difference in kind that America, in contrast with Europe and as a "new" nation, hoped to achieve, and this idealism appealed to the idealism of the Adams who had strayed into the Gilded Age.

So in the beginning of the *History*, we find the description of the American character and the American aspiration, and Jefferson's hope that, with the restraints common to older societies now removed, man would not only improve his material lot but his spiritual nature: the conquest of the continent and the conquest of his own soul—that would be the destiny of the American. But Jefferson, once he was President, found his faith and his theory put to the test of circumstances, and in the most dramatic instance of such a conflict, he bought Louisiana. In so doing he violated, in full awareness, his basic principles of government. And so, also, for Madison, Jefferson's successor as President. Both men seemed caught and borne along in the stream of history, nothing more than "mere grasshoppers kicking and gesticulating" on their way into darkness.

Adams does not pretend to decide how much of the failure of Jefferson and Madison to impress their principles upon American life and institutions was the result of a moral collapse and how much was due to historical forces. But he was already considering a theory of "naturalistic" history as may be seen in a letter to his great fellow historian Francis Parkman in which he predicted a "new science of history": "I am satisfied that the purely mechanical development of the human mind in society must appear in a great democracy so clearly, for want of disturbing elements, that in another generation

psychology, physiology, and history will join in proving man to have as fixed and necessary development as that of a tree; and almost as unconscious."

At the same time Adams was continuing to nurse the idea of moral responsibility in political action and to ask what, after the compromises made by idealism, could remain of the American "mission." With the ideal mission gone, what remained for America except to be, as Israel became in replacing the prophets by a king,[4] "like all the nations," engaged in the old game of power. Some force was afoot beyond the humanistic ideals of Jefferson, and America, like Israel, had rejected God to choose the path to power. The "people," as John Quincy Adams, the nonbeliever in perfectibility, wrote in the age of Jackson, had gone "the way of the world." So from Jefferson to Senator Ratcliffe would be but a step, with both Madeleine Lee and Henry Adams suffering from "shaken" nerves.

By the time the last of the six volumes of the *History* had come out (1891), "Clover" Adams was dead, with St. Gaudens' magnificent and inscrutable monument over her grave in Rock Creek Cemetery in Washington, and Adams had become a wanderer, to Japan, the Rockies, France, Russia, China, Samoa, Tahiti. In 1895 he discovered the "meaning" (for him) of the Gothic cathedrals. Of Coutances and Mont-Saint-Michel he said: "They are noble, both in spirit and execution. . . . They [the builders] knew their own force perfectly well; measured it to a hair; gave to the ideal all it had a right to expect, and looked out for the actual with a cool head." He identified himself with the Norman spirit, imagining himself back into a Norman skin, some vassal of the Church, perhaps a farmer doing military service for his fief. But at the same time he drew New England into this complex identification: "I have rarely felt New England at its highest ideal power as

---

[4] See Samuel 8. The shadow of this chapter hangs in the background of Adams' history. See also "The Conflict of Convictions," by Melville, reprinted in our text.

it appeared to me, beautified and glorified, in the Cathedral of Coutances."

Unity, simplicity, power, beauty—the balance of the ideal and the actual: these were the elements of the vision[5] represented by Coutances and, later, by Mont-Saint-Michel and Chartres. They were the things he found lacking in the world he lived in, fragmented, secular, pluralistic, and confused, and in his own life as a wanderer, the man who could find no mission, the bystander watching his friends and contemporaries making their marks in science, art, and politics, the sufferer from inner loneliness made more poignant by a gift for friendship. But both he and his friends, too, for all their successes, were of the age of aimlessness, fragmentation, and pluralism, and, again thinking of Coutances, he could say: "The squirming Devils under the feet of the stone Apostles looked uncommonly like me and my generation." So, by 1904, the book that stemmed from these musings of a dozen years before was written: *Mont-Saint-Michel and Chartres*. It was printed privately for distribution among a few friends. That was a way of spitting in the world's eye.

The book, outside the accepted categories, was puzzling. It was a work of history, a work of aesthetics, a work of philosophy, and a work of theology, but one thing seemed to flow into another and to defy the rules of chronology and the rules of reason; and all was throbbing with an undeclared personal life. The book was, indeed, like a symbolist poem, progressing by association but at the same time always reaching backward and spreading outward, by the intersection of auras of meaning rather than by logic, existing in time but declaring itself outside of time.

What the book intended to convey—rather, in a poetic sense, to embody—was the various spiritual dimensions of the age specified in the title, with the overarching unity in the fact of spirit. The book was, in fact, a poem celebrating the fact that spirit could give unity, purpose, mis-

sion, and fullness of experience to an individual, a society, and an age, the age being that period in France, from 1150 to 1250, when lord and serf might tug at the same rope to drag the great stone from quarry to building site, for the greater glory of God and the merciful smile of the Virgin. Living in his own fragmented world, where, as Yeats was to put it, the "best lack all conviction," Adams had written to William James that his book was an "anchor" for him, a point of meaningfulness to which he might refer in the ruck of history. It was, to paraphrase the end of Eliot's *Waste Land*, a fragment that he had shored against his ruins. No—perhaps, after all, it was not a "fragment" of any literal past that he might shore against his ruinous experience of modernity, but only a dream of the might-have-been-but-never-to-be that floated before him as a constant rebuke to the actual? not history at all, but vision?

As Adams, in the *History*, had tried to catch the inner light of faith that had guided the early American, so in *Mont-Saint-Michel and Chartres* he tries, more ambitiously, to catch the inner light of an earlier time when men, as he dreamed, had been fulfilled in relation, not to a future hope of human possibility, but to an actual faith, society, and self. Undoubtedly, Adams shared to some degree in the sentimental yearning for the Middle Ages that, in the late nineteenth century, following a world fashion, swept upper-class New England and, as the historian Froude said of the Oxford Movement, "disseminated the priggism that to be an Anglican, if not a Papist, is essential to being a gentleman."

Here, however, as in the *History*, the creation of a vision was not merely a flight of unsatisfied fancy and irrelevant snobbery, but a reasoned criticism of the present and the assertion of an ideal as a challenge to an age. It stood in much the same relation to its time as did Matthew Arnold's poem "The Scholar Gypsy," which bewails the "divided aims" of the modern world, or Melville's *Clarel*, or Eliot's *The Waste Land*, or Faulkner's *The Sound and the Fury*. It was no accident that the work, in spite of being published privately to a meager distribution, should have found its fame, as the

---

[5] The existence of this vision has been questioned, for example, by Meyer Schapiro in his essay "On the Aesthetic Attitude in Romanesque Art," collected in *Art and Thought* (1947).

Education did, after the First World War when knowledge of the fragmentation and inner paradoxes of the modern world was no longer the privilege of the learned, subtle, and disenchanted mind of the aged Adams, but was appropriated by the romantic melancholy of a generation of college sophomores as well as by that of their elders.

The *Education* was finished in 1906, when Adams was sixty-eight years old. He had been everywhere; had known everybody that he wanted to know, politicians, artists, writers, scientists, and charming ladies; was adored by distinguished friends strategically scattered in the great cities of the world so that he was at home wherever he went; and at home he lived surrounded by objects of art collected in his travels and by massive furniture built somewhat low so as not to dwarf the master of the house, who, though not a dwarf, was not very big—in a temple of taste of which Santayana, once a visitor there, got the "impression that, if most things were illusions, having money and spending money were great realities."

Here, with all passion and ambition fading, proud and, when irony failed him, peevish as he confronted his "failures," he was witty, handsome, and charming (except occasionally to a distinguished Jew[6]), with impeccably civilized

[6] There was a streak of ambiguous anti-Semitism in Adams, as illustrated by his friendship with Bernard Berenson, the art historian and critic, much younger than he, who, of humble origins, had made by brilliance and charm a financial and literary success that was an affront to Adams' chronic sense of failure. Ernest Samuels, in *Henry Adams: The Major Phase*, gives an anecdote:

> Once in Washington after Berenson and his wife left, Adams burst out, "I *can't* bear it. There is in the Jew deprecation, something that no weary sinner ought to stand. I rarely murder. By nature I am humane. . . . Yet I did murder Berenson [sic]. . . . In my own house I ought not to have done so. I tried to do it gently, without temper or violence of manner. Alas! murder will out!"

But Berenson, in spite of whatever veiled but insulting irony Adams had visited upon him, continued the friendship. He later said that they had much in common, but Adams "could not forget that he was an Adams and was always more embarrassed than I that I happened

discriminations, an *éminence grise* rising above the mudflats of corruption and the parched prairies of barbarous mediocrity of a world which he had certainly never made and for which he cherished only a contempt that he was often too well-bred to express. Now summoning up his last aging energies, in a combination of self-depreciation and self-vindication, he wrote the great book which consolidated his fame.

Education, Adams says, in a language that echoes his theory that human conduct could be understood in purely scientific terms, should "train minds to react, not at haphazard, but by choice, on the lines of force that attract their world"—such a force, for instance, as that represented by the Virgin as he had described her or the "dynamo" as he had found it at the Chicago World's Fair, the emblem of modern scientific energy. "The sum of force attracts; the feeble atom or molecule called man is attracted; he suffers education or growth; he is the sum of the forces that attract him; his body and his thought are alike their product. . . ." The educated man can "react with vigor and economy," for he knows his world and his proper relation to it. This was what Adams felt that he himself had not done. He was not, therefore, educated. But why not?

The nub of the answer to this question is that Adams, by reason of the very privileges to which he was born, was underprivileged. Puritan idealism, the belief that life is meaningful, the faith in the "old Ciceronian idea of government by the best," the notion that politics should represent moral law, the belief that education was "divine"—it developed that such things would, in the modern world, turn out to be handicaps. He began life, he says, "nearer the year 1 than to the year 1900." But the initial handicap was to be compounded by a series of failures.

But whose failures?

to be a Jew." And he should have added: "And a success."

Among other lesser breeds without the law, Adams could class Filipinos, who were, to him, the "usual worthless Malay types."

Adams failed to get educated, but the world also failed to educate him, and this equivocation is the root irony of the book. Adams sought meaning all his life but he found it nowhere, not as a young journalist trying to reform democracy; not in the doctrine of Darwin, for evolution turned out to be just another "religion," a faith and not a fact morally or socially significant; not in the history of America, or of mankind, which had led to multiplicity and meaninglessness; not in human love, with all its frailty before the hazards of nature (though Adams did not treat that aspect of his own life); not in religion or art, for at the end of *Mont-Saint-Michel and Chartres* we find that such a moment of unity and fulfillment was based, as all societies are always based, on a fiction, an illusion, and could not last. He had found no truth to give meaning to the multiplicity of life. The last hope to give meaning—though a chilling and impersonal one—would be the idea that the discovery of some natural law of history would bring what seemed multiplicity into a unified order—that is, a determined universe would be for him, as it had been for the philosopher Spinoza, the equivalent of God. The last part of the *Education* is devoted to this question; but a solution here, though it might give satisfaction to Adams as a philosopher, would not, presumably, give satisfaction to him as moralist; it would not give meaning to the act of will, being able to explain only the irrelevance, the illusion, of will.

In his long quest, as he himself implies in discussing the part of his education before the Civil War, Adams had simply been acting in accordance with his Puritan intellectual tradition. The Puritan had assumed the working out of God's will in nature and in history, and Adams, as the critic Yvor Winters has said, was "as passionate an allegorist as [Cotton] Mather had been; instead of seeing God's meaning in every event, he saw the meaninglessness of a godless universe, but with a Calvinistic intensity of vision."

Not only the Puritan fathers stood behind the *Education*, but Saint Augustine's *Confessions*, that first real autobiography in history,

the first story of a soul. As Ernest Samuels, in *Henry Adams: The Major Phase*, puts it, the parallels between Augustine and Adams are so persuasive that he could hardly have missed them. Both came at a moment in history when society had lost its old sanctions. Both had been passionately committed to success. Both had a very limited faith in human possibility, and both lived with a constant feeling of self-condemnation. Both, though seekers after a faith, had a deep vein of skepticism. Both had known love and bereavement. And to come to a small detail, both had been professors who freed themselves from such obligations in order to pursue a literary career. Furthermore, Adams found in Augustine the psychological concern with the meaning of consciousness and memory that lay behind his own work, as when Augustine wrote: "Great is the power of memory, a deep and boundless manifoldness, and this thing is the mind, and this am I myself." So Augustine in plunging into memory was seeking to encounter the self. And this was what Adams was doing. He found in that first autobiographer what James Russell Lowell called the "introversion of mind" that marked modernity.

The *Education* is not merely a personal and philosophical record; it is, in another dimension, a work of art, and if this dimension had not existed, the impact of the work would never have been felt. As a work of art it has the urgency of personal experience and the commanding force of a dramatic structure. To Henry James, who proclaimed the *Education* a "superlatively precious achievement," Adams replied, in a self-deprecation that was characteristic, and characteristically both ironical and pathological, that his work was "rotten," and that of all the great autobiographers only Augustine had an "idea of literary form—a notion of writing a story with an end and an object, not for the sake of the object, but for the form, like a romance." Thus he implied the ideal that he had aspired to and, according to his rejection of the praise of James, failed to achieve.

It is now a widespread conviction that he did not fail to achieve it, and certainly the key factor contributing to such success would be the point of view—the creation of "Adams" as a fictional device, a mask, a *persona*. And here the word "romance," in the remark to James, is significant. Adams had already written two "romances" on the obsessive theme of his life and of the *Education,* the quest for a meaning to validate life. In *Democracy* and *Esther* he had written his "romances," which, as novels, proposed an existence "not for the sake of the object [that is, the purpose], but for the form." In these novels he had, indeed, failed to achieve the inward "form" he sought, and the basic reason why this "form" eluded him was that the questers, Madeleine and Esther, for all Adams' intuitive sympathy for, and appreciation of, women, are not realized as characters; they are "written about," but they do not exist except in the "aboutness" of a schema. Adams had, no doubt, projected his own experience into fiction as a way of forming it, and into women as a way of giving the distance to his experience necessary for the forming; but in so doing he had lost the intensity of the experiencer's existence that would give meaning and form—form-as-felt—to the experience. Now with the fictional "Adams" as a mask he could achieve the necessary distance for focus and control to achieve form and at the same time profit from the reality of the character that, as a poor novelist, he could not create.

After the *Education* Adams published three more books, two of which were a continuation of the "Dynamic Theory of History" outlined in the last part of the great work. He hoped that the natural law would be discovered that governs the thought and behavior of man and the movements of the "stellar universe." Such a law would give him, he thought, the unity his soul craved. He could not face, as did his friend William James, the idea of a world of multiplicity, nor face the effort of trying to frame a philosophy in such terms. So he clung to his theory, but prophesying in terms of this theory and its rigid determinism, he saw little chance for other than a tragic end for human endeavor—no more chance, in fact, than did

his brother Brooks Adams, the author of *The Law of Civilization and Decay,* to whom we have previously referred.

The last book of Adams was a brief memorial biography of the young poet George Cabot Lodge, the son of Senator Henry Cabot Lodge and a sort of protégé of Adams, an intelligent and sensitive young man, who, disgusted with the materialism of America, had staked his life on being a poet. Adams had no illusions about the value of his work, but in writing the critically discreet memorial he would inevitably see the dead man as, somehow, a victim of crass modernity. As Edith Wharton was afterward to say, the young poet was, rather, the victim of "the slightly rarefied atmosphere of mutual admiration, and disdain of the rest of the world, that prevailed in his immediate surroundings," where the "dominating spirits were Henry Adams and [Senator] Cabot Lodge." She added that these "influences kept Bay [the nickname of the poet] in a state of brilliant immaturity."

Mutual admiration and disdain of the rest of the world—she was aptly describing something of the faintly miasmal atmosphere of the circle Adams was the center of, an atmosphere that may have contributed to the "state of brilliant immaturity" that sometimes strikes one about Adams himself. But then Adams, unlike poor "Bay," was a genius, and the true mark of genius is the capacity to make something out of the most crippling limitations.

The last days of Adams were grim. Reading the autobiography of Henry James, which pictured the world he had grown up in, he burst out: "Why did we live? Was that all?" But the grimness was sometimes relieved by mordant flashes of irony, that laughter of the mind corresponding to the wilder laughter with which Mark Twain greeted his despairs and his own sense of failure and guilt. Adams, like Mark Twain, had gone beyond the mere conquest by laughter. In the "Adams" of the *Education,* both as a record and as a creation, he had given an image that more and more has served to sum up, in human urgency and anguish, the spirit of a disordered and questioning age.

Adams died in Washington, in 1918, before the end of the war that he had predicted as one of the catastrophes to mark the break-up of the civilization he had known. He was buried beside his wife in the Rock Creek Cemetery. By his direction, his grave there was unmarked.

It was his final way of spitting in the world's eye.

BIOGRAPHICAL CHART

1838   Born, February 16, in Boston, Massachusetts, fourth of five children of Charles Francis Adams and Abigail Brown Brooks

1854–58   Attends Harvard College, contributes to the *Harvard Magazine*, and gives the Class Day Oration, June, 1858

1858–60   Studies law at the University of Berlin; travels in Europe; does sporadic journalism, including an interview with Garibaldi

1860   Returns to the United States in October; to Washington as private secretary to his father

1861–68   Goes to London as private secretary to his father, minister to Great Britain; works as anonymous correspondent to the New York *Times*; first attempts at historical writing, three articles in the *North American Review* of 1867

1868–70   Goes to Washington, as free-lance political journalist

1870   Becomes assistant professor of medieval history at Harvard and editor of the *North American Review*

1872   Marries Marian Hooper, June 27; year-long wedding trip includes Europe and a trip up the Nile

1876   Edits *Essays in Anglo-Saxon Law*; resigns editorship of the *North American Review*

1877   Moves to Washington

1879   *The Life of Albert Gallatin*; work on the *History of the United States During the Administrations of Jefferson and Madison*

1880   *Democracy: An American Novel* published anonymously, his most popular work during his lifetime

1882   *John Randolph*, in the American Statesmen Series

1884   *Esther*, under the pseudonym Frances Snow Compton

1885   Wife commits suicide December 6, in Washington

1886   Travels to Japan with the painter John La Farge

1889–91   First two volumes of the trade edition of the *History*; four more volumes issued the following year; the last three in January, 1891

1890–92   Travels with La Farge to Hawaii, Samoa, Tahiti, Fiji, Australia, Ceylon, and Europe

1891   *Historical Essays*, mostly a reprinting of earlier pieces

1893   Elected, in absentia, president of the American Historical Association for 1894

1902   *Mont-Saint-Michel and Chartres* completed in December; privately printed in 1904; trade edition in 1913

1906   Finishes *The Education of Henry Adams*; a few copies printed the following year and sent to friends and persons mentioned in the text

1908   *The Rule of Phase Applied to History* written and offered to the *American Historical Review* early in 1909; refused for publication

1910   *A Letter to American Teachers of History* printed and sent to professors of history at various universities; few replies

1911   *The Life of George Cabot Lodge*

1914   In France at the outbreak of the First World War; escapes to England

1918   Dies, March 27, in Washington; buried beside his wife in Rock Creek Cemetery

FURTHER READINGS

There is no standard edition of Adams' works. The reader is referred to the individual works mentioned in the biographical chart.

Worthington C. Ford, ed., *Letters* (1930–38)

Carl Becker, *Every Man His Own Historian* (1935)
R. P. Blackmur, "The Harmony of True Liberalism: Henry Adams' *Mont-Saint-Michel and Chartres*," *Sewanee Review* (Summer, 1952)

Van Wyck Brooks, *New England: Indian Summer* (1940)
George Hochfield, *Henry Adams: An Introduction and Interpretation* (1962)
Irving Howe, *Politics and the Novel* (1957)
William H. Jordy, *Henry Adams: Scientific Historian* (1951)
J. C. Levenson, *The Mind and Art of Henry James* (1957)
Jay Martin, *Harvests of Change* (1967)

Paul Elmer More, *A New England Group and Others:*
  Shelburne Essays, Eleventh Series (1921)
Ernest Samuels, *The Young Henry Adams* (1948)
———, *Henry Adams: The Middle Years* (1958)

———, *Henry Adams: The Major Phase* (1964)
Elizabeth Stevenson, *Henry Adams, a Biography* (1956)
Yvor Winters, *In Defense of Reason* (1947)

From Mont-Saint-Michel and Chartres (1904)

CHAPTER 6: THE VIRGIN OF CHARTRES

We must take ten minutes to accustom our eyes to the light, and we had better use them to seek the reason why we come to Chartres rather than to Rheims or Amiens or Bourges, for the cathedral that fills our ideal. The truth is, there are several reasons; there generally are, for doing the things we like; and after you have studied Chartres to the ground, and got your reasons settled, you will never find an antiquarian to agree with you; the architects will probably listen to you with contempt; and even these excellent priests, whose kindness is great, whose patience is heavenly, and whose good opinion you would so gladly gain, will turn from you with pain, if not with horror. The Gothic is singular in this; one seems easily at home in the Renaissance; one is not too strange in the Byzantine; as for the Roman, it is ourselves; and we could walk blindfolded through every chink and cranny of the Greek mind; all these styles seem modern, when we come close to them; but the Gothic gets away. No two men think alike about it, and no woman agrees with either man. The Church itself never agreed about it, and the architects agree even less than the priests. To most minds it casts too many shadows; it wraps itself in mystery; and when people talk of mystery, they commonly mean fear. To others, the Gothic seems hoary with age and decrepitude, and its shadows mean death. What is curious to watch is the fanatical conviction of the Gothic enthusiast, to whom the twelfth century means exuberant youth, the eternal child of Wordsworth, over whom its immortality broods like the day; it is so simple and yet so complicated; it sees so much and so little; it loves so many toys and cares for so few necessities; its youth is so young, its age so old, and its youthful yearning for old thought is so disconcerting, like the mysterious senility of the baby that—

> Deaf and silent, reads the eternal deep,
> Haunted forever by the eternal mind.

One need not take it more seriously than one takes the baby itself. Our amusement is to play with it, and to catch its meaning in its smile; and whatever Chartres may be now, when young it was a smile. To the Church, no doubt, its cathedral here has a fixed and administrative meaning, which is the same as that of every other bishop's seat and with which we have nothing whatever to do. To us, it is a child's fancy; a toy-house to please the Queen of Heaven,—to please her so much that she would be happy in it,—to charm her till she smiled.

The Queen Mother was as majestic as you like; she was absolute; she could be stern; she was not above being angry; but she was still a woman, who loved grace, beauty, ornament,—her toilette, robes, jewels;—who considered the arrangements of her palace with attention, and liked both light and colour; who kept a keen eye on her Court, and exacted prompt and willing obedience from king and archbishops as well as from beggars and drunken priests. She protected her friends and punished her enemies. She required space, beyond what was known in the Courts of kings, because she was liable at all times to have ten thousand people begging her for favours—mostly inconsistent with law—and deaf to refusal. She was extremely sensitive to neglect, to disagreeable impressions, to want of intelligence in her surroundings. She was the greatest artist, as she was the greatest philosopher and musician and theologist, that ever lived on earth, except her Son, Who, at Chartres, is still an Infant under her guardianship. Her taste was infallible; her silence eternally final. This church was built for her in this spirit of simple-minded, practical, utilitarian faith,—in this singleness of thought, exactly as a little girl sets up a doll-house for her favourite blonde doll. Unless you can go back to your dolls, you are out of place here. If you can go back to them, and get rid of one small hour of the weight of custom, you shall see Chartres in glory.

The palaces of earthly queens were hovels compared with these palaces of the Queen of Heaven at Chartres, Paris, Laon, Noyon, Rheims, Amiens, Rouen, Bayeux, Coutances,—a list that might be stretched into a volume. The nearest approach we have made to a palace was the Merveille at Mont-Saint-Michel, but no Queen had a palace equal to that. The Merveille was built, or designed, about the year 1200; toward the year 1500, Louis XI built a great castle at Loches in Touraine, and there Queen Anne de Bretagne had apartments which still exist, and which we will visit. At Blois you shall see the residence which served for Catherine de Medicis till her death in 1589. Anne de Bretagne was trebly queen, and Catherine de Medicis took her standard of comfort from the luxury of Florence. At Versailles you can see the apartments which the queens of the Bourbon line occupied through their century of magnificence. All put together, and then trebled in importance, could not rival the splendour of any single cathedral dedicated to Queen Mary in the thirteenth century; and of them all, Chartres was built to be peculiarly and exceptionally her delight.

One has grown so used to this sort of loose comparison, this reckless waste of words, that one no longer adopts an idea unless it is driven in with hammers of statistics and columns of figures. With the irritating demand for literal exactness and perfectly straight lines which lights up every truly American eye, you will certainly ask when this exaltation of Mary began, and unless you get the dates, you will doubt the facts. It is your own fault if they are tiresome; you might easily read them all in the "Iconographie de la Sainte Vierge," by M. Rohault de Fleury, published in 1878. You can start at Byzantium with the Empress Helena in 326, or with the Council of Ephesus in 431. You will find the Virgin acting as the patron saint of Constantinople and of the Imperial residence, under as many names as Artemis or Aphrodite had borne. As Godmother ($\Theta\epsilon o\mu\eta\tau\eta\rho$), Deipara ($\Theta\epsilon o\tau o\kappa o\varsigma$), Pathfinder ('$O\delta\eta\gamma\eta\tau\rho\iota\alpha$), she was the chief favourite of the Eastern Empire, and her picture was carried at the head of every procession and hung on the wall of every hut and hovel, as it is still wherever the Greek Church goes. In the year 610, when Heraclius sailed from Carthage to dethrone Phocas at Constantinople, his ships carried the image of the Virgin at their mastheads. In 1143, just before the flèche on the Chartres clocher was begun, the Basileus John Comnenus died, and so devoted was he to the Virgin that, on a triumphal entry into Constantinople, he put the image of the Mother of God in his chariot, while

he himself walked. In the Western Church the Virgin had always been highly honoured, but it was not until the crusades that she began to over-shadow the Trinity itself. Then her miracles became more frequent and her shrines more frequented, so that Chartres, soon after 1100, was rich enough to build its western portal with Byzantine splendour. A proof of the new outburst can be read in the story of Citeaux. For us, Citeaux means Saint Bernard, who joined the Order in 1112, and in 1115 founded his Abbey of Clairvaux in the territory of Troyes. In him, the religious emotion of the half-century between the first and second crusades (1095–1145) centred as in no one else. He was a French precursor of Saint Francis of Assisi who lived a century later. If we were to plunge into the story of Citeaux and Saint Bernard we should never escape, for Saint Bernard incarnates what we are trying to understand, and his mind is further from us than the architecture. You would lose hold of everything actual, if you could comprehend in its contradictions the strange mixture of passion and caution, the austerity, the self-abandonment, the vehemence, the restraint, the love, the hate, the miracles, and the scepticism of Saint Bernard. The Cistercian Order, which was founded in 1098, from the first put all its churches under the special protection of the Virgin, and Saint Bernard in his time was regarded as the apple of the Virgin's eye. Tradition as old as the twelfth century, which long afterwards gave to Murillo the subject of a famous painting, told that once, when he was reciting before her statue the "Ave Maris Stella," and came to the words, "Monstra te esse Matrem," the image, pressing its breast, dropped on the lips of her servant three drops of the milk which had nourished the Saviour. The same miracle, in various forms, was told of many other persons, both saints and sinners; but it made so much impression on the mind of the age that, in the fourteenth century, Dante, seeking in Paradise for some official introduction to the foot of the Throne, found no intercessor with the Queen of Heaven more potent than Saint Bernard. You can still read Bernard's hymns to the Virgin, and even his sermons, if you like. To him she was the great mediator. In the eyes of a culpable humanity, Christ was too sublime, too terrible, too just, but not even the weakest human frailty could fear to approach his Mother. Her attribute was humility; her love and pity were infinite. "Let him deny your mercy who can say that he has ever asked it in vain."

Saint Bernard was emotional and to a certain degree mystical, like Adam de Saint-Victor, whose hymns were equally famous, but the emotional saints and mystical poets were not by any means allowed to establish exclusive rights to the Virgin's favour. Abélard was as devoted as they were, and wrote hymns as well. Philosophy claimed her, and Albert the Great, the head of scholasticism, the teacher of Thomas Aquinas, decided in her favour the question: "Whether the Blessed Virgin possessed perfectly the seven liberal arts." The Church at Chartres had decided it a hundred years before by putting the seven liberal arts next her throne, with Aristotle himself to witness; but Albertus gave the reason: "I hold that she did, for it is written, 'Wisdom has built herself a house, and has sculptured seven columns.' That house is the blessed Virgin; the seven columns are the seven liberal arts. Mary, therefore, had perfect mastery of science." Naturally she had also perfect mastery of economics, and most of her great churches were built in economic centres. The guilds were, if possible, more devoted to her than the monks; the bourgeoisie of Paris, Rouen, Amiens, Laon, spend money by millions to gain her favour. Most surprising of all, the great military class was perhaps the most vociferous. Of all inappropriate haunts for the gentle, courteous, pitying Mary, a field of battle seems to be the worst, if not distinctly blasphemous; yet the greatest French warriors insisted on her leading them into battle, and in the actual mêlée when men were killing each other, on every battle-field in Europe, for at least five hundred years, Mary was present, leading both sides. The battle-cry of the famous Constable du Guesclin was "Notre-Dame-Guesclin"; "Notre-Dame-Coucy" was the cry of the great Sires de Coucy; "Notre-Dame-Auxerre"; "Notre-Dame-Sancerre"; "Notre-Dame-Hainault"; "Notre-Dame-Gueldres"; "Notre-Dame-Bourbon"; "Notre-Dame-Bearn";—all well-known battle-cries. The King's own battle at one time cried, "Notre-Dame-Saint-Denis-Montjoie"; the Dukes of Burgundy cried, "Notre-Dame-Bourgogne"; and even the soldiers of the Pope were said to cry, "Notre-Dame-Saint-Pierre."

The measure of this devotion, which proves to any religious American mind, beyond possible cavil, its serious and practical reality, is the money it cost. According to statistics, in the single century between 1170 and 1270, the French built eighty cathedrals and nearly five hundred churches of the cathedral class, which would have cost, according to an estimate made in 1840, more than five thou-

sand millions to replace. Five thousand million francs is a thousand million dollars, and this covered only the great churches of a single century. The same scale of expenditure had been going on since the year 1000, and almost every parish in France had rebuilt its church in stone; to this day France is strewn with the ruins of this architecture, and yet the still preserved churches of the eleventh and twelfth centuries, among the churches that belong to the Romanesque and Transition period, are numbered by hundreds until they reach well into the thousands. The share of this capital which was—if one may use a commercial figure—invested in the Virgin cannot be fixed, any more than the total sum given to religious objects between 1000 and 1300; but in a spiritual and artistic sense, it was almost the whole, and expressed an intensity of conviction never again reached by any passion, whether of religion, of loyalty, of patriotism, or of wealth; perhaps never even parallelled by any single economic effort, except in war. Nearly every great church of the twelfth and thirteenth centuries belonged to Mary, until in France one asks for the church of Notre Dame as though it meant cathedral; but, not satisfied with this, she contracted the habit of requiring in all churches a chapel of her own, called in English the "Lady Chapel," which was apt to be as large as the church but was always meant to be handsomer; and there, behind the high altar, in her own private apartment, Mary sat, receiving her innumerable suppliants, and ready at any moment to step up upon the high altar itself to support the tottering authority of the local saint.

Expenditure like this rests invariably on an economic idea. Just as the French of the nineteenth century invested their surplus capital in a railway system in the belief that they would make money by it in this life, in the thirteenth they trusted their money to the Queen of Heaven because of their belief in her power to repay it with interest in the life to come. The investment was based on the power of Mary as Queen rather than on any orthodox Church conception of the Virgin's legitimate station. Papal Rome never greatly loved Byzantine empresses or French queens. The Virgin of Chartres was never wholly sympathetic to the Roman Curia. To this day the Church writers—like the Abbé Bulteau or M. Rohault de Fleury—are singularly shy of the true Virgin of majesty, whether at Chartres or at Byzantium or wherever she is seen. The fathers Martin and Cahier at Bourges alone left her true value. Had the Church controlled her, the Virgin would perhaps have remained prostrate at the foot of the Cross. Dragged by a Byzantine Court, backed by popular insistence and impelled by overpowering self-interest, the Church accepted the Virgin throned and crowned, seated by Christ, the Judge throned and crowned; but even this did not wholly satisfy the French of the thirteenth century who seemed bent on absorbing Christ in His Mother, and making the

> O salutaris Virgo Stella Maris
> Generans prolem, Æquitatis solem,
> Lucis auctorem, Retinens pudorem,
>   Suscipe laudem!
>
> Celi Regina Per quam medicina
> Datur ægrotis, Gratia devotis,
> Gaudium molstis, Mundo lux cœlestis,
>   Spesque salutis;
>
> Aula regalis, Virgo specialis,
> Posce medelam Nobis et tutelam,
> Suscipe vota, Precibusque cuncta
>   Pelle molesta!

As the lyrical poet of the twelfth century, Adam de Saint-Victor seems to have held rank higher if possible than that of Saint Bernard, and his hymns

> Imperatrix supernorum!
> Superatrix infernorum!
> Eligenda via cœli,
> Retinenda spe fideli,
> Separatos a te longe
> Revocatos ad te junge
>   Tuorum collegio!

To delight in the childish jingle of the mediæval Latin is a sign of a futile mind, no doubt, and I beg pardon of you and of the Church for wasting your precious summer day on poetry which was regarded as mystical in its age and which now

> Salve, Mater Salvatoris!
> Vas electum! Vas honoris!
>   Vas cœlestis Gratiæ!
> Ab æterno Vas provisum!
> Vas insigne! Vas excisum
>   Manu sapientiæ!
>
> Salve, Mater pietatis,
> Et totius Trinitatis
>   Nobile Triclinium!
> Verbi tamen incarnati
> Speciale majestati
>   Præparans hospitium!

Mother the Church, and Christ the Symbol.

The Church had crowned and enthroned her almost from the beginning, and could not have dethroned her if it would. In all Christian art—sculpture or mosaic, painting or poetry—the Virgin's rank was expressly asserted. Saint Bernard, like John Comnenus, and probably at the same time (1120–40), chanted hymns to the Virgin as Queen:—

> O saviour Virgin, Star of Sea,
> Who bore for child the Son of Justice,
> The source of Light, Virgin always
>   Hear our praise!
>
> Queen of Heaven who have given
> Medicine to the sick, Grace to the devout,
> Joy to the sad, Heaven's light to the world
>   And hope of salvation;
>
> Court royal, Virgin typical,
> Grant us cure and guard,
> Accept our vows, and by prayers
>   Drive all griefs away!

on the Virgin are certainly quite as emphatic an assertion of her majesty:—

> Empress of the highest,
> Mistress over the lowest,
> Chosen path of Heaven,
> Held fast by faithful hope,
> Those separated from you far,
> Recalled to you, unite
>   In your fold!

sounds like a nursery rhyme; but a verse or two of Adam's hymn on the Assumption of the Virgin completes the record of her rank, and goes to complete also the documentary proof of her majesty at Chartres:—

> Mother of our Saviour, hail!
> Chosen vessel! Sacred Grail!
>   Font of celestial grace!
> From eternity forethought!
> By the hand of Wisdom wrought!
>   Precious, faultless Vase!
>
> Hail, Mother of Divinity!
> Hail, Temple of the Trinity!
>   Home of the Triune God!
> In whom the Incarnate Word hath birth,
> The King! to whom you gave on earth
>   Imperial abode.

O Maria! Stella maris!
Dignitate singularis,
Super omnes ordinaris
    Ordines cœlestium!
In supremo sita poli
Nos commenda tuæ proli,
Ne terrores sive doli
    Nos supplantent hostium!

Oh, Maria! Constellation!
Inspiration! Elevation!
Rule and Law and Ordination
    Of the angels' host!
Highest height of God's Creation,
Pray your Son's commiseration,
Lest, by fear or fraud, salvation
    For our souls be lost!

Constantly—one might better say at once, officially, she was addressed in these terms of supreme majesty; "Imperatrix supernorum!" "Cœli Regina!" "Aula regalis!" but the twelfth century seemed determined to carry the idea out to its logical conclusion in defiance of dogma. Not only was the Son absorbed in the Mother, or represented as under her guardianship, but the Father fared no better, and the Holy Ghost followed. The poets regarded the Virgin as the "Templum Trinitatis"; "totius Trinitatis nobile Triclinium." She was the refectory of the Trinity—the "Triclinium"—because the refectory was the largest room and contained the whole of the members, and was divided in three parts by two rows of columns. She was the "Templum Trinitatis," the Church itself, with its triple aisle. The Trinity was absorbed in her.

This is a delicate subject in the Church, and you must feel it with delicacy, without brutally insisting on its necessary contradictions. All theology and all philosophy are full of contradictions quite as flagrant and far less sympathetic. This particular variety of religious faith is simply human, and has made its appearance in one form or another in nearly all religions; but though the twelfth century carried it to an extreme, and at Chartres you see it in its most charming expression, we have got always to make allowances for what was going on beneath the surface in men's minds, consciously or unconsciously, and for the latent scepticism which lurks behind all faith. The Church itself never quite accepted the full claims of what was called Mariolatry. One may be sure, too, that the bourgeois capitalist and the student of the schools, each from his own point of view, watched the Virgin with anxious interest. The bourgeois had put an enormous share of his capital into what was in fact an economical speculation, not unlike the South Sea Scheme, or the railway system of our own time; except that in one case the energy was devoted to shortening the road to Heaven; in the other, to shortening the road to Paris; but no serious schoolman could have felt entirely convinced that God would enter into a business partnership with man, to establish a sort of joint-stock society for altering the operation of divine and universal laws. The bourgeois cared little for the philosophical doubt if the economical result proved to be good, but he watched this result with his usual practical sagacity, and required an experience of only about three generations (1200–1300) to satisfy himself that relics were not certain in their effects; that the Saints were not always able or willing to help; that Mary herself could not certainly be bought or bribed; that prayer without money seemed to be quite as efficacious as prayer with money; and that neither the road to Heaven nor Heaven itself had been made surer or brought nearer by an investment of capital which amounted to the best part of the wealth of France. Economically speaking, he became satisfied that his enormous money-investment had proved to be an almost total loss, and the reaction on his mind was as violent as the emotion. For three hundred years it prostrated France. The efforts of the bourgeoisie and the peasantry to recover their property, so far as it was recoverable, have lasted to the present day and we had best take care not to get mixed in those passions.

If you are to get the full enjoyment of Chartres, you must, for the time, believe in Mary as Bernard and Adam did, and feel her presence as the architects did, in every stone they placed, and every touch they chiselled. You must try first to rid your mind of the traditional idea that the Gothic is an intentional expression of religious gloom. The necessity for light was the motive of the Gothic architects. They needed light and always more light, until they sacrificed safety and common sense in trying to get it. They converted their walls into windows, raised their vaults, diminished their piers, until their churches could no longer stand. You will see the limits at Beauvais; at Chartres we have not got so far, but even here, in places where the Virgin wanted it,—as above the high altar,—the architect has taken all the light there was to take. For the same reason, fenestration became the most important part of the Gothic architect's work, and at Chartres was uncommonly interesting because the architect was obliged to design a new system, which should at the same time satisfy the laws of construction and the taste and imagination of Mary. No doubt the first command of the Queen of Heaven was for light, but the second, at least equally imperative, was for colour. Any earthly queen, even though she were not Byzantine in taste, loved colour; and the truest of queens— the only true Queen of Queens—had richer and finer taste in colour than the queens of fifty earthly kingdoms, as you will see when we come to the immense effort to gratify her in the glass of her windows. Illusion for illusion,—granting for the moment that Mary was an illusion,—the Virgin Mother in this instance repaid to her worshippers a larger return for their money than the capitalist has ever been able to get, at least in this world, from any other illusion of wealth which he has tried to make a source of pleasure and profit.

The next point on which Mary evidently insisted was the arrangement for her private apartments, the apse, as distinguished from her throne-room, the choir; both being quite distinct from the hall, or reception-room of the public, which was the nave with its enlargements in the transepts. This arrangement marks the distinction between churches built as shrines for the deity and churches built as halls of worship for the public. The difference is chiefly in the apse, and the apse of Chartres is the most interesting of all apses from this point of view.

The Virgin required chiefly these three things, or, if you like, these four: space, light, convenience; and colour decoration to unite and harmonize the whole. This concerns the interior; on the exterior she required statuary, and the only complete system of decorative sculpture that existed seems to belong to her churches:—Paris, Rheims, Amiens, and Chartres. Mary required all this magnificence at Chartres for herself alone, not for the public. As far as one can see into the spirit of the builders, Chartres was exclusively intended for the Virgin, as the Temple of Abydos was intended for Osiris. The wants of man, beyond a mere roof-cover, and perhaps space to some degree, enter to no very great extent into the problem of Chartres. Man came to render homage or to ask favours. The Queen received him in her palace, where she alone was at home, and alone gave commands.

The artist's second thought was to exclude from his work everything that could displease Mary; and

since Mary differed from living queens only in infinitely greater majesty and refinement, the artist could admit only what pleased the actual taste of the great ladies who dictated taste at the Courts of France and England, which surrounded the little Court of the Counts of Chartres. What they were—these women of the twelfth and thirteenth centuries—we shall have to see or seek in other directions; but Chartres is perhaps the most magnificent and permanent monument they left of their taste, and we can begin here with learning certain things which they were not.

In the first place, they were not in the least vague, dreamy, or mystical in a modern sense;—far from it! They seemed anxious only to throw the mysteries into a blaze of light; not so much physical, perhaps,—since they, like all women, liked moderate shadow for their toilettes,—but luminous in the sense of faith. There is nothing about Chartres that you would think mystical, who know your Lohengrin, Siegfried, and Parsifal. If you care to make a study of the whole literature of the subject, read M. Mâle's "Art Religieux du XIIIe Siècle en France," and use it for a guide-book. Here you need only note how symbolic and how simple the sculpture is, on the portals and porches. Even what seems a grotesque or an abstract idea is no more than the simplest child's personification. On the walls you may have noticed the *Ane qui vielle*,— the ass playing the lyre; and on all the old churches you can see "bestiaries," as they were called, of fabulous animals, symbolic or not; but the symbolism is as simple as the realism of the oxen at Laon. It gave play to the artist in his effort for variety of decoration, and it amused the people, —probably the Virgin also was not above being amused;—now and then it seems about to suggest what you would call an esoteric meaning, that is to say, a meaning which each one of us can consider private property reserved for our own amusement, and from which the public is excluded; yet, in truth, in the Virgin's churches the public is never excluded, but invited. The Virgin even had the additional charm of the public that she was popularly supposed to have no very marked fancy for priests as such; she was a queen, a woman, and a mother, functions, all, which priests could not perform. Accordingly, she seems to have had little taste for mysteries of any sort, and even the symbols that seem most mysterious were clear to every old peasant-woman in her church. The most pleasing and promising of them all is the woman's figure you saw on the front of the cathedral in Paris; her eyes bandaged; her head bent down; her crown falling; without cloak or royal robe; holding in her hand a guidon or banner with its staff broken in more than one place. On the opposite pier stands another woman, with royal mantle, erect and commanding. The symbol is so graceful that one is quite eager to know its meaning; but every child in the Middle Ages would have instantly told you that the woman with the falling crown meant only the Jewish Synagogue, as the one with the royal robe meant the Church of Christ.

Another matter for which the female taste seemed not much to care was theology in the metaphysical sense. Mary troubled herself little about theology except when she retired into the south transept with Pierre de Dreux. Even there one finds little said about the Trinity, always the most metaphysical subtlety of the Church. Indeed, you might find much amusement here in searching the cathedral for any distinct expression at all of the Trinity as a dogma recognized by Mary. One cannot take seriously the idea that the three doors, the three portals, and the three aisles express the Trinity, because, in the first place, there was no rule about it; churches might have what portals and aisles they pleased; both Paris and Bourges have five; the doors themselves are not allotted to the three members of the Trinity, nor are the portals; while another more serious objection is that the side doors and aisles are not of equal importance with the central, but mere adjuncts and dependencies, so that the architect who had misled the ignorant public into accepting so black a heresy would have deserved the stake, and would probably have gone to it. Even this suggestion of trinity is wanting in the transepts, which have only one aisle, and in the choir, which has five, as well as five or seven chapels, and, as far as an ignorant mind can penetrate, no triplets whatever. Occasionally, no doubt, you will discover in some sculpture or window, a symbol of the Trinity, but this discovery itself amounts to an admission of its absence as a controlling idea, for the ordinary worshipper must have been at least as blind as we are, and to him, as to us, it would have seemed a wholly subordinate detail. Even if the Trinity, too, is anywhere expressed, you will hardly find here an attempt to explain its metaphysical meaning—not even a mystic triangle.

The church is wholly given up to the Mother and the Son. The Father seldom appears; the Holy Ghost still more rarely. At least, this is the impression made on an ordinary visitor who has no motive to be orthodox; and it must have been the same with the thirteenth-century worshipper who came here with his mind absorbed in the perfections of Mary. Chartres represents, not the Trinity, but the identity of the Mother and Son. The Son represents the Trinity, which is thus absorbed in the Mother. The idea is not orthodox, but this is no affair of ours. The Church watches over its own.

The Virgin's wants and tastes, positive and negative, ought now to be clear to enable you to feel the artist's sincerity in trying to satisfy them; but first you have still to convince yourselves of the people's sincerity in employing the artists. This point is the easiest of all, for the evidence is express. In the year 1145 when the old flèche was begun,—the year before Saint Bernard preached the second crusade at Vézelay,—Abbot Haimon, of Saint-Pierre-sur-Dives in Normandy, wrote to the monks of Tutbury Abbey in England a famous letter to tell of the great work which the Virgin was doing in France and which began at the Church of Chartres. "Hujus sacræ institutionis ritus apud Carnotensem, ecclesiam est inchoatus." From Chartres it had spread through Normandy, where it produced among other things the beautiful spire which we saw at Saint-Pierre-sur-Dives. "Postremo per totam fere Normanniam longe lateque convaluit ac loca per singula Matri misericordiæ dicata præcipue occupavit." The movement affected especially the places devoted to Mary, but ran through all Normandy, far and wide. Of all Mary's miracles, the best attested, next to the preservation of her church, is the building of it; not so much because it surprises us as because it surprised even more the people of the time and the men who were its instruments. Such deep popular movements are always surprising, and at Chartres the miracle seems to have occurred three times, coinciding more or less with the dates of the crusades, and taking the organization of a crusade, as Archbishop Hugo of Rouen described it in a letter to Bishop Thierry of Amiens. The most interesting part of this letter is the evident astonishment of the writer, who might be talking to us to-day, so modern is he:—

The inhabitants of Chartres have combined to aid in the construction of their church by transporting the materials; our Lord has rewarded their humble zeal by miracles which have roused the Normans to imitate the piety of their neighbours. . . . Since then the faithful of our diocese and of other neighbouring regions have formed associations for the same object; they admit no one into their company unless he has been to confession, has renounced enmities and revenges, and has reconciled himself with his enemies. That done, they elect a chief, under whose direction they conduct their waggons in silence and with humility.

The quarries at Berchères-l'Evêque are about five miles from Chartres. The stone is excessively hard, and was cut in blocks of considerable size, as you can see for yourselves; blocks which required great effort to transport and lay in place. The work was done with feverish rapidity, as it still shows, but it is the solidist building of the age, and without a sign of weakness yet. The Abbot told, with more surprise than pride, of the spirit which was built into the cathedral with the stone:—

Who has ever seen!—Who has ever heard tell, in times past, that powerful princes of the world, that men brought up in honour and in wealth, that nobles, men and women, have bent their proud and haughty necks to the harness of carts, and that, like beasts of burden, they have dragged to the abode of Christ these waggons, loaded with wines, grains, oil, stone, wood, and all that is necessary for the wants of life, or for the construction of the church? But while they draw these burdens, there is one thing admirable to observe; it is that often when a thousand persons and more are attached to the chariots,— so great is the difficulty,—yet they march in such silence that not a murmur is heard, and truly if one did not see the thing with one's eyes, one might believe that among such a multitude there was hardly a person present. When they halt on the road, nothing is heard but the confession of sins, and pure and suppliant prayer to God to obtain pardon. At the voice of the priests who exhort their hearts to peace, they forget all hatred, discord is thrown far aside, debts are remitted, the unity of hearts is established. But if any one is so far advanced in evil as to be unwilling to pardon an offender, or if he rejects the counsel of the priest who has piously advised him, his offering is instantly thrown from the wagon

as impure, and he himself ignominiously and shamefully excluded from the society of the holy. There one sees the priests who preside over each chariot exhort every one to penitence, to confession of faults, to the resolution of better life! There one sees old people, young people, little children, calling on the Lord with a suppliant voice, and uttering to Him, from the depth of the heart, sobs and sighs with words of glory and praise! After the people, warned by the sound of trumpets and the sight of banners, have resumed their road, the march is made with such ease that no obstacle can retard it. . . . When they have reached the church they arrange the wagons about it like a spiritual camp, and during the whole night they celebrate the watch by hymns and canticles. On each waggon they light tapers and lamps; they place there the infirm and sick, and bring them the precious relics of the Saints for their relief. Afterwards the priests and clerics close the ceremony by processions which the people follow with devout heart, imploring the clemency of the Lord and of his Blessed Mother for the recovery of the sick.

Of course, the Virgin was actually and constantly present during all this labour, and gave her assistance to it, but you would get no light on the architecture from listening to an account of her miracles, nor do they heighten the effect of popular faith. Without the conviction of her personal presence, men would not have been inspired; but, to us, it is rather the inspiration of the art which proves the Virgin's presence, and we can better see the conviction of it in the work than in the words. Every day, as the work went on, the Virgin was present, directing the architects, and it is this direction that we are going to study, if you have now got a realizing sense of what it meant. Without this sense, the church is dead. Most persons of a deeply religious nature would tell you emphatically that nine churches out of ten actually were dead-born, after the thirteenth century, and that church architecture became a pure matter of mechanism and mathematics; but that is a question for you to decide when you come to it; and the pleasure consists not in seeing the death, but in feeling the life.

Now let us look about!

From The Education of Henry Adams (1907)

CHAPTER I: QUINCY (1838–1848)

Under the shadow of Boston State House, turning its back on the house of John Hancock, the little passage called Hancock Avenue runs, or ran, from Beacon Street, skirting the State House grounds, to Mount Vernon Street, on the summit of Beacon Hill; and there, in the third house below Mount Vernon Place, February 16, 1838, a child was born, and christened later by his uncle, the minister of the First Church after the tenets of Boston Unitarianism, as Henry Brooks Adams.

Had he been born in Jerusalem under the shadow of the Temple and circumcized in the Synagogue by his uncle the high priest, under the name of Israel Cohen, he would scarcely have been more distinctly branded, and not much more heavily handicapped in the races of the coming century, in running for such stakes as the century was to offer; but, on the other hand, the ordinary traveller, who does not enter the field of racing, finds advantage in being, so to speak, ticketed through life, with the safeguards of an old, established traffic. Safeguards are often irksome, but sometimes convenient, and if one needs them at all, one is apt to need them badly. A hundred years earlier, such safeguards as his would have secured any young man's success; and although in 1838 their value was not very great compared with what they would have had in 1738, yet the mere accident of starting a twentieth-century career from a nest of associations so colonial—so troglodytic—as the First Church, the Boston State House, Beacon Hill, John Hancock and John Adams, Mount Vernon Street and Quincy, all crowding on ten pounds of unconscious babyhood, was so queer as to offer a subject of curious speculation to the baby long after he had witnessed the solution. What could become of such a child of the seventeenth and eighteenth centuries, when he should wake up to find himself required to play the game of the twentieth? Had he been consulted, would he have cared to play the game at all, holding such cards as he held, and suspecting that the game was to be one of which neither he nor any one else back to the beginning of time knew the rules or the risks or the stakes? He was not consulted and was not responsible, but had he been taken into the confidence of his parents, he would certainly have told them to change nothing as far as concerned him. He

would have been astounded by his own luck. Probably no child, born in the year, held better cards than he. Whether life was an honest game of chance, or whether the cards were marked and forced, he could not refuse to play his excellent hand. He could never make the usual plea of irresponsibility. He accepted the situation as though he had been a party to it, and under the same circumstances would do it again, the more readily for knowing the exact values. To his life as a whole he was a consenting, contracting party and partner from the moment he was born to the moment he died. Only with that understanding—as a consciously assenting member in full partnership with the society of his age—had his education an interest to himself or to others.

As it happened, he never got to the point of playing the game at all; he lost himself in the study of it, watching the errors of the players; but this is the only interest in the story, which otherwise has no moral and little incident. A story of education—seventy years of it—the practical value remains to the end in doubt, like other values about which men have disputed since the birth of Cain and Abel; but the practical value of the universe has never been stated in dollars. Although every one cannot be a Gargantua-Napoleon-Bismarck and walk off with the great bells of Notre Dame, every one must bear his own universe, and most persons are moderately interested in learning how their neighbors have managed to carry theirs.

. . .

The atmosphere of education in which he lived was colonial, revolutionary, almost Cromwellian, as though he were steeped, from his greatest grandmother's birth, in the odor of political crime. Resistance to something was the law of New England nature; the boy looked out on the world with the instinct of resistance; for numberless generations his predecessors had viewed the world chiefly as a thing to be reformed, filled with evil forces to be abolished, and they saw no reason to suppose that they had wholly succeeded in the abolition; the duty was unchanged. That duty implied not only resistance to evil, but hatred of it. Boys naturally look on all force as an enemy, and generally find it

Puritan hate

so, but the New Englander, whether boy or man, in his long struggle with a stingy or hostile universe, had learned also to love the pleasure of hating; his joys were few.

Politics, as a practice, whatever its professions, had always been the systematic organization of hatreds, and Massachusetts politics had been as harsh as the climate. The chief charm of New England was harshness of contrasts and extremes of sensibility—a cold that froze the blood, and a heat that boiled it—so that the pleasure of hating—one's self if no better victim offered—was not its rarest amusement; but the charm was a true and natural child of the soil, not a cultivated weed of the ancients. The violence of the contrast was real and made the strongest motive of education. The double exterior nature gave life its relative values. Winter and summer, cold and heat, town and country, force and freedom, marked two modes of life and thought, balanced like lobes of the brain. Town was winter confinement, school, rule, discipline; straight, gloomy streets, piled with six feet of snow in the middle; frosts that made the snow sing under wheels or runners; thaws when the streets became dangerous to cross; society of uncles, aunts, and cousins who expected children to behave themselves, and who were not always gratified; above all else, winter represented the desire to escape and go free. Town was restraint, law, unity. Country, only seven miles away, was liberty, diversity, outlawry, the endless delight of mere sense impressions given by nature for nothing, and breathed by boys without knowing it.

. . .

Winter and summer were two hostile lives and bred two separate natures. Winter was always the effort to live; summer was tropical license. Whether the children rolled in the grass, or waded in the brook, or swam in the salt ocean, or sailed in the bay, or fished for smelts in the creeks, or netted minnows in the salt-marshes, or took to the pine-woods and the granite quarries, or chased muskrats and hunted snapping-turtles in the swamps, or mushrooms or nuts on the autumn hills, summer and country were always sensual living, while winter was always compulsory learning. Summer was the multiplicity of nature; winter was school.

The bearing of the two seasons on the education of Henry Adams was no fancy; it was the most decisive force he ever knew; it ran through life, and made the division between its perplexing, warring, irreconcilable problems, irreducible opposites, with growing emphasis to the last year of study. From earliest childhood the boy was accustomed to feel that, for him, life was double. Winter and summer, town and country, law and liberty, were hostile, and the man who pretended they were not, was in his eyes a schoolmaster—that is, a man employed to tell lies to little boys. Though Quincy was but two hours' walk from Beacon Hill, it belonged in a different world. For two hundred years, every Adams, from father to son, had lived within sight of State Street, and sometimes had lived in it, yet none had ever taken kindly to the town, or been taken kindly by it. The boy inherited his double nature. He knew as yet nothing about his great-grandfather, who had died a dozen years before his own birth; he took for granted that any great-grandfather of his must have always been good, and his enemies wicked; but he divined his great-grandfather's character from his own. Never for a moment did he connect the two ideas of Boston and John Adams; they were separate and antagonistic; the idea of John Adams went with Quincy. He knew his grandfather John Quincy Adams only as an old man of seventy-five or eighty who was friendly and gentle with him, but except that he heard his grandfather always called "the President," and his grandmother "the Madam," he had no reason to suppose that his Adams grandfather differed in character from his Brooks grandfather who was equally kind and benevolent. He liked the Adams side best, but for no other reason than that it reminded him of the country, the summer, and the absence of restraint. Yet he felt also that Quincy was in a way inferior to Boston, and that socially Boston looked down on Quincy. The reason was clear enough even to a five-year old child. Quincy had no Boston style. Little enough style had either; a simpler manner of life and thought could hardly exist, short of cave-dwelling. The flint-and-steel with which his grandfather Adams used to light his own fires in the early morning was still on the mantel-piece of his study. The idea of a livery or even a dress for servants, or of an evening toilette, was next to blasphemy. Bathrooms, water-supplies, lighting, heating, and the whole array of domestic comforts, were unknown at Quincy. Boston had already a bathroom, a water-supply, a furnace, and gas. The superiority of Boston was evident, but a child liked it no better for that.

The magnificence of his grandfather Brooks's house in Pearl Street or South Street has long ago disappeared, but perhaps his country house at Medford may still remain to show what impressed the mind of a boy in 1845 with the idea of city splendor. The President's place at Quincy was the larger and older and far the more interesting of the two; but a boy felt at once its inferiority in fashion. It showed plainly enough its want of wealth. It smacked of colonial age, but not of Boston style or plush curtains. To the end of his life he never quite overcame the prejudice thus drawn in with his childish breath. He never could compel himself to care for nineteenth-century style. He was never able to adopt it, any more than his father or grandfather or great-grandfather had done. Not that he felt it as particularly hostile, for he reconciled himself to much that was worse; but because, for some remote reason, he was born an eighteenth-century child. The old house at Quincy was eighteenth century. What style it had was in its Queen Anne mahogany panels and its Louis Seize chairs and sofas. The panels belonged to an old colonial Vassall who built the house; the furniture had been brought back from Paris in 1789 or 1801 or 1817, along with porcelain and books and much else of old diplomatic remnants; and neither of the two eighteenth-century styles—neither English Queen Anne nor French Louis Seize—was comfortable for a boy, or for any one else. The dark mahogany had been painted white to suit daily life in winter gloom. Nothing seemed to favor, for a child's objects, the older forms. On the contrary, most boys, as well as grown-up people, preferred the new, with good reason, and the child felt himself distinctly at a disadvantage for the taste.

. . .

The attachment to Quincy was not altogether sentimental or wholly sympathetic. Quincy was not a bed of thornless roses. Even there the curse of Cain set its mark. There as elsewhere a cruel universe combined to crush a child. As though three or four vigorous brothers and sisters, with the best will, were not enough to crush any child, every one else conspired towards an education which he hated. From cradle to grave this problem of running order through chaos, direction through space, discipline through freedom, unity through multiplicity, has always been, and must always be, the task of education, as it is the moral of religion, philosophy, science, art, politics, and economy; but a boy's will is his life, and he dies when it is broken, as the colt dies in harness, taking a new nature in becoming tame. Rarely has the boy felt kindly towards his tamers. Between him and his master has always been war. Henry Adams never knew a boy of his generation to like a master, and the task of remaining on friendly terms with one's own family, in such a relation, was never easy.

All the more singular it seemed afterwards to him that his first serious contact with the President should have been a struggle of will, in which the old man almost necessarily defeated the boy, but instead of leaving, as usual in such defeats, a lifelong sting, left rather an impression of as fair treatment as could be expected from a natural enemy. The boy met seldom with such restraint. He could not have been much more than six years old at the time—seven at the utmost—and his mother had taken him to Quincy for a long stay with the President during the summer. What became of the rest of the family he quite forgot; but he distinctly remembered standing at the house door one summer morning in a passionate outburst of rebellion against going to school. Naturally his mother was the immediate victim of his rage; that is what mothers are for, and boys also; but in this case the boy had his mother at unfair disadvantage, for she was a guest, and had no means of enforcing obedience. Henry showed a certain tactical ability by refusing to start, and he met all efforts at compulsion by successful, though too vehement protest. He was in fair way to win, and was holding his own, with sufficient energy, at the bottom of the long staircase which led up to the door of the President's library, when the door opened, and the old man slowly came down. Putting on his hat, he took the boy's hand without a word, and walked with him, paralyzed by awe, up the road to the town. After the first moments of consternation at this interference in a domestic dispute, the boy reflected that an old gentleman close on eighty would never trouble himself to walk near a mile on a hot summer morning over a shadeless road to take a boy to school, and that it would be strange if a lad imbued with the passion of freedom could not find a corner to dodge around, somewhere before reaching the school door. Then and always, the boy insisted that this reasoning justified his apparent submission; but the old man did not stop, and the boy saw all his strategical points turned, one after another, until he found himself seated inside the school, and obviously the centre of curious if not malevolent criticism. Not till then did the President release his hand and depart.

The point was that this act, contrary to the inalienable rights of boys, and nullifying the social compact, ought to have made him dislike his grandfather for life. He could not recall that it had this effect even for a moment. With a certain maturity of mind, the child must have recognized that the President, though a tool of tyranny, had done his disreputable work with a certain intelligence. He had shown no temper, no irritation, no personal feeling, and had made no display of force. Above all, he had held his tongue. During their long walk he had said nothing; he had uttered no syllable of revolting cant about the duty of obedience and the wickedness of resistance to law; he had shown no concern in the matter; hardly even a consciousness of the boy's existence. Probably his mind at that moment was actually troubling itself little about his grandson's iniquities, and much about the iniquities of President Polk, but the boy could scarcely at that age feel the whole satisfaction of thinking that President Polk was to be vicarious victim of his own sins, and he gave his grandfather credit for intelligent silence. For this forbearance he felt instinctive respect. He admitted force as a form of right; he admitted even temper, under protest; but the seeds of a moral education would at that moment have fallen on the stoniest soil in Quincy, which is, as every one knows, the stoniest glacial and tidal drift known in any Puritan land.

Neither party to this momentary disagreement can have felt rancor, for during these three or four summers the old President's relations with the boy were friendly and almost intimate. Whether his older brothers and sisters were still more favored he failed to remember, but he was himself admitted to a sort of familiarity which, when in his turn he had reached old age, rather shocked him, for it must have sometimes tried the President's patience. He hung about the library; handled the books; deranged the papers; ransacked the drawers; searched the old purses and pocket-books for foreign coins; drew the sword-cane; snapped the travelling-pistols; upset everything in the corners, and penetrated the President's dressing-closet where a row of tumblers, inverted on the shelf, covered caterpillars which were supposed to become moths or butterflies, but never did. The Madam bore with fortitude the loss of the tumblers which her husband purloined for these hatcheries; but she made protest when he carried off her best cut-glass bowls to plant with acorns or peachstones that he might see the roots grow, but which, she said, he commonly forgot like the caterpillars.

At that time the President rode the hobby of tree-culture, and some fine old trees should still remain to witness it, unless they have been improved off the ground; but his was a restless mind, and although he took his hobbies seriously and would have been annoyed had his grandchild asked whether he was bored like an English duke, he probably cared more for the processes than for the results, so that his grandson was saddened by the sight and smell of peaches and pears, the best of their kind, which he brought up from the garden to rot on his shelves for seed. With the inherited virtues of his Puritan ancestors, the little boy Henry conscientiously brought up to him in his study the finest peaches he found in the garden, and ate only the less perfect. Naturally he ate more by way of compensation, but the act showed that he bore no grudge. As for his grandfather, it is even possible that he may have felt a certain self-reproach for his temporary rôle of schoolmaster—seeing that his own career did not offer proof of the worldly advantages of docile obedience—for there still exists somewhere a little volume of critically edited Nursery Rhymes with the boy's name in full written in the President's trembling hand on the fly-leaf. Of course there was also the Bible, given to each child at birth, with the proper inscription in the President's hand on the fly-leaf; while their grandfather Brooks supplied the silver mugs.

So many Bibles and silver mugs had to be supplied, that a new house, or cottage, was built to hold them. It was "on the hill," five minutes' walk above "the old house," with a far view eastward over Quincy Bay, and northward over Boston. Till his twelfth year, the child passed his summers there, and his pleasures of childhood mostly centered in it. Of education he had as yet little to complain. Country schools were not very serious. Nothing stuck to the mind except home impressions, and the sharpest were those of kindred children; but as influences that warped a mind, none compared with the mere effect of the back of the President's bald head, as he sat in his pew on Sundays, in line with that of President Quincy, who, though some ten years younger, seemed to children about the same age. Before railways entered the New England town, every parish church showed half-a-dozen of these leading citizens, with gray hair, who sat on the main aisle in the best pews, and had sat there, or in some equivalent dignity, since the time of St. Augustine, if not since the glacial epoch. It was unusual for boys to sit behind a President grandfather, and to read over his head the tablet in memory of a President great-grandfather, who had "pledged his life, his fortune, and his sacred honor" to secure the independence of his country and so forth; but boys naturally supposed, without much reasoning, that other boys had the equivalent of President grandfathers, and that churches would always go on, with the bald-headed leading citizens on the main aisle, and Presidents or their equivalents on the walls. The Irish gardener once said to the child: "You'll be thinkin' you'll be President too!" The casualty of the remark made so strong an impression on his mind that he never forgot it. He could not remember ever to have thought on the subject; to him, that there should be a doubt of his being President was a new idea. What had been would continue to be. He doubted neither about Presidents nor about Churches, and no one suggested at that time a doubt whether a system of society which had lasted since Adam would outlast one Adams more.

. . .

CHAPTER 25: THE DYNAMO AND THE VIRGIN (1900)

Until the Great Exposition of 1900 closed its doors in November, Adams haunted it, aching to absorb knowledge, and helpless to find it. He would have liked to know how much of it could have been grasped by the best-informed man in the world. While he was thus meditating chaos, Langley[1] came by, and showed it to him. At Langley's behest, the Exhibition dropped its superfluous rags and stripped itself to the skin, for Langley knew what to study, and why, and how; while Adams might as well have stood outside in the night, staring at the Milky Way. Yet Langley said nothing new, and taught nothing that one might not have learned from Lord Bacon, three hundred years before; but though one should have known the "Advancement of Science" as well as one knew the "Comedy of Errors," the literary knowledge counted for nothing until some teacher should show how to apply it. Bacon took a vast deal of trouble in teaching King James I and his subjects, American

[1] Samuel Pierpont Langley (1834–1906), director of the Smithsonian Institution from 1887 to 1906, inventor of the bolometer, a device used to measure the solar spectrum, and of the steam-driven airplane, a pilotless craft. Langley also contributed to knowledge of lift and drag on a plane moving at measured speed.

or other, towards the year 1620, that true science was the development or economy of forces; yet an elderly American in 1900 knew neither the formula nor the forces; or even so much as to say to himself that his historical business in the Exposition concerned only the economies or developments of force since 1893, when he began the study at Chicago.

Nothing in education is so astonishing as the amount of ignorance it accumulates in the form of inert facts. Adams had looked at most of the accumulations of art in the storehouses called Art Museums; yet he did not know how to look at the art exhibits of 1900. He had studied Karl Marx and his doctrines of history with profound attention, yet he could not apply them at Paris. Langley, with the ease of a great master of experiment, threw out of the field every exhibit that did not reveal a new application of force, and naturally threw out, to begin with, almost the whole art exhibit. Equally, he ignored almost the whole industrial exhibit. He led his pupil directly to the forces. His chief interest was in new motors to make his airship feasible, and he taught Adams the astonishing complexities of the new Daimler motor, and of the automobile, which, since 1893, had become a nightmare at a hundred kilometres an hour, almost as destructive as the electric tram which was only ten years older; and threatening to become as terrible as the locomotive steam-engine itself, which was almost exactly Adam's own age.

Then he showed his scholar the great hall of dynamos, and explained how little he knew about electricity or force of any kind, even of his own special sun, which spouted heat in inconceivable volume, but which, as far as he knew, might spout less or more, at any time, for all the certainty he felt in it. To him, the dynamo itself was but an ingenious channel for conveying somewhere the heat latent in a few tons of poor coal hidden in a dirty engine-house carefully kept out of sight; but to Adams the dynamo became a symbol of infinity. As he grew accustomed to the great gallery of machines, he began to feel the forty-foot dynamos as a moral force, much as the early Christians felt the Cross. The planet itself seemed less impressive, in its old-fashioned, deliberate, annual or daily revolution, than this huge wheel, revolving within arm's-length at some vertiginous speed, and barely murmuring—scarcely humming an audible warning to stand a hair's-breadth further for respect of power—while it would not wake the baby lying close against its frame. Before the end, one began to pray to it; inherited instinct taught the natural expression of man before silent and infinite force. Among the thousand symbols of ultimate energy, the dynamo was not so human as some, but it was the most expressive.

Yet the dynamo, next to the steam-engine, was the most familiar of exhibits. For Adams's objects its value lay chiefly in its occult mechanism. Between the dynamo in the gallery of machines and the engine-house outside, the break of continuity amounted to abysmal fracture for a historian's objects. No more relation could he discover between the steam and the electric current than between the Cross and the cathedral. The forces were interchangeable if not reversible, but he could see only an absolute *fiat* in electricity as in faith. Langley could not help him. Indeed, Langley seemed to be worried by the same trouble, for he constantly repeated that the new forces were anarchical, and specially that he was not responsible for the new rays, that were little short of parricidal in their wicked spirit towards science. His own rays, with which he had doubled the solar spectrum, were altogether harmless and beneficent; but Radium denied its God—or, what was to Langley the same thing, denied the truths of his Science. The force was wholly new.

A historian who asked only to learn enough to be as futile as Langley or Kelvin, made rapid progress under this teaching, and mixed himself up in the tangle of ideas until he achieved a sort of Paradise of ignorance vastly consoling to his fatigued senses. He wrapped himself in vibrations and rays which were new, and he would have hugged Marconi and Branly had he met them, as he hugged the dynamo; while he lost his arithmetic in trying to figure out the equation between the discoveries and the economies of force. The economies, like the discoveries, were absolute, supersensual, occult; incapable of expression in horsepower. What mathematical equivalent could he suggest as the value of a Branly coherer? Frozen air, or the electric furnace, had some scale of measurement, no doubt, if somebody could invent a thermometer adequate to the purpose; but X-rays had played no part whatever in man's consciousness, and the atom itself had figured only as a fiction of thought. In these seven years man had translated himself into a new universe which had no common scale of measurement with the old. He had entered a supersensual world, in which he could measure nothing except by chance collisions of movements imperceptible to his senses,

perhaps even imperceptible to his instruments, but perceptible to each other, and so to some known ray at the end of the scale. Langley seemed prepared for anything, even for an indeterminable number of universes interfused—physics stark mad in metaphysics.

Historians undertake to arrange sequences,—called stories, or histories—assuming in silence a relation of cause and effect. These assumptions, hidden in the depths of dusty libraries, have been astounding, but commonly unconscious and childlike; so much so, that if any captious critic were to drag them to light, historians would probably reply, with one voice, that they had never supposed themselves required to know what they were talking about. Adams, for one, had toiled in vain to find out what he meant. He had even published a dozen volumes of American history for no other purpose than to satisfy himself whether, by the severest process of stating, with the least possible comment, such facts as seemed sure, in such order as seemed rigorously consequent, he could fix for a familiar moment a necessary sequence of human movement. The result had satisfied him as little as at Harvard College. Where he saw sequence, other men saw something quite different, and no one saw the same unit of measure. He cared little about his experiments and less about his statesmen, who seemed to him quite as ignorant as himself and, as a rule, no more honest; but he insisted on a relation of sequence, and if he could not reach it by one method, he would try as many methods as science knew. Satisfied that the sequence of men led to nothing and that the sequence of their society could lead no further, while the mere sequence of time was artificial, and the sequence of thought was chaos, he turned at last to the sequence of force; and thus it happened that, after ten years' pursuit, he found himself lying in the Gallery of Machines at the Great Exposition of 1900, his historical neck broken by the sudden irruption of forces totally new.

Since no one else showed much concern, an elderly person without other cares had no need to betray alarm. The year 1900 was not the first to upset schoolmasters. Copernicus and Galileo had broken many professional necks about 1600; Columbus had stood the world on its head towards 1500; but the nearest approach to the revolution of 1900 was that of 310, when Constantine set up the Cross. The rays that Langley disowned, as well as those which he fathered, were occult, supersensual, irrational; they were a revelation of mysterious energy like that of the Cross; they were what, in terms of mediæval science, were called ⟨immediate modes of the divine substance.⟩

The historian was thus reduced to his last resources. Clearly if he was bound to reduce all these forces to a common value, this common value could have⟨no measure but that of their attraction on his own mind.⟩He must treat them as they had been felt; as convertible, reversible, interchangeable attractions on thought. He made up his mind to venture it; he would risk translating rays into faith. Such a reversible process would vastly amuse a chemist, but the chemist could not deny that he, or some of his fellow physicists, could feel the force of both. When Adams was a boy in Boston, the best chemist in the place had probably never heard of Venus except by way of scandal, or of the Virgin except as idolatry; neither had he heard of dynamos or automobiles or radium; yet his mind was ready to feel the force of all, though the rays were unborn and the women were dead.

Here opened another totally new education, which promised to be by far the most hazardous of all. The knife-edge along which he must crawl, like Sir Lancelot in the twelfth century, divided two kingdoms of force which had nothing in common but attraction. They were as different as a magnet is from gravitation, supposing one knew what a magnet was, or gravitation, or love. The force of the Virgin was still felt at Lourdes, and seemed to be as potent as X-rays; but in America neither Venus nor Virgin ever had value as force—at most as sentiment. No American had ever been truly afraid of either.

This problem in dynamics gravely perplexed an American historian. The Woman had once been supreme; in France she still seemed potent, not merely as a sentiment, but as a force. Why was she unknown in America? For evidently America was ashamed of her, and she was ashamed of herself, otherwise they would not have strewn fig-leaves so profusely all over her. When she was a true force, she was ignorant of fig-leaves, but the monthly-magazine-made American female had not a feature that would have been recognized by Adam. The trait was notorious, and often humorous, but any one brought up among Puritans knew that sex was sin. In any previous age, sex was strength. Neither art nor beauty was needed. Every one, even among Puritans, knew that neither Diana of the Ephesians nor any of the Oriental goddesses was worshipped for her beauty. She was goddess because of her force; she was the animated dy-

namo; she was reproduction—the greatest and most mysterious of all energies; all she needed was to be fecund. Singularly enough, not one of Adams's many schools of education had ever drawn his attention to the opening lines of Lucretius, though they were perhaps the finest in all Latin literature, where the poet invoked Venus exactly as Dante invoked the Virgin:—

"Quae quoniam rerum naturam *sola* gubernas."
[Since therefore you alone govern the nature of things.]

The Venus of Epicurean philosophy survived in the Virgin of the Schools:—

"Donna, sei tanto grande, e tanto vali,
Che qual vuol grazia, e a te non ricorre,
Sua disianza vuol volar senz' ali."

[Lady, you are so great and so prevailing
That whoever wishes grace and does not turn to you,
His desire wishes to fly without wings.]

All this was to American thought as though it had never existed. The true American knew something of the facts, but nothing of the feelings; he read the letter, but he never felt the law. Before this historical chasm, a mind like that of Adams felt itself helpless; he turned from the Virgin to the Dynamo as though he were a Branly coherer. On one side, at the Louvre and at Chartres, as he knew by the record of work actually done and still before his eyes, was the highest energy ever known to man, the creator of four-fifths of his noblest art, exercising vastly more attraction over the human mind than all the steam-engines and dynamos ever dreamed of; and yet this energy was unknown to the American mind. An American Virgin would never dare command; an American Venus would never dare exist.

The question, which to any plain American of the nineteenth century seemed as remote as it did to Adams, drew him almost violently to study, once it was posed; and on this point Langleys were as useless as though they were Herbert Spencers or dynamos. The idea survived only as art. There one turned as naturally as though the artist were himself a woman. Adams began to ponder, asking himself whether he knew of any American artist who had ever insisted on the power of sex, as every classic had always done; but he could think only of Walt Whitman; Bret Harte, as far as the magazines would let him venture; and one or two painters, for the flesh-tones. All the rest had used sex for sentiment, never for force; to them, Eve was a tender flower, and Herodias an unfeminine horror. American art, like the American language and American education, was as far as possible sexless. Society regarded this victory over sex as its greatest triumph, and the historian readily admitted it, since the moral issue, for the moment, did not concern one who was studying the relations of un-moral force. He cared nothing for the sex of the dynamo until he could measure its energy.

Vaguely seeking a clue, he wandered through the art exhibit, and, in his stroll, stopped almost every day before St. Gaudens's General Sherman, which had been given the central post of honor. St. Gaudens himself was in Paris, putting on the work his usual interminable last touches, and listening to the usual contradictory suggestions of brother sculptors. Of all the American artists who gave to American art whatever life it breathed in the seventies, St. Gaudens was perhaps the most sympathetic, but certainly the most inarticulate. General Grant or Don Cameron had scarcely less instinct of rhetoric than he. All the others—the Hunts, Richardsons, John La Farge, Stanford White —were exuberant; only St. Gaudens could never discuss or dilate on an emotion, or suggest artistic arguments for giving to his work the forms that he felt. He never laid down the law, or affected the despot, or became brutalized like Whistler by the brutalities of his world. He required no incense; he was no egoist; his simplicity of thought was excessive; he could not imitate, or give any form but his own to the creations of his hand. No one felt more strongly than he the strength of other men, but the idea that they could affect him never stirred an image in his mind.

This summer his health was poor and his spirits were low. For such a temper, Adams was not the best companion, since his own gaiety was not *folle*; but he risked going now and then to the studio on Mont Parnasse to draw him out for a stroll in the Bois de Boulogne, or dinner as pleased his moods, and in return St. Gaudens sometimes let Adams go about in his company.

Once St. Gaudens took him down to Amiens, with a party of Frenchmen, to see the cathedral. Not until they found themselves actually studying the sculpture of the western portal, did it dawn on Adams's mind that, for his purposes, St. Gaudens on that spot had more interest to him than the cathedral itself. Great men before great monu-

ments express great truths, provided they are not taken too solemnly. Adams never tired of quoting the supreme phrase of his idol Gibbon, before the Gothic cathedrals: "I darted a contemptuous look on the stately monuments of superstition." Even in the footnotes of his history, Gibbon had never inserted a bit of humor more human than this, and one would have paid largely for a photograph of the fat little historian, on the background of Notre Dame of Amiens, trying to persuade his readers—perhaps himself—that he was darting a contemptuous look on the stately monument, for which he felt in fact the respect which every man of his vast study and active mind always feels before objects worthy of it; but besides the humor, one felt also the relation. Gibbon ignored the Virgin, because in 1789 religious monuments were out of fashion. In 1900 his remark sounded fresh and simple as the green fields to ears that had heard a hundred years of other remarks, mostly no more fresh and certainly less simple. Without malice, one might find it more instructive than a whole lecture of Ruskin. One sees what one brings, and at that moment Gibbon brought the French Revolution. Ruskin brought reaction against the Revolution. St. Gaudens had passed beyond all. He liked the stately monuments much more than he liked Gibbon or Ruskin; he loved their dignity; their unity; their scale; their lines; their lights and shadows; their decorative sculpture; but he was even less conscious than they of the force that created it all—the Virgin, the Woman—by whose genius "the stately monuments of superstition" were built, through which she was expressed. He would have seen more meaning in Isis with the cow's horns, at Edfoo, who expressed the same thought. The art remained, but the energy was lost even upon the artist.

Yet in mind and person St. Gaudens was a survival of the 1500; he bore the stamp of the Renaissance, and should have carried an image of the Virgin round his neck, or stuck in his hat, like Louis XI. In mere time he was a lost soul that had strayed by chance into the twentieth century, and forgotten where it came from. He writhed and cursed at his ignorance, much as Adams did at his own, but in the opposite sense. St. Gaudens was a child of Benvenuto Cellini, smothered in an American cradle. Adams was a quintessence of Boston, devoured by curiosity to think like Benvenuto. St. Gaudens's art was starved from birth, and Adams's instinct was blighted from babyhood. Each had but half of a nature, and when they came together before the Virgin of Amiens they ought both to have felt in her the force that made them one; but it was not so. To Adams she became more than ever a channel of force; to St. Gaudens she remained as before a channel of taste.

OLIVER WENDELL HOLMES, JR. (1841–1935)

Oliver Wendell Holmes, Jr., was born on March 8, 1841, under the presidency of General William Henry Harrison, and died on March 5, 1935, under the presidency of Franklin D. Roosevelt. He lived with furious energy and ruthless ambition, and accomplished much, but the literal achievements were somehow absorbed into his great fame, and in the end, even among legal specialists who could assess the mark he had made in his profession, he had become a symbol honored not so much for what he had done as for what he stood for.

But what did he symbolize? First of all, he symbolized some principle of continuity in our national life, the persistence of old vitality and old virtue. The face of the erect old man with the aggressive hawk-nose and the bristling cavalryman's mustache might have looked out of a daguerreotype of the Civil War. But Holmes also symbolized some principle of change, not merely of adjustment to change but the will to participate in it. Holmes, in himself and in his career, dramatized the eternal tension between these two poles of life, continuity and change, and this fact is what underlay his role as a symbol, as, in fact, a culture hero. He symbolized the old America *and* the new. Through many vicissitudes, crises, and failures of nerve, he embodied a famous utterance of his: "life is action and passion." But if life was to be lived with such full commitment, it was also to be regarded with a calm irony, beyond any illusion: man was an "experiment" of nature.

Dr. Oliver Wendell Holmes had defined the "Brahmin" of Boston (see pp. 631–33), and his son was clearly conscious of being of that order. "All my three names designate families from which I am descended," he wrote in his autobiographical sketch in the album of the Harvard class of 1861, and then proceeded to document the statement. Holmes's awareness of blood and position, however, fired ambitious energy rather than flattered easy complacency, from the time he split the Greek prize at Harvard, in 1861, to the time, in 1933, when the new President came to call and found the ninety-one-year-old justice reading Plato to "improve" his mind.

When the Civil War came, Holmes, twenty years old, volunteered as a private and, as we have said, took his final examinations in uniform. Then the war, and his real education, began. He was wounded three times—at Ball's Bluff, Antietam, and Marye's Heights—and each time returned to active duty. During his service, his beliefs were to run through several phases. He had volunteered as an abolitionist, seeing the war as the "Christian crusade of the 19th century," and he could say, years later, that "in our youth our hearts were touched with fire." But, as Melville put it, "What like a bullet can undeceive?" In a little time, in the reality of war and disgusted by the armchair ferocity and cut-rate idealism of civilians, particularly, it would seem, by that of his father (who was, however, no abolitionist), Holmes could say that he had no hope of the "subjugation (for that is what it is) of a great civilized nation" and was willing to trust to the idea that if the North did represent progress and a better civilization, these things would "conquer in the long run . . . and will stand a better chance in their proper province—peace—than in war, the brother of slavery. . . ."

Holmes stayed on, however, even after the

third wound, through the Wilderness, Spotsylvania, and Cold Harbor—where troops, not expecting to survive, went into action with their names pinned to their uniforms. He fought well and honorably, but by June, 1864, the young lieutenant colonel (brevetted at Chancellorsville) had had enough: "I am now a man and I have been coming to the conclusion for the last six months that my duty has changed."

There is no way to know what went on in his soul. In later years Holmes hated to read about the war or to talk about it, but he had the habit of noting the anniversaries of the battles in which he was wounded, the soldierly discipline had sunk deep into him, and in 1895, speaking on the occasion where he received an honorary LL.D. from Harvard, he could shock his audience with his vision of the meaning of military experience. Holmes knew the reality of pain, funk, and tears, and what it was "to pass a night on the ground in the rain with your bowels out of order," but—and here is where he administered the shock—he added:

> I do not know the meaning of the universe. But in the midst of doubt, in the collapse of creeds, there is one thing I do not doubt, that no man who lives in the same world with most of us can doubt, and that is that the faith is true and adorable which leads a soldier to throw away his life in obedience to a blindly accepted duty, in a cause which he little understands, in a plan of campaign of which he has no notion, under tactics of which he does not see the use. ("The Soldier's Faith")

In the same speech from which we have just quoted, Holmes asks who could endure a life without the "divine folly of honor" that sustains the soldier; he also asks who could endure without the "senseless passion for knowledge." Having known the first, Holmes now turned to the second to sustain him. He was, for the next few years, one of a brilliant group of young men who knew that the old order had passed away and who were trying to discover the nature of—no, to create—the one to come. William James, as we have seen, was one of the group,

perhaps the person closest to Holmes at the time, but there were also among them Henry James and the mathematician and philosopher Charles Peirce, who was to influence William James so profoundly. With them and their friends Holmes debated the great questions, for from the start Holmes knew that if one wanted to be more than a technician of the law, one had to understand the nature of the world in which the law was conceived and the nature of the men who conceived it. In a world where the study of law usually was a "thick fog of details—in a black and frozen night," he said to himself: "law is human—it is a part of man, and of one world with the rest." Furthermore, law was not of divine origin nor a creation of philosophers. It was a development in history, in response to human needs and passions. As he was to put it at the opening of his great work *The Common Law*: "The life of the law has not been logic: it has been experience." This was his great insight.

Holmes was admitted to the bar in 1867. For fifteen years he practiced law, taught as an instructor at Harvard, and worked at his research to document his great insight. He had a great gusto for living, he had a fascinating and devoted wife, he was generally sought after and admired, but his passion was for his work, and he pursued that passion ruthlessly. By 1876, William James, writing to Henry about their old friend, said: "He is a powerful battery, formed like a planing machine to gouge a deep self-beneficial groove through life. . . ." Even earlier James had noted in his friend a "cold-blooded, conscious egotism," and another associate had observed that Holmes was lacking "in the noblest region of human character—selfish, vain, thoughtless of others." Holmes was determined to make Holmes great. He wanted to feel that when he came to the end he would know that he had "touched the superlative," and no price would be too high to pay for that valedictory satisfaction.

When, in 1881, *The Common Law* appeared, Holmes's name was made, in both America and England. He himself knew its merits and remarked that it would make him, in sequence, chief justice of the Supreme Court of Massachusetts, and justice of the Supreme Court of the United States. First, it made him, in 1882, a full professor of the Harvard Law School, and then, within months, a justice of the Supreme Court of Massachusetts. He had to wait seventeen years before he was chief justice. He had to wait three more before he was justice of the Supreme Court of the United States.

In the twenty years before the call to Washington, Holmes was a diner-out, a brilliant conversationalist, witty, paradoxical, epigrammatic, with a keen eye for female beauty, a self-conscious *beau garçon*, in fact, who, at ninety, seeing a handsome lady pass in the street, was to exclaim, "Oh, to be eighty again!" At the same time, with unremitting energy, he was making himself the kind of reputation as a judge that he had made as a scholar and philosopher of law. For certain peculiar reasons that we shall come to, he was also getting the name of a liberal—even, in some very conservative corners, the name of a communist—and rather enjoyed singeing the whiskers of the masters of big business. The most famous instance of this spirit is the case of *Vegelahn* v. *Guntner*, in which Holmes, to the outrage of much of respectable Boston, wrote a dissent defending the right of strikers to picket.

It was such a reputation that made Theodore Roosevelt name Holmes to the Supreme Court. The President, as he had put it in a letter to Senator Henry Cabot Lodge, wanted a man "absolutely sane and sound on the great national policies"—which meant a justice who would support his "trust-busting"; and presumably Lodge gave a satisfying report. So the President, who was the apostle of the strenuous life, an aristocrat, a man of letters, and an admirer of literature and the arts,[1] took to his heart and the dinner table at the White House the new justice, who had shed his blood on three battlefields, knew the Odyssey in Greek and the work of the shocking new French novelist Zola (whom, at a delighted dinner party

in Boston, he had termed "dull, but improving"), wrote a brilliant prose, and was a connoisseur of etchings. But Holmes was nobody's man and was soon to take a sly relish, no doubt, in writing a dissent from the decision that dissolved the Northern Securities holding company and thus blocked the merger of the Northern Pacific and the Great Northern railroads. Roosevelt was outraged: "I could carve out of a banana," he exclaimed, so the story goes, "a justice with more backbone than that." So ended Holmes's friendship with the man who was, as he later described him, "very likeable, a big figure, a rather ordinary intellect, with extraordinary gifts, a shrewd and I think pretty unscrupulous politician. He played all his cards—if not more."

If Holmes did, in his first big case, side with the conservatives on the court, he went on, for thirty years on the bench, to make himself known as the "Great Dissenter" who was the defender of liberalism and human rights, from the dissent in the *Lochner* case of 1905 (in which Holmes supported the right of individual states to legislate the maximum number of hours in a work week, bargaining power for labor, and such social experiments), on to famous civil liberty cases such as *Abrams* (1919), *Gitlow* (1925), and *Schwimmer* (1928).

Taken in isolation such cases would seem to label Holmes as one of what he termed the "*New Republic* crowd"—referring to that magazine of liberal protest. Nothing could, ultimately, be wider of the truth. But the truth here is complex.

We must start with the fact that Holmes was, as we have said, very much the Brahmin, the self-conscious aristocrat. He belonged, he declared, to the group of only a few thousand people in the world who led a truly civilized life and whose special civilization would be extinguished by economic leveling—without, he maintained, doing any good to anybody. Membership in this group of gentlemen would, he held, be impossible for southerners,[2] and even

---

[1] One of Roosevelt's literary achievements was to promote the reputation of Edwin Arlington Robinson. (See the introduction to Robinson.)

[2] In a letter to Albert J. Beveridge, the Senator and historian, he wrote: "I hope that time will explode the humbug of the Southern Gentleman in your mind—not

Philadelphians were decidedly "second-rate." New York and points west were not worth discussing. As well as breeding and taste, Holmes demanded, for membership in this group, character and intellectual capacity, and here we see the clue to the special fondness that Holmes had for certain Jews, such as his fellow justices Louis D. Brandeis and Benjamin Cardozo, and the scholar Harold Laski. We must note that mere wealth is no more relevant to membership in Holmes's club of the "great swells," than it was for his father's definition of a Brahmin. In fact, Holmes felt little more than contempt for the businessman,[3] for the activity of making money, and on this ground the conservative aristocrat was able to clasp hands with liberalism and labor. It is true that, over the years, his sympathies may have been broadened by the social idealism of Brandeis (even if Brandeis could never persuade him to work at economics), but in any case, Holmes sat on the bench with no predisposition in favor of the "merely" rich.

Next to his sense of class and the obligations of his class, Holmes's experience in the Civil War was the most decisive factor in his career. He had volunteered in a "Christian crusade," but with his first wound he encountered a "conversion" from whatever lingering shreds of Christianity he held. Shortly afterward, he described the rationale of the event:

> but then I said—by Jove, I die like a soldier anyhow . . . then I thought I wouldn't be

---

that there weren't a few—and not that their comparatively primitive intellectual condition didn't sometimes give a sort of religious purity of type, rarer in the more civilized and therefore more sceptical northerner. But the southern gentlemen generally were an arrogant crew who knew nothing of the ideas that make the life of a few thousand that may be called civilized."

[3] Charles Francis Adams, the brother of Henry, expressed the Brahmin's view of businessmen: "As I approach the end, I am more than a little puzzled to account for the instances I have seen of business success —money getting. It comes from a rather low instinct. Certainly . . . it is rarely met with in combination with the finer or more interesting traits of character." (*Autobiography*)

guilty of a deathbed recantation . . . it generally meant nothing but a cowardly giving way to fear. . . . Then came in my Philosophy—I am to take a leap in the dark—but now as ever I believe that whatever shall happen is best—for it is in accordance with a general law—and *good and universal* (or *general law*) are synonymous terms on the universe. . . .

From this point on Holmes was prepared to say that the "good" was merely what happened, was what offered survival value; and here was the germ of his pragmatic approach to the law, and to life. Therefore, as a justice, he was concerned not to treat his "preferences" as ethically "good." Society had to be free to determine by experiment what would make for survival. Society might, of course, make errors of judgment in such a process, but it was not the place of Justice Holmes to thwart this vital process. The essence of law was not logic, but life.

The war had also given Holmes the overarching image that summarized life itself and that embodied his social Darwinism. It was merely sentimental to assume that life was other than struggle, as it was to assume that man was "at present" other than a "predatory animal": society, he repeated more than once, rests on the "death of men." Nature had her own way, as does history, of weeding out the unfit and of breeding the qualities that Holmes admired: courage, fortitude, steadfastness of purpose, the capacity for command and self-command, the will to take risks.

Here we shall see is the ground of his argument in the famous case of *Vegelahn* v. *Guntner* in support of the right to picket: to picket is labor's weapon against capital, and to deprive labor of that weapon would be to defeat the natural process of competition. It was the same principle of competition that led Holmes to give the apparently contradictory opinion in the *Northern Securities* case, when he held that to prevent the effective merger of the railroads was to penalize the strong for having strength. But of course, if society should, in the end, wish to penalize the strong, it could do so, for it was stronger. Furthermore, Holmes saw the rise of "bigness" in both capital and labor as inevitable in modern society and would have held William James's abhorrence of it as mere sentimentality.

On this same general basis Holmes grounded his views of the freedom of speech and intellectual freedom, a question that had concerned powerful minds from Plato through Milton to John Stuart Mill. Holmes argued that only in the fair competition of the market place, by the clash and mutual criticism of opinions, could "truth" be determined. But the argument from competition was double-edged: a society could not be expected not to defend itself against an opinion that constituted a "clear and present danger." That is, freedom of speech is not an absolute to be defended under all circumstances and at any cost. It must be considered in the context of a world of struggle, and if things come to the final struggle, the winner not only writes the loser's history, he defines the standard of "truth" by which the loser will be judged.

In this general connection, it may be observed that Holmes had a special revulsion from the man with a burning certainty of his "truth." Communists, "some" Catholics, " 'Drys' apropos of the 18th amendment," all exhibited, he said, what he "had come to loathe in the abolitionists—the conviction that anyone who did not agree with them was a knave or a fool. . . . I detest a man who knows that he knows." The clash of conflict would define "truth," but

pragmatist relativism

Holmes would postpone the moment of decision by violence as long as possible, unless, of course, there was a "clear and present danger." He wanted to give reason her innings against passion and dogmatism and to permit an "atmosphere of intellectual freedom in which one can breathe."

In his old age Holmes became, in the popular view, a sort of national landmark, like the Grand Canyon or the Washington Monument. But his real mass, like that of the iceberg, was largely under water: the layman knew that Holmes was great, yet he had little understanding of the great man's importance in the history of constitutional law. Even so, the layman knew that a dissent recorded by Holmes might well come to be the accepted view of the court. More than that, Holmes's career seemed to indicate that logic, realism, courage, and impartiality might serve society as well as the frenzy of the partisan or the passion of the idealist, real or synthetic. He had worked hard for his greatness, to be a "great swell," to live in history, calculating every sentence in a decision or in a letter, envisioning all in the collected works; joy was duty, he had long maintained, and joy and duty had long since coalesced with ambition, and he had achieved greatness. It was an icy and rugged greatness, like a snow peak in the moonlight.

When he died, he was buried at Arlington, as befitted a soldier whose flesh had felt the hot lead.

BIOGRAPHICAL CHART

1841   Born, March 8, son of Dr. Oliver Wendell Holmes and Amelia Jackson Holmes
1857   Enters Harvard
1861   Graduates Harvard; class poet; shares Greek prize; volunteers for Union service
1861–64   Military service; wounded at three different battles; mustered out June, 1864, as a lieutenant colonel
1867   Admitted to the bar in Massachusetts
1867–82   Practices law in Boston; teaches at Harvard
1872   Marries Fannie Dixwell
1881   *The Common Law*
1882   Appointed Professor of Law at Harvard

1882–99   Justice of Supreme Court of Massachusetts
1895   Receives honorary LL.D. from Harvard; delivers address "The Soldier's Faith"
1896   Dissents in *Vegelahn* v. *Guntner* and *Plant* v. *Woods*
1899–1902   Chief Justice of Supreme Court of Massachusetts
1902   Appointed Justice of United States Supreme Court by Theodore Roosevelt
1904   Dissents in *Northern Securities* case, antagonizing Roosevelt
1905   Dissents in *Lochner*
1919   Dissents in *Abrams*

FURTHER READINGS

Mark DeWolfe Howe, ed., *The Common Law* (1963)
————, ed., *Holmes-Laski Letters* (1963)
————, ed., *Holmes-Pollock Letters* (1961)
A. Lief, ed., *The Dissenting Opinions of Mr. Justice Holmes* (1929)
————, ed., *Representative Opinions of Mister Justice Holmes* (1931)
J. J. Marke, ed., *The Holmes Reader* (1964)

Catherine Drinker Bowen, *Yankee from Olympus* (1944)
Felix Frankfurter, ed., *Mr. Justice Holmes* (1931)
————, ed., *Mister Justice Holmes and the Supreme Court* (1938)
Mark DeWolfe Howe, *Justice Oliver Wendell Holmes* (2 vols.; 1957–63)
Harold J. Laski, *The Danger of Being a Gentleman* (1940)

The Soldier's Faith (1895)

This speech was delivered on Memorial Day, at Harvard University. Holmes saw war, at least in any foreseeable future, as an inevitable condition of human life. He did not have the hope of William James that there would soon be a "moral equivalent of war." He hated war, not the least because it was "organized boredom," and he loathed the easy patriotism and cant of those ignorant of the brutal facts of war. But he also loathed the love of ease, the self-indulgence, and the lack of discipline he saw in a plutocratic society around him.

Holmes sent a copy of the speech to Henry James, who wrote his brother William: "It is ever so fine to read, but with the always strange something, unreal or meager his things have for me." No two men were ever more unlike.

———

Any day in Washington Street, when the throng is greatest and busiest, you may see a blind man playing a flute. I suppose that someone hears him. Perhaps also my pipe may reach the heart of some passer in the crowd.

I once heard a man say, "Where Vanderbilt sits, there is the head of the table. I teach my son to be rich." He said what many think. For although the generation born about 1840, and now governing the world, has fought two at least of the greatest wars in history, and has witnessed others, war is out of fashion, and the man who commands the attention of his fellows is the man of wealth. Commerce is the great power. The aspirations of the world are those of commerce. Moralists and philosophers, following its lead, declare that war is wicked, foolish, and soon to disappear.

The society for which many philanthropists, labor reformers, and men of fashion unite in longing is one in which they may be comfortable and may shine without much trouble or any danger. The unfortunately growing hatred of the poor for the rich seems to me to rest on the belief that money is the main thing (a belief in which the poor have been encouraged by the rich), more than on any grievance. Most of my hearers would rather that their daughters or their sisters should marry a son of one of the great rich families than a regular army officer, were he as beautiful, brave, and gifted as Sir William Napier. I have heard the question asked whether our war was worth fighting, after all. There are many, poor and rich, who think that love of country is an old wife's tale, to be replaced by interest in a labor union, or, under the name of cosmopolitanism, by a rootless self-seeking search for a place where the most enjoyment may be had at the least cost.

Meantime we have learned the doctrine that evil means pain, and the revolt against pain in all its forms has grown more and more marked. From societies for the prevention of cruelty to animals up to socialism, we express in numberless ways the

* *patriotism, fascism + centralization*

[handwritten: national pride]

notion that suffering is a wrong which can be and ought to be prevented, and a whole literature of sympathy has sprung into being which points out in story and in verse how hard it is to be wounded in the battle of life, how terrible, how unjust it is that any one should fail.

Even science has had its part in the tendencies which we observe. It has shaken established religion in the minds of very many. It has pursued analysis until at last this thrilling world of colors and sounds and passions has seemed fatally to resolve itself into one vast network of vibrations endlessly weaving an aimless web, and the rainbow flush of cathedral windows, which once to enraptured eyes appeared the very smile of God, fades slowly out into the pale irony of the void.

And yet from vast orchestras still comes the music of mighty symphonies. Our painters even now are spreading along the walls of our Library glowing symbols of mysteries still real, and the hardly silenced cannon of the East proclaim once more that combat and pain still are the portion of man. For my own part, I believe that the struggle for life is the order of the world, at which it is vain to repine. I can imagine the burden changed in the way in which it is to be borne, but I cannot imagine that it ever will be lifted from men's backs. I can imagine a future in which science shall have passed from the combative to the dogmatic stage, and shall have gained such catholic acceptance that it shall take control of life, and condemn at once with instant execution what now is left for nature to destroy. But we are far from such a future, and we cannot stop to amuse or to terrify ourselves with dreams. Now, at least, and perhaps as long as man dwells upon the globe, his destiny is battle, and he has to take the chances of war If it is our business to fight, the book for the army is a war-song, not a hospital-sketch. It is not well for soldiers to think much about wounds. Sooner or later we shall fall; but meantime it is for us to fix our eyes upon the point to be stormed, and to get there if we can. *[handwritten: ?]*

Behind every scheme to make the world over, lies the question, What kind of world do you want? The ideals of the past for men have been drawn from war, as those for women have been drawn from motherhood. For all our prophecies, I doubt if we are ready to give up our inheritance. Who is there who would not like to be thought a gentleman? Yet what has that name been built on but the soldier's choice of honor rather than life? To be a soldier or descended from soldiers, in time

[handwritten: Socrates, Jesus]

of peace to be ready to give one's life rather than to suffer disgrace, that is what the world has meant; and if we try to claim it at less cost than a splendid carelessness for life, we are trying to steal the good will without the responsibilities of the place. We will not dispute about tastes. The man of the future may want something different. But who of us could endure a world, although cut up into five-acre lots and having no man upon it who was not well fed and well housed, without the divine folly of honor, without the senseless passion for knowledge outreaching the flaming bounds of the possible, without ideals the essence of which is that they never can be achieved? I do not know what is true. I do not know the meaning of the universe. But in the midst of doubt, in the collapse of creeds, there is one thing I do not doubt, that no man who lives in the same world with most of us can doubt, and that is that the faith is true and adorable which leads a soldier to throw away his life in obedience to a blindly accepted duty, in a cause which he little understands, in a plan of campaign of which he has no notion, under tactics of which he does not see the use.

[handwritten: of modern warfare]

[handwritten: beautiful illusions]

[handwritten: ! of my country right or wrong ...]

Most men who know battle know the cynic force with which the thoughts of common sense will assail them in times of stress; but they know that in their greatest moments faith has trampled those thoughts under foot. If you have been in line, suppose on Tremont Street Mall, ordered simply to wait and to do nothing, and have watched the enemy bring their guns to bear upon you down a gentle slope like that from Beacon Street, have seen the puff of the firing, have felt the burst of the spherical case-shot as it came toward you, have heard and seen the shrieking fragments go tearing through your company, and have known that the next or the next shot carries your fate; if you have advanced in line and have seen ahead of you the spot which you must pass where the rifle bullets are striking; if you have ridden by night at a walk toward the blue line of fire at the dead angle of Spotsylvania, where for twenty-four hours the soldiers were fighting on the two sides of an earthwork, and in the morning the dead and dying lay piled in a row six deep, and as you rode have heard the bullets splashing in the mud and earth about you; if you have been on the picketline at night in a black and unknown wood, have heard the spat of the bullets upon the trees, and as you moved have felt your foot slip upon a dead man's body; if you have had a blind fierce gallop against the enemy, with your blood up and a pace that left no time for fear—if, in short, as some,⟨I hope many,⟩ who hear me, have known, you have known the ⟨vicissitudes of terror⟩ and of triumph in war, you know that there is such a thing as the faith I spoke of. You know your own weakness and are modest; but you know that man has in him that unspeakable somewhat which makes him capable of miracle, able to lift himself by the might of his own soul, unaided, able to face annihilation for a blind belief.

From the beginning, to us, children of the North, life has seemed a place hung about by dark mists, out of which come the pale shine of dragon's scales, and the cry of fighting men, and the sound of swords. Beowulf, Milton, Dürer, Rembrandt, Schopenhauer, Turner, Tennyson, from the first war-song of our race to the stall-fed poetry of modern English drawing-rooms, all have had the same vision, and all have had a glimpse of a light to be followed. "The end of worldly life awaits us all. Let him who may, gain honor ere death. That is best for a warrior when he is dead." So spoke Beowulf a thousand years ago.

Not of the sunlight,
Not of the moonlight,
Not of the starlight!
O young Mariner,
Down to the haven,
Call your companions,
Launch your vessel,
And crowd your canvas,
And, ere it vanishes
Over the margin,
After it, follow it,
Follow The Gleam.

[handwritten: cf. Krishna]

So sang Tennyson in the voice of the dying Merlin.

When I went to the war I thought that soldiers were old men. I remembered a picture of the revolutionary soldier which some of you may have seen, representing a white-haired man with his flintlock slung across his back. I remembered one or two living examples of revolutionary soldiers whom I had met, and I took no account of the lapse of time. It was not until long after, in winter quarters, as I was listening to some of the sentimental songs in vogue, such as—

Farewell, Mother, you may never
See your darling boy again,

that it came over me that the army was made up of what I now should call ⟨very young men.⟩ I dare say that my illusion has been shared by some of those now present, as they have looked at us upon whose heads the white shadows have begun to fall. But the truth is that war is the business of youth and early middle age. You who called this assemblage together, not we, would be the soldiers of another war, if we should have one, and we speak to you as the dying Merlin did in the verse which I just quoted. Would that the blind man's pipe might be transfigured by Merlin's magic, to make you hear the bugles as once we heard them beneath the morning stars! For to you it is that now is sung the Song of the Sword:—

The War-Thing, the Comrade,
Father of honor
And giver of kingship,
The fame-smith, the song master.

. . .

Priest (saith the Lord)
Of his marriage with victory.

. . .

Clear singing, clean slicing;
Sweet spoken, soft finishing;
Making death beautiful,
Life but a coin
To be staked in the pastime
Whose playing is more
Than the transfer of being;
Arch-anarch, chief builder,
Prince and evangelist,
I am the Will of God:
I am the Sword.

War, when you are at it, is horrible and dull. It is only when time has passed that you see that ⟨its message was divine.⟩ I hope it may be long before we are called again to sit at that master's feet. But some teacher of the kind we all need. In this snug, over-safe corner of the world we need it, that we may realize that our comfortable routine is no eternal necessity of things, but merely a little space of calm in the midst of the tempestuous untamed streaming of the world, and in order that we may be ready for danger. We need it in this time of ⟨individualist negations,⟩ with its literature of French and American humor, revolting at discipline, loving fleshpots, and denying that anything is worthy of reverence,—in order that we may remember all that buffoons forget. We need it everywhere and at all times. For high and dangerous action teaches us to believe as right beyond dispute things for which our doubting minds are slow to find words of proof. Out of heroism grows faith in the worth of heroism. The proof comes later, and even may never come. Therefore I rejoice at every dangerous sport which I see pursued. The students at Heidelberg, with their sword-slashed faces, inspire me with sincere respect. I gaze with delight upon our poloplayers. If once in a while in our rough riding a neck is broken, I regard it, not as a waste, but as a price well paid for the breeding of a race fit for headship and command.

We do not save our traditions, in this country. The regiments whose battle-flags were not large enough to hold the names of the battles they had fought, vanished with the surrender of Lee, although their memories inherited would have made heroes for a century. It is the more necessary to learn the lesson afresh from perils newly sought, and perhaps it is not vain for us to tell the new generation what we learned in our day, and what we still believe. That the joy of life is living, is to put out all one's powers as far as they will go; that the measure of power is obstacles overcome; to ride boldly at what is in front of you, be it fence or enemy; to pray, not for comfort, but for combat; to keep the soldier's faith against the doubts of civil life, more besetting and harder to overcome than all the misgivings of the battle-field, and to remember that duty is not to be proved in the evil day, but then to be obeyed unquestioning; to love glory more than the temptations of wallowing ease, but to know that one's final judge and only rival is oneself—with all our failures in act and thought, these things we learned from noble enemies in Virginia or Georgia or on the Mississippi, thirty years ago; these things we believe to be true.

"Life is not lost," said she, "for which is bought Endlesse renown."

We learned also, and we still believe, that love of country is not yet an idle name.

> Deare countrey! O how dearely deare
> Ought thy remembraunce, and perpetuall band
> Be to thy foster-child, that from thy hand
> Did commun breath and nouriture receave!
> How brutish is it not to understand

> How much to her we owe, that all us gave;
> That gave unto us all, whatever good we have!

As for us, our days of combat are over. Our swords are rust. Our guns will thunder no more. The vultures that once wheeled over our heads are buried with their prey. Whatever of glory yet remains for us to win must be won in the council or the closet, never again in the field. I do not repine. We have shared the incommunicable experience of war; we have felt, we still feel, the passion of life to its top.

Three years ago died the old colonel of my regiment, the Twentieth Massachusetts. He gave our regiment its soul. No man could falter who heard his "Forward, Twentieth!" I went to his funeral. From a side door of the church a body of little choir-boys came in like a flight of careless doves. At the same time the doors opened at the front, and up the main aisle advanced his coffin, followed by the few gray heads who stood for the men of the Twentieth, the rank and file whom he had loved, and whom he led for the last time. The church was empty. No one remembered the old man whom we were burying, no one save those next to him, and us. And I said to myself, The Twentieth has shrunk to a skeleton, a ghost, a memory, a forgotten name which we other old men alone keep in our hearts. And then I thought: It is right. It is as the colonel would have had it. This also is part of the soldier's faith: Having known great things, to be content with silence. Just then there fell into my hands a little song sung by a warlike people on the Danube, which seemed to me fit for a soldier's last word, another song of the sword, but a song of the sword in its scabbard, a song of oblivion and peace.

A soldier has been buried on the battle-field.

> And when the wind in the tree-tops roared,
> The soldier asked from the deep dark grave:
>   "Did the banner flutter then?"
> "Not so, my hero," the wind replied,
> "The fight is done, but the banner won,
> Thy comrades of old have borne it hence,
>   Have borne it in triumph hence."
> Then the soldier spake from the deep dark grave:
>   "I am content."

. . .

> Then he heareth the lovers laughing pass,
>   And the soldier asks once more:

"Are these not the voices of them that love,
  That love—and remember me?"
"Not so, my hero," the lovers say,
  "We are those that remember not;

For the spring has come and the earth has smiled,
  And the dead must be forgot."
Then the soldier spake from the deep dark grave:
  "I am content."

Natural Law (1918)

It is not enough for the knight of romance that you agree that his lady is a very nice girl—if you do not admit that she is the best that God ever made or will make, you must fight. There is in all men a demand for the superlative, so much so that the poor devil who has no other way of reaching it attains it by getting drunk. It seems to me that this demand is at the bottom of the philosopher's effort to prove that truth is absolute and of the jurist's search for criteria of universal validity which he collects under the head of natural law.

I used to say, when I was young, that truth was the majority vote of that nation that could lick all others. Certainly we may expect that the received opinion about the present war will depend a good deal upon which side wins (I hope with all my soul it will be mine), and I think that the statement was correct in so far as it implied that our test of truth is a reference to either a present or an imagined future majority in favor of our view. If, as I have suggested elsewhere, the truth may be defined as the system of my (intellectual) limitations, what gives it objectivity is the fact that I find my fellow man to a greater or less extent (never wholly) subject to the same *Can't Helps*. If I think that I am sitting at a table I find that the other persons present agree with me; so if I say that the sum of the angles of a triangle is equal to two right angles. If I am in a minority of one they send for a doctor or lock me up; and I am so far able to transcend the to me convincing testimony of my senses or my reason as to recognize that if I am alone probably something is wrong with my works.

Certitude is not the test of certainty. We have been cock-sure of many things that were not so. If I may quote myself again, property, friendship, and truth have a common root in time. One can not be wrenched from the rocky crevices into which one has grown for many years without feeling that one is attacked in one's life. What we most love and revere generally is determined by early associations. I love granite rocks and barberry bushes, no doubt because with them were my earliest joys that reach back through the past eternity of my life. But while one's experience thus makes certain preferences dogmatic for oneself, recognition of how they came to be so leaves one able to see that others, poor souls, may be equally dogmatic about something else. And this again means scepticism. Not that one's belief or love does not remain. Not that we would not fight and die for it if important—we all, whether we know it or not, are fighting to make the kind of a world that we should like—but that we have learned to recognize that others will fight and die to make a different world, with equal sincerity or belief. Deep-seated preferences can not be argued about —you can not argue a man into liking a glass of beer—and therefore. when differences are sufficiently far reaching, we try to kill the other man rather than let him have his way. But that is perfectly consistent with admitting that, so far as appears, his grounds are just as good as ours.

The jurists who believe in natural law seem to me to be in that naïve state of mind that accepts what has been familiar and accepted by them and their neighbors as something that must be accepted by all men everywhere. No doubt it is true that, so far as we can see ahead, some arrangements and the rudiments of familiar institutions seem to be necessary elements in any society that may spring from our own and that would seem to us to be civilized—some form of permanent association between the sexes—some residue of property individually owned—some mode of binding oneself to specified future conduct—at the bottom of all, some protection for the person. But without speculating whether a group is imaginable in which all but the last of these might disappear and the last be subject to qualifications that most of us would abhor, the question remains as to the *Ought* of natural law.

It is true that beliefs and wishes have a transcendental basis in the sense that their foundation is arbitrary. You can not help entertaining and feeling them, and there is an end of it. As an arbitrary fact people wish to live, and we say with vari-

* Cf. Question of mediation:
Constitution vs. Cosmopolitanism
                    (p. 1508)

ous degrees of certainty that they can do so only on certain conditions. To do it they must eat and drink. That necessity is absolute. It is a necessity of less degree but practically general that they should live in society. If they live in society, so far as we can see, there are further conditions. Reason working on experience does tell us, no doubt, that if our wish to live continues, we can do it only on those terms. But that seems to me the whole of the matter. I see no *a priori* duty to live with others and in that way, but simply a statement of what I must do if I wish to remain alive. If I do live with others they tell me that I must do and abstain from doing various things or they will put the screws on to me. I believe that they will, and being of the same mind as to their conduct I not only accept the rules but come in time to accept them with sympathy and emotional affirmation and begin to talk about duties and rights. But for legal purposes a <u>right</u> is only the hypostasis of a prophecy—the imagination of a substance supporting the fact that the public force will be brought to bear upon those who do things said to contravene it—just as we talk of the <u>force</u> of gravitation accounting for the conduct of bodies in space. One phrase adds no more than the other to what we know without it. No doubt behind these legal rights is the fighting will of the subject to maintain them, and the spread of his emotions to the general rules by which they are maintained; but that does not seem to me the same thing as the supposed *a priori* discernment of a duty or the assertion of a pre-existing right. A dog will fight for his bone. *Cf. a soldier's faith*

The most fundamental of the supposed pre-existing rights—the right to life—is sacrificed without a scruple not only in war, but whenever the interest of society, that is, of the predominant power in the community, is thought to demand it. Whether that interest is the interest of mankind in the long run no one can tell, and as, in any event, to those who do not think with Kant and Hegel it is only an interest, the sanctity disappears. I remember a very tender-hearted judge being of opinion that closing a hatch to stop a fire and the destruction of a cargo was justified even if it was known that doing so would stifle a man below. It is idle to illustrate further, because to those who agree with me I am uttering commonplaces and to those who disagree I am ignoring the necessary foundations of thought. The *a priori* men generally call the dissentients superficial. But I do agree with them in believing that one's attitude on these

matters is closely connected with one's general attitude toward the universe. Proximately, as has been suggested, it is determined largely by early associations and temperament, coupled with the desire to have an absolute guide. Men to a great extent believe what they want to—although I see in that *voluntism* no basis for a philosophy that tells us what we should want to want.

Now when we come to our attitude toward the universe I do not see any rational <u>ground</u> for demanding the superlative—for being dissatisfied unless we are assured that our truth is cosmic truth, if there is such a thing—that the ultimates of a little creature on this little earth are the last word of the unimaginable whole. If a man sees no reason for believing that significance, consciousness and ideals are more than marks of the finite, that does not justify what has been familiar in French sceptics; getting upon a pedestal and professing to look with haughty scorn upon a world in ruins. The real conclusion is that the part can not swallow the whole—that our categories are not, or may not be, adequate to formulate what we cannot know. If we believe that we come out of the universe, not it out of us, we must admit that we do not know what we are talking about when we speak of brute matter. We do know that a certain complex of energies can wag its tail and another can make syllogisms. These are among the powers of the unknown, and if, as may be, it has still greater powers that we cannot understand, as Fabre in his studies of instinct would have us believe, studies that gave Bergson one of the strongest strands for his philosophy and enable Maeterlinck to make us fancy for a moment that we heard a clang from behind phenomena—if this be true, why should we not be content? Why should we employ the energy that is furnished to us by the cosmos to defy it and shake our fist at the sky? It seems to me silly. *cf. Hardy*

That the universe has in it more than we understand, that the private soldiers have not been told the plan of campaign, or even that there is one, rather than some vaster unthinkable to which every predicate is an impertinence, has no bearing upon our conduct. We still shall fight—all of us because we want to live, some, at least, because we want to realize our spontaneity and prove our powers, for the joy of it, and we may leave to the unknown the supposed final valuation of that which in any event has value to us. It is enough for us that the universe has produced us and has within it, as less than it, all that we believe and love. If we think

[handwritten margin notes: relativism vs Kantian reason; which?]

of our existence not as that of a little god outside, but as that of a ganglion within, we have the infinite behind us. It gives us our only but our adequate significance. A grain of sand has the same, but what competent person supposes that he understands a grain of sand? That is as much beyond our grasp as man. If our imagination is strong enough to accept the vision of ourselves as parts inseverable from the rest, and to extend our final interest beyond the boundary of our skins, it justi-fies the sacrifice even of our lives for ends outside of ourselves. The motive, to be sure, is the common wants and ideals that we find in man. Philosophy does not furnish motives, but it shows men that they are not fools for doing what they already want to do. It opens to the forlorn hopes on which we throw ourselves away, the vista of the farthest stretch of human thought, the chords of a harmony that breathes from the unknown.

Vegelahn v. Guntner (1896)

This case came at the height of the struggle between capital and labor, less than three years after the panic of 1893. The issue in Vegelahn's attempt to get an injunction against the picketing was whether the fact of picketing itself, construed as a threat of violence, was to be equated with violence. The court granted the injunction, but Holmes's dissent made history. It is germinal for his philosophy of law.

Holmes, J., dissenting:

In a case like the present, it seems to me that, whatever the true result may be, it will be of advantage to sound thinking to have the less popular view of the law stated, and therefore, although when I have been unable to bring my brethren to share my convictions my almost invariable practice is to defer to them in silence, I depart from that practice in this case, notwithstanding my unwillingness to do so in support of an already rendered judgment of my own.

In the first place, a word or two should be said as to the meaning of the report. I assume that my brethren construe it as I meant it to be construed, and that, if they were not prepared to do so, they would give an opportunity to the defendants to have it amended in accordance with what I state my meaning to be. There was no proof of any threat or danger of a patrol exceeding two men, and as of course an injunction is not granted except with reference to what there is reason to expect in its absence, the question on that point is whether a patrol of two men should be enjoined. Again, the defendants are enjoined by the final decree from intimidating by threats, express or implied, of physical harm to body or property, any person who may be desirous of entering into the employment of the plaintiff so far as to prevent him from entering the same. In order to test the correctness of the refusal to go further, it must be assumed that the defendants obey the express prohibition of the decree. If they do not, they fall within the injunction as it now stands, and are liable to summary punishment. The important difference between the preliminary and the final injunction is that the former goes further, and forbids the defendants to interfere with the plaintiff's business "by any scheme . . . organized for the purpose of . . . preventing any person or persons who now are or may hereafter be . . . desirous of entering the [plaintiff's employment] from entering it." I quote only a part, and the part which seems to me most objectionable. This includes refusal of social intercourse, and even organized persuasion or argument, although free from any threat of violence, either express or implied. And this is with reference to persons who have a legal right to contract or not to contract with the plaintiff, as they may see fit. Interference with existing contracts is forbidden by the final decree. I wish to insist a little that the only point of difference which involves a difference of principle between the final decree and the preliminary injunction which it is proposed to restore, is what I have mentioned, in order that it may be seen exactly what we are to discuss. It appears to me that the judgment of the majority turns in part on the assumption that the patrol necessarily carries with it a threat of bodily harm. That assumption I think unwarranted, for the reasons which I have given. Furthermore, it cannot be said, I think, that two men, walking together up and down a sidewalk and speaking to those who enter a certain shop, do necessarily and always thereby convey a threat of force. I do not think it possible to discriminate, and to say that two workmen, or even two representatives of an organization of workmen, do— especially when they are, and are known to be, under the injunction of this court not to do so. See Stimson, *Labor Law*, 60, especially pages 290, 298–300; *Reg.* v. *Shepherd*, 11 Cox, Cr. Cas. 325. I may add, that I think the more intelligent workingmen believe as fully as I do that they no more can be permitted to usurp the State's prerogative of force than can their opponents in their controversies. But if I am wrong, then the decree as it stands reaches the patrol, since it applies to all threats of force. With this I pass to the real difference between the interlocutory and the final decree.

I agree, whatever may be the law in the case of a single defendant, *Rice* v. *Albee*, 164 Mass. 88, that when a plaintiff proves that several persons have combined and conspired to injure his business, and have done acts producing that effect, he shows temporal damage and a cause of action, unless the facts disclose, or the defendants prove, some ground of excuse or justification. And I take it to be settled, and rightly settled, that doing that damage by combined persuasion is actionable, as well as doing it by falsehood or by force. *Walter* v. *Cronin*, 107 Mass. 55.

Nevertheless, in numberless instances the law warrants the intentional infliction of temporal damage because it regards it as justified. It is on the question of what shall amount to a justification, and more especially on the nature of the considerations which really determine or ought to determine the answer to that question, that judicial reasoning seems to me often to be inadequate. The true grounds of decision are considerations of policy and of social advantage, and it is vain to suppose that solutions can be attained merely by logic and the general propositions of law which nobody disputes. Propositions as to public policy rarely are unanimously accepted, and still more rarely, if ever, are capable of unanswerable proof. They require a special training to enable anyone even to form an intelligent opinion about them. In the early stages of law, at least, they generally are acted on rather as inarticulate instincts than as definite ideas for which a rational defence is ready.

. . .

If it be true that workingmen may combine with a view, among other things, to getting as much as they can for their labor, just as capital may combine with a view to getting the greatest possible return, it must be true that when combined they have the same liberty that combined capital has to support their interests by argument, persuasion, and the bestowal or refusal of those advantages which they otherwise lawfully control. I can remember when many people thought that, apart from violence or breach of contract, strikes were wicked, as organized refusals to work. I suppose that intelligent economists and legislators have given up that notion today. I feel pretty confident that they equally will abandon the idea that an organized refusal by workmen of social intercourse with a man who shall enter their antagonist's employ is wrong, if it is dissociated from any threat of violence, and is made for the sole object of prevailing if possible in a contest with their employer about the rate of wages. The fact, that the immediate object of the act by which the benefit to themselves is to be gained is to injure their antagonist, does not necessarily make it unlawful, any more than when a great house lowers the price of goods for the purpose, and with the effect of driving a smaller antagonist from the business. Indeed, the question seems to have been decided as long ago as 1842 by the good sense of Chief Justice Shaw, in *Com.* v. *Hunt*, 4 Metc. (Mass.) 111. I repeat, at the end, as I said at the beginning, that this is the point of difference in principle, and the only one, between the interlocutory and final decree.

Abrams v. United States (1919)

This case was tried in the midst of the excitement of the then recent Russian Revolution, under the Espionage Act. A Russian emigrant, one Jacob Abrams, scattered leaflets from a roof in New York and was convicted and sentenced to twenty years. The nub of the case was that Abrams had advocated reduced production of war materiel (this while the war with Germany was continuing). The United States argued that to reduce production in order to prevent an American intervention in Russia would necessarily involve a reduction of arms for the prosecution of the war with Germany. The majority of the court held that such would be the necessary result of the "intent" of Abrams. On this point Holmes held that the argument was indirect. Holmes position is not unassailable, clearly, but the dissent is one of his great statements. It is an example, too, of his willingness to fly in the face of widespread public prejudice.

A letter to Laski, in October, 1919, is closely related to the dissent:

I fear we have less freedom of speech here than they have in England. Little as I believe in it as a theory, I hope I would die for it and I go as far as anyone whom I regard as competent to form an opinion in favor of it. Of course, when I say I don't believe in it as a theory I don't mean that I do believe in the opposite as a theory. But on their premises it seems logical to me in the Catholic Church to kill heretics and the Puritans to whip Quakers—and I see nothing more wrong in it from our ultimate standards than I do in killing Germans when we are at war. When you are thoroughly convinced that you are right—wholeheartedly desire an end—and have no doubt of your power to accomplish it—I see nothing but municipal regulations to interfere with your using your power to accomplish it. The sacredness of human life is a formula that is good inside a system of law.

Holmes, J., dissenting:

This indictment is founded wholly upon the publication of two leaflets which I shall describe in a moment. The first count charges a conspiracy pending the war with Germany to publish abusive language about the form of government of the United States, laying the preparation and publishing of the first leaflet as overt acts. The second count charges a conspiracy pending the war to publish language intended to bring the form of government into contempt, laying the preparation and publishing of the two leaflets as overt acts. The third count alleges a conspiracy to encourage resistance to the United States in the same war and to attempt to effectuate the purpose by publishing the same leaflets. The fourth count lays a conspiracy to incite curtailment of production of things

necessary to the prosecution of the war and to attempt to accomplish it by publishing the second leaflet to which I have referred.

The first of these leaflets says that the President's cowardly silence about the intervention in Russia reveals the hypocrisy of the plutocratic gang in Washington. It intimates that "German militarism combined with Allied capitalism to crush the Russian revolution," goes on that the tyrants of the world fight each other until they see a common enemy—working-class enlightenment—when they combine to crush it; and that now militarism and capitalism combined, though not openly, to crush the Russian revolution. It says that there is only one enemy of the workers of the world and that is capitalism; that it is a crime for workers of America, &c., to fight the workers' republic of Russia, and ends "Awake! Awake, you workers of the world!" Signed "Revolutionists." A note adds, "It is absurd to call us pro-German. We hate and despise German militarism more than do you hypocritical tyrants. We have more reasons for denouncing German militarism than has the coward of the White House."

The other leaflet, headed "Workers—Wake Up," with abusive language says that America together with the Allies will march for Russia to help the Czecho-Slovaks in their struggle against the Bolsheviki, and that this time the hypocrites shall not fool the Russian emigrants and friends of Russia in America. It tells the Russian emigrants that they now must spit in the face of false military propaganda by which their sympathy and help to the prosecution of the war have been called forth and says that with the money they have lent or are going to lend "they will make bullets not only for the Germans but also for the Workers' Soviets of Russia," and further, "Workers in the ammunition factories, you are producing bullets, bayonets, cannon, to murder not only the Germans but also your dearest, best, who are in Russia fighting for freedom." It then appeals to the same Russian emigrants at some length not to consent to the "inquisitionary expedition to Russia," and says that the destruction of the Russian revolution is "the politics of the march on Russia." The leaflet winds up by saying "Workers, our reply to this barbaric intervention has to be a general strike!" and after a few words on the spirit of revolution, exhortations not to be afraid, and some usual tall talk, ends "Woe unto those who will be in the way of progress. Let solidarity live! The Rebels."

No argument seems to me necessary to show

that these pronunciamentos in no way attack the form of government of the United States, or that they do not support either of the first two counts. What little I have to say about the third count may be postponed until I have considered the fourth. With regard to that it seems too plain to be denied that the suggestion to workers in ammunition factories that they are producing bullets to murder their dearest, and the further advocacy of a general strike, both in the second leaflet, do urge curtailment of production of things necessary to the prosecution of the war within the meaning of the Act of May 16, 1918, c. 75, 40 Stat. 553, amending § 3 of the earlier Act of 1917. But to make the conduct criminal that statute requires that it should be "with intent by such curtailment to cripple or hinder the United States in the prosecution of the war." It seems to me that no such intent is proved.

I am aware of course that the word intent as vaguely used in ordinary legal discussion means no more than knowledge at the time of the act that the consequences said to be intended will ensue. Even less than that will satisfy the general principle of civil and criminal liability. A man may have to pay damages, may be sent to prison, at common law might be hanged, if at the time of his act he knew facts from which common experience showed that the consequences would follow, whether he individually could foresee them or not. But, when words are used exactly, a deed is not done with intent to produce a consequence unless that consequence is the aim of deed. It may be obvious, and obvious to the actor, that the consequence will follow, and he may be liable for it even if he forgets it, but he does not do the act with intent to produce it unless the aim to produce it is the proximate motive of the specific act, although there may be some deeper motive behind.

It seems to me that this statute must be taken to use its words in a strict and accurate sense. They would be absurd in any other. A patriot might think that we were wasting money on aeroplanes, or making more cannon of a certain kind than we needed, and might advocate curtailment with success, yet even if it turned out that the curtailment hindered and was thought by other minds to have been obviously likely to hinder the United States in the prosecution of the war, no one would hold such conduct a crime. I admit that my illustration does not answer all that might be said but it is enough to show what I think and to let me pass to a more important aspect of the case. I refer to

the First Amendment to the Constitution that Congress shall make no law abridging the freedom of speech.

I never have seen any reason to doubt that the questions of law that alone were before this Court in the cases of *Schenck, Frohwerk* and *Debs*, were rightly decided. I do not doubt for a moment that by the same reasoning that would justify punishing persuasion to murder, the United States constitutionally may punish speech that produces or is intended to produce a clear and imminent danger that it will bring about forthwith certain substantive evils that the United States constitutionally may seek to prevent. The power undoubtedly is greater in time of war than in time of peace because war opens dangers that do not exist at other times.

But as against dangers peculiar to war, as against others, the principle of the right to free speech is always the same. It is only the present danger of immediate evil or an intent to bring it about that warrants Congress in setting a limit to the expression of opinion where private rights are not concerned. Congress certainly cannot forbid all effort to change the mind of the country. Now nobody can suppose that the surreptitious publishing of a silly leaflet by an unknown man, without more, would present any immediate danger that its opinions would hinder the success of the Government arms or have any appreciable tendency to do so. Publishing these opinions for the very purpose of obstructing, however, might indicate a greater danger and at any rate would have the quality of an attempt. So I assume that the second leaflet, if published for the purpose alleged in the fourth count, might be punishable. But it seems pretty clear to me that nothing less than that would bring these papers within the scope of this law. An actual intent in the sense that I have explained is necessary to constitute an attempt, where a further act of the same individual is required to complete the substantive crime, for reasons given in *Swift & Co.* v. *United States*, 196 U. S. 375, 396. It is necessary where the success of the attempt depends upon others, because if that intent is not present the actor's aim may be accomplished without bringing about the evils sought to be checked. An intent to prevent interference with the revolution in Russia might have been satisfied without any hindrance to carrying on the war in which we were engaged.

I do not see how anyone can find the intent required by the statute in any of the defendants'

* hermeneutics meets ideology

words. The second leaflet is the only one that affords even a foundation for the charge, and there, without invoking the hatred of German militarism expressed in the former one, it is evident from the beginning to the end that the only object of the paper is to help Russia and stop American intervention there against the popular government—not to impede the United States in the war that it was carrying on. To say that two phrases taken literally might import a suggestion of conduct that would have interference with the war as an indirected and probably undesired effect seems to me by no means enough to show an attempt to produce that effect.

I return for a moment to the third count. That charges an intent to provoke resistance to the United States in its war with Germany. Taking the clause in the statute that deals with that in connection with the other elaborate provisions of the Act, I think that resistance to the United States means some forcible act of opposition to some proceeding of the United States in pursuance of the war. I think the intent must be the specific intent that I have described and for the reasons that I have given. I think that no such intent was proved or existed in fact. I also think that there is no hint at resistance to the United States as I construe the phrase.

In this case sentences of twenty years' imprisonment have been imposed for the publishing of two leaflets that I believe the defendants had as much right to publish as the Government has to publish the Constitution of the United States now vainly invoked by them. Even if I am technically wrong and enough can be squeezed from these poor and puny anonymities to turn the color of legal litmus paper—I will add, even if what I think the necessary intent were shown—the most nominal punishment seems to me all that possibly could be inflicted, unless the defendants are to be made to suffer not for what the indictment alleges but for the creed that they avow—a creed that I believe to be the creed of ignorance and immaturity when honestly held, as I see no reason to doubt that it was held here, but which, although made the subject of examination at the trial, no one has a right even to consider in dealing with the charges before the Court.

Persecution for the expression of opinions seems to me perfectly logical. If you have no doubt of your premises or your power and want a certain result with all your heart you naturally express your wishes in law and sweep away all opposition. To allow opposition by speech seems to indicate that you think the speech impotent, as when a man says that he has squared the circle, or that you do not care wholeheartedly for the result, or that you doubt either your power or your premises. But when men have realized that time has upset many fighting faiths, they may come to believe even more than they believe the very foundations of their own conduct that the ultimate good desired is better reached by free trade in ideas—that the best test of truth is the power of the thought to get itself accepted in the competition of the market, and that truth is the only ground upon which their wishes safely can be carried out. That, at any rate, is the theory of our Constitution. It is an experiment, as all life is an experiment. Every year if not every day we have to wager our salvation upon some prophecy based upon imperfect knowledge. While that experiment is part of our system I think that we should be eternally vigilant against attempts to check the expression of opinions that we loathe and believe to be fraught with death, unless they so imminently threaten immediate interference with the lawful and pressing purposes of the law that an immediate check is required to save the country.

United States *v.* Schwimmer (1928)

Rosiak Schwimmer, an avowed pacifist who had persuaded Henry Ford to his Peace Ship project in 1915, had later appealed for citizenship and been refused because she would not swear to bear arms in defense of the United States. Holmes, as we have seen, was antipacifist to the bone, but he opposed the use of the naturalization process as a device to control opinion. Brandeis again voted with Holmes.

Holmes, J., dissenting:

The applicant seems to be a woman of superior character and intelligence, obviously more than ordinarily desirable as a citizen of the United

States. It is agreed that she is qualified for citizenship except so far as the views set forth in a statement of facts "may show that the applicant is not attached to the principles of the Constitution of the United States and well disposed to the good order and happiness of the same, and except in so far as the same may show that she cannot take the oath of allegiance without a mental reservation." The views referred to are an extreme opinion in favor of pacifism and a statement that she would not bear arms to defend the Constitution. So far as the adequacy of her oath is concerned, I hardly can see how it is affected by the statement, inasmuch as she is a woman over fifty years of age, and would not be allowed to bear arms if she wanted to. And as to the opinion the whole examination of the applicant shows that she holds none of the now-dreaded creeds, but thoroughly believes in organized government and prefers that of the United States to any other in the world. Surely it cannot show lack of attachment to the principles of the Constitution that she thinks it can be improved. I suppose that most intelligent people think that it might be. Her particular improvement looking to the abolition of war seems to me not materially different in its bearing on this case from a wish to establish cabinet government as in England, or a single house, or one term of seven years for the President. To touch a more burning question, only a judge mad with partisanship would exclude because the applicant thought that the Eighteenth Amendment should be repealed.

Of course the fear is that if a war came the applicant would exert activities such as were dealt with in *Schenck* v. *United States*, 249 U.S. 47. But that seems to me unfounded. Her position and motives are wholly different from those of Schenck. She is an optimist and states in strong and, I do not doubt, sincere words her belief that war will disappear and that the impending destiny of mankind is to unite in peaceful leagues. I do not share that optimism nor do I think that a philosophic view of the world would regard war as absurd. But most people who have known it regard it with horror, as a last resort, and, even if not yet ready for cosmopolitan efforts, would welcome any practicable combination that would increase the power on the side of peace. The notion that the applicant's optimistic anticipations would make her a worse citizen is sufficiently answered by her examination, which seems to me a better argument for her admission than any I can offer. Some of her answers might excite popular prejudice, but if there is any principle of the Constitution that more imperatively calls for attachment than any other it is the principle of free thought—not free thought for those who agree with us but freedom for the thought that we hate. I think that we should adhere to that principle with regard to admission into, as well as to life within, this country. And, recurring to the opinion that bars this applicant's way, I would suggest that the Quakers have done their share to make the country what it is, that many citizens agree with the applicant's belief, and that I had not supposed hitherto that we regretted our inability to expel them because they believe more than some of us do in the teachings of the Sermon on the Mount.

please, not too Christian

WILLIAM JAMES (1842–1910)

The first William James, as we have already seen, emigrated from Ireland to settle in Albany, New York, and made one of the most splendid fortunes in America. His son Henry, the father of the philosopher William and the novelist Henry, as well as of three other children, profited from the first William's business acumen by using his leisure to study religion and philosophy and to write on those subjects. He was a man of learning, noble character, and deep family feeling and, in keeping with his own individualistic spirit, gave his children an unconventional and remarkable education. By the time he was grown, William, born in 1842, had traveled widely, knew several languages fluently, had read seriously in literature, philosophy, history, and science, and was studying to be a painter. Suddenly, though competent judges asserted that he had talent, he threw over that project. This was in Newport, Rhode

Island, that focus of wealth and fashion, in the middle of the Civil War, and place and time, along with the fact that two brothers were off fighting, may have conspired to make William feel that art was superfluous.

So he turned to the study of chemistry and biology, then to medicine, at Harvard. He went on a scientific expedition to Brazil with the great Louis Agassiz, to discover that he "was cut out for a speculative rather than an active life"; studied physiology in Germany; returned to finish his medical degree. He had already suffered from one nervous breakdown, and now another, with increasing depression and hallucinations, incapacitated him for some five years. He was saved by discovering the French philosopher Charles Renouvier's argument for free will, which he paraphrased for himself: "My first act of free will shall be to believe in free will." Thus he repeated the experience of his own father, who had escaped from a severe breakdown by a religious conversion;[1] for if the son was not religious in a doctrinal sense, his conversion was religious in its depth, massiveness, and psychological pattern. The experience was the germ of William James's subsequent career.

In the external sense that career was uneventful: teaching (at Harvard, where he began as an instructor in physiology), writing, marrying and raising a family, traveling, enjoying social life. Long since, in Germany, he had decided that he did not have the stamina for laboratory research, and this liability of uncertain health, coupled with the breakdown, may well have been what canalized his powers toward his great achievements. Though he could not stand the laboratory, his restless intelligence and his own experience drove him to the probing of psychological and philosophical problems. The solutions of such problems were *vitally* important in the strict sense of the word; they were, quite literally, his way to life.

There was, in fact, something unprofessional in James's attitude toward his work. He had

come on his key concerns almost by accident: "I originally studied medicine in order to be a physiologist, but I drifted into psychology and philosophy from a sort of fatality. I never had any philosophic instruction, the first lecture on psychology I ever heard being the first I ever gave." He was a sort of amateur, weak in mathematics and logic, as not a few philosophers and psychologists were to point out; but with such limitation he had the true amateur's passionate devotion and the amateur's lack of reverence for professionally received opinion. As Huck Finn shocked Tom Sawyer's sense of propriety by always wanting to start things "fresh," so James shocked the professionals. This personal quality, however, seems to have made James a superb teacher: he was a "learner" rather than a "teacher," an "asker" rather than a "teller," and he dramatized for his students the learner's, the asker's, mind in action.

James's lack of professional sense is further indicated by the fact that he did not publish a book until he was forty-eight years old. But that book, his *Principles of Psychology*, of 1890, though conceived as merely a textbook, made him famous almost overnight. Early in his career, while in Germany, he had imagined, he wrote to his father, that the "border ground of physiology and psychology overlapping both" would be his appropriate province, and this turned out to be the case; James's training in physiology provided a background for his psychological speculations, for instance, in what is known as the James-Lange theory of emotions, the idea that actual physical changes follow on perception and that what we know as emotion is the felt concomitant of such physical changes ("we feel sorry because we cry," as he put it, "angry because we strike"). Long back he had begun to conceive of psychology as a science, not as a form of philosophical speculation, and his book was the fruit of his early studies and of his work in the laboratory of experimental psychology that he had founded at Harvard. He looked forward, he said, to the discovery of the scientific laws of the mind as of chemistry and physics, with resulting prediction and control.

---

[1] The younger Henry, too, was a sufferer from what the father called "vastations" and, too, was able to absorb them into a new vision. See pp. 1375–76.

James, however, was, as we have observed, unfitted for the laboratory, not only by precarious health but by temperament, and his notion of psychology embraced far more than laboratory findings. Late in life he was to say that he had regarded "official psychology" as merely a "part of the larger science of human beings . . . a very *small* part." For James, as his disciple Ralph Barton Perry puts it, "psychology meant seeing man in the round," not merely in the laboratory, and therefore James was "willing to learn about man from any source, including psychologists both proper and improper." And the improper ones might include faith healers, mediums, evangelists, the Society for Psychical Research, and, later, Freud and Jung, who were not eagerly embraced by James's colleagues in the profession. More specifically, in going beyond the laboratory, James was framing a theory that developed the germ that had lain in his own experience when he asserted free will by the act of believing in free will and thus healed himself. In other words, insofar as the laboratory meant scientific determinism and even his own expressed hope of discovering laws that would permit prediction and control, he, paradoxically enough, turned from it to seek a more dynamic conception.

This he did by adapting Darwin to the study of psychology. In explaining the adaptation of a creature to environment, Darwin had appealed to positive variation rather than to passive adjustment, and now James assumed such a role for the mind. The mind was not, he urged, the *tabula rasa* of Locke, but a creative force such as had been proclaimed by Coleridge. "Mental interests, hypotheses, postulates," James asserted in an essay criticizing Herbert Spencer, "so far as they are the basis for human action—action which to a great extent transforms the world—help to *make* the truth which they declare." And he added that the mind possesses "from its birth upward a spontaneity, a vote." That is, the human mind is a tool for changing environment, and all mental life—consciousness itself—exists only as targeted toward action, and the targeting always implies choice. "Consciousness," he declared, "is a fighter for ends." Will,

therefore, is at the center of consciousness, for attention itself is an act of will.

James's conception of consciousness was, generally, revolutionary.[2] The notion usually held was that from simple sensation the mind develops its characteristic processes and creates its knowledge, and James totally rejected this view. He held that consciousness, from the start, is "a teeming multiplicity of objects and relations, and what we call simple sensations are results of discriminative attention." In this "wonderful stream of our consciousness," as James called it, relationships are perceived and drifts of interest are felt as a context for what may emerge into sharper focus—as a "twilight region that surrounds the clearly lighted center of experience." This purposive "thinking" toward ends never ceases and proceeds at different levels of awareness and in incalculable complexity.

As *The Principles of Psychology* had its germ in the breakdown, so James's later line of development had its germ in a period of aimlessness and depression that followed the completion of that work. The essay "The Will to Believe," which was the title piece of a collection published in 1897, returned James to the old, and now new, problem of his salvation, as did *The Varieties of Religious Experience* (1902). In investigating the grounds for religious belief, James returns to the doctrines of *The Principles of Psychology* concerning consciousness and will. "Dumb conviction" lies behind all action. A scientist, for example, with all the rigor of his training, is acting on faith when he stakes himself on his hypothesis. The gamble that the scientist takes is simply one of the tissue of gambles that any man lives by. Every act of life, large and small, is a gamble—a more or less calculated risk, and it is belief, faith, that sets up the action for the test of reality. All life, as we hear repeated by Justice Holmes, is, by this token, an experiment.

---

[2] The notion of "consciousness" was, it might be said, an obsession of the James family. The elder Henry would elevate "consciousness" over conscience, and the younger Henry was concerned with that "huge spider-web of the finest silken thread suspended in the chamber of consciousness."

The justification of a belief comes from its effect. Religion justifies itself, for example, by the kind of life it makes possible for the believer. James had taken his own gamble in free will and had survived, and he "knew" that this belief was, therefore, "true" for him. But he did not intend to suggest that belief is to be dictated merely by whim or can be justified merely as a dream of wish fulfillment. If it requires nerve to take a gamble, it also requires judgment to take the right gamble. The will to believe implies risk, but it counsels a calculated risk. James can say, "as the essence of courage is to stake one's life on a possibility, so the essence of faith is to believe that the possibility exists"; but he can also say that the "world resists some lines of attack . . . and opens herself to others, so that we must go with the grain of her willingness." In short—and this must be emphasized—*possibility* must be regarded in the light of *probability*, and risk by the degree of desperation in the choice between that choice and nonchoice.

As for religion, James was later specifically to declare:

What keeps religion going is something else than abstract definitions and systems of logically concatenated adjectives, and something different from faculties of theology and their professors. All these things are after-effects, secondary accretions upon a mass of concrete religious experiences, connecting themselves with feelings and conduct that renew themselves *in saecula saeculorum* [forever and ever] in the lives of humble private men. If you ask what these experiences are, they are conversations with the unseen, voices and visions, responses to prayer, changes of heart, deliverances from fear, inflowings of help, assurances of support, whenever certain persons set their own internal attitude in certain appropriate ways.

The effect is the justification. James wanted, he said, to put philosophy in touch with the "character of vulgar reality," and here the reality could only be the experience of the religious man.

In his later years James set out to write what he hoped would be a closely reasoned, formal work embodying his general philosophy. It was never written. After 1900 his health was very poor, and his mercurial, ranging temperament had never been such as to conduce to the fulfillment of this kind of project. But he came to fulfill himself, and that was far better than the writing of the great systematic work. Certainly, by the standards of his philosophy this would be true, and it was in the philosophy of pragmatism that James's fulfillment came.

The book *Pragmatism* (1907) brought into focus and summed up James's whole career, as man and thinker. When he said that his effort in psychology was to adapt the theory of evolution to the study of the mind, he was simply stating a particular example of a principle he was to apply in various ways and then, at the end, generalize. His concern was with life as process, as a movement into a future, and with the relation of values to this fact: "The ancients did things by doing the business of their own day, not by gaping at their grandfathers' tombs —and the normal man today will do likewise."

Such an attitude implies the grounding on a certain view of the universe. James rejected the notion of the universe as being in two "editions," one the ideal and one the actual: the "eternal edition [the ideal] complete from the start, in which there is no growth or novelty; and an inferior, sideshow, temporal edition [the actual] in which things seem illusorily to be achieving and growing into that perfection which really preexists."

James wanted no part of the idealistic philosophy that had been central to the thinking of the transcendentalists. Emerson had said in "Spiritual Laws," that "only the finite" has "wrought and suffered," while the "infinite lies stretched in smiling repose," and James, in his attack on such philosophies, in "What Pragmatism Means," would seem to be making an ironical parody of the passage: "He [the Absolute] gives you indeed assurance that all is well with

Him, and for his eternal way of thinking; but thereupon he leaves you to be finitely saved by your own temporal devices." [3] James held that the "eternal edition" of Reality was really nothing more than a construct of the human mind, dictated (as all such constructs are) by certain human needs or interests, and that even the monistic universe[4] of the kind the scientist accepts, the kind implied by the idea of natural law, tends to dissolve under scrutiny. The universe, James maintained, is really pluralistic, not all of one tidy piece and reasonably organized, with many kinds of incidental unities absorbed reasonably into the great unity, but with the unpredictable and indeterminate and untidy always haunting the whole thing.

James saw the universe less like a perfect machine than like an imperfect society: "plurality of individuals, with relations partly external, partly intimate, like and unlike, different in origins, in aims, yet keeping house together, interfering, coalescing, compromising, finding new purposes to arise, getting gradually into more stable habits, winning order, weeding out." Such a universe is fluid, with its only absolute law the law of change, existing as a principle of growth. If will is significant in such a universe, as James insisted, this does not suggest that success is guaranteed; unpredictability and indeterminacy are to be reckoned with, and every act carries an element of risk:

> So far as man stands for anything . . . his entire vital function may be said to have to deal with maybes. Not a victory is gained, not a deed of faithfulness or courage is done, except upon a maybe; not a service, not a sally of generosity, not a scientific exploration or experiment or textbook, that may not be a mistake. It is only by risking our persons from

[3] But James was deeply influenced by Emerson's ideas of self-reliance and of the creative power of mind in the face of theories of scientific determinism and may well have found validation for his own salvation by an act of will in the fact that Emerson had experienced a breakdown and restored himself by "self-reliance."

[4] See James's essay "The One and the Many" for his discussion of the doctrine of monism in general.

one hour to another that we live at all. And often enough our faith beforehand in an uncertified result *is the only thing that makes the results come true.*

James imagined the creator inviting man to participate in life on the following terms: "It [life] is a social scheme of cooperative work genuinely to be done. Will you join the procession? Will you trust yourself and trust other agents enough to take the risk?"

In such a universe and on such terms the nature of truth becomes in a sense provisional; for the truth, as James puts it, *"is the name of whatever proves itself to be good in the way of belief, and good, too, for definite assignable reasons."* We should believe *"what is better for us* to believe"—what, that is, best promotes life and suggests the future. Truth, then, is determined by what "works," by what offers "cash-value in experiential terms." Truth is, in one sense, only what *becomes* true.

If we try to understand what James means by "truth" as what "works," or what has "cash-value," we are likely to conclude that there is an ambiguity in his thinking. On the one hand, in a scientific experiment, for instance, what "works" may indeed be the "truth"—that is, the experiment may confirm the hypothesis on which it was based. But this is a very different kind of "working" from that in the notion that the "lie" that "works"—that makes money, or gets a criminal off in a law court—is a "truth." And it is this second interpretation that is often meant by such a phrase as a "pragmatic approach" as opposed to a moral, or principled, approach.

One way to deal with the ambiguity would be to note that "truth," in James's usage, is applicable to beliefs, not to facts (a fact simply "is"—though, of course, there may be belief about the *is-ness* or *is-not-ness* of a presumed fact); and that, moreover, in assessing what "to work" means, one belief cannot be taken in isolation. A belief must be related to other beliefs. Beliefs—and values—are in constant competition. Life is not systematic and tidy, and a value that in itself is admirable may be incompatible with a value that may be ranked higher. Some values may coexist, some may not, or may not under certain circumstances. In Shakespeare's *King Lear*, for instance, the tragedy arises from the fact that Cordelia's passion for speaking the truth is not compatible with the life of her father and the safety of the kingdom. Or to take another example, would you murder a man whom you regarded as worthless to get money to put your son through medical school, even if his education seemed otherwise impossible, and even with the firm belief that your son would be a benefactor to mankind?

Let us turn to the matter of the "fluid" universe and the question of how belief may "become" true. James says that man must not go "against the grain" of the universe in his beliefs. For instance, no intensity of belief will make two plus two equal five, or a one-legged man become an Olympic champion in pole-vaulting. In some respects the universe is not fluid or open-ended. But in some respects it is —or may be. A father's faith in his son may help to create the son he believes in. Or a man's confidence in himself may, in certain instances, provide the extra release of energy needed for success. James is no mystic.

In all matters, James would return us to experience for determining values. Life "transacts itself" only in the process of living, and not in some "logical dimension"; and if you forget this, you are likely to indulge the "sentimental fallacy," which is to "shed tears over abstract justice and generosity, beauty, etc., and never to know these qualities when you meet them in the street, because the circumstances make them vulgar." By the same line of thought James finds cruelty particularly heinous when associated with noble causes and high ideals— that is, when the abstract good is used as a mask, or justification, for the concrete evil.

When we turn to social questions, to matters of law, politics, and economics, James appeals to the criterion of experience.[5] Institutions

exist, he echoes Jefferson, to serve human needs, individual needs, and he insists that even the social order most successful in satisfying such needs is bound to thwart many other needs, to provoke what Freud calls the "discontents" of civilization. Such thwarted needs are always pressing under the lid of any social order, and thus providing a dynamic of change, for there can never be a final equilibrium of "goods"; and a society, to exist, must be responsive to change and must decide, in the only way possible—that is, by experiment—"how much more outcry or how much more appeasement" will occur in the attempt to reach a new equilibrium. As society should be responsive, so the individual should recognize the possible obligation to risk the "breaking of rules which have grown too narrow for the actual case." At the same time with his sympathy for change and revolution, James set his hopes on the American attitude of "fierce and merciless resentment toward any man or set of men who break the public peace." In other words, he hoped that democracy, in an interaction of social responsiveness and individual courage, would provide a dialectic of orderly change.

At any given moment, the best social order would be the "one that most cherishes the men who represent the residual interests, the one that leaves the highest scope for their peculiarities"—and in holding this view James found himself at odds with the rise of big organizations and the stereotype of what we now call the organization man. He was, he said, "against all big organization as such, national ones first and foremost; against all big successes and big results," for he found the American addiction to bigness had bred the "exclusive worship of the bitch-goddess success."

Here James was, of course, flying in the face of historical developments. "Organization" had been the secret of the conquest of the continent,

---

5 On this central point, James is in direct opposition to Theodore Parker who, in his essay "Transcendentalism," says that a man should "look not to the con-

sequences of virtue," for virtue is an "absolute good, to be loved not for what it brings, but is," and who would repudiate experience (that is, the study of consequences) as a guide and depend on the pure intuition.

and the secret of American prosperity. It had also been the secret of the northern victory in the Civil War, which, in turn, had bred the "big" corporations, and the "big" structure of finance capitalism, and, biggest of all, the "big" centralized nation that the United States had overnight become. James did recognize that in the Civil War, as in all victories, "something drastic and bitter" was left "in the cup," but he assumed that in the conflict of "goods," the victory to be "prayed for" is always for the side with the "more inclusive good." But he did not try to square this view with his views about the curse of bigness, and, in his basic optimism, he did not face the irony of this situation as Melville did, most explicitly in "The Conflict of Convictions," when he says that in victory, and the creation of the great power state, the "founders' dream may flee." James was, of course, deeply opposed to slavery, and we assume that the "inclusive" good to be set against other "goods" in competition with it would be emancipation. But at the same time, he remarked of the Civil War that it was not the solution that God would have chosen.

When it came to the Spanish-American War and the annexation of the Philippines, James did invoke, quite eloquently, his views on bigness. Like Mark Twain, William Dean Howells, and W. E. B. Du Bois, he was appalled by the rise of American imperialism, which, he thought, could bring nothing but evil, both by external injustice and internal corruption. It was, he held, incompatible with democracy.

Not only might bigness and the worship of the bitch-goddess corrupt democracy through the swamping of the concept of the individual, through big organization, and through imperialism, but by debasing the public mind by "big" journalism, with its concentration of power over opinion: "Now illiteracy has an enormous literary organization, and power is sophistical; and the result is necessarily a new phenomenon in history—involving every kind of diseased sensationalism and insincerity in the collective mind." James did not, of course, originate this attitude; we have already found it forcefully expressed by James Fenimore Cooper. (See pp. 320–22). Nor was James to be the last to harbor dire apprehensions on this score. With the growth of big advertising, of the expertise of public relations, and of the big media of news and entertainment, with the increasing concentration of financial control, the question has become more and more acute, and the results for democracy more and more dubious.

When William James died, in 1910 (the year of the death of Mark Twain), his reputation was enormous, and his influence was to continue. Detractors are likely to say that his fame was based on the fact that his philosophy flattered the average man by praising what he had always, innocently or cynically, held to be true—that the proof of the pudding is in the eating, that ends justify means, that success is all. This is, of course, an unfair reading of James's position, but it does indicate a truth about him, the fact that, in spite of his background of privilege, his aristocratic education, and his refined taste, he had a special rapport with the main, common thrust of life in his age and was, indeed, a sort of nerve center for its impulses.

In its simplest terms the great problem for the men who were yet young just after the Civil War was to find some principle of continuity between the philosophical ideas, the ethical values, the conception of democratic idealism, the social assumptions, and the economic system in which they had been raised to the new and explosive order. Some men could commit themselves to the new order of ruthless competition and amoral grab, either by cynical opportunism or by invoking some version of Social Darwinism. Some, seeing nothing but the law of the jungle and the death of democracy, could simply withdraw into despair or sardonic laughter, as, finally, did Mark Twain, or take refuge in a religion of taste or a theory of historical determinism, as did Henry Adams.

William James, with his roots (in a peculiar way) in Emerson, in his father's religious attitude toward life, in his own scientific training, and in his taste for art, was trying to work out a philosophy that might carry the old values of moral will, social responsibility, democratic conviction, and religious faith into a period that, with scientific positivism on the one hand and cynical opportunism on the other, seemed to deny all such values. For James, in fact, recognized the constructive virtue of energy in the world of cynical opportunism and exploitation, and the virtue of intellectual rigor in the dedication to science. Though he was a man of cultivation and taste, he was not afraid of the "character of vulgar reality," but sought to renew philosophy by making contact with that "reality." By accepting the law of change in a pluralistic universe (and in a society of ethnic and social pluralism and economic flux, at a moment of technological revolution), he strove to create a viable definition of truth and a norm of moral good.

The problem he was striving to deal with was the same that in one form or another every citizen of more than rudimentary consciousness or primitive moral sensibility was forced to confront. James did have something to say to the ordinary citizen, even if what he said often came at secondhand. But his appeal was more than a clarity in the formulation of current issues; the issues had been for him a matter of vital importance, quite literally of life and death, and the aura of this fact gave urgency and dramatic force to his ideas. In psychological theory, in education, in law and social reforms, and in politics, the influence of James was to become pervasive. By an ironical perversion, he was even to be invoked by Mussolini as a philosopher of fascism.

Here, however, we are particularly concerned with James in relation to literature. The relation is both important and complex. It has to do not only with influences, more or less direct, but with James as an exemplar and interpreter of the world that the literature of the age necessarily dealt with, and with the effect of James's psychological theory on the understanding of literature in any period.

Let us take the last topic first, as being of the broader reference. James's theory of consciousness, especially his notion of the dynamic unity of the mind, has a fundamental importance for literary theory. The notion that there is a continuity from the most marginal flicker of mood straight to action offers, by implication, a theory of the unity of a literary work in relation to imagery and meaning. This is not to say that James initiated a literary technique. Long before 1890, when *The Principles of Psychology* was published, Keats had written the "Ode to Autumn." In the "Ode" we have a series of items presented that suggest "autumn-ness," with only two lines that hint at a "meaning":

Where are the songs of Spring? Ay, where are
    they?
  Ask not of them, thou hast thy music too.

And even this "meaning," that autumn, too, has a "music," does not explicitly go beyond the accumulation of mere "autumn-nesses." But the fact that in content the poem does not go beyond the mere mood, this "feel" of "autumn-ness," does not mean that the poem does not have a "meaning." This meaning is a certain attitude toward life, toward time—an attitude that may be characterized as a generally joyful acceptance of the possibility of fulfillment in the process of life itself. In the "Ode," in other words, we have a clear example of the projection from mood to meaning, of the dynamic unity of consciousness.[6]

Certainly, James could not have "influenced" Keats, and Keats himself was merely using a poetic method (and a psychological truth) always potential in human experience. But James has influenced the spirit in which poetry has been approached in our century, even poetry of the past, and more specifically the spirit in which poetry has been written in our time. This does not suggest that the critics and poets of this century have all read *The Principles of Psychology*, but rather that James has been so

---

[6] We have used a simple example of a principle that is illustrated in the literature of all times, has many ramifications, and involves fundamental questions concerning metaphor, symbolism, and dramatic action.

absorbed that he is part of the inevitable atmosphere. And what applies to the poets and the critics of poetry also applies to the writers and critics of fiction.

To turn to our second concern, that of James as an exemplar and interpreter of the world that literature dealt with at a certain time, we can, for instance, bring Melville and Mark Twain much more clearly into focus if we see them in the light of intellectual problems that James was more abstractly concerned with. For one thing, James—and, as we have seen, Justice Holmes and Henry Adams—were concerned with the grounds of action, and this was a central concern of Melville's *Battle-Pieces*, *Clarel*, and *Billy Budd*. To realize that James is struggling for an intellectual formulation of the same issues that dramatically engaged Melville gives greater density and force to the work of both men—as does the biographical accident that both men had to endure, and deal with in their work, the most severe psychological crises. The same issues, both thematic and psychological, are to be found in Mark Twain. The fact that all three men came out with different versions of the efficacy of will and the nature of moral responsibility merely emphasizes the community of concern in which they lived and worked. And what applies to Melville and Mark Twain applies, as we shall see, to many other writers.

In various other ways James can enlighten us about the age. His own life and career constitute, as we have said, an attempt to carry over the basic values of the pre–Civil War, agrarian, religious America into the new industrial, secular order, and his intellectual struggle sheds light on, and is illuminated by, a poem like *Snow-Bound*, which represents Whittier's similar struggle, or by Melville's *Clarel*. To take another factor in the work of James, his emphasis on the "vulgar reality," his appeal to the experience of "humble private men" (as in his investigation of religion), and his feeling of repugnance for people addicted to the "sentimental fallacy," who would shed tears over "abstract justice, generosity, beauty, etc.," but never know these qualities when encountered in the com-

mon street—such things make James a philosopher of the rise of realism, of naturalism, even. James would have understood Dreiser in this spirit and, we may add, Dreiser's sympathy for all the deprived yearners of the world, those who are crammed under the tight lid of society. At the same time that James could justify realism, he could, by his reasoned antipathy for "bigness" and the "bitch-goddess," give a ground for regional literature, that is, literature of those parts of America and those groups that had been by-passed by progress, urbanism, industrialism, and success.

As for James's more specific influence, direct or indirect, on literature, it has often been pointed out that his theory of consciousness, usually in connection with the theories of Bergson and Freud, has been enormously significant in relation to literary method. For instance, we may look at T. S. Eliot, Joseph Conrad, James Joyce, Virginia Woolf, Dorothy Richardson, and William Faulkner. The idea of the purposiveness in the "twilight region" of the mind, which is extremely important in fiction, appears as early as Dreiser's *Sister Carrie* (1899), when Hurstwood "unconsciously" locks the safe so that he cannot replace the money he holds in his hand; but this idea of James, as far as literary relevance is concerned, was early absorbed into the Freudian idea of unconscious motivation. In a very different way, James's theory of consciousness has a relation to the rise of impressionistic fiction. Again, this is not to argue that he initiated the method, though there may be, we can speculate, a connection between Conrad, the great master of impressionism, and William James through Henry James, who was Conrad's close friend.

Let us take up the topic of James's more specific relation to individual writers. Jay Martin, in *Harvests of Change*, has pointed out that Robert Frost's basic view of poetry can be regarded as an extension of James's philosophy of pragmatism, of the interplay of will and uncertified possibility in the pluralistic universe, of the interplay of courage and the tragic contingencies, of the sense of life as experiment and of value as a projection of desire or need.

In this connection, we may point out that Gertrude Stein, a seminal influence in modern American literature, was a favorite pupil of James at Harvard, and that, specifically, her own theory and practice of writing was conditioned by his notion of the nature of consciousness. (See p. 2225.) Furthermore, she may have been the nexus between James and Hemingway, who, in a certain sense, was the embodiment in action of James's theories. The appeal to experience, for example, is fundamental in Hemingway's conception of fiction. He rejects all the inherited sanctions and the certified values of the world that demonstrated its bankruptcy in the blood bath of the First World War. The typical Hemingway hero faces the need to locate in experience the minimum on which he can stake a life. The drama of "risk" is at the center of the Hemingway story, as at the center of James's philosophy, and "truth" is validated in his fiction in terms of its function for the man who accepts it. In this sense "style"—in literature or in the bullring—is a moral value, a redemptive "truth." James writes in *Pragmatism:* "Doesn't the fact of 'no' stand at the very core of life? . . . I am willing that there should be real losses and real losers, and no total preservation of all that is." And this would describe the universe of Hemingway, haunted by the great "nada" and demanding constant courage to face the challenge of creating one's own values.

As for literary relations, we must certainly not forget Henry James, who, after reading *Pragmatism*, told his brother that he had been pragmatizing all his life—as indeed, in one sense, any man might say. But something more specific would seem to be at stake here. What both William and Henry shared—what, we may hazard, both knew from painful experience—was a sense of the basic necessity of *risk* in human life. Plot after plot in Henry James's novels is pragmatic in the sense of being based on a drama of risks apprehended by an increased heightening of consciousness. Furthermore, James was keenly aware of the fatal risk of *not* taking risks, the risk that haunts some of the novels and is the specific subject of the story called *The Beast in the Jungle.*

To return to the philosopher brother, there is one more fact of fundamental importance in his relation to literature. He was a superb writer. His style is supple, vigorous, and idiomatic, with the varying rhythmic thrusts of passionate or persuasive speech, logical and sinewy, but poetic in the constant assimilation of ideas into images. His style is, in fact, the dramatic embodiment of a powerful mind that glitters with restless, questing life. And his work is, like all true literature, a celebration of life.

BIOGRAPHICAL CHART

1842   Born, January 11, in New York City
1855–60   School and tutors in Europe
1860   Studies painting with W. M. Hunt
1861   Enters Harvard
1864   Enters medical school
1865–66   Goes on expedition to Brazil, with Louis Agassiz
1867–68   Travels in Europe, mainly Germany
1869   Receives M.D. from Harvard
1873   Becomes instructor in anatomy and physiology at Harvard
1875   Teaches psychology at Harvard
1878   Marries; begins *The Principles of Psychology*
1880   Becomes assistant professor of philosophy at Harvard

1882–83   Travels in England and on the continent
1885   Becomes professor of philosophy at Harvard
1890   *The Principles of Psychology*
1891   *The Moral Philosopher and the Moral Life*
1896   *The Will to Believe*
1901–2   Gives Gifford Lectures, Edinburgh
1902   *The Varieties of Religious Experience*
1903   Receives LL.D. from Harvard
1906–7   Gives Lowell Lectures
1907   *Pragmatism*; resigns from Harvard
1908–9   Gives Hibbert Lectures, Oxford
1909   *A Pluralistic Universe; The Meaning of Truth*
1910   *The Moral Equivalent of War*; dies, August 26

FURTHER READINGS

There is no standard edition of James's works. In addition to the writings mentioned in the biographical chart, the reader may find the following useful.

William James, *Collected Essays and Reviews* (1920)

Julius Bixler, *Religion in the Philosophy of William James* (1924)
John Dewey, *Characters and Events* (1929)
George H. Mead, "The Philosophies of Royce, James and Dewey in Their American Setting," *Journal of Ethics* (1929)

G. E. Moore, *Philosophical Studies* (1922)
Paul Elmer More, "William James' Pragmatism," in *Shelburne Essays* (1904–1921)
R. B. Perry, *The Thought and Character of William James* (2 vols.; 1935)
———, *In the Spirit of William James* (1938)
Josiah Royce, *William James and Other Essays* (1911)
George Santayana, *Character and Opinion in the United States* (1920)
F. C. S. Schiller, "William James and the Making of Pragmatism," *Personalist* (1927)

From Pragmatism (1907)

WHAT PRAGMATISM MEANS

Some years ago, being with a camping party in the mountains, I returned from a solitary ramble to find every one engaged in a ferocious metaphysical dispute. The *corpus* of the dispute was a squirrel—a live squirrel supposed to be clinging to one side of a tree-trunk; while over against the tree's opposite side a human being was imagined to stand. This human witness tries to get sight of the squirrel by moving rapidly round the tree, but no matter how fast he goes, the squirrel moves as fast in the opposite direction, and always keeps the tree between himself and the man, so that never a glimpse of him is caught. The resultant metaphysical problem now is this; *Does the man go round the squirrel or not?* He goes round the tree, sure enough, and the squirrel is on the tree; but does he go round the squirrel? In the unlimited leisure of the wilderness, discussion had been worn threadbare. Every one had taken sides, and was obstinate; and the numbers on both sides were even. Each side, when I appeared therefore appealed to me to make it a majority. Mindful of the scholastic adage that whenever you meet a contradiction you must make a distinction, I immediately sought and found one, as follows: "Which party is right," I said, "depends on what you *practically mean* by 'going round' the squirrel. If you mean passing from the north of him to the east, then to the south, then to the west, and then to the north of of him again, obviously the man does go round him, for he occupies these successive positions. But if on the contrary you mean being first in front of him, then on the right of him, then behind him, then on his left, and finally in front again, it is

quite as obvious that the man fails to go round him, for by the compensating movements the squirrel makes, he keeps his belly turned towards the man all the time, and his back turned away. Make the distinction, and there is no occasion for any farther dispute. You are both right and both wrong according as you conceive the verb 'to go round' in one practical fashion or the other."

Although one or two of the hotter disputants called my speech a shuffling evasion, saying they wanted no quibbling or scholastic hair-splitting, but meant just plain honest English 'round,' the majority seemed to think that the distinction had assuaged the dispute.

I tell this trivial anecdote because it is a peculiarly simply example of what I wish now to speak of as *the pragmatic method*. The pragmatic method is primarily a method of settling metaphysical disputes that otherwise might be interminable. Is the world one or many?—fated or free?—material or spiritual?—here are notions either of which may or may not hold good of the world; and disputes over such notions are unending. The pragmatic method in such cases is to try to interpret each notion by tracing its respective practical consequences. What difference would it practically make to any one if this notion rather than that notion were true? If no practical difference whatever can be traced, then the alternatives mean practically the same thing, and all dispute is idle. Whenever a dispute is serious, we ought to be able to show some practical difference that must follow from one side or the other's being right.

A glance at the history of the idea will show you

still better what pragmatism means. The term is derived from the same Greek word πράγμα, meaning action, from which our words 'practice' and 'practical' come. It was first introduced into philosophy by Mr. Charles Peirce in 1878. In an article entitled 'How to Make Our Ideas Clear,' in the 'Popular Science Monthly' for January of that year[1] Mr. Peirce, after pointing out that our beliefs are really rules for action, said that, to develop a thought's meaning, we need only determine what conduct it is fitted to produce: that conduct is for us its sole significance. And the tangible fact at the root of all our thought-distinctions, however subtle, is that there is no one of them so fine as to consist in anything but a possible difference of practice. To attain perfect clearness in our thoughts of an object, then, we need only consider what conceivable effects of a practical kind the object may involve—what sensations we are to expect from it, and what reactions we must prepare. Our conception of these effects, whether immediate or remote, is then for us the whole of our conception of the object, so far as that conception has positive significance at all.

. . .

To take in the importance of Peirce's principle, one must get accustomed to applying it to concrete cases. I found a few years ago that Ostwald, the illustrious Leipzig chemist, had been making perfectly distinct use of the principle of pragmatism in his lectures on the philosophy of science, though he had not called it by that name.

"All realities influence our practice," he wrote me, "and that influence is their meaning for us. I am accustomed to put questions to my classes in this way: In what respects would the world be different if this alternative or that were true? If I can find nothing that would become different, then the alternative has no sense."

That is, the rival views mean practically the same thing, and meaning, other than practical, there is for us none. Ostwald in a published lecture gives this example of what he means. Chemists have long wrangled over the inner constitution of certain bodies called 'tautomerous.' Their properties seemed equally consistent with the notion that an instable hydrogen atom oscillates inside of them, or that they are instable mixtures of two bodies. Controversy raged, but never was decided.

[1] Translated in the *Revue Philosophique* for January, 1879 (vol. vii). [James's footnote]

"It would never have begun," says Ostwald, "if the combatants had asked themselves what particular experimental fact could have been made different by one or the other view being correct. For it would then have appeared that no difference of fact could possibly ensue; and the quarrel was as unreal as if, theorizing in primitive times about the raising of dough by yeast, one party should have invoked a 'brownie,' while another insisted on an 'elf' as the true cause of the phenomenon."

It is astonishing to see how many philosophical disputes collapse into insignificance the moment you subject them to this simple test of tracing a concrete consequence. There can *be* no difference anywhere that doesn't *make* a difference elsewhere —no difference in abstract truth that doesn't express itself in a difference in concrete fact and in conduct consequent upon that fact, imposed on somebody, somehow, somewhere, and somewhen. The whole function of philosophy ought to be to find out what definite difference it will make to you and me, at definite instants of our life, if this world-formula or that world-formula be the true one.

. . .

Pragmatism represents a perfectly familiar attitude in philosophy, the empiricist attitude, but it represents it, as it seems to me, both in a more radical and in a less objectionable form than it has ever yet assumed. A pragmatist turns his back resolutely and once for all upon a lot of inveterate habits dear to professional philosophers. He turns away from abstraction and insufficiency, from verbal solutions, from bad *a priori* reasons, from fixed principles, closed systems, and pretended absolutes and origins. He turns towards concreteness and adequacy, towards facts, towards action and towards power. That means the empiricist temper regnant and the rationalist temper sincerely given up. It means the open air and possibilities of nature, as against dogma, artificiality, and the pretence of finality in truth.

At the same time it does not stand for any special results. It is a method only. But the general triumph of that method would mean an enormous change in what I called in my last lecture the 'temperament' of philosophy. Teachers of the ultra-rationalistic type would be frozen out, much as the courtier type is frozen out in republics, as the ultramontane type of priest is frozen out in protestant lands. Science and metaphysics would come

much nearer together, would in fact work absolutely hand in hand.

Metaphysics has usually followed a very primitive kind of quest. You know how men have always hankered after unlawful magic, and you know what a great part in magic *words* have always played. If you have his name, or the formula of incantation that binds him, you can control the spirit, genie, afrite, or whatever the power may be. Solomon knew the names of all the spirits, and having their names, he held them subject to his will. So the universe has always appeared to the natural mind as a kind of enigma, of which the key must be sought in the shape of some illuminating or power-bringing word or name. That word names the universe's *principle*, and to possess it is after a fashion to possess the universe itself. 'God,' 'Master,' 'Reason,' 'the Absolute,' 'Energy,' are so many solving names. You can rest when you have them. You are at the end of your metaphysical quest.

But if you follow the pragmatic method, you cannot look on any such word as closing your quest. You must bring out of each word its practical cash-value, set it at work within the stream of your experience. It appears less as a solution, then, than as a program for more work, and more particularly as an indication of the ways in which existing realities may be *changed*.

Theories thus become instruments, not answers to enigmas, in which we can rest. We don't lie back upon them, we move forward, and, on occasion, make nature over again by their aid. Pragmatism unstiffens all our theories, limbers them up and sets each one at work. Being nothing essentially new, it harmonizes with many ancient philosophic tendencies. It agrees with nominalism for instance, in always appealing to particulars; with utilitarianism in emphasizing practical aspects; with positivism in its disdain for verbal solutions, useless questions and metaphysical abstractions.

All these, you see, are *anti-intellectualist* tendencies. Against rationalism as a pretension and a method pragmatism is fully armed and militant. But, at the outset, at least, it stands for no particular results. It has no dogmas, and no doctrines save its method. As the young Italian pragmatist Papini has well said, it lies in the midst of our theories, like a corridor in a hotel. Innumerable chambers open out of it. In one you may find a man writing an atheistic volume; in the next some one on his knees praying for faith and strength; in a third a chemist investigating a body's properties. In a

fourth a system of idealistic metaphysics is being excogitated; in a fifth the impossibility of metaphysics is being shown. But they all own the corridor, and all must pass through it if they want a practicable way of getting into or out of their respective rooms.

No particular results then, so far, but only an attitude of orientation, is what the pragmatic method means. *The attitude of looking away from first things, principles, 'categories,' supposed necessities; and of looking towards last things, fruits, consequences, facts.*

So much for the pragmatic method! You may say that I have been praising it rather than explaining it to you, but I shall presently explain it abundantly enough by showing how it works on some familiar problems. Meanwhile the word pragmatism has come to be used in a still wider sense, as meaning also a certain *theory of truth*.

. . .

One of the most successfully cultivated branches of philosophy in our time is what is called inductive logic, the study of the conditions under which our sciences have evolved. Writers on this subject have begun to show a singular unanimity as to what the laws of nature and elements of fact mean, when formulated by mathematicians, physicists and chemists. When the first mathematical, logical, and natural uniformities, the first *laws*, were discovered, men were so carried away by the clearness, beauty and simplification that resulted, that they believed themselves to have deciphered authentically the eternal thoughts of the Almighty. His mind also thundered and reverberated in syllogisms. He also thought in conic sections, squares and roots and ratios, and geometrized like Euclid. He made Kepler's laws for the planets to follow; he made velocity increase proportionally to the time in falling bodies; he made the law of the sines for light to obey when refracted; he established the classes, orders, families and genera of plants and animals, and fixed the distances between them. He thought the archetypes of all things, and devised their variations; and when we rediscover any one of these his wondrous institutions, we seize his mind in its very literal intention.

But as the sciences have developed farther the notion has gained ground that most, perhaps all, of our laws are only approximations. The laws themselves, moreover, have grown so numerous that there is no counting them; and so many rival formulations are proposed in all the branches of science that investigators have become accustomed to the notion that no theory is absolutely a transcript of reality, but that any one of them may from some point of view be useful. Their great use is to summarize old facts and to lead to new ones. They are only a man-made language, a conceptual shorthand, as some one calls them, in which we write our reports of nature; and languages, as is well known, tolerate much choice of expression and many dialects.

.   .   .

Riding now on the front of this wave of scientific logic Messrs. Schiller and Dewey appear with their pragmatistic account of what truth everywhere signifies. Everywhere, these teachers say, 'truth' in our ideas and beliefs means the same thing that it means in science. It means, they say, nothing but this, *that ideas (which themselves are but parts of our experience) become true just in so far as they help us to get into satisfactory relation with other parts of our experience*, to summarize them and get about among them by conceptual short-cuts instead of following the interminable succession of particular phenomena. Any idea upon which we can ride, so to speak; any idea that will carry us prosperously from any one part of our experience of any other part, linking things satisfactorily, working securely, simplifying, saving labor; is true for just so much, true in so far forth, true *instrumentally*.

.   .   .

The observable process which Schiller and Dewey particularly singled out for generalization is the familiar one by which any individual settles into *new opinions*. The process here is always the same. The individual has a stock of old opinions already, but he meets a new experience that puts them to a strain. Somebody contradicts them; or in a reflective moment he discovers that they contradict each other; or he hears of facts with which they are incompatible; or desires arise in him which they cease to satisfy. The result is an inward trouble to which his mind till then had been a stranger, and from which he seeks to escape by modifying his previous mass of opinions. He saves as much of it as he can, for in this matter of belief we are all extreme conservatives. So he tries to change first this opinion, and then that (for they resist change very variously), until at last some new idea comes up which he can graft upon the ancient stock with a

minimum of disturbance of the latter, some idea that mediates between the stock and the new experience and runs them into one another most felicitously and expediently.

This new idea is then adopted as the true one. It preserves the older stock of truths with a minimum of modification, stretching them just enough to make them admit the novelty, but conceiving that in ways as familiar as the case leaves possible. An *outrée* explanation, violating all our preconceptions, would never pass for a true account of a novelty. We should scratch round industriously till we found something less excentric. The most violent revolutions in an individual's beliefs leave most of his old order standing. Time and space, cause and effect, nature and history, and one's own biography remain untouched. New truth is always a go-between, a smoother-over of transitions. It marries old opinion to new fact so as ever to show a minimum of jolt, a maximum of continuity. We hold a theory true just in proportion to its success in solving this 'problem of maxima and minima.' But success in solving this problem is eminently a matter of approximation. We say this theory solves it on the whole more satisfactorily than that theory; but that means more satisfactorily to ourselves, and individuals will emphasize their points of satisfaction differently. To a certain degree, therefore, everything here is plastic.

The point I now urge you to observe particularly is the part played by the older truths. Failure to take account of it is the source of much of the unjust criticism levelled against pragmatism. Their influence is absolutely controlling. Loyalty to them is the first principle—in most cases it is the only principle; for by far the most usual way of handling phenomena so novel that they would make for a serious rearrangement of our preconception is to ignore them altogether, or to abuse those who bear witness for them.

You doubtless wish examples of this process of truth's growth, and the only trouble is their superabundance. The simplest case of new truth is of course the mere numerical addition of new kinds of facts, or of new single facts of old kinds, to our experience—an addition that involves no alteration in the old beliefs. Day follows day, and its contents are simply added. The new contents themselves are not true, they simply *come* and *are*. Truth is *what we say about* them, and when we say that they have come, truth is satisfied by the plain additive formula.

But often the day's contents oblige a rearrangement. If I should now utter piercing shrieks and act like a maniac on this platform, it would make many of you revise your ideas as to the probable worth of my philosophy. 'Radium' came the other day as part of the day's content, and seemed for a moment to contradict our ideas of the whole order of nature, that order having come to be identified with what is called the conservation of energy. The mere sight of radium paying heat away indefinitely out of its own pocket seemed to violate that conservation. What to think? If the radiations from it were nothing but an escape of unsuspected 'potential' energy, pre-existent inside of the atoms, the principle of conservation would be saved. The discovery of 'helium' as the radiation's outcome, opened a way to this belief. So Ramsay's view is generally held to be true, because, although it extends our old ideas of energy, it causes a minimum of alteration in their nature

I need not multiply instances. A new opinion counts as 'true' just in proportion as it gratifies the individual's desire to assimilate the novel in his experience to his beliefs in stock. It must both lean on old truth and grasp new fact; and its success (as I said a moment ago) in doing this, is a matter for the individual's appreciation. When old truth grows, then, by new truth's addition, it is for subjective reasons. We are in the process and obey the reasons. That new idea is truest which performs most felicitously its function of satisfying our double urgency. It makes itself true, gets itself classed as true, by the way it works; grafting itself then upon the ancient body of truth, which thus grows much as a tree grows by the activity of a new layer of cambium.

Now Dewey and Schiller proceed to generalize this observation and to apply it to the most ancient parts of truth. They also once were plastic. They also were called true for human reasons. They also mediated between still earlier truths and what in those days were novel observations. Purely objective truth, truth in whose establishment the function of giving human satisfaction in marrying previous parts of experience with newer parts played no rôle whatever, is nowhere to be found. The reasons why we call things true is the reason why they *are* true, for 'to be true' *means* only to perform this marriage-function.

The trail of the human serpent is thus over everything. Truth independent; truth that we *find* merely; truth no longer malleable to human need; truth incorrigible, in a word; such truth exists indeed superabundantly—or is supposed to exist

by rationalistically minded thinkers; but then it means only the dead heart of the living tree, and its being there means only that truth also has its paleontology, and its 'prescription,' and may grow stiff with years of veteran service and petrified in men's regard by sheer antiquity. But how plastic even the oldest truths nevertheless really are has been vividly shown in our day by the transformation of logical and mathematical ideas, a transformation which seems even to be invading physics. The ancient formulas are reinterpreted as special expressions of much wider principles, principles that our ancestors never got a glimpse of in their present shape and formulation.

. . .

Such then would be the scope of pragmatism—first, a method; and second, a genetic theory of what is meant by truth.

. . .

. . . Pragmatism is uncomfortable away from facts. Rationalism is comfortable only in the presence of abstractions. This pragmatist talk about truths in the plural, about their utility and satisfactoriness, about the success with which they 'work,' etc., suggests to the typical intellectualist mind a sort of coarse lame second-rate makeshift article of truth. Such truths are not real truth. Such tests are merely subjective. As against this, objective truth must be something non-utilitarian, haughty, refined, remote, august, exalted. It must be an absolute correspondence of our thoughts with an equally absolute reality. It must be what we *ought* to think unconditionally. The conditioned ways in which we *do* think are so much irrelevance and matter for psychology. Down with psychology, up with logic, in all this question!

See the exquisite contrast of the types of mind! The pragmatist clings to facts and concreteness, observes truth at its work in particular cases, and generalizes. Truth, for him, becomes a class-name for all sorts of definite working-values in experience. For the rationalist it remains a pure abstraction, to the bare name of which we must defer. When the pragmatist undertakes to show in detail just *why* we must defer, the rationalist is unable to recognize the concretes from which his own abstraction is taken. He accuses us of *denying* truth; whereas we have only sought to trace exactly why people follow it and always ought to follow it. Your typical ultra-abstractionist fairly shudders at

concreteness: other things equal, he positively prefers the pale and spectral. If the two universes
were offered, he would always choose the skinny
outline rather than the rich thicket of reality. It is
so much purer, clearer, nobler.

. . .

Men who are strongly of the fact-loving temperament, you may remember me to have said, are
liable to be kept at a distance by the small sympathy with facts which the philosophy from the
present-day fashion of idealism offers them. It is
far too intellectualistic. Old fashioned theism was
bad enough, with its notion of God as an exalted
monarch, made up of a lot of unintelligible or preposterous 'attributes'; but, so long as it held
strongly by the argument from design, it kept
some touch with concrete realities. Since, however,
darwinism has once for all displaced design from
the minds of the 'scientific,' theism has lost that
foothold; and some kind of an immanent or pan-
theistic deity working *in* things rather than above
them is, if any, the kind recommended to our contemporary imagination. Aspirants to a philosophic
religion turn, as a rule, more hopefully nowadays
towards idealistic pantheism than towards the
older dualistic theism, in spite of the fact that the
latter still counts able defenders.

But . . . the brand of pantheism offered is hard
for them to assimilate if they are lovers of facts, or
empirically minded. It is the absolutistic brand,
spurning the dust and reared upon pure logic. It
keeps no connexion whatever with concreteness.
Affirming the Absolute Mind, which is its substitute for God, to be the rational presupposition
of all particulars of fact, whatever they may be, it
remains supremely indifferent to what the particular facts in our world actually are. Be they what
they may, the Absolute will father them. Like the
sick lion in Esop's fable, all footprints lead into his
den, but *nulla vestigia retrorsum* [no foot tracks
backward]. You cannot redescend into the world
of particulars by the Absolute's aid, or deduce any
necessary consequences of detail important for your
life from your idea of his nature. He gives you indeed the assurance that all is well with *Him*, and
for his eternal way of thinking; but thereupon he
leaves you to be finitely saved by your own temporal devices.

Far be it from me to deny the majesty of this

conception, or its capacity to yield religious comfort to a most respectable class of minds. But from
the human point of view, no one can pretend that
it doesn't suffer from the faults of remoteness and
abstractness. It is eminently a product of what I
have ventured to call the rationalistic temper. It
disdains empiricism's needs. It substitutes a pallid
outline for the real world's richness. It is dapper,
it is noble in the bad sense, in the sense in which
to be noble is to be inapt for humble service. In
this real world of sweat and dirt, it seems to me
that when a view of things is 'noble,' that ought
to count as a presumption against its truth, and as
a philosophic disqualification. The prince of darkness may be a gentleman, as we are told he is, but
whatever the God of earth and heaven is, he can
surely be no gentleman. His menial services are
needed in the dust of our human trials, even more
than his dignity is needed in the empyrean.

Now pragmatism, devoted though she be to
facts, has no such materialistic bias as ordinary
empiricism labors under. Moreover, she has no objection whatever to the realizing of abstractions, so
long as you get about among particulars with their
aid and they actually carry you somewhere. Interested in no conclusions but those which our
minds and our experiences work out together, she
has no *a priori* prejudices against theology. *If theological ideas prove to have a value for concrete life,
they will be true, for pragmatism, in the sense of
being good for so much. For how much more they
are true, will depend entirely on their relations to
the other truths that also have to be acknowledged.*

What I said just now about the Absolute, of
transcendental idealism, is a case in point. First, I
called it majestic and said it yielded religious comfort to a class of minds, and then I accused it of
remoteness and sterility. But so far as it affords
such comfort, it surely is not sterile; it has that
amount of value; it performs a concrete function.
As a good pragmatist, I myself ought to call the
Absolute true 'in so far forth,' then; and I un-
hesitatingly now do so.

But what does *true in so far forth* mean in this
case? To answer, we need only apply the pragmatic
method. What do believers in the Absolute mean
by saying that their belief affords them comfort?
They mean that since, in the Absolute finite evil
is 'overruled' already, we may, therefore, whenever
we wish, treat the temporal as if it were potentially
the eternal, be sure that we can trust its outcome,
and, without sin, dismiss our fear and drop the

worry of our finite responsibility. In short, they mean that we have a right ever and anon to take a moral holiday, to let the world wag in its own way, feeling that its issues are in better hands than ours and are none of our business.

The universe is a system of which the individual members may relax their anxieties occasionally, in which the don't-care mood is also right for men, and moral holidays in order,—that, if I mistake not, is part, at least, of what the Absolute is 'known-as,' that is the great difference in our particular experiences which his being true makes, for us, that is his cash-value when he is pragmatically interpreted. Farther than that the ordinary lay-reader in philosophy who thinks favorably of absolute idealism does not venture to sharpen his conceptions. He can use the Absolute for so much, and so much is very precious. He is pained at hearing you speak incredulously of the Absolute, therefore, and disregards your criticisms because they deal with aspects of the conception that he fails to follow.

If the Absolute means this, and means no more than this, who can possibly deny the truth of it? To deny it would be to insist that men should never relax, and that holidays are never in order.

I am well aware how odd it must seem to some of you to hear me say that an idea is 'true' so long as to believe it is profitable to our lives. That it is *good*, for as much as it profits, you will gladly admit. If what we do by its aid is good, you will allow the idea itself to be good in so far forth, for we are the better for possessing it. But is it not a strange misuse of the word 'truth,' you will say, to call ideas also 'true' for this reason?

. . .

. . . Let me now say only this, that truth is *one species of good*, and not, as is usually supposed, a category distinct from good, and co-ordinate with it. *The true is the name of whatever proves itself to be good in the way of belief, and good, too, for definite, assignable reasons.* Surely you must admit this, that if there were *no* good for life in true ideas, or if the knowledge of them were positively disadvantageous and false ideas the only useful ones, then the current notion that truth is divine and precious, and its pursuit a duty, could never have grown up or become a dogma. In a world like that, our duty would be to *shun* truth, rather. But in this world, just as certain foods are not only agreeable to our taste, but good for our teeth, our

stomach, and our tissues; so certain ideas are not only agreeable to think about, or agreeable as supporting other ideas that we are fond of, but they are also helpful in life's practical struggles. If there be any life that it is really better we should lead, and if there be any idea which, if believed in, would help us to lead that life, then it would be really *better for us* to believe in that idea, *unless, indeed, belief in it incidentally clashed with other greater vital benefits.*

'What would be better for us to believe'! This sounds very like a definition of truth. It comes very near to saying 'what we *ought* to believe': and in *that* definition none of you would find any oddity. Ought we ever not to believe what it is *better for us* to believe? And can we then keep the notion of what is better for us, and what is true for us, permanently apart?

Pragmatism says no, and I fully agree with her. Probably you also agree, so far as the abstract statement goes, but with a suspicion that if we practically did believe everything that made for good in our own personal lives, we should be found indulging all kinds of fancies about this world's affairs, and all kinds of sentimental superstitions about a world hereafter. Your suspicion here is undoubtedly well founded, and it is evident that something happens when you pass from the abstract to the concrete that complicates the situation.

I said just now that what is better for us to believe is true *unless the belief incidentally clashes with some other vital benefit.* Now in real life what vital benefits is any particular belief of ours most liable to clash with? What indeed except the vital benefits yielded by *other beliefs* when these prove incompatible with the first ones? In other words, the greatest enemy of any one of our truths may be the rest of our truths. Truths have once for all this desperate instinct of self-preservation and of desire to extinguish whatever contradicts them. My belief in the Absolute, based on the good it does me, must run the gauntlet of all my other beliefs. Grant that it may be true in giving me a moral holiday. Nevertheless, as I conceive it,—and let me speak now confidentially, as it were, and merely in my own private person,—it clashes with other truths of mine whose benefits I hate to give up on its account. It happens to be associated with a kind of logic of which I am the enemy, I find that it entangles me in metaphysical paradoxes that are inacceptable, etc., etc. But as I have enough trouble in life already without adding the trouble of carrying these intellectual inconsistencies, I personally just give up the Absolute. I just *take* my moral holidays; or else as a professional philosopher, I try to justify them by some other principle.

If I could restrict my notion of the Absolute to its bare holiday-giving value, it wouldn't clash with my other truths. But we can not easily thus restrict our hypotheses. They carry supernumerary features, and these it is that clash so. My disbelief in the Absolute means then disbelief in those other supernumerary features, for I fully believe in the legitimacy of taking moral holidays.

You see by this what I meant when I called pragmatism a mediator and reconciler and said, borrowing the word from Papini, that she 'unstiffens' our theories. She has in fact no prejudices whatever, no obstructive dogmas, no rigid canons of what shall count as proof. She is completely genial. She will entertain any hypothesis, she will consider any evidence. It follows that in the religious field she is at a great advantage both over positivistic empiricism, with its anti-theological bias, and over religious rationalism, with its exclusive interest in the remote, the noble, the simple, and the abstract in the way of conception.

In short, she widens the field of search for God. Rationalism sticks to logic and the empyrean. Empiricism sticks to the external senses. Pragmatism is willing to take anything, to follow either logic or the senses and to count the humblest and most personal experiences. She will count mystical experiences if they have practical consequences. She will take a God who lives in the very dirt of private fact—if that should seem a likely place to find him.

Her only test of probable truth is what works best in the way of leading us, what fits every part of life best and combines with the collectivity of experience's demands, nothing being omitted. If theological ideas should do this, if the notion of God, in particular, should prove to do it, how could pragmatism possibly deny God's existence? She could see no meaning in treating as 'not true' a notion that was pragmatically so successful. What other kind of truth could there be, for her, than all this agreement with concrete reality?

Remarks

If this life be not a real fight, in which something is eternally gained for the universe by success, it is no better than a game of private theatricals from which one may withdraw at will. But it *feels* like a real fight—as if there were something really wild in the universe which we, with all our idealities and faithfulnesses, are needed to redeem; and first of all to redeem our own hearts from atheisms and fears. For such a half-wild, half-saved universe our nature is adapted.

I have often thought that the best way to define a man's character would be to seek out the particular mental or moral attitude in which, when it came upon him, he felt himself most deeply and intensely active and alive. At such moments there is a voice inside which speaks and says: 'This is the real me!'

The impulse to take life strivingly is indestructible in the race.

Be not afraid of life. Believe that life *is* worth living, and your belief will help create the fact.

The aesthetic principles are at bottom such axioms as that a note sounds good with its third and fifth, or that potatoes need salt.

All intellectual work is the same—the artist feeds the public on his own bleeding insides. Kant's *Kritik* is just like a Strauss waltz.

I envy ye the world of Art. Away from it, as we live, we sink into a flatter, blanker kind of consciousness, and indulge in an ostrich-like forgetfulness of all our richest potentialities—and they startle us now and then when by accident some rich human product, pictorial, literary, or architectural, slaps us with its tail.

There is no worse lie than a truth misunderstood by those who hear it.

The essence of good is simply to satisfy demand.

GEORGE SANTAYANA (1863–1952)

The importance of George Santayana for America and American literature comes largely from the fact that he was not an American. He lived in America from 1872 to 1912, was for the most part educated here, and taught at Harvard until he was forty-nine years old, but he remained a Spanish citizen, loathed many aspects of American life, liked best those Americans who were partly Europeanized, found little solace, intellectual or spiritual, at Harvard, and always looked forward to the day when he would shake the Thracian dust from his deracinated feet and return permanently to the civilization of Europe. In America he was always the "outsider"; but an outsider who, however reluctantly, had the strategic position of the "insider" and could know certain disgraceful family secrets—without any loyalty that would prevent him, in the end, from announcing them to the world.

Santayana's father and his maternal grandfather were civil servants in the Spanish colony of the Philippines, but his mother, by a first marriage to a Bostonian of the prominent mercantile family of Sturgis, had formed a connection with America. In 1868, when the boy who was to become the philosopher was five years old, his mother left him in Spain with the father, in order to take her Sturgis children back to Boston for an American education. The boy was left in Avila in a strange and apparently tormented houseful of kin, and, as he puts it in his great autobiography *Persons and Places*, this "crowded, strained, disunited and tragic family life remains for me the type of what life really is: something confused, hideous, and useless." His eyes and ears, he writes, "became accustomed to the unvarnished truth of the world," and it is tempting to surmise that his own personal isolation and his peculiar detachment from life in general can be traced to his acquaintance with what he took to be the "unvarnished truth."

Outside of the tensions of the household, however, he was exposed to the spell of the hard and hieratic city of cathedral and fortified walls, "all grandeur and granite," but "so small as to seem in the country"; and the country was of wheatfields beset by "rocks and windy moors," with the mountains looming starkly in only the middle distance. Avila was the city of Saint Theresa, a city of faith and festivals and tales of miracles, and these memories were as deep in George Santayana as whatever "unvarnished truth" he found inside the walls of the house where he lived; they were, in fact, his chosen life.

When in 1872, the boy, almost nine years old, came to Boston to join his mother, something of the life of Avila was resumed. He respected his mother for her toughness of mind and her stoic indifference to life, and even loved her, but he was not close to her. What warmth he found was in his sister Susana Sturgis, twelve years older than he, and in his Catholicism, which was fostered by his sister and frowned on by his mother. He was, in short, "solitary and unhappy . . . and attached only to a persistent dreamlife, fed on books of fiction, on architecture and on religion." What Avila had begun, Boston finished, and looking back on that time, Santayana writes: "a certain backwardness, or unwilling acceptance of reality, characterizes my whole life and philosophy, not indeed as a maxim but as a sentiment."

As a sophomore at Harvard, just back from a visit to Avila and barely recovered from the smallpox, Santayana went to William James to try to enroll in a course in philosophy. The professor inspected the frail-looking youth with marks of the disease yet on his face, frowned (according to Santayana's later report), and said: "You don't really want to go into philosophy, do you?" This, as though spying out some hidden weakness or moral inadequacy.

Later James was to become Santayana's admiring teacher and his sponsor for the doctorate; friendship and admiration (though of a perilously balanced sort) developed between the two men; and Santayana did become a famous philosopher and a professor at Harvard—though he never, apparently, forgave that first remark. There was much about America he could never forgive.

In 1912, Santayana resigned from Harvard. Most of his friends (and he had acquired a most glittering galaxy of them) were in Europe, his mother was dead, and he felt that he had never been "altogether fit to be a professor." In his autobiography, he says that he had always been "repelled" by the idea: "What I wanted was to go on being a student, and especially to be a travelling student. . . . I could have made a bargain with Mephistopheles, not for youth but for the appearance of youth, so that with its tastes but without its passions, I might have been a wandering student all my life, at Salamanca, at Bologna, in Oxford, in Paris, at Benares, in China, in Persia."[1]

Now, released from academic routine, from what he regarded as the boring provinciality of Cambridge and Boston (where he had sensed resentment at his frequent flights into the great world), from the necessity for a tactful masking of his feelings, and from the irritating awareness of gossip about his private life (or lack of it), he was free to escape permanently into the world of true civilization, where he knew almost all of those who were truly civilized. And there he could be free to be truly himself.

To understand the kind of self that Santayana was, we must remember Avila with its cathedral and Saint Theresa, and the dreams to which there, and in Boston, he fled from the intolerable actualities of existence. We must remember, too, that his first ambition had been to be a poet, and that for years, even as a student and teacher of philosophy, he poured energy

and hope into poetry. But as, in the end, he was a religious man without a religion, with his Catholicism only a "vista for the imagination," so, in the end, in spite of all he had written, he was a poet without poetry. What he had called his poems was the work of a poetic intellect without a poetic sensibility. The poetic sensibility small or large, slight or powerful, is open to the raw concreteness of the world, the "thingness" of the world and all the compelling involvement of men striving in it. This was the period when poets were trying to perceive the modern world and understand their experience in it; when modernity was taking shape with Whitman, Emily Dickinson, Browning, Arnold, Hardy, and the early Robinson and early Frost. The poetry that Santayana associated himself with, as he said in a letter to William Lyon Phelps concerning the echoes of his life in his novel *The Last Puritan*, was by young men like Philip Savage, George Cabot Lodge, and, in his lesser poetry, Trumbull Stickney, men who, according to the diagnosis of Santayana, "were visibly killed by the lack of air to breathe"—that is, by a world that had not adequately appreciated them. But Santayana was wrong; they died from lack of food to eat—that is, from lack of substance that could become poetry. They were extremely cultivated men with all the wrong notions of what poetry "is" as opposed to what poetry "has been"; they were academic versifiers out of touch with both the actuality of their present and what might constitute a vital relation to the past: for them, in their world of pious reverence for bric-a-brac and museum-ism, "tradition" meant imitation and not an inner understanding of what relation the work of the past had had, in the process of being created, to the actualities of its time.[2] As poets, Lodge

---

[1] Also, in *Character and Opinion in the United States*, Santayana says: "The tendency to gather and to breed philosophers in universities does not belong to ages of free and humane reflection: it is scholastic and proper to the Middle Ages and to Germany."

[2] It may be argued that Santayana's idealistic view of poetry cut him off from the nourishment of common reality. In this connection, we observe that though he was to write a novel (and a fascinating one), he apparently had no real interest in prose fiction, no doubt agreeing with Jacques Maritain's Catholic disparagement of its powers of "idealization" as compared with that of poetry. "The [post-Balzacian] novel differs from other forms of literature in having for object not the manufacture of something with its own special beauty in the

et al. starved to death. And so, as a poet, did Santayana.

Santayana, however, had resources other than poetry. He had philosophy, and if he had no talent for poetry, he had a staggering talent for prose which, being fed on the hard thinking of philosophy, could paradoxically revivify his poetic sensibility to an awareness of actuality. In his prose, the imagery, for example, which in verse had been conventional and vague, could become fresh, sharply observed, and precise in metaphorical reference, and the rhythms that had been mechanical and dull could assume the vitality of thought and feeling, and of the literal breath.

In *The Life of Reason* (Vol. 1), Santayana says that a "theory is not an unemotional thing" and continues by explaining that if an act can be full of passion, "with how much more beauty or terror may not a [philosophic] vision be pregnant which brings order and method into everything that we know." In other words, it was always a philosophic vision that, for him, stirred the depth in which poetry lurks.[3] He could move from idea to the truly poignant perception of nature.

If religion and poetry had been the grounding of Santayana's emotional life, nature was, theoretically at least, the grounding for his intellectual life. He was a philosophical naturalist, and saw man as firmly rooted in nature. Furthermore, unlike William James, who held that the world of ideas existed only in the mind, Santayana maintained that "things and truths have also a systematic and more or less static dimension." As he states it elsewhere, under all natural knowledge lies the "assumption that there are things and events prior to the discovery of them and independent of this discovery." But mind does work on the material of perception, which Santayana calls "essences," to create a view of the world. This is, in the fullest sense, the world of imagination, governed by such reference as is possible to the system of nature. But man can never know if that nature to which he refers is totally a system—absolutely coherent. Man cannot—and should not—aspire to the "whole" truth. As Santayana put it in *Realms of Being*,

> man was not created for the sake of discovering the absolute truth. The absolute truth has its own intangible reality, and scorns to be known. The function of mind is rather to increase the wealth of the universe, in this special dimension, by adding appearance to substance and passion to necessity and by creating all those private perspectives, and those emotions of wonder, adventures, curiosity, and laughter which omniscience would exclude.

Thus, as Santayana had early proclaimed in *Interpretations of Poetry and Religion*, "religion and poetry are identical in essence, and differ merely in the way in which they are attached to practical affairs. Poetry is called religion when it intervenes in life, and religion, when it merely supervenes upon life, is seen to be nothing but poetry." In such a process, imagination redeems life, extends it, and guides it by creating the ideals by which it is to be appreciated and judged. And all for what end? Santayana answers the question in an early letter to James, and there is little reason to think that he ever changed his mind: "philosophy seems to me to be its own reward, and its justification lies in the delight and dignity of the art itself." Philosophy, like religion, could be another name for poetry.

Contemplation—what we may consider an aesthetic contemplation by the intellectual eye, the eye of the "travelling student" ranging from one human scene or activity to another—would thus become Santayana's highest good, and the meaning of wisdom. And on this point we see

---

world of *artefacta*, deriving only its elements from human life, but the conduct of human life itself in fiction. . . ." The modern novel is contrasted with antiquity, in which the "*ideal*" was "a deliverance of the imagination." What moderns are seeking "in the cold night of a calculating anarchy, the Primitives possessed . . . in the peace of interior order." See *Art and Scholasticism*.

[3] In his critical discussions of poets, Santayana is always primarily concerned with "idea" and the implications of ideas, not with dramatic content, quality of perception, or powerful or subtle sense of the medium.

the fundamental split between him and his old teacher, for whom all "truth" is determined by the consequence of action and is therefore targeted to action. James, always outraged by the idealists, saw in Santayana, in spite of his protestations, a very imperfect "naturalist," who seemed to use that doctrine as a screen for a Platonic bent. James could admire the "perfection" of Santayana's exposition of his views, but on one occasion exclaimed: "But what a perfection of rottenness in philosophy!"

But long after Santayana had left America, in 1920, in *Character and Opinion in the United States* he made, perhaps unwittingly, his appropriate retort, a retort which, in one sense, came as a compliment. It is scarcely probable, however, that James, who had tried to establish a naturalistic psychology, would relish a compliment that called *The Principles of Psychology* merely a work of "imagination":

This [*The Principles of Psychology*] is a work of the imagination; and the subject as [James] conceived it, which is the flux of immediate experience in men in general, requires imagination to read it at all. It is a literary subject, like autobiography or psychological fiction, and can be treated only poetically; and in this sense Shakespeare is a better psychologist than Locke or Kant. Yet this gift of imagination is not merely literary; it is not useless in divining the truths of science, and it is invaluable in throwing off prejudice and scientific shams. The fresh imagination and vitality of William James led him to break through many false conventions. He saw that experience, as we endure it, is not a mosaic of distinct sensations, nor the expression of separate hostile faculties, such as reason and the passions, or sense and the categories; it is rather a flow of mental discourse, like a dream, in which all divisions and units are vague and shifting, and the whole continually merging together and drifting apart.

After he left America, Santayana lived in many places, in great honor, a world figure strangely detached from the world. The world

as he knew it was passing, as all things pass, and he, who had abjured all passion except that of the poetry of the intellectual eye, could not grieve too deeply. From his philosophic distance, in a strange parallel to the attitude of Yeats in *A Vision*, he could say:

A flood of barbarism from below may soon level all the fair works of our Christian ancestors, as another flood two thousand years ago levelled those of the ancients. Romantic Christendom—picturesque, passionate, unhappy episode—may be coming to an end. Such a catastrophe would be no reason for despair. Nothing lasts forever; but the elasticity of life is wonderful, and even if the world lost its memory it could not lose its youth. Under the deluge, and watered by it, seeds of all sorts would survive against the time to come, even if what might eventually spring from them, under the new circumstances, should wear a strange aspect.

Santayana even considered the possibility that such destruction and restoration were already occurring in America. It was a land full of "callow disrespect" for the past, but its inhabitants were a "fearless people, and free from malice, as you might see in their eyes and gestures, even if their conduct did not prove it." Why might not such a country eventually breed "clear thinking, honest judgment, and rational happiness?"

Meanwhile, he lived on, enjoying the world for what it was and enjoying his fame, to which he continued to add, book by book. The last volume of his autobiography, published after his death, bore the title *My Host the World*, and the title is a good one; for he was, in the end, an outsider, not only to America, but to the world—a guest, hedonistic but never selfish, grateful and appreciative for the smallest favor or delight of mind or eye, always offering exquisite courtesy and melodious conversation on multitudinous matters, never intruding too closely on the serious domestic concerns of his host, knowing when to retire to his room. He was merely the most discreet and rewarding of guests; not a member of the family, and never, therefore, caught in the old, fateful tangle of daily life in the process of being lived.

Santayana's last years were spent in Rome,[4] the capital of "Romantic Christendom" and the "ideal point of vantage in thought," which sometimes stirred old memories of Avila. After Italy entered the Second World War, the old man to whom Catholicism had long been only a "vista of imagination" retired to the nursing home run by the nuns known as the Blue Sisters. He died there in 1952, at the age of

[4] See the poem "To an Old Philosopher in Rome," by Wallace Stevens, reprinted in our text.

eighty-nine, and was buried in the Catholic cemetery, in a plot reserved for Spanish nationals.

Santayana was, legally, a citizen of Spain. But, willy-nilly, he was an American writer, and a splendid one. All his work is in English, and in an English he learned in Boston. If he wrote the language with exceptional elegance, that elegance is, by God's will and Santayana's genius, grounded in the idiom of his daily life, which often he did not enjoy.

Santayana, who did not love America, is nevertheless as much an American writer as Joseph Conrad, who loved England, is an English writer. For love and hate are the two faces that the same thing may wear.

BIOGRAPHICAL CHART

1863 Born, December 16, in Madrid, of Spanish parents; mother previously married to a Bostonian, George Sturgis, for whom this child was named

1872 Carried to Boston to join his mother, who had taken her Sturgis children there

1882 Enters Harvard

1883 Returns to Spain to visit father at Avila; at Harvard

1886 Graduates from Harvard, *summa cum laude;* receives scholarship to study philosophy in Germany; visits England for first time

1887 Visits England again; begins friendship with the second Earl Russell

1888 Returns to Harvard; works on doctorate

1889 Teaches as instructor

1896 *The Sense of Beauty*

1897–98 Advanced student at Cambridge University

1899 *Lucifer,* a poetic drama

1900 *Interpretations of Poetry and Religion*

1905–6 *The Life of Reason;* exchange professor at the Sorbonne

1910 *Three Philosophical Poets*

1911 August 15, "The Genteel Tradition in American Philosophy" given as a lecture at University of California

1912 Mother dies; resigns from Harvard

1912–14 Travels in Europe

1913 *Winds of Doctrine*

1914–18 Resides in England, most of the time at Oxford

1920 *Character and Opinion in the United States*

1922 *Soliloquies in England and Later Soliloquies*

1923 *Skepticism and Animal Faith*

1924 Begins residence in Rome

1925 *Dialogues in Limbo*

1927–40 *Realms of Being*

1935 *The Last Puritan*

1941 Retires to nursing home of the Blue Sisters

1944 *Persons and Places* (first volume of autobiography)

1945 *The Middle Span* (second volume)

1952 Dies, September 28

1953 *My Host the World*

FURTHER READINGS

There is no standard edition of Santayana's works. In addition to the works mentioned in the biographical chart, the following items may be useful.

Daniel Cory, ed., *Letters* (1963)
Irving Singer, ed., *Essays in Literary Criticism* (1956)
Logan Pearsall Smith, ed., *Little Essays* (1922)

Douglas L. Wilson, ed., *The Genteel Tradition: Nine Essays* (1967)

M. M. Kirkwood, *Santayana, Saint of the Imagination* (1961)

Irving Singer, *Santayana's Aesthetics: A Critical Introduction* (1957)

Sonnet (1894)

In my deep heart these chimes would still have rung
To toll your passing, had you not been dead;
For time a sadder mask than death may spread
Over the face that ever should be young.
The bough that falls with all its trophies hung
Falls not too soon, but lays its flower-crowned head
Most royal in the dust, with no leaf shed
Unhallowed or unchiselled or unsung.
And though the after world will never hear
The happy name of one so gently true,   10
Nor chronicles write large this fatal year,
Yet we who loved you, though we be but few,
Keep you in whatsoe'er is good, and rear
In our weak virtues monuments to you.

The Genteel Tradition in American Philosophy (1911)

Though Santayana considered life in America unsatisfying and did not consider himself an American, America stuck not only in his craw but in his bloodstream. It was a subject that he kept trying to come to terms with. The subject was first opened for official discussion on August 15, 1911, at the University of California, at Berkeley, at a time when, apparently, he had determined not to come back to America after a European leave from Harvard that had lately been arranged; and it was opened at a place on the continent at almost the greatest possible distance from Cambridge, and where he felt, as he wrote to his sister, "almost out of America."

In a spiritual sense, Santayana had always been "out of America," and only because he was could he see the woods in spite of the trees and diagnose the disease of American culture while so many Americans could only complain of the symptoms. When Mark Twain, in *The Innocents Abroad*, summarized life on the *Quaker City* as "Solemnity, decorum, dinner, dominoes, prayers, slander," he was rebelling against the genteel tradition, and when Huck fled the ministrations of the Widow Douglas and Miss Watson, he, like his creator, was rebelling against the feminization of life that Santayana refers to in *Character and Opinion in the United States* (in "The Academic Environment"):

The child in America passes very young into a free school, established and managed by the municipal authorities; the teachers, even for the older boys, are chiefly unmarried women, sensitive, faithful, and feeble; their influence helps to establish the separation which is so characteristic of America between things intellectual, which remain wrapped in a feminine veil and, as it were, under glass, and the rough business and passions of life.

Mark Twain, as the "sagebrush Bohemian," was the enemy of the genteel tradition, as was Whitman, the urban Bohemian, but in the eyes of Santayana, Whitman's rebellion, like Mark Twain's, being uninstructed, unphilosophical, and not fully knowing what it was directed against, was bound to be abortive and would, indeed, replace an old evil by a new. So Santayana set out to define the real nature of the genteel tradition, the disease that lurked behind the various symptoms, the focus of infection that would have to be lanced.

Santayana had been educated in Boston and at Harvard, in the very capital of the genteel tradition, and what, years later, he remembered he summed up on the first page of *Character and Opinion in the United States*:

About the middle of the nineteenth century, and the quiet sunshine of provincial prosperity, New England had an Indian summer of the mind; and an agreeable reflective literature showed how brilliant that russet and yellow season could be. . . . But it was all a harvest of leaves; these worthies [the writers] had an expurgated and barren conception of life; theirs was the purity of sweet old age. Some times they made attempts to rejuvenate their minds by broaching native subjects; they wished to prove how much matter for poetry the new world supplied, and they wrote "Rip Van Winkle," "Hiawatha," or "Evangeline"; but the inspiration did not seem much more American than that of Swift or Ossian or Chateaubriand. These cultivated writers lacked native roots and fresh sap because the American intellect itself lacked them. Their culture was half a pious survival, half an intentional acquirement; it was not the inevitable flowering of a fresh experience.

"Rip Van Winkle" was not, of course, written by a New Englander, but the genteel tradition was, unhappily, not home-keeping; as New Englanders accepted the mission of spreading their culture westward, they spread, too, the defect of their very virtue. Santayana, who had traveled in the United States, knew how, as V. K. Parrington put it in *Main Currents in American Thought*, the "inhibitions of the genteel tradition were all-powerful, and the little Boston group set themselves up as a court of final jurisdiction over American literature." For illustration, when Edgar Lee Masters, in the Middle West, came to write *Spoon River Anthology*, he shows his frustrated poet as suffering from the effect of the genteel tradition: he is writing triolets and villanelles, as though he were a pseudo-medievalist in Boston, instead of listening to "Homer and Whitman roar in the pines."

Nor was the genteel tradition confined, it should be clear, to the period of Longfellow's prime, as might be assumed from the quotation above from Santayana. By the time he came to write that passage, he had lived through the Gilded Age and knew from the experience of the young poets who had been his contemporaries, and perhaps from meditation on his own experience, that the blight of genteelism was now even more lethal in the new America. Now the booming vulgarity of a plutocratic society and the gospel of success made sensitive souls shrink even more into themselves or flee their homeland altogether, and some, ashamed of their origins, even invented European backgrounds for themselves. The painter James McNeill Whistler, for instance, replaced the mill town of Lowell, Massachusetts, with St. Peters-

burg, Russia, as his place of birth and concocted an aristocratic past, and Henry Harland, not satisfied with being the editor of the famous *Yellow Book* magazine, the Bible of the new aestheticism in London in the 1890's, let it be assumed that the Emperor Franz Joseph of the Austro-Hungarian Empire was his father.[1]

Santayana, we must observe, admits handsome exceptions to the blight of the genteel tradition in the American literature of his time. Both William and Henry James had been, according to him, "as tightly swaddled in the genteel tradition as any infant geniuses could be" (their father, after all, gave them a European, not an American, education and for an American this would commonly compound the infection). But William escaped, according to his old student, by his vigor and by his sympathy for both the "groping, nervous, half-educated, spiritually disinherited, emotionally hungry individuals of which America is full" and the "normal, practical American"; but we might add that, even more clearly, William James escaped by his sense of the future, his orientation toward action. Henry escaped, in Santayana's diagnosis, "by adopting the point of view of the outer world, and by turning the genteel tradition . . . into a subject-matter for analysis." In other words, Santayana says that Henry escaped the blight by becoming more, not less, European, and from that point of view analyzing the American disease. This is, in part, true; the medicine of Henry James for the national complaint is not the medicine of Whitman or Mark Twain. It would seem, though, that Santayana, in the end, may miss the point

[1] There is some comedy in the parallel, after the Civil War, between the self-aggrandizing myths of New England and those of the South. As the New Englander might flee from the crass prosperity of victory to Europe, where he might dream himself to be European, so the southerner might flee from the dismal poverty of defeat into the dream world of a plantation society now glamorized by nostalgia into an image quite detached from its earthy actual state. In fact, the Confederate daydream had as little reference to actuality as that of Henry Adams in *Mont-Saint-Michel and Chartres* had to the actuality of the thirteenth century. As T. S. Eliot has put it in a different context, "man cannot bear too much reality"—even in history.

here—or if not *the* point, then *a* point. It can be argued that the complex mind of James would feed on the "case" of James himself, so that James himself, as a special sufferer from the genteel tradition, might discover, after all, not absorption into the foreign culture but a collision of cultures; and that, in dramatizing this story, this collision, he might be forced to define, for dramatic purposes if for no other reason,[2] indigenous American values that underlay the froufrou of the genteel tradition.

Santayana also recognizes other exceptions, notably Whitman but also Mark Twain; but he finds here no hope that satisfies him—except perhaps the remote hope, expressed in the preface to *Character and Opinion in the United States*, from which we have quoted, that a new civilization may arise here after the deluge has destroyed that of old Christendom. The fact that Santayana was incapable of appreciating the values of Whitman and Mark Twain goes back to two things: his fundamental approach to poetry through its content of ideas and his distaste for modernity. In 1911 Santayana did not sense the poetry that was rising in New England on the ruins of the genteel tradition, a poetry that, as we find it in Eliot and elsewhere, satirized the genteel tradition, and certainly went far beyond it. He might have found something to his taste in Eliot (and Pound), who, as he was (and perhaps under something of his influence), were concerned with the crisis of culture in the modern world; but again, he might have regarded their actual poetry as in itself merely symptomatic of the disease of modernity. It is likely that he would have regarded Frost as, if not barbarous, at least retrogressive.

Though we may feel that Santayana underrates both Whitman and Twain, nevertheless we must not close our minds to the possibility that he was right in finding in them and in the American culture they represented certain limitations. Furthermore, if Whitman is a great poet, his influence, especially on those who have

directly imitated him, has not been an unmixed blessing; and we can be sure that if he, with his original genius, were living today, he wouldn't write like an imitator of Whitman. There is, too, a certain irony that, though Santayana thought rather poorly of Walt Whitman and Mark Twain, his essay "The Genteel Tradition" became, only a few years after it was delivered at Berkeley, a rallying point for those writers who strove for a native American mode of expression. It has, in this respect, an importance perhaps as great as that of Emerson's "The American Scholar."

Ladies and Gentlemen: The privilege of addressing you to-day is very welcome to me, not merely for the honor of it, which is great, nor for the pleasures of travel, which are many, when it is California that one is visiting for the first time, but also because there is something I have long wanted to say which this occasion seems particularly favorable for saying. America is still a young country, and this part of it is especially so; and it would have been nothing extraordinary if, in this young country, material preoccupations had altogether absorbed people's minds, and they had been too much engrossed in living to reflect upon life, or to have any philosophy. The opposite, however, is the case. Not only have you already found time to philosophize in California, as your society proves, but the eastern colonists from the very beginning were a sophisticated race. As much as in clearing the land and fighting the Indians they were occupied, as they expressed it, in wrestling with the Lord. The country was new, but the race was tried, chastened, and full of solemn memories. It was an old wine in new bottles; and America did not have to wait for its present universities, with their departments of academic philosophy, in order to possess a living philosophy,—to have a distinct vision of the universe and definite convictions about human destiny.

Now this situation is a singular and remarkable one, and has many consequences, not all of which are equally fortunate. America is a young country with an old mentality: it has enjoyed the advantages of a child carefully brought up, and thoroughly indoctrinated; it has been a wise child. But a wise child, an old head on young shoulders, always has a

---

[2] The fact that technical considerations often lead to fundamental insights is one thing that makes literature a source of moral discovery and philosophic enlargement.

comic and an unpromising side. The wisdom is a little thin and verbal, not aware of its full meaning and grounds; and physical and emotional growth may be stunted by it, or even deranged. Or when the child is too vigorous for that, he will develop a fresh mentality of his own, out of his observations and actual instincts; and this fresh mentality will interfere with the traditional mentality, and tend to reduce it to something perfunctory, conventional, and perhaps secretly despised. A philosophy is not genuine unless it inspires and expresses the life of those who cherish it. I do not think the hereditary philosophy of America has done much to atrophy the natural activities of the inhabitants; the wise child has not missed the joys of youth or of manhood; but what has happened is that the hereditary philosophy has grown stale, and that the academic philosophy afterwards developed has caught the stale odor from it. America is not simply, as I said a moment ago, a young country with an old mentality: it is a country with two mentalities, one a survival of the beliefs and standards of the fathers, the other an expression of the instincts, practice, and discoveries of the younger generations. In all the higher things of the mind— in religion, in literature, in the moral emotions—it is the hereditary spirit that still prevails, so much so that Mr. Bernard Shaw finds that America is a hundred years behind the times. The truth is that that one-half of the American mind, that not occupied intensely in practical affairs, has remained, I will not say high-and-dry, but slightly becalmed; it has floated gently in the backwater, while, alongside, in invention and industry and social organization the other half of the mind was leaping down a sort of Niagara Rapids. This division may be found symbolized in American architecture: a neat reproduction of the colonial mansion—with some modern comforts introduced surreptitiously —stands beside the sky-scraper. The American Will inhabits the sky-scraper; the American Intellect inhabits the colonial mansion. The one is the sphere of the American man; the other, at least predominantly, of the American woman. The one is all aggressive enterprise; the other is all genteel tradition.

Now, with your permission, I should like to analyze more fully how this interesting situation has arisen, how it is qualified, and whither it tends. And in the first place we should remember what, precisely, that philosophy was which the first settlers brought with them into the country. In strict-

ness there was more than one; but we may confine our attention to what I will call Calvinism, since it is on this that the current academic philosophy has been grafted. I do not mean exactly the Calvinism of Calvin, or even of Jonathan Edwards; for in their systems there was much that was not pure philosophy, but rather faith in the externals and history of revelation. Jewish and Christian revelation was interpreted by these men, however, in the spirit of a particular philosophy, which might have arisen under any sky, and been associated with any other religion as well as with Protestant Christianity. In fact, the philosophical principle of Calvinism appears also in the Koran, in Spinoza, and in Cardinal Newman; and persons with no very distinctive Christian belief, like Carlyle or like Professor Royce, may be nevertheless, philosophically, perfect Calvinists. Calvinism, taken in this sense, is an expression of the agonized conscience. It is a view of the world which an agonized conscience readily embraces, if it takes itself seriously, as, being agonized, of course it must. Calvinism, essentially, asserts three things: that sin exists, that sin is punished, and that it is beautiful that sin should exist to be punished. The heart of the Calvinist is therefore divided between tragic concern at his own miserable condition, and tragic exultation about the universe at large. He oscillates between a profound abasement and a paradoxical elation of the spirit. To be a Calvinist philosophically is to feel a fierce pleasure in the existence of misery, especially of one's own, in that this misery seems to manifest the fact that the Absolute is irresponsible or infinite or holy. Human nature, it feels, is totally depraved: to have the instincts and motives that we necessarily have is a great scandal, and we must suffer for it; but that scandal is requisite, since otherwise the serious importance of being as we ought to be would not have been vindicated.

To those of us who have not an agonized conscience this system may seem fantastic and even unintelligible; yet it is logically and intently thought out from its emotional premises. It can take permanent possession of a deep mind here and there, and under certain conditions it can become epidemic. Imagine, for instance, a small nation with an intense vitality, but on the verge of ruin, ecstatic and distressful having a strict and minute code of laws, that paint life in sharp and violent chiaroscuro, all pure righteousness and black abominations, and exaggerating the consequences of both perhaps to infinity. Such a people were the Jews after the exile, and again the early Protestants. If such a people is philosophical at all, it will not improbably be Calvinistic. Even in the early American communities many of these conditions were fulfilled. The nation was small and isolated; it lived under pressure and constant trial; it was acquainted with but a small range of goods and evils. Vigilance over conduct and an absolute demand for personal integrity were not merely traditional things, but things that practical sages, like Franklin and Washington, recommended to their countrymen, because they were virtues that justified themselves visibly by their fruits. But soon these happy results themselves helped to relax the pressure of external circumstances, and indirectly the pressure of the agonized conscience within. The nation became numerous; it ceased to be either ecstatic or distressful; the high social morality which on the whole it preserved took another color; people remained honest and helpful out of good sense and good will rather than out of scrupulous adherence to any fixed principles. They retained their instinct for order, and often created order with surprising quickness; but the sanctity of law, to be obeyed for its own sake, began to escape them; it seemed too unpractical a notion, and not quite serious. In fact, the second and native-born American mentality began to take shape. The sense of sin totally evaporated. Nature, in the words of Emerson, was all beauty and commodity; and while operating on it laboriously, and drawing quick returns, the American began to drink in inspiration from it aesthetically. At the same time, in so broad a continent, he had elbow-room. His neighbors helped more than they hindered him; he wished their number to increase. Good-will became the great American virtue; and a passion arose for counting heads, and square miles, and cubic feet, and minutes saved—as if there had been anything to save them for. How strange to the American now that saying of Jonathan Edwards, that men are naturally God's enemies! Yet that is an axiom to any intelligent Calvinist, though the words he uses may be different. If you told the modern American that he is totally depraved, he would think you were joking, as he himself usually is. He is convinced that he always has been, and always will be, victorious and blameless.

Calvinism thus lost its basis in American life. Some emotional natures, indeed, reverted in their religious revivals or private searchings of heart to the sources of the tradition; for any of the radical points of view in philosophy may cease to be prevalent, but none can cease to be possible. Other natures, more sensitive to the moral and literary influences of the world, preferred to abandon parts of their philosophy, hoping thus to reduce the distance which should separate the remainder from real life.

Meantime, if anybody arose with a special sensibility or a technical genius, he was in great straits; not being fed sufficiently by the world, he was driven in upon his own resources. The three American writers whose personal endowment was perhaps the finest—Poe, Hawthorne, and Emerson—had all a certain starved and abstract quality. They could not retail the genteel tradition; they were too keen, too perceptive, and too independent for that. But life offered them little digestible material, nor were they naturally voracious. They were fastidious, and under the circumstances they were starved. Emerson, to be sure, fed on books. There was a great catholicity in his reading; and he showed a fine tact in his comments, and in his way of appropriating what he read. But he read transcendentally, not historically, to learn what he himself felt, not what others might have felt before him. And to feed on books, for a philosopher or a poet, is still to starve. Books can help him to acquire form, or to avoid pitfalls; they cannot supply him with substance, if he is to have any. Therefore the genius of Poe and Hawthorne, and even of Emerson, was employed on a sort of inner play, or digestion of vacancy. It was a refined labor, but it was in danger of being morbid, or tinkling, or self-indulgent. It was a play of intramental rhymes. Their mind was like an old music-box, full of tender echoes and quaint fancies. These fancies expressed their personal genius sincerely, as dreams may; but they were arbitrary fancies in comparison with what a real observer would have said in the premises. Their manner, in a word, was subjective. In their own persons they escaped the mediocrity of the genteel tradition, but they supplied nothing to supplant it in other minds.

The churches, likewise, although they modified their spirit, had no philosophy to offer save a selection or a new emphasis on parts of what Calvinism contained. The theology of Calvin, we must remember, had much in it besides philosophical Calvinism. A Christian tenderness, and a hope of grace for the individual, came to mitigate its sardonic optimism; and it was these evangelical elements that the Calvinistic churches now emphasized, seldom and with blushes referring to hell-fire or infant damnation. Yet philosophic Calvinism, with a theory of life that would perfectly justify hell-fire and infant damnation if they happened to exist, still dominates the traditional metaphysics. It is an ingredient, and the decisive ingredient, in what calls itself idealism. But in order to see just what part Calvinism plays in current idealism, it will be necessary to distinguish the other chief element in that complex system, namely, transcendentalism.

Transcendentalism is the philosophy which the romantic era produced in Germany, and independently, I believe, in America also. Transcendentalism proper, like romanticism, is not any particular set of dogmas about what things exist; it is not a system of the universe regarded as a fact, or as a collection of facts. It is a method, a point of view, from which any world, no matter what it might contain, could be approached by a self-conscious observer. Transcendentalism is a systematic subjectivism. It studies the perspectives of knowledge, as they radiate from the self; it is a plan of those avenues of inference by which our ideas of things must be reached, if they are to afford any systematic or distant vistas. In other words, transcendentalism is the critical logic of science. Knowledge, it says, has a station, as in a watch-tower; it is always seated here and now, in the self of the moment. The past and the future, things inferred and things conceived, lie around it, painted as upon a panorama. They cannot be lighted up save by some centrifugal ray of the mind.

This is hardly the occasion for developing or explaining this delicate insight; suffice it to say, lest you should think later that I disparage transcendentalism, that as a method I regard it as correct and, when once suggested, unforgettable. I regard it as the chief contribution made in modern times to speculation. But it is a method only, an attitude we may always assume if we like and that will always be legitimate. It is no answer, and involves no particular answer, to the question: What exists; in what order is what exists produced; what is to exist in the future? This question must be answered by observing the object, and tracing humbly the movement of the object. It cannot be answered at all by harping on the fact that this

object, if discovered, must be discovered by somebody who has an interest in discovering it. Yet the Germans who first gained the full transcendental insight were romantic people; they were more or less frankly poets; they were colossal egotists, and wished to make not only their own knowledge but the whole universe center about themselves. And full as they were of their romantic isolation and romantic liberty, it occurred to them to imagine that all reality might be a transcendental self and a romantic dreamer like themselves; nay, that it might be just their own transcendental self and their own romantic dreams extended indefinitely. Transcendental logic, the method of discovery for the mind, was to become also the method of evolution in nature and history. Transcendental method, so abused, produced transcendental myth. A conscientious critique of knowledge was turned into a sham system of nature. We must therefore distinguish sharply the transcendental grammar of the intellect, which is significant and potentially correct, from the various transcendental systems of the universe, which are chimeras.

In both its parts, however, transcendentalism had much to recommend it to American philosophers, for the transcendental method appealed to the individualistic and revolutionary temper of their youth, while transcendental myths enabled them to find a new status for their inherited theology, and to give what parts of it they cared to preserve some semblance of philosophical backing. This last was the use to which the transcendental method was put by Kant himself, who first brought it into vogue, before the terrible weapon had got out of hand, and became the instrument of pure romanticism. Kant came, he himself said, to remove knowledge in order to make room for faith, which in his case meant faith in Calvinism. In other words, he applied the transcendental method to matters of fact, reducing them thereby to human ideas, in order to give to the Calvinistic postulates of conscience a metaphysical validity. For Kant had a genteel tradition of his own, which he wished to remove to a place of safety, feeling that the empirical world had become too hot for it; and this place of safety was the region of transcendental myth. I need hardly say how perfectly this expedient suited the needs of philosophers in America, and it is no accident if the influence of Kant soon became dominant here. To embrace this philosophy was regarded as a sign of profound metaphysical insight, although the most mediocre minds found no difficulty in embracing it. In truth it was a sign of having been brought up in the genteel tradition, of feeling it weak, and of wishing to save it.

But the transcendental method, in its way, was also sympathetic to the American mind. It embodied, in a radical form, the spirit of Protestantism as distinguished from its inherited doctrines; it was autonomous, undismayed, calmly revolutionary; it felt that Will was deeper than Intellect; it focused everything here and now, and asked all things to show their credentials at the bar of the young self, and to prove their value for this latest born moment. These things are truly American; they would be characteristic of any young society with a keen and discursive intelligence, and they are strikingly exemplified in the thought and in the person of Emerson. They constitute what he called self-trust. Self-trust, like other transcendental attitudes, may be expressed in metaphysical fables. The romantic spirit may imagine itself to be an absolute force, evoking and molding the plastic world to express its varying moods. But for a pioneer who is actually a world-builder this metaphysical illusion has a partial warrant in historical fact; far more warrant than it could boast of in the fixed and articulated society of Europe, among the moonstruck rebels and sulking poets of the romantic era. Emerson was a shrewd Yankee, by instinct on the winning side; he was a cheery, child-like soul, impervious to the evidence of evil, as of everything that it did not suit his transcendental individuality to appreciate or to notice. More, perhaps, than anybody that has ever lived, he practiced the transcendental method in all its purity. He had no system. He opened his eyes on the world every morning with a fresh sincerity, marking how things seemed to him then, or what they suggested to his spontaneous fancy. This fancy, for being spontaneous, was not always novel; it was guided by the habits and training of his mind, which were those of a preacher. Yet he never insisted on his notions so as to turn them into settled dogmas; he felt in his bones that they were myths. Sometimes, indeed, the bad example of other transcendentalists, less true than he to their method, or the pressing questions of unintelligent people, or the instinct we all have to think our ideas final, led him to the very verge of system-making; but he stopped short. Had he made a system out of his notion of compensa-

tion, or the over-soul, or spiritual laws, the result would have been as thin and forced as it is in other transcendental systems. But he coveted truth; and he returned to experience, to history, to poetry, to the natural science of his day, for new starting-points and hints toward fresh transcendental musings.

To covet truth is a very distinguished passion. Every philosopher says he is pursuing the truth, but this is seldom the case. As Mr. Bertrand Russell has observed, one reason why philosophers often fail to reach the truth is that often they do not desire to reach it Those who are genuinely concerned in discovering what happens to be true are rather the men of science, the naturalists, the historians; and ordinarily they discover it, according to their lights. The truths they find are never complete, and are not always important; but they are integral parts of the truth, facts and circumstances that help to fill in the picture, and that no later interpretation can invalidate or afford to contradict. But professional philosophers are usually only scholastics: that is, they are absorbed in defending some vested illusion or some eloquent idea. Like lawyers or detectives, they study the case for which they are retained, to see how much evidence or semblance of evidence they can gather for the defense, and how much prejudice they can raise against the witnesses for the prosecution; for they know they are defending prisoners suspected by the world, and perhaps by their own good sense, of falsification. They do not covet truth, but victory and the dispelling of their own doubts. What they defend is some system, that is, some view about the totality of things, of which men are actually ignorant. No system would ever have been framed if people had been simply interested in knowing what is true, whatever it may be. What produces systems is the interest in maintaining against all comers that some favorite or inherited idea of ours is sufficient and right. A system may contain an account of many things which, in detail, are true enough; but as a system, covering infinite possibilities that neither our experience nor our logic can prejudge, it must be a work of imagination, and a piece of human soliloquy. It may be expressive of human experience, it may be poetical; but how should any one who really coveted truth suppose that it was true?

Emerson had no system; and his coveting truth had another exceptional consequence: he was detached, unworldly, contemplative. When he came out of the conventicle or the reform meeting, or out of the rapturous close atmosphere of the lecture-room, he heard nature whispering to him: "Why so hot, little sir?" No doubt the spirit or energy of the world is what is acting in us, as the sea is what rises in every little wave; but it passes through us, and cry out as we may, it will move on. Our privilege is to have perceived it as it moves. Our dignity is not in what we do, but in what we understand. The whole world is doing things. We are turning in that vortex; yet within us is silent observation, the speculative eye before which all passes, which bridges the distances and compares the combatants. On this side of his genius Emerson broke away from all conditions of age or country and represented nothing except intelligence itself.

There was another element in Emerson, curiously combined with transcendentalism, namely, his love and respect for Nature. Nature, for the transcendentalist, is precious because it is his own work, a mirror in which he looks at himself and says (like a poet relishing his own verses), "What a genius I am! Who would have thought there was such stuff in me?" And the philosophical egotist finds in his doctrine a ready explanation of whatever beauty and commodity nature actually has. No wonder, he says to himself, that nature is sympathetic, since I made it. And such a view, one-sided and even fatuous as it may be, undoubtedly sharpens the vision of a poet and a moralist to all that is inspiriting and symbolic in the natural world. Emerson was particularly ingenious and clear-sighted in feeling the spiritual uses of fellowship with the elements. This is something in which all Teutonic poetry is rich and which forms, I think, the most genuine and spontaneous part of modern taste, and especially of American taste. Just as some people are naturally enthralled and refreshed by music, so others are by landscape. Music and landscape make up the spiritual resources of those who cannot or dare not express their unfulfilled ideals in words. Serious poetry, profound religion (Calvinism, for instance) are the joys of an unhappiness that confesses itself; but when a genteel tradition forbids people to confess that they are unhappy, serious poetry and profound religion are closed to them by that; and since human life, in its depths, cannot then express itself openly, imagination is driven for comfort into abstract arts, where human circumstances

are lost sight of, and human problems dissolve in a purer medium. The pressure of care is thus relieved, without its quietus being found in intelligence. To understand oneself is the classic form of consolation; to elude oneself is the romantic. In the presence of music or landscape human experience eludes itself; and thus romanticism is the bond between transcendental and naturalistic sentiment.

Have there been, we may ask, any successful efforts to escape from the genteel tradition, and to express something worth expressing behind its back? This might well not have occurred as yet; but America is so precocious, it has been trained by the genteel tradition to be so wise for its years, that some indications of a truly native philosophy and poetry are already to be found. I might mention the humorists, of whom you here in California have had your share. The humorists, however, only half escape the genteel tradition; their humor would lose its savor if they had wholly escaped it. They point to what contradicts it in the facts; but not in order to abandon the genteel tradition, for they have nothing solid to put in its place. When they point out how ill many facts fit into it, they do not clearly conceive that this militates against the standard, but think it a funny perversity in the facts. Of course, did they earnestly respect the genteel tradition, such an incongruity would seem to them sad, rather than ludicrous. Perhaps the prevalence of humor in America, in and out of season, may be taken as one more evidence that the genteel tradition is present pervasively, but everywhere weak. Similarly in Italy, during the Renaissance, the Catholic tradition could not be banished from the intellect, since there was nothing articulate to take its place; yet its hold on the heart was singularly relaxed. The consequence was that humorists could regale themselves with the foibles of monks and of cardinals, with the credulity of fools, and the bogus miracles of the saints; not intending to deny the theory of the church, but caring for it so little at heart, that they could find it infinitely amusing that it should be contradicted in men's lives, and that no harm should come of it. So when Mark Twain says, "I was born of poor but dishonest parents," the humor depends on the parody of the genteel Anglo-Saxon convention that it is disreputable to be poor; but to hint at the hollowness of it would not be amusing if it did not remain at bottom one's habitual conviction.

The one American writer who has left the genteel tradition entirely behind is perhaps Walt Whitman. For this reason educated Americans find him rather an unpalatable person, who they sincerely protest ought not to be taken for a representative of their culture; and he certainly should not, because their culture is so genteel and traditional. But the foreigner may sometimes think otherwise, since he is looking for what may have arisen in America to express, not the polite and conventional American mind, but the spirit and the inarticulate principles that animate the community, on which its own genteel mentality seems to sit rather lightly. When the foreigner opens the pages of Walt Whitman, he thinks that he has come at last upon something representative and original. In Walt Whitman democracy is carried into psychology and morals. The various sights, moods, and emotions are given each one vote; they are declared to be all free and equal, and the innumerable common-place moments of life are suffered to speak like the others. Those moments formerly reputed great are not excluded, but they are made to march in the ranks with their companions,—plain foot-soldiers and servants of the hour. Nor does the refusal to discriminate stop there; we must carry our principle further down, to the animals, to inanimate nature, to the cosmos as a whole. Whitman became a pantheist; but his pantheism, unlike that of the Stoics and of Spinoza, was unintellectual, lazy, and self-indulgent; for he simply felt jovially that everything real was good enough, and that he was good enough himself. In him Bohemia rebelled against the genteel tradition; but the reconstruction that alone can justify revolution did not ensue. His attitude, in principle, was utterly disintegrating; his poetic genius fell back to the lowest level, perhaps, to which it is possible for poetic genius to fall. He reduced his imagination to a passive sensorium for the registering of impressions. No element of construction remained in it, and therefore no element of penetration. But his scope was wide; and his lazy, desultory apprehension was poetical. His work, for the very reason that it is so rudimentary, contains a beginning, or rather many beginnings, that might possibly grow into a noble moral imagination, a worthy filling for the human mind. An American in the nineteenth century who completely disregarded the genteel tradition could hardly have done more.

But there is another distinguished man, lately lost to this country, who has given some rude shocks to this tradition and who, as much as Whitman, may be regarded as representing the genuine, the long silent American mind—I mean William James. He and his brother Henry were as tightly swaddled in the genteel tradition as any infant geniuses could be, for they were born in Cambridge, and in a Swedenborgian household. Yet they burst those bands almost entirely. The ways in which the two brothers freed themselves, however, are interestingly different. Mr. Henry James has done it by adopting the point of view of the outer world, and by turning the genteel American tradition, as he turns everything else, into a subject-matter for analysis.

For him it is a curious habit of mind, intimately comprehended, to be compared with other habits of mind, also well known to him. Thus he has overcome the genteel tradition in the classic way, by understanding it. With William James too this infusion of worldly insight and European sympathies was a potent influence, especially in his earlier days; but the chief source of his liberty was another. It was his personal spontaneity, similar to that of Emerson, and his personal vitality, similar to that of nobody else. Convictions and ideas came to him, so to speak, from the subsoil. He had a prophetic sympathy with the dawning sentiments of the age, with the moods of the dumb majority. His scattered words caught fire in many parts of the world. His way of thinking and feeling represented the true America, and represented in a measure the whole ultra-modern, radical world. Thus he eluded the genteel tradition in the romantic way, by continuing it into its opposite. The romantic mind, glorified in Hegel's dialectic (which is not dialectic at all, but a sort of tragi-comic history of experience), is always rendering its thoughts unrecognizable through the infusion of new insights, and through the insensible transformation of the moral feeling that accompanies them, till at last it has completely reversed its old judgments under cover of expanding them. Thus the genteel tradition was led a merry dance when it fell again into the hands of a genuine and vigorous romanticist, like William James. He restored their revolutionary force to its neutralized elements, by picking them out afresh, and emphasizing them separately, according to his personal predilections.

For one thing, William James kept his mind and heart wide open to all that might seem, to polite minds, odd, personal, or visionary in religion and philosophy. He gave a sincerely respectful hearing to sentimentalists, mystics, spiritualists, wizards, cranks, quacks, and impostors—for it is hard to draw the line, and James was not willing to draw it prematurely. He thought, with his usual modesty, that any of these might have something to teach him. The lame, the halt, the blind, and those speaking with tongues could come to him with the certainty of finding sympathy; and if they were not healed, at least they were comforted, that a famous professor should take them so seriously; and they began to feel that after all to have only one leg, or one hand, or one eye, or to have three, might be in itself no less beauteous than to have just two, like the stolid majority. Thus William James became the friend and helper of those groping, nervous, half-educated, spiritually disinherited, emotionally hungry individuals of which America is full. He became, at the same time, their spokesman and representative before the learned world; and he made it a chief part of his vocation to recast what the learned world has to offer, so that as far as possible it might serve the needs and interests of these people.

Yet the normal practical masculine American, too, had a friend in William James. There is a feeling abroad now, to which biology and Darwinism lend some color, that theory is simply an instrument for practice, and intelligence merely a help toward material survival. Bears, it is said, have fur and claws, but poor naked man is condemned to be intelligent, or he will perish. This feeling William James embodied in that theory of thought and of truth which he called pragmatism. Intelligence, he thought, is no miraculous, idle faculty, by which we mirror passively any or every thing that happens to be true, reduplicating the real world to no purpose. Intelligence has its roots and its issue in the context of events; it is one kind of practical adjustment, an experimental act, a form of vital tension. It does not essentially serve to picture other parts of reality, but to connect them. This view was not worked out by William James in its psychological and historical details; unfortunately he developed it chiefly in controversy against its opposite, which he called intellectualism, and which he hated with all the hatred of which his kind heart was capable. Intellectualism, as he conceived it, was pure pedantry; it impoverished and verbalized everything, and tied up nature in red tape. Ideas and rules that may have been occasionally useful, it put in the place of the full-blooded irra-

tional movement of life which had called them into being; and these abstractions, so soon obsolete, it strove to fix and to worship forever. Thus all creeds and theories and all formal precepts sink in the estimation of the pragmatist to a local and temporary grammar of action; a grammar that must be changed slowly by time, and may be changed quickly by genius. To know things as a whole, or as they are eternally, if there is anything eternal in them, is not only beyond our powers, but would prove worthless, and perhaps even fatal to our lives. Ideas are not mirrors, they are weapons; their function is to prepare us to meet events, as future experience may unroll them. Those ideas that disappoint us are false ideas; those to which events are true are true themselves.

This may seem a very utilitarian view of the mind; and I confess I think it a partial one, since the logical force of beliefs and ideas, their truth or falsehood as assertions, has been overlooked altogether, or confused with the vital force of the material processes which these ideas express. It is an external view only, which marks the place and conditions of the mind in nature, but neglects its specific essence; as if a jewel were defined as a round hole in a ring. Nevertheless, the more materialistically we interpret the pragmatist theory of what the mind is, the more vitalistic our theory of nature will have to become. If the intellect is a device produced in organic bodies to expedite their processes, these organic bodies must have interests and a chosen direction in their life; otherwise their life could not be expedited, nor could anything be useful to it. In other words—and this is a third point at which the philosophy of William James has played havoc with the genteel tradition, while ostensibly defending it—nature must be conceived anthropomorphically and in psychological terms. Its purposes are not to be static harmonies, self-unfolding destinies, the logic of spirit, the spirit of logic, or any other formal method and abstract law; its purposes are to be concrete endeavors, finite efforts of souls living in an environment which they transform and by which they, too, are affected. A spirit, the divine spirit as much as the human, as this new animism conceives it, is a romantic adventurer. Its future is undetermined. Its scope, its duration, and the quality of its life, are all contingent. This spirit grows; it buds and sends forth feelers, sounding the depths around for such other centers of force or life as may exist there. It has a vital momentum, but no predetermined goal. It uses its past as a stepping-stone, or rather as a diving-board, but has an absolutely fresh will at each moment to plunge this way or that into the unknown. The universe is an experiment; it is unfinished. It has no ultimate or total nature, because it has no end. It embodies no formula or stable law; any formula is at best a poor abstraction, describing what, in some region and for some time, may be the most striking characteristic of existence; the law is a description *a posteriori* of the habit things have chosen to acquire, and which they may possibly throw off altogether. What a day may bring forth is uncertain; uncertain even to God. Omniscience is impossible; time is real; what had been omniscience hitherto might discover something more to-day. "There shall be news," William James was fond of saying with rapture, quoting from the unpublished poem of an obscure friend, "there shall be news in heaven!" There is almost certainly, he thought, a God now; there may be several gods, who might exist together, or one after the other. We might, by our conspiring sympathies, help to make a new one. Much in us is doubtless immortal; we survive death for some time in a recognizable form; but what our career and transformations may be in the sequel, we cannot tell, although we may help to determine them by our daily choices. Observation must be continual, if our ideas are to remain true. Eternal vigilance is the price of knowledge; perpetual hazard, perpetual experiment keep quick the edge of life.

This is, so far as I know, a new philosophical vista; it is a conception never before presented, although implied, perhaps, in various quarters, as in Norse and even Greek mythology. It is a vision radically empirical and radically romantic; and as William James himself used to say, the vision and not the arguments of a philosopher is the interesting and influential thing about him. William James, rather too generously, attributed this vision to M. Bergson, and regarded him in consequence as a philosopher of the first rank, whose thought was to be one of the turning-points in history. M. Bergson had killed intellectualism. It was his book on creative evolution, said James with humorous emphasis, that had come at last to *"écraser l'infâme."* We may suspect, notwithstanding, that intellectualism, infamous and crushed, will survive the blow; and if the author of the Book of Ecclesiastes were now alive, and heard that there shall be news in heaven, he would doubtless say that there may possibly be news there, but that under the sun there is nothing new—not even radical empiricism or radical romanticism, which from the beginning of the world has been the philosophy of those who as yet had had little experience; for to the blinking little child it is not merely something in the world that is new daily, but everything is new all day.

I am not concerned with the rights and wrongs of that controversy; my point is only that William James, in this genial evolutionary view of the world, has given a rude shock to the genteel tradition. What! The world a gradual improvization? Creation unpremeditated? God a sort of young poet or struggling artist? William James is an advocate of theism; pragmatism adds one of the evidences of religion; that is excellent. But is not the cool abstract piety of the genteel getting more than it asks for? This empirical naturalistic God is too crude and positive a force; he will work miracles, he will answer prayers, he may inhabit distinct places, and have distinct conditions under which alone he can operate; he is a neighboring being, whom we can act upon, and rely upon for specific aids, as upon a personal friend, or a physician, or an insurance company. How disconcerting! Is not this new theology a little like superstition? And yet how interesting, how exciting, if it should happen to be true! I am far from wishing to suggest that such a view seems to me more probable than conventional idealism or than Christian orthodoxy. All three are in the region of dramatic system-making and myth, to which probabilities are irrelevant. If one man says the moon is sister to the sun, and another that she is his daughter, the question is not which notion is more probable, but whether either of them is at all expressive. The so-called evidences are devised afterwards, when faith and imagination have prejudged the issue. The force of William James's new theology, or romantic cosmology, lies only in this: that it has broken the spell of the genteel tradition, and enticed faith in a new direction, which on second thoughts may prove no less alluring than the old. The important fact is not that the new fancy might possibly be true—who shall know that?—but that it has entered the heart of a leading American to conceive and to cherish it. The genteel tradition cannot be dislodged by these insurrections, there are circles to which it is still congenial, and where it will be preserved. But it has been challenged and (what is perhaps more insidious) it has been discovered. No one need be brow-beaten any longer into accepting it. No one need be afraid, for instance, that his fate is sealed because some young prig may call him a dualist; the pint would call the quart a dualist, if you tried to pour the quart into him. We need not be afraid of being less profound, for being direct and sincere. The intellectual world may be traversed in many directions; the whole has not been surveyed; there is a great career in it open to talent. That is a sort of knell, that tolls the passing of the genteel tradition. Something else is now in the field; something else can appeal to the imagination, and be a thousand times more idealistic than academic idealism, which is often simply a way of white-washing and adoring things as they are. The illegitimate monopoly which the genteel tradition had established over what ought to be assumed and what ought to be hoped for has been broken down by the first-born of the family, by the genius of the race. Henceforth there can hardly be the same peace and the same pleasure in hugging the old proprieties. Hegel will be to the next generation what Sir William Hamilton was to the last. Nothing will have been disproved, but everything will have been abandoned. An honest man has spoken, and the cant of the genteel tradition has become harder for young lips to repeat.

With this I have finished such a sketch as I am here able to offer you of the genteel tradition in American philosophy. The subject is complex, and calls for many an excursus and qualifying footnote; yet I think the main outlines are clear enough. The chief fountains of this tradition were Calvinism and transcendentalism. Both were living fountains; but to keep them alive they required, one an agonized conscience, and the other a radical subjective criticism of knowledge. When these rare metaphysical preoccupations disappeared—and the American atmosphere is not favorable to either of them—the two systems ceased to be inwardly understood; they subsisted as sacred mysteries only; and the combination of the two in some transcendental system of the universe (a contradiction in principle) was doubly artificial. Besides, it could hardly be held with a single mind. Natural science, history, the beliefs implied in labor and invention, could not be disregarded altogether; so that the transcendental philosopher was condemned to a double allegiance, and to not letting his left hand know the bluff that his right hand was putting up. Nevertheless, the difficulty in bringing practical inarticulate convictions to expression is very great, and the genteel tradition has subsisted in the academic mind, for want of anything equally academic to take its place.

The academic mind, however, has had its flanks turned. On the one side came the revolt of the Bohemian temperament, with its poetry of crude naturalism; on the other side came an impassioned empiricism, welcoming popular religious witnesses to the unseen, reducing science to an instrument of success in action, and declaring the universe to be wild and young, and not to be harnessed by the logic of any school.

This revolution, I should think, might well find an echo among you, who live in a thriving society, and in the presence of a virgin and prodigious world. When you transform nature to your uses, when you experiment with her forces, and reduce them to industrial agents, you cannot feel that nature was made by you or for you, for then these adjustments would have been preestablished. You must feel, rather, that you are an offshoot of her life; one brave little force among her immense forces. When you escape, as you love to do, to your forests and your Sierras, I am sure again that you do not feel you made them, or that they were made for you. They have grown, as you have grown, only more massively and more slowly. In their non-human beauty and peace they stir the sub-human depths and the super-human possibilities of your own spirit. It is no transcendental logic that they teach; and they gave no sign of any deliberate morality seated in the world. It is rather the vanity and superficiality of all logic, the needlessness of argument, the finitude of morals, the strength of time, the fertility of matter, the variety, the unspeakable variety, of possible life. Everything is measurable and conditioned, indefinitely repeated, yet in repetition, twisted somewhat from its old form. Everywhere is beauty and nowhere permanence, everywhere an incipient harmony nowhere an intention, nor a responsibility, nor a plan. It is the irresistible suasion of this daily spectacle, it is the daily discipline of contact with things, so different from the verbal discipline of the schools, that will, I trust, inspire the philosophy of your children. A Californian whom I had recently the pleasure of meeting observed that, if the philosophers had lived among your mountains their systems would have been different from what they are. Certainly, I should say, very different from what those systems are from which the European genteel tradition has handed down since Socrates; for these systems are egotistical; directly or indirectly they are anthropocentric, and inspired by the conceited notion that man, or human reason, or the human distinction between good and evil, is the center and pivot of the universe. That is what the mountains and the woods should make you at last ashamed to assert. From what, indeed, does the society of nature liberate you, that you find it so sweet? It is hardly (is it?) that you wish to forget your past, or your friends, or that you have any secret contempt for your present ambitions. You respect these, you respect them perhaps too much; you are not suffered by the genteel tradition to criticize or to reform them at all radically. No; it is the yoke of this genteel tradition itself, your tyrant from the cradle to the grave, that these primeval solitudes lift from your shoulders. They suspend your forced sense of your own importance not merely as individuals, but even as men. They allow you, in one happy moment, at once to play and to worship, to take yourselves simply, humbly, for what you are, and to salute the wild, indiffer-

ent, noncensorious infinity of nature. You are admonished that what you can do avails little materially, and in the end nothing. At the same time, through wonder and pleasure, you are taught speculation. You learn what you are really fitted to do, and where lie your natural dignity and joy, namely, in representing many things, without being them, and in letting your imagination, through sympathy, celebrate and echo their life. Because the peculiarity of man is that his machinery for reaction on external things has involved an imaginative transcript of these things, which is preserved and suspended in his fancy; and the interest and beauty of this inward landscape, rather than any fortunes that may await his body in the outer world, constitute his proper happiness. By their mind, its scope, quality, and temper, we estimate men, for by the mind only do we exist as men, and are more than so many storage-batteries for material energy. Let us therefore be frankly human. Let us be content to live in the mind.

The Poetry of Barbarism (1900)

We should be careful to observe the position from which Santayana moves to his treatment of Whitman—the standard by which Whitman may be considered a "barbarian." There is a paradox here. The earliest poets—those ordinarily taken to belong to a barbarous time—are here regarded as the most "ideal." The poetry of Homeric times, with "those little barbaric towns," was, we are told, the "sweetest and sanest that the world has known," and since that time "we see the power of idealization steadily decline." Even Dante and Shakespeare, in spite of their great powers, represent, for reasons stated in the text, a decline.

Santayana does not leave the matter with this sweepingly general statement. He discriminates in the general decline a particular example in the modern post-Christian world, in which the "spirit of life, innocent of any rationalizing disciple [by which Santayana would mean the classic or Christian system of ideas], and deprived of any authoritative and adequate method of expression, has relapsed into miscellaneous

and shallow exuberance." He takes Whitman as an extreme example of such a world—though, in the turn of time, we have seen much poetry more irrational in method than Whitman, more formless, more realistic in its content, and more grossly naturalistic in attitude.

The key of Santayana's position is the assumption of an absolute norm for poetry—the doctrine of "idealization"—the norm being established by reference to a certain acceptable system of ideas. But later in his career, Santayana was inclined to revise his views and value more the expressive adequacy, the "lyric adequacy," without such a rigorous reference to philosophical values, to admit the possibility of the dramatic appropriateness of the poetic utterance.

In one sense, it may be argued that Santayana's own theory of poetry is an example of the genteel tradition. His theory would remove the criterion of excellence from the flux of life as it is lived with all its stressful changes in the process of time; it would dismiss as irrelevant what was special to an age and a situation—what we would take as the uniquely expressive element in poetry. And this removal of "culture" from the hard actuality of experience is at the very core of the genteel tradition as Santayana himself defined it.

It is an observation at first sight melancholy but in the end, perhaps, enlightening, that the earliest poets are the most ideal, and that primitive ages furnish the most heroic characters and have the clearest vision of a perfect life. The Homeric times must have been full of ignorance and suffering. In those little barbaric towns, in those camps and farms, in those shipyards, there must have been much insecurity and superstition. That age was singularly poor in all that concerns the convenience of life and the entertainment of the mind with arts and sciences. Yet it had a sense for civilization. That machinery of life which men were beginning to devise appealed to them as poetical; they knew its ultimate justification and studied its incipient processes with delight. The poetry of that simple and ignorant age was, accordingly, the sweetest and sanest that the world has known; the most faultless in taste, and the most even and lofty in inspiration. Without lacking variety and homeliness, it bathed all things human in the golden light of morning; it clothed sorrow in a kind of majesty, instinct with both self-control and heroic frankness. Nowhere else can we find so noble a rendering of human nature, so spontaneous a delight in life, so uncompromising a dedication to beauty, and such a gift of seeing beauty in everything. Homer, the first of poets, was also the best and most poetical.

From this beginning, if we look down the history of Occidental literature, we see the power of idealization steadily decline. For while it finds here and there, as in Dante, a more spiritual theme and a subtler and riper intellect, it pays for that advantage by a more than equivalent loss in breadth, sanity, and happy vigour. And if ever imagination bursts out with a greater potency, as in Shakespeare (who excels the patriarch of poetry in depth of passion and vividness of characterization, and in those exquisite bubblings of poetry and humour in which English genius is at its best), yet Shakespeare also pays the price by a notable loss in taste, in sustained inspiration, in consecra-

tion, and in rationality. There is more or less rubbish in his greatest works. When we come down to our own day we find poets of hardly less natural endowment (for in endowment all ages are perhaps alike) and with vastly richer sources of inspiration; for they have many arts and literatures behind them, with the spectacle of a varied and agitated society, a world which is the living microcosm of its own history and presents in one picture many races, arts, and religions. Our poets have more wonderful tragedies of the imagination to depict than had Homer, whose world was innocent of any essential defeat, or Dante, who believed in the world's definitive redemption. Or, if perhaps their inspiration is comic, they have the pageant of mediaeval manners, with its picturesque artifices and passionate fancies, and the long comedy of modern social revolutions, so illusory in their aims and so productive in their aimlessness. They have, moreover, the new and marvellous conception which natural science has given us of the world and of the conditions of human progress.

With all these lessons of experience behind them, however, we find our contemporary poets incapable of any high wisdom, incapable of any imaginative rendering of human life and its meaning. Our poets are things of shreds and patches; they give us episodes and studies, a sketch of this curiosity, a glimpse of that romance; they have no total vision, no grasp of the whole reality, and consequently no capacity for a sane and steady idealization. The comparatively barbarous ages had a poetry of the ideal; they had visions of beauty, order, and perfection. This age of material elaboration has no sense for those things. Its fancy is retrospective, whimsical, and flickering; its ideals, when it has any, are negative and partial; its moral strength is a blind and miscellaneous vehemence. Its poetry, in a word, is the poetry of barbarism.

This poetry should be viewed in relation to the general moral crisis and imaginative disintegration of which it gives a verbal echo; then we shall avoid the injustice of passing it over as insignificant, no less than the imbecility of hailing it as essentially glorious and successful. We must remember that the imagination of our race has been subject to a double discipline. It has been formed partly in the school of classic literature and polity, and partly in the school of Christian piety. This duality of inspiration, this contradiction between the two accepted methods of rationalizing the world, has been a chief source of that incoherence, that romantic indistinctness and imperfection, which largely characterize the products of the modern arts. A man cannot serve two masters; yet the conditions have not been such as to allow him wholly to despise the one or wholly to obey the other. To be wholly Pagan is impossible after the dissolution of that civilization which had seemed universal, and that empire which had believed itself eternal. To be wholly Christian is impossible for a similar reason, now that the illusion and cohesion of Christian ages is lost, and for the further reason that Christianity was itself fundamentally eclectic. Before it could succeed and dominate men even for a time, it was obliged to adjust itself to reality, to incorporate many elements of Pagan wisdom, and to accommodate itself to many habits and passions at variance with its own ideal.

In these latter times, with the prodigious growth of material life in elaboration and of mental life in diffusion, there has supervened upon this old dualism a new faith in man's absolute power, a kind of return to the inexperience and self-assurance of youth. This new inspiration has made many minds indifferent to the two traditional disciplines; neither is seriously accepted by them, for the reason, excellent from their own point of view, that no discipline whatever is needed. The memory of ancient disillusions has faded with time. Ignorance of the past has bred contempt for the lessons which the past might teach. Men prefer to repeat the old experiment without knowing that they repeat it.

. . .

The poetry of barbarism is not without its charm. It can play with sense and passion the more readily and freely in that it does not aspire to subordinate them to a clear thought or a tenable attitude of the will. It can impart the transitive emotions which it expresses; it can find many partial harmonies of mood and fancy; it can, by virtue of its red-hot irrationality, utter wilder cries, surrender itself and us to more absolute passion, and heap up a more indiscriminate wealth of images than belong to poets of seasoned experience or of heavenly inspiration. Irrational stimulation may tire us in the end, but it excites us in the beginning; and how many conventional poets, tender and prolix, have there not been, who tire us now without ever having excited anybody? The power to stimulate is the beginning of greatness, and when the barbarous poet has genius, as he well may have, he stim-

ulates all the more powerfully on account of the crudity of his methods and the recklessness of his emotions. The defects of such art—lack of distinction, absence of beauty, confusion of ideas, incapacity permanently to please—will hardly be felt by the contemporary public, if once its attention is arrested; for no poet is so undisciplined that he will not find many readers, if he finds readers at all, less disciplined than himself.

These considerations may perhaps be best enforced by applying them to two writers of great influence over the present generation who seem to illustrate them on different planes—Robert Browning and Walt Whitman. They are both analytic poets—poets who seek to reveal and express the elemental as opposed to the conventional; but the dissolution has progressed much farther in Whitman than in Browning, doubtless because Whitman began at a much lower stage of moral and intellectual organization; for the good will to be radical was present in both. The elements to which Browning reduces experience are still passions, characters, persons; Whitman carries the disintegration further and knows nothing but moods and particular images. The world of Browning is a world of history with civilization for its setting and with the conventional passions for its motive forces. The world of Whitman is innocent of these things and contains only far simpler and more chaotic elements. In him the barbarism is much more pronounced; it is, indeed, avowed, and the "barbaric yawp" is sent "over the roofs of the world" in full consciousness of its inarticulate character; but in Browning the barbarism is no less real though disguised by a literary and scientific language, since the passions of civilized life with which he deals are treated as so many "barbaric yawps," complex indeed in their conditions, puffings of an intricate engine, but aimless in their vehemence and mere ebullitions of lustiness in adventurous and profoundly ungoverned souls.

Irrationality on this level is viewed by Browning with the same satisfaction with which, on a lower level, it is viewed by Whitman; and the admirers of each hail it as the secret of a new poetry which pierces to the quick and awakens the imagination to a new and genuine vitality. It is in the rebellion against discipline, in the abandonment of the ideals of classic and Christian tradition, that this rejuvenation is found. Both poets represent, therefore, and are admired for representing, what may be called the poetry of barbarism in the most accurate and descriptive sense of this word. For the barbarian is the man who regards his passions as their own excuse for being; who does not domesticate them either by understanding their cause or by conceiving their ideal goal. He is the man who does not know his derivations nor perceive his tendencies, but who merely feels and acts, valuing in his life its force and its filling, but being careless of its purpose and its form. His delight is in abundance and vehemence; his art, like his life, shows an exclusive respect for quantity and splendour of materials. His scorn for what is poorer and weaker than himself is only surpassed by his ignorance of what is higher:

The works of Walt Whitman offer an extreme illustration of this phase of genius, both by their form and by their substance. It was the singularity of his literary form—the challenge it threw to the conventions of verse and of language—that first gave Whitman notoriety: but this notoriety has become fame, because those incapacities and solecisms which glare at us from his pages are only the obverse of a profound inspiration and of a genuine courage. Even the idiosyncrasies of his style have a side which is not mere perversity or affectation; the order of his words, the procession of his images, reproduce the method of a rich, spontaneous, absolutely lazy fancy. In most poets such a natural order is modified by various governing motives—the thought, the metrical form, the echo of other poems in the memory. By Walt Whitman these conventional influences are resolutely banished. We find the swarms of men and objects rendered as they might strike the retina in a sort of waking dream. It is the most sincere possible confession of the lowest—I mean the most primitive—type of perception. All ancient poets are sophisticated in comparison and give proof of longer intellectual and moral training. Walt Whitman has gone back to the innocent style of Adam, when the animals filed before him one by one and he called each of them by its name.

In fact, the influences to which Walt Whitman was subject were as favourable as possible to the imaginary experiment of beginning the world over again. Liberalism and transcendentalism both harboured some illusions on that score; and they were in the air which our poet breathed. Moreover he breathed this air in America, where the newness of the material environment made it easier to ignore the fatal antiquity of human nature. When he afterward became aware that there was or had been a world with a history, he studied that world with curiosity and spoke of it not without a certain shrewdness. But he still regarded it as a foreign world and imagined, as not a few Americans have done, that his own world was a fresh creation, not amenable to the same laws as the old. The difference in the conditions blinded him, in his merely sensuous apprehension, to the identity of the principles.

His parents were farmers in central Long Island and his early years were spent in that district. The family seems to have been not too prosperous and somewhat nomadic; Whitman himself drifted through boyhood without much guidance. We find him now at school, now helping the labourers at the farms, now wandering along the beaches of Long Island, finally at Brooklyn working in an apparently desultory way as a printer and sometimes as a writer for a local newspaper. He must have read or heard something, at this early period, of the English classics; his style often betrays the deep effect made upon him by the grandiloquence of the Bible, of Shakespeare, and of Milton. But his chief interest, if we may trust his account, was already in his own sensations. The aspects of Nature, the forms and habits of animals, the sights of cities, the movement and talk of common people, were his constant delight. His mind was flooded with these images, keenly felt and afterward to be vividly rendered with bold strokes of realism and imagination.

Many poets have had this faculty to seize the elementary aspects of things, but none has had it so exclusively; with Whitman the surface is absolutely all and the underlying structure is without interest and almost without existence. He had had no education and his natural delight in imbibing sensations had not been trained to the uses of practical or theoretical intelligence. He basked in the sunshine of perception and wallowed in the stream of his own sensibility, as later at Camden in the shallows of his favourite brook. Even during the civil war, when he heard the drum-taps so clearly, he could only gaze at the picturesque and terrible aspects of the struggle, and linger among the wounded day after day with a canine devotion; he could not be aroused either to clear thought or to positive action. So also in his poems; a multiplicity of images pass before him and he yields himself to each in turn with absolute passivity. The world has no inside; it is a phantasmagoria of continuous visions, vivid, impressive, but monotonous and hard to distinguish in memory, like the waves of the sea or the decorations of some barbarous temple, sublime only by the infinite aggregation of parts.

This abundance of detail without organization, this wealth of perception without intelligence and of imagination without taste, makes the singularity of Whitman's genius. Full of sympathy and receptivity, with a wonderful gift of graphic characterization and an occasional rare grandeur of diction, he fills us with a sense of the individuality and the universality of what he describes—it is a drop in itself yet a drop in the ocean. The absence of any principle of selection or of a sustained style enables him to render aspects of things and of emotion which would have eluded a trained writer. He is, therefore, interesting even where he is grotesque or perverse. He has accomplished, by the sacrifice of almost every other good quality, something never so well done before. He has approached common life without bringing in his mind any higher standard by which to criticise it; he has seen it, not in contrast with an ideal, but as the expression of forces more indeterminate and elementary than itself; and the vulgar, in this cosmic setting, has appeared to him sublime.

There is clearly some analogy between a mass of images without structure and the notion of an absolute democracy. Whitman, inclined by his genius and habits to see life without relief or organization, believed that his inclination in this respect corresponded with the spirit of his age and country, and that Nature and society, at least in the United States, were constituted after the fashion of his own mind. Being the poet of the average man, he wished all men to be specimens of that average, and being the poet of a fluid Nature, he believed that Nature was or should be a formless flux. This personal bias of Whitman's was further encouraged by the actual absence of distinction in his immediate environment. Surrounded by ugly things and common people, he felt himself happy, ecstatic, overflowing with a kind of patriarchal love. He accordingly came to think that there was a spirit of the New World which he embodied, and which was in complete opposition to that of the Old, and that a literature upon novel principles was needed to express and strengthen this American spirit.

Democracy was not to be merely a constitutional device for the better government of given nations, not merely a movement for the material improvement of the lot of the poorer classes. It was to be a social and a moral democracy and to involve an actual equality among all men. Whatever kept them apart and made it impossible for them to be messmates together was to be discarded. The literature of democracy was to ignore all extraordinary gifts of genius or virtue, all distinction drawn even from great passions or romantic adventures. In Whitman's works, in which this new literature is foreshadowed, there is accordingly not a single character nor a single story. His only hero is Myself, the "single separate person," endowed with the primary impulses, with health, and with sensitiveness to the elementary aspects of Nature. The perfect man of the future, the prolific begetter of other perfect men, is to work with his hands, chanting the poems of some future Walt, some ideally democratic bard. Women are to have as nearly as possible the same character as men: the emphasis is to pass from family life and local ties to the friendship of comrades and the general brotherhood of man. Men are to be vigorous, comfortable, sentimental, and irresponsible.

This dream is, of course, unrealized and unrealizable, in America as elsewhere. Undeniably there are in America many suggestions of such a society and such a national character. But the growing complexity and fixity of institutions necessarily tends to obscure these traits of a primitive and crude democracy. What Whitman seized upon as the promise of the future was in reality the survival of the past. He sings the song of pioneers, but it is in the nature of the pioneer that the greater his success the quicker must be his transformation into something different. When Whitman made the initial and amorphous phase of society his ideal, he became the prophet of a lost cause. That cause was lost, not merely when wealth and intelligence began to take shape in the American Commonwealth, but it was lost at the very foundation of the world, when those laws of evolution were established which Whitman, like Rousseau, failed to understand. If we may trust Mr. Herbert Spencer, these laws involve a passage from the homogeneous to the heterogeneous, and a constant progress at once in differentiation and in organization—all, in a word, that Whitman systematically deprecated or ignored. He is surely not the spokesman of the tendencies of his country, although he describes some aspects of its past and present condition: nor does he appeal to those whom he describes, but rather to the *dilettanti* he despises. He is regarded as representative chiefly by foreigners, who look for some grotesque expression of the genius of so young and prodigious a people.

Whitman, it is true, loved and comprehended men; but this love and comprehension had the same limits as his love and comprehension of Nature. He observed truly and responded to his observation with genuine and pervasive emotion. A great gregariousness, an innocent tolerance of moral weakness, a genuine admiration for bodily health and strength, made him bubble over with affection for the generic human creature. Incapable of an ideal passion, he was full of the milk of human kindness. Yet, for all his acquaintance with the ways and thoughts of the common man of his choice, he did not truly understand him. For to understand people is to go much deeper than they go themselves; to penetrate to their characters and disentangle their inmost ideals. Whitman's insight into man did not go beyond a sensuous sympathy; it consisted in a vicarious satisfaction in their pleasures, and an instinctive love of their persons. It never approached a scientific or imaginative knowledge of their hearts.

Therefore Whitman failed radically in his dearest ambition: he can never be a poet of the people. For the people, like the early races whose poetry was ideal, are natural believers in perfection. They have no doubts about the absolute desirability of wealth and learning and power, none about the worth of pure goodness and pure love. Their chosen poets, if they have any, will be always those who have known how to paint these ideals in lively even if in gaudy colours. Nothing is farther from the common people than the corrupt desire to be primitive. They instinctively look toward a more exalted life, which they imagine to be full of distinction and pleasure, and the idea of that brighter existence fills them with hope or with envy or with humble admiration.

If the people are ever won over to hostility to such ideals, it is only because they are cheated by demagogues who tell them that if all the flowers of civilization were destroyed its fruits would become more abundant. A greater share of happiness, people think, would fall to their lot could they destroy everything beyond their own possible possessions. But they are made thus envious and ignoble only by a deception: what they really desire is an ideal good for themselves which they are told they may secure by depriving others of their preëminence.

Their hope is always to enjoy perfect satisfaction themselves; and therefore a poet who loves the picturesque aspects of labour and vagrancy will hardly be the poet of the poor. He may have described their figure and occupation, in neither of which they are much interested; he will not have read their souls. They will prefer to him any sentimental story-teller, any sensational dramatist, any moralizing poet; for they are hero-worshippers by temperament, and are too wise or too unfortunate to be much enamoured of themselves or of the conditions of their existence.

Fortunately, the political theory that makes Whitman's principle of literary prophecy and criticism does not always inspire his chants, nor is it presented, even in his prose works, quite bare and unadorned. In "Democratic Vistas" we find it clothed with something of the same poetic passion and lighted up with the same flashes of intuition which we admire in the poems. Even there the temperament is finer than the ideas and the poet wiser than the thinker. His ultimate appeal is really to something more primitive and general than any social aspirations, to something more elementary than an ideal of any kind. He speaks to those minds and to those moods in which sensuality is touched with mysticism. When the intellect is in abeyance, when we would "turn and live with the animals, they are so placid and self-contained," when we are weary of conscience and of ambition, and would yield ourselves for a while to the dream of sense, Walt Whitman is a welcome companion. The images he arouses in us, fresh, full of light and health and of a kind of frankness and beauty, are prized all the more at such a time because they are not choice, but drawn perhaps from a hideous and sordid environment. For this circumstance makes them a better means of escape from convention and from that fatigue and despair which lurk not far beneath the surface of conventional life. In casting off with self-assurance and a sense of fresh vitality the distinctions of tradition and reason a man may feel, as he sinks back comfortably to a lower level of sense and instinct, that he is returning to Nature or escaping into the infinite. Mysticism makes us proud and happy to renounce the work of intelligence, both in thought and in life, and persuades us that we become divine by remaining imperfectly human. Walt Whitman gives a new expression to this ancient and multiform tendency. He feels his own cosmic justification and he would lend the sanction of his inspiration to all loafers and holiday-makers. He would be the congenial patron of farmers and factory hands in their crude pleasures and pieties, as Pan was the patron of the shepherds of Arcadia:

for he is sure that in spite of his hairiness and animality, the gods will acknowledge him as one of themselves and smile upon him from the serenity of Olympus.

Emerson (1900)

Those who knew Emerson, or who stood so near to his time and to his circle that they caught some echo of his personal influence, did not judge him merely as a poet or philosopher, nor identify his efficacy with that of his writings. His friends and neighbours, the congregations he preached to in his younger days, the audiences that afterward listened to his lectures, all agreed in a veneration for his person which had nothing to do with their understanding or acceptance of his opinions. They flocked to him and listened to his word, not so much for the sake of its absolute meaning as for the atmosphere of candour, purity, and serenity that hung about it, as about a sort of sacred music. They felt themselves in the presence of a rare and beautiful spirit, who was in communion with a higher world. More than the truth his teaching might express, they valued the sense it gave them of a truth that was inexpressible. They became aware, if we may say so, of the ultra-violet rays of his spectrum, of the inaudible highest notes of his gamut, too pure and thin for common ears.

This effect was by no means due to the possession on the part of Emerson of the secret of the universe, or even of a definite conception of ultimate truth. He was not a prophet who had once for all climbed his Sinai or his Tabor, and having there beheld the transfigured reality, descended again to make authoritative report of it to the world. Far from it. At bottom he had no doctrine at all. The deeper he went and the more he tried to grapple with fundamental conceptions, the vaguer and more elusive they became in his hands. Did he know what he meant by Spirit or the "Over-Soul"? Could he say what he understood by the terms, so constantly on his lips, Nature, Law, God, Benefit, or Beauty? He could not, and the consciousness of that incapacity was so lively within him that he never attempted to give articulation to his philosophy. His finer instinct kept him from doing that violence to his inspiration.

The source of his power lay not in his doctrine, but in his temperament, and the rare quality of his wisdom was due less to his reason than to his

imagination. Reality eluded him; he had neither diligence nor constancy enough to master and possess it; but his mind was open to all philosophic influences, from whatever quarter they might blow; the lessons of science and the hints of poetry worked themselves out in him to a free and personal religion. He differed from the plodding many, not in knowing things better, but in having more ways of knowing them. His grasp was not particularly firm, he was far from being, like a Plato or an Aristotle, past master in the art and the science of life. But his mind was endowed with unusual plasticity, with unusual spontaneity and liberty of movement—it was a fairyland of thoughts and fancies. He was like a young god making experiments in creation: he blotched the work, and always began again on a new and better plan. Every day he said, "Let there be light," and every day the light was new. His sun, like that of Heraclitus, was different every morning.

What seemed, then, to the more earnest and less critical of his hearers a revelation from above was in truth rather an insurrection from beneath, a shaking loose from convention, a disintegration of the normal categories of reason in favour of various imaginative principles, on which the world might have been built, if it had been built differently. This gift of revolutionary thinking allowed new aspects, hints of wider laws, premonitions of unthought-of fundamental unities to spring constantly into view. But such visions were necessarily fleeting, because the human mind had long before settled its grammar, and discovered, after much groping and many defeats, the general forms in which experience will allow itself to be stated. These general forms are the principles of common sense and positive science, no less imaginative in their origin than those notions which we now call transcendental, but grown prosaic, like the metaphors of common speech, by dint of repetition.

Yet authority, even of this rational kind, sat lightly upon Emerson. To reject tradition and think as one might have thought if no man had ever existed before was indeed the aspiration of the

Transcendentalists, and although Emerson hardly regarded himself as a member of that school, he largely shared its tendency and passed for its spokesman. Without protesting against tradition, he smilingly eluded it in his thoughts, untamable in their quiet irresponsibility. He fled to his woods or to his "pleachèd garden," to be the creator of his own worlds in solitude and freedom. No wonder that he brought thence to the tightly conventional minds of his contemporaries a breath as if from paradise. His simplicity in novelty, his profundity, his ingenuous ardour must have seemed to them something heavenly, and they may be excused if they thought they detected inspiration even in his occasional thin paradoxes and guileless whims. They were stifled with conscience and he brought them a breath of Nature; they were surfeited with shallow controversies and he gave them poetic truth.

Imagination, indeed, is his single theme. As a preacher might under every text enforce the same lessons of the gospel, so Emerson traces in every sphere the same spiritual laws of experience—compensation, continuity, the self-expression of the Soul in the forms of Nature and of society, until she finally recognizes herself in her own work and sees its beneficence and beauty. His constant refrain is the omnipotence of imaginative thought; its power first to make the world, then to understand it, and finally to rise above it. All Nature is an embodiment of our native fancy, all history a drama in which the innate possibilities of the spirit are enacted and realized. While the conflict of life and the shocks of experience seem to bring us face to face with an alien and overwhelming power, reflection can humanize and rationalize that power by conceiving its laws; and with this recognition of the rationality of all things comes the sense of their beauty and order. The destruction which Nature seems to prepare for our special hopes is thus seen to be the victory of our impersonal interests. To awaken in us this spiritual insight, an elevation of mind which is at once an act of comprehension and of worship, to substitute it for lower passions and more servile forms of intelligence—that is Emerson's constant effort. All his resources of illustration, observation, and rhetoric are used to deepen and clarify this sort of wisdom.

Such thought is essentially the same that is found in the German romantic or idealistic philosophers, with whom Emerson's affinity is remarkable, all the more as he seems to have borrowed little or nothing from their works. The critics of human nature, in the eighteenth century, had shown how much men's ideas depend on their predispositions, on the character of their senses and the habits of their intelligence. Seizing upon this thought and exaggerating it, the romantic philosophers attributed to the spirit of man the omnipotence which had belonged to God, and felt that in this way they were reasserting the supremacy of mind over matter and establishing it upon a safe and rational basis.

The Germans were great system-makers, and Emerson cannot rival them in the sustained effort of thought by which they sought to reinterpret every sphere of being according to their chosen principles. But he surpassed them in an instinctive sense of what he was doing. He never represented his poetry as science, nor countenanced the formation of a new sect that should nurse the sense of a private and mysterious illumination, and relight the fagots of passion and prejudice. He never tried to seek out and defend the universal implications of his ideas, and never wrote the book he had once planned on the law of compensation, foreseeing we may well believe, the sophistries in which he would have been directly involved. He fortunately preferred a fresh statement on a fresh subject. A suggestion once given, the spirit once aroused to speculation, a glimpse once gained of some ideal harmony, he chose to descend again to common sense and to touch the earth for a moment before another flight. The faculty of idealization was itself what he valued. Philosophy for him was rather a moral energy flowering into sprightliness of thought than a body of serious and defensible doctrines. In practising transcendental speculation only in this poetic and sporadic fashion, Emerson retained its true value and avoided its greatest danger. He secured the freedom and fertility of his thought and did not allow one conception of law or one hint of harmony to sterilize the mind and prevent the subsequent birth within it of other ideas, no less just and imposing than their predecessors. For we are not dealing at all in such a philosophy with matters of fact or with such verifiable truths as exclude their opposites. We are dealing only with imagination, with the art of conception, and with the various forms in which reflection, like a poet, may compose and recompose human experience.

A certain disquiet mingled, however, in the minds of Emerson's contemporaries with the admiration they felt for his purity and genius. They saw that he had forsaken the doctrines of the

Church; and they were not sure whether he held quite unequivocally any doctrine whatever. We may not all of us share the concern for orthodoxy which usually caused this puzzled alarm: we may understand that it was not Emerson's vocation to be definite and dogmatic in religion any more than in philosophy. Yet that disquiet will not, even for us, wholly disappear. It is produced by a defect which naturally accompanies imagination in all but the greatest minds. I mean disorganization. Emerson not only conceived things in new ways, but he seemed to think the new ways might cancel and supersede the old. His imagination was to invalidate the understanding. That inspiration which should come to fulfil seemed too often to come to destroy. If he was able so constantly to stimulate us to fresh thoughts, was it not because he demolished the labour of long ages of reflection? Was not the startling effect of much of his writing due to its contradiction to tradition and to common sense?

So long as he is a poet and in the enjoyment of his poetic license, we can blame this play of mind only by a misunderstanding. It is possible to think otherwise than as common sense thinks; there are other categories beside those of science. When we employ them we enlarge our lives. We add to the world of fact any number of worlds of the imagination in which human nature and the eternal relations of ideas may be nobly expressed. So far our imaginative fertility is only a benefit: it surrounds us with the congenial and necessary radiation of art and religion. It manifests our moral vitality in the bosom of Nature.

But sometimes imagination invades the sphere of understanding and seems to discredit its indispensable work. Common sense, we are allowed to infer, is a shallow affair: true insight changes all that. When so applied, poetic activity is not an unmixed good. It loosens our hold on fact and confuses our intelligence, so that we forget that intelligence has itself every prerogative of imagination, and has besides the sanction of practical validity. We are made to believe that since the understanding is something human and conditioned, something which might have been different, as the senses might have been different, and which we may yet, so to speak, get behind—therefore the understanding ought to be abandoned. We long for higher faculties, neglecting those we have, we yearn for intuition, closing our eyes upon experience. We become mystical.

Mysticism, as we have said, is the surrender of a category of thought because we divine its relativity. As every new category, however, must share this reproach, the mystic is obliged in the end to give them all up, the poetic and moral categories no less than the physical, so that the end of his purification is the atrophy of his whole nature, the emptying of his whole heart and mind to make room, as he thinks, for God. By attacking the authority of the understanding as the organon of knowledge, by substituting itself for it as the herald of a deeper truth, the imagination thus prepares its own destruction. For if the understanding is rejected because it cannot grasp the absolute, the imagination and all its works—art, dogma, worship—must presently be rejected for the same reason. Common sense and poetry must both go by the board, and conscience must follow after: for all these are human and relative. Mysticism will be satisfied only with the absolute, and as the absolute, by its very definition, is not representable by any specific faculty, it must be approached through the abandonment of all. The lights of life must be extinguished that the light of the absolute may shine, and the possession of everything in general must be secured by the surrender of everything in particular.

The same diffidence, however, the same constant renewal of sincerity which kept Emerson's flights of imagination near to experience, kept his mysticism also within bounds. A certain mystical tendency is pervasive with him, but there are only one or two subjects on which he dwells with enough constancy and energy of attention to make his mystical treatment of them pronounced. One of these is the question of the unity of all minds in the single soul of the universe, which is the same in all creatures; another is the question of evil and of its evaporation in the universal harmony of things. Both these ideas suggest themselves at certain turns in every man's experience, and might receive a rational formulation. But they are intricate subjects, obscured by many emotional prejudices, so that the labour, impartiality, and precision which would be needed to elucidate them are to be looked for in scholastic rather than in inspired thinkers, and in Emerson least of all. Before these problems he is alternately ingenuous and rhapsodical, and in both moods equally helpless. Individuals no doubt exist, he says to himself. But, ah! Napoleon is in every schoolboy. In every squatter in the western prairies we shall find an owner—

"Of Caesar's hand and Plato's brain,
Of Lord Christ's heart, and Shakespeare's strain."

But how? we may ask. Potentially? Is it because any mind, were it given the right body and the right experience, were it made over, in a word, into another mind, would resemble that other mind to the point of identity? Or is it that our souls are already so largely similar that we are subject to many kindred promptings and share many ideals unrealizable in our particular circumstances? But then we should simply be saying that if what makes men different were removed, men would be indistinguishable, or that, in so far as they are now alike, they can understand one another by summoning up their respective experiences in the fancy. There would be no mysticism in that, but at the same time, alas, no eloquence, no paradox, and, if we must say the word, no nonsense.

On the question of evil, Emerson's position is of the same kind. There is evil, of course, he tells us. Experience is sad. There is a crack in everything that God has made. But, ah! the laws of the universe are sacred and beneficent. Without them nothing good could arise. All things, then, are in their right places and the universe is perfect above our querulous tears. Perfect? we may ask. But perfect from what point of view, in reference to what ideal? To its own? To that of a man who, renouncing himself and all naturally dear to him, ignoring the injustice, suffering, and impotence in the world, allows his will and his conscience to be hypnotized by the spectacle of a necessary evolution, and lulled into cruelty by the pomp and music of a tragic show? In that case the evil is not explained, it is forgotten; it is not cured, but condoned. We have surrendered the category of the better and the worse, the deepest foundation of life and reason; we have become mystics on the one subject on which, above all others, we ought to be men.

Two forces may be said to have carried Emerson in this mystical direction; one, that freedom of his imagination which we have already noted, and which kept him from the fear of self-contradiction; the other the habit of worship inherited from his clerical ancestors and enforced by his religious education. The spirit of conformity, the unction, the loyalty even unto death inspired by the religion of Jehovah, were dispositions acquired by too long a discipline and rooted in too many forms of speech,

of thought, and of worship for a man like Emerson, who had felt their full force, ever to be able to lose them. The evolutions of his abstract opinions left that habit unchanged. Unless we keep this circumstance in mind, we shall not be able to understand the kind of elation and sacred joy, so characteristic of his eloquence, with which he propounds laws of Nature and aspects of experience which, viewed in themselves, afford but an equivocal support to moral enthusiasm. An optimism so persistent and unclouded as his will seem at variance with the description he himself gives of human life, a description coloured by a poetic idealism, but hardly by an optimistic bias.

We must remember, therefore, that this optimism is a pious tradition, originally justified by the belief in a personal God and in a providential government of affairs for the ultimate and positive good of the elect, and that the habit of worship survived in Emerson as an instinct after those positive beliefs had faded into a recognition of "spiritual laws." We must remember that Calvinism had known how to combine an awestruck devotion to the Supreme Being with no very roseate picture of the destinies of mankind, and for more than two hundred years had been breeding in the stock from which Emerson came a willingness to be, as the phrase is, "damned for the glory of God."

What wonder, then, that when, for the former inexorable dispensation of Providence, Emerson substituted his general spiritual and natural laws, he should not have felt the spirit of worship fail within him? On the contrary, his thought moved in the presence of moral harmonies which seemed to him truer, more beautiful, and more beneficent than those of the old theology. An independent philosopher would not have seen in those harmonies an object of worship or a sufficient basis for optimism. But he was not an independent philosopher, in spite of his belief in independence. He inherited the problems and the preoccupations of the theology from which he started, being in this respect like the German idealists, who, with all their pretence of absolute metaphysics, were in reality only giving elusive and abstract forms to traditional theology. Emerson, too, was not primarily a philosopher, but a Puritan mystic with a poetic fancy and a gift for observation and epigram, and he saw in the laws of Nature, idealized by his imagination, only a more intelligible form of the divinity he had always recognized and adored. His was not a philosophy passing into a religion, but a religion expressing itself as a philosophy and veiled, as at its setting it descended the heavens, in various tints of poetry and science.

If we ask ourselves what was Emerson's relation to the scientific and religious movements of his time, and what place he may claim in the history of opinion, we must answer that he belonged very little to the past, very little to the present, and almost wholly to that abstract sphere into which mystical or philosophic aspiration has carried a few men in all ages. The religious tradition in which he was reared was that of Puritanism, but of a Puritanism which, retaining its moral intensity and metaphysical abstraction, had minimized its doctrinal expression and become Unitarian. Emerson was indeed the Psyche of Puritanism, "the latest-born and fairest vision far" of all that "faded hierarchy." A Puritan whose religion was all poetry, a poet whose only pleasure was thought, he showed in his life and personality the meagreness, the constraint, the frigid and conscious consecration which belonged to his clerical ancestors, while his inmost impersonal spirit ranged abroad over the fields of history and Nature, gathering what ideas it might, and singing its little snatches of inspired song.

The traditional element was thus rather an external and unessential contribution to Emerson's mind; he had the professional tinge, the decorum, the distinction of an old-fashioned divine; he had also the habit of writing sermons, and he had the national pride and hope of a religious people that felt itself providentially chosen to establish a free and godly commonwealth in a new world. For the rest, he separated himself from the ancient creed of the community with a sense rather of relief than of regret. A literal belief in Christian doctrines repelled him as unspiritual, as manifesting no understanding of the meaning which, as allegories, those doctrines might have to a philosophic and poetical spirit. Although as a clergyman he was at first in the habit of referring to the Bible and its lessons as to a supreme authority, he had no instinctive sympathy with the inspiration of either the Old or the New Testament; in Hafiz or Plutarch, in Plato or Shakespeare, he found more congenial stuff.

While he thus preferred to withdraw, without rancour and without contempt, from the ancient fellowship of the church, he assumed an attitude hardly less cool and deprecatory toward the enthusiasms of the new era. The national ideal of democracy and freedom had his entire sympathy; he allowed himself to be drawn into the movement against slavery; he took a curious and smiling interest in the discoveries of natural science and in the material progress of the age. But he could go no farther. His contemplative nature, his religious training, his dispersed reading, made him stand aside from the life of the world, even while he studied it with benevolent attention. His heart was fixed on eternal things, and he was in no sense a prophet for his age or country. He belonged by nature to that mystical company of devout souls that recognize no particular home and are dispersed throughout history, although not without intercommunication. He felt his affinity to the Hindoos and the Persians, to the Platonists and the Stoics. Like them he remains "a friend and aider of those who would live in the spirit." If not a star of the first magnitude, he is certainly a fixed star in the firmament of philosophy. Alone as yet among Americans, he may be said to have won a place there, if not by the originality of his thought, at least by the originality and beauty of the expression he gave to thoughts that are old and imperishable.

New England Twilight

By 1875, the great epoch of New England writing was drawing toward its close. Such long-lived persons as Lowell, Holmes, Parkman, and Harriet Beecher Stowe were still thriving, and Parkman, at least, still had ahead of him one of his handsomest productions, *Montcalm and Wolfe* (1884). None, however, was breaking fresh ground; and meanwhile Hawthorne and Thoreau were long since dead, Emerson was clouded by increasing senility, and Melville (who was of course really a New Yorker, despite his long years in Lenox) was working obscurely in a customs office and writing verses nobody read. The transcendentalist movement had exhausted itself, though vestiges of it could perhaps be discerned in midwestern academies and the discourses of professional philosophers; the fiery old periodicals had fallen silent.

The general loss of cultural momentum was due in good part, to be sure, to the huge and protracted disruption of the Civil War, and the enormous sociological changes that followed in its wake. But there was an interior slackening as well, a shrinkage of vision (not to say an at least temporary shortage of literary genius), a pervasive and melancholy sense of New England's having seen better days.

Henry James caught the atmosphere perfectly in his novel *The Bostonians*, set in exactly this period and surveying a whole pattern of deterioration: physical, economic, moral, and psychological. Within a decade, William Dean Howells—who had been drawn to the region (from Indiana, by way of Venice) as by a magnet—would be describing Boston as a death-in-life and preparing to transfer himself, his family, and his literary career down to New York City. In another metaphor, as we have seen, the Chicago-born novelist Henry B. Fuller would allege retrospectively that Boston had begun to suffer from intellectual and cultural anemia.

But if energies were dissipating in Boston, a sort of twilight literary glow was starting to appear elsewhere in New England. In 1877, a book called *Deephaven* was published, a collection of vivid and supple sketches of New England coastal life by Sarah Orne Jewett. It was a sign that the region still possessed talent worth tapping; further signs were supplied by Rose Terry Cooke and Mary E. Wilkins Freeman; and the work of these three gifted women comprise a significant, if minor, chapter in American literary history. Their shared, continuing, and appropriate theme, moreover, was the decline of life, of character, of opportunity in postwar New England.

About each of these writers, one feels the way Robert Frost (who in some respects may be reckoned as their descendant) did about the "oven bird," in the poem of that name—the mid-wood warbler whom Frost presents as the poet of diminution:

> The bird would cease and be as other birds
> But that he knows in singing not to sing.
> The question that he frames in all but words
> Is what to make of a diminished thing.

Everywhere in the fiction of this New England twilight one is conscious of diminished things. The characters tend to be old, and they tend to be poor. They are old before their time (at twenty-eight, Mrs. Cooke's Lucy Larkin "was no longer young . . . a gentle, faded, pretty woman"), old in some dim awareness of a more hospitable past. They are poor by contrast with a vaguely recalled or rumored prosperity of times "before the war." They inhabit farms that, mysteriously, no longer yield as once they did and seaports that grow moldy from lack of traffic. "In the old days," Captain Littlepage tells the narrator in Miss Jewett's *The Country of the Pointed Firs*, "a good part of the best men here knew a hundred ports. . . . They lived more dignified, and their houses were better within an' without. Shipping's a terrible loss to this part o' New England." If they are not actually and physically isolated from humanity, like "poor Joanna" in the same book, they are, like Captain Littlepage, psychologically so. Nor is religion much of a resource. The old pieties are frozen, with no new vision at hand to requicken them; the persons we meet, when they are not simply nonbelievers, seem to be either literalists or unconscious hypocrites. In writing about such people and such conditions, Miss Jewett and the others did indeed have to learn how "in singing not to sing." The lesson was learned: their song has an enduring if often wistful charm.

Sarah Orne Jewett and her literary colleagues have customarily been identified as "regionalists," and their New England landscapes compared— as to the degree and kind of "local color"—with the small Indiana towns of

Edward Eggleston, the Iowa farms of Hamlin Garland, and the California camps of Bret Harte. Their work, certainly, arises out of an immediate response to their region, and without it we should know much less than we do about the look and feel of life in the remoter sections of New England in the later decades of the nineteenth century and the first years of the present one. It is to a real extent a literature of *place:* one of the more attractive minor genres traditionally available to the literary art. Yet it can be suggested that the stories of Miss Jewett and the others transcend their settings to engage other and larger themes.

As we read them, we think inevitably, for example, of what is perhaps the masterpiece in the fictional portrait of the stunted or wasted life in discouraged New England surroundings: Edith Wharton's *Ethan Frome.* But Edith Wharton, though for a decade she lived a part of each year in the Berkshires (the setting of *Ethan Frome*), was herself a highly civilized product of New York society and was equally at home in the fashionable quarters of Paris and London. What she had in common with Miss Jewett and the others was not the experience of being a New Englander; it was the experience of being a woman—in late nineteenth-century America. For what we realize, when we look more closely at the New England twilight fiction, is that its true underlying theme is not so much the state of affairs in Massachusetts or Maine or Connecticut some eighty or ninety years ago. It is the condition of women.

More often than not, the condition as described is appalling, and the writers we are considering do not always try to disguise their sense of personal, female outrage. In "West Shetucket Railway," Mrs. Cooke speaks of the New England farmer struggling against a rigorous climate and "a soil bitter and barren," leading a life without excitement and without pleasure, becoming "hard, cruel, sensual, vindictive . . . blunted with over-work and under-feeling." Then she goes on to suggest the dreadful effect of all this upon the women of the region:

> When you bring to bear on these poor weak souls, made for love and gentleness and bright outlooks . . . the daily dullness of work, the brutality, stupidness, small craft, and boorish tyranny of husbands to whom they are tied beyond escape, what wonder is it that a third of all the female lunatics in our asylums are farmers' wives, and that domestic tragedies even beyond the scope of a sensational novel, occur daily in these lonely houses, far beyond human help or scope?

"The boorish tyranny of husbands to whom they are tied beyond escape." In "Mrs. Flint's Married Experience," Rose Terry Cooke tells of a sweet-natured widow who remarries to the local deacon and who does manage to escape (to her children) after undergoing her husband's incalculable physical and mental cruelty—only to discover that the community is solidly on the deacon's side. She had "almost died of cold and hunger," but "to find fault with authorities was little less than a sin, and for a wife to leave her husband, a fearful scandal." She writes the church a pitiful note of abject penitence—and dies.

There is of course a sexual and biological element in the husbandly cruelty (the strain of life, Mrs. Cooke pointed out, made the men folk "sensual" as well as "hard" and "vindictive"). In "Freedom Wheeler's Controversy with Providence," one of Mrs. Cooke's strongest stories, Freedom's wife Lowly is driven to the verge of madness and suicide by her husband's insistence that she bear him child after child until (as she never does) she can produce a son that can carry forward his name. Recovering slowly from the birth of another daughter, Lowly finds Freedom unconcerned about her health and only resentful at having had to hire extra help during her confinement. "But his wife did not care now: a dumb and sudden endurance possessed her. She prayed night and morning, with a certain monomaniac persistence, that she and Lovey [the older child] and the baby might die." And to be sure, a congenital fear of sex on the part of women, prior to any experience of husbandly brutishness, is also observed. (This is the rather subtly evoked theme of Mary Wilkins Freeman's "A New England Nun.") But the authority of the husband, in sexual matters as in all others, is regarded as absolute, a part of the very nature of things. "You ain't found out yet we're women-folks, Nanny Penn," the mother of the Penn family tells her daughter in Mrs. Freeman's perceptive tale, "The Revolt of 'Mother.'"

> You ain't seen enough of men-folks yet to. One of these days you'll find it out, an' then you'll know that we know only what men-folks think we do, far as any use of it goes, an' how we'd ought to reckon men-folks in with Providence, an' not complain of what they do any more than we do of the other.

What is striking about that shrewdly contrived statement is that, if it was the kind of thing some women were saying about men in the eighties and nineties, it was also almost exactly what, at the same moment, black Americans were saying—and in some instances are still saying—about white Americans. A black person was a rarity in outlying New England; Mrs. Freeman and the others were not likely to encounter one. Yet they brilliantly, if unconsciously, intuited the parallel between the condition of women vis-à-vis men and that of blacks vis-à-vis whites, a parallel to which endless decades of American social history have borne unhappy witness. From the point of view of a New England farmer's wife eighty years ago the situation of the blacks could have seemed, if anything, rather more comfortable than that of women. The agitation for women's rights, which had of course begun much earlier, had not yet penetrated Mary Wilkins Freeman's western Massachusetts or Rose Terry Cooke's Connecticut hills,[1] but those writers, with Sarah Orne Jewett, having enlarged beyond merely regional concerns to suggest the plight of the female sex in America, could also on occasion enlarge beyond that latter subject to touch on general issues of freedom and oppression that disturbed the heart of the society.

There are, for example, hints of this in "The Revolt of 'Mother.'" For in this story, which moves from grimness to comedy, "Mother" rebels precisely when her dour husband builds a new barn for his livestock, even though the family home is totally dilapidated. He proposes, in short, to give his animals more comfort and consideration than he does the human beings who depend upon him—as white plantation owners and farmers were not inaccurately accused of favoring animals over blacks. "Mother" asserts her rights as a human being, and, while her husband is absent, moves the entire household into the new barn. Another typical hint may be found in our first image of Lowly Mallory, before she marries Freedom Wheeler. She is a delicate girl with "sweet gray eyes"; but "she had already the line of care that marks New England women across the forehead, like a mark of Cain—the signal of a life in which work has murdered health and joy and freedom."

The severely unhappy aspects of the condition of women have been stressed in these remarks, but by no means are all the female characters of the twilight fiction victims—as "Mother" Penn clearly is not. In several stories by Rose Terry Cooke and Mary Wilkins Freeman, indeed, and in the characteristic work of Sarah Orne Jewett (not to mention that of Edith Wharton), there is something stalwart, creative, enduring about the women that is notably lacking in the men. Facing harsher challenges, they are often capable of more vigorous and intelligent responses. When her father collapses into tearful hopelessness, in Mrs. Cooke's "Farmer Finch," young Polly Finch abandons her schoolteaching and her lover and sets to rescuing the farm and the family fortune through sheer strength and determination. Melinda Bassett, who becomes Freedom Wheeler's second wife after poor Lowly gratefully dies, is a much tougher specimen than her predecessor and quite breaks her husband's proud, implacable spirit.

Best and strongest and most splendidly human of all is Mrs. Todd, the narrator's friend and landlady in Sarah Orne Jewett's *The Country of the*

[1] In fact, by one of the more curious twists in the history of civil rights in America, a number of women "liberationists" after the Civil War became antiblack, on the grounds that the blacks were being better treated: that is, they had been granted the suffrage while it was still denied—as it would be until 1920—to women.

Pointed Firs. She is a familiar figure, much valued and loved, in the little Maine seaport town and among the off-shore islands; and no one suspects that she was denied, early, the one great and real love of her life, and that she carries with her a vast burden of inconsolable grief. She speaks of this mutedly to the narrator one afternoon; and when she then moves away to commune with herself, the narrator feels, looking after her, that

> there was something lonely and solitary about her great determined shape. She might have been Antigone alone on the Theban plain. . . . An absolute, archaic grief possessed this country-woman; she seemed like a renewal of some historic soul, with her sorrows and remoteness of a daily life busied with rustic simplicities and the scents of primeval herbs.

Since Rose Terry Cooke (1827–1892) is not represented in our selections, a word about her is in order here. She was Connecticut born and bred, and the Connecticut hills provide the scene of her best stories. Her work began to appear in the *Atlantic* with the first issue of that magazine in 1857. The best of her stories are collected in *Somebody's Neighbors* (1881), *The Sphinx's Children* (1886), and *Huckleberries Gathered from New England Hills* (1891).

The presence we feel in her pages is decidedly attractive: spirited, emotional, with a strong sense of the comic. These qualities play on New England characters, especially male ones, whose own feelings are normally repressed. "The New-England man, saint or sinner," she observes in "Squire Paine's Conversion," "has few words when feeling is strongest." Her amusement flickers openly at certain regional eccentricities—for example, the taste in proper names. Melinda Wheeler calls her first child Chimera Una Vilda, at which Mrs. Cooke remarks: "Give me no credit for imagination here. These are actual names, registered on church records and tombstones, with sundry others of the like sort, such as Secretia, Luelle, Lorilla Allaroila, Lue, Plumy, Antha." Despite moments like that, however, the prevailing atmosphere in these stories is one of pathos, when it is not one of tragedy. Even when hard-souled persons like Squire Paine and Freedom Wheeler undergo a kind of conversion, they do so only after having subjected their wives and families to long, wasted years of wretchedness. "Too Late," the story of Hannah Blair in *The Sphinx's Children*, could almost stand as the title for Rose Terry Cooke's collected fiction.

"I always write impulsively," she told her editor at the *Atlantic*: "—very fast and without much plan." She was just the kind of writer who did not have time to be brief; and one result is that even her best stories tend to be meandering and overlong. It is indeed the unjustifiable length of these tales that has made it impractical to include any one of them in the selections.

MARY E. WILKINS FREEMAN (1852–1930)

Mary Eleanor Wilkins was brought up in western Massachusetts. All of her important writing is set in that area, even though, after marrying Charles Freeman at the age of fifty, she moved with her husband to New Jersey. Her style tended toward the clipped and the sparse, accurately reflecting the sparse and stunted lives she normally depicted. Like Rose Terry Cooke, Mrs. Freeman also had a sense of the comic and sought to reveal, as she put it, "the pathos in the comedy." Her recurrent subject, she remarked in the preface to her novel *Pembroke* (1894), was "the human will in different phases of disease and abnormal development."

A *New England Nun and Other Stories* contains, along with an earlier collection of tales, A *Humble Romance* (1887), Mrs. Freeman's most durable stories.

A New England Nun (1891)

"A New England Nun" may not appear to be about a diseased or abnormally developed will. Yet in its subdued and oblique manner, it does present us with a female psyche that is abnormally terrified by life, by love, by masculine sexuality. The clues to the character of Louisa Ellis are her attitude to the dog Caesar and the conduct of her little yellow canary. Caesar, whom she regards as ferocious, has been kept chained up for fourteen years—exactly the length of time that Louisa's fiancé, Joe Dagget, has been away seeking his fortune; and Louisa's vision of the dog let loose to rampage through the village and attack innocent children contains, of course, her vision of her husband-to-be's onslaught upon her. As to the canary, he always awakes and flutters wildly, beating his wings against the bars of his cage, whenever Joe comes to call. At the story's end, in a paragraph which repays careful study, Louisa thankfully chooses "serenity and placid narrowness," a life innocent, empty, and in sharp contrast to that of the fertile world just outside the window.

It was late in the afternoon, and the light was waning. There was a difference in the look of the tree shadows out in the yard. Somewhere in the distance cows were lowing and a little bell was tinkling; now and then a farm-wagon tilted by, and the dust flew; some blue-shirted laborers with shovels over their shoulders plodded past; little swarms of flies were dancing up and down before the peoples' faces in the soft air. There seemed to be a gentle stir arising over everything for the mere sake of subsidence—a very premonition of rest and hush and night.

This soft diurnal commotion was over Louisa Ellis also. She had been peacefully sewing at her sitting-room window all the afternoon. Now she quilted her needle carefully into her work, which she folded precisely, and laid in a basket with her thimble and thread and scissors. Louisa Ellis could not remember that ever in her life she had mislaid one of these little feminine appurtenances, which had become, from long use and constant association, a very part of her personality.

Louisa tied a green apron round her waist, and got out a flat straw hat with a green ribbon. Then she went into the garden with a little blue crockery bowl, to pick some currants for her tea. After the currants were picked she sat on the back door-step and stemmed them, collecting the stems carefully in her apron, and afterwards throwing them into the hen-coop. She looked sharply at the grass beside the step to see if any had fallen there.

Louisa was slow and still in her movements; it took her a long time to prepare her tea; but when ready it was set forth with as much grace as if she had been a veritable guest to her own self. The little square table stood exactly in the centre of the kitchen, and was covered with a starched linen cloth whose border pattern of flowers glistened. Louisa had a damask napkin on her tea-tray, where were arranged a cut-glass tumbler full of teaspoons, a silver cream-pitcher, a china sugar-bowl, and one pink china cup and saucer. Louisa used china every day—something which none of her neighbors did. They whispered about it among themselves. Their daily tables were laid with common crockery, their sets of best china stayed in the parlor closet, and Louisa Ellis was no richer nor better bred than they. Still she would use the china. She had for her supper a glass dish full of sugared currants, a plate of little cakes, and one of light white biscuits. Also a leaf or two of lettuce, which she cut up daintily. Louisa was very fond of lettuce, which she raised to perfection in her little garden. She ate quite heartily, though in a delicate, pecking way; it seemed almost surprising that any considerable bulk of the food should vanish.

After tea she filled a plate with nicely baked thin corn-cakes, and carried them out into the back-yard.

"Cæsar!" she called. "Cæsar! Cæsar!"

There was a little rush, and the clank of a chain, and a large yellow-and-white dog appeared at the door of his tiny hut, which was half hidden among the tall grasses and flowers. Louisa patted him and gave him the corn-cakes. Then she returned to the house and washed the tea-things, polished the china carefully. The twilight had deepened; the chorus of the frogs floated in at the open window wonderfully loud and shrill, and once in a while a long sharp drone from a tree-toad pierced it. Louisa took off her green gingham apron, disclosing a shorter one of pink and white print. She lighted her lamp, and sat down again with her sewing.

In about half an hour Joe Dagget came. She heard his heavy step on the walk, and rose and took off her pink-and-white apron. Under that was still another—white linen with a little cambric edging on the bottom; that was Louisa's company apron. She never wore it without her calico sewing apron over it unless she had a guest. She had barely folded the pink and white one with methodical haste and laid it in a table-drawer when the door opened and Joe Dagget entered.

He seemed to fill up the whole room. A little yellow canary that had been asleep in his green cage at the south window woke up and fluttered wildly, beating his little yellow wings against the wires. He always did so when Joe Dagget came into the room.

"Good-evening," said Louisa. She extended her hand with a kind of solemn cordiality.

"Good-evening, Louisa," returned the man, in a loud voice.

She placed a chair for him, and they sat facing each other, with the table between them. He sat bolt-upright, toeing out his heavy feet squarely, glancing with a good-humored uneasiness around the room. She sat gently erect, folding her slender hands in her white-linen lap.

"Been a pleasant day," remarked Dagget.

"Real pleasant," Louisa assented, softly. "Have you been haying?" she asked, after a little while.

"Yes, I've been haying all day, down in the ten-acre lot. Pretty hot work."

"It must be."

"Yes, it's pretty hot work in the sun."

"Is your mother well to-day?"

"Yes, mother's pretty well."

"I suppose Lily Dyer's with her now?"

Dagget colored. "Yes, she's with her," he answered, slowly.

He was not very young, but there was a boyish look about his large face. Louisa was not quite as old as he, her face was fairer and smoother, but she gave people the impression of being older.

"I suppose she's a good deal of help to your mother," she said, further.

"I guess she is; I don't know how mother'd get along without her," said Dagget, with a sort of embarrassed warmth.

"She looks like a real capable girl. She's pretty-looking too," remarked Louisa.

"Yes, she is pretty fair looking."

Presently Dagget began fingering the books on the table. There was a square red autograph album, and a Young Lady's Gift-Book which had belonged to Louisa's mother. He took them up one after the other and opened them; then laid them down again, the album on the Gift-Book.

Louisa kept eying them with mild uneasiness. Finally she rose and changed the position of the books, putting the album underneath. That was the way they had been arranged in the first place.

Dagget gave an awkward little laugh. "Now what difference did it make which book was on top?" said he.

Louisa looked at him with a deprecating smile. "I always keep them that way," murmured she.

"You do beat everything," said Dagget, trying to laugh again. His large face was flushed.

He remained about an hour longer, then rose to take leave. Going out, he stumbled over a rug, and trying to recover himself, hit Louisa's work-basket on the table, and knocked it on the floor.

He looked at Louisa, then at the rolling spools; he ducked himself awkwardly toward them, but she stopped him. "Never mind," said she; "I'll pick them up after you're gone."

She spoke with a mild stiffness. Either she was a little disturbed, or his nervousness affected her, and made her seem constrained in her effort to reassure him.

When Joe Dagget was outside he drew in the sweet evening air with a sigh, and felt much as an innocent and perfectly well-intentioned bear might after his exit from a china shop.

Louisa, on her part, felt much as the kind-hearted, long-suffering owner of the china shop might have done after the exit of the bear.

She tied on the pink, then the green apron, picked up all the scattered treasures and replaced them in her work-basket, and straightened the rug. Then she set the lamp on the floor, and began sharply examining the carpet. She even rubbed her fingers over it, and looked at them.

"He's tracked in a good deal of dust," she murmured. "I thought he must have."

Louisa got a dust-pan and brush, and swept Joe Dagget's track carefully.

If he could have known it, it would have increased his perplexity and uneasiness, although it would not have disturbed his loyalty in the least. He came twice a week to see Louisa Ellis, and every time, sitting there in her delicately sweet room, he felt as if surrounded by a hedge of lace. He was afraid to stir lest he should put a clumsy foot or hand through the fairy web, and he had always the consciousness that Louisa was watching fearfully lest he should.

Still the lace and Louisa commanded perforce his perfect respect and patience and loyalty. They were to be married in a month, after a singular courtship which had lasted for a matter of fifteen years. For fourteen out of the fifteen years the two had not once seen each other, and they had seldom exchanged letters. Joe had been all those years in Australia, where he had gone to make his fortune, and where he had stayed until he made it. He would have stayed fifty years if it had taken so long, and come home feeble and tottering, or never come home at all, to marry Louisa.

But the fortune had been made in the fourteen years, and he had come home now to marry the woman who had been patiently and unquestioningly waiting for him all that time.

Shortly after they were engaged he had announced to Louisa his determination to strike out into new fields, and secure a competency before they should be married. She had listened and assented with the sweet serenity which never failed her, not even when her lover set forth on that long and uncertain journey. Joe, buoyed up as he was by his sturdy determination, broke down a little at the last, but Louisa kissed him with a mild blush, and said good-by.

"It won't be for long," poor Joe had said, huskily; but it was fourteen years.

In that length of time much had happened. Louisa's mother and brother had died, and she was all alone in the world. But greatest happening of all—a subtle happening which both were too simple to understand—Louisa's feet had turned into a path, smooth maybe under a calm, serene sky, but so straight and unswerving that it could only meet a check at her grave, and so narrow that there was no room for any one at her side.

Louisa's first emotion when Joe Dagget came home (he had not apprised her of his coming) was consternation, although she would not admit it to herself, and he never dreamed of it. Fifteen years ago she had been in love with him—at least she considered herself to be. Just at that time, gently acquiescing with and falling into the natural drift of girlhood, she had seen marriage ahead as a reasonable feature and a probable desirability of life. She had listened with calm docility to her mother's views upon the subject. Her mother was remarkable for her cool sense and sweet, even temperament. She talked wisely to her daughter when Joe Dagget presented himself, and Louisa accepted him with no hesitation. He was the first lover she had ever had.

She had been faithful to him all these years. She had never dreamed of the possibility of marrying any one else. Her life, especially for the last seven years, had been full of a pleasant peace, she had never felt discontented nor impatient over her lover's absence; still she had always looked forward to his return and their marriage as the inevitable conclusion of things. However, she had fallen into a way of placing it so far in the future that it was almost equal to placing it over the boundaries of another life.

When Joe came she had been expecting him, and expecting to be married for fourteen years, but she was as much surprised and taken aback as if she had never thought of it.

Joe's consternation came later. He eyed Louisa with an instant confirmation of his old admiration. She had changed but little. She still kept her pretty manner and soft grace, and was, he considered, every whit as attractive as ever. As for himself, his stent was done; he had turned his face away from fortune-seeking, and the old winds of romance whistled as loud and sweet as ever through his ears. All the song which he had been wont to hear in them was Louisa; he had for a long time a loyal belief that he heard it still, but finally it seemed to him that although the winds sang always that one song, it had another name. But for Louisa the wind had never more than murmured; now it had gone down, and everything was still. She listened for a little while with half-wistful attention; then she turned quietly away and went to work on her wedding clothes.

Joe had made some extensive and quite magnificent alterations in his house. It was the old homestead; the newly-married couple would live there, for Joe could not desert his mother, who refused to leave her old home. So Louisa must leave hers. Every morning, rising and going about among her neat maidenly possessions, she felt as one looking her last upon the faces of dear friends. It was true that in a measure she could take them with her, but, robbed of their old environments, they would appear in such new guises that they would almost cease to be themselves. Then there were some peculiar features of her happy solitary life which she would probably be obliged to relinquish altogether. Sterner tasks than these graceful but half-needless ones would probably devolve upon her. There would be a large house to care for; there would be company to entertain; there would be Joe's rigorous and feeble old mother to wait upon; and it would be contrary to all thrifty village traditions for her to keep more than one servant. Louisa had a little still, and she used to occupy herself pleasantly in summer weather with distilling the sweet and aromatic essences from roses and peppermint and spearmint. By-and-by her still must be laid away. Her store of essences was already considerable, and there would be no time for her to distil for the mere pleasure of it. Then Joe's mother would think it foolishness; she had already hinted her opinion in the matter. Louisa dearly loved to sew a linen seam, not always for use, but for the simple, mild pleasure which she took in it. She would have been loath to confess how more

than once she had ripped a seam for the mere delight of sewing it together again. Sitting at her window during long sweet afternoons, drawing her needle gently through the dainty fabric, she was peace itself. But there was small chance of such foolish comfort in the future. Joe's mother, domineering, shrewd old matron that she was even in her old age, and very likely even Joe himself, with his honest masculine rudeness, would laugh and frown down all these pretty but senseless old maiden ways.

Louisa had almost the enthusiasm of an artist over the mere order and cleanliness of her solitary home. She had throbs of genuine triumph at the sight of the window-panes which she had polished until they shone like jewels. She gloated gently over her orderly bureau-drawers, with their exquisitely folded contents redolent with lavender and sweet clover and very purity. Could she be sure of the endurance of even this? She had visions, so startling that she half repudiated them as indelicate, of coarse masculine belongings strewn about in endless litter; of dust and disorder arising necessarily from a coarse masculine presence in the midst of all this delicate harmony.

Among her forebodings of disturbance, not the least was with regard to Cæsar. Cæsar was a veritable hermit of a dog. For the greater part of his life he had dwelt in his secluded hut, shut out from the society of his kind and all innocent canine joys. Never had Cæsar since his early youth watched at a woodchuck's hole; never had he known the delights of a stray bone at a neighbor's kitchen door. And it was all on account of a sin committed when hardly out of his puppyhood. No one knew the possible depth of remorse of which this mild-visaged, altogether innocent-looking old dog might be capable; but whether or not he had encountered remorse, he had encountered a full measure of righteous retribution. Old Cæsar seldom lifted up his voice in a growl or a bark; he was fat and sleepy; there were yellow rings which looked like spectacles around his dim old eyes; but there was a neighbor who bore on his hand the imprint of several of Cæsar's sharp white youthful teeth, and for that he had lived at the end of a chain, all alone in a little hut, for fourteen years. The neighbor, who was choleric and smarting with the pain of his wound, had demanded either Cæsar's death or complete ostracism. So Louisa's brother, to whom the dog had belonged, had built him his little kennel and tied him up. It was now fourteen years since, in a flood of youthful spirits, he had inflicted that memorable bite, and with the exception of short excursions, always at the end of the chain, under the strict guardianship of his master or Louisa, the old dog had remained a close prisoner. It is doubtful if, with his limited ambition, he took much pride in the fact, but it is certain that he was possessed of considerable cheap fame. He was regarded by all the children in the village and by many adults as a very monster of ferocity. St. George's dragon could hardly have surpassed in evil repute Louisa Ellis's old yellow dog. Mothers charged their children with solemn emphasis not to go too near to him, and the children listened and believed greedily, with a fascinated appetite for terror, and ran by Louisa's house stealthily, with many sidelong and backward glances at the terrible dog. If perchance he sounded a hoarse bark, there was a panic. Wayfarers chancing into Louisa's yard eyed him with respect, and inquired if the chain were stout. Cæsar at large might have seemed a very ordinary dog, and excited no comment whatever; chained, his reputation overshadowed him, so that he lost his own proper outlines and looked darkly vague and enormous. Joe Dagget, however, with his good-humored sense and shrewdness, saw him as he was. He strode valiantly up to him and patted him on the head, in spite of Louisa's soft clamor of warning, and even attempted to set him loose. Louisa grew so alarmed that he desisted, but kept announcing his opinion in the matter quite forcibly at intervals. "There ain't a better-natured dog in town," he would say, "and it's downright cruel to keep him tied up there. Some day I'm going to take him out."

Louisa had very little hope that he would not, one of these days, when their interests and possessions should be more completely fused in one. She pictured to herself Cæsar on the rampage through the quiet and unguarded village. She saw innocent children bleeding in his path. She was herself very fond of the old dog, because he had belonged to her dead brother, and he was always very gentle with her; still she had great faith in his ferocity. She always warned people not to go too near him. She fed him on ascetic fare of corn-mush and cakes, and never fired his dangerous temper with heating and sanguinary diet of flesh and bones. Louisa looked at the old dog munching his simple fare, and thought of her approaching marriage and trembled. Still no anticipation of disorder and confusion in lieu of sweet peace and harmony, no forebodings of Cæsar on the rampage, no wild flut-

tering of her little yellow canary, were sufficient to turn her a hair's-breadth. Joe Dagget had been fond of her and working for her all these years. It was not for her, whatever came to pass, to prove untrue and break his heart. She put the exquisite little stitches into her wedding-garments, and the time went on until it was only a week before her wedding-day. It was a Tuesday evening, and the wedding was to be a week from Wednesday.

There was a full moon that night. About nine o'clock Louisa strolled down the road a little way. There were harvest-fields on either hand, bordered by low stone walls. Luxuriant clumps of bushes grew beside the wall, and trees—wild cherry and old apple-trees—at intervals. Presently Louisa sat down on the wall and looked about her with mildly sorrowful reflectiveness. Tall shrubs of blueberry and meadow-sweet, all woven together and tangled with blackberry vines and horsebriers, shut her in on either side. She had a little clear space between them. Opposite her, on the other side of the road, was a spreading tree; the moon shone between its boughs, and the leaves twinkled like silver. The road was bespread with a beautiful shifting dapple of silver and shadow; the air was full of a mysterious sweetness. "I wonder if it's wild grapes?" murmured Louisa. She sat there some time. She was just thinking of rising, when she heard footsteps and low voices, and remained quiet. It was a lonely place, and she felt a little timid. She thought she would keep still in the shadow and let the persons, whoever they might be, pass her.

But just before they reached her the voices ceased, and the footsteps. She understood that their owners had also found seats upon the stone wall. She was wondering if she could not steal away unobserved, when the voice broke the stillness. It was Joe Dagget's. She sat still and listened.

The voice was announced by a loud sigh, which was as familiar as itself. "Well," said Dagget, "you've made up your mind, then, I suppose?"

"Yes," returned another voice; "I'm going day after to-morrow."

"That's Lily Dyer," thought Louisa to herself. The voice embodied itself in her mind. She saw a girl tall and full-figured, with a firm, fair face, looking fairer and firmer in the moonlight, her strong yellow hair braided in a close knot. A girl full of a calm rustic strength and bloom, with a masterful way which might have beseemed a princess. Lily Dyer was a favorite with the village folk; she had just the qualities to arouse the admiration. She was good and handsome and smart. Louisa had often heard her praises sounded.

"Well," said Joe Dagget, "I ain't got a word to say."

"I don't know what you could say," returned Lily Dyer.

"Not a word to say," repeated Joe, drawing out the words heavily. Then there was a silence. "I ain't sorry," he began at last, "that that happened yesterday—that we kind of let on how we felt to each other. I guess it's just as well we knew. Of course I can't do anything any different. I'm going right on an' get married next week. I ain't going back on a woman that's waited for me fourteen years, an' break her heart."

"If you should jilt her to-morrow, I wouldn't have you," spoke up the girl, with sudden vehemence.

"Well, I ain't going to give you the chance," said he; "but I don't believe you would, either."

"You'd see I wouldn't. Honor's honor, an' right's right. An' I'd never think anything of any man that went against 'em for me or any other girl; you'd find that out, Joe Dagget."

"Well, you'll find out fast enough that I ain't going against 'em for you or any other girl," returned he. Their voices sounded almost as if they were angry with each other. Louisa was listening eagerly.

"I'm sorry you feel as if you must go away," said Joe, "but I don't know but it's best."

"Of course it's best. I hope you and I have got common-sense."

"Well, I suppose you're right." Suddenly Joe's voice got an undertone of tenderness. "Say, Lily," said he, "I'll get along well enough myself, but I can't bear to think—You don't suppose you're going to fret much over it?"

"I guess you'll find out I sha'n't fret much over a married man."

"Well, I hope you won't—I hope you won't, Lily. God knows I do. And—I hope—one of these days—you'll—come across somebody else—"

"I don't see any reason why I shouldn't." Suddenly her tone changed. She spoke in a sweet, clear voice, so loud that she could have been heard across the street. "No, Joe Dagget," said she, "I'll never marry any other man as long as I live. I've got good sense, an' I ain't going to break my heart nor make a fool of myself; but I'm never going to be married, you can be sure of that. I ain't that sort of a girl to feel this way twice."

Louisa heard an exclamation and a soft commo-

tion behind the bushes; then Lily spoke again—the voice sounded as if she had risen. "This must be put a stop to," said she. "We've stayed here long enough. I'm going home."

Louisa sat there in a daze, listening to their retreating steps. After a while she got up and slunk softly home herself. The next day she did her housework methodically; that was as much a matter of course as breathing; but she did not sew on her wedding-clothes. She sat at her window and meditated. In the evening Joe came. Louisa Ellis had never known that she had any diplomacy in her, but when she came to look for it that night she found it, although meek of its kind, among her little feminine weapons. Even now she could hardly believe that she had heard aright, and that she would not do Joe a terrible injury should she break her troth-plight. She wanted to sound him without betraying too soon her own inclinations in the matter. She did it successfully, and they finally came to an understanding; but it was a difficult thing, for he was as afraid of betraying himself as she.

She never mentioned Lily Dyer. She simply said that while she had no cause of complaint against him, she had lived so long in one way that she shrank from making a change.

"Well, I never shrank, Louisa," said Dagget. "I'm going to be honest enough to say that I think maybe it's better this way; but if you'd wanted to keep on, I'd have stuck to you till my dying day. I hope you know that."

"Yes, I do," said she.

That night she and Joe parted more tenderly than they had done for a long time. Standing in the door, holding each other's hands, a last great wave of regretful memory swept over them.

"Well, this ain't the way we've thought it was all going to end, is it, Louisa?" said Joe.

She shook her head. There was a little quiver on her placid face.

"You let me know if there's ever anything I can do for you," said he. "I ain't ever going to forget you, Louisa." Then he kissed her, and went down the path.

Louisa, all alone by herself that night, wept a little, she hardly knew why; but the next morning, on waking, she felt like a queen who, after fearing lest her domain be wrested away from her, sees it firmly insured in her possession.

Now the tall weeds and grasses might cluster around Cæsar's little hermit hut, the snow might fall on its roof year in and year out, but he never would go on a rampage through the unguarded village. Now the little canary might turn itself into a peaceful yellow ball night after night, and have no need to wake and flutter with wild terror against its bars. Louisa could sew linen seams, and distil roses, and dust and polish and fold away in lavender, as long as she listed. That afternoon she sat with her needle-work at the window, and felt fairly steeped in peace. Lily Dyer, tall and erect and blooming, went past; but she felt no qualm. If Louisa Ellis had sold her birthright she did not know it, the taste of the pottage was so delicious,

and had been her sole satisfaction for so long. Serenity and placid narrowness had become to her as the birthright itself. She gazed ahead through a long reach of future days strung together like pearls in a rosary, every one like the others, and all smooth and flawless and innocent, and her heart went up in thankfulness. Outside was the fervid summer afternoon; the air was filled with the sounds of the busy harvest of men and birds and bees; there were halloos, metallic clatterings, sweet calls, and long hummings. Louisa sat, prayerfully numbering her days, like an uncloistered nun.

SARAH ORNE JEWETT (1849–1909)

Sarah Orne Jewett, Henry James remarked a few years after her death, was "mistress of an art of fiction all her own." Rose Terry Cooke and Mary E. Wilkins Freeman were writers of definite and original talent, and one can return to their stories with considerable pleasure and profit. But though Miss Jewett is correctly associated with them within the cluster of able New England women writers in the later nineteenth century, she is markedly superior. In tales like "A White Heron," in portions of *Deephaven*, in the whole of the beautifully woven *Country of the Pointed Firs*, one is conscious of a maturity of vision, a strength of imagination, a shaping power capable of bringing together and playing off against each other an impressive variety of significant and compelling themes. Miss Jewett is a "minor" fiction writer only in the European sense of the serious and important literary artist whose accomplishment, however enduring, is somewhere below that of the undeniably great.

She was born in South Berwick, Maine, the daughter of a country doctor. Illness kept her from regular schooling during much of her childhood, and she spent many of her days driving about in a dog cart with her father, on his rounds. She thus became intimately acquainted not only with the minutiae of the natural and man-made scenery of the coast and the inland

country roads, but also with the assorted humanity to whom her father ministered—the small, hidden, but wonderfully full and varied lives of the country folk of her region. Meanwhile, Dr. Jewett, who was an uncommonly literate man, spoke to her of books and authors and enticed her into reading a wide range of English, American, and continental literature.

The particular novel which seems to have stung Sarah Orne Jewett into creative efforts of her own was Harriet Beecher Stowe's narrative portrait of fishermen and their families "along the wooded seacoast and by the decaying shipless harbors of Maine"—*The Pearl of Orr's Island* (1862), in which the fourteen-year-old girl found an "exquisite flavor and reality of delight." Her own first published story appeared in the *Atlantic* only a few years later: one of the sketches collected later in *Deephaven* (1877). There followed, among other books which established her reputation, *A Country Doctor* (1884; the doctor in question being a New England woman); *A White Heron and Other Stories* (1886); and the finest and largest of her works, *The Country of the Pointed Firs* (1896).

The narrator, in that latter work, is not herself a product of the coastal area which is its setting. She comes up from Boston for a summer visit; and this was an expression of Sarah Orne Jewett's developed sense of herself and her relation to her "Down East" origins. She had grown far beyond the small-town or backwoods mentality and could now turn back to her region with the eye of one who, in many respects, had become a gregarious cosmopolitan. She had traveled a good deal across the United States, and by 1896 she had made two of four long trips to Europe. In America, she had come to know Howells, Lowell, Whittier, Holmes. Abroad, she met Tennyson, Charles Reade, Kipling, Mark Twain, and eventually Henry James.

Her closest friend and companion, at home and on the travels, was Annie Fields, the cultivated wife of the Boston publisher James T. Fields. Especially after Fields's death in 1881,

Sarah Jewett spent months each year in Mrs. Fields's summer and winter homes. They went everywhere together. It was Annie Fields who introduced her brilliant younger friend to Europe in 1882 and who escorted her about the continent on a series of tours. In 1898, they went down to Lamb House, in Rye, and Miss Jewett met Henry James.

On her fifty-third birthday, in 1902, Sarah Orne Jewett was thrown from her carriage and suffered severe injuries to her head and spine. She wrote almost nothing more, though she could still walk and sail, and even travel a little. She had a stroke in 1909 and survived only long enough to be transported, at her request, back to South Berwick.

BIOGRAPHICAL CHART

1849   Born September 3, in South Berwick, Maine; descendant of sea captains, traders, and physicians; daughter of a country doctor
1856   Chronically ill throughout childhood; drives with her father on his daily rounds of patients; less time in school than outdoors
1865   Graduates Berwick Academy
1877   Encouraged by Howells, collects several early sketches to form her first volume, *Deephaven*
1880   Lifelong friendship established with Annie Fields; begins spending part of each winter at her Boston home, part of each summer at her Manchester-by-the-Sea cottage

1882   Travels to Europe with Annie Fields; meets Tennyson, Charles Reade, Christina Rossetti
1884   *A Country Doctor*
1886   "A White Heron" and "The Dulham Ladies"
1896   *The Country of the Pointed Firs*
1898   Visits France, England; meets Kipling at Rottingdean, Henry James at Rye
1901   *The Tory Lover* published, her only deliberate attempt at a dramatic novel
1902   Seriously injured in fall from carriage on September 3
1909   Dies, June 24, in South Berwick

FURTHER READINGS

There is no standard edition of Sarah Orne Jewett's works. The reader is referred for individual titles to the biographical chart.

Van Wyck Brooks, *New England: Indian Summer*

(1940)
F. O. Matthiessen, *Sarah Orne Jewett* (1929)
Vernon L. Parrington, *Main Currents in American Thought* (1930)

A White Heron (1886)

"A White Heron" is much the best known of Sarah Orne Jewett's short stories, partly because it has been the most often anthologized. The anthologist is always tempted to look for less

familiar and therefore (allegedly) "fresher" writings by the authors he represents—in Miss Jewett's case, for example, "The Dulham Ladies" (a poignantly funny tale about the efforts of two elderly spinsters to change the time), or "Marsh Rosemary." The latter is an especially acute and moving story about a sensible and hard-working seamstress whose shiftless husband is reported drowned at sea. She accepts her loss with dignity and courage; but when she discovers that her husband is in fact living in a nearby town with another woman, she is totally stricken. In our last glimpse of her, Nancy Floyd is sitting down alone to her supper, with the light off—lest anyone come in "to bring unwelcome sympathy." Or one might have chosen "A Business Man," a story set untypically among the very rich of New York City (it provided the basis for two film versions, one starring George Arliss and the second Sidney Greenstreet).

But the fact is that "A White Heron," however often anthologized, is still not nearly as well known as it deserves to be. Henry James's words for *The Country of the Pointed Firs*— "elegant," "exact," and "absolutely true"—apply beautifully here. It is among other things a story of initiation: of the multiple and simultaneous discovery by a young girl of her physical world (she sees the ocean literally for the first time), of natural and human beauty, of love, of the perplexities that life entails. There is also the archetypal American contrast between the city (where the child has spent her first eight years) and the country (which is now her home); and between the appeal of material things and the mysterious imperatives of nature. A ritualistic atmosphere hovers over the long moment when Sylvia, at dawn, climbs the white oak tree and over to the huge pine tree, seeking a point from which she can see the heron's nest—the secret, somehow, of the reality she is coming to know. Yet the story is told with great simplicity, and in utter truth to human feeling: with the art that conceals art.

I

The woods were already filled with shadows one June evening, just before eight o'clock, though a bright sunset still glimmered faintly among the trunks of the trees. A little girl was driving home her cow, a plodding, dilatory, provoking creature in her behavior, but a valued companion for all that. They were going away from whatever light there was, and striking deep into the woods, but their feet were familiar with the path, and it was no matter whether their eyes could see it or not.

There was hardly a night the summer through when the old cow could be found waiting at the pasture bars; on the contrary, it was her greatest pleasure to hide herself away among the huckleberry bushes, and though she wore a loud bell she had made the discovery that if one stood perfectly still it would not ring. So Sylvia had to hunt for her until she found her, and call Co'! Co'! with never an answering Moo, until her childish patience was quite spent. If the creature had not given good milk and plenty of it, the case would have seemed very different to her owners. Besides, Sylvia had all the time there was, and very little use to make of it. Sometimes in pleasant weather it was a consolation to look upon the cow's pranks as an intelligent attempt to play hide and seek, and as the child had no playmates she lent herself to this amusement with a good deal of zest. Though this chase had been so long that the wary animal herself had given an unusual signal of her whereabouts, Sylvia had only laughed when she came upon Mistress Moolly at the swampside, and urged her affectionately homeward with a twig of birch leaves. The old cow was not inclined to wander farther, she even turned in the right direction for once as they left the pasture, and stepped along the road at a good pace. She was quite ready to be milked now, and seldom stopped to browse. Sylvia wondered what her grandmother would say because they were so late. It was a great while since she had left home at half-past five o'clock, but everybody knew the difficulty of making this errand a short one. Mrs. Tilley had chased the hornéd torment too many summer evenings herself to blame any one else for lingering, and was only thankful as she waited that she had Sylvia, nowadays, to give such valuable assistance. The good woman suspected that Sylvia loitered occasionally on her own account; there never was such a child for straying about out-of-doors since the world was made! Everybody said that it was a good change for a little maid who had tried to grow for eight years in a crowded manufacturing town, but as for Sylvia herself, it seemed as if she never had been alive at all before she came to live at the farm. She thought often with wistful compassion of a wretched geranium that belonged to a town neighbor.

" 'Afraid of folks,' " old Mrs. Tilley said to herself, with a smile, after she had made the unlikely choice of Sylvia from her daughter's houseful of children, and was returning to the farm. " 'Afraid of folks,' they said! I guess she won't be troubled no great with 'em up to the old place!" When they reached the door of the lonely house and stopped to unlock it, and the cat came to purr loudly, and rub against them, a deserted pussy, indeed, but fat with young robins, Sylvia whispered that this was a beautiful place to live in, and she never should wish to go home.

The companions followed the shady woodroad, the cow taking slow steps and the child very fast ones. The cow stopped long at the brook to drink, as if the pasture were not half a swamp, and Sylvia stood still and waited, letting her bare feet cool themselves in the shoal water, while the great twilight moths struck softly against her. She waded on through the brook as the cow moved away, and listened to the thrushes with a heart that beat fast with pleasure. There was a stirring in the great boughs overhead. They were full of little birds and beasts that seemed to be wide awake, and going about their world, or else saying good-night to each other in sleepy twitters. Sylvia herself felt sleepy as she walked along. However, it was not much farther to the house, and the air was soft and sweet. She was not often in the woods so late as this, and it made her feel as if she were a part of the gray shadows and the moving leaves. She was just thinking how long it seemed since she first came to the farm a year ago, and wondering if everything went on in the noisy town just the same as when she was there; the thought of the great red-faced boy who used to chase and frighten her made her hurry along the path to escape from the shadow of the trees.

Suddenly this little woods-girl is horror-stricken to hear a clear whistle not very far away. Not a bird's-whistle, which would have a sort of friendliness, but a boy's whistle, determined, and somewhat aggressive. Sylvia left the cow to whatever sad fate might await her, and stepped discreetly aside into the bushes, but she was just too late. The enemy had discovered her, and called out in a very cheerful and persuasive tone, "Halloa, little girl, how far is it to the road?" and trembling Sylvia answered almost inaudibly, "A good ways."

She did not dare to look boldly at the tall young man, who carried a gun over his shoulder, but she came out of her bush and again followed the cow, while he walked alongside.

"I have been hunting for some birds," the stranger said kindly, "and I have lost my way, and need a friend very much. Don't be afraid," he added gallantly. "Speak up and tell me what your name is, and whether you think I can spend the night at your house, and go out gunning early in the morning."

Sylvia was more alarmed than before. Would not her grandmother consider her much to blame? But who could have foreseen such an accident as this? It did not seem to be her fault, and she hung her head as if the stem of it were broken, but managed to answer "Sylvy," with much effort when her companion again asked her name.

Mrs. Tilley was standing in the doorway when the trio came into view. The cow gave a loud moo by way of explanation.

"Yes, you'd better speak up for yourself, you old trial! Where'd she tucked herself away this time, Sylvy?" But Sylvia kept an awed silence; she knew by instinct that her grandmother did not comprehend the gravity of the situation. She must be mistaking the stranger for one of the farmer-lads of the region.

The young man stood his gun beside the door, and dropped a lumpy game-bag beside it; then he bade Mrs. Tilley good-evening, and repeated his wayfarer's story, and asked if he could have a night's lodging.

"Put me anywhere you like," he said. "I must be off early in the morning, before day; but I am very hungry, indeed. You can give me some milk at any rate, that's plain."

"Dear sakes, yes," responded the hostess, whose long slumbering hospitality seemed to be easily awakened. "You might fare better if you went out to the main road a mile or so, but you're welcome to what we've got. I'll milk right off, and you make yourself at home. You can sleep on husks or feathers," she proffered graciously. "I raised them all myself. There's good pasturing for geese just below here towards the ma'sh. Now step round and set a plate for the gentleman, Sylvy!" And Sylvia promptly stepped. She was glad to have something to do, and she was hungry herself.

It was a surprise to find so clean and comfortable a little dwelling in this New England wilderness. The young man had known the horrors of its most primitive housekeeping, and the dreary squalor of that level of society which does not rebel at the companionship of hens. This was the best thrift of an old-fashioned farmstead, though on such a small scale that it seemed like a hermitage. He listened eagerly to the old woman's quaint talk, he watched Sylvia's pale face and shining gray eyes with ever growing enthusiasm, and insisted that this was the best supper he had eaten for a month, and afterward the new-made friends sat down in the doorway together while the moon came up.

Soon it would be berry-time, and Sylvia was a great help at picking. The cow was a good milker, though a plaguy thing to keep track of, the hostess gossiped frankly, adding presently that she had buried four children, so Sylvia's mother, and a son (who might be dead) in California were all the children she had left. "Dan, my boy, was a great hand to go gunning," she explained sadly. "I never wanted for pa'tridges or gray squer'ls while he was to home. He's been a great wand'rer, I expect, and he's no hand to write letters. There, I don't blame him, I'd ha' seen the world myself if it had been so I could."

"Sylvy takes after him," the grandmother continued affectionately, after a minute's pause. "There ain't a foot o' ground she don't know her way over, and the wild creatures counts her one o' themselves. Squer'ls she'll tame to come an' feed right out o' her hands, and all sorts o' birds. Last winter she got the jaybirds to bangeing here, and I believe she'd 'a' scanted herself of her own meals to have plenty to throw out amongst 'em, if I hadn't kep' watch. Anything but crows, I tell her, I'm willin' to help support—though Dan he had a tamed one o' them that did seem to have reason same as folks. It was round here a good spell after he went away. Dan an' his father they didn't hitch,—but he never held up his head ag'in after Dan had dared him an' gone off."

The guest did not notice this hint of family sorrows in his eager interest in something else.

"So Sylvy knows all about birds, does she?" he exclaimed, as he looked round at the little girl who sat, very demure but increasingly sleepy, in the moonlight. "I am making a collection of birds myself. I have been at it ever since I was a boy." (Mrs. Tilley smiled.) "There are two or three very rare ones I have been hunting for these five years. I mean to get them on my own ground if thcy can bc found."

"Do you cage 'em up?" asked Mrs. Tilley doubtfully, in response to this enthusiastic announcement.

"Oh no, they're stuffed and preserved, dozens and dozens of them," said the ornithologist, "and I have shot or snared every one myself. I caught a glimpse of a white heron a few miles from here on Saturday, and I have followed it in this direction. They have never been found in this district at all. The little white heron, it is," and he turned again to look at Sylvia with the hope of discovering that the rare bird was one of her acquaintances.

But Sylvia was watching a hop-toad in the narrow footpath.

"You would know the heron if you saw it," the stranger continued eagerly. "A queer tall white bird with soft feathers and long thin legs. And it would have a nest perhaps in the top of a high tree, made of sticks, something like a hawk's nest."

Sylvia's heart gave a wild beat; she knew that strange white bird, and had once stolen softly near where it stood in some bright green swamp grass, away over at the other side of the woods. There was an open place where the sunshine always seemed strangely yellow and hot, where tall, nodding rushes grew, and her grandmother had warned her that she might sink in the soft black mud underneath and never be heard of more. Not far beyond were the salt marshes and beyond those was the sea, the sea which Sylvia wondered and dreamed about, but never had looked upon, though its great voice could often be heard above the noise of the woods on stormy nights.

"I can't think of anything I should like so much as to find that heron's nest," the handsome stranger was saying. "I would give ten dollars to anybody who could show it to me," he added desperately, "and I mean to spend my whole vacation hunting for it if need be. Perhaps it was only migrating, or had been chased out of its own region by some bird of prey."

Mrs. Tilley gave amazed attention to all this, but Sylvia still watched the toad, not divining, as she might have done at some calmer time, that the creature wished to get to its hole under the door-step, and was much hindered by the unusual spectators at that hour of the evening. No amount of thought, that night, could decide how many wished-for treasures the ten dollars, so lightly spoken of, would buy.

The next day the young sportsman hovered about thc woods, and Sylvia kept him company, having lost her first fear of the friendly lad, who proved to be most kind and sympathetic. He told her many things about the birds and what they knew and where they lived and what they did with themselves. And he gave her a jack-knife, which she thought as great a treasure as if she were a desert-islander. All day long he did not once make her troubled or afraid except when he brought down some unsuspecting singing creature from its bough. Sylvia would have liked him vastly better without his gun; she could not understand why he killed the very birds he seemed to like so much. But as the day waned, Sylvia still watched the young man with loving admiration. She had never seen anybody so charming and delightful; the woman's heart, asleep in the child, was vaguely thrilled by a dream of love. Some premonition of that great power stirred and swayed these young creatures who traversed the solemn woodlands with soft-footed silent care. They stopped to listen to a bird's song; they pressed forward again eagerly, parting the branches—speaking to each other rarely and in whispers; the young man going first and Sylvia following, fascinated, a few steps behind, with her gray eyes dark with excitement.

She grieved because the longed-for white heron was elusive, but she did not lead the guest, she only followed, and there was no such thing as speaking first. The sound of her own unquestioned voice would have terrified her—it was hard enough to answer yes or no when there was need of that. At last evening began to fall, and they drove the cow home together, and Sylvia smiled with pleasure when they came to the place where she heard the whistle and was afraid only the night before.

II

Half a mile from home, at the farther edge of the woods, where the land was highest, a great pine-tree stood, the last of its generation. Whether it was left for a boundary mark, or for what reason, no one could say; the wood-choppers who had felled its mates were dead and gone long ago, and a whole forest of sturdy trees, pines and oaks and maples, had grown again. But the stately head of this old pine towered above them all and made a landmark for sea and shore miles and miles away. Sylvia knew it well. She had always believed that whoever climbed to the top of it could see the ocean; and the little girl had often laid her hand on the great rough trunk and looked up wistfully at those dark boughs that the wind always stirred, no matter how hot and still the air might be below. Now she thought of the tree with a new excitement, for why, if one climbed it at break of

day could not one see all the world, and easily discover from whence the white heron flew, and mark the place, and find the hidden nest?

What a spirit of adventure, what wild ambition! What fancied triumph and delight and glory for the later morning when she could make known the secret! It was almost too real and too great for the childish heart to bear.

All night the door of the little house stood open and the whippoorwills came and sang upon the very step. The young sportsman and his old hostess were sound asleep, but Sylvia's great design kept her broad awake and watching. She forgot to think of sleep. The short summer night seemed as long as the winter darkness, and at last when the whippoorwills ceased, and she was afraid the morning would after all come too soon, she stole out of the house and followed the pasture path through the woods, hastening toward the open ground beyond, listening with a sense of comfort and companionship to the drowsy twitter of a half-awakened bird, whose perch she had jarred in passing. Alas, if the great wave of human interest which flooded for the first time this dull little life should sweep away the satisfactions of an existence heart to heart with nature and the dumb life of the forest!

There was the huge tree asleep yet in the paling moonlight, and small and silly Sylvia began with utmost bravery to mount to the top of it, with tingling, eager blood coursing the channels of her whole frame, with her bare feet and fingers, that pinched and held like bird's claws to the monstrous ladder reaching up, up, almost to the sky itself. First she must mount the white oak tree that grew alongside, where she was almost lost among the dark branches and the green leaves heavy and wet with dew; a bird fluttered off its nest, and a red squirrel ran to and fro and scolded pettishly at the harmless housebreaker. Sylvia felt her way easily. She had often climbed there, and knew that higher still one of the oak's upper branches chafed against the pine trunk, just where its lower boughs were set close together. There, when she made the dangerous pass from one tree to the other, the great enterprise would really begin.

She crept out along the swaying oak limb at last, and took the daring step across into the old pine-tree. The way was harder than she thought; she must reach far and hold fast, the sharp dry twigs caught and held her and scratched her like angry talons, the pitch made her thin little fingers clumsy and stiff as she went round and round the tree's great stem, higher and higher upward. The sparrows and robins in the woods below were beginning to wake and twitter to the dawn, yet it seemed much lighter there aloft in the pine-tree, and the child knew she must hurry if her project were to be of any use.

The tree seemed to lengthen itself out as she went up, and to reach farther and farther upward. It was like a great main-mast to the voyaging earth; it must truly have been amazed that morning through all its ponderous frame as it felt this determined spark of human spirit wending its way from higher branch to branch. Who knows how steadily the least twigs held themselves to advantage this light, weak creature on her way! The old pine must have loved his new dependent. More than all the hawks, and bats, and moths, and even the sweet voiced thrushes, was the brave, beating heart of the solitary gray-eyed child. And the tree stood still and frowned away the winds that June morning while the dawn grew bright in the east.

Sylvia's face was like a pale star, if one had seen it from the ground, when the last thorny bough was past, and she stood trembling and tired but wholly triumphant, high in the tree-top. Yes, there was the sea with the dawning sun making a golden dazzle over it, and toward that glorious east flew two hawks with slow-moving pinions. How low they looked in the air from that height when one had only seen them before far up, and dark against the blue sky. Their gray feathers were as soft as moths; they seemed only a little way from the tree, and Sylvia felt as if she too could go flying away among the clouds. Westward, the woodlands and farms reached miles and miles into the distance; here and there were church steeples, and white villages, truly it was a vast and awesome world!

The birds sang louder and louder. At last the sun came up bewilderingly bright. Sylvia could see the white sails of ships out at sea, and the clouds that were purple and rose-colored and yellow at first began to fade away. Where was the white heron's nest in the sea of green branches, and was this wonderful sight and pageant of the world the only reward for having climbed to such a giddy height? Now look down again, Sylvia, where the green marsh is set among the shining birches and dark hemlocks; there where you saw the white heron once you will see him again; look, look! a white spot of him like a single floating feather comes up from the dead hemlock and grows larger, and rises, and comes close at last, and goes by the landmark pine with steady sweep of wing and outstretched slender neck and crested head. And wait! wait! do not move a foot or a finger, little girl, do not send an arrow of light and consciousness from your two eager eyes, for the heron has perched on a pine bough not far beyond yours, and cries back to his mate on the nest and plumes his feathers for the new day!

The child gives a long sigh a minute later when a company of shouting cat-birds comes also to the tree, and vexed by their fluttering and lawlessness the solemn heron goes away. She knows his secret now, the wild, light, slender bird that floats and wavers, and goes back like an arrow presently to his home in the green world beneath. Then Sylvia, well satisfied, makes her perilous way down again, not daring to look far below the branch she stands on, ready to cry sometimes because her fingers ache and her lamed feet slip. Wondering over and over again what the stranger would say to her, and what he would think when she told him how to find his way straight to the heron's nest.

"Sylvy, Sylvy!" called the busy old grandmother again and again, but nobody answered, and the small husk bed was empty and Sylvia had disappeared.

The guest waked from a dream, and remembering his day's pleasure hurried to dress himself that might it sooner begin. He was sure from the way the shy little girl looked once or twice yesterday that she had at least seen the white heron, and now she must really be made to tell. Here she comes now, paler than ever, and her worn old frock is torn and tattered, and smeared with pine pitch. The grandmother and the sportsman stand in the door together and question her, and the splendid moment has come to speak of the dead hemlock-tree by the green marsh.

But Sylvia does not speak after all, though the old grandmother fretfully rebukes her, and the young man's kind, appealing eyes are looking straight in her own. He can make them rich with money; he has promised it, and they are poor now. He is so well worth making happy, and he waits to hear the story she can tell.

No, she must keep silence! What is it that suddenly forbids her and makes her dumb? Has she been nine years growing and now, when the great world for the first time puts out a hand to her, must she thrust it aside for a bird's sake? The murmur of the pine's green branches is in her ears, she remembers how the white heron came flying through the golden air and how they watched the sea and the morning together, and Sylvia cannot speak; she cannot tell the heron's secret and give its life away.

Dear loyalty, that suffered a sharp pang as the guest went away disappointed later in the day, that could have served and followed him and loved him as a dog loves! Many a night Sylvia heard the echo of his whistle haunting the pasture path as she came home with the loitering cow. She forgot even her sorrow at the sharp report of his gun and the sight of thrushes and sparrows dropping silent to the ground, their songs hushed and their pretty feathers stained and wet with blood. Were the birds better friends than their hunter might have been,—who can tell? whatever treasures were lost to her, woodlands and summer-time, remember! Bring your gifts and graces and tell your secrets to this lonely country child.

From The Country of the Pointed Firs (1896)

Though it is sometimes spoken of as a collection of sketches or tales, and paired in this regard with Miss Jewett's *Deephaven, The Country of the Pointed Firs* is in fact a single and unified work of fiction, and a masterpiece of its kind. It can hardly be called "seamless": further incidents could have been devised and other characters introduced. But it has a clear beginning: the narrator's arrival in the coast town of Dunnet, Maine, where pointed balsam firs crowd the shore; and an ending: the narrator's departure after a deep summer-long immersion in the countryside, the islands, and the scattered human community. It even has a middle of sorts: the chapters about "poor Joanna" Todd, especially as her situation is contrasted with that of the not much less isolated but infinitely more serene and contented Mrs. Blackett.

A deeper unity seems to derive from the unity of life itself—that is, the life rhythms of the village of Dunnet and the outlying districts. The novel is punctuated by the recurring rituals and ceremonies through which the community declares itself: a funeral, a series of visits and outings, the festive reunion of the Bowden clan, the marriage of Mrs. Todd's brother. At such moments, life is enlarged and intensified, and it joins with the broader life of humanity across the ages. Moving with the others toward the grove where the feast has been prepared for the Bowden family, the narrator reflects:

> We might have been a company of ancient Greeks going to celebrate a victory, or to worship the god of harvests in the grove above. It was strangely moving to see this and to make part of it. The sky, the sea, have watched poor humanity at its rites so long; we were no more a New England family celebrating its own existence and simple progress; we carried the tokens and inheritance of all such households from which this had descended, and were only the latest of our line. We possessed the instincts of a far, forgotten childhood; I found myself thinking that we ought to be carrying green branches and singing as we went.

In passages like that, Miss Jewett shows that she has followed the advice of Emerson, who, in his essay "The Poet" fifty-odd years earlier, had instructed the American writer in how to perceive the materials that were given him to deal with. The elements of everyday life in America, Emerson had said, "are flat and dull to dull people, but rest on the same foundations of wonder as the town of Troy and the temple of Delphi, and are as swiftly passing away."

These rituals are the more important for the folk of Dunnet, because their lives are otherwise rather dreary and constricted. *The Country of the Pointed Firs* contains as varied an array of *isolates* as the shorter fiction of Melville.

Joanna Todd, whom the narrator hears about in the chapters we present, is only the most extreme case of isolation in the story. There is also the ancient mariner Captain Littlepage, frozen in his memory of the arctic zone where he had once been stranded and which seemed to him a Limbo between this world and the next, populated by gray flitting shadows. There is Mrs. Blackett, living far away, her gentle-souled son William her only companion. There is Elijah Tilley, maundering on about his dead wife. As for Joanna, with her talk of the unpardonable sin, her recoil from experience, and her total self-exile, she descends clearly enough from that earlier and greatest chronicler of the troubled New England spirit, Nathaniel Hawthorne. But Sarah Orne Jewett's art, as Henry James insisted, was entirely her own.

CHAPTER 13: POOR JOANNA

One evening my ears caught a mysterious allusion which Mrs. Todd made to Shell-heap Island. It was a chilly night of cold northeasterly rain, and I made a fire for the first time in the Franklin stove in my room, and begged my two housemates to come in and keep me company. The weather had convinced Mrs. Todd that it was time to make a supply of cough-drops, and she had been bringing forth herbs from dark and dry hiding-places, until now the pungent dust and odor of them had resolved themselves into one mighty flavor of spearmint that came from a simmering caldron of syrup in the kitchen. She called it done, and well done, and had ostentatiously left it to cool, and taken her knitting-work because Mrs. Fosdick was busy with hers. They sat in the two rocking-chairs, the small woman and the large one, but now and then I could see that Mrs. Todd's thoughts remained with the cough-drops. The time of gathering herbs was nearly over, but the time of syrups and cordials had begun.

The heat of the open fire made us a little drowsy, but something in the way Mrs. Todd spoke of Shell-heap Island waked my interest. I waited to see if she would say any more, and then took a roundabout way back to the subject by saying what was first in my mind: that I wished the Green Island family were there to spend the evening with us,—Mrs. Todd's mother and her brother William.

Mrs. Todd smiled, and drummed on the arm of the rocking-chair. "Might scare William to death," she warned me; and Mrs. Fosdick mentioned her intention of going out to Green Island to stay two or three days, if this wind didn't make too much sea.

"Where is Shell-heap Island?" I ventured to ask, seizing the opportunity.

"Bears nor'east somewheres about three miles from Green Island; right off-shore, I should call it about eight miles out," said Mrs. Todd. "You never was there, dear; 't is off the thoroughfares, and a very bad place to land at best."

"I should think 't was," agreed Mrs. Fosdick, smoothing down her black silk apron. "'T is a place worth visitin' when you once get there. Some o' the old folks was kind o' fearful about it. 'T was 'counted a great place in old Indian times; you can pick up their stone tools 'most any time if you hunt about. There's a beautiful spring o' water, too. Yes, I remember when they used to tell queer stories about Shell-heap Island. Some said 't was a great bangeing-place for the Indians, and an old chief resided there once that ruled the winds; and others said they'd always heard that once the Indians come down from up country an' left a captive there without any bo't, an' 't was too far to swim across to Black Island, so called, an' he lived there till he perished."

"I've heard say he walked the island after that, and sharp-sighted folks could see him an' lose him like one o' them citizens Cap'n Littlepage was acquainted with up to the north pole," announced Mrs. Todd grimly. "Anyway, there was Indians,— you can see their shell-heap that named the island; and I've heard myself that 't was one o' their cannibal places, but I never could believe it. There never was no cannibals on the coast o' Maine. All the Indians o' these regions are tame-looking folks."

"Sakes alive, yes!" exclaimed Mrs. Fosdick. "Ought to see them painted savages I've seen when I was young out in the South Sea Islands! That was the time for folks to travel, 'way back in the old whalin' days!"

"Whalin' must have been dull for a lady, hardly ever makin' a lively port, and not takin' in any mixed cargoes," said Mrs. Todd. "I never desired to go a whalin' v'y'ge myself."

"I used to return feelin' very slack an' behind the times, 't is true," explained Mrs. Fosdick, "but 't was excitin', an' we always done extra well, and felt rich when we did get ashore. I liked the variety. There, how times have changed; how few seafarin' families there are left! What a lot o' queer folks there used to be about here, anyway, when we was young, Almiry. Everybody's just like everybody else, now; nobody to laugh about, and nobody to cry about."

It seemed to me that there were peculiarities of character in the region of Dunnet Landing yet, but I did not like to interrupt.

"Yes," said Mrs. Todd after a moment of meditation, "there was certain a good many curiosities of human natur' in this neighborhood years ago. There was more energy then, and in some the energy took a singular turn. In these days the young folks is all copy-cats, 'fraid to death they won't be all just alike; as for the old folks, they pray for the advantage o' bein' a little different."

"I ain't heard of a copy-cat this great many years," said Mrs. Fosdick, laughing; " 't was a favorite term o' my grandmother's. No, I wa'n't thinking o' those things, but of them strange straying creatur's that used to rove the country. You don't see them now, or the ones that used to hive away in their own houses with some strange notion or other."

I thought again of Captain Littlepage, but my companions were not reminded of his name; and there was brother William at Green Island, whom we all three knew.

"I was talking o' poor Joanna the other day. I hadn't thought of her for a great while," said Mrs. Fosdick abruptly. "Mis' Brayton an' I recalled her as we sat together sewing. She was one o' your peculiar persons, wa'n't she? Speaking of such persons," she turned to explain to me, "there was a sort of a nun or hermit person lived out there for years all alone on Shell-heap Island. Miss Joanna Todd, her name was,—a cousin o' Almiry's late husband."

I expressed my interest, but as I glanced at Mrs. Todd I saw that she was confused by sudden affectionate feeling and unmistakable desire for reticence.

"I never want to hear Joanna laughed about," she said anxiously.

"Nor I," answered Mrs. Fosdick reassuringly. "She was crossed in love,—that was all the matter to begin with; but as I look back, I can see that Joanna was one doomed from the first to fall into a melancholy. She retired from the world for good an' all, though she was a well-off woman. All she wanted was to get away from folks; she thought she wasn't fit to live with anybody, and wanted to be free. Shell-heap Island come to her from her father, and first thing folks knew she'd gone off out there to live, and left word she didn't want no company. 'T was a bad place to get to, unless the

wind an' tide were just right; 't was hard work to make a landing."

"What time of year was this?" I asked.

"Very late in the summer," said Mrs. Fosdick. "No, I never could laugh at Joanna, as some did. She set everything by the young man, an' they were going to marry in about a month, when he got bewitched with a girl 'way up the bay, and married her, and went off to Massachusetts. He wasn't well thought of,—there were those who thought Joanna's money was what had tempted him; but she'd given him her whole heart, an' she wa'n't so young as she had been. All her hopes were built on marryin', an' havin' a real home and somebody to look to; she acted just like a bird when its nest is spoilt. The day after she heard the news she was in dreadful woe, but the next she came to herself very quiet, and took the horse and wagon, and drove fourteen miles to the lawyer's, and signed a paper givin' her half of the farm to her brother. They never had got along very well together, but he didn't want to sign it, till she acted so distressed that he gave in. Edward Todd's wife was a good woman, who felt very bad indeed, and used every argument with Joanna; but Joanna took a poor old boat that had been her father's and lo'ded in a few things, and off she put all alone, with a good land breeze, right out to sea. Edward Todd ran down to the beach, an' stood there cryin' like a boy to see her go, but she was out o' hearin'. She never stepped foot on the mainland again long as she lived."

"How large an island it is? How did she manage in winter?" I asked.

"Perhaps thirty acres, rocks and all," answered Mrs. Todd, taking up the story gravely. "There can't be much of it that the salt spray don't fly over in storms. No, 't is a dreadful small place to make a world of; it has a different look from any of the other islands, but there's a sheltered cove on the south side, with mud-flats across one end of it at low water where there's excellent clams, and the big shell-heap keeps some o' the wind off a little house her father took the trouble to build when he was a young man. They said there was an old house built o' logs there before that, with a kind of natural cellar in the rock under it. He used to stay out there days to a time, and anchor a little sloop he had, and dig clams to fill it, and sail up to Portland. They said the dealers always gave him an extra price, the clams were so noted. Joanna used to go out and stay with him. They were always great companions, so she knew just what 't was out there. There was a few sheep that belonged to her brother an' her, but she bargained for him to come and get them on the edge o' cold weather. Yes, she desired him to come for the sheep; an' his wife thought perhaps Joanna'd return, but he said no, an' lo'ded the bo't with warm things an' what he thought she'd need through the winter. He come home with the sheep an' left the other things by the house, but she never so much as looked out o' the window. She done it for a penance. She must have wanted to see Edward by that time."

Mrs. Fosdick was fidgeting with eagerness to speak.

"Some thought the first cold snap would set her ashore, but she always remained," concluded Mrs. Todd soberly.

"Talk about the men not having any curiosity!" exclaimed Mrs. Fosdick scornfully. "Why, the waters round Shell-heap Island were white with sails all that fall. 'T was never called no great of a fishin'-ground before. Many of 'em made excuse to go ashore to get water at the spring; but at last she spoke to a bo't-load, very dignified and calm, and said that she'd like it better if they'd make a practice of getting water to Black Island or somewheres else and leave her alone, except in case of accident or trouble. But there was one man who had always set everything by her from a boy. He'd have married her if the other hadn't come about an' spoilt his chance, and he used to get close to the island, before light, on his way out fishin', and throw a little bundle 'way up the green slope front o' the house. His sister told me she happened to see, the first time, what a pretty choice he made o' useful things that a woman would feel lost without. He stood off fishin', and could see them in the grass all day, though sometimes she'd come out and walk right by them. There was other bo'ts near, out after mackerel. But early next morning his present was gone. He didn't presume too much, but once he took her a nice firkin o' things he got up to Portland, and when spring come he landed her a hen and chickens in a nice coop. There was a good many old friends had Joanna on their minds."

"Yes," said Mrs. Todd, losing her sad reserve in the growing sympathy of these reminiscences. "How everybody used to notice whether there was smoke out of the chimney! The Black Island folks could see her with their spy-glass, and if they'd ever missed getting some sign o' life they'd have sent notice to her folks. But after the first year or two

Joanna was more and more forgotten as an everyday charge. Folks lived very simple in those days, you know," she continued, as Mrs. Fosdick's knitting was taking much thought at the moment. "I expect there was always plenty of driftwood thrown up, and a poor failin' patch of spruces covered all the north side of the island, so she always had something to burn. She was very fond of workin' in the garden ashore, and that first summer she began to till the little field out there, and raised a nice parcel o' potatoes. She could fish, o' course, and there was all her clams an' lobsters. You can always live well in any wild place by the sea when you'd starve to death up country, except 't was berry time. Joanna had berries out there, blackberries at least, and there was a few herbs in case she needed them. Mullein in great quantities and a plant o' wormwood I remember seeing once when I stayed there, long before she fled out to Shell-heap. Yes, I recall the wormwood, which is always a planted herb, so there must have been folks there before the Todd's day. A growin' bush makes the best gravestone; I expect that wormwood always stood for somebody's solemn monument. Catnip, too, is a very endurin' herb about an old place."

"But what I want to know is what she did for other things," interrupted Mrs. Fosdick. "Almiry, what did she do for clothin' when she needed to replenish, or risin' for her bread, or the piece-bag that no woman can live long without?"

"Or company," suggested Mrs. Todd. "Joanna was one that loved her friends. There must have been a terrible sight o' long winter evenin's that first year."

"There was her hens," suggested Mrs. Fosdick, after reviewing the melancholy situation. "She never wanted the sheep after that first season. There wa'n't no proper pasture for sheep after the June grass was past, and she ascertained the fact and couldn't bear to see them suffer; but the chickens done well. I remember sailin' by one spring afternoon, an' seein' the coops out front o' the house in the sun. How long was it before you went out with the minister? You were the first ones that ever really got ashore to see Joanna."

I had been reflecting upon a state of society which admitted such personal freedom and a voluntary hermitage. There was something mediæval in the behavior of poor Joanna Todd under a disappointment of the heart. The two women had drawn closer together, and were talking on, quite unconscious of a listener.

"Poor Joanna!" said Mrs. Todd again, and sadly shook her head as if there were things one could not speak about.

"I called her a great fool," declared Mrs. Fosdick, with spirit, "but I pitied her then, and I pity her far more now. Some other minister would have been a great help to her,—one that preached self-forgetfulness and doin' for others to cure our own ills; but Parson Dimmick was a vague person, well meanin', but very numb in his feelin's. I don't suppose at that troubled time Joanna could think of any way to mend her troubles except to run off and hide."

"Mother used to say she didn't see how Joanna lived without having nobody to do for, getting her own meals and tending her own poor self day in an' day out," said Mrs. Todd sorrowfully.

"There was the hens," repeated Mrs. Fosdick kindly. "I expect she soon came to makin' folks o' them. No, I never went to work to blame Joanna, as some did. She was full o' feeling, and her troubles hurt her more than she could bear. I see it all now as I couldn't when I was young."

"I suppose in old times they had their shut-up convents for just such folks," said Mrs. Todd, as if she and her friend had disagreed about Joanna once, and were now in happy harmony. She seemed to speak with new openness and freedom. "Oh yes, I was only too pleased when the Reverend Mr. Dimmick invited me to go out with him. He hadn't been very long in the place when Joanna left home and friends. 'T was one day that next summer after she went, and I had been married early in the spring. He felt that he ought to go out and visit her. She was a member of the church, and might wish to have him consider her spiritual state. I wa'n't so sure o' that, but I always liked Joanna, and I'd come to be her cousin by marriage. Nathan an' I had conversed about goin' out to pay her a visit, but he got his chance to sail sooner 'n he expected. He always thought everything of her, and last time he come home, knowing nothing of her change, he brought her a beautiful coral pin from a port he'd touched at somewheres up the Mediterranean. So I wrapped the little box in a nice piece of paper and put it in my pocket, and picked her a bunch of fresh lemon balm, and off we started."

Mrs. Fosdick laughed. "I remember hearin' about your trials on the v'y'ge," she said.

"Why, yes," continued Mrs. Todd in her company manner. "I picked her the balm, an' we started. Why, yes, Susan, the minister liked to

have cost me my life that day. He would fasten the sheet, though I advised against it. He said the rope was rough an' cut his hand. There was a fresh breeze, an' he went on talking rather high flown, an' I felt some interested. All of a sudden there come up a gust, and he give a screech and stood right up and called for help, 'way out there to sea. I knocked him right over into the bottom o' the bo't, getting by to catch hold of the sheet an' untie it. He wasn't but a little man; I helped him right up after the squall passed, and made a handsome apology to him, but he did act kind o' offended."

"I do think they ought not to settle them land-locked folks in parishes where they're liable to be on the water," insisted Mrs. Fosdick. "Think of the families in our parish that was scattered all about the bay, and what a sight o' sails you used to see, in Mr. Dimmick's day, standing across to the mainland on a pleasant Sunday morning, filled with church-going folks, all sure to want him some time or other! You couldn't find no doctor that would stand up in the boat and screech if a flaw struck her."

"Old Dr. Bennett had a beautiful sailboat, didn't he?" responded Mrs. Todd. "And how well he used to brave the weather! Mother always said that in time o' trouble that tall white sail used to look like an angel's wing comin' over the sea to them that was in pain. Well, there's a difference in gifts. Mr. Dimmick was not without light."

"'T was light o' the moon, then," snapped Mrs. Fosdick; "he was pompous enough, but I never could remember a single word he said. There, go on, Mis' Todd; I forget a great deal about that day you went to see poor Joanna."

"I felt she saw us coming, and knew us a great way off; yes, I seemed to feel it within me," said our friend, laying down her knitting. "I kept my seat, and took the bo't inshore without saying a word; there was a short channel that I was sure Mr. Dimmick wasn't acquainted with, and the tide was very low. She never came out to warn us off nor anything, and I thought, as I hauled the bo't up on a wave and let the Reverend Mr. Dimmick step out, that it was somethin' gained to be safe ashore. There was a little smoke out o' the chimney o' Joanna's house, and it did look sort of homelike and pleasant with wild mornin'-glory vines trained up; an' there was a plot o' flowers under the front window, portulacas and things. I believe she'd made a garden once, when she was stopping there with her father, and some things must have seeded in. It looked as if she might have gone over to the other side of the island. 'T was neat and pretty all about the house, and a lovely day in July. We walked up from the beach together very sedate, and I felt for poor Nathan's little pin to see if 't was safe in my dress pocket. All of a sudden Joanna come right to the fore door and stood there, not sayin' a word."

CHAPTER 14: THE HERMITAGE

My companions and I had been so intent upon the subject of the conversation that we had not heard any one open the gate, but at this moment, above the noise of the rain, we heard a loud knocking. We were all startled as we sat by the fire, and Mrs. Todd rose hastily and went to answer the call, leaving her rocking-chair in violent motion. Mrs. Fosdick and I heard an anxious voice at the door speaking of a sick child, and Mrs. Todd's kind, motherly voice inviting the messenger in: then we waited in silence. There was a sound of heavy dropping of rain from the eaves, and the distant roar and undertone of the sea. My thoughts flew back to the lonely woman on her outer island; what separation from humankind she must have felt, what terror and sadness, even in a summer storm like this!

"You send right after the doctor if she ain't better in half an hour," said Mrs. Todd to her worried customer as they parted; and I felt a warm sense of comfort in the evident resources of even so small a neighborhood, but for the poor hermit Joanna there was no neighbor on a winter night.

"How did she look?" demanded Mrs. Fosdick, without preface, as our large hostess returned to the little room with a mist about her from standing long in the wet doorway, and the sudden draught of her coming beat out the smoke and flame from the Franklin stove. "How did poor Joanna look?"

"She was the same as ever, except I thought she looked smaller," answered Mrs. Todd after thinking a moment; perhaps it was only a last considering thought about her patient. "Yes, she was just the same, and looked very nice, Joanna did. I had been married since she left home, an' she treated me like her own folks. I expected she'd look strange, with her hair turned gray in a night or somethin', but she wore a pretty gingham dress I'd often seen her wear before she went away; she must have kept it nice for best in the afternoons. She always had beautiful, quiet manners. I remember

she waited till we were close to her, and then kissed me real affectionate, and inquired for Nathan before she shook hands with the minister, and then she invited us both in. 'T was the same little house her father had built him when he was a bachelor, with one livin'-room, and a little mite of a bedroom out of it where she slept, but 't was neat as a ship's cabin. There was some old chairs, an' a seat made of a long box that might have held boat tackle an' things to lock up in his fishin' days, and a good enough stove so anybody could cook and keep warm in cold weather. I went over once from home and stayed 'most a week with Joanna when we was girls, and those young happy days rose up before me. Her father was busy all day fishin' or clammin'; he was one o' the pleasantest men in the world, but Joanna's mother had the grim streak, and never knew what 't was to be happy. The first minute my eyes fell upon Joanna's face that day I saw how she had grown to look like Mis' Todd. 'T was the mother right over again."

"Oh dear me!" said Mrs. Fosdick.

"Joanna had done one thing very pretty. There was a little piece o' swamp on the island where good rushes grew plenty, and she'd gathered 'em, and braided some beautiful mats for the floor and a thick cushion for the long bunk. She'd showed a good deal of invention; you see there was a nice chance to pick up pieces o' wood and boards that drove ashore, and she'd made good use o' what she found. There wasn't no clock, but she had a few dishes on a shelf, and flowers set about in shells fixed to the walls, so it did look sort of homelike, though so lonely and poor. I couldn't keep the tears out o' my eyes, I felt so sad. I said to myself, I must get mother to come over an' see Joanna; the love in mother's heart would warm her, an' she might be able to advise."

"Oh no, Joanna was dreadful stern," said Mrs. Fosdick.

"We were all settin' down very proper, but Joanna would keep stealin' glances at me as if she was glad I come. She had but little to say; she was real polite an' gentle, and yet forbiddin'. The minister found it hard," confessed Mrs. Todd; "he got embarrassed, an' when he put on his authority and asked her if she felt to enjoy religion in her present situation, an' she replied that she must be excused from answerin', I thought I should fly. She might have made it easier for him; after all, he was the minister and had taken some trouble to come out, though 't was kind of cold an' unfeelin' the way he inquired. I thought he might have seen the little old Bible a-layin' on the shelf close by him, an' I wished he knew enough to just lay his hand on it an' read somethin' kind an' fatherly 'stead of accusin' her, an' then given poor Joanna his blessin' with the hope she might be led to comfort. He did offer prayer, but 't was all about hearin' the voice o' God out o' the whirlwind; and I thought while he was goin' on that anybody that had spent the long cold winter all alone out on Shell-heap Island knew a good deal more about those things than he did. I got so provoked I opened my eyes and stared right at him.

"She didn't take no notice, she kep' a nice respectful manner towards him, and when there come a pause she asked if he had any interest about the old Indian remains, and took down some queer stone gouges and hammers off of one of her shelves and showed them to him same's if he was a boy. He remarked that he'd like to walk over an' see the shell-heap; so she went right to the door and pointed him the way. I see then that she'd made her some kind o' sandal-shoes out o' the fine rushes to wear on her feet; she stepped light an' nice in 'em as shoes."

Mrs. Fosdick leaned back in her rocking-chair and gave a heavy sigh.

"I didn't move at first, but I'd held out just as long as I could," said Mrs. Todd, whose voice trembled a little. "When Joanna returned from the door, an' I could see that man's stupid back departin' among the wild rose bushes, I just ran to her an' caught her in my arms. I wasn't so big as I be now, and she was older than me, but I hugged her tight, just as if she was a child. 'Oh, Joanna dear,' I says, 'won't you come ashore an' live 'long o' me at the Landin', or go over to Green Island to mother's when winter comes? Nobody shall trouble you, an' mother finds it hard bein' alone. I can't bear to leave you here'—and I burst right out crying. I'd had my own trials, young as I was, an' she knew it. Oh, I did entreat her; yes, I entreated Joanna."

"What did she say then?" asked Mrs. Fosdick, much moved.

"She looked the same way, sad an' remote through it all," said Mrs. Todd mournfully. "She took hold of my hand, and we sat down close together; 't was as if she turned round an' made a child of me. 'I haven't got no right to live with folks no more,' she said. 'You must never ask me again, Almiry: I've done the only thing I could do, and I've made my choice. I feel a great comfort in your kindness, but I don't deserve it. I have committed the unpardonable sin; you don't understand,' says she humbly. 'I was in great wrath and trouble, and my thoughts was so wicked towards God that I can't expect ever to be forgiven. I have come to know what it is to have patience, but I have lost my hope. You must tell those that ask how 'tis with me,' she said, 'an' tell them I want to be alone.' I couldn't speak; no, there wa'n't anything I could say, she seemed so above everything common. I was a good deal younger then than I be now, and I got Nathan's little coral pin out o' my pocket and put it into her hand; and when she saw it and I told her where it come from, her face did really light up for a minute, sort of bright an' pleasant. 'Nathan an' I was always good friends; I'm glad he don't think hard of me,' says she. 'I want you to have it, Almiry, an' wear it for love o' both o' us,' and she handed it back to me. 'You give my love to Nathan,—he's a dear good man,' she said; 'an' tell your mother, if I should be sick she mustn't wish I could get well, but I want her to be the one to come.' Then she seemed to have said all she wanted to, as if she was done with the world, and we sat there a few minutes longer together. It was real sweet and quiet except for a good many birds and the sea rollin' up on the beach; but at last she rose, an' I did too, and she kissed me and held my hand in hers a minute, as if to say good-by; then she turned and went right away out o' the door and disappeared."

EDITH WHARTON (1862–1937)

Edith Wharton's long life seems the longer because of the profound changes that occurred during that span of time, not only in America but in the entire Western world. She was born during the Civil War and grew up amid the sedate confines of that small segment of upper-middle-class New York society—"the good old families"—that was the nearest thing to an aristocracy that New York would know. She saw that society overcome by the "new breed" of millionaires—the Astors, Vanderbilts, Morgans, and others—and the long lines of decorous, indistinguishable brownstone houses displaced by the ornate, bulging homes of the newly rich. She was born in the first year of the Civil War. In her youth she drove about in horse-drawn carriages or, in Newport during the summer, in a dogcart; but she was one of the first American women to own a motor car—the first in a series of ever more splendid motor cars; and from her Paris window in 1914 she watched the first military aeroplane circling over the city.

Geographically, Mrs. Wharton's life was not much less far-flung. Just as her old New York gradually sank without trace—to be given a kind of permanent resurrection in her novels and stories—so the rustic and enchanting Newport of her youth slowly gave way to the Gilded Age of the enormous "cottages" the Astors and others had built for them, often by that architect of uncertain genius, Richard Morris Hunt. At this stage, about the turn of the century, she fled Newport and built a sizable "cottage" of her own in the Berkshires, near Lenox, Massachusetts. But meanwhile Europe had been, as she put it, ineradicably in her blood almost since infancy. Before she was five, she had gone abroad with her parents for a stay of six years; when she was eighteen she again went abroad, for two years, and after her marriage to Edward Robbins Wharton of Boston in 1885, she spent part of every year on the continent. Italy was her first love; but in the course of time she was more and more drawn to Paris, and she settled there in 1907, in the old Faubourg St. Germain on the Left Bank. Here, surrounded by princesses and duchesses, novelists and painters and historians, she remained until 1920—returning every summer, until 1911, to her home in Lenox. In 1920, she acquired a villa at St. Brice, outside of Paris, and at Hyères, on the southern coast of France, and these were her homes until her death.

Edith Wharton's fiction derives in considerable part from these experiences—old New York society always in motion, always subtly realigning itself, New York as she lived in it, and then as she looked at it from across the Atlantic and across the (for her) unbridgeable abyss of the First World War; the significant contrasts between the habits, expectancies, and the sense of moral commitment in European and American society. She is the finest social historian in American literature; and if she lacked that clear perception of the timeless issues at work in social conflict, which was the special gift of her friend Henry James, she was more keenly observant of social actualities as they stirred and reformed, so to speak, before her eyes. In her handling of these matters, she was aided by a talent almost equal to that of James for the manipulation of *place*—for presenting a scene or setting, the interior of a brownstone, a mansion on the Hudson, a bleak village near Lenox, the estate of a French nobleman, as a palpable moral and dramatic reality. Her great theme was the interplay between closely examined and expertly described social change and the troubled, or the impoverished, individual life.

Edith Wharton's own personal life was troubled enough, though she was scarcely impoverished, financially speaking. Despite the material comfort of her youth and the huge financial as well as critical success of her fiction from 1905 on—despite the big house in Lenox, the apartments in Paris, the later villas with their magnificent landscaping and their nineteen servants —she was, as someone said about her, a soul in pain. Not that a sense of humor was absent in her: no one liked a good joke (even if it might contain what the French call "les gros mots") more than she did, and her ready, full-throated laughter was a familiar sound to her intimate friends. But the stiff, even chilly exterior she presented to the world, and which alarmed and repelled certain strangers, concealed a sometimes agonizing shyness (into which we may read a disturbing uncertainty as to role and posture) and a nature a little hardened by the long effort at self-control.

Her childhood had been a lonely one. Her

brothers were, respectively, sixteen and twelve years older than she (this was one of the reasons for the apparently false rumor that she was illegitimate, and the daughter in fact of her brothers' young English tutor). Her father, George Frederic Jones, was a kindly but harried and rather baffled man; and from adolescence on, her relations with her mother, the former Lucretia Rhinelander—whose main interest was the annual trunk of new clothes from Paris and the almost daily small dinner party—were cool and distant. Her strong literary enthusiasms, which began at a very young age, puzzled her family and their circle of anti-intellectual and unimaginative friends. When she was twenty, she was briefly engaged to an attractive young man of great expectations (his name was Harry Stevens); but the boy's mother, a commanding figure of the new social breed, was offended by the snubbing she received from Edith's relatives among the good old families, and at her insistence Edith broke the engagement off.

She was then very much drawn to a young law student named Walter Van Rensselaer Berry. Berry remained her close friend and literary mentor until his death in 1927; but neither before her marriage nor after her divorce could he bring himself to ask her to marry him; most of Mrs. Wharton's friends disliked Berry and thought he had a repressive influence upon her. Her marriage to the Bostonian Edward Wharton, an older man of good family and no vocation, was a mistake—not quite the "utterly inconceivable thing" that Henry James would call it, but unfortunate nonetheless.

Edith Wharton began publishing fiction in 1891, and by 1894 her editor at Scribner's was proposing that she put together a volume of short stories—a suggestion which paradoxically contributed to a nervous breakdown. The tensions arising from enforced proximity to her husband, the demands upon her as a busy and efficient hostess, and an uncertainty about her commitment to the creative life were too much for her. It was more than two years before she recovered from this collapse, and she could not be pronounced a healthy woman until she

moved to Lenox in 1902. By this time Teddy Wharton had undergone several breakdowns of his own; he developed symptoms of manic depression which grew steadily worse over the years; and in 1913, after trying hard to hold the marriage together despite Teddy's exceedingly bizarre and possibly vengeful behavior (it took the form of embezzlement and flagrant infidelity), Edith divorced him on grounds of adultery.

How all this affected a woman of Edith Wharton's nature and background was indicated clearly enough in an article she wrote about George Eliot in the spring of 1902. There was, to begin with, the fact of *being* a woman. George Eliot, she observed, had been rebuked for maintaining philosophic and scientific interests of the sort that male intellectuals were praised for having; Mrs. Wharton was aware that her own increasingly high literary ambitions had made her an alien in the only social world she knew. More than that, George Eliot's best fiction sprang from the severe conflict between her moral beliefs and "her personal situation"—her long illicit relationship with George Henry Lewes. The English novelist was "a conservative in ethics," who felt "a deep reverence for the family ties, for the sanctities of tradition," and her characters "shrink with a peculiar dread from any personal happiness acquired at the cost of the social organism; yet her own happiness was acquired at such a cost." In 1902, Edith Wharton had not yet disturbed the social organism, though she would eventually do so; but her instincts and emotions were already urging her to, and against all the force of *her* moral conservatism and her devotion to family ties and the sanctities of tradition.

It is therefore hardly surprising that her fiction should deal so largely with the vicissitudes and dissatisfactions of marriage, the moral challenge of adultery, illegitimacy, the passionate question never asked, the erotic strategy that failed, the fatally bad timing that destroys the hopes of lovers: in short, with almost every variety of the socially defined private relation between men and women in a carefully circumscribed American social set. It is not perhaps a

very broad area for the imagination to work in. But like other literary artists, Edith Wharton knew how to exploit her limitations and to make much out of relatively little. The power of her best work, moreover, arises from her settled belief that moral commitment was absolute, and that to violate it—much as one, nearly by consequence, yearned to—was to endanger the whole fabric of society, perhaps even of civilization. The pathos in her work arises from her parallel conviction that society was all there was. Unlike many of her American predecessors (Hawthorne, Melville, Mark Twain), Edith Wharton could not envisage an alternative to the socially bounded life she knew. One might dream of such a "world elsewhere," but to do so was quite misleading and invited emotional disaster.

Edith Wharton's first work of fiction was a volume of short stories, *The Greater Inclination*, published in 1899, when she was nearly thirty-eight years old. Before her breakdown five years before, she had already settled on a professional writing career, and had in fact written almost enough stories to compose a volume; she did not, therefore, as legend has had it, turn to writing *after* her illness and as a mode of therapy. The stories in *The Greater Inclination* are remarkably good (especially the unhappily titled "Souls Belated" and "The Pelican"), and they were well received. There followed another volume of stories in 1901, and two novellas. Then, in 1902, came a long and most handsomely written historical romance, *The Valley of Decision*, set within the political stirrings and courtly life of eighteenth-century Italy; the central characters are stiff and stylized, but as the portrait of a little known epoch it is probably unmatched in American fiction.

From England, Henry James wrote a long appreciative letter about *The Valley of Decision*, but added with an intense and earnest sincerity his desire

> to admonish you . . . in favour of the *American Subject*. There it is round you. Don't pass it by—the immediate, the real, the one

that's yours, the novelist that it waits for. Take hold of it, and keep hold, and let it pull you where it will. . . . Profit, be warned by my awful example of exile and ignorance. . . . *Do New York!* The 1st hand account is precious.

In similar words, a decade earlier, William Dean Howells had admonished Henry B. Fuller, in effect, to "do Chicago," after Fuller had published two romances set in Italy and France; and in the wake of his own book about Venice, Howells had himself been summoned back to the American subject by Henry James. The importunities to what James, thinking about the French, once (in 1865) called "the famous realistic system" were thus passed along from writer to writer. James's letter contained the best literary advice Edith Wharton ever received, and she proceeded promptly to follow it.[1] In 1905, she produced *The House of Mirth*, in which she "did" New York—that fragment of it that she knew at first hand—with such fullness and vitality that the novel became an immediate critical and commercial success. It sold over 140,000 copies in the first year and a half of its life; and Edith Wharton was, suddenly, a famous American writer.

The House of Mirth is the story of the last phases in the life of young Lily Bart, a relatively impoverished and singularly attractive member of New York society who cannot bring herself to accept any of the coarse or mindless millionaires who pursue her, but also cannot accept the somewhat shabby existence offered by the intelligent and devoted Lawrence Selden. It is Selden who speaks for "the republic of the spirit," an ideal little community of spiritually harmonious persons; but though this appeals strongly to one side of Lily Bart's character, her lust for material comfort prevents her from seeking to enter it with Selden (nor, one imagines, could Mrs. Wharton herself have opted for it on the terms proposed). Lily's hopelessly

[1] It corresponded with her own inclinations. By the time she received it she was well along on a promising novel set mainly in New York. But she abandoned the story, for reasons not wholly clear.

mixed motives lead her from one unfortunate situation to another; and eventually (the timing is characteristic of Edith Wharton's fiction), just as Selden is hurrying to ask her once and for all to marry him, she dies, possibly though not certainly a suicide, from an overdose of a sleeping draught. Women across America sent each other lachrymose cables when the final installment of the novel appeared in *Scribner's*; and though one or two genteel academics murmured that good fiction could never arise from the figure of a woman of doubtful virtue, Edith Wharton's reputation was established.

Over the next thirty-two years, Mrs. Wharton published fourteen more novels, eight volumes of short stories and novellas, two books of poetry (Tennysonian, Browningesque, and uneven, with a few passionately complex gems), and several highly superior "travel books." Her most widely read work was her novel *Ethan Frome*, which she wrote in Paris over about three months from late 1910 to March, 1911. It began as a short story and grew to a 45,000-word novella; and it amused her (as, with habitual self-deprecation, she wrote her good friend, the art historian Bernard Berenson) to sketch the story's setting—bleak little Starkfield, Massachusetts, a remote and dreary village like several she had seen on excursions from Lenox— amid the sumptuous furnishings of her apartment in the Faubourg St. Germain. *Ethan Frome*, for all its grim rusticity and its starved life, is entirely consonant with the vision of human experience that informs Mrs. Wharton's stories of New York and Parisian society. Its theme, as Blake Nevius has remarked in his study of Edith Wharton's fiction, is much the same as that of *The Custom of the Country* and all the other of Mrs. Wharton's best work. It deals with the trapped sensibility, the psychological enslavement of a larger and more generously imaginative character by a smaller and meaner-minded personality; in the case of Ethan Frome, by two such inferior persons, Zeena Frome and Mattie Silver. Never did Edith Wharton's art exact such richness of effect from such meager and intractable materials as in this story whose major crisis springs from, of all

things, a smashed pickle plate; and nowhere is there a more somber display of Mrs. Wharton's almost gruesome interest in the endless years of expiation which, she believed, inevitably resulted from the attempted violation of the moral code.

Edith Wharton's best single work, however, is probably *The Custom of the Country*, which she wrote at fitful intervals during her years of greatest excitement and tribulation, between 1908 and 1913.[2] It is the account of the beautiful and predatory Undine Spragg, and her course through a series of marital relationships. What gives the novel a breadth of suggestion beyond any other that Edith Wharton wrote is that Undine's career of marital wreckage (one husband becomes a suicide, another ends with bewildered fury in a French divorce court) is paralleled by the buccaneering financial career of Elmer Moffatt, her first and fourth husband. The two careers combine like elements in a vast metaphor: a metaphor about the deepest and the strangely similar forces—sex and business— at work to shake and transform the world of American society. And although many readers have felt that *The Custom of the Country* is marred by Mrs. Wharton's hatred of her heroine, a careful look at the novel can lead to the belief that Undine is not altogether to blame for what happens around her, that she is envisioned as the product, even in part the victim, of the society through which she moves like a tornado.

Edith Wharton was an imposing figure in New York and Newport society in her early mature years, and in Paris and London society in her middle years; but she really preferred her "inner circle" of friends, and gradually withdrew into it. She saw something of the avantgarde writer Jean Cocteau before the First

---

[2] James preferred *The Reef* (1912), on the grounds that, so he claimed, it had a structural unity worthy of a play by Racine. It was an odd contention, since what *The Reef* most obviously suffers from is a structural uncertainty at its beginning and its ending. Edith Wharton herself could not stand the thought of the novel once it was published.

World War, and delighted in him; during the war years she had several friendly transactions with André Gide; she was for a time a frequenter of the salons in the old Faubourg, and consorted there with various men and women of letters now mostly forgotten. But her circle was mainly Anglo-American. The aging Henry Adams was much at hand, after she settled in Paris; so, a little later, was Geoffrey Scott, the gifted English scholar; and later still, Berenson's protégé, Kenneth Clark. Percy Lubbock, the James disciple and author of *The Craft of Fiction*, was a regular member for many years; after Mrs. Wharton's death, he wrote a superb "portrait" of her. But from 1903 to the outbreak of the war, the most eminent figure in the circle was, of course, Henry James—whom she came over annually from Paris to visit and to inveigle with very little difficulty (and despite James's comically exaggerated trepidations) into long motor rides. James traveled across France with her and spent weeks at a time in her Paris apartment; he adopted a breathless wonder at the sheer pace of her life and enjoyed himself thoroughly.

Yet Edith Wharton was rightly vexed by "the continued cry that I am an echo of Mr. James." Wrongheaded as the charge is, it refuses to die. One way to put it might be that Mrs. Wharton took from James something of his "verse"—drawing, for instance, on his rhetorical devices[3] —but little of his "poetry," that is, his appraisal of human life and his method of rendering it in fiction.

To continue the comparison of the two writers, we may insist that James, in spite of his revolutionary contribution to the development of the modern psychological novel, was far closer than Edith Wharton to the American romance tradition, to Hawthorne especially, and in some small part even to Melville. Edith Wharton, in fact, found Hawthorne overrated; and (as she said in 1911, when nobody else was reading him) she preferred Melville's *Typee*

and his *Omoo*, to *Moby-Dick*, because the latter was "so much less simple and straightaway in style." On the same basis she could criticize the later work of James, failing to appreciate fully the sense of epochal, almost mythic significance with which James could invest the literal world of the wealthy and the expatriated.

Edith Wharton's writing can better be placed on the line that leads from Howells through Fuller to Dreiser and Sinclair Lewis, and on—though here the line blurs a little—to Scott Fitzgerald. She was, in short, a realist, though with a much finer dedication to the *art* of fiction than most of her fellow practitioners. If she also had something of Howells' moral piety, and a lesser dash of Fitzgerald's fascination with the very rich, she was nonetheless shrewd enough to appreciate Dreiser's accomplishment and to declare her admiration for it (however much, as one suspects, she deplored his actual subject matter).

Mrs. Wharton met Howells several times; and after he reestablished his arrangement with Harper's, he wrote her very courteously and respectfully asking if he might publish some of her work. Lewis dedicated *Babbitt* to her and came to lunch several times in Paris (Mrs. Wharton admired him, but wished he did not drink quite so much); and Fitzgerald reverentially called on her at St. Brice in 1923, but was so nervous that he arrived more than a little drunk and blurted out something about having spent the previous night, with his wife Zelda, in a French bordello (*"Awful!"* Edith Wharton wrote in her diary that evening).[4] But the point is that Mrs. Wharton shared with all three a deep concern for the carefully observed and the minutely described realities of American social life and social change.

---

[3] She also, on occasion, borrowed his proper names: the name Newbold Archer, for example, conjoins the names Isabel Archer (*The Portrait of a Lady*) and Christopher Newman (*The American*).

[4] Accounts differ about this frequently described encounter, but it seems fairly clear that Fitzgerald's remark about the bordello did not have the shock effect intended. Apparently Edith Wharton simply gazed at him in her most imperious manner and after a pause asked: "But you haven't told us what you did in the bordello!" Fitzgerald is reported to have said later, almost in tears, to Zelda: "She beat me! She beat me!"

Edith Wharton's America was, to be sure, not that of Howells or Lewis, though it had something ambiguously in common with that of Fitzgerald. But she shared with all three a compelling concern for the closely inspected and the meticulously described actualities of social life and social change on the American scene; like them all, she had the sense of possibilities denied and aspiration quenched in American society, of forces that seemed to encourage but actually thwarted. Howells initially took a friendlier view than she of American life, though after the Haymarket riot in 1886 he became, as we have seen, conscious of a perhaps ineradicable ugliness in it; Fitzgerald could imagine, more powerfully than any of the others, a life more romantic and attractive than the one that currently presented itself; Mrs. Wharton, by comparison, resorted to satire, like Sinclair Lewis—with mild nostalgia, as in *The Age of Innocence,* or with a kind of masculine ferocity, as in *The Custom of the Country.* But all four rooted their fiction in finely observed details of manners and dress in a carefully identified place and time, in modes of speech, in the look of streets and houses, in allusions to the music and fiction popular at the moment, in matters they had personally experienced, in a keen sense of the strong undercurrents that were at the moment being portrayed sweeping away or casting up the significant elements of social culture.

Again like Howells and Lewis, though not at all like Scott Fitzgerald, Mrs. Wharton lived on a good many years after she had done her best work and produced a series of generally inferior novels from which her reputation continues to suffer. From the end of the First World War to her death in 1937, she was *at* her best only when she was gazing backward at the old New York of her youth or of her parents' day: in *The Age of Innocence* (which won the Pulitzer prize for fiction in 1920); in the collection of novellas called *Old New York* (1924); in her beautifully written autobiographical memoir *A Backward Glance* (1934), so reticent and so revealing, and with its superb description of the conversational methods of Henry James; and in

The Buccaneers, an unfinished and posthumous work which even in its incomplete stage ranks with her five or six major achievements and is in fact so good that (as Blake Nevius has said) it makes one impatient with the often slack and tuneless potboilers she had brought out in the fifteen odd years preceding.

The Age of Innocence, which deals with certain events in the New York social world of the late 1870's, is usually taken as Mrs. Wharton's most representative novel. If it has a technical flaw, it is that the story is almost too symmetrical in composition; the two halves, almost exactly equal in length, dovetail all too perfectly, and in each Edith Wharton's basic pattern—the effort to escape, the defeat of longing, the return to conformity—is reenacted to an identical rhythm. But as the evocation of an age that, from the vantage point of 1920, seemed nearly as far removed as that of the eighteenth century Italy of *The Valley of Decision,* it is something of a masterpiece. Mrs. Wharton wrote a stream of letters from St. Brice to her sister-in-law in New York asking for precise information as to when so-and-so sang *Faust* at the old Academy of Music, the date of the publication in America of George Eliot's *Middlemarch,* the time it took for train and ferry to convey one in 1877 from Washington to Manhattan. The result is the permanent enshrining of a historic moment. And the story itself, though it lacks the muscularity of *The Custom of the Country* and the pathos of *The House of Mirth* or *Ethan Frome,* reveals more clearly than anywhere else Mrs. Wharton's sense of the painful paradoxes of moral commitment and her sense as well of the fatal gap between the hard fact of one's actual (that is, one's social) life and the "real" and interior life of mind and feeling. The latter, she felt, could never be fully realized, and the former never entirely escaped.[5]

---

[5] Edith Wharton's sense that life offered at best alternative modes of entrapment or defeat brought her oddly close to Dreiser, at least in one of his characteristic moods. This can explain Mrs. Wharton's outspoken and otherwise astonishing admiration for Dreiser.

BIOGRAPHICAL CHART

1862   Born, January 24, in New York City, to George and Lucretia Jones
1878   Privately publishes juvenile *Verses*
1885   Marries Edward Wharton
1889   Publishes first poems in *Scribner's Magazine*
1894   Suffers nervous collapse
1897   *The Decoration of Houses,* together with Ogden Codman
1899   First book of stories, *The Greater Inclination*
1902   First novel, *The Valley of Decision*
1902   Begins friendship with Henry James
1905   *The House of Mirth*
1907   Settles in Paris
1908   Edward Wharton suffers nervous breakdown
1911   *Ethan Frome*

1913   Divorced from Edward Wharton
1913   *The Custom of the Country*
1914–18   Devotes herself to hospital and charity work in wartime France
1917   *Summer*
1920   Awarded Pulitzer prize for *The Age of Innocence*
1923   Receives from Yale University honorary award of Doctor of Letters
1926   *Old New York*
1930   Elected to the American Academy of Arts and Letters
1934   *A Backward Glance*
1937   Dies, August 11, in France

FURTHER READINGS

There is no standard edition of Edith Wharton's works. In addition to the writings cited in the biographical chart, the reader may find the following items useful.

The Edith Wharton Reader (1965; with an introduction by Louis Auchincloss)
R. W. B. Lewis, ed., *The Collected Stories of Edith Wharton* (2 vols. 1968)

Louis Auchincloss, *Edith Wharton: A Woman in Her Time* (1971)

Millicent Bell, *Edith Wharton and Henry James: The Story of Their Friendship* (1965)
Olivia Coolidge, *Edith Wharton: 1862–1937* (1964)
Grace Kellogg, *The Two Lives of Edith Wharton* (1965)
Percy Lubbock, *Portrait of Edith Wharton* (1947)
Blake Nevius, *Edith Wharton: A Study of Her Fiction* (1953)

Note: The first full-scale biography of Edith Wharton is being prepared by R. W. B. Lewis

The Other Two (1904)

In *The Writing of Fiction,* Edith Wharton declared that, while the building and development of character are the province of the novel, "situation is the main concern of the short story." She meant by this, as her own best tales indicate, not that the short story should show us how some particular situation gets itself worked out and resolved, but how it is revealed in all its complexity. "The Other Two" fulfills this intention almost perfectly. It has scarcely any plot and consists rather in the leisurely and coolly comic process by which a situation is gradually disclosed. It is disclosed in particular to Waythorn, his wife's third husband, who finds himself in mysterious but indissoluble league with "the other two."

The story, which is possibly Edith Wharton's best, is also an exemplary little comedy of manners and could serve as a model in any effort to define that genre. Everything is communicated by the exact notation of manners, of dress and gesture and expression—from Haskett's "made-up tie attached with an elastic" and Waythorn's uneasy distaste for it to the final moment when Waythorn, with a wry laugh, accepts the third cup of tea his wife has poured and thereby accepts the situation he has slowly come to understand.

Waythorn, on the drawing-room hearth, waited for his wife to come down to dinner.

It was their first night under his own roof, and he was suprised at his thrill of boyish agitation. He was not so old, to be sure—his glass gave him little more than the five-and-thirty years to which his wife confessed—but he had fancied himself already in the temperate zone; yet here he was listening for her step with a tender sense of all it symbolized, with some old trail of verse about the garlanded nuptial doorposts floating through his enjoyment of the pleasant room and the good dinner just beyond it.

They had been hastily recalled from their honeymoon by the illness of Lily Haskett, the child of Mrs. Waythorn's first marriage. The little girl, at Waythorn's desire, had been transferred to his house on the day of her mother's wedding, and the doctor, on their arrival, broke the news that she was ill with typhoid, but declared that all the symptoms were favorable. Lily could show twelve years of unblemished health, and the case promised to be a light one. The nurse spoke as reassuringly, and after a moment of alarm Mrs. Waythorn had adjusted herself to the situation. She was very fond of Lily—her affection for the child had perhaps been her decisive charm in Waythorn's eyes—but she had the perfectly balanced nerves which her little girl had inherited, and no woman ever wasted less tissue in unproductive worry. Waythorn was therefore quite prepared to see her come in presently, a little late because of a last look at Lily, but as serene and well-appointed as if her goodnight kiss had been laid on the brow of health. Her composure was restful to him; it acted as ballast to his somewhat unstable sensibilities. As he pictured her bending over the child's bed he thought how soothing her presence must be in illness: her very step would prognosticate recovery.

His own life had been a gray one, from temperament rather than circumstance, and he had been drawn to her by the unperturbed gaiety which kept her fresh and elastic at an age when most women's activities are growing either slack or febrile. He knew what was said about her; for, popular as she was, there had always been a faint undercurrent of detraction. When she had appeared in New York, nine or ten years earlier, as the pretty Mrs. Haskett whom Gus Varick had unearthed somewhere—was it in Pittsburgh or Utica?—society, while promptly accepting her, had reserved the right to cast a doubt on its own indiscrimination. Inquiry, however, established her undoubted connection with a socially reigning family, and explained her recent divorce as the natural result of a runaway match at seventeen; and as nothing was known of Mr. Haskett it was easy to believe the worst of him.

Alice Haskett's remarriage with Gus Varick was a passport to the set whose recognition she coveted, and for a few years the Varicks were the most popular couple in town. Unfortunately the alliance was brief and stormy, and this time the husband had his champions. Still, even Varick's stanchest supporters admitted that he was not meant for matrimony, and Mrs. Varick's grievances were of a nature to bear the inspection of the New York courts. A New York divorce is in itself a diploma of virtue, and in the semiwidowhood of this second separation Mrs. Varick took on an air of sanctity, and was allowed to confide her wrongs to some of the most scrupulous ears in town. But when it was known that she was to marry Waythorn there was a momentary reaction. Her best friends would have preferred to see her remain in the role of the injured wife, which was as becoming to her as crepe to a rosy complexion. True, a decent time had elapsed, and it was not even suggested that Waythorn had supplanted his predecessor. People shook their heads over him, however, and one grudging friend, to whom he affirmed that he took the step with his eyes open, replied oracularly: "Yes—and with your ears shut."

Waythorn could afford to smile at these innuendoes. In the Wall Street phrase, he had "discounted" them. He knew that society has not yet adapted itself to the consequences of divorce, and that till the adaptation takes place every woman who uses the freedom the law accords her must be her own social justification. Waythorn had an amused confidence in his wife's ability to justify herself. His expectations were fulfilled, and before the wedding took place Alice Varick's group had rallied openly to her support. She took it all imperturbably: she had a way of surmounting obstacles without seeming to be aware of them, and Waythorn looked back with wonder at the trivialities over which he had worn his nerves thin. He had the sense of having found refuge in a richer, warmer nature than his own, and his satisfaction, at the moment, was humorously summed up in the thought that his wife, when she had done all she could for Lily, would not be ashamed to come down and enjoy a good dinner.

The anticipation of such enjoyment was not, however, the sentiment expressed by Mrs. Waythorn's charming face when she presently joined him. Though she had put on her most engaging tea gown she had neglected to assume the smile that went with it, and Waythorn thought he had never seen her look so nearly worried.

"What is it?" he asked. "Is anything wrong with Lily?"

"No; I've just been in and she's still sleeping." Mrs. Waythorn hesitated. "But something tiresome has happened."

He had taken her two hands, and now perceived that he was crushing a paper between them.

"This letter?"

"Yes—Mr. Haskett has written—I mean his lawyer has written."

Waythorn felt himself flush uncomfortably. He dropped his wife's hands.

"What about?"

"About seeing Lily. You know the courts—"

"Yes, yes," he interrupted nervously.

Nothing was known about Haskett in New York. He was vaguely supposed to have remained in the outer darkness from which his wife had been rescued, and Waythorn was one of the few who were aware that he had given up his business in Utica and followed her to New York in order to be near his little girl. In the days of his wooing, Waythorn had often met Lily on the doorstep, rosy and smiling, on her way "to see papa."

"I am so sorry," Mrs. Waythorn murmured.

He roused himself. "What does he want?"

"He wants to see her. You know she goes to him once a week."

"Well—he doesn't expect her to go to him now, does he?"

"No—he has heard of her illness; but he expects to come here."

"*Here?*"

Mrs. Waythorn reddened under his gaze. They looked away from each other.

"I'm afraid he has the right. . . . You'll see. . . ." She made a proffer of the letter.

Waythorn moved away with a gesture of refusal. He stood staring about the softly-lighted room, which a moment before had seemed so full of bridal intimacy.

"I'm so sorry," she repeated. "If Lily could have been moved—"

"That's out of the question," he returned impatiently.

"I suppose so."

Her lip was beginning to tremble, and he felt himself a brute.

"He must come, of course," he said. "When is —his day?"

"I'm afraid—tomorrow."

"Very well. Send a note in the morning."

The butler entered to announce dinner.

Waythorn turned to his wife. "Come—you must be tired. It's beastly, but try to forget about it," he said, drawing her hand through his arm.

"You're so good, dear. I'll try," she whispered back.

Her face cleared at once, and as she looked at him across the flowers, between the rosy candle-shades, he saw her lips waver back into a smile.

"How pretty everything is!" she sighed luxuriously.

He turned to the butler. "The champagne at once, please. Mrs. Waythorn is tired."

In a moment or two their eyes met above the sparkling glasses. Her own were quite clear and untroubled: he saw that she had obeyed his injunction and forgotten.

II

Waythorn, the next morning, went downtown earlier than usual. Haskett was not likely to come till the afternoon, but the instinct of flight drove him forth. He meant to stay away all day—he had thoughts of dining at his club. As his door closed behind him he reflected that before he opened it again it would have admitted another man who had as much right to enter it as himself, and the thought filled him with a physical repugnance.

He caught the elevated at the employees' hour, and found himself crushed between two layers of pendulous humanity. At Eighth Street the man facing him wriggled out, and another took his place. Waythorn glanced up and saw that it was Gus Varick. The men were so close together that it was impossible to ignore the smile of recognition on Varick's handsome overblown face. And after all—why not? They had always been on good terms, and Varick had been divorced before Waythorn's attentions to his wife began. The two exchanged a word on the perennial grievance of the congested trains, and when a seat at their side was miraculously left empty the instinct of self-preservation made Waythorn slip into it after Varick.

The latter drew the stout man's breath of relief. "Lord—I was beginning to feel like a pressed flower." He leaned back, looking unconcernedly at Waythorn. "Sorry to hear that Sellers is knocked out again."

"Sellers?" echoed Waythorn, starting at his partner's name.

Varick looked surprised. "You didn't know he was laid up with the gout?"

"No. I've been away—I only got back last night." Waythorn felt himself reddening in anticipation of the other's smile.

"Ah—yes; to be sure. And Sellers' attack came on two days ago. I'm afraid he's pretty bad. Very awkward for me, as it happens, because he was just putting through a rather important thing for me."

"Ah?" Waythorn wondered vaguely since when Varick had been dealing in "important things." Hitherto he had dabbled only in the shallow pools of speculation, with which Waythorn's office did not usually concern itself.

It occurred to him that Varick might be talking at random, to relieve the strain of their propinquity. That strain was becoming momentarily more apparent to Waythorn, and when, at Cortlandt Street, he caught sight of an acquaintance and had a sudden vision of the picture he and Varick must present to an initiated eye, he jumped up with a muttered excuse.

"I hope you'll find Sellers better," said Varick civilly, and he stammered back: "If I can be of any use to you—" and let the departing crowd sweep him to the platform.

At his office he heard that Sellers was in fact ill with the gout, and would probably not be able to leave the house for some weeks.

"I'm sorry it should have happened so, Mr. Waythorn," the senior clerk said with affable significance. "Mr. Sellers was very much upset at the idea of giving you such a lot of extra work just now."

"Oh, that's no matter," said Waythorn hastily. He secretly welcomed the pressure of additional business, and was glad to think that, when the day's work was over, he would have to call at his partner's on the way home.

He was late for luncheon, and turned in at the nearest restaurant instead of going to his club. The place was full, and the waiter hurried him to the back of the room to capture the only vacant table. In the cloud of cigar smoke Waythorn did not at once distinguish his neighbors: but presently, looking about him, he saw Varick seated a few feet off.

This time, luckily, they were too far apart for conversation, and Varick, who faced another way, had probably not even seen him; but there was an irony in their renewed nearness.

Varick was said to be fond of good living, and as Waythorn sat dispatching his hurried luncheon he looked across half enviously at the other's leisurely degustation of his meal. When Waythorn first saw him he had been helping himself with critical deliberation to a bit of Camembert at the ideal point of liquefaction, and now, the cheese removed, he was just pouring his *café double* from its little two-storied earthen pot. He poured slowly, his ruddy profile bent over the task, and one beringed white hand steadying the lid of the coffeepot; then he stretched his other hand to the decanter of cognac at his elbow, filled a liqueur glass, took a tentative sip, and poured the brandy into his coffee cup.

Waythorn watched him in a kind of fascination. What was he thinking of—only of the flavor of the coffee and the liqueur? Had the morning's meeting left no more trace in his thoughts than on his face? Had his wife so completely passed out of his life that even this odd encounter with her present husband, within a week after her remarriage, was no more than an incident in his day? And as Waythorn mused, another idea struck him: had Haskett ever met Varick as Varick and he had just met? The recollection of Haskett perturbed him, and he rose and left the restaurant, taking a circuitous way out to escape the placid irony of Varick's nod.

It was after seven when Waythorn reached home. He thought the footman who opened the door looked at him oddly.

"How is Miss Lily?" he asked in haste.

"Doing very well, sir. A gentleman—"

"Tell Barlow to put off dinner for half an hour," Waythorn cut him off, hurrying upstairs.

He went straight to his room and dressed without seeing his wife. When he reached the drawing room she was there, fresh and radiant. Lily's day had been good; the doctor was not coming back that evening.

At dinner Waythorn told her of Seller's illness and of the resulting complications. She listened sympathetically, adjuring him not to let himself be overworked, and asking vague feminine questions about the routine of the office. Then she gave him the chronicle of Lily's day; quoted the nurse and doctor, and told him who had called to inquire. He had never seen her more serene and unruffled. It struck him, with a curious pang, that she was very happy in being with him, so happy that she found a childish pleasure in rehearsing the trivial incidents of her day.

After dinner they went to the library, and the servant put the coffee and liqueurs on a low table before her and left the room. She looked singularly soft and girlish in her rosy-pale dress, against the dark leather of one of his bachelor armchairs. A day earlier the contrast would have charmed him.

He turned away now, choosing a cigar with affected deliberation.

"Did Haskett come?" he asked, with his back to her.

"Oh, yes—he came."

"You didn't see him, of course?"

She hesitated a moment. "I let the nurse see him."

That was all. There was nothing more to ask. He swung round toward her, applying a match to his cigar. Well, the thing was over for a week, at any rate. He would try not to think of it. She looked up at him, a trifle rosier than usual, with a smile in her eyes.

"Ready for your coffee, dear?"

He leaned against the mantelpiece, watching her as she lifted the coffeepot. The lamplight struck a gleam from her bracelets and tipped her soft hair with brightness. How light and slender she was, and how each gesture flowed into the next! She seemed a creature all compact of harmonies. As the thought of Haskett receded, Waythorn felt himself yielding again to the joy of possessorship. They were his, those white hands with their flitting motions, his the light haze of hair, the lips and eyes. . . .

She set down the coffeepot, and reaching for the decanter of cognac, measured off a liqueur glass and poured it into his cup.

Waythorn uttered a sudden exclamation.

"What is the matter?" she said, startled.

"Nothing; only—I don't take cognac in my coffee."

"Oh, how stupid of me," she cried.

Their eyes met, and she blushed a sudden agonized red.

III

Ten days later, Mr. Sellers, still housebound, asked Waythorn to call on his way downtown.

The senior partner, with his swaddled foot propped up by the fire, greeted his associate with an air of embarrassment.

"I'm sorry, my dear fellow; I've got to ask you to do an awkward thing for me."

Waythorn waited, and the other went on, after a pause apparently given to the arrangement of his phrases: "The fact is, when I was knocked out I had just gone into a rather complicated piece of business for—Gus Varick."

"Well?" said Waythorn, with an attempt to put him at his ease.

"Well—it's this way: Varick came to me the day before my attack. He had evidently had an inside tip from somebody, and had made about a hundred thousand. He came to me for advice, and I suggested his going in with Vanderlyn."

"Oh, the deuce!" Waythorn exclaimed. He saw in a flash what had happened. The investment was an alluring one, but required negotiation. He listened quietly while Sellers put the case before him, and, the statement ended, he said: "You think I ought to see Varick?"

"I'm afraid I can't as yet. The doctor is obdurate. And this thing can't wait. I hate to ask you, but no one else in the office knows the ins and outs of it."

Waythorn stood silent. He did not care a farthing for the success of Varick's venture, but the honor of the office was to be considered, and he could hardly refuse to oblige his partner.

"Very well," he said, "I'll do it."

That afternoon, apprised by telephone, Varick called at the office. Waythorn, waiting in his private room, wondered what the others thought of it. The newspapers, at the time of Mrs. Waythorn's marriage, had acquainted their readers with every detail of her previous matrimonial ventures, and Waythorn could fancy the clerks smiling behind Varick's back as he was ushered in.

Varick bore himself admirably. He was easy without being undignified, and Waythorn was conscious of cutting a much less impressive figure. Varick had no experience of business, and the talk prolonged itself for nearly an hour while Waythorn set forth with scrupulous precision the details of the proposed transaction.

"I'm awfully obliged to you," Varick said as he rose. "The fact is I'm not used to having much money to look after, and I don't want to make an ass of myself—" He smiled, and Waythorn could not help noticing that there was something pleasant about his smile. "It feels uncommonly queer to have enough cash to pay one's bills. I'd have sold my soul for it a few years ago!"

Waythorn winced at the allusion. He had heard it rumored that a lack of funds had been one of the determining causes of the Varick separation, but it did not occur to him that Varick's words were intentional. It seemed more likely that the desire to keep clear of embarrassing topics had fatally drawn him into one. Waythorn did not wish to be outdone in civility.

"We'll do the best we can for you," he said. "I think this is a good thing you're in."

"Oh, I'm sure it's immense. It's awfully good of you—" Varick broke off, embarrassed. "I suppose the thing's settled now—but if—"

"If anything happens before Sellers is about, I'll see you again," said Waythorn quietly. He was glad, in the end, to appear the more self-possessed of the two.

The course of Lily's illness ran smooth, and as the days passed Waythorn grew used to the idea of Haskett's weekly visit. The first time the day came round, he stayed out late, and questioned his wife as to the visit on his return. She replied at once that Haskett had merely seen the nurse downstairs, as the doctor did not wish anyone in the child's sickroom till after the crisis.

The following week Waythorn was again conscious of the recurrence of the day, but had forgotten it by the time he came home to dinner. The crisis of the disease came a few days later, with a rapid decline of fever, and the little girl was pronounced out of danger. In the rejoicing which ensued the thought of Haskett passed out of Waythorn's mind, and one afternoon, letting himself into the house with a latchkey, he went straight to his library without noticing a shabby hat and umbrella in the hall.

In the library he found a small effaced-looking man with a thinnish gray beard sitting on the edge of a chair. The stranger might have been a piano tuner, or one of those mysteriously efficient persons who are summoned in emergencies to adjust some detail of the domestic machinery. He blinked at Waythorn through a pair of gold-rimmed spectacles and said mildly: "Mr. Waythorn, I presume? I am Lily's father."

Waythorn flushed. "Oh—" he stammered uncomfortably. He broke off, disliking to appear rude. Inwardly he was trying to adjust the actual Haskett to the image of him projected by his wife's reminis-

cences. Waythorn had been allowed to infer that Alice's first husband was a brute.

"I am sorry to intrude," said Haskett, with his over-the-counter politeness.

"Don't mention it," returned Waythorn, collecting himself. "I suppose the nurse has been told?"

"I presume so. I can wait," said Haskett. He had a resigned way of speaking, as though life had worn down his natural powers of resistance.

Waythorn stood on the threshold, nervously pulling off his gloves.

"I'm sorry you've been detained. I will send for the nurse," he said; and as he opened the door he added with an effort: "I'm glad we can give you a good report of Lily." He winced as the *we* slipped out, but Haskett seemed not to notice it.

"Thank you, Mr. Waythorn, It's been an anxious time for me."

"Ah, well, that's past. Soon she'll be able to go to you." Waythorn nodded and passed out.

In his own room he flung himself down with a groan. He hated the womanish sensibility which made him suffer so acutely from the grotesque chances of life. He had known when he married that his wife's former husbands were both living, and that amid the multiplied contacts of modern existence there were a thousand chances to one that he would run against one or the other, yet he found himself as much disturbed by his brief encounter with Haskett as though the law had not obligingly removed all difficulties in the way of their meeting.

Waythorn sprang up and began to pace the room nervously. He had not suffered half as much from his two meetings with Varick. It was Haskett's presence in his own house that made the situation so intolerable. He stood still, hearing steps in the passage.

"This way, please," he heard the nurse say. Haskett was being taken upstairs, then: not a corner of the house but was open to him. Waythorn dropped into another chair, staring vaguely ahead of him. On his dressing table stood a photograph of Alice, taken when he had first known her. She was Alice Varick then—how fine and exquisite he had thought her! Those were Varick's pearls about her neck. At Waythorn's instance they had been returned before her marriage. Had Haskett ever given her any trinkets—and what had become of them, Waythorn wondered? He realized suddenly that he knew very little of Haskett's past or present situation; but from the man's appearance and manner of speech he could reconstruct with curious precision the surroundings of Alice's first marriage. And it startled him to think that she had, in the background of her life, a phase of existence so different from anything with which he had connected her. Varick, whatever his faults, was a gentleman, in the conventional, traditional sense of the term: the sense which at that moment seemed, oddly enough, to have most meaning to Waythorn. He and Varick had the same social habits, spoke the same language, understood the same allusions. But this other man . . . it was grotesquely uppermost in Waythorn's mind that Haskett had worn a made-up tie attached with an elastic. Why should that ridiculous detail symbolize the whole man? Waythorn was exasperated by his own paltriness, but the fact of the tie expanded, forced itself on him, became as it were the key to Alice's past. He could see her, as Mrs. Haskett, sitting in a "front parlor" furnished in plush, with a pianola, and a copy of *Ben Hur* on the center table. He could see her going to the theater with Haskett—or perhaps even to a "Church Sociable"—she in a "picture hat" and Haskett in a black frock coat, a little creased, with the made-up tie on an elastic. On the way home they would stop and look at the illuminated shop windows, lingering over the photographs of New York actresses. On Sunday afternoons Haskett would take her for a walk, pushing Lily ahead of them in a white enameled perambulator, and Waythorn had a vision of the people they would stop and talk to. He could fancy how pretty Alice must have looked, in a dress adroitly constructed from the hints of a New York fashion paper, and how she must have looked down on the other women, chafing at her life, and secretly feeling that she belonged in a bigger place.

For the moment his foremost thought was one of wonder at the way in which she had shed the phase of existence which her marriage with Haskett implied. It was as if her whole aspect, every gesture, every inflection, every allusion, were a studied negation of that period of her life. If she had denied being married to Haskett she could hardly have stood more convicted of duplicity than in this obliteration of the self which had been his wife.

Waythorn started up, checking himself in the analysis of her motives. What right had he to create a fantastic effigy of her and then pass judgment on it? She had spoken vaguely of her first marriage as unhappy, had hinted, with becoming reticence, that Haskett had wrought havoc among her young illusions. . . . It was a pity for Way-

thorn's peace of mind that Haskett's very inoffensiveness shed a new light on the nature of those illusions. A man would rather think that his wife has been brutalized by her first husband than that the process has been reversed.

IV

"Mr. Waythorn, I don't like that French governess of Lily's."

Haskett, subdued and apologetic, stood before Waythorn in the library, revolving his shabby hat in his hand.

Waythorn, surprised in his armchair over the evening paper, stared back perplexedly at his visitor.

"You'll excuse my asking to see you," Haskett continued. "But this is my last visit, and I thought if I could have a word with you it would be a better way than writing to Mrs. Waythorn's lawyer."

Waythorn rose uneasily. He did not like the French governess either; but that was irrelevant.

"I am not so sure of that," he returned stiffly; "but since you wish it I will give your message to —my wife." He always hesitated over the possessive pronoun in addressing Haskett.

The latter sighed. "I don't know as that will help much. She didn't like it when I spoke to her."

Waythorn turned red. "When did you see her?" he asked.

"Not since the first day I came to see Lily—right after she was taken sick. I remarked to her then that I didn't like the governess."

Waythorn made no answer. He remembered distinctly that, after that first visit, he had asked his wife if she had seen Haskett. She had lied to him then, but she had respected his wishes since; and the incident cast a curious light on her character. He was sure she would not have seen Haskett that first day if she had divined that Waythorn would object, and the fact that she did not divine it was almost as disagreeable to the latter as the discovery that she had lied to him.

"I don't like the woman," Haskett was repeating with mild persistency. "She ain't straight, Mr. Waythorn—she'll teach the child to be underhand. I've noticed a change in Lily—she's too anxious to please—and she don't always tell the truth. She used to be the straightest child, Mr. Waythorn—" He broke off, his voice a little thick. "Not but what I want her to have a stylish education," he ended.

Waythorn was touched. "I'm sorry, Mr. Haskett; but frankly, I don't quite see what I can do."

Haskett hesitated. Then he laid his hat on the table, and advanced to the hearthrug, on which Waythorn was standing. There was nothing aggressive in his manner, but he had the solemnity of a timid man resolved on a decisive measure.

"There's just one thing you can do, Mr. Waythorn," he said. "You can remind Mrs. Waythorn that, by the decree of the courts, I am entitled to have a voice in Lily's bringing-up." He paused, and went on more deprecatingly: "I'm not the kind to talk about enforcing my rights, Mr. Waythorn. I don't know as I think a man is entitled to rights he hasn't known how to hold on to; but this business of the child is different. I've never let go there—and I never mean to."

The scene left Waythorn deeply shaken. Shamefacedly, in indirect ways, he had been finding out about Haskett; and all that he had learned was favorable. The little man, in order to be near his daughter, had sold out his share in a profitable business in Utica, and accepted a modest clerkship in a New York manufacturing house. He boarded in a shabby street and had few acquaintances. His passion for Lily filled his life. Waythorn felt that this exploration of Haskett was like groping about with a dark lantern in his wife's past; but he saw now that there were recesses his lantern had not explored. He had never inquired into the exact circumstances of his wife's first matrimonial rupture. On the surface all had been fair. It was she who had obtained the divorce, and the court had given her the child. But Waythorn knew how many ambiguities such a verdict might cover. The mere fact that Haskett retained a right over his daughter implied an unsuspected compromise. Waythorn was an idealist. He always refused to recognize unpleasant contingencies till he found himself confronted with them, and then he saw them followed by a spectral train of consequences. His next days were thus haunted, and he determined to try to lay the ghosts by conjuring them up in his wife's presence.

When he repeated Haskett's request a flame of anger passed over her face; but she subdued it instantly and spoke with a slight quiver of outraged motherhood.

"It is very ungentlemanly of him," she said.

The word grated on Waythorn. "That is neither here nor there. It's a bare question of rights."

She murmured: "It's not as if he could ever be a help to Lily—"

Waythorn flushed. This was even less to his taste. "The question is," he repeated, "what authority has he over her?"

She looked downward, twisting herself a little in her seat. "I am willing to see him—I thought you objected," she faltered.

In a flash he understood that she knew the extent of Haskett's claims. Perhaps it was not the first time she had resisted them.

"My objecting has nothing to do with it," he said coldly; "if Haskett has a right to be consulted you must consult him."

She burst into tears, and he saw that she expected him to regard her as a victim.

Haskett did not abuse his rights. Waythorn had felt miserably sure that he would not. But the governess was dismissed, and from time to time the little man demanded an interview with Alice. After the first outburst she accepted the situation with her usual adaptability. Haskett had once reminded Waythorn of the piano tuner, and Mrs. Waythorn, after a month or two, appeared to class him with that domestic familiar. Waythorn could not but respect the father's tenacity. At first he had tried to cultivate the suspicion that Haskett might be "up to" something, that he had an object in securing a foothold in the house. But in his heart Waythorn was sure of Haskett's single-mindedness; he even guessed in the latter a mild contempt for such advantages as his relation with the Waythorns might offer. Haskett's sincerity of purpose made him invulnerable, and his successor had to accept him as a lien on the property.

Mr. Sellers was sent to Europe to recover from his gout, and Varick's affairs hung on Waythorn's hands. The negotiations were prolonged and complicated; they necessitated frequent conferences between the two men, and the interests of the firm forbade Waythorn's suggesting that his client should transfer his business to another office.

Varick appeared well in the transaction. In moments of relaxation his coarse streak appeared, and Waythorn dreaded his geniality; but in the office he was concise and clear-headed, with a flattering deference to Waythorn's judgment. Their business relations being so affably established, it would have been absurd for the two men to ignore each other in society. The first time they met in a drawing room, Varick took up their intercourse in the same easy key, and his hostess' grateful glance obliged Waythorn to respond to it. After that they ran across each other frequently, and one evening at a ball Waythorn, wandering through the remoter rooms, came upon Varick seated beside his wife. She colored a little, and faltered in what she was saying; but Varick nodded to Waythorn without rising, and the latter strolled on.

In the carriage, on the way home, he broke out nervously: "I didn't know you spoke to Varick."

Her voice trembled a little. "It's the first time—he happened to be standing near me; I didn't know what to do. It's so awkward, meeting everywhere—and he said you had been very kind about some business."

"That's different," said Waythorn.

She paused a moment. "I'll do just as you wish," she returned pliantly. "I thought it would be less awkward to speak to him when we meet."

Her pliancy was beginning to sicken him. Had she really no will of her own—no theory about her relation to these men? She had accepted Haskett—did she mean to accept Varick? It was "less awkward," as she had said, and her instinct was to evade difficulties or to circumvent them. With sudden vividness Waythorn saw how the instinct had developed. She was "as easy as an old shoe"—a shoe that too many feet had worn. Her elasticity was the result of tension in too many different directions. Alice Haskett—Alice Varick—Alice Waythorn—she had been each in turn, and had left hanging to each name a little of her privacy, a little of her personality, a little of the inmost self where the unknown god abides.

"Yes—it's better to speak to Varick," said Waythorn wearily.

V

The winter wore on, and society took advantage of the Waythorns' acceptance of Varick. Harassed hostesses were grateful to them for bridging over a social difficulty, and Mrs. Waythorn was held up as a miracle of good taste. Some experimental spirits could not resist the diversion of throwing Varick and his former wife together, and there were those who thought he found a zest in the propinquity. But Mrs. Waythorn's conduct remained irreproachable. She neither avoided Varick nor sought him out. Even Waythorn could not but admit that she had discovered the solution of the newest social problem.

He had married her without giving much thought to that problem. He had fancied that a woman can shed her past like a man. But now he saw that Alice was bound to hers both by the circumstances which forced her into continued relation with it, and by the traces it had left on her nature. With grim irony Waythorn compared himself to a member of a syndicate. He held so many shares in his wife's personality and his predecessors were his partners in the business. If there had been any element of passion in the transaction he would have felt less deteriorated by it. The fact that Alice took her change of husbands like a change of weather reduced the situation to mediocrity. He could have forgiven her for blunders, for excesses; for resisting Haskett, for yielding to Varick; for anything but her acquiescence and her tact. She reminded him of a juggler tossing knives; but the knives were blunt and she knew they would never cut her.

And then, gradually, habit formed a protecting surface for his sensibilities. If he paid for each day's comfort with the small change of his illusions, he grew daily to value the comfort more and set less store upon the coin. He had drifted into a dulling propinquity with Haskett and Varick and he took refuge in the cheap revenge of satirizing the situation. He even began to reckon up the advantages which accrued from it, to ask himself if it were not better to own a third of a wife who knew how to make a man happy than a whole one who had lacked opportunity to acquire the art. For it *was* an art, and made up, like all others, of concessions, eliminations and embellishments; of lights judiciously thrown and shadows skillfully softened. His wife knew exactly how to manage the lights, and he knew exactly to what training she owed her skill. He even tried to trace the source of his obligations, to discriminate between the influences which had combined to produce his domestic happiness: he perceived that Haskett's commonness had made Alice worship good breeding, while Varick's liberal construction of the marriage bond had taught her to value the conjugal virtues; so that he was directly indebted to his predecessors for the devotion which made his life easy if not inspiring.

From this phase he passed into that of complete acceptance. He ceased to satirize himself because time dulled the irony of the situation and the joke lost its humor with its sting. Even the sight of Haskett's hat on the hall table had ceased to touch the springs of epigram. The hat was often seen there now, for it had been decided that it was better for Lily's father to visit her than for the little girl to go to his boardinghouse. Waythorn, having acquiesced in this arrangement, had been surprised to find how little difference it made. Haskett was never obtrusive, and the few visitors who met him on the stairs were unaware of his identity. Waythorn did not know how often he saw Alice, but with himself Haskett was seldom in contact.

One afternoon, however, he learned on entering that Lily's father was waiting to see him. In the library he found Haskett occupying a chair in his usual provisional way. Waythorn always felt grateful to him for not leaning back.

"I hope you'll excuse me, Mr. Waythorn," he said rising. "I wanted to see Mrs. Waythorn about Lily, and your man asked me to wait here till she came in."

"Of course," said Waythorn, remembering that a sudden leak had that morning given over the drawing room to the plumbers.

He opened his cigar case and held it out to his visitor, and Haskett's acceptance seemed to mark a fresh stage in their intercourse. The spring evening was chilly, and Waythorn invited his guest to draw up his chair to the fire. He meant to find an excuse to leave Haskett in a moment; but he was tired and cold, and after all the little man no longer jarred on him.

The two were enclosed in the intimacy of their blended cigar smoke when the door opened and Varick walked into the room. Waythorn rose abruptly. It was the first time that Varick had come to the house, and the surprise of seeing him, combined with the singular inopportuneness of his arrival, gave a new edge to Waythorn's blunted sensibilities. He stared at his visitor without speaking.

Varick seemed too preoccupied to notice his host's embarrassment.

"My dear fellow," he exclaimed in his most expansive tone, "I must apologize for tumbling in on you in this way, but I was too late to catch you downtown, and so I thought—"

He stopped short, catching sight of Haskett, and his sanguine color deepened to a flush which spread vividly under his scant blond hair. But in a moment he recovered himself and nodded slightly. Haskett returned the bow in silence, and Waythorn was still groping for speech when the footman came in carrying a tea table.

The intrusion offered a welcome vent to Waythorn's nerves. "What the deuce are you bringing this here for?" he said sharply.

"I beg your pardon, sir, but the plumbers are still in the drawing room, and Mrs. Waythorn said she would have tea in the library." The footman's

perfectly respectful tone implied a reflection on Waythorn's reasonableness.

"Oh, very well," said the latter resignedly, and the footman proceeded to open the folding tea table and set out its complicated appointments. While this interminable process continued the three men stood motionless, watching it with a fascinated stare, till Waythorn, to break the silence, said to Varick, "Won't you have a cigar?"

He held out the case he had just tendered to Haskett, and Varick helped himself with a smile. Waythorn looked about for a match, and finding none, proffered a light from his own cigar. Haskett, in the background, held his ground mildly, examining his cigar tip now and then, and stepping forward at the right moment to knock its ashes into the fire.

The footman at last withdrew, and Varick immediately began: "If I could just say half a word to you about this business—"

"Certainly," stammered Waythorn; "in the dining room—"

But as he placed his hand on the door it opened from without, and his wife appeared on the threshold.

She came in fresh and smiling, in her street dress and hat, shedding a fragrance from the boa which she loosened in advancing.

"Shall we have tea in here, dear?" she began; and then she caught sight of Varick. Her smile deepened, veiling a slight tremor of surprise.

"Why, how do you do?" she said with a distinct note of pleasure.

As she shook hands with Varick she saw Haskett standing behind him. Her smile faded for a moment, but she recalled it quickly, with a scarcely perceptible side glance at Waythorn.

"How do you do, Mr. Haskett?" she said, and shook hands with him a shade less cordially.

The three men stood awkwardly before her, till Varick, always the most self-possessed, dashed into an explanatory phrase.

"We—I had to see Waythorn a moment on business," he stammered, brick-red from chin to nape.

Haskett stepped forward with his air of mild obstinacy. "I am sorry to intrude; but you appointed five o'clock—" he directed his resigned glance to the timepiece on the mantel.

She swept aside their embarrassment with a charming gesture of hospitality.

"I'm so sorry—I'm always late; but the afternoon was so lovely." She stood drawing off her gloves, propitiatory and graceful, diffusing about her a sense of ease and familiarity in which the situation lost its grotesqueness. "But before talking business," she added brightly, "I'm sure everyone wants a cup of tea."

The Eyes (1916)

Edith Wharton was remarkably skillful as a writer of ghost stories, and some of her most memorable achievements are in this genre— among them "Kerfol," "Mr. Jones," "Pomegranate Seed," and "The Eyes." These are first-class yarns in their own right and a delight for the *aficionado* of the uncanny and the supernatural. But they also seem to spring from some out-of-the-way corner of Mrs. Wharton's imagination untapped by her fiction about New York and European society. It is here that her lifelong fascination with violence is allowed to have its way; but it is also here, and here only, that one can detect her deeply repressed intuitions about sexual violence and perversion. Like other writers of Victorian temperament, she could write of these things only by setting them off at a temporal or psychological or so to speak a metaphysical distance—as bestirring themselves within the safely remote or the fantastic.

"The Eyes" is as powerful a story as Edith Wharton wrote in any genre, and it is the one of her ghost stories that approaches the classic horror of James's *The Turn of the Screw*, which Mrs. Wharton regarded as the very model of the supernatural tale. As in *The Turn of the Screw*, the ghostliness—or ghastliness—here doubles on itself. The reader remains conscious throughout Culwin's narrative of the presence of young Frenham, listening silent and transfixed to his mentor. As the events uncoil, one realizes that the end of Culwin's reminiscence is by no means the end of Edith Wharton's story.

One or two critics have suggested that the figure of Culwin is based on Edith Wharton's friend and mentor Walter Berry (see our general introduction). If so, Mrs. Wharton was quite unaware of it: in answer to a friend's

She dropped into her low chair by the tea table, and the two visitors, as if drawn by her smile, advanced to receive the cups she held out.

She glanced about for Waythorn, and he took the third cup with a laugh.

praise of "The Eyes," she wrote: "Yes, the story *is* good. Even Walter liked it!" The inference might be that her portrait of a chillingly selfish, obscurely perverse, dilettantish middle-aged bachelor derived wholly from her creative unconscious and had no conscious connection with the man to whom she believed herself entirely devoted.

We had been put in the mood for ghosts, that evening, after an excellent dinner at our old friend Culwin's, by a tale of Fred Murchard's—the narrative of a strange personal visitation.

Seen through the haze of our cigars, and by the drowsy gleam of a coal fire, Culwin's library, with its oak walls and dark old bindings, made a good setting for such evocations; and ghostly experiences at first hand being, after Murchard's opening, the only kind acceptable to us, we proceeded to take stock of our group and tax each member for a contribution. There were eight of us, and seven contrived, in a manner more or less adequate, to fulfill the condition imposed. It surprised us all to find that we could muster such a show of supernatural impressions, for none of us, excepting Murchard himself and young Phil Frenham—whose story was the slightest of the lot—had the habit of sending our souls into the invisible. So that, on the whole, we had every reason to be proud of our seven "exhibits," and none of us would have dreamed of expecting an eighth from our host.

Our old friend, Mr. Andrew Culwin, who had sat back in his armchair, listening and blinking through the smoke circles with the cheerful tolerance of a wise old idol, was not the kind of man likely to be favored with such contacts, though he had imagination enough to enjoy, without envying, the superior privileges of his guests. By age and by education he belonged to the stout Positivist tradition, and his habit of thought had been formed in the days of the epic struggle between physics and metaphysics. But he had been, then and always, essentially a spectator, a humorous detached observer of the immense muddled variety show of life, slipping out of his seat now and then for a brief dip into the convivialities at the back of the house, but never, as far as one knew, showing the least desire to jump on the stage and do a "turn."

Among his contemporaries there lingered a vague tradition of his having, at a remote period, and in a romantic clime, been wounded in a duel; but this legend no more tallied with what we younger men knew of his character than my mother's assertion that he had once been "a charming little man with nice eyes" corresponded to any possible reconstitution of his physiognomy.

"He never can have looked like anything but a bundle of sticks," Murchard had once said of him. "Or a phosphorescent log, rather," some one else amended; and we recognized the happiness of this description of his small squat trunk, with the red blink of the eyes in a face like mottled bark. He had always been possessed of a leisure which he had nursed and protected, instead of squandering it in vain activities. His carefully guarded hours had been devoted to the cultivation of a fine intelligence and a few judiciously chosen habits; and none of the disturbances common to human experience seemed to have crossed his sky. Nevertheless, his dispassionate survey of the universe had not raised his opinion of that costly experiment, and his study of the human race seemed to have resulted in the conclusion that all men were superfluous, and women necessary only because someone had to do the cooking. On the importance of this point his convictions were absolute, and gastronomy was the only science which he revered as a dogma. It must be owned that his little dinners were a strong argument in favor of this view, besides being a reason—though not the main one—for the fidelity of his friends.

Mentally he exercised a hospitality less seductive but no less stimulating. His mind was like a forum, or some open meeting place for the exchange of ideas: somewhat cold and drafty, but light, spacious and orderly—a kind of academic grove from which all the leaves have fallen. In this privileged area a dozen of us were wont to stretch our muscles and expand our lungs; and, as if to prolong as much as possible the tradition of what we felt to be a vanishing institution, one or two neophytes were now and then added to our band.

Young Phil Frenham was the last, and the most interesting, of these recruits, and a good example of Murchard's somewhat morbid assertion that our old friend "liked 'em juicy." It was indeed a fact that Culwin, for all his dryness, specially tasted the lyric qualities in youth. As he was far too good an Epicurean to nip the flowers of soul which he gathered for his garden, his friendship was not a disintegrating influence: on the contrary, it forced the young idea to robuster bloom. And in Phil Frenham he had a good subject for experimentation. The boy was really intelligent, and the soundness of his nature was like the pure paste under a fine glaze. Culwin had fished him out of a fog of family dullness, and pulled him up to a peak in Darien; and the adventure hadn't hurt him a bit. Indeed, the skill with which Culwin had contrived to stimulate his curiosities without robbing them of their bloom of awe seemed to me a sufficient answer to Murchard's ogreish metaphor. There was nothing hectic in Frenham's efflorescence, and his old friend had not laid even a finger tip on the sacred stupidities. One wanted no better proof of that than the fact that Frenham still reverenced them in Culwin.

"There's a side of him you fellows don't see. *I* believe that story about the duel!" he declared; and it was of the very essence of this belief that it should impel him—just as our little party was dispersing—to turn back to our host with the joking demand: "And now you've got to tell us about *your* ghost!"

The outer door had closed on Murchard and the others; only Frenham and I remained; and the devoted servant who presided over Culwin's destinies, having brought a fresh supply of soda water, had been laconically ordered to bed.

Culwin's sociability was a night-blooming flower, and we knew that he expected the nucleus of his group to tighten around him after midnight. But Frenham's appeal seemed to disconcert him comically, and he rose from the chair in which he had just reseated himself after his farewells in the hall.

"*My* ghost? Do you suppose I'm fool enough to go to the expense of keeping one of my own, when there are so many charming ones in my friends' closets? Take another cigar," he said, revolving toward me with a laugh.

Frenham laughed too, pulling up his slender height before the chimney piece as he turned to face his short bristling friend.

"Oh," he said, "you'd never be content to share if you met one you really liked."

Culwin had dropped back into his armchair, his

shock head embedded in the hollow of worn leather, his little eyes glimmering over a fresh cigar.

"Liked—*liked?* Good Lord!" he growled.

"Ah, you *have*, then." Frenham pounced on him in the same instant, with a side glance of victory at me; but Culwin cowered gnomelike among his cushions, dissembling himself in a protective cloud of smoke.

"What's the use of denying it? You've seen everything, so of course you've seen a ghost!" his young friend persisted, talking intrepidly into the cloud. "Or, if you haven't seen one, it's only because you've seen two!"

The form of the challenge seemed to strike our host. He shot his head out of the mist with a queer tortoise-like motion he sometimes had, and blinked approvingly at Frenham.

"That's it," he flung at us on a shrill jerk of laughter; "it's only because I've seen two!"

The words were so unexpected that they dropped down and down into a deep silence, while we continued to stare at each other over Culwin's head, and Culwin stared at his ghosts. At length Frenham, without speaking, threw himself into the chair on the other side of the hearth, and leaned forward with his listening smile. . . .

II

"Oh, of course they're not show ghosts—a collector wouldn't think anything of them. . . . Don't let me raise your hopes . . . their one merit is their numerical strength: the exceptional fact of their being *two*. But, as against this, I'm bound to admit that at any moment I could probably have exorcised them both by asking my doctor for a prescription, or my oculist for a pair of spectacles. Only, as I never could make up my mind whether to go to the doctor or the oculist—whether I was afflicted by an optical or a digestive delusion—I left them to pursue their interesting double life, though at times they made mine exceedingly uncomfortable. . . .

"Yes—uncomfortable; and you know how I hate to be uncomfortable! But it was part of my stupid pride, when the thing began, not to admit that I could be disturbed by the trifling matter of seeing two.

"And then I'd no reason, really, to suppose I was ill. As far as I knew I was simply bored—horribly bored. But it was part of my boredom—I

remember—that I was feeling so uncommonly well, and didn't know how on earth to work off my surplus energy. I had come back from a long journey—down in South America and Mexico—and had settled down for the winter near New York with an old aunt, who had known Washington Irving and corresponded with N. P. Willis. She lived, not far from Irvington, in a damp Gothic villa overhung by Norway spruces and looking exactly like a memorial emblem done in hair. Her personal appearance was in keeping with this image, and her own hair—of which there was little left—might have been sacrificed to the manufacture of the emblem.

"I had just reached the end of an agitated year, with considerable arrears to make up in money and emotion; and theoretically it seemed as though my aunt's mild hospitality would be as beneficial to my nerves as to my purse. But the deuce of it was that as soon as I felt myself safe and sheltered my energy began to revive; and how was I to work it off inside of a memorial emblem? I had, at that time, the illusion that sustained intellectual effort could engage a man's whole activity; and I decided to write a great book—I forget about what. My aunt, impressed by my plan, gave up to me her Gothic library, filled with classics bound in black cloth and daguerreotypes of faded celebrities; and I sat down at my desk to win myself a place among their number. And to facilitate my task she lent me a cousin to copy my manuscript.

"The cousin was a nice girl, and I had an idea that a nice girl was just what I needed to restore my faith in human nature, and principally in myself. She was neither beautiful nor intelligent—poor Alice Nowell!—but it interested me to see any woman content to be so uninteresting, and I wanted to find out the secret of her content. In doing this I handled it rather rashly, and put it out of joint—oh, just for a moment! There's no fatuity in telling you this, for the poor girl had never seen anyone but cousins. . . .

"Well, I was sorry for what I'd done, of course, and confoundedly bothered as to how I should put it straight. She was staying in the house, and one evening, after my aunt had gone to bed, she came down to the library to fetch a book she'd mislaid, like any artless heroine, on the shelves behind us. She was pink-nosed and flustered, and it suddenly occurred to me that her hair, though it was fairly thick and pretty, would look exactly like my aunt's when she grew older. I was glad I had noticed this, for it made it easier for me to decide to do what was right; and when I had found the book she hadn't lost I told her I was leaving for Europe that week.

"Europe was terribly far off in those days, and Alice knew at once what I meant. She didn't take it in the least as I'd expected—it would have been easier if she had. She held her book very tight, and turned away a moment to wind up the lamp on my desk—it had a ground-glass shade with vine leaves, and glass drops around the edge, I remember. Then she came back, held out her hand, and said: 'Good-bye.' And as she said it she looked straight at me and kissed me. I had never felt anything as fresh and shy and brave as her kiss. It was worse than any reproach, and it made me ashamed to deserve a reproach from her. I said to myself: 'I'll marry her, and when my aunt dies she'll leave us this house, and I'll sit here at the desk and go on with my book; and Alice will sit over there with her embroidery and look at me as she's looking now. And life will go on like that for any number of years.' The prospect frightened me a little, but at the time it didn't frighten me as much as doing anything to hurt her; and ten minutes later she had my seal ring on her finger, and my promise that when I went abroad she should go with me.

"You'll wonder why I'm enlarging on this incident. It's because the evening on which it took place was the very evening on which I first saw the queer sight I've spoken of. Being at that time an ardent believer in a necessary sequence between cause and effect, I naturally tried to trace some kind of link between what had just happened to me in my aunt's library, and what was to happen a few hours later on the same night; and so the coincidence between the two events always remained in my mind.

"I went up to bed with rather a heavy heart, for I was bowed under the weight of the first good action I had ever consciously committed; and young as I was, I saw the gravity of my situation. Don't imagine from this that I had hitherto been an instrument of destruction. I had been merely a harmless young man, who had followed his bent and declined all collaboration with Providence. Now I had suddenly undertaken to promote the moral order of the world, and I felt a good deal like the trustful spectator who has given his gold watch to the conjurer, and doesn't know in what shape he'll get it back when the trick is over. . . . Still, a glow of self-righteousness tempered my fears, and I said to myself as I undressed that when I'd got used to being good it probably wouldn't make me as nervous as it did at the start. And by the time I was in bed, and had blown out my candle, I felt that I really *was* getting used to it, and that, as far as I'd got, it was not unlike sinking down into one of my aunt's very softest wool mattresses.

"I closed my eyes on this image, and when I opened them it must have been a good deal later, for my room had grown cold, and intensely still. I was waked by the queer feeling we all know—the feeling that there was something in the room that hadn't been there when I fell asleep. I sat up and strained my eyes into the darkness. The room was pitch black, and at first I saw nothing; but gradually a vague glimmer at the foot of the bed turned into two eyes staring back at me. I couldn't distinguish the features attached to them, but as I looked the eyes grew more and more distinct: they gave out a light of their own.

"The sensation of being thus gazed at was far from pleasant, and you might suppose that my first impulse would have been to jump out of bed and hurl myself on the invisible figure attached to the eyes. But it wasn't—my impulse was simply to lie still. . . . I can't say whether this was due to an immediate sense of the uncanny nature of the apparition—to the certainty that if I did jump out of bed I should hurl myself on nothing—or merely to the benumbing effect of the eyes themselves. They were the very worst eyes I've ever seen: a man's eyes—but what a man! My first thought was that he must be frightfully old. The orbits were sunk, and the thick red-lined lids hung over the eyeballs like blinds of which the cords are broken. One lid drooped a little lower than the other, with the effect of a crooked leer; and between these folds of flesh, with their scant bristle of lashes, the eyes themselves, small glassy disks with an agate-like rim, looked like sea pebbles in the grip of a starfish.

"But the age of the eyes was not the most unpleasant thing about them. What turned me sick was their expression of vicious security. I don't know how else to describe the fact that they seemed to belong to a man who had done a lot of harm in his life, but had always kept just inside the danger lines. They were not the eyes of a coward, but of someone much too clever to take risks; and my gorge rose at their look of base astuteness. Yet even that wasn't the worst; for as we continued to scan each other I saw in them a tinge of derision, and felt myself to be its object.

"At that I was seized by an impulse of rage that

jerked me to my feet and pitched me straight at the unseen figure. But of course there wasn't any figure there, and my fists struck at emptiness. Ashamed and cold, I groped about for a match and lit the candles. The room looked just as usual—as I had known it would; and I crawled back to bed, and blew out the lights.

"As soon as the room was dark again the eyes reappeared; and I now applied myself to explaining them on scientific principles. At first I thought the illusion might have been caused by the glow of the last embers in the chimney; but the fireplace was on the other side of my bed, and so placed that the fire could not be reflected in my toilet glass, which was the only mirror in the room. Then it struck me that I might have been tricked by the reflection of the embers in some polished bit of wood or metal; and though I couldn't discover any object of the sort in my line of vision, I got up again, groped my way to the hearth, and covered what was left of the fire. But as soon as I was back in bed the eyes were back at its foot.

"They were an hallucination, then: that was plain. But the fact that they were not due to any external dupery didn't make them a bit pleasanter. For if they were a projection of my inner consciousness, what the deuce was the matter with that organ? I had gone deeply enough into the mystery of morbid pathological states to picture the conditions under which an exploring mind might lay itself open to such a midnight admonition; but I couldn't fit it to my present case. I had never felt more normal, mentally and physically; and the only unusual fact in my situation—that of having assured the happiness of an amiable girl—did not seem of a kind to summon unclean spirits about my pillow. But there were the eyes still looking at me.

"I shut mine, and tried to evoke a vision of Alice Nowell's. They were not remarkable eyes, but they were as wholesome as fresh water, and if she had more imagination—or longer lashes—their expression might have been interesting. As it was, they did not prove very efficacious, and in a few moments I perceived that they had mysteriously changed into the eyes at the foot of the bed. It exasperated me more to feel these glaring at me through my shut lids than to see them, and I opened my eyes again and looked straight into their hateful stare. . . .

"And so it went on all night. I can't tell you what that night was like, nor how long it lasted. Have you ever lain in bed, hopelessly wide awake, and tried to keep your eyes shut, knowing that if you opened 'em you'd see something you dreaded and loathed? It sounds easy, but it's devilishly hard. Those eyes hung there and drew me. I had the *vertige de l'abime*, and their red lids were the edge of my abyss. . . . I had known nervous hours before: hours when I'd felt the wind of danger in my neck; but never this kind of strain. It wasn't that the eyes were awful; they hadn't the majesty of the powers of darkness. But they had—how shall I say?—a physical effect that was the equivalent of a bad smell: their look left a smear like a snail's. And I didn't see what business they had with me, anyhow—and I stared and stared, trying to find out.

"I don't know what effect they were trying to produce; but the effect they *did* produce was that of making me pack my portmanteau and bolt to town early the next morning. I left a note for my aunt, explaining that I was ill and had gone to see my doctor; and as a matter of fact I did feel uncommonly ill—the night seemed to have pumped all the blood out of me. But when I reached town I didn't go to the doctor's. I went to a friend's rooms, and threw myself on a bed, and slept for ten heavenly hours. When I woke it was the middle of the night, and I turned cold at the thought of what might be waiting for me. I sat up, shaking, and stared into the darkness; but there wasn't a break in its blessed surface, and when I saw that the eyes were not there I dropped back into another long sleep.

"I had left no word for Alice when I fled, because I meant to go back the next morning. But the next morning I was too exhausted to stir. As the day went on the exhaustion increased, instead of wearing off like the fatigue left by an ordinary night of insomnia: the effect of the eyes seemed to be cumulative, and the thought of seeing them again grew intolerable. For two days I fought my dread; and on the third evening I pulled myself together and decided to go back the next morning. I felt a good deal happier as soon as I'd decided, for I knew that my abrupt disappearance, and the strangeness of my not writing, must have been very distressing to poor Alice. I went to bed with an easy mind, and fell asleep at once; but in the middle of the night I woke, and there were the eyes. . . .

"Well, I simply couldn't face them; and instead of going back to my aunt's I bundled a few things into a trunk and jumped aboard the first steamer for England. I was so dead tired when I got on board that I crawled straight into my berth, and slept most of the way over; and I can't tell you the bliss it was to wake from those long dreamless stretches and look fearlessly into the dark, *knowing* that I shouldn't see the eyes. . . .

"I stayed abroad for a year, and then I stayed for another; and during that time I never had a glimpse of them. That was enough reason for prolonging my stay if I'd been on a desert island. Another was, of course, that I had perfectly come to see, on the voyage over, the complete impossibility of my marrying Alice Nowell. The fact that I had been so slow in making this discovery annoyed me, and made me want to avoid explanations. The bliss of escaping at one stroke from the eyes, and from this other embarrassment, gave my freedom an extraordinary zest; and the longer I savored it the better I liked its taste.

"The eyes had burned such a hole in my consciousness that for a long time I went on puzzling over the nature of the apparition, and wondering if it would ever come back. But as time passed I lost this dread, and retained only the precision of the image. Then that faded in its turn.

"The second year found me settled in Rome, where I was planning, I believe, to write another great book—a definitive work on Etruscan influences in Italian art. At any rate, I'd found some pretext of the kind for taking a sunny apartment in the Piazza di Spagna and dabbling about in the Forum; and there, one morning, a charming youth came to me. As he stood there in the warm light, slender and smooth and hyacinthine, he might have stepped from a ruined altar—one to Antinous, say; but he'd come instead from New York, with a letter from (of all people) Alice Nowell. The letter—the first I'd had from her since our break— was simply a line introducing her young cousin, Gilbert Noyes, and appealing to me to befriend him. It appeared, poor lad, that he 'had talent,' and 'wanted to write'; and, an obdurate family having insisted that his calligraphy should take the form of double entry, Alice had intervened to win him six months' respite, during which he was to travel abroad on a meager pittance, and somehow prove his ability to increase it by his pen. The quaint conditions of the test struck me first: it seemed about as conclusive as a medieval 'ordeal.' Then I was touched by her having sent him to me. I had always wanted to do her some service, to justify myself in my own eyes rather than hers; and here was a beautiful occasion.

"I imagine it's safe to lay down the general principle that predestined geniuses don't, as a rule, appear before one in the spring sunshine of the Forum looking like one of its banished gods. At any rate, poor Noyes wasn't a predestined genius. But he *was* beautiful to see, and charming as a comrade. It was only when he began to talk literature that my heart failed me. I knew all the symptoms so well—the things he had 'in him,' and the things outside him that impinged! There's the real test, after all. It was always—punctually, inevitably, with the inexorableness of a mechanical law—it was *always* the wrong thing that struck him. I grew to find a certain fascination in deciding in advance exactly which wrong thing he'd select; and I acquired an astonishing skill at the game. . . .

"The worst of it was that his *bêtise* wasn't of the too obvious sort. Ladies who met him at picnics thought him intellectual; and even at dinners he passed for clever. I, who had him under the microscope, fancied now and then that he might develop some kind of a slim talent, something that he could make 'do' and be happy on; and wasn't that, after all, what I was concerned with? He was so charming—he continued to be so charming—that he called forth all my charity in support of this argument; and for the first few months I really believed there was a chance for him. . . .

"Those months were delightful. Noyes was constantly with me, and the more I saw of him the better I liked him. His stupidity was a natural grace—it was as beautiful, really, as his eyelashes. And he was so gay, so affectionate, and so happy with me, that telling him the truth would have been about as pleasant as slitting the throat of some gentle animal. At first I used to wonder what had put into that radiant head the detestable delusion that it held a brain. Then I began to see that it was simply protective mimicry—an instinctive ruse to get away from family life and an office desk. Not that Gilbert didn't—dear lad!—believe in himself. There wasn't a trace of hypocrisy in him. He was sure that his 'call' was irresistible, while to me it was the saving grace of his situation that it *wasn't*, and that a little money, a little leisure, a little pleasure would have turned him into an inoffensive idler. Unluckily, however, there was no hope of money, and with the alternative of the office desk before him he couldn't postpone his attempt at literature. The stuff he turned out was deplorable, and I see now that I knew it from the first. Still, the absurdity of deciding a man's whole future on a first trial seemed to justify me in withholding my verdict, and perhaps even in encouraging him a little, on the ground that the human plant generally needs warmth to flower.

"At any rate, I proceeded on that principle, and carried it to the point of getting his term of probation extended. When I left Rome he went with me, and we idled away a delicious summer between Capri and Venice. I said to myself: 'If he has anything in him, it will come out now,' and it *did*. He was never more enchanting and enchanted. There were moments of our pilgrimage when beauty born of murmuring sound seemed actually to pass into his face—but only to issue forth in a flood of the palest ink. . . .

"Well, the time came to turn off the tap; and I knew there was no hand but mine to do it. We were back in Rome, and I had taken him to stay with me, not wanting him to be alone in his *pension* when he had to face the necessity of renouncing his ambition. I hadn't, of course, relied solely on my own judgment in deciding to advise him to drop literature. I had sent his stuff to various people—editors and critics—and they had always sent it back with the same chilling lack of comment. Really there was nothing on earth to say.

"I confess I never felt more shabby than I did on the day when I decided to have it out with Gilbert. It was well enough to tell myself that it was my duty to knock the poor boy's hopes into splinters—but I'd like to know what act of gratuitous cruelty hasn't been justified on that plea? I've always shrunk from usurping the functions of Providence, and when I have to exercise them I decidedly prefer it shouldn't be on an errand of destruction. Besides, in the last issue, who was I to decide, even after a year's trial, if poor Gilbert had it in him or not?

"The more I looked at the part I'd resolved to play, the less I liked it; and I liked it still less when Gilbert sat opposite me, with his head thrown back in the lamplight, just as Phil's is now. . . . I'd been going over his last manuscript, and he knew it, and he knew that his future hung on my verdict—we'd tacitly agreed to that. The manuscript lay between us, on my table—a novel, his first novel, if you please!—and he reached over and laid his hand on it, and looked up at me with all his life in the look.

"I stood up and cleared my throat, trying to keep my eyes away from his face and on the manuscript.

"'The fact is, my dear Gilbert,' I began—

"I saw him turn pale, but he was up and facing me in an instant.

"'Oh, look here, don't take on so, my dear fellow! I'm not so awfully cut up as all that!' His hands were on my shoulders, and he was laughing down on me from his full height, with a kind of mortally stricken gaiety that drove the knife into my side.

"He was too beautifully brave for me to keep up any humbug about my duty. And it came over me suddenly how I should hurt others in hurting him: myself first, since sending him home meant losing him; but more particularly poor Alice Nowell, to whom I had so longed to prove my good faith and my desire to serve her. It really seemed like failing her twice to fail Gilbert.

"But my intuition was like one of those lightning flashes that encircle the whole horizon, and in the same instant I saw what I might be letting myself in for if I didn't tell the truth. I said to myself: 'I shall have him for life'—and I'd never yet seen anyone, man or woman, whom I was quite sure of wanting on those terms. Well, this impulse of egotism decided me. I was ashamed of it, and to get away from it I took a leap that landed me straight in Gilbert's arms.

"'The thing's all right, and you're all wrong!' I shouted up at him; and as he hugged me, and I laughed and shook in his clutch, I had for a minute the sense of self-complacency that is supposed to attend the footsteps of the just. Hang it all, making people happy *has* its charms.

"Gilbert, of course, was for celebrating his emancipation in some spectacular manner; but I sent him away alone to explode his emotions, and went to bed to sleep off mine. As I undressed I began to wonder what their aftertaste would be—so many of the finest don't keep! Still, I wasn't sorry, and I meant to empty the bottle, even if it *did* turn a trifle flat.

"After I got into bed I lay for a long time smiling at the memory of his eyes—his blissful eyes. . . . Then I fell asleep, and when I woke the room was deathly cold, and I sat up with a jerk—and there were *the other eyes*. . . .

"It was three years since I'd seen them, but I'd thought of them so often that I fancied they could never take me unawares again. Now, with their red sneer on me, I knew that I had never really believed they would come back, and that I was as defenceless as ever against them. . . . As before, it was the insane irrelevance of their coming that made it so horrible. What the deuce were they after, to leap out at me at such a time? I had lived more or less carelessly in the years since I'd seen them, though my worst indiscretions were not dark enough to invite the searchings of their infernal glare; but at this particular moment I was really in what might have been called a state of grace; and I can't tell you how the fact added to their horror. . . .

"But it's not enough to say they were as bad as before: they were worse. Worse by just so much as I'd learned of life in the interval; by all the damnable implications my wider experience read into them. I saw now what I hadn't seen before: that they were eyes which had grown hideous gradually, which had built up their baseness coral-wise, bit by bit, out of a series of small turpitudes slowly accumulated through the industrious years. Yes—it came to me that what made them so bad was that they'd grown bad so slowly. . . .

"There they hung in the darkness, their swollen lids dropped across the little watery bulbs rolling loose in the orbits, and the puff of flesh making a muddy shadow underneath—and as their stare moved with my movements, there came over me a sense of their tacit complicity, of a deep hidden understanding between us that was worse than the first shock of their strangeness. Not that I understood them; but that they made it so clear that someday I should. . . . Yes, that was the worst part of it, decidedly; and it was the feeling that became stronger each time they came back. . . .

"For they got into the damnable habit of coming back. They reminded me of vampires with a taste for young flesh, they seemed so to gloat over the taste of a good conscience. Every night for a month they came to claim their morsel of mine: since I'd made Gilbert happy they simply wouldn't loosen their fangs. The coincidence almost made me hate him, poor lad, fortuitous as I felt it to be. I puzzled over it a good deal, but couldn't find any hint of an explanation except in the chance of his association with Alice Nowell. But then the eyes had let up on me the moment I had abandoned her, so they could hardly be the emissaries of a woman scorned, even if one could have pictured poor Alice charging such spirits to avenge her. That set me thinking, and I began to wonder if they would let up on me if I abandoned Gilbert. The temptation was insidious, and I had to stiffen myself against it; but really, dear boy! he was too charming to be sacrificed to such demons. And so, after all, I never found out what they wanted. . . ."

III

The fire crumbled, sending up a flash which threw into relief the narrator's gnarled face under its grey-black stubble. Pressed into the hollow of the chair back, it stood out an instant like an intaglio of yellowish red-veined stone, with spots of enamel for the eyes; then the fire sank and it became once more a dim Rembrandtish blur.

Phil Frenham, sitting in a low chair on the opposite side of the hearth, one long arm propped on the table behind him, one hand supporting his thrown-back head, and his eyes fixed on his old friend's face, had not moved since the tale began. He continued to maintain his silent immobility after Culwin had ceased to speak, and it was I who, with a vague sense of disappointment at the sudden drop of the story, finally asked: "But how long did you keep on seeing them?"

Culwin, so sunk into his chair that he seemed like a heap of his own empty clothes, stirred a little, as if in surprise at my question. He appeared to have half-forgotten what he had been telling us.

"How long? Oh, off and on all that winter. It was infernal. I never got used to them. I grew really ill."

Frenham shifted his attitude, and as he did so his elbow struck against a small mirror in a bronze frame standing on the table behind him. He turned and changed its angle slightly; then he resumed his former attitude, his dark head thrown back on his lifted palm, his eyes intent on Culwin's face. Something in his silent gaze embarrassed me, and as if to divert attention from it I pressed on with another question:

"And you never tried sacrificing Noyes?"

"Oh, no. The fact is I didn't have to. He did it for me, poor boy!"

"Did it for you? How do you mean?"

"He wore me out—wore everybody out. He kept on pouring out his lamentable twaddle, and hawking it up and down the place till he became a thing of terror. I tried to wean him from writing—oh, ever so gently, you understand, by throwing him with agreeable people, giving him a chance to make himself felt, to come to a sense of what he *really* had to give. I'd foreseen this solution from the beginning—felt sure that, once the first ardor of authorship was quenched, he'd drop into his place as a charming parasitic thing, the kind of chronic Cherubino for whom, in old societies, there's always a seat at table, and a shelter behind the ladies' skirts. I saw him take his place as 'the poet': the poet who doesn't write. One knows the type in every drawing room. Living in that way doesn't cost much—I'd worked it all out in my mind, and felt sure that, with a little help, he could manage it for the next few years; and meanwhile he'd be sure to marry. I saw him married to a widow, rather older, with a good cook and a well-run house. And I actually had my eye on the widow. . . . Meanwhile I did everything to help the transition—lent him money to ease his conscience, introduced him to pretty women to make him forget his vows. But nothing would do him: he had but one idea in his beautiful obstinate head. He wanted the laurel and not the rose, and he kept on repeating Gautier's axiom and battering and filing at his limp prose till he'd spread it out over Lord knows how many hundred pages. Now and then he would send a barrelful to a publisher, and of course it would always come back.

"At first it didn't matter—he thought he was 'misunderstood.' He took the attitudes of genius, and whenever an opus came home he wrote another to keep it company. Then he had a reaction of despair, and accused me of deceiving him, and Lord knows what. I got angry at that, and told him it was he who had deceived himself. He'd come to me determined to write, and I'd done my best to help him. That was the extent of my offence, and I'd done it for his cousin's sake, not his.

"That seemed to strike home, and he didn't answer for a minute. Then he said: 'My time's up and my money's up. What do you think I'd better do?'

" 'I think you'd better not be an ass,' I said.

" 'What do you mean by being an ass?' he asked.

"I took a letter from my desk and held it out to him.

" 'I mean refusing this offer of Mrs. Ellinger's: to be her secretary at a salary of five thousand dollars. There may be a lot more in it than that.'

"He flung out his hand with a violence that struck the letter from mine. 'Oh, I know well enough what's in it!' he said, red to the roots of his hair.

" 'And what's the answer, if you know?' I asked.

"He made none at the minute, but turned away slowly to the door. There, with his hand on the threshold, he stopped to say, almost under his breath: 'Then you really think my stuff's no good?'

"I was tired and exasperated, and I laughed. I don't defend my laugh—it was in wretched taste. But I must plead in extenuation that the boy was

a fool, and that I'd done my best for him—I really had.

"He went out of the room, shutting the door quietly after him. That afternoon I left for Frascati, where I'd promised to spend the Sunday with some friends. I was glad to escape from Gilbert, and by the same token, as I learned that night, I had also escaped from the eyes. I dropped into the same lethargic sleep that had come to me before when I left off seeing them; and when I woke the next morning in my peaceful room above the ilexes, I felt the utter weariness and deep relief that always followed on that sleep. I put in two blessed nights at Frascati, and when I got back to my rooms in Rome I found that Gilbert had gone. . . . Oh, nothing tragic had happened—the episode never rose to *that*. He'd simply packed his manuscripts and left for America—for his family and the Wall Street desk. He left a decent enough note to tell me of his decision, and behaved altogether, in the circumstances, as little like a fool as it's possible for a fool to behave. . . ."

IV

Culwin paused again, and Frenham still sat motionless, the dusky contour of his young head reflected in the mirror at his back.

"And what became of Noyes afterward?" I finally asked, still disquieted by a sense of incompleteness, by the need of some connecting thread between the parallel lines of the tale.

Culwin twitched his shoulders. "Oh, nothing became of him—because he became nothing. There could be no question of 'becoming' about it. He vegetated in an office, I believe, and finally got a clerkship in a consulate, and married drearily in China. I saw him once in Hong Kong, years afterward. He was fat and hadn't shaved. I was told he drank. He didn't recognize me."

"And the eyes?" I asked, after another pause which Frenham's continued silence made oppressive.

Culwin, stroking his chin, blinked at me meditatively through the shadows. "I never saw them after my last talk with Gilbert. Put two and two together if you can. For my part, I haven't found the link."

He rose, his hands in his pockets, and walked stiffly over to the table on which reviving drinks had been set out.

"You must be parched after this dry tale. Here,

help yourself, my dear fellow. Here, Phil—" He turned back to the hearth.

Frenham made no response to his host's hospitable summons. He still sat in his low chair without moving, but as Culwin advanced toward him, their eyes met in a long look; after which the young man, turning suddenly, flung his arms across the table behind him, and dropped his face upon them.

Culwin, at the unexpected gesture, stopped short, a flush on his face.

"Phil—what the deuce? Why, have the eyes scared *you?* My dear boy—my dear fellow—I never had such a tribute to my literary ability, never!"

He broke into a chuckle at the thought, and halted on the hearth-rug, his hands still in his pockets, gazing at the youth's bowed head. Then, as Frenham still made no answer, he moved a step or two nearer.

"Cheer up, my dear Phil! It's years since I've seen them—apparently I've done nothing lately bad enough to call them out of chaos. Unless my present evocation of them has made *you* see them;

which would be their worst stroke yet!"

His bantering appeal quivered off into an uneasy laugh, and he moved still nearer, bending over Frenham, and laying his gouty hands on the lad's shoulders.

"Phil, my dear boy, really—what's the matter? Why don't you answer? *Have* you seen the eyes?"

Frenham's face was still hidden, and from where I stood behind Culwin I saw the latter, as if under the rebuff of this unaccountable attitude, draw back slowly from his friend. As he did so, the light of the lamp on the table fell full on his congested face, and I caught its reflection in the mirror behind Frenham's head.

Culwin saw the reflection also. He paused, his face level with the mirror, as if scarcely recognizing the countenance in it as his own. But as he looked his expression gradually changed, and for an appreciable space of time he and the image in the glass confronted each other with a glare of slowly gathering hate. Then Culwin let go on Frenham's shoulders, and drew back a step. . . .

Frenham, his face still hidden, did not stir.

From A Backward Glance (1934)

These glimpses of Henry James over a dozen years are taken from two sections of the autobiography Edith Wharton completed, in 1934, at the age of seventy-two. In a portrait that is at once endearing and penetrating, James emerges as a man of undoubted genius, with a devotion to the art of fiction so absolute that he is incapable of dishonesty in criticizing the work even of his closest friends. But he is clearly seen, here, as not bereft of the foibles, eccentricities, and self-delusions (James thought of himself as an expert guide on a motor trip, and he was a disaster) that usually accompany genius.

What is to be stressed, as well, is the enormous sense of comedy, often of sheer fun, with which James was imbued and which he shared with Edith Wharton—something that could erupt even under the spell of a hauntingly beautiful reading of Whitman (whom both, perhaps surprisingly, regarded without reservation as America's greatest poet), or while idling through the English countryside.

Edith Wharton's opinions of the work of

James's "major phase," as recorded in these pages, appear to be mixed. She is willing to rate the recognition scene in *The Golden Bowl* ("Maggie looking in from the terrace at Fawns at the four bridge-players") as superior even to Isabel Archer's long vigil in *The Portrait of a Lady;* but she finds a certain airlessness, and an excessive regard for form, in the later novels. Yet there is no questioning her reverence for James as a literary artist, a reverence further nurtured by her sense of the wealth of humanity in the man.

That humanity is conveyed with a verbal artistry that Edith Wharton had rarely, if ever, achieved before. Her account of James's reminiscences one summer evening (probably in 1910) at The Mount about his Emmet cousins can hardly be much less poetic and evocative, and finally less clear, than the remarkable talk it describes:

Ghostlike indeed at first, wavering and indistinct, [the Emmets] glimmered at us through a series of disconnected ejaculations, epithets, allusions, parenthetical rectifications and re-statements, till not only our brains but the clear night itself seemed filled with a palpable fog; and then, suddenly, by some miracle of shifted lights and accumulated strokes, there they stood before us as they lived, drawn with a million filament-like lines, yet sharp as an Ingres, dense as a Rembrandt; or, to call upon his own art for an analogy, minute and massive as the people of Balzac.

Note: Howard Sturgis, an effeminate yet by unanimous report an uncommonly engaging American living in England, was a close friend of Henry James, and after James introduced him to Edith Wharton he became an important member of her "inner circle." He wrote an interesting autobiographical novel called *Belchamber*, which Edith Wharton tried, without success, to have published in America; but he spent most of his time as a charming host and an expert at needlework. "Qu' acre"—a contraction of Queen's Acre—was his home near Windsor, which James and Mrs. Wharton regularly visited together.

A PORTRAIT OF HENRY JAMES

The Henry James of the early meetings was the bearded Penseroso of Sargent's delicate drawing, soberly fastidious in dress and manner, cut on the approved pattern of the *homme du monde* of the 'eighties; whereas by the time we got to know each other well the compact upright figure had expanded to a rolling and voluminous outline, and the elegance of dress given way to the dictates of comfort, while a clean shave had revealed in all its sculptural beauty the noble Roman mask and the big dramatic mouth. The change typified something deep beneath the surface. In the interval two things had happened: Henry James had taken the measure of the fashionable society which in youth had subjugated his imagination, as it had Balzac's, and was later to subjugate Proust's, and had fled from it to live in the country, carrying with him all the loot his adventure could yield; and in his new solitude he had come to grips with his genius. Exquisite as the early novels are—and in point of perfection probably none can touch "The Portrait

of a Lady"—yet measured by what was to come Henry James, when he wrote them, had but skimmed the surface of life and of his art. Even the man who wrote, in "The Portrait of a Lady," the chapter in which Isabel broods over her fate at night by the fire, was far from the man in whom was already ripening that greater night-piece, the picture of Maggie looking in from the terrace at Fawns at the four bridge-players, and renouncing her vengeance as "nothing nearer to experience than a wild eastern caravan, looming into view with crude colours in the sun, fierce pipes in the air, high spears against the sky . . . but turning off short before it reached her and plunging into other defiles."

But though he had found his genius and broken away from the social routine, he never emancipated himself in small matters from the conformities. Though he now affected to humour the lumbering frame whose physical ease must be considered first, he remained spasmodically fastidious about his dress, and about other trifling social observances, and once when he was motoring with us in France in 1907, and suddenly made up his mind (at Poitiers, of all places!) that he must then and there buy a new hat, almost insuperable difficulties attended its selection. It was not until he had announced his despair of ever making the hatter understand "that what he wanted was a hat like everybody else's," and I had rather impatiently suggested his asking for a head-covering *"pour l'homme moyen sensuel,"* that the joke broke through his indecisions, and to a rich accompaniment of chuckles the hat was bought.

Still more particular about his figure than his dress, he resented any suggestion that his silhouette had lost firmness and acquired volume; and once, when my friend Jacques-Emile Blanche was doing the fine seated profile portrait which is the only one that renders him *as he really was,* he privately implored me to suggest to Blanche "not to lay such stress on the resemblance to Daniel Lambert."

The truth is that he belonged irrevocably to the old America out of which I also came, and of which—almost—it might paradoxically be said that to follow up its last traces one had to come to Europe; as I discovered when my French and English friends told me, on reading "The Age of Innocence," that they had no idea New York life in the 'seventies had been so like that of the English cathedral town, or the French *"ville de province,"* of the same date. As for the nonsense talked by critics of a later generation, who never knew James, much less the world he grew up in, about his having thwarted his genius by living in Europe, and having understood his mistake too late, as a witness of his long sojourns in America in 1904, 1905 and 1910, and of the reactions they produced (expressed in all the letters written at the time), I can affirm that he was never really happy or at home there. He came several times for long visits to the Mount, and during his first visit to America, in 1904–5, he also stayed with us for some time in New York; and responsive as he always was, interested, curious, and heroically hospitable to new ideas, new aspects, new people, the nostalgia of which he speaks so poignantly in one of his letters to Sir Edmund Gosse (written from the Mount) was never for a moment stilled. Henry James was essentially a novelist of manners, and the manners he was qualified by nature and situation to observe were those of the little vanishing group of people among whom he had grown up, or their more picturesque prototypes in older societies. For better or worse he had to seek that food where he could find it, for it was the only food his imagination could fully assimilate. He was acutely conscious of this limitation, and often bewailed to me his total inability to use the "material," financial and industrial, of modern American life. Wall Street, and everything connected with the big business world, remained an impenetrable mystery to him, and knowing this he felt he could never have dealt fully in fiction with the "American scene," and always frankly acknowledged it. The attempt to portray the retired financier in Mr. Verver, and to relate either him or his native "American City" to any sort of concrete reality, is perhaps proof enough of the difficulties James would have found in trying to depict the American money-maker in action.

. . .

Sometimes his chaff was not untinged with malice. I remember a painful moment, during one of his visits, when my husband imprudently blurted out an allusion to "Edith's new story—you've seen it in the last 'Scribner'?" My heart sank; I knew it always embarrassed James to be called on, in the author's presence, for an "appreciation." He was himself so engrossed in questions of technique and construction—and so increasingly detached from the short-story form as a medium—that very few "fictions" (as he called them) but his own were

of interest to him, except indeed Mr. Wells's, for which he once avowed to me an incurable liking, "because everything he writes is so alive and kicking." At any rate I always tried to keep my own work out of his way, and once accused him of ferreting out and reading it just to annoy me—to which charge his sole response was a guilty chuckle. In the present instance, as usual, he instantly replied: "Oh, yes, my dear Edward, I've read the little work—of course I've read it." A gentle pause, which I knew boded no good; then he softly continued: "Admirable, admirable; a masterly little achievement." He turned to me, full of a terrifying benevolence. "Of course so accomplished a mistress of the art would not, without deliberate intention, have given the tale so curiously conventional a treatment. Though indeed, in the given case, no treatment *but* the conventional was possible; which might conceivably, my dear lady, on further consideration, have led you to reject your subject as—er—in itself a totally unsuitable one."

I will not deny that he may have added a silent twinkle to the shout of laughter with which—on that dear wide sunny terrace of the Mount—his fellow-guests greeted my "dressing-down." Yet it would be a mistake to imagine that he had deliberately started out to destroy my wretched tale. He had begun, I am sure, with the sincere intention of praising it; but no sooner had he opened his lips than he was overmastered by the need to speak the truth, and the whole truth, about anything connected with the art which was sacred to him. Simplicity of heart was combined in him with a brain that Mr. Percy Lubbock has justly called robust, and his tender regard for his friends' feelings was equalled only by the faithfulness with which, on literary questions, he gave them his view of their case when they asked for it—and sometimes when they did not. On all subjects but that of letters his sincerity was tempered by an almost exaggerated tenderness; but when *le métier* was in question no gentler emotion prevailed.

Another day—somewhat later in our friendship, since this time the work under his scalpel was "The Custom of the Country"—after prolonged and really generous praise of my book, he suddenly and irrepressibly burst forth: "But of course you know—as how should you, with your infernal keenness of perception, *not* know?—that in doing your tale you had under your hand a magnificent subject, which ought to have been your main theme, and that you used it as a mere incident and then passed it by?"

He meant by this that for him the chief interest of the book, and its most original theme, was that of a crude young woman such as Undine Spragg entering, all unprepared and unperceiving, into the mysterious labyrinth of family life in the old French aristocracy. I saw his point, and recognized that the contact between the Undine Spraggs and the French families they marry into was, as the French themselves would say, an "actuality" of immense interest to the novelist of manners, and one which as yet had been little dealt with; but I argued that in "The Custom of the Country" I was chronicling the career of a particular young woman, and that to whatever hemisphere her fortunes carried her, my task was to record her ravages and pass on to her next phase. This, however, was no argument to James; he had long since lost all interest in the chronicle-novel, and cared only for the elaborate working out on all sides of a central situation, so that he could merely answer, by implication if not openly: "Then, my dear child, you chose the wrong kind of subject."

Once when he was staying with us in Paris I had a still more amusing experience of this irresistible tendency to speak the truth. He had chanced to nose out the fact that, responding to an S.O.S. from the *Revue des Deux Mondes*, for a given number of which a promised translation of one of my tales had not been ready, I had offered to replace it by writing a story myself—in French! I knew what James would feel about such an experiment, and there was nothing I did not do to conceal the horrid secret from him; but he had found it out before arriving, and when in my presence some idiot challenged him with: "Well, Mr. James, don't you think it's remarkable that Mrs. Wharton should have written a story in French for the *Revue?*" the twinkle which began in the corner of his eyes and trickled slowly down to his twitching lips showed that his answer was ready. "Remarkable—most remarkable! An altogether astonishing feat." He swung around on me slowly. "I do congratulate you, my dear, on the way in which you've picked up every old worn-out literary phrase that's been lying about the streets of Paris for the last twenty years, and managed to pack them all into those few pages." To this withering comment, in talking over the story afterward with one of my friends, he added more seriously, and with singular good sense: "A very creditable episode in her career. *But she must never do it again.*"

He knew I enjoyed our literary rough-and-tumbles, and no doubt for that reason scrupled the less to hit straight from the shoulder; but with others, though he tried to be more merciful, what he really thought was no less manifest. My own experience has taught me that nothing is more difficult than to talk indifferently or insincerely on the subject of one's craft. The writer, without much effort, can reel off polite humbug about pictures, the painter about books; but to fib about the art one practises is incredibly painful, and James's overscrupulous conscience, and passionate reverence for letters, while always inclining him to mercy, made deception doubly impossible.

I think it was James who first made me understand that genius is not an indivisible element, but one variously apportioned, so that the popular system of dividing humanity into geniuses and nongeniuses is a singularly inadequate way of estimating human complexity. In connection with this, I once brought him a phrase culled in a literary review. "Mr.——has *almost a streak* of genius." James, always an eager collector of verbal oddities, fell on the phrase with rapture, and earnest requests to every one to define the exact extent of "almost a streak" caused him amusement for months afterward. I mention this because so few people seem to have known in Henry James the ever-budding fountain of fun which was the delight of his intimates.

One of our joys, when the talk touched on any great example of prose or verse, was to get the book from the shelf, and ask one of the company to read the passage aloud. There were some admirable readers in the group, in whose gift I had long delighted; but I had never heard Henry James read aloud—or known that he enjoyed doing so—till one night some one alluded to Emily Brontë's poems, and I said I had never read "Remembrance." Immediately he took the volume from my hand, and, his eyes filling, and some far-away emotion deepening his rich and flexible voice, he began:

Cold in the earth, and deep snow piled above thee,
Far, far removed, cold in the dreary grave,
Have I forgot, my only Love, to love thee,
Severed at last by Time's all-severing wave?

I had never before heard poetry read as he read it; and I never have since. He chanted it, and he was not afraid to chant it, as many good readers are, who, though they instinctively feel that the genius of the English poetical idiom requires it to be spoken *as poetry*, are yet afraid of yielding to their instinct because the present-day fashion is to chatter high verse as though it were colloquial prose. James, on the contrary, far from shirking the rhythmic emphasis, gave it full expression. His stammer ceased as by magic as soon as he began to read, and his ear, so sensitive to the convolutions of an intricate prose style, never allowed him to falter over the most complex prosody, but swept him forward on great rollers of sound till the full weight of his voice fell on the last cadence.

James's reading was a thing apart, an emanation of his inmost self, unaffected by fashion or elocutionary artifice. He read from his soul, and no one who never heard him read poetry knows what that soul was. Another day some one spoke of Whitman, and it was a joy to me to discover that James thought him, as I did, the greatest of American poets. "Leaves of Grass" was put into his hands, and all that evening we sat rapt while he wandered from "The Song of Myself" to "When lilacs last in the door-yard bloomed" (when he read "Lovely and soothing Death" his voice filled the hushed room like an organ adagio), and thence let himself be lured on to the mysterious music of "Out of the Cradle," reading, or rather crooning it in a mood of subdued ecstasy till the fivefold invocation to Death tolled out like the knocks in the opening bars of the Fifth Symphony.

James's admiration of Whitman, his immediate response to that mighty appeal, was a new proof of the way in which, above a certain level, the most divergent intelligences walk together like gods. We talked long that night of "Leaves of Grass," tossing back and forth to each other treasure after treasure; but finally James, in one of his sudden humorous drops from the heights, flung up his hands and cried out with the old stammer and twinkle: "Oh, yes, a great genius; undoubtedly a very great genius! Only one cannot help deploring his too-extensive acquaintance with the foreign languages."

I believe James enjoyed those days at the Mount as much as he did (or could) anything connected with the American scene; and the proof of it is the length of his visits and their frequency. But on one occasion his stay with us coincided with a protracted heat-wave; a wave of such unusual intensity that even the nights, usually cool and airy at the Mount, were as stifling as the days. My own dislike of heat filled me with sympathy for James, whose sufferings were acute and uncontrollable. Like many men of genius he had a singular inability for dealing with the most ordinary

daily incidents, such as giving an order to a servant, deciding what to wear, taking a railway ticket, or getting from one place to another; and I have often smiled to think how far nearer the truth than he could possibly have known was the author of that cataclysmic sketch in the famous "If—" series: "If Henry James had written Bradshaw."

During a heat-wave this curious inadaptability to conditions or situations became positively tragic. His bodily surface, already broad, seemed to expand to meet it, and his imagination to become a part of his body, so that the one dripped words of distress as the other did moisture. Always uneasy about his health, he became visibly anxious in hot weather, and this anxiety added so much to his sufferings that his state was pitiful. Electric fans, iced drinks and cold baths seemed to give no relief; and finally we discovered that the only panacea was incessant motoring. Luckily by that time we had a car which would really go, and go we did, daily, incessantly, over miles and miles of lustrous landscape lying motionless under the still glaze of heat. While we were moving he was refreshed and happy, his spirits rose, the twinkle returned to lips and eyes; and we never halted except for tea on a high hillside, or for a "cooling drink" at a village apothecary's—on one of which occasions he instructed one of us to bring him "something less innocent than Apollinaris," and was enchanted when this was interpreted as meaning an "orange phosphate," a most sophisticated beverage for that day.

On another afternoon we had encamped for tea on a mossy ledge in the shade of great trees, and as he seemed less uneasy than usual somebody pulled out an anthology, and I asked one of the party to read aloud Swinburne's "Triumph of Time," which I knew to be a favourite of James's; but after a stanza or two I saw the twinkle of beatitude fade, and an agonized hand was lifted up. "Perhaps, in view of the abnormal state of the weather, our young friend would have done better to choose a poem of less inordinate length—" and immediately we were all bundled back into the car and started off again on the incessant quest for air.

James was to leave for England in about a fortnight; but his sufferings distressed me so much that, the day after this expedition, feeling sure that there was nothing to detain him in America if he chose to go, I asked a friend who was staying in the house to propose my telephoning for a passage on a Boston steamer which was sailing within two days. My ambassador executed the commission, and hurried back with the report that the mere hint of such a plan had thrown James into a state of helpless perturbation. To change his sailing date at two days' notice—to get from the Mount to Boston (four hours by train) in *two days*—how could I lightly suggest anything so impracticable? And what about his heavy luggage, which was at his brother William's in New Hampshire? And his wash, which had been sent to the laundry only the afternoon before? Between the electric fan clutched in his hand, and the pile of sucked oranges at his elbow, he cowered there, a mountain of misery, repeating in a sort of low despairing chant: "Good God, what a woman—what a woman! Her imagination boggles at nothing! She does not even scruple to project me in a naked flight across the Atlantic . . ." The heat collapse had been as nothing to the depths into which my rash proposal plunged him, and it took several hours to quiet him down and persuade him that, if he preferred enduring the weather to flying from it, we were only too glad to keep him at the Mount.

. . .

In one respect Henry James stood alone among the great talkers I have known, for while he was inexhaustible in repartee, and never had the least tendency to monopolize the talk, yet it was really in monologue that he was most himself. I remember in particular one summer evening, when we sat late on the terrace at the Mount, with the lake shining palely through dark trees, and one of us suddenly said to him (in response to some chance allusion to his Albany relations): "And now tell us about the Emmets—tell us all about them."

The Emmet and Temple families composed, as we knew, the main element of his vast and labyrinthine cousinship—"the Emmetry," as he called it —and for a moment he stood there brooding in the darkness, murmuring over to himself: "Ah, my dear, the Emmets—ah, the Emmets!" Then he began, forgetting us, forgetting the place, forgetting everything but the vision of his lost youth that the question had evoked, the long train of ghosts flung with his enchanter's wand across the wide stage of the summer night. Ghostlike indeed at first, wavering and indistinct, they glimmered at us through a series of disconnected ejaculations, epithets, allusions, parenthetical rectifications and restate-

ments, till not only our brains but the clear night itself seemed filled with a palpable fog; and then, suddenly, by some miracle of shifted light and accumulated strokes, there they stood before us as they lived, drawn with a million filament-like lines, yet sharp as an Ingres, dense as a Rembrandt; or, to call upon his own art for an analogy, minute and massive as the people of Balzac.

I often saw the trick repeated; saw figures obscure or famous summoned to the white square of his magic lantern, flickering and wavering there, and slowly solidifying under the turn of his lens; but never perhaps anything so ample, so sustained, as that summoning to life of dead-and-gone Emmets and Temples, old lovelinesses, old follies, old failures, all long laid away and forgotten under old crumbling grave-stones. I wonder if it may not have been that very night, the place and his re-awakened associations aiding, that they first came to him and constrained him to make them live for us again in the pages of "A Small Boy" and "A Son and Brother"?

. . .

Not infrequently, on my annual visit to Qu'acre, I "took off" from Lamb House, where I also went annually for a visit to Henry James. The motor run between Rye and Windsor being an easy one, I was often accompanied by Henry James, who generally arranged to have his visit to Qu'acre coincide with mine. James, who was a frequent companion on our English motor-trips, was firmly convinced that, because he lived in England, and our chauffeur (an American) did not, it was necessary that the latter should be guided by him through the intricacies of the English country-side. Signposts were rare in England in those days, and for many years afterward, and a truly British reserve seemed to make the local authorities reluctant to communicate with the invading stranger. Indeed, considerable difficulty existed as to the formulating of advice and instructions, and I remember in one village the agitated warning: "Motorists! Beware of the children!"—while in general there was a marked absence of indications as to the whereabouts of the next village.

It chanced, however, that Charles Cook, our faithful and skillful driver, was a born path-finder, while James's sense of direction was non-existent, or rather actively but always erroneously alert; and the consequences of his intervention were always bewildering, and sometimes extremely fatiguing. The first time that my husband and I went to Lamb House by motor (coming from France) James, who had travelled to Folkestone by train to meet us, insisted on seating himself next to Cook, on the plea that the roads across Romney marsh formed such a tangle that only an old inhabitant could guide us to Rye. The suggestion resulted in our turning around and around in our tracks till long after dark, though Rye, conspicuous on its conical hill, was just ahead of us, and Cook could easily have landed us there in time for tea.

Another year we had been motoring in the west country, and on the way back were to spend a night at Malvern. As we approached (at the close of a dark rainy afternoon) I saw James growing restless, and was not surprised to hear him say: "My dear, I once spent a summer at Malvern, and know it very well; and as it is rather difficult to find the way to the hotel, it might be well if Edward were to change places with me, and let me sit beside Cook." My husband of course acceded (though with doubt in his heart), and James having taken his place, we awaited the result. Malvern, if I am not mistaken, is encircled by a sort of upper boulevard, of the kind called in Italy a *strada di circonvallazione*, and for an hour we circled about above the outspread city, while James vainly tried to remember which particular street led down most directly to our hotel. At each corner (literally) he stopped the motor, and we heard a muttering, first confident and then anguished. "This—this, my dear Cook, yes . . . this certainly is the right corner. But no; stay! A moment longer, please—in this light it's so difficult . . . appearances are so misleading . . . It may be . . . yes! I think it *is* the next turn . . . 'a little farther lend thy guiding hand' . . . that is, drive on; but slowly, please, my dear Cook; *very* slowly!" And at the next corner the same agitated monologue would be repeated; till at length Cook, the mildest of men, interrupted gently: "I guess any turn'll get us down into the town, Mr. James, and after that I can ask—" and late, hungry and exhausted we arrived at length at our destination, James still convinced that the next turn would have been the right one, if only we had been more patient.

The most absurd of these episodes occurred on another rainy evening, when James and I chanced to arrive at Windsor long after dark. We must have been driven by a strange chauffeur—perhaps Cook was on a holiday; at any rate, having fallen into the lazy habit of trusting to him to know the way, I found myself at a loss to direct his substitute to the King's Road. While I was hesitating, and peering out into the darkness, James spied an ancient doddering man who had stopped in the rain to gaze at us. "Wait a moment, my dear—I'll ask him where we are"; and leaning out he signalled to the spectator.

"My good man, if you'll be good enough to come here, please; a little nearer—so," and as the old man came up: "My friend, to put it to you in two words, this lady and I have just arrived here from *Slough*; that is to say, to be more strictly accurate, we have recently *passed through* Slough on our way here, having actually motored to Windsor from Rye, which was our point of departure; and the darkness having overtaken us, we should be much obliged if you would tell us where we now are in relation, say, to the High Street, which, as you of course know, leads to the Castle, after leaving on the left hand the turn down to the railway station." .

I was not surprised to have this extraordinary appeal met by silence, and a dazed expression on the old wrinkled face at the window; nor to have James go on: "In short" (his invariable prelude to a fresh series of explanatory ramifications), "in short, my good man, what I want to put to you in a word is this: supposing we have already (as I have reason to think we have) driven past the turn down to the railway station (which, in that case, by the way, would probably not have been on our left hand, but on our right), where are we now in relation to . . ."

"Oh, please," I interrupted, feeling myself utterly unable to sit through another parenthesis, "do ask him where the King's Road is."

"Ah—? The King's Road? Just so! Quite right! Can you, as a matter of fact, my good man, tell us where, in relation to our present position, the King's Road exactly *is*?"

"Ye're in it," said the aged face at the window.

It would be hard to imagine a greater contrast than between the hospitality of Queen's Acre and that of Lamb House. In the former a cheerful lavishness prevailed, and a cook enamoured of her art set a variety of inviting dishes before a tableful of guests, generally reinforced by transients from London or the country. At Lamb House an anxious frugality was combined with the wish that the usually solitary guest (there were never, at most, more than two at a time) should not suffer too greatly from the contrast between his or her supposed habits of luxury, and the privations imposed by the host's conviction that he was on the brink of ruin. If any one in a pecuniary difficulty appealed to James for help, he gave it without counting; but in his daily life he was haunted by the spectre of impoverishment, and the dreary pudding or pie of which a quarter or half had been consumed at dinner reappeared on the table the next day with its ravages unrepaired.

We used to laugh at Howard Sturgis because, when any new subject was touched on in our talks, he always interrupted us to cry out: "Now please remember that I've read nothing, and know nothing, and am not in the least quick or clever or cultivated"; and one day, when I prefaced a remark with "Of course, to people as intelligent as we all are," he broke in with a sort of passionate terror: "Oh, how can you say such things about us, Edith?"—as though my remark had been a challenge to the Furies.

The same scruples weighed on Henry James; but in his case the pride that apes humility concerned itself (oddly enough) with material things. He lived in terror of being thought rich, worldly or luxurious, and was forever contrasting his visitors' supposed opulence and self-indulgence with his own hermit-like asceticism, and apologizing for his poor food while he trembled lest it should be thought too good. I have often since wondered if he did not find our visits more of a burden than a pleasure, and if the hospitality he so conscientiously offered and we so carelessly enjoyed did not give him more sleepless nights than happy days.

I hope not; for some of my richest hours were spent under his roof. From the moment when I turned the corner of the grass-grown street mounting steeply between squat brick houses, and caught sight, at its upper end, of the wide Palladian window of the garden-room, a sense of joyous liberation bore me on. There *he* stood on the doorstep, the white-panelled hall with its old prints and crowded book-cases forming a background to his heavy loosely-clothed figure. Arms outstretched, lips and eyes twinkling, he came down to the car, uttering cries of mock amazement and mock humility at the undeserved honour of my visit. The arrival at Lamb House was an almost ritual performance, from those first ejaculations to the large hug and the two solemn kisses executed in the middle of the hall rug. Then, arm in arm, through the oak-panelled morning-room we wandered out onto the thin worn turf of the garden, with its ancient mulberry tree, its unkempt flower-borders, the gables of Watchbell Street peeping like village gossips over the creeper-clad walls, and the scent of roses spiced with a strong smell of the sea. Up and down the lawn we strolled with many pauses, exchanging news, answering each other's questions, delivering messages from the other members of the group, inspecting the strawberries and lettuces in the tiny kitchen-garden, and the chrysanthemums "coming along" in pots in the green house; till at length the parlour-maid appeared with a tea-tray, and I was led up the rickety outside steps to the garden-room, that stately and unexpected appendage to the unadorned cube of the house.

. . .

At Lamb House my host and I usually kept to ourselves until luncheon. Our working hours were the same, and it was only now and then that we went out before one o'clock to take a look at the green peas in the kitchen-garden, or to stroll down the High Street to the Post Office. But as soon as luncheon was despatched (amid unnecessary apologies for its meagreness, and sarcastic allusions to my own supposed culinary extravagances) the real business of the day began. Henry James, an indifferent walker, and incurably sedentary in his habits, had a passion for motoring. He denied himself (I believe quite needlessly) the pleasure and relaxation which a car of his own might have given him, but took advantage, to the last drop of petrol, of the travelling capacity of any visitor's car. When, a few years after his death, I stayed at Lamb House with the friend who was then its tenant, I got to know for the first time the rosy old town and its sea-blown neighbourhood. In Henry James's day I was never given the chance, for as soon as luncheon was over we were always whirled miles away, throwing out over the country-side what he called our "great loops" of exploration. Sometimes we went off for two or three days. I remember one beautiful pilgrimage to Winchester, Gloucester and beyond; another long day carried us to the ancient house of Brede, to lunch with the Morton Frewens, another to spend a day near Ashford with the Alfred Austins, in their pleasant old house full of books and flowers. Usually, however, to avoid an interruption to the morning's work, we lunched at Lamb House, and starting out immediately afterward pushed our explorations of down and weald and seashore to the last limit of the summer twilight.

James was as jubilant as a child. Everything pleased him—the easy locomotion (which often cradled him into a brief nap), the bosky softness of the landscape, the discovery of towns and villages hitherto beyond his range, the magic of ancient names, quaint or impressive, crabbed or melodious. These he would murmur over and over to himself in a low chant, finally creating characters to fit them, and sometimes whole families, with their domestic complications and matrimonial alliances, such as the Dymmes of Dymchurch, one of whom married a Sparkle, and was the mother of little Scintilla Dymme-Sparkle, subject of much mirth and many anecdotes. Except during his naps, nothing escaped him, and I suppose no one ever felt more imaginatively, or with deeper poetic emotion, the beauty of sea and sky, the serenities of the landscape, the sober charm of villages, manor-houses and humble churches, and all the implications of that much-storied corner of England.

One perfect afternoon we spent at Bodiam—my first visit there. It was still the old spell-bound ruin, unrestored, guarded by great trees, and by a network of lanes which baffled the invading charabancs. Tranquil white clouds hung above it in a windless sky, and the silence and solitude were complete as we sat looking across at the crumbling towers, and at their reflection in a moat starred with water-lilies, and danced over by great blue dragon-flies. For a long time no one spoke; then James turned to me and said solemnly: "Summer afternoon—summer afternoon; to me those have always been the two most beautiful words in the English language." They were the essence of that hushed scene, those ancient walls; and I never hear them spoken without seeing the towers of Bodiam mirrored in their enchanted moat.

The New Realism

In 1891, Melville, the last of the titans of the old time, died, but he had just finished *Billy Budd*. In the last year of the decade appeared *Sister Carrie*, the first novel of the man who was to be a titan of the new century. Between *Billy Budd* and *Sister Carrie* were Stephen Crane's *Maggie: A Girl of the Streets* (1893), *The Red Badge of Courage* (1895), and such glittering stories as "The Open Boat," "The Bride Comes to Yellow Sky," and "The Blue Hotel." Melville's valedictory masterpiece was to lie unread with his papers until 1924, and Dreiser's massive achievement was to become apparent later, with *Sister Carrie*, which sold, when first issued, only 456 copies. So Crane, with his brilliant style, revolutionary vision, and precocious success, was clearly the dominant figure of the decade, with the air of permanence already about his work when he died, in 1900, at the age of twenty-nine.

Crane was, however, only one of a group of writers who in one way or another were associated with what was to be called the "new realism." There were Hamlin Garland, Ambrose Bierce, Jack London, Frank Norris, and Upton Sinclair, to name the most famous, and to understand the quality of Crane, we must understand something of these others. Dreiser was to be known, in the next century, as the apostle of the new realism, but all these men had a hand in the creating of the future.

"Realism" is a slippery word—it is what the practitioner makes of it; and what these writers of the 1890's were making of it was quite different from what Howells had made and was continuing to make. Ambrose Bierce, the sardonic veteran of four bloody years of war, could call Howells "Miss Nancy Howells" and one of the "cameo-makers-in-chief to Her Littleness the Bostonese small virgin." Men like Bierce, Crane, and Dreiser were not as much concerned with representing the recognizable surface of life, and finding their dramas in its commonplace events, as they were with understanding and depicting human behavior in the context of the machine of the natural universe. The element of naturalism, in varying degrees, is important in their work.

It is sometimes said that there can be no such thing as a novelist who is a pure naturalist—for, according to the doctrine of naturalism strictly interpreted, there would be no human character living by human values in the traditional sense, but rather robots. Indeed, there is a paradox in literary naturalism, one term invoking the idea that all behavior is dictated by the laws of nature, and the other invoking the significance of consciousness, will, aspiration, moral judgment, and intellectual discrimination. What is at stake in this paradox will emerge in the works of the various writers to be considered.

Obviously, modern realism and naturalism grew out of the world of science and positivistic philosophy (see pp. 1215–16), but it is not to be assumed that the novelist takes a philosophy and then mechanically works it out in his fiction. The process is bound to be more complex than that and inevitably involves questions of individual temperament and personal experience; and Ambrose Bierce would seem to offer a clear example of this situation.

AMBROSE BIERCE (1842–1914?)

Ambrose Gwinnett Bierce, later to be known as "Bitter Bierce," was born in 1842, in Meigs County, Ohio, the last of ten children in a farm household in which poverty, grinding labor, and Calvinistic rigor were the order of life. He had the most meager education (but did read books) and in the end his sense of deprivation may have been compounded by the fact that his family had touched history, his mother being descended from the famous Puritan William Bradford and his father's brother being distinguished as a general and district attorney and the man who, in a public address, had blessed John Brown's venture in Kansas and provided the sabers with which he was to chop down his captives at the Pottawatomie massacre.

The war that the uncle helped bring on gave

the nineteen-year-old Bierce, an immediate volunteer, his entry into the great world. He saw action in such bloody battles as Shiloh, Chickamauga, and Kenesaw Mountain, and on the March to the Sea; he was mentioned in dispatches for bravery some fifteen times and was brevetted major; and after Appomattox he stayed in the army, serving in the West. The war was for Bierce, as for Justice Holmes, the great formative experience. In many ways, in fact, Bierce and Holmes are close together, both admiring the simple military virtues and both committed to the cold life of fact.

At the end of his military service, Bierce settled in San Francisco, becoming a prominent journalist and, for years, an unprominent writer. As a muckraking reporter he earned the high distinction of having Collis P. Hunting-

ton, of the Southern Pacific Railroad (then engaged in a gigantic tax fraud) ask him his price
for silence; he gave his answer, in print: "My
price is about seventy-five million dollars, to be
handed to the Treasurer of the United States."
In the Gilded Age, Bierce, who had once been,
he declared, "sufficiently zealous for Freedom
to be engaged in a four-year battle for its promotion," and whose last idealism had been dissipated by the spectacle of carpet-bag operations
in Louisiana, found nothing but moral squalor
and now, after his years of fighting for the
Union, could parody the (then) "National Anthem" as the "Rational Anthem," beginning
"My country 'tis of thee, sweet land of felony."

Many decent men shared Bierce's total disgust with American life, but with him this disgust was only one aspect of a more general disgust with all the shams, lies, pretensions, and
brutalities common to human existence, as he
recorded in *The Devil's Dictionary* (originally
called *The Cynic's Wordbook*, 1906):

CYNIC, n. A Blackguard whose faulty vision
sees things as they are, not as they ought to
be. Hence the custom among the Scythians
of plucking out a cynic's eyes to improve his
vision.
DUTY, n. That which sternly impels us in
the direction of profit, along the line of desire.
IMPUNITY, n. Wealth.
PRAY, v. To ask that the laws of the universe be annulled in behalf of a single peti-
tioner confessedly unworthy.

Feeding this disgust—this "realism," we may
say, for it represented what Bierce took to be
real behind the facade of respectability, morality, patriotism, and religion—was an obsession
with death. There is evidence that this obsession was temperamental, with deep roots, and
was manifested long before Bierce saw war service, but the war certainly provided him with
a wealth of violent episodes and vivid images
on which the obsession, with its peculiar ambivalence, its revulsion and attraction, might
batten: "I obtained leave to go down into the

valley of death [at Shiloh] and gratify a reprehensible curiosity," he wrote of a spot of specially horrible carnage of federal troops, and after
specifying the more striking details, added, with
characteristic irony, "I cannot catalogue the
charms of these gallant gentlemen who had got
what they had enlisted for." And here we may
recall, from Melville's poem "Shiloh," the line:
"What like a bullet can undeceive?"

Bierce's stories of the war, in *In the Midst of
Life* (originally *Tales of Soldiers and Civilians*,
1891), are inspired by this obsession and are
marked by horror, sometimes effectively as in
"Chickamauga," and often by a taut irony, as in
"An Occurrence at Owl Creek Bridge." But
the obsession carries over into stories of "civilians" as does the irony, which in the first line
of "An Imperfect Conflagration" almost becomes a comic gag: "Early one June morning
in 1872 I murdered my father—an act which
made a deep impression on me at the time."

The basic irony—the basic comedy, in fact—
of Bierce's work is that death is of the essence
of life, that all men are caught in a vast joke—a
view of life that reminds one of Hemingway and
the great *nada* of his story "A Clean, Well
Lighted Place," and of the scene at the end of
A Farewell to Arms when the hero, awaiting the
death of Catherine, thinks back on an evening
by a campfire, comparing man's condition to
that of ants running back and forth on a burning log on which they are trapped. Only fools,
Bierce says, deny the truth of their situation and
console themselves with illusions.

Bierce could mock his own illusions. He had
once bemused himself with the illusion that
"Freedom" could be gained by a war—and had
come upon the Gilded Age. Now the only values
left for him were the old military ones of courage, discipline, and fidelity, however empty or
merely self-justifying, with which some men
can face the great joke. So, in the end, he especially detested the Union patrioteers who railed
at the South and preened themselves on moral
virtue or demeaned the southern dead. And late
in life, on a tour of his old battlefields, he came
on a Confederate cemetery and, in "A Bivouac
of the Dead," wrote:

They were honest and courageous foemen, having little in common with the political madmen who persuaded them to their doom and the literary bearers of false witness in the aftertime. They did not live through the period of honorable strife into the period of vilification—did not pass from the iron age to the brazen—from the era of the sword to that of the tongue and pen. Among them is no member of the Southern Historical Society. Their valor was not the fury of the non-combatant; they have no voice in the thunder of the civilians and the shouting. Not by them are impaired the dignity and infinite pathos of the Lost Cause.

The dead, even the dead enemy, with whom he had shared battle, not civilians, South or North, were his friends, after all, and when, on the same trip, he saw the body of a dead Confederate soldier just dug up, with rifle by its side, Bierce wrote the poet George Sterling, back in San Francisco, "I am going over to beg his pardon." Bierce saw himself as such a corpse, but an animated one, watching with sardonic glee the antics of the living, as is suggested by the autobiographical story "The Major's Tale" in which the lonely veteran of the Battle of Franklin (Tennessee) says of himself:

Bear with him yet a little while, oh, thrifty generation; he is but one of the horrors of war strayed from his era into yours. He is only the harmless skeleton at your feast and peace-dance, responding to your laughter and your footing it featly, with rattling fingers and bobbing skull.

Bierce did not wait to die among civilians at their peace-dance of grab, felony, and self-delusion. Shortly after the trip on which he wished to beg pardon of the exhumed body of the Confederate soldier, Bierce, then at the age of seventy, disappeared into Mexico, to seek whatever "reality" might be found there. Not many years earlier, he had written a poem praying for release "From the horrors of peace, the horrors of peace," and he was last heard of while riding with Pancho Villa and his rebel army, veterans all.

In general, critics find the reiterated horror and irony of Bierce's fiction mechanical and tiresome, but if he was trapped in his compulsion, many of his pages are astutely observed and brilliantly written, in a style often precise and suggestive and, even when too "correct," never suffering from the vapidity and inflation still common in "literature." And a few of his stories provide haunting images of fate.

But what, we may ask, has this to do with realism? Bierce, indeed, did not regard himself as a realist and was, for example, savagely critical of Stephen Crane: "I had thought there could be only two worse writers than Stephen Crane, namely two Stephen Cranes." And in *The Devil's Dictionary*, he could refer to the realistic regionalists as a "pignoramus crew of malinguists, cacophonologists and apostrophographers who think that they get close to nature by depicting the sterile lives and limited emotions of the gowks and sodhoppers." Furthermore, the kind of material he himself characteristically fastened on—the gruesome, the horrible, the unusual—seems more closely related to the tradition of the Gothic romance, through Charles Brockden Brown and Poe, than to the life of everyday.

But in another and deeper sense, Bierce did contribute to the realistic impulse. Though he was not concerned with the analysis of character that constitutes one aspect of realism, he was concerned with psychological patterns of experience rather than with mere shock. In addition, and more importantly, Bierce, in his disillusioned repudiation of his boyhood ideal, sought to cut through all illusion, through the screen of rationalization and alibi needed by men and institutions, to locate the "real," the lowest common denominator of human behavior. This led him into muckraking journalism (which was a factor in the rise of realism) and even to sponsor certain radical though not always consistent ideas of social reform (for instance, the abolition of the private ownership of land and the limitation of the size of fortunes); but he was led, too, beyond the question of social and moral "reality," into a vision of man in nature, the vision of man as a natural automaton, but one cursed with consciousness and tricked by illusion. He could not develop, as Dreiser and others were to do, the philosophical and dramatic possibilities of this vision, but the vision was there.

Chickamauga (1891)

One sunny autumn afternoon a child strayed away from its rude home in a small field and entered a forest unobserved. It was happy in a new sense of freedom from control, happy in the opportunity of exploration and adventure; for this child's spirit, in bodies of its ancestors, had for thousands of years been trained to memorable feats of discovery and conquest—victories in battles whose critical moments were centuries, whose victors' camps were cities of hewn stone. From the cradle of its race it had conquered its way through two continents and passing a great sea had penetrated a third, there to be born to war and dominion as a heritage.

The child was a boy aged about six years, the son of a poor planter. In his younger manhood the father had been a soldier, and fought against naked savages and followed the flag of his country into the capital of a civilized race to the far South. In the peaceful life of a planter the warrior-fire survived; once kindled, it is never extinguished. The man loved military books and pictures and the boy had understood enough to make himself a wooden sword, though even the eye of his father would hardly have known it for what it was. This weapon he now bore bravely, as became the son of an heroic race, and pausing now and again in the sunny space of the forest assumed, with some exaggeration, the postures of aggression and defense that he had been taught by the engraver's art. Made reckless by the ease with which he overcame invisible foes attempting to stay his advance, he committed the common enough military error of pushing the pursuit to a dangerous extreme, until he found himself upon the margin of a wide but shallow brook, whose rapid waters barred his direct advance against the flying foe that had crossed with illogical ease. But the intrepid victor was not to be baffled; the spirit of the race which had passed the great sea burned unconquerable in that small breast and would not be denied. Finding a place where some bowlders in the bed of the stream lay but a step or a leap apart, he made his way across and fell again upon the rear-guard of his imaginary foe, putting all to the sword.

Now that the battle had been won, prudence required that he withdraw to his base of operations. Alas; like many a mightier conqueror, and like one, the mightiest, he could not

curb the lust for war,
Nor learn that tempted Fate will leave the loftiest star.

Advancing from the bank of the creek he suddenly found himself confronted with a new and more formidable enemy: in the path that he was following, sat, bolt upright, with ears erect and paws suspended before it, a rabbit! With a startled cry the child turned and fled, he knew not in what direction, calling with inarticulate cries for his mother, weeping, stumbling, his tender skin cruelly torn by brambles, his little heart beating hard with terror—breathless, blind with tears—lost in the forest! Then, for more than an hour, he wandered with erring feet through the tangled undergrowth, till at last, overcome by fatigue, he lay down in a narrow space between two rocks, within a few yards of the stream and still grasping his toy sword, no longer a weapon but a companion, sobbed himself to sleep. The wood birds sang merrily above his head; the squirrels, whisking their bravery of tail, ran barking from tree to tree, unconscious of the pity of it, and somewhere far away was a strange, muffled thunder, as if the partridges were drumming in celebration of nature's victory over the son of her immemorial enslavers. And back at the little plantation, where white men and black were hastily searching the fields and hedges in alarm, a mother's heart was breaking for her missing child.

Hours passed, and then the little sleeper rose to his feet. The chill of the evening was in his limbs, the fear of the gloom in his heart. But he had rested, and he no longer wept. With some blind instinct which impelled to action he struggled through the undergrowth about him and came to a more open ground—on his right the brook, to the left a gentle acclivity studded with infrequent trees; over all, the gathering gloom of twilight. A thin, ghostly mist rose along the water. It fright-

ened and repelled him; instead of recrossing, in the
direction whence he had come, he turned his back
upon it, and went forward toward the dark inclosing wood. Suddenly he saw before him a strange
moving object which he took to be some large animal—a dog, a pig—he could not name it; perhaps it
was a bear. He had seen pictures of bears, but
knew of nothing to their discredit and had vaguely
wished to meet one. But something in form or
movement of this object—something in the awkwardness of its approach—told him that it was not
a bear, and curiosity was stayed by fear. He stood
still and as it came slowly on gained courage every
moment, for he saw that at least it had not the
long, menacing ears of the rabbit. Possibly his impressionable mind was half conscious of something familiar in its shambling, awkward gait. Before it had approached near enough to resolve his
doubts he saw that it was followed by another and
another. To right and to left were many more; the
whole open space about him was alive with them—
all moving toward the brook.

They were men. They crept upon their hands
and knees. They used their hands only, dragging
their legs. They used their knees only, their arms
hanging idle at their sides. They strove to rise to
their feet, but fell prone in the attempt. They did
nothing naturally, and nothing alike, save only to
advance foot by foot in the same direction. Singly,
in pairs and in little groups, they came on through
the gloom, some halting now and again while
others crept slowly past them, then resuming their
movement. They came by dozens and by hundreds;
as far on either hand as one could see in the deepening gloom they extended and the black wood behind them appeared to be inexhaustible. The very
ground seemed in motion toward the creek. Occasionally one who had paused did not again go on,
but lay motionless. He was dead. Some, pausing,
made strange gestures with their hands, erected
their arms and lowered them again, clasped their
heads; spread their palms upward, as men are
sometimes seen to do in public prayer.

Not all of this did the child note; it is what
would have been noted by an elder observer; he
saw little but that these were men, yet crept like
babes. Being men, they were not terrible, though
unfamiliarly clad. He moved among them freely,
going from one to another and peering into their
faces with childish curiosity. All their faces were
singularly white and many were streaked and
gouted with red. Something in this—something too,

perhaps, in their grotesque attitudes and movements—reminded him of the painted clown whom
he had seen last summer in the circus, and he
laughed as he watched them. But on and ever on
they crept, these maimed and bleeding men, as
heedless as he of the dramatic contrast between his
laughter and their own ghastly gravity. To him it
was a merry spectacle. He had seen his father's
negroes creep upon their hands and knees for his
amusement—had ridden them so, "making believe"
they were his horses. He now approached one of
these crawling figures from behind and with an
agile movement mounted it astride. The man sank
upon his breast, recovered, flung the small boy
fiercely to the ground as an unbroken colt might
have done, then turned upon him a face that
lacked a lower jaw—from the upper teeth to the
throat was a great red gap fringed with hanging
shreds of flesh and splinters of bone. The unnatural
prominence of nose, the absence of chin, the fierce
eyes, gave this man the appearance of a great bird
of prey crimsoned in throat and breast by the blood
of its quarry. The man rose to his knees, the child
to his feet. The man shook his fist at the child; the
child, terrified at last, ran to a tree near by, got
upon the farther side of it and took a more serious
view of the situation. And so the clumsy multitude
dragged itself slowly and painfully along in hideous
pantomime—moved forward down the slope like a
swarm of great black beetles, with never a sound
of going—in silence profound, absolute.

Instead of darkening, the haunted landscape began to brighten. Through the belt of trees beyond
the brook shone a strange red light, the trunks
and branches of the trees making a black lacework
against it. It struck the creeping figures and gave
them monstrous shadows, which caricatured their
movements on the lit grass. It fell upon their
faces, touching their whiteness with a ruddy tinge,
accentuating the stains with which so many of
them were freaked and maculated. It sparkled on
buttons and bits of metal in their clothing. Instinctively the child turned toward the growing splendor and moved down the slope with his horrible
companions; in a few moments had passed the
foremost of the throng—not much of a feat, considering his advantages. He placed himself in the
lead, his wooden sword still in hand, and solemnly
directed the march, conforming his pace to theirs
and occasionally turning as if to see that his forces
did not straggle. Surely such a leader never before
had such a following.

Scattered about upon the ground now slowly narrowing by the encroachment of this awful march to water, were certain articles to which, in the leader's mind, were coupled no significant associations: an occasional blanket, tightly rolled lengthwise, doubled and the ends bound together with a string; a heavy knapsack here, and there a broken rifle—such things, in short, as are found in the rear of retreating troops, the "spoor" of men flying from their hunters. Everywhere near the creek, which here had a margin of lowland, the earth was trodden into mud by the feet of men and horses. An observer of better experience in the use of his eyes would have noticed that these footprints pointed in both directions; the ground had been twice passed over—in advance and in retreat. A few hours before, these desperate, stricken men, with their more fortunate and now distant comrades, had penetrated the forest in thousands. Their successive battalions, breaking into swarms and reforming in lines, had passed the child on every side —had almost trodden on him as he slept. The rustle and murmur of their march had not awakened him. Almost within a stone's throw of where he lay they had fought a battle; but all unheard by him were the roar of the musketry, the shock of the cannon, "the thunder of the captains and the shouting." He had slept through it all, grasping his little wooden sword with perhaps a tighter clutch in unconscious sympathy with his martial environment, but as heedless of the grandeur of the struggle as the dead who had died to make the glory.

The fire beyond the belt of woods on the farther side of the creek, reflected to earth from the canopy of its own smoke, was now suffusing the whole landscape. It transformed the sinuous line of mist to the vapor of gold. The water gleamed with dashes of red, and red, too, were many of the stones protruding above the surface. But that was blood; the less desperately wounded had stained them in crossing. On them, too, the child now crossed with eager steps; he was going to the fire. As he stood upon the farther bank he turned about to look at the companions of his march. The advance was arriving at the creek. The stronger had already drawn themselves to the brink and plunged their faces into the flood. Three or four who lay without motion appeared to have no heads. At this the child's eyes expanded with wonder; even his hospitable understanding could not accept a phenomenon implying such vitality as that. After slaking their thirst these men had not had the strength to back away from the water, nor to keep their heads above it. They were drowned. In rear of these, the open spaces of the forest showed the leader as many formless figures of his grim command as at first; but not nearly so many were in motion. He waved his cap for their encouragement and smilingly pointed with his weapon in the direction of the guiding light—a pillar of fire to this strange exodus.

Confident of the fidelity of his forces, he now entered the belt of woods, passed through it easily in the red illumination, climbed a fence, ran across a field, turning now and again to coquet with his responsive shadow, and so approached the blazing ruin of a dwelling. Desolation everywhere! In all the wide glare not a living thing was visible. He cared nothing for that; the spectacle pleased, and he danced with glee in imitation of the wavering flames. He ran about, collecting fuel, but every object that he found was too heavy for him to cast in from the distance to which the heat limited his approach. In despair he flung in his sword—a surrender to the superior forces of nature. His military career was at an end.

Shifting his position, his eyes fell upon some outbuildings which had an oddly familiar appearance, as if he had dreamed of them. He stood considering them with wonder, when suddenly the entire plantation, with its inclosing forest, seemed to turn as if upon a pivot. His little world swung half around; the points of the compass were reversed. He recognized the blazing building as his own home!

For a moment he stood stupefied by the power of the revelation, then ran with stumbling feet, making a half-circuit of the ruin. There, conspicuous in the light of the conflagration, lay the dead body of a woman—the white face turned upward, the hands thrown out and clutched full of grass, the clothing deranged, the long dark hair in tangles and full of clotted blood. The greater part of the forehead was torn away, and from the jagged hole the brain protruded, overflowing the temple, a frothy mass of gray, crowned with clusters of crimson bubbles—the work of a shell.

The child moved his little hands, making wild, uncertain gestures. He uttered a series of inarticulate and indescribable cries—something between the chattering of an ape and the gobbling of a turkey —a startling, soulless, unholy sound, the language of a devil. The child was a deaf mute.

Then he stood motionless, with quivering lips, looking down upon the wreck.

Jack London (1876–1916)

Jack London was a considerably more imperfect realist than Bierce, but even the more romantic excesses in his work characteristically involved certain ideas and attitudes that are central to realism. Though he went briefly to both the Oakland High School and the University of California at Berkeley, London was, like Bierce and Dreiser, a homemade intellectual. Born in 1876, in San Francisco, he was the bastard son of a certain W. H. Chaney—on the one hand an astrologer and charlatan and on the other a man of intellectual power. His mother was a neurotic and wildly eccentric woman, a spiritualist, who later married a man named London.

The boyhood of the writer who thus acquired the name of London knew dire poverty, family confusion, spiritualist séances (in which he was trained to assist), the tough waterfront life of the San Francisco Bay, a hitch as an "oyster pirate" robbing the beds by night, and a job on the California Fish Patrol. By the time he was twenty-one he had been a hand on a sailing voyage to Japan, an "advance man" for Kelly's Army (the West Coast equivalent of Coxey's Army,[1] and a prospector in the Klondike gold rush (which had also drawn Hamlin Garland, though only, he said, to find nature, not gold). By then, too, the last dabbling bit of London's formal education was over, but he continued to read prodigiously—many writers on philosophy and science, including the then essential Spencer, Nietzsche, Darwin, Marx, Engels, Haeckel, and Huxley. He read deeply in realistic novelists like Flaubert and Zola, but also read Kipling,

Hardy, Conrad, and—what was remarkable for that time—Melville.

London had unflagging energy, and his writing came in a flood. By 1900, his career was launched with a collection of stories, *The Son of the Wolf*, and three years later, when he was twenty-seven, *The Call of the Wild*, his second book, was making him rich. Books poured out, fifty by the time of his death in 1916. Meanwhile, he had plunged into a life of action, reporting the Russo-Japanese War, disappearing into the slums of London to study firsthand the degradation of a great modern city (from which came *The People of the Abyss*, in 1902), building a yacht and sailing around the world, propagandizing for the socialist revolution, running for mayor of Oakland (twice), creating a model ranch and estate (where the manor Wolf House, which had taken years and a small fortune to build, burned before he could occupy it). His life was a contest between his vast earning power and his genius for spending, losing, or giving away money, and between his iron constitution and whisky; and by the time he was forty, debts, whisky, and illness were clearly winning. His death may have been a suicide.

Meanwhile London's voracious reading gave a context for his writing. Wolf Larsen, the half-brute, half-philosopher sea captain in *The Sea Wolf* (1904), is a projection of the author— or of one aspect of the author (who was to build himself Wolf House as his lair)—in that he is an autodidact who has seized on the ideas of the age. But Larsen, the Nietzschean superman and apostle of materialism, is balanced by the narrator, a civilized man of spiritual sensitivity. As a parallel split, London, though obviously drawn to Darwin and the bleak doctrine of the survival of the fittest, saw the contradiction between this theory and that of Marx, that is, between individualism and social cooperation. Late in life, London was maintaining that in *The Sea Wolf* he had "attacked Nietzsche and his super-man idea," but the novel is certainly ambiguous on this point, for there is no way to know whether Larsen's doom comes because of a short circuit of the powers of a strongly in-

[1] Coxey's Army was a group of about one hundred unemployed persons who set out on foot from Massillon, Ohio, March 25, 1894, for Washington, D.C. Led by Jacob S. Coxey, a self-made businessman, this "army" was the most famous of many such pilgrimages to the national capital in 1894 to popularize the need for economic reform.

dividualistic man in a closed world, or because of the nature of individualism per se. The largely autobiographical novel *Martin Eden* (1908) was too, London claimed, an indictment of individualism: "Had Martin Eden [who commits suicide in the novel] been a socialist, he would not have died—he would have been able to find a meaning in life." But it is hard to avoid the conclusion that what attracted London to Marxism was less the dream of a society perfected in justice than the drama of a class war fulfilling his own need for apocalyptic violence. His zest in the nightmare vision of *The Iron Heel* (1907) as well as his flirtation with the anarchists, including Emma Goldman, would seem to support this view.

Both Darwinism and Marxism, whatever tensions London found between them, are, we should note, "materialistic," but London was, even so, an imperfect materialist; in *White Fang* (1906), for instance, with the conquest of the wolf nature by love, as well as in Martin Eden's own experience, there are elements presented as scarcely explicable on materialistic grounds. But there were even deeper divisions and contradictions in London. On one hand, he proclaimed his brotherhood with all workers of the world; on the other, he was something of a "blond-beast," Anglo-Saxon racist. With the same self-division that we shall find in Dreiser, London, on the one hand, dedicated his life to literature; but, on the other, writing was only a means to an end, and the end was money and lots of it; as his daughter puts it in *Jack London and His Times*, there was something "definitely working-class" in his attitude toward writing, a mere job to get through with. In the later years he was buying story ideas from various people, including the young Sinclair Lewis, to keep his one-man fiction factory supplied with raw material.

Personally, in spite of his political concerns, London was a romantic adventurer, a two-fisted proletarian version of the adventurer Richard Harding Davis, who wrote best sellers on a prodigious scale, reported six wars, set upper-class fashions and taught manners, and was the model of manhood and the dream-self for the male half of American youth and the dream lover for the other half.[2] Stephen Crane resembled London the adventurer, but, as we shall see, there were significant differences. London, born in poverty, went adventuring to escape the grimy limitations of his personal situation, while Crane, born into middle-class comfort, went adventuring, first into the world of poverty, to escape the grimly starched Methodist respectability of his background. Furthermore, when London adventured to the Klondike or the South Seas, he milked the romantic background and experiences of that world to the utmost, while Crane, when he went to the world of romance, say the American West, reversed London's procedure and, as in "The Bride Comes to Yellow Sky" and "The Blue Hotel," de-romanticized the presumably romantic material.

London, we must remember, was bred on the same basic books that nourished Dreiser—Nietzsche, Darwin, Spencer, Huxley *et al.*—but the difference between what he and Dreiser did with those ideas, like the difference between his adventuring and that of Crane, is crucially important. The ideas became, for Dreiser, the fuel for a personal drama. In London they became the fuel for a projected melodrama. To understand ideas and their relation to himself, Dreiser had to create his fiction, to enact as deeply as possible the potentialities of the ideas, but London, even in work as autobiographical

---

[2] Davis was the son of Rebecca Harding Davis (1831–1910), who earned an early and honorable place in the history of American realism. The son was the middlebrow literary and culture hero for the turn of the century—and also for persons of high pretension, including Dr. Oliver Wendell Holmes, who, in his old age, called on the young man, and Julia Ward Howe, who received him and recited "The Battle Hymn of the Republic" for him—the honor of which event was somewhat mitigated by the fact that she would recite it to lamp-posts if no better audience was handy. The figure of Davis stands behind Stephen Crane and Hemingway, particularly Hemingway, who was a boy when Davis was at the peak of his fame and who, in some of his more fraudulent aspects, is very similar. But there is, of course, for both Crane and Hemingway, the vast difference in talent and artistic integrity.

as *Martin Eden,* was, ultimately, little more involved than he was when the locus of the drama was the soul of the dog in *White Fang.*

As for London, the ideas of his time as caught in his fiction have long since lost meaning. He remains a splendid writer of books for boys, but the intellectual significance of *The Call of the Wild* or of *Jerry of the Islands* now seems, except for historians of literature, no greater than that of Edgar Rice Burroughs' books about Tarzan or the exploration of Mars.

Ideas alone were not decisive for realism.

Not even the idea that literature should use ideas to bring about real change in a real world was enough to make Jack London a realist. His temperament triumphed over all his ideas, and the world he created never seemed quite real— particularly when he was writing the books, such as *Martin Eden,* in which he came closest to realistic fiction. Even so, in 1905 when *The Jungle,* Upton Sinclair's novel of the Chicago stockyards, appeared, London hailed it for the realism that he himself had never achieved: "The book we have been waiting for these many years! The Uncle Tom's Cabin of wage-slavery!" And he continued: "It depicts not what man ought to be, but what man is compelled to be in our world, in the Twentieth Century."

Sinclair stood at a polar distance from London, for with him the only reality was in the documentary solidity of the muckraking reportage he converted into fiction, and in one instance at least he did bring about real change in a real world; *The Jungle* provoked a government investigation of meat packing and the passage of the Pure Food Act. *The Brass Check* (1919), however, scarcely abolished yellow journalism nor did *100%* (1920) get Tom Mooney out of San Quentin. But Sinclair's series of fictionalized exposés, including the treatment of the Teapot Dome scandal in *Oil* (1927) and that of the Sacco-Vanzetti case in *Boston* (1928), undoubtedly did have some long-range effect on the public conscience.

Sinclair is an extreme example of the kind of realism urged by Henry B. Fuller, who, feeling that the spirit of the age, with its positivism and sense of social urgency, called upon writers to abandon imaginative fiction and use their fictional skills in the presentation of significant fact—specifically recommending biography as a subject. So in Sinclair the reformist impulse, supported by documentation, became the dominant version of realism. He was, in fact, active in public affairs (especially during the Depression, when he was almost elected Governor of California); no doubt, he always put political concerns ahead of artistic ones. In any case, the limitation of his version of realism is that both the interest in character and philosophical resonance have been sacrificed to propagandistic journalism. But the work does shed some light on the development of Dreiser; for his imagination was also wedded to fact and, in a complex way, his fiction is documentary too.

Frank Norris (1870–1902)

On the campus of the University of California, at Berkeley, the student Frank Norris often ostentatiously carried a novel by Zola, in French, under his arm and was accustomed to cross the bay to study, as Zola might have done, the pullulating life of mean streets; and the novel that even then he was working on, to be published in 1899 under the title *McTeague,* was first called *The People of Polk Street,* his favorite street in San Francisco for literary observation.

Like Crane, Norris romantically discovered the "real" life of the modern city. His father was a very successful speculator in real estate and his mother had been an actress, and he himself had been sent to Paris to study painting under the mastership of the then great Bouguereau (whom Dreiser admired enough to put a "genuine Bouguereau" in the "swell saloon" of *Sister Carrie*). In Paris, Norris had devoted more attention to medieval romance and the study of armor than to painting, and had even composed *Yvernelle,* a long narrative poem celebrating chivalry (published in 1892, at his mother's expense); and concerning Romanticism of a more modern variety, he says that the main character in his now forgotten autobiographical novel *Blix* had "suffered an almost fatal attack of Richard Harding Davis." The disease, though not fatal for Norris, was chronic, and in certain ways he modeled his life on that popular hero, on the one hand playing the role of the dashing young man-about-town and on the other seeking far countries and interesting wars. In South Africa he found the Boer War, and in Cuba the Spanish-American War (where he met and did not like the already famous Crane, two years his junior). To seek experience was the way, he maintained, to tune the "instrument" of the novelist: "Travel is the only way. Travel in any direction, by any means, so only it be far—very, very far."

But upon his return to America after Paris, Norris had discovered the real world. His conversion to realism was not as positive and dramatic as that of Hamlin Garland on his return to the Middle West, and the romantic element in Norris was simply absorbed into realism. For instance, in an essay called "A Plea for Romantic Fiction," he could write (not without some justification) that Zola "has been dubbed a realist, but he is, on the contrary, the very head of Romanticists," and some critics, like Franklin Walker, in his book on Norris, hold that he followed Zola, and naturalistic determinism, only because the "presenting of man as the victim of external laws allowed for big forces and hence for big conflicts."

Big conflict was what the romantic in Norris did want, at least in the three novels for which he is remembered: *McTeague* (1899), *The Octopus* (1901), and *The Pit* (1903). McTeague, a great brute of a man, is destroyed by elements in his nature and in his wife's that he cannot understand, but this study of avarice (the fine film version made by Erich von Stroheim, in 1923, was called *Greed*) is "big," not primarily because of the personal elements, but because of the relation of the personal story to the society in which it occurs. The novel could have been called, with some reason, *An American Tragedy*, for McTeague, like Clyde Griffiths, the hero of Dreiser's masterpiece, is a sort of Horatio Alger tragically *manqué*. Other characters, too, are struggling in the grip of

the American dream of success, and the whole point of the novel, from the early dream of McTeague's mother of making him "respectable" by his fake dental training, through his hanging a great gold tooth outside his office, on to his ironical discovery of gold when, as a murderer in flight, he is dying in the desert, is a criticism of the American gospel. The criticism in *McTeague* would include, too, an attack on another gospel that Norris was later to accept, the notion that in spite of the brutalities of the natural and social process, "Truth," as he puts it in *The Octopus*, "will, in the end, prevail, and all things surely, inevitably, resistlessly work together for good." This disinfected version of Social Darwinism found in Spencer, in William Graham Sumner, and sometimes in Dreiser, is also found in John D. Rockefeller, Andrew Carnegie, and Bishop Lawrence; it was the most comforting thought a Robber Baron could resort to. But to return to Norris, this notion could add another "big" issue to his drama—the conflict of sympathies and values evoked by the spectacle of the great machine of the universe as it crushes the individual in its merciless progress toward "good."

With *The Octopus* and *The Pit*, the first two items in a projected trilogy, another kind of "bigness" is called forth. With the consolidation of the new nation after the Civil War and the appearance of a new kind of rootless and wandering American—of which Mark Twain, Howells, Bierce, Henry James, and Crane are, in their various ways, examples—the idea of a national novel, the "Great American Novel," gripped the general imagination. Just after Theodore Roosevelt had written *The Winning of the West* (1889; 1896) and Frederick Jackson Turner (1893) had analyzed the significance of the frontier in American history and announced that its day was over (see p. 1474), Norris, dwelling on the grandeur of the story of the westward conquest (from the dawn of European history until the present moment), declared:

The plain truth of the matter is that we have neglected our epic—the black shame of it be on us—and no contemporaneous poet or chronicler thought it worth his while to sing the song or tell the tale of the West because literature in the day when the West was being won was a cult indulged in by certain well-bred gentlemen in New England, who looked eastward to the Old World. . . .

A true epic, Norris said, would involve a "great national event." He had found the event, and to this subject of the conquest of the West he would graft the other equally great American subject, the drama of business. What would bind all together would be the theme of wheat, first in *The Octopus*, in the struggle between the ranchers and the Southern Pacific Railroad (one example of a struggle going on all over the Middle West and West); then, in *The Pit*, in the financial struggle for control of the wheat market; and, finally, in *The Wolf*, in the story of the export of American wheat to all the world. The project, Norris confidently announced, would be "B.I.G."

Not only was Norris going to compose the epic, but he was also going to emphasize the epic "bigness" by incorporating in his work the story of how the true grandeur of the theme had been discovered. In *The Octopus* itself, in the middle of the action, he sets a character much like himself, a cultivated man, a poet, an easterner (he had at one time played all these roles, coming back to California from Paris and *Yvernelle*). This character, who has come West with the idea of writing an epic of the traditional sort, is visiting on the ranch of Magnus Derrick, the leader in the fight against the railroad. Here he stumbles upon a great drama being enacted before his eyes; gradually he realizes the proportions of the event and, to understand it, turns to the study of history and economics, to Malthus and Henry George and Russian revolutionists, and thence to throwing an actual bomb. But he passes beyond action to understanding[3]—and to an awareness that

history, though bloody, is, in the end, a beneficent process of forces that the individual may not be able to understand.

This story of the epic within the epic is followed by the more sharply focused story, in *The Pit*, of the strong man who seeks to corner the wheat market (a drama suggested by the exploit of a certain Joseph Leiter, in 1897). Norris's hero, Curtis Jadwin, modeled in part on his father, the real estate operator, is a forerunner of Cowperwood, the hero of Dreiser's trilogy of business. In him Norris tried to reach the same tragic scale that Dreiser, somewhat more successfully, was to aim for; and his intention, verbalized rather than exhibited, appears in the tribute to Jadwin that, at the moment of his failure when other speculators burst into cheers, his chief enemy pronounces:

> They can cheer now, all they want. They didn't do it. It was the wheat itself that beat him; no combination of men could have done it—go on, cheer you damned fools! He was a bigger man than the best of us.

The wheat had beaten Jadwin—the anonymous, inexplicable, inexorable force that had evoked his own force. But the tragic edge of the situation is somewhat blunted by a new version of Norris's idea that incidental evil works for universal good: Jadwin, who, in his passion for success, has been losing his wife's love, now confidently expects to remedy that oversight and find "happiness." The happy ending is a little too easy.

Norris died in 1902, before he could begin the around-the-world travels that would equip him for writing *The Wolf*. He was thirty-two, dying like Crane before the fulfillment of his talent. It is hard to know what that talent

---

[3] In an essay entitled "The Novel with a 'Purpose'" Norris makes a sharp distinction between the "man" and the "artist." The artist *qua* artist must, in the act of creation, transcend the personal involvements: "Do you think that Mrs. Stowe was more interested in the slave question than she was in the writing of 'Uncle Tom's Cabin'? Her book, her manuscript, the page-to-page progress of the narrative, were more absorbing to her than all the Negroes that were ever whipped or sold." This distinction was one of constant grinding concern for Hawthorne and is a perennially important one, with many variants. See the issue in the 1930's, pp. 2402–6. We have already referred to Upton Sinclair in this regard.

would have amounted to. Clearly it was considerable, but in the work already accomplished he lacked the stylistic flair and psychological acuity of his rival. When he died his work did seem to be on an upswing, and he was still showing the possibilities of growth. One cannot, with much confidence, say the same of Crane. Meanwhile, Dreiser, in this decade of brilliant precocity, had finally published his first book, which failed.

STEPHEN CRANE (1871–1900)

When, in 1893, Stephen Crane, then twenty-two years old, published *Maggie: A Girl of the Streets*, he "initiated," as the poet John Berryman put it, "modern American writing." If Mark Twain was, as Faulkner said, "all our grandfather," then Crane was the father. The time gap between Mark Twain and Crane is important. Mark Twain was born in 1835, and by 1871, when Crane was born, he had published *The Innocents Abroad*. If *Huckleberry Finn*, of 1885, seems modern, it is because it has the timelessness of the old agrarian America and enough American readers even now have echoes of that world in their consciousness to make the book significant for them. But *Maggie*, of 1893, is modern in a very different sense. With it, American fiction comes to the big city. There had been, of course, the novels of Howells, who had been shocked into an awareness of the brutality of the new industrial order and who shows young Dryfoos, of *A Hazard of New Fortunes*, being killed in a strike riot, but once we are out of the comfortable bourgeois interiors of Howells' world and into the mean streets, we are merely sightseers or, at the most, welfare case workers. There had been, too, moralizing exposés, such as *How the Other Half Lives*, by Jacob Riis, *The Night Side of City Life*, by Thomas de Witt Talmage, or *The Dangerous Classes of New York*, by Charles Loring Brace; but Crane's motive in dealing with the same kind of material, is, as we shall see, very different.[1]

More than novelty of material is involved in the modernity of *Maggie*, and here again we may compare it with *Huckleberry Finn*. Crane is committed, at least in *Maggie*, to the idea that environment is fate. Maggie is what she is because her world is the way it is; Crane is a child of the new scientific outlook. If Mark Twain, too, was to come to a bleak determinism, his philosophy, even in its bleakness, is not fundamentally "scientific"; a religious tonality remained, for, in the very sense of outrage, the voice denying God was really a voice cursing God. In *Huckleberry Finn*, however, that phase of Twain's thought had not yet emerged, and a sense of human responsibility is at the very center of the work. As the exact opposite of *Maggie*, it is a story of the growth of moral sensibility and philosophical awareness. The whole point is that Huck, the son of old Pap and raised in the most unpromising "environ-

[1] Such novels as Josiah Gilbert Holland's *Sevenoaks* (1875), concerned with the Robber Baron Jim Fisk, or Charles Dudley Warner's *A Little Journey in the World* (1889) do deal with the city, but they represent an interest at the other end of the spectrum from Crane's. In the same year that *Maggie* appeared, Henry B. Fuller, after writing of Europe, turned to Chicago for subject matter and published *The Cliff-Dwellers*, to be followed, in 1895, by *With the Procession*. Dreiser was to say that Fuller, not Crane, was the pioneer of "realism in America"—by realism meaning his own kind of fiction. But Fuller was actually closer to the "realism" of Howells, who, when an old man, said to Fuller: "Can't you see that it is your duty to write, hereafter, my novels for me?" Melville, of course, in *Pierre; or, The Ambiguities* had used the city—though in a hallucinatory way closer to Baudelaire or T. S. Eliot than to the realistic novelists. And Whitman had treated the city in "Song of Myself."

ment," is *not* a victim of it; he can look at things "fresh," as Tom Sawyer says of him, though without meaning to be complimentary, and can become the critic not only of society, but of society as entrenched in his own "conscience." The essence of Twain's tale is the affirmation of the possibility of conquering those things that might be taken to determine the human fate.

To understand what went into *Maggie* we must look at what Crane himself was. His grandfather Crane, for whom he was named, was president of the Colonial Assemblies when the Declaration of Independence was drawn up, but even then the family was already old in the land and had gained honor, as it was to gain more, on the field of battle and in the pulpit. Stephen was born in Newark, New Jersey (which an ancestor had had a hand in founding in 1666). His father was a Methodist minister of some renown, and his mother, the daughter of a minister, was a power in the early Women's Christian Temperance Union and a contributor to a paper called *The Heathen Woman's Friend*; the boy was raised strictly, if lovingly, in puritanical Methodist orthodoxy.

Stephen was brilliant, loved baseball, horses, and swimming, was a good shot, was fascinated by military matters and went to a military school, and early took up smoking, gambling, swearing, and beer-drinking. By the time he was sixteen he had begun his journalistic career as a summer helper to an older brother who ran a news agency at Asbury Park, New Jersey, then a highly respectable and pious resort community. He went to Lafayette College and flunked out after one term. He lasted longer at Syracuse, even though here too much of his education was extracurricular. He was well acquainted with the local brothels and dives, "gloried," as one classmate later put it, "in talking with the shambling figures who lurked in the dark doorways on deserted slum streets," thought the police court the most interesting place in town, and again flunked out. But he had acquired the habit of reading, had been doing some reporting for the New York *Tribune*, and before he left town had finished, in a cold

tower room of the Delta Upsilon fraternity house, a first draft of *Maggie*.

Back in Asbury Park, as a reporter, not quite twenty, Crane was hard at work on his first tales and sketches of back-country Sullivan County, New Jersey. By fall he was in New York trying to get a job on a newspaper and enlarging his acquaintance with low life by hanging around the East Side, occasionally acquiring a black eye in a barroom, and, with a cigarette out of the corner of his mouth, feeling very superior to what he called the "nicely laundered lives" of his Methodist relatives. Within a year he had a piece in the *Cosmopolitan* magazine and had begun his first stories of New York life. During this time, too, he was in love with a married woman, somewhat his senior, Mrs. Lily Munroe, who refused to leave her husband for the decidedly unkempt youth with no visible prospects, but who remained, apparently, the great love of his brief life. Now he was also writing his strange poems and reworking the old manuscript of *Maggie*. By this time, too, with his poverty and irregular life, he was beginning to show the symptoms of the tuberculosis that was to kill him.

Maggie was finding no publisher. "You mean it's too honest?" Crane is reported to have asked the editor of the great *Century* magazine. And it was a shocking book, in much the same way that Dreiser's *Sister Carrie* was to prove shocking to delicate sensibilities even ten years later. *Maggie* was shocking because it indulged in neither sentiment nor moralizing. In terms very like those that Dreiser, years later, was to use about his own work, Crane said that in *Maggie* he had merely wanted "to show people as they seemed to me." And he added: "If that be evil, make the most of it."

For its mere material, *Maggie* was, as we have said, not revolutionary. In fact, Crane himself, in his newspaper sketches, had presented the world of the slums without attracting censure, for his presentations had seemed disinfected by the pious motive of muckraking. But now, in a novel, the same things looked different—they were no longer at the same safe distance, for fiction invites the immediate act of the imagination. Now Crane was trying to realize, to recreate, the inwardness of the life of the slum, and this was the unforgivable thing.

Maggie came from the degraded world that had always attracted the parsonage boy. The parsonage boy, however, had motives other than mere rebellion against excessive virtue and self-conscious respectability. While flunking out of college he had read Zola's *L'Assommoir*, a powerful novel presenting the degradation of a young woman in the Paris slums, and Flaubert's *Madame Bovary*, and both books had sharpened his vision of the brutal world he was adventuring into, as Balzac's work, at that very moment, was sharpening the vision of the young reporter Theodore Dreiser.[2]

Since nobody wanted his much-revised novel, Crane took what remained of a tiny inheritance from his father (he had already lost part at poker), borrowed a little more from a brother, and paid a printer $869 to manufacture eleven hundred copies of a cheaply printed little yellow paperback dignified by no publisher's name and attributed, to spare his brother's embarrassment, to an author by the name of Johnston Smith. But if the book was published nobody seemed to care. Crane was penniless and defeated, ready to give up the idea of being a writer at all. But he had sent a copy to Hamlin Garland, who in his turn had sent it to the great Howells. At this nadir of Crane's fortunes, Howells invited him to tea; and in a borrowed suit, he went and heard his host, the intimate friend of Mark Twain, declare to the assembled guests that "Mr. Crane can do things that Mr. Clemens can't"—a compliment that Crane, who liked only Mark Twain's *Life on the Mississippi*, thought that *Huckleberry Finn* was botched in the end, and once called *A Connect-*

icut Yankee as "inappropriate as a drunken bride," could scarcely have found overwhelming. Two years later, when Howells wrote the preface to a proper edition of *Maggie*, he essayed a higher flight and pleased Crane somewhat more by saying that the book had about it something of Greek tragedy.

Howells' admiration for *Maggie* made no immediate difference in Crane's way of life. He continued to live in what he called the "antique rookery" of the old Art Students League building, where he slept on borrowed beds, kept irregular hours, ate irregular meals, found irregular employment, and met with irregular companions. All the time he carried, in a notebook in his pocket, a quotation from Emerson: "Congratulate yourselves if you have done something strange and extravagant and broken the monotony of a decorous age." The quotation from Emerson in Crane's pocket as he made his rounds in that world of New York imitated from the artistic underworld of Paris— it is an irony of literary history, for Emerson's wildest extravagance would no doubt have seemed to Crane a thing decorous to the point of death.

But with Emerson in his pocket Crane went on his own mysterious course, gregarious but detached, somehow certain of himself but, as Hamlin Garland described him, "self-derisive" —standing, ill-clothed and coughing, in a breadline to get material for a sketch called "Men in the Storm," sleeping in flophouses to prepare for "An Experiment in Misery," prowling Minetta Lane, a black slum where life was at its most drastic markdown, going down into mines in Pennsylvania to do an exposé of the condition of the coal miners, going out West, to New Orleans, to Mexico, following what a friend called his "hobby . . . to know life as it is." He was a thin young man, sickly looking but somehow tough, untidy and disreputable in appearance, a sort of tramp really, "nervous as a race horse fretting to be on the track," as the novelist Willa Cather, who met him in Nebraska when she was a college girl, described him.

By 1895, a volume of Crane's poems—which

2 To pursue a parallel with Dreiser, the famous sections in *Sister Carrie* (see pp. 1880–82) that deal with the "philosophy of clothes" are close to what Crane says of Maggie's yearnings: "She envied elegance and soft palms. She craved those adornments of person which she saw every day on the street, conceiving them to be allies of vast importance to women. Studying faces, she thought many of the women and girls she chanced to meet smiled with serenity as though forever cherished and watched over by those they loved."

he did not call poems, but "lines"—had been published under the title *The Black Riders*. The reception was, in general, adverse, often savagely so; but the advocates were sometimes passionate in their endorsement, and Howells, who at first had been puzzled by the book, finally hailed it as the finest of the year. In other words, the "lines" struck some sort of nerve center of the time. They were shocking, and at least part of the shock came from the fact that the God of Crane's childhood is constantly present—on stage or off—and is the subject of a peculiarly ambivalent and complex response. But Crane was rebelling not only against God; he was as the *Atlantic Monthly* put it, "rebellious and modern in the extreme, occasionally blasphemous to a degree which even cleverness will not reconcile to a liberal taste." But if, as the London *Athenaeum* said, this strange disciple of Emerson was concerned with the "doctrine that every man is a law unto himself," he also rebelled against the idea of any simple definition of man's nature or man's fate. Man is evil and man is good, and in that ambiguity his fate is a struggle toward self-definition.

> I stood upon a high place,
> And saw, below, many devils
> Running, leaping,
> And carousing in sin.
> One looked up, grinning,
> And said, "Comrade! Brother!"

And:

> A man feared that he might find an assassin;
> Another that he might find a victim.
> One was more wise than the other.

Man does not know his own values by any absolute standard; he must arrive at his values in the process of life; but this process itself is ironical:

> A man saw a ball of gold in the sky;
> He climbed for it,
> And eventually he achieved it—
> It was clay.

> Now this is the strange part:
> When the man went to the earth

> And looked again,
> Lo, there was the ball of gold.
> Now this is the strange part:
> It was a ball of gold.
> Ay, by the heavens, it was a ball of gold.

In the poems quoted above the ambiguity is actually specified but here it is implicit:

> On the horizon the peaks assembled;
> And as I looked,
> The march of the mountains began.
> As they marched, they sang,
> "Ay! we come! we come!"

This poem, like so many of Crane's, is a fantasy; the assumed order of the objective world is violated; some conflict is developed between the inner and the outer realm—or rather, both a conflict and a strange rapport. As John Berryman indicates in his book on Crane, there is here a "conflict between the sense of terror communicated and a suggestion of desire," for the "Ay" answers, as it were, a question or entreaty. Furthermore, the poem suggests the notion of some ambiguous relation between mind and nature, both benign and threatening—an impression, as Berryman put it, of a "fatal relation."

Fate and will do, in fact, give the paradox that is continually toyed with in *The Black Riders*, and that same paradox haunts Crane's fiction, with the emphasis on fate (environment) in *Maggie*, and on will, as we shall see, in *The Red Badge of Courage*. Crane's poetry, to sum up what we have been saying, is metaphysical in the sense that the work of Emily Dickinson is.

The paradox of fate and will haunted Crane's actual life as well as his work, for he lived with bursts of demonic energy and wild appetite for experience in contrast to the steady encroachment of his disease, and the most obvious manifestation of the paradox was in the irony which characterized his personal attitudes and that of his work. Uncertainty is implicit in man's situation in the universe and in his own view of himself; there is always a play on contrasts, of reversals, of inversions of fact or feeling.

The most extended example of irony in Crane's poetry is in "War Is Kind." Let us set this poem addressed to all whom war has bereaved against Whitman's poem on bereavement "Come Up from the Fields, Father." Both are powerful poems, but the differences of feeling and method are great. Whitman is concerned with the focusing of emotional response, presenting the very nakedness of the grief. Crane, on the other hand, professes to deny the appropriateness of the grief, for, as he says, "War is kind." Crane's irony here is extremely complex. This is not the relatively simple irony of the individual plight set against the mechanism of society that makes war; nor even the irony of that plight set against the causes (even the noble causes) for which wars may be fought, the kind of irony that often appears in Melville's poetry of the Civil War. In Crane's poems war is "kind" insofar as it fulfills something in man's nature—the need for the "unexplained glory," the "virtue of slaughter," and the "excellence of killing." And here we should notice that it falsifies the poem to assume that the irony here has only one dimension. Men do find an "unexplained glory" in war, beyond their "little souls," and this fact is ironically set against the human costs. But another kind of effect comes with the more sarcastic tone of "Great is the battle-god" and the "excellence of killing." Both views of war are legitimate, that of "glory" and that sarcastically denying "glory"; and this fact means that the consolation offered the bereaved is both literal (if such awareness of "glory" can be considered consolation, or if war is fated by human nature) and ironical.

There are two more general, contextual ironies to be considered here. First, Crane, as the preacher's son, was certainly aware of the forms of pious consolation (that death is God's will, that death brings relief from the pains of life, that death means the heavenly reward) that amount to the assertion that death is "kind"; and so we have here an ironical parody of pious consolation, with the corollary that man's situation, with war or without war, remains the same. The consolation "War is kind" is merely a special application of the consolation "Death is kind."

For the second contextual irony, we recall that Crane himself was obsessed with war, by the need, we may presume, to exorcise fear, by a passion for the "unexplained glory." So, in a sense, the irony of the poem is self-directed, putting the poet's own views in the context of general human suffering. It is a psychological situation not unlike that we find when Faulkner purges his own romantic militarism by projecting it into the figure of Percy Grimm in *Light in August*. And in this connection we may set the ironical complexities of the poem against those of *The Red Badge of Courage*.

"War Is Kind" is clearly Crane's best poem, complex thematically and tonally, and with the powerful image, almost Shakespearean in depth and precision, that brings the whole poem to focus in the commonplace, but shockingly appropriate, "button."[3] But this image, so freighted with feeling, reminds us how bare in this respect Crane's poetry generally is. The interest is commonly anecdotal, situational; the "lines" are little parables, little allegories, with the interest and force not inhering in suggestive depth and dramatic intensity of language but in the metaphysical or psychological issue under consideration. The effect is usually dependent on bareness, starkness, succinctness, and epigrammatic precision, not on vivid realization; and in this connection we may remember that these "lines," which Crane did not call poems, often seem to be cryptic notes for fiction, the sort of thing that Hawthorne, for instance, might (in a different form, of course) put into his notebook to be developed into his metaphysical fables.

But here a peculiar fact emerges. If Crane wrote a poetry that eschewed poetic effects (metaphorical density, elaboration of rhythm, rhyme, and so on) he was, at the same time, developing, especially in *The Red Badge of*

[3] This image of the mother's heart as a button serves the same purpose here that the figure of the mother serves in giving a background to the action of *The Red Badge of Courage*. In fact, the parallel between the poem and the novel is very close, and each serves as a commentary on the other.

Courage, a highly personal prose style that exploits poetic resources.[4] In association with this fact, we may remark, too, that Crane was to write: "Personally I like my little book of poems . . . better than I do *The Red Badge of Courage*. The reason is, I suppose, that the former is the more ambitious effort." By this we may assume that he regarded his "lines" as direct efforts, spontaneous and therefore more honest, at defining his "truth," as an unadorned rendering of the ideas most important to him.

The tale goes that Crane undertook *The Red Badge* on a bet that he could write a better war story than Zola had delivered in *La Débâcle*. He was then twenty-one and had never seen war. But he had *Battles and Leaders of the Civil War*, with its hundreds of photographs, and he did go to Virginia to talk with Confederate veterans; and he had his own peculiar imagination.[5] That imagination had here found the perfect subject, the subject that gripped him at the deepest level. "I deliberately started in to do a pot-boiler," he once remarked, and added: "I couldn't, I couldn't!"

Beginning in December, 1894, a reduced version (some 15,000 words of the 55,000) was syndicated in newspapers, and in 1895 the book was published. Within a year it had run through nine editions. The critical recognition was generally enthusiastic in both America and England. At the age of twenty-four, Crane was famous.

The fact that Howells was very tepid in his review of *The Red Badge* (and was later to call it "possibly his worst book") tells us something about the startling form of the work. Howells could be enthusiastic about *Maggie* because it

flattered his own theory of realism; even if its grimness was of an order beyond his practice, he understood its purpose and method. If he could not respond to *The Red Badge* it was because, in three years, Crane had leaped ahead a whole generation, leaving him behind.

The documentary realism of *Maggie* was, of course, to be practiced by hordes of writers, some good, some bad, but the "realism" of *The Red Badge* is of another sort altogether. It is concerned not with the "environment" as a thing to be reported, but as a thing to be created; the battlefield of Crane's novel is, in one sense, a fantasy, and its truth is a psychological truth. Further, it is not merely a record of Henry's thoughts and feelings that concerns us; we are concerned with penetrating an existence, not with recording it, and the "war" that is central to the novel is the enormously complex internal struggle of the youth to find his manhood. All of this entails a new style, and the premises of that style, which we shall discuss later, could scarcely be more remote from those of the style of Howells. If, in a root sense, Crane was a realist—even a naturalist—the method, and style, he employed was impressionistic, and Joseph Conrad could regard him as the "impressionist par excellence."

The book that *The Red Badge* most resembles is, in fact, one not yet composed when his was published: *Lord Jim*, by Joseph Conrad. Both books are concerned with what Crane called the "psychological portrayal of fear,[6] and both concern a young man who romantically dreams of heroism and seeks out the occasion for it, flunks his test, and must find some way to reinstate himself in his own eyes and in the eyes of the world. Crane, like Conrad, originally conceived of his work as a tale, not a novel, but bit by bit he elaborated the germ situation, trying to handle it in the way that, as Henry James describes such a process, would entail the "most doing." Conrad's "doing" depends on making Jim into a mysterious figure who is trapped in a

---

[4] Another parallel with Hawthorne appears: in his notebooks Hawthorne could deal with the immediate, present world, but could not do so in his fiction, and Crane achieved poetic effects in his prose that escaped him (or were repudiated) in his poetry.

[5] In "A Night Battle, Over a Week Since," in *Specimen Days*, Whitman had written a remarkable account of Chancellorsville, similar to Crane's in not only the rhythm of "skeedaddling" and then fighting back, but in the conjunction of the savagery of combat with the mysterious beauty of nature. Crane could have read it.

[6] Fear and the test of manhood are obsessive themes for both Conrad and Crane (as for Hemingway). Perhaps Crane's finest story, "The Blue Hotel," is, for instance, a "psychological portrayal of fear."

basic human situation, endowing this figure with a massive symbolic significance through a series of glimpses and interpretations offered by various observers, each bringing us nearer to the crucial mystery of Jim's nature and significance.

Crane, on the contrary, keeps the consciousness of Henry Fleming—the "youth"—as the center of the narrative, and the question is not finally what we are to make of Henry (as in Conrad's novel it is what we must make of Jim), but what Henry can make of himself, his alibis and attempts at exculpation,[7] his shame, his reentry into battle, and his almost accidental "redemption." At the same time, Crane's "doing" involves a poetry constantly embodying the interpenetration of Henry's feelings and the objective physical world. If Crane's masterpiece has not the philosophical breadth and complexity of Conrad's, it can, for subtely of delineation, precision of psychological discrimination, and vividness of effects, hold its own in the confrontation.

There is, moreover, another important point of similarity. In *Lord Jim*, Conrad wrote something close to the ultimate in impressionistic fiction; that is, a fiction in which the author works in terms not of a fixed and objectively conceived reality but of a character's (or characters') "impressions" of what is taken to be reality. In *Lord Jim*, we have the series of "impressions" of Jim from different observers; these are then filtered through Marlowe's mind, and we have Marlowe's sorting out of the various views; then, in the end, what is offered by Marlowe is re-sorted by the author, who, however, declines to give a definitive statement.[8]

In *The Red Badge*, however, we have a different method. To begin with, we have Henry's own "impressions," the movement, stated or implied, of his mind and feelings; then, parallel to these

but intimately related to them, even as a primary expression of them, we have the renderings of the objective world as the scene of his experience. In this rendering there are two consciousnesses—two observers—Henry and the author, with fluctuating degrees of identification.

For instance, in Chapter 7, in one of the crucial scenes of the book, Henry, fleeing in funk from the battle, finds himself in the woods. This landscape gives him justification: "He conceived of Nature to be a woman with a deep aversion to tragedy." This is not the language the youth would use, but a language paraphrasing his feelings: Henry, Crane specifically declares, was "feeling that Nature was of his mind." A moment later, Henry enters a glade where the "high arching boughs made a chapel," with "a religious half light." Henry does not declare to himself that this spot is like a chapel; he merely has, we assume, such a response as he might have upon entering a chapel. It is the author who declares the spot a chapel, that is, a place of peace—"natural" peace, as we know from the context.

Now, shockingly, in this chapel of Nature, Henry finds himself face to face with a dead man, sitting propped against a tree. The dead man's uniform had once been blue "but was now faded to a melancholy shade of green." The eyes, once the focus of life, have "changed to the dull hue to be seen on the side of a dead fish," and the red of the mouth has changed to "an appalling yellow." Ants move over the face. And here is the immediate point of the scene. What, at first glance, seems shocking in the chapel of Nature is really to be read as appropriate there. Man, entering nature, becomes a "thing"—an ant can trundle undisturbed "some sort of burden along the upper lip," for the man has become both a source of food and a sort of highway like any other.

Let us probe further into the meaning of the scene—and, in one sense, of the book—in what appears to be merely a fact of description: the blue of the uniform has "faded to a melancholy shade of green." Green, as the living color of nature, is appropriate to the chapel of Nature. Blue is the color of man outside nature

---

[7] The parallelism is extraordinary between the alibis that Henry gives himself and those that Jim offers Marlowe in the powerful section (Chaps. 7–10) in which Marlowe undercuts his attempts at justification.

[8] In American literature, the most important examples of impressionism are William Faulkner's *The Sound and the Fury* and *Absalom, Absalom!*

—of the men in blue uniforms who by their war are violating the peace which Henry has now assumed to be "natural." But when man enters nature—"dies" into nature (and here the craven flight of Henry equates with a "dying": the "dead man and the living man exchange long looks" of mutual recognition, shall we say) —the blue (man's specifically "human" color, denoting discipline, courage, fidelity, and so on) does not become the bright living green of nature, but a "melancholy shade of green," a sad parody of the living hue.

To paraphrase the imagery: man cannot live by the law of nature; if he thinks he can enter nature, he "dies" in one way or another; he must live by the human law, by what Conrad calls "idea." When man tries to live by the law of nature (by the denial of the human law, as in Henry's flight), he ceases to be a man and becomes a thing, for as his body disintegrates in death, so by the denial of human sanctions his spirit disintegrates into nature.[9] *The Red Badge*, like *Lord Jim*, is concerned with the contrast between the "natural man" and man "redeemed," as it might be put, from nature; redeemed, as Conrad would say, by the "idea." We have used the word "redeemed," and this reminds us that Crane, steeped in the theology of his rearing, is merely transferring its basic idea into secular terms: man cannot find refuge in the chapel of Nature because there death confronts him; he must seek a truth beyond nature—in a sense "supernatural."

But where does man (the "youth" as Crane most often calls his hero, indicating his archetypal role rather than his particular individuality[10]) go when he is shocked at finding death presiding in the chapel of Nature? Standing there, Henry suddenly hears the sound of battle

cut across the "hymn of twilight" (now gone ironical, for he confronts the dead man) and suddenly runs toward the battle: "He saw that it was an ironical thing for him to be running thus toward that thing which he had been at such pains to avoid." He gives himself the false explanation that only curiosity draws him, but then he comes upon the long procession of the wounded. In the midst of this pain, the youth encounters the "tattered man," who, "with humble admiration," demands of him, "Was pretty good fight, warn't it?" Then, when this man, with his "homely face . . . suffused with a light of love for the army which was to him all things beautiful and powerful," demands, "Where yeh hit, ol' boy?" the youth feels "instant panic" and slips away in shame: he has no "red badge" of courage to make him worthy.

In the next stage (in the famous ninth chapter), the youth encounters not the anonymous, abstract death in the form of the man in the "chapel," but the actual dying of Jim Conklin of his own company—a process that becomes a kind of comic *danse macabre* and at the same time a celebration of the tenacious will to life; but it is also a "solemn ceremony" and "something rite-like," for Jim has "at last found the place for which he had struggled," the "rendezvous"—that is, his fulfillment in the "unexplained glory."

When Jim falls dead, and the youth sees the previously concealed wound (in the brilliant phrasing, "his side looked as if it had been chewed by wolves"), the youth turns with "livid rage" toward the battlefield, and shakes his fist, exclaiming, "Hell—." He can find no further word to express his rage, and the chapter ends with the famous sentence: "The red sun was pasted in the sky like a wafer." The image brings to focus all the complex fury of Henry facing the essential fate of man.

The content of the image, or at least part of that content, is interpreted by Crane himself in a passage deleted from the final version. There the sun is "fierce," and the wafer, too—the force against which the fist is raised. As for that force, the deleted passage tells us that the fist

[9] This moment in *The Red Badge*, which is central to the thematic structure of the novel, corresponds in meaning and structural importance to the famous moment in *Lord Jim* (Chap. 20) when Stein, analyzing Jim's "disease," describes man as being doomed to live in the "destructive element."

[10] This echoes the method originally conceived for *Maggie*.

raised against the sky was in anger at the "powers of fate" that had "combined to heap misfortune upon him."

War, he said bitterly to the sky, was a makeshift, created because ordinary processes didn't
furnish deaths enough. To seduce her victims
nature had to simulate a beautiful excuse.
She made glory. This made the men willing,
anxious, in haste to come and be killed. . . .
They regarded warfare and courage as holy
things and did not see that nature had placed
them in hearts because virtuous indignation
would not last through a black struggle. Men
would grow tired of it. They would go home.
They must be inspired by some sentiment
that they could call sacred and enshrine in
their hearts, something that could cause them
to regard slaughter as fine and go at it cheerfully; something that could destroy all the
binding of loves and places that tie men's
hearts. She made glory. From his pinnacle of
wisdom, he regarded the armies as large collections of dupes: Nature's dupes, who were
killing each other to carry out some great
scheme of life. They were under the impression that they were fighting for principles and
honor and homes and various things. Well to
be sure, they were.[11]

We should linger here. If, earlier, in a flight
to nature, the youth had found death, now nature pursues him in that flight back to man: it
is "nature," we are told, that dupes men with
the idea of glory, and so on—which means that
men, attributing to themselves high motives,
are merely fulfilling the aggressiveness and blood
lust of human "nature"—the naturalistic doom.

The whole process of the fictional dialectic
here, as in *Lord Jim*, is from illusion, from the
daydream of the boy Henry, who sees heroism
as his natural right, to experience, which in-
structs in the painful and sometimes fatal cost
of every step toward self-knowledge and man-

hood. Man learns something about the range of
human possibility, for good and evil, and about
the enormous capacity for self-deception and
confusion in the definition of good and evil. He
learns, too, something of the nature of the human communion, as when the "tattered man,"
though "gored by battle and faint for blood,
had fretted concerning an imaginary wound in
another [Henry]" and "had loaned his last of
strength and intellect for the tall soldier [Jim
Conklin]," or as when the color-bearer can be
"duped" by devotion to his flag. In short, the
youth, growing up, discovers that though man is
of nature, and though he may seem to be duped
by nature, he must be redeemed from mere
nature. And essentially involved in that redemption is a recognition of what is embodied in the
"tattered soldier's" generosity of spirit, his feeling for the army, for Henry's wound, and for
what Crane here calls the "subtle battle brotherhood more potent even than the cause for
which they were fighting," and what, in "The
Open Boat," referring to the companionship
among the survivors of the *Commodore*, he
calls the "subtle brotherhood of men."[12]

There is a last corollary to this. At the end,
after the battle and his discovery of the possibility of both cowardice and heroism ambiguously in himself, Henry can turn "with a lover's
thirst to images of tranquil skies, fresh meadows,
and cool brooks." That is, now knowing himself
not of "nature" (neither the child nor the
dupe), he can turn to nature as an image of
"soft and eternal peace," and the sun, no longer
the "fierce wafer," gives a golden ray "through
the hosts of leaden rain clouds."

Many critics take it that Henry, in the end as
in the beginning, is still the victim of his illusions, of his egotistical dreams, that, as Charles
C. Walcutt asserts in *American Literary Naturalism*, he "has never been able to evaluate his
conduct," and though he "may have been fearless for moments," his "motives were vain."

---

[11] Compare this passage with the famous paragraph in
Hemingway's *A Farewell to Arms* that begins: "I was
always embarrassed by the words sacred, glorious, and
sacrifice and the expression in vain." See p. 2258.

[12] This idea appears as fundamental in Conrad's fiction—in *Lord Jim*, the "solidarity" that is violated by
Jim—and in certain of the French existential writers,
especially Malraux and Camus.

One of the arguments for this view is that, in general, Crane is concerned with man's capacity to delude himself, that Crane's irony is characteristically directed against man's vanity, and that if man must live by illusion he must frequently die by it.

It is true that illusion and self-delusion are constant concerns in Crane's work, and that they constantly provoke his irony. In the first chapter of *Maggie*, the boys interpret their fight in heroic terms much as Henry thinks of himself at the beginning of *The Red Badge*: little Jimmie has aimed to be "some vague kind of soldier or a man of blood with a sort of sublime license," and he feels humiliated when his father drags him off home. George Kelcey, of *George's Mother* (1896), sees himself as "a stern general pointing a sword at the nervous and abashed horizon." The Swede, in "The Blue Hotel," dies because, first, he holds a dime-novel notion—an illusion—of the Wild West into which he has ventured, and, second, after the fight with the boy, he has the illusion that he is omnipotent and able to impose his ego on the world. Maggie lives in the dreams fostered by "plays in which the dazzling heroine was rescued from the palatial home of her treacherous guardian by the hero with beautiful sentiments," and it is just such dreams that lead to her ruin. Furthermore, we have a story very specifically about the ambiguity of the motives of heroic action in "A Mystery of Heroism," in which a soldier, lying with his comrades safe from a bombardment, remarks that he wants a drink of water, and soon talks himself into the position where, to save face with the world and with himself, he must venture out with the canteens of the others well exposed to shell-fire.

The question is, what do such episodes elsewhere in Crane's work mean in the interpretation of *The Red Badge?* Henry does, indeed, begin as the victim of illusion and vanity; even in the destruction of the first illusion, he embraces new illusions; when he does become a "hero," the event seems to be something that "happens" to him rather than something he deliberately does out of valor and principle—an

event as ambiguous as Fred Collins' act in "A Mystery of Heroism." But we cannot, by assuming mechanically exact parallels to these episodes, argue that Henry's experience has counted for nothing. Crane does, in fact, show us Henry trying to assess the nature of his experience. If he had begun with illusions about the nature of heroism and his own nature, even if now he has escaped from a "land of strange squalling upheavals" and has earned the praise of his fellows as a "hero," his joy in such "gilded images of memory" of his own triumph cannot be simple. He must remember, too, his own shame, his shortcomings in the kind of sympathy and devotion exhibited by the "tattered soldier," and the almost accidental, impersonal quality of his own final "heroism." In the end he could look back on the "brass and bombast of his earlier gospels," on his first illusions, and find that they are now to be "despised":

> With the conviction [about the earlier "gospels"] came a store of assurance. He felt a quiet manhood, non-assertive, but of sturdy and strong blood. He knew that he would never more quail before his guides wherever they should point. He had been to touch the great death, and found that, after all, it was but the great death. He was a man.
>
> So it came to pass that as he trudged from the place of blood and wrath his soul changed. He came from hot plowshares to prospects of clover tranquility, and it was as if hot plowshares were not. Scars faded as flowers.

We cannot, however, take the story as one of simple redemption. The fact that, in the last sentence, sunlight breaks through the rain clouds does not mean that it will never rain again. Scars may fade, but new wounds may be inflicted. No victory is ever final; there is no refuge of "soft and eternal peace" except in death. Life is in the constant process of being defined. This is quite specifically indicated by the fact that in a later story, "The Veteran," Henry is subjected to a new test, with a new definition of courage, a courage beyond the "battle sleep" as Crane calls it—the sleep in which man enacts, as in a dream, his terrors and his glory.

As we have no simple redemption in *The Red Badge of Courage*, by the same token we do not have a simple denial that Henry's experience goes for nothing. Crane's irony is more radical than that. If he could write of Henry's illusion and consequent funk, or write "A Mystery of Heroism" (which we should notice is "A Mystery" and not "*The* Mystery"), he could still write the scene in Chapter 19, where the "corpse [of the color sergeant] will not relinquish its trust," but clings to the flag staff; and in Crane's reporting of actual war, the act of courage, however complex or even dubious its origins may be assumed to be, is respected, and on the record, as at Guantanamo, on June 11, 1898, it is clear that Crane himself was capable of courage. And we have, in such work as "The Monster" and "The Veteran," examples of heroism, simply rendered.

It is important, in interpreting *The Red Badge*, to remember that we are dealing, not only with Henry, a particular recruit, but with the "youth," that is, with a generalized, archetypal figure. If this is true, then we must be prepared to apply whatever interpretation we make to the generality of "men" who, by experience, have passed the stage of "youth." If we hold, as some critics do, that Henry remains the uninstructed victim of his vainglorious illusions, we must hold that this is true of all men. Crane would agree that all men are incorrigibly addicted to illusion, but he would maintain that there are kinds and kinds of illusion: the untested illusion that you are brave is not the same as the illusion that may prompt you to die for a cause—or merely for self-respect. If the "conceit of man," as it is said in "The Blue Hotel," can be taken to be "the very engine of life," man's conceit has many different forms of manifestation; and if there are levels of illusion, then there are, appropriately, levels of irony. And it should be remembered that when we use the word "illusion," we must ask what is the guaranteed reality against which we test illusion. In the end we, or Crane, may be dealing with the irony of the "meaningfulness" of "meaninglessness." In fact, the nature of "illusion" is a basic subject matter of modern literature, from Conrad and Dreiser to Sartre.

If we must guard against a simplistic reading of the irony of illusion in *The Red Badge of Courage*, we must be equally vigilant to guard against a simplistic reading of Crane's attitude toward war. There is the "redemptive" aspect of war (which, we may recall, Hawthorne, Holmes, and William James recognized), but it is set in the full context of horror and suffering, and in this context it is shot through with ironies that tend to cancel out the values affirmed. It would, however, deny the density of the work to maintain that it is merely a protest against war. It is a deeply ambivalent story, and the root irony is that the "glory" remains "unexplained." By the same token, it is not explained away. The story resembles, in its depth of irony, Melville's *Billy Budd*, which is also a story of redemption and reconciliation, but one in which meaning is left in perilous balance.

In the last analysis, however, *The Red Badge* is not about war; or if it is about war, it is war conceived as the image for all life. Certainly, as Crane observed modern society, with the bitter struggle for existence on the one hand and for wealth and prestige on the other, he found the social experience to be a kind of war. He was a Social Darwinian without the label, a far more convinced one than Justice Holmes, for he, as a writer of fiction, dealt with the particulars of the struggle while the other dealt with abstractions; and for the same reason, he was a more bitter protester than Thorstein Veblen. (See the introduction to Intellectual History, 1861–1914.) War was, for Crane, an image of society.

But war was an image for more than life at the social level. It was the image for life at the emotional and metaphysical levels as well. As Philip Young has said, Crane's view of existence was "of man damaged and alone in a hostile violent world, of life as one long war which we seek and challenge in fear and controlled panic."[13] In fact, it is the aloneness rather than the enmity that is the chief threat to man. The aloneness of Henry prepares for the panic, and the cure for the panic comes when he begins to find himself again with other men—when he joins the line of wounded.

But this interpretation should be broadened to include man's place in nature. As we have seen, Henry, in his vanity, regards nature at one moment as kindly, at another as inimical; and this idea of self-reference as determining the interpretation of nature runs through the story. The animistic imagery constantly reminds us of this. When, in camp, Henry lies down on the grass, the "blades tenderly pressed against his cheek," and the "moon had been lighted and was hung in a treetop"—for him, of course. But the campfires of the enemy are "red eyelike gleams . . . set in the low brow of distant hills." Later, as Henry marches, an idea takes hold of him that he "did not relish the landscape": "It threatened him." When the regiment approaches a woods, yellow flames leap out at it, as the "forest" makes "a tremendous objection." From the dark water of a stream, "white bubble eyes" stare up at Henry. In looking back on his experience of battle, Henry feels that he "had dwelt in a land of strange, squalling upheavals"—that is, a land of maniacal violence that was purely "natural," not made by man. The war itself is sometimes assumed to be not against the Confederates but against this inimical nature, as when, looking back on his glory, Henry finds that he has "overcome obstacles which he had admitted to be mountains," but they "had fallen like paper peaks."

This double vision of nature, as kindly or inimical, is, however, merely another illusion, an illusion dictated by the vanity of men who, as it appears in "The Blue Hotel," are "lice" clinging to a "whirling, fire-smitten, ice-locked, disease-stricken, space-lost bulb." Even to assume that nature is inimical implies a recognition of man's importance, but the truth is, as the correspondent realizes in "The Open Boat," that nature is "indifferent, flatly indifferent," and this is the ultimate loneliness.[14] The only cure is for the individual to recognize the common human plight and join, in courage and compassion, the long line of the "wounded."

We have been discussing the general thematic concerns of *The Red Badge*, but it lives by its particularities, including those of style. To sense the effect of the particularities of the embodiment, let us improvise the "lines" that Crane might have written on the same idea and put this stripped version against the actual story:

From the red claw of battle
From the blunt fist of artillery
And the spiteful pin-prick of musket-fire,
The youth ran.
His legs were alert with philosophy
And they carried him to the Chapel of Nature,
Where the air breathed benediction
And the leaves were green.

There sat the dead man.
He was the god of that place because dead,
But his uniform, no longer blue,
Was faded to a melancholy green.
Why was that green not the green of the leaf?
An ant trundled its forage across an upper lip.
The dead man and the live youth stared at each other.

So the youth fled back to the doom of men.
He joined the holy procession of wounded men.
A friend died and he saw his side as though eaten by wolves,
And shook his fist against the sky.

---

[13] *Ernest Hemingway.* There are, of course, great similarities between the two writers. For the moment, however, we should observe that the essence of the question for both is to seek the challenge as the only way of asserting identity. The same is true of Conrad.

[14] The shock to the romantic sensibility of the idea that nature is indifferent to man is a continuing theme in American literature (and elsewhere) in the nineteenth century. We have, for instance, encountered it in Melville, but it appears with great force in both Frost and Hemingway.

The red sun was a wafer in the sky.

In the end he was overcome by his own un-
worthiness.

There was nothing to do but suffer his legs
To take him back to the place of battle.

Other men were there.

Many things are missing here that we find in
the story—for instance, the very important figure
of the mother, whose feelings provide a contrast
to the whole development of the son's experience, even though she knows that her son's
"nature" is not to be denied: as "youth" he
must go. But one thing most significantly missing is the very medium in which the story exists
—the sensibility which informs the whole.

The sensibility of the author is what makes it
possible for us to understand the sensibility of
the youth, the shades of perception and feeling
that constitute his experience and embody the
shifts of thematic values; but it is also what
defines the author's attitude toward the youth,
and the significance of his experience. For instance, as we have already seen, we grasp the
ambiguous relation of Henry to nature chiefly
by the imagery. To consider one effect rendered
through imagery, Crane communicates the developing tension of the story by playing off over-
emphasis from some assumed but never specified
normal base against underemphasis. On one
hand, in the beginning we have the idea of
heroic "Greeklike struggles" enacted hand-to-
hand, set against the soldier's role as a mere
"part of a vast blue demonstration"—and we
notice the blank impersonality of the word
"demonstration," the furthest thing from the
"throat-grappling instinct" of the "Greeklike
struggle." In the understated version of war, the
Rebel pickets were merely a "sun-tanned philosophical lot, who sometimes shot reflectively at
the blue pickets"—with the words "philosophical" and "reflectively" far removed from the
puncture of any literal bullet. At dawn, against
"a yellow patch like a rug laid for the feet of
the coming sun," there looms "black and pat-
tern-like . . . the gigantic figure of the Colonel
on a gigantic horse," but later, in battle, this
gigantic Colonel can only "scold like a wet parrot." And again, in the midst of battle, officers
"neglect" to assume "picturesque attitudes," but
bob to and fro and howl orders, and the "dimensions of their howls were extraordinary";
and it was the guns, not the officers, that
"squatted in a row like savage chiefs," and "argued with abrupt violence" in a "great powwow,"
with the cannoneers as their servants. In contrast to his earlier terror, Henry finally "gawked"
at the battle, which seemed merely a "machine": "Its complexities and power, its grim
processes, fascinated him. He must go closer
and see it produce corpses." Men are merely
"pushed by bullets," though they enact "grotesque agonies" seemingly out of all proportion
to the event. Or they are merely "grunting
bundles of blue" that begin "to drop." And in
this last sentence we observe how apt is the
word "blue": the dead man is, literally, a blue
bundle; because he wears the uniform (is
"blue") he has ceased to be a man—is only a
"part of a vast blue demonstration"—and a
bullet doesn't hurt a bundle.

What we find in the interplay of overempha-
sis and underemphasis is a tension between a
refusal to face fact and an overreaction to fact.
This leads to another and more pervasive irony:
the play of imagery creates, on the one hand,
an extraordinary empathy with the tension of
the soldier's experience, but, on the other, a
kind of comic commentary, a sense of distance
from the agonized participant, a slight contempt for him who cannot trust his own senses
in a reasonable way. The whole effect is of a
vivid tautness of style, of a tension between the
participatory compulsiveness and the ironic
withdrawal, an effect that was, at its time,
unique. Kipling at his best is equally taut, and
often very precise in his ironies, but his psychological range is much more limited.

In later work, such as "The Open Boat," "An
Episode of War," "The Blue Hotel," and "The
Monster," Crane's style becomes more relaxed
and various, but rarely casual, even when he
was ill and writing desperately for money. In
later books with new material, sometimes mate-

rial less obviously dramatic, Crane was expanding his range and often deepening his effects. "The Open Boat" is, in one sense, no story at all; it is, on the face of it, a piece of reportage, scrupulous in detail, never insisting on the dramatic or striking elements, as for instance in the apparently comic comparison of the dinghy to a bathtub. But with all its repudiation of any effort to create suspense, and in its plotlessness, it succeeds in generating an enormous pull of involvement, a hypnotic poem about man's confrontation with death and the discovery of brotherhood in the human plight.

By this time Crane had, in fact, created an implicative style of marvelous subtlety and force that seemed to suggest revolutionary possibilities for fiction. Yet this is not to say that, had he lived, he would have gone on to revolutionize fiction, as Joyce did. But what Crane did do is, like the work of Keats, superlative in its kind. We may say that *Huckleberry Finn* gives one pole for subsequent American fiction, the revelation of the self, and of the nature of selfhood, in an intimate natural language flowing out of the self: the irony of innocence looking wisely outward on the irrationality and delusion of the world. *The Red Badge* gives the other pole, a fiction in which the view is not outward, but inward at the self, a self that is neither innocent nor wise, but concocted of irrationalities and delusions; a fiction rendered in a language of brilliant impressions that, in their very brilliance, exhibit the corruscations of a constantly shifting irony. For all his taste for action and color in the objective world, Crane is one of the writers who have turned the focus of action inward. He created for the first time in English, since Hawthorne—and how differently—and for the first time in its modern form, the story of psychological depth and poetic force.

The interrelation between Crane's life and his work was for him instinctive. His journalism (what he lived and saw) blends into his fiction (what he created), and it is sometimes hard to say how a particular piece of writing should be classified. His career was, in fact, an oscillation between journalism and fiction. It was also an oscillation between two obsessive interests, which found expression in both journalism and fiction. Crane was interested in low life and he was interested in war, and these are the forces that continued to the end to give shape to his career. But they most significantly merged when, in 1896, on his way to report a filibustering expedition by Cuban patriots against the Spanish regime, he stopped in Jacksonville, Florida, visited a "night club" called Hotel de Dream, took up with the hostess Cora E. Stewart, then passing as Cora Taylor (six years older than he but with authentic golden hair), and gave her a copy of *George's Mother*, recently published, inscribed "To an unnamed sweetheart." On the expedition to Cuba the steamer *Commodore* foundered, and Crane had a harrowing experience in a dinghy with the injured captain and three other men. Back in Jacksonville, in waterfront cafés and in the Hotel de Dream, he wrote the masterpiece "The Open Boat."

The Greco-Turkish War gave Crane his first chance to check *The Red Badge* by experience. By April, 1897, he was in Greece as a correspondent, with Cora, who in attaching herself to Crane had discovered her own literary ambitions and had determined to become the first female war correspondent. Out of the *opera bouffe* war of thirty days, in which, however, men actually died, Crane got an indifferent novel called *Active Service*; and Cora got him. She was still married to her second husband, the son of an English baronet who refused to give her a divorce, but now, in England, she passed as Mrs. Crane, enjoyed his fame, the company of Joseph Conrad, Henry James, Ford Madox Hueffer (later Ford), and other literary personages, and the satisfactions of respectability. From this time on Crane was desperately writing to keep up with Cora's social ambitions and his own extravagance, especially after they occupied Brede, a famous and decrepit manor in Sussex.

But before the last terrible period at Brede, Crane, already struggling to stave off bill collectors and bailiffs, managed to escape from debts and domesticity to Cuba to cover the

Spanish-American War, from which came his dispatches and *Wounds in the Rain*, a fictional treatment of his experiences.

With the war over, Crane was loath to go back to England; he had apparently had enough of Cora, his old feeling for Lily Munroe had returned, and he was writing poems about his tangle of feelings. Cora managed, however, to lure him back, but she had to endure the embarrassment of seeing the poems published, as they were in 1899, under the title "Intrigue" in the volume called *War Is Kind*.

On June 5, 1900, Crane died. The body was carried back to America and buried in Hillside, New Jersey.

Poor Cora, with her idiocies, her sincere de-votion, her self-pity, her illusion that she was a writer, and her debts, soon became a nuisance to Crane's friends. Back in Jacksonville, she took up her old profession with a fine establishment called the Court, married a railroad conductor, some years her junior, and set him up as a saloonkeeper. A little later, the saloonkeeper shot her nineteen-year-old lover. She fled to England, taking with her as a companion one of the more refined ladies of her entourage—a lady who, if left behind in Florida, might have testified in court against Cora's gun-happy husband.

In England Cora again tried to enter upon respectability. Henry James wrote her a note that if she called at his rooms, in Cheyne Walk, in London, he would not be at home.

BIOGRAPHICAL CHART

1871 Born, November 1, son of Jonathan Townley Crane and Mary Helen Peck

1880 Enters Claverack College and Hudson River Institute, a military school; father dies; moves to Newark

1888 Works as reporter at his brother's news agency in Asbury Park, New Jersey

1890 Enters Lafayette College; flunks out in December

1891 Enters Syracuse University, January; makes baseball team; begins *Maggie: A Girl of the Streets*; contributes to the New York *Tribune*; flunks out; does reporting in Asbury Park, where he comes to know Hamlin Garland; newspaper work in New York; discovers the Bowery, begins Sullivan County (N.J.) sketches; early poems; mother dies

1892 Returns to Asbury Park; meets Mrs. Lily Brandon Munroe; reworks *Maggie*

1893 *Maggie* (published privately); Garland sends copy to Howells; works on *The Red Badge of Courage*

1894 "An Experiment in Misery"; other New York sketches; exposé of coal mining in Pennsylvania; *The Red Badge* put into final manuscript, and *George's Mother* written; reduced syndicated version of *The Red Badge* published in Philadelphia *Press*, December 3–8

1895 Travels to West, New Orleans, and Mexico for journalistic material; *The Red Badge* received enthusiastically; *The Black Riders*

1896 *George's Mother*; *Maggie* issued by regular publisher; goes to Florida to report filibustering expedition to Cuba; meets Cora Taylor

1897 *Commodore* sinks on January 1; writes "The Open Boat"; goes to Greece as war correspondent, with Cora; settles in England with her; begins literary friendships with Conrad, James, Ford Madox Ford; has financial troubles

1898 Reports Spanish-American War; lingers in Cuba; writes *Intrigue*; sees Lily Munroe; *The Open Boat and Other Tales of Adventure*

1899 Returns to England; financial troubles and failing health; *The Monster and Other Stories*; *War Is Kind* (including "Intrigue"); *Active Service*

1900 Dies, June 5, in Badenweiler, Germany; buried in Hillside, New Jersey; *Whilomville Stories* and *Wounds in the Rain*

FURTHER READINGS

The University Press of Virginia is now in the process of compiling a ten-volume edition of Crane's works to be completed by 1974. This will become the standard (CEAA) edition.

Wilson Follett, ed., *The Works of Stephen Crane* (13 vols.; 1925–27)

James B. Colvert, ed., *The Great Short Works of Ste-*

phen Crane (1968)

Arthur Edelstein, ed., *Three Great Novels by Stephen Crane* (1970)

Ralph Ellison, ed., *The Red Badge of Courage and Four Great Stories* (1960)

Daniel Hoffman, ed., *The Poetry of Stephen Crane* (1957)

Robert W. Stallman, ed., *The Red Badge of Courage* (1960)

————, ed., *Stephen Crane: An Omnibus* (1952)

———— and Lillian Gilkes, eds., *Letters* (1960)

Maurice Bassan, ed., *Stephen Crane: Twentieth Century Views* (1967)

Thomas Beer, *Stephen Crane* (1923)

John Berryman, *Stephen Crane* (1950)

James B. Colvert, "Structure and Theme in Stephen Crane's Fiction," *Modern Fiction Studies* (Fall, 1959)

Joseph Conrad, *Notes on Life and Letters* (1921)

Maxwell Geismar, *Rebels and Ancestors: The American Novel, 1890–1915* (1953)

Lillian Gilkes, *Cora Crane* (1960)

Jay Martin, *Harvests of Change* (1967)

Robert W. Stallman, *Stephen Crane* (1968)

War Is Kind (1896)

Do not weep, maiden, for war is kind.
Because your lover threw wild hands toward the sky
And the affrighted steed ran on alone,
Do not weep.
War is kind.

Hoarse, booming drums of the regiment,
Little souls who thirst for fight,
These men were born to drill and die.
The unexplained glory flies above them,
Great is the battle-god, great, and his kingdom—   10
A field where a thousand corpses lie.

Do not weep, babe, for war is kind.
Because your father tumbled in the yellow trenches,
Raged at his breast, gulped and died,
Do not weep.
War is kind.

Swift blazing flag of the regiment,
Eagle with crest of red and gold,
These men were born to drill and die.
Point for them the virtue of slaughter,   20
Make plain to them the excellence of killing
And a field where a thousand corpses lie.

Mother whose heart hung humble as a button
On the bright splendid shroud of your son,
Do not weep.
War is kind.

There Was Crimson Clash of War (1899)

There was crimson clash of war.
Lands turned black and bare;
Women wept;
Babes ran, wondering.
There came one who understood not these things.

He said, "Why is this?"
Whereupon a million strove to answer him.
There was such intricate clamor of tongues,
That still the reason was not.

I Saw a Man Pursuing (1899)

I saw a man pursuing the horizon;
Round and round they sped.
I was disturbed at this;
I accosted the man.

"It is futile," I said,
"You can never—"

"You lie," he cried,
And ran on.

A Man Said to the Universe (1899)

A man said to the universe:
"Sir, I exist!"
"However," replied the universe,

"The fact has not created in me
"A sense of obligation."

An Episode of War (1898)

The lieutenant's rubber blanket lay on the ground, and upon it he had poured the company's supply of coffee. Corporals and other representatives of the grimy and hot-throated men who lined the breast-work had come for each squad's portion.

The lieutenant was frowning and serious at this task of division. His lips pursed as he drew with his sword various crevices in the heap, until brown squares of coffee, astoundingly equal in size, appeared on the blanket. He was on the verge of a great triumph in mathematics, and the corporals were thronging forward, each to reap a little square, when suddenly the lieutenant cried out and looked quickly at a man near him as if he suspected it was a case of personal assault. The others cried out also when they saw blood upon the lieutenant's sleeve.

He had winced like a man stung, swayed dangerously, and then straightened. The sound of his hoarse breathing was plainly audible. He looked sadly, mystically, over the breast-work at the green face of a wood, where now were many little puffs of white smoke. During this moment the men about him gazed statue-like and silent, astonished and awed by this catastrophe which happened when catastrophes were not expected—when they had leisure to observe it.

As the lieutenant stared at the wood, they too swung their heads, so that for another instant all hands, still silent, contemplated the distant forest as if their minds were fixed upon the mystery of a bullet's journey.

The officer had, of course, been compelled to take his sword into his left hand. He did not hold it by the hilt. He gripped it at the middle of the blade, awkwardly. Turning his eyes from the hostile wood, he looked at the sword as he held it there, and seemed puzzled as to what to do with it, where to put it. In short, this weapon had of a sudden become a strange thing to him. He looked at it in a kind of stupefaction, as if he had been endowed with a trident, a sceptre, or a spade.

Finally he tried to sheathe it. To sheathe a sword held by the left hand, at the middle of the blade, in a scabbard hung at the left hip, is a feat worthy of a sawdust ring. This wounded officer engaged in a desperate struggle with the sword and the wobbling scabbard, and during the time of it he breathed like a wrestler.

But at this instant the men, the spectators, awoke from their stone-like poses and crowded forward sympathetically. The orderly-sergeant took the sword and tenderly placed it in the scabbard. At the time, he leaned nervously backward, and did not allow even his finger to brush the body of the lieutenant. A wound gives strange dignity to him who bears it. Well men shy from his new and terrible majesty. It is as if the wounded man's hand is upon the curtain which hangs before the revelations of all existence—the meaning of ants, potentates, wars, cities, sunshine, snow, a feather dropped from a bird's wing; and the power of it sheds radiance upon a bloody form, and makes the other men understand sometimes that they are little. His comrades look at him with large eyes thoughtfully. Moreover, they fear vaguely that the weight of a finger upon him might send him headlong, precipitate the tragedy, hurl him at once into the dim, grey unknown. And so the orderly-sergeant, while sheathing the sword, leaned nervously backward.

There were others who proffered assistance. One timidly presented his shoulder and asked the lieutenant if he cared to lean upon it, but the latter waved him away mournfully. He wore the look of one who knows he is the victim of a terrible disease and understands his helplessness. He again stared over the breast-work at the forest, and then, turning, went slowly rearward. He held his right wrist tenderly in his left hand as if the wounded arm was made of very brittle glass.

And the men in silence stared at the wood, then at the departing lieutenant; then at the wood, then at the lieutenant.

As the wounded officer passed from the line of battle, he was enabled to see many things which as a participant in the fight were unknown to him. He saw a general on a black horse gazing over the lines of blue infantry at the green woods which veiled his problems. An aide galloped furiously, dragged his horse suddenly to a halt, saluted, and presented a paper. It was, for a wonder, precisely like a historical painting.

To the rear of the general and his staff a group, composed of a bugler, two or three orderlies, and the bearer of the corps standard, all upon maniacal horses, were working like slaves to hold their ground, preserve their respectful interval, while the shells boomed in the air about them, and caused their chargers to make furious quivering leaps.

A battery, a tumultuous and shining mass, was swirling toward the right. The wild thud of hoofs, the cries of the riders shouting blame and praise, menace and encouragement, and, last, the roar of the wheels, the slant of the glistening guns, brought the lieutenant to an intent pause. The battery swept in curves that stirred the heart; it made halts as dramatic as the crash of a wave on the rocks, and when it fled onward this aggregation of wheels, levers, motors had a beautiful unity, as if it were a missile. The sound of it was a war-chorus that reached into the depths of man's emotion.

The lieutenant, still holding his arm as if it were of glass, stood watching this battery until all detail of it was lost, save the figures of the riders, which rose and fell and waved lashes over the black mass.

Later, he turned his eyes toward the battle, where the shooting sometimes crackled like bush-fires, sometimes sputtered with exasperating irregularity, and sometimes reverberated like the thunder. He saw the smoke rolling upward and saw crowds of men who ran and cheered, or stood and blazed away at the inscrutable distance.

He came upon some stragglers, and they told him how to find the field hospital. They described its exact location. In fact, these men, no longer having part in the battle, knew more of it than others. They told the performance of every corps, every division, the opinion of every general. The lieutenant, carrying his wounded arm rearward, looked upon them with wonder.

At the roadside a brigade was making coffee and buzzing with talk like a girls' boarding-school. Several officers came out to him and inquired concerning things of which he knew nothing. One, seeing his arm, began to scold. "Why, man, that's no way to do. You want to fix that thing." He appropriated the lieutenant and the lieutenant's wound. He cut the sleeve and laid bare the arm, every nerve of which softly fluttered under his touch. He bound his handkerchief over the wound, scolding away in the meantime. His tone allowed one to think that he was in the habit of being wounded every day. The lieutenant hung his head, feeling, in this presence, that he did not know how to be correctly wounded.

The low white tents of the hospital were grouped around an old schoolhouse. There was here a singular commotion. In the foreground two ambulances interlocked wheels in the deep mud. The drivers were tossing the blame of it back and forth, gesticulating and berating, while from the ambulances, both crammed with wounded, there came an occasional groan. An interminable crowd of bandaged men were coming and going. Great numbers sat under the trees nursing heads or arms or legs. There was a dispute of some kind raging on the steps of the schoolhouse. Sitting with his back against a tree a man with a face as grey as a new army blanket was serenely smoking a corncob pipe. The lieutenant wished to rush forward and inform him that he was dying.

A busy surgeon was passing near the lieutenant. "Good-morning," he said, with a friendly smile. Then he caught sight of the lieutenant's arm, and his face at once changed. 'Well, let's have a look at it." He seemed possessed suddenly of a great contempt for the lieutenant. This wound evidently placed the latter on a very low social plane. The doctor cried out impatiently: "What mutton-head had tied it up that way anyhow?" The lieutenant answered, "Oh, a man."

When the wound was disclosed the doctor fingered it disdainfully. "Humph," he said. "You come along with me and I'll 'tend to you." His voice contained the same scorn as if he were saying: "You will have to go to jail."

The lieutenant had been very meek, but now his face flushed, and he looked into the doctor's eyes. "I guess I won't have it amputated," he said.

"Nonsense, man! Nonsense! Nonsense!" cried the doctor. "Come along, now. I won't amputate it. Come along. Don't be a baby."

"Let go of me," said the lieutenant, holding back wrathfully, his glance fixed upon the door of the old schoolhouse, as sinister to him as the portals of death.

And this is the story of how the lieutenant lost

his arm. When he reached home, his sisters, his mother, his wife, sobbed for a long time at the sight of the flat sleeve. "Oh, well," he said, standing shamefaced amid these tears, "I don't suppose it matters so much as all that."

The Open Boat (1897)

A Tale Intended to be after the Fact: Being the Experience of Four Men from the Sunk Steamer Commodore

I

None of them knew the colour of the sky. Their eyes glanced level, and were fastened upon the waves that swept toward them. These waves were of the hue of slate, save for the tops, which were of foaming white, and all of the men knew the colours of the sea. The horizon narrowed and widened, and dipped and rose, and at all times its edge was jagged with waves that seemed thrust up in points like rocks.

Many a man ought to have a bathtub larger than the boat which here rode upon the sea. These waves were most wrongfully and barbarously abrupt and tall, and each froth-top was a problem in small-boat navigation.

The cook squatted in the bottom, and looked with both eyes at the six inches of gunwale which separated him from the ocean. His sleeves were rolled over his fat forearms, and the two flaps of his unbuttoned vest dangled as he bent to bail out the boat. Often he said, "Gawd! that was a narrow clip." As he remarked it he invariably gazed eastward over the broken sea.

The oiler, steering with one of the two oars in the boat, sometimes raised himself suddenly to keep clear of water that swirled in over the stern. It was a thin little oar, and it seemed often ready to snap.

The correspondent, pulling at the other oar, watched the waves and wondered why he was there.

The injured captain, lying in the bow, was at this time buried in that profound dejection and indifference which comes, temporarily at least, to even the bravest and most enduring when, willy-nilly, the firm fails, the army loses, the ship goes down. The mind of the master of a vessel is rooted deep in the timbers of her, though he command for a day or a decade; and this captain had on him the stern impression of a scene in the greys of dawn of seven turned faces, and later a stump of a topmast with a white ball on it, that slashed to and fro at the waves, went low and lower, and down. Thereafter there was something strange in his voice. Although steady, it was deep with mourning, and of a quality beyond oration or tears.

"Keep 'er a little more south, Billie," said he.

"A little more south, sir," said the oiler in the stern.

A seat in this boat was not unlike a seat upon a bucking broncho, and by the same token a broncho is not much smaller. The craft pranced and reared and plunged like an animal. As each wave came, and she rose for it, she seemed like a horse making at a fence outrageously high. The manner of her scramble over these walls of water is a mystic thing, and, moreover, at the top of them were ordinarily these problems in white water, the foam racing down from the summit of each wave requiring a new leap, and a leap from the air. Then, after scornfully bumping a crest, she would slide and race and splash down a long incline, and arrive bobbing and nodding in front of the next menace.

A singular disadvantage of the sea lies in the fact that after successfully surmounting one wave you discover that there is another behind it just as important and just as nervously anxious to do something effective in the way of swamping boats. In a ten-foot dinghy one can get an idea of the resources of the sea in the line of waves that is not probable to the average experience which is never at sea in a dinghy. As each slaty wall of water approached, it shut all else from the view of the men in the boat, and it was not difficult to imagine that this particular wave was the final outburst of the ocean, the last effort of the grim water. There was a terrible grace in the move of the waves, and they came in silence, save for the snarling of the crests.

In the wan light the faces of the men must have been grey. Their eyes must have glinted in strange ways as they gazed steadily astern. Viewed from a balcony, the whole thing would doubtless have been weirdly picturesque. But the men in the boat had no time to see it, and if they had had leisure, there were other things to occupy their minds. The sun swung steadily up the sky, and they knew it was broad day because the colour of the sea changed from slate to emerald green streaked with amber lights, and the foam was like tumbling snow. The process of the breaking day was unknown to them. They were aware only of this effect upon the colour of the waves that rolled toward them.

In disjointed sentences the cook and the correspondent argued as to the difference between a life-saving station and a house of refuge. The cook had said: "There's a house of refuge just north of the Mosquito Inlet Light, and as soon as they see us they'll come off in their boat and pick us up."

"As soon as who sees us?" said the correspondent.

"The crew," said the cook.

"Houses of refuge don't have crews," said the correspondent. "As I understand them, they are only places where clothes and grub are stored for the benefit of ship-wrecked people. They don't carry crews."

"Oh, yes, they do," said the cook.

"No, they don't," said the correspondent.

"Well, we're not there yet, anyhow," said the oiler, in the stern.

"Well," said the cook, "perhaps it's not a house of refuge that I'm thinking of as being near Mosquito Inlet Light; perhaps it's a life-saving station."

"We're not there yet," said the oiler in the stern.

II

As the boat bounced from the top of each wave the wind tore through the hair of the hatless men, and as the craft plopped her stern down again the spray slashed past them. The crest of each of these waves was a hill, from the top of which the men surveyed for a moment a broad tumultuous expanse, shining and wind-riven. It was probably splendid, it was probably glorious, this play of the free sea, wild with lights of emerald and white and amber.

"Bully good thing it's an on-shore wind," said the cook. "If not, where would we be? Wouldn't have a show."

"That's right," said the correspondent.

The busy oiler nodded his assent.

Then the captain, in the bow, chuckled in a way that expressed humour, contempt, tragedy, all in one. "Do you think we've got much of a show now, boys?" said he.

Whereupon the three were silent, save for a trifle of hemming and hawing. To express any particular optimism at this time they felt to be childish and stupid, but they all doubtless possessed this sense of the situation in their minds. A young man thinks doggedly at such times. On the other hand, the ethics of their condition was decidedly against any open suggestion of hopelessness. So they were silent.

"Oh, well," said the captain, soothing his children, "we'll get ashore all right."

But there was that in his tone which made them think; so the oiler quoth, "Yes! if this wind holds."

The cook was bailing. "Yes! if we don't catch hell in the surf."

Canton-flannel gulls flew near and far. Sometimes they sat down on the sea, near patches of brown seaweed that rolled over the waves with a movement like carpets on a line in a gale. The birds sat comfortably in groups, and they were envied by some in the dinghy, for the wrath of the sea was no more to them than it was to a covey of prairie chickens a thousand miles inland. Often they came very close and stared at the men with black bead-like eyes. At these times they were uncanny and sinister in their unblinking scrutiny, and the men hooted angrily at them, telling them to be gone. One came, and evidently decided to alight on the top of the captain's head. The bird flew parallel to the boat and did not circle, but made short sidelong jumps in the air in chicken-fashion. His black eyes were wistfully fixed upon the captain's head. "Ugly brute," said the oiler to the bird. "You look as if you were made with a jackknife." The cook and the correspondent swore darkly at the creature. The captain naturally wished to knock it away with the end of the heavy painter, but he did not dare do it, because anything resembling an emphatic gesture would have capsized this freighted boat; and so, with his open hand, the captain gently and carefully waved the gull away. After it had been discouraged from the pursuit the captain breathed easier on account of his hair, and others breathed easier because the bird struck their minds at this time as being somehow gruesome and ominous.

In the meantime the oiler and the correspondent rowed. And also they rowed. They sat together in the same seat, and each rowed an oar. Then the oiler took both oars; then the correspondent took both oars; then the oiler; then the correspondent.

They rowed and they rowed. The very ticklish part of the business was when the time came for the reclining one in the stern to take his turn at the oars. By the very last star of truth, it is easier to steal eggs from under a hen than it was to change seats in the dinghy. First the man in the stern slid his hand along the thwart and moved with care, as if he were of Sèvres. Then the man in the rowing-seat slid his hand along the other thwart. It was all done with the most extraordinary care. As the two sidled past each other, the whole party kept watchful eyes on the coming wave, and the captain cried: "Look out, now! Steady, there!"

The brown mats of seaweed that appeared from time to time were like islands, bits of earth. They were traveling, apparently, neither one way nor the other. They were, to all intents, stationary. They informed them in the boat that it was making progress slowly toward the land.

The captain, rearing cautiously in the bow after the dinghy soared on a great swell, said that he had seen the lighthouse at Mosquito Inlet. Presently the cook remarked that he had seen it. The correspondent was at the oars then, and for some reason he too wished to look at the lighthouse; but his back was toward the far shore, and the waves were important, and for some time he could not seize an opportunity to turn his head. But at last there came a wave more gentle than the others, and when at the crest of it he swiftly scoured the western horizon.

"See it?" said the captain.

"No," said the correspondent, slowly; "I didn't see anything."

"Look again," said the captain. He pointed. "It's exactly in that direction."

At the top of another wave the correspondent did as he was bid, and this time his eyes chanced on a small, still thing on the edge of the swaying horizon. It was precisely like the point of a pin. It took an anxious eye to find a lighthouse so tiny.

"Think we'll make it, Captain?"

"If this wind holds and the boat don't swamp, we can't do much else," said the captain.

The little boat, lifted by each towering sea and splashed viciously by the crests, made progress that in the absence of seaweed was not apparent to those in her. She seemed just a wee thing wallowing, miraculously top up, at the mercy of five oceans. Occasionally a great spread of water, like white flames, swarmed into her.

"Bail her, cook," said the captain, serenely.

"All right, Captain," said the cheerful cook.

III

It would be difficult to describe the subtle brotherhood of men that was here established on the seas. No one said that it was so. No one mentioned it. But it dwelt in the boat, and each man felt it warm him. They were a captain, an oiler, a cook, and a correspondent, and they were friends—friends in a more curiously iron-bound degree than may be common. The hurt captain, lying against the water-jar in the bow, spoke always in a low voice and calmly; but he could never command a more ready and swiftly obedient crew than the motley three of the dinghy. It was more than a mere recognition of what was best for the common safety. There was surely in it a quality that was personal and heart-felt. And after this devotion to the commander of the boat, there was this comradeship, that the correspondent, for instance, who had been taught to be cynical of men, knew even at the time was the best experience of his life. But no one said that it was so. No one mentioned it.

"I wish we had a sail," remarked the captain. "We might try my overcoat on the end of an oar, and give you two boys a chance to rest." So the cook and the correspondent held the mast and spread wide the overcoat; the oiler steered; and the little boat made good way with her new rig. Sometimes the oiler had to scull sharply to keep a sea from breaking into the boat, but otherwise sailing was a success.

Meanwhile the lighthouse had been growing slowly larger. It had now almost assumed colour, and appeared like a little grey shadow on the sky. The man at the oars could not be prevented from turning his head rather often to try for a glimpse of this little grey shadow.

At last, from the top of each wave, the men in the tossing boat could see land. Even as the lighthouse was an upright shadow on the sky, this land seemed but a long black shadow on the sea. It certainly was thinner than paper. "We must be about opposite New Smyrna," said the cook, who had coasted this shore often in schooners. "Captain, by the way, I believe they abandoned that life-saving station there about a year ago."

"Did they?" said the captain.

The wind slowly died away. The cook and the correspondent were not now obliged to slave in order to hold high the oar. But the waves continued their old impetuous swooping at the dinghy, and the little craft, no longer under way, struggled woundily over them. The oiler or the correspondent took the oars again.

Shipwrecks are apropos of nothing. If men could only train them and have them occur when the men had reached pink condition, there would be less drowning at sea. Of the four in the dinghy none had slept any time worth mentioning for two days and two nights previous to embarking in the dinghy, and in the excitement of clambering about the deck of a foundering ship they had also forgotten to eat heartily.

For these reasons, and for others, neither the oiler nor the correspondent was fond of rowing at this time. The correspondent wondered ingenuously how in the name of all that was sane could there be people who thought it amusing to row a boat. It was not an amusement; it was a diabolical punishment, and even a genius of mental aberrations could never conclude that it was anything but a horror to the muscles and a crime against the back. He mentioned to the boat in general how the amusement of rowing struck him, and the weary-faced oiler smiled in full sympathy. Previously to the foundering, by the way, the oiler had worked a double watch in the engine-room of the ship.

"Take her easy now, boys," said the captain. "Don't spend yourselves. If we have to run a surf you'll need all your strength, because we'll sure have to swim for it. Take your time."

Slowly the land arose from the sea. From a black line it became a line of black and a line of white—trees and sand. Finally the captain said that he could make out a house on the shore. "That's the house of refuge, sure," said the cook. "They'll see us before long, and come out after us."

The distant lighthouse reared high. "The keeper ought to be able to make us out now, if he's looking through a glass," said the captain. "He'll notify the life-saving people."

"None of those other boats could have got ashore to give word of this wreck," said the oiler, in a low voice, "else the life-boat would be out hunting us."

Slowly and beautifully the land loomed out of the sea. The wind came again. It had veered from the north-east to the south-east. Finally a new sound struck the ears of the men in the boat. It was the low thunder of the surf on the shore. "We'll never be able to make the lighthouse now," said the captain. "Swing her head a little more north, Billie."

"A little more north, sir," said the oiler.

Whereupon the little boat turned her nose once more down the wind, and all but the oarsman watched the shore grow. Under the influence of this expansion doubt and direful apprehension were leaving the minds of the men. The management of the boat was still more absorbing, but it could not prevent a quiet cheerfulness. In an hour, perhaps, they would be ashore.

Their backbones had become thoroughly used to balancing in the boat, and they now rode this wild colt of a dinghy like circus men. The correspondent thought that he had been drenched to the skin, but happening to feel in the top pocket of his coat, he found therein eight cigars. Four of them were soaked with sea-water; four were perfectly scatheless. After a search, somebody produced three dry matches; and thereupon the four waifs rode impudently in their little boat and, with an assurance of an impending rescue shining in their eyes, puffed at the big cigars, and judged well and ill of all men. Everybody took a drink of water.

IV

"Cook," remarked the captain, "there don't seem to be any signs of life about your house of refuge."

"No," replied the cook. "Funny they don't see us!"

A broad stretch of lowly coast lay before the eyes of the men. It was of low dunes topped with dark vegetation. The roar of the surf was plain, and sometimes they could see the white lip of a wave as it spun up the beach. A tiny house was blocked out black upon the sky. Southward, the slim lighthouse lifted its little grey length.

Tide, wind, and waves were swinging the dinghy northward. "Funny they don't see us," said the men.

The surf's roar was here dulled, but its tone was nevertheless thunderous and mighty. As the boat swam over the great rollers the men sat listening to this roar. "We'll swamp sure," said everybody.

It is fair to say here that there was not a life-saving station within twenty miles in either direction; but the men did not know this fact, and in consequence they made dark and opprobrious remarks concerning the eyesight of the nation's life-savers. Four scowling men sat in the dinghy and surpassed records in the invention of epithets.

"Funny they don't see us."

The light-heartedness of a former time had completely faded. To their sharpened minds it was easy to conjure pictures of all kinds of incompetency and blindness and, indeed, cowardice. There was the shore of the populous land, and it was bitter to them that from it came no sign.

"Well," said the captain, ultimately, "I suppose we'll have to make a try for ourselves. If we stay out here too long, we'll none of us have strength left to swim after the boat swamps."

And so the oiler, who was at the oars, turned the boat straight for the shore. There was a sudden tightening of muscles. There was some thinking.

"If we don't all get ashore," said the captain—"if we don't all get ashore, I suppose you fellows know where to send news of my finish?"

They then briefly exchanged some addresses and admonitions. As for the reflections of the men, there was a great deal of rage in them. Perchance they might be formulated thus: "If I am going to be drowned—if I am going to be drowned—if I am going to be drowned, why, in the name of the seven mad gods who rule the sea, was I allowed to come thus far and contemplate sand and trees? Was I brought here merely to have my nose dragged away as I was about to nibble the sacred cheese of life? It is preposterous. If this old ninny-woman, Fate, cannot do better than this, she should be deprived of the management of men's fortunes. She is an old hen who knows not her intention. If she has decided to drown me, why did she not do it in the beginning and save me all this trouble? The whole affair is absurd.—But no; she cannot mean to drown me. She dare not drown me. She cannot drown me. Not after all this work." Afterward the man might have had an impulse to shake his fist at the clouds. "Just you drown me, now, and then hear what I call you!"

The billows that came at this time were more formidable. They seemed always just about to break and roll over the little boat in a turmoil of foam. There was a preparatory and long growl in the speech of them. No mind unused to the sea would have concluded that the dinghy could ascend these sheer heights in time. The shore was still afar. The oiler was a wily surfman. "Boys," he said swiftly, "she won't live three minutes more, and we're too far out to swim. Shall I take her to sea again, Captain?"

"Yes; go ahead!" said the captain.

This oiler, by a series of quick miracles and fast and steady oarsmanship, turned the boat in the middle of the surf and took her safely to sea again.

There was a considerable silence as the boat bumped over the furrowed sea to deeper water. Then somebody in gloom spoke: "Well, anyhow, they must have seen us from the shore by now."

The gulls went in slanting flight up the wind toward the grey, desolate east. A squall, marked by dingy clouds and clouds brick-red like smoke from a burning building, appeared from the southeast.

"What do you think of those life-saving people? Ain't they peaches?"

"Funny they haven't seen us."

"Maybe they think we're out here for sport! Maybe they think we're fishin'. Maybe they think we're damned fools."

It was a long afternoon. A changed tide tried to force them southward, but wind and wave said northward. Far ahead, where coast-line, sea, and sky formed their mighty angle, there were little dots which seemed to indicate a city on the shore.

"St. Augustine?"

The captain shook his head. "Too near Mosquito Inlet."

And the oiler rowed, and then the correspondent rowed; then the oiler rowed. It was a weary business. The human back can become the seat of more aches and pains than are registered in books for the composite anatomy of a regiment. It is a limited area, but it can become the theatre of innumerable muscular conflicts, tangles, wrenches, knots, and other comforts.

"Did you ever like to row, Billie?" asked the correspondent.

"No," said the oiler; "hang it!"

When one exchanged the rowing-seat for a place in the bottom of the boat, he suffered a bodily depression that caused him to be careless of everything save an obligation to wiggle one finger. There was cold sea-water swashing to and fro in the boat, and he lay in it. His head, pillowed on a thwart, was within an inch of the swirl of a wave-crest, and sometimes a particularly obstreperous sea came inboard and drenched him once more. But these matters did not annoy him. It is almost certain that if the boat had capsized he would have tumbled comfortably out upon the ocean as if he felt sure that it was a great soft mattress.

"Look! There's a man on the shore!"

"Where?"

"There! See 'im? See 'im?"

"Yes, sure! He's walking along."

"Now he's stopped. Look! He's facing us!"

"He's waving at us!"

"So he is! By thunder!"

"Ah, now we're all right! Now we're all right! There'll be a boat out here for us in half an hour."

"He going on. He's running. He's going up to that house there."

The remote beach seemed lower than the sea, and it required a searching glance to discern the little black figure. The captain saw a floating stick, and they rowed to it. A bath towel was by some weird chance in the boat, and, tying this on the stick, the captain waved it. The oarsman did not dare turn his head, so he was obliged to ask questions.

"What's he doing now?"

"He's standing still again. He's looking, I think. —There he goes again—toward the house.—Now he's stopped again."

"Is he waving at us?"

"No, not now; he was, though."

"Look! There comes another man!"

"He's running."

"Look at him go, would you!"

"Why he's on a bicycle. Now he's met the other man. They're both waving at us. Look!"

"There comes something up the beach."

"What the devil is that thing?"

"Why, it looks like a boat."

"Why, certainly, it's a boat."

"No; it's on wheels."

"Yes, so it is. Well, that must be the life-boat. They drag them along shore on a wagon."

"That's the life-boat, sure."

"No, by God, it's—it's an omnibus."

"I tell you it's a life-boat."

"It is not! It's an omnibus. I can see it plain. See? One of these big hotel omnibuses."

"By thunder, you're right. It's an omnibus, sure as fate. What do you suppose they are doing with an omnibus? Maybe they are going around collecting the life-crew, hey?"

"That's it, likely. Look! There's a fellow waving a little black flag. He's standing on the steps of the omnibus. There come those other two fellows. Now they're all talking together. Look at the fellow with the flag. Maybe he ain't waving it!"

"That ain't a flag, is it? That's his coat. Why, certainly, that's his coat."

"So it is; it's his coat. He's taken it off and is waving it around his head. But would you look at him swing it!"

"Oh, say, there isn't any life-saving station there. That's just a winter-resort hotel omnibus that has brought over some of the boarders to see us drown."

"What's that idiot with the coat mean? What's he signalling, anyhow?"

"It looks as if he were trying to tell us to go north. There must be a life-saving station up there."

"No; he thinks we're fishing. Just giving us a merry hand. See? Ah, there, Willie!"

"Well, I wish I could make something out of those signals. What do you suppose he means?"

"He don't mean anything; he's just playing."

"Well, if he'd just signal us to try the surf again, or to go to sea and wait, or go north, or go south, or go to hell, there would be some reason in it. But look at him! He just stands there and keeps his coat revolving like a wheel. The ass!"

"There come more people."

"Now there's quite a mob. Look! Isn't that a boat?"

"Where? Oh, I see where you mean. No, that's no boat."

"That fellow is still waving his coat."

"He must think we like to see him do that. Why don't he quit it? It don't mean anything."

"I don't know. I think he is trying to make us go north. It must be that there's a life-saving station there somewhere."

"Say, he ain't tired yet. Look at 'im wave!"

"Wonder how long he can keep that up. He's been revolving his coat ever since he caught sight of us. He's an idiot. Why aren't they getting men to bring a boat out? A fishing-boat—one of those big yawls—could come out here all right. Why don't he do something?"

"Oh, it's all right now."

"They'll have a boat out here for us in less than no time, now that they've seen us."

A faint yellow tone came into the sky over the low land. The shadows on the sea slowly deepened. The wind bore coldness with it, and the men began to shiver.

"Holy smoke!" said one, allowing his voice to express his impious mood, "if we keep on monkeying out here! If we've got to flounder out here all night!"

"Oh, we'll never have to stay here all night! Don't you worry. They've seen us now, and it won't be long before they'll come chasing out after us."

The shore grew dusky. The man waving a coat

blended gradually into this gloom, and it swallowed in the same manner the omnibus and the group of people. The spray, when it dashed uproariously over the side, made the voyagers shrink and swear like men who were being branded.

"I'd like to catch the chump who waved the coat. I feel like socking him one, just for luck."

"Why? What did he do?"

"Oh, nothing, but then he seemed so damned cheerful."

In the meantime the oiler rowed, and then the correspondent rowed, and then the oiler rowed. Grey-faced and bowed forward, they mechanically, turn by turn, plied the leaden oars. The form of the lighthouse had vanished from the southern horizon, but finally a pale star appeared, just lifting from the sea. The streaked saffron in the west passed before the all-merging darkness, and the sea to the east was black. The land had vanished, and was expressed only by the low and drear thunder of the surf.

"If I am going to be drowned—if I am going to be drowned—if I am going to be drowned, why, in the name of the seven mad gods who rule the sea, was I allowed to come thus far and contemplate sand and trees? Was I brought here merely to have my nose dragged away as I was about to nibble the sacred cheese of life?"

The patient captain, drooped over the water-jar, was sometimes obliged to speak to the oarsman.

"Keep her head up! Keep her head up!"

"Keep her head up, sir." The voices were weary and low.

This was surely a quiet evening. All save the oarsman lay heavily and listlessly in the boat's bottom. As for him, his eyes were just capable of noting the tall black waves that swept forward in a most sinister silence, save for an occasional subdued growl of a crest.

The cook's head was on a thwart, and he looked without interest at the water under his nose. He was deep in other scenes. Finally he spoke. "Billie," he murmured, dreamfully, "what kind of pie do you like best?"

V

"Pie!" said the oiler and the correspondent, agitatedly. "Don't talk about those things, blast you!"

"Well," said the cook, "I was just thinking about ham sandwiches and—"

A night on the sea in an open boat is a long

night. As darkness settled finally, the shine of the light, lifting from the sea in the south, changed to full gold. On the northern horizon a new light appeared, a small bluish gleam on the edge of the waters. These two lights were the furniture of the world. Otherwise there was nothing but waves.

Two men huddled in the stern, and distances were so magnificent in the dinghy that the rower was enabled to keep his feet partly warm by thrusting them under his companions. Their legs indeed extended far under the rowing-seat until they touched the feet of the captain forward. Sometimes, despite the efforts of the tired oarsman, a wave came piling into the boat, an icy wave of the night, and the chilling water soaked them anew. They would twist their bodies for a moment and groan, and sleep the dead sleep once more, while the water in the boat gurgled about them as the craft rocked.

The plan of the oiler and the correspondent was for one to row until he lost the ability, and then arouse the other from his sea-water couch in the bottom of the boat.

The oiler plied the oars until his head drooped forward and the overpowering sleep blinded him; and he rowed yet afterward. Then he touched a man in the bottom of the boat, and called his name. "Will you spell me for a little while?" he said, meekly.

"Sure, Billie," said the correspondent, awaking and dragging himself to a sitting position. They exchanged places carefully, and the oiler, cuddling down in the sea-water at the cook's side, seemed to go to sleep instantly.

The particular violence of the sea had ceased. The waves came without snarling. The obligation of the man at the oars was to keep the boat headed so that the tilt of the rollers would not capsize her, and to preserve her from filling when the crests rushed past. The black waves were silent and hard to be seen in the darkness. Often one was almost upon the boat before the oarsman was aware.

In a low voice the correspondent addressed the captain. He was not sure that the captain was awake, although this iron man seemed to be always awake. "Captain, shall I keep her making for that light north, sir?"

The same steady voice answered him. "Yes. Keep it about two points off the port bow."

The cook had tied a life-belt around himself in order to get even the warmth which this clumsy cork contrivance could donate, and he seemed almost stove-like when a rower, whose teeth invariably chattered wildly as soon as he ceased his labour, dropped down to sleep.

The correspondent, as he rowed, looked down at the two men sleeping underfoot. The cook's arm was around the oiler's shoulders, and, with their fragmentary clothing and haggard faces, they were the babes of the sea—a grotesque rendering of the old babes in the wood.

Later he must have grown stupid at his work, for suddenly there was a growling of water, and a crest came with a roar and a swash into the boat, and it was a wonder that it did not set the cook afloat in his lifebelt. The cook continued to sleep, but the oiler sat up, blinking his eyes and shaking with the new cold.

"Oh, I'm awfully sorry, Billie," said the correspondent, contritely.

"That's all right, old boy," said the oiler, and lay down again and was asleep.

Presently it seemed that even the captain dozed, and the correspondent thought that he was the one man afloat on all the oceans. The wind had a voice as it came over the waves, and it was sadder than the end.

There was a long, loud swishing astern of the boat, and a gleaming trail of phosphorescence, like blue flame, was furrowed on the black waters. It might have been made by a monstrous knife.

Then there came a stillness, while the correspondent breathed with open mouth and looked at the sea.

Suddenly there was another swish and another long flash of bluish light, and this time it was alongside the boat, and might almost have been reached with an oar. The correspondent saw an enormous fin speed like a shadow through the water, hurling the crystalline spray and leaving the long glowing trail.

The correspondent looked over his shoulder at the captain. His face was hidden, and he seemed to be asleep. He looked at the babes of the sea. They certainly were asleep. So, being bereft of sympathy, he leaned a little way to one side and swore softly into the sea.

But the thing did not then leave the vicinity of the boat. Ahead or astern, on one side or the other, at intervals long or short, fled the long sparkling streak, and there was to be heard the *whirroo* of the dark fin. The speed and power of the thing was greatly to be admired. It cut the water like a gigantic and keen projectile.

The presence of this biding thing did not affect the man with the same horror that it would if he had been a picnicker. He simply looked at the sea dully and swore in an undertone.

Nevertheless, it is true that he did not wish to be alone with the thing. He wished one of his companions to awake by chance and keep him company with it. But the captain hung motionless over the water-jar, and the oiler and the cook in the bottom of the boat were plunged in slumber.

VI

"If I am going to be drowned—if I am going to be drowned—if I am going to be drowned, why, in the name of the seven mad gods who rule the sea, was I allowed to come thus far and contemplate sand and trees?"

During this dismal night, it may be remarked that a man would conclude that it was really the intention of the seven mad gods to drown him, despite the abominable injustice of it. For it was certainly an abominable injustice to drown a man who had worked so hard, so hard. The man felt it would be a crime most unnatural. Other people had drowned at sea since galleys swarmed with painted sails, but still—

When it occurs to a man that nature does not regard him as important, and that she feels she would not maim the universe by disposing of him, he at first wishes to throw bricks at the temple, and he hates deeply the fact that there are no bricks and no temples. Any visible expression of nature would surely be pelleted with his jeers.

Then, if there be no tangible thing to hoot, he feels, perhaps, the desire to confront a personification and indulge in pleas, bowed to one knee, and with hands supplicant, saying, "Yes, but I love myself."

A high cold star on a winter's night is the word he feels that she says to him. Thereafter he knows the pathos of his situation.

The men in the dinghy had not discussed these matters, but each had, no doubt, reflected upon them in silence and according to his mind. There was seldom any expression upon their faces save the general one of complete weariness. Speech was devoted to the business of the boat.

To chime the notes of his emotion, a verse mysteriously entered the correspondent's head. He had even forgotten that he had forgotten this verse, but it suddenly was in his mind.

A soldier of the Legion lay dying in Algiers;
There was lack of woman's nursing, there was dearth
  of woman's tears;
But a comrade stood beside him, and he took that
  comrade's hand,
And he said, "I never more shall see my own, my
  native land."

In his childhood the correspondent had been made acquainted with the fact that a soldier of the Legion lay dying in Algiers, but he had never regarded the fact as important. Myriads of his school-fellows had informed him of the soldier's plight, but the dinning had naturally ended by making him perfectly indifferent. He had never considered it his affair that a soldier of the Legion lay dying in Algiers, nor had it appeared to him as a matter for sorrow. It was less to him than the breaking of a pencil's point.

Now, however, it quaintly came to him as a human, living thing. It was no longer merely a picture of a few throes in the breast of a poet, meanwhile drinking tea and warming his feet at the grate; it was an actuality—stern, mournful, and fine.

The correspondent plainly saw the soldier. He lay on the sand with his feet out straight and still. While his pale left hand was upon his chest in an attempt to thwart the going of his life, the blood came between his fingers. In the far Algerian distance, a city of low square forms was set against a sky that was faint with the last sunset hues. The correspondent, plying the oars and dreaming of the slow and slower movements of the lips of the soldier, was moved by a profound and perfectly impersonal comprehension. He was sorry for the soldier of the Legion who lay dying in Algiers.

The thing which had followed the boat and waited had evidently grown bored at the delay. There was no longer to be heard the slash of the cutwater, and there was no longer the flame of the long trail. The light in the north still glimmered, but it was apparently no nearer to the boat. Sometimes the boom of the surf rang in the correspondent's ears, and he turned the craft seaward then and rowed harder. Southward, some one had evidently built a watch-fire on the beach. It was too low and too far to be seen, but it made a shimmering, roseate reflection upon the bluff in back of it, and this could be discerned from the boat. The wind came stronger, and sometimes a wave suddenly raged out like a mountain cat, and there was

to be seen the sheen and sparkle of a broken crest.

The captain, in the bow, moved on his water-jar and sat erect. "Pretty long night," he observed to the correspondent. He looked at the shore. "Those life-saving people take their time."

"Did you see that shark playing around?"

"Yes, I saw him. He was a big fellow, all right."

"Wish I had known you were awake."

Later the correspondent spoke into the bottom of the boat. "Billie!" There was a slow and gradual disentanglement. "Billie, will you spell me?"

"Sure," said the oiler.

As soon as the correspondent touched the cold, comfortable sea-water in the bottom of the boat and had huddled close to the cook's life-belt he was deep in sleep, despite the fact that his teeth played all the popular airs. This sleep was so good to him that it was but a moment before he heard a voice call his name in a tone that demonstrated the last stages of exhaustion. "Will you spell me?"

"Sure, Billie."

The light in the north had mysteriously vanished, but the correspondent took his course from the wide-awake captain.

Later in the night they took the boat farther out to sea, and the captain directed the cook to take one oar at the stern and keep the boat facing the seas. He was to call out if he should hear the thunder of the surf. This plan enabled the oiler and the correspondent to get respite together. "We'll give those boys a chance to get into shape again," said the captain. They curled down and, after a few preliminary chatterings and trembles, slept once more the dead sleep. Neither knew they had bequeathed to the cook the company of another shark, or perhaps the same shark.

As the boat caroused on the waves, spray occasionally bumped over the side and gave them a fresh soaking, but this had no power to break their repose. The ominous slash of the wind and the water affected them as it would have affected mummies.

"Boys," said the cook, with the notes of every reluctance in his voice, "she's drifted in pretty close. I guess one of you had better take her to sea again." The correspondent, aroused, heard the crash of the toppled crests.

As he was rowing, the captain gave him some whisky-and-water, and this steadied the chills out of him. "If I ever get ashore and anybody shows me even a photograph of an oar—"

At last there was a short conversation.

"Billie!—Billie, will you spell me?"

"Sure," said the oiler.

VII

When the correspondent again opened his eyes, the sea and the sky were each of the grey hue of the dawning. Later, carmine and gold was painted upon the waters. The morning appeared finally, in its splendour, with a sky of pure blue, and the sunlight flamed on the tips of the waves.

On the distant dunes were set many little black cottages, and a tall white windmill reared above them. No man, nor dog, nor bicycle appeared on the beach. The cottages might have formed a deserted village.

The voyagers scanned the shore. A conference was held in the boat. "Well," said the captain, "if no help is coming, we might better try a run through the surf right away. If we stay out here much longer we will be too weak to do anything for ourselves at all." The others silently acquiesced in this reasoning. The boat was headed for the beach. The correspondent wondered if none ever ascended the tall wind-tower, and if then they never looked seaward. This tower was a giant, standing with its back to the plight of the ants. It represented in a degree, to the correspondent, the serenity of nature amid the struggles of the individual—nature in the wind, and nature in the vision of men. She did not seem cruel to him then, nor beneficent, nor treacherous, nor wise. But she was indifferent, flatly indifferent. It is, perhaps, plausible that a man in this situation, impressed with the unconcern of the universe, should see the innumerable flaws of his life, and have them taste wickedly in his mind, and wish for another chance. A distinction between right and wrong seems absurdly clear to him, then, in this new ignorance of the grave-edge, and he understands that if he were given another opportunity he would mend his conduct and his words, and be better and brighter during an introduction or at a tea.

"Now, boys," said the captain, "she is going to swamp sure. All we can do is to work her in as far as possible, and then when she swamps, pile out and scramble for the beach. Keep cool now, and don't jump until she swamps sure."

The oiler took the oars. Over his shoulders he scanned the surf. "Captain," he said, "I think I'd better bring her about and keep her head-on to the seas and back her in."

"All right, Billie," said the captain. "Back her in." The oiler swung the boat then, and, seated in the stern, the cook and the correspondent were obliged to look over their shoulders to contemplate the lonely and indifferent shore.

The monstrous inshore rollers heaved the boat high until the men were again enabled to see the white sheets of water scudding up the slanted beach. "We won't get in very close," said the captain. Each time a man could wrest his attention from the rollers, he turned his glance toward the shore, and in the expression of the eyes during this contemplation there was a singular quality. The correspondent, observing the others, knew that they were not afraid, but the full meaning of their glances was shrouded.

As for himself, he was too tired to grapple fundamentally with the fact. He tried to coerce his mind into thinking of it, but the mind was dominated at this time by the muscles, and the muscles said they did not care. It merely occurred to him that if he should drown it would be a shame.

There were no hurried words, no pallor, no plain agitation. The men simply looked at the shore. "Now, remember to get well clear of the boat when you jump," said the captain.

Seaward the crest of a roller suddenly fell with a thunderous crash, and the long white comber came roaring down upon the boat.

"Steady now," said the captain. The men were silent. They turned their eyes from the shore to the comber and waited. The boat slid up the incline, leaped at the furious top, bounced over it, and swung down the long back of the wave. Some water had been shipped, and the cook bailed it out.

But the next crest crashed also. The tumbling, boiling flood of white water caught the boat and whirled it almost perpendicular. Water swarmed in from all sides. The correspondent had his hands on the gunwale at this time, and when the water entered at that place he swiftly withdrew his fingers, as if he objected to wetting them.

The little boat, drunken with this weight of water, reeled and snuggled deeper into the sea.

"Bail her out, cook! Bail her out!" said the captain.

"All right, Captain," said the cook.

"Now boys, the next one will do for us sure," said the oiler. "Mind to jump clear of the boat."

The third wave moved forward, huge, furious, implacable. It fairly swallowed the dinghy, and almost simultaneously the men tumbled into the sea. A piece of life-belt had laid in the bottom of the boat, and as the correspondent went overboard he held this to his chest with his left hand.

The January water was icy, and he reflected immediately that it was colder than he had expected to find it off the coast of Florida. This appeared to his dazed mind as a fact important enough to be noted at the time. The coldness of the water was sad; it was tragic. This fact was somehow mixed and confused with his opinion of his own situation, so that it seemed almost a proper reason for tears. The water was cold.

When he came to the surface he was conscious of little but the noisy water. Afterward he saw his companions in the sea. The oiler was ahead in the race. He was swimming strongly and rapidly. Off to the correspondent's left, the cook's great white and corked back bulged out of the water; and in the rear the captain was hanging with his one good hand to the keel of the overturned dinghy.

There is a certain immovable quality to a shore, and the correspondent wondered at it amid the confusion of the sea.

It seemed also very attractive; but the correspondent knew that it was a long journey, and he paddled leisurely. The piece of life-preserver lay under him, and sometimes he whirled down the incline of a wave as if he were on a hand-sled.

But finally he arrived at a place in the sea where travel was beset with difficulty. He did not pause swimming to inquire what manner of current had caught him, but there his progress ceased. The shore was set before him like a bit of scenery on a stage, and he looked at it and understood with his eyes each detail of it.

As the cook passed, much farther to the left, the captain was calling to him, "Turn over on your back, cook! Turn over on your back and use the oar."

"All right, sir." The cook turned on his back, and, paddling with an oar, went ahead as if he were a canoe.

Presently the boat also passed to the left of the correspondent, with the captain clinging with one hand to the keel. He would have appeared like a man raising himself to look over a board fence if it were not for the extraordinary gymnastics of the boat. The correspondent marvelled that the captain could still hold to it.

They passed on nearer to shore—the oiler, the cook, the captain—and following them went the water-jar, bouncing gaily over the seas.

The correspondent remained in the grip of this strange new enemy—a current. The shore, with its white slope of sand and its green bluff topped with little silent cottages, was spread like a picture before him. It was very near to him then, but he was impressed as one who, in a gallery, looks at a scene from Brittany or Algiers.

He thought: "I am going to drown? Can it be possible? Can it be possible? Can it be possible?" Perhaps an individual must consider his own death to be the final phenomenon of nature.

But later a wave perhaps whirled him out of this small deadly current, for he found suddenly that he could again make progress toward the shore. Later still he was aware that the captain, clinging with one hand to the keel of the dinghy, had his face turned away from the shore and toward him, and was calling his name. "Come to the boat! Come to the boat!"

In his struggle to reach the captain and the boat, he reflected that when one gets properly wearied drowning must really be a comfortable arrangement—a cessation of hostilities accompanied by a large degree of relief; and he was glad of it, for the main thing in his mind for some moments had been horror of the temporary agony. He did not wish to be hurt.

Presently he saw a man running along the shore. He was undressing with most remarkable speed. Coat, trousers, shirt, everything flew magically off him.

"Come to the boat!" called the captain.

"All right, Captain." As the correspondent paddled, he saw the captain let himself down to bottom and leave the boat. Then the correspondent performed his one little marvel of the voyage. A large wave caught him and flung him with ease and supreme speed completely over the boat and far beyond it. It struck him even then as an event in gymnastics and a true miracle of the sea. An overturned boat in the surf is not a plaything to a swimming man.

The correspondent arrived in water that reached only to his waist, but his condition did not enable him to stand for more than a moment. Each wave knocked him into a heap, and the undertow pulled at him.

Then he saw the man who had been running and undressing, and undressing and running, come bounding into the water. He dragged ashore the cook, and then waded toward the captain; but the captain waved him away and sent him to the correspondent. He was naked—naked as a tree in winter; but a halo was about his head, and he shone like a saint. He gave a strong pull, and a long drag, and a bully heave at the correspondent's hand. The correspondent, schooled in the minor formulæ, said, "Thanks, old man." But suddenly the man cried, "What's that?" He pointed a swift finger. The correspondent said, "Go."

In the shallows, face downward, lay the oiler. His forehead touched sand that was periodically, between each wave, clear of the sea.

The correspondent did not know all that transpired afterward. When he achieved safe ground he fell, striking the sand with each particular part of his body. It was as if he had dropped from a roof, but the thud was grateful to him.

It seemed that instantly the beach was populated with men with blankets, clothes, and flasks, and women with coffee-pots and all the remedies sacred to their minds. The welcome of the land to the men from the sea was warm and generous; but a still and dripping shape was carried slowly up the beach, and the land's welcome for it could only be the different and sinister hospitality of the grave.

When it came night, the white waves paced to and fro in the moonlight, and the wind brought the sound of the great sea's voice to the men on the shore, and they felt that they could then be interpreters.

The Bride Comes to Yellow Sky (1898)

I

The great Pullman was whirling onward with such dignity of motion that a glance from the window seemed simply to prove that the plains of Texas were pouring eastward. Vast flats of green grass, dull-hued spaces of mesquit and cactus, little groups of frame houses, woods of light and tender trees, all were sweeping into the east, sweeping over the horizon, a precipice.

A newly married pair had boarded this coach at San Antonio. The man's face was reddened from many days in the wind and sun, and a direct result of his new black clothes was that his brick-coloured hands were constantly performing in a most conscious fashion. From time to time he looked down respectfully at his attire. He sat with a hand on each knee, like a man waiting in a barber's shop. The glances he devoted to other passengers were furtive and shy.

The bride was not pretty, nor was she very young. She wore a dress of blue cashmere, with small reservations of velvet here and there, and with steel buttons abounding. She continually twisted her head to regard her puff sleeves, very stiff, straight, and high. They embarrassed her. It was quite apparent that she had cooked, and that she expected to cook, dutifully. The blushes caused by the careless scrutiny of some passengers as she had entered the car were strange to see upon this plain, under-class countenance, which was drawn in placid, almost emotionless lines.

They were evidently very happy. "Ever been in a parlour-car before?" he asked, smiling with delight.

"No," she answered; "I never was. It's fine, ain't it?"

"Great! And then after a while we'll go forward to the diner, and get a big lay-out. Finest meal in the world. Charge a dollar."

"Oh, do they?" cried the bride. "Charge a dollar? Why, that's too much—for us—ain't it, Jack?"

"Not this trip, anyhow," he answered bravely. "We're going to go the whole thing."

Later he explained to her about the trains. "You see, it's a thousand miles from one end of Texas to the other; and this train runs right across it, and never stops but four times." He had the pride of an owner. He pointed out to her the dazzling fittings of the coach; and in truth her eyes opened wider as she contemplated the sea-green figured velvet, the shining brass, silver, and glass, the wood that gleamed as darkly brilliant as the surface of a pool of oil. At one end a bronze figure sturdily held a support for a separated chamber, and at convenient places on the ceiling were frescos in olive and silver.

To the minds of the pair, their surroundings reflected the glory of their marriage that morning in San Antonio; this was the environment of their new estate; and the man's face in particular beamed with an elation that made him appear ridiculous to the negro porter. This individual at times surveyed them from afar with an amused and superior grin. On other occasions he bullied them with skill in ways that did not make it exactly plain to them that they were being bullied. He subtly used all the manners of the most unconquerable kind of snobbery. He oppressed them; but of this oppression they had small knowledge, and they speedily forgot that infrequently a number of travellers covered them with stares of derisive enjoyment. Historically there was supposed to be something infinitely humorous in their situation.

"We are due in Yellow Sky at 3:42," he said, looking tenderly into her eyes.

"Oh, are we?" she said, as if she had not been aware of it. To evince surprise at her husband's statement was part of her wifely amiability. She took from a pocket a little silver watch; and as she held it before her, and stared at it with a frown of attention, the new husband's face shone.

"I bought it in San Anton' from a friend of mine," he told her gleefully.

"It's seventeen minutes past twelve," she said, looking up at him with a kind of shy and clumsy coquetry. A passenger, noting this play, grew excessively sardonic, and winked at himself in one of the numerous mirrors.

At last they went to the dining-car. Two rows of negro waiters, in glowing white suits, surveyed their entrance with the interest, and also the equanimity, of men who had been forewarned. The pair fell to the lot of a waiter who happened to feel pleasure in steering them through their meal. He viewed them with the manner of a fatherly pilot, his countenance radiant with benevolence. The patronage, entwined with the ordinary deference, was not plain to them. And yet, as they returned to their coach, they showed in their faces a sense of escape.

To the left, miles down a long purple slope, was a little ribbon of mist where moved the keening Rio Grande. The train was approaching it at an angle, and the apex was Yellow Sky. Presently it was apparent that, as the distance from Yellow Sky grew shorter, the husband became commensurately restless. His brick-red hands were more insistent in their prominence. Occasionally he was even rather absent-minded and far-away when the bride leaned forward and addressed him.

As a matter of truth, Jack Potter was beginning to find the shadow of a deed weigh upon him like a leaden slab. He, the town marshal of Yellow Sky, a man known, liked, and feared in his corner, a prominent person, had gone to San Antonio to meet a girl he believed he loved, and there, after the usual prayers, had actually induced her to marry him, without consulting Yellow Sky for any part of the transaction. He was now bringing his bride before an innocent and unsuspecting community.

Of course people in Yellow Sky married as it pleased them, in accordance with a general custom; but such was Potter's thought of his duty to his friends, or of their idea of his duty, or of an unspoken form which does not control men in these matters, that he felt he was heinous. He had committed an extraordinary crime. Face to face with this girl in San Antonio, and spurred by his sharp impulse, he had gone headlong over all the social hedges. At San Antonio he was like a man hidden in the dark. A knife to sever any friendly duty, any form, was easy to his hand in that remote city. But the hour of Yellow Sky—the hour of daylight—was approaching.

He knew full well that his marriage was an important thing to his town. It could only be exceeded by the burning of the new hotel. His friends could not forgive him. Frequently he had reflected on the advisability of telling them by telegraph, but a new cowardice had been upon him. He feared to do it. And now the train was hurrying him toward a scene of amazement, glee, and reproach. He glanced out of the window at the line of haze swinging slowly in toward the train.

Yellow Sky had a kind of brass band, which played painfully, to the delight of the populace. He laughed without heart as he thought of it. If the citizens could dream of his prospective arrival with his bride, they would parade the band at the station and escort them, amid cheers and laughing congratulations, to his adobe home.

He resolved that he would use all the devices of speed and plainscraft in making the journey from the station to his house. Once within that safe citadel, he could issue some sort of vocal bulletin, and then not go among the citizens until they had time to wear off a little of their enthusiasm.

The bride looked anxiously at him. "What's worrying you, Jack?"

He laughed again. "I'm not worrying, girl; I'm only thinking of Yellow Sky."

She flushed in comprehension.

A sense of mutual guilt invaded their minds and developed a finer tenderness. They looked at each other with eyes softly aglow. But Potter often laughed the same nervous laugh; the flush upon the bride's face seemed quite permanent.

The traitor to the feeling of Yellow Sky narrowly watched the speeding landscape. "We're nearly there," he said.

Presently the porter came and announced the proximity of Potter's home. He held a brush in his hand, and, with all his airy superiority gone, he brushed Potter's new clothes as the latter slowly turned this way and that way. Potter fumbled out a coin and gave it to the porter, as he had seen others do. It was a heavy and muscle-bound business, as that of a man shoeing his first horse.

The porter took their bag, and as the train began to slow they moved forward to the hooded platform of the car. Presently the two engines and their long string of coaches rushed into the station of Yellow Sky.

"They have to take water here," said Potter, from a constricted throat and in mournful cadence, as one announcing death. Before the train stopped his eye had swept the length of the platform, and he was glad and astonished to see there was none upon it but the station-agent, who, with a slightly hurried and anxious air, was walking toward the water-tanks. When the train had halted, the porter alighted first, and placed in position a little temporary step.

"Come on, girl," said Potter, hoarsely. As he helped her down they each laughed on a false note. He took the bag from the negro, and bade his wife cling to his arm. As they slunk rapidly away, his hang-dog glance perceived that they were unloading the two trunks, and also that the station-agent, far ahead near the baggage car, had turned and was running toward him, making gestures. He laughed, and groaned as he laughed, when he noted the first effect of his marital bliss upon Yellow Sky. He gripped his wife's arm firmly to his side, and they fled. Behind them the porter stood, chuckling fatuously.

II

The California express on the Southern Railway was due at Yellow Sky in twenty-one minutes. There were six men at the bar of the Weary Gentleman saloon. One was a drummer who talked a great deal and rapidly; three were Texans who did not care to talk at that time; and two were Mexi-can sheep-herders, who did not talk as a general practice in the Weary Gentleman saloon. The barkeeper's dog lay on the board walk that crossed in front of the door. His head was on his paws, and he glanced drowsily here and there with the constant vigilance of a dog that is kicked on occasion. Across the sandy street were some vivid green grassplots, so wonderful in appearance, amid the sands that burned near them in a blazing sun, that they caused a doubt in the mind. They exactly resembled the grass mats used to represent lawns on the stage. At the cooler end of the railway station, a man without a coat sat in a tilted chair and smoked his pipe. The fresh-cut bank of the Rio Grande circled near the town, and there could be seen beyond it a great plum-coloured plain of mesquit.

Save for the busy drummer and his companions in the saloon, Yellow Sky was dozing. The newcomer leaned gracefully upon the bar, and recited many tales with the confidence of a bard who has come upon a new field.

"—and at the moment that the old man fell downstairs with the bureau in his arms, the old woman was coming up with two scuttles of coal, and of course—"

The drummer's tale was interrupted by a young man who suddenly appeared in the open door. He cried: "Scratchy Wilson's drunk, and has turned loose with both hands." The two Mexicans at once set down their glasses and faded out of the rear entrance of the saloon.

The drummer, innocent and jocular, answered: "All right, old man. S'pose he has? Come in and have a drink, anyhow."

But the information had made such an obvious cleft in every skull in the room that the drummer was obliged to see its importance. All had become instantly solemn. "Say," said he, mystified, "what is this?" His three companions made the introductory gesture of eloquent speech; but the young man at the door forestalled them.

"It means, my friend," he answered, as he came into the saloon, "that for the next two hours this town won't be a health resort."

The barkeeper went to the door, and locked and barred it; reaching out of the window, he pulled in heavy wooden shutters, and barred them. Immediately a solemn, chapel-like gloom was upon the place. The drummer was looking from one to another.

"But say," he cried, "what is this, anyhow? You don't mean there is going to be a gun-fight?"

"Don't know whether there'll be a fight or not," answered one man, grimly; "but there'll be some shootin'—some good shootin'."

The young man who had warned them waved his hand. "Oh, there'll be a fight fast enough, if any one wants it. Anybody can get a fight out there in the street. There's a fight just waiting."

The drummer seemed to be swayed between the interest of a foreigner and a perception of personal danger.

"What did you say his name was?" he asked.

"Scratchy Wilson," they answered in chorus.

"And will he kill anybody? What are you going to do? Does this happen often? Does he rampage around like this once a week or so? Can he break in that door?"

"No; he can't break down that door," replied the barkeeper. "He's tried it three times. But when he comes you'd better lay down on the floor, stranger. He's dead sure to shoot at it, and a bullet may come through."

Thereafter the drummer kept a strict eye upon the door. The time had not yet been called for him to hug the floor, but, as a minor precaution, he sidled near to the wall. "Will he kill anybody?" he said again.

The men laughed low and scornfully at the question.

"He's out to shoot, and he's out for trouble. Don't see any good in experimentin' with him."

"But what do you do in a case like this? What do you do?"

A man responded: "Why, he and Jack Potter—"

"But," in chorus the other men interrupted, "Jack Potter's in San Anton'."

"Well, who is he? What's he got to do with it?"

"Oh, he's the town marshal. He goes out and fights Scratchy when he gets on one of these tears."

"Wow!" said the drummer, mopping his brow. "Nice job he's got."

The voices had toned away to mere whisperings. The drummer wished to ask further questions, which were born of an increasing anxiety and bewilderment; but when he attempted them, the men merely look at him in irritation and motioned him to remain silent. A tense waiting hush was upon them. In the deep shadows of the room their eyes shone as they listened for sounds from the street. One man made three gestures at the barkeeper; and the latter, moving like a ghost, handed him a glass and a bottle. The man poured a full glass of whisky, and set down the bottle noiselessly.

He gulped the whisky in a swallow, and turned again toward the door in immovable silence. The drummer saw that the barkeeper, without a sound, had taken a Winchester from beneath the bar. Later he saw this individual beckoning to him, so he tiptoed across the room.

"You better come with me back of the bar."

"No, thanks," said the drummer, perspiring; "I'd rather be where I can make a break for the back door."

Whereupon the man of bottles made a kindly but peremptory gesture. The drummer obeyed it, and, finding himself seated on a box with his head below the level of the bar, balm was laid upon his soul at sight of various zinc and copper fittings that bore a resemblance to armour-plate. The barkeeper took a seat comfortably upon an adjacent box.

"You see," he whispered, "this here Scratchy Wilson is a wonder with a gun—a perfect wonder; and when he goes on the war-trail, we hunt our holes—naturally. He's about the last one of the old gang that used to hang out along the river here. He's a terror when he's drunk. When he's sober he's all right—kind of simple—wouldn't hurt a fly—nicest fellow in town. But when he's drunk—whoo!"

There were periods of stillness. "I wish Jack Potter was back from San Anton'," said the barkeeper. "He shot Wilson up once—in the leg—and he would sail in and pull out the kinks in this thing."

Presently they heard from a distance the sound of a shot, followed by three wild yowls. It instantly removed a bond from the men in the darkened saloon. There was a shuffling of feet. They looked at each other. "Here he comes," they said.

III

A man in a maroon-coloured flannel shirt, which had been purchased for purposes of decoration, and made principally by some Jewish women on the East Side of New York, rounded a corner and walked into the middle of the main street of Yellow Sky. In either hand the man held a long, heavy, blue-black revolver. Often he yelled, and these cries rang through a semblance of a deserted village, shrilly flying over the roofs in a volume that seemed to have no relation to the ordinary vocal strength of a man. It was as if the surrounding stillness formed the arch of a tomb over him. These cries of ferocious challenge rang against walls of silence. And his boots had red tops with gilded imprints, of the kind beloved in winter by little sledding boys on the hillsides of New England.

The man's face flamed in a rage begot of whisky. His eyes, rolling, and yet keen for ambush, hunted the still doorways and windows. He walked with the creeping movement of the midnight cat. As it occurred to him, he roared menacing information. The long revolvers in his hands were as easy as straws; they were moved with an electric swiftness. The little fingers of each hand played sometimes in a musician's way. Plain from the low collar of the shirt, the cords of his neck straightened and sank, straightened and sank, as passion moved him. The only sounds were his terrible invitations. The calm adobes preserved their demeanour at the passing of this small thing in the middle of the street.

There was no offer of fight—no offer of fight. The man called to the sky. There were no attractions. He bellowed and fumed and swayed his revolvers here and everywhere.

The dog of the barkeeper of the Weary Gentleman saloon had not appreciated the advance of events. He yet lay dozing in front of his master's door. At sight of the dog, the man paused and raised his revolver humorously. At sight of the man, the dog sprang up and walked diagonally away, with a sullen head, and growling. The man yelled, and the dog broke into a gallop. As it was about to enter an alley, there was a loud noise, a whistling, and something spat the ground directly before it. The dog screamed, and, wheeling in terror, galloped headlong in a new direction. Again there was a noise, a whistling, and sand was kicked viciously before it. Fear-stricken, the dog turned and flurried like an animal in a pen. The man stood laughing, his weapons at his hips.

Ultimately the man was attracted by the closed door of the Weary Gentleman saloon. He went to it and, hammering with a revolver, demanded drink.

The door remaining imperturbable, he picked a bit of paper from the walk, and nailed it to the framework with a knife. He then turned his back contemptuously upon this popular resort and, walking to the opposite side of the street and spinning there on his heel quickly and lithely, fired at the bit of paper. He missed it by a half-inch. He swore at himself, and went away. Later he comfortably fusilladed the windows of his most intimate friend.

The man was playing with this town; it was a toy for him.

But still there was no offer of fight. The name of Jack Potter, his ancient antagonist, entered his mind, and he concluded that it would be a glad thing if he should go to Potter's house, and by bombardment induce him to come out and fight. He moved in the direction of his desire, chanting Apache scalp-music.

When he arrived at it, Potter's house presented the same still front as had the other adobes. Taking up a strategic position, the man howled a challenge. But this house regarded him as might a great stone god. It gave no sign. After a decent wait, the man howled further challenges, mingling with them wonderful epithets.

Presently there came the spectacle of a man churning himself into deepest rage over the immobility of a house. He fumed at it as the winter wind attacks a prairie cabin in the North. To the distance there should have gone the sound of a tumult like the fighting of two hundred Mexicans. As necessity bade him, he paused for breath or to reload his revolvers.

IV

Potter and his bride walked sheepishly and with speed. Sometimes they laughed together shamefacedly and low.

"Next corner, dear," he said finally.

They put forth the efforts of a pair walking bowed against a strong wind. Potter was about to raise his finger to point the first appearance of the new home when, as they circled the corner, they came face to face with a man in a maroon-coloured shirt, who was feverishly pushing cartridges into a large revolver. Upon the instant the man dropped his revolver to the ground and, like lightning, whipped another from its holster. The second weapon was aimed at the bridegroom's chest.

There was a silence. Potter's mouth seemed to be merely a grave for his tongue. He exhibited an instinct to at once loosen his arm from the woman's grip, and he dropped the bag to the sand. As for the bride, her face had gone as yellow as old cloth. She was a slave to hideous rites, gazing at the apparitional snake.

The two men faced each other at a distance of three paces. He of the revolver smiled with a new and quiet ferocity.

"Tried to sneak up on me," he said. "Tried to sneak up on me!" His eyes grew more baleful. As Potter made a slight movement, the man thrust his revolver venomously forward. "No; don't you do it, Jack Potter. Don't you move a finger toward a gun just yet. Don't you move an eyelash. The time has come for me to settle with you, and I'm goin' to do it my own way, and loaf along with no interferin'. So if you don't want a gun bent on you, just mind what I tell you."

Potter looked at his enemy. "I ain't got a gun on me, Scratchy," he said. "Honest, I ain't." He was stiffening and steadying, but yet somewhere at the back of his mind a vision of the Pullman floated: the sea-green figured velvet, the shining brass, silver, and glass, the wood that gleamed as darkly brilliant as the surface of a pool of oil—all the glory of the marriage, the environment of the new estate. "You know I fight when it comes to fighting, Scratchy Wilson; but I ain't got a gun on me. You'll have to do all the shootin' yourself."

His enemy's face went livid. He stepped forward, and lashed his weapon to and fro before Potter's chest. "Don't you tell me you ain't got no gun on you, you whelp. Don't tell me no lie like that. There ain't a man in Texas ever seen you without no gun. Don't take me for no kid." His eyes blazed with light, and his throat worked like a pump.

"I ain't takin' you for no kid," answered Potter. His heels had not moved an inch backward. "I'm takin' you for a damn fool. I tell you I ain't got a gun, and I ain't. If you're goin' to shoot me up, you better begin now; you'll never get a chance like this again."

So much enforced reasoning had told on Wilson's rage; he was calmer. "If you ain't got a gun, why ain't you got a gun?" he sneered. "Been to Sunday-school?"

"I ain't got a gun because I've just come from San Anton' with my wife. I'm married," said Potter. "And if I'd thought there was going to be any galoots like you prowling around when I brought my wife home, I'd had a gun, and don't you forget it."

"Married!" said Scratchy, not at all comprehending.

"Yes, married. I'm married," said Potter, distinctly.

"Married?" said Scratchy. Seemingly for the first time, he saw the drooping, drowning woman at the other man's side. "No!" he said. He was like a creature allowed a glimpse of another world. He moved a pace backward, and his arm, with the revolver, dropped to his side. "Is this the lady?" he asked.

"Yes; this is the lady," answered Potter.

There was another period of silence.

"Well," said Wilson at last, slowly, "I s'pose it's all off now."

"It's all off if you say so, Scratchy. You know I didn't make the trouble." Potter lifted his valise.

"Well, I 'low it's off, Jack," said Wilson. He was looking at the ground. "Married!" He was not a student of chivalry; it was merely that in the presence of this foreign condition he was a simple child of the earlier plains. He picked up his starboard revolver, and, placing both weapons in their holsters, he went away. His feet made funnel-shaped tracks in the heavy sand.

The Blue Hotel (1898)

I

The Palace Hotel at Fort Romper was painted a light blue, a shade that is on the legs of a kind of heron, causing the bird to declare its position against any background. The Palace Hotel, then, was always screaming and howling in a way that made the dazzling winter landscape of Nebraska seem only a grey swampish hush. It stood alone on the prairie, and when the snow was falling the town two hundred yards away was not visible. But when the traveller alighted at the railway station he was obliged to pass the Palace Hotel before he could come upon the company of low clapboard houses which composed Fort Romper, and it was not to be thought that any traveller could pass the Palace Hotel without looking at it. Pat Scully, the proprietor, had proved himself a master of strategy when he chose his paints. It is true that on clear days, when the great transcontinental expresses, long lines of swaying pullmans, swept through Fort Romper, passengers were overcome at the sight, and the cult that knows the brown-reds and the subdivisions of the dark greens of the East expressed shame, pity, horror, in a laugh. But to the citizens of this prairie town and to the people who would naturally stop there, Pat Scully had performed a feat. With this opulence and splendour, these creeds, classes, egotisms, that streamed through Romper on the rails day after day, they had no colour in common.

As if the displayed delights of such a blue hotel were not sufficiently enticing, it was Scully's habit to go every morning and evening to meet the leisurely trains that stopped at Romper and work his seductions upon any man that he might see wavering, gripsack in hand.

One morning, when a snow-crusted engine dragged its long string of freight cars and its one passenger coach to the station, Scully performed the marvel of catching three men. One was a shaky and quick-eyed Swede, with a great shining cheap valise; one was a tall bronzed cowboy, who was on his way to a ranch near the Dakota line; one was a little silent man from the East, who didn't look it, and didn't announce it. Scully practically made them prisoners. He was so nimble and merry and kindly that each probably felt it would be the height of brutality to try to escape. They trudged off over the creaking board sidewalks in the wake of the eager little Irishman. He wore a heavy fur cap squeezed tightly down on his head. It caused his two red ears to stick out stiffly, as if they were made of tin.

At last, Scully, elaborately, with boisterous hospitality, conducted them through the portals of the blue hotel. The room which they entered was small. It seemed to be merely a proper temple for an enormous stove, which, in the centre, was humming with godlike violence. At various points on its surface the iron had become luminous and glowed yellow from the heat. Beside the stove Scully's son Johnnie was playing High-Five with an old farmer who had whiskers both grey and sandy. They were quarrelling. Frequently the old farmer turned his face toward a box of sawdust—coloured brown from tobacco juice—that was behind the stove, and spat with an air of great impatience and irritation. With a loud flourish of words Scully destroyed the game of cards, and bustled his son upstairs with part of the baggage of the new guests. He himself conducted them to

three basins of the coldest water in the world. The cowboy and the Easterner burnished themselves fiery red with this water, until it seemed to be some kind of metal-polish. The Swede, however, merely dipped his fingers gingerly and with trepidation. It was notable that throughout this series of small ceremonies the three travellers were made to feel that Scully was very benevolent. He was conferring great favours upon them. He handed the towel from one to another with an air of philanthropic impulse.

Afterward they went to the first room, and, sitting about the stove, listened to Scully's officious clamour at his daughters, who were preparing the midday meal. They reflected in the silence of experienced men who tread carefully amid new people. Nevertheless, the old farmer, stationary, invincible in his chair near the warmest part of the stove, turned his face from the sawdust-box frequently and addressed a glowing commonplace to the strangers. Usually he was answered in short but adequate sentences by either the cowboy or the Easterner. The Swede said nothing. He seemed to be occupied in making furtive estimates of each man in the room. One might have thought that he had the sense of silly suspicion which comes to guilt. He resembled a badly frightened man.

Later, at dinner, he spoke a little, addressing his conversation entirely to Scully. He volunteered that he had come from New York, where for ten years he had worked as a tailor. These facts seemed to strike Scully as fascinating, and afterward he volunteered that he had lived at Romper for fourteen years. The Swede asked about the crops and the price of labour. He seemed barely to listen to Scully's extended replies. His eyes continued to rove from man to man.

Finally, with a laugh and a wink, he said that some of these Western communities were very dangerous; and after his statement he straightened his legs under the table, tilted his head, and laughed again, loudly. It was plain that the demonstration had no meaning to the others. They looked at him wondering and in silence.

II

As the men trooped heavily back into the front room, the two little windows presented views of a turmoiling sea of snow. The huge arms of the wind were making attempts—mighty, circular, futile—to embrace the flakes as they sped. A gatepost like a still man with a blanched face stood aghast amid this profligate fury. In a hearty voice Scully announced the presence of a blizzard. The guests of the blue hotel, lighting their pipes, assented with grunts of lazy masculine contentment. No island of the sea could be exempt in the degree of this little room with its humming stove. Johnnie, son of Scully, in a tone which defined his opinion of his ability as a card-player, challenged the old farmer of both grey and sandy whiskers to a game of High-Five. The farmer agreed with a contemptuous and bitter scoff. They sat close to the stove, and squared their knees under a wide board. The cowboy and the Easterner watched the game with interest. The Swede remained near the window, aloof, but with a countenance that showed signs of an inexplicable excitement.

The play of Johnnie and the grey-beard was suddenly ended by another quarrel. The old man arose while casting a look of heated scorn at his adversary. He slowly buttoned his coat, and then stalked with fabulous dignity from the room. In the discreet silence of all the other men the Swede laughed. His laughter rang somehow childish. Men by this time had begun to look at him askance, as if they wished to inquire what ailed him.

A new game was formed jocosely. The cowboy volunteered to become the partner of Johnnie, and they all then turned to ask the Swede to throw in his lot with the little Easterner. He asked some questions about the game, and, learning that it wore many names, and that he had played it when it was under an alias, he accepted the invitation. He strode toward the men nervously, as if he expected to be assaulted. Finally, seated, he gazed from face to face and laughed shrilly. This laugh was so strange that the Easterner looked up quickly, the cowboy sat intent and with his mouth open, and Johnnie paused, holding the cards with still fingers.

Afterward there was a short silence. Then Johnnie said, "Well, let's get at it. Come on now!" They pulled their chairs forward until their knees were bunched under the board. They began to play, and their interest in the game caused the others to forget the manner of the Swede.

The cowboy was a board-whacker. Each time that he held superior cards he whanged them, one by one, with exceeding force, down upon the improvised table, and took the tricks with a glowing air of prowess and pride that sent thrills of indignation into the hearts of his opponents. A game with a board-whacker in it is sure to become intense. The countenance of the Easterner and the Swede were miserable whenever the cowboy thundered down his aces and kings, while Johnnie, his eyes gleaming wth joy, chuckled and chuckled.

Because of the absorbing play none considered the strange ways of the Swede. They paid strict heed to the game. Finally, during a lull caused by a new deal, the Swede suddenly addressed Johnnie: "I suppose there have been a good many men killed in this room." The jaws of the others dropped and they looked at him.

"What in hell are you talking about?" said Johnnie.

The Swede laughed again his blatant laugh, full of a kind of false courage and defiance. "Oh, you know what I mean all right," he answered.

"I'm a liar if I do!" Johnnie protested. The card was halted, and the men stared at the Swede. Johnnie evidently felt that as the son of the proprietor he should make a direct inquiry. "Now, what might you be drivin' at, mister?" he asked. The Swede winked at him. It was a wink full of cunning. His fingers shook on the edge of the board. "Oh, maybe you think I have been to nowheres. Maybe you think I'm a tenderfoot?"

"I don't know nothin' about you," answered Johnnie, "and I don't give a damn where you've been. All I got to say is that I don't know what you're driving at. There hain't never been nobody killed in this room."

The cowboy, who had been steadily gazing at the Swede, then spoke: "What's wrong with you, mister?"

Apparently it seemed to the Swede that he was formidably menaced. He shivered and turned white near the corners of his mouth. He sent an appealing glance in the direction of the little Easterner. During these moments he did not forget to wear his air of advanced pot-valour. "They say they don't know what I mean," he remarked mockingly to the Easterner.

The latter answered after prolonged and cautious reflection. "I don't understand you," he said, impassively.

The Swede made a movement then which announced that he thought he had encountered treachery from the only quarter where he had expected sympathy, if not help. "Oh, I see you are all against me. I see—"

The cowboy was in a state of deep stupefaction. "Say," he cried, as he tumbled the deck violently down upon the board, "say, what are you gittin' at, hey?"

The Swede sprang up with the celerity of a man escaping from a snake on the floor. "I don't want to fight!" he shouted. "I don't want to fight!"

The cowboy stretched his long legs indolently and deliberately. His hands were in his pockets. He spat into the sawdust-box. "Well, who the hell thought you did?" he inquired.

The Swede backed rapidly toward a corner of the room. His hands were out protectingly in front of his chest, but he was making an obvious struggle to control his fright. "Gentlemen," he quavered, "I suppose I am going to be killed before I can leave this house! I suppose I am going to be killed before I can leave this house!" In his eyes was the dying-swan look. Through the windows could be seen the snow turning blue in the shadow of dusk. The wind tore at the house, and some loose thing beat regularly against the clapboards like a spirit tapping.

A door opened, and Scully himself entered. He paused in surprise as he noted the tragic attitude of the Swede. Then he said, "What's the matter here?"

The Swede answered him swiftly and eagerly: "These men are going to kill me."

"Kill you!" ejaculated Scully. "Kill you! What are you talkin'?"

The Swede made the gesture of a martyr.

Scully wheeled sternly upon his son. "What is this, Johnnie?"

The lad had grown sullen. "Damned if I know," he answered. "I can't make no sense to it." He began to shuffle the cards, fluttering them together with an angry snap. "He says a good many men have been killed in this room, or something like that. And he says he's goin' to be killed here too. I don't know what ails him. He's crazy, I shouldn't wonder."

Scully then looked for explanation to the cowboy, but the cowboy simply shrugged his shoulders.

"Kill you?" said Scully again to the Swede. "Kill you? Man, you're off your nut."

"Oh, I know," burst out the Swede. "I know what will happen. Yes, I'm crazy—yes. Yes, of course, I'm crazy—yes. But I know one thing—" There was a sort of sweat of misery and terror upon his face. "I know I won't get out of here alive."

The cowboy drew a deep breath, as if his mind was passing into the last stages of dissolution. "Well, I'm doggoned," he whispered to himself.

Scully wheeled suddenly and faced his son. "You've been troublin' this man!"

Johnnie's voice was loud with its burden of grievance. "Why, good Gawd, I ain't done nothin' to 'im."

The Swede broke in. "Gentlemen, do not disturb yourselves. I will leave this house. I will go away, because"—he accused them dramatically with his glance—"because I do not want to be killed."

Scully was furious with his son. "Will you tell me what is the matter, you young divil? What's the matter, anyhow? Speak out!"

"Blame it!" cried Johnnie in despair, "don't I tell you I don't know? He—he says we want to kill him, and that's all I know. I can't tell what ails him."

The Swede continued to repeat: "Never mind, Mr. Scully; never mind. I will leave this house. I will go away, because I do not wish to be killed. Yes, of course, I am crazy—yes. But I know one thing! I will go away. I will leave this house. Never mind, Mr. Scully; never mind. I will go away."

"You will not go 'way," said Scully. "You will not go 'way until I hear the reason of this business. If anybody has troubled you I will take care of him. This is my house. You are under my roof, and I will not allow any peaceable man to be troubled here." He cast a terrible eye upon Johnnie, the cowboy, and the Easterner.

"Never mind, Mr. Scully; never mind. I will go away. I do not wish to be killed." The Swede moved toward the door which opened upon the stairs. It was evidently his intention to go at once for his baggage.

"No, no," shouted Scully peremptorily; but the white-faced man slid by him and disappeared. "Now," said Scully severely, "what does this mane?"

Johnnie and the cowboy cried together: "Why, we didn't do nothin' to 'im!"

Scully's eyes were cold. "No," he said, "you didn't?"

Johnnie swore a deep oath. "Why, this is the wildest loon I ever see. We didn't do nothin' at all. We were jest sittin' here playin' cards, and he—"

The father suddenly spoke to the Easterner. "Mr. Blanc," he asked, "what has these boys been doin'?"

The Easterner reflected again. "I didn't see anything wrong at all," he said at last, slowly.

Scully began to howl. "But what does it mane?" He stared ferociously at his son. "I have a mind to lather you for this, my boy."

Johnnie was frantic. "Well, what have I done?" he bawled at his father.

III

"I think you are tongue-tied," said Scully finally to his son, the cowboy, and the Easterner; and at the end of this scornful sentence he left the room.

Upstairs the Swede was swiftly fastening the straps of his great valise. Once his back happened to be half turned toward the door, and, hearing a noise there, he wheeled and sprang up, uttering a loud cry. Scully's wrinkled visage showed grimly in the light of the small lamp he carried. This yellow effulgence, streaming upward, coloured only his prominent features, and left his eyes, for instance, in mysterious shadow. He resembled a murderer.

"Man! man!" he exclaimed, "have you gone daffy?"

"Oh, no! Oh, no!" rejoined the other. "There are people in this world who know pretty nearly as much as you do—understand?"

For a moment they stood gazing at each other. Upon the Swede's deathly pale cheeks were two spots brightly crimson and sharply edged, as if they had been carefully painted. Scully placed the light on the table and sat himself on the edge of the bed. He spoke ruminatively. "By cracky, I never heard of such a thing in my life. It's a complete muddle. I can't, for the soul of me, think how you ever got this idea into your head." Presently he lifted his eyes and asked: "And did you sure think they were going to kill you?"

The Swede scanned the old man as if he wished to see into his mind. "I did," he said at last. He obviously suspected that this answer might precipitate an outbreak. As he pulled on a strap his whole arm shook, the elbow wavering like a bit of paper.

Scully banged his hand impressively on the footboard of the bed. "Why, man, we're goin' to have a line of ilictric street-cars in this town next spring."

" 'A line of electric street-cars,' " repeated the Swede, stupidly.

"And," said Scully, "there's a new railroad goin' to be built down from Broken Arm to here. Not to mintion the four churches and the smashin' big brick schoolhouse. Then there's the big factory, too. Why, in two years Romper'll be a met-tro-*pol*-is."

Having finished the preparation of his baggage, the Swede straightened himself, "Mr. Scully," he said, with sudden hardihood, "how much do I owe you?"

"You don't owe me anythin'," said the old man, angrily.

"Yes, I do," retorted the Swede. He took seventy-five cents from his pocket and tendered it to Scully; but the latter snapped his fingers in disdainful refusal. However, it happened that they both stood gazing in a strange fashion at three silver pieces on the Swede's open palm.

"I'll not take your money," said Scully at last. "Not after what's been goin' on here." Then a plan seemed to strike him. "Here," he cried, picking up his lamp and moving toward the door. "Here! Come with me a minute."

"No," said the Swede, in overwhelming alarm.

"Yes," urged the old man. "Come on! I want you to come and see a picter—just across the hall—in my room."

The Swede must have concluded that his hour was come. His jaw dropped and his teeth showed like a dead man's. He ultimately followed Scully across the corridor, but he had the step of one hung in chains.

Scully flashed the light high on the wall of his own chamber. There was revealed a ridiculous photograph of a little girl. She was leaning against a balustrade of gorgeous decoration, and the formidable bang to her hair was prominent. The figure was as graceful as an upright sled-stake, and, withal, it was of the hue of lead. "There," said Scully, tenderly, "that's the picter of my little girl that died. Her name was Carrie. She had the purtiest hair you ever saw! I was that fond of her, she—"

Turning then, he saw that the Swede was not contemplating the picture at all, but, instead, was keeping keen watch on the gloom in the rear.

"Look, man!" cried Scully, heartily. "That's the picter of my little gal that died. Her name was Carrie. And then here's the picter of my oldest boy, Michael. He's a lawyer in Lincoln, an' doin' well. I gave that boy a grand eddication, and I'm glad for it now. He's a fine boy. Look at 'im now. Ain't he bold as blazes, him there in Lincoln, an honoured an' respicted gintleman! An honoured and respicted gintleman," concluded Scully with a flourish. And, so saying, he smote the Swede jovially on the back.

The Swede faintly smiled.

"Now," said the old man, "there's only one more thing." He dropped suddenly to the floor and thrust his head beneath the bed. The Swede could hear his muffled voice. "I'd keep it under me piller if it wasn't for that boy Johnnie. Then there's the old woman—Where is it now? I never put it twice in the same place. Ah, now come out with you!"

Presently he backed clumsily from under the bed, dragging with him an old coat rolled into a bundle. "I've fetched him," he muttered. Kneeling on the floor, he unrolled the coat and extracted from its heart a large yellow-brown whisky-bottle.

His first manœuvre was to hold the bottle up to the light. Reassured, apparently, that nobody had been tampering with it, he thrust it with a generous movement toward the Swede.

The weak-kneed Swede was about to eagerly clutch this element of strength, but he suddenly jerked his hand away and cast a look of horror upon Scully.

"Drink," said the old man affectionately. He had risen to his feet, and now stood facing the Swede.

There was a silence. Then again Scully said: "Drink!"

The Swede laughed wildly. He grabbed the bottle, put it to his mouth; and as his lips curled absurdly around the opening and his throat worked, he kept his glance, burning with hatred, upon the old man's face.

IV

After the departure of Scully the three men, with the card-board still upon their knees, preserved for a long time an astounded silence. Then Johnnie said: "That's the dod-dangedest Swede I ever see."

"He ain't no Swede," said the cowboy, scornfully.

"Well, what is he then?" cried Johnnie. "What is he then?"

"It's my opinion," replied the cowboy deliberately, "he's some kind of a Dutchman." It was a venerable custom of the country to entitle as Swedes all light-haired men who spoke with a heavy tongue. In consequence the idea of the cowboy was not without its daring. "Yes, sir," he repeated. "It's my opinion this feller is some kind of a Dutchman."

"Well, he says he's a Swede, anyhow," muttered Johnnie, sulkily. He turned to the Easterner: "What do you think, Mr. Blanc?"

"Oh, I don't know," replied the Easterner.

"Well, what do you think makes him act that way?" asked the cowboy.

"Why, he's frightened." The Easterner knocked his pipe against a rim of the stove. "He's clear frightened out of his boots."

"What at?" cried Johnnie and the cowboy together.

The Easterner reflected over his answer.

"What at?"— cried the others again.

"Oh, I don't know, but it seems to me this man has been reading dime novels, and he thinks he's right out in the middle of it—the shootin' and stabbin' and all."

"But," said the cowboy, deeply scandalized, "this ain't Wyoming, ner none of them places. This is Nebrasker."

"Yes," added Johnnie, "an' why don't he wait till he gits *out West?*"

The travelled Easterner laughed. "It isn't different there even—not in these days. But he thinks he's right in the middle of hell."

Johnnie and the cowboy mused long.

"It's awful funny," remarked Johnnie at last.

"Yes," said the cowboy. "This is a queer game. I hope we don't git snowed in, because then we'd have to stand this here man bein' around with us all the time. That wouldn't be no good."

"I wish pop would throw him out," said Johnnie.

Presently they heard a loud stamping on the stairs, accompanied by ringing jokes in the voice of old Scully, and laughter, evidently from the Swede. The men around the stove stared vacantly at each other. "Gosh!" said the cowboy. The door flew open, and old Scully, flushed and anecdotal, came into the room. He was jabbering at the Swede, who followed him, laughing bravely. It was the entry of two roisterers from a banquet hall.

"Come now," said Scully sharply to the three seated men, "move up and give us a chance at the stove." The cowboy and the Easterner obediently sidled their chairs to make room for the newcomers. Johnnie, however, simply arranged himself in a more indolent attitude, and then remained motionless.

"Come! Git over, there," said Scully.

"Plenty of room on the other side of the stove," said Johnnie.

"Do you think we want to sit in the draught?" roared the father.

But the Swede here interposed with a grandeur of confidence. "No, no. Let the boy sit where he likes," he cried in a bullying voice to the father.

"All right! All right!" said Scully, deferentially. The cowboy and the Easterner exchanged glances of wonder.

The five chairs were formed in a crescent about one side of the stove. The Swede began to talk; he talked arrogantly, profanely, angrily. Johnnie, the cowboy, and the Easterner maintained a morose silence, while old Scully appeared to be receptive and eager, breaking in constantly with sympathetic ejaculations.

Finally the Swede announced that he was thirsty. He moved in his chair, and said that he would go for a drink of water.

"I'll git it for you," cried Scully at once.

"No," said the Swede, contemptuously. "I'll get it for myself." He arose and stalked with the air of an owner off into the executive parts of the hotel.

As soon as the Swede was out of hearing Scully sprang to his feet and whispered intensely to the others: "Upstairs he thought I was tryin' to poison 'im."

"Say," said Johnnie, "this makes me sick. Why don't you throw 'im out in the snow?"

"Why, he's all right now," declared Scully. "It was only that he was from the East, and he thought this was a tough place. That's all. He's all right now."

The cowboy looked with admiration upon the Easterner. "You were straight," he said. "You were on to that there Dutchman."

"Well," said Johnnie to his father, "he may be all right now, but I don't see it. Other times he was scared, but now he's too fresh."

Scully's speech was always a combination of Irish brogue and idiom, Western twang and idiom, and scraps of curiously formal diction taken from the story-books and newspapers. He now hurled a strange mass of language at the head of his son. "What do I keep? What do I keep? What do I keep?" he demanded, in a voice of thunder. He slapped his knee impressively, to indicate that he himself was going to make reply, and that all should heed. "I keep a hotel," he shouted. "A hotel, do you mind? A guest under my roof has sacred privileges. He is to be intimidated by none. Not one word shall

he hear that would prijudice him in favour of goin' away. I'll not have it. There's no place in this here town where they can say they iver took in a guest of mine because he was afraid to stay here." He wheeled suddenly upon the cowboy and the Easterner. "Am I right?"

"Yes, Mr. Scully," said the cowboy, "I think you're right."

"Yes, Mr. Scully," said the Easterner, "I think you're right."

V

At six o'clock supper, the Swede fizzed like a fire-wheel. He sometimes seemed on the point of bursting into riotous song, and in all his madness he was encouraged by old Scully. The Easterner was encased in reserve; the cowboy sat in wide-mouthed amazement, forgetting to eat, while Johnnie wrathily demolished great plates of food. The daughters of the house, when they were obliged to replenish the biscuits, approached as warily as Indians, and, having succeeded in their purpose fled with ill-concealed trepidation. The Swede domineered the whole feast, and he gave it the appearance of a cruel bacchanal. He seemed to have grown suddenly taller; he gazed, brutally disdainful, into every face. His voice rang through the room. Once when he jabbed out harpoon-fashion with his fork to pinion a biscuit, the weapon nearly impaled the hand of the Easterner, which had been stretched quietly out for the same biscuit.

After supper, as the men filed toward the other room, the Swede smote Scully ruthlessly on the shoulder. "Well, old boy, that was a good, square meal." Johnnie looked hopefully at his father; he knew that shoulder was tender from an old fall; and, indeed, it appeared for a moment as if Scully was going to flame out over the matter, but in the end he smiled a sickly smile and remained silent. The others understood from his manner that he was admitting his responsibility for the Swede's new view-point.

Johnnie, however, addressed his parent in an aside. "Why don't you license somebody to kick you downstairs?" Scully scowled darkly by way of reply.

When they were gathered about the stove, the Swede insisted on another game of High-Five. Scully gently deprecated the plan at first, but the Swede turned a wolfish glare upon him. The old man subsided, and the Swede canvassed the others. In his tone there was always a great threat. The cowboy and the Easterner both remarked indifferently that they would play. Scully said that he would presently have to go to meet the 6.58 train, and so the Swede turned menacingly upon Johnnie. For a moment their glances crossed like blades, and then Johnnie smiled and said, "Yes, I'll play."

They formed a square, with the little board on their knees. The Easterner and the Swede were again partners. As the play went on, it was noticeable that the cowboy was not board-whacking as usual. Meanwhile, Scully, near the lamp, had put on his spectacles and, with an appearance curiously like an old priest, was reading a newspaper. In time he went out to meet the 6.58 train, and, despite his precautions, a gust of polar wind whirled into the room as he opened the door. Besides scattering the cards, it chilled the players to the marrow. The Swede cursed frightfully. When Scully returned, his entrance disturbed a cosy and friendly scene. The Swede again cursed. But presently they were once more intent, their heads bent forward and their hands moving swiftly. The Swede had adopted the fashion of board-whacking.

Scully took up his paper and for a long time remained immersed in matters which were extraordinarily remote from him. The lamp burned badly, and once he stopped to adjust the wick. The newspaper, as he turned from page to page, rustled with a slow and comfortable sound. Then suddenly he heard three terrible words: "You are cheatin'!"

Such scenes often prove that there can be little of dramatic import in environment. Any room can present a tragic front; any room can be comic. This little den was now hideous as a torture-chamber. The new faces of the men themselves had changed it upon the instant. The Swede held a huge fist in front of Johnnie's face, while the latter looked steadily over it into the blazing orbs of his accuser. The Easterner had grown pallid; the cowboy's jaw had dropped in that expression of bovine amazement which was one of his important mannerisms. After the three words, the first sound in the room was made by Scully's paper as it floated forgotten to his feet. His spectacles had also fallen from his nose, but by a clutch he had saved them in air. His hand, grasping the spectacles, now remained poised awkwardly and near his shoulder. He stared at the card-players.

Probably the silence was while a second elapsed. Then, if the floor had been suddenly twitched out from under the men they could not have moved quicker. The five had projected themselves headlong toward a common point. It happened that Johnnie, in rising to hurl himself upon the Swede, had stumbled slightly because of his curiously instinctive care for the cards and the board. The loss of the moment allowed time for the arrival of Scully, and also allowed the cowboy time to give the Swede a great push which sent him staggering back. The men found tongue together, and hoarse shouts of rage, appeal, or fear burst from every throat. The cowboy pushed and jostled feverishly at the Swede, and the Easterner and Scully clung wildly to Johnnie; but through the smoky air, above the swaying bodies of the peace-compellers, the eyes of the two warriors ever sought each other in glances of challenge that were at once hot and steely.

Of course the board had been overturned, and now the whole company of cards was scattered over the floor, where the boots of the men trampled the fat and painted kings and queens as they gazed with their silly eyes at the war that was waging above them.

Scully's voice was dominating the yells. "Stop now! Stop, I say! Stop, now—"

Johnnie, as he struggled to burst through the rank formed by Scully and the Easterner, was crying, "Well, he says I cheated! He says I cheated! I won't allow no man to say I cheated! If he says I cheated, he's a —— ——!"

The cowboy was telling the Swede, "Quit, now! Quit, d'ye hear—"

The screams of the Swede never ceased: "He did cheat! I saw him! I saw him—"

As for the Easterner, he was importuning in a voice that was not heeded: "Wait a moment, can't you? Oh, wait a moment. What's the good of a fight over a game of cards? Wait a moment—"

In this tumult no complete sentences were clear. "Cheat"—"Quit"—"He says"—these fragments pierced the uproar and rang out sharply. It was remarkable that, whereas Scully undoubtedly made the most noise, he was the least heard of any of the riotous band.

Then suddenly there was a great cessation. It was as if each man had paused for breath; and although the room was still lighted with the anger of men, it could be seen that there was no danger of immediate conflict, and at once Johnnie, shouldering his way forward, almost succeeded in confronting the Swede. "What did you say I cheated for? What did you say I cheated for? I don't cheat, and I won't let no man say I do!"

The Swede said, "I saw you! I saw you!"

"Well," cried Johnnie, "I'll fight any man what says I cheat!"

"No, you won't," said the cowboy. "Not here."

"Ah, be still, can't you?" said Scully, coming between them.

The quiet was sufficient to allow the Easterner's voice to be heard. He was repeating, "Oh, wait a moment, can't you? What's the good of a fight over a game of cards? Wait a moment!"

Johnnie, his red face appearing above his father's shoulder, hailed the Swede again. "Did you say I cheated?"

The Swede showed his teeth. "Yes."

"Then," said Johnnie, "we must fight."

"Yes, fight," roared the Swede. He was like a demoniac. "Yes, fight! I'll show you what kind of a man I am! I'll show you who you want to fight! Maybe you think I can't fight! Maybe you think I can't! I'll show you, you skin, you card-sharp! Yes, you cheated! You cheated! You cheated!"

"Well, let's go at it, then, mister," said Johnnie, coolly.

The cowboy's brow was beaded with sweat from his efforts in intercepting all sorts of raids. He turned in despair to Scully. "What are you goin' to do now?"

A change had come over the Celtic visage of the old man. He now seemed all eagerness; his eyes glowed.

"We'll let them fight," he answered, stalwartly. "I can't put up with it any longer. I've stood this damned Swede till I'm sick. We'll let them fight."

VI

The men prepared to go out of doors. The Easterner was so nervous that he had great difficulty in getting his arms into the sleeves of his new leather coat. As the cowboy drew his fur cap down over his ears his hands trembled. In fact, Johnnie and old Scully were the only ones who displayed no agitation. These preliminaries were conducted without words.

Scully threw open the door. "Well, come on," he said. Instantly a terrific wind caused the flame of the lamp to struggle at its wick, while a puff of black smoke sprang from the chimney top. The stove was in mid-current of the blast, and its voice swelled to equal the roar of the storm. Some of the scarred and bedabbled cards were caught up from the floor and dashed helplessly against the farther wall. The men lowered their heads and plunged into the tempest as into a sea.

No snow was falling, but great whirls and clouds of flakes, swept up from the ground by the frantic winds, were screaming southward with the speed of bullets. The covered land was blue with the sheen of an unearthly satin, and there was no other hue save where, at the low, black railway station—which seemed incredibly distant—one light gleamed like a tiny jewel. As the men floundered into a thigh-deep drift, it was known that the Swede was bawling out something. Scully went to him, put a hand on his shoulder, and projected an ear. "What's that you say?" he shouted.

"I say," bawled the Swede again, "I won't stand much show against this gang. I know you'll all pitch on me."

Scully smote him reproachfully on the arm. "Tut, man!" he yelled. The wind tore the words from Scully's lips and scattered them far alee.

"You are all a gang of—" boomed the Swede, but the storm also seized the remainder of this sentence.

Immediately turning their backs upon the wind, the men had swung around a corner to the sheltered side of the hotel. It was the function of the little house to preserve here, amid this great devastation of snow, an irregular V-shape of heavily encrusted grass, which crackled beneath the feet. One could imagine the great drifts piled against the windward side. When the party reached the comparative peace of this spot it was found that the Swede was still bellowing.

"Oh, I know what kind of a thing this is! I know you'll all pitch on me. I can't lick you all!"

Scully turned upon him panther-fashion. "You'll not have to whip all of us. You'll have to whip my son Johnnie. An' the man what troubles you durin' that time will have me to dale with."

The arrangements were swiftly made. The two men faced each other, obedient to the harsh commands of Scully, whose face, in the subtly luminous gloom, could be seen set in the austere impersonal lines that are pictured on the countenances of the Roman veterans. The Easterner's teeth were chattering, and he was hopping up and down like a mechanical toy. The cowboy stood rock-like.

The contestants had not stripped off any clothing. Each was in his ordinary attire. Their fists were up, and they eyed each other in a calm that had the elements of leonine cruelty in it.

During this pause, the Easterner's mind, like a

film, took lasting impressions of three men—the iron-nerved master of the ceremony; the Swede, pale, motionless, terrible; and Johnnie, serene yet ferocious, brutish yet heroic. The entire prelude had in it a tragedy greater than the tragedy of action, and this aspect was accentuated by the long, mellow cry of the blizzard, as it sped the tumbling and wailing flakes into the black abyss of the south.

"Now!" said Scully.

The two combatants leaped forward and crashed together like bullocks. There was heard the cushioned sound of blows, and of a curse squeezing out from between the tight teeth of one.

As for the spectators, the Easterner's pent-up breath exploded from him with a pop of relief, absolute relief from the tension of the preliminaries. The cowboy bounded into the air with a yowl. Scully was immovable as from supreme amazement and fear at the fury of the fight which he himself had permitted and arranged.

For a time the encounter in the darkness was such a perplexity of flying arms that it presented no more detail than would a swiftly revolving wheel. Occasionally a face, as if illumined by a flash of light, would shine out, ghastly and marked with pink spots. A moment later, the men might have been known as shadows, if it were not for the involuntary utterance of oaths that came from them in whispers.

Suddenly a holocaust of warlike desire caught the cowboy, and he bolted forward with the speed of a broncho. "Go it, Johnnie! go it! Kill him! Kill him!"

Scully confronted him. "Kape back," he said; and by his glance the cowboy could tell that this man was Johnnie's father.

To the Easterner there was a monotony of unchangeable fighting that was an abomination. This confused mingling was eternal to his sense, which was concentrated in a longing for the end, the priceless end. Once the fighters lurched near him, and as he scrambled hastily backward he heard them breathe like men on the rack.

"Kill him, Johnnie! Kill him! Kill him! Kill him!" The cowboy's face was contorted like one of those agony masks in museums.

"Keep still," said Scully, icily.

Then there was a sudden loud grunt, incomplete, cut short, and Johnnie's body swung away from the Swede and fell with sickening heaviness to the grass. The cowboy was barely in time to prevent the mad Swede from flinging himself upon his prone adversary. "No, you don't," said the cowboy, interposing an arm. "Wait a second."

Scully was at his son's side. "Johnnie! Johnnie, me boy!" His voice had a quality of melancholy tenderness. "Johnnie! Can you go on with it?" He looked anxiously down into the bloody, pulpy face of his son.

There was a moment of silence, and then Johnnie answered in his ordinary voice, "Yes, I—it—yes."

Assisted by his father he struggled to his feet. "Wait a bit now till you git your wind," said the old man.

A few paces away the cowboy was lecturing the Swede. "No, you don't! Wait a second!"

The Easterner was plucking at Scully's sleeve. "Oh, this is enough," he pleaded. "This is enough! Let it go as it stands. This is enough!"

"Bill," said Scully, "git out of the road." The cowboy stepped aside. "Now." The combatants were actuated by a new caution as they advanced toward collison. They glared at each other, and then the Swede aimed a lightning blow that carried with it his entire weight. Johnnie was evidently half stupid from weakness, but he miraculously dodged, and his fist sent the overbalanced Swede sprawling.

The cowboy, Scully, and the Easterner burst into a cheer that was like a chorus of triumphant soldiery, but before its conclusion the Swede had scuffled agilely to his feet and come in berserk abandon at his foe. There was another perplexity of flying arms, and Johnnie's body again swung away and fell, even as a bundle might fall from a roof. The Swede instantly staggered to a little wind-waved tree and leaned upon it, breathing like an engine, while his savage and flame-lit eyes roamed from face to face as the men bent over Johnnie. There was a splendour of isolation in his situation at this time which the Easterner felt once when, lifting his eyes from the man on the ground, he beheld that mysterious and lonely figure, waiting.

"Are you any good yet, Johnnie?" asked Scully in a broken voice.

The son gasped and opened his eyes languidly. After a moment he answered, "No—I ain't—any good—any—more." Then, from shame and bodily ill, he began to weep, the tears furrowing down through the blood-stains on his face. "He was too—too—too heavy for me."

Scully straightened and addressed the waiting figure. "Stranger," he said, evenly, "it's all up with our side." Then his voice changed into that vibrant huskiness which is commonly the tone of the most simple and deadly announcements. "Johnnie is whipped."

Without replying, the victor moved off on the route to the front door of the hotel.

The cowboy was formulating new and unspellable blasphemies. The Easterner was startled to find that they were out in a wind that seemed to come direct from the shadowed arctic floes. He heard again the wail of the snow as it was flung to its grave in the south. He knew now that all this time the cold had been sinking into him deeper and deeper, and he wondered that he had not perished. He felt indifferent to the condition of the vanquished man.

"Johnnie, can you walk?" asked Scully.

"Did I hurt—hurt him any?" asked the son.

"Can you walk, boy? Can you walk?"

Johnnie's voice was suddenly strong. There was a robust impatience in it. "I asked you whether I hurt him any!"

"Yes, yes, Johnnie," answered the cowboy, consolingly; "he's hurt a good deal."

They raised him from the ground, and as soon as he was on his feet he went tottering off, rebuffing all attempts at assistance. When the party rounded the corner they were fairly blinded by the pelting of the snow. It burned their faces like fire. The cowboy carried Johnnie through the drift to the door. As they entered, some cards again rose from the floor and beat against the wall.

The Easterner rushed to the stove. He was so profoundly chilled that he almost dared to embrace the glowing iron. The Swede was not in the room. Johnnie sank into a chair and, folding his arms on his knees, buried his face in them. Scully, warming one foot and then the other at a rim of the stove, muttered to himself with Celtic mournfulness. The cowboy had removed his fur cap, and with a dazed and rueful air he was running one hand through his tousled locks. From overhead they could hear the creaking of boards, as the Swede tramped here and there in his room.

The sad quiet was broken by the sudden flinging open of a door that led toward the kitchen. It was instantly followed by an inrush of women. They precipitated themselves upon Johnnie amid a chorus of lamentation. Before they carried their prey off to the kitchen, there to be bathed and

harangued with that mixture of sympathy and abuse which is a feat of their sex, the mother straightened herself and fixed old Scully with an eye of stern reproach. "Shame be upon you, Patrick Scully!" she cried. "Your own son, too. Shame be upon you!"

"There, now! Be quiet, now!" said the old man, weakly.

"Shame be upon you, Patrick Scully!" The girls, rallying to this slogan, sniffed disdainfully in the direction of those trembling accomplices, the cowboy and the Easterner. Presently they bore Johnnie away, and left the three men to dismal reflection.

VII

"I'd like to fight this here Dutchman myself," said the cowboy, breaking a long silence.

Scully wagged his head sadly. "No, that wouldn't do. It wouldn't be right. It wouldn't be right."

"Well, why wouldn't it?" argued the cowboy. "I don't see no harm in it."

"No," answered Scully, with mournful heroism. "It wouldn't be right. It was Johnnie's fight, and now we mustn't whip the man just because he whipped Johnnie."

"Yes, that's true enough," said the cowboy; "but —he better not get fresh with me, because I couldn't stand no more of it."

"You'll not say a word to him," commanded Scully, and even then they heard the tread of the Swede on the stairs. His entrance was made theatric. He swept the door back with a bang and swaggered to the middle of the room. No one looked at him. "Well," he cried, insolently, at Scully, "I s'pose you'll tell me now how much I owe you?"

The old man remained stolid. "You don't owe me nothin'."

"Huh!" said the Swede, "huh! Don't owe 'im nothin'."

The cowboy addressed the Swede. "Stranger, I don't see how you come to be so gay around here."

Old Scully was instantly alert. "Stop!" he shouted, holding his hand forth, fingers upward. "Bill, you shut up!"

The cowboy spat carelessly into the sawdust-box. "I didn't say a word, did I?" he asked.

"Mr. Scully," called the Swede, "how much do I owe you?" It was seen that he was attired for departure, and that he had his valise in his hand.

"You don't owe me nothin'," repeated Scully in the same imperturbable way.

"Huh!" said the Swede. "I guess you're right. I guess if it was any way at all, you'd owe me somethin'. That's what I guess." He turned to the cowboy. "'Kill him! Kill him! Kill him!'" he mimicked, and then guffawed victoriously. "'Kill him!'" He was convulsed with ironical humour.

But he might have been jeering the dead. The three men were immovable and silent, staring with glassy eyes at the stove.

The Swede opened the door and passed into the storm, giving one derisive glance backward at the still group.

As soon as the door was closed, Scully and the cowboy leaped to their feet and began to curse. They trampled to and fro, waving their arms and smashing into the air with their fists. "Oh, but that was a hard minute!" wailed Scully. "That was a hard minute! Him there leerin' and scoffin'! One bang at his nose was worth forty dollars to me that minute! How did you stand it, Bill?"

"How did I stand it?" cried the cowboy in a quivering voice. "How did I stand it? Oh!"

The old man burst into sudden brogue. "I'd loike to take that Swade," he wailed, "and hould 'im down on a shtone flure and bate 'im to a jelly wid a shtick!"

The cowboy groaned in sympathy. "I'd like to git him by the neck and ha-ammer him"—he brought his hand down on a chair with a noise like a pistol-shot—"hammer that there Dutchman until he couldn't tell himself from a dead coyote!"

"I'd bate 'im until he—"

"I'd show *him* some things—"

And then together they raised a yearning, fanatic cry—"Oh-o-oh! if we only could—"

"Yes!"

"Yes!"

"And then I'd—"

"O-o-oh!"

VIII

The Swede, tightly gripping his valise, tacked across the face of the storm as if he carried sails. He was following a line of little naked, grasping trees which, he knew, must mark the way of the road. His face, fresh from the pounding of Johnnie's fists, felt more pleasure than pain in the wind and the driving snow. A number of square shapes loomed upon him finally, and he knew them as the houses of the main body of the town. He found a street and made travel along it, leaning heavily upon the wind whenever, at a corner, a terrific blast caught him.

He might have been in a deserted village. We picture the world as thick with conquering and elate humanity, but here, with the bugles of the tempest pealing, it was hard to imagine a peopled earth. One viewed the existence of man then as a marvel, and conceded a glamour of wonder to these lice which were caused to cling to a whirling, fire-smitten, ice-locked, disease-stricken, space-lost bulb. The conceit of man was explained by this storm to be the very engine of life. One was a coxcomb not to die in it. However, the Swede found a saloon.

In front of it an indomitable red light was burning, and the snowflakes were made blood-colour as they flew through the circumscribed territory of the lamp's shining. The Swede pushed open the door of the saloon and entered. A sanded expanse was before him, and at the end of it four men sat about a table drinking. Down one side of the room extended a radiant bar, and its guardian was leaning upon his elbows listening to the talk of the men at the table. The Swede dropped his valise upon the floor and, smiling fraternally upon the barkeeper, said, "Gimme some whisky, will you?" The man placed a bottle, a whisky-glass, and a glass of ice-thick water upon the bar. The Swede poured himself an abnormal portion of whisky and drank it in three gulps. "Pretty bad night," remarked the bartender, indifferently. He was making the pretension of blindness which is usually a distinction of his class; but it could have been seen that he was furtively studying the half-erased blood-stains on the face of the Swede. "Bad night," he said again.

"Oh, it's good enough for me," replied the Swede, hardily, as he poured himself some more whisky. The barkeeper took his coin and manœuvered it through its reception by the highly nickelled cash-machine. A bell rang; a card labelled "20 cts." had appeared.

"No," continued the Swede, "this isn't too bad weather. It's good enough for me."

"So?" murmured the barkeeper, languidly.

The copious drams made the Swede's eyes swim, and he breathed a trifle heavier. "Yes, I like this weather. I like it. It suits me." It was apparently his design to impart a deep significance to these words.

"So?" murmured the bartender again. He turned

to gaze dreamily at the scroll-like birds and bird-like scrolls which had been drawn with soap upon the mirrors in back of the bar.

"Well, I guess I'll take another drink," said the Swede, presently. "Have something?"

"No thanks; I'm not drinkin'," answered the bartender. Afterward he asked, "How did you hurt your face?"

The Swede immediately began to boast loudly. "Why, in a fight, I thumped the soul out of a man down here at Scully's hotel."

The interest of the four men at the table was at last aroused.

"Who was it?" said one.

"Johnnie Scully," blustered the Swede. "Son of the man what runs it. He will be pretty near dead for some weeks, I can tell you. I made a nice thing of him, I did. He couldn't get up. They carried him in the house. Have a drink?"

Instantly the men in some subtle way encased themselves in reserve. "No, thanks," said one. The group was of curious formation. Two were prominent local business men; one was the district attorney; and one was a professional gambler of the kind known as "square." But a scrutiny of the group would not have enabled an observer to pick the gambler from the men of more reputable pursuits. He was, in fact, a man so delicate in manner, when among people of fair class, and so judicious in his choice of victims, that in the strictly masculine part of the town's life he had come to be explicitly trusted and admired. People called him a thoroughbred. The fear and contempt with which his craft was regarded were undoubtedly the reason why his quiet dignity shone conspicuous above the quiet dignity of men who might be merely hatters, billiard-markers, or grocery clerks. Beyond an occasional unwary traveller who came by rail, this gambler was supposed to prey solely upon reckless and senile farmers, who, when flush with good crops, drove into town in all the pride and confidence of an absolutely invulnerable stupidity. Hearing at times in circuitous fashion of the despoilment of such a farmer, the important men of Romper invariably laughed in contempt of the victim, and if they thought of the wolf at all, it was with a kind of pride at the knowledge that he would never dare think of attacking their wisdom and courage. Besides, it was popular that this gambler had a real wife and two real children in a neat cottage in a suburb, where he led an exemplary home life; and when any one even suggested a discrepancy in his character, the crowd immedi-

ately vociferated descriptions of this virtuous family circle. Then men who led exemplary home lives, and men who did not lead exemplary home lives, all subsided in a bunch, remarking that there was nothing more to be said.

However, when a restriction was placed upon him—as, for instance, when a strong clique of members of the new Pollywog Club refused to permit him, even as a spectator, to appear in the rooms of the organization—the candour and gentleness with which he accepted the judgment disarmed many of his foes and made his friends more desperately partisan. He invariably distinguished between himself and a respectable Romper man so quickly and frankly that his manner actually appeared to be a continual broadcast compliment.

And one must not forget to declare the fundamental fact of his entire position in Romper. It is irrefutable that in all affairs outside his business, in all matters that occur eternally and commonly between man and man, this thieving card-player was so generous, so just, so moral, that, in a contest, he could have put to flight the consciences of nine tenths of the citizens of Romper.

And so it happened that he was seated in this saloon with the two prominent local merchants and the district attorney.

The Swede continued to drink raw whisky, meanwhile babbling at the barkeeper and trying to induce him to indulge in potations. "Come on. Have a drink. Come on. What—no? Well, have a little one, then. By gawd, I've whipped a man tonight, and I want to celebrate. I whipped him good, too. Gentlemen," the Swede cried to the men at the table, "have a drink?"

"Ssh!" said the barkeeper.

The group at the table, although furtively attentive, had been pretending to be deep in talk; but now a man lifted his eyes toward the Swede and said, shortly, "Thanks. We don't want any more."

At this reply the Swede ruffled out his chest like a rooster. "Well," he exploded, "it seems I can't get anybody to drink with me in this town. Seems so, don't it? Well!"

"Ssh!" said the barkeeper.

"Say," snarled the Swede, "don't you try to shut me up. I won't have it. I'm a gentleman, and I want people to drink with me. And I want 'em to drink with me now. *Now*—do you understand?" He rapped the bar with his knuckles.

Years of experience had calloused the bartender. He merely grew sulky. "I hear you," he answered.

"Well," cried the Swede, "listen hard then. See

those men over there? Well, they're going to drink with me, and don't you forget it. Now you watch."

"Hi!" yelled the barkeeper, "this won't do!"

"Why won't it?" demanded the Swede. He stalked over to the table, and by chance laid his hand upon the shoulder of the gambler. "How about this?" he asked wrathfully. "I asked you to drink with me."

The gambler simply twisted his head and spoke over his shoulder. "My friend, I don't know you."

"Oh, hell!" answered the Swede, "come and have a drink."

"Now, my boy," advised the gambler, kindly, "take your hand off my shoulder and go 'way and mind your own business." He was a little, slim man, and it seemed strange to hear him use this tone of heroic patronage to the burly Swede. The other men at the table said nothing.

"What! You won't drink with me, you little dude? I'll make you, then! I'll make you!" The Swede had grasped the gambler frenziedly at the throat, and was dragging him from his chair. The other men sprang up. The barkeeper dashed around the corner of his bar. There was a great tumult, and then was seen a long blade in the hand of the gambler. It shot forward, and a human body, this citadel of virtue, wisdom, power, was pierced as easily as if it had been a melon. The Swede fell with a cry of supreme astonishment.

The prominent merchants and the district attorney must have at once tumbled out of the place backward. The bartender found himself hanging limply to the arm of a chair and gazing into the eyes of a murderer.

"Henry," said the latter, as he wiped his knife on one of the towels that hung beneath the bar rail, "you tell 'em where to find me. I'll be home, waiting for 'em." Then he vanished. A moment afterward the barkeeper was in the street dinning through the storm for help and, moreover, companionship.

The corpse of the Swede, alone in the saloon, had its eyes fixed upon a dreadful legend that dwelt atop of the cash-machine: "This registers the amount of your purchase."

IX

Months later, the cowboy was frying pork over the stove of a little ranch near the Dakota line, when there was a quick thud of hoofs outside, and pres-

ently the Easterner entered with the letters and the papers.

"Well," said the Easterner at once, "the chap that killed the Swede has got three years. Wasn't much, was it?"

"He has? Three years?" The cowboy poised his pan of pork, while he ruminated upon the news. "Three years. That ain't much."

"No. It was a light sentence," replied the Easterner as he unbuckled his spurs. "Seems there was a good deal of sympathy for him in Romper."

"If the bartender had been any good," observed the cowboy, thoughtfully, "he would have gone in and cracked that there Dutchman on the head with a bottle in the beginnin' of it and stopped all this here murderin'."

"Yes, a thousand things might have happened," said the Easterner, tartly.

The cowboy returned his pan of pork to the fire, but his philosophy continued. "It's funny, ain't it? If he hadn't said Johnnie was cheatin' he'd be alive this minute. He was an awful fool. Game played for fun, too. Not for money. I believe he was crazy."

"I feel sorry for that gambler," said the Easterner.

"Oh, so do I," said the cowboy. "He don't deserve none of it for killin' who he did."

"The Swede might not have been killed if everything had been square."

"Might not have been killed?" exclaimed the cowboy. "Everythin' square? Why, when he said that Johnnie was cheatin' and acted like such a jackass? And then in the saloon he fairly walked up to git hurt?" With these arguments the cowboy browbeat the Easterner and reduced him to rage.

"You're a fool!" cried the Easterner, viciously. "You're a bigger jackass than the Swede by a million majority. Now let me tell you one thing. Let me tell you something. Listen! Johnnie *was* cheating!"

" 'Johnnie,' " said the cowboy, blankly. There was a minute of silence, and then he said, robustly, "Why, no. The game was only for fun."

"Fun or not," said the Easterner, "Johnnie was cheating. I saw him. I know it. I saw him. And I refused to stand up and be a man. I let the Swede fight it out alone. And you—you were simply puffing around the place and wanting to fight. And then old Scully himself! We are all in it! This poor gambler isn't even a noun. He is kind of an adverb. Every sin is the result of a collaboration. We, five of us, have collaborated in the murder of this Swede. Usually there are from a dozen to forty women really involved in every murder, but in this case it seems to be only five men—you, I, Johnnie, old Scully; and that fool of an unfortunate gambler came merely as a culmination, the apex of a human movement, and gets all the punishment."

The cowboy, injured and rebellious, cried out blindly into this fog of mysterious theory: "Well, I didn't do anythin', did I?"

The Literature of the South

In earlier sections of this book there has been much mention of the South and frequent references to the political pressures exerted by the slave states in the years leading up to the Civil War. Even so, we have presented very little of what might be called an insider's view of the society that produced political thinkers like Jefferson, Fitzhugh, and Calhoun and fighting men like Washington, Lee, and Stonewall Jackson.[1] Southern leadership came (with some important exceptions) basically from the planter class, and though the reader has earlier been given glimpses of life on the southern plantation, as in Byrd's diaries or Kennedy's reminiscences of his uncle's Virginia estate, these scarcely suffice to provide a vivid sense of the character of life on the southern plantation at the outbreak of the war.

The planters with large estates composed only a fraction of the southern population, but they carried out of the Union with them not only the small planters but the yeoman farmers as well, and indeed all the South except some of the mountain areas and occasional poor-white hill counties. (They also detached from the Union good portions of such border states as Maryland, Kentucky, and Missouri; and the Confederate army had in its ranks thousands of men from Illinois and Indiana.)

What then was the quality of life in the antebellum South? In the still popular view, that life is summed up in the plantation, with its white-columned manor house surrounded by hundreds of acres planted to cotton, rice, or sugar cane and supported by the labor of slaves. Long before Holly-

---

[1] Aspects of the nonplanter South have been represented in the preceding sections: accounts of life in the frontier settlements of the Old Southwest (Crockett, Thorpe, Audubon, and Longstreet); the insights afforded by the folk songs of both the whites and the blacks; the observations of travelers like Olmsted; and, with reference to the plantation itself, the testimony of men like Walker and Douglass, who knew slavery from the black man's point of view.

wood put this image in color on a wide cinema screen, it was the stock-in-trade of hundreds of "historical" novels and costume romances, from the 1870's down to the very recent past.

This image easily hardened into a stereotype, one so completely formalized as to lack authenticity and even credibility. Of late there has been a disposition to question whether this kind of Old South ever had any real existence. It may be useful, therefore, to see whether the image can be grounded in reality and humanized. What was life on a plantation in the Old South like? Could people truly human exist in a world which could and did become the stuff of which Hollywood romances were made?

MARY BOYKIN CHESNUT (1823?–1886?)

Mary Boykin Chesnut was thoroughly human—warm, sensitive, and practical. Her *Diary* provides a vivid account of life on one of the great southern plantations on the eve of the Civil War. Mrs. Chesnut was a spirited and intelligent woman and a born writer. Furthermore, she was peculiarly well placed to give an account of what southern plantation life was like. Her father had been Governor of South Carolina and, later, a United States Senator from that state. In 1840, as a girl of seventeen, she had married James Chesnut, Jr., who was himself to become a United States Senator and, after the establishment of the Confederacy, an aide to President Jefferson Davis. Mrs. Chesnut apparently knew everybody of consequence in Charleston and the Low Country of South Carolina and was an indefatigable hostess. Her husband's post put her in touch with all the members of the Confederate cabinet, and she knew many of the principal generals, including Lee, Hood, Beauregard, Joseph E. Johnston, and Wade Hampton.

Yet the very advantages of mind, personality, and social and political position which make the *Diary* fascinating to read also suggest how special was the life depicted there and warn us against assuming that it is typical of the South in general. The Chesnuts owned, for example, not one plantation but six, and hundreds of slaves. At their Mulberry Plantation, Mrs. Chesnut wrote, there were "sixty or seventy people kept here to wait upon this household, two thirds of them too old or too young to be of any use."

One must remember that only a very few slaveholders in the Old South owned as many as a hundred slaves, that most of them owned no more than four or five, and that many of the small slaveholders worked in the fields side by side with their slaves. In fact, at the outbreak of the Civil War, the majority of white southerners owned no slaves at all. General Lee, though of the planter class, had freed all of his personal slaves long before the war broke out, and during the course of the war he also freed those slaves that he had inherited from his wife; on the other hand, the great northern general Ulysses S. Grant, because he had inherited slaves through his wife's family, was actually a slaveholder at the time of the war. Such are the anomalies of history.

In subsequent pages we shall take into account some of the other subregions of the South: French-speaking south Louisiana (Cable and Kate Chopin), the Piedmont region in Georgia (Joel Chandler Harris and Sidney Lanier), the southern Appalachians, the limestone basin of Kentucky and Tennessee, and states such as Arkansas, Alabama, and Mississippi that were carved out of the Old Southwest. From the beginning there were many Souths. The real matter of surprise perhaps ought to be that there was enough cultural homogeneity to allow the various segments to think of themselves as integral parts of one culture. Yet if the reader of Mrs. Chesnut's *Diary* will use caution and not extend the peculiarities of her position into sweeping generalizations about the South as a whole, he can learn something of the mood of the southern people at the outbreak of the Civil War and later, as well as something about the mind of the cultivated slaveholder, including his sometimes contradictory attitudes toward the Union and toward slavery itself. (The *Diary* amounts to some 325,000 words: hence the 3,000 words of it printed below can provide no more than a suggestive sampling of what it contains.) Another fascinating and important account (through family letters) of the plantation South is to be found in *Children of Pride: A True Story of Georgia and the Civil War* (1972), edited by Robert M. Myers.

From A Diary from Dixie (1861–65)

The text printed here is taken from the *Diary* as edited by Ben Ames Williams, published in 1949. The *Diary* was originally published, in a still more abbreviated form, in 1905.

[March 22, 1861] At my aunt's I heard her coachman give her a message. "The ladies say I must tell you they [their] father is behaving shamefully. He is disgracing hisself. He had not tasted whiskey for 15 years. He took some as physic a month ago, and he ain't drawed a sober breath since."

[April 20, 1861] Arranging my photograph book. First page, Colonel Watts. Here goes a sketch of his life, romantic enough, surely. Beaufort Watts, bluest blood, gentleman to the tips of his fingers, chivalry incarnate, and yet this was his fate. He was given in charge a large amount of money, in bank bills. The money belonged to the State and he was only to deposit it in the bank. On the way he was obliged to stay over one night. He put the roll on a table at his bedside, locked himself in and slept the sleep of the righteous. Lo, next day when he awaked, the money was gone. Well, all who knew him believed him innocent, of course. He searched, and they searched, high and low; but to no purpose—the money had vanished. A damaging story, in spite of previous character; a cloud rested on him.

Many years after, the house where he had taken that disastrous sleep was pulled down. In the wall, behind the wainscoting, was his pile of money.

How the rats got it through so narrow a crack it seemed hard to realize. Like the hole mentioned by Mercutio, it was not as deep as a well nor as wide as a barn door, but it did for Beaufort Watts until it was found. Suppose that house had been burned, or the rats had gnawed up the bills past recognition? The people in power understood how this proud man suffered these many years, in silence, while men looked askance at him. They tried to repair the small blunder of blasting a man's character. He was made Secretary of Legation to Russia. He was afterwards made Consul at Sante Fé de Bogotá. And then when he said he was too old to wander so far afield, they made him Secretary to all the governors of South Carolina, in regular succession.

I knew him more than twenty years ago as Secretary to the Governor. He was a made-up old battered dandy. He was the soul of honour, and his eccentricities were all humored. His misfortune had made him sacred. He stood hat in hand before the ladies, and bowed as I suppose Sir Charles Grandison might have done. It was hard not to laugh at the purple and green shades of his too-black hair. He came at that time to show me the sword presented to Colonel Shelton for killing the only Indian who was killed in the Seminole War. We bagged Osceola and Micanopy under a flag of truce; that is, they were snared, not shot on the wing.

To get back to my knight errant. He knelt, handed me the sword, and then kissed my hand. I was barely sixteen, and did not know how to behave under the circumstances. He said, leaning on the sword: "My dear child, learn that it is a much greater liberty to shake hands with a lady than to kiss her hand. I have kissed the Empress of Russia's hand, and she did not make faces at me."

He looks now just as he did then. He is in uniform, covered with epaulettes and aiguillettes, shining in the sun; and with his plumed hat he reins up his war steed and bows low as ever.

May 19 [1861] Back in Montgomery. Mrs. Fitzpatrick said Mr. [Jefferson] Davis is too gloomy for her. He says we must prepare for a long war and unmerciful reverses at first, because they are readier for war, and so much stronger numerically. Men and money count so in war. "As they do everywhere else," said I, doubting her accurate account of Mr. Davis's spoken words, though she tried to give it faithfully We need patience and persistence. There is enough and to spare of pluck and dash among us; the do-and-dare style.

I drove out with Mrs. Davis. She finds playing Mrs. President of this small Confederacy slow work, after leaving friends such as Mrs. Emory, Mrs. Joe Johnston and the like in Washington. I do not blame her. The wrench has been awful with us all. But we don't mean to be turned into pillars of salt.

Mr. Mallory came for us to go to Mrs. Toombs's reception. Mr. Chesnut would not go, and I decided to remain with him, and it proved a wise decision. First Mr. Hunter came. In college they called him, from his initials, R.M.T., Run Mad Tom Hunter. Just now I think he is the sanest, if not the wisest, man in our newborn Confederacy. I remember when I first met him. He sat next to me at some state dinner in Washington. Mr. Clay had taken me in to dinner, but he seemed quite satisfied that my other side should take me off his hands. Mr. Hunter did not know me, nor I him. I suppose he inquired or looked at my card lying on the table, as I did his. At any rate we began a conversation which lasted steadily through the whole thing from soup to dessert. Mr. Hunter, though in evening dress, presented a rather tumbled-up appearance. His waistcoat wanted pulling down and his hair wanted brushing. He delivered unconsciously that day a lecture on English literature which if printed I still think would be a valuable addition to that literature. Since then I have always looked forward to a talk with the Senator from Virginia with undisguised pleasure. Next came Mr. Miles, and Mr. Jamison of South Caro-

lina. The latter was President of our Secession Convention. Also he has written a life of Du Guesclin. Not so bad.

[May 27, 1861] Johnny[1] has gone as a private in Gregg's regiment. He could not stand it at home any longer. Mr. Chesnut was willing for him to go, because those sandhill men said: "This is a rich man's war," and that the rich men could be officers and have an easy time, and the poor ones be privates. So he said: "Let the gentlemen set the example; let them go in the ranks." So John Chesnut is a gentleman private. He took his servant with him, all the same.

.   .   .

[June 10, 1861] The war is making us all tenderly sentimental. No casualties yet, no real mourning, nobody hurt; so it is all parade, fuss and fine feathers. There is no imagination here to forestall woe, and only the excitement and wild awakening from everyday stagnant life is felt; that is, when one gets away from the two or three sensible men who are still left in the world.

.   .   .

In Charleston, a butcher has been clandestinely supplying the Yankee fleet outside of the Bar with beef. They say he gave the information which led to the capture of the *Savannah*. They will hang him. Mr. Petigru alone, in South Carolina, has not seceded. When they pray for our President, he gets up from his knees. He might risk a prayer for Mr. Davis, though I doubt if it would do Mr. Davis any good. Mr. Petigru is too clever to think himself one of the righteous, whose prayers avail so overly much. Mr. Petigru's disciple, Mr. Bryan, followed his example. Mr. Petigru has such a keen sense of the ridiculous, he must be laughing in his sleeve at the hubbub this untimely trait of independence has raised.

[1] Johnny Chesnut was Mrs. Chesnut's nephew. When, soon after the fall of Sumter, Maxey Gregg's regiment was ordered to Virginia, several companies refused to go, saying they had enlisted for service in South Carolina. The companies which did agree to go were promised that when their enlistments expired, on June 30, they would be disbanded; and this was done. Their arrival in Richmond had been marked by such an ovation as Mrs. Chesnut describes [elsewhere in the *Diary*]; when they went home, three weeks before the battle of Manassas [fought on July 21, 1861, known in the North as the Battle of Bull Run], they were abused as cowards and renegades. [Ben Ames Williams]

Harper's Ferry has been evacuated, and we are looking out for a battle at Manassas Station. I am always ill. The name of my disease is a longing to get away from here, and go to Richmond. Good Lord, forgive me! Your commandment I cannot keep. How can I honor what is so dishonorable, or respect what is so little respectable, or love what is so utterly unlovely. Then I must go, indeed; go away from here.[2]

June 22 [1861] Making ready for Richmond. Last night I was awakened by loud talking and candles flashing everywhere, tramping of feet, growls dying away in the distance, loud calls from point to point in the yard. Up I started, my heart in my mouth. Some dreadful thing had happened, a battle, a death, a horrible accident. Mrs. Chesnut[3] was screaming aloft, that is from the top of the stairway, hoarsely like a boatswain in a storm. Colonel Chesnut was storming at the sleepy Negroes, looking for fire, with lighted candles, in closets. I dressed and came upon the scene of action. "What is it? Any news?" "No, no, only Mamma smells a smell. She thinks something is burning, somewhere." The whole yard was alive, literally swarming. There are sixty or seventy people kept here to wait upon this household, two thirds of them too old or too young to be of any use. But families remain intact. Mr. Chesnut has a magnificent voice. I am sure it can be heard for miles. Literally he was roaring from the piazza, giving orders to the busy crowd who were hunting the smell of fire.

Mrs. Chesnut is deaf, so she did not know what a commotion she was creating. She is very sensitive on the subject of bad odors. Candles have to be taken out of the room to be snuffed. Lamps are extinguished only in the porticos or further afield. She finds violets oppressive, can only tolerate a single kind of sweet rose. Tea roses, she will not have in her room.

She was totally innocent of the storm she had raised, and now in a mild sweet voice was suggesting places to be searched. I was weak enough to laugh hysterically. The bombardment of Fort Sumter was nothing to this.

. . .

[June 28, 1861] In Mrs. Davis's drawing-room last night, the President took a seat by me on the

sofa where I sat. He talked for nearly an hour. He laughed at our faith in our own prowess. We are like the British; we think every Southerner equal to three Yankees at least, but we will have to be equivalent to a dozen now. After his experience of the fighting qualities of Southerners in Mexico, Mr. Davis believes that we will do all that can be done by pluck and muscle, endurance and dogged courage, dash and red-hot patriotism, and yet his tone was not sanguine. There was a sad refrain running through it all. For one thing, either way, he thinks it will be a long war. That floored me at once. It has been too long for me already. Then he said that before the end came we would have many a bitter experience. He said only fools doubted the courage of the Yankees, or their willingness to fight when they saw fit. And now we have stung their pride, we have roused them till they will fight like devils. He said Mr. Chesnut's going as aide-de-camp to Beauregard was a mistake, and that he ought to raise a regiment of his own.

[July 11, 1861] The spy, so called, gave us a parting shot. She said Beauregard arrested her brother so that he might take a fine horse aforesaid brother was riding. Why? Beauregard could have at a moment's notice any horse in South Carolina —or Louisiana, for that matter—at a word. The brother was arrested and sent to Richmond, and "will be acquitted as they always are," said Brewster. They send them first to Richmond to see and hear everything there; then they acquit them, and send them out of the country by way of Norfolk to see everything there. But after all, what does it matter? The Yankees have no need of spies. Our newspapers keep no secrets hid. The thoughts of our hearts are all revealed. Everything with us is open and above board. At Bethel, the Yankees fired too high, and every daily is jeering them about it even now. They'll fire low enough next time, but no newspaper man will be there to get the benefit of their improved practice! Alas!

[September 19, 1861] Mr. Chesnut and Uncle John, both *ci-devant* [heretofore] Union men, are now utterly for State's Rights.

Queer how different the same man appears, viewed from different standpoints. "What a perfect gentleman! So fine looking, high-bred, distinguished, easy, free and above all graceful in his bearing. So high-toned! He is always indignant at any symptom of wrong-doing. He is charming, the man of all others I like to have strangers meet, a noble representative of our country." "Yes, every

---

[2] Mrs. Chesnut was not altogether happy living at Mulberry Plantation with her husband's parents.

[3] The diarist's mother-in-law; she refers to her father-in-law as Colonel Chesnut.

word you say is true. He is all that. But then the other side of the picture is true too. You always know where to find him! Wherever there is a looking glass, a bottle or a woman; there will he be also." "My God! And you call yourself his friend." "Yes, but I know him down to the ground."

This conversation I overheard from an upper window while I was looking down on the piazza below. They were discussing a complicated character with what Mrs. Preston calls the refinement spread thin, skin deep only.

Kate came down, as fresh, as sweet, as smiling as a spring morning. She is the proudest and happiest mother. "Mary, tell Auntie your analysis of character at——'s house." "Oh," said the loveliest blonde with the blackest blue eyes, not yet ten years old: "She likes everybody. She is happy and she wants her children to be happy. He dislikes every living soul outside of their own house, and he is miserable if he can't make everybody as wretched as he is."

An iron steamer has run the blockade at Savannah. We raise our wilted heads like flowers after a shower. This drop of good news revives us.

September 24 [1861] The men who went to Society Hill (the Witherspoon home) have come home again with nothing very definite. William and Cousin Betsey's old maid, Rhody, are in jail; strong suspicion but as yet no proof of their guilt. The neighborhood is in a ferment. Evans and Wallace say these Negroes ought to be burnt. Lynching proposed! But it is all idle talk. They will be tried as the law directs, and not otherwise. John Witherspoon will not allow anything wrong or violent to be done. He has a detective there from Charleston.

Hitherto I have never thought of being afraid of Negroes. I had never injured any of them; why should they want to hurt me? Two thirds of my religion consists in trying to be good to Negroes, because they are so in our power, and it would be so easy to be the other thing. Somehow today I feel that the ground is cut away from under my feet. Why should they treat me any better than they have done Cousin Betsey Witherspoon?

Kate and I sat up late and talked it all over. Mrs. Witherspoon was a saint on this earth, and this is her reward. Kate's maid Betsey came in—a strong-built, mulatto woman—dragging in a mattress. "Missis, I have brought my bed to sleep in your room while Mars' David is at Society Hill. You ought not to stay in a room by yourself these times." She went off for more bed gear. "For the

life of me," said Kate gravely, "I cannot make up my mind. Does she mean to take care of me, or to murder me?" I do not think Betsey heard, but when she came back she said: "Missis, as I have a soul to be saved, I will keep you safe. I will guard you." We know Betsey well, but has she soul enough to swear by? She is a great stout, jolly, irresponsible, unreliable, pleasant-tempered, bad-behaved woman, with ever so many good points. Among others, she is so clever she can do anything, and she never loses her temper; but she has no moral sense whatever.

That night, Kate came into my room. She could not sleep. The thought of those black hands strangling and smothering Mrs. Witherspoon's grey head under the counterpane haunted her; we sat up and talked the long night through.

. . .

Went over just now to have a talk with that optimist, my mother-in-law. Blessed are the pure in mind, for they shall see God. Her mind certainly is free from evil thoughts. Someone says, the most unhappy person is the one who has bad thoughts. She ought to be happy. She thinks no evil. And yet, she is the cleverest woman I know. She began to ask me something of Charlotte Temple (I call her this to keep back her true name). "Has she ever had any more children?" "She has one more." "Is she married?" "No." "Is she a bad girl, really?" "Yes." "Oh! Don't say that. Poor thing! Maybe after all she is not really bad, only to be pitied!" I gave it up. I felt like a fool. Here was one thing I had made sure of as a fixed fact. In this world, an unmarried girl with two children was, necessarily, not a good woman. If that can be waved aside, I give up, in utter confusion of mind. Ever since she came here sixty or seventy years ago, as a bride from Philadelphia, Mrs. Chesnut has been trying to make it up to the Negroes for being slaves. Seventeen ninety-six, I think, was the year of her marriage. Today someone asked her about it, when she was describing Mrs. Washington's drawing-room to us. Through her friendship for Nelly Custis, and living very near, and stiff, stern old Martha Washington not liking to have her coach horses taken out for trifles, and Mrs. Cox letting Nelly Custis and Mary Cox have the carriage at their pleasure, Mrs. Chesnut was a great deal thrown with the Washington household. Now she eloquently related for the hundredth time all this. "How came you to leave that pleasant Philadelphia and all its comforts for this half civilized Up-Country and all the horrors of slavery?" "Did you not know that my father owned slaves in Philadelphia? In his will he left me several of them." In the Quaker City, and in the lifetime of a living woman now present, there were slave holders. It is hard to believe. Time works its wonders like enchantment. So quickly we forget.

[October 7, 1861] An appalling list of foreigners in the Yankee army, just as I feared; a rush of all Europe to them, as soon as they raised the cry that this war is for the extirpation of slavery. If our people had read less of Mr. Calhoun's works, and only read the signs of the times a little more; if they had known more of what was going on around them in the world.

[October 13, 1861] I was shocked to hear that dear friends of mine refused to take work for the soldiers because their seamstresses had their winter clothes to make. I told them true patriotesses would be willing to wear the same clothes until our siege was raised. They did not seem to care. They have seen no ragged, dirty, sick and miserable soldiers lying in the hospital, no lack of woman's nursing, no lack of woman's tears, but an awful lack of a proper change in clean clothes. They know nothing of the horrors of war. One has to see to believe. They take it easy, and are not yet willing to make personal sacrifices. The time is coming when they will not be given a choice in the matter. The very few stay-at-home men we have are absorbed as before in plantation affairs; cotton-picking, Negro squabbles, hay stealing, saving the corn from the freshet. They are like the old Jews while Noah was building the Ark.

Woe to those who began this war, if they were not in bitter earnest. Lamar (L.Q.C., and the cleverest man I know) said in Richmond in one of those long talks of ours: "Slavery is too heavy a load for us to carry."

[October 25, 1861] The Yankees' principal spite is against South Carolina. Fifteen war steamers have sailed—or steamed—out against us. Hot work will be cut out for us whenever they elect to land. They hate us, but they fear us too. They do not move now until their force is immense; overwhelming is their word. Enormous preparations and a cautious approach are the lessons we taught them at Manassas.

. . . The President writes asking for particulars of that famous interview on the 13th July. There were present Colonel John S. Preston, General Lee, General Cooper, Mr. Chesnut and the President.

General Beauregard says he sent to the President, by his aid, Colonel Chesnut, a plan of battle which the President rejected. Are we going to be like the Jews when Titus was thundering against their gates? Quarrelling among ourselves makes me faint with fear. I wrote out a copy of Mr. Chesnut's report to Beauregard, written while the guns were firing on the 18th. Surely Beauregard, by stopping a man to write that day, showed he wanted his justification prepared *en cas*. He looked out for his own fame, the eyes of posterity and all that. I remember Mr. Chesnut's talk when he came back to our rooms, his praise of General Lee's clear soldierly views, and his disgust because I would interrupt him to say "how handsome General Lee was, such a splendid looking soldier, but that I liked Smith Lee best."

The Mississippi Regiment which faced the enemy so gallantly at Leesburg was the same which behaved not so well on the 21st July—something like Frederick the Great at his first battle. They asked, this time, for a place of danger and difficulty, so that they might redeem themselves and the name of their regiment.

November 6 [1861] Mr. Chesnut has gone to Charleston, and Kate to Columbia, on her way to Flat Rock. Partings are sorrowful things now. I read Mrs. Shelley's book, "The Last Man." It is written to sell. A filthy man, but the book is not so bad. She used Byron and Shelley and wrote of things she knew.

As for the dunderheads here, I can account for their stolidity only in one way. They have no imagination. They cannot conceive what lies before them. They can only see what actually lies under their noses. To me it is evident that Russell, the Times [of London] correspondent, tries to tell the truth, unpalatable as it is to us. Why should we expect a man who recorded so unflinchingly the wrong-doing in India, to soften matters for our benefit, sensitive as we are to blame. He described slavery in Maryland, but says that it has worse features further South; yet his account of slavery in Maryland might stand as a perfectly accurate picture of it here. God knows I am not inclined to condone it, come what may. His work is very well done for a stranger who comes and in his haste unpacks his three P's—pen, paper, and prejudices—and hurries through his work.

[May 23, 1862] Maria often smoothed a dress for me. She loved to talk of her marital relations. She was so sad and mysterious in her dark revelations, I cannot make them very clear. She was married, her husband ill-used her; he did something very bad, that is very wrong, and he left her and then he died. She had no children. Then she would go off to her family history, which I had heard from Mrs. Preston when we were at the Fauquier White Sulphur. This is not a pretty story, but Maria told it leaving out all ugly words. Her mother died when they were quite young. She belonged to a Scotchman, a doctor. Her master married a white lady who did not like Maria and her two brothers; but she was not bad to them while her husband lived. Then the Scotchman died, and the widow found these white-fathered children in her yard a blot on the Scotchman's escutcheon. She sent them to Columbia to be sold. They were delighted to be sold, for they hated her worse than she hated them. Mrs. Preston bought them.

Before I knew the history of the Walkers (William, Maria, John), I remember a scene which took place at a ball given by Mrs. Preston while Mr. Preston was in Louisiana. Mrs. Preston was resplendent in diamonds, point lace, velvet train, etc. There is a gentle dignity about her which is very attractive, and her voice is low and sweet, and her will is iron. She is an exceedingly well-informed person, but quiet, retiring and reserved. Her apparent gentleness almost amounts to timidity. At that ball, Governor Manning said to me: "Look at sister Caroline! Does she look as if she had the pluck of a heroine?" "How?" "A little while ago, William came to tell her that his brother John was drunk in the cellar, mad with drink, and that he had a carving knife which he was brandishing in his drunken fury and keeping everybody from their business, threatening to kill anyone who dared to go in the basement. They were like a flock of frightened sheep down there. Caroline did not speak to one of us, but followed William down to the basement, holding up her skirts. She found the servants scurrying everywhere, screaming and shouting that John was crazy and going to kill them. John was bellowing like a bull of Basham, knife in hand, chasing them at his pleasure. Caroline walked up to him. 'Give me that knife.' He handed it to her; she laid it on a table. 'And now come with me,' she said, putting her hand on his collar. She led him away to the empty smoke house, and locked him in and put the key in her pocket; and she returned without a ripple on her placid face to show what she had done. She told me of it, smiling and serene as you see her now."

Before the war shut us in, Mr. Preston sent to the lakes for his salmon, to Mississippi for his veni-

son, to England for his mutton and grouse. But the best dish at all of these houses is what the Spanish call "the hearty welcome." Thackeray says at every American table he was first served with "grilled hostess."

February 26 [1864] We went to see Mrs. Breckenridge, who is here with her husband; then we paid our respects to Mrs. Lee. Her room was like an industrial school, with everybody so busy. Her daughters were all there, plying their needles, and also several other ladies. Mrs. Lee showed us a beautiful sword recently sent to the General by some Marylanders now in Paris. On the blade was engraved, "*Aide Toi et Dieu T' Aidera.*" [Help yourself and God will help you.] When we came out, I said: "Did you see how the Lees spend their time? What a rebuke to the taffy parties!" But I like our parties, *tout même*, [all the same].

There is a victory claimed in Mississippi, so no fears are now felt for Mobile, and our papers are jubilant. Beneficent mud! No killed and no killing on hand; no rumbling of wagons laden with dead or dying. We enjoy this reprieve. We snatch a fearful joy. It is a brief interlude of comparative peace.

August 2 [1865] I am old, old, old; the weight of the years that hangs upon my eyelids is of lead. But there is youth in even our world still. I have another letter from my precious Serena.

Dear Aunty—

Tristy Trezevant arrived here last week and says I can send you a letter by Mrs. Johnson. I am in Greenville. Mamma was obliged to send Mamie and me away. Flat Rock was no longer a place for us, after the bushwhackers.[4] Mamma writes me now what a relief it is for her to know that we are safe from such treatment as we received that night. She says such another night would kill her. However a great many of the wretches have been captured, and I hope something may be done to them.

[Mrs. Chesnut quotes the rest of this letter, a letter from Serena to her young friend, Isabella Martin, and Isabella's letter in reply to Serena. Isabella's letter ends:]

I have begun my small school. It is the only way to make brains available. What do you think; I have been requested to write a history of

[4] These were ruffians who took advantage of the lawless state of the countryside to rob, loot, assault, and kill.

the war, the requestor to pay all expenses. If I only could, would I not? I'd give some people such a showing! Your last letters have been of the meagerest. What is the matter?

Toujours—
Isabella

[Mrs. Chesnut writes by way of comment:]

What is the matter? Enough! I will write no more!

[Thus ends the diary, and the writer's concluding words are eloquent: they speak of hopelessness and emotional exhaustion.]

GEORGE WASHINGTON CABLE (1844–1925)

When the Civil War had ended, the writers of the conquered southern states reacted in a variety of predictable ways. There were memoirs of southern leaders and defenses of the southern cause. Typical are those by Alexander Stephens, vice president of the Confederacy, Albert Taylor Bledsoe, professor of mathematics at the University of Virginia, and Robert Lewis Dabney, Presbyterian chaplain on the staff of Stonewall Jackson.[1]

In fiction and in poetry there was, of course, a tendency to look back with longing and regret to the world of the past, now made by the austerities of the present to appear the more pleasant and gracious. The fact that the South had been defeated and was poverty-stricken and humiliated intensified the perennial human impulse to see the past in retrospect as more splendid than it actually was. This impulse, moreover, evoked a complementary impulse in the victorious North. Lost causes are by their very nature more romantically interesting than those which succeed. Southern writers soon found in the North avid and sympathetic readers of their stories and novels that presented an idealized picture of the South before the war. Perhaps the less said the better about the intrinsic literary merit of such fiction; nevertheless its political impact was great. As Paul H. Buck puts it in *The Road to Reunion* (1937),

For better or for worse [Thomas Nelson] Page, [Joel Chandler] Harris, [James Lane] Allen, and their associates of the South, with the aid of Northern editors, critics, magazines, publishing houses, and theaters, had driven completely from the Northern mind the unfriendly picture of the South implanted there in the days of strife. In place of the discarded image they had fixed a far more friendly conception of a land basically American and loyal to the best traditions of the nation, where men and women had lived noble lives and had made heroic sacrifices to great ideals, where Negroes loved "de white folks," where magnolias and roses blossomed over hospitable homes that sheltered lovely maids and brave cadets, where romance of the past still lived, a land where, in short, the nostalgic Northerner could escape the wear and tear of expanding industry and growing cities and dwell in a Dixie of the storybooks which had become the Arcady of American tradition.

Even though this image did not completely eradicate the picture of another South which still lynched its Negroes and under-educated its whites, the cumulative effect of the literature of Southern themes was to soften the tension of sectional relations and produce a popular attitude of complacency to Southern problems.[2]

---

[1] For an excellent summary of such defenses, the student is referred to Richard M. Weaver's *The Southern Tradition at Bay: A History of Post-Bellum Thought* (1968).

[2] This complacency, however, accomplished no improvement of the South's economic condition. Freight-rate differentials were not changed so as to benefit

Buck provides some startling illustrations of the effectiveness of the new image of the South on northern sensibilities. T. W. Higginson, who had commanded a regiment of black infantry during the Civil War, dissolved in tears after reading Page's story "Marse Chan," in which a faithful black servant brings home the body of his young master, slain in the war. In another striking instance, the daughter of Julia Ward Howe, author of "The Battle Hymn of the Republic," after a short sojourn in the South asserted that the Negroes were happier and better off under slavery than with freedom.

This romantic "Confederate" fiction was not polemical in tone—no defiant justification of the antebellum social order. Rather, it was conciliatory and motivated—much of it at least—by a desire for reconciliation and a binding up of wounds. Sentiment and romantic love were to the fore. Countless novels of the period end with the marriage of a Southern belle to a charming Yankee officer, or it might be a Confederate soldier weds a girl from the North.

Most of this literature, by the way, was published in the North—that is where the publishing houses were—and most of the reading public was northern too. Prior to the Civil War the South had had few publishing centers and had paid too little attention to imaginative literature. As Page remarked, "It was for a lack of literature that [the South] was left behind in the great race for outside support, and that at the supreme moment of her existence she found herself arraigned at the bar of the world without an advocate and without a defense." The fact that his editor was in all likelihood a northern man and that the larger part of his audience was also northern undoubtedly conditioned (unconsciously, if not consciously) the southern writer's work. He was presenting to the world outside his own culture, in all its differences and localisms.

This same general situation also underlies local color literature, since it is essentially a literature written by someone inside a culture but aimed at readers who are outside it. The local colorist emphasizes what in his culture will seem to the outlander interesting or quaint or amusing. Obviously, the southern fiction devoted to local color and the fiction glorifying the life of the old South often overlap, but the modes can and ought to be distinguished. In any case, the best of local color fiction does more than merely exploit what is picturesque or quaint in a provincial culture. Nor does it need to treat that culture uncritically, idealizing and sentimentalizing it. The work of George Washington Cable will provide a good illustration of both points.

Cable's stories and novels about the Creoles of New Orleans record for posterity a whole way of life, which Cable thought ought to be recorded before it passed away. But it also presents the errors and prejudices, the blind sides and imperfections, of this way of life. In spite of the charm of the Creole civilization, Cable believed that it exhibited certain moral weaknesses to be found in the South at large.

In the Civil War, Cable had fought loyally for the Confederacy, but as time went on he was to speak out more and more clearly about the inequities of the southern caste system. Yet his stories of Creole culture were bound to seem to the rest of the nation—including southerners except for the inhabitants of southern Louisiana—primarily a matter of local color. Though he was born and brought up in New Orleans, Cable was not a Creole, and to him too the French-Spanish culture was exotic. If the more pejorative associations of local color—the exploitation of the quaint for the amusement of the more sophisticated metropolis—do not apply to Cable's best work, it is because Cable was sufficiently the artist to render in his work an honest and accurate presentation of the social scene without any smug or scornful disparagement of it.

Yet the Creoles felt that Cable had disparaged them. Though Cable found the Creole women charming and delightful in an innocent

---

southern industries nor tariffs lowered so as to benefit southern agriculture. The new friendliness was essentially sentimental and in practical affairs amounted mainly to letting the South attend to problems of race in its own way.

and sometimes even brainless way, he criticized the men as often headstrong and choleric and too fiercely proud of their Creole heritage. At any rate, he managed to offend the Creoles most bitterly.

Cable's personal heritage was that of a rather narrow Puritanism (which mellowed only in his later years). He was, for instance, brought up to disapprove of dancing and card-playing. Consequently, there was a real danger that the stern moralist would get the upper hand over the perceptive artist, particularly when the immediate problem was to present with proper aesthetic detachment a society that was rather dangerously relaxed and even corrupt. In his best work Cable succeeded in holding reasonably in check his moralizing tendencies and in the long run his concern with morality stood him in good stead, for it enabled him, as we have said, to see that the Creole society that attracted him through its grace and charm harbored grave moral faults and that its system of values tended to rob the black man of his humanity.

Two or three of the stories in *Old Creole Days* (1879) have to do with the race problem, but it is in *The Grandissimes* (1880) that it is presented with excruciating force and with full accent on the plight of the slaves and the treatment of people of mixed blood. *The Grandissimes* is regarded as Cable's greatest novel; it has recently been asserted that it is "a novel better than all but Faulkner's greatest." Certainly it is based on a great conception and includes some immensely powerful scenes. The willingness of an inheritor of the genteel tradition to deal with such subject matter and, what is even more daring, of a southerner to expose racial injustice in the South at a time when the South was still smarting from the wounds of war and Reconstruction is admirable, morally and artistically.

Nevertheless, a judicial reader of *The Grandissimes* must ask whether Cable has not permitted Joseph Frowenfeld, the newcomer to New Orleans, to become too obviously the author's mouthpiece. Frowenfeld judges the Creole society, but Cable does not judge Frowenfeld or even examine very closely his motives

and attitudes.[3] Yet, in view of Frowenfeld's remarkable social and financial success—within a year he has established a flourishing business and married a Creole heiress—his inner life ought to be revealed. Louis Rubin has observed that "In place of what might have been a fascinating delineation of the way in which an outsider responds to the attractions of a richly complex, formidable, but ultimately vulnerable society we are given only the high-minded but wooden and lifeless characterization of Joseph Frowenfeld" (*George Washington Cable*, 1969, p. 95). A reader of *The Grandissimes* might be pardoned for drawing the moral that nothing "succeeds" like a combination of strict probity, energy, and sound business methods.

On its publication *The Grandissimes* won high praise, but, as we have suggested, many of the Creoles were not pleased and some felt a fierce resentment at what seemed a biased treatment by an outsider representing another kind of culture. Within a few years Cable left New Orleans for Northampton, Massachusetts, where he spent the rest of his life. In his continuing protest against the treatment of the Negro, Cable wrote such treatises as *The Silent South* (1885), *The Negro Question* (1888), and *The Southern Struggle for Mature Government* (1890). But he also produced more novels that stressed the problems of race and color. A notable instance is *John March, Southerner* (1894), which Cable deliberately set in northern Georgia as more representative than Louisiana of the South as a whole. *John March* is an ambitious book that concerns the rebuilding of the South after the war. Edmund Wilson has condemned it as didactic, filled with pasteboard characters, and no better than a "note-book product"; but it has also been vigorously defended as an honest attempt to deal with difficult and intractable material.

Cable's later novels are usually dismissed as historical romances, written to make money and shaped to the taste of northern editors who

---

[3] See Olmsted's account of Louisiana life (pp. 1077-79). He, too, was an outsider and his views may well be compared with those of Frowenfeld.

were convinced that the public was tired of reading about the problems of the South and the Negro and wanted mere entertainment. This verdict is generally just, but one has to make two qualifications. First, Cable continued in several of these costume romances to write about racial injustice and the moral inadequacy of southern attitudes. See, for example, *Gideon's Band* (1914). Second, it must be conceded that the faults of the later romances—melodramatic situations, forced and creaky plots, and a syrupy treatment of romantic love—are to be found too in the earlier stories and novels, including some of the best of them. Such faults, however, were endemic to the period in which Cable lived, and only a very great artist could have fought free of them.

FURTHER READINGS

Philip Butcher, *George W. Cable: The Northampton Years* (1959)
Guy A. Cardwell, *Twins of Genius* (1953)
Kjell Ekström, *George Washington Cable: A Study of His Early Life and Work* (1950)
Jay Martin, *Harvests of Change: American Literature, 1865–1914* (1967)

Arlin Turner, *George W. Cable: A Biography* (1956)
————, "Introduction," *The Negro Question: A Selection of Writings on Civil Rights in the South by George W. Cable* (1958)

'Sieur George (1879)

"'Sieur George" was Cable's first published story. The reader may be tempted to relegate it to the category of mere local color, and there is some reason to believe that it was so regarded by the editor who accepted it for *Scribner's Monthly*. The scene of the story is exotic and redolent of a certain decadent charm, but the discerning reader will be able to see something beneath the exotic scene and find not sentimental charm but a deft and unflinching examination of horrifying depravity. Cable's 'Sieur George may be a sentimentalist but Cable is not. Yet the import of the story is certainly not flattened into moralization. In fact, the author's judgment on 'Sieur George is never given directly, but is merely implied. Cable renders the situation and leaves it up to his reader to draw whatever inferences he thinks are justified.

One aspect of this process of indirection is the oblique way in which important information is given the reader; another is Cable's willingness to withhold information until it can come with proper dramatic and climactic force.

In short, the reader is put very nearly in the position of Kookoo, the man from whom 'Sieur George rents his small apartment. Like Kookoo's, the reader's curiosity is aroused. What manner of man is 'Sieur George? The reader gets most of his information at the same time that Kookoo gets his, since it is through Kookoo that he receives it. But the reader, one hopes, will be a person more sensitive to the implications than Kookoo is.

The most masterful stroke is the ending. It is quiet and yet it is—granted the foregoing presentation of 'Sieur George's character—inevitable. Nevertheless, the revelation of his final depravity comes with a considerable shock.

———

In the heart of New Orleans stands a large four-story brick building, that has so stood for about three-quarters of a century. Its rooms are rented to a class of persons occupying them simply for lack of activity to find better and cheaper quarters elsewhere. With its gray stucco peeling off in broad patches, it has a solemn look of gentility in rags, and stands, or, as it were, hangs, about the corner of two ancient streets, like a faded fop who pretends to be looking for employment.

Under its main archway is a dingy apothecary-shop. On one street is the bazaar of a *modiste en robes et chapeaux* and other humble shops; on the other, the immense batten doors with gratings over the lintels, barred and bolted with masses of cob-webbed iron, like the door of a donjon, are over-hung by a creaking sign (left by the sheriff), on which is faintly discernible the mention of wines and liquors. A peep through one of the shops reveals a square court within, hung with many lines of wet clothes, its sides hugged by rotten staircases that seem vainly trying to clamber out of the rubbish.

The neighborhood is one long since given up to fifth-rate shops, whose masters and mistresses display such enticing mottoes as *"Au gagne petit!"* Innumerable children swarm about, and, by some charm of the place, are not run over, but obstruct the sidewalks playing their clamorous games.

The building is a thing of many windows, where passably good-looking women appear and disappear, clad in cotton gowns, watering little outside shelves of flowers and cacti, or hanging canaries' cages. Their husbands are keepers in wine-ware-houses, rent-collectors for the agents of old Frenchmen who have been laid up to dry in Paris, custom-house supernumeraries and court-clerks' deputies (for your second-rate Creole is a great seeker for little offices). A decaying cornice hangs over, dropping bits of mortar on passers below, like a boy at a boarding-house.

The landlord is one Kookoo, an ancient Creole of doubtful purity of blood, who in his landlordly old age takes all suggestions of repairs as personal insults. He was but a stripling when his father left him this inheritance, and has grown old and wrinkled and brown, a sort of periodically animate mummy, in the business. He smokes cascarilla, wears velveteen, and is as punctual as an executioner.

To Kookoo's venerable property a certain old man used for many years to come every evening, stumbling through the groups of prattling children who frolicked about in the early moonlight—whose name no one knew, but whom all the neighbors designated by the title of 'Sieur George. It was his wont to be seen taking a straight—too straight—course toward his home, never careening to right or left, but now forcing himself slowly forward, as

though there were a high gale in front, and now scudding briskly ahead at a ridiculous little dog-trot, as if there were a tornado behind. He would go up the main staircase very carefully, sometimes stopping half-way up for thirty or forty minutes' doze, but getting to the landing eventually, and tramping into his room in the second story, with no little elation to find it still there. Were it not for these slight symptoms of potations, he was such a one as you would pick out of a thousand for a miser. A year or two ago he suddenly disappeared.

A great many years ago, when the old house was still new, a young man with no baggage save a small hair-trunk, came and took the room I have mentioned and another adjoining. He supposed he might stay fifty days—and he staid fifty years and over. This was a very fashionable neighborhood, and he kept the rooms on that account month after month.

But when he had been here about a year something happened to him, so it was rumored, that greatly changed the tenor of his life; and from that time on there began to appear in him and to accumulate upon each other in a manner which became the profound study of Kookoo, the symptoms of a decay, whose cause baffled the landlord's limited powers of conjecture for well-nigh half a century. Hints of a duel, of a reason warped, of disinheritance, and many other unauthorized rumors, fluttered up and floated off, while he became recluse, and, some say, began incidentally to betray the unmanly habit which we have already noticed. His neighbors would have continued neighborly had he allowed them, but he never let himself be understood, and *les Américains* are very droll anyhow; so, as they could do nothing else, they cut him.

So exclusive he became that (though it may have been for economy) he never admitted even a housemaid, but kept his apartments himself. Only the merry serenaders, who in those times used to sing under the balconies, would now and then give him a crumb of their feast for pure fun's sake; and after a while, because they could not find out his full name, called him, at hazard, George—but always prefixing Monsieur. Afterward, when he began to be careless in his dress, and the fashion of serenading had passed away, the commoner people dared to shorten the title to " 'Sieur George."

Many seasons came and went. The city changed like a growing boy; gentility and fashion went up-town, but 'Sieur George still retained his rooms.

Every one knew him slightly, and bowed, but no one seemed to know him well, unless it were a brace or so of those convivial fellows in regulation-blue at little Fort St. Charles. He often came home late, with one of these on either arm, all singing different tunes and stopping at every twenty steps to tell secrets. But by and by the fort was demolished, church and government property melted down under the warm demand for building-lots, the city spread like a ringworm,—and one day 'Sieur George steps out of the old house in full regimentals!

The Creole neighbors rush bareheaded into the middle of the street, as though there were an earthquake or a chimney on fire. What to do or say or think they do not know; they are at their wits' ends, therefore well-nigh happy. However, there is a German blacksmith's shop near by, and they watch to see what *Jacob* will do. Jacob steps into the street with every eye upon him; he approaches Monsieur—he addresses to him a few remarks—they shake hands—they engage in some conversation—Monsieur places his hand on his sword!—now Monsieur passes.

The populace crowd around the blacksmith, children clap their hands softly and jump up and down on tiptoes of expectation—'Sieur George is going to the war in Mexico!

"Ah!" says a little girl in the throng, " 'Sieur George's two rooms will be empty; I find that very droll."

The landlord,—this same Kookoo,—is in the group. He hurls himself into the house and up the stairs. "Fifteen years pass since he have been in those room!" He arrives at the door—it is shut—"It is lock!"

In short, further investigation revealed that a youngish lady in black, who had been seen by several neighbors to enter the house, but had not, of course, been suspected of such remarkable intentions, had, in company with a middle-aged slave-woman, taken these two rooms, and now, at the slightly-opened door, proffered a month's rent in advance. What could a landlord do but smile? Yet there was a pretext left; "the rooms must need repairs?"—"No, sir; he could look in and see." Joy! he looked in. All was neatness. The floor unbroken, the walls cracked but a little, and the cracks closed with new plaster, no doubt by the jealous hand of 'Sieur George himself. Kookoo's eyes swept sharply round the two apartments. The furniture was all there. Moreover, there was Monsieur's little hair-trunk. He should not soon forget that trunk. One

day, fifteen years or more before, he had taken hold of that trunk to assist Monsieur to arrange his apartment, and Monsieur had drawn his fist back and cried to him to "drop it!" *Mais!* there it was, looking very suspicious in Kookoo's eyes, and the lady's domestic, as tidy as a yellow-bird, went and sat on it. Could that trunk contain treasure? It might, for Madame wanted to shut the door, and, in fact, did so.

The lady was quite handsome—had been more so, but was still young—spoke the beautiful language, and kept, in the inner room, her discreet and taciturn mulattress, a tall, straight woman, with a fierce eye, but called by the young Creoles of the neighborhood "confound' good lookin'."

Among *les Américaines*, where the new neighbor always expects to be called upon by the older residents, this lady might have made friends in spite of being as reserved as 'Sieur George; but the reverse being the Creole custom, and she being well pleased to keep her own company, chose mystery rather than society.

The poor landlord was sorely troubled; it must not that any thing *de trop* take place in his house. He watched the two rooms narrowly, but without result, save to find that Madame plied her needle for pay, spent her money for little else besides harpstrings, and took good care of the little trunk of Monsieur. This espionage was a good turn to the mistress and maid, for when Kookoo announced that all was proper, no more was said by outsiders. Their landlord never got but one question answered by the middle-aged maid:

"Madame, he feared, was a litt' bit embarrass' *pour* money, eh?"

"*Non;* Mademoiselle [Mademoiselle, you notice!] had some property, but did not want to eat it up."

Sometimes lady-friends came, in very elegant private carriages, to see her, and one or two seemed to beg her—but in vain—to go away with them; but these gradually dropped off, until lady and servant were alone in the world. And so years, and the Mexican war, went by.

The volunteers came home; peace reigned, and the city went on spreading up and down the land; but 'Sieur George did not return. It overran the country like cocoa-grass. Fields, roads, woodlands, that were once 'Sieur George's places of retreat from mankind, were covered all over with little one-story houses in the "Old Third," and fine residences and gardens up in "Lafayette." Streets went slicing like a butcher's knife, through old colonial estates, whose first masters never dreamed of the city reaching them,—and 'Sieur George was still away. The four-story brick got old and ugly, and the surroundings dim and dreamy. Theatres, processions, dry-goods stores, government establishments, banks, hotels, and all spirit of enterprise were gone to Canal Street and beyond, and the very beggars were gone with them. The little trunk got very old and bald, and still its owner lingered; still the lady, somewhat the worse for lapse of time, looked from the balcony-window in the brief southern twilights, and the maid every morning shook a worn rug or two over the dangerous-looking railing; and yet neither had made friends or enemies.

The two rooms, from having been stingily kept at first, were needing repairs half the time, and the occupants were often moving, now into one, now back into the other; yet the hair-trunk was seen only by glimpses, the landlord, to his infinite chagrin, always being a little too late in offering his services, the women, whether it was light or heavy, having already moved it. He thought it significant.

Late one day of a most bitter winter,—that season when, to the ecstatic amazement of a whole city-full of children, snow covered the streets ankle-deep,—there came a soft tap on the corridor-door of this pair of rooms. The lady opened it, and beheld a tall, lank, iron-gray man, a total stranger, standing behind—Monsieur George! Both men were weather-beaten, scarred, and tattered. Across 'Sieur George's crown, leaving a long, bare streak through his white hair, was the souvenir of a Mexican sabre.

The landlord had accompanied them to the door: it was a magnificent opportunity. Mademoiselle asked them all in, and tried to furnish a seat to each; but failing, 'Sieur George went straight across the room and *sat on the hair-trunk*. The action was so conspicuous, the landlord laid it up in his penetrative mind.

'Sieur George was quiet, or, as it appeared, quieted. The mulattress stood near him, and to her he addressed, in an undertone, most of the little he said, leaving Mademoiselle to his companion. The stranger was a warm talker, and seemed to please the lady from the first; but if he pleased, nothing else did. Kookoo, intensely curious, sought some pretext for staying, but found none. They were, altogether, an uncongenial company. The lady seemed to think Kookoo had no business there; 'Sieur George seemed to think the same concerning his companion; and the few words between

Mademoiselle and 'Sieur George were cool enough. The maid appeared nearly satisfied, but could not avoid casting an anxious eye at times upon her mistress. Naturally the visit was short.

The next day but one the two gentlemen came again in better attire. 'Sieur George evidently disliked his companion, yet would not rid himself of him. The stranger was a gesticulating, stagy fellow, much Monsieur's junior, an incessant talker in Creole-French, always excited on small matters and unable to appreciate a great one. Once, as they were leaving, Kookoo,—accidents will happen,—was under the stairs. As they began to descend the tall man was speaking: "—better to bury it,"—the startled landlord heard him say, and held his breath, thinking of the trunk; but no more was uttered.

A week later they came again.

A week later they came again.

A week later they came yet again!

The landlord's eyes began to open. There must be a courtship in progress. It was very plain now why 'Sieur George had wished not to be accompanied by the tall gentleman; but since his visits had become regular and frequent, it was equally plain why he did not get rid of him;—because it would not look well to be going and coming too often alone. Maybe it was only this tender passion that the tall man had thought "better to bury." Lately there often came sounds of gay conversation from the first of the two rooms, which had been turned into a parlor; and as, week after week, the friends came down-stairs, the tall man was always in high spirits and anxious to embrace 'Sieur George, who,—"sly dog," thought the landlord,—would try to look grave, and only smiled in an embarrassed way. "Ah! Monsieur, you tink to be varry conning; *mais* you not so conning as Kookoo, no;" and the inquisitive little man would shake his head and smile, and shake his head again, as a man has a perfect right to do under the conviction that he has been for twenty years baffled by a riddle and is learning to read it at last; he had guessed what was in 'Sieur George's head, he would by and by guess what was in the trunk.

A few months passed quickly away, and it became apparent to every eye in or about the ancient mansion that the landlord's guess was not so bad; in fact, that Mademoiselle was to be married.

On a certain rainy spring afternoon, a single hired hack drove up to the main entrance of the old house, and after some little bustle and the gathering of a crowd of damp children about the big doorway, 'Sieur George, muffled in a newly-repaired overcoat, jumped out and went up-stairs. A moment later he re-appeared, leading Mademoiselle, wreathed and veiled, down the stairway. Very fair was Mademoiselle still. Her beauty was mature,—fully ripe,—maybe a little too much so, but only a little; and as she came down with the ravishing odor of bridal flowers floating about her, she seemed the garlanded victim of a pagan sacrifice. The mulattress in holiday gear followed behind.

The landlord owed a duty to the community. He arrested the maid on the last step: "Your mistress, she goin' *pour marier* 'Sieur George? It makes me glad, glad, glad!"

"Marry 'Sieur George? Non, Monsieur."

"Non? Not marrie 'Sieur George? *Mais comment?*"

"She's going to marry the tall gentleman."

"*Diable!* ze long gentyman!"—With his hands upon his forehead, he watched the carriage trundle away. It passed out of sight through the rain; he turned to enter the house, and all at once tottered under the weight of a tremendous thought—they had left the trunk! He hurled himself up-stairs as he had done seven years before, but again—"Ah, bah!!"—the door was locked, and not a picayune of rent due.

Late that night a small square man, in a wet overcoat, fumbled his way into the damp entrance of the house, stumbled up the cracking stairs, unlocked, after many languid efforts, the door of the two rooms, and falling over the hair-trunk, slept until the morning sunbeams climbed over the balcony and in at the window, and shone full on the back of his head. Old Kookoo, passing the door just then, was surprised to find it slightly ajar—pushed it open silently, and saw, within, 'Sieur George in the act of rising from his knees beside the mysterious trunk! He had come back to be once more the tenant of the two rooms.

'Sieur George, for the second time, was a changed man—changed from bad to worse; from being retired and reticent, he had come, by reason of advancing years, or mayhap that which had left the terrible scar on his face, to be garrulous. When, once in a while, employment sought him (for he never sought employment), whatever remuneration he received went its way for something that left him dingy and threadbare. He now made a lively acquaintance with his landlord, as, indeed, with every soul in the neighborhood, and told all his adventures in Mexican prisons and Cuban cities; including full details of the hardships and perils experienced jointly with the "long gentleman" who had married Mademoiselle, and who was no Mexican or Cuban, but a genuine Louisianian.

"It was he that fancied me," he said, "not I him; but once he had fallen in love with me I hadn't the force to cast him off. How Madame ever should have liked him was one of those woman's freaks that a man mustn't expect to understand. He was 'no more fit for her than rags are fit for a queen; and I could have choked his head off the night he hugged me round the neck and told me what a suicide she had committed. But other fine women are committing that same folly every day, only they don't wait until they're thirty-four or five to do it.—'Why don't I like him?' Well, for one reason, he's a drunkard!" Here Kookoo, whose imperfect knowledge of English prevented his intelligent reception of the story, would laugh as if the joke came in just at this point.

However, with all Monsieur's prattle, he never dropped a word about the man he had been before he went away; and the great hair-trunk puzzle was still the same puzzle, growing greater every day.

Thus the two rooms had been the scene of some events quite queer, if not really strange; but the queerest that ever they presented, I guess, was 'Sieur George coming in there one day, crying like a little child, and bearing in his arms an infant—a girl—the lovely offspring of the drunkard whom he so detested, and poor, robbed, spirit-broken and now dead Madame. He took good care of the orphan, for orphan she was very soon. The long gentleman was pulled out of the Old Basin one morning, and 'Sieur George identified the body at the Trémé station. He never hired a nurse—the father had sold the lady's maid quite out of sight; so he brought her through all the little ills and around all the sharp corners of baby-life and childhood, without a human hand to help him, until one evening, having persistently shut his eyes to it for weeks and months, like one trying to sleep in the sunshine, he awoke to the realization that she was a woman. It was a smoky one in November, the first cool day of autumn. The sunset was dimmed by the smoke of burning prairies, the air was full of the ashes of grass and reeds, ragged urchins were lugging home sticks of cordwood, and when a bit of coal fell from a cart in front of Kookoo's old house, a child was boxed half across the street and robbed of the booty by a *blanchisseuse de fin* from over the way.

The old man came home quite steady. He mounted the stairs smartly without stopping to rest, went with a step unusually light and quiet to his chamber and sat by the window opening upon the rusty balcony.

It was a small room, sadly changed from what it had been in old times; but then so was 'Sieur George. Close and dark it was, the walls stained with dampness and the ceiling full of bald places that showed the lathing. The furniture was cheap and meagre, including conspicuously the small, curious-looking hair-trunk. The floor was of wide slabs fastened down with spikes, and sloping up and down in one or two broad undulations, as if they had drifted far enough down the current of time to feel the tide-swell.

However, the floor was clean, the bed well made, the cypress table in place, and the musty smell of the walls partly neutralized by a geranium on the window-sill.

He so coming in and sitting down, an unseen person called from the room adjoining (of which, also, he was still the rentee), to know if he were he, and being answered in the affirmative, said, "Papa George, guess who was here to-day?"

"Kookoo, for the rent?"

"Yes, but he will not come back."

"No? why not?"

"Because you will not pay him."

"No? and why not?"

"Because I have paid him."

"Impossible! where did you get the money?"

"Cannot guess?—Mother Nativity."

"What, not for embroidery?"

"No? and why not? *Mais oui!*"—saying which, and with a pleasant laugh, the speaker entered the room. She was a girl of sixteen or thereabout, very beautiful, and with very black hair and eyes. A face and form more entirely out of place you could not have found in the whole city. She sat herself at his feet, and, with her interlocked hands upon his knee, and her face, full of childish innocence mingled with womanly wisdom, turned to his, appeared for a time to take principal part in a conversation which, of course, could not be overheard in the corridor outside.

Whatever was said, she presently rose, he opened his arms, and she sat on his knee and kissed him. This done, there was a silence, both smiling pensively and gazing out over the rotten balcony into the street. After a while she started up, saying something about the change of weather, and, slipping away, thrust a match between the bars of the grate. The old man turned about to the fire, and she from her little room brought a low sewing-chair and sat beside him, laying her head on his knee, and he stroking her brow with his brown palm.

And then, in an altered—a low, sad tone—he began a monotonous recital.

Thus they sat, he talking very steadily and she listening, until all the neighborhood was wrapped in slumber,—all the neighbors, but not Kookoo.

Kookoo in his old age had become a great eavesdropper; his ear and eye took turns at the keyhole that night, for he tells things that were not intended for outside hearers. He heard the girl sobbing, and the old man saying, "But you must go now. You cannot stay with me safely or decently, much as I wish it. The Lord only knows how I'm to bear it, or where you're to go; but He's your Lord, child, and He'll make a place for you. I was your grandfather's death; I frittered your poor, dead mother's fortune away: let that be the last damage I do.

"I have always meant every thing for the best," he added half in soliloquy.

From all Kookoo could gather, he must have been telling her the very story just recounted. She had dropped quite to the floor, hiding her face in her hands, and was saying between sobs, "I cannot go, Papa George; oh, Papa George, I cannot go!"

Just then 'Sieur George, having kept a good resolution all day, was encouraged by the orphan's pitiful tones to contemplate the most senseless act he ever attempted to commit. He said to the sobbing girl that she was not of his blood; that she was nothing to him by natural ties; that his covenant was with her grandsire to care for his offspring; and though it had been poorly kept, it might be breaking it worse than ever to turn her out upon ever so kind a world.

"I have tried to be good to you all these years. When I took you, a wee little baby, I took you for better or worse. I intended to do well by you all your childhood-days, and to do best at last. I thought surely we should be living well by this time, and you could choose from a world full of homes and a world full of friends.

"I don't see how I missed it!" Here he paused a moment in meditation, and presently resumed with some suddenness:

"I thought that education, far better than Mother Nativity has given you, should have afforded your sweet charms a noble setting; that good mothers and sisters would be wanting to count you into their families, and that the blossom of a happy womanhood would open perfect and full of sweetness.

"I would have given my life for it. I did give it, such as it was; but it was a very poor concern, I know—my life—and not enough to buy any good thing.

"I have had a thought of something, but I'm afraid to tell it. It didn't come to me to-day or yesterday; it has beset me a long time—for months."

The girl gazed into the embers, listening intensely.

"And oh! dearie, if I could only get you to think the same way, you might stay with me then."

"How long?" she asked, without stirring.

"Oh, as long as heaven should let us. But there is only one chance," he said, as it were feeling his way, "only one way for us to stay together. Do you understand me?"

She looked up at the old man with a glance of painful inquiry.

"If you could be—my wife, dearie?"

She uttered a low, distressful cry, and, gliding swiftly into her room, for the first time in her young life turned the key between them.

And the old man sat and wept.

Then Kookoo, peering through the keyhole, saw that they had been looking into the little trunk. The lid was up, but the back was toward the door, and he could see no more than if it had been closed.

He stooped and stared into the aperture until his dry old knees were ready to crack. It seemed as if 'Sieur George was stone, only stone couldn't weep like that.

Every separate bone in his neck was hot with pain. He would have given ten dollars—ten sweet dollars!—to have seen 'Sieur George get up and turn that trunk around.

There! 'Sieur George rose up—what a face!

He started toward the bed, and as he came to the trunk he paused, looked at it, muttered something about "ruin," and something about "fortune," kicked the lid down and threw himself across the bed.

Small profit to old Kookoo that he went to his own couch; sleep was not for the little landlord. For well-nigh half a century he had suspected his tenant of having a treasure hidden in his house,

and to-night he had heard his own admission that in the little trunk was a fortune. Kookoo had never felt so poor in all his days before. He felt a Creole's anger, too, that a tenant should be the holder of wealth while his landlord suffered poverty.

And he knew very well, too, did Kookoo, what the tenant would do. If he did not know what he kept in the trunk, he knew what he kept behind it, and he knew he would take enough of it to-night to make him sleep soundly.

No one would ever have supposed Kookoo capable of a crime. He was too fearfully impressed with the extra-hazardous risks of dishonesty; he was old, too, and weak, and, besides all, intensely a coward. Nevertheless, while it was yet two or three hours before daybreak, the sleep-forsaken little man arose, shuffled into his garments, and in his stocking-feet sought the corridor leading to 'Sieur George's apartment. The November night, as it often does in that region, had grown warm and clear; the stars were sparkling like diamonds pendent in the deep blue heavens, and at every window and lattice and cranny the broad, bright moon poured down its glittering beams upon the hoary-headed thief, as he crept along the mouldering galleries and down the ancient corridor that led to 'Sieur George's chamber.

'Sieur George's door, though ever so slowly opened, protested with a loud creak. The landlord, wet with cold sweat from head to foot, and shaking till the floor trembled, paused for several minutes, and then entered the moon-lit apartment. The tenant, lying as if he had not moved, was sleeping heavily. And now the poor coward trembled so, that to kneel before the trunk, without falling, he did not know how. Twice, thrice, he was near tumbling headlong. He became as cold as ice. But the sleeper stirred, and the thought of losing his opportunity strung his nerves up in an instant. He went softly down upon his knees, laid his hands upon the lid, lifted it, and let in the intense moonlight. The trunk was full, full, crowded down and running over full, of the tickets of the Havana Lottery!

A little after daybreak, Kookoo from his window saw the orphan, pausing on the corner. She stood for a moment, and then dove into the dense fog which had floated in from the river, and disappeared. He never saw her again.

But her Lord is taking care of her. Once only she has seen 'Sieur George. She had been in the belvedere of the house which she now calls home, looking down upon the outspread city. Far away southward and westward the great river glistened in the sunset. Along its sweeping bends the chimneys of a smoking commerce, the magazines of surplus wealth, the gardens of the opulent, the steeples of a hundred sanctuaries and thousands on thousands of mansions and hovels covered the fertile birthright arpents which 'Sieur George, in his fifty years' stay, had seen tricked away from dull colonial Esaus by their blue-eyed brethren of the North. Nearer by she looked upon the forlornly silent region of lowly dwellings, neglected by legislation and shunned by all lovers of comfort, that once had been the smiling fields of her own grandsire's broad plantation; and but a little way off, trudging across the marshy commons, her eye caught sight of 'Sieur George following the sunset out upon the prairies to find a night's rest in the high grass.

She turned at once, gathered the skirt of her pink calico uniform, and, watching her steps, through her tears, descended the steep winding-stair to her frequent kneeling-place under the fragrant candles of the chapel-altar in Mother Nativity's asylum.

'Sieur George is houseless. He cannot find the orphan. Mother Nativity seems to know nothing of her. If he could find her now, and could get from her the use of ten dollars for but three days, he knows a combination which would repair all the past; it could not fail, he—thinks. But he cannot find her, and the letters he writes—all containing the one scheme—disappear in the mail-box, and there's an end.

KATE CHOPIN (1851–1904)

Another writer for a long time dismissed as a purveyor of local color but who has recently come in for a revised estimate is Kate Chopin. (Chopin is pronounced in the French fashion exactly like the name of the composer.) She was born Kate O'Flaherty, in St. Louis, of Irish and French descent. In 1870 she married a Louisianian, Oscar Chopin, came to New Orleans, and later lived on a plantation near Nachitoches, Louisiana.

The Creoles of New Orleans kept up their connections with Paris, prided themselves on the quality of the French they spoke, and often sent their sons back to France to be educated. The Acadians (corrupted to "Cajuns") who came to Louisiana by way of Canada, lived in the prairie and bayou parishes (counties) west of New Orleans, spoke their own provincial French filled with dialect words from the seafaring provinces of France, and possessed the virtues of a sturdy and vigorous peasantry.

The rich farming country around Nachitoches had its share of Acadians, but there were also French-speaking people of more aristocratic pretensions, black slaves, and, as late-comers, mostly in the hills, some Anglo-Saxons. In addition to these, there were a good many "free men of color," descendants of white Creole fathers and mothers of Negro blood. The free men of color who had settled near Nachitoches had never been slaves. On land that had been given them by their fathers, they themselves became planters. Some of them even owned black slaves.

The two collections of short stories that Mrs. Chopin published in her lifetime are entitled *Bayou Folk* (1894) and *A Night in Acadie* (1897). Their titles suggest their subject matter. They amount to sketches, vignettes, sometimes pathetic, sometimes amusing, and are fairly described as instances of local color writing. The best of them, however, are much more than that. Mrs. Chopin is aware of problems of race and caste and treats them sympathetically, sometimes even poignantly. "Desiree's Baby" is the somber and pathetic story of a happily married couple whose first child shows unmistakable signs that one of its ancestors had Negro blood. Desiree's husband turns against both mother and child and the heart-broken young wife drowns herself and her infant in the near-by bayou. After their death, her husband proceeds to remove every object associated with his wife and infant: the child's crib, its layette, his wife's clothing, and all their love letters. But as he searches for those letters, he finds, stuck in the bottom of a drawer, a letter from his own mother in which she tells his father that she thanks God "that our dear Armand will never know that his mother, who adores him, belongs to a race that is cursed with the brand of slavery."

Such a story indicates that Kate Chopin was capable of using subject matter disturbing to the southerner and to the general American reading public of that period; but "Desiree's Baby" as a work of art is almost too "well made" in the patness of its ending, even if one overlooks the fact that Armand's parents could scarcely have allowed the fatal letter on which the ironic ending depends to have escaped the flames, years before.

Kate Chopin knew her French nineteenth-century authors well, and "Desiree's Baby" indicates how carefully she had studied the short stories of De Maupassant. What she learned from the style of Flaubert was, however, of more consequence to her art. In recent years thoughtful and sensitive readers have accorded high praise to her treatment of the social scene and especially of the theme of sexuality and married love.

By common consent her novel *The Awakening* (1899) is her masterpiece. The heroine has married a sensible businessman who treats her kindly but who has no special passion for her nor she for him. The title of the novel refers to her awakening to sexual passion and to a knowledge of her own deeper self. Romantic love eventually leads her into adultery, despair, and suicide.

The Awakening was much too bold for its time. Mrs. Chopin had difficulty in getting it published and was much hurt by the kind of reception that it got from reviewers and literary critics. By today's standards, it is anything but sensational. What gives the novel its distinction is the subtlety and finesse with which the author presents the psychological development of Mrs. Pontellier and the force and sustained power with which she reveals that development.

Some of these qualities are suggested—at least hinted at—in some of Mrs. Chopin's short stories, for example, "A Respectable Woman," which follows.

FURTHER READINGS

Per Seyersted, ed., *The Complete Works of Kate Chopin* (1969; 2 vols.)

George Arms, "Kate Chopin's *The Awakening* in the Perspective of Her Literary Career," *Essays in American Literature in Honor of J. B. Hubbell*, Clarence Gohdes, ed. (1967)

Daniel S. Rankin, *Kate Chopin and Her Creole Stories* (1932)

Edmund Wilson, *Patriotic Gore* (1962)

A Respectable Woman (1897)

Mrs. Baroda was a little provoked to learn that her husband expected his friend, Gouvernail, up to spend a week or two on the plantation.

They had entertained a good deal during the winter; much of the time had also been passed in New Orleans in various forms of mild dissipation.

She was looking forward to a period of unbroken rest, now, and undisturbed tête-à-tête with her husband, when he informed her that Gouvernail was coming up to stay a week or two.

This was a man she had heard much of but never seen. He had been her husband's college friend; was now a journalist, and in no sense a society man or "a man about town," which were, perhaps, some of the reasons she had never met him. But she had unconsciously formed an image of him in her mind. She pictured him tall, slim, cynical; with eye-glasses, and his hands in his pockets; and she did not like him. Gouvernail was slim enough, but he wasn't very tall nor very cynical; neither did he wear eye-glasses nor carry his hands in his pockets. And she rather liked him when he first presented himself.

But why she liked him she could not explain satisfactorily to herself when she partly attempted to do so. She could discover in him none of those brilliant and promising traits which Gaston, her husband, had often assured her that he possessed. On the contrary, he sat rather mute and receptive before her chatty eagerness to make him feel at home and in face of Gaston's frank and wordy hospitality. His manner was as courteous toward her as the most exacting woman could require; but he made no direct appeal to her approval or even esteem.

Once settled at the plantation he seemed to like to sit upon the wide portico in the shade of one of the big Corinthian pillars, smoking his cigar lazily and listening attentively to Gaston's experience as a sugar planter.

"This is what I call living," he would utter with deep satisfaction, as the air that swept across the sugar field caressed him with its warm and scented velvety touch. It pleased him also to get on familiar terms with the big dogs that came about him, rubbing themselves sociably against his legs. He did not care to fish, and displayed no eagerness to go out and kill grosbecs when Gaston proposed doing so.

Gouvernail's personality puzzled Mrs. Baroda, but she liked him. Indeed, he was a lovable, inoffensive fellow. After a few days, when she could understand him no better than at first, she gave over being puzzled and remained piqued. In this mood she left her husband and her guest, for the most part, alone together. Then finding that Gouvernail took no manner of exception to her action, she imposed her society upon him, accompanying him in his idle strolls to the mill and walks along the batture. She persistently sought to penetrate the reserve in which he had unconsciously enveloped himself.

"When is he going—your friend?" she one day asked her husband. "For my part, he tires me frightfully."

"Not for a week yet, dear. I can't understand; he gives you no trouble."

"No. I should like him better if he did; if he were more like others, and I had to plan somewhat for his comfort and enjoyment."

Gaston took his wife's pretty face between his hands and looked tenderly and laughingly into her troubled eyes. They were making a bit of toilet sociably together in Mrs. Baroda's dressing-room.

"You are full of surprises, ma belle," he said to her. "Even I can never count upon how you are going to act under given conditions." He kissed her and turned to fasten his cravat before the mirror.

"Here you are," he went on, "taking poor Gouvernail seriously and making a commotion over him, the last thing he would desire or expect."

"Commotion!" she hotly resented. "Nonsense! How can you say such a thing? Commotion, indeed! But, you know, you said he was clever."

"So he is. But the poor fellow is run down by overwork now. That's why I asked him here to take a rest."

"You used to say he was a man of ideas," she retorted, unconciliated. "I expected him to be interesting, at least. I'm going to the city in the morning to have my spring gowns fitted. Let me know when Mr. Gouvernail is gone; I shall be at my Aunt Octavie's."

That night she went and sat alone upon a bench that stood beneath a live oak tree at the edge of the gravel walk.

She had never known her thoughts or her intentions to be so confused. She could gather nothing from them but the feeling of a distinct necessity to quit her home in the morning.

Mrs. Baroda heard footsteps crunching the gravel; but could discern in the darkness only the approaching red point of a lighted cigar. She knew it was Gouvernail, for her husband did not smoke. She hoped to remain unnoticed, but her white gown revealed her to him. He threw away his cigar and seated himself upon the bench beside her; without a suspicion that she might object to his presence.

"Your husband told me to bring this to you, Mrs. Baroda," he said, handing her a filmy, white scarf with which she sometimes enveloped her head and shoulders. She accepted the scarf from him with a murmur of thanks, and let it lie in her lap.

He made some commonplace observation upon the baneful effect of the night air at that season. Then as his gaze reached out into the darkness, he murmured, half to himself:

" 'Night of south winds—night of the large few stars!
Still nodding night—' "

She made no reply to this apostrophe to the night, which indeed, was not addressed to her.

Gouvernail was in no sense a diffident man, for he was not a self-conscious one. His periods of reserve were not constitutional, but the result of moods. Sitting there beside Mrs. Baroda, his silence melted for the time.

He talked freely and intimately in a low, hesitating drawl that was not unpleasant to hear. He talked of the old college days when he and Gaston had been a good deal to each other; of the days of keen and blind ambitions and large intentions. Now there was left with him, at least, a philosophic acquiescence to the existing order—only a desire to be permitted to exist, with now and then a little whiff of genuine life, such as he was breathing now.

Her mind only vaguely grasped what he was saying. Her physical being was for the moment predominant. She was not thinking of his words, only drinking in the tones of his voice. She wanted to reach out her hand in the darkness and touch him with the sensitive tips of her fingers upon the face or the lips. She wanted to draw close to him and whisper against his cheek—she did not care what—as she might have done if she had not been a respectable woman.

The stronger the impulse grew to bring herself near him, the further, in fact, did she draw away from him. As soon as she could do so without an appearance of too great rudeness, she rose and left him there alone.

Before she reached the house, Gouvernail had lighted a fresh cigar and ended his apostrophe to the night.

Mrs. Baroda was greatly tempted that night to tell her husband—who was also her friend—of this folly that had seized her. But she did not yield to the temptation. Beside being a respectable woman she was a very sensible one; and she knew there are some battles in life which a human being must fight alone.

When Gaston arose in the morning, his wife had already departed. She had taken an early morning train to the city. She did not return till Gouvernail was gone from under her roof.

There was some talk of having him back during the summer that followed. That is, Gaston greatly desired it; but this desire yielded to his wife's strenuous opposition.

However, before the year ended, she proposed, wholly from herself, to have Gouvernail visit them again. Her husband was surprised and delighted with the suggestion coming from her.

"I am glad, chère amie, to know that you have finally overcome your dislike for him; truly he did not deserve it."

"Oh," she told him, laughingly, after pressing a long, tender kiss upon his lips, "I have overcome everything! you will see. This time I shall be very nice to him."

The reader may want to reflect on the significance of the title of this story and ask himself whether the heroine, in discovering an unexpectedly different Gouvernail, also discovers a side of herself of which she had been unaware. The last paragraph is rather subtly put. Obviously, her husband does not really know what his wife is talking about here and obviously she does not really want him to know.

Though both Cable and Mrs. Chopin were, as we have seen, much more than purveyors of local color, the French-speaking areas of Louisiana did exhibit an exotic and fascinating way of life. But other regions of the South, notably the southern highlands, Charleston ("a West Indian island anchored just off the coast of the United States"), and the South Carolina "low country" that surrounds Charleston, were sufficiently different from the rest of the country to be regarded as picturesque and quaint and thus prime material for local color sketches and fiction. William Fox, Jr., took as his setting for novels such as *The Little Shepherd of Kingdom Come* (1903) and *The Trail of the Lonesome Pine* (1908) the Cumberland mountain region of Kentucky, and the mountainous areas of the neighboring state of Tennessee provide the background for the stories and novels of Mary Noailles Murfree, who wrote under the pen name of Charles Egbert Craddock.

Local color literature that takes its rise in the southern mountains continues to the present day. One thinks of such twentieth-century titles as James Still's *River of Earth* (1940) and *On Troublesome Creek* (1941) or Jesse Stuart's *Head o' W-Hollow* (1936) and *Taps for Private Tussy* (1943). The bluegrass region of Kentucky provided the background for James Lane Allen's once popular novels such as *A Kentucky Cardinal* (1894) and *The Choir Invisible* (1897). As for Charleston and the low country of South Carolina, this subregion is reflected in twentieth-century fiction such as Julia Peterkin's *Black April* (1927) and *Scarlet Sister Mary* (1928) and in DuBose Heyward's *Porgy* (1925). But here local color fiction merges into another special category, fiction about the Negro—the Negro as exotic, interesting because of his differences, and written about from the outside. One ought to add, however, that with Miss Peterkin and Heyward the treatment is sensitive and highly sympathetic. Fiction about the Negro, the southern highlander, and the poor white has had its interest and a certain popularity for a long time and continues in full volume into the present.

As with local color literature, so with the literature about the southern hillman or the southern Negro: the question is whether the character is rendered honestly, with full dramatic sympathy, and without condescension. With the Negro in particular, the white author now makes it plain that he is not undertaking to speak for him or even—as William Faulkner was to put it—to presume that he understands what the black man thinks and feels. For literature that can confidently make that claim, we have had to wait—except for very special and sporadic instances—until the 1920's.

JOEL CHANDLER HARRIS (1848–1908)

An earlier and once very popular writer of fiction about the Negro is Joel Chandler Harris, the creator of Uncle Remus. Uncle Remus is a composite figure, made up of Harris's memories of his boyhood experiences on Turnwold plantation where as a poor boy, at the age of thirteen, he began work in the print shop and newspaper office. Uncle Remus enjoys a privileged place among the Negroes and among the white folks. He is a fountain of folklore and folk wisdom, entertaining the little boy who slips down to the cabin from the big house almost nightly to hear the wonderful stories of Brer B'ar, Brer Rabbit, Brer Fox, and the rest of the creatures.

In the stories told by Uncle Remus, and in those told by Daddy Jack (in the Gullah dialect), it is significant that the hero is usually that weak and defenseless creature, the rabbit. Analogues to the Uncle Remus stories have been found all over the world: in the folklore of the American Indian and in tales told by peasants of northern Europe, of Asia, and of various African peoples. In the European variants, the hero is the cunning fox, but the Negro slave, caught up in his own sense of helplessness, chose—perhaps unconsciously—for his representative a smaller and more helpless animal. Hence it is Brer Rabbit who usually triumphs over his foes, including Brer B'ar, Brer Wolf, and Brer Fox. Significantly perhaps, the critter that most often succeeds in outwitting Brer Rabbit is even less formidable, Brer Tarrypin.

Brer Rabbit is gay, mischievous, resourceful, and he never gives up hope. One could apply to him the heartfelt compliment that Faulkner was later to apply to the Negroes: "They endured." Brer Rabbit endures.[1] He is not the soft

---

[1] Yet the Uncle Remus stories (along with the romances of Thomas Nelson Page and James Lane Allen) may well have had the effect of making for a favorable

furry bunny of the Easter egg tradition. He is cunning and on occasion he can be cruel with a child's ferocity. He drops his enemies into pots of boiling water, sets fire to the bundles of hay that they are carrying on their shoulders, or induces them to stick their heads into tree holes, leaving them to get out as best they can.

In these stories, we are not dealing with the animal world at all, but with that of humanity in its full variety and complexity. Uncle Remus himself is something of a philosopher and through his beast fables he finds a means of making his commentary on the world of human nature, not excluding the world of white human nature.[2] One remembers that, according to tradition, the first of the great tellers of such stories, Aesop the Phrygian, was also a slave.

In spite of Harris's occasional references to this "Uncle Remus trash," and other such self-disparagements, the stories are in the best sense "artistic" productions. They were very carefully worked and reworked, one of them at least sixteen times.[3] Though most of these stories

---

alteration of the northern view of the defeated South and thus promoting the notion that, after all, the South knew best how to deal with the Negro problem and should be allowed a free hand in making its own kind of settlement. Paul H. Buck makes this point in his *Road to Reunion* (1937), and Louis D. Rubin, in *The Writer in the South* (1972), says that "in the eyes of the nation the image of Uncle Remus replaced that of Uncle Tom." Rubin concedes that such may not have been the effect that "Harris consciously intended; it may not even be what the stories themselves say if read by a discerning modern critic; but it was what they were taken to mean." What *undiscerning* readers of the post–Civil War period took the Uncle Remus stories to mean is, of course, part of the historical record and requires noting here. Literary works do have social effects—oftentimes unintended effects.

[2] It might be noted in passing that a strong vein of primitivism in our culture disposes us to accept with delight stories that seem to come out of a simpler, more direct, and childlike world. Several decades ago Roark Bradford's retelling of Biblical stories in Negro dialect (*Ol' Man Adam an' His Chillun*, 1928) enjoyed an immense success and, as tailored into a play by Marc Connelly in 1930, became a Broadway hit. One of the latest manifestations of this appetite for the naive and primitive (as more sincere and authentic) is the vogue for "folk songs."

[3] See Jay Martin, *Harvests of Change* (1967), p. 96.

---

ultimately come from the Negro, either as directly told to Harris as a boy or supplied to him later by friends and acquaintances, they are not simply bits of folklore jotted down. They are carefully and lovingly shaped.

Allen Tate, many years ago, pointed out that one of the handicaps to the southern white man as a literary artist was that only rarely could he see himself in the Negro and thus he could not receive the necessary nourishment from the black peasantry from whom he was too thoroughly cut off. Any literature needs to be fed from the people; and whereas southern writers living in upland sections frequently did find an imaginative resource in the life of the yeoman whites and the hill folk, too often the writer in the Deep South was almost entirely cut off from it. Harris's mode of access was special and limited, but authentic. He was enabled to push past the conventions and disguises that human beings usually wear into a world of primitive and archetypal patterns of behavior which transcend creed, class, and color.

Perhaps Harris, more than most men, stood in need of material derived from the folk, for he had identified himself with the policies of the New South, of whom a fellow editor of the Atlanta *Constitution*, Henry W. Grady, was to become the high priest and fugleman. Harris was well aware that he contained two different selves: the respectable editor, rational, sensible, and dedicated to progress (which depended on reconciliation with the industrial North), and the other self whom he called "that other fellow" and who wrote the beast fables.

Though Uncle Remus is usually dismissed as a stereotype of the old-fashioned "darky," he has a personality of his own and his attitude toward the white folks is more complicated than a careless reading would suggest. But in any case, Harris was aware of other kinds of Negroes and other kinds of relationships of the Negro to his master or to his employer. Harris writes also about cruel masters and mistreated slaves. In "Free Joe and the Rest of the World," we are told how a manumitted Negro's wife, herself still a slave, is deliberately sold away from the community and parted from her husband forever by her hard-hearted master simply because he resents the fact that Joe is a free Negro and can come and go as he likes.

One of Harris's most remarkable stories, in conception at least, is that called "Where's Duncan?" a terrible story of a white man's having begotten a child of one of his slaves. The father at first treats the boy Duncan kindly and sees that he gets an education, but later something causes him to explode in fury at his son and he sells him to a slave dealer. When the reader is first introduced to the son, the Civil War is over and Duncan, now a man, passes for white. (The secret of Duncan's origins and early life are revealed only late in the story.) "Where's Duncan?" ends with a scene that is more than "Faulknerian." In the dining room of a plantation house, the roof of which is now ablaze and ready to fall in, the horrified narrator of the story sees a mulatto woman, brandishing a carving knife, about to assault the man whose servant she is while Duncan, the son of the pair, sits in a chair and eggs her on. With the sudden collapse of the burning roof, father, mother, and son perish in the flames.

In the light of stories like "Where's Duncan?" it is obviously unjust to say that Harris was willing to permit himself a view of only happy, subservient slaves, or, after emancipation, of only happy house servants like Uncle Remus, petted and spoiled by the people for whom they work. Harris evidently knew another side of the South; but the terrible and the tragic were outside his range. ("Where's Duncan?," for example, is not a successful story.) Harris's genius was comic or gently satiric. It is in such stories as those that Uncle Remus tells to the little boy that Harris realizes his characteristic gifts, though some of his other stories are not negligible, whether they be about mountain whites as in the story entitled "At Teague Poteet's," or about the pathetic freedman, as in "Free Joe and the Rest of the World."

FURTHER READINGS

Stella B. Brookes, *Joel Chandler Harris: Folklorist* (1950)
Paul M. Cousins, *Joel Chandler Harris: A Biography* (1968)
Julia F. C. Harris, *The Life and Letters of Joel Chandler Harris* (1918)

Darwin T. Turner, "Daddy Joel Harris and His Old-Time Darkies," *Southern Literary Journal* (1968)
Robert L. Wiggins, *The Life of Joel Chandler Harris* (1918)

Mr. Terrapin Shows His Strength (1880)

"Brer Tarrypin wuz de out'nes' man," said Uncle Remus, rubbing his hands together contemplatively, and chuckling to himself in a very significant manner; "he wuz de out'nes' man er de whole gang. He wuz dat."

The little boy sat perfectly quiet, betraying no impatience when Uncle Remus paused to hunt, first in one pocket and then in another, for enough crumbs of tobacco to replenish his pipe. Presently the old man proceeded:

"One night Miss Meadows en de gals dey gun a candy-pullin', en so many er de neighbors come in 'sponse ter de invite dat dey hatter put de 'lasses in de wash pot en buil' der fier in de yard. Brer B'ar, he holp Miss Meadows bring de wood, Brer Fox, he men' de fier, Brer Wolf, he kep' de dogs off, Brer Rabbit, he grease de bottom er de plates fer ter keep de candy fum stickin', en Brer Tarrypin, he klum up in a cheer, en say he'd watch en see dat de 'lasses didn't bile over. Dey wuz all dere, en dey weren't cuttin' up no didoes, nudder, kaze Miss Meadows, she done put her foot down, she did, en say dat w'en dey come ter her place dey hatter hang up a flag er truce at de front gate en 'bide by it.

"Well, den, w'iles dey wuz all a settin' dar en de 'lasses wuz a bilin' en a blubberin', dey got ter runnin' on talkin' mighty biggity. Brer Rabbit, he say he de swiffes'; but Brer Tarrypin, he rock 'long in de cheer en watch de 'lasses. Brer Fox, he say he de sharpes', but Brer Tarrypin he rock 'long. Brer Wolf, he say he de mos' suvvigus, but Brer Tarrypin, he rock en he rock 'long. Brer B'ar, he say he de mos' stronges', but Brer Tarrypin he rock, en he keep on rockin'. Bimeby he sorter shet one eye, en say, sezee:

"'Hit look like 'periently dat de ole hardshell ain't nowhars 'longside er dis crowd, yit yer I is, en I'm de same man w'at show Brer Rabbit dat he ain't de swiffes'; en I'm de same man w'at kin show Brer B'ar dat he ain't de stronges',' sezee.

"Den dey all laugh en holler, kaze it look like Brer B'ar mo' stronger dan a steer. Bimeby, Miss Meadows, she up'n ax, she did, how he gwine do it.

"'Gimme a good strong rope,' sez Brer Tarrypin, sezee, 'en lemme git in er puddle er water, en den let Brer B'ar see ef he kin pull me out,' sezee.

"Den dey all laugh 'gin, en Brer B'ar, he ups en sez, sezee: 'We ain't got no rope,' sezee.

"'No,' sez Brer Tarrypin, sezee, 'en needer is you got de strenk,' sezee, en den Brer Tarrypin, he rock en rock 'long, en watch de 'lasses a bilin' en a blubberin'.

"After w'ile Miss Meadows, she up en say, she did, dat she'd take'n loan de young men her bed-cord, en w'iles de candy wuz a coolin' in de plates, dey could all go ter de branch en see Brer Tarrypin kyar out his projick. Brer Tarrypin," continued Uncle Remus, in a tone at once confidential and argumentative, "weren't much bigger'n de pa'm er my han', en it look mighty funny fer ter year 'im braggin' 'bout how he kin out-pull Brer B'ar. But dey got de bed-cord atter w'ile, en den dey all put out ter de branch. W'en Brer Tarrypin fin' de place he wanter, he tuck one een' er de bed-cord, en gun de yuther een' to Brer B'ar.

"'Now den, ladies en gents,' sez Brer Tarrypin, sezee, 'you all go wid Brer B'ar up dar in de woods en I'll stay yer, en w'en you year me holler, den's de time fer Brer B'ar fer ter see ef he kin haul in de slack er de rope. You all take keer er dat ar een',' sezee, 'en I'll take keer er dish yer een',' sezee.

"Den dey all put out en lef' Brer Tarrypin at de branch, en w'en dey got good en gone, he dove down inter de water, he did, en tie de bed-cord hard en fas' ter wunner deze yer big clay-roots, en den he riz up en gin a whoop.

"Brer B'ar he wrop de bed-cord roun' his han', en wink at de gals, en wid dat he gin a big juk, but Brer Tarrypin ain't budge. Den he take bof han's en gin a big pull, but, all de same, Brer Tarrypin ain't budge. Den he tu'n 'roun', he did, en put de rope cross his shoulders en try ter walk off wid Brer Tarrypin, but Brer Tarrypin look like he don't feel like walkin'. Den Brer Wolf he put in en hope Brer B'ar pull, but des like he didn't, en den dey all hope 'im, en, bless gracious! w'iles dey wuz all a pullin', Brer Tarrypin, he holler, en ax um w'y dey don't take up de slack. Den w'en Brer Tarrypin feel um quit pullin',' he dove down, he did, en ontie de rope, en by de time dey got ter de branch, Brer Tarrypin, he wuz settin' in de aidge er de water des ez natchul ez de nex' un, en he up'n say, sezee:

"'Dat las' pull er yone wuz a mighty stiff un, en a leetle mo'n you'd er had me,' sezee. 'You er monstus stout, Brer B'ar,' sezee, 'en you pulls like a yoke er steers, but I sorter had de purchis on you,' sezee.

"Den Brer B'ar, bein's his mouf 'gun ter water atter de sweet'nin', he up'n say he speck de candy's ripe, en off dey put atter it!"

"It's a wonder," said the little boy, after a while, "that the rope didn't break."

"Break who?" exclaimed Uncle Remus, with a touch of indignation in his tone—"break who? In dem days, Miss Meadows's bed-cord would a hilt a mule."

This put an end to whatever doubts the child might have entertained.

Brother Rabbit Has Fun at the Ferry (1892)

One night when the little boy ran out to Uncle Remus's house, he heard the old man talking with some of the other Negroes about an accident at Armour's Ferry. The flat, as the ferry-boat was called, had broken the rope which was used to tow it across the Oconee, and had drifted down the river. Two mules, hitched to a wagon, jumped overboard and were drowned.

"Ah, Lord," exclaimed Uncle Remus, when the Negroes had gone. "Ef ole Brer B'ar had been de fe'yman, I lay dey wouldn't er been none er dat kinder gwines on."

"Uncle Johnny Roach is the ferryman now," remarked the little boy, by way of saying something.

"Dat man is ole, mon," said Uncle Remus; "he ole en shaky. He bin dar I dunner how long. He gray en trimbly. 'Twa'n't dat away wid Brer B'ar. He wuz young, en he ain't had a gray ha'r in his head. Folks use ter come 'long dat away, en gi' 'im a sev'mpunce des ter see 'im r'ar back on his footses en snatch dat ar flat 'cross de river. I tell you, mon, dem wuz gay times."

Here Uncle Remus paused, and looked steadily into the fireplace, and sighed. The impression he left on the little boy was that he himself had crossed on the ferry while Brother Bear was in charge. But where was the story? The youngster looked at the old man intently, and waited patiently.

"Brer B'ar wuz a mighty fine fe'yman," said Uncle Remus, after a while, taking off his spectacles and rubbing them gently on his knee. "Dey ain't no two ways 'bout dat. But dey wuz one time when he got outdone. I dunner what time er de day, ner what dey er de mont', but 'twas somers 'twixt two sun-ups. Brer B'ar wuz settin' in de shade, wishin' dat some un' ud come long en drap a sev'mpunce in his pocket. He wuz des 'bout ter doze off when he hear somebody holler.

"Man 'cross de river say, 'Hello!'"

"Brer B'ar raise up en 'low, 'How you like fer somebody ter call you Hello?'"

"Man holler back, 'Come put me 'cross.'"

"Brer B'ar 'spon', 'Ah-yi.'"

"De man wuz ridin' a gray mar', en de mar' had a gray colt wid 'er. Brer B'ar swung de flat on t'er side, en whiles she wuz a-swingin' he 'uz countin' his money.

"Oh, de rope is long, ketch a holt, ketch a holt,
  Oh, de rope is long, ketch a holt—
A dime fer de mar', a dime fer de man,
  En a thrip fer de little gray colt."

"De flat she swung 'roun', en Brer B'ar he sung out, 'Ride in, mister, en make yo'se'f at home.'"

"Right den en dar," continued Uncle Remus, leaning back in his chair and lifting his eyebrows, "right den en dar de trouble begun. Nobody wa'n't ter blame; nobody wa'n't de 'casion un it. Hit des come up dry so, des like de measles did when you had um."

"What trouble was it, Uncle Remus?" the little boy asked.

"Hit des broke out by hit's own 'lonese'f," responded the old man, solemnly. "De man, he cluck ter de mar', en try fer ter ride 'er in de flat, but de mar' she hilt er head down en sorter snort, en 'fuse ter budge. De man try ter coax 'er, but she won't be coaxed. Den he gi' 'er whip en spur, but she whirl 'roun' en 'fuse ter go in de flat. She'd go up, she'd go down, she'd go anywhar en eve'ywhar ceppin' in de flat. Den de man lit en tried ter lead 'er, but de mar' drug 'im 'bout over de san' like he ain't weigh mo'n two poun' en a half. Brer B'ar try ter he'p, but 'tain't do no good. De colt seed dat his mammy wuz skeer'd, en he 'gun ter whicker en squeal en run 'roun' like a pig wid hot dish-water on his back. Dis make a bad matter wuss.

"Dar dey stood. De man, he study, en Brer B'ar, he study, but 'tain't do no good. Bimeby Brer B'ar look 'roun', en who should he see settin' cross-legged on a stump a-watchin' un um, but ole Brer Rabbit? Dar he wuz, des ez natchul ez one er deze yer dagarrytypes. Fum whar he stood Brer B'ar couldn't tell whedder Brer Rabbit wuz laughin' er whedder he wuz cryin', but his face wuz mighty wrinkled up. Brer B'ar call 'im, but Brer Rabbit shuck his head. Brer B'ar ax 'im ter come he'p 'im git de mar' on de flat, but Brer Rabbit shuck his head. Brer B'ar wuz 'bout ter 'buze Brer Rabbit 'fo' comp'ny, but a n'er notion struck 'im, en he tuck en wobbled off ter whar Brer Rabbit wuz settin'. Time he got whar dey could hold er confab, Brer Rabbit 'low:

"'What de name er goodness is you all tryin' ter do down dar? What kinder capers is you cuttin' up? I bin settin' here watchin' you, en des dyin' er laughin' at de way you en de man en dem creeturs been gwine on.'

"Brer B'ar try ter 'splain, but Brer Rabbit keep a-talkin':

"'Go on back down dar, Brer B'ar, an fool 'roun' wid um some mo'. Fer gracious sake lemme have my fun out! Go on, Brer B'ar—go on! Whiles I'm a settin' here chawin' my terbacker, lemme 'joy myse'f, en git de wuth er my holiday. Go joon 'roun' some mo'!'

"Den Brer B'ar up'n tell Brer Rabbit what de matter is, en Brer Rabbit laugh en holler fit ter kill hisse'f. He low: 'My goodness, Brer B'ar, I had de idee dat you all been cuttin' up dem capers a-purpose.'

"Brer B'ar 'low: 'No, bless gracious! Dat man

yonder want ter be put 'cross. He des bleedzd ter be put 'cross, but how I gwine do it, I'll never tell you.'

"Brer Rabbit say, sezee: 'Well, Brer B'ar, ef you let dat bodder you mo'n a minnit, you'll make me b'lieve dat you got dropsy er de head. I hear tell dat lots er folks is gittin' down wid dat kinder sickness.'

"Den Brer B'ar say he speck he got it, kaze he can't make no 'rangement fer ter git dat ole mar' on de flat. Brer Rabbit look at 'im right hard, en sorter wrinkle up his face. He 'low, sezee:

"'Brer B'ar, hit des ez easy ez gwine ter sleep in a swing.'

"Brer B'ar say, sezee: 'Brer Rabbit, how I gwine do! Ef you'll tell me dat, I'll do anything you ax me; you can't ax me nothin' I won't do.'

"Brer Rabbit 'low, sezee: 'Well den, Brer B'ar, all you got ter do is ter shove de colt on de flat, en de mammy'll foller right atter.'

"Old Brer B'ar went a-wobblin' back ter de river, en when he got dar he driv de colt on de flat, en de mar' follered atter, same ez ef she'd a been born en raise on a flat. When Brer B'ar see dat, he 'low, 'Well!'

"De man ax 'im who tol' 'im how ter do dat. Brer B'ar make answer dat 'twuz Brer Rabbit, en den he went on to tell de man 'bout what er soon creetur Brer Rabbit is, dat nobody can't fool 'im, en nobody can't outdo 'im. De man lissen, an den he 'low dat he comin' back dat away in a day er two, en he bet a pot er honey ag'in' a dish er cream dat he kin outdo Brer Rabbit. Brer B'ar tuck de bet, en den dey shuck han's ter make it mo' bindin'.

"Well, 'twa'n't long atter 'fo' here come de man back, en dis time he had two mar's. He wuz ridin one, en leadin' de udder, en dey wuz bofe des ez much alike ez two peas. Dey wuz de same color, de same size, en de same gait. Brer B'ar tuck de man 'cross on t'er side, en den he say dat now is de time fer ter settle de bet. He 'low sezee:

"'One er deze mar's is de mammy, en de udder one is de colt. Now call up Brer Rabbit, en ax 'im ter tell me which is which, en which is de udder. Ax 'im ter tell me which is de mammy, en which is de colt. En he ain't got ter look in der mouf nudder.'

"Brer B'ar look at um mighty close, en den he shake his head.

"Man say, 'Go fetch me my dish er cream.'

"Brer B'ar look, en look, en still he shake his head.

"Man say, 'Go fetch my dish er cream.'

"Brer B'ar feel mighty bad, kaze he smell de pot er honey in de man's saddle-bags, en it make his mouf water.

"Man keep on sayin', 'Go fetch my dish er cream.'

"But Brer B'ar ain't gwine ter give up dat away. He done made de 'rangement fer ter call Brer Rabbit when de man come back, en he went 'pon top er de hill en holler fer 'im. I tell you now, 'twa'n't long 'fo' Brer Rabbit hove in sight. He come a-hoppin' en a-jumpin', he come a-rippin' en a-rarin'.

"Brer B'ar 'low, sezee: 'Ef you know'd what you got ter do, I lay you wouldn't be in sech a hurry.'

"Den he up'n tell Brer Rabbit de whole circumstance er de case. Brer Rabbit laugh, but Brer B'ar he look sollumcolly. Brer Rabbit tuck'n tol' Brer B'ar fer ter git two bunches er grass en put um dar front er de mar's. Brer B'ar do des like Brer Rabbit tell 'im, en den de mar's sot in ter eatin'; but one un um eat 'er bunch fust, en start ter eatin' on t'er bunch. Den de mar' what wuz eatin' on dat bunch helt up 'er head.

"Brer Rabbit 'low, sezee: 'Dat un what holdin' up 'er head, she de mammy.'

"De man he give up. He say dat beat his time, en den he ax Brer Rabbit how kin he tell.

"Brer Rabbit 'low, sezee: 'De colt, bein' ez she is de youngest, is got de bes' toofies. De best toofies eat de grass fust. Den when de mammy see de colt ain't got none, she willin' ter 'vide wid 'er. Ef de mammy had made at de colt's bundle, de colt'd sholy a bit at 'er.'

"De man look 'stonish, but he ain't sati'fied. He gun Brer B'ar de pot er honey, but he say he got n'er pot, en he willin' ter bet dat he kin fool Brer Rabbit nex' time. Brer B'ar tuck de bet.

"Den de man lef' his hosses dar, en tuck a little basket en went off in de woods. He wuz gone a right smart little whet, but bimeby, here he come back. He hilt de basket high, so Brer Rabbit can't see de inside, en den he hung it on a tree lim'. Den he ax Brer Rabbit what de basket got in it.

"Brer Rabbit study, en den he 'low, sezee: 'De sparrer kin tell you.'

"De man look at 'im hard, en den he say, sezee: 'What kinder creetur is you, nohow?'

"He tuck de basket down, he did, en sho nuff, dar wuz a sparrer in it. He gun Brer B'ar de t'er pot, en ez he wuz gwine, he holler back at Brer Rabbit, sezee:

"'You er one er deze yer graveyard rabbits, dat what you is.'

"Brer Rabbit laugh, but he ain't say nothin'. He des dip like it tas'e mighty good."

"Uncle Remus," said the little boy, as the old man paused, "how did Brother Rabbit know there was a sparrow in the basket?"

"Who say he know it, honey?"

"Didn't you say so?"

"Shoo, honey, freshun up yo' 'membunce.

When de man ax Brer Rabbit, What in dar? he make answer dat a sparrer kin tell 'im, kaze a sparrer flyin' 'roun' kin see what in de basket."

"Well," said the little boy, with a sigh, "I thought Brother Rabbit knew."

"Luck tol' 'im, honey; Brer Rabbit wuz a mighty man fer luck."

SIDNEY LANIER (1842–1881)

The difficulties and frustrations suffered by the southern writer of the Reconstruction period are easily illustrated from the life of Sidney Lanier. Instead of being able to go to Germany for postgraduate study as he had planned, he served in the Confederate army until captured and was held prisoner at Point Lookout for four months. His confinement injured his health permanently, and he died of tuberculosis in his fortieth year.

From the beginning, music and letters were Lanier's prime interests, but in the postwar South a literary career was more difficult than it had ever been, and Lanier had to eke out a living for himself and his family by lecturing, playing the flute in a symphony orchestra in Baltimore, and doing such hack work as adaptations for boys of Percy's *Reliques of Ancient English Poetry*, or Malory's *Morte d'Arthur*.

Lanier began his literary career with a curious hodge-podge of a novel, *Tiger Lilies*, published in 1867. It has a strained and melodramatic plot and is filled with swatches of transcendentalism borrowed from Emerson and German writers like Jean Paul Richter and Novalis. *Tiger Lilies* tells us a great deal about Lanier's reading, his aspirations, and the excitement stirred in him by transcendentalism. *Tiger Lilies* also provides an early expression of Lanier's major theme: the stultifying and degrading philosophy of the counting house. The commercial spirit—Lanier usually prefers the word "Trade"—threatens all

that is chivalric and idealistic. Years later, Lanier was to write to a friend:

The peasants learned . . . that a man who could not be a lord by birth, might be one by wealth, & so Trade arose & overthrew Chivalry. Trade has now had possession of the civilized world for four hundred years; it controls all things, it interprets the Bible, it guides our national & almost all our individual life with its maxims; & its oppressions upon the moral existence of man have come to be ten thousand times more grievous than the worst tyrannies of the Feudal System ever were. Thus in the reversals of time, it is *now* the *Gentleman* who must arise & overthrow Trade.

Perhaps this view of the history of Western civilization found the readier acceptance by Lanier because he was a southerner. In certain respects southern culture had made a remarkable regression toward the Middle Ages: it was basically an agricultural society with few cities and had, in black chattel slavery, a thoroughgoing serfdom. It could actually produce a warrior bishop, General Leonidas Polk, Protestant Episcopal bishop of Louisiana, who commanded an army and was killed in action. In England one would have to go back to the Middle Ages to find a like case.

Yet Lanier does not seem to have regarded the war in which he had fought as a struggle between commerce and agriculture (though in one of his letters he does make "Trade" responsible for "hatching" John Brown and adds that Trade "broke the saintly heart of Robert Lee"). In any case, his concept of chivalry as expressed in his writing was quite "literary" and may well have been derived—as Mark Twain thought most such southern notions were derived—from a too fervent reading of Sir Walter Scott and other Romantic authors. Lanier resembles some Victorian men of letters on the other side of the Atlantic and in the northern states who were troubled by the crassness and greed of an increasingly materialistic society and who were haunted by dreams of a roseate medievalism in which the ideals of chivalry tended to define themselves in stained glass attitudes.[1] In any case, Lanier was not a very effective crusader against Trade. To make a dent in the case-hardened Gilded Age one needed a blade of harder metal than Lanier possessed.[2] Satire might draw blood; a rather confused lyricism had no power to sting.

Just three years after Mark Twain and Charles Dudley Warner published the book that gave the Gilded Age its name, the United States celebrated the first century of its independence. A Centennial Committee was appointed to arrange for appropriate ceremonies to be held in Philadelphia on May 10, 1876.

[1] In the North as well as in the South there was much idealization of the Middle Ages, some of it extravagant. See the introduction to the period 1861–1914. See also Twain's *A Connecticut Yankee in King Arthur's Court.* As we have noted earlier, Twain twitted the South for worshiping Sir Walter Scott's romantic account of medieval chivalry. It is an irony of history that Scott also influenced—through his grim Convenantic characters—the militant abolitionists of New England: for example, the Secret Six who backed John Brown's attempt to organize a slave insurrection in the South. See J. C. Furnos, *The Road to Harpers Ferry.*

[2] Jay Martin (*Harvests of Change,* pp. 93–95) gives Lanier high marks, however, for his attack on pitiless competition and claims that in "The Symphony" (published in 1875) Lanier anticipated by nearly ten years Lester Ward's criticism of the business ethic in *Dynamic Sociology* (1884); and that he also anticipated Thorstein Veblen's attack on a "life of self-seeking force, fraud, and mastery."

There were to be speeches, including one by President Grant, and a hymn, an ode, and a cantata, all to be written especially for the occasion. Lanier was commissioned to supply the words for the cantata. He interpreted this deliberate choice of a southern poet as a gesture toward the reconciliation of the sections so lately torn apart by civil war and he responded in kind. It might even appear that in his eagerness to be reconciled, he overreacted here and in "The Psalm of the West," which the editor of *Lippincott's Magazine* asked him to write as the special feature of its July, 1876, number. Lanier brings into his poem the voyages of the Norsemen, Columbus's celebrated landfall, and the arrival of the Mayflower on these shores, but he makes no mention of the settlement of Virginia. The Battle of Lexington and the signing of the Declaration of Independence get, as the occasion demanded, full attention. But the Civil War, in which Lanier and many of those who heard the cantata and read "The Psalm" had fought, is treated not in realistic but allegorical terms. The bloody war becomes a knightly tournament out of the Middle Ages in which the combatants are Heart and Brain. The poet adjures them to cease their strife:

> Heart and Brain! no more be twain;
> Throb and think, one flesh again!
> Lo! they weep, they turn, they run;
> Lo! they kiss; Love, thou art one!

Either as an interpretation of history or of the realities of the time at which he wrote, this quatrain is almost fatuously beside the point.

Lanier's crippling defect, however, lies not in the quality of his ideas but in his misconceptions about the very nature of poetry. He tries much too hard to make his poetry obviously "musical," and thus reveals his confusion as to what constitutes the true music of poetry. Moreover, he either lacked a proper conception of literary "tone," or if he had it, singularly failed to solve the problems of tone in his own work. His poetry tends to be not a true synthesis of thought and emotion, but an uneasy mixture, with the two ingredients always threatening to separate out into preachiness and sentimentality, didacticism and undisciplined emotion.

These probably seem harsh judgments, but one can illustrate specifically what is meant from Lanier's poem "Corn," first published in 1875. The poem will exhibit the typical strengths as well as weaknesses of Lanier's poetry.

FURTHER READINGS

Charles R. Anderson, ed., *The Centennial Edition of the Works of Sidney Lanier* (1945; 10 vols.)

Gay Wilson Allen, *American Prosody* (1935)

Edd Winfield Parks, *Sidney Lanier: The Man, the Poet, the Critic* (1968)

Aubrey H. Starke, *Sidney Lanier: A Biographical and Critical Study* (1933)

Corn (1875)

To-day the woods are trembling through and
    through
With shimmering forms, that flash before my view,
Then melt in green as dawn-stars melt in blue.
    The leaves that wave against my cheek caress
    Like women's hands; the embracing boughs express
        A subtlety of mighty tenderness;
    The copse-depths into little noises start,
    That sound anon like beatings of a heart,
    Anon like talk 'twixt lips not far apart.
    The beech dreams balm, as a dreamer hums a
      song;   10
    Through that vague wafture, expirations strong
    Throb from young hickories breathing deep and
      long
With stress and urgence bold of prisoned spring
      And ecstasy of burgeoning.
    Now, since the dew-plashed road of morn is dry,
    Forth venture odors of more quality
    And heavenlier giving. Like Jove's locks awry,
      Long muscadines
Rich-wreathe the spacious foreheads of great pines,
And breathe ambrosial passion from their
    vines.   20
    I pray with mosses, ferns and flowers shy
    That hide like gentle nuns from human eye
    To lift adoring perfumes to the sky.
I hear faint bridal-sighs of brown and green
Dying to silent hints of kisses keen
As far lights fringe into a pleasant sheen.
    I start at fragmentary whispers, blown
    From undertalks of leafy souls unknown,
    Vague purports sweet, of inarticulate tone.

Dreaming of gods, men, nuns and brides,
      between   30
Old companies of oaks that inward lean
To join their radiant amplitudes of green
    I slowly move, with ranging looks that pass
    Up from the matted miracles of grass
Into yon veined complex of space
Where sky and leafage interlace
    So close, the heaven of blue is seen
    Inwoven with a heaven of green.

I wander to the zigzag-corner fence
Where sassafras, intrenched in brambles
    dense,   40
Contests with stolid vehemence
    The march of culture, setting limb and thorn
    As pikes against the army of the corn.

There, while I pause, my fieldward-faring eyes
Take harvests, where the stately corn-ranks rise,
      Of inward dignities
And large benignities and insights wise,
      Graces and modest majesties.
Thus, without theft, I reap another's field;
Thus, without tilth, I house a wondrous
    yield,   50
And heap my heart with quintuple crops concealed.

Look, out of line one tall corn-captain stands
Advanced beyond the foremost of his bands,
    And waves his blades upon the very edge
    And hottest thicket of the battling hedge.
Thou lustrous stalk, that ne'er mayst walk nor talk,
    Still shalt thou type the poet-soul sublime
    That leads the vanward of his timid time
    And sings up cowards with commanding rhyme—

Soul calm, like thee, yet fain, like thee, to
    grow   60
By double increment, above, below;
    Soul homely, as thou art, yet rich in grace like
      thee,
    Teaching the yeomen selfless chivalry
    That moves in gentle curves of courtesy;
Soul filled like thy long veins with sweetness
    tense,
      By every godlike sense
Transmuted from the four wild elements.
      Drawn to high plans,
    Thou lift'st more stature than a mortal
      man's,
Yet ever piercest downward in the mould   70
    And keepest hold
    Upon the reverend and steadfast earth
      That gave thee birth;
    Yea, standest smiling in thy future grave,
      Serene and brave,
    With unremitting breath
    Inhaling life from death,
Thine epitaph writ fair in fruitage eloquent,
    Thyself thy monument.

        As poets should,   80
Thou hast built up thy hardihood
With universal food,
    Drawn in select proportion fair
    From honest mould and vagabond air;
From darkness of the dreadful night,
      And joyful light;
    From antique ashes, whose departed flame
    In thee has finer life and longer flame;
From wounds and balms,
From storms and calms,   90
From potsherds and dry bones
      And ruin-stones.
Into thy vigorous substance thou hast wrought
Whate'er the hand of Circumstance hath brought;
    Yea, into cool solacing green hast spun
    While radiance hot from out the sun.
So thou dost mutually leaven
Strength of earth with grace of heaven;
    So thou dost marry new and old
    Into a one of higher mould;   100
      So thou dost reconcile the hot and cold,
      The dark and bright,
And many a heart-perplexing opposite,
      And so,
    Akin by blood to high and low,
Fitly thou playest out thy poet's part,
Richly expending thy much-bruised heart

In equal care to nourish lord in hall,
      Or beast in stall:
    Thou took'st from all that thou mightst give to
    all.   110

O steadfast dweller on the selfsame spot
Where thou wast born, that still repinest not—
Type of the home-fond heart, the happy lot!—
    Deeply thy mild content rebukes the land
    Whose flimsy homes, built on the shifting sand
Of trade, for ever rise and fall
With alternation whimsical,
    Enduring scarce a day,
    Then swept away
By swift engulfments of incalculable tides   120
Whereon capricious Commerce rides.
Look, thou substantial spirit of content!
Across this little vale, thy continent,
    To where, beyond the mouldering mill,
    Yon old deserted Georgian hill
Bares to the sun his piteous aged crest
      And seamy breast,
    By restless-hearted children left to lie
    Untended there beneath the heedless sky,
    As barbarous folk expose their old to die.   130
Upon that generous-rounding side,
      With gullies scarified
    Where keen Neglect his lash hath plied,
Dwelt one I knew of old, who played at toil,
And gave to coquette Cotton soul and soil.
    Scorning the slow reward of patient grain,
    He sowed his heart with hopes of swifter gain,
    Then sat him down and waited for the rain.
He sailed in borrowed ships of usury—
A foolish Jason on a treacherous sea,   140
Seeking the Fleece and finding misery.
    Lulled by smooth-rippling loans, in idle trance
    He lay, content that unthrift Circumstance
    Should plough for him the stony field of Chance.
Yea, gathering crops whose worth no man might
    tell,
He staked his life on games of Buy-and-Sell,
And turned each field into a gambler's hell.
    Aye, as each year began,
    My farmer to the neighboring city ran;
Passed with a mournful anxious face   150
Into the banker's inner place;
Parleyed, excused, pleaded for longer grace;
    Railed at the drought, the worm, the rust, the
    grass;
    Protested ne'er again 'twould come to pass;
    With many an *oh* and *if* and *but alas*
Parried or swallowed searching questions rude,

And kissed the dust to soften Dives's mood.
At last, small loans by pledges great renewed,
   He issues smiling from the fatal door,
   And buys with lavish hand his yearly store   160
   Till his small borrowings will yield no more.
Aye, as each year declined,
With bitter heart and ever-brooding mind
He mourned his fate unkind.
   In dust, in rain, with might and main,
   He nursed his cotton, cursed his grain,
   Fretted for news that made him fret again,
Snatched at each telegram of Future Sale,
And thrilled with Bulls' or Bears' alternate wail—
In hope or fear alike for ever pale.   170
   And thus from year to year, through hope and
      fear,
   With many a curse and many a secret tear,
   Striving in vain his cloud of debt to clear,
      At last
He woke to find his foolish dreaming past,
   And all his best-of-life the easy prey
   Of squandering scamps and quacks that lined his
      way
      With vile array,
From rascal statesman down to petty knave;
Himself, at best, for all his bragging brave,   180
A gamester's catspaw and a banker's slave.
   Then, worn and gray, and sick with deep unrest,
   He fled away into the oblivious West,
      Unmourned, unblest.

Old hill! old hill! thou gashed and hairy Lear
Whom the divine Cordelia of the year,
E'en pitying Spring, will vainly strive to cheer—
   King, that no subject man nor beast may own,
   Discrowned, undaughtered and alone—
Yet shall the great God turn thy fate,   190
And bring thee back into thy monarch state
      And majesty immaculate.
   Lo, through hot waverings of the August morn,
   Thou givest from thy vasty sides forlorn
   Visions of golden treasuries of corn—
Ripe largesse lingering for some bolder heart
That manfully shall take thy part,
      And tend thee,
      And defend thee,
With antique sinew and with modern art.   200

Let us try to draw up a balance sheet of strengths and weaknesses in this poem. On the positive side, one would set down a healthy regionalism and even a certain realism. The poet is willing to call things as he sees them. He refers to native plants, to sassafras and hickory, and even uses slang, as in line 169, when he refers to the "bulls" and "bears" of the stock market. Telegrams were not considered "poetic" in 1875, but Lanier refers to them and calls them by name in line 168.

He is willing to try to find the poetic in the ordinary. The common American field grain has no august associations in English poetry. The "corn" of Keats and Shakespeare is wheat, but Lanier finds the field of maize beautiful and worthy of being celebrated for itself and for what it stirs in the imagination. There are a number of passages that show imaginative power. Consider lines 33–38:

   I slowly move, with ranging looks that pass
   Up from the matted miracles of grass
Into yon veined complex of space
Where sky and leafage interlace
   So close, the heaven of blue is seen
   Inwoven with a heaven of green.

Lanier's realism takes in the whole experience of the Georgia farmer, including the economic facts of his life. The poem attacks Trade but the attack is made relevant to his praise of the corn. Corn is good for man and beast. If prices fall, it can still be eaten. But to commit oneself to the cash crop of cotton is to put oneself at the mercy of the vagaries of the stock market. The presence of such a message—or of any message—won't necessarily make a poem a good one. But the implied exhortation to grow corn at least indicates that Lanier knows his subject and that his feet are on the ground, planted in the good Georgia earth.

Lanier is, to use Coleridge's distinction, a *fanciful* rather than an *imaginative* poet. All sorts of analogies occur to him: shy flowers make him think of gentle nuns (lines 21–22); the massed corn stalks look to him like an army, and the sassafras trees at the edge of the field are "intrenched in brambles," like Civil War infantrymen behind the zigzag rail fence (lines 39–43); a particularly tall stalk suggests to him the sublime "poet-soul" who "sings up cowards with commanding rhyme" (lines 52–59). But some of the resemblances are quite far-fetched. For example, cotton culture, against which the poem is a warning, is a frivolous "coquette" luring on the honest farmer to his doom (line 135), and the cotton farmer is thought of as a "foolish Jason" on a voyage to gain the golden fleece; as he sails, he is lulled, not by waves but by "smooth-rippling *loans*" (line 142). In the last stanza the poet fancies that an old hill, gullied out by intensive cotton-farming, is a King Lear, mistreated by his wicked daughters, and that spring, which pities even infertile land and seeks to clothe it with new verdure, is like Lear's good daughter, Cordelia.

Is it wrong for a poet to be ambitious with his comparisons and to risk making them complicated and sometimes startling? By no means. Some very great poets—one thinks of John Donne, for example, and the great Shakespeare himself—gamble with far-fetched comparisons. But it is not sufficient just to risk them: the successful poet must make them work—or convince his more thoughtful readers that most of them do work. In this poem some of the comparisons are successful, but the reader may well decide that a good many do not really pay their way.

Another problem besets the poet who makes use of fanciful comparisons: a special problem in the control of tone. Ingenious and bizarre analogies usually suggest a tone of playfulness. The poet seems not to be ultimately serious and if he wishes to use his apparently playful comparison in a serious context, the reader may be puzzled at how to take the passage, or may laugh at the poet rather than with him. The problem is not insoluble, but the careless poet or the poet who lacks a sure grip on the tonalities of language will probably come to grief. In this poem—one may add in many of his other poems—Lanier seems to lack a sense of humor altogether—or else to fail to modulate from seriousness to levity.

How seriously are we to take the "alternate wail" of the bulls and bears on the exchange floor? And if an ironic smile is appropriate here,

what is our proper attitude toward the fate of the duped farmer who, the poet tells us, has "fled away into the oblivious West,/Unmourned, unblest"?

What is the tone of voice in which the poet addresses the following words to the corn plant?

Fitly thou playest out thy poet's part,
Richly expending thy much-bruised heart
    In equal care to nourish lord in hall.
        Or beast in stall:
    Thou took'st from all that thou mightst give
    to all.

Reduced to plain English, the lines say: You are like the poet in taking from everything around you materials which you transform into nourishment for both high and low, man and beast, and which you dispense impartially and unselfishly, expending yourself in the process. "Much-bruised heart" must allude to the grinding of the corn kernels into meal. This is a pompous and highfalutin treatment of the corn and it renders the compliment to the poet overstated and sentimental.

Lanier asks too much of the corn plant and too much of his reader. It is a pleasant fancy for the poet to say that he "reaps" a "harvest" when he runs his glance over the field of corn—but what a remarkable harvest he gathers:

    Of inward dignities
    And large benignities and insights wise,
    Graces and modest majesties.

It is fine to have a poet's eye and a large imagination, but Lanier will leave many readers unconvinced by his vision.

Some of the faults in this poem, especially failures to choose the exact word and the use of inverted sentence structure and awkward grammar, come from Lanier's willingness to weaken sense in his grasping for effects of rhyme. The reader may see for himself how often it occurs in this poem.

"The Symphony," which draws upon Lanier's experience in the Baltimore symphony orchestra and which constitutes one of Lanier's most vigorous attacks on Trade, is perhaps his most celebrated poem. But the editors of this volume do not find it essentially better than "Corn" and perhaps less interesting as a poem.

Lanier wrote many lyrics, but they are often rather slight and wispy and not free of Lanier's characteristic faults. The most promising direction that he took in his writing was in dialect poetry, but none of these dialect poems really comes to much. Lanier's most finished and most substantial poem is "The Marshes of Glynn," written in 1878. The marshes take their name from Glynn county along the coast of which they lie. Lanier was thoroughly familiar with the region. The long lines of the poem probably reflect the influence of Whitman, whom Lanier had been reading early in 1878. Metrically, "The Marshes of Glynn" is one of Lanier's most interesting and successful poems.

The Marshes of Glynn (1878)

Glooms of the live-oaks, beautiful-braided
    and woven
With intricate shades of the vines that
    myriad-cloven
    Clamber the forks of the multiform
        boughs,—
        Emerald twilights,—
        Virginal shy lights,
Wrought of the leaves to allure to the whis-
    per of vows,
When lovers pace timidly down through the
    green colonnades
Of the dim sweet woods, of the dear dark
    woods,
    Of the heavenly woods and glades,
That run to the radiant marginal sand-beach
    within   10
    The wide sea-marshes of Glynn;—

Beautiful glooms, soft dusks in the noon-day
    fire,—
Wildwood privacies, closets of lone desire,
Chamber from chamber parted with wavering
    arras of leaves,—
Cells for the passionate pleasure of prayer to
    the soul that grieves,
Pure with a sense of the passing of saints
    through the wood,
Cool for the dutiful weighing of ill with
    good;—

O braided dusks of the oak and woven
    shades of the vine,
While the riotous noon-day sun of the June-
    day long did shine
Ye held me fast in your heart and I held you
    fast in mine;   20

But now when the noon is no more, and riot
    is rest,
And the sun is a-wait at the ponderous gate
    of the West,
And the slant yellow beam down the wood-
    aisle doth seem
Like a lane into heaven that leads from a
    dream,—
Ay, now, when my soul all day hath drunken
    the soul of the oak,
And my heart is at ease from men, and the
    wearisome sound of the stroke
    Of the scythe of time and the trowel of
        trade is low,
    And belief overmasters doubt, and I know
        that I know,
    And my spirit is grown to a lordly great
        compass within,
That the length and the breadth and the
    sweep of the marshes of Glynn   30
Will work me no fear like the fear they have
    wrought me of yore
When length was fatigue, and when breadth
    was but bitterness sore,
And when terror and shrinking and dreary
    unnamable pain
Drew over me out of the merciless miles of
    the plain,—

Oh, now, unafraid, I am fain to face
    The vast sweet visage of space.
To the edge of the wood I am drawn, I am
    drawn,
Where the gray beach glimmering runs, as a
    belt of dawn,
    For a mete and a mark

To the forest-dark:—
    So: 40
Affable live-oak, leaning low,—
Thus—with your favor—soft, with a reverent
    hand,
(Not lightly touching your person, Lord of
    the land!)
Bending your beauty aside, with a step I
    stand
On the firm-packed sand,
      Free
By a world of marsh that borders a world of
    sea.
   Sinuous southward and sinuous northward
    the shimmering band
  Of the sand-beach fastens the fringe of the
    marsh to the folds of the land.   50
Inward and outward to northward and south-
    ward the beachlines linger and curl
As a silver-wrought garment that clings to
    and follows the firm sweet limbs of
    a girl.
Vanishing, swerving, evermore curving again
    into sight,
Softly the sand-beach wavers away to a dim
    gray looping of light.
And what if behind me to westward the wall
    of the woods stands high?
The world lies east: how ample, the marsh
    and the sea and the sky!
A league and a league of marsh-grass, waist-
    high, broad in the blade,
Green, and all of a height, and unflecked
    with a light or a shade,
Stretch leisurely off, in a pleasant plain,
To the terminal blue of the main.   60

Oh, what is abroad in the marsh and the
    terminal sea?
  Somehow my soul seems suddenly free
From the weighing of fate and the sad dis-
    cussion of sin,
By the length and the breadth and the sweep
    of the marshes of Glynn.

Ye marshes, how candid and simple and
    nothing-withholding and free
Ye publish yourselves to the sky and offer
    yourselves to the sea!
Tolerant plains, that suffer the sea and the
    rains and the sun,
Ye spread and span like the catholic man
    who hath mightily won

God out of knowledge and good out of in-
    finite pain
And sight out of blindness and purity out of
    a stain.   70

As the marsh-hen secretly builds on the
    watery sod,
Behold I will build me a nest on the great-
    ness of God:
I will fly in the greatness of God as the
    marsh-hen flies
In the freedom that fills all the space 'twixt
    the marsh and the skies:
By so many roots as the marsh-grass sends in
    the sod
I will heartily lay me a-hold on the greatness
    of God:
Oh, like to the greatness of God is the great-
    ness within
The range of the marshes, the liberal marshes
    of Glynn.

And the sea lends large, as the marsh: lo, out
    of his plenty the sea
Pours fast: full soon the time of the flood-
    tide must be: 80
Look how the grace of the sea doth go
About and about through the intricate chan-
    nels that flow
    Here and there,
      Everywhere,
Till his waters have flooded the uttermost
    creeks and the low-lying lanes,
And the marsh is meshed with a million
    veins,
That like as with rosy and silvery essences
    flow
  In the rose-and-silver evening glow.
    Farewell, my lord Sun!
The creeks overflow: a thousand rivulets run   90
'Twixt the roots of the sod; the blades of the
    marsh-grass stir;
Passeth a hurrying sound of wings that west-
    ward whirr;
Passeth, and all is still; and the currents
    cease to run;
And the sea and the marsh are one.

How still the plains of the waters be!
The tide is in his ecstasy.
The tide is at his highest height:
    And it is night.

And now from the Vast of the Lord will the
    waters of sleep
Roll in on the souls of men,   100
But who will reveal to our waking ken
The forms that swim and the shapes that
    creep
        Under the waters of sleep?
And I would I could know what swimmeth
    below when the tide comes in
On the length and the breadth of the mar-
    vellous marshes of Glynn.

We do not have to depend exclusively on southern authors for fictional accounts of conditions in the South during and just after the Civil War. A number of northerners who came down with the federal armies wrote books that reflect their southern experiences. Three of these writers are particularly noteworthy.

John William De Forest, of Connecticut, served in the federal army in Louisiana and Virginia and after the war became head of the Freedman's Bureau in South Carolina. Thus, he had a firsthand knowledge of what was going on in the Reconstruction South. Of his various novels, *Miss Ravenel's Conversion from Secession to Loyalty* (1867) is the one most relevant to our concerns here.

De Forest's account of the South after 1865 is, as we would expect, colored by his own viewpoint. As Edmund Wilson puts it in *Patriotic Gore,* "The moral [of *Miss Ravenel's Conversion*] is very confident. De Forest never has any doubt of the correctness of the Northern position nor has he any real sympathy with Southerners." And Wilson goes on to say that De Forest's "moral judgments are typical of the complacency of the cockily victorious North."

Gordon Haight, however, in his edition of *Miss Ravenel's Conversion* (1955) sees matters otherwise. He writes that "De Forest understood the Southern as well as the Northern point of view and never made his characters good or bad according to which side they were on. He paid sincere tribute to the skill, courage, and honor of the Confederate soldiers.[1] . . . To him the War was more than a crusade to abolish slavery; it was a conflict of cultures springing from basic causes; neither side was blameless."

The attitude taken by Ambrose Bierce toward the South and toward the Civil War generally has already been mentioned. But it is worth reminding ourselves that he regarded the soldiers against whom he fought as heroic men and in his Civil War stories invariably writes very sympathetically about them. It is true that he had scant respect for the southern statesmen, those "political madmen who persuaded [the Confederate soldiers, whom Bierce calls "these blameless gentlemen"] to their doom." But the disillusioned Bierce was scarcely less savage toward the federal government (and toward the world ushered in by the war). For example, he declined a large sum in accumulated back pay with the words "When I hired out as an assassin for my country, that wasn't part of the contract."

One of the most interesting of the northern writers who produced fiction about the wartime and Reconstruction South is Albion W. Tourgée, who, like De Forest and Bierce, took part in some hard fighting, and, like Bierce, was wounded. Also like De Forest, Tourgée spent a good many years in the South during the Reconstruction period. Edmund Wilson, in *Patriotic Gore,* has written a fascinating account of Tourgée's personality and his writings. See pp. 2814–21 below.

We made the point earlier that most southern writers before the Civil War were celebrating a way of life rather than questioning it, and that consequently southern literature lacks an inner tension. It involves no internal conflict as, say, the work of Nathaniel Hawthorne does. In fairness, it should be observed that a good deal of northern literature also suffers from this lack: it too is self-confident or complacent or simply unaware of any alternative to its committed

[1] Daniel Aaron, in *The Unwritten Conflict,* would on this issue side with Haight. Note also Allen Tate's high opinion of the novel, 1173.

values. After all, there are never many Hawthornes or Melvilles anywhere in the world.
But in the South the great literature of self-
questioning was not to come until later—the
greatest, not until the twentieth century.[2]

Another way to put the problem is to say
that great poetry and great fiction are hardly
to be achieved unless the author is both an
"insider" and an "outsider"—that is, in some
real sense within the culture about which he
writes, fully conversant and even committed to
its values, and yet also capable of standing outside it—capable of achieving a certain detachment.

De Forest, Bierce, and Tourgée were obviously outsiders, but Bierce's general disenchantment with any institutions rendered him at
least neutral, and Tourgée's developing rapprochement with his former enemies made him
a kind of insider.

The problem of insiders like Cable, Chopin,
and Harris was just the converse: their problem
was to secure sufficient detachment. Cable,
aided by circumstances, in his best work did
achieve it to a surprising degree. He was born
outside the Creole society and so was detached
from the society he depicts in *The Grandissimes*. But his realization that the Creole views
on race were substantially the same as those of
his own Anglo-Saxon South tended to put him
into the position of an insider.

As for Mrs. Chopin: with regard to the Louisiana scene she was literally an outsider, though
not completely so. Her mother was of French
stock and her St. Louis family was Confederate
in its political leanings and Roman Catholic in
its religion. New Orleans and the Nachitoches
region were stimulating in their difference from
St. Louis, but not shockingly alien. Yet, it has
to be said that the real tension to be found in
her mature work is located in the pressure exerted by her native artistic honesty, sharpened
and reinforced by her reading of novelists like
Flaubert, against her Catholic and Victorian
conservative heritage.

[2] In this general connection, the reader is referred to
Allen Tate's essay, "A Southern Mode of the Imagination," which appears in our text.

Even Joel Chandler Harris was something
of an "outsider." If Turnwold plantation gave
him a favorable view of plantation life and if
later on he was to find himself a spokesman for
the new southern ruling class, he was not himself to the manor born.[3] Perhaps because he
grew up as a poor boy, somewhat outside the
pale, it was easier for him to establish a measure
of detachment from the life he tended to ideal-
ize.

So much for three case histories that illustrate
the importance, but also the difficulty, of the
southern writer's gaining the needed detachment from the culture in which he had lived
and moved and had his being. But even those
southern writers who failed to gain much perspective on their culture were not totally blind
to the issues. We have had too much talk of the
southern writer's being gripped beyond loosening by the dream of an idyllic past. Even one of
the worst offenders in this matter, Thomas Nelson Page, author of *In Ole Virginny* (1887)
and *The Old South* (1892), in his Reconstruction novel *Red Rock* (1898) has Dr. Cary, a
character treated sympathetically in the novel,
warn his friends of the folly of breaking up the
Union. "War is the most terrible of disasters,
except Dishonor," he tells them; and a little
later, after the secession of Virginia, which he
has opposed, he says: "We are at war now—
with the greatest power on earth: the power of
universal progress. It is not the North that we
shall have to fight, but the world. Go home and
make ready. If we have talked like fools, we
shall at least fight like men."

Even the patron of the young Joel Chandler

[3] The society of the antebellum South was much more
fluid than most Americans of our century realize. Men
of talent and spirit, though born in humble circumstances, were able to acquire land, move up the social
ladder, and take up positions of leadership. For example,
the great South Carolinian John C. Calhoun, the intellectual leader of the Old South, did not come from
Charleston or one of the plantations surrounding it, but
from a modest hill farm in the Piedmont; and Jefferson
Davis, of Mississippi, who was to become the President
of the Confederate States, was, like Abraham Lincoln,
born in a log cabin in Kentucky.

Harris, the benign master of Turnwold, who defended slavery in neoclassical couplets reminiscent of Alexander Pope, was no fire-eating secessionist. He opposed Georgia's secession up until the very end. There was more heart-burning and soul-searching in the antebellum South than a present-day reader is likely to suppose. But few southern writers saw the necessity for getting—or had the ability to get—it into their fiction or their poetry.

Black Literature:

From Reconstruction

to the Harlem Renaissance

The black writer James Weldon Johnson once said that the problem of race is not static, that the nature of the issue changes in time. In other words, this question, like all questions, has a context in history, and we can scarcely understand the role of any participant, black or white, in the great and continuing drama of racial conflict if we do not understand, to some degree, the world in which the participant lived and the options open to him. This is not to say that all values are relative, but it is to say that all values are not equally available in a given historical moment. But we must realize, too, on the other side of the question, that a "given historical moment" is not merely something that happens to happen; it comes to pass, in some degree (though to what degree we can never be sure) through the decisions and acts of men. This would imply that the defeated struggle for a value unavailable at a particular moment may have its effect in creating a later moment more favorable for the emergence of that value.

The world of the American South into which the black slave was freed by the surrender at Appomattox was one of physical ruin, financial bankruptcy, and sometimes starvation—except for the federal rations. More than a quarter of a million men had been killed. The maimed were everywhere visible. Some cities—Charleston, South Carolina, for instance—were, literally, desolate, and some regions like a desert. Fields had gone to ruin. Passing armies had seized cattle and work stock. Men, or women, drew the plow. For the whites, this world was one of despair, resentment, stoicism, and outraged pride. For the blacks, it was one of freedom, opportunity, and the promise of joy.

The blacks, however, had had little preparation for that world. In the life of a slave there was not much need for self-discipline, planning, focused ambition. Now, merely to move, to set foot in the big road, to walk away— that was the most obvious mark of freedom and the country was full of wandering blacks, tasting their freedom, jubilating, simply on the move, living off of what came to hand or on handouts from the victorious troops. But when the chance came, we find the touching picture of blacks, even the very old, sitting before some Yankee schoolmarm and puzzling over the blue-back speller. And during the Reconstruction, in the state governments, and elsewhere, a number of black officials and law-makers proved to be intelligent and high-minded men.

BOOKER T. WASHINGTON (1856–1915)

Once held by many, black and white, as a hero in the development of the black race in America, Booker T. Washington is now often regarded as an "Uncle Tom," a "handkerchief-head," and a traitor to his race. Certainly, in the present age, the attitudes that he held and the methods that he employed may seem ridiculously antiquated, or even craven and corrupt, and it is now obvious that, through limitation of vision, stubbornness, and love of power, Washington did undertake to thwart certain developments necessary to the black world and accepted affronts to racial integrity. But we must try to see how the world in which he lived appeared to him; and try to see how accurate was his assessment of the possibilities for action in that world.

The man who became known as Booker T. Washington did not know exactly when or where he was born (though he knew the county in Virginia, and thought that the year was 1858 or 1859) and had only the vague rumor that his father was a white man from a neighboring plantation. He had no name. He had been simply called "Booker" and on impulse added the name "Washington" when, on his first day in school, he discovered that other people had two names.

The first years of his life Washington spent as a slave. Still a child when the war was won, he grew up in the confusion, ignorance, and brutal poverty of that period—but with a sense of the hopes that freedmen held for the future. He was, however, to see the disintegration of those hopes. The factors responsible for that disintegration are numerous, complex, and subject to debate, but it is clear that no serious, sustained, and reasonable effort was willed by the electorate or favored by the federal government. The dominant Republican party was shot through with corruption and incompetence, and even with a candidate, Rutherford B. Hayes, who promised to purge the organization, the vote was so close that the election was in dispute, and violence, even a new civil war, seemed in the offing. The Compromise of 1877, between the Republicans and the Democrats, assured the peaceful inauguration of Hayes at the price of the withdrawal from the South of federal troops of occupation and the liquidation of the black political power.

From this point on, the movement toward disenfranchisement, economic repression, sometimes peonage, and legal segregation developed at an accelerating pace. It is true that many whites even in the South were, for various reasons, opposed to legal segregation, but this policy was a natural extension of the national temper. An abolitionist like James Russell Lowell had come to hold the blacks "incapable of civilization from their own resources," and after his experience with four black freedwomen as housemaids, he uttered the generalization that at least the first generation of ex-slaves was "dirty, lazy, and lying"; he thought, in fact, that the blacks were only fit to become the peasantry of the southern—*not* of the northern—states. E. L. Godkin, editor of the liberal and influential *Nation*, could write: "I do not see . . . how the negro [*sic*] is ever to be worked into a system of government for which . . . I would have much respect." More and more often the question was asked whether what had been achieved in freeing the black slaves was worth the expense of white blood and treasure, and George W. Julian, trying to shame fellow Republicans out of the "vile spirit of caste" by some plain speaking, deliberately let the cat out of the bag: "The real trouble is that *we hate the negro* [*sic*]." It was, after all, the age of imperialism, Kipling, and the "white man's burden," and soon the United States, having reannexed the South, would annex the Philippines, and with the annexation of the Philippines would begin to debate the logicality of allowing citizenship to one group of nonwhites (that is, the blacks in the South) while denying it to one group of nonwhites in its domain (that is, the Philippines).[1] Meanwhile, by 1885 the Supreme Court, in the Civil Rights case, de-

clared unconstitutional the prohibition of discrimination in public accommodations which had been affirmed in the Civil Rights Act of 1875; by 1896, in the famous *Plessy* v. *Ferguson* decision, it upheld public segregation; and in 1898 it upheld the voting test of Mississippi, which effectively disenfranchised the state's black population.

In the face of this situation what course should the black man, generally penniless and uneducated, follow? Washington, knowing the grim world of poverty, ignorance, and hopelessness from which he had come, held that the most effective way was to eschew political action and to cultivate habits of work, self-discipline, cleanliness, and thrift in order to establish a firm economic base. As he understood it, this meant that the black man should accommodate himself to the superior role the white man held in society, North and South, for only with white money and on white sufferance did Washington see any hope of executing his program.

As a matter of fact, the program he laid down was in accordance with the spirit of the age. It was the age of laissez-faire economics, of Horatio Alger, and of the American dream of success, and Washington was simply urging on his race this magic philosophy, while at the same time using the appeal to that philosophy as a device to extort money from those who cherished it most—that is, the self-made rich, who naturally saw their wealth as the reward of virtue. To come closer home, Washington had every reason to believe in that philosophy; he himself was a more startling example of the Horatio Alger story than even a Thomas A. Edison or an Andrew Carnegie. The title of his famous autobiography, *Up from Slavery*, is a perfect Alger title.

From the age of nine, when he went to work in the mines in West Virginia, Washington was consumed with the desire to learn and to get ahead. He managed to get some scanty schooling. When he was a houseboy for the wife of the owner of the mine, a lady from Vermont who terrorized the household staff,

[1] Kipling's poem was published in the London *Times* on February 4, 1899—just in time, according to Kipling's biographer, C. E. Carrington, to harden the decision of the U.S. Senate in regard to the Philippines.

Washington found that what made her such a dragon was the frustration of her demand for Yankee order and cleanliness; so he learned order and cleanliness. With his will and ambition, he could always learn things, and will and ambition got him to the Hampton Institute. After graduation he became a teacher, and a little later head of a new normal school at Tuskegee, Alabama. On arrival there he found that the "school" existed only on paper. But Washington's years of struggle, begging, borrowing, calculated tact, and genius for organization made Tuskegee Institute real—these things, plus the hard physical work of the students, for Washington was determined that the very buildings should be erected by the hands of those who would occupy them, so that students would learn "to see not only the utility of labor, but its beauty and dignity," and to learn "to love work for its own sake." He wanted to teach brick-making, not Greek.

In twenty years Washington built up an institution of well over 1000 students, with a faculty of 125, and with some $3,000,000 of assets. By this time the founder was internationally famous, had played host to one President, William McKinley, had been the guest in the White House of another, Theodore Roosevelt, and had taken tea with Queen Victoria. He had even received an honorary degree from Harvard, and this, by his account, was his most prized mark of recognition:

> As I sat upon my veranda, with this letter in my hand, tears came into my eyes. My whole former life—my life as a slave on the plantation, my work in the coal-mine, the times when I was without food and clothing, when I made my bed under a sidewalk, my struggles for an education, the trying days I had at Tuskegee . . . the ostracism and sometimes oppression of my race—all this passed before me and nearly overcame me.

Underlying this fame was Washington's furious energy, single-mindedness, and mastery of psychology (particularly the psychology of the white man, on whose vanities and prejudices he

could play like a flute), but the fame was brought to focus by the speech he was invited to give in Atlanta, Georgia, on September 18, 1895, at the Cotton States and International Exposition. In that speech of fifteen minutes he lulled both the arrogance and the fears of the white man, North and South, and stilled his conscience; and the great audience was swept by a storm of applause. So was the national press. As the New York *World* put it: "a Negro Moses stood before a great audience of white people and delivered an oration that marks a new epoch in the history of the South." The speech was hailed, further, as the "beginning of a moral revolution in America." The speaker, "tall, bony, straight as a Sioux chief,[2] high forehead, straight nose, heavy jaws, and strong determined mouth, with big white teeth, piercing eyes, and commanding manner," precipitated an uproar of enthusiasm, and the "fairest women of Georgia stood up and cheered." Also, "Most of the Negroes in the audience were crying, perhaps not knowing just why."

Subsequent history has given an inflection of irony to that last sentence. Since that day, a number of blacks have been inclined to interpret those tears as marks of grief at a betrayal of hope rather than of joy at the enunciation of one.

The central, though sometimes secret, content of Washington's career after he had firmly established Tuskegee was the struggle against various factions that found his accommodationism a sell-out of black pride and his theory of education stultifying. On the first point J. Saunders Redding says:

> From white America's point of view, the situation was ideal. White America had raised this man [Washington] up because he espoused a policy which was intended to keep the Negro docile and dumb in regard to civil, social and political rights and privileges. Hav-

---

[2] The comparison "upward" of the black man to the Indian—especially to a Sioux chief—is significant, the Sioux being warlike and the memory of Custer at the Little Big Horn not yet dimmed. See p. 1178.

ing raised him to power, it was in white America's interest to keep him there. All race matters could be referred to him, and all decisions affecting the race would seem to come from him. In this there was much pretense and, plainly, not a little cynicism. There was the pretense, first, that Washington was leader by sanction of the Negro people; and there was the pretense, second, that speaking in the name of his people, he spoke for them.[3]

On the second point, the attacks by W. E. B. Du Bois, in his protracted feud with Washington, best summarize the issues. (See pp. 1756–62.) But it would be a mistake to assume that the black opposition to Washington was universal or immediate. On the question of universality, there is no way to know clearly what views, if any, were generally held in the unlettered, inarticulate mass, and it is clear that the actual attacks had to come from a special segment, the socially elite group of the well-educated. But even the intellectuals among the blacks did not immediately align themselves against Washington. For some fifteen years after the Atlanta speech—that is, up to the founding of the National Association for the Advancement of Colored People (1909), it is probable, as August Meiers puts it in *Negro Thought in America 1880–1915: Racial Ideologies in the Age of Booker T. Washington*, that "Washington's critics consisted of only a minority of the intellectual and professional men." Even W. E. B. Du Bois, who was to become his chief adversary, was for years in the Washington orbit, and the same is true of James Weldon Johnson.

But the resistance finally came, and two factors contributed significantly to its coming. First, the period of Washington's greatest success saw the increasing pressure of discrimination and the loss of previous gains, for if this was the period of "Progressivism," that liberalizing doctrine was, in the South at least, as C. Vann Woodward puts it, for whites only, and the situation in the North was not much differ-

[3] See Ralph Ellison's novel *Invisible Man* for echoes of this situation.

ent: that is, if the blacks, as a result of Washington's policy, were somewhat better off economically, these gains were being offset by losses. The second factor was the increase, in spite of other social losses, in the number of blacks receiving higher education. This class, prepared to compete in the white world, was, generally speaking, ready to thrust for acceptance and integration, or even assimilation, and to agitate for political and social equality. They were impatient of the policy of dependence on economic advance and moral improvement as long-range preparation for their rights.

Behind this conflict between Washington and the "radicals" lay a deeper conflict—that between the will toward racial solidarity and separatism and the drive toward acceptance and integration. Though there is some justification in equating the first impulse (toward racial solidarity and separatism) with Washington (on the grounds that he accepted segregation and strove to create an independent economy for blacks) and in equating the second impulse (toward integration) with the radicals, the real locus of this conflict might well be in the heart of the individual black; he might be torn between these impulses. Even Washington experienced this self-division. For instance, if he publicly repudiated agitation for political solutions and civil rights, he secretly worked against discrimination by using his influence in the federal government, and even by initiating and supplying money for a fight in the courts against peonage, disenfranchisement, segregation on public conveyances, and lily-white juries. In his last phase, furthermore, Washington's famous tact and self-control seemed to crack, and his utterances became more forthright. Du Bois, Washington's stoutest adversary, was even more complex and divided in his attitudes than Washington, as was James Weldon Johnson, whose novel *The Autobiography of an Ex-Colored Man* is basically about the self-division of the blacks. In fact, this conflict, for the individual and the race, was built into the situation, in all aspects of life, cultural, political, social, and economic. At one moment, one line of feeling might be provoked, and one line of strategy might seem to give results, at another moment the other might offer profit. As Gunnar Myrdal puts it in his famous work on race, *The American Dilemma*, "Negroes seem to be held in a state of internal preparedness for a great number of contradictory opinions—ready to accept one type or another depending on how they are driven by pressures or where they see an opportunity." And this diagnosis merely echoes in different language the idea we have repeated from James Weldon Johnson: that the race question is not fixed but fluid. A monolithic attitude does not exist among blacks any more than does one among whites. It may be said that one black attitude approaching the monolithic has finally emerged: a will to fulfillment.

It is easy to believe that Washington was possessed by the will to fulfillment, that discrimination deeply rankled, that, as H. G. Wells observed on a visit to the United States in 1905, the "sense of the overpowering forces of race prejudice" was constantly apparent in him, and that his accommodationism fundamentally represented a strategic cunning.[4] Myrdal has called Washington a "supreme diplomat," and there is no doubt of Washington's genius at political manipulation. But if politics is the art of the possible, then, in assessing Washington's stature, the accuracy of his diagnosis of the "possible" becomes crucial. What values were "available" at that historical moment? And if Washington did achieve what was possible in the short range of the moment, did he sacrifice values not immediately available but in need of affirmation in a long-range view? How do we relate Nat Turner, the rebel, and Washington, the accommodationist? Such questions can never be definitely settled; but we should try to grasp the nature of the issue before making even a tentative judgment.

Some historians, indeed, would suggest that the matter wasn't in any simple sense one of Washington's assessment and choices, that in the deepest sense Washington's success was not due primarily to his political skill or other personal qualities, but to the fact that he so completely incarnated, in his own special way, a way especially dramatic because of the disabilities of race that he had overcome, the values of his age; that as the historian C. Vann Woodward puts it, in *The Origins of the New South, 1877–1913*, Washington's success was due primarily to the "remarkable congeniality between his doctrines and the dominant forces of his age and society, forces that found an eloquent voice in the brown orator."

Washington's success was of his age; but the age came to an end.

The grounds of the conflict between Washington and his black adversaries were not merely theoretical. Washington loved power and was expert in the manipulation of power. There was, it now appears, such a thing as the apparatus that his adversaries called the "Tuskegee machine," an interlocking arrangement of Washington's personal influence, his prestige, and his ability to bestow favors, to direct gifts to other educational institutions, to sway patronage even at the federal level, and to control a considerable segment of the black press. But even the "machine" could not control history. When, in 1915, Washington died, full of honors, he had lived past his age. By 1906, in fact, the race riot in Atlanta, the very scene of his greatest triumph, had dramatized the failure of his policy as a solution.

[4] Arguments from strategic cunning can cut both ways. It has been suggested, for instance, probably with less justification, that Garrison's extremist position (and conduct) on abolition was, too, strategic rather than obsessive. See p. 337.

BIOGRAPHICAL CHART

1856   Born, April 5 or 6, on a plantation in Franklin County, Virginia; his mother, Jane Ferguson, a black cook, and his father believed to be a white man from a neighboring plantation (Washington's own guess was that he had been born in 1858 or 1859)

1866 Family moves to Malden, near Charleston, West Virginia

1872 Enrolls at the Hampton Institute in West Virginia

1875 Graduates from Hampton and teaches in a Negro grammar school in Malden

1878 Attends Wayland Seminary in Washington, D.C., for one year

1881 Starts Tuskegee Institute under a charter from the Alabama state legislature

1882 Marries Fannie N. Smith of Malden, a graduate of Hampton; she dies in 1884 leaving one daughter

1885 Marries Olivia A. Davidson of Ohio, a teacher at Tuskegee; she dies in 1889, leaving two sons

1891 Receives an honorary degree from Harvard

1893 Succeeds Frederick Douglass, upon his death, as the recognized national leader of the Negro people

1893 Marries Margaret J. Murray of Mississippi, then female principal of Tuskegee

1895 Atlanta Exposition Address

1900 *Sowing and Reaping*

1901 *Up from Slavery*; dines with Theodore Roosevelt

1902 *Character Building*

1906 *Putting the Most into Life*

1907 *Frederick Douglass*; *The Negro in Business*

1909 *The Story of the Negro*

1911 *My Larger Education*

1912 *The Man Farthest Down*, R. E. Park coauthor

1915 Dies, November 14, at home in Alabama

FURTHER READINGS

Francis L. Broderick and August Meier, *Negro Protest Thought in the Twentieth Century* (1965)

John Hope Franklin, *From Slavery to Freedom: A History of American Negroes* (1967)

Hugh Hawkins, *Booker T. Washington and His Critics: The Problem of Negro Leadership* (1962)

L. R. Horton, "Booker T. Washington and the White Man's Burden," *American Historical Review* (1961)

Rayford W. Logan, *The Negro in American Life and Thought: The Nadir, 1877–1901* (1954)

Basil Matthews, *Booker T. Washington: Educator and Interracial Interpreter* (1948)

August Meier, *Negro Thought in America, 1880–1915* (1963)

Gunnar Myrdal, *An American Dilemma* (1940)

G. R. Spencer, *Booker T. Washington and the Negro's Place in American Life* (1955)

E. L. Thornbrough, *Booker T. Washington* (1969)

C. Vann Woodward, *Origins of the New South, 1877–1910* (1951)

From Up from Slavery (1901)

Booker T. Washington's autobiography *Up from Slavery* is an example of a literary form peculiarly congenial to the experience of the black man in America. From Gustavus Vassa's *The Interesting Narrative of the Life of Olaudah Equiano, or Gustavus Vassa, The African*, on through Frederick Douglass's *My Bondage and My Freedom*, Washington's *Up from Slavery*, and Richard Wright's *Black Boy*, to Malcolm X's *Autobiography*, the black man's tale of how he survived in a white world, how he affirmed his identity, has been the archetypal story he had to tell. We have said that *Up from Slavery* echoes the Horatio Alger myth, and that fact may have accounted, in part at least, for its great fame. But we should remember that the book is also the factual account of a black man's successful struggle against a world he never made.

CHAPTER 1:
A SLAVE AMONG SLAVES

I was born a slave on a plantation in Franklin County, Virginia. I am not quite sure of the exact place or exact date of my birth, but at any rate I suspect I must have been born somewhere and at some time. As nearly as I have been able to learn, I was born near a cross-roads post-office called Hale's Ford, and the year was 1858 or 1859. I do not know the month or the day. The earliest impressions I can now recall are of the plantation and the slave quarters—the latter being the part of the plantation where the slaves had their cabins.

My life had its beginning in the midst of the most miserable, desolate, and discouraging surroundings. This was so, however, not because my owners were especially cruel, for they were not, as compared with many others. I was born in a typical log cabin, about fourteen by sixteen feet square. In this cabin I lived with my mother and a brother and sister till after the Civil War, when we were all declared free.

Of my ancestry I know almost nothing. In the slave quarters, and even later, I heard whispered conversations among the coloured people of the tortures which the slaves, including, no doubt, my ancestors on my mother's side, suffered in the middle passage of the slave ship while being conveyed from Africa to America. I have been unsuccessful in securing any information that would throw any accurate light upon the history of my family beyond my mother. She, I remember, had a half-brother and a half-sister. In the days of slavery not very much attention was given to family history and family records—that is, black family records. My mother, I suppose, attracted the attention of a purchaser who was afterward my owner and hers. Her addition to the slave family attracted about as much attention as the purchase of a new horse or cow. Of my father I know even less than of my mother. I do not even know his name. I have heard reports to the effect that he was a white man who lived on one of the near-by plantations. Whoever he was, I never heard of his taking the least interest in me or providing in any way for my rearing. But I do not find especial fault with him. He was simply another unfortunate victim of the institution which the Nation unhappily had engrafted upon it at that time.

The cabin was not only our living-place, but was also used as the kitchen for the plantation. My mother was the plantation cook. The cabin was without glass windows; it had only openings in the side which let in the light, and also the cold, chilly air of winter. There was a door to the cabin—that is, something that was called a door—but the uncertain hinges by which it was hung, and the large cracks in it, to say nothing of the fact that it was too small, made the room a very uncomfortable one. In addition to these openings there was, in the lower right-hand corner of the room, the "cat-hole,"—a contrivance which almost every mansion or cabin in Virginia possessed during the antebellum period. The "cat-hole" was a square opening, about seven by eight inches, provided for the purpose of letting the cat pass in and out of the house at will during the night. In the case of our particular cabin I could never understand the necessity for this convenience, since there were at least a half-dozen other places in the cabin that would have accommodated the cats. There was no wooden floor in our cabin, the naked earth being used as a floor. In the centre of the earthen floor there was a large, deep opening covered with boards, which was used as a place in which to store sweet potatoes during the winter. An impression of this potato-hole is very distinctly engraved upon my memory, because I recall that during the process of putting the potatoes in or taking them out I would often come into possession of one or two, which I roasted and thoroughly enjoyed. There was no cooking-stove on our plantation, and all the cooking for the whites and slaves my mother had to do over an open fire place, mostly in pots and "skillets." While the poorly built cabin caused us to suffer with cold in the winter, the heat from the open fireplace in summer was equally trying.

The early years of my life, which were spent in the little cabin, were not very different from those of thousands of other slaves. My mother, of course, had little time in which to give attention to the training of her children during the day. She snatched a few moments for our care in the early morning before her work began, and at night after the day's work was done. One of my earliest recollections is that of my mother cooking a chicken late at night, and awakening her children for the purpose of feeding them. How or where she got it I do not know. I presume, however, it was procured from our owner's farm. Some people may call this theft. If such a thing were to happen now, I should condemn it as theft myself. But taking place at the time it did, and for the reason that it did, no one could ever make me believe that my mother was guilty of thieving. She was simply a victim of the system of slavery. I cannot remember having slept in a bed until after our family was declared free by the Emancipation Proclamation. Three children—John, my older brother, Amanda, my sister, and myself—had a pallet on the dirt floor, or, to be more correct, we slept in and on a bundle of filthy rags laid upon the dirt floor.

I was asked not long ago to tell something about the sports and pastimes that I engaged in during my youth. Until that question was asked it had never occurred to me that there was no period of my life that was devoted to play. From the time that I can remember anything, almost every day of my life has been occupied in some kind of labour; though I think I would now be a more useful man if I had had time for sports. During the period that I spent in slavery I was not large enough to be of much service, still I was occupied most of the time in cleaning the yards, carrying water to the men in the fields, or going to the mill, to which I used to take the corn, once a week, to be ground. The mill was about three miles from the plantation. This work I always dreaded. The heavy bag of corn would be thrown across the back of the horse, and the corn divided about evenly on each side; but in some way, almost without exception, on the trips, the corn would so shift as to become unbalanced and would fall off the horse, and often I would fall with it. As I was not strong enough to reload the corn upon the horse, I would have to wait, sometimes for many hours, till a chance passer-by came along who would help me out of my trouble. The hours while waiting for some one were usually spent in crying. The time consumed in this way made me late in reaching the mill, and by the time I got my corn ground and reached home it would be far into the night. The road was a lonely one, and often led through dense forests. I was always frightened. The woods were said to be full of soldiers who had deserted from the army, and I had been told that the first thing a deserter did to a Negro boy when he found him alone was to cut off his ears. Besides, when I was late in getting home I knew I would always get a severe scolding or a flogging.

I had no schooling whatever while I was a slave, though I remember on several occasions I went as far as the schoolhouse door with one of my young mistresses to carry her books. The picture of several dozen boys and girls in a schoolroom engaged in study made a deep impression upon me, and I had the feeling that to get into a schoolhouse and study in this way would be about the same as getting into paradise.

So far as I can now recall, the first knowledge that I got of the fact that we were slaves, and that freedom of the slaves was being discussed, was early one morning before day, when I was awakened by my mother kneeling over her children and fervently praying that Lincoln and his armies might be successful, and that one day she and her children might be free. In this connection I have never been able to understand how the slaves throughout the South, completely ignorant as were the masses so far as books or newspapers were concerned, were able to keep themselves so accurately and completely informed about the great National questions that were agitating the country. From the time that Garrison, Lovejoy, and others began to agitate for freedom, the slaves throughout the South kept in close touch with the progress of the movement. Though I was a mere child during the preparation for the Civil War and during the war itself, I now recall the many late-at-night whispered discussions that I heard my mother and the other slaves on the plantation indulge in. These discussions showed that they understood the situation, and that they kept themselves informed of events by what was termed the "grape-vine" telegraph.

During the campaign when Lincoln was first a candidate for the Presidency, the slaves on our far-off plantation, miles from any railroad or large city or daily newspapers, knew what the issues involved were. When war was begun between the North and the South, every slave on our plantation felt and knew that, though other issues were discussed, the primal one was that of slavery. Even the most ignorant members of my race on the remote plantations felt in their hearts, with a certainty that admitted of no doubt, that the freedom of the slaves would be the one great result of the war, if the Northern armies conquered. Every success of the Federal armies and every defeat of the Confederate forces was watched with the keenest and most intense interest. Often the slaves got knowledge of the results of great battles before the white people received it. This news was usually gotten from the coloured man who was sent to the post-office for the mail. In our case the post-office was about three miles from the plantation, and the mail came once or twice a week. The man who was sent to the office would linger about the place long enough to get the drift of the conversation from the group of white people who naturally congregated there, after receiving their mail, to discuss the latest news. The mail-carrier on his way back to our master's house would as naturally retail the news that he had secured among the slaves, and in this way they often heard of important events before the white people at the "big house," as the master's house was called.

I cannot remember a single instance during my childhood or early boyhood when our entire family sat down to the table together, and God's blessing was asked, and the family ate a meal in a civilized manner. On the plantation in Virginia, and even later, meals were gotten by the children very much as dumb animals get theirs. It was a piece of bread here and a scrap of meat there. It was a cup of milk at one time and some potatoes at another.

Sometimes a portion of our family would eat out of the skillet or pot, while some one else would eat from a tin plate held on the knees, and often using nothing but the hands with which to hold the food. When I had grown to sufficient size, I was required to go to the "big house" at meal-times to fan the flies from the table by means of a large set of paper fans operated by a pulley. Naturally much of the conversation of the white people turned upon the subject of freedom and the war, and I absorbed a good deal of it. I remember that at one time I saw two of my young mistresses and some lady visitors eating ginger-cakes, in the yard. At that time those cakes seemed to me to be absolutely the most tempting and desirable things that I had ever seen; and I then and there resolved that, if I ever got free, the height of my ambition would be reached if I could get to the point where I could secure and eat ginger-cakes in the way that I saw those ladies doing.

Of course as the war was prolonged the white people, in many cases, often found it difficult to secure food for themselves. I think the slaves felt the deprivation less than the whites, because the usual diet for the slaves was corn bread and pork, and these could be raised on the plantation; but coffee, tea, sugar, and other articles which the whites had been accustomed to use could not be raised on the plantation, and the conditions brought about by the war frequently made it impossible to secure these things. The whites were often in great straits. Parched corn was used for coffee, and a kind of black molasses was used instead of sugar. Many times nothing was used to sweeten the so-called tea and coffee.

The first pair of shoes that I recall wearing were wooden ones. They had rough leather on the top, but the bottoms, which were about an inch thick, were of wood. When I walked they made a fearful noise, and besides this they were very inconvenient, since there was no yielding to the natural pressure of the foot. In wearing them one presented an exceedingly awkward appearance. The most trying ordeal that I was forced to endure as a slave boy, however, was the wearing of a flax shirt. In the portion of Virginia where I lived it was common to use flax as part of the clothing for the slaves. That part of the flax from which our clothing was made was largely the refuse, which of course was the cheapest and roughest part. I can scarcely imagine any torture, except, perhaps, the pulling of a tooth, that is equal to that caused by putting on a new flax shirt for the first time. It is

almost equal to the feeling that one would experience if he had a dozen or more chestnut burrs, or a hundred small pin-points, in contact with his flesh. Even to this day I can recall accurately the tortures that I underwent when putting on one of these garments. The fact that my flesh was soft and tender added to the pain. But I had no choice. I had to wear the flax shirt or none; and had it been left to me to choose, I should have chosen to wear no covering. In connection with the flax shirt, my brother John, who is several years older than I am, performed one of the most generous acts that I ever heard of one slave relative doing for another. On several occasions when I was being forced to wear a new flax shirt, he generously agreed to put it on in my stead and wear it for several days, till it was "broken in." Until I had grown to be quite a youth this single garment was all that I wore.

One may get the idea, from what I have said, that there was bitter feeling toward the white people on the part of my race, because of the fact that most of the white population was away fighting in a war which would result in keeping the Negro in slavery if the South was successful. In the case of the slaves on our place this was not true, and it was not true of any large portion of the slave population in the South where the Negro was treated with anything like decency. During the Civil War one of my young masters was killed, and two were severely wounded. I recall the feeling of sorrow which existed among the slaves when they heard of the death of "Mars' Billy." It was no sham sorrow, but real. Some of the slaves had nursed "Mars' Billy"; others had played with him when he was a child. "Mars' Billy" had begged for mercy in the case of others when the overseer or master was thrashing them. The sorrow in the slave quarter was only second to that in the "big house." When the two young masters were brought home wounded, the sympathy of the slaves was shown in many ways. They were just as anxious to assist in the nursing as the family relatives of the wounded. Some of the slaves would even beg for the privilege of sitting up at night to nurse their wounded masters. This tenderness and sympathy on the part of those held in bondage was a result of their kindly and generous nature. In order to defend and protect the women and children who were left on the plantations when the white males went to war, the slaves would have laid down their lives. The slave who was selected to sleep in the "big house" during the absence of the males was considered to have the place of honour. Any one attempting to harm "young Mistress" or "old Mistress" during the night would have had to cross the dead body of the slave to do so. I do not know how many have noticed it, but I think that it will be found to be true that there are few instances, either in slavery or freedom, in which a member of my race has been known to betray a specific trust.

As a rule, not only did the members of my race entertain no feelings of bitterness against the whites before and during the war, but there are many instances of Negroes tenderly caring for their former masters and mistresses who for some reason have become poor and dependent since the war. I know of instances where the former masters of slaves have for years been supplied with money by their former slaves to keep them from suffering. I have known of still other cases in which the former slaves have assisted in the education of the descendants of their former owners. I know of a case on a large plantation in the South in which a young white man, the son of the former owner of the estate, has become so reduced in purse and self-control by reason of drink that he is a pitiable creature; and yet, notwithstanding the poverty of the coloured people themselves on this plantation, they have for years supplied this young white man with the necessities of life. One sends him a little coffee or sugar, another a little meat, and so on. Nothing that the coloured people possess is too good for the son of "old Mars' Tom," who will perhaps never be permitted to suffer while any remain on the place who knew directly or indirectly of "old Mars' Tom."

I have said that there are few instances of a member of my race betraying a specific trust. One of the best illustrations of this which I know of is in the case of an ex-slave from Virginia whom I met not long ago in a little town in the state of Ohio. I found that this man had made a contract with his master, two or three years previous to the Emancipation Proclamation, to the effect that the slave was to be permitted to buy himself, by paying so much per year for his body; and while he was paying for himself, he was to be permitted to labour where and for whom he pleased. Finding that he could secure better wages in Ohio, he went there. When freedom came, he was still in debt to his master some three hundred dollars. Notwithstanding that the Emancipation Proclamation freed him from any obligation to his master, this black man walked the greater portion of the distance back to where his old master lived in Virginia, and placed the last dollar, with interest, in his hands. In talking to me about this, the man told me that he knew that he did not have to pay the debt, but that he had given his word to his master, and his word he had never broken. He felt that he could not enjoy his freedom till he had fulfilled his promise.

From some things that I have said one may get the idea that some of the slaves did not want freedom. This is not true. I have never seen one who did not want to be free, or one who would return to slavery.

I pity from the bottom of my heart any nation or body of people that is so unfortunate as to get entangled in the net of slavery. I have long since ceased to cherish any spirit of bitterness against the Southern white people on account of the enslavement of my race. No one section of our country was wholly responsible for its introduction, and, besides, it was recognized and protected for years by the General Government. Having once got its tentacles fastened on to the economic and social life of the Republic, it was no easy matter for the country to relieve itself of the institution. Then, when we rid ourselves of prejudice, or racial feeling, and look facts in the face, we must acknowledge that, notwithstanding the cruelty and moral wrong of slavery, the ten million Negroes inhabiting this country, who themselves or whose ancestors went through the school of American slavery, are in a stronger and more hopeful condition, materially, intellectually, morally, and religiously, than is true of an equal number of black people in any other portion of the globe. This is so to such an extent that Negroes in this country, who themselves or whose forefathers went through the school of slavery, are constantly returning to Africa as missionaries to enlighten those who remained in the fatherland. This I say, not to justify slavery—on the other hand, I condemn it as an institution, as we all know that in America it was established for selfish and financial reasons, and not from a missionary motive—but to call attention to a fact, and to show how Providence so often uses men and institutions to accomplish a purpose. When persons ask me in these days how, in the midst of what sometimes seem hopelessly discouraging conditions, I can have such faith in the future of my race in this country, I remind them of the wilderness through which and out of which, a good Providence has already led us.

Ever since I have been old enough to think for

myself, I have entertained the idea that, notwithstanding the cruel wrongs inflicted upon us, the black man got nearly as much out of slavery as the white man did. The hurtful influences of the institution were not by any means confined to the Negro. This was fully illustrated by the life upon our own plantation. The whole machinery of slavery was so constructed as to cause labour, as a rule, to be looked upon as a badge of degradation, of inferiority. Hence labour was something that both races on the slave plantation sought to escape. The slave system on our place, in a large measure, took the spirit of self-reliance and self-help out of the white people. My old master had many boys and girls, but not one, so far as I know, ever mastered a single trade or special line of productive industry. The girls were not taught to cook, sew, or to take care of the house. All of this was left to the slaves. The slaves, of course, had little personal interest in the life of the plantation, and their ignorance prevented them from learning how to do things in the most improved and thorough manner. As a result of the system, fences were out of repair, gates were hanging half off the hinges, doors creaked, window-panes were out, plastering had fallen but was not replaced, weeds grew in the yard. As a rule, there was food for whites and blacks, but inside the house, and on the dining-room table, there was wanting that delicacy and refinement of touch and finish which can make a home the most convenient, comfortable, and attractive place in the world. Withal there was a waste of food and other materials which was sad. When freedom came, the slaves were almost as well fitted to begin life anew as the master, except in the matter of book-learning and ownership of property. The slave owner and his sons had mastered no special industry. They unconsciously had imbibed the feeling that manual labour was not the proper thing for them. On the other hand, the slaves, in many cases, had mastered some handicraft, and none were ashamed, and few unwilling, to labour.

Finally the war closed, and the day of freedom came. It was a momentous and eventful day to all upon our plantation. We had been expecting it. Freedom was in the air, and had been for months. Deserting soldiers returning to their homes were to be seen every day. Others who had been discharged, or whose regiments had been paroled, were constantly passing near our place. The "grapevine telegraph" was kept busy night and day. The news and mutterings of great events were swiftly carried from one plantation to another. In the fear of "Yankee" invasions, the silverware and other valuables were taken from the "big house," buried in the woods, and guarded by trusted slaves. Woe be to any one who would have attempted to disturb the buried treasure. The slaves would give the Yankee soldiers food, drink, clothing—anything but that which had been specifically intrusted to their care and honour. As the great day drew nearer, there was more singing in the slave quarters than usual. It was bolder, had more ring, and lasted later into the nights. Most of the verses of the plantation songs had some reference to freedom. True, they had sung those same verses before, but they had been careful to explain that the "freedom" in these songs referred to the next world, and had no connection with life in this world. Now they gradually threw off the mask, and were not afraid to let it be known that the "freedom" in their songs meant freedom of the body in this world. The night before the eventful day, word was sent to the slave quarters to the effect that something unusual was going to take place at the "big house" the next morning. There was little, if any, sleep that night. All was excitement and expectancy. Early the next morning word was sent to all the slaves, old and young, to gather at the house. In company with my mother, brother, and sister, and a large number of other slaves, I went to the master's house. All of our master's family were either standing or seated on the veranda of the house, where they could see what was to take place and hear what was said. There was a feeling of deep interest, or perhaps sadness, on their faces, but not bitterness. As I now recall the impression they made upon me, they did not at the moment seem to be sad because of the loss of property, but rather because of parting with those whom they had reared and who were in many ways very close to them. The most distinct thing that I now recall in connection with the scene was that some man who seemed to be a stranger (a United States officer, I presume) made a little speech and then read a rather long paper—the Emancipation Proclamation, I think. After the reading we were told that we were all free, and could go when and where we pleased. My mother, who was standing by my side, leaned over and kissed her children, while tears of joy ran down her cheeks. She explained to us what it all meant, that this was the day for which she had been so long praying, but fearing that she would never live to see.

For some minutes there was great rejoicing, and

thanksgiving, and wild scenes of ecstasy. But there was no feeling of bitterness. In fact, there was pity among the slaves for our former owners. The wild rejoicing on the part of the emancipated coloured people lasted but for a brief period, for I noticed that by the time they returned to their cabins there was a change in their feelings. The great responsibility of being free, of having charge of themselves, of having to think and plan for themselves and their children, seemed to take possession of them. It was very much like suddenly turning a youth of ten or twelve years out into the world to provide for himself. In a few hours the great questions with which the Anglo-Saxon race had been grappling for centuries had been thrown upon these people to be solved. These were the questions of a home, a living, the rearing of children, education, citizenship, and the establishment and support of churches. Was it any wonder that within a few hours the wild rejoicing ceased and a feeling of deep gloom seemed to pervade the slave quarters? To some it seemed that, now that they were in actual possession of it, freedom was a more serious thing than they had expected to find it. Some of the slaves were seventy or eighty years old; their best days were gone. They had no strength with which to earn a living in a strange place and among strange people, even if they had been sure where to find a new place of abode. To this class the problem seemed especially hard. Besides, deep down in their hearts there was a strange and peculiar attachment to "old Marster" and "old Missus," and to their children, which they found it hard to think of breaking off. With these they had spent in some cases nearly a half-century, and it was no light thing to think of parting. Gradually, one by one, stealthily at first, the older slaves began to wander from the slave quarters back to the "big house" to have a whispered conversation with their former owners as to the future.

Atlanta Exposition Address (1895)

The following is the text of the speech delivered by Washington in Atlanta, preceded by his brief recollection of the circumstances of its delivery.

When I arose to speak, there was considerable cheering, especially from the coloured people. As I remember it now, the thing that was uppermost in my mind was the desire to say something that would cement the friendship of the races and bring about hearty cooperation between them. So far as my outward surroundings were concerned, the only thing that I recall distinctly now is that when I got up, I saw thousands of eyes looking intently into my face. The following is the address which I delivered:—

Mr. President and Gentlemen of the Board of Directors and Citizens: One-third of the population of the South is of the Negro race. No enterprise seeking the material, civil, or moral welfare of this section can disregard this element of our population and reach the highest success. I but convey to you, Mr. President and Directors, the sentiment of the masses of my race when I say that in no way have the value and manhood of the American Negro been more fittingly and generously recognized than by the managers of this magnificent Exposition at every stage of its progress. It is a recognition that will do more to cement the friendship of the two races than any occurrence since the dawn of our freedom.

Not only this, but the opportunity here afforded will awaken among us a new era of industrial progress. Ignorant and inexperienced, it is not strange that in the first years of our new life we began at the top instead of at the bottom; that a seat in Congress or the state legislature was more sought than real estate or industrial skill; that the political convention or stump speaking had more attractions than starting a dairy farm or truck garden.

A ship lost at sea for many days suddenly sighted a friendly vessel. From the mast of the unfortunate vessel was seen a signal, "Water, water, we die of thirst!" The answer from the friendly vessel at once came back, "Cast down your bucket where you are." A second time the signal, "Water, water; send us water!" ran from the distressed vessel, and was answered, "Cast down your bucket where you are." And a third and fourth signal for water was answered, "Cast down your bucket where you are." The captain of the distressed vessel at last heeding the injunction, cast down his bucket, and it came up full of fresh, sparkling water from the mouth of the Amazon River. To those of my race who depend on bettering their condition in a foreign land or who underestimate the importance of cultivating friendly relations with the Southern white man, who is their next-door neighbour, I would say: "Cast down your bucket where you are"— cast it down in making friends in every manly way of the people of all races by whom we are surrounded.

Cast it down in agriculture, mechanics, in commerce, in domestic service, and in the professions. And in this connection it is well to bear in mind that whatever other sins the South may be called to bear, when it comes to business, pure and simple, it is in the South that the Negro is given a man's chance in the commercial world, and in nothing is this Exposition more eloquent than in emphasizing this chance. Our greatest danger is that in the great leap from slavery to freedom we may overlook the fact that the masses of us are to live by the productions of our hands, and fail to keep in mind that we shall prosper in proportion as we learn to dignify and glorify common labour and put brains and skill into the common occupations of life; shall prosper in proportion as we learn to draw the line between the superficial and the substantial, the ornamental gewgaws of life and the useful. No race can prosper till it learns that there is as much dignity in tilling a field as in writing a poem. It is at the bottom of life we must begin, and not at the top. Nor should we permit our grievances to overshadow our opportunities.

To those of the white race who look to the incoming of those of foreign birth and strange tongue and habits for the prosperity of the South, were I permitted I would repeat what I say to my own race, "Cast down your bucket where you are." Cast it down among the eight millions of Negroes whose habits you know, whose fidelity and love you have tested in days when to have proved treacherous meant the ruin of your firesides. Cast down your bucket among these people who have, without strikes and labour wars, tilled your fields, cleared your forests, builded your railroads and cities, and brought forth treasures from the bowels of the earth, and helped make possible this magnificent representation of the progress of the South. Casting down your bucket among my people, helping and encouraging them as you are doing on these grounds, and to education of head, hand, and heart, you will find that they will buy your surplus land, make blossom the waste places in your fields, and run your factories. While doing this, you can be sure in the future, as in the past, that you and your families will be surrounded by the most patient, faithful, law-abiding, and unresentful people that the world has seen. As we have proved our loyalty to you in the past, in nursing your children, watching by the sick-bed of your mothers and fathers, and often following them with tear-dimmed eyes to their graves, so in the future, in our humble way, we shall stand by you with a devotion that no foreigner can approach, ready to lay down our lives, if need be, in defence of yours, interlacing our industrial, commercial, civil, and religious life with yours in a way that shall make the interests of both races one. In all things that are purely social we can be as separate as the fingers, yet one as the hand in all things essential to mutual progress.

There is no defence or security for any of us except in the highest intelligence and development of all. If anywhere there are efforts tending to curtail the fullest growth of the Negro, let these efforts be turned into stimulating, encouraging, and making him the most useful and intelligent citizen. Effort or means so invested will pay a thousand per cent interest. These efforts will be twice blessed —"blessing him that gives and him that takes."

There is no escape through law of man or God from the inevitable:—

The laws of changeless justice bind
  Oppressor with oppressed;
And close as sin and suffering joined
  We march to fate abreast

Nearly sixteen millions of hands will aid you in pulling the load upward, or they will pull against you the load downward. We shall constitute one-third and more of the ignorance and crime of the South, or one-third its intelligence and progress; we shall contribute one-third to the business and industrial prosperity of the South, or we shall prove a veritable body of death, stagnating, depressing, retarding every effort to advance the body politic.

Gentlemen of the Exposition, as we present to you our humble effort at an exhibition of our progress, you must not expect overmuch. Starting thirty years ago with ownership here and there in a few quilts and pumpkins and chickens (gathered from miscellaneous sources), remember the path that has led from these to the inventions and production of agricultural implements, buggies, steam-engines, newspapers, books, statuary, carving, paintings, the management of drug-stores and banks, has not been trodden without contact with thorns and thistles. While we take pride in what we exhibit as a result of our independent efforts, we do not for a moment forget that our part in this exhibition would fall far short of your expectations but for the constant help that has come to our educational life, not only from the Southern states, but especially from Northern philanthropists, who have made their gifts a constant stream of blessing and encouragement.

The wisest among my race understand that the agitation of questions of social equality is the extremest folly, and that progress in the enjoyment of all the privileges that will come to us must be the result of severe and constant struggle rather than of artificial forcing. No race that has anything to contribute to the markets of the world is long in any degree ostracized. It is important and right that all privileges of the law be ours, but it is vastly more important that we be prepared for the exercises of these privileges. The opportunity to earn a dollar in a factory just now is worth infinitely more than the opportunity to spend a dollar in an opera house.

In conclusion, may I repeat that nothing in thirty years has given us more hope and encouragement, and drawn us so near to you of the white race, as this opportunity offered by the Exposition; and here bending, as it were, over the altar that represents the results of the struggles of your race and mine, both starting practically empty-handed three decades ago. I pledge that in your effort to work out the great and intricate problem which God has laid at the doors of the South, you shall have at all times the patient, sympathetic help of my race; only let this be constantly in mind, that, while from representations in these buildings of the product of field, of forest, of mine, of factory, letters, and art, much good will come, yet far above and beyond material benefits will be that higher good, that, let us pray God, will come, in a blotting out of sectional differences and racial animosities and suspicions, in a determination to administer absolute justice, in a willing obedience among all classes to the mandates of law. This, this, coupled with our material prosperity, will bring into our beloved South a new heaven and a new earth.

PAUL LAURENCE DUNBAR (1872–1906)

Paul Laurence Dunbar is a perfect example of the transitional figure in black literature in America. Born in 1872, he knew slavery only by hearsay, and only by hearsay the period of new hope that had ended with the Compromise of 1877; he grew up in the period when discrimination and segregation were already hardening. It was the period, too, of the maximum influence of Washington's accommodationism. Both Du Bois and James Weldon Johnson were contemporaries of Dunbar, but they lived on into the next phase of black history and, as we shall see, played leading parts in defining it.

Dunbar's father was a slave who had escaped to Canada and later returned to fight in the 55th Massachusetts. Both he and the mother were poor and ignorant, but intelligent, and they were ambitious for the son, for whom the father prophesied greatness. The boy, the only black in his class in the Dayton, Ohio, high school, was president of the literary society and editor of the school paper, and wrote a song for commencement, at the Grand Opera House, which begins:

> Why stirs with sad alarm, the heart,
> For all who meet must some day part?
> So let no useless cavil be;
> True wisdom bows to God's decree.

The talented student shortly became the operator of an elevator.

Elevator operator or not, a teacher remembered him and, when the Western Association of Writers met in Dayton, saw to it that Dunbar, then twenty, was invited to give the address of welcome—a poem. Before long, through the kind offices of members of the association, the great James Whitcomb Riley had seen some of the elevator boy's poems and wrote him a letter of congratulation, reminding him, however, that "God's is the glory, the singer but His very humble instrument." Within a year, Dunbar had, at his own expense, published a book; the next year, thanks to his new friend Frederick Douglass, he read some of his poems at the Chicago World's Fair, on "Negro Day"; and in 1896 he published another volume, which was handsomely reviewed, in *Harper's Weekly*, by William Dean Howells, the review appearing on the poet's birthday.

A little earlier, in a letter, Dunbar had said that his ambition was to "be able to interpret my own people through song and story, and to prove to the many that after all we are more human than African." Now Howells said: "When Burns was least himself, he wrote literary English, and Mr. Dunbar writes literary English when he is least himself." He added that only in the dialect pieces was there a poet with a "direct and fresh authority" and one "expressive of a race-life from within the race."

Howells was right when he said that in certain poems, "except for the Negro face of the author, the reader can not find anything specially notable," for Dunbar was simply writing conventional "white" poetry, even in his "Ode to Ethiopia":

O Mother Race! to thee I bring
This pledge of faith unwavering,
  This tribute to thy glory.
I know the pangs which thou didst feel,
When Slavery crushed thee with its heel,
  With thy dead blood all gory.

It was inevitable that black writers, in their racial "colonialism," should imitate Boston, as Boston was, sometimes, still imitating England. But was dialect, as Howells suggested, the answer?

It was certainly not the answer for Dunbar, who was to declare that black "poetry will not be exotic or differ much from that of the whites.

. . . For two hundred and fifty years the environment of the Negro has been American, in every respect the same as that of all other Americans." The sad fact is that Dunbar's dialect poetry, except for bits of local color, was much nearer to James Whitcomb Riley than to black life. Or it might even be said, nearer to Stephen Foster, as in "The Deserted Plantation," which ends:

Dey have lef' de ole plantation to de swallers,
But it hol's in me a lover till de las';
Fu' I fin' hyeah in de memory dat follers
All dat loved me an' dat I loved in de pas'.

So I'll stay an' watch de deah ole place an'
  tend it
Ez I used to im de happy days gone by.
'Twell de othah Mastah thinks it's time to end
  it,
An' calls me to my quarters in de sky.

Or as in "Goin' Back":

But now I'm goin' back again
To the blue grass medders an' fiel's o' corn
In the dear ol' State whar I was bo'n

.   .   .

Back to my ol' Kaintucky home,
Back to the ol' Kaintucky sights,
Back to the scenes o' my youth's delights.

When we remember that Dunbar's father had followed the North Star in his flight from those same "blue grass medders" and had fought in the 55th Massachusetts, the sentiment here begins to ring a little false.

Dunbar received great recognition. He was *the* "Negro Writer," just as Washington was *the* "Negro Leader." He died in 1906, only thirty-four years old, before the rise of the new "radicalism," but in spite of his official role, he had, as in "We Wear the Mask" and in "The Haunted Oak," a poem about lynching, treated some of the themes of black protest; and in the poem "An Ante-Bellum Sermon" he touched on the world of the spirituals and of James Weldon Johnson's *God's Trombones*.

FURTHER READINGS

Paul Laurence Dunbar, *Complete Poems* (1925)

Benjamin Brawley, *Paul L. Dunbar: Poet of His People* (1936)

Virginia Cunningham, *Paul L. Dunbar and His Songs* (1947)

Addison Gayle, *Oak and Ivy: A Biography of Paul Laurence Dunbar* (1971)

Victor Lawson, *Dunbar Critically Examined* (1941)

Lida K. Wiggins, *The Life and Works of Paul L. Dunbar* (1907)

We Wear the Mask (1896)

We wear the mask that grins and lies,
It hides our cheeks and shades our eyes,
This debt we pay to human guile;
With torn and bleeding hearts we smile,
And mouth with myriad subtleties.

Why should the world be overwise,
In counting all our tears and sighs?
Nay, let them only see us, while
    We wear the mask.

We smile, but, O great Christ, our cries   10
To thee from tortured souls arise.
We sing, but oh, the clay is vile
Beneath our feet, and long the mile;
But let the world dream otherwise,
    We wear the mask.

The Haunted Oak (1900)

Pray why are you so bare, so bare,
  Oh, bough of the old oak-tree;
And why, when I go through the shade you
    throw,
  Runs a shudder over me?

My leaves were green as the best, I trow,
  And sap ran free in my veins,
But I saw in the moonlight dim and weird
  A guiltless victim's pains.

I bent me down to hear his sigh;
  I shook with his gurgling moan,   10
And I trembled sore when they rode away,
  And left him here alone.

They'd charged him with the old, old crime,
  And set him fast in jail:
Oh, why does the dog howl all night long,
  And why does the night wind wail?

He prayed his prayer and he swore his oath,
  And he raised his hand to the sky;
But the beat of hoofs smote on his ear,
  And the steady tread drew nigh.   20

Who is it rides by night, by night,
  Over the moonlit road?
And what is the spur that keeps the pace,
  What is the galling goad?

And now they beat at the prison door,
  "Ho, keeper, do not stay!
We are friends of him whom you hold within,
  And we fain would take him away

"From those who ride fast on our heels
  With mind to do him wrong;   30
They have no care for his innocence,
  And the rope they bear is long."

They have fooled the jailer with lying words,
  They have fooled the man with lies;
The bolts unbar, the locks are drawn,
  And the great door open flies.

Now they have taken him from the jail,
  And hard and fast they ride,
And the leader laughs low down in his throat,
  As they halt my trunk beside.   40

Oh, the judge, he wore a mask of black,
  And the doctor one of white,
And the minister, with his oldest son,
  Was curiously bedight.

Oh, foolish man, why weep you now?
  'T is but a little space,
And the time will come when these shall dread
  The mem'ry of your face.

I feel the rope against my bark,
  And the weight of him in my grain,   50
I feel in the throe of his final woe
  The touch of my own last pain.

And never more shall leaves come forth
  On a bough that bears the ban;
I am burned with dread, I am dried and dead,
  From the curse of a guiltless man.

And ever the judge rides by, rides by,
  And goes to hunt the deer,
And ever another rides his soul
  In the guise of a mortal fear.   60

And ever the man he rides me hard,
  And never a night stays he;
For I feel his curse as a haunted bough,
  On the trunk of a haunted tree.

An Ante-Bellum Sermon (1896)

We is gathahed hyeah, my brothahs,
  In dis howlin' wildaness,
Fu' to speak some words of comfo't
  To each othah in distress.
An' we chooses fu' ouah subjic'
  Dis—we'll 'splain it by an' by;
"An' de Lawd said, 'Moses, Moses,'
  An' de man said, 'Hyeah am I.'"

Now ole Pher'oh, down in Egypt,
  Was de wuss man evah bo'n,   10
An' he had de Hebrew chillun
  Down dah wukin' in his co'n;
'T well de Lawd got tiahed o' his foolin',
  An' sez he: "I'll let him know—
Look hyeah, Moses, go tell Pher'oh
  Fu' to let dem chillun go."

"An' ef he refuse to do it,
  I will make him rue de houah,
Fu' I'll empty down on Egypt
  All de vials of my powah."   20
Yes, he did—an' Pher'oh's ahmy
  Was n't wuth a ha'f a dime;
Fu' de Lawd will he'p his chillun,
  You kin trust him evah time.

An' yo' enemies may 'sail you
  In de back an' in de front;
But de Lawd is all aroun' you,
  Fu' to ba' de battle's brunt.
Dey kin fo'ge yo' chains an' shackles
  F'om de mountains to de sea;   30
But de Lawd will sen' some Moses
  Fu' to set his chillun free.

An' de lan' shall hyeah his thundah,
  Lak a blas' f'om Gab'el's ho'n,
Fu' de Lawd of hosts is mighty
  When he girds his ahmor on.

But fu' feah some one mistakes me,
  I will pause right hyeah to say,
Dat I'm still a-preachin' ancient,
  I ain't talkin' 'bout to-day.   40

But I tell you, fellah christuns,
  Things'll happen mighty strange;
Now, de Lawd done dis fu' Isrul,
  An' his ways don't nevah change,
An' de love he showed to Isrul
  Was n't all on Isrul spent;
Now don't run an' tell yo' mastahs
  Dat I's preachin' discontent.

'Cause I is n't; I'se a-judgin'
  Bible people by deir ac's;   50
I'se a-givin' you de Scriptuah,
  I'se a-handin' you de fac's.
Cose ole Pher'oh b'lieved in slav'ry,
  But de Lawd he let him see,
Dat de people he put bref in,—
  Evah mothah's son was free.

An' dahs othahs thinks lak Pher'oh,
  But dey calls de Scriptuah liar,
Fu' de Bible says "a servant
  Is a-worthy of his hire."   60
An' you cain't git roun' nor thoo dat,
  An' you cain't git ovah it,
Fu' whatevah place you git in,
  Dis hyeah Bible too 'll fit.

So you see de Lawd's intention,
  Evah sence de worl' began,
Was dat His almighty freedom
  Should belong to evah man,
But I think it would be bettah,
  Ef I'd pause agin to say,   70
Dat I'm talkin' 'bout ouah freedom
  In a Bibleistic way.

But de Moses is a-comin',
   An' he's comin', suah and fas'
We kin hyeah his feet a-trompin',
   We kin hyeah his trumpit blas'.
But I want to wa'n you people,
   Don't you git too biggity;
An' don't you git to braggin'
   'Bout dese things, you wait an' see.   80

But when Moses wif his powah
   Comes an' sets us chillun free,
We will praise de gracious Mastah
   Dat has gin us liberty;
An' we'll shout ouah halleluyahs,
   On dat mighty reck'nin' day,
When we'se reco'nised ez citiz'—
   Huh uh! Chillun, let us pray!

CHARLES WADDELL CHESNUTT (1858–1932)

Though born at approximately the same time as Booker T. Washington, and some fourteen years before Paul Laurence Dunbar, Charles Waddell Chesnutt belongs, psychologically, to a much later generation. His work is concerned not with some generalized and simplistic relation to the white world, but with tensions within the black experience.

Chesnutt was born in 1858, in Cleveland, Ohio, of parents from North Carolina, where, not long after his father was demobilized from the Union army, the family returned. Even there, in the Reconstruction, Charles managed to get enough education to enable him to work later as a journalist in New York.

Neither New York nor journalism seems to have long satisfied Chesnutt, and soon, again in Cleveland, he was working as a stenographer while studying, according to the custom of the time, in the office of a lawyer. But before he was thirty, he had begun to write stories and was soon to publish them in various journals, including the *Atlantic Monthly*. In 1899 he published, in addition to a biography of Frederick Douglass, two collections of stories, *The Conjure Woman*, which deals with slave times, and *The Wife of His Youth*, which is primarily concerned, as is the title story included here, with the problems of the black man free in a white world. Within the next six years, Chesnutt published three novels, still dealing with the racial tension—for instance, the struggle of a black woman torn between a white lover and a black man who offers her marriage, and the relationship between two half-sisters, one white and one black. The novels are interesting chiefly as an intelligent social record, but some of the stories go beyond this to true literary achievement. Chesnutt is, in fact, the first successful black writer of fiction. His themes, it may be added, are still fresh today.

FURTHER READINGS

Charles W. Chesnutt, *The Wife of His Youth and Other Stories of the Color Line* (1899)
——, *The House Behind the Cedars* (1900)
——, *The Marrow of Tradition* (1901)
——, *The Colonel's Dream* (1905)

——, *The Conjure Woman* (1899)

Helen M. Chesnutt, *Charles W. Chesnutt: Pioneer of the Color Line* (1952)

The Wife of His Youth (1899)

Mr. Ryder was going to give a ball. There were several reasons why this was an opportune time for such an event.

Mr. Ryder might aptly be called the dean of the Blue Veins. The original Blue Veins were a little society of colored persons organized in a certain Northern city shortly after the war. Its purpose was to establish and maintain correct social standards among a people whose social condition presented almost unlimited room for improvement. By accident, combined perhaps with some natural affinity, the society consisted of individuals who were, generally speaking, more white than black. Some envious outsider made the suggestion that no one was eligible for membership who was not white enough to show blue veins. The suggestion was readily adopted by those who were not of the favored few, and since that time the society, though possessing a longer and more pretentious name, had been known far and wide as the "Blue Vein Society," and its members as the "Blue Veins."

The Blue Veins did not allow that any such requirement existed for admission to their circle, but, on the contrary, declared that character and culture were the only things considered; and that if most of their members were light-colored, it was because such persons, as a rule, had had better opportunities to qualify themselves for membership. Opinions differed, too, as to the usefulness of the society. There were those who had been known to assail it violently as a glaring example of the very prejudice from which the colored race had suffered most; and later, when such critics had succeeded in getting on the inside, they had been heard to maintain with zeal and earnestness that the society was a life-boat, an anchor, a bulwark and a shield—a pillar of cloud by day and of fire by night, to guide their people through the social wilderness. Another alleged prerequisite for Blue Vein membership was that of free birth; and while there was really no such requirement, it is doubtless true that very few of the members would have been unable to meet it if there had been. If there were one or two of the older members who had come up from the South and from slavery, their history presented enough romantic circumstances to rob their servile origin of its grosser aspects.

While there were no such tests of eligibility, it is true that the Blue Veins had their notions on these subjects, and that not all of them were equally liberal in regard to the things they collectively disclaimed. Mr. Ryder was one of the most conservative. Though he had not been among the founders of the society, but had come in later, his genius for social leadership was such that he had speedily become its recognized adviser and head, the custodian of its standards, and the preserver of its traditions. He shaped its social policy, was active in providing for its entertainment, and when the interest fell off, as it sometimes did, he fanned the embers until they burst again into a cheerful flame.

There were still other reasons for his popularity. While he was not as white as some of the Blue Veins, his appearance was such as to confer distinction upon them. His features were of a refined type, his hair was almost straight; he was always neatly dressed; his manners were irreproachable, and his morals above suspicion. He had come to Groveland a young man, and obtaining employment in the office of a railroad company as messenger had in time worked himself up to the position of stationery clerk, having charge of the distribution of the office supplies for the whole company. Although the lack of early training had hindered the orderly development of a naturally fine mind, it had not prevented him from doing a great deal of reading or from forming decidedly literary tastes. Poetry was his passion. He could repeat whole pages of the great English poets; and if his pronunciation was sometimes faulty, his eye, his voice, his gestures, would respond to the changing sentiment with a precision that revealed a poetic soul and disarmed criticism. He was economical, and had saved money; he owned and occupied a very comfortable house on a respectable street. His residence was handsomely furnished, containing among other things a good library, especially rich in poetry, a piano, and some choice engravings. He generally shared his house with some young couple, who looked after his want and were company for him; for Mr. Ryder was a single man. In the early days of his connection with the Blue Veins he had been regarded as quite a catch, and young ladies and their mothers had maneuvered with much ingenuity to capture him. Not, however, until Mrs. Molly Dixon visited Groveland had any woman ever made him wish to change his condition to that of a married man.

Mrs. Dixon had come to Groveland from Washington in the spring, and before the summer was over she had won Mr. Ryder's heart. She possessed many attractive qualities. She was much younger than he; in fact, he was old enough to have been her father, though no one knew exactly how old he was. She was whiter than he, and better educated. She had moved in the best colored society of the country, at Washington, and had taught in the schools of that city. Such a superior person had been eagerly welcomed to the Blue Vein Society, and had taken a leading part in its activities. Mr. Ryder had at first been attracted by her charms of person, for she was very good-looking and not over twenty-five; then by her refined manners and the vivacity of her wit. Her husband had been a government clerk, and at his death had left a considerable life insurance. She was visiting friends in Groveland, and, finding the town and the people to her liking, had prolonged her stay indefinitely. She had not seemed displeased at Mr. Ryder's attentions, but on the contrary had given him every proper encouragement; and indeed, a younger and less cautious man would long since have spoken. But he had made up his mind, and had only to determine the time when he would ask her to be his wife. He decided to give a ball in her honor, and at some time during the evening of the ball to offer her his heart and hand. He had no special fears about the outcome, but, with a little touch of romance, he wanted the surroundings to be in harmony with his own feelings when he should have received the answer he expected.

Mr. Ryder resolved that this ball should mark an epoch in the social history of Groveland. He knew, of course—no one could know better—the entertainments that had taken place in past years, and what must be done to surpass them. His ball must be worthy of the lady in whose honor it was to be given, and must, by the quality of its guests, set an example for the future. He had observed of late a growing liberality, almost a laxity, in social matters, even among members of his own set, and had several times been forced to meet in a social way persons whose complexions and callings in life were hardly up to the standard which he considered proper for the society to maintain. He had a theory of his own.

"I have no race prejudice," he would say, "but we people of mixed blood are ground between the upper and the nether millstone. Our fate lies between absorption by the white race and extinction in the black. The one doesn't want us yet, but

may take us in time. The other would welcome us, but it would be for us a backward step. 'With malice towards none, with charity for all,' we must do the best we can for ourselves and those who are to follow us. Self-preservation is the first law of nature."

His ball would serve by its exclusiveness to counteract leveling tendencies, and his marriage with Mrs. Dixon would help to further the upward process of absorption he had been wishing and waiting for.

2

The ball was to take place on Friday night. The house had been put in order, the carpets covered with canvas, the halls and stairs decorated with palms and potted plants; and in the afternoon Mr. Ryder sat on his front porch, which the shade of a vine running up over a wire netting made a cool and pleasant lounging place. He expected to respond to the toast "The Ladies" at the supper, and from a volume of Tennyson—his favorite poet—was fortifying himself with apt quotations. The volume was open at "A Dream of Fair Women." His eyes fell on these lines, and he read them aloud to judge better of their effect:

At length I saw a lady within call,
   Stiller than chisell'd marble, standing there;
A daughter of the gods, divinely tall,
   And most divinely fair.

He remarked the verse, and turning the page read the stanza beginning

O sweet pale Margaret,
   O rare pale Margaret.

He weighed the passage a moment, and decided that it would not do. Mrs. Dixon was the palest lady he expected at the ball, and she was of a rather ruddy complexion, and of lively disposition and buxom build. So he ran over the leaves until his eyes rested on the description of Queen Guinevere:

She seem'd a part of joyous Spring:
A gown of grass-green silk she wore,
Buckled with golden clasps before;
A light-green tuft of plumes she bore
Closed in a golden ring.

. . .

She look'd so lovely, as she sway'd
The rein with dainty finger-tips,
A man had given all other bliss,
And all his worldly worth for this,
To waste his whole heart in one kiss
Upon her perfect lips.

As Mr. Ryder murmured these words audibly, with an appreciative thrill, he heard the latch of his gate click, and a light footfall sounding on the steps. He turned his head, and saw a woman standing before his door.

She was a little woman, not five feet tall, and proportioned to her height. Although she stood erect, and looked around her with very bright and restless eyes, she seemed quite old; for her face was crossed and recrossed with a hundred wrinkles, and around the edges of her bonnet could be seen protruding here and there a tuft of short gray wool. She wore a blue calico gown of ancient cut, a little red shawl fastened around her shoulders with an old-fashioned brass brooch, and a large bonnet profusely ornamented with faded red and yellow artificial flowers. And she was very black, so that her toothless gums, revealed when she opened her mouth to speak, were not red, but blue. She looked like a bit of the old plantation life, summoned up from the past by the wave of a magician's wand, as the poet's fancy had called into being the gracious shapes of which Mr. Ryder had just been reading.

He rose from his chair and came over to where she stood. "Good afternoon, madam," he said.

"Good evenin', suh," she answered, ducking suddenly with a quaint curtsy. Her voice was shrill and piping, but softened somewhat by age. "Is dis yere whar Mistuh Ryduh lib, suh?" she asked, looking around her doubtfully, and glancing into the open windows, through which some of the preparations for the evening were visible.

"Yes," he replied, with an air of kingly patronage, unconsciously flattered by her manner, "I am Mr. Ryder. Did you want to see me?"

"Yas, suh, ef I ain't 'sturbin' of you too much."

"Not at all. Have a seat over here behind the vine, where it is cool. What can I do for you?"

"'Scuse me, suh," she continued, when she had sat down on the edge of a chair, "'scuse me, suh, I's lookin' for my husban'. I heerd you wuz a big man an' had libbed heah a long time, an' I 'lowed you would n't min' ef I'd come roun' an' ax you ef you'd ever heerd of a merlatter man by de name er Sam Taylor 'quirin' 'round' in de chu'ches ermongs' de people fer his wife 'Liza Jane?"

Mr. Ryder seemed to think for a moment.

"There used to be many such cases right after the war," he said, "but it has been so long that I have forgotten them. There are very few now. But tell me your story, and it may refresh my memory."

She sat back farther in her chair so as to be more comfortable, and folded her withered hands in her lap.

"My name's 'Liza," she began, "'Liza Jane. W'en I wuz young I us'ter b'long ter Marse Bob Smif, down in ole Missoura. I wuz bawn down dere. W'en I wuz a gal I wuz married ter a man named Jim. But Jim died, an' after dat I married a merlatter man named Sam Taylor. Sam wuz free-bawn, but his mammy and daddy died, an' de w'ite folks 'prenticed him ter my marster fer ter work fer 'im 'tel he wuz growed up. Sam worked in de fiel', an' I wuz de cook. One day Ma'y Ann, ole miss's maid, came rushin' out ter de kitchen, an' says she, ''Liza Jane, old marse gwine sell yo' Sam down de ribber.'"

"'Go way f'm yere,' says I; 'my husban's free!'"

"'Don' make no diff'ence. I heard ole marse tell ole miss she wuz gwine take yo' Sam wid 'im termorrow, fer he needed money, an' he knowed whar he could git a t'ousan' dollars fer Sam an' no questions axed.'"

"W'en Sam come home f'm de fiel' dat night, I tole him 'bout ole marse gwine steal 'im, an' Sam run erway. His time wuz mos' up, an' he swo' dat w'en he wuz twenty-one he would come back an' he'p me run erway, er else save up de money ter buy my freedom. An I know he'd 'a' done it, fer he thought a heap er me, Sam did. But w'en he come back he did n' fin' me, fer I wuzn' dere. Ole marse had heerd dat I warned Sam, so he had me whip' an' sol' down de ribber.

"Den de wah broke out, an' w'en it wuz ober de cullud folks wuz scattered. I went back ter de ole home; but Sam wuzn' dere, an' I could n' l'arn nuffin' 'bout 'im. But I knowed he'd be'n dere to look fer me an' had n' foun' me an' had gone erway ter hunt fer me.

"I's be'n lookin' fer 'im eber sence," she added simply, as though twenty-five years were but a couple of weeks, "an' I knows he's be'n lookin' fer me. Fer he sot a heap er sto' by me, Sam did, an' I know he's be'n huntin' fer me all dese years —les'n he's be'n sick er sump'n, so he could n' work, er out'n his head, so he could n' 'member his promise. I went back down de ribber, fer I 'lowed he'd gone down dere lookin' fer me. I's be'n ter Noo Orleens, an' Atlanty, an' Charleston, an'

Richmon'; an' w'en I'd be'n all ober de Souf I come ter de Norf. Fer I knows I'll fin' 'im some er dese days," she said softly, "er he'll fin' me, an' den we'll bofe be as happy in freedom as we wuz in de ole days befo' de wah." A smile stole over her withered countenance as she paused a moment, and her bright eyes softened into a far-away look.

This was the substance of the old woman's story. She had wandered a little here and there. Mr. Ryder was looking at her curiously when she finished.

"How have you lived all these years?" he asked.

"Cookin', suh. I's a good cook. Does you know anybody w'at needs a good cook, suh? I's stoppin' wid a cullud fam'ly roun' de corner yonder 'tel I kin git a place."

"Do you really expect to find your husband? He may be dead long ago."

She shook her head emphatically. "Oh, no, he ain' dead. De signs an' de tokens tells me. I dremp three nights runnin' on'y dis las' week dat I foun' him."

"He may have married another woman. Your slave marriage would not have prevented him, for you never lived with him after the war, and without that your marriage doesn't count."

"Wouldn' make no diff'ence wid Sam. He would n' marry no yuther 'ooman 'tel he foun' out 'bout me. I knows it," she added. "Sump'n's be'n tellin' me all dese years dat I's gwine fin' Sam 'fo' I dies."

"Perhaps he's outgrown you, and climbed up in the world where he wouldn't care to have you find him."

"No, indeed, suh," she replied, "Sam ain' dat kin' er man. He wuz good ter me, Sam wuz, but he wuzn' much good ter nobody e'se, fer he wuz one er de triflin'es' han's on de plantation. I 'spec's ter haf ter suppo't 'im w'en I fin' 'im, fer he nebber would work 'less'n he had ter. But den he wuz free, an' he did n' git no pay fer his work, an' I don' blame 'im much. Mebbe he's done better sence he run erway, but I ain' 'spectin' much."

"You may have passed him on the street a hundred times during the twenty-five years, and not have known him; time works great changes."

She smiled incredulously. "I'd know 'im 'mongs' a hund'ed men. Fer dey wuzn' no yuther merlatter man like my man Sam, an' I could n' be mistook. I's toted his picture roun' wid me twenty-five years."

"May I see it?" asked Mr. Ryder. "It might help me to remember whether I have seen the original."

As she drew a small parcel from her bosom he saw that it was fastened to a string that went around her neck. Removing several wrappers, she brought to light an old-fashioned daguerreotype in a black case. He looked long and intently at the portrait. It was faded with time, but the features were still distinct, and it was easy to see what manner of man it had represented.

He closed the case, and with a slow movement handed it back to her.

"I don't know of any man in town who goes by that name," he said, "nor have I heard of any one making such inquiries. But if you will leave me your address, I will give the matter some attention, and if I find anything I will let you know."

She gave him the number of a house in the neighborhood and went away, after thanking him warmly.

He wrote the address on the fly-leaf of the volume of Tennyson, and, when she had gone, rose to his feet and stood looking after her curiously. As she walked down the street with mincing step, he saw several persons whom she passed turn and look back at her with a smile of kindly amusement. When she had turned the corner, he went upstairs to his bedroom, and stood for a long time before the mirror of his dressing-case, gazing thoughtfully at the reflection of his own face.

3

At eight o'clock the ballroom was a blaze of light and the guests had begun to assemble; for there was a literary programme and some routine business of the society to be gone through with before the dancing. A black servant in evening dress waited at the door and directed the guests to the dressing-rooms.

The occasion was long memorable among the colored people of the city; not alone for the dress and display, but for the high average of intelligence and culture that distinguished the gathering as a whole. There were a number of school teachers, several young doctors, three or four lawyers, some professional singers, an editor, a lieutenant in the United States Army spending his furlough in the city, and others in various polite callings; these were colored, though most of them would not have attracted even a casual glance because of any marked difference from white people. Most of the ladies were in evening costume, and dress coats and dancing pumps were the rule among the

men. A band of string music, stationed in an al-
cove behind a row of palms, played popular airs
while the guests were gathering.

The dancing began at half past nine. At eleven
o'clock supper was served. Mr. Ryder had left the
ballroom some little time before the intermission,
but reappeared at the supper table. The spread was
worthy of the occasion, and the guests did full justice to it. When the coffee had been served, the
toastmaster, Mr. Solomon Sadler, rapped for order.
He made a brief introductory speech, compliment-
ing host and guests, and then presented in their
order the toasts of the evening. They were responded to with a very fair display of after-dinner
wit.

"The last toast," said the toastmaster, when he
reached the end of the list, "is one which must
appeal to us all. There is no one of us of the
sterner sex who is not at some time dependent
upon woman—in infancy for protection, in manhood for companionship, in old age for care and
comforting. Our good host has been trying to live
alone, but the fair faces I see around me tonight
prove that he is too largely dependent upon the
gentler sex for most that makes life worth living—
the society and love of friends—and rumor is at
fault if he does not soon yield entire subjection
to one of them. Mr. Ryder will now respond to
the toast—'The Ladies.' "

There was a pensive look in Mr. Ryder's eyes as
he took the floor and adjusted his eye-glasses. He
began by speaking of woman as the gift of Heaven
to man, and after some general observations on the
relations of the sexes he said: "But perhaps the
quality which most distinguishes woman is her
fidelity and devotion to those she loves. History is
full of examples, but has recorded none more striking than one which only today came under my
notice."

He then related, simply but effectively, the story
told by his visitor of the afternoon. He gave it in
the same soft dialect, which came readily to his
lips, while the company listened attentively and
sympathetically. For the story had awakened a responsive thrill in many hearts. There were some
present who had seen, and others who had heard
their fathers and grandfathers tell, the wrongs and
sufferings of this past generation, and all of them
still felt, in their darker moments, the shadow
hanging over them. Mr. Ryder went on:

"Such devotion and confidence are rare even
among women. There are many who would have
searched a year, some who would have waited five

years, a few who might have hoped ten years; but
for twenty-five years this woman has retained her
affection for and her faith in a man she has not
seen or heard of in all that time.

"She came to me today in hope that I might
be able to help her find this long-lost husband.
And when she was gone I gave my fancy rein, and
imagined a case I will put to you.

"Suppose that this husband, soon after his escape, had learned that his wife had been sold
away, and that such inquiries as he could make
brought no information of her whereabouts. Suppose that he was young, and she much older than
he; that he was light, and she was black; that their
marriage was a slave marriage, and legally binding
only if they chose to make it so after the war. Suppose, too, that he made his way to the North, as
some of us have done, and there, where he had
larger opportunities, had improved them, and had
in the course of all these years grown to be as different from the ignorant boy who ran away from
fear of slavery as the day is from the night. Suppose, even, that he had qualified himself, by industry, by thrift, and by study, to win the friendship
and be considered worthy of the society of such
people as these I see around me to-night, gracing
my board and filling my heart with gladness; for
I am old enough to remember the day when such
a gathering would not have been possible in this
land. Suppose, too, that, as the years went by, this
man's memory of the past grew more and more
indistinct, until at last it was rarely, except in his
dreams, that any image of this bygone period rose
before his mind. And then suppose that accident
should bring to his knowledge the fact that the
wife of his youth, the wife he had left behind him
—not one who had walked by his side and kept
pace with him in his upward struggle, but one
upon whom advancing years and a laborious life
had set their mark—was alive and seeking him, but
that he was absolutely safe from recognition or
discovery, unless he chose to reveal himself. My
friends, what would the man do? I will presume
that he was one who loved honor, and tried to
deal justly with all men. I will even carry the case
further, and suppose that perhaps he had set his
heart upon another, whom he had hoped to call
his own. What would he do, or rather what ought
he to do, in such a crisis of a lifetime?

"It seemed to me that he might hesitate, and
I imagined that I was an old friend, a near friend,
and that he had come to me for advice; and I
argued the case with him. I tried to discuss it im-

partially. After we had looked upon the matter from every point of view, I said to him, in words that we all know

This above all: to thine own self be true,
And it must follow, as the night the day,
Thou canst not then be false to any man.

Then, finally, I put the question to him, 'Shall you acknowledge her?'

"And now, ladies and gentlemen, friends and companions, I ask you, what should he have done?"

There was something in Mr. Ryder's voice that stirred the hearts of those who sat around him. It suggested more than mere sympathy with an imaginary situation; it seemed rather in the nature of a personal appeal. It was observed, too, that his look rested more especially upon Mrs. Dixon, with a mingled expression of renunciation and inquiry.

She had listened, with parted lips and streaming eyes. She was the first to speak: "He should have acknowledged her."

"Yes," they all echoed, "he should have acknowledged her."

"My friends and companions," responded Mr. Ryder, "I thank you, one and all. It is the answer I expected, for I knew your hearts."

He turned and walked toward the closed door of an adjoining room, while every eye followed him in wondering curiosity. He came back in a moment, leading by the hand his visitor of the afternoon, who stood startled and trembling at the sudden plunge into this scene of brilliant gayety. She was neatly dressed in gray, and wore the white cap of an elderly woman.

"Ladies and gentlemen," he said, "this is the woman, and I am the man, whose story I have told you. Permit me to introduce to you the wife of my youth."

W. E. B. DU BOIS (1868–1963)

The hopes, aspirations, and attitudes expressed in religion often reappear in secular forms. For instance, the philosopher Bertrand Russell has pointed out that Christian theology finds a peculiar parallel in Marxism. It is no wonder, then, that a Nat Turner, organizing his famous slave insurrection in 1831, should have been inspired by a messianic role, or that the black world of America, both before and after the Civil War, with its deep-seated religious sense, should have nourished the hope of a secular messiah. William Edward Burghardt Du Bois (whose name is given the anglicized pronunciation), born in 1868, growing up in the age when the religious temper of life was still dominant, seems to have felt that his great talents fitted him for that role for his people.

His situation, however, was very different from that of a man like Booker T. Washington, who, even if he was half white, was born a slave and was raised in the black world of poverty and ignorance. Du Bois' grandfather and father, who could have passed as white,

were torn between the two worlds in a more obvious tension, trying to find a clear vision of their lives, and the father, seemingly even more harried and uncertain of himself than the grandfather, finally wandered away, leaving his wife and son in the little town of Great Barrington, Massachusetts, where the wife's family, the Burghardts, were old settlers. At that time, in Great Barrington, the racial situation was ambiguous, and the brilliant boy did not grow up with a gradually increasing awareness of his situation, but, as he records, discovered it suddenly and traumatically. The immediate result of the discovery was that, even in high school, where he was the only black pupil, and where he became a correspondent for a New York paper, he took it upon himself to urge the blacks to develop self-help, community participation, and political action. In this period of what he was to call the "isolation" of his boyhood, he heard, too, the singers on tour from Hampton Institute offer the then unfamiliar "spirituals" and burst into tears at recognizing "something inherently and deeply my own." But it was not until he went to Tennessee (on a scholarship to Fisk University, in Nashville) that he discovered "blackness"—the people who, as he puts it in the autobiographical *Dusk of Dawn*, "it seemed were bound to me by new and exciting and eternal ties." This discovery of "blackness" was confirmed when, during summers, he taught school—at a black school, of course—in a remote valley in Tennessee.

Other discoveries were to follow. After Fisk, Du Bois went to Harvard, where he took another B.A. degree, studied under William James and Santayana, became the first black American to win a Ph.D. (with an important dissertation on the slave trade to the United States), and then spent two years in Germany for further study. What drove the young Du Bois in his tireless quest for learning was not merely ambition (though that was there in plenty), but a sense of mission; as he wrote in a theme at Harvard, "I believe foolishly perhaps, but sincerely, that I have something to say to the world." He did have something to say, but the story of his life is not only the very process of saying it; it is the long struggle to find out what he most deeply wanted to say.

Du Bois began his career as a teacher of classics at Wilberforce College, in Ohio, and into this institution, operated on a shoe string by the African Methodist Church, where "wild screams, groans, and shrieks" emanated from the chapel at revival time, the small, dapper young man, with his elegant education and aristocratic manners, and "invariably the cane and gloves of the German student," must have dropped as though from the moon. But by 1899, under the auspices of the University of Pennsylvania, Du Bois published *The Philadelphia Negro*, the first attempt at a scientific sociological study of race in America. At this stage, Du Bois' underlying idea was that knowledge—systematic knowledge made available by research—would solve the problems of race. On the one hand, he criticized the black community for what he considered the disorganized family life (of which he himself had

been a victim) that was the heritage of slavery, a tendency toward criminality (a "menace to a civilized people"), self-pity, intellectual torpor, thriftlessness, the deficiency of racial pride and self-reliance, and the lack of will to organized self-help (in contrast to such minorities as the Jews and the Italians). On the other hand, Du Bois was resentfully aware of the shortsighted and brutal discrimination that the black man suffered and of the relation between this fact and the defects he noted in black society. Already, with his faith in knowledge, Du Bois was convinced of the need for higher education for blacks, for the nurturing of what he called the "Talented Tenth" to serve as a vanguard and a symbol. At the same time, he acidly criticized the "black aristocracy" for race betrayal, for fearing to be identified with the black masses, for economic exploitation of those masses, and for vanity and inordinate ostentation—a line of criticism later developed more systematically by Edward F. Frazier in his famous *Black Bourgeoisie*.

Beyond the whole study made by Du Bois lay the tension between two competing impulses, a tension that was to characterize the experience of the black man in America. On one hand, Du Bois envisaged a strong black culture, independent, as far as possible, economically, socially, and artistically. It is clear that he did not believe that color is merely an accident, that a black, red, yellow, or brown man is merely a white man with a different complexion. Each race, he held, has a special spirit, a special genius, and he called the "race spirit" the "greatest invention for human progress." On this basis, he urged that the blacks foster "our physical power, our intellectual endowment, our spiritual ideas." On this basis, too, Du Bois developed his doctrine of "Pan-Africanism," which was, however, unattractive to many black Americans—to Frederick Douglass, for instance, who, when he visited the Chicago World's Fair in 1893 and saw the Dahomey Village, with its straw huts, scanty costumes, and tribal dancing and singing, was horrified and embarrassed that these "repulsive savages" should be exhibited.

On the other hand, in contrast to his race spirit, Du Bois felt himself to be an heir of Western European culture. As he puts it in *The Souls of Black Folk*, by way of a rebuke to racist America:

I sit with Shakespeare and he winces not. Across the color line I move arm in arm with Balzac and Dumas, where smiling men and welcoming women glide in gilded halls. From out of the caves of evening that swim between the strong-limbed earth and the tracery of the stars, I summon Aristotle and Aurelius and what soul I will, and they come all graciously with no scorn nor condescension. So, wed with Truth, I dwell above the Veil [Du Bois's image for discrimination]. Is this the life you grudge us, O knightly America?

In this half of his mind Du Bois envisaged an America in which the blacks could participate, with equality, justice, and harmony, in the common national life. Assuming that the solution of racial issues would come by the diffusion of knowledge, he now counseled calmness, work, and patience. In other words, allowing for obvious differences, it is easy to see how Du Bois, at this stage of his development, could exist in Booker T. Washington's orbit. But the paradox submerged in Washington's feelings was obvious and dramatic in Du Bois. A doubleness—what he called "an inner psychological paradox"—was at the very center of his consciousness: "One feels his two-ness—an American, a Negro, two souls, two thoughts, two unreconciled strivings, two warring ideals in one dark body." And he continues:

The history of the American Negro is the history of this strife—this longing to attain self-conscious manhood, to merge his double self into a better and truer self. . . . He would not Africanize America for America has too much to teach the world and Africa. He would not bleach the Negro soul in a flood of white Americanism, for he knows that Negro blood has a message for the world. He simply wishes to make it possible for a man to be both a Negro and an American, without being cursed and spit upon.

The second phase of Du Bois' thought may, somewhat arbitrarily, be dated from 1897, when he went to Atlanta University, in Georgia, a black institution which, on paper at least, was integrated. Now in the southern environment, and subject to its pressures, Du Bois continued for some years his scientific study of black society. As this work proceeded, and as the post-Reconstruction program for disenfranchisement and discrimination was fulfilled, Du Bois more and more felt that the economic and cultural gains of the blacks were useless unless they could be defended at the ballot box. By 1903, in *The Souls of Black Folk*, he published a chapter called "Of Mr. Booker T. Washington and Others," in which the two key ideas are Washington's betrayal of his race and the conformity of Washington's theory to the "spirit and thought of triumphant commercialism" that dominated the age. By 1905, Du Bois, having achieved a position of leadership, convened a secret meeting of a small group at Fort Erie, Ontario, to discuss the plight of the race; and this meeting gave shape to the "radical" wing of the race, and by creating the "Niagara Movement" laid, indirectly, the foundation for the National Association for the Advancement of Colored People, created in 1909 as a biracial organization totally committed to the struggle for civil rights and social justice. Du Bois found his role as editor of the *Crisis*, the official publication of the NAACP, and for years this was, for all practical purposes, his personal forum. The combat against all that Washington had stood for was now joined.

Du Bois is best remembered as the intellectual leader of black protest for more than a generation. He was learned, had ferocious energy, and was master of a biting polemical style, and no man in the century had a more significant role in the struggle for racial justice than his. But his role was a complex one, with aspects that extended far beyond the matter of simple civil rights. He was, as we have said, an ardent exponent of Pan-Africanism and after a visit to Africa, in 1923, could write:

> The spell of Africa is upon me. The ancient witchery of her medicine is burning my drowsy, dreamy blood. This is not a country, it is a world—a universe of itself and for itself, a thing, Different, Immense, Menacing, Alluring. . . . Africa is the Spiritual Frontier of human kind—oh, the wild and beautiful adventures of its taming!

But with all his romantic passion for Africa, Du Bois was a stout adversary of the Garvey movement, the most significant manifestation of black nationalism ever known in this country.[1] To Du Bois, Garvey was simply a wild demagogue, with no rational program. Furthermore, the black nationalism of the slums offended Du Bois' aesthetic and intellectual temperament. He simply could not understand leadership divorced from intellectual distinction.

Du Bois' relation to Marxism offers some of the same complexity and paradoxicality that we find in his relation to the Garvey movement, and it is by reference to Marxism that we may label the third phase of Du Bois' development. His socialism had been of long and gradual growth. After the Russian Revolution he had said that a socialist order should never be established by "murder," but by 1926, after a visit to Russia, he wrote:

> I stand in astonishment and wonder at the revelation of Russia that has come to me. I may be particularly deceived and half informed. But if what I have seen with my eyes and heard with my ears in Russia is Bolshevism, I am a Bolshevik.

He found, it seemed, the kind of cultural pluralism he had longed for in America, and as for race prejudice, he said: "while in Moscow if I happened to sit beside a white woman, no one seemed to notice me." Even so, Du Bois could never quite make peace between "his blackness" and his Marxism. Even if one of his most famous books, *Black Reconstruction,* is a Marxist interpretation of the post–Civil War period,[2] Du Bois could not help but recognize that the Communists in the United States had been willing to sacrifice blacks for party propaganda, and that the relation between black and white labor in the United States left something to be desired.

Ending his editorship of the *Crisis,* after three decades of struggle, often against the NAACP itself, Du Bois retired briefly to Atlanta to resume his academic life. It was only natural, however, that with the turn of time, with the effects of the Depression and the coming on of the Second World War, he should find the

---

[1] Marcus Mosiah Garvey was born in 1887, in Jamaica. With some education (he was a printer by trade), he undertook, single-handed, a crusade to relieve the condition of black men all over the world. Along the way he became especially interested in Booker T. Washington; however, he grafted on to Washington's views the doctrine of Africa for Africans, the idea of creating a powerful homeland that would command international respect and protect blacks everywhere; to this end Garvey founded the Universal Negro Improvement Association. By the early 1920's, riding the wave of resentment and unrest consequent on the First World War, and the new enthusiasm for Pan-Africanism, Garvey built up a membership for the UNIA of some millions of blacks, so he claimed, in the Indies, Central America, Africa, and the United States, where he had come, in 1916, to establish headquarters. An accomplished showman and psychologist, he set up as a glittering potentate, dispensing titles to his court—an emperor without an empire. But he did have the Universal African Legion (a para-military organization), the Africa Motor Corps, the Black Flying Eagles, the Negro Political Union, and the Black Star Line.

It was this last organization, with its four derelict steamers, that brought him to grief. In raising money for the Black Star Line, Garvey, who was no businessman, laid himself open to charges of "deceptive artifices" in promoting stock sales by mail. In general, black leaders, several officials of the NAACP, A. Philip Randolph and Du Bois among them, closed ranks against Garvey and pushed for his conviction. He was convicted, and it is sometimes maintained by historians that the conviction was primarily political in motivation. The sentence of five years was commuted by President Coolidge, and Garvey was deported.

[2] The general view among historians is that in this work Du Bois simply ignores certain obvious facts in order to make the conduct of both slaves (later freemen) and poor white southerners conform to Marxist theory.

world running past him. More and more disillusioned with white America, he had come to believe that the pluralistic society of his early dream would not be attainable for generations and was staking his practical, more immediate hope on a segregated black world organized according to socialistic and fraternal principles. But for the next twenty years—that is, up into the 1960's, when pressures for separatism again became significant—the dominant drive in the black community would be toward some form of integration. By that time, Du Bois, now an avowed Communist, had shaken the dust of America off his feet and gone to Africa, where he took out Ghanaian citizenship. He died there on August 27, 1963, in Accra.

BIOGRAPHICAL CHART

1868 Born, February 23, in Great Barrington, Massachusetts

1884 Graduates from high school in Great Barrington, valedictorian

1885–88 Attends Fisk University, Nashville, Tennessee, receiving B.A.; teaches in country schools during summers

1888 Enters Harvard as a junior

1890 Receives B.A., *cum laude*; one of six commencement speakers, subject: "Jefferson Davis: Representative of Civilization"; attracts national attention

1892–94 Graduate student at University of Berlin

1894–96 Professor of Greek and Latin, Wilberforce University, Ohio

1896 Receives Ph.D. from Harvard

1896–97 Assistant instructor of sociology, University of Pennsylvania

1897–1910 Professor of economics and history, Atlanta University; organizer of University Studies of the Negro Problem

1900 Secretary, first Pan-African Conference in England

1903 *The Souls of Black Folks: Essays and Sketches*

1905 Founder and general secretary of the Niagara Movement

1909 Among original founders and incorporators of the National Association for the Advancement of Colored People (NAACP)

1910–34 Director of publicity and research, board of directors, NAACP; edits the *Crisis* (until 1934); joins Socialist party

1911 First Universal Races Congress in England

1912 Supports Woodrow Wilson in Presidential campaign; helps organize first significant Negro breakaway from Republican party; resigns from Socialist party

1915 *The Negro*

1917–18 Supports U.S. entry into First World War; fights maltreatment of Negro troops; leads in efforts to enroll Negro officers; leads massive silent protest parade (1917) in New York City, against lynching and jim-crow

1919 Investigates racist treatment of Negro troops in Europe; chief organizer of modern Pan-African movement, with first conference held in Paris

1920 Leader in exposing role of U.S. in Haiti; *Darkwater: Voices from Within the Veil*

1921 Second Pan-African Congress, London, Brussels, and Paris

1923 Spingarn medalist; Special Minister Plenipotentiary and Envoy Extraordinary representing the United States at inauguration of President of Liberia; third Pan-African Congress in London, Paris, and Lisbon

1926 Visits the Soviet Union for the first time

1927 Leader in Negro Renaissance movement; founds the Negro Theatre in Harlem called the "Krigwa Players"; fourth Pan-African Congress in New York

1933 Leading force in undertaking to produce an *Encyclopedia of the Negro*

1934 Resigns from the *Crisis* and Board of NAACP

1934–44 Chairman, Department of Sociology, Atlanta University

1936 Travels around the world

1940 Founds and edits (to 1944) *Phylon* magazine, Atlanta

1944 Returns to NAACP as director of special research

1945 With Walter White, accredited from the NAACP as consultant to founding convention of United Nations; seeks anti-colonial commitment by United States; presides at fifth Pan-African Congress in Manchester, England

1949 Helps organize Cultural and Scientific Conference for World Peace, New York City; attends Paris Peace Congress; attends Moscow Peace Congress

1950 Candidate in New York for U.S. Senator, Progressive party

1958–59 Travels extensively, especially to USSR and China

1961 *The Worlds of Color*; joins Communist party of United States; emigrates to Ghana, becoming Ghanaian citizen

1963 Dies, August 27

FURTHER READINGS

The reader will find individual titles of Du Bois' works in the biographical chart.

W. E. B. Du Bois, *The Autobiography of W. E. B. Du Bois: A Soliloquy on Viewing My Life from the Last Decade of the First Century* (1968)

Francis L. Broderick, *W. E. B. Du Bois: Negro Leader in a Time of Crisis* (1957)

Leslie A. Lacy, *Cheer the Lonesome Traveler: The Life of W. E. B. Du Bois* (1970)

Meyer Weinberg, ed., *W. E. B. Du Bois: A Reader* (1970)

The Song of the Smoke (1921)

I am the smoke king,
I am black.
I am swinging in the sky,
I am ringing worlds on high:
I am the thought of the throbbing mills,
I am the soul toil kills,
I am the ripple of trading rills.

Up I'm curling from the sod,
I am whirling home to God.
I am the smoke king,   10
I am black.

I am the smoke king,
I am black.
I am wreathing broken hearts,
I am sheathing devils' darts;
Dark inspiration of iron times,
Wedding the toil of toiling climes
Shedding the blood of bloodless crimes.

Down I lower in the blue,
Up I tower toward the true,   20
I am the smoke king,
I am black.

I am the smoke king,
I am black.

I am darkening with song,
I am hearkening to wrong;
I will be black as blackness can,
The blacker the mantle the mightier the man,
My purpl'ing midnights no day dawn may ban.

I am carving God in night,   30
I am painting hell in white.
I am the smoke king,
I am black.

I am the smoke king,
I am black.

I am cursing ruddy morn,
I am nursing hearts unborn;
Souls unto me are as mists in the night.
I whiten my blackmen, I beckon my white,
What's the hue of a hide to a man in his might!   40

Sweet Christ, pity toiling lands!
Hail to the smoke king,
Hail to the black!

Of Mr. Booker T. Washington and Others (1903)

*From birth till death enslaved; in word, in deed,
    unmanned!*

* * *

*Hereditary bondsmen! Know ye not
Who would be free themselves must strike the blow?*
                                    BYRON

Easily the most striking thing in the history of the American Negro since 1876 is the ascendancy of Mr. Booker T. Washington. It began at the time when war memories and ideals were rapidly passing; a day of astonishing commercial development was dawning; a sense of doubt and hesitation over-took the freedmen's sons,—then it was that his leading began. Mr. Washington came, with a simple definite programme, at the psychological moment when the nation was a little ashamed of having bestowed so much sentiment on Negroes, and was concentrating its energies on Dollars. His programme of industrial education, conciliation of the South, and submission and silence as to civil and political rights, was not wholly original; the Free Negroes from 1880 up to war-time had striven to build industrial schools, and the American Missionary Association had from the first taught various trades; and Price and others had sought a way of honorable alliance with the best of the South-erners. But Mr. Washington first indissolubly linked these things; he put enthusiasm, unlimited energy, and perfect faith into this programme, and changed it from a by-path into a veritable Way of Life. And the tale of the methods by which he did this is a fascinating study of human life.

It startled the nation to hear a Negro advocating such a programme after many decades of bitter complaint; it startled and won the applause of the South; it interested and won the admiration of the North; and after a confused murmur of pro-tests, it silenced if it did not convert the Negroes themselves.

To gain the sympathy and coöperation of the various elements comprising the white South was Mr. Washington's first task; and this, at the time Tuskegee was founded, seemed, for a black man, well-nigh impossible. And yet ten years later it was done in the word spoken at Atlanta: "In all things purely social we can be as separate as the five fingers, and yet one as the hand in all things essen-tial to mutual progress." This "Atlanta Compro-mise" is by all odds the most notable thing in Mr. Washington's career. The South interpreted it in different ways: the radicals received it as a com-plete surrender of the demand for civil and political equality; the conservatives, as a generously con-ceived working basis for mutual understanding. So both approved it, and to-day its author is certainly the most distinguished Southerner since Jefferson Davis, and the one with the largest personal fol-lowing.

Next to this achievement comes Mr. Washing-ton's work in gaining place and consideration in the North. Others less shrewd and tactful had formerly essayed to sit on these two stools and had fallen between them; but as Mr. Washington knew the heart of the South from birth and train-ing, so by singular insight he intuitively grasped the spirit of the age which was dominating the North. And so thoroughly did he learn the speech and thought of triumphant commercialism, and the ideals of material prosperity, that the picture of a lone black boy poring over a French grammar amid the weeds and dirt of a neglected home soon seemed to him the acme of absurdities. One won-ders what Socrates and St. Francis of Assisi would say to this.

And yet this very singleness of vision and thor-ough oneness with his age is a mark of the suc-cessful man. It is as though Nature must needs make men narrow in order to give them force. So

Mr. Washington's cult has gained unquestioning followers, his work has wonderfully prospered, his friends are legion, and his enemies are confounded. To-day he stands as the one recognized spokesman of his ten million fellows, and one of the most notable figures in a nation of seventy millions. One hesitates, therefore, to criticize a life which, begin-ning with so little, has done so much. And yet the time is come when one may speak in all sincerity and utter courtesy of the mistakes and shortcom-ings of Mr. Washington's career, as well as of his triumphs, without being thought captious or en-vious, and without forgetting that it is easier to do ill than well in the world.

The criticism that has hitherto met Mr. Wash-ington has not always been of this broad character. In the South especially has he had to walk warily to avoid the harshest judgments,—and naturally so, for he is dealing with the one subject of deepest sensitiveness to that section. Twice—once when at the Chicago celebration of the Spanish-American War he alluded to the color-prejudice that is "eat-ing away the vitals of the South," and once when he dined with President Roosevelt—has the result-ing Southern criticism been violent enough to threaten seriously his popularity. In the North the feeling has several times forced itself into words, that Mr. Washington's counsels of submission overlooked certain elements of true mankind, and that his educational programme was unnecessarily narrow. Usually, however, such criticism has not found open expression, although, too, the spiritual sons of the Abolitionists have not been prepared to acknowledge that the schools founded before Tuskegee, by men of broad ideals and self-sacri-ficing spirit, were wholly failures or worthy of ridi-cule. While, then, criticism has not failed to fol-low Mr. Washington, yet the prevailing public opinion of the land has been but too willing to deliver the solution of a wearisome problem into his hands, and say, "If that is all you and your race ask, take it."

Among his own people, however, Mr. Washing-ton has encountered the strongest and most lasting opposition, amounting at times to bitterness, and even to-day continuing strong and insistent even though largely silenced in outward expression by the public opinion of the nation. Some of this opposition is, of course, mere envy; the disappoint-ment of displaced demagogues and the spite of narrow minds. But aside from this, there is among educated and thoughtful colored men in all parts of the land a feeling of deep regret, sorrow, and apprehension at the wide currency and ascendancy which some of Mr. Washington's theories have gained. These same men admire his sincerity of purpose, and are willing to forgive much to honest endeavor which is doing something worth the doing. They coöperate with Mr. Washington as far as they conscientiously can; and, indeed, it is no ordinary tribute to this man's tact and power that, steering as he must between so many diverse interests and opinions, he so largely retains the respect of all.

But the hushing of the criticism of honest opponents is a dangerous thing. It leads some of the best of the critics to unfortunate silence and paralysis of effort, and others to burst into speech so passionately and intemperately as to lose listeners. Honest and earnest criticism from those whose interests are most nearly touched,—criticism of writers by readers, of government by those governed, of leaders by those led,—this is the soul of democracy and the safeguard of modern society. If the best of the American Negroes receive by outer pressure a leader whom they had not recognized before, manifestly there is here a certain palpable gain. Yet there is also irreparable loss,—a loss of that peculiarly valuable education which a group receives when by search and criticism it finds and commissions its own leaders. The way in which this is done is at once the most elementary and the nicest problem of social growth. History is but the record of such group-leadership; and yet how infinitely changeful is its type and character! And of all types and kinds, what can be more instructive than the leadership of a group within a group? —that curious double movement where real progress may be negative and actual advance be relative retrogression. All this is the social student's inspiration and despair.

Now in the past the American Negro has had instructive experience in the choosing of group leaders, founding thus a peculiar dynasty which in the light of present conditions is worth while studying. When sticks and stones and beasts form the sole environment of a people, their attitude is largely one of determined opposition to and conquest of natural forces. But when to earth and brute is added an environment of men and ideas, then the attitude of the imprisoned group may take three main forms,—a feeling of revolt and revenge; an attempt to adjust all thought and action to the will of the greater group; or, finally, a determined effort at self-realization and self-development despite environing opinion. The influence of all of these attitudes at various times can be traced in the history of the American Negro, and in the evolution of his successive leaders.

Before 1750, while the fire of African freedom still burned in the veins of the slaves, there was in all leadership or attempted leadership but the one motive of revolt and revenge, typified in the terrible Maroons, the Danish blacks, and Cato of Stono, and veiling all the Americans in fear of insurrection. The liberalizing tendencies of the latter half of the eighteenth century brought, along with kindlier relations between black and white, thoughts of ultimate adjustment and assimilation. Such aspiration was especially voiced in the earnest songs of Phyllis, in the martyrdom of Attucks, the fighting of Salem and Poor, the intellectual accomplishments of Banneker and Derham, and the political demands of the Cuffes.

Stern financial and social stress after the war cooled much of the previous humanitarian ardor. The disappointment and impatience of the Negroes at the persistence of slavery and serfdom voiced itself in two movements. The slaves in the South, aroused undoubtedly by vague rumors of the Haytian revolt, made three fierce attempts at insurrection,—in 1800 under Gabriel in Virginia, in 1822 under Vesey in Carolina, and in 1831 again in Virginia under the terrible Nat Turner. In the Free States, on the other hand, a new and curious attempt at self-development was made. In Philadelphia and New York color-prescription led to a withdrawal of Negro communicants from white churches and the formation of a peculiar socio-religious institution among the Negroes known as the African Church,—an organization still living and controlling in its various branches over a million of men.

Walker's wild appeal against the trend of the times showed how the world was changing after the coming of the cotton-gin. By 1820 slavery seemed hopelessly fastened on the South, and the slaves thoroughly cowed into submission. The free Negroes of the North, inspired by the mulatto immigrants from the West Indies, began to change the basis of their demands; they recognized the slavery of slaves, but insisted that they themselves were freemen, and sought assimilation and amalgamation with the nation on the same terms with other men. Thus, Forten and Purvis of Philadelphia, Shad of Wilmington, Du Bois of New Haven, Barbadoes of Boston, and others, strove singly and together as men, they said, not as slaves; as "people of color," not as "Negroes." The trend of the times, however, refused them recognition save in individual and exceptional cases, considered them as one with all the despised blacks, and they soon found themselves striving to keep even the rights they formerly had of voting and working and moving as freemen. Schemes of migration and colonization arose among them; but these they refused to entertain, and they eventually turned to the Abolition movement as a final refuge.

Here, led by Remond, Nell, Wells-Brown, and Douglass, a new period of self-assertion and self-development dawned. To be sure, ultimate freedom and assimilation was the ideal before the leaders, but the assertion of the manhood rights of the Negro by himself was the main reliance, and John Brown's raid was the extreme of its logic. After the war and emancipation, the great form of Frederick Douglass, the greatest of American Negro leaders, still led the host. Self-assertion, especially in political lines, was the main programme, and behind Douglass came Elliot, Bruce, and Langston, and the Reconstruction politicians, and, less conspicuous but of greater social significance Alexander Crummell and Bishop Daniel Payne.

Then came the Revolution of 1876, the suppression of the Negro votes, the changing and shifting of ideals, and the seeking of new lights in the great night. Douglass, in his old age, still bravely stood for the ideals of his early manhood, —ultimate assimilation *through* self-assertion, and on no other terms. For a time Price arose as a new leader, destined, it seemed, not to give up, but to re-state the old ideals in a form less repugnant to the white South. But he passed away in his prime. Then came the new leader. Nearly all the former ones had become leaders by the silent suffrage of their fellows, had sought to lead their own people alone, and were usually, save Douglass, little known outside their race. But Booker T. Washington arose as essentially the leader not of one race but of two,—a compromiser between the South, the North, and the Negro. Naturally the Negroes resented, at first bitterly, signs of compromise which surrendered their civil and political rights, even though this was to be exchanged for larger chances of economic development. The rich and dominating North, however, was not only weary of the race problem, but was investing largely in Southern enterprises, and welcomed any method of peaceful coöperation. Thus, by national opinion, the Negroes began to recognize Mr. Washington's leadership; and the voice of criticism was hushed.

Mr. Washington represents in Negro thought the old attitude of adjustment and submission; but adjustment at such a peculiar time as to make his programme unique. This is an age of unusual economic development, and Mr. Washington's programme naturally takes an economic cast, becoming a gospel of Work and Money to such an extent as apparently almost completely to overshadow the higher aims of life. Moreover, this is an age when the more advanced races are coming in closer contact with the less developed races, and the race-feeling is therefore intensified; and Mr. Washington's programme practically accepts the alleged inferiority of the Negro races. Again, in our own land, the reaction from the sentiment of war time has given impetus to race-prejudices against Negroes, and Mr. Washington withdraws many of the high demands of Negroes as men and American citizens. In other periods of intensified prejudice all the Negro's tendency to self-assertion has been called forth; at this period a policy of submission is advocated. In the history of nearly all other races and peoples the doctrine preached at such crises has been that manly self-respect is worth more than lands and houses, and that a people who voluntarily surrender such respect, or cease striving for it, are not worth civilizing.

In answer to this, it has been claimed that the Negro can survive only through submission. Mr. Washington distinctly asks that black people give up, at least for the present, three things,—

First, political power,

Second, insistence on civil rights,

Third, higher education of Negro youth,—
and concentrate all their energies on industrial education, the accumulation of wealth, and the conciliation of the South. This policy has been courageously and insistently advocated for over fifteen years, and has been triumphant for perhaps ten years. As a result of this tender of the palm-branch, what has been the return? In these years there have occurred:

1. The disfranchisement of the Negro.

2. The legal creation of a distinct status of civil inferiority for the Negro.

3. The steady withdrawal of aid from institutions for the higher training of the Negro.

These movements are not, to be sure, direct results of Mr. Washington's teachings; but his propaganda has, without a shadow of doubt, helped their speedier accomplishment. The question then comes: Is it possible, and probable, that nine millions of men can make effective progress in economic lines if they are deprived of political rights, made a servile caste, and allowed only the most meagre chance for developing their exceptional men? If history and reason give any distinct answer to these questions, it is an emphatic No. And Mr. Washington thus faces the triple paradox of his career:

1. He is striving nobly to make Negro artisans business men and property-owners; but it is utterly impossible, under modern competitive methods, for workingmen and property-owners to defend their rights and exist without the right of suffrage.

2. He insists on thrift and self-respect, but at the same time counsels a silent submission to civic inferiority such as is bound to sap the manhood of any race in the long run.

3. He advocates common-school and industrial training, and depreciates institutions of higher learning; but neither the Negro common-schools, nor Tuskegee itself, could remain open a day were it not for teachers trained in Negro colleges, or trained by their graduates.

This triple paradox in Mr. Washington's position is the object of criticism by two classes of colored Americans. One class is spiritually descended from Toussaint the Savior, through Gabriel, Vesey, and Turner, and they represent the attitude of revolt and revenge; they hate the white South blindly and distrust the white race generally, and so far as they agree on definite action, think that the Negro's only hope lies in emigration beyond the borders of the United States. And yet, by the irony of fate, nothing has more effectually made this programme seem hopeless than the recent course of the United States toward weaker and darker peoples in the West Indies, Hawaii, and the Philippines,—for where in the world may we go and be safe from lying and brute force?

The other class of Negroes who cannot agree with Mr. Washington has hitherto said little aloud. They deprecate the sight of scattered counsels, of internal disagreement; and especially they dislike making their just criticism of a useful and earnest man an excuse for a general discharge of venom from small-minded opponents. Nevertheless, the questions involved are so fundamental and serious that it is difficult to see how men like the Grimkes, Kelly Miller, J. W. E. Bowen, and other representatives of this group, can much longer be silent. Such men feel in conscience bound to ask of this nation three things:

1. The right to vote.
2. Civic equality.

3. The education of youth according to ability. They acknowledge Mr. Washington's invaluable service in counselling patience and courtesy in such demands; they do not ask that ignorant black men vote when ignorant whites are debarred, or that any reasonable restrictions in the suffrage should not be applied; they know that the low social level of the mass of the race is responsible for much discrimination against it, but they also know, and the nation knows, that relentless color-prejudice is more often a cause than a result of the Negro's degradation; they seek the abatement of this relic of barbarism, and not its systematic encouragement and pampering by all agencies of social power from the Associated Press to the Church of Christ. They advocate, with Mr. Washington, a broad system of Negro common schools supplemented by thorough industrial training; but they are surprised that a man of Mr. Washington's insight cannot see that no such educational system ever has rested or can rest on any other basis than that of the well-equipped college and university, and they insist that there is a demand for a few such institutions throughout the South to train the best of the Negro youth as teachers, professional men, and leaders.

This group of men honor Mr. Washington for his attitude of conciliation toward the white South; they accept the "Atlanta Compromise" in its broadest interpretation; they recognize, with him, many signs of promise, many men of high purpose and fair judgment, in this section; they know that no easy task has been laid upon a region already tottering under heavy burdens. But, nevertheless, they insist that the way to truth and right lies in straightforward honesty, not in indiscriminate flattery; in praising those of the South who do well and criticising uncompromisingly those who do ill; in taking advantage of the opportunities at hand and urging their fellows to do the same, but at the same time remembering that only a firm adherence to their higher ideals and aspirations will ever keep those ideals within the realm of possibility. They do not expect that the free right to vote, to enjoy civic rights, and to be educated, will come in a moment; they do not expect to see the bias and prejudices of years disappear at the blast of a trumpet; but they are absolutely certain that the way for a people to gain their reasonable rights is not by voluntarily throwing them away and insisting that they do not want them; that the way for a people to gain respect is not by continually belittling and ridiculing themselves; that, on the contrary, Negroes must insist continually, in season and out of season, that voting is necessary to modern manhood, that color discrimination is barbarism, and that black boys need education as well as white boys.

In failing thus to state plainly and unequivocally the legitimate demands of their people, even at the cost of opposing an honored leader, the thinking classes of American Negroes would shirk a heavy responsibility,—a responsibility to themselves, a responsibility to the struggling masses, a responsibility to the darker races of men whose future depends so largely on this American experiment, but especially a responsibility to this nation,—this common Fatherland. It is wrong to encourage a man or a people in evil-doing; it is wrong to aid and abet a national crime simply because it is unpopular not to do so. The growing spirit of kindliness and reconciliation between the North and South after the frightful differences of a generation ago ought to be a source of deep congratulation to all, and especially to those whose mistreatment caused the war; but if that reconciliation is to be marked by the industrial slavery and civic death of those same black men, with permanent legislation into a position of inferiority, then those black men, if they are really men, are called upon by every consideration of patriotism and loyalty to oppose such a course by all civilized methods, even though such opposition involves disagreement with Mr. Booker T. Washington. We have no right to sit silently by while the inevitable seeds are sown for a harvest of disaster to our children, black and white.

First, it is the duty of black men to judge the South discriminatingly. The present generation of Southerners are not responsible for the past, and they should not be blindly hated or blamed for it. Furthermore, to no class is the indiscriminate endorsement of the recent course of the South toward Negroes more nauseating than to the best thought of the South. The South is not "solid"; it is a land in the ferment of social change, wherein forces of all kinds are fighting for supremacy; and to praise the ill the South is to-day perpetrating is just as wrong as to condemn the good. Discriminating and broad-minded criticism is what the South needs, —needs it for the sake of her own white sons and daughters, and for the insurance of robust, healthy mental and moral development.

To-day even the attitude of the Southern whites toward the blacks is not, as so many assume, in all cases the same; the ignorant Southerner hates the Negro, the workingmen fear his competition, the money-makers wish to use him as a laborer, some of the educated see a menace in his upward development, while others—usually the sons of the masters—wish to help him to rise. National opinion has enabled this last class to maintain the Negro common schools, and to protect the Negro partially in property, life, and limb. Through the pressure of the money-makers, the Negro is in danger of being reduced to semi-slavery, especially in the country districts; the workingmen, and those of the educated who fear the Negro, have united to disfranchise him, and some have urged his deportation; while the passions of the ignorant are easily aroused to lynch and abuse any black man. To praise this intricate whirl of thought and prejudice is nonsense; to inveigh indiscriminately against "the South" is unjust; but to use the same breath in praising Governor Aycock, exposing Senator Morgan, arguing with Mr. Thomas Nelson Page, and denouncing Senator Ben Tillman, is not only sane, but the imperative duty of thinking black men.

It would be unjust to Mr. Washington not to acknowledge that in several instances he has opposed movements in the South which were unjust to the Negro; he sent memorials to the Louisiana and Alabama constitutional conventions, he has spoken against lynching, and in other ways has openly or silently set his influence against sinister schemes and unfortunate happenings. Notwithstanding this, it is equally true to assert that on the whole the distinct impression left by Mr. Washington's propaganda is, first, that the South is justified in its present attitude toward the Negro because of the Negro's degradation; secondly, that the prime cause of the Negro's failure to rise more quickly is his wrong education in the past; and, thirdly, that his future rise depends primarily on his own efforts. Each of these propositions is a dangerous half-truth. The supplementary truths must never be lost sight of: first, slavery and race-prejudice are potent if not sufficient causes of the Negro's position; second, industrial and common-school training were necessarily slow in planting because they had to await the black teachers trained by higher institutions,—it being extremely doubtful if any essentially different development was possible, and certainly a Tuskegee was unthinkable before 1880; and, third, while it is a great truth to say that the Negro must strive and strive mightily to help himself, it is equally true that unless his striving be not simply seconded, but rather aroused and encouraged, by the initiative of the richer and wiser environing group, he cannot hope for great success.

In his failure to realize and impress this last point, Mr. Washington is especially to be criticised. His doctrine has tended to make the whites, North and South, shift the burden of the Negro problem to the Negro's shoulders and stand aside as critical and rather pessimistic spectators; when in fact the burden belongs to the nation, and the hands of none of us are clean if we bend not our energies to righting these great wrongs.

The South ought to be led, by candid and honest criticism, to assert her better self and do her full duty to the race she has cruelly wronged and is still wronging. The North—her co-partner in guilt—cannot salve her conscience by plastering it with gold. We cannot settle this problem by diplomacy and suaveness, by "policy" alone. If worse come to worst, can the moral fibre of this country survive the slow throttling and murder of nine millions of men?

The black men of America have a duty to perform, a duty stern and delicate,—a forward movement to oppose a part of the work of their greatest leader. So far as Mr. Washington preaches Thrift, Patience, and Industrial Training for the masses, we must hold up his hands and strive with him, rejoicing in his honors and glorying in the strength of this Joshua called of God and of man to lead the headless host. But so far as Mr. Washington apologizes for injustice, North or South, does not rightly value the privilege and duty of voting, belittles the emasculating effects of caste distinctions, and opposes the higher training and ambition of our brighter minds,—so far as he, the South, or the Nation, does this,—we must unceasingly and firmly oppose them. By every civilized and peaceful method we must strive for the rights which the world accords to men, clinging unwaveringly to those great words which the sons of the Fathers would fain forget: "We hold these truths to be self-evident: That all men are created equal; that they are endowed by their Creator with certain unalienable rights; that among these are life, liberty, and the pursuit of happiness."

Providence as grace vs pride of desert

Of the Sorrow Songs (1903)

> *I walk through the churchyard*
> *To lay this body down;*
> *I know moon-rise, I know star-rise;*
> *I walk in the moonlight, I walk in the starlight;*
> *I'll lie in the grave and stretch out my arms,*
> *I'll go to judgment in the evening of the day,*
> *And my soul and thy soul shall meet that day,*
> *When I lay this body down.*
>
> NEGRO SONG

They that walked in darkness sang songs in the olden days—Sorrow Songs—for they were weary at heart. And so before each thought that I have written in this book I have set a phrase, a haunting echo of these weird old songs in which the soul of the black slave spoke to men. Ever since I was a child these songs have stirred me strangely. They came out of the South unknown to me, one by one, and yet at once I knew them as of me and of mine. Then in after years when I came to Nashville I saw the great temple builded of these songs towering over the pale city. To me Jubilee Hall seemed ever made of the songs themselves, and its bricks were red with the blood and dust of toil.

Out of them rose for me morning, noon, and night, bursts of wonderful melody, full of the voices of my brothers and sisters, full of the voices of the past.

Little of beauty has America given the world save the rude grandeur God himself stamped on her bosom; the human spirit in this new world has expressed itself in vigor and ingenuity rather than in beauty. And so by fateful chance the Negro folk-song—the rhythmic cry of the slave—stands to-day not simply as the sole American music, but as the most beautiful expression of human experience born this side the seas. It has been neglected, it has been, and is, half despised, and above all it has been persistently mistaken and misunderstood; but notwithstanding, it still remains as the singular spiritual heritage of the nation and the greatest gift of the Negro people.

Away back in the thirties the melody of these slave songs stirred the nation, but the songs were soon half forgotten. Some, like "Near the lake where drooped the willow," passed into current airs and their source was forgotten; others were caricatured on the "minstrel" stage and their memory died away. Then in war-time came the singular Port Royal experiment after the capture of Hilton Head, and perhaps for the first time the North met the Southern slave face to face and heart to heart with no third witness. The Sea Islands of the Carolinas, where they met, were filled with a black folk of primitive type, touched and moulded less by the world about them than any others outside the Black Belt. Their appearance was uncouth, their language funny, but their hearts were human and their singing stirred men with a mighty power. Thomas Wentworth Higginson hastened to tell of these songs, and Miss McKim and others urged upon the world their rare beauty. But the world listened only half credulously until the Fisk Jubilee Singers sang the slave songs so deeply into the world's heart that it can never wholly forget them again.

There was once a blacksmith's son born at Cadiz, New York, who in the changes of time taught school in Ohio and helped defend Cincinnati from Kirby Smith. Then he fought at Chancellorsville and Gettysburg and finally served in the Freedman's Bureau at Nashville. Here he formed a Sunday-school class of black children in 1866, and sang with them and taught them to sing. And then they taught him to sing, and when once the glory of the Jubilee songs passed into the soul of George L. White, he knew his life-work was to let those Negroes sing to the world as they had sung to him. So in 1871 the pilgrimage of the Fisk Jubilee Singers began. North to Cincinnati they rode,—four half-clothed black boys and five girl-women,—led by a man with a cause and a purpose. They stopped at Wilberforce, the oldest of Negro schools, where a black bishop blessed them. Then they went, fighting cold and starvation, shut out of hotels, and cheerfully sneered at, ever northward; and ever the magic of their song kept thrilling hearts, until a burst of applause in the Congregational Council at Oberlin revealed them to the world. They came to New York and Henry Ward Beecher dared to welcome them, even though the metropolitan dailies sneered at his "Nigger Minstrels." So their songs conquered till they sang across the land and across the sea, before Queen and Kaiser, in Scotland and Ireland, Holland and Switzerland. Seven years they sang, and brought back a hundred and fifty thousand dollars to found Fisk University.

Since their day they have been imitated—sometimes well, by the singers of Hampton and Atlanta, sometimes ill, by straggling quartettes. Caricature has sought again to spoil the quaint beauty of the music, and has filled the air with many debased melodies which vulgar ears scarce know from the real. But the true Negro folk-song still lives in the hearts of those who have heard them truly sung and in the hearts of the Negro people.

What are these songs, and what do they mean? I know little of music and can say nothing in technical phrase, but I know something of men, and knowing them, I know that these songs are the articulate message of the slave to the world. They tell us in these eager days that life was joyous to the black slave, careless and happy. I can easily believe this of some, of many. But not all the past South, though it rose from the dead, can gainsay the heart-touching witness of these songs. They are the music of an unhappy people, of the children of disappointment; they tell of death and suffering and unvoiced longing toward a truer world, of misty wanderings and hidden ways.

The songs are indeed the siftings of centuries; the music is far more ancient than the words, and in it we can trace here and there signs of development. My grandfather's grandmother was seized by an evil Dutch trader two centuries ago; and coming to the valleys of the Hudson and Housatonic, black, little, and lithe, she shivered and shrank in the harsh north winds, looked longingly at the hills, and often crooned a heathen melody to the child between her knees, thus:

"Do ba-na co-ba, ge-ne me, ge-ne me!
Do ba-na co-ba, ge-ne me, ge-ne me!
Ben d' nu-li, nu-li, nu-li, nu-li, ben d' le."

The child sang it to his children and they to their children's children, and so two hundred years it has travelled down to us and we sing it to our children, knowing as little as our fathers what its words may mean, but knowing well the meaning of its music.

This was primitive African music; it may be seen in larger form in the strange chant which heralds "The Coming of John":

"You may bury me in the East,
You may bury me in the West,
But I'll hear the trumpet sound in that morning,"

—the voice of exile.

Ten master songs, more or less, one may pluck from this forest of melody—songs of undoubted *rock music*

Negro origin and wide popular currency, and songs peculiarly characteristic of the slave. One of these I have just mentioned. Another whose strains begin this book is "Nobody knows the trouble I've seen." When, struck with a sudden poverty, the United States refused to fulfil its promises of land to the freedmen, a brigadier-general went down to the Sea Islands to carry the news. An old woman on the outskirts of the throng began singing this song; all the mass joined with her, swaying. And the soldier wept.

The third song is the cradle-song of death which all men know,—"Swing low, sweet chariot,"—whose bars begin the life story of "Alexander Crummell." Then there is the song of many waters, "Roll, Jordan, roll," a mighty chorus with minor cadences. There were many songs of the fugitive like that which opens "The Wings of Atalanta," and the more familiar "Been a-listening." The seventh is the song of the End and the Beginning—"My Lord, what a mourning! when the stars begin to fall"; a strain of this is placed before "The Dawn of Freedom." The song of groping—"My way's cloudy"—begins "The Meaning of Progress"; the ninth is the song of this chapter—"Wrestlin' Jacob, the day is a-breaking,"—a pæan of hopeful strife. The last master song is the song of songs—"Steal away,"—sprung from "The Faith of the Fathers."

There are many others of the Negro folk-songs as striking and characteristic as these, as, for instance, the three strains in the third, eighth, and ninth chapters; and others I am sure could easily make a selection on more scientific principles. There are, too, songs that seem to me a step removed from the more primitive types: there is the maze-like medley, "Bright sparkles," one phrase of which heads "The Black Belt"; the Easter carol, "Dust, dust and ashes"; the dirge, "My mother's took her flight and gone home"; and that burst of melody hovering over "The Passing of the First-Born"—"I hope my mother will be there in that beautiful world on high."

These represent a third step in the development of the slave song, of which "You may bury me in the East" is the first, and songs like "March on" (chapter six) and "Steal away" are the second. The first is African music, the second Afro-American, while the third is a blending of Negro music with the music heard in the foster land. The result is still distinctively Negro and the method of blending original, but the elements are both Negro and Caucasian. One might go further and find a fourth step in this development, where the songs of white America have been distinctively influenced by the slave songs or have incorporated whole phrases of Negro melody, as "Swanee River" and "Old Black Joe." Side by side, too, with the growth has gone the debasements and imitations—the Negro "minstrel" songs, many of the "gospel" hymns, and some of the contemporary "coon" songs,—a mass of music in which the novice may easily lose himself and never find the real Negro melodies.

In these songs, I have said, the slave spoke to the world. Such a message is naturally veiled and half articulate. Words and music have lost each other and new and cant phrases of a dimly understood theology have displaced the older sentiment. Once in a while we catch a strange word of an unknown tongue, as the "Mighty Myo," which figures as a river of death; more often slight words or mere doggerel are joined to music of singular sweetness. Purely secular songs are few in number, partly because many of them were turned into hymns by a change of words, partly because the frolics were seldom heard by the stranger, and the music less often caught. Of nearly all the songs, however, the music is distinctly sorrowful. The ten master songs I have mentioned tell in word and music of trouble and exile, of strife and hiding; they grope toward some unseen power and sigh for rest in the End.

The words that are left to us are not without interest, and, cleared of evident dross, they conceal much of real poetry and meaning beneath conventional theology and unmeaning rhapsody. Like all primitive folk, the slave stood near to Nature's heart. Life was a "rough and rolling sea" like the brown Atlantic of the Sea Islands; the "Wilderness" was the home of God, and the "lonesome valley" led to the way of life. "Winter'll soon be over," was the picture of life and death to a tropical imagination. The sudden wild thunderstorms of the South awed and impressed the Negroes,—at times the rumbling seemed to them "mournful," at times imperious:

> "My Lord calls me,
> He calls me by the thunder,
> The trumpet sounds it in my soul."

The monotonous toil and exposure is painted in many words. One sees the ploughmen in the hot, moist furrow, singing:

"Dere's no rain to wet you,
Dere's no sun to burn you,
Oh, push along, believer,
I want to go home."

The bowed and bent old man cries, with thrice-repeated wail:

"O Lord, keep me from sinking down,"

and he rebukes the devil of doubt who can whisper:

"Jesus is dead and God's gone away."

Yet the soul-hunger is there, the restlessness of the savage, the wail of the wanderer, and the plaint is put in one little phrase:

"My soul wants something that's new, that's new."

Over the inner thoughts of the slaves and their relations one with another the shadow of fear ever hung, so that we got but glimpses here and there, and also with them, eloquent omissions and silences. Mother and child are sung, but seldom father; fugitive and weary wanderer call for pity and affection, but there is little of wooing and wedding; the rocks and the mountains are well known, but home is unknown. Strange blending of love and helplessness sings through the refrain:

"Yonder's my ole mudder,
Been waggin' at de hill so long;
'Bout time she cross over,
Git home bime-by."

Elsewhere comes the cry of the "motherless" and the "Farewell, farewell, my only child."
Love-songs are scarce and fall into two categories —the frivolous and light, and the sad. Of deep successful love there is ominous silence, and in one of the oldest of these songs there is a depth of history and meaning:

"Poor Ro - sy, poor gal;
Poor Ro - sy, poor gal;
Ro - sy break my poor heart,
Heav'n shall - a - be my home."

A black woman said of the song, "It can't be sung without a full heart and a troubled sperrit." The same voice sings here that sings in the German folk-song:

"Jetz Geh i' an's brunele, trink' aber net."

Of death the Negro showed little fear, but talked of it familiarly and even fondly as simply a crossing of the waters, perhaps—who knows?—back to his ancient forests again. Later days transfigured his fatalism, and amid the dust and dirt the toiler sang:

"Dust, dust and ashes, fly over my grave,
But the Lord shall bear my spirit home."

The things evidently borrowed from the surrounding world undergo characteristic change when they enter the mouth of the slave. Especially is this true of Bible phrases. "Weep, O captive daughter of Zion," is quaintly turned into "Zion, weep-a-low," and the wheels of Ezekiel are turned every way in the mystic dreaming of the slave, till he says:

"There's a little wheel a-turnin' in-a-my heart."

As in olden time, the words of these hymns were improvised by some leading minstrel of the religious band. The circumstances of the gathering, however, the rhythm of the songs, and the limitations of allowable thought, confined the poetry for the most part to single or double lines, and they seldom were expanded to quatrains or longer tales, although there are some few examples of sustained efforts, chiefly paraphrases of the Bible. Three short series of verses have always attracted me,— the one that heads this chapter, of one line of which Thomas Wentworth Higginson has fittingly said, "Never, it seems to me, since man first lived and suffered was his infinite longing for peace uttered more plaintively." The second and third are descriptions of the Last Judgment,—the one a late improvisation, with some traces of outside influence:

"Oh, the stars in the elements are falling,
And the moon drips away into blood,
And the ransomed of the Lord are returning unto
   God,
Blessed be the name of the word."

And the other earlier and homelier picture from the low coast lands:

"Michael, haul the boat ashore,
Then you'll hear the horn they blow,
Then you'll hear the trumpet sound,
Trumpet sound the world around,
Trumpet sound for rich and poor,
Trumpet sound the Jubilee,
Trumpet sound for you and me."

Through all the sorrow of the Sorrow Songs there breathes a hope—a faith in the ultimate justice of things. The minor cadences of despair change often to triumph and calm confidence. Sometimes it is faith in life, sometimes a faith in death, sometimes assurance of boundless justice in some fair world beyond. But whichever it is, the meaning is always clear: that sometime, somewhere, men will judge men by their souls and not by their skins. Is such a hope justified? Do the Sorrow Songs sing true?

The silently growing assumption of this age is that the probation of races is past, and that the backward races of to-day are of proven inefficiency and not worth the saving. Such an assumption is the arrogance of peoples irreverent toward Time and ignorant of the deeds of men. A thousand years ago such an assumption, easily possible, would have made it difficult for the Teuton to prove his right of life. Two thousand years ago such dogmatism, readily welcome, would have scouted the idea of blond races ever leading civilization. So woefully unorganized is sociological knowledge that the meaning of progress, the meaning of "swift" and "slow" in human doing, and the limits of human perfectability, are veiled, unanswered sphinxes on the shores of science. Why should Æschylus have sung two thousand years before Shakespeare was born? Why has civilization flourished in England, and flickered, flamed, and died in Africa? So long as the world stands meekly dumb before such questions, shall this nation proclaim its ignorance and unhallowed prejudices by denying freedom of opportunity to those who brought the Sorrow Songs to the Seats of the Mighty?

Your country? How came it yours? Before the Pilgrims landed we were here. Here we have brought our three gifts and mingled them with yours: a gift of story and song—soft, stirring melody in an ill-harmonized and unmelodious land; the gift of sweat and brawn to beat back the wilderness, conquer the soil, and lay the foundations of this vast economic empire two hundred years earlier than your weak hands could have done it; the third, a gift of the Spirit. Around us the history of the land has centred for thrice a hundred years; out of the nation's heart we have called all that was best to throttle and subdue all that was worst; fire and blood, prayer and sacrifice, have billowed over this people, and they have found peace only in the altars of the God of Right. Nor has our gift of the Spirit been merely passive. Actively we have woven ourselves with the very warp and woof of this nation,—we fought their battles, shared their sorrow, mingled our blood with theirs, and generation after generation have pleaded with a headstrong, careless people to despise not Justice, Mercy, and Truth, lest the nation be smitten with a curse. Our song, our toil, our cheer, and warning have been given to this nation in blood-brotherhood. Are not these gifts worth the giving? Is not this work and striving? Would America have been America without her Negro people?

Even so is the hope that sang in the songs of my fathers well sung. If somewhere in this whirl and chaos of things there dwells Eternal Good, pitiful yet masterful, then anon in His good time America shall rend the Veil and the prisoned shall go free. Free, free as the sunshine trickling down the morning into these high windows of mine, free as yonder fresh young voices welling up to me from the caverns of brick and mortar below—swelling with song, instinct with life, tremulous treble and darkening bass. My children, my little children, are singing to the sunshine, and thus they sing:

> "Let us cheer the wea - ry trav - el - ler, . .
> Cheer the wea - ry trav - el - ler,
> Let us cheer the wea - ry trav - el - ler
> A - long the heav - en - ly way."

And the traveller girds himself, and sets his face toward the Morning, and goes his way.

JAMES WELDON JOHNSON (1871–1938)

James Weldon Johnson (who for "literary advantages" had replaced "William" by "Weldon") was of mixed blood, considerably more white than black, and was the child of parents who had not known slavery. Though born and raised in the South, in Jacksonville, Florida, he did not experience the harsher pressures of race prejudice and segregation and had a family background of middle-class comfort and respectability—the kind of family life that Du Bois hoped would, by morality and manners, cure the "heritage of slavery."[1] Furthermore, Atlanta University gave him an education not significantly different from what a white boy in good circumstances might then receive—fairly solid doses of English, Latin, and mathematics.

The young Johnson was clearly slated to be one of the "Talented Tenth" defined by Du Bois—that is, one of the elite prepared to compete in the white world on its own cultural terms; but at this stage of his life he discovered "blackness." Like Du Bois, he discovered it by teaching in a back-country black school, in Georgia, and the rest of Johnson's life can be thought of at least in one perspective as a continuing exploration of the tension between the will, as one of the Talented Tenth, to master the white culture and the need to identify with "blackness."

But the tension of Johnson's life was not—and could scarcely have been—between such simple and clear-cut options. To begin with, as Johnson himself put it in *Along This Way*, the racial situation is never static; it is constantly changing in certain respects, as his own story amply illustrates. Furthermore, the matter of options is complicated by the fact that the only language in which the discovery of "blackness" could be celebrated was the "white" language, and the career of Johnson, even in his music, was through white culture as a means of making possible his return to "blackness." But that is to get ahead of ourselves.

Johnson, like any young man, had to find his way in the world. After college he went back

to Jacksonville. He taught school. He tried journalism, journalism dedicated to developing a black consciousness. He studied law, in the office of a white man, and by his fine abilities forced admission to the white bar. He wrote in 1900 the lines to a hymn (to which his brother J. Rosamond put the music) to commemorate Lincoln's birthday, "Lift Every Voice and Sing"—which was to become known, unofficially, as "The Negro National Anthem." With his brother and Bob Cole, he founded the songwriting and performing trio of Cole and the Johnson Brothers and made a success in the theatrical world. By 1906, dissatisfied with that career, he entered the consular service, first in Venezuela and then in Nicaragua. In 1914 he reentered journalism, in New York City.

Up to this point, as a friend of Booker T. Washington, Johnson had been more or less under that influence. For instance, some of his "coon songs" had, perhaps unconsciously, accepted stereotypes of the black man that were implicit in Washington's accommodationism, as when the patent medicine man Dr. Hocus Pocus, in Johnson's light opera *Tolosa*, boasts

> . . . a Zulu king so black
> He'd dim the brightest light;
> I rubbed him with my liniment,
> And now the king is white.

Or, in *The Belle*, in the song "I Ain't Gwinter Work No More":

> Labor is tiresome, sho'
> The best occupation is recreation;
> I ain't gwinter work no mo'.

But before going to Venezuela, in New York Johnson had begun a book called *The Autobiography of an Ex-Colored Man*, and as consul he found time, as he said, to gain his "first perspective view of life." This meant primarily a perspective on the implications of being black in the white world. The germ of the book lay in the fact that Johnson's friend and one-time law partner, J. Douglas Wetmore, did, on occasion, pass as white and finally married a white woman. Historically, and in literature, the character of mixed blood has provided the strategic

---

[1] Du Bois, as we have seen, regarded a weak family structure as the most disastrous result of slavery. Later, the Black Muslims, including Malcolm X, were to emphasize the necessity of the firmly based family; in fact, the Black Muslims teach, in general, the standard middle-class virtues of thrift, industriousness, cleanliness, temperance, and a strict sexual morality. But this idea of a weak family structure in black society is not universally accepted. See p. 2726.

double vision of the man who can slip unquestioned from one race to the other, and thus is a device by which the subject of race can be anatomized and its built-in ironies and irrationalities dramatized. The first novel ever written by a black man in America, *Clotel, or the President's Daughter*, by William Wells Brown (1853), had used this as the key of the story.

Whatever the importance of Wetmore for Johnson, the book has, as the title suggests, the form of first-person narration.[2] Johnson's relation to the first-person form is a complex one. Much of the material for *The Autobiography* is drawn from his own experience and observation. Its background includes, for instance, Jacksonville, Atlanta, and New York. But in the literal sense, the story, certainly in its more melodramatic elements, is not a retelling of Johnson's life. What the form provides is a *persona* through which Johnson can inspect his experience, and, strangely enough, this mask seems to make possible a fuller sense of Johnson's life and feeling than the rather tired and perfunctory "real" autobiography *Along This Way*, which was published in 1933.

Though Johnson never shows any instinctive skill for fiction, and in neither *The Autobiography of an Ex-Colored Man* nor *Along This Way* any considerable psychological acumen, the former book has great documentary value. Here we see projected Johnson's developing attitude toward the race question. The hero of *The Autobiography* undergoes various adventures on both sides of the color line, finally marrying a white woman (to whom he has revealed his secret), who, after a brief period of mutual happiness (marred only by his fear that she may "unconsciously attribute some shortcoming" to his "blood rather than to a failing of human nature"), dies, leaving two small children. Now he devotes his life to the children, who do not know his secret, but he sometimes opens the "little box" in which he keeps the "fast yellowing manuscripts" that hold his story.

If the career in the consular service had represented, in a sense, a flight from race, Johnson's life for years thereafter was a movement toward it. After a brief period in black journalism, he began work, as field secretary, for the then relatively new National Association for the Advancement of Colored People; and later, having been nominated by Du Bois, he became secretary, that is, chief executive officer. By embarking on this career Johnson clearly indicated that he had left the orbit of Booker T. Washington's influence and had repudiated the doctrine of accommodationism. His goal now was full equality and full integration, and his hope lay in the cooperation between blacks and the white liberals. On this basis he resisted both Du Bois' effort to move the headquarters of the NAACP to Harlem and Marcus Garvey's more radical program of surrendering the goal of equality and integration and taking refuge in a nationalistic "back-to-Africa" solution.

During his long period with the NAACP, when much of his work was focused on the drive for federal antilynching legislation, Johnson continued as best he could his literary activities. Back in 1913, he had published, in the New York *Times*, a long poem called "Fifty Years" that proclaimed the black man's "right of birth" in America.

Parallel to his tone of militancy in "Fifty Years" (which had actually been modified for publication), Johnson had developed in his literary work the discovery of "blackness," notably in the volume called *God's Trombones* (1927). Here, in a series of sermons rendered as poems,[3] Johnson celebrates the "old time Negro preacher" and the sermons he himself had heard in his childhood and youth. There was, as he points out in the preface, a highly developed folk art of the pulpit; certain sermons on set themes were passed down from preacher to preacher, being elaborated and altered with each rendering, as might happen to a spiritual or a ballad. As for the preacher, Johnson says that

[2] The first-person narrative was, as we have pointed out, the traditional form for accounts of black experience.

[3] See "An Ante-Bellum Sermon," by Paul Laurence Dunbar, earlier in this section.

though he had sometimes been presented as either a comic or pathetic figure, he was of fundamental importance in the development of life under slavery: "It was through him that people of diverse languages and customs who were brought here from diverse parts of Africa and thrown into slavery were given their first sense of unity and solidarity." It was, Johnson admits, the preachers who offered the "narcotic doctrine epitomized in the Spiritual, 'You May Have All Dis World, But Give Me Jesus,'" and who later (as of 1927) made, he insists, the blacks the "most priest-governed group in the country." But strangely enough, Johnson neglects to mention that the Bible, as passed on by the preachers, had provided the basic image of slavery in the story of the sojourn of the Children of Israel in Egypt, and of the flight from bondage, and of a vengeance on "Pharaoh," and that rebels like Nat Turner had drunk the heady brew of Old Testament rhetoric.

On another count the preface is interesting. Johnson's sermons are not in dialect. Dialect, he insists, is the "exact instrument for voicing certain traditional phases of Negro life," but he goes on to assert that the instrument has only two "complete stops"—pathos and humor—and that this is the result of the white man's view that the black must be either a "happy-go-lucky or a forlorn figure." In the face of this situation, dialect is dead, at least until such time as the stereotype of the black man has disappeared. This repudiation of dialect, Johnson admits, will entail a loss, but what is needed is something like "what Synge did for the Irish . . . to find a form that will express the racial spirit by symbols from within rather than by symbols from without—such as the mere mutilation of English spelling and pronunciation."[4]

Johnson is perfectly aware that more is at stake here than mere language, that language springs from an inner situation; but at the level of language what would be called for, by his theory, would be something roughly analogous to the style that Mark Twain developed for Huck, with the flavor of Huck's world and of his sensibility but without dependence on dialect. Furthermore, Johnson would argue, even if the black preacher used dialect in ordinary speech, he would, when he came to the pulpit, saturate it with another temper and vocabulary, drawn from the King James Version, and this would amount to "some kinship with the innate grandiloquence of their old African tongues."

This was what Johnson, in *God's Trombones*, was trying to create. The work was immensely popular (no doubt for a variety of reasons, often ironically contradictory), ran through numerous editions, and established Johnson's fame as a writer. Meanwhile, he had become a force in the burst of black talent in the arts known as the Harlem Renaissance, and as a personage on the general literary scene. But, in one sense, he was not really of that scene. For all his powers of growth and adaptability, he was, like Du Bois, rooted in the earlier period. He was a ground-breaker for, rather than a creator of, the Harlem Renaissance.

After many years with the NAACP, Johnson became, in 1931, a professor at Fisk University, in Nashville, Tennessee. He died in 1938. In the course of his life Johnson had come to the conclusion that there were only two courses open to the black man: integration (with or without racial blending) or the making of "isolation into a religion and the cultivation of a hard, keen, relentless hatred for everything white." Late in life, in his autobiography, he declared that the question was "immediately at hand and imminent." We shall see, in the literature of the Harlem Renaissance, and in the writings of the blacks who followed, the continuing effort to provide an answer to that as yet unanswered question.

---

[4] But in his important collections of spirituals he defends the use of dialect. See p. 1173.

BIOGRAPHICAL CHART

1871   Born, June 17, in Jacksonville, Florida
1887   Finishes Stanton Elementary School; enters Atlanta University as a junior in the Preparatory Department
1891   During the summer teaches school in the backwoods of Georgia
1894   Graduates Atlanta University; becomes principal of Stanton School the following fall
1897   Admitted to the bar, the first Negro member in Florida
1899   With brother, Rosamond, spends the summer in New York City writing for the musical comedy stage
1900   "Lift Every Voice and Sing," for a Lincoln's birthday program in Jacksonville
1901   The Johnson brothers and Bob Cole begin publishing lyrics for musical comedies under the name of Cole and Johnson Brothers
1904   Receives M.A. degree from Atlanta University
1906   Becomes Consul in Venezuela
1909–12   Consul in Nicaragua
1910   Marries Grace Nail of New York City
1912   *The Autobiography of an Ex-Colored Man*

1913   "Fifty Years" published in New York *Times*
1914   Edits the *New York Age*
1916   Becomes field secretary of the National Association for the Advancement of Colored People
1920   Investigates for the NAACP the American misrule of the Black Republic of Haiti
1923   Receives honorary degree of Doctor of Literature from Howard University
1925   Awarded the Spingarn Medal as "author, diplomat, and public servant"
1927   *God's Trombones*
1930   *Black Manhattan*
1931   Joins the faculty of Fisk University
1933   Receives the W. E. B. Du Bois prize of $1,000 for *Black Manhattan* as the outstanding work of nonfiction prose by a Negro writer during the period of 1930–32; *Along This Way* (autobiography); *The Book of American Negro Spirituals*
1934   Appointed Visiting Professor of Creative Literature at New York University; *Negro Americans, What Now?*
1938   Dies, June 26, in Wiscasset, Maine

FURTHER READINGS

The reader will find individual titles of Johnson's works in the biographical chart.

James Weldon Johnson, *Along This Way* (1933)
————, *Lift Every Voice and Sing: Negro National Anthem* (1970)
Brander Matthews, ed., *Fifty Years and Other Poems* (1917)

Stephen H. Bronz, *Roots of Negro Racial Conscious-ness; The 1920's: Three Harlem Renaissance Authors* (1964)
Dorothy Sterling, *Lift Every Voice: The Lives of Booker T. Washington, W. E. B. Du Bois, Mary Church Terrell and James Weldon Johnson* (1965)
Ellen Tarry, *Young Jim: The Early Years of James Weldon Johnson* (1967)
Ernest Tate, *The Social Implications of the Writings and Career of James Weldon Johnson* (1959)

O Black and Unknown Bards (1917)

O black and unknown bards of long ago,
How come your lips to touch the sacred fire?
How, in your darkness, did you come to know
The power and beauty of the minstrel's lyre?
Who first from midst his bonds lifted his eyes?
Who first from out the still watch, lone and long,
Feeling the ancient faith of prophets rise
Within his dark-kept soul, burst into song?

Heart of what slave poured out such melody

As "Steal Away to Jesus"? On its strains   10
His spirit must have nightly floated free,
Though still about his hands he felt his chains.
Who heard great "Jordan roll"? Whose starward eye
Saw chariot "swing low"? And who was he
That breathed that comforting, melodic sigh,
"Nobody Knows de Trouble I See"?

What merely living clod, what captive thing,

Could up toward God through all its darkness
    grope,
And find within its deadened heart to sing
These songs of sorrow, love, and faith, and
    hope?   20
How did it catch that subtle undertone,
That note in music heard not with the ears?
How sound the elusive reed so seldom blown,
Which stirs the soul or melts the heart to
    tears?

Not that great German master in his dream
Of harmonies that thundered amongst the
    stars
At the creation, ever heard a theme
Nobler than "Go Down, Moses." Mark its
    bars,
How like a mighty trumpet-call they stir
The blood. Such are the notes that men have
    sung   30
Going to valorous deeds; such tones there
    were

That helped make history when Time was
    young.
There is a wide, wide wonder in it all,
That from degraded rest and servile toil
The fiery spirit of the seer should call
These simple children of the sun and soil.
O black slave singers, gone, forgot, unfamed,
You—you alone, of all the long, long line
Of those who've sung untaught, unknown,
    unnamed,
Have stretched out upward, seeking the divine.   40

You sang not deeds of heroes or of kings;
No chant of bloody war, no exulting pæan
Of arms-won triumphs; but your humble
    strings
You touched in chord with music empyrean.
You sang far better than you knew; the songs
That for your listeners' hungry hearts sufficed
Still live—but more than this to you belongs:
You sang a race from wood and stone to
    Christ.

The Crucifixion (1927)

Jesus, my gentle Jesus,
Walking in the dark of the Garden—
The Garden of Gethsemane,
Saying to the three disciples:
Sorrow is in my soul—
Even unto death;
Tarry ye here a little while,
And watch with me.

Jesus, my burdened Jesus,
Praying in the dark of the Garden—   10
The Garden of Gethsemane.
Saying: Father,
Oh, Father,
This bitter cup,
This bitter cup,
Let it pass from me.

Jesus, my sorrowing Jesus,
The sweat like drops of blood upon his brow,
Talking with his Father,
While the three disciples slept,   20
Saying: Father,
Oh, Father,
Not as I will,
Not as I will,
But let thy will be done.

Oh, look at black-hearted Judas—
Sneaking through the dark of the Garden—
Leading his crucifying mob.
Oh, God!
Strike him down!   30
Why *don't* you strike him down,
Before he plants his traitor's kiss
Upon my Jesus' cheek?

And they take my blameless Jesus,
And they drag him to the Governor,
To the mighty Roman Governor.
Great Pilate seated in his hall,—
Great Pilate on his judgment seat,
Said: In this man I find no fault,
I find no fault in him.   40
And Pilate washed his hands.

But they cried out, saying:
Crucify him!—
Crucify him!—
Crucify him!—
His blood be on our heads.
And they beat my loving Jesus,
They spit on my precious Jesus;
They dressed him up in a purple robe,
They put a crown of thorns upon his head,   50

And they pressed it down—
Oh, they pressed it down—
And they mocked my sweet King Jesus.

Up Golgotha's rugged road
I see my Jesus go.
I see him sink beneath the load,
I see my drooping Jesus sink.
And then they laid hold on Simon,
Black Simon, yes, black Simon;
They put the cross on Simon,   60
And Simon bore the cross.

On Calvary, on Calvary,
They crucified my Jesus.
They nailed him to the cruel tree,
And the hammer!
The hammer!
The hammer!
Rang through Jerusalem's streets.
The hammer!
The hammer!   70
The hammer!
Rang through Jerusalem's streets.

Jesus, my lamb-like Jesus,
Shivering as the nails go through his hands;
Jesus, my lamb-like Jesus,
Shivering as the nails go through his feet.
Jesus, my darling Jesus,
Groaning as the Roman spear plunged in his
    side;
Jesus, my darling Jesus,

Groaning as the blood came spurting from
    his wound.   80
Oh, look how they done my Jesus.

Mary,
Weeping Mary,
Sees her poor little Jesus on the cross.
Mary,
Weeping Mary,
Sees her sweet, baby Jesus on the cruel cross,
Hanging between two thieves.

And Jesus, my lonesome Jesus,
Called out once more to his Father,   90
Saying:
My God,
My God,
Why hast thou forsaken me?
And he drooped his head and died.

And the veil of the temple was split in two,
The midday sun refused to shine,
The thunder rumbled and the lightning
    wrote
An unknown language in the sky.
What a day! Lord, what a day!   100
When my blessed Jesus died.

Oh, I tremble, yes, I tremble,
It causes me to tremble, tremble,
When I think how Jesus died;
Died on the steeps of Calvary,
How Jesus died for sinners,
Sinners like you and me.

From The Autobiography of an Ex-Colored Man (1912)

As my capital went over the thousand dollar mark, I was puzzled to know what to do with it, how to put it to the most advantageous use. I turned down first one scheme and then another, as though they had been devised for the sole purpose of gobbling up my money. I finally listened to a friend who advised me to put all I had in New York real estate; and under his guidance I took equity in a piece of property on which stood a rickety old tenement-house. I did not regret following this friend's advice, for in something like six months I disposed of my equity for more than double my investment. From that time on I devoted myself to the study of New York real estate, and watched for opportunities to make similar investments. In spite of two or three speculations which did not turn out well, I have been remarkably successful. To-day I am the owner and part-owner of several flat-houses. I have changed my place of employment four times since returning to New York, and each change has been a decided advancement. Concerning the position which I now hold, I shall say nothing except that it pays extremely well.

As my outlook on the world grew brighter, I began to mingle in the social circles of the men with whom I came in contact; and gradually, by a process of elimination, I reached a grade of society of no small degree of culture. My appearance was always good and my ability to play on the piano, especially ragtime, which was then at the height of its vogue, made me a welcome guest. The anomaly of my social position often appealed strongly to my sense of humor. I frequently smiled inwardly at some remark not altogether complimentary to people of color; and more than once I felt like declaiming, "I am a colored man. Do I not disprove the theory that one drop of Negro blood renders a man unfit?" Many a night when I returned to my room after an enjoyable evening, I laughed heartily over what struck me as the capital joke I was playing.

Then I met her, and what I had regarded as a joke was gradually changed into the most serious question of my life. I first saw her at a musical which was given one evening at a house to which I was frequently invited. I did not notice her among the other guests before she came forward and sang two sad little songs. When she began I was out in the hallway where many of the men were gathered; but with the first few notes I crowded with others into the doorway to see who the singer was. When I saw the girl, the surprise which I had felt at the first sound of her voice was heightened; she was almost tall and quite slender, with lustrous yellow hair and eyes so blue as to appear almost black. She was as white as a lily, and she was dressed in white. Indeed, she seemed to me the most dazzlingly white thing I had ever seen. But it was not her delicate beauty which attracted me most; it was her voice, a voice which made one wonder how tones of such passionate color could come from so fragile a body.

I determined that when the programme was over I would seek an introduction to her; but at the moment, instead of being the easy man of the world, I became again the bashful boy of fourteen, and my courage failed me. I contented myself with hovering as near her as politeness would permit; near enough to hear her voice, which in conversation was low, yet thrilling, like the deeper middle tones of a flute. I watched the men gather around her talking and laughing in an easy manner, and wondered how it was possible for them to do it. But destiny, my special destiny, was at work. I was standing ncar, talking with affected gayety to several young ladies, who, however, must have remarked my preoccupation; for my second sense of hearing was alert to what was being said

by the group of which the girl in white was the center, when I heard her say, "I think his playing of Chopin is exquisite." And one of my friends in the group replied, "You haven't met him? Allow me—" then turning to me, "Old man, when you have a moment I wish you to meet Miss ——." I don't know what she said to me or what I said to her. I can remember that I tried to be clever, and experienced a growing conviction that I was making myself appear more and more idiotic. I am certain, too, that, in spite of my Italian-like complexion, I was as red as a beet.

Instead of taking the car I walked home. I needed the air and exercise as a sort of sedative. I am not sure whether my troubled condition of mind was due to the fact that I had been struck by love or to the feeling that I had made a bad impression upon her.

As the weeks went by, and when I had met her several more times, I came to know that I was seriously in love; and then began for me days of worry, for I had more than the usual doubts and fears of a young man in love to contend with.

Up to this time I had assumed and played my rôle as a white man with a certain degree of nonchalance, a carelessness as to the outcome, which made the whole thing more amusing to me than serious; but now I ceased to regard "being a white man" as a sort of practical joke. My acting had called for mere external effects. Now I began to doubt my ability to play the part. I watched her to see if she was scrutinizing me, to see if she was looking for anything in me which made me differ from the other men she knew. In place of an old inward feeling of superiority over many of my friends, I began to doubt myself. I began even to wonder if I really was like the men I associated with; if there was not, after all, an indefinable something which marked a difference.

But, in spite of my doubts and timidity, my affair progressed; and I finally felt sufficiently encouraged to decide to ask her to marry me. Then began the hardest struggle of my life, whether to ask her to marry me under false colors or to tell her the whole truth. My sense of what was exigent made me feel there was no necessity of saying anything; but my inborn sense of honor rebelled at even indirect deception in this case. But however much I moralized on the question, I found it more and more difficult to reach the point of confession. The dread that I might lose her took possession of me each time I sought to speak, and rendered it impossible for me to do so. That moral courage requires more than physical courage is no mere poetic fancy. I am sure I would have found it easier to take the place of a gladiator, no matter how fierce the Numidian lion, than to tell that slender girl that I had Negro blood in my veins. The fact which I had at times wished to cry out, I now wished to hide forever.

During this time we were drawn together a great deal by the mutual bond of music. She loved to hear me play Chopin, and was herself far from being a poor performer of his compositions. I think I carried her every new song that was published which I thought suitable to her voice, and played the accompaniment for her. Over these songs we were like two innocent children with new toys. She had never been anything but innocent; but my innocence was a transformation wrought by my love for her, love which melted away my cynicism and whitened my sullied soul and gave me back the wholesome dreams of my boyhood. There is nothing better in all the world that a man can do for his moral welfare than to love a good woman.

My artistic temperament also underwent an awakening. I spent many hours at my piano, playing over old and new composers. I also wrote several little pieces in a more or less Chopinesque style, which I dedicated to her. And so the weeks and months went by. Often words of love trembled on my lips, but I dared not utter them, because I knew they would have to be followed by other words which I had not the courage to frame. There might have been some other woman in my set with whom I could have fallen in love and asked to marry me without a word of explanation; but the more I knew this girl, the less could I find it in my heart to deceive her. And yet, in spite of this specter that was constantly looming up before me, I could never have believed that life held such happiness as was contained in those dream days of love.

One Saturday afternoon, in early June, I was coming up Fifth Avenue, and at the corner of Twenty-third Street I met her. She had been shopping. We stopped to chat for a moment, and I suggested that we spend half an hour at the Eden Musée. We were standing leaning on the rail in front of a group of figures, more interested in what we had to say to each other than in the group, when my attention became fixed upon a man who stood at my side studying his cata-

logue. It took me only an instant to recognize in him my old friend "Shiny." My first impulse was to change my position at once. As quick as a flash I considered all the risks I might run in speaking to him, and most especially the delicate question of introducing him to her. I must confess that in my embarrassment and confusion I felt small and mean. But before I could decide what to do he looked around at me and, after an instant, said, "Pardon me; but isn't this ——?" The nobler part in me responded to the sound of his voice, and I took his hand in a hearty clasp. Whatever fears I had felt were quickly banished, for he seemed, at a glance, to divine my situation, and let drop no word that would have aroused suspicion as to the truth. With a slight misgiving I presented him to her, and was again relieved of fear. She received the introduction in her usual gracious manner, and without the least hesitancy or embarrassment joined in the conversation. An amusing part about the introduction was that I was upon the point of introducing him as "Shiny," and stammered a second or two before I could recall his name. We chatted for some fifteen minutes. He was spending his vacation North, with the intention of doing four or six weeks' work in one of the summer schools; he was also going to take a bride back with him in the fall. He asked me about myself, but in so diplomatic a way that I found no difficulty in answering him. The polish of his language and the unpedantic manner in which he revealed his culture greatly impressed her; and after we had left the Musée she showed it by questioning me about him. I was surprised at the amount of interest a refined black man could arouse. Even after changes in the conversation she reverted several times to the subject of "Shiny." Whether it was more than mere curiosity I could not tell; but I was convinced that she herself knew very little about prejudice.

Just why it should have done so I do not know; but somehow the "Shiny" incident gave me encouragement and confidence to cast the die of my fate; but I reasoned that since I wanted to marry her only, and since it concerned her alone, I would divulge my secret to no one else, not even her parents.

One evening, a few days afterwards, at her home, we were going over some new songs and compositions, when she asked me, as she often did, to play the "13th Nocturne." When I began she drew a chair near to my right, and sat leaning with her elbow on the end of the piano, her chin resting on her hand, and her eyes reflecting the emotions which the music awoke in her. An impulse which I could not control rushed over me, a wave of exaltation, the music under my fingers sank almost to a whisper, and calling her for the first time by her Christian name, but without daring to look at her, I said, "I love you, I love you, I love you." My fingers were trembling, so that I ceased playing. I felt her hand creep to mine, and when I looked at her her eyes were glistening with tears. I understood, and could scarcely resist the longing to take her in my arms; but I remembered, remembered that which has been the sacrificial altar of so much happiness—Duty; and bending over her hand in mine, I said, "Yes, I love you; but there is something more, too, that I must tell you." Then I told her, in what words I do not know, the truth. I felt her hand grow cold, and when I looked up she was gazing at me with a wild, fixed stare as though I was some object she had never seen. Under the strange light in her eyes I felt that I was growing black and thick-featured and crimp-haired. She appeared not to have comprehended what I had said. Her lips trembled and she attempted to say something to me; but the words stuck in her throat. Then dropping her head on the piano she began to weep with great sobs that shook her frail body. I tried to console her, and blurted out incoherent words of love; but this seemed only to increase her distress, and when I left her she was still weeping.

When I got into the street I felt very much as I did the night after meeting my father and sister at the opera in Paris, even a similar desperate inclination to get drunk; but my self-control was stronger. This was the only time in my life that I ever felt absolute regret at being colored, that I cursed the drops of African blood in my veins, and wished that I were really white. When I reached my rooms I sat and smoked several cigars while I tried to think out the significance of what had occurred. I reviewed the whole history of our acquaintance, recalled each smile she had given me, each word she had said to me that nourished my hope. I went over the scene we had just gone through, trying to draw from it what was in my favor and what was against me. I was rewarded by feeling confident that she loved me, but I could not estimate what was the effect upon her of my confession. At last, nervous and unhappy, I wrote her a letter, which I dropped into the mailbox before going to bed, in which I said:

I understand, understand even better than you, so I suffer even more than you. But why should either of us suffer for what neither of us is to blame? If there is any blame, it belongs to me, and I can only make the old, yet strongest plea that can be offered, I love you; and I know that my love, my great love, infinitely overbalances that blame, and blots it out. What is it that stands in the way of our happiness? It is not what you feel or what I feel; it is not what you are or what I am. It is what others feel and are. But, oh! is that a fair price? In all the endeavors and struggles of life, in all our strivings and longings there is only one thing worth seeking, only one thing worth winning, and that is love. It is not always found; but when it is, there is nothing in all the world for which it can be profitably exchanged.

The second morning after, I received a note from her which stated briefly that she was going up in New Hampshire to spend the summer with relatives there. She made no reference to what had passed between us; nor did she say exactly when she would leave the city. The note contained no single word that gave me any clue to her feelings. I could only gather hope from the fact that she had written at all. On the same evening, with a degree of trepidation which rendered me almost frightened, I went to her house.

I met her mother, who told me that she had left for the country that very afternoon. Her mother treated me in her usual pleasant manner, which fact greatly reassured me; and I left the house with a vague sense of hope stirring in my breast, which sprang from the conviction that she had not yet divulged my secret. But that hope did not remain with me long. I waited one, two, three weeks, nervously examining my mail every day, looking for some word from her. All of the letters received by me seemed so insignificant, so worthless, because there was none from her. The slight buoyancy of spirit which I had felt gradually dissolved into gloomy heartsickness. I became preoccupied, I lost appetite, lost sleep, and lost ambition. Several of my friends intimated to me that perhaps I was working too hard.

She stayed away the whole summer. I did not go to the house, but saw her father at various times, and he was as friendly as ever. Even after

I knew that she was back in town I did not go to see her. I determined to wait for some word or sign. I had finally taken refuge and comfort in my pride, pride which, I suppose, I came by naturally enough.

The first time I saw her after her return was one night at the theater. She and her mother sat in company with a young man who I knew slightly, not many seats away from me. Never did she appear more beautiful; and yet, it may have been my fancy, she seemed a trifle paler and there was a suggestion of haggardness in her countenance. But that only heightened her beauty; the very delicacy of her charm melted down the strength of my pride. My situation made me feel weak and powerless, like a man trying with his bare hands to break the iron bars of his prison cell. When the performance was over I hurried out and placed myself where, unobserved, I could see her as she passed out. The haughtiness of spirit in which I had sought relief was all gone, and I was willing and ready to undergo any humiliation.

Shortly afterward we met at a progressive card party, and during the evening we were thrown together at one of the tables as partners. This was really our first meeting since the eventful night at her house. Strangely enough, in spite of our mutual nervousness, we won every trick of the game, and one of our opponents jokingly quoted the old saw, "Lucky at cards, unlucky in love." Our eyes met, and I am sure that in the momentary glance my whole soul went out to her in one great plea. She lowered her eyes and uttered a nervous little laugh. During the rest of the game I fully merited the unexpressed and expressed abuse of my various partners; for my eyes followed her wherever she was, and I played whatever card my fingers happened to touch.

Later in the evening she went to the piano and began to play very softly, as to herself, the opening bars of the 13th Nocturne. I felt that the psychic moment of my life had come, a moment which if lost could never be called back; and, in as careless a manner as I could assume, I sauntered over to the piano and stood almost bending over her. She continued playing; but, in a voice that was almost a whisper, she called me by my Christian name and said, "I love you, I love you, I love you." I took her place at the piano and played the Nocturne in a manner that silenced the chatter of the company both in and out of the room; involuntarily closing it with the major triad.

We were married the following spring, and went to Europe for several months. It was a double joy for me to be in France again under such conditions.

First there came to us a little girl, with hair and eyes dark like mine, but who is growing to have ways like her mother. Two years later there came a boy, who has my temperament, but is fair like his mother, a little golden-headed god, a face and head that would have delighted the heart of an old Italian master. And this boy, with his mother's eyes and features, occupies an inner sanctuary of my heart; for it was for him that she gave all; and that is the second sacred sorrow of my life.

The few years of our married life were supremely happy, and, perhaps she was even happier than I; for after our marriage, in spite of all the wealth of her love which she lavished upon me, there came a new dread to haunt me, a dread which I cannot explain and which was unfounded, but one that never left me. I was in constant fear that she would discover in me some shortcoming which she would unconsciously attribute to my blood rather than to a failing of human nature. But no cloud ever came to mar our life together; her loss to me is irreparable. My children need a mother's care, but I shall never marry again. It is to my children that I have devoted my life. I no longer have the same fear for myself of my secret being found out; for since my wife's death I have gradually dropped out of social life; but there is nothing I would not suffer to keep the "brand" from being placed upon them.

It is difficult for me to analyze my feelings concerning my present position in the world. Sometimes it seems to me that I have never really been a Negro, that I have been only a privileged spectator of their inner life; at other times I feel that I have been a coward, a deserter, and I am possessed by a strange longing for my mother's people.

Several years ago I attended a great meeting in the interest of Hampton Institute at Carnegie Hall. The Hampton students sang the old songs and awoke memories that left me sad. Among the speakers were R. C. Ogden, Ex-Ambassador Choate, and Mark Twain; but the greatest interest of the audience was centered in Booker T. Washington; and not because he so much surpassed the others in eloquence, but because of what he represented with so much earnestness and faith. And it is this that all of that small but gallant band of colored men who are publicly fighting the cause of their race have behind them. Even those who oppose them know that these men have the eternal principles of right on their side, and they will be victors even though they should go down in defeat. Beside them I feel small and selfish. I am an ordinarily successful white man who has made a little money. They are men who are making history and a race. I, too, might have taken part in a work so glorious.

My love for my children makes me glad that I am what I am, and keeps me from desiring to be otherwise; and yet, when I sometimes open a little box in which I still keep my fast yellowing manuscripts, the only tangible remnants of a vanished dream, a dead ambition, a sacrificed talent, I cannot repress the thought, that, after all, I have chosen the lesser part, that I have sold my birthright for a mess of pottage.

The Folk

The teeming, pushing, various life of the world that arose after the Civil War and that fueled the new literature is, in many aspects, nowhere more faithfully represented than in folk song and folk tale. The old strains of balladry and spiritual persisted in what was left of their old world, but more prominent now were the expressions of the new, glamorous occupations— buffalo hunting, riding the range, building railroads and railroading, lumbering. There were, too, the songs of western outlawry and of the new urban life, and the blues spoke of the lost and defeated man who had no place in the big and thriving world, as did the songs of the hobo. In the midst of this new excitement and new pain, there was, too, a nostalgia for the old certainties, the life of the old farmstead, the devotion of mother, and the comforts of religion.

The Old Chisholm Trail

The old Chisholm Trail ran from San Antonio, Texas, to Montana, and up it Texas-bred longhorns were driven to stock northwestern ranches. Named for Jesse Chisholm, a half-breed Cherokee trader and government agent, the trail first assumed importance right after the Civil War and continued to be the most famous thoroughfare for the cattle industry until 1888, when the combined influence of sheepherders and homesteaders brought the period of the great cattle drives to an abrupt end. By that time, however, the drives had already given birth to many of the songs and stories that were to make the cowboy a romantic figure long after the last drive was over.

The cowboys are supposed to have derived the famous refrain of "The Old Chisholm Trail" from an old Indian war cry that they learned from the Mexican *vaqueros*.

Come along boys and listen to my tale,
I'll tell you of my troubles on the old Chisholm trail.
Chorus:
  Come a ti yi yippee, come a ti yi yea,
  Come a ti yi yippee, come a ti yi yea,

Oh, a ten-dollar hoss and a forty-dollar saddle,
And I'm goin' to punchin' Texas cattle.

I wake in the mornin' afore daylight
And afore I sleep the moon shines bright.

It's cloudy in the west, a-lookin' like rain,
And my durned old slicker's in the wagon again.

No chaps, no slicker, and it's pourin' down rain,
And I swear, by gosh, I'll never night-herd again.

Feet in the stirrups and seat in the saddle,
I hung and rattled with them long-horn cattle.

The wind commenced to blow, and the rain began
to fall,
Hit looked, by grab, like we was goin' to lose 'em
all.

I don't give a darn if they never do stop;
I'll ride as long as an eight-day clock.

We rounded 'em up and put 'em on the cars,
And that was the last of the old Two Bars.

Oh, it's bacon and beans most every day,
I'd as soon be a-eatin' prairie hay.

I went to the boss to draw my roll,
He had it figgered out I was nine dollars in the
hole.

Goin' back to town to draw my money,
Goin' back home to see my honey.

With my knees in the saddle and my seat in the
sky,
I'll quit punchin' cows in the sweet by and by.

Git Along, Little Dogies

As I was a-walking one morning for pleasure,
I spied a young cowpuncher a-riding alone.
His hat was thrown back and his spurs was a-
jingling,
As he approached me a-singing this song.

Chorus:
    Whoopee ti yi yo, git along, little dogies,
    It's your misfortune and none of my own,

Whoopie ti yi yo, git along, little dogies,
For you know Wyoming will be your new
home.

Some fellows goes up the trail for pleasure,
But that's where they've got it most awfully
wrong,
For you haven't an idea the trouble they give us,
As we go a-driving them dogies along.

The Range of the Buffalo

It happened in Jacksboro, boys, in the year of
seventy-three,
A man by the name of Crego came stepping up to
me,
Says, "How do you do, young fellow, and how
would you like to go
And spend one summer season on the range of the
buffalo?"

It's me bein' out of employment, boys, to Crego I
did say,
"This goin' out on the buffalo range depends upon
the pay.
But if you will pay good wages, give transporta-
tion, too,
I think, sir, I will go with you and stay the summer through."

It's now we've crossed Pease River, boys, our
troubles just begun,
The first damned tail I went to rip, Christ, how I
cut my thumb,
While skinning the damned old stinkers our lives
they had no show,
For the Indians waited to pick us off on the range
of the buffalo.

Our hearts were cased in buffalo hocks, our souls
were cased in steel,
The hardship of that summer would nearly make
us reel,
The water was salty as hell fire, the beef I could
not go,
And the Indians waited to pick us off on the range
of the buffalo.

The season being over, boys, old Crego he did say,
That we had been extravagant, were in debt to
  him that day,
We coaxed him and we begged him, but still it
  was no go,
So we left his damned old bones to bleach on the
  range of the buffalo.

It's now we've crossed Pease River, boys, and
  homeward we are bound,
No more in that hellfired country will ever we be
  found,
Go back to our wives and sweethearts, tell others
  not to go,
For God's forsaken the buffalo range, and the
  damned old buffalo.

The Cowboy's Lament

As I walked out in the streets of Laredo,
As I walked out in Laredo one day,
I spied a poor cowboy wrapped up in white linen,
Wrapped up in white linen as cold as the clay.

"Oh, beat the drum slowly and play the fife lowly,
Play the dead march as you carry me along;
Take me to the green valley, there lay the sod o'er
  me,
For I'm a young cowboy and I know I've done
  wrong.

"I see by your outfit that you are a cowboy"—
These words he did say as I boldly stepped by.
"Come sit down beside me and hear my sad story;
I am shot in the breast and I know I must die.

"Let sixteen gamblers come handle my coffin,
Let sixteen cowboys come sing me a song.
Take me to the graveyard and lay the sod o'er me,
For I'm a poor cowboy and I know I've done
  wrong.

"My friends and relations they live in the Nation,
They know not where their boy has gone.
He first came to Texas and hired to a ranchman,
Oh, I'm a young cowboy and I know I've done
  wrong.

"It was once in the saddle I used to go dashing,
It was once in the saddle I used to go gay;
First to the dram-house and then to the card-
  house;

Got shot in the breast and I am dying today.

"Get six jolly cowboys to carry my coffin;
Get six pretty maidens to bear up my pall.
Put bunches of roses all over my coffin,
Put roses to deaden the sods as they fall.

"Then swing your rope slowly and rattle your
  spurs lowly,
And give a wild whoop as you carry me along;
And in the grave throw me and roll the sod o'er me
For I'm a young cowboy and I know I've done
  wrong.

"Oh, bury beside me my knife and six-shooter,
My spurs on my heel, my rifle by my side,
And over my coffin put a bottle of brandy
That the cowboys may drink as they carry me
  along.

"Go bring me a cup, a cup of cold water,
To cool my parched lips," the cowboy then said;
Before I returned his soul had departed,
And gone to the round-up—the cowboy was dead.

We beat the drum slowly and played the fife
  lowly,
And bitterly wept as we bore him along;
For we all loved our comrade, so brave, young, and
  handsome,
We all loved our comrade although he'd done
  wrong.

Drill, Ye Tarriers, Drill ©

In the days after the Civil War, with the epic
building of transcontinental lines, there was a
saying that for every cross-tie there was a dead
Irishman, and this song commemorates the
hardihood of the world from which that saying
sprang. "Tarrier" is, of course, "terrier."

The words of the song were composed by
Thomas Casey and the tune by Charles Con-
nolly, in 1888.

Ev'ry morning at seven o'clock
There's twenty tarriers a-working at the rock.

And the boss comes along and he says, "kape still,
And come down heavy with the cast iron drill."
And drill, ye tarriers, drill!

Chorus:

Drill, ye tarriers, drill. It's work all day for the
    sugar in your tay,
Down behind the railway. And drill, ye tarriers,
    drill, and blast, and fire.

Now our new foreman was Jean McCann,
By God, he was a blame mean man.
Past week, a premature blast went off
And a mile in the air went big Jim Goff,

And drill, ye tarriers, drill!

Now the next time payday comes around,
Jim Goff a dollar short was found.
When asked, "What for?" came this reply,
"You're docked for the time you was up in the
    sky."
And drill, ye tarriers, drill!

Now the boss was a fine man, down to the ground,
And he married a lady, six feet round.
She baked good bread and she baked it well,
But she baked it hard as the holes of hell.
And drill, ye tarriers, drill!

Casey Jones ©

Casey Jones was a real man, John Luther Jones,
born in Missouri in 1864 but raised in Cayce,
Kentucky, a village in the western part of the
state. By 1890, at a tender age for such responsibility, he had become an engineer on the Illinois Central and by 1900 was pulling the New
Orleans Special, the "Cannonball," on the Chicago–New Orleans run. Six feet four, handsome,
well-liked, nondrinking, expert, Casey was at the
top of his profession, with the "whippoorwill
call" of his personal six-note calliope whistle
famous on his section of the run, from Memphis to Canton, Mississippi.

On the night of April 29, 1900, arriving at
Memphis from Canton, he and his black fireman Sim Webb took over for a sick engineer due
for the run on the southbound "Cannonball."
Casey pulled out of Memphis an hour and
thirty-five minutes late, but most of the time
had been made up before he approached the
little town of Vaughn, where two freights and
two passenger locals were on sidings waiting for
him to pass. Because of an accident to an air
hose, four cars—a caboose and three boxcars—
were overlapping on the main line, and the signal lantern and the torpedo did not stop Casey
in time. He ordered his fireman to jump and
hung on to the throttle and air brake, managing
to cut his speed from seventy-odd to around fifty
before barreling into the caboose of the freight
ahead. In his career Casey had never lost a life,
and now, sticking to his post to keep breaking

speed to the last moment, he lost none but his
own. Sim Webb reported that, as he jumped,
Casey opened the whistle to a piercing scream,
trying, according to Sim's guess, to warn the
freight conductor in the caboose. The conductor
was not there.

Tradition has it that the original version of
the song was composed by Wallace Saunders, a
black engine-wiper who had been much attached
to Casey. One day, according to an article
on Casey in the *Erie Railroad Magazine* (1928),
a "songwriter," passing through Jackson, Mississippi, heard Saunders' version and proceeded to
elaborate it.

"Casey Jones"[1] became enormously popular
and widespread, especially in the period before
the First World War, when the romance of the
railroad was still high. The heroism of Casey
appealed to men in other tough callings that,
in a pinch, demand heroism and a raw, simple
devotion to duty. There were numerous variations, adaptations, and parodies, the best known
putting Casey on a run to San Francisco, and

---

[1] It is interesting to set "Casey Jones" beside Whittier's poem celebrating the heroic death of another railroad man "Conductor Bradley" (see pp. 554–55). Whittier's poem is unwittingly comic, in that he treats the
episode in the "official" tone of high poetry and ends
in bathos; Saunders (and the nameless "songwriter")
treats it in the language of the world in which it belongs, innocently and simply, and so the hearer (or
reader) accepts it and renders homage to Casey's heroism.

some with a comic ending in which Mrs. Jones tells the children to hush their crying, they got another poppa on the Salt Lake Line. In the old days, these changes, especially the libel on a devoted wife, aroused resentment in some quarters. Now nobody remembers the facts.

The text below is one of the traditional versions, not having the chorus of the standard popular version generally known.

Come all you rounders for I want you to hear
The story told of a brave engineer;
Casey Jones was the rounder's name
On a heavy six-eight wheeler he rode to fame.

Caller called Jones about half-past four,
Jones kissed his wife at the station door,
Climbed into the cab with the orders in his hand,
Says, "This is my trip to the promised land."

Through South Memphis yards on the fly,
He heard the fireman say, "You've got a white-eye,"[2]
All the switchmen knew by the engine's moans,
That the man at the throttle was Casey Jones.

It had been raining for more than a week,
The railroad track was like the bed of a creek.

[2] The phrase means a clear track, the right of way. The modern equivalent in railroad parlance is "a high green." Interestingly, another version of the song has the fireman telling Casey, "Boy, you've *gotta* white eye," making "white eye" a verb, meaning to go full speed.

They rated him down to a thirty mile gait,
Threw the south-bound mail about eight hours late.

Fireman says, "Casey, you're runnin' too fast,
You run the block signal the last station you passed."
Jones says, "Yes, I think we can make it though,
For she steams much better than ever I know."

Jones says, "Fireman, don't you fret,
Keep knockin' at the fire door, don't give up yet;
I'm goin' to run her till she leaves the rail
Or make it on time with the south-bound mail."

Around the curve and a-down the dump
Two locomotives were a-bound to bump.
Fireman hollered, "Jones, it's just ahead,
We might jump and make it but we'll all be dead."

'Twas around this curve he saw a passenger train;
Something happened in Casey's brain;
Fireman jumped off, but Casey stayed on,
He's a good engineer but he's dead and gone—

Poor Casey was always all right,
He stuck to his post both day and night;
They loved to hear the whistle of old Number Three
As he came into Memphis on the old K.C.

Headaches and heartaches and all kinds of pain
Are not apart from a railroad train;
Tales that are earnest, noble and gran'
Belong to the life of a railroad man.

The Wreck of the Old Ninety-Seven

The wreck celebrated here occurred on September 27, 1903, when Joe Broody, engineer of the Fast Mail of the Southern Railway, running more than an hour behind schedule, was ordered to "put her in Spencer on time" and undertook to do the four-and-a-quarter-hour run from Monroe, Virginia, in a little over three. Coming down grade on a curve and approaching a trestle, the locomotive plunged from the track into the bank of Cherrystone Creek. Immediately after the wreck, a hillman, David Graves George, saw what remained of the train and composed the ballad to the tune of "The Ship That Never Returned," by Henry C. Work,

which had been current in the hills for a generation. Some years later, George heard the song on a phonograph and claimed ownership. Finally the Supreme Court ruled in his favor against other claimants but would not force compensation from the record company.

They give him his orders at Monroe, Virginia,
Say-ing, "Steve, you're way behind time."
This is not Thirty Eight, but it's old Ninety Seven
You must put her in Spencer on time.

He looked round and said to his black greasy fire-man,

"Just shovel in a little more coal,
And when we cross that White Oak Mountain,
You can watch old Ninety-seven roll."

It's a mighty rough road from Lynchburg to Danville,
And a line on a three-mile grade.
It was on that grade that he lost his average,
And you see what a jump he made.

He was going down grade, making ninety miles an hour

When his whistle broke into a scream.
Wooo! Wooo!
He was found in the wreck with his hand on the throttle,
And a-scalded to death with the steam.

Now, ladies, you must take warning,
From this time now and on:
Never speak harsh words to your true loving husband,
He may leave you and never return.

John Henry

The character John Henry appears in hammer songs (a type of work song), in ballads, and in a more or less amorphous legend. The story is of a powerful black "steel-driver" (the man who drives a steel drill into stone with a sledge, to prepare for explosives) who, while working on the Big Bend tunnel of the C & O Railroad, in 1872–73, undertook a drilling contest with a steam hammer and, immediately after victory, died. In the legend John Henry achieves the symbolic aura of the black man in America, as is attested by Guy B. Johnson, in *John Henry: Tracking Down a Negro Legend*, and by Roark Bradford, in his *John Henry*, a literary synthesis of various materials.

Even though word-of-mouth reports had given a very confused and contradictory account of John Henry, it was for a long time assumed (as by Johnson) that a real John Henry had existed and, if he had not literally died after a competition with a steam drill,[1] had distinguished himself in some drilling contest on the C & O job. But research has shown no John Henry among

the workers on the Big Bend tunnel, and there is no evidence that a steam drill (though the possibility remains) was used in the operation.

There was, however, a John Hardy working at the Big Bend tunnel who, more than ten years later, gained fame as a murderer and got himself executed and earned a ballad about himself; and the name John Hardy is that of the hero in the oldest known version of the man-against-steam-drill contest—which, too, was laid at the Big Bend. These versions of John Hardy as a steel-driver significantly carry a stanza that appears in what is probably the first ballad to use the name John Henry in the steam-drill contest, a stanza in which the hero, in infancy, predicts that the C & O is "going to be the death of me."

What comes out of this tangle?

Perhaps, as Johnson suggests, there had been a contest between a man and a steam drill and the man (Hardy or Henry?) won. Work songs developed, then perhaps a brief song involving narrative, then some ballad (perhaps sold on single sheets, as was not uncommon), then a general dissemination with the development of variants. If Hardy had been the original man, his name might disappear as the result of bad memory or of the appearance of a John Henry whose local and temporary fame (for what?) would tend to displace Hardy. In any case, whatever had actually happened was long since lost when the name John Henry first appeared in a ballad—in a fragment, collected in 1905, circulating among mountain whites of eastern Tennessee.

[1] There is nothing inherently improbable about such a contest, or about an expert steel-driver winning it, for the machine was imperfect and official records for single-hand driving in granite are almost incredible—one Montana contest gives a record of 25 and 5/16 inches in 15 minutes. The Montana Irishman, one William Shea, might well have put both John Henry and the steam drill in the shade, for the most claimed in a ballad for John Henry is 27 feet—but in a day. This, on the face of it, would seem, even allowing for the slow pace of protracted work, entirely possible. As for contests between men, they are clearly on record, not uncommonly between Irish and black steel-drivers.

It scarcely matters, in one sense, how the ballad originated. Even if there never was a steeldriver by the name of John Henry, that was the name that entered legend, and if no man, black or white, ever competed with a steam drill, John Henry, in his legend, did. By the 1920's, when Johnson was collecting material for his study, the hero was alive in the imagination of the black pick-and-shovel hand or sledge-hammer hand, fulfilling some deep need of the black men, who found themselves, as men, used as machines or pitted against machines.

John Henry was a li'l baby, un-huh,
Sittin' on his mama's knee, oh, yeah.
Said: "De Big Bend Tunnel on de C. & O. road
Gonna cause de death of me,
Lawd, Lawd, gonna' cause de death of me."

John Henry, he had a woman,
Her name was Mary Magdalene,
She would go to de tunnel and sing for John,
Jes' to hear John Henry's hammer ring,
Lawd, Lawd, jes' to hear John Henry's hammer ring.

John Henry had a li'l woman,
Her name was Lucy Ann,
John Henry took sick an' had to go to bed,
Lucy Ann drove steel like a man,
Lawd, Lawd, Lucy Ann drove steel like a man.

Cap'n says to John Henry,
"Gonna bring me a steam drill 'round,
Gonna take dat steam drill out on de job,
Gonna whop dat steel on down,
Lawd, Lawd, gonna whop dat steel on down."

John Henry tol' his cap'n,
Lightnin' was in his eye:
"Cap'n, bet yo' las' red cent on me,
Fo' I'll beat it to de bottom or I'll die,
Lawd, Lawd, I'll beat it to de bottom or I'll die."

Sun shine hot an' burnin',
Wer'n't no breeze a-tall,
Sweat ran down like water down a hill,
Dat day John Henry let his hammer fall,
Lawd, Lawd, dat day John Henry let his hammer fall.

John Henry went to de tunnel,
An' dey put him in de lead to drive;

De rock so tall an' John Henry so small,
Dat he lied down his hammer an' he cried,
Lawd, Lawd, dat he lied down his hammer an' he cried.

John Henry started on de right hand,
De steam drill started on de lef'—
"Before I'd let dis steam drill beat me down,
I'd hammer my fool self to death,
Lawd, Lawd, I'd hammer my fool self to death."

White man tol' John Henry,
"Nigger, damn yo' soul,
You might beat dis steam an' drill of mine,
When de rocks in dis mountain turn to gol',
Lawd, Lawd, when de rocks in dis mountain turn to gol'."

John Henry said to his shaker,
"Nigger, why don' you sing?
I'm throwin' twelve poun's from my hips on down,
Jes' listen to de col' steel ring,
Lawd, Lawd, jes' listen to de col' steel ring."

Oh, de captain said to John Henry,
"I b'lieve this mountain's shakin' in."
John Henry said to his captain, oh my,
"Ain' nothin' but my hammer suckin' win'.
Lawd, Lawd, ain' nothin' but my hammer suckin' win'."

John Henry tol' his shaker,
"Shaker, you better pray,
For, if I miss dis six-foot steel,
Tomorrow'll be yo' buryin' day,
Lawd, Lawd, tomorrow'll be yo' buryin' day."

John Henry tol' his captain,
"Looka yonder what I see—
Yo' drill's done broke an' yo' hole's done choke,
An' you cain' drive steel like me,
Lawd, Lawd, an' you cain' drive steel like me."

De man dat invented de steam drill,
Thought he was mighty fine.
John Henry drove his fifteen feet,
An' de steam drill only made nine,
Lawd, Lawd, an' de steam drill only made nine.

De hammer dat John Henry swung
It weighed over nine pound;
He broke a rib in his lef'-han' side,
An' his intrels fell on de groun',
Lawd, Lawd, an' his intrels fell on de groun'.

John Henry was hammerin' on de mountain,

An' his hammer was strikin' fire,
He drove so hard till he broke his pore heart,
An' he lied down his hammer an' he died,
Lawd, Lawd, he lied down his hammer and he
    died.

All de womens in de Wes',
When de heared of John Henry's death,
Stood in de rain, flagged de eas'-boun' train,
Goin' where John Henry fell dead,
Lawd, Lawd, goin' where John Henry fell dead.

John Henry's li'l mother,
She was all dressed in red,
She jumped in bed, covered up her head,
Said she didn' know her son was dead,
Lawd, Lawd, didn' know her son was dead.

John Henry had a pretty li'l woman,
An' de dress she wo' was blue,
An' de las' words she said to him:
"John Henry, I've been true to you,
Lawd, Lawd, John Henry, I've been true to you."

Paul Bunyan: Six Tales

The legend of Paul Bunyan illustrates the complications that sometimes arise in the relation of folk material and literature. In this case, which came first?

It has been said that Paul Bunyan the hero was, literally, the invention of the lumber business. In 1910, in the Detroit *News-Tribune*, in a long poem of little merit called "The Round River Drive," Paul Bunyan appears as a minor character, and a little later another doggerel version was printed in the *American Lumberman*, a trade journal. But in 1914, a certain W. B. Laughead wrote a pamphlet in which Paul Bunyan is the central character of a number of tales—that is, he achieves his heroic stature in this publication designed, as the author later said, "merely as a vehicle for advertising" the Red River Lumber Company of Minneapolis. This pamphlet made little impact, but it was followed by more elaborate versions that did catch on, and no doubt did circulate in the camps. Meanwhile, the company began to advertise its "Paul Bunyan Pine"; but the apotheosis of the mythical Minnesota logger came after the First World War, when the owners of the Minneapolis firm, which long back had been operating in the West, founded the Paul Bunyan Lumber Company, of Susquehanna, California. Paul himself had been rising in the world, up from advertising to literature, with, in 1925, a best-selling sequence of his tales written by James Stevens.

In contrast to the theory that Paul was an invention of the lumber business of Minneapolis, with, of course, a certain amount of what is called "downward transmission" into the folk world, there is the idea that Paul was truly a folk creation. Laying aside the perhaps suspect claim of Laughead to authenticity and the more clearly suspect one of Stevens that he himself had been, as a youth "fledging into a camp bard," revising and elaborating "the tales of older bards,"[1] there is evidence, such as that offered by Daniel Hoffman, in *Paul Bunyan: Last of the Frontier Demigods*, that Paul was well known in the Minnesota camps well before the turn of the century. Paul, in fact, has all the earmarks of belonging to that group of heroic figures developed by special occupations in America—like Mike Fink of the keelboats (see pp. 1105–9), Pecos Bill of the cattle ranges, John Henry of the "steel-drivers," and Casey Jones of the railroads. The Bunyan stories carry a sense of their special world of the logger, a sense of the details of the occupation and the human community developed by it, the humor that would sublimate fear, brutal fatigue, and incidental distresses (such as mosquitoes big enough to kill cows and butcher them), and the admiration of brute strength and courage inflated to Homeric proportions but, at the same time, submitted to self-humor.

Paul embodied, too, not only elements found in folklore of far places and times, but the impulse to myth-making that had changed Davy Crockett from a tale-telling, bear-hunting frontier politician of Tennessee into a demigod who,

---

[1] No other students of the folklore of lumbering record or accept this notion of the camp bard; generally a much more informal, around-the-stove notion prevails.

after lighting his pipe by the blaze of the "top-knot" of the rising sun, could walk home, "introducin' people to the fresh daylight with a piece of sunrise in my pocket." There is, it is true, none of the wild poetry and strong characterization of the Crockett tales (see pp. 1094–1100) in those of Paul, but the scale and grotesquerie are the same, and there is the same strain of cunning and "smartness" that Crockett shares with the clever Yankees such as Jack Downing and Sam Slick (see pp. 1091–94) and that reaches back to the guile of the tricksters, like Loki and Mercury, of mythology and legend.

THE BIRTH OF PAUL

Whatever the precise origins of Paul Bunyan, he is long since firmly established in the American folk pantheon. That he is the stuff of which heroes are made is clearly indicated by the fact that early in his westward migration he was adopted from his original occupation into other tough and manly worlds—for instance, into those of oil drilling and of heavy construction.

In what follows Daniel Hoffman compares three versions of the same episode in Paul Bunyan's career in his original world of lumbering and compares them: first, a tale from oral tradition which he simply records; second, a version of the same told by a gifted oral narrator, Perry Allen by name; and third, literary treatment by a Mrs. Shephard, who had collected the original tale and now retells it in her *Paul Bunyan* (1924).

Writing in the *Pacific Review* for December 1921, Mrs. Shephard quotes the following yarn about Paul Bunyan's birth:

Paul Bunyan was born in Maine. When three weeks old he rolled around so much in his sleep that he destroyed four square miles of standing timber. Then they built a floating cradle for him and anchored it off Eastport. When Paul rocked in his cradle it caused a seventy-five foot tide in the Bay of Fundy, and several villages were washed away. It was soon seen that if this kept up Nova Scotia would become an island, and Paul's parents were ordered to take him

away. He couldn't be wakened, however, until the British navy was called out and fired broadsides for seven hours. When Paul stepped out of his cradle he sank seven warships and the British government seized his cradle and used the timber to build seven more. That saved Nova Scotia from becoming an island, but the tides in the Bay of Fundy haven't subsided yet.

Perry Allen naturally would not have seen this tale had it appeared only in a university quarterly. But Mr. Laughead reprinted it in the introduction to *The Marvelous Exploits*; that is the most likely source for Perry's recitation, which uses most of the details of the printed story, but puts the yarn back into the strong vernacular of the skilled oral raconteur:

A lot of people wondered where Paul Bunyan was born. But he was born, in Maine! When he was three weeks old he was such a lummox of a kid that he wallered around so much in his sleep that he rolled down four square miles of standin' timber. Well, the natives wouldn't stand for that so they built him a floatin' cradle and anchored it out at Eastport, Maine. Every time he rocked in that cradle, he caused a seventy-five foot tide in the Bay of Fundy. And it, uh, destroyed several villages and a loss of lots of lives. And when he got asleep, they couldn't wake him however, so they called the British navy out and a-fired broadsides for seven hours. When they did awake him, he was excited ever so much, uh, excitement, that he tumbled overboard into the ocean. And he raised the water so it sank seven war ships. Well the natives wouldn't stand for that, so they captured his cradle, and out of the cradle they made seven more ships. But the tide, in the Bay of Fundy, is a-goin' yet.

See how Perry Allen filled in Mrs. Shephard's ellipsis ("When three weeks old . . ."), eliminated every passive construction ("villages were washed away," "It was soon seen . . .," "parents were ordered," "navy was called out"), and dropped the complicating details about Paul's parents, the government, and Nova Scotia's becoming an island. (Perhaps, in Michigan, Perry did not understand the relevance of this last motif; at any rate his story is stronger for leaving it out.) Note, too, the concreteness of the details he adds: "When he was three weeks old he was such a lummox of a kid";

"destroyed several villages and a loss of lots of lives."

Mrs. Shephard reworked her field notes, too. This is how she fixed up Paul's birth for book publication:

If what they say is true Paul Bunyan was born down in Maine. And he must of been a pretty husky baby, too, just like you'd expect him to be, from knowin' him afterwards.

When he was only three weeks old he rolled around so much in his sleep that he knocked down four square miles of standin' timber and the government got after his folks and told 'em they'd have to move him away.

So then they got some timbers together and made a floatin' cradle for Paul and anchored it off Eastport, but every time Paul rocked in his cradle, if he rocked shoreward, it made such a swell it come near drownin' out all the villages on the coast of Maine, and the waves was so high Nova Scotia come pretty near becomin' an island instead of a peninsula.

And so that wouldn't do, of course, and the government got after 'em again and told 'em they'd have to do somethin' about it. They'd have to move him out of there, and put him somewhere else, they was told, and so they figured they'd better take him home again and keep him in the house for a spell.

But it happened Paul was asleep in his cradle when they went to get him, and they had to send for the British navy and it took seven hours of bombardin' to wake him up. And then when Paul stepped out of his cradle it made such a swell it caused a seventy-five foot tide in the Bay of Fundy and several villages was swept away and seven of the invincible English warships was sunk to the bottom of the sea.

Well, Paul got out of his cradle then, and that saved Nova Scotia from becomin' an island, but the tides in the Bay of Fundy is just as high as they ever was.

And so I guess the old folks must have had their hands full with him all right. And I ought to say, the King of England sent over and confiscated the timbers in Paul's cradle and built seven new warships to take the place of the ones he'd lost.

Note how discursive, undramatic, and generally disorganized Mrs. Shephard's story is now. Compare the dramatic terseness of Perry Allen's; the directness of his opening rhetorical question, in-stead of her rambling introduction. Note his repe-tition of the refrain-like phrase, "Well, the natives wouldn't stand for that"; the logical proximity of causes and effects; the knock-out punch of his last line, where fantasy is overwhelmed—and thus in-tensified—by realism! If Perry Allen got his facts and "figgers" from reading or hearing Mrs. Shep-hard's first version, then this Michigan raconteur has in some measure done for her what Thorpe and Longstreet did for the likes of him a hundred years ago. He has taken the crude outlines of a good story, slashed away the extraneous matter, and whittled the narrative into artistic unity. But it is Mrs. Shephard who should be doing this; in-stead she piles detail on detail, insensitive to the dramatic basis on which the best oral narratives are always erected.

BREAKING THE JAM

Paul B Driving a large Bunch of logs Down the Wisconsin River When the logs Suddenly Jamed. in the Dells. The logs were piled Two Hundred feet high at the head. And were backed up for One mile up river. Paul was at the rear of the Jam with the Blue Oxen And while he was coming to the front the Crew was trying to break the Jam but they couldent Budge it. When Paul Arrived at the Head with the Ox he told them to Stand Back. He put the Ox in the old Wisc [River] in front of the Jam. And then Standing on the Bank Shot the Ox with a 303 Savage Rifle. The ox thought it was flies And began to Switch his Tail. The tail commenced to go around in a circle And up Stream And do you know That Ox Switching his tail forced that Stream to flow Backward And Eventually the Jam floated back also. He took the ox out of the Stream. And let the Stream And logs go on their way.

PAUL FIXES THE MOSQUITOES

Boys, did I ever tell you about the time I drove the Naubinway over to Paul Bunyan's camp on Big Mantisque Lake? Boys, I want to tell you there's some dandy mosquitoes over in that swamp even now, but the modern mosquitoes are nothing like their ancestors.

Well, just as I was pulling into Paul Bunyan's camp that day I heard some terrible droning noise like one of these modern airplanes. Even Paul, big as he was, seemed excited and yelled to me to hurry into his office. So I knew something was wrong.

Then Paul told me that some of the big mosquitoes was loose. He had trapped them several years ago, because they was bothering his cattle. Paul told me that two mosquitoes was trying to kill his prize heifer. They had the critter down and was trying to drag it off, he said, when along came a really big mosquito. The big mosquito simply killed off the other two, picked up the cow, and flew away. So Paul decided then and there to put on a campaign against them. He and his men trapped several of them in live traps, he said, and the rest got scared and flew away.

But this day, when I come to visit Paul, some of the mosquitoes had broken loose. We had barred the doors when we heard the mosquitoes droning overhead. They were landing on the roof. I shook like a leaf, but Paul wasn't scared. Overhead I heard a terrible cracking and looked to see swordlike weapons piercing the roof. Paul said they were mosquito stingers. So he grabbed his sledge and clinched those stingers like a carpenter clinches a nail. Next day he put twelve of his star lumberjacks to executing mosquitoes on that roof. He said he was through showing kindness to the mosquitoes. It didn't pay. They'd stab you in the back.

FREEZING THE LANTERNS

Well, uh, this most particular winter . . . we was lumberin' here up on the Manassee, sixty-eight degrees below zero and each degree was sixteen inches long, froze all the blazes in Paul's lanterns. We couldn't blow 'em out so we hauled 'em off and towed 'em outdoors. In spring when it thawed up, they set the whole north of Michigan afire and burned the Saint Marie's river in two!

THE WHISTLING RIVER

It seems that some years before the winter of the Blue Snow (which every old logger remembers because of a heavy fall of bright blue snow which melted to ink, giving folks the idea of writing stories like these, so they tell) Ol' Paul was logging on what was then known as the Whistling River. It got its name from the fact that every morning, right on the dot, at nineteen minutes after five, and every night at ten minutes past six, it r'ared up to a height of two hundred and seventy-three feet and let loose a whistle that could be heard for

a distance of six hundred and three miles in any direction.

Of course, if one man listening by himself can hear that far, it seems reasonable to suppose that two men listening together can hear it just twice as far. They tell me that even as far away as Alaska, most every camp had from two to four whistle-listeners (as many as were needed to hear the whistle without straining), who got two bits a listen and did nothing but listen for the right time, especially quitting time.

However, it seems that the river was famous for more than its whistling, for it was known as the orneriest river that ever ran between two banks. It seemed to take a fiendish delight in tying whole rafts of good saw logs into more plain and fancy knots than forty-three old sailors even knew the names of. It was an old "side winder" for fair. Even so, it is unlikely that Ol' Paul would ever have bothered with it, if it had left his beard alone.

It happened this way. It seems that Ol' Paul is sitting on a low hill one afternoon, combing his great curly beard with a pine tree, while he plans his winter operations. All of a sudden like, and without a word of warning, the river h'ists itself up on its hind legs and squirts about four thousand five hundred and nineteen gallons of river water straight in the center of Ol' Paul's whiskers.

Naturally Paul's considerably startled, but says nothing, figuring that if he pays it no mind, it'll go 'way and leave him be. But no sooner does he get settled back with his thinking and combing again, than the durn river squirts some more! This time, along with the water, it throws in for good measure a batch of mud turtles, thirteen large carp, a couple of drowned muskrat, and half a raft of last year's saw logs. By this time Ol' Paul is pretty mad, and he jumps up and lets loose a yell that causes a landslide out near Pike's Peak, and startles a barber in Missouri so he cuts half the hair off the minister's toupee, causing somewhat of a stir thereabouts. Paul stomps around waving his arms for a spell, and allows:

"By the Gee-Jumpin' John Henry and the Great Horn Spoon, I'll tame that river or bust a gallus tryin'."

He goes over to another hill and sits down to think out a way to tame a river, forgetting his winter operations entirely. He sits there for three days and forty-seven hours without moving, thinking at top speed all the while, and finally comes to the conclusion that the best thing to do is to take out the kinks. But he knows that taking the kinks out of a river as tricky as this one is apt to be quite a chore, so he keeps on sitting there while he figures out ways and means. Of course, he could dig a new channel and run the river through that, but that was never Paul's way. He liked to figure out new ways of doing things, even if they were harder.

Meanwhile he's gotten a mite hungry, so he hollers down to camp for Sourdough Sam to bring him up a little popcorn, of which he is very fond. So Sam hitches up a four-horse team while his helpers are popping the corn, and soon arrives at Paul's feet with a wagon load.

Paul eats popcorn and thinks. The faster he thinks the faster he eats, and the faster he eats the faster he thinks, until finally his hands are moving so fast that nothing shows but a blur, and they make a wind that is uprooting trees all around him. His chewing sounds like a couple hundred coffee grinders all going at once. In practically no time at all the ground for three miles and a quarter in every direction is covered to a depth of eighteen inches with popcorn scraps, and several thousand small birds and animals, seeing the ground all white and the air filled with what looks like snowflakes, conclude that a blizzard is upon them and immediately freeze to death, furnishing the men with pot pies for some days.

But to get back to Ol' Paul's problem. Just before the popcorn is all gone, he decides that the only practical solution is to hitch Babe, the Mighty Blue Ox, to the river and let him yank it straight.

Babe was so strong that he could pull mighty near anything that could be hitched to. His exact size, as I said before, is not known, for although it is said that he stood ninety-three hands high, it's not known whether that meant ordinary logger's hands, or hands the size of Paul's, which, of course, would be something else again.

However, they tell of an eagle that had been in the habit of roosting on the tip of Babe's right horn, suddenly deciding to fly to the other. Columbus Day, it was, when he started. He flew steadily, so they say, night and day, fair weather and foul, until his wing feathers were worn down to pinfeathers and a new set grew to replace them. In all, he seems to have worn out seventeen sets of feathers on the trip, and from reaching up to brush the sweat out of his eyes so much, had worn all the feathers off the top of his head, becoming completely bald, as are all of his descendants to this day. Finally the courageous bird won through, reaching the brass ball on the tip of the left horn

on the seventeenth of March. He waved a wing weakly at the cheering lumberjacks and 'lowed as how he'd of made it sooner but for the head winds.

But the problem is how to hitch Babe to the river, as it's a well-know fact that an ordinary log chain and skid hook will not hold water. So after a light lunch of three sides of barbecued beef, half a wagon load of potatoes, carrots and a few other odds and ends, Ol' Paul goes down to the blacksmith shop and gets Ole, the Big Swede, to help him look through the big instruction book that came with the woods and tells how to do most everything under the sun. But though Paul reads the book through from front to back twice while Ole reads it from back to front, and they both read it once from bottom to top, they find nary a word about how to hook onto a river. However, they do find an old almanac stuck between the pages and get so busy reading up on the weather for the coming year, and a lot of fancy ailments of one kind and another that it's supper time before they know it, and the problem's still unsolved. So Paul decides that the only practical thing to do is to invent a rigging of some kind himself.

At any rate he has to do something, as every time he hears the river whistle, it makes him so mad he's fit to be tied, which interferes with his work more than something. No one can do their best under such conditions.

Being as how this was sort of a special problem, he thought it out in a special way. Paul was like that. As he always thought best when he walked, he had the men survey a circle about thirty miles in diameter to walk around. This was so that if he was quite a while thinking it out he wouldn't be finding himself way down in Australia when he'd finished.

When everything is ready, he sets his old fur cap tight on his head, clasps his hands behind him, and starts walking and thinking. He thinks and walks. The faster he walks the faster he thinks. He makes a complete circle every half hour. By morning he's worn a path that is knee-deep even on him, and he has to call the men to herd the stock away and keep them from falling in and getting crippled. Three days later he thinks it out, but he's worn himself down so deep that it takes a day and a half to get a ladder built that will reach down that far. When he does get out, he doesn't even wait for breakfast, but whistles for Babe and tears right out across the hills to the north.

The men have no idea what he intends to do, but they know from experience that it'll be good, so they cheer till their throats are so sore they have to stay around the mess hall drinking Paul's private barrel of cough syrup till supper time. And after that they go to bed and sleep very soundly.

Paul and the Ox travel plenty fast, covering twenty-four townships at a stride, and the wind from their passing raises a dust that doesn't even begin to settle for some months. There are those who claim that the present dust storms are nothing more or less than that same dust just beginning to get back to earth—but that's a matter of opinion. About noon, as they near the North Pole, they begin to see blizzard tracks, and in a short time are in the very heart of their summer feeding grounds. Taking a sack from his shoulder, Paul digs out materials for a box trap, which he sets near a well-traveled blizzard trail, and baits with fresh icicles from the top of the North Pole. Then he goes away to eat his lunch, but not until he's carefully brushed out his tracks—a trick he later taught the Indians.

After lunch he amuses himself for a while by throwing huge chunks of ice into the water for Babe to retrieve, but he soon has to whistle the great beast out, as every time he jumps into the water he causes such a splash that a tidal wave threatens Galveston, Texas, which at that time was inhabited by nobody in particular. Some of the ice he threw in is still floating around the ocean, causing plenty of excitement for the iceberg patrol.

About two o'clock he goes back to his blizzard trap and discovers that he has caught seven half-grown blizzards and one grizzled old nor'wester, which is raising considerable fuss and bids fair to trample the young ones before he can get them out. But he finally manages to get a pair of half-grown ones in his sack and turns the others loose.

About midnight he gets back to camp, and hollers at Ole, the Big Swede:

"Build me the biggest log chain that's ever been built, while I stake out these dadblasted blizzards! We're goin' to warp it to 'er proper, come mornin'."

Then he goes down to the foot of the river and pickets one of the blizzards to a tree on the bank, then crosses and ties the other directly opposite. Right away the river begins to freeze. In ten minutes the slush ice reaches nearly from bank to bank, and the blizzards are not yet really warmed to their work, either. Paul watches for a few minutes, and then goes back to camp to warm up, feeling mighty well satisfied with the way things are working out.

In the morning the river has a tough time r'aring up for what it maybe knows to be its last whistle, for its foot is frozen solid for more than seventeen miles. The blizzards have really done the business.

By the time breakfast is over, the great chain's ready and Babe all harnessed. Paul quick-like wraps one end of the chain seventy-two times around the foot of the river, and hitches Babe to the other. Warning the men to stand clear, he shouts at the Ox to pull. But though the great beast strains till his tongue hangs out, pulling the chain out into a solid bar some seven and a half miles long, and sinks knee-deep in the solid rock, the river stubbornly refuses to budge, hanging onto its kinks like a snake in a gopher hole. Seeing this, Ol' Paul grabs the chain and, letting loose a holler that blows the tarpaper off the shacks in the Nebraska sandhills, he and the Ox together give a mighty yank that jerks the river loose from end to end, and start hauling it out across the prairie so fast that it smokes.

After a time Paul comes back and sights along the river, which now is as straight as a gun barrel. But he doesn't have long to admire his work, for he soon finds he has another problem on his hands. You see, it's this way. A straight river is naturally much shorter than a crooked one, and now all the miles and miles of extra river that used to be in the kinks are running wild out on the prairie. This galls the farmers in those parts more than a little. So it looks like Paul had better figure something out, and mighty soon at that, for already he can see clouds of dust the prairie folks are raising as they come at top speed to claim damages.

After three minutes of extra deep thought he sends a crew to camp to bring his big cross-cut saw and a lot of baling wire. He saws the river into nine-mile lengths and the men roll it up like linoleum and tie it with the wire. Some say he used these later when he logged off the desert, rolling out as many lengths as he needed to float his logs. But that's another story.

But his troubles with the Whistling River were not all over. It seems that being straightened sort of took the gimp out of the river, and from that day on it refused to whistle even a bird call. And as Paul had gotten into the habit of depending on the whistle to wake up the men in the morning, things were a mite upset.

First he hired an official getter-upper who rode through the camp on a horse, and beat a triangle.

But the camp was so big that it took three hours and seventy-odd minutes to make the trip. Naturally some of the men were called too early and some too late. It's hard to say what might have happened if Squeaky Swanson hadn't showed up about that time. His speaking voice was a thin squeak, but when he hollered he could be heard clear out to Kansas on a still day. So every morning he stood outside the cookshack and hollered the blankets off every bunk in camp. Naturally the men didn't stay in bed long after the blankets were off them, what with the cold wind and all, so Squeaky was a great success and for years did nothing but holler in the mornings.

WHO MADE PAUL AND WHAT HE DID

Paul, no matter how he originated, was a hero of the folk and one of the best tests of his stature is, paradoxically, the "upward transmission" that has put him into the world of serious art—in a long poem by Carl Sandburg, who, in *The People, Yes*, sees him as a symbol of the durability of the "common man," and in the libretto of the opera *Theodora*, by W. H. Auden, with the music by the English composer Benjamin Britten. Below is Paul as he appears in Sandburg's poem.

Who made Paul Bunyan, who gave him birth as a myth, who joked him into life as the Master Lumberjack, who fashioned him forth as an apparition easing the hours of men amid axes and trees, saws and lumber? The people, the bookless people, they made Paul and had him alive long before he got into the books for those who read. He grew up in shanties, around the hot stoves of winter, among socks and mittens drying, in the smell of tobacco smoke and the roar of laughter mocking the outside weather. And some of Paul came overseas in wooden bunks below decks in sailing vessels. And some of Paul is old as the hills, young as the alphabet.

The Pacific Ocean froze over in the winter of the Blue Snow and Paul Bunyan had long teams of oxen hauling regular white snow over from China. This was the winter Paul gave a party to the Seven Axmen. Paul fixed a granite floor sunk two hundred feet deep for them to dance on. Still, it tipped and tilted as the dance went on. And because the Seven Axmen refused to take off their hob-nailed boots, the sparks from the nails of their dancing feet lit up the place so that Paul didn't light the kerosene lamps. No women being on the Big Onion river at that time the Seven Axmen had to dance with each other, the one left over in each set taking Paul as a partner. The commotion of the dancing that night brought on an earthquake and the Big Onion river moved over three counties to the east.

One year when it rained from St. Patrick's Day till the Fourth of July, Paul Bunyan got disgusted because his celebration of the Fourth was spoiled. He dived into Lake Superior and swam to where a solid pillar of water was coming down. He dived under this pillar, swam up into it and climbed with powerful swimming strokes, was gone about an hour, came splashing down, and as the rain stopped, he explained, "I turned the dam thing off." This is told in the Big North Woods and on the Great Lakes, with many particulars.

Two mosquitoes lighted on one of Paul Bunyan's oxen, killed it, ate it, cleaned the bones, and sat on a grub shanty picking their teeth as Paul came along. Paul sent to Australia for two special bumble bees to kill these mosquitoes. But the bees and the mosquitoes intermarried; their children had stingers on both ends. And things kept getting worse till Paul brought a big boatload of sorghum up from Louisiana and while all the bee-mosquitoes were eating at the sweet sorghum he floated them down to the Gulf of Mexico. They got so fat that it was easy to drown them all between New Orleans and Galveston.

Paul logged on the Little Gimlet in Oregon one winter. The cook stove at that camp covered an acre of ground. They fastened the side of a hog on each snowshoe and four men used to skate on the griddle while the cook flipped the pancakes. The eating table was three miles long; elevators carried the cakes to the ends of the table where boys on bicycles rode back and forth on a path down the center of the table dropping the cakes where called for.

Benny, the Little Blue Ox of Paul Bunyan, grew two feet every time Paul looked at him, when a youngster. The barn was gone one morning and they found it on Benny's back; he grew out of it in a night. One night he kept pawing and bellowing for more pancakes, till there were two hundred men at the cook shanty stove trying to keep him fed. About breakfast time Benny broke loose, tore down the cook shanty, ate all the pancakes piled up for the loggers' breakfast. And after that Benny made his mistake; he ate the red hot stove; and that finished him. This is only one of the hot stove stories told in the North Woods.

Jesse James

Jesse James is the most famous of America's outlaw-heroes. Born on a Missouri farm in 1847, James's childhood was dominated by the bloody conflict over the Free Soil issue, and in 1863, after being seized and lashed by federal militia, he and his brother Frank joined Confederate guerrillas under the command of "Bloody Bill" Anderson. As a result of their exploits, the James brothers were outlawed at the end of the Civil War. Thus began James's fame as America's Robin Hood—a robber of banks and railroads, who, like his American counterparts Sam Bass and Pretty Boy Floyd, "robbed from the rich and gave to the poor." Perhaps the best known tale of James's chivalry relates how, after paying off the mortgage of a poor widow, he then recovered his money by stealing it back from the mortgage owner.

Jesse's fame was secured by his death in 1882, when, under the name of Howard, he was shot in the back by Robert Ford, a member of his own gang. Our memory of Ford as "the dirty little coward" who martyred his leader in exchange for reward money and a police pardon reflects the epitaph inscribed, by his mother's request, on Jesse James's tombstone:

> Murdered by a Traitor and Coward Whose Name Is Not Worthy to Appear Here.

Jesse James was a lad who killed many a man.
He robbed the Glendale train.
He stole from the rich and he gave to the poor,
He'd a hand and a heart and a brain.

Chorus:
  Jesse had a wife to mourn for his life,
  Three children, they were brave,
  But that dirty little coward that shot Mister Howard,

Has laid Jesse James in his grave.

It was Robert Ford, that dirty little coward,
I wonder how he does feel,
For he ate of Jesse's bread and he slept in Jesse's bed,
Then he laid Jesse James in his grave.

Jesse was a man, a friend to the poor.
He'd never see a man suffer pain,
And with his brother Frank he robbed the Chicago bank,
And stopped the Glendale train.

It was on a Wednesday night, the moon was shining bright,
He stopped the Glendale train,
And the people all did say for many miles away,
It was robbed by Frank and Jesse James.

It was on a Saturday night, Jesse was at home,
Talking to his family brave,
Robert Ford came along like a thief in the night,
And laid Jesse James in his grave.

The people held their breath when they heard of Jesse's death,
And wondered how he ever came to die,
It was one of the gang called little Robert Ford,
That shot Jesse James on the sly.

Jesse went to his rest with hand on his breast,
The devil will be upon his knee,
He was born one day in the county of Shea
And he came of a solitary race.

This song was made by Billy Gashade,
As soon as the news did arrive,
He said there was no man with the law in his hand
Could take Jesse James when alive.

Jesse had a wife to mourn for his life,
Three children, they were brave,
But that dirty little coward that shot Mister Howard,
Has laid Jesse James in his grave.

Frankie and Albert

The story of the real-life Frankie Baker and Allen ("Albert" as he liked to be called) Britt was not quite as dramatic as the ballad version, though substantially the same. Frankie is reported, by John Huston, in his *Frankie and Johnny*, as "a beautiful light brown girl" with a "long razor scar down one side of her face" that seems not to have impaired her reputation for beauty in the sporting circles of St. Louis in the 1890's. She was twenty-seven the year of the tragedy—1899—and had "gone partial" on Albert, a handsome "ginger" youth, whom she took to live with her at 212 Targee Street (where she "sat for company"), who presumably served as her "mack" (*maquereau*, or pimp), and on whom she lavished her affection and cash. Albert was ten years her junior, not experienced enough to control his random impulses and not clever enough to guess the kind of woman he was dealing with. A random impulse led him to one Alice Pryar, in whose company Frankie discovered him on the night of October 15. When he came back to Targee Street, the lovers quarreled, and she shot him, presumably when he drew a knife. In any case, she was acquitted. The St. Louis *Post-Despatch* reported the event in the heavily jocular tone reserved for news items about the goings-on in the black under-world. The authorship of the ballad, one of the most popular and powerful ever to appear in America, is unknown. There are many variants, some of which go under the title "Frankie and Johnny."

Frankie and Albert were lovers, O Lordy, how they
    could love.
Swore to be true to each other, true as the stars
    above;
He was her man, but he done her wrong.

Frankie she was a good woman, just like every one
    knows.
She spent a hundred dollars for a suit of Albert's
    clothes.
He was her man, but he done her wrong.

Frankie and Albert went walking, Albert in a
    brand new suit.
"Oh, good Lord," says Frankie, "but don't my
    Albert look cute?"
He was her man, but he done her wrong.

Frankie went down to Memphis, she went on the
    evening train.
She paid one hundred dollars for Albert a watch
    and chain.
He was her man, but he done her wrong.

Frankie lived in the crib house, crib house had
    only two doors;
Gave all her money to Albert, he spent it on those
    call house whores.
He was her man, but he done her wrong.

Albert's mother told him, and she was mighty wise,
"Don't spend Frankie's money on that parlor Alice
    Pry.
You're Frankie's man, and you're doing her wrong."

Frankie and Albert were lovers, they had a quarrel
    one day,
Albert he up and told Frankie, "Bye-bye, babe, I'm
    going away.
I was your man, but I'm just gone."

Frankie went down to the corner to buy a glass of
    beer.
Says to the fat bartender, "Has my lovingest man
    been here?
He was my man, but he's doing me wrong."

"Ain't going to tell you no story, ain't going to tell
    you no lie,
I seen your man 'bout an hour ago with a girl
    named Alice Pry.
If he's your man, he's doing you wrong."

Frankie went down to the pawnshop, she didn't go
    there for fun;
She hocked all of her jewelry, bought a pearl-
    handled forty-four gun
For to get her man who was doing her wrong.

Frankie she went down Broadway, with her gun in
    her hand,
Sayin', "Stand back, all you livin' women, I'm
    a-looking for my gambolin' man.
For he's my man, won't treat me right."

Frankie went down to the hotel, looked in the window so high,
There she saw her loving Albert a-loving up Alice Pry.
Damn his soul, he was mining in coal.

Frankie went down to the hotel, she rang that hotel bell.
"Stand back, all of you chippies, or I'll blow you all to hell.
I want my man, who's doing me wrong."

Frankie threw back her kimono, she took out her forty-four,
Root-a-toot-toot three times she shot right through that hotel door.
She was after her man who was doing her wrong.

Albert grabbed off his Stetson, "Oh, good Lord, Frankie, don't shoot!"
But Frankie pulled the trigger and the gun went root-a-toot-toot.
He was her man, but she shot him down.

Albert he mounted the staircase, crying, "Oh, Frankie, don't you shoot!"
Three times she pulled that forty-four a-root-a-toot-toot-toot-toot.
She shot her man who threw her down.

First time she shot him he staggered, second time she shot him he fell.
Third time she shot him, O Lordy, there was a new man's face in hell.
She killed her man who had done her wrong.

"Roll me over easy, roll me over slow,
Roll me over on my left side for the bullet hurt me so.
I was her man, but I done her wrong."

"Oh my baby, kiss me, once before I go.
Turn me over on my right side, the bullet hurt me so.
I was your man, but I done you wrong."

Albert he was a gambler, he gambled for the gain,
The very last words that Albert said were, "High-low Jack and the game."
He was her man, but he done her wrong.

Frankie heard a rumbling away down in the ground.
Maybe it was Albert where she had shot him down.
He was her man and she done him wrong.

Oh, bring on your rubber-tired hearses, bring on your rubber-tired hacks,

They're taking Albert to the cemetery and they ain't a-bringing him back.
He was her man, but he done her wrong.

Eleven macks a-riding to the graveyard, all in a rubber-tired hack,
Eleven macks a-riding to the graveyard, only ten a-coming back.
He was her man, but he done her wrong.

Frankie went to the coffin, she looked down on Albert's face,
She said, "Oh, Lord, have mercy on me. I wish I could take his place.
He was my man and I done him wrong."

Frankie went to Mrs. Halcomb, she fell down on her knees,
She said to Mrs. Halcomb, "Forgive me if you please.
I've killed my man for doing me wrong."

"Forgive you, Frankie darling, forgive you I never can.
Forgive you, Frankie darling, for killing your only man.
He was your man, though he done you wrong."

The judge said to the jury, "It's as plain as plain can be.
This woman shot her man, it's murder in the second degree.
He was her man, though he done her wrong."

Now it was not murder in the second degree, it was not murder in the third.
The woman simply dropped her man, like a hunter drops his bird.
He was her man and he done her wrong.

"Oh bring a thousand policemen, bring them around today,
Oh, lock me in that dungeon and throw the key away.
I killed my man 'cause he done me wrong."

"Oh, put me in that dungeon. Oh, put me in that cell,
Put me where the northeast wind blows from the southwest corner of hell.
I shot my man 'cause he done me wrong."

Frankie walked up the scaffold, as calm as a girl can be,
And turning her eyes to heaven she said, "Good Lord, I'm coming to thee.
He was my man, and I done him wrong."

Careless Love ©

It's on this railroad bank I stand,
It's on this railroad bank I stand,
It's on this railroad bank I stand,
All for the love of a railroad man.
How I wish that train would come,
How I wish that train would come,
How I wish that train would come,
And take me back where I come from.

Chorus:
    Love, oh, love, oh, careless love,
    Love, oh, love, oh, careless love,
    Love, oh, love, oh, careless love,
    See what careless love has done.

When my apron string will bow,

When my apron string will bow,
When my apron string will bow,
You'll pass my door an' say "hello."
But when my apron string won't pin,
When my apron string won't pin,
When my apron string won't pin,
You'll pass my door an' won't come in.

It's caused me to weep, it's caused me to mourn,
It's caused me to weep, it's caused me to mourn,
It's caused me to weep, it's caused me to mourn,
It's caused me to leave my happy home.
What do you reckon my mama'll say,
What do you reckon my mama'll say,
What do you reckon my mama'll say,
When she hears I've gone astray.

Little Boy Blue

"Little Boy Blue" and the three following items well illustrate the sentimentality of the last phase of the tradition of "fireside poetry" that prevailed up until the shock of the First World War. Eugene Field (1850–1895) was a successful newspaperman, whose column concerning city life was one of the influences that led Theodore Dreiser to be a writer; but his great fame rested on his poetry, which was perfectly attuned to the heart of the new middle class.

The little toy dog is covered with dust,
    But sturdy and stanch he stands;
And the little toy soldier is red with rust,
    And his musket molds in his hand.
Time was when the little toy dog was new
    And the soldier was passing fair,
And that was the time when our Little Boy Blue

Kissed them and put them there.

"Now, don't you go till I come," he said,
    "And don't you make any noise!"
So toddling off to his trundle-bed
    He dreamed of the pretty toys.
And as he was dreaming, an angel song
    Awakened our Little Boy Blue.—
Oh, the years are many, the years are long,
    But the little toy friends are true.

Ay, faithful to Little Boy Blue they stand,
    Each in the same old place,
Awaiting the touch of a little hand,
    The smile of a little face.
And they wonder, as waiting these long years through,
    In the dust of that little chair,
What has become of our Little Boy Blue
    Since he kissed them and put them there.

Little Orphant Annie

James Whitcomb Riley (1849–1916) was a more rural manifestation of the same basic attitudes found in Field, with his exploiting of dialect and the folksy charms of the life on the old homestead in a simpler age. In other words, he appealed to the last backwash of the sentimental nostalgia that had made Whittier's *Snow-Bound* popular with a multitude that were completely incapable of grasping its inner meaning. (See pp. 568–77.)

INSCRIBED

WITH ALL FAITH AND AFFECTION

To all the little children:—The happy ones; and sad ones;
The sober and the silent ones; the boisterous and glad
   ones;
The good ones—Yes, the good ones, too; and all the
   lovely bad ones.

Little Orphant Annie's come to our house to stay,
An' wash the cups an' saucers up, an' brush the
   crumbs away,
An' shoo the chickens off the porch, an' dust the
   hearth, an' sweep,
An' make the fire, an' bake the bread, an' earn her
   board-an'-keep;
An' all us other childern, when the supper-things
   is done,
We set around the kitchen fire an' has the mostest
   fun
A-list'nin' to the witch-tales 'at Annie tells about,
An' the Gobble-uns 'at gits you
         Ef you
            Don't
               Watch
                  Out!

Wunst they wuz a little boy wouldn't say his
   prayers,—
An' when he went to bed at night, away up-stairs,
His Mammy heerd him holler, an' his Daddy heerd
   him bawl,
An' when they turn't the kivvers down, he wuzn't
   there at all!
An' they seeked him in the rafter-room, an' cubby-
   hole, an' press,
An' seeked him up the chimbly-flue, an' ever'-
   wheres, I guess;
But all they ever found wuz thist his pants an'
   roundabout:—
An' the Gobble-uns 'll git you

         Ef you
            Don't
               Watch
                  Out!

An' one time a little girl 'ud allus laugh an' grin,
An' make fun of ever' one, an' all her blood-an'-kin;
An' wunst, when they was "company," an' ole folks
   wuz there,
She mocked 'em an' shocked 'em, an' said she
   didn't care!
An' thist as she kicked her heels, an' turn't to run
   an' hide,
They wuz two great big Black Things a-standin'
   by her side,
An' they snatched her through the ceilin' 'fore she
   knowed what she's about!
An' the Gobble-uns 'll git you
         Ef you
            Don't
               Watch
                  Out!

An' little Orphant Annie says, when the blaze is
   blue,
An' the lamp-wick sputters, an' the wind goes
   woo-oo!
An' you hear the crickets quit, an' the moon is
   gray,
An' the lightnin'-bugs in dew is all squenched
   away,—
You better mind yer parunts, an' yer teachurs fond
   an' dear,
An' churish them 'at loves you, an' dry the orphant's tear,
An' he'p the pore an' needy ones 'at clusters all
   about,
Er the Gobble-uns 'll git you
         Ef you
            Don't
               Watch
                  Out!

On the Banks of the Wabash Far Away ©

Paul Dresser (1857–1911), the older brother of
Theodore Dreiser, was a successful actor and
songwriter who had changed the family name
to something more "American." He was a genial,
warm-hearted bon vivant, hail-fellow-well-met,
and whoremaster, and, in fact, his most famous
song, "My Gal Sal," was written to the madam
of a brothel in Evansville, Illinois, who was for
a time his light o'love; even so, he struck unerringly the tone of the fireside poetry of the

time, with such songs as "On the Banks of the Wabash" and "The Path That Leads the Other Way." In his autobiography, the brother Theodore reports that he composed the verse for the first stanza of "On the Banks of the Wabash."

As a note on literary fame in America, we may point out that Terre Haute, Indiana, proudly lays claim to Paul Dresser and has made a modest shrine of the house where he was, presumably, born. The city fathers are, apparently, ashamed of Theodore, for when the centennial of his birth was celebrated in 1971, they ignored it.

Round my Indiana homestead wave the cornfields,
In the distance loom the woodlands clear and cool.
Often times my thoughts revert to scenes of childhood,
Where I first received my lessons, nature's school.
But one thing there is missing in the picture,

Without her face it seems so incomplete.
I long to see my mother in the doorway,
As she stood there years ago, her boy to greet!

Chorus:
Oh, the moonlight's fair tonight along the Wabash,
From the fields there comes the breath of new mown hay.
Thro' the sycamores the candle lights are gleaming,
On the banks of the Wabash, faraway.

Many years have passed since I strolled by the river,
Arm in arm with sweetheart Mary by my side.
It was there I tried to tell her that I loved her,
It was there I begged of her to be my bride.
Long years have passed since I strolled thro' the churchyard,
She's sleeping there, my angel Mary dear.
I loved her but she thought I didn't mean it,
Still I'd give my future were she only here.

The Sidewalks of New York

In 1894, James W. Blake was a salesman in a hatter's shop in New York. Known locally as a man who had a way with words, he was approached one day by Charlie Lawlor to write lyrics for a melody that Lawlor hummed for him. "I want it to be something about New York," said Lawlor. Between customers, Blake then scribbled his way into the history of American music.

"The Sidewalks of New York" was an immediate success. Its enduring popularity as the unofficial anthem of New York City was attested to in 1928, when New York Governor Alfred E. Smith used it for his presidential campaign.

Down in front of Casey's old brown wooden stoop,
On a summer's evening we formed a merry group.
Boys and girls together, we would sing and waltz
While the Ginnie played the organ on the sidewalks of New York.

Chorus:
East side, west side, all around the town,
The tots sang Ring a Rosie, London bridge is falling down.
Boys and girls together, me and Mamie O'Rourke,
Tripped the light fantastic on the sidewalks of New York.

That's where Johnny Casey and little Jimmy Crowe,
With Jakey Krause, the baker, who always had the dough,
Pretty Nellie Shannon, with a dude as light as cork,
First picked up the waltz step on the sidewalks of New York.

Things have changed since those times, some are up in G.
Others they are on the hog, but they all feel just like me.
They would part with all they've got could they but once more walk
With their best girl and have a twirl on the sidewalks of New York.

Little Black Train Is A-Comin'

When the period of the spirituals was past, the black believers continued to produce songs of faith, which now echoed the new order.

God tole Hezykiah
In a message from on high:
Go set yo' house in ordah,
For thou shalt sholy die.
He turned to the wall an' a-weepin',
Oh! see the King in tears;
He got his bus'ness fixed all right,
God spared him fifteen years.

Chorus:
    Little black train is a-comin',
    Get all yo' bus'ness right;
    Go set yo' house in ordah,
    For the train may be here tonight.

Go tell that ball room lady,

All filled with worldly pride,
That little black train is a-comin',
Prepare to take a ride.
That little black train and engine
An' a little baggage car,
With idle thoughts and wicked deeds,
Must stop at the judgment bar.

There was a po' young man in darkness,
Cared not for the gospel light.
Suddenly a whistle blew
From a little black train in sight.
"Oh, death, will you not spare me?
I'm just in my wicked plight.
Have mercy, Lord, do hear me,
Pray come an' set me right."
But death had fixed his shackles
About his soul so tight,
Just befo' he got his bus'ness fixed,
The train rolled in that night.

Keep Your Hands on That Plow ©

The "Holiness" churches, once confined to the poor whites of the back country but now penetrating the cities, have their roots in the Great Awakening of the eighteenth century and the tradition of orgiastic revivalism that developed thereafter. When the "Spirit" hits, there may be speaking in the unknown tongues, falling on the ground with twitches and jerks, weeping in the straw pen, holy dancing, the handling of "sarpints" (rattlers or copperheads, sometimes with deadly results), and sensational public confessions. And the music is anything but sedate. A song such as the present one may, like other folk creations, have many variants. For instance, this stanza not given in the text:

Mary had a only Son,
The Jews and the Romans had Him hung,
Keep your hands on that plow, hold on.

The "Holiness" folk often, and quite unbiblically, interpreted the "Romans" to mean Roman Catholics.

Got my hands on the gospel plow,
Wouldn't take nothin' for my journey now.
Keep your hands on that plow, hold on.

Chorus:
    Hold on, hold on,
    Keep your hands on that plow, hold on.

Took Paul and Silas, put 'em in the jail,
Had no one to go their bail.
Keep your hands on the plow, hold on.

Paul and Silas, they begin to shout,
Jail doors opened and they walked out.
Keep your hands on the plow, hold on.

Peter was so nice and neat,
Wouldn't let Jesus wash his feet.
Keep your hands on the plow, hold on.

Jesus said, "If I wash them not,
You'll have no father in this lot."
Keep your hands on the plow, hold on.

Peter got anxious and he said,
"Wash my feet, my hands and head."
Keep your hands on the plow, hold on.

The Boll Weevil Song ©

The boll weevil first invaded the United States, through Texas, in 1892; in 1916 the weevil reached Georgia; and, by 1923, his domain stretched across the entire cotton South. Indeed, the devastation that the weevil wreaked upon the South through the mid-1920's was comparable to the Dust Bowl disaster of the 1930's in Oklahoma and Texas. Only a combination of hot, dry summers, with airplanes and insecticides, was able to bring the weevil menace under control.

For some years, however, to take refuge in the grim humor of "The Boll Weevil Song" was about the only thing the farmer could do about the disastrous invasion. In the version printed here, the weevil, at home in ice and fire, lives in painfully comic contrast to the homeless farmer, whose creditors stand ready to take from him what cotton the weevil leaves. The song was popular, and many variants of it were sung by both blacks and whites through the South. Some even attempted to derive some consolation from the depredations of the weevil: for example, in the variant recorded by the great blueswoman Ma Rainey herself, the singer, identifying with the weevil, feels a measure of triumph in the victory of the little black bug over the great white Captain. Such consolation, however, effective as it might be within the blues, still left both black and white farmers facing the need to scrape a living.

Oh, de boll weevil am a little black bug,
  Come from Mexico, dey say,
Come all de way to Texas, jus' a-lookin' foh a
    place to stay,
  Jus' a-lookin' foh a home, jus' a-lookin' foh a
    home.

De first time I seen de boll weevil,
  He was a-settin' on the square.
De next time I seen de boll weevil, he had all of
    his family dere,
  Jus' a-lookin' for a home, jus' a-lookin' foh a
    home.

De farmer say to de weevil:
  "What make yo' head so red?"
De weevil say to de farmer, "It's a wondah I ain't
    dead,
  A-lookin' foh a home, jus' a-lookin' foh a home."

De farmer take de boll weevil,
  An' he put him in de hot san'.
De weevil say: "Dis is mighty hot, but I'll stan' it
    like a man,
  Dis'll be my home, it'll be my home."

De farmer take de boll weevil,
  An' he put him in a lump of ice;
De boll weevil say to de farmer: "Dis is mighty
    cool an' nice,
  It'll be my home, dis'll be my home."

De farmer take de boll weevil,
  An' he put him in de tire.
De boll weevil say to de farmer: "Here I are, here
    I are,
  Dis'll be my home, dis'll be my home."

De boll weevil say to de farmer:
  "You better leave me alone;
I done eat all yo' cotton, now I'm goin' to start
    on yo' corn,
  I'll have a home, I'll have a home."

De merchant got half de cotton,
  De boll weevil got de res'.
Didn't leave de farmer's wife but one old cotton
    dress,
  An' it's full of holes, it's full of holes.

De farmer say to de merchant:
  "We's in an awful fix;
De boll weevil et all de cotton up an' lef' us only
    sticks,
  We's got no home, we's got no home."

De farmer say to de merchant:
  "We ain't made but only one bale,
And befoh we'll give yo' dat one we'll fight an' go
    to jail,
  We'll have a home, we'll have a home."

De cap'n say to de missus:
  "What d' you t'ink o' dat?

De boll weevil done make a nes' in my bes' Sunday
    hat,
    Goin' to have a home, goin' to have a home."

And if anybody should ax you

Who it was dat make dis song,
Jus' tell 'em 'twas a big buck niggah wid a paih o'
    blue duckin's on.
Ain' got no home, ain' got no home.

5

The Moderns:

Founders and Beyond

1914–1945

The period that we are to survey here covers the two great world wars of our century, the interval between them, and the years since the second one. This half century and more is crowded with events, many of them spectacular and some, as we like to say, earth-shattering. In the early twentieth century, America entered the era of big industry and big technology and began to be felt as a world power. This development, however, was simply the result of a process that had been decisively initiated in the Civil War. For after Appomattox, the United States had been committed to centralization, industrialization, scientific progress, plutocratic democracy, and national expansion. The record of what, since 1914, has put America in a dominant position is essentially one of the increasing velocity in these movements. In direction, there has been no significant change. The Civil War remains the turning point in American history. Our poets and novelists have always sensed that fact.[1]

I.e. power, machinery, money, empire

[1] From the very beginning they grasped the deeper import of the war, and it is with its deeper importance with the forces it unleashed rather than its political outcome that we also are concerned in calling it the turning point in American history. Even if the Civil War had not resulted in a victory for the North, the long-range consequences would probably have been the same. If the South had gained its indepen-

The United States, no longer a loose confederation, but truly united in a vast economic pattern, was further advanced in technology and industrialization than any other nation, and, as we have noted earlier, there were, long before 1914, certain telltale indicators of a movement toward world power: the impact of the ideas of William Seward (on territorial expansion), of Admiral Mahan (on seapower), and of Rudyard Kipling (on the white man's burden); our shift-over from the status of a debtor to a creditor nation; and our acquisition of overseas territory, notably Puerto Rico and the Philippine Islands as a result of the Spanish-American War.

But in spite of the impact of such ideas and events, the American people moved into the twentieth century rather reluctantly: our national values and preoccupations were not yet those of a conscious world power. In fact, many of the values, ideas, and prejudices of the earlier days of the Republic had remained substantially unchanged, and in 1914 the man in the street probably found old-fashioned isolationism more congenial than imperialism. He continued to think of the United States as a haven for the oppressed and a model for the rest of the world to follow. He liked to call it "God's country," a phrase that allowed him to express his pride in his own land along with a certain disparagement of less favored regions of the earth. But a cocky self-assurance is not identical with imperialistic ambition, and in fact men such as William James, Mark Twain, and W. E. B. Du Bois spoke out directly against such signs of a growing imperialism as they detected it.

Thus, when the First World War began, there was a strong resistance to any thought of our becoming involved. Woodrow Wilson had been elected on a platform proposing domestic reforms,[2] and he had promised to keep the country out of the war. His election itself was partly the result of a fluke: the Republican party, then by far the larger of the two major parties, had suffered a temporary split.[3]

Yet if the United States was hesitant about intervening in what seemed an exclusively European affair, it emerged from the First World War as a

---

dence, that fact could scarcely have prevented the North from eventually becoming a great industrial world power, though it might have slowed down the process. Moreover, a southern victory would not even have insured the preservation of the southern status quo. Ironically, an independent South just might have become industrialized more rapidly than has been the case. But we are not here concerned with historical might-have-beens.

[2] In his administration, the Clayton Anti-Trust Act was passed; the Federal Reserve System and the Federal Trade Commission were established; and provision was made for a graduated income tax, the prohibition of child labor, and the limitation of the working day to eight hours.

[3] Theodore Roosevelt had fallen out with William Howard Taft, his former protégé, and had run on the "Bull Moose" ticket.

superpower. The European combatants ended the war exhausted, burdened with heavy debts, and threatened with inflation and revolution, whereas for the United States the future looked rosy.

Thus the First World War did not really shake America's optimism. For the European intellectual, on the other hand, the very fact that the war had happened at all was disillusioning. It shocked his expectations for an increasingly rational conduct of affairs, the evolution of a peaceful European society, and liberal, cultural, and scientific development. To be sure, some American writers also experienced a serious disillusionment. Of this group perhaps the archetypal figure was Ernest Hemingway, who used as an epigraph for his first novel Gertrude Stein's pronouncement "You are all a lost generation," and the heroes of whose novels find little more in which to believe than courage and a certain personal dignity as they look out upon a world bereft of meaning. But in the overview the American people, though they grumbled about ever having become involved and refused to allow the nation to enter their President's almost single-handed creation, the League of Nations, had not lost their confidence in their own country. In their minds, they had fought a war to end all war, and if they had failed to accomplish that end, it was because a too naive and idealistic President had been made the cat's paw of Europe's devious statesmen. The American could at least return to his own world and carry out at home the job from which he had been unfortunately diverted.

Beyond its economic and political effects, the war exerted more deeply pervasive influences on American life. It broke down old habits and conventions. It introduced new fashions in dress, manners, behavior, and language. It shook established moral codes, especially those having to do with sex. It was followed immediately by the "jazz age," to use the name that F. Scott Fitzgerald gave it. The American's sense of his relation to his past and to his place seemed fundamentally changed. To sum up, this was a period of fluidity, of questioning, and of experimentation. This was also a time of disillusionment and even cynicism.

In the presidential campaign of 1920 the Republican candidate, Warren G. Harding, promised a "return to normalcy," and that promise proved very attractive to the great majority of the electorate, who were already disillusioned with Wilsonian idealism. They wanted no more foreign intervention and longed to settle down to a period of business growth and prosperity. The administration's general policy favored big business—"What's good for business is good for America"—and business did begin to boom.

But some of it was shady business. Just as after the Civil War there had been corruption in high places, so it was now—and the corruption in high places was matched by crime in somewhat lower places. Harding's regime was characterized by the Teapot Dome scandal, in which the Secretary of the Interior was convicted of accepting bribes in order to have certain government oil reserves thrown open to lease and purchase by private oil companies. In the cities there was gangsterism, including gang wars, executions, and shoot-outs over who was to control the sale of beer, say, or who would control other rackets—in Chicago and in other cities. It was also the era of the speakeasy and of Texas Guinan, who saluted customers entering her famous New York night club with the cheery greeting, "Hi, sucker!"

There were, however, some important and long-lasting effects of American participation in the First World War that were not immediately obvious. For example, thousands of American soldiers had got at least a glimpse of France and perhaps of Germany. Europe had, of course, for a long time been visited by "long-haired Victorian sages," as Robert Lowell has described them, who "accept[ed] the universe/while breezing on their trust funds through the world." But America's new sightseers were a different breed, most of them without much interest in metaphysics and certainly without trust funds to ease their way through life. Many of them had never been out of their home states before, and whatever they made of what they saw, Europe suddenly drew much closer to the American mind.[4] From now on, each summer, hordes of tourists would visit Europe, and young American writers and artists—far more now than in the past—would be living abroad for months and even years. For young men and women interested in the arts, letters, and scholarship, Europe was glamorous and exciting. The culture of the Old World was exotic and yet relaxed. Whereas life at home had been stuffy (Prohibition had come in), in Europe one could legally get a drink, and there, because of the rate of exchange, living was ridiculously cheap.[5]

Another important indirect effect of the war was to introduce to America certain European intellectual influences. One thinks immediately of Sigmund Freud and Sir James Fraser. (There was also, because of the Russian

---

[4] One of the popular songs of the period asked "How're you going to keep 'em down on the farm/After they've seen Paree?" Whether or not Paree had much to do with it, many did not stay on the farm. The migration to the city went forward.

[5] The Eighteenth Amendment, which prohibited the manufacture and sale of intoxicating beverages, was a manifestation of American reformist zeal. In the passage of the Amendment, the Puritan ethic had associated itself with the gospel of efficiency. One argument urged in favor of Prohibition was that drunkenness was an economic liability in a world in which vast numbers of people worked in mills and factories and were now acquiring automobiles: it cut down the worker's efficiency and, at the wheel of his automobile or at the lever of his machine, he might very well, if tipsy, kill himself or someone else.

Revolution, a new and much intensified interest in Karl Marx, to whom we have already referred and about whom we shall have something to say later.) Though Freud had published his first important work in 1899 and, in 1909, had actually visited the United States to give some important lectures at Clark University, Freudianism did not become generally known until after the war. Even then, it was frequently misunderstood as providing a kind of license for easygoing sexual behavior. Once it had got fully into circulation, however, it would be seriously studied, put into practice by psychoanalysts, and taken into account by poets and novelists. For example, in Eugene O'Neill's *Mourning Becomes Electra* (1931) the motivation of the characters is almost nakedly Freudian. (See p. 2009.) Though Fraser had published, in 1890, *The Golden Bough*, his monumental work on myth and ritual, his influence, like that of Freud, was not felt at once. His ideas did not get into general literary and intellectual circulation in the United States until the 1920's. Then, with reference to it in such works as Eliot's *The Waste Land* (1922), its influence spread beyond the world of professional anthropologists and scholars of culture to the whole literary world.

The shock of the experience of war and the exciting, if confusing, period that was its aftermath provided a powerful stimulus to American writing. A vigorous literature will not inevitably ensue on the breaking up of older patterns of manners and morals, but, as proved by the event, the time was now ripe for a literary flowering and the young writers were prepared to respond fruitfully to the stimulus of change. At all events, the decade of the 1920's turned out to be one of our most brilliant eras in literature. The more important of these writers will be treated in detail in their due places in the pages that follow. At this point, in making some general comments on the cultural situation, it may be most useful simply to say something about the variety of the writers who came forward: their regional, or ethnic, or economic, or political identifications.

In this postwar period the voices of new groups of Americans were heard almost for the first time in American literature. Up to this point in our history, the typical American writer had been native-born, white, more or less affluent, Protestant, and Anglo-Saxon. Thenceforward one finds writers who are poor, or immigrants, or Jews,[6] or blacks. It was in the 1920's, in fact, that the Negro made his first general cultural breakthrough, with jazz, the new

---

[6] The first American Jewish writer of consequence, however, was Gertrude Stein, who was not poor or reared in the slums, but wealthy and a Radcliffe graduate. (See p. 2221.) Bret Harte is a special case. (See pp. 1250–51.) Dreiser, as a representative of the immigrant poor, had already begun to publish in 1900, and, as we have already observed, the blacks, with Chesnutt, Dunbar, and Du Bois, had already entered literature.

music that became the special music of the young, provided a name for the era, and soon made a conquest of Europe.

Something should be said in passing about the popular arts and the mass entertainment that the new technology had provided: the movies, the radio, and, later, television. The 1930's and 1940's constituted the great era for radio. Before the end of the 1920's nearly every American family, however poor, owned at least a cheap set and had begun to receive news, listen to favorite commentators, such as Elmer Davis, Edgar Mowrer, or William Shirer, hear popular music, grand opera, radio plays, and comedy acts. The 1920's, 1930's, and 1940's were the great days of the movies. By this time, of course, the movies could scarcely be called a new art, yet it was in these decades that they reached their own characteristic form and became the enormously popular entertainment for the masses. In their own way they became also a powerful educational force, indirectly suggesting to the average American man or woman how a house should be furnished, how a meal should be served, how to make love; and introducing them to remote and exotic settings: the world of the gangster, the movie star, the millionaire, the Hungarian countess; of Nero, the decadent Roman emperor, and Blackbeard the pirate. It was the heyday of Rudolph Valentino, Charlie Chaplin, Greta Garbo, Norma Talmadge, Clara Bow, and Marlene Dietrich.

What would be the eventual social and cultural consequences of a mass entertainment that catered to everyone? Would it vulgarize taste? Would it—for better or worse—homogenize society? The intellectuals were far from certain. In any case, they cast few favoring looks on the solid middle-class citizen whose cultural habits were agreed to be deplorable. Sinclair Lewis paid his respects to the small-town businessman in *Main Street* (1920) and to the go-getters of the growing cities in *Babbitt* (1922). H. L. Mencken in the *American Mercury* (founded in 1924) month by month worked over with special zeal the hapless booboisie.[7]

But in spite of the concern that a gray and mediocre uniformity might result from a diet of radio, movies, and television, the worst has not happened. Mass entertainment has nourished a common faddish lingo, and there has been a powerful drift toward cultural uniformity. Yet America has always had a certain resilience along with a powerful and, in some respects, valuable inertia. A good many people stay put in spite of changing fashions

---

[7] One notes in this period a sharpened division between the intellectual (including the poet and the novelist) and the man in the street. Such a division is implicit in any culture, and since the days of Cooper, Emerson, and Thoreau, American writers have been criticizing with asperity various aspects of American culture.

and fads. Some actually react against cultural pressures. The parts of the country that had their own individuality have managed to retain a surprising amount of it. For illustration, one small but significant instance: after decades of radio, sound movies, and, later, television, and despite the increasing mobility of the population, the various regional accents have managed to hold their own to a degree that many observers in the 1920's had not thought possible.

Earlier, we noted, in the nineteenth century, the development of local color fiction, particularly in the South and the Midwest. In the twentieth century this process of a wide geographical distribution of writers went on apace. Indiana-born Theodore Dreiser published *Sister Carrie,* the story of a young Wisconsin girl who undergoes her initiation in Chicago, as early as 1900 (though the book did not achieve wide circulation until 1912). In 1913 appeared Willa Cather's *O Pioneers!,* a novel with a Nebraska setting. In 1915 Edgar Lee Masters published an account of life in a small Illinois town in a collection of poems entitled *Spoon River Anthology.*

After the First World War, books with settings in the American hinterland came thick and fast. One thinks of Sherwood Anderson's *Winesburg, Ohio* (1919); of the new literature coming out of the South, so different from the local-colorism of the 1880's and 1890's; of the accounts of the far West produced by John Steinbeck, who wrote of farmers, fruit-pickers, and Chicanos; and of those commentaries on a very different sort of Pacific-coast culture: Nathanael West's *The Day of the Locust* (1939) and F. Scott Fitzgerald's *The Last Tycoon* (1941).

Books such as these are not quaintly or coyly "regional." Most of them represent the artist's normal use of material at hand about which he has something to say and do not attempt to glamorize the material with which they deal. They may even be harshly critical. The region, on the other hand, could be used as a point of vantage from which to criticize the national culture, measuring the latter's insipidity or vapid uniformity against the region's tang and color and humanity. Criticism of this sort appears in the poetry of Robert Frost, though Frost is careful to allow the criticism to remain implicit and to make his claim that New Hampshire is the "best state in the nation" somewhat tongue in cheek.

But quite explicit defenses of the regional subcultures appear in the twentieth century, some of them serious and carefully reasoned, not mere expressions of provincial pride. Such reassertions of the value of cultural differences were prompted in great part by the threat of an encroaching cultural uniformity. That threat, however, usually elicited criticism of a different kind, one that focused the attack on the prevailing thinness and banality of the typical best seller, Broadway hit, or popular movie. The more intelligent of these critiques did not condemn the current offerings merely because they were popular but called attention to the sleaziness, the sentimentality, and the arrant escapism of much that was offered to the public at large.

A more serious critical response to the cultural situation went much further than taking note of the trivial and the sensational, the saccharine and the vapid. It turned back to first principles. It refused to take refuge in the genteel tradition. Thus, it did not condemn contemporary poetry merely because it failed to resemble the work of Tennyson and Longfellow. Tennyson and Longfellow themselves were appraised with a sharper eye. Besides, the point was not that good art should be vigorously contemporary and even daringly experimental. More profound questions were being raised. Did art have any role in a scientific society? What should the poet write about in an industrial and urban community? Should he try to relieve the humdrum of the industrial day with tales of the Middle Ages or poems about old Japan? Surely that was not a proper job for the artist who took his work seriously.

The critical discussion thus initiated went on to raise questions about the nature of literature as such. Along with the general repudiation of Victorian culture and morals, there was a reaction against Victorian notions of what literature was and the ways in which it was to be judged. In sum, during the period from roughly 1920 to 1950 there occurred, both in Britain and in America, an intense reexamination of the structure of literature and, as a consequence, of the nature of the critical activity itself. This was stimulated in part by the science of semantics, depth psychology, anthropology, and important new studies in the symbolism of ancient cultures, mythological patterns, and comparative religion. Yet what gave this critical activity point and urgency was the state of the popular arts and the general challenge of the prevailingly scientific climate of ideas. Confronted by what seemed to be a crisis in the culture, both the writer and the critic had to decide just what the function of literature was.

There were plenty of his fellow citizens—once America had been engulfed by the Depression—to urge the writer to become a prophet and provide the culture with inspired ideas or perhaps to act as a skilled propagandist for the ideas of others. The job of mere entertainer seemed trivial in times of such urgency, unless, of course, the writer could demonstrate that his play with words was a serious and valuable kind of playfulness, relevant and even necessary to the health of a culture. So with a new intensity, the literary artists and critics of our century canvassed the nature of literature and the role of the artist—in relation to science, religion, and the life of the mind generally.

We mistake matters utterly if we assume that the debate over criticism that ensued was over mere literary niceties and precious technicalities. Not at all: it grew logically out of the twentieth-century cultural crisis. In one of the later sections of this volume, we shall print some of the more significant discussions of the problem.

A few months after President Herbert Hoover took office, on Friday, October 29, 1929—it speedily came to be known as "Black Friday"—the bottom fell out of the stock market, and shortly thereafter the Depression hit the United States with full force. Though Hoover tried the various expedients that were possible within the limits of his political and economic philosophy, and though later he ventured a few experiments, some of which were to receive further development in the next administration, nothing worked. In the next election Franklin Roosevelt won, hands down. Ever since the Civil War the Democratic party had been the minority party in the country, holding the presidency for only sixteen years during the entire period from 1860 to 1932. Now it was to become the party of the majority, or rather of a coalition of minorities.

Roosevelt brilliantly exploited the political situation by bringing together five "have-not" entities: the South, which had lived for years in a state of chronic depression (Roosevelt was to characterize it as the country's "economic problem number one"); the Roman Catholics, who still formed a minority group in many parts of the country; the blacks, particularly those settled in the urban communities; the Jews; and the labor unions. Labor was especially significant, for now, with a friendly national administration in Washington and with favorable legislative and court action broadening and confirming its rights, it was to become a powerful political force. To this rather improbable coalition that Roosevelt put together should be added another constituency, relatively small in numbers but important in influence: the intellectuals.

Roosevelt thus came into power, not as a doctrinaire political philosopher, but as a political opportunist. He was willing to experiment, to play things by ear, and to change an adviser when his advice didn't pan out. Nevertheless, the reforms carried through under Roosevelt were important and far-reaching in their influence. Roosevelt had inherited a crisis situation and what he effected amounted to a bloodless revolution. Roosevelt gained enormous popularity and was the first, and will presumably be the last,[8] President ever to be elected for four terms. Nevertheless, in spite of all the

---

[8] A constitutional amendment now forbids any President's being elected for a third term.

Roosevelt administration's efforts, the Depression did not come to an end until unemployment was ended by the vast expansion of our armed forces and of the industrial establishment as it tooled up for the Second World War.

The spectacular breakdown of what had seemed the invulnerable American system set the intellectuals (and with them, the men of letters) to speculating about what would be the ideal economic system. They were willing now to question whether, in the second quarter of the twentieth century, any capitalist system could be made to work. More and more of them began to give serious consideration to Karl Marx's analysis of the bankruptcy of capitalism and his prophecies of a communistic society. Though the Communist Manifesto had been published in 1848 and Karl Marx had issued the first volume of *Das Kapital* in 1871, Marxism had made little headway in the United States. The Socialist movement had, to be sure, come to represent a force of some importance. Eugene Debs, as the presidential candidate for the Socialist party, polled nearly nine hundred thousand votes in the 1912 election, and in 1924 Robert LaFollette, running as a Progressive, but receiving Socialist support, got nearly five million. But the Socialist and other allied movements were at this time non-Marxist, deriving from Jeffersonian egalitarianism and democratic idealism. In short, they were developments of native American aspirations and pinned their hopes on man's inherent goodness rather than on theories of the class struggle and of dialectical materialism.

What happened and what failed to happen in the First World War weakened the cause of socialism. (This weakening of socialism is one of the themes of John Dos Passos' trilogy *U.S.A.*) It had been hoped that the workers of one country would refuse to bear arms against their brother workers in other countries, but bear arms they did. Moreover, "the economic consequences of the peace"—to invoke the title of John Maynard Keynes's famous and prophetic book on the subject—brought about economic stagnation in Europe, hardship to the working classes everywhere, and finally a great depression in the United States. American intellectuals were now ready to take seriously radical analyses of their own society and recommendations for drastic solutions.

What Marx invoked for the working class was not sentimental concern or an appeal to a philosophical or religious notion of justice, but the rigor of "scientific" analysis and the inevitable verdict of history. Capitalism, Marx argued, would be ultimately liquidated because of its own internal contradictions. It was inevitable that under the capitalist system production would become more and more concentrated in the hands of a very few owners and that this development would necessarily create a larger and larger number of workers who would become more and more thoroughly exploited. Sooner or later, the workers would take over from the tiny handful of capitalists.[9]

Though Marxism scoffed at sentimental and idealistic illusions, and based itself firmly on a materialistic philosophy, it appealed to many aspects of the old American dream. Marxism too promised a society in which every man would have his own place and dignity, in which social snobbery and economic exploitation could not exist, and in which man would at last live in peace and harmony with his fellows. Its very aura of scientific rigor and no-nonsense practicality appealed to some elements in American culture, for post–Civil War America was in important ways materialistic too and prided itself on the application of scientific methods to all the problems of human life. Finally, Marxism conveniently left the nature of the ultimate millennial state sufficiently vague and unspecified—after all, how could one describe in detail the perfect society to people who had never experienced it? The American idealist could therefore easily accommodate it to the native and familiar American version. The early American Socialists, as we have said, thought of themselves as the heirs of Jefferson, Emerson, and Whitman. Dos Passos, as we shall see, once remarked that he knew no Russian poet as revolutionary as Whitman.

Yet the American idealist who was disturbed by the inequities of the American economic system and was disposed to ally himself with the working class could appeal to more than a merely literary tradition of concern for the oppressed. There was a tradition of American activism too. Whitman himself had learned of the "war of the classes" from Fanny Wright (see pp. 329–30) in New York; and American workingmen had shocked the public by fighting back against the bosses in the Haymarket riot of 1886 and the Homestead steel strike in 1892. Emma Goldman, the anarchist (who because of her agitation was once sentenced to a year in prison), was living in Greenwich Village about 1914 and Theodore Dreiser, the novelist, met her there. So did Henry Miller. These instances illustrate the fact of a native tradition of resistance to finance-capitalism.

[9] At the end of the Middle Ages, so the Marxist argument ran, the feudal aristocracy had been subverted in something like this fashion by a new rising class, the bourgeoisie. The class now rising and destined by history to win was the workers, those who really produced the goods and services for mankind. Thus the triumph of the working class was inevitable. With the disappearance of bourgeois capitalists, a classless society would at last have been achieved. The profit motive would have disappeared. In the new dispensation service would be given by each according to his abilities and goods would be provided to each according to his needs. The utopia that philosophers had long dreamed of would be ushered in—not because man had been persuaded to be good and kind to his fellows, but because the very laws of economic history decreed that it must be so.

It might be argued that since the perfect Communist society was inevitable, there was no need for anyone to toil and sweat to help bring it about; it was bound to arrive anyway. But the inevitability of a future event, far from paralyzing human activity, can actually prove an incentive. We sometimes work harder because we feel that we are on the side of history. Thus, in an earlier day, New England's Calvinism was theoretically a determinism that rendered any human action unnecessary and even vain: God had decreed before history began who would be saved and who would be damned; but in practice, Calvinism produced a society that strove valiantly to bring God's kingdom to pass. Here again the appeal of Marxism found answering traits in American culture.

True, Marxism, even in its twentieth-century triumphs, did not quite work out as Marx had said that it would. The first country to become Communist ought to have been highly industrialized like the United States or Great Britain. Instead, the first country to adopt communism was Russia— backward, largely agricultural, still partially feudalistic in its economic and social patterns. As someone has observed: "Wrong country, wrong time, and for the wrong reasons." But the anomaly did not too much disturb American observers: after all, it *was* a triumph. Communism had been brought from the airy realm of theory down to the here and now. The American John Reed sent this message from revolutionary Russia to his friends: "I have seen the future and it works." In fact, most American intellectuals did not become disillusioned with communism because of the contradictions in Marxist theory. They were disenchanted by particular events such as the pressure exerted on artists and intellectuals, the bloody purges carried out by Stalin, and, most notably, in 1939, the nonaggression pact signed by Hitler and Stalin which freed the Nazis to carry out their invasion of Poland, the overt act that opened the Second World War.

In the pages that follow the reader will find work revealing the impact of Marxism and communism on both critics and fiction writers.[10] It must be added, however, that not many of the novels and stories thus inspired survived the Depression period. They were too one-sided, too frankly propagandistic, to have much literary quality or to contain anything permanent to say to a subsequent generation. There was, of course, the occasional exception: see the account of Michael Gold's *Jews Without Money* (pp. 2385–86).

---

[10] It should be noted that a good many of those who wrote "proletarian" novels during the 1930's did not follow the Communist party line, and not all were even "fellow travelers." Literary people are usually not sufficiently doctrinaire to become good members of any party. The "leftist" writers of the 1930's questioned the established order because they were stirred by the spectacle of men out of work through no fault of their own, or of families without proper food.

At the outset of the war it did not seem that the United States would necessarily be involved; but as Hitler, with apparently invincible power, overran country after country, eventually leaving Great Britain isolated as his only unconquered foe,[11] it began to be clear that the United States would almost certainly have to take a stand. Even so, isolationism died hard. Peace sentiment was strong and peace rallies attracted vast numbers of people. Almost on the verge of our entry into the war, a bill before Congress to extend the draft law and so have at hand some kind of potential army managed to pass by only one vote. But the attack on Pearl Harbor by the Japanese on December 7, 1941, put us squarely in the war.

In 1945, after nearly four years of hard fighting, both Germany and Japan were crushed. The closing days of the campaign against Japan were notable for the use of the atomic bomb, the first being exploded over Hiroshima on August 6, 1945, and, three days later, a second, over Nagasaki. Even though the United States had a major part in drawing up the peace terms, the period that ensued was not one of real peace. Russia had emerged from the war as a superpower, not so strong as the United States, but formidable. Such power vacuums as the peace treaties left, Russian power promptly filled. By the terms of the peace settlement and because of its contiguity with the smaller states of eastern Europe, Russia became master there.

In 1946, Winston Churchill, in a speech delivered at Westminster College in Fulton, Missouri, announced that though the shooting war had ended, the Western nations had to realize that they were engaged in a "Cold War" with the Communist world. For a time, the United States had a monopoly on atomic bombs, but within a few years Russian scientists perfected one of their own and the fact of the Cold War was brought home to everyone as the two superpowers and their allies tried to make sure that the rival group did not upset the precarious balance of power.

The threat of total war is in fact simply an extreme extension of the general threat that had been posed for a long time by the prodigious growth of science. Serious thinkers—for instance, Henry Adams—had not had to wait for the development of missiles with nuclear warheads to be troubled by mankind's having come to possess instruments too powerful for its moral and emotional capabilities. The fault, of course, is not with science, which is neutral and provides, indifferently, the means for good or ill, but lies in man's sense of values and ends having been outstripped by his knowledge of means. It is now clear to all that nuclear war is not the only threat posed by

---

[11] Before we entered the war, Russia had also become a foe of Hitler's, having been invaded in 1942. The enormous power of the German attack and the immense territory it won in the first year emphasized, if anything, the impression of Hitler's power.

this fact. Uncontrolled technological development has given us a polluted atmosphere, "dead" lakes and fouled streams, a gravely threatened ecology; or to turn to social and economic matters: traffic-choked highways, dire poverty, the "problem of the cities," and schools that do not educate.

Because of limitations of space and our present lack of a proper historical perspective, the events of the 1950's and 1960's lie outside the proper scope of this book; but many of them are so important and so many fall within the lifetime of even the youngest reader that it would seem obtuse not to mention them at least briefly, particularly since many of them seem the normal development of tendencies already discussed.

As for the history of this later period a few other developments demand at least cursory attention. The civil rights movement under the brilliant leadership of such men as Martin Luther King succeeded in making its case and eventually winning the support of Congress as well as of the courts. The development of television played an important role in this process. Though we commonly think of it as providing a rather vapid kind of home entertainment, interspersed with commercial messages, it can provide a vivid documentation of events and one that at least in this instance radically altered the American mind on the basic issues. It was one thing to read that demonstrations had occurred and that some demonstrators had been attacked; it was another thing to see it with one's own eyes.[12] Moreover, the courts, and particularly the Supreme Court, had begun to take seriously, indeed quite literally, the Bill of Rights of the Constitution and were forcing American life to conform, in certain ways at least, to the letter of the law.[13]

A matter only peripherally related to civil rights, but one which obviously has had a bearing on the problem, has been the great shift of population to the cities—white as well as black, Puerto Ricans as well as people living in the continental United States. The process—as a particular aspect of industrialization—has been going on for a long time[14] though in recent decades it has accelerated. That acceleration has not been resisted but actively promoted by the federal government. Throughout a series of administrations,

---

[12] Television has indeed introduced a new dimension in the reporting of the news, especially of topical events with strong emotional overtones. Like any other technique, it can be used for good or misused. It is far less objective than language, and in the hands of partisans can be manipulated as a powerful rhetorical instrument. Part of its power derives from the immense size of its audience, far greater than any newspaper can command.

[13] Various legal restrictions on the Negro with regard to his attending certain schools, his registering to vote in certain primaries, his buying houses, and so on, were rapidly struck down. In the wide area of social and economic discrimination, the gains have been less impressive.

and presumably on the best advice of its economic experts, the government has virtually abandoned support of the one-family farm. Price supports have gone to the efficient farmer, the "farmer" who runs what might be called a large grain or cotton or lettuce "factory." In recent years government subsidies to individual farming entrepreneurs have run as high as $250,000 a year. The result has been that for the last several decades more and more small farmers have left their farms for the cities, and particularly for the great cities of the East and Midwest.

This has not been merely an affair of black farmers migrating from the Carolinas to New York and Philadelphia. White farmers from Appalachia also, finding that they could no longer eke out a living on the land, have moved to Akron or Detroit. The result has been a change in the character of the cities, tremendous pressure upon their resources, and obviously a terribly wrenching experience for the uprooted countryman, often ill-equipped to make a living in the city, unused to living under urban conditions, but with literally nowhere else to go. There has probably been nothing like this enforced uprooting and dislocation of human lives since the Enclosure Acts of eighteenth-century England drove the peasantry off the land and into the mills and factories of Manchester and Birmingham.

Such hardships were presumably not intended; and, on abstract economic grounds, the decision to discourage small, inefficient farms may well be sound. But in an organization so complicated as the modern federal government must be, the left hand literally does not know what the right is doing, and a sound decision in one area may have very adverse consequences in others. The misery, anger, and frustration felt by those crowded into the

14 John Steinbeck's *The Grapes of Wrath* (1939) is probably the most famous of the novels that depict the predicament of the small farmer, in this instance the "Okies," people forced out of the Dust Bowl of Oklahoma and Arkansas, who make their way to California in a desperate attempt to find farm jobs. The hardships of the small farmer and the sharecropper have also been recorded in the large mass of documentary reports written during the Depression years. In 1935 the Works Progress Administration was formed under the Roosevelt administration to provide immediate economic relief to various groups, including writers, actors, and artists. The WPA consequently produced a great deal of literary and semiliterary material, including case histories of the plight of the sharecroppers. See, for example, *These Are Our Lives*. (This WPA documentary material was by no means limited to the farm workers, however: it included firsthand studies of social and economic distress in cities and industrial communities as well.)

An important aspect of this documentation of the plight of the underdog consisted in books made up of photographs and text. The most celebrated of these is *Let Us Now Praise Famous Men* (1941), a study of Alabama sharecroppers. The photographs were supplied by Walker Evans; the text, by James Agee.

core areas of our large cities, particularly the blacks, have been eloquently expressed by writers such as Malcolm X, James Baldwin, and Eldridge Cleaver.[15]

The movement for the rights of the black man was followed by the women's liberation movement, by the students' and youth rebellion, and by the hippie revolt against American middle-class standards. It is too early to predict the ultimate consequences of these and related movements, but the general tendency, of which they are all variants, amounts to a challenge to limitations, restrictions, and taboos of every kind, whether sanctioned by custom, tradition, and present or past laws. Thus, for example, the censorship of books, plays, and movies has been practically abrogated. There is a new sexual freedom and radically revised codes of sexual conduct are rapidly coming into acceptance. Society becomes more and more pluralistic and individualistic.

To many people the elimination of all restraints has seemed the logical further course for a society that has long paid lip service to the freedom of the individual. They regard the situation as one in which society is finally making good its heretofore empty promises. Some serious thinkers, however, find that this tendency to get rid of obstacles and inhibitions implies a much more complex situation than appears on the surface. Cries for more and more liberty, they would say, though seeming to express a desire for isolated individualism outside of society—even for anarchy—actually spring from a contrary impulse. They express—though perhaps unconsciously—a hunger for the warmth, friendliness, and human satisfaction that many people miss in our present-day civilization. The sense of community has been lost. The individual has come up against what seems to him a cold, faceless, and inhuman machine.

As a justification for associating the demand for more individual freedom with what might appear to be its opposite, the yearning for community, one could cite such matters as the current vogue for sensitivity training, an activity that promises the reestablishment of warm human relations with others; the urge to live in communes, including those that propose a return to simplicity and "nature"; the need on the part of so many people, particularly the more literate and self-conscious, for psychiatric help; the interest in non-Western religions; and the fact of loneliness and alienation

---

[15] In part perhaps because of the influx of the "disinherited" into the cities, many of the more affluent have moved out to the suburbs, and their own sense of disorientation and worthlessness has been expressed by writers such as John Updike and John Cheever. Still, a recent survey conducted by a prominent magazine indicated that the ambition of the majority of city dwellers is to be able to afford a move to the country.

suffered in the modern world by people who feel that they have somehow lost their way and their very identity. The attempt to find one's identity and to establish a relation with other human beings would in any case seem to be as much a feature of the age as the assertion of pure individuality. Both tendencies are powerfully reflected in our current literature.

A modern poet, W. H. Auden, has some interesting comments to make on the apparently contradictory situation of the man who has shaken off "the traditional beliefs of a closed society," who can "no longer believe simply because his forefathers did," and yet who feels a terrible necessity to find a belief. The critical difficulty of his situation is that he "has found no source or principle of direction to replace" the beliefs that had directed his forefathers. If the man in question is an artist, there are satisfactions that he can derive from the very precariousness of his situation, but if he "is not a genius, [if] he is not sociably gifted, [if] his work is not important or interesting, so that self-love and the thirst for glory cannot motivate his life; if self-consciousness can only turn in destructively on himself, his freedom wastes itself in freakish, arbitrary, spiteful little acts."

In the foregoing comments Auden is referring to the man who reveals himself in Dostoevski's *Notes from the Underground*. Yet Auden is interested in him because this "underground" man is also a twentieth-century type. Auden goes on to say:

> Liberalism is at a loss to know how to handle him, for the only thing liberalism knows to offer is more freedom, and it is precisely freedom in the sense of lack of necessity that is his trouble. When a man knows what he wants, liberalism can help him—when a peasant exploited by his landlord desires a farm of his own, for example, liberalism can fight for land reform. But ask this man what he wants and his only answer is a fantastic daydream.

Auden is not alone among the modern writers who are concerned with the plight of human beings whose self-consciousness is not a source of strength but has become a crippling burden and whose freedom is not a boon but an embarrassment. Such a person's aimlessness and bewildered resentment against some vaguely apprehended inimical system constitute one of the more formidable challenges, not only to liberalism, but to the American notion of progress.[16]

Though the man completely emptied of beliefs can occasionally be found in the United States, and though his negativity points to the dead

---

[16] These remarks are not meant to imply that specific and well-documented grievances do not exist. The task of a reforming liberalism, of course, is far from complete.

end of mere naked individualism, yet he rarely exists in a chemically pure state. Few Americans have made such a clean job of jettisoning their intellectual cargo. In fact, most of us as Americans believe quite a lot. Moreover, some basic beliefs are shared by the radical and conservative alike, by both the youthful rebel and the middle-aging solid citizen of the suburbs.

What, then, are these articles of faith? Is there a definite complex of values and beliefs that can be called distinctively American? With this last question, we come back to the problem that Crèvecoeur attempted to answer in 1782: What is an American?[17]

In the account that follows we shall emphasize only what seem the typical American's core beliefs.[18] First among them is the belief in the new start. If the first colonist did not assume that he achieved a new innocence from contact with the soil of the New World, at least he knew he was being given a second chance—the opportunity to make a new beginning. Europe had its immemorial legends and myths about an innocent earlier world, a golden age, a pastoral Arcadia, now, alas, irrecoverably lost in the past. But the American imagination typically can't concede that it is really lost in the past. F. Scott Fitzgerald's character Gatsby is thus nowhere more American than

---

[17] Many writers have tried to answer Crèvecoeur's question, and there have been a number of formidable attempts in our own century. We have space here to mention only a few. The short life span of Randolph Bourne (see pp. 1474–75) allowed him to do little more than put important questions about American culture and to try to penetrate beneath the superficial notions of what Americanism consisted in. His friend Van Wyck Brooks carried on this general line of inquiry with *The Wine of the Puritans* (1908), *America's Coming of Age* (1915), and *The Ordeal of Mark Twain* (1920), in which he indicted Twain's Calvinistic background and the provincial environment in which he grew up in Missouri for thwarting his genius.

Later, during the 1930's and 1940's, a much mellowed Brooks published five volumes of literary history, the best known of which is *The Flowering of New England, 1815–1865* (1936). But these rather relaxed studies represent celebrations of the American literary achievement rather than stringent intellectual inquiries.

V. K. Parrington attempted an ambitious analysis and evaluation of American intellectual development, calling his work *Main Currents in American Thought* (1929–30). F. O. Matthiessen published an impressive and far more specifically literary work in his *American Renaissance* (1941) and in his *Henry James: The Major Phase* (1944).

The titles cited represent only a few of the major works that have come off presses in the last forty years. There have been numerous individual biographies, special studies, and monographs. A good many of these are referred to in our introduction and in our lists of further readings.

[18] We shall not attempt to set down all the things that Americans believe nor shall we take any special notice of beliefs peculiar to some of America's subcultures. Finally, some of the beliefs to be noticed below are shared by other peoples. After all, America is an offshoot of Europe and represents not a complete departure from, but rather a specialization and intensification of, beliefs that belong to the general Western tradition.

in the answer he gives to a friend who reminds him that he must not expect to be able to repeat the past. Gatsby exclaims: "Can't repeat the past? Why, of course you can!" The American likes to believe that his golden Arcadia of only apparently lost innocence is actually still here and now—somewhere. Maybe you can find it by looking about in some hidden spot—or maybe by just moving farther west into the wilderness.

A second, corollary, and in one sense a contradictory belief is that since the past can be repeated, its pastness is of no account. History is a nightmare that anyone would want to escape (as Joyce's Stephen Dedalus longed to escape it). And the American is certain that he can escape it. History is a sad chronicle of disasters and mistakes. Thank goodness one is not bound by it. Henry Ford spoke for legions of his countrymen when he said that history is bunk.[19] Just as some Americans felt that they could find the lost Arcadia by penetrating deeper into the forests of the new continent, thus transposing the order of time into that of space, so they made a similar transposition in believing that they had left history behind in the Old World and had stepped, disburdened of the past, onto the shores of the New.

As a third article of faith, there remains, though in modified form, the old doctrine of the Inner Light. We don't like spiritual authority; we don't want people telling us what we are to value or believe. Even most church-goers who claim to be orthodox and recite the creeds believe a little more emphatically in the God within than in their Father in Heaven. Moreover, it is not easy for us always to distinguish the voice of the Holy Spirit speaking within us from our own voice. (One hastens to say that this distinction has never been really easy; but the American, because of his special tradition, may encounter more difficulties than most.)

It is true, of course, that, like other people, we are impressed by charm and winning eloquence. We have a weakness for charismatic leaders. We sometimes rush almost like lemmings in one direction, caught in the grip of a fad or joining in a popular crusade. But even here we resist the belief that we have been swept off our feet by personal magnetism or are merely following the crowd. We never tire of congratulating ourselves on our freedom of judgment and freedom of conscience even in the midst of our need for clubs and associations and joinings and our susceptibility to passing fashions. We fondly believe in Emerson's self-reliance.

We are also inveterate technologists, and put our faith in machinery, not only in literal machines but in organizational machinery: in special programs, in the findings of presidential committees, in "taking a course" in something,

---

[19] Ford denied that he used just these words, but he did not disavow the sentiment.

and in technical training of every kind. We want technical training even in matters that are supposed to involve natural functions (see the number of sex manuals advertised and sold).

Does our faith in the Inner Light conflict with our trust in machinery? Not really. The two fit neatly together, as the inner and outer aspects of our lives. For though we believe that we need professional training in the *means* with which to accomplish the ends we seek, we are very chary about being instructed in what our *ends* should be. Here we tend to be amateurs and intense individualists. In choosing our goals, we depend—or think we depend—on the Inner Light, a certain feeling, even a hunch.

Finally, in this brief and sketchy summary it should be observed that though we talk much about the recovery of lost innocence and therefore might appear to be wistful Arcadians, we are in fact—most of us, at least— utopians or millennialists. We have lost our hearts to the Future, not to the Past. The concept of millennialism perhaps provides the simplest way to put into one pattern such "American" phenomena as the attempt to recapture a childlike innocence, the repudiation of history, and the curious way in which we are at once materialists and idealists. The "materialism" with which we are often reproached, when intently inspected, turns out to be an idealism, and, on the other hand, when the "idealism" which we flatter ourselves as possessing is examined, it promptly expresses itself in material things. From whichever pole we start, we quickly arrive at the same realm of wonders, filled with the most efficient machinery, including household appliances. In our dream of the perfect future *everyone* will be able at the touch of a button to satisfy all his wants. The wants that cannot be satisfied by pushing a button usually come in for scant notice in our millennial dream. In our ideal society, everyone will be free and untrammeled, yet the society will be so perfectly organized that nobody can possibly do anything wrong. T. S. Eliot describes the dream of our time in this fashion: Men today "constantly try to escape/From the darkness outside and within/By dreaming of systems so perfect that no one will need to be good."

In this book we have had occasion to mention millennialism again and again, and with good reason, for it has been a powerful force throughout our history and in the millennial concept are mingled some of our greatest strengths and some of our abiding weaknesses. Though the beginnings of this conception of history and human nature can be traced far back into the classical-Christian tradition, we may well begin our summary of millennialism with the arrival of the Puritans in New England.

As we have seen, they were a dedicated people, God-fearing, completely convinced that they ought to establish the kind of ecclesiastical and political arrangement that Christ had ordained. They meant to build this New Jerusalem in the American forest, following the divine model as nearly as fallible and mortal creatures can. They respected this crucial proviso, for the seventeenth-century Puritans were still sufficiently orthodox to believe in man's limitations and original sinfulness.[20] Thus, the tendency toward millennialism in the Puritan culture was counterbalanced by a powerful sense of man's inability to carry out his transcendental ideal. He lived in a tension between the eternal and the temporal.

The shift of the Puritans' interest from the transcendental to the world of here and now relaxed this tension. It occurred gradually as life became more comfortable and the doctrine of original sin lost its hold on men's minds. Prospects for the success of man's secular enterprise began to appear distinctly brighter. By the time of Emerson and Thoreau, the intellectual climate had definitely changed. Yet the Puritan drive toward perfection, one observes, did not weaken with the passage of time. It was simply now directed to a temporal goal.

In American millennialism, one recognizes a great deal that is entirely admirable. No one is going to quarrel with the wish to abolish poverty, to see that children do not develop rickets from malnutrition, or that the aged have proper medical care. Nor is it less than noble to try to abolish war and to increase economic security and freedom for human beings throughout the world. Insofar as the American belief in progress and a certain millennial expectation have spurred us on toward such goals, we must be truly grateful —and grateful, too, for the tonic effect that the pull of the future, like the pull of the great spaces of the continent, exerted on American energies and the American's will to act. Nevertheless, there is another side to millennialism that has to be acknowledged, one that began early in American history in such acts as the hanging of Quakers, the expulsion of people like Anne Hutchinson, and the almost genocidal warfare on the Indians, a process that lasted right down to the twentieth century. It is the arrogance of the fanatic who is willing to impose his judgments on other people because of his confidence that he knows the truth and that the erring brother will really be better off if forced to knuckle under.

One turn of the screw and millennialism demands immediate solutions. Another turn of the screw and it demands whatever violent means may be necessary to achieve its solutions, for the ends can, for the millennialist,

[20] In this matter they had not really given up the classic distinction enunciated by Saint Augustine as between the city of God and the cities of this world. The heavenly city could be realized only in eternity when, in God's providence, time had come to an end. Though the heavenly city was to be the model for man's earthly dwelling place, it was not within man's unaided power to build it. It could come only in God's own time, and when it did, history would be over and redeemed mankind would be living in the light of eternity.

often be taken to sanctify the means. Thus, on this basis, communism and fascism may be considered to be violent and aggressive versions of millennialism, for though we think of them as polar extremes, both show the telltale symptoms: a certainty of the possession of a privileged insight into the meaning of history and a fanatic determination to use that knowledge to set up the perfect society—along with a willingness to liquidate, if necessary, any opposers of the scheme.

American millennialism tends, on the whole, to be less violent, is characterized by a youthful enthusiasm, and is often innocent and guileless. Its characteristic weakness is a somewhat distorted view of reality. One or two examples here will have to suffice: in 1920 we let our concern for the real dangers of alcoholism override our sense of the intractability of human nature and passed the Eighteenth Amendment, attempting to get rid of the human misuse of alcohol by outlawing the thing that was misused, the alcohol itself; in 1928, hoping to avert another war, our then Secretary of State, Frank Kellogg, proposed that the nations should sign a pact outlawing war. It was duly signed by the very nations that would be fighting each other in the Second World War. Ironically, on the day on which our own Senate ratified the pact, it also passed a bill authorizing the construction of fifteen more cruisers. (Granting that the two actions are not *necessarily* contradictory, the timing would seem to suggest that our Senators were either naive or cynical, and scarcely the wise statesmen they were supposed to be.)

To speak more generally, Americans are prone to underestimate the recalcitrance of human nature and the untidiness of history. Confident in the inevitable "rightness" of ourselves, we have got into the habit of demanding "unconditional surrender." Any war that we fight must be deemed a holy war. (It is to be hoped that if we ever have to fight at all, it will be in a good cause;[21] but the danger is that we may try to prove that any war that we engage in is holy.) We do tend to falsify reality, or refuse to inspect it at all. Perhaps it would be more accurate to say that we have a schizophrenic personality. Our Dr. Jekyll self assures us that our motives are pure and that their purity guarantees our success. Meantime, our Mr. Hyde self, who is a tough customer and willing to be devious, makes his own dispositions on the basis that success is the mark of the purity of our motives—if indeed purity has to be considered at all. As a nation we might be more honest and happy if we could achieve an integrated personality, even at the price of moderating our millennial hopes and losing our aura of self-righteousness.

[21] The original version of our national anthem expresses confidence in the victory of our aims "When our cause, it is just." But the line was soon altered to read "For our cause, it is just." Presumably any cause in which we are engaged is assumed to be just.

Foreign critics have for a long time been aware of our millennialism, though they do not always use that term. A friendly critic, Anthony Burgess, the British novelist, writing in 1971 observes:

Attacks on America can be, and usually are, manifestations of concern and affection. Whom the Lord loveth He chastiseth. Mr. Campbell [whose book Burgess is reviewing here] finds individual Americans altogether decent and amiable, as all of us foreigners do. It is the great American myth that has to be assaulted, and, ever since a Declaration of Independence that was conceivably ill advised, America, through her very self-righteousness, has laid herself open to the worst charge that can ever be laid against anyone—hypocrisy. Hypocrisy is not a European disease. Europeans know they are wicked and *haussent* their *épaules* [shrug their shoulders] at it. A European rapist will blame original sin. An American rapist will say it was all for the good of the victim.

Burgess is being playful, but as a reading of the rest of the review will indicate, he is thoroughly serious as to the basic truth of his indictment.

It is tempting to mention just here another important strain in American literature, the apocalyptic, which may be regarded as a kind of reverse image of millennialism. The Apocalypse in the New Testament is the Book of Revelation, in which the faithful are given a vision of "the last things," when time will have ended and the reign of eternity will have begun. If millennialism prophesies the perfect society realized at last on earth, the apocalyptic writer gives us the day of judgment in which the old and corrupt order is abolished—quite literally cast into hell.

A secularized apocalypse need not be treated solemnly or piously. In the last several decades in particular it is usually treated savagely, often with a kind of maniacal mirth. Nathanael West's *The Day of the Locust* (1939) presents a nightmare vision of extreme Protestantism gone finally insane. Joseph Heller's *Catch-22* (1961) takes us into a lunatic Armageddon. But the appetite for apocalyptic writing has earlier manifestations. Even Mark Twain exhibits it, most notably in *A Connecticut Yankee in King Arthur's Court*, and in fact apocalyptic writing, like millennialism, can be traced back to seventeenth-century Puritanism, as in *The Day of Doom*.

The foregoing observations on our millennial streak are descriptive, not prescriptive. They are not intended as a moral lecture. Yet millennialism has to be mentioned, for it is deeply rooted in the American psyche and has an important bearing on American literature. One encounters it as a recurrent theme in our poetry and fiction. Some of our writers take the American dream very seriously and are themselves caught up in it. Some are hard-bitten realists who stand outside it, and all our more sensitive and profound literary artists, even those attracted by the hopeful dream, are aware of the obstacles that lie along the path to the New Jerusalem. On the other hand, even our writers who are skeptical of the millennial vision are often moved by the heroic effort that men are capable of making in their attempts to realize their ideals and indeed this fact determines the irony of Fitzgerald's *The Great Gatsby* and that of Dreiser's *An American Tragedy*.

The most profound literature does not so much advocate a thesis as provide a dramatic rendering of the human effort as men try to live out their ideas. Our Hawthornes and Melvilles may be said to "test" the various ideas that Americans have held by subjecting those ideas to the pressures of history and to the vicissitudes of human experience. Viewed in this perspective, American literature becomes a record of unique value, for in it the reader can live through the fortunes of American idealism as it has had to meet the shock of lived experience.

Native Traditions:

Poets in the American Grain

In speaking of "native traditions in poetry," our first intention is to draw a loose distinction between the poets considered in this section—from Edwin Arlington Robinson to Robert Frost—and those examined in a section following: Amy Lowell, Pound, Eliot, and a number of others. It is a distinction, essentially, between poets who kept pretty much to American settings and experiences, and who drew upon techniques developed by their American predecessors, and poets who engaged European (or even, in the case of Pound, oriental) subjects, and whose imaginations were vivified and focused by poetic methods that had their origins abroad, sometimes in the remote European past. But history, as we have just remarked, is never tidy, and this is nowhere more evident than in American literary history.

So let us begin by muddying the critical waters, as a necessary preliminary to sorting things out. Take the question of "free verse," or *vers libre* as it is often called. The poetry of Edgar Lee Masters, unquestionably a nativist with Whitman in his literary background, drifted toward free verse, and frequently settled there. But Amy Lowell, a leader of the "imagist" movement (see pp. 2043–57) and sometime associate of Ezra Pound, also—as we shall see in the next section—espoused *vers libre*. "We do not insist upon 'free-verse' as the only method of writing poetry," she declared in the preface to an anthology of new poetry she edited in 1915. "We fight for it as a principle of liberty. We believe that the individuality of a poet may often be better expressed in free-verse than in conventional forms." Yet when T. S. Eliot and Ezra Pound first met, in London, in 1914, they found themselves firmly agreed in opposing *both* Amy Lowell and Masters, and in the general proposition "that the dilution of *vers libre*, Amygism, Lee Masterism, general floppiness had gone too far." What was needed, Pound continued, was a return to the ideal of poetic craft, to careful workmanship, to poetry that is shaped and formed. Robert Frost, arriving in England at exactly this time, took to himself these strict creative counsels and exploited them to become the century's major representative of the native, indeed the Yankee, poet.

Free verse, then, does not a native make, nor traditional craft a European. The fact is that Amy Lowell came to *vers libre* out of her allegiance to imagism, a new mode of poetry that was English in its immediate origin and which proclaimed that "image" should replace "statement" in poetry, and images should be allowed, as it were, to develop according to their own natures. Masters, and following him Carl Sandburg, wrote free verse as the American thing to do: they were the conscious heirs of Walt Whitman, and they cheered the attack of Emerson (in his essay "The Poet") on the conventional meters of English-language verse. As to Frost, for all the sustenance he could derive from the England-based devotees of craft, he also had behind him the American example of Edwin Arlington Robinson, one of the few poets (Emerson was another) for whom Frost was willing to admit admiration and a writer as strict in matters of rhyme and meter as any poet who ever lived.

It will be evident from these remarks that even the circumscribed history we are calling "native traditions" is itself untidy, as no doubt it should be. But there is much to be said for hanging on to our basic distinction. It can be pointed out, at a minimum, that each of the poets we now come to attached himself imaginatively to one or another distinctive feature of the American scene: a mill town in Maine; rural life in the Midwest; the city of Chicago; Springfield, Illinois; New England farming country. Beyond that, we find in their work an attachment to certain traditional themes and attitudes that themselves represent a gathering response to experience in America. And if they are remarkably different one from another in poetic technique, the differences depend largely upon which segment of the American literary tradition each has chosen to ally himself with: whether it be, for example, the free-moving verse of Whitman adopted by Masters and Sandburg; the rousing evangelical hymn-singing echoed in Vachel Lindsay; or, as with Robinson, the storytelling methods of realistic fiction.

EDWIN ARLINGTON ROBINSON (1869–1935)

The period from about 1890 to 1910 is one of the hardest to define, and to appraise, in modern American literature. As we have remarked in our discussion of Stephen Crane, there was, on the one hand, a genuine vigor in the area of fiction—though one masterpiece, *Billy Budd*, remained unpublished until the 1920's and another, *Sister Carrie* (1900), was, at the time of its publication, generally ignored. Still Crane flared brilliantly, if briefly, and Henry James was passing through some of the ripest years of his career; and Sarah Orne Jewett and other gifted women were writing quietly in various sections of New England. But the situation in poetry was a good deal murkier: to the literary historian, figures seem to loom in a kind of cultural fog and disappear; reputations are made overnight and as quickly forgotten. Out of this general darkness, the poetic voice that now comes through to us most clearly is that of Edwin Arlington Robinson.

Literary achievement is always to some extent a matter of luck: the luck, quite simply, to have been born at the right time—a time when one's vision coincides with a vocabulary sufficiently alive (and it is sometimes luckier to have at hand a vocabulary in partial decay) to convey that vision in an enduring manner; and when there is an audience equipped to grasp and respond to the vision. Jacques Maritain has spoken of Dante's great good luck in coming to maturity just as the medieval "synthesis," fully realized in the work of the master theologians, became, on the eve of its dissolution, accessible to poetry. And about Emily Dickinson, a lesser poet of course but a great one nonetheless, Allen Tate has made a similar point: that as the formidable New England Protestant vision of human affairs began to dissolve, Emily Dickinson could seize upon its ingredients as symbols for the poetry of terror and ecstasy. Edwin Arlington Robinson had no such luck.

During his most fruitful years, between 1896 and 1916, he suffered a kind of absolute silence and neglect, something explicable only by the murkiness and the chaos of literary standards of the time. There was little for him to draw upon in his cultural environment except a kind of waning and effete idealism, the thin residue of the transcendental theory (which indeed rather hampered than aided his natural poetic instinct); and there was little for him to appeal *to* in the minds and imagination of readers. It was not only that his lack of readership was the source of pain that led him to the brink of suicide; it was also—his biographer Louis O. Coxe has persuasively argued—that the long years of public indifference actually damaged him as a poet. He was a very fine poet; but it is more than possible that he would have been even better if he had been luckier. Considerable success, along with honors and a modest affluence, came to him in the 1920's. But by this time he had virtually abandoned the dramatic and reflective lyric by which he had made his enduring mark in favor of a series of long narrative poems, some of them very popular and prize-winning but not likely, today, to engage many readers. By that time, too, the modern vision, or, as it is sometimes called, "the modern tradition," had taken hold of Anglo-American literary culture, and the important voices in American poetry—Eliot, Pound, and later William Carlos Williams, Wallace Stevens, and Hart Crane—were carrying the art into areas (imagist, symbolist, metaphysical, and in ways to be defined European) from which Robinson was self-excluded. Seen in broad outline, Robinson's career resembles one of his own ironic and compassionate lyrics based on the theme of failure, including the failure of success. Like Miniver Cheevy, he picked the wrong time to be born into.

If Robinson's life sometimes seems a reflection of his poetry, there is no doubt that his finest poems are in part a reflection of his life, and of his darkly troubled family background. He was born in December, 1869, in Head Tide, Maine, the third son of Edward and Mary Palmer Robinson; after going nameless for six months, the child was christened Edwin at the suggestion of a lady from Arlington, Massachusetts, who was then rewarded by having her home town chosen for the middle name. The following September, the family moved to Gardiner, Maine (the Tilbury Town of Robinson's poetry), a burgeoning mill and factory town of some forty-five hundred inhabitants where, except for two years at Harvard, Robinson would live more or less uninterruptedly till 1897, when he moved down to New York ("the town down the river," as Robinson would call it in his wry Yankee way). The Robinsons never quite "made it" in Gardiner, socially or otherwise. Mary Robinson could count the distinguished Dudley family among her ancestry, and Robinson could properly claim to be descended from the New World's first genuine poet, the Mistress Anne Bradstreet who married Governor Dudley. But Edward Robinson, though he amassed a certain amount of wealth through his involvement with local factories and banks and through the manipulation of farm mortgages, and became a citizen of some renown, was known derisively as the Duke of Puddledock and was not invited to the grander mansions on the hill. Still, the years of the poet's childhood were passed in reasonable comfort (though he would later recall that at the age of six he had spent some hours in a rocking chair pondering the question of why he had ever been born) and it was not until late in his adolescence that things began to go, at first mildly, then hideously, awry.

Dean Robinson, Edwin's older brother, had gone to college and medical school and had begun the practice of medicine, a profession for which he was woefully unfitted. He wore himself out at tasks from which he derived no sense of reward, took to morphine to keep himself going, abandoned his practice, and came back to the family home to live out the wreckage of his life. Edwin loved him and admired him extravagantly

("Dean knew more at twenty than I shall ever know," he said later, in sad retrospect); it was his first close experience of desperate failure. The second son, Herman, was to be the financial wizard of the family. He toured the Middle West, speculating in land, mills, railroads, extending his father's resources in a heady effort to multiply them—until the smash came; whereupon he took to drink with bitter and serious determination, became at last a helpless alcoholic, leaving his beautiful wife, the former Emma Shepherd (with whom Edwin has been rumored, probably falsely, to have been in love), and their three daughters largely dependent on the very small and very occasional donations from the youngest brother. When Edward Robinson, the father, died in 1892, he was all but bankrupt, an acrimonious old man vainly demanding explanations from a world that had somehow destroyed him. The culminating horror was the death of Mary Robinson four years later. She was stricken by black diphtheria, and no townsman would even enter the house for fear of contagion. The doctor refused to call, and the dying woman was cared for by the three sons; the pastor intoned a prayer at a safe distance through an open window; and when told that Mrs. Robinson was dead, the undertaker left a coffin on the front porch and departed in haste. The sons (one of them, Dean, more nearly dead than alive himself) saw to their mother's burial in the family plot of the Gardiner graveyard.

For examples of frustration, defeat, wreckage, and in general of the smitten life, Robinson needed thus to look no further than his own family, though he did in fact look beyond it— for his early poems and for years thereafter—at least as far as other secretively troubled residents of Gardiner. And it was experience of the devastations wrought upon those dear to him—his brother Dean and, more ambiguously, his mother —that gave him the oddly detached sympathy which is the strength and perhaps also the limitation of his characteristic poems. The note is struck perfectly in "Reuben Bright":

For when they told him that his wife must die,

He stared at them, and shook with grief and
    fright,
And cried like a great baby half the night,
And made the women cry to see him cry.

The poem is from Robinson's first volume, *The
Torrent and the Night Before,* published in
1896, the year of his mother's death.

His literary education, meanwhile, had been
spurred by the two years (1891–93) he managed
to complete at Harvard before financial disaster
back home made it impossible for him to continue. The Robinson household was not without
books; there was Anne Bradstreet in the background; and Edward Robinson was not opposed
to the reading and even the writing of poetry so
long as it did not interfere with the serious business of life. But the period at Harvard, though it
was not a happy one for Robinson personally,
served to introduce him to a larger world and to
other young literary enthusiasts—like William
Vaughan Moody, of whom Robinson became a
friend, admirer, and wary rival (and in celebration of whose highly successful play, *The Great
Divide,* Robinson would write a poem called
"The White Lights"). He was not a particularly
voracious reader (it might be hazarded that
most American writers who went to college read
rather less than those who did not), nor were
his tastes unusual. He enjoyed the Romantic
writers, but he was also drawn to Latin poetry
(some of which he translated at an early age),
and perhaps something of the gravity and solidity of the Virgilian lyric may be felt amid the
Yankee idiom and tonality of Robinson's own
verse. He was not affected by Browning, whose
"men and women" might otherwise be thought
to have been an obvious influence upon him;
but he did respond to Kipling and, to a lesser
degree, Housman.

Still, as more than one observer of Robinson
has suggested, it is less to previous poetry than
to fiction—especially nineteenth-century American, English, and French fiction—that one must
turn for anything like "sources" for his poetry.
If there was no powerful ongoing movement in
poetry for Robinson to attach himself to in the
nineties, there was a strong movement in fiction, both at home and abroad: that is, the

development of literary realism. The evidence
is inadequate, but one naturally associates
Robinson's poems of New York City life more
with the novels of William Dean Howells than
with the exoticism of his best-known contemporaries in poetry; and "Eros Turannos," one
of Robinson's masterpieces, gazes at the nearly
hidden desperation of a wealthy married woman
in a manner remarkably similar to a short story
by Edith Wharton. There is little doubt that
Robinson was a serious reader of Henry James
during most of his life and that he also seized
upon Hawthorne's tales of dark New England
passion and human fatality. Even his attachment to Emerson seems to have been mainly
to Emerson's effort to restore the pungent
everyday language of street and farm to poetry,
and what appealed to him in Whitman was
what we have described as Whitman's experiments with narrative realism.

All this constitutes a fact of considerable importance. Robinson is not to be reduced to a
single lyrical mode; and yet many of his best
poems—one picks, almost at random, "Reuben
Bright," "The Clerks," "Eros Turannos," "Old
Trails," "The Poor Relation," "Mr. Flood's
Party"—deal with themes, episodes, individual
characters that before Robinson and for the
most part after him were dealt with by writers
of fiction. What is perhaps more surprising,
Robinson scarcely bothered to devise new poetic
forms in order to project his little dramas: he
preferred to reinvigorate the forms that were
available. "Reuben Bright," like "The Clerks,"
is cast in the form of an absolutely conventional
Petrarchan sonnet. The form of the poem con-
strains and tightens the narrative content, while
the narrative movement to some extent loosens
and vitalizes the form.

All but one of the poems in *The Torrent and
the Night Before* were reprinted in *The Children of the Night* (1897). At least half a dozen
of these are very good indeed, and neither volume
went entirely unnoticed; but they did not elicit
from the literary periodicals any demand for
new work. Robinson had a job of sorts at
Harvard in 1898–99 and then moved to New
York City, where he would spend part of every

year for the rest of his life. He wandered the streets, frequenting bars and, from time to time, brothels, and consorted with the bohemian set. By 1902 he had a new volume ready: *Captain Craig*. On this book he rested his poetic case, so to speak; he presented it to the public as his announcement of himself as a mature poet—particularly the long title poem, which memorializes a picaresque figure whom Robinson had come to know in New York (and whose actual name was Alfred Louis), and also in "Isaac and Archibald," which is in fact superior to "Captain Craig" and is one of the handsomest and freshest treatments in American poetry of the theme of initiation. When the volume was received with almost total silence, Robinson was reduced to something like despair.

For a time he threatened to follow the alcoholic path to ruin of his unhappy brother Herman and wrote next to nothing. Then, in March, 1905, he received a letter from the White House: "I have enjoyed your poems . . . so much," wrote President Roosevelt, "that I must write to tell you so." Roosevelt's son Kermit had drawn his father's attention to *The Children of the Night*; and the President followed up his letter not only by having Robinson appointed to the customs house on Wall Street at the then princely salary of two thousand dollars a year, but also by writing an article for the *Outlook* in which he praised Robinson's poetry as giving off "just a little of the light that never was on land or sea." "I am not sure I understand 'Luke Havergal'," Roosevelt remarked, naming one of the strangest and best of Robinson's early poems, "but I am entirely sure I like it."

Roosevelt salvaged Robinson's external situation, and Robinson was now able to come in turn to the aid of his sister-in-law and her three daughters. But the President's public support rather hindered than helped Robinson's standing with the literati of New York, nor did it stimulate Robinson to new creative efforts. He spent his days reading in the customs house office before going back to his room to drink heavily and talk till all hours with his few cronies. When Roosevelt left the White House in 1909, Robinson was out of a job—and, mirac-

ulously, experienced a sudden recovery of power. In 1910, he brought out *The Town Down the River*.

Though there was little immediate acclaim, Robinson's reputation was at last beginning to grow. In 1911, he was invited to the MacDowell Colony in Peterboro, New Hampshire, a haven for serious, indigent writers; it was here that Robinson thereafter did most of his work. Harriet Monroe's *Poetry* was inaugurated in 1912, and Robinson began to appear in it; other magazines were after him; in Boston, the English poet Alfred Noyes proclaimed that Robinson was the best American poet living. When *The Man Against the Sky* was published in 1916, a number of reviewers, and not the least discerning and influential among them, found themselves in agreement with Noyes's estimate.

The Man Against the Sky does contain a group of poems sufficient by themselves to make any poet's lasting reputation—including "Flammonde," "The Gift of God," "Hillcrest," "Eros Turannos," "Old Trails," "Veteran Sirens," and "The Poor Relation." Yet there was something ominous in the intellectually ambitious meditative poem which gave the volume its title, something ominous too in the fact that this was the work singled out by most commentators for special admiration. The intention of "The Man Against the Sky" is indeed admirable; in one perspective, it is noble: nothing less than to confront, through the resources of poetry, the very mystery of the universe—the mystery, that is, of human knowledge, of man's capacity to perceive his relationship with reality. But here again luck was against Robinson. There was simply not enough in his intellectual background and environment to provide him—as Melville and Emily Dickinson in their time *had* been provided—with the instruments necessary for such an inquiry. The terms from which a poet might draw meaningful symbols and images, the ingredients of his poetic discourse, were lacking. The result is a sort of dignified bombast, an earnest but unsuccessful attempt to resurrect an Emersonianism in which Robinson no longer really believed.

But that may be putting the case too simply,

and even (though such is far from being the intention) condescendingly. The fact is that Robinson's relation to Emerson was highly ambiguous. If he was tempted at times to strive after the spiritual freedom Emerson proclaimed, he was also tempted at other times to accept too quickly Emerson's occasional acknowledgment of the element of necessity, or fate, in human experience. Harold Bloom, in *The Ringers in the Tower* (1971), makes the latter point and notes that Robinson read Emerson's essays "Fate" and "Power" as early as 1899, was much struck by them, and said that Emerson walloped the reader "with a big New England shingle," the weapon of fatalism. But however one interprets the matter, one is forced to the conclusion that neither his personal circumstances nor his intellectual environment provided Robinson with the resources to project a persuasive idealism on the one hand, nor on the other a vision of what Hawthorne called the "dark necessity."

Robinson's best poems, nonetheless, are glimpses into the darkness. Some of these are among the lyrics in *The Three Taverns* (1920), *Avon's Harvest* (1921), and his *Collected Poems* (also 1921), which won him the first of three Pulitzer prizes. But the cosmic appetite apparent in "The Man Against the Sky" could be sensed even more strongly in *Merlin* (1917), in the two Arthurian stories in verse which followed over a decade, *Lancelot* and *Tristram*, and in the succession of narrative poems beginning with *The Man Who Died Twice*. The Arthurian poems represented Robinson's attempt, stimulated by the First World War, to wrestle with vast problems of history and politics, but to do so through character, dialogue, patterns of relationship. Conrad Aiken was brilliantly right when he observed, in 1922, that *Merlin* and *Lancelot* "give us a Malory as Henry James might have written and enlarged it," and that in both instances the narrative method is strikingly Jamesian:

> Merlin and Vivien have here all the dim subtleties and delicate mutual awarenesses of the people, let us say, in *The Wings of the Dove*. The story, the poetry, is precisely in these

hoverings and perturbations, these pauses and approaches and flights.

Nothing finer could be said about the Arthurian poems; but at a greater distance in time, *Merlin* and the others strike us as Jamesian only in technique, with not enough of the old master's tough moral substance. As to the other narrative poems, they all now blur together in one's memory, to paraphrase Louis O. Coxe, in one long gray undifferentiated work. There are arresting passages in all of them, especially when, as in *The Man Who Died Twice* (which won the poet the second of his three Pulitzer prizes), Robinson seems to be reflecting on the theme of failure as it relates to his own artistic career. And there is some hint that in *King Jasper*, which was published posthumously in 1936 with a curiously grudging introduction by Robert Frost, the then dying poet was attempting a new narrative idiom.

But Robinson's achievement, and it is very considerable, consists finally not in those large poetic enterprises by which, in his later years, he exercised the role of the Great Poet in a recognizably Georgian manner. It consists in a goodly handful of lyric poems, dramatic or meditative or both, as the case may be. When we think of Robinson, we think of Reuben Bright shaken with grief and fright, of Luke Havergal mysteriously summoned to the western gate, of the clerks grown old without fulfilling the vague bright promise of youth, of Miniver Cheevy dreaming and scratching his head, of the "poor relation" ensconced by her unfeeling family in an apartment perhaps in Yonkers, of old Eben Flood swallowing his drink and singing his quavery song on the hillside at night. We hear a voice, calm and sure, speaking out of and into the darkness, telling us of loneliness, sorrow, defeat, endurance. It may be that Robinson insisted too much on the "light" for which he always waited—that he concealed a little the tragic vision that he really possessed. But the expression of such a vision during Robinson's best years might also have meant a silence on the part of readers even longer drawn out than the one he suffered from. Robinson was a superior poet, but an unlucky one.[1]

William Vaughan Moody (1869–1910)

During the long years when Robinson was earning virtually no critical, not to mention public, recognition, the most highly regarded living American poet was William Vaughan Moody. The same kind of critic who embarrassed Edith Wharton in 1902—by calling her often fascinating but artistically unsuccessful novel *The Valley of Decision* the greatest work of fiction ever written by man or woman on the American continent—said about Moody, in the wake of his *Poems* in 1901, and later of *Poems and Poetic Dramas* in 1912, that "such a poet [has] not been raised up before him in America —or even in the English-speaking world—since the eclipse of the great line of the older singers," and did not scruple to compare him with Milton and Shelley.

Moody—Indiana-born and Harvard-educated, sometime teacher at the University of Chicago, editor and literary historian—was a dramatist as well as a poet; and his enormously successful play of 1906, *The Great Divide*, is almost worthy of Robinson's poetic tribute to it. For all its melodrama and sentimentality (it gets going with an attempted rape in an Arizona cabin and ends with a tearful reconciliation in a Massachusetts mansion), the work not only poises against one another the New England Puritan mentality and the western spirit of independence, it rather artfully reveals the puritanic and the rebellious at odds within each of the two principal characters. It is precisely that sort of tension, or interior quarrel, that is missing from Moody's poetry.

Moody's poetry, today, strikes one as stale and derivative: vaguely allegorical in the early stages, merely abstract in the later ones; and in between, a good deal of public and, worse yet, "cosmic" poetry. His effort to write public verse—about the Spanish-American War, the annexation of the Philippines, the attempted partition of China—should not be scorned; significant achievement in that mode has usually been the sign of genuine cultural health from age to age, and such achievement has almost always been the ultimate ambition of the dedicated poet, from, say, Pindar to Robert Lowell. The trouble, in Moody's instructive case, is that just as he had no inspiriting quarrel with himself, so he had an insufficient quarrel with his country and his culture (of the kind, for example, that we have traced in Poe, in Whittier, in Hawthorne).

Much of Moody's more personal poetry was inspired by his love for Mrs. Harriet Tilden Brainerd, a Chicago divorcee who was some eleven years older than Moody and who became his wife the year before he died. One hazards that Mrs. Brainerd was a surrogate mother for Moody, replacing the actual mother whom he had revered (see his idealizing portrait of her, "The Daguerreotype"); and that, as a result, the figure addressed in poems like "The Moon-Moth" could not, in the nature of things, be a flesh-and-blood object of intimate love and sexual desire, but a representative at once of universal womanhood and motherhood.

But thou, fled heart, who cling'st here close and
    true!
For us the future was, the past will be,
And all the holy human years are new,
And all are tasted of eternally,
And still the eaten fruit shines on the tree.
—Let us go down. . . .
                          Love, we'll not grieve again,
We ne'er shall grieve again, not what we could
    call grief!

So ends "The Moon-Moth," the lyric which,

[1] An anecdote the critic R. P. Blackmur used to tell about Robinson has an almost symbolic quality. Young Blackmur, himself a native of Maine, had been taken to be introduced to Robinson, in Gardiner. Robinson was sitting on the front porch of his house, and as the shadows lengthened Blackmur could no longer clearly make him out. Finally Robinson asked, in a low voice, "What do *you* want to do?" "I want to be a poet," Blackmur answered. After a silence: "Don't!" said the voice out of the darkness.

of all Moody's poems, most threatens to break out into poetry.

A public which extolled Moody could hardly be expected to appreciate Edwin Arlington Robinson, with his coiling surprises, his expressionless ironies—as in the poem "Veteran Sirens" (see headnote and poem below):

> Although they suffer, they may not forswear
> The patient ardor of the unpursued.

Trumbull Stickney (1875–1904)

But neither did the public pay the slightest attention to Trumbull Stickney, a friend of both Moody and Robinson, and a very different writer from either; often a good, sometimes a rather vapid, and once or twice a superb, poet, whose *Dramatic Verses* in 1902 and posthumous *Poems* in 1905 passed instantly into silence.

Stickney—who was known as "Joe" to all his friends—was born in Switzerland, and spent most of his youth moving from Florence and the Italian lakes to Paris and to England. His father was a classical scholar, and young Stickney from his childhood was drawn to what he regarded as the hard realism of the Greek view of life, as against the hazy romanticism of his own time. (In an undergraduate work, *Nature-Worship, Ancient and Modern*, Stickney opts for the tough Euripidean vision over the Wordsworthian one, in which, according to Stickney, nature is invested with vague and unspecified forces.) He entered Harvard in 1891, became friendly with Moody and George Cabot Lodge, and wrote for the *Monthly*; after graduating, he returned to Paris for further study at the Sorbonne. He continued to shift base: "My Goddess is unrest," he once wrote; and by an understandable paradox, the appeal of highly particularized *place* (Cortina d'Ampezzo, Mount Ida, a city garden) is strong in his poetry. He came back to America in 1903, to teach, with very little enthusiasm, at Harvard; and he died, at the age of thirty, the following year.

Trumbull Stickney's poetry is intensely personal—too much so, some critics have thought; and some of the best of it is love poetry: actual and passionate love for an actual and thoroughly individualized woman. There were several women in fact: a married woman during the undergraduate days; a French Jewess, whom Stickney scandalized his parents by pursuing in Paris; Mrs. Elizabeth Cameron, who was the estranged wife of a United States Senator, a friend of Henry Adams, and a highly emotional and impulsive person. Stickney's writings to and about these women sprang, as it were, from a lovers' quarrel:

> No, no, 't is very much too late.
> I thought it mockery that you said
> You loved me; but a certain fate
> Lowers your voice and bows your head.
> I tell you, you desire to wake the dead.
>
> 'T is pitiful so to drag out
> The sorry quarrel in our souls,
> Till even the blood suspends in doubt
> And each full impulse backward rolls.
> Meantime the hour regardless passing tolls.
>
> Yes! think how year on year is gone.
> You went your way and hummed your dreams
> Of passion and oblivion
> In lands where terrible sunbeams
> Shiver upon the leaping arch of streams.

This extract from "Eride"—a name possibly concocted by the scholarly Stickney out of a Greek verb meaning "to strive after"—is part of a long sequence on the ambiguities and ambivalences of the erotic feeling, seemingly addressed to the second of the women mentioned above.

But Stickney also had a sharp and painful awareness of the rending tensions within his own psyche, as these two "fragments" suggest:

> The passions that we fought with and subdued
> Never quite die. In some maimed serpent's coil
> They lurk, ready to spring and vindicate
> That power was once our torture and our Lord.

And:

> Sir, say no more.
> Within me 't is as if

The green and climbing eyesight of a cat
Crawled near my mind's poor birds.

There is no doubt a hint in the latter fragment
of the imagist poetry soon to come; but as two
able editors of Stickney's selected poems have
insisted,[2] Stickney is best taken as *sui generis*,
and as against his own background and personal
experience, rather than as a minor forerunner of
Pound and Eliot, or as the representative of the
literary age in which he lived.

   Far more subjective and, in its way, more
graceful than Robinson's, incomparably more
vitalized than Moody's, Stickney's is the poetry
of love—but of love experienced in beautifully
evoked settings, in gardens, often in the rain,
usually in the autumn; love haunted by memory
and leading to a sense of private desolation. All
these themes and images flow together in the
finest of Stickney's lyrics, and the best-known,
"Mnemosyne":

It's autumn in the country I remember

   [2] James Reeves and Sean Haldane, *Homage to Trumbull Stickney* (1968), a much needed little volume containing a number of poems, and a sensible and informative introduction. Another judicious selection of
Stickney's work has been made by Amberys R. Whittle
in *The Poems of Trumbull Stickney*, which also contains a foreword by Edmund Wilson.

How warm a wind blew here about the ways!
And shadows on the hillside lay to slumber
During the long sun-sweetened summer-days.

It's cold abroad the country I remember.

The swallows veering skimmed the golden grain
At midday with a wing aslant and limber;
And yellow cattle browsed upon the plain

It's empty down the country I remember.

I had a sister lovely in my sight;
Her hair was dark, her eyes were very sombre;
We sang together in the woods at night.

It's lonely in the country I remember.

The babble of our children fills my ears,
And on our hearth I stare the perished ember
To flames that show all starry thro' my years.

It's dark about the country I remember.

There are the mountains where I lived. The
   path
Is slushed with cattle-tracks and fallen timber,
The stumps are twisted by the tempests' wrath.

But that I know these places are my own,
I'd ask how came such wretchedness to cumber
The earth, and I to people it alone.

It rains across the country I remember.

BIOGRAPHICAL CHART

1869 Born, December 22, in Head Tide, Maine, the
third son of Edward and Mary Palmer Robinson
1870 Family moves to Gardiner, Maine
1891–93 Enters Harvard as a "special" student; publishes poems in *The Harvard Advocate*
1893 Family in serious financial difficulties, owing to
bad investments in western real estate
1896 Has printed at his own expense *The Torrent and
the Night Before*; mother dies of "black diphtheria"
1897 *The Children of the Night*
1899 Serves on President Eliot's administrative staff at
Harvard from January to June; returns to New
York
1902 Manuscript of *Captain Craig*, lost for a time by
Small, Maynard and Company editor, finally
published by Houghton, Mifflin Company

1903–4 Employed as a time-checker during the construction of New York's first subway
1905–9 Theodore Roosevelt reads *The Children of the
Night*, is impressed by it, and writes a critical
estimate of the poetry in *The Outlook*; he appoints Robinson to a position in the New York
office of the Collector of Customs, a sinecure
that the poet holds until he resigns, June, 1909
1911 Spends the first of twenty-four summers at the
MacDowell Colony, Peterboro, New Hampshire
1915 *Captain Craig* reprinted
1916 *The Man Against the Sky*
1917 *Merlin*; from 1917 until 1922, receives a gift of
money from anonymous donors
1920 *Lancelot; The Three Taverns*
1921 *Avon's Harvest; Collected Poems* awarded the
Pulitzer prize

1924 *The Man Who Died Twice*; receives his second
      Pulitzer prize
1927 *Tristram*; receives his third Pulitzer prize
1929–34 *Cavender's House*; *The Glory of the Nightin-*

gales; *Selected Poems*; *Matthias at the Door*;
Nicodemus; *Talifer*; *Amaranth*
1935 Dies, April 6, in New York Hospital; *King Jasper*
      published posthumously

FURTHER READINGS

Edwin Arlington Robinson, *Collected Poems* (1961)

Louis O. Coxe, *Edwin Arlington Robinson: The Life
  of Poetry* (1969)
Robert Frost, Foreword to *King Jasper* (1935)
Edwin S. Fussel, *Edwin Arlington Robinson: The Liter-*

ary *Background of a Traditional Poet* (1954)
Emery E. Neff, *Edwin Arlington Robinson* (1948)
Charles Powers Smith, *Where the Light Fails: A Por-
  trait of Edwin Arlington Robinson* (1965)
Yvor Winters, *Edwin Arlington Robinson* (1946)

Luke Havergal (1897)

Robinson grew impatient with the lasting popularity of this poem, which he regarded as a
lucky hit and (which was true) uncharacteristic
of him. It breathes a romantic decadence quite
alien to Robinson's usual laconic directness, and
it may indeed have been written while he was
at Harvard. But it is a fine poem, one of Robinson's best, and its incantational tone, while it
effects a sort of hovering vagueness, does not
blur the ingredients which build firmly into a
total picture: the crimson leaves, the darkness,
the winds, the voice calling.

A poem of this kind scarcely has a "literal
meaning." But it may be ventured that someone
who has died (or, more practically, someone
who knows about death) is urging Luke Havergal to "go to the western gate"—the gate furthest from the east and the rising sun; in short,
to accept the darkness, to accept the fact of loss
and of death. Only by doing so can Luke Havergal be reconciled to the death of "her," presumably his beloved. Only, in fact, by dying can
Luke be reunited with her. "There is yet one
way to where she is, / Bitter . . ." But these are
mysterious messages, the speaker admits: Luke
must not "think to riddle the dead words they
say."

Go to the western gate, Luke Havergal,
There where the vines cling crimson on the wall,

And in the twilight wait for what will come.
The leaves will whisper there of her, and some,
Like flying words, will strike you as they fall;
But go, and if you listen she will call.
Go to the western gate, Luke Havergal—
Luke Havergal.

No, there is not a dawn in eastern skies
To rift the fiery night that's in your eyes;   10
But there, where western glooms are gathering,
The dark will end the dark, if anything:
God slays Himself with every leaf that flies,
And hell is more than half of paradise.
No, there is not a dawn in eastern skies—
In eastern skies.

Out of a grave I come to tell you this,
Out of a grave I come to quench the kiss
That flames upon your forehead with a glow
That blinds you to the way that you must go.   20
Yes, there is yet one way to where she is,
Bitter, but one that faith may never miss.
Out of a grave I come to tell you this—
To tell you this.

There is the western gate, Luke Havergal,
There are the crimson leaves upon the wall.
Go, for the winds are tearing them away,—
Nor think to riddle the dead words they say,
Nor any more to feel them as they fall;
But go, and if you trust her she will call.   30
There is the western gate, Luke Havergal—
Luke Havergal.

The Clerks (1897)

I did not think that I should find them there
When I came back again; but there they stood,
As in the days they dreamed of when young blood
Was in their cheeks and women called them fair.
Be sure, they met me with an ancient air,—
And yes, there was a shop-worn brotherhood
About them; but the men were just as good,
And just as human as they ever were.

And you that ache so much to be sublime,
And you that feed yourselves with your descent,   10
What comes of all your visions and your fears?
Poets and kings are but the clerks of Time,
Tiering the same dull webs of discontent,
Clipping the same sad alnage of the years.

Reuben Bright (1897)

Because he was a butcher and thereby
Did earn an honest living (and did right),
I would not have you think that Reuben Bright
Was any more a brute than you or I;
For when they told him that his wife must die,
He stared at them, and shook with grief and fright,
And cried like a great baby half that night,
And made the women cry to see him cry.

And after she was dead, and he had paid
The singers and the sexton and the rest,   10
He packed a lot of things that she had made
Most mournfully away in an old chest
Of hers, and put some chopped-up cedar boughs
In with them, and tore down the slaughter-house.

The Pity of the Leaves (1897)

As Louis O. Coxe remarks in his study of Robinson, this skillfully packed sonnet links three stages of the New England imagination. The sad wind that is "loud with ancestral shame" harks back to Hawthorne's stories of inherited taint; the poem itself evokes the cold landscape of Robinson's Maine; and it clearly echoes in such poems of Robert Frost as "An Old Man's Winter Night."

Vengeful across the cold November moors,
Loud with ancestral shame there came the
   bleak
Sad wind that shrieked, and answered with a
   shriek
Reverberant through lonely corridors.

The old man heard it; and he heard, perforce,
Words out of lips that were no more to speak—
Words of the past that shook the old man's cheek
Like dead, remembered footsteps on old floors.

And then there were the leaves that plagued
   him so!
The brown, thin leaves that on the stones outside   10
Skipped with a freezing whisper. Now and then
They stopped, and stayed there—just to let him
   know
How dead they were, but if the old man cried,
They fluttered off like withered souls of men.

For a Dead Lady (1910)

Robinson here thinks back to his mother and to her death (though no hint of the peculiar ghastliness of that event enters the poem) and out of his memory composes a meditation on the loss of any beautiful and strong-minded mother. Observations of her shortcomings—"the laugh that love could not forgive"—slide in quietly amid the acknowledgment of "the flowing wonder of her ways" and of her grace and beauty. With all her faults she was an unfor-

gettable woman—or rather, as the poem unfolds
to demonstrate, a *lady*.

No more with overflowing light
Shall fill the eyes that now are faded,
Nor shall another's fringe with night
Their woman-hidden world as they did.
No more shall quiver down the days
The flowing wonder of her ways,
Whereof no language may requite
The shifting and the many-shaded.

The grace, divine, definitive,
Clings only as a faint forestalling;   10

The laugh that love could not forgive
Is hushed, and answers to no calling;
The forehead and the little ears
Have gone where Saturn keeps the years;
The breast where roses could not live
Has done with rising and with falling.

The beauty, shattered by the laws
That have creation in their keeping,
No longer trembles at applause,
Or over children that are sleeping;   20
And we who delve in beauty's lore
Know all that we have known before
Of what inexorable cause
Makes Time so vicious in his reaping.

Miniver Cheevy (1910)

This well-known poem is undoubtedly an ironic,
amused self-portrait. Robinson did not need the
critics to tell him that he had been born at
the wrong moment—for his brand of poetry.

Miniver Cheevy, child of scorn,
    Grew lean while he assailed the seasons;
He wept that he was ever born,
    And he had reasons.

Miniver loved the days of old
    When swords were bright and steeds were
        prancing;
The vision of a warrior bold
    Would set him dancing.

Miniver sighed for what was not,
    And dreamed, and rested from his labors;   10
He dreamed of Thebes and Camelot,
    And Priam's neighbors.

Miniver mourned the ripe renown

That made so many a name so fragrant;
He mourned Romance, now on the town,
    And Art, a vagrant.

Miniver loved the Medici,
    Albeit he had never seen one;
He would have sinned incessantly
    Could he have been one.   20

Miniver cursed the commonplace
    And eyed a khaki suit with loathing;
He missed the mediæval grace
    Of iron clothing.

Miniver scorned the gold he sought,
    But sore annoyed was he without it;
Miniver thought, and thought, and thought,
    And thought about it.

Miniver Cheevy, born too late,
    Scratched his head and kept on thinking;   30
Miniver coughed, and called it fate,
    And kept on drinking.

Eros Turannos (1916)

This poem is not without flaw, but nowhere
does Robinson better reveal his special talent
for compressing within a brief poetic space a
story of such psychological complexity, richness
of characterization, and breadth of human resonance that Henry James might have devoted
a good-sized novella to it. The unnamed fastidious lady and the charming, worthless husband
she fears and cannot live without—these are
immediately recognizable individuals. One imagines them in the spacious mansion on the hill
overlooking the sea, surrounded by a high wall
which conceals from the curious townspeople
the lady's deepening humiliation. He is perhaps

something like Gilbert Osmond in James's *The Portrait of a Lady:*

Tradition, touching all he sees,
  Beguiles and reassures him;

But she is a far more forlorn, confused, doomed Isabel Archer. She is the fated victim of "eros turannos," the tyrannical god of sexual love.

Yvor Winters, who finds in the poem the substance "of a tragic drama" and who believes that in general "the writing seems to me beyond praise," nonetheless regards the fifth stanza as commonplace, and a piece of "provincial cleverness." But what is puzzling is the cascade of rhymes, including the triple rhymes in each stanza—these tumbling echoes seem to draw attention away from the slow disclosure of the situation. It may be argued, however, that they also prepare (as it were, by contrast) with the hard, tight, brief line that concludes almost every stanza, and that puts a sudden and mildly shocking stop to the metrical flow.

She fears him, and will always ask
  What fated her to choose him;
She meets in his engaging mask
  All reasons to refuse him;
But what she meets and what she fears
Are less than are the downward years,
Drawn slowly to the foamless weirs
  Of age, were she to lose him.

Between a blurred sagacity
  That once had power to sound him,   10
And Love, that will not let him be
  The Judas that she found him,

Her pride assuages her almost,
  As if it were alone the cost.—
He sees that he will not be lost,
  And waits and looks around him.

A sense of ocean and old trees
  Envelops and allures him;
Tradition, touching all he sees,
  Beguiles and reassures him;   20
And all her doubts of what he says
Are dimmed with what she knows of days—
Till even prejudice delays
  And fades, and she secures him.

The falling leaf inaugurates
  The reign of her confusion:
The pounding wave reverberates
  The dirge of her illusion;
And home, where passion lived and died,
Becomes a place where she can hide,   30
While all the town and harbor side
  Vibrate with her seclusion.

We tell you, tapping on our brows,
  The story as it should be,—
As if the story of a house
  Were told, or ever could be;
We'll have no kindly veil between
Her visions and those we have seen,—
As if we guessed what hers have been,
  Or what they are or would be.   40

Meanwhile we do no harm; for they
  That with a god have striven,
Not hearing much of what we say,
  Take what the god has given;
Though like waves breaking it may be,
Or like a changed familiar tree,
Or like a stairway to the sea
  Where down the blind are driven.

Old Trails (1916)

This is one of Robinson's richest variations on one of his central themes—the paradoxes of success and of failure. The man whom the poet encounters in lower Manhattan, after a number of years, has failed so far to realize his youthful ambitions—ambitions, perhaps, of artistic or intellectual achievement which he had shared with the poet in the lofts of Greenwich Village at an earlier time. He returns now to go back one last time along those "old trails," back to the old room on Eleventh Street where the ghosts of his former hopes must be exorcised. Then he moves on to a glossy new hotel and a fresh start, and within five years he has "sauntered into fame."

He becomes famous, let us suppose, as a Broadway playwright or producer. The poet is glad enough to find himself proved wrong in predicting future failure for his friend; yet there is something meretricious in the other man's success—something won at too great a cost. So much is hinted by the cryptic allusions to Moussorgsky's opera, *Boris Godunov*, the story of the sixteenth-century Russian leader who rose to absolute power by destroying the past (in the form of heirs and rivals), and against whom the Russian people are at last summoned to revolt. Yet the final stanza may suggest the poet's awareness that his attitude may not be devoid of simple envy.

I met him, as one meets a ghost or two,
Between the gray Arch and the old Hotel.
"King Solomon was right, there's nothing new,"
Said he. "Behold a ruin who meant well."

He led me down familiar steps again,
Appealingly, and set me in a chair.
"My dreams have all come true to other men,"
Said he; "God lives, however, and why care?

"An hour among the ghosts will do no harm."
He laughed, and something glad within me sank.   10
I may have eyed him with a faint alarm,
For now his laugh was lost in what he drank.

"They chill things here with ice from hell," he said;
"I might have known it." And he made a face
That showed again how much of him was dead,
And how much was alive and out of place,

And out of reach. He knew as well as I
That all the words of wise men who are skilled
In using them are not much to defy
What comes when memory meets the unfulfilled. 20

What evil and infirm perversity
Had been at work with him to bring him back?
Never among the ghosts, assuredly,
Would he originate a new attack;

Never among the ghosts, or anywhere,
Till what was dead of him was put away,
Would he attain to his offended share
Of honor among others of his day.

"You ponder like an owl," he said at last;
"You always did, and here you have a cause.   30
For I'm a confirmation of the past,
A vengeance, and a flowering of what was.

"Sorry? Of course you are, though you compress,
With even your most impenetrable fears,
A placid and a proper consciousness
Of anxious angels over my arrears.

"I see them there against me in a book
As large as hope, in ink that shines by night
Surely I see; but now I'd rather look
At you, and you are not a pleasant sight.   40

"Forbear, forgive. Ten years are on my soul,
And on my conscience. I've an incubus:
My one distinction, and a parlous toll
To glory; but hope lives on clamorous.

" 'Twas hope, though heaven I grant you knows of what—
The kind that blinks and rises when it falls,
Whether it sees a reason why or not—
That heard Broadway's hard-throated siren-calls;

" 'Twas hope that brought me through December storms,
To shores again where I'll not have to be   50
A lonely man with only foreign worms
To cheer him in his last obscurity.

"But what it was that hurried me down here
To be among the ghosts, I leave to you.
My thanks are yours, no less, for one thing clear:
Though you are silent, what you say is true.

"There may have been the devil in my feet,
For down I blundered, like a fugitive,
To find the old room in Eleventh Street.
God save us!—I came here again to live."   60

We rose at that, and all the ghosts rose then,
And followed us unseen to his old room.
No longer a good place for living men
We found it, and we shivered in the gloom.

The goods he took away from there were few,
And soon we found ourselves outside once more,
Where now the lamps along the Avenue
Bloomed white for miles above an iron floor.

"Now lead me to the newest of hotels,"
He said, "and let your spleen be undeceived: 70
This ruin is not myself, but some one else;
I haven't failed; I've merely not achieved."

Whether he knew or not, he laughed and dined

With more of an immune regardlessness
Of pits before him and of sands behind
Than many a child at forty would confess;

And after, when the bells in *Boris* rang
Their tumult at the Metropolitan,
He rocked himself, and I believe he sang.
"God lives," he crooned aloud, "and I'm the
    man!"   80

He was. And even though the creature
    spoiled
All prophecies, I cherish his acclaim.
Three weeks he fattened; and five years he
    toiled
In Yonkers,—and then sauntered into fame.

And he may go now to what streets he will—
Eleventh, or the last, and little care;
But he would find the old room very still

Of evenings, and the ghosts would all be
    there.

I doubt if he goes after them; I doubt
If many of them ever come to him.   90
His memories are like lamps, and they go
    out;
Or if they burn, they flicker and are dim.

A light of other gleams he has to-day
And adulations of applauding hosts;
A famous danger, but a safer way
Than growing old alone among the ghosts.

But we may still be glad that we were
    wrong:
He fooled us, and we'd shrivel to deny it;
Though sometimes when old echoes ring too
    long,
I wish the bells in *Boris* would be quiet.   100

Veteran Sirens (1916)

Robinson was at times a hesitant poet—not an indecisive one, but a poet who moved between alternative appraisals of human beings, who seemed to commit himself and then take it back, whose characteristic line started in one direction then apparently reversed itself. "Veteran Sirens" is a highly successful example of this tendency.

These aging ladies of pleasure are at once enhanced and diminished by juxtaposition with Ninon de Lenclos, the glamorous seventeenth-century French courtesan, mistress of La Rochefoucauld and Saint-Evremond among others, patroness of the adolescent and gifted Voltaire, and a genuine power in the French court. The ghost of Ninon makes them seem a definite cut above the common prostitutes whom Robinson had known in Boston and New York; but it also draws attention to their losing battle with time. Further contradictions gather: their vanity is both quaint and brave, their folly self-deceiving and strong. Perhaps the key lines are these:

Although they suffer, they may not forswear
The patient ardor of the unpursued.

That last line, in particular, is of a compassionate irony all compact—the ladies have run out of lovers (or customers), but, while suffering, they hang on, as indeed they must, to an ardor that is nonetheless *patient*.

The ghost of Ninon would be sorry now
To laugh at them, were she to see them
    here,
So brave and so alert for learning how
To fence with reason for another year.

Age offers a far comelier diadem
Than theirs; but anguish has no eye for
    grace,
When time's malicious mercy cautions them
To think a while of number and of space.

The burning hope, the worn expectancy,
The martyred humor, and the maimed allure,   10
Cry out for time to end his levity,
And age to soften its investiture;

But they, though others fade and are still
    fair,
Defy their fairness and are unsubdued;

Although they suffer, they may not forswear
The patient ardor of the unpursued.

Poor flesh, to fight the calendar so long;

The Poor Relation (1916)

Among the surprises and ironies of this poem—
which contains, as Louis O. Coxe has remarked,
"a nearly intolerable intensity of pathos"—is
the fact that this poor relation, this spinster
aunt or sister, inhabits a comfortable apartment
in the heart of New York City (rather than the
little third-floor room in the family house, which
is the convention one expects); and that, indeed, the one thing she is *not* is poor—materially speaking. She has been handsomely established by relatives whose domestic piety is
assuaged by their generous and self-righteous
support of her; she is generously allowed to sit
alone and listen to the city traffic and dream
without rancor of youthful triumphs (of beauty?
of social distinction?) that were "born to be
defeated." In Robinson's canon, the poem is
unmatched for its image of brave but utter
loneliness and of quiet but total despair.

No longer torn by what she knows
And sees within the eyes of others,
Her doubts are when the daylight goes,
Her fears are for the few she bothers.
She tells them it is wholly wrong
Of her to stay alive so long;
And when she smiles her forehead shows
A crinkle that had been her mother's.

Beneath her beauty, blanched with pain,
And wistful yet for being cheated,   10
A child would seem to ask again
A question many times repeated;
But no rebellion has betrayed
Her wonder at what she has paid
For memories that have to stain,
For triumph born to be defeated.

To those who come for what she was—
The few left who know where to find her—
She clings, for they are all she has;
And she may smile when they remind her,   20
As heretofore, of what they know

Poor vanity, so quaint and yet so brave;
Poor folly, so deceived and yet so strong,
So far from Ninon and so near the grave.   20

Of roses that are still to blow
By ways where not so much as grass
Remains of what she sees behind her.

They stay a while, and having done
What penance or the past requires,
They go, and leave her there alone
To count her chimneys and her spires.
Her lip shakes when they go away,
And yet she would not have them stay;   30
She knows as well as anyone
That Pity, having played, soon tires.

But one friend always reappears,
A good ghost, not to be forsaken;
Whereat she laughs and has no fears
Of what a ghost may reawaken,
But welcomes, while she wears and mends
The poor relation's odds and ends,
Her truant from a tomb of years—
Her power of youth so early taken.   40

Poor laugh, more slender than her song
It seems; and there are none to hear it
With even the stopped ears of the strong
For breaking heart or broken spirit.
The friends who clamored for her place,
And would have scratched her for her face,
Have lost her laughter for so long
That none would care enough to fear it.

None live who need fear anything
From her, whose losses are their pleasure;   50
The plover with a wounded wing
Stays not the flight that others measure;
So there she waits, and while she lives,
And death forgets, and faith forgives,
Her memories go foraging
For bits of childhood song they treasure.

And like a giant harp that hums
On always, and is always blending
The coming of what never comes
With what has past and had an ending,   60
The City trembles, throbs, and pounds
Outside, and through a thousand sounds
The small intolerable drums

Of Time are like slow drops descending.

Bereft enough to shame a sage
And given little to long sighing,
With no illusion to assuage

The lonely changelessness of dying,—
Unsought, unthought-of, and unheard,
She sings and watches like a bird,   70
Safe in a comfortable cage
From which there will be no more flying.

The Mill (1920)

It would be instructive to convert this poem
into a prose narrative—to see how long it would
take to render, by the resources of fiction, all
the aspects of the two tragic lives Robinson
summarizes in twenty-four lines of verse. The
miller is sprung into life with a phrase; the enjoyable past is evoked in fourteen words; the
present horror and the one almost certainly to
come are communicated in two sentences. One
lingers over the poem, fascinated and appalled,
gradually making out not only what has happened and is about to happen, but the full
range of the psychological and emotional causes
at work.

The miller's wife had waited long,
  The tea was cold, the fire was dead;
And there might yet be nothing wrong
  In how he went and what he said:

"There are no millers any more,"
  Was all that she had heard him say;
And he had lingered at the door
  So long that it seemed yesterday.

Sick with a fear that had no form
  She knew that she was there at last;   10
And in the mill there was a warm
  And mealy fragrance of the past.
What else there was would only seem
  To say again what he had meant;
And what was hanging from a beam
  Would not have heeded where she went.

And if she thought it followed her,
  She may have reasoned in the dark
That one way of the few there were
  Would hide her and would leave no mark: 20
Black water, smooth above the weir
  Like starry velvet in the night,
Though ruffled once, would soon appear
  The same as ever to the sight.

Mr. Flood's Party (1921)

Robinson did not usually display the capacity
of, say, Robert Frost for shifting tone effectively
in mid-poem or even mid-stanza; reading his
poetry in bulk, one has the distinct impression
of (literally) monotony. To this, "Mr. Flood's
Party" is something of an exception: read aloud,
after thoughtful preparation, it can reveal a
striking suppleness of emotional attitude.

To be sure, the tone here shifts between the
poet's language and feeling and those of old
Eben Flood, the aged Maine farmer who has
outlived all his friends and now drinks by and
to himself, under the harvest moon, on the
empty hill. But there is variety *within* each of
these modes of expression.

Consider only the third and fourth stanzas.
In the third, there is the happy incongruity of
the elderly rustic, tilting the jug of liquor to his
lips as he thinks of his dead friends, compared
with Roland in the medieval epic, *The Song
of Roland*, bringing his horn to his lips to warn
the Emperor Charlemagne that all his rearguard
host has been slain. Mr. Flood's gallant durability is thus established, but at the same time
he is further revealed for what he is—a slightly
drunk, garrulous, and very lonely old man.

In the following stanza, Mr. Flood, as he
tremblingly sets the jug down on the ground, is
likened to a mother laying down her sleeping
child. One aspect of that unsentimental comparison is Mr. Flood's fear that the jug may
break; another is that he is childless—indeed,
his only relative, his only friend, is the precious
jug.

Old Eben Flood, climbing alone one night
Over the hill between the town below
And the forsaken upland hermitage
That held as much as he should ever know
On earth again of home, paused warily.
The road was his with not a native near;
And Eben, having leisure, said aloud,
For no man else in Tilbury Town to hear:

"Well, Mr. Flood, we have the harvest moon
Again, and we may not have many more;   10
The bird is on the wing, the poet says,
And you and I have said it here before.
Drink to the bird." He raised up to the light
The jug that he had gone so far to fill,
And answered huskily: "Well, Mr. Flood,
Since you propose it, I believe I will."

Alone, as if enduring to the end
A valiant armor of scarred hopes outworn,
He stood there in the middle of the road
Like Roland's ghost winding a silent horn.   20
Below him, in the town among the trees,
Where friends of other days had honored him,
A phantom salutation of the dead
Rang thinly till old Eben's eyes were dim.

Then, as a mother lays her sleeping child
Down tenderly, fearing it may awake,
He set the jug down slowly at his feet
With trembling care, knowing that most
    things break;
And only when assured that on firm earth

It stood, as the uncertain lives of men   30
Assuredly did not, he paced away,
And with his hand extended paused again:

"Well, Mr. Flood, we have not met like this
In a long time; and many a change has come
To both of us, I fear, since last it was
We had a drop together. Welcome home!"
Convivially returning with himself,
Again he raised the jug up to the light;
And with an acquiescent quaver said:
"Well, Mr. Flood, if you insist, I might.   40

"Only a very little, Mr. Flood—
For auld lang syne. No more, sir; that will do."
So, for the time, apparently it did,
And Eben evidently thought so too;
For soon amid the silver loneliness
Of night he lifted up his voice and sang,
Secure, with only two moons listening,
Until the whole harmonious landscape rang—

"For auld lang syne." The weary throat gave
    out,
The last word wavered, and the song was done.   50
He raised again the jug regretfully
And shook his head, and was again alone.
There was not much that was ahead of him,
And there was nothing in the town below—
Where strangers would have shut the many
    doors
That many friends had opened long ago.

EDGAR LEE MASTERS (1869–1950)

Though Edwin Arlington Robinson, in the poems for which he is now remembered, had peopled the American literary scene with a number of memorable characters from New England and Manhattan, he occasionally wandered off into the mists of philosophy (in "The Man Against the Sky") and later into the even more remote mists of Camelot and the Arthurian legend ("Merlin" and later long poems). In his most important poetry he was a nativist in *subject matter*, but he had no quarrel with, nor indeed much interest in, the Europeanized poetic developments as they began to be repre-

sented by Pound and Eliot. Robinson, then, was a somewhat imperfect nativist, but others were willing to go further. Just before the First World War another poetic movement started to take shape in the Middle West whose impulse was to carry forward "the native tradition," partly in recoil, as we shall see, against the news from Europe.

The poets chiefly involved at the outset were Edgar Lee Masters, Carl Sandburg, and Vachel Lindsay, all three reared in Illinois (though Masters was born in Kansas). Their combined achievement by the end of the war led some observers to speak (as American observers have periodically spoken) of a "poetic renaissance." They shared in common a dedication to the American scene and character, especially those of "the heartlands," to the American idiom and rhythms of speech; but insofar as they succeeded in creating a renaissance, it was by reason of their affection for Walt Whitman, both as poet and persona.

The Imagists, both here and abroad, were wary of Whitman, who at times seemed to reach for that "cosmic vision" which the imagists programmatically opposed. If Whitman was entirely an American, that fact could count against him. As early as 1909, Pound, after saying that Whitman "*is* America," went on to declare him, almost for that very fact, "disgusting" and an "exceedingly nauseating pill." If the new midwestern voices offended Pound, it was to some extent because of their echo of Whitman: for it was the influence of Whitman that lay behind everything that Pound and Eliot, in 1914, deplored in current poetry—

"*vers libre* . . . Lee Masterism, general floppiness. . . ." [1]

What Pound might have had in mind as a Whitmanian "Lee Masterism" in free verse could be the following, from *Spoon River Anthology* (published in 1915), a little poem called "Knowlt Hoheimer":

[1] Pound's attitude to Whitman, however, was changeable and ambivalent. Even in 1909 he grudgingly admitted that Whitman "accomplishes his mission" and that he "is a genius because he has a vision of what he is and of his function." Four years later, Pound came to a kind of public truce with Whitman:

> I make a pact with you, Walt Whitman—
> I have detested you long enough.
> I come to you as a grown child
> Who has had a pig-headed father;
> I am old enough now to make friends.
> It was you that broke the new wood,
> Now is a time for carving.
> We have one sap and one root—
> Let there be commerce between us.

A more condescending "pact" can hardly be imagined; but at least Pound had the discernment to acknowledge his American heritage from Whitman, while Eliot resolutely refused to acknowledge that he owed Whitman anything.

Knowlt Hoheimer (1915)

I was the first fruits of the battle of Missionary
    Ridge.
When I felt the bullet enter my heart
I wished I had staid at home and gone to jail
For stealing the hogs of Curl Trenary,
Instead of running away and joining the army.
Rather a thousand times the county jail
Than to lie under this marble figure with wings,
And this granite pedestal
Bearing the words, '*Pro Patria*.'
What do they mean, anyway?

Masters knew perfectly well that this kind of easy-moving, colloquial, farm-boy poetry (suspicious even of phrases in a foreign language) was abhorrent to sophisticated literati, especially to those who had attached themselves to European poetic traditions and genres. In "Petit, the Poet," in the same volume, he implicitly defended his mode of verse as being free of conventional styles and themes, of being rooted in the actual and near hand, and of being closer in spirit not only to Whitman but to Homer:

Petit, the Poet (1915)

Seeds in a dry pod, tick, tick, tick,
Tick, tick, tick, like mites in a quarrel—
Faint iambics that the full breeze wakens—
But the pine tree makes a symphony thereof.
Triolets, villanelles, rondels, rondeaus,
Ballades by the score with the same old
    thought:

The snows and the roses of yesterday are vanished;
And what is love but a rose that fades?
Life all around me here in the village:
Tragedy, comedy, valor and truth,   10

Courage, constancy, heroism, failure—
All in the loom, and oh what patterns!
Woodlands, meadows, streams and rivers—
Blind to all of it all my life long.
Triolets, villanelles, rondels, rondeaus,
Seeds in a dry pod, tick, tick, tick,
Tick, tick, tick, what little iambics,
While Homer and Whitman roared in the
    pines?

Away then, Masters announces, with such outmoded and foreign forms as villanelles and ballades (the latter carefully spelled in the archaic manner), with imitations of Provençal verse and of François Villon (the reference to yesterday's snows is an ironic adaptation of the English translation of Villon's most famous line). Conventional iambics are likewise disposed of in a tumbling rhythm similar to the one practiced by Vachel Lindsay, whom Masters greatly esteemed: "Faint iambics that the full breeze wakens." Life, meanwhile, "is all around me here in the village"—though Petit (which of course means "small") had been too small-spirited all his life to take account of it.

Edgar Lee Masters was born in Kansas and moved at an early age to Chicago. He was originally a lawyer by profession, publishing volumes of poetry on the side as early as 1898 and 1902. For some years thereafter Masters was publishing poems of the sort collected in *Spoon River Anthology*, which made him nationally and internationally famous and caused him to devote himself from that moment to a career of writing. *Spoon River* is also by far the most impressive of Masters' nearly twenty books of poetry, and the one that still retains a certain definite vitality, and appeal.[1]

[1] Masters' reputation is currently at its lowest ebb, and perhaps undeservedly so. In *The Oxford Book of American Verse*, in 1950, the editor F. O. Matthiessen included sixteen of Masters' poems. The editors of *American Poetry* in 1965 (Gay Wilson Allen, Walter B.

The New Spoon River, in 1924, in its harsh and embittered manner, does not approach it. Among Masters' other writings, one finds an autobiography (1936), a series of undistinguished novels, a biography denouncing Abraham Lincoln as hypocritical and vindictive, and book-length eulogies of Walt Whitman and Vachel Lindsay.

Spoon River is an "anthology" of monologues, spoken from the graves of a variety of people in a midwestern cemetery. Eventually, the life stories of a good many individuals are revealed, through direct utterance and cross reference. "Practically every ordinary human occupation is covered," Masters claimed later, and all levels of life and varieties of moral character. Masters also liked to claim that the book had a careful and significant structure, in the order of persons introduced: "the fools, the drunkards, and the failures came first, the people of one-birth minds got second place, and the heroes and enlightened spirits came last, a sort of *Divine Comedy*, which some critics were acute enough to point out at once." The Dante parallel is dubious; but we can grant *Spoon River* a progression of sorts, in terms of the degree of the morality, intelligence, and determination of the characters presented.

Such poetry of characterization might seem to relate Masters to Robinson, though Robinson was probably no more widely read in Illinois, in the first decade or so of the century, than he was anywhere else. Thematically, *Spoon River* has affinities with the work of Sarah Orne Jewett (whom, also, Masters almost certainly did not know)—in the poignant vision of loss, diminution, shrinkage. Dim memories of grander ages, stouter-hearted men, stronger faith crowd the pages—as in "Rutherford McDowell."

Rideout, and James K. Robinson) omitted Masters entirely.

Rutherford McDowell (1915)

They brought me ambrotypes
Of the old pioneers to enlarge.
And sometimes one sat for me—

Some one who was in being
When giant hands from the womb of the
    world

Tore the republic.
What was it in their eyes?—
For I could never fathom
That mystical pathos of drooped eyelids,
And the serene sorrow of their eyes.   10
It was like a pool of water,
Amid oak trees at the edge of a forest,
Where the leaves fall,
As you hear the crow of a cock
From a far-off farm house, seen near the hills
Where the third generation lives, and the
     strong men
And the strong women are gone and for-
     gotten.

And these grand-children and great grand-
     children
Of the pioneers!
Truly did my camera record their faces, too,   20
With so much of the old strength gone,
And the old faith gone,
And the old mastery of life gone,
And the old courage gone,
Which labors and loves and suffers and sings
Under the sun!

Another attitude is expressed in such poems as
"Lucinda Matlock" and "Anne Rutledge."

Lucinda Matlock (1915)

I went to the dances at Chandlerville,
And played snap-out at Winchester.
One time we changed partners,
Driving home in the moonlight of middle
     June,
And then I found Davis.
We were married and lived together for
     seventy years,
Enjoying, working, raising the twelve children,
Eight of whom we lost
Ere I had reached the age of sixty.
I spun, I wove, I kept the house, I nursed
     the sick,   10

I made the garden, and for holiday
Rambled over the fields where sang the larks,
And by Spoon River gathering many a shell,
And many a flower and medicinal weed—
Shouting to the wooded hills, singing to the
     green valleys.
At ninety-six I had lived enough, that is all,
And passed to a sweet repose.
What is this I hear of sorrow and weariness,
Anger, discontent and drooping hopes?
Degenerate sons and daughters,   20
Life is too strong for you—
It takes life to love Life.

Anne Rutledge (1915)

Out of me unworthy and unknown
The vibrations of deathless music;
"With malice toward none, with charity
     for all."
Out of me the forgiveness of millions toward
     millions,
And the beneficent face of a nation
Shining with justice and truth.
I am Anne Rutledge who sleep beneath
     these weeds,
Beloved in life of Abraham Lincoln,
Wedded to him, not through union,
But through separation.
Bloom forever, O Republic,   10
From the dust of my bosom!

Finally, however, and consciously, Masters was closest to those fiction writers who had explored and would explore the circumscribed and vaguely aspiring lives of the American heartland—to Hamlin Garland, and even more to Masters' younger associate Sherwood Anderson. *Spoon River* leads directly to the pattern of midwestern small-town lives lyrically described by Anderson in *Winesburg, Ohio* only four years later.

From the outset, Masters said retrospectively, "I was an American, and circumstanced with the most characteristic conditions of American life." His roots, he told an interviewer, were

"The America of Jefferson—of Jeffersonian democracy." He could find his natural ancestor, and inspiration, in Whitman; but as to the modernist poets, Pound and Eliot and others,

Masters regarded them as having virtually betrayed the central American tradition: "They have no principles, no individuality, no moral code and no roots."

CARL SANDBURG (1878–1967)

If the eastern and Europeanized American poets were looking for an unmistakable example of the continuing influence of Whitman, they might well have picked, not a "Lee Masterism,"

but a "Carl Sandburgism," like the following, which appeared in *Poetry* in 1914, just as Pound and Eliot were getting acquainted in London:

Chicago (1914)

Hog Butcher for the World,
Tool Maker, Stacker of Wheat,
Player with Railroads and the Nation's
    Freight Handler;
Stormy, husky, brawling,
City of the Big Shoulders:

They tell me you are wicked and I believe
    them, for I have seen your painted women
    under the gas lamps luring the farm boys.
And they tell me you are crooked and I an-
    swer: Yes, it is true I have seen the gun-
    man kill and go free to kill again.
And they tell me you are brutal and my reply
    is: On the faces of women and children I
    have seen the marks of wanton hunger.
And having answered so I turn once more to
    those who sneer at this my city, and I give
    them back the sneer and say to them:
Come and show me another city with lifted
    head singing so proud to be alive and coarse
    and strong and cunning.   10
Flinging magnetic curses amid the toil of
    piling job on job, here is a tall bold slugger
    set vivid against the little soft cities;
Fierce as a dog with tongue lapping for ac-
    tion, cunning as a savage pitted against the
    wilderness,
        Bareheaded,
        Shoveling,
        Wrecking,
        Planning,

Building, breaking, rebuilding,
Under the smoke, dust all over his mouth,
    laughing with white teeth,
Under the terrible burden of destiny laughing
    as a young man laughs,
Laughing even as an ignorant fighter laughs
    who has never lost a battle,   20
Bragging and laughing that under his wrist is
    the pulse, and under his ribs the heart of
    the people,
        Laughing!
Laughing the stormy, husky, brawling laugh-
    ter of Youth, half-naked, sweating, proud
    to be Hog Butcher, Tool Maker, Stacker of
    Wheat, Player with Railroads and Freight
    Handler to the Nation.

The lines are not without strength, and Sandburg was one of the first after Whitman to catch, in poetry, something of the brute reality of the emerging American city. But, typically of Sandburg, the poem reflects Whitman's wordiness without his sensitivity to the delicately exact image, Whitman's uncoiling line without his grace of movement. And where Whitman, at his best, fuses and reconciles opposing attitudes, Sandburg seems able only to lay side by side an awareness of the brutish and the coarse on the one hand and an ungrounded and sentimental assertion of vitality and warmth of spirit on the other.

Carl Sandburg was born in Galesburg, Illinois, the son of Swedish immigrants. He spent much of his youth as an itinerant workman, wandering through Kansas, Colorado, Nebraska. After a hitch in the Spanish-American War, he returned to Galesburg and worked his way through Lombard College. He went on to dabble in politics, as organizer for the Social-Democrat party in Wisconsin, and in journalism, as associate editor of *System Magazine* in Chicago. *Chicago Poems*, the fruit of these years, appeared in 1916. Observers, while always pointing to the Whitman strain in Sandburg, also paired him with Theodore Dreiser, especially in his capacity (as Rebecca West put it in the preface to Sandburg's *Selected Poems*, 1926) for describing "the inner life of the eager little girls who leave small towns and come to Chicago" and "the inner life of the strong young men who wander about the vast land, proud and yet perplexed." After *Chicago Poems*, probably the most notable (or at least most often quoted from) volumes of verse are *Smoke and Steel* (1920), *Good Morning, America* (1928), and *The People, Yes* (1936).

Sandburg consciously adopted the pose of a latter-day Whitman. "I wear my hat as I please, indoors or out," Whitman insisted in "Song of Myself," as a declaration of psychological independence. And in "Shirt" (from *Smoke and Steel*), Sandburg professed his own similar and derivative liberation. "My shirt is a torch and symbol," Sandburg wrote.

> I can take off my shirt and tear it,
> and so make a ripping razzly noise,
> and the people will say,
> "Look at him tear his shirt."
>
> I can keep my shirt on.
> I can stick around and sing like a little bird
> and look 'em in the eye and never be fazed.
>   I can keep my shirt on.

Occasionally, Sandburg really did approximate Whitman's brand of journalistic but melodic realism. Compare section 8 of "Song of Myself" ("the policeman with his star quickly working his passage to the centre of the crowd") with "Psalm of Those Who Go Forth Before Daylight" (from Sandburg's *Cornhuskers*):

Psalm of Those Who Go Forth Before Daylight (1918)

The policeman buys shoes slow and careful; the teamster buys gloves slow and careful; they take care of their feet and hands; they live on their feet and hands.

The milkman never argues; he works alone and no one speaks to him; the city is asleep when he is on the job; he puts a bottle on six hundred porches and calls it a day's work; he climbs two hundred wooden stairways; two horses are company for him; he never argues.

The rolling-mill men and the sheet-steel men are brothers of cinders; they empty cinders out of their shoes after the day's work; they ask their wives to fix burnt holes in the knees of their trousers; their necks and ears are covered with a smut; they scour their necks and ears; they are brothers of cinders.

Even more than Whitman, Sandburg, in his genuine passion for democracy, was passionately devoted to "the people"—the people as such, what Whitman called "the en masse."

I Am the People, the Mob (1916)

I am the people—the mob—the crowd—the mass.
Do you know that all the great work of the world is done through me?

I am the workingman, the inventor, the maker of the world's food and clothes.
I am the audience that witnesses history. The

Napoleons come from me and the Lincolns. They die. And then I send forth more Napoleons and Lincolns.

I am the seed ground. I am a prairie that will stand for much plowing. Terrible storms pass over me. I forget. The best of me is sucked out and wasted. I forget. Everything but Death comes to me and makes me work and give up what I have. And I forget.

Sometimes I growl, shake myself and spatter a few red drops for history to remember. Then—I forget.

When I, the People, learn to remember, when I, the People, use the lessons of yesterday and no longer forget who robbed me last year, who played me for a fool—then there will be no speaker in all the world say the name: "The People," with any fleck of a sneer in his voice or any far-off smile of derision.

The mob—the crowd—the mass—will arrive then.

Without impugning the poet's grass-roots democratic fervor, what must be remarked about a poem like that is not only Sandburg's customary verbosity and his ungainly swaggering, but the poem's vulnerability to parody. No few declamations about the strength of everyday people, all expressed with a proud uncouthness, have been spawned by Sandburg's poetry; and though he cannot perhaps be blamed for them, they have become a familiar object of burlesque. One may recall, as an example, a fairly recent New York night club comedy routine, in which a tough young proletarian poet angrily informs the world that "we are de truck drivers, we drive de trucks," and assures his audience that they are a bunch of "crummy bastards."

Yet Sandburg's imagination ranged more broadly than these remarks may suggest. He knew a great deal more of his native country than simply the stockyards of Chicago; and he was appreciative of many other poets beyond Whitman (a late volume, *New Section*, contains an unexpectedly attractive and gracious tribute to Emily Dickinson). He was deeply read in American history, and wrote a six-volume life of Abraham Lincoln. Critics and scholars disagree about this achievement; Edmund Wilson once remarked curtly that it represented the second assassination of Lincoln; but no one questions the exhaustive research than went into it. Sandburg, finally, was a figure that has become far more familiar in the decades after the Second World War: the poet as wandering minstrel, composing almost at random his "songs" about the hopes and dangers of America, playing his guitar and crooning the American folk songs he had collected.[1] He saw himself, to the end, as the poet par excellence in the American grain.

[1] And published in *The American Songbag* (1927).

VACHEL LINDSAY (1879–1931)

Vachel Lindsay was also a troubadour poet and made a living for more than a decade by chanting, singing, and shouting his poems in lecture halls across the United States and Europe, sometimes accompanied by deafening percussion instruments. He was an intense and hopelessly immature person, who performed what he rather nicely called "the higher vaudeville" (one likes to think he was teasing the advocates of "the higher consciousness") before wildly enthusiastic audiences.[1] There is something undeniably stirring in Lindsay's exuberant, clownish, pell-mell rant, though what it stirs is anything but the mind. From his dominating mother, Lindsay inherited a strong evangelical strain—she wanted him to become a "Christian cartoonist," whatever that means, and a "war-

[1] At least he did so until his popularity waned, to such a degree, and with such an effect upon him, that he finally took his own life.

rior of God"; and though for all his excessive attachment to his mother Lindsay eschewed both roles, he did bring into his poetry something of the old, rousing, evangelical hymn-singing.

In 1913, Harriet Monroe published Lindsay's "General William Booth Enters into Heaven," and with this thumping salute to the head of the Salvation Army, the Lindsay style was established. Here are the opening stanzas:

From General William Booth Enters into Heaven (1913)

(To be sung to the tune of 'The Blood of the Lamb' with indicated instrument)

1

(Bass drum beaten loudly.)
Booth led boldly with his big bass drum—
(Are you washed in the blood of the Lamb?)
The Saints smiled gravely and they said: 'He's come.'
(Are you washed in the blood of the Lamb?)
Walking lepers followed, rank on rank,
Lurching bravos from the ditches dank,
Drabs from the alleyways and drug fiends pale—
Minds still passion-ridden, soul-powers frail:—
Vermin-eaten saints with moldy breath,
Unwashed legions with the ways of Death—   10
(Are you washed in the blood of the Lamb?)

(Banjos.)
Every slum had sent its half-a-score
The round world over. (Booth had groaned for more.)
Every banner that the wide world flies
Bloomed with glory and transcendent dyes.
Big-voiced lasses made their banjos bang,
Tranced, fanatical they shrieked and sang:—
'Are you washed in the blood of the Lamb?'
Hallelujah! It was queer to see
Bull-necked convicts with that land make free.   20
Loons with trumpets blowed a blare, blare, blare
On, on upward thro' the golden air!
(Are you washed in the blood of the Lamb?)

2

(Bass drum slower and softer.)
Booth died blind and still by faith he trod,
Eyes still dazzled by the ways of God.
Booth led boldly, and he looked the chief
Eagle countenance in sharp relief,
Beard a-flying, air of high command
Unabated in that holy land.

(Sweet flute music.)
Jesus came from out the court-house door,   30
Stretched his hands above the passing poor.
Booth saw not, but led his queer ones there
Round and round the mighty court-house square.
Then, in an instant all that blear review
Marched on spotless, clad in raiment new.
The lame were straightened, withered limbs uncurled
And blind eyes opened on a new, sweet world.

(Bass drum louder.)
Drabs and vixens in a flash made whole!
Gone was the weasel-head, the snout, the jowl!
Sages and sibyls now, and athletes clean,   40
Rulers of empires, and of forests green!

(Grand chorus of all instruments. Tambourines to the foreground.)

The following year Lindsay brought out the highly syncopated and even more popular work "The Congo," in which evangelical zeal and the exuberant getting of religion are enacted as on the dark continent. It erupts like this:

From The Congo (1914)

A Study of the Negro Race

(Being a memorial to Ray Eldred, a Disciple missionary of the Congo River)

1. THEIR BASIC SAVAGERY

Fat black bucks in a wine-barrel room,
Barrel-house kings, with feet unstable,

Sagged and reeled and pounded on
  the table,   *A deep roll-*
Pounded on the table,   *ing bass.*
Beat an empty barrel with the handle
  of a broom,
Hard as they were able,
Boom, boom, Boom,
With a silk umbrella and the handle
  of a broom,
Boomlay, boomlay, boomlay, Boom.
Then I had religion, Then I had a
  vision,   10
I could not turn from their revel in
  derision.
Then I saw the Congo, creeping   *More*
  through the black,   *deliberate.*
Cutting through the forest with   *Solemnly*
  a golden track.   *chanted.*
Then along that riverbank
A thousand miles
Tattooed cannibals danced in files;
Then I heard the boom of the blood-
  lust song

And so on for half a dozen more table-pounding
pages. The critical purist will be in doubt
whether to call "The Congo" a poem at all—
but rather a medley of sounds, rhythmically organized, with a series of flickering indistinct
images, all designed to arouse certain childlike
emotions. The cultural historian, however, has to
credit Lindsay with pioneering in mingling various ingredients (words, jazz rhythms, gesture,
performance) in a way that has increasingly
appealed to younger people. He was America's
first "rock poet."

Probably Lindsay's best work is "Bryan,
Bryan, Bryan, Bryan," which he composed on a
ranch in Colorado in 1919. It is too long for
total inclusion here, but a few selections may
give the reader some sense of it. It is more
coherent, more artistically resolute, and emotionally more subdued and serious than the
others among Lindsay's best-known writings—
and this is due in good part to the poetic stance
Lindsay here assumes. It is that of the forty-
year-old man (Lindsay was born in 1879) recalling the crucial experience of a sixteen-year-old
boy and reliving that experience through the
boy's consciousness. Here, for once, Lindsay's
sustained boyishness found its proper poetic outlet, achieving a prolonged effect not dissimilar
from, and not altogether inferior to, Whitman's
"Out of the Cradle Endlessly Rocking," where
also a forty-year-old man renews himself by returning to an all-important boyhood experience
of loss and defeat. In both cases, the being who
is *observed* by the boy (the mockingbird in the
earlier case, William Jennings Bryan in the
later one) suffers an irreparable loss; yet for the
boy, and for the man he becomes, the experience leads to an immense gain in insight and
psychic power. And though Lindsay's theme is
ostensibly political and economic—Bryan's
evangelical commitment to the cause of free
silver—his real theme, like Whitman's, has to
do with poetry. Bryan is "the one American
Poet who could sing outdoors"; he is a "gigantic
troubadour, speaking like a siege gun." He is

That Homer Bryan, who sang from the West,
Gone to join the shadows with Altgeld the
  Eagle,
Where the kings and the slaves and the trouba-
  dours rest.

His political enemies—McKinley, Mark Hanna
(Ohio Senator and industrialist), Theodore
Roosevelt—have vanished utterly; but Bryan,
with John Peter Altgeld (liberal Governor of
Illinois, defender of radicals), has joined the
kings and the poets.

From Bryan, Bryan, Bryan, Bryan (1919)

The Campaign of Eighteen Ninety-six,
    as Viewed at the Time by a
        Sixteen-Year-Old, etc.

1

In a nation of one hundred fine, mob-hearted,
  lynching, relenting, millions,

There are plenty of sweeping, swinging,
  stinging, gorgeous things to shout about,
And knock your old blue devils out.

I brag and chant of Bryan, Bryan, Bryan,
Candidate for president who sketched a silver Zion,

The one American Poet who could sing out-
doors,
He brought in tides of wonder, of unprece-
dented splendor,
Wild roses from the plains, that made hearts
tender,
All the funny circus silks
Of politics unfurled,   10
Bartlett pears of romance that were honey at
the cores,
And torchlights down the street, to the end
of the world.

There were truths eternal in the gab and tit-
tle-tattle.
There were real heads broken in the fustian
and the rattle.
There were real lines drawn:
Not the silver and the gold,
But Nebraska's cry went eastward against the
dour and old,
The mean and cold.

It was eighteen ninety-six, and I was just
sixteen
And Altgeld ruled in Springfield, Illinois,   20
When there came from the sunset Nebraska's
shout of joy:
In a coat like a deacon, in a black Stetson hat
He scourged the elephant plutocrats
With barbed wire from the Platte.
The scales dropped from their mighty eyes.
They saw that summer's noon
A tribe of wonders coming
To a marching tune.

Oh, the longhorns from Texas,
The jay hawks from Kansas,   30
The plop-eyed bungaroo and giant giassicus,
The varmint, chipmunk, bugaboo,
The horned-toad, prairie-dog and ballyhoo,
From all the newborn states arow,
Bidding the eagles of the west fly on,
Bidding the eagles of the west fly on.
The fawn, prodactyl and thing-a-ma-jig,
The rakaboor, the hellangone,
The whangdoodle, batfowl and pig,
The coyote, wild-cat and grizzly in a glow,   40
In a miracle of health and speed, the whole
breed abreast,
They leaped the Mississippi, blue border of
the West,
From the Gulf to Canada, two thousand
miles long:—

Against the towns of Tubal Cain,
Ah,—sharp was their song.
Against the ways of Tubal Cain, too cunning
for the young,
The longhorn calf, the buffalo and wampus
gave tongue.

. . .

2

When Bryan came to Springfield, and Altgeld
gave him greeting,
Rochester was deserted, Divernon was de-
serted,
Mechanicsburg, Riverton, Chickenbristle,
Cotton Hill,   50
Empty: for all Sangamon drove to the
meeting—
In silver-decked racing cart,
Buggy, buckboard, carryall,
Carriage, phaeton, whatever would haul,
And silver-decked farm wagons gritted,
banged and rolled,
With the new tale of Bryan by the iron tires
told.

The State House loomed afar,
A speck, a hive, a football,
A captive balloon!
And the town was all one spreading wing of
bunting, plumes, and sunshine,   60
Every rag and flag, and Bryan picture sold,
When the rigs in many a dusty line
Jammed our streets at noon,
And joined the wild parade against the power
of gold.

We roamed, we boys from High School,
With mankind,
While Springfield gleamed,
Silk-lined.
Oh, Tom Dines, and Art Fitzgerald,
And the gangs that they could get!   70
I can hear them yelling yet.
Helping the incantation,
Defying aristocracy,
With every bridle gone,
Ridding the world of the low down mean,
Bidding the eagles of the West fly on,
Bidding the eagles of the West fly on,
We were bully, wild and woolly,
Never yet curried below the knees.
We saw flowers in the air,   80
Fair as the Pleiades, bright as Orion,

—Hopes of all mankind,
Made rare, resistless, thrice refined.
Oh, we bucks from every Springfield ward!
Colts of democracy—
Yet time-winds out of Chaos from the star-
  fields of the Lord.

The long parade rolled on. I stood by my
  best girl.
She was a cool young citizen, with wise and
  laughing eyes.
With my necktie by my ear, I was stepping
  on my dear,
But she kept like a pattern, without a shaken
  curl.   90

She wore in her hair a brave prairie rose.
Her gold chums cut her, for that was not
  the pose.
No Gibson Girl would wear it in that fresh
  way.
But we were fairy Democrats, and this was
  our day.

                    . . .

                     5
Election night at midnight:
Boy Bryan's defeat.
Defeat of western silver.
Defeat of the wheat.
Victory of letterfiles
And plutocrats in miles   100
With dollar signs upon their coats,
Diamond watchchains on their vests
And spats on their feet.
Victory of custodians,
Plymouth Rock,
And all that inbred landlord stock.
Victory of the neat.
Defeat of the aspen groves of Colorado
  valleys,
The blue bells of the Rockies,
And blue bonnets of old Texas,   110
By the Pittsburg alleys.
Defeat of alfalfa and the Mariposa lily.
Defeat of the Pacific and the long Mississippi.
Defeat of the young by the old and silly.
Defeat of tornadoes by the poison vats su-
  preme.
Defeat of my boyhood, defeat of my dream.

                     6
Where is McKinley, that respectable
  McKinley,

The man without an angle or a tangle,
Who soothed down the city man and
  soothed down the farmer,
The German, the Irish, the Southerner, the
  Northerner,   120
Who climbed every greasy pole, and slipped
  through every crack;
Who soothed down the gambling hall, the
  bar-room, the church,
The devil vote, the angel vote, the neutral
  vote,
The desperately wicked, and their victims on
  the rack,
The gold vote, the silver vote, the brass
  vote, the lead vote,
Every vote? . . .

Where is McKinley, Mark Hanna's
  McKinley,
His slave, his echo, his suit of clothes?
Gone to join the shadows, with the pomps
  of that time,
And the flame of that summer's prairie rose.   130

Where is Cleveland whom the Democratic
  platform
Read from the party in a glorious hour,
Gone to join the shadows with pitchfork
  Tillman,
And sledge-hammer Altgeld who wrecked his
  power.

Where is Hanna, bulldog Hanna,
Low-browed Hanna, who said: 'Stand pat'?
Gone to his place with old Pierpont Morgan.
Gone somewhere . . . with lean rat Platt.

Where is Roosevelt, the young dude cowboy,
Who hated Bryan, then aped his way?   140
Gone to join the shadows with mighty
  Cromwell
And tall King Saul, till the Judgment day.

Where is Altgeld, brave as the truth,
Whose name the few still say with tears?
Gone to join the ironies with Old John
  Brown,
Whose fame rings loud for a thousand years.

Where is that boy, that Heaven-born Bryan,
That Homer Bryan, who sang from the
  West?
Gone to join the shadows with Altgeld the
  Eagle,
Where the kings and the slaves and the
  troubadours rest.   150

ROBERT FROST (1874–1963)

The geography of Robert Frost's life, especially the first half of it, itself constitutes a minor American saga. This most New England of poets was in fact born in San Francisco in 1874. Both his schoolteaching parents were New Englanders; but his father became so disaffected from the region that in 1873 he took his bride of three months to California; a year later, he displayed his Copperhead sympathies by naming his first-born Robert Lee after the great Confederate general. It was not until he was eleven that young Frost, following the death of his father, came east with his mother and sister, settled in the new family home in Lawrence, Massachusetts, and witnessed his first New England snowstorm. Frost went to school in Lawrence and put in a couple of months at Dartmouth College. He married a schoolmate, Elinor White (with whom he had shared high school graduation honors), and attended Harvard for a year, where he studied under William James, George Santayana, and Barrett Wendell. Then, at the turn of the century, his grandfather generously purchased a farm for him and supplied him with a small annual income. Frost spent a decade chicken-farming and schoolteaching, reading a great deal and writing an occasional poem.

He was more and more absorbed into the New England atmosphere, but he was leading a desultory life which turned his thoughts more than once to suicide (it was from his father, evidently, that Frost inherited an inner turbulence, and a tendency to fits of rage or desperation). As he was nearing forty, Frost took his family to England, hoping at least for better literary luck there than he had experienced in America. He received it: an English publisher brought out his first volume of poetry, *A Boy's Will*, in 1913, with an introduction by Ezra Pound which hailed Frost as "another personality in the realm of verse," and "another American found, as usual, on this side of the water, by

an English publisher long known as a lover of good letters." [1] Frost's second volume, and one of his best, *North of Boston*, was also published in England the following year; and when he returned to America in 1915, the California-born transplant to New England found that his reputation, established at last in the mother country, had preceded him back across the Atlantic.

In fact, and by a not unfamiliar paradox, the English experience, for all its modest triumph, only served to solidify Frost's sense of himself as an American and a New Englander. Pound, a few days after meeting Frost in London and reading some of his poems, wrote an editor of *Poetry* (the recently founded Chicago periodical presided over by the influential Harriet Monroe) that he had "just discovered another Amur'kin. VURRY Amur'kin, with, I think, the seeds of grace." By this, Pound meant that he might lure Frost into the better poetic ways then being formulated in England; he even tried to persuade Frost to experiment with free verse. Frost resisted strenuously. He wrote a friend resentfully that Pound had "made up his mind . . . to add me to his party of American literary refugees in London. Nothing could be more unfair, nothing better calculated to make me an exile for life." It was a shrewd insight, for Frost had now realized that apart from America and especially his adopted region, apart from the nourishment and inspiration they provided, he could be nothing *but* an exile, and would be disempowered as a poet. Besides, he even found himself drawn to the transient Americans in London, for all their absurd tourist costumes. "I'm a Yank from Yankville," he decided, and fell to dreaming about remem-

[1] Pound also repeated, in all innocence, a tissue of romantic nonsense Frost had handed him about being cruelly disinherited by his grandfather and left to starve for the crime of being a poet. Frost, who had simply been exercising his talent at role-playing in spinning this yarn, was appalled.

bered New England scenes: "the snug downhill churning room with the view over five ranges of mountains," as he had once remarked. "There is a pang there that makes poetry."

It was not only his national and regional identity that Frost was working out in the English years; it was also his literary and his poetic ancestry. From his early adolescence on, Bryant and even more Emerson had been the objects of his enthusiasm; Emily Dickinson joined them when her first poems appeared in 1891. Emerson loomed ever larger for Frost over the years, to the point where, in 1959, Frost paid eloquent if easygoing tribute to Emerson as one of the four greatest Americans of all time (with Washington, Jefferson, and Lincoln) (see pp. 687–88). He named *Emerson's Essays and Poems* as one of his ten favorite books, declaring that he found in it "the⟨rapture of idealism⟩either way you have it, in prose or in verse and in brief." Farm life had, meanwhile, taken him back to Thoreau and *Walden*, which he also listed among his ten favorites and pages from which he read aloud to his classes in a New Hampshire school. As early as 1901, according to his biographer Lawrance Thompson, Emerson and Thoreau had become Frost's "patron saints." [2]

To be sure, Frost read, enjoyably, far beyond the boundaries of American literature. Even as a millhand in the mid-nineties (in Lawrence), he relieved the tedium of his life by immersing himself in Shakespeare, making notes in the margins of the plays; and he relished Francis Palgrave's *Golden Treasury* of English songs and lyrics. He was an inveterate reader of the older fiction, and a devotee of Mark Twain (he once endeared himself to his students in a girls' school by reading them Twain's "jumping frog" story, and then dismissing them for the day). He was also an accomplished classicist, with a particular mastery of Latin, which he studied at Harvard, along with philosophy and literature, and taught at several schools. There is a more pronounced Latin strain in Frost's poetry than has usually been observed—not only in its frequent echo of Horace and his odes to his Sabine farm, but in the very texture and cadence (a kind of packed and rhythmic gravity) of some of the verses.

Nonetheless, it was in American writing and particularly in the New England writing of the nineteenth-century "renaissance" that Frost properly located his own line of descent. His growing literary nativism had been spurred, in 1913, by an article in the *Encyclopedia Britannica* in which the author, George Edward Woodberry, denounced the universities for failing to support American writing. This had been Frost's experience at Dartmouth and Harvard, and a main reason why he had not lasted very long at either: the growing awareness that the then-current style of education hampered rather than encouraged an appreciation of American literature, much less the further production of it. Frost determined to ground himself in the living traditions of his own country, and to become, in poetry at least, their contemporary champion.[3]

---

[2] The other books on the list of 1936 were: the *Odyssey*, *Robinson Crusoe*, the tales of Edgar Allan Poe, *The Oxford Book of English Verse*, Louis Untermeyer's *Modern American and British Poetry*, *The Last of the Mohicans*, Anthony Hope's *The Prisoner of Zenda* ("surely one of the very best of our modern best-sellers"), and Kipling's *The Jungle Book* (the first).

[3] Frost was as pugnaciously watchful of his status in the world of letters as would be Hemingway, whom in other regards as well he oddly resembled. His fiercest jealousy was of Edwin Arlington Robinson, his closest competitor, as Frost recognized. He could not but admire much of Robinson's work, but he was enraged when, on first being introduced to him in 1915, their host tactlessly remarked that everyone in America "thinks of Robinson as our greatest poet." Robinson remained well disposed toward Frost, and in 1930 was one of the five members who nominated him to the American Academy of Arts and Letters. Frost learned of this shortly after he had pronounced Robinson a "romantic" and "enervated old soak"; he failed even to acknowledge one of the volumes Robinson sent him, and refused to join in the tribute to Robinson on the latter's fiftieth birthday. Robinson observed mildly, in 1934, that "I'm afraid Frost is a jealous man"; but despite the whole record, Frost, after Robinson's death, insisted stoutly: "I never felt jealous of him at any time." On Frost's introduction to Robinson's posthumous *King Jasper*, see below, pp. 1863–64. It might also be observed that after Robinson's death T. S. Eliot became the prime object of Frost's disparagement.

As to his pair of "patron saints," while there are obvious parallels with Thoreau's knowing observation of natural phenomena and seasonal change (as both may be experienced in the New England countryside), Frost also drew more from Emerson, as he constantly implied, than may at first sight appear. He was a good deal more conservative, politically, than Emerson declared himself to be (at least on paper and in the lecture halls)—and exactly because he was much more conservative intellectually. He had a sturdy Puritan distrust of human nature which led him to look skeptically upon social or political programs rooted in optimistic idealism; in this regard he had more of Hawthorne in him than of Emerson. If he took to himself any portion of the substance of Emerson's vision, it was the occasional and belated but no less vigorous acknowledgment—which Robinson also borrowed—of the limitations and barriers to human aspiration.

But Frost could respond to Emerson's flashing Yankee wit, his capacity for pungent formulation, his affection for racy colloquial speech—to the twang that resounds through so much of Emerson's prose and some of his poetry. More important than that but closely akin is the matter of symbolism. In 1923, in answer to a question about his philosophy, Frost began by recalling that he had been baptized and brought up a Swedenborgian, and though he no longer held to the doctrines of the Swedish thinker—whose ideas pervaded Emerson's generation ("the age is Swedenborg's," Emerson was heard to say)—he still found persuasive Swedenborg's theory of a correspondence between natural facts and the world of spirit. "I am a mystic," he went on, "I believe in symbols. I believe in change and changing symbols." It was in Emerson's *Nature* of 1836 that Frost found the most compelling argument yet written by an American that natural facts are symbols of spiritual facts. Exploiting that conviction in poetry, Frost took as his symbolic examples many of the same ingredients of the New England scene—farms, snowstorms, winds, birds, rivers—that Emerson had deployed for his own purposes.

The major difference, of course, was that for Frost more often than not the natural facts symbolized a darkness, or at least a dark and threatening mystery, at the heart of reality; and sometimes he wondered if they symbolized anything that the human mind could fully comprehend. This puritanic outlook controls the fine and disturbing sonnet "Design," written in 1911 when Frost was wrestling with some of the ideas of William James and the French philosopher Henri Bergson:

I found a dimpled spider, fat and white,
On a white heal-all, holding up a moth
Like a white piece of rigid satin cloth—
Assorted characters of death and blight
Mixed ready to begin the morning right,
Like the ingredients of a witches' broth—
A snow-drop spider, a flower like a froth,
And dead wings carried like a paper kite.

What had that flower to do with being white,
The wayside blue and innocent heal-all?
What brought the kindred spider to that height,
Then steered the white moth thither in the
        night?
What but design of a darkness to appall?—
If design govern in a thing so small.

That perfectly designed poem gathers together three instances of whiteness (one a flower ironically called a "heal-all") to symbolize an appalling design of darkness: that is, if there actually is any design, any rationally discoverable meaning, in nature.

Frost's stance toward the natural world is, obviously, much more shifty than that of Emerson, though perhaps Emerson's (and Thoreau's) usual confidence that nature was his ally and his solace should be kept in mind as a background against which Frost's poetry can be measured. Frost is the kind of late romantic who appears as an antiromantic: if nature for him is sometimes indecipherable, it is in part because the elements of nature have little or no interest in the human situation, in human hope or human grief. This is the burden of "The Need of Being Versed in Country Things," one of Frost's best poems. The scene is a farm, whose house has burned down and which is now abandoned. Birds continue to visit, and they *seem* to share the human sense of loss:

The birds that came to it through the air
At open windows flew out and in,
Their murmur more like the sigh we sigh
From too much thinking on what has been.

In fact, however, far from grieving, the birds are enjoying the renewal of nature, a process that goes on whatever the range of man's defeat—but one has to be privy to the truth about nature ("country things") to understand that fact:

Yet for them the lilac renewed its leaf,
And the aged elm, though touched with fire;
And the dry pump flung up an awkward arm;
And the fence post carried a strand of wire.

For them there was really nothing sad.
But though they rejoiced in the nest they kept,
One had to be versed in country things
Not to believe the phoebes wept.

Nature, when it is not merely indifferent, can be menacing; but in "An Old Man's Winter Night," where that note is struck to awesome effect, it is also suggested fancifully that a certain kind of human condition can be as frightening to nature as nature sometimes is to man. "All out of doors looked darkly in at him," at the aged and isolated farmer—wholly isolated, physically and psychologically; a figure to compare with Melville's lost souls; isolated even from himself. As he moves heavily about his cottage at night, trying to remember what it was he started to do, he thoroughly alarms his environment:

And having scared the cellar under him
In clomping here, he scared it once again
In clomping off;—and scared the outer night,
Which has its sounds, familiar, like the roar
Of trees and crack of branches, common things,
But nothing so like beating on a box.
A light he was to no one but himself
Where now he sat, concerned with he knew what,
A quiet light, and then not even that.

Modern poetry offers no grimmer, or more beautifully worded, image of irredeemable psychic solitude.

Those familiar with the New England countryside will not find in Frost much celebration of certain aspects they remember: the glow of meadows and hills in the summer sunshine, the thick woods in full leaf. Frost is not a celebrant of summer, nor (except as a contrast to human deterioration) of spring rebirth. He is, characteristically, the poet of autumn, of impending winter, of the darkness to come. If he sets his scene in mid-summer, as he does in "The Oven Bird," it is exactly to focus on the passage of summer, the imminence of autumn: what the bird says, in his mid-summer song, is

. . . that leaves are old and that for flowers
Mid-summer is to spring as one to ten—

as one in the afternoon is to ten in the morning. The question the oven bird has to answer is just the question faced by Frost in his best poetry: it is "what to make of a diminished thing."[4]

That motif was sounded early and late in Frost's verse. One of the first poems in which Frost began to find his true voice, "The Quest of the Purple-fringed" in 1896, concludes—after describing the successful search through the meadows for "the far-sought flower"—with these lines:

Then I arose and silently wandered home,
And I for one
Said that the fall might come and whirl of leaves,
For summer was done.

Twenty-three years later, in 1919, Frost wrote what is perhaps his most resonant variation on the theme, "The Onset" (see text of "The Onset," p. 1870).

[4] It is not impossible that one source of "The Oven Bird" was Emily Dickinson's poem "Further in Summer Than the Birds," which Frost read soon after it appeared in the volume of 1891. For Emily Dickinson (see p. 1247), it is the cricket whose solitary chirp at high noon bespeaks the departure of summer; the cricket, mentally, is further along toward the end of summer than any of the birds.

That is quintessential Frost. For Frost is, finally, the poet of the "onset," not only of literal winter and the night, but of the encroachment of spiritual darkness, even of psychic death: the inexorable moving in upon man of ultimate, desperate challenges. (Frost once admitted lightly that he had "an ulteriority complex.") Indeed, his very concept of poetry springs from this view of the confrontations between half-benighted man and the environmental threat. A poem, for Frost, is, precisely, a facing-up to the many-sided danger: an attempt to overcome, or to fend off, or at least to illuminate the danger. So conceived, a poem is a living symbol of the fundamental situation: "an epitome," as Frost put it, "of the great predicament, a figure of the will braving alien entanglements." Similarly, in a little essay called "The Figure a Poem Makes," Frost wrote: "It begins in delight, it inclines to the impulse, it assumes direction with the first line laid down, it runs a course of lucky events, and ends in a clarification of life—not necessarily a great clarification, such as sects and cults are founded on, but in a momentary stay against confusion."

But for all its awareness of "alien entanglements," there is in Frost's poetry a steady tone of wry Yankee humor, and a virtually inexhaustible verbal grace. There is even an amount of sheer playfulness—a playing with notions, images, language. In a late couplet, Frost remarked:

It takes all sorts of in and outdoor schooling
To get adapted to my kind of fooling.

There is a definite streak of fooling amid the bleak chill of "An Old Man's Winter Night," and even when he allowed his vision of impending darkness to deepen into outright apocalyptics, as in "Fire and Ice," Frost meditates the end of the world with a sort of laconic, lip-chewing thoughtfulness (see text of "Fire and Ice," p. 1870).

At Frost's eightieth birthday party in New York City in 1954, Lionel Trilling profoundly shocked a number of Frost's friends and admirers by declaring that Frost was a "terrifying poet," and that the "universe [Frost] conceives is a terrifying universe" ("Design" and "Neither Out Far Nor In Deep" were among the poems cited). There were outraged protests, though it should have been plain that Trilling meant to pay the poet a high compliment; and it was in any case an excellent and long overdue corrective to the cozy, homey Frost of popular legend. But that figure itself was only another instance of Frost's kind of fooling: he was a role-player from young manhood on, and his favorite role, or mask, was that of the easygoing rustic philosopher with a Vermont accent (a role not entirely dissimilar to the one preferred, in his Paris days, by Frost's American predecessor most adept at the game, Benjamin Franklin). This, in the words of Randall Jarrell, was "the only genuine Robert Frost in captivity." Though the terror, in short, is part of the very fiber of Frost's poetry and his vision, it is customarily held in check by the fooling: one way to achieve a momentary stay against confusion.

If the sense of diminution is so prevalent in Frost's verse, it is partly because he saw and felt a kind of shrinking in the section of the country he chose to inhabit. The effect of the Civil War had been to shift power away from New England almost as much as it had shifted it from the Old South. Boston was no longer "the hub of the [American] universe." The power axis of the post–Civil War United States now ran through New York and Chicago. New England retained its fine colleges and great universities, its landmarks of revolutionary history, its mementoes of the great days of the whaling ships and the China clippers. Above all, it retained its intellectual tradition, but it had lost political power and population. In more than one poem Frost descants on lonely farmhouses, townships which were still named on the map but were now without population, and clusters of vine-grown cellar holes that marked where a village had once stood. As if to underline his awareness and acceptance of the general fact of decline, Frost elects to write about those New England states that through the 1930's and 1940's were actually losing population and rarely about more prosperous Massachusetts, Connecticut, and Rhode Island. Significantly, his second volume was entitled *North of Boston*. His fourth volume bears the title *New Hampshire*, and in its title poem the speaker declares that New Hampshire and Vermont are "the two best states in the Union." [5]

Many people would interpret Frost's choice as reflecting a desire to escape into the past. They hold that he felt spiritually more comfortable in the simpler and less sophisticated civilization; and that, besides, he knew that a Currier and Ives America would prove the more attractive to an affluent American who was eager and able to collect early American furniture, bric-a-brac, bottles, china wear—and poetry.

Critics like Yvor Winters and Malcolm Cowley have said as much. Living rooms furnished with rock-maple tables and chairs, with an imitation spinning wheel in one corner and a fake cobbler's bench in the other, included as a normal part of their early American decor a copy of the poems of Robert Frost. This caricature of the poet's purposes has been reinforced by the particular mask that, to repeat, Frost wears in so many of his poems—that of the Yankee philosopher, speaking his aphorisms of homely wisdom to his farmer friends around a pot-bellied, wood-burning stove on a winter's afternoon in a Vermont village general store. Further damage has been done by Frost's own admirers, who have often emphasized what they believed would appeal to readers who are notoriously gun-shy when they come within the range of modern poetry.

Yet to any serious reader it ought to be clear that Frost, in writing about what is left of New England farm and village life, is not escaping into an idyllic world. Even his earliest poems

[5] Frost is thoroughly disarming in telling us why he decided to move to New Hampshire:

When I left Massachusetts years ago
Between two days, the reason why I sought
New Hampshire, not Connecticut,
Rhode Island, New York, or Vermont was this:
Where I was living then, New Hampshire offered
The nearest boundary to escape across.
I hadn't an illusion in my hand-bag
About the people being better there
Than those I left behind. I thought they weren't.
I thought they couldn't be. And yet they were.

made it plain that he is thoroughly aware of the loneliness, the frustration, and the failure to be found in his favorite part of the United States. Frost tells us that a Massachusetts poet (evidently Amy Lowell) said that she had decided to give up her summer place in New Hampshire. When he inquired why, she told him:

. . . she couldn't stand the people in it.

. . .

And when I asked to know what ailed the people,
She said, "Go read your own books and find out."

And Frost in *North of Boston* (1914) and *Mountain Interval* (1916) had not failed to cite instances of lonely despair and degradation. But there are also in these volumes plenty of thoroughly sturdy folk who would not necessarily have pleased Miss Lowell. If Frost believed that on balance the older rural life was a good life, it was not because it was free of hardship and disappointment. Rather, its recommendation would have to be that since the good life is always a matter of self-discipline and moral character, the very asperities of a relatively impoverished society—which was at the same time a true community, concrete, personal, and possessed of a recognizable structure of values—tend to promote the good life. Neither a fabulous Arcadia nor an affluent modern suburb would be so conducive to the formation of character.

The second point to be observed is that Frost is thoroughly aware of what life is like in other parts of the world and specifically in other parts of the United States. Far from running away from it, he is an acute observer and a critic of the quality of life in modern America. That this is the true state of affairs can most clearly be seen in a poem like the rambling, quasi-meditative colloquy entitled "New Hampshire." The poem is, to be sure, half-jocular. The speaker tells us that New Hampshire is the best state in the Union because it entertains no disdain and hasn't been soiled by trade. As for the matter of the dignity of work, the speaker keeps an anchor to windward. When the lady from the South tells him that "None of my family ever worked/Or had a thing to sell," he tells us that he doesn't suppose that the work "Much matters. You may work for all of me./I've seen the time I've had to work myself." As for not having been soiled by trade, as the poet implies California has been, New Hampshire has to thank Nature itself. The poet concludes a long inventory of the state's meager natural resources, by mentioning its trace of radium, remarking:

But trust New Hampshire not to have enough
Of radium or anything to sell.

He had earlier observed that

> Just specimens is all New Hampshire has,
> One each of everything as in a show-case
> Which naturally she doesn't care to sell.

Nevertheless, in spite of sly reservations and qualification, the celebration of New Hampshire is seriously meant. Its virtues are never spelled out, but they are clearly implied. Horace on his Sabine farm would have understood and endorsed them.

There is another justification for using the older culture of rural New England as a vantage point from which to comment on a highly industrialized urban society. One gains a special perspective by putting the complicated problems into a simpler and less abstract context. Such is the essence of the pastoral mode, as William Empson pointed out a number of years ago. Indeed, the important fact about a pastoral poem is not that the characters are shepherds—they need not be—but that the concerns of a complex world are treated in terms of a world more primitive.

In this connection, it may be well to remember that the father of pastoral poetry, Theocritus, wrote his pastorals at the elegant court of Ptolemy in Greek-speaking Alexandria, and that the greatest Latin pastoralist, Virgil, also wrote an epic about the legendary founder of Rome and enjoyed the patronage of the Emperor Augustus. From the beginning pastorals have been written by sophisticated men of the cities.

The deeper import of the pastoral may be more shrewd than its innocent surfaces would suggest.[6]

All of this is not to say that Frost did not know New England farming and village life from the inside out. Our point in calling Frost a pastoralist is not to suggest that the world depicted in his poetry is charmingly unrealistic, but rather that in choosing to write about "The Death of the Hired Man" or "Evening in a Sugar Orchard," or Brad McLaughlin, the "under-ticket-agent" at a village railroad station who had "failed at hugger-mugger farming," Frost has not relaxed his grip on what most suburban or urban Americans now regard as "real."

Frost's regionalism finds its parallel in other writers of our day. Dylan Thomas got a certain leverage on the problems of modern man by basing himself in his native Wales; so did Thomas Hardy, by writing about his native West Country in England; so also did William Butler Yeats, by making his native Ireland the bedrock of his poetry. Coming closer home, William Faulkner, as we shall see later, located most of his work—and certainly most of his best work—in a mythical Mississippi county which he named Yoknapatawpha. In doing so, Faulkner was not running away from the real world and its problems, or indulging in mere antiquarianism. Frost's New England has also been called "mythical," and so it is—in almost the same sense as Faulkner's Yoknapatawpha.

Frost's career after 1915 was one of immense productivity and steadily widening popularity. Lawrance Thompson calls his biographical volume that covers the period 1915–38 *The Years of Triumph*; but the triumph, far from stopping in 1938, continued on for more than two decades, through Frost's reading of "The Gift Outright" at the inauguration of President Kennedy in 1961 to the poet's death, as he was nearing ninety, in 1963. There were, to be sure, severe domestic disturbances and inner stresses: Frost, as he said in one of his poems, was "acquainted with the night." The Frosts' first-born child,

6 Readers interested in this aspect of Frost might profitably consult John F. Lynen's *The Pastoral Art of Robert Frost* (1960).

Elliott, had died of cholera at the age of four in 1900; "Home Burial" is a somber memory of the days after that shattering event. In 1920, Frost's sister Jean, always an edgy and sometimes a hysterical and paranoid personality with whom Frost never managed to communicate, was arrested (in Portland, Maine) by police officers she accused of being white-slavers; she was placed in an asylum for the insane and died there nine years later. His daughter Majorie died of tuberculosis before she was thirty; a son committed suicide; and most wearing of all was the constant tension between Frost and his wife Elinor. "Elinor has never been of any earthly use to me," Frost wrote Untermeyer in 1917. "She has resisted every inch of the way my efforts to get money. She is not too sure that she cares about my reputation." The letter is bitter, but it is also ambiguous: it reflects a curious pride in his wife's unmanageable temperament; at Elinor's death in 1938, Frost was utterly stricken.

But meanwhile over the years the volumes had appeared and the honors had piled up: among them no less than four Pulitzer prizes, for *New Hampshire* (1924), *Collected Poems* (1931), *A Further Range* (1936), and *A Witness Tree* (1943). Frost read and talked about his poems in lecture halls and on campuses all across the country, to enormous effect. Or rather, as he preferred it, he "said" his poems; in his vocal performances as in his verse itself, Frost always sought to catch the sound of the normal conversational human voice. He taught on and off at Amherst College before settling there for a stay of twelve years in 1926. He put in two teaching stints at the University of Michigan; and from 1939 to 1942 he occupied the remarkably appropriate position of Ralph Waldo Emerson Fellow in Poetry at Harvard. During most of this time, his family home was a farm in South Shaftsbury, Vermont.

In spite of the ongoing praise and popularity, when *A Further Range* appeared in 1936 it met with a good deal of hostile criticism. Frost was indicted for poor form or else for insignificant content. That extraordinarily able critic

R. P. Blackmur urged both charges. He asserted in the *Nation* that Frost was really not a poet at all, but "at heart, an easygoing versifier of all that comes to hand, and hence never lacks either a subject or the sense of its mastery." Blackmur, whose critical enthusiasms at the time were all for the writings of Eliot, Pound, Wallace Stevens, and Hart Crane, also found in Frost a willfully escapist strain (as, we have remarked, so did Cowley and others). But far more severe was the onslaught of the politically minded critics of liberal or left-wing persuasion. They pressed hard the charge that Frost was an ⟨ escapist or, worse still, a political reactionary. ⟩

The volume in question contained some of Frost's best and also his most tough-minded poems (like "Desert Places" and "Provide, Provide"); but the further range it aspired to was into the realm of political commentary, in particular some sardonic and skeptical allusions to Franklin D. Roosevelt's New Deal and the reformist spirit which had swept the land. It was upon this element in the volume that critics as cultivated and knowing as Newton Arvin and F. O. Matthiessen came down hardest. In speaking of Frost's preface to Robinson's *King Jasper*, Arvin had cited Frost's complaint about the absence of woes in American life for a poet to write about[7] and added: "both that passage and the present preface have the effect of placing an astronomical distance between him and us." Turning to *A Further Range*, Arvin discerned in it nothing but "the New England of nasalized

[7] Frost had said: "How can we write/The Russian novel in America/As long as life goes so unterribly?" This was clearly an echo, partly playful, of William Dean Howells' contention that "the smiling aspects" of America forbade her novelists from imitating their Russian counterparts. Howells, incidentally, greeted both *A Boy's Will* and *North of Boston* with his customary perceptive generosity and took the occasion to berate imagism and other "foreign" poetic developments: "Here is no *vers libre*, no shredded prose, but very sweet rhyme and pleasant rhythm." Six years later, in 1921, Frost from a sickbed wrote a peculiarly warm tribute for a memorial service following Howells' death: "I am tempted to accept your invitation for the chance it would give me, the only one I may ever have, to discharge in downright prose the great debt I owe Howells." The debt was then lavishly discharged.

negations, monosyllabic uncertainties, and non-committal rejoinders," and a "philosophy [that] seems as profitless as a dried-up well." Horace Gregory, observing rather nastily that "it has always been Mr. Frost's particular virtue to make molehills out of mountains," declared that Frost's attempt to expand his subject was a mistake; and Rolfe Humphries, writing in the radical *New Masses*, entitled his review "A Further Shrinking."

But the age of reform gave way to the Second World War; and Frost (to borrow a phrase from Faulkner in a rather different context) not only survived but prevailed. There were more volumes, including the *Complete Poems* of 1949; more honors, including honorary degrees at both Oxford and Cambridge; another year of teaching (at Dartmouth); and, finally, the vastness of his achievement became so visible that even Arvin and Blackmur changed their opinions. When, in 1951, John Crowe Ransom came to rank the English and American poets of the century, Frost was one of four he was willing to classify as "major."

It is hardly surprising that Frost's preface to *King Jasper* should arouse profound hostility in certain literary and politico-literary circles in the America of the mid-thirties. With a kind of merciless blandness, Frost took on, first, the entire theory and practice of political liberalism; and, second, the entire chapter of experimentation in poetry. (Robinson, it has to be said, got rather lost in the battle, though Frost added some kindly words in revision.) As to liberalism, Frost spared no punches:

The day of perfection waits on unanimous social action. Two or three more national elections should do the business. It has been similarly urged on us to give up courage, make cowardice a virtue, and see if that won't end war and the need of courage. Desert religion for science, clean out the holes and corners of the residual unknown, and there will be no more need for religion. (Religion is merely consolation for what we don't know.) But

suppose there was some mistake; and the evil stood siege, the war didn't end, and something remained unknowable. Our having disarmed would make our case worse than it had ever been before.

Frost had never spoken in a more staunchly and unyieldingly puritanic voice; nor has the age of war that historically followed, and the mysteries that have remained ("the residual unknown"), done much to refute his ironic case.

But these slaps at the New Deal were essentially asides. What Frost really wanted to press was his insistent *literary* conservatism—to argue in favor of "The Old Way to Be New," as he called the first of his six Norton Lectures, given at Harvard in the spring of 1938 before overflow and hugely sympathetic crowds (the series was an elaboration of the *King Jasper* preface). "It may come to the notice of posterity (and then again it may not)," he began, "that this our age ran wild in the quest of new ways to be new. The one old way to be new no longer served."

Science put it into our heads that there must be new ways to be new. Those tried were largely by subtraction—elimination. Poetry for example was tried without punctuation. It was tried without capital letters. It was tried without metric frame on which to measure the rhythms. It was tried without any images but those to the eye, and a loud general intoning had to be kept up to cover the total loss of specific images to the ear, those dramatic tones of voice which had hitherto constituted the better half-tone of poetry. It was tried without content under the trade name of poesie pure.

And so on.

Moving toward his own deepest conviction, he recalled the first discussion he had held with Robinson, over drinks in Boston. "The sense of the meeting was, we didn't care how arrant a reformer or experimentalist a man was if he gave us real poems. For ourselves, we would hate to be read for any theory upon which we might be supposed to write. . . . Poems are all that matter." That is probably as sound a theory as any truly dedicated poet would want or need. Frost held to it for better than sixty years; and over that long time he gave us an enduring abundance of real poems, poems that mattered and continue to matter.

BIOGRAPHICAL CHART

1874 Born, March 26, in San Francisco, California, son of William Prescott Frost, Jr., and Isabelle Moodie Frost

1885 Father dies; family moves to Lawrence, Massachusetts

1892 Graduates from Lawrence High School, co-valedictorian with Elinor White

1893–94 Matriculates at Dartmouth College

1894 "My Butterfly," first published poem, appears in the *Independent*

1895 Marries Elinor Miriam White, his high school sweetheart

1897–99 Attends Harvard College

1900 Moves to farm near West Derry, New Hampshire

1905 Writes "The Black Cottage," "The Housekeeper," "The Death of the Hired Man"

1912 Takes his family to England, farms and writes poetry in Buckinghamshire and Herefordshire

1913 David Nutt, London, publishes Frost's first book of poetry, *A Boy's Will*

1914 David Nutt publishes Frost's *North of Boston*

1915 Brings his family to farm near Franconia, New Hampshire; *A Boy's Will*

1916 Reads "The Bonfire" at Phi Beta Kappa Day, Harvard; *Mountain Interval*; elected to National Institute of Arts and Letters

1917–20 Serves as professor of English, Amherst College

1919 Moves to farm near South Shaftsbury, Vermont

1921–23 Serves as Poet in Residence, University of Michigan, Ann Arbor

1923 *Selected Poems; New Hampshire*

1924 Receives Pulitzer prize for *New Hampshire*

1928 *West-Running Brook*

1930 *Collected Poems*

1936 *A Further Range*; serves as Charles Eliot Norton Professor of Poetry, Harvard University

1937 Receives Pulitzer prize for *A Further Range*; awarded an honorary Doctor of Letters by Harvard

1938 Elinor White Frost dies; resigns from Amherst College

1939 *Collected Poems*; The National Institute of Arts and Letters awards Frost its Gold Medal for Poetry

1939–42 Serves as Ralph Waldo Emerson Fellow in Poetry, Harvard University

1940 Buys farm near Ripton, Vermont, and house in Cambridge, Massachusetts

1942 *A Witness Tree*

1943 Receives Pulitzer prize for *A Witness Tree*

1943–49 Serves as Ticknor Fellow in the Humanities, Dartmouth College

1945 *A Masque of Reason*

1947 *Steeple Bush; A Masque of Mercy*

1948 Amherst College awards Frost the Doctor of Letters

1949 *Complete Poems*; Amherst College appoints Frost as Simpson Lecturer in Literature

1950 The United States Senate passes resolution commending Frost on event of his seventy-fifth birthday

1958 Serves as Consultant in Poetry to Library of Congress

1959 Honored by publishers, friends, and government officials on anniversary of his eighty-fifth birthday; United States Senate passes resolution commending Frost

1961 Reads "The Gift Outright" at inauguration of President John F. Kennedy

1963 Awarded the Bollingen prize for poetry; dies, January 29, in Boston, aged eighty-eight

FURTHER READINGS

Robert Frost, *Complete Poems* (1967)
Lawrance Thompson, ed., *Selected Letters* (1964)

Reuben A. Brower, *The Poetry of Robert Frost* (1963)
James Cox, "Robert Frost and the Edge of the Clearing," *Virginia Quarterly Review* (Winter, 1959)
———, ed., *Robert Frost: Twentieth Century Views* (1962)

Vivian Hopkins, "Robert Frost: Out Far and in Deep," *Western Humanities Review* (Summer, 1960)
Randall Jarrell, *Poetry and the Age* (1955)
Edward C. Latham, *Interviews with Robert Frost* (1966)
J. F. Lynen, *The Pastoral Art of Robert Frost* (1960)
Lawrance Thompson, *Robert Frost: The Early Years, 1874–1915* (1966)

————, *Robert Frost: The Years of Triumph, 1915–1938* (1970)
Yvor Winters, *On Modern Poets* (1959)

These poems are presented in the chronological order of the volumes in which they appeared. This does not mean in all cases the order in which they were written. Frost, who wanted each of his volumes to have a significant structure, sometimes held a poem back until it could form part of such a structure. For the interested, Lawrance Thompson's biography dates the writing of most of Frost's work.

Some of the poems selected here have been discussed in the introduction, and further comment is unnecessary.

Note: The poem "The Gift Outright" (from *A Witness Tree*, 1942) appears, and is commented on, at the beginning of our first volume, where it supplies a central theme for our opening section. "New Hampshire," the title poem for its volume of 1923, is discussed in a certain detail in the introduction to Frost but is too long to be included here.

The Pasture (1913)

The title of Frost's first book of verse comes from Longfellow's "My Lost Childhood":

A boy's will is the wind's will,
And the thoughts of youth are long, long
    thoughts.

The thirty-eight-year-old poet organized his initial volume in such a way, so he hoped, as to dramatize the thoughts of a young person facing up to the psychological and emotional problems of maturity.

"The Pasture" was carefully placed by Frost at the beginning of *A Boy's Will*. It can be taken as a ⟨friendly invitation⟩ to join him in some small farming undertakings—and also as

an invitation to join in the poetic experience offered by the entire book. Its actual origin was a gesture of reconciliation by Frost to his wife Elinor, a sort of poetic lovemaking, after a period of domestic strain.

I'm going out to clean the pasture spring;
I'll only stop to rake the leaves away
(And wait to watch the water clear, I may):
I shan't be gone long.—You come too.

I'm going out to fetch the little calf
That's standing by the mother. It's so young
It totters when she licks it with her tongue.
I shan't be gone long.—You come too.

The Death of the Hired Man (1905–6)

This poem is to be dated from 1905–6 when Frost farmed at Derry, New Hampshire. It was not published until many years later in *North of Boston* (1914). One of the most interesting things about this poem is the way in which Frost has handled the pathos of the hired man's situation. Pride keeps him from going back to his prosperous brother. Now, old and sick and tired, he has come back to the farm on which he had worked—whose farmer he had actually left in the lurch. Here too we find him trying to

preserve his pride, by not appealing for help, but to do his employers a favor.

The hired man is not treated as a tragic figure, merely as pathetic. It is interesting to see how Frost has kept the pathos pure and has kept the poem from dissolving into sentimentality. His realism; his honesty, in not concealing from his reader the hired man's faults and weaknesses; his indirection (we never see the hired man or hear him speak directly); and the use of dramatic dialogue as the husband and wife debate

his case—all of these serve to make us feel that
our pity for the lonely old man has been earned
by the poet, not illegitimately imposed upon a
situation that does not warrant it.

Mary sat musing on the lamp-flame at the
    table,
Waiting for Warren. When she heard his
    step,
She ran on tiptoe down the darkened passage
To meet him in the doorway with the news
And put him on his guard. "Silas is back."
She pushed him outward with her through
    the door
And shut it after her. "Be kind," she said.
She took the market things from Warren's
    arms
And set them on the porch, then drew him
    down
To sit beside her on the wooden steps.   10

"When was I ever anything but kind to
    him?
But I'll not have the fellow back," he said.
"I told him so last haying, didn't I?
If he left then, I said, that ended it.
What good is he? Who else will harbor him
At his age for the little he can do?
What help he is there's no depending on.
Off he goes always when I need him most.
He thinks he ought to earn a little pay,
Enough at least to buy tobacco with,   20
So he won't have to beg and be beholden.
'All right,' I say, 'I can't afford to pay
Any fixed wages, though I wish I could.'
'Someone else can.' 'Then someone else will
    have to.'
I shouldn't mind his bettering himself
If that was what it was. You can be certain,
When he begins like that, there's someone at
    him
Trying to coax him off with pocket money—
In haying time, when any help is scarce.
In winter he comes back to us. I'm done."   30

"Sh! not so loud: he'll hear you," Mary said.

"I want him to: he'll have to soon or late."

"He's worn out. He's asleep beside the stove.
When I came up from Rowe's I found him
    here,
Huddled against the barn door fast asleep,
A miserable sight, and frightening, too—

You needn't smile—I didn't recognize him—
I wasn't looking for him—and he's changed.
Wait till you see."

        "Where did you say he'd been?"

"He didn't say. I dragged him to the house,   40
And gave him tea and tried to make him
    smoke.
I tried to make him talk about his travels.
Nothing would do: he just kept nodding
    off."

"What did he say? Did he say anything?"

"But little."

        "Anything? Mary, confess
He said he'd come to ditch the meadow for
    me."

"Warren!"

        "But did he? I just want to know."

"Of course he did. What would you have
    him say?
Surely you wouldn't grudge the poor old
    man
Some humble way to save his self-respect.   50
He added, if you really care to know,
He meant to clear the upper pasture, too.
That sounds like something you have heard
    before?
Warren, I wish you could have heard the
    way
He jumbled everything. I stopped to look
Two or three times—he made me feel so
    queer—
To see if he was talking in his sleep.
He ran on Harold Wilson—you remember—
The boy you had in haying four years since.
He's finished school, and teaching in his
    college.   60
Silas declares you'll have to get him back.
He says they two will make a team for work:
Between them they will lay this farm as
    smooth!
The way he mixed that in with other things.
He thinks young Wilson a likely lad, though
    daft
On education—you know how they fought
All through July under the blazing sun,
Silas up on the cart to build the load,
Harold along beside to pitch it on."

"Yes, I took care to keep well out of earshot."   70

"Well, those days trouble Silas like a dream.
You wouldn't think they would. How some
     things linger!
Harold's young college-boy's assurance piqued
     him.
After so many years he still keeps finding
Good arguments he sees he might have used.
I sympathize. I know just how it feels
To think of the right thing to say too late.
Harold's associated in his mind with Latin.
He asked me what I thought of Harold's
     saying
He studied Latin, like the violin,   80
Because he liked it—that an argument!
He said he couldn't make the boy believe
He could find water with a hazel prong—
Which showed how much good school had
     ever done him.
He wanted to go over that. But most of all
He thinks if he could have another chance
To teach him how to build a load of hay——"

"I know, that's Silas' one accomplishment.
He bundles every forkful in its place,
And tags and numbers it for future reference,   90
So he can find and easily dislodge it
In the unloading. Silas does that well.
He takes it out in bunches like big birds'
     nests.
You never see him standing on the hay
He's trying to lift, straining to lift himself."

"He thinks if he could teach him that, he'd
     be
Some good perhaps to someone in the world.
He hates to see a boy the fool of books.
Poor Silas, so concerned for other folk,
And nothing to look backward to with pride,   100
And nothing to look forward to with hope,
So now and never any different."

Part of a moon was falling down the west,
Dragging the whole sky with it to the hills.
Its light poured softly in her lap. She saw it
And spread her apron to it. She put out her
     hand
Among the harplike morning-glory strings,
Taut with the dew from garden bed to eaves,
As if she played unheard some tenderness
That wrought on him beside her in the night.   110
"Warren," she said, "he has come home to
     die:
You needn't be afraid he'll leave you this
     time."

"Home," he mocked gently.

                    "Yes, what else but home?
It all depends on what you mean by home.
Of course he's nothing to us, any more
Than was the hound that came a stranger
     to us
Out of the woods, worn out upon the trail."

"Home is the place where, when you have
     to go there,
They have to take you in."

                    "I should have called it
Something you somehow haven't to deserve."   120

Warren leaned out and took a step or two,
Picked up a little stick, and brought it back
And broke it in his hand and tossed it by.
"Silas has better claim on us you think
Than on his brother? Thirteen little miles
As the road winds would bring him to his
     door.
Silas has walked that far no doubt today.
Why doesn't he go there? His brother's rich,
A somebody—director in the bank."

"He never told us that."

                    "We know it though."   130

"I think his brother ought to help, of course.
I'll see to that if there is need. He ought of
     right
To take him in, and might be willing to—
He may be better than appearances.
But have some pity on Silas. Do you think
If he had any pride in claiming kin
Or anything he looked for from his brother,
He'd keep so still about him all this time?"

"I wonder what's between them."

                    "I can tell you.
Silas is what he is—we wouldn't mind him—   140
But just the kind that kinsfolk can't abide.
He never did a thing so very bad.
He don't know why he isn't quite as good
As anybody. Worthless though he is,
He won't be made ashamed to please his
     brother."

"I can't think Si ever hurt anyone."

"No, but he hurt my heart the way he lay
And rolled his old head on that sharp-edged
     chair-back.

He wouldn't let me put him on the lounge.
You must go in and see what you can do.   150
I made the bed up for him there tonight.
You'll be surprised at him—how much he's
  broken.
His working days are done; I'm sure of it."

"I'd not be in a hurry to say that."

"I haven't been. Go, look, see for yourself.
But, Warren, please remember how it is:
He's come to help you ditch the meadow.
He has a plan. You mustn't laugh at him.
He may not speak of it, and then he may.
I'll sit and see if that small sailing cloud   160

Will hit or miss the moon."

                    It hit the moon.
Then there were three there, making a dim
  row,
The moon, the little silver cloud, and she.

Warren returned—too soon, it seemed to
  her,
Slipped to her side, caught up her hand and
  waited.

"Warren?" she questioned.

            "Dead," was all he answered.

After Apple-Picking (1914)

Here is another instance of the poet—in his persona as farmer—experiencing the onset of evening, darkness, sleep: "Essence of winter sleep is on the night"—and on the poem too. On this occasion, the experience is gentle, even pleasurable, an easy drift into a perhaps brief or perhaps prolonged oblivion.

The rhyme scheme itself in this quietly artful poem contributes to the sense of easy drift and so does the unemphatic variety of line length. A more insistent rhyme scheme—say, *abab cdcd*, and so on, throughout—would have conveyed the sense of experience tightly controlled by a wide-awake participant; but it is just the gradual loss of control and of consciousness that Frost is presenting. A rhyming word may thus wait five lines or more for its faintly whispering echo, and the final word, "sleep," rhymes with a word seven lines above. By this time the poet is so drowsy that rhyme has become nearly inaudible.

My long two-pointed ladder's sticking through
  a tree
Toward heaven still,
And there's a barrel that I didn't fill
Beside it, and there may be two or three
Apples I didn't pick upon some bough.
But I am done with apple-picking now.
Essence of winter sleep is on the night,
The scent of apples: I am drowsing off.
I cannot rub the strangeness from my sight
I got from looking through a pane of glass   10

I skimmed this morning from the drinking
  trough
And held against the world of hoary grass.
It melted, and I let it fall and break.
But I was well
Upon my way to sleep before it fell,
And I could tell
What form my dreaming was about to take.
Magnified apples appear and disappear,
Stem end and blossom end,
And every fleck of russet showing clear.   20
My instep arch not only keeps the ache,
It keeps the pressure of a ladder-round.
I feel the ladder sway as the boughs bend.
And I keep hearing from the cellar bin
The rumbling sound
Of load on load of apples coming in.
For I have had too much
Of apple-picking: I am overtired
Of the great harvest I myself desired.
There were ten thousand thousand fruit to
  touch,   30
Cherish in hand, lift down, and not let fall.
For all
That struck the earth,
No matter if not bruised or spiked with
  stubble,
Went surely to the cider-apple heap
As of no worth.
One can see what will trouble
This sleep of mine, whatever sleep it is.
Were he not gone,
The woodchuck could say whether it's like his   40
Long sleep, as I describe its coming on,
Or just some human sleep.

The Oven Bird (1916)

There is a singer everyone has heard,
Loud, a mid-summer and a mid-wood bird,
Who makes the solid tree trunks sound again.
He says that leaves are old and that for flowers
Mid-summer is to spring as one to ten.
He says the early petal-fall is past
When pear and cherry bloom went down in
    showers

On sunny days a moment overcast;
And comes that other fall we name the fall.
He says the highway dust is over all.   10
The bird would cease and be as other birds
But that he knows in singing not to sing.
The question that he frames in all but words
Is what to make of a diminished thing.

Fire and Ice (1923)

Some say the world will end in fire,
Some say in ice.
From what I've tasted of desire
I hold with those who favor fire.
But if it had to perish twice,

I think I know enough of hate
To say that for destruction ice
Is also great
And would suffice.

Stopping by Woods on a Snowy Evening (1923)

Probably no other of Frost's lyrics, perhaps no
other English-language poem in this century,
has been more often anthologized, dissected, and
commented upon than this poem. Yet it retains
its capacity to engage the reader and, what is
more remarkable, to surprise and even to per-
plex him.

As a single example of the beguilingly unre-
solvable mystery that haunts these sixteen short
lines, take the start of the last stanza. Are the
snow-covered woods lovely *and* dark *and* deep?
Or are they, rather, lovely *because* they are dark
and deep: is the loveliness the product of the
dark depth? In the latter case, the phrase "dark
and deep" is grammatically in apposition to
"lovely," an explanation of it. The punctuation
of the line, at least, does not undercut such an
interpretation.

Whose woods these are I think I know.
His house is in the village though;
He will not see me stopping here
To watch his woods fill up with snow.

My little horse must think it queer
To stop without a farmhouse near
Between the woods and frozen lake
The darkest evening of the year.

He gives his harness bells a shake
To ask if there is some mistake.   10
The only other sound's the sweep
Of easy wind and downy flake.

The woods are lovely, dark, and deep,
But I have promises to keep,
And miles to go before I sleep,
And miles to go before I sleep.

The Onset (1919)

Always the same when on a fated night
At last the gathered snow lets down as white
As may be in dark woods, and with a song
It shall not make again all winter long—
Of hissing on the yet uncovered ground—

I almost stumble looking up and round,
As one, who, overtaken by the end,
Gives up his errand and lets death descend
Upon him where he is, with nothing done
To evil, no important triumph won   10

More than if life had never been begun.

Yet all the precedent is on my side:
I know that winter-death has never tried
The earth but it has failed; the snow may heap
In long storms an undrifted four feet deep
As measured against maple, birch or oak,
It cannot check the Peeper's silver croak;

And I shall see the snow all go down hill
In water of a slender April rill
That flashes tail through last year's withered
  brake
And dead weed like a disappearing snake.
Nothing will be left white but here a birch
And there a clump of houses with a church.

20

[handwritten: natural. moral polarity]

The Need of Being Versed in Country Things (1923)

The house had gone to bring again *[handwritten: soft apocalypse]*
To the midnight sky a sunset glow.
Now the chimney was all of the house that
  stood,
Like a pistil after the petals go.

The barn opposed across the way,
That would have joined the house in flame
Had it been the will of the wind, was left
To bear forsaken the place's name.

No more it opened with all one end
For teams that came by the stony road   10
To drum on the floor with scurrying hoofs
And brush the mow with the summer load.

The birds that came to it through the air
At broken windows flew out and in,
Their murmur more like the sigh we sigh
From too much dwelling on what has been.

Yet for them the lilac renewed its leaf,
And the aged elm, though touched with fire;
And the dry pump flung up an awkward arm;
And the fence post carried a strand of wire.   20

For them there was really nothing sad.
But though they rejoiced in the nest they
  kept,
One had to be versed in country things
Not to believe the phoebes wept.

Once by the Pacific (1928)

This apocalyptic poem is rooted in Frost's memory of his childhood days in San Francisco and, in particular, it seems, of an evening when his father led the family down to Pacific beach after dinner for a walk along the shore. Young Frost got separated from the others, and had time to experience a kind of terror at the roaring waves and threatening skies before he was found.

    That event is here enlarged into one of Frost's recurring visions of the end of the world—with the same God who began the creation by saying "Let There Be Light" now sending down the opposite and final imperative.

The shattered water made a misty din.

Great waves looked over others coming in,
And thought of doing something to the shore
That water never did to land before.
The clouds were low and hairy in the skies,
Like locks blown forward in the gleam of
  eyes.
You could not tell, and yet it looked as if
The shore was lucky in being backed by cliff,
The cliff in being backed by continent;
It looked as if a night of dark intent   10
Was coming, and not only a night, an age.
Someone had better be prepared for rage.
There would be more than ocean-water broken
Before God's last *Put out the Light* was
  spoken.

Acquainted with the Night (1928)

For a change, this characteristic acknowledgment of the darkness surrounding human experience is given a city setting. It is as though Frost were saying that a man can be as solitary

in the darkened streets of a city as on a remote farm on a winter night: the phrase "saddest city *lane*" fuses the two settings.

Frost was a master, among other things, of internal rhyming. Notice how "dropped" part way into line six is echoed by "stopped" further along in the next line. The rhyming actions contain much of the speaker's attitude to, or better his oddly deliberate involvement with, the darkness and the separation of man from man.

I have been one acquainted with the night.
I have walked out in rain—and back in rain.
I have outwalked the furthest city light.

I have looked down the saddest city lane.
I have passed by the watchman on his beat
And dropped my eyes, unwilling to explain.

I have stood still and stopped the sound of feet
When far away an interrupted cry
Came over houses from another street,

But not to call me back or say good-by;   10
And further still at an unearthly height
One luminary clock against the sky

Proclaimed the time was neither wrong nor right.
I have been one acquainted with the night.

Two Tramps in Mud Time (1936)

Frost read this poem at the Rocky Mountain Writers' Conference in Colorado, in the summer of 1935, as part of a general talk on the relation between poetry and social reform. The poem annoyed some members of the audience, as the entire volume in which it later appeared would annoy the liberal and radical literary critics. "It is not the business of the poet to cry for reform," Frost said flatly; and in the poem, he suggested that however pressing the need of the tramps might be for a paying job, he would not offer them his own—since it satisfied both his need and his love. Whether Frost knew it or not, the principle he invoked—"Only where love and need are one . . . is the deed ever really done"—was central to the Fourierite socialist theory about "attractive labor" which had gotten some play in New England a century earlier. But of course, in speaking of the enjoyment of wood-chopping, Frost is finally talking about his vocation as a poet.

Out of the mud two strangers came
And caught me splitting wood in the yard.
And one of them put me off my aim
By hailing cheerily "Hit them hard!"
I knew pretty well why he dropped behind
And let the other go on a way.
I knew pretty well what he had in mind:
He wanted to take my job for pay.

Good blocks of oak it was I split,

As large around as the chopping block;   10
And every piece I squarely hit
Fell splinterless as a cloven rock.
The blows that a life of self-control
Spares to strike for the common good,
That day, giving a loose to my soul,
I spent on the unimportant wood.

The sun was warm but the wind was chill.
You know how it is with an April day
When the sun is out and the wind is still,
You're one month on in the middle of May.   20
But if you so much as dare to speak,
A cloud comes over the sunlit arch,
A wind comes off a frozen peak,
And you're two months back in the middle of March.

A bluebird comes tenderly up to alight
And turns to the wind to unruffle a plume,
His song so pitched as not to excite
A single flower as yet to bloom.
It is snowing a flake: and he half knew
Winter was only playing possum.   30
Except in color he isn't blue,
But he wouldn't advise a thing to blossom.

The water for which we may have to look
In summertime with a witching wand,
In every wheelrut's now a brook,
In every print of a hoof a pond.
Be glad of water, but don't forget
The lurking frost in the earth beneath
That will steal forth after the sun is set
And show on the water its crystal teeth.   40

The time when most I loved my task
These two must make me love it more
By coming with what they came to ask.
You'd think I never had felt before
The weight of an ax-head poised aloft,
The grip on earth of outspread feet,
The life of muscles rocking soft
And smooth and moist in vernal heat.

Out of the woods two hulking tramps
(From sleeping God knows where last night,   50
But not long since in the lumber camps).
They thought all chopping was theirs of right.
Men of the woods and lumberjacks,
They judged me by their appropriate tool.
Except as a fellow handled an ax
They had no way of knowing a fool.

Nothing on either side was said.
They knew they had but to stay their stay
And all their logic would fill my head:
As that I had no right to play   60
With what was another man's work for gain.
My right might be love but theirs was need.
And where the two exist in twain
Theirs was the better right—agreed.

But yield who will to their separation,
My object in living is to unite
My avocation and my vocation
As my two eyes make one in sight.
Only where love and need are one,
And the work is play for mortal stakes,   70
Is the deed ever really done
For Heaven and the future's sakes.

Desert Places (1936)

Again, the darkness and, worse, the emptiness of the human spirit are felt as almost more alarming than the dark emptiness of nature or the universe. Notice how, in the third stanza, the sheer *absence* within the natural setting paradoxically enlarges and intensifies into sheer meaninglessness.

Snow falling and night falling fast, oh, fast
In a field I looked into going past,
And the ground almost covered smooth in snow,
But a few weeds and stubble showing last.

The woods around it have it—it is theirs.
All animals are smothered in their lairs.
I am too absent-spirited to count;
The loneliness includes me unawares.

And lonely as it is that loneliness
Will be more lonely ere it will be less—   10
A blanker whiteness of benighted snow
With no expression, nothing to express.

They cannot scare me with their empty spaces
Between stars—on stars where no human race is.
I have it in me so much nearer home
To scare myself with my own desert places.

Neither Out Far Nor In Deep (1936)

This curiously unsettling poem might gain further meaning by juxtaposing it with Ishmael's remarks at the start of *Moby-Dick* about the sea as "the ungraspable phantom of life." Ishmael gazes far and plunges deep before his adventure is over; the people here observed sit on the shore and look out a little way. They may not see much and they may be looking the wrong way; Frost does not quite say so; his poem accepts them as a portion of human reality.

The people along the sand
All turn and look one way.

They turn their back on the land.
They look at the sea all day.

As long as it takes to pass
A ship keeps raising its hull;
The wetter ground like glass
Reflects a standing gull.

The land may vary more;
But wherever the truth may be—   10
The water comes ashore,
And the people look at the sea.

They cannot look out far.
They cannot look in deep.
But when was that ever a bar
To any watch they keep?

[handwritten margin note: limits of human vision]

Design (1936)

I found a dimpled spider, fat and white,
On a white heal-all, holding up a moth
Like a white piece of rigid satin cloth—
Assorted characters of death and blight
Mixed ready to begin the morning right,
Like the ingredients of a witches' broth—
A snow-drop spider, a flower like a froth,
And dead wings carried like a paper kite.

[handwritten: pattern as meaning?]

What had that flower to do with being white,
The wayside blue and innocent heal-all?   10
What brought the kindred spider to that height,
Then steered the white moth thither in the night?
What but design of darkness to appall?—
If design govern in a thing so small.

Provide, Provide (1936)

Frost's habitual playful irony here seems to deepen into downright cynicism. Yet that quality is so subtly interwoven with clarity of perception and stored up wisdom that one is (enjoyably) at a loss as to whether the cynicism is intensified or palliated by the context.

It operates, anyhow, as a sort of unexpected counterstatement to piety. For example, after the lines "Some have relied on what they knew, /Others on being simply true," one expects some Polonius-like cliché about the rewards that invariably follow being true to one's self and to others. Frost only remarks laconically: "What worked for them might work for you."

Again, to the phrase "Better to go down dignified"—a familiarly pious beginning—Frost adds abruptly: "With boughten friendship at your side." In New England, "boughten" is used to indicate something bought at a store rather than prepared at home—artificial or canned or bottled, rather than freshly made; "boughten" as against homemade butter, for example. So the dignity which Frost dryly urges is made possible only, as it were, by a purchased and pseudo-friendship.

The witch that came (the withered hag)
To wash the steps with pail and rag
Was once the beauty Abishag,

The picture pride of Hollywood.
Too many fall from great and good
For you to doubt the likelihood.

Die early and avoid the fate.
Or if predestined to die late,
Make up your mind to die in state.

Make the whole stock exchange your own!   10
If need be occupy a throne,
Where nobody can call *you* crone.

Some have relied on what they knew,
Others on being simply true.
What worked for them might work for you.

No memory of having starred
Atones for later disregard
Or keeps the end from being hard.

Better to go down dignified
With boughten friendship at your side   20
Than none at all. Provide, provide!

Come In (1942)

Here the stance is that of the poet, surrounded by dusk, peering into the darkness, wondering whether to enter it and become unequivocally a poet of darkness and grief ("lament"). He refuses to do so; but in a typical twist at the end, he also admits that the thrush had not been singing to him to begin with. The bird is oblivious of the man, as nature and its inhabitants so often are in Frost's poetry. The line "Almost like a call to come in" resembles in suggestiveness the lines "Their murmur more like the sigh we sigh/From too much dwelling on what has been" in "The Need of Being Versed in Country Things"; both allusions reflect the human temptation to believe in a communication, a psychic sharing, with nature.

As I came to the edge of the woods,
Thrush music—hark!
Now if it was dusk outside,
Inside it was dark.

Too dark in the woods for a bird
By sleight of wing
To better its perch for the night,

Though it still could sing.

The last of the light of the sun
That had died in the west   10
Still lived for one song more
In a thrush's breast.

Far in the pillared dark
Thrush music went—
Almost like a call to come in
To the dark and lament.

But no, I was out for stars:
I would not come in.
I meant not even if asked,
And I hadn't been.   20

The Most of It (1942)

Here is another and powerful variant on the theme of the relation between the individual and nature. The poem was originally written as a sort of reply to some verses by a former student of Frost's at the University of Michigan, a young man for whom Frost had some real hopes. The initial title was "Making the Most of It," and Frost's point was that a would-be poet living by himself (as his student had been) in the wilderness should make the most of what nature had to offer and not yield to any sentimental distress that human companionship could not be included in the offering.

As an example of making "the most of it," poetically, consider the last five lines of this poem:

He thought he kept the universe alone;
For all the voice in answer he could wake
Was but the mocking echo of his own
From some tree-hidden cliff across the lake.
Some morning from the boulder-broken beach
He would cry out on life, that what it wants

Is not its own love back in copy speech,
But counter-love, original response.
And nothing ever came of what he cried
Unless it was the embodiment that crashed   10
In the cliff's talus on the other side,
And then in the far distant water splashed,
But after a time allowed for it to swim,
Instead of proving human when it neared
And someone else additional to him.
As a great buck it powerfully appeared,
Pushing the crumpled water up ahead,
And landed pouring like a waterfall,
And stumbled through the rocks with horny
     tread,
And forced the underbrush—and that was all. 20

A poet thus responsive to natural phenomena, and capable of catching them with such verbal artistry ("the *crumpled* water"), should not, Frost and the poem imply, waste time lamenting the absence of other satisfactions. But as for the matter of nature's ability or inability to make some response to man, one might compare "The Most of It" with the poem just before.

Away (1962)

Even when announcing his impending departure from this life, at the age of eighty-eight, Frost cannot hold back from his kind of fooling. The playfulness, in this case, consists in a mingling of archaic and colloquial language, the one fancifully elevating the commonplace (the poet's shoe and stocking, for example), the other puncturing the mythic (as of Adam and

Eve). Even his death, at the end, provides Frost with the occasion for a joking but still meaningful threat.

Now I out walking
The world desert,
And my shoe and my stocking
Do me no hurt.

I leave behind
Good friends in town.
Let them get well-wined
And go lie down.

Don't think I leave
For the outer dark   10

Like Adam and Eve
Put out of the Park.

Forget the myth.
There is no one I
Am put out with
Or put out by.

Unless I'm wrong
I but obey
The urge of a song:
"I'm—bound—away!"   20

And I may return
If dissatisfied
With what I learn
From having died.

Realism and the American Dream

THEODORE DREISER (1871–1945)

Theodore Dreiser was the first American writer not of the old American tradition. Though born in America, he was definitely the outsider, the yearner, and that fact determines the basic emotion of his work.

John Paul Dreiser, from Germany, a weaver by trade, had come to America well before the Civil War, gone to Ohio, and there married the illiterate, sixteen-year-old daughter of a Moravian farm family. He seemed on the way to the classic success of the industrious immigrant, but his woolen mill burned, with no insurance on it, and shortly thereafter he was himself injured. After the disaster, John Paul, with eight children, moved on to Terre Haute, Indiana, where, in 1871, Theodore was born. From this time on, the family sank deeper into poverty, and John Paul found refuge in his Catholicism. As the children yearned for the colorful life beyond the range of his tyranny, fear and contempt became, apparently, their dominant reactions to the father whom Dreiser was to describe as "a thin grasshopper of a man, brooding wearily." Less to the influence of Nietzsche and Darwin than to contempt for the father, the son may have owed his admiration for the ruthless superman whom

he was to celebrate in several novels and would sometimes try, in his personal life, to emulate. But to the father, too, the son may, in the complexity of things, have owed his deep ambivalence toward success.

In almost schematic precision, the mother of Theodore was the opposite of John Paul Dreiser: large, maternal, instinctual, feeling that people were hard-driven by life and might be permitted what small compensatory pleasures could be snatched along the way. She was, as Dreiser says in *Dawn*, one of his autobiographical works, "beyond or behind good and evil." Her morality, in any case, was based on sympathy and pity, and it was from her that Dreiser, as a small child, learned those qualities that characterize his work. We even have his account of the birth of pity:

I recall her lounging in a white dressing-sacque, a pair of worn slippers on her feet. In my playful peregrinations I came to her feet and began smoothing her toes. I can hear her now. "See poor mother's shoes? Aren't you sorry she has to wear such worn shoes? See the hole here?" She reached down to show me, and in the wonder and final pity—evoked by the tone of her voice which so long controlled me—I began to examine, growing more and more sorrowful as I did so. And then finally, a sudden, swelling sense of pity that ended in tears.

Sarah Dreiser tried to hold the family of ten children together, but it was a losing battle against poverty and, even, the threat of starvation. One of the sons, after being jailed for forgery, eluded his father's plan to make him into a priest by running off with a minstrel troupe, to return later with a fur overcoat and a gold-headed cane, a successful actor and songwriter bearing the name of Paul Dresser. He took the miserable family to Evansville, Indiana, where they were installed in a cottage owned by his then mistress, the madam of a brothel, whom he was later to celebrate in the song "My Gal Sal."

Evansville was simply a momentary pause on the downward spiral of poverty and humiliation. One sister had been seduced, by a politician in Terre Haute, and when she became pregnant was discarded; that child was stillborn, but when somewhat later another sister bore an illegitimate child, it fell to the care of Sarah Dreiser. Meanwhile, the family was on the move, trying place after place, even Chicago.

During these years Dreiser was a weak, spindly boy, cowardly in the rough and tumble of boyhood. But, as his mother's pet, he felt that, for all his weakness, dreaminess, and ugliness, he was especially chosen to be great, and the refrain of his inner life was "No common man am I." Two teachers, sensing some unusual quality in the young Dreiser, confirmed his dream of himself as one of the chosen; a few years later, when Dreiser had a dead-end job as a stock boy in a hardware store in Chicago, one of them, Mildred Fielding, sought him out and sent him to Indiana University.

At the university Dreiser, poorly prepared, did not do well in his studies and felt himself cut off from the gaiety of student life: the confirmed outsider. The next year he went back

to Chicago; and as Melville said that the deck of a whaler was his Harvard and Yale, so Dreiser might have said the same of the raw and bustling city into which, still in his teens, he was plunged.

In *Dawn*, looking back on the excitement of that world, Dreiser says: "Hail, Chicago! First of the daughters of the new world! Strange illusion of hope and happiness that resounded as a paean by your lake of blue! . . . Of what dreams and songs were your walls and ways compounded!"

But the city had another, and contradictory, face. If it smiled on the strong or the lucky, it was pitiless to those who failed. Later, in *A Book About Myself*, Dreiser would describe that other face as "gross and cruel and mechanical." It is the contrast between these two faces—the face of dream and the face of reality—that provides a profound and recurring drama for his work.

In the beginning it was the face of dream that enthralled Dreiser, and even in a series of menial jobs (in one of which he embezzled twenty-five dollars to buy a snappy overcoat) he saw himself as one of "the real rulers of the world." But the youth who saw himself in that role was of unpromising aspect—height six feet one and a half inches, weight one hundred and thirty-seven pounds, with a squint in the left eye, buck teeth, bulbous irregular features, and no compensatory grace of bearing. His education was miserable. He was, he records, "blazing with sex," a ferocious masturbator, and was consumed by yearnings for wealth, display, and power, as well as by deep social resentments. One way to become a "ruler" was to marry into the charmed circle of power, and so in the deep confusion of dreams of sexuality and those of power there was the image of the girl who was both sensual and rich. Meanwhile, not finding her, Dreiser used such poor girls as he could find to his purpose and callously disposed of each when she had served his need. He was, in other words, forecasting the story of his greatest work, *An American Tragedy*.

No rich girls available, Dreiser chose another way to power and enacted another daydream common to yearning youth; he would be a writer. He got a job on a newspaper, and his fate was sealed.

As a newspaperman, Dreiser had certain glaring deficiencies. For one thing, he was barely literate, with only the faintest notion of syntax. For another, though his imagination fed on fact, he had, as a reporter, a curious contempt for it—as he was to have in other connections all his life, being, to put it nakedly, a born liar. But these deficiencies did not prevent him from being effective at feature stories about the seamy side of city life. That is, his sense of fact was novelistic and not reportorial.

In this decade Dreiser practiced his craft in Chicago, St. Louis, Toledo, Cleveland, Pittsburgh, and New York. He came to know the underside of the cities—skid rows, flophouses, saloons, brothels, theaters (he sometimes served as a drama critic, of sorts), hotels, and night spots. And he knew, too, the mines in Pennsylvania, and the bloody troubles accompanying the rise of organized labor, and how, in Pittsburgh, the money of the steelmasters controlled all life and all news. So he came to ask certain corrosive questions: "Here then was a part of the work of an omnipotent God, who nevertheless tolerated, apparently, a most industrious devil. Why did he do it? Why did nature, when left to itself, devise such astounding slums and human muck heaps?"

In that age of the beginning of modern journalism, when individualism and intellectual curiosity were often a mark of the guild, he met men who read Nietzsche and Machiavelli and introduced him to the doctrine of the superman, a doctrine that seemed to justify the ruthlessness of the Robber Barons like Vanderbilt, Diamond Jim Brady, Carnegie, and Rockefeller, and to justify his own daydream of being a "ruler." He learned, too, about the shocking new scientists and philosophers, such as Darwin, Thomas Huxley, and Herbert Spencer, and his course of reading in them destroyed the last vestige of his religious training, confirming him in his contempt for his fanatical and feckless father. But if Machiavelli's *Prince* and Darwin's theory of the survival of the fittest might flatter his arrogant daydreams, he also found in the new reading ideas that, paradoxically enough, struck a blow at his egotistical sense of power. Spencer, he says, "showed me that I was a chemical atom in a whirl of unknown forces; the realization clouded my mind."

What was Theodore Dreiser to be? A superman or a chemical atom? Was he all will, or was he a will-less pawn in a blind process? In either case, what was the moral content of experience? The torturous answer to such questions does not lie in his work. It *is* his work.

Putting such questions aside for the moment, each of the competing views, that of Nietzsche and that of Spencer, gave him an image for one pole of the modern world. In it certain men were merciless predators, monsters of will. But in it, too, a man might feel himself nothing, without personal meaning or value, totally alienated. In the end, even the successful predator might come to this. These competing images lie behind the fiction Dreiser was to write.

We must not assume, however, that, in any simple sense, Dreiser took his ideas from Machiavelli, Spencer, Huxley, and Darwin. Reading them merely gave form to ideas that Dreiser had, year after year, been living into. The reading that did affect him more directly was Balzac, who, in his massive fictions about the life of Paris, gave Dreiser a new sense of the cities that he himself knew. He was not yet a novelist, but Balzac gave him a way to look at his cities, a new meaning to the lowly reporter's dreary routine of "police and city hall." But Balzac did an even greater service. Dreiser says that Balzac's portraits of "the brooding, seeking, ambitious beginner in life" were, simply, himself. Balzac not only made Dreiser see the world; he also made him see himself in that world. Dreiser's only story was always to be that of "the brooding, seeking, ambitious beginner." But he was to put that story of the young man derived from Balzac in the context derived from Spencer: the dream of glory was dreamed in a world where the dreamer might wake to find that he himself was nothing.

Meanwhile, Dreiser became a magazine editor and a writer of articles for the best-known magazines. It did not matter that the articles were hastily worked up, full of errors and plagiarisms, and miserably written; he was making money. He was making enough money, in fact, to marry a fiancée whom he had long since ceased to desire and with whom matrimony was, as he put it, merely the "pale flame of duty."

No match could have been more inappropriate. Sara White, nicknamed "Jug," was a pretty, well-brought-up, conventional woman, raised on a prosperous farm in Missouri, somewhat older than the bridegroom. Dreiser was, by his own account, incapable of loving anybody except, perhaps, the mother whose worn shoes he had once caressed and who was long since dead. Still outraged at old deprivations, haunted by a sense of insufficiency and inferiority, suspicious, totally self-centered, brutally selfish, and fearful of impotence, Dreiser had long since found that only a stream of different women could solace his mortally wounded ego. In the end Sara, whose name was, ironically, the same as that of the dead mother, took on the mother's role. She served him, too, by correcting and rewriting his work; for she had been a schoolteacher and knew all about grammar. But she also served his work in another way, as the wife Angela Blue in his autobiographical novel *The "Genius,"* and in a more shadowy way as the model for Roberta in *An American Tragedy.*

In the summer of 1899, Dreiser wrote the words *Sister Carrie* at the top of a sheet of paper. He had no idea what the story was to be, but he knew the old yearnings of his sisters and how they had been caught by the glitter of a world beyond them. So we see Carrie, a country girl on a train, on her way to Chicago for work, full of unformulated desires and with no firm moral principles, and see her meet the drummer Drouet, a cheap ladykiller in flashy clothes. Dreiser remembered not only his sisters but himself and his own enchantment by Chicago and his own experience as the yearning "beginner," the outsider suffering the primal pain of wanting and not having.

Carrie, after a dreary round of job-hunting, with the sense of lostness and depersonalization

in the swarming city, is easy prey to Drouet. So, later, with her blind aspiration toward something more glittering and more real, she is an easy prey to Hurstwood—the manager of a saloon, a "way-up, swell place," as Drouet puts it—who stands at a higher level than Drouet, closer to some center of power, wealth, and joy that poor Carrie cannot actually conceive but merely senses.

But the great Hurstwood is, in a way, a victim, too—merely one of Spencer's "chemical atoms." Even when Hurstwood takes ten thousand dollars from the safe of his employers (an episode based on the fact that the lover of one of Dreiser's sisters had stolen from his employer and fled with the girl), the event is, in a sense, an accident. He is debating the theft, when the lock of the safe clicks. Had he pushed the door? He does not know. Is the slamming of the door an accident or an alibi, a trap of fate or a masking of the unconscious decision to steal? In *An American Tragedy*, that deeper study of guilt, we shall find the same ambiguity in the murder of Roberta.

It can reasonably be held that this sense of moral ambiguity is central for *Sister Carrie*, as it is central for *An American Tragedy*. In one perspective the whole story of Carrie and her lovers is a study of the mechanical process of success and failure—a process that to Dreiser appears as unrelated to morality as a chemical experiment. Hurstwood sinks to ruin, Carrie rises to be a theatrical star, but success and failure are both aspects of a morally neutral process.

Sex, love, appetite, loyalty—all feelings seem to shrivel to meaninglessness before the cold objective law of success and failure. Stage by stage, we observe Hurstwood on the "road downward" that "has but few landings and level places," and, stage by stage, we see Carrie pass from the first moment of boredom to indifference, then to disgust, to contempt and cruelty, to a coldly mechanical act of desertion, and, in the end, into a blank forgetfulness. In other words, Hurstwood is, bit by bit, robbed of reality. Failure is a kind of death that precedes the mortal death, and the mortal death will be, ironically enough, merely the shadow of the earlier death. Several years before *Sister Carrie* was written, in an editorial in his first magazine *Ev'ry Month*, while commenting on the current money panic and the suffering entailed by it, Dreiser had said: "In this world generally failure opens wide the gates to mortal onslaught, and the invariable result is death." It is this brutal editorial, with its theme of vulgarized Darwinism and the idea of a "psychosomatic" relation between the hard world of economic competition and the physiological fate, that finds a dramatic projection in poor Hurstwood—especially in the night scene in which, having decided to commit suicide, he goes past the theater to take a last look at Carrie's name in "incandescent fire" and, continuing on his way, slips and falls in the snow outside the splendor of the Waldorf, where she now lives.

Long since, in the long process of the decay of their relation, both Carrie and Hurstwood have recognized the law of success and failure. From the opening of the novel Carrie has, in fact, been instinctively aware of the mechanism of success. Dreiser calls her a "little soldier of fortune," and that is literally what she is, an adventuress with an eye to the main chance, as undistracted by sex or love as by moral scruples. When Drouet gives Carrie her first pretty clothes, Dreiser presents, for example, a little scene of remarkable psychological insight. Admiring herself, Carrie caught "her little red lip with her teeth and felt her first thrill of power," and here the biting of her own lip, with its charge of narcissistic sexuality, is fused with the "thrill of power." And at the moment of her marriage to Hurstwood, Dreiser is quite specific: "There was no great passion in her, but the drift of things and this man's proximity created a semblance of affection." Thus what Dreiser called "material" success could absorb all other aspects of life. And here we may recall that the success-mad Dreiser could say that he had never loved anybody except perhaps his mother, that he had loved women merely in the "abstract."

The feelings of sex, love, and affection do not prevail against the cold mechanism of success and failure. But even beyond this fact, and beyond the pathos of yearning, of wanting and not having, there is another range of feeling in the novel, an ambivalent criticism of success, even a rejection of it, a conviction that success is bound to be empty and meaningless, an unformulated awareness that success is sought so desperately only as a compensation for some irremediable deprivation or failure, and that no success can ever be a surrogate for what has been denied. So we find Dreiser, even in the full tide of his drive for success, suffering the shock of the encounter with Herbert Spencer, and saying of himself: "Up to this time there had been a blazing and unchecked desire to get on, the feeling that in doing so we did get somewhere; now in its place was the definite conviction that spiritually one got nowhere. . . ."

There is, then, a pathos of success as well as of failure, and as Hurstwood exemplifies one, so Carrie exemplifies the other. This contrast provides, structurally, the poles of the action. As Hurstwood has been doomed to failure, so Carrie has been doomed to success, and at the end we see her in the apartment at the Waldorf:

Oh, Carrie, Carrie! Oh, blind strivings of the human heart! Onward, onward, it saith, and where beauty leads, there it follows. Whether it be the tinkle of a lone sheep bell o'er some quiet landscape, or the glimmer of beauty in sylvan places, or the show of soul in some passing eye, the heart knows and makes answer, following. It is when the feet weary and hope seems in vain that the heartaches and the longings arise. Know, then, that for you is neither surfeit nor content. In your rocking-chair, by your window dreaming, shall you long alone. In your rocking-chair, by your window, shall you dream such happiness as you may never feel.

Carrie has everything, and yet has nothing, and the rocking chair—a motion without progress, life spent in mere repetition, a hypnotic dream without content—is a perfect image of the success that "got nowhere." It is the image of the pathos of success—and to sit rocking by the hour was one of Dreiser's characteristic habits. To sit rocking while over and over again he would fold and unfold a handkerchief.

This last scene of Carrie in her chair is, then, an image of Dreiser. He was a powerful artist, but his artistic ambition was painfully intermingled with his ambition for money and fine clothes; in fact, he often saw his literary work as only an instrument to satisfy his grossest aspirations. It is only natural, then, that success of the artist should seem as fragile and infected as that of Cowperwood, the hero of Dreiser's future trilogy about high finance, or any real-life Robber Baron. Let us remember that it is as an "artist" that Carrie succeeds, and it is an artist who sits in the rocking chair that goes nowhere. Is Carrie the image, after all, not of artist-as-artist but of artist-as-golddigger?

Sister Carrie, though a historical and social document and a record of the psychology of Dreiser, is also a vivid and absorbing work of art. In dealing with a novelist, the most obvious question is what kind of world stimulates his imagination. For Dreiser this was the world he lived in and the world he *was*, and by accepting as fully as possible this limitation, he enlarged, willy-nilly, by a kind of historical accident if you will, the range of American literature. The same kind of compulsive veracity that made him record such details of his own life as masturbation and theft made him struggle to convert into fiction substances of experience at both the social and the personal level that had not been earlier absorbed.

The kind of realism that is associated with William Dean Howells had little relation to the depths that Dreiser inhabited. What was shocking in *Sister Carrie* was not only Dreiser's failure to punish vice and reward virtue, but the implication that vice and virtue are, in themselves, mere accidents, mere irrelevancies in the process of human life, and that the world is a great machine, morally indifferent. Ultimately, what shocked readers of Dreiser was not so much the things that he presented as the fact that he himself was *not* shocked by them.

Sister Carrie introduced into American fiction a novelty of method as well as of material and attitude, but the method was generated out of the material so spontaneously that it scarcely seems a method at all, merely a natural event.

At first glance, the novel appears to be simply a loose chronicle, the kind of narrative furthest removed from the well-made novel of a carefully wrought plot with close logical interreactions and an increasing intensity that moves to a summarizing climax. But Dreiser, even in violating the logic of the well-made plot, has developed a deeper thematic logic, with psychological grounding, to give both thrust and structure to the work. If we analyze the psychological and thematic significance of the key elements in Carrie's career, from the first meeting with Drouet to the scene of the rocking chair, we find that we have a very compelling thrust and a coherent structure: Carrie's movement upward, like Hurstwood's movement downward, sets up its characteristic suspense, and at the same time the movement is marked by stages that convert chronological flow into closely articulated structure. Furthermore, the two movements are in structural counterpoint, each being enriched and reinforced by ironic parallels and contrasts in the other, these parallels and contrasts constituting a dialectical progression, a development of the thematic logic. Further, the appearance of Drouet at the beginning and at the end serves to bracket the main action in a simple structural fashion; but Drouet serves a deeper purpose as well, offering a counterpoint to both lives, to the high success of Carrie and the ruin of Hurstwood. He, Drouet, is the casual by-product, the drifter on the tide of things, significant in his insignificance, pitiful in his psychological and animal complacencies. To sum up, the apparently casual structure of mere chronicle is set against a very firm and complex structure of thematic contrast and parallelism and in the tension between these two principles of structure—the narrative and the thematic— the vital rhythm of the novel is defined.

Frank Norris, the brilliantly successful young novelist who was an editor at Doubleday, Page and Company, had used all his powers to persuade others in the firm of the great merit of *Sister Carrie*, but when Mrs. Doubleday finally read the book the firm tried to renege on the contract to publish it. Dreiser held to his legal rights. But the novel sold only 456 copies and netted the author only $68.40.

The publishers, however reluctantly, had fulfilled their contract, but in Dreiser's paranoid imaginings, the failure of *Sister Carrie* was the result of a deliberate conspiracy, and his romantic tale of high-handed and purblind abuse became the generally accepted version. *Sister Carrie* became a *cause célèbre*. It became a battle cry of the young and a symbol of the new freedom.

Meanwhile, in spite of the critical (but not financial) success of the novel in England, Dreiser fell into a frightful depression. He found it difficult to write or place articles. He did have a small advance against a projected novel, *Jennie Gerhardt*, but he could not get on with it. A period of wandering ensued. Relations with his wife went from bad to worse, and finally he sent her back to her family, returning penniless to New York. He was near starvation and felt himself verging toward insanity or suicide. All the terrors of failure that had been projected into Hurstwood were now his own fate.

But his brother Paul, by a chance encounter, found him and put him on a "health farm" to rebuild his strength and morale. In spite of fits of depression, Dreiser was soon successful beyond his wildest dreams, not as a writer but as a magazine editor, first for pulp publications and later for the Butterick publications, the *Delineator*, the *New Idea Woman's Magazine*, and the *Designer*. These were "women's magazines," devoted to fashion, household concerns, child-rearing, and society, with a smattering of stories and articles; but all this was merely bait, the real function of the Butterick publications being to sell dress patterns.

"Success is what counts in the world," Dreiser had once written in an editorial, "and it is little matter how success is won." With Machiavelli, Dreiser recognized, too, that not only the strength of the lion may be necessary for success, but also the cunning of the fox; so, as the fox, he wrote a statement of the editorial policy for the best-known of these magazines:

The *Delineator's* message is human better-ment. Its appeal is to the one great harmonizing force of humanity—womanhood. To sustain it, to broaden it, to refine it, to inspire it, is our aim. Our theme is one that a woman may carry into her house, her church and her social affairs—the theme of the ready smile, the theme of the ungrudged helping hand.

He added that the purpose of the *Delineator* was to strengthen every woman "in her moral fight for righteousness in the world."

To gain success Dreiser gagged at nothing, not the Tiny Wren Club organized to sell patterns for doll clothes, not articles on the "joys of motherhood," not the Santa Claus Association, not even the campaign against the Teddy Bear undertaken because bears, unlike dolls, don't need dress patterns ("Bring your babies back to dollies or you will have weaned the grown-ups of the future from the babies that will never be"). He did not even gag at the fiction selected in strict conformity with his editorial instructions: "We like sentiment, we like humor, we like realism, but it must be tinged with sufficient idealism to make it all of a truly uplifting character. . . . We cannot admit stories which deal with false or immoral relations. . . ." Meanwhile, Dreiser was trying to seduce the seventeen-year-old daughter of a female member of his staff.

In October, 1910, thanks to the outraged mother of the young girl whom he called "Flower-face," Dreiser was summarily fired, and the firing turned the editor back into a novelist. Now he could, at last, get back to *Jennie Gerhardt*. Seated at a desk made from the old rosewood piano that had belonged to his now dead brother Paul, an object that could evoke his early visions of success and all the tangle of envy, admiration, and resentment in his attitude toward the successful brother, he drove himself mercilessly. The novel was finished in January, 1911. It was published the following October.

Jennie Gerhardt is, in a deep and complex way, a parallel to *Sister Carrie*. Like *Sister Carrie*, though with greater fidelity in detail, it echoes the story of the Dreiser family, in which two daughters had borne illegitimate children. Jennie, like Carrie, comes from a poor family and, like Carrie, enters, by seduction, the glittering world of wealth and privilege. But more important than such direct parallels are the parallels by contrast, for Jennie is a sort of mirror image of Carrie, everything the same, but reversed. Dreiser had set out to rework the same basic materials but in the process developed, consciously or unconsciously, a contrasting order of intellectual and emotional values, of new and contradictory possibilities of meaning.

For example, though Jennie enters the world of wealth by seduction, she, unlike Carrie, is not seduced by the glitter of wealth. She is no golddigger, and the men who are drawn to her —the middle-aged Senator Brander and the rich young man Lester Kane—are, in significant contrast to Drouet and Hurstwood, drawn by some intuition of Jennie's capacity for sympathy, unselfishness, and love. Though Jennie is so far beneath him in the social scale, Senator Brander, when Jennie is carrying his child, is happily preparing to marry her and is only prevented by death; and later, Lester Kane, even after he knows the paternity of the child, feels a deep satisfaction in the day-to-day life with Jennie. Sexuality is the appeal fraudulently offered by the cold-hearted Carrie, but sexuality is only a component of the appeal offered by Jennie; the "capacity for deep feeling" is what Senator Brander finds in her, and that is what Lester Kane finds too.

This is not to say that Jennie is unaware of the "material" base of life. She knows, as only the poor can know and as Dreiser knew, the value of money, but she can translate that value into other values—into what money can mean for the good of those she loves, her mother, her brothers and sisters, and even her father, for whom, in spite of his tyrannical and bigoted nature, she has feeling. In the end, when Robert Kane, Lester's "successful" and conventional brother, gives him the choice of marrying Jennie, with a modest guaranteed income, or leaving her, again with a guarantee of security for her, to resume his place in the world, it is Jen-

nie who forces the issue. What is remarkable is that Dreiser can portray her generosities without making her into a saccharine saint. She makes her renunciation with full awareness of the cost, but with no masochistic satisfactions, self-pity, or self-righteousness; Dreiser conveys this by offering such acts as a natural reflex of her full nature, not isolated, we might say, as individual moral decisions.

There is another factor to be considered here. In *Sister Carrie* we have referred to the recognition of the merciless "natural" law of success and failure. Here, in a different context and with a different tonality, Dreiser shows that Jennie also recognizes in the workings of society such a law, or doom, that can contravene love, devotion, and justice. In one perspective, her renunciation is a recognition of this law, a recognition early prepared for when, in Egypt, Jennie and Lester encounter his old flame, who, as Jennie, with painful clairvoyance, recognizes, is the proper wife for him; and this objective recognition works to disinfect her renunciation of sentimentality.

At this point it is instructive to recall that in the first version of the novel, the end was a happy marriage for Lester and Jennie, with Jennie's daughter well and happy too. We have no way of knowing whether Dreiser had become the victim of his own editorials for the *Delineator* or whether, as one of his friends suggested, he had tacked on the happy and moral ending to placate the reviewers who had attacked *Sister Carrie*; but in any case, Dreiser soon realized that the happy ending violated the logic of his material and its pervasive feeling. So Lester obeys Jennie and marries the appropriate and quite doting wife, and sinks into a life of expensively coddled torpor, the life of unreality from which he had fled to Jennie. Jennie is, however, called to visit him on his deathbed, and in a scene of restrained but masterfully rendered emotional implications, the meaning of their relation is summarized. After his death, Jennie, veiled, is at the railroad station to see the casket loaded on the baggage car to be carried back to Cleveland; she lives on, only to lose her daughter and then find solace in an adopted child and

in her overflowing sense of sympathetic fulfillment in life. As *Sister Carrie* tells a sardonic
tale of the pitilessly blank world dominated by
the two obsessions of success and failure, so the
story of Jennie is concerned with the discovery
of meaning beyond that world, a meaningfulness that, even in the face of failure, may be
affirmed in the individual's intuition of life as
a human community of sympathy and compassion.

Jennie Gerhardt is, in one sense, the most
personal of Dreiser's novels. Here the man
who is obsessed with sexuality and unable to
regard a woman as other than a physiological
convenience, the man who, by his own admission, was incapable of love, sets out to write a
novel about the definition of love. Here the
man who is obsessed with success, haunted by
the fear of failure and an irremediable anxiety
about money, hag-ridden by vanity, and tortured by suspicion sets out to write a novel
about an inner peace achieved, outside the
world of success and failure, by a triumph of
spirit. In other words, the deepest drama of the
novel is the confrontation of the self of the
novelist and the anti-self; and herein lies its
deep paradox. If Jennie first appears as the outsider, the yearner, in the end she is the insider,
secure in a charmed place to which the inhabitants of the loud world cannot penetrate. If
Dreiser is characteristically the poet of the poor
and deprived who yearn to enter the glittering
world, in this novel he changes his role to become another and more deprived kind of outsider, and the deep yearning that permeates the
novel is that of the worldling who can dream
the secret of peace but cannot enter where it
abides.

Jennie Gerhardt, in spite of prolixity and the
frequent grossness of the writing, received considerable acclaim. Mencken, for instance, pronounced it the best American novel, "with the
Himalayan exception of *Huck Finn*." But even
if the sales were a distinct disappointment, Dreiser had already begun work on two more novels.

The books that Dreiser already had under
way illustrate a deep cleft in his nature. *Sister
Carrie*, delineating the blankness of the world
obsessed with success and failure, and *Jennie
Gerhardt*, affirming a spiritual meaning beyond
that world, can be thought of as written under the
aegis of the mother, as the negative and positive
aspects of an inspiration derived from her. But
the two books that Dreiser now had in mind,
The "Genius" and *The Financier*, affirming the
values of the practical world and advertising the
grandeur of the superman, can be thought of as
written under the aegis of the father. That is,
in revulsion from, in contempt of, the bigoted,
sex-hating failure that was John Paul Dreiser,
the son now proceeded to celebrate untrammeled sexuality and the ruthless pursuit of success; and here he projects the cherished image
of himself as conqueror, with echoes of Balzac,
Spencer, and Darwin, and of the incantation
of the boyhood dreams, "No common man am
I."

The "Genius" was a thinly disguised version
of Dreiser's ambitious career, his marriage, his
promiscuous love affairs, of the passion he had
for the young girl Thelma Cudlipp, and of the
vengeful ruin visited upon him by her mother.
Though still married, and living with his wife,
Dreiser made the new novel a justification of
the freedom the "genius" sought from the restricting conventionality and stupidity of a
small-town girl, and in the process gave a cruelly
embarrassing account of the intimate details of
his relationship to Jug, from the early infatuation through the dreary sense of obligation that
led to marriage, on through the long sequel of
betrayals and reconciliations. This sadistic exercise was performed, literally, in his wife's
daily presence. Under her unwitting gaze, Dreiser was contriving a time bomb to explode some
day and settle the hash of Sara White, the silly
prig who hadn't been willing to go to bed with
him until she had the ring on. He was going to
settle the hash of Thelma Cudlipp, too, whom
in real life he called Flower-face and who in fiction retains that name, and who never got to
bed with him at all. And we may surmise that
all this business of settling hash and all the
elements of self-indulgence and self-vindication

that appear so nakedly in *The "Genius"* constitute one of the reasons, perhaps the basic reason,
for the book's being the crashing bore that it is.
It helps to defeat the very purpose of fiction—
to create and explore a world. *The "Genius"*
was personal and reportorial in a disastrous way.

The other novel that Dreiser was projecting
was personal only in the deep way that all fiction must be personal in order to be good. *The
Financier*, the first of Dreiser's trilogy about
business, was, in fact, grounded in journalism,
and though Dreiser may have been a most untrustworthy reporter, he did have to a superlative degree the journalistic instinct for the hot
topic. Both *Sister Carrie* and *Jennie Gerhardt*
touched nerves that led deep into American life,
and the period when Dreiser was beginning his
career as a journalist and brooding toward his
massive work about business was the period when
that subject was becoming more and more
the storm center of public concern.

The money panics of the age, the rapacity of
the Robber Barons, the increasing violence of
the labor wars, the growth of the great slums,
the fear of the middle class that, with the concentration of wealth on the one hand and the
threat of socialism on the other, they would be
liquidated—all these factors led to protest and
reform, to Populism, William Jennings Bryan,
Teddy Roosevelt, the Sherman Anti-Trust Act.
A part of this impulse was manifested in the
work of the "muckrakers," which found its first
great document in H. D. Lloyd's *Wealth
Against Commonwealth*, in 1894. This was, too,
the period when William Dean Howells, editor
of the *Atlantic*, had caught, under the influence
of Tolstoi, the passion for social justice, and the
period of the magazines of exposé, such as the
Forum, the *Cosmopolitan*, *Muncey's*, and *Mc-
Clure's*. It was the period of the rise of Thor-
stein Veblen, Jacob Riis, Jack London, Ida
Tarbell, Lincoln Steffens, Upton Sinclair, and
Gustavus Myers, with his *History of the Great
American Fortunes*. And as early as 1875 there
had been a novel about a Robber Baron, Jim
Fisk, in Josiah Gilbert Holland's *Sevenoaks*.
Whatever originality and significance lies in

Dreiser's trilogy does not lie in the fact that
he saw business as a crucial concern of American life and as a threat to democracy. This had
been clearly demonstrated, as we have said, by a
great body of writing. Dreiser's originality and
significance lie in his ability to see under—and
over—what reformers, muckrakers, and politicians saw, to relate the world of business to
other elements and attitudes in American life
and to the philosophy of an age, and finally to
inform the tale of American business with a
deeply complex and contradictory personal emotion. The descriptive title "A Trilogy of Desire"
that Dreiser early gave to his projected work
hints at the nature of what he dreamed.

The trilogy—*The Financier, The Titan*, and
The Stoic—was projected as a fictional version
of the life of Charles Tyson Yerkes, who, just
after the Civil War, began his career as a manipulator of the streetcar system of Philadelphia,
made a fortune, crashed, and went to prison,
and then proceeded to fantastic triumphs in
Chicago, New York, and London. He was, too,
a collector of art and of women; and to arrange
the legal and financial details for the dismissal,
usually amicable, of mistresses or casual ladies
of whom he had tired, he retained a staff of
lawyers at the annual cost of $150,000. If the
fictional Eugene Witla, in *The "Genius,"* had
been a projection of Dreiser's image of himself,
that of the real Yerkes gave an even grander
scope for self-indulgent daydreams of identification with the Nietzschean superman. In fact,
when in 1911 Dreiser explained to the British
publisher Grant Richards his need to go to
Europe to finish preparation for *The Financier*,
he did not talk about getting a sense of the
background for the European adventures of
Yerkes, but of his desire to move in the same
circles and, prospectively, to know the same
kind of women who had caught his hero's fancy
—in short, to relive the life of Yerkes. In the
daydream thus projected, the cold logic of fact
—the difference between his poverty and the
fabulous wealth of Yerkes, between his stumbling uncouthness and the superman's worldly

and hypnotic self-assurance—meant nothing. The sense of identification was too complete to admit any such awareness.

The superman whom Dreiser saw in his hero —and in himself—was justified as a creature of nature, an exemplification of Darwinist theory: "Nature is unscrupulous! She takes her own way, regardless of the suffering caused, and the fittest survive." He longed, he said, to see a race "who like Niccolò Machiavelli could look life in the face," and saw his own role as that of an awakener who would make such a race possible. As a corollary, he saw the great businessmen as conscious of the "poetry" and "romance" of their work.

If Dreiser was willing, by his identification with the new breed of businessmen beyond good and evil, to take the responsibility for their deeds, he would, at the same time, give those deeds a moral justification. On the whole, he affirmed, these predators "have been a blessing to the rest of us," and their services absolve them from blame. "It's because of Vanderbilt that we can now ride to Chicago in eighteen hours. It's because of Rockefeller that we get oil at the present price." In general, he said, "America is great not because of, but in spite of, her pieties and her moralities"—great, because the great businessmen had been strong enough to "do as they pleased."

The age was, in fact, shot through with deep ambivalences toward the Robber Barons. We have already observed the doubleness of Mark Twain; and even such famous muckrakers as Ida Tarbell and Lincoln Steffens had more than a sneaking admiration for the villains in the story. In Justice Holmes, who had read Herbert Spencer as a student at Harvard and not as a cub reporter in a newspaper office, and whose intellectual history is so central to the age, we find a similar split of feeling. On the one hand, there was the Holmes adored by the liberals, but, on the other, there was the Holmes who could enunciate the grim social Darwinism of a famous letter to Sir Frederick Pollock: "I think that the sacredness of human life is a purely municipal ideal of no validity outside the juris-diction . . . every society rests on the death of men."

Clearly, Holmes would have understood the meaning of the parabolic moment in *The Financier* when the boy Frank Cowperwood stares into the tank where a lobster and a squid are exhibited and where, at last, the lobster eats the squid. Young Frank ponders the event: "Things lived on each other—that was it. Lobsters lived on squids and other things. What lived on lobsters? Men, of course! Sure, that was it! And what lived on men?" Frank finds the answer: "Sure, men lived on men."

The boy Frank, having learned his basic lesson by staring into the fishmonger's tank, and an important corollary in the local brothels, is ready for life, and the first novel of the "Trilogy of Desire" is a record of his precocious conquest of the streetcar system of Philadelphia up to the time when, in 1871, as a backlash of the Chicago fire, his speculations with public funds are revealed and he serves a short sentence in the penitentiary (as did Dreiser's model Yerkes). "He was not," Dreiser says of Cowperwood in the early stages of his career, "a man who was inherently troubled with conscientious scruples. At the same time he still believed himself financially honest." But a little later this analysis is modified and elaborated: ". . . by this time his financial morality had become special and local in its character. He did not think it was wise for any one to steal anything from anybody where the act of taking or profiting was directly and plainly considered stealing. . . . Morality varied, in his mind at least, with conditions, and climates." The word "right" for Cowperwood, as for Holmes in his role not of man but philosopher, might be considered a matter of "municipal jurisdiction," and the municipality in which Cowperwood operated was the politically corrupt Philadelphia of the Gilded Age. If he happens to wind up in the penitentiary, that is little more than an industrial accident.

Cowperwood's spirit is no more broken than shamed by the accident. If anything, it is confirmed in both its sense of high destiny and the philosophy that was becoming more explicit as he inspected the logic of experience, a philosophy to be summed up by the motto, "I satisfy myself." Pardoned, he leaves the penitentiary, steeled for new struggles; and when, on September 13, 1873, the great Philadelphia firm of Jay Cooke & Company fails and the panic is on, Cowperwood knows that this is his moment, and with lethal certainty proceeds to batten on the general ruin. He is now ready, at the end of the first novel, to move to Chicago, where the sky is the limit.

Along with the financial education of the hero goes his *éducation sentimentale*. After the women of the brothels have begun to pall, the young Cowperwood develops a passion for the widow of a middle-aged friend—a woman five years his senior, but young-looking, tall and shapely, of pale waxen complexion, gray-blue eyes, and a face "artistically narrow," and with a calm, sometimes brooding dignity, a dignity that Cowperwood later discovers to spring from stupidity. With Lillian Semple it was, first, her seeming indifference, or even the dignity, that fired his combative instinct. That "pale, uncertain, lymphatic body extracted a form of dynamic energy from him." He gets the woman, builds her a new house, has a son in whom he takes pleasure (the "idea of self-duplication" being almost acquisitive), but his growing interest in art and his ambitions are far beyond her imagination.

Then Aileen Butler appears. She is only a girl, the daughter of the restricted Catholic household of a crude Irish contractor who has become a political power, but Cowperwood sees in her the capacity for passion, the strength of will, the deep contempt for convention, and the sensibility and intelligence to match his own qualities. She becomes his mistress, and even in his apparent ruin, she retains, unlike his wife, her faith in his great destiny. When he leaves for Chicago at the end of the novel, it is with the understanding that she will join him there, to become his wife as soon as he is free.

The Financier would seem, then, to have, in its own way, a happy ending. The superman has found the appropriate mate to share his labors and conquests. But with *The Titan* it does not work out quite this way. The labors are performed, and the conquests are made—at least Cowperwood acquires a great fortune, becomes a national figure, and moves on to New York, where he builds a mansion crammed with his collection of art. But in Chicago his name has become synonymous with political corruption, and in New York, no more than in Chicago, can he breach the inner defenses of society. At the end of *The Titan*, he is still the outsider, the marauder, now preparing to attack the citadel of Europe.

Aileen, however, is no longer significant in his life. A dozen women, all kinds, have passed through his hands, each captured by the hard, assertive, "glazed" blue stare. Aileen is still married to him and still, even in her outrage, in love with him; but when, by chance, she sees him with the latest of his loves, a young girl at whom he looks with "soul-hunger," that look drives her to a protracted orgy with a man for whom she cares nothing. Later, when Cowperwood declares that the "thing I used to feel I cannot feel any more," she attempts suicide. Even then Cowperwood remains unmoved.

Now, in a moment of political reverse, the girl at whom he had stared with "soul-hunger" but on whom he had not yet laid a finger, comes to him. She is, he feels, the woman who will sum up life for him, who is the "ultimate end of fame, power, vigor."

She steps into his arms:

"Berenice!" he smothered her cheeks and hair.

"Not so close, please. And there aren't to be any other ladies, unless you want me to change my mind."

"Not another one, as I hope to keep you. You will share everything I have. . . ."

For answer—

How strange are realities as opposed to illusion!

So this novel, like the previous one, seems to have a happy ending—one here eminently fit, except for the small matter of a legal ceremony, for the Butterick publications.

There is, however, a brief epilogue in which appears the following passage:

Anew the old urgent thirst for life, and only its partial quenchment. In Dresden, a palace for one woman, in Rome a second for another. In London a third for his beloved Berenice, the lure of beauty ever in his eye. The lives of two women wrecked, a score of victims despoiled; Berenice herself weary, yet brilliant, turning to others for recompense for her lost youth.

In one sense, "In Retrospect," as the epilogue to *The Titan* is called, renders *The Stoic* superfluous. For the remaining years of Cowperwood's life, *The Stoic* adds little beyond documentation, drearily repetitious, of his financial operations in London and of the love affairs forecast in the epilogue of *The Titan*. On the verge of success in his last great foray, Cowperwood dies and his fortune is picked to pieces in litigations, as though by jackals—providing symbolic balance to the fact that, long ago in Philadelphia, it had been founded on the ruin of Jay Cooke. Cowperwood's projects of an art museum and a charity hospital go unfulfilled.

The trilogy was massively researched. But the research indicates, too, a significant aspect of the fiction. Cowperwood is not a fictional creation based on Yerkes. Rather he is, insofar as Dreiser could make him, the image of Yerkes. And this fact of fidelity to historical fact sets the trilogy off, paradoxically, from the ordinary historical novel; for the historicity of the ordinary historical novel lies in situation and decor into which the actors, with their "perennial humanity," are introduced.[1] But Cowperwood, the Yerkes-image, is not introduced into historical situation and decor merely to act out his "perennial humanity"; he is there because he himself *is* the history; he is his own validation.

Here we may ask why Dreiser, after considering other models, chose Yerkes and not Vanderbilt, Frick, Fisk, Brady, Carnegie, or Rocke-

feller—one of the men who now bulk so much larger than Yerkes in our consciousness. But our consciousness is not Dreiser's—nor that of the general public at the time Dreiser was meditating his work; for the dramatic quality of Yerkes's manipulations gave them something of the popular interest of a sporting event. Furthermore, the death of Yerkes came at a dramatic point in his career and was an event that, in its massive and simple irony, came ready-made for the folk-consciousness.

But most importantly of all, Yerkes gave Dreiser the combination of factors he needed for his projected work: the strongly individualized man fulfilling himself in the realms of finance, love, and art. And this collocation was fundamental for Dreiser's conception; it constitutes, as we shall later see, another kind of trilogy of desire. For Dreiser was undertaking to reveal a more dire secret than the muckraker had ever suspected; he was undertaking to give the true "inside" story of the "financier," to show the workings of his mind and soul, to show how his acquisitiveness, sex, and "art-dreams" flowed into one another, to place him not only in society but in nature, in the economy of the universe. If Dreiser was to be a muckraker, he was to be a cosmic muckraker. To achieve this end he needed to analyze the most perfectly formed specimen of "financier" available.

As such a specimen, Cowperwood is strongly outlined in his ruthless self-certainty, but from this self-certainty emerges a kind of grandeur to give a hint of the tragic dimension. This depth and complexity of effect derive, in the end, from Dreiser's ambivalence toward his hero, but most immediately it is dependent upon Cowperwood's self-knowledge. He is not merely an automaton acting out his role in society and in nature, but is the self-conscious predator-as-philosopher who analyzes his own role and who speculates concerning his own place in the universe.

The kind of grandeur that the predator-as-philosopher can achieve is best illustrated by the scene in *The Financier* where Cowperwood, in the penitentiary, his career apparently blasted, stares up at the stars:

---

[1] In the ordinary historical novel, literal historical figures usually become, for all practical purposes, part of the decor, or examples of the "perennial humanity."

he thought of the earth floating like a little ball in the immeasurable reaches of ether. His own life appeared very trivial in view of these things, and he found himself asking whether it was all really of any significance or importance. He shook these moods off with ease, however, for the man was possessed of a sense of grandeur, largely in relation to himself and his affairs. . . .

As a kind of gloss on this passage, we may take Cowperwood's attitude when, for the first time after beginning his sentence, wearing his prison clothes, he must confront Aileen: "Only a stoic sense of his own soul-dignity aided him here." He is, in other words, himself, no matter where he is, or what he wears. In part, of course, this comes from his certainty of superior endowments and his will to persist, but more, as we shall see when the two passages are juxtaposed, is involved. To be himself, in the face of personal disaster *and* in the face of the indifferent constellations: in both the practical and the metaphysical sense, a man must create the self by the assertion of "soul-dignity." Such values may be in contrast with those of society; but more fundamentally, they are inevitably in contrast with the blankness of the universe.

The hero who is instructed in the nature of things and can face his knowledge knows that values find their sanction only in the passion of their assertion. He is aware of the root-irony that even he, the man of will, is part of the machine of the universe and is, like the veriest weakling, a creature of "chemisms." Cowperwood has used the idea of determinism as extenuation for his infidelities to Aileen as when he tells her that it is not his fault that he cannot feel what once he felt, that "love is not a bunch of coals that can be blown by an artificial bellows into flame"; but, by the same token, he must in the end recognize that even the act of will, and therefore the sense of "soul-dignity," is ultimately an illusion.

Illusion—it is the key word for Dreiser. And on this basis we may see the deeper relationship he would find in his predator's self-assertion on one hand and love and art on the other. It is true, as critics have pointed out, that a woman may be nothing more than a convenience or a status symbol for the "financier," and that the Robber Barons characteristically collected art not for art's sake, but as a mark of culture, privilege, and prestige—and for investment. Dreiser gives full weight to such realistic motives, but behind such motives of self-aggrandizement, convenience, and profit, taken at a realistic level, Dreiser would expose a more metaphysical truth. As the "financier" yearning for meaning in the meaningless universe of indifferent stars finds it in the illusion of will, so he seeks meaning in the other primary illusions, love and art. Cowperwood can stare at the beautiful woman or the beautiful picture with "soul-hunger," for both, in their beauty, seem annunciations of meaning. But both, like the act of will, are illusions.

Cowperwood as predator lives in the driving force of his "chemisms," but Cowperwood as philosopher lives in a skepticism that finds its fullest expression in his doctrine of illusion. No, the fullest expression of his skepticism is his discovery that even the philosopher needs "truth"—even if it is illusion. Cowperwood lives on, "resigned and yet not" to the fate of the man who, though "drawn by chemisms," can truly live only by illusion. If the wall of the world is blank, yet man can project upon it a vision of "amethyst and gold," and it does not matter that this projection is the product of "some mulch of chemistry" in the makeup of the visionary. If even the self is created by the illusory act of will, it may, as the blazing trajectory of Cowperwood is described at the end of *The Titan*, briefly "illuminate the terror and wonder of individuality."

The ultimate wisdom, Dreiser would seem to say, is to be unillusioned, but to know, in a strange paradoxical doubleness, the necessity of illusion: "Woe be to him who places his faith in illusion—the only reality—and woe to him who does not." For only by the acceptance of the illusion that creates individuality can it be said, to quote the last words of *The Titan*, "Thou hast lived."

An American Tragedy, Dreiser's next novel, was not to appear until 1925, more than ten years after *The Titan*. That period was full of distractions, confusions, and blind alleys, for Dreiser was now experiencing the new ideas characteristic of the time. He took up with political radicalism and with psychoanalysis, knew Dr. Abraham Brill, the local apostle of the cult, and suffered severe depression from reading the doctor's expositions. He cultivated, a little later, the acquaintance of Dr. Jacques Loeb,[2] the great physiological researcher of the Rockefeller Institute, who was one of the pioneers in the effort to establish the explanation of life by physicochemical laws subject to exploration by methods of the laboratory. He consorted with intellectuals of various stripes, who almost universally regarded him as a child; even if some did recognize his force, they, being accustomed to treat ideas as counters in their characteristic game, could not understand the man who automatically absorbed ideas into the blood stream of his passionate being. Dreiser was not concerned with consistency within a logical frame, with the rules of the game; he was concerned with how an idea "felt."[3] Mencken, who thought that Dreiser was wasting his time among the frauds of Greenwich Village, was right when he declared that Dreiser's "ideas always seem to be deduced from his feelings"; they seemed to be deduced from the feelings because ideas that signified anything to him were absorbed, were in a strange, innocent voracity ingurgitated and assimilated. They had to be dramatized in his own experience or they were of no worth. One corollary of this fact was that Dreiser, always unstable in love and friendship, could not be sure of his own feelings. Like Cowperwood, he could not be sure of the difference between sincerity and the illusion of sincerity; as the critic Randolph Bourne remarked of him, he had to "discover his own sincerity." He had only one way of doing that—by dramatization; and in this

process the ideas absorbed into his blood stream found their significance and their logic.

Two things did occur, however, to give some stability to Dreiser's life. First, a new publishing house, Boni and Liveright, sought Dreiser out with the hope of assembling his scattered literary properties under one publisher's imprint. Second, there was a certain Helen Richardson, née Patges, who was twenty-five years old, very good-looking, a disappointed actress now working as a stenographer; she was, too, the novelist's second cousin and, on the strength of this kinship, presented herself at his door, and two nights later was lyrically in his bed. For the rest of Dreiser's life, in spite of outrage on outrage, she was in and out of that bed, and in the end he married her.

Now she wanted to go to Hollywood, and they went.

During this middle decade Dreiser's literary work, superficially at least, was as confused as the rest of his life, but the central concern of this period seems to have been a probing back into his own past. As early as 1914, he had seriously begun work on what was projected as a multivolume autobiography, and by 1916, in the midst of his other occupations, he had finished the first volume *Dawn*, which, because of the revelations of the early lives of his sisters, was not published until 1931. The second volume, *A Book About Myself*, was finished by 1919, but delayed in publication until 1922. Two other works of autobiographical importance belong to the period, *A Hoosier Holiday* and *A Gallery of Women*.

Looking back on these middle years, we can detect a pattern. In *Sister Carrie* and *Jennie Gerhardt*, Dreiser, beginning his career in fiction, had written *out of* his life but not *about* his life. These books were out of his life not only in that they embodied observed life and told the stories of his sisters and his family, but also in that they emphasized his deep obsessive concerns, the first novel in its story of failure-in-success, the second in the story of success-in-failure. Now, with the second period of his work, the concern with the self becomes more overt. In *The "Genius"* and the trilogy, Dreiser

---

[2] Who appears as Max Gottlieb in *Arrowsmith*, by Sinclair Lewis. See p. 1948.

[3] In this, as in many other aspects of his personality, and his work, Dreiser resembles Dostoevski.

is dealing with the dream-self—the superman, the success. In the autobiographical works he is dealing with, or trying to deal with, the literal self, whether success or failure; with the actual self, however that self might be evaluated. In the next phase, in *An American Tragedy*, he was to deal, not with the dream-self, but with the nightmare-self. Over the years he had been engaged in the long struggle to define the self and its contradictory potentialities—in the effort, as we have suggested, to "discover his own sincerity."

An American Tragedy had a long history. As early as 1892 and 1893 Dreiser began to collect clippings on murder cases, always cases in which a girl is killed by her lover, always with ambition as the motive. He made false starts at writing the obsessive story, and as late as 1919 was working on a version based on the case of a Baptist minister who seduced a girl and then, out of ambition, poisoned her when she became pregnant. Finally, out of this slow, mulling process, Dreiser found the focus for his murder story, and the particular story elected was one that had been collected years earlier, in 1906, the murder of the pregnant Grace ("Billie") Brown by young Chester Gillette.

Chester was the son of a fanatically devout couple who had run a mission. Born in the West, he had wound up, after two years at Oberlin College and much wandering, in Cortland, in upper New York. There an uncle owned a shirt factory, where Chester got a job and promptly seduced one of the girls employed there. Meanwhile, he had penetrated the world of "society" in Cortland. At this juncture Billie announced her pregnancy, and as her seducer withdrew into his more elegant life, she wrote him the letters that were to bring jurors to tears. With Billie insisting on marriage, Chester saw only one solution. He persuaded her to go on a trip with him, presumably to be married. At Big Moose Lake, he took her out in a rowboat, hit her on the head with a tennis racket, and, when she fell into the water, left her to drown. A straw hat (an extra provided for the occasion) floated on the water to announce his

death. He was captured and, in March, 1908, executed.

The objective story of Chester is very close to that of Clyde, and Dreiser, rather than trying to disguise similarities, often insisted on them. He kept, for example, the initials of Chester Gillette for Clyde Griffiths, and the "B" of the nickname of Grace Brown for Bert, the nickname of Roberta Alden. For Clyde he kept the pseudonym of Carl Graham, which Chester had used on the death trip with Billie. Big Moose Lake, where Billie died, becomes Big Bittern Lake. The tennis racket of Chester (an improbable object for a jaunt in a rowboat) is transformed into a camera, but both items are accouterments of a vacation. The poor but respectable family of Roberta is like the Brown family. With only a little editing, the letters from Billie, which unstrung the jurors in the Herkimer County court house, become the letters of Roberta which unstring the jurors in the Cataraqui County court house.

Furthermore, Dreiser made a preparatory tour of the region where Chester had acted out his sleazy drama. He saw the pushing little cities, the rutted roads and isolated farms, the very lake where, years back, Billie Brown had died, the dark woods into which Chester had fled, the Herkimer County court house, where Chester had been convicted. Dreiser heard the cry of the wier-wier bird that Chester must have heard and that Clyde was to hear. Dreiser's imagination fed on fact: this was where *it* had happened, and this was where *it* had to happen now. Fact is doom, the ultimate, irreversible doom, and he was writing a story of doom.

The factual scene becomes, in Dreiser's imagination, the action: in its factuality it becomes, as the city had become in *Sister Carrie*, the image of doom, fulfilled and complete in the moment when Clyde, after the deed, disappears into the shadow of trees.

The nightmare-self had long needed to find its story, for we know how far back goes the file of clippings. But so much had to be understood before Dreiser could make the final effort of self-understanding that would be *An American Tragedy*. There had to be the antithesis between the world of Carrie and that of Jennie. There had to be the self-glorification in *The "Genius"* and the trilogy. There had to be the long exploration of the autobiographies. There had to be, perhaps, Freud, with his gospel of the meaning of the past in the living self. But Dreiser finally came into the time when he could recognize what the story of Chester Gillette really meant.

But Dreiser was not trying to tell Chester's story. He was trying to tell his own. It was his own story—a murder story with no literal murder—that he had begun to tell long ago. In *Dawn* he had told it—the story of his own growing up, as the deprived one, the yearner. It is the story of the young Dreiser up through *A Book About Myself*, which follows *Dawn* and which ends with the marriage of Jug—"after the first flare of love had thinned down to the pale flame of duty."

The tale had begun, as we must remember, long before Dreiser ever laid eyes on Jug. First, there is the boy "flaming with sex," masturbating, tortured by fear of "imaginary sex weakness." Next, there is the episode of the nameless little "reckless and adventure-looking Italian girl of not more than sixteen or seventeen," who in "an idle or adventuring mood" comes into the real estate office where the boy is alone for the afternoon and lures and badgers him into the back room. Then comes the time when, heartened by the fact that the little Italian girl had seized him "convulsively and even affectionately" before lying back in "a smiling calm," he embarks on his own sexual adventures and establishes the pattern of his subsequent life—over which presides the archetypal figure of that girl who comes out of nowhere, as though summoned by a dream, to give herself and, after the spasm, affectionate embrace, and smiling calm, disappears into nowhere, nameless and undemanding.

In this third phase, at the same time when the boy Dreiser, presumably freed from the fears of impotence, is seeking sex, he has the "giddy dreams" of the world of wealth, elegance, social position, and ostentation. As a laundry boy making deliveries at rich houses in Chicago,

he had peered through doorways "into boudoirs and reception rooms," to catch "flashy touches of social superiority and social supremacy," and could vision himself "in golden chambers," giving himself "over to what luxuries and delights." He longed to "succeed financially by marriage with some beautiful and wealthy girl," but he never met the dream girl who was both "rich" and "sensual."

What he met was little Nellie MacPherson, behind the cashier's desk in the laundry. She was pretty, gay, good-natured, quick at repartee, and sweet, but she was "embedded in a conservative and wholly religious family—Scotch Presbyterian"—as he was to find Jug embedded in her Missouri Methodism. In any case, Nellie was not the girl Dreiser would have chosen from the "veritable garden of femininity" that the laundry room was. She was merely what he, in his uncertainty, had to make do with. The best he could do was to act out the charade of a love affair with her and go regularly to her house, where, though secretly preferring a younger sister, he spent endless hours cuddling Nellie and talking of their married bliss to come and systematically trying to seduce her. Though she was not "lustful" like the nameless little Italian girl, she was "passionate enough within her conventional tether," and now and then he almost "over-ran her good judgement." He had no intention of marrying her. His vainglorious ambitions lay elsewhere, even in the realm of intellectual achievement, and in *Dawn*, like Cowperwood looking back with pity on the "passionate illusion" of Aileen's girlhood love for him, Dreiser could write:

I think I must have been her first serious affair. The pity of it was that she had no understanding of the type of youth she was dealing with, any more than I had of myself, and soon believed in the gushing phrases I lavished upon her.

It was all a charade. Even at the time when Dreiser was lavishing the "gushing phrases" on Nellie, he was trying them out on Alice. So we have the beginning of the pattern of the double (or multiple) romance which was to continue for Dreiser's life, and which is the central fact of the story of Clyde.

When at last Dreiser left Alice, he went to St. Louis to a better newspaper job, and the letter she wrote him there had all the pathos of those of Billie Brown, or Roberta Alden. Dreiser, suffering loneliness, remorse, and self-pity, wrote her that he loved her and that her letter had torn his heart. But in looking back on that moment, he says, in *A Book About Myself*, of his letter: "But I could not write it as effectually as I might have, for I was haunted by the idea that I should never keep my word. Something kept telling me that it was not wise, that I didn't really want to."

The "something" was always there, pronouncing his doom. He yearned for love, but only, as he put it, "after I had the prosperity and fame that somehow I falsely fancied commanded love." If he was "blazing with sex," he was also blazing with the "desire for material and social supremacy—to have wealth, to be in society." That "something" was the voice of the anguishingly uncertain ego that had to have "prosperity and fame" before it could feel itself even to exist—or if existing, to be worthy of love. And the voice was so cold and commanding that it seemed the very voice of destiny. It was the voice that Clyde finally heard, as we shall see, the voice of the "Efrit."[4] The voice, for Dreiser as for Clyde, seemed detached from the self, and thus to exculpate the self:

> I saw myself a stormy petrel hanging over the yellowish-black waves of life and never really resting anywhere. I could not; my mind would not let me. I saw too much, felt too much, knew too much. What was I, what anyone, but a small bit of seaweed on an endless sea, flotsam, jetsam, being moved hither and thither—by what subterranean tides?[5]

[4] In some translations of *The Arabian Nights* the word "Efrit" is used instead of "genii." It was the form Dreiser used.

[5] Notice how, in this passage, the images combine the notions of power and freedom (petrel) with innocent victimization (seaweed). But both notions are detached from the "self."

By what subterranean tides? That is the question underlying *An American Tragedy*.

The same psychic trick that allows Dreiser to exculpate the self as a victim of the subterranean tides allows him to pity the self; and in the next stage, to pity and bless Alice ("She wanted to unite with me for this little span of existence, to go with me hand and hand into the ultimate nothingness")—or Nellie, who had not understood the grip of the subterranean tides on Theodore Dreiser, or Roberta, who had not understood their grip on Clyde Griffiths.

There is, however, a third and most important stage in the natural history of pity. In *A Book About Myself*, at the end of the paragraph from which we have quoted the sentence on "prosperity and fame," Dreiser says: ". . . at the same time I was horribly depressed by the thought that I should never have them [prosperity, fame, love], never; and that thought, for the most part has been fulfilled." But after this self-pity, in the next paragraph, in the very next sentence we find:

> In addition to this, I was filled with an intense sympathy for the woes of others, life in all its helpless degradation and poverty, the unsatisfied dreams of people, their sweaty labors, the things they were compelled to endure—nameless impositions, curses, brutalities,—the things they would never have, their hungers, half-formed dreams of pleasure, their gibbering insanities and beaten resignations at the end.

This paragraph continues with a Whitmanesque catalogue of human sufferings and Dreiser's confession of the literal tears which we must believe he shed. But the next two paragraphs return to the young man's preoccupation with his own defects and limitations, his obsessive fear of failure, his yearning looks into the house of "some kindly family" or through the "windows of some successful business firm" and his "aches and pains that went with all this, the amazing depression, all but suicidal." The whole passage has its own deep intrinsic interest, but holds another interest, one that provides the background for the analysis of Clyde's stages of pity when he finds his sister in the lonely room, pregnant and abandoned.

To sum up, what appears from *Dawn* and the first twenty-two chapters of *A Book About Myself* is not only Dreiser's basic personality and life pattern, but the basic characters, situations, and issues of *An American Tragedy*. All is ready. Life is there, ready for the understanding that will make art possible and the art that will make understanding possible.

But there was to be an essential, intermediate stage in the process. Up to this moment, the elements that were to reappear in Dreiser's great masterpiece and, indeed, in his fiction in general had been floating, not brought to focus in experience. The entrance of Sara White—poor Jug, who could not understand the "subterranean tides"—was to do this. In an extremely interesting book *The Two Dreisers*, the author Ellen Moers insists on Jug's importance in the background of *An American Tragedy*. Her presence had dominated the second half of *A Book About Myself*, and her story brings to focus all that had been diffused in Dreiser's earlier experience. Looking back on this moment, Dreiser wrote:

> She would never give herself to me without marriage, and here I was, lonely and financially unable to take her, and spiritually unable to justify my marriage to her even if I were. The tangle of life, its unfairness and indifference to the moods and longings of any individual, swept over me once more, weighing me down far beyond the power of expression.

Life's "unfairness and indifference to the moods and longings of any individual": the generalization of pity in the phrase "of any individual" is a mask for the self-pity. If we lift the mask we find that the phrase reads: *Life's unfairness and indifference to the moods and longings of Theodore Dreiser—or Clyde Griffiths.* This would imply the premise: *The moods and longings of Theodore Dreiser* (or *of Clyde Griffiths*) *are the measure of justice.* And from this premise would flow the inexorable conclusion: *Those who would contravene these sacred moods and longings shall have justice visited upon them.*

Poor Jug. Poor Roberta.

An American Tragedy is the work in which Dreiser could look backward from the distance of middle age and evaluate his own experience of success and failure, the burden of personal pathos, the echo of the personal struggle to purge the unworthy aspirations, to discover his own sincerity. We also feel a historical moment, the moment of the Great Boom which climaxed the period from Grant to Coolidge, the half century in which the new America of industry and finance-capitalism was hardening into shape and its secret forces were emerging to dominate all life. In other words, *An American Tragedy* can be taken as a document, both personal and historical, and it is often admired, and defended, in these terms.

As a document, it is indeed powerful, but the weight of Dreiser's experience and of the historical moment are, in the strange metabolism of creation, absorbed and transmuted into fictional idea, fictional analogy, fictional illusion. The book is "created" and therefore generates its own power as art.

The thing in *The American Tragedy* most obviously created is Clyde Griffiths himself. The fact that Dreiser chose a model for Clyde does not make Clyde less of a creation. Rather, it emphasizes that he *is* a creation; and the contrast between the dreary factuality of an old newspaper account and the inwardness of the personal story may well have served as a mirror for the contrast that always touched Dreiser's feelings and fired his imagination—the contrast between the grinding impersonality of the machine of the world and the pathos of the personal experience. Indeed, the novel begins and ends with an image of this contrast: the family of street preachers, in the beginning with the boy Clyde and in the end with the illegitimate son of Clyde's sister Esta, stands lost between the "tall walls of the commercial heart of an American city" and lift up their hymn "against the vast skepticism and apathy of life." The image of the boy Clyde looking up at the "tall walls" of the world is the key image of the novel. And of Dreiser's life.

The creation of the character of Clyde is begun by a scrupulous accretion of detail. We are early caught in the dawning logic of these details. We see the sidewise glances of yearning. We see how, when he discovers his sister Esta in the secret room, pregnant and abandoned, his first reaction is selfish; how only when she refers to "poor Mamma" does his own sympathy stir; how this sympathy is converted suddenly into a sense of world-pathos, and then, in the end, turns back into self-pity. We see him staring at the rich house of his uncle, and again when for the first time he lays eyes on Sondra, with "a curiously stinging sense of what it was to want and not to have." We see his real sadness at Roberta's jealousy, which he, also one of the deprived, can feel himself into, but we know that his pity for her is, at root, self-pity. We see him open the *Times-Union* to read the headline: *Accidental Double Tragedy at Pass Lake.* We see all this, and so much more, and remember his mother's letter to him after his flight from Kansas City: ". . . for well I know how the devil tempts and pursues all of us mortals, and particularly just such a child as you." And what a stroke it is to fuse the reader's foreboding interest with the anxiety of the mother!

But Dreiser's method of presenting the character is far deeper and more subtle than that of mere accretion. The method is an enlargement and a clarifying, slow and merciless, of a dimly envisaged possibility. We gradually see the inward truth of the mother's clairvoyant phrase, "such a child as you." The story of Clyde is the documentation of this phrase.

A thousand strands run backward and forward in this documentation, converting what is a process in time into a logic outside of time. When back in Kansas City we see Clyde's sexual fear and masochism in relation to the cold, cunning Hortense, we are laying the basis for our understanding of what will come later, the repetition with Sondra of the old relationship and the avenging of it on the defenseless Roberta. When in the room of women where Clyde is foreman, he looks wistfully out the window on the summer river, we are being prepared for the moment when he first encounters Roberta at the pleasure lake, and for the grimmer moment to come on Big Bittern Lake. When, on the night after the first meeting with Sondra, Clyde does not go to Roberta, we know that this is a shadowy rehearsal for the last betrayal and murder.

It is not only that we find, in an analytic sense, the logic of character displayed; in such instances we find this logic transliterated into a thousand intermingling images, into a poetry of destiny. We see the process moving toward climax when, on the train, on the death ride with Roberta, Clyde flees from his own inner turmoil into the objective observations which, in their irrelevancy, are the mark of destiny: *Those nine black and white cows on that green hillside,* or *Those three automobiles out there running almost as fast as the train.* And we find the climax of the process in the "weird, contemptuous, mocking, lonely" call of the wierwier bird which offers a commentary on the execution, as it had on the birth, of the murderous impulse.

This transliteration of logic into a poetry of destiny is what accounts for our peculiar involvement in the story of Clyde. What man, short of saint or sage, does not understand, in some secret way however different from Clyde's way, the story of Clyde, and does not find it something deeper than a mere comment on the values of American culture? Furthermore, the mere fact that our suspense is not about the *what* but about the *how* and the *when* emphasizes our involvement. No, to be more specific, our *entrapment.* We are living out a destiny, painfully waiting for a doom. We live into Clyde's doom, and in the process live our own secret sense of doom which is the backdrop of our favorite dramas of the will.

How deep is our involvement—or entrapment—is indicated by the sudden sense of lassitude, even relief, once the murder is committed; all is now fulfilled, and all tension is released. With the act thus consummated, we may even detach ourselves, at least for the moment, from the youth now "making his way through a dark, uninhabited woods, a dry straw hat upon his head, a bag in his hand. . . ."

As a commentary of Dreiser's art, we can note how, after this sentence that closes Book 2, Dreiser jerks back his camera from that lonely figure and begins Book 3 by withdrawing into magisterial distance for a panoramic sweep of the lens: "Cataraqui County extending from the northernmost line of the village known as Three Mile Bay on the south to the Canadian border, on the north a distance of fifty miles. Its greater portion covered by uninhabited forests. . . ." The whole effect is that of detachment; and with this we are restored, after a long painful while, to the role of observer, interested and critical, but not now involved.

But we shall not be long permitted to keep this comfortable role. Soon the camera will come to sharp focus on the cell where Clyde waits. And in such alternation of focus, the constant shifting from involvement to detachment and back, we find one of the deep art principles of the work, one of the principles of its compelling rhythm. It is compelling because the shift of focus is never arbitrary; it grows out of the expressive needs of the narrative as Dreiser has conceived it, and out of the prior fact that the narrative is conceived as a drama between the individual and the universe.

Many critics will find it absurd to discuss "Dreiser's art," and even critics who admire Dreiser will, with few exceptions, concede that he lacks "art," or apologetically explain that Dreiser's ineptitudes somehow have the value of stylistic decorum and can be taken as a manifestation of his groping honesty, and will then push on to stake their case on his "power" and "compassion." But ultimately how do we know the "power" or the "compassion"—know them differently, that is, from the power or compassion we may read into a news story—except by Dreiser's control? Except, in other words, by his grasp of the human materials and his rhythmic organization of them, the vibrance that

is the life of fictional illusion, that mutual interpenetration in meaning of part and whole that gives us the sense of preternatural fulfillment? Except, in short, by art?

There is a tendency to freeze the question of Dreiser as an artist at the question of prose style. As for prose style, Dreiser is a split writer. There is the "literary" writer whose style is often abominable. But there is another writer, too, a writer who can write a scene with fidelity if not always with felicity. But sometimes there is the felicity, a felicity of dramatic baldness: the letters of Mrs. Griffiths or Roberta; the scene of Roberta back home, in her mother's house, looking out at the ruined fields; the scene when Clyde first sees Sondra, with that "curiously stinging sense of what it is to want and not to have."

Words are what we have on the page of a novel, and words are not only a threshold, a set of signs, but a fundamental aspect of meaning, absorbed into everything else. Words, however, are not the only language of fiction. There is the language of the unfolding scenes, what Dreiser, in the course of composing the novel, called the "procession and selection of events," the language of the imagery of enactment, with all its primitive massiveness—the movie in our heads, with all the entailed questions of psychological veracity and subtlety, of symbolic densities and rhythmic complexities. We are trying here to indicate something of the weight of this language, or better, languages, as an aspect of Dreiser's art.

With this intention we can return to the question of the rhythm between detachment and involvement, which manifests itself in shifts of pace and scale. But we may find the basis for another rhythm in the fact that the personal story of Clyde is set in a whole series of shifting perspectives. Here perspective does not mean a point of view in the ordinary technical sense. It means what may be called an angle of interest. For instance, the picture of the organization of the collar factory in Lycurgus gives a perspective on life and on the fate of Clyde; this is another contrast between a mechanism and man, a symbolic rendering of the ground idea of the novel.

But there are many perspectives. There is the perspective of the religious belief of the family, which returns in the end to frame the whole story; that of the world of the bellhop's bench in the hotel; that of sex and "chemism"; that of the stamping room in the factory with its mixture of sex, social differences, power, and money; that of the economic order of Lycurgus which stands as a mirror for the world outside; that of the jealousies and intrigues of the young social set of the town, jealousies and intrigues which, ironically enough, make it possible for Clyde to enter that charmed circle; that of justice and law in relation to the political structure of Cataraqui County; that of the death house.

Sometimes a perspective comes as an idea boldly stated, sometimes as implicit in a situation or person. In fact, all the persons of the novel, even the most incidental, are carriers of ideas and represent significant perspectives in which the story may be viewed. In the enormous cast there are no walk-ons; each actor has a role in the structure of the unfolding dialectic. And it is the pervasive sense of this participation, however unformulated, that gives the novel its density, the weight of destiny.

If, as a matter of fact, the dialectic were insisted upon as dialectic, we should not find this force; and this is the great difference in method from the trilogy. We find that now the force develops as the dialectic unfolds in personality, in the presentation of personality not as a carrier of idea but as a thing of inner vibrance. The mother, for instance, is a small masterpiece of characterization. She is the carrier of "religion," but with her own inner contradictions; she exists in her full and suffering actuality, an actuality that, at the end when she comes to join Clyde, affirms itself by her effect on everyone around. Roberta is fully rendered, not only in her place in the social and economic order and in her role as victim, but with the complexity of her humanity. When her friend Grace catches her in a lie about Clyde, she stiffens with "resentment," and this conversion of her self-anger into the relief of anger at her friend

is a telling index, given in a flash, of the depth and anguish of her scarcely formulated inner struggle. She does not quite tell the truth to her mother about why she moves out of her first room. In the midst of her as yet submerged moral struggle, she deceives even herself as to why she selects a room in the new house downstairs and with an outside door. She is a sufferer, but she is not beyond the flash of jealous anger when Clyde, with unconscious brutality, remarks that Sondra dresses well: "If I had as much money as that, I could too." And the scene in which Clyde tries to persuade her to let him come to her room is of extraordinary depth, coming to climax when he turns sullenly away, and she, overwhelmed by her fear and pain at her own rebelliousness, feels the "first, flashing, blinding, bleeding stab of love."

Even minor characters have more than their relation to the dialectic. The prosecuting attorney and the defending lawyers have their own depth, and their roles are defined by their personal histories. A character like Hortense may be merely sketched in, but she takes on a new significance when we see her, like Rita, as an earlier image of Sondra, who is—and let us dwell on the adjectives—"as smart and vain and sweet a girl as Clyde had ever laid eyes on." And if at first Sondra herself seems scarcely more than another example of the particular type of *femme fatale* destined to work Clyde's ruin, let us remember how Clyde, in his cell, receives the letter beginning: "Clyde—This is so that you will not think someone once dear to you has utterly forgotten you. . . ." The letter, typewritten, is unsigned, but with it, in all the mixture of human feeling and falsity, Sondra, retroactively as it were, leaps to life.

As every person enters the story with a role in the dialectic, so every person enters with a human need which seeks fulfillment in the story. The delineation of this need—for instance, the portrait of the socially ambitious clerk in Lycurgus or the history of the prosecuting attorney Mason—serves to distract our interest from Clyde's personal story, to provide another kind of distancing for the main line of narrative. At the same time, in the extraordinary coherence of the novel, we finally see that such apparent digressions are really mirrors held up to Clyde's story, in fact to Clyde himself: in this world of mirrors, complicity is the common doom. So here we have another version, in distraction of interest and realization of complicity, of the rhythm of approach and withdrawal.

There is, indeed, another sense in which the delineation of each new need compensates, in the end, for the distraction it has provoked. Each new need introduced into the novel serves as a booster to the thrust of narrative, each providing a new energy that, though at first a distraction, is absorbed into the central drive; and in the rhythm of these thrusts, we find another principle of the organization of the whole. Or to change our image, in the braiding together of these needs with the need of Clyde, we find a rhythm of pause and acceleration, the pulse of creative life. To put the matter in another way, the delineation of each new perspective, each new person, each new need acts as a new energy absorbed into the dynamism of the story; for instance, the psychological makeup of the prosecutor, his frustrations and yearnings, is a part of the explanation of the course of justice. The delineation of each new perspective, each new person, each new need reveals a new factor of motive; there is a progressive "unmasking" of the secret springs of the action, related in the end to the "unmasking" of life as a mechanism cursed with consciousness, and something of our own resistance to unmasking enters into the whole response to the story. This resistance, set against our natural commitment to the narrative, creates another sort of frustrating tension, and another sort of rhythm of withdrawal and approach. Furthermore, over against the unmasking of the mechanism of life is set the feel of life itself being lived in the urgency of its illusions; and the play between the elements of this contrast gives us another principle of rhythm, another principle by which the form unfolds.

We have spoken of the marked moment of withdrawal at the beginning of Book 3, after we have left Clyde walking away from the scene of Roberta's death, into the forest. Our commitment to the movement of narrative leading to Roberta's death has been so complete that now, with that accomplished, the story of the crime seems, for the moment at least, to split off from the subsequent story of consequences; and Dreiser, by the moment of withdrawal into distance, emphasizes the split. The split, coming about two thirds of the way through the novel, has been felt, by some readers, as a grave flaw in the structure. The split is indeed real—a real break in emotional continuity. But we must ask ourselves whether or not this split may not serve to emphasize a deeper thematic continuity.

The story is one of crime and punishment. In the first two books we see the forces that converge toward the death of Roberta, and in Book 3 we see the forces that are triggered into action by her death; that is, we see the relation of the individual personality, and individual fate, to such forces as a continuing theme. What, in other words, is the nature of responsibility in this world of shadowy complicities, where all things seem to conspire in evil? The shadowiness of the outer world is matched by the shadowiness of the inner world; at the very last moment in the boat Clyde does not "will" to strike Roberta—even her death is an "accident." Then after the accident, this shadowiness of the inner world merges again with that of the outer. For instance, Jephson, one of the lawyers defending Clyde, creates a version of the accident; and then Clyde is persuaded, without much resistance, to testify to a "lie" in order to establish, as Jephson put it, the "truth."

This scene of the "persuasion" of Clyde is balanced by a later scene of "persuasion" in which, after Clyde's conviction, the young preacher McMillan strips Clyde of all his alibis and equivocations and prepares him for repentance and salvation. But just before the execution, even as Clyde assures his mother that God has heard his prayers, he is asking himself: "Had he?" And Clyde goes to his death unsure of what he really knows or feels, or what he has done. The theme of ambiguity, as of complicity, in varying manifestations, runs throughout. Clyde lives in the ambiguous mists of a dream, and the most important thing shrouded from his sight is his own identity.

At the end, on death row, there is a little episode that returns us to the notion of dream and identity in the novel. One of the condemned awaiting death is a man named Nicholson, a lawyer who has poisoned a client to gain control of his estate. Nicholson is clearly a man of breeding and education, and in spite of his criminality has courage, humor, kindliness, and dignity. In short, he has a self that can survive his own criminality and its consequences. His role in the story is a thematic one. He is set in contrast to Clyde—who has no "self"—and undertakes to instruct him in the rudimentary dignity of having an identity. When he is to be executed, he sends two books to Clyde, *Robinson Crusoe* and the *Arabian Nights*.

Here we find repeated the little device with which Dreiser indicates his meaning when he gives us the last glimpse of Carrie, sitting in her rocking chair with a copy of *Père Goriot* on her lap. As the novel of Balzac (whose fiction long ago had made Dreiser aware of his own role as the "ambitious beginner") summarizes the theme of *Sister Carrie*, so the gifts of Nicholson summarize the theme of *An American Tragedy*. His two books provide the poles of Clyde's story.

The significance of *Robinson Crusoe* is clear. It gives the image of a man who is totally self-reliant, who, alone and out of nothing, can create a life for himself, a world. Even in shipwreck—in disaster—he asserts and fulfills the self (as, we may say, Nicholson does).

As for the *Arabian Nights*, Dreiser does not have to rely on the reader for a last-minute interpretation. At the trial, while Jephson, one of the defending lawyers, is leading Clyde in his testimony, we find the following passage:

"I see! I see!" went on Jephson, oratorically and loudly, having the jury and audience in mind. "A case of the *Arabian Nights*, of the enscorcelled and the enscorcellor."

"I don't think I know what you mean," said Clyde.

"A case of being bewitched, my poor boy—by beauty, love, wealth, by things that we sometimes think we want very, very much, and cannot ever have—that is what I mean, and that is what much of the love in the world amounts to."

In this passage Jephson summarizes the whole story of Clyde, but the summary has long since been prepared for in the novel. At the very beginning of his worldly career, in his "imaginary flights," the hotel where he was a bellhop seemed a magic world, "Aladdinish, really": "It meant that you did what you pleased." And this Aladdinish world appears again at the very crucial moment of the novel when Clyde contemplates the death of Roberta: the Efrit of his "darkest" side says: "And would you escape from the demands of Roberta that but now and unto this hour have appeared unescapable to you? Behold! I bring you a way."

This is the world where dream is law, where every wish is fulfilled effortlessly and innocently. The first Aladdinish dream, back in the Green-Davidson in Kansas City, had merely been to be like the guests of the hotel: "That you possessed all of these luxuries. That you went where and when you pleased." Now the dream is different and dire.

The fact that Dreiser divides the novel into only three books falsifies the intrinsic structure and blurs the fundamental theme. There are really four basic movements of the narrative, and there should be four books: the story up to the flight from Kansas City, that of the preparation; the story of the temptation leading to the death of Roberta; the story of the conviction, that of the ambiguities of justice; and the story of the search, as death draws near, for salvation and certainty as contrasted with ambiguity. In other words, the present Book 3 should be divided; and then in the latter half, related to other themes, especially to that of Aladdin, but more deeply grounded, the theme of identity would be specific and dominant.

Throughout the whole novel this theme has been emerging. If in the world of complicities and ambiguities it is hard to understand responsibility, then how, ultimately, can one understand the self? If one's dream is to "have things done for you," if one is passive, how can there be a self? In fact, in this world of shadows Clyde has always sought to flee from the self. In all his self-absorption and selfishness, he has sought to repudiate the deepest meaning of self. He had longed to enter the "tall walls" of the world and find there a dream-self, a self-to-be-created, a role to play in the rich and thrilling world—a *role*, we may say, to take the place of a *self*. The very end of Book 1, which has described Clyde's first attempt to enter the world, shows him fleeing from the wreck of the borrowed car: ". . . he hoped to hide—to lose himself and so escape. . . ." He wishes to escape responsibility and punishment; he does "lose himself," and early in Book 2 we learn that he has lost his name, to reassume it only when he can use it to advantage with his rich uncle from Lycurgus.

All the rest of Clyde's sleazy career can be regarded as an attempt to repudiate the old self. And the repudiation of self is associated with Clyde's readiness to repudiate others: he is ashamed of his family; he drops new friends—Dillard and Rita, for example—as soon as he makes contact with his rich relations; he ends by murdering Roberta. Or it may be put that Clyde, having no sense of the reality of self, can have no sense of the reality of others: for instance, when he assists Roberta into the boat that is to take her to her death, she seems "an almost nebulous figure . . . stepping down into an unsubstantial rowboat, upon a purely ideational lake." And even his pity for others is always, as we have seen, a covert self-pity or a pity for the self that could not be, truly, a self.

At the end, in his last desperation, Clyde is forced by McMillan to recognize the truth that he has fled from responsibility and self. But even now, as Clyde tries to recognize this fact and thus discover and accept a self, he cannot be sure of who or what he is. His "tragedy" is that of namelessness, and this is one aspect of its being an American tragedy, the story of the individual without identity, whose responsible

self has been absorbed by the great machine of modern industrial secularized society and reduced to a cog, a cipher, an abstraction. Many critics have emphasized the social determinism in *An American Tragedy*, and James T. Farrell succinctly summarizes this view: "To him [Dreiser] evil is social: all his novels are concerned with social history, the social process of evil. Ambition, yearning, aspiration—these all revolve around this problem, and it in turn revolves around the role of money. He has related social causation . . . to the individual pattern of destiny."

Dreiser did indeed relate social causation to the individual pattern of destiny, but deeper than this story of the individual set against the great machine of the secularized society is the story of the individual set against the great machine of the universe—the story we find in the image of Cowperwood, in prison, staring up at the stars, or in that of Clyde, after the death of Roberta, moving into the darkness of the woods.

These images are not, however, adequate to focus the issue as it appears in *An American Tragedy*. For man is not merely *set against* the machine of the universe, he is *part* of it; he himself is a machine. This was the doctrine that in the years leading up to the novel Dreiser had been absorbing from Jacques Loeb. Under the tutelage of Loeb, Dreiser had come to feel that the stars that are indifferent to man, or would cross him, are not in the sky but in his blood stream and nerve cells and genes; and that man himself is the dark wood in which he wanders. Loeb had confirmed Dreiser in the belief that consciousness itself is merely a product of the physicochemical process. And this brings us back to Dreiser's theme of illusion.

Success, power, place, wealth, religion, art, love—over and over, in one way or another, in fiction or autobiography, Dreiser had defined each of these things as an "illusion." Now, in *An American Tragedy*, he specifically comes upon his final subject, the illusion of the self. The "mulch of chemistry" that gives man all his other illusions gives him this, the primary illusion; whatever its origin, consciousness, with its aspirations and desires, exists and the drama of self-definition remains crucial. The last anguish is the yearning for identity, for the illusion that is the fundamental "truth," and at the end of *An American Tragedy* Clyde Griffiths, now past all the other empty yearnings that had merely been masks for this deepest yearning, longs for this certainty as he walks down the corridor toward the door that would close upon "all the earthly life he had ever known."

As soon as *An American Tragedy* was off the press, people began to ask what kind of tragedy, if any, it was. Clyde Griffiths scarcely seemed to be a tragic hero. He had not fallen from a great place. He was not of great scale. Rather than being a man of action, he was acted upon. By what criteria might he be called tragic? Even readers who felt the power of the novel were troubled by the title.

The puzzlement was compounded by the notion that, if Dreiser had used this title for his trilogy (of which only two volumes had then appeared), nobody would have been surprised. Cowperwood, that is, appeared to be every inch the stuff of tragedy. If not of kingly blood, he was, like Tamburlaine, the stuff of which kings are made. His scale was beyond dispute, his power over men, women, and events preternatural. As for his ability to act, he was will incarnate in action.

The comparison of Cowperwood and Clyde is essential for an understanding of what Dreiser is about in *An American Tragedy*; and it is reasonably clear that Dreiser himself was thinking and feeling in these terms. The hard, hypnotic, blazing blue gaze of Cowperwood, before which men quailed and women shivered delightedly, is the central fact of his image, insisted upon again and again. Clyde's eyes, too, are central for his image. In the very beginning, even as we are told that Clyde was "as vain and proud as he was poor," and was "one of those interesting individuals who looked upon himself as a thing apart" (as the young Dreiser had sung the refrain to himself, "No common man am I"), we see him studying his assets in a mirror: "a straight, well-cut nose, high, white forehead,

wavy, glossy black hair, eyes that were black and rather melancholy at times." It is those "deep and rather appealing eyes" that, when a girl cashier in a drugstore notices him, put him in the way of his first good job, in the Green-Davidson hotel. And when the other bellhops take him to his first brothel, the prostitute, trying to overcome his timidity, says, "I like your eyes. You're not like those other fellows. You're more refined, kinda."

Many others, including, of course, Sondra, are to feel the peculiar attraction of his eyes, but this attraction is most obviously important in the affair with Roberta. There is the moment when she first becomes aware of the "darkness and melancholy and lure of his eyes" and, at the first kiss, of the "dark, hungry eyes held very close to hers." Then, in the magnificent scene when, after she has refused to let him come to her room and he leaves her standing in the dark street, she, in the "first, flashing, blinding, bleeding stab of love," thinks: "His beautiful face, his beautiful hands. His eyes." At last, on Big Bittern Lake, trying to steel himself to the deed: "And his dark, liquid, nervous eyes, looking anywhere but at her." And in the instant when she becomes aware of his strange expression and makes her fateful movement toward him in the boat: "And in the meantime his eyes—the pupils of the same growing momentarily larger and more lurid. . . ."

The hard, blaze-blue glance of Cowperwood is the index of unrelenting, self-assertive male force. The dark melancholy gaze of Clyde is not an index of force: rather, of weakness, a device of blackmail by which, somehow, his weakness feeds on the kindly or guilty weakness of others so that pity is in the end converted into complicity. In *Dawn* Dreiser says that he himself gave way "to the whining notion that if something were done for me—much—I would amount to a great deal—a whimper which had taken its rise out of my self-exaggerated deprivations. . . . And which of us is not anxious, or at least willing, to have things done for him?"

Cowperwood's glance is the mark of naked self-assertion, Clyde's gaze is a confession of the non-self—blank desire, a primal need to "have things done for him." The self of Clyde does not exist except in terms of desire— at root the desire to create a self worthy of the fulfillment of desire, to take the place of the sniveling worthless self. When Clyde sees girls "accompanied by some man in evening suit, dress shirt, high hat, bow tie, white kid gloves and patent leather shoes," he thinks: "To be able to wear such a suit with such ease and air!" And if he did attain such raiment, would he not be "well set upon the path that leads to all the blisses?" And so Dreiser develops, not by a woman but by a man, Clyde or himself, the philosophy of clothes that he had begun in *Sister Carrie:* now at a deeper level, an existential level, a level at which we understand the inwardness of the sad little tale of his embezzlement of twenty-five dollars for the snappy overcoat and of his passion for fame, both as manifestations of the need to create a worthy self, or to conceal the unworthy self.

To sum up, Cowperwood, with his brutal self-sufficiency, could make his way with women, but Clyde was like Dreiser, who could say of himself: "I was too cowardly to make my way with women readily; rather they made their way with me." So we see, for example, that Hortense, Rita, and Sondra "make their way" with Clyde; they have reasons for using him, Hortense for money, Sondra to spite the Griffithses of Lycurgus. Clyde, with his dark, melancholy eyes, merely happens to be handy. Roberta, too, in her own fashion, makes her way with him, as Dreiser quite explicitly puts it, for she has been seized by the "very virus of ambition and unrest that afflicted him."

Her own purposes, however shadowy and unadmitted to herself, are at work, but these purposes are transformed into love, while the purposes of Clyde, in his shadowy inner world of self-concern and self-deception, are not. Since Roberta is in love, and he is not, he can dominate her. But there is another factor involved here. Sondra is in love with Clyde too, and he does not dominate her; rather, with her he remains the passive yearner, the one who must "have things done for him," and it is appropriate that she talk baby talk to him. Under-

lying the difference between his dominance of Roberta and his subservience to Sondra is, too, the difference in social scale. To Sondra, Clyde feels socially inferior, this feeling of social inferiority fusing with his other feelings of weakness, but he has sensed that Roberta accepts him as a social superior who stoops to her, who can "do something" for her, and this feeling fuses with his satisfaction in a sexual dominance here achieved for the first time.

So we find, in the instant when Roberta, alarmed by the expression on her lover's face, moves toward him in the boat, this fundamentally significant sentence: "And Clyde, as instantly sensing the profoundness of his own failure, his own cowardice and inadequateness for such an occasion, as instantly yielding to a tide of submerged hate, not only for himself, but for Roberta—her power—or that of life to restrain him in this way." Roberta, the one woman whom he, as a male, has been able to dominate, now seeks to dominate him: she would thwart his desire. And in this instant of her return to the old role all women had had with him, he senses the "profoundness" of his own failure—that is, his life-failure, his sexual failure—and the "submerged hate" bursts forth, and poor Roberta pays for all the pent-up and undecipherable hatred and self-hatred Clyde had found in those other relationships.

The hate that bursts forth from its secret hiding place does not, it must be emphasized, eventuate in an act of will. Dreiser is explicit: "And yet fearing to act in any way. . . ." If the hand holding the camera flies out, the gesture is one of revulsion and self-protection, and of flight that somehow has sexual overtones. If Roberta falls into the water and drowns, he is innocent. And here we are concerned with something different from a mere illustration of unconscious motive, for the episode has a deeper and more ironical implication in which the psychological dimension merges into the metaphysical. Clyde, the blackmailer with the dark, melancholy eyes, Clyde who wants things done for him, Clyde who trusts the Aladdin with the magic lamp—in this, the great crisis of his life, he finds that his deepest wish comes true. The

Efrit has served him faithfully to the end: "For despite your fear, your cowardice, this—this—has been done for you."

His wish is his doom.

To return to our question, if Clyde is merely the passive yearner who "wants things done for him," in what sense is his story a tragedy? The first stage toward an answer may be in the adjective "American," which is best explained by a remark, in *A Hoosier Holiday*, about the atmosphere of American cities: the "crude, sweet illusion about the importance of things material"—the importance, as he puts it elsewhere in a passage already quoted, of "getting on." But behind this illusion is the illusion that in terms of "getting on" a self may be created, or an unworthy self concealed and redeemed. So here, again, as in the trilogy, illusion is the key. With Cowperwood the tragic effect lies in the fact that the hero of great scale and force spends himself on illusion—the illusions of will, love, and art. But the hero who seems so self-sufficient, whose "blazing trail . . . did for the hour illuminate the terrors and wonders of individuality," is in the end only, as Dreiser puts it in the epilogue to *The Financier*, the "prince of a world of dreams whose reality was disillusion." So Dreiser, in Clyde Griffiths, turns his attention to another "prince of dreams." What does it matter if Clyde cannot achieve the "soul-dignity," the sense of identity, that Cowperwood could feel even when, in prison, he stared up at the indifferent constellations, for even that sense of "soul-dignity," though it is the illusion that is the only "truth," is but an illusion.

In the story of Clyde, Dreiser is trying to write the root tragedy. It is a tragedy concerned, as tragedy must be, with the nature of destiny, but, as the root tragedy, it seeks the lowest common denominator of tragic effect, an effect grounded in the essential human situation. It is a type of tragedy based on the notion that, on whatever scale, man's lot is always the same. He is the mechanism envisioned by Jacques Loeb, but he is a mechanism with consciousness. His tragedy lies in the doubleness of his nature. He is doomed, as mechanism, to enact a certain role. As a consciousness, he is doomed to seek self-definition in the "terrors and wonders of individuality," the last illusion and the source of final pain.

In December, 1925, *An American Tragedy* was published, in two volumes. Dreiser, fearing a bad press, had fled New York for Florida, taking Helen with him. But the book was a success. He was rich from the novel, the movie rights, and the play, for which, on the opening night, a hired claque yelled "Bravo, Dreiser!" He set himself up, with Helen, in a luxurious apartment, hired a butler, and had Thursday evenings "at home." He played the stock market. He went to Russia as a guest of the government and found the masses "as Asiatic and dreadful as ever," quarreled with cab drivers, and ended up by writing a trivial and slovenly book about his impressions in which he plagiarized from Dorothy Thompson. He built an eccentric and expensive house in the country. He continued to pursue, sometimes successfully, all sorts of ladies and, in general, tortured Helen. He dabbled in spiritualism. He lost the Nobel prize to Sinclair Lewis.

Meanwhile had come the stock market crash of 1929 and the Depression. Now Dreiser became involved in social and economic questions, matters on which he had violent and often contradictory opinions, and was, at the same time, working on a book intended to be a systematic presentation of his philosophy. A streak of religiosity was beginning to appear in his nature—an echo of old John Paul, but turning him to Quakerism rather than to Catholicism; he was, too, flirting with communism and in 1932 even tried to join the party, which, much to his outrage, turned him down. Meanwhile, he had written a disastrously bad book called *Tragic America* and continued deep in causes, committees, and campaigns—for example, leading a group to investigate conditions in the coal fields in Harlan County, Kentucky (where he got indicted on two counts, criminal syndicalism and adultery). He had lunch with President Roosevelt on the subject of relief for Spain, now in the midst of the Franco revolution. He loathed the English and when, in 1939, the Berlin-Moscow Pact was signed, praised Hitler's wisdom and goodness. When war began, and Roosevelt favored the Allies, he wrote: "I begin to suspect that Hitler is correct. The president may be part Jewish." He also began to cherish the notion that the firm currently suffering as his publishers, Simon and Schuster, was in a Jewish plot to suppress his works. He joined the American Peace Mobilization and made a violently anti-English speech in Washington to an outdoor mass rally. When, after difficulties, he succeeded in getting a printer for his rabid and incoherent book *America Is Worth Saving* (a title changed at the last minute from *Is America Worth Saving?*), he sent an autographed copy to Joseph Stalin. At the news of Hitler's attack on Russia, Dreiser simply retreated to his bed.

Dreiser's health was not good, and clearly his mind was failing. He felt defeated and forgotten. But he managed to do some work on his fiction, for he was still nursing an old Quaker novel, *The Bulwark*, and the last item of the trilogy, *The Stoic*. He wrote a pietistic essay called "My Creator," which indicated the drift his fiction was taking. *The Bulwark*, which, in fact, had started out years ago as an attack on religion, was becoming a story of Job in modern dress, and Dreiser even attended church (Congregational, not Catholic) and took communion. Shortly afterward, however, he applied again for membership in the Communist party (in a letter written for him by party-trained hands expert with the language of propaganda) and was accepted. Even with ill health, he still found energy for his sexual intrigues, including (after he had again fled to California) a ten-day honeymoon in a Los Angeles hotel with an admirer whom he had never seen but whom he had lured West from Detroit. But on June 13, 1944, he married Helen.

It was the last phase. *The Bulwark* finished and turned over to one of the faithful lady editors, Dreiser resumed work on *The Stoic*, dictating to Helen. His strength was failing fast. On December 27, 1945, in accordance with suggestions from James Farrell, who had read the manuscript for him, Dreiser revised the penultimate chapter of the trilogy. Before dawn, he suffered an attack and was put in an oxygen tent. In the afternoon, a Congregational minister came to pray at the bedside. A little later, the death occurred.

Just before he died, Dreiser asked Helen to kiss him.

Dreiser was buried in Forest Lawn Cemetery, in Los Angeles, among the movie moguls and movie stars and their hangers-on, for which final glory he had, no doubt, yearned. At the funeral ceremony, the Congregational minister who had prayed by the bedside spoke; then, John Howard Lawson, a successful movie writer who had shepherded Dreiser into the Communist party. In conclusion, Charlie Chaplin read Dreiser's poem "The Road I Came."

> Ah, what is this
> That knows
> The road I came
> And go again?
> Matter?
> Instinct?
> Energy?
> Nature?
> That whispers of paths
> Beyond these
> Which now I seem to know
> Yet do not;
> Wastes,
> Planes,
> Immensities,
> In remote consciousness,
> Where there is no breath of self,
> Such as I witness here,
> Yet of which
> To be conscious
> Is wisdom—
> Power, perhaps,
> Creative strength.
>
> Oh, inorganic
> Yet breathing
> The organic,—
> Inarticulate,
> Yet voicing itself
> Articulate

In heights,
Depths,
To which we rise
Or sink—
Yet infinite
And from which we take our rise.

Oh, space!
Change!
Toward which we run
So gladly,
Or from which we retreat
In terror—
Yet that promises to bear us
In itself
Forever.

Oh, what is this
That knows the road I came?

At the time of Dreiser's death, his reputation was at a low ebb. His defects were obvious and his virtues were often misunderstood. But as the literature of the first half of the century falls into perspective, Dreiser's fiction gains in stature. The intellectual complexity and coherence of his work, the psychological subtlety, and the structural principles begin to emerge. And most impressively, the creative vigor. In the novel, only Faulkner, in this century, is of the same scale.

BIOGRAPHICAL CHART

1871   Born, August 27, in Terre Haute, Indiana, son of John Paul Dreiser and Sarah Schänäb
1879   Family broken up, never to be permanently reassembled; Dreiser and some of the other children live with mother in various localities—Vincennes, Sullivan, and Evansville
1887–89   Dreiser in Chicago alone; does menial labor; found by Mildred Fielding, his old teacher
1889–90   Attends Indiana University, at Bloomington
1890   Mother dies, November 14
1892   Begins work as reporter on Chicago *Globe*; then St. Louis *Globe-Democrat* and *Republic*
1893   Meets Sara White ("Jug")
1894   Works on newspapers in Toledo, Cleveland, Pittsburgh, New York; edits *Ev'ry Month* and is successful as writer of articles
1898   Marries Jug
1899   Begins work on *Sister Carrie*, in Maumee, Ohio
1900   *Sister Carrie* published; a failure
1901–3   First separated from Jug; has nervous collapse; saved by Paul, who puts him on Muldoon's health farm
1904–6   Resumes editorial career; Street and Smith magazines, *Smith's Magazine*, *Broadway Magazine*
1907   *Sister Carrie* republished; literary success begins; edits Butterick publications—*Delineator*, *New Idea Woman's Magazine*, and *Designer*
1909   *Jennie Gerhardt* begun
1910   Fired, October 15, from Butterick editorship, on account of pursuit of young daughter of a woman employee; works full time on *Jennie Gerhardt*
1911   *Jennie Gerhardt* published to respectful press; travels to Europe to gather material for trilogy based on Charles Tyson Yerkes
1912   *The Financier*; *Sister Carrie* again published, by Harper and Brothers; does research on Yerkes in Chicago; acquainted wth literary and artistic group, including Edgar Lee Masters, Floyd Dell, Margaret Anderson, and actress Kirah Markham, who was to become a mistress
1913   *A Traveler at Forty*
1914   *The Titan*, published less successfully than *The Financier*
1915   *The "Genius"*; banned for obscenity and withdrawn; gets publicity and plays role of literary hero
1918   Dreiser's new publisher, Boni and Liveright, brings out *Free, and Other Stories*, *The Hand of the Potter* (play), and *Twelve Men* (sketches)
1919   Begins liaison with Helen Patges Richardson; leaves for Hollywood with Helen, beginning period there till late 1922; begins *An American Tragedy*
1920   *Hey, Rub-A-Dub-Dub* (philosophical essays)
1922   *A Book About Myself* (autobiography) published, with miserable sale
1923   Works seriously on *An American Tragedy*
1925   *An American Tragedy* appears, with prodigious success; begins life of luxury
1927   Visits Russia; *Chains* (stories)
1928   *Moods, Cadenced and Declaimed* (poems) and *Dreiser Looks at Russia*
1929   *A Gallery of Women*
1931   *Dawn* published, many years after composition; and *A Book About Myself* republished with new title *Newspaper Days*; *Tragic America*

1932–34 Contributing editor of the *American Spectator*, edited by George Jean Nathan and Ernest Boyd
1941 *America Is Worth Saving*
1942 Jug dies
1944 Award of Merit from American Academy of Arts and Letters; marries Helen

1945 Application for membership in Communist party granted; dies, December 28, in Hollywood; buried in Forest Lawn Cemetery
1946 *The Bulwark*
1947 *The Stoic*, last of the trilogy

FURTHER READINGS

There is no standard edition of Dreiser's work. The reader will find the publication dates of many individual titles in the biographical chart and may also find the following books useful.

Robert H. Elias, ed., *Letters* (1959; 3 vols.)
James T. Farrell, introd., *Best Short Stories* (1956)

Helen Dreiser, *My Life with Dreiser* (1951)
Dorothy Dudley, *Dreiser and the Land of the Free* (1932)
Robert H. Elias, *Theodore Dreiser: Apostle of Nature* (1949)
Philip Gerber, *Theodore Dreiser* (1964)
Richard Lehan, *Theodore Dreiser: His World and His Novels* (1969)

John Lydenberg, ed., *Theodore Dreiser: A Collection of Critical Essays* (1971)
F. O. Matthiessen, *Theodore Dreiser* (1951)
John J. McAleer, *Theodore Dreiser: An Introduction and Interpretation* (1968)
Ellen Moers, *The Two Dreisers: The Man and the Novelist As Revealed in His Two Most Important Works* (1969)
Charles Shapiro, *Theodore Dreiser: Our Bitter Patriot* (1962)
——— and Alfred Kazin, *The Stature of Theodore Dreiser* (1955)
W. A. Swanberg, *Dreiser* (1965)
Robert Penn Warren, *Homage to Theodore Dreiser* (1971)

From An American Tragedy (1925)

This selection begins near the end of Chapter 44, shortly after Clyde's reading of a newspaper account of an accidental drowning at Pass Lake has set in train the desire to murder Roberta.

———

But, good God! What was he thinking of anyhow? He, Clyde Griffiths! The nephew of Samuel Griffiths! What was "getting into" him? Murder! That's what it was. This terrible item—this devil's accident or machination that was constantly putting it before him! A most horrible crime, and one for which they electrocuted people if they were caught. Besides, he could not murder anybody—not Roberta, anyhow. Oh, no! Surely not after all that had been between them. And yet—this other world!—Sondra —which he was certain to lose now unless he acted in some way——

His hands shook, his eyelids twitched—then his hair at the roots tingled and over his body ran chill nervous titillations in waves. Murder! Or upsetting a boat at any rate in deep water, which of course might happen anywhere, and by accident, as at Pass Lake. And Roberta could not swim. He knew that. But she might save herself at that—scream—cling to the boat—and then—if there were any to hear—and she told afterwards! An icy perspiration now sprang to his forehead; his lips trembled and suddenly his throat felt parched and dry. To prevent a thing like that he would have to—to—but no—he was not like that. He could not do a thing like that—hit any one—a girl—Roberta—and when drowning or struggling. Oh, no, no—no such thing as that! Impossible.

He took his straw hat and went out, almost before any one heard him *think*, as he would have phrased it to himself, such horrible, terrible thoughts. He could not and would not think them from now on. He was no such person. And yet—and yet—these thoughts. The solution—if he wanted one. The way to stay here—not leave—marry Sondra —be rid of Roberta and all—all—for the price of a little courage or daring. But no!

He walked and walked—away from Lycurgus— out on a road to the southeast which passed through a poor and decidedly unfrequented rural section, and so left him alone to think—or, as he felt, not to be heard in his thinking.

Day was fading into dark. Lamps were beginning to glow in the cottages here and there. Trees in groups in fields or along the road were beginning to blur or smokily blend. And although it was warm—the air lifeless and lethargic—he walked fast, thinking, and perspiring as he did so, as though he were seeking to outwalk and outthink or divert some inner self that preferred to be still and think.

That gloomy, lonely lake up there!

That island to the south!

Who would see?

Who could hear?

That station at Gun Lodge with a bus running to it at this season of the year. (Ah, he remembered that, did he? The deuce!) A terrible thing, to remember a thing like that in connection with such a thought as this! But if he were going to think of such a thing as this at all, he had better think well—he could tell himself that—or stop thinking about it now—once and forever—forever. But Sondra! Roberta! If ever he were caught—electrocuted! And yet the actual misery of his present state. The difficulty! The danger of losing Sondra. And yet, murder—

He wiped his hot and wet face, and paused and gazed at a group of trees across a field which somehow reminded him of the trees of . . . well . . . he didn't like this road. It was getting too dark out here. He had better turn and go back. But that road at the south and leading to Three Mile Bay and Greys Lake—if one chose to go that way—to Sharon and the Cranston Lodge—whither he would be going afterwards if he did go that way. God! Big Bittern—the trees along there after dark would be like that—blurred and gloomy. It would have to be toward evening, of course. No one would think of trying to . . . well . . . in the morning, when there was so much light. Only a fool would do that. But at night, toward dusk, as it was now, or a little later. But, damn it, he would not listen to such thoughts. Yet no one would be likely to see him or Roberta either—would they—there? It would be so easy to go to a place like Big Bittern—for an alleged wedding trip—would it not—over the Fourth, say—or after the fourth or fifth, when there would be fewer people. And to register as some one else —not himself—so that he could never be traced that way. And then, again, it would be so easy to get back to Sharon and the Cranstons' by midnight, or the morning of the next day, maybe, and then, once there he could pretend also that he had come north on that early morning train that arrived about ten o'clock. And then . . .

Confound it—why should his mind keep dwelling on this idea? Was he actually planning to do a thing like this? But he was not! He could not be! He, Clyde Griffiths, could not be serious about a thing like this. That was not possible. He could not be. Of course! It was all too impossible, too wicked, to imagine that he, Clyde Griffiths, could bring himself to execute a deed like that. And yet . . . .

And forthwith an uncanny feeling of wretchedness and insufficiency for so dark a crime insisted on thrusting itself forward. He decided to retrace his steps toward Lycurgus, where at least he could be among people.

There are moments when in connection with the sensitively imaginative or morbidly anachronistic— the mentality assailed and the same not of any great strength and the problem confronting it of sufficient force and complexity—the reason not actually toppling from its throne, still totters or is warped or shaken—the mind befuddled to the extent that for the time being, at least, unreason or disorder and mistaken or erroneous counsel would appear to hold against all else. In such instances the will and the courage confronted by some great difficulty which it can neither master nor endure, appears in some to recede in precipitate flight, leaving only panic and temporary unreason in its wake.

And in this instance, the mind of Clyde might well have been compared to a small and routed army in full flight before a major one, yet at various times in its precipitate departure, pausing for a moment to meditate on some way of escaping complete destruction and in the coincident panic of such a state, resorting to the weirdest and most haphazard of schemes of escaping from an impending and yet wholly unescapable fate. The strained and bedeviled look in his eyes at moments—the manner in which, from moment to moment and hour to hour, he went over and over his hitherto poorly balanced actions and thoughts but with no smallest door of escape anywhere. And yet again at moments the solution suggested by the item in *The Times-Union* again thrusting itself forward, psychogenetically, born of his own turbulent, eager and disappointed seeking. And hence persisting.

Indeed, it was now as though from the depths of some lower or higher world never before guessed or plumbed by him . . . a region otherwise than in life or death and peopled by creatures otherwise than himself . . . there had now suddenly appeared, as the genie at the accidental rubbing of Aladdin's lamp—as the efrit emerging as smoke from the mystic jar in the net of the fisherman— the very substance of some leering and diabolic wish or wisdom concealed in his own nature, and that now abhorrent and yet compelling, leering and yet intriguing, friendly and yet cruel, offered him a choice between an evil which threatened to destroy him (and against his deepest opposition) and a second evil which, however it might disgust or sear or terrify, still provided for freedom and success and love.

Indeed the center or mentating section of his brain at this time might well have been compared to a sealed and silent hall in which alone and undisturbed, and that in spite of himself, he now sat thinking on the mystic or evil and terrifying desires or advice of some darker or primordial and unregenerate nature of his own, and without the power to drive the same forth or himself to decamp, and yet also without the courage to act upon anything.

For now the genie of his darkest and weakest side was speaking. And it said: "And would you escape from the demands of Roberta that but now and unto this hour have appeared unescapable to you? Behold! I bring you a way. It is the way of the lake—Pass Lake. This item that you have read— do you think it was placed in your hands for nothing? Remember Big Bittern, the deep, blue-black water, the island to the south, the lone road to Three Mile Bay? How suitable to your needs! A row-boat or a canoe upset in such a lake and Roberta would pass forever from your life. She cannot swim! The lake—the lake—that you have seen—that I have shown you—is it not ideal for the purpose? So removed and so little frequented and yet comparatively near—but a hundred miles from here. And how easy for you and Roberta to go there—not directly but indirectly—on this purely imaginative marriage-trip that you have already agreed to. And all that you need do now is to change your name —and hers—or let her keep her own and you use yours. You have never permitted her to speak of you and this relationship, and she never has. You have written her but formal notes. And now if you should meet her somewhere as you have already agreed to, and without any one seeing you, you might travel with her, as in the past to Fonda, to Big Bittern—or some point near there."

"But there is no hotel at Big Bittern," at once

corrected Clyde. "A mere shack that entertains but few people and that not very well."

"All the better. The less people are likely to be there."

"But we might be seen on the train going up together. I would be identified as having been with her."

"Were you seen at Fonda, Gloversville, Little Falls? Have you not ridden in separate cars or seats before and could you not do so now? Is it not presumably to be a secret marriage? Then why not a secret honeymoon?"

"True enough—true enough."

"And once you have arranged for that and arrive at Big Bittern or some lake like it—there are so many there—how easy to row out on such a lake? No questions. No registry under your own name or hers. A boat rented for an hour or half-day or day. You saw the island far to the south on that lone lake. Is it not beautiful? It is well worth seeing. Why should you not go there on such a pleasure trip before marriage? Would she not be happy so to do—as weary and distressed as she is now—an outing—a rest before the ordeal of the new life? Is not that sensible—plausible? And neither of you will ever return presumably. You will both be drowned, will you not? Who is to see? A guide or two—the man who rents you the boat—the innkeeper once, as you go. But how are they to know who you are? Or who she is? And you heard the depth of the water."

"But I do not want to kill her. I do not want to kill her. I do not want to injure her in any way. If she will but let me go and she go her own way, I will be so glad and so happy never to see her more."

"But she will not let you go or go her way unless you accompany her. And if you go yours, it will be without Sondra and all that she represents, as well as all this pleasant life here—your standing with your uncle, his friends, their cars, the dances, visits to the lodges on the lakes. And what then? A small job! Small pay! Another such period of wandering as followed that accident at Kansas City. Never another chance like this anywhere. Do you prefer that?"

"But might there not be some accident here, destroying all my dreams—my future—as there was in Kansas City?"

"An accident, to be sure—but not the same. In this instance the plan is in your hands. You can arrange it all as you will. And how easy! So many boats upsetting every summer—the occupants of them drowning, because in most cases they cannot swim. And will it ever be known whether the man who was with Roberta Alden on Big Bittern could swim? And of all deaths, drowning is the easiest—no noise—no outcry—perhaps the accidental blow of an oar—the side of a boat. And then silence! Freedom—a body that no one may ever find. Or if found and identified, will it not be easy, if you but trouble to plan, to make it appear that you were elsewhere, visiting at one of the other lakes before you decided to go to Twelfth Lake. What is wrong with it? Where is the flaw?"

"But assuming that I should upset the boat and that she should not drown, then what? Should cling to it, cry out, be saved and relate afterward that . . . But no, I cannot do that—will not do it. I will not hit her. That would be too terrible . . . too vile."

"But a little blow—any little blow under such circumstances would be sufficient to confuse and complete her undoing. Sad, yes, but she has an opportunity to go her own way, has she not? And she will not, nor let you go yours. Well, then, is this so terribly unfair? And do not forget that afterwards there is Sondra—the beautiful—a home with her in Lycurgus—wealth, a high position such as elsewhere you may never obtain again—never—never. Love and happiness—the equal of any one here—superior even to your cousin Gilbert."

The voice ceased temporarily, trailing off into shadow,—silence, dreams.

And Clyde, contemplating all that had been said, was still unconvinced. Darker fears or better impulses supplanted the counsel of the voice in the great hall. But presently thinking of Sondra and all that she represented, and then of Roberta, the dark personality would as suddenly and swiftly return and with amplified suavity and subtlety.

"Ah, still thinking on the matter. And you have not found a way out and you will not. I have truly pointed out to you and in all helpfulness the only way—the only way—It is a long lake. And would it not be easy in rowing about to eventually find some secluded spot—some invisible nook near that south shore where the water is deep? And from there how easy to walk through the woods to Three Mile Bay and Upper Greys Lake? And from there to the Cranstons'? There is a boat from there, as you know. Pah—how cowardly—how lacking in courage to win the thing that above all things you desire—beauty—wealth—position—the solution of your every material and spiritual desire.

And with poverty, commonplace, hard and poor work as the alternative to all this.

"But you must choose—choose! And then act. You must! You must! You must!"

Thus the voice in parting, echoing from some remote part of the enormous chamber.

And Clyde, listening at first with horror and in terror, later with a detached and philosophic calm as one who, entirely apart from what he may think or do, is still entitled to consider even the wildest and most desperate proposals for his release, at last, because of his own mental and material weakness before pleasures and dreams which he could not bring himself to forego, psychically intrigued to the point where he was beginning to think that it might be possible. Why not? Was it not even as the voice said—a possible and plausible way—all his desires and dreams to be made real by this one evil thing? Yet in his case, because of flaws and weaknesses in his own unstable and highly variable will, the problem was not to be solved by thinking thus—then—nor for the next ten days for that matter.

He could not really act on such a matter for himself and would not. It remained as usual for him to be forced either to act or to abandon this most *wild* and terrible thought. Yet during this time a series of letters—seven from Roberta, five from Sondra—in which in somber tones in so far as Roberta was concerned—in gay and colorful ones in those which came from Sondra—was painted the now so sharply contrasting phases of the black rebus which lay before him. To Roberta's pleadings, argumentative and threatening as they were, Clyde did not trust himself to reply, not even by telephone. For now he reasoned that to answer would be only to lure Roberta to her doom—or to the attempted drastic conclusion of his difficulties as outlined by the tragedy at Pass Lake.

At the same time, in several notes addressed to Sondra, he gave vent to the most impassioned declarations of love—his darling—his wonder girl—how eager he was to be at Twelfth Lake by the morning of the Fourth, if he could, and so thrilled to see her there again. Yet, alas, as he also wrote now, so uncertain was he, even now, as to how he was to do, there were certain details in connection with his work here that might delay him a day or two or three—he could not tell as yet—but would write her by the second at the latest, when he would know positively. Yet saying to himself as he wrote this, if she but knew what those details were—if she but knew. Yet in penning this, and without having as yet answered the last importunate letter from Roberta, he was also saying to himself that this did not mean that he was planning to go to Roberta at all, or that if he did, it did not mean that he was going to attempt to kill her. Never once did he honestly, or to put it more accurately, forthrightly and courageously or coldly face the thought of committing so grim a crime. On the contrary, the nearer he approached a final resolution or the need for one in connection with all this, the more hideous and terrible seemed the idea—hideous and difficult, and hence the more improbable it seemed that he should ever commit it. It was true that from moment to moment—arguing with himself as he constantly was—sweating mental sweats and fleeing from moral and social terrors in connection with it all, he was thinking from time to time that he might go to Big Bittern in order to quiet her in connection with these present importunities and threats and hence (once more evasion—tergiversation with himself) give himself more time in which to conclude what his true course must be.

The way of the Lake.

The way of the Lake.

But once there—whether it would then be advisable so to do—or not—well who could tell. He might even yet be able to convert Roberta to some other point of view. For, say what you would, she was certainly acting very unfairly and captiously in all this. She was, as he saw it in connection with his very vital dream of Sondra, making a mountain —an immense terror—out of a state that when all was said and done, was not so different from Esta's. And Esta had not compelled any one to marry her. And how much better were the Aldens to his own parents—poor farmers as compared to poor preachers. And why should he be so concerned as to what they would think when Esta had not troubled to think what her parents would feel?

In spite of all that Roberta had said about blame, was she so entirely lacking in blame herself? To be sure, he had sought to entice or seduce her, as you will, but even so, could she be held entirely blameless? Could she not have refused, if she was so positive at the time that she was so very moral? But she had not. And as to all this, all that he had done, had he not done all he could to help her out of it? And he had so little money, too. And was placed in such a difficult position. She was just as much to blame as he was. And yet now she was so

determined to drive him this way. To insist on his marrying her, whereas if she would only go her own way—as she could with his help—she might still save both of them all this trouble.

But no, she would not, and he would not marry her and that was all there was to it. She need not think that she could make him. No, no, no! At times, when in such moods, he felt that he could do anything—drown her easily enough, and she would only have herself to blame.

Then again his more cowering sense of what society would think and do, if it knew, what he himself would be compelled to think of himself afterwards, fairly well satisfied him that as much as he desired to stay, he was not the one to do anything at all and in consequence must flee.

And so it was that Tuesday, Wednesday and Thursday following Roberta's letter received on Monday, had passed. And then, on Thursday night, following a most torturesome mental day on his and Roberta's part for that matter, this is what he received:

Biltz, Wednesday, June 30th.

DEAR CLYDE:

This is to tell you that unless I hear from you either by telephone or letter before noon, Friday, I shall be in Lycurgus that same night, and the world will know how you have treated me. I cannot and will not wait and suffer one more hour. I regret to be compelled to take this step, but you have allowed all this time to go in silence really, and Saturday is the third, and without any plans of any kind. My whole life is ruined and so will yours be in a measure, but I cannot feel that I am entirely to blame. I have done all I possibly could to make this burden as easy for you as possible and I certainly regret all the misery it will cause my parents and friends and all whom you know and hold dear. But I will not wait and suffer one hour more.

ROBERTA.

And with this in his hands, he was finally all but numbed by the fact that now decidedly he must act. She was actually coming! Unless he could soothe or restrain her in some manner she would be here to-morrow—the second. And yet the second, or the third, or any time until after the Fourth, was no time to leave with her. The holiday crowds would be too great. There would be too many people to see—to encounter. There must be more secrecy. He must have at least a little more time in which to get ready. He must think now quickly and then act. Great God! Get ready. Could he not telephone her and say that he had been sick or so worried on account of the necessary money or something that he could not write—and that besides his uncle had sent for him to come to Greenwood Lake over the Fourth. His uncle! His uncle! No, that would not do. He had used his name too much. What difference should it make to him or her now, whether he saw his uncle once more or not? He was leaving once and for all, or so he had been telling her, on her account, was he not? And so he had better say that he was going to his uncle, in order to give a reason why he was going away so that, possibly, he might be able to return in a year or so. She might believe that. At any rate he must tell her something that would quiet her until after the Fourth—make her stay up there until at least he could perfect some plan— bring himself to the place where he could do one thing or the other. One thing or the other.

Without pausing to plan anything more than just this at this time, he hurried to the nearest telephone where he was least likely to be overheard. And, getting her once more, began one of those long and evasive and, in this instance, ingratiating explanations which eventually, after he had insisted that he had actually been sick—confined to his room with a fever and hence not able to get to a telephone—and because, as he now said, he had finally decided that it would be best if he were to make some explanation to his uncle, so that he might return some time in the future, if necessary —he, by using the most pleading, if not actually affectionate, tones and asking her to consider what a state he had been in, too, was able not only to make her believe that there was some excuse for his delay and silence, but also to introduce the plan that he now had in mind; which was if only she could wait until the sixth, then assuredly, without fail as to any particular, he would meet her at any place she would choose to come—Homer, Fonda, Lycurgus, Little Falls—only since they were trying to keep everything so secret, he would suggest that she come to Fonda on the morning of the sixth in order to make the noon train for Utica. There they could spend the night since they could not very well discuss and decide on their plans over the telephone, now, and then they could act upon whatever they had decided. Besides he could tell her better then just how he thought they

ought to do. He had an idea—a little trip maybe, somewhere before they got married or after, just as she wished, but—something nice anyhow—(his voice grew husky and his knees and hands shook slightly as he said this, only Roberta could not detect the sudden perturbation within him). But she must not ask him now. He could not tell her over the phone. But as sure as anything, at noon on the sixth, he would be on the station platform at Fonda. All she had to do after seeing him was to buy her ticket to Utica and get in one coach, and he would buy his separately and get in an- other—the one just ahead or behind hers. On the way down, if she didn't see him at the station beforehand, he would pass through her car for a drink so that she could see that he was there—no more than that—but she mustn't speak to him. Then once in Utica, she should check her bag and he would follow her out to the nearest quiet corner. After that he would go and get her bag, and then they could go to some little hotel and he would take care of all the rest.

But she must do this. Would she have that much faith in him? If so, he would call her up on the third—the very next day—and on the morning of the sixth—sure, so that both he and she would know that everything was all right—that she was starting and that he would be there. What was that? Her trunk? The little one? Sure. If she needed it, certainly bring it. Only, if he were she, he would not trouble to try to bring too much now, because once she was settled somewhere, it would be easy enough to send for anything else that she really needed.

As Clyde stood at the telephone in a small outlying drug store and talked—the lonely proprietor buried in a silly romance among his pots and phials at the back—it seemed as though the Giant Efrit that had previously materialized in the silent halls of his brain, was once more here at his elbow —that he himself, cold and numb and fearsome, was being talked through—not actually talking himself.

Go to the lake which you visited with Sondra!

Get travel folders of the region there from either the Lycurgus House here or the depot.

Go to the south end of it and from there walk south, afterwards.

Pick a boat that will upset easily—one with a round bottom, such as those you have seen here at Crum Lake and up there.

Buy a new and different hat and leave that on

the water—one that cannot be traced to you. You might even tear the lining out of it so that it cannot be traced.

Pack all of your things in your trunk here, but leave it, so that swiftly, in the event that anything goes wrong, you can return here and get it and depart.

And take only such things with you as will make it seem as though you were going for an outing to Twelfth Lake—not away, so that should you be sought at Twelfth Lake, it will look as though you had gone only there, not elsewhere.

Tell her that you intend to marry her, but *after* you return from this outing, not before.

And if necessary strike a light blow, so as to stun her—no more—so that falling in the water, she will drown the more easily.

Do not fear!

Do not be weak!

Walk through the woods by night, not by day—so that when seen again you will be in Three Mile Bay or Sharon—and can say that you came from Racquette or Long Lake south, or from Lycurgus north.

Use a false name and alter your handwriting as much as possible.

Assume that you will be successful.

And whisper, whisper—let your language be soft, your tone tender, loving, even. It must be, if you are to win her to your will now.

So the Efrit of his own darker self.

And then at noon on Tuesday, July sixth, the station platform of the railroad running from Fonda to Utica, with Roberta stepping down from the train which came south from Biltz to await Clyde, for the train that was to take them to Utica was not due for another half hour. And fifteen minutes later Clyde himself coming from a side street and approaching the station from the south, from which position Roberta could not see him but from where, after turning the west corner of the depot and stationing himself behind a pile of crates, he could see her. How thin and pale indeed! By contrast with Sondra, how illy-dressed in the blue traveling suit and small brown hat with which she had equipped herself for this occasion—the promise of a restricted and difficult life as contrasted with that offered by Sondra. And she was thinking of compelling him to give up Sondra in order to marry her, and from which union he might never be able to extricate himself until such

time as would make Sondra and all she represented a mere recollection. The difference between the attitudes of these two girls—Sondra with everything offering all—asking nothing of him; Roberta, with nothing, asking all.

A feeling of dark and bitter resentment swept over him and he could not help but feel sympathetic toward that unknown man at Pass Lake and secretly wish that he had been successful. Perhaps he, too, had been confronted by a situation just like this. And perhaps he had done right, too, after all, and that was why it had not been found out. His nerves twitched. His eyes were somber, resentful and yet nervous. Could it not happen again successfully in this case?

But here he was now upon the same platform with her as the result of her persistent and illogical demands, and he must be thinking how, and boldly, he must carry out the plans which, for four days, or ever since he had telephoned her, and in a dimmer way for the ten preceding those, he had been planning. This settled course must not be interfered with now. He must act! He must not let fear influence him to anything less than he had now planned.

And so it was that he now stepped forth in order that she might see him, at the same time giving her a wise and seemingly friendly and informative look as if to say, "You see I am here." But behind the look! If only she could have pierced beneath the surface and sensed that dark and tortured mood, how speedily she would have fled. But now seeing him actually present, a heavy shadow that was lurking in her eyes lifted, the somewhat down-turned corners of her mouth reversed themselves, and without appearing to recognize him, she nevertheless brightened and at once proceeded to the window to purchase her ticket to Utica, as he had instructed her to do.

And she was now thinking that at last, at last he had come. And he was going to take her away. And hence a kind of gratefulness for this welling up in her. For they were to be together for seven or eight months at the least. And while it might take tact and patience to adjust things, still it might and probably could be done. From now on she must be the very soul of caution—not do or say anything that would irritate him in any way, since naturally he would not be in the best mood because of this. But he must have changed some—perhaps he was seeing her in a more kindly light—sympathizing with her a little, since he now appeared at last to have most gracefully and genially succumbed to the unavoidable. And at the same time noting his light gray suit, his new straw hat, his brightly polished shoes and the dark tan suit-case and (strange, equivocal, frivolous erraticism of his in this instance) the tripod of a recently pur-chased camera together with his tennis racquet in its canvas case strapped to the side—more than anything to conceal the initials C. G.—she was seized with much of her old-time mood and desire in regard to his looks and temperament. He was still, and despite his present indifference to her, her Clyde.

Having seen her secure her ticket, he now went to get his own, and then, with another knowing look in her direction, which said that everything was now all right, he returned to the eastern end of the platform, while she returned to her position at the forward end.

(*Why was that old man in that old brown win-ter suit and hat and carrying that bird cage in a brown paper looking at him so? Could he sense anything? Did he know him? Had he ever worked in Lycurgus or seen him before?*)

He was going to buy a second straw hat in Utica to-day—he must remember that—a straw hat with a Utica label, which he would wear instead of his present one. Then, when she was not looking, he would put the old one in his bag with his other things. That was why he would have to leave her for a little while after they reached Utica—at the depot or library or somewhere—perhaps as was his first plan, take her to some small hotel somewhere and register as Mr. and Mrs. Carl Graham or Clif-ford Golden or Gehring (there was a girl in the factory by that name) so if they were ever traced in any way, it would be assumed that she had gone away with some man of that name.

(*That whistle of a train afar off. It must be coming now. His watch said twelve-twenty-seven.*)

And again he must decide what his manner to-ward her in Utica must be—whether very cordial or the opposite. For over the telephone, of course, he had talked very soft and genial-like because he had to. Perhaps it would be best to keep that up, otherwise she might become angry or suspicious or stubborn and that would make it hard.

(*Would that train never get here?*)

At the same time it was going to be very hard on him to be so very pleasant when, after all, she was driving him as she was—expecting him to do all that she was asking him to do and yet be nice to her. Damn! And yet if he weren't?—Supposing she should sense something of his thoughts in connection with this—really refuse to go through with it this way and spoil his plans.

(*If only his knees and hands wouldn't tremble so at times.*)

But no, how was she to be able to detect any-thing of that kind, when he himself had not quite made up his mind as to whether he would be able to go through with it or not? He only knew he was not going away with her, and that was all there was to that. He might not upset the boat, as he had decided on the day before, but just the same he was not going away with her.

But here now was the train. And there was Roberta lifting her bag. Was it too heavy for her in her present state? It probably was. Well, too bad. It was very hot to-day, too. At any rate he would help her with it later, when they were where no one could see them. She was looking toward him to be sure he was getting on—so like her these days, in her suspicious, doubtful mood in regard to him. But here was a seat in the rear of the car on the shady side, too. That was not so bad. He would settle himself comfortably and look out. For just outside Fonda, a mile or two beyond, was that same Mohawk that ran through Lycurgus and past the factory, and along the banks of which the year before, he and Roberta had walked about this time. But the memory of that being far from pleasant now, he turned his eyes to a paper he had bought, and behind which he could shield himself as much as possible, while he once more began to observe the details of the more inward scene which now so much more concerned him—the nature of the lake country around Big Bittern, which ever since that final important conversation with Ro-berta over the telephone, had been interesting him more than any other geography of the world.

For on Friday, after the conversation, he had stopped in at the Lycurgus House and secured three different folders relating to hotels, lodges, inns and other camps in the more remote region beyond Big Bittern and Long Lake. (If only there were some way to get to one of those completely deserted lakes described by that guide at Big Bittern—only, perhaps, there might not be any row-boats on any of these lakes at all!) And again on Saturday, had he not secured four more circulars from the rack at the depot (they were in his pocket now)? Had they not proved how many small lakes and inns there were along this same railroad, which ran north to Big Bittern, to which he and Roberta might resort for a day or two if she would —a night, anyhow, before going to Big Bittern and Grass Lake—had he not noted that in particular—a beautiful lake it had said—near the station, and with at least three attractive lodges or country home inns where two could stay for as low as twenty dollars a week. That meant that two could stay for one night surely for as little as five dollars. It must be so surely—and so he was going to say to her, as he had already planned these several days, that she needed a little rest before going away to a strange place. That it would not cost very much—about fifteen dollars for fares and all, so the circulars said—if they went to Grass Lake for a night— this same night after reaching Utica—or on the morrow, anyhow. And he would have to picture it all to her as a sort of honeymoon journey—a little pleasant outing—before getting married. And it would not do to succumb to any plan of hers to get married before they did this—that would never do.

(*Those five birds winging toward that patch of trees over there—below that hill.*)

It certainly would not do to go direct to Big Bittern from Utica for a boat ride—just one day— seventy miles. That would not sound right to her, or to any one. It would make her suspicious, maybe. It might be better, since he would have to get away from her to buy a hat in Utica, to spend this first night there at some inexpensive, inconspicuous hotel, and once there, suggest going up to Grass Lake. And from there they could go to Big Bittern in the morning. He could say that Big Bittern was nicer—or that they would go down to Three Mile Bay—a hamlet really as he knew— where they could be married, but en route stop at Big Bittern as a sort of lark. He would say that he wanted to show her the lake—take some pictures of her and himself. He had brought his camera for that and for other pictures of Sondra later.

The blackness of this plot of his!

(*Those nine black and white cows on that green hillside.*)

But again, strapping that tripod along with his tennis racquet to the side of his suitcase, might not that cause people to imagine that they were passing tourists from some distant point, maybe, and if they both disappeared, well, then, they were not people from anywhere around here, were they? Didn't the guide say that the water in the lake was all of seventy-five feet deep—like that water at Pass Lake? And as for Roberta's grip—oh, yes, what about that? He hadn't even thought about that as yet, really.

(*Those three automobiles out there running almost as fast as this train.*)

Well, in coming down from Grass Lake after one night there (he could say that he was going to marry her at Three Mile Bay at the north end of Greys Lake, where a minister lived whom he had met), he would induce her to leave her bag at that Gun Lodge station, where they took the bus over to Big Bittern, while he took his with him. He could just say to some one—the boatman, maybe, or the driver, that he was taking his camera in his bag, and ask where the best views were. Or maybe a lunch. Was that not a better idea—to take a lunch and so deceive Roberta, too, perhaps? And that would tend to mislead the driver, also, would it not? People did carry cameras in bags when they went out on lakes, at times. At any rate it was most necessary for him to carry his bag in this instance. Else why the plan to go south to that island and from thence through the woods?

(*Oh, the grimness and the terror of this plan! Could he really execute it?*)

But that strange cry of that bird at Big Bittern. He had not liked that, or seeing that guide up there who might remember him now. He had not talked to him at all—had not even gotten out of the car, but had only looked out at him through the window; and in so far as he could recall the guide had not even once looked at him—had merely talked to Grant Cranston and Harley Baggott, who had gotten out and had done all the talking. But supposing this guide should be there and remember him? But how could that be when he really had not seen him? This guide would probably not remember him at all—might not even be there. But why should his hands and face be damp all the time now—wet almost, and cold—his knees shaky?

(*This train was following the exact curve of this stream—and last summer he and Roberta. But no—*)

As soon as they reached Utica now this was the way he would do—and must keep it well in mind and not get rattled in any way. He must not—he must not. He must let her walk up the street before him, say a hundred feet or so between them, so that no one would think he was following her, of course. And then when they were quite alone somewhere he would catch up with her and explain all about this—be very nice as though he cared for her as much as ever now—he would have to—if he were to get her to do as he wanted. And then—and then, oh, yes, have her wait while he went for that extra straw hat that he was going to— well, leave on the water, maybe. And the oars, too, of course. And her hat—and—well—

(*The long, sad sounding whistle of this train. Damn. He was getting nervous already.*)

But before going to the hotel, he must go back to the depot and put his new hat in the bag, or better yet, carry it while he looked for the sort of hotel he wanted, and then, before going to Roberta, take the hat and put it in his bag. Then he would go and find her and have her come to the entrance of the hotel he had found and wait for him, while he got the bags. And, of course, if there was no one around or very few, they would enter together, only she could wait in the ladies' parlor somewhere, while he went and registered as Charles Golden, maybe, this time. And then, well, in the morning, if she agreed, or to-night, for that matter, if there were any trains—he would have to find out about that—they could go up to Grass Lake in separate cars until they were past Twelfth Lake and Sharon, at any rate.

(*The beautiful Cranston Lodge there and Sondra.*)

And then—and then—

. . .

And then the next day at noon, Gun Lodge and Big Bittern itself and Clyde climbing down from the train at Gun Lodge and escorting Roberta to the waiting bus, the while he assured her that since they were coming back this way, it would be best if she were to leave her bag here, while he, because of his camera as well as the lunch done up at Grass Lake and crowded into his suitcase, would take his own with him, because they would lunch on the lake. But on reaching the bus, he was dismayed by the fact that the driver was the same guide whom he had heard talk at Big Bittern.

What if it should prove now that this guide had seen and remembered him! Would he not at least recall the handsome Finchley car—Bertine and Stuart on the front seat—himself and Sondra at the back—Grant and that Harley Baggott talking to him outside?

At once that cold perspiration that had marked his more nervous and terrified moods for weeks past, now burst forth on his face and hands. Of what had he been thinking, anyhow? How planning? In God's name, how expect to carry a thing like this through, if he were going to think so poorly? It was like his failing to wear his cap from Lycurgus to Utica, or at least getting it out of his bag before he tried to buy that straw hat; it was like not buying the straw hat before he went to Utica at all.

Yet the guide did not remember him, thank God! On the contrary he inquired rather curiously, and as of a total stranger: "Goin' over to the lodge at Big Bittern? First time up here?" And Clyde, enormously relieved and yet really tremulous, replied: "Yes," and then in his nervous excitement asked: "Many people over there to-day?" a question which the moment he had propounded it, seemed almost insane. Why, why, of all questions, should he ask that? Oh, God, would his silly, self-destructive mistakes never cease?

So troubled was he indeed, now, that he scarcely heard the guide's reply, or, if at all, as a voice speaking from a long way off. "Not so many. About seven or eight, I guess. We did have about thirty over the Fourth, but most o' them went down yesterday."

The stillness of these pines lining this damp yellow road along which they were traveling; the cool and the silence; the dark shadows and purple and gray depths and nooks in them, even at high noon. If one were slipping away at night or by day, who would encounter one here? A blue-jay far in the depths somewhere uttered its metallic shriek; a field sparrow, tremulous upon some distant twig, filled the silver shadows with its perfect song. And Roberta, as this heavy, covered bus crossed rill and thin stream, and then rough wooden bridges here and there, commented on the clarity and sparkle of the water: "Isn't that wonderful in there? Do you hear the tinkling of that water, Clyde? Oh, the freshness of this air!"

And yet she was going to die so soon!

God!

But supposing now, at Big Bittern—the lodge and boathouse there—there were many people. Or that the lake, peradventure, was literally dotted with those that were there—all fishermen and all fishing here and there, each one separate and alone —no privacy or a deserted spot anywhere. And how strange he had not thought of that. This lake was probably not nearly as deserted as he had imagined, or would not be to-day, any more than Grass Lake had proved. And then what?

Well, flight then—flight—and let it go at that. This strain was too much—hell—he would die, thinking thoughts like these. How could he have dreamed to better his fortunes by any so wild and brutal a scheme as this anyhow—to kill and then run away—or rather to kill and pretend that he and she had drowned—while he—the real murderer —slipped away to life and happiness. What a horrible plan! And yet how else? How? Had he not come all this way to do this? And was he going to turn back now?

And all this time Roberta at his side was imagining that she was not going to anything but marriage—to-morrow morning sure; and now only to the passing pleasure of seeing this beautiful lake of which he had been talking—talking, as though it were something more important and delectable than any that had as yet been in her or his life for that matter.

But now the guide was speaking again, and to him: "You're not mindin' to stay over, I suppose. I see you left the young lady's bag over there." He nodded in the direction of Gun Lodge.

"No, we're going on down to-night—on that 8:10. You take people over to that?"

"Oh, sure."

"They said you did—at Grass Lake."

But now why should he have added that reference to Grass Lake, for that showed that he and Roberta had been there before coming here. But this fool with his reference to "the young lady's bag"! And leaving it at Gun Lodge. The Devil! Why shouldn't he mind his own business? Or why should he have decided that he and Roberta were not married? Or had he so decided? At any rate, why such a question when they were carrying two bags and he had brought one? Strange! The effrontery! How should he know or guess or what? But what harm could it do—married or unmarried? If she were not found—"married or unmarried" would make no difference, would it? And if she were, and it was discovered that she was not married, would that not prove that she was off with some one else? Of course! So why worry over that now?

And Roberta asking: "Are there any hotels or boarding houses on the lake besides this one we're going to?"

"Not a one, miss, outside o' the inn that we're goin' to. There was a crowd of young fellers and girls campin' over on the east shore, yisterday, I believe, about a mile from the inn—but whether they're there now or not, I dunno. Ain't seen none of 'em to-day."

A crowd of young fellows and girls! For God's sake! And might not they now be out on the water —all of them—rowing—or sailing—or what? And he here with her! Maybe some of them from Twelfth Lake! Just as he and Sondra and Harriet and Stuart and Bertine had come up two weeks before— some of them friends of the Cranstons, Harriets, Finchleys or others who had come up here to play and who would remember him, of course. And again, then, there must be a road to the east of this lake. And all this knowledge and their presence there now might make this trip of his useless. Such silly plotting! Such pointless planning as this —when at least he might have taken more time— chosen a lake still farther away and should have —only so tortured had he been for these last many days, that he could scarcely think how to think. Well, all he could do now was to go and see. If there were many he must think of some way to row to some real lonely spot or maybe turn and return to Grass Lake—or where? Oh, what could or would he do—if there were many over here?

But just then a long aisle of green trees giving out at the far end as he now recalled upon a square of lawn, and the lake itself, the little inn with its pillared verandah, facing the dark blue waters of Big Bittern. And that low, small red-roofed boathouse to the right on the water that he had seen before when he was here. And Roberta exclaiming on sight, "Oh, it is pretty, isn't it—just beautiful." And Clyde surveying that dark, low island in the distance, to the south, and seeing but few people about—none on the lake itself—exclaimed nervously, "Yes, it is, you bet." But feeling half choked as he said it.

And now the host of the inn himself appearing and approaching—a medium-sized, red-faced, broad-shouldered man who was saying most intriguingly, "Staying over for a few days?"

But Clyde, irritated by this new development and after paying the guide a dollar, replying crustily and irritably, "No, no—just came over for the afternoon. We're going on down to-night."

"You'll be staying over for dinner then, I suppose? The train doesn't leave till eight-fifteen."

"Oh, yes—that's so. Sure. Yes, well, in that case, we will." . . . For, of course, Roberta on her honeymoon—the day before her wedding and on a trip like this, would be expecting her dinner. Damn this stocky, red-faced fool, anyway.

"Well, then, I'll just take your bag and you can register. Your wife'll probably be wanting to freshen up a bit anyway."

He led the way, bag in hand, although Clyde's greatest desire was to snatch it from him. For he had not expected to register here—nor leave his bag either. And would not. He would recapture it and hire a boat. But on top of that, being compelled "for the register's sake," as Boniface phrased it, to sign Clifford Golden and wife—before he could take his bag again.

And then to add to the nervousness and confusion engendered by all this, thoughts as to what additional developments or persons, even, he might encounter before leaving on his climacteric errand —Roberta announcing that because of the heat and the fact that they were coming back to dinner, she would leave her hat and coat—a hat in which he had already seen the label of Braunstein in Lycurgus—and which at the time caused him to meditate as to the wisdom of leaving or extracting it. But he had decided that perhaps afterwards— afterwards—if he should really do this—it might not make any difference whether it was there or not. Was she not likely to be identified anyhow, if found, and if not found, who was to know who she was?

In a confused and turbulent state mentally, scarcely realizing the clarity or import of any particular thought or movement or act now, he took up his bag and led the way to the boathouse platform. And then, after dropping the bag into the boat, asking of the boathouse keeper if he knew where the best views were, that he wanted to photograph them. And this done—the meaningless explanation over, assisting Roberta (an almost nebulous figure, she now seemed, stepping down into an insubstantial row-boat upon a purely ideational lake), he now stepped in after her, seating himself in the center and taking the oars.

The quiet, glassy, iridescent surface of this lake that now to both seemed, not so much like water as oil—like molten glass that, of enormous bulk and weight, resting upon the substantial earth so very far below. And the lightness and freshness and intoxication of the gentle air blowing here and there, yet scarcely rippling the surface of the lake.

And the softness and furry thickness of the tall pines about the shore. Everywhere pines—tall and spearlike. And above them the humped backs of the dark and distant Adirondacks beyond. Not a rower to be seen. Not a house or cabin. He sought to distinguish the camp of which the guide had spoken. He could not. He sought to distinguish the voices of those who might be there—or any voices. Yet, except for the lock-lock of his own oars as he rowed and the voice of the boathouse keeper and the guide in converse two hundred, three hundred, five hundred, a thousand feet behind, there was no sound.

"Isn't it still and peaceful?" It was Roberta talking. "It seems to be so restful here. I think it's beautiful, truly, so much more beautiful than that other lake. These trees are so tall, aren't they? And those mountains. I was thinking all the way over how cool and silent that road was, even if it was a little rough."

"Did you talk to any one in the inn there just now?"

"Why, no; what makes you ask?"

"Oh, I thought you might have run into some one. There don't seem to be very many people up here to-day, though, does there?"

"No, I don't see any one on the lake. I saw two men in that billiard room at the back there, and there was a girl in the ladies' room, that was all. Isn't this water cold?" She had put her hand over the side and was trailing it in the blue-black ripples made by his oars.

"Is it? I haven't felt it yet."

He paused in his rowing and put out his hand, then resumed. He would not row directly to that island to the south. It was—too far—too early. She might think it odd. Better a little delay. A little time in which to think—a little while in which to reconnoiter. Roberta would be wanting to eat her lunch (her lunch!) and there was a charming looking point of land there to the west about a mile further on. They could go there and eat first—or she could—for he would not be eating to-day. And then—and then——

She was looking at the very same point of land that he was—a curved horn of land that bent to the south and yet reached quite far out into the water and combed with tall pines. And now she added:

"Have you any spot in mind, dear, where we could stop and eat? I'm getting a little hungry, aren't you?" (If she would only not call him *dear*, here and now!)

The little inn and the boathouse to the north were growing momentarily smaller,–looking now, like that other boathouse and pavilion on Crum Lake the day he had first rowed there, and when he had been wishing that he might come to such a lake as this in the Adirondacks, dreaming of such a lake–and wishing to meet such a girl as Roberta –then—— And overhead was one of those identical woolly clouds that had sailed above him at Crum Lake on that fateful day.

The horror of this effort!

They might look for water-lilies here to-day to kill time a little, before–to kill time . . . to kill, (God)–he must quit thinking of that, if he were going to do it at all. He needn't be thinking of it now, at any rate.

At the point of land favored by Roberta, into a minute protected bay with a small, curved, honey-colored beach, and safe from all prying eyes north or east. And then he and she stepping out normally enough. And Roberta, after Clyde had extracted the lunch most cautiously from his bag, spreading it on a newspaper on the shore, while he walked here and there, making strained and yet admiring comments on the beauty of the scene– the pines and the curve of this small bay, yet thinking–thinking, thinking of the island farther on and the bay below that again somewhere, where somehow, and in the face of a weakening courage for it, he must still execute this grim and terrible business before him–not allow this carefully planned opportunity to go for nothing–if–if–he were to not really run away and leave all that he most desired to keep.

And yet the horror of this business and the danger, now that it was so close at hand–the danger of making a mistake of some kind–if nothing more, of not upsetting the boat right–of not being able to–to–oh, God! And subsequently, maybe, to be proved to be what he would be–then–a murderer. Arrested! Tried. (He could not, he would not, go through with it. No, no, no!)

And yet Roberta, sitting here with him now on the sand, feeling quite at peace with all the world as he could see. And she was beginning to hum a little, and then to make advisory and practical references to the nature of their coming adventure together–their material and financial state from now on–how and where they would go from here –Syracuse, most likely–since Clyde seemed to have no objection to that–and what, once there, they would do. For Roberta had heard from her brother-in-law, Fred Gabel, of a new collar and shirt fac-

tory that was just starting up in Syracuse. Might it not be possible for Clyde, for the time being at least, to get himself a position with that firm at once? And then later, when her own worst trouble was over, might not she connect herself with some company, or some other? And temporarily, since they had so little money, could they not take a small room together, somewhere in some family home, or if he did not like that, since they were by no means so close temperamentally as they once had been, then two small adjoining rooms, maybe. She could still feel his unrelenting opposition under all this present show of courtesy and consideration.

And he thinking, Oh, well, what difference such talk now? And whether he agreed or whether he did not. What difference since he was not going–or she either–that way. Great God! But here he was talking as though to-morrow she would be here still. And she would not be.

If only his knees would not tremble so; his hands and face and body continue so damp.

And after that, farther on down the west shore of this small lake in this little boat, to that island, with Clyde looking nervously and wearily here and there to see that there was no one–no one–not anywhere in sight on land or water–no one. It was so still and deserted here, thank God. Here–or anywhere near here might do, really,–if only he had the courage so to do now, which he had not,– yet. Roberta trailing her hand in the water, asking him if he thought they might find some water-lilies or wild flowers somewhere on shore. Water-lilies! Wild flowers! And he convincing himself as he went that there were no roads, cabins, tents, paths, anything in the form of a habitation among these tall, close, ranking pines–no trace of any little boat on the widespread surface of this beautiful lake on this beautiful day. Yet might there not be some lone, solitary hunter and trapper or guide or fisherman in these woods or along these banks? Might there not be? And supposing there were one here now somewhere? And watching!

Fate!

Destruction!

Death! Yet no sound and no smoke. Only–only –these tall, dark, green pines–spear-shaped and still, with here and there a dead one–ashen pale in the hard afternoon sun, its gaunt, sapless arms almost menacingly outstretched.

Death!

And the sharp metallic cry of a blue-jay speeding in the depths of these woods. Or the lone and ghostly tap-tap-tap of some solitary woodpecker, with now and then the red line of a flying tanager, the yellow and black of a yellow-shouldered blackbird.

"Oh, the sun shines bright in my old Kentucky home."

It was Roberta singing cheerfully, one hand in the deep blue water.

And then a little later—"I'll be there Sunday if you will," one of the popular dance pieces of the day.

And then at last, after fully an hour of rowing, brooding, singing, stopping to look at some charming point of land, reconnoitering some receding inlet which promised water-lilies, and with Roberta already saying that they must watch the time and not stay out too long—the bay, south of the island itself—a beautiful and yet most funereally pine-encircled and land delimited bit of water—more like a smaller lake, connected by an inlet or passage to the larger one, and yet itself a respectable body of water of perhaps twenty acres of surface and almost circular in form. The manner in which to the east, the north, the south, the west, even, except for the passage by which the island to the north of it was separated from the mainland, this pool or tarn was encircled by trees! And cat-tails and water-lilies here and there—a few along its shores. And somehow suggesting an especially arranged pool or tarn to which one who was weary of life and cares—anxious to be away from the strife and contentions of the world, might most wisely and yet gloomily repair.

And as they glided into this, this still dark water seemed to grip Clyde as nothing here or anywhere before this ever had—to change his mood. For once here he seemed to be fairly pulled or lured along into it, and having encircled its quiet banks, to be drifting, drifting—in endless space where was no end of anything—no plots—no plans—no practical problems to be solved—nothing. The insidious beauty of this place! Truly, it seemed to mock him —this strangeness—this dark pool, surrounded on all sides by those wonderful, soft, fir trees. And the water itself looking like a huge, black pearl cast by some mighty hand, in anger possibly, in sport or phantasy maybe, into the bosom of this valley of dark, green plush—and which seemed bottomless as he gazed into it.

And yet, what did it all suggest so strongly? Death! Death! More definitely than anything he had ever seen before. Death! But also a still, quiet, unprotesting type of death into which one, by

reason of choice or hypnosis or unutterable weariness, might joyfully and gratefully sink. So quiet— so shaded—so serene. Even Roberta exclaimed over this. And he now felt for the first time the grip of some seemingly strong, and yet friendly sympathetic, hands laid firmly on his shoulders. The comfort of them! The warmth! The strength! For now they seemed to have a steadying effect on him and he liked them—their reassurance—their support. If only they would not be removed! If only they would remain always—the hand of this friend! For where had he ever known this comforting and almost tender sensation before in all his life? Not anywhere—and somehow this calmed him and he seemed to slip away from the reality of all things.

To be sure, there was Roberta over there, but by now she had faded to a shadow or thought really, a form of illusion more vaporous than real. And while there was something about her in color, form that suggested reality—still she was very insubstantial—so very—and once more now he felt strangely alone. For the hands of the friend of firm grip had vanished also. And Clyde was alone, so very much alone and forlorn, in this somber, beautiful realm to which apparently he had been led, and then deserted. Also he felt strangely cold —the spell of this strange beauty overwhelming him with a kind of chill.

He had come here for what?

And he must do what?

Kill Roberta? Oh, no!

And again he lowered his head and gazed into the fascinating and yet treacherous depths of that magnetic, bluish, purple pool, which, as he continued to gaze, seemed to change its form kaleidoscopically to a large, crystalline ball. But what was that moving about in this crystal? A form! It came nearer—clearer—and as it did so, he recognized Roberta struggling and waving her thin white arms out of the water and reaching toward him! God! How terrible! The expression on her face! What in God's name was he thinking of anyway? Death! Murder!

And suddenly becoming conscious that his courage, on which he had counted so much this long while to sustain him here, was leaving him, and he instantly and consciously plumbing the depths of his being in a vain search to recapture it.

Kit, kit, kit, Ca-a-a-ah!
Kit, kit, kit, Ca-a-a-ah!
Kit, kit, kit, Ca-a-a-ah!

(The weird, haunting cry of that unearthly bird

again. So cold, so harsh! Here it was once more to startle him out of his soul flight into a realization of the real or unreal immediate problem with all of its torturesome angles that lay before him.)

He must face this thing! He must!

Kit, kit, kit, Ca-a-a-ah!
Kit, kit, kit, Ca-a-a-ah!

What was it sounding—a warning—a protest—condemnation? The same bird that had marked the very birth of this miserable plan. For there it was now upon that dead tree—that wretched bird. And now it was flying to another one—as dead—a little farther inland and crying as it did so. God!

And then to the shore again in spite of himself. For Clyde, in order to justify his having brought his bag, now must suggest that pictures of this be taken—and of Roberta—and of himself, possibly—on land and water. For that would bring her into the boat again, without his bag, which would be safe and dry on land. And once on shore, actually pretending to be seeking out various special views here and there, while he fixed in his mind the exact tree at the base of which he might leave his bag against his return—which must be soon now—must be soon. They would not come on shore again together. Never! Never! And that in spite of Roberta protesting that she was getting tired; and did he not think they ought to be starting back pretty soon? It must be after five, surely. And Clyde, assuring her that presently they would—after he had made one or two more pictures of her in the boat with those wonderful trees—that island and this dark water around and beneath her.

His wet, damp, nervous hands!

And his dark, liquid, nervous eyes, looking anywhere but at her.

And then once more on the water again—about five hundred feet from shore, the while he fumbled aimlessly with the hard and heavy and yet small camera that he now held, as the boat floated out nearer the center. And then, at this point and time looking fearfully about. For now—now—in spite of himself, the long evaded and yet commanding moment. And no voice or figure or sound on shore. No road or cabin or smoke! And the moment which he or something had planned for him, and which was now to decide his fate at hand! The moment of action—of crisis! All that he needed to do now was to turn swiftly and savagely to one side or the other—leap up—upon the left wale or

right and upset the boat; or, failing that, rock it swiftly, and if Roberta protested too much, strike her with the camera in his hand, or one of the oars at his right. It could be done—it could be done—swiftly and simply, were he now of the mind and heart, or lack of it—with him swimming swiftly away thereafter to freedom—to success—of course—to Sondra and happiness—a new and greater and sweeter life than any he had ever known.

Yet why was he waiting now?

What was the matter with him, anyhow?

Why was he waiting?

At this cataclysmic moment, and in the face of the utmost, the most urgent need of action, a sudden palsy of the will—of courage—of hate or rage sufficient; and with Roberta from her seat in the stern of the boat gazing at his troubled and then suddenly distorted and fulgurous, yet weak and even unbalanced face—a face of a sudden, instead of angry, ferocious, demoniac—confused and all but meaningless in its registration of a balanced combat between fear (a chemic revulsion against death or murderous brutality that would bring death) and a harried and restless and yet self-repressed desire to do—to do—to do—yet temporarily unbreakable here and now—a static between a powerful compulsion to do and yet not to do.

And in the meantime his eyes—the pupils of the same growing momentarily larger and more lurid; his face and body and hands tense and contracted—the stillness of his position, the balanced immobility of the mood more and more ominous, yet in truth not suggesting a brutal, courageous power to destroy, but the imminence of trance or spasm.

And Roberta, suddenly noticing the strangeness of it all—the something of eerie unreason or physical and mental indetermination so strangely and painfully contrasting with this scene, exclaiming: "Why, Clyde! Clyde! What is it? Whatever is the matter with you anyhow? You look so—so strange —so—so—Why, I never saw you look like this before. What is it?" And suddenly rising, or rather leaning forward, and by crawling along the even keel, attempting to approach him, since he looked as though he was about to fall forward into the boat—or to one side and out into the water. And Clyde, as instantly sensing the profoundness of his own failure, his own cowardice or inadequateness for such an occasion, as instantly yielding to a tide of submerged hate, not only for himself, but Roberta—her power—or that of life to restrain him in this way. And yet fearing to act in any way—being unwilling to—being willing only to say that never,

never would he marry her—that never, even should she expose him, would he leave here with her to marry her—that he was in love with Sondra and would cling only to her—and yet not being able to say that even. But angry and confused and glowering. And then, as she drew near him, seeking to take his hand in hers and the camera from him in order to put it in the boat, he flinging out at her, but not even then with any intention to do other than free himself of her—her touch—her pleading —consoling sympathy—her presence forever—God!

Yet (the camera still unconsciously held tight) pushing at her with so much vehemence as not only to strike her lips and nose and chin with it, but to throw her back sidewise toward the left wale which caused the boat to careen to the very water's edge. And then he, stirred by her sharp scream, (as much due to the lurch of the boat, as the cut on her nose and lip), rising and reaching half to assist or recapture her and half to apologize for the unintended blow—yet in so doing completely capsizing the boat—himself and Roberta being as instantly thrown into the water. And the left wale of the boat as it turned, striking Roberta on the head as she sank and then rose for the first time, her frantic, contorted face turned to Clyde, who by now had righted himself. For she was stunned, horror-struck, unintelligible with pain and fear—her lifelong fear of water and drowning and the blow he had so accidentally and all but unconsciously administered.

"Help! Help!

"Oh, my God, I'm drowning, I'm drowning. Help! Oh, my God!

"Clyde, Clyde!"

And then the voice at his ear!

"But this—this—is not this that which you have been thinking and wishing for this while—you in your great need? And behold! For despite your fear, your cowardice, this—this—has been done for you. An accident—an accident—an unintentional blow on your part is now saving you the labor of what you sought, and yet did not have the courage to do! But will you now, and when you need not, since it is an accident, by going to her rescue, once more plunge yourself in the horror of that defeat and failure which has so tortured you and from which this now releases you? You might save her. But again you might not! For see how she strikes about. She is stunned. She herself is unable to save

herself and by her erratic terror, if you draw near her now, may bring about your own death also. But you desire to live! And her living will make your life not worth while from now on. Rest but a moment—a fraction of a minute! Wait—wait— ignore the pity of that appeal. And then—then —But there! Behold. It is over. She is sinking now. You will never, never see her alive any more—ever. And there is your own hat upon the water—as you wished. And upon the boat, clinging to that row-lock a veil belonging to her. Leave it. Will it not show that this was an accident?"

And apart from that, nothing—a few ripples— the peace and solemnity of this wondrous scene. And then once more the voice of that weird, contemptuous, mocking, lonely bird,

Kit, kit, kit, Ca-a-a-ah!
Kit, kit, kit, Ca-a-a-ah!
Kit, kit, kit, Ca-a-a-ah!

The cry of that devilish bird upon that dead limb—the wier-wier.

And then Clyde, with the sound of Roberta's cries still in his ears, that last frantic, white, appealing look in her eyes, swimming heavily, gloomily and darkly to shore. And the thought that, after all, he had not really killed her. No, no. Thank God for that. He had not. And yet (stepping up on the near-by bank and shaking the water from his clothes) had he? Or, had he not? For had he not refused to go to her rescue, and when he might have saved her, and when the fault for casting her in the water, however accidentally, was so truly his? And yet—and yet—

The dusk and silence of a closing day. A concealed spot in the depths of the same sheltering woods where alone and dripping, his dry bag near, Clyde stood, and by waiting, sought to dry himself. But in the interim, removing from the side of the bag the unused tripod of his camera and seeking an obscure, dead log farther in the woods, hiding it. Had any one seen? Was any one looking? Then returning and wondering as to the direction! He must go west and then south. He must not get turned about! But the repeated cry of that bird,—harsh, nerve shaking. And then the gloom, in spite of the summer stars. And a youth making his way through a dark, uninhabited wood, a dry straw hat upon his head, a bag in his hand, walking briskly and yet warily—south—south.

SHERWOOD ANDERSON (1876–1941)

One day in November, 1912, in the prosperous little Ohio city of Elyria, Sherwood Anderson, sitting in the office of the president of a successful paint manufacturing company, looked down at his feet and, much to the surprise of his secretary, said: "I have been wading in a long river, and my feet are wet." With that he got up and walked out and kept on walking. At least, that is the account given by Sherwood Anderson, after he had become a famous writer, of how he broke with the world of business and the American mystique of success and took to literature. Anderson was a notoriously undependable autobiographer, but, in any case, a few days after he had left his office he was found wandering in a confused condition on the streets of Cleveland, was hospitalized, and upon recovery moved to Chicago and sought out the writers and artists who were then creating the "Chicago renaissance."

The walking out on the paint business—and on a wife, too—was simply the climax of a tension that had been building up in Anderson; but this tension also epitomized a crisis in American life, and so Anderson became, in much the same way as Dreiser, a symbolic figure. Both enacted in their personal lives the drama of their time, the glamor and the failure of the Horatio Alger story.

Anderson, born in 1876, in the village of Clyde, Ohio, was the son of a cavalryman who had fought in the federal army in the Civil War, but Anderson, in his autobiography, made him somewhat more romantic by referring to him as a "ruined Southern dandy." The father was a harness-maker by vocation and a boozer and tale-teller by avocation, but as factory-made harnesses put independent craftsmen out of business, the avocation more and more replaced the vocation, and the Anderson family sank in the social scale until the mother was taking in washing. All of the seven Anderson children were energetic and ambitious, but Sherwood,

from childhood on, was notable for his enterprise and push and earned the nickname of Jobby. After serving in the Spanish-American War, from which he emerged a corporal, he became an advertising salesman, then a copywriter, was something of a dude and, as he later described it, a "smooth son-of-a-bitch." He married a girl who had been to college, was a member of a sorority, and had taken the European tour. Anderson cast himself as the star in a Horatio Alger story, and his first literary efforts, published in trade journals, hymned "boosterism" and the business ethic—as Dreiser, in the 1890's, had done in editorials in his pulp magazines, asserting, for instance, that "Success is what counts in the world, and it little matters how success is won."

But along the way, something came over the man who was president of the Anderson Manufacturing Company and a happy husband and father, and he began to drink and make passes at women other than his wife, got careless in dress, and wrote a novel. He even claimed, later, to have written a book called *Why I Am a Socialist*—but that may have been one of his "stretchers," as Huck Finn called them: it was one of the things it would have been nice to have done.

Anderson had been a successful advertising man in Chicago, with the advertising mentality, but when, in 1913, after his nervous breakdown, he went back to that city, he moved into an entirely different world. He again wrote copy, it is true, but he lived with people who read things he had never even heard of, George Bernard Shaw, D'Annunzio, Yeats, and Gorky, and talked about Freud, free love, and socialism; he even knew people who ran magazines, like Harriet Monroe, with her *Poetry: A Magazine of Verse*, in which Ezra Pound, Marianne Moore, T. S. Eliot, and other young people were appearing, and Margaret Anderson (no relation), with her *Little Review*; he knew, too, writers like Carl Sandburg, Vachel Lindsay, and Theodore Dreiser, who by this time, like Anderson, had been a business success and, unlike Anderson, a literary success, at least for the radicals who championed the "new realism."

Anderson had little education (a year at a small Lutheran academy), had read little, and knew nothing of the literary world, but he was eager for instruction, was attractive to women, and could tell a tale as well as ever his old drunken father could. Chicago gave him his literary education, an audience, and a new wife appropriate for this phase of his career, Tennessee Mitchell, a "new woman" who, even after the marriage rite, kept an establishment of her own.

Among the manuscripts that Anderson had brought to Chicago was *Windy McPherson's Son*, and by 1916 this novel was published. The story represented, for Anderson himself, both a history of his life and a prophecy. As for history, *Windy* is a vindictive portrait of Anderson's own father, a blowhard, braggart, and liar, whom the son, Sam McPherson, tries to kill. After this episode, strangely parallel to Huck Finn's "virtual" killing of Pap, which releases him to go out into the world, Sam escapes, goes to Chicago, makes a success, and marries upward. So much for the history, a shadowy recapitulation of the author's own. As for prophecy, in this novel, written while Anderson was still in Elyria, the hero, afflicted with loneliness in his childless marriage (Anderson had children, however) and with the emptiness of his Horatio Alger success, flees to seek "meaning," for "American men and women have not learned to be clean and noble and natural, like their forests and the wide, clean plains." In the end, as a solution to the problem of life, Sam picks up three waifs and with these children comes back to his wife.

Considered in a different light, the novel has two quite distinct elements that correspond to two strains in Anderson's subsequent work. The first element, dealing with the youth of Sam, pictures the small town of Caxton, Iowa, with the pathos of loneliness and groping aspiration that was later to characterize *Winesburg, Ohio*, Anderson's most famous book, and the best of

his short stories. The second element is the account of the man who repudiates success to seek "meaning." In handling the first theme, Anderson turns back to the world of his childhood to try to penetrate to the reality of people around him. In handling the second, he becomes self-centered, trying to penetrate the nature of his own adult experience, and this appears most disastrously in *Marching Men* (1917), Anderson's second novel, in which the problem of life is to be resolved in some mystique of collective action.

In exploring the first theme, Anderson was to discover his true gift, and it was, no doubt, the period in Chicago that made the discovery possible. One discovers home by leaving home, and often the fundamental discovery made by the aspiring young who fled to the bohemia of Chicago, Greenwich Village, or the Left Bank in Paris was the discovery of the busy little cities, small towns, and farms from which they had fled. In one sense, in fact, it is important to remember about regionalism that there was no "small town" until there was the "big city." The unresolved ambivalences of Mark Twain toward Hannibal was the archetypal situation, and the poetry of boyhood and nature that Huck embodied and uttered was balanced against the cruelties of the adult community that Huck came to know and criticize.[1] In any

---

[1] It is instructive to note that Stephen Crane, who began his literary career by treating the urban slum which he had penetrated merely by observation and imagination, not by personal experience, had no great admiration for Mark Twain. When Crane came to write his later stories (see p. 1650), which do not have an urban setting, he derived little or nothing from the matter of Hannibal, and "The Monster," the best of those stories, though it was savage enough to have satisfied the Mark Twain who loathed the "damned human race," had a very different tonality from, say, "The Man That Corrupted Hadleyburg"—which in itself is far from the world of sunrise on the Mississippi. For one thing, in "The Monster" there is a good man to give the lie to Mark Twain's absolute view of human depravity.

It should also be noted that with Sinclair Lewis's *Main Street* another attitude toward the small town appears, one derived straight from the big city world—this, even though Lewis was from Sauk Centre, Minnesota.

case, it was after Anderson had entered the bohemia of Chicago and its freedom, that he discovered Winesburg.

Three discoveries, more narrowly literary, led to Winesburg. In 1915 *Spoon River Anthology*, by Edgar Lee Masters, appeared, with its complex gallery of the characters of a small town, and when Anderson got his hands on the book, he sat up all night. Here was Caxton, Iowa (or Clyde, Ohio, or Elyria) rendered in and for itself, not used as a mere way-station for Sam McPherson (or Sherwood Anderson) in a quest for "meaning." Here was an unfolding pattern of secret lives, and here, too, the projection of an ambivalence toward that world, for if there was Archibald Higbie who prayed to be reborn with all of Spoon River "Routed out of my soul," there was also Lucinda Matlock, who conquered life and found happiness in Spoon River.

The second literary discovery came when Anderson's brother Karl, who had set up in Chicago as a painter, gave him a copy of Gertrude Stein's *Tender Buttons*, which, after the first shock, excited him, he records, "as one might grow excited in going into a new and wonderful country where everything is strange." The very shock of Stein's wrenching of words from their function as a mere set of counters for meaning to independent, self-assertive existence gave Anderson, as it gave various other writers, a new freedom, a new sense of stylistic purity and flexibility, and a chance to achieve, however fitfully, what Edmund Wilson defines as a "naiveté of language, often passing into the colloquialism of the character dealt with, which serves actually to convey profound emotions and complex states of mind." We must remember, however, that here the influence of Stein did not operate in isolation; it fused with the language that Mark Twain had invented for Huck, which, too, can be described by the passage just quoted from Wilson. And to this fusion of the influence of Stein and Mark Twain is to be added that of the Bible, for the pagan esthetes of Chicago had set Anderson to reading that—for its style, of course. But to return to the influence of Stein, out of the innocence of effect contrived

by her own subtle and highly trained mind, this star pupil of William James and medical student from Johns Hopkins University taught Anderson how to use his own quite natural innocence and, even, ignorance. In the stories in her *Three Lives* she could give him models, too, for fiction concerning simple people and a model for simplicity of style that could sometimes create a depth of emotional involvement almost hypnotic.

In any case, *Winesburg, Ohio* got written and, published in 1919, when Anderson was forty-three years old, made his reputation; two years later it was the first work to win the award given by the *Dial* magazine (the second being Eliot's *Waste Land*). With reputation came the need to classify the book. Very early, *Winesburg*, because of its locale, was lumped with Masters' *Spoon River* and Lewis's *Main Street* as part of the "revolt against the village." Because of commonplace background and the sexual elements, it was also lumped with the work of Dreiser as an example of the new realism, or naturalism (those terms being used almost interchangeably by reviewers). Again because of the sexual element, it was taken as an example of Freud's theories or D. H. Lawrence's doctrines. As a matter of fact, *Winesburg* cannot comfortably wear any of these labels, though all have a certain superficial plausibility.

The first step toward understanding *Winesburg* is to remind ourselves that it is as much a return to, as a revolt from, the village and as such represents a release of the burden of memory, a burden toward which, as we have said, the author is characteristically ambivalent. This return meant, for the self-obsessed Anderson, the discovery of "others" in his work. In his novels, over and over, we have the rebel, the renegade, the quester who goes forth to seek reality and who usually tries to find it by establishing a relation to others—to find solace in the company of "marching men" or in the arms of compliant women, who promise some mystic fulfillment. But in the novels this discovery of "others" is commonly abstract; the emphasis is always on the discoverer, and the self-applauding effort to discover, not on what is discovered. Anderson had come to have some understanding of this situation, and *Winesburg* represented, according to his own report, an effort to break out of it. He says that in this period he wanted to "get out of myself, truly into others, the others I met constantly in the streets of the city . . . and still others remembered out of my childhood."

To whom does Anderson reach out? The book is introduced by a sketch that—as though Anderson had asked himself the question—gives the answer to it. In the sketch, entitled "The Book of the Grotesque," an old writer offers a fable that describes the content of *Winesburg*: in the early days of mankind, there were many vague thoughts but no truths; then men learned to put thoughts together to make a "truth"; people then seized on what truth, or truths, they fancied, and the moment a man "took one of the truths to himself . . . and tried to live by it, he became a grotesque and the truth he embraced became a falsehood." This fable would suggest that the grotesque is a person who, by taking a truth out of the context of other truths and fanatically clinging to it, distorts his own nature and cuts himself off from others; he is, we are told in the story "Paper Pills," like the ill-shaped and blemished apples rejected by the pickers, that are often much sweeter than the perfectly marketable fruit.

Anderson's reaching out toward the grotesques is not indicated merely by their presence as subject matter, for here the author adopts a *persona*, a young newspaper reporter, George Willard, who plays Anderson's role. George, scarcely beyond adolescence, groping to find his own nature and his own fate, is open to experience, has not yet accepted the values of the public world to which the grotesques fail to conform, and is seeking the secret of life. It is the grotesques who may have this "secret," the sweetness of the rejected fruit, and so he turns to them. The alienated ones, in turn, come to him as the one person to whom, because of his uncorrupted innocence, they may speak. Thematically, the book is unified by the fact that all characters are suffering from various forms of "grotesqueness," of loneliness, but the figure of George provides an objective device of unifica-

tion. The solitaries are grouped around him, each, including his own mother, having a secret need and hoping for some significant response.

The grotesques are presented, not by the ordinary devices of characterization and not in the ordinary unfolding of narrative, certainly not in sharply defined dramatic encounters (except at the climax of the story "Queer"). They tend to be summarized, or tagged, by some habit or mannerism: in "Hands," there is the furtive, suppressed motion of the hands of the schoolteacher ruined by the suspicion of homosexuality because he had now and then tousled the hair of some student, or in "Paper Pills" the doctor's habit of scribbling down thoughts that could not be uttered and making little wads, or "pills," to stuff into his pocket. The characteristic focus of a story is the moment of unmasking—or rather, of the attempt at unmasking. In other words, the emphasis is on the role and the revelation rather than on the ordinary fictional process of documentary development and dramatic contact. Anderson tends not to present action, but to absorb action into the process of the telling, the tone of voice, the flow of feeling *about* the action being narrated; and it is sometimes said that this emphasis in his fiction relates it to the oral tradition in which he was raised and in which his father was a local expert.

What we have been saying about the method of *Winesburg* applies primarily to the treatment of the grotesques. With George himself there is, indeed, more of the ordinary fictional suspense. He is in motion, he is trying to find meaning, and his responses represent stages in his preparation for an entry into the great world. The growth of his awareness comes to climax with the story "Sophistication," for here he sees himself caught in the common process of life, and for the first time can take a backward look at his own experience and realize that he himself has been "merely a leaf blown by the wind through the streets of his village" toward his own natural end, with "death calling." It is this awareness that brings him to his understanding of the grotesques, for now he too feels the need "to come close to some other human, touch someone with all his hands." Now he knows why they have reached out to him, and why he has, unwittingly, reached out to them.

What we learn from George's experience is that the world is not, in the end, divided into grotesques and "normal" people. All men, caught in the common fate, need "to come close to some other human," and the grotesque is merely one whose normal need had been short-circuited. Indeed, the apparently normal person who does not deeply feel such a need may, in the last analysis, be the most completely grotesque of all.

It has sometimes been said that *Winesburg* is not a veracious picture of life in a small town —or elsewhere—but is merely a gallery of freaks. One retort to this criticism has been given above: the freak simply embodies in an obvious or exaggerated form the common human story. But another retort can be drawn from Anderson's conception of realism. By what standard, he would ask, can you determine the correct percentage of freaks for a Winesburg? How do you know, to begin with, who is, and who is not a freak, except by the act of imagination? In a lecture called "A Writer's Conception of Realism," Anderson says that even if imagination must feed "from the life of reality," it "will always remain separate from the life of reality." Strangely enough, in that lecture, what Anderson objects to is that people had called *Winesburg* "an exact picture of Ohio village life." He goes on to say that *Winesburg* was "written in a crowded tenement district of Chicago" and that the model "for almost every character was taken from my fellow lodgers in a large roominghouse, many of whom had never lived in a village."

Even if Anderson does not clarify the relation between imagination and reality, he does indicate that the work created is to be judged as much by its coherence and force as an expression of the author's attitude toward life as by its accuracy in reporting the objective world with statistical accuracy. And this leads us to the idea that *Winesburg* is as much a poem of Anderson's obsessive theme of loneliness and alienation as it is an account of life in an Ohio village. The power of the work largely comes, in fact, from a certain atmosphere best exemplified by the night scenes in which the grotesques emerge to seek contact with George, and from the evocation, dependent in part at least on style, of a characteristic emotion that involves both yearning and the pity for yearning.

The fact that *Winesburg* is at root a lyric expression accounts for a criticism not infrequently offered against the book: that it, like Anderson's novels, lacks dramatic action. This criticism does indeed apply to the novels, for in them he undertakes to give an account of protracted action, which would logically imply crucial collisions between characters and dialogue that would have an inner tension and forward thrust. But the criticism does not apply to *Winesburg*; here we are dealing with a series of moments of revelation representing variations on a theme rather than a progression, and the form of the book as a series of short stories accommodates the individual moments of revelation without forcing them into an overall dramatic structure that would strain Anderson's natural talent. Except for the line of George Willard's personal development, this structure involves merely a series of subtly shaded emotional variations on the theme, rather than a plot.

Whatever may be said of *Winesburg, Ohio*, it struck for the first time a certain deep chord in American experience. It is to be bracketed with *The Adventures of Huckleberry Finn*, *Spoon River Anthology*, and *Main Street*—books that have shown Americans the potentials of emotion and meaning in those little towns from which so many have sprung. In its modest way, it came as a revelation, with something like the "low fine music" that Anderson himself had found in the work of the Russian Turgenev, but here endowed with his own tonality—a music that entered into American literature and is to be heard again, for example, in Thornton Wilder's moving play *Our Town*.

When the young poet Hart Crane reviewed *Winesburg, Ohio*, he called it the "Bible of the American consciousness." It is scarcely that, but it is one of the indispensable documents of that consciousness.

Though, generally speaking, Anderson's novels

are much inferior to his stories, one of them often touches his best level. *Poor White* (1920) opens in Mudcat Landing, Missouri, which is clearly descended from Hannibal, with the main character, now a boy, the son of a drunken bum whose whole existence has been little more than an "animal-like stupor." But if Hugh McVey is descended from Huck and if the poetry of the great river is here repeated, Anderson manages to infuse this world with new life and with his own tonality so different from Mark Twain's.

Furthermore, Hugh McVey is not only a version of Huck, he is also a version of the boy Anderson remembered himself to have been, and of the world he had inhabited, the world on the verge of the great industrial expansion. "There was this talk," Anderson says in the lecture already quoted from, "heard on all sides, of America being the great land of opportunity," and "such talk pretty much meant getting on, if possible, growing rich, getting to be something big in the world." Though Hugh is a born lummox, the yearning outsider brooding in loneliness, his very isolation makes him "something big in the world." His locked-in energies drive him to tinkering, to inventing. He is typical of a moment of the industrial history of America, the time of the self-taught mechanical genius, the McCormick, the Edison, the Wright, the Ford, but his very success, the product of his alienation, confirms that alienation. He embodies a crisis in our history.

If Hugh McVey is different from the other Alger heroes of Anderson's novels in that here the nature of the success is grounded on the groping loneliness and alienation, Anderson does not know, even here, what to do with the man who has achieved success and finds that it does not answer to his deepest need. The trouble is simply that Anderson did not know what his own need was. He had the psychology of the rebel and the yearner, but beyond that neither the man nor the writer could go. So this novel, like the others, bleeds off into the undramatic and the irrelevant.

In the 1920's Anderson achieved a very con-siderable reputation. Even the very poor novels *Many Marriages* and *Dark Laughter* touched the representative interests of the moment and found readers—though not enough to make Anderson financially independent. Meanwhile two collections of stories, *The Triumph of the Egg* (1921) and *Death in the Woods* (1933), confirmed his solid achievement in that form. But the last twenty years of Anderson's life, between *Winesburg* and his death, were a period of groping and fumbling. In New York he entered the literary world and made friends but was never at home there. He visited Europe, found that his fame had penetrated to Paris, and visited Gertrude Stein, who admired his "fine dark, Italian eyes" and with whom he established an enduring mutual admiration society documented by more than a decade of correspondence. He lived in New Orleans, in the French Quarter, where he knew and encouraged the young Faulkner. Later he settled in the hills of Virginia, where he edited a country newspaper and tried to renew his feeling for back-country life.

He wrote an autobiography, in fact two, and more and worse fiction. The Depression came on, and he wrote social commentary and studies of the plight of the southern textile worker. He involved himself in textile strikes and protests of various kinds and briefly flirted with the Communist party. But he was not, as he put it, a "politically-minded man" and, in fact, never bothered to work at understanding either theories or issues. He was a romantic rebel to his death, a sentimental wanderer seeking something never quite defined, somehow deriving force from the feeling that what he had missed in his short life, America had missed in its history. He was seeking a vision and a gospel that eluded him. "I hardly know what I can teach," he wrote to Karl, the brother who had set out to be a painter, "except anti-success." In that way, at least, he was a disciple of William James, who hated the "bitch-goddess success" and was suspicious of all things "big."

Meanwhile, Anderson had run his marriage count up to four, for apparently no woman could lead him to the vision he sought. During the Depression his popularity declined; his poetry of village loneliness, his dream of the old agrarian order, his true simplicities and his often spurious folksiness—all of it seemed oddly dated amid the arguments about dialectical materialism and New Deal policies. But now those arguments seem oddly dated, and Anderson's stories survive.

Anderson died in 1941, while on a tour of South America, under the auspices of the state department.

BIOGRAPHICAL CHART

1876	Born, September 13, in Camden, Ohio, third of seven children of Irvin and Emma Anderson
1884	Family settles in Clyde, Ohio, the prototype of Winesburg
1896	Works as laborer in Chicago warehouse
1898	Joins army for service in Spanish-American War
1899	Enrolls, in September, in Wittenberg Academy, graduating the following June
1900	Becomes advertising salesman and copywriter in Chicago
1904	Marries Cornelia Lane
1906–12	In Cleveland, then Elyria, Ohio, a success in business; writes in secret
1912	Has breakdown; leaves paint business
1913–16	Lives in Chicago; associates with Ben Hecht, Floyd Dell, Theodore Dreiser, Carl Sandburg, and Eunice Tietjens in Chicago renaissance; contributes to *Little Review*
1916	Divorced from Cornelia Lane; marries Tennessee Mitchell; first novel published, *Windy McPherson's Son*
1917	*Marching Men*
1918	*Mid-American Chants*
1919	*Winesburg, Ohio*
1921	Meets Hemingway, whose work he is to influence; travels to Europe; meets Gertrude Stein, Joyce, Ford Madox Ford *et al.*; wins first *Dial* award; *The Triumph of the Egg*

1922	Travels to New Orleans; *Many Marriages*
1923	*Horses and Men*
1924–25	Divorced from Tennessee Mitchell; marries Elizabeth Prall; *A Story-Teller's Story*; second period in New Orleans, where he encourages Faulkner to become a novelist
1926	*Tar: A Midwest Childhood*
1927	Settles in Marion, Virginia; buys two local newspapers; *A New Testament*
1929	Divorced from Elizabeth Prall; *Hello, Towns*
1931	Supports strike at Danville; begins social involvement
1932	Joins Dreiser, Dos Passos, Edmund Wilson, Malcolm Cowley, and others in demanding a "new order" and a "temporary dictatorship of the proletariat"; *Beyond Desire*
1933	Marries Eleanor Copenhaver; *Death in the Woods*
1935	*Puzzled America*, social essays
1936	*Kit Brandon*
1937	Elected to National Institute of Arts and Letters; *Plays* ("Winesburg," "Triumph of the Egg," "Mother," and "They Married Later")
1940	*Home Town*
1941	Dies, March 8, in Colon, Panama, on good-will tour of South America, under auspices of state department
1942	*Memoirs*

FURTHER READINGS

There is no standard edition of Anderson's works. In addition to the writings mentioned in the biographical chart, the reader may find the following items useful.

Maxwell Geismar, ed., *Short Stories* (1962)
Horace Gregory, ed., *The Portable Sherwood Anderson* (1949)
Howard Mumford Jones and Walter B. Rideout, eds., *Letters* (1953)
Paul Rosenfeld, ed., *The Sherwood Anderson Reader* (1947)
Edmund Wilson, ed., "Letters to Van Wyck Brooks," in *The Shock of Recognition* (1943)

David D. Anderson, *Sherwood Anderson: An Introduction and Interpretation* (1967)

Paul P. Appel, ed., *Homage to Sherwood Anderson* (1970)
Cleanth Brooks and Robert Penn Warren, *Understanding Fiction* (1943)
Rex Burbank, *Sherwood Anderson* (1964)
Bernard Duffey, *The Chicago Renaissance in American Letters* (1954)
Maxwell Geismar, *The Last of the Provincials* (1949)
Granville Hicks, *The Great Tradition* (1933)
Irving Howe, *Sherwood Anderson* (1951)
Alfred Kazin, *On Native Grounds* (1942)
Simon Lesser, *Fiction and the Unconscious* (1962)
Paul Rosenfeld, *Port of New York* (1924)
Arthur Sherbo, " 'I Want to Know Why' and Brooks and Warren," *College English* (March, 1954)
Lionel Trilling, *The Liberal Imagination* (1948)

"Queer" (1919)

From his seat on a box in the rough board shed that stuck like a burr on the rear of Cowley & Son's store in Winesburg, Elmer Cowley, the junior member of the firm, could see through a dirty window into the printshop of the *Winesburg Eagle*. Elmer was putting new shoelaces in his shoes. They did not go in readily and he had to take the shoes off. With the shoes in his hand he sat looking at a large hole in the heel of one of his stockings. Then looking quickly up he saw George Willard, the only newspaper reporter in Winesburg, standing at the back door of the *Eagle* printshop and staring absent-mindedly about. "Well, well, what next!" exclaimed the young man with the shoes in his hand, jumping to his feet and creeping away from the window.

A flush crept into Elmer Cowley's face and his hands began to tremble. In Cowley & Son's store a Jewish traveling salesman stood by the counter talking to his father. He imagined the reporter could hear what was being said and the thought made him furious. With one of the shoes still held in his hand he stood in a corner of the shed and stamped with a stockinged foot upon the board floor.

Cowley & Son's store did not face the main street of Winesburg. The front was on Maumee Street and beyond it was Voight's wagon shop and a shed for the sheltering of farmers' horses. Beside the store an alleyway ran behind the main street stores and all day drays and delivery wagons, intent on bringing in and taking out goods, passed up and down. The store itself was indescribable. Will Henderson once said of it that it sold everything and nothing. In the window facing Maumee Street stood a chunk of coal as large as an apple barrel, to indicate that orders for coal were taken, and beside the black mass of the coal stood three combs of honey grown brown and dirty in their wooden frames.

The honey had stood in the store window for six months. It was for sale as were also the coat hangers, patent suspender buttons, cans of roof paint, bottles of rheumatism cure and a substitute for coffee that companioned the honey in its patient willingness to serve the public.

Ebenezer Cowley, the man who stood in the store listening to the eager patter of words that fell from the lips of the traveling man, was tall and lean and looked unwashed. On his scrawny neck was a large wen partially covered by a grey beard. He wore a long Prince Albert coat. The coat had been purchased to serve as a wedding garment. Before he became a merchant Ebenezer was a farmer and after his marriage he wore the Prince Albert coat to church on Sundays and on Saturday afternoons when he came into town to trade. When he sold the farm to become a merchant he wore the coat constantly. It had become brown with age and was covered with grease spots, but in it Ebenezer always felt dressed up and ready for the day in town.

As a merchant Ebenezer was not happily placed in life and he had not been happily placed as a farmer. Still he existed. His family, consisting of a daughter named Mabel and the son, lived with him in rooms above the store and it did not cost them much to live. His troubles were not financial. His unhappiness as a merchant lay in the fact that when a traveling man with wares to be sold came in at the front door he was afraid. Behind the counter he stood shaking his head. He was afraid, first that he would stubbornly refuse to buy and thus lose the opportunity to sell again; second that he would not be stubborn enough and would in a moment of weakness buy what could not be sold.

In the store on the morning when Elmer Cowley saw George Willard standing and apparently listening at the back door of the *Eagle* printshop, a situation had arisen that always stirred the son's wrath. The traveling man talked and Ebenezer listened, his whole figure expressing uncertainty. "You see how quickly it is done," said the traveling man who had for sale a small flat metal substitute for collar buttons. With one hand he quickly unfastened a collar from his shirt and then fastened it on again. He assumed a flattering wheedling tone. "I tell you what, men have come to the end of all this fooling with collar buttons and you are the man to make money out of the change that is coming. I am offering you the exclusive agency for this town. Take twenty dozen of these fasteners and I'll not visit any other store. I'll leave the field to you."

The traveling man leaned over the counter and tapped with his finger on Ebenezer's breast. "It's an opportunity and I want you to take it," he urged. "A friend of mine told me about you. 'See that man Cowley,' he said. 'He's a live one.'"

The traveling man paused and waited. Taking a

book from his pocket he began writing out the order. Still holding the shoe in his hand Elmer Cowley went through the store, past the two absorbed men, to a glass showcase near the front door. He took a cheap revolver from the case and began to wave it about. "You get out of here!" he shrieked. "We don't want any collar fasteners here." An idea came to him. "Mind, I'm not making any threat," he added. "I don't say I'll shoot. Maybe I just took this gun out of the case to look at it. But you better get out. Yes sir, I'll say that. You better grab up your things and get out."

The young storekeeper's voice rose to a scream and going behind the counter he began to advance upon the two men. "We're through being fools here!" he cried. "We ain't going to buy any more stuff until we begin to sell. We ain't going to keep on being queer and have folks staring and listening. You get out of here!"

The traveling man left. Raking the samples of collar fasteners off the counter into a black leather bag, he ran. He was a small man and very bowlegged and he ran awkwardly. The black bag caught against the door and he stumbled and fell. "Crazy, that's what he is—crazy!" he sputtered as he arose from the sidewalk and hurried away.

In the store Elmer Cowley and his father stared at each other. Now that the immediate object of his wrath had fled, the younger man was embarrassed. "Well, I meant it. I think we've been queer long enough," he declared, going to the showcase and replacing the revolver. Sitting on a barrel he pulled on and fastened the shoe he had been holding in his hand. He was waiting for some word of understanding from his father but when Ebenezer spoke his words only served to reawaken the wrath in the son and the young man ran out of the store without replying. Scratching his grey beard with his long dirty fingers, the merchant looked at his son with the same wavering uncertain stare with which he had confronted the traveling man. "I'll be starched," he said softly. "Well, well, I'll be washed and ironed and starched!"

Elmer Cowley went out of Winesburg and along a country road that paralleled the railroad track. He did not know where he was going or what he was going to do. In the shelter of a deep cut where the road, after turning sharply to the right, dipped under the tracks he stopped and the passion that had been the cause of his outburst in the store began to again find expression. "I will not be queer—one to be looked at and listened to," he declared

aloud. "I'll be like other people. I'll show that George Willard. He'll find out. I'll show him!"

The distraught young man stood in the middle of the road and glared back at the town. He did not know the reporter George Willard and had no special feeling concerning the tall boy who ran about town gathering the town news. The reporter had merely come, by his presence in the office and in the printshop of the *Winesburg Eagle*, to stand for something in the young merchant's mind. He thought the boy who passed and repassed Cowley & Son's store and who stopped to talk to people in the street must be thinking of him and perhaps laughing at him. George Willard, he felt, belonged to the town, typified the town, represented in his person the spirit of the town. Elmer Cowley could not have believed that George Willard had also his days of unhappiness, that vague hungers and secret unnamable desires visited also his mind. Did he not represent public opinion and had not the public opinion of Winesburg condemned the Cowleys to queerness? Did he not walk whistling and laughing through Main Street? Might not one by striking his person strike also the greater enemy—the thing that smiled and went its own way—the judgment of Winesburg?

Elmer Cowley was extraordinarily tall and his arms were long and powerful. His hair, his eyebrows, and the downy beard that had begun to grow upon his chin, were pale almost to whiteness. His teeth protruded from between his lips and his eyes were blue with the colorless blueness of the marbles called "aggies" that the boys of Winesburg carried in their pockets. Elmer had lived in Winesburg for a year and had made no friends. He was, he felt, one condemned to go through life without friends and he hated the thought.

Sullenly the tall young man tramped along the road with his hands stuffed into his trouser pockets. The day was cold with a raw wind, but presently the sun began to shine and the road became soft and muddy. The tops of the ridges of frozen mud that formed the road began to melt and the mud clung to Elmer's shoes. His feet became cold. When he had gone several miles he turned off the road, crossed a field and entered a wood. In the wood he gathered sticks to build a fire by which he sat trying to warm himself, miserable in body and in mind.

For two hours he sat on the log by the fire and then, arising and creeping cautiously through a mass of underbrush, he went to a fence and looked across fields to a small farmhouse surrounded by low sheds. A smile came to his lips and he began making motions with his long arms to a man who was husking corn in one of the fields.

In his hour of misery the young merchant had returned to the farm where he had lived through boyhood and where there was another human being to whom he felt he could explain himself. The man on the farm was a half-witted old fellow named Mook. He had once been employed by Ebenezer Cowley and had stayed on the farm when it was sold. The old man lived in one of the unpainted sheds back of the farmhouse and puttered about all day in the fields.

Mook the half-wit lived happily. With childlike faith he believed in the intelligence of the animals that lived in the sheds with him, and when he was lonely held long conversations with the cows, the pigs, and even with the chickens that ran about the barnyard. He it was who had put the expression regarding being "laundered" into the mouth of his former employer. When excited or surprised by anything he smiled vaguely and muttered: "I'll be washed and ironed. Well, well, I'll be washed and ironed and starched."

When the half-witted old man left his husking of corn and came into the wood to meet Elmer Cowley, he was neither surprised nor especially interested in the sudden appearance of the young man. His feet also were cold and he sat on the log by the fire, grateful for the warmth and apparently indifferent to what Elmer had to say.

Elmer talked earnestly and with great freedom, walking up and down and waving his arms about. "You don't understand what's the matter with me so of course you don't care," he declared. "With me it's different. Look how it has always been with me. Father is queer and mother was queer, too. Even the clothes mother used to wear were not like other people's clothes, and look at that coat in which father goes about there in town, thinking he's dressed up, too. Why don't he get a new one? It wouldn't cost much. I'll tell you why. Father doesn't know and when mother was alive she didn't know either. Mabel is different. She knows but she won't say anything. I will, though. I'm not going to be stared at any longer. Why look here, Mook, father doesn't know that his store there in town is just a queer jumble, that he'll never sell the stuff he buys. He knows nothing about it. Sometimes he's a little worried that trade doesn't come and then he goes and buys something else. In the evenings he sits by the fire upstairs and says trade will come after a while. He

isn't worried. He's queer. He doesn't know enough to be worried."

The excited young man became more excited. "He don't know but I know," he shouted, stopping to gaze down into the dumb, unresponsive face of the half-wit. "I know too well. I can't stand it. When we lived out here it was different. I worked and at night I went to bed and slept. I wasn't always seeing people and thinking as I am now. In the evening, there in town, I go to the post office or to the depot to see the train come in, and no one says anything to me. Everyone stands around and laughs and they talk but they say nothing to me. Then I feel so queer that I can't talk either. I go away. I don't say anything. I can't."

The fury of the young man became uncontrollable. "I won't stand it," he yelled, looking up at the bare branches of the trees. "I'm not made to stand it."

Maddened by the dull face of the man on the log by the fire, Elmer turned and glared at him as he had glared back along the road at the town of Winesburg. "Go on back to work," he screamed. "What good does it do me to talk to you?" A thought came to him and his voice dropped. "I'm a coward too, eh?" he muttered. "Do you know why I came clear out here afoot? I had to tell some one and you were the only one I could tell. I hunted out another queer one, you see. I ran away, that's what I did. I couldn't stand up to some one like that George Willard. I had to come to you. I ought to tell him and I will."

Again his voice arose to a shout and his arms flew about. "I will tell him. I won't be queer. I don't care what they think. I won't stand it."

Elmer Cowley ran out of the woods leaving the half-wit sitting on the log before the fire. Presently the old man arose and climbing over the fence went back to his work in the corn. "I'll be washed and ironed and starched," he declared. "Well, well, I'll be washed and ironed." Mook was interested. He went along a lane to a field where two cows stood nibbling at a straw stack. "Elmer was here," he said to the cows. "Elmer is crazy. You better get behind the stack where he don't see you. He'll hurt someone yet, Elmer will."

At eight o'clock that evening Elmer Cowley put his head in at the front door of the office of the *Winesburg Eagle* where George Willard sat writing. His cap was pulled down over his eyes and a sullen determined look was on his face. "You come on outside with me," he said, stepping in and closing the door. He kept his hand on the knob as though prepared to resist anyone else coming in. "You just come along outside. I want to see you."

George Willard and Elmer Cowley walked through the main street of Winesburg. The night was cold and George Willard had on a new overcoat and looked very spruce and dressed up. He thrust his hands into the overcoat pockets **and** looked inquiringly at his companion. He had long been wanting to make friends with the young merchant and find out what was in his mind. Now he thought he saw a chance and was delighted. "I wonder what he's up to? Perhaps he thinks he has a piece of news for the paper. It can't be a fire because I haven't heard the fire bell and there isn't anyone running," he thought.

In the main street of Winesburg, on the cold November evening, but few citizens appeared and these hurried along bent on getting to the stove at the back of some store. The windows of the stores were frosted and the wind rattled the tin sign that hung over the entrance to the stairway leading to Doctor Welling's office. Before Hearn's Grocery a basket of apples and a rack filled with new brooms stood on the sidewalk. Elmer Cowley stopped and stood facing George Willard. He tried to talk and his arms began to pump up and down. His face worked spasmodically. He seemed about to shout. "Oh, you go on back," he cried. "Don't stay out here with me. I ain't got anything to tell you. I don't want to see you at all."

For three hours the distracted young merchant wandered through the resident streets of Winesburg blind with anger, brought on by his failure to declare his determination not to be queer. Bitterly the sense of defeat settled upon him and he wanted to weep. After the hours of futile sputtering at nothingness that had occupied the afternoon and his failure in the presence of the young reporter, he thought he could see no hope of a future for himself.

And then a new idea dawned for him. In the darkness that surrounded him he began to see a light. Going to the now darkened store, where Cowley & Son had for over a year waited vainly for trade to come, he crept stealthily in and felt about in a barrel that stood by the stove at the rear. In the barrel beneath shavings lay a tin box containing Cowley & Son's cash. Every evening Ebenezer Cowley put the box in the barrel when he closed the store and went upstairs to bed. "They wouldn't never think of a careless place like that," he told himself, thinking of robbers.

Elmer took twenty dollars, two ten dollar bills, from the little roll containing perhaps four hundred dollars, the cash left from the sale of the farm. Then replacing the box beneath the shavings he went quietly out at the front door and walked again in the streets.

The idea that he thought might put an end to all of his unhappiness was very simple. "I will get out of here, run away from home," he told himself. He knew that a local freight train passed through Winesburg at midnight and went on to Cleveland where it arrived at dawn. He would steal a ride on the local and when he got to Cleveland would lose himself in the crowds there. He would get work in some shop and become friends with the other workmen. Gradually he would become like other men and would be indistinguishable. Then he could talk and laugh. He would no longer be queer and would make friends. Life would begin to have warmth and meaning for him as it had for others.

The tall awkward young man, striding through the streets, laughed at himself because he had been angry and had been half afraid of George Willard. He decided he would have his talk with the young reporter before he left town, that he would tell him about things, perhaps challenge him, challenge all of Winesburg through him.

Aglow with new confidence Elmer went to the office of the New Willard House and pounded on the door. A sleep-eyed boy slept on a cot in the office. He received no salary but was fed at the hotel table and bore with pride the title of "night clerk." Before the boy Elmer was bold, insistent. "You wake him up," he commanded. "You tell him to come down by the depot. I got to see him and I'm going away on the local. Tell him to dress and come on down. I ain't got much time."

The midnight local had finished its work in Winesburg and the trainsmen were coupling cars, swinging lanterns and preparing to resume their flight east. George Willard, rubbing his eyes and again wearing the new overcoat, ran down to the station platform afire with curiosity. "Well, here I am. What do you want? You've got something to tell me, eh?" he said.

Elmer tried to explain. He wet his lips with his tongue and looked at the train that had begun to groan and get under way. "Well, you see," he began, and then lost control of his tongue. "I'll be washed and ironed. I'll be washed and ironed and starched," he muttered half incoherently.

Elmer Cowley danced with fury beside the

groaning train in the darkness on the station platform. Lights leaped into the air and bobbed up
and down before his eyes. Taking the two ten
dollar bills from his pocket he thrust them into
George Willard's hand. "Take them," he cried.
"I don't want them. Give them to father. I stole
them." With a snarl of rage he turned and his
long arms began to flay the air. Like one struggling for release from hands that held him he
struck out, hitting George Willard blow after blow

on the breast, the neck, the mouth. The young
reporter rolled over on the platform half unconscious, stunned by the terrific force of the blows.
Springing aboard the passing train and running
over the tops of cars, Elmer sprang down to a flat
car and lying on his face looked back, trying to see
the fallen man in the darkness. Pride surged up in
him. "I showed him," he cried. "I guess I showed
him. I ain't so queer. I guess I showed him I ain't
so queer."

I Want to Know Why (1921)

We got up at four in the morning, that first day
in the East. On the evening before, we had
climbed off a freight train at the edge of town
and with the true instinct of Kentucky boys had
found our way across town and to the race track
and the stables at once. Then we knew we were
all right. Hanley Turner right away found a nigger
we knew. It was Bildad Johnson, who in the
winter works at Ed Becker's livery barn in our
home town, Beckersville. Bildad is a good cook as
almost all our niggers are and of course he, like
everyone in our part of Kentucky who is anyone
at all, likes the horses. In the spring Bildad begins
to scratch around. A nigger from our country can
flatter and wheedle anyone into letting him do
most anything he wants. Bildad wheedles the
stable men and the trainers from the horse farms
in our country around Lexington. The trainers
come into town in the evening to stand around
and talk and maybe get into a poker game. Bildad
gets in with them. He is always doing little favors
and telling about things to eat, chicken browned
in a pan, and how is the best way to cook sweet
potatoes and corn bread. It makes your mouth
water to hear him.

When the racing season comes on and the
horses go to the races and there is all the talk on
the streets in the evenings about the new colts,
and everyone says when they are going over to
Lexington or to the spring meeting at Churchill
Downs or to Latonia, and the horsemen that have
been down to New Orleans or maybe at the winter
meeting at Havana in Cuba come home to spend
a week before they start out again, at such a time
when everything talked about in Beckersville is
just horses and nothing else and the outfits start
out and horse racing is in every breath of air you
breathe, Bildad shows up with a job as cook for

some outfit. Often when I think about it, his always going all season to the races and working in
the livery barn in the winter where horses are and
where men like to come and talk about horses, I
wish I was a nigger. It's a foolish thing to say, but
that's the way I am about being around horses,
just crazy. I can't help it.

Well, I must tell you about what we did and
let you in on what I'm talking about. Four of us
boys from Beckersville, all whites and sons of men
who live in Beckersville regular, made up our
minds we were going to the races, not just to Lexington or Louisville, I don't mean, but to the big
Eastern track we were always hearing our Beckersville men talk about, to Saratoga. We were all
pretty young then. I was just turned fifteen and I
was the oldest of the four. It was my scheme. I
admit that, and I talked the others into trying it.
There was Hanley Turner and Henry Rieback and
Tom Tumberton and myself. I had thirty-seven
dollars I had earned during the winter working
nights and Saturdays in Enoch Myer's grocery.
Henry Rieback had eleven dollars and the others,
Hanley and Tom, had only a dollar or two each.
We fixed it all up and laid low until the Kentucky
spring meetings were over and some of our men,
the sportiest ones, the ones we envied the most,
had cut out. Then we cut out too.

I won't tell you the trouble we had beating our
way on freights and all. We went through Cleveland and Buffalo and other cities and saw Niagara
Falls. We bought things there, souvenirs and
spoons and cards and shells with pictures of the
falls on them for our sisters and mothers, but
thought we had better not send any of the things
home. We didn't want to put the folks on our
trail and maybe be nabbed.

We got into Saratoga as I said at night and

went to the track. Bildad fed us up. He showed us a place to sleep in hay over a shed and promised to keep still. Niggers are all right about things like that. They won't squeal on you. Often a white man you might meet, when you had run away from home like that, might appear to be all right and give you a quarter or a half dollar or something, and then go right and give you away. White men will do that, but not a nigger. You can trust them. They are squarer with kids. I don't know why.

At the Saratoga meeting that year there were a lot of men from home. Dave Williams and Arthur Mulford and Jerry Myers and others. Then there was a lot from Louisville and Lexington Henry Rieback knew but I didn't. They were professional gamblers and Henry Rieback's father is one too. He is what is called a sheet writer and goes away most of the year to tracks. In the winter when he is home in Beckersville he don't stay there much but goes away to cities and deals faro. He is a nice man and generous, is always sending Henry presents, a bicycle and a gold watch and a boy scout suit of clothes and things like that.

My own father is a lawyer. He's all right, but don't make much money and can't buy me things, and anyway I'm getting so old now I don't expect it. He never said nothing to me against Henry, but Hanley Turner and Tom Tumberton's fathers did. They said to their boys that money so come by is no good and they didn't want their boys brought up to hear gamblers' talk and be thinking about such things and maybe embrace them.

That's all right and I guess the men know what they are talking about, but I don't see what it's got to do with Henry or with horses either. That's what I'm writing this story about. I'm puzzled. I'm getting to be a man and want to think straight and be O. K., and there's something I saw at the race meeting at the Eastern track I can't figure out.

I can't help it, I'm crazy about thoroughbred horses. I've always been that way. When I was ten years old and saw I was growing to be big and couldn't be a rider I was so sorry I nearly died. Harry Hellinfinger in Beckersville, whose father is Postmaster, is grown up and too lazy to work, but likes to stand around in the street and get up jokes on boys like sending them to a hardware store for a gimlet to bore square holes and other jokes like that. He played one on me. He told me that if I would eat a half a cigar I would be stunted and not grow any more and maybe could

be a rider. I did it. When father wasn't looking I took a cigar out of his pocket and gagged it down some way. It made me awful sick and the doctor had to be sent for, and then it did no good. I kept right on growing. It was a joke. When I told what I had done and why, most fathers would have whipped me, but mine didn't.

Well, I didn't get stunted and didn't die. It serves Harry Hellinfinger right. Then I made up my mind I would like to be a stableboy, but had to give that up too. Mostly niggers do that work and I knew father wouldn't let me go into it. No use to ask him.

If you've never been crazy about thoroughbreds, it's because you've never been around where they are much and don't know any better. They're beautiful. There isn't anything so lovely and clean and full of spunk and honest and everything as some race horses. On the big horse farms that are all around our town Beckersville there are tracks, and the horses run in the early morning. More than a thousand times I've got out of bed before daylight and walked two or three miles to the tracks. Mother wouldn't of let me go, but father always says, "Let him alone." So I got some bread out of the breadbox and some butter and jam, gobbled it and lit out.

At the tracks you sit on the fence with men, whites and niggers, and they chew tobacco and talk, and then the colts are brought out. It's early and the grass is covered with shiny dew and in another field a man is plowing and they are frying things in a shed where the track niggers sleep, and you know how a nigger can giggle and laugh and say things that make you laugh. A white man can't do it and some niggers can't, but a track nigger can every time.

And so the colts are brought out and some are just galloped by stableboys, but almost every morning on a big track owned by a rich man who lives maybe in New York, there are always, nearly every morning, a few colts and some of the old race horses and geldings and mares that are cut loose.

It brings a lump up into my throat when a horse runs. I don't mean all horses, but some. I can pick them nearly every time. It's in my blood like in the blood of race track niggers and trainers. Even when they just go slop-jogging along with a little nigger on their backs, I can tell a winner. If my throat hurts and it's hard for me to swallow, that's him. He'll run like Sam Hill when you let him out. If he don't win every time it'll be a wonder and because they've got him in a pocket behind another or he was pulled or got off bad at the post or something. If I wanted to be a gambler like Henry Rieback's father I could get rich. I know I could and Henry says so too. All I would have to do is to wait till that hurt comes when I see a horse and then bet every cent. That's what I would do if I wanted to be a gambler, but I don't.

When you're at the tracks in the morning—not the race tracks but the training tracks around Beckersville—you don't see a horse, the kind I've been talking about, very often, but it's nice anyway. Any thoroughbred, that is sired right and out of a good mare and trained by a man that knows how, can run. If he couldn't, what would he be there for and not pulling a plow?

Well, out of the stables they come and the boys are on their backs and it's lovely to be there. You hunch down on top of the fence and itch inside you. Over in the sheds the niggers giggle and sing. Bacon is being fried and coffee made. Everything smells lovely. Nothing smells better than coffee and manure and horses and niggers and bacon frying and pipes being smoked out of doors on a morning like that. It just gets you, that's what it does.

But about Saratoga. We was there six days and not a soul from home seen us and everything came off just as we wanted it to, fine weather and horses and races and all. We beat our way home and Bildad gave us a basket with fried chicken and bread and other eatables in it, and I had eighteen dollars when we got back to Beckersville. Mother jawed and cried, but Pop didn't say much. I told everything we done, except one thing. I did and saw that alone. That's what I'm writing about. It got me upset. I think about it at night. Here it is.

At Saratoga we laid up nights in the hay in the shed Bildad had showed us and ate with the niggers early and at night when the race people had all gone away. The men from home stayed mostly in the grandstand and betting field and didn't come out around the places where the horses are kept except to the paddocks just before a race when the horses are saddled. At Saratoga they don't have paddocks under an open shed as at Lexington and Churchill Downs and other tracks down in our country, but saddle the horses right out in an open place under trees on a lawn as smooth and nice as Banker Bohon's front yard here in Beckersville. It's lovely. The horses are sweaty and nervous and shine and the men come out and smoke cigars and look at them and the trainers are there and the owners, and your heart thumps so you can hardly breathe.

Then the bugle blows for post and the boys that ride come running out with their silk clothes on and you run to get a place by the fence with the niggers.

I always am wanting to be a trainer or owner, and at the risk of being seen and caught and sent home I went to the paddocks before every race. The other boys didn't, but I did.

We got to Saratoga on a Friday, and on Wednesday the next week the big Mulford Handicap was to be run. Middlestride was in it and Sunstreak. The weather was fine and the track fast. I couldn't sleep the night before.

What had happened was that both these horses are the kind it makes my throat hurt to see. Middlestride is long and looks awkward and is a gelding. He belongs to Joe Thompson, a little owner from home who only has a half dozen horses. The Mulford Handicap is for a mile and Middlestride can't untrack fast. He goes away slow and is always 'way back at the half, then he begins to run and if the race is a mile and a quarter he'll just eat up everything and get there.

Sunstreak is different. He is a stallion and nervous and belongs on the biggest farm we've got in our country, the Van Riddle place that belongs to Mr. Van Riddle of New York. Sunstreak is like a girl you think about sometimes but never see. He is hard all over and lovely too. When you look at his head you want to kiss him. He is trained by Jerry Tillford who knows me and has been good to me lots of times, lets me walk into a horse's stall to look at him close and other things. There isn't anything as sweet as that horse. He stands at the post quiet and not letting on, but he is just burning up inside. Then when the barrier goes up he is off like his name, Sunstreak. It makes you ache to see him. It hurts you. He just lays down and runs like a bird dog. There can't anything I ever see run like him except Middlestride when he gets untraced and stretches himself.

Gee! I ached to see that race and those two horses run, ached and dreaded it too. I didn't want to see either of our horses beaten. We had never sent a pair like that to the races before. Old men in Beckersville said so and the niggers said so. It was a fact.

Before the race, I went over to the paddocks to see. I looked a last look at Middlestride, who isn't such a much standing in a paddock that way, then I went to see Sunstreak.

It was his day. I knew when I seen him. I forgot all about being seen myself and walked right up. All the men from Beckersville were there and no one noticed me except Jerry Tillford. He saw me and something happened. I'll tell you about that.

I was standing looking at that horse and aching. In some way, I can't tell how, I knew just how Sunstreak felt inside. He was quiet and letting the niggers rub his legs and Mr. Van Riddle himself put the saddle on, but he was just a raging torrent inside. He was like the water in the river at Niagara Falls just before its goes plunk down. That horse wasn't thinking about running. He don't have to think about that. He was just thinking about holding himself back till the time for the running came. I knew that. I could just in a way see right inside him. He was going to do some awful running and I knew it. He wasn't bragging or letting on much or prancing or making a fuss, but just waiting. I knew it and Jerry Tillford his trainer knew. I look up, and then that man and I looked into each other's eyes. Something happened to me. I guess I loved the man as much as I did the horse because he knew what I knew. Seemed to me there wasn't anything in the world but that man and the horse and me. I cried and Jerry Tillford had a shine in his eyes. Then I came away to the fence to wait for the race. The horse was better than me, more steadier and, now I know, better than Jerry. He was the quietest and he had to do the running.

Sunstreak ran first of course and he busted the world's record for a mile. I've seen that if I never see anything more. Everything came out just as I expected. Middlestride got left at the post and was 'way back and closed up to be second, just as I knew he would. He'll get a world's record too some day. They can't skin the Beckersville country on horses.

I watched the race calm because I knew what would happen. I was sure. Hanley Turner and Henry Rieback and Tom Tumberton were all more excited than me.

A funny thing had happened to me. I was thinking about Jerry Tillford the trainer and how happy he was all through the race. I liked him that afternoon even more than I ever liked my own father. I almost forgot the horses thinking that way about him. It was because of what I had seen in his eyes as he stood in the paddocks beside Sunstreak before the race started. I knew he had been watching and working with Sunstreak since the horse was a baby colt, had taught him to run and be patient and when to let himself out and not to quit, never. I knew that for him it was like a mother seeing her child do something brave or wonderful. It was the first time I ever felt for a man like that.

After the race that night I cut out from Tom and Hanley and Henry. I wanted to be by myself and I wanted to be near Jerry Tillford if I could work it. Here is what happened.

The track in Saratoga is near the edge of town. It is all polished up and trees around, the evergreen kind, and grass and everything painted and nice. If you go past the track you get to a hard road made of asphalt for automobiles, and if you go along this for a few miles there is a road turns off to a little rummy-looking farmhouse set in a yard.

That night after the race I went along that road because I had seen Jerry and some other men go that way in an automobile. I didn't expect to find them. I walked for a ways and then sat down by a fence to think. It was the direction they went in. I wanted to be as near Jerry as I could. I felt close to him. Pretty soon I went up the side road—I don't know why—and came to the rummy farmhouse. I was just lonesome to see Jerry, like wanting to see your father at night when you are a young kid. Just then an automobile came along and turned in. Jerry was in it and Henry Rieback's father, and Arthur Bedford from home, and Dave Williams and two other men I didn't know. They got out of the car and went into the house, all but Henry Rieback's father who quarreled with them and said he wouldn't go. It was only about nine o'clock, but they were all drunk and the rummy-looking farmhouse was a place for bad women to stay in. That's what it was. I crept up along a fence and looked through a window and saw.

It's what give me the fantods. I can't make it out. The women in the house were all ugly mean-looking women, not nice to look at or be near. They were homely too, except one who was tall and looked a little like the gelding Middlestride, but not clean like him, but with a hard ugly mouth. She had red hair. I saw everything plain. I got up by an old rosebush by an open window and looked. The women had on loose dresses and sat around in chairs. The men came in and some sat on the women's laps. The place smelled rotten and there was rotten talk, the kind a kid hears around a livery stable in a town like Beckersville in the winter but don't ever expect to hear talked when there are women around. It was rotten. A nigger wouldn't go into such a place.

I looked at Jerry Tillford. I've told you how I had been feeling about him on account of his knowing what was going on inside of Sunstreak in the minute before he went to the post for the race in which he made a world's record.

Jerry bragged in that bad woman house as I know Sunstreak wouldn't never have bragged. He said that he made that horse, that it was him that won the race and made the record. He lied and bragged like a fool. I never heard such silly talk.

And, then, what do you suppose he did! He looked at the woman in there, the one that was lean and hard-mouthed and looked a little like the gelding Middlestride but not clean like him, and his eyes began to shine just as they did when he looked at me and at Sunstreak in the paddocks at the track in the afternoon. I stood there by the window—gee!—but I wished I hadn't gone away from the tracks, but had stayed with the boys and the niggers and the horses. The tall rotten-looking woman was between us just as Sunstreak was in the paddocks in the afternoon.

Then, all of a sudden, I began to hate that man. I wanted to scream and rush in the room and kill him. I never had such a feeling before. I was so mad clean through that I cried and my fists were doubled up so my fingernails cut my hands.

And Jerry's eyes kept shining and he waved back and forth, and then he went and kissed that woman and I crept away and went back to the tracks and to bed and didn't sleep hardly any, and then next day I got the other kids to start home with me and never told them anything I seen.

I been thinking about it ever since. I can't make it out. Spring has come again and I'm nearly sixteen and go to the tracks mornings same as always, and I see Sunstreak and Middlestride and a new colt named Strident I'll bet will lay them all out, but no one thinks so but me and two or three niggers.

But things are different. At the tracks the air don't taste as good or smell as good. It's because a man like Jerry Tillford, who knows what he does, could see a horse like Sunstreak run, and kiss a woman like that the same day. I can't make it out. Darn him, what did he want to do like that for? I keep thinking about it and it spoils looking at horses and smelling things and hearing niggers laugh and everything. Sometimes I'm so mad about it I want to fight someone. It gives me the fantods. What did he do it for? I want to know why.

Death in the Woods (1933)

She was an old woman and lived on a farm near the town in which I lived. All country and small-town people have seen such old women, but no one knows much about them. Such an old woman comes into town driving an old worn-out horse or she comes afoot carrying a basket. She may own a few hens and have eggs to sell. She brings them in a basket and takes them to a grocer. There she trades them in. She gets some salt pork and some beans. Then she gets a pound or two of sugar and some flour.

Afterwards she goes to the butcher's and asks for some dog meat. She may spend ten or fifteen cents, but when she does she asks for something. Formerly the butchers gave liver to anyone who wanted to carry it away. In our family we were always having it. Once one of my brothers got a whole cow's liver at the slaughterhouse near the fairgrounds in our town. We had it until we were sick of it. It never cost a cent. I have hated the thought of it ever since.

The old farm woman got some liver and a soup-bone. She never visited with anyone, and as soon as she got what she wanted she lit out for home. It made quite a load for such an old body. No one gave her a lift. People drive right down a road and never notice an old woman like that.

There was such an old woman who used to come into town past our house one summer and fall when I was a young boy and was sick with what was called inflammatory rheumatism. She went home later carrying a heavy pack on her back. Two or three large gaunt-looking dogs followed at her heels.

The old woman was nothing special. She was one of the nameless ones that hardly anyone knows, but she got into my thoughts. I have just suddenly now, after all these years, remembered her and what happened. It is a story. Her name was Grimes, and she lived with her husband and son in a small unpainted house on the bank of a small creek four miles from town.

The husband and son were a tough lot. Although the son was but twenty-one, he had already served a term in jail. It was whispered about that the woman's husband stole horses and ran them off to some other county. Now and then, when a horse turned up missing, the man had also disappeared. No one ever caught him. Once, when I was loafing at Tom Whitehead's livery barn, the man came there and sat on the bench in front. Two or three other men were there, but no one spoke to him. He sat for a few minutes and then got up and went away. When he was leaving he turned around and stared at the men. There was a look of defiance in his eyes. "Well, I have tried to be friendly. You don't want to talk to me. It has been so wherever I have gone in this town. If, some day, one of your fine horses turns up missing, well, then what?" He did not say anything actually. "I'd like to bust one of you on the jaw," was about what his eyes said. I remember how the look in his eyes made me shiver.

The old man belonged to a family that had had money once. His name was Jake Grimes. It all comes back clearly now. His father, John Grimes, had owned a sawmill when the country was new, and had made money. Then he got to drinking and running after women. When he died there wasn't much left.

Jake blew in the rest. Pretty soon there wasn't any more lumber to cut and his land was nearly all gone.

He got his wife off a German farmer, for whom he went to work one June day in the wheat harvest. She was a young thing then and scared to death. You see, the farmer was up to something with the girl—she was, I think, a bound girl and his wife had her suspicions. She took it out on the girl when the man wasn't around. Then, when the wife had to go off to town for supplies, the farmer got after her. She told young Jake that nothing really ever happened, but he didn't know whether to believe it or not.

He got her pretty easy himself, the first time he was out with her. He wouldn't have married her if the German farmer hadn't tried to tell him where to get off. He got her to go riding with him in his buggy one night when he was threshing on the place, and then he came for her the next Sunday night.

She managed to get out of the house without her employer's seeing, but when she was getting into the buggy he showed up. It was almost dark, and he just popped up suddenly at the horse's head. He grabbed the horse by the bridle and Jake got out his buggy whip.

They had it out all right! The German was a tough one. Maybe he didn't care whether his wife knew or not. Jake hit him over the face and shoulders with the buggy whip, but the horse got to acting up and he had to get out.

Then the two men went for it. The girl didn't see it. The horse started to run away and went nearly a mile down the road before the girl got him stopped. Then she managed to tie him to a tree beside the road. (I wonder how I know all this. It must have stuck in my mind from small-town tales when I was a boy.) Jake found her there after he got through with the German. She was huddled up in the buggy seat, crying, scared to death. She told Jake a lot of stuff, how the German had tried to get her, how he chased her once into the barn, how another time, when they happened to be alone in the house together, he tore her dress open clear down the front. The German, she said, might have got her that time if he hadn't heard his old woman drive in at the gate. She had been off to town for supplies. Well, she would be putting the horse in the barn. The German managed to sneak off to the fields without his wife seeing. He told the girl he would kill her if she told. What could she do? She told a lie about ripping her dress in the barn when she was feeding the stock. I remember now that she was a bound girl and did not know where her father and mother were. Maybe she did not have any father. You know what I mean.

Such bound children were often enough cruelly treated. They were children who had no parents, slaves really. There were very few orphan homes then. They were legally bound into some home. It was a matter of pure luck how it came out.

II

She married Jake and had a son and a daughter, but the daughter died.

Then she settled down to feed stock. That was her job. At the German's place she had cooked the food for the German and his wife. The wife was a strong woman with big hips and worked most of the time in the fields with her husband. She fed them and fed the cows in the barn, fed the pigs, the horses and the chickens. Every moment of every day, as a young girl, was spent feeding something.

Then she married Jake Grimes and he had to be fed. She was a slight thing, and when she had been married for three or four years, and after the two children were born, her slender shoulders became stooped.

Jake always had a lot of big dogs around the house, that stood near the unused sawmill near the creek. He was always trading horses when he wasn't stealing something and had a lot of poor bony ones about. Also he kept three or four pigs and a cow. They were all pastured in the few acres left of the Grimes place and Jake did little enough work.

He went into debt for a threshing outfit and ran it for several years, but it did not pay. People did not trust him. They were afraid he would steal the grain at night. He had to go a long way off to get work and it cost too much to get there. In the winter he hunted and cut a little firewood, to be sold in some nearby town. When the son grew up he was just like the father. They got drunk together. If there wasn't anything to eat in the house when they came home the old man gave his old woman a cut over the head. She had a few chickens of her own and had to kill one of them in a hurry. When they were all killed she wouldn't have any eggs to sell when she went to town, and then what would she do?

She had to scheme all her life about getting things fed, getting the pigs fed so they would grow fat and could be butchered in the fall. When they were butchered her husband took most of the meat off to town and sold it. If he did not do it first, the boy did. They fought sometimes and when they fought the old woman stood aside trembling.

She had got the habit of silence anyway—that was fixed. Sometimes, when she began to look old —she wasn't forty yet—and when the husband and son were both off, trading horses or drinking or hunting or stealing, she went around the house and the barnyard muttering to herself.

How was she going to get everything fed?—that was her problem. The dogs had to be fed. There wasn't enough hay in the barn for the horses and the cow. If she didn't feed the chickens how could they lay eggs? Without eggs to sell how could she get things in town, things she had to have to keep the life of the farm going? Thank heaven, she did not have to feed her husband—in a certain way.

That hadn't lasted long after their marriage and after the babies came. Where he went on his long trips she did not know. Sometimes he was gone from home for weeks, and after the boy grew up they went off together.

They left everything at home for her to manage and she had no money. She knew no one. No one ever talked to her in town. When it was winter she had to gather sticks of wood for her fire, had to try to keep the stock fed with very little grain.

The stock in the barn cried to her hungrily, the dogs followed her about. In the winter the hens laid few enough eggs. They huddled in the corners of the barn and she kept watching them. If a hen lays an egg in the barn in the winter and you do not find it, it freezes and breaks.

One day in winter the old woman went off to town with a few eggs and the dogs followed her. She did not get started until nearly three o'clock and the snow was heavy. She hadn't been feeling very well for several days and so she went muttering along, scantily clad, her shoulders stooped. She had an old grain bag in which she carried her eggs, tucked away down in the bottom. There weren't many of them, but in winter the price of eggs is up. She would get a little meat in exchange for the eggs, some salt pork, a little sugar, and some coffee perhaps. It might be the butcher would give her a piece of liver.

When she had got to town and was trading in her eggs the dogs lay by the door outside. She did pretty well, got the things she needed, more than she had hoped. Then she went to the butcher and he gave her some liver and some dog meat.

It was the first time anyone had spoken to her in a friendly way for a long time. The butcher was alone in his shop when she came in and was annoyed by the thought of such a sick-looking old woman out on such a day. It was bitter cold and the snow, that had let up during the afternoon, was falling again. The butcher said something about her husband and her son, swore at them, and the old woman stared at him, a look of mild surprise in her eyes as he talked. He said that if either the husband or the son were going to get any of the liver or the heavy bones with scraps of meat hanging to them that he had put into the grain bag, he'd see him starve first.

Starve, eh? Well, things had to be fed. Men had to be fed, and the horses that weren't any good but maybe could be traded off, and the poor thin cow that hadn't given any milk for three months.

Horses, cows, pigs, dogs, men.

III

The old woman had to get back before darkness came if she could. The dogs followed at her heels, sniffing at the heavy grain bag she had fastened on her back. When she got to the edge of town she stopped by a fence and tied the bag on her back with a piece of rope she had carried in her dress pocket for just that purpose. That was an easier way to carry it. Her arms ached. It was hard when she had to crawl over fences and once she fell over and landed in the snow. The dogs went frisking about. She had to struggle to get to her feet again, but she made it. The point of climbing over the fences was that there was a short cut over a hill and through a woods. She might have gone around by the road, but it was a mile farther that way. She was afraid she couldn't make it. And then, besides, the stock had to be fed. There was a little hay left and a little corn. Perhaps her husband and son would bring some home when they came. They had driven off in the only buggy the Grimes family had, a rickety thing, a rickety horse hitched to the buggy, two other rickety horses led by halters. They were going to trade horses, get a little money if they could. They might come home drunk. It would be well to have something in the house when they came back.

The son had an affair on with a woman at the county seat, fifteen miles away. She was a rough enough woman, a tough one. Once, in the summer, the son had brought her to the house. Both she and the son had been drinking. Jake Grimes was away and the son and his woman ordered the old woman about like a servant. She didn't mind much; she was used to it. Whatever happened she never said anything. That was her way of getting along. She had managed that way when she was a young girl at the German's and ever since she had married Jake. That time her son brought his woman to the house they stayed all night, sleeping together just as though they were married. It hadn't shocked the old woman, not much. She had got past being shocked early in life.

With the pack on her back she went painfully along across an open field, wading in the deep snow, and got into the woods.

There was a path, but it was hard to follow. Just beyond the top of the hill, where the woods was thickest, there was a small clearing. Had someone once thought of building a house there? The clearing was as large as a building lot in town, large enough for a house and a garden. The path ran along the side of the clearing, and when she got there the old woman sat down to rest at the foot of a tree.

It was a foolish thing to do. When she got herself placed, the pack against the tree's trunk, it was nice, but what about getting up again? She worried about that for a moment and then quietly closed her eyes.

She must have slept for a time. When you are about so cold you can't get any colder. The afternoon grew a little warmer and the snow came thicker than ever. Then after a time the weather cleared. The moon even came out.

There were four Grimes dogs that had followed Mrs. Grimes into town, all tall gaunt fellows. Such men as Jake Grimes and his son always keep just such dogs. They kick and abuse them, but they stay. The Grimes dogs, in order to keep from starving, had to do a lot of foraging for themselves, and they had been at it while the old woman slept with her back to the tree at the side of the clearing. They had been chasing rabbits in the woods and in adjoining fields and in their ranging had picked up three other farm dogs.

After a time all the dogs came back to the clearing. They were excited about something. Such nights, cold and clear and with a moon, do things to dogs. It may be that some old instinct, come down from the time when they were wolves and ranged the woods in packs on winter nights, comes back into them.

The dogs in the clearing, before the old woman, had caught two or three rabbits and their immediate hunger had been satisfied. They began to play, running in circles in the clearing. Round and round they ran, each dog's nose at the tail of the next dog. In the clearing, under the snow-laden trees and under the wintry moon they made a strange picture, running thus silently, in a circle their running had beaten in the soft snow. The dogs made no sound. They ran around and around in the circle.

It may have been that the old woman saw them doing that before she died. She may have awakened once or twice and looked at the strange sight with dim old eyes.

She wouldn't be very cold now, just drowsy. Life hangs on a long time. Perhaps the old woman was out of her head. She may have dreamed of her girlhood, at the German's, and before that, when she was a child and before her mother lit out and left her.

Her dreams couldn't have been very pleasant.

Not many pleasant things have happened to her. Now and then one of the Grimes dogs left the running circle and came to stand before her. The dog thrust his face close to her face. His red tongue was hanging out.

The running of the dogs may have been a kind of death ceremony. It may have been that the primitive instinct of the wolf, having been aroused in the dogs by the night and the running, made them somehow afraid.

"Now we are no longer wolves. We are dogs, the servants of men. Keep alive, man! When man dies we become wolves again."

When one of the dogs came to where the old woman sat with her back against the tree and thrust his nose close to her face he seemed satisfied and went back to run with the pack. All the Grimes dogs did it at some time during the evening, before she died. I knew all about it afterward, when I grew to be a man, because once in a woods in Illinois, on another winter night, I saw a pack of dogs act just like that. The dogs were waiting for me to die as they had waited for the old woman that night when I was a child, but when it happened to me I was a young man and had no intention whatever of dying.

The old woman died softly and quietly. When she was dead and when one of the Grimes dogs had come to her and had found her dead all the dogs stopped running.

They gathered about her.

Well, she was dead now. She had fed the Grimes dogs when she was alive, what about now?

There was the pack on her back, the grain bag containing the piece of salt pork, the liver the butcher had given her, the dog meat, the soupbones. The butcher in town, having been suddenly overcome with a feeling of pity, had loaded her grain bag heavily. It had been a big haul for the old woman.

It was a big haul for the dogs now.

IV

One of the Grimes dogs sprang suddenly out from among the others and began worrying the pack on the old woman's back. Had the dogs really been wolves, that one would have been the leader of the pack. What he did, all the others did.

All of them sank their teeth into the grain bag the old woman had fastened with ropes to her back.

They dragged the old woman's body out into the open clearing. The worn-out dress was quickly torn from her shoulders. When she was found, a day or two later, the dress had been torn from her body clear to the hips, but the dogs had not touched her body. They had got the meat out of the grain bag, that was all. Her body was frozen stiff when it was found, and the shoulders were so narrow and the body so slight that in death it looked like the body of some charming young girl.

Such things happened in towns of the Middle West, on farms near town, when I was a boy. A hunter out after rabbits found the old woman's body and did not touch it. Something, the beaten round path in the little snow-covered clearing, the silence of the place, the place where the dogs had worried the body trying to pull the grain bag away or tear it open—something startled the man and he hurried off to town.

I was in Main Street with one of my brothers who was town newsboy and who was taking the afternoon papers to the stores. It was almost night.

The hunter came into a grocery and told his story. Then he went to a hardware shop and into a drugstore. Men began to gather on the sidewalks. Then they started out along the road to the place in the woods.

My brother should have gone on about his business of distributing papers but he didn't. Everyone was going to the woods. The undertaker went and the town marshal. Several men got on a dray and rode out to where the path left the road and went into the woods, but the horses weren't very sharply shod and slid about on the slippery roads. They made no better time than those of us who walked.

The town marshal was a large man whose leg had been injured in the Civil War. He carried a heavy cane and limped rapidly along the road. My brother and I followed at his heels, and as we went other men and boys joined the crowd.

It had grown dark by the time we got to where the old woman had left the road, but the moon had come out. The marshal was thinking there might have been a murder. He kept asking the hunter questions. The hunter went along with his gun across his shoulders, a dog following at his heels. It isn't often a rabbit hunter has a chance to be so conspicuous. He was taking full advantage of it, leading the procession with the town marshal. "I didn't see any wounds. She was a beautiful young girl. Her face was buried in the snow. No, I didn't know her." As a matter of fact, the hunter had not looked closely at the body. He had been frightened. She might have been murdered and someone might spring out from behind a tree and murder him. In a woods, in the late afternoon, when the trees are all bare and there is white snow on the ground, when all is silent, something creepy steals over the mind and body. If something strange or uncanny has happened in the neighborhood all you think about is getting away from there as fast as you can.

The crowd of men and boys had got to where the old woman had crossed the field and went, following the marshal and the hunter, up the slight incline and into the woods.

My brother and I were silent. He had his bundle of papers in a bag slung across his shoulder. When he got back to town he would have to go on distributing his papers before he went home to supper. If I went along, as he had no doubt already determined I should, we would both be late. Either Mother or our older sister would have to warm our supper.

Well, we would have something to tell. A boy did not get such a chance very often. It was lucky we just happened to go into the grocery when the hunter came in. The hunter was a country fellow. Neither of us had ever seen him before.

Now the crowd of men and boys had got to the clearing. Darkness comes quickly on such winter nights, but the full moon made everything clear. My brother and I stood near the tree beneath which the old woman had died.

She did not look old, lying there in that light, frozen and still. One of the men turned her over in the snow and I saw everything. My body trembled with some strange mystical feeling and so did my brother's. It might have been the cold.

Neither of us had ever seen a woman's body before. It may have been the snow, clinging to the frozen flesh, that made it look so white and lovely, so like marble. No woman had come with the party from town; but one of the men, he was the town blacksmith, took off his overcoat and spread it over her. Then he gathered her into his arms and started off to town, all the others following silently. At that time no one knew who she was.

V

I had seen everything, had seen the oval in the snow, like a miniature race track, where the dogs

had run, had seen how the men were mystified, had seen the white bare young-looking shoulders, had heard the whispered comments of the men.

The men were simply mystified. They took the body to the undertaker's, and when the blacksmith, the hunter, the marshal and several others had got inside they closed the door. If Father had been there perhaps he could have got in, but we boys couldn't.

I went with my brother to distribute the rest of his papers and when we got home it was my brother who told the story.

I kept silent and went to bed early. It may have been I was not satisfied with the way he told it.

Later, in the town, I must have heard other fragments of the old woman's story. She was recognized the next day and there was an investigation.

The husband and son were found somewhere and brought to town and there was an attempt to connect them with the woman's death, but it did not work. They had perfect enough alibis.

However, the town was against them. They had to get out. Where they went I never heard.

I remember only the picture there in the forest, the men standing about, the naked girlish-looking figure, face down in the snow, the tracks made by the running dogs and the clear cold winter sky above. White fragments of clouds were drifting across the sky. They went racing across the little open space among the trees.

The scene in the forest had become for me, without my knowing it, the foundation for the real story I am now trying to tell. The fragments, you see, had to be picked up slowly, long afterward.

Things happened. When I was a young man I worked on the farm of a German. The hired girl was afraid of her employer. The farmer's wife hated her.

I saw things at that place. Once later, I had a half-uncanny, mystical adventure with dogs in an Illinois forest on a clear, moonlit winter night. When I was a schoolboy, and on a summer day, I went with a boy friend out along a creek some miles from town and came to the house where the old woman had lived. No one had lived in the house since her death. The doors were broken from the hinges; the window lights were all broken. As the boy and I stood in the road outside, two dogs, just roving farm dogs no doubt, came running around the corner of the house. The dogs were tall, gaunt fellows and came down to the fence and glared through at us, standing in the road.

The whole thing, the story of the old woman's death, was to me as I grew older like music heard from far off. The notes had to be picked up slowly one at a time. Something had to be understood.

The woman who died was one destined to feed animal life. Anyway, that is all she ever did. She was feeding animal life before she was born, as a child, as a young woman working on the farm of the German, after she married, when she grew old and when she died. She fed animal life in cows, in chickens, in pigs, in horses, in dogs, in men. Her daughter had died in childhood and with her one son she had no articulate relations. On the night when she died she was hurrying homeward, bearing on her body food for animal life.

She died in the clearing in the woods and even after her death continued feeding animal life.

You see it is likely that, when my brother told the story, that night when we got home and my mother and sister sat listening, I did not think he got the point. He was too young and so was I. A thing so complete has its own beauty.

I shall not try to emphasize the point. I am only explaining why I was dissatisfied then and have been ever since. I speak of that only that you may understand why I have been impelled to try to tell the simple story over again.

SINCLAIR LEWIS (1885–1951)

Realism of a meticulous and almost scientific kind mingles, in the fiction of Sinclair Lewis, with a vein of nostalgia that in his best work expressed itself obliquely as satire. The nostalgia was for a pattern of values that seemed to Lewis to be disintegrating: self-trust, the companionship of independent individuals, a total commitment to freedom of spirit and of thought. Lewis found the most eloquent American statement of those values in the writings of Thoreau, which he revered and carried with him. Like Thoreau, he saw the impulse to freedom beset by the sources of repression—in particular, during the second and third decade of this century by the complex and unvillainous, yet lethal power of middle-class conventionality—but he was far less confident than Thoreau that the American individual, under the modern circumstances, could resist that all-enveloping opposition. Lewis's work characteristically depicts his "heroes" as resenting the pressure to conform, then in open rebellion against, and making the effort to escape, conformity; and, finally, the effort having failed, returning to the undaring kind of existence they had originally found intolerable.[1]

[1] In American fiction this pattern is as old as Hawthorne's *Scarlet Letter* and—for Lewis—as recent as the work of Edith Wharton (see pp. 1592–93).

It was not only that the old nineteenth-century dream seemed no longer operable amid the drabness of the small town or the commercial bustle of the expanding city. The dream was no longer perceived very clearly; it had gotten blurred and shrunken and misapplied. It should be added that Lewis himself shared to some degree—in his later years to a serious degree—in this loss of moral and intellectual coherence. One cannot always be sure about the precise target of his satire—whether, for example, in his imaginative vision he deplores or rather honors Babbitt's return to the fold. Nonetheless, in the best of his novels he seems, clearly enough, to be describing with very considerable art an American society which no longer understands and aspires to a freshness of experience, a beauty in life, or the dignity of a sustained freedom of spirit.

He was born Harry Sinclair Lewis—and called Harry, Hal, and most often (because of the tinge of his hair) "Red"—the son of a doctor in the small, brand-new town of Sauk Centre, Minnesota, in 1885. He was an unattractive youth: gangly and graceless, wholly inept at sport. His home life was cheerless, his circle of friends nonexistent. Things were not much better at Yale, which he entered in 1903. His classmates found him intrusive and unappealing, though some of the teachers of literature were kind to him and he earned some kind of acceptance by his contributions to the *Yale Literary Magazine*. He dropped out for awhile and tried to earn a living in New York and Panama; then (not entirely unlike some of his later characters) he came back to graduate with the class of 1908.

For awhile, he made a few dollars selling plot outlines to Jack London; later, he took a job with a New York publishing house. During this period (he had married Grace Hegger, an editor of *Vogue*, and was living on Long Island) he continued his own writing, often on the train to and from work, and on weekends. In 1914, Harper published his first novel, *Our Mr. Wrenn*, which was favorably if not enthusiastically received. There followed *The Trail of the Hawk* in 1915, which won a letter of characteristic warmth from Howells ("It was all good, BETTER, BEST"),[2] and which asserted without any equivocation the possibility of carrying forward the old virtues. It was for the hero Carl Ericson, Lewis declared, "to carry on the American destiny of extending the western horizon; . . . to restore the wintry Pilgrim virtues . . . to add, in his own or another generation, new American aspirations for beauty." In *The Job* (1917), two novels later, aspiration has been replaced by a sense of the dreariness at the heart of the American scene.

During the several years that Lewis was at work on *Main Street*, his next novel, he also managed to write a sufficient number of short stories and serialized longer ones to earn him an annual income of nearly ten thousand dollars, a very considerable sum half a century ago; the image of the starving but dauntless and dedicated writer was somebody's later invention. He had become a professional writer, and he was a popular one; as his biographer Mark Schorer points out, Lewis's narrative style was

shaped in this period by the demands of his large audience for the straightforward, the explicit, the carefully documented. During that period he traveled about the continent incessantly and sometimes aimlessly—the entire movement of his life, Schorer suggests, was a passage from "the unsatisfactory elsewhere" to "the inadequate nowhere." But he was also searching constantly for fresh material, new settings, new kinds of Americans; though for *Main Street*, at last, he returned to Sauk Centre to make an exact recording of all the old materials.

Main Street, published in 1920, was an explosive literary event. The publishers had dared hope for a sale of twenty thousand copies, but the count rapidly soared into the hundreds of thousands. The book was loudly acclaimed: Vachel Lindsay campaigned for it in Illinois, and letters poured in from enthusiasts, both here and abroad. It was heatedly attacked: Hamlin Garland, whose *Main-Travelled Roads* had been an element in its inspiration but who had long since turned away from that kind of fiction, tried to stir up a countercampaign on the curious grounds that Lewis had belittled "the descendants of the old frontier." But there was no doubt that with *Main Street* Lewis had leaped into prominence as the major figure in the American literary world (Howells, almost symbolically, had very recently died), and that he had done so exactly by heaping scorn on just those moral and psychological convictions he had put forward in *The Trail of the Hawk*. It may be that in Lewis's case, as in that of Garland some thirty years earlier, it was the return to the childhood environment—after the experience of the wider America from California to New York—that opened his imagination to the cramp and the ugliness of life he was to describe.

The novel itself does not stand up quite as well as it once did. The exposure of the stifling, antiaesthetic nature of the small-town Minnesota life Lewis had miserably known in his youth suffers from the uncertain handling of the confusedly rebellious heroine, Carol Kennicott. H. L. Mencken, Lewis's most effectively vociferous champion, assumed that she too was

---

[2] Lewis had met Howells briefly in Florida; on this occasion Howells kept talking about someone named "Pussy Jones"—who, Lewis learned much later, was his friend-to-be Edith Wharton.

an object of satire, and that Lewis had adroitly shown that her "superior culture is, after all, chiefly bogus." He may have done that, but it was not his conscious intention; for Lewis, Carol was "sensitive and articulate" and drawn in part from his wife Grace and in part from himself. "Carol is 'Red' Lewis," he said on a later occasion: "always groping for something she isn't capable of attaining . . . intolerant of her surroundings, yet lacking any clearly defined vision of what she really wants to do or be." Lewis's own lack of a clearly defined vision was obviously a literary weakness, but it was also an odd source of strength: it permitted him to sympathize, in some degree to identify, with the characters whose limitations he was so well describing. In any event, *Main Street* seemed to countless readers to be the first truthful picture of a heart-shriveling bleakness that had been experienced by many Americans without their having fully appreciated the quiet horror of it.

To be sure, there was a native tradition in this mode going back at least to Edward Eggleston in the 1870's, but it had not taken hold, as such, on the American imagination, and Lewis himself was only partially and intermittently aware of it. He felt some affinity with the early Garland, and with Edgar Lee Masters, Theodore Dreiser, and Sherwood Anderson; but he seems not to have ventured much beyond them in the varieties of realistic fiction, and besides he was also open to stimulus from the comic extravagances of Mark Twain, the fantasies of James Branch Cabell and of Edith Wharton's careful depiction of the mannered life. *Main Street* evoked by its very title what Americans ever since have seen as part of the truth about themselves.

So did *Babbitt*, which appeared two years later in 1922. It is no small thing, one reflects in passing, to have contributed, as Lewis did, a number of proper names and phrases which have become fixed in the country's vocabulary of archetypes. Even now the list of such terms is quite short. In addition to Lewis's contributions it would contain only Rip Van Winkle, Ahab and Moby-Dick, Tom Sawyer and Huckle-berry Finn, Daisy Miller, and the tribe of the Snopeses (see pp. 2580–81). Even after he had passed his prime, Lewis, in a novel not otherwise very compelling, supplied a phrase which went into the international conversation about fascism: "It can't happen here." An archetypal intuition of this sort does not by itself indicate a writer of the very first order; but no writer possessed of it is likely to pass into total oblivion.

Babbitt, though the seventh of Lewis's novels, was, following *Main Street*, the second of the five novels which constituted his "major phase" —a period that extended, conveniently enough, from the appearance of *Main Street* in 1920 to Lewis's acceptance speech of the Nobel prize for literature in Stockholm, Sweden, in December, 1930. This story of a middle-aged real estate salesman was dedicated to Edith Wharton, a singularly attractive gesture since the year previously *The Age of Innocence* had won the Pulitzer prize after the authorities at Columbia had overruled the committee of judges (including a reluctant Hamlin Garland), which had voted for *Main Street*.[3]

There were good reasons for the dedication, apart from (typical) good sportsmanship. Lewis was dealing with the solidly middle-class citizenry of a growing midwestern city (Cincinnati, where Lewis stayed while writing the book, provided the actual model, though four other cities proudly put in a claim); Edith Wharton usually dealt with a small segment of upper-class New York. But their essential theme was the

_____

[3] Lewis had written Edith Wharton a letter of congratulation not long after she received the award. Mrs. Wharton was deeply touched. "What you say is so kind, so generous & so unexpected, that I don't know where to begin to answer. It is the first sign I have ever had—literally—that 'les jeunes' at home had ever read a word of me. . . . As for the Columbia prize . . . when I discovered that I was being rewarded—by one of our leading Universities—for uplifting American morals [such were the technical terms of the prize] I confess I *did* despair. Subsequently, when I found the prize sh[oul]d really have been yours, but was withdrawn because your book (I quote from memory) had 'offended a number of prominent persons in the Middle West,' disgust was added to despair."

same, and it was one they shared with Anderson, among others: the impulse to freedom in conflict with the forces of social convention. Both writers found that impulse almost invariably defeated ("They've licked me; licked me to a finish!" Babbitt whimpers, at the end of the novel). Lewis's Babbitt and Edith Wharton's Newland Archer both retreat into a sad and tolerant conformity, illuminated only by the dim hope that their sons may be permitted a more expansive life than themselves. And to this theme, Lewis, like Mrs. Wharton, brought a satirical talent well suited to expose the banalities and shibboleths, the complacent limits of mind and imagination, the dull obsessive rituals of the nearly invincible social order.

Lewis, too, had as sharp an eye as Edith Wharton for the symbols of social change. However, for example, in *Silas Lapham*, had been one of the first to take an ordinary businessman as hero—to show a businessman actually going about his affairs, pursuing those transactions which bring him his wealth. That was in 1885; somewhat later Dreiser, in his trilogy, presented another type of businessman, the ruthless Robber Baron Frank Cowperwood. But Lewis, writing after the First World War, perceived that the average American's notion of the mythical hero of business had become the sales manager. In the smoking compartment of a Pullman en route to New York, Babbitt joins his fellow travelers in discussing the new hero of romance:

They went profoundly into the science of business, and indicated that the purpose of manufacturing a plow or a brick was so that it might be sold. To them, the Romantic Hero was no longer the knight, the wandering poet, the cowpuncher, the aviator, nor the brave young district attorney, but the great sales manager, who had an Analysis of Merchandising Problems on his glass-topped desk, whose title of nobility was "Go-getter," and who devoted himself and all his young samurai to the cosmic purpose of Selling—not of selling anything in particular, for or to anybody in particular, but Selling.

This replacement of archetypes affects every phase of life in the Zenith of Lewis's Babbitt. Go-getting pure and simple, go-getting for its own sake, is what motivates Babbitt's entire circle of friends (except Paul Riesling, who is destroyed by his hatred of it) and motivates Babbitt too until he makes his stumbling bid to escape. It impels the local minister as much as the elderly millionaire, the neighbor's wife no less than the bootlegger.

There seems no real alternative to the go-getting life in the world of this novel. In *A World Elsewhere* (1966), Richard Poirier describes the ways in which American novelists in the nineteenth and twentieth centuries have suggested some better alternative to the kind of life their characters are leading: the idyllic existence aboard a raft on the Mississippi, for example, as experienced by Huck and Jim in *Huckleberry Finn;* or the ideal society, and a possible new relation between men and women, brooded upon by Hester Prynne in *The Scarlet Letter.* That image of a better alternative dimmed fairly steadily from the Gilded Age onward, as options seemed to be inexorably closing out: the sense of such a possibility is less visible in James than in Hawthorne, and, again, less visible in Dreiser than in James. Some sort of minimum is reached in *Babbitt.* As against the world of buying and selling in Zenith, the morning sounds of the milk trucks, furnace-men and cars starting up, Babbitt has only his fleeting predawn dream—the wavering, sentimental image of a slender fairy child crouching next to him on a hillside.

By way of compensation, Babbitt and his associates seek to invest their real life with heroic and poetic qualities: a process Lewis treats in a kindly but knowingly mock-epic manner. The blanket Babbitt buys for a camping trip represents "freedom and heroism"; his automobile "was poetry and tragedy, love and heroism"; the drama involved daily in parking the car downtown is "a virile adventure." By background and temperament, Lewis was peculiarly alert to such displacements: the muddled desires to find in the secular and material world elements upon which, in this case, Babbitt's yearning to worship and to love, to experience some kind of ultimate reality, can be lavished. Looking up at the Second National Tower, early in the book, Babbitt solemnly and comfortingly sees it as "a temple spire of the religion of business."

It is Lewis's sympathetic, if acute, understanding of these wistful beliefs, and his skillful portrayal of them, that lifts *Babbitt* far above the pure documentary it might otherwise have been. For no novel was more thoroughly worked up as to its detail. Lewis always took the most elaborate pains to get his facts straight; while working on a novel, he would make maps of the areas where the action was to occur, and blueprints of the houses; he walked the streets with notebook in hand, lingered watchfully in hotel lounges, sat in the waiting rooms of business offices. He was realism's devoted agent; yet in Lewis, realistic fiction—which had begun entangled with the older pieties and had divested itself of those pieties in Crane, Dreiser, and others—now took on the new glow of a spurious yet appealing romanticism.

During the twenties, Lewis regularly proposed writing a large-scale "labor novel," and to this end he saw a good deal of the indomitable Eugene Debs. The novel never got written: Lewis had neither the mind, the historical knowledge, nor the imagination to cope with that intricate subject and its crowding contradictions. He turned instead to other themes closer to his experience. In *Arrowsmith* (1925) he explored the tensions that most interested him—particularly the tension between idealism and hypocrisy—in the setting of the American medical profession. Lewis's father, uncle, and brother had all been doctors; and in writing the new novel, he had the close assistance of a young medical researcher he had met in New York, Paul de Kruif (later known as the author of *Men Against Death*). The unmistakable accuracy of the scientific data lent a much needed credibility to the story of Martin Arrowsmith's capacity to resist and survive the bland hypocrisy of the leaders of the medical establishment.

Arrowsmith was awarded the Pulitzer prize, but after the affair involving Edith Wharton's novel, and after *Babbitt* had been voted down in favor of Willa Cather's *One of Ours* (see below), Lewis rejected the award in a trenchant letter written well in advance of the news. The letter makes it clear that *Arrowsmith* had reflected as much Lewis's sense of his own relation to the American literary powers as his hero's to the medical profession. Citing an earlier instance of his refusal to accept a literary honor (as evidence that he did not act out of personal pique), Lewis remarked:

Between the Pulitzer Prizes, the American Academy of Arts and Letters, amateur boards of censorship, and the inquisition of earnest literary ladies, every compulsion is put upon writers to become safe, polite, obedient, and sterile. In protest, I declined election to the National Institute of Arts and Letters some years ago (1921), and now I must decline the Pulitzer Prize.[4]

Whatever its motives, the action roused the kind of storm Lewis was growing used to; and it spurred the sales to new heights.

About *Elmer Gantry* (1927), Mark Schorer has said that in some ways it is "the novel that gives us the purest Lewis" and that it is "perhaps the most underestimated of Lewis' major works." For in this episodic story of a rogue's progress—that of the brutally powerful Elmer Gantry from Baptist to evangelist to prophet of New Thought to Methodist, each phase punctuated by sexual conquest and destruction—there emerges, Schorer believes, "a world of total death, of social monsters without shadow." Lewis used to say that his ambition had been to become an Episcopal bishop; and while this was probably mockery, it remains true that he was fascinated by, and very knowing about, every phase of religion in America—that is, by every kind of decay in genuine religious energy

---

[4] As a matter of fact Lewis did accept membership in the Institute in 1935 and proceeded to the Academy in 1937.

and by every sign of the deflection thereof into other areas (commercial, sexual, technological). *Elmer Gantry*, the harshest of his satires, is quite devoid of that vein of sentimentality which flaws his other work in this genre. The book was of course banned in Boston, as well as in many other parts of the country; a party of Virginians offered to lynch the author; one clergyman suggested sending Lewis to jail for five years. The sales were tremendous.

In *Dodsworth* (1929) Lewis introduced a wealthier, better established, and more intelligent George Babbitt. Dodsworth embodies, but is not altogether at the mercy of, the bourgeois conventions. For instance, he is capable of leaving his pretentious wife to find fulfillment in another woman. *Dodsworth* is the one novel among Lewis's serious efforts that plumps unmistakably for the middle-class American virtues: solid and unimaginative, untinged by home-grown boosterism on the one hand or on the other by an equally false Europeanization. In the figure of Sam Dodsworth, George Babbitt has really come to some kind of maturity, but one wonders whether Babbitt, that oddly appealing character, would have altogether relished growing up.

Yet when, in the following year, Lewis was the first American to be given the Nobel prize in literature (there had been a good deal of unsuccessful lobbying for Henry James and Edith Wharton in earlier years), he reverted in his acceptance speech to his more iconoclastic period. He denounced American academics and critics and quite unfairly laid the blame for the pervasive current gentility in American letters upon the influence of William Dean Howells. He selected for praise the work of Dreiser and Anderson and the quite unknown Thomas Wolfe. If he was ungenerous to Howells, he was wonderfully generous to other and younger writers; and he seemed, as it were, to establish at a stroke a great fact that both America and the rest of the world had taken far too long to recognize—that American writing was a living and a very powerful literary force to be everywhere and permanently reckoned with. On that day, Mark Schorer has said, Lewis was "the

spokesman—what Walt Whitman had called the 'literatus'—for the literary culture of the United States."

Lewis-watchers, in whom the country and its periodicals abounded, had wondered, to begin with, on what terms he could justify accepting the Nobel prize after publicly rejecting previous honors. Now, following the acceptance speech, the familiar storm burst out again. It was not calmed very much by the statement of Calvin Coolidge that "No necessity exists for becoming excited."

In 1930, Sinclair Lewis, at the peak of his literary prestige and, apparently, of his powers, was in fact also moving toward nostalgia. It was not, in his case, a yearning for some particular historical period: if Willa Cather's view of history was reductive, Lewis's was nonexistent. But what he increasingly missed were certain values: kindness, tolerance, and especially individualism. The latter quality was not held in much esteem in the thirties; and the more it was denigrated, the more Lewis celebrated it.

The creative fire was burning out. Soon after he received the word, to his stunned surprise, that he had won the Nobel prize, he was heard to say: "This is the end of me. This is fatal. I cannot live up to it." It was not the end of him as a producer, but it did coincide with the ebbing of the strong if confused vision that had sustained him through the powerful novels of the twenties. Indeed Lewis, like Howells and Edith Wharton, had the misfortune—so far as his later reputation is concerned—to live many years after he had passed his creative prime and to write many more novels. Their titles, their characters, the successive aspects of American life they explore—these remain blurred in one's memory. There was *Ann Vickers* and her forays into radical thought and prison reform work; *Work of Art*, in which hotel management is extolled as an art superior to poetry;[5] *The*

---

[5] It may be that Lewis's work owed something of its popularity to his passion for delineating how institutions work, even as he condemned their effect on the individual.

Prodigal Parents, where the problem of the generation gap is resolved entirely in favor of the conservative older folk; *Bethel Merriday*, about the stage; *Gideon Planish*, about philanthropy; *Cass Timberlane* (the best of these later novels and in parts very good indeed), about American marriages; and *Kingsblood Royal*, an inept if blunderingly sympathetic attempt to examine the situation of the Negro in American life.

Somewhat earlier than the last items on this list, *It Can't Happen Here* (1935) aroused an outburst of liberal approval by its picture of the coming of fascism to America; but it was not liberal progressivism that the book was sponsoring. Even here Lewis had been writing from his now settled belief in the old-fashioned virtues; and *It Can't Happen Here* is an infinitely less cunning analysis of the fascist mentality than the brilliant satirical fantasy that just the year before had been produced to the attention of nobody—Nathanael West's *A Cool Million*.

The thirties and forties were contradictory times for Sinclair Lewis. He was world famous and commercially successful almost beyond calculation. But he was increasingly out of touch with the authentic literary currents—which is also to say, with the authentic social and intellectual currents—of the day. Influential critics, with the exception of Edmund Wilson in a review of *Cass Timberlane* in the *New Yorker*, had little good to say about him; Thomas Wolfe, whom he had cited for special mention at Stockholm, drew a portrait of him in *You Can't Go Home Again* that, for all its moving exposure of the contradictions in Lewis's personality, leaves the impression of a faint, lingering contempt. He became an intermittent al-

coholic; his second marriage, to the distinguished journalist Dorothy Thompson, broke up in an incredible tempest of drunken recriminations. There were absurd liaisons with young actresses and absurd attempts to write plays for them. Lewis exiled himself to Italy after the Second World War, and there, in Rome, he died in early 1951.

Yet during all those nearly catastrophic years, there remained something singularly taking about the man, an ever-ready generosity of spirit, a sort of battered nobility. People *liked* Red Lewis to the end and often found him delightful company—witty, warm, decent, open. In some obscure way they also respected him, even those most disconcerted by his self-destructive behavior and those most aware of the frequent aesthetic awkwardness of his novels, the best as well as the worst. By way of a measure of his overall literary achievement, Mark Schorer suggests that, though Lewis was not a great writer, he was "the major figure . . . in what is called the liberation of modern American literature." Our literature has been liberated as often as the Italian peninsula: it was liberated by Emerson, then by Howells and Mark Twain, then by Crane and Dreiser. After the great breakthrough in the twenties—in which Lewis undoubtedly played an important part—it was liberated politically by writers in the thirties; more recently, it has been liberated by novelists who have searched out the limits of sexual candor. Within that tradition of recurring emancipation, Lewis was one of the crucial channels through which the great imaginative currents of the later nineteenth century flowed down to our own time.

BIOGRAPHICAL CHART

1885   Born, February 7, in Sauk Centre, Minnesota, to Edwin J. Lewis and Emma Kermott Lewis
1891   Mother dies
1890–1902 Attends public schools in Sauk Centre
1903–6 Attends Yale; contributes to Yale *Literary Magazine* and *Courant*; serves as editor of *Literary Magazine*
1906   Leaves Yale, spends October–November at Helicon Hall, Upton Sinclair's utopian colony at Englewood, New Jersey, as man-of-all-work

1907–8 Returns to Yale; receives degree
1908–10 Sells short-story plots to Jack London
1910–15 Holds number of positions in New York City connected with publishing: manuscript reader, editor, advertising manager, reviewer
1914 Marries Grace Livingstone Hegger in New York; *Our Mr. Wrenn* published
1915 *The Trail of the Hawk;* resigns position with George H. Doran Company to devote full time to writing
1920 *Main Street*
1922 *Babbitt*
1923 Travels with Paul de Kruif, collecting material for *Arrowsmith; Arrowsmith* written in France, revised in London, 1923–24
1925 *Arrowsmith*
1926 Refuses Pulitzer prize for *Arrowsmith*
1927 *Elmer Gantry*
1928 Divorced from Grace Hegger Lewis; in May, marries Dorothy Thompson

1929 *Dodsworth*
1930 Awarded Nobel prize for literature; travels to Stockholm to accept award
1933 *Ann Vickers*
1934 *Work of Art*
1935 *It Can't Happen Here*
1936 Awarded honorary degree by Yale
1938 *The Prodigal Parents*
1940 *Bethel Merriday;* conducts writing class at University of Wisconsin
1942 Divorced from Dorothy Thompson; special lecturer in English at University of Minnesota
1942–46 Resides intermittently in Minnesota, with extended trips to New York and elsewhere
1945 *Cass Timberlane*
1946–49 When not traveling, resides at Thorvale Farm near Williamstown, Massachusetts
1947 *Kingsblood Royal*
1951 Dies, January 10, in Rome of heart disease

FURTHER READINGS

There is no standard edition of Lewis's works. In addition to the works mentioned in the biographical chart, the reader may find the following items useful.

Sinclair Lewis, *Selected Short Stories* (1935)
Harry E. Maule and Melville H. Cane, eds., *The Man from Main Street: A Sinclair Lewis Reader* (1953)

Alfred Kazin, *On Native Grounds* (1942)
Perry Miller, "The Incorruptible Sinclair Lewis," *Atlantic* (April, 1951)
Mark Schorer, ed., *Sinclair Lewis: A Collection of Critical Essays* (1970)
———, *Sinclair Lewis: An American Life* (1961)
———, *Society and Self in the Novel: English Institute Essays* (1956)

From Babbitt (1922)

George F. Babbitt of Zenith was originally baptized G. T. Pumphrey of Monarch City; if Lewis had stuck to his original names, "Pumphreyism" would have become as familiar in our vocabulary as "Babbitry" now is. "I planned," Lewis told the literary editor of the New York *Herald* a year after the novel appeared, "to make the whole novel twenty-four hours in his life, from alarm clock to alarm clock. The rest came more or less unconsciously." In fact, the round of the day carries only through the first six chapters, about one fourth of the whole.

The rest of the novel consists in a series of set pieces, each designed to illustrate one phase of life in Zenith or of Babbitt's growing restiveness—to the point where he rebels a little and falls in with a fast-moving group, until domestic circumstances pull him back to home and an acceptance of things.

We present here the first stages of Babbitt's day.

CHAPTER I

I

The towers of Zenith aspired above the morning mist; austere towers of steel and cement and limestone, sturdy as cliffs and delicate as silver rods. They were neither citadels nor churches, but frankly and beautifully office-buildings.

The mist took pity on the fretted structures of earlier generations: the Post Office with its shingle-tortured mansard, the red brick minarets of hulking old houses, factories with stingy and sooted windows, wooden tenements colored like mud. The city was full of such grotesqueries, but the clean towers were thrusting them from the business center, and on the farther hills were shining new houses, homes—they seemed—for laughter and tranquillity.

Over a concrete bridge fled a limousine of long sleek hood and noiseless engine. These people in evening clothes were returning from an all-night rehearsal of a Little Theater play, an artistic adventure considerably illuminated by champagne. Below the bridge curved a railroad, a maze of green and crimson lights. The New York Flyer boomed past, and twenty lines of polished steel leaped into the glare.

In one of the skyscrapers the wires of the Associated Press were closing down. The telegraph operators wearily raised their celluloid eye-shades after a night of talking with Paris and Peking. Through the building crawled the scrubwomen, yawning, their old shoes slapping. The dawn mist spun away. Cues of men with lunch-boxes clumped toward the immensity of new factories, sheets of glass and hollow tile, glittering shops where five thousand men worked beneath one roof, pouring out the honest wares that would be sold up the Euphrates and across the veldt. The whistles rolled out in greeting a chorus cheerful as the April dawn; the song of labor in a city built—it seemed—for giants.

II

There was nothing of the giant in the aspect of the man who was beginning to awaken on the sleeping-porch of a Dutch Colonial house in that residential district of Zenith known as Floral Heights.

His name was George F. Babbitt. He was forty-six years old now, in April, 1920, and he made nothing in particular, neither butter nor shoes nor poetry, but he was nimble in the calling of selling houses for more than people could afford to pay.

His large head was pink, his brown hair thin and dry. His face was babyish in slumber, despite his wrinkles and the red spectacle-dents on the slopes of his nose. He was not fat but he was exceedingly well fed; his cheeks were pads, and the unroughened hand which lay helpless upon the khaki-colored blanket was slightly puffy. He seemed prosperous, extremely married and unromantic; and altogether unromantic appeared this sleeping-porch,

which looked on one sizable elm, two respectable grass-plots, a cement driveway, and a corrugated iron garage. Yet Babbitt was again dreaming of the fairy child, a dream more romantic than scarlet pagodas by a silver sea.

For years the fairy child had come to him. Where others saw but George Babbitt, she discerned gallant youth. She waited for him, in the darkness beyond mysterious groves. When at last he could slip away from the crowded house he darted to her. His wife, his clamoring friends, sought to follow, but he escaped, the girl fleet beside him, and they crouched together on a shadowy hillside. She was so slim, so white, so eager! She cried that he was gay and valiant, that she would wait for him, that they would sail—

Rumble and bang of the milk-truck.

Babbitt moaned, turned over, struggled back toward his dream. He could see only her face now, beyond misty waters. The furnace-man slammed the basement door. A dog barked in the next yard. As Babbitt sank blissfully into a dim warm tide, the paper-carrier went by whistling, and the rolled-up *Advocate* thumped the front door. Babbitt roused, his stomach constricted with alarm. As he relaxed, he was pierced by the familiar and irritating rattle of some one cranking a Ford: snap-ah-ah, snap-ah-ah, snap-ah-ah. Himself a pious motorist, Babbitt cranked with the unseen driver, with him waited through taut hours for the roar of the starting engine, with him agonized as the roar ceased and again began the infernal patient snap-ah-ah—a round, flat sound, a shivering cold-morning sound, a sound infuriating and inescapable. Not till the rising voice of the motor told him that the Ford was moving was he released from the panting tension. He glanced once at his favorite tree, elm twigs against the gold patina of sky, and fumbled for sleep as for a drug. He who had been a boy very credulous of life was no longer greatly interested in the possible and improbable adventures of each new day.

He escaped from reality till the alarm-clock rang, at seven-twenty.

III

It was the best of nationally advertised and quantitatively produced alarm-clocks, with all modern attachments, including cathedral chime, intermittent alarm, and a phosphorescent dial. Babbitt was proud of being awakened by such a rich device. Socially it was almost as creditable as buying expensive cord tires.

He sulkily admitted now that there was no more escape, but he lay and detested the grind of the real-estate business, and disliked his family, and disliked himself for disliking them. The evening before, he had played poker at Vergil Gunch's till midnight, and after such holidays he was irritable before breakfast. It may have been the tremendous home-brewed beer of the prohibition-era and the cigars to which that beer enticed him; it may have been resentment of return from this fine, bold man-world to a restricted region of wives and stenographers, and of suggestions not to smoke so much.

From the bedroom beside the sleeping-porch, his wife's detestably cheerful "Time to get up, Georgie boy," and the itchy sound, the brisk and scratchy sound, of combing hairs out of a stiff brush.

He grunted; he dragged his thick legs, in faded baby-blue pajamas, from under the khaki blanket; he sat on the edge of the cot, running his fingers through his wild hair, while his plump feet mechanically felt for his slippers. He looked regretfully at the blanket—forever a suggestion to him of freedom and heroism. He had bought it for a camping trip which had never come off. It symbolized gorgeous loafing, gorgeous cursing, virile flannel shirts.

He creaked to his feet, groaning at the waves of pain which passed behind his eyeballs. Though he waited for their scorching recurrence, he looked blurrily out at the yard. It delighted him, as always; it was the neat yard of a successful business man of Zenith, that is, it was perfection, and made him also perfect. He regarded the corrugated iron garage. For the three-hundred-and-sixty-fifth time in a year he reflected, "No class to that tin shack. Have to build me a frame garage. But by golly it's the only thing on the place that isn't up-to-date!" While he stared he thought of a community garage for his acreage development, Glen Oriole. He stopped puffing and jiggling. His arms were akimbo. His petulant, sleep-swollen face was set in harder lines. He suddenly seemed capable, an official, a man to contrive, to direct, to get things done.

On the vigor of his idea he was carried down the hard, clean, unused-looking hall into the bathroom.

Though the house was not large it had, like all houses on Floral Heights, an altogether royal bathroom of porcelain and glazed tile and metal sleek as silver. The towel-rack was a rod of clear glass set in nickel. The tub was long enough for a Prussian Guard, and above the set bowl was a sensational exhibit of tooth-brush holder, shaving-brush holder, soap-dish, sponge-dish, and medicine-cabinet, so glittering and so ingenious that they resembled an electrical instrument-board. But the Babbitt whose god was Modern Appliances was not pleased. The air of the bathroom was thick with the smell of a heathen toothpaste. "Verona been at it again! 'Stead of sticking to Lilidol, like I've re-peat-ed-ly asked her, she's gone and gotten some confounded stinkum stuff that makes you sick!"

The bath-mat was wrinkled and the floor was wet. (His daughter Verona eccentrically took baths in the morning, now and then.) He slipped on the mat, and slid against the tub. He said "Damn!" Furiously he snatched up his tube of shaving-cream, furiously he lathered, with a belligerent slapping of the unctuous brush, furiously he raked his plump cheeks with a safety-razor. It pulled. The blade was dull. He said, "Damn—oh—oh—damn it!"

He hunted through the medicine-cabinet for a packet of new razor-blades (reflecting, as invariably, "Be cheaper to buy one of these dinguses and strop your own blades,") and when he discovered the packet, behind the round box of bicarbonate of soda, he thought ill of his wife for putting it there and very well of himself for not saying "Damn." But he did say it, immediately afterward, when with wet and soap-slippery fingers he tried to remove the horrible little envelope and crisp cling-ing oiled paper from the new blade.

Then there was the problem, oft-pondered, never solved, of what to do with the old blade, which might imperil the fingers of his young. As usual, he tossed it on top of the medicine-cabinet, with a mental note that some day he must remove the fifty or sixty other blades that were also temporarily, piled up there. He finished his shaving in a growing testiness increased by his spinning head-ache and by the emptiness in his stomach. When he was done, his round face smooth and streamy and his eyes stinging from soapy water, he reached for a towel. The family towels were wet, wet and clammy and vile, all of them wet, he found, as he blindly snatched them—his own face-towel, his wife's, Verona's, Ted's, Tinka's, and the lone bath-towel with the huge welt of initial. Then George F. Babbitt did a dismaying thing. He wiped his face on the guest-towel! It was a pansy-embroidered trifle which always hung there to indicate that the Babbitts were in the best Floral Heights society.

No one had ever used it. No guest had ever dared to. Guests secretively took a corner of the nearest regular towel.

He was raging, "By golly, here they go and use up all the towels, every doggone one of 'em, and they use 'em and get 'em all wet and sopping, and never put out a dry one for me—of course, I'm the goat!—and then I want one and— I'm the only person in the doggone house that's got the slightest doggone bit of consideration for other people and thoughtfulness and consider there may be others that may want to use the doggone bathroom after me and consider—"

He was pitching the chill abominations into the bath-tub, pleased by the vindictiveness of that desolate flapping sound; and in the midst his wife serenely trotted in, observed serenely, "Why Georgie dear, what are you doing? Are you going to wash out the towels? Why, you needn't wash out the towels. Oh, Georgie, you didn't go and use the guest-towel, did you?"

It is not recorded that he was able to answer.

For the first time in weeks he was sufficiently roused by his wife to look at her.

IV

Myra Babbitt—Mrs. George F. Babbitt—was definitely mature. She had creases from the corners of her mouth to the bottom of her chin, and her plump neck bagged. But the thing that marked her as having passed the line was that she no longer had reticences before her husband, and no longer worried about not having reticences. She was in a petticoat now, and corsets which bulged, and unaware of being seen in bulgy corsets. She had become so dully habituated to married life that in her full matronliness she was as sexless as an anemic nun. She was a good woman, a kind woman, a diligent woman, but no one, save perhaps Tinka her ten-year-old, was at all interested in her or entirely aware that she was alive.

After a rather thorough discussion of all the domestic and social aspects of towels she apologized to Babbitt for his having an alcoholic headache; and he recovered enough to endure the search for a B.V.D. undershirt which had, he pointed out, malevolently been concealed among his clean pajamas.

He was fairly amiable in the conference on the brown suit.

"What do you think, Myra?" He pawed at the clothes hunched on a chair in their bedroom, while she moved about mysteriously adjusting and patting her petticoat and, to his jaundiced eye, never seeming to get on with her dressing. "How about it? Shall I wear the brown suit another day?"

"Well, it looks awfully nice on you."

"I know, but gosh, it needs pressing."

"That's so. Perhaps it does."

"It certainly could stand being pressed, all right."

"Yes, perhaps it wouldn't hurt it to be pressed."

"But gee, the coat doesn't need pressing. No sense in having the whole darn suit pressed, when the coat doesn't need it."

"That's so."

"But the pants certainly need it, all right. Look at them—look at those wrinkles—the pants certainly do need pressing."

"That's so. Oh, George, why couldn't you wear the brown coat with the blue trousers we were wondering what we'd do with them?"

"Good Lord! Did you ever in all my life know me to wear the coat of one suit and the pants of another? What do you think I am? A busted book-keeper?"

"Well, why don't you put on the dark gray suit to-day, and stop in at the tailor and leave the brown trousers?"

"Well, they certainly need— Now where the devil is that gray suit? Oh, yes, here we are."

He was able to get through the other crises of dressing with comparative resoluteness and calm.

His first adornment was the sleeveless dimity B.V.D. undershirt, in which he resembled a small boy humorlessly wearing a cheesecloth tabard at a civic pageant. He never put on B.V.D.'s without thanking the God of Progress that he didn't wear tight, long, old-fashioned undergarments, like his father-in-law and partner, Henry Thompson. His second embellishment was combing and slicking back his hair. It gave him a tremendous forehead, arching up two inches beyond the former hair-line. But most wonder-working of all was the donning of his spectacles.

There is character in spectacles—the pretentious tortoise-shell, the meek pince-nez of the school teacher, the twisted silver-framed glasses of the old villager. Babbitt's spectacles had huge, circular, frameless lenses of the very best glass; the earpieces were thin bars of gold. In them he was the modern business man; one who gave orders to clerks and drove a car and played occasional golf and was scholarly in regard to Salesmanship. His head suddenly appeared not babyish but weighty, and you noted his heavy, blunt nose, his straight mouth and thick, long upper lip, his chin over-fleshy but strong; with respect you beheld him put on the rest of his uniform as a Solid Citizen.

The gray suit was well cut, well made, and completely undistinguished. It was a standard suit. White piping on the V of the vest added a flavor of law and learning. His shoes were black laced boots, good boots, honest boots, standard boots, extraordinarily uninteresting boots. The only frivolity was in his purple knitted scarf. With considerable comment on the matter to Mrs. Babbitt (who, acrobatically fastening the back of her blouse to her skirt with a safety-pin, did not hear a word he said), he chose between the purple scarf and a tapestry effect with stringless brown harps among blown palms, and into it he thrust a snake-head pin with opal eyes.

A sensational event was changing from the brown suit to the gray the contents of his pockets. He was earnest about these objects. They were of eternal importance, like baseball or the Republican Party. They included a fountain pen and a silver pencil (always lacking a supply of new leads) which belonged in the righthand upper vest pocket. Without them he would have felt naked. On his watch-chain were a gold penknife, silver cigar-cutter, seven keys (the use of two of which he had forgotten), and incidentally a good watch. Depending from the chain was a large, yellowish elk's-tooth—proclamation of his membership in the Brotherly and Protective Order of Elks. Most significant of all was his loose-leaf pocket note-book, that modern and efficient note-book which contained the addresses of people whom he had forgotten, prudent memoranda of postal money-orders which had reached their destination months ago, stamps which had lost their mucilage, clippings of verses by T. Cholmondeley Frink and of the newspaper editorials from which Babbitt got his opinions and his polysyllables, notes to be sure and do things which he did not intend to do, and one curious inscription—D.S.S.D.M.Y.P.D.F.

But he had no cigarette-case. No one had ever happened to give him one, so he hadn't the habit, and people who carried cigarette-cases he regarded as effeminate.

Last, he stuck in his lapel the Boosters' Club button. With the conciseness of great art the button displayed two words: "Boosters—Pep!" It made Babbitt feel loyal and important. It associated him with Good Fellows, with men who were nice and human, and important in business circles. It was his V.C., his Legion of Honor ribbon, his Phi Beta Kappa key.

With the subtleties of dressing ran other complex worries. "I feel kind of punk this morning," he said. "I think I had too much dinner last evening. You oughtn't to serve those heavy banana fritters."

"But you asked me to have some."

"I know, but— I tell you, when a fellow gets past forty he has to look after his digestion. There's a lot of fellows that don't take proper care of themselves. I tell you at forty a man's a fool or his doctor—I mean, his own doctor. Folks don't give enough attention to this matter of dieting. Now I think— Course a man ought to have a good meal after the day's work, but it would be a good thing for both of us if we took lighter lunches."

"But Georgie, here at home I always do have a light lunch."

"Mean to imply I make a hog of myself, eating down-town? Yes, sure! You'd have a swell time if you had to eat the truck that new steward hands out to us at the Athletic Club! But I certainly do feel out of sorts, this morning. Funny, got a pain down here on the left side—but no, that wouldn't be appendicitis, would it? Last night, when I was driving over to Verg Gunch's, I felt a pain in my stomach, too. Right here it was—kind of a sharp shooting pain. I— Where'd that dime go to? Why don't you serve more prunes at breakfast? Of course I eat an apple every evening—an apple a day keeps the doctor away—but still, you ought to have more prunes, and not all these fancy doodads."

"The last time I had prunes you didn't eat them."

"Well, I didn't feel like eating 'em, I suppose. Matter of fact, I think I did eat some of 'em. Anyway— I tell you it's mighty important to— I was saying to Verg Gunch, just last evening, most people don't take sufficient care of their diges—"

"Shall we have the Gunches for our dinner, next week?"

"Why sure; you bet."

"Now see here, George: I want you to put on your nice dinner-jacket that evening."

"Rats! The rest of 'em won't want to dress."

"Of course they will. You remember when you didn't dress for the Littlefields' supper-party, and all the rest did, and how embarrassed you were."

"Embarrassed, hell! I wasn't embarrassed. Everybody knows I can put on as expensive a Tux. as anybody else, and I should worry if I don't happen to have it on sometimes. All a darn nuisance, anyway. All right for a woman, that stays around the house all the time, but when a fellow's worked like the dickens all day, he doesn't want to go and hustle his head off getting into the soup-and-fish for a lot of folks that he's seen in just reg'lar ordinary clothes that same day."

"You know you enjoy being seen in one. The other evening you admitted you were glad I'd insisted on your dressing. You said you felt a lot better for it. And oh, Georgie, I do wish you wouldn't say 'Tux.' It's 'dinner-jacket.'"

"Rats, what's the odds?"

"Well, it's what all the nice folks say. Suppose Lucile McKelvey heard you calling it a 'Tux.'"

"Well, that's all right now! Lucile McKelvey can't pull anything on me! Her folks are common as mud, even if her husband and her dad are millionaires! I suppose you're trying to rub in *your* exalted social position! Well, let me tell you that your revered paternal ancestor, Henry T., doesn't even call it a 'Tux.'! He calls it a 'bobtail jacket for a ringtail monkey,' and you couldn't get him into one unless you chloroformed him!"

"Now don't be horrid, George."

"Well, I don't want to be horrid, but Lord! you're getting as fussy as Verona. Ever since she got out of college she's been too rambunctious to live with—doesn't know what she wants—well, I know what she wants!—all she wants is to marry a millionaire, and live in Europe, and hold some preacher's hand, and simultaneously at the same time stay right here in Zenith and be some blooming kind of a socialist agitator or boss charity-worker or some damn thing! Lord, and Ted is just as bad! He wants to go to college, and he doesn't want to go to college. Only one of the three that knows her own mind is Tinka. Simply can't understand how I ever came to have a pair of shilly-shallying children like Rone and Ted. I may not be any Rockefeller or James J. Shakespeare, but I certainly do know my own mind, and I do keep right on plugging along in the office and— Do you know the latest? Far as I can figure out, Ted's new bee is he'd like to be a movie actor and— And here I've told him a hundred times, if he'll go to college and law-school and make good, I'll set him up in business and— Verona just exactly as bad. Doesn't know what she wants. Well, well, come on! Aren't you ready yet? The girl rang the bell three minutes ago."

V

Before he followed his wife, Babbitt stood at the westernmost window of their room. This residential settlement, Floral Heights, was on a rise; and though the center of the city was three miles away —Zenith had between three and four hundred thousand inhabitants now—he could see the top of the Second National Tower, an Indiana limestone building of thirty-five stories.

Its shining walls rose against April sky to a simple cornice like a streak of white fire. Integrity was in the tower, and decision. It bore its strength lightly as a tall soldier. As Babbitt stared, the nervousness was soothed from his face, his slack chin lifted in reverence. All he articulated was "That's one lovely sight!" but he was inspired by the rhythm of the city; his love of it renewed. He beheld the tower as a temple-spire of the religion of business, a faith passionate, exalted, surpassing common men; and as he clumped down to breakfast he whistled the ballad "Oh, by gee, by gosh, by jingo" as though it were a hymn melancholy and noble.

CHAPTER 11

I

Relieved of Babbitt's bumbling and the soft grunts with which his wife expressed the sympathy she was too experienced to feel and much too experienced not to show, their bedroom settled instantly into impersonality.

It gave on the sleeping-porch. It served both of them as dressing-room, and on the coldest nights Babbitt luxuriously gave up the duty of being manly and retreated to the bed inside, to curl his toes in the warmth and laugh at the January gale.

The room displayed a modest and pleasant color-scheme, after one of the best standard designs of the decorator who "did the interiors" for most of the speculative-builders' houses in Zenith. The walls were gray, the woodwork white, the rug a serene blue; and very much like mahogany was the furniture—the bureau with its great clear mirror, Mrs. Babbitt's dressing-table with toilet-articles of almost solid silver, the plain twin beds, between them a small table holding a standard electric bedside lamp, a glass for water, and a standard bedside book with colored illustrations—what particular book it was cannot be ascertained, since no one had ever opened it. The mattresses were firm but not hard, triumphant modern mattresses which had cost a great deal of money; the hot-water radiator was of exactly the proper scientific surface for the cubic contents of the room. The windows were large and easily opened, with the best catches and cords, and Holland roller-shades guaranteed not to crack. It was a masterpiece among bedrooms, right out of Cheerful Modern Houses for Medium Incomes. Only it had nothing to do with the Babbitts, nor with any one else. If people had ever lived and loved here, read thrillers at midnight and lain in beautiful indolence on a Sunday morning, there were no signs of it. It had the air of being a very good room in a very good hotel. One expected the chambermaid to come in and make it ready for people who would stay but one night, go without looking back, and never think of it again.

Every second house in Floral Heights had a bedroom precisely like this.

The Babbitts' house was five years old. It was all as competent and glossy as this bedroom. It had the best of taste, the best of inexpensive rugs, a simple and laudable architecture, and the latest conveniences. Throughout, electricity took the place of candles and slatternly hearth-fires. Along the bedroom baseboard were three plugs for electric lamps, concealed by little brass doors. In the halls were plugs for the vacuum cleaner, and in the living-room plugs for the piano lamp, for the electric fan. The trim dining-room (with its admirable oak buffet, its leaded-glass cupboard, its creamy plaster walls, its modest scene of a salmon expiring upon a pile of oysters) had plugs which supplied the electric percolator and the electric toaster.

In fact there was but one thing wrong with the Babbitt house: It was not a home.

II

Often of a morning Babbitt came bouncing and jesting in to breakfast. But things were mysteriously awry to-day. As he pontifically tread the upper hall he looked into Verona's bedroom and protested, "What's the use of giving the family a high-class house when they don't appreciate it and tend to business and get down to brass tacks?"

He marched upon them: Verona, a dumpy brown-haired girl of twenty-two, just out of Bryn Mawr, given to solicitudes about duty and sex and God and the unconquerable bagginess of the gray

sports-suit she was now wearing. Ted—Theodore Roosevelt Babbitt—a decorative boy of seventeen. Tinka—Katherine—still a baby at ten, with radiant red hair and a thin skin which hinted of too much candy and too many ice cream sodas. Babbitt did not show his vague irritation as he tramped in. He really disliked being a family tyrant, and his nagging was as meaningless as it was frequent. He shouted at Tinka, "Well, kittiedoolie!" It was the only pet name in his vocabulary, except the "dear" and "hon." with which he recognized his wife, and he flung it at Tinka every morning.

He gulped a cup of coffee in the hope of pacifying his stomach and his soul. His stomach ceased to feel as though it did not belong to him, but Verona began to be conscientious and annoying, and abruptly there returned to Babbitt the doubts regarding life and families and business which had clawed at him when his dream-life and the slim fairy girl had fled.

Verona had for six months been filing-clerk at the Gruensberg Leather Company offices, with a prospect of becoming secretary to Mr. Gruensberg and thus, as Babbitt defined it, "getting some good out of your expensive college education till you're ready to marry and settle down."

But now said Verona: "Father! I was talking to a classmate of mine that's working for the Associated Charities—oh, Dad, there's the sweetest little babies that come to the milk-station there!— and I feel as though I ought to be doing something worth while like that."

"What do you mean 'worth while'? If you get to be Gruensberg's secretary—and maybe you would, if you kept up your shorthand and didn't go sneaking off to concerts and talkfests every evening—I guess you'll find thirty-five or forty bones a week worth while!"

"I know, but—oh, I want to—contribute— I wish I were working in a settlement-house. I wonder if I could get one of the department-stores to let me put in a welfare-department with a nice rest-room and chintzes and wicker chairs and so on and so forth. Or I could—"

"Now you look here! The first thing you got to understand is that all this uplift and flipflop and settlement-work and recreation is nothing in God's world but the entering wedge for socialism. The sooner a man learns he isn't going to be coddled, and he needn't expect a lot of free grub and, uh, all these free classes and flipflop and doodads for his kids unless he earns 'em, why, the sooner he'll get on the job and produce—produce—produce!

That's what the country needs, and not all this fancy stuff that just enfeebles the will-power of the working man and gives his kids a lot of notions above their class. And you—if you'd tend to business instead of fooling and fussing— All the time! When I was a young man I made up my mind what I wanted to do, and stuck to it through thick and thin, and that's why I'm where I am to-day, and—Myra! What do you let the girl chop the toast up into these dinky little chunks for? Can't get your fist onto 'em. Half cold, anyway!"

Ted Babbitt, junior in the great East Side High School, had been making hiccup-like sounds of interruption. He blurted now, "Say, Rone, you going to—"

Verona whirled. "Ted! Will you kindly not interrupt us when we're talking about serious matters!"

"Aw punk," said Ted judicially. "Ever since somebody slipped up and let you out of college, Ammonia, you been pulling these nut conversations about what-nots and so-on-and-so-forths. Are you going to— I want to use the car tonight."

Babbitt snorted, "Oh, you do! May want it myself!" Verona protested, "Oh, you do, Mr. Smarty! I'm going to take it myself!" Tinka wailed, "Oh, papa, you said maybe you'd drive us down to Rosedale!" and Mrs. Babbitt, "Careful, Tinka, your sleeve is in the butter." They glared, and Verona hurled, "Ted, you're a perfect pig about the car!"

"Course you're not! Not a-tall!" Ted could be maddeningly bland. "You just want to grab it off, right after dinner, and leave it in front of some skirt's house all evening while you sit and gas about lite'ature and the highbrows you're going to marry—if they only propose!"

"Well, Dad oughtn't to *ever* let you have it! You and those beastly Jones boys drive like maniacs. The idea of your taking the turn on Chautauqua Place at forty miles an hour!"

"Aw, where do you get that stuff! You're so darn scared of the car that you drive up-hill with the emergency brake on!"

"I do not! And you— Always talking about how much you know about motors, and Eunice Littlefield told me you said the battery fed the generator!"

"You—why, my good woman, you don't know a generator from a differential." Not unreasonably was Ted lofty with her. He was a natural mechanic, a maker and tinkerer of machines; he lisped in blueprints for the blueprints came.

"That'll do now!" Babbitt flung in mechani-cally, as he lighted the gloriously satisfying first cigar of the day and tasted the exhilarating drug of the *Advocate-Times* headlines.

Ted negotiated: "Gee, honest, Rone, I don't want to take the old boat, but I promised couple o' girls in my class I'd drive 'em down to the rehearsal of the school chorus, and, gee, I don't want to, but a gentleman's got to keep his social engagements."

"Well, upon my word! You and your social engagements! In high school!"

"Oh, ain't we select since we went to that hen college! Let me tell you there isn't a private school in the state that's got as swell a bunch as we got in Gamma Digamma this year. There's two fellows that their dads are millionaires. Say, gee, I ought to have a car of my own, like lots of the fellows."

Babbitt almost rose. "A car of your own! Don't you want a yacht, and a house and lot? That pretty nearly takes the cake! A boy that can't pass his Latin examinations, like any other boy ought to, and he expects me to give him a motor-car, and I suppose a chauffeur, and an aeroplane maybe, as a reward for the hard work he puts in going to the movies with Eunice Littlefield! Well, when you see me giving you—"

Somewhat later, after diplomacies, Ted persuaded Verona to admit that she was merely going to the Armory, that evening, to see the dog and cat show. She was then, Ted planned, to park the car in front of the candy-store across from the Armory and he would pick it up. There were masterly arrangements regarding leaving the key, and having the gasoline tank filled; and passionately, devotees of the Great God Motor, they hymned the patch on the spare inner-tube, and the lost jack-handle.

Their truce dissolving, Ted observed that her friends were "a scream of a bunch—stuck-up gabby four-flushers." His friends, she indicated, were "disgusting imitation sports, and horrid little shrieking ignorant girls." Further: "It's disgusting of you to smoke cigarettes, and so on and so forth, and those clothes you've got on this morning, they're too utterly ridiculous—honestly, simply disgusting."

Ted balanced over to the low beveled mirror in the buffet, regarded his charms, and smirked. His suit, the latest thing in Old Eli Togs, was skin-tight, with skimpy trousers to the tops of his glaring tan boots, a chorus-man waistline, pattern of an agitated check, and across the back a belt which belted nothing. His scarf was an enormous black silk wad. His flaxen hair was ice-smooth,

pasted back without parting. When he went to school he would add a cap with a long vizor like a shovel-blade. Proudest of all was his waistcoat, saved for, begged for, plotted for; a real Fancy Vest of fawn with polka dots of a decayed red, the points astoundingly long. On the lower edge of it he wore a high-school button, a class button, and a fraternity pin.

And none of it mattered. He was supple and swift and flushed; his eyes (which he believed to be cynical) were candidly eager. But he was not over-gentle. He waved his hand at poor dumpy Verona and drawled: "Yes, I guess we're pretty ridiculous and disgusticulus, and I rather guess our new necktie is some smear!"

Babbitt barked: "It is! And while you're admiring yourself, let me tell you it might add to your manly beauty if you wiped some of that egg off your mouth!"

Verona giggled, momentary victor in the greatest of Great Wars, which is the family war. Ted looked at her hopelessly, then shrieked at Tinka: "For the love o' Pete, quit pouring the whole sugar bowl on your corn flakes!"

When Verona and Ted were gone and Tinka upstairs, Babbitt groaned to his wife: "Nice family, I must say! I don't pretend to be any baa-lamb, and maybe I'm a little cross-grained at breakfast sometimes, but the way they go on jab-jab-jabbering, I simply can't stand it. I swear, I feel like going off some place where I can get a little peace. I do think after a man's spent his lifetime trying to give his kids a chance and a decent education, it's pretty discouraging to hear them all the time scrapping like a bunch of hyenas and never—and never— Curious; here in the paper it says— Never silent for one mom— Seen the morning paper yet?"

"No, dear." In twenty-three years of married life, Mrs. Babbitt had seen the paper before her husband just sixty-seven times.

"Lots of news. Terrible big tornado in the South. Hard luck, all right. But this, say, this is corking! Beginning of the end for those fellows! New York Assembly has passed some bills that ought to completely outlaw the socialists! And there's an elevator-runners' strike in New York and a lot of college boys are taking their places. That's the stuff! And a mass-meeting in Birmingham's demanded that this Mick agitator, this fellow De Valera, be deported. Dead right, by golly! All these agitators paid with German gold anyway. And we got no business interfering with the Irish

or any other foreign government. Keep our hands strictly off. And there's another well-authenticated rumor from Russia that Lenin is dead. That's fine. It's beyond me why we don't just step in there and kick those Bolshevik cusses out."

"That's so," said Mrs. Babbitt.

"And it says here a fellow was inaugurated mayor in overalls—a preacher, too! What do you think of that!"

"Humph! Well!"

He searched for an attitude, but neither as a Republican, a Presbyterian, an Elk, nor a real-estate broker did he have any doctrine about preacher-mayors laid down for him, so he grunted and went on. She looked sympathetic and did not hear a word. Later she would read the headlines, the society columns, and the department-store advertisements.

"What do you know about this! Charley McKelvey still doing the sassiety stunt as heavy as ever. Here's what that gushy woman reporter says about last night:

Never is Society with the big, big S more flattered than when they are bidden to partake of good cheer at the distinguished and hospitable residence of Mr. and Mrs. Charles L. McKelvey as they were last night. Set in its spacious lawns and landscaping, one of the notable sights crowning Royal Ridge, but merry and homelike despite its mighty stone walls and its vast rooms famed for their decoration, their home was thrown open last night for a dance in honor of Mrs. McKelvey's notable guest, Miss J. Sneeth of Washington. The wide hall is so generous in its proportions that it made a perfect ballroom, its hardwood floor reflecting the charming pageant above its polished surface. Even the delights of dancing paled before the alluring opportunities for tête-à-têtes that invited the soul to loaf in the long library before the baronial fireplace, or in the drawing-room with its deep comfy armchairs, its shaded lamps just made for a sly whisper of pretty nothings all a deux; or even in the billiard room where one could take a cue and show a prowess at still another game than that sponsored by Cupid and Terpsichore.

There was more, a great deal more, in the best urban journalistic style of Miss Elnora Pearl Bates, the popular society editor of the *Advocate-Times*. But Babbitt could not abide it. He grunted. He wrinkled the newspaper. He protested: "Can you

beat it! I'm willing to hand a lot of credit to Charley McKelvey. When we were in college together,
he was just as hard up as any of us, and he's made
a million good bucks out of contracting and hasn't
been any dishonester or bought any more city
councils than was necessary. And that's a good
house of his—though it ain't any 'mighty stone
walls' and it ain't worth the ninety thousand it
cost him. But when it comes to talking as though
Charley McKelvey and all that booze-hoisting set
of his are any blooming bunch of of, of Vanderbilts, why, it makes me tired!"

Timidly from Mrs. Babbitt: "I would like to see
the inside of their house though. It must be lovely.
I've never been inside."

"Well, I have! Lots of—couple of times. To see
Chaz about business deals, in the evening. It's not
so much. I wouldn't *want* to go there to dinner
with that gang of, high-binders. And I'll bet I
make a whole lot more money than some of those
tin-horns that spend all they got on dress-suits and
haven't got a decent suit of underwear to their
name! Hey! What do you think of this!"

Mrs. Babbitt was strangely unmoved by the tid-
ings from the Real Estate and Building column of
the *Advocate-Times*:

Ashtabula Street, 496—J. K. Dawson to Thomas
Mullally, April 17, 15.7x112.2, mtg. $4000 . . . .
Nom.

And this morning Babbitt was too disquieted to
entertain her with items from Mechanics' Liens,
Mortgages Recorded, and Contracts Awarded. He
rose. As he looked at her his eyebrows seemed
shaggier than usual. Suddenly:

"Yes, maybe— Kind of shame to not keep in
touch with folks like the McKelveys. We might
try inviting them to dinner, some evening. Oh,
thunder, let's not waste our good time thinking
about 'em! Our little bunch has a lot liver times
than all those plutes. Just compare a real human
like you with these neurotic birds like Lucile Mc-
Kelvey—all highbrow talk and dressed up like a
plush horse! You're a great old girl, hon.!"

He covered his betrayal of softness with a complaining: "Say, don't let Tinka go and eat any
more of that poison nut-fudge. For Heaven's sake,
try to keep her from ruining her digestion. I tell
you, most folks don't appreciate how important
it is to have a good digestion and regular habits.
Be back 'bout usual time, I guess."

He kissed her—he didn't quite kiss her—he laid
unmoving lips against her unflushing cheek. He

hurried out to the garage, muttering: "Lord, what
a family! And now Myra is going to get pathetic
on me because we don't train with this millionaire
outfit. Oh, Lord, sometimes I'd like to quit the
whole game. And the office worry and detail just
as bad. And I act cranky and— I don't mean to,
but I get— So darn tired!"

CHAPTER III

I

To George F. Babbitt, as to most prosperous citizens of Zenith, his motor car was poetry and tragedy, love and heroism. The office was his pirate
ship but the car his perilous excursion ashore.

Among the tremendous crises of each day none
was more dramatic than starting the engine. It was
slow on cold mornings; there was the long, anxious
whirr of the starter; and sometimes he had to drip
ether into the cocks of the cylinders, which was so
very interesting that at lunch he would chronicle it
drop by drop, and orally calculate how much each
drop had cost him.

This morning he was darkly prepared to find
something wrong, and he felt belittled when the
mixture exploded sweet and strong, and the car
didn't even brush the door-jamb, gouged and
splintery with many bruisings by fenders, as he
backed out of the garage. He was confused. He
shouted "Morning!" to Sam Doppelbrau with
more cordiality than he had intended.

Babbitt's green and white Dutch Colonial house
was one of three in that block on Chatham Road.
To the left of it was the residence of Mr. Samuel
Doppelbrau, secretary of an excellent firm of bath-
room-fixture jobbers. His was a comfortable house
with no architectural manners whatever; a large
wooden box with a squat tower, a broad porch,
and glossy paint yellow as a yolk. Babbitt disapproved of Mr. and Mrs. Doppelbrau as "Bohemian." From their house came midnight music
and obscene laughter; there were neighborhood
rumors of bootlegged whisky and fast motor rides.
They furnished Babbitt with many happy evenings
of discussion, during which he announced firmly,
"I'm not straitlaced, and I don't mind seeing a
fellow throw in a drink once in a while, but when
it comes to deliberately trying to get away with a
lot of hell-raising all the while like the Doppel-
braus do, it's too rich for my blood!"

On the other side of Babbitt lived Howard Littlefield, Ph.D., in a strictly modern house whereof

the lower part was dark red tapestry brick, with a leaded oriel, the upper part of pale stucco like spattered clay, and the roof red-tiled. Littlefield was the Great Scholar of the neighborhood; the authority on everything in the world except babies, cooking and motors. He was a Bachelor of Arts of Blodgett College, and a Doctor of Philosophy in economics of Yale. He was the employment-manager and publicity-counsel of the Zenith Street Traction Company. He could, on ten hours' notice, appear before the board of aldermen or the state legislature and prove, absolutely, with figures all in rows and with precedents from Poland and New Zealand, that the street-car company loved the Public and yearned over its employees; that all its stock was owned by Widows and Orphans; and that whatever it desired to do would benefit property-owners by increasing rental values, and help the poor by lowering rents. All his acquaintances turned to Littlefield when they desired to know the date of the battle of Saragossa, the definition of the word "sabotage," the future of the German mark, the translation of "*hinc illæ lachrimæ*," or the number of products of coal tar. He awed Babbitt by confessing that he often sat up till midnight reading the figures and footnotes in Government reports, or skimming (with amusement at the author's mistakes) the latest volumes of chemistry, archeology, and ichthyology.

But Littlefield's great value was as a spiritual example. Despite his strange learnings he was as strict a Presbyterian and as firm a Republican as George F. Babbitt. He confirmed the business men in the faith. Where they knew only by passionate instinct that their system of industry and manners was perfect, Dr. Howard Littlefield proved it to them, out of history, economics, and the confessions of reformed radicals.

Babbitt had a good deal of honest pride in being the neighbor of such a savant, and in Ted's intimacy with Eunice Littlefield. At sixteen Eunice was interested in no statistics save those regarding the ages and salaries of motion-picture stars, but—as Babbitt definitively put it—"she was her father's daughter."

The difference between a light man like Sam Doppelbrau and a really fine character like Littlefield was revealed in their appearances. Doppelbrau was disturbingly young for a man of forty-eight. He wore his derby on the back of his head, and his red face was wrinkled with meaningless laughter. But Littlefield was old for a man of forty-two. He was tall, broad, thick; his gold-rimmed spectacles were engulfed in the folds of his long face; his hair was a tossed mass of greasy blackness; he puffed and rumbled as he talked; his Phi Beta Kappa key shone against a spotty black vest; he smelled of old pipes; he was altogether funereal and archidiaconal; and to real-estate brokerage and the jobbing of bathroom-fixtures he added an aroma of sanctity.

This morning he was in front of his house, inspecting the grass parking between the curb and the broad cement sidewalk. Babbitt stopped his car and leaned out to shout "Mornin'!" Littlefield lumbered over and stood with one foot up on the running-board.

"Fine morning," said Babbitt, lighting—illegally early—his second cigar of the day.

"Yes, it's a mighty fine morning," said Littlefield.

"Spring coming along fast now."

"Yes, it's real spring now, all right," said Littlefield.

"Still cold nights, though. Had to have a couple blankets, on the sleeping-porch last night."

WILLA CATHER (1873–1947)

Among those who sent Lewis congratulations on winning the Nobel award was Willa Cather, who admitted candidly that she wished she had been the recipient, but, failing that, felt that he was the best choice. Lewis had been an admirer of Willa Cather's work; they had met in New York in 1922, and soon afterward Lewis agreed to review her novel *One of Ours* for the New York *Post*. After reading it, he told Mencken he was "damnably disappointed"—the book was a "thin second-rate account of the war" and revealed a "wobbly indecisiveness." He acknowledged his disappointment in the review, but muted it: the writer from small-town Minnesota had a strong fellow feeling for the writer from small-town Nebraska, and in *One of Ours* he discovered "moments of beauty which reveal not an American West of obvious heroisms but the actual grain-brightened, wind-sharpened land of today; moments out of serene October afternoons and eager April mornings and cold-grasping winter nights." He ranked her with Edith Wharton as a literary artist (though instantly spoiling that remark by adding the names of Booth Tarkington and Joseph Hergesheimer) and declared that "of the . . . fabulous Middle West not even Mr. Hamlin Garland has given a more valid and beautiful expression than has Miss Cather."

If there was a conscious irony in the latter allusion, there were in the review other ironies of which Lewis was quite unconscious. The fact is, *One of Ours* is virtually unique among Willa Cather's most serious efforts in that it did deal with the actualities of the present or very immediate past. From *O, Pioneers!* in 1913 to her last novel, *Sapphira and the Slave Girl*, in 1940, Willa Cather's subject (as Hamlin Garland's had become) was the "obvious heroisms" of the older American West, and her obsessive theme the decline of those heroisms in the sterile and uncreative age of the machine. Nor can she be reckoned among the realists. Within a year after Lewis's review, Willa Cather wrote an essay called "The Novel Demeublé" (her one venture, as she said, into "the dim wilderness of theory"), in which she deplored the tendency of novelists from Balzac onward to furnish their stories with an abundance of social and sociological fact, to impair artistic form in the interest of sheer documentation. With all that, she said, the true novelist had nothing to do with; neither the banking system nor the Stock Exchange had any place in fiction—neither, she added interestingly enough, did "physical sensation." One can scarcely miss an echo there of the writer whom she once praised as having "surely the keenest mind any American had ever devoted to the craft of fiction"—Henry James.

But if her theory was simplistic, her work,

like her personality, was more interestingly complex and tension-ridden than the theory would lead one to expect. She was born in Virginia farming country in 1873, in a community thick with relatives and in-laws. A decade later, her father took the family to Nebraska (to which some of those relatives had already removed) and settled in Red Cloud, a town founded only fourteen years earlier by a band of sturdy souls coming down from Omaha. It was still decidedly pioneer country, a new, hard-working society: a rich mixture of older American families with Swedes, Danes, Bohemians, Germans, and Swiss. If, under the leaden skies of winter, it was, as Willa Cather would say, the loneliest country in the world, there was a sense of abounding vitality in spring and drowsy charm in summer.

There was something boyish about Willa Cather as a girl, just as there would be something mannish about her as a woman. Even her early intellectual interests were those then normally pursued by young males: though she read fairly widely—in Parkman, and in Victorian fiction and poetry—she was determined upon a scientific career (in high school, she gave a speech extolling the rigors of scientific investigation). But soon after she entered the University of Nebraska, in 1890, an essay she had written on Carlyle was published in a newspaper in Lincoln; she decided then and there that writing was her métier and began to talk about the supremacy of art, the lonely dedication of the artist, and the merits of Henry James.

She was slow, however, slower even than Edith Wharton, to commit herself fully to the profession of writing. After graduating from Lincoln, she spent a decade in Pittsburgh. In 1905, she published a volume of shorter fiction, *The Troll Garden*. S. S. McClure, the editor of *McClure's Magazine*, came out from New York to talk with her and persuaded her to join his staff. The magazine was engaged in a mode of journalism that had made it nationally famous, highly influential, and much feared—the publishing of vigorous, but not usually malicious, exposés of the ties between business, politics, and crime. After one cluster of these, a number of hard-hitting articles by David Graham Phillips called "The Treason of the Senate" (in which democracy was pictured as gravely endangered by ruthless senatorial conspiracies), Theodore Roosevelt, in rage, added a new noun to the American vocabulary: "The men with the muckrakes are often indispensable to the well-being of society, but only if they know how to stop raking the muck, and to look upward to the celestial crown above them, to the crown of worthy endeavor." In fact, "muckraking" had been going on for more than a decade (see p. 1213), and many of Roosevelt's own reformist policies had been stimulated by the revelations of the various muckraking magazines. It was Willa Cather, as managing editor, who helped guide *McClure's* through its muckraking days, with remarkable efficiency and a keenly discriminating eye.

When, in 1912, Willa Cather resigned from the magazine to work on the novel that became *O, Pioneers!*, she had behind her a good many years of practical journalism, and a journalism that had addressed itself to just those tough social actualities she would later rule out of the art of fiction. It may even be—for it is otherwise hard to explain her change of heart and direction—that she went back in fact and in fictional memory to the early Nebraska years out of a revulsion against the eastern world of criminal greed and political shenanigans. In any event, there is in both *The Bohemian Girl*, a novella of 1912, and *O, Pioneers!*, a year later, a start toward reconciliation with the Nebraska scene she had fled in the mid-nineties as stiflingly repressive of the creative impulse. Contemplating Alexandra Bergson, the Scandinavian heroine of *O, Pioneers!*, as Alexandra herself looks out almost reverently upon the Divide (the plains country Willa Cather had known, between the Republican and the Platte rivers), Willa Cather writes:

For the first time, perhaps, since that land emerged from the waters of geologic ages, a human face was set toward it with love and yearning. It seemed beautiful to her, rich and strong and glorious. Her eyes drank in the breadth of it, until her tears blinded her.

Yet even in these stories, a distinction is beginning to emerge—between the old pioneer Nebraska and its twentieth-century descendant. The hero of *The Bohemian Girl* is frank to confess that he finds the grandparents in the community more lively and stimulating than the young folk; and Alexandra, after she has conquered her resistant land and turned it into a domain of "milk and honey" and rich crops, yearns for the untamed countryside—"I liked the old country better," she says. "This is all very splendid in its way, but there was something about this country when it was a wild old beast that has haunted me all these years." Deep affection for the wild old beast, or its human equivalents, would mingle in the novels that followed with an increasing hostility to what had replaced it.

There was in all this something of the Parkman Willa Cather so admired, something of Parkman's nostalgia for the vanished days of hardship, courageous endurance, unremitting but rewarding struggle; and there were affinities, too, conscious or not, with the different kinds of nostalgia (or, to use one critic's word, of "backwardness") voiced by Cooper and Mark Twain.

Willa Cather herself, for all her reverence for Henry James, found her own literary model in Sarah Orne Jewett. She had met Miss Jewett in the winter of 1908, when she came up to Boston on an assignment for *McClure's*, in the house of Mrs. James T. Fields, widow of the eminent publisher and friend of Longfellow, Lowell, Holmes, and other Brahmins. She recognized the similarity between Sarah Orne Jewett's deteriorating Maine coastal towns and her own Red Cloud; she honored and sought to emulate Miss Jewett's delicate and evocative artistry; and she took completely to heart the counsel she received from the older writer not long before the latter's death: "You must find a quiet place. You must find your own quiet center of life and write from that. . . . The thing that teases the mind over and over for years, and at last gets itself put down on paper —whether little or great, it belongs to Literature."

What teased Willa Cather's mind over and over was the grandeur of the past and the repulsiveness of the present. If this double theme —with emphasis on the first half of it—permeates *My Ántonia* (1918, the story of the heroic and fertile daughter of an immigrant Nebraska family), it received its most compelling formulation in *A Lost Lady* (1923). In this novel, a brilliant and quietly harrowing study of the interaction between personality and social environment, the lady in question is Marian Forrester. She first appears as the wife of an elderly member of the midwestern "railroad aristocracy" (Willa Cather put the pioneering railroad tycoons on the level of great creative artists); Mrs. Forrester then becomes the mistress of another figure in that aristocracy; her husband goes honorably bankrupt during the financial crisis of the nineties, has a stroke, and eventually dies; his widow falls into the hands of a pushy young businessman, who seduces her, marries someone else, and gains possession of the Forrester home. Marian Forrester manages, somehow, to keep intact much of her graciousness and charm; she is still a "lady" even if she is in a manner "lost"; but her story enacts the decline and end of an era.

As the twenties wore on, Willa Cather felt steadily more estranged from her contemporary world: "the world broke in two in 1922 or thereabout," she said later—meaning perhaps that the full effect of the First World War was felt only then; and also, just possibly, meaning that something in her personal life gave way at that time.[1] Her response, at any rate, was to retreat

ever further into the past. *The Professor's House* (1925), a subtly if sparsely woven meditation on death, is set in a period close to the present; but *Death Comes for the Archbishop* (1927) goes back to the American Southwest and the pre–Civil War days of Kit Carson; *Shadows on the Rock* (1931), which depends heavily on Parkman, retreats as far as seventeenth-century Quebec; and *Sapphira and the Slave Girl* (1940) explores the Virginia society of Willa Cather's grandparents in the 1850's. In a collection of items called *Not Under Forty*, in 1936, Willa Cather in effect signed off from the machine civilization of the twentieth century and declaimed that no one born later than the turn of that century would understand or appreciate what she had to say.

This is not to suggest that her work was unpopular or that she lacked admiring critics. The liberals, needless to say, attacked her in the thirties, especially for her rejection of contemporary social fact as the stuff of fiction. But her novels sold very widely, and none more than those which peered furthest into the past. Throughout the twenties, she was regarded as one of the best living American writers (a poll taken in 1929 ranked her first in "general literary merit," with Edith Wharton the runner-up). It could plausibly be argued that nostalgia became her: a nostalgia at once for a lost heroic past and for a lost commitment to the craft of fiction. Her view of American history and the nature and sources of social change was drastically oversimplified. But she was another of those gifted American women whose subject, to borrow Robert Frost's phrase again, was "what to make of a diminished thing." Morton D. Zabel, in an essay (1940) as judicious as it is astute, concludes quite rightly that "in her best work Willa Cather brought to a kind of climax and epic vision the work of the American women [writing on this subject] who preceded her—Rose Terry Cooke, Sarah Orne Jewett, Mrs. [Mary Wilkins] Freeman."

---

[1] In *Literary Biography* (1957), Leon Edel offers an extremely suggestive psychoanalytic commentary on *The Professor's House* of 1925, in which he relates the professor's addiction to his former house and his attic room to certain profound psychic and emotional stresses in Willa Cather's life in the years just preceding the book and to her desire to hide herself away from the world.

Neighbour Rosicky (1932)

I

When Doctor Burleigh told neighbour Rosicky he had a bad heart, Rosicky protested.

"So? No, I guess my heart was always pretty good. I got a little asthma, maybe. Just a awful short breath when I was pitchin' hay last summer, dat's all."

"Well now, Rosicky, if you know more about it than I do, what did you come to me for? It's your heart that makes you short of breath, I tell you. You're sixty-five years old, and you've always worked hard, and your heart's tired. You've got to be careful from now on, and you can't do heavy work any more. You've got five boys at home to do it for you."

The old farmer looked up at the Doctor with a gleam of amusement in his queer, triangular-shaped eyes. His eyes were large and lively, but the lids were caught up in the middle in a curious way, so that they formed a triangle. He did not look like a sick man. His brown face was creased but not wrinkled, he had a ruddy colour in his smooth-shaven cheeks and in his lips, under his long brown moustache. His hair was thin and ragged around his ears, but very little grey. His forehead, naturally high and crossed by deep parallel lines, now ran all the way up to his pointed crown. Rosicky's face had the habit of looking interested,—suggested a contented disposition and a reflective quality that was gay rather than grave. This gave him a certain detachment, the easy manner of an on-looker and observer.

"Well, I guess you ain't got no pills for a bad heart, Doctor Ed. I guess the only thing is fur me to git me a new one."

Doctor Burleigh swung round in his desk-chair and frowned at the old farmer. "I think if I were you I'd take a little care of the old one, Rosicky."

Rosicky shrugged. "Maybe I don't know how. I expect you mean fur me not to drink my coffee no more."

"I wouldn't, in your place. But you'll do as you choose about that. I've never yet been able to separate a Bohemian from his coffee or his pipe. I've quit trying. But the sure thing is you've got to cut out farm work. You can feed the stock and do chores about the barn, but you can't do anything in the fields that makes you short of breath."

"How about shelling corn?"

"Of course not!"

Rosicky considered with puckered brows.

"I can't make my heart go no longer'n it wants to, can I, Doctor Ed?"

"I think it's good for five or six years yet, maybe more, if you'll take the strain off it. Sit around the house and help Mary. If I had a good wife like yours, I'd want to stay around the house."

His patient chuckled. "It ain't no place fur a man. I don't like no old man hanging round the kitchen too much. An' my wife, she's a awful hard worker her own self."

"That's it; you can help her a little. My Lord, Rosicky, you are one of the few men I know who has a family he can get some comfort out of; happy dispositions, never quarrel among themselves, and they treat you right. I want to see you live a few years and enjoy them."

"Oh, they're good kids, all right," Rosicky assented.

The Doctor wrote him a prescription and asked him how his oldest son, Rudolph, who had married in the spring, was getting on. Rudolph had struck out for himself, on rented land. "And how's Polly? I was afraid Mary mightn't like an American daughter-in-law, but it seems to be working out all right."

"Yes, she's a fine girl. Dat widder woman bring her daughters up very nice. Polly got lots of spunk, an' she got some style, too. Da's nice, for young folks to have some style." Rosicky inclined his head gallantly. His voice and his twinkly smile were an affectionate compliment to his daughter-in-law.

"It looks like a storm, and you'd better be getting home before it comes. In town in the car?" Doctor Burleigh rose.

"No, I'm in de wagon. When you got five boys, you ain't got much chance to ride round in de Ford. I ain't much for cars, noway."

"Well, it's a good road out to your place; but I don't want you bumping around in a wagon much. And never again on a hay-rake, remember!"

Rosicky placed the Doctor's fee delicately behind the desk-telephone, looking the other way, as if this were an absent-minded gesture. He put on his plush cap and his corduroy jacket with a sheep-skin collar, and went out.

The Doctor picked up his stethoscope and frowned at it as if he were seriously annoyed with the instrument. He wished it had been telling tales about some other man's heart, some old man who didn't look the Doctor in the eye so knowingly, or hold out such a warm brown hand when he said good-bye. Doctor Burleigh had been a poor boy in the country before he went away to medical school; he had known Rosicky almost ever since he could remember, and he had a deep affection for Mrs. Rosicky.

Only last winter he had had such a good breakfast at Rosicky's, and that when he needed it. He had been out all night on a long, hard confinement case at Tom Marshall's,—a big rich farm where there was plenty of stock and plenty of feed and a great deal of expensive farm machinery of the newest model, and no comfort whatever. The woman had too many children and too much work, and she was no manager. When the baby was born at last, and handed over to the assisting neighbour woman, and the mother was properly attended to, Burleigh refused any breakfast in that slovenly house, and drove his buggy—the snow was too deep for a car—eight miles to Anton Rosicky's place. He didn't know another farm-house where a man could get such a warm welcome, and such good strong coffee with rich cream. No wonder the old chap didn't want to give up his coffee!

He had driven in just when the boys had come back from the barn and were washing up for breakfast. The long table, covered with a bright oilcloth, was set out with dishes waiting for them, and the warm kitchen was full of the smell of coffee and hot biscuit and sausage. Five big handsome boys, running from twenty to twelve, all with what Burleigh called natural good manners,—they hadn't a bit of the painful self-consciousness he himself had to struggle with when he was a lad. One ran to put his horse away, another helped him off with his fur coat and hung it up, and Josephine, the youngest child and the only daughter, quickly set another place under her mother's direction.

With Mary, to feed creatures was the natural expression of affection,—her chickens, the calves, her big hungry boys. It was a rare pleasure to feed a young man whom she seldom saw and of whom she was as proud as if he belonged to her. Some country housekeepers would have stopped to spread a white cloth over the oilcloth, to change the thick cups and plates for their best china, and the wooden-handled knives for plated ones. But not Mary.

"You must take us as you find us, Doctor Ed. I'd be glad to put out my good things for you if you was expected, but I'm glad to get you any way at all."

He knew she was glad,—she threw back her head and spoke out as if she were announcing him to the whole prairie. Rosicky hadn't said anything at all; he merely smiled his twinkling smile, put some more coal on the fire, and went into his own room to pour the Doctor a little drink in a medicine glass. When they were all seated, he watched his wife's face from his end of the table and spoke to her in Czech. Then, with the instinct of politeness which seldom failed him, he turned to the Doctor and said slyly, "I was just tellin' her not to ask you no questions about Mrs. Marshall till you eat some breakfast. My wife, she's terrible fur to ask questions."

The boys laughed, and so did Mary. She watched the Doctor devour her biscuit and sausage, too much excited to eat anything herself. She drank her coffee and sat taking in everything about her visitor. She had known him when he was a poor country boy, and was boastfully proud of his success, always saying: "What do people go to Omaha for, to see a doctor, when we got the best one in the State right here?" If Mary liked people at all, she felt physical pleasure in the sight of them, personal exultation in any good fortune that came to them. Burleigh didn't know many women like that, but he knew she was like that.

When his hunger was satisfied, he did, of course, have to tell them about Mrs. Marshall, and he noticed what a friendly interest the boys took in the matter.

Rudolph, the oldest one (he was still living at home then), said: "The last time I was over there, she was lifting them big heavy milk-cans, and I knew she ought not to be doing it."

"Yes, Rudolph told me about that when he come home, and I said it wasn't right," Mary put in warmly. "It was all right for me to do them things up to the last, for I was terrible strong, but that woman's weakly. And do you think she'll be able to nurse it, Ed?" She sometimes forgot to give him the title she was so proud of. "And to think of your being up all night and then not able to get a decent breakfast! I don't know what's the matter with such people."

"Why, mother," said one of the boys, "if Doctor Ed had got breakfast there, we wouldn't have him here. So you ought to be glad."

"He knows I'm glad to have him, John, any

time. But I'm sorry for that poor woman, how bad she'll feel the Doctor had to go away in the cold without his breakfast."

"I wish I'd been in practice when these were getting born." The doctor looked down the row of close-clipped heads. "I missed some good breakfasts by not being."

The boys began to laugh at their mother because she flushed so red, but she stood her ground and threw up her head. "I don't care, you wouldn't have got away from this house without breakfast. No doctor ever did. I'd have had something ready fixed that Anton could warm up for you."

The boys laughed harder than ever, and exclaimed at her: "I'll bet you would!" "She would, that!"

"Father, did you get breakfast for the doctor when we were born?"

"Yes, and he used to bring me my breakfast, too, mighty nice. I was always awful hungry!" Mary admitted with a guilty laugh.

While the boys were getting the Doctor's horse, he went to the window to examine the house plants. "What do you do to your geraniums to keep them blooming all winter, Mary? I never pass this house that from the road I don't see your windows full of flowers."

She snapped off a dark red one, and a ruffled new green leaf, and put them in his buttonhole. "There, that looks better. You look too solemn for a young man, Ed. Why don't you git married? I'm worried about you. Settin' at breakfast, I looked at you real hard, and I seen you've got some grey hairs already."

"Oh, yes! They're coming. Maybe they'd come faster if I married."

"Don't talk so. You'll ruin your health eating at the hotel. I could send your wife a nice loaf of nut bread, if you only had one. I don't like to see a young man getting grey. I'll tell you something, Ed; you make some strong black tea and keep it handy in a bowl, and every morning just brush it into your hair, an' it'll keep the grey from showin' much. That's the way I do!"

Sometimes the Doctor heard the gossipers in the drugstore wondering why Rosicky didn't get on faster. He was industrious, and so were his boys, but they were rather free and easy, weren't pushers, and they didn't always show good judgment. They were comfortable, they were out of debt, but they didn't get much ahead. Maybe, Doctor Burleigh reflected, people as generous and warmhearted and affectionate as the Rosickys never got ahead much; maybe you could not enjoy your life and put it into the bank, too.

II

When Rosicky left Doctor Burleigh's office, he went into the farm-implement store to light his pipe and put on his glasses and read over the list Mary had given him. Then he went into the general merchandise place next door and stood about until the pretty girl with the plucked eyebrows, who always waited on him, was free. Those eyebrows, two thin India-ink strokes, amused him, because he remembered how they used to be. Rosicky always prolonged his shopping by a little joking; the girl knew the old fellow admired her, and she liked to chaff with him.

"Seems to me about every other week you buy ticking, Mr. Rosicky, and always the best quality," she remarked as she measured off the heavy bolt with red stripes.

"You see, my wife is always makin' goose-fedder pillows, an de' thin stuff don't hold in dem little down-fedders."

"You must have lots of pillows at your house."

"Sure. She makes quilts of dem, too. We sleeps easy. Now she's makin' a fedder quilt for my son's wife. You know Polly, that married my Rudolph. How much my bill, Miss Pearl?"

"Eight eighty-five."

"Chust make it nine, and put in some candy fur de women."

"As usual. I never did see a man buy so much candy for his wife. First thing you know, she'll be getting too fat."

"I'd like dat. I ain't much fur all dem slim women like what de style is now."

"That's one for me, I suppose, Mr. Bohunk!" Pearl sniffed and elevated her India-ink strokes.

When Rosicky went out to his wagon, it was beginning to snow,—the first snow of the season, and he was glad to see it. He rattled out of town and along the highway through a wonderfully rich stretch of country, the finest farms in the country. He admired this High Prairie, as it was called, and always liked to drive through it. His own place lay in a rougher territory, where there was some clay in the soil and it was not so productive. When he bought his land, he hadn't the money to buy on High Prairie; so he told his boys, when they grumbled, that if their land hadn't some clay in it, they wouldn't own it at all. All the same, he enjoyed looking at these fine farms, as he enjoyed looking at a prize bull.

After he had gone eight miles, he came to the graveyard, which lay just at the edge of his own hay-land. There he stopped his horses and sat still on his wagon seat, looking about at the snowfall. Over yonder on the hill he could see his own house, crouching low, with the clump of orchard behind and the windmill before, and all down the gentle hill-slope the rows of pale gold cornstalks stood out against the white field. The snow was falling over the cornfield and the pasture and the hay-land, steadily, with very little wind,—a nice dry snow. The graveyard had only a light wire fence about it and was all overgrown with long red grass. The fine snow, settling into this red grass and upon the few little evergreens and the headstones, looked very pretty.

It was a nice graveyard, Rosicky reflected, sort of snug and homelike, not cramped or mournful,—a big sweep all around it. A man could lie down in the long grass and see the complete arch of the sky over him, hear the wagons go by; in summer the mowing-machine rattled right up to the wire fence. And it was so near home. Over there across the cornstalks his own roof and windmill looked so good to him that he promised himself to mind the Doctor and take care of himself. He was awful fond of his place, he admitted. He wasn't anxious to leave it. And it was a comfort to think that he would never have to go farther than the edge of his own hayfield. The snow, falling over his barn-yard and the graveyard, seemed to draw things to-gether like. And they were all old neighbours in the graveyard, most of them friends; there was nothing to feel awkward or embarrassed about. Em-barrassment was the most disagreeable feeling Rosicky knew. He didn't often have it,—only with certain people whom he didn't understand at all.

Well, it was a nice snowstorm; a fine sight to see the snow falling so quietly and graciously over so much open country. On his cap and shoulders, on the horses' backs and manes, light, delicate, mys-terious it fell; and with it a dry cool fragrance was released into the air. It meant rest for vegetation and men and beasts, for the ground itself; a season of long nights for sleep, leisurely breakfasts, peace by the fire. This and much more went through Rosicky's mind, but he merely told himself that winter was coming, clucked to his horses, and drove on.

When he reached home, John, the youngest boy, ran out to put away his team for him, and he met Mary coming up from the outside cellar with her apron full of carrots. They went into the house together. On the table, covered with oilcloth fig-ured with clusters of blue grapes, a place was set, and he smelled hot coffee cake of some kind. An-ton never lunched in town; he thought that ex-travagant, and anyhow he didn't like the food. So Mary always had something ready for him when he got home.

After he was settled in his chair, stirring his coffee in a big cup, Mary took out of the oven a pan of *kolache* stuffed with apricots, examined them anxiously to see whether they had got too dry, put them beside his plate, and then sat down opposite him.

Rosicky asked her in Czech if she wasn't going to have any coffee.

She replied in English, as being somehow the right language for transacting business: "Now what did Doctor Ed say, Anton? You tell me just what."

"He said I was to tell you some compliments, but I forgot 'em." Rosicky's eyes twinkled.

"About you, I mean. What did he say about your asthma?"

"He says I ain't got no asthma." Rosicky took one of the little rolls in his broad brown fingers. The thickened nail of his right thumb told the story of his past.

"Well, what is the matter? And don't try to put me off."

"He don't say nothing much, only I'm a little older, and my heart ain't so good like it used to be."

Mary started and brushed her hair back from her temples with both hands as if she were a little out of her mind. From the way she glared, she might have been in a rage with him.

"He says there's something the matter with your heart? Doctor Ed says so?"

"Now don't yell at me like I was a hog in de garden, Mary. You know I always did like to hear a woman talk soft. He didn't say anything de matter wid my heart, only it ain't so young like it used to be, an' he tell me not to pitch hay or run de corn-sheller."

Mary wanted to jump up, but she sat still. She admired the way he never under any circumstances raised his voice or spoke roughly. He was city-bred, and she was country-bred; she often said she wanted her boys to have their papa's nice ways.

"You never have no pain there, do you? It's your breathing and your stomach that's been wrong. I wouldn't believe nobody but Doctor Ed about it. I guess I'll go see him myself. Didn't he give you no advice?"

"Chust to take it easy like, an' stay round de house dis winter. I guess you got some carpenter work for me to do. I kin make some new shelves for you, and I want dis long time to build a closet in de boys' room and make dem two little fellers keep dere clo'es hung up."

Rosicky drank his coffee from time to time, while he considered. His moustache was of the soft long variety and came down over his mouth like the teeth of a buggy-rake over a bundle of hay. Each time he put down his cup, he ran his blue handkerchief over his lips. When he took a drink of water, he managed very neatly with the back of his hand.

Mary sat watching him intently, trying to find any change in his face. It is hard to see anyone who has become like your own body to you. Yes, his hair had got thin, and his high forehead had deep lines running from left to right. But his neck, always clean-shaved except in the busiest seasons, was not loose or baggy. It was burned a dark reddish brown, and there were deep creases in it, but it looked firm and full of blood. His cheeks had a good colour. On either side of his mouth there was a half-moon down the length of his cheek, not wrinkles, but two lines that had come there from his habitual expression. He was shorter and broader than when she married him; his back had grown broad and curved, a good deal like the shell of an old turtle, and his arms and legs were short.

He was fifteen years older than Mary, but she had hardly ever thought about it before. He was her man, and the kind of man she liked. She was rough, and he was gentle,—city-bred, as she always said. They had been shipmates on a rough voyage and had stood by each other in trying times. Life had gone well with them because, at bottom, they had the same ideas about life. They agreed, without discussion, as to what was most important and what was secondary. They didn't often exchange opinions, even in Czech,—it was as if they had thought the same thought together. A good deal had to be sacrificed and thrown overboard in a hard life like theirs, and they had never disagreed as to the things that could go. It had been a hard life, and a soft life, too. There wasn't anything brutal in the short, broad-backed man with the three-cornered eyes and the forehead that went on to the top of his skull. He was a city man, a gentle man, and though he had married a rough farm

girl, he had never touched her without gentleness.

They had been at one accord not to hurry through life, not to be always skimping and saving. They saw their neighbours buy more land and feed more stock than they did, without discontent. Once when the creamery agent came to the Rosickys to persuade them to sell him their cream, he told them how much money the Fasslers, their nearest neighbours, had made on their cream last year.

"Yes," said Mary, "and look at them Fassler children! Pale, pinched little things, they look like skimmed milk. I had rather put some colour into my children's faces than put money into the bank."

The agent shrugged and turned to Anton.

"I guess we'll do like she says," said Rosicky.

III

Mary very soon got into town to see Doctor Ed, and then she had a talk with her boys and set a guard over Rosicky. Even John, the youngest, had his father on his mind. If Rosicky went to throw hay down from the loft, one of the boys ran up the ladder and took the fork from him. He sometimes complained that though he was getting to be an old man, he wasn't an old woman yet.

That winter he stayed in the house in the afternoons and carpentered, or sat in the chair between the window full of plants and the wooden bench where the two pails of drinking-water stood. This spot was called "Father's corner," though it was not a corner at all. He had a shelf there, where he kept his Bohemian papers and his pipes and tobacco, and his shears and needles and thread and tailor's thimble. Having been a tailor in his youth, he couldn't bear to see a woman patching at his clothes, or at the boys'. He liked tailoring, and always patched all the overalls and jackets and work shirts. Occasionally he made over a pair of pants one of the older boys had outgrown, for the little fellow.

While he sewed, he let his mind run back over his life. He had a good deal to remember, really; life in three countries. The only part of his youth he didn't like to remember was the two years he had spent in London, in Cheapside, working for a German tailor who was wretchedly poor. Those days, when he was nearly always hungry, when his clothes were dropping off him for dirt, and the sound of a strange language kept him in continual bewilderment, had left a sore spot in his mind that wouldn't bear touching.

He was twenty when he landed at Castle Garden in New York, and he had a protector who got him work in a tailor shop in Vesey Street, down near the Washington Market. He looked upon that part of his life as very happy. He became a good workman, he was industrious, and his wages were increased from time to time. He minded his own business and envied nobody's good fortune. He went to night school and learned to read English. He often did overtime work and was well paid for it, but somehow he never saved anything. He couldn't refuse a loan to a friend, and he was self-indulgent. He liked a good dinner, and a little went for beer, a little for tobacco; a good deal went to the girls. He often stood through an opera on Saturday nights; he could get standing-room for a dollar. Those were the great days of opera in New York, and it gave a fellow something to think about for the rest of the week. Rosicky had a quick ear, and a childish love of all the stage splendour; the scenery, the costumes, the ballet. He usually went with a chum, and after the performance they had beer and maybe some oysters somewhere. It was a fine life; for the first five years or so it satisfied him completely. He was never hungry or cold or dirty, and everything amused him: a fire, a dog fight, a parade, a storm, a ferry ride. He thought New York the finest, richest, friendliest city in the world.

Moreover, he had what he called a happy home life. Very near the tailor shop was a small furniture-factory, where an old Austrian, Loeffler, employed a few skilled men and made unusual furniture, most of it to order, for the rich German housewives uptown. The top floor of Loeffler's five-story factory was a loft, where he kept his choice lumber and stored the odd pieces of furniture left on his hands. One of the young workmen he employed was a Czech, and he and Rosicky became fast friends. They persuaded Loeffler to let them have a sleeping-room in one corner of the loft. They bought good beds and bedding and had their pick of the furniture kept up there. The loft was low-pitched, but light and airy, full of windows, and good-smelling by reason of the fine lumber put up there to season. Old Loeffler used to go down to the docks and buy wood from South America and the East from the sea captains. The young men were as foolish about their house as a bridal pair. Zichec, the young cabinet-maker, devised every sort of convenience, and Rosicky kept their clothes in order. At night and on Sundays, when the quiver of machinery underneath was still, it was the quietest place in the world, and on summer nights all the sea winds blew in. Zichec often practiced on his flute in the evening. They were both fond of music and went to the opera together. Rosicky thought he wanted to live like that forever.

But as the years passed, all alike, he began to get a little restless. When spring came round, he would begin to feel fretted, and he got to drinking. He was likely to drink too much of a Saturday night. On Sunday he was languid and heavy, getting over his spree. On Monday he plunged into work again. So he never had time to figure out what ailed him, though he knew something did. When the grass turned green in Park Place, and the lilac hedge at the back of Trinity churchyard put out its blossoms, he was tormented by a longing to run away. That was why he drank too much; to get a temporary illusion of freedom and wide horizons.

Rosicky, the old Rosicky, could remember as if it were yesterday the day when the young Rosicky found out what was the matter with him. It was on a Fourth of July afternoon, and he was sitting in Park Place in the sun. The lower part of New York was empty. Wall Street, Liberty Street, Broadway, all empty. So much stone and asphalt with nothing going on, so many empty windows. The emptiness was intense, like the stillness in a great factory when the machinery stops and the belts and bands cease running. It was too great a change, it took all the strength out of one. Those blank buildings, without the stream of life pouring through them, were like empty jails. It struck young Rosicky that this was the trouble with big cities; they built you in from the earth itself, cemented you away from any contact with the ground. You lived in an unnatural world, like the fish in an aquarium, who were probably much more comfortable than they ever were in the sea.

On that very day he began to think seriously about the articles he had read in the Bohemian papers, describing prosperous Czech farming communities in the West. He believed he would like to go out there as a farmhand; it was hardly possible that he could ever have land of his own. His people had always been workmen; his father and grandfather had worked in shops. His mother's parents had lived in the country, but they rented their farm and had a hard time to get along. Nobody in his family had ever owned any land,—that belonged to a different station of life altogether. Anton's mother died when he was little, and he was sent into the country to her parents. He stayed with them until he was twelve, and formed those ties with the earth and the farm animals and growing things which are never made at all unless they are made early. After his grandfather died, he went back to live with his father and stepmother, but she was very hard on him, and his father helped him to get passage to London.

After that Fourth of July day in Park Place, the desire to return to the country never left him. To work on another man's farm would be all he asked; to see the sun rise and set and to plant things and watch them grow. He was a very simple man. He was like a tree that has not many roots, but one tap-root that goes down deep. He subscribed for a Bohemian paper printed in Chicago, then for one printed in Omaha. His mind got farther and farther west. He began to save a little money to buy his liberty. When he was thirty-five, there was a great meeting in New York of Bohemian athletic societies, and Rosicky left the tailor shop and went home with the Omaha delegates to try his fortune in another part of the world.

IV

Perhaps the fact that his own youth was well over before he began to have a family was one reason why Rosicky was so fond of his boys. He had almost a grandfather's indulgence for them. He had never had to worry about any of them—except, just now, a little about Rudolph.

On Saturday night the boys always piled into the Ford, took little Josephine, and went to town to the moving-picture show. One Saturday morning they were talking at the breakfast table about starting early that evening, so that they would have an hour or so to see the Christmas things in the stores before the show began. Rosicky looked down the table.

"I hope you boys ain't disappointed, but I want you to let me have de car tonight. Maybe some of you can go in with de neighbours."

Their faces fell. They worked hard all week, and they were still like children. A new jack-knife or a box of candy pleased the older ones as much as the little fellow.

"If you and Mother are going to town," Frank said, "maybe you could take a couple of us along with you, anyway."

"No, I want to take de car down to Rudolph's, and let him an' Polly go in to de show. She don't git into town enough, an' I'm afraid she's gittin' lonesome, an' he can't afford no car yet."

That settled it. The boys were a good deal dashed. Their father took another piece of apple-cake and went on: "Maybe next Saturday night de two little fellers can go along wid dem."

"Oh, is Rudolph going to have the car every Saturday night?"

Rosicky did not reply at once; then he began to speak seriously: "Listen, boys; Polly ain't lookin' so good. I don't like to see nobody lookin' sad. It comes hard fur a town girl to be a farmer's wife. I don't want no trouble to start in Rudolph's family. When it starts, it ain't so easy to stop. An American girl don't git used to our ways all at once. I like to tell Polly she and Rudolph can have the car every Saturday night till after New Year's, if it's all right with you boys."

"Sure it's all right, Papa," Mary cut in. "And it's good you thought about that. Town girls is used to more than country girls. I lay awake nights, scared she'll make Rudolph discontented with the farm."

The boys put as good a face on it as they could. They surely looked forward to their Saturday nights in town. That evening Rosicky drove the car the half-mile down the road to Rudolph's new, bare little house.

Polly was in a short-sleeved gingham dress, clearing away the supper dishes. She was a trim, slim little thing, with blue eyes and shingled yellow hair, and her eyebrows were reduced to a mere brush-stroke, like Miss Pearl's.

"Good evening, Mr. Rosicky. Rudolph's at the barn, I guess." She never called him father, or Mary mother. She was sensitive about having married a foreigner. She never in the world would have done it if Rudolph hadn't been such a handsome, persuasive fellow and such a gallant lover. He had graduated in her class in the high school in town, and their friendship began in the ninth grade.

Rosicky went in, though he wasn't exactly asked. "My boys ain't goin' to town to-night, an' I brought de car over fur you two to go in to de picture show."

Polly, carrying dishes to the sink, looked over her shoulder at him. "Thank you. But I'm late with my work tonight, and pretty tired. Maybe Rudolph would like to go in with you."

"Oh, I don't go to de shows! I'm too old-fashioned. You won't feel so tired after you ride in de air a ways. It's a nice clear night, an' it ain't cold. You go an' fix yourself up, Polly, an' I'll wash de dishes an' leave everything nice fur you."

Polly blushed and tossed her bob. "I couldn't let you do that, Mr. Rosicky. I wouldn't think of it."

Rosicky said nothing. He found a bib apron on a nail behind the kitchen door. He slipped it over his head and then took Polly by her two elbows and pushed her gently toward the door of her own room. "I washed up de kitchen many times for my wife, when de babies was sick or somethin'. You go an' make yourself look nice. I like you to look prettier'n any of dem town girls when you go in. De young folks must have some fun, an' I'm goin' to look out fur you, Polly."

That kind, reassuring grip on her elbows, the old man's funny bright eyes, made Polly want to drop her head on his shoulder for a second. She restrained herself, but she lingered in his grasp at the door of her room, murmuring tearfully: "You always lived in the city when you were young, didn't you? Don't you ever get lonesome out here?"

As she turned round to him, her hand fell naturally into his, and he stood holding it and smiling into her face with his peculiar, knowing, indulgent smile without a shadow of reproach in it. "Dem big cities is all right fur de rich, but dey is terrible hard fur de poor."

"I don't know. Sometimes I think I'd like to take a chance. You lived in New York, didn't you?"

"An' London. Da's bigger still. I learned my trade dere. Here's Rudolph comin', you better hurry."

"Will you tell me about London sometime?"

"Maybe. Only I ain't no talker, Polly. Run an' dress yourself up."

The bedroom door closed behind her, and Rudolph came in from the outside, looking anxious. He had seen the car and was sorry any of his family should come just then. Supper hadn't been a very pleasant occasion. Halting in the doorway, he saw his father in a kitchen apron, carrying dishes to the sink. He flushed crimson and something flashed in his eye. Rosicky held up a warning finger.

"I brought de car over fur you an' Polly to go to de picture show, an' I made her let me finish here so you won't be late. You go put on a clean shirt, quick!"

"But don't the boys want the car, father?"

"Not tonight dey don't." Rosicky fumbled under his apron and found his pants pocket. He took out a silver dollar and said in a hurried whisper: "You go an' buy dat girl some ice cream an' candy tonight, like you was courtin'. She's awful good friends wid me."

Rudolph was very short of cash, but he took the money as if it hurt him. There had been a crop failure all over the country. He had more than once been sorry he'd married this year.

In a few minutes the young people came out, looking clean and a little stiff. Rosicky hurried them off, and then he took his own time with the dishes. He scoured the pots and pans and put away the milk and swept the kitchen. He put some coal in the stove and shut off the draughts, so the place would be warm for them when they got home late at night. Then he sat down and had a pipe and listened to the clock tick.

Generally speaking, marrying an American girl was certainly a risk. A Czech should marry a Czech. It was lucky that Polly was the daughter of a poor widow woman; Rudolph was proud, and if she had a prosperous family to throw up at him, they could never make it go. Polly was one of four sisters, and they all worked; one was book-keeper in the bank, one taught music, and Polly and her younger sister had been clerks, like Miss Pearl. All four of them were musical, had pretty voices, and sang in the Methodist choir, which the eldest sister directed.

Polly missed the sociability of a store position. She missed the choir, and the company of her sisters. She didn't dislike housework, but she disliked so much of it. Rosicky was a little anxious about this pair. He was afraid Polly would grow so discontented that Rudy would quit the farm and take a factory job in Omaha. He had worked for a winter up there, two years ago, to get money to marry on. He had done very well, and they would always take him back at the stockyards. But to Rosicky that meant the end of everything for his son. To be a landless man was to be a wage-earner, a slave, all your life; to have nothing, to be nothing.

Rosicky thought he would come over and do a little carpentering for Polly after the New Year. He guessed she needed jollying. Rudolph was a serious sort of chap, serious in love and serious about his work.

Rosicky shook out his pipe and walked home across the fields. Ahead of him the lamplight shone from his kitchen windows. Suppose he were still in a tailor shop on Vesey Street, with a bunch of pale, narrow-chested sons working on machines, all coming home tired and sullen to eat supper in a kitchen that was a parlour also; with another crowded, angry family quarrelling just across the dumb-waiter shaft, and squeaking pulleys at the windows where dirty washings hung on dirty lines above a court full of old brooms and mops and ash-cans. . . .

He stopped by the windmill to look up at the frosty winter stars and draw a long breath before he went inside. That kitchen with the shining windows was dear to him; but the sleeping fields and bright stars and the noble darkness were dearer still.

V

On the day before Christmas the weather set in very cold; no snow, but a bitter, biting wind that whistled and sang over the flat land and lashed one's face like fine wires. There was baking going on in the Rosicky kitchen all day, and Rosicky sat inside, making over a coat that Albert had outgrown into an overcoat for John. Mary had a big red geranium in bloom for Christmas, and a row of Jerusalem cherry trees, full of berries. It was the first year she had ever grown these; Doctor Ed brought her the seeds from Omaha when he went to some medical convention. They reminded Rosicky of plants he had seen in England; and all afternoon, as he stitched, he sat thinking about those two years in London, which his mind usually shrank from even after all this while.

He was a lad of eighteen when he dropped down into London, with no money and no connexions except the address of a cousin who was supposed to be working at a confectioner's. When he went to the pastry shop, however, he found that the cousin had gone to America. Anton tramped the streets for several days, sleeping in doorways and on the Embankment, until he was in utter despair. He knew no English, and the sound of the strange language all about him confused him. By chance he met a poor German tailor who had learned his trade in Vienna, and could speak a little Czech. This tailor, Lifschnitz, kept a repair shop in a Cheapside basement, underneath a cobbler. He didn't much need an apprentice, but he was sorry for the boy and took him in for no wages but his keep and what he could pick up. The pickings were supposed to be coppers given you when you took work home to a customer. But most of the customers called for their clothes themselves,

and the coppers that came Anton's way were very few. He had, however, a place to sleep. The tailor's family lived upstairs in three rooms; a kitchen, a bedroom, where Lifschnitz and his wife and five children slept, and a living-room. Two corners of this living-room were curtained off for lodgers; in one Rosicky slept on an old horsehair sofa, with a feather quilt to wrap himself in. The other corner was rented to a wretched, dirty boy, who was studying the violin. He actually practised there. Rosicky was dirty, too. There was no way to be anything else. Mrs. Lifschnitz got the water she cooked and washed with from a pump in a brick court, four flights down. There were bugs in the place, and multitudes of fleas, though the poor woman did the best she could. Rosicky knew she often went empty to give another potato or a spoonful of drippings to the two hungry, sad-eyed boys who lodged with her. He used to think he would never get out of there, never get a clean shirt to his back again. What would he do, he wondered, when his clothes actually dropped to pieces and the worn cloth wouldn't hold patches any longer?

It was still early when the old farmer put aside his sewing and his recollections. The sky had been a dark grey all day, with not a gleam of sun, and the light failed at four o'clock. He went to shave and change his shirt while the turkey was roasting. Rudolph and Polly were coming over for supper.

After supper they sat round in the kitchen, and the younger boys were saying how sorry they were it hadn't snowed. Everybody was sorry. They wanted a deep snow that would lie long and keep the wheat warm, and leave the ground soaked when it melted.

"Yes, sir!" Rudolph broke out fiercely; "if we have another dry year like last year, there's going to be hard times in this country."

Rosicky filled his pipe. "You boys don't know what hard times is. You don't owe nobody, you got plenty to eat an' keep warm, an' plenty water to keep clean. When you got them, you can't have it very hard."

Rudolph frowned, opened and shut his big right hand, and dropped it clenched upon his knee. "I've got to have a good deal more than that, Father, or I'll quit this farming gamble. I can always make good wages railroading or at the packing house, and be sure of my money."

"Maybe so," his father answered dryly.

Mary, who had just come in from the pantry and was wiping her hands on the roller towel, thought Rudy and his father were getting too serious. She brought her darning-basket and sat down in the middle of the group.

"I ain't much afraid of hard times, Rudy," she said heartily. "We've had a plenty, but we've always come through. Your father wouldn't never take nothing very hard, not even hard times. I got a mind to tell you a story on him. Maybe you boys can't hardly remember the year we had that terrible hot wind, that burned everything up on the Fourth of July? All the corn an' the gardens. An' that was in the days when we didn't have alfalfa yet,—I guess it wasn't invented.

"Well, that very day your father was out cultivatin' corn, and I was here in the kitchen makin' plum preserves. We had bushels of plums that year. I noticed it was terrible hot, but it's always hot in the kitchen when you're preservin', an' I was too busy with my plums to mind. Anton come in from the field about three o'clock, an' I asked him what was the matter.

"'Nothin',' he says, 'but it's pretty hot, an' I think I won't work no more today.' He stood round for a few minutes, an' then he says: 'Ain't you near through? I want you should git up a nice supper for us tonight. It's Fourth of July.'

"I told him to git along, that I was right in the middle of preservin', but the plums would taste good on hot biscuit. 'I'm goin' to have fried chicken, too,' he says, and he went off an' killed a couple. You three oldest boys was little fellers, playin' round outside, real hot an' sweaty, an' your father took you to the horse tank down by the windmill an' took off your clothes an' put you in. Them two box-elder trees was little then, but they made shade over the tank. Then he took off all his own clothes, an' got in with you. While he was playin' in the water with you, the Methodist preacher drove into our place to say how all the neighbours was goin' to meet at the schoolhouse that night, to pray for rain. He drove right to the windmill, of course, and there was your father and you three with no clothes on. I was in the kitchen door, an' I had to laugh, for the preacher acted like he ain't never seen a naked man before. He surely was embarrassed, an' your father couldn't git to his clothes; they was all hangin' up on the windmill to let the sweat dry out of 'em. So he laid in the tank where he was, an' put one of you boys on top of him to cover him up a little, an' talked to the preacher.

"When you got through playin' in the water, he put clean clothes on you and a clean shirt on himself, and by that time I'd begun to get supper. He says: 'It's too hot in here to eat comfortable. Let's have a picnic in the orchard. We'll eat our supper behind the mulberry hedge, under them linden trees.'

"So he carried our supper down, an' a bottle of my wild-grape wine, an' everything tasted good, I can tell you. The wind got cooler as the sun was goin' down, and it turned out pleasant, only I noticed how the leaves was curled up on the linden trees. That made me think, an' I asked your father if that hot wind all day hadn't been terrible hard on the gardens an' the corn.

"'Corn,' he says, 'there ain't no corn.'

"'What you talkin' about?' I said. 'Ain't we got forty acres?'

"'We ain't got an ear,' he says, 'nor nobody else ain't got none. All the corn in this country was cooked by three o'clock today, like you'd roasted it in an oven.'

"'You mean you won't get no crop at all?' I asked him. I couldn't believe it, after he'd worked so hard.

"'No crop this year,' he says. 'That's why we're havin' a picnic. We might as well enjoy what we got.'

"An' that's how your father behaved, when all the neighbours was so discouraged they couldn't look you in the face. An' we enjoyed ourselves that year, poor as we was, an' our neighbours wasn't a bit better off for bein' miserable. Some of 'em grieved till they got poor digestions and couldn't relish what they did have."

The younger boys said they thought their father had the best of it. But Rudolph was thinking that, all the same, the neighbours had managed to get ahead more, in the fifteen years since that time. There must be something wrong about his father's way of doing things. He wished he knew what was going on in the back of Polly's mind. He knew she liked his father, but he knew, too, that she was afraid of something. When his mother sent over coffee-cake or prune tarts or a loaf of fresh bread, Polly seemed to regard them with a certain suspicion. When she observed to him that his brothers had nice manners, her tone implied that it was remarkable they should have. With his mother she was still stiff and on her guard. Mary's hearty frankness and gusts of good humour irritated her. Polly was afraid of being unusual or conspicuous in any way, of being "ordinary," as she said!

When Mary had finished her story, Rosicky laid aside his pipe.

"You boys like me to tell you about some of dem hard times I been through in London?" Warmly encouraged, he sat rubbing his forehead along the deep creases. It was bothersome to tell a long story in English (he nearly always talked to the boys in Czech), but he wanted Polly to hear this one.

"Well, you know about dat tailor shop I worked in in London? I had one Christmas dere I ain't never forgot. Times was awful bad before Christmas; de boss ain't got much work, an' have it awful hard to pay his rent. It ain't so much fun, bein' poor in a big city like London, I'll say! All de windows is full of good t'ings to eat, an' all de push-carts in de streets is full, an' you smell 'em all de time, an' you ain't got no money,—not a damn bit. I didn't mind de cold so much, though I didn't have no overcoat, chust a short jacket I'd out-growed so it wouldn't meet on me, an' my hands was chapped raw. But I always had a good appe-tite, like you all know, an' de sight of dem pork pies in de windows was awful fur me!

"Day before Christmas was terrible foggy dat year, an' dat fog gits into your bones and makes you all damp like. Mrs. Lifschnitz didn't give us nothin' but a little bread an' drippin' for supper, because she was savin' to try for to give us a good dinner on Christmas Day. After supper de boss say I can go an' enjoy myself, so I went into de streets to listen to de Christmas singers. Dey sing old songs an' make very nice music, an' I run round after dem a good ways, till I got awful hungry. I t'ink maybe if I go home, I can sleep till mornin' an' forgit my belly.

"I went into my corner real quiet, and roll up in my fedder quilt. But I ain't got my head down, till I smell somet'ing good. Seem like it git stronger an' stronger, an' I can't git to sleep noway. I can't understand dat smell. Dere was a gas light in a hall across de court, dat always shine in at my window a little. I got up an' look round. I got a little wooden box in my corner fur a stool, 'cause I ain't got no chair. I picks up dat box, and under it dere is a roast goose on a platter! I can't believe my eyes. I carry it to de window where de light comes in, an' touch it and smell it to find out, an' den I taste it to be sure. I say, I will eat chust one little bite of dat goose, so I can go to sleep, and tomorrow I won't eat none at all. But I tell you, boys, when I stop, one half of dat goose was gone!"

The narrator bowed his head, and the boys shouted. But little Josephine slipped behind his chair and kissed him on the neck beneath his ear.

"Poor little Papa, I don't want him to be hun-gry!"

"Da's long ago, child. I ain't never been hungry since I had your mudder to cook fur me."

"Go on and tell us the rest, please," said Polly.

"Well, when I come to realize what I done, of course, I felt terrible. I felt better in de stomach, but very bad in de heart. I set on my bed wid dat platter on my knees, an' it all come to me; how hard dat poor woman save to buy dat goose, and how she get some neighbour to cook it dat got more fire, an' how she put it in my corner to keep it away from dem hungry children. Dey was an old carpet hung up to shut my corner off, an' de children wasn't allowed to go in dere. An' I know she put it in my corner because she trust me more'n she did de violin boy. I can't stand it to face her after I spoil de Christmas. So I put on my shoes and go out into de city. I tell myself I better throw myself in de river; but I guess I ain't dat kind of a boy.

"It was after twelve o'clock, an' terrible cold, an' I start out to walk about London all night. I walk along de river awhile, but dey was lots of drunks all along; men, and women too. I chust move along to keep away from the police. I git onto de Strand, an' den over to New Oxford Street, where dere was a big German restaurant on de ground floor, wid big windows all fixed up fine, an' I could see de people havin' parties inside. While I was lookin' in, two men and two ladies come out, laughin' and talkin' and feelin' happy about all dey been eatin' an' drinkin', and dey was speakin' Czech,—not like de Austrians, but like de home folks talk it.

"I guess I went crazy, an' I done what I ain't never done before nor since. I went right up to dem gay people an' begun to beg dem: 'Fellow countrymen, for God's sake give me money enough to buy a goose!'

"Dey laugh, of course, but de ladies speak awful kind to me, an' dey take me back into de res-taurant and give me hot coffee and cakes, an' make me tell all about how I happened to come to London, an' what I was doin' dere. Dey take my name and where I work down on paper, an' both of dem ladies give me ten shillings.

"De big market at Covent Garden ain't very far away, an' by dat time it was open. I go dere an' buy a big goose an' some pork pies, an' potatoes and onions, an' cakes an' oranges fur de children, —all I could carry! When I git home, everybody is still asleep. I pile all I bought on de kitchen table, an' go in an' lay down on my bed, an' I ain't waken up till I hear dat woman scream when she come out into her kitchen. My goodness, but she was surprise! She laugh an' cry at de same time, an' hug me and waken all de children. She ain't stop fur no breakfast; she git de Christmas dinner ready dat morning, and we all sit down an' eat all we can hold. I ain't never seen dat violin boy have all he can hold before.

"Two three days after dat, de two men come to hunt me up, an' dey ask my boss, and he give me a good report an' tell dem I was a steady boy all right. One of dem Bohemians was very smart an' run a Bohemian newspaper in New York, an' de odder was a rich man, in de importing business, an' dey been travelling togedder. Dey told me how t'ings was easier in New York, an' offered to pay my passage when dey was goin' home soon on a boat. My boss say to me: 'You go. You ain't got no chance here, an' I like to see you git ahead, fur you always been a good boy to my woman, and fur dat fine Christmas dinner you give us all.' An' da's how I got to New York."

That night when Rudolph and Polly, arm in arm, were running home across the fields with the bitter wind at their backs, his heart leaped for joy when she said she thought they might have his family come over for supper on New Year's Eve. "Let's get up a nice supper, and not let your mother help at all; make her be company for once."

"That would be lovely of you, Polly," he said humbly. He was a very simple, modest boy, and he, too, felt vaguely that Polly and her sisters were more experienced and worldly than his people.

VI

The winter turned out badly for farmers. It was bitterly cold, and after the first light snows before Christmas there was no snow at all,—and no rain. March was as bitter as February. On those days when the wind fairly punished the country, Rosicky sat by his window. In the fall he and the boys had put in a big wheat planting, and now the seed had frozen in the ground. All that land would have to be ploughed up and planted over again, planted in corn. It had happened before, but he was younger then, and he never worried about what had to be. He was sure of himself and of Mary; he knew they could bear what they had to bear, that they would always pull through some-how. But he was not so sure about the young ones,

and he felt troubled because Rudolph and Polly were having such a hard start.

Sitting beside his flowering window while the panes rattled and the wind blew in under the door, Rosicky gave himself to reflection as he had not done since those Sundays in the loft of the furniture-factory in New York, long ago. Then he was trying to find what he wanted in life for himself; now he was trying to find what he wanted for his boys, and why it was he so hungered to feel sure they would be here, working this very land, after he was gone.

They would have to work hard on the farm, and probably they would never do much more than make a living. But if he could think of them as staying here on the land, he wouldn't have to fear any great unkindness for them. Hardships, certainly; it was a hardship to have the wheat freeze in the ground when seed was so high; and to have to sell your stock because you had no feed. But there would be other years when everything came along right, and you caught up. And what you had was your own. You didn't have to choose between bosses and strikers, and go wrong either way. You didn't have to do with dishonest and cruel people. They were the only things in his experience he had found terrifying and horrible; the look in the eyes of a dishonest and crafty man, of a scheming and rapacious woman.

In the country, if you had a mean neighbour, you could keep off his land and make him keep off yours. But in the city, all the foulness and misery and brutality of your neighbours was part of your life. The worst things he had come upon in his journey through the world were human,—depraved and poisonous specimens of man. To this day he could recall certain terrible faces in the London streets. There were mean people everywhere, to be sure, even in their own country town here. But they weren't tempered, hardened, sharpened, like the treacherous people in cities who live by grinding or cheating or poisoning their fellow-men. He had helped to bury two of his fellow-workmen in the tailoring trade, and he was distrustful of the organized industries that see one out of the world in big cities. Here, if you were sick, you had Doctor Ed to look after you; and if you died, fat Mr. Haycock, the kindest man in the world, buried you.

It seemed to Rosicky that for good, honest boys like his, the worst they could do on the farm was better than the best they would be likely to do in the city. If he'd had a mean boy, now, one who was crooked and sharp and tried to put anything over on his brothers, then town would be the place for him. But he had no such boy. As for Rudolph, the discontented one, he would give the shirt off his back to anyone who touched his heart. What Rosicky really hoped for his boys was that they could get through the world without ever knowing much about the cruelty of human beings. "Their mother an' me ain't prepared them for that," he sometimes said to himself.

These thoughts brought him back to a grateful consideration of his own case. What an escape he had had, to be sure! He, too, in his time, had had to take money for repair work from the hand of a hungry child who let it go so wistfully; because it was money due his boss. And now, in all these years, he had never had to take a cent from anyone in bitter need,—never had to look at the face of a woman become like a wolf's from struggle and famine. When he thought of these things, Rosicky would put on his cap and jacket and slip down to the barn and give his work-horses a little extra oats, letting them eat it out of his hand in their slobbery fashion. It was his way of expressing what he felt, and made him chuckle with pleasure.

The spring came warm, with blue skies,—but dry, dry as a bone. The boys began ploughing up the wheat-fields to plant them over in corn. Rosicky would stand at the fence corner and watch them, and the earth was so dry it blew up in clouds of brown dust that hid the horses and the sulky plough and the driver. It was a bad outlook.

The big alfalfa-field that lay between the home place and Rudolph's came up green, but Rosicky was worried because during that open windy winter a great many Russian thistle plants had blown in there and lodged. He kept asking the boys to rake them out; he was afraid that their seed would root and "take the alfalfa." Rudolph said that was nonsense. The boys were working so hard planting corn, their father felt he couldn't insist about the thistles, but he set great store by that big alfalfa field. It was a feed you could depend on,—and there was some deeper reason, vague, but strong. The peculiar green of that clover woke early memories in old Rosicky, went back to something in his childhood in the old world. When he was a little boy, he had played in fields of that strong blue-green colour.

One morning, when Rudolph had gone to town in the car, leaving a work-team idle in his barn, Rosicky went over to his son's place, put the horses to the buggy rake, and set about quietly raking up those thistles. He behaved with guilty caution, and rather enjoyed stealing a march on Doctor Ed, who was just then taking his first vacation in seven years of practice and was attending a clinic in Chicago. Rosicky got the thistles raked up, but did not stop to burn them. That would take some time, and his breath was pretty short, so he thought he had better get the horses back to the barn.

He got them into the barn and to their stalls, but the pain had come on so sharp in his chest that he didn't try to take the harness off. He started for the house, bending lower with every step. The cramp in his chest was shutting him up like a jack-knife. When he reached the windmill, he swayed and caught at the ladder. He saw Polly coming down the hill, running with the swiftness of a slim greyhound. In a flash she had her shoulder under his armpit.

"Lean on me, Father, hard! Don't be afraid. We can get to the house all right."

Somehow they did, though Rosicky became blind with pain; he could keep on his legs, but he couldn't steer his course. The next thing he was conscious of was lying on Polly's bed, and Polly bending over him wringing out bath towels in hot water and putting them on his chest. She stopped only to throw coal into the stove, and she kept the tea-kettle and the black pot going. She put these hot applications on him for nearly an hour, she told him afterwards, and all that time he was drawn up stiff and blue, with the sweat pouring off him.

As the pain gradually loosed its grip, the stiffness went out of his jaws, the black circles round his eyes disappeared, and a little of his natural colour came back. When his daughter-in-law buttoned his shirt over his chest at last, he sighed.

"Da's fine, de way I feel now, Polly. It was a awful bad spell, an' I was so sorry it all come on you like it did."

Polly was flushed and excited. "Is the pain really gone? Can I leave you long enough to telephone over to your place?"

Rosicky's eyelids fluttered. "Don't telephone, Polly. It ain't no use to scare my wife. It's nice and quiet here, an' if I ain't too much trouble to you, just let me lay still till I feel like myself. I ain't got no pain now. It's nice here."

Polly bent over him and wiped the moisture from his face. "Oh, I'm so glad it's over!" she broke out impulsively. "It just broke my heart to see you suffer so, Father."

Rosicky motioned her to sit down on the chair

where the tea-kettle had been, and looked up at her with that lively affectionate gleam in his eyes. "You was awful good to me, I won't ever forgit dat. I hate it to be sick on you like dis. Down at de barn I say to myself, dat young girl ain't had much experience in sickness, I don't want to scare her, an' maybe she's got a baby comin' or some-t'ing."

Polly took his hand. He was looking at her so intently and affectionately and confidingly; his eyes seemed to caress her face, to regard it with plea-sure. She frowned with her funny streaks of eye-brows, and then smiled back at him.

"I guess maybe there is something of that kind going to happen. But I haven't told anyone yet, not my mother or Rudolph. You'll be the first to know."

His hand pressed hers. She noticed that it was warm again. The twinkle in his yellow-brown eyes seemed to come nearer.

"I like mighty well to see dat little child, Polly," was all he said. Then he closed his eyes and lay half-smiling. But Polly sat still, thinking hard. She had a sudden feeling that nobody in the world, not her mother, not Rudolph, or anyone, really loved her as much as old Rosicky did. It perplexed her. She sat frowning and trying to puzzle it out. It was as if Rosicky had a special gift for loving people, something that was like an ear for music or an eye for colour. It was quiet, unobtrusive; it was merely there. You saw it in his eyes,—perhaps that was why they were merry. You felt it in his hands, too. After he dropped off to sleep, she sat holding his warm, broad, flexible brown hand. She had never seen another in the least like it. She wondered if it wasn't a kind of gypsy hand, it was so alive and quick and light in its communications, —very strange in a farmer. Nearly all the farmers she knew had huge lumps of fists, like mauls, or they were knotty and bony and uncomfortable-looking, with stiff fingers. But Rosicky's hand was like quicksilver, flexible, muscular, about the colour of a pale cigar, with deep, deep creases across the palm. It wasn't nervous, it wasn't a stupid lump; it was a warm brown human hand, with some cleverness in it, a great deal of generosity, and something else which Polly could only call "gypsy-like,"—something nimble and lively and sure, in the way that animals are.

Polly remembered that hour long afterward; it had been like an awakening to her. It seemed to her that she had never learned so much about life from anything as from old Rosicky's hand. It

brought her to herself; it communicated some direct and untranslatable message.

When she heard Rudolph coming in the car, she ran out to meet him.

"Oh, Rudy, your father's been awful sick! He raked up those thistles he's been worrying about, and afterwards he could hardly get to the house. He suffered so I was afraid he was going to die."

Rudolph jumped to the ground. "Where is he now?"

"On the bed. He's asleep. I was terribly scared, because, you know, I'm so fond of your father." She slipped her arm through his and they went into the house. That afternoon they took Rosicky home and put him to bed, though he protested that he was quite well again.

The next morning he got up and dressed and sat down to breakfast with his family. He told Mary that his coffee tasted better than usual to him, and he warned the boys not to bear any tales to Doctor Ed when he got home. After breakfast he sat down by his window to do some patching and asked Mary to thread several needles for him before she went to feed her chickens,—her eyes were better than his, and her hands steadier. He lit his pipe and took up John's overalls. Mary had been watching him anxiously all morning, and as she went out of the door with her bucket of scraps, she saw that he was smiling. He was thinking, in-deed, about Polly, and how he might never have known what a tender heart she had if he hadn't got sick over there. Girls nowadays didn't wear their heart on their sleeve. But now he knew Polly would make a fine woman after the foolishness wore off. Either a woman had that sweetness at her heart or she hadn't. You couldn't always tell by the look of them; but if they had that, everything came out right in the end.

After he had taken a few stitches, the cramp be-gan in his chest, like yesterday. He put his pipe cautiously down on the window-sill and bent over to ease the pull. No use,—he had better try to get to his bed if he could. He rose and groped his way across the familiar floor, which was rising and falling like the deck of a ship. At the door he fell. When Mary came in, she found him lying there, and the moment she touched him she knew that he was gone.

Doctor Ed was away when Rosicky died, and for the first few weeks after he got home he was hard driven. Every day he said to himself that he must get out to see the family that had lost their father.

One soft, warm moonlight night in early summer he started for the farm. His mind was on other things, and not until his road ran by the graveyard did he realize that Rosicky wasn't over there on the hill where the red lamplight shone, but here, in the moonlight. He stopped his car, shut off the engine, and sat there for a while.

A sudden hush had fallen on his soul. Everything here seemed strangely moving and significant, though signifying what, he did not know. Close by the wire fence stood Rosicky's mowing-machine, where one of the boys had been cutting hay that afternoon; his own work-horses had been going up and down there. The new-cut hay perfumed all the night air. The moonlight silvered the long, billowy grass that grew over the graves and hid the fence; the few little evergreens stood out black in it, like shadows in a pool. The sky was very blue and soft, the stars rather faint because the moon was full.

For the first time it struck Doctor Ed that this was really a beautiful graveyard. He thought of city cemeteries; acres of shrubbery and heavy stone, so arranged and lonely and unlike anything in the living world. Cities of the dead, indeed; cities of the forgotten, of the "put away." But this was open and free, this little square of long grass which the wind for ever stirred. Nothing but the sky overhead, and the many-coloured fields running on until they met that sky. The horses worked here in summer; the neighbours passed on their way to town; and over yonder, in the cornfield, Rosicky's own cattle would be eating fodder as winter came on. Nothing could be more undeathlike than this place; nothing could be more right for a man who had helped to do the work of great cities and had always longed for the open country and had got to it at last. Rosicky's life seemed to him complete and beautiful.

THOMAS WOLFE (1900–1938)

Until late in his rather short life Thomas Wolfe was convinced that the American dream was less an inheritance from the splendid past than something that lay in the future, yet to be achieved. The twentieth century was to be the century of destiny; and the fact that he had been born in 1900 gave him an inspiriting confidence that his personal destiny was closely interwoven with it—he would be the one to utter, in large fictions, the tremendous secret and to reveal to his generation its essential grandeur of spirit.

Wolfe grew up in Asheville, North Carolina (a mountain town fairly high up in the Smokies), and went to the state university at Chapel Hill. Because of his temperamental orientation toward the future, he was less concerned with ancestry than many other southern writers—Faulkner, for example. For awhile in the thirties, as we shall see, he entertained the heady notion of writing a series of volumes which would encompass a vast amount of American history and regional lore. But he had little

genuine historical sense; he did not feel, as Faulkner and others did, what C. Vann Woodward has called "the burden of Southern history"; the past was not a living force coloring and shaping the present. This is perhaps another way of saying that Wolfe also lacked a tragic sense: he used the word "tragic" frequently, even lavishly, but it had for him a romantic and personal flavor—it denoted private frustration and defeat.

These are by no means intended as denigrations, but simply as sources of identification; and indeed Wolfe's deepening sense of frustration —though compounded at the end by a slackening of faith in America—was caused chiefly by the magnitude of his literary ambition. "Tom Wolfe," Faulkner would say after Wolfe's death, "was trying to say everything, the world plus 'I,' or filtered through 'I' or the effort of 'I' to embrace the world in which he was born and walked a little while and then lay down again."[1]

[1] And when Faulkner was asked to rank the writers of fiction contemporary with him, he replied at once

Wolfe was the youngest of seven children, each of whom, along with the parents, had a distinct role to play in his first and best novel, *Look Homeward, Angel*. Several members of the family (dead before the novel was written) appear under their own names. There is Wolfe's father, W. O., Pennsylvania-born, of Dutch-German descent, who had wandered down to Asheville and settled there, almost by accident, to ply his stonecutter's trade: strong, violent-natured, given to bouts of ferocious drinking, but also oddly pious, with a smothered artistic soul and a capacity for intense affection. There was Grover, a promising child who died at the age of twelve in 1904; and above all Grover's twin brother Ben, a quiet, intense, and perhaps brilliant young man with whom Tom Wolfe had a very intimate bond, and who was working for a local newspaper when he died, just after Tom had gone off to college. His death is the climax of *Look Homeward, Angel*, if that free-flowing work can be said to have a climax; and Tom felt it to be the climax of that part of his life. "The Asheville I knew died for me when Ben died," he would say. Ben's death was a main reason why, upon leaving for graduate study at Harvard in 1920, Tom Wolfe knew (and in the hallucinatory final scene of *Look Homeward, Angel* so tells Ben's ghost) that he would never again return permanently to Asheville. It may also have released something in the younger brother that eventually permitted him to look homeward on Asheville with, or partly with, the eyes of a creative alien.[2]

Among the others in the quite well-to-do but socially aloof and inwardly turbulent Wolfe family, the dominating figure was Wolfe's mother, the former Julia Westfall, whose ancestors (of British stock) had come to the area in the later eighteenth century. No less shrewd and no less talkative, but rather more endearing than Eliza Gant, the character in Wolfe's novel for whom she served as prototype, Julia Wolfe kept the family going, if anyone did. But in 1906, after one of W. O.'s more exhausting alcoholic performances, she bought another house in town, turned it into a boarding house named "The Old Kentucky Home," and moved into it, taking Tom with her. Finally, there was Tom's sister Mabel—Helen in the novel: "almost six feet high: a tall thin girl, with large hands and feet, big-boned, generous features, behind which the hysteria of constant excitement lurked."

These are characteristically sure strokes of description and characterization (Mabel-Helen is six feet "high" rather than "tall"). For all its surging romanticism and its flights of breathless meditation, *Look Homeward, Angel* comprises as carefully evoked a family portrait as one can find in modern American fiction (outside of fiction, it is rivaled in this regard only by Eugene O'Neill's *Long Day's Journey into Night*). If Wolfe was a romantic, he was also decidedly a realist, concerned all his life to get at the literal truth of experience, in his own phrase, to "get it right." He may best be identified as a poetic realist (not entirely unlike Anderson in this regard); such was implied retrospectively by Scott Fitzgerald, when he remarked that "the more valuable parts of Tom were . . . those moments when his lyricism was best combined with his powers of observation."

The first person to sense those powers was Margaret Roberts (the fictional Mrs. Leonard), who persuaded the Wolfes to send the boy to the school she and her husband opened in 1912, and who nursed him along in his efforts, despite his atrocious handwriting and lack of paragraphing. Wolfe arrived at Chapel Hill in 1916—Pulpit Hill was Wolfe's minimal rebaptizing of the place—better equipped in a literary way than most of his classmates; and it was his literary talent that, by his senior year, made him one of the most imposing figures on campus. Helpless at athletics, socially awkward (except when prowling through the various establishments of the town at night, in search of

---

that Wolfe's name must go at the head of the list: greatness, he said, can only be measured by the extent of the failure, and Wolfe had failed the most because he had attempted the most.

[2] For a discussion of the kind of southern writer who is at once an "insider" and an "outsider," see below, pp. 1696–97.

companionship and copy), Wolfe nonetheless loomed over the campus scene as the influential editor of and contributor to the college paper, *The Tar Heel.*

Thomas Wolfe, in fact, passed a far more satisfactory undergraduate career than did Eugene Gant in *Look Homeward, Angel,* and here we observe one of the ways in which Wolfe's portrait of himself as a young would-be artist differed from the actualities of his life. Looking homeward, the writer reshaped those actualities to make them conform to romantic expectations. Thus, where Wolfe had been successful and fairly contented at college, Eugene Gant becomes steadily estranged, feeling within himself some special quality that sets him apart from and above the mediocrities of his classmates and the banalities of the classroom. Similarly, during one of his vacations, Wolfe was much in the company of a young woman some years older than he, Clara Paul, who was staying at his mother's boarding house; the relationship did not develop, but in the novel Laura James (another minimal renaming) yields to Gene's sexual approaches in a haze of retarded wish-fulfillment: "He grew into her young Maenad's body, his heart numbed deliciously against the pressure of her narrow breasts" (whereupon Wolfe soars again into his rhapsodic appeal—"Come up into the hills, O my young love. Return! O lost, and by the wind grieved, ghost, come back again. . . .").

Something *was,* nevertheless, beginning to churn in Wolfe's spirit as he finished at Chapel Hill and went on, with his mother's financial help, to graduate study at Harvard. He was beginning to feel, we may suppose, the way all truly alive young men are alleged to feel in *The Web and the Rock.* "What is it that a young man wants?" the author bursts out, and goes on: "Where is the central source of that wild fury that boils up in him, that goads and drives and lashes him, that explodes his energies and strews his purpose to the wind of a thousand instant and chaotic impulses?" Later in his life, Wolfe would realize that not every gifted and imaginative person was goaded and lashed by a wild fury; but he clung to his personal preference—as he said to Fitzgerald—for novels "that *boil* and *pour*," citing *The Brothers Karamazov* and *Tristram Shandy,* among others. Wolfe himself remained a boiler and a pourer and (as he also told Fitzgerald) a "putter-inner" in fiction, rather than a "leaver-outer," like Flaubert and Fitzgerald.

Wolfe chose an odd area of study at Harvard —George Pierce Baker's celebrated course in drama and playwriting, the "47 Workshop" as it was familiarly known; Eugene O'Neill and Edward Sheldon had been among its more notable members. Such dramatic sense as Wolfe had was always overwhelmed by his creative exuberance. His own best production for Baker was a play originally called *Niggertown* (later softened to the ironic *Welcome to Our City*), dealing—via the seduction of a black girl by a young white and the subsequent murder of the girl's father—with what Wolfe called "the sore spot in our life here in the South—the forbidden fruit of conversation and exposure." This was Wolfe both at his most southern and his most emancipated; but the play ran for four hours and involved seven changes of set and thirty characters plus a mob. "Some day," Wolfe wrote Baker confidently, "I'm going to write a play with fifty, eighty, a hundred people—a whole town, a whole race, a whole epoch—for my soul's ease and comfort." He would find that writing about a whole race required a different and much more expansive medium.[3]

Wolfe, by this time, was extremely well acquainted with the medium in which he might most suitably test himself—that of the novel. In addition to having surveyed the entire range of English poetry, and a good deal of drama, criticism, and intellectual history, he had taken courses in eighteenth- and nineteenth-century English fiction. In *The Web and the Rock* much space is given to a sort of Homeric catalogue of writers and writings the young hero had delved into. But the novelists about whom he grew most enthusiastic were ones he read

---

[3] It should be said, however, that Thornton Wilder's *The Skin of Our Teeth* (see p. 2322) fulfills one part of Wolfe's playwriting ambition, and Tennessee Williams' *Camino Real* another.

on his own: Dostoevski and Joyce, Dickens and Laurence Sterne. As to American literature, Wolfe took an allegedly dull course in the subject at Harvard, which left no mark. Only after the critics of *Look Homeward, Angel* made out the strong presences in that novel of Melville and Whitman was Wolfe led to read them. He spoke later of Whitman as being of the same stature as Homer; but it was Melville's *Moby-Dick* that was to become, along with Joyce's *Ulysses*, a sort of Bible.

In the winter of 1924 Wolfe accepted a teaching job, in writing, at New York University. Self-centered though he was, he became, according to his students, an unforgettable teacher, given to writing a commentary rather longer than the piece being criticized. But the following fall, he interrupted his university work for a trip to Europe, an experience faithfully recorded in *Of Time and the River*, including a curious *ménage à quatre* in Paris with two American girls and a former college friend who turned out to be a homosexual. It was on the voyage back, in August, 1926, that he met the woman to whom he would dedicate *Look Homeward, Angel*, and who would be the central human force in his life during the composition of that book.

She was Aline Bernstein, a graduate of Hunter College, the wife of a steady-going broker and mother of two children, and, at the same time, a highly regarded designer of sets and costumes for the Broadway theater. She was also eighteen years older than Wolfe, which was only somewhat above average in the pattern of Wolfe's erotic relationships, Wolfe following the European, rather than the American, tradition, in choosing older women to conduct his sexual education. The pattern may possibly be traced back to Julia Wolfe's possessiveness in keeping Tom in long hair, and in her bed in the Asheville rooming house, till he was nine years old. There had been, in any event, a succession of accommodating landladies of uncertain years, and bountiful widows here and abroad, to look after Wolfe's various interests.

Aline Bernstein was, of course, a very different figure from any of these. Her ancestry was Jewish and mixed European; and it showed itself in her gentleness and vivacity, her slightly exotic charm, her quickness of perception, her capacity to give of her whole nature. She mothered Wolfe, fed him (superbly), kept him in funds, including money for a trip to Europe; listened to him, encouraged him, brought him into the New York dramatic and literary circles, and quarreled with him.

It was a tempestuous affair, from start to finish, with idyllic moments and violent struggles. Aline brought to the surface some of Wolfe's most convulsive contradictions—his stupendous need for love and his remarkable fund of tenderness; his irrepressible cruelty; his need of direction and smoldering hatred of anyone who supplied the direction; his ambivalence toward Jews. As to the latter, when Wolfe, in his first months at New York University, wrote a friend: "I teach! I teach! Jews! Jews!" he may have intended to express excitement over the stimulating qualities of his Jewish students. But it does not quite come through that way when transferred to the pages of *Of Time and the River*, where Gant recoils from the "shrieking, shouting tides of dark amber Jewish flesh" in his classrooms. In the thirties, Wolfe was slow to realize, if he ever did fully realize, the hideous plight of the Jews in his beloved Germany—and this despite the severe beating he took from a gang of proto-Nazi toughs in a Munich beerhall during the Oktoberfest in 1927. Yet he was fascinated by Jewishness and helplessly drawn to it. So he alternately taunted and caressed Aline Bernstein as "my dear Jew," and loved and hated her for her racial origins.

This explosion of contradictory feelings, however devastating for Aline, seems to have been the source of the immense effort which, by mid-1927, had produced more than 350,000 words of a novel then called *O Lost*. When the work faltered the following year, Wolfe took out his frustrations on the available Mrs. Bernstein. Early in 1929, Wolfe came into the orbit of Maxwell Perkins, the distinguished editor at Scribner's; and as he worked under Perkins' reassuring guidance, the relationship with Aline

Bernstein once more became (relatively) calm and happy. It was only after the novel was published to no small acclaim that Wolfe turned against his mistress with what developed into a sort of obsessive savagery. The relationship did drag on a little longer, but it had, in effect, died by the time the novel dedicated to her appeared. In the wake of Wolfe's subsequent break with Perkins, Aline Bernstein would reflect upon Wolfe's "advancement from one thing to another in himself, the mighty stride of his changes, and his cruel and relentless disentanglement from all that bound him."

The role of Wolfe's principal editors—Maxwell Perkins at Scribner's, and later Edward Aswell at Harper's—points up several perplexing questions about Wolfe's literary career, and, by extension, about certain phenomena in modern American literature generally. Surveying the evidence, one wonders, to begin with, exactly who is responsible for each of Wolfe's four "novels," an uncertainty that only deepens as book follows book.[4] Perkins' work on *Look Homeward, Angel* consisted chiefly in persuading Wolfe to cut back the manuscript from eleven hundred pages to about eight hundred. This was done by deleting separate chunks, including several of Eugene's comical fantasies of high heroism (of the sort, presumably, that freshen the pages of *The Web and the Rock*), and parodies of literary styles. The book could have stood some of those lighter touches. But in 1934, with the manuscript of what would be *Of Time and the River*, Perkins became very nearly a collaborator, so much so that Wolfe, who dedicated the book to him, remarked that his editor could claim to have himself written at least one novel. The evolution of *Of Time and the River* between 1930 and 1935 was a process complicated and confused almost beyond description, and Perkins

[4] For much of the information in this discussion of Wolfe and his editors, we are indebted to John Halberstadt and to *The Window of Memory: The Literary Career of Thomas Wolfe* (1962; slightly revised 1968), by Richard S. Kennedy, an exemplary work of judicious scholarship.

undoubtedly had a formidable editorial challenge. He was, certainly, one of the great editors; but he seems to have been motivated by a desire to hurry publication and to squeeze Wolfe's huge typescript into something resembling a conventional and publicly acceptable novel, no less than to bring to fulfillment Wolfe's own creative aims.

Late in 1937 Wolfe, enraged by the report that he was unable to write without the help of Perkins, broke with Scribner's and moved over to Harper's. That, anyhow, is one version of the shift. According to another version, the people at Scribner's were much offended because Wolfe, having landed the firm in a suit for libel (because of a character he had perhaps drawn too closely from real life), failed to appear in court on the day of the trial. Scribner's may have been willing to let Wolfe go, or possibly he guiltily suspected they were. In any event, during the remaining months of his life Wolfe showered Harper's with gobbets of manuscript and enormous outlines of the big novel to come, receiving in return telegrams of praise and encouragement from his new editor, Edward Aswell. But when Wolfe died in mid-September, 1938 (of tuberculosis of the brain), Aswell found on his hands a huge chaotic bundle of writing, in which the meandering hero appeared under seven different names, and his mistress under four separate first names and several different married names.

The whole of this jumble was to be called *The Web and the Rock*, and into it Wolfe had planned to pour not only his personal career from 1925 (where, effectively, *Of Time and the River* had left off) to 1937, but also many bits and pieces written along the way over the years —reminiscences, anecdotes, parodies, period pieces, sections dropped from previous novels, items published as short stories. Of the four large original parts, Aswell detached the first (ancestral explorations), held back the last for a later volume, and put together a book consisting of the second and third parts: the love affair between George Webber and Esther Jack (that is, Wolfe and Aline Bernstein), and Webber's later wanderings in Europe, to the moment he is roughed up in the Munich beer-hall. The stitching required Aswell to revise some of Wolfe's prose, and to add some paragraphs of his own. *The Web and the Rock*, as it appeared in 1939, is a combination of Wolfe's writing and Aswell's editorial decisions —the latter taken painfully over eight months of extremely hard work.

With what was left over, Aswell constructed the work called *You Can't Go Home Again*. The phrase was Wolfe's and derived from his feelings about returning to Asheville in the summer of 1937; but it was intended as the title of the final portion of the original *Web and the Rock*. The idea of cutting off that material and making it into another book was entirely Aswell's—though to be sure, had Wolfe lived, he might have agreed to it. But in the present case, Aswell revised quite heavily, seeking in particular to bring Wolfe's earlier style— as it showed in sections written up to eight years before—in line with the somewhat more sober style of the last couple of years of his life. Aswell also added a fair amount of his own prose, imitating as best he might (on the whole, successfully) Wolfe's literary manner.

In the face of all this—and our account is in fact much foreshortened—one wonders, to repeat, just what it is we are engaged with when we read a novel by Thomas Wolfe. That question is least worrisome with *Look Homeward, Angel*, but the doubts increase with each successive book. The critic concerned mainly with matters of form and structure can content himself with observing the relative sloppiness of the last three books, whatever their source; and many critics have done so. But if we are interested in the biographical or psychic origins of the literary work, what are we to do with Wolfe's fictions? We can exaggerate the case to make the point. Wolfe is usually taken to be the most persistently autobiographical of writers —yet, for example, in the decision to exclude the Esther Jack affair from *Of Time and the River* (where it initially belonged), whose autobiography is at work, Wolfe's or Max Perkins'? Are the emphases palpable in *You Can't Go Home Again* to be traced back to Wolfe's life

experiences or to Aswell's, and if to both, in what degree of mix? These are questions by no means lacking in importance in our day, as the publisher's editor takes an ever more active hand in shaping the author's final product.[5]

There is, further, the question of novelistic form. It can easily be argued that the books from *Of Time and the River* onward (and *Look Homeward, Angel*, too, though less so) suffer from lack of form, if that word is taken in its classical meaning of an action leading from a beginning through a well-placed middle to an end. It was the purpose of both Perkins and Aswell to prod Wolfe's manuscripts into something at least remotely approaching such a form. But it can also be argued that, for better or worse, Wolfe knew what he wanted to do, and it was not exactly what his editors wanted. In novellas like *A Portrait of Bascom Hawke*—published separately and then rather unluckily imbedded in *Of Time and the River* —and *The Web of Earth* (included in the collection *From Death to Morning*), as well as in several shorter pieces, Wolfe had demonstrated that he could command a fine rhythmic structure when he cared to. He was also well acquainted with the most beautifully constructed novels. As he indicated to Scott Fitzgerald, he was quite aware of that latter mode and conscious that *his* vision of fiction was something very different—and with a distinguished ancestry.

Wolfe, in fact, preferred to talk about his

[5] A great deal of cutting and patching was also done by other hands on Theodore Dreiser's manuscripts— though in this case not so much by his editors as by various female associates.

But as to the general point, it may be remarked that in former days, an author's writing, once accepted, was published quickly, with virtually no changes from the manuscript as submitted. On one occasion, according to legend, Henry James, by request, wrote an article for the *Times Literary Supplement* which the editors found perhaps fifty words too long (for the fit of the page). It never occurred to them to make the necessary deletions themselves; instead they fearfully begged James, by messenger, to do the trifling job himself. James did so, after several hours' labor, and sent the article back with the comment: "Yours is a butcher's trade."

"books" rather than his "novels," and often to talk about his *book*, much as Whitman spoke all his life about his one book, the unfolding *Leaves of Grass*. Somewhere amid the enormous debris of Wolfe's published works and unpublished scraps is a single gigantic work of fiction. It might have been an utter catastrophe; but it was what Wolfe wanted to create. Perhaps within Wolfe's egotistic jealousy of Perkins, there also lay the artist's more justifiable depression at having allowed himself to be deflected from his own true course.

Published in 1929, *Look Homeward, Angel* (that title, happily replacing *O Lost*, was taken by Wolfe from Milton's *Lycidas*) is the one among Wolfe's longer writings that continues to meet the challenge of time, though several of his shorter pieces may some day work themselves loose from their surroundings and become permanent if minor contributions to American literature. The novel's appeal does not derive from the "ideas" brooded over periodically through the pages, ideas about the "life force" and other vaguenesses (which Richard S. Kennedy has examined in useful detail); but the ideas, in fact, strike one today as the least interesting and coherent aspect of the book. Wolfe had audited some courses in philosophy at Harvard and had been looking into Freudian theory; but thinking was not what he did best. The strength of *Look Homeward, Angel* lies in the sinewy account of the life of Eugene Gant from his earliest years in "Altamont" to his graduation from "Pulpit Hill"; in the series of vigorously etched portraits of members of his family, other individuals in the town, teachers and friends at college; in the passions, quarrels, surging energies, and intense affections of the Gant family life; and in the prose which—when it is not philosophizing or rhapsodizing—wells up through these persons and incidents. The book may not have been what Stringfellow Barr, a fellow southerner writing in the *Virginia Quarterly*, claimed for it—"the South's first contribution to world literature" (*The Sound and the Fury*, published the same year, would now

seem to offer a more formidable claim to that title)—but in many respects it was, as Barr said, "a work of genius," aspiring to, if not always achieving, "epic proportions."

The novel was a considerable, if not an electrifying, critical and commercial success; and on the basis of it, Wolfe won a Guggenheim grant and went to Europe to meditate his next novel. He told the Guggenheim authorities—who are to be congratulated for seeing through the statement to a hard imaginative purpose—that the theme of the new work would be "why Americans are a nomad race (as this writer believes); why they are touched with a powerful and obscure homesickness wherever they go, both at home and abroad." But in Europe and after he came back to New York, he seems to have lost his direction. He was writing steadily, thousands of words a day, often leaning down from his great height on the top of his refrigerator to scribble on whatever scraps of paper were at hand. But for several years what might be called "the American theme" refused to come to the surface. He recovered balance, finally, and with the tireless cooperation of Perkins (if that is how one chooses to read the evidence) *Of Time and the River* got itself finished and into print, with a note that announced the full range of the American theme, in novels written and to come.

The note, prepared by the publishers at Wolfe's request, was the following:

This novel is the second in a series of six of which the first four have now been written and the first two published. The title of the whole work, when complete, will be the same as that of the present book, "Of Time and the River." The titles of the six books, in the order of their appearance, together with the time plan which each follows, are:

Look Homeward, Angel (1884–1920)
Of Time and the River (1920–1925)
The October Fair (1925–1928)
The Hills Beyond Pentland (1838–1926)
The Death of the Enemy (1928–1933)
Pacific End (1791–1884)

Wolfe thus proposed a staggeringly ambitious saga which would cover the period from the later eighteenth century through the nineteenth and up to the Depression years of the present epoch. The center of it was to be the development of an individual artist (Wolfe himself, of course), but that career was to parallel and be involved with the life of the artist's family; and both were to be seen emerging from a long span of American national and regional history.

The scheme was, ostensibly, a marked departure from *Look Homeward, Angel*, and indeed Wolfe hesitated before including his first novel as part of the saga. *Look Homeward, Angel* had been consciously conceived as an autobiographical novel, a long retrospective inward journey through his own psyche during the three stages (as a notebook entry put it) of infancy, childhood, and young manhood—with that journey balanced against what Wolfe called "another time element," the marriage of his parents and the lives of the older children. Now he seemed to be enlarging far beyond the personal self, to take in nothing less than the history and the essence of America. "I want," he told the poet John Hall Wheelock, whom he met at Scribner's, "to get the whole wilderness of the American continent into my work." If anyone ever aimed to write the long awaited "Great American Novel," it was Thomas Wolfe in the early thirties.[6]

The grandiose conception was never realized, though the turgid outline of *The Web and the Rock* suggests that Wolfe never entirely abandoned hope for it. But the fact was that Wolfe did not possess the kind of historical imagination the intended saga required. He could spin tales about any portion of American history he was familiar with and could find beguiling characters in any place or time. But he had almost no sense of history as process, of history

as image—the kind of awareness displayed by Faulkner in *Absalom, Absalom!* where the personal career of Thomas Sutpen is so interwoven with the life of the slaveholding society about him that if both derives its own meaning from and sheds light back upon the history of the South before, during, and after the Civil War. What Wolfe could do most compellingly was to chart the responses of a developing ego to a highly charged environment. The chart consisted of private reminiscences, embellished, exaggerated, often artfully distorted. *Of Time and the River* carries Eugene Gant from Harvard through the European experience to the remembered moment when Wolfe first met Aline Bernstein. *The Web and the Rock*, after circling back to earlier days, relives the stormy love affair, with Eugene Gant now being replaced by George Webber as Wolfe's alter ego, and continues through the composition of *Look Homeward, Angel*. *You Can't Go Home Again* begins with the events of 1929 and moves into the thirties.

Of Time and the River was a stunning success; Wolfe, at thirty-five, had become a major figure in the world of letters, and especially in the New York literary scene; and the Wolfe legend expanded. It was the legend of a very tall man—six and a half feet and only just beginning to fill out—striding through life, bursting with vitality, shouting with laughter, roaring with rage; making love casually to some young woman he might meet at a party and later asking what her name was; firing off stories to the magazines; rocketing from pinnacle to pinnacle. He felt, himself, that he was a kind of Gulliver, that he lived uncomfortably "in the world of six feet six," where clothes, beds, and low ceilings provided a constant challenge, but where a curious kind of wisdom could be achieved. "In an extraordinary way," he wrote, "a tall man comes to know things about the world as other people do not, cannot know them."

But it was a "lonely wisdom," he said in the same essay ("Gulliver"); and he also saw himself as "God's Lonely Man" and the spokesman

---

[6] Wolfe may have aspired to follow the example of James Joyce, who had moved on from his *Portrait of the Artist as a Young Man* to a work, *Ulysses*, in which the young artist's later career is entwined with the entire life of Dublin, and of Ireland. Wolfe admired *Ulysses* extravagantly, carried it about with him, and scoured its pages for rhetorical inspiration.

for all the lonely ones in the world. "If my experience of loneliness has not been different in kind from that of other men, I suspect it has been sharper in intensity. This gives me the best authority in the world to write about this, our general complaint." Wolfe's lonely wisdom comprised a faith in "humanity," in "man's fundamental goodness," and always by implication in America's nobility of spirit.

The 1930's were an unhappy period for anyone who held to such beliefs. As the decade moved forward, Wolfe was too close an observer of the American scene not to acknowledge the ugliness that was spreading across it, and he decried the scene with a passion deeper than that of the disenchanted Whitman in *Democratic Vistas:*

Is it not true that having known faith and freedom in this land, and an image of free institutions, the very words that once gave life and hope to us have been so befouled and slobbered over by the politicians getting votes, that they have now gone dead and stale and foul for us? . . . Is it not true that . . . even the *promise* of that high and glorious fulfillment has been so aborted, corrupted, made dropsical with disease, that its ancient and primeval lineaments are no more to be seen?

Wolfe continued to insist that "the artist who makes his art the vehicle for political dogma and intolerant propaganda is a lost man," and though he was vociferously on the side of "the working classes," he steadfastly refused to place his art at the service of social justice.

In the last years of his life (1937 and 1938) his own failing health (an affliction of the lung was slowly working its way up into his brain), along with a kind of rising frustration over the distance between his ambition and his accomplishment, may well have darkened his outlook. In any event, he grew by the month more appalled at the social, political, and economic scene—at what seemed to be happening to the very fiber of the culture—to the point where he could exclaim: "We've got to *loathe* America, as we loathe ourselves. With loathing, horror, shame and anguish of the soul unspeakable—as well as with love—we've got to face the total horror of our self-betrayal, the way America has betrayed itself." Wolfe's indictment of his country was as hyperbolic as his praise. He could never really loathe America, though he could question it with an urgency that bespoke an anguished questioning of himself. But as to the old promise of "high and glorious fulfillment," those old outlines of a greatness to be, Wolfe knew at the end that you can't go back to that again, either.

BIOGRAPHICAL CHART

1900   Born, October 3, in Asheville, North Carolina
1916   Enters the University of North Carolina, where he becomes editor of the college paper and magazine
1920   Enrolls in the "47 Workshop" at Harvard University to study theater after graduating from North Carolina
1923   *Welcome to Our City*, a play, is produced at Harvard; moves to New York City
1924   Teaches at the Washington Square College of New York University
1925   Travels to Europe
1926   Begins work on *Look Homeward, Angel*; spends more time in Europe; on trip back meets Aline Bernstein
1928   Returns to Europe (until January, 1929); revises

manuscript of novel with Maxwell Perkins of Scribner's
1929   *Look Homeward, Angel* published
1930   Resigns teaching position to devote himself full time to writing; goes to Paris on a Guggenheim Fellowship
1931   Returns to the United States
1935   *Of Time and the River; From Death to Morning*; visits Europe again
1936   *The Story of a Novel*
1937   Breaks with Perkins and Scribner's and moves to Harper's
1938   Dies, September 15, in Baltimore
1939   *The Web and the Rock*
1940   *You Can't Go Home Again*
1941   *The Hills Beyond*

FURTHER READINGS

Leslie A. Field, *Thomas Wolfe: Three Decades of Criticism* (1968)

C. Hugh Holman, *Thomas Wolfe* (1960)

———, ed., *The World of Thomas Wolfe: A Scribner Research Anthology* (1962)

Richard S. Kennedy, *The Window of Memory: The Literary Career of Thomas Wolfe* (1962)

Bruce R. McElderry, *Thomas Wolfe* (1964)

Herbert Muller, *Thomas Wolfe* (1947)

Thomas C. Pollock and Oscar Cargill, eds., *Thomas Wolfe at Washington Square* (1954)

Louis D. Rubin, *Thomas Wolfe: The Weather of His Youth* (1955)

Andrew Turnbull, *Thomas Wolfe* (1967)

Richard G. Walser, ed., *The Enigma of Thomas Wolfe* (1953)

———, *Thomas Wolfe: An Introduction and Interpretation* (1961)

Floyd C. Watkins, *Thomas Wolfe's Characters: Portraits from Life* (1957)

From Look Homeward, Angel (1929)

It is not easy to make a representative selection from Wolfe's writing. None of the best of his shorter works is really short enough for inclusion: brevity, one is inclined to say, was something Wolfe had little fondness for. By the same token, it is impossible to suggest, by offering a section or two from one of his novels, the expanding rush that characterizes the longer writings. Paradoxically, however, his most bulging novels seem at times to be anthologies of short stories, even anecdotes—the large canvasses were made up of myriad brief sketches. There follows one from *Look Homeward, Angel*.

It catches the eleven-year-old Eugene Gant exercising his fantasies on the world about him, gives a glimpse of the Gant family life, and—in the report on the Gants' financial affairs—shows Wolfe the realist getting his facts straight: three phases of Wolfe's narrative method. The story then moves on to the discovery of Eugene's literary talent by Margaret Leonard, and the boy's admission to the Leonards' school. In real life the two schoolteachers were Margaret and J. M. Roberts; and the former, who had lavished her devotion on Tom Wolfe, was stricken by the account Wolfe gave of her husband in this section: "He talked to the children aimlessly, pompously, dully for twenty minutes each morning," and so on. Wolfe, typically, was totally unprepared for Mrs. Roberts' reaction.

CHAPTER 15

The mountains were his masters. They rimmed in life. They were the cup of reality, beyond growth, beyond struggle and death. They were his absolute unity in the midst of eternal change. Old haunt-eyed faces glimmered in his memory. He thought of Swain's cow, St. Louis, death, himself in the cradle. He was the haunter of himself, trying for a moment to recover what he had been part of. He did not understand change, he did not understand growth. He stared at his framed baby picture in the parlor, and turned away sick with fear and the effort to touch, retain, grasp himself for only a moment.

And these bodiless phantoms of his life appeared with terrible precision, with all the mad nearness of a vision. That which was five years gone came within the touch of his hand, and he ceased at that moment to believe in his own existence. He expected some one to wake him; he would hear Gant's great voice below the laden vines, would gaze sleepily from the porch into the rich low moon, and go obediently to bed. But still there would be all that he remembered before that and what if— Cause flowed ceaselessly into cause.

He heard the ghostly ticking of his life; his powerful clairvoyance, the wild Scotch gift of Eliza, burned inward back across the phantom years, plucking out of the ghostly shadows a million gleams of light—a little station by the rails at dawn, the road cleft through the pineland seen at twilight, a smoky cabin-light below the trestles, a boy who ran among the bounding calves, a wisp-haired slattern, with snuff-sticked mouth, framed in a door, floury negroes unloading sacks from freight-cars on a shed, the man who drove the Fair Grounds bus at Saint Louis, a cool-lipped lake at dawn.

His life coiled back into the brown murk of the past like a twined filament of electric wire; he gave life, a pattern, and movement to these million sensations that Chance, the loss or gain of a moment, the turn of the head, the enormous and aimless impulsion of accident, had thrust into the blazing heat of him. His mind picked out in white living brightness these pinpoints of experience and the ghostliness of all things else became more awful because of them. So many of the sensations that returned to open haunting vistas of fantasy and imagining had been caught from a whirling landscape through the windows of the train.

And it was this that awed him—the weird combination of fixity and change, the terrible moment of immobility stamped with eternity in which, passing life at great speed, both the observer and the observed seem frozen in time. There was one moment of timeless suspension when the land did not move, the train did not move, the slattern in the doorway did not move, he did not move. It was as if God had lifted his baton sharply above the endless orchestration of the seas, and the eternal movement had stopped, suspended in the timeless architecture of the absolute. Or like those motion-pictures that describe the movements of a swimmer making a dive, or a horse taking a hedge —movement is petrified suddenly in mid-air, the inexorable completion of an act is arrested. Then, completing its parabola, the suspended body plops down into the pool. Only, these images that burnt in him existed without beginning or ending, without the essential structure of time. Fixed in no-time, the slattern vanished, fixed, without a moment of transition.

His sense of unreality came from time and movement, from imagining the woman, when the train had passed, as walking back into the house, lifting a kettle from the hearth embers. Thus life turned shadow, the living lights went ghost again. The boy among the calves. Where later? Where now?

I am, he thought, a part of all that I have touched and that has touched me, which, having for me no existence save that which I gave to it, became other than itself by being mixed with what I then was, and is now still otherwise, having fused with what I now am, which is itself a cumulation of what I have been becoming. Why here? Why there? Why now? Why then?

The fusion of the two strong egotisms, Eliza's inbrooding and Gant's expanding outward, made of him a fanatical zealot in the religion of Chance. Beyond all misuse, waste, pain, tragedy, death, confusion, unswerving necessity was on the rails; not a sparrow fell through the air but that its repercussion acted on his life, and the lonely light that fell upon the viscous and interminable seas at dawn awoke sea-changes washing life to him. The fish swam upward from the depth.

The seed of our destruction will blossom in the desert, the alexin of our cure grows by a mountain rock, and our lives are haunted by a Georgia slattern because a London cut-purse went unhung. Through Chance, we are each a ghost to all the others, and our only reality; through Chance, the huge hinge of the world, and a grain of dust; the stone that starts an avalanche, the pebble whose concentric circles widen across the seas.

He believed himself thus at the centre of life; he believed the mountains rimmed the heart of the world; he believed that from all the chaos of accident the inevitable event came at the inexorable moment to add to the sum of his life.

Against the hidden other flanks of the immutable hills the world washed like a vast and shadowy sea, alive with the great fish of his imagining. Variety, in this unvisited world, was unending, but order and purpose certain: there would be no wastage in adventure—courage would be rewarded with beauty, talent with success, all merit with its true deserving. There would be peril, there would be toil, there would be struggle. But there would not be confusion and waste. There would not be groping. For collected Fate would fall, on its chosen moment, like a plum. There was no disorder in enchantment.

Spring lay abroad through all the garden of this world. Beyond the hills the land bayed out to other hills, to golden cities, to rich meadows, to deep forests, to the sea. Forever and forever.

Beyond the hills were the mines of King Solomon, the toy republics of Central America, and little tinkling fountains in a court; beyond, the moonlit roofs of Bagdad, the little grated blinds of Samarkand, the moonlit camels of Bythinia, the Spanish ranch-house of the Triple Z, and J. B. Montgomery and his lovely daughter stepping from their private car upon a western track; and the castle-haunted crags of Graustark; the fortune-yielding casino of Monte Carlo; and the blue eternal Mediterranean, mother of empires. And instant wealth ticked out upon a tape, and the first stage of the Eiffel Tower where the restaurant was, and Frenchmen setting fire to their whiskers, and a farm in Devon, white cream, brown ale, the winter's chimney merriment, and *Lorna Doone*; and the hanging gardens of Babylon, and supper in the sunset with the queens, and the slow slide of the barge upon the Nile, or the wise rich bodies of Egyptian women couched on moonlit balustrades, and the thunder of the chariots of great kings, and tomb-treasure sought at midnight, and the wine-rich chateau land of France, and calico warm legs in hay.

Upon a field in Thrace Queen Helen lay, her lovely body dappled in the sun.

Meanwhile, business had been fairly good. Eliza's earning power the first few years at Dixieland had been injured by her illnesses. Now, however, she had recovered, and had paid off the last installment on the house. It was entirely hers. The property at this time was worth perhaps $12,000. In addition she had borrowed $3,500 on a twenty-year $5,000 life insurance policy that had only two years more to run, and had made extensive alterations: she had added a large sleeping-porch upstairs, tacked on two rooms, a bath, and a hallway on one side, and extended a hallway, adding three bedrooms, two baths, and a watercloset, on the other. Downstairs she had widened the veranda, put in a large sun-parlor under the sleeping-porch, knocked out the archway in the dining-room, which she prepared to use as a big bedroom in the slack season, scooped out a small pantry, in which the family was to eat, and added a tiny room beside the kitchen for her own occupancy.

The construction was after her own plans, and of the cheapest material: it never lost the smell of raw wood, cheap varnish, and flimsy rough plastering, but she had added eight or ten rooms at a cost of only $3,000. The year before she had banked almost $2,000—her bank account was almost $5,000. In addition, she owned jointly with Gant the shop on the Square, which had thirty feet of frontage, and was valued at $20,000, from which he got $65 a month in rent: $20 from Jannadeau, $25 from the McLean Plumbing Company in the basement, and $20 from the J. N. Gillespie Printing Co., which occupied all of the second story.

There were, besides, three good building-lots on Merrion Avenue valued at $2,000 apiece, or at $5,500 for all three; the house on Woodson Street valued at $5,000; 110 acres of wooded mountainside with a farmhouse, several hundred peach, apple and cherry trees, and a few acres of arable ground for which Gant received $120 a year in rent, and which they valued at $50 an acre, $5,500; two houses, one on Carter Street, and one on Duncan, rented to railway people, for which they received $25 a month apiece, and which they valued together at $4,500; forty-eight acres of land two miles above Biltburn, and four from Altamont, upon the important Reynoldsville Road, which they valued at $210 an acre, or $10,000; three houses in Niggertown—one on lower Valley Street, one on Beaumont Crescent, just below the negro Johnson's big house, and one on Short Oak, valued at $600, $900, and $1,600 respectively, and drawing a room-rental of $8, $12, and $17 a month (total: $3,100 and $37 rental); two houses across the river, four miles away in West Altamont, valued at $2,750 and at $3,500, drawing a rental of $22 and $30 a month; three lots, lost in the growth of a rough hillside, a mile from the main highway through West Altamont, $500; and a house, unoccupied, object of Gantian anathema, on Lower Hatton Avenue, $4,500.

In addition, Gant held 10 shares, which were already worth $200 each ($2,000), in the newly organized Fidelity Bank; his stock of stones, monuments, and fly-specked angels represented an investment of $2,700, although he could not have sold them outright for so much; and he had about $3,000 deposited in the Fidelity, the Merchants, and the Battery Hill banks.

Thus, at the beginning of 1912, before the rapid and intensive development of Southern industry, and the consequent tripling of Altamont's population, and before the multiplication of her land values, the wealth of Gant and Eliza amounted to about $100,000, the great bulk of which was solidly founded in juicy well chosen pieces of property of Eliza's selection, yielding them a monthly rental of more than $200, which, added to their own earning capacities at the shop and Dixieland, gave them a combined yearly income of $8,000 or $10,000. Although Gant often cried out bitterly against his business and declared, when he was not attacking property, that he had never made even a bare living from his tombstones, he was rarely short of ready money: he usually had one or two small commissions from country people, and he always carried a well-filled purse, containing $150 or $200 in five and ten-dollar bills, which he allowed Eugene to count out frequently, enjoying his son's delight, and the feel of abundance.

Eliza had suffered one or two losses in her investments, led astray by a strain of wild romanticism which destroyed for the moment her shrewd caution. She invested $1,200 in the Missouri Utopia of a colonizer, and received nothing for her money but a weekly copy of the man's newspaper, several beautiful prospectuses of the look of things when finished, and a piece of clay sculpture, eight inches in height, showing Big Brother with his little sisters Jenny and Kate, the last with thumb in her mouth.

"By God," said Gant, who made savage fun of the proceeding, "she ought to have it on her nose."

And Ben sneered, jerking his head toward it, saying:

"There's her $1,200."

But Eliza was preparing to go on by herself. She saw that cooperation with Gant in the purchase of land was becoming more difficult each year. And with something like pain, something assuredly like hunger, she saw various rich plums fall into other hands or go unbought. She realized that in a very short time land values would soar beyond her present means. And she proposed to be on hand when the pie was cut.

Across the street from Dixieland was the Brunswick, a well-built red brick house of twenty rooms. The marble facings had been done by Gant himself twenty years before, the hardwood floors and oak timbering by Will Pentland. It was an ugly gabled Victorian house, the marriage gift of a rich Northerner to his daughter, who died of tuberculosis.

"Not a better built house in town," said Gant. Nevertheless he refused to buy it with Eliza, and with an aching heart she saw it go to S. Greenberg, the rich junk-man, for $8,500. Within a year he had sold off five lots at the back, on the Yancey Street side, for $1,000 each, and was holding the house for $20,000.

"We could have had our money back by now three times over," Eliza fretted.

She did not have enough money at the time for any important investment. She saved and she waited.

Will Pentland's fortune at this time was vaguely estimated at from $500,000 to $700,000. It was mainly in property, a great deal of which was situated—warehouses and buildings—near the passenger depot of the railway.

Sometimes Altamont people, particularly the young men who loafed about Collister's drug-store, and who spent long dreamy hours estimating the wealth of the native plutocracy, called Will Pent-

land a millionaire. At this time it was a distinction in American life to be a millionaire. There were only six or eight thousand. But Will Pentland wasn't one. He was really worth only a half million.

Mr. Goulderbilt was a millionaire. He was driven into town in a big Packard, but he got out and went along the streets like other men.

One time Gant pointed him out to Eugene. He was about to enter a bank.

"There he is," whispered Gant. "Do you see him?"

Eugene nodded, wagging his head mechanically. He was unable to speak. Mr. Goulderbilt was a small dapper man, with black hair, black clothes, and a black mustache. His hands and feet were small.

"He's got over $50,000,000," said Gant. "You'd never think it to look at him, would you?"

And Eugene dreamed of these money princes living in a princely fashion. He wanted to see them riding down a street in a crested coach around which rode a teetering guard of liveried outriders. He wanted their fingers to be heavily gemmed, their clothes trimmed with ermine, their women coroneted with flashing mosaics of amethyst, beryl, ruby, topaz, sapphire, opal, emerald, and wearing thick ropes of pearls. And he wanted to see them living in palaces of alabaster columns, eating in vast halls upon an immense creamy table from vessels of old silver—eating strange fabulous foods—swelling unctuous paps of a fat pregnant sow, oiled mushrooms, calvered salmon, jugged hare, the beards of barbels dressed with an exquisite and poignant sauce, carps' tongues, dormice and camels' heels, with spoons of amber headed with diamond and carbuncle, and cups of agate, studded with emeralds, hyacinths, and rubies—everything, in fact, for which Epicure Mammon wished.

Eugene met only one millionaire whose performances in public satisfied him, and he, unhappily, was crazy. His name was Simon.

Simon, when Eugene first saw him, was a man of almost fifty years. He had a strong, rather heavy figure of middling height, a lean brown face, with shadowy hollows across the cheeks, always closely shaven, but sometimes badly scarred by his gouging fingernails, and a long thin mouth that curved slightly downward, subtle, sensitive, lighting his whole face at times with blazing demoniac glee. He had straight abundant hair, heavily grayed, which he kept smartly brushed and flattened at the sides. His clothing was loose and well cut: he wore a dark coat above baggy gray flannels, silk shirts rayed with broad stripes, a collar to match, and a generous loosely knotted tie. His waistcoats were of a ruddy-brown chequered pattern. He had an appearance of great distinction.

Simon and his two keepers first came to Dixieland when difficulties with several of the Altamont hotels forced them to look for private quarters. The men took two rooms and a sleeping-porch, and paid generously.

"Why, pshaw!" said Eliza persuasively to Helen, "I don't believe there's a thing wrong with him. He's as quiet and well-behaved as you please."

At this moment there was a piercing yell upstairs, followed by a long peal of diabolical laughter. Eugene bounded up and down the hall in his exultancy and delight, producing little squealing noises in his throat. Ben, scowling, with a quick flicker of his mouth, drew back his hard white hand swiftly as if to cuff his brother. Instead, he jerked his head sideways to Eliza, and said with a soft, scornful laugh: "By God, mama, I don't see why you have to take them in. You've got enough of them in the family already."

"Mama, in heaven's name—" Helen began furiously. At this moment Gant strode in out of the dusk, carrying a mottled package of pork chops, and muttering rhetorically to himself. There was another long peal of laughter above. He halted abruptly, startled, and lifted his head. Luke, listening attentively at the foot of the stairs, exploded in a loud boisterous guffaw, and the girl, her annoyance changing at once to angry amusement, walked toward her father's inquiring face, and prodded him several times in the ribs.

"Hey?" he said startled. "What is it?"

"Miss Eliza's got a crazy man upstairs," she sniggered, enjoying his amazement.

"Jesus God!" Gant yelled frantically, wetting his big thumb swiftly on his tongue, and glancing up toward his Maker with an attitude of exaggerated supplication in his small gray eyes and the thrust of his huge bladelike nose. Then, letting his arms slap heavily at his sides, in a gesture of defeat, he began to walk rapidly back and forth, clucking his deprecation loudly. Eliza stood solidly, looking from one to another, her lips working rapidly, her white face hurt and bitter.

There was another long howl of mirth above. Gant paused, caught Helen's eye, and began to grin suddenly in an unwilling sheepish manner. "God have mercy on us," he chuckled. "She'll

have the place filled with all of Barnum's freaks the next thing you know."

At this moment, Simon, self-contained, distinguished and grave in his manner, descended the steps with Mr. Gilroy and Mr. Flannagan, his companions. The two guards were red in the face, and breathed stertorously as if from some recent exertion. Simon, however, preserved his habitual appearance of immaculate and well-washed urbanity.

"Good evening," he remarked suavely. "I hope I have not kept you waiting long." He caught sight of Eugene.

"Come here, my boy," he said very kindly.

"It's all right," remarked Mr. Gilroy, encouragingly. "He wouldn't hurt a fly."

Eugene moved into the presence.

"And what is your name, young man?" said Simon with his beautiful devil's smile.

"Eugene."

"That's a very fine name," said Simon. "Always try to live up to it." He trust his hand carelessly and magnificently into his coat pocket, drawing out under the boy's astonished eyes, a handful of shining five and ten-cent pieces.

"Always be good to the birds, my boy," said Simon, and he poured the money into Eugene's cupped hands.

Every one looked doubtfully at Mr. Gilroy.

"Oh, that's all right!" said Mr. Gilroy cheerfully. "He'll never miss it. There's lots more where that came from."

"He's a mul-tye-millionaire," Mr. Flannagan explained proudly. "We give him four or five dollars in small change every morning just to throw away."

Simon caught sight of Gant for the first time.

"Look out for the Stingaree," he cried. "Remember the Maine."

"I tell you what," said Eliza laughing. "He's not so crazy as you think."

"That's right," said Mr. Gilroy, noting Gant's grin. "The Stingaree's a fish. They have them in Florida."

"Don't forget the birds, my friends," said Simon, going out with his companions. "Be good to the birds."

They became very fond of him. Somehow he fitted into the pattern of their life. None of them was uncomfortable in the presence of madness. In the flowering darkness of Spring, prisoned in a room, his satanic laughter burst suddenly out: Eugene listened, thrilled, and slept, unable to forget the smile of dark flowering evil, the loose pocket chinking heavily with coins.

Night, the myriad rustle of tiny wings. Heard lapping water of the inland seas.

—And the air will be filled with warm-throated plum-dropping bird-notes. He was almost twelve. He was done with childhood. As that Spring ripened he felt entirely, for the first time, the full delight of loneliness. Sheeted in his thin night-gown, he stood in darkness by the orchard window of the back room at Gant's, drinking the sweet air down, exulting in his isolation in darkness, hearing the strange wail of the whistle going west.

The prison walls of self had closed entirely round him; he was walled completely by the esym-plastic power of his imagination—he had learned by now to project mechanically, before the world, an acceptable counterfeit of himself which would protect him from intrusion. He no longer went through the torment of the recess flight and pursuit. He was now in one of the upper grades of grammar school, he was one of the Big Boys. His hair had been cut when he was nine years old, after a bitter siege against Eliza's obstinacy. He no longer suffered because of the curls. But he had grown like a weed, he already topped his mother by an inch or two; his body was big-boned but very thin and fragile, with no meat on it; his legs were absurdly long, thin, and straight, giving him a curious scissored look as he walked with long bounding strides.

Stuck on a thin undeveloped neck beneath a big wide-browed head covered thickly by curling hair which had changed, since his infancy, from a light maple to dark brown-black, was a face so small, and so delicately sculptured, that it seemed not to belong to its body. The strangeness, the remote quality of this face was enhanced by its brooding fabulous concentration, by its passionate dark intensity, across which every splinter of thought or sensation flashed like a streak of light across a pool. The mouth was full, sensual, extraordinarily mobile, the lower lip deeply scooped and pouting. His rapt dreaming intensity set the face usually in an expression of almost sullen contemplation; he smiled, oftener than he laughed, inwardly, at some extravagant invention, or some recollection of the absurd, now fully appreciated for the first time. He did not open his lips to smile—there was a swift twisted flicker across his mouth. His thick heavily

arched eyebrows grew straight across the base of his nose.

That Spring he was more alone than ever. Eliza's departure for Dixieland three or four years before, and the disruption of established life at Gant's, had begun the loosening of his first friendships with the neighborhood boys, Harry Tarkinton, Max Isaacs, and the others, and had now almost completely severed them. Occasionally he saw these boys again, occasionally he resumed again, at sporadic intervals, his association with them, but he now had no steady companionship, he had only a series of associations with children whose parents stayed for a time at Dixieland, with Tim O'Doyle, whose mother ran the Brunswick, with children here and there who briefly held his interest.

But he became passionately bored with them, plunged into a miasmic swamp of weariness and horror, after a time, because of the dullness and ugliness of their lives, their minds, their amusements. Dull people filled him with terror: he was never so much frightened by tedium in his own life as in the lives of others—his early distaste for Pett Pentland and her grim rusty aunts came from submerged memories of the old house on Central Avenue, the smell of mellow apples and medicine in the hot room, the swooping howl of the wind outside, and the endless monotone of their conversation on disease, death, and misery. He was filled with terror and anger against them because they were able to live, to thrive, in this horrible depression that sickened him.

Thus, the entire landscape, the whole physical background of his life, was now dappled by powerful prejudices of liking and distaste formed, God knows how, or by what intangible affinities of thought, feeling and connotation. Thus, one street would seem to him to be a "good street"—to exist in the rich light of cheerful, abundant, and high-hearted living; another, inexplicably, a "bad street," touching him somehow with fear, hopelessness, depression.

Perhaps the cold red light of some remembered winter's afternoon, waning pallidly over a playing-field, with all its mockery of Spring, while lights flared up smokily in houses, the rabble-rout of children dirtily went in to supper, and men came back to the dull but warm imprisonment of home, oil lamps (which he hated), and bedtime, clotted in him a hatred of the place which remained even when the sensations that caused it were forgotten.

Or, returning from some country walk in late

autumn, he would come back from Cove or Valley with dewy nose, clotted boots, the smell of a mashed persimmon on his knee, and the odor of wet earth and grass on the palms of his hands, and with a stubborn dislike and suspicion of the scene he had visited, and fear of the people who lived there.

He had the most extraordinary love of incandescence. He hated dull lights, smoky lights, soft, or sombre lights. At night he wanted to be in rooms brilliantly illuminated with beautiful, blazing, sharp, poignant lights. After that, the dark.

He played games badly, although he took a violent interest in sports. Max Isaacs continued to interest him as an athlete long after he had ceased to interest him as a person. The game Max Isaacs excelled in was baseball. Usually he played one of the outfield positions, ranging easily about in his field, when a ball was hit to him, with the speed of a panther, making impossible catches with effortless grace. He was a terrific hitter, standing at the plate casually but alertly, and meeting the ball squarely with a level swinging smack of his heavy shoulders. Eugene tried vainly to imitate the precision and power of this movement, which drove the ball in a smoking arc out of the lot, but he was never able: he chopped down clumsily and blindly, knocking a futile bounder to some nimble baseman. In the field he was equally useless: he never learned to play in a team, to become a limb of that single animal which united telepathically in a concerted movement. He became nervous, highly excited, and erratic in team-play, but he spent hours alone with another boy, or, after the mid-day meal, with Ben, passing a ball back and forth.

He developed blinding speed, bending all the young suppleness of his long thin body behind the ball, exulting as it smoked into the pocket of the mitt with a loud smack, or streaked up with a sharp dropping curve. Ben, taken by surprise by a fast drop, would curse him savagely, and in a rage hurl the ball back into his thin gloved hand. In the Spring and Summer he went as often as he could afford it, or was invited, to the baseball games in the district league, a fanatic partisan of the town club and its best players, making a fantasy constantly of himself in a heroic game-saving rôle.

But he was in no way able to submit himself to the discipline, the hard labor, the acceptance of defeat and failure that make a good athlete; he

wanted always to win, he wanted always to be the general, the heroic spear-head of victory. And after that he wanted to be loved. Victory and love. In all of his swarming fantasies Eugene saw himself like this—unbeaten and beloved. But moments of clear vision returned to him when all the defeat and misery of his life was revealed. He saw his gangling and absurd figure, his remote unpractical brooding face, too like a dark strange flower to arouse any feeling among his companions and his kin, he thought, but discomfort, bitterness, and mockery; he remembered, with a drained sick heart, the countless humiliations, physical and verbal, he had endured, at the hands of school and family, before the world, and as he thought, the horns of victory died within the wood, the battle-drums of triumph stopped, the proud clangor of the gongs quivered away in silence. His eagles had flown; he saw himself, in a moment of reason, as a madman playing Cæsar. He craned his head aside and covered his face with his hand.

CHAPTER 16

The Spring grew ripe. There was at mid-day a soft drowsiness in the sun. Warm sporting gusts of wind howled faintly at the eaves; the young grass bent; the daisies twinkled.

He pressed his high knees uncomfortably against the bottom of his desk, grew nostalgic on his dreams. Bessie Barnes scrawled vigorously two rows away, displaying her long full silken leg. Open for me the gates of delight. Behind her sat a girl named Ruth, dark, with milk-white skin, eyes as gentle as her name, and thick black hair, parted in the middle. He thought of a wild life with Bessie and of a later resurrection, a pure holy life, with Ruth.

One day, after the noon recess, they were marshalled by the teachers—all of the children in the three upper grades—and marched upstairs to the big assembly hall. They were excited, and gossiped in low voices as they went. They had never been called upstairs at this hour. Quite often the bells rang in the halls: they sprang quickly into line and were marched out in double files. That was fire drill. They liked that. Once they emptied the building in four minutes.

This was something new. They marched into the big room and sat down in blocks of seats assigned to each class: they sat with a seat between each of them. In a moment the door of the principal's office on the left—where little boys were beaten—was opened, and the principal came out. He walked around the corner of the big room and stepped softly up on the platform. He began to talk.

He was a new principal. Young Armstrong, who had smelled the flower so delicately, and who had visited Daisy, and who once had almost beaten Eugene because of the smutty rhymes, was gone. The new principal was older. He was about thirty-eight years old. He was a strong rather heavy man a little under six feet tall; he was one of a large family who had grown up on a Tennessee farm. His father was poor but he had helped his children to get an education. All this Eugene knew already, because the principal made long talks to them in the morning and said he had never had their advantages. He pointed to himself with some pride. And he urged the little boys, playfully but earnestly, to "be not like dumb driven cattle, be a hero in the strife." That was poetry, Longfellow.

The principal had thick powerful shoulders; clumsy white arms, knotted with big awkward country muscles. Eugene had seen him once hoeing in the schoolyard; each of them had been given a plant to set out. He got those muscles on the farm. The boys said he beat very hard. He walked with a clumsy stealthy tread—awkward and comical enough, it is true, but he could be up at a boy's back before you knew it. Otto Krause called him Creeping Jesus. The name stuck, among the tough crowd. Eugene was a little shocked by it.

The principal had a white face of waxen transparency, with deep flat cheeks like the Pentlands, a pallid nose, a trifle deeper in its color than his face, and a thin slightly-bowed mouth. His hair was coarse, black, and thick, but he never let it grow too long. He had short dry hands, strong, and always coated deeply with chalk. When he passed near by, Eugene got the odor of chalk and of the schoolhouse: his heart grew cold with excitement and fear. The sanctity of chalk and school hovered about the man's flesh. He was the one who could touch without being touched, beat without being beaten. Eugene had terrible fantasies of resistance, shuddering with horror as he thought of the awful consequences of fighting back: something like God's fist in lightning. Then he looked around cautiously to see if any one had noticed.

The principal's name was Leonard. He made

long speeches to the children every morning, after a ten-minute prayer. He had a high sonorous countrified voice which often trailed off in a comical drawl; he got lost very easily in revery, would pause in the middle of a sentence, gaze absently off with his mouth half-open and an expression of stupefaction on his face, and return presently to the business before him, his mind still loose, with witless distracted laugh.

He talked to the children aimlessly, pompously, dully for twenty minutes every morning: the teachers yawned carefully behind their hands, the students made furtive drawings, or passed notes. He spoke to them of "the higher life" and of "the things of the mind." He assured them that they were the leaders of to-morrow and the hope of the world. Then he quoted Longfellow.

He was a good man, a dull man, a man of honor. He had a broad streak of coarse earthy brutality in him. He loved a farm better than anything in the world except a school. He had rented a big dilapidated house in a grove of lordly oaks on the outskirts of town: he lived there with his wife and his two children. He had a cow—he was never without a cow: he would go out at night and morning to milk her, laughing his vacant silly laugh, and giving her a good smacking kick in the belly to make her come round into position.

He was a heavy-handed master. He put down rebellion with good cornfield violence. If a boy was impudent to him he would rip him powerfully from his seat, drag his wriggling figure into his office, breathing stertorously as he walked along at his clumsy rapid gait, and saying roundly, in tones of scathing contempt: "Why, you young upstart, we'll just see who's master here. I'll just show you, my sonny, if I'm to be dictated to by every two-by-four whippersnapper who comes along." And once within the office, with the glazed door shut, he published the stern warning of his justice by the loud exertion of his breathing, the cutting swish of his rattan, and the yowls of pain and terror that he exacted from his captive.

He had called the school together that day to command it to write him a composition. The children sat, staring dumbly up at him as he made a rambling explanation of what he wanted. Finally he announced a prize. He would give five dollars from his own pocket to the student who wrote the best paper. That aroused them. There was a rustle of interest.

They were to write a paper on the meaning of a

French picture called The Song of the Lark. It represented a French peasant girl, barefooted, with a sickle in one hand, and with face upturned in the morning-light of the fields as she listened to the bird-song. They were asked to describe what they saw in the expression of the girl's face. They were asked to tell what the picture meant to them. It had been reproduced in one of their readers. A larger print was now hung up on the platform for their inspection. Sheets of yellow paper were given them. They stared, thoughtfully masticating their pencils. Finally, the room was silent save for a minute scratching on paper.

The warm wind spouted about the eaves; the grasses bent, whistling gently.

Eugene wrote: "The girl is hearing the song of the first lark. She knows that it means Spring has come. She is about seventeen or eighteen years old. Her people are very poor, she has never been anywhere. In the winter she wears wooden shoes. She is making out as if she was going to whistle. But she doesn't let on to the bird that she has heard him. The rest of her people are behind her, coming down the field, but we do not see them. She has a father, a mother, and two brothers. They have worked hard all their life. The girl is the youngest child. She thinks she would like to go away somewhere and see the world. Sometimes she hears the whistle of a train that is going to Paris. She has never ridden on a train in her life. She would like to go to Paris. She would like to have some fine clothes, she would like to travel. Perhaps she would like to start life new in America, the Land of Opportunity. The girl has had a hard time. Her people do not understand her. If they saw her listening to the lark they would poke fun at her. She has never had the advantages of a good education, her people are so poor, but she would profit by her opportunity if she did, more than some people who have. You can tell by looking at her that she's intelligent."

It was early in May; examinations came in another two weeks. He thought of them with excitement and pleasure—he liked the period of hard cramming, the long reviews, the delight of emptying out abundantly on paper his stored knowledge. The big assembly room had about it the odor of completion, of sharp nervous ecstasy. All through the summer it would be drowsy-warm; if only here, alone, with the big plaster cast of Minerva, himself and Bessie Barnes, or Miss—Miss——

"We want this boy," said Margaret Leonard. She handed Eugene's paper over to her husband.

They were starting a private school for boys. That was what the paper had been for.

Leonard took the paper, pretended to read half a page, looked off absently into eternity, and began to rub his chin reflectively, leaving a slight coating of chalk-dust on his face. Then, catching her eye, he laughed idiotically, and said: "Why, that little rascal! Huh? Do you suppose——?"

Feeling delightfully scattered, he bent over with a long suction of whining laughter, slapping his knee and leaving a chalk print, making a slobbering noise in his mouth.

"The Lord have mercy!" he gasped.

"Here! Never you mind about that," she said, laughing with tender sharp amusement. "Pull yourself together and see this boy's people." She loved the man dearly, and he loved her.

A few days later Leonard assembled the children a second time. He made a rambling speech, the purport of which was to inform them that one of them had won the prize, but to conceal the winner's name. Then, after several divagations, which he thoroughly enjoyed, he read Eugene's paper, announced his name, and called him forward.

Chalkface took chalkhand. The boy's heart thundered against his ribs. The proud horns blared, he tasted glory.

Patiently, all through the summer, Leonard laid siege to Gant and Eliza. Gant fidgeted, spoke shiftily, finally said:

"You'll have to see his mother." Privately he was bitterly scornful, roared the merits of the public school as an incubator of citizenship. The family was contemptuous. Private school! Mr. Vanderbilt! Ruin him for good!

Which made Eliza reflective. She had a good streak of snobbism. Mr. Vanderbilt? She was as good as any of them. They'd just see.

"Who are you going to have?" she asked. "Have you drummed any one up yet?"

Leonard mentioned the sons of several fashionable and wealthy people,—of Dr. Kitchen, the eye, ear, nose and throat man, Mr. Arthur, the corporation lawyer, and Bishop Raper, of the Episcopal diocese.

Eliza grew more reflective. She thought of Pett. She needn't give herself airs.

"How much are you asking?" she said.

He told her the tuition was one hundred dollars a year. She pursed her lips lingeringly before she answered.

"Hm-m!" she began, with a bantering smile, as she looked at Eugene. "That's a whole lot of money. You know," she continued with her tremulous smile, "as the darkey says, we're pore-folks."

Eugene squirmed.

"Well what about it, boy?" said Eliza banteringly. "Do you think you're worth that much money?"

Mr. Leonard placed his white dry hand upon Eugene's shoulders, affectionately sliding it down his back and across his kidneys, leaving white chalk prints everywhere. Then he clamped his meaty palm tightly around the slender bracelet of boy-arm.

"That boy's worth it," he said, shaking him gently to and fro. "Yes, sir!"

Eugene smiled painfully. Eliza continued to purse her lips. She felt a strong psychic relation to Leonard. They both took time.

"Say," she said, rubbing her broad red nose, and smiling slyly, "I used to be a school-teacher. You didn't know that, did you? But I didn't get any such prices as you're asking," she added. "I thought myself mighty lucky if I got my board and twenty dollars a month."

"Is that so, Mrs. Gant?" said Mr. Leonard with great interest. "Well, sir!" He began to laugh in a vague whine, pulling Eugene about more violently and deadening his arm under his crushing grip.

"Yes," said Eliza, "I remember my father—it was long before you were born, boy," she said to Eugene, "for I hadn't laid eyes on your papa—as the feller says, you were nothing but a dish-rag hanging out in heaven—I'd have laughed at any one who suggested marriage then— Well, I tell you what [she shook her head with a sad pursed deprecating mouth], we were mighty poor at the time, I can tell you.—I was thinking about it the other day—many's the time we didn't have food in the house for the next meal.—Well, as I was saying, your grandfather [addressing Eugene] came home one night and said—Look here, what about it?—Who do you suppose I saw to-day?—I remember him just as plain as if I saw him standing here—I had a feeling—[addressing Leonard with a doubtful smile] I don't know what you'd call it but it's pretty strange when you come to think about it, isn't it?—I had just finished helping Aunt Jane set the table—she had come all the way from Yancey County to visit your grandmother—when all of a sudden it flashed over me—mind you [to Leonard] I never looked out the window or anything but I knew just as well as I knew anything that he was coming—mercy I cried—here he comes—why what on earth are you talking about, Eliza? said your

grandma—I remember she went to the door and looked out down the path—there's no one there—He's acoming, I said—wait and see—Who? said your grandmother—Why, father, I said—he's carrying something on his shoulder—and sure enough—I had no sooner got the words out of my mouth than there he was just acoming it for all he was worth, up the path, with a tow-sack full of apples on his back—you could tell by the way he walked that he had news of some sort—well—sure enough—without stopping to say howdy-do—I remembered he began to talk almost before he got into the house—O father, I called out—you've brought the apples—it was the year after I had almost died of pneumonia—I'd been spitting up blood ever since—and having hemorrhages—and I asked him to bring me some apples—Well sir, mother said to him, and she looked mighty queer, I can tell you—that's the strangest thing I ever heard of—and she told him what had happened—Well, he looked pretty serious and said—Yes, I'll never forget the way he said it—I reckon she saw me. I wasn't there but I was thinking of being there and coming up the path at that very moment—I've got news for you he said—who do you suppose I saw to-day—why, I've no idea, I said—why old Professor Truman—he came rushing up to me in town and said, see here: where's Eliza—I've got a job for her if she wants it, teaching school this winter out on Beaver-dam—why, pshaw, said your grandfather, she's never taught school a day in her life—and Professor Truman laughed just as big as you please and said never you mind about that—Eliza can do anything she sets her mind on—well sir, that's the way it all came about." High-sorrowful and sad, she paused for a moment, adrift, her white face slanting her life back through the aisled grove of years.

"Well, sir!" said Mr. Leonard vaguely, rubbing his chin. "You young rascal, you!" he said, giving Eugene another jerk, and beginning to laugh with narcissistic pleasure.

Eliza pursed her lips slowly.

"Well," she said, "I'll send him to you for a year." That was the way she did business. Tides run deep in Sargasso.

So, on the hairline of million-minded impulse, destiny bore down on his life again.

Mr. Leonard had leased an old pre-war house, set on a hill wooded by magnificent trees. It faced west and south, looking toward Biltburn, and abruptly down on South End, and the negro flats that stretched to the depot. One day early in September he took Eugene there. They walked across town, talking weightily of politics, across the Square, down Hatton Avenue, south into Church, and southwesterly along the bending road that ended in the schoolhouse on the abutting hill.

The huge trees made sad autumn music as they entered the grounds. In the broad hall of the squat rambling old house Eugene for the first time saw Margaret Leonard. She held a broom in her hands, and was aproned. But his first impression was of her shocking fragility.

Margaret Leonard at this time was thirty-four years old. She had borne two children, a son who was now six years old, and a daughter who was two. As she stood there, with her long slender fingers splayed about the broomstick, he noted, with a momentary cold nausea, that the tip of her right index finger was flattened out as if it had been crushed beyond healing by a hammer. But it was years before he knew that tuberculars sometimes have such fingers.

Margaret Leonard was of middling height, five feet six inches perhaps. As the giddiness of his embarrassment wore off, he saw that she could not weigh more than eighty or ninety pounds. He had heard of the children. Now he remembered them, and Leonard's white muscular bulk, with a sense of horror. His swift vision leaped at once to the sexual relation, and something in him twisted aside, incredulous and afraid.

She had on a dress of crisp gray gingham, not loose or lapping round her wasted figure, but hiding every line in her body, like a draped stick.

As his mind groped out of the pain of impression he heard her voice and, still feeling within him the strange convulsive shame, he lifted his eyes to her face. It was the most tranquil and the most passionate face he had ever seen. The skin was sallow with a dead ashen tinge; beneath, the delicate bone-carving of face and skull traced itself clearly: the cadaverous tightness of those who are about to die had been checked. She had won her way back just far enough to balance carefully in the scales of disease and recovery. It was necessary for her to measure everything she did.

Her thin face was given a touch of shrewdness and decision by the straight line of her nose, the fine long carving of her chin. Beneath the sallow minutely pitted skin in her cheeks, and about her mouth, several frayed nerve-centres twitched from moment to moment, jarring the skin slightly without contorting or destroying the passionate calm beauty that fed her inexhaustibly from within.

This face was the constant field of conflict, nearly always calm, but always reflecting the incessant struggle and victory of the enormous energy that inhabited her, over the thousand jangling devils of depletion and weariness that tried to pull her apart. There was always written upon her the epic poetry of beauty and repose out of struggle— he never ceased to feel that she had her hand around the reins of her heart, that gathered into her grasp were all the straining wires and sinews of disunion which would scatter and unjoint her members, once she let go. Literally, physically, he felt that, the great tide of valiance once flowed out of her, she would immediately go to pieces.

She was like some great general, famous, tranquil, wounded unto death, who, with his fingers clamped across a severed artery, stops for an hour the ebbing of his life—sends on the battle.

Her hair was coarse and dull-brown, fairly abundant, tinged lightly with gray: it was combed evenly in the middle and bound tightly in a knot behind. Everything about her was very clean, like a scrubbed kitchen board: she took his hand, he felt the firm nervous vitality of her fingers, and he noticed how clean and scrubbed her thin somewhat labor-worn hands were. If he noticed her emaciation at all now, it was only with a sense of her purification: he felt himself in union with disease, but with the greatest health he had ever known. She made a high music in him. His heart lifted.

"This," said Mr. Leonard, stroking him gently across the kidneys, "is Mister Eugene Gant."

"Well, sir," she said, in a low voice, in which a vibrant wire was thrumming, "I'm glad to know you." The voice had in it that quality of quiet wonder that he had sometimes heard in the voices of people who had seen or were told of some strange event, or coincidence, that seemed to reach beyond life, beyond nature—a note of acceptance; and suddenly he knew that all life seemed eternally strange to this woman, that she looked directly into the beauty and the mystery and the tragedy in the hearts of men, and that he seemed beautiful to her.

Her face darkened with the strange passionate vitality that left no print, that lived there bodiless like life; her brown eyes darkened into black as if a bird had flown through them and left the shadow of its wings. She saw his small remote face burning strangely at the end of his long unfleshed body, she saw the straight thin shanks, the big feet turned awkwardly inward, the dusty patches on his stockings at the knees, and his thin wristy arms that stuck out painfully below his cheap ill-fitting jacket; she saw the thin hunched line of his shoulders, the tangled mass of hair—and she did not laugh.

He turned his face up to her as a prisoner who recovers light, as a man long pent in darkness who bathes himself in the great pool of dawn, as a blind man who feels upon his eyes the white core and essence of immutable brightness. His body drank in her great light as a famished castaway the rain: he closed his eyes and let the great light bathe him, and when he opened them again, he saw that her own were luminous and wet.

Then she began to laugh. "Why, Mr. Leonard," she said, "what in the world! He's almost as tall as you. Here, boy. Stand up here while I measure." Deft-fingered, she put them back to back. Mr. Leonard was two or three inches taller than Eugene. He began to whine with laughter.

"Why, the rascal," he said. "That little shaver."

"How old are you, boy?" she asked.

"I'll be twelve next month," he said.

"Well, what do you know about that!" she said wonderingly. "I tell you what, though," she continued. "We've got to get some meat on those bones. You can't go around like that. I don't like the way you look." She shook her head.

He was uncomfortable, disturbed, vaguely resentful. It embarrassed and frightened him to be told that he was "delicate"; it touched sharply on his pride.

She took him into a big room on the left that had been fitted out as a living-room and library. She watched his face light with eagerness as he saw the fifteen hundred or two thousand books shelved away in various places. He sat down clumsily in a wicker chair by the table and waited until she returned, bringing him a plate of sandwiches and a tall glass full of clabber, which he had never tasted before.

When he had finished, she drew a chair near to his, and sat down. She had previously sent Leonard out on some barnyard errands; he could be heard from time to time shouting in an authoritative country voice to his live stock.

"Well, tell me boy," she said, "what have you been reading?"

Craftily he picked his way across the waste land of printery naming as his favorites those books which he felt would win her approval. As he had read everything, good and bad, that the town library contained, he was able to make an impressive showing. Sometimes she stopped him to question

about a book—he rebuilt the story richly with a blazing tenacity of detail that satisfied her wholly. She was excited and eager—she saw at once how abundantly she could feed this ravenous hunger for knowledge, experience, wisdom. And he knew suddenly the joy of obedience: the wild ignorant groping, the blind hunt, the desperate baffled desire was now to be ruddered, guided, controlled. The way through the passage to India, that he had never been able to find, would now be charted for him. Before he went away she had given him a fat volume of nine hundred pages, shot through with spirited engravings of love and battle, of the period he loved best.

He was drowned deep at midnight in the destiny of the man who killed the bear, the burner of windmills and the scourge of banditry, in all the life of road and tavern in the Middle Ages, in valiant and beautiful Gerard, the seed of genius, the father of Erasmus. Eugene thought *The Cloister and the Hearth* the best story he had ever read.

The Altamont Fitting School was the greatest venture of their lives. All the delayed success that Leonard had dreamed of as a younger man he hoped to realize now. For him the school was independence, mastership, power, and, he hoped, prosperity. For her, teaching was its own exceeding great reward—her lyric music, her life, the world in which plastically she built to beauty what was good, the lord of her soul that gave her spirit life while he broke her body.

In the cruel volcano of the boy's mind, the little brief moths of his idolatry wavered in to their strange marriage and were consumed. One by one the merciless years reaped down his gods and captains. What had lived up to hope? What had withstood the scourge of growth and memory? Why had the gold become so dim? All of his life, it seemed, his blazing loyalties began with men and ended with images; the life he leaned on melted below his weight, and looking down, he saw he clasped a statue; but enduring, a victorious reality amid his shadow-haunted heart, she remained, who first had touched his blinded eyes with light, who nested his hooded houseless soul. She remained.

O death in life that turns our men to stone! O change that levels down our gods! If only one lives yet, above the cinders of the consuming years, shall not this dust awaken, shall not dead faith revive, shall we not see God again, as once in morning, on the mountain? Who walks with us on the hills?

EUGENE O'NEILL (1888–1953)

In the work of Eugene O'Neill, as in that of Dreiser, the notion of the American *dream* gave way again to the notion of the necessity and the fatality of *illusion*—particularly the kind of illusion (as to the possibility of heroic achievement, material success, self-fulfillment) generated by life in America. For Dreiser, we have suggested, the ultimate wisdom is to know the necessity of illusion while yet somehow remaining unillusioned. In *The Iceman Cometh*, the relatively unillusioned Larry Slade speaks for all the denizens of Harry Hope's saloon—and hence for modern man generally, in O'Neill's view of him—when he says: "The truth has no bearing on anything. It's irrelevant and immaterial, as the lawyers say. The lie of a pipe-dream is what gives life to the whole misbegotten mad lot of us, drunk or sober." Between Dreiser and O'Neill, there are a number of important similarities;[1] but there are also some large differences, and among the latter the most obvious may seem to be the fact that Dreiser wrote novels and O'Neill wrote plays. Yet that difference may, for reasons to be explained, turn out to be more apparent than real.

If O'Neill set his two finest plays, *The Iceman Cometh* and *Long Day's Journey into Night,* in the year 1912, it was because it was in that year that he first set out to become a playwright. For a young man of creative urgings, this decision was, at the time, a surprising one, even if the young man in question was the son of a famous and popular actor, had grown up close to the theater, and had himself been on stage once or twice. But it was not the lure of the footlights that drew O'Neill on, then or

later; it was the desire to express himself in the form of dramatic literature—and that was not a form which, in 1912, appealed very much to the American imagination. Prior to O'Neill's arrival, drama in America had been for the most part an undistinguished affair. Plays had been written in this country, to be sure, since Royall Tyler's *The Contrast* in 1787; but unlike poetry and fiction (and indeed unlike some of the "nonliterary" modes), drama had failed to develop its own native tradition and its own appropriate conventions. This is not easy to explain, especially since one of the great strengths of American fiction—as may be seen in the works of Cooper, Hawthorne, Melville, and Henry James—had been precisely its dramatic quality: its ability to manipulate large and significant actions, to deal with the intensities of human conflict, with what James (whose most emphatic advice to himself as a novelist was "dramatize, dramatize, dramatize!") called "the lunging of ego against ego." Some of the most compelling American poetry, moreover, had been decidedly dramatic: witness the intense little spiritual dramas of Emily Dickinson, the more metaphysical actions that animated Melville's verses, and Edwin Arlington Robinson's desperate or pathetic verse-tales.

It may even be that the American dramatic energy was, as it were, exhausted before it ever got to the theater. Certainly the dire paucity of good plays before the second decade of this century cannot be laid to any lingering Puritan distrust of the stage as such, or any lack of interest in the art of theater. Irving, Howells, and James (to name three) all wrote for the stage, though with indifferent success; and the cultural scene across the nineteenth century is littered with the remains of brief-lived offerings by scores, perhaps hundreds, of other aspiring playwrights. Their names lie buried—most of them entirely forgotten, though a few still stirring a faint memory—in learned histories of the

---

[1] As early as 1930, Francis Fergusson recognized that O'Neill, along with Dreiser, Sherwood Anderson, and H. L. Mencken, was a member of a group which was "impatient of tradition and convention," deeply anti-Puritan, and concerned primarily with personal emotional needs ("Eugene O'Neill," in *Hound and Horn*, January, 1930).

genre: Augustin Daly, Bronson Howard, James A. Herne, David Belasco, Augustus Thomas, Clyde Fitch.[2] Proposals to establish an American repertory theater to resurrect a number of those vanished scripts made little headway.[3]

It is not our purpose, nor is it within our competence, to tell the story of theater-writing in America: a history that must take into account social and financial considerations, the talents and styles of an assortment of actors and actresses, the eccentricities and biases of individual producers, and above all perhaps the long-standing and overwhelming influence of English drama. That story has been told elsewhere and belongs in any case to a history quite different, for the most part, from the one we are pursuing. Our concern is *literary*: that is, with the relation between theater-writing and the mainstreams of American literature proper. And in this regard, it must be said that playwriting in America approached the level of literature only belatedly, and as an appendage to large-scale accomplishments in fiction; and this, on the whole, has been true up to the present moment. For example, forty years after Howells had opened the American novel to the methods of realistic fiction, and twenty years after Stephen Crane's *Maggie* had inaugurated the "new realism," American drama, more often than not, remained sentimental, melodramatic, mid-Victorian and imitative.

The occasional play of the early 1900's that still seems to have some enduring value tends to remind one, in its general makeup, of the first ventures into fictional realism. Langdon Mitchell's *The New York Idea* (1906), for instance, and William Vaughan Moody's *The Great Divide* (1909) both, in their different ways, combine a certain freshness of actuality with a

dependence on the old pieties.[4] The average playwright in the early 1900's, like the novelist in the 1870's, tended to be more concerned with the old conventions of his art than with the life which his art was to give shape and meaning to; and the average playwright was further limited (from our literary point of view) by the need of designing his works for particular actors, as audiences were really interested in actors rather than in dramas: in William Gillette playing Sherlock Holmes, Joseph Jefferson playing Rip Van Winkle, James O'Neill (Eugene's father) playing the Count of Monte Cristo.

Both lessons—the primacy of convention, and of the actor—were borne in upon a gloomily attendant Eugene O'Neill in a drama class at Harvard in 1914, when a visiting playwright, Augustus Thomas, demonstrated how to compose a Broadway hit in seconds flat. "Suggest the name of a star," Thomas told the class, which came up with the name of a certain Margaret Anglin.

> "All right," said Thomas, "we'll write a play for Anglin. She's broad of hip, well-developed —so our story will have to fit a woman of that physical type. She's no longer young and beautiful, so it must be a role for an older woman—a woman with deep emotions; we'll make her a mother—and since we have to have drama—a mother threatened with losing her child." (Arthur and Barbara Gelb, *O'Neill*, 1962, p. 271)

And on, through an evolving story of New England, adultery, a struggle over possession, and the like. If O'Neill did make the first serious breakthrough in American drama, it was because (as someone acutely said about him), while others were thinking of life in terms of the conventions of drama, O'Neill began to think

---

[2] Arthur Hobson Quinn's *History of the American Drama* (1936), in its account of such figures, makes melancholy reading, despite the author's admirable effort to persuade us of the power and vitality of the works discussed.

[3] For example, Edmund Wilson, writing in the *New York Review of Books* (1969), listed a dozen plays which he believed would make an attractive permanent program for such a theater. The idea was not followed up.

[4] The "idea" of Mitchell's title is divorce—the fashionable thing to do in the upper-class New York society Mitchell is portraying. His work is a still readable, and perhaps still playable, comedy of manners somewhat in the style of Edith Wharton (who was a good friend of the playwright's father, the physician-novelist S. Weir Mitchell).

about drama in terms of the life it was to represent.

Despite the generally discouraging condition of things, the year 1912 was not an entirely inopportune time for a young American determined to write plays of genuine artistic merit. There were stirrings on the far edges of the New York theatrical world, particularly in Greenwich Village. A number of people took to meeting together in a bookstore in Washington Square, to voice their contempt for the arrant commercialism of the Broadway stage and to discuss the possibility of writing and producing work of their own—work, as one of them said, in which "a young and growing culture could find its voice"—and of bringing in examples of avant-garde European writing. The Washington Square Players became a reality in 1915 and immediately began presenting plays by some of its members, as well as imports by Chekhov, Maeterlinck, and others. The productions were invariably one-acters, that being the form, then as now, easiest to experiment with. But when the group turned down a little comedy called *Suppressed Desires*, a relatively uninhibited spoof of contemporary theories about sex, the authors of that work broke away and formed their own company in Provincetown, Massachusetts. (The Washington Square Players was eventually transformed into the Theater Guild.) The Provincetown Players converted an old fishhouse into the twenty-five-foot-square Wharf Theater and opened for business in the summer of 1916. One of the first plays it put on was *Bound East for Cardiff*, Eugene O'Neill's debut, and a work that as much as any has a claim to mark the birth of modern American drama.

Within the span of O'Neill's life and career, the year 1912 had another, deeper significance than its marking of his decision to write plays. It was in the fall of that year that O'Neill—twenty-four years old, a recent attempted suicide, suddenly afflicted with tuberculosis—took stock not only of himself, but also of his father, his mother, and his older brother Jamie: in short, of his entire personal and domestic world. It was that world, with its often intolerably

severe tensions and its sometimes violent mixture of love, hatred, guilt, and resentment, that would be the obsessive subject of almost every important play that O'Neill was thereafter to write. If O'Neill moved on to the theater after an explosive showdown with his family, what he contributed to the theater was a constant retelling and reinterpretation of that showdown, ever more thinly disguised until he produced the remorselessly naked account in *Long Day's Journey into Night*, in 1941.

O'Neill's father, James, had been a dashingly handsome man from an immigrant Irish Catholic family. He was an actor of high potential and at one time seemed destined to become one of the country's most gifted performers (after playing Iago to O'Neill's Othello in 1874, Edwin Booth, America's leading actor, exclaimed: "That young man is playing Othello better than I ever did!"). But with an irony Dreiser would have appreciated, enormous success proved to be the source of life-long failure. In 1880, O'Neill was thrust abruptly into the title role of *The Count of Monte Cristo*, an adaptation of Alexander Dumas's romance. His performance became fantastically popular all across the country and abroad, and O'Neill was trapped in the part forever. He played it more than six thousand times; he bought the rights for next to nothing and earned close to a million dollars. In *Long Day's Journey*, the sixty-five-year-old actor (called James Tyrone in the play) confesses the failure he had made of his career to his son Edmund (that is, Eugene):

That God-damned play I bought for a song and made such a success in—a great money success—it ruined me with its promise of an easy fortune. I didn't want to do anything else, and by the time I woke up to the fact I'd become a slave to the damned thing and did try other plays, it was too late. They had identified me with that one part, and didn't want me in anything else. They were right, too. I'd lost the great talent I once had through years of easy repetition, never learning a new part, never really working hard. Thirty-five to forty thousand dollars net profit a season like snapping your fingers! It was too great a temptation.

In O'Neill's diagnosis of his father, a main reason for the older man's yielding to the temptation was the extreme penury of his youth. As a consequence, for all his acquired wealth, James O'Neill was exceedingly tight-fisted and begrudged every penny he was forced to spend on his children; and one of the things that most bitterly rankled in Eugene was the fact that after his tuberculous condition was discovered, his father had him sent to a state hospital to save the expenses of a sanatorium.[5]

In 1877, James married Ella Quinlan, the plumply pretty daughter of reasonably affluent middle-class Irish Catholic parents. She was a girl of somewhat vague religious aspirations, who passed her adolescent years in a convent school and thought of becoming a nun; but she also had a fund of gayety and even sensuality, and it was this side of her that responded to the romantic lead-performer in *Monte Cristo*. Her parents were shocked by her marrying an actor, and her parents' friends immediately dropped her. If Eugene O'Neill is to be believed, his father and mother genuinely loved each other all their lives; but Ella O'Neill clearly resented the social consequences of her marriage, and she greatly disliked the unsettled nature of an actor's life—the succession of hotel rooms, the pre-breakfast train rides, the suitcases carried like manacles. A first child, Jamie, was born, and a second, Edmund; and it was while Ella was on a road tour with her husband in 1885 that Edmund, only eighteen months old, died of measles. The inevitable guilt feelings Ella suffered over her "neglect" of the infant took the form of alternately blaming James for dragging her away from home and Jamie for deliberately infecting his little brother (all this is rehearsed in *Long Day's Journey*). Ella was in a state of mounting depression when she gave birth to Eugene in October, 1888, in a New York hotel.

[5] In *Long Day's Journey*, James Tyrone does first propose sending Edmund to a state institution, but then is shamed by his son's accusation of heartless penny-pinching into changing his mind.

It was a difficult delivery, and the doctor in attendance gave Ella morphine to overcome the pain. In time she became addicted to the drug, retreating periodically, after an injection, into a fog of unreality, from within which she would murmur incoherent reminiscences of her convent days and her courtship. As *Monte Cristo* comprised the prison into which James O'Neill locked himself, so drugs were the prison of his wife.

The fourth member of this bedeviled family, Jamie, remains something of an enigma, even though Eugene devoted an entire play—*A Moon for the Misbegotten*—to a description of his shattered and tragic last days in 1923. As a youth, he had talent, energy, and charm; but later he seemed to oscillate between an earthy ebullience and a paralyzing indecisiveness. Like his father and brother, he drank heavily, often for days at a time, but he lacked their capacity to carry it off and get on with the job at hand. (James, who customarily began the day with a couple of stiff drinks, boasted accurately that he had never once missed a performance because of alcohol.) Jamie was desperately proud of Eugene's success, yet mixed with his admiration and intense affection was a consuming envy and a portion of hatred. He is made to confess as much, drunkenly, in the closing moments of *Long Day's Journey*. "Want to warn you—against me," he tells his brother.

I've been rotten bad influence. And worst of it is, I did it on purpose. . . . Did it on purpose to make a bum of you. Or part of me did. A big part. That part of me that's been dead so long. That hates life. My putting you wise so you'd learn from my mistakes. Believed that myself at times, but it's a fake. Made my mistakes look good. Made getting drunk romantic. . . . Never wanted you succeed and make me look even worse by comparison. Wanted you to fail. Always jealous of you. . . . And it was your being born that started Mama on dope. I know that's not your fault, but all the same, God damn you, I can't help hating your guts—! . . . But don't get wrong idea, Kid. I love you more than I hate you. My saying what I'm telling you now proves it. I run the risk you'll hate me—and you're all I have left.

Eugene O'Neill went to a parochial school in the Bronx, and then to Catholic Institute in Manhattan. Between them, these schools made their contribution to one of the continuing dramas of O'Neill's personal life; for as late as his play *Days Without End*, in the early thirties, he was still wrestling with the challenge and the appeal of Catholic Christianity, and there are marked liturgical and Biblical overtones in *The Iceman Cometh*. O'Neill went on to a private school in Stamford, Connecticut, which he rather enjoyed; and in the fall of 1906, he entered Princeton. (The previous summer, when he was between school and college, is described in the surprisingly amiable domestic comedy *Ah, Wilderness!*, 1932, in which O'Neill appears as young Richard Miller.) He lasted less than a year in college: the academic study of literature bored and obscurely frightened him (he said later that he had been "afraid" of Shakespeare when forced to study him in class). He was drawn, on his own, to writers like Jack London and Conrad; and it was Conrad's *The Nigger of the "Narcissus"* that, more than anything else, inspired him to take the step, in the spring of 1910, of signing on to the *Charles Racine*, a Norwegian four-rigger bound out of Boston for Buenos Aires.

We might, paraphrasing Ishmael's remark in *Moby-Dick*, say that for O'Neill a cargo vessel was his real Princeton and his Harvard. His departure was a profoundly symbolic act. For seven months, he had been touring with his father as a bit-actor and assistant manager in F. Marion Crawford's lachrymose melodrama *The White Sister*;[6] and the experience had convinced him once and for all that if he were to have a career in the theater, it would have to be rooted in a direct knowledge of life. He admitted later that he had "wanted to be a he-man," and he more than held his own in the

rough and tumble with his sailing companions, with some of whom he became fast friends. He also, of course, wanted to escape the exacerbations of the O'Neill family situation. But above all, according to his lyrical recollection in *Long Day's Journey*, what energized him was the sheer beauty and power of physical nature:

I lay on the bowsprit, facing astern, with the water foaming into spume under me, the masts with every sail white in the moonlight, towering high above me. I became drunk with the beauty and singing rhythm of it, and for a moment I lost myself—actually lost my life. I was set free! I dissolved in the sea, became white sails and flying spray, became beauty and rhythm, became moonlight and the ship and the high dim-starred sky! I belonged, without past or future, within peace and unity and wild joy, within something greater than my own life, or the life of Man, to Life itself! To God, if you want to put it that way.

("There's the making of a poet in you all right," his father says, staring.)

The *Charles Racine* took sixty-five days to crawl down to Buenos Aires. O'Neill spent ten months "on the beach" in the Argentina capital, collecting experience, listening to sailors' yarns, and drinking. In May, 1911, he made his way back home on the British tramp *Ikalis*, and a month later a drinking partner named Driscoll persuaded him to join the *New York* en route to Great Britain. He returned on the *Philadelphia* in August—and settled down to an aimless, alcoholic existence in the dim recesses of a New York saloon known as Jimmy-the-Priest's (it would contribute part of the background in *The Iceman Cometh*).

Some such haunted, passive, liquor-drenched period was evidently necessary, as it seems in retrospect, before the voyaging could be absorbed into his imagination and projected in dramatic form. At home, things were worse than ever. O'Neill was worried about his brother; Ella had been sent to a sanitorium for a cure, and Eugene was horrified at the thought of her

---

[6] James O'Neill had accepted a minor role in the play—that of a bishop—in one last pathetic attempt to succeed in a part other than that of Edmund Dantes.

humiliation; as his biographers put it, "he was filled with helpless rage over what his family had done to each other." As he sat somberly drinking, he received the news that his friend Driscoll had committed suicide. Soon after that, his roommate in a waterfront hotel plunged from the window to his death, whereupon O'Neill promptly bought several doses of veronal and made a pass at killing himself—probably more of a dark histrionic gesture than a real attempt. His friends found him unconscious in his room and restored him with coffee.

It was the summer of 1912. O'Neill went up to the family summer home in New London (the only place that remotely resembled a "home" for the O'Neills). Here the family foregathered to indulge presumably in the endless round of recriminations O'Neill set down in *Long Day's Journey into Night*—exchanges of wounding charges which nonetheless led occasionally to precarious reconciliations. Eugene had a continuing "bad cold" which turned out to be tuberculosis, and in the late fall his father escorted him to the Fairfield County State Sanatorium. He stayed only two miserable days there before his doctor persuaded James to take him to the eminently superior, smaller, cleaner, and better-equipped Gaylord Farm in nearby Wallingford. When he was released the following June, he felt quite literally reborn (he makes it clear in *Long Day's Journey* that he had more than half expected to die).

Back in New London, perhaps as a result of this series of confrontations, O'Neill began to show a much increased understanding of, and even love for, his parents; they, in turn, grew closer together. The combination of events—including, too, the suicide attempt and the ravaging illness—had, it appears, brought O'Neill to the point where he could contemplate life with a certain amount of objectivity: that kind of imaginative objectivity, by no means unmixed with a sense of emotional involvement, which his art would require. And "art" was a word O'Neill was now beginning, resolutely, to use. During his enforced inactivity at Gaylord Farm, he had worked on a variety of one-act plays, and though several of them grappled with

what would be one of his major themes—the way an individual willfully connives at his own doom—he knew they were melodramatic and poorly constructed and that they lacked the authentic touch of life. In the summer of 1914, he wrote to Professor George Pierce Baker, who had been giving an increasingly famous graduate seminar in drama at Harvard (the "47 Workshop"), asking to be admitted. "With my present training," he said, "I might hope to become a mediocre journeyman playwright. It is just because I do not wish to be one, because I want to be an artist or nothing, that I am writing to you."

Baker's seminar did little to help O'Neill fulfill his ambition, though, as we have seen, it usefully helped confirm his distaste for contemporary American playwriting. There followed another period—symbolically enough lasting just nine months—during which O'Neill lay fallow, not to say drunk, in a Greenwich Village saloon-hotel popularly referred to as the Hell Hole—where he met the prototypes of such characters as Hickey and Larry Slade, in *The Iceman Cometh*. But this time O'Neill was sustained by an awareness that something was stirring within him. In the spring of 1916, he drifted up to Cape Cod and, after looking on warily for awhile, approached the Provincetown Players with the manuscript of the one-act play of which he felt most confident, *Bound East for Cardiff*. The company was enthusiastic and at once produced the play in the dilapidated Wharf Theater. Conrad had contributed again to O'Neill's career. *Bound East for Cardiff* condenses the action of *The Nigger of the "Narcissus"*—essentially, the slow death on shipboard of the black man, James Waite—into a brief mood-piece centering on the death of a garrulous old sailor named Yank.

O'Neill was now twenty-eight years old, and he was about to embark upon a twenty-five-year period of productivity unexampled in the history of the American theater—an achievement that has earned him almost universal recognition as the most powerful playwright this country has yet seen. Surveying that achievement, we make out a fairly persistent movement—with occasional divagations, to be sure—toward a direct and conscious dramatic confrontation of himself in relation to his family which is at the same time a movement toward dramatic realism, of the kind practiced in fiction by Crane and Dreiser. One of the first tenets of fictional realism was that the novelist should ground his work in personal experience, and O'Neill declared his allegiance to this principle when he said: "I have never written anything which did not come directly or indirectly from some event or impression of my own." After several more sea plays that arose directly from personal life (they were artfully strung together in the excellent film *The Long Voyage Home*, directed by John Ford), O'Neill moved on to work that sprang more *indirectly* from his experience—and which represented a sometimes uneasy mingling of the personal with the symbolic, the abstract, and the ritualistic.

From the outset there was no doubting O'Neill's ambition to be a *literary* artist. He referred to *Beyond the Horizon*—which opened in February, 1920, to the first thunderous applause O'Neill had received, and which won him the first of four Pulitzer prizes—as a "novelplay," and he prided himself on having deployed the resources of the theater to trace the development of character in a manner worthy of a novelist. The two main characters, in fact—two brothers, Robert and Andrew Mayo—develop in conflict and by contrast with each other, as to a considerable extent Eugene and Jamie had done. The setting is a farm on northern Cape Cod, and in the course of a rather elementary plot Robert Mayo abandons his dream of going to sea and marries the girl his brother is also in love with: having rejected the opportunity truly to live, and to grow, he then dies of tuberculosis. It is Andrew who goes adventuring, to the cold fury of his father James Mayo, but he lacks his brother's imaginative ability to appreciate the experience. The sets suggested a larger contrast, meanwhile, by alternating between the out of doors and indoors: six alternations in all, to the annoyance of some of the critics. But O'Neill felt, correctly, that setting (or place) was one of the elements

that might most valuably be manipulated for dramatic purposes, and that in the present case "One scene is out of doors, showing the horizon, suggesting [Robert's] desire and dream. The other is indoors, the horizon gone, suggesting what has come between him and his dream. In that way I tried to get the rhythm, the alternation of longing and loss."

In *The Emperor Jones* (also 1920), O'Neill added further novelties to the American stage. In the figure of Brutus Jones—a pullman porter who flees the country after killing a man and holds imperial sway over a native island until the natives revolt and murder him—O'Neill presented American audiences with their first black tragic hero; the entire play is a single long monologue spoken by Jones as he struggles through the jungle; and the ghosts of his pursuers, whom his agonized imagination conjures up, are made physically present.[7] The play, with its steadily intensifying Congo drumbeat, made a stunning impact, and no work of O'Neill's has been revived more frequently.

Pursuing his effort to get closer, dramatically, to the reality of human relationships, O'Neill hit upon the notion (or rather it was suggested to him by his costume designer) of introducing masks into *The Hairy Ape* (1921), a play in eight scenes about the psychological and physical destruction of a ship's stoker named Yank Smith—a character based on O'Neill's unfortunate friend Driscoll. They were used to render faceless a crowd emerging from a church service: the coldly aloof aristocratic society whose representative, a haughty young woman called Mildred, drives Yank to a violent death by referring to him as nothing more than a "filthy beast." For *The Great God Brown*, four years later, O'Neill deployed masks more variously. The main character, Dion Anthony, for example, wears a mask before his wife to indicate—in a manner not unlike that in Hawthorne's "The

---

[7] The idea of casting the play in the form of a monologue was derived in part by O'Neill from the Swedish dramatist August Strindberg, the playwright to whom O'Neill felt most akin and whom he regarded as a mentor. As for presenting ghosts on stage, O'Neill could of course find that device in Shakespeare.

Minister's Black Veil"—that his soul is possessed of a torment his wife cannot understand; in the company of a prostitute, Dion, unmasked, can reveal himself totally. His wife is unmasked and vulnerable before her husband, but masked before the uncomprehending world.

These experiments were of the utmost value in expanding the possibilities of American stagecraft, as comparable technical experiments were doing in the same years for the arts of poetry and fiction. For the use of masks O'Neill had the great example of the stiffly masked figures in Greek drama, but such devices remained artifices, almost gimmicks—challenging but finally unsatisfying, and only adding to the confusion of purpose from which *The Great God Brown* suffers. Yet the experiment was perhaps a necessary step in O'Neill's development toward the potent realism of his best work.

James O'Neill had died of cancer in August, 1920. He and Eugene had enjoyed a genuine closeness in the last year of his life and had spent a number of weeks together in a relationship nourished by Eugene's undefensive affection and James's loving pride in his son's career. The old actor's widow, Ella, immediately went off drugs, took much greater care of her appearance, and enlarged her circle of friends in New London. Jamie, astonished by his mother's rejuvenation, swore off drinking and became a model son and companion. This happy state of affairs lasted for nearly two years. Then, on a visit with Jamie to Los Angeles in February, 1922, Ella was suddenly stricken with the effects of a brain tumor and within a fortnight died. Her death was the end of Jamie. He got hopelessly and continuously drunk; escorting his mother's body back from California by train, he paid a prostitute fifty dollars a night (as he told Eugene) to help him forget "what was in the baggage car ahead." A little more than a year later, Jamie too was dead in a New Jersey sanatorium to which he had been delivered several months earlier in a pitiable state of delirium tremens.

Although Eugene O'Neill was repelled by his brother's behavior on the trip from Los Angeles (when the train reached Grand Central Station, Jamie was too drunk to locate the casket, and Eugene had to go in search of it), and later much disturbed by Jamie's drunken misery, he was beginning to see his dead parents in clearer perspective. The first evidence of this was the play *All God's Chillun Got Wings*, in 1924. The drama has to do with a marriage between a black man and a white woman, and it was taken—according to the viewpoint—as a daring or a disgusting study of miscegenation. But the husband and wife are named Jim and Ella (Harris), and, as the Gelbs remark, the play offers a compassionate firsthand observation of the intolerable strain of a marriage clouded by misunderstanding and prejudice. O'Neill again attempted to convey a sense of the psychic rhythm by shifts in the physical set: the New York apartment in which the marital relationship slowly congeals grows literally smaller, scene by scene, before one's eyes.

Desire Under the Elms, written and produced in 1924, achieved the firmest grasp O'Neill had yet shown on his obsessive theme and is probably the best of his plays before *The Iceman Cometh* in 1939. One thing O'Neill had strikingly in common with Ephraim Cabot, the hero of *Desire Under the Elms*, was that he was married three times and had three children by his first two wives and none by his third. O'Neill had been briefly married to Kathleen Jenkins, a good-looking New York socialite, who bore him a son—Eugene O'Neill, Jr.—before the marriage was broken up by an irate James O'Neill in the climactic year 1912. Six years later Eugene married Agnes Boulton, a slender, attractive, and intelligent young woman he met in the Greenwich Village theater circles. It was a love match, and Agnes bore him a second son, Shane, and a daughter, Oona; but strains developed between them remarkably similar to those that afflicted O'Neill's parents—and all the more severely after the death of his parents. O'Neill took to spending more and more time away from Agnes and the children and to paying a kind of anguished court to Carlotta Monterey, a minor actress and one of the most beautiful women in America (she had recently divorced her third husband). One day in the fall of 1926, according to Miss Monterey, O'Neill came to her apartment with a bad head-cold and "looked at me with those tragic eyes and said, 'I need you.' He kept saying, 'I need you, I need you'— never 'I love you. I think you are wonderful'— just 'I need you, I need you.' Sometimes it was a bit frightening. Nobody had ever gritted their teeth at me that way and said they needed me. And he did need me, I discovered." They were married in 1929, soon after the opening of *Strange Interlude*, and despite tiffs and estrangements, Carlotta remained O'Neill's wife until his death twenty-four years later.

There had been several other women along the way, especially in earlier years, and it is perhaps not surprising that *Strange Interlude*— written as one marriage was breaking up and another forming—should present as its main character a person who passes through an exhausting series of family problems, marital and extramarital. The person is Nina Leeds, and O'Neill referred to the work as his "woman-play," but in Nina's endless tortuous involvements we can discern something of the pattern of O'Neill's private life.

Though *Strange Interlude* was a major theatrical event in 1928, it strikes one today as curiously banal. There were, however, some interesting features to it, and to O'Neill's conception of it. It was, for one thing, much the longest play yet produced in this country. It consisted of no less than nine acts, covering a period of twenty-five years in Nina's busy emotional life; the daily performance began at 5:30 in the afternoon and continued, with an eighty-minute break for supper, until nearly midnight. This "woman-play," much more than *Beyond the Horizon*, was also patently a "novel-play." O'Neill was stretching the conventions of the theater beyond anything he had previously attempted in order to encompass within the dramatic medium what had customarily been engaged only by long fiction. He was indeed seeking, by his own example, to make drama *supplant* the novel as the chief available artistic instrument for giving meaningful shape to life.

It was at just this time that he wrote one of his most perceptive admirers, the critic Joseph Wood Krutch, about what he regarded as the failure of modern fiction:

Even the best of modern novels strike me as a dire failure. . . . They are all . . . so padded with the unimportant and insignificant, so obsessed with the trivial meaning of trivialities that the authors appear to me as mere timid recorders of life, dodging the responsibility of that ruthless selection and deletion and concentration on the emotional which is the test of an artist—the forcing of significant form upon experience.

With that appraisal—at a moment when Dreiser and Edith Wharton were only just past their peak, Sinclair Lewis and Willa Cather were in their prime, and Wolfe, Fitzgerald, Faulkner, and Hemingway beginning to appear —one may well quarrel. But with the basic principle enunciated, even so devoted a craftsman as Henry James would have entirely agreed (though he might have winced at the verbal "forcing"). After his plays had failed on the London stage, James, in fact, had tried successfully to enrich the art of fiction by exploiting the resources of drama—on grounds quite comparable to those on which O'Neill was now attempting an exactly reverse process. Each, as an artist, wanted to give form to experience by applying to a massive impression of life the techniques of "selection," "deletion," and "concentration." The parallel can be carried further, for O'Neill set greater store, finally, by the published versions of his plays than by their stage productions. He became notably less interested, as the years passed, in actual performances of his work, and no longer bothered to attend rehearsals or even the Broadway opening. After completing *The Iceman Cometh* in 1939, he let the manuscript lie in his desk for seven years before allowing it to be put on; and it is doubtful whether, during the period (1939-41) that he was writing *Long Day's Journey into Night*, he even envisaged its appearance on stage (it was produced in 1956, several years after his death).

He grew into the firm conviction, as one of his editors has remarked, that it was in its published form that his work would live, and he worked even harder revising the galley proofs of his plays than he had with the playing scripts.

The most obvious instance in *Strange Interlude* of O'Neill's determination to grant drama the same privileges as fiction was the introduction of "asides"—monologues uttered by the various characters, inaudible to the rest of the cast and intended to reveal hidden and unsuspected thoughts and feelings. That device had, of course, been a staple of the Elizabethan theater—one thinks at once of Hamlet's several monologues—but O'Neill was probably borrowing less from Shakespeare than from the kind of inner musing perfected in fiction by Henry James. But the asides in *Strange Interlude*, though, like the masks, a useful experiment, point up one of the main difficulties in the attempt to be a novelist on the stage. In *The Portrait of a Lady*, for example, the action continues unimpeded during Isabel Archer's long brooding vigil before the fire—indeed, James felt the vigil thrust the action forward more surely than any melodramatic incident could have done. But the requirements of stage performance resist such an effect: the only method O'Neill and his associates could invent to handle the "asides" was to have all the other characters freeze, remaining stiff and motionless while one person gave voice to his or her inner reactions.

By the time, in late 1929, that O'Neill was well along with *Mourning Becomes Electra*, he had resolved to dispense not only with asides ("'Interludian' technique," as he called it) in the new play, but with all his other theatrical experiments. He felt that for too many years he had gotten "terribly messed up searching for new ways and means and styles" and was now determined to write "with the utmost simplicity and naturalness." Thus after more than a decade of several kinds of innovations, O'Neill had found the road to dramatic realism and was moving directly toward his greatest achievements.

He had, as a matter of fact, discovered that road five years earlier in *Desire Under the Elms*, but he had lost his way in the histrionic trickiness of *Strange Interlude* and several other plays in the intervening period. *Mourning Becomes Electra* (produced in 1931) had in common with the latter play only the fact that it too was constructed in nine acts and took almost seven hours to perform. But like *Desire Under the Elms*, *Mourning Becomes Electra* was set in the New England of seventy years earlier, and once again O'Neill was bent on Americanizing and modernizing a Greek tragedy—in this case the story of Electra and her doomed family, largely as rendered in the *Oresteia* of Aeschylus. Agamemnon reappears as Ezra Mannon, a northern general returning home from the Civil War; Clytemnestra as Christine, Ezra's unfaithful wife; Aegisthus as Adam Brant, Christine's lover; Electra is renamed Lavinia, and Orestes becomes Orin. Returning to the Greek-style tragedy of family life, O'Neill could return as well to the grand old themes: uncontrollable passion, adultery, incest, murder, and suicide. O'Neill followed fairly carefully the broad outlines of the Greek legend: the murder of Ezra by the guilty couple, Christine and Adam; the revenge-murder of Adam by Orin and Lavinia; the suicide of Christine, followed by that of Orin.

Lavinia at the end is left chillingly alone, and as she reenters the family home and closes the door behind her, she pronounces her own peculiar doom:

> I'll never go out to see anyone! I'll have the shutters nailed closed so no sunlight can ever get in. I'll live alone with the dead, and keep their secrets, and let them hound me, until the curse is paid out and the last Mannon is left to die!

So O'Neill must sometimes have felt, for all the externally satisfying conditions of his life at the time, as he sat keeping the secrets of his dead father, mother, and brother—hounded by them till the curse was exorcised in the writing of *Long Day's Journey into Night*. As before, a tremendous personal involvement gave special dramatic charge and power to the work; and one feels about *Mourning Becomes Electra* much as

Joseph Wood Krutch had felt in 1924 about all the best of O'Neill's writing, after the play *Desire Under the Elms*. Krutch descried the tendency to seek "ideas" and messages in O'Neill's plays:

It was not thought that drove him, as a young man, to seek adventure among the roughest men he could find, and it was not thought which he brought back from this and other experiments in life. . . . The meaning and unity of his work lies not in any controlling intellectual idea and certainly not in a "message," but merely in the fact that each play is an experience of extraordinary intensity.

Through the decade of the twenties and into the thirties, O'Neill was very much a public personality—a role that, despite his deep psychological need of privacy, he developed a certain zest for. He became a familiar and indeed a magnetic figure in the New York theater and literary worlds, with his saturnine good looks and the brilliant play of his mind. The newspapers watched his every move, and he was rarely loath to offer a fresh pronouncement upon the cultural state of things and his own shifting dramatic ambitions. It must be admitted that events would not leave him alone: in 1929, he went abroad with Carlotta to escape the throngs and work on *Mourning Becomes Electra*; but his lavish existence in several palatial European chateaus drew much comment in the press; and three days after his return to New York in May, 1930, reporters were hammering at the door of the hotel suite where he and Carlotta were trying to hide out, asking for the O'Neills' reaction to the suicide of Ralph Barton, Carlotta's third husband.

There were public honors, as well. In 1921, O'Neill received a second Pulitzer prize for *Anna Christie*, a waterfront drama about a reformed prostitute which became a memorable film vehicle for Greta Garbo, but which O'Neill disowned early on as a piece of mere trickery. He won a third Pulitzer in 1928 for *Strange Interlude*, which turned out to be his greatest success, running for 414 long nights and netting

him $275,000. In 1926, there had been an honorary degree from Yale—a distinction which highly gratified the former drop-out from Princeton and sometime graduate student at Harvard (George Pierce Baker had by this time transferred down to Yale and was instrumental in arranging the award). In both 1929 and 1930, there were rumors that the Nobel prize in literature would for the first time go to an American, and that the leading candidates were O'Neill, Dreiser, and Sinclair Lewis. Thomas Mann was given the prize in 1929, but in 1930 it did go to Lewis—who took the occasion to belabor the American literary scene for its lingering gentility and its failure to recognize new and different kinds of artistic genius. If the Nobel committee had chosen Dreiser, Lewis told his audience in Stockholm, "you would have heard" (that is, from commentators back home) "that his style . . . is cumbersome, his choice of words insensitive."

And had you chosen Eugene O'Neill, who has done nothing much in the American drama save to transform it utterly in ten or twelve years from a false world of neat and competent trickery to a world of splendor, fear and greatness, you would have been reminded that he had done something worse than scoffing, that he had seen life as something not to be neatly arranged in a study, but as terrifying, magnificent and often quite horrible, a thing akin to a tornado, an earthquake or a devastating fire.

Lewis thus expressed his solidarity with his artistic generation, and at the same time offered a shrewd and characteristically generous assessment of his rival.

Six years later, the O'Neill household overlooking Puget Sound in Washington—where O'Neill had repaired for peace and quiet and to do research for a new play to be set in that region—was enlivened by the news that he had at last been awarded the Nobel prize. In his acceptance speech in December, 1936, O'Neill touched gracefully on "the debt my work owes to that greatest genius of all modern dramatists, your August Strindberg. . . . I am only too proud of my debt to Strindberg, only too happy to have this opportunity to proclaim it to his people." No other living English-language playwright had been more widely honored, save possibly George Bernard Shaw—about whose accomplishments O'Neill was always a trifle wary.[8]

But by 1936, O'Neill's fortunes had begun to change, and he himself had begun to withdraw from the public world—withdraw into himself and into the past. The enormous acclaim for *Mourning Becomes Electra* was not repeated for *Days Without End* in 1933, a play in which O'Neill wrestled unsuccessfully but challengingly with the dilemmas and possibilities of religious faith. "The critics didn't understand it," he said later, "and also it wasn't very good." O'Neill's mind, however, was already fixed on a different and incalculably more ambitious undertaking. Both *Desire Under the Elms* and *Mourning Becomes Electra* had carried his imagination back to an earlier period of American and New England history; and O'Neill now proposed writing a cycle of plays—perhaps as many as half a dozen—which would cover a much broader span of that history, going back possibly as far as the Revolution and then moving forward to the present. The project rather resembled the huge work confusedly envisaged and chaotically outlined by Thomas Wolfe in those same years; and like Wolfe's gigantic novel-in-progress, O'Neill's cycle was never completed.

O'Neill in fact finished only one phase of the cycle, *A Touch of the Poet*, written between 1935 and 1942. From this work, though it is set in early nineteenth-century Boston and has to do with an ex-officer (in the Napoleonic wars) who becomes a saloon-keeper, it is evident, as the Gelbs observe, that the entire cycle would again be a rehearsal of the O'Neill family history. While thus groping in his personal and re-

gional past, O'Neill found further cause to remove himself from social intercourse. In 1936 he was beset by the first stages of an illness that would grow steadily worse for the remaining seventeen years of his life and which forced the former public figure into a seclusion almost as total as that of Emily Dickinson. In addition to kidney trouble and neuritis, he suffered from a nervous disorder which spread from a severe tremor of the hands to a sometimes complete loss of control over his entire body, a disease at first wrongly diagnosed as Parkinson's disease, later as something so rare as not to have a proper name. There were moments when O'Neill's hands or feet would fly in directions unintended, and at times he had to use his left hand to guide his right even in writing his name. But his mind remained untouched, and there were times when his imagination worked with an intensity and a vigor he had never before achieved, especially in the period from 1939 through 1941 when O'Neill was writing, in astonishing succession, *The Iceman Cometh* and *Long Day's Journey into Night*. With the latter work a part of O'Neill must have known that he had reached his artistic zenith and had probed with an all-compelling finality into his obsessive story. With the first of those plays, O'Neill felt that "I had locked myself in with my own memories"—in a way uncannily reminiscent of the last glimpse of Lavinia in *Mourning Becomes Electra,* locking the door behind her and nailing the shutters to live with her dead. He was opposed to production of *Iceman*, fearing the torment of a public airing of his memories; but he was induced out of retirement in 1946 to attend rehearsals, though he stayed at home during the generally successful opening.

The following year he managed to compose *A Moon for the Misbegotten*, dealing, as has been said, with the final desperate days of his brother Jamie. He let himself be persuaded to have it produced, and it was an almost unmixed disaster. He did no more writing of any consequence and spent his concluding years for the most part staring out silently onto the Atlantic from the cottage Carlotta had found for them

---

[8] In 1931, during an interview in the Theater Guild offices, O'Neill pointed to a picture of Shaw hanging on the wall and said, smiling: "I wish they would take that down; the old gentleman seems to be laughing at me."

in Marblehead Neck, near Boston. In 1943, his daughter Oona had married Charlie Chaplin, to Carlotta's pleasure though not to her husband's, who never forgave Oona or spoke to or about her again. (For reasons unclear, O'Neill nurtured a detestation of Chaplin.) In 1950, his son Eugene, Jr.—at one time a classical scholar and a teacher of great promise—killed himself. That event, the last of the acts of self-destruction with which O'Neill's life was so constantly punctuated, may have borne it in upon him that he had been as unnatural a father to his three children as, in his view, James O'Neill had sometimes been. (The title of his son Shane's autobiography was *The Curse of the Misbegotten*.)

In 1951, O'Neill suffered a succession of strange and small accidents and was hospitalized. Later he was able to move to a hotel in Boston, where Carlotta nursed and protected him with a devotion that had outlived their many troubles together. He died in November, 1953.

O'Neill's will stipulated that *Long Day's Journey into Night* not be released for twenty-five years after his death. But it also stipulated that Carlotta O'Neill could dispose of his work as she saw fit, and in 1956 the play was published by the Yale University Press. The same year it was produced in Stockholm with international reverberations of praise. Carlotta had hesitated to have it put on in America, but after José Quintero's splendid revival of *The Iceman*

Cometh in a small Broadway theater in 1956 (with Jason Robards as an unforgettable Hickey), she gave *Long Day's Journey* to Quintero and his associates. It won O'Neill a fourth Pulitzer prize and is now generally reckoned the strongest play yet written by an American.

It is hard not to believe that Arthur Miller did not have *Long Day's Journey* close at hand when he was writing *All My Sons* in 1947 and *Death of a Salesman* two years later, but as the facts above indicate, such could not have been the case. O'Neill's "influence" on later American playwrights is, indeed, much more pervasive and general than any particular notation would suggest. As Sinclair Lewis remarked, he virtually established the American theater, especially by relating it to Strindberg on the one hand and Greek tragedy on the other. O'Neill's major subject matter—the tension-ridden family—and his major theme, the power of illusion, continue to be the major subject matter and the major theme; both reappear, handsomely fused, in Edward Albee's *Who's Afraid of Virginia Woolf* (1962). O'Neill's was the major impetus toward innovation and experimentation, though he might well have regretted some of the extremes to which certain playwrights have gone in this regard. Above all, there was the enormous force of his example: as Clifford Odets acknowledged, it was "the awesome sense" of O'Neill—his sheer achievement, rather than any individual work—that most inspired him when he was beginning his career.

BIOGRAPHICAL CHART

1888   Born, October 16, to Ella Quinlan and James O'Neill, the celebrated actor-manager

1906–7   Attends Princeton

1909   Marries Kathleen Jenkins (divorced 1912); one son, Eugene O'Neill, Jr.; prospects for gold in Honduras; at sea for two years; lives in a waterfront dive, "Jimmy-the-Priest's" in New York City, which became the locale for *Anna Christie* and *The Iceman Cometh*

1912   Just before Christmas develops mild case of tuberculosis; spends five months at the Gaylord Farm Sanatorium at Wallingford, Connecticut; reads Strindberg and the Greek tragic poets

1912–13   Convalesces from tuberculosis; during this period writes eleven one-act and two long plays and tears up all but six of the one-act plays.

1914–15   Attends George Pierce Baker's "47 Workshop" at Harvard

1916   Moves to Provincetown, Massachusetts; *Bound East for Cardiff* (one-act play) successfully produced by the Provincetown Players at Wharf Theater, Provincetown

1917   *In the Zone* (one-act play) produced by the Washington Square Players; *The Long Voyage Home* (one-act play) produced by the Provincetown Players

1918	Marries Agnes Boulton (divorced 1929); two children, Shane and Oona (Mrs. Charles Chaplin); moves to Cape Cod, occupying a former Coast Guard station; *The Moon of the Caribbees* (one-act play) produced by the Provincetown Players
1920	Awarded Pulitzer prize for *Beyond the Horizon; Chris Christopherson* (first version of *Anna Christie*); *The Emperor Jones*
1921	Awarded Pulitzer prize for *Anna Christie*
1922	*The Hairy Ape*
1924	*All God's Chillun Got Wings; S. S. Glencairn; Desire Under the Elms*
1926	*The Great God Brown;* receives honorary Litt.D from Yale
1928	*Marco Millions;* awarded Pulitzer prize for *Strange Interlude; Lazarus Laughed*
1929	*Dynamo;* marries Carlotta Monterey
1931	*Mourning Becomes Electra*

1932	*Ah, Wilderness!*
1934	*Days Without End*
1936	Receives Nobel prize for literature
1946	*The Iceman Cometh*
1947	Stricken with a disorder of the nervous system; *A Moon for the Misbegotten*
1953	Dies, November 27
1955	*A Long Day's Journey into Night,* world premiere at the Royal Dramatic Theatre, Stockholm
1956	Broadway opening of *A Long Day's Journey into Night;* Pulitzer prize awarded posthumously
1957	Broadway opening of *A Moon for the Misbegotten*
1958	World premiere of *A Touch of the Poet* at the Royal Dramatic Theatre, Stockholm, March 29; Broadway premiere October 12
1962	World premiere of an adaptation of *More Stately Mansions* (left in rough draft by O'Neill) at the Royal Dramatic Theatre, Stockholm.

FURTHER READINGS

Collected Works (3 vols. 1959)

Doris Alexander, *The Tempering of Eugene O'Neill* (1962)

———, "Eugene O'Neill as Social Critic," *American Quarterly* (Winter, 1954)

Brooks Atkinson, "The Iceman Cometh," in *Broadway Scrapbook* (1947)

Eric Bentley, "A Moon for the Misbegotten," in *The Dramatic Event* (1954)

Anita Block, *The Changing World in Plays and Theatre* (1939)

Travis Bogard, *Contour in Time* (1972)

Agnes Boulton, *Part of a Long Story* (1958)

Croswell Bowen and Shane O'Neill, *The Curse of the Misbegotten: A Tale of the House of O'Neill* (1959)

Oscar Cargill, *O'Neill and His Plays: Four Decades of Criticism* (1961)

Barrett H. Clark, *Eugene O'Neill* (1947)

Leon Edel, "Eugene O'Neill: The Face and the Mask," *University of Toronto Quarterly* (October, 1937)

Edwin A. Engel, *The Haunted Heroes of Eugene O'Neill* (1953)

Doris Falk, *Eugene O'Neill and the Tragic Tension: An Interpretative Study of the Plays* (1958)

John Gassner, *Eugene O'Neill* (1965)

———, *O'Neill: A Collection of Critical Essays* (1964)

Arthur and Barbara Gelb, *O'Neill* (1962)

Albert Rothenberg, "The Iceman Changeth: Toward an Empirical Approach to Creativity," in *The Journal of the American Psychoanalytic Association,* XVII, 549–607

Richard Dana Skinner, *Eugene O'Neill: A Poet's Quest* (1935)

Sophus Keith Winther, *Eugene O'Neill: A Critical Study* (1934)

Desire Under the Elms (1924)

Part of the artistic accomplishment in *Desire Under the Elms* is due to O'Neill's confident fusing of sources and resources he had tended hitherto to draw upon seriatim. Distance was achieved by setting the drama back in 1850, and intimacy by locating it in the Connecticut farmland where O'Neill himself was now living—he has recently bought a thirty-acre estate called Brook Farm (O'Neill seems not to have been aware of the historic Brook Farm, nor of his literary ancestor Hawthorne's association with it), in Ridgefield, about fifty miles north of New York. This time, as he grappled once more with the theme of family, O'Neill succeeded in bringing to bear upon it several crucially valuable elements. His long immersion in Greek tragedy had taught him not only that *its* theme too was the devouring tensions of family relations—husband and wife, parents and children, brother and sister—but that Sophocles, Aeschylus, and Euripides had bodied forth those tensions in the most extreme and violent forms. With the Greek dramatists as his warrant, O'Neill did not scruple, in *Desire Under the Elms,* to portray modes of incest and infanticide, nor to mention the murderous hatred of a son for his father. All this suited one aspect of O'Neill's artistic temperament—his incurable addiction to the melodramatic, a legacy from his father's long entrapment in the archetypal melodrama, *The Count of Monte Cristo.*

But the personally grounded motifs, the model of Greek tragedy, and the melodramatic trappings were also fused with another element which gave the play its compelling modernity and its basic intellectual coherence. In one of his not infrequent discourses upon the ideal the modern theater should aspire to, O'Neill laid it down that "The theater should give us what the church no longer gives us—a meaning. In brief, it should return to the spirit of Greek grandeur. And if we have no Gods or heroes to portray, we have the subconscious, the mother of all gods and heroes." There speaks the lapsed Catholic who had never managed to escape the faith of his childhood and the cast of mind that faith gave rise to: religious significance must still be striven for, but, as O'Neill believed at this time, it would return to literature by way of the doctrines of Freud and Jung.

The household in *Desire Under the Elms* is, accordingly, at once an unmistakably *real* household, realistically portrayed, and at the same time a theater in which conflicting subconscious desires are presented as actual happenings participated in by flesh-and-blood characters. Ephraim Cabot, an aging, flinty-hearted farmer, returns to his Connecticut home after a brief absence, bringing with him a new wife, a buxom and ambitious former housemaid, much younger than he, named Abbie Putnam. This essentially father-daughter relationship is invaded by Ephraim's third son, Eben, who is smolderingly convinced that Ephraim had killed his former wife—Eben's mother—by years of overwork. Eben's

revenge takes the form of an affair, both adulterous and incestuous, with Abbie, who eventually has a child by him. Eben then persuades himself that a child was all Abbie had wanted of him, as an assurance of possessing the farm after Ephraim dies. He denounces her and makes ready to leave. Abbie, now deeply in love with her husband's young son, thereupon strangles the baby in order to prove to Eben the truth of her feelings. In a daze of horror and outrage, Eben reports the crime to the police; but after Abbie is arrested, Eben discovers he cannot bear to be separated from her either in guilt or in love and gives himself up as equally culpable.

The plot as thus recapitulated cannot but sound almost grotesquely melodramatic, yet the play as experienced does not convey that impression. The tragic action unfolds at a leisurely yet inexorable pace, and one becomes gradually conscious of a host of accumulating contrasts, parallels, and complexities. Eben constantly asserts that he is his mother's son and virtually refuses to acknowledge Ephraim as his Pa; yet everyone tells him he is the spitting image of his father. For much of the play, it is indeed the paternal side of him that is in command: he lusts after and has sexual relations both with Ephraim's prostitute, Minnie, and his third wife; he steals the very money Ephraim had stolen from his own brother some years before; his rejection of Abbie has a sort of inherited puritanic fury in it. A similar conflict—what Doris Falk has called "tragic tension"—becomes apparent in Abbie and Ephraim as well. If Abbie at first rather resembles Ephraim in her calculating acquisitiveness (Ephraim had married his previous wife precisely to get hold of the farm), under the influence of love she comes to seem more like Eben's mother; and Ephraim's stern and forbidding nature becomes pliant, submissive, and wistful under Abbie's domination.

At the center of this thickening pattern is the character of Eben—so much so that Ephraim and Abbie, however fully and handsomely realized, function, one ends by suspecting, mainly as externalizations of Eben's inner conflicts. In other words, *Desire Under the Elms* from one vantage point may be seen as the elaborate dramatization of the search for a harmony of self, and it concludes—when Eben, imprisoned yet liberated, arrives at peace with Abbie and his own soul—with what Jung has defined as the integration of the personality. The self in question, needless to say, is, when all is said and done, that of Eugene O'Neill—a psychic entity that he did not restrict to Eben, but artfully distributed among his father and step-mother as well. It was indeed about Ephraim rather than Eben that O'Neill said later: "He's so autobiographical!"[1] What remains obvious, in any case, is that in the wake of his parents' death, O'Neill was able—if only temporarily—to come to terms with himself and to find the dramatic method whereby that difficult and potentially tragic process might be projected.

CHARACTERS

EPHRAIM CABOT

SIMEON
PETER   } *His sons*
EBEN

ABBIE PUTNAM

Young Girl, Two Farmers, The Fiddler, A Sheriff, and other folk from the neighboring farms.

The action of the entire play takes place in, and immediately outside of, the Cabot farmhouse in New England, in the year 1850. The south end of the house faces front to a stone wall with a wooden gate at center opening on a country road. The house is in good condition but in need of paint. Its walls are a sickly grayish, the green of the shutters faded. Two enormous elms are on each side of the house. They bend their trailing branches down over the roof. They appear to protect and at the same time subdue. There is a sinister maternity in their aspect, a crushing, jealous absorption. They

[1] The remark partly undercuts and partly confirms the findings of Dr. Philip Weissman, a cultivated psychiatrist who maintained, in an article of 1957, that *Desire Under the Elms* was O'Neill's "unconscious autobiography"—and a play written "by someone who was recently in the midst of the most intense personal mourning for his mother"—while *Long Day's Journey* was the "conscious autobiography."

have developed from their intimate contact with the life of man in the house an appalling humanness. They brood oppressively over the house. They are like exhausted women resting their sagging breasts and hands and hair on its roof, and when it rains their tears trickle down monotonously and rot on the shingles.

There is a path running from the gate around the right corner of the house to the front door. A narrow porch is on this side. The end wall facing us has two windows in its upper story, two larger ones on the floor below. The two upper are those of the father's bedroom and that of the brothers. On the left, ground floor, is the kitchen—on the right, the parlor, the shades of which are always drawn down.

PART ONE • SCENE ONE

Exterior of the farmhouse. It is sunset of a day at the beginning of summer in the year 1850. There is no wind and everything is still. The sky above the roof is suffused with deep colors, the green of the elms glows, but the house is in shadow, seeming pale and washed out by contrast.

A door opens and EBEN CABOT *comes to the end of the porch and stands looking down the road to the right. He has a large bell in his hand and this he swings mechanically, awakening a deafening clangor. Then he puts his hands on his hips and stares up at the sky. He sighs with a puzzled awe and blurts out with halting appreciation.*

EBEN: God! Purty! (*His eyes fall and he stares about him frowningly. He is twenty-five, tall and sinewy. His face is well-formed, good-looking, but its expression is resentful and defensive. His defiant, dark eyes remind one of a wild animal's in captivity. Each day is a cage in which he finds himself trapped but inwardly unsubdued. There is a fierce repressed vitality about him. He has black hair, mustache, a thin curly trace of beard. He is dressed in rough farm clothes.*

He spits on the ground with intense disgust, turns and goes back into the house.

SIMEON *and* PETER *come in from their work in the fields. They are tall men, much older than their half-brother [*SIMEON *is thirty-nine and* PETER *thirty-seven], built on a squarer, simpler model, fleshier in body, more bovine and homelier in face, shrewder and more practical. Their shoulders stoop a bit from years of farm work. They clump heavily* along in their clumsy thick-soled boots caked with earth. Their clothes, their faces, hands, bare arms and throats are earth-stained. They smell of earth. They stand together for a moment in front of the house and, as if with the one impulse, stare dumbly up at the sky, leaning on their hoes. Their faces have a compressed, unresigned expression. As they look upward, this softens.)

SIMEON (*grudgingly*): Purty.

PETER: Ay-eh.

SIMEON (*suddenly*): Eighteen years ago.

PETER: What?

SIMEON: Jenn. My woman. She died.

PETER: I'd fergot.

SIMEON: I rec'lect—now an' agin. Makes it lonesome. She'd hair long's a hoss' tail—an' yaller like gold!

PETER: Waal—she's gone. (*This with indifferent finality—then after a pause*) They's gold in the West, Sim.

SIMEON (*still under the influence of sunset—vaguely*): In the sky?

PETER: Waal—in a manner o' speakin'—thar's the promise. (*Growing excited*) Gold in the sky—in the West—Golden Gate—Californi-a!—Goldest West!—fields o' gold!

SIMEON (*excited in his turn*): Fortunes layin' just atop o' the ground waitin' t' be picked! Solomon's mines, they says! (*For a moment they continue looking up at the sky—then their eyes drop*).

PETER (*with sardonic bitterness*): Here—it's stones atop o' the ground—stones atop o' stones—makin' stone walls—year atop o' year—him 'n' yew 'n' me 'n' then Eben—makin' stone walls fur him to fence us in!

SIMEON: We've wuked. Give our strength. Give our years. Plowed 'em under in the ground,—(*he stamps rebelliously*)—rottin'—makin' soil for his crops! (*A pause*) Waal—the farm pays good for hereabouts.

PETER: If we plowed in Californi-a, they'd be lumps o' gold in the furrow!

SIMEON: Californi-a's t'other side o' earth, a'most. We got t' calc'late—

PETER (*after a pause*): 'Twould be hard fur me, too, to give up what we've 'arned here by our sweat. (*A pause.* EBEN *sticks his head out of the dining-room window, listening.*)

SIMEON: Ay-eh. (*A pause*) Mebbe—he'll die soon.

PETER (*doubtfully*): Mebbe.

SIMEON: Mebbe—fur all we knows—he's dead now.

PETER: Ye'd need proof.

SIMEON: He's been gone two months—with no word.

PETER: Left us in the fields an evenin' like this. Hitched up an' druv off into the West. That's plum onnateral. He hain't never been off this farm 'ceptin' t' the village in thirty year or more, not since he married Eben's maw. (*A pause. Shrewdly*) I calc'late we might git him declared crazy by the court.

SIMEON: He skinned 'em too slick. He got the best o' all on 'em. They'd never b'lieve him crazy. (*A pause*) We got t' wait—till he's under ground.

EBEN (*with a sardonic chuckle*): Honor thy father! (*They turn, startled, and stare at him. He grins, then scowls*) I pray he's died. (*They stare at him. He continues matter-of-factly*) Supper's ready.

SIMEON *and* PETER (*together*): Ay-eh.

EBEN (*gazing up at the sky*): Sun's downin' purty.

SIMEON *and* PETER (*together*): Ay-eh. They's gold in the West.

EBEN: Ay-eh. (*Pointing*) Yonder atop o' the hill pasture, ye mean?

SIMEON *and* PETER (*together*): In Californi-a!

EBEN: Hunh? (*Stares at them indifferently for a second, then drawls*) Waal—supper's gittin' cold. (*He turns back into kitchen.*)

SIMEON (*startled—smacks his lips*): I air hungry!

PETER (*sniffing*): I smells bacon!

SIMEON (*with hungry appreciation*): Bacon's good!

PETER (*in same tone*): Bacon's bacon! (*They turn, shouldering each other, their bodies bumping and rubbing together as they hurry clumsily to their food, like two friendly oxen toward their evening meal. They disappear around the right corner of house and can be heard entering the door.*)

SCENE TWO

The color fades from the sky. Twilight begins. The interior of the kitchen is now visible. A pine table is at center, a cookstove in the right rear corner, four rough wooden chairs, a tallow candle on the table. In the middle of the rear wall is fastened a big advertizing poster with a ship in full sail and the word "California" in big letters. Kitchen utensils hang from nails. Everything is neat and in order but the atmosphere is of a men's camp kitchen rather than that of a home.

Places for three are laid. EBEN *takes boiled pota-*

toes and bacon from the stove and puts them on the table, also a loaf of bread and a crock of water. SIMEON *and* PETER *shoulder in, slump down in their chairs without a word.* EBEN *joins them. The three eat in silence for a moment, the two elder as naturally unrestrained as beasts of the field,* EBEN *picking at his food without appetite, glancing at them with a tolerant dislike.*

SIMEON (*suddenly turns to* EBEN): Looky here! Ye'd oughtn't t' said that, Eben.

PETER: 'Twa'n't righteous.

EBEN: What?

SIMEON: Ye prayed he'd died.

EBEN: Waal—don't yew pray it? (*A pause.*)

PETER: He's our Paw.

EBEN (*violently*): Not mine!

SIMEON (*dryly*): Ye'd not let no one else say that about yer Maw! Ha! (*He gives one abrupt sardonic guffaw.* PETER *grins.*)

EBEN (*very pale*): I meant—I hain't his'n—I hain't like him—he hain't me!

PETER (*dryly*): Wait till ye've growed his age!

EBEN (*intensely*): I'm Maw—every drop o' blood! (*A pause. They stare at him with indifferent curiosity.*)

PETER (*reminiscently*): She was good t' Sim 'n' me. A good step-maw's scurse.

SIMEON: She was good t' everyone.

EBEN (*greatly moved, gets to his feet and makes an awkward bow to each of them—stammering*): I be thankful t' ye. I'm her—her heir. (*He sits down in confusion.*)

PETER (*after a pause—judicially*): She was good even t' him.

EBEN (*fiercely*): An' fur thanks he killed her!

SIMEON (*after a pause*): No one never kills nobody. It's allus some thin'. That's the murderer.

EBEN: Didn't he slave Maw t' death?

PETER: He's slaved himself t' death. He's slaved Sim 'n' me 'n' yew t' death—on'y none o' us hain't died—yit.

SIMEON: It's somethin'—drivin' him—t' drive us!

EBEN (*vengefully*): Waal—I hold him t' jedgment! (*Then scornfully*) Somethin'! What's somethin'?

SIMEON: Dunno.

EBEN (*sardonically*): What's drivin' yew to Californi-a, mebbe? (*They look at him in surprise*) Oh, I've heerd ye! (*Then, after a pause*) But ye'll never go t' the gold fields!

PETER (*assertively*): Mebbe!

EBEN: Whar'll ye git the money?

PETER: We kin walk. It's an a'mighty ways—Californi-a—but if yew was t' put all the steps we've walked on this farm end t' end we'd be in the moon!

EBEN: The Injuns'll skulp ye on the plains.

SIMEON (*with grim humor*): We'll mebbe make 'em pay a hair fur a hair!

EBEN (*decisively*): But t'aint that. Ye won't never go because ye'll wait here fur yer share o' the farm, thinkin' allus he'll die soon.

SIMEON (*after a pause*): We've a right.

PETER: Two-thirds belong t' us.

EBEN (*jumping to his feet*): Ye've no right! She wa'n't yewr Maw! It was her farm! Didn't he steal it from her? She's dead. It's my farm.

SIMEON (*sardonically*): Tell that t' Paw—when he comes! I'll bet ye a dollar he'll laugh—fur once in his life. Ha! (*He laughs himself in one single mirthless bark.*)

PETER (*amused in turn, echoes his brother*): Ha!

SIMEON (*after a pause*): What've ye got held agin us, Eben? Year arter year it's skulked in yer eye—somethin'.

PETER: Ay-eh.

EBEN: Ay-eh. They's somethin'. (*Suddenly exploding*) Why didn't ye never stand between him 'n' my Maw when he was slavin' her to her grave—t' pay her back fur the kindness she done t' yew? (*There is a long pause. They stare at him in surprise.*)

SIMEON: Waal—the stock's got t' be watered.

PETER: 'R they was woodin' t' do.

SIMEON: 'R plowin'.

PETER: 'R hayin'.

SIMEON: 'R spreadin' manure.

PETER: 'R weedin'.

SIMEON: 'R prunin'.

PETER: 'R milkin'.

EBEN (*breaking in harshly*): An' makin' walls—stone atop o' stone—makin' walls till yer heart's a stone ye heft up out o' the way o' growth onto a stone wall t' wall in yer heart!

SIMEON (*matter-of-factly*): We never had no time t' meddle.

PETER (*to* EBEN): Yew was fifteen afore yer Maw died—an' big fur yer age. Why didn't ye never do nothin'?

EBEN (*harshly*): They was chores t' do, wa'n't they? (*A pause—then slowly*) It was on'y arter she died I come to think o' it. Me cookin'—doin' her work—that made me know her, suffer her sufferin'—she'd come back t' help—come back t' bile potatoes—come back t' fry bacon—come back t' bake biscuits—come back all cramped up t' shake the fire, an' carry ashes, her eyes weepin' an' bloody with smoke an' cinders same's they used t' be. She still comes back—stands by the stove thar in the evenin'—she can't find it nateral sleepin' an' restin' in peace. She can't git used t' bein' free—even in her grave.

SIMEON: She never complained none.

EBEN: She'd got too tired. She'd got too used t' bein' too tired. That was what he done. (*With vengeful passion*) An' sooner'r later, I'll meddle. I'll say the thin's I didn't say then t' him! I'll yell 'em at the top o' my lungs. I'll see t' it my Maw gits some rest an' sleep in her grave! (*He sits down again, relapsing into a brooding silence. They look at him with a queer indifferent curiosity.*)

PETER (*after a pause*): Whar in tarnation d'ye s'pose he went, Sim?

SIMEON: Dunno. He druv off in the buggy, all spick an' span, with the mare all breshed an' shiny, druv off clackin' his tongue an' wavin' his whip. I remember it right well. I was finishin' plowin', it was spring an' May an' sunset, an' gold in the West, an' he druv off into it. I yells "Whar ye goin', Paw?" an' he hauls up by the stone wall a jiffy. His old snake's eyes was glitterin' in the sun like he'd been drinkin' a jugful an' he says with a mule's grin: "Don't ye run away till I come back!"

PETER: Wonder if he knowed we was wantin' fur Californi-a?

SIMEON: Mebbe. I didn't say nothin' and he says, lookin' kinder queer an' sick: "I been hearin' the hens cluckin' an' the roosters crowin' all the durn day. I been listenin' t' the cows lowin' an' everythin' else kickin' up till I can't stand it no more. It's spring an' I'm feelin' damned," he says. "Damned like an old bare hickory tree fit on'y fur burnin'," he says. An' then I calc'late I must've looked a mite hopeful, fur he adds real spry and vicious: "But don't git no fool idee I'm dead. I've sworn t' live a hundred an' I'll do it, if on'y t' spite yer sinful greed! An' now I'm ridin' out t' learn God's message t' me in the spring, like the prophets done. An' yew git back t' yer plowin'," he says. An' he druv off singin' a hymn. I thought he was drunk—'r I'd stopped him goin'.

EBEN (*scornfully*): No, ye wouldn't! Ye're scared o' him. He's stronger—inside—than both o' ye put together!

PETER (*sardonically*): An' yew—be yew Samson?

EBEN: I'm gittin' stronger. I kin feel it growin' in me—growin' an' growin'—till it'll bust out—! (*He gets up and puts on his coat and a hat. They watch him, gradually breaking into grins. EBEN avoids their eyes sheepishly*) I'm goin' out fur a spell—up the road.

PETER: T' the village?

SIMEON: T' the village?

SIMEON: T' see Minnie?

EBEN (*defiantly*): Ay-eh?

PETER (*jeeringly*): The Scarlet Woman!

SIMEON: Lust—that's what's growin' in ye!

EBEN: Waal—she's purty!

PETER: She's been purty fur twenty year!

SIMEON: A new coat o' paint'll make a heifer out of forty.

EBEN: She hain't forty!

PETER: If she hain't, she's teeterin' on the edge.

EBEN (*desperately*): What d'yew know—

PETER: All they is . . . Sim knew her—an' then me arter—

SIMEON: An' Paw kin tell yew somethin' too! He was fust!

EBEN: D'ye mean t' say he . . . ?

SIMEON (*with a grin*): Ay-eh! We air his heirs in everythin'!

EBEN (*intensely*): That's more to it! That grows on it! It'll bust soon! (*Then violently*) I'll go smash my fist in her face! (*He pulls open the door in rear violently.*)

SIMEON (*with a wink at PETER—drawlingly*): Mebbe—but the night's wa'm—purty—by the time ye git thar mebbe ye'll kiss her instead!

PETER: Sart'n he will! (*They both roar with coarse laughter. EBEN rushes out and slams the door—then the outside front door—comes around the corner of the house and stands still by the gate, staring up at the sky.*)

SIMEON (*looking after him*): Like his Paw.

PETER: Dead spit an' image!

SIMEON: Dog'll eat dog!

PETER: Ay-eh. (*Pause. With yearning*) Mebbe a year from now we'll be in Californi-a.

SIMEON: Ay-eh. (*A pause. Both yawn*) Let's git t' bed. (*He blows out the candle. They go out door in rear. EBEN stretches his arms up to the sky—rebelliously.*)

EBEN: Waal—thar's a star, an' somewhar's they's him, an' here's me, an' thar's Min up the road—in the same night. What if I does kiss her? She's like t'night, she's soft 'n' wa'm, her eyes kin wink like a star, her mouth's wa'm, her arms're wa'm, she smells like a wa'm plowed field, she's purty . . . Ay-eh! By God A'mighty she's purty, an' I don't give a damn how many sins she's sinned afore mine or who she's sinned 'em with, my sin's as purty as any one of 'em! (*He strides off down the road to the left.*)

SCENE THREE

It is the pitch darkness just before dawn. EBEN *comes in from the left and goes around to the porch, feeling his way, chuckling bitterly and cursing half-aloud to himself.*

EBEN: The cussed old miser! (*He can be heard going in the front door. There is a pause as he goes upstairs, then a loud knock on the bedroom door of the brothers*) Wake up!

SIMEON (*startedly*): Who's thar?

EBEN (*pushing open the door and coming in, a lighted candle in his hand. The bedroom of the brothers is revealed. Its ceiling is the sloping roof. They can stand upright only close to the center dividing wall of the upstairs.* SIMEON *and* PETER *are in a double bed, front.* EBEN'S *cot is to the rear.* EBEN *has a mixture of a silly grin and vicious scowl on his face*): I be!

PETER (*angrily*): What in hell's-fire . . . ?

EBEN: I got news fur ye! Ha! (*He gives one abrupt sardonic guffaw.*)

SIMEON (*angrily*): Couldn't ye hold it 'til we'd got our sleep?

EBEN: It's nigh sunup. (*Then explosively*) He's gone an' married agen!

SIMEON *and* PETER (*explosively*): Paw?

EBEN: Got himself hitched to a female 'bout thirty-five—an' purty, they says . . .

SIMEON (*aghast*): It's a durn lie!

PETER: Who says?

SIMEON: They been stringin' ye!

EBEN: Think I'm a dunce, do ye? The hull village says. The preacher from New Dover, he brung the news—told it t' our preacher—New Dover, that's whar the old loon got himself hitched—that's whar the woman lived—

PETER (*no longer doubting—stunned*): Waal . . . !

SIMEON (*the same*): Waal . . . !

EBEN (*sitting down on a bed—with vicious hatred*): Ain't he a devil out o' hell? It's jest t' spite us—the damned old mule!

PETER (*after a pause*): Everythin'll go t' her now.

SIMEON: Ay-eh. (*A pause—dully*) Waal—if it's done—

PETER: It's done us. (*Pause—then persuasively*) They's gold in the fields o' Californi-a, Sim. No good a-stayin' here now.

SIMEON: Jest what I was a-thinkin'. (*Then with decision*) S'well fust's last! Let's light out and git this mornin'.

PETER: Suits me.

EBEN: Ye must like walkin'.

SIMEON (*sardonically*): If ye'd grow wings on us we'd fly thar!

EBEN: Ye'd like ridin' better—on a boat, wouldn't ye? (*Fumbles in his pocket and takes out a crumpled sheet of foolscap*) Waal, if ye sign this ye kin ride on a boat. I've had it writ out an' ready in case ye'd ever go. It says fur three hundred dollars t' each ye agree yewr shares o' the farm is sold t' me. (*They look suspiciously at the paper. A pause.*)

SIMEON (*wonderingly*): But if he's hitched agen—

PETER: An' whar'd yew git that sum o' money, anyways?

EBEN (*cunningly*): I know whar it's hid. I been waitin'—Maw told me. She knew whar it lay fur years, but she was waitin' . . . It's her'n—the money he hoarded from her farm an' hid from Maw. It's my money by rights now.

PETER: Whar's it hid?

EBEN (*cunningly*): Whar yew won't never find it without me. Maw spied on him—'r she'd never knowed. (*A pause. They look at him suspiciously, and he at them*) Waal, is it fa'r trade?

SIMEON: Dunno.

PETER: Dunno.

SIMEON (*looking at window*): Sky's grayin'.

PETER: Ye better start the fire, Eben.

SIMEON: An' fix some vittles.

EBEN: Ay-eh. (*Then with a forced jocular heartiness*) I'll git ye a good one. If ye're startin' t' hoof it t' Californi-a ye'll need somethin' that'll stick t' yer ribs. (*He turns to the door, adding meaningly*) But ye kin ride on a boat if ye'll swap. (*He stops at the door and pauses. They stare at him.*)

SIMEON (*suspiciously*): Whar was ye all night?

EBEN (*defiantly*): Up t' Min's. (*Then slowly*) Walkin' thar, fust I felt 's if I'd kiss her; then I got a-thinkin' o' what ye'd said o' him an' her an' I says, I'll bust her nose fur that! Then I got t' the village an' heerd the news an' I got madder'n hell an' run all the way t' Min's not knowin' what I'd do—(*He pauses—then sheepishly but more defiantly*) Waal—when I seen her, I didn't hit her—nor I didn't kiss her nuther—I begun t' beller like a calf an' cuss at the same time, I was so durn mad—an' she got scared—an' I jest grabbed holt an' tuk her! (*Proudly*) Yes, sirree! I tuk her. She may've been his'n—an' your'n, too—but she's mine now!

SIMEON (*dryly*): In love, air yew?

EBEN (*with lofty scorn*): Love! I don't take no stock in sech slop!

PETER (*winking at* SIMEON): Mebbe Eben's aimin' t' marry, too.

SIMEON: Min'd make a true faithful he'pmeet! (*They snicker.*)

EBEN: What do I care fur her—'ceptin' she's round an' wa'm? The p'int is she was his'n—an' now she b'longs t' me! (*He goes to the door—then turns—rebelliously*) An' Min hain't sech a bad un. They's worse'n Min in the world, I'll bet ye! Wait'll we see this cow the Old Man's hitched t'! She'll beat Min, I got a notion! (*He starts to go out.*)

SIMEON (*suddenly*): Mebbe ye'll try t' make her your'n, too?

PETER: Ha! (*He gives a sardonic laugh of relish at this idea.*)

EBEN (*spitting with disgust*): Her—here—sleepin' with him—stealin' my Maw's farm! I'd as soon pet a skunk 'r kiss a snake! (*He goes out. The two stare after him suspiciously. A pause. They listen to his steps receding.*)

PETER: He's startin' the fire.

SIMEON: I'd like t' ride t' Californi-a—but—

PETER: Min might o' put some scheme in his head.

SIMEON: Mebbe it's all a lie 'bout Paw marryin'. We'd best wait an' see the bride.

PETER: An' don't sign nothin' till we does!

SIMEON: Nor till we've tested it's good money! (*Then with a grin*) But if Paw's hitched we'd be sellin' Eben somethin' we'd never git nohow!

PETER: We'll wait an' see. (*Then with sudden vindictive anger*) An' till he comes, let's yew 'n' me not wuk a lick, let Eben tend to thin's if he's a mind t', let's us jest sleep an' eat an' drink likker an' let the hull damned farm go t' blazes!

SIMEON (*excitedly*): By God, we've 'arned a rest! We'll play rich fur a change. I hain't a-going to stir outa bed till breakfast's ready.

PETER: An' on the table!

SIMEON (*after a pause—thoughtfully*): What d'ye calc'late she'll be like—our new Maw? Like Eben thinks?

PETER: More'n' likely.

SIMEON (*vindictively*): Waal—I hope she's a she-devil that'll make him wish he was dead an' livin' in the pit o' hell fur comfort!

PETER (*fervently*): Amen!

SIMEON (*imitating his father's voice*): "I'm ridin' out t' learn God's message t' me in the spring like the prophets done," he says. I'll bet right then an' thar he knew plumb well he was goin' whorin', the stinkin' old hypocrite!

SCENE FOUR

Same as Scene Two—shows the interior of the kitchen with a lighted candle on table. It is gray dawn outside. SIMEON *and* PETER *are just finishing their breakfast.* EBEN *sits before his plate of untouched food, brooding frowningly.*

PETER (*glancing at him rather irritably*): Lookin' glum don't help none.

SIMEON (*sarcastically*): Sorrowin' over his lust o' the flesh!

PETER (*with a grin*): Was she yer fust?

EBEN (*angrily*): None o' yer business. (*A pause*) I was thinkin' o' him. I got a notion he's gittin' near—I kin feel him comin' on like yew kin feel malaria chill afore it takes ye.

PETER: It's too early yet.

SIMEON: Dunno. He'd like t' catch us nappin'—jest t' have somethin' t' hoss us 'round over.

PETER (*mechanically gets to his feet.* SIMEON *does the same*): Waal—let's git t' wuk. (*They both plod mechanically toward the door before they realize. Then they stop short.*)

SIMEON (*grinning*): Ye're a cussed fool, Pete—and I be wuss! Let him see we hain't wukin'! We don't give a durn!

PETER (*as they go back to the table*): Not a damned durn! It'll serve t' show him we're done with him. (*They sit down again.* EBEN *stares from one to the other with surprise.*)

SIMEON (*grins at him*): We're aimin' t' start bein' lilies o' the field.

PETER: Nary a toil 'r spin 'r lick o' wuk do we put in!

SIMEON: Ye're sole owner—till he comes—that's what ye wanted. Waal, ye got t' be sole hand, too.

PETER: The cows air bellerin'. Ye better hustle at the milkin'.

EBEN (*with excited joy*): Ye mean ye'll sign the paper?

SIMEON (*dryly*): Mebbe.

PETER: Mebbe.

SIMEON: We're considerin'. (*Peremptorily*) Ye better git t' wuk.

EBEN (*with queer excitement*): It's Maw's farm agen! It's my farm! Them's my cows! I'll milk my durn fingers off fur cows o' mine! (*He goes out door in rear, they stare after him indifferently.*)

SIMEON: Like his Paw.

PETER: Dead spit 'n' image!

SIMEON: Waal—let dog eat dog! (EBEN *comes out of front door and around the corner of the house. The sky is beginning to grow flushed with sunrise.* EBEN *stops by the gate and stares around him with glowing, possessive eyes. He takes in the whole farm with his embracing glance of desire.*)

EBEN: It's purty! It's damned purty! It's mine! (*He suddenly throws his head back boldly and glares with hard, defiant eyes at the sky*) Mine, d'ye hear? Mine! (*He turns and walks quickly off left, rear, toward the barn. The two brothers light their pipes.*)

SIMEON (*putting his muddy boots up on the table, tilting back his chair, and puffing defiantly*): Waal—this air solid comfort—fur once.

PETER: Ay-eh. (*He follows suit. A pause. Unconsciously they both sigh.*)

SIMEON (*suddenly*): He never was much o' a hand at milkin', Eben wa'n't.

PETER (*with a snort*): His hands air like hoofs! (*A pause.*)

SIMEON: Reach down the jug thar! Let's take a swaller. I'm feelin' kind o' low.

PETER: Good idee! (*He does so—gets two glasses —they pour out drinks of whisky*) Here's t' the gold in Californi-a!

SIMEON: An' luck t' find it! (*They drink—puff resolutely—sigh—take their feet down from the table.*)

PETER: Likker don't 'pear t' sot right.

SIMEON: We hain't used t' it this early. (*A pause. They become very restless.*)

PETER: Gittin' close in this kitchen.

SIMEON (*with immense relief*): Let's git a breath o' air. (*They arise briskly and go out rear—appear around house and stop by the gate. They stare up at the sky with a numbed appreciation.*)

PETER: Purty!

SIMEON: Ay-eh. Gold's t' the East now.

PETER: Sun's startin' with us fur the Golden West.

SIMEON (*staring around the farm, his compressed face tightened, unable to conceal his emotion*): Waal—it's our last mornin'—mebbe.

PETER (*the same*): Ay-eh.

SIMEON (*stamps his foot on the earth and addresses it desperately*): Waal—ye've thirty year o' me buried in ye—spread out over ye—blood an' bone an' sweat—rotted away—fertilizin' ye—richin' yer soul—prime manure, by God, that's what I been t' ye!

PETER: Ay-eh! An' me!

SIMEON: An' yew, Peter. (*He sighs—then spits*) Waal—no use'n cryin' over spilt milk.

PETER: They's gold in the West—an' freedom, mebbe. We been slaves t' stone walls here.

SIMEON (*defiantly*): We hain't nobody's slaves from this out—nor no thin's slaves nuther. (*A pause—restlessly*) Speakin' o' milk, wonder how Eben's managin'?

PETER: I s'pose he's managin'.

SIMEON: Mebbe we'd ought t' help—this once.

PETER: Mebbe. The cows know us.

SIMEON: An' likes us. They don't know him much.

PETER: An' the hosses, an' pigs, an' chickens. They don't know him much.

SIMEON: They knows us like brothers—an' likes us! (*Proudly*) Hain't we raised 'em t' be fust-rate, number one prize stock?

PETER: We hain't—not no more.

SIMEON (*dully*): I was fergittin'. (*Then resignedly*) Waal, let's go help Eben a spell an' git waked up.

PETER: Suits me. (*They are starting off down left, rear, for the barn when* EBEN *appears from there hurrying toward them, his face excited.*)

EBEN (*breathlessly*): Waal—thar they be! The old mule an' the bride! I seen 'em from the barn down below at the turnin'.

PETER: How could ye tell that far?

EBEN: Hain't I as far-sight as he's near-sight? Don't I know the mare 'n' buggy, an' two people settin' in it? Who else . . . ? An' I tell ye I kin feel 'em a-comin', too! (*He squirms as if he had the itch.*)

PETER (*beginning to be angry*): Waal—let him do his own unhitchin'!

SIMEON (*angry in his turn*): Let's hustle in an' git our bundles an' be a-goin' as he's a-comin'. I don't want never t' step inside the door agen arter he's back. (*They both start back around the corner of the house.* EBEN *follows them.*)

EBEN (*anxiously*): Will ye sign it afore ye go?

PETER: Let's see the color o' the old skinflint's money an' we'll sign. (*They disappear left. The two brothers clump upstairs to get their bundles.* EBEN *appears in the kitchen, runs to window, peers out, comes back and pulls up a strip of flooring in under stove, takes out a canvas bag and puts it on table, then sets the floorboard back in place. The two brothers appear a moment after. They carry old carpetbags.*)

EBEN (*puts his hand on bag guardingly*): Have ye signed?

SIMEON (*shows paper in his hand*): Ay-eh. (*Greedily*) Be that the money?

EBEN (*opens bag and pours out pile of twenty-dollar gold pieces*): Twenty-dollar pieces—thirty of 'em. Count 'em. (*Peter does so, arranging them in stacks of five, biting one or two to test them.*)

PETER: Six hundred. (*He puts them in bag and puts it inside his shirt carefully.*)

SIMEON (*handing paper to* EBEN): Har ye be.

EBEN (*after a glance, folds it carefully and hides it under his shirt—gratefully*): Thank yew.

PETER: Thank yew fur the ride.

SIMEON: We'll send ye a lump o' gold fur Christmas. (*A pause.* EBEN *stares at them and they at him.*)

PETER (*awkwardly*): Waal—we're a-goin'.

SIMEON: Comin' out t' the yard?

EBEN: No. I'm waitin' in here a spell. (*Another silence. The brothers edge awkwardly to door in rear—then turn and stand.*)

SIMEON: Waal—good-by.

PETER: Good-by.

EBEN: Good-by. (*They go out. He sits down at the table, faces the stove and pulls out the paper. He looks from it to the stove. His face, lighted up by the shaft of sunlight from the window, has an expression of trance. His lips move. The two brothers come out to the gate.*)

PETER (*looking off toward barn*): Thar he be—unhitchin'.

SIMEON (*with a chuckle*): I'll bet ye he's riled!

PETER: An' thar she be.

SIMEON: Let's wait 'n' see what our new Maw looks like.

PETER (*with a grin*): An' give him our partin' cuss!

SIMEON (*grinning*): I feel like raisin' fun. I feel light in my head an' feet.

PETER: Me, too. I feel like laffin' till I'd split up the middle.

SIMEON: Reckon it's the likker?

PETER: No. My feet feel itchin' t' walk an' walk —an' jump high over thin's—an'. . . .

SIMEON: Dance? (*A pause.*)

PETER (*puzzled*): It's plumb onnateral.

SIMEON (*a light coming over his face*): I cal-c'late it's 'cause school's out. It's holiday. Fur once we're free!

PETER (*dazedly*): Free?

SIMEON: The halter's broke—the harness is busted —the fence bars is down—the stone walls air crum-blin' an' tumblin'! We'll be kickin' up an' tearin' away down the road!

PETER (*drawing a deep breath—oratorically*): Anybody that wants this stinkin' old rock-pile of a farm kin hev it. T'ain't our'n, no sirree!

SIMEON (*takes the gate off its hinges and puts it under his arm*): We harby 'bolishes shet gates, an' open gates, an' all gates, by thunder!

PETER: We'll take it with us fur luck an' let 'er sail free down some river.

SIMEON (*as a sound of voices comes from left, rear*): Har they comes! (*The two brothers congeal into two stiff, grim-visaged statues.* EPHRAIM CABOT *and* ABBIE PUTNAM *come in.* CABOT *is seventy-five, tall and gaunt, with great, wiry, concentrated power, but stoop-shouldered from toil. His face is as hard as if it were hewn out of a boulder, yet there is a weakness in it, a petty pride in its own narrow strength. His eyes are small, close together, and extremely near-sighted, blinking continually in the effort to focus on objects, their stare having a straining, ingrowing quality. He is dressed in his dismal black Sunday suit.* ABBIE *is thirty-five, buxom, full of vitality. Her round face is pretty but marred by its rather gross sensuality. There is strength and obstinacy in her jaw, a hard determination in her eyes, and about her whole personality the same unsettled, untamed, desperate quality which is so apparent in* EBEN.)

CABOT (*as they enter—a queer strangled emotion in his dry cracking voice*): Har we be t' hum, Abbie.

ABBIE (*with lust for the word*): Hum! (*Her eyes gloating on the house without seeming to see the two stiff figures at the gate*) It's purty—purty! I can't b'lieve it's r'ally mine.

CABOT (*sharply*): Yewr'n? Mine! (*He stares at her penetratingly, she stares back. He adds relentingly*) Our'n—mebbe! It was lonesome too long. I was growin' old in the spring. A hum's got t' hev a woman.

ABBIE (*her voice taking possession*): A woman's got t' hev a hum!

CABOT (*nodding uncertainly*): Ay-eh. (*Then irritably*) Whar be they? Ain't thar nobody about— 'r wukin'—'r nothin'?

ABBIE (*sees the brothers. She returns their stare of cold appraising contempt with interest—slowly*): Thar's two men loafin' at the gate an' starin' at me like a couple o' strayed hogs.

CABOT (*straining his eyes*): I kin see 'em—but I can't make out. . . .

SIMEON: It's Simeon.

PETER: It's Peter.

CABOT (*exploding*): Why hain't ye wukin'?

SIMEON (*dryly*): We're waitin' t' welcome ye hum—yew an' the bride!

CABOT (*confusedly*): Huh? Waal—this be yer new Maw, boys. (*She stares at them and they at her.*)

SIMEON (*turns away and spits contemptuously*): I see her!

PETER (*spits also*): An' I see her!

ABBIE (*with the conqueror's conscious superiority*): I'll go in an' look at *my* house. (*She goes slowly around to porch.*)

SIMEON (*with a snort*): Her house!

PETER (*calls after her*): Ye'll find Eben inside. Ye better not tell him it's yewr house.

ABBIE (*mouthing the name*): Eben. (*Then quietly*) I'll tell Eben.

CABOT (*with a contemptuous sneer*): Ye needn't heed Eben. Eben's a dumb fool—like his Maw—soft an' simple!

SIMEON (*with his sardonic burst of laughter*): Ha! Eben's a chip o' yew—spit 'n' image—hard 'n' bitter's a hickory tree! Dog'll eat dog. He'll eat ye yet, old man!

CABOT (*commandingly*): Ye git t' wuk!

SIMEON (*as ABBIE disappears in house—winks at PETER and says tauntingly*): So that thar's our new Maw, be it? Whar in hell did ye dig her up? (*He and PETER laugh.*)

PETER: Ha! Ye'd better turn her in the pen with the other sows. (*They laugh uproariously, slapping their thighs.*)

CABOT (*so amazed at their effrontery that he stutters in confusion*): Simeon! Peter! What's come over ye? Air ye drunk?

SIMEON: We're free, old man—free o' yew an' the hull damned farm! (*They grow more and more hilarious and excited.*)

PETER: An' we're startin' out fur the gold fields o' Californi-a!

SIMEON: Ye kin take this place an' burn it!

PETER: An' bury it—fur all we cares!

SIMEON: We're free, old man! (*He cuts a caper.*)

PETER: Free! (*He gives a kick in the air.*)

SIMEON (*in a frenzy*): Whoop!

PETER: Whoop! (*They do an absurd Indian war dance about the old man who is petrified between rage and the fear that they are insane.*)

SIMEON: We're free as Injuns! Lucky we don't skulp ye!

PETER: An' burn yer barn an' kill the stock!

SIMEON: An' rape yer new woman! Whoop! (*He

and PETER stop their dance, holding their sides, rocking with wild laughter.*)

CABOT (*edging away*): Lust fur gold—fur the sinful, easy gold o' Californi-a! It's made ye mad!

SIMEON (*tauntingly*): Wouldn't ye like us to send ye back some sinful gold, ye old sinner?

PETER: They's gold besides what's in Californi-a! (*He retreats back beyond the vision of the old man and takes the bag of money and flaunts it in the air above his head, laughing.*)

SIMEON: And sinfuller, too!

PETER: We'll be voyagin' on the sea! Whoop! (*He leaps up and down.*)

SIMEON: Livin' free! Whoop! (*He leaps in turn.*)

CABOT (*suddenly roaring with rage*): My cuss on ye!

SIMEON: Take our'n in trade fur it! Whoop!

CABOT: I'll hev ye both chained up in the asylum!

PETER: Ye old skinflint! Good-by!

SIMEON: Ye old blood sucker! Good-by!

CABOT: Go afore I . . . !

PETER: Whoop! (*He picks a stone from the road. SIMEON does the same.*)

SIMEON: Maw'll be in the parlor.

PETER: Ay-eh! One! Two!

CABOT (*frightened*): What air ye . . . ?

PETER: Three! (*They both throw, the stones hitting the parlor window with a crash of glass, tearing the shade.*)

SIMEON: Whoop!

PETER: Whoop!

CABOT (*in a fury now, rushing toward them*): If I kin lay hands on ye—I'll break yer bones fur ye! (*But they beat a capering retreat before him, SIMEON with the gate still under his arm. CABOT comes back, panting with impotent rage. Their voices as they go off take up the song of the gold-seekers to the old tune of "Oh, Susannah!"*)

> "I jumped aboard the Liza ship,
> And traveled on the sea.
> And every time I thought of home
> I wished it wasn't me!
> Oh! Californi-a,
> That's the land fur me!
> I'm off to Californi-a!
> With my wash bowl on my knee."

(*In the meantime, the window of the upper bedroom on right is raised and ABBIE sticks her head out. She looks down at CABOT—with a sigh of relief*).

ABBIE: Waal—that's the last o' them two, hain't it? (*He doesn't answer. Then in possessive tones*) This here's a nice bedroom, Ephraim. It's a r'al nice bed. Is it my room, Ephraim?

CABOT (*grimly—without looking up*): Our'n! (*She cannot control a grimace of aversion and pulls back her head slowly and shuts the window. A sudden horrible thought seems to enter* CABOT's *head*) They been up to somethin'! Mebbe—mebbe they've pizened the stock—'r somethin'! (*He almost runs off down toward the barn. A moment later the kitchen door is slowly pushed open and* ABBIE *enters. For a moment she stands looking at* EBEN. *He does not notice her at first. Her eyes take him in penetratingly with a calculating appraisal of his strength as against hers. But under this her desire is dimly awakened by his youth and good looks. Suddenly he becomes conscious of her presence and looks up. Their eyes meet. He leaps to his feet, glowering at her speechlessly.*)

ABBIE (*in her most seductive tones which she uses all through this scene*): Be you—Eben? I'm Abbie—(*she laughs*) I mean, I'm yer new Maw.

EBEN (*viciously*): No, damn ye!

ABBIE (*as if she hadn't heard—with a queer smile*): Yer Paw's spoke a lot o' yew. . . .

EBEN: Ha!

ABBIE: Ye mustn't mind him. He's an old man. (*A long pause. They stare at each other*) I don't want t' pretend playin' Maw t' ye, Eben. (*Admiringly*) Ye're too big an' too strong fur that. I want t' be frens with ye. Mebbe with me fur a fren ye'd find ye'd like livin' here better. I kin make it easy fur ye with him, mebbe. (*With a scornful sense of power*) I calc'late I kin git him t' do most anythin' fur me.

EBEN (*with bitter scorn*): Ha! (*They stare again,* EBEN *obscurely moved, physically attracted to her—in forced stilted tones*) Yew kin go t' the devil!

ABBIE (*calmly*): If cussin' me does ye good, cuss all ye've a mind t'. I'm all prepared t' have ye agin me—at fust. I don't blame ye nuther. I'd feel the same at any stranger comin' t' take my Maw's place. (*He shudders. She is watching him carefully*) Yew must've cared a lot fur yewr Maw, didn't ye? My Maw died afore I'd growed. I don't remember her none. (*A pause*) But yew won't hate me long, Eben. I'm not the wust in the world —an' yew an' me've got a lot in common. I kin tell that by lookin' at ye. Waal—I've had a hard life, too—oceans o' trouble an' nuthin' but wuk fur reward. I was a orphan early an' had t' wuk fur others in other folks' hums. Then I married an' he turned out a drunken spreer an' so he had to wuk fur others an' me too agen in other folks' hums, an' the baby died, an' my husband got sick an' died too, an' I was glad sayin' now I'm free fur once, on'y I diskivered right away all I was free fur was t' wuk agen in other folks' hums, doin' other folks' wuk till I'd most give up hope o' ever doin' my own wuk in my own hum, an' then your Paw come. . . . (CABOT *appears returning from the barn. He comes to the gate and looks down the road the brothers have gone. A faint strain of their retreating voices is heard: "Oh, Californi-a! That's the place for me." He stands glowering, his fist clenched, his face grim with rage.*)

EBEN (*fighting against his growing attraction and sympathy—harshly*): An' bought yew—like a harlot! (*She is stung and flushes angrily. She has been sincerely moved by the recital of her troubles. He adds furiously*) An' the price he's payin' ye—this farm—was my Maw's, damn ye!—an' mine now!

ABBIE (*with a cool laugh of confidence*): Yewr'n? We'll see 'bout that! (*Then strongly*) Waal—what if I did need a hum? What else'd I marry an old man like him fur?

EBEN (*maliciously*): I'll tell him ye said that!

ABBIE (*smiling*): I'll say ye're lyin' a-purpose—an' he'll drive ye off the place!

EBEN: Ye devil!

ABBIE (*defying him*): This be my farm—this be my hum—this be my kitchen—!

EBEN (*furiously, as if he were going to attack her*): Shut up, damn ye!

ABBIE (*walks up to him—a queer coarse expression of desire in her face and body—slowly*): An' upstairs—that be my bedroom—an' my bed! (*He stares into her eyes, terribly confused and torn. She adds softly*) I hain't bad nor mean—'ceptin' fur an enemy—but I got t' fight fur what's due me out o' life, if I ever 'spect t' git it. (*Then putting her hand on his arm—seductively*) Let's yew 'n' me be frens, Eben.

EBEN (*stupidly—as if hypnotized*): Ay-eh. (*Then furiously flinging off her arm*) No, ye durned old witch! I hate ye! (*He rushes out the door.*)

ABBIE (*looks after him smiling satisfiedly—then half to herself, mouthing the word*): Eben's nice. (*She looks at the table, proudly*) I'll wash up *my* dishes now. (EBEN *appears outside, slamming the door behind him. He comes around corner, stops on seeing his father, and stands staring at him with hate.*)

CABOT (*raising his arms to heaven in the fury he can no longer control*): Lord God o' Hosts, smite the undutiful sons with Thy wust cuss!

EBEN (*breaking in violently*): Yew 'n' yewr God! Allus cussin' folks—allus naggin' em!

CABOT (*oblivious to him—summoningly*): God o' the old! God o' the lonesome!

EBEN (*mockingly*): Naggin' His sheep t' sin! T' hell with yewr God! (CABOT *turns. He and* EBEN *glower at each other.*)

CABOT (*harshly*): So it's yew. I might've knowed it. (*Shaking his finger threateningly at him*) Blasphemin' fool! (*Then quickly*) Why hain't ye t' wuk?

EBEN: Why hain't yew? They've went. I can't wuk it all alone.

CABOT (*contemptuously*): Nor noways! I'm wuth ten o' ye yit, old's I be! Ye'll never be more'n half a man! (*Then, matter-of-factly*) Waal—let's git t' the barn. (*They go. A last faint note of the "Cali-forni-a" song is heard from the distance.* ABBIE *is washing her dishes.*)

PART TWO • SCENE ONE

The exterior of the farmhouse, as in Part One—a hot Sunday afternoon two months later. ABBIE, *dressed in her best, is discovered sitting in a rocker at the end of the porch. She rocks listlessly, enervated by the heat, staring in front of her with bored, half-closed eyes.*

EBEN *sticks his head out of his bedroom window. He looks around furtively and tries to see—or hear—if anyone is on the porch, but although he has been careful to make no noise,* ABBIE *has sensed his movement. She stops rocking, her face grows animated and eager, she waits attentively.* EBEN *seems to feel her presence, he scowls back his thoughts of her and spits with exaggerated disdain—then withdraws back into the room.* ABBIE *waits, holding her breath as she listens with passionate eagerness for every sound within the house.*

EBEN *comes out. Their eyes meet. His falter, he is confused, he turns away and slams the door resentfully. At this gesture,* ABBIE *laughs tantalizingly, amused but at the same time piqued and irritated. He scowls, strides off the porch to the path and starts to walk past her to the road with a grand swagger of ignoring her existence. He is dressed in his store suit, spruced up, his face shines from soap and water.* ABBIE *leans forward on her chair, her eyes hard and angry now, and, as he passes her, gives a sneering, taunting chuckle.*

EBEN (*stung—turns on her furiously*): What air yew cacklin' 'bout?

ABBIE (*triumphant*): Yew!

EBEN: What about me?

ABBIE: Ye look all slicked up like a prize bull.

EBEN (*with a sneer*): Waal—ye hain't so durned purty yerself, be ye? (*They stare into each other's eyes, his held by hers in spite of himself, hers glowingly possessive. Their physical attraction becomes a palpable force quivering in the hot air.*)

ABBIE (*softly*): Ye don't mean that, Eben. Ye may think ye mean it, mebbe, but ye don't. Ye can't. It's agin nature, Eben. Ye been fightin' yer nature ever since the day I come—tryin' t' tell yerself I hain't purty t'ye. (*She laughs a low humid laugh without taking her eyes from his. A pause—her body squirms desirously—she murmurs languorously*) Hain't the sun strong an' hot? Ye kin feel it burnin' into the earth—Nature—makin' thin's grow—bigger 'n' bigger—burnin' inside ye—makin' ye want t' grow—into somethin' else—till ye're jined with it—an' it's your'n—but it owns ye, too—an' makes ye grow bigger—like a tree—like them elums—(*She laughs again softly, holding his eyes. He takes a step toward her, compelled against his will*) Nature'll beat ye, Eben. Ye might's well own up t' it fust 's last.

EBEN (*trying to break from her spell—confusedly*): If Paw'd hear ye goin' on. . . . (*Resentfully*) But ye've made such a damned idjit out o' the old devil . . . ! (ABBIE *laughs.*)

ABBIE: Waal—hain't it easier fur yew with him changed softer?

EBEN (*defiantly*): No. I'm fightin' him—fightin' yew—fightin' fur Maw's rights t' her hum! (*This breaks her spell for him. He glowers at her*) An' I'm onto ye. Ye hain't foolin' me a mite. Ye're aimin' t' swaller up everythin' an' make it your'n. Waal, you'll find I'm a heap sight bigger hunk nor yew kin chew! (*He turns from her with a sneer.*)

ABBIE (*trying to regain her ascendancy—seductively*): Eben!

EBEN: Leave me be! (*He starts to walk away.*)

ABBIE (*more commandingly*): Eben!

EBEN (*stops—resentfully*): What d'ye want?

ABBIE (*trying to conceal a growing excitement*): Whar air ye goin'?

EBEN (*with malicious nonchalance*): Oh—up the road a spell.

ABBIE: T' the village?

EBEN (*airily*): Mebbe.

ABBIE (*excitedly*): T' see that Min, I s'pose?

EBEN: Mebbe.

ABBIE (*weakly*): What d'ye want t' waste time on her fur?

EBEN (*revenging himself now—grinning at her*): Ye can't beat Nature, didn't ye say? (*He laughs and again starts to walk away.*)

ABBIE (*bursting out*): An ugly old hake!

EBEN (*with a tantalizing sneer*): She's purtier'n yew be!

ABBIE: That every wuthless drunk in the country has. . . .

EBEN (*tauntingly*): Mebbe—but she's better'n yew. She owns up fa'r 'n' squar' t' her doin's.

ABBIE (*furiously*): Don't ye dare compare. . . .

EBEN: She don't go sneakin' an' stealin'—what's mine.

ABBIE (*savagely seizing on his weak point*): Your'n? Yew mean—my farm?

EBEN: I mean the farm yew sold yerself fur like any other old whore—my farm!

ABBIE (*stung—fiercely*): Ye'll never live t' see the day when even a stinkin' weed on it 'll belong t' ye! (*Then in a scream*) Git out o' my sight! Go on t' yer slut—disgracin' yer Paw 'n' me! I'll git yer Paw t' horsewhip ye off the place if I want t'! Ye're only livin' here 'cause I tolerate ye! Git along! I hate the sight o' ye! (*She stops panting and glaring at him.*)

EBEN (*returning her glance in kind*): An' I hate the sight o' yew! (*He turns and strides off up the road. She follows his retreating figure with concentrated hate. Old* CABOT *appears coming up from the barn. The hard, grim expression of his face has changed. He seems in some queer way softened, mellowed. His eyes have taken on a strange, incongruous dreamy quality. Yet there is not a hint of physical weakness about him—rather he looks more robust and younger.* ABBIE *sees him and turns away quickly with unconcealed aversion. He comes slowly up to her.*)

CABOT (*mildly*): War yew an' Eben quarrelin' agen?

ABBIE (*shortly*): No.

CABOT: Ye was talkin' a'mighty loud. (*He sits down on the edge of porch.*)

ABBIE (*snappishly*): If ye heerd us they hain't no need askin' questions.

CABOT: I didn't hear what ye said.

ABBIE (*relieved*): Waal—it wa'n't nothin' t' speak on.

CABOT (*after a pause*): Eben's queer.

ABBIE (*bitterly*): He's the dead spit 'n' image o' yew!

CABOT (*queerly interested*): D'ye think so, Abbie? (*After a pause, ruminatingly*) Me 'n' Eben's allus fit 'n' fit. I never could b'ar him noways. He's so thunderin' soft—like his Maw.

ABBIE (*scornfully*): Ay-eh! 'Bout as soft as yew be!

CABOT (*as if he hadn't heard*): Mebbe I been too hard on him.

ABBIE (*jeeringly*): Waal—ye're gittin' soft now—soft as slop! That's what Eben was sayin'.

CABOT (*his face instantly grim and ominous*): Eben was sayin'? Waal, he'd best not do nothin' t' try me 'r he'll soon diskiver. . . . (*A pause. She keeps her face turned away. His gradually softens. He stares up at the sky*) Purty, hain't it?

ABBIE (*crossly*): I don't see nothin' purty.

CABOT: The sky. Feels like a wa'm field up thar.

ABBIE (*sarcastically*): Air yew aimin' t' buy up over the farm too? (*She snickers contemptuously.*)

CABOT (*strangely*): I'd like t' own my place up thar. (*A pause*) I'm gittin' old, Abbie. I'm gittin' ripe on the bough. (*A pause. She stares at him mystified. He goes on*) It's allus lonesome cold in the house—even when it's bilin' hot outside. Hain't yew noticed?

ABBIE: No.

CABOT: It's wa'm down t' the barn—nice smellin' an' warm—with the cows. (*A pause*) Cows is queer.

ABBIE: Like yew?

CABOT: Like Eben. (*A pause*) I'm gittin' t' feel resigned t' Eben—jest as I got t' feel 'bout his Maw. I'm gittin' t' learn to b'ar his softness—jest like her'n. I calc'late I c'd a'most take t' him—if he wa'n't sech a dumb fool! (*A pause*) I s'pose it's old age a'creepin' in my bones.

ABBIE (*indifferently*): Waal—ye hain't dead yet.

CABOT (*roused*): No, I hain't, yew bet—not by a hell of a sight—I'm sound 'n' tough as hickory! (*Then moodily*) But arter three score and ten the Lord warns ye t' prepare. (*A pause*) That's why Eben's come in my head. Now that his cussed sinful brothers is gone their path t' hell, they's no one left but Eben.

ABBIE (*resentfully*): They's me, hain't they? (*Agitatedly*) What's all this sudden likin' ye've tuk to Eben? Why don't ye say nothin' 'bout me? Hain't I yer lawful wife?

CABOT (*simply*): Ay-eh. Ye be. (*A pause—he stares at her desirously—his eyes grow avid—then with a sudden movement he seizes her hands and squeezes them, declaiming in a queer camp-meeting preacher's tempo*) Yew air my Rose o' Sharon! Behold, yew air fair; yer eyes air doves; yer lips air like scarlet; yer two breasts air like two fawns; yer navel be like a round goblet; yer belly be like a heap o' wheat. . . . (*He covers her hand with kisses. She does not seem to notice. She stares before her with hard angry eyes.*)

ABBIE (*jerking her hands away—harshly*): So ye're plannin' t' leave the farm t' Eben, air ye?

CABOT (*dazedly*): Leave . . . ? (*Then with resentful obstinacy*) I hain't a-givin' it t' no one!

ABBIE (*remorselessly*): Ye can't take it with ye.

CABOT (*thinks a moment—then reluctantly*): No, I calc'late not. (*After a pause—with a strange passion*) But if I could, I would, by the Etarnal! 'R if I could, in my dyin' hour, I'd set it afire an' watch it burn—this house an' every ear o' corn an' every tree down t' the last blade o' hay! I'd sit an' know it was all a-dying with me an' no one else'd ever own what was mine, what I'd made out o' nothin' with my own sweat 'n' blood! (*A pause—then he adds with a queer affection*) 'Ceptin' the cows. Them I'd turn free.

ABBIE (*harshly*): An' me?

CABOT (*with a queer smile*): Ye'd be turned free, too.

ABBIE (*furiously*): So that's the thanks I git fur marryin' ye—t' have ye change kind to Eben who hates ye, an' talk o' turnin' me out in the road.

CABOT (*hastily*): Abbie! Ye know I wa'n't. . . .

ABBIE (*vengefully*): Just let me tell ye a thing or two 'bout Eben! Whar's he gone? T' see that harlot, Min! I tried fur t' stop him. Disgracin' yew an' me—on the Sabbath, too!

CABOT (*rather guiltily*): He's a sinner—nateral-born. It's lust eatin' his heart.

ABBIE (*enraged beyond endurance—wildly vindictive*): An' his lust fur me! Kin ye find excuses fur that?

CABOT (*stares at her—after a dead pause*): Lust —fur yew?

ABBIE (*defiantly*): He was tryin' t' make love t' me—when ye heerd us quarrelin'.

CABOT (*stares at her—then a terrible expression of rage comes over his face—he springs to his feet shaking all over*): By the A'mighty God—I'll end him!

ABBIE (*frightened now for EBEN*): No! Don't ye!

CABOT (*violently*): I'll git the shotgun an' blow his soft brains t' the top o' them elums!

ABBIE (*throwing her arms around him*): No, Ephraim!

CABOT (*pushing her away violently*): I will, by God!

ABBIE (*in a quieting tone*): Listen, Ephraim. 'Twa'n't nothin' bad—on'y a boy's foolin'—'twa'n't meant serious—jest jokin' an' teasin'. . . .

CABOT: Then why did ye say—lust?

ABBIE: It must hev sounded wusser'n I meant. An' I was mad at thinkin'—ye'd leave him the farm.

CABOT (*quieter but still grim and cruel*): Waal then, I'll horsewhip him off the place if that much'll content ye.

ABBIE (*reaching out and taking his hand*): No. Don't think o' me! Ye mustn't drive him off. 'Tain't sensible. Who'll ye get to help ye on the farm? They's no one hereabouts.

CABOT (*considers this—then nodding his appreciation*): Ye got a head on ye. (*Then irritably*) Waal, let him stay. (*He sits down on the edge of the porch. She sits beside him. He murmurs contemptuously*) I oughtn't t' git riled so—at that 'ere fool calf. (*A pause*) But har's the p'int. What son o' mine'll keep on here t' the farm—when the Lord does call me? Simeon an' Peter air gone t' hell— an' Eben's follerin' 'em.

ABBIE: They's me.

CABOT: Ye're on'y a woman.

ABBIE: I'm yewr wife.

CABOT: That hain't me. A son is me—my blood —mine. Mine ought t' git mine. An' then it's still mine—even though I be six foot under. D'ye see?

ABBIE (*giving him a look of hatred*): Ay-eh. I see. (*She becomes very thoughtful, her face growing shrewd, her eyes studying* CABOT *craftily.*)

CABOT: I'm gittin' old—ripe on the bough. (*Then with a sudden forced reassurance*) Not but what I hain't a hard nut t' crack even yet—an' fur many a year t' come! By the Etarnal, I kin break most o' the young fellers' backs at any kind o' work any day o' the year!

ABBIE (*suddenly*): Mebbe the Lord'll give *us* a son.

CABOT (*turns and stares at her eagerly*): Ye mean—a son—t' me 'n' yew?

ABBIE (*with a cajoling smile*): Ye're a strong man yet, hain't ye? 'Tain't noways impossible, be it? We know that. Why d'ye stare so? Hain't ye never thought o' that afore? I been thinkin' o' it all along. Ay-eh—an' I been prayin' it'd happen, too.

CABOT (*his face growing full of joyous pride and a sort of religious ecstasy*): Ye been prayin', Abbie?—fur a son?—t' us?

ABBIE: Ay-eh. (*With a grim resolution*) I want a son now.

CABOT (*excitedly clutching both of her hands in his*): It'd be the blessin' o' God, Abbie—the blessin' o' God A'mighty on me—in my old age—in my lonesomeness! They hain't nothin' I wouldn't do fur ye then, Abbie. Ye'd hev on'y t' ask it—anythin' ye'd a mind t'!

ABBIE (*interrupting*): Would ye will the farm t' me then—t' me an' it . . . ?

CABOT (*vehemently*): I'd do anythin' ye axed, I tell ye! I swar it! May I be everlastin' damned t' hell if I wouldn't! (*He sinks to his knees pulling her down with him. He trembles all over with the fervor of his hopes*) Pray t' the Lord agen, Abbie. It's the Sabbath! I'll jine ye! Two prayers air better nor one. "An' God hearkened unto Rachel"! An' God hearkened unto Abbie! Pray, Abbie! Pray fur him to hearken! (*He bows his head, mumbling. She pretends to do likewise but gives him a side glance of scorn and triumph.*)

SCENE TWO

About eight in the evening. The interior of the two bedrooms on the top floor is shown. EBEN *is sitting on the side of his bed in the room on the left. On account of the heat he has taken off everything but his undershirt and pants. His feet are bare. He faces front, brooding moodily, his chin propped on his hands, a desperate expression on his face.*

In the other room CABOT *and* ABBIE *are sitting side by side on the edge of their bed, an old four-poster with feather mattress. He is in his night shirt, she in her nightdress. He is still in the queer, excited mood into which the notion of a son has thrown him. Both rooms are lighted dimly and flickeringly by tallow candles.*

CABOT: The farm needs a son.

ABBIE: I need a son.

CABOT: Ay-eh. Sometimes ye air the farm an' sometimes the farm be yew. That's why I clove t' ye in my lonesomeness. (*A pause. He pounds his knee with his fist*) Me an' the farm has got t' beget a son!

ABBIE: Ye'd best go t' sleep. Ye're gittin' thin's all mixed.

CABOT (*with an impatient gesture*): No, I hain't. My mind's clear's a well. Ye don't know me, that's it. (*He stares hopelessly at the floor.*)

ABBIE (*indifferently*): Mebbe. (*In the next room* EBEN *gets up and paces up and down distractedly.* ABBIE *hears him. Her eyes fasten on the intervening wall with concentrated attention.* EBEN *stops and stares. Their hot glances seem to meet through the wall. Unconsciously he stretches out his arms for her and she half rises. Then aware, he mutters a curse at himself and flings himself face downward on the bed, his clenched fists above his head, his face buried in the pillow.* ABBIE *relaxes with a faint sigh but her eyes remain fixed on the wall; she listens with all her attention for some movement from* EBEN.)

CABOT (*suddenly raises his head and looks at her —scornfully*): Will ye ever know me—'r will any man 'r woman? (*Shaking his head*) No. I calc'late 't wa'n't t' be. (*He turns away.* ABBIE *looks at the wall. Then, evidently unable to keep silent about his thoughts without looking at his wife, he puts out his hand and clutches her knee. She starts violently, looks at him, sees he is not watching her, concentrates again on the wall and pays no attention to what he says*) Listen, Abbie. When I come here fifty odd year ago—I was jest twenty an' the strongest an' hardest ye ever seen—ten times as strong an' fifty times as hard as Eben. Waal—this place was nothin' but fields o' stones. Folks laughed when I tuk it. They couldn't know what I knowed. When ye kin make corn sprout out o' stones, God's livin' in yew! They wa'n't strong enuf fur that! They reckoned God was easy. They laughed. They don't laugh no more. Some died hereabouts. Some went West an' died. They're all under ground—fur follerin' arter an easy God. God hain't easy. (*He shakes his head slowly*) An' I growed hard. Folks kept allus sayin' he's a hard man like 'twas sinful t' be hard, so's at last I said back at 'em: Waal then, by thunder, ye'll git me hard an' see how ye like it! (*Then suddenly*) But I give in t' weakness once. 'Twas arter I'd been here two year. I got weak—despairful—they was so many stones. They was a party leavin', givin' up, goin' West. I jined 'em. We tracked on 'n' on. We come t' broad medders, plains, whar the soil was black an' rich as gold. Nary a stone. Easy. Ye'd on'y to plow an' sow an' then set an' smoke yer pipe an' watch thin's grow. I could o' been a rich man—but somethin' in me fit me an' fit me—the voice o' God sayin': "This hain't wuth nothin' t' Me. Git ye back t' hum!" I got afeered o' that voice an' I lit out back t' hum here, leavin' my claim an' crops t' whoever'd a mind t' take 'em. Ay-eh. I actoolly give up what was rightful mine! God's hard, not easy! God's in the stones! Build my church on a rock—out o' stones an' I'll be in them! That's what He meant t' Peter! (*He sighs heavily —a pause*) Stones. I picked 'em up an' piled 'em into walls. Ye kin read the years o' my life in them walls, every day a hefted stone, climbin' over the hills up and down, fencin' in the fields that was mine, whar I'd made thin's grow out o' nothin'— like the will o' God, like the servant o' His hand. It wa'n't easy. It was hard an' He made me hard fur it. (*He pauses*) All the time I kept gittin' lonesomer. I tuk a wife. She bore Simeon an' Peter. She was a good woman. She wuked hard. We was married twenty year. She never knowed me. She helped but she never knowed what she was helpin'. I was allus lonesome. She died. After that it wa'n't so lonesome fur a spell. (*A pause*) I lost count o' the years. I had no time t' fool away countin' 'em. Sim an' Peter helped. The farm growed. It was all mine! When I thought o' that I didn't feel lonesome. (*A pause*) But ye can't hitch yer mind t' one thin' day an' night. I tuk another wife— Eben's Maw. Her folks was contestin' me at law over my deeds t' the farm—my farm! That's why Eben keeps a-talkin' his fool talk o' this bein' his Maw's farm. She bore Eben. She was purty—but soft. She tried t' be hard. She couldn't. She never knowed me nor nothin'. It was lonesomer 'n hell with her. After a matter o' sixteen odd years, she died. (*A pause*) I lived with the boys. They hated me 'cause I was hard. I hated them 'cause they was soft. They coveted the farm without knowin' what it meant. It made me bitter 'n wormwood. It aged me—them coveting what I'd made fur mine. Then this spring the call come—the voice o' God cryin' in my wilderness, in my lonesomeness—t' go out an' seek an' find! (*Turning to her with strange passion*) I sought ye an' I found ye! Yew air my Rose o' Sharon! Yer eyes air like. . . . (*She has turned a blank face, resentful eyes to his. He stares at her for a moment—then harshly*) Air ye any the wiser fur all I've told ye?

ABBIE (*confusedly*): Mebbe.

CABOT (*pushing her away from him—angrily*): Ye don't know nothin'—nor never will. If ye don't hev a son t' redeem ye. . . . (*This in a tone of cold threat.*)

ABBIE (*resentfully*): I've prayed, hain't I?

CABOT (*bitterly*): Pray agen—fur understandin'!

ABBIE (*a veiled threat in her tone*): Ye'll have a son out o' me, I promise ye.

CABOT: How kin ye promise?

ABBIE: I got second-sight mebbe. I kin foretell. (*She gives a queer smile.*)

CABOT: I believe ye have. Ye give me the chills sometimes. (*He shivers*) It's cold in this house. It's oneasy. They's thin's pokin' about in the dark —in the corners. (*He pulls on his trousers, tucking in his night shirt, and pulls on his boots.*)

ABBIE (*surprised*): Whar air ye goin'?

CABOT (*queerly*): Down whar it's restful—whar it's warm down t' the barn. (*Bitterly*) I kin talk t' the cows. They know. They know the farm an' me. They'll give me peace. (*He turns to go out the door.*)

ABBIE (*a bit frightenedly*): Air ye ailin' tonight, Ephraim?

CABOT: Growin'. Growin' ripe on the bough. (*He turns and goes, his boots clumping down the stairs.* EBEN *sits up with a start, listening.* ABBIE *is conscious of his movement and stares at the wall.* CABOT *comes out of the house around the corner and stands by the gate, blinking at the sky. He stretches up his hands in a tortured gesture*) God A'mighty, call from the dark! (*He listens as if expecting an answer. Then his arms drop, he shakes his head and plods off toward the barn.* EBEN *and* ABBIE *stare at each other through the wall.* EBEN *sighs heavily and* ABBIE *echoes it. Both become terribly nervous, uneasy. Finally* ABBIE *gets up and listens, her ear to the wall. He acts as if he saw every move she was making, he becomes resolutely still. She seems driven into a decision—goes out the door in rear determinedly. His eyes follow her. Then as the door of his room is opened softly, he turns away, waits in an attitude of strained fixity.* ABBIE *stands for a second staring at him, her eyes burning with desire. Then with a little cry she runs over and throws her arms about his neck, she pulls his head back and covers his mouth with kisses. At first, he submits dumbly; then he puts his arms about her neck and returns her kisses, but finally, suddenly aware of his hatred, he hurls her away from him, springing to his feet. They stand speechless and breathless, panting like two animals.*)

ABBIE (*at last—painfully*): Ye shouldn't, Eben— ye shouldn't—I'd make ye happy!

EBEN (*harshly*): I don't want t' be happy—from yew!

ABBIE (*helplessly*): Ye do, Eben! Ye do! Why d'ye lie?

EBEN (*viciously*): I don't take t'ye, I tell ye! I hate the sight o' ye!

ABBIE (*with an uncertain troubled laugh*): Waal, I kissed ye anyways—an' ye kissed back—yer lips was burnin'—ye can't lie 'bout that! (*Intensely*) If ye don't care, why did ye kiss me back—why was yer lips burnin'?

EBEN (*wiping his mouth*): It was like pizen on 'em. (*Then tauntingly*) When I kissed ye back, mebbe I thought 'twas someone else.

ABBIE (*wildly*): Min?

EBEN: Mebbe.

ABBIE (*torturedly*): Did ye go t' see her? Did ye r'ally go? I thought ye mightn't. Is that why ye throwed me off jest now?

EBEN (*sneeringly*): What if it be?

ABBIE (*raging*): Then ye're a dog, Eben Cabot!

EBEN (*threateningly*): Ye can't talk that way t' me!

ABBIE (*with a shrill laugh*): Can't I? Did ye think I was in love with ye—a weak thin' like yew? Not much! I on'y wanted ye fur a purpose o' my own—an' I'll hev ye fur it yet 'cause I'm stronger'n yew be!

EBEN (*resentfully*): I knowed well it was on'y part o' yer plan t' swaller everythin'!

ABBIE (*tauntingly*): Mebbe!

EBEN (*furious*): Git out o' my room!

ABBIE: This air my room an' ye're on'y hired help!

EBEN (*threateningly*): Git out afore I murder ye!

ABBIE (*quite confident now*): I hain't a mite afeerd. Ye want me, don't ye? Yes, ye do! An' yer Paw's son'll never kill what he wants! Look at yer eyes! They's lust fur me in 'em, burnin' 'em up! Look at yer lips now! They're tremblin' an' longin' t' kiss me, an' yer teeth t' bite! (*He is watching her now with a horrible fascination. She laughs a crazy triumphant laugh*) I'm a-goin' t' make all o' this hum my hum! They's one room hain't mine yet, but it's a-goin' t' be tonight. I'm a-goin' down now an' light up! (*She makes him a mocking bow*) Won't ye come courtin' me in the best parlor, Mister Cabot?

EBEN (*staring at her—horribly confused—dully*): Don't ye dare! It hain't been opened since Maw died an' was laid out thar! Don't ye . . . ! (*But her eyes are fixed on his so burningly that his will seems to wither before hers. He stands swaying toward her helplessly.*)

ABBIE (*holding his eyes and putting all her will into her words as she backs out the door*): I'll expect ye afore long, Eben.

EBEN (*stares after her for a while, walking toward the door. A light appears in the parlor window. He murmurs*): In the parlor? (*This seems to arouse connotations for he comes back and puts on his white shirt, collar, half ties the tie mechanically, puts on coat, takes his hat, stands barefooted looking about him in bewilderment, mutters wonderingly*) Maw! Whar air yew? (*Then goes slowly toward the door in rear.*)

SCENE THREE

A few minutes later. The interior of the parlor is shown. A grim, repressed room like a tomb in which the family has been interred alive. ABBIE *sits on the edge of the horsehair sofa. She has lighted all the candles and the room is revealed in all its preserved ugliness. A change has come over the woman. She looks awed and frightened now, ready to run away.*

The door is opened and EBEN *appears. His face wears an expression of obsessed confusion. He stands staring at her, his arms hanging disjointedly from his shoulders, his feet bare, his hat in his hand.*

ABBIE (*after a pause—with a nervous, formal politeness*): Won't ye set?

EBEN (*dully*): Ay-eh. (*Mechanically he places his hat carefully on the floor near the door and sits stiffly beside her on the edge of the sofa. A pause. They both remain rigid, looking straight ahead with eyes full of fear.*)

ABBIE: When I fust come in—in the dark—they seemed somethin' here.

EBEN (*simply*): Maw.

ABBIE: I kin still feel—somethin'. . . .

EBEN: It's Maw.

ABBIE: At fust I was feered o' it. I wanted t' yell an' run. Now—since yew come—seems like it's growin' soft an' kind t' me. (*Addressing the air—queerly*) Thank yew.

EBEN: Maw allus loved me.

ABBIE: Mebbe it knows I love yew, too. Mebbe that makes it kind t' me.

EBEN (*dully*): I dunno. I should think she'd hate ye.

ABBIE (*with certainty*): No. I kin feel it don't—not no more.

EBEN: Hate ye fur stealin' her place—here in her hum—settin' in her parlor whar she was laid—(*He suddenly stops, staring stupidly before him.*)

ABBIE: What is it, Eben?

EBEN (*in a whisper*): Seems like Maw didn't want me t' remind ye.

ABBIE (*excitedly*): I knowed, Eben! It's kind t' me! It don't b'ar me no grudges fur what I never knowed an' couldn't help!

EBEN: Maw b'ars him a grudge.

ABBIE: Waal, so does all o' us.

EBEN: Ay-eh. (*With passion*) I does, by God!

ABBIE (*taking one of his hands in hers and patting it*): Thar! Don't git riled thinkin' o' him. Think o' yer Maw who's kind t' us. Tell me about yer Maw, Eben.

EBEN: They hain't nothin' much. She was kind. She was good.

ABBIE (*putting one arm over his shoulder. He does not seem to notice—passionately*): I'll be kind an' good t' ye!

EBEN: Sometimes she used t' sing fur me.

ABBIE: I'll sing fur ye!

EBEN: This was her hum. This was her farm.

ABBIE: This is my hum! This is my farm!

EBEN: He married her t' steal 'em. She was soft an' easy. He couldn't 'preciate her.

ABBIE: He can't 'preciate me!

EBEN: He murdered her with his hardness.

ABBIE: He's murderin' me!

EBEN: She died. (*A pause*) Sometimes she used to sing fur me. (*He bursts into a fit of sobbing.*)

ABBIE (*both her arms around him—with wild passion*): I'll sing fur ye! I'll die fur ye! (*In spite of her overwhelming desire for him, there is a sincere maternal love in her manner and voice—a horribly frank mixture of lust and mother love*) Don't cry, Eben! I'll take yer Maw's place! I'll be everythin' she was t' ye! Let me kiss ye, Eben! (*She pulls his head around. He makes a bewildered pretense of resistance. She is tender*) Don't be afeered! I'll kiss ye pure, Eben—same 's if I was a Maw t' ye—an' ye kin kiss me back 's if yew was my son—my boy—sayin' good-night t' me! Kiss me, Eben. (*They kiss in restrained fashion. Then suddenly wild passion overcomes her. She kisses him lustfully again and again and he flings his arms about her and returns her kisses. Suddenly, as in the bedroom, he frees himself from her violently and springs to his feet. He is trembling all over, in a strange state of terror.* ABBIE *strains her arms toward him with fierce pleading*) Don't ye leave me, Eben! Can't ye see it hain't enuf—lovin' ye like a Maw—can't ye see it's got t' be that an' more—much more—a hundred times more—fur me t' be happy—fur yew t' be happy?

EBEN (*to the presence he feels in the room*): Maw! Maw! What d'ye want? What air ye tellin' me?

ABBIE: She's tellin' ye t' love me. She knows I love ye an' I'll be good t' ye. Can't ye feel it? Don't ye know? She's tellin' ye t' love me, Eben!

EBEN: Ay-eh. I feel—mebbe she—but—I can't figger out—why—when ye've stole her place—here in her hum—in the parlor whar she was—

ABBIE (*fiercely*): She knows I love ye!

EBEN (*his face suddenly lighting up with a fierce, triumphant grin*): I see it! I see why. It's her vengeance on him—so's she kin rest quiet in her grave!

ABBIE (*wildly*): Vengeance o' God on the hull o' us! What d'we give a durn? I love ye, Eben! God knows I love ye! (*She stretches out her arms for him.*)

EBEN (*throws himself on his knees beside the sofa and grabs her in his arms—releasing all his pent-up passion*): An' I love yew, Abbie!—now I kin say it! I been dyin' fur want o' ye—every hour since ye come! I love ye! (*Their lips meet in a fierce, bruising kiss.*)

SCENE FOUR

Exterior of the farmhouse. It is just dawn. The front door at right is opened and EBEN *comes out and walks around to the gate. He is dressed in his working clothes. He seems changed. His face wears a bold and confident expression, he is grinning to himself with evident satisfaction. As he gets near the gate, the window of the parlor is heard opening and the shutters are flung back and* ABBIE *sticks her head out. Her hair tumbles over her shoulders in disarray, her face is flushed, she looks at* EBEN *with tender, languorous eyes and calls softly.*

ABBIE: Eben. (*As he turns—playfully*) Jest one more kiss afore ye go. I'm goin' to miss ye fearful all day.

EBEN: An' me yew, ye kin bet! (*He goes to her. They kiss several times. He draws away, laughingly*) Thar. That's enuf, hain't it? Ye won't hev none left fur next time.

ABBIE: I got a million o' 'em left fur yew! (*Then a bit anxiously*) D'ye r'ally love me, Eben?

EBEN (*emphatically*): I like ye better'n any gal I ever knowed! That's gospel!

ABBIE: Likin' hain't lovin'.

EBEN: Waal then—I love ye. Now air yew satisfied?

ABBIE: Ay-eh, I be. (*She smiles at him adoringly.*)

EBEN: I better git t' the barn. The old critter's liable t' suspicion an' come sneakin' up.

ABBIE (*with a confident laugh*): Let him! I kin allus pull the wool over his eyes. I'm goin' t' leave the shutters open and let in the sun 'n' air. This room's been dead long enuf. Now it's goin' t' be my room!

EBEN (*frowning*): Ay-eh.

ABBIE (*hastily*): I meant—our room.

EBEN: Ay-eh.

ABBIE: We made it our'n last night, didn't we? We give it life—our lovin' did. (*A pause.*)

EBEN (*with a strange look*): Maw's gone back t' her grave. She kin sleep now.

ABBIE: May she rest in peace! (*Then tenderly rebuking*) Ye oughtn't t' talk o' sad thin's—this mornin'.

EBEN: It jest come up in my mind o' itself.

ABBIE: Don't let it. (*He doesn't answer. She yawns*) Waal, I'm a-goin' t' steal a wink o' sleep. I'll tell the Old Man I hain't feelin' pert. Let him git his own vittles.

EBEN: I see him comin' from the barn. Ye better look smart an' git upstairs.

ABBIE: Ay-eh. Good-by. Don't ferget me. (*She throws him a kiss. He grins—then squares his shoulders and awaits his father confidently. CABOT walks slowly up from the left, staring up at the sky with a vague face.*)

EBEN (*jovially*): Mornin', Paw. Star-gazin' in daylight?

CABOT: Purty, hain't it?

EBEN (*looking around him possessively*): It's a durned purty farm.

CABOT: I mean the sky.

EBEN (*grinning*): How d'ye know? Them eyes o' your'n can't see that fur. (*This tickles his humor and he slaps his thigh and laughs*) Ho-ho! That's a good un!

CABOT (*grimly sarcastic*): Ye're feelin' right chipper, hain't ye? Whar'd ye steal the likker?

EBEN (*good-naturedly*): 'Tain't likker. Jest life. (*Suddenly holding out his hand—soberly*) Yew 'n' me is quits. Let's shake hands.

CABOT (*suspiciously*): What's come over ye?

EBEN: Then don't. Mebbe it's jest as well. (*A moment's pause*) What's come over me? (*Queerly*) Didn't ye feel her passin'—goin' back t' her grave?

CABOT (*dully*): Who?

EBEN: Maw. She kin rest now an' sleep content. She's quit with ye.

CABOT (*confusedly*): I rested. I slept good—down with the cows. They know how t' sleep. They're teachin' me.

EBEN (*suddenly jovial again*): Good fur the cows! Waal—ye better git t' work.

CABOT (*grimly amused*): Air ye bossin' me, ye calf?

EBEN (*beginning to laugh*): Ay-eh! I'm bossin' yew! Ha-ha-ha! See how ye like it! Ha-ha-ha! I'm the prize rooster o' this roost. Ha-ha-ha! (*He goes off toward the barn laughing.*)

CABOT (*looks after him with scornful pity*): Soft-headed. Like his Maw. Dead spit 'n' image. No hope in him! (*He spits with contemptuous disgust*) A born fool! (*Then matter-of-factly*) Waal—I'm gittin' peckish. (*He goes toward door.*)

PART THREE • SCENE ONE

A *night in late spring the following year. The kitchen and the two bedrooms upstairs are shown. The two bedrooms are dimly lighted by a tallow candle in each.* EBEN *is sitting on the side of the bed in his room, his chin propped on his fists, his face a study of the struggle he is making to understand his conflicting emotions. The noisy laughter and music from below where a kitchen dance is in progress annoy and distract him. He scowls at the floor.*

In *the next room a cradle stands beside the double bed.*

In *the kitchen all is festivity. The stove has been taken down to give more room to the dancers. The chairs, with wooden benches added, have been pushed back against the walls. On these are seated, squeezed in tight against one another, farmers and their wives and their young folks of both sexes from the neighboring farms. They are all chattering and laughing loudly. They evidently have some secret joke in common. There is no end of winking, of nudging, of meaning nods of the head toward* CABOT *who, in a state of extreme hilarious excitement increased by the amount he has drunk, is standing near the rear door where there is a small keg of whisky and serving drinks to all the men. In the left corner, front, dividing the attention with her husband,* ABBIE *is sitting in a rocking chair, a shawl wrapped about her shoulders. She is very pale, her face is thin and drawn, her eyes are fixed anxiously on the open door in rear as if waiting for someone.*

The *musician is tuning up his fiddle, seated in the far right corner. He is a lanky young fellow with a long, weak face. His pale eyes blink incessantly and he grins about him slyly with a greedy malice.*

ABBIE (*suddenly turning to a young girl on her right*): Whar's Eben?

YOUNG GIRL (*eying her scornfully*): I dunno, Mrs. Cabot. I hain't seen Eben in ages. (*Meaningly*) Seems like he's spent most o' his time t' hum since yew come.

ABBIE (*vaguely*): I tuk his Maw's place.

YOUNG GIRL: Ay-eh. So I've heerd. (*She turns away to retail this bit of gossip to her mother sitting next to her.* ABBIE *turns to her left to a big stoutish middle-aged man whose flushed face and starting eyes show the amount of "likker" he has consumed.*)

ABBIE: Ye hain't seen Eben, hev ye?

MAN: No, I hain't. (*Then he adds with a wink*) If yew hain't, who would?

ABBIE: He's the best dancer in the county. He'd ought t' come an' dance.

MAN (*with a wink*): Mebbe he's doin' the dutiful an' walkin' the kid t' sleep. It's a boy, hain't it?

ABBIE (*nodding vaguely*): Ay-eh—born two weeks back—purty's a picter.

MAN: They all is—t' their Maws. (*Then in a whisper, with a nudge and a leer*) Listen, Abbie—if ye ever git tired o' Eben, remember me! Don't fergit now! (*He looks at her uncomprehending face for a second—then grunts disgustedly*) Waal—guess I'll likker agin. (*He goes over and joins* CABOT *who is arguing noisily with an old farmer over cows. They all drink.*)

ABBIE (*this time appealing to nobody in particular*): Wonder what Eben's a-doin'? (*Her remark is repeated down the line with many a guffaw and titter until it reaches the fiddler. He fastens his blinking eyes on* ABBIE.)

FIDDLER (*raising his voice*): Bet I kin tell ye, Abbie, what Eben's doin'! He's down t' the church offerin' up prayers o' thanksgivin'. (*They all titter expectantly.*)

A MAN: What fur? (*Another titter.*)

FIDDLER: 'Cause unto him a— (*He hesitates just long enough*) brother is born! (*A roar of laughter. They all look from* ABBIE *to* CABOT. *She is oblivious, staring at the door.* CABOT, *although he hasn't heard the words, is irritated by the laughter and steps forward, glaring about him. There is an immediate silence.*)

CABOT: What're ye all bleatin' about—like a flock o' goats? Why don't ye dance, damn ye?

I axed ye here t' dance—t' eat, drink an' be merry—an' thar ye set cacklin' like a lot o' wet hens with the pip! Ye've swilled my likker an' guzzled my vittles like hogs, hain't ye? Then dance fur me, can't ye? That's fa'r an' squar', hain't it? (*A grumble of resentment goes around but they are all evidently in too much awe of him to express it openly.*)

FIDDLER (*slyly*): We're waitin' fur Eben. (*A suppressed laugh.*)

CABOT (*with a fierce exultation*): T'hell with Eben! Eben's done fur now! I got a new son! (*His mood switching with drunken suddenness*) But ye needn't t' laugh at Eben, none o' ye! He's my blood, if he be a dumb fool. He's better nor any o' yew! He kin do a day's work a'most up t' what I kin—an' that'd put any o' yew pore critters t' shame!

FIDDLER: An' he kin do a good night's work too! (*A roar of laughter.*)

CABOT: Laugh, ye damn fools! Ye're right jist the same, Fiddler. He kin work day an' night too, like I kin, if need be!

OLD FARMER (*from behind the keg where he is weaving drunkenly back and forth—with great simplicity*): They hain't many t' touch ye, Ephraim—a son at seventy-six. That's a hard man fur ye! I be on'y sixty-eight an' I couldn't do it. (*A roar of laughter in which* CABOT *joins uproariously.*)

CABOT (*slapping him on the back*): I'm sorry fur ye, Hi. I'd never suspicion sech weakness from a boy like yew!

OLD FARMER: An' I never reckoned yew had it in ye nuther, Ephraim. (*There is another laugh.*)

CABOT (*suddenly grim*): I got a lot in me—a hell of a lot—folks don't know on. (*Turning to the fiddler*) Fiddle 'er up, durn ye! Give 'em somethin' t' dance t'! What air ye, an ornament? Hain't this a celebration? Then grease yer elbow an' go it!

FIDDLER (*seizes a drink which the* OLD FARMER *holds out to him and downs it*): Here goes! (*He starts to fiddle "Lady of the Lake." Four young fellows and four girls form in two lines and dance a square dance. The* FIDDLER *shouts directions for the different movements, keeping his words in the rhythm of the music and interspersing them with jocular personal remarks to the dancers themselves. The people seated along the walls stamp their feet and clap their hands in unison.* CABOT *is especially active in this respect. Only* ABBIE *remains apathetic, staring at the door as if she were alone in a silent room.*)

FIDDLER: Swing your partner t' the right! That's it, Jim! Give her a b'ar hug! Her Maw hain't lookin'. (*Laughter*) Change partners! That suits ye, don't it, Essie, now ye got Reub afore ye? Look at her redden up, will ye? Waal, life is short an' so's love, as the feller says. (*Laughter.*)

CABOT (*excitedly, stamping his foot*): Go it, boys! Go it, gals!

FIDDLER (*with a wink at the others*): Ye're the spryest seventy-six ever I sees, Ephraim! Now if ye'd on'y good eye-sight . . . ! (*Suppressed laughter. He gives* CABOT *no chance to retort but roars*) Promenade! Ye're walkin' like a bride down the aisle, Sarah! Waal, while they's life they's allus hope, I've heerd tell. Swing your partner to the left! Gosh A'mighty, look at Johnny Cook high-steppin'! They hain't goin' t'be much strength left fur howin' in the corn lot t'morrow. (*Laughter.*)

CABOT: Go it! Go it! (*Then suddenly, unable to restrain himself any longer, he prances into the midst of the dancers, scattering them, waving his arms about wildly*) Ye're all hoofs! Git out o' my road! Give me room! I'll show ye dancin'. Ye're all too soft! (*He pushes them roughly away. They crowd back toward the walls, muttering, looking at him resentfully.*)

FIDDLER (*jeeringly*): Go it, Ephraim! Go it! (*He starts "Pop Goes the Weasel," increasing the tempo with every verse until at the end he is fiddling crazily as fast as he can go.*)

CABOT (*starts to dance, which he does very well and with tremendous vigor. Then he begins to improvise, cuts incredibly grotesque capers, leaping up and cracking his heels together, prancing around in a circle with body bent in an Indian war dance, then suddenly straightening up and kicking as high as he can with both legs. He is like a monkey on a string. And all the while he intersperses his antics with shouts and derisive comments*): Whoop! Here's dancin' fur ye! Whoop! See that! Seventy-six, if I'm a day! Hard as iron yet! Beatin' the young 'uns like I allus done! Look at me! I'd invite ye t' dance on my hundredth birthday on'y ye'll all be dead by then. Ye're a sickly generation! Yer hearts air pink, not red! Yer veins is full o' mud an' water! I be the on'y man in the county! Whoop! See that! I'm a Injun! I've killed Injuns in the West afore ye was born—an' skulped 'em too! They's a arrer wound on my backside I c'd show ye! The hull tribe chased me. I outrun 'em all—with the arrer stuck in me! An' I tuk vengeance on 'em. Ten eyes fur an eye, that was my motter! Whoop! Look at me! I kin kick the ceilin' off the room! Whoop!

FIDDLER (*stops playing—exhaustedly*): God A'-mighty, I got enuf. Ye got the devil's strength in ye.

CABOT (*delightedly*): Did I beat yew, too? Wa'al, ye played smart. Hev a swig. (*He pours whisky for himself and* FIDDLER. *They drink. The others watch* CABOT *silently with cold, hostile eyes. There is a dead pause. The* FIDDLER *rests.* CABOT *leans against the keg, panting, glaring around him confusedly. In the room above,* EBEN *gets to his feet and tiptoes out the door in rear, appearing a moment later in the other bedroom. He moves silently, even frightenedly, toward the cradle and stands there looking down at the baby. His face is as vague as his reactions are confused, but there is a trace of tenderness, of interested discovery. At the same moment that he reaches the cradle,* ABBIE *seems to sense something. She gets up weakly and goes to* CABOT.)

ABBIE: I'm goin' up t' the baby.

CABOT (*with real solicitation*): Air ye able fur the stairs? D'ye want me t' help ye, Abbie?

ABBIE: No. I'm able. I'll be down agen soon.

CABOT: Don't ye git wore out! He needs ye, remember—our son does! (*He grins affectionately, patting her on the back. She shrinks from his touch.*)

ABBIE (*dully*): Don't—tech me. I'm goin'—up. (*She goes.* CABOT *looks after her. A whisper goes around the room.* CABOT *turns. It ceases. He wipes his forehead streaming with sweat. He is breathing pantingly.*)

CABOT: I'm a-goin' out t' git fresh air. I'm feelin' a mite dizzy. Fiddle up thar! Dance, all o' ye! Here's likker fur them as wants it. Enjoy yerselves. I'll be back. (*He goes, closing the door behind him.*)

FIDDLER (*sarcastically*): Don't hurry none on our account! (*A suppressed laugh. He imitates* ABBIE) Whar's Eben? (*More laughter.*)

A WOMAN (*loudly*): What's happened in this house is plain as the nose on yer face! (ABBIE *appears in the doorway upstairs and stands looking in surprise and adoration at* EBEN *who does not see her.*)

A MAN: Ssshh! He's li-ble t' be listenin' at the door. That'd be like him. (*Their voices die to an intensive whispering. Their faces are concentrated on this gossip. A noise as of dead leaves in the wind comes from the room.* CABOT *has come out from the porch and stands by the gate, leaning on it, staring at the sky blinkingly.* ABBIE *comes across the room silently.* EBEN *does not notice her until quite near.*)

EBEN (*starting*): Abbie!

ABBIE: Ssshh! (*She throws her arms around him. They kiss—then bend over the cradle together*) Ain't he purty?—dead spit 'n' image o' yew!

EBEN (*pleased*): Air he? I can't tell none.

ABBIE: E-zactly like!

EBEN (*frowningly*): I don't like this. I don't like lettin' on what's mine's his'n. I been doin' that all my life. I'm gittin' t' the end o' b'arin' it!

ABBIE (*putting her finger on his lips*): We're doin' the best we kin. We got t' wait. Somethin's bound t' happen. (*She puts her arms around him*) I got t' go back.

EBEN: I'm goin' out. I can't b'ar it with the fiddle playin' an' the laughin'.

ABBIE: Don't git feelin' low. I love ye, Eben. Kiss me. (*He kisses her. They remain in each other's arms.*)

CABOT (*at the gate, confusedly*): Even the music can't drive it out—somethin'. Ye kin feel it droppin' off the elums, climbin' up the roof, sneakin' down the chimney, pokin' in the corners! They's no peace in houses, they's no rest livin' with folks. Somethin's always livin' with ye. (*With a deep sigh*) I'll go t' the barn an' rest a spell. (*He goes wearily toward the barn.*)

FIDDLER (*tuning up*): Let's celebrate the old skunk gittin' fooled! We kin have some fun now he's went. (*He starts to fiddle "Turkey in the Straw." There is real merriment now. The young folks get up to dance.*)

SCENE TWO

*A half-hour later—Exterior—*EBEN *is standing by the gate looking up at the sky, an expression of dumb pain bewildered by itself on his face.* CABOT *appears, returning from the barn, walking wearily, his eyes on the ground. He sees* EBEN *and his whole mood immediately changes. He becomes excited, a cruel, triumphant grin comes to his lips, he strides up and slaps* EBEN *on the back. From within comes the whining of the fiddle and the noise of stamping feet and laughing voices.*

CABOT: So har ye be!

EBEN (*startled, stares at him with hatred for a moment—then dully*): Ay-eh.

CABOT (*surveying him jeeringly*): Why hain't ye been in t' dance? They was all axin' fur ye.

EBEN: Let 'em ax!

CABOT: They's a hull passel o' purty gals.

EBEN: T' hell with 'em!

CABOT: Ye'd ought t' be marryin' one o' 'em soon.

EBEN: I hain't marryin' no one.

CABOT: Ye might 'arn a share o' a farm that way.

EBEN (*with a sneer*): Like yew did, ye mean? I hain't that kind.

CABOT (*stung*): Ye lie! 'Twas yer Maw's folks aimed t' steal my farm from me.

EBEN: Other folks don't say so. (*After a pause—defiantly*) An' I got a farm, anyways!

CABOT (*derisively*): Whar?

EBEN (*stamps a foot on the ground*): Har!

CABOT (*throws his head back and laughs coarsely*): Ho-ho! Ye hev, hev ye? Waal, that's a good un!

EBEN (*controlling himself—grimly*): Ye'll see!

CABOT (*stares at him suspiciously, trying to make him out—a pause—then with scornful confidence*): Ay-eh. I'll see. So'll ye. It's ye that's blind—blind as a mole underground. (EBEN *suddenly laughs, one short sardonic bark: "Ha." A pause.* CABOT *peers at him with renewed suspicion*) Whar air ye hawin' 'bout? (EBEN *turns away without answering.* CABOT *grows angry*) God A'mighty, yew air a dumb dunce! They's nothin' in that thick skull o' your'n but noise—like a empty keg it be! (EBEN *doesn't seem to hear.* CABOT's *rage grows*) Yewr farm! God A'mighty! If ye wa'n't a born donkey ye'd know ye'll never own stick nor stone on it, specially now arter him bein' born. It's his'n, I tell ye—his'n arter I die—but I'll live a hundred jest t' fool ye all—an' he'll be growed then—yewr age a'most! (EBEN *laughs again his sardonic "Ha." This drives* CABOT *into a fury*) Ha? Ye think ye kin git 'round that someways, do ye? Waal, it'll be her'n, too—Abbie's—ye won't git 'round her—she knows yer tricks—she'll be too much fur ye—she wants the farm her'n—she was afeerd o' ye—she told me ye was sneakin' 'round tryin' t' make love t' her t' git her on yer side . . . ye . . . ye mad fool, ye! (*He raises his clenched fists threateningly.*)

EBEN (*is confronting him choking with rage*): Ye lie, ye old skunk! Abbie never said no sech thing!

CABOT (*suddenly triumphant when he sees how shaken* EBEN *is*): She did. An' I says, I'll blow his brains t' the top o' them elums—an' she says no, that hain't sense, who'll ye git t'help ye on the farm in his place—an' then she says yew'n me ought t' have a son—I know we kin, she says—an' I says, if we do, ye kin have anythin' I've got ye've a mind t'. An' she says, I wants Eben cut off so's this farm'll be mine when ye die! (*With terrible gloating*) An that's what's happened, hain't it? An' the farm's her'n! An' the dust o' the road— that's you'rn! Ha! Now who's hawin'?

EBEN (*has been listening, petrified with grief and rage—suddenly laughs wildly and brokenly*): Ha-ha-ha! So that's her sneakin' game—all along!— like I suspicioned at fust—t' swaller it all—an' me, too . . . ! (*Madly*) I'll murder her! (*He springs toward the porch but* CABOT *is quicker and gets in between.*)

CABOT: No, ye don't!

EBEN: Git out o' my road! (*He tries to throw* CABOT *aside. They grapple in what becomes immediately a murderous struggle. The old man's concentrated strength is too much for* EBEN. CABOT *gets one hand on his throat and presses him back across the stone well. At the same moment,* ABBIE *comes out on the porch. With a stifled cry she runs toward them.*)

ABBIE: Eben! Ephraim! (*She tugs at the hand on* EBEN's *throat*) Let go, Ephraim! Ye're chokin' him!

CABOT (*removes his hand and flings* EBEN *sideways full length on the grass, gasping and choking. With a cry,* ABBIE *kneels beside him, trying to take his head on her lap, but he pushes her away.* CABOT *stands looking down with fierce triumph*): Ye needn't t've fret, Abbie, I wa'n't aimin' t' kill him. He hain't wuth hangin' fur—not by a hell of a sight! (*More and more triumphantly*) Seventy-six an' him not thirty yit—an' look whar he be fur thinkin' his Paw was easy! No, by God, I hain't easy! An' him upstairs, I'll raise him t' be like me! (*He turns to leave them*) I'm goin' in an' dance! —sing an' celebrate! (*He walks to the porch—then turns with a great grin*) I don't calc'late it's left in him, but if he gits pesky, Abbie, ye jest sing out. I'll come a-runnin' an' by the Etarnal, I'll put him across my knee an' birch him! Ha-ha-ha! (*He goes into the house laughing. A moment later his loud "whoop" is heard.*)

ABBIE (*tenderly*): Eben. Air ye hurt? (*She tries to kiss him but he pushes her violently away and struggles to a sitting position.*)

EBEN (*gaspingly*): T' hell—with ye!

ABBIE (*not believing her ears*): It's me, Eben— Abbie—don't ye know me?

EBEN (*glowering at her with hatred*): Ay-eh—I know ye—now! (*He suddenly breaks down, sobbing weakly.*)

ABBIE (*fearfully*): Eben—what's happened t' ye— why did ye look at me 's if ye hated me?

EBEN (*violently, between sobs and gasps*): I do hate ye! Ye're a whore—a damn trickin' whore!

ABBIE (*shrinking back horrified*): Eben! Ye don't know what ye're sayin'!

EBEN (*scrambling to his feet and following her— accusingly*): Ye're nothin' but a stinkin' passel o' lies! Ye've been lyin' t' me every word ye spoke, day an' night, since we fust—done it. Ye've kept sayin' ye loved me. . . .

ABBIE (*frantically*): I do love ye! (*She takes his hand but he flings hers away.*)

EBEN (*unheeding*): Ye've made a fool o' me—a sick, dumb fool—a-purpose! Ye've been on'y playin' yer sneakin', stealin' game all along—gittin' me t' lie with ye so's ye'd hev a son he'd think was his'n, an' makin' him promise he'd give ye the farm and let me eat dust, if ye did git him a son! (*Staring at her with anguished, bewildered eyes*) They must be a devil livin' in ye! T'ain't human t' be as bad as that be!

ABBIE (*stunned—dully*): He told yew . . . ?

EBEN: Hain't it true? It hain't no good in yew lyin'.

ABBIE (*pleadingly*): Eben, listen—ye must listen —it was long ago—afore we done nothin'—yew was scornin' me—goin' t' see Min—when I was lovin' ye —an' I said it t' him t' git vengeance on ye!

EBEN (*unheedingly. With tortured passion*): I wish ye was dead! I wish I was dead along with ye afore this come! (*Ragingly*) But I'll git my vengeance too! I'll pray Maw t' come back t' help me —t' put her cuss on yew an' him!

ABBIE (*brokenly*): Don't ye, Eben! Don't ye! (*She throws herself on her knees before him, weeping*) I didn't mean t' do bad t' ye! Fergive me, won't ye?

EBEN (*not seeming to hear her—fiercely*): I'll git squar' with the old skunk—an' yew! I'll tell him the truth 'bout the son he's so proud o'! Then I'll leave ye here t' pizen each other—with Maw comin' out o' her grave at nights—an' I'll go t' the gold fields o' Californi-a whar Sim an' Peter be!

ABBIE (*terrified*): Ye won't—leave me? Ye can't!

EBEN (*with fierce determination*): I'm a-goin', I tell ye! I'll git rich thar an' come back an' fight him fur the farm he stole—an' I'll kick ye both out in the road—t' beg an' sleep in the woods—an' yer son along with ye—t' starve an' die! (*He is hysterical at the end.*)

ABBIE (*with a shudder—humbly*): He's yewr son, too, Eben.

EBEN (*torturedly*): I wish he never was born! I wish he'd die this minit! I wish I'd never sot eyes on him! It's him—yew havin' him—a-purpose t' steal—that's changed everythin'!

ABBIE (*gently*): Did ye believe I loved ye—afore he come?

EBEN: Ay-eh—like a dumb ox!

ABBIE: An' ye don't believe no more?

EBEN: B'lieve a lyin' thief! Ha!

ABBIE (*shudders—then humbly*): An' did ye r'ally love me afore?

EBEN (*brokenly*): Ay-eh—an' ye was trickin' me!

ABBIE: An' ye don't love me now!

EBEN (*violently*): I hate ye, I tell ye!

ABBIE: An' ye're truly goin' West—goin' t' leave me—all account o' him being born?

EBEN: I'm a-goin' in the mornin'—or may God strike me t' hell!

ABBIE (*after a pause—with a dreadful cold intensity—slowly*): If that's what his comin 's done t' me—killin' yewr love—takin' yew away—my on'y joy—the on'y joy I ever knowed—like heaven t' me—purtier'n heaven—then I hate him, too, even if I be his Maw!

EBEN (*bitterly*): Lies! Ye love him! He'll steal the farm fur ye! (*Brokenly*) But t'ain't the farm so much—not no more—it's yew foolin' me—gittin' me t' love ye—lyin' yew loved me—jest t' git a son t' steal!

ABBIE (*distractedly*): He won't steal! I'd kill him fust! I do love ye! I'll prove t' ye . . . !

EBEN (*harshly*): T'ain't no use lyin' no more. I'm deaf t' ye! (*He turns away*) I hain't seein' ye agen. Good-by!

ABBIE (*pale with anguish*): Hain't ye even goin' t' kiss me—not once—arter all we loved?

EBEN (*in a hard voice*): I hain't wantin' t' kiss ye never agen! I'm wantin' t' forgit I ever sot eyes on ye!

ABBIE: Eben!—ye mustn't—wait a spell—I want t' tell ye. . . .

EBEN: I'm a-goin' in t' git drunk. I'm a-goin' t' dance.

ABBIE (*clinging to his arm—with passionate earnestness*): If I could make it—'s if he'd never come up between us—if I could prove t' ye I wa'n't schemin' t' steal from ye—so's everythin' could be jest the same with us, lovin' each other jest the same, kissin' an' happy the same's we've been happy afore he come—if I could do it—ye'd love me agen, wouldn't ye? Ye'd kiss me agen? Ye wouldn't never leave me, would ye?

EBEN (*moved*): I calc'late not. (*Then shaking her hand off his arm—with a bitter smile*) But ye hain't God, be ye?

ABBIE (*exultantly*): Remember ye've promised! (*Then with strange intensity*) Mebbe I kin take back one thin' God does!

EBEN (*peering at her*): Ye're gittin' cracked, hain't ye? (*Then going towards door*) I'm a-goin t' dance.

ABBIE (*calls after him intensely*): I'll prove t' ye! I'll prove I love ye better'n. . . . (*He goes in the door, not seeming to hear. She remains standing where she is, looking after him—then she finishes desperately*) Bettern' everythin' else in the world!

SCENE THREE

Just before dawn in the morning—shows the kitchen and CABOT's *bedroom. In the kitchen, by the light of a tallow candle on the table,* EBEN *is sitting, his chin propped on his hands, his drawn face blank and expressionless. His carpetbag is on the floor beside him. In the bedroom, dimly lighted by a small whale-oil lamp,* CABOT *lies asleep.* ABBIE *is bending over the cradle, listening, her face full of terror yet with an undercurrent of desperate triumph. Suddenly, she breaks down and sobs, appears about to throw herself on her knees beside the cradle; but the old man turns restlessly, groaning in his sleep, and she controls herself, and shrinking away from the cradle with a gesture of horror, backs swiftly toward the door in rear and goes out. A moment later she comes into the kitchen and, running to* EBEN, *flings her arms about his neck and kisses him wildly. He hardens himself, he remains unmoved and cold, he keeps his eyes straight ahead.*

ABBIE (*hysterically*): I done it, Eben! I told ye I'd do it! I've proved I love ye—better'n everythin'—so's ye can't never doubt me no more!

EBEN (*dully*): Whatever ye done, it hain't no good now.

ABBIE (*wildly*): Don't ye say that! Kiss me, Eben, won't ye? I need ye t' kiss me arter what I done! I need ye t' say ye love me!

EBEN (*kisses her without emotion—dully*): That's fur good-by. I'm a-goin' soon.

ABBIE: No! No! Ye won't go—not now!

EBEN (*going on with his own thoughts*): I been a-thinkin'—an' I hain't goin' t' tell Paw nothin'. I'll leave Maw t' take vengeance on ye. If I told him, the old skunk'd jest be stinkin' mean enuf to take it out on that baby. (*His voice showing emotion in spite of him*) An' I don't want nothin' bad t' happen t' him. He hain't t' blame fur yew. (*He adds with a certain queer pride*) An' he looks like me! An' by God, he's mine! An' some day I'll be a-comin' back an' . . . !

ABBIE (*too absorbed in her own thoughts to listen to him—pleadingly*): They's no cause fur ye t' go now—they's no sense—it's all the same's it was —they's nothin' come b'tween us now—arter what I done!

EBEN (*something in her voice arouses him. He stares at her a bit frightenedly*): Ye look mad, Abbie. What did ye do?

ABBIE: I—I killed him, Eben.

EBEN (*amazed*): Ye killed him?

ABBIE (*dully*): Ay-eh.

EBEN (*recovering from his astonishment—savagely*): An' serves him right! But we got t' do somethin' quick t' make it look 's if the old skunk'd killed himself when he was drunk. We kin prove by 'em all how drunk he got.

ABBIE (*wildly*): No! No! Not him! (*Laughing distractedly*) But that's what I ought t' done, hain't it? I oughter killed him instead! Why didn't ye tell me?

EBEN (*appalled*): Instead? What d'ye mean?

ABBIE: Not him.

EBEN (*his face grown ghastly*): Not—not that baby!

ABBIE (*dully*): Ay-eh?

EBEN (*falls to his knees as if he'd been struck —his voice trembling with horror*): Oh, God A'mighty! A'mighty God! Maw, whar was ye, why didn't ye stop her?

ABBIE (*simply*): She went back t' her grave that night we fust done it, remember? I hain't felt her about since. (*A pause.* EBEN *hides his head in his hands, trembling all over as if he had the ague. She goes on dully*) I left the piller over his little face. Then he killed himself. He stopped breathin'. (*She begins to weep softly.*)

EBEN (*rage beginning to mingle with grief*): He looked like me. He was mine, damn ye!

ABBIE (*slowly and brokenly*): I didn't want t' do it. I hated myself fur doin' it. I loved him. He was so purty—dead spit 'n' image o' yew. But I loved yew more—an' yew was goin' away—far off whar I'd never see ye agen, never kiss ye, never feel ye pressed agin me agen—an' ye said ye hated me fur havin' him—ye said ye hated him an' wished he was dead—ye said if it hadn't been fur him comin' it'd be the same's afore between us.

EBEN (*unable to endure this, springs to his feet in a fury, threatening her, his twitching fingers seeming to reach out for her throat*): Ye lie! I never said—I never dreamed ye'd—I'd cut off my head afore I'd hurt his finger!

ABBIE (*piteously, sinking on her knees*): Eben, don't ye look at me like that—hatin' me—not after what I done fur ye—fur us—so's we could be happy agen—

EBEN (*furiously now*): Shut up, or I'll kill ye! I see yer game now—the same old sneakin' trick— ye're aimin' t' blame me fur the murder ye done!

ABBIE (*moaning—putting her hands over her ears*): Don't ye, Eben! Don't ye! (*She grasps his legs.*)

EBEN (*his mood suddenly changing to horror, shrinks away from her*): Don't ye tech me! Ye're pizen! How could ye—t' murder a pore little critter —Ye must've swapped yer soul t' hell! (*Suddenly raging*) Ha! I kin see why ye done it! Not the lies ye jest told—but 'cause ye wanted t' steal agen— steal the last thin' ye'd left me—my part o' him— no, the hull o' him—ye saw he looked like me—ye knowed he was all mine—an' ye couldn't b'ar it—I know ye! Ye killed him fur bein' mine! (*All this has driven him almost insane. He makes a rush past her for the door—then turns—shaking both fists at her, violently*) But I'll take vengeance now! I'll git the Sheriff! I'll tell him everythin'! Then I'll sing "I'm off to Californi-a!" an' go—gold— Golden Gate—gold sun—fields o' gold in the West! (*This last he half shouts, half croons incoherently, suddenly breaking off passionately*) I'm a-goin' fur the Sheriff t' come an' git ye! I want ye tuk away, locked up from me! I can't stand t' luk at ye! Murderer an' thief 'r not, ye still tempt me! I'll give ye up t' the Sheriff. (*He turns and runs out, around the corner of house, panting and sobbing, and breaks into a swerving sprint down the road.*)

ABBIE (*struggling to her feet, runs to the door, calling after him*): I love ye, Eben! I love ye! (*She stops at the door weakly, swaying, about to fall*) I don't care what ye do—if ye'll on'y love me agen —(*She falls limply to the floor in a faint.*)

SCENE FOUR

About an hour later. Same as Scene Three. Shows the kitchen and CABOT'S *bedroom. It is after dawn. The sky is brilliant with the sunrise. In the kitchen,* ABBIE *sits at the table, her body limp and exhausted, her head bowed down over her arms, her face hidden. Upstairs,* CABOT *is still asleep but awakens with a start. He looks toward the window and gives a snort of surprise and irritation—throws back the covers and begins hurriedly pulling on his clothes. Without looking behind him, he begins talking to* ABBIE *whom he supposes beside him.*

CABOT: Thunder 'n' lightin', Abbie! I hain't slept this late in fifty year! Looks 's if the sun was full riz a'most. Must've been the dancin' an' likker. Must be gittin' old. I hope Eben's t' wuk. Ye might've tuk the trouble t' rouse me, Abbie. (*He turns—sees no one there—surprised*) Waal—whar air she? Gittin' vittles, I calc'late. (*He tiptoes to the cradle and peers down—proudly*) Mornin', sonny. Purty's a picture! Sleepin' sound. He don't beller all night like most o' 'em. (*He goes quietly out the door in rear—a few moments later enters kitchen—sees* ABBIE—*with satisfaction*) So thar ye be. Ye got any vittles cooked?

ABBIE (*without moving*): No.

CABOT (*coming to her, almost sympathetically*): Ye feelin' sick?

ABBIE: No.

CABOT (*pats her on shoulder. She shudders*): Ye'd best lie down a spell. (*Half jocularly*) Yer son'll be needin' ye soon. He'd ought t' wake up with a gnashin' appetite, the sound way he's sleepin'.

ABBIE (*shudders—then in a dead voice*): He hain't never goin' t' wake up.

CABOT (*jokingly*): Takes after me this mornin'. I hain't slept so late in . . .

ABBIE: He's dead.

CABOT (*stares at her—bewilderedly*): What. . . .

ABBIE: I killed him.

CABOT (*stepping back from her—aghast*): Air ye drunk— 'r crazy—'r . . . !

ABBIE (*suddenly lifts her head and turns on him—wildly*): I killed him, I tell ye! I smothered him. Go up an' see if ye don't b'lieve me! (CABOT *stares at her a second, then bolts out the rear door—can be heard bounding up the stairs—and rushes into the bedroom and over to the cradle.* ABBIE *has sunk back lifelessly into her former position.* CABOT *puts his hand down on the body in the crib. An expression of fear and horror comes over his face.*)

CABOT (*shrinking away—tremblingly*): God A'mighty! God A'mighty. (*He stumbles out the door—in a short while returns to the kitchen—comes to* ABBIE, *the stunned expression still on his face—hoarsely*) Why did ye do it? Why? (*As she doesn't answer, he grabs her violently by the shoulder and shakes her*) I ax ye why ye done it! Ye'd better tell me 'r . . . !

ABBIE (*gives him a furious push which sends him staggering back and springs to her feet—with wild rage and hatred*): Don't ye dare tech me! What right hev ye t' question me 'bout him? He wa'n't yewr son! Think I'd have a son by yew? I'd die fust! I hate the sight o' ye an' allus did! It's yew I should've murdered, if I'd had good sense! I hate ye! I love Eben. I did from the fust. An' he was Eben's son—mine an' Eben's—not your'n!

CABOT (*stands looking at her dazedly—a pause—finding his words with an effort—dully*): That was it—what I felt—pokin' round the corners—while ye lied—holdin' yerself from me—sayin' ye'd a'ready conceived—(*He lapses into crushed silence—then with a strange emotion*) He's dead, sart'n. I felt his heart. Pore little critter! (*He blinks back one tear, wiping his sleeve across his nose.*)

ABBIE (*hysterically*): Don't ye! Don't ye! (*She sobs unrestrainedly.*)

CABOT (*with a concentrated effort that stiffens his body into a rigid line and hardens his face into a stony mask—through his teeth to himself*): I got t' be—like a stone—a rock o' jedgment! (*A pause. He gets complete control over himself—harshly*) If he was Eben's, I be glad he air gone! An' mebbe I suspicioned it all along. I felt they was somethin' onnateral—somewhars—the house got so lonesome —an' cold—drivin' me down t' the barn—t' the beasts o' the field. . . . Ay-eh. I must've suspicioned—somethin'. Ye didn't fool me—not altogether, leastways—I'm too old a bird—growin' ripe on the bough. . . . (*He becomes aware he is wandering, straightens again, looks at* ABBIE *with a cruel grin*) So ye'd like t' hev murdered me 'stead o' him, would ye? Waal, I'll live to a hundred! I'll live t' see ye hung! I'll deliver ye up t' the jedgment o' God an' the law! I'll git the Sheriff now. (*Starts for the door.*)

ABBIE (*dully*): Ye needn't. Eben's gone fur him.

CABOT (*amazed*): Eben—gone fur the Sheriff?

ABBIE: Ay-eh.

CABOT: T' inform agen ye?

ABBIE: Ay-eh.

CABOT (*considers this—a pause—then in a hard voice*): Waal, I'm thankful fur him savin' me the trouble. I'll git t' wuk. (*He goes to the door—then turns—in a voice full of strange emotion*) He'd ought t' been my son, Abbie. Ye'd ought t' loved me. I'm a man. If ye'd loved me, I'd never told no Sheriff on ye no matter what ye did, if they was t' brile me alive!

ABBIE (*defensively*): They's more to it nor yew know, makes him tell.

CABOT (*dryly*): Fur yewr sake, I hope they be. (*He goes out—comes around to the gate—stares up at the sky. His control relaxes. For a moment he is old and weary. He murmurs despairingly)* God A'mighty, I be lonesomer'n ever! *(He hears running footsteps from the left, immediately is himself again.* EBEN *runs in, panting exhaustedly, wild-eyed and mad looking. He lurches through the gate.* CABOT *grabs him by the shoulder.* EBEN *stares at him dumbly)* Did ye tell the Sheriff?

EBEN *(nodding stupidly)*: Ay-eh.

CABOT *(gives him a push away that sends him sprawling—laughing with withering contempt)*: Good fur ye! A prime chip o' yer Maw ye be! *(He goes toward the barn, laughing harshly.* EBEN *scrambles to his feet. Suddenly* CABOT *turns—grimly threatening)* Git off this farm when the Sheriff takes her—or, by God, he'll have t' come back an' git me fur murder, too! *(He stalks off.* EBEN *does not appear to have heard him. He runs to the door and comes into the kitchen.* ABBIE *looks up with a cry of anguished joy.* EBEN *stumbles over and throws himself on his knees beside her—sobbing brokenly.)*

EBEN: Fergive me!

ABBIE *(happily)*: Eben! *(She kisses him and pulls his head over against her breast.)*

EBEN: I love ye! Fergive me!

ABBIE *(ecstatically)*: I'd fergive ye all the sins in hell fur sayin' that! *(She kisses his head, pressing it to her with a fierce passion of possession.)*

EBEN *(brokenly)*: But I told the Sheriff. He's comin' fur ye!

ABBIE: I kin b'ar what happens t' me—now!

EBEN: I woke him up. I told him. He says, wait 'til I git dressed. I was waiting. I got to thinkin' o' yew. I got to thinkin' how I'd loved ye. It hurt like somethin' was bustin' in my chest an' head. I got t' cryin'. I knowed sudden I loved ye yet, an' allus would love ye!

ABBIE *(caressing his hair—tenderly)*: My boy, hain't ye?

EBEN: I begun t' run back. I cut across the fields an' through the woods. I thought ye might have time t' run away—with me—an' . . .

ABBIE *(shaking her head)*: I got t' take my punishment—t' pay fur my sin.

EBEN: Then I want t' share it with ye.

ABBIE: Ye didn't do nothin'.

EBEN: I put it in yer head. I wisht he was dead! I as much as urged ye t' do it!

ABBIE: No. It was me alone!

EBEN: I'm as guilty as yew be! He was the child o' our sin.

ABBIE *(lifting her head as if defying God)*: I

don't repent that sin! I hain't askin' God t' fergive that!

EBEN: Nor me—but it led up t' the other—an' the murder ye did, ye did 'count o' me—an' it's my murder, too, I'll tell the Sheriff—an' if ye deny it, I'll say we planned it t'gether—an' they'll all b'lieve me, fur they suspicion everythin' we've done, an' it'll seem likely an' true to 'em. An' it is true—way down. I did help ye—somehow.

ABBIE *(laying her head on his—sobbing)*: No! I don't want yew t' suffer!

EBEN: I got t' pay fur my part o' the sin! An' I'd suffer wust leavin' ye, goin' West, thinkin' o' ye day an' night, bein' out when yew was in— *(Lowering his voice)* 'r bein' alive when yew was dead. *(A pause)* I want t' share with ye, Abbie—prison 'r death 'r hell 'r anythin'! *(He looks into her eyes and forces a trembling smile)* If I'm sharin' with ye, I won't feel lonesome, leastways.

ABBIE *(weakly)*: Eben! I won't let ye! I can't let ye!

EBEN *(kissing her—tenderly)*: Ye can't he'p yerself. I got ye beat fur once!

ABBIE *(forcing a smile—adoringly)*: I hain't beat —s'long's I got ye!

EBEN *(hears the sound of feet outside)*: Ssshh! Listen! They've come t' take us!

ABBIE: No, it's him. Don't give him no chance to fight ye, Eben. Don't say nothin'—no matter what he says. An' I won't neither. *(It is* CABOT. *He comes up from the barn in a great state of excitement and strides into the house and then into the kitchen.* EBEN *is kneeling beside* ABBIE, *his arm around her, hers around him. They stare straight ahead.)*

CABOT *(stares at them, his face hard. A long pause—vindictively)*: Ye make a slick pair o' murderin' turtle doves! Ye'd ought t' be both hung on the same limb an' left thar t' swing in the breeze an' rot—a warnin' t' old fools like me t' b'ar their lonesomeness alone—an' fur young fools like ye t' hobble their lust. *(A pause. The excitement returns to his face, his eyes snap, he looks a bit crazy)* I couldn't work today. I couldn't take no interest. T' hell with the farm! I'm leavin' it! I've turned the cows an' other stock loose! I've druv 'em into the woods whar they kin be free! By freein' 'em, I'm freein' myself! I'm quittin' here today! I'll set fire t' house an' barn an' watch 'em burn, an' I'll leave yer Maw t' haunt the ashes, an' I'll will the fields back t' God, so that nothin' human kin never touch 'em! I'll be a-goin' to Californi-a—t' jine Simeon an' Peter—true sons o' mine if they be dumb fools—an' the Cabots'll find Solomon's Mines t'gether! (*He suddenly cuts a mad caper*) Whoop! What was the song they sung? "Oh, Californi-a! That's the land fur me." (*He sings this—then gets on his knees by the floor-board under which the money was hid*) An' I'll sail thar on one o' the finest clippers I kin find! I've got the money! Pity ye didn't know whar this was hidden so's ye could steal. . . . (*He has pulled up the board. He stares—feels—stares again. A pause of dead silence. He slowly turns, slumping into a sitting position on the floor, his eyes like those of a dead fish, his face the sickly green of an attack of nausea. He swallows painfully several times—forces a weak smile at last*) So—ye did steal it!

EBEN (*emotionlessly*): I swapped it t' Sim an' Peter fur their share o' the farm—t' pay their passage t' Californi-a.

CABOT (*with one sardonic*): Ha! (*He begins to recover. Gets slowly to his feet—strangely*) I calc'late God give it to 'em—not yew! God's hard, not easy! Mebbe they's easy gold in the West but it hain't God's gold. It hain't fur me. I kin hear His voice warnin' me agen t' be hard an' stay on my farm. I kin see his hand usin' Eben t' steal t' keep me from weakness. I kin feel I be in the palm o' His hand, His fingers guidin' me. (*A pause—then he mutters sadly*) It's a-goin' t' be lonesomer now than ever it war afore—an' I'm gittin' old, Lord—ripe on the bough. . . . (*Then stiffening*) Waal —what d'ye want? God's lonesome, hain't He? God's hard an' lonesome! (*A pause. The Sheriff with two men comes up the road from the left. They move cautiously to the door. The Sheriff knocks on it with the butt of his pistol.*)

SHERIFF: Open in the name o' the law! (*They start.*)

CABOT: They've come fur ye. (*He goes to the rear door*) Come in, Jim! (*The three men enter.* CABOT *meets them in doorway*) Jest a minit, Jim. I got 'em safe here. (*The Sheriff nods. He and his companions remain in the doorway.*)

EBEN (*suddenly calls*): I lied this mornin', Jim. I helped her do it. Ye kin take me, too.

ABBIE (*brokenly*): No!

CABOT: Take 'em both. (*He comes forward— stares at* EBEN *with a trace of grudging admiration*) Purty good—fur yew! Waal, I got t' round up the stock. Good-by.

EBEN: Good-by.

ABBIE: Good-by. (CABOT *turns and strides past the men—comes out and around the corner of the house, his shoulders squared, his face stony, and stalks grimly toward the barn. In the meantime the Sheriff and men have come into the room.*)

SHERIFF (*embarrassedly*): Waal—we'd best start.

ABBIE: Wait. (*Turns to* EBEN) I love ye, Eben.

EBEN: I love ye, Abbie. (*They kiss. The three men grin and shuffle embarrassedly.* EBEN *takes* ABBIE's *hand. They go out the door in rear, the men following, and come from the house, walking hand in hand to the gate.* EBEN *stops there and points to the sunrise sky*) Sun's a-rizin'. Purty, hain't it?

ABBIE: Ay-eh. (*They both stand for a moment looking up raptly in attitudes strangely aloof and devout.*)

SHERIFF (*looking around at the farm enviously— to his companion*): It's a jim-dandy farm, no denyin'. Wished I owned it!

From Imagism to Symbolism:
The Crisis in Culture

We have earlier discussed what we called the nativist branch of twentieth-century American poetry. But another very important branch developed not in America but in London. Some of the influential theorists who helped to shape it were English, men like T. E. Hulme and Ford Madox Ford, and two of its most influential American practitioners, T. S. Eliot and Ezra Pound, were living in London prior to the outbreak of the First World War. In fact, London at this time was one of the most active centers of the new American movements.[1]

By the end of the nineteenth century, Victorian literature[2] was visibly in decay. There is nothing surprising in this. The possibilities of the set of assumptions that underlay Victorian literature had had plenty of time to be worked out and indeed to be worked threadbare. Like other fashions, literary fashions are constantly changing, and sometimes they change for no better

---

[1] A comparable reconsideration of the proper aims and methods of fiction was undertaken by Gertrude Stein in Paris. See pp. 2223–32.

[2] Though the term applies literally only to the literature of Great Britain written during the reign of Queen Victoria (1837–1901), it is convenient to apply it to American literature of this period, which shows many of the same characteristics. Moreover, the Victorian period—if we are to be technical—ended with the death of Queen Victoria and was followed by the Edwardian period (1901–10), which takes its title from the name of the reigning sovereign, Edward VII. But there is little harm done here in disregarding the differences between Victorian and Edwardian poetry, since the Pound-Eliot revolution was a radical subversion of both—and even of "Georgian" poetry as represented in *Georgian Poetry*, the first volume of which was published in 1912, early in the reign of George V.

reason, it seems, than that people get tired of one mode and demand something novel.

Yet the breakdown of Victorian poetry was more special and raised
deeper issues, some of which touch on the very quick of literature itself. To
take up only one of them here: the Victorian poet's mode of "saying" what
he wanted to "say" became increasingly suspect. The realm of "statement"
had been compromised by the rapid progress of science: what science "said"
was true and, to some people, it clearly was the only authentic truth that
there was. The special devices of poetry therefore began to look more and
more like elegant, or prettified, but certainly needlessly roundabout, ways for
saying what could be said more simply and directly. In short, the man of
common sense began to wonder whether the "poetic" was anything more
than the emptily "rhetorical." The special diction of poetry and its avoidance of ordinary speech came to seem either mincing or pompous. Even the
basic poetic devices of meter and imagery looked more and more like mere
"ornaments." If "true" statements were necessarily of the order of "scientific" statements, then most of the paraphernalia of poetry was really inessential and had to be regarded as mere decoration.

artificiality of poetry

Thus, when Victorian poetry went to seed, one was led to ask what kind
of "statement" poetry made and whether it dealt in truth at all. Unless one
could show that science did not have a monopoly on truth, then didn't
the poet who wanted to tell the truth have to trudge very warily behind,
and more or less in, the footsteps of the scientist? For centuries the poet had
been regarded as the prime truth-teller, endowed with wisdom and even the
gift of prophecy. From time to time, to be sure, doubts had arisen and
attacks had been made on the validity of poetry, but in the day of Thomas
Huxley and Charles Darwin the crisis of poetry became more formidable.

Yet at the beginning, and certainly to the more superficial observer, dissatisfaction with late nineteenth-century poetry primarily had to do with its
conventions, which had come to seem tiresome and artificial. Why should a
poet have to go through such stupid circumlocutions in order to say something that was perfectly obvious? Was the only alternative to using the same
worn epithets over and over again the expedient of using even more strained
and out-of-the-way metaphors? As for meter, poets like Algernon Swinburne
seemed to have exhausted all the possibilities of even the more intricate
metrical forms. And even in Swinburne's skillful hands, the meter was now
making so much noise—melodious though it might be—that the reader could
hardly make out what the poem was saying.

One way of dealing with a too insistent and too artificial metrical beat
is to loosen the metrical pattern and bring it back closer to the rhythms of
ordinary speech; another is to abandon altogether a set metrical pattern and

to allow the play of thought and emotion to dictate the cadences. Even in the nineteenth century there were poets in England like Matthew Arnold who occasionally wrote poems in what came to be called *free verse* (that is, verse without a formal metrical pattern). On the American side, of course, there was the signal example of Walt Whitman and, later in the century, that of Stephen Crane. But free verse began to be used programmatically only in the twentieth century.

The "Imagist" movement had a great deal to do with promoting experiments with free verse, although Imagism as such did not demand its use; it is possible to write Imagist verse in traditional meters. Conversely, Stephen Crane's poems written in free verse bear no close resemblance to what came to be called Imagist poems. Imagism, as its name implies, stresses the primacy of the image, the concrete particular. Images, not general statements, are, by this theory, the fundamental building blocks of poetry. As Ezra Pound was to put it in 1914: "The point of Imagism is that it does not use images as *ornaments*. The image itself is the speech."

Imagism found its first theorist in the person of T. E. Hulme, who had studied philosophy at Cambridge University and later on the continent. Though Hulme, a casualty of the First World War, died young (in 1917), he had already gathered around him a group of young writers who met to discuss poetry and aesthetics. Hulme was quite clear in his own mind as to what was wrong with the traditional poetry of his time: it made use of words that had had all their particularity rubbed off and had been smoothed down to abstract bits of notation. Hulme argued that poetry ought to return to the concrete images out of which language itself had originated. For poetry, according to Hulme, "always endeavors to arrest you, and to make you continuously see a physical thing, to prevent you gliding through an abstract process."

It may not be self-evident that language works normally by making one "see a physical thing," but Hulme's attack on vagueness, high-level abstraction, windy rhetoric, and Victorian moralization was pertinent and useful. Moreover, one can, if he prefers, restate Hulme's position rather easily in terms consonant with recent criticism. Thus, we can say that poetry is not a system of abstract notation like mathematics. It tries to deal with another dimension, that of emotion and human valuation. Hence *metaphor*—a *transaction* between different "things" (love is a rose, love is a fire)—is essential to the poetic process. Or, if we are not stressing the *transfer* of qualities and associations from one word to another, we can say that poetry is essentially *symbolic*: that is, a concrete particular comes to "stand for" something other than itself. For example, the image of a rose, placed in a certain context, implies the quality of love or perhaps the quality of the loved one. However

[handwritten marginalia: cf. allegory vs imagism]

[handwritten marginalia: concretion vs abstraction]

[handwritten marginalia: cf. Symbolist correspondences]

we choose to put it, Hulme's insistence that poetry is "not a counter[3] language but a visual concrete one" was calculated to move poetry back toward its original qualities.[4]

Hulme, having made his own diagnosis of the breakdown of poetry in his time, went on to predict that the poetry of the future would be "dry, cheerful, and classical." Late Victorian poetry had been emotional, often melancholy, and generally highfalutin: Hulme complained that too much of Romantic poetry had been "a raid on the absolute," and in another telling phrase he had dismissed it as "spilt religion." The poetry to come would be less vague, more accurate in its references, and more modest in its assertions and in its claims. (The reader may well ask whether Hulme's prediction actually came true. Scarcely at all, would be our answer, and we would prefer a rather different set of terms with which to describe the kind of poetry that did ensue. At all events, the new poetry was certainly radically different from that of the past.)

Hulme's Poets' Club began to meet in a London restaurant in the spring of 1908. Very shortly after (in February of the next year), a young American expatriate, Ezra Pound,[5] was introduced to Hulme and the club. Pound speedily became a vigorous proponent of the new poetry and one of its ablest theorists. In a volume of poems published in 1912 and called *Ripostes*, Pound included as an appendix "The Complete Poetical Works of T. E. Hulme." Pound's title was half-jesting, for the poems in question were the little handful that Hulme had produced as illustrations of his theories. Here are two of them:

---

[3] Hulme means by "counter" something like a "token" or "imitation coin," the value of which does not reside in the silver or gold that it contains but in the figure stamped on it.

[4] Since such were the original qualities, they were not the discoveries of modern criticism. By and large, poetic practice has always recognized that poetry is a concrete figurative language, and the critics of the past have from time to time rediscovered these qualities and found it necessary to stress them once more. Thus the German Johann Gottfried von Herder (1744–1803), who was the first critic to break with the neoclassical past, asserted that primitive man thinks in terms of metaphors and symbols and by combining them makes fables and myths—in short, that language itself begins as metaphor. To go further back in time—to the very beginnings of criticism—Aristotle pointed out that mastery of metaphor is the great poetic gift, something that cannot be learned from someone else.

[5] Though born in Hailey, Idaho—"born/In a half savage country," Pound was to write of himself later—nearly all of his early life was spent in Philadelphia. He attended there the University of Pennsylvania, next Hamilton College, and then returned to the University of Pennsylvania for graduate work. But before he attained his Ph.D., his passionate interest in Provençal poetry brought him to Europe, first to Italy and then, in 1908, for a long stay in London.

Autumn (1912)

A touch of cold in the Autumn night
I walked abroad,
And saw the ruddy moon lean over a hedge
Like a red-faced farmer.
I did not stop to speak, but nodded;
And round about were the wistful stars
With white faces like town children.

The Embankment (1912)

(*The fantasia of a fallen gentleman on a
cold, bitter night*)

Once, in finesse of fiddles found I ecstasy,
In a flash of gold heels on the hard pavement.
Now see I
That warmth's the very stuff of poesy.
Oh, God, make small
The old star-eaten blanket of the sky,
That I may fold it round me and in comfort lie.

Hulme's "Autumn," written in free verse, gives an impression of the moon and stars on an autumn night. Though the images as such make their effect, what is even more heavily stressed is the element of comparison: the images are really full-blown similes. In "The Embankment" the element of comparison is also stressed: the poem concludes with a complicated and perhaps strained metaphor. Neither poem seems to be precisely revolutionary.

Hulme's poetry, however, largely on account of its use of developed simile, differs rather sharply from what we think of as typically Imagist poetry—for example, the poems of H. D. Hilda Doolittle was an American girl whom Pound had known when they were both students at the University of Pennsylvania. In 1912 H. D. showed Pound a group of poems which, thanks to him, were to be published in the January, 1913, issue of *Poetry: A Magazine of Verse*. One of these was "Orchard" (originally titled "Priapus"):

Orchard (1913)

I saw the first pear
as it fell—
the honey-seeking, golden-banded,
the yellow swarm

was not more fleet than I,
(spare us from loveliness)
and I fell prostrate,
crying:
you have flayed us
with your blossoms,   10
spare us the beauty
of fruit-trees.

The honey-seeking
paused not,
the air thundered their song,
and I alone was prostrate.

O rough-hewn
god of the orchard,
I bring an offering—
do you, alone unbeautiful,   20
son of the god,
spare us from loveliness:

these fallen hazel-nuts,
stripped late of their green sheaths,
grapes, red-purple
their berries
dripping with wine,
pomegranates already broken,
and shrunken figs
and quinces untouched,   30
I bring you as offering.

H. D.'s poem "Oread" defines far more specifically than "Orchard" the
quality that Pound seized on as representing the kind of laconic intensity
which should be the character of Imagist poetry.

Oread (1914)

Whirl up, sea—
whirl your pointed pines,
splash your great pines
on our rocks,
hurl your green over us,
cover us with your pools of fir.

Like "Orchard," the setting of this poem is Greek: an oread is a Greek mountain nymph. But in the poem she is treated as if she were a sea nymph. (Or is a sea nymph being described here in terms of a mountain nymph? For the purposes of the poem, does it matter?) The poem, by the way, leans rather heavily on Milton's *Paradise Lost* (Bk. 9, lines 1088–90): "Cover me ye Pines,/Ye Cedars, with innumerable boughs/Hide me. . . ." Early Imagist poetry is often surprisingly "literary" in its origins.

When Pound sent H. D.'s poems to Harriet Monroe, the editor of *Poetry*, he wrote that "This is the sort of American stuff that I can show here [in London] and in Paris without its being ridiculed. Objective—no slither; direct—no excessive use of adjectives, no metaphors that won't permit examination. It's straight talk, straight as the Greek!"

H. D. had studied Greek at the University of Pennsylvania, and her poetry was much influenced by the Greek lyric. From the very first, we observe, one of the features of Imagist poetry was its eclecticism. The French symbolist poets were one powerful influence; another influence came from the Chinese and Japanese poets. Pound's poem "In a Station of the Metro," for example, uses the form of the Japanese *haiku*, which consists of exactly seventeen syllables. To Pound and H. D., and to many other poets associated with them in the burgeoning Imagist movement, the poetry of the English-speaking nations had become too insular—too much shut away from the rest of the world. Ford Madox Ford, the British poet and novelist, who was a friend of Pound and of Hulme, praised the new poetry because it was free of what he called "the polysyllabic, honey-dripping and derivative adjectives that, distinguishing the works of most of their contemporaries, makes nineteenth-century poetry as a whole seem greasy and close, like the air of a room." Windows were to be opened. Fresh ideas and forms from the non-English-speaking world were to be admitted.[6]

Most of the early pronouncements made by the Imagist poets are protests against decadent Victorian poetry and are thus essentially negative. Pound's little document "A Few Don'ts of an Imagiste" (1913) is characteristic. Such also is the nature of the comments he made in a letter to Harriet Monroe in 1915:

Rhythm *must* have meaning. It can't be merely a careless dash off, with no

[6] In this matter of international influence, there are clear affinities between the Imagist movement and theorists of the novel like Henry James. A more international outlook joined with a concern to get back to first principles and with a renewed stress on craftsmanship reminds us of James's efforts to apply the lessons of Flaubert to the novel written in English, or of Ford Madox Ford's collaborations with the Polish-born novelist Joseph Conrad, and of Stephen Crane's revolutionary experiments in both fiction and poetry.

grip and no real hold to the words and sense, a tumpy tum tumpy tum tum ta.

There must be no clichés, set phrases, stereotyped journalese. . . . Objectivity and again objectivity, and expression: no hindside-beforeness, no straddled adjectives (as "addled mosses dank"), no Tennysonianness of speech; nothing—nothing that you couldn't, in some circumstances, in the stress of some emotion, actually say. . . . Language is made out of concrete things. . . .

Such a reaction against the vague and pretentiously literary in the new poetry beginning to emerge about 1913 has its counterpart in the fiction that was to be written a decade or so later. For example, Ernest Hemingway developed a prose style that was stripped of ornament, lean, muscled, and—to use one of Hemingway's favorite adjectives—"accurate."[7]

Yet among his "Don'ts," Pound did include a brief positive definition of the image: "an 'image' is that which presents an intellectual and emotional complex in an instant of time." Pound fixes on the image because it represents for him a hunk of undivided reality—of reality not yet separated into intellectual and emotional segments.[8] The phrase "in an instant of time" is awkward: presumably Pound means to say that the intellectual and emotional components of the complex are simultaneously present. But the Imagist movement did not require a crystal-clear definition of its positive aims in order to attract poets. Plenty of talented young men and women, tired of a poetry now evidently gone to seed, were happy to experiment with a poetry founded on "images" without inquiring too precisely just what these were.

In 1914 Pound got together an anthology entitled *Des Imagistes*. It included ten poets—among the Americans, H. D., Amy Lowell, and William Carlos Williams. Of these, Amy Lowell was soon to become a vigorous propagandist for the movement. She herself issued anthologies entitled *Some Imagist Poets* in 1915, 1916, and 1917. Her 1915 volume included six poets, of whom the Americans in addition to herself were H. D. and John Gould Fletcher. Pound preferred not to appear; he had his own quarrel with Amy Lowell and with her conception of imagism (which he derisively nicknamed "Amygism"). But his refusal to appear in further Imagist anthologies did not mean, of course, any slackening of his interest in "images" or in working

[7] The return to simplicity, concision, "the language actually spoken by men" is a recurrent phenomenon in all literary history. But it will not be difficult to find native American roots for the return to lean and "accurate" writing. The Puritan writers of New England had laid heavy stress on a "plain" style, and in the nineteenth century Emerson had insisted on making "the word one with the thing."

[8] The deeper implications of this phrase and its relation to the split between head and heart, science and poetry, the objective and the subjective, will be discussed later.

out his own concept of what poetry ought to be. We shall return to these matters on a later page.

In the preface to her 1915 anthology, Amy Lowell printed an Imagist manifesto. It consisted of six articles.

1. To use the language of common speech, but to employ the *exact* word, not the nearly-exact, nor the merely decorative word.

2. To create new rhythms—as the expression of new moods—and not to copy old rhythms, which merely echo old moods. We do not insist upon "free-verse" as the only method of writing poetry. We fight for it as a principle of liberty. We believe that the individuality of a poet may often be better expressed in free-verse than in conventional forms. In poetry, a new cadence means a new idea.

3. To allow absolute freedom in the choice of subject. It is not good art to write badly about aeroplanes and automobiles; nor is it necessarily bad art to write well about the past. We believe passionately in the artistic value of modern life, but we wish to point out that there is nothing so uninspiring nor so old-fashioned as an aeroplane of the year 1911.

4. To present an image (hence the name: "Imagist"). We are not a school of painters, but we believe that poetry should render particulars exactly and not deal in vague generalities, however magnificent and sonorous. It is for this reason that we oppose the cosmic poet, who seems to us to shirk the real difficulties of his art.

5. To produce poetry that is hard and clear, never blurred nor indefinite.

6. Finally, most of us believe that concentration is of the very essence of poetry.

As the Imagists themselves pointed out, the principles set forth were not new. For example, over a century earlier William Wordsworth had repudiated meaningless ornament and a specifically "poetic" diction. Perhaps the Imagists went somewhat farther in arguing that nothing was to be considered as intrinsically "poetic"—neither words nor objects. So also perhaps in holding that poetry might dispense with any particular metrical pattern. The Imagists are, in their stress at least, most nearly original in condemning "vague generalities, however magnificent and sonorous." Their negative prescriptions are sound enough.

But when we come to the "dos" rather than the "don'ts," the case is not so obvious. For example, what is meant by "hard and clear" poetry? And what is meant by "the exact word"? In what sense, exact? If one took the principles fairly literally, he might have to discard some very great poetry of the past. Thus, can one say that Keats's "Ode to a Nightingale" is "hard and clear, never blurred or indefinite"? (It's possible to argue that it *is* hard and clear, and since Amy Lowell herself wrote an admiring biography of Keats, perhaps she would have endorsed such an argument; but in that case, the choice of such terms as "hard and clear" is not a very happy one.)

Again, with a glance at the first article, did Shakespeare make use of "the language of common speech" when he wrote "the multitudinous seas incarnadine"? One could argue that neither "multitudinous" nor "incarnadine" in this context is a "merely decorative word," but it would be difficult to claim that either was ever a part of the "language of common speech"— even in 1605 or 1606 when Shakespeare wrote *Macbeth*. In framing their manifesto, the Imagists were not always themselves careful to use the exact word.

One's misgivings about the limitations of the 1915 manifesto are deepened when he looks at the kind of poetry actually written at this time by the Imagists. What do terms like "hard," "clear," and "exact" mean in relation to a poem like Amy Lowell's "Night Clouds."

Night Clouds (1925)

The white mares of the moon rush along the sky
Beating their golden hoofs upon the glass Heavens;
The white mares of the moon are all standing on their hind legs
Pawing at the green porcelain doors of the remote Heavens.
Fly, Mares!
Strain your utmost,
Scatter the milky dust of stars,
Or the tiger sun will leap upon you and destroy you
With one lick of his vermilion tongue.

Despite the Imagists' disclaimer that they were not "a school of painters," this little poem comes very close to competing with the painter—that is, attempting to do something that the painter can by virtue of his very medium always do better than the poet. Moreover, some of the words in the poem do seem to be "merely decorative." As a matter of fact, if we try to visualize the scene, it looks like nothing so much as the decorations of a Hollywood bathroom. At best, the poem indulges a mannered fantasy; it does not give any real sense of a moonlit sky.

The stress on concentration in poetry (article 6) is probably that with which fewest people would quarrel; yet it is just on the matter of scale that Imagist poems most often are defective. Some are too brief, too limited in context, to build up any real sense of significance and power. Worse still, by restricting themselves to a mere sequence of images the poets of this school often dissipate whatever impression of dramatic continuity they might otherwise have developed. Consider the following poem by H. D.

Lais (1924)

Let her who walks in Paphos
take the glass,
let Paphos take the mirror
and the work of frosted fruit,
gold apples set
with silver apple-leaf,
white leaf of silver
wrought with vein of gilt.

Let Paphos lift the mirror;
let her look   10
into the polished center of the disk.
Let Paphos take the mirror:
did she press
flowerlet of flame-flower
to the lustrous white
of the white forehead?
Did the dark veins beat
a deeper purple
than the wine-deep tint
of the dark flower?

Did she deck black hair,   20
one evening, with the winter-white
flower of the winter-berry?
Did she look (reft of her lover)
at a face gone white
under the chaplet
of white virgin-breath?

Lais, exultant, tyrannizing Greece,
Lais who kept her lovers in the porch,
lover on lover waiting
(but to creep   30
where the robe brushed the threshold
where still sleeps Lais),

> so she creeps, Lais,
> to lay her mirror at the feet
> of her who reigns in Paphos.
>
> Lais has left her mirror,
> for she sees no longer in its depth
> the Lais' self
> that laughed exultant,
> tyrannizing Greece.   40
>
> Lais has left her mirror,
> for she weeps no longer,
> finding in its depth
> a face, but other
> than dark flame and white
> feature of perfect marble.
>
> *Lais has left her mirror*
> *(so one wrote)*
> *to her who reigns in Paphos;*
> *Lais who laughed a tyrant over Greece,*   50
> *Lais who turned the lovers from the porch,*
> *that swarm for whom now*
> *Lais has no use;*
> *Lais is now no lover of the glass,*
> *seeing no more the face as once it was,*
> *wishing to see that face and finding this.*

The real drama of this poem is concentrated in the lines printed in italic at the end: all that goes before is simply a dilution of this core passage. The core passage itself is an expansion of a celebrated Greek poem (H. D. refers to it in the phrase "so one wrote") attributed, probably incorrectly, to Plato. Here follows a modern translation of that poem:

> I Lais whose laughter was scornful in Hellas,
> Whose doorways were thronged daily with young lovers,
> I dedicate my mirror to Aphroditê:
>
> For I will not see myself as I am now,
> And can not see myself as once I was.[9]

The Greek poet has been willing to leave to the reader's imagination what the American needlessly elaborates.

[9] *Poems from the Greek Anthology* (1956), translated by Dudley Fitts.

The real deficiency in Imagist theory and the besetting sin of much Imagist practice is a lack of dynamic quality. The most nearly "pure" Imagist poems are starved of verbs. Too often the Imagist poet is content to offer little more than a hint of description, a bit of detail, an isolated vignette. Typically he builds his poem out of nouns and noun phrases, stacked one upon another.[10] Even when the organization of the poem is more elaborate and there is a series of verbs, as in H. D.'s "Lais," the same monotony often prevails: "Let her . . . take the glass," "Did she deck black hair," and so on. The constant repetition is calculated to slow down any sense of movement: the structure is static.[11] Yet the greatest of poetry is dynamic, and its concentration and intensity are linked with action—physical or mental. (Pound's choice of the term "vortex" in 1914 to characterize his post-Imagist stance— he defined "vortex" as a "Mass of whirling fluid, esp. whirlpool"—is perhaps a recognition of the static quality of Imagism and an assertion of the need for dynamic energy in art.)

Another real deficiency in Imagist theory and practice is the tendency to rely on images as mere surfaces and to neglect their symbolic quality. Human beings demand meanings, and if the image presented is a mere surface, the poem will remain curiously flat and two-dimensional. One is tempted to call Imagism a symbolism *manqué*; that is, it is a symbolist poetry that never manages to develop its implicit symbolism.[12] It was well and good to ask poetry to be "hard" and "clear," but not at the expense of its overtones and symbolic implications.

The best poetry produced by the Imagists turns out in fact to be symbolist poetry. Consider, for example, Amy Lowell's "Meeting-House Hill."

---

[10] It is in this matter of the method of construction that the later Pound would come to differ most radically with the "pure" Imagists.

[11] In its reaction against Victorian rhetorical "statement," the Imagist poets and those associated with them tend to go back to simpler and more primitive ways of unifying their work: repetition and simple juxtaposition; that is, placing the "images" alongside each other and allowing the reader to make a meaningful connection—if he can. Such methods can be very effective, as fifteenth-century folk ballads and some of Wordsworth's Lucy poems show. But there is always the threat that such poetry will prove to be a regression from the more complex and sophisticated methods employed, say, by the Elizabethan poets and dramatists. Such a slip back into false innocence and faked simplicity is essentially what Yvor Winters deplored in his *Primitivism and Decadence* (1937).

[12] René Taupin, in his *L'Influence du symbolisme français sur la poésie américaine (de 1910 à 1920)*, 1929, writes that "between the 'image' of the Imagists and the 'symbol' of the [French] Symbolists there is a difference only of precision" (p. 98). In saying so he is, however, overgenerous to most of the Imagists; but Taupin is surely right in stressing the basic resemblance between the two schools.

Meeting-House Hill (1925)

I must be mad, or very tired,
When the curve of a blue bay beyond a railroad track
Is shrill and sweet to me like the sudden springing of a tune,
And the sight of a white church above thin trees in a city square
Amazes my eyes as though it were the Parthenon.
Clear, reticent, superbly final,
With the pillars of its portico refined to a cautious elegance,
It dominates the weak trees,
And the shot of its spire
Is cool and candid,   10
Rising into an unresisting sky.

Strange meeting-house
Pausing a moment upon a squalid hill-top.
I watch the spire sweeping the sky,
I am dizzy with the movement of the sky;
I might be watching a mast
With its royals set full
Straining before a two-reef breeze.
I might be sighting a tea-clipper,
Tacking into the blue bay,   20
Just back from Canton
With her hold full of green and blue porcelain
And a Chinese coolie leaning over the rail
Gazing at the white spire
With dull, sea-spent eyes.

There is a sufficiency of images here: that of the meeting-house itself, the squalid district that has grown up around it, the bay and the railroad track, and the imagined clipper ship just in from China—even the "green and blue porcelain" down in the clipper's hold. At first glance these images may appear to be only loosely associated in a kind of stream-of-consciousness and the poem itself to lack any internal logic. That is, we seem to have no more than two stacks of images, the meeting-house group and the ship group, connected by a fancied analogy between church spire and ship's mast. But the poem does have an internal logic and the cluster of images "says" something—about the speaker and about her relation to present and past. The meeting-house and the clipper ship represent two significant forces in the older New England culture. The contrast between the eighteenth-century meeting-house, now preserved as a cultural monument in the midst of the squalor of twentieth-century Boston, suggests, unobtrusively but powerfully, the contrast between what New England once was and what it is now. What this contrast means to the "I" of the poem, the context makes perfectly plain. The meeting-house, she realizes, has now become as strange to her as it must have seemed a century ago to the eyes of a Chinese coolie as he viewed for the first time this curious temple of an alien faith, the cultural center of a foreign civilization.

The poem is not static. Despite its Imagistic technique, it is not just an arrangement of surfaces. To the sensitive reader, willing to use his imagination, it is richer in emotion and shows more "concentration" than any other of Miss Lowell's poems.

If an Imagist poem when *fully* realized becomes a symbolist poem, then the poet need not forgo shimmering overtones and symbolic resonances under a mistaken notion that his poem might thereby become "blurred" and "indefinite." No wonder that poets like Pound and William Carlos Williams broke through the constriction of narrow interpretations of "hard and clear" to experiment further, to use bits of Imagist poetry as the building blocks of larger structures, and to develop their work far beyond any strict interpretation of the original Imagist credo.

A recent short history of the Imagist movement, William Pratt's introduction to *The Imagist Poem* (1963), makes just this point. He writes that

> after 1917 . . . Imagism was no longer a movement: it had become a tool, which each poet could adapt to his own use. Younger poets like E. E. Cummings and Archibald MacLeish would make new poems of the Imagist type, but without forming any association or publishing further rules. . . . Older poets, who had already forged their weapons in the Imagist fire, would use them to fight bigger wars than the strict Imagist poem permitted.

A SHEAF OF IMAGIST POEMS

H. D. [HILDA DOOLITTLE]
(1886–1961)

Heat (1916)

O wind, rend open the heat,
cut apart the heat,
rend it to tatters.

Fruit cannot drop
through this thick air—
fruit cannot fall into heat
that presses up and blunts
the points of pears
and rounds the grapes.

Cut the heat—
plough through it,

10

turning it on either side
of your path.

Pear Tree (1916)

Silver dust,
lifted from the earth,
higher than my arms reach,
you have mounted,
O, silver,
higher than my arms reach,
you front us with great mass;

no flower ever opened
so staunch a white leaf,
no flower ever parted silver   10
from such rare silver:
O, white pear,
your flower-tufts
thick on the branch
bring summer and ripe fruits
in their purple hearts.

Sea Rose (1916)

Rose, harsh rose,
marred and with stint of petals,
meagre flower, thin,
sparse of leaf,

more precious
than a wet rose,
single on a stem—
you are caught in the drift.

Stunted, with small leaf,
you are flung on the sands,   10
you are lifted
in the crisp sand
that drives in the wind.

Can the spice-rose
drip such acrid fragrance
hardened in a leaf?

AMY LOWELL (1874–1925)

A Lady (1914)

You are beautiful and faded
Like an old opera tune
Played upon a harpsichord;

Or like the sun-flooded silks
Of an eighteenth-century boudoir.
In your eyes
Smolder the fallen roses of out-lived minutes,
And the perfume of your soul
Is vague and suffusing,
With the pungence of sealed spice-jars.   10
Your half-tones delight me,
And I grow mad with gazing
At your blent colors.

My vigor is a new-minted penny,
Which I cast at your feet.
Gather it up from the dust,
That its sparkle may amuse you.

A Decade (1919)

When you came, you were like red wine and
    honey,
And the taste of you burnt my mouth with
    its sweetness.
Now you are like morning bread,
Smooth and pleasant.
I hardly taste you at all, for I know your savor;
But I am completely nourished.

Lilacs (1925)

Lilacs,
False blue,
White,
Purple,
Colour of lilac,
Your great puffs of flowers
Are everywhere in this my New England.
Among your heart-shaped leaves
Orange orioles hop like music-box birds and
    sing
Their little weak soft songs;   10
In the crooks of your branches
The bright eyes of song sparrows sitting on
    spotted eggs
Peer restlessly through the light and shadow
Of all Springs.

Lilacs in dooryards
Holding quiet conversations with an early
    moon;
Lilacs watching a deserted house
Settling sideways into the grass of an old
    road;

Lilacs, wind-beaten, staggering under a lop-
    sided shock of bloom
Above a cellar dug into a hill.   20
You are everywhere.
You were everywhere.
You tapped the window when the preacher
    preached his sermon,
And ran along the road beside the boy going
    to school.
You stood by pasture-bars to give the cows
    good milking,
You persuaded the housewife that her dish
    pan was of silver
And her husband an image of pure gold.
You flaunted the fragrance of your blossoms
Through the wide doors of Custom Houses—
You, and sandal-wood, and tea,   30
Charging the noses of quill-driving clerks
When a ship was in from China.
You called to them: "Goose-quill men, goose-
    quill men,
May is a month for flitting."
Until they writhed on their high stools
And wrote poetry on their letter-sheets be-
    hind the propped-up ledgers.
Paradoxical New England clerks,
Writing inventories in ledgers, reading the
    "Song of Solomon" at night,
So many verses before bed-time,
Because it was the Bible.   40
The dead fed you
Amid the slant stones of graveyards.
Pale ghosts who planted you
Came in the night-time
And let their thin hair blow through your
    clustered stems.
You are of the green sea,
And of the stone hills which reach a long
    distance.
You are of elm-shaded streets with little
    shops where they sell kites and marbles,
You are of great parks where everyone walks
    and nobody is at home.
You cover the blind sides of greenhouses   50
And lean over the top to say a hurry-word
    through the glass
To your friends, the grapes, inside.

Lilacs,
False blue,
White,
Purple,
Colour of lilac,

You have forgotten your Eastern origin,
The veiled women with eyes like panthers,
The swollen, aggressive turbans of jewelled
    Pashas.   60
Now you are a very decent flower,
A reticent flower,
A curiously clear-cut, candid flower,
Standing beside clean doorways,
Friendly to a house-cat and a pair of spectacles,
Making poetry out of a bit of moonlight
And a hundred or two sharp blossoms.

Maine knows you,
Has for years and years;
New Hampshire knows you,   70
And Massachusetts
And Vermont.
Cape Cod starts you along the beaches to
    Rhode Island;
Connecticut takes you from a river to the
    sea.
You are brighter than apples,
Sweeter than tulips,
You are the great flood of our souls
Bursting above the leaf-shapes of our hearts,
You are the smell of all Summers,
The love of wives and children,   80
The recollection of the gardens of little
    children,
You are State Houses and Charters
And the familiar treading of the foot to and
    fro on a road it knows.
May is lilac here in New England,
May is a thrush singing "Sun up!" on a tip-
    top ash-tree,
May is white clouds behind pine-trees
Puffed out and marching upon a blue sky.
May is a green as no other,
May is much sun through small leaves,
May is soft earth,   90
And apple-blossoms,
And windows open to a South wind.
May is full light wind of lilac
From Canada to Narragansett Bay.

Lilacs,
False blue,
White,
Purple,
Colour of lilac.
Heart-leaves of lilac all over New England,   100
Roots of lilac under all the soil of New
    England,

Lilac in me because I am New England,
Because my roots are in it,
Because my leaves are of it,
Because my flowers are for it,
Because it is my country
And I speak to it of itself
And sing of it with my own voice
Since certainly it is mine.

JOHN GOULD FLETCHER
(1886–1950)

Fletcher, born in Arkansas and educated at Harvard, resided in London from 1918 to 1933.

From Irradiations (1915)

3

Over the roof-tops race the shadows of clouds;
Like horses the shadows of clouds charge
    down the street.

Whirlpools of purple and gold,
Winds from the mountains of cinnabar,
Lacquered mandarin moments, palanquins
    swaying and balancing
Amid vermilion pavilions, against the jade
    balustrades.
Glint of the glittering wings of dragon-flies in
    the light:
Silver filaments, golden flakes settling down-
    wards,
Rippling, quivering flutters, repulse and sur-
    render,
The sun broidered upon the rain,   10
The rain rustling with the sun.

Over the roof-tops race the shadows of clouds;
Like horses the shadows of clouds charge
    down the street.

5

Flickering of incessant rain
On flashing pavements:
Sudden scurry of umbrellas:
Bending, recurved blossoms of the storm.

The winds come clanging and clattering
From long white highroads shipping in rib-
    bons up summits:
They strew upon the city gusty wafts of ap-
    ple-blossom,

And the rustling of innumerable translucent
    leaves.
Uneven tinkling, the lazy rain
Dripping from the eaves.   10

The Skaters (1916)

Black swallows swooping or gliding
In a flurry of entangled loops and curves;
The skaters skim over the frozen river.
And the grinding click of their skates as they im-
    pinge upon the surface,
Is like the brushing together of thin wing-tips of
    silver.

ADELAIDE CRAPSEY (1878–1914)

The following poems are *cinquains*, a form invented by the author on the analogy of Japanese
forms like the *tanka* and the *haiku*. A cinquain
consists of twenty-two syllables, broken into five
lines, of two, four, six, eight, and two syllables,
respectively.

The Warning (1915)

Just now,
Out of the strange
Still dusk . . . as strange, as still . . .
A white moth flew. Why am I grown
So cold?

Triad (1915)

These be
Three silent things:
The falling snow . . . the hour
Before the dawn . . . the mouth of one
Just dead.

November Night (1915)

Listen . . .
With faint dry sound,
Like steps of passing ghosts,
The leaves, frost-crisp'd, break from the trees
And fall.

EZRA POUND (1885–1972)

A discussion of Pound's later poems, with representative examples, will be found on pp. 2063–89.

The Jewel Stairs' Grievance (1915)

The jewelled steps are already quite white with
    dew,
It is so late that the dew soaks my gauze stockings,
And I let down the crystal curtain
And watch the moon through the clear autumn.

Note. —*Jewel stairs, therefore a palace. Grievance, therefore there is something to complain of. Gauze stockings, therefore a court lady, not a servant who complains. Clear autumn, therefore he has no excuse on account of weather. Also she has come early, for the dew has not merely whitened the stairs, but has soaked her stockings. The poem is especially prized because she utters no direct reproach.*[1]

In a Station of the Metro (1916)

The apparition of these faces in the crowd:
Petals, on a wet, black bough.

Pound has provided the following account of the genesis and development of this poem:

I got out of a "metro" train at La Concorde, and saw suddenly a beautiful face, and then another beautiful woman, and I tried all that day to find words for what this had meant to me, and I could not find any words that seemed to me worthy, or as lovely as that sudden emotion. And that evening, as I went home along the rue Raynouard, I was still trying and I found, suddenly, the expression. I do not mean that I found words, but there came an equation . . . not in speech, but in little splotches of colour. It was just that—a

"pattern," or hardly a pattern, if by "pattern" you mean something with a "repeat" in it. But it was a word, the beginning, for me, of a language in colour. . . .

That evening in the rue Raynouard, I realized quite vividly that if I were a painter, or if I had, often, *that kind* of emotion, or even if I had the energy to get paints and brushes and keep at it, I might found a new school of painting, of "non-representative" painting, a painting that would speak only by arrangements in colour. . . . That is to say, my experience in Paris should have gone into paint. If instead of colour I had perceived sound or planes in relation, I should have expressed it in music or in sculpture. Colour was, in that instance, the "primary pigment"; I mean that it was the first adequate equation that came into consciousness. . . . All poetic language is the language of exploration. Since the beginning of bad writing, writers have used images as ornaments. The point of Imagisme is that it does not use images *as ornaments*. The image is itself the speech. The image is the word beyond formulated language. . . . The "one-image poem" is a form of super-position, that is to say, it is one idea set on top of another. I found it useful in getting out of the impasse in which I had been left by my metro emotion. I wrote a thirty-line poem, and destroyed it because it was what we call work "of second intensity." Six months later I made a poem half that length; a year later I made the following hokku-like sentence [which constitutes the poem]:[2]

MARIANNE MOORE (1887–1972)

An introduction to Marianne Moore, and a selection of her poems, will be found on pp. 2169–79.

---

[1] Pound is not praising himself here. The poem is a "translation" of a poem by Rihaku (Li Po), and it is prized by the Chinese poet's fellow countrymen.

[2] Quoted by Charles Norman in *Ezra Pound* (1960), pp. 98–99. For a somewhat different account, see that quoted by Noel Stock in *The Life of Ezra Pound* (1970), p. 136.

To a Chameleon (1921)

Hid by the august foliage and fruit
  of the grape-vine
    twine
      your anatomy
        round the pruned and polished stem,
          Chameleon.
          Fire laid upon
        an emerald as long as
      the Dark King's massy one,
could not snap the spectrum up for food   10
  as you have done.

E. E. CUMMINGS (1894–1962)

An introduction to Cummings, and a selection
of his poems, will be found on pp. 2179–85.

Tumbling-hair (1923)

If the second of the two flower-pickers is
death, then it is plain that the poet has tried to
give a fresh image of what the cliché calls "the
grim reaper."

Tumbling-hair
        picker of buttercups
              violets
dandelions
And the big bullying daisies
           through the field wonderful
with eyes a little sorry
Another comes
      also picking flowers

i was considering how (1923)

i was considering how
within night's loose
sack a star's
nibbling in-

fin
-i-
tes-
i

-mal-
ly devours   10

darkness the
hungry star
which
will e
-ven
tu-
al
-ly jiggle
the bait of
dawn and be jerked   20

into

eternity.   when over my head a
shooting
star
Bur   s

          (t
             into a stale shriek
like an alarm-clock)

WILLIAM CARLOS WILLIAMS (1883–1963)

An introduction to Williams, and a selection of
his poems, will be found on pp. 2142–53.

Nantucket (1934)

Nantucket, an island just off the Massachusetts coast, was once a great whaling port but is
now a quaint spot for summer tourists. The
reader ought to ask himself: What is the poet
trying to describe? What do the images "do"?

Flowers through the window
lavender and yellow

changed by white curtains—
Smell of cleanliness—

Sunshine of late afternoon—
On the glass tray

a glass pitcher, the tumbler
turned down, by which

a key is lying—And the
immaculate white bed

Flowers by the Sea (1935)

When over the flowery, sharp pasture's
edge, unseen, the salt ocean

lifts its form—chicory and daisies
tied, released, seem hardly flowers alone

but color and the movement—or the shape
perhaps—of restlessness, whereas

the sea is circled and sways
peacefully upon its plantlike stem

EZRA POUND (1885–1972)

Ezra Pound's share in the development of Imagism and his related speculations about the nature of literature and particularly of poetry have
been discussed on earlier pages. Pound was a
born teacher—in spite of his rejection of aca-
demicism and his scorn of the study of literature
as conducted in the typical American graduate
school. Pound was also an extremely well-read
man. Before he departed for Europe, he had
become interested in medieval poetry and especially that of the poets of Provence. These
studies he continued and extended during his
years in London, 1908 to 1920, and later in Paris
and in Italy. Before long Pound had included in
the range of literatures in which he was interested not only those of the Western tradition
from classical times onward, but Oriental literature as well. He translated Ernest Fenollosa's
essay "The Chinese Written Characters as a
Medium for Poetry," and, making use of Fenollosa's notes, he turned the poems of Li Po into
English (*Cathay*, 1915).

Pound's translations have from the beginning
come in for sharp attacks. He has been derided
for making downright howlers and reproved for
straying, in his concern to render it into live and
idiomatic English, too far from the letter of the
text. But these eminently readable "translations" have also received high praise from many
of Pound's literary peers. What needs to be
stressed at this point is Pound's knowledge of,
and interest in, so many literatures. First, there
is the matter of their influences on Pound's own

style. Second, cultural history, primarily as reflected in these literatures, eventually came to
constitute the subject matter of his later and
more ambitious work.

Pound's very stance as an American living
abroad gave him, as it had earlier given to
Henry James, a special perspective on the cultural modes of the older world. Pound's mature
poetry became a diagnosis of cultural worth. He
celebrates the glory of those periods in the past
which he found admirable, or he angrily denounces those in which civilization had become
coarse, weak, or corrupt. Pound's passionate
concern for civilization led him into a study of
history and economics; but the state of literature and the arts remained for him the best
gauge of cultural health and well-being.[1]

The way in which Pound's concern for literature led him inevitably into the concern for the
good society and the healthy civilization comes
out very clearly in the suite of poems entitled
Hugh Selwyn Mauberley: Life and Contacts,
published in 1920. The work is a summary of
Pound's literary career in London from 1908 to
1920, in which year he shook the dust of the
London pavements from his shoes and left for
the continent. The poem is also a condensed

---

[1] After finally meeting Pound in January of 1939,
George Santayana wrote his secretary that Pound "reminded me of several old friends (young, when I knew
them) who were spasmodic rebels, but decent by tradition, emulators of Thoreau, full of scraps of culture
but lost, lost, lost in the intellectual world. . . ."

review of the literary and art history of London from the time of the pre-Raphaelite poets up to the First World War. Forming part of this history is a partial roll call of Pound's friends and of his pet aversions on the London literary scene. We must not be surprised then to see the poetry of Pound, the restorer of objectivity in verse, become autobiographical and even "private." It was not for nothing that Pound added "Life and Contacts" as a subtitle for the poem —these were his own life and contacts. The era is seen (naturally) through Pound's own eyes, and the poem makes as a consequence heavy demands upon the reader: he must become acquainted with Pound's friends, know (or be willing to learn) the history of the time, read what Pound has himself read, and be prepared to recognize all sorts of out-of-the-way literary allusions. *Hugh Selwyn Mauberley* is, of course, much more than a highly personal document, but it is at the least that.[2]

So much for the sources of Pound's first major poem. The judgment that the poem makes on the modern age may be partially summarized as follows:

Modern civilization, as represented by London, has no place for the artist, for it cannot recognize what he is trying to do or by what principles he lives. In the speaker's embittered gaze, much more is involved than an indifference to the arts bred by the desire to make money or to live by commercial values. Those values themselves destroy not only art but with it human integrity. They make the good life— on any level—impossible to live. The speaker predicts that "a tawdry cheapness/Shall outlast our days."

As for the immediate past: the catastrophe of the First World War was a consequence of the rotting out of humanistic values. The youth of England and of Europe were made to walk "eye-deep in hell" because they believed "in old men's lies." Then, "unbelieving," they "came home, home to a lie/Home to many deceits/Home to old lies and new infamy;/Usury age-old and age-thick/And liars in public places." The young men had indeed died for nothing better than "an old bitch gone in the teeth,/For a botched civilization. . . ./For two gross of broken statues,/For a few thousand battered books."

The point is not the disparagement of the broken torsos like those of the Elgin marbles in the British Museum or the early editions of Homer, Virgil, and Dante that are carefully guarded in the great libraries of the world; rather it is that a civilization that regards such books and statues only as valuable antiques and curiosities, a civilization that is incapable of understanding what they mean, derives no spiritual nourishment from them and is unable to produce art and literature of its own, is indeed a "botched civilization." In that case, all that it has received from the past becomes in effect mere collectors' items, lifeless antiquarian junk.

Pound's conception of art is thus anything but "arty"; it is manly and healthy. He does not exalt art at the expense of every other human activity. For him, authentic art has a direct relation to human society: it is the symptom of a healthy society, and in a corrupt society it may become a means of directing attention to the causes of the malady.

By the time of *Mauberley* Pound had discovered what he took to be the prime corrupting force: it was the misuse of the power of money. Significantly, he names usury, "age-old and age-thick," among the horrors to which the young veterans of the First World War returned. He came to this belief largely under the influence of the writings of Professor Silvio Gesell and Major C. H. Douglas, of Social Credit fame.[3]

---

[2] In this respect, of course, Pound is not alone. James Joyce's work reveals the same kind of construction: if we want to understand *Finnegans Wake* (or even *Ulysses*) we shall have to deal with a great deal of personal and even quite private material. T. S. Eliot's work too, as we shall see, is to a considerable degree built out of Eliot's reading of literature: the "fragments" that the protagonist "has shored against [his] ruins" are out of the funded experience of the race—as expressed in art, literature, dogma, rite, and cultural history.

[3] Pound's hatred of usury would have been reinforced—perhaps in the first instance was instigated—by his studies in the poetry of Dante, who provided a special place for usurers in the sixth circle of the Inferno. In his prose, Pound places great stress on the

(Pound was, however, able to document the case, to his own satisfaction at least, from the writings of the American founding fathers—Adams, Jefferson, Washington, and others.)

Responsibility for the corruption of a civilization lay primarily, Pound maintained, with its discount bankers and with its "usurers" generally. In the twentieth century the chief villains were, for Pound, the international banker and his henchmen, the munitions maker, and the demogogic politician. So clearly was usury the root evil that Pound claimed that by looking at the fineness or the thickness of an artist's line, he could calculate the interest rate during the age in which the artist worked.

This is already extravagant; yet Pound became more and more extreme in his views. Thus, a traditional caricature of the Jew made him out to be a moneylender, with no roots in the community, producing nothing, a kind of parasite on the local or national society; and Pound apparently had no difficulty in assimilating this ancient stereotype to his already grossly oversimplified economics. If usury was the root evil in the culture, then the wicked international bankers who profited from moneylending must, of course, be largely Jews. Pound went further still: nationalism must be invoked to oppose a destructive internationalism, and so Pound accepted Italian fascism. Since Mussolini promised to do away with the "usurocrats," Pound saw in him a new Thomas Jefferson. Pound's involvement in Italian fascism (including broadcasts deploring our entrance into the Second World War) caused him, after the collapse of Mussolini's government in 1945, to be indicted for treason against the United States. Government psychiatrists, however, reported him mentally unfit to stand trial. He was committed to St. Elizabeth's Hospital in Washington, D.C.,[4] and remained there

from 1945 until April, 1958, when the indictment against him was quashed and he was released. He returned to Italy and lived there until his death on November 1, 1972.

Robert Frost, who along with other American writers sought to obtain Pound's release, read a statement to the court which said, among other things:

> [Pound] went very wrongheaded in his egotism, but he insists it was from patriotism—love of America. He has never admitted that he went over to the enemy any more than the writers at home who have despaired of the Republic. I hate such nonsense and can only

medieval church's teachings on economics, particularly on its condemnation of usury and its concern for establishing and maintaining the just price for every commodity.

[4] In 1949 an award jury consisting of the Fellows in American Letters of the Library of Congress voted the first annual Bollingen Prize in Poetry to Ezra Pound for his *Pisan Cantos*, which had been published in 1948. This prize had been set up by the Bollingen Foundation in 1948 to honor the highest achievement in American poetry for each year. As might have been expected, the choice of Pound, under the special circumstances, created an uproar. The Fellows were praised by some for their courage in daring to follow their literary judgment and accused by others of being soft on treason or of condoning anti-Semitism. Congress forthwith dissociated itself entirely from future awards of literary prizes. (The Bollingen Prize henceforth was awarded by a committee chosen by the Yale University Library.)

In spite of the resort to personalities and the use of the occasion to settle some scores in literary politics, some sensible voices were heard who attempted to get to the real issues. Some of these may be stated as follows: Can a poet be mad and yet write some "sane" poetry? Can he be misguided or even wickedly wrong-headed and yet write worthy poetry? What is the relation of a poem's "content" (intellectual, political, moral) to its "form"? Can one separate content from form?

The statement that form (considered as mere decoration) is all important obviously reduces poetry to triviality. But to say that poetic worth is determined by raw content in effect reduces poetry to mere morality or politics. Obviously, a theory of literature that takes literature seriously must find some way to avoid either of these extremes. Such a conception of literature—Pound's Bollingen award quite aside—is important for the reader of this book and we trust is implicit in our various discussions of particular works. As for the Pound award as such, the reader may want to consult some of the articles contained in *The Case of Ezra Pound* (1948), by Charles Norman, *The Case Against the Saturday Review of Literature* (1949), issued by the Fellows of the Library of Congress in American Literature, *A Casebook on Ezra Pound* (1959), by William Van O'Connor and Edward Stone, and *This Difficult Individual, Ezra Pound* (1961), by Eustace Mullins.

listen to it as an evidence of mental disorder. But mental disorder is what we are considering. I rest the case on Dr. Overholser's pronouncement that Ezra Pound is not too dangerous to go free in his wife's care, and too insane ever to be tried—a very nice discrimination.

Frost's estimate of the situation seems a wise one, but in any case, we should make a careful distinction between Pound's basic principles and his application of those principles. Pound's view of mankind is an exalted one, and his notion of the just society far from ignoble. But his way of arguing from his principles to specific cases is open to doubt and worse than doubt. Pound's failure in practical logic may indeed smack of psychic aberration rather than a primary moral viciousness—though morally vicious attitudes may result from a failure in logic.[5]

We have grossly oversimplified *Hugh Selwyn Mauberley* by talking about it thus far as if it were only the indictment of an age and as if that indictment itself had been put into explicit terms. Some of the passages in the poem do have bitterly harsh things to say about the civilization, but even these passages are placed in an elaborate context; they obviously are to be "spoken" in a particular tone of voice as coming from a particular kind of observer; and they are anchored to quite concrete particulars. For example, with reference to the young men who went out to die in the First World War, the author does not regard all of them as deceived by old men's lies: as he puts it, "some [went] for adventure,/some from fear of weakness,/some

from fear of censure,/some for love of slaughter, in imagination. . . ."

Some of them did indeed die for their country: "Died some, pro patria," though the poet hastily adds "non 'dulce' non 'et decor'. . . ." (It was Horace, the Latin poet, who wrote that it is sweet and fitting—"dulce et decor"—to die for one's country.) Was it ever sweet to do so? Perhaps it was, if one's country was a true community, bound together by genuine ties. But the modern poet is insisting here that it is not sweet or fitting to die to keep up an interest rate or to assure some manufacturer a profit.[6]

Hugh Selwyn Mauberley is, in fact, such an intricate tissue of echoes from Pound's reading and reminiscences of his life in London that only the unusually well-read reader (unless he has elaborate notes) can hope to encompass the poem. But such notes may wait until we come to a reading of this poem.

In this introduction one ought to say something about the more ambitious work, the *Cantos*, with which Pound closed his literary career. *Hugh Selwyn Mauberley* in many respects prefigures the *Cantos*. The first three cantos were published in *Poetry* (August, 1917). In 1918 Pound told William Butler Yeats that he meant to write one hundred cantos and that "when the hundredth canto is finished, [the series will] display a structure like that of a Bach fugue. There will be no plot, no chronicle of events, no logic of discourse, but two themes, the Descent into Hades from Homer, a Metamorphosis from Ovid, and mixed with these, medieval or modern historical characters" (*A Vision*, 1937, p. 4). At the time of his death, Pound had completed 117 cantos, but for most readers the unity of this poem remains problematic.

Some literary authorities claim to discern in the *Cantos* an intricate and rather exact structure.[7] Others argue that the poem is nothing

[5] One is tempted to say also that Pound may show himself most "American" just here. A genuine idealist, possessing an overweening confidence in his own intelligence and in his own purity of intentions, may, if he is touched by American millennialism, plump for doctrinaire solutions to complicated and all-but-insoluble problems. When people do not agree with his solutions, he may then assume that conspiracies exist to suppress the truth. This is not to say that the typical American idealist is paranoid, but Pound, special case though he may be, is not the first, nor will he prove to be the last American, to believe that only wicked people in high places with their own ends to serve could fail to accept what *he knows* to be obviously reasonable and clearly true.

[6] Pound writes that "Wars are made to create debts" ("America and the Second World War," *Impact*, 1960, p. 193). Pound's attitude toward the First World War is close to that of George Bernard Shaw and the so-called Revisionist historians.

[7] See, for example, Hugh Kenner, *The Poetry of Ezra Pound* (1964).

more than a glorious ragbag of snips and scraps of Pound's experiences,[8] his reading, his retelling of various legends and historical events, jesting comments on his friends, fierce denunciations of those persons whom he regards as public enemies, the events of the day as recorded in the press, some of them now so thoroughly dated and apparently insignificant that it takes considerable research to make a proper identification of them.

One of the cantos (LXXV) consists largely of a musical score. There are scatalogical cantos describing Pound's hell inhabited principally by munitions makers, owners of newspapers, and English bishops. There are others that glow with an unearthly radiance as Pound describes a seascape or the descent of one of the Greek gods, or a chorus of nymphs. There are still others which are full of what can only be called good talk, including literary gossip, some of it of a high order; some of it trivial.

The authors of this book do not at this point intend to try to resolve the question of whether or not the *Cantos* possess a unity. We want to avoid any appearance of a snap judgment; yet to present the material necessary to a reasoned judgment would require space far greater than this book affords. But it may be proper to point out here some of the difficulties in making sense of the *Cantos*—at least on the level of surface meaning. In his book *Reading the Cantos* (1966), Noel Stock tells us that "[Pound's] subject-matter is mostly simple and straightforward and could be communicated without undue strain if the poet saw his task in this light. But two things intervene: a personal quirk and a theory about poetry."

Of the quirk, Stock has this to say:

[Pound] takes it for granted that the rest of the world somehow shares his own knowledge of his own life and experiences. It does not occur to him that his own views of his own encounters, especially mere passing incidents in far-off times and places, are not available to

the world unless he re-creates them. We cannot see what he saw in a certain unrecorded situation in Spain in 1906, unless he tells us about it. We cannot see what he saw in the eyes of a figure from a fresco in Siena unless he gives us some idea—holds out some very definite, universal and intelligible thing independent of the fresco, yet related to it, through which we may grasp the significance of what he is trying to communicate.

When Pound gives only a mere fragment of some incident which he has never, or barely, referred to in some other place, I do not think that he is simply being cantankerous. Often for him the fragment is not a fragment any more than a key phrase known among youths who have been at college together, or a signal between husband and wife, is fragmentary. The fragment tells a story— for those who know. It is Pound's peculiarity to think that because he knows something *therefore* we know it too. . . . We encounter [this peculiar notion of Pound's] . . . in the first canto. After two pages of fairly straightforward narrative, during which Odysseus descends into the underworld and Tiresias delivers his soothsay, we are suddenly confronted with "Lie quiet Divus. I mean, that is Andreas Divus, In officina Wecheli, 1538, out of Homer." We may suppose that most people guess immediately who this Divus is (the Latin translator through whom Pound has rendered Homer into "Anglo-Saxon") because they have already heard about him from some commentator or read about him in the second part of Pound's "Early Translators of Homer" first published in the *Egoist* of September, 1918, and available later in *Make It New* (1934) and the *Literary Essays* (1954):

In the year of grace 1906, 1908, or 1910 I picked up from the Paris quais a Latin version of the *Odyssey* by Andreas Divus Justinopolitanus (Parisiis, In officina Christiani Wecheli, MDXXXVIII), the volume containing also the *Batrachomyomachia*, by Aldus Manutius, and the *Hymni Deorum* rendered by Georgius Dartona Cretensis. I lost a Latin *Iliads* for the economy of four

---

[8] See, for example, Allen Tate, *Essays of Four Decades* (1968), pp. 364–71.

francs, these coins being at that time scarcer with me than they should be with any man of my tastes and abilities.

But I cannot help wondering how long it would take us to work it out unaided. Even the additional phrase, "plucked from a Paris stall," which was included in an earlier cancelled version of canto I, does not bridge the essential gap between Pound and his reader; does not tell us who Divus is, or why he is there.

Stock cites other examples from the *Cantos* in which Pound's prose does not provide the necessary data for us and which, therefore, are inaccessible, not merely to the common reader but even to most scholars. With reference to a very obscure passage in Canto XCIII he writes (p. 102) as follows:

⌈ Now it is not enough to know a little about these matters if we are to understand what Pound is talking about. We have to have read the books, pamphlets and cuttings, and to have heard the stories. Everything about the ⌊ passage above, including the tone, depends upon our knowing the facts and having some definite appreciation of the atmosphere in which it was written. Until we actually look into the sources, handle the books, place ourselves in Pound's situation and see as nearly as possible through his eyes, we cannot even begin to know how the material is supposed to function. But function is too serious a word. It suggests the working out of a poetic design. Pound is not here composing poetry, he is keeping a kind of mental diary which includes snatches of poetry. And in this sense, and this sense alone, the matter and form are one.[9]

[9] In his *Life of Ezra Pound* (1970), Stock prints the following fragment of a conversation between Pound and Daniel Cory in Venice, in October, 1966. Cory brought up the subject of the *Cantos* and the conflicting opinions they had aroused. Pound intervened firmly, describing the work as "a botch." And when Cory persisted, "You mean it didn't come off?" the poet replied: "Of course it didn't. That's what I mean when I say I botched it." He then went on to describe a shop window full of various objects: "I picked out this and that thing that interested me,

One must concede the difficulties in reading the *Cantos*—at least with reference to the names of people, places, incidents, and literary allusions—are formidable. But most readers will at the least agree that the *Cantos* is filled with particular passages, some extending to two or three lines, others amounting to a hundred or more, of great power and beauty. Consider, for example, the following:

From Canto II (Tyro was a nymph possessed by the Greek sea-god, Poseidon):

And by the beach-run, Tyro,
    Twisted arms of the sea-god,
Lithe sinews of water, gripping her, cross-hold,
And the blue-gray glass of the wave tents them,
Glare azure of water, cold-welter, close cover.
Quiet sun-tawny sand-stretch
The gulls broad out their wings,
    nipping between the splay feathers. . . .

From Canto IV (the passage describes the dance of the nymphs [choros nympharum]):

Dawn, to our waking, drifts in the green cool light;
Dew-haze blurs, in the grass, pale ankles moving.
Beat, beat, whirr, thud, in the soft turf
    under the apple trees,
Choros nympharum, goat-foot, with the pale foot alternate;
Crescent of blue-shot waters, green-gold in the shallows,
A black cock crows in the sea-foam;

From Canto XVII (the wine-god Bacchus was mistaken for a mortal youth by Greek pirates and brought aboard their vessel to be sold as a

and then jumbled them into a bag. But that's not the way," he said, "to make"—and here he paused—"*a work of art.*"
The reader may feel that this quotation from Pound settles the matter, and perhaps it does. But, of course, it could be argued that Pound made this statement when he was old, ill, and perhaps in a fit of depression. If we wish to deny unity to the *Cantos*, we are on far stronger ground when we base our judgment on a reading of the cantos themselves. This is in fact where Stock bases his case and not on what the poet is reported to have said about his own work.

slave; this passage presents a seascape as seen from the ship after the god has asserted his powers):

> . . . cliff green-gray in the far,
> In the near, the gate-cliffs of amber,
> And the wave
> > green clear, and blue clear,
> And the cave salt-white, and glare-purple,
> > cool, porphyry smooth,
> > the rock sea-worn.
> No gull-cry, no sound of porpoise,
> Sand as of malachite, and no cold there,
> > the light not of the sun.

From Canto XVII (a brief vignette of gold shining in subdued light):

> "In the gloom the gold
> Gathers the light about it" . . . .

From Canto XLV (even when the passage makes "statements," the poet has found images to give them precision and power; *usura* is, of course, usury; note how all the images in this brief passage have to do with the wool trade—from sheep-raising to making the yarn):

> WITH USURA
> wool comes not to market
> sheep bringeth no gain with usura
> Usura is a murrain, usura
> blunteth the needle in the maid's hand
> and stoppeth the spinner's cunning.

One observes that Pound has not given up his "imagist" methods. The cantos are sprinkled with images that seize on our attention and hold it with their exactness and fineness of line, and frequently too are surrounded by a nimbus of symbolic meaning. In fact, in order to understand fully what Pound had in mind when he spoke of the possibilities of "Imagism"—as opposed to "Amygism"—one has to look at a few of the great passages in the *Cantos*.

BIOGRAPHICAL CHART

1885   Born, October 30, in Hailey, Idaho
1887   Family moves to Wyncote, Pennsylvania
1901–5   Attends University of Pennsylvania and Hamilton College
1906   First travels to Europe
1907   Teaches Romance languages and literature at Wabash College, Indiana; arrives in Italy
1908   *A Lume Spento*
1909   *Personae; Exultations;* lectures at Regent Street Polytechnic, London
1910   *The Spirit of Romance*
1912   *Sonnets and Ballads of Guido Cavalcanti; Ripostes*
1913–14   Secretary to William Butler Yeats
1914   Marries Dorothy Shakespear
1915   *Cathay;* begins work on the *Cantos*
1916   *Certain Noble Plays of Japan; Lustra*
1920   *Hugh Selwyn Mauberley*
1921   *Poems, 1918–1921* (includes *Cantos IV–VII*)

1925   Arrives in Rapallo; *A Draft of XVI Cantos*
1930   *A Draft of XXX Cantos*
1935   *Jefferson and/or Mussolini*
1939   Visits the United States
1940   Broadcasts for Radio Rome; *Cantos LII–LXXI*
1943   Indicted for treason by the United States
1945   May through November, imprisoned at Pisa; removed to Washington
1946   Committed to St. Elizabeth's Hospital as "of unsound mind"
1948   *The Pisan Cantos* in *The Cantos of Ezra Pound*
1949   Awarded the Bollingen Prize for Poetry
1955   *Section Rock-Drill: 85–95 de los Cantares*
1958   Treason charges dropped; released from St. Elizabeth's; arrives in Italy
1959   *Thrones: 96–109 de los cantares*
1968   *Drafts and Fragments of Cantos CX–CXVII*
1972   Dies, November 1, in Italy

FURTHER READINGS

A B C of Reading (1960)
Gaudier-Brzeska: A Memoir (rev. ed., 1960)
Donald Gallup, *Bibliography of Ezra Pound* (1963)

D. D. Paige, ed., *The Letters of Ezra Pound, 1907–1941* (1951)

Donald Davie, *Ezra Pound: Poet as Sculptor* (1964)

John Hamilton Edwards and William W. Vosse, *Annotated Index to the Cantos of Ezra Pound, Cantos I–LXXXIV* (1959)

John J. Espey, *Ezra Pound's Mauberley: A Study in Composition* (1955)

Patricia Hutchins, *Ezra Pound's Kensington: An Exploration, 1885–1913* (1965)

Hugh Kenner, *The Pound Era* (1972)

Lewis Leary, ed., *Motive and Method in the Cantos of Ezra Pound* (1954)

Daniel D. Pearlman, *The Barb of Time* (1971)

Sister M. Bernetta Quinn, *The Metamorphic Tradition in Modern Poetry* (1955)

Herbert Schneidau, *Ezra Pound: The Image and the Real* (1971)

The Seafarer (1911)

Pound is a great translator and some of his finest work is to be found in his "translations," never very literal and often best described as lively and vigorous paraphrases of the poems that excited him. The original text is preserved in the famous Exeter Book, a manuscript to be dated toward the end of the tenth century though the composition of the poem may be much earlier.

Pound has made use of the alliteration which is the normal binding device in Anglo-Saxon poetry. The influence of Anglo-Saxon verse, seen clearly in this poem, carries over into Pound's Canto I; that is, he has given something of an Anglo-Saxon cast to his translation of Book 12 of Homer's *Odyssey*. Pound has written of "The Seafarer" that it "alone in the works of our forebears . . . [is] fit to compare with Homer."

Pound's free translation of the poem was published in 1911 in *The New Age* and in 1915 in *Cathay* with the following title: "The Seafarer (from the early Anglo-Saxon Text)."

May I for my own self song's truth reckon,
Journey's jargon, how I in harsh days
Hardship endured oft.
Bitter breast-cares have I abided,
Known on my keel many a care's hold,
And dire sea-surge, and there I oft spent
Narrow nightwatch nigh the ship's head
While she tossed close to cliffs. Coldly
  afflicted,
My feet were by frost benumbed.
Chill its chains are; chafing sighs   10
Hew my heart round and hunger begot
Mere-weary mood. Lest man know not
That he on dry land loveliest liveth,

List how I, care-wretched, on ice-cold sea,
Weathered the winter, wretched outcast
Deprived of my kinsmen;
Hung with hard ice-flakes, where hail-scur
  flew,
There I heard naught save the harsh sea
And ice-cold wave, at whiles the swan cries,
Did for my games the gannet's clamour.   20
Sea-fowls' loudness was for me laughter,
The mews' singing all my mead-drink.
Storms, on the stone-cliffs beaten, fell on the
  stern
In icy feathers; full oft the eagle screamed
With spray on his pinion.
                    Not any protector
May make merry man faring needy.
This he little believes, who aye in winsome
  life
Abides 'mid burghers some heavy business,
Wealthy and wine-flushed, how I weary oft
Must bide above brine.   30
Neareth nightshade, snoweth from north,
Frost froze the land, hail fell on earth then,
Corn of the coldest. Nathless there knocketh
  now
The heart's thought that I on high streams
The salt-wavy tumult traverse alone.
Moaneth alway my mind's lust
That I fare forth, that I afar hence
Seek out a foreign fastness.
For this there's no mood-lofty man over
  earth's midst,
Not though he be given his good, but will
  have in his youth greed;   40
Nor his deed to the daring, nor his king to the
  faithful
But shall have his sorrow for sea-fare
Whatever his lord will.
He hath not heart for harping, nor in
  ring-having
Nor winsomeness to wife, nor world's delight
Nor any whit else save the wave's slash,

Yet longing comes upon him to fare forth
    on the water.
Bosque taketh blossom, cometh beauty of
    berries,
Fields to fairness, land fares brisker,
All this admonisheth man eager of mood,   50
The heart turns to travel so that he then
    thinks
On flood-ways to be far departing.
Cuckoo calleth with gloomy crying,
He singeth summerward, bodeth sorrow,
The bitter heart's blood. Burgher knows not—
He the prosperous man—what some perform
Where wandering them widest draweth.
So that but now my heart burst from my
    breastlock,
My mood 'mid the mere-flood,
Over the whale's acre, would wander wide.   60
On earth's shelter cometh oft to me,
Eager and ready, the crying lone-flyer,
Whets for the whale-path the heart
    irresistibly,
O'er tracks of ocean; seeing that anyhow
My lord deems to me this dead life
On loan and on land, I believe not
That any earth-weal eternal standeth
Save there be somewhat calamitous
That, ere a man's tide go, turn it to twain.
Disease or oldness or sword-hate   70
Beats out the breath from doom-gripped
    body.
And for this, every earl whatever, for those
    speaking after—

Laud of the living, boasteth some last word,
That he will work ere he pass onward,
Frame on the fair earth 'gainst foes his
    malice,
Daring ado, . . .
So that all men shall honour him after
And his laud beyond them remain 'mid
    the English,
Aye, for ever, a lasting life's-blast,
Delight 'mid the doughty.
                 Days little durable,   80
And all arrogance of earthen riches,
There come now no kings nor Caesars
Nor gold-giving lords like those gone.
Howe'er in mirth most magnified,
Whoe'er lived in life most lordliest,
Drear all this excellence, delights undurable!
Waneth the watch, but the world holdeth.
Tomb hideth trouble. The blade is layed low.
Earthly glory ageth and seareth.
No man at all going the earth's gait,   90
But age fares against him, his face paleth,
Grey-haired he groaneth, knows gone
    companions,
Lordly men, are to earth o'ergiven,
Nor may he then the flesh-cover, whose
    life ceaseth,
Nor eat the sweet nor feel the sorry,
Nor stir hand nor think in mid heart,
And though he strew the grave with gold,
His born brothers, their buried bodies
Be an unlikely treasure hoard.

Portrait d'Une Femme (1912)

This poem is another that comes out of Pound's
London experience. The Sargasso Sea is an area
in the Atlantic, relatively windless, where ships
in the old sailing days might remain becalmed
for weeks and where, according to the fable,
one might find derelict ships centuries old
though still afloat. The sargasso is a seaweed
that covers much of this sea.

Your mind and you are our Sargasso Sea,
London has swept about you this score years
And bright ships left you this or that in fee:
Ideas, old gossip, oddments of all things,
Strange spars of knowledge and dimmed wares
    of price.
Great minds have sought you—lacking some-
    one else.
You have been second always. Tragical?
No. You preferred it to the usual thing:
One dull man, dulling and uxorious,
One average mind—with one thought less each
    year.   10
Oh, you are patient, I have seen you sit
Hours, where something might have floated
    up.
And now you pay one. Yes, you richly pay.
You are a person of some interest, one comes
    to you

And takes strange gain away:
Trophies fished up; some curious suggestion;
Fact that leads nowhere; and a tale or two,
Pregnant with mandrakes, or with something
    else
That might prove useful and yet never proves,
That never fits a corner or shows use,   20
Or finds its hour upon the loom of days:
The tarnished, gaudy, wonderful old work;
Idols and ambergris and rare inlays,

These are your riches, your great store; and
    yet
For all this sea-hoard of deciduous things,
Strange woods half sodden, and new brighter
    stuff:
In the slow float of differing light and deep,
No! there is nothing! In the whole and all,
Nothing that's quite your own.

                Yet this is you.   30

The Garden (1913)

Pound lived in Kensington for a number of
years: there is an interesting account of his life
there in *Ezra Pound's Kensington* (1965), by
Patricia Hutchins.

Like a skein of loose silk blown against a wall
She walks by the railing of a path in Kensing-
    ton Gardens,
And she is dying piece-meal
    of a sort of emotional anaemia.

And round about there is a rabble
Of the filthy, sturdy, unkillable infants of the
    very poor.
They shall inherit the earth.

In her is the end of breeding.
Her boredom is exquisite and excessive.
She would like some one to speak to her,   10
And is almost afraid that I
    will commit that indiscretion.

The River Merchant's Wife: A Letter (1915)

This poem was first published in *Cathay* with
the title, "The River Merchant's Wife: A Letter. By Rihaku." Rihaku is the Japanese form
of the name of the Chinese poet Li Po (701–
62). Though he writes "By Rihaku," Pound has
made an adaptation rather than a strict translation.

    The poem is a fine example of the method
of Imagism, but one in which the images have
been developed into full symbols. In her lonesomeness, the young wife recalls to her absent
husband their first meeting as children, and
their marriage and the growth of her love for
him. Her desire to see him is expressed with
shy restraint, a restraint that is quite in character. (The poem very skillfully gives us a sense
of her character.)

    In keeping with her restraint, the young wife
uses intimation and suggestion rather than direct
statement: for example, her comment that "the
monkeys make sorrowful noise overhead" is ob-

viously a projection of her own sorrow. She does
not say that her husband was reluctant to leave
her, but she does remember that "you dragged
your feet when you went out." The gate by
which he went out has not had much traffic
since. There the moss has grown "too deep to
clear . . . away!" It looks to be an early autumn: the leaves are already falling and she notices "the paired butterflies are already yellow
with August." We are given specific concrete
details, but these images are not opaque: they
transmit delicately but firmly the young
woman's emotions.

While my hair was still cut straight across my
    forehead
Played I about the front gate, pulling flowers.
You came by on bamboo stilts, playing horse,
You walked about my seat, playing with blue
    plums.

And we went on living in the village of
  Chokan:
Two small people, without dislike or suspicion.

At fourteen I married My Lord you.
I never laughed, being bashful.
Lowering my head, I looked at the wall.
Called to, a thousand times, I never looked
  back.   10

At fifteen I stopped scowling,
I desired my dust to be mingled with yours
Forever and forever and forever.
Why should I climb the lookout?

At sixteen you departed,
You went into far Ku-to-yen, by the river of
  swirling eddies,

And you have been gone five months.
The monkeys make sorrowful noise overhead.

You dragged your feet when you went out.
By the gate now, the moss is grown, the dif-
  ferent mosses,   20
Too deep to clear them away!
The leaves fall early this autumn, in wind.
The paired butterflies are already yellow with
  August
Over the grass in the West garden;
They hurt me. I grow older.
If you are coming down through the narrows
  of the river Kiang,
Please let me know beforehand,
And I will come out to meet you
              As far as Cho-fu-Sa.

Hugh Selwyn Mauberley (1920)

We have already touched lightly on *Hugh Selwyn Mauberley* as a record of Pound's life in
London during the second decade of the twentieth century and of his estimate of what was
wrong with the literature of the period. But the
poem can be read in a number of other ways.
For example, it is a distillation of Pound's reading—a rich, intricate tissue of literary references.
It is possible, of course, to appreciate much of
the poem without recognizing all the echoes
from the literature of the nineteenth century
and earlier, literatures that are woven into the
fabric of Pound's poem. Yet it would be disin-
genuous to underestimate the difficulties that
the reader will encounter in trying to understand what is going on specifically in certain
passages.

  John J. Espey, in his *Ezra Pound's Mauberley:
A Study in Composition*,[1] devotes a great deal
of space to running down the sources of
Mauberley and identifying some of the works
that Pound is echoing. His book pays a great

deal of attention to Pound's debt to the French
nineteenth-century writers such as Théophile
Gautier and Remy de Gourmont, to English
writers of the nineties like Victor Plarr, Edward
Dowson, and Lionel Johnson; and to the expatriate American Henry James. Indeed, Pound
says that his *Mauberley* is "an attempt to condense the [Henry] James novel."

  The student who wants to see the virtues of
this poem and at the same time the weighty
burden that Pound sometimes places on his
reader should consult Espey's volume. Considerations of space allow in the notes that follow this
poem not much more than the identification
of names and places and the translation of some
foreign words.

"vocat aestus in umbram"

Nemesianus Ec. IV.

E. P. ODE POUR L'ELECTION
DE SON SEPULCHRE

For three years, out of key with his time,
He strove to resuscitate the dead art

---

[1] Espey, of course, builds upon earlier Pound scholarship, notably that of Kimon Friar (*Modern Poetry:
American and British* 1951, edited by Kimon Friar
and J. M. Brinnin), to whom Pound himself gave notes
on the poem, and that of Hugh Kenner (*The Poetry of
Ezra Pound*).

Of poetry; to maintain "the sublime"
In the old sense. Wrong from the start—

No, hardly, but seeing he had been born
In a half savage country, out of date;
Bent resolutely on wringing lilies from the
   acorn;
Capaneus; trout for factitious bait;

"Ἴδμεν γάρ τοι πάνθ', ὅσ'ἐνί Τροίῃ
Caught in the unstopped ear;
Giving the rocks small lee-way   10
The chopped seas held him, therefore, that
   year.

His true Penelope was Flaubert,
He fished by obstinate isles;
Observed the elegance of Circe's hair
Rather than the mottoes on sun-dials.

Unaffected by "the march of events,"
He passed from men's memory in *l'an
   trentiesme*
De son eage; the case presents
No adjunct to the Muses' diadem.   20

2

The age demanded an image   *cf. H. Adams*
Of its accelerated grimace,
Something for the modern stage,
Not, at any rate, an Attic grace;

Not, not certainly, the obscure reveries
Of the inward gaze;
Better mendacities
Than the classics in paraphrase!

The "age demanded" chiefly a mould in
   plaster,
Made with no loss of time,
A prose kinema, not, not assuredly, alabaster   30
Or the "sculpture" of rhyme.

3

The tea-rose tea-gown, etc.
Supplants the mousseline of Cos,
The pianola "replaces"
Sappho's barbitos.

Christ follows Dionysus,
Phallic and ambrosial
Made way for macerations;
Caliban casts out Ariel.   40

All things are a flowing,

Sage Heracleitus says;
But a tawdry cheapness
Shall outlast our days.

Even the Christian beauty
Defects—after Samothrace;
We see τὸ καλόν
Decreed in the market place.

Faun's flesh is not to us,   *loss of ritual*
Nor the saint's vision.
We have the press for wafer;   50
Franchise for circumcision.

All men, in law, are equals.   *demagogic democracy*
Free of Pisistratus,
We choose a knave or an eunuch
To rule over us.

O bright Apollo,
τίν' ἄνδρα, τίν' ἥρωα, τίνα θεόν,
What god, man, or hero
Shall I place a tin wreath upon!   60

4   *WW I*

These fought in any case,
and some believing,
            pro domo, in any case . . .

Some quick to arm,
some for adventure,
some from fear of weakness,
some from fear of censure,
some for love of slaughter, in imagination,
learning later . . .
some in fear, learning love of slaughter;   70

Died some, pro patria,
            non "dulce" non "et decor". . .
walked eye-deep in hell
believing in old men's lies, then unbelieving
came home, home to a lie,
home to many deceits,
home to old lies and new infamy;   *
usury age-old and age-thick
and liars in public places.

Daring as never before, wastage as never
   before.   80
Young blood and high blood,
fair cheeks, and fine bodies;

fortitude as never before

frankness as never before,
disillusions as never told in the old days,

* *Lusitania as munitions vessel*

hysterias, trench confessions,
laughter out of dead bellies.

5

There died a myriad,
And of the best, among them,
For an old bitch gone in the teeth,   90
For a botched civilization,

Charm, smiling at the good mouth,
Quick eyes gone under earth's lid,

For two gross of broken statues,
For a few thousand battered books.

YEUX GLAUQUES   *sea-green eyes*

Gladstone was still respected,
When John Ruskin produced
"Kings' Treasuries"; Swinburne
And Rossetti still abused.

Fœtid Buchanan lifted up his voice   100
When that faun's head of hers
Became a pastime for
Painters and adulterers.

The Burne-Jones cartons
Have preserved her eyes;
Still, at the Tate, they teach
Cophetua to rhapsodize;

Thin like brook-water,
With a vacant gaze.
The English Rubaiyat was still-born   110
In those days.

The thin, clear gaze, the same
Still darts out faunlike from the half-ruin'd
   face,
Questing and passive. . . .
"Ah, poor Jenny's case". . .

Bewildered that a world
Shows no surprise
At her last maquero's
Adulteries.

"SIENA MI FE'; DISFECEMI MAREMMA"

Among the pickled fœtuses and bottled bones,   120
Engaged in perfecting the catalogue,

I found the last scion of the
Senatorial families of Strasbourg, Monsieur
   Verog.

For two hours he talked of Galliffet;
Of Dowson; of the Rhymers' Club;
Told me how Johnson (Lionel) died
By falling from a high stool in a pub . . .

But showed no trace of alcohol
At the autopsy, privately performed—
Tissue preserved—the pure mind
Arose toward Newman as the whiskey   130
   warmed.

Dowson found harlots cheaper than hotels;
Headlam for uplift; Image impartially imbued
With raptures for Bacchus, Terpsichore and
   the Church.
So spoke the author of "The Dorian Mood,"

M. Verog, out of step with the decade,
Detached from his contemporaries,
Neglected by the young,
Because of these reveries.

BRENNBAUM

The skylike limpid eyes,   140
The circular infant's face,
The stiffness from spats to collar
‹ Never relaxing into grace;

The heavy memories of Horeb, Sinai and
   the forty years,
Showed only when the daylight fell
Level across the face
Of Brennbaum "The Impeccable."

MR. NIXON   *art as commodity*

In the cream gilded cabin of his steam yacht
Mr. Nixon advised me kindly, to advance
   with fewer
Dangers of delay. "Consider   150
         "Carefully the reviewer.

"I was as poor as you are;
"When I began I got, of course,
"Advance on royalties, fifty at first," said
   Mr. Nixon,
"Follow me, and take a column,
"Even if you have to work free.

"Butter reviewers. From fifty to three hun-
    dred
"I rose in eighteen months;
"The hardest nut I had to crack
"Was Dr. Dundas.   160

"I never mentioned a man but with the view
"Of selling my own works.
"The tip's a good one, as for literature
"It gives no man a sinecure.

"And no one knows, at sight, a masterpiece.
"And give up verse, my boy,
"There's nothing in it."

                  *   *   *   *

Likewise a friend of Bloughram's once ad-
    vised me:
Don't kick against the pricks,
Accept opinion. The "Nineties" tried your
    game   170
And died, there's nothing in it.

                  10
Beneath the sagging roof
The stylist has taken shelter,
Unpaid, uncelebrated,
At last from the world's welter

Nature receives him;
With a placid and uneducated mistress
He exercises his talents
And the soil meets his distress.

The haven from sophistications and
    contentions   180
Leaks through its thatch;
He offers succulent cooking;
The door has a creaking latch.

                  11
"Conservatrix of Milésien"
Habits of mind and feeling,
Possibly. But in Ealing
With the most bank-clerkly of Englishmen?

No, "Milesian" is an exaggeration.
No instinct has survived in her
Older than those her grandmother   190
Told her would fit her station.

                  12
"Daphne with her thighs in bark
"Stretches toward me her leafy hands,"—

Subjectively. In the stuffed-satin drawing-
    room
I await The Lady Valentine's commands,

Knowing my coat has never been
Of precisely the fashion
To stimulate, in her,
A durable passion;

Doubtful, somewhat, of the value   200
Of well-gowned approbation
Of literary effort,
But never of The Lady Valentine's vocation:

Poetry, her border of ideas,
The edge, uncertain, but a means of blending
With other strata
Where the lower and higher have ending;

A hook to catch the Lady Jane's attention,
A modulation toward the theatre,
Also, in the case of revolution,   210
A possible friend and comforter.

                  *   *   *   *

Conduct, on the other hand, the soul
"Which the highest cultures have nourished"
To Fleet St. where
Dr. Johnson flourished;

Beside this thoroughfare
The sale of half-hose has
Long since superseded the cultivation
Of Pierian roses.

ENVOI (1919)

Go, dumb-born book,   220
Tell her that sang me once that song of
    Lawes:
Hadst thou but song
As thou hast subjects known,
Then were there cause in thee that should
    condone
Even my faults that heavy upon me lie,
And build her glories their longevity.

Tell her that sheds
Such treasure in the air,
Recking naught else but that her graces give
Life to the moment,   230
I would bid them live
As roses might, in magic amber laid,
Red overwrought with orange and all made

One substance and one colour
Braving time.

Tell her that goes
With song upon her lips
But sings not out the song, nor knows
The maker of it, some other mouth,
May be as fair as hers,   240
Might, in new ages, gain her worshippers,
When our two dusts with Waller's shall be
*   laid,*
Siftings on siftings in oblivion,
Till change hath broken down
All things save Beauty alone.

MAUBERLEY (1920)

"Vacuos exercet aera morsus."

Turned from the "eau-forte
Par Jacquemart"
To the strait head
Of Messalina:

"His true Penelope   250
Was Flaubert,"
And his tool
The engraver's.

Firmness,
Not the full smile,
His art, but an art
In profile;

Colourless
Pier Francesca,
Pisanello lacking the skill   260
To forge Achaia.

2

"Qu'est ce qu'ils savent de l'amour, et qu'est ce
qu'ils peuvent comprendre?
S'ils ne comprennent pas la poésie, s'ils ne sen-
tent pas la musique, qu'est ce qu'ils peuvent com-
prendre de cette passion en comparaison avec
laquelle la rose est grossière et le parfum des
violettes un tonnerre?" CAID ALI

For three years, diabolus in the scale,
He drank ambrosia
All passes, ANANGKE prevails,
Came end, at last, to that Arcadia.

He had moved amid her phantasmagoria,

Amid her galaxies,
NUKTOS AGALMA

* * * *

Drifted . . . drifted precipitate,
Asking time to be rid of . . .   270
Of his bewilderment; to designate
His new found orchid. . . .

To be certain . . . certain . . .
(Amid ærial flowers) . . . time for
    arrangements—
Drifted on
To the final estrangement;

Unable in the supervening blankness
To sift TO AGATHON from the chaff
Until he found his sieve . . .
Ultimately, his seismograph: 280

—Given that is his "fundamental passion,"
This urge to convey the relation
Of eye-lid and cheek-bone
By verbal manifestations;

To present the series
Of curious heads in medallion—

He had passed, inconscient, full gaze,
The wide-banded irides
And botticellian sprays implied
In their diastasis;   290

Which anæsthesis, noted a year late,
And weighed, revealed his great affect,
(Orchid), mandate
Of Eros, a retrospect.

* * * *

Mouths biting empty air,
The still stone dogs,
Caught in metamorphosis, were
Left him as epilogues.

"THE AGE DEMANDED"

Vide Poem II, Page 119

For this agility chance found
Him of all men, unfit   300
As the red-beaked steeds of
The Cytheræan for a chain bit.

The glow of porcelain

Brought no reforming sense
To his perception
Of the social inconsequence.

Thus, if her colour
Came against his gaze,
Tempered as if
It were through a perfect glaze   310

He made no immediate application
Of this to relation of the state
To the individual, the month was more
    temperate
Because this beauty had been.

    The coral isle, the lion-coloured sand
    Burst in upon the porcelain revery:
    Impetuous troubling
    Of his imagery.

Mildness, amid the neo-Nietzschean clatter,
His sense of graduations,   320
Quite out of place amid
Resistance to current exacerbations,

Invitation, mere invitation to perceptivity
Gradually led him to the isolation
Which these presents place
Under a more tolerant, perhaps, examination.

By constant elimination
The manifest universe
Yielded an armour
Against utter consternation,   330

A Minoan undulation,
Seen, we admit, amid ambrosial circumstances
Strengthened him against
The discouraging doctrine of chances,

And his desire for survival,
Faint in the most strenuous moods,
Became an Olympian *apathein*
In the presence of selected perceptions.

A pale gold, in the aforesaid pattern,
The unexpected palms   340
Destroying, certainly, the artist's urge,
Left him delighted with imaginary
Audition of the phantasmal sea-surge,
Incapable of the least utterance or com-
    position,
Emendation, conservation of the "better
    tradition,"
Refinement of medium, elimination of
    superfluities,
August attraction or concentration.

Nothing, in brief, but maudlin confession,
Irresponse to human aggression,
Amid the precipitation, down-float   350
Of insubstantial manna,
Lifting the faint susurrus
Of his subjective hosannah.

Ultimate affronts to
Human redundancies;

Non-esteem of self-styled "his betters"
Leading, as he well knew,
To his final
Exclusion from the world of letters.

4

Scattered Moluccas   360
Not knowing, day to day,
The first day's end, in the next noon;
The placid water
Unbroken by the Simoon;

Thick foliage
Placid beneath warm suns,
Tawn fore-shores
Washed in the cobalt of oblivions;

Or through dawn-mist
The grey and rose   370
Of the juridical
Flamingoes;

A consciousness disjunct,
Being but this overblotted
Series
Of intermittences;

Coracle of Pacific voyages,
The unforecasted beach;
Then on an oar
Read this: 380

"I was
"And I no more exist;
"Here drifted
"An hedonist."

MEDALLION

Luini in porcelain!
The grand piano
Utters a profane
Protest with her clear soprano.

The sleek head emerges
From the gold-yellow frock   390

As Anadyomene in the opening
Pages of Reinach.

Honey-red, closing the face-oval,
A basket-work of braids which seem as if
   they were
Spun in King Minos' hall
From metal, or intractable amber;

The face-oval beneath the glaze,
Bright in its suave bounding-line, as,
Beneath half-watt rays,
The eyes turn topaz.   400

NOTES

Epigraph: "vocat aestus in umbram," quoted from a perfectly conventional pastoral poem, may be translated: "The heat calls [us] into the shade." There seems to be no obvious reason for Pound's choosing it as an epigraph for this poem. Perhaps the clue is in the fact that Nemesianus, though a poet who wrote in Latin, did not come from Rome but from the provincial city of Carthage. Early in the poem Pound refers to himself as a provincial ("born/In a half savage country"). Now he is preparing to leave London, the literary capital of the world of English letters, where he has failed to make his mark ("the case presents/No adjunct to the Muses' diadem"). High time to retire into obscurity.

E. P. Ode, etc.: that is, "Ezra Pound's Ode on the Choice of His Tomb." Pound is not to be confused with Mauberley, the character whose name furnishes the title of the poem as a whole. Mauberley may be best viewed as the man that an artist like Pound might conceivably have become, for like Pound, Mauberley refused as an artist to comply with the demands of the age. But unlike Pound, Mauberley let himself be shouldered aside by the Philistines and dismissed as a mere esthete.

In this first section of the poem Pound writes about himself as he feels he must have appeared to the London literary world: wrong-headed, obstinate, and a failure—"wrong from the start. . . ."

Line 7: Pound is ironically regarded here as a kind of poetic Luther Burbank, the plant expert, but a Burbank silly enough to believe that he could breed lilies from oak trees.

Line 8: Capaneus figures in the Greek story of the Seven against Thebes. He was so impious that he declared that he would take Thebes whether Zeus, king of the gods, liked it or not. Zeus killed him with a thunderbolt. Dante puts him in the seventh circle of Hell as one of those "violent against God" (*Inferno*, Canto 16, line 63).

Line 9: this line, taken from the *Odyssey* (Bk. 12, line 189), is to be translated "for we know all the things that [are] in Troy. . . ." It is the song of the Sirens who tried to lure Odysseus (or Ulysses) into their power. In this stanza and the next, Pound is compared to Odysseus trying to get back from Troy to his home in Ithaca and his faithful wife, Penelope. One of the adventures of Odysseus was with the goddess Circe. But the goal toward which Pound the poet strives (comparable to Odysseus' Penelope) is Gustave Flaubert, the great French novelist who insisted on achieving perfection in his art and also insisted on exposing the shams of the age in which he lived.

Line 16: these usually remind the viewer of the swift passage of time and advise him to make prudent use of it.

Lines 18–19: in the first line of his *Grand Testament* François Villon, the great medieval poet, tells us that in the "thirtieth year of [his] age [he] had drunk all [his] shames."

Line 34: the Latin poet Propertius refers to the silks of the island of Cos. *Mousseline*, the French word for *muslin*, is a very finely woven cloth.

Line 36: Sappho of Lesbos was the celebrated Greek woman poet who was born about the middle of the seventh century B.C. Her barbitos was a kind of lyre or lute.

Line 46: Samothrace is a Greek island, best known to modern readers for the famous Winged Victory of Samothrace (now in the Louvre), erected by the Rhodians to commemorate a naval victory c. 190 B.C. But this battle had little effect on Greek cultural history and there seems to be no connection between it and the "defection" of Christian beauty. Samothrace was the home of the great mystery cult of the Greeks, but again there seems no evident connection with the quality of Christian beauty.

Line 47: Greek for "the beautiful."

Line 51: the wafer is the consecrated bread offered in the Eucharist. Nowadays the public press serves as our substitute for it. The modern world wants neither pagan beauty nor Christian holiness.

Line 54: that is, free of dictatorship: Pisistratus, who three times made himself master of Athens, is referred to here as a kind of archetype of the tyrant.

Line 58: somewhat misquoted from Pindar's "Second Olympian Ode": "What man, what hero, what god [shall we praise]?" Pound's use of "tin" two lines later is a scornful play on the Greek word Τίν meaning "what."

Line 63: the Latin signifying "for home."

Lines 71–72: Horace wrote (*Ode: 12, 2, 13*): "*Dulce et decorum est pro patria mori*" (It is sweet and fitting to die for one's native land).

Yeux Glauques: sea-green eyes. Espey has shown that the phrase is probably derived from Théophile Gautier. It is applied here to Elizabeth Eleanor Siddal, whose features appear in a number of pre-Raphaelite paintings and who became Gabriel Dante Rossetti's wife.

Line 100: Robert Williams Buchanan published in 1871 an article in the *Contemporary Review* in which he attacked what he called "the fleshly school of poetry." Buchanan singled out for special malediction a poem of Rossetti's about a prostitute named Jenny.

Lines 104–6: Sir Edmund Burne-Jones did drawings of Elizabeth Siddal (that is, his "cartons have preserved her eyes") and used her also as his model for the beggar maid in his painting "Cophetua and the Beggar Maid," which hangs in the Tate Gallery in London.

Line 110: Edward Fitzgerald's translation of *The Rubaiyat of Omar Khayyam* was almost unnoticed on its publication in 1859. Such a failure constituted in Pound's eyes another symptom of the degradation of taste in the mid-Victorian period.

Line 115: Rossetti had chosen as an epigraph for his poem "Jenny" a passage from *The Merry Wives of Windsor* (4.1.64): "Vengeance of Jenny's case! Fie on her! Never name her, child. . . ." The passage in the play goes on to read "if she be a whore!" Pound, in his turn, has altered the epigraph to "Ah, poor Jenny's case," as if to suggest that the face that looks out at the viewer from the Burne-Jones cartons (and from "Cophetua and the Beggar Maid") is that of a girl named Jenny who was somewhat like the prostitute of Rossetti's poem. She has a "faun's head" and eyes, "thin like brook-water." (It is to be noted that there is no biographical warrant for linking Elizabeth Siddal with the girl who may have suggested to Rossetti the story of "Jenny.")

Line 118: a maquero is a pimp.

Siena mi fe, etc.: "Siena made me, Maremma undid me," from Dante's *Purgatorio* (Canto 5, line 135). In this half-riddling way, one of the female characters that Dante meets in purgatory laconically gives the main facts of her life: the place of her birth and the place of her death. (Eliot echoes this passage in *The Waste Land*: see lines 293–94.) The student may be forgiven for thinking this a rather oblique way of indicating the fact that this section of the poem will have to do with a life, namely, that of M. Verog.

Lines 123–26: in real life Victor Gustave Plarr. Plarr came of an Alsatian family that had removed to Britain after the Franco-Prussian war. It is natural, therefore, that he should have talked to Pound—this section of the poem is plainly autobiographical—of Galliffet, a French general who led a cavalry charge at the battle of Sedan, where the French were defeated and lost the 1870 war to the Prussians. And since Plarr was also a literary man and a poet, the author of a book of verse entitled *In the Dorian Mode*, he might also have been expected to talk of poets like Ernest Dowson (1867–1900) and Lionel Johnson (1867–1902), both of them alcoholics and both converts to Roman Catholicism. Pound's friend William Butler Yeats regarded Dowson and Johnson as men of great sensitivity and talent, shipwrecked by the crassness of the age. Presumably Pound shared this opinion. Pound "found" Plarr among the "pickled foetuses and bottled bones" because Plarr was at this time librarian to the Royal College of Surgeons.

Line 125: the Rhymers' Club, founded in 1891, included among others Dowson and Johnson, Yeats, Arthur Symons, and Headlam (see below).

Line 132: the Rev. Stewart Headlam was an Anglican priest who had a wide acquaintance in the literary and artistic world. Selwyn Image was an editor and artist of the period. As Pound indicates in line 133, he could find delight quite impartially in drink, dance, and religion.

Line 147: if M. Verog was "out of step with the decade," obviously Brennbaum was not. Espey has located (in Pound's essay on Remy de Gourmont) the phrase "the impeccable Beerbohm" and in view of line 147, one would assume that Max Beerbohm was the real life figure standing behind Brennbaum. But Espey points out that Pound was mistaken if he thought that Beerbohm possessed any Jewish blood.

Line 149: Pound wrote to Kimon Friar that a real person is alluded to under the name of Mr. Nixon. Hugh Kenner suggests that the person might well be Arnold Bennett, the popular British novelist of the first part of the twentieth century. The suggestion is thoroughly plausible.

Line 173: Kenner also suggests that the novelist may have been Ford Madox Ford, whom Pound venerated as a stylist and superb craftsman whom the age did not appreciate. Ford mentions a visit that Pound paid him in Sussex: "Mr. Pound appeared, aloft on the seat of my immensely high dogcart, like a bewildered Stuart pretender visiting a repellent portion of his realms. For Mr. Pound hated the country, though I will put it on record that he can carve a suckling pig as few others can."

Line 184: Pound is remembering here a passage from Remy de Gourmont: "Désirs grenades pleins de rubis," etc. A rather free translation might read: "Desires, pomegranates filled with imprisoned rubies, from which one puncture of a tooth makes bedazzlement spill forth— one bite of a woman's tooth. Some women, encountered in just the right place, know how to bite. They are not to be despised, these preservers of Milesian [that is, voluptuous] traditions." But this modern woman living in lower-middle-class Ealing (a district of greater London), whose husband is "the most bank-clerkly of Englishmen," can hardly be expected to have preserved very much of any voluptuous habits or instincts. If the reader feels that Pound's own modification of the Gourmont phrase ("Conservatrix of Milésien") is here made to bear a very heavy burden of meaning and that there will be few readers capable of recognizing such an unfamiliar passage, he has our full sympathy. Pound does demand a great deal of his reader—not only in the matter of picking up hints and suggestions, but of knowing intimately the literature of the late nineteenth century— French, British, and American.

Lines 192–93: Pound's rather free translation of two lines from Gautier's *Le Château du Souvenir*. The reference is to the Greek myth which tells how the nymph Daphne was transformed into a laurel tree when Apollo pursued and caught her. If Daphne felt such awe and even terror at the approach of the god of poetry, the fashionable London hostess, Lady Valentine, obviously feels no awe at all. For her, the cultivation of the arts is an amusement, a kind of literary slumming, a way of meeting those dubious bohemians of the artistic world.

Line 214: the street in London associated with journalism and the publishing industry. In the eighteenth century Dr. Samuel Johnson, the acknowledged Great Cham of literature, lived in Fleet Street.

Line 219: Pieria in Thessaly was associated with the Muses.

Line 221: Henry Lawes (1596–1662) was a celebrated composer and musician. He set to music "Go, Lovely Rose," by Edmund Waller (1606–1687), the poem that Pound echoes in the "Envoi":

> Go, lovely Rose!
> Tell her that wastes her time and me
> That now she knows,
> When I resemble her to thee,
> How sweet and fair she seems to be.

Tell her that's young,
And shuns to have her graces spied,
That hadst thou sprung
In deserts, where no men abide,
Thou must have uncommended died.

Small is the worth
Of beauty from the light retired;
Bid her come forth,
Suffer herself to be desired,
And not blush so to be admired.

Then die! that she
The common fate of all things rare
May read in thee;
How small a part of time they share
That are so wondrous sweet and fair!

The "Envoi" is Pound's proud and triumphant salute to poetry as the preserver of beauty and a demonstration of his own superb command of the art. Charles Norman records that when he asked Pound for the name of the lady who "sang [you] once that song of Lawes," Pound replied: "Your question is the kind of damn fool enquiry into what is nobody's damn business."

Mauberley (1920): the poem from this point onward has to do specifically with Hugh Selwyn Mauberley, Pound's antithetical self, the poet that Pound might have been had he been content to dwindle into a half-poet, a pure aesthete, unwilling to accept the crass demands of the ages, and yet not willing to penetrate its shams or to make any connection between his concern to create sound art and a concern for the "relation of the state/To the individual. . . ."

Epigraph: "*Vacuos exercet*," etc.: borrowed from Ovid's *Metamorphoses* (Bk. 7, line 786). The passage in Ovid, by the way, reads "vacuos exercet *in* aera morsus" (italics ours), or (in the earlier manuscripts) "Vanos exercet in aera motus"; that is, "[the dog] makes vain leaps into the air."

Line 247: that is, an etching executed by Jacquemart. "Eau-forte" means "acid," and the reference is to an engraving etched with acid as distinguished from a "dry-point" engraving. Espey has shown that Pound probably borrowed the phrase from the title page of the 1884 edition of Gautier's *Emaux et Camées*. The title page records that this is the "Édition Définitive /Avec une eau-forte par J. Jacquemart."

Line 249: the notoriously dissolute wife of the Emperor Claudius.

Lines 250–51: compare the fourth stanza of "E. P. Ode," etc. Mauberley, like Pound, may have claimed to revere Flaubert, but Mauberley's art, as this section of the poem takes pains to point out, was "but an art/In profile."

Line 259: Kimon Friar has pointed out that Salomon Reinach, the French archeologist, in his *Apollo: A General History of the Plastic Arts*—Reinach is mentioned in "Medallion" below—refers to the work of Piero della Francesca (1416?–1492) as being "cold and impersonal."

Line 260: Vittore Pisaro (1397–1455), called Pisanello, had his workshop in Verona and was famous for the medals that he struck. Pound mentions him in the *Cantos*. Mauberley was a Pisanello who lacked the skills "to forge Achaia." Achaia is the ancient name for Greece and Pound must mean to say that Mauberley was unable to achieve the authentic Greek character as Pisanello, though also living in a later time, was able to do.

"Qu'est ce qu'ils," etc.: "What do they know about love and what can they understand? If they don't understand poetry, if they have no feeling for music, what can they understand of that passion in comparison with which the rose is a grossness, the perfume of violets, a thunder clap?" Kimon Friar reports that Pound told him that Caid Ali is a pseudonym for himself.

Line 262: this refers to the augmented fourth, an interval difficult for the musician to manage. But it is characteristic of Mauberley that he should set himself just such difficult technical problems.

Line 264: Greek for "necessity."

Line 266: Hugh Kenner has pointed out that Pound is probably echoing here a remark made by one of the characters in Henry James's *The Ambassadors:* "Of course I moved among miracles. It was all a phantasmagoria. . . ."

Line 268: Greek for "glory of night." Espey locates the phrase in a verse fragment of the Greek pastoral poet Bion. There the phrase is applied to Hesperus, the evening star, that is, the planet Venus.

Line 278: *to agathon* is Greek for "the good."

Line 288: irides is the plural (the Greek form) of the word "iris" and refers primarily to the colored portion of the eye (though the word "iris" can also refer to a variety of flower). "Diastasis" is a Greek word meaning "distance," but the dictionaries do not record the meaning in which Pound uses it here, that is, the distance between the eyes—eyes set wide apart. By a very neat piece of literary detective work, Espey shows how Pound derived this meaning principally from Poliziano's *La Giostra*, which is the literary source of the painter Botticelli's picture, "The Birth of Venus."

Line 291: Pound uses what is usually a technical medical term here to mean a lack of feeling or sensibility: as noted earlier, Mauberley is "inconscient" and doesn't see what is right before his eyes.

Line 292: "affect" seems to be used in its now obsolete Elizabethan sense of "general disposition," "prevailing temperament."

Lines 295–96: the fit emblem of Mauberley is a dog turned to stone whose mouth is open to snap but who is biting only the empty air, that is, Mauberley can't get his teeth into anything.

Lines 301–2: the chariot of the Cytherean, Venus, goddess of love, was drawn by doves. One needs a chain bit to hold in a spirited horse but hardly for steeds as light and airy as these.

Line 331: perhaps "Minoan" suggested to Pound a rather pleasant, charming, slightly decadent, and highly mannered civilization, which, protected as was the Minoan civilization of Crete by its seapower, did not need to defend its cities with walls. Pound had undoubtedly seen the charming statuettes and mural fragments unearthed from Knossos by Sir Arthur Evans in the first years of the twentieth century.

Line 337: the Greek word meaning "not to feel." Olympian because Pound is thinking of the Greek gods on their remote Olympus, detached from mankind and untroubled by the sorrows and violence of the human world.

Line 360: the spice islands in the South Seas, between Celebes and New Guinea.

Lines 379–84: when Odysseus reached the land of the dead he met there the spirit of his shipmate, Elpenor, who begged Odysseus to set up his oar on the beach as a memorial to him and to inscribe on it: "A man of no fortune, and with a name to come."

Medallion: we are told in lines 285–86 that Mauberley's artistic ambition was "to present the series/Of curious heads in medallion. . . ." Here is one of his curious heads, that of a woman. Mauberley's work is not without merit: it is fastidious and carefully wrought. It possesses a certain charm, but it reveals the limitations and weaknesses of a mannered and artificial art.

Line 385: Bernadino Luini (1475?–1532?) was one of the pupils of Leonardo da Vinci. He painted in oils, but Mauberley's productions are more brittle still; as if an artist like Luini were working in porcelain.

Line 389: compare "To the strait head/Of Messalina. . . ." (lines 248–49).

Line 391: the Venus Anadyomene is Venus portrayed as rising from the sea.

Line 392: for Reinach, see l. 259.

Canto I (1925)

And then went down to the ship,
Set keel to breakers, forth on the godly sea, and
We set up mast and sail on that swart ship,
Bore sheep aboard her, and our bodies also
Heavy with weeping, and winds from stern-
    ward
Bore us out onward with bellying canvas,
Circe's this craft, the trim-coifed goddess.
Then sat we amidships, wind jamming the
    tiller,
Thus with stretched sail, we went over sea till
    day's end.
Sun to his slumber, shadows o'er all the ocean,   10

Came we then to the bounds of deepest water,
To the Kimmerian lands, and peopled cities
Covered with close-webbed mist, unpierced ever
With glitter of sun-rays
Nor with stars stretched, nor looking back from heaven
Swartest night stretched over wretched men there.
The ocean flowing backward, came we then to the place
Aforesaid by Circe.
Here did they rites, Perimedes and Eurylochus,
And drawing sword from my hip   20
I dug the ell-square pitkin;
Poured we libations unto each the dead,
First mead and then sweet wine, water mixed with white flour.
Then prayed I many a prayer to the sickly death's-heads;
As set in Ithaca, sterile bulls of the best
For sacrifice, heaping the pyre with goods,
A sheep to Tiresias only, black and a bell-sheep.
Dark blood flowed in the fosse,
Souls out of Erebus, cadaverous dead, of brides
Of youths and of the old who had borne much;   30
Souls stained with recent tears, girls tender,
Men many, mauled with bronze lance heads,
Battle spoil, bearing yet dreory arms,
These many crowded about me; with shouting,
Pallor upon me, cried to my men for more beasts;
Slaughtered the herds, sheep slain of bronze;
Poured ointment, cried to the gods,
To Pluto the strong, and praised Proserpine;
Unsheathed the narrow sword,
I sat to keep off the impetuous impotent dead, 40
Till I should hear Tiresias.
But first Elpenor came, our friend Elpenor,
Unburied, cast on the wide earth,
Limbs that we left in the house of Circe,
Unwept, unwrapped in sepulchre, since toils urged other.
Pitiful spirit. And I cried in hurried speech:
"Elpenor, how art thou come to this dark coast?
"Cam'st thou afoot, outstripping seamen?"
            And he in heavy speech:
"Ill fate and abundant wine. I slept in Circe's ingle.   50
"Going down the long ladder unguarded,

"I fell against the buttress,
"Shattered the nape-nerve, the soul sought Avernus.
"But thou, O King, I bid remember me, unwept, unburied,
"Heap up mine arms, be tomb by sea-bord, and inscribed:
"A *man of no fortune, and with a name to come.*
"And set my oar up, that I swung mid fellows."

And Anticlea came, whom I beat off, and then Tiresias Theban,
Holding his golden wand, knew me, and spoke first:
"A second time? why? man of ill star,   60
"Facing the sunless dead and this joyless region?
"Stand from the fosse, leave me my bloody bever
"For soothsay."
            And I stepped back,
And he strong with the blood, said then: "Odysseus
"Shalt return through spiteful Neptune, over dark seas,
"Lose all companions." And then Anticlea came.
Lie quiet Divus. I mean, that is Andreas Divus,
In officina Wecheli, 1538, out of Homer.
And he sailed, by Sirens and thence outward and away   70
And unto Circe.
            Venerandam,
In the Cretan's phrase, with the golden crown, Aphrodite,
Cypri munimenta sortita est, mirthful, oricalchi, with golden
Girdles and breast bands, thou with dark eyelids
Bearing the golden bough of Argicida. So that:

NOTES

Lines 1–7: Pound's rather free rendering of lines 1–78 of Book II of the *Odyssey*. Ulysses has persuaded the goddess Circe, on whose island he has been sojourning, to let him depart for home. Circe insists that, before making for home, he visit the land of the dead to consult the shade of the prophet Tiresias.

Line 7: by "Circe's this craft" Ulysses means to say that the ship sails under Circe's patronage and has been given a favoring wind through her magic arts.

Line 19: Perimedes and Eurylochus are two of Ulysses' companions.

Line 21: a pitkin is literally a little pit. (Ulysses is here following instructions given him by Circe.)

Line 33: Pound spells "dreory" as he does because he wants to emphasize the Anglo-Saxon word from which it derives, *dreorig,* which literally meant "bloody," and not merely "sad" or "mournful."

Lines 42–57: these lines tell the story of the death of Elpenor on Circe's island. Though they have left his body behind them, the shade of Elpenor, traveling as no living man can, is already waiting for them in the land of the dead.

Line 58: Anticlea was the mother of Ulysses. She had died after he left his home in Ithaca. Though he loves her, Ulysses keeps his main purpose in mind and therefore beats her away from the blood until Tiresias has drunk and has thus received enough "life" to be able to utter his prophecy to the living. Only then, with his mission fulfilled, does Ulysses permit his mother's shade to drink of the blood. (See line 67.)

Line 62: "bever" means "drink." It is the price of the soothsay, the telling of truth which Tiresias will give him.

Line 66: the seagod Neptune, whose son, the Cyclops, Ulysses had blinded, sought to prevent Ulysses' getting home.

Lines 69–70: the narrative from the *Odyssey,* though much condensed, resumes.

Lines 72–76: "Venerandam" (Latin) means "compelling adoration" (literally, "that which must be regarded with awe"). Pound took the word from a Latin translation of the second Homeric hymn to Aphrodite (Greek). The

first two lines read as follows:

Venerandam auream coronam habentem pulchram Venerem
Canam, quae totius Cypri munimenta sortita est

which may be translated "I shall sing of beautiful Venus, crowned with gold, compelling adoration, to whom has been awarded the citadels of all Cyprus. . . ."

Just as Pound has preferred to use the Latin translation of the *Odyssey,* so here again he has preferred to use a Latin translation (by Gorgius Dartona Cretensis) of the original Greek hymn. The word "oricalchi" means literally "of copper" and again is taken from Dartona's translation, where he refers to "a votive gift *of copper.*" Except for the phrase "with dark eyelids" all the rest of the descriptive details come from Dartona's translation of the second Homeric hymn.

Line 76: "Bearing the golden bough of Argicida" offers more special problems. "Argicida" is the Latin translation of the Greek "argeiphontes," slayer of Argus (which is an epithet that occurs frequently in the *first* Homeric hymn to Aphrodite but is there applied to Hermes, the messenger of the gods, not to Aphrodite herself). But just what the golden bough is and why it should belong to Hermes— the golden bough is usually associated with Diana's grave at Nemi—and why it should be borne in this instance by Aphrodite are not clear.

E. M. Glynn, writing in the *Analyst* (No. 8), conjectures that "So that" represents Pound's translation of a Latin "ut" found in the Latin of either Divus or Dartona. But if so, what does "So that" mean? And what does it look forward to? Such an abrupt breaking off of a canto, however, is not uncharacteristic of Pound's manner.

From Canto VII (1925)

The old men's voices, beneath the columns of
    false marble,

The modish and darkish walls,
Discreeter gilding, and the panelled wood

Suggested, for the leasehold is
Touched with an imprecision . . . about
   three squares;
The house too thick, the paintings
a shade too oiled.
And the great domed head, *con gli occhi
   onesti e tardi*
Moves before me, phantom with weighted
   motion,
Grave incessu, drinking the tone of things,   10
And the old voice lifts itself
         weaving an endless sentence.
We also made ghostly visits, and the stair
That knew us, found us again on the turn
   of it,
Knocking at empty rooms, seeking for buried
   beauty;
And the sun-tanned, gracious and well-formed
   fingers
Lift no latch of bent bronze, no Empire
   handle
Twists for the knocker's fall; no voice to
   answer.
A strange concierge, in place of the gouty-
   footed.
Sceptic against all this one seeks the living,   20
Stubborn against the fact. The wilted flowers
Brushed out a seven year since, of no effect.
Damn the partition! Paper, dark brown and
   stretched,
Flimsy and damned partition.
         Ione, dead the long year
My lintel, and Liu Ch'e's lintel.
Time blacked out with the rubber.

NOTES

The following notes are derived from "A Guide
to Ezra Pound's *Canto VII*," by Robert Schneideman, published in the *Analyst* (No. 4).

This part of Canto VII is a meditation on
the artist's problem of bringing the past back
to life, with special reference to particular artists who have done so, notably such a writer as
Henry James.

Line 1: "The old men's voices" probably
echoes the passage in the *Iliad* (Bk. 3, lines
151–52), where the old men on the walls of
Troy sit chirping like grasshoppers as Helen approaches them. Mr. Schneideman thinks that

throughout this canto the "old men" are the
death-in-life inhabitants of Pound's "waste
land" and that they are contrasted through
Canto VII with such living forces as Helen's
beauty, Henry James's art, and Pound's own
imagination. But Pound is here also echoing an
earlier poem of his own, "I Vecchi" ("the old
men"), which is Number 7 of a series entitled
"Moeurs Contemporaines," first published in
the *Little Review* in 1908. This poem begins:

> They will come no more;
> The old men with beautiful manners.

It ends:

> Old men with beautiful manners,
> Sitting in the Row of a morning;
> Walking on the Chelsea Embankment.

The Chelsea Embankment is along the Thames
in London. "I Vecchi," like Canto VII, contains a portrait of Henry James. In fact it is
with Pound's account of James that we are here
most concerned.

Lines 1–7: the house referred to here has been
identified as the Polytechnic Institute in London where Pound lectured in 1910. The building
was an old London mansion that had been converted into classrooms.

Lines 8–11: Pound's impression of Henry
James. The phrase "con gli occhi onesti e tardi"
(Italian for "with eyes stately and slow") is
taken from Dante's *Purgatorio* (Canto 6, line
63). There Dante describes the shade of Sor-
dello (c. 1180–1255), a Provençal poet. Browning wrote a poem about him and he appears
frequently in the *Cantos*.

Line 10: *Grave incessu* (Latin, "with stately
pace") comes from Virgil's *Aeneid*: Aeneas
knows, by her gait, that the woman who approaches him is actually a goddess. "We" refers
to Pound himself. Like James, he has made
"ghostly visits" and sought for "buried beauty"
in empty rooms. Mr. Schneideman suggests
that Pound may have had in mind the "ghostly
visits" made by the heroes in James's novel *The
Sense of the Past* and his story "The Jolly Corner," the text of which is printed in this book.
In each instance the hero wanders through the

house and meditates on its past, trying not only to understand the house but himself and his past.

Marianne Moore, the poet, has made the following comment on lines 19–21: ". . . Mr. Pound lived in Paris at one time. On returning after seven years, he is told by 'a strange concierge, in place of the gouty-footed,' that the friend he asks about is dead. For the altar of the friendship of one long dead

> Dry casques of departed locusts
> speaking a shell of speech . . .

are not a substitute" (*Poetry*, 1931, p. 37). The lines "Dry casques . . . shell of speech" occur later on in Canto VII.

Line 23: Schneideman writes: "Pound is speaking of the obliteration of the true picture by time and means, figuratively, that the artist is constantly struggling to break through a partition of imprecision which settles between him and the object he seeks to find and portray."

Line 25: Pound here quotes the title of one of his early poems, first printed in 1914. Ione was one of the Nereides of Greek mythology, but in Pound's poem she is evidently simply a mortal woman whose loveliness the poet tries to recapture in his poem.

Line 26: the poet associates himself with Liu Ch'e (156–87 B.C.), a Chinese emperor, philosopher, and poet. The modern poet and the long-dead Chinese poet have the same problem (line 27): to "black out" time with the eraser. If this smudge of time could be removed, the image would once more shine forth, fresh and new. It has been argued, however, that line 27 means that objects of the past—such as Liu Ch'e's lintel—are blacked out by the rubber of the intervening years. But it may be objected that in this interpretation the modern poet's lintel (not yet an object of the past) is equated with that of the ancient Chinese poet. A problem with either of these interpretations has to do with whether a "rubber" (eraser) *blacks out* anything.

An earlier poem by Pound entitled "Liu Ch'e" was first published in *Lustra* (1916). Like the poem on Ione, Liu Ch'e commemorates a beautiful woman now dead. The last lines read

And she the rejoicer of the heart is beneath [the
    leaves]:
A wet leaf that clings to the threshold.

The threshold is obviously the lintel that Pound and Liu Ch'e share.

From Canto LXXXI (1947)

Canto LXXXI is one of the Pisan Cantos, so named because they were written while Pound was a prisoner, awaiting trial for treason, in an American military camp near Pisa, Italy. The passage which follows is often interpreted as Pound's own profession of humility as he contemplates his past career from his position as a prisoner. It is true that the concluding lines, with their personal reference to the poet's relation with Blunt (line 36; see below) will sustain such an interpretation. Nevertheless, one must not miss the fact that Pound may not be addressing only himself when he says "Pull down thy vanity." He may be including along with himself man in general, man who has forgotten his place in the order of being, the worth

of which is not limited to himself. Lines 11–19 constitute a brilliant disquisition on the hierarchy of being. Paquin (line 18) is the famous Parisian couturier. Wilfred Seawen Blunt (1840–1922) was an English poet, diplomat, and traveler. Pound very properly saw in Blunt a representative of the best of the older English tradition. Blunt's integrity showed itself in his stand against imperialism, in his fearless defense of truth, and in his dedication to literature. As this passage indicates, Blunt had received Pound as a man worthy of his friendship.

The ant's a centaur in his dragon world.
Pull down thy vanity, it is not man

Made courage, or made order, or made grace,
    Pull down thy vanity, I say pull down.
Learn of the green world what can be thy
        place
In scaled invention or true artistry,
Pull down thy vanity,
            Paquin pull down!
The green casque has outdone your elegance.

"Master thyself, then others shall thee beare"   10
    Pull down thy vanity
Thou art a beaten dog beneath the hail,
A swollen magpie in a fitful sun,
Half black half white
Nor knowst'ou wing from tail
Pull down thy vanity
         How mean thy hates

Fostered in falsity,
          Pull down thy vanity,
Rathe to destroy, niggard in charity,   20
Pull down thy vanity,
          I say pull down.

But to have done instead of not doing
         this is not vanity
To have, with decency, knocked
That a Blunt should open
       To have gathered from the air a live
         tradition
or from a fine old eye the unconquered flame
This is not vanity.
     Here error is all in the not done,   30
all in the diffidence that faltered,

From Canto LXXXIII (1947)

This is another of the Pisan Cantos. In the passage that follows, Pound refers to a time between 1913 and 1916 in which he and William Butler Yeats spend a good deal of time together at Stone Cottage, Coleman's Hatch, in Sussex. At this time Pound was acting as Yeats's secretary. Pound wrote to one of his friends about trying, during this period, to get Yeats to read a little of Robert Burns's poetry aloud. Yeats was unable to read except according to his own singsong rhythm. Pound continues: "I had a half hour of unmitigated glee in hearing 'Saw ye bonnie Alexander' and 'The Birks o Averfeld' *keened*, wailed with infinite difficulty and many pauses and restarts to *The Wind Among the Reeds*."

There is fatigue deep as the grave.
The Kakemono grows in flat land out of mist
    sun rises lop-sided over the mountain
        so that I recalled the noise in the
         chimney
as it were the wind in the chimney
        but was in reality Uncle William

downstairs composing
that had made a great Peeeeacock
    in the proide ov his oiye
        had made a great peeeeeeecock in the . . .   10

made a great peacock
    in the proide of his oyyee

proide ov his oy-ee
as indeed he had, and perdurable

a great peacock aere perennius
    or as in the advice to the young man to
breed and get married (or not)
        as you choose to regard it

at Stone Cottage in Sussex by the waste moor
(or whatever) and the holly bush   20
    who would not eat ham for dinner
because peasants eat ham for dinner
    despite the excellent quality
and the pleasure of having it hot

well those days are gone forever
      and the traveling rug with the coon-
      skin tabs
and his hearing nearly all Wordsworth
    for the sake of his conscience but
preferring Ennemosor on Witches

NOTES

Line 2: a Kakemono is a Japanese picture done on silk or paper and put on rollers so that it can be rolled up when not in use. Presumably a Kakemono hung on the wall of the cottage.
    Line 8: the poem on which Yeats must have

been at work was "The Peacock." It was published in May, 1914. It reads:

> What's riches to him
> That has made a great peacock
> With the pride of his eye?
> The wind-beaten, stone-grey,
> And desolate Three Rock
> Would nourish his whim.
> Live he or die
> And mid wet rocks and heather,
> His ghost will be gay
> Adding feather to feather
> For the pride of his eye.

Pound's mode of spelling some of Yeats's lines reflects his attempt to imitate Yeats's Irish accent.

Line 15: "aere perennius" is from Horace's Ode XXX, Book 3. The Latin poet promises in his verse to erect something "more lasting than brass."

Lines 16–17: the reference here is to Shakespeare's Sonnet 55, where the poet also claims to be building in verse something perdurable:

> Not marble, nor the gilded monuments
> Of princes, shall outlive this powerful rhyme.
> . . .

Lines 20–29: Donald Davie, in his *Ezra Pound: Poet as Sculptor* (1964), comments as follows on Pound's picture of Yeats: "The whole man, Yeats, is carried before us; we delight, as the poet has delighted, in his alien mode of being. His foibles, recorded with affectionate and amused indulgence—his way of *keening* rather than reading poetry, his 'Gothick' interests ('preferring Ennemosor on Witches'), his preposterous snobbery ('because peasants eat ham for dinner')—do not in the least detract from, they only substantiate, the perception of his greatness."

Line 29: Joseph Ennemoser (1787–1854), author of *Geschichte des thierischen Magnetismus* (1844), translated as *The History of Magic* (1854), by William Howitt. Throughout his life Yeats was interested in magic and the occult.

T. S. ELIOT (1888–1965)

T. S. Eliot was born in St. Louis where the Eliot family had been settled for two generations. They were of New England stock, however, and in due course Eliot went back East, to the Milton School in Cambridge and on to Harvard University. There he studied philosophy, literature, and languages, including Sanskrit. After taking his B.A., Eliot attended the Sorbonne for a year and then returned to Harvard to begin work on a Ph.D. in philosophy; but in 1913, having won a traveling fellowship, he was once more abroad, in residence at Merton College, Oxford, where he pursued work on the English philosopher, F. H. Bradley. Many years later Eliot was to write that "on going down from Oxford in 1915 I made the decision to stay in England. . . ."[1] He did not, however, become a British citizen for another twelve years.

Why did Eliot decide to remain in England? The reasons were probably complex and the editors do not pretend to know in detail what they were, but in 1928 Eliot did provide a friend with an interesting and suggestive rationale.

> Some day I want to write an essay about the point of view of an American who wasn't an American, because he was born in the South

[1] See Eliot's preface to *Knowledge and Experience in the Philosophy of F. H. Bradley*, his doctoral dissertation. He brought it to completion and it was accepted by Harvard, but he never returned to stand his doctoral examination and consequently was never awarded the degree. The work was not published until 1964.

and went to school in New England as a small boy with a nigger drawl, but who wasn't a southerner in the South because his people were northerners in a border state and looked down on all southerners and Virginians, and who so was never anything anywhere and who therefore felt himself to be more a Frenchman than an American and more an Englishman than a Frenchman and yet felt that the U.S.A. up to a hundred years ago was a family extension. It is almost too difficult even for H. J. [Henry James], who for that matter wasn't an American at all, in that sense.[2]

Whatever Eliot's ultimate reason, the decision to remain in England obviously involved some difficulties. He had his living to make and, since in 1915 he had got married, there were two persons to provide for rather than one. Eliot became a schoolmaster, did some book-reviewing on the side, and later worked in a bank, where his knowledge of languages was useful in handling foreign accounts.

In choosing to remain in England, he had also chosen not to pursue an academic career but to become a poet and man of letters. It was this young man whom Pound encountered in London in 1914.[3] Later Pound was to write that Eliot

. . . displayed great tact, or enjoyed good fortune, in arriving in London at a particular date with a formed style of his own. He also participated in a movement to which no name has ever been given.

That is to say, at a particular date in a particular room, two authors, neither engaged in picking the other's pocket, decided that the dilutation of *vers libre*, Amygism, Lee Masterism, general floppiness had gone too far and that some counter-current must be set going.

[2] T. S. Eliot, *The Man and His Work* (1966), edited by Allen Tate, p. 15. The recipient of the letter was Sir Herbert Read.

[3] See Donald Gallup, "T. S. Eliot and Ezra Pound: Collaboration in Letters," *Atlantic Monthly* (January, 1970). This is a fascinating and authoritative account of the relation of the two men.

. . . Remedy prescribed [Théophile Gautier's] "Emaux et Camées" (or the Bay State Hymn Book). Rhyme and regular strophes.

Results: Poems in Mr. Eliot's *second* volume, not contained in his first, . . . also "H. S. Mauberley." Divergence later. (*Criterion*, July, 1932; reprinted in Pound's *Polite Essays*, 1937)

This brief excerpt from Pound obviously bears upon such poems of Eliot as "Whispers of Immortality" and "Sweeney Among the Nightingales." More generally, it touches upon Eliot's attitude toward verse. He was to say "No *vers* is *libre* for the man who wants to do a good job" —though in his later work Eliot did develop very complicated verse patterns which at times seem almost as fluid and "unmetrical" as free verse.

The friendship between the two poets lasted through their lives. It was Pound to whom Eliot sent the manuscript of *The Waste Land* and to whose suggestions Eliot deferred when he came to shortening and remodeling that poem. Moreover, in spite of very different personalities and in spite of somewhat divergent conceptions of poetry, the two men had much in common.

Out of his vast, specialized, and sometimes even eccentric reading, each man built much of his own poetry: as a consequence their poetry is a mosaic of literary and historical fragments from past authors. The very fact that both men chose to construct their poetry out of such fragments—which can be regarded as "images" of a special sort—implies a special awareness of and a concern for the crisis in our culture. But Eliot's diagnosis of the malady of our civilization is—and this should be emphasized—quite different from Pound's, less simple and less optimistic.

The general cultural problem inherited by Pound and Eliot had its beginnings in a time long antecedent to the Victorian period. Ultimately one can trace it back to the seventeenth century, to René Descartes, a philosopher notorious for having—inadvertently, of course—"cut the throat of poetry." His act was to make a distinction between the world outside ourselves, which can be measured scientifically and is therefore objective, and our inner, subjective world of emotions and values. The separation effected by Descartes proved to be immensely beneficial to science, which needed to eliminate the "personal equation" from its description of reality. Science, now that its scope and methods had been clarified, went on from victory to victory. But poetry, having been effectually detached from the objective world, gradually came to be disparaged as merely subjective, precious, and finally trivial.   *positivism, scientism*

The split between the realm of scientific measurement and that of human valuation has persisted to this day and the problems it entails for mankind have become more rather than less acute. Bertrand Russell, one of the coauthors of *Principia Mathematica*, in his *The Scientific Outlook* (1931) defines science as "power knowledge," and carefully distinguishes it from the "love knowledge" sought by the mystic, the lover, and the poet. He regards the outlook for our time as ominous, since science as power knowledge is becoming increasingly dominant. Russell warns us that ". . . it is only in so far as we renounce the world as its lovers that we can conquer it as its technicians. But this division in the soul is fatal to what is best in man."

Problems concerning the value and relevance of poetry began to emerge quite clearly in the early nineteenth century. Wordsworth, for example, was concerned about the drying up of human values and associated this spiritual aridity with the growth of science: in one of his poems he chides the man who would "peek and botanize upon his mother's grave." Yet Wordsworth had no intention of rejecting science out of hand. As a student at Cambridge he had got a sound notion of Newtonian physics and found a place for it in his poetry; he had adopted the new "scientific" psychology of the time, David Hartley's associationism, and found a place for it too in his early poetry. Wordsworth in fact looked forward to the eventual absorption of scientific material into poetry: "If the time should ever come when what is now called science . . .

should be ready to put on . . . a form of flesh and blood," the poet, he promised, would be ready to "lend his divine spirit to aid the transfiguration."

Yet, in his own poetry Wordsworth usually wrote about the parts of the world least affected by the impact of science, whether theoretical or applied. His characteristic scene is that of untouched and untroubled nature, and his typical characters are the peasant, the shepherd, the villager, the child, the wanderer—people who live "in the eye of nature" and whose inner life in some sense mirrors the nature that lies about them. With such people the gap between the scientifically measurable world and the inner world of emotion is most easily bridged. (Perhaps it would be more accurate to say that it has never been seriously breached.)

Wordsworth's concern for poetry, it is plain, was far more than a self-serving interest. He identified the cause of poetry with the spiritual health of mankind. Though it was not necessary for all men to become poets, yet their ability to participate in the life of the imagination was crucial. The death of the imagination—and of poetry—would signify a mortal sickness of the culture itself.

Wordsworth's response to the cultural situation as he understood it produced some very great poetry, and so did the related responses of his fellow Romantics, who had arrived at their own special definitions of the critical issues. But by the twentieth century a new assessment of the cultural situation was required. Science, theoretical and applied, had drastically altered man's psyche and his culture, and the vitality of the Romantic movement had lost itself in the sands of late Victorianism.

The cultural problem as it presented itself to Eliot demanded a more radical solution. Eliot had come to the conclusion that the ultimate values by which men live could not be derived from science or supplied from a study of history —at least as objectively conducted—or even garnered from the poet's insights. Thus, Eliot's decision in 1927 to go into the Church of England, one may conjecture, was influenced by his

* cf. faith, hope, + charity
    symbolism idealism sympathy

skepticism about secularistic and humanistic solutions such as Pound's essentially were. Eliot's comments on Matthew Arnold, that great pro-consul of Victorian culture, are relevant here— the more so since there has been a disposition to regard Eliot as the Matthew Arnold of our own epoch and therefore to find it surprising that he should handle Arnold as sharply as he does.

In Arnold's estimate, the findings of science had rendered religion obsolete. Yet, though religion (and Arnold was thinking particularly of Christianity) could no longer be believed, he apparently felt no disposition to go beyond its value system. As Eliot puts it in his 1930 essay "Arnold and Pater," Arnold's writings amount to an affirmation "that the emotions of Christianity can and must be preserved without the belief. . . . The effect of Arnold's religious campaign [thus was] to divorce religion from thought." Indeed, religion becomes for Arnold simply—to use his own words—"morality touched by emotion." With Victorians of a different personality—Walter Pater, for instance —religion dissolves into poetry or poetry itself becomes a religion. Eliot, however, was convinced that poetry could not replace religion and went so far as to write in 1933 that "if you find that you must do without something, such as religious faith or philosophical belief, then you must just do without it." Eliot believed that a culture could not do without religion, but of course most of his literary friends, including Pound, felt that it could and must. Pound was later to twit Eliot from time to time for talking "a lot of cod about a dead god." At most, the church might help in training simple people in certain basic values until they became sufficiently sophisticated to discard what Pound regarded as a supernatural crutch.

We have said in an earlier paragraph that Eliot did not believe that men's fundamental values could be derived even from the poet's insight or from imaginative vision but must come from "revelation." Yet is not revelation a form of imaginative insight? Matthew Arnold and the Arnoldians in general would certainly hold that it was. But for Eliot, the poet is only incidentally—if at all—a prophet, or Joyce's "priest of the eternal imagination." The revelation that Eliot accepts is special. It comes through divine inspiration, is enshrined in a sacred book, has been so defined as to guard against heretical misinterpretations, and is mediated through a teaching church which has developed doctrine through its councils and its traditional experience.

For most moderns, terms like "supernatural" and "sacred" beg the very question to be proved. But we are not concerned here to justify Eliot's position but rather to indicate what it was and was not and to suggest its relation to some of the intellectual trends of the last century—scientific positivism, the Arnoldian prophecy as to the future of poetry, aestheticism, and others. Though Eliot has exercised a great influence on the poetry of our time, his solution of the problem of knowledge and value has attracted few other men of letters. Yet it ought to be plain that Eliot's reinstatement of religion was not for him gratuitous or simply a matter of highly emotional and personal associations. His way of solving the poetic problem involved a total world view, including the relation of science to poetry, to philosophy, and to religion.

It might be pointed out that Eliot's developed theological and religious position was not uninformed by philosophy. His careful study of Bradley has been mentioned earlier. Bradley was not a theist, but his philosophical position, one which greatly influenced Eliot's view of reality, could, without much strain, be made to accommodate theism. Two other names are worth mentioning in relation to Eliot's philosophical education, those of Bertrand Russell and George Santayana.

In view of their later differences, it may seem strange to mention Russell here at all. Yet the young Eliot worked hard at the older man's writings and for some years could call him his intimate friend. Professor Brand Blanshard of Yale, who was at Oxford with Eliot in 1914–15, reports that at this time all of Eliot's talk "was in the realm of philosophy" and that, night after night, Eliot could be seen absorbed in Russell's *Principia Mathematica.* (See the *Yale Review,* Summer, 1965.) Eliot had first met Russell when Russell was a visiting professor at Harvard. After Eliot settled in England he saw much of Russell, and for some years Eliot and his young wife lived as guests in Russell's London flat. The relationship was to cool, and Eliot would later print some sharp things about Russell's *A Free Man's Worship,* but the two always felt a mutual respect, and Eliot was in touch with Russell as late as 1955.

While Eliot was a student at Harvard, he took two courses under Santayana. Robert Lowell has amusingly but accurately called Santayana a "free-thinking Catholic infidel . . . who'd found/the Church too good to be believed." Yet Santayana had warned—and at about the period when Eliot was studying with him—of the/perils of modernism in religion:⟩

> In a supernaturalism [he wrote], in a tight clericalism, not in a pleasant secularization, lies the sole hope of the church. Its sole dignity also lies there. It will not convert the world; it never did and it never could. It will remain a voice crying in the wilderness; but it will believe what it cries and there will be some to listen to it in the future, as there have been many in the past. As to modernism, it is suicide. . . . It concedes everything; for it conceives of everything in Christianity, as Christians hold it, as an illusion.

Santayana himself took it to be an illusion, though a beautiful, and, to him, aesthetically satisfying, illusion. But his warning was seriously meant.

At any rate, Eliot was to reject such positions as the Victorian compromise, liberal Protestantism, and humanism and to move back into the orthodoxy of a doctrinal church, thus reversing the course taken by his Unitarian forebears and the New England Puritanism from which they had descended. In his own special terms, then, Eliot too had broken with the genteel tradition as described by Santayana.

Whatever we make of the logic of Eliot's philosophical and religious position,[4] his poetry addresses itself quite directly to the problems of a culture more and more affected by applied as well as theoretical science. Eliot's early work concerns itself directly with the urban scene. In a very interesting passage from an essay entitled "What Dante Means to Me" he writes:

> I think that from Baudelaire I learned first, a precedent for the poetical possibilities, never developed by any poet writing in my own language, the more sordid aspects of the modern metropolis, of the possibility of fusion between the sordidly realistic and the phantasmagoric, the possibility of the juxtaposition of the matter-of-fact and the fantastic. From him, as from Laforgue, I learned that the sort of material that I had, the sort of experience that an adolescent had had, in an industrial city in America, could be the material for poetry; and that the source of new poetry might be found in what had been regarded hitherto as the impossible, the sterile, the intractably unpoetic. That, in fact, the business of the poet was to make poetry out of the unexplored resources of the unpoetical; that the poet, in fact, was committed by his profession to turn the unpoetical into poetry. A great poet can give a younger poet everything that he has to give him in a very few lines. It may be that I am indebted to Baudelaire chiefly for half a dozen lines out of the whole of *Fleurs du Mal;* and that his significance for me is summed up in the lines:

> *Fourmillante cité, cité pleine de rêves,*
> *Où le spectre en plein jour raccroche le*
>   *passant!*

> I knew what *that* meant, because I had lived it before I knew that I wanted to turn it into verse on my own account.

These comments on his "material" are important; equally important is what Eliot says in

---

[4] An attempt to sketch the whole range of influences that shaped Eliot's position would have to include much more than we have noticed here, including some of the French intellectuals of the nineteenth and twentieth centuries.

this passage about his method. Obviously, he considers poetry to be a fusion of opposites— in this instance a fusion of "the sordidly realistic and the phantasmagoric," of "the matter-of-fact and the fantastic." Indeed, what Eliot does in a great deal of his poetry is to discover a relationship between items ordinarily thought of as completely disparate. The relationship may even be one of strong tension, in which the materials pull against each other and resist any easy reconciliation.

In this general connection it is interesting to refer to another passage in which Eliot discusses the use in poetry of what the Victorians sometimes regarded as hopelessly unpromising. After quoting Matthew Arnold's rather prim observation to the effect that "no one can deny that it is of advantage to a poet to deal with a beautiful world,"[5] Eliot suddenly rounds on the great nineteenth-century critic and denies flatly his basic assumption: "the essential advantage for a poet," he declares, is not that of having a beautiful world with which to deal, but rather the ability "to be able to see beneath both beauty and ugliness; to see the boredom, and the horror, and the glory. The vision of the horror and the glory," Eliot rather acidly concludes, "was denied to Arnold, but he knew something of the boredom" (*The Use of Poetry*, 1933, pp. 98–99).

Eliot also knew something of the boredom. What his poetry describes in the modern world, along with the possibility of either horror or glory, is the boredom. Many of his vignettes of urban life describe men and women caught in a world of monotonous repetition, a world of aimless circling about, without end or purpose. Eliot's early poetry is full of this sort of thing:

The morning comes to consciousness
Of faint stale smells of beer
From the sawdust-trampled street
With all its muddy feet that press
To early coffee-stands.
With the other masquerades

That time resumes,
One thinks of all the hands
That are raising dingy shades
In a thousand furnished rooms. ("Preludes")

They are rattling breakfast plates in basement
    kitchens,
And along the trampled edges of the street
I am aware of the damp souls of housemaids
Sprouting despondently at area gates.
                    ("Morning at the Window")

At the violet hour, the evening hour that strives
Homeward, and brings the sailor home from sea,
The typist home at teatime, clears her breakfast,
    lights
Her stove, and lays out food in tins.
                        (*The Waste Land*)

Let us go, through certain half-deserted streets,
The muttering retreats
Of restless nights in one-night cheap hotels
And sawdust restaurants with oyster-shells:
Streets that follow like a tedious argument
Of insidious intent. . . .
        ("The Love Song of J. Alfred Prufrock")[6]

The wanderer moving through the deserted city streets long past midnight walks through a genuine nightmare in which

> the floors of memory
> And all its clear relations
> Its divisions and precisions,

are dissolved, a fantastic world in which every street lamp that one passes

> Beats like a fatalistic drum . . .

Yet when the wanderer turns to his own door, and enters his own bedroom, he steps out of one horror into a worse horror:

'The bed is open; the tooth-brush hangs on the
    wall,
Put your shoes at the door, sleep, prepare for
    life.'

---

[5] The lengths to which Arnold's sense of poetic propriety could take him is amusingly illustrated by his throwing down in disgust Lincoln's "Gettysburg Address" when he came upon the word "proposition."

[6] Hart Crane, in part under Eliot's influence, also treats the modern city in his poetry. A comparison between his poetry of the city and Eliot's will bring out not only parallels but important differences in tone.

*Cf.
world-machine*

The last twist of the knife.
                    ("Rhapsody on a Windy Night")

The wound in which this knife is twisted is modern man's loss of meaning and purpose. When life to which one expects to rise after sleep—a daylight world of clear plans and purposes—turns out to be simply a kind of automatism, as absurd as the bizarre world of the nightmare streets, the knife in the wound is given a final agonizing twist. For a further instance, the reader might look at the Song of the third Thames Daughter in *The Waste Land* (p. 2116).

Modern man's loss of purpose is put more explicitly in the raffish Sweeney's recital of his philosophy—a view of life held, incidentally, by many of Sweeney's betters.

Birth, and copulation, and death.
That's all the facts when you come to brass
    tacks:
Birth, and copulation, and death.
I've been born, and once is enough.

"Sweeney Agonistes," from which this passage comes, can serve as a useful reminder of Eliot's ability to treat the emptiness of the modern world in more than one tone of voice. The fact doesn't necessarily have to be stated "solemnly" and in Eliot's poetry it is usually not "stated" at all. It is dramatized through concrete imagery and it is, as here, presented not as abstract formulation but as a dramatic projection in which the very rhythms testify to a personality and an attitude.

In the world depicted in Eliot's poetry those who have been drugged and numbed by their life in the modern world can only with difficulty be awakened to full consciousness of their condition. They are tempted to cling to their partial oblivion. This is why April, with its promise of new life, and its threat to awaken them, is "the cruellest month." The chorus of old women in *Murder in the Cathedral* "do not wish anything to happen." They prefer to keep on living quietly, "avoiding notice,/Living and partly liv-

ing." The benumbed may also be certain well-bred inhabitants of a city like Boston:

. . . evening quickens faintly in the street,
Wakening the appetites of life in some
And to others bringing the *Boston Evening
    Transcript.* . . .

Or they may be the bored drawing-room characters in "The Love Song of J. Alfred Prufrock" whom Prufrock would like to confront with the truth about themselves. He would like to say to them:

. . . "I am Lazarus, come from the dead,
Come back to tell you all, I shall tell you all."

But he well knows that these overcivilized and desiccated people would not be impressed by the Lazarus of the New Testament, much less by a self-conscious man "with a bald spot in the middle of [his] hair," a man aware of the fact that he wears a "necktie rich and modest, but asserted by a simple pin." In any case, these people would not understand the talk of a man who had experienced real death or real life.

The themes that run through so much of Eliot's poetry—life that is only a half-life because it cannot come to terms with death, the liberation into true living that comes from the acceptance of death, the ecstatic moment in the hyacinth garden (lines 38–41 of *The Waste Land*) that partakes of both life and death:

                    . . . I could not
Speak, and my eyes failed, I was neither
Living nor dead, and I knew nothing,
Looking into the heart of light, the silence—

these, and the other themes that recur in Eliot's poetry, bear a close relation to his concern with the boredom and the horror—and the possibility of glory—that he finds in our contemporary metropolitan life. They also bear a close relation to the unreality that pervades a world which for Eliot has lost the rhythm of the seasons, has lost a sense of community, and, most of all, has lost a sense of purpose. Such a world *is* unreal: the sordid and the matter-of-fact, far from erasing the phantasmagoric, accentuate it. The

*diseased
imagination*

specter does indeed in broad daylight reach out to grasp the passer-by. London, "under the brown fog of a winter noon" as well as "under the brown fog of a winter dawn," is seen as an "Unreal City," and the crowds flowing across London Bridge might be in Dante's Hell:

I had not thought death had undone so many.
Sighs, short and infrequent, were exhaled,
And each man fixed his eyes before his feet.

Eliot has sometimes been reproached for hating the present, sentimentalizing the past, and sighing after vanished glories. There are certain things in the present that are evidently repugnant to him as there are certain things in it repugnant to most of us. But the issue is not the degree of enthusiasm that a modern poet feels for the present day but rather his willingness to face up to the present reality and his ability to render it with honesty and conviction in his poetry. Eliot has remarked that in prose—he means expository or argumentative prose—we may state our ideals or argue for them, but that in our poetry (in which he would include imaginative fiction) we must deal with reality. We have already quoted his remark that the poet must "be able to see beneath both beauty and ugliness." But if the ugliness is a part of the reality, it must not be glossed over or denied. If it is in effect denied, then the poet's deeper vision, whether of horror or glory, will seem simply an imposed subjective interpretation, a vision that has not been earned.

Thus, though Eliot obviously deplores the forces in the modern world that turn a man into a machine, in his poetry he must make us "see" the human being as a machine:

At the violet hour, when the eyes and back
Turn upward from the desk, when the human
    engine waits
Like a taxi throbbing waiting. . . .

In rendering the present reality, Eliot skillfully uses his rhythms as well as his images. Thus, the rhythms in which he describes the house agent's clerk's visit to the typist emphasize the mechanical and perfunctory "love-making." The metronomic beat of the meter is insistent. There is no passion here; sexual love has been made trivial by a world that can attach no significance to it.

The time is now propitious, as he guesses,
The meal is ended, she is bored and tired,
Endeavours to engage her in caresses
Which still are unreproved, if undesired.
Flushed and decided, he assaults at once;
Exploring hands encounter no defence;
His vanity requires no response,
And makes a welcome of indifference.

If the modern world has lost its sense of communication and community, the poet must render that loss dramatically, not as observed from the outside but as felt from the inside. He has done so not only in the nightmare passages of *The Waste Land*:

There is not even solitude in the mountains
But red sullen faces sneer and snarl
From doors of mudcracked houses—

but also in the realistic passages:

"My nerves are bad to-night. Yes, bad. Stay
    with me.
"Speak to me. Why do you never speak. Speak.
    "What are you thinking of? What thinking?
    What?
"I never know what you are thinking. Think."

But he has also on occasion rendered the sense of community in positive terms—not as something lost but as a surviving reality:

O City city, I can sometimes hear
Beside a public bar in Lower Thames Street,
The pleasant whining of a mandoline
And a clatter and a chatter from within
Where fishmen lounge at noon. . . .

As for the sense of unreality, that too is rendered concretely, not merely asserted. It is also associated with visions of a world that is disintegrating. In *The Waste Land* the cities of the dissolving civilization are inverted like those seen in a mirage. The parched traveler asks:

What is the city over the mountains

Cracks and reforms and bursts in the violet air
Falling towers—

but these cities are also like those seen in a mirage in that they are upside down; and the passage that follows shows everything turned topsy-turvy:

. . . bats with baby faces in the violet light
Whistled, and beat their wings
And crawled head downward down a blackened
    wall
And upside down in air were towers
Tolling reminiscent bells, that kept the hours
And voices singing out of empty cisterns and
    exhausted wells.

Eliot also uses the empty whirl in order to suggest the breakup of civilization. There is such a vision at the end of "Gerontion" in which people, whose surnames (De Bailhache, Fresca, Cammel) suggest that the disintegration is international and worldwide, are whirled "in fractured atoms." The last section of "The Hollow Men" ends with the hollow men who have finally realized that they are not "lost/Violent souls," but only "stuffed men," dancing around the prickly pear singing "This is the way the world ends/Not with a bang but a whimper." Again, in "Burnt Norton," there is a description of "men and bits of paper, whirled by the cold wind/That blows before and after time. . . ."

The empty whirl, the purposeless moving in a circle, is Eliot's recurrent symbol of deadening monotony, of boredom. Even in a poem like "Sweeney Agonistes," where we have a spoof on the movies' stereotype of the modern golden age, life on a South Sea island, "where the Gauguin maids . . . Wear palmleaf drapery," there is boredom too.

Two songs describe the delights of life on this island—a life which seems to consist of making love under the "breadfruit, banyan, palmleaf/Or bamboo tree." ("Any old tree will do for me/Any old wood is just as good/Any old isle is just my style. . . .") But a character named Doris exclaims: "That's not life, that's no life/Why I'd just as soon be dead." The context makes it plain that Doris is, in the Victorian

phraseology, a young woman who is no better than she should be, but in this essential matter she shows a great deal more discernment than Mr. Prufrock's companions, the ladies who "come and go/Talking of Michelangelo."

On an earlier page, we discussed the modern poet's reaction against Victorian rhetoric, moralizing, and "statements" of every kind, and we have noted that out of this reaction the Imagist movement was born. Eliot does not say that the basic mode of poetry is the presentation of an image. He had his own way of putting the matter. In 1919 he wrote: "The only way of expressing emotion in the form of art is by finding an 'objective correlative'; in other words, a set of objects, a situation, a chain of events which will be the formula of that *particular* emotion; such as when the external facts which must terminate in sensory experience are given, the emotion is immediately evoked."[7]

This formulation has been questioned[8] because it seems to imply that the poet can transfer intact a precise emotion to his reader, whereas a poet usually discovers what he really wants to say only through the process of trying to formulate it; moreover, no reader will in fact ever receive from the poem exactly what the poet at some point may have had in mind. Such objections to Eliot's account of the matter are well taken. Yet what is important in Eliot's notion of the objective correlative can be shorn of these unnecessary embarrassments. Eliot himself stated the core of the theory two years later in his essay "The Metaphysical Poets" (included in this text) when he wrote that at their best the metaphysicals were "engaged in the task of trying to

7 "Hamlet and His Problems," *Selected Essays*, pp. 124–25. One might compare Pound's definition of poetry (1915): "Poetry is a sort of inspired mathematics, which gives us equations, not for abstract figures, triangles, spheres, and the like, but equations for the human emotions. If one have a mind which inclines to magic rather than science, one will prefer to speak of these equations as spells or incantations; it sounds more arcane, mysterious, recondite" (*Spirit of Romance*, p. 5).

8 Notably by Eliseo Vivas: see his "The Objective Correlative of T. S. Eliot," *Critiques and Essays in Criticism* (1949), edited by R. W. Stallman.

find the verbal equivalent for states of mind and feeling."

"Verbal equivalent" is probably a safer way of putting matters than is "objective correlative" —though in practice they come to the same thing: for the poet's private and personal experience is being "objectified"—not in objects, to be sure, but in a structure of words. Moreover, the phrase "states of mind and feeling" is at once more cautious and more accurate than "a particular emotion." In any case, the conjunction of mind *and* feeling is important, as other passages in "The Metaphysical Poets" make clear. Thus, Eliot asserts in this essay that in poets like Chapman and John Donne "there is a direct sensuous apprehension of thought, or a recreation of thought into feeling. . . ." Quite clearly Eliot here is himself making use of metaphorical (and not strictly philosophical) language. So also when he writes that later poets like Tennyson and Browning "do not feel their thoughts as immediately as the odour of a rose." Yet how, save in metaphorical language, is one going to describe the quality of that earlier pre-Cartesian poetry in view of the fact that anyone writing today is forced to employ the language of a world in which thought and feeling seem to have been irrecoverably split apart? We may carp if we like at expressions such as "feeling" a "thought." Nevertheless, Eliot is right in claiming that a special quality of Elizabethan and Jacobean poetry—however we may want to describe it—did disappear from English poetry later on in the seventeenth century.

There occurred, Eliot conjectures, a "dissociation of sensibility."[9] This notion has been sharply criticized, notably by Frank Kermode in *Romantic Image* (1957), but in the light of the context in which Eliot employs it, it is not too difficult to come at his meaning. Though the term "sensibility" may be cloudy and

though "dissociation" may raise questions that the phrase "separation of thought from feeling" would not, the lesion that Eliot points to here is essentially that effected by Descartes. Decisively in favor of such an interpretation is Eliot's remark that early "in the eighteenth century" the "sentimental age began." For sentimentality characteristically occurs when the poet purges his experience of the realistic, the recalcitrant, the rational, and indeed of all those elements that the metaphysical poets assimilated in virtue of what Eliot calls a "sensibility which could devour any kind of experience." Sentimentality, in short, is emotion not disciplined by the intellect—emotion indulged in for its own sake.

Pound's formulation of the "image," one recalls, was an attempt to reunite intellect and emotion in poetry (he called an image "an intellectual and emotional complex"). Eliot's description of metaphysical poetry is his own way of dealing with the same problem. Pound's Imagism derived in part from the example of the French symbolist poets. One of Eliot's most important insights was to discern a resemblance between the French symbolists and the English metaphysicals.[10] Since, as he put it, "Jules Laforgue and Tristan Corbière in many of his poems [were] nearer to the 'school of Donne' than any modern English poet," the modern poet trying to find "the verbal equivalent" of his contemporary experience could learn from both schools. The influence of the school of Donne on Eliot's poetry, particularly on his earlier poetry, is clear. Because Donne's poetry was intellectual, witty, and dramatic (as was, for instance, the poetry of Corbière), it served to correct the Imagist tendency toward the piling up of merely static images. In his essays Eliot insists that *all* poetry is dramatic[11] and his own poetry is intensely so.

So much for Eliot's forging or reforging of his poetic instrument. Yet, as we have indicated

[9] Eliot, writing in the *New Statesman*, in 1965, admitted that he was "not quite sure of what [he] meant thirty-five years ago." This apologetic note is of a piece with the tone of much of Eliot's writing during his later years—writing in which he sought to soften what he took to be too polemical earlier statements or to modify remarks that now seemed to him to smack of the pontifical.

[10] Eliot makes the resemblance precisely this fusion of intellect and emotion: ". . . they have the same essential quality of transmuting ideas into sensations. . . ." See Eliot's essay "The Metaphysical Poets" printed below.

[11] See, for example, "A Dialogue of Dramatic Poetry," *Selected Essays*, p. 38.

earlier, Eliot's speculations in the realm of poetics have the closest of relations to his analysis of the problems of contemporary civilization.

The twentieth-century world in which Eliot found himself had been blasted by a catastrophic war in which the new power-knowledge of science had revealed just how powerful it was. But more important still, the new knowledge, even with peace restored, seemed to blight all the traditional values and the age-old pieties. Head

and heart, intellect and emotion, had to be brought—if such were in fact possible—into working relation again. Thus the crisis in poetry presented in little what the crisis in culture presented in its largest form, and indeed the lesser crisis was continuous with and counted finally as simply one aspect of the greater. This crisis also provided the grounding, directly or indirectly, for much of American fiction of the 1920's and later.

BIOGRAPHICAL CHART

1888   Born, September 26, in St. Louis
1898–1906   Attends Smith Academy and Milton Academy
1906–10   Undergraduate (class of 1909) and graduate student at Harvard
1910–11   Studies at the Sorbonne in Paris
1911–14   Continues graduate studies at Harvard in philosophy; begins friendship with Bertrand Russell
1914   Traveling fellowship to Germany interrupted by First World War; goes to Merton College, Oxford; begins close association with Ezra Pound in London
1915   Marries Vivienne Haigh-Wood, teaches school, works at Lloyd's Bank
1922   Becomes editor of the *Criterion*; *The Waste Land*; wins $2000 Dial Award

1925   Joins publishing house of Faber and Gwyer (later Faber and Faber)
1927   Becomes British citizen and member of the Church of England
1930   *Ash-Wednesday*; *Animula*; *Dante*
1934   Returns to America as Charles Eliot Norton Professor of Poetry, Harvard University
1935–39   *Murder in the Cathedral*; *Burnt Norton*; *Family Reunion*; the *Criterion* discontinued
1942   *Four Quartets* completed with publication of *Little Gidding*
1947   Wife dies after years of illness
1948   Nobel prize and the Order of Merit; *The Cocktail Party*
1957   Marries Valerie Fletcher
1959   *The Elder Statesman*
1965   Dies, January 5, in London

FURTHER READINGS

The Collected Plays (1962)
The Complete Poems and Plays (1952)
The Idea of a Christian Society (1940)
Knowledge and Experience in the Philosophy of F. H. Bradley (1964)
On Poetry and Poets (1957)
Selected Essays, 1917–1932 (1932)

Donald Gallup, *T. S. Eliot: A Bibliography* (1953)
Elizabeth Drew, *T. S. Eliot: The Design of His Poetry* (1949)
Helen Louise Gardner, *The Art of T. S. Eliot* (1949)

Herbert Howarth, *Some Figures Behind T. S. Eliot* (1964)
Hugh Kenner, *The Invisible Poet: T. S. Eliot* (1959)
———, ed., *T. S. Eliot: A Collection of Critical Essays* (1962)
Grover A. Smith, Jr., *T. S. Eliot's Poetry and Plays: A Study in Sources and Meaning* (1956)
Allen Tate, ed., *T. S. Eliot: The Man and His Work* (1966)
Leonard Unger, *T. S. Eliot: A Selected Critique* (1948)
———, "Laforgue, Conrad, and Eliot," in *The Man in the Name* (1956)

The Love Song of J. Alfred Prufrock (1917)

The poem takes the form of a dramatic monologue, in this matter at least harking back to

Robert Browning who is the most famous employer of this mode. But otherwise how un-

Browningesque is the poem. Though it comes at the very beginning of his career, it shows Eliot already making use of his characteristic themes and symbols. Prufrock is the fine flower of an "overrefined" society. He is sensitive and self-conscious and moves in the best circles; but the important matter is that he himself moves in a closed circle: his life is without purpose and meaning, monotonous, and finally boring.

Prufrock himself is aware that he is not truly alive. He is afraid of sexual love; his love song is finally unsingable. He can only yearn toward a vision of vital beauty. In fact, at the close of the poem, as he ruefully admits to himself, there is no fear of his suffering a death by water in the "chambers of the sea." It is "human voices" that in waking him from his reverie cause him to "drown." It is in the everyday world in which he lives and moves and has his being that he cannot get his breath.

It is also worth remarking that in this poem, as in so many of his later poems, Eliot brings in both halves of the modern urban world. Prufrock, wearing his "morning coat" and his "necktie rich and modest," and his companions, the ladies whose "arms . . . are braceleted and white and bare," represent the elegant, literate, upper-class world. But the poem acknowledges that other world of "sawdust restaurants with oyster-shells" and "lonely men in shirt-sleeves" (see lines 4-8 and 70-72). The same blight of listlessness and lack of purpose rests upon it too.

This early poem is also rather typical of what were to be Eliot's characteristic techniques. He makes much use of literary references, like those to Hamlet and Michelangelo, or to more recondite ones, like that to Hesiod's poem, *Works and Days* (line 20). There are abrupt shifts and breaks in the continuity. Thus, lines 73-74 at first glance seem to be utterly unconnected with what immediately precedes or follows. There is a great deal of wit play: the fog is elaborately described in terms of catlike behavior (lines 15-22); there are witty metaphors, for example, "I have measured out my life with coffee spoons" (line 51); and there is verbal wit as the poet chimes the sounds of words, for example, "And

time yet for a hundred *indecisions,*/And for a hundred *visions* and *revisions* . . ." (lines 32-33, italics ours).

The epigraph gives a useful lead into the poem. It is taken from Dante's *Inferno* (Canto 27, lines 61-66). The speech comes from the mouth of the spirit of Guido da Montefeltro, one of the Evil Counselors tormented in this part of Hell. He is encased in flame and when he speaks his voice issues from the tip of the flame, which shakes and wavers like a tongue. When Dante asks him who he is, the proud Guido tells him that he would refuse to answer except that he is confident that the man who asks this question can never return to earth; that is, the secret of his infamy is safe. Thus he says: "If I believed that my answer were to someone who might ever go back to the world, this flame would shake no more. But since, if I hear truth, no one ever returned alive from this pit, I respond to you without fear of infamy."

The relevance of this quotation to the present poem becomes apparent if we realize that the "you" in the first sentence of the poem is the person who is now reading this poem; that is, *you,* the present reader. For in this poem the painfully self-conscious Prufrock is making a confession about himself—about his timidity, about his failure of nerve, about his lack of any sense of purpose. But like Guido, he wouldn't be exposing himself in this fashion but for the fact that he knows that his reader, as a fellow creature in the modern world, is also damned. To confide in a fellow sufferer involves no shame.

Poets have frequently compared a peaceful evening to something sleeping, and at line 75 the poet tells us that this particular evening "sleeps so peacefully!" (though he is to hint a few lines later that the sleep may be less peaceful than he had first surmised, for he adds "or it malingers . . ."). Yet peaceful is hardly the way to characterize the sleep described in line 3. The phrase "etherised upon a table" suggests something else: a sleep artificially induced in a patient lying on an operating table. This figure of anaesthesia and the operating room has much to do with the mood of the poem and prepares for the subsequent development of the theme.

The poet has chosen to have the women talking of Michelangelo (lines 14 and 36) and not Marcel Proust or Virginia Woolf. The reader might ponder why, and might ask whether it would make any difference—rhyme and meter aside—if either of these names were substituted.

An early critic declared the poem stupid or worse because the poet wishes he had been a lobster and not a man. Surely the crustacean in question is a crab. But lobster or crab, what Prufrock says, metaphorically, is that, rather than be the kind of desiccated man he actually is, he would be better off if he were some primitive creature of the sea floor—alive even if only as instinctive brute force. Perhaps to this self-conscious oversensitive man, the crab's hard armor would seem particularly attractive.

The Lazarus to whom Prufrock refers is the beggar in Luke 16. The beggar died and was carried by angels to Abraham's bosom, and the rich man under whose table Lazarus would "fain have gathered up the crumbs" in time also died and went to hell. The rich man, seeing Lazarus in bliss, asks his forefather Abraham to send Lazarus to him with water for his parched tongue, but Abraham replies that this is impossible. The rich man then asks that Lazarus at least be sent to warn his five brothers of what might happen to them if they withhold their charity. Abraham replies that the brothers had already had the prophets warn them. When the rich man protests, "Nay, father Abraham, but if one went unto them from the dead," Abraham tells him: "If they hear not Moses and the prophets neither will they be persuaded, though one rose from the dead." The clear implication is that the people in Prufrock's society are no more capable than the rich man's brothers of being roused from the living death of their meaningless lives.[1]

---

[1] A reader may be disposed to ask: why couldn't the Lazarus referred to be the brother of Mary and Martha, whom Jesus raised from the dead (see John 11). Since he was brought back from the dead presumably he could have told living men what it was like, even though there is no record in the Bible that he ever did so. In the context of this poem, however, the story from Luke

A little earlier (line 82) there is another Biblical reference. John the Baptist was beheaded by King Herod at the request of Salome, the king's stepdaughter, and the head was brought to her on a platter. It is well to ask in what sense does Prufrock mean that he has seen his own head brought in on a platter.

Prufrock is too timid—too self-conscious—to summon the courage required to tell his companions what is wrong with them and their society. Yet if Prufrock is timid, he is honest. He will not pretend that he is a Prince Hamlet. Hamlet, one remembers, discovered that "something was rotten" in his own society, though he is appalled by the notion that he should have to cut out the rotten core: "Oh cursed spite, that I was ever born to set it right." If Hamlet, as some critics have argued, was incapable of decision, at least his debates of conscience had to do with great issues. There is a big difference between daring to kill a king and daring to eat a peach. Prufrock's one virtue is his honesty. He does not see himself as a person of sufficient stature to sustain a tragic and heroic role.

It is significant that the first appearance of a scene of vitality and beauty in this poem is that which depicts Prufrock's imaginative vision of the mermaids (lines 126–28). We are here for the first time in the poem away from the streets that "follow like a tedious argument/Of insidious intent" and from those "narrow streets" from which Prufrock has seen "lonely men in shirt-sleeves, leaning out of windows." We are also out of the atmosphere of literary chatter at a literary tea. The mermaids seem to mean to Prufrock not merely a romantic daydream but a living force. It is amusing to speculate on what would happen if Prufrock came back into the drawing room to report that he had heard "the mermaids singing, each to each"—and to tell of a realm of transcendent beauty and power. One can imagine what the lady, "settling a pillow by her head," would say about that. And what

---

has more point, for in this poem, what is stressed is the obtuseness of people who simply cannot be made to see the truth about themselves.

would she say about Prufrock after he left the room?[2]

In Joseph Conrad's *Lord Jim* one of the characters exclaims: "A man that is born falls into a dream like a man falls into the sea. If he tries to climb out into the air as inexperienced people endeavour to do, he drowns. . . . The way is to the destructive element submit yourself, and with the exertion of your hands and feet . . . make the deep, deep sea keep you up." Eliot knew his Conrad well,[3] and though there is no evidence to show that he is remembering this passage, it makes a very apposite commentary on Prufrock's plight. He would have done better to have remained true to his dream of the mermaids, to have risked death by water, rather than have "waked" to "drown" in the half-life of a desiccated society.

S'io credessi che mia risposta fosse
a persona che mai tornasse al mondo,
questa fiamma staria senza piu scosse.
Ma per cid che giammai di questo fondo
non torno vivo alcun, s'i'odo il vero,
senza tema d'infamia ti rispondo.

Let us go then, you and I,
When the evening is spread out against the
 sky
Like a patient etherised upon a table;
Let us go, through certain half-deserted
 streets,
The muttering retreats
Of restless nights in one-night cheap hotels
And sawdust restaurants with oyster-shells:
Streets that follow like a tedious argument
Of insidious intent
To lead you to an overwhelming question . . .   10
Oh, do not ask, "What is it?"
Let us go and make our visit.

In the room the women come and go
Talking of Michelangelo.

[2] Let us remark that, in this poem, the sea is the element of both the crab and the mermaid—that is, of the two extremes of life: brute force and transcendent meaning. The woman, living in her enervated and meaningless world, would be as much appalled by the one as by the other.
[3] The epigraph of "The Hollow Men"—"Mistah Kurtz—he dead"—is from Conrad's *Heart of Darkness*.

The yellow fog that rubs its back upon the
 window-panes,
The yellow smoke that rubs its muzzle on
 the window-panes,
Licked its tongue into the corners of the
 evening,
Lingered upon the pools that stand in drains,
Let fall upon its back the soot that falls
 from chimneys,
Slipped by the terrace, made a sudden leap,   20
And seeing that it was a soft October night,
Curled once about the house, and fell asleep.

And indeed there will be time
For the yellow smoke that slides along the
 street
Rubbing its back upon the window-panes;
There will be time, there will be time
To prepare a face to meet the faces that
 you meet;
There will be time to murder and create,
And time for all the works and days of hands
That lift and drop a question on your plate;   30
Time for you and time for me,
And time yet for a hundred indecisions,
And for a hundred visions and revisions,
Before the taking of a toast and tea.

In the room the women come and go
Talking of Michelangelo.

And indeed there will be time
To wonder, "Do I dare?" and, "Do I dare?"
Time to turn back and descend the stair,
With a bald spot in the middle of my hair—   40
[They will say: "How his hair is growing
 thin!"]
My morning coat, my collar mounting firmly
 to the chin,
My necktie rich and modest, but asserted by
 a simple pin—
[They will say: "But how his arms and legs
 are thin!"]
Do I dare
Disturb the universe?
In a minute there is time
For decisions and revisions which a minute
 will reverse.

For I have known them all already, known
 them all—
Have known the evenings, mornings, afternoons,   50

I have measured out my life with coffee
  spoons;
I know the voices dying with a dying fall
Beneath the music from a farther room.
    So how should I presume?

And I have known the eyes already, known
  them all—
The eyes that fix you in a formulated phrase,
And when I am formulated, sprawling on a
  pin,
When I am pinned and wriggling on the
  wall,
Then how should I begin
To spit out all the butt-ends of my days and
  ways?   60
    And how should I presume?

And I have known the arms already, known
  them all—
Arms that are braceleted and white and bare
[But in the lamplight, downed with light
  brown hair!]
Is it perfume from a dress
That makes me so digress?
Arms that lie along a table, or wrap about a
  shawl.
    And should I then presume?
    And how should I begin?

          . . . . .

Shall I say, I have gone at dusk through narrow streets   70
And watched the smoke that rises from the
  pipes
Of lonely men in shirt-sleeves, leaning out of
  windows? . . .

    I should have been a pair of ragged claws
Scuttling across the floors of silent seas.

          . . . . .

And the afternoon, the evening, sleeps so
  peacefully!
Smoothed by long fingers,
Asleep . . . tired . . . or it malingers,
Stretched on the floor, here beside you and
  me.
Should I, after tea and cakes and ices,
Have the strength to force the moment to its
  crisis?   80
But though I have wept and fasted, wept and
  prayed,

Though I have seen my head [grown slightly
  bald] brought in upon a platter,
I am no prophet—and here's no great matter;
I have seen the moment of my greatness
  flicker,
And I have seen the eternal Footman hold
  my coat, and snicker,
And in short, I was afraid.

And would it have been worth it, after all,
After the cups, the marmalade, the tea,
Among the porcelain, among some talk of
  you and me,
Would it have been worth while,   90
To have bitten off the matter with a smile,
To have squeezed the universe into a ball
To roll it toward some overwhelming ques-
  tion,
To say: "I am Lazarus, come from the dead,
Come back to tell you all, I shall tell you
  all"—
If one, settling a pillow by her head,
    Should say: "That is not what I meant at
      all.
    That is not it, at all."

And would it have been worth it, after all,
Would it have been worth while,   100
After the sunsets and the dooryards and the
  sprinkled streets,
After the novels, after the teacups, after the
  skirts that trail along the floor—
And this, and so much more?—
It is impossible to say just what I mean!
But as if a magic lantern threw the nerves in
  patterns on a screen:
Would it have been worth while
If one, settling a pillow or throwing off a
  shawl,
And turning toward the window, should say:
    "That is not it at all,
    That is not what I meant, at all."   110

          . . . . .

No! I am not Prince Hamlet, nor was meant
  to be;
Am an attendant lord, one that will do
To swell a progress, start a scene or two,
Advise the prince; no doubt, an easy tool,
Deferential, glad to be of use,
Politic, cautious, and meticulous;

Full of high sentence, but a bit obtuse;
At times, indeed, almost ridiculous—
Almost, at times, the Fool.

I grow old . . . I grow old . . .   120
I shall wear the bottoms of my trousers rolled.

Shall I part my hair behind? Do I dare to
    eat a peach?
I shall wear white flannel trousers, and walk
    upon the beach.
I have heard the mermaids singing, each to
    each.

I do not think that they will sing to me.

I have seen them riding seaward on the
    waves
Combing the white hair of the waves blown
    back
When the wind blows the water white and
    black.

We have lingered in the chambers of the
    sea
By sea-girls wreathed with seaweed red and
    brown   130
Till human voices wake us, and we drown.

Sweeney Among the Nightingales (1920)

This poem is another one of Eliot's wry commentaries on the modern world. Our world prides itself on its frankness and honesty and on the absence of all illusions. In such a world, how would one relate a story of intrigue—say, that of Agamemnon murdered by his wife? If you are forced to treat these lordly personages as merely biological mechanisms, what will you have to say of lesser fry?

Sweeney is in a dive where one of the bar girls is making a pass at him, presumably to get him drunk or give him knockout drops and roll him for his wallet. Sweeney is described in almost purely animal terms, with allusions to the ape, zebra, and giraffe. He is aggressively "physical" and so are his gestures. The silent man in mocha brown is also (if other than Sweeney) described in biological terms: he is a "vertebrate," a classification which includes everything from men to mammoths and marmosets. Rachel has "paws" and her companion, "the person in the Spanish cape," is described almost as if she were a brainless automaton (see lines 17–20).

If this is the stress that the poet intends, then why all the literary folderol in the poem? The epigraph, from the *Agamemnon* of Aeschylus, is used for ironic contrast. (Agamemnon, having been axed by his wife after he has entered his palace, cries: "Oh me, I have been dealt a mortal blow within" (that is, inside the house). But why is there reference to Death and the

Raven? Why the rather luridly Poe-esque atmosphere?

In view of what follows, the Raven must be the constellation Corvo. Orion, two lines on, is the constellation thus named, and the Dog is presumably Canis Major. The poet is obviously providing a mock-epic background for his antihero, Sweeney.

Agamemnon's world, a world of gods and demigods and heroes, has been canceled. Apeneck Sweeney, of course, has never heard of it. Even the reader, who has, must now relegate it to obsolete "literary" bric-a-brac. The modern seas are indeed "shrunken" (line 10), though Eliot wrote this poem long before the advent of the jet plane, which now carries us across the seas in a few hours. To put the plot against Sweeney in the exalted terminology of an older mythical world is one way of sharpening our sense of the difference between that world and our own.

The second stanza provides a good example. The first two lines describe the moon with a ring around it (foretelling bad weather), moving on its natural course from east to west, toward the River Plate in South America—though the Mississippi or the Mekong would have pointed the proper direction just as well. To say that "Death and the Raven drift above" is a rather highfalutin way of expressing the foreboding. "And Sweeney guards the horned gate" is a mockingly grandiose way of saying that Sweeney himself is suspicious. In Homer's *Odyssey* we are told that when dreams are released from the underworld, the false ones come through the gates of ivory, but the dreams that foretell what is really going to happen make their way out through the gates of horn. Sweeney presumably does not know anything about the *Odyssey*, but he is here properly suspicious of the women. He is on his guard and stationed at the proper gate —the one through which the true intimations of what is going to happen issue forth.

To sum up, the poem presents modern man, without illusions, the most intelligent of the mammals (but merely that), operating in a mechanistic world; yet the poet employs for background echoes of intrigue as enacted in the old-fashioned mythopoetic world.

One asks himself what the nightingales are doing in this poem. They occupy the climactic position and they lend their name to its title. The nightingales, we may say, represent nature, with which mankind in the past has associated all sorts of spiritual qualities and which the poet Wordsworth, only a century and a half ago, wanted to believe actually sympathized with man. But modern man faces a neutralized nature—pure mechanism, beautiful if one wants to indulge the fancy that it is so, but in fact pitiless and indifferent. The nightingales sing as sweet an obbligato to the intrigue against Sweeney as they sang thousands of years ago to the assassination of Agamemnon. Actually they neither know nor care about the human world: they let their "liquid siftings fall" as impartially on the murdered king's shroud as they formerly let their melodious song fall on his living ears. In Keats's "Ode to a Nightingale," the song of the bird remains the same through the ages, though falling impartially on the ears of "emperor" or "clown."

ὤμοι, πέπλημαι καιρίαν πληγὴν ἔσω.

Whispers of Immortality (1920)

English literature of the early seventeenth century reflects an overpowering consciousness of

Apeneck Sweeney spreads his knees
Letting his arms hang down to laugh,
The zebra stripes along his jaw
Swelling to maculate giraffe.

The circles of the stormy moon
Slide westward toward the River Plate,
Death and the Raven drift above
And Sweeney guards the horned gate.

Gloomy Orion and the Dog
Are veiled; and hushed the shrunken seas;   10
The person in the Spanish cape
Tries to sit on Sweeney's knees

Slips and pulls the table cloth
Overturns a coffee-cup,
Reorganized upon the floor
She yawns and draws a stocking up;

The silent man in mocha brown
Sprawls at the window-sill and gapes;
The waiter brings in oranges
Bananas figs and hothouse grapes;   20

The silent vertebrate in brown
Contracts and concentrates, withdraws;
Rachel *née* Rabinovitch
Tears at the grapes with murderous paws;

She and the lady in the cape
Are suspect, thought to be in league;
Therefore the man with heavy eyes
Declines the gambit, shows fatigue,

Leaves the room and reappears
Outside the window, leaning in,   30
Branches of wistaria
Circumscribe a golden grin;

The host with someone indistinct
Converses at the door apart,
The nightingales are singing near
The Convent of the Sacred Heart,

And sang within the bloody wood
When Agamemnon cried aloud,
And let their liquid siftings fall
To stain the stiff dishonoured shroud.   40

death. John Webster (1580?–1625?), the dramatist, and John Donne (1571–1631), the great "metaphysical" poet, later Dean of St. Paul's, are striking instances.[1] But if their obsession with death contains an ingredient of terror, it apparently gave them also a heightened awareness of experience and particularly of sensuous experience. ("Luxuries" in line 8 of Eliot's poem carries something of its original meaning of "lechery."[2] But the intensification of the sensual did not for these poets exclude thought: rather thought itself took on a sensual character. Eliot has stated his belief that the metaphysical poets achieved in their work "a direct sensuous apprehension of thought, or recreation of thought into feeling. . . ."

These observations on and illustrations of a quality of mind in which thinking and feeling interpenetrate each other are abruptly broken off at the end of the fourth stanza, for stanza 5 presents a modern and contrasting picture, one of pure amiable sensuality. Grishkin is no "breastless creature under ground." She possesses a "friendly bust," she is very much alive, and her animality suffuses the atmosphere of any room in which she stands.

The speaker of the poem pays due respect to her magnetic attraction—and to his own altered intellectual situation. He is no Donne or Webster. Thought has now separated itself from feeling—and this is a serious loss. For even the Abstract Entities such as spirit, truth, beatitude yearn toward some concrete embodiment. As it is, they walk warily—the poet's term is "circumambulate"—around Grishkin's charm, much like aging men, now more or less impotent, but who nevertheless evidently respond to her sensuous invitation.

Perhaps one shouldn't press this last point too

hard, but it is interesting that for Webster the dead limbs seem to atract thought, which curls around them, and for Donne the bones have marrow and even suffer fever, as if in his day even the most nearly mineral part of man seemed alive with a deep passion and yearning. But the ribs between which it is the lot of us, the moderns, to "crawl" are dry, and the implication of the last line is that the metaphysics that we entertain are not really kept very warm: they offer a very chilly comfort indeed.

The clash between the two halves of the poem is brilliantly presented and makes its shocking impact. The reader's problem will be to see whether the two halves do more than clash, and whether it is possible to unify them in a total meaning.

We have suggested earlier that Eliot is here concerned with the difference between the intellectual climate of the seventeenth and twentieth centuries. In "The Metaphysical Poets" he goes on to say that after the collapse of metaphysical poetry there occurred a "dissociation of sensibility." Perhaps this is what is being described and illustrated in the last four stanzas. In any case, we do seem to have the polarization of the modern world: Grishkin in her maisonette and the metaphysician in his study. The poem might even be said to dramatize the Cartesian split.

Webster was much possessed by death
And saw the skull beneath the skin;
And breastless creatures under ground
Leaned backward with a lipless grin.

Daffodil bulbs instead of balls
Stared from the sockets of the eyes!
He knew that thought clings round dead limbs
Tightening its lusts and luxuries.

Donne, I suppose, was such another
Who found no substitute for sense,   10
To seize and clutch and penetrate;
Expert beyond experience,

He knew the anguish of the marrow
The ague of the skeleton;
No contact possible to flesh
Allayed the fever of the bone.

.   .   .   .

[1] Webster's plays are filled with images of death: for example, "Millions are now in graves, which at last day/ Like mandrakes shall rise shrieking" or "Thou art undone;/And thou hast ta'en that massy sheet of lead/ That hid thy husband's bones, and folded it/About thy heart." Donne often juxtaposes love and death: "And all your graces no more use shall have/Than a sun-dial in a grave" or "When my grave is broke up again/ . . . And he that digs it, spies/A bracelet of bright hair about the bone. . . ."

[2] See Emily Dickinson's similar use of this meaning of the word in her poem "Wild Nights — Wild Nights!" (p. 1242).

Grishkin is nice: her Russian eye
Is underlined for emphasis;
Uncorseted, her friendly bust
Gives promise of pneumatic bliss.   20

The couched Brazilian jaguar
Compels the scampering marmoset
With subtle effluence of cat;
Grishkin has a maisonette;

The sleek Brazilian jaguar
Does not in its arboreal gloom
Distil so rank a feline smell
As Grishkin in a drawing-room.

And even the Abstract Entities
Circumambulate her charm;   30
But our lot crawls between dry ribs
To keep our metaphysics warm.

Gerontion (1920)

"Gerontion" is a poem that deals with themes embodied in other forms in "Prufrock" and perhaps in "Whispers of Immortality." The title character (*gerontion* is the Greek word meaning "little old man") looks back on a lifetime in which he has been involved in no significant action and in which the sum of human history has revealed itself as yielding no meaning. Now as an impotent old man, living in memories which add up to nothing, he waits for death.

The epigraph from Shakespeare's *Measure for Measure* (3. 1. 32–34) provides a proper introduction to the theme and to the character of the man whose reverie makes up the stuff of the poem. In this passage from Shakespeare's play, Claudio, who has been condemned to death, is being prepared for death by a friar (actually the Duke of Vienna in disguise). The friar's "consolation" amounts to an argument that Claudio ought not to dread dying since living, when carefully considered, is revealed as worthless. As so often with Eliot, it is useful to quote further from the passage that he uses for an epigraph or to which he alludes. The friar's speech continues as follows:

>   for all thy blessed youth
> Becomes as aged, and doth beg the alms
> Of palsied eld: and when thou art old and rich,
> Thou hast neither heat, affection, limb, nor
>   beauty,
> To make thy riches pleasant. What's yet in this
> That bears the name of life? Yet in this life
> Lie hid more thousand deaths; yet death we
>   fear,
> That makes these odds all even.

Whatever the merit of the argument, and whatever the propriety of its application to Claudio, it beautifully represents Gerontion's own state of mind. Eliot obviously refers to it in lines 41–42 and 58–61.

The reader may find an even more useful lead into the poem in certain passages from Henry Adams' autobiography, *The Education of Henry Adams*. (See pp. 1495–1503.) In this work, the former Harvard history professor insists that his life-long attempt to educate himself has been a failure. He has discovered that history shows no meaning and that it was from a myth, a mere illusion, that men in an earlier and more naive period like the Middle Ages had drawn their power to make beautiful works of art and satisfying philosophy. As for himself, after sixty years he has found that the "ultimate triumph [of science was] the kinetic theory of gases; which seems to cover all motion in space, and to furnish the measure of time." To such an analysis "all matter whatever was reducible, and the only difference of opinion in science regarded the doubt whether a still deeper analysis would reduce the atom of gas to pure motion" may not be true. (In our time, of course, this deeper analysis—or something like it—has now been made. Analysis has reduced the atom to various particles of electrical energy.) So far as Adams is concerned, "the kinetic theory of gases" amounts to a theory of dispersal and disintegration: the universe, like a great machine, is simply running down. Such, for him, were the fruits of a lifetime of study. Now he finds himself to be "an ignorant old man [who] felt no motive for trying to escape [from the abyss of nothingness], seeing that the only escape possible lay in the form of *vis a tergo* [a push from behind] commonly called Death."

In a later, and characteristic, passage, Adams says: ". . . the human mind has always struggled . . . to escape the chaos which caged it" —the human mind which had appeared

> suddenly and inexplicably out of some unknown and unimaginable void; passing half its known life in the mental chaos of sleep; victim even when awake, to its own ill-adjustment, to disease, to age, to external suggestion, to nature's compulsion; doubting its own sensations, and, in that last resort, trusting only to instruments and averages—after sixty or seventy years of growing astonishment, the mind wakes to find itself looking blankly into the void of death.

Yet though the life and work of Henry Adams must have influenced this poem, we are not to assume that Gerontion *is* Adams. Gerontion is obviously a fictional figure and Eliot has given him his own quality, dramatizing his plight in a characteristically Eliotic way.

For example, Gerontion not only finds himself in "a dry month" but in a dry age: his whole meditation (which constitutes the poem) is dismissed in the last line as "thoughts of a dry brain in a dry season." He is an uprooted man living in a rented house, and the owner of the house is significantly himself a member of an uprooted people. The same blight affects his world that affects the world of Prufrock. Both characters are living a mere semblance of life, not the real thing. Like the speaker in "Rhapsody on a Windy Night," Gerontion's world has become empty and meaningless, his life no better than "an after dinner sleep."

> *Thou hast nor youth nor age*
> *But as it were an after dinner sleep*
> *Dreaming of both.*

Here I am, an old man in a dry month,
Being read to by a boy, waiting for rain.
I was neither at the hot gates
Nor fought in the warm rain
Nor knee deep in the salt marsh, heaving a
  cutlass,

Bitten by flies, fought.
My house is a decayed house,
And the jew squats on the window sill, the
  owner,
Spawned in some estaminet of Antwerp,
Blistered in Brussels, patched and peeled in
  London.   10
The goat coughs at night in the field over-
  head;
Rocks, moss, stonecrop, iron, merds.
The woman keeps the kitchen, makes tea,
Sneezes at evening, poking the peevish gutter.
                              I an old man,
A dull head among windy spaces.

Signs are taken for wonders. "We would see
  a sign!"
The word within a word, unable to speak a
  word,
Swaddled with darkness. In the juvescence of
  the year
Came Christ the tiger   20

In depraved May, dogwood and chestnut,
  flowering judas,
To be eaten, to be divided, to be drunk
Among whispers; by Mr. Silvero
With caressing hands, at Limoges
Who walked all night in the next room;

By Hakagawa, bowing among the Titians;
By Madame de Tornquist, in the dark room
Shifting the candles: Fräulein von Kulp
Who turned in the hall, one hand on the
  door.
    Vacant shuttles   30
Weave the wind. I have no ghosts,
An old man in a draughty house
Under a windy knob.

After such knowledge, what forgiveness? Think
  now
History has many cunning passages, contrived
  corridors
And issues, deceives with whispering ambitions,
Guides us by vanities. Think now
She gives when our attention is distracted
And what she gives, gives with such supple
  confusions
That the giving famishes the craving. Gives
  too late   40
What's not believed in, or if still believed,
In memory only, reconsidered passion. Gives
  too soon

Into weak hands, what's thought can be dis-
    pensed with
Till the refusal propagates a fear. Think
Neither fear nor courage saves us. Unnatural
    vices
Are fathered by our heroism. Virtues
Are forced upon us by our impudent crimes.
These tears are shaken from the wrath-bearing
    tree.

The tiger springs in the new year. Us he
    devours. Think at last
We have not reached conclusion, when I   50
Stiffen in a rented house. Think at last
I have not made this show purposelessly
And it is not by any concitation
Of the backward devils.
I would meet you upon this honestly.
I that was near your heart was removed there-
    from
To lose beauty in terror, terror in inquisition.
I have lost my passion: why should I need to
    keep it
Since what is kept must be adulterated?
I have lost my sight, smell, hearing, taste and
    touch: 60
How should I use them for your closer contact?

These with a thousand small deliberations
Protract the profit of their chilled delirium,
Excite the membrane, when the sense has
    cooled,
With pungent sauces, multiply variety
In a wilderness of mirrors. What will the spider
    do,
Suspend its operations, will the weevil
Delay? De Bailhache, Fresca, Mrs. Cammel,
    whirled
Beyond the circuit of the shuddering Bear
In fractured atoms. Gull against the wind, in
    the windy straits   70
Of Belle Isle, or running on the Horn.
White feathers in the snow, the Gulf claims,
And an old man driven by the Trades
To a sleepy corner.

               Tenants of the house,
Thoughts of a dry brain in a dry season.

NOTES

Line 1: Eliot is here following A. C. Benson's life of Edward Fitzgerald, the "translator" of *The Rubaiyat of Omar Khayyam,* who is described as sitting "in a dry month, old and blind, being read to by a country boy, and longing for rain."

Line 3: the "hot gates" translates the Greek place name Thermopylae where in 480 B.C. three hundred Spartans for three days held the narrow pass against the Persian host of Xerxes.

Line 13: Benson quotes from a letter that Fitzgerald wrote to Frederick Tennyson in which he described the place in which he was living: a "doleful place with a good fire, a cat and dog on the rug, an old woman in the kitchen. This is all my live-stock. The house is yet damp as last year; one of the great events of this winter is my putting up a trough around the eaves to carry off the wet."

Line 17: "An evil and adulterous generation seeks for a sign; but no sign shall be given to it except the sign of the prophet Jonah. For as Jonah was three days and three nights in the belly of the whale, so will the Son of Man be three days and three nights in the heart of the earth" (Matthew 12:39). That is, the sign to be given is that of Christ's own crucifixion, burial, and resurrection. But Christ, in the grave, "swaddled with darkness," brings to Eliot's (and to Gerontion's) mind a passage from a sermon by Lancelot Andrewes (1555–1626), a passage that Eliot has quoted in his essay on Andrewes. Andrewes is here preaching not about Christ in the tomb, but the Christ child in the manger, and he writes: "Signs are taken for wonders. 'Master, we would feign see a sign,' that is a miracle. And in this sense it is a sign to wonder at. Indeed, every word here is a wonder. . . . Verbum infans, the Word without a word; the eternal Word not able to speak a word; 1. a wonder sure. 2. And . . . swaddled; and that a wonder too."

Line 20: Christ is seen here not as the meek infant, but as the dynamic force that reshaped the nature of Western civilization. But he came not to prey upon human beings—to devour them—but to be eaten by them in the sacrament of Communion.

Lines 23–29: Mr. Silvero is one of those to whom Christ's flesh is offered. So also are Hakagawa, Madame de Tornquist, and Fräulein von Kulp; that is, Christ's flesh was offered to the whole world, as the international flavor of the names suggests. But the brief glimpses of these people suggest something other: that the sacramental meaning has been lost—that religion has become empty ritual, "art," spiritualism, or even perversion.

Eliot told F. O. Matthiessen that in inventing the names for such characters as Mr. Silvero and in presenting them in very brief vignettes, his purpose was "to give the *exact* perceived detail, without comment, and let that picture carry its own connotations." Eliot also said that "the images here are 'consciously concrete'; they correspond as closely as possible to something he has actually seen and remembered. But he also believes that if they are clearly rendered, they will stand for something larger than themselves; they will not depend for their apprehension upon any private references, but will become 'unconsciously general.' "

The whole passage is highly interesting as exhibiting the influence of the "Imagists" on Eliot. That is, we are not to expect to find Madame de Tornquist in any biographical dictionary but to catch her gesture as she shifts the candles in the dark room along with such implications as may reverberate from this scene. Does it suggest religion gone esoteric and "private"? Could Madame de Tornquist, for example, be a spirit medium?

Line 34: in an essay entitled "The Humanism of Irving Babbitt" Eliot writes of his old Harvard professor: "Professor Babbitt knows too much; and by that I do not mean merely erudition or information or scholarship. I mean that he knows too many religions and philosophies, has assimilated their spirit too thoroughly . . . to be able to give himself to any." The passage says in effect that one's knowing so many religions, having so many options, can prevent a person's making a commitment to any. Though it is commitment that is involved here and not forgiveness, the passage may throw some light on what Gerontion realizes is his own prime difficulty. He knows too much to believe in anything, and though Irving Babbitt is not any

more to be made the prototype of Gerontion than is Henry Adams, perhaps a little of Irving Babbitt went into the making of Gerontion.

Line 35: Henry Adams uses the phrase "the corridors of chaos" (*Education*, p. 402). The issue here is whether one can derive any values from history. Clearly one can, up to a point, test his values by seeing how they fare in the course of history. But to try to derive values from history is more difficult. The facts may not speak for themselves. Event A was caused by Event B, B was caused by C, C was caused by D, and on in infinite regression. But how can one hope to get back to the ultimate cause? Or even be clear as to the meaning of the concept of cause?

Line 48: this is usually interpreted as the tree of the knowledge of good and evil from which came the forbidden fruit eaten by Adam and Eve.

Line 49: Christ the tiger gave his body to be eaten; but rejected, he now springs and devours us. The truth which we are enjoined to follow, if denied exacts its penalty. Gerontion's is an evil generation without faith; see the note on line 17 above.

Lines 51–61: lines 34–50 have amounted to a meditation on the vanities and ironies of history as secularly conceived. With line 51 we observe a sudden shift in address to an unspecified "you." It might be claimed, of course, that here the "you" is to be understood merely as those of "us," the readers, who suffer the same spiritual malaise that Gerontion reflects on. But we should observe that in lines 23–28, in leading up to his generalizing meditations on history, Gerontion has referred to specific persons like Mr. Silvers, Hakagawa, Madame de Tornquist, and Fräulein von Kulp, personages presumably out of his own past, and that he will do so again (see line 68). It is thus not illogical to suppose that the "you" addressed with such sudden urgency and sharp emphasis represents a specific, though unnamed, person, the lost beloved of Gerontion, and a literal drama.

The details of that drama are not given, but we do witness the anguish and despair of the process of separation, and its painful conse-

quence he has become a mere thinking ma-
spiritual meaning in life, has lost too the capacity to experience the physical world. In consequence he has become a mere thinking machine—"a dull head among windy spaces." One
is tempted to say that Gerontion, now reduced
to "a dull head," is here addressing his lost
"heart"—the passionate former self. In any case,
the address has the emotional and sexual
timbre of a man speaking to a woman with
whom he was once in love and with whom he
became one flesh.

Incidentally, lines 51–61 may reflect something out of Eliot's personal experience—his
misery and despair during his first marriage.
Such anguished relations as are suggested by
this passage may well have existed at the time
of the poem's composition between the poet
and his first wife, who soon after the marriage
began to develop the "hysterical psychoses to
which she finally succumbed." The words are
those of Eliot's friend Sir Herbert Read, who
goes on to say that "Eliot's sufferings in these
years were acute." In fact, in 1921 the poet was
to suffer a severe nervous breakdown (see p.
2112).

Finally, we may point out that a literary
source for this passage is suggested by Eliot's
singling out for praise a section from Thomas
Middleton's *The Changeling* in his essay on
Middleton. That section begins: "I that am of
your blood was taken from you. . . ." See line
56 of "Gerontion."

Line 67: though it is clear that Gerontion will
continue to shuffle his dry thoughts without ever
reaching any conclusion, the spider and the
weevil will not wait. The forces of disintegration will end Gerontion's fruitless meditation,
whether it reaches a conclusion or not.

Line 68: this clump of names has an international flavor like those in lines 23–28 above. The
basic suggestion is the same: the whole civilization is breaking up. Death and disintegration
are no respecters of persons and Gerontion imagines Frenchmen, Spaniards, Englishmen, all participating in the whirl into interstellar spaces.

Line 69: Eliot here is remembering a passage
from George Chapman's play *Bussy d'Ambois*.
One of the characters speaks of men living in
the torrid zone and in the Arctic:

> where men feel
> The burning axle-tree, or those that suffer
> Under the chariot of the snowy Bear.

The snowy Bear is the constellation Ursa Major,
which in the Northern Hemisphere never sets
but seems to revolve around the pole star.

Line 70: in order to understand this figure,
one has to visualize a basic weather map of our
globe. In the temperate zones, the prevailing
westerlies blow. Between them and the equator,
the prevailing winds are the trade winds, in the
Northern Hemisphere blowing from the northeast to the southwest and in the Southern Hemisphere, from the southeast to the northwest. As
the trade winds approach the equator, their
warm air rises and the surface of the sea is calm.
This is the region of the doldrums, where sailing
ships sometimes waited for weeks for a wind to
fill their sails.

Both the straits of Belle Isle at the mouth of
the St. Lawrence River in the Northern Hemisphere and Cape Horn in the Southern Hemisphere are high up in the temperate regions and
have cold and bracing weather. In contrast to
the situation of Gerontion in his "doldrums,"
an old man "driven by the Trade/To a sleepy
corner," the poet imagines the gull, whether in
a high northern or a high southern latitude, flying "against the wind," an image of vitality and
grace. (Compare the vision of the mermaids
at the end of "The Love Song of J. Alfred
Prufrock.") True, the Gulf will eventually claim
the gull as it eventually claims every living thing.
The abyss of death claims all and will finally
claim Gerontion too. But the life of the gull has
power and beauty and presents a sharp contrast
to the "after dinner sleep" of Gerontion, who,
though "living," is not properly alive at all.

The Waste Land (1922)

In 1921 Eliot had suffered a breakdown that forced him to take leave from his work at Lloyd's Bank in London and to enter a sanatorium in Lausanne, Switzerland. There, much of *The Waste Land* was written. The original poem was much longer than the version published in the following year. In 1922 the manuscript was acquired by John Quinn, the New York lawyer and collector, and subsequently disappeared from sight. In 1968 it turned up among Quinn's papers in the Berg collection in the New York Public Library and was edited by the poet's widow and published in 1971 (*T. S. Eliot: The Waste Land. A Facsimile and Transcript of the Original Drafts including the Annotations of Ezra Pound*, edited by Valerie Eliot). A comparison of the manuscript version with *The Waste Land* as published in 1922 reveals how extensive were the excisions and revisions that Pound recommended, to most of which—though certainly not to all—Eliot agreed.

Pound's letters to Eliot in 1921 on the subject of the poem are amusing as well as informative. Pound playfully boasts to his friend that "on each Occasion" of the poem's parturitional difficulties "Ezra performed the Caesarean Operation." (See *The Letters of Ezra Pound*, 1950, edited by D. D. Paige.)

On its appearance in 1922 in the *Dial*, *The Waste Land* created something of a sensation. Some critics proclaimed that it expressed the disillusion of a generation, an intention emphatically denied by Eliot in 1934. Though today there is a substantial agreement about its meaning, the poem still presents some difficulties and they are reflected in the considerable variations in its interpretation.

"Prufrock" provides a good general introduction to *The Waste Land*, for the two poems have a similar theme, though in *The Waste Land* Eliot greatly extends and develops the techniques of presentation used in the earlier poem. The reader may well begin by assuming that he will find in *The Waste Land* the world of "Prufrock" as seen under a metaphor derived from the cursed land of the medieval legend. The reader should also keep in mind what has been said about "Gerontion" and what is said in that poem itself. Eliot, in fact, first planned to print "Gerontion" as a "prelude" to *The Waste Land*, but Pound suggested that he not. (See *The Letters of Ezra Pound*, p. 151.)

"Nam Sibyllam quidem Cumis ego ipse oculis meis vidi in ampulla pendere, et cum illi pueri dicerent: Σίβυλλα τί θέλεις; respondebat illa: ἀποθανεῖν θέλω."

> For Ezra Pound
> *il miglior fabbro.*

I. THE BURIAL OF THE DEAD

April is the cruellest month, breeding
Lilacs out of the dead land, mixing
Memory and desire, stirring
Dull roots with spring rain.
Winter kept us warm, covering
Earth in forgetful snow, feeding
A little life with dried tubers.
Summer surprised us, coming over the
    Starnbergersee
With a shower of rain; we stopped in
    the colonnade,
And went on in sunlight, into the Hofgarten,   10
And drank coffee, and talked for an hour.
Bin gar keine Russin, stamm' aus Litauen,
    echt deutsch.
And when we were children, staying at
    the arch-duke's,
My cousin's, he took me out on a sled,
And I was frightened. He said, Marie,
Marie, hold on tight. And down we went.
In the mountains, there you feel free.
I read, much of the night, and go south
    in the winter.

What are the roots that clutch, what
    branches grow
Out of this stony rubbish? Son of man,   20
You cannot say, or guess, for you know only
A heap of broken images, where the sun beats,

And the dead tree gives no shelter, the
 cricket no relief,
And the dry stone no sound of water. Only
There is shadow under this red rock,
(Come in under the shadow of this
 red rock),
And I will show you something different
 from either
Your shadow at morning striding behind you
Or your shadow at evening rising to
 meet you;
I will show you fear in a handful of dust. 30
    Frisch weht der Wind
    Der Heimat zu
    Mein Irisch Kind,
    Wo weilest du?
"You gave my hyacinths first a year ago;
"They called me the hyacinth girl."
—Yet when we came back, late, from the
 hyacinth garden,
Your arms full, and your hair wet, I
 could not
Speak, and my eyes failed, I was neither
Living nor dead, and I knew nothing, 40
Looking into the heart of light, the silence.
Oed' und leer das Meer.

Madame Sosostris, famous clairvoyante,
Had a bad cold, nevertheless
Is known to be the wisest woman in Europe,
With a wicked pack of cards. Here, said she,
Is your card, the drowned Phoenician Sailor,
(Those are pearls that were his eyes. Look!)
Here is Belladonna, the Lady of the Rocks,
The lady of situations. 50
Here is the man with three staves,
 and here the Wheel,
And here is the one-eyed merchant,
 and this card,
Which is blank, is something he carries
 on his back,
Which I am forbidden to see. I do not find
The Hanged Man. Fear death by water.
I see crowds of people, walking round
 in a ring.
Thank you. If you see dear Mrs. Equitone,
Tell her I bring the horoscope myself:
One must be so careful these days.

Unreal City, 60
Under the brown fog of a winter dawn,
A crowd flowed over London Bridge,
 so many,

I had not thought death had undone
 so many.
Sighs, short and infrequent, were exhaled,
And each man fixed his eyes before his feet.
Flowed up the hill and down King
 William Street,
To where Saint Mary Woolnoth kept
 the hours
With a dead sound on the final stroke
 of nine.
There I saw one I knew, and stopped him,
 crying: "Stetson!
"You who were with me in the ships
 at Mylae! 70
"That corpse you planted last year in
 your garden,
"Has it begun to sprout? Will it bloom
 this year?
"Or has the sudden frost disturbed its bed?
"O keep the Dog far hence, that's friend
 to men,
"Or with his nails he'll dig it up again!
"You! hypocrite lecteur!—mon semblable,
 —mon frère!"

II. A GAME OF CHESS

The Chair she sat in, like a burnished
 throne,
Glowed on the marble, where the glass
Held up by standards wrought with
 fruited vines
From which a golden Cupidon peeped out 80
(Another hid his eyes behind his wing)
Doubled the flames of sevenbranched
 candelabra
Reflecting light upon the table as
The glitter of her jewels rose to meet it,
From satin cases poured in rich profusion.
In vials of ivory and coloured glass
Unstoppered, lurked her strange synthetic
 perfumes,
Unguent, powdered, or liquid—troubled,
 confused
And drowned the sense in odours;
 stirred by the air
That freshened from the window, these
 ascended 90
In fattening the prolonged candle-flames,
Flung their smoke into the laquearia,
Stirring the pattern on the coffered ceiling.
Huge sea-wood fed with copper

Burned green and orange, framed by the
    coloured stone,
In which sad light a carvèd dolphin swam.
Above the antique mantel was displayed
As though a window gave upon the
    sylvan scene
The change of Philomel, by the barbarous
    king
So rudely forced; yet there the nightingale   100
Filled all the desert with inviolable voice
And still she cried, and still the world
    pursues,
"Jug Jug" to dirty ears.
And other withered stumps of time
Were told upon the walls; staring forms
Leaned out, leaning, hushing the room
    enclosed.
Footsteps shuffled on the stair.
Under the firelight, under the brush, her hair
Spread out in fiery points
Glowed into words, then would be
    savagely still.   110

"My nerves are bad to-night. Yes, bad.
    Stay with me.
"Speak to me. Why do you never speak.
    Speak.
   "What are you thinking of? What thinking?
    What?
"I never know what you are thinking. Think."

I think we are in rats' alley
Where the dead men lost their bones.

"What is that noise?"
                The wind under the door.
"What is that noise now? What is the
    wind doing?"
                Nothing again nothing.   120
                    "Do
"You know nothing? Do you see nothing?
    Do you remember
"Nothing?"

    I remember
Those are pearls that were his eyes.
"Are you alive, or not? Is there nothing
    in your head?"
                         But
O O O O that Shakespeherian Rag—
It's so elegant
So intelligent   130
"What shall I do now? What shall I do?"

"I shall rush out as I am, and walk the street
"With my hair down, so. What shall we
    do to-morrow?
"What shall we ever do?"
                      The hot water at ten.
And if it rains, a closed car at four.
And we shall play a game of chess,
Pressing lidless eyes and waiting for a
    knock upon the door.

When Lil's husband got demobbed,
    I said—
I didn't mince my words, I said to her
    myself,   140
HURRY UP PLEASE ITS TIME
Now Albert's coming back, make yourself
    a bit smart.
He'll want to know what you done with
    that money he gave you
To get yourself some teeth. He did,
    I was there.
You have them all out, Lil, and get a
    nice set,
He said, I swear, I can't bear to look at you.
And no more can't I, I said, and think
    of poor Albert,
He's been in the army four years, he wants
    a good time,
And if you don't give it him, there's others
    will, I said.
Oh is there, she said. Something o' that,
    I said.   150
Then I'll know who to thank, she said,
    and give me a straight look.
HURRY UP PLEASE ITS TIME
If you don't like it you can get on with it,
    I said.
Others can pick and choose if you can't.
But if Albert makes off, it won't be for
    lack of telling.
You ought to be ashamed, I said, to look
    so antique.
(And her only thirty one.)
I can't help it, she said, pulling a long face,
It's them pills I took, to bring it off, she said.
(She's had five already, and nearly died of
    young George.)   160
The chemist said it would be all right, but
    I've never been the same.
You are a proper fool, I said.
Well, if Albert won't leave you alone,
    there it is, I said,

What you get married for if you don't
    want children?
HURRY UP PLEASE ITS TIME
Well, that Sunday Albert was home, they
    had a hot gammon,
And they asked me in to dinner, to get the
    beauty of it hot—
HURRY UP PLEASE ITS TIME
HURRY UP PLEASE ITS TIME
Goonight Bill. Goonight Lou. Goonight
    May. Goonight.   170
Ta ta. Goonight. Goonight.
Good night, ladies, good night, sweet ladies,
    good night, good night.

III. THE FIRE SERMON

The river's tent is broken; the last fingers
    of leaf
Clutch and sink into the wet bank. The wind
Crosses the brown land, unheard. The
    nymphs are departed.
Sweet Thames, run softly, till I end my song.
The river bears no empty bottles, sandwich
    papers,
Silk handkerchiefs, cardboard boxes,
    cigarette ends
Or other testimony of summer nights. The
    nymphs are departed.
And their friends, the loitering heirs of
    City directors;   180
Departed, have left no addresses.
By the waters of Leman I sat down and
    wept . . .
Sweet Thames, run softly till I end my song,
Sweet Thames, run softly, for I speak not
    loud or long.
But at my back in a cold blast I hear
The rattle of the bones, and chuckle spread
    from ear to ear.
A rat crept softly through the vegetation
Dragging its slimy belly on the bank
While I was fishing in the dull canal
On a winter evening round behind the
    gashouse   190
Musing upon the king my brother's wreck
And on the king my father's death before him.
White bodies naked on the low damp ground
And bones cast in a little low dry garret,
Rattled by the rat's foot only, year to year.
But at my back from time to time I hear

The sound of horns and motors, which shall
    bring
Sweeney to Mrs. Porter in the spring.
O the moon shone bright on Mrs. Porter
And on her daughter   200
They wash their feet in soda water
*Et O ces voix d'enfants, chantant dans
    la coupole!*

Twit twit twit
Jug jug jug jug jug jug
So rudely forc'd.
Tereu

Unreal City
Under the brown fog of a winter noon
Mr. Eugenides, the Smyrna merchant
Unshaven, with a pocket full of currants   210
C.i.f. London: documents at sight,
Asked me in demotic French
To luncheon at the Cannon Street Hotel
Followed by a weekend at the Metropole.

At the violet hour, when the eyes and back
Turn upward from the desk, when the
    human engine waits
Like a taxi throbbing waiting,
I Tiresias, though blind, throbbing
    between two lives,
Old man with wrinkled female breasts, can see
At the violet hour, the evening hour that
    strives   220
Homeward, and brings the sailor home
    from sea,
The typist home at teatime, clears her
    breakfast, lights
Her stove, and lays out food in tins.
Out of the window perilously spread
Her drying combinations touched by the
    sun's last rays,
On the divan are piled (at night her bed)
Stockings, slippers, camisoles, and stays.
I Tiresias, old man with wrinkled dugs
Perceived the scene, and foretold the rest—
I too awaited the expected guest.   230
He, the young man carbuncular, arrives,
A small house agent's clerk, with one
    bold stare,
One of the low on whom assurance sits
As a silk hat on a Bradford millionaire.
The time is now propitious, as he guesses,
The meal is ended, she is bored and tired,
Endeavours to engage her in caresses

Which still are unreproved, if undesired.
Flushed and decided, he assaults at once;
Exploring hands encounter no defence;   240
His vanity requires no response,
And makes a welcome of indifference.
(And I Tiresias have foresuffered all
Enacted on this same divan or bed;
I who have sat by Thebes below the wall
And walked among the lowest of the dead.)
Bestows one final patronising kiss,
And gropes his way, finding the stairs
     unlit . . .

She turns and looks a moment in the glass,
Hardly aware of her departed lover;   250
Her brain allows one half-formed thought
     to pass.
"Well now that's done: and I'm glad it's over."
When lovely woman stoops to folly and
Paces about her room again, alone,
She smoothes her hair with automatic hand,
And puts a record on the gramophone.

"This music crept by me upon the waters"
And along the Strand, up Queen Victoria
     Street.
O City city, I can sometimes hear
Beside a public bar in Lower Thames Street,   260
The pleasant whining of a mandoline
And a clatter and a chatter from within
Where fishmen lounge at noon: where
     the walls
Of Magnus Martyr hold
Inexplicable splendour of Ionian white
     and gold.

          The river sweats
          Oil and tar
          The barges drift
          With the turning tide
          Red sails   270
          Wide
          To leeward, swing on the heavy spar.
          The barges wash
          Drifting logs
          Down Greenwich reach
          Past the Isle of Dogs.
               Weialala leia
               Wallala leialala

          Elizabeth and Leicester
          Beating oars   280
          The stern was formed
          A gilded shell

          Red and gold
          The brisk swell
          Rippled both shores
          Southwest wind
          Carried down stream
          The peal of bells
          White towers
               Weialala leia   290
               Wallala leialala

"Trams and dusty trees.
Highbury bore me. Richmond and Kew
Undid me. By Richmond I raised
     my knees
Supine on the floor of a narrow canoe."

"My feet are at Moorgate, and
     my heart
Under my feet. After the event
He wept. He promised 'a new start.'
I made no comment. What should
     I resent?"

"On Margate Sands.   300
I can connect
Nothing with nothing.
The broken fingernails of dirty hands.
My people humble people who expect
Nothing."
          la la

To Carthage then I came

Burning burning burning burning
O Lord Thou pluckest me out
O Lord Thou pluckest   310

burning

IV. DEATH BY WATER

Phlebas the Phoenician, a fortnight dead,
Forgot the cry of gulls, and the deep sea swell
And the profit and loss.
               A current under sea
Picked his bones in whispers. As he rose
     and fell
He passed the stages of his age and youth
Entering the whirlpool.
               Gentile or Jew
O you who turn the wheel and look to
     windward,   320
Consider Phlebas, who was once handsome
     and tall as you.

V. WHAT THE THUNDER SAID

After the torchlight red on sweaty faces
After the frosty silence in the gardens
After the agony in stony places
The shouting and the crying
Prison and palace and reverberation
Of thunder of spring over distant mountains
He who was living is now dead
We who were living are now dying
With a little patience   330

Here is no water but only rock
Rock and no water and the sandy road
The road winding above among the mountains
Which are mountains of rock without water
If there were water we should stop and drink
Amongst the rock one cannot stop or think
Sweat is dry and feet are in the sand
If there were only water amongst the rock
Dead mountain mouth of carious teeth
      that cannot spit
Here one can neither stand nor lie nor sit   340
There is not even silence in the mountains
But dry sterile thunder without rain
There is not even solitude in the mountains
But red sullen faces sneer and snarl
From doors of mudcracked houses
                        If there were water
      And no rock
      If there were rock
      And also water
      And water   350
      A spring
      A pool among the rock
      If there were the sound of water only
      Not the cicada
      And dry grass singing
      But sound of water over a rock
      Where the hermit-thrush sings in the
          pine trees
      Drip drop drip drop drop drop drop
      But there is no water

Who is the third who walks always
      beside you?   360
When I count, there are only you and I
      together
But when I look ahead up the white road
There is always another one walking
      beside you
Gliding wrapt in a brown mantle, hooded
I do not know whether a man or a woman
—But who is that on the other side of you?

What is that sound high in the air
Murmur of maternal lamentation
Who are those hooded hordes swarming
Over endless plains, stumbling in cracked earth   370
Ringed by the flat horizon only
What is the city over the mountains
Cracks and reforms and bursts in the violet air
Falling towers
Jerusalem Athens Alexandria
Vienna London
Unreal

A woman drew her long black hair out tight
And fiddled whisper music on those strings
And bats with baby faces in the violet light   380
Whistled, and beat their wings
And crawled head downward down a
          blackened wall
And upside down in air were towers
Tolling reminiscent bells, that kept the hours
And voices singing out of empty cisterns
      and exhausted wells.

In this decayed hole among the mountains
In the faint moonlight, the grass is singing
Over the tumbled graves, about the chapel
There is the empty chapel, only the
          wind's home.
It has no windows, and the door swings,   390
Dry bones can harm no one.
Only a cock stood on the rooftree
Co co rico co co rico
In a flash of lightning. Then a damp gust
Bringing rain

Ganga was sunken, and the limp leaves
Waited for rain, while the black clouds
Gathered far distant, over Himavant.
The jungle crouched, humped in silence.
Then spoke the thunder   400
DA
Datta: what have we given?
My friend, blood shaking my heart
The awful daring of a moment's surrender
Which an age of prudence can never retract
By this, and this only, we have existed
Which is not to be found in our obituaries
Or in memories draped by the beneficent
          spider
Or under seals broken by the lean solicitor
In our empty rooms   410
DA
Dayadhvam: I have heard the key
Turn in the door once and turn once only

We think of the key, each in his prison
Thinking of the key, each confirms a prison
Only at nightfall, aethereal rumours
Revive for a moment a broken Coriolanus
Dᴀ
Damyata: The boat responded
Gaily, to the hand expert with sail and oar
The sea was calm, your heart would have   420
    responded
Gaily, when invited, beating obedient
To controlling hands

            I sat upon the shore
Fishing, with the arid plain behind me
Shall I at least set my lands in order?
London Bridge is falling down falling down
    falling down
Poi s'ascose nel foco che gli affina
Quando fiam uti chelidon—O swallow swallow
Le Prince d'Aquitaine à la tour abolie
These fragments I have shored against   430
    my ruins
Why then Ile fit you. Hieronymo's mad
    againe.
Datta. Dayadhvam. Damyata.
        Shantih   shantih   shantih

NOTES

When *The Waste Land* first appeared, it made its chief impact on the young. This impact was the result, of course, of its intrinsic power—those who read it for the first time found the local excitement of particular scenes, passages, and even individual lines enough to grip the imagination. This is not to say, however, that the notes which accompanied the poem were excess baggage. After his first encounter, the reader found that the notes at the least provided a dramatic context giving new dimensions of meaning to the poem by setting it in a long historical perspective. This dramatic context may well be the most important contribution the notes made. But more specifically, they elucidated, by their reference to Jesse Weston, the basic image suggested in the title and developed in the body of the poem.

Nowadays, the notes are sometimes too airily dismissed. If Eliot had not supplied a single note, his readers would eventually have done so,

for *The Waste Land*, with its highly charged material, is very much a poem of this age—an age in which most readers of poetry have at least a smattering of anthropology, depth psychology, and comparative religion. The readers themselves would have soon begun to note down ironic parallels and teasing juxtapositions, to develop hints of symbolism, and put back together *disjecta membra*.

The legend, from which the title of the poem derives, has to do with the parched land ruled over by a maimed and impotent king. His castle stands on the banks of a river and he is called the Fisher King. The fate of the land is bound up with the fate of its lord. Until he is healed, the land will remain under the curse: cattle will not breed; the crops will not grow. The curse may be removed only if a knight is bold enough to make his way to the castle and inquire as to the meanings of the various objects that will be shown to him.

In her book *From Ritual to Romance*,[1] Miss Jessie Weston argues that the Fisher King was originally the vegetation god whose death was mourned in the dying year, but whose triumphant return as expressed in the renewed life of nature was celebrated in the spring. According to Miss Weston this fertility cult was widely disseminated through Europe, and the principal carriers of its mysteries were soldiers and Syrian merchants. The story of the Fisher King was later Christianized in the Grail legends which show that they are reminiscent of an initiation rite. The candidate's courage was tested by making a journey to the Perilous Chapel, around which demons seemed to howl. Moreover, when the candidate arrived at the Castle of the Fisher King, he had to take the initiative in seeking the truth—had to demand the meaning of the various symbols, if the secret doctrine was to be revealed. What was then disclosed to him was the interrelation of death and birth with its

---

[1] In his notes on the poem, Eliot writes: "Not only the title, but the plan and a good deal of the symbolism of the poem were suggested by" this book. "I recommend it . . . to any who think . . . elucidation of the poem worth the trouble."

corollary truth that the way into life was through death.

The waste-land symbolism is echoed in a number of incidents in the poem, for example, in the fortune-telling scene (lines 43–59) where Madame Sosostris uses the Tarot pack. Miss Weston traces the symbols used on the Tarot cards back to the symbolism of the fertility cult. The cards were probably used in ancient Egypt to predict the rise of the waters upon which the prosperity of a whole people depended. (We may also see the fortune-telling scene as the presentation of the symbols whose meaning the questing knight must ask if the curse is to be lifted.)

The waste-land symbolism is reflected also in the reference to Mr. Eugenides (line 209). He is a modern descendant of the Syrian merchants who, like Phlebas the Phoenician (section 4), once brought the mysteries to faraway Britain. "Eugenides" means "son of the well born," but his function is now degraded. His invitation to a "weekend at the Metropole" does not promise initiation into the secret of life but into a cult of empty, and perhaps perverted, pleasure. The agonized journey to the chapel (section 5) alludes to the journey to the Perilous Chapel, which was part of the initiation ceremony.

For the reader of this poem, the waste-land legend has a special relevance. The poet is attempting to dramatize for us what it feels like to live in a secularized world—a world emptied of religious meaning. But the prime difficulty for the modern reader is that he may be himself so thoroughly numbed by secularization that he cannot see what the poet is talking about. The poet has therefore adopted the device of putting the reader into something of the position of the knight in the Grail legends. The knight in the story was able to remove the curse only if he questioned what he saw—only if he demanded meanings of the symbols shown to him. If he merely marveled at them, the truth was not revealed to him. If we are to experience the poem —as opposed to being merely "told" about the theme—we must be alert for the significance of what we see. Otherwise we shall find a mere

jumble of fragments that can be tied together in terms of an abstract and arbitrary scheme, but which never unite in felt significance.

Eliot finds in the Bible and in Dante further analogues for what he considers to be the state of the contemporary world. He takes the phrase "Son of man" (line 20) from Ezekiel 2. The relevant passage reads:

1. And he said unto me, Son of man, stand upon thy feet, and I will speak unto thee. 2. And the spirit entered into me when he spake unto me and set me upon my feet, that I heard him that spake unto me. 3. And he said unto me, Son of man, I send thee to the children of Israel, to a rebellious nation that hath rebelled against me: they and their fathers have transgressed against me, even unto this very day.

Though Eliot in the notes he appended to *The Waste Land* does not refer to Ezekiel 37, it too bears upon the poem, for there the prophet describes his vision of a waste land—a valley of dry bones. He is asked (verse 3), "Son of man, can these bones live? And I answered, O Lord God, thou knowest [verse 4]. Again he said unto me, Prophesy over these bones, and say unto them, O ye dry bones, hear the word of the Lord."

Ecclesiastes 12 (to which Eliot's note on line 23 refers) also describes a parched and nightmare world:

1. Remember now thy Creator in the days of thy youth, while the evil days come not, nor the years draw nigh, when thou shalt say, I have no pleasure in them; 2. While the sun, or the light, or the moon, or the stars, be not darkened, nor the clouds return after the rain; 3. In the day when the keepers of the house shall tremble, and the strong men shall bow themselves, and the grinders cease because they are few, and those that look out of the windows be darkened, 4. And the doors shall be shut in the streets, when the sound of the grinding is low, and he shall rise up at the voice of the bird, and all the daughters of music shall be brought low; 5. Also when

they shall be afraid of that which is high, and fears shall be in the way, and the almond tree shall flourish, and the grasshopper shall be a burden, and desire shall fail: because man goeth to his long home, and the mourners go about the streets; 6. Or ever the silver cord be loosed, or the golden bowl be broken, or the pitcher be broken at the fountain, or the wheel broken at the cistern. 7. Then shall the dust return to the earth as it was: and the spirit shall return unto God who gave it. 8. Vanity of vanities, saith the preacher; all is vanity.

This vision also matches the landscape described in section 5 of *The Waste Land* and various details of the poem seem to have been drawn from it.

The modern waste land also resembles Dante's Hell. Eliot's notes on line 63 refer us to Canto 3 of the *Inferno*; his note on line 64, to Canto 4. Canto 3 describes the place of those who on earth had "lived without praise or blame." They share this antechamber of hell with the angels "who were not rebels, nor were faithful to God, but were for themselves." These then are the "trimmers," those who make no commitment. Now they bewail the fact that they "have no hope of death." But though they may not hope for death,[2] Dante scornfully calls them "these unfortunate who never were alive." To have real life demands a kind of commitment which men too fearful of death can never make.[3]

[2] This is the hopeless wish of the Sibyl in the epigraph at the beginning of the poem. The passage is from the *Satyricon* of Petronius. "For indeed I saw with my own eyes the Sibyl at Cumae, hanging in a cage, and when the boys would say to her, 'Sibyl, what do you want'; she would answer, 'I want to die.' " The Sibyl was a prophetess to whom the god Apollo had granted a thousand years of life, but she had forgotten to ask for youth as well.

[3] The following passage from the work of a modern psychiatrist bears on this point. He writes: "During the last war I had frequent occasion to note that those who vegetate more than they live [see lines 1–6 of *The Waste Land*] were the most afraid and the first to run for the shelters during air raids. Panic was always greatest in hospitals for incurable cases and homes for old

Keeping in mind the three realms of negation and sterility (as described in the Grail legend, the Bible, and Dante), let us see how Eliot has developed his poem. In section 1, there pass through the speaker's mind glimpses of a world that is tired and timid, bored and yet uneasy, preferring the half-life of winter to the violent renewal of the energies of spring. It is a world that fears death as the greatest evil, but is disturbed by the idea of birth, and certainly sees birth and death as utterly distinct. There are reflections on the character of this world (lines 1–7; 20–30) intermingled with memories of specific scenes (lines 8–18; 35–41). These are interspersed with scraps of song or remembered bits of poetry.

It is a world apprehensive of the future and eager for signs and portents, even though it cannot believe in them. The hero has his fortune told, and in contrast to the almost prophetic injunction of line 30, "I will show you fear in a handful of dust," is admonished by the fortune-teller to "Fear death by water."

The crowds going over London Bridge on their way to work in the foggy winter dawn remind the protagonist of the multitude of the

people." So writes Ignatz Lepp, in *Death and Its Mysteries* (1968, pp. 38–39). He goes on to tell of a house servant in his employ whose life was miserable. Her drunkard husband beat her and she suffered from a terminal disease. Yet she was the first to race for the shelter, for the thought of death terrified her, and especially the thought of a violent death.

On the other hand, Lepp says that he "observed that those whose lives were full and exciting faced death calmly and courageously." He tells of a very pretty girl, twenty-one, a good student, deeply in love, who in spite of her parents' remonstrances risked death every day during the raids. "She was well aware of the danger. Nor was there any question in her case of heroism or temerity. She simply did what she took to be her duty."

The fact that the old woman was killed in a cellar where she had been hiding whereas the young woman survived the war, as Lepp properly points out, "obviously proves nothing, unless it might be that panic fear is far from being a certain indication of the instinct for preservation." And he adds that it "is only apparently paradoxical that those in love with life are less afraid of death than those who live superficially. On a deeper psychological view, this is perfectly normal."

dead whom Dante saw in his vision of Hell. These people in their meaningless activity are dead, not really alive.

The theme of death, sterility, and meaninglessness receives a more complicated treatment in the closing lines of section 1. In the age of the fertility cults the ritual burial of the god was undertaken in the confidence that his energies, like those of nature, would revive again. The life of nature was not only dependent on the god's powers: it offered a specific example of his powers. Bury the seed of corn and the corn would spring up again. But now the burial of the dead is without hope. The jeering question about the possibilities of the sprouting of that "corpse you planted in your garden" implies its answer.

Modern man, like his ancient ancestors, has indeed "buried" the god—the fertility god, the Christian God, indeed the very conception of divinity; and the god has died at man's own hands. (In a celebrated pronouncement Friedrich Nietzsche told us that "we have murdered" God.) The "you" of line 71 (like that of line 76) is addressed to the reader: each of us in our secularized age has buried god in our garden, doesn't expect the corpse to sprout, and would feel consternation if it did.

Line 74 parodies a line from the dirge in John Webster's play *The White Devil:*

Call for the robin-redbreast and the wren,
Since o'er shady groves they hover,
And with leaves and flowers do cover
The friendless bodies of unburied men.
    Call unto his funeral dole
    The ant, the field-mouse, and the mole,
To rear him hillocks that shall keep him warm,
And, when gay tombs are robbed, sustain no
        harm;
But keep the wolf far thence, that's foe to men,
For with his nails he'll dig them up again.

Webster's dirge does not have to do with the burial of the fertility god, but is an invocation to nature to cover the "friendless bodies of unburied men," men who have died in the wilderness and have been deprived of Christian rites

of burial. In the Christian scheme, man is a fallen creature and he has involved nature in his fall; even so, man has not lost all contact with God; nor has nature. Most important of all, in this conception, the world of nature has not been "neutralized"—to use I. A. Richards' term. Nature contains both the robin-redbreast and the wolf "that's foe to men," and one can sometimes appeal to it against the malignancy of wicked men. A Jacobean poet like Webster or Shakespeare can, without any sense of contradiction, call a wicked human being "unnatural." In Webster's poem nature still retains some of its energies and mysterious powers.

Not so in the suburban garden in which the secularized man has "planted" the corpse, which appears here as suggesting both that of the fertility god and that of any ordinary human being. In any case, all our patented fertilizers can't be expected to make it bloom. Nature has, indeed, been neutralized; and even the wolf has been domesticated into the friendly dog. Man has tamed him along with taming nature. The real enemy to the god's resurrection lies precisely here: Fido will scratch up the body out of pure friendliness. Man's belief that he can totally master nature and make it a mere extension of his powers is part of the process of secularization.

In this first section the one scene of ecstasy and beauty is the memory of the incident outside the hyacinth garden. It recalls a moment not of half-life but of full life; and yet the protagonist says that in that moment "I was neither /Living nor dead." But *ecstasy* means a state of being that lies outside normal life. Far from being "lifeless," it is surcharged with life. Compare "I could not/Speak . . . and I knew nothing" in this passage with "Do/You know nothing? Do you see nothing?" (lines 121–22) in the next section. The passages register with entirely different effect.

Section 2 is in a sense the most easily comprehended section of the poem. We have in it two vignettes of life in the waste land, having to do with two women from opposite ends of the social scale: the woman in the rich room, and Lil, who is discussed by her two Cockney friends in the pub. But both women are frustrated and unhappy; for both, "love" is a problem—for the one whose nerves are bad and who threatens to rush out into the street, and for the other who has had an abortion and dreads the return to childbearing now that her husband has been demobilized. Both are symbols of the spiritual sterility of the modern secular world though they represent opposed aspects of the modern world: the degradation of the slum and the neuroticism of the drawing room.

Lines 77–78 associate the first woman with Cleopatra as she first appeared to Antony on the River Cydnus (see Shakespeare, *Antony and Cleopatra,* 2. 2. 190). But the richness of the room simply comments ironically upon the essential emptiness of the woman's life. The decoration of the room reflects the richness of the cultural heritage; but the symbols are meaningless to her and the past is dead; so that the poem suddenly dismisses the rest of the decor of the room at line 104 as "other withered stumps of time." There is no real communication between her and her lover (or husband) who sits in the room with her. She finally demands desperately, "Are you alive, or not? Is there nothing in your head?" She can see in her life no purpose—only a monotonous round of activities: "The hot water at ten./And if it rains, a closed car at four." The meaning of her life is as arbitrary as that of a game of chess.

The pathetic sordidness of Lil's life comes out as her friends discuss her over their beer. The barman's notice that it is closing time is heard more and more urgently, until finally he manages to hustle the women out of the pub.

The river dominates section 3: the modern river, its banks littered with debris, and the Elizabethan river as described in Spenser's "Prothalamion," the scene of stately bridals. The protagonist walks through the city down to the river front, and the river is seen again, the modern river, sweating "oil and tar," the river on which Queen Elizabeth rode in her barge of state, and, once more, the modern river, the scene of sordid love affairs.

The love theme suggested in the river scenes finds explicit development in the central episode of this section: the meeting of the typist and the carbuncular young man, whose love affair has no meaning beyond the action of biological mechanism. The automatism is reflected even in the verse. The young woman "stoops to folly," but she is not betrayed because she is not deluded, expects nothing, and thus loses nothing. The poet's rewriting of Goldsmith's poem, with the alteration of theme, mood, and even the quality of rhythm, conveys brilliantly the contrast between two radically different conceptions of the same act. She is not stricken with horror and remorse. She doesn't feel anything at all. Her automatic gesture of smoothing her hair as she puts a record on the gramophone signifies that the act of love for her is meaningless.

Philomela, the maiden who in the Greek legend was raped and mutilated by her brother-in-law and later was transformed into a nightingale, achieved her music through suffering; through her violation comes the "inviolable voice" (line 101). The typist, of course, is not violated, but there is no inviolable music either—simply the automatic music of the gramophone.

One other allusion of considerable importance figures in this third section. It is the song from Shakespeare's *Tempest,* "Full fathom five thy father lies." Here, as in the Philomela story, the song promises that hurt and loss will be transmuted to richness and beauty. In the fertility cult, death was transformed into life: the seed was buried to flourish again as a plant; the god died to rise again. In Shakespeare's play, the young Prince Ferdinand wanders disconsolately along the shores of Prospero's island after the shipwreck, sorrowing over his father's death (see line 192). As he wanders there, he hears Ariel's song, "Full fathom five thy father lies," music which seems to him to come from no mortal source. Led on by the music, he finds Miranda and love, and later will find his father alive and transformed by his experience on the island.

Fragments of this song have haunted the speaker through the day. At the fortuneteller's, mention of the card of the drowned "Phoenician sailor" brings into his head the line "Those are pearls that were his eyes" (line 48); and in

section 2, when he is asked "Do you see nothing? Do you remember/Nothing?" he remembers inconsequentially "Those are pearls that were his eyes" (line 125). Now, as he walks behind the gashouse, he remembers Prince Ferdinand's sorrowful wandering, but death presents to his mind no bones turned to coral or eyes to pearls. There has been no transformation "into something rich and strange," only dry bones "Rattled by the rat's foot only, year to year" (line 195). And the music that creeps by him on the waters (line 257) is that from the typist's gramophone.

In the monotonous world of the waste land, even time has a different character. Consciousness of time is not felt as an insistent urgency to action as in Andrew Marvell's "To His Coy Mistress." Marvell, at his back, "always" hears "Time's winged Chariot"; the protagonist hears "From time to time" (line 196), not "Time's winged Chariot" but the sound of "horns and motors" (line 197), the noise of the London traffic.

Perhaps in this section the one modern scene that possesses vitality and beauty is that described in lines 260–65. The magnificent church built by Christopher Wren is now surrounded by squalid buildings; but the whining mandolin is "pleasant," and the fishmen are alive ("a clatter and a chatter from within"), and the church still holds "Inexplicable splendour of Ionian white and gold." There is here the sense of a life quite other than the half-life that dominates the other scenes. At the literal level, these poor fishmen have vitality; at the symbolic level, they are associated with the fish, symbol of fertility. Section 3 ends with the "burning" and the world portrayed in this section is depicted as burning with sterile lust.

The brief lyric interlude furnished by section 4 presents a contrast: not sterile burning, but drowning; not half-death, but actual death; and not the dry bones in the low dry garret, but bones picked by the sea currents in whispers. Though one may be tempted to take this passage as merely a simple contrast—a shift in tone and mood—the passage is heavily "charged" by the three sections that precede it. Phlebas is

one of the Syrian merchants. This is a "death by water" that Madame Sosostris had admonished the hero to fear. Whether or not Phlebas here suffers a "sea change/Into something rich and strange," there is at least a sense of peace and forgetfulness. Profit and loss no longer disturb him. He has returned to the source of all life, the sea, and there is even the sense of regression—"passed the stages of his age and youth"—as if he were now retracing his journey from the womb.

This section, like section 1, ends in an address to all men: "O you who turn the wheel and look to windward"—that is, you who like Phlebas steer your ship and watch the weather signs —you who think that you direct your own course and are confident that you are not merely turning helplessly on the "wheel," moving in meaningless circles—do not forget that Phlebas, once as strong as you, could not avoid the whirlpool. Death is a fact that cannot be evaded.

Section 5 gives the sense of a painful journey through a landscape of nightmare. The god has died. Lines 322–23 suggest Christ's agony in the Garden of Gethsemane; lines 324–25, his trial before Pilate and his crucifixion: "He who was living is now dead." But for those who cannot believe in him, he is now in a special sense dead; and the unbelievers, being the people of the waste land, are themselves not really alive: "We who were living are now dying/With a little patience" (lines 329–30).

The lines that follow suggest an experience in which the drought-tormented traveler suffers from delirium. The speaker is haunted by the sense of an unseen presence. The two apostles on the road to Emmaus (Luke 24:13–31) after the crucifixion found themselves walking beside a stranger who later revealed himself to them as the risen Christ. Here no revelation is made, and the sense of hallucination is extended into a nightmare vision of a topsy-turvy world. The city, like a city seen inverted as in a mirage, "Cracks and reforms and bursts in the violet air." The towers are "upside down in air," the bells which ring from them are "reminiscent," and voices sing out of "exhausted wells."

The civilization is breaking up; reality and

unreality seem to mix. The woman who exclaimed "I shall rush out as I am, and walk the street/With my hair down, so" (lines 132–33) reappears, and having drawn "her long black hair out tight/ . . . [fiddles] whisper music from those strings" (lines 378–79). The bats with "baby faces" and the voices "singing out of empty cisterns and exhausted wells" point to a nightmare of sterile longing.

The nightmare journey is made to take on the character of the initiate's journey to the Perilous Chapel. The Chapel is deserted and apparently abandoned, and made the more ominous thereby. But the cock upon the rooftree, as the lightning flashes, crows: and there is "a damp gust/ Bringing rain," the promise of relief.

The lightning flash is followed by the clap of thunder. The sound of the thunder is represented by the onomatopoeic syllable "da." But the poet takes advantage of its occurrence as the first syllable of the Sanskrit words "datta" (give), "dayadhvam" (sympathize), and "damyata" (control).[4] What the thunder says contains the secret for removing the curse. The unwillingness to give of oneself—to make a positive commitment—is bound up with the sense of isolation and with the paralysis of action which are the special characteristics of the waste land. "Give," "sympathize," and "control" answer to the situation, point by point.

The passages that follow each of these words comment upon them and relate them to situations presented earlier in the poem. Man cannot be absolutely self-regarding. Even the propagation of the race calls for a commitment and surrender. To live demands belief in something more than "life."

The surrender to something outside the self is an attempt (whether on the sexual level or some other) to transcend one's essential isolation. We are each of us shut up within the private world of our thoughts and sensations just as Count Ugolino was locked within his tower (see *Inferno*, Canto 33). Only "for a moment" can the "broken Coriolanus" be revived. (For

Coriolanus as a figure of pride, see Shakespeare's play of that name.)

The comment on the thunder's third command echoes, and contrasts with, "Death by Water." Instead of the passivity of the drowned sailor, Phlebas, rising and falling with the sea currents, here the sailor dominates the boat so thoroughly that it seems an extension of his own will. It responds "gaily." To say "your heart would have responded gaily" implies that the heart has not. The speaker's condition has been negative. (The command to give prompts in him the question: "what have we given?" The command to sympathize reminds him that he has heard the key turn "once only." There must be a second turning of the key if his prison is to be unlocked.)

By interpreting the rumbling of the thunder in terms of Sanskrit words, the poet extends his reference back to the earliest history of the race. The fable of the meaning of the thunder is found in one of the Upanishads and thus the ancient wisdom can be found couched in the earliest surviving form of the primordial language from which most of the modern European languages are finally derived.

The poem does not end, however, with a downpour of the reviving rain. The speaker's perception of the ancient wisdom cannot in itself lift the general curse. Yet if secularization has destroyed or is likely to destroy modern civilization, the speaker has his own private obligations to fulfill. Even if London Bridge is falling down, "Shall I at least set my lands in order?"

"The fragments" which the protagonist has "shored against [his] ruins" may seem to furnish a difficult and unsatisfactory ending for the poem. But if we know from what they are taken and of what they are fragments, we shall find that though they measure the desperate plight of the protagonist, they are more than a jumble: they shore up his ruins to some purpose. Line 428, to be translated "Then he hid him in the fire which refines them," is spoken in Dante's *Purgatorio* by the poet Arnaut who says to Dante, "I am Arnaut that weep and go a-singing; in thought I see my past madness, and I

---

[4] The onomatopoeic effect is not, of course, limited to the syllable "da." "Dayadhvam," for example, admirably suggests the rolling thunder peal.

see with joy the day which I await before me." His is no meaningless suffering and he steps back into the refining fire with joy.[5]

Line 429 ("When shall I be like the swallow") is taken from the *Pervigilium Veneris*, a late Latin poem. That poem too ends on a note of hope with the refrain "Tomorrow may he who has never loved and he who has loved, make love." (Our translation of these lines is by Allen Tate.)

Line 430 ("The Prince of Aquitaine at the ruined tower") is taken from "El Desdichado" (The Disinherited), a sonnet by Gerard de Nerval. The poem ends with lines that may be translated: "I have twice crossed Acheron [the river of Hell] victorious: modulating upon the lyre of Orpheus, by turns, the sighs of the saints and the cries of the fay." Like him, the protagonist in *The Waste Land* has come back from Hell. The ruined tower is the Perilous Chapel, and it is also the whole tradition in decay. The protagonist resolves to claim his tradition and rehabilitate it. "Why then Ile fit you" in line 432 comes from an Elizabethan play, *The Spanish Tragedy*, the subtitle of which is "Hieronymo's mad againe." In order to avenge the murder of his son, Hieronymo feigns madness. When he is asked to write a play for the court's entertainment, he replies:

Why then, I'll fit you; say no more.
When I was young, I gave my mind
And plied myself to fruitless poetry;
Which though it profit the professor naught,
Yet it is passing pleasing to the world.

He sees that the play will give him the opportunity he has been seeking to avenge his son's murder. Like Hieronymo (and like Arnaut and El Desdichado), the protagonist has now found his theme; what he is about to perform is not "fruitless."

The various parts in Hieronymo's play are written in various foreign tongues (compare the cluster of quotations with which this poem ends). When the courtiers protest that this device will make the play "a mere confusion," Hieronymo persists; and his odd scheme is accepted, presumably in order to humor his madness.

The poet's manner of proceeding here may seem mad in the same way, the poem ending in a "mere confusion." But if we understand that the poem is about the breakup of a culture and if we have seen the importance of the fact of convergence of many cultures upon a common theme, then the method makes sense. There is a further justification for this ending: the protagonist is conscious that the words with which the poem closes will seem to many to be a meaningless babbling, though they contain the oldest and most permanent truth of the race:[6] "Datta. Dayadhvam. Damyata." There is one more roll of the thunder: "Shantih Shantih Shantih." Eliot's note tells us that these Sanskrit words as repeated here are equivalent to our "The Peace that passeth understanding."

In the preceding account of the poem we have neglected many incidental allusions and special references. These will be identified in the notes that conclude this section.

The basic method used in *The Waste Land* may be described as follows: the poet works in terms of surface parallelisms which in reality make ironical contrasts, and in terms of surface contrasts which in reality constitute parallelisms. The fortunetelling of "The Burial of the Dead" will illustrate the general method. On the surface of the poem the poet reproduces the patter of the charlatan, Madame Sosostris, and there is the surface irony: that is, the contrast between the original use of the Tarot cards and the use made by Madame Sosostris. But each of the details assumes a new meaning in the general context of the poem. The "fortunetelling,"

---

[5] The third of the Thames daughters (lines 293–94) also echoes a passage from the *Purgatorio*, the speech of Pia, Canto 5, but here the reference to the *Purgatorio* provides an ironical contrast. For like Arnaut's, Pia's suffering is a purgation; she has hope, whereas the first of the Thames daughters speaks in dejected hopelessness.

[6] One may compare in a later work by Eliot, *The Family Reunion*, the speech made by Harry toward the end of the play: "It is very hard, when one has just recovered sanity,/And not yet assured of its possession, that is when/One begins to seem the maddest to other people."

which is taken *ironically* by a twentieth-century audience, becomes *true* as the poem develops— true in a sense in which Madame Sosostris herself does not believe it true. In the context of her speech, the items have only one reference: the "man with three staves," the "one-eyed merchant," the "crowds of people, walking round in a ring," and so on. But transferred to other contexts they become loaded with special meanings. To sum up, all the central symbols of the poem head up here; but here, in the only section in which they are explicitly bound together, the binding is slight and accidental. The deeper lines of association emerge only in terms of the total context as the poem develops—and this is, of course, exactly the effect to be sought.

The melting of the characters into each other, on which Eliot remarks in his notes, is, of course, an aspect of this general process. Queen Elizabeth and the girl born at Highbury both ride on the Thames, one in the barge of state, the other supine in a narrow canoe. The girl is a Thames-nymph, who has been violated and thus is like the Rhine-nymphs (see note on line 266 below), who have also been violated. With the characters as with the other symbols, the surface relationships may be accidental and apparently trivial and they may be made either ironically or through random association or in hallucination, but in the total context of the poem the deeper relationships are revealed. The effect is a sense of the oneness of experience, and of the unity of all periods, and with this, a sense that the general theme is being generated out of the poem, that the theme has not been imposed, but has been revealed.

This complication of parallelisms and contrasts makes, of course, for ambiguity, but the ambiguity, in part, resides in the poet's fidelity to the complexity of experience. The symbols resist complete equation with a simple meaning. To take an example, "rock" throughout the poem seems to be one of the "desert" symbols. The "dry stone" gives "no sound of water"; woman in the waste land is "the Lady of the Rocks"; and most pointed of all, there is the long delirium passage in "What the Thunder Said": "Here is no water but only rock." But in

lines 24–26 "Only/There is shadow under this red rock,/(Come in under the shadow of this red rock)," the rock is a place of refuge.

For a more striking instance of this ambiguous use of symbols, consider the lines which occur in the hyacinth girl passage. The vision gives obviously a sense of the richness and beauty of life. It is a moment of ecstasy (the basic imagery is obviously sexual); but the moment in its intensity is like death. The protagonist looks in that moment into the "heart of light, the silence," and so looks into—not richness—but blankness: he is neither "living nor dead." The symbol of life stands also for a kind of death. This duality of function may, of course, extend to a whole passage. For example, consider: "Where fishmen lounge at noon: where the walls/Of Magnus Martyr hold/Inexplicable splendour of Ionian white and gold." The function of the passage is to indicate the poverty into which religion has fallen: the splendid church now surrounded by the poorer districts. But the passage has an opposed effect also: the fishmen in the "public bar in Lower Thames Street" next to the church have a meaningful life which has been largely lost to the secularized upper and middle classes.

The poem would undoubtedly be "clearer" if every symbol had a single, unequivocal meaning; but the poem would be thinner, and less honest. For the poet has not been content to develop a didactic allegory in which the symbols are two-dimensional items adding up directly to the sum of the general scheme. They represent dramatized instances of the theme, embodying in their own nature the fundamental paradox of the theme.

We have been speaking as if the poet were a strategist trying to win acceptance from a hostile audience. But of course this is true only in a sense. The poet himself is audience as well as speaker; we state the problem more exactly if we state it in terms of the poet's integrity rather than in terms of his strategy. He is so much a man of his own age that he can indicate his attitude toward the Christian tradition without falsity only in terms of the difficulties of a rehabilitation; and he is so much a poet and so little a propagandist that he can be sincere only as he presents his theme concretely and dramatically.

In making a more detailed examination of the poem, the reader may need to take into account the following notes (which, incidentally, absorb the substance of the notes that Eliot himself provided for the poem).

Lines 8–18: the Starnbergersee is a lake to the south of Munich. Eliot's knowledge of Munich and Bavaria and the importance of this locale for the poem have been elaborately discussed by Herbert Knust in a monograph entitled "Wagner, the King, and 'The Waste Land'" (1967). G. L. K. Morris, in an article entitled "Marie, Marie, Hold on Tight," *Partisan Review* (March–April, 1954), identifies the Marie of line 15 with the Countess Marie Larisch, who had a home on the Starnbergersee, whose cousins were archdukes, and whose account of the life style of the decadent Bavarian-Austrian aristocracy was published in her memoir, *My Past*. Morris had naturally assumed that Eliot had read this book. But Mrs. Eliot has recently told us that, in fact, Eliot "had met the author (when and where is not known), and his description of the sledding, for example, was taken verbatim from a conversation he had with this niece and confidante of the Austrian Empress Elizabeth." (See *T. S. Eliot: The Waste Land. A Facsimile*, 1971, p. 126.) Like the girl from Lithuania (line 12) who insists that she is not Russian but pure German, the Austrian countess is an essentially uprooted person.

Lines 31–34: translated as "Fresh blows the wind to the homeland. My Irish child, where dost thou tarry." From Wagner's *Tristan und Isolde* (act 1, verses 5–8). It is a song sung by a young sailor aboard the ship which is bringing Isolde to Cornwall.

Line 42: translated as "Empty and wide the sea." From *Tristan und Isolde* (act 3, verse 24). The reply of the watcher to the wounded Tristan, who hopes that Isolde will come to him, and who has asked whether there is any sight of a ship that may be bearing her to him. Note that these two quotations from the opera frame the hyacinth-garden passage.

Line 49: Belladonna, literally "beautiful lady."

Line 51: the man with three staves is a card in the Tarot pack, with which Eliot says that he quite arbitrarily associates the Fisher King; the Wheel is a symbol throughout the poem of purposeless activity—the monotonous round of aimless life.

Line 52: the one-eyed merchant is literally a card with the face presented in profile. But as associated with Mr. Eugenides (line 209), "one-eyed" suggests the function of the *seer* in decay. Compare with the fortuneteller's bad cold.

Line 53: "Which is blank," etc. The secret that the merchant is supposed to carry.

Line 55: The Hanged Man (a card in the Tarot pack). Here it stands as a type of the god who dies for his people; the hanged god of Frazer's *Golden Bough* including Christ.

Line 60: Eliot adds the note: "Cf. Baudelaire: 'Fourmillante cité, cité plein de rêves,/Où le spectre en plein jour raccroche le passant'" (Swarming city, city full of dreams, where the specter in broad daylight seizes on the passerby).

Line 66: King William Street runs north from London Bridge to the heart of the "City" of London.

Line 67: Saint Mary Woolnoth, a church on the corner of King William and Lombard streets.

Line 69: Oscar Cargill, having in mind Ezra Pound's black sombrero hat and his reputation during his London years for being a Wild Westerner, says that Stetson is "clearly a portrait of Ezra Pound." See "Death in a Handful of Dust," *Criticism* (Summer, 1969). The whole article is very interesting in throwing light on incidents in *The Waste Land* that may be connected with incidents in Eliot's personal life.

Line 70: Mylae, 200 B.C., a naval battle fought between the Romans and the Carthaginians in the First Punic War. We expect the protagonist to hail his friend as a comrade in some battle of the First World War, but the souls in Hell are gathered from every age. All the pasts mingle there, ancient and recent; and in the modern waste land, all wars seem to be essentially the same.

Line 76: translated as "You! hypocritical reader!—my likeness,—my brother!" from Baudelaire's preface to *Fleurs de Mal*. Here the reader is suddenly addressed directly. Compare the "you" in "Prufrock" and note in particular this use of "you" in "Gerontion."

Line 92: laquearia, the hollow spaces between the intersecting cross beams of a ceiling. Eliot takes the word from the *Aeneid* (1. 726), where it is used in the description of the scene in which Dido entertains Aeneas at a great feast. The setting for this interview is thus meant to suggest not only the meeting of Antony and Cleopatra, but that of Dido and Aeneas, another great tragic love story of the past.

Line 98: sylvan scene: Eliot's note indicates that the phrase is taken from Milton's description in *Paradise Lost* (4. 140) of the mountain on which the Garden of Eden was located.

Line 103: "Jug Jug": the Elizabethans sometimes represented bird songs by these—to our ears—outlandish syllables.

Line 110: note that it is the hair here that speaks. The hair is an immemorial fertility symbol.

Line 137: in the original version of the poem this line was followed by "The ivory men make company between us." We are told in *T. S. Eliot: The Waste Land. A Facsimile* (p. 126) that "This line was omitted at Vivian Eliot's request. The author restored it, from memory, when he made a fair copy of the poem for the sale in aid of the London Library in June 1960."

Line 138: Eliot gives a note: "Cf. the game of chess in Middleton's *Women Beware Women*." In that play the chess game is used as a device to keep the widow occupied while her daughter-in-law is being seduced. The seduction, through a series of *double-entendres*, is described in terms of the game.

Line 172: from *Hamlet* (4. 5). Ophelia, driven mad by her sorrow, sings her pathetic song and then speaks this line as she takes her leave of the company in the room. Like Philomela, her music has come from her suffering. Here the line counterpoints ironically the goodnights of

the company in the pub.

Line 180: city directors, that is, directors of corporations. The "City" in London is the financial district.

Line 182: from Psalm 137. It is a song of mourning for Zion, sung by those carried away into Babylonian captivity. The waste land is such a Babylonian captivity.

Line 191: compare the lines spoken by Prince Ferdinand ("Weeping again the king my father's wreck") in Shakespeare's *Tempest* (1. 2), just after he has heard Ariel's first song.

Line 195: see line 115.

Line 197: Eliot gives the note: "Cf. Day, *Parliament of Bees*, 'When of a sudden, listening you shall hear,/A noise of horns and hunting, which shall bring/Actaeon to Diana in the spring,/Where all shall see her naked skin. . . .'" Actaeon, a hunter, caught a glimpse of Diana, goddess of chastity, bathing. For this sacrilege he was turned into a stag and killed by his own hunting dogs. But here nakedness is put upon exhibition. Actaeon becomes Sweeney, and Diana, the hardly chaste Mrs. Porter.

Line 199: from a ballad reported to Eliot from Sydney, Australia.

Line 202: translated as "And O the voices of children singing in the cupola," from Verlaine's *Parsifal*. The story of Parsifal is one of the Grail legends. Just before the healing of Amfortas (the Fisher King) by Parsifal there is heard the clear song of the children in the choirloft of the Grail Chapel.

Line 204: see line 103.

Line 205: see line 100.

Line 207: see line 60.

Line 211: "C.i.f. London: documents at sight" means carriage and insurance free to London, and the Bill of Lading, and so on, were to be handed to the buyer upon payment of the sight draft.

Line 214: the Metropole is a luxury hotel in the resort town of Brighton.

Line 218: Tiresias, the blind Greek prophet who is one of the characters in Sophocles' *Oedipus Rex*. When the land of Thebes lay under a curse—another "waste land" parallel—it was Tiresias who discerned the cause of the curse.

Eliot's note states that "What Tiresias *sees* . . . is the substance of the poem." He sees here the life-giving act turned into something meaningless. The allusion to his "wrinkled female breasts" refers to the legend that he had been changed by the gods into a woman and then, after seven years, turned back into a man.

Line 221: this line is an alteration of lines by Sappho: "Hesperus [the evening star], you bring home all things bright morning scattered; you bring the sheep, you bring the goat, you bring the child to the mother."

Line 234: Bradford is an industrial town in north England.

Line 257: spoken by Prince Ferdinand (*Tempest*, 1. 2) just after he has heard Ariel's first song. See also line 191.

Line 258: the Strand is one of the great thoroughfares of London, running from the West End to the "City" of London; Queen Victoria Street connects the "City" with Victoria wharf.

Line 260: Lower Thames Street runs alongside Billingsgate Market, the central fish market of London.

Line 266: from here through line 306 we have the songs of the three Thames daughters. The songs are patterned upon those of the Rhine daughters in Wagner's *Götterdämmerung* (act 3, scene 1). These were the nymphs of the Rhine, whose treasure, the Rhine gold, was stolen from them. Like the Rhine daughters, the Thames daughters here sing of the violation of the river, and as they sing in turn (lines 292–306), they tell of other violations.

Line 279: the Earl of Leicester was one of Queen Elizabeth's great favorites, and Eliot's note quotes from a letter which describes her dalliance with Leicester on the Queen's barge.

Line 293: Highbury, Richmond, and Kew are suburbs of London.

Line 296: Moorgate is a slum district in the heart of the "City."

Line 300: Margate is a popular, unfashionable resort town in Kent at the end of the Thames estuary.

Line 307: from St. Augustine's *Confessions*: "To Carthage then I came, where a cauldron

of unholy loves sang all about my ears."

Line 308: from Buddha's *Fire Sermon*. The following excerpts will suggest its nature: "Everything, O priests, is burning. . . . The eye, O priests, is burning; visible things are burning. . . . I declare unto you that it is burning with the fire of lust, with the fire of anger. . . . The ear is burning. . . . The tongue is burning. . . ." and so on.

Line 309: from St. Augustine's *Confessions* (according to Eliot's note). Compare also Zechariah 3:2, Psalms 25:15, and Amos 4:11.

Line 369: for this and the lines that immediately follow, compare these lines from Eliot's play, *The Family Reunion*: "The sudden solitude in a crowded desert/In a thick smoke, many creatures moving/Without direction, for no direction/Leads anywhere but round and round that vapor. . . ."

Line 378: one of the "daughters of music"; see Ecclesiastes 12:4.

Line 380: violet is the liturgical color for repentance. See also lines 220 and 372.

Line 383: compare the towers and the bells (in the next line) with lines 288–89.

Line 393: the cock was believed to scare away evil spirits. Ariel's first song in *The Tempest* (1. 2) ends with the lines, "O hear/The strain of strutting chanticleer/Cry, cock-a-doodle-do."

Line 408: Eliot gives a note: "Cf. Webster, *The White Devil*, V, vi: '. . . They'll remarry/Ere the worm pierce your winding-sheet, ere the spider/Make a thin curtain for your epitaphs.'"

Line 412: in connection with this passage Eliot quotes from F. H. Bradley's *Appearance and Reality*, p. 346: "My external sensations are no less private to myself than are my thoughts or my feelings. In either case my experience falls within my own circle, a circle closed on the outside; and, with all its elements alike, every sphere is opaque to the others which surround it. . . . In brief, regarded as an existence which appears in a soul, the whole world for each is peculiar and private to that soul."

Line 429: the swallow is the bird of summer. Philomela's sister Procne was transformed into a swallow. See line 100 and the later references to Philomela.

Little Gidding (1942)

"Little Gidding" is the last of the four poems that make up *Four Quartets*. In choosing this title for his poem, Eliot seems to have had in mind an analogy with Beethoven's late quartets, which he much admired. He did not conceive of the four-part poem, however, until some years after "Burnt Norton" (1935), which was to become the first section of it, had been published.

"Burnt Norton" takes its name from a country house in Gloucestershire that Eliot once visited. The second poem of the suite, "East Coker," is the name of a village in Somersetshire in which the Eliot family lived in the seventeenth century before emigrating to America. The third, "The Dry Salvages" [it rhymes with "Hal rages"], is named for "a small group of rocks, with a beacon, off the N.E. coast of Cape Ann, Massachusetts," to make use of Eliot's own description. As a child, Eliot had spent summer holidays on this coast. "Little Gidding" is a village in Huntingdonshire where Nicholas Ferrar in 1625 set up an Anglican religious community. The community was not monastic, but was composed of Ferrar's family and some of his friends. (Subsequent notes on "Little Gidding" will suggest why the community had special meaning for the poet.)

The four major divisions of the poem correspond to the four elements: air, earth, water, and fire. It has also been pointed out that they emphasize, in succession, God the Father, God the Son, the Virgin Mary, and the Holy Ghost. "Little Gidding," with which we shall here be particularly concerned, constitutes the fire section and makes specific references to the descent of the Holy Spirit in tongues of flame at the Feast of Pentecost: see Acts 2.

The foregoing brief remarks on *Four Quartets* can do no more than suggest the elaborate ordering of motifs and themes, the contrapuntal "musical" effects, and the richness and intricacy of the structure of this poem. Yet the general theme of *Four Quartets* can be put quite simply: it has to do with how to find one's way home. We are told in "Little Gidding" that

> . . . the end of all our exploring
> Will be to arrive where we started
> And know the place for the first time.

Alternatively, we can say that the general theme is the possibility of an apprehension of the eternal—even though man is a creature of time and his life is immersed in the world of time. Scattered throughout *Four Quartets* are hints and glimpses of the world of eternity, moments, necessarily moments *in time*, which yet seem to partake of something outside time. The poet, in "Burnt Norton," describes the quality of such moments thus:

> . . . release from action and suffering, release from the inner
> And the outer compulsion, yet surrounded
> By a grace of sense, a white light still and moving,
>
>   . . .
>
>   Time past and time future
> Allow but a little consciousness.
> To be conscious is not to be in time
> But only in time can the moment in the rose-garden,
> The moment in the arbour where the rain beat,
> The moment in the draughty church at smoke-fall
> Be remembered; involved with past and future.

In developing this theme, the speaker does not pretend to have a mystic's power of vision. He classes himself with the rest of us, people who have to be content with these evanescent intimations, which are at best "only hints and guesses,/Hints followed by guesses. . . ." To apprehend "The point of intersection of the timeless/With time . . ." is an "occupation only" for the saint. Thus the poet speaks in the third part of the poem, "The Dry Salvages."

Still another way to describe the general import of the poem is to say that it treats of Incarnation. That is, the poem assumes that the world of time implies and embodies the world of eternity. Nature is not to be regarded as merely a process of physical events following each other in endless succession. Nor is history simply an infinite series of happenings which have only a cause-and-effect relation to one another. Human decisions made in the world of time need not be dismissed as no more than conditioned responses, items in an endless sequence of cause and effect. Yet, as the speaker confesses, it is not easy to see through to the eternal meanings. To do so may require a lifetime's discipline and humility of spirit. As he says in "The Dry Salvages," knowledge derived from experience

      . . . imposes a pattern and falsifies,
For the pattern is new in every moment
And every moment is a new and shocking
Valuation of all we have been.

1

Midwinter spring is its own season
Sempiternal though sodden towards sundown,
Suspended in time, between pole and tropic.
When the short day is brightest, with
    frost and fire,
The brief sun flames the ice, on pond
    and ditches,
In windless cold that is the heart's heat,
Reflecting in a watery mirror
A glare that is blindness in the early
    afternoon.
And glow more intense than blaze of
    branch, or brazier,
Stirs the dumb spirit: no wind, but
    pentecostal fire   10
In the dark time of the year. Between
    melting and freezing
The soul's sap quivers. There is no earth smell
Or smell of living thing. This is the
    spring time
But not in time's covenant. Now the
    hedgerow
Is blanched for an hour with transitory
    blossom
Of snow, a bloom more sudden
Than that of summer, neither budding
    nor fading,
Not in the scheme of generation.
Where is the summer, the unimaginable
Zero summer?   20

        If you came this way,
Taking the route you would be likely to take
From the place you would be likely to
    come from,
If you came this way in may time, you
    would find the hedges
White again, in May, with voluptuary
    sweetness.
It would be the same at the end of the
    journey,
If you came at night like a broken king,
If you came by day not knowing what
    you came for,
It would be the same, when you leave the
    rough road
And turn behind the pig-sty to the dull façade   30
And the tombstone. And what you thought
    you came for
Is only a shell, a husk of meaning
From which the purpose breaks only when
    it is fulfilled
If at all. Either you had no purpose
Or the purpose is beyond the end you figured
And is altered in fulfilment. There are
    other places
Which also are the world's end, some at
    the sea jaws,
Or over a dark lake, in a desert or a city—
But this is the nearest, in place and time,
Now and in England.   40

        If you came this way,
Taking any route, starting from anywhere,
At any time or at any season,
It would always be the same: you would
    have to put off
Sense and notion. You are not here to verify,
Instruct yourself, or inform curiosity
Or carry report. You are here to kneel
Where prayer has been valid. And prayer
    is more
Than an order of words, the conscious
    occupation
Of the praying mind, or the sound of the
    voice praying.   50
And what the dead had no speech for,
    when living,
They can tell you, being dead: the
    communication
Of the dead is tongued with fire beyond
    the language of the living.
Here, the intersection of the timeless moment
Is England and nowhere. Never and always.

2

Ash on an old man's sleeve
Is all the ash the burnt roses leave.
Dust in the air suspended
Marks the place where a story ended.
Dust inbreathed was a house—   60
The wall, the wainscot and the mouse.
The death of hope and despair,
This is the death of air.

There are flood and drouth
Over the eyes and in the mouth,
Dead water and dead sand
Contending for the upper hand.
The parched eviscerate soil
Gapes at the vanity of toil,
Laughs without mirth.   70
This is the death of earth.

Water and fire succeed
The town, the pasture and the weed.
Water and fire deride
The sacrifice that we denied.
Water and fire shall rot
The marred foundations we forgot,
Of sanctuary and choir.
This is the death of water and fire.

In the uncertain hour before the morning   80
Near the ending of interminable night
At the recurrent end of the unending
After the dark dove with the flickering tongue
Had passed below the horizon of his homing
While the dead leaves still rattled on like tin
Over the asphalt where no other sound was
Between three districts whence the smoke
arose
I met one walking, loitering and hurried
As if blown towards me like the metal leaves
Before the urban dawn wind unresisting.   90
And as I fixed upon the down-turned face
That pointed scrutiny with which we challenge
The first-met stranger in the waning dusk
I caught the sudden look of some dead master
Whom I had known, forgotten, half recalled
Both one and many; in the brown baked
features
The eyes of a familiar compound ghost
Both intimate and unidentifiable.
So I assumed a double part, and cried
And heard another's voice cry: 'What!
are *you* here?'   100
Although we were not. I was still the same,

Knowing myself yet being someone other—
And he a face still forming; yet the
words sufficed
To compel the recognition they preceded.
And so, compliant to the common wind,
Too strange to each other for
misunderstanding,
In concord at this intersection time
Of meeting nowhere, no before and after,
We trod the pavement in a dead patrol.
I said: 'The wonder that I feel is easy,   110
Yet ease is cause of wonder. Therefore speak:
I may not comprehend, may not remember.'
And he: 'I am not eager to rehearse
My thought and theory which you have
forgotten.
These things have served their purpose:
let them be.
So with your own, and pray they be forgiven
By others, as I pray you to forgive
Both bad and good. Last season's fruit
is eaten
And the fullfed beast shall kick the empty pail.
For last year's words belong to last year's
language   120
And next year's words await another voice.
But, as the passage now presents no hindrance
To the spirit unappeased and peregrine
Between two worlds become much like
each other,
So I find words I never thought to speak
In streets I never thought I should revisit
When I left my body on a distant shore.
Since our concern was speech, and speech
impelled us
To purify the dialect of the tribe
And urge the mind to aftersight and
foresight,   130
Let me disclose the gifts reserved for age
To set a crown upon your lifetime's effort.
First, the cold friction of expiring sense
Without enchantment, offering no promise
But bitter tastelessness of shadow fruit
As body and soul begin to fall asunder.
Second, the conscious impotence of rage
At human folly, and the laceration
Of laughter at what ceases to amuse.
And last, the rending pain of re-enactment   140
Of all that you have done, and been;
the shame
Of motives late revealed, and the awareness
Of things ill done and done to others' harm
Which once you took for exercise of virtue.

Then fools' approval stings, and honour
    stains.
From wrong to wrong the exasperated spirit
    Proceeds, unless restored by that refining fire
    Where you must move in measure,
        like a dancer.'
The day was breaking. In the disfigured street
    He left me, with a kind of valediction,   150
    And faded on the blowing of the horn.

3

There are three conditions which often
    look alike
Yet differ completely, flourish in the same
    hedgerow:
Attachment to self and to things and to
    persons, detachment
From self and from things and from persons;
    and, growing between them, indifference
Which resembles the others as death
    resembles life,
Being between two lives—unflowering, between
The live and the dead nettle. This is the
    use of memory:
For liberation—not less of love but expanding
Of love beyond desire, and so liberation   160
From the future as well as the past.
        Thus, love of a country
Begins as attachment to our own field of action
And comes to find that action of little
    importance
Though never indifferent. History may
    be servitude,
History may be freedom. See, now they vanish,
The faces and places, with the self which,
    as it could, loved them,
To become renewed, transfigured, in
    another pattern.

Sin is Behovely, but
All shall be well, and
All manner of thing shall be well.   170
If I think, again, of this place,
And of people, not wholly commendable,
Of no immediate kin or kindness,
But some of peculiar genius,
All touched by a common genius,
United in the strife which divided them;
If I think of a king at nightfall,
Of three men, and more, on the scaffold
And a few who died forgotten
In other places, here and abroad,   180
And of one who died blind and quiet,

Why should we celebrate
These dead men more than the dying?
It is not to ring the bell backward
Nor is it an incantation
To summon the spectre of a Rose.
We cannot revive old factions
We cannot restore old policies
Or follow an antique drum.
These men, and those who opposed them   190
And those whom they opposed
Accept the constitution of silence
And are folded in a single party.
Whatever we inherit from the fortunate
We have taken from the defeated
What they had to leave us—a symbol:
A symbol perfected in death.
And all shall be well and
All manner of thing shall be well
By the purification of the motive   200
In the ground of our beseeching.

4

The dove descending breaks the air
With flame of incandescent terror
Of which the tongues declare
The one discharge from sin and error.
The only hope, or else despair
    Lies in the choice of pyre or pyre—
    To be redeemed from fire by fire.

Who then devised the torment? Love.
Love is the unfamiliar Name   210
Behind the hands that wove
The intolerable shirt of flame
Which human power cannot remove.
    We only live, only suspire
    Consumed by either fire or fire.

5

What we call the beginning is often the end
And to make an end is to make a beginning.
The end is where we start from. And
    every phrase
And sentence that is right (where every word
    is at home,
Taking its place to support the others,   220
The word neither diffident nor ostentatious,
An easy commerce of the old and the new,
The common word exact without vulgarity,
The formal word precise but not pedantic,
The complete consort dancing together)
Every phrase and every sentence is an end
    and a beginning,

Every poem an epitaph. And any action
Is a step to the block, to the fire, down
    the sea's throat
Or to an illegible stone: and that is where
    we start.
We die with the dying: 230
See, they depart, and we go with them.
We are born with the dead:
See, they return, and bring us with them.
The moment of the rose and the moment
    of the yew-tree
Are of equal duration. A people without history
Is not redeemed from time, for history is
    a pattern
Of timeless moments. So, while the light fails
On a winter's afternoon, in a secluded chapel
History is now and England.

With the drawing of this Love and the
    voice of this Calling   240

We shall not cease from exploration
And the end of all our exploring
Will be to arrive where we started
And know the place for the first time.
Through the unknown, remembered gate
When the last of earth left to discover
Is that which was the beginning;
At the source of the longest river
The voice of the hidden waterfall
And the children in the apple-tree   250
Not known, because not looked for
But heard, half-heard, in the stillness
Between two waves of the sea.
Quick now, here, now, always—
A condition of complete simplicity
(Costing not less than everything)
And all shall be well and
All manner of thing shall be well
When the tongues of flame are in-folded
Into the crowned knot of fire   260
And the fire and the rose are one.

NOTES

One of the most formidable problems that the poet faces with a topic of this sort is how to express what is by definition inexpressible: how is one to describe what it is like to experience eternity when one's readers are, like oneself, creatures of time, and when the language to be used is the product of temporal experience? The speaker must rely on hint, suggestion, and metaphor, and this he does.

"Little Gidding" begins with such an attempt: to persuade us to imagine "the unimaginable"—the "Zero summer." A blazingly bright winter day may seem, in its strangeness, to be "its own season," "Suspended in time." It has no "earth smell" or other smell "of living thing." It is "not in the scheme of generation." Yet, just because it is not, its "windless cold" is like "the heart's heat" and its "glow more intense than blaze of branch or brazier" is like "pentecostal fire."

Yet, the speaker goes on to say, the season in which one journeys to "Little Gidding" does not matter. At any time or season the road is rough and the look of the place unprepossessing as one turns "behind the pig-sty to the dull façade/And the tombstone." Yet, this place "is the nearest, in place and time,/Now and in England."

"Nearest" to what? To the experience of transcendence, the context would suggest. But such an experience is not actually promised—as, in terms of the speaker's assumptions, it cannot be. The Ferrars presumably did achieve it, but the sojourner (including the poet himself) must simply accept his role of humility and kneel here "Where prayer has been valid."

Section 2 begins with a lyrical passage composed of three stanzas which sums up the various kinds of death treated in the preceding Quartets: the death of air, of earth, of water, and of fire. Lines 58–62 refer to Eliot's experience as a fire-watcher during the blitz in London. The "dust in the air suspended" marks the place where a direct bomb hit occurred. The "Dust inbreathed" is literally "a house."

In the rest of section 2, the poet is fire-watching, walking the streets before the dawn, and finds himself in a nightmare world which resembles Dante's Hell. The poet has reinforced the Dantesque atmosphere by the versification that he uses (a modified unrhymed terza rima) and by descriptive detail such as "the brown baked features" of the "dead master" whose ghost he meets (compare Dante's description of his friend Brunetto Latini, *Inferno*, Canto 15). In such a hallucinated atmosphere, it does not seem odd for the fire-watcher to be treading "the pavement in a dead patrol" with a "familiar compound ghost."

Since the ghost is "compound," it seems idle to try to identify him with any one particular master. But commentators have nevertheless made guesses—the master is Joyce, or he is Yeats. But the master may be a scholar rather than a creative artist. His reference to "My thought and theory which you have forgotten" (line 114) and his statement that "our concern was speech" (line 128) seem to point in that direction. Remembering that he has left his "body on a distant shore" (line 127), we suggest that one of Eliot's revered Harvard professors, Irving Babbitt (see pp. 2781–82), contributes a principal element to the compound. (Line 129 translates a line from Mallarmé's "Le Tombeau d'Edgar Poe"—"To give a purer meaning to the words of the tribe.")

What the shade of the dead master says of the gifts reserved for age repeats a note sounded earlier in *Four Quartets*: a disillusionment with old men's wisdom and with any wisdom founded merely on experience. Reality is more complicated: it retains its mystery and has its surprises.

Line 151 echoes a line in *Hamlet* (1. 1. 157), in which the ghost of Hamlet's father "faded on the crowing of the cock." The blast, in this case, is that sounding the All Clear.

Section 3, through a very effective metaphor, makes a distinction between attachment to, detachment from, and indifference to self, things, and persons. Indifference is as different from the other two attitudes as death is from life. (Note that the term "dead nettle," line 158, does not mean a dead plant. It is a special kind of living plant—a nettle that is not "live," that is, stinging.) The poet does not scorn attachment to self and to things and to persons. One begins with attachments to what is local and near. A proper love of country can grow out of parochial and even selfish attachment, but growth ought to occur. It is the function of memory (lines 157–60) to accomplish this liberation—this detachment.

Lines 168–70 are a quotation from the writ-

ing of a fourteenth-century recluse, Lady Julian of Norwich. She was troubled about the problem of evil. How could a good God allow his creature, man, to fall into sin? Later, she was able to resolve the question and wrote in her *Shewings* that sin is "behovely," that is, needful. Lady Julian was not urging people to sin that grace might abound. What she was arguing was that out of sin good could come—that evil could be redeemed.

Little Gidding has for the speaker a particular association with the English civil wars of the seventeenth century. In line 27 the "broken king" alludes to Charles I, who had twice visited the Ferrars' community and now, after his disastrous defeat at the battle of Naseby, paid a third and last visit. Later, the Ferrars' community at Little Gidding was destroyed by the Roundheads.

What follows of section 3 has to do with the king and the king's friends and foes in the Civil War. The "king at nightfall" (line 177) is Charles I. Line 178 (". . . three men, and more, on the scaffold") refers to the beheading of Charles; Strafford, his chief minister; Laud, the Archbishop; and others involved in the conflict. The "one who died blind and quiet" (line 181) is Milton, who had written against the king and had been a great pamphleteer for the Puritan cause, but who was not molested when the monarchy was restored.

In line 183 the poet asks why should we celebrate "These dead men" more than the "dying," that is, those now dying in the fire raids or elsewhere in the present war. It is not, he says, because we want to reverse history or to recover by magic a lost era or to fight over again the issues that convulsed the nation in the seventeenth century. Our justification is that we who inherit not only from those who won but also from those who lost, can take from the dead "A symbol perfected in death" (line 197). What we can learn, it is implied, is what Lady Julian had learned: that violence and conflict are "behovely."

Section 4 is a brief lyrical moment in the poem. One may ask whether the dove descending with its "flame of incandescent terror" is a

German bomber over London or the spirit of the Holy Ghost (so often depicted by Renaissance painters as a dove), descending with its pentecostal flame. Whichever it is, the choice offered seems a desperate one: the choice of "pyre or pyre." Since fire—pain and suffering—are inevitable, the only choice is that between meaningless and sterile suffering and a suffering that does have meaning because it refines the spirit. (Line 427 of *The Waste Land* is a quotation from the *Purgatorio* in which Dante describes the poet Arnaut joyfully leaping back into the fire "that refines" souls in Purgatory.)

Yet who could have devised such a choice, a tormenting one, since one suffers, whichever the fire! The shocking answer is that love devised it. This is an answer always hard, but peculiarly hard for modern man, to accept. The poet provides an analogy from the story of Hercules. His wife, Deianira, innocently gave him the shirt of the Centaur Nessus, who had earlier been killed by Hercules' envenomed arrows. Hercules, suffering intolerable pain, could not pull the shirt off. Knowing that he was doomed, he built a funeral pyre, ascended it, and died in its flames.

Dante, on whom Eliot levies so heavily in *Four Quartets*, also attempted to provide in his *Divine Comedy* a justification of the ways of God to man and to answer the hard question of why love can permit suffering. Over the gates of Hell (*Inferno*, Canto 3) Dante tells us is written (John Ciardi translation):

Sacred justice moved my Architect:
I was raised here by Divine Omnipotence,
Primordial Love and Ultimate Intellect.

.   .   .

Abandon all hope you, who enter here.

Love is not indifferent; it makes its demands. Since it is the greatest good, those who reject it bring down torment on themselves.

Since Section 5 concludes not only "Little Gidding," but the *Four Quartets* conceived as a total poem, it gathers up motifs from the rest of the poem. (The reader who wishes to partici-

pate in its full richness will need to read the three Quartets which precede it.)

Lines 216–18 use "end" not only in the sense of "termination" but of "purposeful goal." To "make an end" is a meaningful act, for its purpose is implied in its beginning.

Lines 218–27 provide a magnificent account of how the words in a great poem work together. The passage picks up once more the theme of poetry, a theme which has occurred several times earlier in the *Quartets*.

Lines 227–33 resume the theme of the relation of the living to the dead: the living and dead constitute one community. The living cannot disown the past. We are part of it.

Lines 234–35 state a paradox: the moment of the fragile rose of a day is of equal duration with the moment of the centuries-old yew tree, for the apprehension of the perfect pattern affords a glimpse of eternity in which all time is gathered up.

Lines 235–39 bring up again the theme of incarnation. History is not mere duration, an endless and meaningless succession of events, but has meaning, and its meaning is given through events which have to be regarded as outside the mere sequence of time. Moreover, the human being can reach through to the world of eternity by making decisions that transcend the temporal. That is why history is not just something past, but *now*, and something that can be located in space: "History is now and England" (line 239).

Line 240 is a quotation from *The Cloud of Unknowing*, an anonymous mystical work of the fourteenth century.

Lines 241–47 bring the theme of exploration to a conclusion: more than exploration into the unknown is involved. One discovers that he had come home "through the unknown, remembered gate" and is miraculously back at his beginning.

Lines 249–50: "The voice of the hidden waterfall" and the voices of the "children in the apple-tree"—sounds mentioned earlier in *Four Quartets*—carry intimations of the transcendent and the eternal.

Lines 257–58 repeat part of the quotation (in

lines 168–70 above) from *The Shewings* of Lady Julian.

Lines 259–61 may also, as Elizabeth Drew has pointed out, echo another passage from *The Cloud of Unknowing*: "The Author of *The Cloud of Unknowing*" says that renunciation and humility "will at the last help thee to knit a ghostly knot of burning love betwixt thee and thy God in ghostly one head" (*T. S. Eliot: The Design of His Poetry*, 1949).

Other works which may be consulted for commentary on *Four Quartets* (and for Eliot's work generally) are Helen Gardner, *The Art of T. S. Eliot* (1949); Raymond Preston, *Four Quartets Rehearsed* (1947); and George Williamson, *A Reader's Guide to T. S. Eliot* (1953).

CONRAD AIKEN (1889–1973)

Conrad Aiken was born in Savannah, Georgia, but of a New England family whose history goes back to early colonial times. His parents died under tragic circumstances while he was still a young boy, and he returned to New England to live with relatives in New Bedford, Massachusetts. He entered Harvard and became one of T. S. Eliot's closest friends during the years in which Eliot was doing graduate work at Harvard.

Many of the same forces, literary and cultural, that impinged on Eliot and Pound also touched Aiken. Like Eliot and Pound, he came to England as a young man and lived there for many years. He and Eliot remained good friends, and some of the most interesting glimpses of the young Eliot are to be found in Aiken's autobiographical work entitled *Ushant* (1952). In *Ushant*, Eliot is referred to as the Tsetse; that is, his initials doubled spell the name of the dreaded fly whose bite infects with African sleeping sickness. (Is the joke that Eliot is a gadfly with a difference?) Ezra Pound is sardonically named after Browning's hero, Rabbi Ben Ezra; Aiken himself is D., and so on.

Ushant contains vignettes of life at Harvard in the early years of the century. Aiken recalls spending "a whole cerulean winter reading Shelley with Santayana." For Aiken, he was "that Merlin, that Prospero, with his wizard's mantle from Spain." There are glimpses of Aiken's first trip to Europe: in the summer of 1910 he had visited Italy and then came to Paris to join Eliot. The two young men have "*sirop des fraises* and soda at the sidewalk café" and much talk about "all that had gone on during the year at Harvard, and the Sorbonne [Eliot was spending the academic year 1910–11 there]. . . . And then the . . . making of plans. Bergson, and *L'Évolution Créatrice*, and the Tsetse's intention to return to Harvard for a study of Sanskrit."

Of particular interest is Aiken's report of conversations between the two young Americans about the advantages and risks of living in Europe and pursuing a literary career abroad rather than at home. At this time Eliot had a special interest in France: "The early Tsetse, early inoculated by the subtle creative venoms of Laforgue and Vildrac, looked rather to France than to England: an editor of the [Harvard] Advocate had returned from Paris, after a year, in exotic Left-Bank clothing, and with his hair parted behind: it had made a sensation." (Was Eliot's Prufrock modeled in part on this young Harvard editor? Or has Aiken chosen to describe him with a phrase borrowed from Eliot's poem? It doesn't matter, but it is useful to remind ourselves of the kind of world out of which the early poems of Eliot and Aiken come.) The upshot of that "prolonged debate," about where to live their lives was the eventual choice of England by both, Eliot finally settling down in London; Aiken, at Rye, the little town on the south coast where Henry James had his English residence from 1898 to 1916.

Aiken became interested very early in the

new depth psychology, not only that of Freud but later that of Jung and of other savants as well. He was sure that the psychoanalytic studies would prove a great new resource for the poet and the novelist, all the more so since he believed that literature was destined to become increasingly introspective. Modern man must recognize clearly what had always been implicit: namely, that poetry was essentially a discovery of the self. Since that was the nature of authentic poetry, only through a facing of the real truth about one's self, without exception or reservation, could one attain a just sense of one's self and of reality.

Yet Aiken has always avoided the excesses of what later was to be known as "confessional poetry." Though the poet must be prepared to reveal anything about himself, complete frankness did not imply slipshod work or lack of self-criticism. Poetry was not a mere letting go. It had to be well disciplined, and Aiken, despite his openness to ideas from the modern world, resisted any impulse to spill his guts in the delusion that telling it all without let or restraint would result in poetry.

Aiken was suspicious of all kinds of short cuts. Imagism seemed a reprehensible loosening of the rules. Aiken's verse has always been "formed"; he is highly aware of the importance of the verbal factor as such, and perfectly willing to exploit it. One finds in his poetry, as in that of Eliot, verbal wit and even serious puns.

Yet Aiken's poetry, for all its conscious attempt to absorb what was new and lively in the twentieth-century world, is in several senses deeply traditional. One does not find in his work, for example, the almost calculated disorder and discontinuity of, say, *The Waste Land*, nor, at another extreme, the vehement, often strained, rhetoric of Hart Crane's more apocalyptic poems.

Thus, in spite of his use of verbal wit, his Freudianism, his interest in myth and archetypal pattern, and his exploitation of the rituals and liturgies of the past, Aiken's is an old-fashioned romanticism. In Aiken's view of things, man finds himself alone in a beautiful but meaningless universe. Man's very consciousness, which

is at once his burden and his glory, is the result of a mere cosmic accident. No creator of the universe planned it: it simply happened. In any case, man's only salvation is to widen and deepen his consciousness and so to come to terms with himself. His only stay against confusion and oblivion is to be found in art.

Since this is a view of man's relation to nature and to art (*ars longa, vita brevis*) that goes back to the very beginnings of the Western literary tradition and one that has proved attractive and plausible to many men of letters today, it may seem rather odd to term it old-fashioned. But it is implicit in the Romantic poets of 150 years ago, and, as expressed in Aiken, aspects of it are clearly traceable to Aiken's New England literary forebears, notably to Emerson and the transcendentalists. Other aspects can be referred to continental figures like Arthur Schopenhauer and Friedrich Nietzsche, whose impact on men of letters generally, especially toward the end of the nineteenth century, was immense.

In matters of this sort Aiken sharply differs from his old Harvard classmate, Eliot, but the differences have to do not merely with what kind of poetry one should try to write (or what kinds it is possible nowadays to write) but with the nature of civilization and the nature of man. In *Ushant* and elsewhere, Aiken indicates that in spite of his great respect for Eliot's literary intelligence and power, he is forced to condemn what seemed to him a dangerously regressive step taken when Eliot broke with the tradition of New England transcendentalism and his family's tradition of Unitarianism, and went back to a doctrinal church and subscribed to a formal creed.

One of the most interesting things to note about Aiken's poems and critical essays is his attempt to come to terms with his own American heritage. He tries to make his self-imposed exile from America yield a perspective which will allow him to discern its quality more accurately and to penetrate to its special meaning. In a long late poem entitled "The Kid," Aiken's summarizing image of the American is that of a folk hero like Billy the Kid, the sandy-haired, blue-eyed boy riding "a pinto without no bit," and packing the fastest gun in the West. To Aiken Billy is clearly the archetypal American, and in the poem Aiken discovers ways to relate to him such diverse American figures as Anne Bradstreet, Audubon, Crèvecoeur, Thoreau, the poet and essayist John Jay Chapman, Paul Revere, Benjamin Franklin, the scientist William Gibbs, Henry Adams, Brooks Adams, Walt Whitman, and Emily Dickinson. "The Kid" is an interesting and ambitious poem, full of resource and surprise, and in many respects brilliantly executed. For obvious reasons it ought to be of particular interest to the reader of this volume. Unfortunately, it cannot be adequately represented by fragments and it is much too long to be printed entire in our text.

BIOGRAPHICAL CHART

1889   Born August 5, in Savannah, Georgia, of parents who were transplanted New Englanders
1900   Discovers father and mother dead after murder-suicide; goes to live with a great-great-aunt in New Bedford, Massachusetts
1907   Enters Harvard University
1912   Receives Harvard degree; marries a few days later
1922   Settles in England
1930   Receives Pulitzer prize for *Selected Poems* (published in 1929)
1934   Begins "London Letter" to the *New Yorker* (to 1936), under pseudonym of Samuel Leake, Jr.
1950–51   Chair of Poetry, Library of Congress
1953   *Collected Poems* wins National Book Award as most distinguished volume of poems published that year
1956   Wins the Bollingen prize for poetry
1958   Receives the Gold Medal in Poetry from the American Academy of Arts and Letters

FURTHER READINGS

Collected Poems (1953)
A Letter from Li Po and Other Poems (1955)
Sheepfold Hill: Fifteen Poems (1958)
The Short Stories of Conrad Aiken (1950)

Joseph Warren Beech, "Conrad Aiken and T. S. Eliot: Echoes and Overtones," *PMLA* (1959)
Calvin Brown, "The Poetry of Conrad Aiken," *Georgia Review* (1954)
Jay Martin, *Conrad Aiken: A Life of His Art* (1962)

From Preludes for Memnon (1931)

The subtitle for *Preludes for Memnon* is "Preludes to Attitude," and the phrase suggests the subject matter of this suite of poems. The basic question pondered concerns the controlling attitude that man in our time ought to take toward the world about him and toward himself. Aiken has told us that *Preludes for Memnon* and *Time in the Rock*, excerpts from which follow, are to be regarded as one poem.

19

Watch long enough, and you will see the leaf
Fall from the bough. Without a sound it falls:
And soundless meets the grass . . . And so you have
A bare bough, and a dead leaf in dead grass.
Something has come and gone. And that is all.

But what were all the tumults in this action?
What wars of atoms in the twig, what ruins,
Fiery and disastrous, in the leaf?
Timeless the tumult was, but gave no sign.
Only, the leaf fell, and the bough is bare.   10

This is the world: there is no more than this.
The unseen and disastrous prelude, shaking
The trivial act from the terrific action.
Speak: and the ghosts of change, past and to come,

Throng the brief word. The maelstrom has
    us all.

                    20

So, in the evening, to the simple cloister:
This place of boughs, where sounds of water,
    softly,
Lap on the stones. And this is what you are:
Here, in this dusty room, to which you climb
By four steep flights of stairs. The door is
    closed:
The furies of the city howl behind you:
The last bell plunges rock-like to the sea:
The horns of taxis wail in vain. You come
Once more, at evening, to this simple cloister;

Hushed by the quiet walls, you stand at peace.   10

What ferns of thought are these, the cool
    and green,
Dripping with moisture, that festoon
    these walls?
What water-lights are these, whose pallid rings
Dance with the leaves, or speckle the pale
    stones?
What spring is this, that bubbles the cold sand,
Urging the sluggish grains of white and
    gold? . . .
Peace. The delicious silence throngs
    with ghosts
Of winged sound and shadow. These are you.

From Time in the Rock (1936)

The subtitle for *Time in the Rock*, "Preludes
to Definition," states quite explicitly some of
Aiken's beliefs about mankind and reality. In
section 11, which follows, God is seen as within
us: we create the divine in our own consciousness. Mysticism is good, but ought to be regarded as a "flower"—a spontaneous generation
of our consciousness, appreciated, enjoyed for
the moment, then discarded. The mystic illumination ought not to be frozen into dogma or
made to yield a fixed creed.

used for our needs with selfish simplicity,
broken for love and as soon forgotten;

and let the churches be our houses
defiled daily, loud with discord,—
where the dead gods that were our selves
    may hang,
our outgrown gods on every wall;
Christ on the mantelpiece, with downcast eyes;
Buddha above the stove;
the Holy Ghost by the hatrack, and God
    himself
staring like Narcissus from the mirror,   20
clad in a raincoat, and with hat and gloves.

                    11

Mysticism, but let us have no words,
angels, but let us have no fantasies,
churches, but let us have no creeds,
no dead gods hung on crosses in a shop,
nor beads nor prayers nor faith nor sin
    nor penance:
and yet, let us believe, let us believe.

Let it be the flower
seen by the child for the first time,
    plucked without thought
broken for love and as soon forgotten:

and the angels, let them be our friends,   10

Mysticism, but let it be a flower,
let it be the hand that reaches for the flower,
let it be the flower that imagined the
    first hand,
let it be the space that removed itself to
    give place
for the hand that reaches, the flower to be
    reached—
let it be self displacing self
as quietly as a child lifts a pebble,
as softly as a flower decides to fall,—
self replacing self   30
as seed follows flower to earth.

From A Letter from Li Po (1955)

Li Po (701–62) was a great Chinese poet. Pound
adapted and translated a good many of his

poems, though his attribution of them is to
Rihaku, the Japanese transliteration of Li Po's

name. In this poem, Aiken is making the point that all humanity is one, that all men are brothers, and that the great function of art is to commemorate that fact. The twentieth-century American poet chooses here to take his representative poet from a distant time and from a completely different civilization. In other words, Aiken wants for his purposes a figure who will stand in the sharpest contrast to the Quaker graveyard and the New England meetinghouse. (In *Ushant*, Aiken mentions Cousin Abiel, the Quaker, who was a "sly wag and iconoclast" and who lived in a cottage on Cape Cod, and the Quaker graveyard at South Yarmouth, Massachusetts, in which some of Aiken's ancestors are buried.) The selection printed below is the conclusion of a poem of over 400 lines.

12

Northwest by north. The grasshopper weathervane
bares to the moon his golden breastplate,
swings
in his predicted circle, gilded legs and wings
bright with frost, predicting frost. The tide
scales with moon-silver, floods the marsh,
fulfils
Payne Creek and Quivett Creek, rises to lift
the fishing-boats against a jetty wall;
and past them floods the plankton and the
weed
and limp sea-lettuce for the horseshoe crab
who sleeps till daybreak in his nest of reed.   10
The hour is open as the mind is open.
Closed as the mind is closed. Opens as the
hand opens
to receive the ghostly snowflakes of the moon,
closes
to feel the sunbeams of the bloodstream warm
our human inheritance of touch. The air
tonight
brings back to the all-remembering world, its
ghosts,
home from the Great Year on the Wind
Wheel Circle.
On that invisible wave we lift, we too,
and drag at secret moorings,
stirred by the ancient currents that gave us
birth.   20

And they are here, Li Po and all the others,
our fathers and our mothers: the dead leaf's
footstep
touches the grass: those who were lost at sea
and those the innocents the too-soon dead:
                                  all mankind
and all it ever knew is here in-gathered,
held in our hands, and in the wind
breathed by the pines on Sheepfold Hill.
                                  How still
the Quaker Graveyard, the Meeting House
how still,   30
where Cousin Abiel, on a night like this,
now long since dead, but then how young,
how young,
scuffing among the dead leaves after frost
looked up and saw the Wine Star, listened
and heard
borne from all quarters the Wind Wheel
Circle word:
the father within him, the mother within him,
the self
coming to self through love of each for each.
In this small mute democracy of stones
is it Abiel or Li Po who lies
and lends us against death our speech?   40
They are the same, and it is both who teach.
The poets and the prophecies are ours:
and these are with us as we turn, in turn,
the leaves of love that fill the Book of Change.

From The Crystal (1958)

The first line of *The Crystal* reads "What time is it now, brother Pythagoras, by the pale stone. . . ." Pythagoras is the celebrated Greek philosopher, born *c.* 582 B.C. His knowledge of medicine, mathematics, and music brought him fame throughout the Greek world, and his reputation as a wise man and seer gathered about him a group of disciples. In this poem (like that above) Aiken again wants a representative of the archetypal poet, a poet from the misty early beginnings of Western literature, but who nevertheless, since Aiken's contention is that mankind does not change and that poetry does not change, is a man who can be saluted by the modern poet as "brother." Again, as in *A Letter from Li Po*, the poem comes to rest in a New England scene, the "ancient farmhouse" in which the poet now writes. The time is that of our own century.

5

What is the voyage and who is the voyager?
Who is it now hoisting the sail
casting off the rope and running out the oars
the helmsman with his hand on the tiller
and his eyes turned to windward? What time
    is it now
in the westward pour of the worlds and the
    westward
pour of the mind? Like a centipede on a
    mirror
the galley stands still in a blaze of light
and yet swims forward: on the mirror of
    eternity
glitters like a golden scarab: and the ranked
    oars   10
strike down in harmony beat down in unison
churn up the water to phosphor and foam

and yet like the galley are still.
                    So you
still stand there, your hand on the tiller,
at the center of your thought, which is
    timeless,
yourself become crystal. While we,
still locked in the west, yet are present before
    you,
and wait and are silent.
                    In the ancient
                            farmhouse
which has now become your temple
we listen again to the caucus of robins   20
the whistle of migrant voices and wings
the turn of the great glass of season.
You taught the migration of souls: all things
must continue, since numbers are deathless:
the mind, like these migrants, crosses all
    seasons,
and thought, like these cries, is immortal.
The cocktails sparkle, are an oblation.
We pour for the gods, and will always,
you there, we here, and the others who follow,
pour thus in communion. Separate in time,   30
and yet not separate. Making oblation
in a single moment of consciousness
to the endless forever-together.
                            This night
we all set sail for the west.

WILLIAM CARLOS WILLIAMS (1883–1963)

We have earlier scrutinized William Carlos Williams' credentials as an Imagist. He was a friend of Ezra Pound and of H. D. from the time that all three were students at the University of Pennsylvania. Williams contributed poems to the first Imagist anthology, *Des Imag-* *istes,* in 1914. But whereas H. D. usually limits herself to a Greek setting and Amy Lowell in her Imagist poems also often uses an exotic rather than a native setting, Williams' poems are from the beginning pretty well tied to the local scene that he knew well.

The Red Wheelbarrow (1923)

so much depends
upon

a red wheel
barrow

glazed with rain
water

beside the white
chickens.

Philip Wheelwright makes the following comment on this poem:

A classical case (and apparently a classical failure) of the attempt to convey a simple experience through sheer simplicity of statement is to be found in Section xxi of William Carlos Williams' *Spring and All*. The eight short lines of the section, although they bear no distinguishing title, form an independent unit with no imagistic or thematic outside connections, and it may therefore be treated (as its author has, in fact, publicly spoken of it) as a single poem. [Wheelwright then quotes the poem and writes:] That is all. To most readers it will be accepted as a pleasant pastiche with no more than a fanciful justification for the opening words. To Dr. Williams, however, as he has repeatedly declared, the small remembered scene is of arresting and retaining importance. But quite obviously the personal associations and bubbles of memory that have stirred the poet's sensitive recollections are not shared by a reader whose only clues are to be found in the poem itself. The trouble is that in these lines the poet has tried to convey the simplicity of the remembered experience by a plain simplicity of utterance —by a simple simplicity, one might say, as opposed to a contextual simplicity. The attempt was bound to fail. Simplicity, when it is fresh and not banal, can scarcely be conveyed to another mind, except in rare instances where, by happy accident, two diverse sensitivities happen to be attuned in just that respect. (*Metaphor and Reality*, 1962, pp. 159–60)

Other readers, however, have tried to find a justification for the opening words "so much depends," and for the apparently matter-of-fact presentation of the wheelbarrow itself. Hillis Miller, for instance, writes as follows:

The wheelbarrow, in a famous poem, does not stand for anything or mean anything. It is an object in space dissociated from the objects around it, without reference beyond itself. It is what it is. The aim of the poem is to make it stand there for the reader in its separateness, as the words of the poem stand on the page. (*Poets of Reality*, 1965, p. 307)

Yet some readers might be disposed to wonder whether Miller is right in thus describing the poet's aim. If he is, then a good color photograph of the wheelbarrow in the backyard might do the specified job even better than words. (Best of all, of course, would be to present the red wheelbarrow itself—as a toy or full size.)

Like his friend Ezra Pound, Williams fairly early became dissatisfied with Imagism in favor of what he and some of the disciples of Ezra Pound called "Objectivism." Williams wrote that "We had had 'imagism' . . . which ran quickly out. That, though it had been useful in ridding the field of verbiage, had no formal necessity implicit in it. It had already dribbled off into so-called 'free verse' which, as we saw, was a misnomer. There is no such thing as free verse! Verse is measure of some sort."[1] Yet Williams found it easier to indicate his dissatisfaction with the formlessness and aimlessness of Imagism rather than to give a positive account of Objectivism.

He tells us that a poem is an object—like a Cubist painting or a symphony—and that therefore it has to have form, but it needs a new form, one "consonant" with our times. To say all this is well enough, but the definition is too vague to be of much help. What Williams meant by Objectivism can be more profitably inferred from his most successful poems rather than from the statements of Williams speaking as theorist. Williams' preferences for concrete particulars and his notions of America and American poetry will be more helpful here than his abstract specifications.

The influence of Whitman[2] upon Williams was early and powerful. Characteristically, Williams writes of the America of the present and of urban and industrialized America. We have

[1] Quoted from John Malcolm Brinnin, *William Carlos Williams* (1963), p. 30.
[2] See, for example, James E. Breslin, "Whitman and the Early Development of William Carlos Williams," *PMLA* (1967).

already noted that he likes to write about white leghorns in suburban backyards and about weeds like Queen Anne's lace, that flourish on suburban lots as well as on old pasture land. But most of all he likes to write about people, working people, second-generation immigrants such as live in the industrial cities of northern New Jersey. These interests and this subject matter find expression in his stories and novels as well as in his poetry.

Williams has a Whitmanesque hostility toward the European muse and toward the forms and conventions of traditional poetry. He has an aggressively theoretical (as well as a practical and instinctive) concern for the local. He tells us over and over again that "there are no ideas but in things." His method, indeed, is a kind of symbolism turned upside down: instead of embodying his ideas in things so that the things become symbols of those ideas, he undertakes to present things so accurately and so convincingly that the ideas that reside in them will inevitably rise up to our apprehension without any sense of conscious intervention by the poet.[3]

Richard Ellman a number of years ago put the matter very well in a review (*Kenyon Review*, Summer, 1952) in which he ascribes to Williams "the gift of *gaucherie*. He portrays himself struggling through the world of life and letters, typewriter in one hand and stethoscope in the other, delivering poems dextrously between triplets." But Ellman goes on to remark that Williams' pursuit of the naked truth has its drawbacks. "The danger of keeping one's clothes off is suffering from exposure. Dr. Williams' detestation of philosophy, of abstraction, of generalization is so strong that it affects his

work adversely. His method is to amass particulars until generalizations form themselves, but they don't necessarily do so." The method resembles that of Pound in the *Cantos*, though, of course, Pound had ideas and sometimes began with them.

Williams not only insists that there are no ideas but in things. A corollary proposition would hold that for the contemporary American poet there are no ideas except in contemporary American things. Williams' almost fanatical stress on this point helps account for his hostility to one of Ezra Pound's other old and close friends, T. S. Eliot.

In his *Autobiography*, Williams tells us that the appearance of T. S. Eliot's *The Waste Land* in 1922 "wiped out our world as if an atom bomb had been dropped upon it. . . ." The vehemence with which Williams rejects Eliot's achievement suggests the extent of Williams' emotional investment in America as the promise of the future and his extreme repugnance to anything that smacked of an attachment to the Old World. Clearly, Williams' response to the publication of *The Waste Land* was a feeling of betrayal. He tells us that he "felt at once that it had set me back twenty years, and I'm sure it did. Critically Eliot returned us to the classroom just at the moment when I felt that we were on the point of an escape to matters much closer to the essence of a new art form itself—rooted in the locality which should give it fruit. I knew at once that in certain ways I was most defeated." Williams remarks even more caustically: "I had to watch [Eliot] carry my world off with him, the fool, to the enemy." The note of grievance is very like Browning's complaint against Wordsworth in his poem entitled "The Lost Leader": "Just for a handful of silver he left us/ Just for a ribbon to stick in his cloak."

The justice of Williams' remarks must wait, of course, on the reader's ultimate judgment of what Eliot's *The Waste Land* actually means and on his estimate of what Eliot's attitude toward human experience and history is worth. Even so, it is useful to record at this point the shock that Williams experienced when *The*

---

[3] This conception of poetry goes back at least as early as the poetry of William Wordsworth. Like Williams, Wordsworth sometimes simply juxtaposes images and trusts that something like spontaneous combustion will occur in the mind of the reader: the poetry will flame up without the poet's having to strike a single match. Like Williams, Wordsworth on occasion wrote poems of a blank and artless honesty—poems presumably based on experiences that meant much to him—but which elicit from the reader not much more than a puzzled and uncomprehending stare.

Waste Land appeared. A good many of Williams' contemporaries, one may add, were affected in the same way.

Perhaps Williams' best presentation of the subject matter with which he worked lovingly and patiently through a lifetime is to be found in his long poem *Paterson* which appeared in five books from 1946 through 1958. As he tells us in his *Autobiography* (p. 390), he started to write this poem because "a man is indeed a city. . . ." As he puts it: "The poet does not . . . permit himself to go beyond the thought to be discovered in the context of that with which he is dealing: no ideas but in things. The poet thinks with his poem, in that lies his thought, and that in itself is the profundity. The thought is *Paterson*, to be discovered there."

This lyrical-historical-poetic-prosaical-quotidian-eternal account of what Williams thought of as a completely typical American small city gave Williams exactly the proper receptacle for his notion of American material. It is his major opus and it is as typical of his spirit as Pound's *Cantos* are of Pound's. Like the *Cantos*, *Pater-*

son has been praised by some readers as a brilliantly integrated work and characterized by others as a mere ragbag into which the poet has crammed all sorts of uneven and unlikely materials. Meditation, biography, and history are juxtaposed; prose and poetry lie side by side. The poem is much too long to print here, but some notion of a few of its themes may be gathered from a reading of "Paterson: The Falls" (p. 2150).

Putting aside the question of the unity of *Paterson*, where is Williams at his characteristic best as a poet? What sort of "form" does this poet achieve since he is so aggressively "artless" and so disdainful of abstractions, ideas, and indeed anything that smacks of a contrived rhetoric?

There is, of course, no really formless poem. Whatever his apparently every-which-way manner, his unaffectedness, his aura of *gaucherie*, Williams' authentic poetry achieved form—and achieved it in even some kind of traditional sense. Consider the following poem. The poet disarmingly entitles it "A Sort of a Song."

A Sort of a Song (1944)

Let the snake wait under
his weed
and the writing
be of words, slow and quick, sharp
to strike, quiet to wait,
sleepless.

—through metaphor to reconcile
the people and the stones.
Compose. (No ideas
but in things) Invent!   10
Saxifrage is my flower that splits
the rocks.

The poem is of course a ⟨poem about poetry.⟩ An old-fashioned conventional poet might have written: Let my writing imitate a snake that can wait under his weed with infinite patience; let my writing be like the snake, that throughout its waiting remains sleepless and ready to

strike. But Williams—quite properly—sees no reason to spell out the <u>analogy</u>. He takes it for granted that his reader can find it.

The second part of the poem indicates the purpose of the poem: it is to reconcile—through metaphor—the people and the stones. What does Williams mean by reconciling people and stones? If the collocation is surprising and even shocking, it is also very rich. Think of all the things that stones represent: the least lifelike things around us, the solid material of our buildings, things relatively eternal as compared with our quickly aging and crumbling bodies, and so on. The poem closes with admonitions to the poet: "Compose." That is, put things in a pattern so that the ideas will emerge from them. "Invent," that is, discover-create ("invent" can mean either).

Finally the poet closes with an intimation that the poem is the flower that can grow among the stones and that can break even these mute heavy apparently meaningless objects. Saxi-frage, by the way, is the name of a particular flower and it means literally a "rock-breaker."

Or consider as another example the following "Song."

Song (1962)

beauty is a shell
from the sea
where she rules triumphant
till love has had its way with her

scallops and
lion's paws
sculptured to the
tune of retreating waves

undying accents
repeated till   10
the ear and the eye lie
down together in the same bed

This poem shows how richly allusive Williams can be—in spite of his apparent literal inconsequence. The first stanza clearly is an allusion to Botticelli's painting "The Birth of Venus." The Italian quattrocento painter depicting an incident from the legend of Venus, the goddess of beauty, who is born of the sea foam, shows her riding in a great shell over the waves, being blown by the sea breezes to shore. The scallops and lion's paws are suggested—though Williams is letting his imagination play in his way of interpreting them—in the modeling that Botticelli gives to the shell.

Finally the poet wishes to indicate how in a good poem the images of the poem and its music become one. He has presented an image of the shell of beauty riding triumphantly over the waves and he has mentioned the "tune" of the retreating waves. Now he brings them together—as, he implies, they must be brought together in a good poem. But in order to make his point he employs a metaphor: the accents must be repeated until

> the ear and the eye lie
> down together in the same bed.

The figure is a bold one. The eye and the ear are married—lie down in the same bed.

Such marriages of matter and form are most easily illustrated from short poems like the two we have just discussed. But Williams can achieve such formal intensity in his larger poems also, as, for example, in his pictures of American life past and present as it moves around him and particularly in some of his meditative poems, a number of which he wrote toward the end of his life, such as "Asphodel, That Greeny Flower."

Randall Jarrell, who became one of Williams' most zealous champions, has provided us with an account of Williams' strengths and weaknesses. He writes that Williams

is a *very* good but *very* limited poet, particularly in vertical range. He is a notably unreasoning intuitive writer—is not, of course, an intellectual at all, in either the best or the worst sense of the word; and he has further limited himself by volunteering for and organizing a long dreary imaginary war in which America and the Present are fighting against Europe and the Past. But go a few hundred years back inside the most American American and it is Europe: Dr. Williams is just as much Darkest Europe as any of us, way down there in the middle of his past.

In his long one-sided war with Eliot Dr. Williams seems to me to come off surprisingly badly—particularly so when we compare the whole of *Paterson* with the *Four Quartets*. When we read the *Four Quartets* we are reading the long poem of a poet so temperamentally isolated that he does not even put another character, another human being treated at length, into the whole poem; and yet the poem (probably the best since the *Duino Elegies*) impresses us not with its limitations but with its range and elevation, with how much it knows not simply about men but about Man—not simply about one city or one country but about the West, that West of which America is no more than the last part. (*Partisan Review*, November–December, 1951, p. 700)

Jarrell's summation does not, of course, represent a consensus. Other observers ought to be heard from, particularly critics whose special interest is to define the particular quality that Williams sought to achieve in his own poetry. Here follows a passage in which John Malcolm Brinnin describes Williams' pioneering spirit, his "refreshing ability to surprise himself."

Most poets who have reached an artistic maturity as advanced as Williams' have long ago defined for themselves an area in which [even those] poems inspired by new experience and the surprise encounters of everyday existence quite naturally find a place. If they have not come to a settled view of life, they at least are marked by attitudes that color their thinking and lend a consistent tone to its expression. These poets have achieved a style of language that identifies them as surely as the clothes they wear. When their individual interests are repeated and developed in the course of many poems, their predilections, like their uses of language, tend to fall into patterns. Once a pattern has become clear, its rhythms obvious and its figures familiar, it takes on the character of a territory staked out and settled. The poet's authority there is both natural and appropriate: he has found a local habitation and created a world of such distinctive character that any sensitive reader knows at once into just what territory he has ventured. The worlds of Frost and Stevens and Cummings can be recognized at the threshold; and while, in each case, objects that loom beyond may vary enormously, they are always harmonious with their settings and obedient to laws of sensibility that are seldom relaxed.

In the case of Williams, the sense of a large controlling spirit, on the one hand, and

of an essentially homogeneous landscape, on the other hand, is comparatively minor. He has maintained a refreshing ability to surprise himself as often as he is surprised by what he meets, but since the element of chance is the liveliest agent in his purview, Williams' vision remains expectant and unsettled. Where other poets tend to swell in wonder, Williams, refusing to stay put, makes wonder the vehicle on which he rides. His creative life depends upon his being alive to contingencies; and since these recur with a relentlessness that keeps him always newly addressed to his task, he gives the appearance of a man forever trying to transmute base metals into gold or to re-invent the umbrella. He has never given up the attempt to capture the thing that cannot be captured, to do the work that is never done. Unlike the master craftsman who apportions his energies with an inherent sense of economy, Williams spends his with profligacy. Since he is less interested in arriving anywhere than he is in maintaining the journey at a high pitch of movement and purposiveness, his career has the quality of a vector that continually points a direction that needs no goal. (*William Carlos Williams*, 1965, pp. 30–32)

Finally, we print a short selection from Hugh Kenner, who is here particularly concerned with Williams' conception of poetry as a "drama of utterance: not a statement . . . but a miraculous action" in which a poem is "identical with its own paraphrase."

Kenner illustrates by quoting the following poem by Williams.

As the cat
climbed over
the top of

the jamcloset
first the right
forefoot

carefully
then the hind
stepped down

into the pit of
the empty
flowerpot

This poem is a simple example of the act Williams is always ambitious of performing: the reduction to zero of the space between the words the poet writes and the words that will convey the thing that happened, leaving paraphrase no elbow room whatever; and the corresponding intensification of our interest in the tensions of predication that affirm word after word. Tennyson wrote,

> I held it truth, with him who sings
> To one clear harp in divers tones,
> That men may rise on stepping-stones
> Of their dead selves to higher things;

and it is a common place observation that if we shake and wring out the statement this contains, writing for instance, "I agreed with another poet that people are capable of improving themselves by wise use of past experience," the poetry gets lost, and the introduction of the other poet, which was the most striking feature of the first version, becomes fatuous (we are apt to take an irrelevant interest in a footnote informing us that it was Goethe). But it is intolerable to Dr. Williams that the poem and the direct statement shall not coincide.

> Is this the counterfoil to sweetest
>
> music? The source of poetry that
> seeing the clock stopped, says
> The clock has stopped
>
> that ticked yesterday so well?

and hears the sound of lakewater splashing—that is now stone.

He presents to us, then, the continuous fascination of watching word succeed word like the sections of a telescope opening, as though nothing more mysterious were at work than natural discourse; and simultaneously of observing the whole sequence of words arch through space and vanish with a single echo in a way no natural discourse can manage. There is nothing for commentary to do, except once in a while remove some simple impediment to understanding or supply for instance such a quotation as the following, from the poet's *Autobiography:*

Day in day out when the inarticulate patient struggles to lay himself bare for you . . . so caught off balance that he reveals some secret twist of a whole community's pathetic way of thought, a man is suddenly seized again with a desire to speak of the underground stream which for a moment has come up just under the surface. . . . We begin to see that the underlying meaning of all that they want to tell us and have always failed to communicate is the poem, the poem which their lives are being lived to realize. No one will believe it. And it is the actual words, as we hear them spoken under all circumstances, which contain it. It is actually there, in the life before us, every minute that we are listening, a rarest element—not in our imagination but there, there in fact. ("The Drama of Utterance," *Massachusetts Review,* Winter, 1962, pp. 329–30)

BIOGRAPHICAL CHART

1920–23 With Robert McAlmon edits the first *Contact*

1925 *In the American Grain*

1928 *A Voyage to Pagany*, dedicated to "the first of all of us, my old friend Ezra Pound"

1934 *Collected Poems 1921–1931*, with preface by Wallace Stevens

1937 *White Mule*, a novel

1946 *Paterson: Book 1*

1948 *Paterson: Book 2; A Dream of Love: A Play in Three Acts and Eight Scenes*

1949 *Selected Poems*, with introduction by Randall Jarrell; *Paterson: Book 3*

1950 *The Collected Later Poems*; elected to the National Institute of Arts and Letters

1951 *The Collected Earlier Poems; Paterson: Book 4; Autobiography*; suffers first stroke; retires from medical practice; *The Desert Music and Other Poems*

1954 *Selected Essays*

1957 *The Selected Letters of William Carlos Williams*

1958 *Paterson: Book 5; I Wanted to Write a Poem*; elected to the American Academy of Arts and Letters

1962 *Pictures from Breughel and Other Poems*

1963 Receives Pulitzer prize for *Pictures from Breughel; The Collected Later Poems* (revised edition); dies, March 4, in Rutherford, New Jersey; *Paterson*, including notes for Book 6

FURTHER READINGS

The reader will find individual titles of Williams' works in the biographical chart.

John Malcolm Brinnin, *William Carlos Williams* (1963)
Randall Jarrell, *Poetry and the Age* (1953)
Vivienne Koch, *William Carlos Williams* (1950)
J. Hillis Miller, *Poets of Reality* (1965)

Alan Ostrum, *The Poetic World of William Carlos Williams* (1966)
Walter S. Peterson, *An Approach to Paterson* (1967)
Linda W. Wagner, *The Poems of William Carlos Williams* (1964)
Mike Weaver, *William Carlos Williams: The American Background* (1971)

By the Road to the Contagious Hospital (1923)

This poem appeared in *Spring and All*. Williams thought it one of his best poems and even Yvor Winters, who wrote that Williams "was a foolish and ignorant man, [though] at moments a fine stylist," admired the poem.

By the road to the contagious hospital
under the surge of the blue
mottled clouds driven from the
northeast—cold wind. Beyond, the
waste of broad, muddy fields
brown with dried weeds, standing and fallen

patches of standing water
the scattering of tall trees.

All along the road the reddish
purplish, forked, upstanding, twiggy   10
stuff of brushes and small trees

with dead, brown leaves under them
leafless vines—

Lifeless in appearance, sluggish
dazed spring approaches—

They enter the new world naked,
cold, uncertain of all
save that they enter. All about them
the cold, familiar wind—

Now the grass, tomorrow   20
the stiff curl of wild-carrot leaf

One by one objects are defined—
It quickens: clarity, outline of leaf

But now the stark dignity of
entrance—Still, the profound change
has come upon them; rooted, they
grip down and begin to awaken

The Dance (1944)

This poem appeared in a volume entitled *The Wedge*. Pieter Breughel (1525?–1569) was one of the great Flemish painters. A kermess is an outdoor fair held in the Low Countries. "The Dance" is deceptively simple: though we are apparently being presented with mere description, the poet has managed to convey a quality of life and an attitude toward that life.

In Breughel's great picture, The Kermess,

the dancers go round, they go round and around, the squeal and the blare and the tweedle of bagpipes, a bugle and fiddles tipping their bellies (round as the thick-sided glasses whose wash they impound) their hips and their bellies off balance to turn them. Kicking and rolling about the Fair Grounds, swinging their butts, those shanks must be sound to bear up under such   10 rollicking measures, prance as they dance in Breughel's great picture, The Kermess.

Paterson: The Falls (1944)

This poem is a prospectus to Williams' long poem *Paterson* in five books, the first of which was published in 1946. Though Williams was born in Rutherford, New Jersey, and practiced medicine there, he chose for the setting of his poem the nearby city of Paterson, in part perhaps because of the falls of the Passaic River and because events in its history provided him with the materials that he needed. In this poem Williams mentions only four sections of the longer poem, for Book 5 was an afterthought. (Notes for a sixth book were found among Williams' papers after his death.)

Williams saw in the river an emblem of time and heard in the falls an attempt to speak. His poem is an attempt to understand that language and thus come to understand reality. Paterson, the city, is conceived as a man, a giant listening to the roar of the falls. The "shirt-sleeved Evangelist" with his call to repentance and his promise of eternal life appears in Book 2. Alexander Hamilton saw in the falls a source of power for industry and wished Paterson to become a great manufacturing city. (It has today large silk mills, and power for these has drawn off water from the falls.) The eels which are hatched in the warm waters of the Sargasso Sea, even further south of Hamilton's birthplace on St. Croix, migrate, as Hamilton did, to the waters of the Atlantic coast, but can go up the Passaic no further than the falls. Book 4 deals with the

modern city—broken apart from nature and from learning.[1]

analysis

What common language to unravel?
The Falls, combed into straight lines
from that rafter of a rock's
lip. Strike in! the middle of

some trenchant phrase, some
well packed clause. Then . . .
This is my plan. 4 sections: First,
the archaic persons of the drama.

An eternity of bird and bush,
resolved. An unraveling: 10
the confused streams aligned, side
by side, speaking! Sound

married to strength, a strength
of falling—from a height! The wild

[1] Richard Gustafson (in "William Carlos Williams' *Paterson*," *College English*, 1965, pp. 532–34, 39) summarizes Williams' plan as follows:

Book I, "The Delineaments of the Giants," shows how the schemes and plots of the past have become dead history. Book II, "Sunday in the Park," shows how the present tries to find beauty in mere self-indulgence. Book III, "The Library," shows how the present seeks escape in history and philosophy. Book IV, "The Run to the Sea," shows how the present finds beauty in its posterity. Book V, untitled but dedicated to Toulouse-Lautrec, shows that the only beauty that persists is art.

The rest of Gustafson's article is devoted to a more minute analysis of the detail of the five books.

voice of the shirt-sleeved
Evangelist rivaling, Hear

me! I am the Resurrection
and the Life! echoing
among the bass and pickerel, slim
eels from Barbados, Sargasso   20

Sea, working up the coast to that
bounty, ponds and wild streams—
Third, the old town: Alexander Hamilton
working up from St. Croix,

from that sea! and a deeper, whence
he came! stopped cold
by that unmoving roar, fastened

there: the rocks silent

but the water, married to the stone,
voluble, though frozen; the water   30
even when and though frozen
still whispers and moans—

And in the brittle air
a factory bell clangs, at dawn, and
snow whines under their feet. Fourth,
the modern town, a

disembodied roar! the cataract and
its clamor broken apart—and from
all learning, the empty
ear struck from within, roaring . . .   40

Asphodel, That Greeny Flower: Coda (1955)

This long poem is divided into three short "books" and a coda. The asphodel is an actual flower growing in Mediterranean lands but the Greek and Latin poets also placed it in the afterworld. The virtuous and happy dead walked in the Elysian fields through meadows of asphodel.

It is the appropriate flower for a poem about the close of life and impending death. As the opening lines of Book 1 indicate, the poem is addressed to the poet's wife.

The poem is written in the triadic stanza which is found so frequently in Williams' last poems, and it also makes use of what Williams called the "variable foot." In a letter (quoted by John Malcolm Brinnin) Williams gave the following examples:

(1) The smell of the heat is boxwood
    (2) when rousing us
        (3) a movement of the air
(4) stirs our thoughts
    (5) that had no life in them
        (6) to a life, a life in which
(or)
(1) Mother of God! Our Lady!
    (2) the heart
        (3) is an unruly master:
(4) Forgive us our sins
    (5) as we
        (6) forgive.

(7) those who have sinned against

"Count a single beat to each numeral. You may not agree with my ear, but that is the way I count the line. Over the whole poem it gives a pattern to the meter that can be felt as a new measure. It gives resources to the ear which result in a language which we hear spoken about us every day." (*Williams Carlos Williams*, 1963, p. 34)

But, Brinnin writes,

as an explanation, and an attempted demonstration of the "variable foot" as meticulous as any Williams has made, this account nevertheless gives a reader or critic little more than a statement of intention. Williams anticipates the difficulty when he says, "You may not agree with my ear, but that is the way I count the line." His count is arbitrary, applied to lines that may ring with an authentic music in his ears, but which are apt to register with an entirely different measure, and consequently a different music, on the ears of anyone else. The way in which one hears naturally determines the way one writes, but the enormous variability in the capacity to hear, plus all the intricacies of selection that set one hearer apart from another, gives Williams' theory so much latitude that it becomes all but useless for analysis or for emulation.

That this method works for him is indisputable. But if it is to work for anyone else, its pretensions as theory and method must be put aside in favor of the unique pragmatic ingenuity which gives his poetry its character."
(PP. 34–35)

Inseparable from the fire
    its light
        takes precedence over it.
Then follows
    what we have dreaded—
        but it can never
overcome what has gone before.
    In the huge gap
        between the flash
and the thunderstroke
    spring has come in 10
        or a deep snow fallen.
Call it old age.
    In that stretch
        we have lived to see
a colt kick up his heels.
    Do not hasten
        laugh and play
in an eternity
    the heat will not overtake the light 20
        That's sure.
That gelds the bomb,
    permitting
        that the mind contain it.
This is that interval,
    that sweetest interval,
        when love will blossom,
come early, come late
    and give itself to the lover.
Only the imagination is real! 30
    I have declared it
        time without end.
If a man die
    it is because death
        has first
possessed his imagination.
    But if he refuse death—
        no greater evil
can befall him
    unless it be the death of love 40
        meet him
in full career.
    Then indeed
        for him

the light has gone out.
But love and the imagination
    are of a piece,
        swift as the light
to avoid destruction.
    So we come to watch time's flight 50
        as we might watch
summer lightning
    or fireflies, secure,
        by grace of the
            imagination,
safe in its care.
    For if
        the light itself
has escaped,
    the whole edifice opposed to it
        goes down. 60
Light, the imagination
    and love,
        in our age,
by natural law,
    which we worship,
        maintain
all of a piece
    their dominance.
So let us love
    confident as is the light 70
        in its struggle with
            darkness
that there is as much to say
    and more
        for the one side
and that not the darker
    which John Donne
        for instance
among many men
    presents to us.
        In the controversy 80
touching the younger
    and the older Tolstoi,
        Villon, St. Anthony, Kung
            [Confucius],
Rimbaud, Buddha
    and Abraham Lincoln
        the palm goes
always to the light;
    Who most shall advance the light—
        call it what you may!
The light 90
    for all time shall outspeed
        the thunder crack.
Medieval pageantry

[Handwritten marginal annotations: "light over heat in lightning"; "violence w/o oblivion"; "between birth + death"; "transcend w/ freedom of imagination"; "moment of redemption"; "death as failure of will"; "footnotes?"; "neo-romanticism"; "light as foundation"]

is human and we enjoy
                the rumor of it
as in our world we enjoy
                the reading of Chaucer,
                                likewise
a priest's raiment
                (or that of a savage chieftain).   100
                It is all
a celebration of the light.
                All the pomp and ceremony
                                of weddings,
"Sweet Thames, run softly
                till I end
                                my song,"—   *[handwritten: Spenser's Prothalamion]*
are of an equal sort.
For our wedding, too,
                the light was wakened   110
                                and shone. The light!
the light stood before us
                waiting!
                                I thought the world   *[handwritten: sweetest interval]*
stood still.
                At the altar
                                so intent was I

before my vows,
                so moved by your presence
                                a girl so pale   120
and ready to faint
                that I pitied
                                and wanted to protect you.
As I think of it now,
                after a lifetime,
                                it is as if
a sweet-scented flower
                were poised
                                and for me did open.
Asphodel   *[handwritten: 130 unheard melodies are sweeter]*
                has no odor
                                save to the imagination
but it too
                celebrates the light.
                                It is late
but an odor
                as from our wedding
                                has revived for me
and begun again to penetrate
                into all crevices   140
                                of my world.

WALLACE STEVENS (1879–1955)

Poems by Wallace Stevens began to appear in the magazines as early as 1913, though he did not bring out a volume until 1923. For a time many people were so intrigued with the notion that a lawyer who was an officer in a big Hartford insurance company wanted to write poetry that they paid less attention to the poetry than to the startling circumstances of its production. It is true that Wallace Stevens' first volume, *Harmonium*, made a resounding impact on some of the poets and the critics of the time, but then there ensued a long silence before the next volume, *Ideas of Order*, which was not published until 1935. Thus Stevens' poetry, though it never dropped completely out of sight, was regarded as a very special dish, an aesthetician's parfait.

That impression was strengthened by the surface quality of the poetry itself. Wallace Stevens had gone to school to the French symbolist poets of the nineteenth century. More than that, the particular "mask" that Stevens adopted was the mask of connoisseur, the man who cultivates elegant trifles, even the mask of the dandy. Some readers confused the mask with the man himself and found in the poet's careful manipulation of verbal nuance and association a measure of his lack of passion and conviction. The Depression years made such poetry seem even less relevant to humanity.

Prejudices and misapprehensions of this sort have been thoroughly swept away in the last decades. Today Wallace Stevens is regarded as one of the major American poets of the twentieth century. Roy Harvey Pearce finds in Stevens a realization of Emerson's hope "for a writer of the future who would take upon himself the duties of poet, philosopher, and priest" (*The Continuity of American Poetry*, 1961).

As to the basic facts of the cultural situation, Stevens and Eliot are in substantial agreement, though they were to react to it in opposite ways. Stevens puts his position thus: "In an age of disbelief, it is for the poet to supply the satisfac-

tions of belief, in his measure and in his style." A useful way of interpreting Stevens' poems is to say that they attempt to supply "the satisfactions of [religious] belief."

In his very first volume, one can find more than one poem that faces up to a world emptied of the gods. Thus, in "Sunday Morning," a woman sits over a late breakfast on a sunny porch. She is evidently not going to church this morning.

Sunday Morning (1923)

[handwritten: Death of God as a poetic failure: failure of imagination]

1

Complacencies of the peignoir, and late
Coffee and oranges in a sunny chair,
And the green freedom of a cockatoo
Upon a rug mingle to dissipate
The holy hush of ancient sacrifice.
She dreams a little, and she feels the dark
Encroachment of that old catastrophe,
As a calm darkens among water-lights.
The pungent oranges and bright, green wings
Seem things in some procession of the dead,　10
Winding across wide water, without sound.
The day is like wide water, without sound,
Stilled for the passing of her dreaming feet
Over the seas, to silent Palestine,
Dominion of the blood and sepulchre.

2

Why should she give her bounty to the dead?
What is divinity if it can come
Only in silent shadows and in dreams?
Shall she not find in comforts of the sun,
In pungent fruit and bright, green wings, or
　else　20
In any balm or beauty of the earth,
Things to be cherished like the thought of
　heaven?
Divinity must live within herself:
Passions of rain, or moods in falling snow;
Grievings in loneliness, or unsubdued
Elations when the forest blooms; gusty
Emotions on wet roads on autumn nights;
All pleasures and all pains, remembering
The bough of summer and the winter branch.
These are the measures destined for her soul.　30

3

Jove in the clouds had his inhuman birth.
No mother suckled him, no sweet land gave

[handwritten: power of pagan divinity]

Large-mannered motions to his mythy mind
He moved among us, as a muttering king,
Magnificent, would move among his hinds,
Until our blood, commingling, virginal,
With heaven, brought such requital to desire
The very hinds discerned it, in a star.
Shall our blood fail? Or shall it come to be
The blood of paradise? And shall the earth　40
Seem all of paradise that we shall know?
The sky will be much friendlier then than
　now,
A part of labor and a part of pain,
And next in glory to enduring love,
Not this dividing and indifferent blue.

4

[handwritten: impermanence]

She says, "I am content when wakened birds,
Before they fly, test the reality
Of misty fields, by their sweet questionings;
But when the birds are gone, and their warm
　fields
Return no more, where, then, is paradise?"　50
There is not any haunt of prophecy,
Nor any old chimera of the grave,
Neither the golden underground, nor isle
Melodious, where spirits gat them home,
Nor visionary south, nor cloudy palm
Remote on heaven's hill, that has endured
As April's green endures; or will endure
Like her remembrance of awakened birds,
Or her desire for June and evening, tipped
By the consummation of the swallow's wings.　60

5

She says, "But in contentment I still feel
The need of some imperishable bliss."
Death is the mother of beauty; hence from
　her,
Alone, shall come fulfilment to our dreams

[handwritten: eternal bliss]

[handwritten: vs changing world]

And our desires. Although she strews the
  leaves
Of sure obliteration on our paths,
The path sick sorrow took, the many paths
Where triumph rang its brassy phrase, or
  love
Whispered a little out of tenderness,
She makes the willow shiver in the sun   70
For maidens who were wont to sit and gaze
Upon the grass, relinquished to their feet.
She causes boys to pile new plums and pears
On disregarded plate. The maidens taste
And stray impassioned in the littering leaves.

6

Is there no change of death in paradise?
Does ripe fruit never fall? Or do the boughs
Hang always heavy in that perfect sky,
Unchanging, yet so like our perishing earth,
With rivers like our own that seek for seas   80
They never find, the same receding shores
That never touch with inarticulate pang?
Why set the pear upon those river-banks
Or spice the shores with odors of the plum?
Alas, that they should wear our colors there, *7 error of imagining transcend divinity*
The silken weavings of our afternoons,
And pick the strings of our insipid lutes!
Death is the mother of beauty, mystical,
Within whose burning bosom we devise
Our earthly mothers waiting, sleeplessly.   90

7

Supple and turbulent, a ring of men
Shall chant in orgy on a summer morn
Their boisterous devotion to the sun, *new participatory divinity*
Not as a god, but as a god might be,
Naked among them, like a savage source.
Their chant shall be a chant of paradise,
Out of their blood, returning to the sky;
And in their chant shall enter, voice by
  voice,
The windy lake wherein their lord delights,
The trees, like serafin, and echoing hills,   100
That choir among themselves long afterward.
They shall know well the heavenly fellowship
Of men that perish and of summer morn.
And whence they came and whither they
  shall go
The dew upon their feet shall manifest.

8

She hears, upon that water without sound,
A voice that cries, "The tomb in Palestine
Is not the porch of spirits lingering.

2 not a retrospective salvation

It is the grave of Jesus, where he lay."
We live in an old chaos of the sun, *119 burden of meaning*
Or old dependency of day and night,
Or island solitude, unsponsored, free,
Of that wide water, inescapable.
Deer walk upon our mountains, and the quail
Whistle about us their spontaneous cries;
Sweet berries ripen in the wilderness;
And, in the isolation of the sky,
At evening, casual flocks of pigeons make
Ambiguous undulations as they sink,
Downward to darkness, on extended wings.   120

Her reverie takes the following course: Why should she give her bounty to the dead (line 16)? (The proof that the divinity is dead is that it can express itself only in "silent shadows and in dreams"—not appear in full daylight. She—and the poet himself—insist on their allegiance to the sun.)

Jove "had his inhuman birth"—"inhuman" because he really is a projection of men's minds. *?* Since "No mother suckled him," he has always remained apart from men, "a muttering king." Lines 36–38 apparently make reference to the Christian doctrine of the Incarnation, where there is commingling of "our blood" in the person of the Virgin Mary "with heaven." Men's response to the notion of an incarnation indicates a deep yearning to find godhood in themselves. The yearning is so powerful that "the very hinds [the shepherds who came to the manger in Bethlehem] discerned it, in a star."[1] *modern death of God*

The woman asks herself: Why should our human blood fail now? Surely our mortal blood will some day become "The blood of paradise." For it is only on this earth that we shall ever *?* find paradise. When that happens, "The sky will be much friendlier then than now" (line 42), for no longer will it be the habitation of some Jove far up "in the clouds."

She tells herself (stanza 4) that she is content with the world of nature, and yet (stanza 5), she still feels the need of "some imperishable bliss" (line 62). Yet on further reflection she

---

[1] It was, of course, the wise men from the East, not the shepherds ("hinds") who were attracted to Bethlehem by the star.

realizes that any imperishable bliss would be static—inhuman and without the charm of a world flickering with change, with fruit that ripens and falls and boughs that wave. Death is part of the process of a rich and meaningful life; so she is willing to say (line 63): "Death is the mother of beauty" and to repeat it in line 88.

Stanza 7 provides a vision of nature which, though emptied of the gods, can incite and sustain rituals that satisfy men's deepest impulses. The woman imagines a ring of men chanting "in orgy on a summer morn/Their boisterous devotions to the sun/Not as a god, but as a god might be,/Naked among them, like a savage source." These qualifications, so carefully made, are important to Stevens. The sun, to which devotion is paid, is not thought of here as a manifestation of a sun god like the Egyptian Ra or the Greek Apollo. It is only the natural sun, but filled with all the energies and powers that have for past ages prompted in the human breast some notion of godhead. In this "natural" heaven, there will be no angels, but the trees will be "like serafin" and the hills will constitute a "choir" like that of the fabled heavenly host. But the men chanting their devotions will accept their mortality and their fellowship will be a heavenly fellowship "of men that perish. . . ."

The poem closes with a vision of the acceptable and accepted natural "heaven" (lines 114–20), a world of change from season to season and of change from day to night. The vision of the pigeons, sinking "Downward to darkness, on extended wings," brings the poem to a close and perhaps suggests also the woman's contentment to make, in her due time, that descent into the darkness of death.

In trying to put briefly the "argument" of the poem, we have had to neglect its flesh and blood, the massive richness of the imagery, the music of phrases variously modulated or repeated in altered contexts. We have, in short, not dealt properly with what Morton Zabel calls "the richness of [the poem's] imagery and the sustained authority of [Stevens'] rhetoric." "Sunday Morning" ought to be read aloud and it ought to be read and reread with an eye and ear for these qualities.

We have cited "Sunday Morning" primarily as an example of Stevens' view of the cultural "situation," an age of unbelief. But, of course, as our commentary has suggested, Stevens has found his solution: man can discover in his own human resources, in his powers of imagination, all that he needs in order to cope with the crisis in culture.

The theme of the imagination is so pervasive in Stevens' poetry that one ought to note some of the special variations that it receives. One might very well begin with a rather tiny poem—again an early one—in which the effect of the imagination is to transform a landscape.

Anecdote of the Jar (1923)

I placed a jar in Tennessee,
And round it was, upon a hill.
It made the slovenly wilderness
Surround that hill.

The wilderness rose up to it,
And sprawled around, no longer wild.
The jar was round upon the ground
And tall and of a port in air.

It took dominion everywhere.
The jar was gray and bare.   10
It did not give of bird or bush,
Like nothing else in Tennessee.

This poem begins with what seems a rather whimsical and pointless action. After the first shock of surprise, the reader may very well put the question: "So what?" But whimsy should not be allowed to rule out the presence of significant action and certainly not the presence of poetry.

The speaker stresses not the motive of his action, but what happened to the landscape after he had placed the jar on the hill. Once there, it dominates the landscape. It makes the wilderness "surround" the hill. In the second stanza, the poet tells us that the jar tamed the wilderness so that it "sprawled around, no longer wild."

It may help us to understand what is going on if we substitute another object for the jar. Suppose that the poet had planted a maple tree on the hill. The magic would not have worked, for the maple tree would have been absorbed by the wilderness; indeed, it would simply have become another tree growing in the wilderness. In the third stanza the poet is careful to say of the jar that "It did not give of bird or bush,/Like nothing else in Tennessee." Precisely; for the magic to work, the object placed upon the hill would have to be something different from the wilderness, something "unnatural," something man-made. This jar, the poet tells us, was "gray and bare," not glittering or ornamented. But no one would mistake it for a *natural* object.

The jar makes its impress upon the mental eye and upon man's imagination, because all of us require a point of reference. A point of reference confers shape and order on the world. In the Canadian wilds, for example, it is the hunter's camp and campfire, no matter how small it is, that for him gives bearing and orientation. He kills the moose *three miles north of camp*. He loses a favorite hunting-knife *a hundred yards or so to the west of camp*.

The theme of the imagination informs nearly all of Stevens' poetry, but there is a great variety in the directness or obliquity with which Stevens approaches it. There is also a great variety in the tones of the voice in which he talks about the way the imagination shapes our notion of reality. For example, consider "Bantams in Pine-Woods":

Bantams in Pine-Woods (1923)

Chieftain Iffucan of Azcan in caftan
Of tan with henna hackles, halt!

Damned universal cock, as if the sun
Was blackamoor to bear your blazing tail.

Fat! Fat! Fat! Fat! I am the personal.
Your world is you. I am my world.

You ten-foot poet among inchlings. Fat!
Begone! An inchling bristles in these pines,

Bristles, and points their Appalachian tangs,
And fears not portly Azcan nor his hoos.   10

The poet is obviously enjoying himself here; the opening lines are done with gusto. The bantam rooster is a chieftain. He is "Iffucan," a name with a vaguely Indian sound, though plainly it is composed of the three English words *if you can*—just as "Azcan," part of his title, resolves into *as can*. The reader need not concern himself too much with whether "caftan" (a long-sleeved gown worn in the Middle East) is overspecific

or whether it is the best way of describing the bantam cock's feathers; Stevens is here primarily playing with the possibilities of the *-an* syllable. The bird's coloring is certainly evoked for us, and, more important, the sense of the bustling importance and cocky arrogance that he exudes.

If the poet is amused, he is also admiring and understanding: each of us makes his own world: "I am the personal," the poet says. But he recognizes that "Your world is you." For the bantam cock makes his world also and sees it in terms of himself. He is a poet too. In his arrogance, the cock becomes a "ten-foot poet among inchlings." But the human being who has met him on the path, nevertheless shoos him out of the way. "If you can" conducts himself *as if he can* —as one able to dispute the path with the human "inchling" who is in fact, but only *in fact*, so much taller than he.

The theme of the imagination is greatly extended and given one of its more elaborate developments in "The Idea of Order at Key West."

The Idea of Order at Key West (1935)

[handwritten: cf. Jar shaping the landscape]

[handwritten: Shelley: artist as heroic cosmogenist]

She sang beyond the genius of the sea.   *[handwritten: sea beyond mind]*
The water never formed to mind or voice,
Like a body wholly body, fluttering
Its empty sleeves; and yet its mimic motion
Made constant cry, caused constantly a cry,
That was not ours although we understood,   *[handwritten: mysterious voice]*
Inhuman, of the veritable ocean.

The sea was not a mask. No more was she.   *[handwritten: not pure mimesis]*
The song and water were not medleyed sound
Even if what she sang was what she heard,   10
Since what she sang was uttered word by
    word.
It may be that in all her phrases stirred
The grinding water and the gasping wind;   *[handwritten: artist's made identity]*
But it was she and not the sea we heard.

For she was the maker of the song she sang.
The ever-hooded, tragic-gestured sea
Was merely a place by which she walked to
    sing.
Whose spirit is this? we said, because we
    knew
It was the spirit that we sought and knew
That we should ask this often as she sang.   20

If it was only the dark voice of the sea
That rose, or even colored by many waves;
If it was only the outer voice of sky
And cloud, of the sunken coral water-walled,
However clear, it would have been deep air,
The heaving speech of air, a summer sound
Repeated in a summer without end
And sound alone. But it was more than that,
More even than her voice, and ours, among   *[handwritten: surplus of art]*
The meaningless plungings of water and the
    wind,   30
Theatrical distances, bronze shadows heaped
On high horizons, mountainous atmospheres
Of sky and sea.
                    It was her voice that made
The sky acutest at its vanishing.   *[handwritten: contextual dynamic]*
She measured to the hour its solitude.
She was the single artificer of the world
In which she sang. And when she sang, the
    sea,
Whatever self it had, became the self
That was her song, for she was the maker.
    Then we,
As we beheld her striding there alone,   40

Knew that there never was a world for her
Except the one she sang and, singing, made.

Ramon Fernandez, tell me, if you know,
Why, when the singing ended and we turned   *[handwritten: illuminating power]*
Toward the town, tell why the glassy lights,
The lights in the fishing boats at anchor
    there,
As the night descended, tilting in the air,
Mastered the night and portioned out the sea,
Fixing emblazoned zones and fiery poles,
Arranging, deepening, enchanting night.   50

Oh! Blessed rage for order, pale Ramon,
The maker's rage to order words of the sea,
Words of the fragrant portals, dimly-starred,
And of ourselves and of our origins,
In ghostlier demarcations, keener sounds.

The scene of the poem is taken presumably from one of Stevens' trips South. (Florida, the Mississippi Gulf coast, and Mexico come into his poems very often.) A girl is singing by the sea and her song causes the poet to meditate on the whole problem of the relation of poetry to reality and the power of the imagination. The poem begins with a number of careful definitions and rejections. The first line tells us that the girl sang "beyond the genius of the sea." The older Romantic poetry would simply say that she expressed the genius, or the spirit, of the sea. But this is not exact enough for the poet here. He carefully distinguishes between the voice of the sea and the voice of the girl. The sea has its own noises and makes its constant cry. It is a cry which may remind us of a human cry but it is not human (line 6), even though we understand it. It is not "ours" but the sound of the ocean itself.

The poet also rejects another Romantic theme: that the spirit speaking through the ocean is also speaking through the girl. Line 8 says that the sea was not a mask, though adding "no more was she." Moreover, the girl's song and the water didn't mix themselves together in "medleyed sound." Even if the girl thought that she was simply expressing the ocean's voice—even if she were singing "what she heard"—still, it was not the ocean's voice, for "what she sang was uttered word by word."

The word, for Stevens, is the specifically human thing: it is the mode in which the human imagination in poetry bodies forth itself. The poet is willing (stanza 2) to make all the proper concessions. He tells us that it may be that in the girl's phrases stirred "the grinding water and the gasping wind." Nevertheless he maintains that it was *she* "and not the sea we heard."

Why is the poet so careful to reject all of these other accounts of the relation between the girl's song and the sea? Because the girl here stands for the poet. We are told (line 15) that "she was the maker of the song she sang." "Maker" is used here in the sense of fabricator, but one remembers that in an earlier period of our language the word "maker" was the word for "poet." It is in the poet's making that the speaker of this poem exults.

The "tragic-gestured sea" is merely a place by which the girl walked to sing. What was the spirit, then, that played through her song? Again, the poet is careful to make almost pedantic reservations and exceptions. He takes the trouble to explain why it was not merely "the dark voice of the sea" and not merely "the outer voice of the sky and cloud" that expressed themselves through her song.

In lines 33–34 Stevens triumphantly declares: "It was her voice that made/The sky acutest at its vanishing." The girl's song gives ordered significance to the scene. The poet goes on to say: "She measured to the hour its solitude." But the poet is bolder still: "She was the single artificer of the world/In which she sang."

This is a high claim, but one that Stevens makes over and over again in his poetry. The world which the girl is expressing in her song— the world informed by her values and her meanings—is a world of which she is the sole artificer: she herself has constructed that world. And so the poet can proclaim that "when she sang, the sea,/Whatever self it had"—for Stevens is entirely too tough-minded a modern to deny that

the sea may very well have its own self—"became the self/That was her song, for she was the maker." Here the word "maker" clearly has its older significance of "poet." It is indeed the poet that Stevens celebrates in the closing lines of this section of the poem in which he says that we, overhearing the girl's song, "Knew that there never was a world for her/Except the one she sang, and, singing, made."

In line 43 the speaker directly addresses Ramon Fernandez. Wallace Stevens once told someone that Ramon Fernandez was simply a name that he had made up—that he had no special person in mind. Perhaps so, and there is no reason to believe that that is not the way he remembered it. But it is almost too good to be true that Ramon Fernandez should turn out to be a flesh-and-blood philosopher. (Probably on some forgotten occasion that name had been deposited in the back of Stevens' mind and when he came to need a name for his poem, he found that of Fernandez' waiting for him.) Still, Stevens is quite right in insisting that in this instance a made-up name would serve. For we don't need to read Fernandez's works in order to understand this poem. What Stevens needed at this point was to address a particular man by name—a man who presumably had thought about these matters and to whom the poet had once appealed. At any rate, the speaker of the poem does appeal to Fernandez now to tell him why "the lights in the fishing boats . . . /Mastered the night and portioned out the sea."

The lights here perform the function of the jar in Tennessee. They master the night even as the jar on the hill tames the wilderness. It is true that the lights perform their function under the spell of the girl's song, but that is simply to say that the lights as points of reference "deepen" and "arrange" the night through the effort of the imagination, and that the imagination of the listener has been stimulated and sensitized by the girl's singing, since her singing performs precisely just that function.

The last five lines rise to a great hymn in praise of the imagination. The poet, the "maker," is possessed by a "rage for order," a rage "to order words of the sea." Why of the sea? Because the sea, in its ever-changing panorama, its ever-shifting moods and sights and sounds, constitutes a perfect example of the chaotic and disordered world of our experience which the poet needs to arrange, deepen, enchant, and put into order.

The fragrant portals mentioned in line 53 are the doorways into deeper experience, doorways through which we enter into the world of ourselves, our deeper selves, that is, "and of our origins."

"The Idea of Order" is one of the most eloquent poems of the modern period, and it is one of Stevens' finest tributes to the power of the imagination, the great ordering force which, through the peculiar attribute of the poet, is an essential aspect of all human life.

Stevens is a master of tone—dazzling in the way in which he can run the gamut from trifling whimsy to the self-deprecatory, the mock-heroic, the ironic, and on up to the exalted strain of rapture. He is also willing to take his risks in making rapid shifts from one tone into another or in complicating the dominant tone. Stevens is also a master of the image. His poems are grounded in the concrete and abound in metaphor. One is not surprised to hear him say in one of the poems, "The greatest poverty is not to live/In a physical world." As we have seen in "Sunday Morning," a nonphysical heaven holds no charm for him. Stevens makes this point emphatically in one of his essays, writing that "Poetry must resist the intelligence almost successfully." Stevens, of course, is not advocating a brainless poetry of pure emotionality. (Moreover, he is careful to make plain that the resistance must not be *fully* successful.) His point is that poetry is not a matter of discursive reasoning or abstract logic, and in his reaction against the discursive Stevens shows his affinity with the Imagists.

With all of his praise of the imagination, and the way in which it shapes our notions of the world, Stevens is tremendously interested in the brute fact of the world. Other poets might entitle a poem "Of Mere Being"—in view of his "The Meaning of Life" and "The Meaning of

Death" Allen Tate might—but what other poet can one think of who would entitle a poem "The Pleasures of Merely Circulating"? One finds in Stevens a poet at home in his world and indeed at home in *the* world.

Randall Jarrell, himself a fine poet, sums up this side of Stevens very well, both in its limitations and in its positive qualities. He points out

> how little there is in Stevens, ordinarily, of the narrative, dramatic, immediately active side of life, of harried actors compelled, impelled, in ignorant hope. But how much there is of the man who looks, feels, meditates, in the freedom of removedness, of disinterested imagining, of thoughtful love! (*The Third Book of Criticism*, 1969, p. 63)

Jarrell goes on to say:

> Few poets have made a more interesting rhetoric out of just fooling around: turning things upsidedown, looking at them from under the sofa. . . . (p. 64)

The reason for his having been able to do so is this:

> At the bottom of Stevens' poetry there is wonder and delight, the child's or animal's or savage's—man's—joy in his own existence, and thankfulness for it. He is the poet of well-being: "One might have thought of sight, but who could think/Of what it sees, for all the ill it sees?" This sigh of awe, of wondering pleasure, is underneath all these poems that show us the "celestial possible," everything that has not yet been transformed into the infernal impossibilities of our everyday earth. Stevens is full of the natural or Aristotelian virtues; he is, in the terms of Hopkins' poem, all windhover and no Jesuit. There is about him, under the translucent glazes, a Dutch solidity and weight: he sits surrounded by all the good things of this earth, with rosy cheeks and fresh clear blue eyes, eyes not going out to you but shining in their place, like fixed stars—or else he moves off, like the bishop in his poem, "globed in today and tomorrow." If he were an animal he would be, without a

doubt, that rational, magnanimous, voluminous animal, the elephant. (p. 67)

Stevens is certainly not a tragic poet. No one agonizes in his poems. There are meditations and rich ponderings, but not much of Yeats's "quarrel with the self." He is the poet of the sun: even his night poems are in some profound sense optimistic and cheerful. Perhaps it would be more accurate to say that they too issue from tolerant well-being, and that Stevens' more exalted poems rise out of a joyful realization that human nature has the resources to make of the present world a place in which it is satisfactory to live. Louis Martz puts that matter very well in defining the kind of meditation so often found in Stevens' poems as an "attentive thinking about concrete things with the aim of developing an affectionate understanding of how good it is to be alive." Frank Kermode, who quotes with approval this comment of Martz's, adds: "In the end that is the subject of Stevens: living without God and finding it good, because of the survival of the power that once made Him suffice."

In sum, Stevens is a naturalist, a humanist, and a poet fully in the Romantic tradition. René Wellek has recently restated the common factors in Romanticism. All the Romantics, he says, "see the implication of imagination, symbol, myth, and organic nature and see it as part of the great endeavor to overcome the split between subject and object, the self and the world, the conscious and the unconscious. This is the central creed of the great Romantic poets in England, Germany, and France" (*Concepts of Criticism*, 1963, p. 220).

To heal this split between subject and object, the self and the world, is obviously Stevens' abiding concern.[2] The means is the imagination, which in one of his essays Stevens defines as "the sum of our faculties" and to which he has applied the term "intelligence" (the "acute intelligence of the imagination"). No wonder, then, that Roy Harvey Pearce finds in Stevens something perhaps transcending poetry: "Even if Stevens' later writing is not quite poetry, we must attend closely to it. Perhaps it is something beyond poetry. In any case, it is, for good and for bad, one of the most elaborate apologies for poetry conceived of in modern times. More important, it is as a consequence one of the most elaborate apologies for man."

This is heady stuff, and the editors of this text beg to be excused from deposing on it. Pearce, of course, may be right, but even if he is right, we are content to praise Stevens the poet, and find in his poetry sufficient merit to make him a major figure in our twentieth-century literature.

[2] This concern is no mere matter of poetry, but of philosophy as well, and Stevens has sometimes been taxed with "philosophizing" in some of his extended late poems, particularly in the volume entitled *Auroras of Autumn*. Thus, Randall Jarrell writes in *Poetry and the Age* (1953): "The habit of philosophizing in poetry— or of seeming to philosophize, of using a philosophical tone, images, constructions, of having quasi-philosophical daydreams, has been unfortunate for Stevens. . . . [He] is never more philosophical, abstract, rational than when telling us to put our faith in nothing but immediate sensation, perceptions, aesthetic particulars. . . ." Yet Stevens has not lacked defenders on this point, and Helen Vendler in *On Extended Wings: Wallace Stevens' Longer Poems* (1969) regards *Auroras of Autumn* as his greatest poem.

BIOGRAPHICAL CHART

1879	Born, October 2, in Reading, Pennsylvania
1897–1900	Attends Harvard as undergraduate
1900–1	Reporter for New York *Herald Tribune*
1901	Enters New York Law School
1909	Marries Elsie V. Kachel
1916	Joins legal staff of Hartford Accident and Indemnity Company
1923	*Harmonium*
1934	Becomes vice president of Hartford Accident and Indemnity Company
1935	*Ideas of Order*
1937	*The Man with the Blue Guitar*
1946	Member of the National Institute of Arts and Letters

1947 *Transport to Summer*
1950 *The Auroras of Autumn;* awarded Bollingen Prize in Poetry
1951 *The Necessary Angel: Essays on Reality and the Imagination*

1954 *The Collected Poems of Wallace Stevens*
1955 Pulitzer prize for poetry and National Book Award; dies, August 2
1957 *Opus Posthumous*

FURTHER READINGS

Samuel French Morse, Jackson R. Bryer, and Joseph N. Riddel, *Wallace Stevens Checklist and Bibliography of Stevens Criticism* (1963)
Holly Stevens, ed., *Letters of Wallace Stevens* (1967)

Marie Borroff, *Wallace Stevens* (1963)
Ashley Brown and Robert S. Haller, eds., *The Achievement of Wallace Stevens* (1962)
Frank Doggett, *Stevens' Poetry of Thought* (1966)

Daniel Fuchs, *The Comic Spirit of Wallace Stevens* (1963)
Randall Jarrell, *Poetry and the Age* (1953)
Frank Kermode, *Wallace Stevens* (1961)
Louis Martz, *The Poem of the Mind* (1966)
Robert Pack, *Wallace Stevens* (1958)
Helen Vendler, *On Extended Wings: Wallace Stevens' Longer Poems* (1969)

Disillusionment of Ten O'Clock (1923)

This charming poem is thoroughly characteristic of Stevens' way of teasing the bourgeoisie. There are no ghosts in these prim suburban houses except human beings clad in white nightgowns, and no dreams except those appropriate to the wearer of a white nightgown.

The houses are haunted
By white night-gowns.
None are green,

Or purple with green rings,
Or green with yellow rings,
Or yellow with blue rings.
None of them are strange,
With socks of lace
And beaded ceintures.
People are not going   10
To dream of baboons and periwinkles.
Only, here and there, an old sailor,
Drunk and asleep in his boots,
Catches tigers
In red weather.

Evening Without Angels (1935)

against life denial

The epigraph that Stevens chooses for this poem is obviously one after his own heart. What has been said earlier about "Sunday Morning" will serve as a general note for this poem. In line 12 Stevens seems to have in mind something parallel to Christ's statement that "the Sabbath was made for man and not man for the Sabbath" (Mark 2:27).

> *the great interests of man: air and light, the joy of having a body, the voluptuousness of looking*
> —Mario Rossi

Why seraphim like lutanists arranged

Above the trees? And why the poet as
Eternal *chef d'orchestre?*

        Air is air,
Its vacancy glitters round us everywhere.
Its sounds are not angelic syllables
But our unfashioned spirits realized
More sharply in more furious selves.

        And light
That fosters seraphim and is to them   10
Coiffeur of haloes, fecund jeweller—
〈Was the sun concoct for angels or for men?〉
Sad men made angels of the sun, and of
The moon they made their own attendant
        ghosts,

Which led them back to angels, after death.

Let this be clear that we are men of sun
And men of day and never of pointed night,
Men that repeat antiquest sounds of air
In an accord of repetitions. Yet,
If we repeat, it is because the wind   20
Encircling us, speaks always with our speech.

Light, too, encrusts us making visible
The motions of the mind and giving form
To moodiest nothings, as, desire for day
Accomplished in the immensely flashing East,
Desire for rest, in that descending sea
Of dark, which in its very darkening

Is rest and silence spreading into sleep.

. . . Evening, when the measure skips a beat
And then another, one by one, and all   30
To a seething minor swiftly modulate.
Bare night is best. Bare earth is best. Bare,
        bare,
Except for our own houses, huddled low
Beneath the arches and their spangled air,
Beneath the rhapsodies of fire and fire,
Where the voice that is in us makes a true
        response,
Where the voice that is great within us rises
        up,
As we stand gazing at the rounded moon.

Of Modern Poetry (1942)

This poem, like the preceding poem, is about the situation in which the modern poet finds himself. Indeed "Of Modern Poetry" may help explain the full meaning of the question put in lines 2–3 of "Evening Without Angels."

The poem of the mind in the act of finding
What will suffice. It has not always had
To find: the scene was set; it repeated what
Was in the script.
                Then the theatre was changed
To something else. Its past was a souvenir.
It has to be living, to learn the speech of the
    place.
It has to face the men of the time and to
    meet
The women of the time. It has to think about
    war
And it has to find what will suffice. It has
To construct a new stage. It has to be on that
    stage   10

And, like an insatiable actor, slowly and
With meditation, speak words that in the ear,
In the delicatest ear of the mind, repeat,
Exactly, that which it wants to hear, at the
    sound
Of which, an invisible audience listens,
Not to the play, but to itself, expressed
In an emotion as of two people, as of two
Emotions becoming one. The actor is
A metaphysician in the dark, twanging
An instrument, twanging a wiry string that
    gives   20
Sounds passing through sudden rightnesses,
    wholly
Containing the mind, below which it cannot
    descend,
Beyond which it has no will to rise.
                        It must
Be the finding of a satisfaction, and may
Be of a man skating, a woman dancing, a
    woman
Combing. The poem of the act of the mind.

The Snow Man (1923)

This poem is a wonderfully evocative disquisition on the nature of "nothingness"—or rather, on what it would feel like to experience complete nothingness. What does the snow man, himself a kind of nothing, with "a mind of winter," see and hear in the bleak scene? What would it be like to be such a snow man?

One must have a mind of winter
To regard the frost and the boughs
Of the pine-trees crusted with snow;

And have been cold a long time
To behold the junipers shagged with ice,
The spruces rough in the distant glitter

Of the January sun; and not to think
Of any misery in the sound of the wind,
In the sound of a few leaves,

Which is the sound of the land   10
Full of the same wind

That is blowing in the same bare place

For the listener, who listens in the snow,
And, nothing himself, beholds
Nothing that is not there and the nothing
    that is.

No Possum, No Sop, No Taters (1947)

It will be interesting to compare this poem with
the preceding poem, which also makes use of
a bleak winter scene but for a somewhat different effect.

He is not here, the old sun,
As absent as if we were asleep.

The field is frozen. The leaves are dry.
Bad is final in this light.

In this bleak air the broken stalks
Have arms without hands. They have trunks

Without legs or, for that, without heads.
They have heads in which a captive cry

Is merely the moving of a tongue.
Snow sparkles like eyesight falling to earth,   10

Like seeing fallen brightly away.
The leaves hop, scraping on the ground.

It is deep January. The sky is hard.
The stalks are firmly rooted in ice.

It is in this solitude, a syllable,
Out of these gawky flitterings,

Intones its single emptiness,
The savagest hollow of winter-sound.

It is here, in this bad, that we reach
The last purity of the knowledge of good.   20

The crow looks rusty as he rises up.
Bright is the malice in his eye . . .

One joins him there for company,
But at a distance, in another tree.

Peter Quince at the Clavier (1923)

In Shakespeare's *A Midsummer Night's Dream*,
Peter Quince is one of the company of journey-
men and rustics who are preparing to act a play
at the duke's court. Peter seems to be the playwright and director of the group. The speaker
in this poem does not presume on the title of
"poet": he is content to call himself a Peter
Quince.

    With his fingers on the keyboard and his eyes
on the loved one, the speaker moves through a
kind of reverie, touching on the relation of
music to emotion, his feelings for the loved one,
and then on to the strain of emotion awakened
by thinking of Susanna's beauty, and of the
Elders, who spied on her bathing. The story of
the old men's lust for the young woman and
how their plot against her was thwarted by the

prophet Daniel is told in one of the Apocry-
phal books of the Bible.

    The speaker's stream of consciousness moves
in slow eddies around the details of the Susanna
story—continuing to express all the emotions in
musical terms—until in the fourth section of
the poem he makes some bold assertions about
the nature of beauty and its immortality. Surprisingly, he locates the immortality of beauty,
not in a kind of Platonic idea, abstract and
changeless in the mind, but in the flesh itself—
not, to be sure, in the flesh of one particular
person such as that of the Susanna of Biblical
days, but in the realm of nature, where death
is a necessary part of the continuing process. He
uses a number of brilliant figures to make his
point, chief among them the metaphor of a

wave of the sea. In a wave, the actual molecules of water travel hardly at all, yet the wave, passing through the water, continues "interminably."

1

Just as my fingers on these keys
Make music, so the selfsame sounds
On my spirit make a music, too.

Music is feeling, then, not sound;
And thus it is that what I feel,
Here in this room, desiring you,

Thinking of your blue-shadowed silk,
Is music. It is like the strain
Waked in the elders by Susanna.

Of a green evening, clear and warm,   10
She bathed in her still garden, while
The red-eyed elders watching, felt

The basses of their beings throb
In witching chords, and their thin blood
Pulse pizzicati of Hosanna.

2

In the green water, clear and warm,
Susanna lay.
She searched
The touch of springs,
And found   20
Concealed imaginings.
She sighed,
For so much melody.

Upon the bank, she stood
In the cool
Of spent emotions.
She felt, among the leaves,
The dew
Of old devotions.

She walked upon the grass,   30

Still quavering.
The winds were like her maids,
On timid feet,
Fetching her woven scarves,
Yet wavering.

A breath upon her hand
Muted the night.
She turned—
A cymbal crashed,
And roaring horns.   40

3

Soon, with a noise like tambourines,
Came her attendant Byzantines.

They wondered why Susanna cried
Against the elders by her side;

And as they whispered, the refrain
Was like a willow swept by rain.

Anon, their lamps' uplifted flame
Revealed Susanna and her shame.

And then, the simpering Byzantines
Fled, with a noise like tambourines.   50

4

Beauty is momentary in the mind—
The fitful tracing of a portal;
But in the flesh it is immortal.
The body dies; the body's beauty lives.
So evenings die, in their green going,
A wave, interminably flowing.
So gardens die, their meek breath scenting
The cowl of winter, done repenting.
So maidens die, to the auroral
Celebration of a maiden's choral.   60
Susanna's music touched the bawdy strings
Of those white elders; but, escaping,
Left only Death's ironic scraping.
Now, in its immortality, it plays
On the clear viol of her memory,
And makes a constant sacrament of praise.

Asides on the Oboe (1942)

In this philosophical poem, Stevens canvasses once more the situation in which man stands in a universe emptied of the gods. The poet affirms again that man's imagination is enough.

François Boucher (1703–1770) was a French artist of the rococo and a court painter to Louis

XV. Boucher killed the gods by prettifying and trivializing them so that one could no longer take them seriously. In line 13 the "impossible possible philosophers' man" is the man that the future must bring forth—the ideal person that man may become when he has thought long enough about, and become fully responsive to, the world in which he finds himself. Stevens describes this "philosophers' man" as "a mirror with a voice" and therefore (in the last line of the poem) calls him "the glass man, without external reference."

The prologues are over. It is a question, now,
Of final belief. So, say that final belief
Must be in a fiction. It is time to choose.

1

That obsolete fiction of the wide river in
An empty land; the gods that Boucher killed;
And the metal heroes that time granulates—
The philosophers' man alone still walks in
   dew,
Still by the sea-side mutters milky lines
Concerning an immaculate imagery.
If you say on the hautboy man is not enough, 10
Can never stand as god, is ever wrong
In the end, however naked, tall, there is still
The impossible possible philosophers' man,
The man who has had the time to think
   enough,
The central man, the human globe, responsive
As a mirror with a voice, the man of glass,
Who in a million diamonds sums us up.

2

He is the transparence of the place in which
He is and in his poems we find peace.
He sets this peddler's pie and cries in summer, 20
The glass man, cold and numbered, dewily
   cries,
"Thou art not August unless I make thee so."
Clandestine steps upon imagined stairs
Climb through the night, because his cuckoos
   call.

3

One year, death and war prevented the jas-
   mine scent
And the jasmine islands were bloody martyr-
   doms.
How was it then with the central man? Did
   we
Find peace? We found the sum of men. We
   found,
If we found the central evil, the central good.
We buried the fallen without jasmine crowns. 30
There was nothing he did not suffer, no; nor
   we.

It was not as if the jasmine ever returned.
But we and the diamond globe at last were
   one.
We had always been partly one. It was as we
   came
To see him, that we were wholly one, as we
   heard
Him chanting for those buried in their blood,
In the jasmine haunted forests, that we knew
The glass man, without external reference.

To an Old Philosopher in Rome (1954)

The old philosopher is George Santayana (see pp. 1537–64), who spent his last years in Rome in a nursing home maintained by the Blue Nuns. Santayana once remarked that he was a Roman Catholic in everything except faith. Robert Lowell, in his poem on Santayana, calls him a "free-thinking Catholic infidel,/stray spirit, who'd found/the Church too good to be believed."

Santayana died in 1952. Stevens' poem describes him in his last years, still at work, still correcting proofs, with the nuns moving about, carrying out their duties, and outside the noises of the present-day Eternal City.

Small wonder that Stevens' imagination takes fire at this scene, for Santayana, with his fine sensitivity, his antipuritanical attitudes, his acceptance of the world of the flesh, and his conviction that all "beliefs" are ultimately grounded in what he called "animal faith," was a living monument to the philosophical imagination. Santayana, in his works and in his own character as a person, had built an edifice in which man's spirit could find its proper exaltation.

Stevens wrote in one of his prose works that Santayana had given his life the shape of a "deliberate work of art or letters. We have only to think of this present phase of it, in which, in his old age, he dwells in the head of the world, in the company of devoted women, in their convent, and in the company of familiar saints, whose presence does so much to make any convent an appropriate refuge for a generous and human philosopher" (*The Necessary Angel*, 1951, pp. 147–48).

On the threshold of heaven, the figures in the
   street
Become the figures of heaven, the majestic
   movement
Of men growing small in the distances of
   space,
Singing, with smaller and still smaller sound,
Unintelligible absolution and an end—

The threshold, Rome, and that more merciful
   Rome
Beyond, the two alike in the make of the
   mind.
It is as if in a human dignity
Two parallels become one, a perspective, of
   which
Men are part both in the inch and in the
   mile.   10

How easily the blown banners change to
   wings . . .
Things dark on the horizons of perception,
Become accompaniments of fortune, but
Of the fortune of the spirit, beyond the eye,
Not of its sphere, and yet not far beyond,

The human end in the spirit's greatest reach,
The extreme of the known in the presence of
   the extreme
Of the unknown. The newsboys' muttering
Becomes another murmuring; the smell
Of medicine, a fragrantness not to be
   spoiled . . .   20

The bed, the books, the chair, the moving
   nuns,
The candle as it evades the sight, these are
The sources of happiness in the shape of
   Rome,
A shape within the ancient circles of shapes,
And these beneath the shadow of a shape

In a confusion on bed and books, a portent
On the chair, a moving transparence on the
   nuns,
A light on the candle tearing against the wick
To join a hovering excellence, to escape
From fire and be part only of that of which   30

Fire is the symbol: the celestial possible.
Speak to your pillow as if it was yourself.
Be orator but with an accurate tongue
And without eloquence, O, half-asleep,
Of the pity that is the memorial of this room,

So that we feel, in this illumined large,
The veritable small, so that each of us
Beholds himself in you, and hears his voice
In yours, master and commiserable man,
Intent on your particles of nether-do,   40

Your dozing in the depths of wakefulness,
In the warmth of your bed, at the edge of
   your chair, alive
Yet living in two worlds, impenitent
As to one, and, as to one, most penitent,
Impatient for the grandeur that you need

In so much misery; and yet finding it
Only in misery, the afflatus of ruin,
Profound poetry of the poor and of the dead,
As in the last drop of the deepest blood,
As it falls from the heart and lies there to be
   seen,   50

Even as the blood of an empire, it might be,
For a citizen of heaven though still of Rome.
It is poverty's speech that seeks us out the
   most.
It is older than the oldest speech of Rome.
This is the tragic accent of the scene.

And you—it is you that speak it, without
   speech,
The loftiest syllables among loftiest things,
The one invulnerable man among
Crude captains, the naked majesty, if you like,
Of bird-nest arches and of rain-stained-vaults.   60

The sounds drift in. The buildings are
   remembered.
The life of the city never lets go, nor do you
Ever want it to. It is part of the life in your
   room.
Its domes are the architecture of your bed.
The bells keep on repeating solemn names
In choruses and choirs of choruses,
Unwilling that mercy should be a mystery
Of silence, that any solitude of sense
Should give you more than their peculiar
   chords
And reverberations clinging to whisper still.   70

It is a kind of total grandeur at the end,

With every visible thing enlarged and yet
No more than a bed, a chair and moving
   nuns,
The immensest theatre, the pillared porch,
The book and candle in your ambered room,

Total grandeur of a total edifice,
Chosen by an inquisitor of structures
For himself. He stops upon this threshold,
As if the design of all his words takes form
And frame from thinking and is realized.   80

The World as Meditation (1954)

The epigraph may be translated "I have spent too much time playing my violin to travel. But the essential activity of a composer—meditation—has never been suspended in me. . . . I live in a permanent dream, which doesn't stop night or day."

The scene is in Penelope's bedroom. Her husband, Ulysses, who was away from her for twenty years—ten during the siege of Troy and ten more trying to get home—has not yet returned. The poet imagines how Penelope sustained herself in his absence.

The best gloss on this fine poem has been provided by Louis Martz. He writes:

There is, we see, a "savage presence" outside her, the primitive force of the sun, which arouses within her a "barbarous strength," some primitive human power that makes it possible for her to compose a self, with the sun's encouragement; and so she dwells in a world of belief created by her will. This sounds like the conception found at the close of Stevens' essay "The Noble Rider" (1942), where he mentions a certain nobility of mind that constitutes "a violence from within that protects us from a violence without. It is the imagination pressing back against the pressure of reality." Thus the violence of the sun might have aroused Penelope to the violent, ugly pressure of those outward suitors [the suitors who insisted that her husband was dead and tried to persuade her to choose one of them for a second husband]; but her imagination of Ulysses, her constant meditation of reunion with the man she constantly creates in her mind, this power presses back, composes within herself a world of value and order. Thus, as Stevens concludes in that essay, imagination "seems, in the last analysis, to have something to do with our self-preser-

vation." (*The Poem of the Mind*, 1966, pp. 201–2)

J'ai passé trop de temps à travailler mon violon, à voyager. Mais l'exercice essentiel du compositeur—la méditation—rien ne l'a jamais suspendu en moi . . . Je vis un rêve permanent, qui ne s'arrête ni nuit ni jour.—Georges Enesco

Is it Ulysses that approaches from the east,
The interminable adventurer? The trees are
   mended.
That winter is washed away. Someone is
   moving

On the horizon and lifting himself up above
   it.
A form of fire approaches the cretonnes of
   Penelope,
Whose mere savage presence awakens the
   world in which she dwells.

She has composed, so long, a self with which
   to welcome him,
Companion to his self for her, which she
   imagined,
Two in a deep-founded sheltering, friend and
   dear friend.

The trees had been mended, as an essential
   exercise   10
In an inhuman meditation, larger than her
   own.
No winds like dogs watched over her at night.

She wanted nothing he could not bring her
   by coming alone.
She wanted no fetchings. His arms would be
   her necklace
And her belt, the final fortune of their desire.

But was it Ulysses? Or was it only the warmth
   of the sun
On her pillow? The thought kept beating in
   her like her heart.
The two kept beating together. It was only
   day.

It was Ulysses and it was not. Yet they had
    met,
Friend and dear friend and a planet's encour-
    agement.   20
The barbarous strength within her would
    never fail.

She would talk a little to herself as she
    combed her hair,
Repeating his name with its patient syllables,
Never forgetting him that kept coming con-
    stantly so near.

MARIANNE MOORE (1887–1972)

The relationship of Marianne Moore's poetry to the Imagists is clear. To begin with, she has a sharp eye for the thinginess of things. One could illustrate almost endlessly. In her vision, the Egyptian desert rat, the jerboa, becomes a "pillar body erect/On a three-cornered smooth-working Chippendale claw"; for her the ostrich wears on his "great neck" a "comic duckling head"; she watches the frigate pelican glide a hundred feet, then quiver about "As charred paper behaves. . . ." William Carlos Williams wrote of her in 1948 that he didn't think that there "was a better poet writing in America"; and because, like Williams, she finds a virtue in things and respects their integrity, she would seem to be closer to Williams than to Eliot.

Yet Eliot also has given high praise to her poetry and with due recognition of her "Imagist" perspective. He has written that "the aim of 'Imagism,' so far as I understand it, or so far as it ever had any, was to induce a peculiar concentration upon something visual, and to set in motion an expanding succession of concentric feelings." Eliot finds that in spite of Miss Moore's rather special subject matter and her apparently dry and spare treatment of it, the emotions generated—"release[d]" is Eliot's term —may yet be "major."

Readers put off by her studiedly laconic style may question, however, whether the virtues that Miss Moore's writing displays are not simply the virtues of prose. At some level, they surely are. As we noted earlier, Ezra Pound in 1913 asked that poetry should be at least as well written as prose. Marianne Moore is of a like mind. She

has evidently been concerned that her work be well written rather than that it seem poetic— which is to put first things first.[1] Eliot has written that she "seems to have saturated her mind in the perfections of prose, in its precision rather than its purple; and to have found her rhythm, her poetry, her appreciation of the individual word, for herself." This is well said, but we shall misunderstand it entirely if we interpret it as a polite way of withholding from her the title of poet. Her best and characteristic work is poetry. Only the reader who approaches it with the wrong preconceptions and expectations will find in it merely an eccentric prose.

Before examining the verse measures and stanzaic patterns used by Marianne Moore, it may be useful to comment further on her subject matter and her attitude toward the world about her. In the first place, her poetry is—or seems to be—descriptive. Her poems are, to be sure, very different from the set pieces of local-descriptive poetry such as one finds in Sir John Denham's "Cooper's Hill" or in William Collins' "Ode to Evening," with its landscape of "hamlets brown, and dim-discovered spires," or even in the work of twentieth-century poets like W. S. Blunt or Harold Monro. Though Miss Moore has written poems on Ireland, on the

[1] She shares in that tendency to simplify and intensify expression which we have remarked in earlier pages as characterizing American fiction writers of the 1920's as well as the poets. One thinks at once of Hemingway, and though her personality could not possibly be more different from his, there are some resemblances to be found in their work: both can make one "see" an object or a scene.

state of Virginia, on England, and on New York City, what she really like to describe are things such as the "Smooth Gnarled Crepe Myrtle" or "Nine Nectarines," or mechanical contrivances like steam rollers, or more delicately fabricated ones like "Four Quartz Crystal Clocks." But most of all she likes to describe birds, reptiles, and mammals. Her *Collected Poems* displays a whole zoo of them—snakes, mongooses, monkeys, elephants, snails, including such rare and curious creatures as the pangolin and even fabulous beasts like the unicorn. Miss Moore has hinted at the reason for her fondness for animals, for in "The Pangolin" she says: "Among animals, one has a/Sense of humor./Humor saves a few steps. It saves years."

This statement is very compact, and taken in isolation, it is riddling. But even a desultory run through Marianne Moore's poems suggests why the world of the creatures holds her special interest. The world of nonhuman animate life can illuminate our human world—by comparison and by contrast. It can even beget a sense of humility in mankind. For it must be emphasized that Marianne Moore does not view the creatures about her as mere caricatures of human types—Tom, Dick, and Harry dressed up in animal skins. She refuses to condescend to her beasts. She is scrupulous in allowing them their own dignity. The sense of humor that one has "among animals" does not prompt laughter at their expense, but the smile that goes with a due sense of proportion about ourselves.

Whatever her motives in choosing her favorite subject matter, she examines it with a gimlet eye. As the poet Elizabeth Bishop has remarked, Marianne Moore is "The World's Greatest Living Observer." The statement is just possibly literally true. One is moved to add that Marianne Moore is also constantly making "observations"—that is, succinct comments on what she describes. Thus one finds her remarking that "heroism is exhausting"; that "[Superiority] has never been confined to one locality"; that "Discreet behavior is not now the sum/Of statesmanlike good sense"; and that "There is a great amount of poetry in unconscious fastidiousness."

What is the relation of these pithy generalizations to the descriptions of things in which they are embedded or to which they may be more loosely attached? A fellow poet has, seriously and admiringly, called Miss Moore a "moralist"; and yet most of her admirers would want to deny that, in passages such as these, she is "moralizing." Does Miss Moore believe, with William Carlos Williams, that ideas inhere in things? And do these tersely phrased statements embody the ideas that she finds in things? The answer will surely have to be yes *and* no. Her comments do indeed have a relation to what she observes in the monkey puzzle or the ostrich or a Swedish carriage, but the relationship between thing and idea—and, more largely, between the raw subject matter and the meaning of the formed poem—is delicate and indirect.

We are compelled to return then to the question of whether—and in what sense—she is a poet. One cannot hope to say anything really pertinent to this matter without going a stage further and talking about the whole matter of "form" in Miss Moore's poetry; and an examination of that form will have to include her versification and her use of rhythm as well as her treatment of image and idea. For her rather special and even eccentric handling of the problems of rhythm and meter may give us some inkling about how she regards, and wishes us to regard, her writing. Since she usually develops very elaborate stanzaic patterns, she evidently does not think of her poems as merely prose. Her characteristic verse is syllabic; that is, the line is not composed of so many feet, each with its accented syllable. Instead, the count is of syllables *as such*: for example, in "No Swan So Fine," we find the following pattern: the first line has seven syllables, the second eight, the third six, and so on, with lines of eight, five, and nine syllables. But since English is a heavily accentual language, the effect that Miss Moore gets out of her syllabic lines is delicate, and by the hasty reader may not be heard at all. Her "metrical" effects are best thought of as a kind of counterpoint set against the prose rhythms. So it is with the use of the other conventional devices associated with verse. She is not only sparing with rhyme but often uses half rhymes or rhymes that involve lightly accented words. Thus, in the first stanza of "The Jerboa" the first two lines of the stanza rhyme, but the rhyme involves the article "an" and the unaccented second syllable of "freedman." (Miss Moore, however, sometimes does use emphatic rhymes, particularly in some of her later work.)[2]

Yet though the formal devices used by Miss Moore may at first acquaintance seem arbitrary and their effects quite muted, they do exercise a controlling function over the shape of her utterance. They indicate phrasings and emphases and in general act to "formalize" the whole. Their effect on the tone is even more definite. They help establish a tone that only rarely breaks down into mere fussiness or owl-eyed solemnity or sentimentality.

In these precisely formed verbal contexts, even the generalizations which Miss Moore allows herself partake of the kind of individuality and precision with which she perceives the details of the world about her. Randall Jarrell has put his finger right on the point when he remarks that "Because of their exact seriousness of utterance, their complete individuality of embodiment, these generalizations of hers seem almost more particular than the particulars."

Jarrell is also very good in defining the tone of her poetry in general. He calls it a "tone of much wit and precision and intelligence, of irony and forbearance, of unusual moral penetration—[it] is plainly the voice of a person of good taste and good sense and good will, of a genuinely human being."

How important it is to maintain this tone becomes apparent when we read the occasional poem of Miss Moore's that fails. Charles Tomlinson singles out as an example her wartime poem entitled "In Distrust of Merits." He calls it a failure

> because the feeling is no longer contained [by her characteristic form]. Her characteristic and remarkable achievements derive from an impersonality in the means of the poetry which, in fact, permits the fusion of both personal and impersonal in their most significant form. There occurs invitation to "feeling" because the means do not admit of such.

The poet herself was later to concur in this judgment, with a fine honesty, saying of this poem that it was "Just a protest—disjointed, exclamatory. Emotion overpowered me—first one thought and then that."

Marianne Moore is a poet's poet. Few others of our time have drawn such plaudits from their fellows. In recent years she acquired a larger public and became something of an institution—in good part because of her more relaxed efforts, such as poems in praise of the Brooklyn Dodgers baseball team (before they had moved out to Los Angeles). What is lacking in these poems but what is present in her best has been well summarized by Hugh Kenner:

> Counting her syllables, revealing and concealing her rhymes, setting down her finely particularized exempla for elucidation by tone alone, putting "unconscious elegance" into tension against "sophistication" and showing how art, a third thing, can endorse the former without false entanglement in the latter, she has accomplished things of general import to the maintenance of language that no one else has had the patience, the skill, the discipline, or the perfect unselfconscious conviction to adumbrate.

[2] For a systematic discussion of Marianne Moore's prosody, the reader is referred to Robert Beloof's "Prosody and Tone: The 'Mathematics' of Marianne Moore," *Kenyon Review* (Winter, 1958); reprinted in Charles Tomlinson, *Marianne Moore* (1969).

BIOGRAPHICAL CHART

1887 Born, November 15, in Kirkwood, a suburb of St. Louis
1905–9 Attends Bryn Mawr College (Hilda Doolittle is among her fellow students)
1911–15 Teaches "commercial subjects" at the United States Indian School in Carlisle, Pennsylvania
1916 Moves with her mother to Chatham, New Jersey, to keep house for her brother John, a Presbyterian minister
1920 Work begins to appear in the *Dial*

FURTHER READINGS

The reader will find individual titles of Miss Moore's works in the biographical chart.

Eugene P. Sheehy and Kenneth A. Lohf, *The Achievement of Marianne Moore: A Bibliography, 1907–1957* (1958)

Jean Garrigue, *Marianne Moore* (1965)

Randall Jarrell, *Poetry and the Age* (1953)

Wallace Stevens, "A Poet That Matters," in *Opus Posthumous* (1957)

Charles Tomlinson, *Marianne Moore* (1969)

Poetry (1921)

Miss Moore has supplied notes (as did Eliot for *The Waste Land*) indicating the sources of allusions and quotations used in her poems. For "Poetry" she cites the following passage from Tolstoi's diary: "Where the boundary between prose and poetry lies, I shall never be able to understand. The question is raised in manuals of style, yet the answer to it lies beyond me. Poetry is verse: prose is not verse. Or else poetry is everything with the exception of business documents and school books."

She also indicates that the phrase "literalists of the imagination" comes from W. B. Yeats's essay "William Blake and the Illustrations to *The Divine Comedy*." Miss Moore quotes the following passage: "The limitation of his view was from the very intensity of his vision; he was a too literal realist of imagination, as others are of nature; and because he believed that the figures seen by the mind's eye, when exalted by inspiration, were 'eternal existences,' symbols of divine essences, he hated every grace of style that might obscure their lineaments."

This rather early poem dismisses what too often passed (and still passes) for poetry. With it should be compared a poem written much later, "Armor's Undermining Modesty," where the poet approached the subject from a different angle. The following lines are particularly relevant to the lines with which "Poetry" opens:

> No wonder we hate poetry,
> and stars and harps and the new moon. If trib-
>   utes cannot be implicit,
>   give me diatribes and the fragrance of iodine,
>   the cork oak acorn grown in Spain;
>   the pale-ale-eyed impersonal look
>   which the sales-placard gives the bock beer
>   buck.
> What is more precise than precision? Illusion.

For the sixth line quoted from "Armor's Undermining Modesty," Miss Moore supplies the amusingly overspecific note: "Poster unsigned, distributed by Eastern Beverage Corporation, Hammonton, New Jersey."

In her *Complete Poems* (1967) Miss Moore cut down "Poetry" to the first three lines of the original text that we print here.

> I, too, dislike it: there are things that are im-
>   portant beyond all this fiddle.
>   Reading it, however, with a perfect con-
>   tempt for it, one discovers in

it after all, a place for the genuine.
    Hands that can grasp, eyes
      that can dilate, hair that can rise
        if it must, these things are important
          not because a

high-sounding interpretation can be put upon
        them but because they are
    useful. When they become so derivative as
        to become unintelligible,
    the same thing may be said for all of us,
        that we
    do not admire what   10
    we cannot understand: the bat
      holding on upside down or in quest of
        something to

eat, elephants pushing, a wild horse taking
      a roll, a tireless wolf under
a tree, the immovable critic twitching his
      skin like a horse that feels a flea,
      the base-
ball fan, the statistician—
    nor is it valid

to discriminate against 'business doc-
    uments and

school-books'; all these phenomena are im-
      portant. One must make a dis-
      tinction
    however: when dragged into prominence
      by half poets, the result is not
      poetry,
nor till the poets among us can be   20
    'literalists of
    the imagination'—above
      insolence and triviality and can
      present

for inspection, 'imaginary gardens with real
      toads in them', shall we have
    it. In the meantime, if you demand on
      the one hand,
    the raw material of poetry in
      all its rawness and
    that which is on the other hand
      genuine, you are interested in poetry.

Silence (1924)

This poem is written in free verse and not in
Miss Moore's more usual syllabic verse. In her
note she identifies the two quoted passages.
The first, she tells us, is from Miss A. M. Ho-
mans: "My father used to say, 'Superior people
never make long visits. When I am visiting, I
like to go about by myself. I never had to be
shown Longfellow's grave or the glass flowers of
Harvard.'"

    The second quotation, Miss Moore indicates,
is taken from Sir James Prior's *Life of Edmund
Burke:* " 'Throw yourself into a coach,' said he.
'Come down and make my house your inn.' "

My father used to say,

"Superior people never make long visits,
have to be shown Longfellow's grave
or the glass flowers at Harvard.
Self-reliant like the cat—
that takes its prey to privacy,
the mouse's limp tail hanging like a shoelace
    from its mouth—
they sometimes enjoy solitude,
and can be robbed of speech
by speech which has delighted them.   10
The deepest feeling always shows itself in
    silence;
not in silence, but restraint."
Nor was he insincere in saying, "Make my
    house your inn."
Inns are not residences.

The Steeple-Jack (1961)

The text of this poem, as revised in 1961, is
taken from *Collected Poems.* A useful brief
account of "The Steeple-Jack" is given by A. K.

Weatherhead in *The Edge of the Image* (1967;
pp. 59–61). He calls attention to the contrasts
of points of view: first, the town as seen from

aloft in a comprehensive and romantically picturesque view; and, after the storm which destroys the romantic picture, a more realistic
view of the town as seen by an observer standing on the ground. The two views are really
complementary: after all, it is the same town;
and if the storm has altered the sentimental
view of the town and disturbed the "star" on
the steeple of the church, no permanent damage
has been done. An efficient and prudent steeple-
jack—he has put out a Danger sign on the sidewalk above which he is working—is now repairing the star on the church that "stands for
hope."

Dürer would have seen a reason for living
    in a town like this, with eight stranded
      whales
to look at; with the sweet sea air coming into
    your house
on a fine day, from water etched
    with waves as formal as the scales
on a fish.

One by one in two's and three's, the seagulls
    keep
    flying back and forth over the town
      clock,
or sailing around the lighthouse without mov-
    ing their wings—
rising steadily with a slight   10
    quiver of the body—or flock
mewing where

a sea the purple of the peacock's neck is
    paled to greenish azure as Dürer changed
the pine green of the Tyrol to peacock blue
    and guinea
gray. You can see a twenty-five-
    pound lobster; and fish nets arranged
to dry. The

whirlwind fife-and-drum of the storm bends
    the salt
    marsh grass, disturbs stars in the sky and
      the   20
star on the steeple; it is a privilege to see so
much confusion. Disguised by what
    might seem the opposite, the sea-
side flowers and

trees are favored by the fog so that you have
    the tropics at first hand: the trumpet
      vine,
foxglove, giant snapdragon, a salpiglossis that
    has
spots and stripes; morning-glories, gourds,
    or moon-vines trained on fishing twine
at the back door: 30

cattails, flags, blueberries and spiderwort,
    striped grass, lichens, sunflowers, asters,
      daisies—
yellow and crab-claw ragged sailors with green
      bracts—toad-plant,
petunias, ferns; pink lilies, blue
    ones, tigers; poppies; black sweet-peas.
The climate

is not right for the banyan, frangipani, or
    jack-fruit trees; or for exotic serpent
life. Ring lizard and snakeskin for the foot, if
    you see fit;
but here they've cats, not cobras, to   40
    keep down the rats. The diffident
little newt

with white pin-dots on black horizontal spaced-
    out bands lives here; yet there is nothing
      that
ambition can buy or take away. The college
    student
named Ambrose sits on the hillside
    with his not-native books and hat
and sees boats

at sea progress white and rigid as if in
    a groove. Liking an elegance of which   50
the source is not bravado, he knows by heart
    the antique
sugar-bowl shaped summerhouse of
    interlacing slats, and the pitch
of the church

spire, not true, from which a man in scarlet
    lets
    down a rope as a spider spins a thread;
he might be part of a novel, but on the side-
    walk a
sign says C. J. Poole, Steeple Jack,
    in black and white; and one in red
and white says   60

Danger. The church portico has four fluted
    columns, each a single piece of stone,
    made

modester by whitewash. This would be a fit
        haven for
waifs, children, animals, prisoners,
        and presidents who have repaid
sin-driven

senators by not thinking about them. The
        place has a schoolhouse, a post-office in a
store, fish-houses, hen-houses, a three-masted
        schooner on

the stocks. The hero, the student,   70
        the steeple jack, each in his way,
is at home.

It could not be dangerous to be living
        in a town like this, of simple people,
who have a steeple-jack placing danger signs
        by the church
while he is gilding the solid-
        pointed star, which on a steeple
stands for hope.

The Frigate Pelican (1935)

The text is taken from the longer version of the poem as published in *Selected Poems* (1935). Miss Moore's first note reads: "*Fregata aquila*. The Frigate Pelican of Audubon." Audubon also refers to it as the "Frigate Bird." In his *Ornithological Biography* he writes of seeing it between "Cuba and the Floridas," "ranging high overhead in the azure, cloudless sky." The bird here described is the Man-o'-War bird (*fregata magnificens rothschildi*). It has a scissor tail and a wingspread of seven and a half feet. As the poet herself tells us in the first line of the third stanza, "he is not a pelican."

Rasselas, referred to in line 2, is the hero of Dr. Samuel Johnson's *Rasselas* (1759). Chapter 6 is called "A dissertation on the art of flying." Rasselas hopes to escape from the "happy valley" in which he is confined by means of "a sailing chariot." Rasselas "visited the work from time to time, observed its progress, and remarked many ingenious contrivances to facilitate motion, and unite levity with strength."

Miss Moore's second note refers to line 64 and reads: "*Giant tame armadillo*. Photograph and description by W. Stephen Thomas of New York." Miss Moore has been teased with being pedantically specific with regard to her source, but she tells us (*Collected Poems*, p. 262) that she wants to be honest in acknowledging all her borrowings.

She supplies a note on line 66: "*Red-spotted orchids*. The blood, supposedly, of natives slain by Pizarro." (In line 82 "Festina lente" is Latin for "make haste slowly.") Miss Moore's fourth and last note applies to lines 83–85: " 'If I do well, I am blessed,' etc. Hindoo saying."

Rapidly cruising or lying on the air there is a
        bird
        that realizes Rasselas's friend's project
of wings uniting levity with strength. This
        hell-diver, frigate-bird, hurricane-
bird; unless swift is the proper word
        for him, the storm omen when
        he flies close to the waves, should be seen
                fishing, although oftener
                he appears to prefer

to take, on the wing, from industrious cruder-
        winged species   10
        the fish they have caught, and is seldom
                successless.
        A marvel of grace, no matter how fast his
                victim may fly or how often may
turn, the dishonest pelican's ease
        in pursuit, bears him away
with the fish that the badgered bird drops.
        A kind of superlative
        swallow, that likes to live

on food caught while flying, he is not a
        pelican. The toe
        with slight web, air-boned body, and
                very long wings   20
        with the spread of a swan's—duplicating a
        bow-string as he floats overhead—feel
the changing V-shaped scissor swallow-
        tail direct the rigid keel.
        And steering beak to windward always,
                the fleetest foremost fairy
                among birds, outflies the

aeroplane which cannot flap its wings nor
    alter any quill-
  tip. For him, the feeling in a hand, in fins, is
in his unbent downbent crafty oar. With him   30
    other pelicans aimlessly soar
as he does; separating, until
  not flapping they rise once more,
  closing in without looking and move
    outward again to the top
    of the circle and stop

and blow back, allowing the wind to reverse
    their direction.
  This is not the stalwart swan that can
    ferry the
woodcutter's two children home; no.
    Make hay; keep
  the shop; I have one sheep; were a less   40
limber animal's mottoes. This one
  finds sticks for the swan's-down dress
of his child to rest upon and would
    not know Gretel from Hänsel.
    As impassioned Handel—

meant for a lawyer and a masculine
    German domestic
career—clandestinely studied the harpsichord
and never was known to have fallen in love,
  the unconfiding frigate-bird hides
in the height and in the majestic   50
    display of his art. He glides
a hundred feet or quivers about
    as charred paper behaves—full
    of feints; and an eagle

of vigilance, earns the term aquiline;
    keeping at a height
so great the feathers look black and the
    beak does not
show. It is not retreat but exclusion from
  which he looks down and observes
    what went
secretly, as it thought, out of sight
  among dense jungle plants. Sent   60
ahead of the rest, there goes the true
    knight in his jointed coat that
    covers all but his bat

ears; a-trot, with stiff pig gait—our tame
    armadillo, loosed by
his master and as pleased as a dog. Beside the
spattered blood—that orchid which the
    native fears—

the fer-de-lance lies sleeping; centaur-
like, this harmful couple's amity
  is apropos. A jaguar
and crocodile are fighting. Sharp-shinned   70
  hawks and peacock-freckled small
  cats, like the literal

merry-go-round, come wandering within
    the circular view
of the high bird for whom from the air
    they are ants
keeping house all their lives in the crack of a
  crag with no view from the top. And here,
unlikely animals learning to
  dance, crouch on two steeds that rear
behind a leopard with a frantic
    face, tamed by an Artemis   80
    who wears a dress like his,

and hampering haymaker's hat. *Festina lente*.
    Be gay
civilly. How so? 'If I do well I am blessed
whether any bless me or not, and if I do
  ill I am cursed'. We watch the moon rise
on the Susquehanna. In his way
  this most romantic bird, flies
to a more mundane place, the mangrove
  swamp, to sleep. He wastes the moon.
    But he, and others, soon   90

rise from the bough, and though flying are
    able to foil the tired
moment of danger, that lays on heart
    and lungs the
weight of the python that crushes to powder.
  The tune's illiterate footsteps fail;
the steam hacks are not to be admired.
  These, unturbulent, avail
themselves of turbulence to fly—pleased
    with the faint wind's varyings,
    on which to spread fixed wings.

The reticent lugubrious ragged immense
    minuet   100
  descending to leeward, ascending to
    windward
again without flapping, in what seems to be
  a way of resting, are now nearer,
but as seemingly bodiless yet
    as they were. Theirs are sombre
  quills for so wide and lightboned a bird
    as the frigate pelican
    of the Caribbean.

The Paper Nautilus (1940)

The paper nautilus is a cephalopod and thus is, as the poet remarks in lines 18–19, a kind of devil fish or octopus. Lines 21–23 refer to the second labor of Hercules, his destruction of the Lernaean Hydra. When Hercules tried to kill this many-headed monster, two new heads grew in place of every head that he destroyed. He solved the problem by having his friend Iolaus burn each neck as soon as he had dealt with it and thus cauterized it against any new growth. The goddess Juno, Hercules' enemy, sent an enormous crab to attack Hercules as he fought the Hydra. It nipped Hercules' foot and this is what caused him first to summon Iolaus to help him. This is presumably what Miss Moore has in mind: had Hercules not been "hindered" by the crab, he might not have called for the aid that was necessary if he was to succeed.

In line 29 a chiton is a kind of tunic worn in ancient Greece. The poet is thinking of the delicate lines in Greek sculpture that represent the foldings. The "Parthenon horse" of line 31 refers to the horses in the bas relief of the Panathenaic procession which adorned the Parthenon at Athens.

> For authorities whose hopes
> are shaped by mercenaries?
>   Writers entrapped by
>   teatime fame and by

commuters' comforts? Not for these
    the paper nautilus
    constructs her thin glass shell.

Giving her perishable
souvenir of hope, a dull
    white outside and smooth-   10
    edged inner surface
glossy as the sea, the watchful
    maker of it guards it
    day and night; she scarcely

    eats until the eggs are hatched.
Buried eightfold in her eight
    arms, for she is in
    a sense a devil-
fish, her glass ram's-horn-cradled freight
    is hid but is not crushed;   20
    as Hercules, bitten

by a crab loyal to the hydra,
was hindered to succeed,
    the intensively
    watched eggs coming from
the shell free it when they are freed—
    leaving its wasp-nest flaws
    of white on white, and close-

    laid Ionic chiton-folds
like the lines in the mane of   30
    a Parthenon horse,
    round which the arms had
wound themselves as if they knew love
    is the only fortress
    strong enough to trust to.

No Swan So Fine (1935)

The quotation which begins the poem comes, as Miss Moore's note tells us, from the *New York Times Magazine*, May 10, 1931, where Percy Philips writes: "There is no water so still as the dead fountains of Versailles." A second note identifies the Louis XV candelabra. She writes: "A pair of Louis XV candelabra with Dresden figures of swans belonging to Lord Balfour." Yet though these notes suggest what probably stimulated the creation of the poem,

its meaning will have to come out of our own attempt to read it.

Like Keats's "Ode on a Grecian Urn," this poem meditates the relation of nature and art. How is the porcelain swan finer than any flesh-and-blood swan? How is the poet's statement to be taken? Literally, or with some note of irony? The "chintz china" swan is certainly a very fine swan indeed—though of course it is not alive, and yet could one say that it was "dead"—as is Louis XV who presumably commissioned its making.

It has been confidently urged that the meaning of this poem is that art can kill. But it is possible to read the poem otherwise: Louis XV is dead, long dead, and so is the flesh-and-blood swan that the artist copied in order to make the candelabra. As artifact, the china swan preserves for us what would have otherwise utterly perished. Whatever the special inflection that the poet gives to her account of the paradoxical nature of art, we can be very sure that this paradox of something "dead" which is also deathless was not lost on her. Notice, for example, line 11. Everlastings are immortelles or straw flowers, the blossoms of which retain their form and color when dried. But in this rococo art work even the everlastings themselves

had been rendered longer-lasting still, turned into "polished sculptured/flowers—at ease and tall."

"No water so still as the
    dead fountains of Versailles." No swan,
with swart blind look askance
and gondoliering legs, so fine
    as the chintz china one with fawn-
brown eyes and toothed gold
collar on to show whose bird it was.

Lodged in the Louis Fifteenth
    candelabrum-tree of cockscomb-
tinted buttons, dahlias,   10
sea urchins, and everlastings,
    it perches on the branching foam
of polished sculptured
flowers—at ease and tall. The king is dead.

Bird-Witted (1941)

As her note on this poem indicates, the title is borrowed from a phrase of Sir Francis Bacon's. The passage occurs in Book 2 of *The Advancement of Learning* (1605) and reads: "If a child be bird-witted, that is, hath not the faculty of attention, the Mathematics giveth a remedy thereunto."

With innocent wide penguin eyes, three
    large fledgling mockingbirds below
the pussy-willow tree,
    stand in a row,
wings touching, feebly solemn,
till they see
        their no longer larger
        mother bringing
something which will partially
feed one of them.   10

Toward the high-keyed intermittent squeak
    of broken carriage springs, made by
the three similar, meek-
    coated bird's-eye
freckled forms she comes; and when
from the beak
        of one, the still living
        beetle has dropped

out, she picks it up and puts
it in again.   20

Standing in the shade till they have dressed
    their thickly filamented, pale
pussy-willow-surfaced
    coats, they spread tail
and wings, showing one by one,
the modest
        white stripe lengthwise on the
        tail and crosswise
underneath the wing, and the
accordion   30

is closed again. What delightful note
    with rapid unexpected flute
sounds leaping from the throat
    of the astute
grown bird, comes back to one from
the remote
        unenergetic sun-
        lit air before
the brood was here? How harsh
the bird's voice has become.   40

A piebald cat observing them,
    is slowly creeping toward the trim
trio on the tree stem.
        Unused to him

the three make room—uneasy
new problem.
    A dangling foot that missed
      its grasp, is raised
and finds the twig on which it
planned to perch. The   50

parent darting down, nerved by what chills
    the blood, and by hope rewarded—

of toil—since nothing fills
    squeaking unfed
mouths, wages deadly combat,
and half kills
    with bayonet beak and
    cruel wings, the
intellectual cautious-
ly creeping cat.   60

E. E. CUMMINGS (1894–1962)

Edward Eslin Cummings, though never an avowed Imagist, shows in his poetry that he has been influenced by the Imagist movement. Many of his poems are technically Imagistic; and even those poems that incorporate an anecdote or make a statement or conduct an argument are usually focused on specific images and derive their energy and driving power from the images. Cummings was, by the way, a painter of considerable distinction. Perhaps this fact kept him free of the temptation to "paint" with words, the weakness of some of the more doctrinaire Imagist poets. Cummings never confuses the modes.

What hits the eye in looking at a Cummings poem is the odd typography and format. Words may be broken up and their parts scattered over the page. Capitalization is not used conventionally and if it occurs at all serves only for emphasis. But beneath the eccentricity the poet manifests a singularly pure lyric impulse. The typography bristles like a kind of barbed-wire fence as if to forbid the old-fashioned reader to enter into the poem. But the reader who is willing to make the attempt often finds inside a simple and charming poem about springtime or love or the beauty of the earth. A great many of Cummings' poems are celebrations of joy.

Such is one side of Cummings' work. The other side is rather direct and simple too. The poems of this other side express Cummings' contempt for those who would soil love or violate innocence and for those who cheapen lyric poetry by pretentious faking. Thus, Cummings' poems are sometimes irreverent, quite occasionally bawdy, and at times scathingly bitter. For example, in "POEM, OR BEAUTY HURTS MR. VINAL," Cummings takes off the pseudo-poetry of the O-God-the-pain girls and boys. In "next to of course god america i" he parodies the flatulently rhetorical politician. In "the Cambridge ladies who live in furnished souls," Cummings pays his respects to "culture" that has become overrefined and anemic—to the world of J. Alfred Prufrock.

Cummings has a real zest for the American idiom, including its different subdialects such as those heard in cities like Boston and New York. He has, in fact, a generally fine ear for the rhythms of American speech, and one test of this is that when his typographical oddities distract and confuse the reader (as they sometimes do) all is set right by simply reading the poem aloud. Cummings' rhythms, too, are important for the meanings of his poems. Thus, in "Buffalo Bill" the dazzling vitality of the old Wild West bronco-buster and crack pistol shot is conveyed as much by the rhythm of the poem as by the imagery:

[he] used to
ride a watersmooth-silver
                stallion
and break onetwothreefourfive pigeonsjustlike
    that
      Jesus

he was a handsome man

But a fashionable lady in her limousine moves to a very different rhythm. Her car

> oozes in fashionable traffic, just
> a halfsmile (for society's sweet sake)

The poem beginning "mr youse" has the very intonation and accent of the tough young man whose utterance it is supposed to be. The politician's speech that begins "next to of course god" beautifully mimics the rhythm as well as the clichés of a political hack.

Cummings is, incidentally, one of our most accomplished poets of the city. Like Whitman and Eliot, he provides shockingly realistic vignettes of urban life. A barber pole:

> the wisti-twisti barber
> -pole is climbing
>
> people high,up-in
>
> tenements talk.in sawdust Voices

A brothel:

when you rang at Dick Mid's Place
the madam was a bulb stuck in the door.
a fang of wincing gas showed how

hair, in two fists of shrill colour
clutched the dull volume of her tumbling face

McSorley's saloon:

i was sitting in mcsorley's. outside it was New
    York and beautifully snowing.

Cummings shows little or no development during the course of his poetic career. To make such a statement with reference to most poets would imply a serious defect—a lack of growth and maturity. But this ordinarily disparaging observation has to be heavily qualified in view of the character of Cummings' earliest poems. They are not at all fumbling and awkward, but graceful and accomplished. Indeed, the first poems that Cummings published are usually as good—and as characteristic—as any that he was to write later. Compare "in Just-" (published in 1923) with "nine birds(rising" (published in 1950). That there was no particular development from this early and brilliant start does point to a limitation of a sort: Cummings' range of topics and attitudes is rather narrow and his later years did little to widen it. (But see p. 2184.) To sum up: Cummings found almost immediately what he wanted to do and did it, often well, sometimes brilliantly, and continued to do so throughout a lifetime.

BIOGRAPHICAL CHART

1894 Born, October 14, in Cambridge, Massachusetts
1915 Graduates from Harvard, *magna cum laude*
1917 With his friend Slater Brown, joins Norton Harjes Ambulance Corps, American Red Cross, in France; from September to December held in a French prison camp at La Ferté Macé
1921 First sojourns in Paris; lives in Paris intermittently throughout the 1920's and makes at least five trips abroad thereafter
1922 *The Enormous Room*, based on experiences at La Ferté Macé
1923 *Tulips and Chimneys* (poems)
1925 *&* [*And*] and *XLI Poems*
1931 Travels to Russia, described in *Eimi* (1933); twenty-nine paintings exhibited at Painters and Sculptors Gallery
1935 *Tom*, a ballet based on *Uncle Tom's Cabin*

1949 One-man show of paintings, American British Art Centre; elected to the National Institute of Arts and Letters
1950 Awarded Fellowship of the Academy of American Poets for "great achievement"; *XAIPE*
1952–53 Charles Eliot Norton lecturer at Harvard (published as *Six Nonlectures*); elected to the American Academy of Arts and Letters
1954 *Poems 1923–1954*
1955 Receives special citation by National Book Awards Committee for *Poems, 1923–1954*
1957 Receives Bollingen prize in poetry and Boston Arts Festival poetry award
1959 One-man show, Rochester Memorial Art Gallery
1962 Dies, September 3, in North Conway, New Hampshire

FURTHER READINGS

F. W. Dupee and George State, eds., *Selected Letters of E. E. Cummings* (1969)

George J. Firmage, *E. E. Cummings: A Bibliography* (1960)

S. V. Baum, ed., *ΕΣΤΙ: E. E. Cummings and the Critics* (1962)

Norman Friedman, *E. E. Cummings: The Art of His Poetry* (1960)

————, *E. E. Cummings: The Growth of a Writer* (1964)

Barry A. Marks, *E. E. Cummings* (1964)

Charles Norman, *E. E. Cummings: The Magic-Maker* (1958)

in Just- (1923)

The reader might ask himself why the poet wrote "eddieandbill" rather than "little boys" and "bettyandisbel" rather than "little girls." The balloonman is called "goat-footed" presumably to suggest a clubfoot or a partially crippled limb that would account for an awkward gait. But Pan, the Greek god of nature, one remembers, was literally goat-footed.

in Just-
spring   when the world is mud-
luscious the little
lame balloonman

whistles   far   and wee

and eddieandbill come
running from marbles and
piracies and it's

spring

when the world is puddle-wonderful   10

the queer
old balloonman whistles
far   and   wee
and bettyandisbel come dancing

from hop-scotch and jump-rope and
it's
spring
and
    the
           goat-footed   20

balloonMan   whistles
far
and
wee

O sweet spontaneous (1923)

In this poet's view, those who try to make the natural spontaneity of earth fit their abstract schemes are likened to dirty old men. The earth suffers them but in fact remains faithful to the couch of her true lover—death. Compare Wallace Stevens' "Sunday Morning" (p. 2154) where death is regarded as the parent of natural beauty.

O sweet spontaneous
earth how often have
the
doting
      fingers of

prurient philosophers pinched
and
poked

thee
, has the naughty thumb   10
of science prodded
thy

     beauty   . how
often have religions taken
thee upon their scraggy knees
squeezing and

buffeting thee that thou mightest conceive
gods

(but   thou answerest
true   20

to the incomparable   them only with
couch of death thy
rhythmic
lover   spring)

the Cambridge ladies who live in furnished souls (1923)

The last lines may seem extravagant, but they
can be readily justified. The moon (obviously
here an unromantic gibbous moon) objects to
being treated as a piece of romantic confection-
ery. But the ladies of Cambridge, Massachusetts, are too well insulated from nature to hear
its protest, even when it rattles its box as loud
as it can.

the Cambridge ladies who live in furnished
    souls
are unbeautiful and have comfortable minds

(also, with the church's protestant blessings
daughters, unscented shapeless spirited)
they believe in Christ and Longfellow, both
    dead,
are invariably interested in so many things—
at the present writing one still finds
delighted fingers knitting for the is it Poles?
perhaps. While permanent faces coyly bandy
scandal of Mrs. N and Professor D   10
. . . . the Cambridge ladies do not care,
    above
Cambridge if sometimes in its box of
sky lavender and cornerless, the
moon rattles like a fragment of angry candy

come, gaze with me upon this dome (1926)

In this poem Cummings takes note—not altogether unsympathetically, since he had been
involved in it—of the callowness of youthful
American idealism. Stanza 1 echoes Shelley's
"Adonis," and 2, Emerson's "Voluntaries," part
III: "When duty whispers low, Thou must,/The
youth replies, I can." The third line of the last
stanza is the opening line of a well-known hymn,
in which the "Son of Man" is Christ.

   Cummings had firsthand experience of the
First World War. Before the United States declared war, he was in France serving as an ambulance driver with the French army. He spent
part of his wartime years in a French prison
camp, though he was later cleared of the charges
against him. He fashioned this experience into
a brilliant book, *The Enormous Room* (1922).

come, gaze with me upon this dome
of many coloured glass, and see
his mother's pride, his father's joy,
unto whom duty whispers low

"thou must!" and who replies "I can!"
—yon clean upstanding well dressed boy
that with his peers full oft hath quaffed
the wine of life and found it sweet—

a tear within his stern blue eye,
upon his firm white lips a smile,
one thought a!one: to do or die
for God for country and for Yale   10

above his blond determined head
the sacred flag of truth unfurled,
in the bright heyday of his youth
the upper class American

unsullied stands, before the world:
with manly heart and conscience free,
upon the front steps of her home
by the high minded pure young girl
                                              20

much kissed, by loving relatives
well fed, and fully photographed
the son of man goes forth to war
with trumpets clap and syphilis

since feeling is first (1926)

This poem is a nice instance of Cummings' ability to combine wit with tenderness. One notices particularly the play with terms having to do with grammar and punctuation. With reference to the last line: one eventually *closes* a parenthesis and *resumes* his principal narrative. Not so, with death.

since feeling is first
who pays any attention
to the syntax of things
will never wholly kiss you;

wholly to be a fool
while Spring is in the world

my blood approves,
and kisses are a better fate
than wisdom
lady i swear by all flowers. Don't cry   10
—the best gesture of my brain is less than
your eyelids' flutter which says

we are for each other: then
laugh, leaning back in my arms
for life's not a paragraph

And death i think is no parenthesis

the first president to be loved by his (1931)

Warren Gamaliel Harding (1865–1923), twenty-ninth President of the United States, died suddenly, while on a visit to the West Coast, of an illness never quite identified. H. L. Mencken declared that Harding's prose was the worst he had ever encountered.

the first president to be loved by his
bitterest enemies" is dead

the only man woman or child who wrote

a simple declarative sentence with seven
     grammatical
errors "is dead"
beautiful Warren Gamaliel Harding
"is" dead
he's
"dead"
if he wouldn't have eaten them Yapanese
     Craps   10

somebody might hardly never not have been
                    unsorry,perhaps

somewhere i have never travelled,gladly beyond (1931)

The imagery in this poem is more consistent than a first glance would indicate and very deftly used—especially the imagery having to do with opening and closing (skillfully, mysteriously, things of excessive delicacy by instruments that are themselves delicate and fragile). It is interesting to contemplate the relation of such imagery to the brilliant last line.

somewhere i have never travelled,gladly
     beyond
any experience,your eyes have their silence:
in your most frail gesture are things which en-
     close me,

or which i cannot touch because they are too
     near

your slightest look easily will unclose me
though i have closed myself as fingers,
you open always petal by petal myself as
     Spring opens
(touching skilfully,mysteriously)her first rose

or if your wish be to close me,i and
my life will shut very beautifully,suddenly,   10
as when the heart of this flower imagines
the snow carefully everywhere descending;

nothing which we are to perceive in this world
     equals

the power of your intense fragility:whose
   texture
compels me with the colour of its countries,
rendering death and forever with each
   breathing

(i do not know what it is about you that closes
and opens;only something in me understands
the voice of your eyes is deeper than all roses)
nobody,not even the rain,has such small hands   20

my father moved through dooms of love (1940)

We have remarked earlier that Cummings'
career shows little development, but the following poem reveals enlarging sympathies not revealed in the poet's earlier work. His father was
a Unitarian pastor. Though many of Cummings'
poems, particularly of his earlier period, tend
to jeer at Boston respectability and middle-class
refinements, Cummings apparently wrote very
moving tributes to his father (as here) and to
his mother. The language of the poem may offer
some initial difficulty to the reader: what, for
example, are we to make of such wrenched language as "dooms of love," "sames of am" and
"haves of give"? "Doom" is the old word for
"judgments." Presumably his father's *dooms*
were "judgments" made by love—that is, not
condemnations at all; "sames of am" is an emphatic way of saying "a uniformity of the self"—
his father was always the same; and "haves of
give" must be translated as "possession of the
spirit of giving." For his father to own something was to consider it as something to be
given to someone else. Not all of Cummings'
uses of this device are successful; but some
clearly are, and in any case the device does not
necessarily render the poem unintelligible.

?

– ⇢ +

my father moved through dooms of love
through sames of am through haves of give,
singing each morning out of each night
my father moved through depths of height

this motionless forgetful where
turned at his glance to shining here;
that if(so timid air is firm)
under his eyes would stir and squirm

newly as from unburied which
floats the first who,his april touch   10

drove sleeping selves to swarm their fates
woke dreamers to their ghostly roots

and should some why completely weep
my father's fingers brought her sleep:
vainly no smallest voice might cry
for he could feel the mountains grow.

Lifting the valleys of the sea
my father moved through griefs of joy;
praising a forehead called the moon
singing desire into begin   20

joy was his song and joy so pure
a heart of star by him could steer
and pure so now and now so yes
the wrists of twilight would rejoice

keen as midsummer's keen beyond
conceiving mind of sun will stand,
so strictly(over utmost him
so hugely)stood my father's dream

his flesh was flesh his blood was blood:
no hungry man but wished him food;   30
no cripple wouldn't creep one mile
uphill to only see him smile.

Scorning the pomp of must and shall
my father moved through dooms of feel;
his anger was as right as rain
his pity was as green as grain

septembering arms of year extend
less humbly wealth to foe and friend
than he to foolish and to wise
offered immeasurable is   40

proudly and(by octobering flame
beckoned)as earth will downward climb,
so naked for immortal work
his shoulders marched against the dark

his sorrow was as true as bread:
no liar looked him in the head;
if every friend became his foe
he'd laugh and build a world with snow.

My father moved through theys of we,
singing each new leaf out of each tree   50
(and every child was sure that spring
danced when she heard my father sing)

then let men kill which cannot share,
let blood and flesh be mud and mire,
scheming imagine,passion willed,
freedom a drug that's bought and sold

giving to steal and cruel kind,
a heart to fear, to doubt a mind,
to differ a disease of same,
conform the pinnacle of am   60

though dull were all we taste as bright,
bitter all utterly things sweet,
maggoty minus and dumb death
all we inherit,all bequeath

and nothing quite so least as truth
—i say though hate were why men breathe—
because my father lived his soul
love is the whole and more than all

plato told (1944)

What all the sages of the East and West told
him was what General William Tecumseh Sherman told him: "War is hell." But it took a
piece of hot steel to get the message through his
thick head. The steel was a "nipponized bit
of/the old sixth/avenue/el[evated railroad]":
the United States government had continued to
sell scrap-iron to Japan in the late 1930's though
it was evident that Japan was arming herself
for war, probably against the United States.

plato told

him:he couldn't
believe it(jesus

told him;he
wouldn't believe
it)lao

tsze

certainly told
him,and general
(yes   10

mam)
sherman;
and even
(believe it
or

not)you
told him:i told
him;we told him
(he didn't believe it, no

sir)it took   20
a nipponized bit of
the old sixth

avenue
el;in the top of his head:to tell

him

nine birds (1950)

nine birds(rising

through a gold moment)climb:
ing i

-nto
wintry
twi-

light
(all together a

manying
one

-ness)nine
souls
only alive with a single mys-

tery(liftingly
caught upon falling)silent!

ly living the dying of glory

ARCHIBALD MAC LEISH (1892–   )

Though Archibald MacLeish was not one of the original Imagists, his early poems show Imagist influence—in his occasional use of free verse, but more importantly in his anchoring his poetry, even that which has a strong narrative line, to key images. Moreover, he has the distinction of having written one of the finest of the poems using an Imagist technique and one which also expresses most succinctly the conception of poetry implied in a strict and pure use of that technique.

Ars Poetica (1926)

A poem should be palpable and mute
As a globed fruit,

Dumb
As old medallions to the thumb,

Silent as the sleeve-worn stone
Of casement ledges where the moss has grown—

A poem should be wordless
As the flight of birds.

A poem should be motionless in time
As the moon climbs,   10

Leaving, as the moon releases
Twig by twig the night-entangled trees,

Leaving, as the moon behind the winter leaves,
Memory by memory the mind—

A poem should be motionless in time
As the moon climbs.

A poem should be equal to:
Not true.

For all the history of grief
An empty doorway and a maple leaf.   20

For love
The leaning grasses and two lights above the
    sea—

A poem should not mean
But be.

This poem dramatizes through appropriate images the Imagists' attack on "wordiness"; that is, the poem practices here what it preaches. The statement that a poem should be "palpable," "mute," "silent,"—and most perverse of all—"wordless" is literally self-contradictory. For how can a bit of discourse, necessarily framed in words, be *wordless?* Yet the poet's real point is intimated by the images that he has chosen. In a good poem the words do not call attention to themselves stridently and noisily. They take their quiet place as elements in a structure, a structure that will resemble, in its solidity and massiveness, a thing—a thing like a fruit, or a medallion, or a smooth casement ledge.

In "Ars Poetica" the static quality implied by a strict Imagist theory is accepted and made a resource of strength. *This* poem ought not to seem to move, and again the chosen image makes the point: though the moon does move, we can't see the motion, and the moon in the process of climbing gives the illusion of standing still. Action is arrested in a frozen moment.

Lastly, the poem should not "state" but should imply and suggest. Its task is not to relate the history of grief but to capture that history in an image. The maple leaf, dropped from the autumnal tree, and now sliding across the open doorway, symbolizes the end of another year, with the doorway still empty, still awaiting the beloved person's return. Again, the two lights above the sea at evening imply two lovers, though if we prefer to take the lights as merely lights, setting a scene, building a mood, we are at liberty to do so.

Yet, even accepting what has just been said, how can we swallow the poet's explicit denial to poetry of "truth" and "meaning"? Because the context provided by the poem indicates the appropriate specialization of these terms. The poem need not be true in a scientific or historical sense; nor does it need to have a meaning that can be abstracted to provide, say, a political article. Rather, the authentic poem has the kind of truth and meaning that are continuous with its very structure. Form and content are merged and the form of the poem *is* its meaning, the choice and arrangement of images presenting a whole state of mind.[1]

The qualities of poetry defined by, and given concrete body in, "Ars Poetica" occur throughout MacLeish's poetry; they are to be found even in his long narrative and historical poems. *Frescoes for Mr. Rockefeller's City* (see below) will provide examples.

The poem has a thesis of sorts. MacLeish rejoices in the concrete stuff of the American experience, which stubbornly resists every attempt to reduce it to an abstraction. On the one hand, he makes his satiric thrust at the millionaire Robber Barons who would have liked to reduce the American landscape itself to a value on the stock exchange; and on the other, at the doctrinaire revolutionaries who wanted to reduce the American experience to an illustration of the Marxian formula. It is particularly proper, therefore, that the power of the poem comes from the images, these irreducible, concrete modes of experience.

Thus, in Part 5, MacLeish attempts to suggest to his reader the spirit of Meriwether Lewis's letter sent back to President Jefferson from the

Pacific coast, to which the Lewis and Clark expedition had finally penetrated. MacLeish has made use of the original letter, but through some remarkable compressions he has managed to suggest in brief compass Lewis's awe at the size of the Louisiana Territory and the sense of loneliness felt by the little band of explorers waiting out the winter on the coast where the Columbia River enters the Pacific. (See pp. 185–89.)

And we here on the back of this beach behold-
  ing the
Other ocean—two years gone and the cold
Breaking with rain the third spring since St.
  Louis,
The crows at the fishbones on the frozen
  dunes. . . .

The crows trying to pick a few more dried shreds of nourishment from the fishbones frozen into the sand dunes provide a telling symbol of desolation.

Again, in order to suggest a sense of the vast territory in which the small exploring expedition is almost swallowed up, MacLeish has Lewis write:

The wind was west in the evenings, and no dew
  and the
Morning Star larger and whiter than usual—

The winter rattling in the brittle haws. . . .

MacLeish employs images of such effectiveness not merely in the more lyrical passages but also in the bitter and satirical sections of the poem. See, for example, the following lines, in which he pays his respects to Josiah Perham and J. P. Morgan as "Empire Builders":

It was all prices to them: they never looked at
  it:
Why should they look at the land? they were
  Empire Builders:
It was all in the bid and the asked and the ink
  on their books. . . .

MacLeish is a man of varied talents and many interests. In the course of his career he has

---

[1] MacLeish here is probably remembering Eliot's famous description of poetry as providing an objective correlative. See p. 2097. Yet the extreme position as literally stated in "Ars Poetica" may have come to cause MacLeish misgivings and to play its part in his later insistence on a more "public" utterance. See pp. 2188–90.

served on the editorial board of *Fortune* magazine, as Librarian of Congress, as an Assistant Secretary of State, and as a university professor (at Harvard). As such a career would suggest, MacLeish has always had a tremendous interest in public affairs, in politics, and particularly in international relations. He has always believed that the poet is also a citizen and that he should take an active and positive interest in the life that goes on around him. Thus, increasingly, and particularly as the Nazi menace to Western civilization began to make itself apparent in the 1930's, MacLeish was drawn away from lyrics of the kind one associates with Imagism and became more and more attracted to what he was to call "public speech."

Though MacLeish resisted the pressure of the Marxists of the 1930's to view all art as a political instrument by which to bring on the revolution, and though he jeered at such an interpretation of art in his "Invocation to the Social Muse," he decided that he must use his own poetic gifts to arouse America to its danger from Hitler.

MacLeish's article "Public Speech and Private Speech in Poetry" (1938) was an attempt to clarify the issues involved. Though he meant to chart a different course for himself, MacLeish was careful to do justice to that taken by his literary masters: Yeats, Pound, and Eliot. These poets, he argued, had indeed been revolutionaries in breaking with the decadent Victorian poetry under which they had grown up. They had sought to turn poetry back toward the world of reality, but their poetry had not in fact achieved that aim. It had to be regarded as no more than "a transition towards a poetry capable of accepting a political and revolutionary era upon its own terms . . . a transition capable of restoring a poetry of public speech."

This is generous in its acknowledgment of a debt owed to great predecessors and MacLeish has always been generous, even to Pound, whose Fascist position he detested. (See, for example, his poem "Ezry," printed below.) It is also an adroit rhetorical maneuver; but it hardly gets down to the basic issues. It does not, for example, do justice to Yeats's account of the role

of the poet or to Yeats's analysis of the modern world. Nor does it do justice to Eliot on either of these counts. Eliot has been discussed earlier; a comment here about Yeats—whom MacLeish has declared to be "the best of modern poets"—may be worth making. Yeats as man and citizen believed that the poet should speak to issues, but he had little faith that poetry could be used as an instrument for social rehabilitation or an incitement to revolution.

In this connection it is worth remembering Yeats's observation that it is only out of our quarrel with ourselves that we make poetry. Our quarrel with others will yield no better than rhetoric. Most of MacLeish's "public speech" is rhetoric, some of it eloquent and surely nearly all of it rhetoric devoted to a good cause; but its quarrel is obviously with "others" as the poet scolds or admonishes or castigates the enemies of mankind or his own bemused or cowardly countrymen. "America Was Promises" (1939) and "Colloquy for the States" (1943) will illustrate.[2]

If, as seems likely, MacLeish's poem "Hypocrite Auteur"[3] is to be considered a late and perhaps final reply to Eliot, then MacLeish's ultimate position on Eliot's general stance is not so very different from that of William Carlos Williams (see p. 2144). MacLeish's poem reproaches "our epoch" for taking "a voluptuous satisfaction" in seeing our civilization as dying—"Not that we love death," not really, that is, but that we do like to pose as

---

[2] The issue, let us repeat, is not whether MacLeish as man and citizen was wrong to speak out on public issues or whether the "speeches" (whether in poetry or prose) were effective or ineffective. The issue is whether the "public" character of such utterances made them better poetry than they otherwise would have been. All honor to the citizen who acts according to his deepest convictions. Perhaps even more honor is due to the poet who risks deserting his special vocation in order to get a practical (and prosaic) job done!

[3] Line 76 of *The Waste Land* reads "You! hypocrite lecteur!—mon semblable,—mon frère!" Compare also MacLeish's description of *The Waste Land* as "a poem which sees the contemporary world as the wreckage and scattered ruin of many great and fallen cities. . . . Nothing could follow it but darkness and silence. Or a new beginning" ("Nevertheless One Debt," 1931).

those about to die, posed in a theatrical tableau just before the final curtain falls. The men of our age are happy to play the role of "Victim, rebel, convert, stoic/Every role but the heroic—." But the poem insists that civilization is not dead. Though "A world ends when its metaphor has died," the life-giving metaphor of a new world already struggles to be born:

The journey of our history has not ceased:
Earth turns us still toward the rising east,
The metaphor still struggles in the stone. . . .

The poets are challenged to provide us with a metaphor that will give civilization the imaginative energy to achieve rebirth.

Poets, deserted by the world before,
Turn round into the actual air:
Invent the age! Invent the metaphor!

MacLeish's assumption is that all the great cultures of the past have found their dynamic in a great sustaining myth, a controlling metaphor, and that the great poets of the past— Chaucer, Dante, Shakespeare—were "public" figures and gave the fullest and richest expression to their cultures. MacLeish's third assumption seems to be that the poet's expression of his world is a process of creation—he brings the underlying "metaphor" to a focus that it never had before. Therefore, it is the poet who can invent (create, find? "invent" can mean either) the animating metaphor that will "invent" the age. It is a stirring appeal.

But did Dante "invent" the Christian synthesis of the high Middle Ages? Or did Shakespeare invent the English Renaissance? Even Yeats, who was never bashful in assigning the poet a lofty role in his civilization, never went so far as this. In fact, Yeats tells us that we are "given" our metaphors. Art cannot simply be willed.

There is a further point to be made. Though Dante and Shakespeare did give the richest and most powerful expression to the values of their respective cultures, to the great "myths" which articulated the fundamental beliefs of those cultures, they did something more than merely express them. It might be claimed that they "judged" them too. Dante subjected the great Christian myth to the hurly-burly of actuality, for his *Divine Comedy* included an *Inferno* and a *Purgatorio* as well as a *Paradiso*. The Christian drama caused destruction to some men as well as bringing the beatific vision to others. Not all were saved, and the culture itself could deteriorate and perish. As for Shakespeare, in his tragedies he questioned the secular myths of his time, showed what they "cost" in human terms, and rebuked the very things encouraged by those myths. Shakespeare accomplished this in the very process of exhibiting the power and grandeur of those myths. Self-knowledge is a great good. It would be a wonderful thing to understand the meaning of one's own epoch, but knowledge will not necessarily save a culture or alter history. Moreover, the full knowledge of what the great poets were really saying about their own culture is usually realized only after that culture has perished.

Nowhere else is MacLeish more the American than here in his proposal that the poet be prophet and perhaps priest as well. The true believers in the American dream[4] hold that, granted the know-how, granted an unshakable determination, and granted a deep faith in himself, the American can accomplish literally anything. But can even a determined American by sheer will power compel that notoriously fickle and capricious goddess, the Muse?

Some of the difficulties of writing a public poem, a poem of heroic stance, are revealed in MacLeish's *Conquistador* (1932), a retelling of the Spanish conquest of Mexico. The subject matter and the scope of the poem would seem to be epic, and MacLeish's handling of the description of the preparations for the expedition, of landscapes in Mexico, of scenes of battles, slaughter, or of village life, are often brilliantly done. The vignettes come alive. The sense of the actual is vivid. But as Allen Tate pointed out in a review of the poem in 1932, the spirit

---

[4] MacLeish's heroes among the founding fathers of the Republic include Jefferson and Tom Paine. Paine comes in for special mention in *America Was Promises*, and "Brave New World" is addressed to Jefferson.

of the poem is not epic, but lyric—beautifully so. The poem is also "modern" in a very particular sense. For the story of the conquest is told by one of the soldiers, Bernál Díaz,[5] now in his old age, and his special pathos is the sense of his own frustration as he witnesses the imminent perishing of what he had experienced so vividly: for this experience is now at the mercy of the "quilled professors," who will distort it out of carelessness or out of flattery to "bishops rich men generals." Even his personal hold on the experience is at the mercy of death.

Tate writes:

We get the peculiarly modern situation: the personality of one man is dramatized against an historical setting. "What have they written of us: the poor soldiers"—what can the private sensibility get out of history to sustain it? What can Bernál get out of his past? Nothing appears in the story that Bernál did not see; it is all enriched by memory. Although Bernál announces his subject as "That which I have myself seen and the fighting," there is little fighting; there is little action; for the dramatic tension of the poem grows out of the narrator-hero's fear of death upon the gradual disappearance of sensation. The dramatic quality of the poem—a quality that has little to do with the story as such—lies thus in the hero's anxiety to recover his sensuous early years, upon which his identity as a person, and hence his life, depends.

In short, the tone of *Conquistador* is not epic, but elegiac. An epic would give us the story of a hero who typifies a people and whose career provides us with a sense of the history of a people

enacted and of a civilization realized or transformed: for example, Virgil's account of Aeneas, the Trojan, finding his way through vast difficulties to Latium and founding the Roman state. But there are no overarching and "public" values to which Bernál, the hero of MacLeish's poem, can commit himself. His values are personal and subjective. For him, the conquest of Mexico means very little more than, say, the First World War and its issues means for Hemingway's Lieutenant Henry in *A Farewell to Arms*. If one wants to argue that we now know that *all* wars are in fact meaningless slaughters and that the epic poets of the past, including Virgil, were deluded in thinking that they were not, the basic issue here is unaffected. One has simply said in different language that the epic in its old public sense is, for a modern poet—and perhaps for a modern reader—dead, and that the only possible modern response is what personal and subjective emotions he can glean from the horror.

Tate observes that it is thus

a mistake to suppose that MacLeish has offered a "way out" of the introspective indecision of the school of T. S. Eliot, affirming a faith in heroic action against the moral paralysis presumably suffered by the best minds of that older generation. Not only is there, in the poem, a lack of belief in any kind of action that we might imitate; the poet does not evince much interest in the action implied by the reminiscences that support the narrative.

Yet, considered in its own terms and for itself, *Conquistador* is a brilliant performance. Many of its scenes are fresh, powerful, and evocative. In short, in spite of the fact that it proposes to deal with a "great public" occasion, it remains "private speech," after all—poetry in some essential sense of an extremely high order.

[5] MacLeish draws the character, and his situation, from history. Bernál Díaz del Castillo (1492–1581?) authored *The True History of the Conquest of New Spain, Written in the Year 1568 by Captain Bernál Díaz del Castillo, One of the Conquerors.*

BIOGRAPHICAL CHART

1892   Born, May 7, in Glencoe, Illinois
1907–11   Attends the Hotchkiss School
1915   Graduates from Yale

1916   Marries Ada Hitchcock
1917–18   Moves from private to captain, United States Army, France

1919   Receives L.L.B. from Harvard; teaches constitutional law and international law at Harvard
1920   Admitted to Massachusetts Bar and practices law
1923–28   Lives in France, working on poetry
1924   *The Happy Marriage*
1925   *The Pot of Earth*
1926   *Streets in the Moon*
1928   Returns to America to farm at Conway, Massachusetts; *The Hamlet of A. MacLeish*
1928–29   Makes trip to Mexico on foot and muleback, following route of Cortés
1930   *New Found Land*
1930–38   Joins editorial board, *Fortune* magazine
1932   *Conquistador*, for which he was awarded Pulitzer prize in 1933
1933   *Poems 1924–33; Frescoes for Mr. Rockefeller's City*; elected to National Institute of Arts and Letters
1936   *Public Speech*
1939   *America Was Promises*
1939–44   Librarian of Congress
1940   *The Irresponsibles*
1941–42   Director, Office of Facts and Figures; assistant director, Office of War Information

1944–45   Assistant Secretary of State
1945   Chairman, United States Delegation, London Conference of United Nations to found United Nations Educational Scientific and Cultural Organization (UNESCO)
1946   Chairman, American Delegation, First General Conference, UNESCO, Paris; elected to the American Academy of Arts and Letters
1948   *Actfive*
1949–62   Boylston Professor of Rhetoric and Oratory at Harvard
1950   *Poetry and Opinion*
1952   *Collected Poems, 1917–1952; Trojan Horse*
1953   Awarded Pulitzer prize for poetry; Bollingen Prize for Poetry; Shelley Memorial Award; National Book Award in Poetry
1953–56   President, American Academy of Arts and Letters
1954   *Songs for Eve*
1959   *J.B.* (a verse play), for which he was awarded a Pulitzer prize in drama
1961   *Poetry and Experience*

FURTHER READINGS

Signi Lenea Falk, *Archibald MacLeish* (1965)
Archibald MacLeish and Elia Kazan, "The Staging of the Play 'J.B.,'" *Esquire* (May, 1959)
Arthur Mizener, "The Poetry of Archibald MacLeish," *Sewanee Review* (October–December, 1938)

Morton D. Zabel, "The Poet on Capitol Hill," *Partisan Review* (January and March, 1941)

You, Andrew Marvell (1930)

The rather cryptic and highly memorable title of this hypnotic poem might be expanded in something like this fashion: "You, Andrew Marvell, who wrote 'But at my back I always hear/ Time's winged chariot hurrying near,' would understand this poem in which I try to portray the slow, inexorable—but also swift—movement of time."

It is interesting to see the devices the poet has used to give his reader the sense of the gradual advance of the shadow of night. The reader might notice how many infinitives (noun forms of the verb) are used instead of active verbs, and he might like to count the "ands." But he will also want to notice how the poet in the last two lines suddenly speeds up the sense of the coming of the night.

And here face down beneath the sun
And here upon earth's noonward height
To feel the always coming on
The always rising of the night:

To feel creep up the curving cast
The earthy chill of dusk and slow
Upon those under lands the vast
And ever climbing shadow grow

And strange at Ecbatan the trees
Take leaf by leaf the evening strange   10
The flooding dark about their knees
The mountains over Persia change

And now at Kermanshah the gate
Dark empty and the withered grass
And through the twilight now the late
Few travelers in the westward pass

And Baghdad darken and the bridge
Across the silent river gone
And through Arabia the edge
Of evening widen and steal on   20

And deepen on Palmyra's street
The wheel rut in the ruined stone
And Lebanon fade out and Crete
High through the clouds and overblown

And over Sicily the air
Still flashing with the landward gulls
And loom and slowly disappear
The sails above the shadowy hulls

And Spain go under and the shore
Of Africa the gilded sand   30
And evening vanish and no more
The low pale light across that land

Nor now the long light on the sea:

And here face downward in the sun
To feel how swift how secretly
The shadow of the night comes on . . .

Memorial Rain (1926)

Kenneth MacLeish, who died in 1918 in the
First World War, was the poet's brother. Technically, this is one of the most brilliant of Mac-
Leish's shorter poems: in its contrast of the
formal and outer occasion and the personal and
inward emotion and in its very effective control
of speech rhythms, including the parody of the
ambassador's speech.

Ambassador Puser the ambassador
Reminds himself in French, felicitous tongue,
What these (young men no longer) lie here
     for
In rows that once, and somewhere else, were
     young . . .

All night in Brussels the wind had tugged
     at my door:
I had heard the wind at my door and the
     trees strung
Taut, and to me who had never been before
In that country it was a strange wind,
     blowing
Steadily, stiffening the walls, the floor,
The roof of my room. I had not slept for
     knowing   10
He too, dead, was a stranger in that land
And felt beneath the earth in the wind's
     flowing
A tightening of roots and would not under-
     stand,
Remembering lake winds in Illinois,
That strange wind. I had felt his bones in
     the sand
Listening.

          . . . Reflects that these enjoy
Their country's gratitude, that deep repose,
That peace no pain can break, no hurt destroy,
That rest, that sleep . . .

               At Ghent the wind rose.
There was a smell of rain and a heavy drag
Of wind in the hedges but not as the wind   20
     blows
Over fresh water when the waves lag
Foaming and the willows huddle and it will
     rain:
I felt him waiting.

          . . . Indicates the flag
Which (may he say) ensiles in Flanders plain
This little field these happy, happy dead
Have made America . . .

               In the ripe grain
The wind coiled glistening, darted, fled,
Dragging its heavy body: at Waereghem
The wind coiled in the grass above his head: 30
Waiting—listening . . .

          . . . Dedicates to them
This earth their bones have hallowed, this last
     gift
A grateful country . . .

               Under the dry grass stem

The words are blurred, are thickened, the
   words sift
Confused by the rasp of the wind, by the
   thin grating
Of ants under the grass, the minute shift
And tumble of dusty sand separating
From dusty sand. The roots of the grass
   strain,
Tighten, the earth is rigid, waits—he is
   waiting—

And suddenly, and all at once, the rain!   40

The text printed above is from the 1963 edition
of the *Collected Poems*. The original text concluded with these additional lines:

The living scatter, they run into houses, the
   wind
Is trampled under the rain, shakes free, is again
Trampled. The rain gathers, running in thinned
Spurts of water that ravel in the dry sand,
Seeping in the sand under the grass roots, seeping
Between cracked boards to the bones of a
   clenched hand:
The earth relaxes, loosens; he is sleeping,
He rests, he is quiet, he sleeps in a strange land.

The reader may find it interesting to speculate
on why the poet decided to omit these lines and
whether he agrees with that decision.

From Conquistador (1932)

Conquistador was based, MacLeish tells us, on
"the historical chronicles of the Conquest of
Mexico." The poet writes that he has "followed
the account given by Bernál Díaz del Castillo,
one of the Conquerors, in his *True History of
the Conquest of New Spain*," but that he has
"altered and transposed and invented incidents."

The Conquistador under whom Bernál served
was Hernando Cortés (1485–1547), who deposed and killed Montezuma (1480?–1520), the
last Aztec emperor of Mexico.

It would be interesting for the reader to try to
determine how the influence of Pound appears
in this poem (especially in "The Argument")
and how well it has been assimilated.

Bernál Díaz' Preface to His Book

"That which I have myself seen and the
   fighting". . . .

And I am an ignorant man: and this priest
   this
Gómara with the school-taught skip to his
   writing

The pompous Latin the appropriate feasts
The big names the imperial decorations
The beautiful battles and the brave deceased

The onward marches the wild Indian nations
The conquests sieges sorties wars campaigns
(And one eye always on the live relations)—

He with his famous history of New Spain   10
This priest is a learned man: is not ignorant:
And I am poor: without gold: gainless:

My lands deserts in Guatemala: my fig-tree
   the
Spiked bush: my grapes thorns: my children
Half-grown: sons with beards: the big one

Breaking the small of his back in the brothel
   thills
And a girl to be married and all of them
   snarling at home
With the Indian look in their eyes like a cat
   killing:

And·this Professor Francisco López de
   Gómara
Childless; not poor: and I am old: over
   eighty: 20
Stupid with sleepless nights: unused to the
   combing of

Words clean of the wool while the tale
   waits:
And he is a youthful man: a sound one:
   lightened with
Good sleep: skilled in the pen's plaiting—

I am an ignorant old sick man: blind with the
Shadow of death on my face and my hands
   to lead me:
And he not ignorant: not sick—
                    but I

Fought in those battles! These were my own
   deeds!
These names he writes of mouthing them
   out as a man would
Names in Herodotus—dead and their wars to
   read—   30

These were my friends: these dead my com-
   panions:
I: Bernál Díaz: called del Castíllo:
Called in the time of my first fights El Galán:

I here in the turn of the day in the feel of
Darkness to come now: moving my chair
   with the change:
Thinking too much these times how the
   doves would wheel at

Evening over my youth and the air's strange-
   ness:
Thinking too much of my old town of
   Medina
And the Spanish dust and the smell of the
   true rain:

I: poor: blind in the sun: I have seen   40
With these eyes those battles: I saw
   Montezúma:
I saw the armies of Mexico marching the
   leaning

Wind in their garments: the painted faces:
   the plumes
Blown on the light air: I saw that city:
I walked at night on those stones: in the
   shadowy rooms

I have heard the chink of my heel and the
   bats twittering:
I: poor as I am: I was young in that country:
These words were my life: these letters written

Cold on the page with the split ink and the
   shunt of the

Stubborn thumb: these marks at my fingers: 50
These are the shape of my own life. . . .
                    and I hunted the

Unknown birds in the west with their beautiful wings!

Old men should die with their time's span:
The sad thing is not death: the sad thing

Is the life's loss out of earth when the living
   vanish:
All that was good in the throat: the hard
   going:
The marching singing in sunshine: the
   showery land:

The quick loves: the sleep: the waking: the
   blowing of
Winds over us: all this that we knew:
All this goes out at the end as the flowing of   60

Water carries the leaves down: and the few—
Three or four there are of us still that re-
   member it—
Perish: and that time's stopt like a stale tune:

And the bright young masters with their bitter
   treble
Understanding it all like an old game!
And the pucker of art on their lips like the
   pip of a lemon!—

"The tedious veteran jealous of his fame!"
What is my fame or the fame of these my
   companions?
Their tombs are the bellies of Indians: theirs
   are the shameful

Graves in the wild earth: in the Godless
   sand: 70
None know the place of their bones: as for
   mine
Strangers will dig my grave in a stony land:

Even my sons have the strangeness of dark
   kind in them:
Indian dogs will bark at dusk by my
   sepulchre:
What is my fame! But those days: the shine
   of the

Sun in that time: the wind then: the step
Of the moon over those leaf-fallen nights:
   the sleet in the
Dry grass: the smell of the dust where we
   slept—

These things were real: these suns had heat
    in them:
This was brine in the mouth: bitterest foam: 80
Earth: water to drink: bread to be eaten—

Not the sound of a word like the writing of
    Gómara:
Not a past time: a year: the name of a
Battle lost—"and the Emperor Charles came
    home

"That year: and that was the year the same
"They fought in Flanders and the Duke was
    hung—"
The dates of empire: the dry skull of fame!

No but our lives: the days of our lives: we
    were young then:
The strong sun was standing in deep trees:
We drank at the springs: the thongs of our
    swords unslung to it: 90

We saw that city on the inland sea:
Towers between: and the green-crowned
    Montezúma
Walking the gardens of shade: and the
    staggering bees:

And the girls bearing the woven baskets of
    bloom on their
Black hair: their breasts alive: and the hunters
Shouldering dangling herons with their ruffled
    plumes:

We were the first that found that famous
    country:
We marched by a king's name: we crossed
    the sierras:
Unknown hardships we suffered: hunger:

Death by the stone knife: thirst: we fared by
    the   100
Bitter streams: we came at last to that water:
Towers were steep upon the fluttering air:

We were the lords of it all. . . .
               Now time has taught us:
Death has mastered us most: sorrow and pain
Sickness and evil days are our lives' lot:

Now even the time of our youth has been
    taken:
Now are our deeds words: our lives chronicles:
Afterwards none will think of the night
    rain. . . .

How shall a man endure the will of God
    and the
Days and the silence!
                  In the world before us   110
Neither in Cuba nor the isles beyond—

Not Fonséca himself the sagging whore—
Not the Council the Audience even the
    Indians—
Knew of a land to the west: they skirted the
    Floridas:

They ran the islands on the bare-pole winds:
They touched the Old Main and the mid-
    land shores:
They saw the sun go down at the gulf's
    beginning:

None had sailed to the west and returned till
    Córdova:
I went in that ship: Alvarez handled her:
Trusting to luck: keeping the evening before
    him: 120

Sighting after the third week land
And no report of a land there in that ocean:
The Indians clean: wearing the delicate
    bands:

Cape Catoche we called it: *conës catoche*—
So they cried to us over the sea flood:
Many idols they had for their devotion

Some of women: some coupled in sodomy
So we sailed on: we came to Campéchë:
There by the sweet pool they kindled the
    wood-fire:

Words they were saying like *Castilán* in
    their speech: 130
They warned us by signs to be gone when
    the logs charred:
So we turned from them down to the smooth
    beaches:

The boats followed us close in: we departed:
Afterwards there was a *nortë* with fine haze:
We stood for Pontonchán through the boil
    of the narrows:

There they attacked us crossing the green of
    the maize fields:
Me they struck thrice and they killed fifty
And all were hurt and two taken crazy with

Much pain and it blew and the dust lifted

And the thirst cracked the tongues in our
mouths and before us the   140
Sea-corrupted pools where the river drifts:

And we turned back and the wind drove us
to Florida:
There in the scooped sand in the withered
bed—
There by the sea they encountered us threatening war:

So we returned to the islands half dead:
And Córdova did die: and we wrote to
Velásquez—
Diégo the Governor—writing it out: and we
said—

"Excellence: there are lands in the west: the
pass is
"Clean sailing: the scuts of the men are
covered:
"The houses are masonry: gold they have:
baskets   150
"Painted with herbs: the women are chaste
in love"—
Much else of the kind I cannot remember:
And Velásquez took the credit for this
discovery:

And all we had was our wounds: and enough
of them:
And Fonséca Bishop of Búrgos (for so he was
called)
President of the Council: he write to the
Emperor

Telling the wonderful news in a mule's volley
And not a word of our deeds or our pains or
our battles:
And Charles gone: and Joanna the poor queen
stalled

In Tordesíllas shaking the peas in a rattle: 160
And Barbarossa licking his chin in Algiers:
And trouble enough in Spain with all that

And the Cardinal dying and Sicily over the
ears—
Trouble enough without new lands to be conquered and
Naked Indians taken and wild sheep sheared:

But as for us that returned from that westward country—
We could not lie in our towns for the sound
of the sea:

We could not rest at all in our thoughts: we
were young then:

We looked to the west: we remembered the
foreign trees
Borne out on the tide from the unknown
rivers   170
And the clouds like hills in the air our eyes
had seen:

And Grijálva sailed next and we that were
living—
We that had gear to our flesh and the gold
to find
And an old pike in the stall with the haft to
it slivered—

We signed on and we sailed by the first tide:
And we fought at Potonchán that voyage: I
remember
The locusts covered the earth like a false
shine to it:

They flew with a shrill sound like the arrow
stem:
Often we took the whir of the darts for the
locusts:
Often we left our shields from our mouths
as they came: 180

I remember our fighting was much marred
by the locusts:
And that voyage we came to the river
Tabasco:
We saw the nets as we came in and the
smoke of the

Sea over the bar: and we filled the casks
there:
There first we heard of the farther land—
"Colúa" they said "Méjico"—we that were
asking the

Gold there on that shore on the evening
sand—
"Colúa" they said: pointing on toward the
sunset:
They made a sign on the air with their
solemn hands:

Afterward: north: on the sea: and the ships
running   190
We saw the steep snow mountain on the sky:
We stared as dream-awakened men in wonder:

And that voyage it was we came to the island:

Well I remember the shore and the sound
of that place

And the smoke smell on the dunes and the
wind dying:

Well I remember the walls and the rusty
taste of the

New-spilled blood in the air: many among us

Seeing the priests with their small and arrogant faces:

Seeing the dead boy's breasts and the idols
hung with the

Dried shells of the hearts like the husks of
cicadas   200

And their human eyeballs and their painted
tongues

Cried out to the Holy Mother of God for it:

And some that stood there bore themselves
the stone:

And some were eaten of wild beasts of their
bodies:

And none of us all but had his heart fore-
known the

Evil to come would have turned from the
land then:

But the lives of men are covered and not
shown—

Only late to the old at their time's ending

The land shows backward and the way is
there:

And the next day we sailed and the sea was
against us   210

And our bread was dirty with weevils and
grown scarce and the

Rains began and the beans stank in the ovens

And we soldiers were thoroughly tired of seafaring:

So we returned from that voyage with God's
love:

And they talked about nothing else in the
whole of Cuba:

And gentlemen sold their farms to go on discoveries:

And we that had fought in the marshes with
no food—

We sat by the palms in the square in the
green gloaming

With the delicate girls on our knees and the
night to lose:

We that had fought in those lands. . . .
                    and the eloquent Gómara: 220

The quilled professors: the taught tongues of
fame:

What have they written of us: the poor
soldiers:

We that were wounded often for no pay:

We that died and were dumped cold in the
bread sacks:

Bellies up: the birds at us: floating for days

And none remembering which it was that
was dead there

Whether of Búrgos or Yúste or Villalár:

Where have they written our names? What
have they said of us?

They call the towns for the kings that bear
no scars:

They keep the names of the great for time to
stare at—   230

The bishops rich-men generals cocks-at-arms:

Those with the glaze in their eyes and the
fine bearing:

The born leaders of men: the resonant
voices:

They give them the lands for their tombs:
they call it America!

(And who has heard of Vespucci in this soil
Or down by the lee of the coast or toward
the Havana?)

And we that fought here: that with heavy
toil

Earthed up the powerful cities of this land—

What are we? When will our fame come?

An old man in a hill town
                              a handful of   240

Dust under the dry grass at Otúmba

Unknown names
                    hands vanished
                                        faces

Many gone from the day
                              unspeakable numbers

Lives forgotten
                    deeds honored in strangers

"That which I have myself seen and the
fighting" . . .

The True History of Bernál Díaz

THE ARGUMENT

Of that world's conquest and the fortunate
    wars:
Of the great report and expectation of honor:
How in their youth they stretched sail: how
    fared they

Westward under the wind: by wave wandered:
Shoaled ship at the last at the ends of ocean:
How they were marching in the lands beyond:

Of the difficult ways there were and the
    winter's snow:
Of the city they found in the good lands: how
    they lay in it:
How there were always the leaves and the days
    going:

Of the fear they had in their hearts for their
    lives' sake: 10

How there was neither the night nor the day
    sure: and the
Gage they took for their guard: and how evil
    came of it:

How they were dead and driven and endured:
How they returned with arms in the wet
    month:
How they destroyed that city: and the gourds
    were

Bitter with blood: and they made their roofs
    with the gun stocks:

Of that world's conquest and the fortunate
    wars. . . .

From The First Book

So does a man's voice speak from the dream
    that bears his

Sleeping body with it and the cry
Comes from a great way off as over water—   20
As the sea-bell's that the veering wind
    divides. . . .

Now is it Díaz in the Book—
        . . . . where
               lost in the . . . .
Santiágo de Cuba it was: I remember. . . .

Hoisted over the. . . .
        king's arms and a cross on it. . . .

Cortés I mean and the pleat of his purse
    empty:
And they made him captain: Duéro did: and
    the split-up
Three ways and as for the Governor. . . .
                slept. . . .

November and warm in. . . .
        surf. . . .
           the dry winter:

Palms ragged with sea-gust. . . .
               all careened with the
Weed in the rusty chains and the keelsons
    splintered. . . .   30

Bleaching with sun and the. . . .
        nights in. . . .
           elegant knees like the
Girls in Spain and the sand still hot from the
    sun and the
Surf slow. . . .
        wind over. . . .
           palm-trees sweeping the

Stars into darkness. . . .
        weeks. . . .
           waited. . . .
             the guns

Brassy in. . . .
        loading the cobbed maize and the
           pigs and
Powder enough for a . . .
        ropes on the. . . .
           eight tons:

And we launched the last of them well out
and the brigantine
Cocked in the poop like a Genoa. . . .
　　　　　　　　　　　sixteen horses:
Alvarádo's the mare the sorrel the big one:

Montéjo's the galled gelding: his rump sore
with it: 40
Puertocarréro's grey that the captain bought
him:
A fast dark chestnut horse of de Mórla's:

Ortíz the musician's stallion: well taught:
Clever under the bit: the mare La Rabóna:
The captain's hack that died of the foul water:

Láres the excellent horseman a strong roan:
Gonzálo de Sandovál's La Motílla: the best of
them:
A chestnut bearing a white star: and the loan
of a. . . .

And we lay by for the beans and they told
Cortés . . .
Governor knew of the. . . .
　　　　　　　　wild and the writ signed   50
And the sergeants out in the King's square to
arrest him:

And the captain heard it at dusk and the wind
rising
And he ordered the lot of us down to the
ships by dark
And the chains short. . . .
　　　　　　　bucking the. . . .
　　　　　　　　　all that night. . . .

Sentries at. . . .
　　　　waked and beachward and still stars
and the

Governor riding his white horse on the fish
nets
Big in the fault of the light and his men armed

And the palms back of him black and the
leaves threshing:
We cold on the dew-wet decks: yawning: our
Mouths sour with sleep: the pimpling flesh   60

Crawling under the thin cloths: and at dawn
the
Captain out in the oared boat: and we hoisted
the
Jibs on the rest of them: getting the low airs:
yawing

Wide to the ruffle of squalls and we cleared
the buoys
And we luffed up by the quay with the gear
rolling
And Velásquez cried to him there in his bull's
voice—

"How is it O my Compadre I see you go?
"Is this the right way to take leave of the
Governor?"
Hollow it was on the gale as a conch blowing:

And Cortés below there and the quay above: 70
And he stood to the swing of the sea in the
boat's stern
Baring his head and the tune of his voice like
a lover's—

"Señor! there are some things in this sinful
world
"Best done before they're thought of! At your
orders!"
And they stared across the water with no
words:

From Frescoes for Mr. Rockefeller's City (1933)

This poem was occasioned by the commission-
ing of the Mexican artist Diego Rivera to provide murals for the walls of one of the buildings
of Rockefeller Center in New York City. Rivera's work proved too belligerently Marxist for
the Rockefellers, and though the artist was paid
his fee, the murals were removed. The poet,
therefore, undertakes to provide appropriate
murals, done this time, however, not in pig-
ments but in words.

The poem is in six parts, to correspond with
the original six panels of murals. We print below the fifth and sixth parts. The Empire Builders
mentioned are Edward Henry Harriman (1848–
1909) and Cornelius Vanderbilt (1794–1877),
both railroad magnates; J. P. Morgan (1837–

1913), international banker; Andrew Mellon (1855–1937), financier and founder of the Aluminum Company of America; and Bruce Barton (1886–   ), member of one of the great advertising firms of the 1920's.

The poet assumes the mask of a museum attendant who is showing the murals to visitors. Hidden "under the Panel Paint" is an account of the real empire builders, men like Meriwether Lewis and William Clark, who explored the newly acquired Louisiana Territory. MacLeish has versified passages out of the report that

Lewis sent back to Thomas Jefferson from the Pacific coast, in which he described the spacious lands to the west which had been purchased.

The fifth section ends with another glance at the finance capitalists who, the poet indicates, were not interested in the land, but in its exploitation.

The sixth section indicts the doctrinaire revolutionists for also treating America as an "abstraction," not as a complex and finally mysterious reality.

Empire Builders

THE MUSEUM ATTENDANT

This is *The Making of America in Five Panels:*

This is Mister Harriman making America:
Mister-Harriman-is-buying-the-
    Union-Pacific-at-Seventy:
The Santa Fe is shining on his hair.

This is Commodore Vanderbilt making
    America:
Mister-Vanderbilt-is-eliminating-the-short-
    interest-in-Hudson:
Observe the carving on the rocking chair.

This is J. P. Morgan making America:
(The Tennessee Coal is behind to the left
    of the Steel Company.)
Those in mauve are braces he is wearing.   10

This is Mister Mellon making America:
Mister-Mellon-is-represented-as-a-symbolical-
    figure-in-aluminum-
Strewing-bank-stocks-on-a-burnished-stair.

This is the Bruce is the Barton making
    America:
Mister-Barton-is-selling-us-Doctor's-
    Deliciousest-Dentifrice.
This is he in beige with the canary.

You have just beheld the Makers making
    America:
This is The Making of America in
    Five Panels:
America lies to the west-southwest
    of the switch-tower:
There is nothing to see of America but land.   20

THE ORIGINAL DOCUMENT UNDER THE PANEL PAINT:

"To Thos. Jefferson Esq. his obd't serv't
M. Lewis: captain: detached:
                    Sir:

Having in mind your repeated commands
    in this matter,
And the worst half of it done and the
    streams mapped,

And we here on the back of this beach
    beholding the
Other ocean—two years gone and the cold

Breaking with rain for the third spring
    since St. Louis,
The crows at the fishbones on the
    frozen dunes,

The first cranes going over from south north,
And the river down by a mark of the pole
    since the morning,   10

And time near to return, and a ship
    (Spanish)
Lying in for the salmon: and fearing
    chance or the

Drought or the Sioux should deprive you
    of these discoveries—
Therefore we send by sea in this writing.

                    Above the
Platte there were long plains and a clay
    country:

Rim of the sky far off, grass under it,

Dung for the cook fires by the sulphur licks.
After that there were low hills and the
   sycamores,

And we poled up by the Great Bend
   in the skiffs:
The honey bees left us after the Osage River: 20

The wind was west in the evenings, and
   no dew and the
Morning Star larger and whiter than usual—

The winter rattling in the brittle haws.
The second year there was sage and the
   quail calling.

All that valley is good land by the river:
Three thousand miles and the clay cliffs and

Rue and beargrass by the water banks
And many birds and the brant going over
   and tracks of

Bear, elk, wolves, marten: the buffalo
Numberless so that the cloud of their dust
   covers them: 30

The antelope fording the fall creeks, and
   the mountains and

Grazing lands and the meadow lands
   and the ground

Sweet and open and well-drained.
              We advise you to
Settle troops at the forks and to issue licenses:

Many men will have living on these lands.
There is wealth in the earth for them all
   and the wood standing

And wild birds on the water where they sleep.
There is stone in the hills for the towns
   of a great people . . ."

You have just beheld the Makers Making
   America:

They screwed her scrawny and gaunt with
   their seven-year panics: 40
They bought her back on their mortgages
   old-whore-cheap:
They fattened their bonds at her breasts till
   the thin blood ran from them.
Men have forgotten how full clear and deep
The Yellowstone moved on the gravel
   and the grass grew
When the land lay waiting for her
   westward people!

Background with Revolutionaries

      And the corn singing Millennium!
      Lenin! Millennium! Lennium!

*When they're shunting the cars on the Katy
   a mile off
When they're shunting the cars when they're
   shunting the cars on the Katy
You can hear the clank of the couplings
   riding away.*

Also Comrade Devine who writes of America
Most instructively having in 'Seventy-four
Crossed to the Hoboken side on the
   Barclay Street Ferry.

*She sits on a settle in the State of
   North Dakota,
O she sits on a settle in the State of
   North Dakota,
She can hear the engines whistle over
   Iowa and Idaho.*

Also Comrade Edward Remington Ridge   10
Who has prayed God since the April of
   'Seventeen
To replace in his life his lost (M.E.) religion.

*And The New York Daily Worker goes
   a'blowing over Arkansas,
The New York Daily Worker goes a'blowing
   over Arkansas,
The grasses let it go along the Ozarks
   over Arkansas.*

Even Comrade Grenadine Grilt who has
   tried since
August tenth for something to feel about
   strongly in
Verses—his personal passions having tired.

*I can tell my land by the jays in the
   apple-trees,
Tell my land by the jays in the apple-trees,*   20

*I can tell my people by the blue-jays in
    the apple-trees.*

Aindt you read in d' books you are all
    brudders?
D' glassic historic objective broves you
    are brudders!
You and d' Wops and d' Chinks you are
    all brudders!
Havend't you got it d' same ideology?
    Havend't you?

*When it's yesterday in Oregon it's
    one A M in Maine
And she slides: and the day slides: and
    it runs: runs over us:
And the bells strike twelve strike twelve
    strike twelve
In Marblehead in Buffalo in Cheyenne
    in Cherokee:
Yesterday runs on the states like a crow's
    shadow.*   30

For Marx has said to us, Workers what
    do you need?

And Stalin has said to us, Starvers what
    do you need?
You need the Dialectical Materialism!

*She's a tough land under the corn, mister:
She has changed the bone in the cheeks
    of many races:
She has winced the eyes of the soft Slavs
    with her sun on them:
She has tried the fat from the round
    rumps of Italians:
Even the voice of the English has gone dry
And hard on the tongue and alive in the
    throat speaking.*

She's a tough land under the oak-trees, mister: 40
*It may be she can change the word
    in the book
As she changes the bone of a man's head
    in his children:
It may be that the earth and the men
    remain . . .*

*There is too much sun on the lids of my eyes
    to be listening.*

Ezry (1951)

This poem is a tribute to Ezra Pound. The
"Grove" referred to in the first line is the sacred
grove consecrated to poetry. It is referred to in
the last stanza as "the Muses' Wood."

    A bench mark is cut by a surveyor into a
stone or other permanent surface to indicate a
known elevation above sea level. The mark can
then be used to establish other elevations in the
neighborhood.

    Perhaps the most famous bench mark in this
country is that carved by George Washington,
when he surveyed the Natural Bridge in Virginia. It is still plainly visible, high above the
stream in the gorge.

Maybe you ranted in the Grove—
Maybe!—but you found the mark

That measures altitude above
Sea-level for a poet's work.

Mad if you were or fool instead
You found the bench-mark in the stone—
Horizon over arrow-head—
Alder and dock had overgrown.

These later and more cautious critics
Think themselves high if they look down   10
From Rome's or England's steeple—spit
On fools below them in the town:

Not you! Although the absolute sea
Is far down from the Muses' Wood,
You gauged the steep declivity,
Giddy with grandeur where you stood.

HART CRANE (1899–1932)

Hart Crane's brilliant poetic career was brief but meteoric, and the record of his career constitutes a significant chapter in the literary history of the first half of our century. His appearance in this particular section of the book may seem somewhat anomalous for, like many midwesterners, he had strong natural affinities with Whitman and the nativist tradition. Yet he early became intensely interested in the French symbolist poets—he has been called the American Rimbaud[1]—and he made the same connection that Eliot had made between the methods and qualities of the symbolists and the English Elizabethan and seventeenth-century metaphysicals (see p. 2097). He was himself heavily influenced by Eliot's poetry and adopted some of Eliot's techniques, but he found Eliot's general position negative and pessimistic, and early in his career wrote to Allen Tate, his close friend, that he hoped to go *"through* [Eliot] toward a *different goal."* This tension between a Whitmanesque "content" and symbolist "methods" was determinative for the development of Crane's poetry.

Crane had a rather sketchy formal education, but he was precocious—most of all precocious in his aptitude for literature. He knew what to read in order to nourish his own creative sensibility, and he absorbed very rapidly the literary point and the technical values of whatever he read. Tate tells us: "He read for shock, for language. It was reading for sensibility."

A major turning point in Crane's life was the moment, about Easter of 1923, when he left his grandmother's house in Cleveland and went to New York City, there to settle more or less for good. He had spent his childhood in the town of Warren, Ohio, but from 1908 to 1923 he was mostly in Cleveland, with an occasional east-ward excursion. His youth was beset by family turmoil, by the quarrels, separations, and reconciliations between his parents: his father, Clarence Crane, an increasingly successful manufacturer of chocolate candy; and his neurotic mother, the former Grace Hart, of Chicago. Soon after their divorce in 1916 Crane wrote his mother that "I don't want to fling accusations, etc., at anybody, but I think it's time you realized that for the last eight years my youth has been a rather bloody battleground for yours and father's sex life and troubles." When he felt ready to launch out on his own, he was drawn naturally—not, as were other midwesterners like Sandburg and Anderson, to Chicago—to Manhattan, and to the literary currents and literary wars of that artistically lively city.

Yet when Crane examined the New York scene, especially in his long poem *The Bridge,* he sought to transform that discordant and mechanized world into a dream of pastoral purity, evoking the hills and rivers of his Ohio boyhood. He was for some time torn between the kind of writing espoused by Edgar Lee Masters and Sherwood Anderson—in a review of *Winesburg, Ohio,* he praised that book as "the Bible of the American consciousness"—and its polar opposite, the poetry practiced and championed by Pound and Eliot and the French poets like Rimbaud and Laforgue.[2]

At the outset Crane had even tried his hand at the free verse urged by Amy Lowell and exemplified by Masters—verse, as he put it in a poem called "Forgetfulness," that wanders "freed from beat and measure." But he was soon working away from "the current impres-

---

[1] Arthur Rimbaud (1854–1891), a French symbolist poet who practiced what he called the "systematic derangement of the senses" through alcohol, drugs, and other means, in the interest of what would be called today an "expansion" of his consciousness.

[2] In 1920, Crane translated three of Laforgue's *Locutions des Pierrots* ("Asides," as it were, spoken by the poet assuming the persona of the traditional French clown, Pierrot) and published them in the *Double Dealer.* It is suggestive of Crane's development that only a few years later he was dismissing Laforgue's work as fastidious whimpering.

sionism," as he termed it in a letter of 1921, and was being "carried back into 'rime and meter'"—not into the "swinging" meters of Vachel Lindsay, but the strong, declamatory rhythms he heard in the Jacobean verse drama that Eliot was brilliantly analyzing in his essays.[3] Crane often, though not always, used these rhythms in verse along with distinctly audible alternating rhymes.

"Black Tambourine" of the same year was symptomatic:

The interests of a black man in a cellar
Mark tardy judgment on the world's closed
  door.
Gnats toss in the shadow of a bottle,
And a roach spans a crevice in the floor.

It is worth noting that this interesting poem reflects what was becoming Crane's major theme: the poet in the modern world. For in the course of obliquely describing the humiliation of the black man in American society, Crane was perhaps also describing the humiliation of the poet; "Black Tambourine" presents the poet as a kind of "white black man."

A better poem, and a step forward in Crane's treatment of the theme and the development of his powers, was "Chaplinesque," also of 1921, in which he presents the poet as clown. "Chaplinesque" was inspired by Charlie Chaplin and his recent film *The Kid* ("comedy has never reached a higher level in this country before," Crane wrote a friend excitedly); and Crane was moved by the felt analogy between Chaplin and the poet—the figure threadbare and homeless, sliding his way through a hostile and derisive world with fleet ingratiating smiles and frequent pratfalls. The poem ends, however, with the first clear example of what would become Crane's characteristic poetic mode—that of visionary transformation:

The game enforces smirks; but we have seen
The moon in lonely alleys make

[3] These were later collected in a volume entitled *Elizabethan Essays* (1934). But they can also be found in Eliot's *Selected Essays* (1932).

A grail of laughter of an empty ash can,
And through all sound of gaiety and quest
Have heard a kitten in the wilderness.

This is obviously an example of what Emerson meant by seeing "the miraculous in the common": an ash can in a slum alley perceived by moonlight as a holy grail—more than that, as a grail holding not the blood of Christ but "laughter."

Yet before the visionary and apocalyptic became dominant in Crane's poetry, he produced one more poem in measured quatrains—restrained, understated, even "classical" in character. This was an elegy entitled "Praise for an Urn," written late in 1921. In its poise and balance, its precise but delicately evocative phrasing, and its grasp of moral complexities, it remains one of Crane's very finest accomplishments. But it was the last of Crane's work of this sort. For early in 1922 he began work on a three-part poem of some 140 lines entitled "For the Marriage of Faustus and Helen" and thus entered fully into his attempt to claim for the alchemy of transforming vision the world of twentieth-century industrial man. The poet's imagination would dare to make out even in the confused and frustrating world of the 1920's the old high promise of the future. America was still the America of hope and the new day.[4]

The title that Crane chose for his poem is significant. Faustus is the philosopher who, in Christopher Marlowe's play (and Goethe's), sells his soul to the devil to gain a renewal of his youth and the gift of power through sorcery and magic. Crane was also familiar with Oswald Spengler's appropriation of the name to form the adjective "Faustian" which he applied to our present civilization of the West, with its scientific power and its ambition to transform nature. (In writing to a friend, Crane indicated

[4] It ought to be noted, however, that even here Crane's purpose is not as far from Eliot as might be supposed. Eliot did not believe that the poet could "transform" the civilization by an act of the imagination but he did believe that it was the poet's obligation to see the "glory" possible in the modern world, as well as the obvious horror and the boredom.

that he thought his poem on Faustus and Helen should be "Promethean" in mood.)[5]

The Helen of the poem is, of course, Helen of Troy, the archetype of love and beauty. In Marlowe's *Doctor Faustus*, Faustus has Mephistopheles call Helen back to life to be his paramour. Crane's poem, then, is about the possibility of wedding modern industrial man to eternal beauty—that is, about the possibility of a marriage between science and art. The union of Faustus with Helen, as Marlowe told the story, was finally an unhappy one, impermanent, perhaps merely an illusion, and Faustus the great sorcerer was damned. Crane is more optimistic. He will retell the story in a more hopeful mood and he will set it down in modern America and use (especially in Part 2) a jazz idiom; but he will also hint at something like Elizabethan opulence of language and a glittering rhetoric even if the modern Faustus first sees his Helen seated across the aisle of a streetcar.

The poem won warm praise and congratulations from Crane's friends. Waldo Frank wrote to him to say that the poem was "a sort of marriage of heaven and hell . . . the hell of our modern mechanized world suddenly bearing as its essence an antique beauty which certain Elizabethans glimpsed for our language. . ."

In spite of the highly contemporary setting, "For the Marriage of Faustus and Helen" embodies a traditional Romantic theme. Sidney Colvin's summary of John Keats's *Endymion* can be applied to Crane's poem: "a parable of the poetic soul in man seeking communion with the spirit of essential beauty in the world." Crane, it should be said, takes the matter of "in this world" very seriously. The act of transcendence would seem to be heroic, for in Part 1 of the poem, the imagination must rise from the hot sidewalks of, say, Cleveland, Ohio, to some cooler domain from which the journeying spirit can catch a glimpse of another world, the realm of Helen, or beauty incarnate:

There is the world dimensional for

[5] See John Unterecker, *Voyager: A Life of Hart Crane* (1969), p. 257.

those untwisted by the love of things irreconcilable.

This other world is accessible to all those not wedded "by the love of things" or who think that man's dream is "irreconcilable" with the truth of life. Yet, once having perceived that other world, the imagination (in Crane's view) does not rest in it, but returns to trace its outlines in the actual world. The last lines of the final section of "Faustus and Helen" declare as much. The reader is admonished to

Distinctly praise the years, whose volatile
Blamed bleeding hands extend and thresh the
  height
The imagination spans beyond despair,
Outpacing bargain, vocable and prayer.[6]

There are almost tortured complexities in these packed lines, but at the least one notes Crane's insistence on praise for "the years"—for the world of time—if only because the imagination sees it as touching on (and perhaps being redeemed by) the higher world of the timeless.

Fully aware, as it seems, that he had arrived at a crucial new stage in his career, Crane, within weeks of finishing "Faustus and Helen," had left the house in Cleveland and settled, with every expectation of permanence, in New York. He had, he wrote his friend Gorham Munson at just this time, "lost the last shreds of philosophical pessimism during the last few months," and now felt himself "directly connected with Whitman . . . in currents that are positively awesome in their extent and possibilities."

A climactic moment in this development had occurred about a year earlier, when, seated in a dentist's chair and under ether, his mind had (so he told Munson) "spiraled to a kind of seventh heaven of consciousness." He heard a voice

[6] Crane's complicated language offers real difficulties even to a sensitive and careful reader. Barbara Herman's "The Language of Hart Crane," *Sewanee Review* (Winter, 1950), is well worth consulting. She discusses Crane's view of language and its potentialities and, by way of illustration, analyzes specific passages.

saying: "You have the higher consciousness. . . . This is what is called genius." And "a happiness, ecstatic such as I have known only twice in 'inspirations' came over me. I felt the two worlds. And at once." It was this simultaneous apprehension of the two worlds, or dimensions of experience, that drew Crane so close to Whitman and that, at the same time, led him to diverge sharply from what he took to be the poetic road of T. S. Eliot. Crane's letter to Munson (of January 5, 1923) deserves to be quoted at some length; it describes very well the Romantic—and the American nativist—opposition to Eliot and all that he represented.

There is no one writing in English who can command so much respect, to my mind, as Eliot. However, I take Eliot as a point of departure toward an almost complete reverse of direction. His pessimism is amply justified, in his own case. But I would apply as much of his erudition and technique as I can absorb and assemble toward a more positive, or (if [I] must put it so in a sceptical age) ecstatic goal. I should not think of this if a kind of rhythm and ecstasy were not (at odd moments, and rare!) a very real thing to me. I feel that Eliot ignores certain spiritual events and possibilities as real and powerful now as, say, in the time of Blake. Certainly the man has dug the ground and buried hope as deep and direfully as it can ever be done. He has outclassed Baudelaire with a devastating humor that the earlier poet lacked.

After this perfection of death—nothing is possible in motion but a resurrection of some kind. Or else, as everyone persists in announcing in the deep and dirgeful *Dial*, the fruits of civilization are entirely harvested. Everyone, of course, wants to die as soon and as painlessly as possible! Now is the time for humor, and the Dance of Death. All I know through very much suffering and dullness (somehow I seem to twinge more all the time) is that it interests me to still affirm certain things. That will be the persisting theme of the last part of "F[austus] and H[elen]" as it has been all along. (Brom Weber, ed., *The Letters of Hart Crane*, 1952, pp. 114–15)

A second major turning point in Crane's life may be located in the summer of 1926 when, in little more than a month, he wrote or revised ten of the fifteen separable "poems" in his major work *The Bridge* and made a good start on two of the others. This represented one of the most extraordinary outbursts of creative energy in the history of American poetry—though Crane's energy thereupon abruptly gave out, and *The Bridge* was not in fact completed and published until April, 1930.

During the three previous years, in Manhattan and in a series of rural retreats in upstate New York, Crane had composed enough lyrics to make up his first volume, *White Buildings*—the title coming from the fourth stanza of the poem "Recitative":

Look steadily—how the wind feasts and spins
The brain's disk shivered against lust. Then watch
While darkness, like an ape's face, falls away,
And gradually white buildings answer day.

Crane's title, indeed, indicates the central theme of the book: the felt relation, as here, between the divided self ("the brain's disk shivered") and the divided world, and the intense effort to move in spirit not only from darkness to day, but from a shattered condition to one of restored wholeness and harmony. Such harmony is splendidly described in the resounding conclusion of "Recitative":

In alternating bells have you not heard
All hours clapped dense into a single stride?
Forgive me for an echo of these things,
And let us walk through time with equal pride.

Several of the best poems in *White Buildings* are presented and commented on later. Here only two or three general aspects of the book need be mentioned. The most obvious one is the sheer difficulty of these poems. Some of the first readers found Crane's poetry so opaque as to arouse a suspicion of fraudulence; and even today critics differ almost violently in their interpretation of individual lines and stanzas, not to say entire poems. But when the poems written after "Faustus and Helen" are read as a group, a good many of the difficulties disappear. The poems clarify and reinforce each other; and the reader begins to notice not only recurring postures and emphases and cadences, but also recurring allusions—to sight and hearing, to the wind, to the color white, to fire, to memory, to tears and laughter—all of which accumulate into a pattern of symbolism, something expressive both of private urgencies and of a traditionally Romantic view of experience.

One realizes, too, that if Crane was now writing out of an increasingly close spiritual conjunction with Whitman, he was also writing (and more definitely than perhaps he knew) in the shadow of Emerson. The last pages of Emerson's *Nature* remain the best single account of the aim and drive of Crane's imagination, particularly Emerson's argument that "The problem of restoring to the world original and eternal beauty is solved by the redemption of the soul. . . . The reason why the world lacks unity, and lies broken and in heaps, is because man is disunited with himself."

Another aspect to be noted is Crane's *moral* attitude toward the division he felt within himself. Though anything but effeminate, Crane was a vigorously practicing homosexual; and it is sometimes suggested that his sense of guilt in this regard (the "lust" against which his brain was "shivered") was at the heart of his verse. This explanation, however, seems not really or usually applicable: Crane was extremely cheerful about his sexual conduct; and his typical attitude, as voiced in "Legend," was:

> I am not ready for repentance;
> Nor to match regrets.

Again Crane follows the example of Whitman, and especially of the strenuously anti-Calvinist spirit of Crane's favorite among Whitman's poems, "Passage to India":

Chanting our chant of pleasant exploration,
With laugh and many a kiss
(Let others deprecate, let others weep for sin, remorse, humiliation,)
O soul, thou pleasest me, I thee.[7]

[7] One also recalls Whitman, in "Song of Myself," demanding contemptuously, "What blurt is this about

But Crane's most succinct formulation of his moral position can be found in the following lines from the otherwise almost insurmountably difficult "Lachrymae Christi":

> And the nights opening
> Chant pyramids,—
> Anoint with innocence—recall
> To music and retrieve what perjuries
> Had galvanized the eyes.
>   While chime
> Beneath and all around
> Distilling clemencies,—worms'
> Inaudible whistle, tunneling
> Not penitence
> But song. . . .

The power of song (of chanting, music, chiming bells) can dissipate not only the sense of guilt, but the very principle of guilt; it anoints, recalls, retrieves, forgives.[8]

The major motif of Crane's lyric poetry, however, is implied in the phrase above about "perjuries" having "galvanized the eyes." What disturbed Crane, if anything did, about his riotous living was not that it was an offense to conscience, but that it sometimes tended to impair his poetic vision—to "galvanize" it (coat it over, metallically). Put most simply, too much wine and too much sexual activity got in the way of writing poetry. But by the same token, the writing of a new poem (like "Lachrymae Christi") was a triumph over the self-induced obstacles to it. The best poems in *White Buildings*—among them, the "Voyages" sequence, "The Wine Menagerie," "At Melville's Tomb," and "Repose of Rivers"—are recurring celebrations of poetry and imaginative vision. Such

---

virtue and about vice," and saying that he was inclined to "turn and live with animals" because they "do not lie awake in the dark and weep for their sins," and "do not make me sick discussing their duty to God."

[8] Crane's very title involves something of this sort. *Lachrymae Christi* (Latin) means "tears of Christ," but *lacrima Christi* (Italian), which means literally "tear of Christ," is the name of a famous Italian white wine. Thus, the title of the poem implies that the true tears of the Savior are to be associated, not with sorrow, but with joyous intoxication.

celebration, Crane believed, can unite and redeem the self and the world.

Crane continued hard at work on *The Bridge*, and several independent lyrics, into the summer of 1927. Then, somehow, his life seems to have lost its rhythm. He recovered enough in the fall of 1929 to complete *The Bridge*; and he had a last surge in the spring of 1932, when he composed "The Broken Tower." But for the rest, these were the years when Crane's reputation for wildly unpredictable behavior—for getting into fights with sailors, for smashing his typewriter in a spasm of rage, for reeling drunkenly down the streets shouting that he was Blake, he was Marlowe, he was Christ—became established. This lurid reputation, as we have said, has blurred a true understanding of Crane's

character, and of his visionary, often sweet-spirited and always love-oriented poetry.

In March, 1931, Crane was granted a Guggenheim fellowship, and left for a year in Mexico. A year later, sailing north, he disappeared over the side of the S.S. *Orizaba*, presumably, though not certainly, a suicide. He had been drunk and belligerent the night before and had lost all his money. He told his companion Peggy Baird that he felt "utterly disgraced." Miss Baird said many years later that she had been sure his threat of suicide (one he frequently made) had only "been a threat—to get a reaction." On a stone in the cemetery at Garrettsville, Ohio, Crane's relatives inscribed the simple phrase "Lost at Sea."

BIOGRAPHICAL CHART

1899　Born, July 21, in Garrettsville, Ohio
1908　Family moves to Cleveland, Ohio, where his father organizes a chain of retail candy shops
1916　"C-33" (poem) in *Bruno's Weekly*, a small Greenwich Village magazine; parents begin divorce proceedings; comes to live in New York City
1919　Works in one of his father's candy shops, Akron, Ohio
1920–23　Lives in Cleveland, working for his father and in advertising
1923　"For the Marriage of Faustus and Helen," his

first major poem; begins writing *The Bridge*; returns to New York City
1926　*White Buildings*; continues work on *The Bridge* while living on his grandmother's plantation on the Isle of Pines, Cuba
1928–29　Travels in Europe for several months
1930　*The Bridge*
1931　Awarded a Guggenheim fellowship; takes up residence in Mexico
1932　April 27, leaps to his death from a ship traveling from Mexico to New York
1933　*The Collected Poems of Hart Crane*

FURTHER READINGS

H. D. Rowe, *Hart Crane: A Bibliography* (1955)
Brom Weber, ed., *The Letters of Hart Crane, 1916–1932* (1952)

L. S. Dembo, *Hart Crane's Sanskrit Charge: A Study of The Bridge* (1960)
Paul Friedman, "*The Bridge*: A Study in Symbolism," *Psychoanalytic Quarterly* (1952)

Philip Horton, *Hart Crane: The Life of an American Poet* (1937)
R. W. B. Lewis, *The Poetry of Hart Crane: A Critical Study* (1967)
Allen Tate, *Essays of Four Decades* (1968)
John Unterecker, *Voyager: A Life of Hart Crane* (1969)
Brom Weber, *Hart Crane: A Biographical and Critical Study* (1948)

Praise for an Urn (1926)

In 1922 Ernest Nelson, born in Norway (hence "northern face"), now in his fifties, had been

struck by a passing automobile and killed. Crane had come to know him and called him "one of the best-read people I ever met," a man of "wonderful kindliness and tolerance and a true Nietzschean." Crane was a pallbearer at Nelson's funeral, and since the body was cremated and his ashes placed in an urn, Crane's title for his poem is thoroughly appropriate.

Pierrot, one of the stock characters in French pantomime, is in love with Pierrette but often frustrated in that love. His sentimental poses and his ineffectuality render him a comic figure. Gargantua (in Rabelais's *Gargantua and Pantagruel*) is an amiable giant with an enormous love for food and drink. He is everything that Pierrot is not—sensual rather than ethereal, earthy rather than poetic. Crane's friend combined the extremes of human nature.

In Memoriam: Ernest Nelson

It was a kind and northern face
That mingled in such exile guise
The everlasting eyes of Pierrot

And, of Gargantua, the laughter.

His thoughts, delivered to me
From the white coverlet and pillow,
I see now, were inheritances—
Delicate riders of the storm.

The slant moon on the slanting hill
Once moved us toward presentiments   10
Of what the dead keep, living still,
And such assessments of the soul

As, perched in the crematory lobby,
The insistent clock commented on,
Touching as well upon our praise
Of glories proper to the time.

Still, having in mind gold hair,
I cannot see that broken brow
And miss the dry sound of bees
Stretching across a lucid space.   20

Scatter these well-meant idioms
Into the smoky spring that fills
The suburbs, where they will be lost.
They are no trophies of the sun.

Repose of Rivers (1926)

The willows carried a slow sound,
A sarabande the wind mowed on the mead.
I could never remember
That seething, steady leveling of the marshes
Till age had brought me to the sea.

Flags, weeds. And remembrance of steep alcoves
Where cypresses shared the noon's
Tyranny; they drew me into hades almost.
And mammoth turtles climbing sulphur dreams
Yielded, while sun-silt rippled them   10
Asunder . . .

How much I would have bartered! the black gorge

And all the singular nestings in the hills
Where beavers learn stitch and tooth.
The pond I entered once and quickly fled—
I remember now its singing willow rim.

And finally, in that memory all things nurse;
After the city that I finally passed
With scalding unguents spread and smoking darts
The monsoon cut across the delta   20
At gulf gates . . . There, beyond the dykes

I heard wind flaking sapphire, like this summer,
And willows could not hold more steady sound.

At Melville's Tomb (1926)

When Crane sent this poem to *Poetry: A Magazine of Verse* in 1926, the editor, Harriet Monroe, put some questions to him about the meaning of certain lines. The following excerpts from

Crane's letter of reply to her will suggest the way in which he justified his imagery. Miss Monroe had asked "How *dice* can *bequeath an embassy* (or anything else); and how a calyx (*of death's bounty* or anything else) can give back a *scattered chapter, livid hieroglyph*; and how, if it does, such a *portent* can be *wound in corridors* (of shells or anything else)."

Crane replied in part as follows:

. . . I'll . . . come at once to the explanations you requested on the Melville poem:

"The dice of drowned men's bones he saw
    bequeath
An embassy."

Dice bequeath an embassy, in the first place, by being ground (in this connection only, of course) in little cubes from the bones of drowned men by the action of the sea, and are finally thrown up on the sand, having "numbers" but no identification. These being the bones of dead men who never completed their voyage, it seems legitimate to refer to them as the only surviving evidence of certain messages undelivered, mute evidence of certain things, experiences that the dead mariners might have had to deliver. Dice as a symbol of chance and circumstance is also implied.

"The calyx of death's bounty giving back,"
    etc.

This calyx refers in a double ironic sense both to a cornucopia and the vortex made by a sinking vessel. As soon as the water has closed over a ship this whirlpool sends up broken spars, wreckage, etc., which can be alluded to as *livid hieroglyphs*, making a *scattered chapter* so far as any complete record of the recent ship and her crew is concerned. In fact, about as much definite knowledge might come from all this as anyone might gain from the roar of his own veins, which is easily heard (haven't you ever done it?) by holding a shell close to one's ear.

"Frosted eyes lift altars"

refers simply to a conviction that a man, not knowing perhaps a definite god yet being endowed with a reverence for deity—such a man naturally postulates a deity somehow, and the altar of that deity by the very *action* of the eyes *lifted* in searching.

"Compass, quadrant and sextant contrive no
    farther tides."

Hasn't it often occurred that instruments originally invented for record and computation have inadvertently so extended the concepts of the entity they were invented to measure (concepts of space, etc.) in the mind and imagination that employed them, that they may metaphorically be said to have extended the original boundaries of the entity measured? This little bit of "relativity" ought not to be discredited in poetry now that scientists are proceeding to measure the universe on principles of pure *ratio*, quite as metaphorical, so far as previous standards of scientific methods extended. . . .

The difficult but beautiful last line of Crane's poem might be paraphrased as follows: Melville's imagination was so vividly engaged by the sea and he saw such grandeur in man's struggle with the sea that though Melville's body has been buried in the earth, his spirit surely can find its real resting place only in the sea. It is reasonable to associate the last line of this poem with Crane's own death at sea.

Often beneath the wave, wide from this ledge
The dice of drowned men's bones he saw
    bequeath
An embassy. Their numbers as he watched,
Beat on the dusty shore and were obscured.

And wrecks passed without sound of bells,
The calyx of death's bounty giving back
A scattered chapter, livid hieroglyph,
The portent wound in corridors of shells.

Then in the circuit calm of one vast coil,
Its lashings charmed and malice reconciled,   10
Frosted eyes there were that lifted altars;
And silent answers crept across the stars.

Compass, quadrant and sextant contrive
No farther tides . . . High in the azure steeps
Monody shall not wake the mariner.
This fabulous shadow only the sea keeps.

Voyages: II (1926)

"Voyages" is a suite of six poems, of which we print below II and VI. These are love poems and both are dominated by the image of the sea as a nature goddess who is also the love goddess. The poem is addressed, however, to the loved one, who, like the speaker, is a "prodigal." The beloved is urged to a complete commitment to change and flux and mutability, for reality is like the sea, changeless only in its constant change, and its goddess respects only the spontaneous outpouring of love. To try to find stability in this life is to attempt the impossible and indeed to invite destruction by the goddess, who "rends" everything except "the pieties of lovers' hands."

The rhetoric is in places difficult. Crane has put on record what he meant by line 5 of stanza 3:

> When . . . I speak of "adagios of islands," the reference is to the motion of a boat through islands clustered thickly, the rhythm of the motion, etc. And it seems a much more direct and creative statement than any more logical employment of words such as "coasting slowly through the islands," besides ushering in a whole world of music. (Unterecker, p. 378)

(By the last phrase, Crane means that since *adagio* is a musical term, its occurrence brings in a suggestion of music and thus enriches the texture of the poem.)

The reader should notice how in the first stanza the poet stresses the completely unlimited and infinite character of the sea; and how, in the fourth stanza, he powerfully suggests that the sea is not subject to time but dominates time. The sea circles the globe and actually creates time, as the sea goddess's "turning shoulders wind the hours."

The closing image, though very beautiful and rich, may require a note. What is the seal's "spindrift gaze toward paradise"? Presumably the seal, immersed in its natural element, free in a world that supports it and that it dominates,

is already in paradise. Therefore, in any direction that it looks, it sees its perfect natural home, simply *more* of its paradise. Even if its eyes are blurred by blown spray, what does that matter? For paradise is all around it, seen or unseen. But an apparently contradictory notion seems to be also implied. In the image of the seal there is almost bound to be an anthropomorphic element—as though, manlike, the seal had eyes fixed on a "paradise" beyond his natural world. Man, too, is a creature of nature, in his "sea"—but yearning beyond nature. And could there be in the background here the famous passage from Conrad's *Lord Jim* about the "destructive elements"? We find in this image one of the most memorable expressions of Crane's mysticism.

The poet is asking the loved one to trust love's spontaneity in a world of change, to surrender to the flux as the seal does, and thus win paradise by not even seeking it.

—And yet this great wink of eternity,
Of rimless floods, unfettered leewardings,
Samite sheeted and processioned where
Her undinal vast belly moonward bends,
Laughing the wrapt inflections of our love;

Take this Sea, whose diapason knells
On scrolls of silver snowy sentences,
The sceptred terror of whose sessions rends
As her demeanors motion well or ill,
All but the pieties of lovers' hands.   10

And onward, as bells off San Salvador
Salute the crocus lustres of the stars,
In these poinsettia meadows of her tides,—
Adagios of islands, O my Prodigal,
Complete the dark confessions her veins spell.

Mark how her turning shoulders wind
    the hours,
And hasten while her penniless rich palms
Pass superscription of bent foam and wave,—
Hasten, while they are true,—sleep,
    death, desire,
Close round one instant in one floating flower.   20

Bind us in time, O Seasons clear, and awe.
O minstrel galleons of Carib fire,
Bequeath us to no earthly shore until

Is answered in the vortex of our grave
The seal's wide spindrift gaze toward paradise.

Voyages: VI (1926)

In "Voyages: VI," as in "II," Crane counts on his reader's remembering that Aphrodite, the Greek goddess of love, was, according to the myth, born of the sea, arising out of the foam. Crane may also have in mind—and may hope that his reader has in mind—the notion, long embodied in various myths and now confirmed by science, that all life arose in the sea. Thus in the sixth stanza the "lounged goddess" is Aphrodite, the love goddess as she rose from the foam.

In the first stanza the "ocean rivers" are currents like the Gulf Stream, which runs for thousands of miles through the sea, keeping their own temperature and definite direction and even having a color different from that of the surrounding sea water.

One way to regard this poem is to see that it is a prayer to the sea goddess as the principle of love and creation, a prayer asking that she extend her grace to the poet. Lost and unseeing ("Thy derelict and blinded guest"), he cannot claim to be the prophet and seer. He will be content if the sea goddess simply acknowledges him as her poet by whatever humble name. It will be enough if she accords him only a "splintered" laureate garland by rearing up her savage waves. But he does wait "afire" for her sign, for he has committed himself wholly to her world of flux and sea change and has been accorded the vision of the deeper changeless world that it masks, the "imaged Word" itself. Thus he establishes his title to being called her poet.

Where icy and bright dungeons lift
Of swimmers their lost morning eyes,
And ocean rivers, churning, shift
Green borders under stranger skies,

Steadily as a shell secretes
Its beating leagues of monotone,
Or as many waters trough the sun's
Red kelson past the cape's wet stone;

O rivers mingling toward the sky
And harbor of the phœnix's breast—   10
My eyes pressed black against the prow,
—Thy derelict and blinded guest

Waiting, afire, what name, unspoke,
I cannot claim: let thy waves rear
More savage than the death of kings,
Some splintered garland for the seer.

Beyond siroccos harvesting
The solstice thunders, crept away,
Like a cliff swinging or a sail
Flung into April's inmost day—   20

Creation's blithe and petalled word
To the lounged goddess when she rose
Conceding dialogue with eyes
That smile unsearchable repose—

Still fervid covenant, Belle Isle,
—Unfolded floating dais before
Which rainbows twine continual hair—
Belle Isle, white echo of the oar!

The imaged Word, it is, that holds
Hushed willows anchored in its glow.   30
It is the unbetrayable reply
Whose accent no farewell can know.

The Broken Tower (1932)

Crane's friend Lesley Simpson has this to say about the beginnings of this poem:

I was with Hart Crane in Taxco, Mexico, the morning of January 27th, this year [1932], when he first conceived the idea of 'The Broken Tower.' The night before, being troubled with insomnia, he had risen before daybreak and walked down to the village square. . . . Hart met the old Indian bell-ringer who

was on his way to the church. He and Hart
were old friends, and he brought Hart up into
the tower with him to help ring the bells. As
Hart was swinging the clapper of the great
bell, half drunk with its mighty music, the
swift tropical dawn broke over the mountains.
The sublimity of the scene and the thunder of
the bells woke in Hart one of those gusts of
joy of which only he was capable.

"The Broken Tower" is Crane's last big poem.
It is particularly rich, and though it has its difficulties, the main theme becomes clear enough
on sufficient reading. It is a poem about art and
the artist's life—a kind of parable about the
poet's triumph and despair. There is the poet
with his animal body, subject to time and eventually to death, and there is his art, which, when
achieved, seems deathless and timeless. Wonderfully, the mortal creature actually molds and
gives shape to a music that transcends time. In
other words, there is a "paradise"—of imagination, of art—to which man, awash in his natural
element, yearns.

Though the poet rejoices in the great sound
that he can evoke by pulling his bell rope, he
also often feels that he has been used and then
abandoned by the creative power. He is the servant of the bells, their "sexton slave!"

The poem, however, modulates—in stanzas 5
through 7—into a fine humility. The poet is content with his role. In the concluding stanzas,
there is a final development of the poem: the
creation of an authentic work of art does affect
the artist after all. It heals him, it makes him
complete and pure, and builds within him a
tower not, like the bell tower, made of stone,
but a tower of the spirit. "The Broken Tower"
is perhaps Crane's most "religious" poem. In
one sense it resembles Stevens' "The Idea of
Order at Key West."

The bell-rope that gathers God at dawn
Dispatches me as though I dropped down
     the knell
Of a spent day—to wander the cathedral lawn

From pit to crucifix, feet chill on steps
     from hell.

Have you not heard, have you not seen
     that corps
Of shadows in the tower, whose shoulders
     sway
Antiphonal carillons launched before
The stars are caught and hived in the sun's ray?

The bells, I say, the bells break down
     their tower;
And swing I know not where. Their
     tongues engrave   10
Membrane through marrow, my
     long-scattered score
Of broken intervals . . . And I, their
     sexton slave!

Oval encyclicals in canyons heaping
The impasse high with choir. Banked
     voices slain!
Pagodas, campaniles with reveilles outleaping—
O terraced echoes prostrate on the plain! . . .

And so it was I entered the broken world
To trace the visionary company of love,
     its voice
An instant in the wind (I know not
     whither hurled)
But not for long to hold each desperate choice.   20

My word I poured. But was it cognate, scored
Of that tribunal monarch of the air
Whose thigh embronzes earth, strikes
     crystal Word
In wounds pledged once to hope—
     cleft to despair?

The steep encroachments of my blood left me
No answer (could blood hold such a
     lofty tower
As flings the question true?)—or is it she
Whose sweet mortality stirs latent power?—

And through whose pulse I hear, counting
     the strokes
My veins recall and add, revived and sure   30
The angelus of wars my chest evokes:
What I hold healed, original now, and
     pure . . .

And builds, within, a tower that is not stone
(Not stone can jacket heaven)—but slip
Of pebbles,—visible wings of silence sown
In azure circles, widening as they dip

The matrix of the heart, lift down the eye
That shrines the quiet lake and swells
    a tower . . .

The commodious, tall decorum of that sky
Unseals her earth, and lifts love in
    its shower.   40

From The Bridge (1930)

The Bridge is a poem in fifteen parts. In a letter
to his patron, Otto H. Kahn, September 12,
1927, Crane gave an account of the poem as he
saw it at that time. Though some modifications
in the plan were made before the poem was
published and though the reader must not
take it to represent a full and final account
of what Crane planned to do, it is well worth
reading in full. (See *The Letters of Hart Crane*,
pp. 304–9.)

Immediately below we print "To Brooklyn

Bridge," which Crane refers to as a "Proem,"
that is, a verse introduction. It announces clearly
the main theme of the poem proper.

Brooklyn Bridge has the beauty of a fine piece
of engineering; it thus becomes for the poet a
symbol of what modern industrial America at
its best can be. But the poet sees in it something
more transcendental: the bridge takes on an almost religious significance, for it expresses man's
aspiration and suggests the great spiritual bridges
which must connect our present with the future.

Proem: To Brooklyn Bridge

How many dawns, chill from his rippling rest
The seagull's wings shall dip and pivot him,
Shedding white rings of tumult, building high
Over the chained bay waters Liberty—

Then, with inviolate curve, forsake our eyes
As apparitional as sails that cross
Some page of figures to be filed away;
—Till elevators drop us from our day . . .

I think of cinemas, panoramic sleights
With multitudes bent toward some flashing
    scene   10
Never disclosed, but hastened to again,
Foretold to other eyes on the same screen;

And Thee, across the harbor, silver-paced
As though the sun took step of thee, yet left
Some motion ever unspent in thy stride,—
Implicitly thy freedom staying thee!

Out of some subway scuttle, cell or loft
A bedlamite speeds to thy parapets,
Tilting there momently, shrill shirt ballooning,
A jest falls from the speechless caravan.[1]   20

Down Wall, from girder into street noon leaks,
A rip-tooth of the sky's acetylene;
All afternoon the cloud-flown derricks
    turn . . .
Thy cables breathe the North Atlantic still.

And obscure as that heaven of the Jews,
Thy guerdon . . . Accolade thou dost bestow
Of anonymity time cannot raise:
Vibrant reprieve and pardon thou dost show

O harp and altar, of the fury fused,
(How could mere toil align thy choiring
    strings!)   30
Terrific threshold of the prophet's pledge,
Prayer of pariah, and the lover's cry,—

Again the traffic lights that skim thy swift
Unfractioned idiom, immaculate sigh of stars,
Beading thy path—condense eternity:
And we have seen night lifted in thine arms.

Under thy shadow by the piers I waited;

---

[1] It may be useful to paraphrase this stanza in order
to make plain to the reader an aspect of the poem
likely to be missed and yet important for Crane's full
sense of reality. If the bridge in its majesty and in its
symbolic promise is capable of lending "a myth to God,"
it can also provide for people distracted and maddened
by the inhuman hurry and rush of the great city a
means to suicide. The "bedlamite" in his crazed state
hurries up to the parapets of the bridge to jump off.
The wind makes his shirt balloon. The caravan of
pedestrians is arrested by the sight and waits speechless
to see what he will do until—such is the callousness of
such crowds—one of them makes a joke about the man
about to kill himself.

Only in darkness is thy shadow clear.
The City's fiery parcels all undone,
Already snow submerges an iron year . . .   40

O Sleepless as the river under thee,
Vaulting the sea, the prairies' dreaming sod,
Unto us lowliest sometime sweep, descend
And of the curveship lend a myth to God.

Section 1 of *The Bridge*, "Ave Maria," takes the reader back to Columbus's discovery of the New World. Section 2, "Powhatan's Daughter," begins with a subsection called "The Harbor Dawn." The scene is New York City in the 1920's. This is followed by a subsection entitled "Van Winkle," which shows him to be still very much alive in modern America. Rip is now sweeping "a tenement way down on Avenue A." The movement of the poem through "Van Winkle" and forward into the first parts of "The River" (the third subsection of "Powhatan's Daughter") is a movement away from the eastern seaboard to the great central valley and a corresponding regression in time from the twentieth century to De Soto's death and burial in the Mississippi in the sixteenth century. For the river described in this section is our great continental river, the Mississippi.

In "The River" we meet the typical American wanderers, wandering still, hoboes "riding the rods" as well as more elegant folk taking their breakfast in the Pullman dining car.

From The River

Behind

My father's cannery works I used to see
Rail-squatters ranged in nomad raillery,
The ancient men—wifeless or runaway
Hobo-trekkers that forever search
An empire wilderness of freight and rails.
Each seemed a child, like me, on a loose perch,
Holding to childhood like some termless play.
John, Jake or Charley, hopping the slow freight
—Memphis to Tallahassee—riding the rods,   10
Blind fists of nothing, humpty-dumpty clods.

but who have touched her,
knowing her without name

Yet they touch something like a key perhaps.
From pole to pole across the hills, the states
—They know a body under the wide rain;
Youngsters with eyes like fjords, old reprobates
With racetrack jargon,—dotting immensity
They lurk across her, knowing her yonder
  breast
Snow-silvered, sumac-stained or smoky blue—
Is past the valley-sleepers, south or west.
—As I have trod the rumorous midnights, too,   20

And past the circuit of the lamp's thin flame
(O Nights that brought me to her body bare!)
Have dreamed beyond the print that bound
  her name.
Trains sounding the long blizzards out—I heard
Wail into distances I knew were hers.

Papooses crying on the wind's long mane
Screamed redskin dynasties that fled the brain,
—Dead echoes! But I knew her body there,
Time like a serpent down her shoulder, dark,
And space, an eaglet's wing, laid on her hair.   30

nor the myths of her fathers . . .

Under the Ozarks, domed by Iron Mountain,
The old gods of the rain lie wrapped in pools
Where eyeless fish curvet a sunken fountain
And re-descend with corn from querulous crows.
Such pilferings make up their timeless eatage,
Propitiate them for their timber torn
By iron, iron—always the iron dealt cleavage!
They doze now, below axe and powder horn.

And Pullman breakfasters glide glistening steel
From tunnel into field—iron strides the dew—   40
Straddles the hill, a dance of wheel on wheel.
You have a half-hour's wait at Siskiyou,
Or stay the night and take the next train
  through.
Southward, near Cairo passing, you can see
The Ohio merging,—borne down Tennessee;
And if it's summer and the sun's in dusk
Maybe the breeze will lift the River's musk
—As though the waters breathed that you
  might know
Memphis Johnny, Steamboat Bill, Missouri Joe.
Oh, lean from the window, if the train
  slows down,   50

As though you touched hands with some
   ancient clown,
—A little while gaze absently below
And hum *Deep River* with them while they go.

Yes, turn again and sniff once more—look see,
O Sheriff, Brakeman and Authority—
Hitch up your pants and crunch another quid,
For you, too, feed the River timelessly.
And few evade full measure of their fate;
Always they smile out eerily what they seem.
I could believe he joked at heaven's gate—   60
Dan Midland—jolted from the cold brake-beam.

Down, down—born pioneers in time's despite,
Grimed tributaries to an ancient flow—
They win no frontier by their wayward plight,
But drift in stillness, as from Jordan's brow.

You will not hear it as the sea; even stone
Is not more hushed by gravity . . . But slow,
As loth to take more tribute—sliding prone
Like one whose eyes were buried long ago
The River, spreading, flows—and spends
   your dream.   70
What are you, lost within this tideless spell?
You are your father's father, and the stream—
A liquid theme that floating niggers swell.

Damp tonnage and alluvial march of days—
Nights turbid, vascular with silted shale
And roots surrendered down of moraine clays:
The Mississippi drinks the farthest dale.

O quarrying passion, undertowed sunlight!
The basalt surface drags a jungle grace
Ochreous and lynx-barred in lengthening
   might;   80
Patience! and you shall reach the biding place!

Over De Soto's bones the freighted floors
Throb past the City storied of three thrones.[2]
Down two more turns the Mississippi pours
(Anon tall ironsides up from salt lagoons)

And flows within itself, heaps itself free.
All fades but one thin skyline 'round . . .
   Ahead
No embrace opens but the stinging sea;
The River lifts itself from its long bed,

Poised wholly on its dream, a mustard glow   90
Tortured with history, its one will—flow!

  [2] New Orleans, which acknowledged the sovereignty
of French kings, then Spanish, and finally Napoleon as
emperor, before being ceded to the United States.

—The Passion spreads in wide tongues,
   choked and slow,
Meeting the Gulf, hosannas silently below.

After the long Section 2 ("Powhatan's Daughter") follows a short third section, "Cutty Sark," which takes its epigraph from Melville and celebrates the American clipper ships and whalers of the nineteenth century. Then follows Section 4, "Cape Hatteras," from which the excerpt that follows is taken.

"Cape Hatteras" celebrates the Wright brothers and their first successful flight at Kitty Hawk, near Cape Hatteras, North Carolina. But the section also pays special tribute to Walt Whitman as the poet who prophesied the American conquest of space: "Passage to India," and other such "passages." It is he particularly that Crane would emulate.

In the excerpt that follows, beginning at line 32 and ending with line 47, occurs one of the most condensed and perhaps contorted examples of Crane's rhetoric. Yet it may be possible to discern in the passage a certain logic of imagination of the sort that Crane believed the poet could properly use. Since few readers will question the tremendous verve and imaginative stimulation achieved, the effort to see the passage as also coherent may be worth making.

The poet celebrates in pride and awe—perhaps even with a trace of terror—the gigantic powerhouse and the mammoth dynamos that whir inside it. (See pp. 1497–1501.)

Boys "whip" tops in a game, but here power, with what seems like a carelessness, sets spinning, not merely the dynamos that whine nasally, but by means of them, a whole new universe. The pillars of the smokestacks spout smoke which leaves its tracks ("spoor") on the evening sky. Having in mind what these looming stacks imply, the viewer's eyes are now pricked —stung as with ammonia—by the stars. Men have always looked at the stars, but now the stars no longer seem to utter well-worn statements of traditional wisdom, but suddenly sting the eyes with new truths—proverbs that are as sharp as ammonia. After all, man, with his heightened sense of the powers of electric energy, now sees the stars themselves as great whirlpools of such energy.

Thus the stars provide new truths, new "inklings" of truth, that can be heard in the "velvet humming" of the dynamos. The figure in ". . . where hearing's leash is strummed. . . ." is difficult to visualize. A dog or other animal pulling tight on a leash may make it taut enough to vibrate, like a banjo string. Is the metaphor saying that the sound of the dynamos tugs at the sense of hearing as the man listening tries to hear a sound implicit in the humming but just below the threshold of the ear, something that he imperfectly senses as not true sound but a sort of physical vibration? Maybe so, maybe not. Perhaps the poet has got beyond himself: the reader will have to decide.

With "Power's script," we return to an easier figure. What the dynamos are doing is to write out the notation of power—but also winding it up as if it were a scroll and, in the process, "refining" it. Whether or not this image is really implicit, the poet quickly shifts to a new suggestion: the "refining" of this power amounts to putting an edge on it as if someone were sharpening a razor on an enormous leather strop.

These confusedly mingled images are combined with a powerful sense of onomatopoeia: "stropped to the slap of belts on booming spools" brilliantly echoes the sounds themselves as the belts feed power to the dynamos. How is one to describe condensed power, concentrated electrical energy, piled up and, as it were, stored? Perhaps "harnessed jelly of the stars" is about as well as can be done, remembering that a few lines earlier the stars have been seen as whirlpools of energy.

Yet though the observer feels shaken and stunned by the amount and quality of the sound, the dynamos themselves seem imperturbable, oblivious to any observer, obsessed with their own tranced action. His attention fixes on them, and the poetry shifts from stress on sound to sight. The glint of the bearings catches his eye, as they shine in "oilrinsed circles," quite "murmurless."

The glinting "bearings" are of course the ball bearings held in the steel shell that forms an annular track to keep them in place as they provide a cushion between the spinning shaft and the bearing within which it revolves. Anyone who has gone frog giggling around a pond at night—as Crane presumably had as a boy in Ohio—knows that in the beam of a flashlight the eyes of the frogs do make points of light. But can frogs' eyes be said to giggle? In any case, would they want to giggle, having now been swallowed and lying packed together in a monstrous gizzard?

Yet it is just this insane gleefulness that makes the figure work. The dynamo does seem to possess a life of its own and appears to be some kind of monstrous animal,[3] with its own inhuman vitality. Though it is the creation of man, the dynamo seems to have cut itself loose from him, now his master rather than his slave. If it appears to our imagination as possessing a consciousness of its own, it is a consciousness in which there is no place for man's sensibility. It is caught up in its own ecstatic rapture, like some incarnate demonic power.

[3] This way of thinking of the machine has now of course become common. Henry Adams entitles one of the chapters in his *Education*, "The Virgin and the Dynamo"; a character in one of Eugene O'Neill's plays comes at last to pray to the dynamo. In recent decades, the cover of *Time* has more than once presented drawings in which a machine was portrayed as an animal or a man. But Crane's treatment is early—and effective.

From Cape Hatteras

But that star-glistered salver of infinity,
The circle, blind crucible of endless space,
Is sluiced by motion,—subjugated never.
Adam and Adam's answer in the forest
Left Hesperus mirrored in the lucid pool.
Now the eagle dominates our days, is jurist
Of the ambiguous cloud. We know the
　　strident rule

Of wings imperious . . . Space, instantaneous,
Flickers a moment, consumes us in its smile:
A flash over the horizon—shifting gears—   10
And we have laughter, or more sudden tears.
Dream cancels dream in this new realm of fact
From which we wake into the dream of act;
Seeing himself an atom in a shroud—
Man hears himself an engine in a cloud!

"—Recorders ages hence"—ah, syllables
    of faith!
Walt, tell me, Walt Whitman, if infinity
Be still the same as when you walked the beach
Near Paumanok—your lone patrol—and
    heard the wraith
Through surf, its bird note there a long
    time falling . . .   20
For you, the panoramas and this breed
    of towers,
Of you—the theme that's statured in the cliff.
O Saunterer on free ways still ahead!
Not this our empire yet, but labyrinth
Wherein your eyes, like the Great Navigator's
    without ship,
Gleam from the great stones of each prison
    crypt
Of canyoned traffic . . . Confronting the
    Exchange,
Surviving in a world of stocks,—they also range
Across the hills where second timber strays
Back over Connecticut farms, abandoned
    pastures,—   30
Sea eyes and tidal, undenying, bright
    with myth!

The nasal whine of power whips a new
    universe . . .
Where spouting pillars spoor the evening sky,
Under the looming stacks of the gigantic
    power house
Stars prick the eyes with sharp ammoniac
    proverbs,
New verities, new inklings in the velvet
    hummed
Of dynamos, where hearing's leash is
    strummed . . .
Power's script,—wound, bobbin-bound,
    refined—
Is stropped to the slap of belts on booming
    spools, spurred
Into the bulging bouillon, harnessed jelly
    of the stars.   40
Towards what? The forked crash of split
    thunder parts

Our hearing momentwise; but fast in
    whirling armatures,
As bright as frogs' eyes, giggling in the girth
Of steely gizzards—axle-bound, confined
In coiled precision, bunched in mutual glee
The bearings glint,—O murmurless and shined
In oilrinsed circles of blind ecstasy!

Stars scribble on our eyes the frosty sagas,
The gleaming cantos of unvanquished
    space . . .
O sinewy silver biplane, nudging the wind's
    withers!   50
There, from Kill Devils Hill at Kitty Hawk
Two brothers in their twinship left the dune;
Warping the gale, the Wright windwrestlers
    veered
Capeward, then blading the wind's flank,
    banked and spun
What ciphers risen from prophetic script,
What marathons new-set between the stars!
The soul, by naphtha fledged into new reaches
Already knows the closer clasp of Mars,—
New latitudes, unknotting, soon give place
To what fierce schedules, rife of doom apace!   60

Section 5 of *The Bridge* is entitled "Three Songs." The first of these, "Southern Cross," apostrophizes the eternal woman in her various manifestations as Eve, Magdalene, and Mary. The second song, "National Winter Garden," treats woman in her animality, seen as a burlesque dancer. The third song describes the "nice" girl named Mary, who works in an office, and evokes from the poet a lyrical celebration of freshness and young love.

A long section 6, entitled "Quaker Hill," comes next in the poem and then Section 7, "The Tunnel," an excerpt from which follows below.

The hell of the modern city is the subway. At any rate, it is on a subway ride that the poet can most intensely sense its hellishness. In the excerpt we print below we have the stream of consciousness of the protagonist as he sits in a subway car. From time to time there impinges on his consciousness scraps of conversation from other passengers. In hallucinated vision, he suddenly recognizes Edgar Allan Poe riding on the car as a straphanger, his eyes "just below the toothpaste and the dandruff ads" that are affixed to the upper walls of the car.

"The Tunnel" section owes a great deal in its structure of presentation to Eliot's *The Waste Land*. It also contains some of Crane's most powerful imagery—terribly complicated as in lines 10–14, where the pattern of nerves in man is likened to the pattern of tracks in the subway system itself. Yet some of the images are brilliantly hit off with relatively little complication, as in lines 2–3, where love flashes its brief puny flame before it winks out like a burnt match skating on the ceramic sides of the public urinal —a sardonic account of the sordid triviality of ⟨meaningless lust.⟩

[handwritten: of linkage of greed-lust-violence]

From The Tunnel

The phonographs of hades in the brain
Are tunnels that re-wind themselves, and love
A burnt match skating in a urinal—
Somewhere above Fourteenth
   TAKE THE EXPRESS
To brush some new presentiment of pain—

[handwritten: premonition]

"But I want service in this office SERVICE
I said—after
the show she cried a little afterwards but—"

Whose head is swinging from the swollen
   strap?
Whose body smokes along the bitten rails,   10
Bursts from a smoldering bundle far behind
In back forks of the chasms of the brain,—
Puffs from a river stump far out behind
In interborough fissures of the mind . . . ?

[handwritten: urban design as lower brain embodied]

And why do I often meet your visage here,
Your eyes like agate lanterns—on and on
Below the toothpaste and the dandruff ads?
—And did their riding eyes right through
   your side,
And did their eyes like unwashed platters ride?
And Death, aloft,—gigantically down   20
Probing through you—toward me, O evermore!
And when they dragged your retching flesh,
Your trembling hands that night through
   Baltimore—
That last night on the ballot rounds, did you
Shaking, did you deny the ticket, Poe?

[handwritten: alcoholic]

For Gravesend Manor change at Chambers
   Street.
The platform hurries along to a dead stop.

The Bridge concludes with Section 8, entitled "Atlantis," the name of the legendary city that long ago sank beneath the waves. Plato was the first to use the name Atlantis, and the epigraph for this section is taken from Plato. The poet's final optimism has not been erased by his recognition of the problems of Western man or the cheapness and venality of so many aspects of American life. Brooklyn Bridge remains a "steeled cognizance" and "Deity's glittering Pledge." It remains an emblem of what America may be, and will be, a passageway to new truths.

Allen Tate, who was one of Crane's earliest admirers and remained his friend, wrote one of the most decidedly negative accounts of *The Bridge* when he reviewed it in 1930. Crane was obviously disappointed that Tate could not see the poem as a success and as a victory over disorder. But his letter to Tate written after he had read the review makes it clear that he did not question Tate's motives nor did he break off their friendship.

The reader might well take the trouble to read Tate's review (in *Essays of Four Decades*, 1968) in full, for the point of Tate's indictment of the poem was not to impugn Crane's genius or his mastery of certain qualities of style. It was rather to point out the general difficulties of writing an epic poem, a long poem, or even an "objective" poem in our time.

What Tate felt unsatisfactory in *The Bridge* was essentially what he deemed unsatisfactory in MacLeish's *Conquistador* (pp. 2193–2199): the modern poet lacks objective ideas and communally held values which he can dramatize in his poem. His poem thus tends to be lyrical and subjective. It expresses the poet's personal reactions to the world, for in an age of unbelief, his personal reactions are the only things in which he can really believe.

Tate points out that in the great epic and philosophical works of our tradition—Dante's *Divine Comedy* would be an example—we are given "the complete articulation of the idea down to the slightest detail, and we are given it objectively apart from anything that the poet is going to say about it. When the poet extends his perception, there is a further extension of the groundwork ready to meet it and discipline it and to compel the sensibility of the poet to stick to the subject." Tate uses an analogy: writing such a poem is like playing a game of chess; neither side can make a move without taking into account the other. "Crane's difficulty," Tate points out, "is that of modern poets generally: they played a game with half of the men, the men of sensibility, and because sensibility can make any move, the significance of all moves is obscure."

Crane took as his basic theme "the Greatness of America"—a proper enough theme; but how is the poet to articulate it? Crane believed that "America stands for a passage into new truths," and perhaps it does; but which America stands for this? And what events in American history show it? Unless the poet has a plot to unfold or a tale to tell, he will find that he has left for his subject matter only an abstract idea, which in itself provides no progression, no development, but simply a series of analogies. America is like a bridge *in this way*. It is also like a bridge *in that way*, and so on. Thus the poem has to keep starting over again and again.

Tate points out that Crane would have gained "an overwhelming advantage by choosing a single period [of American history] or episode, a concrete event with all its dramatic causes, and by following it up minutely, and being bound to it. In short, he would have gained an advantage could he have found a subject to stick to." Virgil in writing the Aeneid elected to tell the story of Aeneas' journey from burning Troy, through various adventures and difficulties, to the founding of Rome in Italy. The story of the man becomes, as Virgil's imagination forms it, the story of Rome and a prefiguring of the Roman virtues and the Roman concept of order.

The point made by Tate really goes to the heart of "Imagism" as a technique. Is the method, as we have suggested earlier in this section, basically static? Did Crane, in spite of his interest in the nativist tradition and in spite of his interest in Whitman, ever really break with a highly personal Imagist and symbolist technique? Did he ever really come clear of the influence of T. S. Eliot? Incidentally, did Eliot himself move beyond a static symbolist method? What is the structure of *The Waste Land*—which also seems relatively plotless and to be weak in narrative line? If *The Waste Land* is not vulnerable to the objections that Tate raises against *The Bridge*, why is it not? (Apparently Tate did not regard it as vulnerable.) Wherein lies the difference?

This is a whole basketful of questions. How they are to be answered—or whether they can be answered at all—are matters that must finally be left to the reader's judgment. But the questions we have raised may, if pondered, tell one a great deal about the strengths and weaknesses of American poetry in the twentieth century and they may suggest the kinds of poetry that are possible in our time and those that are not. But in any case, the problems are not peculiar to the poetry of Crane. In the very review we have been discussing, Tate is emphatic in his praise of Crane's great powers. Some twenty years after his review of *The Bridge*, he published an essay with the title "Crane: The Poet as Hero," in which he calls Crane "the most gifted poet of his generation." The praise is emphatic but it remains judicious and considered: it is for his lyric poetry that Tate praises him.

The Cult of Experience

and the Gospel of Style

GERTRUDE STEIN (1874–1946)

Ordinarily, the idea of the expatriate American is associated with Paris in the 1920's, but the expatriate was, in fact, a very old phenomenon. In the first half of the nineteenth century many thousands of Americans lived in Italy, chiefly in Rome and Florence, and after the Civil War, Paris, as was most famously illustrated in *The Ambassadors*, by Henry James, became a center for Americans. England—"Our Old Home," as Hawthorne called it in the title of the book about his long stay there—had, of course, always drawn Americans, and just before the First World War Pound, Eliot, and other American writers had been in London, where Eliot was to remain as the most celebrated American expatriate.

The First World War was, if not the cause, the occasion for Paris' becoming the center of expatriate life. Many thousands of young Americans had been there under the auspices of the A.E.F. and had liked what they saw. The French capital was, as Gertrude Stein described it, "the place that suited those of us that were to create the twentieth century art and litera-

ture . . . France could be civilized without having progress on her mind, she could believe in civilization in and for itself, and so she was the natural background for this period." Paris was, especially, a place where, in a setting of the great monuments of the past, the art of the future could be pursued with intensity, where that pursuit was conditioned by a current of vital ideas, scientific and humanistic, flowing naturally and unacademically into life, and where life itself might be lived with a maximum of personal freedom.

When the young American expatriate-to-be arrived in Paris he found already established there and in full charge a heavy, middle-aged, formidable, eagle-eyed American female, looking rather like a squat Aztec idol in a corduroy skirt—a sort of combination of sibyl and concierge of the arts. She had been there at 27 rue de Fleurus ever since 1903, but a full generation later she could affirm "I have never been called an expatriate and that is the thing I am proud of." She was an American in the sense that James Joyce was an Irishman, and she remained one to the end, once a week eating a good solid American meal prepared by her companion Alice B. Toklas.

As she said of herself in her own idiom, Gertrude Stein "always remained firmly born in Allegheny Pennsylvania"—that event having occurred on February 3, 1874. She was born of solid, energetic, intelligent, middle-class, and by-and-large very successful German-Jewish stock (she was to become the first Jewish writer in America, Bret Harte being a special case; see pp. 1250–51), and though she lived most of her life in the midst of the most famous "bohemia" in the world, where *épater le bourgeois* [to shock the bourgeoisie] was the favorite sport, she stoutly defended that class which, as she said, had "rejected" her: "I simply contend that the middle-class ideal which demands that people be affectionate, responsible, honest and content, that they avoid excitements and cultivate serenity is the ideal that appeals to me, it is in short the ideal of affectionate family life, of honorable business methods." One of Stein's earliest and most famous books *The Making of Americans* (1925) recounts—"relives" might be a more accurate word here—the lives of three generations of the class from which she had sprung as represented by her own family.

Daniel Stein, Gertrude's father, something of a wanderer and not as solidly successful as most of the clan, took the family to Vienna, Baltimore, and Oakland, California, where Gertrude spent her childhood in a country rather than a city way. Orphaned early, she grew up into a lonely and bookish but practical girl, massively unwieldy (weighing over two hundred pounds when she went to college), with a hard, piercing glance, a strong, original mind, and, strangely enough, a streak of dependence on men, or rather on some individual man, at that time her intellectual brother Leo. She attended college at the Harvard Annex (now Radcliffe College) and became a favorite pupil of William James, who, she proclaimed worshipfully, stood "firmly, nobly for the dignity of man." On the day of his final examination in her senior year, she read the questions over, and then wrote: "Dear Professor James, I am so sorry but really I do not feel like an examination paper in philosophy today." James's answer ran: "Dear Miss Stein, I understand perfectly how you feel. I often feel like that myself." She got the highest possible mark.

With the idea of becoming a psychologist, Gertrude entered medical school at Johns Hopkins, in 1897. Here, in spite of her ability, her reputation for originality in research, and the admiration of the great Dr. Osler, other interests began to intrude upon her medical studies, and one professor who set a final examination at the end of her senior year proved less understanding than had William James. He flunked her, and she refused the formality of a retake that would give the M.D. The course was obstetrics.

Now free to pursue her destiny, she went to Europe to join Leo, the learned and wildly neurotic brother who was pursuing his own destiny in the study of art and aesthetics and nursing the obsession that he would, miraculously, turn into a painter. In 1902 the pair lived in London, and Gertrude spent her time in the British Museum reading room, deep in the English classics, jotting down in a notebook phrases that pleased her. The next year, with Leo still in the grip of his obsession, they settled in Paris at the address they would make famous, 27 rue de Fleurus.

The time of the arrival in Paris was right. The great names of modern painting were not yet great, and Leo had the eye, the passion for discovery, and the money (though not a great deal was needed then), to gather the paintings that were to give him the name, among some art historians at least, of being one of the really significant collectors of the early twentieth century. Beginning with a small Cézanne, he soon acquired work by Renoir, Gauguin, Picasso, and many others, not to mention more canvases by Cézanne. In this period, Leo dominated Gertrude in the choice of paintings, as in other things, regarding her as a somewhat dull ward whose education was, willy-nilly, entrusted to him. But very early she did become the friend of Picasso—*her* discovery—and it was her portrait that Picasso painted.

She had Picasso and she began to have her writing, which was a way to find her own identity. Indeed, it may even be supposed that her inordinate egotism was a necessary ground for achieving her freedom, as Leo, who all his life disparaged her writing and patronized its author, seems to have half-intuited: "Gertrude's sort of massive self-admiration, and, in part self-assurance, enabled her to build something rather effective on her foundation"—a foundation for work for which he had, as he said after her death, no "respect."

In any case, Gertrude began to write, and in writing made two discoveries. The first was that when Leo was "explaining" she did not now have to listen—and "This had never happened to me before up to that time." The second was that "slowly I was knowing that I was a genius." She had already written a novel, unpublished, that was much influenced by Henry James, but now she was working from Cézanne, with his emancipated clarity of vision, and Flaubert, with his doctrine of style, whose *Trois Contes* she had been translating (a task set by Leo) in the early time in Paris. Specifically, it was one of the *contes*, "A Simple Heart," the story of a simple-minded servant woman totally absorbed in the lives of others, that provided the immediate suggestion for Gertrude Stein's *Three Lives* (1909).

The influence of Flaubert is clear, but Stein's originality is equally clear. First, the Americanism of the *Lives* comes sharply through, with the type of German-American servant woman in "The Good Anna" and "The Gentle Lena," but most of all with the heroine of "Melanctha," a black woman in Baltimore. Second, the fictional method is far different from that of Flaubert. He is basically detached and analytical in his treatment of Felicité, who is the "simple heart," while Stein seeks to develop a method that is, one might say, almost a nonmethod—a method that seeks to be absorbed as totally as possible into the subject, to irradiate the feeling of the subject, and verbally to "utter" the subject, to sink into the language and rhythm of the character and the character's world. Even in the rare moments when certain words that are not "simple" appear, as with the phrase "vague distrusts and complicated disillusions," in the following passage, they are absorbed into the characteristic tone, punctuated by repetition, exhibiting verbal dislocations, and uncoiling in the slow, self-fulfilling rhythm.

From Three Lives (1909)

Melanctha Herbert was always losing what she had in wanting all the things she saw. Melanctha was always being left when she was not leaving others.

Melanctha Herbert always loved too hard and much too often. She was always full with mystery and subtle movements and denials and vague distrusts and complicated disillusions. Then Melanctha would be sudden and impulsive and unbounded in some faith, and then she would suffer and be strong in her repression.

Melanctha Herbert was always seeking rest and quiet, and always she could only find new ways to be in trouble.

Melanctha wondered often how it was she did not kill herself when she was so blue. Often she thought this would be really the best way for her to do.

Melanctha Herbert had been raised to be religious, by her mother. Melanctha had not liked her mother very well. This mother, 'Mis' Herbert, as her neighbors called her, had been a sweet appearing and dignified and pleasant pale yellow, colored woman. 'Mis' Herbert had always been a little wandering and mysterious and uncertain in her ways.

Melanctha was pale yellow and mysterious and a little pleasant like her mother, but the real power in Melanctha's nature came through her robust and unpleasant and very unendurable black father.

Melanctha's father only used to come to where Melanctha and her mother lived, once in a while.

It was many years now that Melanctha had not heard or seen or known of anything her father did.

Melanctha Herbert almost always hated her

black father, but she loved very well the power in herself that came through him. And so her feeling was really closer to her black coarse father, than her feeling had ever been toward her pale yellow, sweet-appearing mother. The things she had in her of her mother never made her feel respect.

Melanctha Herbert had not loved herself in childhood. All of her youth was bitter to remember.

Melanctha had not loved her father and her mother and they had found it very troublesome to have her.

Melanctha's mother and her father had been regularly married. Melanctha's father was a big black virile negro. He only came once in a while to where Melanctha and her mother lived, but always that pleasant, sweet-appearing, pale yellow woman, mysterious and uncertain and wandering in her ways, was close in sympathy and thinking to her big black virile husband.

James Herbert was a common, decent enough, colored workman, brutal and rough to his one daughter, but then she was a most disturbing child to manage.

The young Melanctha did not love her father and her mother, and she had a break neck courage, and a tongue that could be very nasty. Then, too, Melanctha went to school and was very quick in all the learning, and she knew very well how to use this knowledge to annoy her parents who knew nothing.

Melanctha Herbert had always had a break neck courage. Melanctha always loved to be with horses; she loved to do wild things, to ride the horses and to break and tame them.

Melanctha, when she was a little girl, had had a good chance to live with horses. Near where Melanctha and her mother lived was the stable of the Bishops, a rich family who always had fine horses.

John, the Bishops' coachman, liked Melanctha very well and he always let her do anything she wanted with the horses. John was a decent, vigorous mulatto with a prosperous house and wife and children. Melanctha Herbert was older than any of his children. She was now a well grown girl of twelve and just beginning as a woman.

James Herbert, Melanctha's father, knew this John, the Bishops' coachman very well.

One day James Herbert came to where his wife and daughter lived, and he was furious.

"Where's that Melanctha girl of yours," he said fiercely, "if she is to the Bishops' stables again, with that man John, I swear I kill her. Why don't

you see to that girl better you, you're her mother."

James Herbert was a powerful, loose built, hard handed, black, angry negro. Herbert never was a joyous negro. Even when he drank with other men, and he did that very often, he was never really joyous. In the days when he had been most young and free and open, he had never had the wide abandoned laughter that gives the broad glow to negro sunshine.

His daughter, Melanctha Herbert, later always made a hard forced laughter. She was only strong and sweet and in her nature when she was really deep in trouble, when she was fighting so with all she really had, that she did not use her laughter. This was always true of poor Melanctha who was so certain that she hated trouble. Melanctha Herbert was always seeking peace and quiet, and she could always only find new ways to get excited.

James Herbert was often a very angry negro. He was fierce and serious, and he was very certain that he often had good reason to be angry with Melanctha, who knew so well how to be nasty, and to use her learning with a father who knew nothing.

———

What Stein is seeking here is an effect of immediacy—the isolation of a clear, simple, self-contained effect. The immediacy is even more striking when, with the apparent simplicity of method—or nonmethod—the rendering is of a complicated emotional state, as here of the lover of Melanctha:

Jeff Campbell never knew very well these days what it was that was going on inside him. All he knew was, he was uneasy now always to be with Melanctha. All he knew was, that he was always uneasy when he was with Melanctha, not the way he used to be from just not being very understanding, but now because he never could be honest with her, because he was now knowing always her strong suffering, in her, because he knew now he was having a straight, good feeling with her, but she went so fast, and he was so slow to her; Jeff knew his right feeling never got a chance to show itself as strong, to her.

When Stein sent her first book to William James, he wrote (though he hated to read novels and hadn't read it all) that it was "a fine new kind of realism." His remark sets the book in a reasonable context. The realism of Howells was already a settled matter; more recently there had been Hamlin Garland, Stephen Crane, and, with *Sister Carrie*, Theodore Dreiser, and now there was Stein. *Three Lives*, like much of the post-Howells realism, did treat the lower classes, and "Melanctha" was to come to be regarded as a sort of breakthrough in the treatment of black life. James Weldon Johnson affirmed that here was the first "white writer to write a story of love between a Negro man and woman and deal with them as normal members of the human family"; and years later, Richard Wright, disturbed when left-wing critics regarded Stein as antirevolutionary, read "Melanctha" aloud to a "group of semi-literate Negro stockyard workers," who, he reports, "slapped their thighs, howled, laughed, stomped, and interrupted . . . to comment upon the characters."

Stein was not, however, a revolutionary, not in the sense Wright meant, and not, finally, a realist or naturalist—not in any ordinary sense of the words. For one thing, subject matter as such was never of much concern to her, even this early, and was to become programmatically of much less: "form," as she understood the term, was to become all. For a second thing, there is a crucial difference between her book and the work of naturalistic writers in the treatment of process and time. Some realists and all naturalists see man set in the natural process— see his life as conditioned by the past and enacted in a present in constant flux, with a thrust toward a future which will be the fulfillment of the past. With Stein, on the contrary, there is a peculiar lack of movement, of flow, of a sense of continuity. There is a peculiar plotlessness, with character conceived as basically passive, not as embodying will, as a *given* and not as a development, the exfoliation of being rather than a process of becoming, and the characteristic movement, insofar as movement exists beyond the minimal action, is circular, a returning upon the self, a sense of repetitive refrain. The

reiteration of what *is* is the key to this fiction. For instance, we find very early, in the quotation above, the key to the *is*-ness of Melanctha, and the body of the story is an elaboration of that. We start, in a sense, at the end. The same action of Melanctha—approach and withdrawal —is repeated over and over: it *is* Melanctha. Or rather, she cannot "be"—cannot fulfill an action and find a self; and unable to connect with life (or love) she dies in a sanatorium for consumptives—simply withers, fades, disintegrating in a slow un-being. And with this we come to another aspect of the immediacy to which we have referred.

What is at stake here becomes clearer as we see how more and more radically Stein develops her original impulse: even now the germinal importance of William James is emerging in her fiction. The germ is James's theory of consciousness. We can really know, according to his notion, only the unique instant of consciousness, there being no higher self, no "transcendent" self, to which consciousness can be referred; each instant is discrete and is succeeded by another equally discrete. James maintained that the "only states of consciousness that we naturally deal with are found in personal consciousnesses, minds, selves, concrete particular I's and you's." All else, including will and choice, is dependent on inference—and, in fact, on the metaphor of a stream of consciousness to describe a unity of being.

Stein, we must observe, focused her attention on the instant of consciousness of James's theory, *not* on the stream, and sought to make the realization of the instant the mark of reality; with the result that the basic time for a story would be, as she called it, a "continuous present." Furthermore, she worked from James's account of identity: "Resemblance among the parts of a continuum of feeling (especially bodily feelings) experienced along with things widely different in other regards thus constitutes the real and verifiable 'personal identity' which we feel." So if we put together the notion of the moment of consciousness and that of resemblance as the basis of identity, we have the elements of Stein's continuous present as manifested in repetition, reiteration, circular movement, and exfoliation of the *given*.

A much fuller rendering of this stage of Stein's development appears in *The Making of Americans*, her longest (one thousand pages) and most ambitious book, which, after a struggle of years, was completed in 1908 but did not find publication until 1925, when Robert McAlmon, an American living in Paris, brought it out in his Contact Press (which presented early work of many writers who were to become famous, including Hemingway, Pound, H. D., and William Carlos Williams). *The Making of Americans*, the history of Stein's own family, was, in one sense, an example of that popular form of fiction, the family chronicle, of which *The Forsyte Saga*, by John Galsworthy, is a famous example, but the resemblance between Stein and a writer like Galsworthy simply accentuates the differences. The differences are a logical extension of the method of *Three Lives*, particularly of "Melanctha," now more

elaborately developed. *The Making of Americans* is a history, but one in which time is denied in the way of the telling, and in which the texture of life is denied in the ambition to tell the "essential truth," and the recognizable details of the individual are scraped off like moss from a stone in order that a conception—a schema—of the essence of character may be visible.

Stein, in fact, repudiates all elements that create the fictional illusion—or keeps only such as may be necessary to establish points of reference for her special kind of fiction, to give it some mooring, however tenuous, in the world of actuality. Her method, with all its returns and repetitions, is like hypnosis; if the reader submits himself, he will lose the outline of the actuality he has known and move into a new landscape and a new range of ghostly feeling that takes the place of daily needs and passions.

The essence of character was what Stein sought to give. Here is the young girl Julia growing up:

From The Making of Americans (1925)

. . . One day he was out walking and his daughter was with him. "Julia hadn't you better be a little careful how much you encourage that young Hersland."

Mr. Dehning, always, in his working, began very far away from a thing he meant later to be firmly attacking. And always in such a far away beginning, he would be looking sharply, out from him, in a sidelong, piercing, deprecating, challenging, fashion, the kind of a way he had always of looking when his wife, who, by her more than equal living, as it often is with a woman, had not in any kind of a way any fear in her of him, could be going to rebuke him. And this way he had of looking, always made him an old man to his children, and mostly there was a fear then in them, only now Julia was strong, other things were bright and glowing, and she could not now feel it in him, the old grown man's sharp outward looking that, closing him, went always so straight into them.

And so, now, filled full with her new warm imagining, Julia Dehning had not any kind of a fear from him, the kind of a fear a young grown

woman has almost always from an old man's looking.

"Why papa!" she had eagerly quickly demanded of him.

"I say Julia I don't know anything against him. Yes, I say to you Julia I don't know of anything there is against him. I have looked up all the record there is yet of him and I haven't heard anything against him but Julia, I say, somehow I don't quite like him. His family are alright, I know a man who knows all Gossols, and I asked him, he says yes the family are all successful and well appearing, I say Julia I don't say anything against him only I don't altogether trust him. I know all about his father, everybody has heard of David Hersland, he is the richest man they ever had in Gossols, I know too how he made his own money out there, and everybody says he is alright and he made his own money by his own work; I don't say anything against him, only Julia I think you better be a little careful with him, somehow I don't altogether like him." "Isn't that papa because he plays the piano and parts his hair that way in the middle." Julia was eager in her questioning. The father laughed, "I guess there is some reason in your question Julia, I don't like that kind of thing much in a man, that's right. It's foolish in a man who wants to make a success making a living, it's foolish to do things that make other men feel they don't want to trust him. It's alright if he was just doing nothing, only I never would want you to tie up with a man who didn't know how to take care of himself to make a living, but Hersland has got ambition, he wants to be a lawyer who makes a big success with his living, I know him, and that don't seem to me the kind of a way to make a good beginning, but may be I am wrong, you young ones always think you know everything. Anyhow Julia I think you better be a little careful with him." Mr. Dehning paused, and they walked on a little while and she said nothing.

"You know Julia" Mr. Dehning went on after a silent interval of walking when they had each been pretty busy with their own thinking, "you know Julia, your mother doesn't like him." "Oh! mamma!" Julia broke out, "you know how mamma is, he talks about love and beauty and mamma thinks it ought to be all wedding dresses and a fine house when it isn't money and business. She would be the same about anybody that I would want."

"Yes Julia, those are your literary notions but a lawyer has got to be a business man now and you like success and money as well as any one. You have always had everything you wanted and you don't want to get along without it. Literary effects and modern improvements are alright for women but with Hersland it ought to be different, it ought to be that he has the kind of sense he needs in his business. I don't say he hasn't got good sense in him to make a success in him and you want to be careful I say Julia, how far you go with him." "I know papa just what you mean, and that's alright papa, I know it, but you know yourself papa it isn't everything, now, is it. I know papa how you feel about it, you think we young ones are all wrong the way we look at it, but you say yourself papa how different things are nowadays from the way they used to be when you began with it, and surely papa it can't hurt a man to be interesting even if he wants to make a success in his business."

Mr. Dehning shook his head but he did not so carry much conviction to his daughter and on this day they said no more about the matter.

And so Julia began and surely she would win in the struggle. She worked every day and very hard, and slowly she began to bring her father to it. Mrs. Dehning would have to agree if he said she could have it and no one else's opinion in the matter was important.

Time and again Julia would be sure she had succeeded, for her father always listened to her "yes papa I know it, I know what you mean and it's alright, only you know yourself everything nowadays is very different, you know that yourself papa, you know you always say it," and he liked to hear her say it, and he listened with amusement, and he approved when she knew how to do it, when she brought out with great fervor and with much repeating, great arguments against all his objections. He always openly admired the bright way she had then to make clear to him all her theories and convictions, the new faith in her, the new ideas she had of life and business.

And then Julia would be sure she had convinced him, for how could a reasonable man ever resist it, she knew she had good reasons in her.

And each day when their talk was ending and she was saying to him, "you know papa you say yourself now that it's all different, I know what you mean papa, always, I know how you want me to do it, but papa, really, I am not talking without thinking hard about it, you know I listen to you and want to understand it but you know papa, now don't you, that it will be alright and that I am alright just the way you like to have me do it," and then he would have stopped listening to her and his mind would have sort of shut up away from her, and she still held his arm for they had been walking all this time up and down as was their custom every afternoon together, and yet he then himself had quite slipped away from her, and now he would be looking at her with that sharp completed look that, always so full of his own understanding, could not leave it open any way to her to reach inside to him to let in any other kind of a meaning.

And then he would for that time altogether leave her and the last thing he always would say to her, with the quick movement he had when he felt no more time in him then for her. "Alright, yes, well to-morrow is another day Julia I say to-morrow is another day Julia and you think it all over and we will talk about it further, perhaps to-morrow, I say to-morrow is another day Julia. There is your mother there now Julia, you better go in now to her."

It was hard for Julia to have such a kind of resistance fighting against her. It was hard for an impatient and eager temper to endure the kind of a way her father always finished off his long talks with her. It was hard for Julia to have to always begin over every time she started to talk about it with her father. But he was very proud of her, she knew very well his feeling for her, she knew very well too how to win him to agree in the end with her. She loved it in a way the struggle he made each day a new one for her. They loved and admired and respected each other very much this daughter and her father. They understood very well both of them how to please while they were combating with each other. And so each to-morrow they met, and Julia was sturdy and had strong faith in her, and always, her father, a long time each day listened to her.

So Julia struggled every day, to have him, arguing discoursing explaining and appealing. She was always winning but it was slow progress like that in very steep and slippery climbing. For every forward movement of three feet she always slipped back two, sometimes all three and often four and five and six and seven. It was long eager steady fighting but the father was slowly understanding that his daughter wanted this thing enough to stand hard by it and with such a feeling and no real fact against the man, such a father was bound to let her some time get married to him.

"I tell you what Julia what I been thinking. When we all get back to town you can tell better whether you do really want him. I say we better leave off all this talking and just wait till we get home now again. I don't say no Julia and I don't say yes to you. When everybody gets back to town and you are busy and running around with your girls and talking and meeting all the other people and the other kinds of young men, you can tell much better then whether all this business is not all just talking with you. I say now Julia we will wait and just see how you feel about it later. I say we will talk it all over when we get home and you are altogether with all your friends there. I say Julia I don't say no to you and I don't say yes yet to you. I say when we get home we will talk it over again all together and then if nothing turns up new against him, and you still want him, I say if then you still want him enough to trust to him and to trust to your own judgment about him, we will see what we can do about him." "Alright papa," Julia said to him, "alright I won't even see Alfy any more till we get back to town then, and papa I won't say another word to you about it. I'll

just go and ride around the country and think hard the way you like to have me do it about what we both have said about it."

And always every day it came and always every day when it was ending it would be the same. "Yes I certainly do care for him and I do know him, And he and I will live our lives together always learning things and doing things, good things they will be for us whatever other people may think or say."

And so at last, filled full with faith and hope and fine new joy she went back to her busy city life, strong in the passion of her eager young imagining.

It was good solid riches in the Dehning house, a parlor full of ornate marbles placed on yellow onyx stands, chairs gold and white of various size and shape, a delicate blue silk brocaded covering on the walls and a ceiling painted pink with angels and cupids all about, a dining room all dark and gold, a living room all rich and gold and red with built-in-couches, glass-covered book-cases and paintings of well washed peasants of the german school, and large and dressed up bedrooms all light and blue and white. (All this was twenty years ago in the dark age, you know, before the passion for the simple line and the toned burlap on the wall and wooden panelling all classic and severe.) Marbles and bronzes and crystal chandeliers and gas logs finished out each room. And always everywhere there were complicated ways to wash, and dressing tables filled full of brushes, sponges, instruments, and ways to make one clean, and to help out all the special doctors in their work.

It was good riches in this house and here it was that Julia Dehning dreamed of other worlds and here each day she grew more firm in her resolve for that free wide and cultured life to which for her young Hersland had the key.

At last it was agreed that these two young people should become engaged, but not be married for a year to come, and if nothing new had then turned up, the father said he would then no longer interfere. And so the marriage now was made for with these kind of people an engagement always meant a marriage excepting only for the gravest cause. And Alfred Hersland and Julia had this time to learn each other's natures and prepare themselves for the event.

When the twelve months had passed away no grave cause had come to make a reason why this marriage should not be. Julia was twelve months older now, and wiser, and through this wisdom had in general a little more distrusting in her, but never in any kind of a way was she changing about the new world she needed now to content her and she was firm always in her intention to marry Alfred Hersland. She loved him then with all the strength of her eager young imagining, though dimly, somewhere, in her head and heart now there was sometimes a vague dread that comes of ignorance and a beginning wisdom, a distrust she could not then yet seize and look on so that she could really know it, but a distrust that often was there, somewhere in the background, somehow sometimes mixed there to her sense, in with her energy, her new faith, and her feeling.

For a girl like Julia Dehning, all men, excepting those of an outside unknown world, these one read about in books and never really could believe in, for it is a strange feeling one has in one's later living, when one finds the story-books really have truth in them, for one loved the story-books earlier, one loved to read them but one never really believed there was truth in them, and later when one by living has gained a new illusion and a kind of wisdom, and one reads again in them, there it is, the things we have learned since to believe in, there it is and we know then that the man or the woman who wrote them had just the same kind of wisdom in them we have been spending our lives winning, and this shows to any one wise in learning that no young people can learn wisdom from the talking of the older ones around them. If they cannot believe the things they read in the story-books where it is all made life-like, real and interesting for them, how should they ever learn things from older people's talking. It's foolish to expect such things of them. No let them read the story-books we write for them, they don't learn much, to be sure, but more than they can from their fathers', mothers', aunts' and uncles' talking. Yes from their fathers' and their mothers' living they can get some wisdom, yes supply them with a tradition by your lives, you grown men and women, and for the rest let them come to us for their teaching.

But now to come back to Julia Dehning. As I was saying, to a girl like Julia Dehning, all men, excepting those of an outside unknown world, those one reads about in books and never really can believe in, or men like Jameson to whom one never could belong and whom one always knows, now after having once begun with one's living, for what they are whenever one met with them, I say for a girl like Julia Dehning, with the family with

which she had all her life been living, to her all men that could be counted as men by her and could be thought of as belonging ever to her, they must be, all, good strong gentle creatures, honest and honorable and honoring. For her to doubt this of all men, of decent men, of men whom she could ever know well or belong to, to doubt this would be for her to recreate the world and make one all from her own head. Surely, of course, she knew it, there were the men one could read of in the books and hear of in the scandal of the daily news, but never could such things be true of men of her own world. For her to think it in herself as real any such a thing would be for her to imagine a vain thing, to recreate the world and make a new one all out of her own head.

No, this was a thought that could not come to her to really think, and so for her the warnings of her father carried no real truth. Of course Alfred Hersland was a good and honest man. All decent men, all men who belonged to her own kind and to whom she could by any chance belong, were good and straight. They had this as they had all simple rights in a sane and simple world. Hersland had besides that he was brilliant, that he knew that there were things of beauty in the world, and that he was in his bearing and appearance a distinguished man. And then over and above all this, he was so freely passionate in his fervent love.

And so the marriage was really to be made. Mrs. Dehning now all reconciled and eager, began the trousseau and the preparation of the house that the young couple were to have as a wedding portion from the elder Dehnings.

In dresses, hats and shoes and gloves and underwear, and jewel ornaments, Julia was very ready to follow her mother in her choice and to agree with her in all variety and richness of trimming in material, but in the furnishing of her own house it must be as she wished, taught as she now had been that there were things of beauty in the world and that decoration should be strange and like old fashions, not be in the new. To have the older things themselves had not yet come to her to know, not just how old was the best time that they should be. It was queer in its results this mingling of old taste and new desire.

The mother was all disgusted, half-impressed; she sneered at these new notions to her daughter and bragged of it to all of her acquaintance. She followed Julia about now from store to store, struggling to put in a little her own way, but always she was beaten back and overborne by the eagerness of knowing and the hardness of unconsidering disregard with which her daughter met her words.

Julia Dehning's new house was in arrangement a small edition of her mother's. In ways to wash, to help out all the special doctors in their work, in sponges, brushes, running water everywhere, in hygienic ways to air things and keep one's self and everything all clean, this house that Julia was to make fit for her new life which was to come, in this it was very like the old one she had lived in, but always here there were more plunges, douches, showers, ways to get cold water, luxury in freezing, in hardening, than her mother's house had ever afforded to them. In her mother's house there were many ways to get clean but they mostly suggested warm water and a certain comfort, here in the new house was a sterner feeling, it must be a cold world, that one could keep one's soul high and clean in.

All through this new house there were no solid warm substantial riches. There were no silks in curtains, no blue brocade here, no glass chandeliers to make prisms and give tinklings. Here the parlor was covered with modern sombre tapestry, the ceiling all in tone the chairs as near to good colonial as modern imitation can effect, and all about dark aesthetic ornaments from China and Japan. Paintings there were none, only carbon photographs framed close, in dull and wooden frames.

The dining room was without brilliancy, for there can be no brilliance in a real aesthetic aspiration. The chairs were made after some old french fashion, not very certain what, and covered with dull tapestry, copied without life from old designs, the room was all a discreet green with simple oaken wood-work underneath. The living rooms were a prevailing red, that certain shade of red like that certain shade of green, dull, without hope, the shade that so completely bodies forth the ethically aesthetic aspiration of the spare American emotion. Everywhere were carbon photographs upon the walls sadly framed in painted wooden frames. Free couches, open book-cases, and fire places with really burning logs, finished out each room.

These were triumphant days for Julia. Every day she led her family a new flight and they followed after agape with wonder disapproval and with pride. The mother almost lost all sense of her creation of this original and brilliant daughter, she was almost ready to admit the obedience and defeat she now had in her. Sometimes she still had a little resistance to her but mostly she was swelling inside and to all around her with her admiration and her pride in this new wonderful kind of a daughter.

The father had always been convinced and proud even when he had disapproved the opinions of his daughter. He now took a solid satisfaction in the completeness of accomplishment she now had in her. To her father, to know well what one wanted, and to win it, by patient steady fighting for it, was the best act a man or woman could accomplish, and well had his daughter done it. She had won it, she knew very well what she wanted and she had it. He still shook his head at her new fangled notions, her literary effects, the artistic kind of new improvement, as he called it, that she put into her new house to make it perfect. He did not understand it and he always said it, but he was very proud to see her do it, and he bragged to everybody and made them listen to it, of his daughter and the wonderful new kind of a house she had, and the bright way she knew how to do it.

After *The Making of Americans*, however, such a narrative with its moorings in actuality was to disappear from Stein's writing. Other influences than those of Flaubert and James had been at work, and her long immersion in painting and her intimate friendship with Picasso, which had begun long before his fame, were having the profound effect that would lead her, long afterward, to declare that both of them—she in writing and he in painting—had been doing the same thing.

What Picasso (along with Braque and some who were generally called cubists and others who were to be known as futurists) was doing was to replace representational painting by nonrepresentational. The change was not sudden, but gradual, with its own internal logic. For example, at one stage the elements of the human face—eyes, ears, nose, mouth—might appear in distorted relationships but still belonging to the overall structure of the face; at a later stage, still recognizable as individual elements of a face, they might appear detached, not as parts of a face but belonging to another structure, that of the picture; later the teasing resemblance of individual items to actuality—that of a detached eye, for instance—would disappear, with only a shape or line now forming part of the whole structure that was the picture, the individual items and the picture withdrawn totally from actuality—abstract.

The reaction against the traditional art of the actual was not, of course, confined to painting. There was in Europe a strong reaction against realism in the theater, a reaction later felt in America, most strongly in the work of Eugene O'Neill, with his experiments in modes of abstractness, such as masks, asides, and symbolically shifting stage sets. There was, too, the doctrine of "pure" poetry. Such poetry was being rendered necessary, it was argued, by the rise of science and technology, which could do better certain things that poetry had traditionally done. Who would now turn to poetry for history or philosophy or instruction in agriculture? Such kinds of "truth," once sought in poetry, would no longer be expected there, and no writer would be insane enough to try to put them there. And who would turn to poetry for "story" when the movies were so much more immediate and compelling—or reportage, with its guarantee of fact? The French poet Paul Valéry—of Stein's generation—puts the argument succinctly:

Sometimes I think that there will be place in the future for a literature the nature of which will singularly resemble that of a sport.

Let us subtract from literary possibilities everything which today, by the direct expression of things and the direct stimulation of the sensibility by new means—motion pictures, omnipresent music, etc.—is being rendered useless or ineffective for the art of language.

Let us also subtract a whole category of subjects—psychological, sociological, etc.—which the growing precision of the sciences will render it difficult to treat freely. There will remain to letters a private domain: that of symbolic expression and of imaginative values due to the free combination of the elements of language.

The "free combination of the elements of language"—that was what Stein was moving toward after *The Making of Americans*, the patterning of words wrenched from meaning to become units in a syntax of no-sense. And so, after a series of compositions that she called "portraits"—compositions to suggest nondescriptively but in words the essence of a personality— came the even more radical volume *Tender Buttons*, published in 1914.

From Tender Buttons (1914)

A CARAFE THAT IS A BLIND GLASS

A kind in glass and a cousin, a spectacle and nothing strange single hurt color and an arrangement in a system to pointing. All this and not ordinary, not unordered in not resembling. The difference is spreading.

DIRT AND NOT COPPER

Dirt and not copper makes a color darker. It makes the shape so heavy and makes no melody harder.

It makes a mercy and relaxation and even a strength to spread a table fuller. There are more places not empty. They see cover.

A FRIGHTFUL RELEASE

A bag which was left and not only taken but turned away was not found. The place was shown to be very like the last time. A piece was not exchanged, not a bit of it, a piece was left over. The rest was missing.

A TABLE

A table means does it not my dear it means a whole steadiness. Is it likely that a change.

A table means more than a glass even a looking glass is tall. A table means necessary places and a revision a revision of a little thing it means it does mean that there has been a stand, a stand where it did shake.

Here, however, in spite of all the abstracting of the elements of language from their ordinary function and all the wrenching and isolating of words, the "purity" of the final stage of cubism —and of abstract art in general—is not achieved, the stage in which the "eye" or "nose" is no longer eye or nose but merely a line or shape in a pattern created without reference to actuality. With Stein the word is still a word, with its burden of denotation and connotation, and the contrast, the tension, between this aura of "sense" and the "no-sense" of the relations into which they are cast is, finally, what gives these compositions their teasing interest, the portentous suggestion of discovery never quite realized. This point comes clear if we set Stein's poems against poems that do indeed go all the way toward abstraction—poems in which the "eye," to speak metaphorically, is merely a mark or shape.

J. Drootan-Sussting Benn
Mill-down Leduren N.
   Telamba-taras oderwainto weiring
Awersey zet bidreen
Ownd istellester sween
   Lithabian tweet ablissood owdswown stiering
Apleven aswetsen sestinal
Yintomen I adaits afurf I gallas Ball.

Here the word has really disappeared into sound, but sound without any burden of meaning, self-sufficient in its "meaning" and self-sustaining in its "identity." However much or little this poem may interest us, it suddenly becomes different, and for most readers, much more interesting, when we learn that this is a "dummy" of the fifteenth stanza of Milton's "Hymn on the Morning of Christ's Nativity":

Yea Truth, and Justice then
Will down return to men,
   Orb'd in a Rain-bow; and like glories wearing
Mercy will sit between,
Thron'd in Celestial sheen,
   With radiant feet the tissued clouds down
      stearing,
And Heav'n as at some Festivall,

Will open wide the Gates of her high Palace Hall.

Such a "poem" taken in itself is, then, a structure abstracted from among other structures (linguistic, syntactical, metaphorical, rhetorical, and so on) of Milton's poem; but once we become aware of its relation to Milton's poem, the abstracted one cannot be taken purely in itself, for we are inevitably aware, even if in a shadowy way, of the tensions of this abstracted structure against the others—and perhaps more acutely aware, too, of the tensions among the other structures that work to give Milton's composition its overall form.[1]

For years, except by a few friends, Gertrude Stein was regarded merely as an egotistical eccentric who consorted with bohemians and artists and who collected pictures. *Three Lives* did not appear until 1909, in New York, where it had not found a regular publisher but was printed at the author's expense. *Tender Buttons* (New York, 1914) did appear with a regular publisher, even if a fugitive house devoted to "exotic" tastes, and did make some impression on the literary world. Far off in Chicago, Sherwood Anderson read it, as excited, he said, "as one might grow excited in going into a new and wonderful country where everything is strange." The distortion of language gave him a new sense of language, and in the naiveté (or, rather, calculated naiveté, or pseudo-naiveté) that seemed to reduce the word to a bare minimum, there appeared an irreducible, primal value. It scarcely seems an accident that the writers most strongly affected by Stein's practice were Anderson and Hemingway, both of whom were trying to find a new ground for a new start outside of what they regarded, in their different ways and for their different reasons, as the outworn clutter of social and literary tradition. The new ground was to be a direct perception—the notion of perception as reality in the "continuous present"—and the new start was to be an escape from the "big

[1] See *Practical Criticism*, by I. A. Richards, pp. 225–34.

words" that Hemingway was later to call "obscene." Stein thought that Anderson wrote the most "beautiful sentences" in America, and Hemingway, in his early time in Paris, when he first came into her orbit, had set himself to learn to write "a simple, declarative sentence." The immediacy of the sentence was what all three strove for. What, in the end, each was to *make* of his *sentences* is another matter.

Stein's impact on Hemingway was fundamentally conditioned by the historical context—was dependent for its force, that is, on the nature of the European world into which the young man was suddenly plunged. It was a world of both great confusion and great promise. Over thirteen million men had died in the war; the world was shaken by revolutions; the economic system was a shambles; but two dreams flourished, that of a new social order and that of a new art. Sometimes the two dreams were related, but sometimes they were quite distinct, even antipathetic.

In the arts it was a period of cults, schools, and movements (some of them—it must be emphasized—with roots going back well before the war): cubism, futurism, expressionism, and, with its special *succès de scandale*, dadaism. Dada, founded in 1916, in Zurich, by the Rumanian Tristan Tzara, and later supported by such French talents as André Breton and Louis Aragon, proposed an art of lunacy and farce as the only mirror of, and protest against, a world ruled by lunatics, and advertised an individualism of final absurdity in an absurd world. Surrealism, following shortly after, with its grounding in the new psychology rather than in the new politics of protest, offered another art repudiating tradition and, like all the other movements we have mentioned, represented at least a distortion, if not a denial, of the world of actuality. Out of this ferment, with its numberless self-indulgences, vanities, posturings, idiocies, and tragedies, emerged, directly or indirectly, the modern spirit; and modern American literature, because of its earlier isolation and provincialism, has a special debt to Paris. Almost all of the younger writers of the 1920's who were to make distinguished, or even not quite so

distinguished, names had direct contact with the Left Bank in the period between the First World War and the Depression, and their recollections, in such books as *Exile's Return*, by Malcolm Cowley, and *Being Geniuses Together*, by Robert McAlmon and Kay Boyle, constitute an important chapter in our history. It is true that Faulkner took one look at Paris and decided it was not the place for him, but he had, indirectly, his own debt, through Joyce and, even, Stein.

It was in this context of confusion and promise that, in 1922, Hemingway came to Paris, seeking his identity as a man and a writer; and in Stein he found someone who personally and dramatically stood for the "new," who, to adopt the phrasing of Pound (who was also to become a mentor of Hemingway), said "make it new." Furthermore, and more specifically right for Hemingway, her work was an attempt to get at and celebrate the germinal moment in experience. Whatever of William James's psychological theories was hers became his—perhaps with no mention of the name of the old teacher —and somehow, with or without the nexus of Stein, Hemingway, in his own terms and allowing for all differences, became as pure an instance as we can imagine of the dramatist of pragmatism.

Whatever the precise range and depth of Stein's influence on Hemingway, he found something fundamental there. It was he who, presumably out of admiration and gratitude, was responsible for the publication of *The Making of Americans*. Later, too, he was to tell John Peale Bishop that Ezra Pound was "right half the time, and when he was wrong, he was so wrong you were never in any doubt about it," but that "Stein was always right." But even if she was always "right" and was the godmother of his first son to boot, Hemingway was not going to have her, or anybody else, for a literary godmother. The friendship was doomed from the start: the meeting of two such egos was bound to develop into the collision of the irresistible force with the immovable object. In the end, Hemingway declared that he had been the teacher, that he had taught Stein how to write "conversation." And she retorted that if he should ever write his real story, it would be about being "yellow,"[2] and later, in an interview, interpreted his obsessive "tough-boy" pose as springing from a fear of impotence.

When *The Making of Americans* appeared, it found some distinguished admirers. Marianne Moore said: "We have here a truly psychological exposition of American living—an account of that happiness and of that unhappiness which is, for those experiencing it, as fortuitous as it is to those who have an understanding of heredity and environment, natural and inevitable." And Katherine Anne Porter, whose final and famous judgment on Stein was harsh ("The Wooden Umbrella," in *Collected Essays*), could say, in 1927, that *The Making of Americans* was a "very necessary book" and that to shorten its great length "would be to mutilate its vitals."

By this time, too, the poet Edith Sitwell had taken Stein up and could call her work "important" and "beautiful," and had sponsored triumphal lectures at Oxford and Cambridge. But the climax of Stein's success did not come until 1933, when she published *The Autobiography of Alice B. Toklas*, a vastly amusing and often witty account of the life of art and literature in Paris and a vastly successful job of self-promotion, as in the following extract:[3]

Observation and construction make imagination, that is granting the possession of imagination, is what she has taught many young writers. Once when Hemingway wrote in one of his stories that Gertrude Stein always knew what was good in a Cézanne, she looked at him and said, Hemingway, remarks are not literature.

The young often when they have learnt all they can learn accuse her of an inordinate pride. She says yes of course. She realises that in english literature in her time she is the only one. She has always known it and now she says it.

She understands very well the basis of creation and therefore her advice and criticism is invaluable to all her friends. How often have I heard Picasso say to her when she has said something about a picture of his and then illustrated by something she was trying to do, racontez-moi cela. In other words tell me about it. These two even to-day have long solitary conversations. They sit in two little low chairs up in his apartment studio, knee to knee and Picasso says, expliquez-moi cela. And they explain to each other. They talk about everything, about pictures, about dogs, about death, about unhappiness. Because Picasso is a spaniard and life is tragic and bitter and unhappy. Gertrude Stein often comes down to me and says, Pablo has been persuading me that I am as unhappy as he is. He insists that I am and with as much cause. But are you, I ask. Well I don't think I look it, do I, and she laughs. He says, she says, that I don't look it because I have more courage, but I don't think I am, she says, no I don't think I am.

"But God what a liar she is!" exclaimed her brother Leo when he read the *Autobiography*. Leo may have had deep and complicated motives for holding such a view, but others who might be regarded as more objective were inclined to agree with him. Edith Sitwell and her brother Osbert, an eminent writer also, were inclined to hold that, in general, to believe any thing Stein said was a hazardous enterprise; and when it came to the particulars of the *Autobiography*, there was an epidemic of outrage in the world of art and letters. Eugene and Maria Jolas, who edited *transition*, the enormously important avant-garde magazine in Paris, and who had befriended Stein's work (*Four Saints in Three Acts* had appeared in *transition* in 1929), issued a special supplement called "Testimony Against Gertrude Stein," in which the testifiers included the impressive

---

[2] As various critics have pointed out, Hemingway's stories are characteristically about being "yellow"—about the conquest or exorcism of "yellowness."

[3] Since the work is supposed to be by Toklas, Stein, as will be observed, appears in the third person—a not too subtle device for muting the note of self-adulation.

names of Matisse, Braque, André Salmon, and Tristan Tzara. Eugene Jolas introduced the sheaf of testimonies, summing it up: "There is a uniformity of opinion that she had no understanding of what really was happening around her." Matisse corrected her on the history of cubist painting, giving Braque the honor of having done the first example of the school; he declared that Sarah Stein (the wife of Gertrude's oldest brother Michael and herself a painter), unmentioned by the *Autobiography*, was the "really intelligently sensitive member of the family," and described Gertrude as "without taste and without relation to reality." Tzara regarded the book as the symptom of a "clinical case of megalomania" and continued:

To tell the truth, all this would have no importance if it took place in the family circle between two maiden ladies greedy for fame and publicity. . . . They tell us the infinite pains they took to lure to their house, where their collection of canvases constituted an irresistible bait, people who might be useful to them in publishing an article in this or that review. I have no objection to their revealing the secrets of their literary kitchen, if they feel inclined to do so.

Braque echoed Jolas's opinion that she understood "nothing of what went on around her."

But nothing succeeds like success. The *Autobiography* was a best seller and the author was newspaper copy of a high order, and headlines and money conspired to salve wounded feelings. There was, too, the public success of *Four Saints in Three Acts* as an opera with music composed by Virgil Thompson, and shortly afterward, later in 1934, there was the lecture tour in America, with a series of intoxicating triumphs on the platform: she was a public figure, something of a combination of a top presidential candidate, a movie queen, and an overblown Grandma Moses.

Stein had long been institutionalized in Paris. For fifteen years the young expatriates, many seeking for genius to rub off on them, and American sightseers eager to gawk, reverenti-

ally or with secret snickers, had made their way to the rue de Fleurus. Among the young men had been F. Scott Fitzgerald, Ezra Pound, William Carlos Williams, Glenway Wescott, Paul Bowles, Hart Crane, the composers Virgil Thompson and George Anthiel, the painters George Biddle and Pavel Tchelitchew, the black singer Paul Robeson, and, late in the story, the black writer Richard Wright.

Once, back in the 1920's, even that most famous of all young literary men, T. S. Eliot, in his fresh glory as author of *The Waste Land*, had come to the rue de Fleurus and had asked the chatelaine for a contribution to his magazine the *Criterion*—and had got it, a "portrait" of himself. He was later to say of her work that "it is not improving, it is not amusing, it is not interesting, it is not good for one's mind." But he added that "its rhythms have a peculiar hypnotic power not met with before." That guarded praise was quickly discounted: "If this is the future, then the future is, as it very likely is, of the barbarians. But this is the future in which we ought not to be interested."[4]

Now, in that "future" that may, indeed, be "of the barbarians," we can look back with the perspective of half a century and see that Stein and Eliot, for all their differences, were closer together than either would have imagined. There was some truth in the intuition of uninstructed readers that both those new books *Tender Buttons* and *The Waste Land* were destroying old, sanctified ways of seeing and feeling and old ways of saying what you saw and felt. And, perhaps more importantly, Eliot, for all his concern with ideas, religious and social, was, along with the scandalous, motley crew of Pound, Joyce, Yeats, Hemingway, Fitzgerald, West, and, of course, Stein, an apostle of the cult of style. For them all, the "saying" of a work of art was its "being."

Gertrude Stein died July 27, 1946, in Paris, after an operation. Coming out from anesthesia,

[4] The young Pound, whose ego, temperament, and will to instruct had early clashed with Stein's, was less rhetorical than Eliot in expressing his disapproval; he simply called her an "old tub of guts."

she asked, "What is the answer?" To this, no-body had an answer, and so she uttered her last words: "In that case, what is the question?"

She was speaking in riddles to the end.

As for her work, though it has evoked guffaws and contempt, it has also evoked fanatical admiration. And it is hard to believe that at least *Three Lives* and *The Making of Americans* will not be "permanent"—unless the next "future" turns out to be one even more "of the barbarians" than this has turned out to be.

It is true, however, that Stein's great effort ended in failure. The medium of painting is not the medium of literature, and if her experiment proved anything it proved that her hypothesis was mistaken, that a nonrepresentational literature is not, in any final form, possible. But that is not the point. Some of the "failures" will continue to tease readers—and writers, too—to the very verge of the possibilities of language, and in so doing provide a shock, and a liberation. They will also suggest that, though literature cannot be "nonrepresentational," it cannot be "representational" either. For literature is, in one sense, a process by which "about-ness" is converted into "is-ness"—but an "is-ness" that miraculously becomes another kind of "about-ness."

BIOGRAPHICAL CHART

1874 Born, in Allegheny, Pennsylvania, February 3, daughter of Donald Stein and Amelia Keyser

1876–79 After Vienna and Paris, family settles in Oakland, California

1893–97 Enrolls at Harvard Annex (later Radcliffe College); studies with William James; travels in Europe with Leo Stein

1897–1902 Attends Johns Hopkins Medical School; flunks a final examination and joins Leo in Italy; spends winter in London

1903 Settles in Paris, 27 rue de Fleurus; translates Flaubert; new interest in painting; writes *Three Lives*

1905 Meets Picasso; portrait of Stein by Picasso begun

1906 Begins friendship with Alice B. Toklas

1906–8 Writes *The Making of Americans*

1909 *Three Lives*

1912 Begins *Tender Buttons*; breaks with Leo

1913 Visits England; meets Roger Fry

1914 *Tender Buttons*

1914–18 Spends war years in France

1918–37 Plays role of sibyl of modernism and hostess of the young

1924 Begins friendship with Edith Sitwell

1925 *The Making of Americans*

1926 Meets with Virgil Thompson, who was to turn *Four Saints in Three Acts* into an opera; lectures at Cambridge and Oxford

1933 *The Autobiography of Alice B. Toklas*

1934 *Four Saints* successfully produced as opera at Hartford, Connecticut, and in New York; makes triumphant lecture tour in America

1934–35 "Testimony Against Gertrude Stein," as supplement to *transition*, by Georges Braque, Matisse, André Salmon, Tristan Tzara, and Eugene and Maria Jolas: violent reaction to *The Autobiography*

1936 *The Geographical History of America*

1937 Leaves 27 rue de Fleurus

1939–45 Spends war years in France; plays role as welcomer of American troops; tours bases occupied in Germany

1946 Dies, July 27, in Paris

FURTHER READINGS

There is no standard edition of Stein's writings. The reader may consult the biographical chart for publication dates of major works.

Carl Van Vechten, ed., *Selected Writings* (1946)

John Malcolm Brinnin, *The Third Rose: Gertrude Stein and Her World* (1959)

Bravig Imbs, *Confessions of Another Young Man* (1936)

Rosalind S. Miller, *Gertrude Stein: Form and Intelligibility* (1949)

Marianne Moore, "The Spare American Emotion," *Dial* (February, 1926)

Katherine Anne Porter, "Gertrude Stein: Three Views," in *The Days Before* (1952)

B. L. Reid, *Art by Subtraction—A Dissenting Opinion of Gertrude Stein* (1958)

W. G. Rogers, *When This You See Remember Me* (1948)

B. F. Skinner, "Has Gertrude Stein a Secret?" *Atlantic Monthly* (1934)

Elizabeth Sprigge, *Gertrude Stein: Her Life and Work* (1957)

Leo Stein, *Journey into the Self* (1950), Edmund Fuller, ed.

Donald Sutherland, *Gertrude Stein: A Biography of Her Work* (1951)

Thornton Wilder, Introduction to *The Geographical History of America* (1936)

———, Introduction to *Four in America* (1947)

Edmund Wilson, "Gertrude Stein," in *Axel's Castle* (1931)

HENRY MILLER (1891–   )

In many ways Gertrude Stein's career is paralleled by Henry Miller's. They both became monuments of expatriate Paris. Both found recognition late, and the recognition of both, when it came, was as much that of a role—in both cases a prophetic role—as of achieved work. As for the recognition of the work, that was in both cases as much a success by scandal as by esteem. Both were regarded, in many quarters, as scandalous anarchists, but there was a difference in the kind of anarchy involved: Stein was regarded as an anarchist of language and logic, Miller of sexual morality and social stability.

If Stein may be said to be the first of the between-the-wars expatriates, then Miller may be regarded as the last. He did not even make his first trip to Paris until 1928, just before the cold blast of the Depression began to depopulate the Left Bank, and he did not settle there until the process was well under way. He did not, in fact, much resemble either the writers or the hangers-on of the 1920's, being of a different heritage and education, and his tastes ran rather to the grimness of the true slum than to the sometimes theatrical poverty of bohemia. The Paris he writes about has little relation to that of *The Sun Also Rises* and Hemingway's "lost generation."

Miller was older than most of the writers and would-be writers who flocked to Paris after the First World War. Born in 1891, he had already had a marriage, two children, and a good foothold in business (personnel manager of Western Union in New York) before he decided, as Sherwood Anderson had done, to walk out on everything and be a writer. He confirmed his decision by getting a divorce and taking up with a taxi-dancer, the Mona of his books. As for background, he was of German blood, his father a merchant tailor, prosperous enough in the beginning but steadily losing ground to ready-made clothes, just as the home neighborhood of solid German comfort in Brooklyn was losing ground to the hordes of new immigrants of various nationalities. Henry went to high school, and even to college for two months, but he was a born rebel, and his education was in the streets. Of the home street, in *Tropic of Capricorn*, he writes:

It was the most enchanting street I have ever seen in all my life. It was the ideal street—for a boy, a lover, a maniac, a drunkard, a crook, a lecher, a thief, an astronomer, a musician, a poet, a tailor, a shoemaker, a politician. In fact, this was just the sort of street it was, containing just such representatives of the human race, each one a world unto himself and all living together harmoniously and unharmoniously, *but together*, a solid corporation, a close knit human spore which could not disintegrate unless the street itself disintegrated.

Miller was always a "city man through and

through," as he was to say; and added: "I hate nature, just as I hate 'classics.'"

But if Miller hated "classics," there was, even with the turbulent life of the street, the life of the mind. He was a voracious but scarcely a discriminating reader, with H. Rider Haggard (a writer of adventure stories) and Nietzsche entering as equals into his consciousness. But Whitman, with his celebration of the body and the ego, became permanently important for him. So did Thoreau and Emerson, as rebels, antinomians, and defenders of the self against society—and strange masters they are for Miller, with his raucous comedy of the obscene. Aside from these three (later to be joined by Melville), American literature had very little meaning for Miller—nor had English literature, for, as his admirer Lawrence Durrell points out, he did not read such writers as Shakespeare, Milton, Donne, and Pope, and, though "cultivated," was certainly not "cultured." The writers that early caught him were Balzac, Dostoevski, Stirner, Giono, Mann, and Nietzsche.

But it was the complex and sometimes revolutionary tradition of the ghetto (to which he did not belong but into which he penetrated) of the new immigrants that gave Miller his literary orientation; and his youthful immersion in socialist and anarchist theory, as William A. Gordon has pointed out in *The Mind and Art of Henry Miller*, provided an objective frame to his instinctive distrust of the values of the world beyond the streets, the tailor shop, and the Brooklyn Public Library. So when, in 1913, in San Diego, he met Emma Goldman, who, as a good anarchist, saw the moral conscience as little more than a built-in device for social and economic enslavement, government as tyranny, and natural law as confirming overt sexuality and free love, Miller wrote in his autobiographical notes: "turning point in life." But along with his anarchism, instinctive and philosophical, went a contradictory strain derived from a long reading in Oriental mysticism, perhaps inspired by Emerson and Thoreau. There is another element in Miller and his work not derived from any reading—a demonic energy that manifested itself in his study of music and his athleticism, and, in his later work, in a wild Rabelaisian comedy.

Miller would write of his life as a young man:

Those were the days, drunk or sober, I always rose at 5 A.M. sharp to take a spin on my Bohemian racing wheel to Coney Island and back. Sometimes, skeetering over the thin ice of a dark winter morning, the fierce wind carrying me along like an iceboat, I would be shaking with laughter over the events of the night before . . . This Spartan regime, combined with the feasts and festivities, the one man study course, the pleasure reading, the arguments and discussions, the clowning and buffoonery, the fights and wrestling bouts, the hockey games, the six-day races at the Garden, the low dance halls, the piano playing and piano teaching, the disastrous love affairs, the perpetual lack of money, the contempt for work, the goings on in the tailor shop, the solitary promenades to the reservoir, to the cemetery . . . this unilateral, multilingual, sesquipedalian activity night and day, morning, noon, and night, in season and out, drunk or sober, or drunk and sober, always in the crowd, always milling around, always searching, struggling, prying, peeping . . . completely gregarious yet utterly solitary . . . well there it was, a sort of caricature of Elizabethan times, all gathered up and played out in the shabby purlieus of Brooklyn, Manhattan and the Bronx, the foulest city in the world . . .

Later, like a good anarchist summing up the world, with the youthful passion and energy discounted, Miller writes:

Civilization is drugs, alcohol, engines of war, prostitution, machines and machine slaves, low wages, bad food, bad taste, prisons, reformatories, lunatic asylums, divorce, perversion, brutal sports, suicides, infanticides, cinema, quackery, demagoguery, strikes, lockouts, revolutions, putsches, colonization, electric chairs, guillotines, sabotage, floods, famine, disease, gangsters, money barons, horse racing, fashion shows, poodle dogs, chow dogs, Siamese cats, condoms, pessaries, syphilis, gonorrhea, insanity, neuroses, etc. etc.

We have here, in the two quotations just given, what may be called the poles of Miller's work. Even when, in the most sordid or disgusting detail, Miller writes about society and the degradation of the lower depths,[1] that grimness is often not the memorable thing; in opposition to the grimness, what comes through is often the joy in manic energy and the élan of creation manifested in a comic vision.

The subject of Miller's work is Miller.[2] Or rather, it is Miller the hero-and-ham, philosopher and shameless bum, vis-à-vis the lunatic world. When, in 1924, he gave up his good executive job with Western Union, left his family, and took up with Mona, he set out, as a writer, on a double quest: to discover what sort of man he had been and what sort he might become. He had the past, or rather he had the raw material out of which he would construct the past, but in 1927, by his account, he had, too, the vision of a massive autobiography—or autonovel—even if the vision had to be incomplete, for much of the life to be dealt with had not yet been lived.

By then, however, he did know what he took to be the theme of his life: that through "being crucified one may be resurrected—or 'transformed,' if you like"—and that the work was to be entitled *The Rosy Crucifixion*, which now is the title of the trilogy, *Sexus*, *Plexus*, and *Nexus*. The "resurrection" is, of course, the repudiation of the world of ordered society in the search for meaning in personal life and the discovery of the self as the "roving cultural desperado"—and writer. He set out to make his personal story into a myth for his time.

The first of Miller's books, *Tropic of Cancer*, (1934, in Paris), though autobiography, is not part of *The Rosy Crucifixion*. It is an account of his life after going abroad to live, unplotted, random, projected from one association to another, emerging from the ruck of consciousness. It begins:

---

[1] In this respect Miller's work resembles that of Djuna Barnes, another expatriate resident of Paris during the period, though no two writers could have more different styles. Miller is all apparent artlessness, while Barnes's best-known novel, *Nightwood*, is a highly structured example of impressionism.

[2] The epigraph of *Tropic of Cancer* is from Emerson: "These novels will give way, by and by, to diaries or autobiographies—captivating books, if only a man knew how to choose among what he calls his experiences that which is really his experience, and how to record truth truly." The epigraph is apt: it describes what Miller was trying to do. It is also significantly Emersonian. As Emerson eschewed the rigor of logical form and converted philosophy into a series of intuitions epigrammatically expressed—a sequence of explosions celebrating a theme—so he distrusted the imaginative form. He wanted neither logical structure nor imaginative structure—only the bursts of truth. He is an early prophet of the death of the novel—which, to date, has not obligingly died.

From Tropic of Cancer (1934)

I am living at the Villa Borghese. There is not a crumb of dirt anywhere, nor a chair misplaced. We are all alone here and we are dead.

Last night Boris discovered that he was lousy. I had to shave his armpits and even then the itching did not stop. How can one get lousy in a beautiful place like this? But no matter. We might never have known each other so intimately, Boris and I, had it not been for the lice.

Boris has just given me a summary of his views. He is a weather prophet. The weather will continue bad, he says. There will be more calamities, more death, more despair. Not the slightest indication of a change anywhere. The cancer of time is eating us away. Our heroes have killed themselves, or are killing themselves. The hero, then, is not Time, but Timelessness. We must get in step, a lock step, toward the prison of death. There is no escape. The weather will not change.

It is now the fall of my second year in Paris. I was sent here for a reason I have not yet been able to fathom.

I have no money, no resources, no hopes. I am the happiest man alive. A year ago, six months ago, I thought that I was an artist. I no longer think about it, I *am*. Everything that was literature has fallen from me. There are no more books to be written, thank God.

This then? This is not a book. This is libel, slander, defamation of character. This is not a book, in the ordinary sense of the word. No, this is a prolonged insult, a gob of spit in the face of Art, a kick in the pants to God, Man, Destiny, Time, Love, Beauty . . . what you will. I am going to sing for you, a little off key perhaps, but I will sing. I will sing while you croak, I will dance over your dirty corpse. . . .

Miller is soon to announce: "There is only one thing that interests me vitally now, and that is the recording of all that is omitted in books."[3] He is, he avows elsewhere, against "literature," that is, against the "formed," the "organized," the "ritualized," the "framed." This book is not framed like a picture and so has no organization distinct from the flux of life. Life flows into the unframed picture, and the picture bleeds off into life. At least, that is the illusion created by Miller's method—and the words "illusion" and "method" are justified when we realize that, after all, the end is not merely a stopping, it is a focus of feeling, a summarizing moment of vision. Out of the randomness, a sense of structure, of meaning, has emerged.

Meanwhile, in the very beginning, characters appear or are remembered, then disappear, pop in for a moment, perhaps to reappear as randomly at a later date. As does Moldorf, the suffering Jew:

It is the caricature of a man which Moldorf first presents. Thyroid eyes. Michelin lips. Voice like pea soup. Under his vest he carries a little pear. However you look at him it is always the same

panorama: netsuke snuffbox, ivory handle, chess piece, fan, temple motif. He has fermented so long now that he is amorphous. Yeast despoiled of its vitamins. Vase without a rubber plant.

The females were sired twice in the ninth century, and again during the Renaissance. He was carried through the great dispersions under yellow bellies and white. Long before the Exodus a Tatar spat in his blood.

His dilemma is that of the dwarf. With his pineal eye he sees his silhouette projected on a screen of incommensurable size. His voice, synchronized to the shadow of a pinhead, intoxicates him. He hears a roar where others hear only a squeak.

There is his mind. It is an amphitheater in which the actor gives a protean performance. Moldorf, multiform and unerring, goes through his roles—clown, juggler, contortionist, priest, lecher, mountebank. The amphitheater is too small. He puts dynamite to it. The audience is drugged. He scotches it.

I am trying ineffectually to approach Moldorf. It is like trying to approach God, for Moldorf *is* God—he has never been anything else. I am merely putting down words. . . .

I have had opinions about him which I have discarded; I have had other opinions which I am revising. I have pinned him down only to find that it was not a dungbeetle I had in my hands, but a dragonfly. He has offended me by his coarseness and then overwhelmed me with his delicacy. He has been voluble to the point of suffocation, then quiet as the Jordan.

When I see him trotting forward to greet me, his little paws outstretched, his eyes perspiring, I feel that I am meeting. . . . No, this is not the way to go about it!

"*Comme un œuf dansant sur un jet d'eau.*" [Like an egg dancing on a jet of water]

He has only one cane—a mediocre one. In his pocket scraps of paper containing prescriptions for *Weltschmerz*. He is cured now, and the little German girl who washed his feet is breaking her heart. It is like Mr. Nonentity toting his Gujarati dictionary everywhere. "*Inevitable for everyone*"— meaning, no doubt, *indispensable*. Borowski would find all this incomprehensible. Borowski has a different cane for each day in the week, and one for Easter.

We have so many points in common that it is like looking at myself in a cracked mirror.

[3] American writers have traditionally been concerned with freedom and fullness of expression. Melville, in reviewing Hawthorne's *Mosses from an Old Manse*, had argued that the "Declaration of Independence makes a difference" and that writers would be free to say what they would and face up to the unknown life, and a little later, in "Song of Myself," Whitman was to advertise some of the forbidden elements of the unknown life; later, in "The Art of Fiction," even Henry James was to complain about Victorian prudery and envy the freedom of the French.

I have been looking over my manuscripts, pages scrawled with revisions. Pages of *literature*. This frightens me a little. It is so much like Moldorf. Only I am a Gentile, and Gentiles have a different way of suffering. They suffer without neuroses and, as Sylvester says, a man who has never been afflicted with a neurosis does not know the meaning of suffering.

I recall distinctly how I enjoyed my suffering. It was like taking a cub to bed with you. Once in a while he clawed you—and then you really were frightened. Ordinarily you had no fear—you could always turn him loose, or chop his head off.

There are people who cannot resist the desire to get into a cage with wild beasts and be mangled. They go in even without revolver or whip. Fear makes them fearless. . . . For the Jew the world is a cage filled with wild beasts. The door is locked and he is there without whip or revolver. His courage is so great that he does not even smell the dung in the corner. The spectators applaud but he does not hear. The drama, he thinks, is going on inside the cage. The cage, he thinks, is the world. Standing there alone and helpless, the door locked, he finds that the lions do not understand his language. Not one lion has ever heard of Spinoza. Spinoza? Why they can't even get their teeth into him. "Give us meat!" they roar, while he stands there petrified, his ideas frozen, his *Weltanschauung* a trapeze out of reach. A single blow of the lion's paw and his cosmogony is smashed.

The lions, too, are disappointed. They expected blood, bones, gristle, sinews. They chew and chew, but the words are chicle and chicle is indigestible. Chicle is a base over which you sprinkle sugar, pepsin, thyme, licorice. Chicle, when it is gathered by *chicleros*, is O.K. The *chicleros* came over on the ridge of a sunken continent. They brought with them an algebraic language. In the Arizona desert they met the Mongols of the North, glazed like eggplants. Time shortly after the earth had taken its gyroscopic lean—when the Gulf Stream was parting ways with the Japanese current. In the heart of the soil they found tufa rock. They embroidered the very bowels of the earth with their language. They ate one another's entrails and the forest closed in on them, on their bones and skulls, on their lace tufa. Their language was lost. Here and there one still finds the remnants of a menagerie, a brain plate covered with figures.

What has all this to do with you, Moldorf? The word in your mouth is anarchy. Say it, Mol-

dorf, I am waiting for it. Nobody knows, when we shake hands, the rivers that pour through our sweat. Whilst you are framing your words, your lips half parted, the saliva gurgling in your cheeks, I have jumped halfway across Asia. Were I to take your cane, mediocre as it is, and poke a little hole in your side, I could collect enough material to fill the British Museum. We stand on five minutes and devour centuries. You are the sieve through which my anarchy strains, resolves itself into words. Behind the word is chaos. Each word a stripe, a bar, but there are not and never will be enough bars to make the mesh.

In my absence the window curtains have been hung. They have the appearance of Tyrolean table-cloths dipped in lysol. The room sparkles. I sit on the bed in a daze, thinking about man before his birth. Suddenly bells begin to toll, a weird, unearthly music, as if I had been translated to the steppes of Central Asia. Some ring out with a long, lingering roll, some erupt drunkenly, maudlinly. And now it is quiet again, except for a last note that barely grazes the silence of the night—just a faint, high gong snuffed out like a flame.

I have made a silent compact with myself not to change a line of what I write. I am not interested in perfecting my thoughts, nor my actions. Beside the perfection of Turgenev I put the perfection of Dostoevski. (Is there anything more perfect than *The Eternal Husband?*) Here, then, in one and the same medium, we have two kinds of perfection. But in Van Gogh's letters there is a perfection beyond either of these. It is the triumph of the individual over art.

Or take the episode, a few pages later, when Boris, who has just rented, to a Mr. Wren, the apartment where he and Miller have been living, is celebrating the deal by offering wine:

. . . I have a bottle between my legs and I'm shoving the corkscrew in. Mrs. Wren has her mouth parted expectantly. The wine is splashing between my legs, the sun is splashing through the bay window, and inside my veins there is a bubble and splash of a thousand crazy things that commence to gush out of me now pell-mell. I'm telling them everything that comes to mind, everything that was bottled up inside me and which Mrs. Wren's loose laugh has somehow released. With that bottle between my legs and the sun splashing through the window I experience once again the splendor of those miserable days when I first arrived in Paris, a bewildered, poverty-stricken individual who haunted the streets like a ghost at a banquet. Everything comes back to me in a rush— the toilets that wouldn't work, the prince who shined my shoes, the Cinema Splendide where I slept on the patron's overcoat, the bars in the window, the feeling of suffocation, the fat cockroaches, the drinking and carousing that went on between times, Rose Cannaque and Naples dying in the sunlight. Dancing the streets on an empty belly and now and then calling on strange people —Madame Delorme, for instance. How I ever got to Madame Delorme's, I can't imagine any more. But I got there, got inside somehow, past the butler, past the maid with her little white apron, got right inside the palace with my corduroy trousers and my hunting jacket—and not a button on my fly. Even now I can taste again the golden ambiance of that room where Madame Delorme sat upon a throne in her mannish rig, the goldfish in the bowls, the maps of the ancient world, the beautifully bound books; I can feel again her heavy hand resting upon my shoulder, frightening me a little with her heavy Lesbian air. More comfortable down below in that thick stew pouring into the Gare St. Lazare, the whores in the doorways, seltzer bottles on every table; a thick tide of semen flooding the gutters. Nothing better between five and seven than to be pushed around in that throng, to follow a leg or a beautiful bust, to move along with the tide and everything whirling in your brain. A weird sort of contentment in those days. No appointments, no invitations for dinner, no program, no dough. The golden period, when I had not a single friend. Each morning the dreary walk to the American Express, and each morning the inevitable answer from the clerk. Dashing here and there like a bedbug, gathering butts now and then, sometimes furtively, sometimes brazenly; sitting down on a bench and squeezing my guts to stop the gnawing, or walking through the Jardin des Tuileries and getting an erection looking at the dumb statues. Or wandering along the Seine at night, wandering and wandering, and going mad with the beauty of it, the trees leaning to, the broken images in the water, the rush of the current under the bloody lights of the bridges, the women sleeping in doorways, sleeping on newspapers, sleeping in the rain; everywhere the musty porches of the cathedrals and beggars and lice and old hags full of St. Vitus'

dance; pushcarts stacked up like wine barrels in the side streets, the smell of berries in the market place and the old church surrounded with vegetables and blue arc lights, the gutters slippery with garbage and women in satin pumps staggering through the filth and vermin at the end of an all-night souse. The Place St. Sulpice, so quiet and deserted, where toward midnight there came every night the woman with the busted umbrella and the crazy veil; every night she slept there on a bench under her torn umbrella, the ribs hanging down, her dress turning green, her bony fingers and the odor of decay oozing from her body; and in the morning I'd be sitting there myself, taking a quiet snooze in the sunshine, cursing the goddamned pigeons gathering up the crumbs everywhere. St. Sulpice! The fat belfries, the garish posters over the door, the candles flaming inside. The Square so beloved of Anatole France, with that drone and buzz from the altar, the splash of the fountain, the pigeons cooing, the crumbs disappearing like magic and only a dull rumbling in the hollow of the guts. Here I would sit day after day thinking of Germaine and that dirty little street near the Bastille where she lived, and that buzz-buzz going on behind the altar, the buses whizzing by, the sun beating down into the asphalt and the asphalt working into me and Germaine, into the asphalt and all Paris in the big fat belfries.

And it was down the Rue Bonaparte that only a year before Mona and I used to walk every night, after we had taken leave of Borowski. St. Sulpice not meaning much to me then, nor anything in Paris. Washed out with talk. Sick of faces. Fed up with cathedrals and squares and menageries and what not. Picking up a book in the red bedroom and the cane chair uncomfortable; tired of sitting on my ass all day long, tired of red wallpaper, tired of seeing so many people jabbering away about nothing. The red bedroom and the trunk always open; her gowns lying about in a delirium of disorder. The red bedroom with my galoshes and canes, the notebooks I never touched, the manuscripts lying cold and dead.

———————

This recollection flows into the recollection— with obscene interludes—of the night when he and Mona, after the first visit to Paris, were celebrating their impending departure, and this recollection flows into another, of Mona's return to him after an absence—the famous scene of lyric love comically mixed with bedbugs:

———

We look out on the courtyard where the bicycles are parked, and there is the little room up above, under the attic, where some smart young Alec played the phonograph all day long and repeated clever little things at the top of his voice. I say "we" but I'm getting ahead of myself, because Mona has been away a long time and it's just to-day that I'm meeting her at the Gare St. Lazare. Toward evening I'm standing there with my face squeezed between the bars, but there's no Mona, and I read the cable over again but it doesn't help any. I go back to the Quarter and just the same I put away a hearty meal. Strolling past the Dôme a little later suddenly I see a pale, heavy face and burning eyes—and the little velvet suit that I al-ways adore because under the soft velvet there were always her warm breasts, the marble legs, cool, firm, muscular. She rises up out of a sea of faces and embraces me, embraces me passionately—a thou-sand eyes, noses, fingers, legs, bottles, windows, purses, saucers all glaring at us and we in each other's arm oblivious. I sit down beside her and she talks—a flood of talk. Wild consumptive notes of hysteria, perversion, leprosy. I hear not a word because she is beautiful and I love her and now I am happy and willing to die.

We walk down the Rue du Château, looking for Eugene. Walk over the railroad bridge where I used to watch the trains pulling out and feel all sick inside wondering where the hell she could be. Everything soft and enchanting as we walk over the bridge. Smoke coming up between our legs, the tracks creaking, semaphores in our blood. I feel her body close to mine—all mine now—and I stop to rub my hands over the warm velvet. Everything around us is crumbling, crumbling and the warm body under the warm velvet is aching for me. . . .

Back in the very same room and fifty francs to the good, thanks to Eugene. I look out on the court but the phonograph is silent. The trunk is open and her things are lying around everywhere just as before. She lies down on the bed with her clothes on. Once, twice, three times, four times . . . I'm afraid she'll go mad . . . in bed, under the blankets, how good to feel her body again! But for how long? Will it last this time? Already I have a presentiment that it won't.

She talks to me so feverishly—as if there will be no tomorrow. "Be quiet, Mona! Just look at me . . . *don't talk!*" Finally she drops off and I pull my arm from under her. My eyes close. Her body is there beside me . . . it will be there till morn-ing surely. . . . It was in February I pulled out of the harbor in a blinding snowstorm. The last glimpse I had of her was in the window waving good-bye to me. A man standing on the other side of the street, at the corner, his hat pulled down over his eyes, his jowls resting on his lapels. A fetus watching me. A fetus with a cigar in its mouth. Mona at the window waving good-bye. White heavy face, hair streaming wild. And now it is a heavy bedroom, breathing regularly through the gills, sap still oozing from between her legs, a warm feline odor and her hair in my mouth. My eyes are closed. We breathe warmly into each other's mouth. Close together, America three thou-sand miles away. I never want to see it again. To have her here in bed with me, breathing on me, her hair in my mouth—I count that something of a miracle. Nothing can happen now till morning. . . .

I wake from a deep slumber to look at her. A pale light is trickling in. I look at her beautiful wild hair. I feel something crawling down my neck. I look at her again, closely. Her hair is alive. I pull back the sheet—more of them. They are swarming over the pillow.

It is a little after daybreak. We pack hurriedly and sneak out of the hotel. The cafés are still closed. We walk, and as we walk we scratch our-selves. The day opens in milky whiteness, streaks of salmon-pink sky, snails leaving their shells. Paris. Paris. Everything happens here. Old, crum-bling walls and the pleasant sound of water run-ning in the urinals. Men licking their mustaches at the bar. Shutters going up with a bang and lit-tle streams purling in the gutters. *Amer Picon* in huge scarlet letters. *Zigzag.* Which way will we go and why or where or what?

Mona is hungry, her dress is thin. Nothing but evening wraps, bottles of perfume, barbaric ear-rings, bracelets, depilatories. We sit down in a bil-liard parlor on the Avenue du Maine and order hot coffee. The toilet is out of order. We shall have to sit some time before we can go to another hotel. Meanwhile we pick bedbugs out of each other's hair. Nervous. Mona is losing her temper. Must have a bath. Must have this. Must have that. Must, must, must. . .

"How much money have you left?"

Money! Forgot all about that.

Hôtel des Etats-Unis. An *ascenseur*. We go to bed in broad daylight. When we get up it is dark and the first thing to do is to raise enough dough to send a cable to America. A cable to the fetus with the long juicy cigar in his mouth. Meanwhile there is the Spanish woman on the Boulevard Raspail—she's always good for a warm meal. By morning something will happen. At least we're going to bed together. No more bedbugs now. The rainy season has commenced. The sheets are immaculate. . . .

Though Miller is the central character in *Tropic of Cancer*, as in his other work, there are dozens of others, eccentric, absurd, wicked, or pitiful. There is the sex-obsessed Van Norden (in a sense the foil of Miller and Miller's point of view), through whose grimy room numberless women pass, but who is totally devoid of passion in his mechanical charade of copulation. There is the absurd Russian princess. There is the young Hindu:

A pompous, vain little devil to boot! He had decked himself out in a corduroy suit, a beret, a cane, a Windsor tie; he had bought himself two fountain pens, a kodak, and some fancy underwear. The money he was spending was a gift from the merchants of Bombay; they were sending him to England to spread the gospel of Gandhi.

Meanwhile, before he goes to spread the gospel, he is being conducted by Miller to two brothels —where he disastrously, and comically, mistakes the function of a bidet.

The picaresque wanderings of the author-hero take him to brothels, bistros, boîtes, waterfront dives, and once, after an all-night debauch, at dawn, to a church:

The night before I left we had a good time. About dawn it began to snow: we walked about from one quarter to another taking a last look at Paris. Passing through the Rue St. Dominique we suddenly fell upon a little square and there was the Eglise Ste.-Clotilde. People were going to mass. Fillmore, whose head was still a little cloudy, was bent on going to mass too. "For the fun of it!" as he put it. I felt somewhat uneasy about it; in the first

place I had never attended a mass, and in the second place I looked seedy and felt seedy. Fillmore, too, looked rather battered, even more disreputable than myself; his big slouch hat was on assways and his overcoat was still full of sawdust from the last joint we had been in. However, we marched in. The worst they could do would be to throw us out.

I was so astounded by the sight that greeted my eyes that I lost all uneasiness. It took me a little while to get adjusted to the dim light. I stumbled around behind Fillmore, holding his sleeve. A weird, unearthly noise assailed my ears, a sort of hollow drone that rose up out of the cold flagging. A huge, dismal tomb it was with mourners shuffling in and out. A sort of antechamber to the world below. Temperature about 55 or 60 Fahrenheit. No music except this undefinable dirge manufactured in the subcellar—like a million heads of cauliflower wailing in the dark. People in shrouds were chewing away with that hopeless, dejected look of beggars who hold out their hands in a trance and mumble an unintelligible appeal.

That this sort of thing existed I knew, but then one also knows that there are slaughterhouses and morgues and dissecting rooms. One instinctively avoids such places. In the street I had often passed a priest with a little prayer book in his hands laboriously memorizing his lines. *Idiot*, I would say to myself, and let it go at that. In the street one meets with all forms of dementia and the priest is by no means the most striking. Two thousand years of it has deadened us to the idiocy of it. However, when you are suddenly transported to the very midst of his realm, when you see the little world in which the priest functions like an alarm clock, you are apt to have entirely different sensations.

For a moment all this slaver and twitching of the lips almost began to have a meaning. Something was going on, some kind of dumb show which, not rendering me wholly stupefied, held me spellbound. All over the world, wherever there are these dim-lit tombs, you have this incredible spectacle—the same mean temperature, the same crepuscular glow, the same buzz and drone. All over Christendom, at certain stipulated hours, people in black are groveling before the altar where the priest stands up with a little book in one hand and a dinner bell or atomizer in the other and mumbles to them in a language which, even if it were comprehensible, no longer contains a shred of meaning. Blessing them, most likely. Blessing the country, blessing the ruler, blessing the firearms and the battleships and the ammunition and the hand grenades. Surrounding him on the altar are little boys dressed like angels of the Lord who sing alto and soprano. Innocent lambs. All in skirts, sexless, like the priest himself who is usually flat-footed and nearsighted to boot. A fine epicene caterwauling. Sex in a jockstrap, to the tune of J-mol.

I was taking it in as best I could in the dim light. Fascinating and stupefying at the same time. All over the civilized world, I thought to myself. All over the world. Marvelous. Rain or shine, hail, sleet, snow, thunder, lightning, war, famine, pestilence—makes not the slightest difference. Always the same mean temperature, the same mumbo jumbo, the same high-laced shoes and the little angels of the Lord singing soprano and alto. Near the exit a little slot-box—to carry on the heavenly work. So that God's blessing may rain down upon king and country and battleships and high explosives and tanks and airplanes, so that the worker may have more strength in his arms, strength to slaughter horses and cows and sheep, strength to punch holes in iron girders, strength to sew buttons on other people's pants, strength to sell carrots and sewing machines and automobiles, strength to exterminate insects and clean stables and unload garbage cans and scrub lavatories, strength to write headlines and chop tickets in the subway. Strength . . . strength. All that lip chewing and hornswoggling just to furnish a little strength!

We were moving about from one spot to another, surveying the scene with that clearheadedness which comes after an all-night session. We must have made ourselves pretty conspicuous shuffling about that way with our coat collars turned up and never once crossing ourselves and never once moving our lips except to whisper some callous remark. Perhaps everything would have passed off without notice if Fillmore hadn't insisted on walking past the altar in the midst of the ceremony. He was looking for the exit, and he thought while he was at it, I suppose, that he would take a good squint at the holy of holies, get a close-up on it, as it were. We had gotten safely by and were marching toward a crack of light which must have been the way out when a priest suddenly stepped out of the gloom and blocked our path. Wanted to know where we were going and what we were doing. We told him politely enough that we were looking for the exit. We said "exit" because at the moment we were so flabber-

gasted that we couldn't think of the French for exit. Without a word of response he took us firmly by the arm and, opening the door, a side door it was, he gave us a push and out we tumbled into the blinding light of day. It happened so suddenly and unexpectedly that when we hit the sidewalk we were in a daze. We walked a few paces, blinking our eyes, and then instinctively we both turned round; the priest was still standing on the steps, pale as a ghost and scowling like the devil himself. He must have been sore as hell. Later, thinking back on it, I couldn't blame him for it. But at that moment, seeing him with his long skirts and the little skull cap on his cranium, he looked so ridiculous that I burst out laughing. I looked at Fillmore and he began to laugh too. For a full minute we stood there laughing right in the poor bugger's face. He was so bewildered, I guess, that for a moment he didn't know what to do; suddenly, however, he started down the steps on the run, shaking his fist at us as if he were in earnest. When he swung out of the enclosure he was on the gallop. By this time some preservative instinct warned me to get a move on. I grabbed Fillmore by the coat sleeve and started to run. He was saying, like an idiot: "No, no! I won't run!"—"Come on!" I yelled, "we'd better get out of here. That guy's mad clean through." And off we ran, beating it as fast as our legs would carry us.

So now they are outside in the snow—outside history, outside society.

Two themes run through *Tropic of Cancer*. One theme is that of the birth of the artist, outside the cruelties, lunacies, and hypocrisies of society:[4]

[4] The general theme of the birth of the artist is an old one in world literature and recurs with particular frequency in the Anglo-American romantic tradition. In this country, the motif can perhaps first be made out within the imaginative action of Whitman's "Song of Myself," though one can find allusions to it in the writings of Emerson and Thoreau. In the past fifty years it has perhaps been most pronounced in various poems by Hart Crane ("For the Marriage of Faustus and Helen," for example) and in the work of Thomas Wolfe. In this and other regards, Miller clearly belongs to the same tradition; but his special and revealing stance is less the familiar one of opposition to a crass and materialistic world (in which the artist alone deserves to be honored), than that of a being outside—as though emancipated from—a savage and lunatic society.

Once I thought that to be human was the highest aim a man could have, but I see now that it was meant to destroy me. Today I am proud to say that I am *inhuman*, that I belong not to men and governments, that I have nothing to do with creeds and principles. I have nothing to do with the creaking machinery of humanity—I belong to the earth! I say that lying on my pillow and I can feel the horns sprouting from my temples. I can see about me all those cracked forebears of mine dancing around the bed, consoling me, egging me on, lashing me with their serpent tongues, grinning and leering at me with their skulking skulls. *I am inhuman!* I say it with a mad, hallucinated grin, and I will keep on saying it though it rain crocodiles. Behind my words are all those grinning, leering, skulking skulls, some dead and grinning a long time, some grinning as if they had lockjaw, some grinning with the grimace of a grin, the foretaste and aftermath of what is always going on. Clearer than all I see my own grinning skull, see the skeleton dancing in the wind, serpents issuing from the rotted tongue and the bloated pages of ecstasy slimed with excrement. And I join my slime, my excrement, my madness, my ecstasy to the great circuit which flows through the subterranean vaults of the flesh. All this unbidden, unwanted, drunken vomit will flow on endlessly through the minds of those to come in the inexhaustible vessel that contains the history of the race. Side by side with the human race there runs another race of beings, the inhuman ones, the race of artists who, goaded by unknown impulses, take the lifeless mass of humanity and by the fever and ferment with which they imbue it turn this soggy dough into bread and the bread into wine and the wine into song. Out of the dead compost and the inert slag they breed a song that contaminates. I see this other race of individuals ransacking the universe, turning everything upside down, their feet always moving in blood and tears, their hands always empty, always clutching and grasping for the beyond, for the god out of reach: slaying everything within reach in order to quiet the monster that gnaws at their vitals. I see that when they tear their hair with the effort to comprehend, to seize this forever unattainable, I see that when they bellow like crazed beasts and rip and gore, I see that this is right, that there is no other path to pursue. A man who belongs to this race must stand up on the high place with gibberish in his mouth and rip out his entrails. It is right and just, because he must! And anything that falls short of this frightening spec-

tacle, anything less shuddering, less terrifying, less mad, less intoxicated, less contaminating, is not art. The rest is counterfeit. The rest is human. The rest belongs to life and lifelessness.

When I think of Stavrogin for example, I think of some divine monster standing on a high place and flinging to us his torn bowels. In *The Possessed* the earth quakes: it is not the catastrophe that befalls the imaginative individual, but a cataclysm in which a large portion of humanity is buried, wiped out forever. Stavrogin was Dostoevski and Dostoevski was the sum of all those contradictions which either paralyze a man or lead him to the heights. There was no world too low for him to enter, no place too high for him to fear to ascend. He went the whole gamut, from the abyss to the stars. It is a pity that we shall never again have the opportunity to see a man placed at the very core of mystery and, by his flashes, illuminating for us the depth and immensity of the darkness.

Today I am aware of my lineage. I have no need to consult my horoscope or my genealogical chart. What is written in the stars, or in my blood, I know nothing of. I know that I spring from the mythological founders of the race. The man who raises the holy bottle to his lips, the criminal who kneels in the marketplace, the innocent one who discovers that *all* corpses stink, the madman who dances with lightning in his hands, the friar who lifts his skirts to pee over the world, the fanatic who ransacks libraries in order to find the World—all these are fused in me, all these make my confusion, my ecstasy. If I am inhuman it is because my world has slopped over its human bounds, because to be human seems like a poor, sorry, miserable affair, limited by the senses, restricted by moralities and codes, defined by platitudes and isms. I am pouring the juice of the grape down my gullet and I find wisdom in it, but my wisdom is not born of the grape, my intoxication owes nothing to wine. . . .

The other theme is that of the celebration of sexuality. This theme is directed not toward pornographic provocation, certainly not toward the exploiting of the charming, the beautiful, the subtle, the appealing, the titillating, the seductive. The celebration tends, rather, toward the ugly, the crude, the debased, as though the dignity of the sexual principle must be shown to surpass and survive all vessels and all contexts—even the comedy of sex and the slapstick of the sexual act. But more than comedy is involved here, a universal pathos, too—the pathos of sexual yearning in the middle of the great, grinding machine of the modern world, and of the emptiness of time:

The silence descends in volcanic chutes. Yonder, in the barren hills, rolling onward toward the great metallurgical regions, the locomotives are pulling their merchant products. Over steel and iron beds they roll, the ground sown with slag and cinders and purple ore. In the baggage car, kelps, fishplate, rolled iron, sleepers, wire rods, plates and sheets, laminated articles, hot rolled hoops, splints and mortar carriages, and Zorès ore. The wheels U-80 millimeters or over. Pass splendid specimens of Anglo-Norman architecture, pass pedestrians and pederasts, open hearth furnaces, basic Bessemer mills, dynamos and transformers, pig iron castings and steel ingots. The public at large, pedestrians and pederasts, goldfish and spun-glass palm trees, donkeys sobbing, all circulating freely through quincuncial alleys. At the Place du Brésil a lavender eye.

Going back in a flash over the women I've known. It's like a chain which I've forged out of my own misery. Each one bound to the other. A fear of living separate, of staying born. The door of the womb always on the latch. Dread and longing. Deep in the blood the pull of paradise. The beyond. Always the beyond. It must have all started with the navel. They cut the umbilical cord, give you a slap on the ass, and presto! you're out in the world, adrift, a ship without a rudder. You look at the stars and then you look at your navel. You grow eyes everywhere—in the armpits, between the lips, in the roots of your hair, on the soles of your feet. What is distant becomes near, what is near becomes distant. Inner-outer, a constant flux, a shedding of skins, a turning inside out. You drift around like that for years and years, until you find yourself in the dead center, and there you slowly rot, slowly crumble to pieces, get dispersed again. Only your name remains.

Beyond both themes, a third emerges, absorbing both: the idea of the creation of the true self. According to Miller, the artist is simply engaged in the effort to create the self, to free it from the throttling limitations proposed by society, and in this effort the artist is not to be distinguished, ultimately, from any man who recognizes and attempts to transcend his plight.[5] So, as Miller puts it in our second quotation from *Tropic of Cancer*, Van Gogh's letters have a "perfection" different from that of the work of Turgenev and Dostoevski—"the triumph of the individual over art." As for the theme of sexuality, the same idea of self-discovery appears. Only insofar as sex is freed from the distortions and repressions of society can identity be developed—or, to go one step further, can there be the full recognition of another person's identity requisite for love.

On these two themes and, in fact, on the book as a whole, the last scene gives a very strange and unexpected perspective:

Suddenly it occurred to me that if I wanted I could go to America myself. It was the first time the opportunity had ever presented itself. I asked myself—"do you want to go?" There was no answer. My thoughts drifted out, toward the sea, toward the other side where, taking a last look back, I had seen the skyscrapers fading out in a flurry of snowflakes. I saw them looming up again, in that same ghostly way as when I left. Saw the lights creeping through their ribs. I saw the whole city spread out, from Harlem to the Battery, the streets choked with ants, the elevated rushing by, the theaters emptying. I wondered in a vague way what had ever happened to my wife.

After everything had quietly sifted through my head a great peace came over me. Here, where the river gently winds through the girdle of hills, lies a soil so saturated with the past that however far back the mind roams one can never detach it from its human background. Christ, before my eyes there shimmered such a golden peace that only a neurotic could dream of turning his head away. So quietly flows the Seine that one hardly notices its presence. It is always there, quiet and unobtrusive, like a great artery running through the human

---

[5] Miller shares this theme with, among others, Anaïs Nin, a life-long friend and, particularly during his years in Paris, literary adviser. Nin expounds the theme most effectively in her voluminous diary, four volumes of which have been published to date, though she is also the author of a number of short novels and stories.

body. In the wonderful peace that fell over me it seemed as if I had climbed to the top of a high mountain; for a little while I would be able to look around me, to take in the meaning of the landscape.

Human beings make a strange fauna and flora. From a distance they appear negligible; close up they are apt to appear ugly and malicious. More than anything they need to be surrounded with sufficient space—space even more than time.

The sun is setting. I feel this river flowing through me—its past, its ancient soil, the changing climate. The hills gently girdle it about: its course is fixed.

Miller had not soaked himself in Oriental mysticism for nothing.

The 1930's were for Miller in Paris, as for Faulkner in far-off Mississippi, the great creative decade. In addition to *Tropic of Cancer*, he wrote *Black Spring* and *Tropic of Capricorn* (two other autobiographical works earlier than *The Rosy Crucifixion*, but going back in time to the Brooklyn period and to the job with the "Cosmodemonic Telegraph Company" and the "resurrection"); and *Max and the White Phagocytes*, *Aller Retour New York*, and *The Wisdom of the Heart*, dealing not only with autobiographical but with descriptive, critical, and philosophical materials.

The Second World War drove Miller back to the United States. There he wrote *The Colossus*, concerning a period in Greece with his admirer Lawrence Durrell. His salute to the homeland was *The Air-Conditioned Nightmare*,[6] the record of a long, wandering journey by secondhand Buick to reacquaint himself with the country. The title declares what he found—a blasphemous parody of all the "natural" values he admired and those professed in the Declaration of Independence as well. While carrying on his guerrilla war with the United States, and the world of modern technology at large, Miller was also working at last on *The Rosy Crucifixion*, which he had envisioned back in 1927 and

which, when completed, repeated and elaborated the personal story of *Black Spring* and *Tropic of Capricorn*.

There are brilliant passages in *The Rosy Crucifixion*, but there are many dull ones, and often sections that are dull in a repetitive, conventional way. The chief interest lies in the character of Mona, but even so, she, like the "truth" that she had led Miller to discover, remains mysterious and somehow unrealized. We do know, however, that this Beatrice to Miller's Dante is almost totally amoral, a pathological liar and daydreamer, seeking in lies a redeemed self, with lesbian traits. She was, however, capable of providing the sexual revelation to Miller that somehow created the writer and the new man. Perhaps the point is that in our dispensation, as contrasted with Dante's, only such a Beatrice can, as Dante put it, call one "out of the vulgar herd."[7]

In spite of incidental virtues, fine passages, and the character of Mona, Miller's inspiration had run out. By now he had started a new life in California, in the Big Sur country, marrying, begetting two more children, getting a divorce, marrying again, painting his watercolors. His fame was constantly increasing. He was a guru on a high hilltop against the magnificent backdrop of California mountains, sea, and sky, uttering wisdom that, as it became more abstract, became more silly. He was a hermit beset by would-be disciples, mostly crackpots seeking metaphysical solutions or admission into the mystic Sex Circle or whatever they thought was on the hill, and not recognizing the real nature of the master's achievement.

What was that achievement?

Miller sneers at the tidy artistry of Hemingway and the "insufferable, the obsessional lucidity," and the "mortuary odor" not only of traditional writers but of the great masters of

---

[6] As has been remarked, the vision of America announced in *The Air-Conditioned Nightmare* is anticipated in the work of Edgar Allan Poe.

[7] Among the better work of Miller's later years is *The Smile at the Foot of the Ladder*, a wistfully attractive little parable, or fairy tale, about an aspiring clown. The image of the clown seems particularly attractive as a subject to writers of the past fifty years. (See Nathanael West, E. E. Cummings, Hart Crane, and others.)

the new literature of the twentieth century—sparing only D. H. Lawrence. His own obsession has not been "lucidity," but what we may call "authenticity." He professes the superior literary practice of opening his spirit—and typewriter—to the flow of inner reality. But what sometimes comes out—in the best work, at least—has the peculiar lambent aura of what we take to be art.

For the guru has turned out, after all, to be an artist, and the message he has to give—even if he abhors the cult of style—inheres in the compelling quality of his art.

The early work of Miller was published in Paris, by the Obelisk Press, which supported the ideal of literary freedom by catering to the tourist smut trade. By 1941 Miller had been published in America, but not with the kind of work that had given him his notoriety; and *The Air-Conditioned Nightmare*, though offensive to patriots, did not provoke the Watch and Ward Society to effective action. The "hot" work continued to be published in Paris, even if *Sexus*, the first section of *The Rosy Crucifixion*, was sensational enough, even in the eyes of the normally permissive French authorities, to get the publisher haled into court and convicted. But by 1961 *Tropic of Cancer* was legally published in the United States, and, with the backlist of the erstwhile "obscene" works to draw on, Miller was soon on the way to becoming one of the more solvent writers in America.

A good part of Miller's fame, as well as of his solvency, is no doubt to be attributed to the fact that he was billed in the public mind as "dirty." But from the beginning some discerning readers recognized other qualities. Pound, for instance, was originally responsible for the publication of *Tropic of Cancer*, and the then young man Lawrence Durrell was soon to hail the author as a master. Suggestible admirers began to regard him as another Jean Jacques Rousseau, and, more recently, in the introduction to the American edition of *Tropic of Cancer*, the poet Karl Shapiro calls him the "greatest living author."

Miller's influence has been seminal. It is to be recognized in the writing and attitudes of the Beats, such as Jack Kerouac and Allen Ginsberg, in Heller's *Catch-22*, the novels of Pynchon and Barth, in Norman Mailer, with his "personalized" journalism and his ad hoc fiction, and in two quite contradictory aspects of contemporary poetry, the "confessional" and the "neosurrealistic." Even so, time may show Miller more important as a social phenomenon than as a writer, for more and more in the contemporary world the attitudes of the "cultural desperado" that Miller called himself are becoming common. He makes personal virtue, as he makes literary achievement, seem "easy." And the easy is always attractive.

But the work remains, and the productions of the great decade, as well as a few of the later works, show real power—and a not narrow streak of genius. The work should survive, even, the label of sociological significance.

BIOGRAPHICAL CHART

1891 Born, December 26, in New York City, the only son of a lower-middle-class German-American family

1892 Family moves to Williamsburg section of Brooklyn

1905–9 Attends Eastern District High School in Brooklyn; studies piano and reads widely; spends two months at City College of New York

1910–13 Employed in clerical jobs; travels to West Coast and works at odd jobs there

1914–16 In New York, work in father's tailor shop, then at a variety of menial jobs

1917 Marries Beatrice Wickens

1920–24 Works as messenger for Western Union, then three years as messenger employment manager; writing begins

1924 Divorced from Beatrice Wickens and marries June Smith [Mansfield] the "Mona" of the novels; unsuccessful at commercial writing

1925–28 Works as door-to-door salesman, a clerk in own "speakeasy," and beggar; unpublished stories and novel

1928–29 Tours Europe with wife on money provided by her friend

1930–32 Returns to Europe; marginal existence in Paris; writes *Tropic of Cancer*
1933 Lives in Clichy with Alfred Perlès; writes *Black Spring*
1934 Returns to New York; *Tropic of Cancer* published in Paris (book denied entry into the United States)
1935 Divorced from second wife
1936 *Black Spring* published in Paris
1937–39 Lives in Paris; *Tropic of Capricorn* completed and published there
1940 Returns to New York in January; writes book on

travels in Greece, *The Colossus of Maroussi* (1941); makes auto tour of the United States
1942 Settles in Los Angeles; painting and writing
1944 Marries Janina Lepska; settles in Big Sur, California
1945 Completes *Sexus* and *Air-Conditioned Nightmare*
1952 Divorced from third wife
1953 Tours Europe; marries Eve McClure
1958–60 Lives in Big Sur; *Nexus*
1961 Separates from fourth wife; *Tropic of Cancer* first published in the United States—best seller and subject of dozens of local censorship cases

FURTHER READINGS

There is no standard edition of Miller's writings. The reader may consult the biographical chart for the publication dates of his major works.

Lawrence Durrell and Alfred Perlès, *Art and Outrage* (1959)
William A. Gordon, *The Mind and Art of Henry Miller* (1967)
Ihab Hassan, *The Literature of Silence: Henry Miller and Samuel Beckett* (1968)

Norman Mailer, *The Prisoner of Sex* (1971)
Anaïs Nin, *The Diary of Anaïs Nin*, Gunther Stuhlmann, ed. (1966– ; 4 vols. to date)
Alfred Perlès, *My Friend, Henry Miller* (1955)
George Wickes, "Henry Miller," in *Writers at Work: The Paris Review Interviews* (1963)
————, *Henry Miller and the Critics* (1963)
————, *Henry Miller* (1966)

ERNEST HEMINGWAY (1899–1961)

With Ernest Hemingway, we have the example of a type of writer who is more and more common in America since the Civil War—the writer who deliberately projects his own personality and life as central to his work (even though in a fashion more oblique or masked than that of Henry Miller). Such a writer—and such an attitude toward the nature and role of the writer—is fairly recent in history. The first clear-cut instance would probably be Byron, the archetypal "romantic" exploiting his own personality for material. But in the contemporary world the interest in the romantic personality has become fused with other elements. As the intellectual orientation has become increasingly positivistic, the accepted role of the literary artist has involved a growing emphasis on reportage and less on imaginative creation. When Whitman wrote, "I am the man, I suf-

fered, I was there," he fused the two elements, the romantic observer or spokesman (in his case the poet with a special persona) and the positivist (who reported the realistic material in his poetry). So reportage, documentary fiction, and autobiography more and more tended to merge, as with Richard Harding Davis, Stephen Crane, Dreiser, Sherwood Anderson, and, more recently, Hemingway. With Hemingway, this special relation of man and work, or of man and artist, raises questions concerning the nature of fiction in our time and concerning the relation of the writer to his public.

Ernest Hemingway was born July 21, 1899, in the pleasant Chicago suburb of Oak Park, the son of a prosperous physician, and lived what seemed to be the ideal American boyhood. He was strong, handsome, and intelligent, played football in high school and boxed, and in the summers, in northern Michigan, became, under the tutelage of his father, a fisherman, hunter, and woodsman. Then, at the age of eighteen, he was a cub reporter on the Kansas City *Star*, at fifteen dollars a week, observing the underside of life and reading poetry. The next year, in 1918, he was in Italy as an ambulance driver, was badly wounded and, though wounded, saved a man's life; in the hospital he was baptized, almost accidentally, by an Abruzzese priest, who, along with a doctor met there, reappears in *A Farewell to Arms*. There, too, he fell in love with a nurse who gave him the model for Catherine, the heroine of the same novel. The first American wounded in Italy, he was decorated by the Italian government.

The next year Hemingway was back home in Chicago, then on the Toronto *Star*, and a year later, in 1921, he was married and on his way to Paris preceded by a letter of introduction to Gertrude Stein (from Sherwood Anderson, whom he had met in Chicago). In Paris, he worked as a foreign correspondent for the *Star*, covering international conferences and brush-fire wars, but his ambition was to be a writer, and his program, as he put it, was to write "the truest sentence that you know," the straight presentation of unvarnished fact to give a "true simple declarative sentence." In this was not only his program for education as a writer, but the germ of his "philosophy." Meanwhile, he knew Gertrude Stein, Ezra Pound, Ford Madox Ford, and F. Scott Fitzgerald, already precociously famous, and from each of them, in different ways, drew what he needed for his development, for part of his genius was the instinct to locate and seize on precisely what— and what person—was useful to him. Another part of his genius was his energy, another his conviction that he would be great, and another his totally ruthless concentration, strangely like that of Justice Holmes, on his ambition: with these qualities was another, even less amiable, the need to repudiate and avenge himself on anyone who had been useful to him.

Out of this period came the creation, almost

instinctive, of Hemingway's persona, that of the observer, the "eye," seemingly emotionless, but suggesting, by the very intensity of attention and the precision of report, a tightly suppressed emotional force. Furthermore, the persona might select only a certain kind of fact for this preternatural intensity of attention, the fact of violence; and always the fact behind a fact, the story within a story, was the relation between the unspecified inner tension of the observer and the nature of the object observed. It was as though the inner tension of the see-er might be alleviated only in the transference effected by the act of seeing.

Carlos Baker, Hemingway's biographer, reports that in 1922 the young writer wrote out on telegraph blanks, as though composing a correspondent's report to the home paper, a summary of his "seeing" for the first months in Paris, and this is the germ of all his subsequent work:

I have seen the favourite crash into the Bulfinch and come down in a heap kicking, while the rest of the field swooped over the jump . . . and the crowd raced across the pelouze to see the horses come into the stretch. . . . I have seen Peggy Joyce at 2 A.M. in a Dancing in the Rue Camartin quarreling with the shellac-haired young Chilean who had manicured finger nails, blew a puff of cigarette smoke into her face, wrote something in a notebook, and shot himself at 3:30 the same morning. . . . I have watched the police charge the crowd with swords as they milled back into Paris through the Porte Maillot on the first of May and seen the frightened proud look on the white beaten-up face of the sixteen year old kid who looked like a prep school quarter back and had just shot two policemen. . . . I have stood on the crowded back platform of a seven o'clock Batignolles bus as it lurched along the wet lamp-lit street while men who were going home to supper never looked up from their newspapers as we passed Notre Dame grey and dripping in the rain. . . . I have seen the one legged street walker who works the

Boulevard Madelaine between the Rue Cambon and Bernheim Jeune's limping along the pavement through the crowd on a rainy night with a beefy red-faced Episcopal clergyman holding an umbrella over her. . . . I have watched two Senegalese soldiers in the dim light of the snake house of the Jardin des Plantes teasing the King Cobra who swayed and tightened in tense erect rage as one of the little brown men crouched and feinted at him with his red fez.

Meanwhile Hemingway was creating the personal legend. He was the boxer and expert on boxing, the trout fisherman who handled a fly rod with the delicacy of a virtuoso's fiddle bow, the unerring wing-shot and killer of the kudu and the lion, the connoisseur of art, cookery, wines, and women, the aficionado of the bullring and the pal of name matadors, the crack skier, the warrior and military theorist. He was, indeed, a young man of prodigal energies, perfect coordination, exquisite timing, total courage, iron will, and high intelligence. In addition, he had great good looks, and a boyish charm that was to survive well past his youth, to survive, even, his rather calculated use of it; and people were drawn to him instinctively, even against the evidence of fact and their own better judgment.

There was, indeed, a deep streak of cruelty in Hemingway. Physically he was a bully, and weakness seemed to incite his savagery, as though the weakness of another man had to be punished as a way of expunging the possibility in himself. Furthermore, one of the surest ways of inciting Hemingway's cruelty was to do him a service or fruitfully influence his work, as hosts of his friends would come to testify. Again, the pattern for him seemed to be that to receive a service or influence implied a weakness that had to be expunged if the self-image was to remain untarnished. Often mixed with the outbursts of cruelty were suicidal moments and, more and more as the years passed, a proneness to accident.

Nothing, no achievement, no fame, no devotion, was ever enough for the glittering young (or later, aging) demigod, and lies had to be evoked to make everything seem better, to redeem some terrible uncertainty and gnawing emptiness; and he himself had to learn to believe all the lies that were constantly being placed as burnt offerings to some secret and implacable idol-image of the self.

By 1923, Hemingway's first book was out, *Three Stories and Ten Poems*, published by Robert McAlmon, a fellow expatriate with a rich wife who established the Contact Press and for whom Hemingway nourished a not-too-secret contempt. Before the year was out, *In Our Time* appeared from the Three Mountains Press in Paris. Both books were published in severely limited editions, but certain critics of influence, such as Edmund Wilson, read them, and the second, in an enlarged edition, shortly appeared in America. Meanwhile, since it had been remarked that his stories owed something to Anderson, Hemingway wrote a savage parody of his benefactor's novel *Dark Laughter*, called *Torrents of Spring*, which came out in 1926.

The stories had made a limited impact, but with *The Sun Also Rises*, Hemingway found a general public, convinced the critics that he was a writer of magnitude, and achieved overnight the role of spokesman for a generation. A remark attributed to Gertrude Stein, "You are all a lost generation," appears as the epigraph, and the novel celebrated the young people, no longer quite young, who had been maimed by the First World War, literally or spiritually—characters who are thinly disguised versions of Hemingway's friends of the Left Bank. This world of the drifters, the maimed, and the wastrels is contrasted with the world of the bullring, the contrast, in the protracted section of the novel embodying it, being an account, again only thinly disguised, of an expedition Hemingway and his wife had taken with a group of friends to the fiesta at Pamplona. The strangest of the disguises is that of Hemingway, the exhibitionistic apostle of virility, as Jake Barnes, the young newspaperman who had been castrated by a wound received in the war.

The Sun Also Rises was, on a minor scale,

one of those literary works, like Goethe's *The Sorrows of Werther*, Byron's *Childe Harold*, or Fitzgerald's *This Side of Paradise*, that reveals an age to itself, that has a visionary quality—that becomes, in short, more significant in its repercussions than it may be in itself. Though the novel was not greeted with universal applause, Hemingway was clearly a force to be reckoned with, a powerfully individual writer obsessed by a disturbing vision, and his readership was growing and the ground was prepared for a great acclaim. It came with *A Farewell to Arms*, in 1929. The new novel did, in fact, have a much broader base of appeal than the earlier work. Here was the classic story of true love ending in death. The main characters, though they might offend strict morality, were young, beautiful, and devoted; Frederick Henry and Catherine were freely compared to Romeo and Juliet. As Malcolm Cowley summed it up in his review, Hemingway was saying farewell to a "period, an attitude, and perhaps to a method also." The reviewer, though later to make one of the most perceptive analyses of Hemingway's work, was here wrong: *A Farewell to Arms*, rather than leaving the world of *The Sun Also Rises*, simply probes the events that made that world historically possible.

Hemingway was thirty years old when fame came. His first marriage had been wrecked when his wife's best friend, back in 1926, decided that Hemingway was the man for her, and when he, after much anguish and some suicidal meditations, finally decided that she was right. He had decided, too, that since he, by the accident of getting sprinkled by a Catholic priest back in 1918, must be a Catholic, his first marriage was invalid, and he was free to contract a Catholic marriage with Pauline Pfeiffer. The marriage was particularly inviting in that she had promised him that he could have his way all the time, and that she would never cross him; and this much of Pauline, at least, was to get into the heroine of *A Farewell to Arms*, Catherine Barkley, who promises the hero, Frederick Henry, exactly the same thing in almost the exact words.

By the time of his success, Hemingway had become more sadistic and was more and more inclined to indulge fantasies of self-aggrandizement. Meanwhile, his father, in poor health and worried about money, had shot himself, and his mother, the disappointed opera star whom the son had come, apparently with some justification, to regard as a prime "bitch," had sent him, along with some of her paintings (she was a painter, too, as well as a singer), a chocolate cake and the Civil War revolver used in the suicide. The father, Hemingway decided, hadn't been tough enough to deal with his wife. This was not a mistake he was ever likely to make.

A Farewell to Arms marked not only the change of Hemingway's role from that of the promising young writer to that of the "success," but it also marked the change of the world in which he lived. The Depression (which, in relation to Hemingway, we discuss later) was on, and concern with the individual fate was being replaced by concern for the social fate, at a bread-and-meat level as well as at the level of fashion, journalism, and book reviewing. Hemingway, with his individualistic code, invited attack, but three factors worked in his favor: he was fully established when the Depression took deep hold—at the height of his fame, in fact; his cynical view of the First World War corroborated, within limits, the Marxist view of history; and his fictional method and style, unlike Faulkner's, for example, was "easy" and attracted readers from the wide public. Hemingway's integrity did not, however, allow him to adapt to the new climate in which "social relevance," mechanically interpreted, was too often taken to be the only criterion of literary virtue.

Hemingway's first reaction to the new world was, indeed, to flee it, to seek his materials and meanings in places quite different. His first flight was to Spain, with *Death in the Afternoon* (1932), a book about bull-fighting, the mystique and the aesthetic of the sport liberally larded with the author's view of life, letters, and himself. But hunting expeditions to the American West and to Africa, and fishing in the Caribbean, offered even more positive flights from the Depression world of politics and ideology; and *The Green Hills of Africa* (1935), which the author referred to as "true autobiography," commemorated his exploits on a safari and gave a background for personal anecdote, literary criticism, and a strange theory of history that things are always good until men come. Meanwhile, a collection of stories, *Men Without Women* (1927), though it contained some of his best work, was severely criticized for its lack of relevance and for self-imitation.

By 1937, however, Hemingway had succumbed to the pressure of friends, reviewers, and the logic of history, and was in Spain, as a correspondent covering the Civil War. Even though he made no pretense of impartiality in the task, being now committed to the Loyalist cause, he could, unlike some observers, offer tribute to the bravery of the Fascist troops when he encountered it. In the same year appeared the novel *To Have and Have Not*, which presumably announced his discovery of a social conscience.

An actual war was, however, the sort of thing that Hemingway could still look at and write some "true sentences" about. If the Spanish war gave him a bad play called *The Fifth Column*, it also gave him the novel *For Whom the Bell Tolls* (1940), which was widely proclaimed as a master work, made a great deal of money, and, for the moment, wiped out some of the anger, bitterness, and frustration of the years since the appearance of *A Farewell to Arms* had seemed to announce a millennium of unbroken triumphs. In 1940, too, Hemingway received his divorce from Pauline and married a beautiful, blond, and political-minded young journalist named Martha Gellhorn, whom later, in the novel *Across the River and into the Trees* (1950), he described as having "more ambition than Napoleon and about the talent of the average High School Valedictorian."

Three new triumphs awaited Hemingway. The first was his career as a correspondent in the Second World War, when he lived in a euphoria of heroic adventure, real and imaginary, and crowned his exploits by liberating the Ritz Bar in Paris. The second was the reception of *The Old Man and the Sea* (1952). The third was the Nobel prize (1954). During the war he had met another newspaperwoman, Mary Welch by name, who became Martha Gellhorn's successor, and who managed to give some stability to his life.

His reputation had solidified. He was now a great public figure, his picture appeared on the cover of *Time*, and a magnificent photograph of the grizzled, leonine head was on the back cover of another and more elegant periodical called *Wisdom*—with Picasso on the front. He fished for marlin off the coast of Cuba and was photographed so doing. He again hunted in Africa, where he was almost killed in an air crash and, in fact, was reported dead. He made a nostalgic and triumphant return to Spain. He became an addict of Venice and the friend of Italian aristocrats. He bought a house at Ketchum, Idaho, for he loved the country there.

Nothing went well, however. His health was bad. Delusions of grandeur and fits of depression alternated. He began to lose the capacity for work. Twice he underwent shock treatment at the Mayo Clinic, in Minnesota. Back in Ketchum from the second stay at the clinic, early on Sunday morning, on July 2, 1961, he shot his head off with both charges from a double-barreled shotgun.

One of the most fruitful questions to ask about a writer is "What is his world like?" The English country houses of Henry James imply something of the kinds of people and the kinds of issues that concern him. The forests of Cooper imply something of the story he has to tell.

The world of Hemingway is characteristically violent and often brutal, the world of war, of crime, of dissipation, of the bullring and prize ring, of big game hunting and deep sea fishing; it is also a world of failures, bums, punch-drunk prize fighters, homosexuals, drunkards, writers who have betrayed their talent, opera singers at whom the audience throws things, bull-fighters who have lost their nerve. It is a world of fear and despair—and the despair is sometimes metaphysical, a world in which a man cannot find meaning, a world of nothingness. The typical character always stands under the shadow of ruin, and the ruin has not only the obvious objective aspect, but an inner aspect, too, that of spiritual ruin, of a disintegration of the self.

The issue for the Hemingway character is always to make terms with the two threats, the outer and the inner. The story itself has two characteristic forms: that of the initiation, in which the youth discovers the nature of the world and, sometimes, the saving reaction toward it; and that of the test, in which the man who thinks he knows the secret is set in a crucial situation. The title of one of Hemingway's collections of stories is *Winner Take Nothing*, a perfect title for stories about a world which, as the hero puts it in *A Farewell to Arms*, always "breaks" you. In such a situation what can the "winner" win? Only himself. The characteristic Hemingway hero is not a squealer, weeper, welcher, compromiser, or coward, and in the face of the inevitable defeat, he realizes that the stance a man may take, the stoic endurance, the stiff upper lip, may mean a kind of winning, after all. If the hero is to be defeated, it is to be upon his own terms, and on those terms, even in defeat, he maintains some definition, formulated or unformulated, of how a man should behave, some ideal of the self, some loyalty to a code. This conception of honor, to use the old word, is what distinguishes the Hemingway hero from men who merely follow their natural impulses and random desires, and who are, by consequence, "messy."

So we have the old bull-fighter in the story "The Undefeated" who, incompetently and in spite of the jeers of the crowd, continues until the bull is dead and he himself is mortally wounded. And in "The Short Happy Life of Francis Macomber," the rich young sportsman who, though he has funked it and bolted before a wounded lion, at last learns what the code of the hunter demands—that he go into the bush after an animal he has wounded. And Brett, the heroine of *The Sun Also Rises*, who, after giving up her destructive love affair with the young bull-fighter Romero, says to Jake: "I'm not going to be one of those bitches that ruins children . . . I'm not going to be that way. I feel rather good, you know. I feel rather set up."

It is, in other words, the discipline, the code, that gives man his full humanity. The discipline is a way of giving order and meaning to the confusion of the world; and so the discipline of the soldier, the form of the athlete, the gameness of the sportsman, the technique of the artist, achieve a moral significance. Here we see how Hemingway's concern with war and sport merges with his concern for literary style. If a writer can get the kind of style at which Hemingway, in *The Green Hills of Africa*, professes to aim, then "nothing else matters." Such a style is, ultimately, a moral achievement, and to get it is "more important than anything else he [a writer] can do."

We may put this conception in an even broader context, by seeing it as a response to two ideas current in modern times. The first is the naturalistic view of life, the scientific view of the universe as, to use Bertrand Russell's phrase, "secular hurryings through space," the sense of the world as "God-abandoned." At one time the order in the universe had been taken as a manifestation of Divine Intelligence, but Hemingway, in "A Natural History of the Dead," considers that argument as quoted from the traveler Mungo Park, who, naked and starving in an African desert, observed a beautiful moss flower and meditated:

Can the Being who planted, watered, and brought to perfection, in this obscure part of the world, a thing which appears of so small importance, look with unconcern upon the situation and suffering of creatures formed after his own image? Surely not.

But Hemingway continues:

With a disposition to wonder and adore in like manner, as Bishop Stanley [the author of *A Familiar History of Birds*] says, can any branch of Natural History be studied without increasing that faith, love and hope which we also, every one of us, need in our journey through the wilderness of life? Let us therefore see what inspiration we may derive from the dead.

Then Hemingway presents the picture of a modern battlefield, where the decaying bodies afford a perfect example of the natural order of chemistry—but scarcely an argument for an order of faith, hope, and love. If nature can be, at times, beautiful and charming, and seem to represent a promise of meaning for the universe, it can also be blindly destructive or blankly meaningless. Nature, as Herman Melville puts it in a poem, is "no man's ally." It is ambivalent, double-faced, deceptive, or empty. Nature in *A Farewell to Arms* is, as we shall see, a back upon himself. (See the discussion of the "cathedral" of "nature" in *The Red Badge of Courage*, pp. 1643–44.)

The second idea, which had special impact just after the First World War, is that man, thrown back upon himself, has ended with a bankrupt civilization, and that history, instead of exhibiting a meaningful progress, has wound up in a great blood bath. Over and over again in Hemingway's work, the monuments of the past are objects of contempt—the "two gross of broken statues" and the "few thousand battered books" of Ezra Pound's poem *Hugh Selwyn Mauberley*. The words that stand for traditional values, such as "sacred," "glorious," and "sacrifice," are regarded as obscene, as in the famous passage in *A Farewell to Arms*. (See p. 2258.) And the Hemingway hero is characteristically without a past he considers important and, we should add, without a future.

In the face of a world meaningless in either Divine or human terms, man is alone. The story "A Clean, Well-Lighted Place" can be considered as, perhaps, a central statement of this situation that underlies Hemingway's world of violent action. The story is simple and brief. Two waiters, one old and one young, in a clean little Spanish café, are speaking of an old man who sits alone, every night, until closing time. When the first waiter remarks that the old man has, just the past week, tried to commit suicide, the second and older waiter asks why. The

old man, the first waiter says, had been in despair—but despair, as emerges on further questioning, about "nothing." So the old waiter demands how it is known that the old man had been in despair about nothing. "He has plenty of money," the young waiter says.[1]

The nature of this despair beyond plenty of money—or beyond all the gifts of the world—becomes clearer at the end of the story when the old waiter, too, is left alone, reluctant to leave the haven of the clean, well-lighted place, still carrying on the conversation but now with himself:

What did he [the old waiter] fear? It was not fear or dread. It was a nothing that he knew too well. It was a nothing and a man was nothing too. It was only that and light was all it needed and a certain cleanness and order. Some lived in it and never felt it but he knew it all was nada y pues nada y nada y pues nada.[2] Our nada who art in nada, nada be thy name thy kingdom nada thy will be nada in nada as it is in nada. Give us this nada our daily nada and nada us our nada as we nada our nadas and nada us not into nada but deliver us from nada; pues nada. Hail nothing full of nothing, nothing is with thee. He smiled and stood before a bar with a shining steam pressure coffee machine.
   "What's yous?" asked the barman.
   "Nada."

At last the old waiter is ready to leave the clean, well-lighted place, even though knowing that he will lie awake until daylight. After all, he comforts himself, "it is probably only in-

---

[1] John V. Hagopian has argued that this speech has to be assigned to the *old* waiter. For a discussion as to whether the earlier printings of the story confuse the assignment of the speeches—Scribner's in its recent printings of the story has adopted Hagopian's assignments—see "Tidying Up Hemingway's 'Clean, Well-Lighted Place,'" *Studies in Short Fiction* (Winter, 1964). But see also a vigorous rebuttal by Charles E. May, "Is Hemingway's 'Well-Lighted Place' Really Clean Now?" *Studies in Short Fiction* (Spring, 1971).

[2] Spanish for "nothing and then nothing and nothing and then nothing." This is followed by a parody of the Lord's Prayer, which indicates the nature of the ultimate question the Hemingway hero faces.

somnia." And adds to himself: "Many must have it."

The old waiter is a brother under the skin to the young and dashing Frederick Henry of *A Farewell to Arms* and other heroes—and to Hemingway himself.

In the face of the world without meaning, the first impulse is to ask what certainty, if any, is available to man. Even in the early stories of *In Our Time* this question finds an answer implied in the scrupulous attention to sensation, the most obvious data of consciousness, which underlie and undercut all the big words and big ideas that Hemingway had repudiated. For instance, we have Nick, in the "Big Two-Hearted River," who has been wading in a trout stream: "Nick climbed out onto the meadow and stood, water running down his trousers and out of his shoes, his shoes squelchy. He went over and sat on the logs. He did not want to rush his sensations any." The careful relish of sensation—that is what counts. Over and over again, we find an idea, such as that of happiness, that is traditionally connected with a complicated state of being, associated with notions of virtue, achievement, and so on, equated here with a set of merely agreeable sensations: as though the sensations offer the nearest thing to "happiness" available to man.

The careful relishing of the world of the senses comes to a climax in drink and sex. Drink is the "giant-killer," the weapon against man's awareness of *nada*. And so is sex, and the typical Hemingway hero is a man of Monel-metal stomach and Homeric prowess in the arts of love. And the typical situation is love, with some drinking, against the background of *nada*—of civilization gone to pot, of war and death. But it is important to observe here that the cult of sensation—even at the level of drinking and mere sexuality—is a self-conscious act, not a random gratification of appetite or impulse. We see this quite clearly in *The Sun Also Rises*, in the contrast between Cohn, who is the random dabbler in the world of sensation, and the initiates like Brett and Jake, who are aware of *nada*, and whose dissipations, therefore, have a philosophical overtone.

The cult of sensation may pass over into the cult of true love—and the word "cult" is appropriate here, for in both the attention to sensation and the experience of true love, the quest is for certitude, and in the second for a certitude as full and profound as that offered by religion. No matter how full and profound the certitude offered by true love, love is still presented in terms of the cult of sensation (and *A Farewell to Arms* is, in one aspect, a study of the transition from the cult of sensation to that of love). In all the love stories, it is the moment of sensation that is emphasized, not the massiveness of experience; and the love story is without a past or future, and outside of society, with the lovers alone against the world, enacting their drama against the background, as we have said, of *nada*.

But what is the significance of violence in the Hemingway world? It embodies, of course, the great threat of *nada*, of physical death. But in another dimension, it also involves the threat of *nada* as spiritual death, for if the hero cannot summon up courage and discipline to face the threat of physical death, he will die the death of the spirit. If the characters of the Hemingway world appear tough and insensitive, the hero recognizes his obligation to the code, to the demands of the spirit; his sensitivity is to honor, and not only his own, for he recognizes the code of honor in others and responds to it. Just as there is a margin of victory in the defeat suffered by the Hemingway character, so there is a margin of sensitivity in their brutal and insensitive world—the streak of poetry or pathos in "The Pursuit Race," "The Killers," or "My Old Man." The contrast between the apparent toughness, in the face of the threat of *nada* or in the minimal statement of a felt pity, is summed up in an old cartoon in the *New Yorker* showing a brawny, muscle-knotted arm and a hairy hand that clutches a rose.

Hemingway's celebrated style is based, too, on the same notion of the "marginal" that drove him back to seek in sensation the root certitude of life. The famous key statement on this point appears in *A Farewell to Arms*, when Frederick, the hero, is filled with nausea at the big words used to justify the violence and meaninglessness of the war:

> I was always embarrassed by the words sacred, glorious, and sacrifice and the expression in vain. We had heard them sometimes standing in the rain almost out of earshot, so that only the shouted words came through, and had read them, on proclamations that were slapped up by billposters over other proclamations, now for a long time, and I had seen nothing sacred, and the things that were glorious had no glory and the sacrifices were like the stockyards in Chicago if nothing was done with the meat except to bury it. There were many words that you could not stand to hear and finally only the names of places had dignity . . . abstract words such as glory, honor, courage, or hallow were obscene beside the concrete names of villages, the numbers of roads, the names of rivers, the numbers of regiments and the dates.

The big abstract words stand for a civilization going to pot in the war, for all the sanctions and justifications summoned up to justify the butcheries, for the big lie of the past. By returning to the "concrete names" of things, as by returning to sensation as the root of knowledge, Hemingway sought to be able to write a "true sentence." The name of a thing—the noun—is at the base of Hemingway's style, and it is strange to discover that in a writer whose specialty is the rendering of action, the verb,[3] the dynamic part of speech, is minimal, and that often, as Harry Levin points out in an important essay "The Style of Ernest Hemingway," we find verbs converted into verbal nouns: "Instead of writing 'they fought' or 'we did not feel,' Hemingway writes 'there was fighting' and 'there was not the feeling of a storm coming.'" Hemingway could, as Levin says, "get along on the so-called 'operators' of Basic English, the sixteen monosyllabic verbs that stem from movements of the body."

Aside from this reliance on the noun, with

the repudiation of the adjective and the discriminations possible by a range of verbs and by inflections, the simplification of syntax is another characteristic, and here, again, the impulse underlying the style is the need to return to the root of knowledge—the simple sensation or perception embodied in a declarative sentence. So if we conceive of experience as basically a sequence, style becomes a series of simple declarative sentences, or a linking together of such sentences to make a compound.

Such sequential compounds are indeed the simplest order of syntactical structure, but Hemingway is capable of developing from it very elaborate and expressive rhythmical structures. Or sometimes, from the base of an ordinary complex (though not *too* complex) sentence, Hemingway will erect a rhythmic structure developed from a sequence. For example, in the story "Now I Lay Me," the insomniac Nick, now a soldier, after trying to put himself to sleep by imagining that he is fishing over all the trout streams he has ever known, will try to pray for all the people he has ever known:

> That took up a great amount of time, for if you try to remember all the people you have ever known, going back to the earliest thing you remember—which was, with me, the attic of the house where I was born and my mother's and father's wedding-cake in a tin box hanging from one of the rafters, and, in the attic, jars of snakes and other specimens that my father had collected as a boy and preserved in alcohol so the backs of some of the snakes and specimens were exposed and had turned white—if you thought back that far, you remembered a great many people.

Here it is, we see, the rhythmic structure that really holds the sentence together; the syntactical structure gets lost in the sequence, and the sentence ends with a desperate effort to put things back in order; and this, we observe, is in itself an image of the desperate effort of the insomniac mind to affirm control over itself.

Even with such elaborations, the simple declarative sentence remains basic for Hemingway;

---

[3] See the parallel situation in the verblessness of Imagist poetry: p. 2055.

and if the elements of experience itself are not given a structure of emphasis and subordination, then the style has little use for conjunctions other than the simple *and*—and certainly little use for subordinating conjunctions establishing complex relationships. So the style itself, in tending to discard discrimination among elements, expresses the rejection of civilization and history, with the complex intellectual structures that have turned out to be "lies." This is not to say that Hemingway does not express ideas, and sometimes very complex ones, but he avoids expressing them analytically; he expresses them tangentially, elliptically, metaphorically, or reduced to some simple root form in image or drama, with a syntax fractured or flowing. That is, an idea must emerge in the texture of experience, as a function of the concrete.

We have said that the typical Hemingway hero is without a past. That is not quite true. In the stories of *In Our Time* we find, as Philip Young has demonstrated, a continuing narrative about the growing up of Nick Adams. Each story exhibits him, from early boyhood onward, in the process of being exposed to one of the shocks of evil or despair that life holds. But the book has a very significant feature in brief interchapters, often not more than a paragraph, that give vivid snapshots of shocking scenes of violence, usually from the First World War. Ordinarily these scenes have no reference to Nick except insofar as we sense that Nick, grown up and now a soldier, has witnessed them. But one scene does specifically and crucially involve Nick. Here, in a town just taken, Nick sits propped against a wall, with a spinal wound, both legs sticking out unnaturally. A friend named Rinaldi—that is all we know of him—lies face down by the wall. To continue:

Up the street were other dead. Things were getting forward in the town. It was getting well. Stretcher bearers would be along any time now. Nick turned his head carefully and looked at Rinaldi. "Senta, Rinaldi, Senta. You and me, we've made a separate peace." Rinaldi lay still in the sun breathing with difficulty. "Not patriots." Nick turned his

head carefully away smiling sweatily. Rinaldi was a disappointing audience.[4]

So with this scene we have Nick Adams brought up to the point where he has completed his initiation. With his wound, he is ready to step outside of society and the obligations of society: he is no "patriot." In his "separate peace," he is to make his terms with life, develop his private code. Thus with Nick, at least, we do have a character with a past—the past that leads to the philosophy of total individualism and the repudiation of the past.

The story of Nick is a retelling of the story of Hemingway's own life as he interpreted it, culminating in the wound and the separate peace. It was the story he continued to tell, over and over again, the story of a literal and a psychic wound; the story of fear of death and of impotence and of meaninglessness and that of the conquest of fear. Among all the obsessive retellings, *A Farewell to Arms* is the most obviously autobiographical version and, at the same time, the version that most fully transcends the personal obsession and achieves a general reference of meaning.[5]

---

[4] We observe here three elements that enter *A Farewell to Arms*: the wound, the "separate peace," and the name Rinaldi for the friend. And, of course, the special ironic tone: the attack goes forward well, but Rinaldi is propped against the wall; and Nick has been wounded in the spine.

[5] Hemingway incorporated into *A Farewell to Arms* two quite different sets of events and people. The first set belong to his war years in Italy, including his wound, the nurse, the doctor, and the priest, and, of course, a massive body of feeling provoked by the experiences of that period. The second set belong to the period of the actual writing, a decade later, including a painful accident, religious confusion, Pauline's difficult childbirth, and, no doubt, Hemingway's deep ambivalence about family life and children, and perhaps about women, a bitter heritage from the household at Oak Park, Illinois.

It can be surmised that Hemingway's need, and perhaps even intention, in writing the novel was—by conjoining these two crucial periods in his life—to capture some harmony and some felt continuity in his own experience, and in himself. If this is true, Hemingway was similar to Henry James, who, on occasion, sought to renew himself by reviewing himself. (See pp. 1393, 1398, and 1400.)

At first glance A *Farewell to Arms* seems to be the simplest kind of novel: a straightforward narrative, told in the first person, of the hero's adventures, little more than a sequence of events without much differentiation in shading, a mere chronicle. In fact, Hemingway sometimes seems to insist on the impression of the mere chronicle, especially in Book 1, where the general atmosphere of the novel is being established. For instance, in the opening sentence: "In the late summer of that year we lived in a house in a village that looked across the river and the plain to the mountains." What year?— we do not know. Nor what village, river, or even country. The next chapter begins: "The next year there were many victories." In this unspecified place and at this unspecified time, the apparently aimless, undifferentiated sequence of events proceeds, indifferent to victory or defeat.

Later, when the place, time, and war are identified, we find the same attitude, the sense of events of long ago and far away, without immediate relevance. For instance, there is the British major (Chap. 21), who regards the war with perfect detachment and equanimity, even as he says that everybody is "cooked" but that the "last country to realize they were cooked would win the war"—a victory meaningless because they, the victors, would, of course, be cooked too. Or take the scene (Chap. 35) when Frederick and Count Greffi discuss the war over a billiard game: now Henry has withdrawn from history and has no further interest in how things go, and the war for him, as for the count because of his age, has simply ceased to exist except as a tale. When we turn to Frederick's personal story, the method of chronicle, of mere sequence, still seems to prevail, the personal chronicle set against the general chronicle of the war. But in regard to the personal story, this method only "seems" to prevail, and the simplicity and apparent naiveté of the chronicle are in contrast to the subtlety of the development of the internal logic of the story.

The first factor in the contrast between the apparent naiveté of the chronicle and the subtlety of the development of the inner logic is the relation of the narrator-Frederick to the actor-Frederick. The novel is, after all, a first-person narrative, but not one simple and objective; it is what we may call a retrospective evaluation of the experience of the actor-Frederick which has ended in the creation of a new self, the narrator-Frederick, regenerated and instructed in the nature of the world and therefore able to tell the story. Though in the course of the novel we are mainly acquainted with the naive, uninstructed actor Frederick, and learn about him through the naive chronicle, the author has carefully planted indications of the relation between the naive actor-Frederick and the instructed narrator-Frederick.

The character of the priest serves as the main "indicator," and in relation to the priest, to whom we shall soon return, we find the specific statement (Chap. 3) that defines the fundamental drama between the actor and the narrator: "He [the priest] had always known what I did not know and what, when I learned it, I was always able to forget. But I did not know that *then*, although I learned it *later* [italics ours]." In A *Farewell to Arms* the drama of the "learning" that the hero must undergo is more specifically defined and made more central than in *The Sun Also Rises*, but the process of learning is also what gives form to the earlier book, in which Jake Barnes does state very precisely the nature of the "learning" that must be undergone in order to live in the world: "I did not care what it [the world] was all about. All I wanted to know was how to live in it. Maybe if you found out how to live in it, you learned from that what it was all about."[6]

The irony of the contrast between actor-Frederick and narrator-Frederick provides a constant resonance in A *Farewell to Arms*, but

---

[6] This is, in a nut shell, a perfect statement of the philosophy of pragmatism of William James—that is, that meaning is essentially derived from action. (See pp. 1528–36.) One may entertain the notion that even if Hemingway had probably not read James, Gertrude Stein, who had been one of James's more brilliant pupils, may well have instructed Hemingway—who was one of her most brilliant pupils.

what the actor actually learns constitutes the theme of the novel and interprets the apparently naive drift of the personal chronicle. Insofar as the personal chronicle is exhibited as "aimed" rather than aimless, it provides another irony in its contrast with the general chronicle which gives the "meaningless" historical and social backdrop for the individual story.

The personal story, as "aimed," proceeds by logical stages of thematic development, each stage indicated by one of the five "books" into which the novel is divided. Hemingway does not affix labels to the books, but their nature is clear and we may label them: (1) definition of the problem: out of the wound comes the possibility of "learning" the "truth"; (2) birth of love: but the lovers still in the world; (3) baptism of the hero: the repudiation of the world; (4) flight of the lovers from the world: human love promises entrance into the "Abruzzi"—the country of natural and spiritual harmony; (5) the "False Abruzzi": the hero learns the final lesson.

To understand properly the implications of the structure by books, we must see this in relation to another structural element in the novel, that of the pattern—or we may say "deployment"—of the characters. Frederick and Catherine are, of course, central in the ordinary sense of plot, but thematically the priest and Rinaldi loom large, for they are the fundamental indicators of the meaning of Frederick's relation to Catherine.[7] Furthermore, we cannot understand the thematic "roles" of the priest and Rinaldi if we do not take them in the special *setting* provided in the early chapters—and this fact indicates the resonance of implication, and the technical virtuosity, of the novel.

The most obvious setting in *A Farewell to Arms* is physical nature, and in the first three chapters the natural world receives significant emphasis. The beauty of the natural world is the backdrop for the filthy business of war. This contrast eventuates in two key images, with both literal and metaphorical significance. The first (Chap. 2) is that of the redemptive snow falling on the battle-scarred landscape—a contrast emphasized by the "paths in the snow going back to the latrines behind the trenches," the mark of man's filth. The second (Chap. 3) appears when, after his return from his leave, Frederick realizes, in some deep way (indicating his desire for a life of spiritual meaning), that he had wanted to go to the Abruzzi, the home province of the priest, to which he had been invited. He says: "I had gone to no such place where the roads were frozen and hard as iron, where it was clear cold and dry and the snow was dry and powdery and hare-tracks in the snow and the peasants took off their hats and called you Lord and there was good hunting."

Thus far it would seem that nature appears as literal beauty, literal blessedness, which develops into a metaphor of spiritual fulfillment. But even in the second paragraph of the novel, we find hints of the doubleness of nature.[8] Beyond the beautiful plain, the hero could see at night flashes of artillery, but in the dark "it was like summer lightning"—in other words, the mark of the filth of man seemed to merge into the "natural" lightning. And when, down in the rich valley, the artillery is drawn past, the green branches and vines that camouflage the guns and tractors not only imply a contrast but a merging.

With this much of the setting of nature, we can grasp something of the roles of Rinaldi and the priest. Rinaldi is, shall we say, the poet, even the priest, of nature—gay, witty, charming, devoted to natural pleasure but fastidious, warm, and sympathetic. It is, significantly, he who introduces Frederick to Catherine, the "priest of nature" who presides over the "natural" marriage rites of the couple who are young,

---

[7] It can be argued that Frederick is the main character, that Catherine is significant only in relation to him, is not characterized in any full sense, and is little more than a thematic indicator like the priest or Rinaldi; that it is Frederick's experience that we follow, his growth of awareness, and that Catherine is a vessel of meaning rather than a person. See later in this essay.

[8] In this connection see the discussion above of the story "A Natural History of the Dead," which specifically treats the idea of the doubleness of nature.

beautiful, and devoted. He is, too, a kind of Mercutio standing outside the wall of the garden where Romeo and Juliet meet, with his melange of "natural" poetry and bawdy jokes.

The priest, too, is concerned with love, but what he offers, in contrast to the "profane love" —to use the old theological phrase—is "sacred love." The roles of the priest and Rinaldi come quite clear in the balanced scenes of their visits to the wounded Frederick in the hospital. Both Rinaldi and the priest talk of love. Rinaldi says: "With your priest and your English girl, and really you are just like me underneath." That is, Rinaldi says that Frederick is, after all, only a creature of nature, for whom only "natural" pleasure has significance: "I tell you something about your good women. Your goddesses. There is only one difference between taking a girl who has always been good and a woman. With a girl it is painful. That's all I know." The word "know" here is important: what can be "known" is only the natural, and everything else is illusion, self-deception, or merely hope. And the question of what can be "known" is, we remember, the basis of Hemingway's philosophy as it is of his style.

We must notice that even if Rinaldi is the opposite of the priest in his doctrine, he is, up to this point, sympathetic with him. As he says to Frederick: "It isn't me that makes fun of him. It is the captain. I like him. If you must have a priest have that priest." In other words, Rinaldi understands the need that makes people of fiber less logical than his seek out values beyond mere nature and also recognizes the natural values in the priest. With this we have an important distinction between Rinaldi on one hand and the captain who baits the priest on the other. Though Rinaldi is the spokesman for nature, he still feels that the *merely* natural life is squalid and meaningless; it must be redeemed by awareness, wit, poetry, and discipline. His professional discipline, his pride in being a "lovely surgeon," is a redemptive fact that sets him off from those men who are *merely* natural, who drift ignorantly through life and do not see the tragic emptiness with which the "aware" man must deal. On the same basis, Rinaldi

finds his sympathy with the priest, who "sees through" the natural world and who lives by a rigorous discipline. But there remains an important distinction: for the priest the discipline is an expression of man's love of God and is therefore justified by the belief in God; for Rinaldi the discipline is self-justifying.

Here, with Rinaldi and the priest, we find, in the deployment of characters, the life-options that the young Frederick must confront. When we first see him individualized (Chap. 2), he is sitting in the window of the bawdy house with a friend (one of the officers of the mess), while the priest passes in the falling snow[9] and smiles up at them. In other words, Frederick is here sunk into the aimless world of those who "do not see through it"; but we learn, a page later, that he has some sort of secret rapport with the priest, for while the officers of the mess bait the priest, Frederick and he exchange smiles "across the candle light." This scene, then, develops almost schematically, as in an old morality play, into a struggle for Frederick's soul between the forces of Good and those of Evil, between the priest and the officers of the mess. Here, the officers of the mess are urging Frederick to go for his leave to "centres of culture and civilization," and have "beautiful young girls," and the priest urges him to go to the Abruzzi, where there is "good hunting" in a cold, clean, high country. Even as the priest utters the invitation,

---

[9] The snow in this scene is very important. The most obvious reading of the scene is that Frederick Henry in the bawdy house gives an image of human filth in contrast with the image of the priest in the snow, an image of purity at both the natural and the supernatural level. To support this view, at the end of the preceding paragraph, we find the contrast between the natural purity of the snow and the human filth of the latrines. At this point the contrast is between the human filth and the purity of nature; we have not yet reached the theme of the "doubleness" of nature. Structurally, we must set this scene of the priest in the snow (that fuses supernatural and natural purity) against the end of the novel where Frederick has thought to find "purity"— that is, total meaningfulness—in Switzerland as the "true Abruzzi" (the Abruzzi being the homeland of the priest where life is meaningful), but finds only the "false Abruzzi," where there is no redemption in nature, after all.

the scene ends: " 'Come on,' said the captain. 'We go whore-house before it shuts.' "

The affair between Frederick and Catherine begins, of course, at the natural level—as indicated by the reason she gives for slapping him. Then she, who has lost her fiancé in the war, shifts the level of the relationship: after allowing Frederick to kiss her, she says, as though addressing a true lover, "You will be good to me, won't you?" But the affair, even for her, is still meaningless: Frederick is not real, only a shadowy surrogate for the "very nice boy" who had been going to marry her but who is now dead. She has been merely enacting a charade, a futile attempt to rise above the most primitive natural level, and it is important to realize, in relation to the structure and meaning of the novel, that in this attempt we have a preliminary indication of the basic theme of the work. As for Frederick, he, for the moment, desires nothing more than animal satisfaction, as is indicated by Rinaldi's remark when he sees Frederick enter their room that night: "You have the pleasant air of a dog in heat."

The main body of *A Farewell to Arms* is the account of how, from these beginnings, Frederick seeks meaning in the experience of love; and by "meaning" here we must understand the kind of life justification the priest exhibits. This is clearly suggested by the role of the priest and by Frederick's rapport with him, as later by the conversation with the priest at the visit to the hospital when Frederick admits that though he does not "love God," he is "afraid of him in the night sometimes." In fact, from the very beginning of the novel, there is an aura of religion about the love affair. For instance, when Frederick tells Catherine good-by before going on the mission on which he is wounded, she gives him a Saint Anthony to wear—even though they are not Catholic; and after the wound, in Book 2, which is concerned with the "Birth of Love," she says to him, "You're my religion." The theme is reemphasized, after Frederick's flight from the army, when old Count Greffi says to him that "love is a religious feeling."

To sum up, the lovers are attempting to find in love a substitute for the spiritual certainties of religion. In this attempt we see repeated one of the impulses that appears in both the life and literature of the nineteenth century, and even earlier: in the Age of Faith, human love had been taken to be an image of Divine love, but with the decline of faith, it was taken more and more as a substitute for religious certainties—the most famous literary example of this attitude being in Matthew Arnold's poem "Dover Beach":

Ah, love, let us be true
To one another! for the world, which seems
To lie about us like a land of dreams,
So various, so beautiful, so new,
Hath really neither joy, nor love, nor light,
Nor certitude, nor peace, nor help for pain;
And we are here as on a darkling plain
Swept with confused alarms of struggle and
    flight,
Where ignorant armies clash by night.

In Arnold's poem the lovers find their love the only refuge from the aimless violence of the world, but if in the poem the "ignorant armies" that "clash by night" are merely metaphorical, they are, in the novel, all too literal before they are metaphorical; and a developing theme is the growing alienation of the lovers from, first, the literal world of war, and second, by extension, from society in all its institutions. The war, in fact, is the image of the bankruptcy of Western civilization that now tries to justify the bloody debacle by slogans, big words, and outworn ideas, as we have seen in the famous passage (Chap. 24) already quoted.

This passage has importance—a structural importance, for one thing—far greater than that of a commentary on the groundings of Hemingway's philosophy and style. Coming at almost the mathematical center of the novel, before the Battle of Caporetto, it provides the emotional center of gravity of the novel. All the elements around this passage support it, document it, or flow into it. Frederick has now recovered from his wound and rejoined his command to find that by this time many people have, in the words of the priest, "realized the war"—its aimlessness and horror—and do not "believe in victory any more." They do not, as Frederick says, believe in defeat either and have simply come to accept meaninglessness. Rinaldi, too, now appears in a new light. He has taken refuge in his work and has become, he says, a "lovely surgeon"; his discipline is all he can now cling to in the general debacle. But bitterness has replaced wit and sympathy (he now baits the priest, too), and now on him, who had been, like Mercutio, the witty spokesman for the joy and poetry of nature, nature has played a dirty trick: he is treating himself for syphilis.

The increasing bitterness summarized in Frederick's attitude toward the "big words" leads up to the retreat after the defeat at Caporetto, with the confusion of a world gone completely to pot. In this chaos, as an image of the lunacy of the world, there is the lunacy of the battle-police (all "young men" busy "saving their country"), who seize officers from the rout, briefly question them, and then execute them on the spot. Frederick is seized, but jerks free and dives into the swollen Tagliamento River and escapes:

Anger was washed away in the river along with any obligation. Although that ceased when the carabiniere put his hands on my collar. I would like to have had the uniform off although I did not care much about the outward forms. I had taken off the stars, but that was for convenience. It was no point of honor. I was not against them. I was through. I wished them all the luck. There were the good ones, and the brave ones, and the calm ones and the sensible ones, and they deserved it. But it was not my show any more. . . .

Frederick has made, he says, a "separate peace." He has been baptized, as it were, into a new state of being—as Huck Finn is baptized when the steamboat runs his raft down. Frederick is now the individual, alone except for Catherine, in the meaningless violence of the world. He and she are outside history and society, "alone against the others"—though occasionally

they recognize, or are recognized by, other individuals, such as the friendly barman or Count Greffi—by an "elite," the members of a secret club, by those, in other words, who understand the true nature of the human plight. Understanding that plight, the lovers flee from the world of war and meaninglessness to Switzerland—a land of mountains and snow and clear cold, like the Abruzzi of the priest—there to find total meaning in their love for each other. We observe here that the expected child (Catherine is now pregnant) is not welcomed as a meaningful aspect of their love projected into time, but is regarded as nothing more than an interruption of their pleasure in each other.

Book 5 presents, first, the idyllic life in Switzerland, about which Catherine can exclaim, "Don't we have a fine time?" But then comes the caesarean operation with the child dead, and the death of Catherine. Switzerland proves to be the "false Abruzzi"; the dream of meaning beyond nature has come to nothing, or even less, for if love is, as Count Greffi had said, "a religious feeling," it has turned out to be only a "feeling" tied to the necessities of the flesh. This is the "end of the trap," and what happens to Catherine is "just nature giving her hell." There is no exit from the trap of nature except death, and here we find the famous episode, which Frederick recollects, of the ants on the log of a campfire. The ants had run back and forth, some swarming on the cool end until they fell off, and Frederick remembers thinking at the time that it was like the end of the world and a splendid chance to play messiah. But instead, to empty a cup for his whisky, he poured water on the log. This, he thinks, had probably steamed the ants.[10]

Beyond this naturalistic vision, what catharsis —if any—is implicit? We have, to begin with,

---

[10] This may be an echo from a speech in *King Lear*:
    As flies to wanton boys, are we to the gods,
    They kill us for their sport.
Or it may be an echo of a scene in Mark Twain's "The Mysterious Stranger," in which the Stranger tortures the minuscule human-looking creatures of his making. Or it may be, of course, merely what it professes to be—a recollection.

Catherine's words about her impending death: "I'm not a bit afraid. It's just a dirty trick." The catharsis suggested is the oldest, simplest, and most primitive: courage, the assertion of self at the moment of annihilation. This has been earlier stated in the novel (and implied in the body of Hemingway's previous work) in the scene (Chap. 16) when Frederick and Catherine are talking about the meaning of their love. Frederick says that the world can never come between them because she is "too brave." And adds: "Nothing ever happens to the brave." To which she retorts: "They die of course." As, of course, she will.

At the end of the scene, which may be taken as Catherine's instruction to her lover in the nature of heroism, she, playing off the quotation, "The coward dies a thousand deaths, the brave but one," sums up the "code" that it is her role to impart: "The brave dies perhaps two thousand deaths if he's intelligent. He simply doesn't mention them."

Or if he mentions death, the brave man, like Catherine, refers to it merely as a "dirty trick." One of the significant strokes of art in *A Farewell to Arms* is to provide, absorbed into the narrative, the statement that gives background for the dying Catherine's understatement. Then, in turn, the last interchange between Catherine and Frederick gives the background for the last, brief paragraph that Hemingway rewrote over and over to pare it down to the minimum that could, because of that preparation, suggest all.

Another aspect of the preparation lies in the idea, earlier developed, that the lovers have been against all the "others," the inimical world. Here at the end, Frederick again encounters the "others" in the persons of the nurses, who would try to prevent the lovers being together for their last tryst: he again confronts the "others" and again wins against them. But even with his victory against the "others" he has lost against nature and is alone, not together with Catherine, against the world. She is no more than a "statue."

We have already asked what emerges beyond the naturalistic vision, and the question emerges again in relation to Frederick. We have already been told by Frederick that the "night can be a dreadful time for lonely people once their loneliness has started" (Chap. 24). What, we ask, is the difference between the loneliness that he has suffered before and this more terrible loneliness of absolute loss? He has, presumably, learned through Catherine, the "brave" one, the true condition of man in nature and the only way of dealing with it: by the stoic discipline, the "code" that will enable him to walk out into the night rain, alone.

What *A Farewell to Arms* amounts to, then, is the most fully rendered of Hemingway's various stories of the initiation. It is the story of how Frederick Henry comes to see through the sanctions, official comforts, big words, and illusions of history and society, and to emerge as the man alone, able at last to confront his fate in nature. It is the old mythological story of the "birth of the hero."

This hero is a very special one—the modern man in his loneliness in nature.

A Farewell to Arms appeared just before the great stock market crash that ended the Coolidge boom and ushered in the Depression. In a deep sense, the novel summed up better than any other single work, not excluding *The Great Gatsby* and *An American Tragedy*, the special spirit of a period—the disillusionment with the Wilsonian idealism, the genteel tradition, religious orthodoxy, the nationalistic doctrine of Manifest Destiny, the progressive hope of salvation by social reform, and the gospel of the bitch-goddess Success. Hemingway was a strong and often subtle artist and his attitudes were dramatized in such a hypnotically compelling fashion that his very limitations sometimes appeared as virtues; and his appeal went beyond mere artistic power. The Hemingway hero provided a personal model, and what is now sometimes called a "life style," to a generation of Americans, many of whom had scarcely read Hemingway, or anything else. Furthermore, Hemingway's general influence was worldwide —or, rather, he found a way of touching off and bringing to focus certain feelings latent in countries as diverse as Fascist Italy, Communist Russia, and liberal Sweden.

Though, after *A Farewell to Arms*, Hemingway's international reputation continued to grow, the Depression, as we have mentioned, occasioned a sharp reassessment, sometimes intelligent and sometimes stupid, of his work and its underlying assumptions. At that historical moment, the immediate and overriding problem, in the midst of massive human suffering, was to make the economic system function again, with violent conflict among various social theories, with Stalinist communism at one extreme and fascism at the other, as to how this would be done.[11] Naturally, in the context of this emphasis on social action and collectivism of one sort or another, Hemingway's individualism, which amounted to a resignation from history and society, was, as we have said earlier, highly suspect, especially among critics who held or were well-disposed to Marxist doctrine. Even in the novel *To Have and Have Not* (1937), which was proclaimed by some critics as showing the birth of a social conscience in Hemingway, the hero turns out to be nothing more than a criminal adventurer who happens to exhibit the characteristic virtues applauded by Hemingway. When he lies in his launch dying of gunshot wounds, he utters a speech that was supposed to embody a serious social message: "One man alone ain't got. No man alone now. No matter how a man alone ain't got no bloody . . . chance." But the only practical action the death speech would seem to suggest would be the need to organize a Smuggler's Union, perhaps in the then-rising C.I.O. *To Have and Have Not* may have an element

of protest against the social order, but, as the Russian critic Nemerovskaya puts it, the protest "discloses no perspective, remains sterile and merely aggravates the pessimistic character of his work." More generally it may be said that, though from the beginning, war, revolution, and social disorder had provided the material of Hemingway's fiction, he had, out of a psychological need, drawn away from the significance of the material, to present only the personal drama and personal gesture. As the Russian Kashkeen declares, Hemingway's heroes remain "lonely sportsmen."

It would seem that Kashkeen's diagnosis is correct, but when, in 1940, *For Whom the Bell Tolls* appeared, it was generally said that now Hemingway had *really* developed a social conscience and was dedicating his genius to the fight against fascism. It was true, of course, that Hemingway, as a correspondent in Spain during the civil war, was anti-Fascist, but it is also true that his new hero Robert Jordan, like the hero of *To Have and Have Not*, is the typical old-style individualist long since baptized in the waters of the Tagliamento River, that the particular war he is engaged in is a highly personal guerrilla action, and that the love story is little changed from that of *A Farewell to Arms*, except for the name of the lady and the setting, which is now outdoors, with the characteristic couch of bliss now a sleeping bag and not a hospital bed.

The most effective and memorable things in the novel are the things that had always evoked Hemingway's special talent, the poetry of the natural world, the sense of physical action, the air of heroic decision. Robert Jordan is as much outside society as Frederick Henry ever was, and one of the most striking sections of narrative comes when he enters briefly the world of "official" war to find the same horror and disillusionment that Frederick had found. After *For Whom the Bell Tolls*, Hemingway apparently abandoned the effort to establish a direct relation between his work and the world of political action and general ideas.

After *For Whom the Bell Tolls*, three works of fiction by Hemingway appeared: *Across the*

---

[11] Communism was a highly organized force working both officially as a political party and propaganda agency and underground as an influence, sometimes in connection with what was called a Popular Front. The effect, direct or indirect, of communism on literature was enormous, on both writers and publishers. In the United States fascism was not an officially organized force, though there were such groups as the German Bund and the home-grown Silver Shirts and America-Firsters. In general, fascism operated as a pervasive influence on ordinary right-wing opinion and had little connection with literature.

River and into the Trees (1950), *The Old Man and the Sea* (1952), and *Islands in the Stream* (posthumous, 1970). All return to Hemingway's old concerns. *Across the River and into the Trees* and *Islands in the Stream* have large elements of autobiography even more thinly disguised than usual, and more embarrassing than usual in their self-adulation; and both, in spite of patches of fine narration, are simply bad, the former disastrously so.

The Old Man and the Sea was, however, generally hailed as the crown of the author's career. Faulkner said of it: "Time may show it to be the best single piece of any of us," and Bernard Berenson, the art historian, called it "this short but not small masterpiece." The story made strong men weep, and the author himself came to stand in awe before it, in much the same way as Harriet Beecher Stowe came to stand in awe of *Uncle Tom's Cabin* and Julia Ward Howe of "The Battle Hymn of the Republic"; but Hemingway's youngest son regarded it as sentimental slop. Now, some years later, it appears that the disillusioned son was the most perceptive of the various critics. The work seems little more than an expert but uninspired recapitulation of earlier fiction—with expertise taking the place of fresh perception and stylistic élan, in what one critic has called "a slick fake-biblical style which retains the mannerisms and omits the virtues" of the best stories and the first two novels.

A Moveable Feast (posthumous, 1964), an autobiographical work dealing with the early days in Paris, again has sections of fine narration and atmospheric re-creations of place and time, but it is embarrassingly marred by the need to settle old scores (mostly imaginary) and to embellish the personal legend of the demigod.

The death of Hemingway seemed to mark the end of an era, for he, like T. S. Eliot, had become, over the years, as much a culture-hero as a writer. But the era, like Hemingway the writer, had ended long before he took down the shotgun to perform the act that certain uncharitable commentators took to be the mark of the bankruptcy of the values which he had undertaken to embody.

The decade of the 1960's were to prove even more inhospitable to Hemingway's values than the 1930's. If Hemingway's special brand of individualism seemed anachronistic in the 1930's, in that world of social emphasis, the concept of heroism was, nevertheless, still available; more recently, however, the very concept of heroism had, in some circles, fallen into disrepute, and the antihero, rather than the hero, more commonly dominates literature. Perhaps even more significant is the change in attitude toward sex. In the age of Hemingway, and certainly in his works, sex was treated romantically; this would be just as true of sex-as-debauch as of sex-as-true-love, for in either case there was an aura of significance, quite different from the casualness —sometimes the contemptuous casualness—that is now not uncommon in regard to sex, and is indicated by the diminishing of sexual differences recently fashionable.

We should recognize, however, that the basic criticism of Hemingway is not the result of a mere change in time and fashion. It was clear from the start that Hemingway was incapable of dealing with great tracts of experience. The problem was not that Hemingway had only one basic theme; it may well be argued, in fact, that all *good* writers—and *great* writers, too—have only one basic theme. The problem was that Hemingway did not try to explore very deeply the dramatic and moral implications of his theme. A basic theme may lead to a great variety of interests and effects. For instance, the number and variety of the explorations of heroism in Shakespeare's work are astounding; and to take two writers at a less world-dominating level, Faulkner and Conrad are deeply concerned with heroism, and with them we find examples of very complex relations of motive, act, and occasion that are almost totally lacking in Hemingway.

This fact is associated with the fact that Hemingway, in his self-absorption, was not really interested in character; "we are confronted," as Edmund Wilson put it as far back as 1940, "with the paradox that Hemingway, who possesses so remarkable a mimetic gift in getting the tone of social and national types and in making his people talk appropriately, has not shown any very solid sense of character, or, indeed, any real interest in it." This limitation is most marked in his love stories, for not only are the heroines of most stories and all the novels identical, but they are little more than pin-up girls, ⟨targets for the projection of adolescent fantasy,⟩ and the most obvious characteristic is a lack of character—a total sexual obligingness.[12] To love or to be loved implies an identity of some sort, but the ladies in Hemingway's fiction rather make a point of having no identity: Catherine Barkley, in *A Farewell to Arms*, who says "I'll do anything you want," also says, "There isn't any me."

It has been argued that women of this type do, actually, exist; but, granting this, the fact remains that this is the only type, with the exception of Brett, in *The Sun Also Rises*, and Pilar, in *For Whom the Bell Tolls*, that Hemingway could, or would, create.[13] Waiving the psychological question, we must insist that this fact proposes a severe limitation on the possibility of dramatic development in Hemingway's work. If one of the lovers is both totally obliging and totally nonexistent, there can be no problems of time—which means in effect that we have bypassed the human condition. If the beloved is no more than a lovely dream of unearthly bliss, there can be no story—certainly not in the sense of a continuing development, in time, of a relationship. And this situation is fundamentally associated with Hemingway's repudiation of history, and with his anti-intellectualism: the repudiation, in other words, of any concern with the process by which values emerge in time. There is no place for a Hemingway story to go; it has to end quickly; it has to get outside of the problems of time. With Hemingway, as with Poe, the lover is not in love with the lady, but with death. For the lady must die, be absorbed into death, in order to continue to be loved.[14]

What would happen, really, if at the end of *A Farewell to Arms* mother and child were doing well? Would Frederick go back to America to get a job? Or would he stay in Europe to become an artist or journalist? At least we know how that second story would come out; it would come out the way Hemingway's personal story came out, and that is very different from the end of *A Farewell to Arms*, and very unlike *Romeo and Juliet* to boot.[15]

The Hemingway story—that is, the stories he wrote—are characteristically without past and without future. The story appears as an archetypal moment outside of time, and outside of society. It has only one actor, the "self" of the hero, who, in the vast ⟨solipsistic dream⟩ that is Hemingway's fiction, moves among other figures that, ultimately, are shadows. Allowing for all differences, Hemingway, with his total repudiation of history and society and scientific culture, and his glorification of the self and of personal intuition, is the ultimate in the American dream of self-validating identity. Hemingway was, indeed, a sort of transcendentalist

[12] As we have seen, Hemingway's second wife seems to have won him by a repudiation of identity.

[13] Pilar, according to some critics, is little different from a man in skirts, and this might well be said of Brett.

[14] The similarity on this point between the Hemingway lover and Quentin Compson, of Faulkner's *The Sound and the Fury*, with his incestuous attachment to his sister, is striking and complex. Both Quentin and the Hemingway lover are strange modern exemplars of the tradition of "courtly love" of the Provençal troubadours and of Petrarch and his imitators. The courtly lover is to be debarred from the lady, but, even so, he can indulge his role as the lover—without the threat of responsibility. His love is, ultimately, Manichean Puritanism. See C. S. Lewis, *The Allegory of Love* (1936); Denis de Rougemont, *Love in the Western World* (1957) and his *Love Declared: Essays on the Myths of Love* (1963); Leslie Fiedler, *Love and Death in the American Novel* (1966). To return to Petrarch, the relation between Petrarch and his Laura is similar to that between Frederick and Catherine. It is true that Frederick does get to bed with his love, but she, like Laura, has her real function in leading her lover to "salvation" and is more significant in death than in life—as Petrarch indicates in the two divisions of his great sequence of poems, "In Life" and "In Death."

[15] As a matter of fact, Hemingway, in "A Very Short Story," an early piece about a wounded man and a nurse who are in love, does treat the dwindling away of such a relationship as that between Frederick and Catherine: another kind of "death."

manqué, with the same short-circuited religiosity; his Brook Farm of choice spirits was the floating community of the elite, those who "see through" society and trust their intuition—in bars or bullrings, or more cozily isolated in the lion-country of the African veldt, or on his *Anita*, on the open sea, with an eye out for marlin.[16]

Could Hemingway have known how much of the dream life of America flowed into him?

Hemingway's story of the lonely hero is sometimes fantastically successful. But it succeeds only when the lonely hero partakes of the archetypal—when we can be persuaded that this is the paradigmatic story underlying our experience, when we can be persuaded to dismiss our ordinary concern with the details of individual character, and when we are not invited to use the hero as a peg on which to hang the details of the personality and achievements of the Success-Boy from Oak Park, Illinois.

Indeed, it has long since been noted by various critics that when the personal Hemingway merges with the Hemingway hero something often distasteful and sometimes disastrous occurs. Elements of the bully, the exhibitionist, the braggart, the self-made and self-admiring ignoramus, and a self-nominated demigod fleetingly appear and are paraded as points of virtue. The personal elements in *Death in the Afternoon* and *The Green Hills of Africa* are constantly distracting, but the situation is much worse in fiction, for instance, in *Across the River and into the Trees*. Hemingway achieves his art when he conquers the temptation to indulge his vanity and self-centeredness and when his obsessive theme becomes a personal intensity objectified in a formal rigor.

[16] A fundamental point of contrast between Hemingway and Faulkner is that, unlike Hemingway, Faulkner is basically concerned with man in society. The moral identity of the individual is, of course, a crucial part of the Faulknerian story, as is the question of man's relation to nature, but the overarching story is the history of a society—specifically, the South—and the "doom" involved is the result of a crime (slavery) that violates the human bond, that is, the social ideal. In the stories of individual men the question of moral identity appears in the social context.

The art of Hemingway is essentially a lyric art, not a dramatic art, and depends for success on precision and coherence in structure, on rigorous exclusiveness in its rendered world, and on an intensity and purity of emotional effect. In a strange way, Hemingway's theory of literature is very close to Poe's[17]; both aimed at an intensity of emotional effect based on rigorous selection and arrangement of materials, and the effect both aimed at is, in the end, a sublimation of terror (a terror, as Poe put it, "not of Germany but of the soul"), a sublimation accomplished, in part at least, by the tightness of technical control. Hemingway, unlike Poe, was an accomplished ironist, but his irony is the element in his work operating under the most rigorous limitations[18] so that it may accent, but not impair, the characteristic emotional effect. As another aspect of the emphasis on the purity of emotional effect, we find another parallel; Poe could not conceive of the long poem except as a compendium of short poems, and this is very close to Hemingway's practice—even though his practice did not square with his intentions and ambitions. Hemingway's novels, in the end, tend to split up into units like stories or to feel like expanded stories, the one exception being, perhaps, *A Farewell to Arms*, which, as we have argued, has a highly organized structure. To sum up, the personal and lyric nature of Hemingway's creative impulse has given critics a ground for a revision of his former great reputation. But within that range there is a characteristic power possible.

There is a sort of natural history of literary reputations. Inevitably, there is a reassessment; the reassessment is, in the first phase, almost inevitably a scaling down—there is always a

[17] See pp. 426–27. There is also a parallel not in theory, but in practice, and in emotional bias, between Hemingway and Kipling and Stephen Crane.

[18] Only in *For Whom the Bell Tolls* is there what might be called a dramatic irony, an irony in which the theme itself is called into question, and here only because it is involved in the contrast between the Hemingway hero with his individualism and the social and political aspect of the material.

killing off of the fathers. If a reputation has come early, with almost the authority of a revelation, as was the case with Hemingway, the reassessment is usually more immediate and drastic than is ordinary. But it is hard to believe that, given the turn of time, we will not see a rediscovery of Hemingway. He is, after all, a master narrator. What if his range of concern is limited? The question is, how much abiding validity resides within that limitation. It is hard to believe that the concern for honor, no matter what fashionable changes of name for it there may be, or what changes in the characteristic arena of its testing, is dead. Within the limits of Hemingway's concern, the coherence of dramatization and the intensity of effect are remarkable; and that intensity will evoke some answering resonance as long as the terror which is "not of Germany but of the soul" remains a part of human experience.

Furthermore, as a crucial part of that coherence of dramatization, there remains Hemingway's style. It is true that, as the critic Dwight Macdonald says, the style was "a kind of inspired baby talk when he was going good," but when "he was not going good, it was just baby talk." But not infrequently in his best years, Hemingway was "inspired," and his "baby talk" was deeply rooted in the historical moment from which it sprang, as was the "baby talk" of Gertrude Stein, Ezra Pound, James Joyce, and T. S. Eliot. Hemingway, too, was a purifier of the language of the tribe. And, in any case, when baby talk is inspired, it is often the language of saints, sages, and poets.

BIOGRAPHICAL CHART

1899   Born, July 21, in Oak Park, Illinois
1917   Works in Kansas City as local reporter for the *Star*
1918   Volunteers for military service in Europe as a member of the ambulance corps in the Italian army; is seriously wounded and spends three months in hospital; discharged as fit, joins the Italian Infantry, soon promoted to Lieutenant
1919   Returns to America
1920   Works in Toronto on the *Star Weekly*, then in Chicago on the Chicago *Tribune*
1921   Marries Hadley Richardson; travels to Paris, with a letter of introduction to Gertrude Stein
1923   *Three Stories and Ten Poems*
1924   *In Our Time*; first marriage is dissolved
1926   *Torrents of Spring*; marries Pauline Pfeiffer; *The Sun Also Rises* published and achieves immediate success
1927   *Men Without Women*
1928   Father commits suicide
1929   *A Farewell to Arms*
1932   *Death in the Afternoon*
1933   *Winner Take Nothing*; hunting expedition through Africa lasting five months

1935   *Green Hills of Africa*
1936   As war correspondent in the Spanish Civil War, supports the cause of the Spanish Republic
1937   *To Have and Have Not*
1938   *The Fifth Column and the First Forty-Nine Stories*
1940   Acquires the estate of "Finca Vigia" in Cuba; second marriage ends in divorce; *For Whom the Bell Tolls*
1941   Marries Martha Gellhorn
1944   Third marriage ends in divorce; marries Mary Walsh; war correspondent at the French front; cited for bravery
1950   *Across the River and into the Trees*
1952   *The Old Man and the Sea*; commissioned by *Look* magazine, flies to Africa and is involved in two air crashes
1954   Nobel prize for literature
1961   Dies, a suicide, July 2, at Ketchum, Idaho
1964   *A Moveable Feast*
1970   *Islands in the Stream*

FURTHER READINGS

There is no standard edition of Hemingway's works.

John Aldridge, *After the Lost Generation* (1951)

John A. Atkins, *The Art of Ernest Hemingway: His Work and Personality* (1952)
Carlos Baker, *Ernest Hemingway: A Life Story* (1969)

————, *Hemingway: The Writer as Artist* (1952)

————, ed., *Hemingway and His Critics: An International Anthology* (1961)

John Peale Bishop, "Homage to Hemingway," *Collected Essays* (1948), edited by Edmund Wilson

John P. Bury, "Hemingway in Spain," *Contemporary Review* (February, 1959)

Malcolm Cowley, *Exile's Return* (1951)

————, introd., *The Portable Hemingway* (1944)

Charles A. Fenton, *The Apprenticeship of Ernest Hemingway: The Early Years* (1954)

W. M. Frohock, *The Novel of Violence in America, 1920–1950* (1950)

Maxwell Geismar, *Writers in Crisis: The American Novel Between Two Wars* (1942)

John Graham, "Ernest Hemingway: The Meaning of Style," *Modern Fiction Studies* (Winter, 1960–61)

E. M. Halliday, "Hemingway's Ambiguity: Symbolism and Irony," *American Literature* (1950)

Leicester Hemingway, *My Brother, Ernest Hemingway* (1962)

Frederick Hoffman, *The Modern Novel in America, 1900–1950* (1951)

A. E. Hotchner, *Papa Hemingway: A Personal Memoir* (1966)

Ivan Kashkeen, "Ernest Hemingway: Tragedy in Craftsmanship," *International Literature* (1934)

Alfred Kazin, *On Native Grounds* (1942)

Earle Labor, "Crane and Hemingway: Anatomy of Trauma," *Renascence* (Summer, 1959)

Harry Levin, "Observations on the Style of Ernest Hemingway," *Kenyon Review* (Fall, 1951)

Wyndham Lewis, *Men Without Art* (1934)

John K. M. McCaffery, ed., *Ernest Hemingway: The Man and His Work* (1950)

Wright Morris, "The Ability to Function: A Reappraisal of Fitzgerald and Hemingway," *New World Writing* (June, 1958)

Sean O'Faolain, *The Vanishing Hero: Studies of the Hero in the Modern Novel* (1956)

Reynolds Price, "For Ernest Hemingway," in *Things Themselves* (1972)

Isaac Rosenfeld, "A Farewell to Hemingway," *Kenyon Review* (1951)

Lillian Ross, *Portrait of Hemingway* (1961)

Marcelline Hemingway Sanford, *At the Hemingways* (1961)

Mark Spilka, "The Death of Love in *The Sun Also Rises*," *Twelve Original Essays on Great American Novels* (1958), edited by Charles Shapiro

Gertrude Stein, *The Autobiography of Alice B. Toklas* (1933)

Robert Penn Warren, "Ernest Hemingway," *Selected Essays* (1958)

Edmund Wilson, "Hemingway: Bourdon Gauge of Morale," in *The Wound and the Bow* (1941)

Virginia Woolf, "An Essay in Criticism," New York *Herald Tribune* (October 8, 1927)

Philip Young, *Ernest Hemingway* (1952)

————, *Three Bags Full: Essays in American Fiction* (1972)

The Snows of Kilimanjaro (1936)

Kilimanjaro is a snow covered mountain 19,710 feet high, and is said to be the highest mountain in Africa. Its western summit is called the Masai "Ngàje Ngài," the House of God. Close to the western summit there is the dried and frozen carcass of a leopard. No one has explained what the leopard was seeking at that altitude.

"The marvellous thing is that it's painless," he said. "That's how you know when it starts."

"Is it really?"

"Absolutely. I'm awfully sorry about the odor though. That must bother you."

"Don't! Please don't."

"Look at them," he said. "Now is it sight or is it scent that brings them like that?"

The cot the man lay on was in the wide shade of a mimosa trce and as he looked out past the shade onto the glare of the plain there were three of the big birds squatted obscenely, while in the sky a dozen more sailed, making quick-moving shadows as they passed.

"They've been there since the day the truck broke down," he said. "Today's the first time any have lit on the ground. I watched the way they sailed very carefully at first in case I ever wanted to use them in a story. That's funny now."

"I wish you wouldn't," she said.

"I'm only talking," he said. "It's much easier if I talk. But I don't want to bother you."

"You know it doesn't bother me," she said. "It's that I've gotten so very nervous not being able to do anything. I think we might make it as easy as we can until the plane comes."

"Or until the plane doesn't come."

"Please tell me what I can do. There must be something I can do."

"You can take the leg off and that might stop it, though I doubt it. Or you can shoot me. You're a good shot now. I taught you to shoot didn't I?"

"Please don't talk that way. Couldn't I read to you?"

"Read what?"

"Anything in the book bag that we haven't read."

"I can't listen to it," he said. "Talking is the easiest. We quarrel and that makes the time pass."

"I don't quarrel. I never want to quarrel. Let's not quarrel any more. No matter how nervous we get. Maybe they will be back with another truck today. Maybe the plane will come."

"I don't want to move," the man said. "There is no sense in moving now except to make it easier for you."

"That's cowardly."

"Can't you let a man die as comfortably as he can without calling him names? What's the use of slanging me?"

"You're not going to die."

"Don't be silly. I'm dying now. Ask those bastards." He looked over to where the huge, filthy birds sat, their naked heads sunk in the hunched feathers. A fourth planed down, to run quick-legged and then waddle slowly toward the others.

"They are around every camp. You never notice them. You can't die if you don't give up."

"Where did you read that? You're such a bloody fool."

"You might think about some one else."

"For Christ's sake," he said, "That's been my trade."

He lay then and was quiet for a while and looked across the heat shimmer of the plain to the edge of the bush. There were a few Tommies that showed minute and white against the yellow and, far off, he saw a herd of zebra, white against the green of the bush. This was a pleasant camp under big trees against a hill, with good water, and close by, a nearly dry water hole where sand grouse flighted in the mornings.

"Wouldn't you like me to read?" she asked. She was sitting on a canvas chair beside his cot. "There's a breeze coming up."

"No thanks."

"Maybe the truck will come."

"I don't give a damn about the truck."

"I do."

"You give a damn about so many things that I don't."

"Not so many, Harry."

"What about a drink."

"It's supposesd to be bad for you. It said in Black's to avoid all alcohol. You shouldn't drink."

"Molo!" he shouted.

"Yes Bwana."

"Bring whiskey-soda."

"Yes Bwana."

"You shouldn't," she said. "That's what I mean by giving up. It says it's bad for you. I know it's bad for you."

"No," he said. "It's good for me."

So now it was all over, he thought. So now he would never have a chance to finish it. So this was the way it ended in a bickering over a drink. Since the gangrene started in his right leg he had no pain and with the pain the horror had gone and all he felt now was a great tiredness and anger that this was the end of it. For this, that now was coming, he had very little curiosity. For years it had obsessed him; but now it meant nothing in itself. It was strange how easy being tired enough made it.

Now he would never write the things that he had saved to write until he knew enough to write them well. Well, he would not have to fail at trying to write them either. Maybe you could never write them, and that was why you put them off and delayed the starting. Well he would never know, now.

"I wish we'd never come," the woman said. She was looking at him holding the glass and biting her lip. "You never would have gotten anything like this in Paris. You always said you loved Paris. We could have stayed in Paris or gone anywhere. I'd have gone anywhere. I said I'd go anywhere you wanted. If you wanted to shoot we could have gone shooting in Hungary and been comfortable."

"Your bloody money," he said.

"That's not fair," she said. "It was always yours as much as mine. I left everything and I went wherever you wanted to go and I've done what you wanted to do. But I wish we'd never come here."

"You said you loved it."

"I did when you were all right. But now I hate it. I don't see why that had to happen to your leg. What have we done to have that happen to us?"

"I suppose what I did was to forget to put iodine on it when I first scratched it. Then I didn't pay any attention to it because I never infect. Then, later, when it got bad, it was probably using that weak carbolic solution when the other antiseptics ran out that paralyzed the minute blood vessels and started the gangrene." He looked at her, "What else?"

"I don't mean that."

"If we would have hired a good mechanic instead of a half baked kikúyu driver, he would have checked the oil and never burned out that bearing in the truck."

"I don't mean that."

"If you hadn't left your own people, your god-damned Old Westbury, Saratoga, Palm Beach people to take me on——"

"Why, I loved you. That's not fair. I love you now. I'll always love you. Don't you love me?"

"No," said the man. "I don't think so. I never have."

"Harry, what are you saying? You're out of your head."

"No. I haven't any head to go out of."

"Don't drink that," she said. "Darling, please don't drink that. We have to do everything we can."

"You do it," he said. "I'm tired." ⟩

Now in his mind he saw a railway station at Karagatch and he was standing with his pack and that was the headlight of the Simplon-Orient cutting the dark now and he was leaving Thrace then after the retreat. That was one of the things he had saved to write, with, in the morning at breakfast, looking out the window and seeing snow on the mountains in Bulgaria and Nansen's Secretary asking the old man if it were snow and the old man looking at it and saying, No, that's not snow. It's too early for snow. And the Secretary repeating to the other girls, No, you see. It's not snow and them all saying, It's not snow we were mistaken. But it was the snow all right and he sent them on into it when he evolved exchange of populations. And it was snow they tramped along in until they died that winter.

It was snow too that fell all Christmas week that year up in the Gauertal, that year they lived in the woodcutter's house with the big square porcelain stove that filled half the room, and they slept on mattresses filled with beech leaves, the time the deserter came with his feet bloody in the snow. He said the police were right behind him and they gave him woolen socks and held the gendarmes talking until the tracks had drifted over.

In Schrunz, on Christmas day, the snow was so bright it hurt your eyes when you looked out from the weinstube and saw every one coming home from church. That was where they walked up the sleigh-smoothed urine-yellowed road along the river with the steep pine hills, skis heavy on the shoulder, and where they ran that great run down the glacier above the Madlener-haus, the snow as smooth to see as cake frosting and as light as powder and he remembered the noiseless rush the speed made as you dropped down like a bird.

They were snow-bound a week in the Madlener-haus that time in the blizzard playing cards in the smoke by the lantern light and the stakes were higher all the time as Herr Lent lost more. Finally he lost it all. Everything, the skischule money and all the season's profit and then his capital. He could see him with his long nose, picking up the cards and then opening, "Sans Voir." There was always gambling then. When there was no snow you gambled and when there was too much you gambled. He thought of all the time in his life he had spent gambling. ⟩

But he had never written a line of that, nor of that cold, bright Christmas day with the mountains showing across the plain that Barker had flown across the lines to bomb the Austrian officers' leave train, machine-gunning them as they scattered and ran. He remembered Barker afterwards coming into the mess and starting to tell about it. And how quiet it got and then somebody saying, "You bloody murderous bastard."

Those were the same Austrians they killed then that he skied with later. No not the same. Hans, that he skied with all that year, had been in the Kaiser-Jägers and when they went hunting hares together up the little valley above the saw-mill they had talked of the fighting on Pasubio and of the attack on Pertica and Asalone and he had never written a word of that. Nor of Monte Corno, nor the Siete Commun, nor of Arsiedo.

How many winters had he lived in the Voralberg and the Arlberg? It was four and then he remembered the man who had the fox to sell when they had walked into Bludenz, that time to buy presents, and the cherry-pit taste of good kirsch, the fast-slipping rush of running powder-snow on crust, singing "Hi! Ho! said Rolly!" as you ran down the last stretch to the steep drop, taking it straight, then running the orchard in three turns and out across the ditch and onto the icy road behind the inn. Knocking your bindings loose, kicking the skis free and leaning them up against the wooden wall of the inn, the lamp-light coming from the window, where inside, in the smoky, new-wine smelling warmth, they were playing the accordion.

"Where did we stay in Paris?" he asked the

woman who was sitting by him in a canvas chair, now, in Africa.

"At the Crillon. You know that."

"Why do I know that?"

"That's where we always stayed."

"No. Not always."

"There and at the Pavillion Henri-Quatre in St. Germain. You said you loved it there."

"Love is a dunghill," said Harry. "And I'm the cock that gets on it to crow."

"If you have to go away," she said, "is it absolutely necessary to kill off everything you leave behind? I mean do you have to take away everything? Do you have to kill your horse, and your wife and burn your saddle and your armour?"

"Yes," he said. "Your damned money was my armour. My Swift and my Armour."

"Don't."

"All right. I'll stop that. I don't want to hurt you."

"It's a little bit late now."

"All right then. I'll go on hurting you. It's more amusing. The only thing I ever really liked to do with you I can't do now."

"No, that's not true. You liked to do many things and everything you wanted to do I did."

"Oh, for Christ sake stop bragging, will you?"

He looked at her and saw her crying.

"Listen," he said. "Do you think that it is fun to do this? I don't know why I'm doing it. It's trying to kill to keep yourself alive, I imagine. I was all right when we started talking. I didn't mean to start this, and now I'm crazy as a coot and being as cruel to you as I can be. Don't pay any attention, darling, to what I say. I love you, really. You know I love you. I've never loved any one else the way I love you."

He slipped into the familiar lie he made his bread and butter by.

"You're sweet to me."

"You bitch," he said. "You rich bitch. That's poetry. I'm full of poetry now. Rot and poetry. Rotten poetry."

"Stop it. Harry, why do you have to turn into a devil now?"

"I don't like to leave anything," the man said. "I don't like to leave things behind."

* * *

It was evening now and he had been asleep. The sun was gone behind the hill and there was a shadow all across the plain and the small animals were feeding close to camp; quick dropping heads and switching tails, he watched them keeping well out away from the bush now. The birds no longer waited on the ground. They were all perched heavily in a tree. There were many more of them. His personal boy was sitting by the bed.

"Memsahib's gone to shoot," the boy said. "Does Bwana want?"

"Nothing."

She had gone to kill a piece of meat and, knowing how he liked to watch the game, she had gone well away so she would not disturb this little pocket of the plain that he could see. She was always thoughtful, he thought. On anything she knew about, or had read, or that she had ever heard.

It was not her fault that when he went to her he was already over. How could a woman know that you meant nothing that you said; that you spoke only from habit and to be comfortable? After he no longer meant what he said, his lies were more successful with women than when he had told them the truth.

It was not so much that he lied as that there was no truth to tell. He had had his life and it was over and then he went on living it again with different people and more money, with the best of the same places, and some new ones.

You kept from thinking and it was all marvellous. You were equipped with good insides so that you did not go to pieces that way, the way most of them had, and you made an attitude that you cared nothing for the work you used to do, now that you could no longer do it. But, in yourself, you said that you would write about these people; about the very rich; that you were really not of them but a spy in their country; that you would leave it and write of it and for once it would be written by some one who knew what he was writing of. But he would never do it, because each day of not writing, of comfort, of being that which he despised, dulled his ability and softened his will to work so that, finally, he did no work at all. The people he knew now were all much more comfortable when he did not work. Africa was where he had been happiest in the good time of his life, so he had come out here to start again. They had made this safari with the minimum of comfort. There was no hardship; but there was no luxury and he had thought that he could get back into training that way. That in some way he could work the fat off his soul the way a fighter went into the mountains to work and train in order to burn it out of his body.

Rocky III

She had liked it. She said she loved it. She loved anything that was exciting, that involved a change of scene, where there were new people and where things were pleasant. And he had felt the illusion of returning strength of will to work. Now if this was how it ended, and he knew it was, he must not turn like some snake biting itself because its back was broken. It wasn't this woman's fault. If it had not been she it would have been another. If he lived by a lie he should try to die by it. He heard a shot beyond the hill.

She shot very well this good, this rich bitch, this kindly caretaker and destroyer of his talent. Nonsense. He had destroyed his talent himself. Why should be blame this woman because she kept him well? He had destroyed his talent by not using it, by betrayals of himself and what he believed in, by drinking so much that he blunted the edge of his perceptions, by laziness, by sloth, and by snobbery, by pride and by prejudice, by hook and by crook. What was this? A catalogue of old books? What was his talent anyway? It was a talent all right but instead of using it, he had traded on it. It was never what he had done, but always what he could do. And he had chosen to make his living with something else instead of a pen or a pencil. It was strange, too, wasn't it, that when he fell in love with another woman, that woman should always have more money than the last one? But when he no longer was in love, when he was only lying, as to this woman, now, who had the most money of all, who had all the money there was, who had had a husband and children, who had taken lovers and been dissatisfied with them, and who loved him dearly as a writer, as a man, as a companion and as a proud possession; it was strange that when he did not love her at all and was lying, that he should be able to give her more for her money than when he had really loved.

We must all be cut out for what we do, he thought. However you make your living is where your talent lies. He had sold vitality, in one form or another, all his life and when your affections are not too involved you give much better value for the money. He had found that out but he would never write that, now, either. No, he would not write that, although it was well worth writing.

Now she came in sight, walking across the open toward the camp. She was wearing jodphurs and carrying her rifle. The two boys had a Tommie slung and they were coming along behind her. She was still a good-looking woman, he thought, and she had a pleasant body. She had a great talent and appreciation for the bed, she was not pretty, but he liked her face, she read enormously, liked to ride and shoot and, certainly, she drank too much. Her husband had died when she was still a comparatively young woman and for a while she had devoted herself to her two just-grown children, who did not need her and were embarrassed at having her about, to her stable of horses, to books, and to bottles. She liked to read in the evening before dinner and she drank Scotch and soda while she read. By dinner she was fairly drunk and after a bottle of wine at dinner she was usually drunk enough to sleep.

That was before the lovers. After she had the lovers she did not drink so much because she did not have to be drunk to sleep. But the lovers bored her. She had been married to a man who had never bored her and these people bored her very much.

Then one of her two children was killed in a plane crash and after that was over she did not want the lovers, and drink being no anæsthetic she had to make another life. Suddenly, she had been acutely frightened of being alone. But she wanted some one that she respected with her.

It had begun very simply. She liked what he wrote and she had always envied the life he led. She thought he did exactly what he wanted to. The steps by which she had acquired him and the way in which she had fallen in love with him were all part of a regular progression in which she had built herself a new life and he had traded away what remained of his old life.

He had traded it for security, for comfort too, there was no denying that, and for what else? He did not know. She would have bought him anything he wanted. He knew that. She was a damned nice woman too. He would as soon be in bed with her as any one; rather with her, because she was richer, because she was very pleasant and appreciative and because she never made scenes. And now this life that she had built again was coming to a term because he had not used iodine two weeks ago when a thorn had scratched his knee as they moved forward trying to photograph a herd of waterbuck standing, their heads up, peering while their nostrils searched the air, their ears spread wide to hear the first noise that would send them rushing into the bush. They had bolted, too, before he got the picture.

Here she came now.

He turned his head on the cot to look toward her. "Hello," he said.

*

macho·complement:
image as artifice

"I shot a Tommy ram," she told him. "He'll make you good broth and I'll have them mash some potatoes with the Klim. How do you feel?"

"Much better."

"Isn't that lovely? You know I thought perhaps you would. You were sleeping when I left."

"I had a good sleep. Did you walk far?"

"No. Just around behind the hill. I made quite a good shot on the Tommy."

"You shoot marvellously, you know."

"I love it. I've loved Africa. Really. If *you're* all right it's the most fun that I've ever had. You don't know the fun it's been to shoot with you. I've loved the country."

"I love it too."

"Darling, you don't know how marvellous it is to see you feeling better. I couldn't stand it when you felt that way. You won't talk to me like that again, will you? Promise me?"

"No," he said. "I don't remember what I said."

"You don't have to destroy me. Do you? I'm only a middle-aged woman who loves you and wants to do what you want to do. I've been destroyed two or three times already. You wouldn't want to destroy me again, would you?"

"I'd like to destroy you a few times in bed," he said.

"Yes. That's the good destruction. That's the way we're made to be destroyed. The plane will be here tomorrow."

"How do you know?"

"I'm sure. It's bound to come. The boys have the wood all ready and the grass to make the smudge. I went down and looked at it again today. There's plenty of room to land and we have the smudges ready at both ends."

"What makes you think it will come tomorrow?"

"I'm sure it will. It's overdue now. Then, in town, they will fix up your leg and then we will have some good destruction. Not that dreadful talking kind."

"Should we have a drink? The sun is down."

"Do you think you should?"

"I'm having one."

"We'll have one together. *Molo, letti dui whiskey-soda!*" she called.

"You'd better put on your mosquito boots," he told her.

"I'll wait till I bathe . . ."

While it grew dark they drank and just before it was dark and there was no longer enough light to shoot, a hyena crossed the open on his way around the hill.

"That bastard crosses there every night," the man said. "Every night for two weeks."

"He's the one makes the noise at night. I don't mind it. They're a filthy animal though."

Drinking together, with no pain now except the discomfort of lying in the one position, the boys lighting a fire, its shadow jumping on the tents, he could feel the return of acquiescence in this life of pleasant surrender. She *was* very good to him. He had been cruel and unjust in the afternoon. She was a fine woman, marvellous really. And just then it occurred to him that he was going to die.

It came with a rush; not as a rush of water nor of wind; but of a sudden evil-smelling emptiness and the odd thing was that the hyena slipped lightly along the edge of it.

"What is it, Harry?" she asked him.

"Nothing," he said. "You had better move over to the other side. To windward."

"Did Molo change the dressing?"

"Yes. I'm just using the boric now."

"How do you feel?"

"A little wobbly."

"I'm going in to bathe," she said. "I'll be right out. I'll eat with you and then we'll put the cot in."

So, he said to himself, we did well to stop the quarrelling. He had never quarrelled much with this woman, while with the woman that he loved he had quarrelled so much they had finally, always, with the corrosion of the quarrelling, killed what they had together. He had loved too much, demanded too much, and he wore it all out.

He thought about alone in Constantinople that time, having quarrelled in Paris before he had gone out. He had whored the whole time and then, when that was over, and he had failed to kill his loneliness, but only made it worse, he had written her, the first one, the one who left him, a letter telling her how he had never been able to kill it. . . . How when he thought he saw her outside the Regence one time it made him go all faint and sick inside, and that he would follow a woman who looked like her in some way, along the Boulevard, afraid to see it was not she, afraid to lose the feeling it gave him. How every one he had slept with had only made him miss her more. How what she had done could never matter since he knew he could not cure himself of loving her. He wrote this letter at the Club, cold sober, and mailed it to New York asking her to write him at the office in Paris. That seemed safe. And that night missing her so much it made him feel hollow sick inside, he wandered up past Taxim's, picked a girl up and took her out to supper. He had gone to a place to dance with her afterward, she danced badly, and left her for a hot Armenian slut, that swung her belly against him so it almost scalded. He took her away from a British gunner subaltern after a row. The gunner asked him outside and they fought in the street on the cobbles in the dark. He'd hit him twice, hard, on the side of the jaw and when he didn't go down he knew he was in for a fight. The gunner hit him in the body, then beside his eye. He swung with his left again and landed and the gunner fell on him and grabbed his coat and tore the sleeve off and he clubbed him twice behind the ear and then smashed him with his right as he pushed him away. When the gunner went down his head hit first and he ran with the girl because they heard the M. P.'s coming. They got into a taxi and drove out to Rimmily Hissa along the Bosphorus, and around, and back in the cool night and went to bed and she felt as over-ripe as she looked but smooth, rose-petal, syrupy, smooth-bellied, big-breasted and needed no pillow under her buttocks, and he left her before she was awake looking blousy enough in the first daylight and turned up at the Pera Palace with a black eye, carrying his coat because one sleeve was missing.

That same night he left for Anatolia and he remembered, later on that trip, riding all day through fields of the poppies that they raised for opium and how strange it made you feel, finally, and all the distances seemed wrong, to where they had made the attack with the newly arrived Constantine officers, that did not know a god-damned thing, and the artillery had fired into the troops and the British observer had cried like a child.

That was the day he'd first seen dead men wearing white ballet skirts and upturned shoes with pompons on them. The Turks had come steadily and lumpily and he had seen the skirted men running and the officers shooting into them and running then themselves and he and the British observer had run too until his lungs ached and his mouth was full of the taste of pennies and they stopped behind some rocks and there were the Turks coming as lumpily as ever. Later he had seen the things that he could never think of and later still he had seen much worse. So when he got back to Paris that time he could not talk about it or stand to have it mentioned. And there in the café as he passed was that American poet with a pile of saucers in front of him and a stupid look

on his potato face talking about the Dada movement with a Roumanian who said his name was Tristan Tzara, who always wore a monocle and had a headache, and, back at the apartment with his wife that now he loved again, the quarrel all over, the madness all over, glad to be home, the office sent his mail up to the flat. So then the letter in answer to the one he'd written came in on a platter one morning and when he saw the handwriting he went cold all over and tried to slip the letter underneath another. But his wife said, "Who is that letter from, dear?" and that was the end of the beginning of that.

He remembered the good times with them all, and the quarrels. They always picked the finest places to have the quarrels. And why had they always quarrelled when he was feeling best? He had never written any of that because, at first, he never wanted to hurt any one and then it seemed as though there was enough to write without it. But he had always thought that he would write it finally. There was so much to write. He had seen the world change; not just the events; although he had seen many of them and had watched the people, but he had seen the subtler change and he could remember how the people were at different times. He had been in it and he had watched it and it was his duty to write of it; but now he never would.

"How do you feel?" she said. She had come out from the tent now after her bath.

"All right."

"Could you eat now?" He saw Molo behind her with the folding table and the other boy with the dishes.

"I want to write," he said.

"You ought to take some broth to keep your strength up."

"I'm going to die tonight," he said. "I don't need my strength up."

"Don't be melodramatic, Harry, please," she said.

"Why don't you use your nose? I'm rotted half way up my thigh now. What the hell should I fool with broth for? Molo bring whiskey-soda."

"Please take the broth," she said gently.

"All right."

The broth was too hot. He had to hold it in the cup until it cooled enough to take it and then he just got it down without gagging.

"You're a fine woman," he said. "Don't pay any attention to me."

She looked at him with her well-known, well-loved face from *Spur* and *Town and Country*, only a little the worse for drink, only a little the worse for bed, but *Town and Country* never showed those good breasts and those useful thighs and those lightly small-of-back-caressing hands, and as he looked and saw her well known pleasant smile, he felt death come again. This time there was no rush. It was a puff, as of a wind that makes a candle flicker and the flame go tall.

"They can bring my net out later and hang it from the tree and build the fire up. I'm not going in the tent tonight. It's not worth moving. It's a clear night. There won't be any rain."

So this was how you died, in whispers that you did not hear. Well, there would be no more quarrelling. He could promise that. The one experience that he had never had he was not going to spoil now. He probably would. You spoiled everything. But perhaps he wouldn't.

"You can't take dictation, can you?"

"I never learned," she told him.

"That's all right."

There wasn't time, of course, although it seemed as though it telescoped so that you might put it all into one paragraph if you could get it right.

There was a log house, chinked white with mortar, on a hill above the lake. There was a bell on a pole by the door to call the people in to meals. Behind the house were fields and behind the fields was the timber. A line of lombardy poplars ran from the house to the dock. Other poplars ran along the point. A road went up to the hills along the edge of the timber and along that road he picked blackberries. Then that log house was burned down and all the guns that had been on deer foot racks above the open fire place were burned and afterwards their barrels, with the lead melted in the magazines, and the stocks burned away, lay out on the heap of ashes that were used to make lye for the big iron soap kettles, and you asked Grandfather if you could have them to play with, and he said, no. You see they were his guns still and he never bought any others. Nor did he hunt any more. The house was rebuilt in the same place out of lumber now and painted white and from its porch you saw the poplars and the lake beyond; but there were never any more guns. The barrels of the guns that had hung on the deer feet on the wall of the log house lay out there on the heap of ashes and no one ever touched them.

In the Black Forest, after the war, we rented a trout stream and there were two ways to walk to it. One was down the valley from Triberg and around the valley road in the shade of the trees that bordered the white road, and then up a side road that went up through the hills past many small farms, with the big Schwarzwald houses, until that road crossed the stream. That was where our fishing began.

The other way was to climb steeply up to the edge of the woods and then go across the top of the hills through the pine woods, and then out to the edge of a meadow and down across this meadow to the bridge. There were birches along the stream and it was not big, but narrow, clear and fast, with pools where it had cut under the roots of the birches. At the Hotel in Triberg the proprietor had a fine season. It was very pleasant and we were all great friends. The next year came the inflation and the money he had made the year before was not enough to buy supplies to open the hotel and he hanged himself.

You could dictate that, but you could not dictate the Place Contrescarpe where the flower sellers dyed their flowers in the street and the dye ran over the paving where the autobus started and the old men and the women, always drunk on wine and bad marc; and the children with their noses running in the cold; the smell of dirty sweat and poverty and drunkenness at the Café des Amateurs and the whores at the Bal Musette they lived above. The Concierge who entertained the trooper of the Garde Républicaine in her loge, his horse-hair-plumed helmet on a chair. The locataire across the hall whose husband was a bicycle racer and her joy that morning at the Cremerie when she had opened L'Auto and seen where he placed third in Paris-Tours, his first big race. She had blushed and laughed and then gone upstairs crying with the yellow sporting paper in her hand. The husband of the woman who ran the Bal Musette drove a taxi and when he, Harry, had to take an early plane the husband knocked upon the door to wake him and they each drank a glass of white wine at the zinc of the bar before they started. He knew his neighbors in that quarter then because they all were poor.

Around that Place there were two kinds; the drunkards and the sportifs. The drunkards killed their poverty that way; the sportifs took it out in exercise. They were the descendants of the Communards and it was no struggle for them to know their politics. They knew who had shot their fathers, their relatives, their brothers, and their friends when the Versailles troops came in and took the town after the Commune and executed any one they could catch with calloused hands, or who wore a cap, or carried any other sign he was a working man. And in that poverty, and in that quarter across the street from a Boucherie Chevaline and a wine co-operative he had written the start of all he was to do. There never was another part of Paris that he loved like that, the sprawling trees, the old white plastered houses painted brown below, the long green of the autobus in that round square, the purple flower dye upon the paving, the sudden drop down the hill of the rue Cardinal Lemoine to the River, and the other way the narrow crowded world of the rue Mouffetard. The street that ran up toward the Pantheon and the other that he always took with the bicycle, the only asphalted street in all that quarter, smooth under the tires, with the high narrow houses and the cheap tall hotel where Paul Verlaine had died. There were only two rooms in the apartment where they lived and he had a room on the top floor of that hotel that cost him sixty francs a month where he did his writing, and from it he could see the roofs and chimney pots and all the hills of Paris.

From the apartment you could only see the wood and coal man's place. He sold wine too, bad wine. The golden horse's head outside the Boucherie Chevaline where the carcasses hung yellow gold and red in the open window, and the green painted co-operative where they bought their wine; good wine and cheap. The rest was plaster walls and the windows of the neighbors. The neighbors who, at night, when some one lay drunk in the street, moaning and groaning in that typical French ivresse that you were propaganded to believe did not exist, would open their windows and then the murmur of talk.

"Where is the policeman? When you don't want him the bugger is always there. He's sleeping with some concierge. Get the Agent." Till some one threw a bucket of water from a window and the moaning stopped. "What's that? Water. Ah, that's intelligent." And the windows shutting. Marie, his femme de menage, protesting against the eight-hour day saying, "If a husband works until six he gets only a little drunk on the way home and does not waste too much. If he works only until five he is drunk every night and one has

no money. It is the wife of the working man who suffers from this shortening of hours."

"Wouldn't you like some more broth?" the woman asked him now.

"No, thank you very much. It is awfully good."

"Try just a little."

"I would like a whiskey-soda."

"It's not good for you."

"No. It's bad for me. Cole Porter wrote the words and the music. This knowledge that you're going mad for me."

"You know I like you to drink."

"Oh yes. Only it's bad for me."

When she goes, he thought, I'll have all I want. Not all I want but all there is. Ayee he was tired. Too tired. He was going to sleep a little while. He lay still and death was not there. It must have gone around another street. It went in pairs, on bicycles, and moved absolutely silently on the pavements.

No, he had never written about Paris. Not the Paris that he cared about. But what about the rest that he had never written?

What about the ranch and the silvered gray of the sage brush, the quick, clear water in the irrigation ditches, and the heavy green of the alfalfa. The trail went up into the hills and the cattle in the summer were shy as deer. The bawling and the steady noise and slow moving mass raising a dust as you brought them down in the fall. And behind the mountains, the clear sharpness of the peak in the evening light and, riding down along the trail in the moonlight, bright across the valley. Now he remembered coming down through the timber in the dark holding the horse's tail when you could not see and all the stories that he meant to write.

About the half-wit chore boy who was left at the ranch that time and told not to let any one get any hay, and that old bastard from the Forks who had beaten the boy when he had worked for him stopping to get some feed. The boy refusing and the old man saying he would beat him again. The boy got the rifle from the kitchen and shot him when he tried to come into the barn and when they came back to the ranch he'd been dead a week, frozen in the corral, and the dogs had eaten part of him. But what was left you packed on a sled wrapped in a blanket and roped on and you got the boy to help you haul it, and the two

[margin annotation: empty outer life / richer inner life of memory]

of you took it out over the road on skis, and sixty miles down to town to turn the boy over. He having no idea that he would be arrested. Thinking he had done his duty and that you were his friend and he would be rewarded. He'd helped to haul the old man in so everybody could know how bad the old man had been and how he'd tried to steal some feed that didn't belong to him, and when the sheriff put the handcuffs on the boy he couldn't believe it. Then he'd started to cry. That was one story he had saved to write. He knew at least twenty good stories from out there and he had never written one. Why?

"You tell them why," he said.

"Why what, dear?"

"Why nothing."

She didn't drink so much, now, since she had him. But if he lived he would never write about her, he knew that now. Nor about any of them. The rich were dull and they drank too much, or they played too much backgammon. They were dull and they were repetitious. He remembered poor Julian and his romantic awe of them and how he had started a story once that began, "The very rich are different from you and me." And how some one had said to Julian, Yes, they have more money. But that was not humorous to Julian. He thought they were a special glamorous race and when he found they weren't it wrecked him just as much as any other thing that wrecked him.

He had been contemptuous of those who wrecked. You did not have to like it because you understood it. He could beat anything, he thought, because no thing could hurt him if he did not care.

All right. Now he would not care for death. One thing he had always dreaded was the pain. He could stand pain as well as any man, until it went on too long, and wore him out, but here he had something that had hurt frightfully and just when he had felt it breaking him, the pain had stopped.

He remembered long ago when Williamson, the bombing officer, had been hit by a stick bomb some one in a German patrol had thrown as he was coming in through the wire that night and, screaming, had begged every one to kill him. He was a fat man, very brave, and a good officer, although addicted to fantastic shows. But that night he was caught in the wire, with a flare lighting him up and his bowels spilled out into the wire, so when they brought him in, alive, they had to

cut him loose. Shoot me, Harry. For Christ sake shoot me. They had had an argument one time about our Lord never sending you anything you could not bear and some one's theory had been that meant that at a certain time the pain passed you out automatically. But he had always remembered Williamson, that night. Nothing passed out Williamson until he gave him all his morphine tablets that he had always saved to use himself and then they did not work right away.

Still this now, that he had, was very easy; and if it was no worse as it went on there was nothing to worry about. Except that he would rather be in better company.

He thought a little about the company that he would like to have.

No, he thought, when everything you do, you do too long, and do too late, you can't expect to find the people still there. The people all are gone. The party's over and you are with your hostess now.

I'm getting as bored with dying as with everything else, he thought.

"It's a bore," he said out loud.

"What is, my dear?"

"Anything you do too bloody long."

He looked at her face between him and the fire. She was leaning back in the chair and the firelight shone on her pleasantly lined face and he could see that she was sleepy. He heard the hyena make a noise just outside the range of the fire.

"I've been writing," he said. "But I got tired."

"Do you think you will be able to sleep?"

"Pretty sure. Why don't you turn in?"

"I like to sit here with you."

"Do you feel anything strange?" he asked her.

"No. Just a little sleepy."

"I do," he said.

He had just felt death come by again.

"You know the only thing I've never lost is curiosity," he said to her.

"You've never lost anything. You're the most complete man I've ever known."

"Christ," he said. "How little a woman knows. What is that? Your intuition?"

Because, just then, death had come and rested its head on the foot of the cot and he could smell its breath.

"Never believe any of that about a scythe and a skull," he told her. "It can be two bicycle policemen as easily, or be a bird. Or it can have a wide snout like a hyena."

It had moved up on him now, but it had no shape any more. It simply occupied space.

"Tell it to go away."

It did not go away but moved a little closer.

"You've got a hell of a breath," he told it. "You stinking bastard."

It moved up closer to him still and now he could not speak to it, and when it saw he could not speak it came a little closer, and now he tried to send it away without speaking, but it moved in on him so its weight was all upon his chest, and while it crouched there and he could not move, or speak, he heard the woman say, "Bwana is asleep now. Take the cot up very gently and carry it into the tent."

He could not speak to tell her to make it go away and it crouched now, heavier, so he could not breathe. And then, while they lifted the cot, suddenly it was all right and the weight went from his chest.

It was morning and had been morning for some time and he heard the plane. It showed very tiny and then made a wide circle and the boys ran out and lit the fires, using kerosene, and piled on grass so there were two big smudges at each end of the level place and the morning breeze blew them toward the camp and the plane circled twice more, low this time, and then glided down and levelled off and landed smoothly and, coming walking toward him, was old Compton in slacks, a tweed jacket and a brown felt hat.

"What's the matter, old cock?" Compton said.

"Bad leg," he told him. "Will you have some breakfast?"

"Thanks. I'll just have some tea. It's the Puss Moth you know. I won't be able to take the Memsahib. There's only room for one. Your lorry is on the way."

Helen had taken Compton aside and was speaking to him. Compton came back more cheery than ever.

"We'll get you right in," he said. "I'll be back for the Mem. Now I'm afraid I'll have to stop at Arusha to refuel. We'd better get going."

"What about the tea?"

"I don't really care about it you know."

The boys had picked up the cot and carried it around the green tents and down along the rock and out onto the plain and along past the smudges that were burning brightly now, the grass all consumed, and the wind fanning the fire, to the little plane. It was difficult getting him in, but once in he lay back in the leather seat, and the leg was stuck straight out to one side of the seat where Compton sat. Compton started the motor and got in. He waved to Helen and to the boys and, as the clatter moved into the old familiar roar, they swung around with Compie watching for wart-hog holes and roared, bumping, along the stretch between the fires and with the last bump rose and he saw them all standing below, waving, and the camp beside the hill, flattening now, and the plain spreading, clumps of trees, and the bush flattening, while the game trails ran now smoothly to the dry waterholes, and there was a new water that he had never known of. The zebra, small rounded backs now, and the wildebeeste, big-headed dots seeming to climb as they moved in long fingers across the plain, now scattering as the shadow came toward them, they were tiny now, and the movement had no gallop, and the plain as far as you could see, gray-yellow now and ahead old Compie's tweed back and the brown felt hat. Then they were over the first hills and the wildebeeste were trailing up them, and then they were over mountains with sudden depths of green-rising forest and the solid bamboo slopes, and then the heavy forest again, sculptured into peaks and hollows until they crossed, and hills sloped down and then another plain, hot now, and purple brown, bumpy with heat and Compie looking back to see how he was riding. Then there were other mountains dark ahead.

And then instead of going on to Arusha they turned left, he evidently figured that they had the gas, and looking down he saw a pink sifting cloud, moving over the ground, and in the air, like the first snow in a blizzard, that comes from nowhere, and he knew the locusts were coming up from the South. Then they began to climb and they were going to the East it seemed, and then it darkened and they were in a storm, the rain so thick it seemed like flying through a waterfall, and then they were out and Compie turned his head and grinned and pointed and there, ahead, all he could see, as wide as all the world, great, high, and unbelievably white in the sun, was the square top of Kilimanjaro. And then he knew that there was where he was going. *"Snow man"* 7

Just then the hyena stopped whimpering in the night and started to make a strange, human, almost crying sound. The woman heard it and stirred uneasily. She did not wake. In her dream she was at the house on Long Island and it was the night before her daughter's début. Somehow her father was there and he had been very rude. Then the noise the hyena made was so loud she woke and for a moment she did not know where she was and she was very afraid. Then she took the flashlight and shone it on the other cot that they had carried in after Harry had gone to sleep. She could see his bulk under the mosquito bar but somehow he had gotten his leg out and it hung down along-side the cot. The dressings had all come down and she could not look at it.

"Molo," she called, "Molo! Molo!"

Then she said, "Harry, Harry!" Then her voice rising, "Harry! Please, Oh Harry!"

There was no answer and she could not hear him breathing.

Outside the tent the hyena made the same strange noise that had awakened her. But she did not hear him for the beating of her heart.

F. SCOTT FITZGERALD (1896–1940)

F. Scott Fitzgerald had the capacity (and the curse) of being able to immerse himself in the life of his age. He had a basic faith in the dignity of his vocation as a writer, and a somewhat more flickering faith in his own gifts. And he could regard himself and his work with a mordant, and sometimes morbid, candor. These qualities were essential components of his genius. At times they almost seemed, in fact, to be his genius.

"I am half black Irish," Fitzgerald once wrote, "and half old American stock with the usual exaggerated ancestral pretensions. The black Irish half of the family had the money and looked down upon the Maryland side of the family who had, and really had, that certain screen of reticences and obligations that go under the poor old shattered word 'breeding' (modern form 'inhibitions')." The Maryland Fitzgeralds boasted Irish nobility (which the rich Irish side could lay no claim to), colonial aristocracy, Francis Scott Key with "The Star Spangled Banner," and Confederate romanticism; but Edward, the father of the novelist, had come west, to St. Paul, Minnesota, where, with his good manners, he married the granddaughter of the self-made and very rich Philip F. McQuillan, born in Ireland. The Fitzgerald father gave the son his literary taste and his romantic nostalgia and set him a model of drink and failure—and of the romance of failure. The McQuillan mother spoiled the handsome son with devouring affection, and the McQuillan relatives ended by supporting the Fitzgerald family, paying for Scott's education and giving him, as he put it, a "two-cylinder inferiority complex"—and perhaps the paradoxical attitude toward wealth that marks his life and work.

The boy Scott was not accepted by other boys, and being spoiled beyond description, was rather an undisciplined failure at school work. The early refuge of his damaged self-esteem was in daydreams—dreams of being popular and of being a football hero—and in writing about those dreams. But the writing became, too, the source of another daydream, that of being a writer, successful and rich. By the time he was a freshman at Princeton he could remark to his fellow student Edmund Wilson: "I want to be one of the greatest writers that ever lived, don't you?" Even as he entered his teens, Scott had set himself to studying and imitating the stories in popular magazines.

At the Roman Catholic Newman School in New Jersey, where Scott was sent to prepare for Princeton, things were, in general, a little better. In his second year he earned letters in football and track, and he wound up with a play—about the Civil War—that was given a production in St. Paul. It was only an amateur production, but his name got on the front page of the local newspapers.

Thoroughly stage-struck, Scott, at Princeton, devoted himself primarily to the Triangle Club, the dramatic organization. He wrote a Triangle musical show, *Fie, Fie, Fi-Fi*, and the lyrics for another, by Edmund Wilson, which, in honor of the native son, who not only had done the lyrics but was cast as the female lead, was scheduled to venture as far west as St. Paul.

But when Edmund Wilson's *The Evil Eye* appeared in St. Paul, the native son was incapacitated by failing grades and a physical breakdown. When, in 1916, he came back to repeat his junior year, his new show was rejected and he turned, by way of compensation, to the *Nassau Literary Magazine*. Here the editor Edmund Wilson, who was introducing modern literature to Princeton, published his friend's stories and poems; and another friend, John Peale Bishop,[1] gave him private seminars in poetry—Keats, Shakespeare, and Verlaine.

As the novelist Glenway Wescott has said, Fitzgerald must have been one of the worst educated writers in the world, but he did have Wilson and Bishop for friends, and for all practical purposes, they could give him the kind of education he needed most. They were extraordinarily intelligent young men, they felt the modern spirit in their bones, and they both had strong literary talents. Scott may have come to Princeton with the conviction that he was a genius, but it was Bishop and Wilson who gave him his sense of what vocation means, and all his life he would turn to them, especially to Wilson, to renew his "literary conscience."

But now in the fall of 1917, with America in the war, Fitzgerald, in the beginning of his senior year, left Princeton with orders to report to Fort Leavenworth, Kansas, for officer's training. Already, he had begun a novel about his own growing up, apparently entitled "The Romantic Egotist"; and now he continued to work ferociously at it. Scribner's rejected it and then, after Fitzgerald had done some rewriting, rejected it again.

[1] Bishop (1892–1944) was a fine poet and talented writer of fiction. His *Collected Poems*, edited by Allen Tate, and his *Collected Essays*, edited by Edmund Wilson, were published in 1948.

Fitzgerald, who yearned to distinguish himself as a hero in the uniform of the A.E.F. as once he had yearned, fruitlessly, to distinguish himself in the football uniform of the Princeton Tigers, was stationed, after his training, at Camp Sheridan, in Alabama, where he fell in love. Zelda Sayre was a belle of Montgomery, of good family (her father was a judge on the supreme court of the state), with no money and a wild desire for excitement, luxury, and distinction. She might have said of herself what Rosalind, the girl in Fitzgerald's first novel, *This Side of Paradise*, says to her suitor: "You know I'm old in some ways—in others—well, I'm just a little girl. I like sunshine and pretty things and cheerfulness—and I dread responsibility. . . ."

And there is another passage in the novel, not spoken by Rosalind but about her, that is instructive about Zelda and, in fact, about Fitzgerald himself:

> She wants what she wants when she wants it and she is prone to make every one else around her pretty miserable when she doesn't get it —but in the true sense she is not spoiled. Her fresh enthusiasm, her will to grow—learn, her endless faith in the inexhaustibility of romance, her courage and fundamental honesty —these things are not spoiled.

Before he married her, Fitzgerald, who himself remained a spoiled child almost all his life, could write these diagnostic passages about Zelda, with the strange mixture of clear perception and exculpation that was to characterize his later views of her. He early saw the hard core of her nature, but insisted that she was not spoiled —this merely because of her faith that mirrored his own "endless faith in the inexhaustibility of romance." This faith became the theme of his most enduring work.

The Zelda who, "in the true sense," was not spoiled and who, according to her lights, was in love with Fitzgerald, knew herself well enough to break her engagement when he didn't seem to be getting ahead at a satisfactory speed. Not even a contract for the novel, now after a third rewriting known as *This Side of Paradise*, and a series of stories in the *Saturday Evening Post* won her over. But a movie sale did. By the time of the marriage, on April 3, 1920, the novel was clearly bound for a spectacular success, and the author, at the age of twenty-three, was famous.

This Side of Paradise is an example of the *Bildungsroman*—a novel about growing up, specifically about the growing up of Amory Blaine, whose childhood and youth are closely parallel to the life of Fitzgerald up through Princeton. The *Bildungsroman* is most famously represented by Goethe's *The Sorrows of Werther*, and in our century by James Joyce's *A Portrait of the Artist as a Young Man*, but the models for Fitzgerald were Compton MacKenzie's *Youth's Encounter* and *Mean Street*, models not only for Fitzgerald's hero, but, along with Keats, for a certain floridity of style. But another model also served Fitzgerald—strangely enough, *The Education of Henry Adams*, whose author Fitzgerald had once met. The incongruity between MacKenzie and Adams is compounded by the fact that onto the narrative based on MacKenzie, Fitzgerald grafted certain ideas—for instance, that of Fabian socialism—derived from H. G. Wells and placed them, inappropriately, on the lips of Amory Blaine. Or rather, on the lips of the golden boy and prophet of the Jazz Age, Fitzgerald himself, for whom Amory Blaine is only a mask.

In one sense *This Side of Paradise* is very undistinguished, even for a first novel. Long ago Edmund Wilson said that the novel is "not really about anything"; and it is true that if we try to define the significance of Amory's experience, we are likely to feel rather baffled. Amory is, as we have said, little more than a transparent mask for Fitzgerald himself, and this fact seems to have robbed Fitzgerald of perspective on the materials of the novel—that is, on his own experience. His immersion was too complete.

Paradoxically, however, in *This Side of Paradise* this very defect of uncritical identification may be associated with the success of the novel. It was the *immediacy* of the rendering of mere experience that caught the readers of 1920.

Furthermore, Amory Blaine gave a report from the new world of the young—the revolutionaries who flouted all the old sanctions, mores, and morality, raced through the night in high-powered cars, and drank illegal liquor from monogrammed silver hip-flasks. Fitzgerald, who invented the "flapper" and the "sheik," knew that this was a new world, and Amory knew it too, for he "saw girls doing things that even in his memory would have been impossible." It was a postwar world in which direction and justification for life had been lost, nothing was sacred, and the driving force was an exhibitionistic need for excitement which sometimes had a suicidal undertone—"one vast juvenile intrigue," a world where the young found "all Gods dead, all wars fought, all faiths in man shaken."

Historically, the 1920's were not only an age of disillusionment and frenetic excitement; they were also an age of vital creativity and intellectual development. But that aspect of the age meant little to Fitzgerald. He could fruitfully know only what he himself had personally experienced; and with his self-indulgence, his somewhat tawdry social ambitions, his small capacity for abstract thought, his painfully limited curiosity about history, politics, and ideas in general, what he did experience was severely restricted. But the world in which he did immerse himself he reported as faithfully, and came to judge as honestly, as he could. If he was relatively ignorant of the great forces that were shaking that world, he did have an acute sense for "felt" history, for the tremors that those forces set up in the unconscious of individuals and of society; it is significant that T. S. Eliot, the author of *The Waste Land*, was a devoted admirer of *The Great Gatsby*, Fitzgerald's third and best novel.

If Fitzgerald was, as Edmund Wilson has said, "wrapped up in the dream of himself," this "self" was a representative one, and the dream was prophetic. It even became a communal dream, for *This Side of Paradise* not only reported a generation, it created one. Fitzgerald gave romantic substance and form to the inarticulate yearnings of those who longed for something a little less heroic than the dream Hemingway was to offer, and Fitzgerald's genius shed a magic light in which even the most tawdry objects of desire glittered like pure gold. He appealed to, and justified, that streak in poor Clyde Griffiths that is in everyone.

This Side of Paradise was a considerable financial success, but Fitzgerald and Zelda, who set out to enact as spectacularly as possible the spirit of the Jazz Age, had a splendid talent for spending, sometimes alloyed by self-accusation and regret, but never by any trace of prudence. Even Fitzgerald's ambition to be an artist had no substantial effect on his way of life; he tried living in the country and, for a time, in St. Paul, but the lure of the world of excitement and fashion was too strong, and by the fall of 1922 he was established on Long Island, living the frenetic life to be described in *The Great Gatsby*. But he did manage to work, and by 1922 the second novel, *The Beautiful and Damned*, had appeared, and a number of stories.

In the new novel, with the picture of the young Anthony Patch brought to grief on the "shoals of dissipation," we see that Fitzgerald intended to go beyond the glitter of the life he had written about (and was living) to some moral vision. The novel does not, however, fully show action that vitally embodies such a vision; as Edmund Wilson said at the time of the book's appearance, there is a "succession of catastrophes so arbitrary that, beside them, the perversities of Hardy seemed the working out of natural laws." But if there remains in *The Beautiful and Damned* a fundamental incoherence of theme and action, there is a unity of tone, a ground swell of feeling that informs the whole composition. Critics have made much of the romantic nostalgia in Fitzgerald's life and work, and of the moment when, at the height of his first success, married to Zelda, riding in a taxi down a street in New York, he burst into tears because he knew that he would never again be so happy. He was like Mark Twain, who, tasting his first success, just married to his Livy and living in the mansion his rich father-in-law had just given him as a wedding present, called himself "Little Sammy in Fairy Land." Further-

more like Mark Twain, Fitzgerald was haunted by a sense of doom, morbidly haunted by his early Catholicism as Mark Twain was by his Presbyterian conscience, with the "problem of evil" appropriately "solidified," as Fitzgerald says of Amory Blaine, "into the problem of sex."

So, in Fitzgerald's world, according to some superstitious logic, guilt and failure necessarily follow from success. In Fitzgerald's world the "beautiful" *are* indeed "damned"—damned merely for being beautiful. And later, looking back on the heyday of his precocious success, Fitzgerald could say: "All the stories that came into my head had a touch of disaster in them—the lovely young creatures in my novels went to ruin, the dream mountains of my short stories blew up, my millionaires were as beautiful and damned as Thomas Hardy's peasants." So *The Beautiful and Damned* is bathed in what the critic William Troy called the "atmosphere of failure."

In *The Beautiful and Damned* begins to emerge, however cloudily, with self-pity and romantic self-indulgence, the feeling that later would lead Fitzgerald to write to his daughter that a grasp of the tragic sense of life was the only sound basis for happiness. Here, too, begins to emerge the fundamental duality of Fitzgerald's nature, the tensions that provide the spring, and the subject matter, of his work. But the issues of life did not now come to him in such abstract terms. It was not until near the end, in an essay called "The Crack-Up," that he could see his own situation and remark that the "test of a first-rate intelligence is the ability to hold two opposed ideas in the mind at the same time, and still retain the ability to function." It can scarcely be maintained that Fitzgerald had, in any ordinary sense, a first-rate intelligence, but in an extraordinary sense, he did have the ability to hold, at the same time, two opposed ideas, and two opposed sets of feelings, and still function—which, in his case, meant the ability to dramatize, and in the act of dramatization to resolve, that tension. That tension, that "duality," which first appears in *The Beautiful and Damned*, may have torn him apart in the end, but without it he would have had little worth dramatizing.

The duality in Fitzgerald's work most obviously appears in the fact that he wrote two entirely different kinds of fiction. On one hand, he was developing a slick story that exploited the "new" generation at a very superficial level; and by and large this kind, often expert but always trivial, constitutes the main body of his production. It supported, thanks to the *Saturday Evening Post* and *Liberty Magazine*, his style of life and gave him the reputation of Prince of the Jazz Age. On the other hand, beginning with "The Jelly Bean" (1920), there came a series of stories in which he treats serious issues implicit in the same material used in the pot-boilers. In "The Jelly Bean," for instance, we find the first fully rendered "flapper," clearly modeled on Zelda; but more significant as an indication of the seriousness of his talent is the dramatization of the conflict between modernity and traditional southern values, a dramatization that suggests certain elements in Faulkner's early novels, particularly *Soldier's Pay* and *Sartoris* (which did not come until toward the end of the decade).

The fact of being serious sets stories like "The Jelly Bean" off from the pot-boilers, but the nature of the seriousness in such fictions as "May Day," "Absolution," "The Diamond as Big as the Ritz," "Winter Dreams," "The Rich Boy," and supremely *The Great Gatsby* is even more important to an understanding of the split in Fitzgerald's nature, and of his basic theme. "May Day," which belongs to the winter of 1919–20, is a striking picture of the disorganization of life just after the First World War, but what is basically important is that the world portrayed here made the "flapper" and the "sheik" possible. Furthermore, "Absolution," dealing with the struggle enacted by an adolescent boy and a priest, between the glamor of the world and the demands of faith, a story that may be an echo of Fitzgerald's own life, gives support to the notion that Fitzgerald was a worldling who, in the depth of his nature, had contempt for the world, an immoralist whose dissipations were devised as a torture for an incorrigible

morality. "The Diamond as Big as the Ritz," though much inferior to the other stories mentioned, has, too, great thematic significance; it is a fantasy portraying a world of indescribable wealth and luxury that ends, literally, in a vast suicidal explosion, and we may recall that Fitzgerald was later to generalize this image—"the dream mountains of my short stories blew up" —to describe the sense of doom that hung over his work.

Fitzgerald regarded "Winter Dreams," a trial run for *The Great Gatsby*, as "pretty bad stuff," but it remains one of the best stories he ever wrote, and the first in which he fully engaged his commanding theme. Written during the experiment of living back in St. Paul, the story is located in Minnesota. Dexter Green, as a poor boy caddying for a rich and beautiful young girl, falls madly in love with her—or with a dream of her—precociously makes a fortune, becomes engaged to her, gets jilted, and then takes her back when she, in her vanity and aimlessness, which he thoroughly recognizes, cries out, "I'm more beautiful than anybody, why can't I be happy?" But she again jilts him. A few years later, now a financial power in New York, he learns from a casual business acquaintance that the girl has married, has children, is mistreated by her husband, and has lost her looks and her spirit. Alone in his office, Dexter Green realizes that a dream is dead:

Even the grief he could have borne was left behind in the country of illusion, of youth, of the richness of life, where his winter dreams had flourished.

"Long ago," he said, "long ago there was something in me but now that thing is gone. Now that thing is gone, that thing is gone. I cannot cry. I cannot care. That thing will come back no more."

Three years later, when Fitzgerald was finishing *The Great Gatsby*, he would almost repeat those words in describing the burden of that novel: "the loss of those illusions that give such color to the world that you don't care whether things are true or false so long as they partake of the magical glory." But Fitzgerald, in half of his nature, did care whether "things" were "true or false."

In 1922 Fitzgerald wrote to his editor Maxwell Perkins that he was going to write "something new, something extraordinarily beautiful and simple and intricately patterned"—which is what he was aiming for in *The Great Gatsby*. But before that was to emerge, Fitzgerald was to try for a Broadway success with *The Vegetable*, a disastrously bad play, and was to write a number of stories, mostly undertaken for quick money. Finally, he fled to France, where he holed up in a villa near St. Raphaël, on the Mediterranean. There, while Zelda and the baby daughter basked on the beach (and Zelda, as is suggested by her novel *Save Me the Waltz*, may have been dabbling in adultery with a man vaguely resembling Nicole's lover in *Tender Is the Night*), Fitzgerald immersed himself in his work. *The Great Gatsby* was published in 1925.

The basic story of the novel is simple. James Gatz, a poor boy in the Middle West, is driven to try to realize a dream of success and elegance —a theme that had underlain almost all of Fitzgerald's work (and life), and had been overtly stated in "Absolution," in the story of little Rudolph and his dream-self Blatchford Sarmemington. By the time America entered the First World War, James Gatz had become Jay Gatsby, a lieutenant stationed at Camp Taylor, Kentucky, and had a Louisville girl, a certain Daisy Fay, the first "nice girl," as he puts it, whom he had ever known, and who was to embody all his dreams. But he went to France and the girl married Tom Buchanan of Chicago, an athlete, handsome and fabulously rich with new Chicago money.

After the war, Tom and Daisy are occupying a great house on Long Island, leading a reckless and idle life, with Tom seeking excitement in his adulteries. Gatsby, now rich from underworld connections, and still obsessed with Daisy, takes a house near the Buchanan place, near enough so that at night he can see the "green light" on Daisy's dock. He begins to give preposterous wild parties for the heterogeneous

floating population of the Jazz Age—all the while hoping to snatch Daisy from what he assumes to be her miserable life with Tom, and thus recapture the past and his dream. He does manage to encounter Daisy, does persuade her, for the moment, that the past can be recaptured, and almost persuades her that she had never, in any sense, loved Tom. But in the showdown scene with both, he is exposed for the shabby charlatan that, in one sense, he is.

The same afternoon, Daisy, driving Gatsby's car, accidentally runs down and kills Tom's current mistress, the wife of a garage keeper on the road to West Egg. In the sequel Tom manages to convince the garageman, now mad with grief and jealousy and already suspecting that Gatsby had been his wife's lover, that Gatsby had killed the woman. Later, Gatsby, waiting for some word from Daisy, is shot to death by the garageman, who then commits suicide. Tom and Daisy, immune in "their money and their vast carelessness," disappear and "let other people clean up the mess they have made."

The factual summary above is of the action which the novel presents—action as distinguished from plot, plot being the order of treatment of action. In certain novels, this distinction is more theoretical than actual and its importance minimal, but for *The Great Gatsby* it is crucial. The essential meaning of the action, the interpretation, here depends on the treatment, and it is by the special treatment that Fitzgerald creates his masterpiece.

The key to the treatment is a character placed in the novel as an "observer," through whose gradually increasing knowledge of the facts we, the readers, follow the story and sense its significance—a character whose reactions serve as an index to meaning. By such a treatment the interest of the basic story is constantly being fortified by the process of discovery, and thus the interpretation is saved from being a mere footnote, as it were, to the whole and is converted into a constantly expanding aspect of the actual narrative.

So in the role of observer and narrator we find Nick Carraway, the son of a wealthy family in the Middle West, a graduate of Yale, recently

an officer in the A.E.F. but now a bond salesman in New York, who, bit by bit, moves into
the fabulously rich, idle, and self-indulgent
world of Tom and Daisy. He has his own relation to that world and his own little abortive
love story with a young sportswoman named
Jordan Baker, but his technical function is to
give focus and form to the story of Gatsby, the
mysterious neighbor occupying a mansion that
towers over a forty-acre estate next to his bun-
galow. Nick is in a strategic position to assemble bits of the jigsaw puzzle that is the story of
Gatsby and Daisy and even contributes to the
story by bringing them together again after the
five years of separation, thus initiating the immediate action of the novel. And he ends by
burying Gatsby, thus asserting himself as the
agent that defines the form of the novel. That
form, as distinguished from the mere narrative,
is extraordinarily complex, and one aspect of
form that gives vitality to the whole is the contrast and tension between the simple story of
Gatsby, as it might be if related chronologically,
and the complexity of the process of discovery.

The first movement, or section, of the novel
gives the setting of the immediate action
—the Buchanan mansion, Gatsby's mansion, the
dreary wasteland of ash heaps where stands the
garage of the husband of Tom's mistress, dominated by the great eyes of an oculist's advertisement on a billboard, and the apartment in
New York where Tom keeps his trysts. Each
of the settings involves a scene—a probing into
a crucial element of the story. As for action,
this first section presents the life of Tom and
Daisy, and then Jordan Baker as part of that
world; the relation of Tom and his mistress
Myrtle Wilson, with his brutality and arrogance
and her vulgarity; and the mysterious image of
Gatsby, with at the end the portrait of Jordan
as the "most dishonest person" Nick had ever
known.

The second section is composed of Chapters
4, 5, and 6. Chapter 4 is concerned with Gatsby
and his world, including the racketeer and gambler Wolfsheim. It develops Gatsby's dream of
himself, how he wants to appear, with his false
autobiography and the account Jordan gives of

Gatsby, which is also, in a sense, false, in that
it is merely about Gatsby and ignores the nature of "Gatsby." Chapter 5, which is the
mathematical center of the book, concerns the
meeting of Gatsby and Daisy, and his showing
off his new success to her and his attempt to
evoke for her the old dream. Here, for a moment, in the dusk, with rain and a "faint flow of
thunder along the Sound," with the improbable
fellow Klipspringer (a hanger-on of Gatsby)
playing songs popular at the time of the old
romance in Louisville, Gatsby succeeds in his
endeavor to seize a reality beyond time, to make
his illusion come true. If Chapter 5 represents
the conquest of time and actuality, Chapter 6
brackets the out-of-time scene in Chapter 5 by
balancing the "false" biography of Gatsby in
Chapter 4 by the "true" biography of Gatz.
Then, still in Chapter 6, in contrast to the story
of Gatz, we find the last of Gatsby's parties,
this one, finally, attended by Tom and Daisy.
The vulgar scene of the party is concluded by
Gatsby's statement to Nick that he intends to
make Daisy tell Tom that she had never, in
fact, loved him, that he—Gatsby—is "going to
fix everything just the way it was before," and
as, in his dream, it still is.

The third and final section, Chapters 7, 8,
and 9, presents the tragic miscarriage of Gatsby's attempt to reverse the clock and relive the
past. In Chapter 7, after a maniacal drive into
the city, in a suite in the Plaza Hotel, in the
presence of Nick and Jordan, Gatsby tries to
make Daisy tell her husband that she has never
loved him; but Tom confronts him with what
he has discovered of his underworld associations; and, partly from this and partly from her
confusion of feeling about Tom himself, Daisy
cannot take the final step that Gatsby needs to
make his dream come true. On the way back
to West Egg, Daisy, driving Gatsby's car, runs
down Myrtle, and the chapter ends with Gatsby
waiting in the dark outside the Buchanan house,
thinking that Daisy may need him. But she had
never needed him, for, as Nick discovers, she
and Tom are sitting in their kitchen, not
"happy" nor "unhappy," but with "an unmistakable air of intimacy" that somehow declares

that they belong together. Gatsby's dream is in vain. Chapter 8 returns to the "true" biography of Gatz, the origin of his dream of being Gatsby, followed by a brief scene of Wilson's mourning, and then the report of the murder of Gatsby and the suicide.

Chapter 9 has, as far as action is concerned, two elements. First, there is the arrival of poor old Mr. Gatz, the father of the dead dreamer, with a ragged copy of *Hopalong Cassidy* in which Gatsby, as a boy already committed to his "Platonic conception of himself," had written down on a flyleaf the heroic schedule that was to work the magic of success. There are such entries as: "Rise from bed . . . 6:00"; "Dumbell exercises and wall scaling—6:15–6:30"; "Study electricity, etc.—7:15–8:15"; and "Practice elocution, poise and how to attain it—5:00–6:00." The second element of the action is the funeral, with no mourners. Gatsby, the party-giver, is abandoned except for Nick and one stray: "The party was over." So here, in the last chapter, we find juxtaposed the beginning of Gatsby's dream and the end.

In addition to the visit of the old father and the funeral, there is, in the last chapter of *The Great Gatsby*, another element, one having nothing to do with the action as such but of great importance in the interpretation of the novel. To fully understand this importance we must consider the thematic aspects of the role of Nick.

Nick, like Gatsby on the one hand, whom he observes and tries to understand, and like Fitzgerald on the other, whose surrogate observer he is, comes from the Middle West, drawn by the glamor of the East. To this extent Nick, representing Fitzgerald, understands and identifies with Gatsby. He sees "something gorgeous about him, some heightened sensitivity to the promises of life"—"an extraordinary gift for hope." But, at the same time, he is a critic of Gatsby and can state, at the beginning, that Gatsby represents everything for which he had "an unaffected scorn." In the end, Nick can resolve the ambivalence by making a distinction between Gatsby, "who turned out all right,"

and "what preyed on Gatsby, what foul dust floated in the wake of his dream." In other words, the progress of Nick is thematically toward this distinction; at the time of the telling of the story, as distinguished from the time of the action, Nick has repudiated the glamor of the corrupting East and returned to his native region, where he wants the world "to be in uniform and at a sort of moral attention forever"; but at the same time he has reached an understanding of what Gatsby embodies of human experience in general, and of American experience in particular.

As for what Gatsby embodies of human experience in general, we may profitably look at the two writers, Dreiser and Conrad, who, by Fitzgerald's own avowal, most influenced him. In a letter to President Hibben of Princeton, in 1920, Fitzgerald wrote that his own view of life was the "view of Theodore Dreiser and of Joseph Conrad—that life is too strong and remorseless for the sons of man"; but if the remorselessness of life belongs to the conception of those two masters, they shared a belief even more significant and personally characteristic, that the secret of life is illusion.[2] Over against

---

[2] Critics have recognized the great debt that Fitzgerald owes Conrad as a technician, but have let the broader matter of his philosophical indebtedness rest with the remark of 1920. But at this time Fitzgerald was only fumbling toward his theory of illusion. The theme runs, in fact, throughout American literature for more than a century. It is not, of course, confined to American literature, and it may have at least one of its roots in the need, with the decline of faith in religion as revelation, to found values on a naturalistic base. Values so founded must, in one sense, always be "illusions," at least, in one perspective. But it may be that there is a special American inflection to the theme. America was, in a way not found in any other country, a dream—or rather, a tissue of dreams—and the dreams were always being put to the test of actuality, over and over again. (The reader may recall our observation of the fact, and the announcement of the theme, as early as the discussion of Thomas Jefferson. See p. 158.) And, in a parallel fashion, the Alger dream of success would be constantly under the criticism of actuality; and sometimes under the most corrosive criticism possible—that is, the criticism that success achieved makes of the success that had been dreamed. In Dreiser this is one of the clear components of his theory of illusion. (See pp. 1881, 1890.) But the theme, as we have said, is pervasive,

his avowed skepticism, Conrad placed his doctrine that the "Idea" redeems all—the "Idea" that Lord Jim betrays and then, in the end, dies to affirm, the "Idea" that Marlow affirms by his "lie," at the end of *Heart of Darkness*, when he tells Kurtz's "intended" that he had died murmuring her name. It is only "illusion" that here gives life meaning, the "good lie" that prevents the world from being altogether "too dark." As for Dreiser, his trilogy and *An American Tragedy*[3] are quite specific in affirming a similar doctrine of illusion, which he sums up in the paradox: "Woe be to him who places his faith in illusion—the only reality—and woe to him who does not."[4]

To return to Gatsby, it is only because he has the capacity to create a dream and remain faithful to it that Nick can say of him, at the moment of the breakup of hope, "You're worth the whole damn bunch put together." The "bunch"—the Buchanans and all the other people around—cannot "dream." And this notion is what gives the haunting and cryptic resonance to the remark made by Gatsby that, even if "just for a minute, when they were first married," Daisy might have loved Tom, "it was just personal." Here for "personal" we must read "trivial, accidental, mechanical, meaningless"—because outside the magisterial significance of the dream, everything is merely part of the drift of the world. As though, we may add, even Daisy, when she stepped outside the dream, was not real, and what she had done was not real: only "personal."

It is natural, however, to ask about the content of Gatsby's dream. Is that content so much more worthy than the literal world inhabited by

the "bunch"? Scarcely, for Gatsby's aspiration has been, from the first days in Louisville, simply to enter that world, which was a "dream" only because inaccessible to him—like Daisy's house, with a "ripe mystery" and "hints of gay and radiant activities . . . of romances that were not musty and laid away already in lavender, but fresh and breathing and redolent of this year's shining motor-cars and of dances whose flowers were scarcely withered." There is little nobility or generosity of spirit in this dream, and only the fact of distance and yearning, the fact of its *being* a dream, endows the content with dignity, worth, and poetry. This is precisely the point.

By the time he wrote *The Great Gatsby*, Fitzgerald was perfectly aware of the deep division of his own nature, and his own ambivalence toward wealth, privilege, and self-indulgence. If he yearned toward that world, he also confessed to a deep hatred for the arrogant and careless lords of creation who populated it, a hatred that was the obverse of a certain toadyism and social insecurity. How deep-seated in his inner life was this hatred may be guessed not only from his boyhood position as a poor relation, but from the fact that poverty almost cost him Zelda; after that moment, he could never, he said, "stop wondering where my friends' money came from, nor . . . stop thinking that at one time a sort of *droit de seigneur* might have been exercised to give one of them my girl." And if Fitzgerald's moral revulsion from the world of wealth and privilege, which is manifested in Nick's return home, may legitimately be traced to puritanical Catholicism, we cannot ignore the instinctive and totally amoral hatred that provided a fuel and dynamism for the moral judgment.[5] For he was a moralist and in the end knew it: "I guess I am . . . a moralist at heart, and really want to preach at people in some acceptable form, rather than to entertain them."

---

as in Melville, Stephen Crane, Anderson, Hemingway, Sinclair Lewis, O'Neill, and Nathanael West. For further discussion in relation to West, see pp. 2352–58.

[3] The hero of Dreiser's novel, which, significantly, appeared in the middle of the Coolidge boom, in the same year as *The Great Gatsby*, is, like Gatz, the arriviste trying to live out the American Dream.

[4] The famous passage in *Lord Jim* (Chap. 22) about the "destructive element" is a precise parallel to this statement by Dreiser, and to Nick's remark that Gatsby is "worth the whole damn bunch put together."

[5] With his basic honesty, Fitzgerald refused, even in the depth of the Depression, and with all the real urgencies of the situation and the synthetic urgencies of fashion, to use the politics of the "left" as a façade for his personal rancor.

As we have already observed, Fitzgerald, late in his career, declared that the "test of a first-rate intelligence is the ability to hold two opposed ideas in the mind at the same time, and still retain the ability to function," and it is this principle that is crucial for the story of Gatsby. On one hand, Fitzgerald presents the poetry of Gatsby's dream, and on the other the moral sleaziness of the content of the dream—a sleaziness which he saw quite as clearly as Dreiser saw the content of Clyde Griffiths' dream.[6] It is only because we understand that the *content of the dream is indeed worthless and the means of achieving it criminal, that we can, paradoxically, understand the full worth of the mere act of dreaming.* To dream—to accept illusion as the essence of the creation of the self and of all values—is the characteristic act of man. "Where there is no vision, the people perish"—and in the midst of shadowy nonpersons like Tom and Daisy and the hordes of nameless guests, in a comic pseudo-castle set in a landscape of ashes as barren as Melville's *Encantadas* (see p. 829) and reigned over only by the painted eyes of Dr. T. J. Eckelberg's billboard and not by the eye of God, Gatsby alone possesses the rudimentary human power. He keeps his gaze faithfully on the green light across the dark water.

Such is Gatsby's mythic role in its most generalized form, but more specifically he has a mythic role in the American story. In its simplest form, this role is hinted at by the fact, remarked on by Nick, that he himself, Tom, Daisy, and Gatsby are all from the Middle West and have come east drawn by their illusion. Even the tragic conclusion of the novel is set against the far-off "dark fields of the Republic" stretching westward into the night. In Gatsby himself are fused the various versions of the American dream, on one hand the vulgar story of Horatio Alger with the worship of what William James called the "bitch-goddess, Success," and on the other hand the hope of the founding fathers, the millennial expectation of earthly perfection to be achieved by democracy, American know-how, technology, hard work, and Manifest Destiny—the Edenic vision with the American as the New Adam. In Gatsby, in fact, is the embodiment of the richly ambiguous American story, and the novel comes to rest with the green light of Daisy's dock merging with the first glimpse the Dutch sailors had of Long Island—the "fresh green breast of the New World," which, "for the last time in history," appeared to the stolid seaman as "something commensurate to his capacity for wonder."[7]

As a way of emphasizing the theme of illusion in *The Great Gatsby*, we may remark how the novel is related to "Winter Dreams," which comes just before it, and to "The Rich Boy," which comes just after. In the earlier story, Dexter, like Gatz, dreams a "Platonic self," finds the girl who will symbolize all his dreams, and, like Gatsby, loses her. But Dexter survives his loss and goes on to his (legitimate) financial triumphs, and merely becomes aware, as we have seen, that his dreams have been "left behind in the country of illusion." Dexter is a literal, not a mythic, figure.

In "The Rich Boy," a mirror image of "Winter Dreams," Anson Hunter is born rich; he is one of those who, according to a famous remark in the introduction to the story, "are different from you and me. They possess and enjoy early, and it does something to them, makes them soft where we are hard, and cynical where we are trustful." In other words, the rich, with no need for the "hard" energy to achieve success, have no faith in its mystic efficacy. Beyond illusion, they have no "capacity for wonder." Over against Anson, as over against Dexter, Gatsby stands in incorruptible illusion, and, in that incorruptibility, is of mythic scale.

The fact of Gatsby's mythic dimension is closely related to the method of the novel. Critics have sometimes maintained that the character of Gatsby is unsatisfactorily rendered,

---

[6] We must remind ourselves that Gatsby is, after all, a criminal; and if he is so enraptured by his dream that all judgment is wiped out, that does not mean that Fitzgerald intended us to be deceived.

[7] We have remarked elsewhere that the phrase echoes one of Whitman's in *Democratic Vistas*.

and Fitzgerald himself wrote John Peale Bishop agreeing with his friend's criticism that Gatsby was "blurred and patchy." But Fitzgerald was almost pathologically ready to agree with such criticism as Bishop had made. As a matter of fact, Fitzgerald's problem and its solution are here precisely the same as those of his master Conrad in *Heart of Darkness* and in *Lord Jim*; in both works Conrad found the dynamic not in the presentation of the main character, but in the "approach" to him. Furthermore, the approach, for Conrad, was not primarily to the literal man—to the "rounded" presentation—but to the mythic significance. And it was primarily from Conrad (and somewhat more remotely from Henry James, in such works as *The Ambassadors* and *The Portrait of a Lady*) that Fitzgerald derived the method that made it possible for him to develop the mythic presentation we have here.

The Great Gatsby does have certain faults. For example, the trip into New York for the confrontation of Gatsby and Daisy in the Plaza Hotel is peculiarly weak in motivation. Fitzgerald needed to arrange things so that the killing of Myrtle would coincide, in time, with the confrontation, and needed, too, to have Gatsby's yellow car, with Daisy at the wheel, as the lethal instrument; he simply couldn't work out a way less obviously dependent on coincidence. But there is such a deep resonance of the American experience in Gatsby's personal fate that we tend to forgive such incidental slips. For Gatsby is a late exemplar of the romantic individualist, the perverted idealist who earlier appears as Hawthorne's Ethan Brand, Melville's Ahab or Pierre, Mark Twain's Yankee, Dreiser's Cowperwood, and, ten years later, Faulkner's Sutpen in *Absalom, Absalom!*

The Great Gatsby won critical acclaim, notably from T. S. Eliot, who, forgetting or misreading Stephen Crane and Theodore Dreiser, called it "the first step the American novel has taken since Henry James." But Fitzgerald felt that even the most friendly critic had not the "slightest idea what the book is about." Doomed to the drudgery of writing stories that, with

rare exceptions like "Babylon Revisited," less and less commanded his faith and enthusiasm, tortured by Zelda's jealousy and encroaching madness, and caught in his own dissipations, he could not get on with a new novel. It was not until after the Depression had come to demolish the Jazz Age, Zelda had been put into a hospital, and he himself had had a breakdown, that Fitzgerald got seriously to work on the novel that, in the end, was to be known as *Tender Is the Night*.

It was finished—if a book in such need of revision could be called finished—in time for publication in the spring of 1934. The press was generally unfriendly and the public apathetic. Public interest was in economic and political matters, in social reform or revolution, and the story of how rich and deranged expatriates went to pot on the Riviera provoked little more from reviewers than the moralistic comment that it served them right. But *Tender Is the Night* exhibits, though fitfully, the gift that makes *The Great Gatsby* so memorable, and over the years since its publication, it has established itself as an indispensable item in the literary as well as the social record.

Tender Is the Night tells the same story as *The Great Gatsby*, in a new dimension and with a new emphasis: the story of the young man of obscure origins who commits himself to the pursuit of an illusion. But here Fitzgerald undertakes, as he does not do in the story of Gatsby, to give the hero the girl who embodies the illusion. He then proceeds to a detailed psychological portrait of the hero and, indirectly, to a moral analysis. In other ways, too, the story of Dick Diver is different. Though poor, his father, an Episcopal minister, is of Virginia blood, a fact echoing Fitzgerald's own family story, and has had, like Fitzgerald, a good education, not at Princeton but at Yale and Oxford, followed by medical and psychiatric studies on the continent. Like Fitzgerald, Diver has precocious standing in his profession. And he has great charm, charm based not on social expertness, but on intuition and sympathy—and here again, there is something of Fitzgerald, who had natural charm, and knew

it, and knew it to be, in the end, a dangerous gift.

As we have indicated, not only an obsessive idea, but Fitzgerald's actual life, is evident in *Tender Is the Night*, and this fact is powerfully underscored by Zelda's novel, *Save Me the Waltz*, a scarcely disguised account of her marriage with Fitzgerald as she, in her madness, understood it. In her jealousy-ridden version, written in the Johns Hopkins Hospital, the husband appears as monstrously overbearing; and the final conception of his own novel was apparently conditioned by the shocking encounter that *Save Me the Waltz* precipitated with his personal past. In one sense, *Tender Is the Night*, in its acknowledgment of failure and disintegration, corroborates Zelda's record; but in another it is a partial rebuttal and extenuation, for Diver is endowed with the capacity to love and the wish to protect and save Nicole.

To summarize: in Switzerland, Dick Diver, a brilliant young physician and psychiatric theorist, has as a patient a beautiful and baronially rich young American girl, Nicole Warren, suffering from schizophrenia brought on, as we later learn, by seduction by her own father. Dick falls in love with her, and in violation of all psychiatric principles and professional ethics, marries her. He undertakes a triple program, to protect and heal Nicole, to devote himself to psychiatric research, and to create a world of aesthetic elegance and cultivation.[8] For a time the program, executed in a villa of expensive simplicity, on a cliff overhanging the Mediterranean, seems to prosper; but bit by bit, it is corrupted by the aimlessness, waste, and self-indulgence of the world of expatriates in which the Divers move as well as by the deep am-

biguities in Dick's nature and motivation; he becomes little more than a shadowman, with charm disintegrating from self-disgust and dissipation, kept by a rich wife, in a situation of general ruin that echoes entries such as these from Fitzgerald's own day book: "July—Drinking and general unpleasantness—first trip jail; August—second trip jail—general carelessness and boredom." In the end, Nicole is "cured" —that is, she no longer needs Dick to sustain her, and so can leave him for a lover, a virile soldier of fortune. Dick disappears, to follow a downward spiral in the hinterland of upstate New York.

Fitzgerald apparently intended this story to embody a number of themes, to be a condensation of the meanings he had found in his own experience and in that of his generation. There was the theme of the dangerous gift of charm; of the commitment to illusion; of the ambiguity and corruption of motive; of the ambiguity of love. But there are other more peripheral themes; for instance, a pervasive but not clearly integrated theme of religion (summed up in the parody of papal blessing that Diver gives the beach world, the "carnival by the sea," as he prepares to leave it forever), and as in *The Great Gatsby*, the theme of America, clearly indicated in the early description of Nicole as "this scarcely saved waif of disaster bringing here the essence of a continent." To the theme of America, the "New World," is closely related the theme of time. The garden of the Diver villa is a new Eden, out of time—that is, built literally on the ruins of an old village, triumphing over history, an image of the Platonic moment heroically sought by Gatsby that would annul the passage of time.

The theme of time may, too, absorb that of America, as when Nicole is described as perpetually young, somehow a child, unable to grow up into responsibility: "enough ridden by the current youth worship, the moving pictures with their myriad faces of girl-children blandly represented as carrying on the work and wisdom of the world, to find a jealousy of youth." Again related to the theme of America, but distinguishable from it, is that of social criticism, in-

---

[8] For this aesthetic aspect of the novel the wealthy and cultivated American expatriate Gerald Murphy served as a model for Diver. Murphy was trained as a landscape architect, was a painter of talent, owned a famously beautiful villa near Antibes, was acquainted with the great and near-great of the world of art and letters, and was a celebrated host. With the Murphy-Diver was fused the Fitzgerald-Diver—to give a fusion not always perfectly without seam.

volving Fitzgerald's old attitude toward the callousness and carelessness of the rich. But now Fitzgerald's old envious hatred and moralistic criticism have been given, by the climate of the 1930's, a new aspect, most clearly stated in this famous passage:

> Nicole was the product of much ingenuity and toil. For her sake trains began their run at Chicago and traversed the round belly of the continent to California; chicle factories fumed and link belts grew link by link in factories; men mixed toothpaste in vats and drew mouthwash out of copper hogsheads; girls canned tomatoes quickly in August or worked rudely at the Five-and-Tens on Christmas Eve; half-breed Indians toiled on Brazilian coffee plantations and dreamers were muscled out of patent rights in new tractors —these were some of the people who gave a tithe to Nicole. . . .

The multiplicity of themes and perspectives of meaning in *Tender Is the Night* does sometimes give the novel range and depth, but at other times it merely makes for distraction. The root of the difficulty seems to be technical. We have remarked how in *The Great Gatsby* the use of the observer-narrator dramatizes the process of discovery, to give a control of the story of the hero and a focus for his significance; but in *Tender Is the Night* there is no such principle of unity. It is true that a brilliant use is made of the young actress Rosemary Hoyt in the first section; by his effect on her Diver's charm and the aesthetic appeal of the little world he has created is established; and this vision of the new Eden seen from the outside by Rosemary gives a dramatic basis for the contrast, gradually revealed, between this outer vision and the inner reality. But Fitzgerald never discovers a consistent method, a fundamental principle of control, for presenting and anatomizing that inner reality, and in spite of certain strongly rendered sections, the general effect is one of drift and improvisation. Furthermore, there is no return at the end to some method of objective rendering which would give depth and

architectural balance to the Rosemary Hoyt section that opens the book.[9]

In *Tender Is the Night*, Fitzgerald was heroically attempting a work that would distill the meaning of his own disastrous experience. He failed. Perhaps, in this climactic effort, he remained too entangled in the spirit of the decade, in his own experience; here, too, the "double vision" that had given power to *The Great Gatsby* deserted him. But by fits and starts something of the heroism of the effort shows through, and even if there is a certain blur in the moral and psychological issue that confronts Diver, the book still creates, in a more compelling way than *The Beautiful and Damned*, the sense of what it means to fall in love, in the end, with one's own ruin. And, too, *Tender Is the Night* is an appropriate monument, and epitaph, to an age.

In the last phase of his life, from *Tender Is the Night* to his death, Fitzgerald was struggling against debt, failing health, depression (with two attempts at suicide), and the problems posed by Zelda's condition. His talent, however, managed to survive, though surviving, in part at least, by feeding off his own ruin. In a series of essays originally published in *Esquire* magazine, Fitzgerald turned from the analysis of the semifictional Dick Diver to that of the painfully real self. To support himself during this period, Fitzgerald worked in Hollywood as a script writer, but he found the experience frustrating; it did, however, provide him with the material for *The Last Tycoon*, based on the life of Irving Thalberg, the young genius who had general charge of the Metro-Goldwyn-Mayer studio, with the main female character drawn from Sheilah Graham, an English journalist with whom Fitzgerald had fallen in love. As he wrote of the last struggles of the dying Monroe Stahr, the character based on Thalberg, he himself was propped up in bed. On December 21, 1940, in the living room of

---

[9] Fitzgerald was fully aware of the problem, and in one edition he tried the desperate solution of putting the early life of Diver before the Rosemary Hoyt section. The original order is now generally accepted.

Sheilah Graham's apartment, he died of a heart attack.

Though unfinished, *The Last Tycoon*, edited by Edmund Wilson, was published in 1941. Certain responsible critics, including Wilson, have felt that this novel would have been Fitzgerald's crowning achievement, that it marked a new maturity of feeling and a deeper sense of tragedy, and gave promise of the control of form so lacking in *Tender Is the Night*. Some of those claims seem inflated. It is hard, for instance, to believe that *The Last Tycoon* affords a more significant vision of Hollywood than *The Day of the Locust*, by Nathanael West, which preceded it by some years (see pp. 2359–73); and those who praise it as the finest novel about business organization must not have read *The Financier* and *The Titan* by Dreiser. As for the tragic sense, some readers, even those who feel the pathos of Stahr's story, would argue that the tragic scale is exactly what the story of Stahr lacks—the sense of the hero's personal force and of general significance, the qualities that are more obvious in Dreiser's Cowperwood or Faulkner's Sutpen.

In any case, *The Last Tycoon* is not finished. And if, even in its promise, it is less to be admired than some have asserted, Fitzgerald can still offer the enduring fascination of *The Great Gatsby*, the true, if fitful, power of *Tender Is the Night*, and a half dozen stories that are inexpungable items in the American record.

BIOGRAPHICAL CHART

1896　Born, September 24, in St. Paul, Minnesota, son of Edward Fitzgerald and Mollie (formal name Mary) McQuillan, daughter of a rich merchant of Irish blood

1911–13　Attends Newman Academy, in New Jersey; interested in fiction and stage

1913–17　Attends Princeton; member of Triangle Club; begins novel to be *This Side of Paradise*; begins officers' training at Fort Leavenworth, Kansas

1918　Sent to Camp Sheridan, Alabama; falls in love with Zelda Sayre

1920　Stories successful; movie sale; *This Side of Paradise* published to great acclaim; marries Zelda; *Flappers and Philosophers*

1922　*The Beautiful and Damned* and *Tales of the Jazz Age*; lives in St. Paul; returns East to Great Neck, Long Island

1923　*The Vegetable*, a play, fails on Broadway

1924　Flees to France; lives in St. Raphaël and works on *The Great Gatsby*

1925　*The Great Gatsby* a critical success, but financially disappointing

1926　*All the Sad Young Men*

1927　First works in Hollywood; returns East to "Ellerslie," near Wilmington; heavy drinking and disorder of life

1928　Returns to Paris; inability to work and dissipation; Zelda's work at ballet, and deterioration

1930　Zelda collapses and is hospitalized

1931　Works again in Hollywood

1932　Zelda's novel *Save Me the Waltz*, written in Johns Hopkins Hospital, published; lives back East, at "La Paix," near Baltimore; struggles to write and maintain a household

1934　*Tender Is the Night* receives poor reception

1937　Last phase, Hollywood; love affair with Sheilah Graham

1940　Dies, December 21; buried in Rockville, Maryland

1941　*The Last Tycoon*

1945　*The Crack-Up*

FURTHER READINGS

There is no standard edition of Fitzgerald's works.

Andrew Turnbull, ed., *The Letters of F. Scott Fitzgerald* (1963)

Malcolm Cowley, *The Short Stories of F. Scott Fitzgerald* (1951)

John Berryman, "F. Scott Fitzgerald," *Kenyon Review* (Winter, 1946)

Matthew J. Bruccoli, *The Composition of Tender Is the Night* (1963)

Richard Chase, *The American Novel and Its Tradition* (1957)

Malcolm Cowley, *Exile's Return* (1951)
Maxwell Geismar, *The Last of the Provincials* (1943)
Sheilah Graham and Gerold Frank, *Beloved Infidel* (1958)
Ernest Hemingway, *A Moveable Feast* (1964)
F. J. Hoffman, *The Twenties* (1955)
———, ed., *The Great Gatsby: A Study* (1962) 1962
Alfred Kazin, ed., *F. Scott Fitzgerald: The Man and His Work* (1951)
Frank Kinahan, "Focus on F. Scott Fitzgerald's *Tender Is the Night*," in *American Dreams, American Nightmares* (1970), edited by David Madden
Aaton Latham, *Crazy Sundays: F. Scott Fitzgerald in Hollywood* (1971)
Richard Lehan, *F. Scott Fitzgerald* (1966)
Nancy Mitford, *Zelda* (1970)

James E. Miller, *F. Scott Fitzgerald: His Art and His Technique* (1964)
Arthur Mizener, *The Far Side of Paradise* (1951)
———, ed., *F. Scott Fitzgerald: A Collection of Critical Articles* (1963)
Wright Morris, "The Ability to Function: A Reappraisal of Fitzgerald and Hemingway," *New World Writing* (June, 1958)
Sergio Perosa, *The Art of F. Scott Fitzgerald* (1965)
Henry Dan Piper, *F. Scott Fitzgerald: A Candid Portrait* (1963)
Calvin Tompkins, *Living Well Is the Best Revenge* (1971)
Andrew Turnbull, *Scott Fitzgerald* (1962)
Edmund Wilson, ed., *Collected Essays of John Peale Bishop* (1948)

The Rich Boy (1926)

Begin with an individual, and before you know it you find that you have created a type; begin with a type, and you find that you have created—nothing. That is because we are all queer fish, queerer behind our faces and voices than we want any one to know or than we know ourselves. When I hear a man proclaiming himself an "average, honest, open fellow," I feel pretty sure that he has some definite and perhaps terrible abnormality which he has agreed to conceal—and his protestation of being average and honest and open is his way of reminding himself of his misprision.

There are no types, no plurals. There is a rich boy, and this is his and not his brothers' story. All my life I have lived among his brothers but this one has been my friend. Besides, if I wrote about his brothers I should have to begin by attacking all the lies that the poor have told about the rich and the rich have told about themselves—such a wild structure they have erected that when we pick up a book about the rich, some instinct prepares us for unreality. Even the intelligent and impassioned reporters of life have made the country of the rich as unreal as fairy-land.

Let me tell you about the very rich. They are different from you and me. They possess and enjoy early, and it does something to them, makes them soft where we are hard, and cynical where we are trustful, in a way that, unless you were born rich, it is very difficult to understand. They think, deep in their hearts, that they are better than we are because we had to discover the compensations and refuges of life for ourselves. Even when they enter deep into our world or sink below us, they still think that they are better than we are. They are different. The only way I can describe young Anson Hunter is to approach him as if he were a foreigner and cling stubbornly to my point of view. If I accept his for a moment I am lost—I have nothing to show but a preposterous movie.

II

Anson was the eldest of six children who would some day divide a fortune of fifteen million dollars, and he reached the age of reason—is it seven?—at the beginning of the century when daring young women were already gliding along Fifth Avenue in electric "mobiles." In those days he and his brother had an English governess who spoke the language very clearly and crisply and well, so that the two boys grew to speak as she did—their words and sentences were all crisp and clear and not run together as ours are. They didn't talk exactly like English children but acquired an accent that is peculiar to fashionable people in the city of New York.

In the summer the six children were moved from the house on 71st Street to a big estate in northern Connecticut. It was not a fashionable locality—Anson's father wanted to delay as long as possible his children's knowledge of that side of life. He was a man somewhat superior to his class, which composed New York society, and to his period, which was the snobbish and formalized vulgarity of the Gilded Age, and he wanted his sons to learn habits of concentration and have sound constitutions and grow up into right-living and successful men. He and his wife kept an eye on them as well as they were able until the two older boys went away to school, but in huge establishments this is difficult—it was much simpler in the series of small and medium-sized houses in which my own youth was spent—I was never far out of the reach of my mother's voice, of the sense of her presence, her approval or disapproval.

Anson's first sense of his superiority came to him when he realized the half-grudging American deference that was paid to him in the Connecticut village. The parents of the boys he played with always inquired after his father and mother, and were vaguely excited when their own children were asked to the Hunters' house. He accepted this as the natural state of things, and a sort of impatience with all groups of which he was not the centre—in money, in position, in authority—remained with him for the rest of his life. He disdained to struggle with other boys for precedence—he expected it to be given him freely, and when it wasn't he withdrew into his family. His family was sufficient, for in the East money is still a somewhat feudal thing, a clan-forming thing. In the snobbish West, money separates families to form "sets."

At eighteen, when he went to New Haven, Anson was tall and thick-set, with a clear complexion and a healthy color from the ordered life he had led in school. His hair was yellow and grew in a funny way on his head, his nose was beaked—these two things kept him from being handsome—but he had a confident charm and a certain brusque style, and the upper-class men who passed him on the street knew without being told that he was a rich boy and had gone to one of the best schools. Nevertheless, his very superiority kept him from being a success in college—the independence was mistaken for egotism, and the refusal to accept Yale standards with the proper awe seemed to belittle all those who had. So, long before he graduated, he began to shift the centre of his life to New York.

He was at home in New York—there was his own house with "the kind of servants you can't get any more"—and his own family, of which, because of his good humor and a certain ability to make things go, he was rapidly becoming the centre, and the débutante parties, and the correct manly world of the men's clubs, and the occasional wild spree with the gallant girls whom New Haven only knew from the fifth row. His aspirations were conventional enough—they included even the irreproachable shadow he would some day marry, but they differed from the aspirations of the majority of young men in that there was no mist over them, none of that quality which is variously known as "idealism" or "illusion." Anson accepted without reservation the world of high finance and high extravagance, of divorce and dissipation, of snobbery and of privilege. Most of our lives end as a compromise—it was as a compromise that his life began.

He and I first met in the late summer of 1917 when he was just out of Yale, and, like the rest of us, was swept up into the systematized hysteria of the war. In the blue-green uniform of the naval aviation he came down to Pensacola, where the hotel orchestras played "I'm sorry, dear," and we young officers danced with the girls. Every one liked him, and though he ran with the drinkers and wasn't an especially good pilot, even the instructors treated him with a certain respect. He was always having long talks with them in his confident, logical voice—talks which ended by his getting himself, or, more frequently, another officer, out of some impending trouble. He was convivial, bawdy, robustly avid for pleasure, and we were all surprised when he fell in love with a conservative and rather proper girl.

Her name was Paula Legendre, a dark, serious beauty from somewhere in California. Her family kept a winter residence just outside of town, and in spite of her primness she was enormously popular; there is a large class of men whose egotism can't endure humor in a woman. But Anson wasn't that sort, and I couldn't understand the attraction of her "sincerity"—that was the thing to say about her—for his keen and somewhat sardonic mind.

Nevertheless, they fell in love—and on her terms. He no longer joined the twilight gathering at the De Soto bar, and whenever they were seen together they were engaged in a long, serious dialogue, which must have gone on several weeks. Long afterward he told me that it was not about anything in particular but was composed on both sides of immature and even meaningless statements —the emotional content that gradually came to fill it grew up not out of the words but out of its enormous seriousness. It was a sort of hypnosis. Often it was interrupted, giving way to that emasculated humor we call fun; when they were alone it was resumed again, solemn, low-keyed, and pitched so as to give each other a sense of unity in feeling and thought. They came to resent any interruptions of it, to be unresponsive to facetiousness about life, even to the mild cynicism of their contemporaries. They were only happy when the dialogue was going on, and its seriousness bathed them like the amber glow of an open fire. Toward the end there came an interruption they did not resent—it began to be interrupted by passion.

Oddly enough, Anson was as engrossed in the dialogue as she was and as profoundly affected by it, yet at the same time aware that on his side much was insincere, and on hers much was merely simple. At first, too, he despised her emotional simplicity as well, but with his love her nature deepened and blossomed, and he could despise it no longer. He felt that if he could enter into Paula's warm safe life he would be happy. The long preparation of the dialogue removed any constraint—he taught her some of what he had learned from more adventurous women, and she responded with a rapt holy intensity. One evening after a dance they agreed to marry, and he wrote a long letter about her to his mother. The next day Paula told him that she was rich, that she had a personal fortune of nearly a million dollars.

III

It was exactly as if they could say "Neither of us has anything: we shall be poor together"—just as delightful that they should be rich instead. It gave them the same communion of adventure. Yet when Anson got leave in April, and Paula and her mother accompanied him North, she was impressed with the standing of his family in New York and with the scale on which they lived. Alone with Anson for the first time in the rooms where he had played as a boy, she was filled with a comfortable emotion, as though she were pre-eminently safe and taken care of. The pictures of Anson in a skull cap at his first school, of Anson on horseback with the sweetheart of a mysterious forgotten summer, of Anson in a gay group of ushers and bridesmaids at a wedding, made her jealous of his life apart from her in the past, and so completely did his authoritative person seem to sum up and typify these possessions of his that she was inspired with the idea of being married immediately and returning to Pensacola as his wife.

But an immediate marriage wasn't discussed—even the engagement was to be secret until after the war. When she realized that only two days of

his leave remained, her dissatisfaction crystallized in the intention of making him as unwilling to wait as she was. They were driving to the country for dinner, and she determined to force the issue that night.

Now a cousin of Paula's was staying with them at the Ritz, a severe, bitter girl who loved Paula but was somewhat jealous of her impressive engagement, and as Paula was late in dressing, the cousin, who wasn't going to the party, received Anson in the parlor of the suite.

Anson had met friends at five o'clock and drunk freely and indiscreetly with them for an hour. He left the Yale Club at a proper time, and his mother's chauffeur drove him to the Ritz, but his usual capacity was not in evidence, and the impact of the steam-heated sitting-room made him suddenly dizzy. He knew it, and he was both amused and sorry.

Paula's cousin was twenty-five, but she was exceptionally naïve, and at first failed to realize what was up. She had never met Anson before, and she was surprised when he mumbled strange information and nearly fell off his chair, but until Paula appeared it didn't occur to her that what she had taken for the odor of a dry-cleaned uniform was really whiskey. But Paula understood as soon as she appeared; her only thought was to get Anson away before her mother saw him, and at the look in her eyes the cousin understood too.

When Paula and Anson descended to the limousine they found two men inside, both asleep; they were the men with whom he had been drinking at the Yale Club, and they were also going to the party. He had entirely forgotten their presence in the car. On the way to Hempstead they awoke and sang. Some of the songs were rough, and though Paula tried to reconcile herself to the fact that Anson had few verbal inhibitions, her lips tightened with shame and distaste.

Back at the hotel the cousin, confused and agitated, considered the incident, and then walked into Mrs. Legendre's bedroom, saying: "Isn't he funny?"

"Who is funny?"

"Why—Mr. Hunter. He seemed so funny."

Mrs. Legendre looked at her sharply.

"How is he funny?"

"Why, he said he was French. I didn't know he was French."

"That's absurd. You must have misunderstood." She smiled: "It was a joke."

The cousin shook her head stubbornly.

"No. He said he was brought up in France. He said he couldn't speak any English, and that's why he couldn't talk to me. And he couldn't!"

Mrs. Legendre looked away with impatience just as the cousin added thoughtfully, "Perhaps it was because he was so drunk," and walked out of the room.

This curious report was true. Anson, finding his voice thick and uncontrollable, had taken the unusual refuge of announcing that he spoke no English. Years afterwards he used to tell that part of the story, and he invariably communicated the uproarious laughter which the memory aroused in him.

Five times in the next hour Mrs. Legendre tried to get Hempstead on the phone. When she succeeded, there was a ten-minute delay before she heard Paula's voice on the wire.

"Cousin Jo told me Anson was intoxicated."

"Oh, no. . . ."

"Oh, yes. Cousin Jo says he was intoxicated. He told her he was French, and fell off his chair and behaved as if he was very intoxicated. I don't want you to come home with him."

"Mother, he's all right! Please don't worry about——"

"But I do worry. I think it's dreadful. I want you to promise me not to come home with him."

"I'll take care of it, mother. . . ."

"I don't want you to come home with him."

"All right, mother. Good-by."

"Be sure now, Paula. Ask some one to bring you."

Deliberately Paula took the receiver from her ear and hung it up. Her face was flushed with helpless annoyance. Anson was stretched out asleep in a bedroom up-stairs, while the dinner-party below was proceeding lamely toward conclusion.

The hour's drive had sobered him somewhat—his arrival was merely hilarious—and Paula hoped that the evening was not spoiled, after all, but two imprudent cocktails before dinner completed the disaster. He talked boisterously and somewhat offensively to the party at large for fifteen minutes, and then slid silently under the table; like a man in an old print—but, unlike an old print, it was rather horrible without being at all quaint. None of the young girls present remarked upon the incident—it seemed to merit only silence. His uncle and two other men carried him up-stairs, and it was just after this that Paula was called to the phone.

An hour later Anson awoke in a fog of nervous agony, through which he perceived after a moment the figure of his uncle Robert standing by the door.

". . . I said are you better?"

"What?"

"Do you feel better, old man?"

"Terrible," said Anson.

"I'm going to try you on another bromo-seltzer. If you can hold it down, it'll do you good to sleep."

With an effort Anson slid his legs from the bed and stood up.

"I'm all right," he said dully.

"Take it easy."

"I thin' if you gave me a glassbrandy I could go down-stairs."

"Oh, no——"

"Yes, that's the only thin'. I'm all right now. . . . I suppose I'm in Dutch dow' there."

"They know you're a little under the weather," said his uncle deprecatingly. "But don't worry about it. Schuyler didn't even get here. He passed away in the locker-room over at the Links."

Indifferent to any opinion, except Paula's, Anson was nevertheless determined to save the débris of the evening, but when after a cold bath he made his appearance most of the party had already left. Paula got up immediately to go home.

In the limousine the old serious dialogue began. She had known that he drank, she admitted, but she had never expected anything like this—it seemed to her that perhaps they were not suited to each other, after all. Their ideas about life were too different, and so forth. When she finished speaking, Anson spoke in turn, very soberly. Then Paula said she'd have to think it over; she wouldn't decide tonight; she was not angry but she was terribly sorry. Nor would she let him come into the hotel with her, but just before she got out of the car she leaned and kissed him unhappily on the cheek.

The next afternoon Anson had a long talk with Mrs. Legendre while Paula sat listening in silence. It was agreed that Paula was to brood over the incident for a proper period and then, if mother and daughter thought it best, they would follow Anson to Pensacola. On his part he apologized with sincerity and dignity—that was all; with every card in her hand Mrs. Legendre was unable to establish any advantage over him. He made no promises, showed no humility, only delivered a few serious comments on life which brought him off with rather a moral superiority at the end. When they came South three weeks later, neither

Anson in his satisfaction nor Paula in her relief at the reunion realized that the psychological moment had passed forever.

IV

He dominated and attracted her, and at the same time filled her with anxiety. Confused by his mixture of solidarity and self-indulgence, of sentiment and cynicism—incongruities which her gentle mind was unable to resolve—Paula grew to think of him as two alternating personalities. When she saw him alone, or at a formal party, or with his casual inferiors, she felt a tremendous pride in his strong, attractive presence, the paternal, understanding stature of his mind. In other company she became uneasy when what had been a fine imperviousness to mere gentility showed its other face. The other face was gross, humorous, reckless of everything but pleasure. It startled her mind temporarily away from him, even led her into a short covert experiment with an old beau, but it was no use—after four months of Anson's enveloping vitality there was an anæmic pallor in all other men.

In July he was ordered abroad, and their tenderness and desire reached a crescendo. Paula considered a last-minute marriage—decided against it only because there were always cocktails on his breath now, but the parting itself made her physically ill with grief. After his departure she wrote him long letters of regret for the days of love they had missed by waiting. In August Anson's plane slipped down into the North Sea. He was pulled onto a destroyer after a night in the water and sent to hospital with pneumonia; the armistice was signed before he was finally sent home.

Then, with every opportunity given back to them, with no material obstacle to overcome, the secret weavings of their temperaments came between them, drying up their kisses and their tears, making their voices less loud to one another, muffling the intimate chatter of their hearts until the old communication was only possible by letters, from far away. One afternoon a society reporter waited for two hours in the Hunters' house for a confirmation of their engagement. Anson denied it; nevertheless an early issue carried the report as a leading paragraph—they were "constantly seen together at Southhampton, Hot Springs, and Tuxedo Park." But the serious dialogue had turned a corner into a long-sustained quarrel, and the affair was almost played out. Anson got drunk flagrantly

and missed an engagement with her, whereupon Paula made certain behavioristic demands. His despair was helpless before his pride and his knowledge of himself: the engagement was definitely broken.

"Dearest," said their letters now, "Dearest, Dearest, when I wake up in the middle of the night and realize that after all it was not to be, I feel that I want to die. I can't go on living any more. Perhaps when we meet this summer we may talk things over and decide differently—we were so excited and sad that day, and I don't feel that I can live all my life without you. You speak of other people. Don't you know there are no other people for me, but only you. . . ."

But as Paula drifted here and there around the East she would sometimes mention her gaieties to make him wonder. Anson was too acute to wonder. When he saw a man's name in her letters he felt more sure of her and a little disdainful—he was always superior to such things. But he still hoped that they would some day marry.

Meanwhile he plunged vigorously into all the movement and glitter of post-bellum New York, entering a brokerage house, joining half a dozen clubs, dancing late, and moving in three worlds— his own world, the world of young Yale graduates, and that section of the half-world which rests one end on Broadway. But there was always a thorough and infractible eight hours devoted to his work in Wall Street, where the combination of his influential family connection, his sharp intelligence, and his abundance of sheer physical energy brought him almost immediately forward. He had one of those invaluable minds with partitions in it; sometimes he appeared at his office refreshed by less than an hour's sleep, but such occurrences were rare. So early as 1920 his income in salary and commissions exceeded twelve thousand dollars.

As the Yale tradition slipped into the past he became more and more of a popular figure among his classmates in New York, more popular than he had ever been in college. He lived in a great house, and had the means of introducing young men into other great houses. Moreover, his life already seemed secure, while theirs, for the most part, had arrived again at precarious beginnings. They commenced to turn to him for amusement and escape, and Anson responded readily, taking pleasure in helping people and arranging their affairs.

There were no men in Paula's letters now, but a note of tenderness ran through them that had not been there before. From several sources he heard that she had "a heavy beau," Lowell Thayer, a Bostonian of wealth and position, and though he was sure she still loved him, it made him uneasy to think that he might lose her, after all. Save for one unsatisfactory day she had not been in New York for almost five months, and as the rumors multiplied he became increasingly anxious to see her. In February he took his vacation and went down to Florida.

Palm Beach sprawled plump and opulent between the sparkling sapphire of Lake Worth, flawed here and there by house-boats at anchor, and the great turquoise bar of the Atlantic Ocean. The huge bulks of the Breakers and the Royal Poinciana rose as twin paunches from the bright level of the sand, and around them clustered the Dancing Glade, Bradley's House of Chance, and a dozen modistes and milliners with goods at triple prices from New York. Upon the trellised veranda of the Breakers two hundred women stepped right, stepped left, wheeled, and slid in that then celebrated calisthenic known as the double-shuffle, while in half-time to the music two thousand bracelets clicked up and down on two hundred arms.

At the Everglades Club after dark Paula and Lowell Thayer and Anson and a casual fourth played bridge with hot cards. It seemed to Anson that her kind, serious face was wan and tired—she had been around now for four, five, years. He had known her for three.

"Two spades."

"Cigarette? . . . Oh, I beg your pardon. By me."

"By."

"I'll double three spades."

There were a dozen tables of bridge in the room, which was filling up with smoke. Anson's eyes met Paula's, held them persistently even when Thayer's glance fell between them. . . .

"What was bid?" he asked abstractedly.

"Rose of Washington Square"

sang the young people in the corners:

> *"I'm withering there*
> *In basement air———"*

The smoke banked like fog, and the opening of a door filled the room with blown swirls of ectoplasm. Little Bright Eyes streaked past the tables seeking Mr. Conan Doyle among the Englishmen who were posing as Englishmen about the lobby.

"You could cut it with a knife."

". . . cut it with a knife."

". . . a knife."

At the end of the rubber Paula suddenly got up and spoke to Anson in a tense, low voice. With scarcely a glance at Lowell Thayer, they walked out the door and descended a long flight of stone steps—in a moment they were walking hand in hand along the moonlit beach.

"Darling, darling. . . ." They embraced recklessly, passionately, in a shadow. . . . Then Paula drew back her face to let his lips say what she wanted to hear—she could feel the words forming as they kissed again. . . . Again she broke away, listening, but as he pulled her close once more she realized that he had said nothing—only *"Darling! Darling!"* in that deep, sad whisper that always made her cry. Humbly, obediently, her emotions yielded to him and the tears streamed down her face, but her heart kept on crying: "Ask me—oh, Anson, dearest, ask me!"

"Paula. . . . *Paula!*"

The words wrung her heart like hands, and Anson, feeling her tremble, knew that emotion was enough. He need say no more, commit their destinies to no practical enigma. Why should he, when he might hold her so, biding his own time, for another year—forever? He was considering them both, her more than himself. For a moment, when she said suddenly that she must go back to her hotel, he hesitated, thinking, first, "This is the moment, after all," and then: "No, let it wait—she is mine. . . ."

He had forgotten that Paula too was worn away inside with the strain of three years. Her mood passed forever in the night.

He went back to New York next morning filled with a certain restless dissatisfaction. Late in April, without warning, he received a telegram from Bar Harbor in which Paula told him that she was engaged to Lowell Thayer, and that they would be married immediately in Boston. What he never really believed could happen had happened at last.

Anson filled himself with whiskey that morning, and going to the office, carried on his work without a break—rather with a fear of what would happen if he stopped. In the evening he went out as usual, saying nothing of what had occurred; he was cordial, humorous, unabstracted. But one thing he could not help—for three days, in any place, in any company, he would suddenly bend his head into his hands and cry like a child.

V

In 1922 when Anson went abroad with the junior partner to investigate some London loans, the journey intimated that he was to be taken into the firm. He was twenty-seven now, a little heavy without being definitely stout, and with a manner older than his years. Old people and young people liked him and trusted him, and mothers felt safe when their daughters were in his charge, for he had a way, when he came into a room, of putting himself on a footing with the oldest and most conservative people there. "You and I," he seemed to say, "we're solid. We understand."

He had an instinctive and rather charitable knowledge of the weaknesses of men and women, and, like a priest, it made him the more concerned for the maintenance of outward forms. It was typical of him that every Sunday morning he taught in a fashionable Episcopal Sunday-school—even though a cold shower and a quick change into a cutaway coat were all that separated him from the wild night before.

After his father's death he was the practical head of his family, and, in effect, guided the destinies of the younger children. Through a complication his authority did not extend to his father's estate, which was administered by his Uncle Robert, who was the horsey member of the family, a good-natured, hard-drinking member of that set which centres about Wheatley Hills.

Uncle Robert and his wife, Edna, had been great friends of Anson's youth, and the former was disappointed when his nephew's superiority failed to take a horsey form. He backed him for a city club which was the most difficult in America to enter—one could only join if one's family had "helped to build up New York" (or, in other words, were rich before 1880)—and when Anson, after his election, neglected it for the Yale Club, Uncle Robert gave him a little talk on the subject. But when on top of that Anson declined to enter Robert Hunter's own conservative and somewhat neglected brokerage house, his manner grew cooler. Like a primary teacher who has taught all he knew, he slipped out of Anson's life.

There were so many friends in Anson's life—scarcely one for whom he had not done some unusual kindness and scarcely one whom he did not occasionally embarrass by his bursts of rough conversation or his habit of getting drunk whenever and however he liked. It annoyed him when any one else blundered in that regard—about his own lapses he was always humorous. Odd things happened to him and he told them with infectious laughter.

I was working in New York that spring, and I used to lunch with him at the Yale Club, which my university was sharing until the completion of our own. I had read of Paula's marriage, and one afternoon, when I asked him about her, something moved him to tell me the story. After that he frequently invited me to family dinners at his house and behaved as though there was a special relation between us, as though with his confidence a little of that consuming memory had passed into me.

I found that despite the trusting mothers, his attitude toward girls was not indiscriminately protective. It was up to the girl—if she showed an inclination toward looseness, she must take care of herself, even with him.

"Life," he would explain sometimes, "has made a cynic of me."

By life he meant Paula. Sometimes, especially when he was drinking, it became a little twisted in his mind, and he thought that she had callously thrown him over.

This "cynicism," or rather his realization that naturally fast girls were not worth sparing, led to his affair with Dolly Karger. It wasn't his only affair in those years, but it came nearest to touching him deeply, and it had a profound effect upon his attitude toward life.

Dolly was the daughter of a notorious "publicist" who had married into society. She herself grew up into the Junior League, came out at the Plaza, and went to the Assembly; and only a few old families like the Hunters could question whether or not she "belonged," for her picture was often in the papers, and she had more enviable attention than many girls who undoubtedly did. She was dark-haired, with carmine lips and a high, lovely color, which she concealed under pinkish-gray powder all through the first year out, because high color was unfashionable—Victorian-pale was the thing to be. She wore black, severe suits and stood with her hands in her pockets leaning a little forward, with a humorous restraint on her face. She danced exquisitely—better than anything she liked to dance—better than anything except making love. Since she was ten she had always been in love, and, usually, with some boy who didn't respond to her. Those who did—and there were many—bored her after a brief encounter, but for her failures she reserved the warmest spot in her heart. When she met them she would always try once more—sometimes she succeeded, more often she failed.

It never occurred to this gypsy of the unattainable that there was a certain resemblance in those who refused to love her—they shared a hard intuition that saw through to her weakness, not a weakness of emotion but a weakness of rudder. Anson perceived this when he first met her, less than a month after Paula's marriage. He was drinking rather heavily, and he pretended for a week that he was falling in love with her. Then he dropped her abruptly and forgot—immediately he took up the commanding position in her heart.

Like so many girls of that day Dolly was slackly and indiscreetly wild. The unconventionality of a slightly older generation had been simply one facet of a post-war movement to discredit obsolete manners—Dolly's was both older and shabbier, and she saw in Anson the two extremes which the emotionally shiftless woman seeks, an abandon to indulgence alternating with a protective strength. In his character she felt both the sybarite and the solid rock, and these two satisfied every need of her nature.

She felt that it was going to be difficult, but she mistook the reason—she thought that Anson and his family expected a more spectacular marriage, but she guessed immediately that her advantage lay in his tendency to drink.

They met at the large débutante dances, but as her infatuation increased they managed to be more and more together. Like most mothers, Mrs. Karger believed that Anson was exceptionally reliable, so she allowed Dolly to go with him to distant country clubs and suburban houses without inquiring closely into their activities or questioning her explanations when they came in late. At first these explanations might have been accurate, but Dolly's worldly ideas of capturing Anson were soon engulfed in the rising sweep of her emotion. Kisses in the back of taxis and motor-cars were no longer enough; they did a curious thing:

They dropped out of their world for a while and made another world just beneath it where Anson's tippling and Dolly's irregular hours would be less noticed and commented on. It was composed, this world, of varying elements—several of Anson's Yale friends and their wives, two or three young brokers and bond salesmen and a handful of unattached men, fresh from college, with money and a propensity to dissipation. What this world lacked in spaciousness and scale it made up for by allowing them a liberty that it scarcely permitted itself. Moreover, it centred around them and permitted Dolly the pleasure of a faint condescension —a pleasure which Anson, whose whole life was a condescension from the certitudes of his childhood, was unable to share.

He was not in love with her, and in the long feverish winter of their affair he frequently told her so. In the spring he was weary—he wanted to renew his life at some other source—moreover, he saw that either he must break with her now or accept the responsibility of a definite seduction. Her family's encouraging attitude precipitated his decision—one evening when Mr. Karger knocked discreetly at the library door to announce that he had left a bottle of old brandy in the dining-room, Anson felt that life was hemming him in. That night he wrote her a short letter in which he told her that he was going on his vacation, and that in view of all the circumstances they had better meet no more.

It was June. His family had closed up the house and gone to the country, so he was living temporarily at the Yale Club. I had heard about his affair with Dolly as it developed—accounts salted with humor, for he despised unstable women, and granted them no place in the social edifice in which he believed—and when he told me that night that he was definitely breaking with her I was glad. I had seen Dolly here and there, and each time with a feeling of pity at the hopelessness of her struggle, and of shame at knowing so much about her that I had no right to know. She was what is known as "a pretty little thing," but there was a certain recklessness which rather fascinated me. Her dedication to the goddess of waste would have been less obvious had she been less spirited—she would most certainly throw herself away, but I was glad when I heard that the sacrifice would not be consummated in my sight.

Anson was going to leave the letter of farewell at her house next morning. It was one of the few houses left open in the Fifth Avenue district, and he knew that the Kargers, acting upon erroneous information from Dolly, had foregone a trip abroad to give their daughter her chance. As he stepped out the door of the Yale Club into Madison Avenue the postman passed him, and he followed back inside. The first letter that caught his eye was in Dolly's hand.

He knew what it would be—a lonely and tragic monologue, full of the reproaches he knew, the invoked memories, the "I wonder if's"—all the immemorial intimacies that he had communicated to Paula Legendre in what seemed another age. Thumbing over some bills, he brought it on top again and opened it. To his surprise it was a short, somewhat formal note, which said that Dolly would be unable to go to the country with him for the week-end, because Perry Hull from Chicago had unexpectedly come to town. It added that Anson had brought this on himself: "—if I felt you loved me as I love you I would go with you at any time, any place, but Perry is *so* nice, and he so much wants me to marry him——"

Anson smiled contemptuously—he had had experience with such decoy epistles. Moreover, he knew how Dolly had labored over this plan, probably sent for the faithful Perry and calculated the time of his arrival—even labored over the note so that it would make him jealous without driving him away. Like most compromises, it had neither force nor vitality but only a timorous despair.

Suddenly he was angry. He sat down in the lobby and read it again. Then he went to the phone, called Dolly and told her in his clear, compelling voice that he had received her note and would call for her at five o'clock as they had previously planned. Scarcely waiting for the pretended uncertainty of her "Perhaps I can see you for an hour," he hung up the receiver and went down to his office. On the way he tore his own letter into bits and dropped it in the street.

He was not jealous—she meant nothing to him—but at her pathetic ruse everything stubborn and self-indulgent in him came to the surface. It was a presumption from a mental inferior and it could not be overlooked. If she wanted to know to whom she belonged she would see.

He was on the door-step at quarter past five. Dolly was dressed for the street, and he listened in silence to the paragraph of "I can only see you for an hour," which she had begun on the phone.

"Put on your hat, Dolly," he said, "we'll take a walk."

They strolled up Madison Avenue and over to Fifth while Anson's shirt dampened upon his portly body in the deep heat. He talked little, scolding her, making no love to her, but before they had walked six blocks she was his again, apologizing for the note, offering not to see Perry at all as an atonement, offering anything. She thought that he had come because he was beginning to love her.

"I'm hot," he said when they reached 71st Street. "This is a winter suit. If I stop by the house and change, would you mind waiting for me downstairs? I'll only be a minute."

She was happy; the intimacy of his being hot, of any physical fact about him, thrilled her. When they came to the iron-grated door and Anson took out his key she experienced a sort of delight.

Down-stairs it was dark, and after he ascended in the lift Dolly raised a curtain and looked out through opaque lace at the houses over the way. She heard the lift machinery stop, and with the notion of teasing him pressed the button that brought it down. Then on what was more than an impulse she got into it and sent it up to what she guessed was his floor.

"Anson," she called, laughing a little.

"Just a minute," he answered from his bedroom . . . then after a brief delay: "Now you can come in."

He had changed and was buttoning his vest.

"This is my room," he said lightly. "How do you like it?"

She caught sight of Paula's picture on the wall and stared at it in fascination, just as Paula had stared at the pictures of Anson's childish sweethearts five years before. She knew something about Paula—sometimes she tortured herself with fragments of the story.

Suddenly she came close to Anson, raising her arms. They embraced. Outside the area window a soft artificial twilight already hovered, though the sun was still bright on a back roof across the way. In half an hour the room would be quite dark. The uncalculated opportunity overwhelmed them, made them both breathless, and they clung more closely. It was imminent, inevitable. Still holding one another, they raised their heads—their eyes fell together upon Paula's picture, staring down at them from the wall.

Suddenly Anson dropped his arms, and sitting down at his desk tried the drawer with a bunch of keys.

"Like a drink?" he asked in a gruff voice.

"No, Anson."

He poured himself half a tumbler of whiskey, swallowed it, and then opened the door into the hall.

"Come on," he said.

Dolly hesitated.

"Anson—I'm going to the country with you to-night, after all. You understand that, don't you?"

"Of course," he answered brusquely.

In Dolly's car they rode on to Long Island,

closer in their emotions than they had ever been before. They knew what would happen—not with Paula's face to remind them that something was lacking, but when they were alone in the still, hot Long Island night they did not care.

The estate in Port Washington where they were to spend the week-end belonged to a cousin of Anson's who had married a Montana copper operator. An interminable drive began at the lodge and twisted under imported poplar saplings toward a huge, pink Spanish house. Anson had often visited there before.

After dinner they danced at the Linx Club. About midnight Anson assured himself that his cousins would not leave before two—then he explained that Dolly was tired; he would take her home and return to the dance later. Trembling a little with excitement, they got into a borrowed car together and drove to Port Washington. As they reached the lodge he stopped and spoke to the night-watchman.

"When are you making a round, Carl?"

"Right away."

"Then you'll be here till everybody's in?"

"Yes, sir."

"All right. Listen: if any automobile, no matter whose it is, turns in at this gate, I want you to phone the house immediately." He put a five-dollar bill into Carl's hand. "Is that clear?"

"Yes, Mr. Anson." Being of the Old World, he neither winked nor smiled. Yet Dolly sat with her face turned slightly away.

Anson had a key. Once inside he poured a drink for both of them—Dolly left hers untouched—then he ascertained definitely the location of the phone, and found that it was within easy hearing distance of their rooms, both of which were on the first floor.

Five minutes later he knocked at the door of Dolly's room.

"Anson?" He went in, closing the door behind him. She was in bed, leaning up anxiously with elbows on the pillow; sitting beside her he took her in his arms.

"Anson, darling."

He didn't answer.

"Anson. . . . Anson! I love you. . . . Say you love me. Say it now—can't you say it now? Even if you don't mean it?"

He did not listen. Over her head he perceived that the picture of Paula was hanging here upon this wall.

He got up and went close to it. The frame gleamed faintly with thrice-reflected moonlight—within was a blurred shadow of a face that he saw he did not know. Almost sobbing, he turned around and stared with abomination at the little figure on the bed.

"This is all foolishness," he said thickly. "I don't know what I was thinking about. I don't love you and you'd better wait for somebody that loves you. I don't love you a bit, can't you understand?"

His voice broke, and he went hurriedly out. Back in the salon he was pouring himself a drink with uneasy fingers, when the front door opened suddenly, and his cousin came in.

"Why, Anson, I hear Dolly's sick," she began solicitously. "I hear she's sick. . . ."

"It was nothing," he interrupted, raising his voice so that it would carry into Dolly's room. "She was a little tired. She went to bed."

For a long time afterward Anson believed that a protective God sometimes interfered in human affairs. But Dolly Karger, lying awake and staring at the ceiling, never again believed in anything at all.

VI

When Dolly married during the following autumn, Anson was in London on business. Like Paula's marriage, it was sudden, but it affected him in a different way. At first he felt that it was funny, and had an inclination to laugh when he thought of it. Later it depressed him—it made him feel old.

There was something repetitive about it—why, Paula and Dolly had belonged to different generations. He had a foretaste of the sensation of a man of forty who hears that the daughter of an old flame has married. He wired congratulations and, as was not the case with Paula, they were sincere—he had never really hoped that Paula would be happy.

When he returned to New York, he was made a partner in the firm, and, as his responsibilities increased, he had less time on his hands. The refusal of a life-insurance company to issue him a policy made such an impression on him that he stopped drinking for a year, and claimed that he felt better physically, though I think he missed the convivial recounting of those Celliniesque adventures which, in his early twenties, had played such a part in his life. But he never abandoned the Yale Club. He was a figure there, a personality, and the tendency of his class, who were now seven years out of college, to drift away to more sober haunts was checked by his presence.

His day was never too full nor his mind too weary to give any sort of aid to any one who asked it. What had been done at first through pride and superiority had become a habit and a passion. And there was always something—a younger brother in trouble at New Haven, a quarrel to be patched up between a friend and his wife, a position to be found for this man, an investment for that. But his specialty was the solving of problems for young married people. Young married people fascinated him and their apartments were almost sacred to him—he knew the story of their love-affair, advised them where to live and how, and remembered their babies' names. Toward young wives his attitude was circumspect: he never abused the trust which their husbands—strangely enough in view of his unconcealed irregularities—invariably reposed in him.

He came to take a vicarious pleasure in happy marriages, and to be inspired to an almost equally pleasant melancholy by those that went astray. Not a season passed that he did not witness the collapse of an affair that perhaps he himself had fathered. When Paula was divorced and almost immediately remarried to another Bostonian, he talked about her to me all one afternoon. He would never love any one as he had loved Paula, but he insisted that he no longer cared.

"I'll never marry," he came to say; "I've seen too much of it, and I know a happy marriage is a very rare thing. Besides, I'm too old."

But he did believe in marriage. Like all men who spring from a happy and successful marriage, he believed in it passionately—nothing he had seen would change his belief, his cynicism dissolved upon it like air. But he did really believe he was too old. At twenty-eight he began to accept with equanimity the prospect of marrying without romantic love; he resolutely chose a New York girl of his own class, pretty, intelligent, congenial, above reproach—and set about falling in love with her. The things he had said to Paula with sincerity, to other girls with grace, he could no longer say at all without smiling, or with the force necessary to convince.

"When I'm forty," he told his friends, "I'll be ripe. I'll fall for some chorus girl like the rest."

Nevertheless, he persisted in his attempt. His mother wanted to see him married, and he could now well afford it—he had a seat on the Stock Exchange, and his earned income came to twenty-five thousand a year. The idea was agreeable: when his friends—he spent most of his time with the set he and Dolly had evolved—closed themselves in behind domestic doors at night, he no longer rejoiced in his freedom. He even wondered if he should have married Dolly. Not even Paula had loved him more, and he was learning the rarity, in a single life, of encountering true emotion.

Just as this mood began to creep over him a disquieting story reached his ear. His Aunt Edna, a woman just this side of forty, was carrying on an open intrigue with a dissolute, hard-drinking young man named Cary Sloane. Every one knew of it except Anson's Uncle Robert, who for fifteen years had talked long in clubs and taken his wife for granted.

Anson heard the story again and again with increasing annoyance. Something of his old feeling for his uncle came back to him, a feeling that was more than personal, a reversion toward that family solidarity on which he had based his pride. His intuition singled out the essential point of the affair, which was that his uncle shouldn't be hurt. It was his first experiment in unsolicited meddling, but with his knowledge of Edna's character he felt that he could handle the matter better than a district judge or his uncle.

His uncle was in Hot Springs. Anson traced down the sources of the scandal so that there should be no possibility of mistake and then he called Edna and asked her to lunch with him at the Plaza next day. Something in his tone must have frightened her, for she was reluctant, but he insisted, putting off the date until she had no excuse for refusing.

She met him at the appointed time in the Plaza lobby, a lovely, faded, gray-eyed blonde in a coat of Russian sable. Five great rings, cold with diamonds and emeralds, sparkled on her slender hands. It occurred to Anson that it was his father's intelligence and not his uncle's that had earned the fur and the stones, the rich brilliance that buoyed up her passing beauty.

Though Edna scented his hostility, she was unprepared for the directness of his approach.

"Edna, I'm astonished at the way you've been acting," he said in a strong, frank voice. "At first I couldn't believe it."

"Believe what?" she demanded sharply.

"You needn't pretend with me, Edna. I'm talking about Cary Sloane. Aside from any other consideration, I didn't think you could treat Uncle Robert——"

"Now look here, Anson—" she began angrily, but his peremptory voice broke through hers:

"—and your children in such a way. You've been married eighteen years, and you're old enough to know better."

"You can't talk to me like that! You——"

"Yes, I can. Uncle Robert has always been my best friend." He was tremendously moved. He felt a real distress about his uncle, about his three young cousins.

Edna stood up, leaving her crab-flake cocktail untasted.

"This is the silliest thing——"

"Very well, if you won't listen to me I'll go to Uncle Robert and tell him the whole story—he's bound to hear it sooner or later. And afterward I'll got to old Moses Sloane."

Edna faltered back into her chair.

"Don't talk so loud," she begged him. Her eyes blurred with tears. "You have no idea how your voice carries. You might have chosen a less public place to make all these crazy accusations."

He didn't answer.

"Oh, you never liked me, I know," she went on. "You're just taking advantage of some silly gossip to try and break up the only interesting friendship I've ever had. What did I ever do to make you hate me so?"

Still Anson waited. There would be the appeal to his chivalry, then to his pity, finally to his superior sophistication—when he had shouldered his way through all these there would be admissions, and he could come to grips with her. By being silent, by being impervious, by returning constantly to his main weapon, which was his own true emotion, he bullied her into frantic despair as the luncheon hour slipped away. At two o'clock she took out a mirror and a handkerchief, shined away the marks of her tears and powdered the slight hollows where they had lain. She had agreed to meet him at her own house at five.

When he arrived she was stretched on a *chaise-longue* which was covered with cretonne for the summer, and the tears he had called up at luncheon seemed still to be standing in her eyes. Then he was aware of Cary Sloane's dark anxious presence upon the cold hearth.

"What's this idea of yours?" broke out Sloane immediately. "I understand you invited Edna to lunch and then threatened her on the basis of some cheap scandal."

Anson sat down.

"I have no reason to think it's only scandal."

"I hear you're going to take it to Robert Hunter, and to my father."

Anson nodded.

"Either you break it off—or I will," he said.

"What God damned business is it of yours, Hunter?"

"Don't lose your temper, Cary," said Edna nervously. "It's only a question of showing him how absurd——"

"For one thing, it's my name that's being handed around," interrupted Anson. "That's all that concerns you, Cary."

"Edna isn't a member of your family."

"She most certainly is!" His anger mounted. "Why—she owes this house and the rings on her fingers to my father's brains. When Uncle Robert married her she didn't have a penny."

They all looked at the rings as if they had a significant bearing on the situation. Edna made a gesture to take them from her hand.

"I guess they're not the only rings in the world," said Sloane.

"Oh, this is absurd," cried Edna. "Anson, will you listen to me? I've found out how the silly story started. It was a maid I discharged who went right to the Chilicheffs—all these Russians pump things out of their servants and then put a false meaning on them." She brought down her fist angrily on the table: "And after Robert lent them the limousine for a whole month when we were South last winter——"

"Do you see?" demanded Sloane eagerly. "This maid got hold of the wrong end of the thing. She knew that Edna and I were friends, and she carried it to the Chilicheffs. In Russia they assume that if a man and a woman——"

He enlarged the theme to a disquisition upon social relations in the Caucasus.

"If that's the case it better be explained to Uncle Robert," said Anson dryly, "so that when the rumors do reach him he'll know they're not true."

Adopting the method he had followed with Edna at luncheon he let them explain it all away. He knew that they were guilty and that presently they would cross the line from explanation into justification and convict themselves more definitely than he could ever do. By seven they had taken the desperate step of telling him the truth—Robert Hunter's neglect, Edna's empty life, the casual dalliance that had flamed up into passion—but like so many true stories it had the misfortune of being old, and its enfeebled body beat helplessly against the armor of Anson's will. The threat to go to Sloane's father sealed their helplessness, for the latter, a retired cotton broker out of Alabama, was a notorious fundamentalist who controlled his son by a rigid allowance and the promise that at his next vagary the allowance would stop forever.

They dined at a small French restaurant, and the discussion continued—at one time Sloane resorted to physical threats, a little later they were both imploring him to give them time. But Anson was obdurate. He saw that Edna was breaking up, and that her spirit must not be refreshed by any renewal of their passion.

At two o'clock in a small night-club on 53d Street, Edna's nerves suddenly collapsed, and she cried to go home. Sloane had been drinking heavily all evening, and he was faintly maudlin, leaning on the table and weeping a little with his face in his hands. Quickly Anson gave them his terms. Sloane was to leave town for six months, and he must be gone within forty-eight hours. When he returned there was to be no resumption of the affair, but at the end of a year Edna might, if she wished, tell Robert Hunter that she wanted a divorce and go about it in the usual way.

He paused, gaining confidence from their faces for his final word.

"Or there's another thing you can do," he said slowly, "if Edna wants to leave her children, there's nothing I can do to prevent your running off together."

"I want to go home!" cried Edna again. "Oh, haven't you done enough to us for one day?"

Outside it was dark, save for a blurred glow from Sixth Avenue down the street. In that light those two who had been lovers looked for the last time into each other's tragic faces, realizing that between them there was not enough youth and strength to avert their eternal parting. Sloane walked suddenly off down the street and Anson tapped a dozing taxi-driver on the arm.

It was almost four; there was a patient flow of cleaning water along the ghostly pavement of Fifth Avenue, and the shadows of two night women flitted over the dark façade of St. Thomas's church. Then the desolate shrubbery of Central Park where Anson had often played as a child, and the mounting numbers, significant as names, of the marching streets. This was his city, he thought, where his name had flourished through five generations. No change could alter the permanence of its place here, for change itself was the essential substratum by which he and those of his name identified themselves with the spirit of New York. Resourcefulness and a powerful will—for his threats in weaker hands would have been less than nothing—had beaten the gathering dust from his uncle's name, from the name of his family, from even this shivering figure that sat beside him in the car.

Cary Sloane's body was found next morning on the lower shelf of a pillar of Queensboro Bridge. In the darkness and in his excitement he had thought that it was the water flowing black beneath him, but in less than a second it made no possible difference—unless he had planned to think one last thought of Edna, and call out her name as he struggled feebly in the water.

VII

Anson never blamed himself for his part in this affair—the situation which brought it about had not been of his making. But the just suffer with the unjust, and he found that his oldest and somehow his most precious friendship was over. He never knew what distorted story Edna told, but he was welcome in his uncle's house no longer.

Just before Christmas Mrs. Hunter retired to a select Episcopal heaven, and Anson became the responsible head of his family. An unmarried aunt who had lived with them for years ran the house, and attempted with helpless inefficiency to chaperone the younger girls. All the children were less self-reliant than Anson, more conventional both in their virtues and in their shortcomings. Mrs. Hunter's death had postponed the début of one daughter and the wedding of another. Also it had taken something deeply material from all of them, for with her passing the quiet, expensive superiority of the Hunters came to an end.

For one thing, the estate, considerably diminished by two inheritance taxes and soon to be divided among six children, was not a notable fortune any more. Anson saw a tendency in his youngest sisters to speak rather respectfully of families that hadn't "existed" twenty years ago. His own feeling of precedence was not echoed in them—sometimes they were conventionally snobbish, that was all. For another thing, this was the last summer they would spend on the Connecticut estate; the clamor against it was too loud: "Who wants to waste the best months of the year shut up in that dead old town?" Reluctantly he yielded—the house would go into the market in the fall, and next summer they would rent a smaller place in Westchester County. It was a step down from the expensive simplicity of his father's idea, and, while he sympathized with the revolt, it also annoyed him; during his mother's lifetime he had gone up there at least every other week-end—even in the gayest summers.

Yet he himself was part of this change, and his strong instinct for life had turned him in his twenties from the hollow obsequies of that abortive leisure class. He did not see this clearly—he still felt that there was a norm, a standard of society. But there was no norm, it was doubtful if there ever had been a true norm in New York. The few who still paid and fought to enter a particular set succeeded only to find that as a society it scarcely functioned—or, what was more alarming, that the Bohemia from which they fled sat above them at table.

At twenty-nine Anson's chief concern was his own growing loneliness. He was sure now that he would never marry. The number of weddings at which he had officiated as best man or usher was past all counting—there was a drawer at home that bulged with the official neckties of this or that wedding-party, neckties standing for romances that had not endured a year, for couples who had passed completely from his life. Scarf-pins, gold pencils, cuff-buttons, presents from a generation of grooms had passed through his jewel-box and been lost—and with every ceremony he was less and less able to imagine himself in the groom's place. Under his hearty good-will toward all those marriages there was despair about his own.

And as he neared thirty he became not a little depressed at the inroads that marriage, especially lately, had made upon his friendships. Groups of people had a disconcerting tendency to dissolve and disappear. The men from his own college— and it was upon them he had expended the most time and affection—were the most elusive of all. Most of them were drawn deep into domesticity, two were dead, one lived abroad, one was in Hollywood writing continuities for pictures that Anson went faithfully to see.

Most of them, however, were permanent commuters with an intricate family life centring around some suburban country club, and it was from these that he felt his estrangement most keenly.

In the early days of their married life they had all needed him; he gave them advice about their slim finances, he exorcised their doubts about the advisability of bringing a baby into two rooms and a bath, especially he stood for the great world outside. But now their financial troubles were in the past and the fearfully expected child had evolved into an absorbing family. They were always glad to see old Anson, but they dressed up for him and tried to impress him with their present importance, and kept their troubles to themselves. They needed him no longer.

A few weeks before his thirtieth birthday the last of his early and intimate friends was married. Anson acted in his usual rôle of best man, gave his usual silver tea-service, and went down to the usual *Homeric* to say good-by. It was a hot Friday afternoon in May, and as he walked from the pier he realized that Saturday closing had begun and he was free until Monday morning.

"Go where?" he asked himself.

The Yale Club, of course; bridge until dinner, then four or five raw cocktails in somebody's room and a pleasant confused evening. He regretted that this afternoon's groom wouldn't be along—they had always been able to cram so much into such nights: they knew how to attach women and how to get rid of them, how much consideration any girl deserved from their intelligent hedonism. A party was an adjusted thing—you took certain girls to certain places and spent just so much on their amusement; you drank a little, not much, more than you ought to drink, and at a certain time in the morning you stood up and said you were going home. You avoided college boys, sponges, future engagements, fights, sentiment, and indiscretions. That was the way it was done. All the rest was dissipation.

In the morning you were never violently sorry— you made no resolutions, but if you had overdone it and your heart was slightly out of order, you went on the wagon for a few days without saying anything about it, and waited until an accumulation of nervous boredom projected you into another party.

The lobby of the Yale Club was unpopulated. In the bar three very young alumni looked up at him, momentarily and without curiosity.

"Hello, there, Oscar," he said to the bartender. "Mr. Cahill been around this afternoon?"

"Mr. Cahill's gone to New Haven."

"Oh . . . that so?"

"Gone to the ball game. Lot of men gone up."

Anson looked once again into the lobby, considered for a moment, and then walked out and over to Fifth Avenue. From the broad window of one of his clubs—one that he had scarcely visited in five years—a gray man with watery eyes stared down at him. Anson looked quickly away—that figure sitting in vacant resignation, in supercilious solitude, depressed him. He stopped and, retracing his steps, started over 47th Street toward Teak Warden's apartment. Teak and his wife had once been his most familiar friends—it was a household where he and Dolly Karger had been used to go in the days of their affair. But Teak had taken to drink, and his wife had remarked publicly that Anson was a bad influence on him. The remark reached Anson in an exaggerated form—when it was finally cleared up, the delicate spell of intimacy was broken, never to be renewed.

"Is Mr. Warden at home?" he inquired.

"They've gone to the country."

The fact unexpectedly cut at him. They were gone to the country and he hadn't known. Two years before he would have known the date, the hour, come up at the last moment for a final drink, and planned his first visit to them. Now they had gone without a word.

Anson looked at his watch and considered a week-end with his family, but the only train was a local that would jolt through the aggressive heat for three hours. And to-morrow in the country, and Sunday—he was in no mood for porch-bridge with polite undergraduates, and dancing after dinner at a rural roadhouse, a diminutive of gaiety which his father had estimated too well.

"Oh, no," he said to himself. . . . "No."

He was a dignified, impressive young man, rather stout now, but otherwise unmarked by dissipation. He could have been cast for a pillar of something—at times you were sure it was not society, at others nothing else—for the law, for the church. He stood for a few minutes motionless on the sidewalk in front of a 47th Street apartment-house; for almost the first time in his life he had nothing whatever to do.

Then he began to walk briskly up Fifth Avenue, as if he had just been reminded of an important engagement there. The necessity of dissimulation is one of the few characteristics that we share with dogs, and I think of Anson on that day as some well-bred specimen who had been disappointed at a familiar back door. He was going to see Nick, once a fashionable bartender in demand at all private dances, and now employed in cooling non-alcoholic champagne among the labyrinthine cellars of the Plaza Hotel.

"Nick," he said "what's happened to everything?"

"Dead," Nick said.

"Make me a whiskey sour." Anson handed a pint bottle over the counter. "Nick, the girls are different; I had a little girl in Brooklyn and she got married last week without letting me know."

"That a fact? Ha-ha-ha," responded Nick diplomatically. "Slipped it over on you."

"Absolutely," said Anson. "And I was out with her the night before."

"Ha-ha-ha," said Nick, "ha-ha-ha!"

"Do you remember the wedding, Nick, in Hot Springs where I had the waiters and the musicians singing 'God save the King'?"

"Now where was that, Mr. Hunter?" Nick concentrated doubtfully. "Seems to me that was——"

"Next time they were back for more, and I began to wonder how much I'd paid them," continued Anson.

"—seems to me that was at Mr. Trenholm's wedding."

"Don't know him," said Anson decisively. He was offended that a strange name should intrude upon his reminiscences; Nick perceived this.

"Na—aw—" he admitted, "I ought to know that. It was one of *your* crowd—Brakins . . . Baker——"

"Bicker Baker," said Anson responsively. "They put me in a hearse after it was over and covered me up with flowers and drove me away."

"Ha-ha-ha," said Nick. "Ha-ha-ha."

Nick's simulation of the old family servant paled presently and Anson went up-stairs to the lobby. He looked around—his eyes met the glance of an unfamiliar clerk at the desk, then fell upon a flower from the morning's marriage hesitating in the mouth of a brass cuspidor. He went out and walked slowly toward the blood-red sun over Columbus Circle. Suddenly he turned around and, retracing his steps to the Plaza, immured himself in a telephone-booth.

Later he said that he tried to get me three times that afternoon, that he tried every one who might be in New York—men and girls he had not seen for years, an artist's model of his college days whose faded number was still in his address book —Central told him that even the exchange existed no longer. At length his quest roved into the country, and he held brief disappointing conversations with emphatic butlers and maids. So-and-so was out, riding, swimming, playing golf, sailed to Europe last week. Who shall I say phoned?

It was intolerable that he should pass the evening alone—the private reckonings which one plans for a moment of leisure lose every charm when the solitude is enforced. There were always women of a sort, but the ones he knew had temporarily vanished, and to pass a New York evening in the hired company of a stranger never occurred to him —he would have considered that that was something shameful and secret, the diversion of a travelling salesman in a strange town.

Anson paid the telephone bill—the girl tried unsuccessfully to joke with him about its size—and for the second time that afternoon started to leave the Plaza and go he knew not where. Near the revolving door the figure of a woman, obviously with child, stood sideways to the light—a sheer beige cape fluttered at her shoulders when the door turned and, each time, she looked impatiently toward it as if she were weary of waiting. At the first sight of her a strong nervous thrill of familiarity went over him, but not until he was within five feet of her did he realize that it was Paula.

"Why, Anson Hunter!"

His heart turned over.

"Why, Paula——"

"Why, this is wonderful. I can't believe it, *Anson!*"

She took both his hands, and he saw in the freedom of the gesture that the memory of him had lost poignancy to her. But not to him—he felt that old mood that she evoked in him stealing over his brain, that gentleness with which he had always met her optimism as if afraid to mar its surface.

"We're at Rye for the summer. Pete had to come East on business—you know of course I'm Mrs. Peter Hagerty now—so we brought the children and took a house. You've got to come out and see us."

"Can I?" he asked directly. "When?"

"When you like. Here's Pete." The revolving door functioned, giving up a fine tall man of thirty with a tanned face and a trim mustache. His immaculate fitness made a sharp contrast with Anson's increasing bulk, which was obvious under the faintly tight cut-away coat.

"You oughtn't to be standing," said Hagerty to his wife. "Let's sit down here." He indicated lobby chairs, but Paula hesitated.

"I've got to go right home," she said. "Anson, why don't you—why don't you come out and have dinner with us to-night? We're just getting settled, but if you can stand that——"

Hagerty confirmed the invitation cordially.

"Come out for the night."

Their car waited in front of the hotel, and Paula with a tired gesture sank back against silk cushions in the corner.

"There's so much I want to talk to you about," she said, "it seems hopeless."

"I want to hear about you."

"Well"—she smiled at Hagerty—"that would take a long time too. I have three children—by my first marriage. The oldest is five, then four, then three." She smiled again. "I didn't waste much time having them, did I?"

"Boys?"

"A boy and two girls. Then—oh, a lot of things happened, and I got a divorce in Paris a year ago and married Pete. That's all—except that I'm awfully happy."

In Rye they drove up to a large house near the Beach Club, from which there issued presently three dark, slim children who broke from an English governess and approached them with an esoteric cry. Abstractedly and with difficulty Paula took each one into her arms, a caress which they accepted stiffly, as they had evidently been told not to bump into Mummy. Even against their fresh faces Paula's skin showed scarcely any weariness—for all her physical languor she seemed younger than when he had last seen her at Palm Beach seven years ago.

At dinner she was preoccupied, and afterward, during the homage to the radio, she lay with closed eyes on the sofa, until Anson wondered if his presence at this time were not an intrusion. But at nine o'clock, when Hagerty rose and said pleasantly that he was going to leave them by themselves for a while, she began to talk slowly about herself and the past.

"My first baby," she said—"the one we call Darling, the biggest little girl—I wanted to die when I knew I was going to have her, because Lowell was like a stranger to me. It didn't seem as though she could be my own. I wrote you a letter and tore it up. Oh, you were *so* bad to me, Anson."

It was the dialogue again, rising and falling. Anson felt a sudden quickening of memory.

"Weren't you engaged once?" she asked—"a girl named Dolly something?"

"I wasn't ever engaged. I tried to be engaged, but I never loved anybody but you, Paula."

"Oh," she said. Then after a moment: "This

baby is the first one I ever really wanted. You see, I'm in love now—at last."

He didn't answer, shocked at the treachery of her remembrance. She must have seen that the "at last" bruised him, for she continued:

"I was infatuated with you, Anson—you could make me do anything you liked. But we wouldn't have been happy. I'm not smart enough for you. I don't like things to be complicated like you do." She paused. "You'll never settle down," she said.

The phrase struck at him from behind—it was an accusation that of all accusations he had never merited.

"I could settle down if women were different," he said. "If I didn't understand so much about them, if women didn't spoil you for other women, if they had only a little pride. If I could go to sleep for a while and wake up into a home that was really mine—why, that's what I'm made for, Paula, that's what women have seen in me and liked in me. It's only that I can't get through the preliminaries any more."

Hagerty came in a little before eleven; after a whiskey Paula stood up and announced that she was going to bed. She went over and stood by her husband.

"Where did you go, dearest?" she demanded.

"I had a drink with Ed Saunders."

"I was worried. I thought maybe you'd run away."

She rested her head against his coat.

"He's sweet, isn't he, Anson?" she demanded.

"Absolutely," said Anson, laughing.

She raised her face to her husband.

"Well, I'm ready," she said. She turned to Anson: "Do you want to see our family gymnastic stunt?"

"Yes," he said in an interested voice.

"All right. Here we go!"

Hagerty picked her up easily in his arms.

"This is called the family acrobatic stunt," said Paula. "He carries me upstairs. Isn't it sweet of him?"

"Yes," said Anson.

Hagerty bent his head slightly until his face touched Paula's.

"And I love him," she said. "I've just been telling you, haven't I, Anson?"

"Yes," he said.

"He's the dearest thing that ever lived in this world; aren't you, darling? . . . Well, good night. Here we go. Isn't he strong?"

"Yes," Anson said.

"You'll find a pair of Pete's pajamas laid out for you. Sweet dreams—see you at breakfast."

"Yes," Anson said.

VIII

The older members of the firm insisted that Anson should go abroad for the summer. He had scarcely had a vacation in seven years, they said. He was stale and needed a change. Anson resisted.

"If I go," he declared, "I won't come back any more."

"That's absurd, old man. You'll be back in three months with all this depression gone. Fit as ever."

"No." He shook his head stubbornly. "If I stop, I won't go back to work. If I stop, that means I've given up—I'm through."

"We'll take a chance on that. Stay six months if you like—we're not afraid you'll leave us. Why, you'd be miserable if you didn't work."

They arranged his passage for him. They liked Anson—every one liked Anson—and the change that had been coming over him cast a sort of pall over the office. The enthusiasm that had invariably signalled up business, the consideration toward his equals and his inferiors, the lift of his vital presence—within the past four months his intense nervousness had melted down these qualities into the fussy pessimism of a man of forty. On every transaction in which he was involved he acted as a drag and a strain.

"If I go I'll never come back," he said.

Three days before he sailed Paula Legendre Hagerty died in childbirth. I was with him a great deal then, for we were crossing together, but for the first time in our friendship he told me not a word of how he felt, nor did I see the slightest sign of emotion. His chief preoccupation was with the fact that he was thirty years old—he would turn the conversation to the point where he could remind you of it and then fall silent, as if he assumed that the statement would start a chain of thought sufficient to itself. Like his partners, I was amazed at the change in him, and I was glad when the *Paris* moved off into the wet space between the worlds, leaving his principality behind.

"How about a drink?" he suggested.

We walked into the bar with that defiant feeling that characterizes the day of departure and ordered four Martinis. After one cocktail a change came over him—he suddenly reached across and slapped my knee with the first joviality I had seen him exhibit for months.

"Did you see that girl in the red tam?" he demanded, "the one with the high color who had the two police dogs down to bid her good-by."

"She's pretty," I agreed.

"I looked her up in the purser's office and found out that she's alone. I'm going down to see the steward in a few minutes. We'll have dinner with her to-night."

After a while he left me, and within an hour he was walking up and down the deck with her, talking to her in his strong, clear voice. Her red tam was a bright spot of color against the steel-green sea, and from time to time she looked up with a flashing bob of her head, and smiled with amusement and interest, and anticipation. At dinner we had champagne, and were very joyous—afterward Anson ran the pool with infectious gusto, and several people who had seen me with him asked me his name. He and the girl were talking and laughing together on a lounge in the bar when I went to bed.

I saw less of him on the trip than I had hoped. He wanted to arrange a foursome, but there was no one available, so I saw him only at meals. Sometimes, though, he would have a cocktail in the bar, and he told me about the girl in the red tam, and his adventures with her, making them all bizarre and amusing, as he had a way of doing, and I was glad that he was himself again, or at least the self that I knew, and with which I felt at home. I don't think he was ever happy unless some one was in love with him, responding to him like filings to a magnet, helping him to explain himself, promising him something. What it was I do not know. Perhaps they promised that there would always be women in the world who would spend their brightest, freshest, rarest hours to nurse and protect that superiority he cherished in his heart.

The Crack-Up (1945)

Of course all life is a process of breaking down, but the blows that do the dramatic side of the work—the big sudden blows that come, or seem to come, from outside—the ones you remember and blame things on and, in moments of weakness, tell your friends about, don't show their effect all at once. There is another sort of blow that comes from within—that you don't feel until it's too late to do anything about it, until you realize with finality that in some regard you will never be as good a man again. The first sort of breakage seems to happen quick—the second kind happens almost without your knowing it but is realized suddenly indeed.

Before I go on with this short history let me make a general observation—the test of a first-rate intelligence is the ability to hold two opposed ideas in the mind at the same time, and still retain the ability to function. One should, for example, be able to see that things are hopeless and yet be determined to make them otherwise. This philosophy fitted on to my early adult life, when I saw the improbable, the implausible, often the "impossible" come true. Life was something you dominated if you were any good. Life yielded easily to intelligence and effort, or to what proportion could be mustered of both. It seemed a romantic business to be a successful literary man—you were not ever going to be as famous as a movie star but what note you had was probably longer-lived—you were never going to have the power of a man of strong political or religious convictions but you were certainly more independent. Of course within the practice of your trade you were forever unsatisfied—but I, for one, would not have chosen any other.

As the twenties passed, with my own twenties marching a little ahead of them, my two juvenile regrets—at not being big enough (or good enough) to play football in college, and at not getting overseas during the war—resolved themselves into childish waking dreams of imaginary heroism that were good enough to go to sleep on in restless nights. The big problems of life seemed to solve themselves, and if the business of fixing them was difficult, it made one too tired to think of more general problems.

Life, ten years ago, was largely a personal matter. I must hold in balance the sense of the futility of effort and the sense of the necessity to struggle; the conviction of the inevitability of failure and still the determination to "succeed"—and, more than these, the contradiction between the dead hand of the past and the high intentions of the future. If I could do this through the common ills —domestic, professional and personal—then the ego would continue as an arrow shot from nothingness to nothingness with such force that only gravity would bring it to earth at last.

For seventeen years, with a year of deliberate loafing and resting out in the center—things went on like that, with a new chore only a nice prospect for the next day. I was living hard too, but: "Up to forty-nine it'll be all right," I said. "I can count on that. For a man who's lived as I have, that's all you could ask."

—And then, ten years this side of forty-nine, I suddenly realized that I had prematurely cracked.

II

Now a man can crack in many ways—can crack in the head—in which case the power of decision is taken from you by others; or in the body when one can but submit to the white hospital world— or in the nerves. William Seabrook in an unsympathetic book tells, with some pride and a movie ending, of how he became a public charge. What led to his alcoholism or was bound up with it, was a collapse of his nervous system. Though the present writer was not so entangled—having at the time not tasted so much as a glass of beer for six months —it was his nervous reflexes that were giving way— too much anger and too many tears.

Moreover, to go back to my thesis that life has a varying offensive, the realization of having cracked was not simultaneous with a blow, but with a reprieve.

Not long before, I had sat in the office of a great doctor and listened to a grave sentence. With what, in retrospect, seems some equanimity, I had gone on about my affairs in the city where I was then living, not caring much, not thinking how much had been left undone, or what would become of this and that responsibility, like people do in books; I was well insured and anyhow I had been only a mediocre caretaker of most of the things left in my hands, even of my talent.

But I had a strong sudden instinct that I must be alone. I didn't want to see any people at all. I had seen so many people all my life—I was an average mixer, but more than average in a tendency to identify myself, my ideas, my destiny with those of all classes that I came in contact with. I was always saving or being saved—in a single morning I would go through the emotions ascribable to Wellington at Waterloo. I lived in a world of inscrutable hostiles and unalienable friends and supporters.

But now I wanted to be absolutely alone and so arranged a certain insulation from ordinary cares.

It was not an unhappy time. I went away and there were fewer people. I found I was good-and-tired. I could lie around and was glad to, sleeping or dozing sometimes twenty hours a day and in the intervals trying resolutely not to think—instead I made lists—made lists and tore them up, hundreds of lists: of cavalry leaders and football players and cities, and popular tunes and pitchers, and happy times, and hobbies and houses lived in and how many suits since I left the army and how many pairs of shoes (I didn't count the suit I brought in Sorrento that shrunk, nor the the pumps and dress shirt and collar that I carried around for years and never wore because the pumps got damp and grainy and the shirt and collar got yellow and starch-rotted). And lists of women I'd liked, and of the times I had let myself be snubbed by people who had not been my betters in character or ability.

—And then suddenly, surprisingly I got better.

—And cracked like an old plate as soon as I heard the news.

That is the real end of this story. What was to be done about it will have to rest in what used to be called the "womb of time." Suffice it to say that after about an hour of solitary pillow-hugging, I began to realize that for two years my life had been a drawing on resources that I did not possess, that I had been mortgaging myself physically and spiritually up to the hilt. What was the small gift of life given back in comparison to that?—when there had once been a pride of direction and a confidence in enduring independence.

I realized that in those two years in order to preserve something—an inner hush maybe, maybe not—I had weaned myself from all the things I used to love—that every act of life from the morning toothbrush to the friend at dinner had become an effort. I saw that for a long time I had not liked people and things, but only followed the rickety old pretense of liking. I saw that even my love for those closest to me was become only an attempt to love, that my casual relations—with an editor, a tobacco seller, the child of a friend, were only what I remembered I *should* do, from other days. All in the same month I became bitter about such things as the sound of the radio, the advertisements in the magazines, the screech of tracks, the dead silence of the country—contemptuous at human softness, immediately (if secretively) quarrelsome toward hardness—hating the night when I couldn't sleep and hating the day because it went toward night. I slept on the heart side now because I knew that the sooner I could tire that out, even a little, the sooner would come that blessed hour of nightmare which, like a catharsis, would enable me to better meet the new day.

There were certain spots, certain faces I could look at. Like most middle-westerners I have never had any but the vaguest race prejudices—I always had a secret yen for the lovely Scandinavian blondes who sat on porches in St. Paul but hadn't emerged enough economically to be part of what was then society. They were too nice to be "chickens" and too quickly off the farmlands to seize a place in the sun, but I remember going round blocks to catch a single glimpse of shining hair—the bright shock of a girl I'd never know. This is urban, unpopular talk. It strays afield from the fact that in these latter days I couldn't stand the sight of Celts, English, Politicians, Strangers, Virginians, Negroes (light or dark), Hunting People, all retail clerks, and middlemen in general, all writers (I avoided writers very carefully because they can perpetuate trouble as no one else can)— and all the classes as classes and most of them as members of their class . . .

Trying to cling to something, I liked doctors and girl children up to the age of about thirteen and well-brought-up boy children from about eight years old on. I could have peace and happiness with these few categories of people. I forgot to add that I liked old men—men over seventy, sometimes over sixty if their faces looked seasoned. I liked Katharine Hepburn's face on the screen, no matter what was said about her pretentiousness, and Miriam Hopkins' face, and old friends if I only saw them once a year and could remember their ghosts.

All rather inhuman and undernourished, isn't it? Well, that, children, is the true sign of cracking up.

It is not a pretty picture. Inevitably it was carted here and there within its frame and exposed to various critics. One of them can only be described as a person whose life makes other people's lives

seem like death—even this time when she was cast in the usually unappealing role of Job's comforter. In spite of the fact that this story is over, let me append our conversation as a sort of postscript:

"Instead of being so sorry for yourself, listen—" she said. (She always says "Listen," because she thinks while she talks—*really* thinks.) So she said: "Listen. Suppose this wasn't a crack in you—suppose it was a crack in the Grand Canyon."

"The crack's in me," I said heroically.

"Listen! The world only exists in your eyes— your conception of it: You can make it as big or as small as you want to. And you're trying to be a little puny individual. By God, if I ever cracked I'd try to make the world crack with me. Listen! The world only exists through your apprehension of it, and so it's much better to say that it's not you that's cracked—it's the Grand Canyon."

"Baby et up all her Spinoza?"

"I don't know anything about Spinoza. I know —" She spoke, then, of old woes of her own, that seemed, in the telling, to have been more dolorous than mine, and how she had met them, overridden them, beaten them.

I felt a certain reaction to what she said, but I am a slow-thinking man, and it occurred to me simultaneously that of all natural forces, vitality is the incommunicable one. In days when juice came into one as an article without duty, one tried to distribute it—but always without success; to further mix metaphors, vitality never "takes." You have it or you haven't it, like health or brown eyes or honor or a baritone voice. I might have asked some of it from her, neatly wrapped and ready for home cooking and digestion, but I could never have got it—not if I'd waited around for a thousand hours with the tin cup of self-pity. I could only walk from her door, holding myself very carefully like cracked crockery, and go away into the world of bitterness, where I was making a home with such materials as are found there—and quote to myself after I left her door:

"*Ye are the salt of the earth. But if the salt hath lost its savour, wherewith shall it be salted?*"
Matthew 5-13.

From the Notebooks

Fitzgerald was a devoted keeper of notebooks, jottings, observations, memoranda and sketches that might go into fiction. In his later life he organized all this material under alphabetical headings, such as A—Anecdotes, B—Bright Clippings, C—Conversations and things overheard.

"Oh, have you got an engagement with your drug-taking friend in Monte Carlo?"

He sat down and began putting on his shoes.

"I shouldn't have told you that. I suppose you think he'll convert me to the habit."

"I certainly don't think it's a very profitable association."

"Oh, yes it is. It's not everybody who can get the dope habit from a prominent moving picture director. In fact, it's begun already. At this very moment I'm full of dope. He started me on cocaine, and we're working slowly up to heroin."

"That isn't really funny, Francis."

"Excuse me. I was trying to be funny and I know you don't like my way of being funny."

She countered his growing bitterness by adopting a tone of calm patience.

"Learn young about hard work and good manners—and you'll be through the whole dirty mess and nicely dead again before you know it."

"Francis says he wants to go away and try his personality on a lot of new people."

Far out past the breakers he could survey the green-and-brown line of the Old Dominion with the pleasant impersonality of a porpoise. The burden of his wretched marriage fell away with the buoyant tumble of his body among the swells, and he would begin to move in a child's dream of space. Sometimes remembered playmates of his youth swam with him; sometimes, with his two sons beside him, he seemed to be setting off along the bright pathway to the moon. Americans, he liked to say, should be born with fins, and perhaps they were—perhaps money was a form of fin. In England, property begot a strong place sense, but Americans, restless and with shallow roots, needed fins and wings. There was even a recurrent idea in America about an education that would leave out history and the past, that should be a sort of equipment for aerial adventure, weighed down by none of the stowaways of inheritance or tradition.

Cannes in the season—he was filling the café, the light which blazed against the white poplar bark and green leaves, with sprightlier motes of his own creation—he saw it vivid with dresses just down from Paris and giving off a sweet pungent odor of flowers and chartreuse and fresh black coffee and cigarettes, and mingled with these another scent, the mysterious thrilling scent of love. Hands touched jewelled hands over the white tables; the vivid gowns and the shirt fronts swayed together and matches were held, trembling a little, for slow-lighting cigarettes.

The battered hacks waiting at the station; the snow-covered campus, the big open fires in the club houses.

Zelda's worn places in yard and hammock.

A man says to another man: "I'd certainly like to steal your girl." Second man: "I'd give her to you, but she's part of a set."

They have more money. (Ernest's wisecrack.)[1]

In the light of four strong pocket flashlights, borne by four sailors in spotless white, a gentleman was shaving himself, standing clad only in athletic underwear upon the sand. Before his eyes an irreproachable valet held a silver mirror, which gave back the soapy reflection of his face. To right and left stood two additional menservants, one with a dinner coat and trousers hanging from his arm and the other bearing a white stiff shirt, whose studs glistened in the glow of the electric lamps. There was not a sound except the dull scrape of the razor along its wielder's face and the intermittent groaning sound that blew in out of the sea.

For Esther M[urphy]: In memory of an old friendship or a prolonged quarrel that has gone on so long and accumulated so much moss that it is much the same thing.

She wanted to crawl into his pocket and be safe forever.

She found the appalling truth. She could never love him, never while he lived. It was as if he had charged her to react negatively and so long as the current flowed she had no choice. Passionately she tried to think back to a few minutes before when the world had been tragic and glorious, but the moment was gone. He was alive, and as she heard his feet take up the chase again, the wings of her mind were already preening themselves for flight.

She was not more than eighteen—a dark little beauty with the fine crystal gloss over her that, in brunettes, takes the place of a blond's bright glow.

He imagined Kay and Arthur Busch progressing through the afternoon. Kay would cry a great deal and the situation would seem harsh and unexpected to them at first, but the tender closing of

---

[1] Fitzgerald had said, "The rich are different from you and me." Hemingway had replied, "Yes, they have more money."

the day would draw them together. They would turn inevitably toward each other and he would slip more and more into the position of the enemy outside.

She was eighteen, with such a skin as the Italian painters of the decadence used for corner angels, and all the wishing in the world glistening in her grey eyes.

A girl who could send tear-stained telegrams.

* * * * is still a flapper. Fashions, names, manners, customs and morals change, but for * * * * it is still 1920. This concerns me, for there is no doubt that she originally patterned herself upon certain immature and unfortunate writings of mine, so I have a special indulgence for * * * * as for one who has lost an arm or leg in one's service.

They swayed suddenly and childishly together.

She was desperately adaptable, desperately sweet-natured.

Her childish beauty was lustful and sad about being so rich and sixteen.

Ernest Hemingway—until we began trying to walk over each other with cleats.

His features were well-formed against the flat canvas of his face.

Women read a couple of books and see a few pictures because they haven't got anything else to do, and then they say they're finer in grain than you are, and to prove it they take the bit in their teeth and tear off for a fare-you-well—just about as sensitive as a fire horse.

A panama hat, under which burned fierce, undefeated Southern eyes.

Harlot in glasses.

Jews lose clarity. They get to look like old melted candles as if their bodies were preparing to waddle. Irish get slovenly and dirty. Anglo-Saxons get frayed and worn.

As an incorrigible masturbator, he was usually in a state of disgust with life. It came through, however, etc.

Idea about Nicole [that she] can do everything, extroverts toward everything save people. So earth, flowers, pictures, voices, comparisons. [She] seems to writhe—no rest wherever she turns, like a tom-

tom beat. Escapes over the line, where in fantasy alone she finds rest.

He was wearing old white duck trousers with a Spanish flare and a few strange coins nodding at their seams, and a striped Riviera sweater, and straw shoes from the Bahamas, and an ancient Mexican hat. It was, for him, a typical costume, Diana thought. Always at Christmas she arranged to get him some odd foreign importation from parts as far away as possible from Loudoun County.

When I like men I want to be like them—I want to lose the outer qualities that give me my individuality and be like them. I don't want the man; I want to absorb into myself all the qualities that make him attractive and leave him out. I cling to my own innards. When I like women I want to own them, to dominate them, to have them admire me.

As to Ernest as a boy: reckless, adventurous, etc. Yet it is undeniable that the dark was peopled for him. His bravery and acquired characteristics.

Books are like brothers. I am an only child. Gatsby my imaginary eldest brother, Amory my younger, Anthony my worry, Dick my comparatively good brother, but all of them far from home. When I have the courage to put the old white light on the home of my heart, then . . .

Didn't Hemingway say this in effect: If Tom Wolfe ever learns to separate what he gets from books from what he gets from life, he will be an original. All you can get from books is rhythm and technique. He's half-grown artistically—this is truer than what Ernest said about him. But when I've criticized him (several times in talk), I've felt mad afterwards. Putting sharp weapons in the hands of his inferiors.

I talk with the authority of failure—Ernest with the authority of success. We could never sit across the same table again.

She was asleep—he stood for a moment beside her bed, sorry for her, because she was asleep, and because she had set her slippers beside her bed.

The silence was coming from some deep place in Mrs. Ives' heart.

Our fathers died. Suddenly in the night they died and in the morning we knew.

Ernest Hemingway, while careful to avoid clichés

in his work, fairly revels in them in his private life, his favorite being *"Parbleu!"* ("So what?"—French), and "Yes, We Have No Bananas." Contrary to popular opinion, he is not as tall as Thomas Wolfe, standing only six feet five in his health belt. He is naturally clumsy with his body, but shooting from a blind or from adequate cover, makes a fine figure of a man. We are happy to announce that his work will appear in future exclusively on United States postage stamps.

I have never wished there was a God to call on —I have often wished that there was a God to thank.

Do you know what your affair was founded on? On sorrow. You got sorry for each other.

You can't take the son of a plough manufacturer, clip off his testicles and make an artist of him.

She had never done anything for love before. She didn't know what it meant. When her hand struck the bulb she still didn't know it, nor while the shattered glass made a nuisance by the bedside.

A young man phoned from a city far off, then from a city near by, then from downtown, informing me that he was coming to call, though he had never seen me. He arrived eventually with a great ripping up of garden borders, a four-ply rip in a new lawn, a watch pointing accurately and unforgivably at 3 A.M. But he was prepared to disarm me with the force of his compliment, the intensity of the impulse that had brought him to my door. "Here I am at last," he said, teetering triumphantly. "I had to see you. I feel I owe you more than I can say. I feel that you formed my life."

In Hendersonville:[2] I am living very cheaply.

[2] North Carolina, from one of the periods when Fitzgerald was at the lowest ebb.

Today I am in comparative affluence, but Monday and Tuesday I had two tins of potted meat, three oranges and a box of Uneedas and two cans of beer. For the food, that totalled eighteen cents a day—and when I think of the thousand meals I've sent back untasted in the last two years. It was fun to be poor—especially when you haven't enough liver power for an appetite. But the air is fine here, and I liked what I had—and there was nothing to do about it anyhow because I was afraid to cash any checks, and I had to save enough for postage for the story. But it was funny coming into the hotel and the very deferential clerk not knowing that I was not only thousands, nay tens of thousands in debt, but had less than forty cents cash in the world and probably a deficit at my bank. I gallantly gave Scotty my last ten when I left her and of course the Flynns, etc., had no idea and wondered why I didn't just "jump into a taxi" (four dollars and tip) and run over for dinner.

Enough of this bankrupt's comedy—I suppose it has been enacted all over the U.S. in the last four years, plenty of times.

Nevertheless, I haven't told you the half of it— i.e., my underwear I started with was a pair of pyjama pants—*just that*. It was only today I could replace them with a union suit. I washed my two handkerchiefs and my shirt every night, but the pyjama trousers I had to wear all the time, and I am presenting it to the Hendersonville Museum. My socks would have been equally notorious save there was not enough of them left, for they served double duty as slippers at night. The final irony was when a drunk man in the shop where I bought my can of ale said in a voice obviously intended for me, "These city dudes from the East come down here with their millions. Why don't they support us?"

My great grandmother visited Dolly Madison.

THORNTON WILDER (1897–   )

Thornton Wilder has had a long and distinguished career as both novelist and playwright. At almost the beginning of that career he won the Pulitzer prize for his novel *The Bridge of San Luis Rey* (1927), and two of his plays— *Our Town* (1938) and *The Skin of Our Teeth*

(1942)—have also been Pulitzer prize winners.

He was born in Madison, Wisconsin, but while he was still a small boy his father was appointed Consul General to Hong Kong and the family then lived for a number of years in China. At nine, Wilder began to attend a school in Hong Kong conducted by German nationals. After some six months there he was sent to school in California, but in 1911 he was back in China, this time in an English mission school at Chefoo. His college work was begun at Oberlin and completed at Yale.

After service in the First World War—he also served in Europe in the Second World War—he was for a year at the American Academy in Rome, studying archeology. When he returned to America it was as a teacher of French at the Lawrenceville School. His knowledge of the modern languages, his association from time to time with American universities, and his frequent visits to Europe throughout a lifetime have kept him in touch with literary experiments in fiction and in the theater abroad. In view of his personal experience, then, it is not surprising that his earlier fiction finds its setting outside the United States.

His first novel, *The Cabala* (1926), reflects a very special segment of Roman society early in this century; *The Bridge of San Luis Rey*, that of seventeenth-century Peru; and *The Woman of Andros* (1930), life in the first century B.C. on one of the Greek islands. Wilder's propensity for using foreign scenes and the past was severely criticized during the Depression years by Michael Gold (see p. 2385) and others who insisted on proletarian realism and who accused Wilder of having retreated into mannered and snobbish preciosity. But Wilder was never concerned with the pastness of the past; rather, with the persistence of the past into the present and the continuity of human nature through all the ages. Thus, it was not at all a reaction to hostile criticism that caused Wilder to return to contemporary America as he did in *Heaven's My Destination* (1935), a novel that has its setting in the Midwest of the 1930's, or in plays such as *Our Town* and *The Skin of Our Teeth*.

Our Town, perhaps his best-known play and the one most frequently performed, has as its setting a small New England village in 1901. It has certain affinities with other literary works of the early twentieth century, works such as Edgar Lee Masters' *Spoon River Anthology* (1915) and Sherwood Anderson's *Winesburg, Ohio* (1919). Yet in important respects Wilder's treatment of the American small town differs sharply from that of Masters and that of Anderson, just as his background differs from theirs. Masters began his career as a midwestern lawyer; Anderson began his as a midwestern business man. Both men were largely self-educated, and their strength lies in their immersion in the local culture in which they grew up. By contrast, Wilder's sensibility is cosmopolitan, and from his boyhood he was made aware of the international scene. Consequently he brought to his novels and plays not only a powerful sense of the literary tradition, but a first-hand acquaintance with cultures other than those within the borders of our country.

Our Town, then, is not a bit of latter-day local color, the exploitation of American folksiness, meant to appeal to a contemporary auditor's nostalgia for the past. On the contrary, it represents an interesting application to provincial subject matter of sophisticated dramatic and theatrical techniques and employs them the better to present a universal theme. As for the theme: Wilder has told us in his preface to *Three Plays* (1959) that "*Our Town* is not offered as a picture of life in a New Hampshire village. . . . It is an attempt to find a value above all price for the smallest events in our daily life. I have made the claim as preposterous as possible, for I set the village against the largest dimensions of time and place." Wilder's assertion that the smallest events of our lives are infinitely precious may be said to take the form of an *a fortiori* argument: that is, if the dramatist can show the supreme value of the smallest incidents in a life as apparently humdrum as that lived in Grover's Corners, then he will have shown that value for life everywhere. Surely this is what Wilder means in writing that he has "made the claim as preposterous as possible," for he obviously considers his claim not actually preposterous, but true.

The plot of *Our Town* is as ordinary as one could make it. It amounts to not much more than boy meets girl; they fall in love, get married and have a child, and die, as all human beings must. In this instance it is the wife who dies first, as a still very young woman.

Wilder's way of urging his claim about the value of the smallest events is properly reserved for the last act, and he has cunningly prepared for that last act by his way of rendering the small events that make up the two acts that precede it. Here his special mode of presentation, although it looks simple, is really enormously artful. A discerning reading of the play will reveal that he has found an acceptable way to skim rapidly over certain events, to provide panoramic views where they are desirable, and summary or shorthand accounts of matters that are not important enough to demand much stress, thus saving time for the truly significant happenings. The method has a further advantage: it provides the playwright with a device for indicating the important scenes by the way in which they are made to stand out from the common run of events.

One significant part of the technique is the simplification of the stage and the use of few stage properties—properties that, by their very meagerness, invite us to use our imaginations. The summaries, the shorthand accounts that allow the playwright to get over ground rapidly, the lightning transitions from one scene to another, may well owe something to Wilder's experience as a novelist, for the novelist must in such fashion constantly manipulate the scale and pace of his narration. Wilder's techniques of presentation may also owe something to the movies.

In speaking of the absence of elaborate sets and stage properties, we have stressed what may be called the negative aspect of Wilder's technique—that is, what is left out to the advantage of the play. A positive aspect is his use in *Our Town* of the "stage manager." Wilder establishes him from the first moment as the man in charge, who announces the title of the play, the names of the dramatis personae, the place and time of the action, and who speaks what amounts to a prologue. He knows everything about the town and what happens there. He can provide background for a character; he can shift the scene by a casual reference or by actually moving a few stage properties; he can act as chorus, commenting on the action, connecting it with universal life patterns and with the experience of the audience. He can even step in and take the part of a minor character, as, for example, in the drugstore scene, where he dispenses sodas, or in the wedding scene, where he becomes the officiating minister. In short, he is as omniscient as God and as ubiquitous, but he is not in the least solemn. He is colloquial, even folksy, as easy and comfortable as an old shoe.

Effective dramatic and theatrical devices are thoroughly characteristic of Wilder. At an early period he became aware of what was happening on the new European stage. For example, he learned something from the plays of André Obey, whose experiments were staged by the Compagnie de Quinze in Paris, where Wilder lived for a time. In Paris too he knew Gertrude Stein (see p. 2220) to whose wisdom and insight he has paid high tribute, with special emphasis on her keen observations about human nature and her experiments with language. Her influence, as we have already noted, was directed toward simplicity—even naiveté—and at the cutting away from language of irrelevant and stultifying associations. (Sherwood Anderson, as we have already seen, also knew her work and profited from her experiments.) The new French experimental drama was also concerned to get away from the bourgeois theater, with its well-made plays, its elaborate stage sets, and its special insulation of art from life.

Thornton Wilder's plays are meant to engage life, to reveal it, to penetrate to its core. His technical resourcefulness has been developed solely to realize this purpose—never to provide an exhibition of mere technique.

BIOGRAPHICAL CHART

1897 Born April 17, in Madison, Wisconsin
1905–9 Lives in Shanghai and Hong Kong during father's term as consul general
1915 First three-minute plays in *The Angel That Troubled the Waters*, written in Berkeley
1919–20 First full-length play, *The Trumpet Shall Sound*, published serially in the *Yale Literary Magazine*
1920 Receives A.B. from Yale; leaves for Europe
1920–21 Studies archeology at American Academy in Rome; impressions later recorded in *The Cabala*
1926 *The Cabala*
1927 *The Bridge of San Luis Rey*
1928 *The Angel That Troubled the Waters*; receives first Pulitzer prize—for *The Bridge*
1930 *The Woman of Andros*
1931 *The Long Christmas Dinner and Other Plays*
1935 Invites Gertrude Stein to lecture at Chicago; *Heaven's My Destination*
1936 Leaves University of Chicago; begins career as serious dramatist

1938 *Our Town* first performed, in Princeton, New Jersey; *The Merchant of Yonkers* first produced, in Boston; awarded Pulitzer prize for *Our Town*
1941 Lectures on James Joyce
1942–45 *The Skin of Our Teeth* first performed, in New Haven; enlists in U.S. Air Force; serves in U.S.A., North Africa, and Italy
1943 Receives third Pulitzer prize, for *Skin of Our Teeth*
1948 Translates Sartre's *Morts sans sepulture* (*The Victors*) for American stage; *The Ides of March*
1950–51 Gives Charles Eliot Norton lectures at Harvard on Thoreau, Melville, and Emily Dickinson
1952 Awarded Gold Medal for Fiction by Academy of Arts and Letters
1955 *A Life in the Sun* (*The Alcestiad*) performed at Edinburgh Festival
1967 *The Eighth Day*

FURTHER READINGS

There is no standard edition of Wilder's work. The reader may consult the biographical chart for the publication dates of his major works.

Malcolm Cowley, *Exile's Return* (1951)
———, Introduction to *A Thornton Wilder Trio* (1956)
———, ed., *Writers at Work: The Paris Review Interviews* (1958)

Francis Fergusson, "Three Allegorists: Brecht, Wilder, and Eliot," *Sewanee Review* (Fall, 1956)
Joseph Firebaugh, "The Humanism of Thornton Wilder," *Pacific Spectator* (Autumn, 1950)
Edmund Wilson, *The Shores of Light* (1952)
———, "The Antrobuses and the Earwickers," *Nation* (1943)

The Skin of Our Teeth (1942)

The Skin of Our Teeth is as resourceful in theatrical technique as is *Our Town*. The dramatist deliberately scrambles the various epochs of history in a series of momentarily bewildering anachronisms: a radio announcer gives us news bulletins about the advance of the polar ice cap into the temperate zone, a catastrophe that most recently occurred at least 40,000 years ago; a telegram arrives telling us that the hero of the play, Mr. Antrobus, is making progress toward perfecting the alphabet. The anachronisms are, to be sure, used for their momentary shock value and for incidental comic effect, but they also rather quickly drive home to the audience that the play being witnessed is a dramatized fable about man's ability to endure catastrophes of nature as well as those of his own making, about his powers of recuperation, and about his willingness to try again. All times constitute one time; the *essential* story is always the same—whether the threat is that of a new ice age or a global war.

The theme is reinforced by having the play end as it began—with Sabina, the character whose first speech opened the play, repeating the same speech as the play ends. Having done so, Sabina steps out of the play proper by coming down to the footlights to address the audience directly with the words: "This is where you came in. We have to go on for ages and ages yet. You can go home. The end of this play isn't written yet." Drama and reality are thus made to merge. We are given to understand that the activity which has been bodied forth on the stage is the age-old life of mankind, a life that will go on, with its basic triumphs and defeats, for a long, long time to come.

Mr. Antrobus (the Greek word for man is *anthropus*) is Adam and also Cadmus, the man who in Greek myth invented the alphabet, and also Noah, who saved the remnant of mankind from the universal flood and thus insured a new chance for the human race.

Mrs. Antrobus is Eve: on page 2324 we are told that it was "she who invented the apron [of fig leaves, presumably] on which so many interesting changes have been rung since." Sabina is obviously Lilith, the primal "other woman." (In Hebrew folklore she is Adam's first wife.) Henry bears on his brow the mark of Cain, who was the first murderer according to the story in Genesis.

Yet, in spite of the archetypal characteristics of the dramatis personae, it is important that the playwright be able to locate them firmly in the here-and-now of our own time. Since Mr. Antrobus in Wilder's dramatized fable is universal man, he must not be limited to the role of Adam, the "gardener" of the Genesis story, or to that of Noah, who built the Ark. Instead, he must be given a specific residence in the United States—and in our present time—in a house "conveniently situated near a public school, a Methodist church, and a firehouse. . . ."

Most of all, if a play with such a theme is to succeed, the characters must not be treated solemnly. There must be room for realism and for comedy. Though the story of man is finally one of heroic courage and endurance, individual human beings have from the beginnings of recorded history been guilty of folly, delusions of grandeur, bad temper, and general cantankerousness. Mr. Antrobus is no exception. Besides,

in this play, Mr. Antrobus is first presented to us in the setting of his home, and no one is a hero to his valet—or to his housemaid—and, perhaps least of all, to his wife.

Yet Mr. Antrobus does have his solid merit. If he occasionally breaks a minor law, his veneration for Moses, the primal law-giver, is genuine. Even when the times become really desperate, he will nevertheless spare a place by the fire and some food for the arts and sciences, the poet and the philosopher. If he occasionally falls for the other woman, eventually he remembers his promise and comes back to his wife, Eva Antrobus.

Wilder's very theme, then, demands the scrambling of historic epochs, fantastic juxtapositions (such as Noah's flood and the Atlantic City boardwalk), and the comic clash between man's archetypal role, grand and sometimes heroic, and his all-too-human day-to-day gaucheries and pratfalls.

One of the sources of comedy is the constant use of clichés in this play. Nearly everybody rattles off, at one time or another, threadbare expressions—platitudes, bits of tarnished political rhetoric, and other tired expressions. Thus, when Antrobus is called on for a speech, he says: "Friends, Cousins. Four score and ten billion years ago our forefathers brought forth upon this planet the spark of life." Mrs. Antrobus, when her husband complains of their son's conduct, replies with the typical mother's age-old defence: "George, he's only four thousand years old." As for Sabina, her whole conversation is a tireless cascade of clichés: "Pray God nothing serious has happened to [Mr. Antrobus] crossing the Hudson River. If anything happened to him, we would certainly be inconsolable and have to move into a less desirable district. . . . But I'm not surprised. The whole world's at sixes and sevens, and why the house hasn't fallen down about our ears is a miracle to me."

The incongruity between the worn-out phrases and the situations that call them forth is often genuinely funny. But in addition to these incidentally comic effects, the clichés serve to underline the theme of the play. They suggest that human beings have changed little in a thousand, or four thousand, years—that the same proverbs are mouthed, the same oratorical flourishes flourished, and the same hyperboles continue to oppress the ear. In short, the very language used by the characters stresses the point that human nature remains stable. The differences between historical epochs are ultimately unimportant: they are made to blur out.

The difference between art and life is also made to blur out in this play. Sabina in particular is continually stepping out of her role in the play, ceasing to be the fictional character and becoming Miss Somerset, the rather stupid young woman who regrets being in the play at all and occasionally frankly tells the audience so. We have earlier referred to one important passage in which this moving out of the framework of the play into the realm of the actual present is effective: when Sabina, in the closing lines of the play, "comes down to the footlights" and dismisses the audience with the words "You can go home. The end of this play isn't written yet." Here she is plainly telling the men and women who have been watching the stage performance that it is not merely a stage performance but an action that is real and ongoing. (Act I ends in much the same way: Sabina appeals directly to the audience to help save the human race. The Antrobus' fire must not be allowed to die out. Therefore, "Pass up your chairs [for firewood], everybody. Save the human race.")

The breaking out of the stage illusion occurs with special frequency early in the play. Thus, there is a hitch in the performance, and we hear the voice of the prompter urging Sabina to improvise. Sabina makes the effort for a moment, and then "*Suddenly flings pretense to the winds and coming downstage says with indignation*" that she hates the play, and confesses: "As for me, I don't understand a single word of it— all about the troubles the human race has gone through, there's a subject for you.

"Besides the author hasn't made up his silly mind as to whether we're all living back in caves or in New Jersey today, and that's the way it is all the way through."

Later, when the advancing glaciers threaten to freeze the human race to death, Sabina says "(*energetically, to the audience*) Ladies and gentlemen! Don't take this play serious. The world's not coming to an end. You know it's not." And she goes on to try to reassure her auditors.

What is accomplished by such mocking exposures of the theatrical conventions? Doesn't such undercutting of the stage illusion threaten to destroy the credibility of the play? On the contrary. It provides a justification for the evident anachronisms and the confusion of historical eras, for it shows that the confusions and anachronisms are not inadvertent blunders but are deliberate and therefore meaningful. In short, in the first few minutes of the play, we can learn—if we are willing to listen to the rather hare-brained and not too bright young woman who is attempting to play Sabina— that there is method in the muddles that bewilder her and that the playwright is not offering us nonsense but essential truth.

CHARACTERS (*in the order of their appearance*)

ANNOUNCER	GLADYS	MISS E. MUSE	SIX CONVEENERS
SABINA	HENRY	MISS T. MUSE	BROADCAST OFFICIAL
MR. FITZPATRICK	MR. ANTROBUS	MISS M. MUSE	DEFEATED CANDIDATE
MRS. ANTROBUS	DOCTOR	TWO USHERS	MR. TREMAYNE
DINOSAUR	PROFESSOR	TWO DRUM MAJORETTES	HESTER
MAMMOTH	JUDGE	FORTUNE TELLER	IVY
TELEGRAPH BOY	HOMER	TWO CHAIR PUSHERS	FRED BAILEY

Act. I.   Home, Excelsior, New Jersey.
Act. II.   Atlantic City Boardwalk.
Act. III.   Home, Excelsior, New Jersey.

ACT I

A projection screen in the middle of the curtain. The first lantern slide: the name of the theatre, and the words: NEWS EVENTS OF THE WORLD. An ANNOUNCER'S *voice is heard.*

ANNOUNCER: The management takes pleasure in bringing to you—The News Events of the World: *Slide of the sun appearing above the horizon.*

Freeport, Long Island:
The sun rose this morning at 6:32 A.M. This gratifying event was first reported by Mrs. Dorothy Stetson of Freeport, Long Island, who promptly telephoned the Mayor.

The Society for Affirming the End of the World at once went into a special session and postponed the arrival of that event for TWENTY-FOUR HOURS.

All honor to Mrs. Stetson for her public spirit.

New York City: *Slide of the front doors of the theatre in which this play is playing; three cleaning* WOMEN *with mops and pails.*

The X Theatre. During the daily cleaning of this theatre a number of lost objects were collected as usual by Mesdames Simpson, Pateslewski, and Moriarty.

Among these objects found today was a wedding ring, inscribed: To Eva from Adam. Genesis II:18.
The ring will be restored to the owner or owners, if their credentials are satisfactory.

Tippehatchee, Vermont: *Slide representing a glacier.*

The unprecedented cold weather of this summer has produced a condition that has not yet been satisfactorily explained. There is a report that a wall of ice is moving southward across these counties. The disruption of communications by the cold wave now crossing the country has rendered exact information difficult, but little credence is given to the rumor that the ice had pushed the Cathedral of Montreal as far as St. Albans, Vermont.

For further information see your daily papers.

Excelsior, New Jersey: *Slide of a modest suburban home.*

The home of Mr. George Antrobus, the inventor of the wheel. The discovery of the wheel, follow-ing so closely on the discovery of the lever, has centered the attention of the country on Mr. Antrobus of this attractive suburban residence district. This is his home, a commodious seven-room house, conveniently situated near a public school, a Methodist church, and a firehouse; it is right handy to an A. and P. *Slide of* MR. ANTROBUS *on his front steps, smiling and lifting his straw hat. He holds a wheel.*

Mr. Antrobus, himself. He comes of very old stock and has made his way up from next to nothing.

It is reported that he was once a gardener, but left that situation under circumstances that have been variously reported.

Mr. Antrobus is a veteran of foreign wars, and bears a number of scars, front and back. *Slide of* MRS. ANTROBUS, *holding some roses.*

This is Mrs. Antrobus, the charming and gracious president of the Excelsior Mothers' Club.

Mrs. Antrobus is an excellent needlewoman; it is she who invented the apron on which so many interesting changes have been rung since. *Slide of the* FAMILY *and* SABINA.

Here we see the Antrobuses with their two children, Henry and Gladys, and friend. The friend in the rear, is Lily Sabina, the maid.

I know we all want to congratulate this typical American family on its enterprise. We all wish Mr. Antrobus a successful future. Now the management takes you to the interior of this home for a brief visit. *Curtain rises. Living room of a commuter's home.* SABINA—*straw-blonde, over-rouged—is standing by the window back center, a feather duster under her elbow.*

SABINA: Oh, oh, oh! Six o'clock and the master not home yet.

Pray God nothing serious has happened to him crossing the Hudson River. If anything happened to him, we would certainly be inconsolable and have to move into a less desirable residence district.

The fact is I don't know what'll become of us. Here it is the middle of August and the coldest day of the year. It's simply freezing; the dogs are sticking to the sidewalks; can anybody explain that? No.

But I'm not surprised. The whole world's at sixes and sevens, and why the house hasn't fallen down about our ears long ago is a miracle to me. *A fragment of the right wall leans precariously over the stage.* SABINA *looks at it nervously and it slowly rights itself.*

Every night this same anxiety as to whether the master will get home safely: whether he'll bring home anything to eat. In the midst of life we are in the midst of death, a truer word was never said. *The fragment of scenery flies up into the lofts.* SABINA *is struck dumb with surprise, shrugs her shoulders and starts dusting* MR. ANTROBUS' *chair, including the under side.*

Of course, Mr. Antrobus is a very fine man, an excellent husband and father, a pillar of the church, and has all the best interests of the community at heart. Of course, every muscle goes tight every time he passes a policeman; but what I think is that there are certain charges that ought not to be made, and I think I may add, ought not to be allowed to be made; we're all human; who isn't? *She dusts* MRS. ANTROBUS' *rocking chair.*

Mrs. Antrobus is as fine a woman as you could hope to see. She lives only for her children; and if it would be any benefit to her children she'd see the rest of us stretched out dead at her feet without turning a hair,—that's the truth. If you want to know anything more about Mrs. Antrobus, just go and look at a tigress, and look hard.

As to the children—

Well, Henry Antrobus is a real, clean-cut American boy. He'll graduate from High School one of these days, if they make the alphabet any easier.— Henry, when he has a stone in his hand, has a perfect aim; he can hit anything from a bird to an older brother—Oh! I didn't mean to say that!— but it certainly was an unfortunate accident, and it was very hard getting the police out of the house.

Mr. and Mrs. Antrobus' daughter is named Gladys. She'll make some good man a good wife some day, if he'll just come down off the movie screen and ask her.

So here we are!

We've managed to survive for some time now, catch as catch can, the fat and the lean, and if the dinosaurs don't trample us to death, and if the grasshoppers don't eat up our garden, we'll all live to see better days, knock on wood.

Each new child that's born to the Antrobuses seems to them to be sufficient reason for the whole universe's being set in motion; and each new child that dies seems to them to have been spared a whole world of sorrow, and what the end of it will be is still very much an open question.

We've rattled along, hot and cold, for some time now—*A portion of the wall above the door, right, flies up into the air and disappears.* —and my advice to you is not to inquire into why or whither, but just enjoy your ice cream while it's on your plate,—that's my philosophy.

Don't forget that a few years ago we came through the depression by the skin of our teeth! One more tight squeeze like that and where will we be? *This is a cue line.* SABINA *looks angrily at the kitchen door and repeats* . . . we came through the depression by the skin of our teeth; one more tight squeeze like that and where will we be? *Flustered, she looks through the opening in the right wall; then goes to the window and reopens the Act.*

Oh, oh, oh! Six o'clock and the master not home yet. Pray God nothing has happened to him crossing the Hudson. Here it is the middle of August and the coldest day of the year. It's simply freezing; the dogs are sticking. One more tight squeeze like that and where will we be?

VOICE, *off stage:* Make up something! Invent something!

SABINA: Well . . . uh . . . this certainly is a fine American home . . . and—uh . . . everybody's very happy . . . and—uh . . . *Suddenly flings pretense to the winds and coming downstage says with indignation:* I can't invent any words for this play, and I'm glad I can't. I hate this play and every word in it.

As for me, I don't understand a single word of it, anyway,—all about the troubles the human race has gone through, there's a subject for you.

Besides, the author hasn't made up his silly mind as to whether we're all living back in caves or in New Jersey today, and that's the way it is all through.

Oh—why can't we have plays like we used to have—*Peg o' My Heart*, and *Smilin' Thru*, and *The Bat*—good entertainment with a message you can take home with you?

I took this hateful job because I had to. For two years I've sat up in my living room living on a sandwich and a cup of tea a day, waiting for better times in the theatre. And look at me now: I—I who've played *Rain* and *The Barretts of Wimpole Street* and *First Lady*—God in Heaven! *The* STAGE MANAGER *puts his head out from the hole in the scenery.*

MR. FITZPATRICK: Miss Somerset! Miss Somerset!

SABINA: Oh! Anyway!—nothing matters! It'll all be the same in a hundred years. *Loudly,* We came through the depression by the skin of our teeth,— that's true!—one more tight squeeze like that and where will we be? *Enter* MRS. ANTROBUS, *a mother.*

MRS. ANTROBUS: Sabina, you've let the fire go out.

SABINA, *in a lather:* One-thing-and-another; don't-know-whether-my-wits-are-upside-or-down; might-as-well-be-dead-as-alive-in-a-house-all-sixes-and-sevens. . . .

MRS. ANTROBUS: You've let the fire go out. Here it is the coldest day of the year right in the middle of August, and you've let the fire go out.

SABINA: Mrs. Antrobus, I'd like to give my two weeks' notice, Mrs. Antrobus. A girl like I can get a situation in a home where they're rich enough to have a fire in every room, Mrs. Antrobus, and a girl don't have to carry the responsibility of the whole house on her two shoulders. And a home without children, Mrs. Antrobus, because children are a thing only a parent can understand, and a truer word was never said; and a home, Mrs. Antrobus, where the master of the house don't pinch decent, self-respecting girls when he meets them in a dark corridor. I mention no names and make no charges. So you have my notice, Mrs. Antrobus. I hope that's perfectly clear.

MRS. ANTROBUS: You've let the fire go out!—Have you milked the mammoth?

SABINA: I don't understand a word of this play.—Yes, I've milked the mammoth.

MRS. ANTROBUS: Until Mr. Antrobus comes home we have no food and we have no fire. You'd better go over to the neighbors and borrow some fire.

SABINA: Mrs. Antrobus! I can't! I'd die on the way, you know I would. It's worse than January. The dogs are sticking to the sidewalks. I'd die.

MRS. ANTROBUS: Very well, I'll go.

SABINA, *even more distraught, coming forward and sinking on her knees:* You'd never come back alive; we'd all perish; if you weren't here, we'd just perish. How do we know Mr. Antrobus'll be back? We don't know. If you go out, I'll just kill myself.

MRS. ANTROBUS: Get up, Sabina.

SABINA: Every night it's the same thing. Will he come back safe, or won't he? Will we starve to death, or freeze to death, or boil to death or will we be killed by burglars? I don't know why we go on living. I don't know why we go on living at all. It's easier being dead. *She flings her arms on the table and buries her head in them. In each of the succeeding speeches she flings her head up—and sometimes her hands—then quickly buries her head again.*

MRS. ANTROBUS: The same thing! Always throwing up the sponge, Sabina. Always announcing your own death. But give you a new hat—or a plate of ice cream—or a ticket to the movies, and you want to live forever.

SABINA: You don't care whether we live or die; all you care about is those children. If it would be any benefit to them you'd be glad to see us all stretched out dead.

MRS. ANTROBUS: Well, maybe I would.

SABINA: And what do they care about? Themselves—that's all they care about. *Shrilly.* They make fun of you behind your back. Don't tell me: they're ashamed of you. Half the time, they pretend they're someone else's children. Little thanks you get from them.

MRS. ANTROBUS: I'm not asking for any thanks.

SABINA: And Mr. Antrobus—you don't understand *him.* All that work he does—trying to discover the alphabet and the multiplication table. Whenever he tries to learn anything you fight against it.

MRS. ANTROBUS: Oh Sabina, I know you.

When Mr. Antrobus raped you home from your Sabine hills, he did it to insult me.

He did it for your pretty face, and to insult me.

You were the new wife, weren't you?

For a year or two you lay on your bed all day and polished the nails on your hands and feet:

You made puff-balls of the combings of your hair and you blew them up to the ceiling.

And I washed your underclothes and I made you chicken broths.

I bore children and between my very groans I stirred the cream that you'd put on your face.

But I knew you wouldn't last.

You didn't last.

SABINA: But it was I who encouraged Mr. Antrobus to make the alphabet. I'm sorry to say it, Mrs. Antrobus, but you're not a beautiful woman, and you can never know what a man could do if he tried. It's girls like I who inspire the multiplication table.

I'm sorry to say it, but you're not a beautiful woman, Mrs. Antrobus, and that's the God's truth.

MRS. ANTROBUS: And you didn't last—you sank to the kitchen. And what do you do there? *You let the fire go out!*

No wonder to you it seems easier being dead.

Reading and writing and counting on your fingers is all very well in their way,—but I keep the home going.

MRS. ANTROBUS: —There's that dinosaur on the front lawn again.—Shoo! Go away. Go away. *The baby* DINOSAUR *puts his head in the window.*

DINOSAUR: It's cold.

MRS. ANTROBUS: You go around to the back of the house where you belong.

DINOSAUR: It's cold. *The* DINOSAUR *disappears.* MRS. ANTROBUS *goes calmly out.* SABINA *slowly raises her head and speaks to the audience. The central portion of the center wall rises, pauses, and disappears into the loft.*

SABINA: Now that you audience are listening to this, too, I understand it a little better.

I wish eleven o'clock were here; I don't want to be dragged through this whole play again. *The* TELEGRAPH BOY *is seen entering along the back wall of the stage from the right. She catches sight of him and calls:* Mrs. Antrobus! Mrs. Antrobus! Help! There's a strange man coming to the house. He's coming up the walk, help! *Enter* MRS. ANTROBUS *in alarm, but efficient.*

MRS. ANTROBUS: Help me quick! *They barricade the door by piling the furniture against it.* Who is it? What do you want?

TELEGRAPH BOY: A telegram for Mrs. Antrobus from Mr. Antrobus in the city.

SABINA: Are you sure, are you sure? Maybe it's just a trap!

MRS. ANTROBUS: I know his voice, Sabina. We can open the door. *Enter the* TELEGRAPH BOY, 12 *years old, in uniform. The* DINOSAUR *and* MAMMOTH *slip by him into the room and settle down front right.* I'm sorry we kept you waiting. We have to be careful, you know. *To the* ANIMALS. Hm! . . . Will you be quiet? *They nod.* Have you had your supper? *They nod.* Are you ready to come in? *They nod.* Young man, have you any fire with you? Then light the grate, will you? *He nods, produces something like a briquet; and kneels by the imagined fireplace, footlights center. Pause.* What are people saying about this cold weather? *He makes a doubtful shrug with his shoulders.* Sabina, take this stick and go and light the stove.

SABINA: Like I told you, Mrs. Antrobus; two weeks. That's the law. I hope that's perfectly clear. *Exit.*

MRS. ANTROBUS: What about this cold weather?

TELEGRAPH BOY, *lowered eyes:* Of course, I don't know anything . . . but they say there's a wall of ice moving down from the North, that's what they say. We can't get Boston by telegraph, and they're burning pianos in Hartford.

. . . It moves everything in front of it, churches and post offices and city halls.

I live in Brooklyn, myself.

MRS. ANTROBUS: What are people doing about it?

TELEGRAPH BOY: Well . . . uh . . . Talking, mostly.

Or just what you'd do a day in February.

There are some that are trying to go South and the roads are crowded; but you can't take old people and children very far in a cold like this.

MRS. ANTROBUS: —What's this telegram you have for me?

TELEGRAPH BOY, *fingertips to his forehead:* If you wait just a minute; I've got to remember it. *The* ANIMALS *have left their corner and are nosing him. Presently they take places on either side of him, leaning against his hips, like heraldic beasts.*

This telegram was flashed from Murray Hill to University Heights! And then by puffs of smoke from University Heights to Staten Island.

And then by lantern from Staten Island to Plainfield, New Jersey. What hath God wrought! *He clears his throat.*

"To Mrs. Antrobus, Excelsior, New Jersey:

"My dear wife, will be an hour late. Busy day at the office. Don't worry the children about the cold just keep them warm burn everything except Shakespeare." *Pause.*

MRS. ANTROBUS: Men!—He knows I'd burn ten Shakespeares to prevent a child of mine from having one cold in the head. What does it say next? *Enter* SABINA.

TELEGRAPH BOY: "Have made great discoveries today have separated em from en."

SABINA: I know what that is, that's the alphabet, yes it is. Mr. Antrobus is just the cleverest man. Why, when the alphabet's finished, we'll be able to tell the future and everything.

TELEGRAPH BOY: Then listen to this: "Ten tens make a hundred semi-colon consequences far-reaching." *Watches for effect.*

MRS. ANTROBUS: The earth's turning to ice, and all he can do is to make up new numbers.

TELEGRAPH BOY: Well, Mrs. Antrobus, like the head man at our office said: a few more discoveries like that and we'll be worth freezing.

MRS. ANTROBUS: What does he say next?

TELEGRAPH BOY: I . . . I can't do this last part very well. *He clears his throat and sings.* "Happy w'dding ann'vers'ry to you, Happy ann'vers'ry to you—" *The* ANIMALS *begin to howl soulfully;* SABINA *screams with pleasure.*

MRS. ANTROBUS: Dolly! Frederick! Be quiet.

TELEGRAPH BOY, *above the din:* "Happy w'dding ann'vers'ry, dear Eva; happy w'dding ann'vers'ry to you."

MRS. ANTROBUS: Is that in the telegram? Are

they singing telegrams now? *He nods.* The earth's getting so silly no wonder the sun turns cold.

SABINA: Mrs. Antrobus, I want to take back the notice I gave you. Mrs. Antrobus, I don't want to leave a house that gets such interesting telegrams and I'm sorry for anything I said. I really am.

MRS. ANTROBUS: Young man, I'd like to give you something for all this trouble; Mr. Antrobus isn't home yet and I have no money and no food in the house—

TELEGRAPH BOY: Mrs. Antrobus . . . I don't like to . . . appear to . . . ask for anything, but . . .

MRS. ANTROBUS: What is it you'd like?

TELEGRAPH BOY: Do you happen to have an old needle you could spare? My wife just sits home all day thinking about needles.

SABINA, *shrilly*: We only got two in the house. Mrs. Antrobus, you know we only got two in the house.

MRS. ANTROBUS, *after a look at* SABINA *taking a needle from her collar*: Why yes, I can spare this.

TELEGRAPH BOY, *lowered eyes*: Thank you, Mrs. Antrobus. Mrs. Antrobus, can I ask you something else? I have two sons of my own; if the cold gets worse, what should I do?

SABINA: I think we'll all perish, that's what I think. Cold like this in August is just the end of the whole world. *Silence.*

MRS. ANTROBUS: I don't know. After all, what does one do about anything? Just keep as warm as you can. And don't let your wife and children see that you're worried.

TELEGRAPH BOY: Yes . . . Thank you, Mrs. Antrobus. Well, I'd better be going.—Oh, I forgot! There's one more sentence in the telegram. "Three cheers have invented the wheel."

MRS. ANTROBUS: A wheel? What's a wheel?

TELEGRAPH BOY: I don't know. That's what it said. The sign for it is like this. Well, goodbye. *The* WOMEN *see him to the door, with goodbyes and injunctions to keep warm.*

SABINA, *apron to her eyes, wailing*: Mrs. Antrobus, it looks to me like all the nice men in the world are already married; I don't know what that is. *Exit.*

MRS. ANTROBUS, *thoughtful; to the* ANIMALS: Do you ever remember hearing tell of any cold like this in August? *The* ANIMALS *shake their heads.* From your grandmothers or anyone? *They shake their heads.* Have you any suggestions? *They shake their heads. She pulls her shawl around, goes to the front door and opening it an inch calls*: HENRY. GLADYS. CHILDREN. Come right in and get warm. No, no, when mama says a thing she means it.

Henry! HENRY. Put down that stone. You know what happened last time. *Shriek.* HENRY! Put down that stone!

Gladys! Put down your dress!! Try and be a lady. *The* CHILDREN *bound in and dash to the fire. They take off their winter things and leave them in heaps on the floor.*

GLADYS: Mama, I'm hungry. Mama, why is it so cold?

HENRY, *at the same time*: Mama, why doesn't it snow? Mama, when's supper ready? Maybe, it'll snow and we can make snowballs.

GLADYS: Mama, it's so cold that in one more minute I just couldn't of stood it.

MRS. ANTROBUS: Settle down, both of you, I want to talk to you. *She draws up a hassock and sits front center over the orchestra pit before the imaginary fire. The* CHILDREN *stretch out on the floor, leaning against her lap. Tableau by Raphael. The* ANIMALS *edge up and complete the triangle.*

It's just a cold spell of some kind. Now listen to what I'm saying:

When your father comes home I want you to be extra quiet. He's had a hard day at the office and I don't know but what he may have one of his moods.

I just got a telegram from him very happy and excited, and you know what that means. Your father's temper's uneven; I guess you know that. *Shriek.*

Henry! Henry!

Why—why can't you remember to keep your hair down over your forehead? You must keep that scar covered up. Don't you know that when your father sees it he loses all control over himself? He goes crazy. He wants to die. *After a moment's despair she collects herself decisively, wets the hem of her apron in her mouth and starts polishing his forehead vigorously.*

Lift your head up. Stop squirming. Blessed me, sometimes I think that it's going away—and then there it is; just as red as ever.

HENRY: Mama, today at school two teachers forgot and called me by my old name. They forgot, Mama. You'd better write another letter to the principal, so that he'll tell them I've changed my name. Right out in class they called me: Cain.

MRS. ANTROBUS, *putting her hand on his mouth, too late; hoarsely*: Don't say it. *Polishing feverishly.* If you're good they'll forget it. Henry, you didn't hit anyone . . . today, did you?

HENRY: Oh . . . no-o-o!

MRS. ANTROBUS, *still working, not looking at Gladys*: And, Gladys, I want you to be especially nice to your father tonight. You know what he calls you when you're good—his little angel, his little star. Keep your dress down like a little lady. And keep your voice nice and low. Gladys Antrobus!! What's that red stuff you have on your face? *Slaps her*. You're a filthy detestable child! *Rises in real, though temporary, repudiation and despair*. Get away from me, both of you! I wish I'd never seen sight or sound of you. Let the cold come! I can't stand it. I don't want to go on. *She walks away*.

GLADYS, *weeping*: All the girls at school do, Mama.

MRS. ANTROBUS, *shrieking*: I'm through with you, that's all!—Sabina! Sabina!—Don't you know your father'd go crazy if he saw that paint on your face? Don't you know your father thinks you're perfect? Don't you know he couldn't live if he didn't think you were perfect?—Sabina! *Enter* SABINA.

SABINA: Yes, Mrs. Antrobus!

MRS. ANTROBUS: Take this girl out into the kitchen and wash her face with the scrubbing brush.

MR. ANTROBUS, *outside, roaring*: "I've been working on the railroad, all the livelong day . . . etc." *The* ANIMALS *start running around in circles, bellowing*. SABINA *rushes to the window*.

MRS. ANTROBUS: Sabina, what's that noise outside?

SABINA: Oh, it's a drunken tramp. It's a giant, Mrs. Antrobus. We'll all be killed in our beds, I know it!

MRS. ANTROBUS: Help me quick. Quick. Everybody. *Again they stack all the furniture against the door*. MR. ANTROBUS *pounds and bellows*. Who is it? What do you want?—Sabina, have you any boiling water ready?—Who is it?

MR. ANTROBUS: Broken-down camel of a pig's snout, open this door.

MRS. ANTROBUS: God be praised! It's your father.—Just a minute, George!—Sabina, clear the door, quick. Gladys, come here while I clean your nasty face!

MR. ANTROBUS: She-bitch of a goat's gizzard, I'll break every bone in your body. Let me in or I'll tear the whole house down.

MRS. ANTROBUS: Just a minute, George, something's the matter with the lock.

MR. ANTROBUS: Open the door or I'll tear your

livers out. I'll smash your brains on the ceiling, and Devil take the hindmost.

MRS. ANTROBUS: Now, you can open the door, Sabina. I'm ready. *The door is flung open. Silence*. MR. ANTROBUS—*face of a Keystone Comedy Cop—stands there in fur cap and blanket. His arms are full of parcels, including a large stone wheel with a center in it. One hand carries a railroad man's lantern. Suddenly he bursts into joyous roar*.

MR. ANTROBUS: Well, how's the whole crooked family? *Relief. Laughter. Tears. Jumping up and down*. ANIMALS *cavorting*. ANTROBUS *throws the parcels on the ground. Hurls his cap and blanket after them. Heroic embraces. Melee of* HUMANS *and* ANIMALS, SABINA *included*. I'll be scalded and tarred if a man can't get a little welcome when he comes home. Well, Maggie, you old gunny-sack, how's the broken down old weather hen?—Sabina, old fishbait, old skunkpot.—And the children,—how've the little smellers been?

GLADYS: Papa, Papa, Papa, Papa, Papa.

MR. ANTROBUS: How've they been, Maggie?

MRS. ANTROBUS: Well, I must say, they've been as good as gold. I haven't had to raise my voice once. I don't know what's the matter with them.

ANTROBUS, *kneeling before* GLADYS: Papa's little weasel, eh?—Sabina, there's some food for you.—Papa's little gopher?

GLADYS, *her arm around his neck*: Papa, you're always teasing me.

ANTROBUS: And Henry? Nothing rash today, I hope. Nothing rash?

HENRY: No, Papa.

ANTROBUS, *roaring*: Well that's good, that's good—I'll bet Sabina let the fire go out.

SABINA: Mr. Antrobus, I've given my notice. I'm leaving two weeks from today. I'm sorry, but I'm leaving.

ANTROBUS, *roar*: Well, if you leave now you'll freeze to death, so go and cook the dinner.

SABINA: Two weeks, that's the law. *Exit*.

ANTROBUS: Did you get my telegram?

MRS. ANTROBUS: Yes.—What's a wheel? *He indicates the wheel with a glance*. HENRY *is rolling it around the floor. Rapid, hoarse interchange*: MRS. ANTROBUS: What does this cold weather mean? It's below freezing. ANTROBUS: Not before the children! MRS. ANTROBUS: Shouldn't we do something about it?—start off, move? ANTROBUS: Not before the children!!! *He gives* HENRY *a sharp slap*.

HENRY: Papa, you hit me!

ANTROBUS: Well, remember it. That's to make you remember today. Today. The day the alphabet's finished; and the day that we *saw* the hundred—the hundred, the hundred, the hundred, the hundred, the hundred—there's no end to 'em.

I've had a day at the office!

Take a look at that wheel, Maggie—when I've got that to rights: you'll see a sight.

There's a reward there for all the walking you've done.

MRS. ANTROBUS: How do you mean?

ANTROBUS, *on the hassock looking into the fire; with awe:* Maggie, we've reached the top of the wave. There's not much more to be done. We're there!

MRS. ANTROBUS, *cutting across his mood sharply:* And the ice?

ANTROBUS: The ice!

HENRY, *playing with the wheel:* Papa, you could put a chair on this.

ANTROBUS, *broodingly:* Ye-e-s, any booby can fool with it now,—but I thought of it first.

MRS. ANTROBUS: Children, go out in the kitchen. I want to talk to your father alone. *The CHILDREN go out.* ANTROBUS *has moved to his chair up left. He takes the goldfish bowl on his lap; pulls the canary cage down to the level of his face. Both the* ANIMALS *put their paws up on the arm of his chair.* MRS. ANTROBUS *faces him across the room, like a judge.*

MRS. ANTROBUS: Well?

ANTROBUS, *shortly:* It's cold.—How things been, eh? Keck, keck, keck.—And you, Millicent?

MRS. ANTROBUS: I know it's cold.

ANTROBUS, *to the canary:* No spilling of sunflower seed, eh? No singing after lights-out, y'know what I mean?

MRS. ANTROBUS: You can try and prevent us freezing to death, can't you? You can do something? We can start moving. Or we can go on the animals' backs?

ANTROBUS: The best thing about animals is that they don't talk much.

MAMMOTH: It's cold.

ANTROBUS: Eh, eh, eh! Watch that!—

—By midnight we'd turn to ice. The roads are full of people now who can scarcely lift a foot from the ground. The grass out in front is like iron,—which reminds me, I have another needle for you.—The people up north—where are they?

Frozen . . . crushed. . . .

MRS. ANTROBUS: Is that what's going to happen to us?—Will you answer me?

ANTROBUS: I don't know. I don't know anything.

Some say that the ice is going slower. Some say that it's stopped. The sun's growing cold. What can I do about that? Nothing we can do but burn everything in the house, and the fenceposts and the barn. Keep the fire going. When we have no more fire, we die.

MRS. ANTROBUS: Well, why didn't you say so in the first place? MRS. ANTROBUS *is about to march off when she catches sight of two* REFUGEES, *men, who have appeared against the back wall of the theatre and who are soon joined by others.*

REFUGEES: Mr. Antrobus! Mr. Antrobus! Mr. An-nn-tro-bus!

MRS. ANTROBUS: Who's that? Who's that calling you?

ANTROBUS, *clearing his throat guiltily:* Hm—let me see. *Two* REFUGEES *come up to the window.*

REFUGEE: Could we warm our hands for a moment, Mr. Antrobus. It's very cold, Mr. Antrobus.

ANOTHER REFUGEE: Mr. Antrobus, I wonder if you have a piece of bread or something that you could spare. *Silence. They wait humbly.* MRS. ANTROBUS *stands rooted to the spot. Suddenly a knock at the door, then another hand knocking in short rapid blows.*

MRS. ANTROBUS: Who are these people? Why, they're all over the front yard. What have they come *here* for? *Enter* SABINA.

SABINA: Mrs. Antrobus! There are some tramps knocking at the back door.

MRS. ANTROBUS: George, tell these people to go away. Tell them to move right along. I'll go and send them away from the back door. Sabina come with me. *She goes out energetically.*

ANTROBUS: Sabina! Stay here! I have something to say to you. *He goes to the door and opens it a crack and talks through it.* Ladies and gentlemen! I'll have to ask you to wait a few minutes longer. It'll be all right . . . while you're waiting you might each one pull up a stake of the fence. We'll need them all for the fireplace. There'll be coffee and sandwiches in a moment. SABINA *looks out door over his shoulder and suddenly extends her arm pointing, with a scream.*

SABINA: Mr. Antrobus, what's that??—that big white thing? Mr. Antrobus, it's ICE. It's ICE!!

ANTROBUS: Sabina, I want you to go in the kitchen and make a lot of coffee. Make a whole pail full.

SABINA: Pail full!!

ANTROBUS, *with gesture:* And sandwiches . . . piles of them . . . like this.

SABINA: Mr. An . . . !! *Suddenly she drops the play, and says in her own person as* MISS SOMERSET, *with surprise.* Oh, I see what this part of the play means now! This means refugees. *She starts to cross to the proscenium.* Oh, I don't like it. I don't like it. *She leans against the proscenium and bursts into tears.*

ANTROBUS: Miss Somerset!

Voice of the STAGE MANAGER: Miss Somerset!

SABINA, *energetically, to the audience:* Ladies and gentlemen! Don't take this play serious. The world's not coming to an end. You know it's not. People exaggerate! Most people really have enough to eat and a roof over their heads. Nobody actually starves—you can always eat grass or something. That ice-business—why, it was a long, long time ago. Besides they were only savages. Savages don't love their families—not like we do.

ANTROBUS *and* STAGE MANAGER: Miss Somerset!! *There is renewed knocking at the door.*

SABINA: All right. I'll say the lines, but I won't think about the play. *Enter* MRS. ANTROBUS.

SABINA, *parting thrust at the audience:* And I advise *you* not to think about the play, either. *Exit* SABINA.

MRS. ANTROBUS: George, these tramps say that you asked them to come to the house. What does this mean? *Knocking at the door.*

ANTROBUS: Just . . . uh . . . There are a few friends, Maggie, I met on the road. Real nice, real useful people. . . .

MRS. ANTROBUS, *back to the door:* Now, don't you ask them in!

George Antrobus, not another soul comes in here over my dead body.

ANTROBUS: Maggie, there's a doctor there. Never hurts to have a good doctor in the house. We've lost a peck of children, one way and another. You can never tell when a child's throat will get stopped up. What you and I have seen—!!! *He puts his fingers on his throat, and imitates diphtheria.*

MRS. ANTROBUS: Well, just one person then, the Doctor. The others can go right along the road.

ANTROBUS: Maggie, there's an old man, particular friend of mine—

MRS. ANTROBUS: I won't listen to you—

ANTROBUS: It was he that really started off the A.B.C.'s.

MRS. ANTROBUS: I don't care if he perishes. We can do without reading or writing. We can't do without food.

ANTROBUS: Then let the ice come!! Drink your coffee!! I don't want any coffee if I can't drink it with some good people.

MRS. ANTROBUS: Stop shouting. Who else is there trying to push us off the cliff?

ANTROBUS: Well, there's the man . . . who makes all the laws. Judge Moses!

MRS. ANTROBUS: Judges can't help us now.

ANTROBUS: And if the ice melts? . . . and if we pull through? Have you and I been able to bring up Henry? What have we done?

MRS. ANTROBUS: Who are those old women?

ANTROBUS, *coughs:* Up in town there are nine sisters. There are three or four of them here. They're sort of music teachers . . . and one of them recites and one of them—

MRS. ANTROBUS: That's the end. A singing troupe! Well, take your choice, live or die. Starve your own children before your face.

ANTROBUS, *gently:* These people don't take much. They're used to starving. They'll sleep on the floor. Besides, Maggie, listen: no, listen:

Who've we got in the house, but Sabina? Sabina's always afraid the worst will happen. Whose spirits can she keep up? Maggie, these people never give up. They think they'll live and work forever.

MRS. ANTROBUS, *walks slowly to the middle of the room:* All right, let them in. Let them in. You're master here. *Softly.*—But these animals must go. Enough's enough. They'll soon be big enough to push the walls down, anyway. Take them away.

ANTROBUS, *sadly:* All right. The dinosaur and mammoth—! Come on, baby, come on Frederick. Come for a walk. That's a good little fellow.

DINOSAUR: It's cold.

ANTROBUS: Yes, nice cold fresh air. Bracing. *He holds the door open and the* ANIMALS *go out. He beckons to his friends. The* REFUGEES *are typical elderly out-of-works from the streets of New York today.* JUDGE MOSES *wears a skull cap.* HOMER *is a blind beggar with a guitar. The seedy crowd shuffles in and waits humbly and expectantly.* ANTROBUS *introduces them to his wife who bows to each with a stately bend of her head.* Make yourself at home, Maggie, this the doctor . . . m . . . Coffee'll be here in a minute. . . . Professor, this is my wife. . . . And: . . . Judge . . . Maggie, you know the Judge. *An old blind man with a guitar.* Maggie, you know . . . you know Homer?—Come right in, Judge.—Miss Muse—are some of your sisters here? Come right in. . . . Miss E. Muse; Miss T. Muse, Miss M. Muse.

MRS. ANTROBUS: Pleased to meet you. Just . . . make yourself comfortable. Supper'll be ready in a minute. *She goes out, abruptly.*

ANTROBUS: Make yourself at home, friends. I'll be right back. *He goes out. The* REFUGEES *stare about them in awe. Presently several voices start whispering* Homer! Homer! *All take it up.* HOMER *strikes a chord or two on his guitar, then starts to speak:*

HOMER:

"Μῆνιν ἄειδε, θεά, Πηληϊάδεω Ἀχιλῆος, οὐλομένην, ἣ μυρί' Ἀχαιοῖς ἄλγε' ἔθηκεν, πολλὰς δ' ἰφθίμους ψυχὰς—"

HOMER'S *face shows he is lost in thought and memory and the words die away on his lips. The* REFUGEES *likewise nod in dreamy recollection. Soon the whisper* Moses, Moses! *goes around. An aged Jew parts his beard and recites dramatically:*

MOSES:

בְּרֵאשִׁית בָּרָא אֱלֹהִים אֵת הַשָּׁמַיִם וְאֵת הָאָרֶץ: וְהָאָרֶץ הָיְתָה תֹהוּ וָבֹהוּ וְחֹשֶׁךְ עַל־פְּנֵי תְהוֹם וְרוּחַ אֱלֹהִים מְרַחֶפֶת עַל־פְּנֵי הַמָּיִם:

The same dying away of the words takes place, and on the part of the REFUGEES *the same retreat into recollection. Some of them murmur,* Yes, yes. *The mood is broken by the abrupt entrance of* MR. *and* MRS. ANTROBUS *and* SABINA *bearing platters of sandwiches and a pail of coffee.* SABINA *stops and stares at the guests.*

MR. ANTROBUS: Sabina, pass the sandwiches.

SABINA: I thought I was working in a respectable house that had respectable guests. I'm giving my notice, Mr. Antrobus: two weeks, that's the law.

MR. ANTROBUS: Sabina! Pass the sandwiches.

SABINA: Two weeks, that's the law.

MR. ANTROBUS: There's the law. That's Moses.

SABINA, *stares:* The Ten Commandments—FAUGH!!—(*To Audience*) That's the worst line I've ever had to say on any stage.

ANTROBUS: I think the best thing to do is just not to stand on ceremony, but pass the sandwiches around from left to right.—Judge, help yourself to one of these.

MRS. ANTROBUS: The roads are crowded, I hear?

THE GUESTS, *all talking at once:* Oh, ma'am, you can't imagine. . . . You can hardly put one foot before you . . . people are trampling one another. *Sudden silence.*

MRS. ANTROBUS: Well, you know what I think it is,—I think it's sun-spots!

THE GUESTS, *discreet hubbub:* Oh, you're right,

Mrs. Antrobus . . . that's what it is. . . . That's what I was saying the other day. *Sudden silence.*

ANTROBUS: Well, I don't believe the whole world's going to turn to ice. *All eyes are fixed on him, waiting.* I can't believe it. Judge! Have we worked for nothing? Professor! Have we just failed in the whole thing?

MRS. ANTROBUS: It is certainly very strange—well fortunately on both sides of the family we come of very hearty stock.—Doctor, I want you to meet my children. They're eating their supper now. And of course I want them to meet you.

MISS M. MUSE: How many children have you, Mrs. Antrobus?

MRS. ANTROBUS: I have two,—a boy and a girl.

MOSES, *softly:* I understand you had two sons, Mrs. Antrobus. MRS. ANTROBUS *in blind suffering; she walks toward the footlights.*

MRS. ANTROBUS, *in a low voice:* Abel, Abel, my son, my son, Abel, my son, Abel, Abel, my son. *The* REFUGEES *move with few steps toward her as though in comfort murmuring words in Greek, Hebrew, German, et cetera. A piercing shriek from the kitchen,—* SABINA'S *voice. All heads turn.*

ANTROBUS: What's that? SABINA *enters, bursting with indignation, pulling on her gloves.*

SABINA: Mr. Antrobus—that son of yours, that boy Henry Antrobus—I don't stay in this house another moment!—He's not fit to live among respectable folks and that's a fact.

MRS. ANTROBUS: Don't say another word, Sabina. I'll be right back. *Without waiting for an answer she goes past her into the kitchen.*

SABINA: Mr. Antrobus, Henry has thrown a stone again and if he hasn't killed the boy that lives next door, I'm very much mistaken. He finished his supper and went out to play; and I heard such a fight; and then I saw it. I saw it with my own eyes. And it looked to me like stark murder. MRS. ANTROBUS *appears at the kitchen door, shielding* HENRY *who follows her. When she steps aside, we see on* HENRY'S *forehead a large ochre and scarlet scar in the shape of a C.* MR. ANTROBUS *starts toward him. A pause.* HENRY *is heard saying under his breath:*

HENRY: He was going to take the wheel away from me. He started to throw a stone at me first.

MRS. ANTROBUS: George, it was just a boyish impulse. Remember how young he is. *Louder, in an urgent wail.* George, he's only four thousand years old.

SABINA: And everything was going along so nicely! *Silence.*

ANTROBUS *goes back to the fireplace.*

ANTROBUS: Put out the fire! Put out all the fires. *Violently.* No wonder the sun grows cold. *He starts stamping on the fireplace.*

MRS. ANTROBUS: Doctor! Judge! Help me!— George, have you lost your mind?

ANTROBUS: There is no mind. We'll not try to live. *To the guests.* Give it up. Give up trying. MRS. ANTROBUS *seizes him.*

SABINA: Mr. Antrobus! I'm downright ashamed of you.

MRS. ANTROBUS: George, have some more coffee. —Gladys! Where's Gladys gone? GLADYS *steps in, frightened.*

GLADYS: Here I am, Mama.

MRS. ANTROBUS: Go upstairs and bring your father's slippers. How could you forget a thing like that, when you know how tired he is? ANTROBUS *sits in his chair. He covers his face with his hands.* MRS. ANTROBUS *turns to the* REFUGEES: Can't some of you sing? It's your business in life to sing, isn't it? Sabina! *Several of the women clear their throats tentatively, and with frightened faces gather around* HOMER's *guitar. He establishes a few chords. Almost inaudibly they start singing, led by* SABINA: Jingle Bells. MRS. ANTROBUS *continues to* ANTROBUS *in a low voice, while taking off his shoes:* George, remember all the other times. When the volcanoes came right up in the front yard.

And the time the grasshoppers ate every single leaf and blade of grass, and all the grain and spinach you'd grown with your own hands. And the summer there were earthquakes every night.

ANTROBUS: Henry! Henry! *Puts his hand on his forehead.* Myself. All of us, we're covered with blood.

MRS. ANTROBUS: Then remember all the times you were pleased with him and when you were proud of yourself.— Henry! Henry! Come here and recite to your father the multiplication table that you do so nicely. HENRY *kneels on one knee beside his father and starts whispering the multiplication table.*

HENRY, *finally:* Two times six is twelve; three times six is eighteen—I don't think I know the sixes. *Enter* GLADYS *with the slippers.* MRS. ANTROBUS *makes stern gestures to her:* Go in there and do your best. *The* GUESTS *are now singing* Tenting Tonight.

GLADYS, *putting slippers on his feet:* Papa . . . papa . . . I was very good in school today. Miss Conover said right out in class that if all the girls had as good manners as Gladys Antrobus, that the world would be a very different place to live in.

MRS. ANTROBUS: You recited a piece at assembly, didn't you? Recite it to your father.

GLADYS: Papa, do you want to hear what I recited in class? *Fierce directional glance from her mother.* "THE STAR" by Henry Wadsworth LONGFELLOW.

MRS. ANTROBUS: Wait!!! The fire's going out. There isn't enough wood! Henry, go upstairs and bring down the chairs and start breaking up the beds. *Exit* HENRY. *The singers return to* Jingle Bells, *still very softly.*

GLADYS: Look, Papa, here's my report card. Lookit. Conduct A! Look, Papa. Papa, do you want to hear the Star, by Henry Wadsworth Longfellow? Papa, you're not mad at me, are you?—I know it'll get warmer. Soon it'll be just like spring, and we can go to a picnic at the Hibernian Picnic Grounds like you always like to do, don't you remember? Papa, just look at me once. *Enter* HENRY *with some chairs.*

ANTROBUS: You recited in assembly, did you? *She nods eagerly.* You didn't forget it?

GLADYS: No!!! I was perfect. *Pause. Then* ANTROBUS *rises, goes to the front door and opens it. The* REFUGEES *draw back timidly; the song stops; he peers out of the door, then closes it.*

ANTROBUS, *with decision, suddenly:* Build up the fire. It's cold. Build up the fire. We'll do what we can. Sabina, get some more wood. Come around the fire, everybody. At least the young ones may pull through. Henry, have you eaten something?

HENRY: Yes, papa.

ANTROBUS: Gladys, have you had some supper?

GLADYS: I ate in the kitchen, papa.

ANTROBUS: If you do come through this—what'll you be able to do? What do you know? Henry, did you take a good look at that wheel?

HENRY: Yes, papa.

ANTROBUS, *sitting down in his chair:* Six times two are—

HENRY: —twelve; six times three are eighteen; six times four are—Papa, it's hot and cold. It makes my head all funny. It makes me sleepy.

ANTROBUS, *gives him a cuff:* Wake up. I don't care if your head is sleepy. Six times four are twenty-four. Six times five are—

HENRY: Thirty. Papa!

ANTROBUS: Maggie, put something into Gladys' head on the chance she can use it.

MRS. ANTROBUS: What do you mean, George?

ANTROBUS: Six times six are thirty-six. Teach her the beginnings of the Bible.

GLADYS: But, Mama, it's so cold and close. HENRY *has all but drowsed off. His father slaps him sharply and the lesson goes on.*

MRS. ANTROBUS: "In the beginning God created the heavens and the earth; and the earth was waste and void; and the darkness was upon the face of the deep—" *The singing starts up again louder.* SABINA *has returned with wood.*

SABINA, *after placing wood on the fireplace comes down to the footlights and addresses the audience:* Will you please start handing up your chairs? We'll need everything for this fire. Save the human race.—Ushers, will you pass the chairs up here? Thank you.

HENRY: Six times nine are fifty-four; six times ten are sixty. *In the back of the auditorium the sound of chairs being ripped up can be heard.* USHERS *rush down the aisles with chairs and hand them over.*

GLADYS: "And God called the light Day and the darkness he called Night."

SABINA: Pass up your chairs, everybody. Save the human race.

ACT II

Toward the end of the intermission, though with the house-lights still up, lantern slide projections begin to appear on the curtain. Timetables for trains leaving Pennsylvania Station for Atlantic City. Advertisements of Atlantic City hotels, drug-stores, churches, rug merchants; fortune tellers, Bingo parlors.

When the house-lights go down, the voice of an ANNOUNCER *is heard.*

ANNOUNCER: The Management now brings you the News Events of the World. Atlantic City, New Jersey: *Projection of a chrome postcard of the waterfront, trimmed in mica with the legend:* FUN AT THE BEACH.

This great convention city is playing host this week to the anniversary convocation of that great fraternal order,—the Ancient and Honorable Order of Mammals, Subdivision Humans. This great fraternal, militant and burial society is celebrating on the Boardwalk, ladies and gentlemen, its six hundred thousandth Annual Convention.

It has just elected its president for the ensuing term,—*Projection of Mr. and Mrs. Antrobus posed as they will be shown a few moments later.*

Mr. George Antrobus of Excelsior, New Jersey. We show you President Antrobus and his gracious and charming wife, every inch a mammal. Mr. Antrobus has had a long and chequered career. Credit has been paid to him for many useful enterprises including the introduction of the lever, of the wheel and the brewing of beer. Credit has also been extended to President Antrobus's gracious and charming wife for many practical suggestions, including the hem, the gore, and the gusset; and the novelty of the year,—frying in oil. Before we show you Mr. Antrobus accepting the nomination, we have an important announcement to make. As many of you know, this great celebration of the Order of the Mammals has received delegations from the other rival Orders,—or shall we say: esteemed concurrent Orders: the WINGS, the FINS, the SHELLS, and so on. These Orders are holding their conventions also, in various parts of the world, and have sent representatives to our own, two of a kind.

Later in the day we will show you President Antrobus broadcasting his words of greeting and congratulation to the collected assemblies of the whole natural world.

Ladies and Gentlemen! We give you President Antrobus! *The screen becomes a Transparency.* MR. ANTROBUS *stands beside a pedestal;* MRS. ANTROBUS *is seated wearing a corsage of orchids.* ANTROBUS *wears an untidy Prince Albert; spats; from a red rosette in his buttonhole hangs a fine long purple ribbon of honor. He wears a gay lodge hat,—something between a fez and a legionnaire's cap.*

ANTROBUS: Fellow-mammals, fellow vertebrates, fellow-humans, I thank you. Little did my dear parents think,—when they told me to stand on my own two feet,—that I'd arrive at this place.

My friends, we have come a long way.

During this week of happy celebration it is perhaps not fitting that we dwell on some of the difficult times we have been through. The dinosaur is extinct— *Applause.* —the ice has retreated; and the common cold is being pursued by every means within our power. MRS. ANTROBUS *sneezes, laughs prettily, and murmurs:* I beg your pardon.

In our memorial service yesterday we did honor to all our friends and relatives who are no longer with us, by reason of cold, earthquakes, plagues and . . . and . . . *Coughs.* differences of opinion.

As our Bishop so ably said . . . uh . . . so ably said. . . .

MRS. ANTROBUS, *closed lips:* Gone, but not forgotten.

ANTROBUS: "They are gone, but not forgotten."

I think I can say, I think I can prophesy with complete . . . uh . . . with complete. . . .

MRS. ANTROBUS: Confidence.

ANTROBUS: Thank you, my dear,—With complete lack of confidence, that a new day of security is about to dawn.

The watchword of the closing year was: Work. I give you the watchword for the future: Enjoy Yourselves.

MRS. ANTROBUS: George, sit down!

ANTROBUS: Before I close, however, I wish to answer one of those unjust and malicious accusations that were brought against me during this last electoral campaign.

Ladies and gentlemen, the charge was made that at various points in my career I leaned toward joining some of the rival orders,—that's a lie.

As I told reporters of the *Atlantic City Herald,* I do not deny that a few months before my birth I hesitated between . . . uh . . . between pin-feathers and gill-breathing,—and so did many of us here,—but for the last million years I have been viviparous, hairy and diaphragmatic. *Applause. Cries of Good old Antrobus, The Prince chap! Georgie, etc.*

ANNOUNCER: Thank you. Thank you very much, Mr. Antrobus.

Now I know that our visitors will wish to hear a word from that gracious and charming mammal, Mrs. Antrobus, wife and mother,—Mrs. Antrobus!

MRS. ANTROBUS *rises, lays her program on her chair, bows and says:*

MRS. ANTROBUS: Dear friends, I don't really think I should say anything. After all, it was my husband who was elected and not I.

Perhaps, as president of the Womens Auxiliary Bed and Board Society,—I had some notes here, oh, yes, here they are:—I should give a short report from some of our committees that have been meeting in this beautiful city.

Perhaps it may interest you to know that it has at last been decided that the tomato is edible. Can you all hear me? The tomato *is* edible.

A delegate from across the sea reports that the thread woven by the silkworm gives a cloth . . . I have a sample of it here . . . can you see it? smooth, elastic. I should say that it's rather attractive,—though personally I prefer less shiny surfaces. Should the windows of a sleeping apartment be open or shut? I know all mothers will follow our debates on this matter with close interest. I am sorry to say that the most expert authorities have not yet decided. It does seem to me that the night air would be bound to be unhealthy for our children, but there are many distinguished authorities

on both sides. Well, I could go on talking forever, —as Shakespeare says: a woman's work is seldom done; but I think I'd better join my husband in saying thank you, and sit down. Thank you. *She sits down.*

ANNOUNCER: Oh, Mrs. Antrobus!

MRS. ANTROBUS: Yes?

ANNOUNCER: We understand that you are about to celebrate a wedding anniversary. I know our listeners would like to extend their felicitations and hear a few words from you on that subject.

MRS. ANTROBUS: I have been asked by this kind gentleman . . . yes, my friends, this Spring Mr. Antrobus and I will be celebrating our five thousandth wedding anniversary.

I don't know if I speak for my husband, but I can say that, as for me, I regret every moment of it. *Laughter of confusion.* I beg your pardon. What I *mean* to say is that I do not regret one moment of it. I hope none of you catch my cold. We have two children. We've always had two children, though it hasn't always been the same two. But as I say, we have two fine children, and we're very grateful for that. Yes, Mr. Antrobus and I have been married five thousand years. Each wedding anniversary reminds me of the times when there were no weddings. We had to crusade for marriage. Perhaps there are some women within the sound of my voice who remember that crusade and those struggles; we fought for it, didn't we? We chained ourselves to lampposts and we made disturbances in the Senate,—anyway, at last we women got the ring.

A few men helped us, but I must say that most men blocked our way at every step: they said we were unfeminine.

I only bring up these unpleasant memories, because I see some signs of backsliding from that great victory.

Oh, my fellow mammals, keep hold of that.

My husband says that the watchword for the year is Enjoy Yourselves. I think that's very open to misunderstanding. My watchword for the year is: Save the Family. It's held together for over five thousand years: Save it! Thank you.

ANNOUNCER: Thank you, Mrs. Antrobus. *The transparency disappears.* We had hoped to show you the Beauty Contest that took place here today.

President Antrobus, an experienced judge of pretty girls, gave the title of Miss Atlantic City 1942, to Miss Lily-Sabina Fairweather, charming hostess of our Boardwalk Bingo Parlor.

Unfortunately, however, our time is up, and I

must take you to some views of the Convention City and conveeners,—enjoying themselves.

A burst of music; the curtain rises.

The Boardwalk. The audience is sitting in the ocean. A hand rail of scarlet cord stretches across the front of the stage. A ramp—also with scarlet hand rail—descends to the right corner of the orchestra pit where a great scarlet beach umbrella or a cabana stands. Front and right stage left are benches facing the sea; attached to each bench is a streetlamp.

The only scenery is two cardboard cut-outs six feet high, representing shops at the back of the stage. Reading from left to right they are: SALT WATER TAFFY; FORTUNE TELLER; *then the blank space;* BINGO PARLOR; TURKISH BATH. *They have practical doors, that of the Fortune Teller's being hung with bright gypsy curtains.*

By the left proscenium and rising from the orchestra pit is the weather signal; it is like the mast of a ship with cross bars. From time to time black discs are hung on it to indicate the storm and hurricane warnings. Three roller chairs, pushed by melancholy NEGROES *file by empty. Throughout the act they traverse the stage in both directions.*

From time to time, CONVEENERS, *dressed like* MR. ANTROBUS, *cross the stage. Some walk sedately by; others engage in inane horseplay. The old gypsy* FORTUNE TELLER *is seated at the door of her shop, smoking a corncob pipe.*

From the Bingo Parlor comes the voice of the CALLER.

BINGO CALLER: A-Nine; A-Nine. C-Twenty-six; C-Twenty-six. A-Four; A-Four. B-Twelve.

CHORUS, *back-stage:* Bingo!!! *The front of the Bingo parlor shudders, rises a few feet in the air and returns to the ground trembling.*

FORTUNE TELLER, *mechanically, to the unconscious back of a passerby, pointing with her pipe:* Bright's disease! Your partner's deceiving you in that Kansas City deal. You'll have six grandchildren. Avoid high places. *She rises and shouts after another:* Cirrhosis of the liver! SABINA *appears at the door of the Bingo Parlor. She hugs about her a blue raincoat that almost conceals her red bathing suit. She tries to catch the* FORTUNE TELLER'S *attention.*

SABINA: Sssssst! Esmeralda! Sssssst!

FORTUNE TELLER: Keck!

SABINA: Has President Antrobus come along yet?

FORTUNE TELLER: No, no, no. Get back there. Hide yourself.

SABINA: I'm afraid I'll miss him. Oh, Esmeralda, if I fail in this, I'll die; I know I'll die. President Antrobus!!! And I'll be his wife! If it's the last thing I'll do, I'll be Mrs. George Antrobus.—Esmeralda, tell me my future.

FORTUNE TELLER: Keck!

SABINA: All right, I'll tell *you* my future. *Laughing dreamily and tracing it out with one finger on the palm of her hand.* I've won the Beauty Contest in Atlantic City,—well, I'll win the Beauty Contest of the whole world. I'll take President Antrobus away from that wife of his. Then I'll take every man away from his wife. I'll turn the whole earth upside down.

FORTUNE TELLER: Keck!

SABINA: When all those husbands just think about me they'll get dizzy. They'll faint in the streets. They'll have to lean against lampposts.—Esmeralda, who was Helen of Troy?

FORTUNE TELLER, *furiously:* Shut your foolish mouth. When Mr. Antrobus comes along you can see what you can do. Until then,—go away. SABINA *laughs. As she returns to the door of her Bingo Parlor a group of* COVEENERS *rush over and smother her with attention:* Oh, Miss Lily, you know me. You've known me for years.

SABINA: Go away, boys, go away. I'm after bigger fry than you are.—Why, Mr. Simpson!! How *dare* you!! I expect that even you nobodies must have girls to amuse you; but where you find them and what you do with them, is of absolutely no interest to me. *Exit. The* CONVEENERS *squeal with pleasure and stumble in after her. The* FORTUNE TELLER *rises, puts her pipe down on the stool, unfurls her voluminous skirts, gives a sharp wrench to her bodice and strolls towards the audience, swinging her hips like a young woman.*

FORTUNE TELLER: I tell the future. Keck. Nothing easier. Everybody's future is in their face. Nothing easier.

But who can tell your past,—eh? Nobody!

Your youth,—where did it go? It slipped away while you weren't looking. While you were asleep. While you were drunk? Puh! You're like our friend, Mr. and Mrs. Antrobus; you lie awake nights trying to know your past. What did it mean? What was it trying to say to you?

Think! Think! Split your heads. I can't tell the past and neither can you. If anybody tries to tell you the past, take my word for it, they're charlatans! Charlatans! But I can tell you the future. *She suddenly barks at a passing chair-pusher.* Apoplexy! *She returns to the audience.* Nobody listens.—Keck! I see a face among you now—I won't embarrass him by pointing him out, but, listen, it may be you: Next year the watchsprings inside you will crumple up. Death by regret,—Type Y. It's in the corners of your mouth. You'll decide that you should have lived for pleasure, but that you missed it. Death by regret,—Type Y. . . . Avoid mirrors. You'll try to be angry,—but no!—no anger. *Far forward, confidentially.* And now what's the immediate future of our friends, the Antrobuses? Oh, you've seen it as well as I have, keck,— that dizziness of the head; that Great Man dizziness? The inventor of beer and gunpowder? The sudden fits of temper and then the long stretches of inertia? I'm a sultan; let my slave-girls fan me?

You know as well as I do what's coming. Rain. Rain. Rain in floods. The deluge. But first you'll see shameful things—shameful things. Some of you will be saying: Let him drown. He's not worth saving. Give the whole thing up. I can see it in your faces. But you're wrong. Keep your doubts and desires to yourselves.

Again there'll be the narrow escape. The survival of a handful. From destruction,—total destruction. *She points sweeping with her hand to the stage.* Even of the animals, a few will be saved: two of a kind, male and female, two of a kind. *The heads of* CONVEENERS *appear about the stage and in the orchestra pit, jeering at her.*

CONVEENERS: Charlatan! Madam Kill-joy! Mrs. Jeremiah! Charlatan!

FORTUNE TELLER: And *you!* Mark my words before it's too late. Where'll *you* be?

CONVEENERS: The croaking raven. Old dust and ashes. Rags, bottles, sacks.

FORTUNE TELLER: Yes, stick out your tongues. You can't stick your tongues out far enough to lick the death-sweat from your foreheads. It's too late to work now—bail out the flood with your soup spoons. You've had your chance and you've lost.

CONVEENERS: Enjoy yourselves!!! *They disappear. The* FORTUNE TELLER *looks off left and puts her finger on her lip.*

FORTUNE TELLER: They're coming—the Antrobuses. Keck. Your hope. Your despair. Your selves. *Enter from the left,* MR. *and* MRS. ANTROBUS *and* GLADYS.

MRS. ANTROBUS: Gladys Antrobus, stick your stummick in.

GLADYS: But it's easier this way.

MRS. ANTROBUS: Well, it's too bad the new president has such a clumsy daughter, that's all I can say. Try and be a lady.

FORTUNE TELLER: Aijah! That's been said a hundred billion times.

MRS. ANTROBUS: Goodness! Where's Henry? He was here just a minute ago. Henry! *Sudden violent stir. A roller-chair appears from the left. About it are dancing in great excitement* HENRY *and a* NEGRO CHAIR-PUSHER.

HENRY, *slingshot in hand:* I'll put your eye out. I'll make you yell, like you never yelled before.

NEGRO, *at the same time:* Now, I warns you. I warns you. If you make me mad, you'll get hurt.

ANTROBUS: Henry! What is this? Put down that slingshot.

MRS. ANTROBUS, *at the same time:* Henry! HENRY! Behave yourself.

FORTUNE TELLER: That's right, young man. There are too many people in the world as it is. Everybody's in the way, except one's self.

HENRY: All I wanted to do was—have some fun.

NEGRO: Nobody can't touch my chair, nobody, without I allow 'em to. You get clean away from me and you get away fast. *He pushes his chair off, muttering.*

ANTROBUS: What were you doing, Henry?

HENRY: Everybody's always getting mad. Everybody's always trying to push you around. I'll make him sorry for this; I'll make him sorry.

ANTROBUS: Give me that slingshot.

HENRY: I won't. I'm sorry I came to this place. I wish I weren't here. I wish I weren't anywhere.

MRS. ANTROBUS: Now, Henry, don't get so excited about nothing. I declare I don't know what we're going to do with you. Put your slingshot in your pocket, and don't try to take hold of things that don't belong to you.

ANTROBUS: After this you can stay home. I wash my hands of you.

MRS. ANTROBUS: Come now, let's forget all about it. Everybody take a good breath of that sea air and calm down. *A passing* CONVEENER *bows to* ANTROBUS *who nods to him.* Who was that you spoke to, George?

ANTROBUS: Nobody, Maggie. Just the candidate who ran against me in the election.

MRS. ANTROBUS: The man who ran against you in the election!! *She turns and waves her umbrella after the disappearing* CONVEENER. My husband didn't speak to you and he never will speak to you.

ANTROBUS: Now, Maggie.

MRS. ANTROBUS: After those lies you told about him in your speeches! Lies, that's what they were.

GLADYS AND HENRY: Mama, everybody's looking at you. Everybody's laughing at you.

MRS. ANTROBUS: If you must know, my husband's a SAINT, a downright SAINT, and you're not fit to speak to him on the street.

ANTROBUS: Now, Maggie, now, Maggie, that's enough of that.

MRS. ANTROBUS: George Antrobus, you're a perfect worm. If you won't stand up for yourself, I will.

GLADYS: Mama, you just act awful in public.

MRS. ANTROBUS, *laughing:* Well, I must say I enjoyed it. I feel better. Wish his wife had been there to hear it. Children, what do you want to do?

GLADYS: Papa, can we ride in one of those chairs? Mama, I want to ride in one of those chairs.

MRS. ANTROBUS: No, sir. If you're tired you just sit where you are. We have no money to spend on foolishness.

ANTROBUS: I guess we have enough for a thing like that. It's one of the things you do at Atlantic City.

MRS. ANTROBUS: Oh, we have? I tell you it's a miracle my children have shoes to stand up in. I didn't think I'd ever live to see them pushed around in chairs.

ANTROBUS: We're on a vacation, aren't we? We have a right to some treats, I guess. Maggie, some day you're going to drive me crazy.

MRS. ANTROBUS: All right, go. I'll just sit here and laugh at you. And you can give me my dollar right in my hand. Mark my words, a rainy day is coming. There's a rainy day ahead of us. I feel it in my bones. Go on, throw your money around. I can starve. I've starved before. I know how. *A* CONVEENER *puts his head through Turkish Bath window, and says with raised eyebrows:*

CONVEENER: Hello, George. How are ya? I see where you brought the WHOLE family along.

MRS. ANTROBUS: And what do you mean by that? CONVEENER *withdraws head and closes window.*

ANTROBUS: Maggie, I tell you there's a limit to what I can stand. God's Heaven, haven't I worked *enough?* Don't I get *any* vacation? Can't I even give my children so much as a ride in a roller-chair?

MRS. ANTROBUS, *putting her hand out for raindrops:* Anyway, it's going to rain very soon and you have your broadcast to make.

ANTROBUS: Now, Maggie, I warn you. A man can stand a family only just so long. I'm warning you. *Enter* SABINA *from the Bingo Parlor. She wears a flounced red silk bathing suit, 1905. Red*

stockings, shoes, parasol. *She bows demurely to* ANTROBUS *and starts down the ramp.* ANTROBUS *and the* CHILDREN *stare at her.* ANTROBUS *bows gallantly.*

MRS. ANTROBUS: Why, George Antrobus, how can you say such a thing! You have the best family in the world.

ANTROBUS: Good morning, Miss Fairweather. SABINA *finally disappears behind the beach umbrella or in a cabana in the orchestra pit.*

MRS. ANTROBUS: Who on earth was that you spoke to, George?

ANTROBUS, *complacent; mock-modest:* Hm . . . m . . . just a . . . solambaka keray.

MRS. ANTROBUS: What? I can't understand you.

GLADYS: Mama, wasn't she beautiful?

HENRY: Papa, introduce her to me.

MRS. ANTROBUS: Children, will you be quiet while I ask your father a simple question?—Who did you say it was, George?

ANTROBUS: Why-uh . . . a friend of mine. Very nice refined girl.

MRS. ANTROBUS: I'm waiting.

ANTROBUS: Maggie, that's the girl I gave the prize to in the beauty contest,—that's Miss Atlantic City 1942.

MRS. ANTROBUS: Hm! She looked like Sabina to me.

HENRY, *at the railing:* Mama, the life-guard knows her, too. Mama, he knows her well.

ANTROBUS: Henry, come here.—She's a very nice girl in every way and the sole support of her aged mother.

MRS. ANTROBUS: So was Sabina, so was Sabina; and it took a wall of ice to open your eyes about Sabina.—Henry, come over and sit down on this bench.

ANTROBUS: She's a very different matter from Sabina. Miss Fairweather is a college graduate, Phi Beta Kappa.

MRS. ANTROBUS: Henry, you sit here by mama. Gladys—

ANTROBUS, *sitting:* Reduced circumstances have required her taking a position as hostess in a Bingo Parlor; but there isn't a girl with higher principles in the country.

MRS. ANTROBUS: Well, let's not talk about it.— Henry, I haven't seen a whale yet.

ANTROBUS: She speaks seven languages and has more culture in her little finger than you've acquired in a lifetime.

MRS. ANTROBUS, *assuming amiability:* All right,

all right, George. I'm glad to know there are such superior girls in the Bingo Parlors.—Henry, what's that? *Pointing at the storm signal, which has one black disk.*

HENRY: What is it, Papa?

ANTROBUS: What? Oh, that's the storm signal. One of those black disks means bad weather; two means storm; three means hurricane; and four means the end of the world. *As they watch it a second black disk rolls into place.*

MRS. ANTROBUS: Goodness! I'm going this very minute to buy you all some raincoats.

GLADYS, *putting her cheek against her father's shoulder:* Mama, don't go yet. I like sitting this way. And the ocean coming in and coming in. Papa, don't you like it?

MRS. ANTROBUS: Well, there's only one thing I lack to make me a perfectly happy woman: I'd like to see a whale.

HENRY: Mama, we saw two. Right out there. They're delegates to the convention. I'll find you one.

GLADYS: Papa, ask me something. Ask me a question.

ANTROBUS: Well . . . how big's the ocean?

GLADYS: Papa, you're teasing me. It's — three-hundred and sixty million square-miles — and — it — covers — three-fourths — of — the — earth's — surface — and — its — deepest-place — is — five — and — a — half — miles — deep — and — its — average — depth — is — twelve-thousand — feet. No, Papa, ask me something hard, real hard.

MRS. ANTROBUS, *rising:* Now I'm going off to buy those raincoats. I think that bad weather's going to get worse and worse. I hope it doesn't come before your broadcast. I should think we have about an hour or so.

HENRY: I hope it comes and zzzzzz everything before it. I hope it—

MRS. ANTROBUS: Henry!—George, I think . . . maybe, it's one of those storms that are just as bad on land as on the sea. When you're just as safe and safer in a good stout boat.

HENRY: There's a boat out at the end of the pier.

MRS. ANTROBUS: Well, keep your eye on it. George, you shut your eyes and get a good rest before the broadcast.

ANTROBUS: Thundering Judas, do I have to be told when to open and shut my eyes? Go and buy your raincoats.

MRS. ANTROBUS: Now, children, you have ten minutes to walk around. Ten minutes. And,

Henry: control yourself. Gladys, stick by your brother and don't get lost. *They run off.*

MRS. ANTROBUS: Will you be all right, George? CONVEENERS *suddenly stick their heads out of the Bingo Parlor and Salt Water Taffy store, and voices rise from the orchestra pit.*

CONVEENERS: George. Geo-r-r-rge! George! Leave the old hen-coop at home, George. Do-mes-ticated Georgie!

MRS. ANTROBUS, *shaking her umbrella:* Low common oafs! That's what they are. Guess a man has a right to bring his wife to a convention, if he wants to. *She starts off.* What's the matter with a family, I'd like to know. What else have they got to offer? *Exit.* ANTROBUS *has closed his eyes. The* FORTUNE TELLER *comes out of her shop and goes over to the left proscenium. She leans against it watching* SABINA *quizzically:*

FORTUNE TELLER: Heh! Here she comes!

SABINA, *loud whisper:* What's he doing?

FORTUNE TELLER: Oh, he's ready for you. Bite your lips, dear, take a long breath and come on up.

SABINA: I'm nervous. My whole future depends on this. I'm nervous.

FORTUNE TELLER: Don't be a fool. What more could you want? He's forty-five. His head's a little dizzy. He's just been elected president. He's never known any other woman than his wife. Whenever he looks at her he realizes that she knows every foolish thing he's ever done.

SABINA, *still whispering:* I don't know why it is, but every time I start one of these I'm nervous. *The* FORTUNE TELLER *stands in the center of the stage watching the following:*

SABINA: First tell me my fortune. *The* FORTUNE TELLER *laughs drily and makes the gesture of brushing away a nonsensical question.* SABINA *coughs and says:* Oh, Mr. Antrobus,—dare I speak to you for a moment?

ANTROBUS: What?—Oh, certainly, certainly, Miss Fairweather.

SABINA: Mr. Antrobus . . . I've been so unhappy. I've wanted . . . I've wanted to make sure that you don't think that I'm the kind of girl who goes out for beauty contests.

FORTUNE TELLER: That's the way!

ANTROBUS: Oh, I understand. I understand perfectly.

FORTUNE TELLER: Give it a little more. Lean on it.

SABINA: I knew you would. My mother said to

me this morning: Lily, she said, that fine Mr. Antrobus gave you the prize because he saw at once
that you weren't the kind of girl who'd go in for a
thing like that. But, honestly, Mr. Antrobus, in
this world, honestly, a good girl doesn't know
where to turn.

FORTUNE TELLER: Now you've gone too far.

ANTROBUS: My dear Miss Fairweather!

SABINA: You wouldn't know how hard it is.
With that lovely wife and daughter you have. Oh,
I think Mrs. Antrobus is the finest woman I ever
saw. I wish I were like her.

ANTROBUS: There, there. There's . . . uh . . .
room for all kinds of people in the world, Miss
Fairweather.

SABINA: How wonderful of you to say that. How
generous!—Mr. Antrobus, have you a moment free?
. . . I'm afraid I may be a little conspicuous here
. . . could you come down, for just a moment, to
my beach cabana . . . ?

ANTROBUS: Why-uh . . . yes, certainly . . . for
a moment . . . just for a moment.

SABINA: There's a deck chair there. Because: you
know you *do* look tired. Just this morning my
mother said to me: Lily, she said, I hope Mr. Antrobus is getting a good rest. His fine strong face
has deep deep lines in it. Now isn't it true, Mr.
Antrobus: you work too hard?

FORTUNE TELLER: Bingo! *She goes into her
shop.*

SABINA: Now you will just stretch out. No, I
shan't say a word, not a word. I shall just sit there,
—privileged. That's what I am.

ANTROBUS, *taking her hand:* Miss Fairweather
. . . you'll . . . spoil me.

SABINA: Just a moment. I have something I wish
to say to the audience.—Ladies and gentlemen. I'm
not going to play this particular scene tonight. It's
just a short scene and we're going to skip it. But
I'll tell you what takes place and then we can
continue the play from there on. Now in this
scene—

ANTROBUS, *between his teeth:* But, Miss Somerset!

SABINA: I'm sorry. I'm sorry. But I have to skip
it. In this scene, I talk to Mr. Antrobus, and at
the end of it he decides to leave his wife, get a
divorce at Reno and marry me. That's all.

ANTROBUS: Fitz!—Fitz!

SABINA: So that now I've told you we can jump
to the end of it,—where you say: *Enter in fury* MR.
FITZPATRICK, *the stage manager.*

MR. FITZPATRICK: Miss Somerset, we insist on
your playing this scene.

SABINA: I'm sorry, Mr. Fitzpatrick, but I can't
and I won't. I've told the audience all they need
to know and now we can go on. *Other* ACTORS *begin to appear on the stage, listening.*

MR. FITZPATRICK: And why *can't* you play it?

SABINA: Because there are some lines in that
scene that would hurt some people's feelings and
I don't think the theatre is a place where people's
feelings ought to be hurt.

MR. FITZPATRICK: Miss Somerset, you can pack
your things and go home. I shall call the understudy and I shall report you to Equity.

SABINA: I sent the understudy up to the corner
for a cup of coffee and if Equity tries to penalize
me I'll drag the case right up to the Supreme
Court. Now listen, everybody, there's no need to
get excited.

MR. FITZPATRICK *and* ANTROBUS: Why can't you
play it . . . what's the matter with the scene?

SABINA: Well, if you must know, I have a personal guest in the audience tonight. Her life hasn't
been exactly a happy one. I wouldn't have my
friend hear some of these lines for the whole
world. I don't suppose it occurred to the author
that some other women might have gone through
the experience of losing their husbands like this.
Wild horses wouldn't drag from me the details of
my friend's life . . . well, they'd been married
twenty years, and before he got rich, why, she'd
done the washing and everything.

MR. FITZPATRICK: Miss Somerset, your friend
will forgive you. We must play this scene.

SABINA: Nothing, nothing will make me say
some of those lines . . . about "a man outgrows a
wife every seven years" and . . . and that one
about "the Mohammedans being the only people
who looked the subject square in the face." Nothing.

MR. FITZPATRICK: Miss Somerset! Go to your
dressing room. I'll *read* your lines.

SABINA: Now everybody's nerves are on edge.

MR. ANTROBUS: Skip the scene. MR. FITZPATRICK
and the other ACTORS *go off.*

SABINA: Thank you. I knew you'd understand.
We'll do just what I said. So Mr. Antrobus is going to divorce his wife and marry me. Mr. Antrobus, you say: "It won't be easy to lay all this before my wife." *The* ACTORS *withdraw.* ANTROBUS
walks about, his hand to his forehead, muttering:

ANTROBUS: Wait a minute. I can't get back into
it as easily as all that. "My wife is a very obstinate

woman." Hm . . . then you say . . . hm . . . Miss Fairweather, I mean Lily, it won't be easy to lay all this before my wife. It'll hurt her feelings a little.

SABINA: Listen, George: *other* people haven't got feelings. Not in the same way that we have,—we who are presidents like you and prize-winners like me. Listen, other people haven't got feelings; they just imagine they have. Within two weeks they go back to playing bridge and going to the movies. Listen, dear: everybody in the world except a few people like you and me are just people of straw. Most people have no insides at all. Now that you're president you'll see that. Listen, darling, there's a kind of secret society at the top of the world,—like you and me,—that know this. The world was made for us. What's life anyway? Except for two things, pleasure and power, what is life? Boredom! Foolishness. You know it is. Except for those two things, life's nau-se-at-ing. So,—come here! *She moves close. They kiss.* So.

Now when your wife comes, it's really very simple; just tell her.

ANTROBUS: Lily, Lily: you're a wonderful woman.

SABINA: Of course I am. *They enter the cabana and it hides them from view. Distant roll of thunder. A third black disk appears on the weather signal. Distant thunder is heard.* MRS. ANTROBUS *appears carrying parcels. She looks about, seats herself on the bench left, and fans herself with her handkerchief. Enter* GLADYS *right, followed by two* CONVEENERS. *She is wearing red stockings.*

MRS. ANTROBUS: Gladys!

GLADYS: Mama, here I am.

MRS. ANTROBUS: Gladys Antrobus!!! Where did you get those dreadful things?

GLADYS: Wh-a-t? Papa liked the color.

MRS. ANTROBUS: You go back to the hotel this minute!

GLADYS: I won't. I won't. Papa liked the color.

MRS. ANTROBUS: All right. All right. You stay here. I've a good mind to let your father see you that way. You stay right here.

GLADYS: I . . . I don't want to stay . . . if you don't think he'd like it.

MRS. ANTROBUS: Oh . . . it's all one to me. I don't care what happens. I don't care if the biggest storm in the whole world comes. Let it come. *She folds her hands.* Where's your brother?

GLADYS, *in a small voice:* He'll be here.

MRS. ANTROBUS: Will he? Well, let him get into trouble. I don't care. I don't know where your

father is, I'm sure. *Laughter from the cabana.*

GLADYS, *leaning over the rail:* I think he's . . . Mama, he's talking to the lady in the red dress.

MRS. ANTROBUS: Is that so? *Pause.* We'll wait till he's through. Sit down here beside me and stop fidgeting . . . what are you crying about? *Distant thunder. She covers* GLADYS's *stockings with a raincoat.*

GLADYS: You don't like my stockings. *Two* CONVEENERS *rush in with a microphone on a standard and various paraphernalia. The* FORTUNE TELLER *appears at the door of her shop. Other characters gradually gather.*

BROADCAST OFFICIAL: Mrs. Antrobus! Thank God we've found you at last. Where's Mr. Antrobus? We've been hunting everywhere for him. It's about time for the broadcast to the conventions of the world.

MRS. ANTROBUS, *calm:* I expect he'll be here in a minute.

BROADCAST OFFICIAL: Mrs. Antrobus, if he doesn't show up in time, I hope you will consent to broadcast in his place. It's the most important broadcast of the year. SABINA *enters from the cabana followed by* ANTROBUS.

MRS. ANTROBUS: No, I shan't. I haven't one single thing to say.

BROADCAST OFFICIAL: Then won't you help us find him, Mrs. Antrobus? A storm's coming up. A hurricane. A deluge!

SECOND CONVEENER, *who has sighted* ANTROBUS *over the rail:* Joe! Joe! Here he is.

BROADCAST OFFICIAL: In the name of God, Mr. Antrobus, you're on the air in five minutes. Will you kindly please come and test the instrument? That's all we ask. If you just please begin the alphabet slowly. ANTROBUS, *with set face, comes ponderously up the ramp. He stops at the point where his waist is level with the stage and speaks authoritatively to the* OFFICIALS.

ANTROBUS: I'll be ready when the time comes. Until then, move away. Go away. I have something I wish to say to my wife.

BROADCAST OFFICIAL, *whimpering:* Mr. Antrobus! This is the most important broadcast of the year. *The* OFFICIALS *withdraw to the edge of the stage.* SABINA *glides up the ramp behind* ANTROBUS.

SABINA, *whispering:* Don't let her argue. Remember arguments have nothing to do with it.

ANTROBUS: Maggie, I'm moving out of the hotel. In fact, I'm moving out of everything. For good. I'm going to marry Miss Fairweather. I shall provide generously for you and the children. In a few years you'll be able to see that it's all for the best. That's all I have to say.

BROADCAST OFFICIAL: Mr. Antrobus! I hope you'll be ready. This is the most important broadcast of the year.

GLADYS: What did Papa say, Mama? I didn't hear what Papa said.

BROADCAST OFFICIAL: Mr. Antrobus. All we want to do is test your voice with the alphabet.

BINGO ANNOUNCER: A—nine; A—nine. D—forty-two; D—forty-two. C—thirty; C—thirty.

B—seventeen; B—seventeen. C—forty; C—forty.

CHORUS: Bingo!!

ANTROBUS: Go away. Clear out.

MRS. ANTROBUS, *composedly with lowered eyes:* George, I can't talk to you until you wipe those silly red marks off your face.

ANTROBUS: I think there's nothing to talk about. I've said what I have to say.

SABINA: Splendid!!

ANTROBUS: You're a fine woman, Maggie, but . . . but a man has his own life to lead in the world.

MRS. ANTROBUS: Well, after living with you for five thousand years I guess I have a right to a word or two, haven't I?

ANTROBUS, *to* SABINA: What can I answer to that?

SABINA: Tell her that conversation would only hurt her feelings. It's-kinder-in-the-long-run-to-do-it-short-and-quick.

ANTROBUS: I want to spare your feelings in every way I can, Maggie.

BROADCAST OFFICIAL: Mr. Antrobus, the hurricane signal's gone up. We could begin right now.

MRS. ANTROBUS, *calmly, almost dreamily:* I didn't marry you because you were perfect. I didn't even marry you because I loved you. I married you because you gave me a promise. *She takes off her ring and looks at it.* That promise made up for your faults. And the promise I gave you made up for mine. Two imperfect people got married and it was the promise that made the marriage.

ANTROBUS: Maggie, . . . I was only nineteen.

MRS. ANTROBUS, *she puts her ring back on her finger:* And when our children were growing up, it wasn't a house that protected them; and it wasn't our love, that protected them—it was that promise.

And when that promise is broken—this can happen! *With a sweep of the hand she removes the raincoat from* GLADYS' *stockings.*

ANTROBUS, *stretches out his arm, apoplectic:* Gladys!! Have you gone crazy? Has everyone gone crazy? *Turning on* SABINA. You did this. You gave them to her.

SABINA: I never said a word to her.

ANTROBUS, *to* GLADYS: You go back to the hotel and take those horrible things off.

GLADYS, *pert:* Before I go, I've got something to tell you,—it's about Henry.

MRS. ANTROBUS, *claps her hands peremptorily:* Stop your noise,—I'm taking her back to the hotel, George. Before I go I have a letter. . . . I have a message to throw into the ocean. *Fumbling in her handbag.* Where is the plagued thing? Here it is. *She flings something—invisible to us—far over the heads of the audience to the back of the auditorium.* It's a bottle. And in the bottle's a letter. And in the letter is written all the things that a woman knows.

It's never been told to any man and it's never been told to any woman, and if it finds its destination, a new time will come. We're not what books and plays say we are. We're not what advertisements say we are. We're not in the movies and we're not on the radio.

We're not what you're all told and what you think we are: We're ourselves. And if any man can find one of us he'll learn why the whole universe was set in motion. And if any man harm any one of us, his soul—the only soul he's got—had better be at the bottom of that ocean,—and that's the only way to put it. Gladys, come here. We're going back to the hotel. *She drags* GLADYS *firmly off by the hand, but* GLADYS *breaks away and comes down to speak to her father.*

SABINA: Such goings-on. Don't give it a minute's thought.

GLADYS: Anyway, I think you ought to know that Henry hit a man with a stone. He hit one of those colored men that push the chairs and the man's very sick. Henry ran away and hid and some policemen are looking for him very hard. And I don't care a bit if you don't want to have anything to do with mama and me, because I'll never like you again and I hope nobody ever likes you again, —so there! *She runs off.* ANTROBUS *starts after her.*

ANTROBUS: I . . . I have to go and see what I can do about this.

SABINA: You stay right here. Don't go now while

you're excited. Gracious sakes, all these things will be forgotten in a hundred years. Come, now, you're on the air. Just say anything,—it doesn't matter what. Just a lot of birds and fishes and things.

BROADCAST OFFICIAL: Thank you, Miss Fairweather. Thank you very much. Ready, Mr. Antrobus.

ANTROBUS, *touching the microphone:* What is it, what is it? Who am I talking to?

BROADCAST OFFICIAL: Why, Mr. Antrobus! To our order and to all the other orders.

ANTROBUS, *raising his head:* What are all those birds doing?

BROADCAST OFFICIAL: Those are just a few of the birds. Those are the delegates to our convention,—two of a kind.

ANTROBUS, *pointing into the audience:* Look at the water. Look at them all. Those fishes jumping. The children should see this!—There's Maggie's whales!! Here are your whales, Maggie!!

BROADCAST OFFICIAL: I hope you're ready, Mr. Antrobus.

ANTROBUS: And look on the beach! You didn't tell me these would be here!

SABINA: Yes, George. Those are the animals.

BROADCAST OFFICIAL, *busy with the apparatus:* Yes, Mr. Antrobus, those are the vertebrates. We hope the lion will have a word to say when you're through. Step right up, Mr. Antrobus, we're ready. We'll just have time before the storm. *Pause. In a hoarse whisper:* They're wait-ing. *It has grown dark. Soon after he speaks a high whistling noise begins. Strange veering lights start whirling about the stage. The other characters disappear from the stage.*

ANTROBUS: Friends. Cousins. Four score and ten billion years ago our forefather brought forth upon this planet the spark of life,— *He is drowned out by thunder. When the thunder stops the* FORTUNE TELLER *is seen standing beside him.*

FORTUNE TELLER: Antrobus, there's not a minute to be lost. Don't you see the four disks on the weather signal? Take your family into that boat at the end of the pier.

ANTROBUS: My family? I have no family. Maggie! Maggie! They won't come.

FORTUNE TELLER: They'll come.—Antrobus! Take these animals into that boat with you. All of them,—two of each kind.

SABINA: George, what's the matter with you? This is just a storm like any other storm.

ANTROBUS: Maggie!

SABINA: Stay with me, we'll go . . . *Losing conviction.* This is just another thunderstorm,—isn't it? Isn't it?

ANTROBUS: Maggie!!! MRS. ANTROBUS *appears beside him with* GLADYS.

MRS. ANTROBUS, *matter-of-fact:* Here I am and here's Gladys.

ANTROBUS: Where've you been? Where have you been? Quick, we're going into that boat out there.

MRS. ANTROBUS: I know we are. But I haven't found Henry. *She wanders off into the darkness calling* Henry!

SABINA, *low urgent babbling, only occasionally raising her voice:* I don't believe it. I don't believe it's anything at all. I've seen hundreds of storms like this.

FORTUNE TELLER: There's no time to lose. Go. Push the animals along before you. Start a new world. Begin again.

SABINA: Esmeralda! George! Tell me,—is it really serious?

ANTROBUS, *suddenly very busy:* Elephants first. Gently, gently.—Look where you're going.

GLADYS, *leaning over the ramp and striking an animal on the back:* Stop it or you'll be left behind!

ANTROBUS: Is the Kangaroo there? *There* you are! Take those turtles in your pouch, will you? *To some other animals, pointing to his shoulder.* Here! You jump up here. You'll be trampled on.

GLADYS, *to her father, pointing below:* Papa, look,—the snakes!

MRS. ANTROBUS: I can't find Henry. Hen-ry!

ANTROBUS: Go along. Go along. Climb on their backs.—Wolves! Jackals,—whatever you are,—tend to your own business!

GLADYS, *pointing, tenderly:* Papa,—look.

SABINA: Mr. Antrobus—take me with you. Don't leave me here. I'll work. I'll help. I'll do anything. THREE CONVEENERS *cross the stage, marching with a banner.*

CONVEENERS: George! What are you scared of? —George! Fellas, it looks like rain.—"Maggie, where's my umbrella?"—George, setting up for Barnum and Bailey.

ANTROBUS, *again catching his wife's hand:* Come on now, Maggie,—the pier's going to break any minute.

MRS. ANTROBUS: I'm not going a step without Henry. Henry!

GLADYS, *on the ramp:* Mama! Papa! Hurry. The

pier's cracking, Mama. It's going to break.

MRS. ANTROBUS: Henry! Cain! CAIN! *HENRY dashes into the stage and joins his mother.*

HENRY: Here I am, Mama.

MRS. ANTROBUS: Thank God!—now come quick.

HENRY: I didn't think you wanted me.

MRS. ANTROBUS: Quick! *She pushes him down before her into the aisle.*

SABINA, *all the* ANTROBUSES *are now in the theatre aisle.* SABINA *stands at the top of the ramp:* Mrs. Antrobus, take me. Don't you remember me? I'll work. I'll help. Don't leave me here!

MRS. ANTROBUS, *impatiently, but as though it were of no importance:* Yes, yes. There's a lot of work to be done. Only hurry.

FORTUNE TELLER, *now dominating the stage. To* SABINA *with a grim smile:* Yes, go—back to the kitchen with you.

SABINA, *half-down the ramp. To* FORTUNE TELLER: I don't know why my life's always being interrupted—just when everything's going fine!! *She dashes up the aisle. Now the* CONVEENERS *emerge doing a serpentine dance on the stage. They jeer at the* FORTUNE TELLER.

CONVEENERS: Get a canoe—there's not a minute to be lost! Tell me my future, Mrs. Croaker.

FORTUNE TELLER: Paddle in the water, boys—enjoy yourselves.

VOICE *from the* BINGO PARLOR: A-nine; A-nine. C-Twenty-four. C-Twenty-four.

CONVEENERS: Rags, bottles, and sacks.

FORTUNE TELLER: Go back and climb on your roofs. Put rags in the cracks under your doors.—Nothing will keep out the flood. You've had your chance. You've had your day. You've failed. You've lost.

VOICE *from the* BINGO PARLOR: B-Fifteen. B-Fifteen.

FORTUNE TELLER, *shading her eyes and looking out to sea:* They're safe. George Antrobus! Think it over! A new world to make.—think it over!

ACT III

Just before the curtain rises, two sounds are heard from the stage: a cracked bugle call.

The curtain rises on almost total darkness. Almost all the flats composing the walls of MR. ANTROBUS's *house, as of Act I, are up, but they lean helter-skelter against one another, leaving irregular gaps. Among the flats missing are two in the back wall, leaving the frames of the window and door crazily*

out of line. *Off stage, back right, some red Roman fire is burning. The bugle call is repeated. Enter* SABINA *through the tilted door. She is dressed as a Napoleonic camp follower, "la fille du regiment," in begrimed reds and blues.*

SABINA: Mrs. Antrobus! Gladys! Where are you? The war's over. The war's over. You can come out. The peace treaty's been signed.

Where are they?—Hmpf! Are they dead, too? Mrs. Annnntrobus! Glaaaadus! Mr. Antrobus'll be here this afternoon. I just saw him downtown. Huuuurry and put things in order. He says that now that the war's over we'll all have to settle down and be perfect. *Enter* MR. FITZPATRICK, *the stage manager, followed by the whole company, who stand waiting at the edges of the stage.* MR. FITZPATRICK *tries to interrupt* SABINA.

MR. FITZPATRICK: Miss Somerset, we have to stop a moment.

SABINA: They may be hiding out in the back—

MR. FITZPATRICK: Miss Somerset! We have to stop a moment.

SABINA: What's the matter?

MR. FITZPATRICK: There's an explanation we have to make to the audience.—Lights, please. *To the actor who plays* MR. ANTROBUS, Will you explain the matter to the audience? *The lights go up. We now see that a balcony or elevated runway has been erected at the back of the stage, back of the wall of the Antrobus house. From its extreme right and left ends ladder-like steps descend to the floor of the stage.*

ANTROBUS: Ladies and gentlemen, an unfortunate accident has taken place back stage. Perhaps I should say *another* unfortunate accident.

SABINA: I'm sorry. I'm sorry.

ANTROBUS: The management feels, in fact, we all feel that you are due an apology. And now we have to ask your indulgence for the most serious mishap of all. Seven of our actors have . . . have been taken ill. Apparently, it was something they ate. I'm not exactly clear what happened. *All the* ACTORS *start to talk at once.* ANTROBUS *raises his hand.* Now, now—not all at once. Fitz, do you know what it was?

MR. FITZPATRICK: Why, it's perfectly clear. These seven actors had dinner together, and they ate something that disagreed with them.

SABINA: Disagreed with them!!! They have ptomaine poisoning. They're in Bellevue Hospital this very minute in agony. They're having their stomachs pumped out this very minute, in perfect agony.

ANTROBUS: Fortunately, we've just heard they'll all recover.

SABINA: It'll be a miracle if they do, a downright miracle. It was the lemon meringue pie.

ACTORS: It was the fish . . . it was the canned tomatoes . . . it was the fish.

SABINA: It was the lemon meringue pie. I saw it with my own eyes; it had blue mould all over the bottom of it.

ANTROBUS: Whatever it was, they're in no condition to take part in this performance. Naturally, we haven't enough understudies to fill all those roles; but we do have a number of splendid volunteers who have kindly consented to help us out. These friends have watched our rehearsals, and they assure me that they know the lines and the business very well. Let me introduce them to you— my dresser, Mr. Tremayne,—himself a distinguished Shakespearean actor for many years; our wardrobe mistress, Hester; Miss Somerset's maid, Ivy; and Fred Bailey, captain of the ushers in this theatre. *These persons bow modestly.* IVY *and* HESTER *are colored girls.* Now this scene takes place near the end of the act. And I'm sorry to say we'll need a short rehearsal, just a short run-through. And as some of it takes place in the auditorium, we'll have to keep the curtain up. Those of you who wish can go out in the lobby and smoke some more. The rest of you can listen to us, or . . . or just talk quietly among yourselves, as you choose. Thank you. Now will you take it over, Mr. Fitzpatrick?

MR. FITZPATRICK: Thank you.—Now for those of you who are listening perhaps I should explain that at the end of this act, the men have come back from the War and the family's settled down in the house. And the author wants to show the hours of the night passing by over their heads, and the planets crossing the sky . . . uh . . . over their heads. And he says—this is hard to explain— that each of the hours of the night is a philosopher, or a great thinker. Eleven o'clock, for instance, is Aristotle. And nine o'clock is Spinoza. Like that. I don't suppose it means anything. It's just a kind of poetic effect.

SABINA: Not mean anything! Why, it certainly does. Twelve o'clock goes by saying those wonderful things. I think it means that when people are asleep they have all those lovely thoughts, much better than when they're awake.

IVY: Excuse me, I think it means,—excuse me, Mr. Fitzpatrick—

SABINA: What were you going to say, Ivy?

IVY: Mr. Fitzpatrick, you let my father come to a rehearsal; and my father's a Baptist minister, and he said that the author meant that—just like the hours and stars go by over our heads at night, in the same way the ideas and thoughts of the great men are in the air around us all the time and they're working on us, even when we don't know it.

MR. FITZPATRICK: Well, well, maybe that's it. Thank you, Ivy. Anyway,—the hours of the night are philosophers. My friends, are you ready? Ivy, can you be eleven o'clock? "This good estate of the mind possessing its object in energy we call divine." Aristotle.

IVY: Yes, sir. I know that and I know twelve o'clock and I know nine o'clock.

MR. FITZPATRICK: Twelve o'clock? Mr. Tremayne, the Bible.

TREMAYNE: Yes.

MR. FITZPATRICK: Ten o'clock? Hester,—Plato? *She nods eagerly.* Nine o'clock, Spinoza,—Fred?

BAILEY: Yes, *sir.* FRED BAILEY *picks up a great gilded cardboard numeral IX and starts up the steps to the platform.* MR. FITZPATRICK *strikes his forehead.*

MR. FITZPATRICK: The planets!! We forgot all about the planets.

SABINA: O my God! The planets! Are they sick too? ACTORS *nod.*

MR. FITZPATRICK: Ladies and gentlemen, the planets are singers. Of course, we can't replace them, so you'll have to imagine them singing in this scene. Saturn sings from the orchestra pit down here. The Moon is way up there. And Mars with a red lantern in his hand, stands in the aisle over there—Tz-tz-tz. It's too bad; it all makes a very fine effect. However! Ready—nine o'clock: Spinoza.

BAILEY, *walking slowly across the balcony, left to right:* "After experience had taught me that the common occurrences of daily life are vain and futile—"

FITZPATRICK: Louder, Fred. "And I saw that all the objects of my desire and fear—"

BAILEY: "And I saw that all the objects of my desire and fear were in themselves nothing good nor bad save insofar as the mind was affected by them—"

FITZPATRICK: Do you know the rest? All right. Ten o'clock. Hester. Plato.

HESTER: "Then tell me, O Critias, how will a man choose the ruler that shall rule over him? Will he not—"

FITZPATRICK: Thank you. Skip to the end, Hester.

HESTER: ". . . can be multiplied a thousand fold in its effects among the citizens."

FITZPATRICK: Thank you.—Aristotle, Ivy?

IVY: "This good estate of the mind possessing its object in energy we call divine. This we mortals have occasionally and it is this energy which is pleasantest and best. But God has it always. It is wonderful in us; but in Him how much more wonderful."

FITZPATRICK: Midnight. Midnight, Mr. Tremayne. That's right,—you've done it before.—All right, everybody. You know what you have to do. —Lower the curtain. House lights up. Act Three of THE SKIN OF OUR TEETH. *As the curtain descends he is heard saying:* You volunteers, just wear what you have on. Don't try to put on the costumes today. *House lights go down. The Act begins again. The Bugle call. Curtain rises. Enter* SABINA.

SABINA: Mrs. Antrobus! Gladys! Where are you? The war's over.—You've heard all this—*She gabbles the main points.* Where—are—they? Are—they— dead, too, et cetera. I—just—saw—Mr.—Antrobus— down town, et cetera. *Slowing up:* He says that now that the war's over we'll all have to settle down and be perfect. They may be hiding out in the back somewhere. Mrs. An-tro-bus. *She wanders off. It has grown lighter. A trapdoor is cautiously raised and* MRS. ANTROBUS *emerges waist-high and listens. She is disheveled and worn; she wears a tattered dress and a shawl half covers her head. She talks down through the trapdoor.*

MRS. ANTROBUS: It's getting light. There's still something burning over there—Newark, or Jersey City. What? Yes, I could swear I heard someone moving about up here. But I can't see anybody. I say: I can't see anybody. *She starts to move about the stage.* GLADYS' *head appears at the trapdoor. She is holding a* BABY.

GLADYS: Oh, Mama. Be careful.

MRS. ANTROBUS: Now, Gladys, you stay out of sight.

GLADYS: Well, let me stay here just a minute. I want the baby to get some of this fresh air.

MRS. ANTROBUS: All right, but keep your eyes open. I'll see what I can find. I'll have a good hot plate of soup for you before you can say Jack Robinson. Gladys Antrobus! Do you know what I think I see? There's old Mr. Hawkins sweeping the sidewalk in front of his A. and P. store. Sweeping it with a broom. Why, he must have gone crazy, like the others! I see some other people moving about, too.

GLADYS: Mama, come back, come back. MRS. ANTROBUS *returns to the trapdoor and listens.*

MRS. ANTROBUS: Gladys, there's something in the air. Everybody's movement's sort of different. I see some women walking right out in the middle of the street.

SABINA'S VOICE: Mrs. An-tro-bus!

MRS. ANTROBUS AND GLADYS: What's that?!!

SABINA'S VOICE: Glaaaadys! Mrs. An-tro-bus! *Enter* SABINA.

MRS. ANTROBUS: Gladys, that's Sabina's voice as sure as I live.—Sabina! Sabina!—Are you alive?!!

SABINA: Of course, I'm alive. How've you girls been?—Don't try and kiss me. I never want to kiss another human being as long as I live. Sh'sh, there's nothing to get emotional about. Pull yourself together, the war's over. Take a deep breath,— the war's over.

MRS. ANTROBUS: The war's over!! I don't believe you. I don't believe you. I can't believe you.

GLADYS: Mama!

SABINA: Who's that?

MRS. ANTROBUS: That's Gladys and her baby. I don't believe you. Gladys, Sabina says the war's over. Oh, Sabina.

SABINA, *leaning over the* BABY: Goodness! Are there any babies left in the world! Can it *see?* And can it cry and everything?

GLADYS: Yes, he can. He notices everything very well.

SABINA: Where on earth did you get it? Oh, I won't ask.—Lord, I've lived all these seven years around camp and I've forgotten how to behave.— Now we've got to think about the men coming home.—Mrs. Antrobus, go and wash your face, I'm ashamed of you. Put your best clothes on. Mr. Antrobus'll be here this afternoon. I just saw him downtown.

MRS. ANTROBUS AND GLADYS: He's alive!! He'll be here!! Sabina, you're not joking?

MRS. ANTROBUS: And Henry?

SABINA, *dryly:* Yes, Henry's alive, too, that's what they say. Now don't stop to talk. Get yourselves fixed up. Gladys, you look terrible. Have you any decent clothes? SABINA *has pushed them toward the trapdoor.*

MRS. ANTROBUS, *half down:* Yes, I've something to wear just for this very day. But, Sabina,—who won the war?

SABINA: Don't stop now,—just wash your face. *A whistle sounds in the distance.* Oh, my God, what's that silly little noise?

MRS. ANTROBUS: Why, it sounds like . . . it

sounds like what used to be the noon whistle at the shoe-polish factory. *Exit.*

SABINA: That's what it is. Seems to me like peacetime's coming along pretty fast—shoe polish!

GLADYS, *half down:* Sabina, how soon after peacetime begins does the milkman start coming to the door?

SABINA: As soon as he catches a cow. Give him time to catch a cow, dear. *Exit* GLADYS. SABINA *walks about a moment, thinking.* Shoe polish! My, I'd forgotten what peacetime was like. *She shakes her head, then sits down by the trapdoor and starts talking down the hole.* Mrs. Antrobus, guess what I saw Mr. Antrobus doing this morning at dawn. He was tacking up a piece of paper on the door of the Town Hall. You'll die when you hear: it was a recipe for grass soup, for a grass soup that doesn't give you the diarrhea. Mr. Antrobus is still thinking up new things.—He told me to give you his love. He's got all sorts of ideas for peacetime, he says. No more laziness and idiocy, he says. And oh, yes! Where are his books? What? Well, pass them up. The first thing he wants to see are his books. He says if you've burnt those books, or if the rats have eaten them, he says it isn't worthwhile starting over again. Everybody's going to be beautiful, he says, and diligent, and very intelligent. *A hand reaches up with two volumes.* What language is that? Pu-u-gh,—mold! And he's got such plans for you, Mrs. Antrobus. You're going to study history and algebra—and so are Gladys and I—and philosophy. You should hear him talk: *Taking two more volumes.* Well, these are in English, anyway.—To hear him talk, seems like he expects you to be a combination, Mrs. Antrobus, of a saint and a college professor, and a dancehall hostess, if you know what I mean. *Two more volumes.* Ugh. German! *She is lying on the floor; one elbow bent, her cheek on her hand, meditatively.* Yes, peace will be here before we know it. In a week or two we'll be asking the Perkinses in for a quiet evening of bridge. We'll turn on the radio and hear how to be big successes with a new toothpaste. We'll trot down to the movies and see how girls with wax faces live—all that will begin again. Oh, Mrs. Antrobus, God forgive me but I enjoyed the war. Everybody's at their best in wartime. I'm sorry it's over. And, oh, I forgot! Mr. Antrobus sent you another message—can you hear me?— *Enter* HENRY, *blackened and sullen. He is wearing torn overalls, but has one gaudy admiral's epaulette hanging by a thread from his right shoulder, and there are vestiges of gold and scarlet braid running*

down his left trouser leg. He stands listening. Listen! Henry's never to put foot in this house again, he says. He'll kill Henry on sight, if he sees him.

You don't know about Henry??? Well, where have you been? What? Well, Henry rose right to the top. Top of *what?* Listen, I'm telling you. Henry rose from corporal to captain, to major, to general. —I don't know how to say it, but the enemy is *Henry;* Henry *is* the enemy. Everybody knows that.

HENRY: He'll kill me, will he?

SABINA: Who are *you?* I'm not afraid of you. The war's over.

HENRY: I'll kill him so fast. I've spent seven years trying to find him; the others I killed were just substitutes.

SABINA: Goodness! It's Henry!—*He makes an angry gesture.* Oh, I'm not afraid of you. The war's over, Henry Antrobus, and you're not any more important than any other unemployed. You go away and hide yourself, until we calm your father down.

HENRY: The first thing to do is to burn up those old books; it's the ideas he gets out of those old books that . . . that makes the whole world so you can't live in it. *He reels forward and starts kicking the books about, but suddenly falls down in a sitting position.*

SABINA: You leave those books alone!! Mr. Antrobus is looking forward to them a-special.—Gracious sakes, Henry, you're so tired you can't stand up. Your mother and sister'll be here in a minute and we'll think what to do about you.

HENRY: What did they ever care about me?

SABINA: There's that old whine again. All you people think you're not loved enough, nobody loves you. Well, you start being lovable and we'll love you.

HENRY, *outraged:* I don't want anybody to love me.

SABINA: Then stop talking about it all the time.

HENRY: I *never* talk about it. The last thing I want is anybody to pay any attention to me.

SABINA: I can hear it behind every word you say.

HENRY: I want everybody to hate me.

SABINA: Yes, you've decided that's second best, but it's still the same thing.—Mrs. Antrobus! Henry's here. He's so tired he can't stand up. MRS. ANTROBUS *and* GLADYS, *with her* BABY, *emerge. They are dressed as in Act I.* MRS. ANTROBUS *carries some objects in her apron, and* GLADYS *has a blanket over her shoulder.*

MRS. ANTROBUS AND GLADYS: Henry! Henry! Henry!

HENRY, *glaring at them:* Have you anything to eat?

MRS. ANTROBUS: Yes, I have, Henry. I've been saving it for this very day,—two good baked potatoes. No! Henry! one of them's for your father. Henry!! Give me that other potato back this minute. SABINA *sidles up behind him and snatches the other potato away.*

SABINA: He's so dog-tired he doesn't know what he's doing.

MRS. ANTROBUS: Now you just rest there, Henry, until I can get your room ready. Eat that potato good and slow, so you can get all the nourishment out of it.

HENRY: You all might as well know right now that I haven't come back here to live.

MRS. ANTROBUS: Sh. . . . I'll put this coat over you. Your room's hardly damaged at all. Your football trophies are a little tarnished, but Sabina and I will polish them up tomorrow.

HENRY: Did you hear me? I don't live here. I don't belong to anybody.

MRS. ANTROBUS: Why, how can you say a thing like that! You certainly do belong right here. Where else would you want to go? Your forehead's feverish, Henry, seems to me. You'd better give me that gun, Henry. You won't need that any more.

GLADYS, *whispering:* Look, he's fallen asleep already, with his potato half-chewed.

SABINA: Puh! The terror of the world.

MRS. ANTROBUS: Sabina, you mind your own business, and start putting the room to rights. HENRY *has turned his face to the back of the sofa.* MRS. ANTROBUS *gingerly puts the revolver in her apron pocket, then helps* SABINA. SABINA *has found a rope hanging from the ceiling. Grunting, she hangs all her weight on it, and as she pulls the walls begin to move into their right places.* MRS. ANTROBUS *brings the overturned tables, chairs and hassock into the positions of Act I.*

SABINA: That's all we can do—always beginning again! Over and over again. Always beginning again. *She pulls on the rope and a part of the wall moves into place. She stops. Meditatively:* How do we know that it'll be any better than before? Why do we go on pretending? Some day the whole earth's going to have to turn cold anyway, and until that time all these other things'll be happening again: it will be more wars and more walls of ice and floods and earthquakes.

MRS. ANTROBUS: Sabina!! Stop arguing and go on with your work.

SABINA: All right. I'll go on just out of *habit,* but I won't believe in it.

MRS. ANTROBUS, *aroused:* Now, Sabina. I've let you talk long enough. I don't want to hear any more of it. Do I have to explain to you what everybody knows,—everybody who keeps a home going? Do I have to say to you what nobody should ever *have* to say, because they can read it in each other's eyes?

Now listen to me: MRS. ANTROBUS *takes hold of the rope.* I could live for seventy years in a cellar and make soup out of grass and bark, without ever doubting that this world has a work to do and will do it.

Do you hear me?

SABINA, *frightened:* Yes, Mrs. Antrobus.

MRS. ANTROBUS: Sabina, do you see this house,— 216 Cedar Street,—do you see it?

SABINA: Yes, Mrs. Antrobus.

MRS. ANTROBUS: Well, just to have known this house is to have seen the idea of what we can do someday if we keep our wits about us. Too many people have suffered and died for my children for us to start reneging now. So we'll start putting this house to rights. Now, Sabina, go and see what you can do in the kitchen.

SABINA: Kitchen! Why is it that however far I go away, I always find myself back in the kitchen? *Exit.*

MRS. ANTROBUS, *still thinking over her last speech, relaxes and says with a reminiscent smile:* Goodness gracious, wouldn't you know that my father was a person? It was just like I heard his own voice speaking and he's been dead five thousand years. There! I've gone and almost waked Henry up.

HENRY, *talking in his sleep, indistinctly:* Fellows . . . what have they done for us? . . . Blocked our way at every step. Kept everything in their own hands. And you've stood it. When are you going to wake up?

MRS. ANTROBUS: Sh, Henry. Go to sleep. Go to sleep. Go to sleep.—Well, that looks better. Now let's go and help Sabina.

GLADYS: Mama, I'm going out into the backyard and hold the baby right up in the air. And show him that we don't have to be afraid any more. *Exit* GLADYS *to the kitchen.* MRS. ANTROBUS *glances at* HENRY, *exits into kitchen.* HENRY *thrashes about in his sleep. Enter* ANTROBUS, *his arms full of bundles, chewing the end of a carrot. He has a slight limp. Over the suit of Act I he is wearing an overcoat too long for him, its skirts trailing on the ground. He lets his bundles fall and stands looking about. Presently his attention is fixed on* HENRY, *whose words grow clearer.*

HENRY: All right! What have you got to lose? What have they done for us? That's right—nothing. Tear everything down. I don't care what you smash. We'll begin again and we'll show 'em. ANTROBUS *takes out his revolver and holds it pointing downwards. With his back towards the audience he moves toward the footlights.* HENRY'S *voice grows louder and he wakes with a start. They stare at one another. Then* HENRY *sits up quickly. Throughout the following scene* HENRY *is played, not as a misunderstood or misguided young man, but as a representation of strong unreconciled evil.* All right! Do something. *Pause.* Don't think I'm afraid of you, either. All right, do what you were going to do. Do it. *Furiously.* Shoot me, I tell you. You don't have to think I'm any relation of yours. I haven't got any father or any mother, or brothers or sisters. And I don't want any. And what's more I haven't got anybody over me; and I never will have. I'm alone, and that's all I want to be: alone. So you can shoot me.

ANTROBUS: You're the last person I wanted to see. The sight of you dries up all my plans and hopes. I wish I were back at war still, because it's easier to fight you than to live with you. War's a pleasure—do you hear me?—War's a pleasure compared to what faces us now: trying to build up a peacetime with you in the middle of it. ANTROBUS *walks up to the window.*

HENRY: I'm not going to be a part of any peacetime of yours. I'm going a long way from here and make my own world that's fit for a man to live in. Where a man can be free, and have a chance, and do what he wants to do in his own way.

ANTROBUS, *his attention arrested; thoughtfully. He throws the gun out of the window and turns with hope:* . . . Henry, let's try again.

HENRY: Try what? Living *here?*—Speaking polite downtown to all the old men like you? Standing like a sheep at the street corner until the red light turns to green? Being a good boy and a good sheep, like all the stinking ideas you get out of your books? Oh, no. I'll make a world, and I'll show you.

ANTROBUS, *hard:* How can you make a world for people to live in, unless you've first put order in

yourself? Mark my words: I shall continue fighting you until my last breath as long as you mix up your idea of liberty with your idea of hogging everything for yourself. I shall have no pity on you. I shall pursue you to the far corners of the earth. You and I want the same thing; but until you think of it as something that everyone has a right to, you are my deadly enemy and I will destroy you.—I hear your mother's voice in the kitchen. Have you seen her?

HENRY: I have no mother. Get it into your head. I don't belong here. I have nothing to do here. I have no home.

ANTROBUS: Then why did you come here? With the whole world to choose from, why did you come to this one place: 216 Cedar Street, Excelsior, New Jersey. . . . Well?

HENRY: What if I did? What if I wanted to look at it once more, to see if—

ANTROBUS: Oh, you're related, all right—When your mother comes in you must behave yourself. Do you hear me?

HENRY, *wildly:* What is this?—*must behave* yourself. Don't you say *must* to me.

ANTROBUS: Quiet! *Enter* MRS. ANTROBUS *and* SABINA.

HENRY: Nobody can say *must* to me. All my life everybody's been crossing me,—everybody, everything, all of you. I'm going to be free, even if I have to kill half the world for it. Right now, too. Let me get my hands on his throat. I'll show him. *He advances toward* ANTROBUS. *Suddenly,* SABINA *jumps between them and calls out in her own person:*

SABINA: Stop! Stop! Don't play this scene. You know what happened last night. Stop the play. *The men fall back, panting.* HENRY *covers his face with his hands.* Last night you almost strangled him. You became a regular savage. Stop it!

HENRY: It's true. I'm sorry. I don't know what comes over me. I have nothing against him personally. I respect him very much . . . I . . . I admire him. But something comes over me. It's like I become fifteen years old again. I . . . I . . . listen: my own father used to whip me and lock me up every Saturday night. I never had enough to eat. He never let me have enough money to buy decent clothes. I was ashamed to go downtown. I never could go to the dances. My father and my uncle put rules in the way of everything I wanted to do. They tried to prevent my living at all.—I'm sorry. I'm sorry.

MRS. ANTROBUS, *quickly*: No, go on. Finish what you were saying. Say it all.

HENRY: In this scene it's as though I were back in High School again. It's like I had some big emptiness inside me,—the emptiness of being hated and blocked at every turn. And the emptiness fills up with the one thought that you have to strike and fight and kill. Listen, it's as though you have to kill somebody else so as not to end up killing yourself.

SABINA: That's not true. I knew your father and your uncle and your mother. You imagined all that. Why, they did everything they could for you. How can you say things like that? They didn't lock you up.

HENRY: They did. They did. They wished I hadn't been born.

SABINA: That's not true.

ANTROBUS, *in his own person, with self-condemnation, but cold and proud*: Wait a minute. I have something to say, too. It's not wholly his fault that he wants to strangle me in this scene. It's my fault, too. He wouldn't feel that way unless there were something in me that reminded him of all that. He talks about an emptiness. Well, there's an emptiness in me, too. Yes,—work, work, work,—that's all I do. I've ceased to *live*. No wonder he feels that anger coming over him.

MRS. ANTROBUS: There! At least you've said it.

SABINA: We're all just as wicked as we can be, and that's the God's truth.

MRS ANTROBUS, *nods a moment, then comes forward; quietly*: Come. Come and put your head under some cold water.

SABINA, *in a whisper*: I'll go with him. I've known him a long while. You have to go on with the play. Come with me. HENRY *starts out with* SABINA, *but turns at the exit and says to* ANTROBUS:

HENRY: Thanks. Thanks for what you said. I'll be all right tomorrow. I won't lose control in that place. I promise. *Exeunt* HENRY *and* SABINA. ANTROBUS *starts toward the front door, fastens it.* MRS. ANTROBUS *goes up stage and places the chair close to table.*

MRS. ANTROBUS: George, do I see you limping?

ANTROBUS: Yes, a little. My old wound from the other war started smarting again. I can manage.

MRS. ANTROBUS, *looking out of the window*: Some lights are coming on,—the first in seven years. People are walking up and down looking at them. Over in Hawkins' open lot they've built a bonfire to celebrate the peace. They're dancing around it like scarecrows.

ANTROBUS: A bonfire! As though they hadn't seen enough things burning.—Maggie,—the dog died?

MRS. ANTROBUS: Oh, yes. Long ago. There are no dogs left in Excelsior.—You're back again! All these years. I gave up counting on letters. The few that arrived were anywhere from six months to a year late.

ANTROBUS: Yes, the ocean's full of letters, along with the other things.

MRS. ANTROBUS: George, sit down, you're tired.

ANTROBUS: No, you sit down. I'm tired but I'm restless. *Suddenly, as she comes forward*: Maggie! I've lost it. I've lost it.

MRS. ANTROBUS: What, George? What have you lost?

ANTROBUS: The most important thing of all: The desire to begin again, to start building.

MRS. ANTROBUS, *sitting in the chair right of the table*: Well, it will come back.

ANTROBUS, *at the window*: I've lost it. This minute I feel like all those people dancing around the bonfire—just relief. Just the desire to settle down; to slip into the old grooves and keep the neighbors from walking over my lawn.—Hm. But during the war,—in the middle of all that blood and dirt and hot and cold—every day and night, I'd have moments, Maggie, when I *saw* the things that we could do when it was over. When you're at war you think about a better life; when you're at peace you think about a more comfortable one. I've lost it. I feel sick and tired.

MRS. ANTROBUS: Listen! The baby's crying.

I hear Gladys talking. Probably she's quieting Henry again. George, while Gladys and I were living here—like moles, like rats, and when we were at our wits' end to save the baby's life—the only thought we clung to was that you were going to bring something good out of this suffering. In the night, in the dark, we'd whisper about it, starving and sick.—Oh, George, you'll have to get it back again. Think! What else kept us alive all these years? Even now, it's not comfort we want. We can suffer whatever's necessary; only give us back that promise. *Enter* SABINA *with a lighted lamp. She is dressed as in Act I.*

SABINA: Mrs. Antrobus . . .

MRS. ANTROBUS: Yes, Sabina?

SABINA: Will you need me?

MRS. ANTROBUS: No, Sabina, you can go to bed.

SABINA: Mrs. Antrobus, if it's all right with you, I'd like to go to the bonfire and celebrate seeing the war's over. And, Mrs. Antrobus, they've opened the Gem Movie Theatre and they're giving away a hand-painted soup tureen to every lady, and I thought one of us ought to go.

ANTROBUS: Well, Sabina, I haven't any money. I haven't seen any money for quite a while.

SABINA: Oh, you don't need money. They're taking anything you can give them. And I have some . . . some . . . Mrs. Antrobus, promise you won't tell anyone. It's a little against the law. But I'll give you some, too.

ANTROBUS: What is it?

SABINA: I'll give you some, too. Yesterday I picked up a lot of . . . beef-cubes! MRS. ANTROBUS *turns and says calmly*:

MRS. ANTROBUS: But, Sabina, you know you ought to give that in to the Center downtown. They know who needs them most.

SABINA, *outburst*: Mrs. Antrobus, I didn't make this war. I didn't ask for it. And, in my opinion, after anybody's gone through what we've gone through, they have a right to grab what they can find. You're a very nice man, Mr. Antrobus, but you'd have got on better in the world if you'd realized that dog-eat-dog was the rule in the beginning and always will be. And most of all now. *In tears.* Oh, the world's an awful place, and you know it is. I used to think something could be done about it; but I know better now. I hate it. I hate it. *She comes forward slowly and brings six cubes from the bag.* All right. All right. You can have them.

ANTROBUS: Thank you, Sabina.

SABINA: Can I have . . . can I have one to go to the movies? ANTROBUS *in silence gives her one.* Thank you.

ANTROBUS: Good night, Sabina.

SABINA: Mr. Antrobus, don't mind what I say. I'm just an ordinary girl, you know what I mean, I'm just an ordinary girl. But you're a bright man, you're a very bright man, and of course you invented the alphabet and the wheel, and, my God, a lot of things . . . and if you've got any other plans, my God, don't let me upset them. Only every now and then I've got to go to the movies. I mean my nerves can't stand it. But if you have any ideas about improving the crazy old world, I'm really with you. I really am. Because it's . . . it's . . . Good night. *She goes out.* ANTROBUS *starts laughing softly with exhilaration.*

ANTROBUS: Now I remember what three things always went together when I was able to see things most clearly: three things. Three things: *He points to where* SABINA *has gone out.* The voice of the

people in their confusion and their need. And the thought of you and the children and this house . . . And . . . Maggie! I didn't dare ask you: my books! They haven't been lost, have they?

MRS. ANTROBUS: No. There are some of them right here. Kind of tattered.

ANTROBUS: Yes.—Remember, Maggie, we almost lost them once before? And when we finally did collect a few torn copies out of old cellars they ran in everyone's head like a fever. They as good as rebuilt the world. *Pauses, book in hand, and looks up.* Oh, I've never forgotten for long at a time that living is struggle. I know that every good and excellent thing in the world stands moment by moment on the razor-edge of danger and must be fought for—whether it's a field, or a home, or a country. All I ask is the chance to build new worlds and God has always given us that. And has given us *opening the book* voices to guide us; and the memory of our mistakes to warn us. Maggie, you and I will remember in peacetime all the resolves that were so clear to us in the days of war. We've come a long ways. We've learned. We're learning. And the steps of our journey are marked for us here. *He stands by the table turning the leaves of a book.* Sometimes out there in the war,— standing all night on a hill—I'd try and remember some of the words in these books. Parts of them and phrases would come back to me. And after a while I used to give names to the hours of the night. *He sits, hunting for a passage in the book.* Nine o'clock I used to call Spinoza. Where is it: After experience had taught me—*The back wall has disappeared, revealing the platform.* FRED BAILEY *carrying his numeral has started from left to right.* MRS. ANTROBUS *sits by the table sewing.*

BAILEY: "After experience had taught me that the common occurrences of daily life are vain and futile; and I saw that all the objects of my desire and fear were in themselves nothing good nor bad save insofar as the mind was affected by them; I at length determined to search out whether there was something truly good and communicable to man." *Almost without break* HESTER, *carrying a large Roman numeral ten, starts crossing the platform.* GLADYS *appears at the kitchen door and moves toward her mother's chair.*

HESTER: "Then tell me, O Critias, how will a man choose the ruler that shall rule over him? Will he not choose a man who has first established order in himself, knowing that any decision that has its spring from anger or pride or vanity can be multiplied a thousand fold in its effects upon the citizens?" HESTER *disappears and* IVY, *as eleven o'clock starts speaking.*

IVY: "This good estate of the mind possessing its object in energy we call divine. This we mortals have occasionally and it is this energy which is pleasantest and best. But God has it always. It is wonderful in us; but in Him how much more wonderful." *As* MR. TREMAYNE *starts to speak,* HENRY *appears at the edge of the scene, brooding and unreconciled, but present.*

TREMAYNE: "In the beginning, God created the Heavens and the Earth; and the Earth was waste and void; And the darkness was upon the face of the deep. And the Lord said let there be light and there was light." *Sudden black-out and silence, except for the last strokes of the midnight bell. Then*

just as suddenly the lights go up, and SABINA *is standing at the window, as at the opening of the play.*

SABINA: Oh, oh, oh. Six o'clock and the master not home yet. Pray God nothing serious has happened to him crossing the Hudson River. But I wouldn't be surprised. The whole world's at sixes and sevens, and why the house hasn't fallen down about our ears long ago is a miracle to me. *She comes down to the footlights.* This is where you came in. We have to go on for ages and ages yet.

You go home.

The end of this play isn't written yet.

Mr. and Mrs. Antrobus! Their heads are full of plans and they're as confident as the first day they began,—and they told me to tell you: good night.

NATHANAEL WEST (1903–1940)

Though he died in 1940 (at the age of thirty-seven), and though all his fiction was written during the thirties, Nathanael West can be regarded as the first of the post–Second World War novelists. As an imaginative artist, he has recognizably more in common with writers like John Barth, Thomas Pynchon, and Ralph Ellison than with most of his own contemporaries—especially such determined realists as James T. Farrell and Richard Wright. Indeed, West's four short novels began the trend away from realism and toward the modes of fantasy and allegory that have appeared in the past two decades, and in this regard West appears as one of the major "swing" figures in modern American literary history. West was, as he knew, the creator of a "peculiar half world," a darkening scene devoid of that other half of reality, those "sincere, honest people," of whose existence in his actual world West was quite aware. Fictional half-worlds, since West's death, have multiplied with such regularity as to become a commonplace of the contemporary American novel.

West viewed his world satirically. He was, however, conscious that he lacked the traditional satirist's major resource—a firm vision of a way of life superior to the one depicted (there was in his books, West once admitted, "nothing to root for"). He also viewed it apocalyptically, with the constant apprehension of some colossal disaster just ahead. A sense of violence was at the heart of West's narrow, tense vision; violence was what he saw everywhere when he looked around him. Anticipating by three decades a remark made by a black spokesman in the sixties (who found violence as American as apple pie), West observed that "In America, violence is idiomatic. . . . In America violence is daily." These elements in his work are combined in a literary genre which we may call apocalyptic satire, a mixed mode which can claim for its distinguished American ancestors Melville's *The Confidence Man* and Mark Twain's *The Mysterious Stranger:* and far behind them, one is conscious of the unsmiling apocalyptics of Jonathan Edwards and the earlier Puritans: for in America the apocalyptic imagination, whether infused with comedy or not, will always show a kinship to Puritanism.

Yet if West had such affinities with past literature, and if he opened the way to future writing, he was nonetheless decidedly a writer of the thirties. He took on, and made peculiarly his own, a portion of contemporary experience that no other writer was dealing with. While his friend Jack Conroy, for example, was addressing himself to the actualities of unemployment, the harsh frustrated lives of "the disinherited," West was giving narrative form to what Nathan Scott (in a monograph on West) has called "a time of cultural and religious disinheritance." We remark elsewhere that a great many Americans responded to the economic disaster not by aggressive counteraction but by willful self-deception and a flight into a world of fantasy, illusion, dream. This is West's real subject. His first book was called *The Dream Life of Balso Snell*, and all his books are about dream lives. It is the tortured aspiration of the newspaper columnist in *Miss Lonelyhearts* to speak to all those people whose "dreams . . . have been made puerile by the movies, radio and newspapers"; and while West himself had no such foolish ambition, he did seek to disclose the sometimes puerile, sometimes ferocious daydreaming in which his countrymen were indulging, and on the basis of which they took preposterous or violent action. The novels of Nathanael West are authentic works of art —an art that originated in caricatures of one phase of the American mentality during the Depression years.

Nathan Weinstein, as he was originally named, was born in New York in 1903, the son of Max and Anna Weinstein, who had come to this country from Kovna in western Russia after the passage of certain imperial laws which drastically curtailed the rights of the Lithuanian Jews. In school he became known as "Pep," largely because, athletically speaking, he lacked that quality. He did not bother to finish high school, but managed nonetheless to be admitted to Tufts College in Massachusetts by doctoring his school transcript and according himself an array of credits in courses he never took. At Tufts, he preferred reading Joyce and Dostoevski, Eliot and Pound, to doing regular class

work, and he was flunked out after a few months. By a piece of expert chicanery, or perhaps only through bureaucratic confusion, West then succeeded in transferring to Brown University, with a year and a half of advance standing—because the transcript forwarded to Brown was in fact that of another and far more industrious Nathan Weinstein, also enrolled at Tufts, as a science major. Eventually, having sailed ahead with a series of invented or borrowed credits, West received the degree of Ph.B. in 1924.

It was in 1926, on the eve of departing for a six-month stay in Paris, that he had his name legally changed to Nathanael West. He liked the Biblical sound, and spelling, of Nathanael, and the combination struck him as containing invigorating overtones of colonial New England. There was, obviously, an intense concern with the *self*, though something less than an "identity crisis," in the change of name and in the cultural associations. West was not so much denying his Jewishness as he was seeking to reestablish it in a new, a modern, an American context. A friend of West, remarking that West tended to deny "that such a thing as a Jew exists," said that "he did not regard himself as a Jew at all, but as an American." This oversimplifies the case. As his biographer Jay Martin points out, West enjoyed and drew upon his Jewish heritage; but he felt that being a Jew in twentieth-century New York was so different from being a Jew in old Russia that nothing short of a different—but distinctly echoing—name could suffice. Martin quotes the comment of the historian Stuart E. Rosenberg on the racial and cultural phenomenon represented by Nathanael West. Highly intellectual Jews who accept the modernism of the modern world, Rosenberg writes, "do so most radically," and with remarkable results. They "brought with them the intellectual vitality, the moral perplexity, the religious optimism, the sound and the fury of a great awakening . . . [and] attained a cultural and intellectual richness in New York greater than any in Eastern Europe."

It should be added that West showed uncommon perceptiveness in sensing a closeness between the New England and the Jewish character. This is a significant fact which has been mainly forgotten by Gentile and Jew alike, and only belatedly explored by students of American cultural history.[1] The first Puritan settlers identified themselves with the Israelites looking for the Promised Land and saw each other as Old Testament figures reincarnated; the very notion of the New World as the site of a divinely ordained mission is, of course, profoundly Hebraic in origin. In *Oldtown Folks*, Harriet Beecher Stowe recalled the Beecher family prayers presided over by her grandfather. "They were Hebraistic in their form; they spoke of Zion and Jerusalem, of the God of Israel, the God of Jacob, as much as if my grandfather had been a veritable Jew." Harriet's husband, Calvin Stowe, grew a beard and wore a rabbinical skull cap; Harriet referred to him as "my old rabbi," or "old rab." James Russell Lowell, the very type of Boston Brahmin, was a monomaniac on the subject of the Jews and would hold forth for hours about their history, their language, their omnipresence, and their enormous power in the world—with an intense admiration combined with a profound fear that they would soon control the planet.[2] Barrett Wendell, Harvard professor and purest Anglo-Saxon, wrote his father (in 1891) that "It is wholly possible . . . that the Yankee Puritan, with all his Old Testament feeling, was really, without knowing it, largely Jewish in blood."

After a heady few months in Paris—an obligatory undertaking, in those days, for the aspiring American writer—West came back to New York and a job as assistant manager of the Hotel Kenmore. He remained there for three years, until 1930, working at odd moments on

his first substantial piece of fiction. *The Dream Life of Balso Snell*, which runs to little more than sixty pages, appeared in 1931: a weird, entertaining little book that is essentially a parody of the literary styles and of writers most in fashion during the twenties. A poet named Balso Snell, wandering through the tall grass outside the city of Troy, comes upon the Trojan Horse, enters it through its wooden posterior, and explores its internal terrain. It is populated, he discovers, "solely by writers in search of an audience," each of whom forces on Balso an example of his work. By this easy device, West has his sport with Dostoevski (via a possibly insane killer called John Roskolnikov Gilson), Rimbaud and Baudelaire, Joyce (through mimicry of the closing words of *A Portrait of the Artist as a Young Man*: "O Beer! O Meyerbeer! O Bach! O Offenbach! Stand me now as ever in good stead"), Ezra Pound, the dadaists, and a good many other poets, novelists, and literary movements. The exercise concludes with a triumphant orgasm—a signal, in retrospect, that West, having made his playful tribute to all that he had absorbed in his reading and conversations, was now ready to move on to his own mode of expression.

That mode found its singular outlet in the small masterpiece, *Miss Lonelyhearts*, in 1933. Whether or not this book might otherwise have achieved something of a success (which is not likely), its fate was entangled with the financial battles of its publisher, and most copies of it were seized and held back by creditors. Since then, however, *Miss Lonelyhearts* has settled slowly into its secure place as one of the most arresting imaginative acts of modern American fiction.

It had its origin on a spring evening in 1929, when the greatly gifted humorist S. J. Perelman —who was courting West's sister Laura—introduced him to a young man who wrote advice for the troubled and lovelorn in a Brooklyn newspaper. "Susan Chester," as he called himself, showed West some of the bizarre and poignant letters he received; and West, with the peculiar slant of his mind, saw at once that they could provide him with the makings of a story.

[1] See, for example, Edmund Wilson's essay "The Jews," in *A Piece of My Mind* (1956). See also the book to which Wilson acknowledges indebtedness: *The Hebrew Impact on Western Civilization* (1961), edited by Dagobert D. Runes.

[2] See also p. 1253 in regard to Lowell's relations with Twain and Harte and p. 1483 in regard to Henry Adams' relation with Berenson.

The letters received by the young man who becomes the hero, or hapless antihero, of *Miss Lonelyhearts* are even more touching and grotesque ("I would like to have boy friends like the other girls and go out on Saturday nites, but no boy will take me because I was born without a nose—although I am a good dancer and have a nice shape and my father buys me pretty clothes"). Gradually, he becomes deeply unsettled by the miseries disclosed by his correspondents—as he tries, in vain, to explain to his girl friend Betty:

> A man is hired to give advice to the readers of a newspaper. The job is a circulation stunt and the whole staff considers it a joke. He welcomes the job, for it might lead to a gossip column, and anyway he's tired of being a leg man. He too considers the job a joke, but after several months of it, the joke begins to escape him. He sees that the majority of the letters are profoundly humble pleas for moral and spiritual advice, that they are inarticulate expressions of genuine suffering. He also discovers that his correspondents take him seriously. For the first time in his life, he is forced to examine the values by which he lives. The examination shows him that he is the victim of the joke and not its perpetrator.

The half-world of *Miss Lonelyhearts* is not one in which the examination of moral and spiritual values can make much headway. It is presided over by the demonic editor Shrike, who taunts Miss Lonelyhearts brilliantly with parodies of the latter's yearning toward a Christlike conduct: "Soul of Miss L, glorify me. Body of Miss L, nourish me. Blood of Miss L, intoxicate me," and so on. Shrike, indeed, represents for West the fundamental condition of this world, in which humanity has turned into a hideous and unredeemable parody of itself; and so the narrative, which proceeds through discrete episodes deliberately imitative of the comic strip, is a parody of the traditional myth of the quest, in particular of *Pilgrim's Progress* (as the title of one of the chapters—"Miss Lonelyhearts in the Dismal Swamp"—indicates). This baffled pilgrim progresses only toward greater confusion and frustration. He oscillates between the sane, unimaginative Betty, who assumes he must be "sick," and Shrike's sexually exhausting wife. He falls in with Fay Doyle, the wife of a crippled homosexual reader of gas meters. Finally, feverish and unbalanced, he attempts to make a gesture of warmly compassionate friendship toward Pete Doyle, and is accidentally shot and killed by Pete.

That juxtaposition of love and violence is perhaps the central theme of this remarkable tale. The actuality of violence and the fevered dream of love are the seed components of West's vision. It is that very actuality which makes the dream seem puerile—for one must agree with Nathan Scott that Miss Lonelyhearts's dream, if morally worthier, is not much more mature or coherent than the dreams of his correspondents. There is a perfect condensation of all this— what the critic Kenneth Burke would call a "representative anecdote"—in the moment when Miss Lonelyhearts, standing slightly drunk at a bar, has a memory of an evening in his childhood when he played Mozart on the piano and his eight-year-old sister danced to it, gravely and carefully.

> As Miss Lonelyhearts stood at the bar, swaying slightly to the remembered music, he thought of children dancing. Square replacing oblong and being replaced by circle. Every child, everywhere; in the whole world there was not one child who was not gravely, sweetly dancing.
>
>   He stepped away from the bar and accidentally collided with a man holding a glass of beer. When he turned to beg the man's pardon, he received a punch in the mouth.

The same year that *Miss Lonelyhearts* was published, West went to Hollywood for a six-month stint as a script writer for Columbia pictures. Back in the East again, and staying on a farm in Pennsylvania, West turned to his third short novel, *A Cool Million*, which came out in 1934. (It was bought by Columbia, but never produced; its book earnings amounted to $780.) This is the most antic and unrestrainedly fantastic of West's writings. It is in part a rambunctious satire on the Horatio Alger mythology, which was then so large an element in middle-class America's sense of itself—the image of the resourceful young American who, seizing each opportunity, rises smoothly from rags to riches. Lemuel Pitkin, driven by this image, sets out to make his fortune, and in the course of his misadventures—the subtitle of the book is "The Dismantling of Lemuel Pitkin"—succeeds in losing a leg and an eye and most of his teeth, and in being scalped; his sweetheart Betty is raped time and again, and installed in a brothel; and Lemuel is finally shot dead by a hired assassin. But *A Cool Million* is equally and simultaneously concerned with the "mantling" of Shagpoke Whipple, the very embodiment of home-grown, corn-fed American fascism. Whipple really does rise to wealth and power, supreme power, as leader of the National Revolutionary party. The triumph of this party, Whipple intones at a Fifth Avenue parade in honor of Lemuel's memory, has delivered America "from sophistication, Marxism and International Capitalism," and has returned the country to its true self.

Such manifestations of political lunacy were, as West brilliantly perceived, another mode, the most dangerous mode of all, of daydreaming, and one to which Americans—habitual searchers after scapegoats—were peculiarly prone. This is one reason why *A Cool Million* is so far superior to Sinclair Lewis's narrative account of the advent of fascism in America, *It Can't Happen Here*, which appeared the following year. Lewis's novel is hurried and journalistic; it stays close to the surfaces of things—that is, to the immediate political and economic preoccupations of the Depression years; and the only values Lewis opposes to the totalitarian impulse are wobbly and archaic. West, by resorting to the ludicrously fabulous, composed a mock allegory that bears upon every period in which American society drifts toward its own native version of fascism. *A Cool Million* speaks to the American condition, say, of the early seventies at least as much as it did to that of the early

thirties, for it speaks to the recurring tendency, in America, to anti-intellectualism, thoughtless cruelty, fear, suspicion, and the paranoid.[3]

By the spring of 1935, West was in Hollywood once again, jobless and relatively miserable but enjoying the company of a rich assortment of people (including William Faulkner, with whom he shared a passion for hunting). Early in 1936, however, he signed on with Republic Productions and stayed with that company for the last years of his short life. Writing for the film industry, in this generation and later, was a parallel of sorts to the newspaper work by which, in earlier years, indigent writers had supported and in part trained themselves. West was good at it and earned a healthy income out of such potboilers as *I Stole a Million*. Amid the disorders of a Hollywood studio, however, script writing had a far slighter relation to serious fiction than did journalism; but how little West's talent had been corrupted by his screen assignments is indicated by *The Day of the Locust*, which, published in 1939, draws markedly upon the California experience.

The volume containing *The Complete Works of Nathanael West* (1957) amounts to little more than four hundred pages. It can also be noted that West's lifelong royalties from these astonishing literary performances added up to less than $1300. The last thing that most Americans, daydreaming their way through an age of distress, wanted to read was a devastatingly accurate analysis of themselves. Of West's four "novels," *The Day of the Locust* is the longest and encompasses the most. It moves closer to the realistic mode than the others—though this fact is hidden behind West's decision to deal with the bizarre underside of Hollywood and California society: with dwarfs and clowns, brothel-keepers and part-time call girls, with frantic solitaries, and with the scowling indistinguishable faces of those hordes who have come to California to die. And West—ever in

[3] See Richard Hofstadter's excellent article "The Paranoid Style in American Politics," *Harper's* (November, 1964).

pursuit of what had happened, squalidly or ludicrously, to an earlier and nobler kind of American dreaming—stresses the illusory and deceitful qualities of his chosen domain: here movie actors dress up as French generals, ordinary citizens are garbed as Tyrolean hunters, a hill on a movie set, as its supports give way, rips the canvas of which it is composed to show the hollowness within.

The Day of the Locust may be the best place to examine what W. H. Auden—"in honor of the man who spent his life studying it"—calls "West's disease." This, according to Auden, "is a disease of consciousness which renders it incapable of converting wishes into desires"; and almost everybody in the novel is afflicted by it. The silent people who wait for some disaster—an airplane crash, perhaps—are wishing, not desiring; Faye Greener, the would-be actress who moonlights occasionally in the local bordello, lies on her bed sorting through her pack of fantasies, drowsily convinced that "any dream was better than none and beggars couldn't be choosers"; Homer Simpson sits motionless in his new home, his consciousness too paralyzed even to shape itself into a wish. From these varieties of unreality, Auden points out in his diagnosis, "a man can only be delivered by some physical or mental explosion outside his voluntary control."

This whole conception is a final twist or refinement of the theme of illusion which, as we have seen, was so prevalent in twentieth-century writing—in the work of Dreiser, O'Neill, Lewis, Wilder, and Fitzgerald, to name only a few. In West, the illusion itself is, so to speak, merely an illusion and has nothing to do with action. We have noticed how powerful illusion can be in the vision of Dreiser and O'Neill; it is yoked to will and can at times become an energetic source of motivation—partly because those writers saw it battering itself against a fully perceived reality. But for West, reality had grown dim and frail (this relates, obviously, to his move *away* from literary realism); he was not himself the victim of illusion, but in his own words he was able to imagine and project nothing more than a "peculiar half world," within which the psyche lay listlessly in the soft grip of the illusory. Only, as Auden formulates it, by an explosion *outside his voluntary control* could a person be taken out of that condition.

In none of West's novels is the dumb yearning for such an explosion more intense than in *The Day of the Locust*—and, by the same token, in none of them is the satire more robust and searching, the apocalyptic vision more fully developed. (The book's title is presumably Biblical and perhaps echoes both the allusion in Exodus to the Lord laying waste the land of Egypt by a swarm of locusts, and the image in the Book of Revelation of God sending locusts to destroy "those men who have not the seal of God upon their foreheads.") At one moment, Tod Hackett, the young painter who is the main and sanest figure in the book, lies partly drunk on a clump of wild mustard, dreaming his own dream about the invasion of California by "the cream of America's madmen" and deciding that "the milk from which it had been skimmed was just as rich in violence. The Angelenos would be first, but their comrades all over the country would follow. There would be a civil war." The beginnings of that war, as it may be, erupt in the riot with which the novel closes, but its full scope is suggested by Tod Hackett's apocalyptic painting, which is also described in the final chapter. Violence and hatred, greed and lust are the sources of the forthcoming Armageddon: and these qualities are rooted in West's version of the profound apathy into which so many of his contemporaries had sunk, and which, as he sketches it, takes the form of a national *acedia*, an ultimate boredom, a freezing of the humane impulse.

West's satiric eye is particularly sharp in detecting the intimate connection in America between the destructive tendency and radical religiosity, an extreme Protestantism gone finally insane. Tod Hackett finds a special ferocity in the people who gather in the temples and churches of the lunatic-fringe cults of California. As he watches them "writhe on the hard seats of their churches," his painter's imagination reflects how well the artist Magnasco (one of West's favorites) "would dramatize the contrast between their drained-out feeble bodies and their wild disordered minds." He is determined to paint "their fury with respect, appreciating its awful, anarchic power, and aware that they had it in them to destroy civilization." Thus West's own intense but utterly nondoctrinal religious imagination, which had first shaped the blind religious gropings of Miss Lonelyhearts, illuminates the spreading menace of "religion" wholly disinherited from the Judaeo-Christian tradition.

In the spring of 1940, West was married to Eileen McKenney, who had become something of a celebrity through Ruth McKenney's sprightly stories about her in the *New Yorker;* a play based upon the stories, *My Sister Eileen,* would open on Broadway on Christmas Eve of that year. In Hollywood, the Wests saw a good deal of Scott Fitzgerald, who admired the younger writer and thought of him as a protégé. Fitzgerald, too, was at work on a novel about the movie scene, *The Last Tycoon,* which was left unfinished, as we have remarked, when he died of a heart attack on December 21. West was informed of the event in Mexico, where he had gone on a hunting trip with his wife. Driving north toward Los Angeles the following afternoon, the Wests' car collided with another. Nathanael and Eileen were fatally injured, and died within two hours.

BIOGRAPHICAL CHART

1903   Born Nathan Weinstein, October 17, in New York City
1920   Leaves DeWitt Clinton High School after three years' attendance
1921   Enters Tufts College; flunks out
1922   Transfers to Brown University, falsifying his transcript; rooms with S. J. Perelman
1923–24   Publishes in *Casements* and *Brown Jug,* college magazines
1924   Graduates from Brown
1926   Changes name to Nathanael West
1926–27   Lives in Paris; works on *The Dream Life of Balso Snell*
1931   *The Dream Life of Balso Snell*

1933   *Miss Lonelyhearts;* becomes junior writer at Columbia Studios in Hollywood
1934   *A Cool Million*
1936   Writes scripts at Republic Studios; continues as screenwriter for Republic and other studios until his death
1938   *Good Hunting,* a play written in collaboration with Joseph Schrank, closes after two performances
1939   *The Day of the Locust*
1940   Marries Eileen McKenney in Beverly Hills; dies, December 22, with his wife, in an automobile accident

FURTHER READINGS

The Complete Works of Nathanael West (1957) (no editor cited)
William White, "Nathanael West: A Bibliography," *Studies in Bibliography,* 11 (1958), 207–24
————, "Nathanael West: Further Bibliographical Notes," *Serif,* 2 (1965), 28–31

Victor Comerchero, *Nathanael West: The Ironic Prophet* (1964)

Stanley Edgar Hyman, *Nathanael West* (1962)
James F. Light, *Nathanael West: An Interpretive Study* (1961)
Jay Martin, *Nathanael West: The Art of His Life* (1970)
————, ed., *Nathanael West: A Collection of Critical Essays* (1971)
Randall Reid, *The Fiction of Nathanael West: No Redeemer, No Promised Land* (1971)

From The Day of the Locust (1939)

We offer here the first five chapters and parts of the sixth of the novel and its final scene. The latter speaks for itself: it presents the largest of those "explosions" which, as has been said, West believed modern Americans found necessary as an escape from unreality. Here the explosion affects an entire society. It may also be observed that Tod's painting—and we are supposed to believe that it will be a great one—indicates the two weapons by which West thought it possible to counter the horror. These are: art and comedy; the art that, as Henry James said, makes life, reveals importance, and can discover meaning even in a society marching noisily to disaster; and the comedy that assuages and humanizes—that restores proportion.

In the opening scenes, what may be underlined is the novel's "choreography." As a single example, consider the seemingly random sequence of the pornographic film at Mrs. Jenning's, and the newspaper account of Harry Greener's vaudeville act. Both items, in fact, describe, as modes of comedy, the victimization of one person by several others—indeed by a close group, for instance, a family. Marie, the "distracted maid" in the movie, is grabbed at by the several members of the French family; the clown Harry Greener is mishandled by a family of acrobats known as "The Flying Lings." Between them, these two passages begin to create West's image of the human situation in the half-world of the novel.

1

Around quitting time, Tod Hackett heard a great din on the road outside his office. The groan of leather mingled with the jangle of iron and over all beat the tattoo of a thousand hooves. He hurried to the window.

An army of cavalry and foot was passing. It moved like a mob; its lines broken, as though fleeing from some terrible defeat. The dolmans of the hussars, the heavy shakos of the guards, Hanoverian light horse, with their flat leather caps and flowing red plumes, were all jumbled together in bobbing disorder. Behind the cavalry came the infantry, a wild sea of waving sabretaches, sloped muskets, crossed shoulder belts and swinging cartridge boxes. Tod recognized the scarlet infantry of England with their white shoulder pads, the black infantry of the Duke of Brunswick, the French grenadiers with their enormous white gaiters, the Scotch with bare knees under plaid skirts.

While he watched, a little fat man, wearing a cork sun-helmet, polo shirt and knickers, darted around the corner of the building in pursuit of the army.

"Stage Nine—you bastards—Stage Nine!" he screamed through a small megaphone.

The cavalry put spur to their horses and the infantry broke into a dogtrot. The little man in the cork hat ran after them, shaking his fist and cursing.

Tod watched until they had disappeared behind half a Mississippi steamboat, then put away his pencils and drawing board, and left the office. On the sidewalk outside the studio he stood for a moment trying to decide whether to walk home or take a streetcar. He had been in Hollywood less than three months and still found it a very exciting place, but he was lazy and didn't like to walk. He decided to take the streetcar as far as Vine Street and walk the rest of the way.

A talent scout for National Films had brought Tod to the Coast after seeing some of his drawings in an exhibit of undergraduate work at the Yale School of Fine Arts. He had been hired by telegram. If the scout had met Tod, he probably wouldn't have sent him to Hollywood to learn set and costume designing. His large, sprawling body, his slow blue eyes and sloppy grin made him seem completely without talent, almost doltish in fact.

Yes, despite his appearance, he was really a very complicated young man with a whole set of personalities, one inside the other like a nest of Chinese boxes. And "The Burning of Los Angeles," a picture he was soon to paint, definitely proved he had talent.

He left the car at Vine Street. As he walked along, he examined the evening crowd. A great many of the people wore sports clothes which were not really sports clothes. Their sweaters, knickers, slacks, blue flannel jackets with brass buttons were fancy dress. The fat lady in the yachting cap was going shopping, not boating; the man in the Norfolk jacket and Tyrolean hat was returning, not from a mountain, but an insurance office; and the girl in slacks and sneaks with a bandanna around her head had just left a switchboard, not a tennis court.

Scattered among these masquerades were people of a different type. Their clothing was somber and badly cut, bought from mail-order houses. While the others moved rapidly, darting into stores and cocktail bars, they loitered on the corners or stood with their backs to the shop windows and stared at everyone who passed. When their stare was returned, their eyes filled with hatred. At this time Tod knew very little about them except that they had come to California to die.

He was determined to learn much more. They were the people he felt he must paint. He would never again do a fat red barn, old stone wall or sturdy Nantucket fisherman. From the moment he had seen them, he had known that, despite his race, training and heritage, neither Winslow Homer nor Thomas Ryder could be his masters and he turned to Goya and Daumier.

He had learned this just in time. During his last year in art school, he had begun to think that he might give up painting completely. The pleasures he received from the problems of composition and color had decreased as his facility had increased and he had realized that he was going the way of all his classmates toward illustration or mere handsomeness. When the Hollywood job had come along, he had grabbed it despite the arguments of his friends who were certain that he was selling out and would never paint again.

He reached the end of Vine Street and began the climb into Pinyon Canyon. Night had started to fall.

The edges of the trees burned with a pale violet light and their centers gradually turned from deep purple to black. The same violet piping, like a Neon tube, outlined the tops of the ugly, humpbacked hills and they were almost beautiful.

But not even the soft wash of dusk could help the houses. Only dynamite would be of any use against the Mexican ranch houses, Samoan huts, Mediterranean villas, Egyptian and Japanese temples, Swiss chalets, Tudor cottages, and every possible combination of these styles that lined the slopes of the canyon.

When he noticed that they were all of plaster,

lath and paper, he was charitable and blamed their shape on the materials used. Steel, stone and brick curb a builder's fancy a little, forcing him to distribute his stresses and weights and to keep his corners plumb, but plaster and paper know no law, not even that of gravity.

On the corner of La Huerta Road was a miniature Rhine castle with tarpaper turrets pierced for archers. Next to it was a little highly colored shack with domes and minarets out of the *Arabian Nights*. Again he was charitable. Both houses were comic, but he didn't laugh. Their desire to startle was so eager and guileless.

It is hard to laugh at the need for beauty and romance, no matter how tasteless, even horrible, the results of that need are. But it is easy to sigh. Few things are sadder than the truly monstrous.

2

The house he lived in was a nondescript affair called the San Bernardino Arms. It was an oblong three stories high, the back and sides of which were of plain, unpainted stucco, broken by even rows of unadorned windows. The façade was the color of diluted mustard and its windows, all double, were framed by pink Moorish columns which supported turnip-shaped lintels.

His room was on the third floor, but he paused for a moment on the landing of the second. It was on that floor that Faye Greener lived, in 208. When someone laughed in one of the apartments he started guiltily and continued upstairs.

As he opened his door a card fluttered to the floor. "Honest Abe Kusich," it said in large type, then underneath in smaller italics were several endorsements, printed to look like press notices.

"*. . . the Lloyds of Hollywood*"—Stanley Rose.

"*Abe's word is better than Morgan's bonds*"—Gail Brenshaw.

On the other side was a penciled message:

"Kingpin fourth, Solitair sixth. You can make some real dough on those nags."

After opening the window, he took off his jacket and lay down on the bed. Through the window he could see a square of enameled sky and a spray of eucalyptus. A light breeze stirred its long, narrow leaves, making them show first their green side, then their silver one.

He began to think of "Honest Abe Kusich" in order not to think of Faye Greener. He felt comfortable and wanted to remain that way.

Abe was an important figure in a set of lithographs called "The Dancers" on which Tod was working. He was one of the dancers. Faye Greener was another and her father, Harry, still another. They changed with each plate, but the group of uneasy people who formed their audience remained the same. They stood staring at the performers in just the way that they stared at the masqueraders on Vine Street. It was their stare that drove Abe and the others to spin crazily and leap into the air with twisted backs like hooked trout.

Despite the sincere indignation that Abe's grotesque depravity aroused in him, he welcomed his company. The little man excited him and in that way made him feel certain of his need to paint.

He had first met Abe when he was living on Ivar Street, in a hotel called the Chateau Mirabella. Another name for Ivar Street was "Lysol Alley," and the Chateau was mainly inhabited by hustlers, their managers, trainers and advance agents.

In the morning its halls reeked of antiseptic. Tod didn't like this odor. Moreover, the rent was high because it included police protection, a service for which he had no need. He wanted to move, but inertia and the fact that he didn't know where to go kept him in the Chateau until he met Abe. The meeting was accidental.

He was on the way to his room late one night when he saw what he supposed was a pile of soiled laundry lying in front of the door across the hall from his own. Just as he was passing it, the bundle moved and made a peculiar noise. He struck a match, thinking it might be a dog wrapped in a blanket. When the light flared up, he saw it was a tiny man.

The match went out and he hastily lit another. It was a male dwarf rolled up in a woman's flannel bathrobe. The round thing at the end was his slightly hydrocephalic head. A slow, choked snore bubbled from it.

The hall was cold and draughty. Tod decided to wake the man and stirred him with his toe. He groaned and opened his eyes.

"You oughtn't to sleep there."

"The hell you say," said the dwarf, closing his eyes again.

"You'll catch cold."

This friendly observation angered the little man still more.

"I want my clothes!" he bellowed.

The bottom of the door next to which he was lying filled with light. Tod decided to take a chance and knock. A few seconds later a woman opened it part way.

"What the hell do you want?" she demanded.

"There's a friend of yours out here who . . ."

Neither of them let him finish.

"So what!" she barked, slamming the door.

"Give me my clothes, you bitch!" roared the dwarf.

She opened the door again and began to hurl things into the hall. A jacket and trousers, a shirt, socks, shoes and underwear, a tie and hat followed each other through the air in rapid succession. With each article went a special curse.

Tod whistled with amazement.

"Some gal!"

"You bet," said the dwarf. "A lollapalooza—all slut and a yard wide."

He laughed at his own joke, using a high-pitched cackle more dwarflike than anything that had come from him so far, then struggled to his feet and arranged the voluminous robe so that he could walk without tripping. Tod helped him gather his scattered clothing.

"Say, mister," he asked, "could I dress in your place?"

Tod let him into his bathroom. While waiting for him to reappear, he couldn't help imagining what had happened in the woman's apartment. He began to feel sorry for having interfered. But when the dwarf came out wearing his hat, Tod felt better.

The little man's hat fixed almost everything. That year Tyrolean hats were being worn a great deal along Hollywood Boulevard and the dwarf's was a fine specimen. It was the proper magic green color and had a high, conical crown. There should have been a brass buckle on the front, but otherwise it was quite perfect.

The rest of his outfit didn't go well with the hat. Instead of shoes with long points and a leather apron, he wore a blue, double-breasted suit and a black shirt with a yellow tie. Instead of a crooked thorn stick, he carried a rolled copy of the *Daily Running Horse*.

"That's what I get for fooling with four-bit broads," he said by way of greeting.

Tod nodded and tried to concentrate on the green hat. His ready acquiescence seemed to irritate the little man.

"No quiff can give Abe Kusich the fingeroo and get away with it," he said bitterly. "Not when I can get her leg broke for twenty bucks and I got twenty."

He took out a thick billfold and shook it at Tod.

"So she thinks she can give me the fingeroo, hah? Well, let me tell . . ."

Tod broke in hastily.

"You're right, Mr. Kusich."

The dwarf came over to where Tod was sitting and for a moment Tod thought he was going to climb into his lap, but he only asked his name and shook hands. The little man had a powerful grip.

"Let me tell you something, Hackett, if you hadn't come along, I'da broke in the door. That dame thinks she can give me the fingeroo, but she's got another thinkola coming. But thanks anyway."

"Forget it."

"I don't forget nothing. I remember. I remember those who do me dirt and those who do me favors."

He wrinkled his brow and was silent for a moment.

"Listen," he finally said, "seeing as you helped me, I got to return it. I don't want anybody going around saying Abe Kusich owes him anything. So I'll tell you what. I'll give you a good one for the fifth at Caliente. You put a fiver on its nose and it'll get you twenty smackeroos. What I'm telling you is strictly correct."

Tod didn't know how to answer and his hesitation offended the little man.

"Would I give you a bum steer?" he demanded, scowling. "Would I?"

Tod walked toward the door to get rid of him.

"No," he said.

"Then why won't you bet, hah?"

"What's the name of the horse?" Tod asked, hoping to calm him.

The dwarf had followed him to the door, pulling the bathrobe after him by one sleeve. Hat and all, he came to a foot below Tod's belt.

"Tragopan. He's a certain, sure winner. I know the guy who owns him and he gave me the office."

"Is he a Greek?" Tod asked.

He was being pleasant in order to hide the attempt he was making to maneuver the dwarf through the door.

"Yeh, he's a Greek. Do you know him?"

"No."

"No?"

"No," said Tod with finality.

"Keep your drawers on," ordered the dwarf, "all I want to know is how you know he's a Greek if you don't know him?"

His eyes narrowed with suspicion and he clenched his fists.

Tod smiled to placate him.

"I just guessed it."

"You did?"

The dwarf hunched his shoulders as though he were going to pull a gun or throw a punch. Tod backed off and tried to explain.

"I guessed he was a Greek because Tragopan is a Greek word that means pheasant."

The dwarf was far from satisfied.

"How do you know what it means? You ain't a Greek?"

"No, but I know a few Greek words."

"So you're a wise guy, hah, a know-it-all."

He took a short step forward, moving on his toes, and Tod got set to block a punch.

"A college man, hah? Well, let me tell . . ."

His foot caught in the wrapper and he fell forward on his hands. He forgot Tod and cursed the bathrobe, then got started on the woman again.

"So she thinks she can give me the fingeroo."

He kept poking himself in the chest with his thumbs.

"Who gave her forty bucks for an abortion? Who? And another ten to go to the country for a rest that time. To a ranch I sent her. And who got her fiddle out of hock that time in Santa Monica? Who?"

"That's right," Tod said, getting ready to give him a quick shove through the door.

But he didn't have to shove him. The little man suddenly darted out of the room and ran down the hall, dragging the bathrobe after him.

A few days later, Tod went into a stationary store on Vine Street to buy a magazine. While he was looking through the rack, he felt a tug at the bottom of his jacket. It was Abe Kusich, the dwarf, again.

"How's things?" he demanded.

Tod was surprised to find that he was just as truculent as he had been the other night. Later, when he got to know him better, he discovered that Abe's pugnacity was often a joke. When he used it on his friends, they played with him like one does with a growling puppy, staving off his mad rushes and then baiting him to rush again.

"Fair enough," Tod said, "but I think I'll move."

He had spent most of Sunday looking for a place to live and was full of the subject. The moment he mentioned it, however, he knew that he had made a mistake. He tried to end the matter by turning away, but the little man blocked him. He evidently considered himself an expert on the housing situation. After naming and discarding a dozen possibilities without a word from Tod, he finally hit on the San Bernardino Arms.

"That's the place for you, the San Berdoo. I live there, so I ought to know. The owner's strictly from hunger. Come on, I'll get you fixed up swell."

"I don't know, I . . ." Tod began.

The dwarf bridled instantly, and appeared to be mortally offended.

"I suppose it ain't good enough for you. Well, let me tell you something, you . . ."

Tod allowed himself to be bullied and went with the dwarf to Pinyon Canyon. The rooms in the San Berdoo were small and not very clean. He rented one without hesitation, however, when he saw Faye Greener in the hall.

3

Tod had fallen asleep. When he woke again, it was after eight o'clock. He took a bath and shaved, then dressed in front of the bureau mirror. He tried to watch his fingers as he fixed his collar and tie, but his eyes kept straying to the photograph that was pushed into the upper corner of the frame.

It was a picture of Faye Greener, a still from a two-reel farce in which she had worked as an extra. She had given him the photograph willingly enough, had even autographed it in a large, wild hand, "Affectionately yours, Faye Greener," but she refused his friendship, or, rather, insisted on keeping it impersonal. She had told him why. He had nothing to offer her, neither money nor looks, and she could only love a handsome man and would only let a wealthy man love her. Tod was a "good-hearted man," and she liked "good-hearted men," but only as friends. She wasn't hard-boiled. It was just that she put love on a special plane, where a man without money or looks couldn't move.

Tod grunted with annoyance as he turned to the photograph. In it she was wearing a harem costume, full Turkish trousers, breastplates and a monkey jacket, and lay stretched out on a silken divan. One hand held a beer bottle and the other a pewter stein.

He had gone all the way to Glendale to see her in that movie. It was about an American drummer who gets lost in the seraglio of a Damascus mer-

chant and has a lot of fun with the female inmates. Faye played one of the dancing girls. She had only one line to speak, "Oh, Mr. Smith!" and spoke it badly.

She was a tall girl with wide, straight shoulders and long, swordlike legs. Her neck was long, too, and columnar. Her face was much fuller than the rest of her body would lead you to expect and much larger. It was a moon face, wide at the cheek bones and narrow at chin and brow. She wore her "platinum" hair long, letting it fall almost to her shoulders in back, but kept it away from her face and ears with a narrow blue ribbon that went under it and was tied on top of her head with a little bow.

She was supposed to look drunk and she did, but not with alcohol. She lay stretched out on the divan with her arms and legs spread, as though welcoming a lover, and her lips were parted in a heavy, sullen smile. She was supposed to look inviting, but the invitation wasn't to pleasure.

Tod lit a cigarette and inhaled with a nervous gasp. He started to fool with his tie again, but had to go back to the photograph.

Her invitation wasn't to pleasure, but to struggle, hard and sharp, closer to murder than to love. If you threw yourself on her, it would be like throwing yourself from the parapet of a skyscraper. You would do it with a scream. You couldn't expect to rise again. Your teeth would be driven into your skull like nails into a pine board and your back would be broken. You wouldn't even have time to sweat or close your eyes.

He managed to laugh at his language, but it wasn't a real laugh and nothing was destroyed by it.

If she would only let him, he would be glad to throw himself, no matter what the cost. But she wouldn't have him. She didn't love him and he couldn't further her career. She wasn't sentimental and she had no need for tenderness, even if he were capable of it.

When he had finished dressing, he hurried out of the room. He had promised to go to a party at Claude Estee's.

4

Claude was a successful screen writer who lived in a big house that was an exact reproduction of the old Dupuy mansion near Biloxi, Mississippi. When

Tod came up the walk between the boxwood hedges, he greeted him from the enormous, two-story porch by doing the impersonation that went with the Southern colonial architecture. He teetered back and forth on his heels like a Civil War colonel and made believe he had a large belly.

He had no belly at all. He was a dried-up little man with the rubbed features and stooped shoulders of a postal clerk. The shiny mohair coat and nondescript trousers of that official would have become him, but he was dressed, as always, elaborately. In the buttonhole of his brown jacket was a lemon flower. His trousers were of reddish Harris tweed with a hound tooth check and on his feet were a pair of magnificent, rust-colored blüchers. His shirt was ivory flannel and his knitted tie a red that was almost black.

While Tod mounted the steps to reach his outstretched hand, he shouted to the butler.

"Here, you black rascal! A mint julep."

A Chinese servant came running with a Scotch and soda.

After talking to Tod for a moment, Claude started him in the direction of Alice, his wife, who was at the other end of the porch.

"Don't run off," he whispered. "We're going to a sporting house."

Alice was sitting in a wicker swing with a woman named Mrs. Joan Schwartzen. When she asked him if he was playing any tennis, Mrs. Schwartzen interrupted her.

"How silly, batting an inoffensive ball across something that ought to be used to catch fish on account of millions are starving for a bite of herring."

"Joan's a female tennis champ," Alice explained.

Mrs. Schwartzen was a big girl with large hands and feet and square, bony shoulders. She had a pretty, eighteen-year-old face and a thirty-five-year-old neck that was veined and sinewy. Her deep sunburn, ruby colored with a slight blue tint, kept the contrast between her face and neck from being too startling.

"Well, I wish we were going to a brothel this minute," she said. "I adore them."

She turned to Tod and fluttered her eyelids.

"Don't you, Mr. Hackett?"

"That's right, Joan darling," Alice answered for him. "Nothing like a bagnio to set a fellow up. Hair of the dog that bit you."

"How dare you insult me!"

She stood up and took Tod's arm.

"Convoy me over there."

She pointed to the group of men with whom Claude was standing.

"For God's sake, convoy her," Alice said. "She thinks they're telling dirty stories."

Mrs. Schwartzen pushed right among them, dragging Tod after her.

"Are you talking smut?" she asked. "I adore smut."

They all laughed politely.

"No, shop," said someone.

"I don't believe it. I can tell from the beast in your voices. Go ahead, do say something obscene."

This time no one laughed.

Tod dried to disengage her arm, but she kept a firm grip on it. There was a moment of awkward silence, then the man she had interrupted tried to make a fresh start.

"The picture business is too humble," he said. "We ought to resent people like Coombes."

"That's right," said another man. "Guys like that come out here, make a lot of money, grouse all the time about the place, flop on their assignments, then go back East and tell dialect stories about producers they've never met."

"My God," Mrs. Schwartzen said to Tod in a loud, stagey whisper, "they *are* talking shop."

"Let's look for the man with the drinks," Tod said.

"No. Take me into the garden. Have you seen what's in the swimming pool?"

She pulled him along.

The air of the garden was heavy with the odor of mimosa and honeysuckle. Through a slit in the blue serge sky poked a grained moon that looked like an enormous bone button. A little flagstone path, made narrow by its border of oleander, led to the edge of the sunken pool. On the bottom, near the deep end, he could see a heavy, black mass of some kind.

"What is it?" he asked.

She kicked a switch that was hidden at the base of a shrub and a row of submerged floodlights illuminated the green water. The thing was a dead horse, or, rather, a life-size, realistic reproduction of one. Its legs stuck up stiff and straight and it had an enormous, distended belly. Its hammerhead lay twisted to one side and from its mouth, which was set in an agonized grin, hung a heavy, black tongue.

"Isn't it marvelous!" exclaimed Mrs. Schwartzen,

clapping her hands and jumping up and down excitedly like a little girl.

"What's it made of?"

"Then you weren't fooled? How impolite! It's rubber, of course. It cost lots of money."

"But why?"

"To amuse. We were looking at the pool one day and somebody, Jerry Appis, I think, said that it needed a dead horse on the bottom, so Alice got one. Don't you think it looks cute?"

"Very."

"You're just an old meanie. Think how happy the Estees must feel, showing it to people and listening to their merriment and their oh's and ah's of unconfined delight."

She stood on the edge of the pool and "ohed and ahed" rapidly several times in succession.

"Is it still there?" someone called.

Tod turned and saw two women and a man coming down the path.

"I think its belly's going to burst," Mrs. Schwartzen shouted to them gleefully.

"Goody," said the man, hurrying to look.

"But it's only full of air," said one of the women.

Mrs. Schwartzen made believe she was going to cry.

"You're just like that mean Mr. Hackett. You just won't let me cherish my illusions."

Tod was halfway to the house when she called after him. He waved but kept going.

The men with Claude were still talking shop.

"But how are you going to get rid of the illiterate mockies that run it? They've got a strangle hold on the industry. Maybe they're intellectual stumblebums, but they're damn good businessmen. Or at least they know how to go into receivership and come up with a gold watch in their teeth."

"They ought to put some of the millions they make back into the business again. Like Rockefeller does with his Foundation. People used to hate the Rockefellers, but now instead of hollering about their ill-gotten oil dough, everybody praises them for what the Foundation does. It's a swell stunt and pictures could do the same thing. Have a Cinema Foundation and make contributions to Science and Art. You know, give the racket a front."

Tod took Claude to one side to say good night, but he wouldn't let him go. He led him into the library and mixed two double Scotches. They sat down on the couch facing the fireplace.

"You haven't been to Audrey Jenning's place?" Claude asked.

"No, but I've heard tell of it."

"Then you've got to come along."

"I don't like pro-sport."

"We won't indulge in any. We're just going to see a movie."

"I get depressed."

"Not at Jenning's you won't. She makes vice attractive by skillful packaging. Her dive's a triumph of industrial design."

Tod liked to hear him talk. He was master of an involved comic rhetoric that permitted him to express his moral indignation and still keep his reputation for worldliness and wit.

Tod fed him another lead. "I don't care how much cellophane she wraps it in," he said—"nautch joints are depressing, like all places for deposit, banks, mail boxes, tombs, vending machines."

"Love is like a vending machine, eh? Not bad. You insert a coin and press home the lever. There's some mechanical activity inside the bowels of the device. You receive a small sweet, frown at yourself in the dirty mirror, adjust your hat, take a firm grip on your umbrella and walk away, trying to look as though nothing had happened. It's good, but it's not for pictures."

Tod played straight again.

"That's not it. I've been chasing a girl and it's like carrying something a little too large to conceal in your pocket, like a briefcase or a small valise. It's uncomfortable."

"I know, I know. It's always uncomfortable. First your right hand gets tired, then your left. You put the valise down and sit on it, but people are surprised and stop to stare at you, so you move on. You hide it behind a tree and hurry away, but someone finds it and runs after you to return it. It's a small valise when you leave home in the morning, cheap and with a bad handle, but by evening it's a trunk with brass corners and many foreign labels. I know. It's good, but it won't film. You've got to remember your audience. What about the barber in Purdue? He's been cutting hair all day and he's tired. He doesn't want to see some dope carrying a valise or fooling with a nickel machine. What the barber wants is amour and glamor."

The last part was for himself and he sighed heavily. He was about to begin again when the Chinese servant came in and said that the others were ready to leave for Mrs. Jenning's.

5

They started out in several cars. Tod rode in the front of the one Claude drove and as they went down Sunset Boulevard he described Mrs. Jenning for him. She had been a fairly prominent actress in the days of silent films, but sound made it impossible for her to get work. Instead of becoming an extra or a bit player like many other old stars, she had shown excellent business sense and had opened a callhouse. She wasn't vicious. Far from it. She ran her business just as other women run lending libraries, shrewdly and with taste.

None of the girls lived on the premises. You telephoned and she sent a girl over. The charge was thirty dollars for a single night of sport and Mrs. Jenning kept fifteen of it. Some people might think that fifty per cent is a high brokerage fee, but she really earned every cent of it. There was a big overhead. She maintained a beautiful house for the girls to wait in and a car and a chauffeur to deliver them to the clients.

Then, too, she had to move in the kind of society where she could make the right contacts. After all, not every man can afford thirty dollars. She permitted her girls to service only men of wealth and position, not to say taste and discretion. She was so particular that she insisted on meeting the prospective sportsman before servicing him. She had often said, and truthfully, that she would not let a girl of hers go to a man with whom she herself would not be willing to sleep.

And she was really cultured. All the most distinguished visitors considered it quite a lark to meet her. They were disappointed, however, when they discovered how refined she was. They wanted to talk about certain lively matters of universal interest, but she insisted on discussing Gertrude Stein and Juan Gris. No matter how hard the distinguished visitor tried, and some had been known to go to really great lengths, he could never find a flaw in her refinement or make a breach in her culture.

Claude was still using his peculiar rhetoric on Mrs. Jenning when she came to the door of her house to greet them.

"It's so nice to see you again," she said. "I was telling Mrs. Prince at tea only yesterday—the Estees are my favorite couple."

She was a handsome woman, smooth and buttery, with fair hair and a red complexion.

She led them into a small drawing room whose color scheme was violet, gray and rose. The Venetian blinds were rose, as was the ceiling, and the walls were covered with a pale gray paper that had a tiny, widely spaced flower design in violet. On one wall hung a silver screen, the kind that rolls up, and against the opposite wall, on each side of a cherrywood table, was a row of chairs covered with rose and gray, glazed chintz bound in violet piping. There was a small projection machine on the table and a young man in evening dress was fumbling with it.

She waved them to their seats. A waiter then came in and asked what they wanted to drink. When their orders had been taken and filled, she flipped the light switch and the young man started his machine. It whirred merrily, but he had trouble in getting it focused.

"What are we going to see first?" Mrs. Schwartzen asked.

"*Le Predicament de Marie.*"

"That sounds ducky."

"It's charming, utterly charming," said Mrs. Jenning.

"Yes," said the cameraman, who was still having trouble. "I love *Le Predicament de Marie*. It has a marvelous quality that is too exciting."

There was a long delay, during which he fussed desperately with his machine. Mrs. Schwartzen started to whistle and stamp her feet and the others joined in. They imitated a rowdy audience in the days of the nickelodeon.

"Get a move on, slow poke."

"What's your hurry? Here's your hat."

"Get a horse!"

"Get out and get under!"

The young man finally found the screen with his light beam and the film began.

LE PREDICAMENT DE MARIE
ou
LA BONNE DISTRAITE

Marie, the "bonne," was a buxom young girl in a tight-fitting black silk uniform with very short skirts. On her head was a tiny lace cap. In the first scene, she was shown serving dinner to a middle-class family in an oak-paneled dining room full of heavy, carved furniture. The family was very respectable and consisted of a bearded, frock-coated father, a mother with a whalebone collar and a cameo brooch, a tall, thin son with a long mustache and almost no chin and a little girl wearing a large bow in her hair and a crucifix on a gold chain around her neck.

After some low comedy with father's beard and

the soup, the actors settled down seriously to their theme. It was evident that while the whole family desired Marie, she only desired the young girl. Using his napkin to hide his activities, the old man pinched Marie, the son tried to look down the neck of her dress and the mother patted her knee. Marie, for her part, surreptitiously fondled the child.

The scene changed to Marie's room. She undressed and got into a chiffon negligee, leaving on only her black silk stockings and high-heeled shoes. She was making an elaborate night toilet when the child entered. Marie took her on her lap and started to kiss her. There was a knock on the door. Consternation. She hid the child in the closet and let in the bearded father. He was suspicious and she had to accept his advances. He was embracing her when there was another knock. Again consternation and tableau. This time it was the mustachioed son. Marie hid the father under the bed. No sooner had the son begun to grow warm than there was another knock. Marie made him climb into a large blanket chest. The new caller was the lady of the house. She, too, was just settling down to work when there was another knock.

Who could it be? A telegram? A policeman? Frantically Marie counted the different hiding places. The whole family was present. She tiptoed to the door and listened.

"Who can it be that wishes to enter now?" read the title card.

And there the machine stuck. The young man in evening dress became as frantic as Marie. When he got it running again, there was a flash of light and the film whizzed through the apparatus until it had all run out.

"I'm sorry, extremely," he said. "I'll have to rewind."

"It's a frameup," someone yelled.

"Fake!"

"Cheat!"

"The old teaser routine!"

They stamped their feet and whistled.

Under cover of the mock riot, Tod sneaked out. He wanted to get some fresh air. The waiter, whom he found loitering in the hall, showed him to the patio in back of the house.

On his return, he peeked into the different rooms. In one of them he found a large number of miniature dogs in a curio cabinet. There were glass pointers, silver beagles, porcelain schnauzers, stone dachshunds, aluminum bulldogs, onyx whippets, china bassets, wooden spaniels. Every recognized breed was represented and almost every material that could be sculptured, cast or carved.

While he was admiring the little figures, he heard a girl singing. He thought he recognized her voice and peeked into the hall. It was Mary Dove, one of Faye Greener's best friends.

Perhaps Faye also worked for Mrs. Jenning. If so, for thirty dollars . . .

He went back to see the rest of the film.

6

Tod's hope that he could end his trouble by paying a small fee didn't last long. When he got Claude to ask Mrs. Jenning about Faye, that lady said she had never heard of the girl. Claude then asked her to inquire through Mary Dove. A few days later she phoned him to say there was nothing doing. The girl wasn't available.

Tod wasn't really disappointed. He didn't want Fay that way, not at least while he still had a chance some other way. Lately, he had begun to think he had a good one. Harry, her father, was sick and that gave him an excuse for hanging around their apartment. He ran errands and kept the old man company. To repay his kindness, she permitted him the intimacies of a family friend. He hoped to deepen her gratitude and make it serious.

Apart from this purpose, he was interested in Harry and enjoyed visiting him. The old man was a clown and Tod had all the painter's usual love of clowns. But what was more important, he felt that his clownship was a clue to the people who stared (a painter's clue, that is—a clue in the form of a symbol), just as Faye's dreams were another.

He sat near Harry's bed and listened to his stories by the hour. Forty years in vaudeville and burlesque had provided him with an infinite number of them. As he put it, his life had consisted of a lightning series of "nip-ups," "high-gruesomes," "flying-W's" and "hundred-and-eights" done to escape a barrage of "exploding stoves." An "exploding stove" was any catastrophe, natural or human, from a flood in Medicine Hat, Wyoming, to an angry policeman in Moose Factory, Ontario.

When Harry had first begun his stage career, he had probably restricted his clowning to the boards, but now he clowned continuously. It was his sole method of defense. Most people, he had discovered, won't go out of their way to punish a clown.

He used a set of elegant gestures to accent the

comedy of his bent, hopeless figure and wore a special costume, dressing like a banker, a cheap, unconvincing, imitation banker. The costume consisted of a greasy derby with an unusually high crown, a wing collar and polka dot four-in-hand, a shiny double-breasted jacket and gray-striped trousers. His outfit fooled no one, but then he didn't intend it to fool anyone. His slyness was of a different sort.

On the stage he was a complete failure and knew it. Yet he claimed to have once come very close to success. To prove how close, he made Tod read an old clipping from the theatrical section of the Sunday *Times*.

"BEDRAGGLED HARLEQUIN," it was headed.

"The commedia del' arte is not dead, but lives on in Brooklyn, or was living there last week on the stage of the Oglethorpe Theatre in the person of one Harry Greener. Mr. Greener is of a troupe called 'The Flying Lings,' who, by the time this reaches you, have probably moved on to Mystic, Connecticut, or some other place more fitting than the borough of large families. If you have the time and really love the theatre, by all means seek out the Lings wherever they may be.

"Mr. Greener, the bedraggled Harlequin of our caption, is not bedraggled but clean, neat and sweet when he first comes on. By the time the Lings, four muscular Orientals, finish with him, however, he is plenty bedraggled. He is tattered and bloody, but still sweet.

"When Mr. Greener enters the trumpets are properly silent. Mama Ling is spinning a plate on the end of a stick held in her mouth, Papa Ling is doing cartwheels, Sister Ling is juggling fans and Sonny Ling is hanging from the proscenium arch by his pigtail. As he inspects his strenuous colleagues, Mr. Greener tries to hide his confusion under some much too obvious worldliness. He ventures to tickle Sister and receives a powerful kick in the belly in return for this innocent attention. Having been kicked, he is on familiar ground and begins to tell a dull joke. Father Ling sneaks up behind him and tosses him to Brother, who looks the other way. Mr. Greener lands on the back of his neck. He shows his mettle by finishing his dull story from a recumbent position. When he stands up, the audience, which failed to laugh at his joke, laughs at his limp, so he continues lame for the rest of the act.

"Mr. Greener begins another story, even longer and duller than his first. Just before he arrives at the gag line, the orchestra blares loudly and drowns him out. He is very patient and very brave. He begins again, but the orchestra will not let him finish. The pain that almost, not quite, thank God, crumples his stiff little figure would be unbearable if it were not obviously make-believe. It is gloriously funny.

"The finale is superb. While the Ling Family flies through the air, Mr. Greener, held to the ground by his sense of reality and his knowledge of gravitation, tries hard to make the audience think that he is neither surprised nor worried by the rocketing Orientals. It's familiar stuff, his hands signal, but his face denies this. As time goes on and no one is hurt, he regains his assurance. The acrobats ignore him, so he ignores the acrobats. His is the final victory; the applause is for him.

"My first thought was that some producer should put Mr. Greener into a big revue against a background of beautiful girls and glittering curtains. But my second was that this would be a mistake. I am afraid that Mr. Greener, like certain humble field plants which die when transferred to richer soil, had better be left to bloom in vaudeville against a background of ventriloquists and lady bicycle riders."

Harry had more than a dozen copies of this article, several on rag paper. After trying to get a job by inserting a small advertisement in *Variety* (". . . 'some producer should put Mr. Greener into a big revue . . .' The *Times*"), he had come to Hollywood, thinking to earn a living playing comedy bits in films. There proved to be little demand for his talents, however. As he himself put it, he "stank from hunger." To supplement his meager income from the studios, he peddled silver polish which he made in the bathroom of the apartment out of chalk, soap and yellow axle grease. When Faye wasn't at Central Casting, she took him around on his peddling trips in her Model T Ford. It was on their last expedition together that he had fallen sick.

. . .

27

When Tod reached the street, he saw a dozen great violet shafts of light moving across the evening sky in wide crazy sweeps. Whenever one of the fiery columns reached the lowest point of its arc, it lit for a moment the rose-colored domes and delicate minarets of Kahn's Persian Palace Theatre. The purpose of this display was to signal the world premiere of a new picture.

Turning his back on the searchlights, he started in the opposite direction, toward Homer's[1] place. Before he had gone very far, he saw a clock that read a quarter past six and changed his mind about going back just yet. He might as well let the poor fellow sleep for another hour and kill some time by looking at the crowds.

When still a block from the theatre, he saw an enormous electric sign that hung over the middle of the street. In letters ten feet high he read that—

"MR. KAHN A PLEASURE DOME DECREED"

Although it was still several hours before the celebrities would arrive, thousands of people had already gathered. They stood facing the theatre with their backs toward the gutter in a thick line hundreds of feet long. A big squad of policemen was trying to keep a lane open between the front rank of the crowd and the façade of the theatre.

Tod entered the lane while the policeman guarding it was busy with a woman whose parcel had torn open, dropping oranges all over the place. Another policeman shouted for him to get the hell across the street, but he took a chance and kept going. They had enough to do without chasing him. He noticed how worried they looked and how careful they tried to be. If they had to arrest someone, they joked good-naturedly with the culprit, making light of it until they got him around the corner, then they whaled him with their clubs. Only so long as the man was actually part of the crowd did they have to be gentle.

Tod had walked only a short distance along the narrow lane when he began to get frightened. People shouted, commenting on his hat, his carriage, and his clothing. There was a continuous roar of catcalls, laughter and yells, pierced occasionally by a scream. The scream was usually followed by a sudden movement in the dense mass and part of it would surge forward wherever the police line was weakest. As soon as that part was rammed back, the bulge would pop out somewhere else.

The police force would have to be doubled when the stars started to arrive. At the sight of their heroes and heroines, the crowd would turn demoniac. Some little gesture, either too pleasing or too offensive, would start it moving and then nothing but machine guns would stop it. Individu-

[1] Homer Simpson, a middle-aged admirer of Faye, who suffers acutely from "West's disease" (see p. 2357).

ally the purpose of its members might simply be to get a souvenir, but collectively it would grab and rend.

A young man with a portable microphone was describing the scene. His rapid, hysterical voice was like that of a revivalist preacher whipping his congregation toward the ecstasy of fits.

"What a crowd, folks! What a crowd! There must be ten thousand excited, screaming fans outside Kahn's Persian tonight. The police can't hold them. Here, listen to them roar."

He held the microphone out and those near it obligingly roared for him.

"Did you hear it? It's a bedlam, folks. A veritable bedlam! What excitement! Of all the premières I've attended, this is the most . . . the most . . . stupendous, folks. Can the police hold them? Can they? It doesn't look so, folks . . ."

Another squad of police came charging up. The sergeant pleaded with the announcer to stand further back so the people couldn't hear him. His men threw themselves at the crowd. It allowed itself to be hustled and shoved out of habit and because it lacked an objective. It tolerated the police, just as a bull elephant does when he allows a small boy to drive him with a light stick.

Tod could see very few people who looked tough, nor could he see any working men. The crowd was made up of the lower middle classes, every other person one of his torchbearers.

Just as he came near the end of the lane, it closed in front of him with a heave, and he had to fight his way through. Someone knocked his hat off and when he stooped to pick it up, someone kicked him. He whirled around angrily and found himself surrounded by people who were laughing at him. He knew enough to laugh with them. The crowd became sympathetic. A stout woman slapped him on the back, while a man handed him his hat, first brushing it carefully with his sleeve. Still another man shouted for a way to be cleared.

By a great deal of pushing and squirming, always trying to look as though he were enjoying himself, Tod finally managed to break into the open. After rearranging his clothes, he went over to a parking lot and sat down on the low retaining wall that ran along the front of it.

New groups, whole families, kept arriving. He could see a change come over them as soon as they had become part of the crowd. Until they reached the line, they looked diffident, almost furtive, but the moment they had become part of it, they turned arrogant and pugnacious. It was a mistake to think them harmless curiosity seekers. They were savage and bitter, especially the middle-aged and the old, and had been made so by boredom and disappointment.

All their lives they had slaved at some kind of dull, heavy labor, behind desks and counters, in the fields and at tedious machines of all sorts, saving their pennies and dreaming of the leisure that would be theirs when they had enough. Finally that day came. They could draw a weekly income of ten or fifteen dollars. Where else should they go but California, the land of sunshine and oranges?

Once there, they discover that sunshine isn't enough. They get tired of oranges, even of avocado pears and passion fruit. Nothing happens. They don't know what to do with their time. They haven't the mental equipment for leisure, the money nor the physical equipment for pleasure. Did they slave so long just to go to an occasional Iowa picnic? What else is there? They watch the waves come in at Venice. There wasn't any ocean where most of them came from, but after you've seen one wave, you've seen them all. The same is true of the airplanes at Glendale. If only a plane would crash once in a while so that they could watch the passengers being consumed in a "holocaust of flame," as the newspapers put it. But the planes never crash.

Their boredom becomes more and more terrible. They realize that they've been tricked and burn with resentment. Every day of their lives they read the newspapers and went to the movies. Both fed them on lynchings, murder, sex crimes, explosions, wrecks, love nests, fires, miracles, revolutions, wars. This daily diet made sophisticates of them. The sun is a joke. Oranges can't titillate their jaded palates. Nothing can ever be violent enough to make taut their slack minds and bodies. They have been cheated and betrayed. They have slaved and saved for nothing.

Tod stood up. During the ten minutes he had been sitting on the wall, the crowd had grown thirty feet and he was afraid that his escape might be cut off if he loitered much longer. He crossed to the other side of the street and started back.

He was trying to figure what to do if he were unable to wake Homer when, suddenly he saw his head bobbing above the crowd. He hurried toward him. From his appearance, it was evident that there was something definitely wrong.

Homer walked more than ever like a badly made automaton and his features were set in a rigid, mechanical grin. He had his trousers on over his nightgown and part of it hung out of his open fly. In both of his hands were suitcases. With each step, he lurched to one side then the other, using the suitcases for balance weights.

Tod stopped directly in front of him, blocking his way.

"Where're you going?"

"Wayneville," he replied, using an extraordinary amount of jaw movement to get out this single word.

"That's fine. But you can't walk to the station from here. It's in Los Angeles."

Homer tried to get around him, but he caught his arm.

"We'll get a taxi. I'll go with you."

The cabs were all being routed around the block because of the preview. He explained this to Homer and tried to get him to walk to the corner.

"Come on, we're sure to get one on the next street."

Once Tod got him into a cab, he intended to tell the driver to go to the nearest hospital. But Homer wouldn't budge, no matter how hard he yanked and pleaded. People stopped to watch them, others turned their heads curiously. He decided to leave him and get a cab.

"I'll come right back," he said.

He couldn't tell from either Homer's eyes or expression whether he heard, for they both were empty of everything, even annoyance. At the corner he looked around and saw that Homer had started to cross the street, moving blindly. Brakes screeched and twice he was almost run over, but he didn't swerve or hurry. He moved in a straight diagonal. When he reached the other curb, he tried to get on the sidewalk at a point where the crowd was very thick and was shoved violently back. He made another attempt and this time a policeman grabbed him by the back of the neck and hustled him to the end of the line. When the policeman let go of him, he kept on walking as though nothing had happened.

Tod tried to get over to him, but was unable to cross until the traffic lights changed. When he reached the other side, he found Homer sitting on a bench, fifty or sixty feet from the outskirts of the crowd.

He put his arm around Homer's shoulder and suggested that they walk a few blocks further. When Homer didn't answer, he reached over to pick up one of the valises. Homer held on to it.

"I'll carry it for you," he said, tugging gently.

"Thief!"

Before Homer could repeat the shout, he jumped away. It would be extremely embarrassing if Homer shouted thief in front of a cop. He thought of phoning for an ambulance. But then, after all, how could he be sure that Homer was crazy? He was sitting quietly on the bench, minding his own business.

Tod decided to wait, then try again to get him into a cab. The crowd was growing in size all the time, but it would be at least half an hour before it over-ran the bench. Before that happened, he would think of some plan. He moved a short distance away and stood with his back to a store window so that he could watch Homer without attracting attention.

About ten feet from where Homer was sitting grew a large eucalyptus tree and behind the trunk of the tree was a little boy. Tod saw him peer around it with great caution, then suddenly jerk his head back. A minute later he repeated the maneuver. At first Tod thought he was playing hide and seek, then noticed that he had a string in his hand which was attached to an old purse that lay in front of Homer's bench. Every once in a while the child would jerk the string, making the purse hop like a sluggish toad. Its torn lining hung from its iron mouth like a furry tongue and a few uncertain flies hovered over it.

Tod knew the game the child was playing. He used to play it himself when he was small. If Homer reached to pick up the purse, thinking there was money in it, he would yank it away and scream with laughter.

When Tod went over to the tree, he was surprised to discover that it was Adore Loomis, the kid who lived across the street from Homer. Tod tried to chase him, but he dodged around the tree, thumbing his nose. He gave up and went back to his original position. The moment he left, Adore got busy with his purse again. Homer wasn't paying any attention to the child, so Tod decided to let him alone.

Mrs. Loomis must be somewhere in the crowd, he thought. Tonight when she found Adore, she would give him a hiding. He had torn the pocket of his jacket and his Buster Brown collar was smeared with grease.

Adore had a nasty temper. The completeness with which Homer ignored both him and his pocketbook made him frantic. He gave up dancing

it at the end of the string and approached the bench on tiptoes, making ferocious faces, yet ready to run at Homer's first move. He stopped when about four feet away and stuck his tongue out. Homer ignored him. He took another step forward and ran through a series of insulting gestures.

If Tod had known that the boy held a stone in his hand, he would have interfered. But he felt sure that Homer wouldn't hurt the child and was waiting to see if he wouldn't move because of his pestering. When Adore raised his arm, it was too late. The stone hit Homer in the face. The boy turned to flee, but tripped and fell. Before he could scramble away, Homer landed on his back with both feet, then jumped again.

Tod yelled for him to stop and tried to yank him away. He shoved Tod and went on using his heels. Tod hit him as hard as he could, first in the belly, then in the face. He ignored the blows and continued to stamp on the boy. Tod hit him again and again, then threw both arms around him and tried to pull him off. He couldn't budge him. He was like a stone column.

The next thing Tod knew, he was torn loose from Homer and sent to his knees by a blow in the back of the head that spun him sideways. The crowd in front of the theatre had charged. He was surrounded by churning legs and feet. He pulled himself erect by grabbing a man's coat then let himself be carried along backwards in a long, curving swoop. He saw Homer rise above the mass for a moment, shoved against the sky, his jaw hanging as though he wanted to scream but couldn't. A hand reached up and caught him by his open mouth and pulled him forward and down.

There was another dizzy rush. Tod closed his eyes and fought to keep upright. He was jostled about in a hacking cross surf of shoulders and backs, carried rapidly in one direction and then in the opposite. He kept pushing and hitting out at the people around him, trying to face in the direction he was going. Being carried backwards terrified him.

Using the eucalyptus tree as a landmark, he tried to work toward it by slipping sideways against the tide, pushing hard when carried away from it and riding the current when it moved toward his objective. He was within only a few feet of the tree when a sudden, driving rush carried him far past it. He struggled desperately for a moment, then gave up and let himself be swept along. He was the spearhead of a flying wedge when it collided with a mass going in the opposite direction. The impact turned him around. As the two forces ground against each other, he was turned again and again, like a grain between millstones. This didn't stop until he became part of the opposing force. The pressure continued to increase until he thought he must collapse. He was slowly being pushed into the air. Although relief for his cracking ribs could be gotten by continuing to rise, he fought to keep his feet on the ground. Not being able to touch was an even more dreadful sensation than being carried backwards.

There was another rush, shorter this time, and he found himself in a dead spot where the pressure was less and equal. He became conscious of a terrible pain in his left leg, just above the ankle, and tried to work it into a more comfortable position. He couldn't turn his body, but managed to get his head around. A very skinny boy, wearing a Western Union cap, had his back wedged against his shoulder. The pain continued to grow and his whole leg as high as the groin throbbed. He finally got his left arm free and took the back of the boy's neck in his fingers. He twisted as hard as he could. The boy began to jump up and down in his clothes. He managed to straighten his elbow, by pushing at the back of the boy's head, and to turn halfway around and free his leg. The pain didn't grow less.

There was another wild surge forward that ended in another dead spot. He now faced a young girl who was sobbing steadily. Her silk print dress had been torn down the front and her tiny brassiere hung from one strap. He tried by pressing back to give her room, but she moved with him every time he moved. Now and then, she would jerk violently and he wondered if she was going to have a fit. One of her thighs was between his legs. He struggled to get free of her, but she clung to him, moving with him and pressing against him.

She turned her head and said, "Stop, stop," to someone behind her.

He saw what the trouble was. An old man, wearing a Panama hat and horn-rimmed glasses, was hugging her. He had one of his hands inside her dress and was biting her neck.

Tod freed his right arm with a heave, reached over the girl and brought his fist down on the man's head. He couldn't hit very hard but managed to knock the man's hat off, also his glasses. The man tried to bury his face in the girl's shoulder, but Tod grabbed one of his ears and yanked. They started to move again. Tod held on

to the ear as long as he could hoping that it would come away in his hand. The girl managed to twist under his arm. A piece of her dress tore, but she was free of her attacker.

Another spasm passed through the mob and he was carried toward the curb. He fought toward a lamp-post, but he was swept by before he could grasp it. He saw another man catch the girl with the torn dress. She screamed for help. He tried to get to her, but was carried in the opposite direction. This rush also ended in a dead spot. Here his neighbors were all shorter than he was. He turned his head upward toward the sky and tried to pull some fresh air into his aching lungs, but it was all heavily tainted with sweat.

In this part of the mob no one was hysterical. In fact, most of the people seemed to be enjoying themselves. Near him was a stout woman with a man pressing hard against her from in front. His chin was on her shoulder, and his arms were around her. She paid no attention to him and went on talking to the woman at her side.

"The first thing I knew," Tod heard her say, "there was a rush and I was in the middle."

"Yeah. Somebody hollered, 'Here comes Gary Cooper,' and then wham!"

"That ain't it," said a little man wearing a cloth cap and pullover sweater. "This is a riot you're in."

"Yeah," said a third woman, whose snaky gray hair was hanging over her face and shoulders. "A pervert attacked a child."

"He ought to be lynched."

Everybody agreed vehemently.

"I come from St. Louis," announced the stout woman, "and we had one of them pervert fellers in our neighborhood once. He ripped up a girl with a pair of scissors."

"He must have been crazy," said the man in the cap. "What kind of fun is that?"

Everybody laughed. The stout woman spoke to the man who was hugging her.

"Hey, you," she said. "I ain't no pillow."

The man smiled beatifically but didn't move. She laughed, making no effort to get out of his embrace.

"A fresh guy," she said.

The other woman laughed.

"Yeah," she said, "this is a regular free-for-all."

The man in the cap and sweater thought there was another laugh in his comment about the pervert.

"Ripping up a girl with scissors. That's the wrong tool."

He was right. They laughed even louder than the first time.

"You'd a done it different, eh, kid?" said a young man with a kidney-shaped head and waxed mustaches.

The two women laughed. This encouraged the man in the cap and he reached over and pinched the stout woman's friend. She squealed.

"Lay off that," she said good-naturedly.

"I was shoved," he said.

An ambulance siren screamed in the street. Its wailing moan started the crowd moving again and Tod was carried along in a slow, steady push. He closed his eyes and tried to protect his throbbing leg. This time, when the movement ended, he found himself with his back to the theatre wall. He kept his eyes closed and stood on his good leg. After what seemed like hours, the pack began to loosen and move again with a churning motion. It gathered momentum and rushed. He rode it until he was slammed against the base of an iron rail which fenced the driveway of the theatre from the street. He had the wind knocked out of him by the impact, but managed to cling to the rail. He held on desperately, fighting to keep from being sucked back. A woman caught him around the waist and tried to hang on. She was sobbing rhythmically. Tod felt his fingers slipping from the rail and kicked backwards as hard as he could. The woman let go.

Despite the agony in his leg, he was able to think clearly about his picture, "The Burning of Los Angeles." After his quarrel with Faye, he had worked on it continually to escape tormenting himself, and the way to it in his mind had become almost automatic.

As he stood on his good leg, clinging desperately to the iron rail, he could see all the rough charcoal strokes with which he had blocked it out on the big canvas. Across the top, parallel with the frame, he had drawn the burning city, a great bonfire of architectural styles, ranging from Egyptian to Cape Cod colonial. Through the center, winding from left to right, was a long hill street and down it, spilling into the middle foreground, came the mob carrying baseball bats and torches. For the faces of its members, he was using the innumerable sketches he had made of the people who come to California to die; the cultists of all sorts, economic as well as religious, the wave, airplane, funeral and preview watchers—all those poor devils who can only be stirred by the promise of miracles and then only to violence. A super "Dr. Know-All Pierce-All" had

made the necessary promise and they were marching behind his banner in a great united front of screwballs and screwboxes to purify the land. No longer bored, they sang and danced joyously in the red light of the flames.

In the lower foreground, men and women fled wildly before the vanguard of the crusading mob. Among them were Faye, Harry, Homer, Claude and himself. Faye ran proudly, throwing her knees high. Harry stumbled along behind her, holding on to his beloved derby hat with both hands. Homer seemed to be falling out of the canvas, his face half-asleep, his big hands clawing the air in anguished pantomime. Claude turned his head as he ran to thumb his nose at his pursuers. Tod himself picked up a small stone to throw before continuing his flight.

He had almost forgotten both his leg and his predicament, and to make his escape still more complete he stood on a chair and worked at the flames in an upper corner of the canvas, modeling the tongues of fire so that they licked even more avidly at a corinthian column that held up the palmleaf roof of a nutburger stand.

He had finished one flame and was starting on another when he was brought back by someone shouting in his ear. He opened his eyes and saw a policeman trying to reach him from behind the rail to which he was clinging. He let go with his left hand and raised his arm. The policeman caught him by the wrist, but couldn't lift him. Tod was afraid to let go until another man came to aid the policeman and caught him by the back of his jacket. He let go of the rail and they hauled him up and over it.

When they saw that he couldn't stand, they let him down easily to the ground. He was in the theatre driveway. On the curb next to him sat a woman crying into her skirt. Along the wall were groups of other disheveled people. At the end of the driveway was an ambulance. A policeman asked him if he wanted to go to the hospital. He shook his head no. He then offered him a lift home. Tod had the presence of mind to give Claude's address.

He was carried through the exit to the back street and lifted into a police car. The siren began to scream and at first he thought he was making the noise himself. He felt his lips with his hands. They were clamped tight. He knew then it was the siren. For some reason this made him laugh and he began to imitate the siren as loud as he could.

JOHN O'HARA (1905-1970)

John O'Hara is another name on the long list of American writers whose fictional methods have been closely allied to the arts of journalism —arts, in O'Hara's case, which he practiced for some years in his native region of eastern Pennsylvania and in New York City. Like other figures on that list, O'Hara always showed in his creative work a passion for factual precision not only in recording manners and speech, but in describing accouterments of life, no matter how trivial. If one should want to know the make and model of car favored by a rich young blade in the 1920's, the spiffiest speakeasy in Manhattan, or the most elegant bootmaker in London, he may well begin his search in the pages of O'Hara.

O'Hara was also a remarkably prolific writer. His first novel, *Appointment in Samarra* (1934), immediately marked him as a figure of great literary promise. To many readers the novel seemed to sum up one phase of the thirties (the more affluent phase) in the same way, though with less artistic power, that Hemingway's *The Sun Also Rises* had summed up an important part of the twenties. In the next thirty-five years O'Hara produced no less than eleven novels and ten volumes of short stories, with the highly successful musical comedy *Pal Joey* being derived by him from the volume of that name.

Anyone who writes as much as that is bound to come in for a certain amount of condescension in some critical quarters, and O'Hara sometimes found himself dismissed as one who wrote much too easily and quickly, and who did no more than describe the life style of the "emancipated speakeasy set." Such a judgment involves, to begin with, questionable aesthetics —as if one could damn a writer merely because he wrote rapidly or because of the material he used, without any regard for the quality of what he produced. It also misapprehends the motive behind O'Hara's productivity—his professional dedication to his métier, his conviction that it

is the business of a writer of fiction to keep writing and to write as well as he can. And finally it simply overlooks what should be obvious to any discerning reader—O'Hara's very real talents as a literary craftsman and observer of his chosen world.

O'Hara's material does include the speakeasy and the nightclub set, though with an accuracy and perception not suggested by the disparaging formula quoted above. Nelson Algren has remarked that O'Hara was "one of the few people who are really in touch with what a bartender does when he goes broke . . . with the aging woman who comes in and sits on a barstool and expresses her loneliness one way or another." (O'Hara's compassionate understanding of loneliness, as in the story we have selected, is one of his finest traits.) But O'Hara is by no means limited to that scene. In his own special way, he can even be regarded as a sort of regionalist. He knew—none better—the eastern end of Pennsylvania, especially the area around Pottsville, the "Gibbsville" of his fiction. Many readers would argue that his best novels and stories have their setting in what has become known as the "O'Hara country" (and again, it is no small achievement to have brought a region so fully to life that it is named after one). And here, too, there is a wide variety in the types treated —small-town lawyers, hardware merchants, city politicians, and Pennsylvania housewives, to name a few.

A great deal of his best-known fiction, however, does have its setting quite outside the O'Hara country, and depicts what may be called, for want of a better term, the region that lies along the Broadway-Hollywood axis. The characters range from aging movie stars to burnt-out newspaper feature writers; from playgirls to junior executives living with their wives in Westchester County or the more fashionable parts of Long Island.

As an ironic commentator on these strata of

American society, O'Hara is quite often superb. When the American Academy of Arts and Letters in 1964 presented him with its Award of Merit for achievement in the novel, the citation included the observation that his "ear for the American language in dialogue is unsurpassed." And to match his ear for conversation, he had a keen eye for nuances of manners and behavior. O'Hara's very expertness as a reporter sometimes caused him to be undervalued. He was, in fact, far more than a reporter accepting uncritically what he describes and was obviously interested in something far deeper than the mere surfaces. He was interested in human beings and concerned with what makes them human. He was, too, an ironist, and his ironies were based on the contrast between the mere surfaces he so scrupulously reported and the inner life of the characters involved.

It is when one comes to question the *basis* of O'Hara's interest, his final attitude toward his characters and reality itself, that the author suffers to some extent by comparison with others we have considered in this section.

Unlike Fitzgerald and Hemingway, whom he much admired, O'Hara lacked a fundamental and controlling vision to give depth and imaginative resonance to his account of the human predicament.

Not infrequently, however, O'Hara may provide a sense of the pathos and even the tragedy of existence. In "The Bonfire," for instance, his attitude toward a young widow's attempt to re-enter life after her husband's death is richly complex and profoundly moving. In the culminating scene of the story the woman, still young, still in love with life, has put her young children to bed and steps out on the beach. She hears the laughter and singing going on around a bonfire that has been lighted further down the beach. She is sure that she knows some of the people, some not much younger than herself. The bonfire attracts her out of the darkness to its light and warmth. Yet what appears to her ears as the "harsh and frightening chorus of . . . baritone derision and alto contempt and soprano coquetry" repels her and "she [runs] all the way home." In a passage like this, O'Hara finds an imaginative language and a beautifully conclusive resolving figure with which to gather up the meaning of his story.

FURTHER READINGS

John O'Hara, *Appointment in Samarra* (1934)
————, *Butterfield 8* (1935)
————, *The Ewings* (1972)
————, *From the Terrace* (1958)
————, *The Lockwood Concern* (1965)
————, *Sermons and Soda-Water* (1960)
————, *Ten North Frederick* (1955)
————, *The Time Element and Other Stories* (1972)

John Peale Bishop, "The Missing All," *Virginia Quarterly Review* (January, 1937)

E. Russell Carson, *The Fiction of John O'Hara* (1961)
Sheldon N. Grebstein, *John O'Hara* (1966)
Alfred Kazin, *On Native Grounds* (1942)
Arthur Mizener, "Afterword," in *Appointment in Samarra* (1963)
Lionel Trilling, "Introduction," to *Selected Short Stories of John O'Hara* (1956)
Charles C. Walcutt, *John O'Hara* (1969)

The Bonfire (1952)

Kitty Bull said the final goodnights to the children, the final "no, no more stories" to the older two and paid a silent visit to the baby's room (for she firmly believed that a one-year-old can sense a break in his routine even when he is asleep). The cook and the maid were at the early movie in Southampton. The Bannings and their guests—a noisy cocktail party—had taken off for a dinner party in Wainscott, leaving all the lights on in the house next door but leaving, too, a merciful silence. The ocean was reasonably subdued, pounding the beach at long intervals and with only enough force to keep you from forgetting that it was there, that it had been angry most of the day and could be angry again.

She kicked off her Belgian slippers and went out and stood on the top of the dune. There was still enough light for a visibility of five miles, three miles, six miles. Make it three miles. It was about three miles to the Inlet, and she could see two white dots that would be fishing boats heading for the Inlet in a race against the coming darkness. The sand squishing through her toes made her wish she could run down and go for a brief swim, but she could not leave the house so soon. This was the first half hour, when Jeanie might be naughty and find some excuse to call her. She would pay no attention to the first call, and Jeanie might give up; but sometimes Jeanie would be insistent and repeat her call, louder and often, and disturb the other children.

She thanked God for the children. She thanked God . . .

Now she could not see the white dots and she would have to suppose that the fishing boats had got inside the Inlet. The visibility, whatever it had been, was now to be estimated in yards, not miles, and far far out, where the horizon had been, there were three twinkling lights, the riding lights of three other fishing boats that she had not seen before. They would be out there all night and if she got up early enough—five o'clock in the morning—they would still be there, but at six o'clock they would be gone. They were professional fishing boats, bunker boats that filled their nets, loaded up, and returned to Islip or to Baltimore with catches that would be converted into some kind of fertilizer. That, at least, was what Jerry had told her five years ago. Five years ago. Six years ago. *Seven* years ago, when they had first come to this house. Could it be seven years? Almost a fifth of her life? One wave, heavier than all the others had been, struck the beach like thunder and she picked up her slippers and went inside.

In her bare feet she went upstairs and stood outside the children's rooms and listened. There was not a sound from them. She opened the door of the baby's room. She could not see him, but when she caught the rhythm of his breathing she closed the door and went downstairs again. The first half hour was more than gone, and for a moment she thought of going for a swim; but that was something she had promised Jerry never to do. Never go in that ocean alone, but especially at night. He had never permitted her to go in alone at night even when he was there in the house, watching a ball game on the TV. It isn't a question of how good a swimmer you are, or of keeping your head, he had told her. Naturally you would have sense enough to conserve your energy, and try to keep the lights of the beach cottages in front of you. But who could see *you* in the dark? Never go in alone at night, he had said; and then one night a year ago, a little tight and just arrived from the hot city, he had broken all his own rules. He had stopped for dinner at Rothman's on the way down, and you did not stop at Rothman's if you were alone, but she guessed whom he had dined with. It was not a clever guess. It was not a guess at all. It was an assumption based as much on instinct as on the things she had heard. "I feel as if I'd been dipped in oatmeal," he had said.

"You've been dipping in something stronger than oatmeal," she said.

"A few. Not enough to do any damage. I'm going for a swim."

"I can't go for a swim. Dr. Mando said not to for a while."

"That's all right. I just want to dunk."

"Why don't you just take a shower?"

"Because I want to go in the ocean! My God, Kitty."

"Well, you're always the one that says—"

"I'm *not* planning to swim to *Brazil*. If you're going to make a federal case of it, I won't go in. But my God, Kitty."

"Oh, go ahead," she said.

She could have stopped him. For a year she had told herself that she could have stopped him, and many times during the second half of that year she had wondered why she had not stopped him. She had given in to him and to his irritability and his stubbornness, but had there not been some irritability, some jealousy, on her part? Four days later they found his body near the Inlet, confirming his identity through his dental history, an X-ray photograph of a shoulder he had broken in college, and physical measurements that matched his in the Navy files. It was he, all right, beyond any reasonable doubt, and it was not necessary for her to look at him. His mother and father had been perfectly wonderful, and so had his brother. The only unpleasantness had been created by his sister, when he had been dead six months.

"You don't mind talking about Jerry, do you, Kitty?" said Edna.

"Not a bit. Why?"

"Well, because he was always against going in the ocean at night. It was so *unlike* him."

"Your father brought that up. Your mother did too."

"I know they did, and you tried to stop him. I know that, too. But can you think of any reason why Jerry would do such a complete about-face? I mean, he was my brother and we were very close."

"I know."

"I adored him. I really did."

"I know you did, Edna."

"But I wasn't blinded to his imperfections," said Edna.

"He had a few. Who hasn't?"

"Yes, who hasn't? Francine Barrow, for instance. You know what she's saying, of course."

"Yes, I do. But I didn't expect you to repeat anything Francine Barrow said. Jerry didn't commit suicide over Francine Barrow. He didn't commit suicide over anyone or anything. He was quite tight that night."

"You might have thought the cold water would have sobered him up."

"It doesn't always work that way. In fact, almost never. Haven't you ever been to a beach party where there was a lot of drinking? I haven't noticed that going in the ocean sobered them up. Quite the contrary, in some cases. I remember one night when you were tight and you went in and came out without your bikini."

"I've never been allowed to forget that," said Edna.

"Well, I only bring it up now to show that cold salt water doesn't necessarily sober you up. Jerry himself said you were really bagged that night. And you were."

"I'm perfectly willing to change the subject, if that's what you want to do, Kitty."

"No, I'd rather have this out. I knew about Francine. It started the last few months I was having the baby, and it continued for the same reason after the baby was born."

"Did you quarrel with him about it?"

"We had some minor quarrels, not over Francine. Although I suppose that was at the bottom of it. I didn't like it. You wouldn't like it if Mike slept with someone else while you were in the midst of having a baby. My first two pregnancies were fairly simple, but not this one. I was having a hard time, and Jerry wasn't much help to my morale. I've always thought Francine was one of the worst tramps on Long Island anyway."

"So do I, for that matter."

"Well then why do you help her spread that story? Jerry did not commit suicide. I would have known if he'd had any such intentions. The only reason he came down that night was because he was playing in a tournament at the National the next day. That was on his mind, not committing suicide."

"All right, Kitty. I'm sorry I had to bring this up, but I had to."

"Yes I suppose you did," said Kitty, and the weariness in her voice surprised her. Acute grief had gone and now there was weariness that she had not suspected, and it remained with her for many months. It was much worse than the acute grief. The doctor had told her that she need not worry about having the strength to recover from her pregnancy and take care of the children. Nature is very reliable, he had said; when something like that happened to you, a shock, a dramatic episode, Nature responded. But when the acute grief began to wear off and the postponed weariness set in, that was the time to be careful. She went to see him, and because he was a good man she told him about her sister-in-law's conversation.

"I was afraid there'd be something like that," he said. "She hit you with it at just the wrong time. I'm going to send you up to the hospital for a G.I. series."

"Is that the barium thing? I haven't got an ulcer."

"Let's make sure," said the doctor.

She saw him again in a few days. "Now you can be glad I made you swallow all the barium," he said. "There's no sign of an ulcer."

"I knew there wouldn't be," she said.

"Did you indeed?" he said. He smiled.

"Well, I was right, wasn't I?" she said.

"Gloating, hey?" He had a pencil in his hand and he began sketching on a prescription blank.

"Now what, Dr. Mando? I always know there's something when you start drawing those little pictures. Are they my insides that you're drawing, or just anyone's?"

"You're pretty fresh. I think you're greatly relieved at my good news."

"Well, why shouldn't I be? I'd *hate* to have an ulcer. But come on, Doctor, what's on your mind?"

"*You* are, Mrs. Bull. Four cigarettes just since you've been here. I'm sure your internist has spoken to you about them. I *know* he has, because we had a conversation this morning. He had the first look at your X-ray pictures, you know."

"Yes, you two keep me up in the air like a shuttlecock."

"Badminton," said the doctor.

"Don't tell me I'm not going to be able to play games."

"No, that isn't what's on my mind. You can start swimming any time you feel like it, and golf or tennis, if you're planning to go South."

"I'm staying in New York, but there are places where I can swim and play squash."

"Exercise will be good for you. Dr. Randolph will tell you that, too."

"Fine, and now you tell me what's got you drawing those pictures."

He put down his pencil and sat back in his chair, his hands folded across his chest and reminding her of a spiritual adviser. "Is there any chance that you might be getting married fairly soon?"

"No," she said. "Is there any reason why I shouldn't?"

"On the contrary, there is every reason why you should, from my point of view."

"I haven't thought about it, at least not very much. And there's no man in the offing. Some day I suppose I will. Some day my prince will come." Suddenly, inexplicably, the sound of her words made her burst into tears. The doctor bent forward and gave her one of his large, hand-rolled handkerchiefs.

"Good Lord," she said. She dried her eyes and blew her nose.

"Mm-hmm," the doctor muttered.

"May I keep the handkerchief? I'll send it back to you," she said.

"Of course," said the doctor. He opened his desk drawer and took out a silver cigarette box. "I keep these out of sight nowadays. Have one?"

"Thanks," she said. He lit it for her. "I remember that lighter," she said.

"Yes, it's quite a beautiful piece of workmanship," he said. He looked at it and put it back in his pocket, and resumed his clerical attitude.

"It was the words of that song," she said.

"Yes, but it wasn't only the words of the song, Mrs. Bull. You know that."

"I do now. I hadn't realized that I was in any such state. But I guess I am, aren't I?"

"Be very strange if you weren't. I've known you pretty well these last six or seven years."

"Well, what do you suggest?" she said.

"I suggest that you start going out a little bit."

"In the hope of meeting some man," she said.

"Naturally."

"And having an affair with him, even if I don't fall in love with him?"

"You may have to wait a long time before you'll admit that you're in love with anyone."

"Yes, you're right," she said.

"In fact, you could conceivably go through the rest of your life without falling in love again."

"Yes," she said.

"Your husband left you three children, and the circumstances of his death. No other man will be able to make that deep an impression on you. On your life. On your memories. So don't expect anyone to."

"You didn't like my husband, did you, Dr. Mando?"

"That's not a very nice question to ask me, young woman. And I'm not going to answer it. But if he were my own son I'd still give you the same advice. You're in your early thirties and most of your life lies ahead of you. That includes having children, if you want any more. And you should, or these nice children you have now will become something that they shouldn't."

"What's that?"

"Walking reminder of your husband, of course. Making it impossible for you to start your new life. I hope you'll meet an interesting man and marry him and have children right away."

"I don't think that's going to happen," she said.

"It won't if you don't give it a chance," said the doctor. "Well, when do you want to see me again?"

"When do *you* want to see *me*?"

"In about three months. Miss Murphy will give you an appointment."

"Not till then? That's the longest I've ever gone without seeing you. Aren't you going to miss me?"

He smiled. "Yes, as a matter of fact I will. But it'll do you good to stay out of here for a while. Save you money too."

"You're such a lovely man, Dr. Mando. You really are," she said.

"Of course I am," he said. "My patients are nice, too. Some of them."

"Me?"

"Go on, young woman. There are women waiting," he said. "And I have to clean out this ash tray."

There was no "interesting" man at any of the small dinner parties she went to. Among the new men there were the pitiers, depressing fellows who acted as though Jerry had died last week; there were the others who were so determinedly cheerful that they seemed to deny that Jerry had ever lived at all. Among the men she had known in the past there were the instant patriarchs, contemporaries of Jerry's who took it upon themselves to plan her life for her; and, not surprisingly, there were two who were ready to move into her life. One of them was a dirty talker, who had never talked dirty to her while Jerry was alive; and the other was Edna's husband, Mike, who had always looked at her from the edges of groups with a dumb lechery that he now expressed in terms of love. "I think you've always known how I felt about you, Kitty," he said.

"Not exactly," she said. It was malicious, drawing him out, but she had not forgiven Edna for her inquisition.

"Maybe not exactly, but you must have had some idea," said Mike.

"Some idea, more or less," she said.

"Invite me to dinner some night. Just me."

"Without Edna?"

"That's the general idea," he said. "I suppose you're going to say that's impossible, but it isn't."

"But it is. If I invited you alone, there could only be one interpretation of that. There isn't any other interpretation."

"Oh, I see. You mean that you'd be the aggressor?"

"Not only the aggressor, but—well, yes, the aggressor. The troublemaker."

"Would you go away with me? If we went in my car, I'd be the aggressor, if that's what you object to. What I'm trying to tell you is—we've gotten sidetracked with this aggressor talk. I want you to see me without Edna, without anyone. To get used to me. And if I can convince you—to marry me."

"Oh."

"I know you're not all that anxious to get married again so soon. But it would take time in any case. Unfortunately people don't just say 'I've had it' and end a marriage that way. But I've been in love with you for a long time. We would have had this conversation sooner or later, even if Jerry had lived."

"I wonder," she said.

"You needn't. He kept you pregnant most of the time or I'd have spoken up sooner."

"That was very considerate of you, Mike."

"Is that sarcasm?"

"Not at all," she said.

"The week after next I'm going to Pinehurst. Come with me. I'm taking my car because it's more convenient. I'm making stops on the way down and then circling back through West Virginia, Ohio, and Pennsylvania. I'll be in Pinehurst for three days, a business convention, and you probably wouldn't want to do that, but you could join me when the convention's over, and we could have the better part of a week together. The most I'd have to spend with my business acquaintances would be two or three hours a day, and you like to read. What do you say?"

"Oh, you know what I'm going to say, Mike. How could I nip off for a week, leaving three small children and telling the nurse that I'd be at such-and-such a motel?"

"You're so practical," he said. "What if I sent Edna away, that is, gave her a trip abroad?"

"I don't know. Yes, I do know. I think that when I'm ready to do anything in that department, I *am* going to have to be the aggressor. I'm the only one that will know when I'm ready—and I'm not ready now."

"That Jerry. He's still got a tight grip on you, hasn't he?"

"Or I have a tight grip on myself. One or the other, or maybe both."

"When you loosen up a little, will you let me know? I'm serious. You can trust me, you know."

"You mean if I just wanted to have sex?"

"Yes. Don't you ever want sex? You've had a lot of it. With Jerry, I mean."

"And for seven years with no one else. So, when the time comes—I'm awfully tired of the word—but I'll be the aggressor. I much prefer 'on the make.'"

"You'll never go on the make, Kitty."

"Except that I did with Jerry. I wanted him, I went after him, and I got him. And I've lost him."

She would have been more abrupt and far more cruel with Mike if she had not realized, midway in the conversation, that the conversation was useful to the clarification of her problems. Mike was in no sense a stimulating man, but he had helped her to see that the next man in her life would have to be one she chose. Whimsically she told herself that she owed something to Mike for his collaboration, and in that mood she thought of inviting him to spend a night with her. But he was a clod and he would be around again and again, believing himself to be in love with her and upsetting the lives of too many people. Nevertheless she felt better for having come even that remotely close. Very tentatively, a toe in the water, she was back in life once more.

It was enough to go on for a while, and there were other things to keep her busy. At home there were the children, uncomprehending of the mystery of death or, in the case of the baby, petulantly demanding that she keep him alive. The older two were forgetting about their father. Kitty put a cabinet-size photograph of Jerry in a silver frame and set it on a table in the livingroom of the New York apartment. It was two days before Jeanie noticed it. She stood in front of the picture for a moment, and Kitty waited for her comment.

"That's Daddy," said Jeanie.

"Yes. It's my favorite picture of him. Do you like it?"

"I guess so."

"But not very much," said Kitty. "What is there that you don't like about it?"

"He's so serious, Mum."

"And that's not the way you remember him? Well, that's because when he was with you and your little brothers he *wasn't* very serious. Nearly always laughing. Little jokes and so forth."

"Didn't he have jokes with you too?"

"Oh, yes. Lots of them."

"Tell me one," said the child.

"A joke that he told me? Well, let me think. A joke that he told me. There was one that Grandfather Bull told him. About an oyster?"

"Tell it to me."

"It's sort of a riddle. What kind of a noise annoys an oyster? Do you know the answer?"

"What?"

"A *noisy* noise annoys an oyster."

"Oh, that's old."

"It sure is. See if I can think of another. Most of his jokes with me were about people. I'll think of some and write them down so I won't forget them. And I'll see if I can find a picture of him smiling. Where shall we put it, if I find one?"

"I don't know. Over there, I guess. Mummy, can I watch TV after supper?"

"Nope. Before supper, yes. After supper, off it goes."

The older boy, Timothy, was only three, cheerful and strong and increasingly able to take his own part when his sister bullied him. The Irish nurse would say to him, "You're the man of the house, Timothy."

"I yam not a man. I'm a boy, silly."

"You'll be a man soon enough, then."

"You're silly, Margaret. You're silly, silly, silly. You think a boy is a man. *You're* a man. You have a moustache."

"For that somebody gets no pudding this supper."

"It isn't pudding, it's junket, and I hate junket. So yah!"

And there was the baby, now old enough to follow her with his eyes when he was serene and to scream for her and only for her when he was not.

There was more money than she had expected, and many more lawyers to see. There were certain financial advantages to be gained by a delay in settling Jerry's estate. "This could drag on for another year at least," said her lawyer. "But we want it to. Now for instance, Mrs. Bull, there's the matter of your husband's insurance. He carried a lot of insurance, much more than young men usually do nowadays. But he could afford it, so he did. The interesting thing here is that we've been arguing with the insurance company about the circumstances of your husband's death. We feel that accidental drowning may change the picture to your advantage. On the other hand *they* feel—I have to say this—that the possibility of suicide alters the picture in their favor. The medical examiner's report said accidental death by drowning, but the insurance company is trying to inject the element of suicide, not because they think they can get away with it, but maybe in the hope that we won't collect anything extra, like double indemnity. Give and take, you know. That's their position. But they know perfectly well that we're prepared to go to court. And by prepared I mean that you have enough money without insurance to not have to make a quick settlement. By the way, who is a Mrs. Barrow? Francine Barrow? She wasn't at your house the night your husband lost his life, was she?"

"No. She was a friend of his. And mine, I suppose. My husband had dinner with her early that evening, over on the North Shore. But she wasn't in our house. She's never been in our house."

"No, I shouldn't think so. In a very roundabout way we found out that the insurance company is basing its whole argument on some story of hers."

"Well, she's a congenital liar, among other things."

"That's a good thing to know," said Mr. Hastings. "You understand, Mrs. Bull, that if we collect a large amount of insurance, it'll go a long way toward paying your inheritance taxes. In fact we may come out a little ahead of the game. You'd have no objection to suing the insurance company, I hope?"

"None whatever," said Kitty. "Especially if Mrs. Barrow is on their side."

"When Mrs. Barrow understands a little better what could happen to her in court, she may not want to testify. I know if I were her lawyer I'd tell her to think twice."

"She doesn't embarrass very easily, Mr. Hastings. In plain language, she's a tramp."

"It's a curious thing, though, Mrs. Bull. There's something about a courtroom. The austerity of the furniture. The flag. The judge's robe. The strange language. It produces an atmosphere that's the next thing to a church, and it's intended to. And a woman like this Mrs. Barrow, although she may be shameless in her everyday life, when she gets in court a remarkable change comes over her. They fight like the devil to stay respectable. The insurance companies have very good lawyers. None better. And I seriously doubt that they'd want her to testify. In short, Mrs. Bull, her lawyer will advise her to shut up, and the insurance lawyers won't want her. But I have to give you the whole picture, to explain why we're moving so slowly."

"I'm in no hurry," said Kitty.

"That's good, that's fine. I'm sorry you have to come down here so often. I could save you some of these trips. There's probably a notary public in your neighborhood."

"I like coming down here. It's almost that same atmosphere you just described, the courtroom. And it makes me feel useful, as though I were doing it for my children. Although I'm not."

"Yes you are," said Mr. Hastings.

"Well, maybe I am," she said. "But doing things for them is the same as doing them for myself. It's what I like."

She put on a sweater and went out again and sat on the top of a dune. There were stars but no moon and down the beach at someone's cottage—she was not sure whose—there was a sizable bonfire and moving about it, like comical figures in some pagan rite, were the members of a beach picnic. They were too far away to be recognizable, even to be distinguishable as to sex. It seemed to be a fairly good-sized party and she was glad that the noise they would make was no closer to her house. It was a party of the young, that much she could determine by their frenetic activity. A great deal of running about, chasing, and, as she watched, two of the figures picked up a third figure by the hands

and feet and carried it to the ocean and dropped it in. This might go on all night. It was at the McDades', the only cottage in that section that would be having that kind of party for the young.

The young. *She* was young. She had been a young wife, she was a young widow, and people like Dr. Mando continually called her "young woman." She would still be young, really, when those children now asleep in her cottage would be having beach picnics like the McDades'. She was old to them now, as a parent is old to all young children; but to Jerry's father and mother she was so young that they had worried about her ability to cope. She was too young to have been invited to any of the Bannings' noisy parties. She was only four or five years older than some of the members of the McDade picnic. Angus McDade was twenty-six, George Lasswell was twenty-six or seven. Harry Stephenson had been one of Jerry's favorite golfing companions. They would all be at the McDades' picnic.

Something got her to her feet, and she knew what it was. She denied it angrily, then admitted it so that she could dismiss it. It was a word that had first come up in her conversation with Mike, and the word had stayed with her. Aggressor. Well, she was not quite being an aggressor if she was being drawn to the beach bonfire like a moth to a flame. They would be nice to her, they would offer her food and drink, and they would admire her in the ways that she was used to being admired. She would sit with them and drink beer out of a can and smoke a cigarette and in a little while they would start singing and she would sing with them. She would only stay a little while.

She kicked off her slippers. It would make her seem more like one of them if she arrived in her bare feet. She walked down to where the sand was hardest, at the dry edge of the beach that was not being licked by the tide. She turned and headed toward the bonfire, and she was almost very sure of herself, and her step was light. She did not feel that she was leaving footprints on the hard sand.

It was a long way, and she could make out the figures before she could hear them. She was so close to the ocean that its sounds were all she could hear for the first fifty yards, the first seventy-five yards, the first hundred. And then the voices began to penetrate the sounds of the ocean. She walked on and the voices grew more distinct, the voices of young women and young men, a harsh and frightening chorus of people who did not want her. She stopped to listen. Now she could hear baritone derision and alto contempt and soprano coquetry answered by the baritone derision, and though they were ignorant of her existence they were commanding her to stay away.

She turned and for a terrifying second her eyes, so long focused on the bonfire, looked into black-

ness. She could not move. Then she looked up at the sky until she could see a star, and then there were more stars and to her left were the lights of the cottages on the dunes. She ran all the way home.

Poverty, Politics,
and the Artistic Impulse

Looked at from a certain distance, American literature—fiction and poetry alike—seems to benefit from a tension between writing that clings to the native scene and draws upon national or local traditions and writing nourished by European or yet more exotic resources, and which looks abroad for its settings and even its base of operation. While Hawthorne was exploring the history and the psychological landscape of New England, Melville was converting into narrative his reminiscences of far-flung sea journeys and packing his rhetoric with images drawn from Europe and its literature. A generation later, the first fictional treatment of the American Middle West (Indiana, Iowa, Chicago), in the first wave of realism, was contemporaneous with Henry James's permanent removal to England and his development of the novel of international manners. Edwin Arlington Robinson was just coming into his own as the poet of Tilbury Town (that is, Gardiner, Maine) and New York City, and Masters was sketching the little lives along the midwestern Spoon River, when, partly as a counterattack, Pound, Eliot, and others among those whom Frost would call "literary refugees" in London were proposing new departures for poetry under the influence of certain great traditions of European thought and literary practice. And the impact of postwar Europe (Paris, Spain, the Riviera) upon Hemingway and Fitzgerald, and even to an extent upon Nathanael West, had scarcely been recorded before other voices began commenting on conditions and scenes back home. These latter writers—some of whom represent a sort of extreme of fictional realism—are the ones we now come to.

The untidiness of literary history, to which we have more than once referred, prevents us from pressing too hard on the basic distinction between
the "nativist" and the partly "Europeanized" writer. A good writer transcends
the category into which the critical historian may put him, and this is perhaps especially true in America, where schools, movements, and literary
theories have never truly flourished. In addition, as we shall see in a moment,
"nativist" hardly serves to define the first writers here dealt with. Nor do
these writers whom we inspect constitute a group, even as loosely as did the
early realists.

What the present cluster of novelists have in common (again, with one
or two exceptions) is the theme, more often than not based upon experience, of poverty. For the most part, they deal with the poor, often the very
poor indeed—the poor in the New York ghettos, the poor who have been
evicted from their western farms, the poor who have migrated to the vineyards of California, the poor—in Dos Passos' *U.S.A.*—all across the land.[1]
Poverty, of course, had long been a fact of American life and a phenomenon
in American literature (one thinks of Hepzibah Pyncheon in *The House of
Seven Gables,* and some of the figures described by Sarah Orne Jewett and
her New England contemporaries); but there had been nothing really like
the economic and social "bottom dogs"—to borrow Edward Dahlberg's title
—that we encounter in these writings.

But there is still another chronological and sociological distinction to be
made, and it is the basis for the division of this section into its two parts.
Writing about Michael Gold's *Jews Without Money,* Michael Harrington
has observed (in 1964) that the poverty of the American sixties, to which
we can now add the seventies, made it possible to understand by contrast "what a distinctive, and in many ways hopeful, misery existed in the
various Lower East Sides of the United States at the turn of the century,"
when it was always possible to dream, at least, of escaping the ghetto. It is
just that essentially hopeful misery that we discover in the fictionalized recollections of Michael Gold and Henry Roth—though decidedly and significantly *not* in the autobiographical novel of Edward Dahlberg. Poverty
today, Harrington goes on, "is all the more tenacious because it has fewer
internal resources than in Gold's day." That view is sound enough basically,
but it is limited in several important ways. For one thing, it leaves out of
account the experience of the blacks—for whom the issue of race and racial
hostility has always been interwoven with economic exploitation and a low

---

[1] Somewhat different from most of these phenomena was the marginal life of the
poor whites in Georgia and South Carolina, as portrayed by Erskine Caldwell in his
funny, grotesque, violent, and sentimental novel of 1934, *God's Little Acre.* Or, indeed, of the poor—white and black—of Faulkner's Mississippi (see pp. 2480 and 2559).

social status. The crucial additional factor of race—that is, specifically, of blackness—made it incalculably harder for blacks even seventy years ago to find much hopefulness in their misery than it was for Jews or any other ethnic group. At the same time (the point is related but not identical) the blacks—unlike the Jews or Chinese, for example—had no obvious and clearly articulated cultural tradition, and no national history, on which to build their hopes, or in terms of which to express their dream of escape. This is one of the reasons for the successive efforts to create, as it were *ex nihilo*, a "black nation," as illustrated by Marcus Garvey (see p. 1754).

There is another vital distinction to be made within the history of poverty in this century. If the poverty of the pre–First World War Jewish immigrant was different in kind, and in the emotions it engendered, from that of certain afflicted urban areas in the sixties, it was also different from the condition described by Jack Conroy and indicated by the title of his novel, *The Disinherited*. Conroy's characters, if they had not known anything approaching affluence, had known a certain minimal economic well-being, and it was of this that they were deprived when the mines closed down and the jobs disappeared. Where the poverty of the East Side Jew had been marked by pervasive but by no means disempowering sadness, the joblessness of the disemployed of the Depression was marked by shock, anger, and frustration. John Steinbeck had reason to choose as his best known title the militant old phrase *The Grapes of Wrath*. Writing such as this in the 1930's dramatized poverty as the occasion and the cause for aggressive political action; and what we shall eventually want to notice is how both the poverty and the politics might be presented in literature.

The Immigrant Imagination

MICHAEL GOLD (1894–1967)

Jews Without Money (1930)—another immediately communicative and ironic title—tells of what it meant to be Jewish, poor, and the child of immigrants on Manhattan's East Side in the years before the First World War. Gold's parents had come to New York from Rumania; and he himself was born into the ghetto in 1894, as Irving Granach. After the childhood and adolescence recounted in the novel, Gold celebrated his coming of age by joining the Socialist party (this after an incident in which, having innocently wandered into a demonstration in Union Square, he was gratuitously knocked down by a policeman). Later he would become a Communist. He wrote tirelessly for the *Masses*, the *New Masses*, the *Liberator*, the

Daily Worker; a collection of his articles appeared in 1937 as *Change the World*. Through a long-embattled life, Gold remained the most doctrinally unyielding, but at the same time, perhaps, the most widely respected and trusted, of American Communists. No denial of his past or political tale-telling marred his career; yet Gold unfortunately fell prey to the Stalinist theory (especially after the Stalinist takeover of the *New Masses* in 1928, when Gold became editor-in-chief) that writers on the left must be judged exclusively by their devotion to the Communist cause. This view was shared for a while by critics like Granville Hicks, but it was stoutly resisted by other left-minded writers like James T. Farrell and Richard Wright, and the editors of the *Partisan Review*, Philip Rahv and William Phillips: and neither Malcolm Cowley nor Kenneth Burke found the straight party line on literature acceptable.

Jews Without Money was thus written after Gold was solidly committed to the propagandistic kind of "proletarian literature" which he had been urging for a decade. The book ends, after a bitter recollection of poverty and hopelessness, with a salute to the revolution:

> O workers' Revolution, you brought hope to me, a lonely suicidal boy. You are the true Messiah. You will destroy the East Side when you come, and build there a garden for the human spirit.

> O Revolution, that forced me to think, to struggle and to live.
> O great beginning!

But except for those last lines (which sound, as Gold elsewhere tends to sound, like an unconscious parody of Whitman), *Jews Without Money* is an almost entirely nonpolitical book. It evokes, often with a kind of tender tolerance, the reality encountered by immigrant Jews coming to the New World with their own Semitic dream of Eden. "The Jews had fled from the European pogroms; with thanksgiving and solemn faith from a new Egypt into a New Promised Land. They found awaiting them the sweatshops, the bawdy houses and Tammany Hall. There were hundreds of prostitutes on my street." It is a story about a small boy's hunger; about street fights; about the Jewish fear of Christians, except for "the good ones"; about family quarrels and family love. Handsomely belying Gold's politico-literary theory, the novel presents us with a human being in a particular time and place achieving his own brand of humanity, and only on the last page is that brand revealed as revolutionary.

Gold's quick and effectively nervous narrative style, with its mixture of the lyrical and the hardheaded, and his growing consciousness of Jewishness, poverty, and the ghetto environment, are here represented by an early chapter from *Jews Without Money*.

From Jews Without Money (1930)

CHAPTER 3: A GANG OF LITTLE YIDS

1

I first admired Nigger in school, when I was new there. He banged the teacher on the nose.

School is a jail for children. One's crime is youth, and the jailers punish one for it. I hated school at first; I missed the street. It made me nervous to sit stiffly in a room while New York blazed with autumn.

I was always in hot water. The fat old maid teacher (weight about 250 pounds), with a sniffle, and eyeglasses, and the waddle of a ruptured person, was my enemy.

She was shocked by the dirty word I, a six-year-old villain, once used. She washed my mouth with yellow lye soap. I submitted. She stood me in the corner for the day to serve as an example of anarchy to a class of fifty scared kids.

Soap eating is nasty. But my parents objected because soap is made of Christian fat, is not kosher. I was being forced into pork-eating, a crime against the Mosaic law. They complained to the Principal.

O irritable, starched old maid teacher, O stupid, proper, unimaginative despot, O cow with no milk or calf or bull, it was torture to you, Ku Kluxer before your time, to teach in a Jewish neighborhood.

I knew no English when handed to you. I was a little savage and lover of the street. I used no tooth-brush. I slept in my underwear, I was lousy, maybe. To sit on a bench made me restless, my body hated coffins. But Teacher! O Teacher for little slaves. O ruptured American virgin of fifty-five, you should not have called me "Little Kike."

Nigger banged you on the nose for that. I should have been as brave. It was Justice.

2

Ku Klux moralizers say the gangster system is not American. They say it was brought here by "low-class" European immigrants. What nonsense! There never were any Jewish gangsters in Europe. The Jews there were a timid bookish lot. The Jews have done no killing since Jerusalem fell. That's why the Christians have called us the "peculiar people." But it is America that has taught the sons of tubercular Jewish tailors how to kill.

Nigger was a virile boy, the best pitcher, fighter and crapshooter in my gang. He was George Washington when our army annihilated the redcoats. He rode the mustangs, and shot the most buffalo among the tenements. He scalped Indians, and was our stern General in war.

Some of the gang have become famous. Al Levy was known to us simply as "Stinker"; now he writes wealthy musical comedies.

Abe Sugarman is a proud movie director. He also has become a Spanish nobleman. His Hollywood name is Arturo De Sagaar, no less.

Lew Moses shoots craps with high stakes, with skyscrapers; he is a big real estate speculator.

Others of the boys are humbler comedians. Jake Gottlieb is a taxi driver, and feeds his three kids every day. Harry Weintraub is a clothing cutter. Some of the boys are dead.

There was always something for boys to see in the free enormous circus of the East Side. Always a funeral, a riot, a quarrel between two fat mommas, or an accident, or wedding. Day after day we explored the street, we wandered in this remarkable dream of a million Jews.

Our gang played the universal games, tag, prisoner's base, duck on a rock. Like boys in Africa and Peru, we followed the seasons religiously for kites, tops and marbles.

One of the most exciting games was invented by Nigger. It was the stealing game. Nigger ran the fastest, so he would march up to a pushcart and boldly steal a piece of fruit. The outraged peddler chased him, of course, which was the signal for us to grab fruit and run the other way.

With a penny one could buy much; a hot dog, or a cup of cocoa, or one of thirty varieties of poisoned candies. Watermelon, apples, and old world delicacies like Turkish *halvah* and *lakoom;* liver *knishes;* Russian sunflower seeds; Roumanian pastry; pickled tomatoes. For a nickel a mixture of five of these street luxuries produced amazing Jewish nightmares.

We turned on the fire hydrant in summer, and splashed in the street, shoes, clothes and all. Or went swimming from the docks. Our East River is a sun-spangled open sewer running with oily scum and garbage. It should be underground, like a sewer. It stinks with the many deaths of New York. Often while swimming I had to push dead swollen dogs and vegetables from my face. In our set it was considered humor to slyly paddle ordure at another boy when he was swimming.

What a dirty way of getting clean. But the sun was shining, the tugboats passed, puffing like bulldogs, the freight boats passed, their pale stokers hanging over the rails, looking at us, the river flowed and glittered, the sky was blue, it was all good.

Nigger taught us how to swim. His method was to throw a boy from the steep pier. If the boy swam, well and good. If he sank and screamed for help, Nigger laughed and rescued him.

Jack Korbin died that way, I almost drowned, too.

But it was good. We were naked, free and coocoo with youngness. Anything done in the sun is good. The sun, the jolly old sun who is every one's poppa, looked down as affectionately on his little riffraff Yids as he did on his syphilitic millionaires at Palm Beach, I am sure.

3

Let me tell of a trait we boys showed: the hunger for country things.

New York is a devil's dream, the most urbanized

city in the world. It is all geometry angles and stone. It is mythical, a city buried by a volcano. No grass is found in this petrified city, no big living trees, no flowers, no bird but the drab little lecherous sparrow, no soil, loam, earth; fresh earth to smell, earth to walk on, to roll on, and love like a woman.

Just stone. It is the ruins of Pompeii, except that seven million animals full of earth-love must dwell in the dead lava streets.

Each week at public school there was an hour called Nature Study. The old maid teacher fetched from a dark closet a collection of banal objects: bird-nests, cornstalks, minerals, autumn leaves and other poor withered corpses. On these she lectured tediously, and bade us admire Nature.

What an insult. We twisted on our benches, and ached for the outdoors. It was as if a starving bum were offered snapshots of food, and expected to feel grateful. It was like lecturing a cage of young monkeys on the jungle joys.

"Lady, gimme a flower! Gimme a flower! Me, me, me!"

In summer, if a slummer or settlement house lady walked on our street with flowers in her hand, we attacked her, begging for the flowers. We rioted and yelled, yanked at her skirt, and frightened her to the point of hysteria.

Once Jake Gottlieb and I discovered grass struggling between the sidewalk cracks near the livery stable. We were amazed by this miracle. We guarded this treasure, allowed no one to step on it. Every hour the gang studied "our" grass, to try to catch it growing. It died, of course, after a few days; only children are hardy enough to grow on the East Side.

The Italians raised red and pink geraniums in tomato cans. The Jews could have, too, but hadn't the desire. When an excavation was being dug for a new tenement, the Italians swarmed there with pots, hungry for the new earth. Some of them grew bean vines and morning glories.

America is so rich and fat, because it has eaten the tragedy of millions of immigrants.

To understand this, you should have seen at twilight, after the day's work, one of our pick and shovel wops watering his can of beloved flowers. Brown peasant, son of thirty generations of peasants, in a sweaty undershirt by a tenement window, feeling the lost poetry. Uprooted! Lost! Betrayed!

A white butterfly once blundered into our street. We chased it, and Joey Cohen caught it under his cap. But when he lifted his cap, the butterfly was dead. Joey felt bad about this for days.

4

To come back to Nigger.

He was built for power like a tugboat, squat and solid. His eyes, even then, had the contemptuous glare of the criminal and genius. His nose had been squashed at birth, and with his black hair and murky face, made inevitable the East Side nickname: "Nigger."

He was bold, tameless, untouchable, like a little gypsy. He was always in motion, planning mischief. He was suspicious like a cat, quick to sidestep every sudden kick from his enemy, the world. The East Side breeds this wariness. East Side prize fighters have always been of the lightning type; they learn to move fast dodging cops and street cars.

The East Side, for children, was a world plunged in eternal war. It was suicide to walk into the next block. Each block was a separate nation, and when a strange boy appeared, the patriots swarmed.

"What streeter?" was demanded, furiously.

"Chrystie Street," was the trembling reply.

Bang! This was the signal for a mass assault on the unlucky foreigner, with sticks, stones, fists and feet. The beating was cruel and bloody as that of grown-ups, no mercy was shown. I have had three holes in my head, and many black eyes and puffed lips from our street wars. We did it to others, they did it to us. It was patriotism, though what difference there was between one East Side block and another is now hard to see. Each was the same theosophist's fantasy of tenements, demons, old hats, Jews, pushcarts, angels, urine smells, shadows, featherbeds and bananas. The same gray lava streets.

One had to join a gang in self-protection, and be loyal. And one had to be brave. Even I was brave, an odd child cursed with introspection.

Joey Cohen, a dreamy boy with spectacles, was brave. Stinker claimed to be brave, and Jake Gottlieb was brave, and Abie, Izzy, Fat, Maxie, Pishteppel, Harry, all were indubitably brave. We often boasted about our remarkable bravery to each other. But Nigger was bravest of the brave, the chieftain of our brave savage tribe.

Nigger would fight guys twice his age, he would fight men and cops. He put his head down and tore in with flying arms, face bloody, eyes puffed by punching, lips curled back from the teeth, a snarling iron machine, an animal bred for centuries to fighting, yet his father was a meek sick little tailor.

Nigger began to hate cops at an early age. The cops on our street were no worse than most cops, and no better. They loafed around the saloon back-doors, guzzling free beer. They were intimate with the prostitutes, and with all the thieves, cokefiends, pimps and gamblers of the neighborhood. They took graft everywhere, even from the humblest shoelace peddler.

Every one knew what cops were like. Why, then, did they adopt such an attitude of stern virtue toward the small boys? It was as if we were the biggest criminals of the region. They broke up our baseball games, confiscated our bats. They beat us for splashing under the fire hydrant. They cursed us, growled and chased us for any reason. They hated to see us having fun.

We were absorbed in a crap game one day. Suddenly Fat yelled: "Cheese it, the cop!" Every one scattered like rabbits, leaving around 15 pennies on the sidewalk. The cops usually pocketed this small change. It was one of our grievances. We often suspected them of being moralists for the sake of this petty graft.

Nigger didn't run. He bent down calmly and picked up the pennies. He was defying the cop. The cop swelled up like a turkey with purple rage. He slammed Nigger with his club across the spine. Nigger was knocked to the sidewalk. The cop forced the pennies out of Nigger's hand.

"Yuh little bastard," said the cop, "I'll ship yuh to the reformatory yet!"

Nigger stood up quietly, and walked away. His face was hard. Five minutes later a brick dropped from the sky and just missed the cop's skull.

It was Nigger's grim reply. The cop rushed up to the roof, and chased Nigger. But Nigger was too daring to be caught. He leaped gaps between the tenements like a mountain goat. He was ready to die for justice. The cop was not as brave.

For months Nigger remembered to drop bricks, bundles of garbage and paper bags filled with water on this cop's head. It drove the man crazy. But he could never catch the somber little ghost. But he spread the word that Nigger was a bad egg, due for the reformatory. This cop's name was Murph. It was he who later tipped the balances that swung Nigger into his career of gangster.

5

Delancey Street was being torn up to be converted into Schiff Parkway, and there were acres of empty lots there.

On our East Side, suffocated with miles of tenements, an open space was a fairy-tale gift to children.

Air, space, weeds, elbow room, one sickened for space on the East Side, any kind of marsh or wasteland to testify that the world was still young, and wild and free.

My gang seized upon one of these Delancey Street lots, and turned it, with the power of imagination, into a vast western plain.

We buried pirate treasure there, and built snow forts. We played football and baseball through the long beautiful days. We dug caves, and with Peary explored the North Pole. We camped there at night under the stars, roasting sweet potatoes that were sweeter because stolen.

It was there I vomited over my first tobacco, and first marveled at the profundities of sex. It was there I first came to look at the sky.

The elevated train anger was not heard there. The shouting of peddlers like an idiot asylum, the East Side danger and traffic rumble and pain, all were shut by a magic fence out of this boy's Nirvana.

Shabby old ground, ripped like a battlefield by workers' picks and shovels, little garbage dump lying forgotten in the midst of tall tenements, O home of all the twisted junk, rusty baby carriages, lumber, bottles, boxes, moldy pants and dead cats of the neighborhood—every one spat and held the nostrils when passing you. But in my mind you still blaze in a halo of childish romance. No place will ever seem as wonderful again.

We had to defend our playground by force of arms. This made it even more romantic.

One April day, Abie, Jakie, Stinker and I were playing tipcat under the blue sky. The air was warm. Yellow mutts moved dreamily on the garbage. The sun covered the tenements with gold. Pools of melted snow shone in the mud. An old man smoked his pipe and watched us.

Boys feel the moment of beauty, but can't express it except through a crazy exuberance. We were happy. Suddenly a bomb shattered the peace.

The Forsythe Street boys, our enemies, whooped down like a band of Indians. They were led by

Butch, that dark fearless boy whose "rep" was as formidable as Nigger's.

They proceeded to massacre us. There were about fifteen of them. Abie and Jake were buried under a football pyramid of arms and legs. Stinker, who had earned his nickname because he would whine, beg, weep and stool-pigeon his way out of any bad mess, howled for mercy. Butch worked on me. It was a duel between a cockroach and a subway train.

At last they permitted us to get to our feet.

"Listen, you guys," said Butch, sneering as he wiped his hand on his seat, "this dump belongs to us Forsythe streeters, see? Get the hell out."

We ran off, glad to escape alive. Our shirts were torn, our stockings chewed off, we were muddy and wounded and in disgrace. We found Nigger. He was loaded with an immense bundle of men's coats which he was bringing to his family from the factory. His family worked at home; this was his daily chore.

He turned pale with rage when he heard of the massacre. All that afternoon strategy was discussed. We spied on the Forsythe streeters, we visited the Eldridge streeters and formed an alliance against the common enemy.

The very next day the historic battle was fought. Some of our boys stole tops of washboilers at home, and used them as shields. Others had tin swords, sticks, blackjacks. The two armies slaughtered each other in the street. Bottles were thrown, heads cut open. Nigger was bravest of the brave.

We won back our playground. And after that we posted sentries, and enjoyed passwords, drills, and other military ritual. The old maid teachers would have been horrified to see us practice their principal teaching: War. War.

6

But the Schiff Parkway was an opponent we could not defeat. It robbed us of our playground at last.

A long concrete patch was laid out, with anemic trees and lines of benches where jobless workers sit in summer.

We went back to our crowded street. Joey Cohen was killed by the horse car not long afterward.

He had stolen a ride, and in jumping, fell under the wheels. The people around saw the flash of his body, and then heard a last scream of pain.

The car rolled on. The people rushed to the tracks and picked up the broken body of my playmate.

O what a horrible joke happened. The head was missing. Policemen arrived, Joey's father and mother screamed and moaned, every one searched, but the head could not be found.

Later it was discovered under the car, hanging from the bloody axle.

Our gang was depressed by this accident. Jake Gottlieb said he would never steal another ride on a horse car. But Nigger, to show how brave he was, stole a ride that very afternoon.

Joey was the dreamy boy in spectacles who was so sorry when he killed the butterfly. He was always reading books, and had many queer ideas. It was he who put the notion in my head of becoming a doctor. I had always imagined I wanted to be a fireman.

EDWARD DAHLBERG (1900–   )

Edward Dahlberg's *Bottom Dogs* appeared in the same year, 1930, which saw the publication of *Jews Without Money*. Like the latter, Dahlberg's novel deals with personal experiences in the period before the First World War, and poverty in his special Jewish world. Yet no two books could, otherwise, be more dissimilar. *Bottom Dogs* presents as fiction part of the early life which Dahlberg was to rehearse in his quite remarkable autobiography of 1964, *Because I Was Flesh*. Dahlberg, born in 1900, was, like his fictional Lorry Lewis, the illegitimate child of a lady barber in Kansas City—a young woman, according to Dahlberg's own report, of impressive physical proportions and striking if wayward personality. Dahlberg also spent several years in a Jewish orphanage in Cleveland, as Lewis does, and later bummed about the country. But where Lewis is devoid of any life purpose and a stranger to hope, Dahlberg himself possessed an intense intellectual drive which brought him to the University of California in 1922, and later to Columbia.

He flirted with communism in the early thirties, but soon moved away from it to develop his own highly personal, even idiosyncratic, view of life. He made Europe his home and developed gradually into one of the most vigorous and learned, as well as one of the thorniest, of American men of letters. Several other novels followed *Bottom Dogs*, but Dahlberg's real strength has revealed itself in a uniquely personal kind of literary criticism, and in excursions into cultural history—heavily buttressed by abstruse knowledge—in which he assaults modern civilization with a sort of savage joy (for example, *The Sorrows of Priapus*, an aptly named book of 1957). If this quirky, original, and uncompromising writer has not yet received his due, it is partly because he escapes or violates the usual literary categories. It seems possible that he may now be coming into his own.

In his introduction to *Bottom Dogs*, D. H. Lawrence confessed a horrid fascination with the book and remarked: "I don't want to read any more books like this. But I am glad to have read this one, just to know what is the last word in repulsive consciousness, consciousness in a state of repulsion." Lawrence, a humorless writer himself, failed to detect the potent comic sense at work in the novel (as he missed the extravagant comic dimensions in Melville and Whitman), and especially in the scenes he most admired and which most appalled him —those in the orphanage. But with his firm grasp of some of the main aspects of American literary history, Lawrence could perceive at once the chief disturbing features of *Bottom Dogs*: an atmosphere in which individual human beings are not only psychically divided from, but deeply repugnant to, each other; and the absence of sheer consciousness in the make-up of the characters.

They are brutally and deliberately unaware. They have no hopes, no desires even. They have even no will-to-exist, for existence even is too high a term. They have a strange, stony will-to-persist, that is all. And they persist by reaction, because they feel the repulsiveness of each other, of everything, even of themselves.

Lorry Lewis, as he pursues his radically aimless gray adventures through the Middle West and in California, perfectly exemplifies Lawrence's profile. What Lawrence does not make sufficiently clear is that the perspective and tone of the book are contrivances of art. Dahlberg has *created* an attitude toward experience that is beneath despair, a psychic emptiness that is without anger as it is without hope or the memory of hope. The colloquial style derives at some distance from *Huckleberry Finn*, and by it, one supposes, Dahlberg is asking us to imagine a Huck Finn stripped of ebullience and moral complexity, robbed of anything except (as Lawrence says) an animal awareness. In *Bottom Dogs*—and dismal as it is, it represents a considerable literary achievement—there is only the very thinnest and most fleeting consciousness of a different and richer mode of existence. In discussing Sinclair Lewis, we suggested that in *Babbitt* the old American dream-image of an alternative and better way of life— Huck and Jim on the raft, Hester Prynne meditating a more just social order—reached some sort of minimum with Babbitt's insubstantial fairy child. With Dahlberg, to borrow the adjective from his title, that image touches bottom, somewhere beneath humanity.

Bottom Dogs is a bleak parody of the traditional story of initiation. Characteristically, this kind of story follows the central figure through a moral and psychological education that leads him to some enduring insight into human life and his own nature. Dahlberg's novel systematically and knowingly undercuts this pattern: young Lorry arrives merely at the knowledge that nothing at all is in store for him. "Perhaps, he would go east, get out of it all," he thinks vaguely in the book's last paragraph, wandering through the streets of Los Angeles. Or perhaps, if he is careless enough with the city's whores, he would contract a venereal disease. And here an image of purification, of moral change, touches his mind only to vanish on an instant as his fading thought concludes the novel:

> He would go to the Los Angeles City Hospital; maybe, those enamelled iron beds, the white sheets, the medical immaculateness of it all, might do something for him. Something had to happen; and he knew nothing would. . . .

Our selection cuts in at the point where Lorry Lewis has just arrived at the Cleveland orphanage. The narrative style here, as throughout, is like that of a tape recorder faithfully taking down the tuneless repetitions, the flat unsalted slang, the wearily unresentful thoughts of escape of this born loser—one of the first and one of the most curiously memorable "antiheroes" in American fiction.

FURTHER READINGS

Edward Dahlberg, *Alms for Oblivion* (1964)
———, *Because I Was Flesh* (1964)
———, *Bottom Dogs* (1930)
———, *Can These Bones Live* (1960)
———, *The Confessions of Edward Dahlberg* (1971)
———, *The Edward Dahlberg Reader* (1967)

Harold Billings, ed., *Edward Dahlberg, American Ish-*
mael of Letters: Selected Critical Essays with an Introduction* (1968)
Ford Madox Ford, "The Fate of the Semiclassic," *Forum*, Vol. 98, No. 3 (September, 1937)
Ihab Hassan, "The Sorrows of Edward Dahlberg," *Massachusetts Review*, Vol. 5, No. 3 (Spring, 1964)
Fred Moramarco, *Edward Dahlberg* (1972)

From Bottom Dogs (1930)

It soon got around that you could do anything to that newcumber, Lorry, and he wouldn't even wake up to say how-de-doo to the fellows who were takin' the trouble to maul him and make him a real orphan. Shrimp said it was a waste of time foolin' around with a dead guy like that, and, that anyway, he didn't know he was living probably. When Dan Maxwell got the story, he came down especially every night for a week from the little kids' dormitory, where he was the head monitor to see that that fool of a newcumber got a well-worked-up mauling.

Well, Lorry was starting to get downright miserable, and wanted to run away; he hardly left the playroom, and took to sitting on the steam pipes that ran around the playroom or moping on the cement window sill looking out through the bars into the court. When Dan got wise to this, he stalled around the court, whittled a fine point on the edge of a long broomstick, and stood around layin' low, till Lorry got to taking on that heartbreakin' look. Then he ran the point of his broomstick into his ribs, and if Lorry talked back, he flew into the playroom, and whacking him on the knuckles, said he'd show a newcumber whether he could answer back an eighth grader.

Lorry felt he had taken all he could, and wrote home to his mother that they were starving him and that the orphan asylum kids would be running him into pneumonia or something if he had to stick in that crazy asylum any longer. His mother was all taken up, but Henry said the kid was just lonesome, and that it would do him good to get a few hard knocks. However, she sent him a dime a week, which she enclosed in a letter, but the superintendent, who opened all the letters, said it was not right to send money to them, as it made the others jealous, and besides, he wrote they had everything they wanted.

As fall came on Lorry got to going round with some of the smaller sixth graders, and had gotten on far enough to be in whack with a seventh grader who found out he was getting some money from the outside now and then. A few days before school began again in September, he was forced into a fight with the assistant head wardrobe boy who belonged, besides, to the literary club, wore a necktie, and was one of Mr. G.'s pets.

Lorry had gotten all the pastin' he was looking for those first few months, and he sure wasn't going to go out of his way to get himself mixed up with one of Miss W.'s head helpers. Lorry was awfully hard on stockings, and he often skinned them at the knees, foolin' about with fourth and fifth graders on the roofs of chicken coops at the edge of the back grounds. Anyway, this here wardrobe guy told him one day he was sick and tired making out a new list for him every time he ripped his pants or ruined his stocking knees so that the sewing girls couldn't patch them.

Well, he started to order him around and gave Lorry a push.

Lorry had heard, anyhow, that those wardrobe boys thought they were too much, and although he wasn't for making trouble over a little bit of a push, he said back to him, "Aw, go on, ya wardrobe boy!"

Well, a guy who had been a wardrobe boy for three years, and been in the home for eight, wasn't going to take that kinda gab from a green newcumber, so he stepped on his foot and folded his arms and bucked him harder, and Lorry, who wasn't intendin' to get serious, sort of nudged him with one shoulder; as long as there were no fists in it, he didn't mind playing along just sort of sore-like.

That got the wardrobe boy all in a huff, and he tried to give him a kick in the shins, but Lorry side-stepped, and tripped him up. The wardrobe boy went down flat on his face. That sure scared Lorry; he wanted to run, but he stood there; there was no place to run to, not for long anyway.

Well, the wardrobe boy was all hot, and about to give him a real lickin', when the whistle blew: "All in."

"Yu jest wait till after supper," he whispered as Mr. G. went by, "I'll jus knock the holy stuffings out of ya!"

"All right, I'll wait; no you won't!" came back Lorry who didn't know exactly what he was saying.

In the dining hall it got around that that newcumber, Lorry, was goin' to try to fight with the assistant head wardrobe boy, who sat at the table across from him and who yelled over so that all the big kids could hear: "Lissun, newcumber, dontcha ferget, I challenge yu, in the playroom after supper, and don't think yu kin back out; I've already told Pinky, the door monitor, to keep yu in that playroom."

Well, Lorry didn't say a word; he saw he was in for it. All the kids at his table said their prayers way out loud before and after supper, and kept winking at Lorry. The big kid at the head of the table said it was about time somethin' was happening around the home; as far as he could see, the fellows weren't the killers they used to be, when he first came to the home.

Well, he said, he would referee, and he'd be glad to show a newcumber who sat at his own table a step or two. He went through the motions at the table and told Lorry to meet him downstairs in the washroom for a few minutes' workout just before the scrap.

Lorry didn't say nuthin'; he didn't know what to say; he was all flushed, couldn't eat, and felt all crampy and hollow inside, and wanted to get up and go to the toilet. But he didn't move; he didn't dare; everybody would hiss at him if he left the dining hall that way and yell he was running off. He could see he was done for; they weren't kiddin'; they were all for a killin' maul to the end.

He thought of running away from the orphan asylum; it was no use staying there any longer and always getting beat up; if he only knew where the depot was, he would walk down Woodland Avenue to Superior and get on a train and go back to Kansas City; maybe the conductor would let him ride free. But he didn't know how to find his way around in a big city like Cleveland, and besides, if a cop saw him in that asylum uniform out on the street asking the way to the depot, they would probably lock him up or send him back, and he would get expelled, and he'd be disgraced for life.

Everybody was staring at him; the kids at the table across were putting wads of doughy biscuit in water and placing it on the handle of the spoon, which they thumped down with their hands and which kept clipping him on the back of the neck. His mouth was all twisted up, and Mush Tate, who was feelin' kinda soft about the newcumber asked him if he wanted his biscuit.

Shrimp told Mush Tate to lay off, and said to Lorry that he'd better eat up as much as he could so that he could take on as much weight as possible before the fight.

Lorry gave Mush his biscuit, and Mush told him not to get eaten up about that wardrobe boy, that he was a lot of goulash anyway, and full of bull.

The big guy at the head of the table kept playing up the washroom workout to Lorry, and when he didn't come across, he got up from his chair, reached way over the table, stuck his head in Lorry's face, passing a fork across it, and pressing it up against his nose, growled, "Lissen, newcumber, I'm referee'n this here fight, and I'm seein' it comes off right, get me."

"Aw, let 'im alone," said Mush Tate, counting and stacking the raisins in his biscuit.

"How's that!" yowled the big guy.

"Oh, cow's ass, my eye!" came back Mush Tate, digging into the biscuit for more raisins.

"Yu'd better dry up, Mush Tate, I haven't given yu a lickin' for a long time!" returned the big guy.

"Forget it, Barrutt, you fat ass," yelled over Dan Maxwell, who sat at the seventh- and eighth-grade table, and who was listening to the gab, "dontch yu go monkeying round with that there newcumber. I had 'im signed up the first day he came here; if ther's goin' to be any workout, I'll take ker of it, get me, hollerhead?"

That sort of cooled the big guy off and there was nuthin' more said about the newcumber; when the dining hall got to prayin' again, the big guy winked at the other kids, while Mush Tate had his head low, his nose touching the oilcloth, while he packed the raisins in his shirt pocket.

Well, the gong had rung, the prayers were over, and the kids were running down to the basement playroom; the wardrobe boy took his time, pushed his way through, casual-like, the fellows hanging around outside the door waiting to see Lorry.

Some of the fifth graders waved at him, "Go easy with him, Gabby, he's got to be confirmed some day, yu know."

The wardrobe boy pulled up his suspenders and closed one eye good-naturedly.

Down in the playroom a crowd of fellows were standing around Lorry; the wardrobe boy was in no hurry to get down; he had some work to get off for Miss W. he told one of his helpers, which couldn't wait, and as for that sixth grade newcumber, he could clean him up at any time.

Dan Maxwell was around and tried to spar with him, and Watermelon, who was looking on, got in the way; and when a guy hit his fist up against that louse's head, he was crippled for weeks. Dan ran to the washroom, put his knuckles under the hot water faucet, picked up a plunger standing in the corner, and chased the hell out of Watermelonhead, cracking him on top of the head with the rubber every time he was in reach.

Watermelon was looking crazily for horseshoes, but couldn't find any, and Bucket, who was slippery as they make them, jumped on Dan's back and couldn't be thrown.

Mush Tate was argufying with Prunes, Shrimp, Spunk, and all the goulashes, he said, in the wardrobe, put together. He hadn't warmed up yet and wasn't referring to his dictionary, which he always carried with him. He was recitin' from memory and said he was willing to take on the whole

orphan asylum including Doc's hobnails and the mayor.

Everybody was excited and waiting for the wardrobe boy to come down. Lorry was all splintered up inside; he still had the cramps, and the waiting besides was killin'; he was about ready to hold out his face to the wardrobe boy, take his lickin', anything as long as he could get it over with.

Finally the wardrobe boy came down, took off his coat, neatly folded it and laid it down on the back of the bench, walked over to Lorry, took off his glasses for him, and spitting in his hands, stepped back, to give him time to put out his arms to guard.

Mush Tate held Lorry's signet ring for him; at least Lorry thought he had handed it to him, but he wasn't sure; he was too flustered at the time; anyway, some one told him it was against Queensbury rules fightin' with rings on. Anyway, he never saw the signet ring again, and Mush Tate said he must have given it to Bucket.

The wardrobe boy waded in, and Lorry backing away, fell over Spunk's back; Spunk, who had been kneeling down waiting for Lorry, got a kick in the rump by Dan Maxwell, who didn't want to see the show broken up that way. Governors were bad enough that way, he said, and he wasn't goin' to have an orphan play a dirty trick like that on him.

Lorry got up and tried to walk away; he felt he had no chance; then Mush Tate butted in, got a rope, which he tied onto the two columns and playroom benches, and made everybody get behind it.

The wardrobe boy came in again and clipped Lorry on the back of the ear, and Lorry, putting his left out half-heartedly, grazed the wardrobe boy's nose. Mush Tate started to megaphone through his hands and got some rooters for the newcumber.

The wardrobe boy brushed back his hair, crouched scientifically, and hit Lorry on the back of the head, stinging him.

Suddenly realizing that he was still on his feet and not hurt he came to and doubled up his guard, pasting the wardrobe boy one in the left kidney.

Bucket yelled out, "Wow!" and Mush Tate said, trying to get on the nerves of the wardrobe boy, "Sickem, goulash."

Everybody laughed, and the wardrobe boy, getting out of sorts, decided to finish it right then and there.

He ran into Lorry, with open arms, as though

he was swinging Indian clubs, and Lorry mussed up his hair with his right and stung him on the ear with a left. A loud cheer went up, and the wardrobe boy, his face like hell's bells ringing, stamped into him, jumping on the playroom boards with a lot of noise, and Lorry, a bit blinded by the swinging of arms under the electric bulbs and unnerved by a fellow stamping his feet against the boards, got a grazing left across his cheek.

"Go on, Gabby!" cried a few wardrobe followers; but Lorry, who had been half-closing his eyes every time the other fellow came in, opened them up, and saw that he wasn't guarding at all. He left-jabbed the wardrobe boy in the stomach and shook up his teeth with a right as he stamped in again.

The wardrobe boy, losing all of his haberdashery sureness, kept running in, offering his face, as the pascal lamb on the altar, and Lorry, smashing out, caught him between the eyes.

"Wot a sock!" yelled a kid who had just gotten angry at the wardrobe boy that morning.

The wardrobe boy wasn't looking any more and threw his arms about, like straight broomsticks, as he stampeded in, and Lorry got more calculating.

Dan, who had to go off to the engine room,

didn't stay till the finish, and the big guy, who sat at the head of the sixth-grade table, stopped the fight; he wasn't going to stand around and watch a newcumber put it over a fellow of the home; he stepped between them, told the wardrobe boy to go to the washroom and wash up, and gave Lorry a sock in the eye, because, he said, he didn't want him to be getting too much around the home.

Well, after that, the wardrobe boy didn't have much to say to Lorry and Lorry didn't go about boasting either; he didn't want any more socks in the eye; besides, he sort of felt sorry for the comedown it meant to the wardrobe boy to be licked by a green newcumber.

However, the wardrobe boy seemed to have heard that Lorry had a signet ring, and he went around and said that he'd been fightin' with it on; that started to get around, and some other wardrobe helpers had it that that looney newcumber had had a big spike inside his fist, and another kid, who had once gotten hurt foolin' with Watermelonhead, said he was standin' behind the ropes right next to Bucket and that Mush Tate had slipped that newcumber a piece of a horseshoe as big as four knuckles.

HENRY ROTH (1906–   )

Henry Roth's *Call It Sleep* (1934) is incomparably the best of those novels which, from the perspective of the thirties, looked back on the ghetto life and the immigrant Jewish community of several decades before. It is indeed, to speak without equivocation, one of the classic American novels; and its history says a good deal about the vicissitudes of literary response in this country. It was warmly praised by several critics when published; but it contained no warm welcome to the cause of social revolution —it strangely evaded the conventions of the ghetto novel—and it quickly disappeared from view. It was reprinted in a paperback edition in 1960, with more critical approval but hardly greater popular success. But a second reprinting, in 1964, was greeted with a critical acclaim by Irving Howe, Leslie Fiedler, Alfred Kazin,

Walter Allen, and other influential commentators that forced it at last upon the attention of the public. By 1970, a million copies were in print, and *Call It Sleep* had doggedly established itself as a major literary accomplishment.[1]

The novel gives us what Henry James thought every serious novel should give: "an impression of life," and one conveyed in a wonderfully flexible prose style which can shift easily between scraps of tough dialogue, graceful eloquence, and hallucinatory intensity. The life rendered is that of David Schearl, an Austrian Jewish immigrant child, between his sixth and

[1] One notices, however, that the usually invaluable 1965 edition of *The Oxford Companion to American Literature*, while bestowing sixteen lines upon Philip Roth, does not see fit to mention the Henry of that surname.

eighth years, first in the Brownsville section of Brooklyn, and then on the East Side of New York. Much of this presumably recapitulates Henry Roth's early years, though Roth was born in New York rather than in Austria. Roth himself has spoken of the composition of *Call It Sleep* as an almost dreamlike experience, as though he had been for a time possessed by an imagination which did his work for him. He has not since recaptured that condition. He made a start on a second novel, but it refused to move and he abandoned it. A few years later, perhaps discouraged by the relative failure of *Call It Sleep* or perhaps simply feeling that he had no more to contribute to literature, he moved to New England, eventually to Augusta, Maine, where he has made a living as a water-fowl farmer, breeding ducks and geese, and occasionally teaching Latin and mathematics to the boys in the neighborhood. "I don't think I'll write again," he has remarked, though in fact the reemergence of his novel has elicited a few articles and stories. One can only echo Walter Allen's rejoinder to the remark quoted: "More than one can say, one hopes that time will prove him wrong."

But as Allen also says, *Call It Sleep* is almost enough for a lifetime's devotion to the art of fiction. The novel is at once a child's vision of life, a rich family portrait, and the evocation of a community. The point of view is mainly that of David—the view, in Irving Howe's words, of "an overwrought, phobic and dangerously imaginative little boy"; and nothing is more artful than Roth's revelation of the limitations and distortions of the boy's outlook, his fears and fantasies, his ability at once to absorb and to falsify the world. In the foreground of his vision are the elder Schearls: David's fury-driven, accident-prone father, devoured by love for and wildly impatient of the family, and Genya, the mother, one of the truest females in our fiction —every inch a woman, with an inner graciousness of spirit, a modest but irrepressible sexuality, and a habitual bewilderment before the alien turbulence of the city. (Roth gains one of his best effects by bringing this tall beautiful figure, queenly in her own home for all her wariness of her husband's temper, out into the noisy English-speaking clutter of the streets where she is only a frantic and inarticulate mother.)

Outside the family, there is a wealth of palpable reality: slum tenements, darkly menacing rat-infested cellars; a ferocious Rabbi teacher ("May your skull be dark! . . . and your eyes be dark and your fate be such that you will call a poppyseed the sun and a carraway the moon"), beefy, friendly Irish cops, and a candidly profane visiting aunt who surely belongs in the pantheon of comic characters. Parallel to this crowding vitality is an astonishing assortment of dialects, all perfectly controlled, never quaint or condescended to, but always rendered with detachment and accuracy as living ingredients of the impression of life: Irish, Italo-American, and a pure-flowing English speech which Roth offers as the equivalent of speech— particularly Genya's—actually in the Yiddish tongue.

The first of our two selections contains the opening chapters of *Call It Sleep*. They follow a prologue in which David and his mother arrive at Ellis Island in 1907, where they have been met by the characteristically out-of-temper Schearl, who has come to America before them. Brief as it is, this selection can perhaps suggest Roth's way of characterizing David and each of his parents, his variety of speech and of dialect, the contrast between the security of the home and the world just outside it.

FURTHER READINGS

Henry Roth, *Call It Sleep* (1934, 1964)

Maxwell Geismar, "A Critical Introduction to *Call It Sleep*" (in the 1964 edition of the novel)

From Call It Sleep (1934)

I

Standing before the kitchen sink and regarding the bright brass faucets that gleamed so far away, each with a bead of water at its nose, slowly swelling, falling, David again became aware that this world had been created without thought of him. He was thirsty, but the iron hip of the sink rested on legs tall almost as his own body, and by no stretch of arm, no leap, could he ever reach the distant tap. Where did the water come from that lurked so secretly in the curve of the brass? Where did it go, gurgling in the drain? What a strange world must be hidden behind the walls of a house! But he was thirsty.

"Mama!" he called, his voice rising above the hiss of sweeping in the frontroom. "Mama, I want a drink."

The unseen broom stopped to listen. "I'll be there in a moment," his mother answered. A chair squealed on its castors; a window chuckled down; his mother's approaching tread.

Standing in the doorway on the top step (two steps led up into the frontroom) his mother smilingly surveyed him. She looked as tall as a tower. The old grey dress she wore rose straight from strong bare ankle to waist, curved round the deep bosom and over the wide shoulders, and set her full throat in a frame of frayed lace. Her smooth, sloping face was flushed now with her work, but faintly so, diffused, the color of a hand beneath wax. She had mild, full lips, brown hair. A vague, fugitive darkness blurred the hollow above her cheekbone, giving to her face and to her large brown eyes, set in their white ovals, a reserved and almost mournful air.

"I want a drink, mama," he repeated.

"I know," she answered, coming down the stairs. "I heard you." And casting a quick, sidelong glance at him, she went over to the sink and turned the tap. The water spouted noisily down. She stood there a moment, smiling obscurely, one finger parting the turbulent jet, waiting for the water to cool. Then filling a glass, she handed it down to him.

"When am I going to be big enough?" he asked resentfully as he took the glass in both hands.

"There will come a time," she answered, smil-

ing. She rarely smiled broadly; instead the thin furrow along her upper lip would deepen. "Have little fear."

With eyes still fixed on his mother, he drank the water in breathless, uneven gulps, then returned the glass to her, surprised to see its contents scarcely diminished.

"Why can't I talk with my mouth in the water?"

"No one would hear you. Have you had your fill?"

He nodded, murmuring contentedly.

"And is that all?" she asked. Her voice held a faint challenge.

"Yes," he said hesitantly, meanwhile scanning her face for some clue

"I thought so," she drew her head back in droll disappointment.

"What?"

"It is summer," she pointed to the window, "the weather grows warm. Whom will you refresh with the icy lips the water lent you?"

"Oh!" he lifted his smiling face.

"You remember nothing," she reproached him, and with a throaty chuckle, lifted him in her arms.

Sinking his fingers in her hair, David kissed her brow. The faint familiar warmth and odor of her skin and hair.

"There!" she laughed, nuzzling his cheek, "but you've waited too long; the sweet chill has dulled. Lips for me," she reminded him, "must always be cool as the water that wet them." She put him down.

"Sometime I'm going to eat some ice," he said warningly, "then you'll like it."

She laughed. And then soberly, "Aren't you ever going down into the street? The morning grows old."

"Aaa!"

"You'd better go. Just for a little while. I'm going to sweep here, you know."

"I want my calendar first," he pouted, invoking his privilege against the evil hour.

"Get it then. But you've got to go down afterwards."

He dragged a chair over beneath the calendar on the wall, clambered up, plucked off the outworn leaf, and fingered the remaining ones to see how far off the next red day was. Red days were

Sundays, days his father was home. It always gave David a little qualm of dread to watch them draw near.

"Now you have your leaf," his mother reminded him. "Come." She stretched out her arms.

He held back. "Show me where my birthday is."

"Woe is me!" She exclaimed with an impatient chuckle. "I've shown it to you every day for weeks now."

"Show me again."

She rumpled the pad, lifted a thin plaque of leaves. "July—" she murmured, "July 12th . . . There!" She found it. "July 12th, 1911. You'll be six then."

David regarded the strange figures gravely. "Lots of pages still," he informed her.

"Yes."

"And a black day too."

"On the calendar," she laughed, "only on the calendar. Now do come down!"

Grasping her arm, he jumped down from the chair. "I must hide it now." He explained.

"So you must. I see I'll never finish my work today."

Too absorbed in his own affairs to pay much heed to hers, he went over to the pantry beneath the cupboard, opened the door and drew out a shoe-box, his treasure chest.

"See how many I've got already?" he pointed proudly to the fat sheaf of rumpled leaves inside the box.

"Wonderful!" She glanced at the box in perfunctory admiration. "You peel off the year as one might a cabbage. Are you ready for your journey?"

"Yes." He put away the box without a trace of alacrity.

"Where is your sailor blouse?" she murmured looking about. "With the white strings in it? What have I—" She found it. "There is still a little wind."

David held up his arms for her to slip the blouse over his head.

"Now, my own," she said, kissing his reemerging face. "Go down and play." She led him toward the door and opened it. "Not too far. And remember if I don't call you, wait until the whistle blows."

He went out into the hallway. Behind him, like an eyelid shutting, the soft closing of the door winked out the light. He assayed the stairs, lapsing below him into darkness, and grasping one by one each slender upright to the bannister, went down. David never found himself alone on these stairs,

but he wished there were no carpet covering them. How could you hear the sound of your own feet in the dark if a carpet muffled every step you took? And if you couldn't hear the sound of your own feet and couldn't see anything either, how could you be sure you were actually there and not dreaming? A few steps from the bottom landing, he paused and stared rigidly at the cellar door. It bulged with darkness. Would it hold? . . . It held! He jumped from the last steps and raced through the narrow hallway to the light of the street. Flying through the doorway was like butting a wave. A dazzling breaker of sunlight burst over his head, swamped him in reeling blur of brilliance, and then receded . . . A row of frame houses half in thin shade, a pitted gutter, a yawning ashcan, flotsam on the shore, his street.

Blinking and almost shaken, he waited on the low stoop a moment, until his whirling vision steadied. Then for the first time, he noticed that seated on the curbstone near the house was a boy, whom an instant later, he recognized. It was Yussie who had just moved into David's house and who lived on the floor above. Yussie had a very red, fat face. His big sister walked with a limp and wore strange iron slats on one of her legs. What was he doing, David wondered, what did he have in his hands? Stepping down from the stoop, he drew near, and totally disregarded, stood beside him.

Yussie had stripped off the outer shell of an alarm-clock. Exposed, the brassy, geometric vitals ticked when prodded, whirred and jingled falteringly.

"It still c'n go," Yussie gravely enlightened him.

David sat down. Fascinated, he stared at the shining cogs that moved without moving their hearts of light. "So wot makes id?" he asked. In the street David spoke English.

"Kentcha see? Id's coz id's a machine."

"Oh!"

"It wakes op mine fodder in de mawning."

"It wakes op mine fodder too."

"It tells yuh w'en yuh sh'd eat an' w'en yuh have tuh go tuh sleep. It shows yuh w'ea, but I tooked it off."

"I god a calenduh opstai's," David informed him.

"Puh! Who ain' god a calenduh?"

"I save mine. I godda big book outa dem, wit numbuhs on id."

"Who can't do dat?"

"But mine fodder made it," David drove home the one unique point about it all.

"Wot's your fodder?"

"Mine fodder is a printer."

"Mine fodder woiks inna joolery shop. In Brooklyn. Didja ever live in Brooklyn?"

"No." David shook his head.

"We usetuh—right near my fodder's joolery shop on Rainey Avenyuh. W'ea does your fodder woik?"

David tried to think. "I don't know." He finally confessed, hoping that Yussie would not pursue the subject further.

He didn't. Instead "I don' like Brownsville," he said. "I like Brooklyn bedder."

David felt relieved.

"We usetuh find cigahs innuh gudduh," Yussie continued. "An we usetuh t'row 'em on de ladies, an we usetuh run. Who you like bedder, ladies or gents?"

"Ladies."

"I like mine fodder bedder," said Yussie. "My mudder always holluhs on me." He pried a nail between two wheels. A bright yellow gear suddenly snapped off and fell to the gutter at his feet. He picked it up, blew the dust off, and rose. "Yuh want?"

"Yea," David reached for it.

Yussie was about to drop it into his outstretched palm, but on second thought, drew back. "No. Id's liddle like a penny. Maybe I c'n pud id inna slod machine 'n' gid gum. Hea, yuh c'n take dis one." He fished a larger gear out of his pocket, gave it to David. "Id's a quarter. Yuh wanna come?"

David hesitated. "I godduh waid hea till duh wissle blows."

"W'a wissle?"

"By de fectory. All togedder."

"So?"

"So den I c'n go opstai's."

"So w'y?"

"Cuz dey blow on twelve a'clock an' den dey blow on five a'clock. Den I c'n go op."

Yussie eyed him curiously. "I'm gonna gid gum," he said, shrugging off his perplexity. "In duh slod machine." And he ambled off in the direction of the candy store on the corner.

Holding the little wheel in his hand, David wondered again why it was that every boy on the street knew where his father worked except himself. His father had so many jobs. No sooner did you learn where he was working then he was working somewhere else. And why was he always saying, "They look at me crookedly, with mockery in their eyes! How much can a man endure? May the

fire of God consume them!" A terrifying picture rose in David's mind—the memory of how once at the supper table his mother had dared to say that perhaps the men weren't really looking at him crookedly, perhaps he was only imagining it. His father had snarled then. And with one sudden sweep of his arm had sent food and dishes crashing to the floor. And other pictures came in its train, pictures of the door being kicked open and his father coming in looking pale and savage and sitting down like old men sit down, one trembling hand behind him groping for the chair. He wouldn't speak. His jaws, and even his joints, seemed to become fused together by a withering rage. David often dreamed of his father's footsteps booming on the stairs, of the glistening door-knob turning, and of himself clutching at knives he couldn't lift from the table.

Brooding, engrossed in his thoughts, engrossed in the rhythmic, accurate teeth of the yellow cog in his hand, the thin bright circles whirling restlessly without motion, David was unaware that a little group of girls had gathered in the gutter some distance away. But when they began to sing, he started and looked up. Their faces were sober, their hands locked in one anothers; circling slowly in a ring they chanted in a plaintive nasal chorus:

"Waltuh, Waltuh, Wiuhlflowuh,
Growin' up so high;
So we are all young ladies,
An' we are ready to die."

Again and again, they repeated their burden. Their words obscure at first, emerged at last, gathered meaning. The song troubled David strangely. Walter Wildflower was a little boy. David knew him. He lived in Europe, far away, where David's mother said he was born. He had seen him standing on a hill, far away. Filled with a warm, nostalgic mournfulness, he shut his eyes. Fragments of forgotten rivers floated under the lids, dusty roads, fathomless curve of trees, a branch in a window under flawless light. A world somewhere, somewhere else.

"Waltuh, Waltuh, Wiuhlflowuh,
Growin' up so high,

His body relaxed, yielding to the rhythm of the song and to the golden June sunlight. He seemed to rise and fall on waves somewhere without him. Within him a voice spoke with no words but with the shift of slow flame. . . .

"So we are all young ladies,
An' we are ready to die."

From the limp, uncurling fingers, the cog rolled
to the ground, rang like a coin, fell over on its
side. The sudden sound moored him again, fixed
him to the quiet, suburban street, the curbstone.
The inarticulate flame that had pulsed within him,
wavered and went out. He sighed, bent over and
picked up the wheel.

When would the whistle blow he wondered. It
took long to-day. . . .

II

As far back as he could remember, this was the
first time that he had ever gone any where alone
with his father, and already he felt desolated, stirred
with dismal forebodings, longing desperately for
his mother. His father was so silent and so remote
that he felt as though he were alone even at his
side. What if his father should abandon him, leave
him in some lonely street. The thought sent
shudders of horror through his body. No! No! He
couldn't do that!

At last they reached the trolley lines. The sight
of people cheered him again, dispelling his fear for
a while. They boarded a car, rode what seemed to
him a long time and then got off in a crowded
street under an elevated. Nervously gripping David's
arm, his father guided him across the street. They
stopped before the stretched iron wicker of a
closed theater. Colored billboards on either side of
them, the odor of stale perfume behind. People
hurrying, trains roaring. David gazed about him
frightened. To the right of the theatre, in the window of an ice cream parlor, gaudy, colored popcorn danced and drifted, blown by a fan. He
looked up apprehensively at his father. He was
pale, grim. The fine veins in his nose stood out like
a pink cobweb.

"Do you see that door?" He shook him into attention. "In the grey house. See? That man just
came out of there."

"Yes, Papa."

"Now you go in there and go up the stairs and
you'll see another door. Go right in. And to the
first man you see inside, say this: I'm Albert
Schearl's son. He wants you to give me the clothes
in his locker and the money that's coming to him.
Do you understand? When they've given it to you
bring it down here. I'll be waiting for you. Now
what will you say?" he demanded abruptly.

David began to repeat his instructions in Yiddish.

"Say it in English, you fool!"

He rendered them in English. And when he had
satisfied his father that he knew them, he was
sent in.

"And don't tell them I'm out here," he was
warned as he left. "Remember you came alone!"

Full of misgivings, unnerved at the ordeal of
facing strangers alone, strangers of whom his own
father seemed apprehensive, he entered the hallway, climbed the stairs. One flight up, he pushed
open the door and entered a small room, an office.
From somewhere back of this office, machinery
clanked and rattled. A bald-headed man smoking
a cigar looked up as he came in.

"Well, my boy," he asked smiling, "what do
you want?"

For a moment all of his instructions flew out of
his head. "My—my fodder sent me hea." He
faltered.

"Your father? Who's he?"

"I—I'm Albert Schearl's son," he blurted out.
"He sent me I shuh ged his clo's f'om de locker
an' his money you owing him."

"Oh, you're Albert Schearl's son," said the man,
his expression changing. "And he wants his money,
eh?" He nodded with the short vibrating motion
of a bell. "You've got some father, my boy. You
can tell him that for me. I didn't get a chance.
He's crazy. Anybody who—What does he do at
home?"

David shook his head guiltily, "Nuttin."

"No?" he chuckled. "Nothin', hey?—Well—" he
broke off and went over to a small arched window
in the rear. "Joe!" he called. "Oh Joe! Come here
a minute, will you?"

In a few seconds a gray-haired man in overalls
came in.

"Call me, Mr. Lobe?"

"Yea, will you get Schearl's things out of his
locker and wrap 'em up for me. His kid's here."

The other man's face broke into a wide, brown-
toothed grin. "Is zat his kid?" As if to keep from
laughing his tongue worried the quid of tobacco in
his cheek.

"Yea."

"He don' look crazy." He burst into a laugh.

"No." Mr. Lobe subdued him with a wave of
the hand. "He's a nice kid."

"Your ol' man near brained me wid a hammer,"
said the man addressing David. "Don' know wot
happened, nobody said nuttin." He grinned. "Never
saw such a guy, Mr. Lobe. Holy Jesus, he looked
like he wuz boinin' up. Didja see de rail he twisted

wid his hands? Maybe I oughta to give it to 'im fer a souvenir?"

Mr. Lobe grinned. "Let the kid alone," he said quietly. "Get his stuff."

"O.K." Still chuckling, the gray-haired man went out.

"Sit down, my boy," said Mr. Lobe, pointing to a seat. "We'll have your father's things here in a few minutes."

David sat down. In a few minutes, a girl, bearing a paper in her hand, came into the office.

"Say, Marge," said Mr. Lobe, "find out what Schearl gets, will you."

"Yes, Mr. Lobe." She regarded David, "What's that, his boy?"

"Mmm."

"Looks like him, don't he?"

"Maybe."

"I'd have him arrested," said the girl opening up a large ledger.

"What good would that do?"

"I don't know, it might put some sense into his head."

Mr. Lobe shrugged. "I'm only too glad he didn't kill anybody."

"He ought to be in a padded cell," said the girl scribbling something on a paper.

Mr. Lobe made no response.

"He gets Six sixty-two." She put down her pencil. "Shall I get it?"

"Mmm."

The girl went over to a large black safe in a corner, drew out a box, and when she had counted out some money, put it into a small envelope and gave it to Mr. Lobe.

"Come here," he said to David. "What's your name?"

"David."

"David and Goliath," he smiled. "Well, David have you got a good deep pocket? Let's see." He picked up the tails of David's jacket. "There, that's the one I want." And fingering the small watch-pocket at the waist. "We'll put it in there." He folded the envelope and wedged it in. "Now don't take it out. Don't tell anybody you've got it till you get home, understand? The idea, sending a kid his age on an errand like this."

David, staring ahead of him, under Mr. Lobe's arm, was aware of two faces, peering in at the little window in the back. The eyes of both were fastened on him, regarding him with a curious and amused scrutiny of men beholding for the first time some astonishing freak. They both grinned

when the girl, happening to turn in their direction, saw them; one of the men winked and cranked his temple with his hand. As Mr. Lobe turned, both disappeared. A moment later, the gray-haired man returned with a paper wrapped bundle.

"Here's all I c'n find, Mr. Lobe. His towel, and his shoit an' a jacket."

"All right, Joe," Mr. Lobe took the package from him and turned to David. "Here you are, my boy. Put it under your arm and don't lose it." He tucked it under David's arm. "Not heavy, is it? No? That's good." He opened the door to let David pass. "Good bye." A dry smile whisked over his features. "Pretty tough for you."

Grasping the bundle firmly under his arm, David went slowly down the stairs. So that was how his father quit a place! He held a hammer in hand, he would have killed somebody. David could almost see him, the hammer raised over his head, his face contorted in terrific wrath, the rest cringing away. He shuddered at the image in his mind, stopped motionless on the stair, terrified at having to confront the reality. But he must go down; he must meet him; it would be worse for him if he remained on the stair any longer. He didn't want to go, but he had to. If only the stairs were twice as high.

He hurried down, came out into the street. His father, his back pressed close to the iron wicker, was waiting for him, and when he saw him come out, motioned to him to hurry and began walking away. David ran after him, caught up to him finally, and his father, without slackening his pace, relieved him of the bundle.

"They took long enough," he said, casting a malevolent glance over his shoulder. It was evident from his face that he had worked himself into a rage during the interval that David had left him. "They gave you the money?"

"Yes, Papa."

"How much?"

"Six—six dollars, the girl—"

"Did they say anything to you?" His teeth clenched grimly, "About me?"

"No, Papa," he answered hurriedly. "Nothing papa. They just gave me the—the money and I went down."

"Where is it?"

"Over here," he pointed to the pocket.

"Well, give it to me!"

With difficulty, David uprooted the envelope from his pocket. His father snatched it from him, counted the money.

"And so they said nothing, eh?" He seemed to demand a final confirmation. "None of the men spoke to you, did they? Only that bald-headed pig with the glasses?" He was watching him narrowly.

"No, papa. Only that man. He just gave me the money." He knew that while his father's eyes rested on him he must look frank, he must look wide-eyed, simple.

"Very well!" His lips stretched for a brief instant in fleeting satisfaction. "Good!"

They stopped at the corner and waited for the trolley . . .

David never said anything to anyone of what he had discovered, not even to his mother—it was all too terrifying, too unreal to share with someone else. He brooded about it till it entered his sleep, till he no longer could tell where his father was flesh and where dream. Who would believe him if he said, I saw my father lift a hammer; he was standing on a high roof of darkness, and below him were faces uplifted, so many, they stretched like white cobbles to the end of the world; who would believe him? He dared not.

Our second selection consists of the final paragraphs of the novel, where the book's title is arrived at as a kind of drowsy revelation. David has had an accident, a serious but curable leg injury, and his father, baffled and shaken, has gone out to buy the medicine recommended by the doctor. Utterly different in content and tone as it is, David's dissolving flow of consciousness bears a certain comparison—as poetic summary and affirmation—with the final interior monologue of the novel Roth most greatly reveres, Joyce's *Ulysses*.

David listened to his father's dull, unresilient footfall cross the kitchen floor. The door was opened, closed. A vague, remote pity stirred within his breast like a wreathing, raveling smoke tenuously dispersed within his being, a kind of torpid heartbreak he had felt sometimes in winter awakened deep in the night and hearing that dull tread descend the stairs.

"Perhaps you'll be hungry in a little while," his mother said persuasively. "After you've rested a bit and we've put the medicine on your foot. And then some milk and a boiled egg. You'd like that?" Her question was sufficiently shored by statement to require no answer. "And then you'll go to sleep and forget it all." She paused. Her dark, unswerving eyes sought his. "Sleepy, beloved?"

"Yes, mama."

He might as well call it sleep. It was only toward sleep that every wink of the eyelids could strike a spark into the cloudy tinder of the dark, kindle out of shadowy corners of the bedroom such myriad and such vivid jets of images—of the glint on tilted beards, of the uneven shine on roller skates, of the dry light on grey stone stops, of the tapering glitter of rails, of the oily sheen on the night-smooth rivers, of the glow on thin blonde hair, red faces, of the glow on the outstretched, open palms of legions upon legions of hands hurtling toward him. He might as well call it sleep. It was only toward sleep that ears had power to cull again and reassemble the shrill cry, the hoarse voice, the scream of fear, the bells, the thick-breathing, the roar of crowds and all sounds that lay fermenting in the vats of silence and the past. It was only toward sleep one knew himself still lying on the cobbles, felt the cobbles under him, and over him and scudding ever toward him like a black foam, the perpetual blur of shod and running feet, the broken shoes, new shoes, stubby, pointed, caked, polished, bunyiony, pavement-beveled, lumpish, under skirts, under trousers, shoes, over one and through one, and feel them all and feel, not pain, not terror, but strangest triumph, strangest acquiescence. One might as well call it sleep. He shut his eyes.

Depression Themes

For many Americans, the Depression years—essentially the decade of the thirties—were a period of searching, sometimes desperate appraisal and reappraisal of their country: of its economic structure, its characterizing ideas, its priorities, its psychology, its geography, its history, its great men and its villains. For many others, of course, the economic disaster led simply to apathy, a shriveling of social and economic ambition, or a self-deceiving refusal to confront the hard facts of life. In a story of 1936, William Saroyan, after rejoicing ironically that "ten million unemployed continue law-abiding," concluded that "Hardly anybody is interested in anything much. Hardly anybody *is* at all." And another writer, after traveling across the continent, reported bitterly that nothing had disgusted him so much as the "American addiction to make-believe. Apparently, not even empty bellies can cure it."[1] But elsewhere energies rose to meet the crisis, to explore it in depth, and to suggest or dramatize ways to resolve it.

It was a time of large-scale novels which attempted to encompass vast segments of the national scene: Dos Passos' *U.S.A.*, James T. Farrell's *Studs Lonigan*, Steinbeck's *The Grapes of Wrath* (as well as the differently motivated but equally expansive work of Thomas Wolfe and William Faulkner). Before coming to them, however, we should consider another phenomenon of the period, a "secondary literature" of sorts, which provided an enormous amount of raw materials for those "primary" writers to refine upon. This is something best described as documentary nonfiction. In *On Native Grounds* (1942), a very useful and sometimes controversial survey of the epoch, Alfred Kazin has remarked that the documentaries of the thirties comprised "a vast body of writing that is perhaps the fullest expression of the American consciousness after 1930." It was an urgent, often a passionate, response to the physical, economic, and psychological dislocations caused by the Depression, and, as Kazin pointed out, it had profoundly tragic overtones.

Here, in the revealing—especially revealing because it was so often mechanical —effort of so many American writers to seek out the reality of America in a time of crisis, is an authentic and curiously unconscious characterization of a tragic period. Here, in the vast granary of facts on life in America put away by the WPA writers, the documentary reporters, the folklorists preparing an American mythology, the explorers who went hunting through darkest America with notebook and camera, the new army of biographers and historians—here, stocked away like a reserve against bad times, is the raw stuff of the contemporary mass record.

[1] Both these passages are quoted by Harvey Swados in the introduction to his excellent anthology, *The American Writer and the Great Depression* (1966). Other extremely useful compilations on the period are *The Strenuous Decade: A Social and Intellectual Record of the Nineteen-Thirties* (1970), edited by Daniel Aaron and Robert Bendiner, and *Hard Times, An Oral History of the Great Depression* (1970), compiled by Louis (Studs) Terkel.

There were—to spell out Kazin's catalogue a little—the myriad guides, commissioned by the Works Project Administration as a device for employment, of the states and highways of the country. There were the accumulating and scientifically documented, firsthand studies of social and economic distress: among the rubber workers in Akron, Ohio (Ruth McKenney's *Industrial Valley*); in various urban centers (George Leighton's *Five Cities*); amid the dispossessed sharecroppers of the South (the W.P.A. case histories, *These Are Our Lives*). There were also—and this was one of the most invaluable enterprises of the W.P.A.—a great many interviews with former slaves: a treasure of historical and psychological material, for years available only (except for a small selection in B. A. Botkin's *Lay My Burden Down*) in the thirty-odd volumes of bound typescript in the Library of Congress, but recently published and made available to the public.

There was, too, the rapidly developing genre of the "picture book"—collections of photographs of the dispossessed, in camps and mills and fields, accompanied by captions and sometimes by texts. The begetters of these books claimed to be originating a new genre, and to some extent they were right. In one of the best of them, *An American Exodus*—an inquiry by Dorothea Lange and Paul S. Taylor into the plight of migratory workers from Oklahoma and Arkansas—the authors maintained that theirs was neither a commentary with illustrations nor a mere book of pictures. "Upon a tripod of photographs, captions, and text," they argued, "we rest themes evolved out of long observations in the field." It is true, as Kazin shrewdly noted, that there was a danger in letting the camera do the work of the mind, in simply recording things as they flatly were without relating them to the needs of body and spirit. But the picture books produced an immensely valuable shock to the sensibility of more fortunate Americans—*An American Exodus* came out the same year as *The Grapes of Wrath* and set off much larger vibrations. They led to at least one authentic masterpiece, *Let Us Now Praise Famous Men* (1941), a hauntingly effective study of the Alabama sharecroppers, with a poetic and intricately composed text by James Agee fusing beautifully with the photographic works of art of Walker Evans.[2]

There was, meanwhile, in the thirties, an outpouring of books which explicitly announced their troubled concern with America in general—*Per-*

---

[2] The most striking development beyond the picture books, in recent years, has been the television documentary—on hunger and poverty in America, for instance, or on the swollen public relations budget of the defense department. The television documentary, in addition to evolving what amounts to a new language of communication, is immediately accessible to millions of viewers and reaches an audience undreamed of by the authors of the earlier printed works.

plexed America (Sherwood Anderson), *Tragic America* (Theodore Dreiser), *The American Jitters* (Edmund Wilson), *Say, Is This the U.S.A.?* (Erskine Caldwell). And as part of the effort to get at the origins of the perplexed and tragic condition of the country, there was a sudden increase of research into the American past: historical studies of every variety, which sought out the defining traditions of the native culture; surveys of the growth of American thought and literature; biographies of the country's vanished great.

In the eyes of a good many concerned writers and intellectuals, the economic crisis could be explained by Karl Marx's historical analyses of class warfare and the workings of the capitalist system; and for these same individuals the Soviet Union stood as a model of social organization—all the more as its seeming opposite, fascism, seized iron control in Germany and Italy. At home, many literary people announced their fervent support of the American working class. Speaking to the first American Writers Congress in 1935, where Communist theory was beginning to hold sway, Malcolm Cowley declared: "The interests of my own class lie in a close alliance with the proletariat, and I believe that writers especially can profit by this alliance." Looking back, thirty years later, and referring to the second congress in 1937, Harvey Swados has movingly recalled the feel of things for a young writer:

> In addition to a passionate attachment to the mystique of the proletariat and a perfect Soviet state, there were also tremendous pressures—moral, psychological, even physical—to keep writers in line. The depression would not end, fascism would not go away, Hitler grew stronger. All your friends and associates were committed to the common struggle; Newton Arvin, Van Wyck Brooks, Erskine Caldwell, Marc Connelly, Malcolm Cowley, Waldo Frank, Langston Hughes, Archibald MacLeish, Lewis Mumford, Clifford Odets, Upton Sinclair, and Carl Van Doren were among those who issued the call to the second national congress of American writers, and thousands were turned away from the opening session at Carnegie Hall; where would you be, *who* would you be, if you were to question them and thus isolate yourself?

In fact, not a few writers did, from the first, question the Communist, as well as the Fascist, vision of the past and the future. By the later 1930's, many writers, card-carrying members of the Communist party or fellow travelers, had been disenchanted by the Stalinist purges and by what the followers of the exiled Trotsky regarded as the betrayal of the Revolution. This disenchantment was compounded in 1939 by Stalin's alliance with Hitler, and later by the revelation of Communist atrocities in Poland. In the late 1940's the pressures of the Cold War and the Red-baiting of Senator Joe McCarthy provoked additional recantations of Communism, often accompanied by the unhappy spectacle of finger-pointing at former friends and political associates.

Undoubtedly, Marxism had vastly sharpened the American awareness of the deep interrelation of economic and other forces in society, and sharpened the sense of the complexity of the democratic tradition. After the Depression American writers inevitably saw new dimensions in the drama of life in this country. But the truth is that Marxism left curiously little direct imprint upon American literature. It can be discovered in book reviews, leaves from private journals, addresses to public forums, assorted calls to arms;[3] but not in such fiction and poetry as have survived the thirties. The writing that *has* survived is, as always, work that transcends the blinding immediacies of a particular social, political, or economic situation to disclose an image of common humanity and human destiny.[4]

---

[3] See, for example, the attacks by left-wing critics on Robert Frost's A *Further Range* in 1937 (pp. 1863–64 above). William Faulkner suffered even more than did Frost from that brand of criticism. His work was generally dismissed with passing references to its fascistic or decadent qualities.

[4] One may be reminded of the later nineteenth-century literary movement known as "critical realism." As espoused by Howells, critical realism seemed to press the American writer into the cause of immediate social change; but what it really aimed at was an enlarged concern with the issue of justice and the masks of hypocrisy in modern civilization.

JACK CONROY (1899–   )

A case in point, though not perhaps a very imposing one, is Jack Conroy's novel of 1933, *The Disinherited*. It is virtually the only "proletarian novel" that is still readable as a work of some literary appeal in its own right. For all the endless—and from this distance, boring—discussion about the need for an American proletarian literature, it was never clear exactly who was to create it or who was to read it. But Conroy's credentials in this regard were impeccable. He was born in Moberly, Missouri, the son of a miner and himself a member of the working class. He belonged to a self-styled group of "rebel poets" and had edited a magazine, *Anvil*, devoted to proletarian fiction. In a novel called *A World to Win* (1935), Conroy was openly doctrinaire about the role of economic forces in the shaping of American life, and in *They Seek a City* (written with Arna Bontemps in 1945), he explored the plight of the homeless American black. But in *The Disinherited* a certain artistic impulse was in the ascendancy. The book, which is essentially autobiographical, carries the narrator from the early 1900's into the first years of the Depression; and the human image it stirs into being derives (by a familiar paradox of art) from a fidelity to the concretenesses of remembered life—mining camps and midwestern cities, the lynching of antiwar speakers in 1918, long cold winters of racking poverty and dwindling hope; sexual adventures, male friendships, marital failures.

For all the misery experienced, and all the bitterness felt in the contrast between present impoverishment and oppression and past stability and aspiration, the novel ends on a note of extremely cautious optimism. In the final episode the local sheriff holds an auction of the meager possessions of an evicted farmer. But the latter's friends and neighbors band together and force the auctioneer to sell them the furnishings for eight cents, after which they sell them back to the farmer, Ben, for another few pennies—which they laconically offer to loan him. But the wary hopefulness which arises from the episode is not in any summons to programmatic action or any vision of a highly organized revolution to come. It is rooted in a low-keyed revelation of human decency and of communal feeling and fellowship.

KENNETH FEARING (1902–1961)

We are mainly concerned, in this section, with prose writing; but as a reminder that other literary arts were also touched by social conscience, we may consider the work of Kenneth Fearing, the poet par excellence of the American thirties. Fearing was born in Oak Park, Illinois (the birthplace, as well, of Ernest Hemingway). After a stint of journalism, he went to the University of Wisconsin and began to immerse himself in contemporary writing. Fearing was responsive to the poetry of T. S. Eliot and E. E. Cummings, and even the early writing of Wallace Stevens; but he was more taken with Robinson's verse portraits of metropolitan failures, and Sandburg's blustering images of the industrial city. Fearing's sympathies were inalienably with the poor and the victimized, but his taste was for the satirical; and he was particularly stimulated by H. L. Mencken's journalistic bombardments of the current absurdities and potent falsities in American culture.

Both Fearing's compassion and his comic sense, often handsomely fused, became evident in his second volume, *Poems* (1935). In "No Credit," for example, the tone is nicely set in the opening clause, with its cozy evocation of a pleasant dinner and of apartment windows brightened—by gunfire in the street outside. Fearing's poetry in this mood somewhat resembles the fiction of Nathanael West (whose *A Cool Million* had appeared the year before); both found sources of dark laughter in an apocalyptic situation. "No Credit" moves through an offbeat catalogue of the ridiculous and the horrifying to a closing image of the only entity that was immune to the destructive efforts of fools, brokers, scabs, sheriffs, and bayonet-wielding troopers—the side-show robot with the welded breast. One senses in a poem like this something of the satirical glee that invests many of the poems of E. E. Cummings; but there is also a potentiality for rage (almost never realized, to be sure) absent from Cummings.

Fearing's is typically a poetry of comment. However faithful he was to Emily Dickinson's notion that a poet should "tell it slant," he usually arrived, by indirection, at a particular observation about a particular historical condition. On occasion, however, he could marshal his resources to convey a more generalized response to life—as in "Devil's Dream" (from *Dead Reckoning*, 1938), where cadence, language, and even syntax intensify toward a sensation of ultimate and absolute terror. As against that, finally, we offer the no less characteristic but much more light-fingered exercise, "Homage" (written in 1940), which suggests how, across the ages, man's commercial instinct might have reacted to man's greatest achievements.

The thirties were Fearing's natural habitat. He kept himself informed of the radical attacks upon the objects of his own outrage; but he was too independent and too humorous to take part in them. In later years, he tended to repeat himself (though he also wrote a first-class thriller, *The Big Clock*, in 1946); and seemed less capable of the muted, half-smiling fury that produced his most memorable work. He died in June of 1961.

No Credit (1935)

Whether dinner was pleasant, with the windows lit by gunfire, and no one disagreed;
or whether, later, we argued in the park, and there was a touch of vomit-gas in the evening air;
Whether we found a greater, deeper, more perfect love, by courtesy of Camels, over NBC; whether the comics amused us, or the newspapers carried a hunger death and a White House prayer for mother's day;
Whether the bills were paid or not, whether or not we had our doubts, whether we spoke our minds at Joe's, and the receipt said "Not Returnable," and the cash-register rang up "No Sale,"
Whether the truth was then, or later, or whether the best had already gone—

Nevertheless, we know; as every turn is measured; as every unavoidable risk is known;
As nevertheless, the flesh grows old, dies, dies in its only life, is gone;
The reflection goes from the mirror, as the shadow, of even a rebel, is gone from the wall;
As nevertheless, the current is thrown and the wheels revolve; and nevertheless, as the word is spoken and the wheat grows tall and the ships sail on—

None but the fool is paid in full; none but the broker, none but the scab is certain of profit;
The sheriff alone may attend a third degree in formal attire; alone, the academy artists multiply in dignity as trooper's bayonet guards the door;   10
Only Steve, the side-show robot, knows content; only Steve, the mechanical man in love with a photo-electric beam, remains aloof; only Steve, who sits and smokes or stands in salute, is secure;
Steve, whose shoebutton eyes are blind to terror, whose painted ears are deaf to appeal, whose welded breast will never be slashed by bullets, whose armature soul can hold no fear.

Devil's Dream (1938)

But it could never be true;
How could it ever happen, if it never did before, and it's not so now?

But suppose that the face behind those steel prison bars—
Why do you dream about a face lying cold in the trenches streaked with rain and dirt and blood?
Is it the very same face seen so often in the mirror?
Just as though it could be true—

But what if it is, what if it is, what if it is, what if the thing that cannot happen really happens just the same.
Suppose the fever goes a hundred, then a hundred and one,
What if Holy Savings Trust goes from 98 to 88 to 78 to 68, then drops down to 28 and 8 and out of sight,
And the fever shoots a hundred two, a hundred three, a hundred four, then a hundred five and out?   10

But now there's only the wind and the sky and sunlight and the clouds,
With everyday people walking and talking as they always have before along the everyday street,

Doing ordinary things with ordinary faces and
    ordinary voices in the ordinary way,
Just as they always will—

Then why does it feel like a bomb, why does
    it feel like a target,
Like standing on the gallows with the trap
    about to drop,

Why does it feel like a thunderbolt the sec-
    ond before it strikes, why does it feel like
    a tight-rope walk high over hell?

Because it is not, will not, never could be true
That the whole wide, bright, green, warm,
    calm world goes:
CRASH.   20

Homage (1940)

They said to him, "It is a very good thing
that you have done, yes, both good and
great, proving this other passage to the
Indies. Marvelous," they said. "Very. But
where, Señor, is the gold?"

They said: "We like it, we admire it very
much, don't misunderstand us, in fact we
think it's almost great. But isn't there, well,
a little too much of this Prince of Denmark? After all, there is no one quite like
you in your lighter vein."

"Astonishing," they said. "Who would have
thought you had it in you, Orville?" They
said, "Wilbur, this machine of yours is
amazing, if it works, and perhaps some day
we can use it to distribute eggs, or to
advertise."

And they were good people, too. Decent
people.
They did not beat their wives. They went to
church. And they kept the law.

CLIFFORD ODETS (1906–1963)

The early plays of Clifford Odets are a further
reminder that the most divisive social issues
during the Depression years were reflected not
only in fiction but in all the modes of literary
expression. Indeed, Odets, whose first and still
best-known stage success, *Waiting for Lefty*,
was produced in January, 1935, was to feel
trapped within the period of the thirties—to
feel, that is, that the public image of him as a
playwright was unfairly limited to that of a
Depression writer. He became, and to his discomfort he tended to remain, what one critic,
borrowing the title of another of his plays,
called "the 'Golden Boy' of the Left Theater."[1]

    Through the forties and into the fifties,
Odets continued to write plays of considerable
merit, and we find in them themes drawn from

[1] Daniel Aaron in *Writers on the Left* (1967), a
study which contains the handiest appraisal of left-
wing theater in the thirties.

Odets' experience after and apart from the Depression. At the same time, we make out a
persistence of theme from Odets' earliest to his
later plays that, as we shall see, has little to do
finally with the actualities of social distress,
a theme at once more personal and more
universal than a concern for immediate social
reform. It is therefore far from our intention to
revive the old cliché about Odets and to restrict
him to a particular moment in American history. It must nonetheless be acknowledged that
in several ways Odets *was* a phenomenon of the
thirties, and we have chosen, as our selection,
the work that first established him as such—in
full recognition that it is not his best.

    Odets, in fact, is one of those writers who
seemed for a moment to be enacting the allegory of his own time. The year 1935 was as
significant for him as the year 1912 had been

for Eugene O'Neill. (See pp. 2000–2.) In the course of 1935, Odets saw no less than four of his plays produced on the New York stage and saw himself catapulted into fame as the country's newest dramatic genius and O'Neill's successor—a person, in Odets' own words to an interviewer, "who receives fantastic offers from Hollywood, invitations to address ladies' clubs, one hundred and fifty telephone calls a day and a lot of solemn consideration from guys who write pieces for the dramatic page." During the same year Odets reached the peak of his rather brief participation in the Communist party and began to move swiftly toward disengagement. Before the year was out he had left New York, had in effect moved away from the left theater, and was settled in Hollywood writing film scripts at a salary of twenty-five hundred dollars a week. One way to formulate the basic motif of several of the plays he went on to compose—particularly *Golden Boy* of 1937 and *The Big Knife* of 1948—is that of a tension between some mode of creative or moral or social idealism and the compulsive desire for fame and money. It is, obviously, a motif that springs directly out of the contradictory experiences of the year 1935.

Odets was twenty-nine at this time. He had been born in Philadelphia in 1906, the eldest child of Jewish parents, Louis and Pearl Geisinger Odets. Clifford Odets has even been named as "the first in a line of emerging American Jewish writers of importance" and linked in this regard with Arthur Miller, Bernard Malamud, Saul Bellow, and Philip Roth.[2] As we have seen, however, Gertrude Stein had been writing work of a very high order since literally the year Odets was born, and in the several years before *Waiting for Lefty* there had been the conspicuously and handsomely Jewish writing of Michael Gold and Henry Roth. Nevertheless, there remains an element of truth in the remark just quoted. Gold and Henry Roth, if not Gertrude Stein, were dealing primarily with Jewish *immigrant* experience—the Jew, as it were, confronting the New World of American urban

society—while Odets, especially in *Awake and Sing!* (1935), may well have been the first to give artistic expression to American Jewish middle-class family life, with its longing for security and respectability.[3]

To what extent *Awake and Sing!* and Odets' other plays about the strains of family life—for example, *Golden Boy* and *The Flowering Peach* (1954)—are based upon Odets' childhood and adolescent recollections is unclear. He once denied quite vehemently that *Awake and Sing!* had anything to do with the Odets household. "I never came from such a family," he insisted. "I never lived such a life. My mother was a strange and nunlike woman"—entirely unlike the possessive and dictatorial "Jewish mother" Bessie Berger in *Awake and Sing!*—"who had to live with two brawling, trigger-tempered men in the house—my father and myself." Odets retained a good deal of affection for both his parents, as for his two sisters, and dedicated *Six Plays* in 1939 to his mother. There appears to be little in Odets' experience or his work that resembles O'Neill's lifelong obsession with the tensions and clashing personalities of his own family.

After being acclaimed as the first talented "proletarian playwright," Odets sometimes liked to identify himself as "a worker's son," but this too was misleading and part of the odd pattern of quasi-deception and self-deception that characterized his career. It is true that Louis Odets once sold newspapers, and his wife worked in a stocking factory. But before Clifford was six, the family had moved to New York where Louis had a good job in a print shop—of which, in due time, he became the owner; when he retired in 1936, he sold the shop for more than $200,000—which in current values would approximate $1,000,000. Odets had some difficulties with these facts in attempting to explain his attraction to communism before the House Committee on Un-American Activities during the worst of the Senator Joseph McCarthy period in 1952.

If Odets was not seriously impoverished in his

[2] Morris Friedman, in the introduction to *Clifford Odets* (1969), by Michael J. Mendelsohn.

[3] Robert Warshow has argued this point effectively in *The Immediate Experience* (1962).

youth, he was undoubtedly neurotic: there was something deeply restive and dissatisfied about him, a sort of unfocused rebelliousness; according to his own possibly exaggerated report, he tried to commit suicide a number of times during his young manhood. But like many of his contemporaries, he tended to locate the source of his inner turmoil not in any personal factor —creative frustration, for example—but in the severe dislocations and inequities of American society. The chances are, as one or two critics have suggested, that Odets was drawn to the Communist party in 1934 for much the same reason that he had joined the Group Theater in New York a few years earlier—because he detected in both entities an emphatically optimistic vision of the future possibilities for social man. He might almost have said, as Michael Gold did at the end of his novel *Jews Without Money*, "O workers' Revolution, you brought hope to me, a lonely suicidal boy. You are the true Messiah." Unlike Gold, however, Odets moved in and out of the Communist association fairly hurriedly. The influence of the Group Theater lasted much longer.

The Group Theater had been formed in 1930–31, a by-product of the Theater Guild (itself, it may be recalled, the successor to the old Washington Square Players), by Harold Clurman, Lee Strasberg, and Cheryl Crawford. Though by no means doctrinaire along political lines, the members of the new enterprise implicitly extended the concept of "group" to apply not only to themselves as a closely knit gathering of theater folk but also to society at large as a collective being. In his well-named and highly informative account of the Group Theater, *The Fervent Years* (1945), Harold Clurman recalls that among its operative ideas were both the principle that "a unified method should be employed by the triumvirate of directors in order to mold the actors into a single organism" and the injunction that "a philosophy of life should guide the work of the Group and even pervade all the plays." The philosophy in question was a sort of vague but hopeful socialism, and in view of it playwrights whose work was produced by the theater (like Paul Green and Maxwell Anderson) were persuaded to tack on cheerful endings to incipient tragedies, and Odets, as he later remarked, "to make the materials of my plays say something that they were really not saying." It was, philosophically speaking, a somewhat crude version of the "critical realism" borrowed forty-odd years earlier by William Dean Howells from various European writers (Tolstoi and Zola among them); but the Group Theater contributed a crucial chapter to American dramatic history on the basis of it, and it contained at one time what was arguably the most accomplished list of actors and actresses the American stage has ever seen.[4]

The Theater's biggest commercial success was Sidney Kingsley's slickly built play about the medical profession, *Men in White*, in 1933; but its most memorable occasion, for those who witnessed it, was the opening of *Waiting for Lefty* on January 5, 1935. When the curtain rang down, according to the reviewer in the left-wing *New Masses*, "the audience cheered, whistled and screamed with applause." For Harold Clurman, the choral shout that concluded the one-acter—"STRIKE, STRIKE, STRIKE!!!"— was "the birth cry of the thirties"; and looking back on the opening night almost three decades later, Malcolm Cowley reflected on the degree of excitement that the particular historical moment had lent the play. "To recapture the effect of its first performance," Cowley wrote (in "While They Waited for Lefty," in 1964), ". . . one would have to reconstitute the audience that remembered five years of depression, the banks closing, the landlord at the door, and that shouted "Strike!" with a sense of release . . . as it raised a thousand clenched fists." In the months following, *Waiting for Lefty* played in more than a hundred cities, often against the strenuous opposition of conservative or antilabor elements in those areas.

[4] The cast of Odets' *Golden Boy*, in 1937, for example, included (in order of appearance) Frances Farmer, Luther Adler, Lee J. Cobb, Jules Garfield (whose movie name was John Garfield), Morris Carnovsky, Elia Kazan, Howard Da Silva, and Karl Malden. Stella Adler also played several roles in Group Theater productions.

Waiting for Lefty, which deals with the decision of members of a cab-drivers union to go on strike, was based loosely on a New York taxi strike of 1934. Reconsidering it today, one is likely to find it only too deeply entangled in the labor politics of the time, in union organization, espionage, double-dealing, and rough stuff. But divested of its historical trappings (and its sometimes badly dated dialogue), the play reveals what is probably Odets' major theme—the confrontation of the moment of decision. Behind the clamorous vote of the union members, there is the decision of young Joe to demonstrate his manhood to his wife by joining the strike, of Sid to take the possibly dangerous action which may make it possible for him to marry the girl Florence, of the laboratory assistant Miller to reject the well-greased invitation of an industrialist to work on the preparation of a poison gas, and so on. Whatever one may think of these somewhat hackneyed instances of the theme, there is no doubt that the fundamental motif—the arrival at decision—has an authentic and traditional dramatic power.

In *Awake and Sing!*, which opened a month after *Waiting for Lefty*, the theme is given a somewhat richer and more complex treatment. The ingredients of this drama about a Brooklyn Jewish household are again banal or melodramatic, and uncomfortably suggestive, in a contemporary perspective of a television serial; yet the play is curiously compelling, if only because all members of the family are caught up in the moment of crisis, each according to his or her character. While the mother, Bessie, continues to insist on family solidarity (under her dominion), respectability, and saving for a rainy day, the daughter Hennie abandons the man with whom she has been forced into marriage and departs with her lover, the grandfather commits suicide so that the children will receive an inheritance that can insure their freedom,[5] and the son Ralph announces (not altogether persuasively) his intention to stay and enlist in the struggle for the rights of workers.

[5] An action also taken by Arthur Miller's Willy Loman in the more effective *Death of a Salesman*.

The closing glimpse of Ralph standing "full and strong in the doorway" (according to the stage direction) is presumably an instance of Odets' being coerced into making his materials "say something that they were really not saying." In two more plays of 1935—*Till the Day I Die* and *Paradise Lost*—Odets again yielded to the optimistic vision of the Group Theater, producing in the second a concluding manifesto of faith in man and human progress that the deplorably messy circumstances of the play up to that point make quite incredible. But the Hollywood experience over the next two years, far from corrupting Odets' talent, seems actually to have strengthened it—in particular by drawing him away from the political or labor-movement theme that was not, as it turned out, really congenial to him. His departure from the Communist party in 1936—though in the eyes of his associates it constituted a characteristic bourgeois betrayal of the revolution for the fleshpots of California—was another step in the process of Odets' self-liberation.

The strength of *Golden Boy* (1937) is due in part, one surmises, to the fact that it derives more immediately than anything Odets had yet written from his own inner tensions. The choice confronted by the protagonist Joe Bonaparte—whether to pursue an artistic career, as a concert violinist, or the materially more rewarding career in the prize ring—clearly reflects Odets' sense of the alternatives he himself was facing and to each of which a portion of him was deeply drawn: a commitment to the art of drama or to the riches available to the complaisant hack writer. (Odets, incidentally, was a serious devotee of classical music and once thought of writing a play about Beethoven.) But what is most striking about *Golden Boy* is that the major decisions are not arrived at, with large histrionic gestures, in the last five minutes of the drama, as in both *Waiting for Lefty* and *Awake and Sing!* Rather, the widening implications of the alternatives permeate the play's entire atmosphere, and instead of a work poised on a single and all-determining overt act we have the relentless probing of a complex situation, somewhat in the manner of Chekhov or the later O'Neill.[6] The play is constructed with the most admirable craftsmanship—Odets was never more in command of his resources—and its subtle, slow, persistent movement is all in the direction of death. Joe Bonaparte and his fiancée are literally killed in an automobile crash; but this, one feels, is the inevitable culmination of a process and not a melodramatic device to solve a plot problem. And the process in question, so the play gradually discloses, is not after all one of decision-making: it is a quest for an identity of which the alternative careers are merely external guises; and it is a quest that tragically fails.

Odets put in three stretches in Hollywood: 1936–38, 1943–47, and 1955–61. After each visit, he returned to New York, and after the second he produced a play which is precisely *about* a man desperately trying to escape from Hollywood and get back to the New York stage. In *The Big Knife*, Charlie Castle, an enormously popular screen actor, is faced with the alternative of attempting a problematic career in the Broadway theater or staying in Hollywood in fulfillment of a contract which would net him three million dollars: a dilemma Castle finds so

intolerable that he kills himself. *The Big Knife* is, in short, a very contrived piece of work, for all its moments of characteristically intense and eloquent dialogue; and what it points up is not only Odets' frequent failure of imagination— that is, of an imagination capable of genuinely grasping its subject—but also his uncertainty about the dramatic mode in which he was attempting to write. He had none of O'Neill's taste for modernizing Greek tragedy and little of O'Neill's daring in theatrical innovation; he seems indeed never to have been very clear about the possible relation between drama and the rest of literature. What he aimed at—most successfully in *Golden Boy*—was to use the framework of the well-made play, something familiar and attractive to New York audiences, in order to build a far-reaching dramatic statement about human experience.

The Country Girl, which Odets himself directed with considerable success in 1950, was something of a recovery. In the figure of Frank Elgin—an alcoholic actor who is given one last chance, both in the theater and in his marriage to the country-bred Georgie—Odets projected his personal apprehensions, with the passing years, about his position in the American theater. (Odets, it may be noted, was anything but an alcoholic.) The apprehensions were not unfounded. *The Country Girl* was a tremendous hit and was turned into a prize-winning and money-making movie; but it defined the terms, as it were, of Odets' achievement. He was and would remain as accomplished an artist as one could be within the confines of show business. His work is an authentic though marginal contribution to American literature. It is also and perhaps more importantly a reflection, at one period, of our social history, and at a later period of the history of taste.

---

[6] Odets was ambivalent about Chekhov, sometimes happily acknowledging his influence, sometimes stoutly denying it. There is no doubt, however, that Chekhov's influence, whatever it amounted to, was a healthy one, and helped Odets grow beyond the plot-ridden soap-opera kind of work to which he was early addicted, and toward a dramatized exploration of certain aspects of the human condition.

As to O'Neill, Odets later in his life paid him a graceful and, from all one can tell, completely accurate tribute:

I admired O'Neill. I am influenced by O'Neill in terms of aspiration, in terms of becoming a big American playwright.

FURTHER READINGS

Michael J. Mendelsohn, *Clifford Odets: Human Dramatist* (1969)

Edward Murray, *Clifford Odets: The Thirties and After* (1968)

Arthur H. Quinn, *A History of the American Drama* (1936)

R. Baird Shuman, *Clifford Odets* (1962)

Gerald Weales, *Clifford Odets: Playwright* (1971)

Waiting for Lefty (1935)

CHARACTERS

FATT	SID
JOE	CLAYTON
EDNA	AGATE KELLER
MILLER	HENCHMAN
FAYETTE	DR. BARNES
IRV	DR. BENJAMIN
FLORRIE	A MAN

As the curtain goes up we see a bare stage. On it are sitting six or seven men in a semi-circle. Lolling against the proscenium down left is a young man chewing a toothpick: a gunman. A fat man of porcine appearance is talking directly to the audience. In other words he is the head of a union and the men ranged behind him are a committee of workers. They are now seated in interesting different attitudes and present a wide diversity of type, as we shall soon see. The fat man is hot and heavy under the collar, near the end of a long talk, but not too hot: he is well fed and confident. His name is HARRY FATT.

FATT: You're so wrong I ain't laughing. Any guy with eyes to read knows it. Look at the textile strike—out like lions and in like lambs. Take the San Francisco tie-up—starvation and broken heads. The steel boys wanted to walk out too, but they changed their minds. It's the trend of the times, that's what it is. All we workers got a good man behind us now. He's top man of the country—looking out for our interests—the man in the White House is the one I'm referrin' to. That's why the times ain't ripe for a strike. He's working day and night—

VOICE (*from the audience*): For who? (*The* GUNMAN *stirs himself.*)

FATT: For you! The records prove it. If this was the Hoover régime, would I say don't go out, boys? Not on your tin-type! But things is different now. You read the papers as well as me. You know it. And that's why I'm against the strike. Because we gotta stand behind the man who's standin' behind us! The whole country—

ANOTHER VOICE: Is on the blink! (*The* GUNMAN *looks grave.*)

FATT: Stand up and show yourself, you damn red! Be a man, let's see what you look like! (*Waits in vain.*) Yellow from the word go! Red and yellow makes a dirty color, boys. I got my eyes on four or five of them in the union here. What the hell'll they do for you? Pull you out and run away when trouble starts. Give those birds a chance and they'll have your sisters and wives in the whore houses, like they done in Russia. They'll tear Christ off his bleeding cross. They'll wreck your homes and throw your babies in the river. You think that's bunk? Read the papers! Now listen, we can't stay here all night. I gave you the facts in the case. You boys got hot suppers to go to and—

ANOTHER VOICE: Says you!

GUNMAN: Sit down, Punk!

ANOTHER VOICE: Where's Lefty? (*Now this question is taken up by the others in unison.* FATT *pounds with gavel.*)

FATT: That's what I wanna know. Where's your pal, Lefty? You elected him chairman—where the hell did he disappear?

VOICES: We want Lefty! Lefty! Lefty!

FATT (*pounding*): What the hell is this—a circus? You got the committee here. This bunch of cowboys you elected. (*Pointing to man on extreme right end.*)

MAN: Benjamin.

FATT: Yeah, Doc Benjamin. (*Pointing to other men in circle in seated order*): Benjamin, Miller, Stein, Mitchell, Phillips, Keller. It ain't my fault Lefty took a run-out powder. If you guys—

A GOOD VOICE: What's the committee say?

OTHERS: The committee! Let's hear from the committee! (FATT *tries to quiet the crowd, but one of the seated men suddenly comes to the front. The* GUNMAN *moves over to center stage, but* FATT *says:*)

FATT: Sure, let him talk. Let's hear what the red boys gotta say! (*Various shouts are coming from the audience.* FATT *insolently goes back to his seat in the middle of the circle. He sits on his raised platform and relights his cigar. The* GUNMAN *goes back to his post.* JOE, *the new speaker, raises his hand for quiet. Gets it quickly. He is sore.*)

JOE: You boys know me. I ain't a red boy one bit! Here I'm carryin' a shrapnel that I picked up in the war. And maybe I don't know it when it rains! Don't tell me red! You know what we are? The black and blue boys! We been kicked around so long we're black and blue from head to toes. But I guess anyone who says straight out he don't like it, he's a red boy to the leaders of the union. What's this crap about goin' home to hot suppers?

I'm asking to your faces how many's got hot suppers to go home to? Anyone who's sure of his next meal, raise your hand! A certain gent sitting behind me can raise them both. But not in front here! And that's why we're talking strike—to get a living wage!

VOICE: Where's Lefty?

JOE: I honest to God don't know, but he didn't take no run-out powder. That Wop's got more guts than a slaughter house. Maybe a traffic jam got him, but he'll be here. But don't let this red stuff scare you. Unless fighting for a living scares you. We gotta make up our minds. My wife made up my mind last week, if you want the truth. It's plain as the nose on Sol Feinberg's face we need a strike. There's us comin' home every night—eight, ten hours on the cab. "God," the wife says, "eighty cents ain't money—don't buy beans almost. You're workin' for the company," she says to me, "Joe! you ain't workin' for me or the family no more!" She says to me, "If you don't start . . ."

I. JOE AND EDNA

The lights fade out and a white spot picks out the playing space within the space of seated men. The seated men are very dimly visible in the outer dark, but more prominent is FATT *smoking his cigar and often blowing the smoke in the lighted circle.*

A tired but attractive woman of thirty comes into the room, drying her hands on an apron. She stands there sullenly as JOE *comes in from the other side, home from work. For a moment they stand and look at each other in silence.*

JOE: Where's all the furniture, honey?
EDNA: They took it away. No installments paid.
JOE: When?
EDNA: Three o'clock.
JOE: They can't do that.
EDNA: Can't? They did it.
JOE: Why, the palookas, we paid three-quarters.
EDNA: The man said read the contract.
JOE: We must have signed a phoney. . . .
EDNA: It's a regular contract and you signed it.
JOE: Don't be so sour, Edna. . . . (*Tries to embrace her.*)
EDNA: Do it in the Movies, Joe—they pay Clark Gable big money for it.
JOE: This is a helluva house to come home to. Take my word!

EDNA: Take MY word! Whose fault is it?
JOE: Must you start that stuff again?
EDNA: Maybe you'd like to talk about books?
JOE: I'd like to slap you in the mouth!
EDNA: No you won't.
JOE (*sheepishly*): Jeez, Edna, you get me sore some time. . . .
EDNA: But just look at me—I'm laughing all over!
JOE: Don't insult me. Can I help it if times are bad? What the hell do you want me to do, jump off a bridge or something?
EDNA: Don't yell. I just put the kids to bed so they won't know they missed a meal. If I don't have Emmy's shoes soled tomorrow, she can't go to school. In the meantime let her sleep.
JOE: Honey, I rode the wheels off the chariot today. I cruised around five hours without a call. It's conditions.
EDNA: Tell it to the A & P!
JOE: I booked two-twenty on the clock. A lady with a dog was lit . . . she gave me a quarter tip by mistake. If you'd only listen to me—we're rolling in wealth.
EDNA: Yeah? How much?
JOE: I had "coffee and—" in a beanery. (*Hands her silver coins.*) A buck four.
EDNA: The second month's rent is due tomorrow.
JOE: Don't look at me that way, Edna.
EDNA: I'm looking through you, not at you. . . . Everything was gonna be so ducky! A cottage by the waterfall, roses in Picardy. You're a four-starbust! If you think I'm standing for it much longer, you're crazy as a bedbug.
JOE: I'd get another job if I could. There's no work—you know it.
EDNA: I only know we're at the bottom of the ocean.
JOE: What can I do?
EDNA: Who's the man in the family, you or me?
JOE: That's no answer. Get down to brass tacks. Christ, gimme a break, too! A coffee and java all day. I'm hungry, too, Babe. I'd work my fingers to the bone if—
EDNA: I'll open a can of salmon.
JOE: Not now. Tell me what to do!
EDNA: I'm not God!
JOE: Jeez, I wish I was a kid again and didn't have to think about the next minute.
EDNA: But you're not a kid and you do have to think about the next minute. You got two blondie kids sleeping in the next room. They need food and clothes. I'm not mentioning anything else—But we're stalled like a flivver in the snow. For five

years I laid awake at night listening to my heart pound. For God's sake, do something, Joe, get wise. Maybe get your buddies together, maybe go on strike for better money. Poppa did it during the war and they won out. I'm turning into a sour old nag.

JOE (*defending himself*): Strikes don't work!

EDNA: Who told you?

JOE: Besides that means not a nickel a week while we're out. Then when it's over they don't take you back.

EDNA: Suppose they don't! What's to lose?

JOE: Well, we're averaging six-seven dollars a week now.

EDNA: That just pays for the rent.

JOE: That is something, Edna.

EDNA: It isn't. They'll push you down to three and four a week before you know it. Then you'll say, "That's somethin'," too!

JOE: There's too many cabs on the street, that's the whole damn trouble.

EDNA: Let the company worry about that, you big fool! If their cabs didn't make a profit, they'd take them off the streets. Or maybe you think they're in business just to pay Joe Mitchell's rent!

JOE: You don't know a-b-c, Edna.

EDNA: I know this—your boss is making suckers outa you boys every minute. Yes, and suckers out of all the wives and the poor innocent kids who'll grow up with crooked spines and sick bones. Sure, I see it in the papers, how good orange juice is for kids. But damnit our kids get colds one on top of the other. They look like little ghosts. Betty never saw a grapefruit. I took her to the store last week and she pointed to a stack of grapefruits. "What's that!" she said. My God, Joe—the world is supposed to be for all of us.

JOE: You'll wake them up.

EDNA: I don't care, as long as I can maybe wake you up.

JOE: Don't insult me. One man can't make a strike.

EDNA: Who says one? You got hundreds in your rotten union!

JOE: The union ain't rotten.

EDNA: No? Then what are they doing? Collecting dues and patting your back?

JOE: They're making plans.

EDNA: What kind?

JOE: They don't tell us.

EDNA: It's too damn bad about you. They don't tell little Joey what's happening in his bitsie witsie union. What do you think it is—a ping pong game?

JOE: You know they're racketeers. The guys at the top would shoot you for a nickel.

EDNA: Why do you stand for that stuff?

JOE: Don't you wanna see me alive?

EDNA (*after a deep pause*): No . . . I don't think I do, Joe. Not if you can lift a finger to do something about it, and don't. No, I don't care.

JOE: Honey, you don't understand what—

EDNA: And any other hackie that won't fight . . . let them all be ground to hamburger!

JOE: It's one thing to—

EDNA: Take your hand away! Only they don't grind me to little pieces! I got different plans. (*Starts to take off her apron.*)

JOE: Where are you going?

EDNA: None of your business.

JOE: What's up your sleeve?

EDNA: My arm'd be up my sleeve, darling, if I had a sleeve to wear. (*Puts neatly folded apron on back of chair.*)

JOE: Tell me!

EDNA: Tell you what?

JOE: Where are you going?

EDNA: Don't you remember my old boy friend?

JOE: Who?

EDNA: Bud Haas. He still has my picture in his watch. He earns a living.

JOE: What the hell are you talking about?

EDNA: I heard worse than I'm talking about.

JOE: Have you seen Bud since we got married?

EDNA: Maybe.

JOE: If I thought . . . (*He stands looking at her.*)

EDNA: See much? Listen, boy friend, if you think I won't do this it just means you can't see straight.

JOE: Stop talking bull!

EDNA: This isn't five years ago, Joe.

JOE: You mean you'd leave me and the kids?

EDNA: I'd leave *you* like a shot!

JOE: No. . . .

EDNA: Yes! (JOE *turns away, sitting in a chair with his back to her. Outside the lighted circle of the playing stage we hear the other seated members of the strike committee. "She will . . . she will . . . it happens that way," etc. This group should be used throughout for various comments, political, emotional and as general chorus. Whispering. . . . The fat boss now blows a heavy cloud of smoke into the scene.*)

JOE (*finally*): Well, I guess I ain't got a leg to stand on.

EDNA: No?

JOE (*suddenly mad*): No, you lousy tart, no!

Get the hell out of here. Go pick up that bull-thrower on the corner and stop at some cushy hotel downtown. He's probably been coming here every morning and laying you while I hacked my guts out!

EDNA: You're crawling like a worm!

JOE: You'll be crawling in a minute.

EDNA: You don't scare me that much! (*Indicates a half inch on her finger.*)

JOE: This is what I slaved for!

EDNA: Tell it to your boss!

JOE: He don't give a damn for you or me!

EDNA: That's what I say.

JOE: Don't change the subject!

EDNA: This is the subject, the *exact subject!* Your boss makes this subject. I never saw him in my life, but he's putting ideas in my head a mile a minute. He's giving your kids that fancy disease called the rickets. He's making a jelly-fish outa you and putting wrinkles in my face. This is the subject every inch of the way! He's throwing me into Bud Haas' lap. When in hell will you get wise—

JOE: I'm not so dumb as you think! But you are talking like a red.

EDNA: I don't know what that means. But when a man knocks you down you get up and kiss his fist! You gutless piece of boloney.

JOE: One man can't—

EDNA (*with great joy*): I don't say one man! I say a hundred, a thousand, a whole million, I say. But start in your own union. Get those hack boys together! Sweep out those racketeers like a pile of dirt! Stand up like men and fight for the crying kids and wives. Goddamnit! I'm tired of slavery and sleepless nights.

JOE (*with her*): Sure, sure! . . .

EDNA: Yes, Get brass toes on your shoes and know where to kick!

JOE (*suddenly jumping up and kissing his wife full on the mouth*): Listen, Edna, I'm goin' down to 147th Street to look up Lefty Costello. Left was saying the other day . . . (*He suddenly stops.*) How about this Haas guy?

EDNA: Get out of here!

JOE: I'll be back! (*Runs out. For a moment* EDNA *stands triumphant. There is a blackout and when the regular lights come up,* JOE MITCHELL *is concluding what he has been saying*):

JOE: You guys know this stuff better than me. We gotta walk out! (*Abruptly he turns and goes back to his seat.*)

Blackout

II. LAB ASSISTANT EPISODE

Discovered: MILLER, *a lab assistant, looking around; and* FAYETTE, *an industrialist.*

FAY: Like it?

MILLER: Very much. I've never seen an office like this outside the movies.

FAY: Yes, I often wonder if interior decorators and bathroom fixture people don't get all their ideas from Hollywood. Our country's extraordinary that way. Soap, cosmetics, electric refrigerators—just let Mrs. Consumer know they're used by the Crawfords and Garbos—more volume of sale than one plant can handle!

MILL: I'm afraid it isn't that easy, Mr. Fayette.

FAY: No, you're right—gross exaggeration on my part. Competition is cutthroat today. Market's up flush against a stone wall. The astronomers had better hurry—open Mars to trade expansion.

MILL: Or it will be just too bad!

FAY: Cigar?

MILL: Thank you, don't smoke.

FAY: Drink?

MILL: Ditto, Mr. Fayette.

FAY: I like sobriety in my workers . . . the trained ones, I mean. The pollacks and niggers, they're better drunk—keeps them out of mischief. Wondering why I had you come over?

MILL: If you don't mind my saying—very much.

FAY (*patting him on the knee*): I like your work.

MILL: Thanks.

FAY: No reason why a talented young man like yourself shouldn't string along with us—a growing concern. Loyalty is well repaid in our organization. Did you see Siegfried this morning?

MILL: He hasn't been in the laboratory all day.

FAY: I told him yesterday to raise you twenty dollars a month. Starts this week.

MILL: You don't know how happy my wife'll be.

FAY: Oh, I can appreciate it. (*He laughs.*)

MILL: Was that all, Mr. Fayette?

FAY: Yes, except that we're switching you to laboratory A tomorrow. Siegfried knows about it. That's why I had you in. The new work is very important. Siegfried recommended you very highly as a man to trust. You'll work directly under Dr. Brenner. Make you happy?

MILL: Very. He's an important chemist!

FAY (*leaning over seriously*): We think so, Miller. We think so to the extent of asking you to stay within the building throughout the time you work with him.

MILL: You mean sleep and eat in?

FAY: Yes . . .

MILL: It can be arranged.

FAY: Fine. You'll go far, Miller.

MILL: May I ask the nature of the new work?

FAY (*looking around first*): Poison gas. . . .

MILL: Poison!

FAY: Orders from above. I don't have to tell you from where. New type poison gas for modern warfare.

MILL: I see.

FAY: You didn't know a new war was that close, did you?

MILL: I guess I didn't.

FAY: I don't have to stress the importance of absolute secrecy.

MILL: I understand.

FAY: The world is an armed camp today. One match sets the whole world blazing in forty-eight hours. Uncle Sam won't be caught napping!

MILL (*addressing his pencil*): They say 12 million men were killed in that last one and 20 million more wounded or missing.

FAY: That's not our worry. If big business went sentimental over human life there wouldn't be big business of any sort!

MILL: My brother and two cousins went in the last one.

FAY: They died in a good cause.

MILL: My mother says "no!"

FAY: She won't worry about you this time. You're too valuable behind the front.

MILL: That's right.

FAY: All right, Miller. See Siegfried for further orders.

MILL: You should have seen my brother—he could ride a bike without hands. . . .

FAY: You'd better move some clothes and shaving tools in tomorrow. Remember what I said—you're with a growing organization.

MILL: He could run the hundred yards in 9:8 flat. . . .

FAY: Who?

MILL: My brother. He's in the Meuse-Argonne Cemetery. Mama went there in 1926. . . .

FAY: Yes, those things stick. How's your handwriting, Miller, fairly legible?

MILL: Fairly so.

FAY: Once a week I'd like a little report from you.

MILL: What sort of report?

FAY: Just a few hundred words once a week on Dr. Brenner's progress.

MILL: Don't you think it might be better coming from the Doctor?

FAY: I didn't ask you that.

MILL: Sorry.

FAY: I want to know what progress he's making, the reports to be purely confidential—between you and me.

MILL: You mean I'm to watch him?

FAY: Yes!

MILL: I guess I can't do that. . . .

FAY: Thirty a month raise . . .

MILL: You said twenty. . . .

FAY: Thirty!

MILL: Guess I'm not built that way.

FAY: Forty. . . .

MILL: Spying's not in my line, Mr. Fayette!

FAY: You use ugly words, Mr. Miller!

MILL: For ugly activity? Yes!

FAY: Think about it, Miller. Your chances are excellent. . . .

MILL: No.

FAY: You're doing something for your country. Assuring the United States that when those goddamn Japs start a ruckus we'll have offensive weapons to back us up! Don't you read your newspapers, Miller?

MILL: Nothing but Andy Gump.

FAY: If you were on the inside you'd know I'm talking cold sober truth! Now, I'm not asking you to make up your mind on the spot. Think about it over your lunch period.

MILL: No.

FAY: Made up your mind already?

MILL: Afraid so.

FAY: You understand the consequences?

MILL: I lose my raise—

Simultaneously: { MILL: And my job!
                    FAY: And your job!
                    MILL: You misunderstand—

MILL: Rather dig ditches first!

FAY: That's a big job for foreigners.

MILL: But sneaking—and making poison gas—that's for Americans?

FAY: It's up to you.

MILL: My mind's made up.

FAY: No hard feelings?

MILL: Sure hard feelings! I'm not the civilized type, Mr. Fayette. Nothing suave or sophisticated about me. Plenty of hard feelings! Enough to want to bust you and all your kind square in the mouth! (*Does exactly that.*)

Blackout

III. THE YOUNG HACK AND HIS GIRL

Opens with girl and brother. FLORENCE *waiting for* SID *to take her to a dance.*

FLOR: I gotta right to have something out of life. I don't smoke, I don't drink. So if Sid wants to take me to a dance, I'll go. Maybe if you was in love you wouldn't talk so hard.

IRV: I'm saying it for your good.

FLOR: Don't be so good to me.

IRV: Mom's sick in bed and you'll be worryin' her to the grave. She don't want that boy hanging around the house and she don't want you meeting him in Crotona Park.

FLOR: I'll meet him anytime I like!

IRV: If you do, yours truly'll take care of it in his own way. With just one hand, too!

FLOR: Why are you all so set against him?

IRV: Mom told you ten times—it ain't him. It's that he ain't got nothing. Sure, we know he's serious, that he's stuck on you. But that don't cut no ice.

FLOR: Taxi drivers used to make good money.

IRV: Today they're makin' five and six dollars a week. Maybe you wanta raise a family on that. Then you'll be back here living with us again and I'll be supporting two families in one. Well . . . over my dead body.

FLOR: Irv, I don't care—I love him!

IRV: You're a little kid with half-baked ideas!

FLOR: I stand there behind the counter the whole day. I think about him—

IRV: If you thought more about Mom it would be better.

FLOR: Don't I take care of her every night when I come home? Don't I cook supper and iron your shirts and . . . you give me a pain in the neck, too. Don't try to shut me up! I bring a few dollars in the house, too. Don't you see I want something else out of life. Sure, I want romance, love, babies. I want everything in life I can get.

IRV: You take care of Mom and watch your step!

FLOR: And if I don't?

IRV: Yours truly'll watch it for you!

FLOR: You can talk that way to a girl. . . .

IRV: I'll talk that way to your boy friend, too, and it won't be with words! Florrie, if you had a pair of eyes you'd see it's for your own good we're talking. This ain't no time to get married. Maybe later—

FLOR: "Maybe Later" never comes for me, though. Why don't we send Mom to a hospital? She can die in peace there instead of looking at the clock on the mantelpiece all day.

IRV: That needs money. Which we don't have!

FLOR: Money, Money, Money!

IRV: Don't change the subject.

FLOR: This is the subject!

IRV: You gonna stop seeing him? (*She turns away.*) Jesus, kiddie, I remember when you were a baby with curls down your back. Now I gotta stand here yellin' at you like this.

FLOR: I'll talk to him, Irv.

IRV: When?

FLOR: I asked him to come here tonight. We'll talk it over.

IRV: Don't get soft with him. Nowadays is no time to be soft. You gotta be hard as a rock or go under.

FLOR: I found that out. There's the bell. Take the egg off the stove I boiled for Mom. Leave us alone Irv. (SID *comes in—the two men look at each other for a second.* IRV *exits.*)

SID (*enters*): Hello, Florrie.

FLOR: Hello, Honey. You're looking tired.

SID: Naw, I just need a shave.

FLOR: Well, draw your chair up to the fire and I'll ring for brandy and soda . . . like in the movies.

SID: If this was the movies I'd bring a big bunch of roses.

FLOR: How big?

SID: Fifty or sixty dozen—the kind with long, long stems—big as that. . . .

FLOR: You dope. . . .

SID: Your Paris gown is beautiful.

FLOR (*acting grandly*): Yes, Percy, velvet panels are coming back again. Madame La Farge told me today that Queen Marie herself designed it.

SID: Gee . . . !

FLOR: Every princess in the Balkans is wearing one like this. (*Poses grandly.*)

SID: Hold it. (*Does a nose camera—thumbing nose and imitating grinding of camera with other hand. Suddenly she falls out of the posture and swiftly goes to him, to embrace him, to kiss him with love. Finally*):

SID: You look tired, Florrie.

FLOR: Naw, I just need a shave. (*She laughs tremulously.*)

SID: You worried about your mother?

FLOR: No.

SID: What's on your mind?

FLOR: The French and Indian War.

SID: What's on your mind?

FLOR: I got us on my mind, Sid. Night and day, Sid!

SID: I smacked a beer truck today. Did I get hell! I was driving along thinking of US, too. You don't have to say it—I know what's on your mind. I'm rat poison around here.

FLOR: Not to me. . . .

SID: I know to who . . . and I know why. I don't blame them. We're engaged now for three years. . . .

FLOR: That's a long time. . . .

SID: My brother Sam joined the navy this morning—get a break that way. They'll send him down to Cuba with the hootchy-kootchy girls. He don't know from nothing, that dumb basketball player!

FLOR: Don't you do that.

SID: Don't you worry, I'm not the kind who runs away. But I'm so tired of being a dog, Baby, I could choke. I don't even have to ask what's going on in your mind. I know from the word go, 'cause I'm thinking the same things, too.

FLOR: It's yes or no—nothing in between.

SID: The answer is no—a big electric sign looking down on Broadway!

FLOR: We wanted to have kids. . . .

SID: But that sort of life ain't for the dogs which is us. Christ, Baby! I get like thunder in my chest when we're together. If we went off together I could maybe look the world straight in the face, spit in its eye like a man should do. Goddamnit, it's trying to be a man on the earth. Two in life together.

FLOR: But something wants us to be lonely like that—crawling alone in the dark. Or they want us trapped.

SID: Sure, the big shot money men want us like that.

FLOR: Highly insulting us—

SID: Keeping us in the dark about what is wrong with us in the money sense. They got the power and mean to be damn sure they keep it. They know if they give in just an inch, all the dogs like us will be down on them together—an ocean knocking them to hell and back and each singing cuckoo with stars coming from their nose and ears. I'm not raving, Florrie—

FLOR: I know you're not, I know.

SID: I don't have the words to tell you what I feel. I never finished school. . . .

FLOR: I know. . . .

SID: But it's relative, like the professors say. We worked like hell to send him to college—my kid brother Sam, I mean—and look what he done—joined the navy! The damn fool don't see the cards is stacked for all of us. The money man dealing himself a hot royal flush. Then giving you and me a phony hand like a pair of tens or something. Then keep on losing the pots 'cause the cards is stacked against you. Then he says, what's the matter you can't win—no stuff on the ball, he says to you. And kids like my brother believe it 'cause they don't know better. For all their education, they don't know from nothing. But wait a minute! Don't he come around and say to you—this millionaire with a jazz band—listen Sam or Sid or what's-your-name, you're no good, but here's a chance. The whole world'll know who you are. Yes sir, he says, get up on that ship and fight those bastards who's making the world a lousy place to live in. The Japs, the Turks, the Greeks. Take this gun—kill the slobs like a real hero, he says, a real American. Be a hero! And the guy you're poking at? A real louse, just like you, 'cause they don't let him catch more than a pair of tens, too. On that foreign soil he's a guy like me and Sam, a guy who wants his baby like you and hot sun on his face! They'll teach Sam to point the guns the wrong way, that dumb basketball player!

FLOR: I got a lump in my throat, Honey.

SID: You and me—we never even had a room to sit in somewhere.

FLOR: The park was nice . . .

SID: In winter? The hallways . . . I'm glad we never got together. This way we don't know what we missed.

FLOR (*in a burst*): Sid, I'll go with you—we'll get a room somewhere.

SID: Naw . . . they're right. If we can't climb higher than this together—we better stay apart.

FLOR: I swear to God I wouldn't care.

SID: You would, you would—in a year, two years, you'd curse the day. I seen it happen.

FLOR: Oh, Sid. . . .

SID: Sure, I know. We got the blues, Babe—the 1935 blues. I'm talkin' this way 'cause I love you. If I didn't, I wouldn't care. . . .

FLOR: We'll work together, we'll—

SID: How about the backwash? Your family needs your nine bucks. My family—

FLOR: I don't care for them!

SID: You're making it up, Florrie. Little Florrie Canary in a cage.

FLOR: Don't make fun of me.

SID: I'm not, Baby.

FLOR: Yes, you're laughing at me.

SID: I'm not. (*They stand looking at each other, unable to speak. Finally, he turns to a small portable phonograph and plays a cheap, sad, dance tune. He makes a motion with his hand; she comes to him. They begin to dance slowly. They hold each other tightly, almost as though they would merge into each other. The music stops, but the scratching record continues to the end of the scene. They stop dancing. He finally looses her clutch and seats her on the couch, where she sits, tense and expectant.*)

SID: Hello, Babe.

FLOR: Hello. (*For a brief time they stand as though in a dream.*)

SID (*finally*): Good-bye, Babe. (*He waits for an answer, but she is silent. They look at each other.*)

SID: Did you ever see my Pat Rooney imitation? (*He whistles Rosy O'Grady and soft-shoes to it. Stops. He asks:*)

SID: Don't you like it?

FLOR (*finally*): No. (*Buries her face in her hands. Suddenly he falls on his knees and buries his face in her lap.*)

Blackout

IV. LABOR SPY EPISODE

FATT: You don't know how we work for you. Shooting off your mouth won't help. Hell, don't you guys ever look at the records like me? Look in your own industry. See what happened when the hacks walked out in Philly three months ago! Where's Philly? A thousand miles away? An hour's ride on the train.

VOICE: Two hours!!

FATT: Two hours . . . what the hell's the difference. Let's hear from someone who's got the practical experience to back him up. Fellers, there's a man here who's seen the whole parade in Philly, walked out with his pals, got knocked down like the rest—and blacklisted after they went back. That's why he's here. He's got a mighty interestin' word to say. (*Announces*): Tom Clayton! (*As* CLAYTON *starts up from the audience,* FATT *gives him a hand which is sparsely followed in the audience.* CLAYTON *comes forward.*)

Fellers, this is a man with practical strike experience—Tom Clayton from little ole Philly.

CLAYTON (*a thin, modest individual*): Fellers, I don't mind your booing. If I thought it would help us hacks get better living conditions, I'd let you walk all over me, cut me up to little pieces. I'm one of you myself. But what I wanna say is

that Harry Fatt's right. I only been working here in the big town five weeks, but I know conditions just like the rest of you. You know how it is—don't take long to feel the sore spots, no matter where you park.

CLEAR VOICE (*from audience*): Sit down!

CLAYTON: But Fatt's right. Our officers is right. The time ain't ripe. Like a fruit don't fall off the tree until it's ripe.

CLEAR VOICE: Sit down, you fruit!

FATT (*on his feet*): Take care of him, boys.

VOICE (*in audience, struggling*): No one takes care of me. (*Struggle in house and finally the owner of the voice runs up on stage, says to speaker*):

SAME VOICE: Where the hell did you pick up that name! Clayton! This rat's name is Clancy, from the old Clancys, way back! Fruit! I almost wet myself listening to that one!

FATT (*gunman with him*): This ain't a barn! What the hell do you think you're doing here!

SAME VOICE: Exposing a rat!

FATT: You can't get away with this. Throw him the hell outa here.

VOICE (*preparing to stand his grounds*): Try it yourself. . . . When this bozo throws that slop around. You know who he is? That's a company spy.

FATT: Who the hell are you to make—

VOICE: I paid dues in this union for four years, that's who's me! I gotta right and this pussy-footed rat ain't coming in here with ideas like that. You know his record. Lemme say it out—

FATT: You'll prove all this or I'll bust you in every hack outfit in town!

VOICE: I gotta right. I gotta right. Looka *him*, he don't say boo!

CLAYTON: You're a liar and I never seen you before in my life!

VOICE: Boys, he spent two years in the coal fields breaking up any organization he touched. Fifty guys he put in jail. He's ranged up and down the east coast—shipping, textiles, steel—he's been in everything you can name. Right now—

CLAYTON: That's a lie!

VOICE: Right now he's working for that Bergman outfit on Columbus Circle who furnishes rats for any outfit in the country, before, during, and after strikes. (*The man who is the hero of the next episode goes down to his side with other committee men.*)

CLAYTON: He's trying to break up the meeting, fellers!

VOICE: We won't search you for credentials. . . .

CLAYTON: I got nothing to hide. Your own secretary knows I'm straight.

VOICE: Sure. Boys, you know who this sonovabitch is?

CLAYTON: I never seen you before in my life!!

VOICE: Boys, I slept with him in the same bed sixteen years. HE'S MY OWN LOUSY BROTHER!!

FATT (*after pause*): Is this true? (*No answer from* CLAYTON.)

VOICE (*to* CLAYTON): Scram, before I break your neck! (CLAYTON *scrams down center aisle.* VOICE *says, watching him*): Remember his map—he can't change that—Clancy! (*Standing in his place says*): Too bad you didn't know about this, Fatt! (*After a pause.*) The Clancy family tree is bearing nuts! (*Standing isolated clear on the stage is the hero of the next episode.*)

Blackout

V. INTERNE EPISODE

Dr. Barnes, an elderly distinguished man, is speaking on the telephone. He wears a white coat.

DR. BARNES: No, I gave you my opinion twice. You outvoted me. You did this to Dr. Benjamin yourself. That is why you can tell him yourself. (*Hangs up phone, angrily. As he is about to pour himself a drink from a bottle on the table, a knock is heard.*)

BARNES: Who is it?

BENJAMIN (*without*): Can I see you a minute, please?

BARNES (*hiding the bottle*): Come in, Dr. Benjamin, come in.

BENJ: It's important—excuse me—they've got Leeds up there in my place—He's operating on Mrs. Lewis—the hysterectomy—it's my job. I washed up, prepared . . . they told me at the last minute. I don't mind being replaced, Doctor, but Leeds is a damn fool! He shouldn't be permitted—

BARNES (*dryly*): Leeds is the nephew of Senator Leeds.

BENJ: He's incompetent as hell.

BARNES (*obviously changing subject, picks up lab. jar*): They're doing splendid work in brain surgery these days. This is a very fine specimen. . . .

BENJ: I'm sorry. I thought you might be interested.

BARNES (*still examining jar*): Well, I am, young man, I am! Only remember it's a charity case!

BENJ: Of course. They wouldn't allow it for a second, otherwise.

BARNES: Her life is in danger?

BENJ: Of course! You know how serious the case is!

BARNES: Turn your gimlet eyes elsewhere, Doctor. Jigging around like a cricket on a hot grill won't help. Doctors don't run these hospitals. He's the Senator's nephew and there he stays.

BENJ: It's too bad.

BARNES: I'm not calling you down either. (*Plopping down jar suddenly.*) Goddamnit, do you think it's my fault?

BENJ (*about to leave*): I know . . . I'm sorry.

BARNES: Just a minute. Sit down.

BENJ: Sorry, I can't sit.

BARNES: Stand then!

BENJ (*sits*): Understand, Dr. Barnes, I don't mind being replaced at the last minute this way, but . . . well, this flagrant bit of class distinction—because she's poor—

BARNES: Be careful of words like that—"class distinction." Don't belong here. Lots of energy, you brilliant young men, but idiots. Discretion! Ever hear that word?

BENJ: Too radical?

BARNES: Precisely. And some day like in Germany, it might cost you your head.

BENJ: Not to mention my job.

BARNES: So they told you?

BENJ: Told me what?

BARNES: They're closing Ward C next month. I don't have to tell you the hospital isn't self-supporting. Until last year that board of trustees met deficits. . . . You can guess the rest. At a board meeting Tuesday, our fine feathered friends discovered they couldn't meet the last quarter's deficit—a neat little sum well over $100,000. If the hospital is to continue at all, its damn—

BENJ: Necessary to close another charity ward!

BARNES: So they say. . . . (*A wait.*)

BENJ: But that's not all?

BARNES (*ashamed*): Have to cut down on staff too. . . .

BENJ: That's too bad. Does it touch me?

BARNES: Afraid it does.

BENJ: But after all I'm top man here. I don't mean I'm better than others, but I've worked harder.

BARNES: And shown more promise. . . .

BENJ: I always supposed they'd cut from the bottom first.

BARNES: Usually.

BENJ: But in this case?

BARNES: Complications.

BENJ: For instance? (BARNES *hesitant.*)

BARNES: I like you, Benjamin. It's one ripping shame.

BENJ: I'm no sensitive plant—what's the answer?

BARNES: An old disease, malignant, tumescent. We need an antitoxin for it.

BENJ: I see.

BARNES: What?

BENJ: I met that disease before—at Harvard first.

BARNES: You have seniority here, Benjamin.

BENJ: But I'm a Jew! (BARNES *nods his head in agreement.* BENJ *stands there a moment and blows his nose.*)

BARNES (*blows his nose*): Microbes!

BENJ: Pressure from above?

BARNES: Don't think Kennedy and I didn't fight for you!

BENJ: Such discrimination, with all those wealthy brother Jews on the board?

BARNES: I've remarked before—doesn't seem to be much difference between wealthy Jews and rich Gentiles. Cut from the same piece!

BENJ: For myself I don't feel sorry. My parents gave up an awful lot to get me this far. They ran a little dry goods shop in the Bronx until their pitiful savings went in the crash last year. Poppa's peddling neckties. . . . Saul Ezra Benjamin—a man who's read Spinoza all his life.

BARNES: Doctors don't run medicine in this country. The men who know their jobs don't run anything here, except the motormen on trolley cars. I've seen medicine change—plenty—anesthesia, sterilization—but not because of rich men—in *spite* of them! In a rich man's country your true self's buried deep. Microbes! Less. . . . Vermin! See this ankle, this delicate sensitive hand? Four hundred years to breed that. Out of a revolutionary background! Spirit of '76! Ancestors froze at Valley Forge! What's it all mean! Slops! The honest workers were sold out then, in '76. The Constitution's for rich men then and now. Slops! (*The phone rings.*)

BARNES (*angrily*): Dr. Barnes. (*Listens a moment, looks at* BENJAMIN.) I see. (*Hangs up, turns slowly to the younger Doctor.*) They lost your patient. (BENJ *stands solid with the shock of this news but finally hurls his operation gloves to the floor.*)

BARNES: That's right . . . that's right. Young, hot, go and do it! I'm very ancient, fossil, but life's ahead of you, Dr. Benjamin, and when you fire the first shot say, "This one's for old Doc Barnes!" Too much dignity—bullets. Don't shoot vermin! Step on them! If I didn't have an invalid daughter—

(BARNES *goes back to his seat, blows his nose in silence*): I have said my piece, Benjamin.

BENJ: Lots of things I wasn't certain of. Many things these radicals say . . . you don't believe theories until they happen to you.

BARNES: You lost a lot today, but you won a great point.

BENJ: Yes, to know I'm right? To really begin believing in something? Not to say, "What a world," but to say, "Change the world!" I wanted to go to Russia. Last week I was thinking about it—the wonderful opportunity to do good work in their socialized medicine—

BARNES: Beautiful, beautiful!

BENJ: To be able to work—

BARNES: Why don't you go? I might be able—

BENJ: Nothing's nearer what I'd like to do!

BARNES: Do it!

BENJ: No! Our work's here—America! I'm scared. . . . What future's ahead, I don't know. Get some job to keep alive—maybe drive a cab—and study and work and learn my place—

BARNES: And step down hard!

BENJ: Fight! Maybe get killed, but goddamn! We'll go ahead! (BENJAMIN *stands with clenched fist raised high.*)

Blackout

AGATE: *Ladies and Gentlemen,* and don't let anyone tell you we ain't got some ladies in this sea of upturned faces! Only they're wearin' pants. Well, maybe I don't know a thing; maybe I fell outa the cradle when I was a kid, and ain't been right since—you can't tell!

VOICE: Sit down, cockeye!

AGATE: Who's paying you for those remarks, Buddy?—Moscow Gold? Maybe I got a *glass eye,* but it come from working in a factory at the age of eleven. They hooked it out because they didn't have a shield on the works. But I wear it like a medal 'cause it tells the world where I belong— deep down in the working class! We had delegates in the union there—all kinds of secretaries and treasurers . . . walkin' delegates, but not with blisters on their feet! Oh no! On their fat little ass from sitting on cushions and raking in mazuma. (SECRETARY *and* GUNMAN *remonstrate in words and actions here.*) Sit down, boys. I'm just sayin' that about unions in general. I know it ain't true here! Why no, our officers is all aces. Why, I seen our own secretary Fatt walk outa his way not to step on a cockroach. No boys, don't think—

FATT (*breaking in*): You're out of order!

AGATE (*to audience*): Am I outa order?

ALL: No, no. Speak. Go on, etc.

AGATE: Yes, our officers is all aces. But I'm a member here—and no experience in Philly either! Today I couldn't wear my union button. The damnest thing happened. When I take the old coat off the wall, I see she's smoking. I'm a sonova-gun if the old union button isn't on fire! Yep, the old celluloid was makin' the most god-awful stink: the landlady come up and give me hell! You know what happened? That old union button just blushed itself to death! Ashamed! Can you beat it?

FATT: Sit down, Keller! Nobody's interested!

AGATE: Yes they are!

GUNMAN: Sit down like he tells you!

AGATE (*continuing to audience*): And when I finish—(*His speech is broken by* FATT *and* GUNMAN *who physically handle him. He breaks away and gets to other side of stage. The two are about to make for him when some of the committee men come forward and get in between the struggling parties.* AGATE's *shirt has been torn.*)

AGATE (*to audience*): What's the answer boys? The answer is, if we're reds because we wanna strike, then we take over their salute too! Know how they do it? (*Makes Communist salute.*) What is it? An uppercut! The good old uppercut to the chin! Hell, some of us boys ain't even got a shirt to our backs. What's the boss class tryin' to do— make a nudist colony outa us? (*The audience laughs and suddenly* AGATE *comes to the middle of the stage so that the other cabmen back him up in a strong clump.*)

AGATE: Don't laugh! Nothing's funny! This is your life and mine! It's skull and bones every incha the road! Christ, we're dyin' by inches! For what? For the debutant-ees to have their sweet comin' out parties in the Ritz! Poppa's got a daughter she's gotta get her picture in the papers. Christ, they make 'em with our blood, Joe said it. Slow

death or fight. It's war! (*Throughout this whole speech* AGATE *is backed up by the other six workers, so that from their activity it is plain that the whole group of them are saying these things. Several of them may take alternate lines out of this long last speech.*)

You Edna, God love your mouth! Sid and Flor-rie, the other boys, old Doc Barnes—fight with us for right! It's war! Working class, unite and fight! Tear down the slaughter house of our old lives! Let freedom really ring.

These slick slobs stand there telling us about bogeymen. That's a new one for the kids—the reds is bogeymen! But the man who got me food in 1932, he called me Comrade! The one who picked me up where I bled—he called me Comrade too! What are we waiting for. . . . Don't wait for Lefty! He might never come. Every minute—(*This is broken into by a man who has dashed up the center aisle from the back of the house. He runs up on stage, says*):

MAN: Boys, they just found Lefty!

OTHERS: What? What? What?

SOME: Shhh. . . . Shhh. . . .

MAN: They found Lefty. . . .

AGATE: Where?

MAN: Behind the car barns with a bullet in his head!

AGATE (*crying*): Hear it, boys, hear it? Hell, listen to me! Coast to coast! HELLO AMERICA! HELLO. WE'RE STORM-BIRDS OF THE WORKING-CLASS. WORKERS OF THE WORLD. . . . OUR BONES AND BLOOD! And when we die they'll know what we did to make a new world! Christ, cut us up to little pieces. We'll die for what is right! put fruit trees where our ashes are!

(*To audience*): Well, what's the answer?

ALL: STRIKE!

AGATE: LOUDER!

ALL: STRIKE!

AGATE and OTHERS on Stage: AGAIN!

ALL: STRIKE, STRIKE, STRIKE!!

JAMES T. FARRELL (1904–   )

Among those sanely and strongly opposing the American Communist theory of "literature for the revolution" in the mid-thirties was James T.

Farrell: a Chicago-born Irish-Catholic writer, whose main characters are the first convincing literary representation of this significant breed.

At this time, Farrell was willing to describe himself as a Marxist in the sense that he believed finance capital to be the determining factor in American life. But the margin left over—the margin in which the individual human will might learn to exert itself—made all the difference. Social environment in Farrell's novels—often exemplified by the Chicago South Side he had grown up in—is an exceedingly powerful force, but it is not everything. If society shapes the individual, the individual also has his share in shaping society—and, perhaps more important, in shaping his own destiny. "Freedom is my concern," Farrell once wrote; ". . . the dream that each and all have the opportunity to rise to the full stature of their potential humanity." The difference between such characters as Studs Lonigan, Danny O'Neill, and Bernard Carr is exactly the degree to which each rises to his full human stature.

Farrell's grandparents on both sides were Irish immigrants and working-class people. His father, "Big Jim" Farrell, was a vigorous and ambitious man; but he was unable to earn enough as a teamster to keep his growing family (there were six surviving children) in any kind of comfort, and when young Farrell was three he was taken to live with his mother's parents, the Dalys. This was not, perhaps, a traumatic experience for the child, who found plentiful affection and a reasonably endowed life in the Daly household (eventually located in Chicago's Washington Park). Socially and economically, it was a move up, from the cramped lower class to at least the lower middle; and these distinctions of surrounding and opportunity would not be lost upon Farrell the writer. But to judge from Farrell's re-creation of the event in his account of Danny O'Neill's earliest years (*No Star Is Lost*, 1938), it was also decidedly unsettling and led to long inner questioning about identity, family relationships, and modes of authority.

Farrell went to several parochial schools in Chicago and later, after several tries, managed to complete eight quarters at the University. He intended to major in the social sciences, but course work bored him, and he dropped out periodically to look for a job. His classes in writing were the only thing he found interesting, and it was in one of these, in the spring of 1929, that he wrote a story called "Studs," in which the narrator attends the wake of a youth from the neighborhood, and, as he listens to the dead man's friends talking in aimless clichés about life and death and their own trivial activities, falls to thinking (in Farrell's own summary) "how these fellows, who are now corpulent and sunk in the trivialities of day-to-day living, were once adventurous boys." The instructor, James Weber Linn, was enthusiastic about the story, but suggested that it could be elaborated. Farrell began at once on what became the trilogy of *Young Lonigan* (1932), finished during a year in Paris; *The Young Manhood of Studs Lonigan* (1934), and *Judgment Day* (1935). The trilogy ends at a point just before the original story had begun, with Studs in his mid-twenties dead of physical debauchery and a failure of will.

Of the thirty-odd volumes of fiction (about evenly divided between novels and collections of stories) Farrell has written to date, eleven are given over to the careers of the three figures already mentioned—Lonigan, O'Neill, and Carr (or Clare as he was called in the first book about him, before a law suit forced Farrell to change the name). The best claim for these novels, and indeed for the whole body of Farrell's work, has been made by Edgar M. Branch, in a monograph of 1963. "[Farrell's] novels and stories, following one after the other," Branch contends in a nice image, "are like a group of islands in the sea. Each is separate yet all rise out of one land mass below the ocean's surface, and when seen from above they form an impressive pattern." Branch's helpful overview finds a suggestive development in the sequence formed by the Lonigan trilogy, the O'Neill pentalogy and the Carr trilogy.

This sequence is the pattern made by an individual human will slowly breaking free from environmental restrictions, misconceptions, and false allegiances and finding its true course and its appropriate setting. Studs Lonigan is defeated by his inability to see beyond the adolescent desire to be a leader of the neighborhood gang—"to be strong, and tough, and the real stuff," in the closing words of *The Young Manhood*. He never understands that there is no human resonance in that ambition, no outlet for the better and more grasping qualities he does in fact possess. Danny O'Neill, whose life Farrell follows (it is the closest of these various lives to that of Farrell himself) from 1909 to 1927, emerges from the background from which Studs Lonigan has come and faces the same threats to his selfhood; but he has enough intellectual and artistic determination to escape Chicago, and heads for New York—as Farrell did for keeps after 1932—and the distant promise of a literary career. Bernard Carr, whose story begins in 1927 where Danny's had broken off, establishes himself in New York, explores the literary and the radical political worlds of the city, and becomes a successful and respected writer (again, as Farrell did at least for a period), and a contented husband and father.

The growth of political insight from character to character and book to book, while real and important, is also a large metaphor for spiritual growth. In his introduction to the Modern Library edition of *Studs Lonigan: A Trilogy*, Farrell was at pains to insist that his subject was spiritual and not economic poverty, and that this was why he set his story in "a neighborhood several steps removed from the slums and dire economic want." One sign of Studs's meagerness of spirit is his slender political awareness—particularly of the radical movement which, it is hinted in *Judgment Day*, might have brought some sustenance into stunted lives like his own. But two sets of novels later, Bernard Carr, who had taken part in the Communist parade on May Day in 1932, watches the 1936 parade from the sidelines, reflecting to himself that marchers are themselves trapped within the false social vision they would impose upon the country.[1]

[1] *Yet Other Waters* (1952). Farrell by this time had entirely shaken off his Socialist views and in that same year was an ardent supporter of Adlai E. Stevenson, as he was later of John F. Kennedy.

In a somewhat analogous manner, Farrell as a writer had, over the same span of years, been moving steadily away from the fictional vision sometimes referred to as "naturalism." As we have implied, Farrell was never really a naturalist, in the "deterministic" meaning of that slippery literary term (see above, pp. 1215–16); he always perceived in experience a certain margin for individual trial and error. But here we have to confess that Farrell's narrative style rarely does justice to his view of things, especially to his profound belief in freedom and his conviction (which one may be surprised to find he shared with André Malraux and Albert Camus) that the supreme feature of literature is that it "humanizes the world." Flat at best, leaden and awkward at worst, Farrell's style *sounds* like the agent of naturalism: what possible horizons of hope, what spontaneous exercise of will can such stubbornly graceless prose be aiming to reveal? If such a style is attuned to anything, it is to the depleted psyche and the fatally indecisive character of Studs Lonigan. The processes of history and of the aimless immediate present exert their pressure upon the unresisting Studs (via Farrell's use of newspaper headlines, advertisements, and snatches of currently popular songs, in the synthesizing manner perfected by John Dos Passos); and he lurches to his doom encased in a prose style that sadly becomes him. And this is why the Studs Lonigan trilogy remains, on balance, Farrell's most satisfactory literary accomplishment. The later novels communicate a happier image of man; and in almost all of them one finds, amid their swarming casts of characters, individuals who embody recognizable moments in American social history. But more than anywhere else in Farrell's fiction, *Studs Lonigan* is the product of a binding, if disconsolate, marriage of language and content.

The characteristic power which that marriage occasionally made possible is indicated in our selection, which is taken from the last chapter of *The Young Manhood of Studs Lonigan*. Considered purely as a drunk scene, it invites comparison with the episode in Howells'

A *Modern Instance* which the whisky-loving Mark Twain found so gloriously true to life. Farrell's New Year's Eve party (the year is 1929) is no less true to life—that is, to the dregs of a ruined life; a life of vomiting and rape and mindless cruelty; a chaos of blurred images and flickering identities. The reader need not bother about the identity of Red, Shorty Leach, Joe Moonan, Les, Tommy, and all the others—though he can, of course, find out who some of them are by reading the entire novel; but it is just the jumble of undiscriminated drunks that Farrell, not inartistically, is trying to describe. And the muted pervasive irony lies in this: that the start of the new year coincides with the full disclosure of what young Lonigan, who once dreamed of the adventurous life, has finally come to.

BIOGRAPHICAL CHART

1904 Born, February 27, in Chicago, to Mary Daly Farrell and James Francis Farrell

1907 Taken to live with his grandparents, John and Julia Brown Daly, Chicago

1911 Enters first grade at Corpus Christi Parochial Grammar School

1915 Moves with the Dalys into the neighborhood depicted in first two volumes of *Studs Lonigan*; enters fourth grade at St. Anselm's Parochial Grammar School

1924 Takes one semester, beginning in September, as pre-law student at De Paul University night school

1925 Begins work as service-station attendant; matriculates in June at University of Chicago; continues through spring quarter, 1926

1926 Resumes studies at University of Chicago in October; continues through winter quarter, 1927

1927 Takes Professor Linn's English 210, Advanced English Composition

1928 Returns to Chicago in January; completes several stories

1929 Works as reporter for Chicago *Herald Examiner*; writes "Studs" in spring; enrolls for spring quarter, his last

1930 "Studs" published in *This Quarter* (July–August–September)

1931 Marries Dorothy Patricia Butler; leaves for Paris; Vanguard Press accepts *Young Lonigan*

1932 Returns from Paris; takes up residence in New York; *Young Lonigan* published

1934 *The Young Manhood of Studs Lonigan*

1935 *Judgment Day*; separates from Dorothy Farrell; *Studs Lonigan: A Trilogy*

1936 Wins $2,500 Guggenheim Fellowship for 1936–1937 in creative writing; *A Note on Literary Criticism*; meets H. L. Mencken and Theodore Dreiser; later supports Socialist ticket; *A World I Never Made*, first Danny O'Neill novel

1937 Book of the Month Club Fellowship Award of $2,500 for *Studs Lonigan*

1940 Divorced from Dorothy Farrell

1941 Marries Hortense Alden; elected to the National Institute of Arts and Letters

1946 *Bernard Clare*, the first Bernard Carr novel

1955 Divorced from Hortense Farrell and remarries Dorothy Farrell

1965 *The Collected Poems of James T. Farrell*

FURTHER READINGS

There is no standard edition of Farrell's work. Individual titles are cited in the biographical chart.

Edgar M. Branch, *James T. Farrell* (1963)

William M. Frohoch, "James Farrell: The Precise Content," *The Novel of Violence in America* (1958)

Alfred Kazin, *On Native Grounds* (1942)

Charles C. Walcutt, "James T. Farrell: Aspects of Telling the Whole Truth," *American Literary Naturalism* (1956)

From The Young Manhood of Studs Lonigan (1934)

CHAPTER 24

I

A voice within Studs, that wasn't his voice, and that perhaps maybe might have been the voice of conscience, said reiteratively, as if in a hoarse accusing tone:

You're nothing but a slob. You're getting to be a great big fat slob. Nothing on the ball any more. Slob! Slob! Fat slob! Double slob!

"I'm drunk. Happy New Year. Whoops!" Studs yelled loudly: he staggered backwards and forwards with the utterance of each syllable.

Slob! Slob! Double Slob!

He looked at the street. It seemed familiar. What was the name?

The voice said:

You don't know your fanny from a hole in the ground!

He ran to escape that voice that kept hammering at him, in his heavy, heavy, twirling head. He ran, thinking he was running straight, and with form. He halted after about a hundreds yards and thought that he'd run a block.

He knew the street as well as he knew his name. His name was Lonigan, the great Studs Lonigan.

Slob Lonigan! that voice said.

He stared bleary-eyed up and down the street. There was light mist, and the street lamps seemed lopsided.

An automobile passed. Studs eyed it intently.

"Hey, where's . . . fire?"

He looked at three-story buildings. They seemed like he saw them and had seen them before. Where, oh, where is my wandering street tonight? Where, oh, where can it be?

The street rolled under him like a ship in a storm. His head spun like a top that was in perpetual motion. The street went up, whoops, and slow, slowly, evenly, it went down, whoops, just like a see-saw.

He shoved his hat on the back of his head.

He stared across the street, and it went up, whoops, and it went down, whoops, and the building came towards him, whoops, like a railroad engine coming forwards on a screen, growing nearer and nearer. Whoops! The building stopped. That was funny.

You're drunk, you clown, drunk as a lord.

He walked, like a paralytic, head down, his body loose, his nervous control deadened. He raised his feet high, as if in a caricature of Germans in a movie comedy doing the goosestep. He halted, threw out his chest, tossed back his head, and almost fell over backwards. His hat slipped to the sidewalk. He turned around in a circle, wondering where, oh, where was his wandering hat tonight.

He saw the hat lying as big as a balloon on the sidewalk. He pulled out a stick that had somehow and somewhere been stuck in his overcoat pocket, and held it over the hat as if it were a fishing pole. He jerked with both hands, like a man dragging in a huge fish, and he tottered backwards for about three yards before he gained a precarious balance. He looked at the end of the stick. No fishee, no hattee! Whoops!

He laughed, and tossed the stick away. He snuck up on his hat, tiptoe, shshing his right index finger to his lips. He circled, continuing to shssh his finger to his lips. He quietly snuck three feet from the hat. He dove for it, clumsily, like a green football player falling on the ball. He lay on the sidewalk. It was cold. Struggling, and by degrees, he achieved his feet again.

Slob Lonigan! Slob Lonigan! You're no goddamn good any more. Got an alderman. Alderman on your gut, and couldn't even get yourself a decent girl. Slob! Slob! Double Slob!

"Who's a slob?" he shouted.

You're a slob, the voice said.

He hauled off on the air, and went for a head-first dive in the hard, cold dirt by the walk. He lay there and looked at the world go around. The buildings spun about as if on a swiftly propelled merry-go-round. An automobile coming along went uphill and then downhill. Whoops! He arose, and ran around in circles in the middle of the street, trying to catch the buildings.

A taxi came skidding along. It stopped.

"You goddamned fool, get off the road!"

Studs uttered some inarticulate sound which seemed like uuuuhhhh.

The driver jumped out, and asked what did he say. Studs cursed him. The taxi driver pushed Studs back over the curb, and drove away. Studs fought to his feet, and rushed in the middle of the street, yelling after the vanished taxi.

Studs staggered, and draped his arms tightly around a lampost. He vomited.

"I'm sick. I want Lucy. I love Lucy. I want Lucy. I want Lucy," he cried aloud, a large tear splattered on his check. The vomiting caused a violent contraction and pressure, as if a hammer were in his head.

"I'm sick! Lucy, please love Studs!" he cried.

A light flurry of snow commenced. Studs tenderly kissed the cold lamppost, which suddenly seemed to be Lucy.

"I always loved you, Lucy!"

Tears rolled down his drunken, dirty face.

II

Weary Reilley went to the Bourbon Palace to get a pickup to take to the party the old boys from Fifty-eighth Street were throwing. There was a huge crowd at the dance hall. He moved about, and danced with several girls. One of them wouldn't sock it in. Another couldn't dance well enough to please him. A third laughed as if she were an idiot. The fourth girl was pretty in a chubby way with brown eyes and a quiet manner. He guessed, though, that here was a case of still waters running deep. She was his meat. She weighed about a hundred and twenty-five pounds, nice figure, got a guy hot just looking at her, straight, small hard breasts, nice legs, meat on them and on the thighs. Just his speed! He danced three successive times with her, and she seemed to like him. At first she drew back when he got her in the corners, but then she laid it right up to him, and they socked it in plenty. That made him sure that she was what he wanted. She had everything. He was going to give it to her like she'd never gotten it before. Dancing with her, he thought of what he would do to her, direct, crude images of brutalized sex.

"You're a pretty good dancer," she said.

"You're keen too," he said, working against her. "Shake that thing," he added.

"That's not . . . nice," she said, blushing as her eyes dropped.

"Come on, sister!" he said, aggressively.

She smiled, and let herself go against him.

"Do you come up here often?" she asked, hanging on his arm, and walking off the floor at the conclusion of the dance.

"I haven't got time for it," he said.

"Umm. Swell people. I suppose you go to the South Shore Country Club."

"No. There's too many pigs, and no-do's around here."

"Am I to take that as a compliment?"

"You're the real stuff, girlie."

"You'd be surprised."

"Meaning which?" he said, looking unflinchingly into her dark eyes.

"Maybe I'm not."

"I can take care of that."

"You're not confident, are you?"

"I pick my women, baby."

"Just like that! You're not what they call an . . . egotistical."

"Listen, want to go to a party?"

"Oh, I couldn't."

"How come?"

"Why, I don't even know you?"

"Come on, never mind that. This damn joint is too crowded. There's too many no-do's here. Come on, baby, and can the stalling. You don't want to be wasting your time with these imitation Valentinos up here."

"But what will my girl friend say?"

"Hell, she can find some guy to look after her, and if she can't, that is just tough."

"But. . . ."

"Listen, Irene. You know you want to come, and you're just playing around before you say yes. I don't like that stuff."

"You're a frank fellow, I see," she said.

"Come on," he said, grabbing her arm. They walked down the stairs to the cloak rooms.

III

The party was held in a suite of three rooms at a disreputable hotel on Grand Boulevard in the black belt.

"Here, Pat, have a drink of my stuff," Red Kelly said to Carrigan, as they stood in a corner of the crowded room.

After drinking, Pat Carrigan coughed and grimaced. He smiled that broad, happy, good-natured, chubby-faced smile of his.

"Ah, good stuff," he said, rubbing his belly.

"Damn tootin'."

"Where'd you get it?"

"Never mind. It's good stuff."

A jazz record was put on the portable victrola.

"Here now, Red. Have some of mine," young Carrigan said.

"Don't care if I do."

Pat handed Red the bottle, and Red took a big drink. Pat tried to take as big a drink, but couldn't. He put the bottle aside, coughing and sneezing.

"You'll learn how to take it in time," Red said.

"Say, I had too much already. Jesus, I'm drunk as a loon. I'm drunk, Kelly. Drunk," Carrigan said.

"Sure, I know how it is."

"But why shouldn't I be drunk? Ain't it New Year's Eve," argued Carrigan.

"Don't crap me now."

"Hey, Leach, commere."

"What the hell you want, you drunken Irishman?" Shorty Leach sourly asked.

"What day is it?"

"What's this, a joke?"

"I'm trying to tell Kelly here what day it is, and he won't believe that it's New Year's Eve."

"Jesus, that's tough tiddy. Give me a drink," said Shorty.

"Sure. Happy New Year," said Carrigan, handing him the bottle.

IV

"Don't say that I'm not a lady, you bastard," the exotic dark girl said.

"But say, kid. The ladies do it, and so do the birds. Don't you know that song, I love the birds, and the bees, and the trees, because they all do it too," Wils Gillen said.

"Well, don't say that I ain't a lady," she said.

"You know what I think you are?" said Wils.

"What?" she muttered, slobbering over the small glass of gin she had in her hand.

"I think you're a man."

"Look at me, then!" she said, laughing raucously.

"I'm from Missouri, kid. Show me!"

"Goddamn you, I will!" she said.

She ripped off her clothes.

"Now you sonofabitch, do you believe me?" she shouted.

"Yeah, I guess you are."

"Now, you goddamn dirty skunk, show me that you're a man."

"I always aim to please."

"Come on over here, and show me. I had plenty, and I'm particular. Particular, I said. You got to prove it to me," she said, looking him over with a sneer.

"You got the right telephone number this time, girlie."

V

"Hey, Swede, don't. Lay off that bitch. She's got a dose."

"Listen, you ain't a man till you got it," Swede said.

"Well, don't say I didn't warn you."

Swede took the pig into one of the bedrooms.

VI

"Say, Dan," said Vinc Curley.

"Yeah," said O'Doul, as he stood in a corner, sheiked out, and unrumpled.

"Want to go to the Tivoli tomorrow afternoon?"

"For Christ sake, hop in the bowl."

Dapper Dan turned his back. Vinc looked puzzled.

VII

"Say, kiddo, listen! Give Doyle here a break!" Slug commanded.

"You know. I can't," Slug's blond jane protested.

"It ain't nothin'."

"I don't mind you, dearie, when I'm this way because I love you, but nobody else. That goes!"

"Come on, kid. I won't hurt you," Tommy Doyle said, his drunken face full of lust.

"No!"

"Go ahead, and do it, or it's the gate!" Slug said, shoving her.

She looked at him with eyes of meek protest.

"Hear me!" snapped Slug.

She went into a bedroom with Tommy.

VIII

"I'll tell you why I'm drunk," Shorty Leach said, letting the tears stream down his cheek.

"Sing 'em!" Joe Moonan said.

"You didn't know my girl, Pearl. Well, I love Pearl. I love her."

Joe vanished. Shorty buttonholed Les, who looked thin and pale.

"Here, kid, have a drink and brace up," said Les.

Shorty took the bottle and drank.

"I love Pearl. And she's out with Jack Morgan tonight. Now Morgan stole my girl. He's a nice guy, and I always liked him, but he's out with Pearl, and I'm crazy about her."

"Sing 'em, kid!"

"Have you ever been in love? Well, I have. You know I was out riding with Pearl. And she took and held my head in her hands and she looked into my eyes, and she said: 'There's something about you that makes me crazy. That's what she said. And I tell you, if you've never been in love, you don't know how I felt. And then I looked out at the moon, and she did, and Jesus, I've never had a feeling like that before. And I thought she was straight, and now she went out with Morgan."

"Here, kid, have a drink, and brace up. The first hundred years is the hardest."

Shorty drank.

"But I tell you I wouldn't be drunk if I was with Pearl because I love and respect her too much. I love that girl," sobbed Shorty, putting his head on Les' shoulder.

IX

"Whoops!" yelled Studs, standing in the doorway.

They wished him Happy New Year. Slug handed him a bottle, and said bottoms up. Studs drank. The New Year bells rang. Everybody drank, and shouted, and a naked girl rushed from one of the bedrooms to kiss everyone. They had to hold Vinc while she kissed him.

"Whoops! It's 1929!" yelled Studs, raising an empty gin bottle with an unsteady arm.

X

"Where you going, Joe?" asked Red.

"I can't telephone here with this noise, and I want to call my mother. I do every New Year's."

"Wish her a Happy New Year for me," said Red.

Moonan went out.

XI

Vinc heard a moan. Then, he heard a girl sobbing. He rushed through the opened door of a bedroom, and turned on the light. He saw Benny Taite and a girl.

"Is there anything wrong?" he said, breathless and embarrassed.

"For Christ sake, who let you in, monkey face?" the girl asked.

"You goddamn idiot!" said Taite.

Taite went at Vinc. He socked Vinc. Vinc lost his temper, and rushed Taite like a bull, socked him, knocked him down, and stood over him, yelling:

"Come on! Come on!"

A crowd gathered. Some of them laughed. Red dragged Vinc off, and told him to get the hell out of the place.

"But he hit me!" said Vinc.

"I told you to blow!"

"He hit me. And I paid my money. I won't."

"Will you shut up, you bastard?"

"Gimme my money back, or I'll call the police," whined Vinc.

"Let me handle the mutt," said Slug.

"Listen, seal your tray and there's the door," Slug said.

"I'm gonna tell my mother!" he said, surlily from the door.

Taite sat in a corner nursing a shiner.

XII

Mickey Flannagan slept in the corner with a stupid expression on his face. He snored. Barney Keefe folded his hands, and placed a soggy Merry Widow in them.

XIII

"Daddy, you're a man. What a man! Daddy!" the exotic dark girl said to Wils Gillen.

"As Napoleon said, don't give up the ship," Wils said.

XIV

The blond girl rushed from a bedroom yelling that she'd been raped. She opened a window, screamed that she'd been raped, and threatened to jump.

Red pulled her back. She stood looking about the shocked group, her face distorted and insane.

Tommy appeared, asking what the hell was eating her.

"He! He! He!" she shouted, missing Tommy's head with a gin bottle; it ricocheted off the wall, and hit Mickey in the bean. He continued to sleep.

Slug walked over to the girl amidst a tense silence. He slapped her face. She cowered.

"One more bat out of you and you won't have to jump!"

XV

Shorty Leach sat fully clothed in a bathtub of water, droning:

The pal that I loved, stole the gal that I loved,
    and took all my sunshine and joy;
Nobody but he was a buddy to me, since we played
    on the floor with our toys.
I just can't believe my old pal would deceive. Gee,
    but I'm heartsick and sore,
The pal that I loved, stole the gal that I loved,
    that's why we're not pals anymore.

XVI

"I shouldn't be drinking. I'm sick. I just came out of the hospital, and the doc he says to me, 'Les, cut it out, or you'll be picking daisies!' "

"Shut up, fool!" Barney mocked.

"But I don't care. There ain't nothin' in life for me. I'm just a goddamn expressman for the Express Company. I ain't got no future."

Tears rolled down his thin, red face; he drank.

"Listen, heel, what's the idea of holding out?" said Keefe.

"Here, pal!"

"Barney, I had a vocation to be a priest. I should be a priest. And look at me! Look at me! Look at me!" Les said, while Barney guzzled.

"I am looking!"

"Ain't I a wreck?"

"Sure, you're the Wreck of the Hesperus."

"Barney, I might be dead next New Year's. The doc said so. He said: 'Kid, lay off the liquor.' But why should I? I'm nothin'. A goddamn teameo for John Continental. Here, gimme a drink," he said, snatching back his bottle and drinking.

Les sneered, looking at a lamp.

"That goddamn thing, I don't like it!" he said. He kicked it over.

Barney pulled out a little bottle and raised it aloft, saying:

"To myself; good men are scarce."

XVII

There was a sharp rap on the door and a command to open up. Two burly, monkey-faced cops entered.

"What the hell do you call this?" one said.

The other drew a gat. A girl fainted.

"Call the wagon," said the cop, holding the gat on them.

"Who's running this party?" asked the other cop.

"We all are," said Carrigan.

"All who? Speak up, you birds!"

"What the hell, Officer. It's New Year's. We're just havin' a little party," Slug said.

"Yeah, so I see," said the cop ironically.

"Pipe down, you!" said the cop with the drawn gun.

"Me?"

"Yeah, you!"

"Say, what's the idea?" Slug asked.

"Stand back, or I'll shoot."

"Drop that gun, and talk!" Slug commanded.

"Just a minute, Officer," Joe Moonan said, appearing, and flashing his star. Red followed, showing his bailiff's star.

He and Red talked to the officers, and Red told them his old man had been a sergeant.

"Sure, this is just a party. You know, all the boys having a good time," Joe said.

"Well, we got a complaint, and we had to come."

"Want a drink, Officer?" Red asked.

"Sure."

Red gave them a couple of drinks.

"And say, listen, you know Moonan, kind of ask the lads to pipe down on the noise. We don't like to be gettin' calls like this."

"Sure."

"Here, take this along," Red said, handing one of them a bottle of gin.

XVIII

"Say, Slug, that goddamn broad in there has made a wreck out of me. Jesus, I'm a wreck. Christ sake, please help me out," Wils said.

"Sure thing, kid," said Slug disappearing.

"I just wanna lay down and die," Wils said, dropping on the floor.

XIX

"Come on, let's play football," said Nate Klein, squatting. Red yelled to cut it out.

"Sixteen, nineteen, twenty-four, Fifty-eighth Street. Cardinals hike!" he yelled, springing against the wall.

Red and Weary grabbed him from behind, and told him to cut it out. He struggled free, squatted, flung himself at the wall again. He bounced back, moaning, holding his hand. Red took him into the bathroom to soak it in hot water.

XX

"Come on, it won't hurt you," Weary coaxed.

"I better go," she said.

"Irene, come on. Don't pull that stuff," he said sharply.

"No. I've never drank. I'm not that kind of a girl."

"Listen! Don't kid me!"

"Please, I'm afraid of you," she said, drawing back.

He took her in a corner, kissed her, pushed her head back and poured the gin down her throat. She coughed.

"Please, take me home!"

"Come on, we'll dance."

He dragged her half-willing, to the victrola. He put on a record and yelled for them to pipe down. They danced, and Weary shimmied. She stood in the center of the floor, an abandoned look on her face, her abdomen pressed forwards, her arms loose, her head flung backwards, shimmying.

XXI

Mickey Flannagan lay in a corner, still out.

XXII

"I got mine from that broad," said Mahoney.

"I thought she was a virgin," said Fluke.

"She was!"

"Well, how did you do it?"

"I got her blind. She's out."

"Where is she?"

"She's in the second bedroom. She passed out, and I carried her there. She's out like a light."

"Mind if I try my luck?"

"Go to it, Fluke," said Mahoney.

XXIII

"Come here, bitch!" Studs said to one of the pigs.

"After a while," she said.

"Come on, bitch!" said Studs.

He pawed at her. She gave him a shove, and he was so drunk that he stumbled backwards. Taite laughed at him. The girl ran into the bathroom. Studs staggered to the door, and tried to open it. It was locked. He pounded the door.

XXIV

"Listen, Irene is my broad. Don't you be monkeying around her," Weary said to Dapper Dan O'Doul.

"I was only dancing with her."

"Listen, rat, you're all together. If you want to stay that way, don't monkey around her," said Weary.

"I'm sorry."

"You heard me!"

XXV

Barney crawled on his hands and knees looking for his false teeth. Slug gave him a slight boot in the tail. They laughed. Barney cursed. Everybody laughed again.

XXVI

"Let's drink this one for poor Shrimp Haggerty," said Les.

"Yeah!" said Studs.

"Poor Shrimp is dying in Fort Wayne. I'll be dead, too, maybe by next year," said Les.

"Yeah!"

Les raised the bottle. Tommy Doyle grabbed it, and told Les he'd better lay off.

"All right, Tommy, but will you and Studs drink to poor Shrimp, our dying buddy?"

"To our buddy Shrimp, may he be guzzling with us next year," said Tommy, drinking.

"Yeah," muttered Studs, taking the bottle.

He raised the bottle and drank, most of the gin pouring down his chin and shirt.

"Studs is so drunk we'll have to hold his head while he drinks," said Tommy: he laughed.

XXVII

"Jesus, Joe, let's get some of these guys out of here. This is getting to be too much of a goddamn mess. If we don't, something's going to happen," said Red.

"Yeah," said Joe.

"Hey, punk," Joe said.

"What's the matter?" O'Doul asked.

"See the door? Blow!"

"But I ain't doing nothing!"

Red told some other punks to blow.

"Some goddamn thing is gonna happen if we don't get some of these drunks out," Red said.

"Tommy, can you get Les out? He's sick and needs air, and we want to cut it down. Then you and him come back," said Joe.

"Sure. Les is my cousin. I stick by my cousin Les."

"All right, do it, Tommy."

XXVIII

Three of the girls staggered away drunk.

XXIX

Studs floundered over to Irene like a listing ship.

"Come on, bitch!" he muttered, clutching her arm.

"All right, Lonigan, hands off!" Weary commanded.

"Aw, gimme the bitch!" Studs said.

Weary socked Studs in the eye with a right. Studs went back against the wall, and bounced off, his eye swelling. Weary caught him in the nose as he rebounded. He grabbed Studs by the coat lapel with his left, smacked him in the eye with his right, and then gave him a last one on the button. Studs sagged to the floor, and lay there, his nose bleeding profusely.

XXX

"Please let's go. Everybody else is gone," Irene said.

"He's here," Weary said, pointing at unconscious Mickey Flannagan.

"Please?"

"Have another drink!"

"Then will we go?"

"Sure!"

"Promise me?"

He nodded. She sipped from his bottle.

"Now get my coat," she said, shrinking, as she saw the expression on his face.

"Oh, please! Please! Please! I'll scream. . . ."

"Commere, goddamn you! And shut up!"

She cowered with fright. He tried to kiss her. She fought off his thrusting mouth with her hand. He knocked it aside, and pressed his lips against her shaking forehead. He encircled her with his arms, and dragged her towards the bed where Mickey lay. He flung her towards the wall, and rolled Mickey off. She ran to the door. He tackled her.

"OOOH, my ankle!" she sobbed.

"Will you come across now," he said, towering over her, while she sat on the floor, holding her ankle.

She screamed. He grabbed for a pillow slip, and tore a strip off it. She hobbled out of the room on her sprained ankle, screaming. He caught her from behind, and as she twisted and tore, he got the pillow slip tied around her mouth. She raised her hand to tear it off, and he twisted her arm. He could see the pain on her face:

"Will you come across?"

She nodded.

He released her. She tore the rag off her mouth. He smothered her scream with his hand, and she hit and scratched. He gave her an uppercut, and she toppled to the floor. She started to rise unsteadily, and he was on her, holding her mouth, using his other hand to ward off her scratching hands. She slumped back limp, breathing heavily. Her hair was down. Her dress was torn.

"Please. I never done it before. Please, lemme go. Please!"

"I won't hurt you. For Christ sake, cut out the stalling."

"Honest to God, please, I never did this. Please. . . ."

"Can that! You're comin' across if I have to kill you!"

"Please . . . you might act like a . . . gentleman."

"Come on, for Christ sake!"

He half smothered her scream. He stuck his knee in her stomach, and slapped her viciously with his left hand.

"Oh, you will, will you!" he said, punching her jaw after she again flashed her teeth.

He carried her unconscious to the bed.

XXXI

Her face was black and blue, and her coat thrown over her torn dress. She winced with each step, and sobbed hysterically, shook all over.

"Now don' try that game on a guy again!" he said, shoving her out the door of the suite.

He left the bloody sheets soaking in the bathtub. Coming from the bathroom, he saw Micky Flannagan stagger out and he smiled.

He was awakened by the cops, who had been let into the suite by the night clerk.

"This is gonna be a tough rap to beat for you, fellow!"

"You ain't got nothin' on me."

"No! She's beat up pretty bad!"

"She was drunk and fell down!"

"Maybe you can prove that alibi."

The other cop came from the bathroom with the dripping, bloody sheets and asked what about them.

"I don't know nothin' about them."

"Where did you get your puss scratched?"

"I had a fight."

"Yeah!"

"Yeah!" said Weary, challengingly.

"Listen, everybody isn't a helpless girl. Watch the way you talk."

"Listen, they sent you to get me. Here I am. Call a cab and I'll pay the bill. But don't try pullin' nothin' on me!" Weary said with clenched fists.

"Shall I let him have it, Joe?" asked the other cop.

"Don't soil your mitts on him."

Weary sneered. He walked out with them. As they went through the door, he made a gesture and said:

"She ain't got no kick. She only got that much!"

XXXII

The dirty gray dawn of the New Year came slowly. It was snowing. There was a drunken figure, huddled by the curb near the fireplug at Fifty-eighth and Prairie. A passing Negro reveler studied it. He saw that the fellow wasn't dead. He rolled it over, and saw it was a young man with a broad face, the eyes puffed black, the nose swollen and bent. He saw that the suit and coat were bloody, dirty, odorous with vomit. He laughed, the drunk stirred as the Negro said:

"Boy, you all has been celebratin' a-plenty."

He searched the unconscious drunk and pocketed eight dollars. He walked on.

The gray dawn spread, lightened. Snow fell more rapidly from the muggy sky of the New Year.

It was Studs Lonigan, who had once, as a boy, stood before Charley Bathcellar's poolroom thinking that some day, he would grow up to be strong, and tough, and the real stuff.

NELSON ALGREN (1909–   )

Nelson Algren's best-known novels, *The Man with the Golden Arm* and *A Walk on the Wild Side,* appeared, respectively, in 1949 and 1956; and he first won general recognition with the stories collected under the striking title of *The Neon Wilderness* in 1946. In this regard, he is a "post-1945" writer; there is a certain modernity of tone in his fiction that locates Algren further along in the century, say, than James T. Farrell and a consciousness of social phenomena —like drug addiction, and the hustler tactics of racetrack confidence men—that belongs more obviously to a later than to an earlier period. Still, Algren's first book, *Somebody in Boots* (partly based on Algren's minor brush with the law in Alpine, Texas), was completed in 1935, and his imagination grew out of the experience of the Depression years and the slum life of the lower South Side of Chicago. He seems to feel himself closest, as a writer, to Dreiser, especially the Dreiser who (in Algren's words) "became very strong as he grew older . . . against capitalism," to Farrell, and to Richard Wright. It will not, we hope, twist too much his literary identity to consider him in the present context.

Algren is of mixed Swedish, German, and Jewish descent—the latter element entering the family when his grandfather, a Stockholm resident named Nels Ahlgren, turned Jew, changed his name to Isaac Ben Abraham, came to this country and married a German-Jewish servant girl. It was Nelson Algren who recovered the original name (minus the "h") when, as a writer, he dropped the "Abraham" as unsuitable for the grand advertisements he half-mockingly looked forward to. Algren was born in Detroit, in 1909; but both his parents (his father was a machinist) were Chicagoans, and they moved back to the city when Algren was three. The boy grew up amid ghetto surroundings, some twenty blocks south of the neighborhood where Farrell had been taken into the Dalys' household. He worked his way through the University of Illinois, reading fairly widely in English literature, but also much drawn to sociological studies: the combination led to a degree in journalism in 1931. After that, he hitchhiked through the South, spent a few months in a Texas jail and a few more as a salesman in New Orleans. Algren drew on this period; as we have said, for *Somebody in Boots* and then, from 1936 to 1940, did writing chores

for the W.P.A. In the Second World War he served as a private, and the only hurt he suffered was from being hit on the head with a shoe, in Marseilles, in a scuffle after the armistice.

The discharged soldier became a more or less full-time writer, and there followed quickly more short stories, and *The Man with the Golden Arm*, which was the first recipient of the National Book Award. Algren was lured to Hollywood, as script writer for the film of his novel; and he has described that brief, unlucky chapter in his life as a kind of fall from innocence. He had, meanwhile, become an intimate friend of the French writer, Simone de Beauvoir, whom he first met in a Chicago café. He traveled with her in this country and visited her in Paris, where he caught glimpses of Jean Paul Sartre and other intellectuals (and seems to have been most taken with the *chanteuse* Juliette Greco); Algren kept the liaison entirely to himself, until Mlle. de Beauvoir gave a graphic fictionalized account of it in her novel *The Mandarins* (1954). At the same time, from his permanent home in Chicago, Algren had all along been a conscientious, if often skeptical, activist for a wide number of libertarian causes.

But Algren is first and last a writer, and it may not be stretching things to say that action occupies the place in Algren's life that it does in the ideal life of Emerson's "American Scholar" —as something that is necessary but occasional, and finally subordinate to the creative experience. He has his gallery of American political and social heroes, from Jefferson to Eugene Debs; and he associates himself, as has been said, with "radical writers" (as he calls them) like Dreiser and Farrell, behind them Stephen Crane, and further back still, Walt Whitman. Like them, Algren is a free spirit; and his dealings with the Communists in the thirties were bound to be unsatisfactory on both sides.

In *Conversations with Nelson Algren* (1964), a fascinating series of long taped interviews by H. E. F. Donahue, Algren gives this account of his Communist involvement (he was at no time a member of the party):

From Conversations with Nelson Algren (1964)

Q: Before the war, in the thirties, were you a Socialist, a left-winger?

ALGREN: Oh not a Socialist, no. I might have started out as a Socialist, but I'd say I was a Communist.

Q: Did you ever join the Communist Party?

ALGREN: No, I never joined the Party, but I did a lot of work for them.

Q: When did you stop doing that? When did that cool off?

ALGREN: During the Civil War in Spain.

Q: O.K. You say the disenchantment with the Communists came during the Civil War in Spain. Why? What happened?

ALGREN: Well, my disenchantment wasn't, I didn't share the disenchantment that some Communists felt when they swung to the Trotskyists' or Anarchists' line. My disenchantment was not an ideological one. I had gone into the Communist Party because I believed the world was changing and I wanted to help change it.

Q: Now what do you mean when you say that you went into the Communist Party. You were not a member?

ALGREN: I went into the Communist movement; that is, everybody I knew was a Communist and I worked knowingly with Communists and I belonged to a Writers' League in which there were many leading Communists. I worked with them and whenever there was a demonstration organized by the Communists against the Italian invasion, the Italian bombing of Ethiopia, I marched with the Communists. I thought they were right on that issue. I thought they were right on many issues and I thought they were right on the issue in Spain. What I did run into was a certain kind of rigidity, and a kind of authoritarian attitude toward people who, like myself, were doing the leg work, for the League of American Writers of Chicago, as Chairman of the Chicago Chapter or something, which meant that I got money for Spain and attended and organized meetings around here. But I didn't like being told by the Secretary of the New York Chapter, through a letter, that he heard, that he'd been informed that I and another member of the League of American Writers had been drunk and disorderly. He felt it was his duty to remind me that, with my present responsibilities, it would look better if I'd try to be a little bit more austere in my conduct. My reaction to this was simply to tell him that my conduct was

no concern of his and he could find somebody else to do this work because if he was going to interfere with my drinking and disorderliness, I wasn't going to let that interfere. I put it in a way that would offend him because he didn't answer the question of "How do you know?" I mean, what kind of operation is it when somebody will write to New York and say somebody else was drunk? This went against me. There wasn't anybody I knew who wasn't friendly, but obviously I was with people who had a higher obligation than a personal one; that is, the personal obligation to inform, to keep the other people thinking the same as they did, which I thought was what we were fighting the war against. A meeting of writers was organized, of artists and writers, and I was expected to be there and I didn't go there because I didn't want to go through a lot of bureaucratic parliamentarianism, and then I was told by one of the organizers of the meeting, very abruptly, "Where were you Thursday night?" Well, I wanted to know what concern it was of his where I was Thursday night. I said, "Where were you *Tuesday* night?" So my disenchantment was based on the purely personal thing that there was something morally wrong to me about being at anybody's behest. They were simply little bureaucratic functionaries so I simply moved away from them and got started thinking more about writing.

"So I simply moved away from them and got started thinking more about writing." *The Man with the Golden Arm* suggests the kind of thinking Algren indulged in. It is a kaleidoscopic novel, held together firmly by a sort of prehensile prose: the story of the final stages in the life of Frankie Machine (formerly Majcinek), a South Side gambler—possessed of a crippled wife and a devoted mistress, and, during a lucky streak, of a "golden arm"—who fights a valiant losing struggle against drug addiction. The novel moves swiftly in and out of gambling dens, slum boarding houses, drug centers, police headquarters—all the darkened treacherous corners of the inescapable city scene. In *Conversations with Nelson Algren*, the author reflects on why he wrote the book and others like it; and in lieu of a selection from *The Man with the Golden Arm* (which, in view of its tight texture, would be next to impossible without an explanatory note of equal length), we cannot do better than quote his words:

Q: What did you write?

ALGREN: I put that *Neon Wilderness* together, which I had started before the war. I finished it then and then I wrote *The Man with the Golden Arm*.

Q: Writing *The Man with the Golden Arm* took you up to 1950—what did you write then?

ALGREN: I wrote that *Chicago: City on the Make* thing.

Q: When did you write *Walk on the Wild Side?*

ALGREN: From 1954 through 1955.

Q: Why have you written the books you've written?

ALGREN: Well, I wrote the books I wrote because, because I was living in the middle of these books when, before they were books, when they were merely scenes in which human beings were involved in conflict, I was in the middle of them and simply recorded my own reactions and tried to catch the emotional ebb and flow and something of the fear and the terror and the dangers and the kind of life that multitudes of people had been forced into with no recognition that such a world existed. They lived in a world which is very plain, which anybody could see, which is lived in the streets of the city, but which the people who didn't live in this world said, "It doesn't exist, they aren't there, we know that they aren't there, and if they are there, it doesn't matter, because we're here and we don't live in that sort of world." And in this, although I was confident at the time of making a dent in this, by writing books about it, books which were accepted and spoken of in reviews and even honored one way or another—I thought I'd make a dent—I didn't make the least dent, because there is no way of convincing or even making the slightest impression on the American middle class that there are people who have no alternative, that there are people who live in horror, that there are people whose lives are nightmares. This is not accepted. The world of the drug addict doesn't exist. The world of the criminal doesn't exist. The world of the murderer doesn't exist. Nothing that does not touch the person individually exists.

Q: At the time you thought you could make a dent?

ALGREN: I thought that there was a certain sentience. I thought there was something you could reach. Now I don't think it can be reached. When such a book comes along more recently, such as *The Naked Lunch*, which I don't think is a great book or anything, but it does tell what a mess a man's life can be, an American life, just a nightmare—I've seen many people live through this nightmare—it immediately becomes a literary confection of some kind. Nobody really believes that this is so. It *is* so. Mary McCarthy says it's a great book and somebody else will say it's not even reviewable, but it simply is a literary event, something that sells for six bucks a copy. It isn't going to change much.

Q: Yeah, but I was primarily interested in why you wrote it at the time.

ALGREN: Well, because, uh . . .

Q: Weren't you doing something new? Was that important to you?

ALGREN: Of course there's a tradition, Dreiser, and certainly at the turn of the century Stephen Crane. He said it does exist in *Maggie: A Girl of the Streets*. He broke out of the middle-class world into the world that the book reviewers largely panned him for and he persisted in it.

Q: Who else besides Dreiser and Crane? Of your day—

ALGREN: Céline.

Q: —of the thirties? Who else was doing what you wanted to do in the thirties?

ALGREN: Well, just Dick Wright, that's all. That's the only one I know of in the thirties who was writing, who wrote anything that was not just from the bottom of American society but a bottom where a tremendous number of people lived inarticulately and I had known Wright and had seen that he had made these multitudes articulate to himself. They had become articulate to him and, well, even before I knew Wright I had this source. I had already established quite a sort of wellspring with the people who didn't belong to American civilization: to the people of the underworld, to the outcasts.

Conversations with Nelson Algren is, among other things, a treasury of shrewd and wittily prejudiced comments on Algren's younger contemporaries: Joseph Heller (whose *Catch-22* Algren admires extravagantly), James Baldwin (with whom Algren had an entertaining encounter), Norman Mailer, Saul Bellow, William Styron, Jack Kerouac, William Burroughs, and a good many others. These judgments lead the interviewer to ask Algren what he thinks American literature really *is*. What it *isn't*, Algren replies, is one writer corresponding or quarreling with another in public, or the life styles of assorted literary eccentrics. All that is coterie gossip. American literature, Algren declares, is a seizure of American life at moments of sharpest revelation:

Q: What *is* it?

ALGREN: Actually American literature isn't anybody phoning to anybody or anybody writing about anybody. American literature is the woman in the courtroom who, finding herself undefended on a charge, asked, "Isn't anybody on my side?" It's also the phrase I used that was once used in court of a kid who, on being sentenced to death, said, "I knew I'd never get to be twenty-one anyhow." More recently I think American literature is also the fifteen-year-old who, after he had stabbed somebody, said, "Put me in the electric chair—my mother can watch me burn." Even *more* recently, American literature is a seventeen-year-old kid picked up on a double murder charge, two killings in a boat, in a ship off Miami, who said he was very glad it happened, he had absolutely no regrets, his only fear was that he might not get the electric chair. He had no vindictiveness toward those two people he killed. He said they were pretty good about it. They didn't know, they had no idea, that he was going to come up with a knife. He had, in fact, a little bit of admiration for their coolness. One of them, finding himself stabbed, said, "Why?" He wanted to know. He said, "I can't tell them why." But I know he's been trying to get out of it since he's six years old. This is an honors student, you understand, this is a bright boy from a respectable home. He never remembers a time when he wasn't fully convinced that death was better than life. And now he was

very contented, his only worry being that he might not get the electric chair. He's afraid of that. That's the only fear he has, that he might have to continue to live. I think that's American literature. I think it's also the thirty-five-year-old Negro who told me recently, "The only times I ever felt human is when I've been in jail." The other times he's been on guard, on guard day and night. He says, "There's no such thing as a friend and you can't afford love. The only time I've ever let down, let myself have a relationship with any other person, is when I've been in jail." I think it's also the girl who says, "It don't matter what happens to me because it's really happening to somebody else. I'm not really here." I think American literature consists of these people. It doesn't consist of the, of the contrivers of literature who, after a certain number of years on campus, are entitled to grow a beard to look like Hemingway although they opposed Hemingway all the time he was alive. And I don't think it's the public performers. I don't think it's the stunt men. This is the very reason I like somebody like O'Hara, because he deals with Americans who seem to me to be all around. He seems to be one of the few people who are really in touch with what a bartender does when he goes broke, with what the relationship is with the woman, with the aging woman who comes in and sits on a barstool and expresses her loneliness one way or another. American literature is also the suspect, picked up for carrying an unregistered gun, who answers, when asked, "If you didn't steal this pistol somewhere, why don't you let us have your fingerprints anyhow, just in case you actually steal one someday," with, "Why should I want to steal a pistol when I have eleven thousand dollars in my pocket?" O'Hara is one of the very few people who is writing about something that goes on, and who himself knows *how* it goes on. He didn't send anybody either. At least he's not writing *about* other writers.

JOHN DOS PASSOS (1896–1970)

John Dos Passos was a contemporary of Hemingway and Fitzgerald, and like them he served in the military in the First World War. Like

them, also, he first began to publish in the twenties. Yet it is in many ways more useful to regard him as a writer of the thirties; in fact, it is tempting to say that the *life* experience of John Dos Passos constitutes the paradigm of the politically concerned writer in the thirties and later. This is not to disparage the work itself: the fifteen hundred pages of *U.S.A.*— though some of them have begun to curl at the edges—add up to a work of considerable literary magnitude, in some sense the representative accomplishment of the period, using the adjective in Emerson's meaning of the best of its kind. But there is also something unmistakably archetypal in the way Dos Passos moved through the successive available stages of belief and commitment: the early angry idealism, the association with the downtrodden, the burning hostility to the economic and political establishment, the somewhat confused support of the Communist party (for whom Dos Passos was briefly the literary hero), the growing disenchantment with the tactics and spokesmen of radicalism, the gradual shift to a conservative position, his acclaim by the leaders of reaction.

About the later Dos Passos, it should be said at once that, as Daniel Aaron has put it, he was "never guilty of the unpardonable impiety. He has changed his politics without slandering himself or his past." At the same time, in giving fictional form to the course of social history in his lifetime, he demonstrated more clearly than any of his contemporaries how the radical temper of the twentieth century was rooted in the old idealism of the century before—in the writings of Emerson and Whitman, and in the Jeffersonian tradition. Dos Passos' inner steadfastness sprang in good part from an abiding idealism.

John Dos Passos was born in Chicago, of a well-to-do Spanish-American family, in 1896. He attended the sternly exclusive Choate School and went on to Harvard College; but before he had graduated (which he did with distinction in 1916), he was giving voice to a sort of high-spirited rage. After watching what he described to a friend as "the cossack tactics of the New York police force" during a riot, he found himself suddenly antagonistic to his own social class and drawn instead to the East Side Jews and other "foreigners" (he used the word favorably,

in conscious reversal of the connotation given it by his peers). These people struck him as closer to life than the young men turned out by "these stupid colleges of ours," by "these instillers of stodginess—every form of bastard culture, middle-class snobbism."

And what are we fit for when they turn us out of Harvard [he asked, warming to the question]? We're too intelligent to be successful businessmen and we haven't the sand or the energy to be anything else—

Until Widener is blown up, and [Harvard President] A. Lawrence Lowell assassinated and the Business School destroyed and its site sowed with salt—no good will come out of Cambridge.[1]

Thus, with apocalyptic enthusiasm, did one solid member of the high American bourgeoisie turn upon his own social culture—and join in spirit with the residents of the ghetto.

It was in this state of mind, having moved on from a detestation of Harvard to a hatred of the entire business world, that Dos Passos joined the Norton-Harjes volunteer ambulance unit and embarked for France. Observers with a penchant for psychoanalysis have alleged a personal source for Dos Passos' rebellious attitude. (The circumstances of his birth show a technical irregularity.) Did Dos Passos' resentment of his father become a general animosity toward established authority? Insofar as this may be true, it would not set Dos Passos apart from all other radicals in the thirties or later: Murray Kempton, in *A Part of Our Time* (1955), has demonstrated how often a private and nonpolitical motive can lead a middle-class individual to embrace the radical left; and examples thereof continue to accumulate today.[2]

[1] For these and other quotations, we are grateful to Daniel Aaron.
[2] The nonpolitical origin of a political attitude by no means casts doubt on the sincerity or urgency of the latter, but it is always important and always worth considering. Lenin once referred to a certain pathological element within radical political thought. And it can be argued that one source of abolitionist rage in nineteenth-century America was the rumored sexual license in the

Dos Passos' experience in France and later in Italy filled him with disgust—at the military authorities, but much more with the atrocities and the hideous ugliness of war itself (as he described it in *Three Soldiers*, 1921), and the blundering and greedy dishonesty which had permitted it to happen. He was sent back to the United States because of his antiwar views, very much of a mind, as he wrote, to "disturb with laughter the religious halo of the holocaust." His assorted hostilities deepened during the twenties and helped give shape and significance to his first clear literary accomplishment, the novel *Manhattan Transfer* in 1925, which was also the first novel cast in the manner of *U.S.A.*, juxtaposing scenes from many kinds and levels of life to present a picture of the shifting reality of the city itself. But his friend Edmund Wilson wondered in print whether something more profound and all-consuming than hostility to capitalism was not at work in *Manhattan Transfer* —whether Dos Passos was not developing "a distaste for all the beings who compose" American society. Not only the rich but all of humanity, Wilson felt, seemed to come off badly in the novel; Dos Passos tended to damn "the sufferers along with the disease." Twelve years later, Michael Gold, rereading *U.S.A.*, was struck by the same thing. By this time, Gold believed, it was communism that Dos Passos detested; but "like the Frenchman Céline, Dos Passos hates Communists because organically he hates the human race."

It was after the execution of Sacco and Vanzetti in 1927 that Dos Passos declared he had "privately seceded" from the United States. That event was also the germ of *U.S.A.*, though it is treated only toward the end of the third and final volume of that sad fictional epic. The first volume, *The 42nd Parallel*, appeared in

1930; the second, *1919*, two years later; and *The Big Money* in 1936. Two thirds or more of *U.S.A.* were written during Dos Passos' most strenuous involvement with radical politics. He never joined the Communist party, but he supported it vigorously—between 1927 and 1932— lending his name to its manifestos and his energies to its undertakings (like the New Playwrights Theater). He spoke urgently of the need for "socially creative ideas . . . the new myth that's got to be created to replace the imperialist prosperity myth if the machinery of American life is ever to be gotten under social control." He insisted that a new American theater must come into being which will "draw its life and ideas from the conscious sections of the industrial and white-collar working classes which are out to get control of the great flabby mass of capitalist society and mould it to their own destiny."

The Communists offered Dos Passos as the prime example of the correctly dedicated American writer. Yet as early as 1934, after Dos Passos had severely criticized "the disruptive action of the Communists" at a Socialist rally in Madison Square Garden, there had been some suspicion that Dos Passos' "orientation" was "not revolutionary." When Dos Passos returned from the war in Spain in 1937, denouncing the bombs and the bloodshed, and the hounding of anarchists by Stalinist forces, the Communists took another look at his work and found it the product of a powerful but perhaps hopelessly confused talent. Only a year after the publication of *The Big Money*, disenchantment on both sides was moving toward the final stage.

Politically detached readers of *U.S.A.* should not have been surprised. Even in *The Big Money*, the radical leaders can strike one as dehumanized, with only the occasional solitary individual (like the vagabond—"vag"—with whom the trilogy closes) regarded with sympathy. The fact was that before the decade was half over, Dos Passos had, in his own phrase, "rejoined the United States," in the belief that its form of democratic government best protected the rights of the poor and lonely individual. Answering a questionnaire sent around by the *Partisan*

---

southern plantations—as against the repressive mores of northern society.

As to Dos Passos' "apocalyptic enthusiasm"—blow up Widener library, assassinate the president of Harvard— it would find its echo at Harvard and on a great many other campuses in the sixties. The rhetoric of the embattled young seems to remain oddly consistent, even though its immediate causes may change drastically.

Review in the summer of 1939, Dos Passos wrote:

> My sympathies, for some reason, lie with the private in the front line against the brass hat; with the hodcarrier against the strawboss, or the walking delegate for that matter; with the laboratory worker against the stuffed shirt in a mortarboard; with the criminal against the cop.

His conviction grew in these years, and those immediately following, that such individualism, such concern for "the little man," lay at the heart of the American democratic tradition—as he sought to demonstrate in his introduction to *The Living Thoughts of Tom Paine* (1940) and *The Ground We Stand On* (1941). The ground Americans stood on, Dos Passos argued in the latter volume, was the democratic heritage reflected in the writings of Roger Williams, Benjamin Franklin, Thomas Jefferson, and Joel Barlow, a legacy that contrasted sharply with the emergent tyrannies in Europe. And always close to the center of Dos Passos' consciousness were the voices of Walt Whitman and (somewhat less so) of Emerson.

Answering an earlier questionnaire (in 1932) from the *Modern Quarterly,* which asked in part about the possibility of a proletarian literature in America, Dos Passos—after praising Dreiser, Anderson, and Jack London—remarked: "We have had a proletarian literature for years, and are about the only country that has. It hasn't been a revolutionary literature, exactly, though it seems to me that Walt Whitman's a hell of a lot more revolutionary than any Russian poet I've ever heard of." And in the forty-sixth "Camera Eye" in *The Big Money*, Dos Passos pauses in the midst of the Whitmanian meditation to wonder "what leverage might pry the owners loose from power and bring back (I too Walt Whitman) our storybook democracy." In this regard, Dos Passos revealed his close affinity with the literary radicals of the earlier, prewar generation. Looking back on those relatively innocent days, one spokesman for the left recalled that:

Fifty years after the first publication of *Leaves of Grass*, the words of Whitman—and of Emerson—were the neutral air we breathed, whether we had read them or not. . . . It is really hard to overestimate how much we depended upon transcendental optimism, how much we were under the spell, politically, of Lincoln, Thoreau, Emerson, Jefferson, Rousseau, and the German sentimental poets of a century earlier, and correspondingly in for disillusion.

Max Eastman, editor of the *Masses* and one of the most intelligent and incisive members of the movement, acknowledged that "we have drunk of the universe in Walt Whitman's poetry," and Van Wyck Brooks said that it was Whitman who had "retrieved our civilization" and "released personality."

It was this link with the liberal and idealistic American tradition, along with a capacity to be nourished by it, that at least in part disappeared in the thirties. And Dos Passos, forging the link anew for his own individual purposes in the late thirties and early forties, went on to feel that it was precisely that tradition that contemporary America was betraying. Big government, Dos Passos argued stoutly, was by this time betraying both the underdog and the spirit of Whitman and Jefferson as big business had in the twenties; he charged that both institutions had taken "the clean words our fathers spoke and made them slimy and foul." This view of things was adumbrated in the political essay *The Prospect Before Us* in 1950 (the prospect was a gloomy one), and then given full-scale fictional treatment, in the manner of *U.S.A.*, in *Midcentury*, in 1961.

Midcentury, like *U.S.A.*, ends in exhaustion and disgust: "Man drowns in his own scum." Only such valiant, frustrated, and unswervingly conservative figures as General MacArthur and Senator Robert Taft are singled out for glum tribute. There is no reason to doubt Dos Passos' sincerity or his integrity, as there is no reason to deny a certain consistency in his viewpoint over the decades. Moving from an involvement with radical politics through a deepening distrust of radicalism to an endorsement of the specifically American tradition, Dos Passos had in a sense never "moved" at all. He held fast to his commitment to the private, the hodcarrier, the laboratory worker, the individual. What must be doubted is that the new conservative affiliations fired Dos Passos' imagination as the old radicalism had done. In Daniel Aaron's perceptive summary, written before the writer's death, Dos Passos "never sold out his principles. He is not a turncoat, the informer, who took the safe course. He remains the oppositionist and seeker who refuses to make his peace. But he spent his talents too lavishly and too emotionally on causes he has since repudiated. He left the best of his literary self behind."

The best of that self is contained in *U.S.A.* Dos Passos' trilogy follows a large cast of characters—who appear and disappear, and many of whom never know each other—from the dawn of the twentieth century to the beginning of the great Depression. At its literal center are the First World War and the peace negotiations at Versailles—the setting of the middle volume, *1919*. But Dos Passos, drawing upon his own grim memories of the war and its aftermath, suggests that what this history is moving toward is the execution in 1927 of the two nonviolent (or "philosophical") anarchists, Sacco and Vanzetti, after their conviction on the charge of murdering a paymaster in Bridgewater County, Massachusetts. This execution, the climactic event in *The Big Money*, gives final and desperate significance to the myriad developments over the years, the thrust and counterthrust of social conflict, the various lives and relationships forged by history. *U.S.A.*, Alfred Kazin has remarked, is the epic of the great American sell-out.[3] But one last perspec-

tive was necessary to bring the entire picture into focus, and this was provided by the stock market crash in 1929 and the spreading misery of the Depression years. Only then did it begin to appear to many Americans that the society had suffered a calamitous division—between rich and poor, the powerful and the powerless. The division was in fact not as great or as irremediable as alleged (or as certain disruptive forces tried to make it); there was still a sufficient sense of national community for Franklin D. Roosevelt's political and economic program to make real headway in pulling the country together. But the *feeling* of a fatal split is very well conveyed toward the end of *U.S.A.*: "all right we are two nations."

What is most obviously striking about *U.S.A.* is the multiplicity of narrative methods and devices. Dos Passos was much praised for extending the art of narrative by these techniques, and deservedly so. Yet these are essentially fictional uses of techniques that were simultaneously being developed in nonfictional writing, and they reflect interests and urgencies brought into play by the Depression.

The massive documentation in *U.S.A.*, for example, is of a kind with the documentary studies mentioned earlier—the case histories sponsored by the W.P.A. of economic privation on the farms and in the cities, and even the commissioned chartings of the country's highways. The "Camera Eye" has its origin in what we have called the "picture-book"; and the "Newsreel" derives, of course, from the actual and popular "Pathé News" of the day. And the sudden intensifying of curiosity about the lives of representative Americans shows up in the potted biographies Dos Passos periodically offers of men like Frank Lloyd Wright, Thorstein

---

[3] Most of those who have studied the Sacco-Vanzetti case with care have become convinced that the two men did *not* receive anything like a fair trial, and that the absence of fairness was due in good part to the agitated antiradicalism in high places during the period. Such a conviction does not necessarily carry with it, as corol-

lary, a belief in the condemned men's innocence. One continuing suggestion is that Vanzetti was innocent and Sacco guilty. Our own immediate concern is not with the historical truth of this enormously tangled matter, but with the impact of the case on a very large group of observers. It is the record of that impact that Dos Passos has movingly presented.

Veblen, and Henry Ford. But the literary art of Dos Passos lies in his ability to make these elements—each meaningful in its own right—comment ironically upon each other.

The newsreels record the onward sweep of contemporary history as echoed in actual quotations from newspapers and from political and business speeches, lines from folk songs and hit tunes of the moment. But they often focus on historical figures who are famous examples of the activity in which one or another *fictional* character is involved. In the first newsreel of our selection below, Lindbergh is seen returning from his pioneer flight to Paris in 1927—the most revered hero in that airplane industry in which the fictional Charlie Anderson (who does not happen to appear in our section) is pursuing his incoherent but moneymaking career. The following newsreel reveals the American panic at events in Soviet Russia, something that helps explain the deadly prejudice against Sacco and Vanzetti. Frank Lloyd Wright is described as engaged in a creative cause that parallels, and is indeed allied with, the cause of the political radicals: that of building "a new clean construction from the ground up, based on uses and needs," "building the lives of the workers." And he does so as the artistic heir of Whitman: "his blueprints, as once Walt Whitman's words, stir the young men." In this regard, he is also akin to the speaker in the "Camera Eye"—John Dos Passos, to some extent, but the voice might be that of any wandering, aspiring American individual. Mary French, finally, whose life has previously been sketched from her childhood to her arrival in New York, is just the kind of forlorn idealistic young person drifting on historical currents toward the Communist party.

In the story of Mary French, as in the narratives of the many other invented characters in *U.S.A.*, the level of perception and the degree of articulateness are precisely those of the person whose story is unfolding. There are as many narrative points of view and styles in the trilogy as there are characters. But Dos Passos chose not to include a single figure of genuine sensitivity or of real intelligence—no one whose mind Henry James would have thought worthy to command our attention; and the cumulative effect is discouraging. One has the sense of spiritual flatness, of irredeemable limitation. There are the real-life heroes, some of them truly heroic (and some of them shams or villains); but the created characters are a sorry lot. The sufferers, as Edmund Wilson said about Dos Passos' earlier novel, seem to be condemned along with the social sickness that afflicts them.

Our selection is a portion of the last stage of *The Big Money*. It is not perhaps the most arresting moment in the trilogy; and it is indeed arguable whether *1919* rather than *The Big Money* may not be the peak not only of *U.S.A.* but of Dos Passos' entire literary career. But our section does contain the lyrical lament over Sacco and Vanzetti, and the famous pronouncement that America had now revealed itself as divided into two nations. It also demonstrates as well as any other section Dos Passos' skillful mingling of narrative devices, though, for the reasons mentioned in the preceding paragraph, we have chosen to omit the chapter dealing with the "created" character, Mary French.

FURTHER READINGS

John Dos Passos, *The Big Money* (1936)
——, *District of Columbia* (trilogy composed of *Adventures of a Young Man, Number One, The Grand Design*) (1952)
——, *The 42nd Parallel* (1930)
——, *The Living Thoughts of Tom Paine* (1940)
——, *Manhattan Transfer* (1925)
——, *The Men Who Made the Nation* (1957)
——, *Midcentury* (1961)
——, *Nineteen Nineteen* (1932)

——, *One Man's Initiation: Nineteen Seventeen* (1920)
——, *Three Soldiers* (1921)
——, *U.S.A.* (trilogy composed of *The 42nd Parallel, Nineteen Nineteen, The Big Money*) (1937)
Jack Potter, *A Bibliography of John Dos Passos* (1950)

John Peale Bishop, "Three Brilliant Young Novelists," in *The Collected Essays of John Peale Bishop* (1948), Edmund Wilson, ed.

Robert G. Davis, *John Dos Passos* (1962)
Alfred Kazin, *On Native Grounds* (1942)
Jean-Paul Sartre, "John Dos Passos and *Nineteen Nineteen*," in *Literary and Philosophical Essays* (1955)

Edmund Wilson, *Shores of Light* (1952)
————, *The Triple Thinkers* (1948)
J. H. Wrenn, *John Dos Passos* (1961)

From The Big Money (1936)

NEWSREEL LXIII

but a few minutes later this false land disappeared as quickly and as mysteriously as it had come and I found before me the long stretch of the silent sea with not a single sign of life in sight

> *Whippoorwills call*
> *And evening is nigh*
> *I hurry to . . . my blue heaven*

LINDBERGH IN PERIL AS WAVE TRAPS HIM
IN CRUISER'S BOW

Down in the Tennessee mountains
Away from the sins of the world
Old Dan Kelly's son there he leaned on his gun
Athinkin' of Zeb Turney's girl

ACCLAIMED BY HUGE CROWDS IN THE
STREETS

SNAPS PICTURES FROM DIZZY YARDARM

Dan was a hotblooded youngster
His Dad raised him up sturdy an' right

ENTHRALLED BY DARING DEED CITY
CHEERS FROM DEPTHS OF ITS HEART

FLYER SPORTS IN AIR

His heart in a whirl with his love for the girl
He loaded his doublebarreled gun

LEADERS OF PUBLIC LIFE BREAK INTO
UPROAR AT SIGHT OF FLYER

CONFUSION IN HOTEL

AVIATOR NEARLY HURLED FROM AUTO AS
IT LEAPS FORWARD THROUGH GAP IN
CROWD

Over the mountains he wandered
This son of a Tennessee man
With fire in his eye and his gun by his side
Alooking for Zeb Turney's clan

SHRINERS PARADE IN DELUGE OF RAIN

PAPER BLIZZARD CHOKES BROADWAY

Shots ringin' out through the mountain
Shots ringin' out through the breeze

LINDY TO HEAD BIG AIRLINE

The story of Dan Kelly's moonshine
Is spread far and wide o'er the world
How Dan killed the clan shot them down to a man
And brought back old Zeb Turney's girl

a short, partly bald man, his face set in tense emotion, ran out from a mass of people where he had been concealed and climbed quickly into the plane as if afraid he might be stopped. He had on ordinary clothes and a leather vest instead of a coat. He was bareheaded. He crowded down beside Chamberlin, looking neither at the crowd nor at his own wife who stood a little in front of the plane and at one side, her eyes big with wonder. The motor roared and the plane started down the runway, stopped and came back again and then took off perfectly

ARCHITECT

A muggy day in late spring in eighteen-eightyseven a tall youngster of eighteen, with fine eyes and a handsome arrogant way of carrying his head, arrived in Chicago with seven dollars left in his pocket from buying his ticket from Madison with some cash he'd got by pawning Plutarch's *Lives*, a Gibbon's *Decline and Fall of the Roman Empire*, and an old furcollared coat.

Before leaving home to make himself a career in an architect's office (there was no architecture course at Wisconsin to clutter his mind with stale Beaux-Arts drawings), the youngster had seen the dome of the new State Capitol in Madison collapse on account of bad rubblework in the piers, some thieving contractors' skimping materials to save the politicians their rakeoff, and perhaps a trifling but deadly error in the architect's plans;

he never forgot the roar of burst masonry, the flying plaster, the soaring dustcloud, the mashed bodies of the dead and dying being carried out, set faces livid with plasterdust.

Walking round downtown Chicago, crossing and recrossing the bridges over the Chicago River in the jingle and clatter of traffic, the rattle of vans and loaded wagons and the stamping of big drayhorses and the hooting of towboats with barges and the rumbling whistle of lakesteamers waiting for the draw,

he thought of the great continent stretching a thousand miles east and south and north, three thousand miles west, and everywhere, at mineheads, on the shores of newlydredged harbors, along watercourses, at the intersections of railroads, sprouting

shacks roundhouses tipples grainelevators stores warehouses tenements, great houses for the wealthy set in broad treeshaded lawns, domed statehouses on hills, hotels churches operahouses auditoriums.

He walked with long eager steps

toward the untrammeled future opening in every direction for a young man who'd keep his hands to his work and his wits sharp to invent.

The same day he landed a job in an architect's office.

Frank Lloyd Wright was the grandson of a Welsh hatter and preacher who'd settled in a rich Wisconsin valley, Spring Valley, and raised a big family of farmers and preachers and schoolteachers there. Wright's father was a preacher too, a restless illadjusted New Englander who studied medicine, preached in a Baptist church in Weymouth, Massachusetts, and then as a Unitarian in the Middle West, taught music, read Sanskrit and finally walked out on his family.

Young Wright was born on his grandfather's farm, went to school in Weymouth and Madison, worked summers on a farm of his uncle's in Wisconsin.

His training in architecture was the reading of Viollet le Duc, the apostle of the thirteenth century and of the pure structural mathematics of Gothic stonemasonry, and the seven years he worked with Louis Sullivan in the office of Adler and Sullivan in Chicago. (It was Louis Sullivan who, after Richardson, invented whatever was invented in nineteenthcentury architecture in America.)

When Frank Lloyd Wright left Sullivan, he had already launched a distinctive style, prairie architecture. In Oak Park he built broad suburban dwellings for rich men that were the first buildings to break the hold on American builders' minds of centuries of pastward routine, of the wornout capital and plinth and pediment dragged through the centuries from the Acropolis and the jaded traditional stencils of Roman masonry, the halfobliterated Palladian copybooks.

Frank Lloyd Wright was cutting out a new avenue that led toward the swift constructions in glassbricks and steel

foreshadowed today.

Delightedly he reached out for the new materials, steel in tension, glass, concrete, the million new metals and alloys.

The son and grandson of preachers, he became a preacher in blueprints,

projecting constructions in the American future instead of the European past.

Inventor of plans,

plotter of tomorrow's girderwork phrases,

he preaches to the young men coming of age in the time of oppression, cooped up by the plasterboard partitions of finance routine, their lives and plans made poor by feudal levies of parasite money standing astride every process to shake down progress for the cutting of coupons:

The properly citified citizen has become a broker, dealing chiefly in human frailties or the ideas and inventions of others, a puller of levers, a presser of buttons of vicarious power, his by way of machine craft . . . and over beside him and beneath him, even in his heart as he sleeps, is the taximeter of rent, in some form to goad this anxious consumer's unceasing struggle for or against more or less merciful or merciless money increment.

To the young men who spend their days and nights drafting the plans for new *rented aggregates of rental cells upended on hard pavements*, he preaches

the horizons of his boyhood,

a future that is not the rise of a few points in a hundred selected stocks, or an increase in carloadings, or a multiplication of credit in the bank or a rise in the rate on callmoney,

but a new clean construction, from the ground up, based on uses and needs,

toward the American future instead of toward the painsmeared past of Europe and Asia. Usonia he calls the broad teeming band of this new nation across the enormous continent between Atlantic and Pacific. He preaches a project for Usonia:

It is easy to realize how the complexity of crude utilitarian construction in the mechanical infancy of our growth, like the crude scaffolding for some noble building, did violence to the landscape. . . . The crude purpose of pioneering days has been accomplished. The scaffolding may be taken down and the true work, the culture of a civilization, may appear.

Like the life of many a preacher, prophet, exhorter, Frank Lloyd Wright's life has been stormy. He has raised children, had rows with wives, overstepped boundaries, got into difficulties with the law, divorcecourts, bankruptcy, always the yellow press yapping at his heels, his misfortunes yelled out in headlines in the evening papers: affairs with women, the nightmare horror of the burning of his house in Wisconsin.

By a curious irony

the building that is most completely his is the Imperial Hotel in Tokyo that was one of the few structures to come unharmed through the earthquake of 1923 (the day the cable came telling him that the building had stood saving so many hundreds of lives he writes was one of his happiest days)

and it was reading in German that most Americans first learned of his work.

His life has been full of arrogant projects unaccomplished. (How often does the preacher hear his voice echo back hollow from the empty hall, the draftsman watch the dust fuzz over the carefullycontrived plans, the architect see the rolledup blueprints curl yellowing and brittle in the filingcabinet.)

Twice he's rebuilt the house where he works in his grandfather's valley in Wisconsin after fires and disasters that would have smashed most men forever.

He works in Wisconsin,

an erect spare whitehaired man, his sons are architects, apprentices from all over the world come to work with him,

drafting the new city (he calls it Broadacre City).

Near and Far are beaten (to imagine the new city you must blot out every ingrained habit of the past, build a nation from the ground up with the new tools). For the architect there are only uses:

the incredible multiplication of functions, strength and tension in metal,

the dynamo, the electric coil, radio, the photoelectric cell, the internalcombustion motor,

glass

concrete;

and needs. (Tell us, doctors of philosophy, what are the needs of a man. At least a man needs to be notjailed notafraid nothungry notcold not without love, not a worker for a power he has never seen

that cares nothing for the uses and needs of a man or a woman or a child.)

Building a building is building the lives of the workers and dwellers in the building.

The buildings determine civilization as the cells in the honeycomb the functions of bees.

Perhaps in spite of himself the arrogant draftsman, the dilettante in concrete, the bohemian artist for wealthy ladies desiring to pay for prominence with the startling elaboration of their homes has been forced by the logic of uses and needs, by the lifelong struggle against the dragging undertow of money in mortmain,

to draft plans that demand for their fulfillment a new life;

only in freedom can we build the Usonian city. His plans are coming to life. His blueprints, as once Walt Whitman's words, stir the young men:—

Frank Lloyd Wright,

patriarch of the new building,

not without honor except in his own country.

NEWSREEL LXIV

WEIRD FISH DRAWN FROM SARGASSO SEA

by night when the rest of the plant was still dim figures ugly in gasmasks worked in the long low building back of the research laboratory

RUM RING LINKS NATIONS

All around the water tank
Waitin' for a train

WOMAN SLAIN MATE HELD

BUSINESS MEN NOT ALARMED OVER COMING ELECTION

GRAVE FOREBODING UNSETTLES MOSCOW

LABOR CHIEFS RULED OUT OF PULPITS

imagination boggles at the reports from Moscow. These murderers have put themselves beyond the pale. They have shown themselves to be the mad dogs of the world

WALLSTREET EMPLOYERS BANISH
CHRISTMAS WORRIES AS BONUSES ROLL IN

Left my girl in the mountains
Left her standin' in the rain

OUR AIR SUPREMACY ACCLAIMED

LAND SO MOUNTAINOUS IT STANDS ON END

Got myself in trouble
An' shot a county sheriff down

In the stealth of the night have you heard
padded feet creeping toward you?

TROTZKY OPENS ATTACK ON STALIN

STRANGLED MAN DEAD IN STREET

Moanin' low . . .
My sweet man's gonna go

HUNT HATCHET WOMAN WHO ATTACKED
SOCIETY MATRON

CLASPS HANDS OF HEROES

GIRL DYING IN MYSTERY PLUNGE

He's the kind of man that needs the kind of
woman like me

COMPLETELY LOST IN FOG OVER MEXICO

ASSERT RUSSIA RISING

For I'm dancin' with tears in my eyes
'Cause the girl in my arms isn't you

SIX HUNDRED PUT TO DEATH AT ONCE
IN CANTON

SEE BOOM YEAR AHEAD

this checking we do for you in our investors
consulting service, we analyze every individual security you own and give you an impartial report
and rating thereon. Periodically through the year
we keep you posted on important developments. If
danger signals suddenly develop, we advise you
promptly

THE CAMERA EYE (49)

walking from Plymouth to North Plymouth through
the raw air of Massachusetts Bay at each step a
small cold squudge through the sole of one shoe
    looking out past the gray frame houses under
the robin's-egg April sky across the white dories
anchored in the bottle-clear shallows across the yellow sandbars and the slaty bay ruffling to blue to
the eastward
    this is where the immigrants landed the round-
heads the sackers of castles the kingkillers haters
of oppression this is where they stood in a cluster
after landing from the crowded ship that stank of
bilge   on the beach that belonged to no one
between the ocean that belonged to no one and
the enormous forest that belonged to no one that
stretched over the hills where the deertracks were
up the green rivervalleys where the redskins grew
their tall corn in patches forever into the incredible west
    for threehundred years the immigrants toiled
into the west
    and now today
    walking from Plymouth to North Plymouth sud-
denly round a bend in the road beyond a little
pond and yellowtwigged willows hazy with green
you see the Cordage   huge sheds and buildings
companyhouses all the same size all grimed the
same color a great square chimney long roofs sharp
ranked squares and oblongs cutting off the sea the
Plymouth Cordage   this is where another immigrant worked hater of oppression who wanted a
world unfenced   when they fired him from the
Cordage he peddled fish   the immigrants in the
dark framehouses knew him   bought his fish
listened to his talk following his cart around from
door to door   you ask them What was he
like?   why are they scared to talk of Bart scared
because they knew him scared eyes narrowing black
with fright?   a barber the man in the little gro-
cerystore the woman he boarded with   in scared
voices they ask Why won't they believe? We
knew him   We seen him every day Why won't
they believe that day we buy the eels?
    only the boy isn't scared
    pencil scrawls in my notebook the scraps of rec-
ollection the broken halfphrases the effort to in-
tersect word with word to dovetail clause with clause
to rebuild out of mangled memories unshakably
(Oh Pontius Pilate) the truth
    the boy walks shyly browneyed beside me to the
station talks about how Bart helped him with his
homework wants to get ahead   why should it
hurt him to have known Bart? wants to go to
Boston University   we shake hands   don't let
them scare you
    accustomed the smokingcar   accustomed the
jumble of faces rumble cozily homelike toward

Boston through the gathering dark   how can I make them feel how our fathers our uncles haters of oppression came to this coast   how say Don't let them scare you   make them feel who are your oppressors America

rebuild the ruined words worn slimy in the mouths of lawyers districtattorneys collegepresidents judges   without the old words the immigrants haters of oppression brought to Plymouth how can you know who are your betrayers America   or that this fishpeddler you have in Charlestown Jail is one of your founders Massachusetts?

NEWSREEL LXV

STORM TIES UP SUBWAY; FLOODS AND
LIGHTNING DARKEN CITY

Love oh love oh careless love
Like a thief comes in the night

ONLOOKERS CRY HALLELUJAH AS PEACE
DOVE LIGHTS; SAID TO HAVE SPLIT A
HUNDRED THOUSAND DOLLARS

CRASH UPSETS EXCHANGE

CHICAGO NIPPLE SLUMP HITS TRADING
ON CURB

Bring me a pillow for my poor head
A hammer for to knock out my brains
For the whiskey has ruined this body of mine
And the red lights have run me insane

FAITH PLACED IN RUBBER BOATS

But I'll love my baby till the sea runs dry

This great new searchlight sunburns you two
miles away

Till the rocks all dissolve by the sun
Oh ain't it hard?

Smythe according to the petition was employed testing the viscosity of lubricating oil in the Okmulgee plant of the company on July 12, 1924. One of his duties was to pour benzol on a hot vat where it was boiled down so that the residue could be examined. Day after day he breathed the not unpleasant fumes from the vat.

One morning about a year later Smythe cut his face while shaving and noticed that the blood flowed for hours in copious quantities from the tiny wound. His teeth also began to bleed when he

brushed them and when the flow failed to stop after several days he consulted a doctor. The diagnosis was that the benzol fumes had broken down the walls of his blood vessels.

After eighteen months in bed, during which he slept only under the effect of opiates, Smythe's spleen and tonsils were removed. Meanwhile the periodic blood transfusions were resorted to in an effort to keep his blood supply near normal.

In all more than thirty-six pints of blood were infused through his arms until when the veins had been destroyed it was necessary to cut into his body to open other veins. During the whole time up to eight hours before his death, the complaint recited, he was conscious and in pain.

There follows a long chapter dramatizing the radicalization of the alienated and idealistic Mary French. The process is set against the background of the futile efforts by the various factions of the political left to free Sacco and Vanzetti and culminates with Mary French being beaten by police at a protest only blocks from the jail where Sacco and Vanzetti are held. The chapter concludes with "Mary [forgetting] everything as her voice joined . . . all their voices, the voices of the crowds being driven back across the bridge in singing:
Arise, ye prisoners of starvation . . ."

NEWSREEL LXVI

HOLMES DENIES STAY

A better world's in birth

Tiny wasps imported from Korea in battle to death with Asiatic beetle

BOY CARRIED MILE DOWN SEWER; SHOT
OUT ALIVE

CHICAGO BARS MEETINGS

For justice thunders condemnation

WASHINGTON KEEPS EYE ON RADICALS

Arise rejected of the earth

PARIS BRUSSELS MOSCOW GENEVA ADD
THEIR VOICES

It is the final conflict
Let each stand in his place

GEOLOGIST LOST IN CAVE SIX DAYS

The International Party

SACCO AND VANZETTI MUST DIE

Shall be the human race

Much I thought of you when I was lying in the death house—the singing, the kind tender voices of the children from the playground where there was all the life and the joy of liberty—just one step from the wall that contains the buried agony of three buried souls. It would remind me so often of you and of your sister and I wish I could see you every moment, but I feel better that you will not come to the death house so that you could not see the horrible picture of three living in agony waiting to be electrocuted.

THE CAMERA EYE (50)

they have clubbed us off the streets   they are stronger   they are rich   they hire and fire the politicians the newspapereditors the old judges the small men with reputations the collegepresidents the wardheelers (listen businessmen collegepresidents judges America will not forget her betrayers) they hire the men with guns   the uniforms the policecars the patrolwagons

all right you have won   you will kill the brave men our friends tonight

there is nothing left to do   we are beaten   we the beaten crowd together in these old dingy schoolrooms on Salem Street   shuffle up and down the gritty creaking stairs sit hunched with bowed heads on benches and hear the old words of the haters of oppression   made new in sweat and agony tonight

our work is over   the scribbled phrases   the nights typing releases the smell of the printshop the sharp reek of newprinted leaflets the rush for Western Union stringing words into wires the search for stinging words to make you feel who are your oppressors America

America our nation has been beaten by strangers who have turned our language inside out who have taken the clean words our fathers spoke and made them slimy and foul

their hired men sit on the judge's bench they sit back with their feet on the tables under the dome of the State House they are ignorant of our beliefs they have the dollars the guns the armed forces the powerplants

they have built the electricchair and hired the executioner to throw the switch

all right we are two nations

America our nation has been beaten by strangers who have bought the laws and fenced off the meadows and cut down the woods for pulp and turned our pleasant cities into slums and sweated the wealth out of our people and when they want to they hire the executioner to throw the switch

but do they know that the old words of the immigrants are being renewed in blood and agony tonight do they know that the old American speech of the haters of oppression is new tonight in the mouth of an old woman from Pittsburgh of a husky boilermaker from Frisco who hopped freights clear from the Coast to come here in the mouth of a Back Bay socialworker in the mouth of an Italian printer of a hobo from Arkansas   the language of the beaten nation is not forgotten in our ears tonight

the men in the deathhouse made the old words new before they died

If it had not been for these things, I might have lived out my life talking at streetcorners to scorning men. I might have died unknown, unmarked, a failure. This is our career and our triumph. Never in our full life can we hope to do such work for tolerance, for justice, for man's understanding of man as now we do by an accident.

now their work is over   the immigrants haters of oppression lie quiet in black suits in the little undertaking parlor in the North End   the city is quiet   the men of the conquering nation are not to be seen on the streets

they have won why are they scared to be seen on the streets? on the streets you see only the downcast faces of the beaten   the streets belong to the beaten nation all the way to the cemetery where the bodies of the immigrants are to be burned   we line the curbs in the drizzling rain we crowd the wet sidewalks elbow to elbow silent pale looking with scared eyes at the coffins

we stand defeated America

JOHN STEINBECK (1902–1968)

John Steinbeck and John Dos Passos provide two major examples of the relation between politics and the literary art—more particularly, between the political and social movements that grew out of the economic distress of the thirties (with such background causes as then became apparent) and the efforts by American novelists to give those movements shape and meaning. The lesson may turn out to be a rather melancholy one; but it is differently so in the two instances; and if the final product of both seems colored by failure, it is a failure that contains no few victories along the way.

Steinbeck, who was born in California in 1902 and attended Stanford at various times during the early twenties, was not, of course, the first writer to examine the California scene. But he was the writer who, in his own generation, most firmly established California as a fertile domain for the novelistic imagination. He had a clear consciousness, as we shall see, of the movement from the American East to the Far West as both a significant historical reality and a symbolic action—in California, a number of American traditions, literary and otherwise, could refresh themselves and take on new forms. For this reason, Steinbeck may best be approached within a fairly large context of American literary history. But the new forms he envisaged contained, or were necessarily drawn toward, the tragic; and for a writer in the thirties, they were almost inevitably imbued with the political. Given Steinbeck's temperament, the combination invited trouble.

It is a complex case, but also an exemplary one; and to clarify things a little, we may begin by distinguishing two basic motifs in Steinbeck's fiction over his prime years. The first may be called the American motif: a celebrational sense of *life*, a sense of promise and possibility and of as yet unspoiled novelty in man and his habitation, a mystical sympathy both for the individual and for what Whitman called the "en-masse." In short, a vision, if that is not too rarefied and romantic a word for it, which was of New England and the American East in its nineteenth-century origins and which Steinbeck naturalized in his native California and translated into its idiom.

The second is the contemporary motif: something so close in substance to the American motif that it can be seen as growing organically out of it, and yet something which also appears in the fiction of other contemporary languages and countries. It appears in the fiction, for example, of Silone in Italy, of Malraux and Camus in France, and, to some extent, of Graham Greene in England. This motif springs from the awareness of the fateful division between man and man; and of that division as a central feature of the mutilated life of which it is the novelist's business to give a direct impression.

The sense of division leads naturally to the political theme. It leads, that is, to the intuition that the form which the human struggle currently assumes, the representative plot of contemporary experience and the soul of its tragedy, is political in design. The political theme consists of a revolt against the forces that keep men separated, and its heart tends to beat to the formula of Albert Camus: I rebel, therefore we are. Or it pulses yet more movingly to the rhythm suggested by Ignazio Silone: "What determined my rebellion was the choice of companions."

Steinbeck has made his contribution to the theme and its heart-beat, especially in *The Grapes of Wrath*. "This is the beginning," he says there, flatly, in his own voice, "from 'I' to 'we.'" But the relation between the elements —the felt division, the rebellion, and the ordering power of art—is extremely complex. It is partly Steinbeck's habit of oversimplifying both life and art that has kept him from seeing and taking hold of the complex entirety. The elements rarely fuse in his fiction; they tend rather to jar against each other. The same may be said of the two leading motifs. The evolution of the contemporary motif from the American motif may be seen within the development of American literature itself, in the movement from Emerson to Hawthorne and from all of them to Henry James; a movement from the happy evocation of "the simple separate person" and the sturdy conviction that the world was, or could be seen as, young and uncorrupted, to the gradual sense of self-isolation, of darkness and bewilderment. Later still there ensues the perception that the form of human experience was exactly the strenuous, perhaps desperate, need and effort of separated individuals to draw close to one another, to enjoy an experience of life by means of a human relationship, in what Henry James was to call "the great greasy sea" of the anarchic modern world.

There is no such coherent and meaningful evolution in Steinbeck's work, though he began reasonably enough in the recognizably American vein and went on to identify, and respond boldly to, the contemporary challenge. The motifs did not so much meet together as collide, in a struggle, as it were, between poetry and politics. For Steinbeck's poetry, the truly creative side of him, remained American while his engrossing theme became contemporary and political. As it turned out it was the poetry which suffered, which is simply a way of referring again to Steinbeck's intermittent novelistic achievement.

The American theme announces itself regularly in Steinbeck's stories in a recurring image of a movement west, a movement particularly to California. Steinbeck's first novel, *To a God Unknown*, begins with the departure of Joseph Wayne, the book's indistinctly godlike hero, from the family home in New England, near Pittsford, Vermont, for the green hills of California. "I've been reading about the West and the good cheap land there," he tells his father; "I've a hunger for the land, sir." "It's not just restlessness," his father replies. "You may go to the West. You are finished here with me."

The process is repeated, through dialogue rather less stagey, in *East of Eden*, when Adam Trask leaves his Connecticut home and heads for California. "It's nice there, sun all the time and beautiful." And the Joad family in *The Grapes of Wrath*, though starting much farther west, in Oklahoma, similarly sets off for the Pacific coast not only to find work and a place to live but to find a new world of hope and opportunity after the destruction of their old world.

Steinbeck's instinct at these initial moments was altogether sound; he was knowingly possessing himself of a native theme and a native resource, a resource both of history and of literature. It is the traditional American impulse to withdraw into the terrain of freedom in order to find or refind one's identity and one's purpose as a human being; to dissociate from the given, the orthodox, the habitual, from whatever passes at the time for civilization. "Aunt Polly she's going to . . . civilize me, and I can't stand it. I been there before," Huck Finn says on the last page of his memoirs. He determines accordingly to "light out for the territories." The same impulse, of course, received its most eloquent treatment in the recorded withdrawal of Henry David Thoreau from the quiet desperation of civilized Concord to the unfallen nature and fertile solitude of Walden Pond, a few miles away. But we remember also Cooper's Natty Bumppo lighting out for the uncomplicated forest from the oppressive society of the town of Templeton, and Herman Melville, in fact and fiction, jumping ship to reflect unfavorably upon the evils of civilization from the Eden-atmosphere of the Taipi valley in the South Seas. Such was the form that rebellion originally took in American literature.

But in seeing his native Salinas Valley in California as a new Eden, the scene of a new chance for man and for men, and in transporting his heroes thither from the exhausted East, Steinbeck is not only continuing in an American tradition, enacting again an old American dream. He is also suggesting that the dream itself has moved west and has settled there, that it is now California which stimulates in its inhabitants the intoxicating sense of fresh beginnings and untroubled potentialities which the eastern scene once stimulated in Emerson, in Thoreau, in Whitman. This is the point and purpose of the prefatory incantations of *East of Eden,* where the local California countryside is observed and named as though by the first man at the dawn of time.

One of Steinbeck's editors has accurately noted in him "an expression of the joy of living." The difficulty with Steinbeck's peculiar brand of joyfulness is not so much that it can easily turn fuzzy or mawkish (a kind of melting process observable in the development, or the decline, from *Tortilla Flat* to *Cannery Row* and *Sweet Thursday*). The difficulty is rather that he was constitutionally unequipped to deal with the more somber reality a man must come up against, in these times or in any times, if he is honest and alert.

Steinbeck was up against a part of that reality during the years between 1936 and 1942 when he was writing *In Dubious Battle, The Grapes of Wrath,* and *The Moon Is Down,* and when he was also writing the one work in which his trapped demon did squirm out and get almost completely into the language—*Of Mice and Men.* With the important exception of the last-named book, the work of those years is characterized by, among other things, a seeming refusal, or perhaps an inability, to confront tragic truth. The result of having done so might have been a considerable enlargement of Steinbeck's art; the transformation, for instance, of the earlier earthy humor into what Hawthorne once called "the tragic power of laughter."

But the work of those years was characterized, too, by a relatively superficial analysis and a makeshift solution of the case, whether it was social injustice or Fascist invasion and oppression. To have looked more searchingly into those phenomena would have been to discover their tragic implications for the nature of man— the proper concern of the artist if not of the politician or the sociologist. *The Moon Is Down,* for example, is intended as a consoling image of heroism—that of a number of European villagers in a town occupied by the Nazi forces. But it is woefully limited by the absence of anything but the slightest hint that the fault, the guilt, the fascism itself, is a manifestation of the human heart, and so detectable on all sides of the conflict. Steinbeck typically permits a portion of goodness to modify the badness of some of the invaders—especially the commanding officer, the book's one interesting characterization—but none of the invaders' badness is reflected in the hearts of the staunch and faithful villagers. Be good, sweet maids and men, Steinbeck seems to be telling them, and let who will be Fascist.

We are not now raising the somewhat tired issue of the artist's responsibility. We are sure that the responsibility is a great one, but we are talking about the form it can most suitably and effectively take—and that is the prophetic form, penetrating to hidden realities and not reflecting mere appearances. Neither *The Grapes of Wrath* nor *In Dubious Battle,* the novels where Steinbeck's rebellious sympathy for the wretched and the luckless is most evident, succeeds in arriving at that form; and in the absence of the prophetic we are left with the merely political. There are many fine, pungent and moving things in each of these books, and Steinbeck has given *The Grapes of Wrath* momentum, an inner drive, which in its generation only Faulkner —and he only a few times—has equaled. It also has a sweetness which never once goes sticky. Yet neither book quite touches bottom, quite manages to expose beneath the particular miseries and misfortunes the existence of what used to be called fate, what now is called the human condition—that twist or flaw in the very nature of things which Steinbeck has himself laid poetic hold on and expressed in the very similar phrases which conclude *The Red Pony* and *Of Mice and Men,* and which refer to two very similar acts of destruction: "I had to do it—had to" and "You hadda, George, I swear you hadda." *In Dubious Battle* and *The Grapes of Wrath* have, as it were, everything but that simple acknowledgment of the secret cause of our suffering and our violence. The secret cause is the ally of the poetic impulse, but these novels reach only as deep as the political cause, and politics in its usual meaning is the enemy of poetry, or, at any rate, of Steinbeck's poetry.

The Grapes of Wrath does not manage to transcend its political theme because the question "What is man?" is not really accepted by Steinbeck as the root question. He could not bring himself to believe that there is anything really wrong with the human heart, so that the causes of the wrongs observed must be other—practical, even mechanical; political, in short. The point here is that the application of Steinbeck's special and happy-natured poetry to his newly discovered and unhappy historical materials could only result in a defeat of the poetry. It would have taken a different brand of poetry, something with a more tragic thrust to it, to have survived. The Grapes of Wrath remains with the political answer, the same political theme—unity—of In Dubious Battle, but what it does is to expand on that theme.

To the story of Tom Joad and his family—their long, rickety journey westward, their exhausted efforts to make a living in California, and the bitter resistance they encounter among the rich, frightened, and greedy landowners—Steinbeck has added a large sky-blue vision of things which is not only like the vision of Emerson, but is straight out of Emerson. It is his notion of the over-soul, the world-soul of which each individual has his modest and particular share. Jim Casy, the former preacher and future martyr, pronounces this idea: "Maybe all men got one big soul and everybody's a part of it." He had come to this vision during his retirement into the hills: "There was the hills, an' there was me, an' we wasn't separate no more. We was one big thing. An' that one thing was holy. That's the Holy Spirit—the human spirit—the whole shebang. An' it on'y got unholy when one mis'able little fella got the bit in his teeth, an' run off his own way . . . Fella like that bust the holiness."

The doctrine of the whole shebang is the warrant for all the desperate organizational efforts, the violence and the heroism which follow later; they are all efforts to reconstruct the busted holiness, to mend once more the unity of the one

soul of mankind. That doctrine also is the philosophical basis for the famous speech that Tom Joad makes to his mother after Casy has been killed—those words which rang bravely and beautifully in 1939 but which seem to have lost a little of their glow since. Tom Joad is about to leave, to continue the whole struggle in hiding. His mother asks: "How'm I gonna know about you? They might kill ya an' I wouldn' know."

Tom laughed uneasily. "Well, maybe like Casy says, a fella ain't got a soul of his own, but on'y a piece of a big one—an then . . . then it don't matter. Then I'll be all aroun' in the dark. I'll be ever'where—wherever you look. Wherever they's a fight so hungry people can eat, I'll be there. Wherever they's a cop beatin' up a guy, I'll be there. If Casy knowed, why, I'll be in the way guys yell when they're mad an'—I'll be in the way kids laugh when they're hungry an' they know supper's ready. An' when our folks eat the stuff they raise an' live in the houses they build—why, I'll be there. See?"

What gets lost amidst the genuinely lyrical flow of that passage and in its infectious hopefulness is the element on which not only the social struggle but the art of narrative depend—the image of the sharply outlined, resolutely differentiated, concretely individual personality. The political movements of the 1930's did tend to submerge the individual in the group, whether or not at the behest of the over-soul, but in reflecting that fact in his fiction Steinbeck again yielded up his poetry to his politics. And his poetry is not saved by superadding to that political tendency a metaphysical principle which, even were it true, is totally unsuited for the craft of fiction. Fiction deals with individuals. A modern philosopher has wisely said that relationship depends upon distance. What may be needed, both for society and for art, is not unity, which dissolves the individuals within it, but community, which is a sharing among distinct human persons. What may be needed is not group-men but companions. Steinbeck always had trouble focusing on individuals, and he always knew it. "You have never known a person," Joseph Wayne's sister-in-law says to him; and we feel it is Steinbeck admonishing himself. "You aren't aware of persons, Joseph; only people. You can't see units, Joseph, only the whole." Therefore it is heartening as well as a trifle surprising to come at last, in *East of Eden*, upon the long-awaited awareness, the long-delayed perception; to arrive in Steinbeck's pages at the revelation withheld from Joseph Wayne and even from Doc Burton and Jim Casy. And this occurs in a passage not wholly justified by the immediate context, but erupting with a fierceness of feeling reminiscent of the explosive and superficially irrelevant ode to democracy which pops up in the early pages of *Moby-Dick*. "And this I believe," Steinbeck's voice suddenly announces to us:

> And this I believe. That the free, exploring mind of the individual human is the most valuable thing in the world. And this I would fight for: the freedom of the mind to take any direction it wishes, undirected. And this I must fight against: an idea, religion or government which limits or destroys the individual. This is what I am and what I am about. I can understand why a system built on a pattern must try to destroy the free mind, for this is one thing which can by inspection destroy such a system. Surely I can understand this, and I hate it and I will fight against it to preserve the one thing that separates us from the uncreative beasts. If the glory can be killed, we are lost.

It can no doubt be explained that such a belief and the passion behind it have been generated by revolt against the peculiar misbehaviors, the conformist pressures, of the 1950's, just as the emphasis on unity and the world-soul were stimulated by the ruggedly destructive individualism of the 1920's. But this time Steinbeck's rebellious impulse has produced a theme which goes beyond politics; which is, very simply, human; which is the actual stuff of the art of narrative.

Steinbeck did not live to write the novel worthy of that trans-political theme. *The Winter of Our Discontent* (1961) was uncharacteristically set in mid-century New England and dealt uncharacteristically with moral confusion and decay; it is readable enough, but a minor effort. It may be, paradoxically, that Steinbeck's most spirited book in the later years was a work written as a contribution to Adlai Stevenson's campaign for the presidency—it was just Stevenson's transpolitical nature that Steinbeck reveled in. *Travels with Charley: In Search of America* (1962) suggested that Steinbeck, though still a liberal, was, in the familiar manner, edging to the right. It may have been only a coincidence that he was promptly awarded the Nobel prize for literature the same year, the seventh American recipient of that award.

BIOGRAPHICAL CHART

1902	Born, February 27, in Salinas, California
1920	Enters Stanford University, contributing occasionally to the college periodicals; never a degree candidate
1925	Goes to New York, working as a reporter and bricklayer
1927	Returns to California; works as a caretaker on a private estate
1929	*Cup of Gold*
1930	Marries Carol Henning
1932	*Pastures of Heaven*
1933	*To a God Unknown*
1935	*Tortilla Flat* published, attracting considerable attention and acclaim
1936	*In Dubious Battle*; visits Mexico
1937	*The Red Pony*; *Of Mice and Men* (novel and drama); visits Europe
1938	*The Long Valley*
1939	*The Grapes of Wrath* evokes great critical response; elected to the National Institute of Arts and Letters
1940	Wins Pulitzer prize for *The Grapes of Wrath*
1942	*The Moon Is Down* (drama)
1943	Covers action on the Italian and African fronts for the New York *Herald-Tribune*; divorced from Carol Henning; marries Gwyn Conger
1945	*Cannery Row*; *The Red Pony* reprinted and enlarged
1947	*The Pearl*; *The Wayward Bus*; invited to visit Russia, which he does

1948   Divorced from Gwyn Conger; elected to the American Academy of Arts and Letters
1950   Marries Elaine Scott; *Burning Bright*
1952   *East of Eden*
1955   *Pipe Dream* produced, a musical based on his *Sweet Thursday*, written by Rodgers and Hammerstein

1961   *The Winter of Our Discontent*
1962   *Travels with Charley*; awarded the Nobel prize for literature
1966   *America and Americans*; lives in South Vietnam, writing a syndicated column about his experiences
1968   Dies, December 20

FURTHER READINGS

There is no standard edition of Steinbeck's works. Individual titles are cited in the biographical chart.

Richard Astro and Hayashii Tetsumaro, *Steinbeck: The Man and His Work* (1970)
Warren G. French, *John Steinbeck* (1961)
R. W. B. Lewis, "The Steinbeck Perspective," in *The Picaresque Saint* (1958)

Peter Lisca, *The Wide World of John Steinbeck* (1958)
Lester Jay Marks, *Thematic Design in the Novels of John Steinbeck* (1969)
Richard O'Connor, *John Steinbeck* (1970)
Ernest W. Tedlock, Jr., and C. V. Wicher, eds., *Steinbeck and His Critics: A Record of Twenty-Five Years* (1957)
Frank William Watt, *John Steinbeck* (1962)

From The Grapes of Wrath (1939)

The Grapes of Wrath divides fairly tidily into four large sections, which might be given the following ritualistic labels: Departure (Chapters 1 through 10); Journey (Chapters 11 through 18); Arrival (Chapters 19 through 24); Death, Disappearance, and the New Life (final six chapters). The slow, painful departure is from the Joad family's dust-swept Oklahoma farm, and the long journey is westward to California.

Our selection begins at the moment the Joads have entered the great California valley. What they first encounter here, in the promised land, is the fear and hatred of the established authorities. Later, in the camp at Weedpitch they will come upon a community life and human kindness and decency. At the end of this large-scale novel, the Joad group is partly dispersed: Jim Casy, the itinerant preacher, has been killed, and Tom Joad, the book's main character, is forced to go into hiding. But in the closing scene there are hints of life continuing.

In this section, Steinbeck can be seen deploying his characteristic fictional resources: a meditation on American history and the conditions of life in his native California; a rapid, almost dreamlike evocation (as of talk overheard or remembered) of human need and human cruelty; direct narration, as the Joads make inquiries about local possibilities; and a conversation between the two figures, Casy and Tom Joad, who carry the novel's burden, respectively, of interpretive thought and significant action.

CHAPTER 19

Once California belonged to Mexico and its land to Mexicans; and a horde of tattered feverish Americans poured in. And such was their hunger for land that they took the land—stole Sutter's land, Guerrero's land, took the grants and broke them up and growled and quarreled over them, those frantic hungry men; and they guarded with guns the land they had stolen. They put up houses and barns, they turned the earth and planted crops. And these things were possession, and possession was ownership.

The Mexicans were weak and fed. They could not resist, because they wanted nothing in the world as frantically as the Americans wanted land.

Then, with time, the squatters were no longer squatters, but owners; and their children grew up and had children on the land. And the hunger was gone from them, the feral hunger, the gnawing, tearing hunger for land, for water and earth and the good sky over it, for the green thrusting grass, for the swelling roots. They had these things so completely that they did not know about them any more. They had no more the stomach-tearing lust for a rich acre and a shining blade to plow it, for seed and a windmill beating its wings in the air. They arose in the dark no more to hear the sleepy birds' first chittering, and the morning wind around the house while they waited for the first light to go out to the dear acres. These things were lost, and crops were reckoned in dollars, and land was valued by principal plus interest, and crops were bought and sold before they were planted. Then crop failure, drought, and flood were no longer little deaths within life, but simple losses of money. And all their love was thinned with money, and all their fierceness dribbled away in interest until they were no longer farmers at all, but little shopkeepers of crops, little manufacturers who must sell before they can make. Then those farmers who were not good shopkeepers lost their land to good shopkeepers. No matter how clever, how loving a man might be with earth and growing things, he could not survive if he were not also a good shopkeeper. And as time went on, the business men had the farms, and the farms grew larger, but there were fewer of them.

Now farming became industry, and the owners followed Rome, although they did not know it. They imported slaves, although they did not call them slaves: Chinese, Japanese, Mexicans, Filipinos. They live on rice and beans, the business men said. They don't need much. They wouldn't know what to do with good wages. Why, look how they live. Why, look what they eat. And if they get funny—deport them.

And all the time the farms grew larger and the owners fewer. And there were pitifully few farmers on the land any more. And the imported serfs were beaten and frightened and starved until some went home again, and some grew fierce and were killed or driven from the country. And the farms grew larger and the owners fewer.

And the crops changed. Fruit trees took the place of grain fields, and vegetables to feed the world spread out on the bottoms: lettuce, cauliflower, artichokes, potatoes—stoop crops. A man may stand to use a scythe, a plow, a pitchfork: but he must crawl like a bug between the rows of lettuce, he must bend his back and pull his long bag between the cotton rows, he must go on his knees like a penitent across a cauliflower patch.

And it came about that owners no longer worked on their farms. They farmed on paper; and they forgot the land, the smell, the feel of it, and re-membered only that they owned it, remembered only what they gained and lost by it. And some of the farms grew so large that one man could not even conceive of them any more, so large that it took batteries of bookkeepers to keep track of interest and gain and loss; chemists to test the soil, to replenish; straw bosses to see that the stooping men were moving along the rows as swiftly as the material of their bodies could stand. Then such a farmer really became a storekeeper, and kept a store. He paid the men, and sold them food, and took the money back. And after a while he did not pay the men at all, and saved bookkeeping. These farms gave food on credit. A man might work and feed himself; and when the work was done, he might find that he owed money to the company. And the owners not only did not work the farms any more, many of them had never seen the farms they owned.

And then the dispossessed were drawn west—from Kansas, Oklahoma, Texas, New Mexico; from Nevada and Arkansas families, tribes, dusted out, tractored out. Carloads, caravans, homeless and hungry; twenty thousand and fifty thousand and a hundred thousand and two hundred thousand. They streamed over the mountains, hungry and restless—restless as ants, scurrying to find work to do—to lift, to push, to pull, to pick, to cut—anything, any burden to bear, for food. The kids are hungry. We got no place to live. Like ants scurrying for work, for food, and most of all for land.

We ain't foreign. Seven generations back Americans, and beyond that Irish, Scotch, English, German. One of our folks in the Revolution, an' they was lots of our folks in the Civil War—both sides. Americans.

They were hungry, and they were fierce. And they had hoped to find a home, and they found only hatred. Okies—the owners hated them because the owners knew they were soft and the Okies strong, that they were fed and the Okies hungry; and perhaps the owners had heard from their grandfathers how easy it is to steal land from a soft man if you are fierce and hungry and armed. The owners hated them. And in the towns, the storekeepers hated them because they had no money to spend. There is no shorter path to a storekeeper's contempt, and all his admirations are exactly opposite. The town men, little bankers, hated Okies because there was nothing to gain from them. They had nothing. And the laboring people hated Okies because a hungry man must work, and if he must work, if he has to work, the wage payer automatically gives him less for his work; and then no one can get more.

And the dispossessed, the migrants, flowed into California, two hundred and fifty thousand, and three hundred thousand. Behind them new tractors were going on the land and the tenants were being forced off. And new waves were on the way, new waves of the dispossessed and the homeless, hardened, intent, and dangerous.

And while the Californians wanted many things, accumulation, social success, amusement, luxury, and a curious banking security, the new barbarians wanted only two things—land and food; and to them the two were one. And whereas the wants of the Californians were nebulous and undefined, the wants of the Okies were beside the roads, lying there to be seen and coveted: the good fields with water to be dug for, the good green fields, earth to crumble experimentally in the hand, grass to smell, oaten stalks to chew until the sharp sweetness was in the throat. A man might look at a fallow field and know, and see in his mind that his own bending back and his own straining arms would bring the cabbages into the light, and the golden eating corn, the turnips and carrots.

And a homeless hungry man, driving the roads with his wife beside him and his thin children in the back seat, could look at the fallow fields which might produce food but not profit, and that man could know how a fallow field is a sin and the unused land a crime against the thin children. And such a man drove along the roads and knew temptation at every field, and knew the lust to take these fields and make them grow strength for his children and a little comfort for his wife. The temptation was before him always. The fields goaded him, and the company ditches with good water flowing were a goad to him.

And in the south he saw the golden oranges hanging on the trees, the little golden oranges on the dark green trees; and guards with shotguns patrolling the lines so a man might not pick an orange for a thin child, oranges to be dumped if the price was low.

He drove his old car into a town. He scoured the farms for work. Where can we sleep the night?

Well, there's Hooverville on the edge of the river. There's a whole raft of Okies there.

He drove his old car to Hooverville. He never asked again, for there was a Hooverville on the edge of every town.

The rag town lay close to water; and the houses were tents, and weed-thatched enclosures, paper houses, a great junk pile. The man drove his family in and became a citizen of Hooverville—always they were called Hooverville. The man put up his own tent as near to water as he could get; or if he had no tent, he went to the city dump and brought back cartons and built a house of corrugated paper. And when the rains came the house melted and washed away. He settled in Hooverville and he scoured the countryside for work, and the little money he had went for gasoline to look for work. In the evening the men gathered and talked together. Squatting on their hams they talked of the land they had seen.

There's thirty thousan' acres, out west of here. Layin' there. Jesus, what I could do with that, with five acres of that! Why, hell, I'd have ever'thing to eat.

Notice one thing? They ain't no vegetables nor chickens nor pigs at the farms. They raise one thing—cotton, say, or peaches, or lettuce. 'Nother place'll be all chickens. They buy the stuff they could raise in the dooryard.

Jesus, what I could do with a couple pigs!

Well, it ain't yourn, an' it ain't gonna be yourn.

What we gonna do? The kids can't grow up this way.

In the camps the word would come whispering. There's work at Shafter. And the cars would be loaded in the night, the highways crowded—a gold rush for work. At Shafter the people would pile up, five times too many to do the work. A gold rush for work. They stole away in the night, frantic for work. And along the roads lay the temptations, the fields that could bear food.

That's owned. That ain't our'n.

Well, maybe we could get a little piece of her. Maybe—a little piece. Right down there—a patch. Jimson weed now. Christ, I could git enough potatoes off'n that little patch to feed my whole family!

It ain't our'n. It got to have Jimson weeds.

Now and then a man tried; crept on the land and cleared a piece, trying like a thief to steal a little richness from the earth. Secret gardens hidden in the weeds. A package of carrot seeds and a few turnips. Planted potato skins, crept out in the evening secretly to hoe in the stolen earth.

Leave the weeds around the edge—then nobody can see what we're a-doin'. Leave some weeds, big tall ones, in the middle.

Secret gardening in the evenings, and water carried in a rusty can.

And then one day a deputy sheriff: Well, what you think you're doin'?

I ain't doin' no harm.

I had my eye on you. This ain't your land. You're trespassing.

The land ain't plowed, an' I ain't hurtin' it none.

You goddamned squatters. Pretty soon you'd think you owned it. You'd be sore as hell. Think you owned it. Get off now.

And the little green carrot tops were kicked off and the turnip greens trampled. And then the Jimson weed moved back in. But the cop was right. A crop raised—why, that makes ownership. Land hoed and the carrots eaten—a man might fight for land he's taken food from. Get him off quick! He'll think he owns it. He might even die fighting for the little plot among the Jimson weeds.

Did ya see his face when we kicked them turnips out? Why, he'd kill a fella soon's he'd look at him. We got to keep these here people down or they'll take the country. They'll take the country.

Outlanders, foreigners.

Sure, they talk the same language, but they ain't the same. Look how they live. Think any of us folks'd live like that? Hell, no!

In the evenings, squatting and talking. And an excited man: Whyn't twenty of us take a piece of lan'? We got guns. Take it an' say, "Put us off if you can." Whyn't we do that?

They'd jus' shoot us like rats.

Well, which'd you ruther be, dead or here? Under groun' or in a house all made of gunny sacks? Which'd you ruther for your kids, dead now or dead in two years with what they call malnutrition? Know what we et all week? Biled nettles an' fried dough! Know where we got the flour for the dough? Swep' the floor of a boxcar.

Talking in the camps, and the deputies, fat-assed men with guns slung on fat hips, swaggering through the camps: Give 'em somepin to think about. Got to keep 'em in line or Christ only knows what they'll do! Why, Jesus, they're as dangerous as niggers in the South! If they ever get together there ain't nothin' that'll stop 'em.

Quote: In Lawrenceville a deputy sheriff evicted a squatter, and the squatter resisted, making it necessary for the officer to use force. The eleven-year-old son of the squatter shot and killed the deputy with a .22 rifle.

Rattlesnakes! Don't take chances with 'em, an' if they argue, shoot first. If a kid'll kill a cop, what'll the men do? Thing is, get tougher'n they are. Treat 'em rough. Scare 'em.

What if they won't scare? What if they stand up and take it and shoot back? These men were armed when they were children. A gun is an extension of themselves. What if they won't scare? What if some time an army of them marches on the land as the Lombards did in Italy, as the Germans did on Gaul and the Turks did on Byzantium? They were land-hungry, ill-armed hordes too, and the legions could not stop them. Slaughter and terror did not stop them. How can you frighten a man whose hunger is not only in his own cramped stomach but in the wretched bellies of his children? You can't scare him—he has known a fear beyond every other.

In Hooverville the men talking: Grampa took his lan' from the Injuns.

Now, this ain't right. We're a-talkin' here. This here you're talkin' about is stealin'. I ain't no thief.

No? You stole a bottle of milk from a porch night before last. An' you stole some copper wire and sold it for a piece of meat.

Yeah, but the kids was hungry.

It's stealin', though.

Know how the Fairfiel' ranch was got? I'll tell ya. It was all gov'ment lan', an' could be took up. Ol' Fairfiel', he went into San Francisco to the bars, an' he got him three hundred stew bums. Them bums took up the lan'. Fairfiel' kep' 'em in food an' whisky, an' then when they'd proved the lan', ol' Fairfiel' took it from 'em. He used to say the lan' cost him a pint of rotgut an acre. Would you say that was stealin'?

Well, it wasn't right, but he never went to jail for it.

No, he never went to jail for it. An' the fella that put a boat in a wagon an' made his report like it was all under water 'cause he went in a boat—he never went to jail neither. An' the fellas that bribed congressmen and the legislatures never went to jail neither.

All over the State, jabbering in the Hoovervilles.

And then the raids—the swoop of armed deputies on the squatters' camps. Get out. Department of Health orders. This camp is a menace to health.

Where we gonna go?

That's none of our business. We got orders to get you out of here. In half an hour we set fire to the camp.

They's typhoid down the line. You want ta spread it all over?

We got orders to get you out of here. Now get! In half an hour we burn the camp.

In half an hour the smoke of paper houses, of weed-thatched huts, rising to the sky, and the people in their cars rolling over the highways, looking for another Hooverville.

And in Kansas and Arkansas, in Oklahoma and Texas and New Mexico, the tractors moved in and pushed the tenants out.

Three hundred thousand in California and more coming. And in California the roads full of frantic people running like ants to pull, to push, to lift, to work. For every manload to lift, five pairs of arms extended to lift it; for every stomachful of food available, five mouths open.

And the great owners, who must lose their land in an upheaval, the great owners with access to history, with eyes to read history and to know the great fact: when property accumulates in too few hands it is taken away. And that companion fact: when a majority of the people are hungry and cold they will take by force what they need. And the little screaming fact that sounds through all history: repression works only to strengthen and knit the repressed. The great owners ignored the three cries of history. The land fell into fewer hands, the number of the dispossessed increased, and every effort of the great owners was directed at repression. The money was spent for arms, for gas to protect the great holdings, and spies were sent to catch the murmuring of revolt so that it might be stamped out. The changing economy was ignored, plans for the change ignored; and only means to destroy revolt were considered, while the causes of revolt went on.

The tractors which throw men out of work, the belt lines which carry loads, the machines which produce, all were increased; and more and more families scampered on the highways, looking for crumbs from the great holdings, lusting after the land beside the roads. The great owners formed associations for protection and they met to discuss ways to intimidate, to kill, to gas. And always they were in fear of a principal—three hundred thousand—if they ever move under a leader—the end. Three hundred thousand, hungry and miserable; if they ever know themselves, the land will be theirs and all the gas, all the rifles in the world won't stop them. And the great owners, who had become through their holdings both more and less than

men, ran to their destruction, and used every means that in the long run would destroy them. Every little means, every violence, every raid on a Hooverville, every deputy swaggering through a ragged camp put off the day a little and cemented the inevitability of the day.

The men squatted on their hams, sharp-faced men, lean from hunger and hard from resisting it, sullen eyes and hard jaws. And the rich land was around them.

D'ja hear about the kid in that fourth tent down?

No, I jus' come in.

Well, that kid's been a-cryin' in his sleep an' a-rollin' in his sleep. Them folks thought he got worms. So they give him a blaster, an' he died. It was what they call black-tongue the kid had. Comes from not gettin' good things to eat.

Poor little fella.

Yeah, but them folks can't bury him. Got to go to the county stone orchard.

Well, hell.

And hands went into pockets and little coins came out. In front of the tent a little heap of silver grew. And the family found it there.

Our people are good people; our people are kind people. Pray God some day kind people won't all be poor. Pray God some day a kid can eat.

And the associations of owners knew that some day the praying would stop.

And there's the end.

CHAPTER 20

The family, on top of the load, the children and Connie and Rose of Sharon and the preacher were stiff and cramped. They had sat in the heat in front of the coroner's office in Bakersfield while Pa and Ma and Uncle John went in. Then a basket was brought out and the long bundle lifted down from the truck. And they sat in the sun while the examination went on, while the cause of death was found and the certificate signed.

Al and Tom strolled along the street and looked in store windows and watched the strange people on the sidewalks.

And at last Pa and Ma and Uncle John came out, and they were subdued and quiet. Uncle John climbed up on the load. Pa and Ma got in the seat. Tom and Al strolled back and Tom got under the steering wheel. He sat there silently, waiting for some instruction. Pa looked straight ahead, his dark hat pulled low. Ma rubbed the sides of her mouth with her fingers, and her eyes were far away and lost, dead with weariness.

Pa sighed deeply. "They wasn't nothin' else to do," he said.

"I know," said Ma. "She would a liked a nice funeral, though. She always wanted one."

Tom looked sideways at them. "County?" he asked.

"Yeah," Pa shook his head quickly, as though to get back to some reality. "We didn't have enough. We couldn' of done it." He turned to Ma. "You ain't to feel bad. We couldn' no matter how hard we tried, no matter what we done. We jus' didn' have it; embalming, an' a coffin an' a preacher, an' a plot in a graveyard. It would of took ten times what we got. We done the bes' we could."

"I know," Ma said. "I jus' can't get it outa my head what store she set by a nice funeral. Got to forget it." She sighed deeply and rubbed the side of her mouth. "That was a purty nice fella in there. Awful bossy, but he was purty nice."

"Yeah," Pa said. "He give us the straight talk, awright."

Ma brushed her hair back with her hand. Her jaw tightened. "We got to git," she said. "We got to find a place to stay. We got to get work an' settle down. No use a-lettin' the little fellas go hungry. That wasn't never Granma's way. She always et a good meal at a funeral."

"Where we goin'?" Tom asked.

Pa raised his hat and scratched among his hair. "Camp," he said. "We ain't gonna spen' what little's lef' till we got work. Drive out in the country."

Tom started the car and they rolled through the streets and out toward the country. And by a bridge they saw a collection of tents and shacks. Tom said, "Might's well stop here. Find out what's doin', an' where at the work is." He drove down a steep dirt incline and parked on the edge of the encampment.

There was no order in the camp; little gray tents, shacks, cars were scattered about at random. The first house was nondescript. The south wall was made of three sheets of rusty corrugated iron, the east wall a square of moldy carpet tacked between two boards, the north wall a strip of roofing paper and a strip of tattered canvas, and the west wall six pieces of gunny sacking. Over the square frame, on untrimmed willow limbs, grass had been

piled, not thatched, but heaped up in a low mound. The entrance, on the gunny-sack side, was cluttered with equipment. A five-gallon kerosene can served for a stove. It was laid on its side, with a section of rusty stovepipe thrust in one end. A wash boiler rested on its side against the wall; and a collection of boxes lay about, boxes to sit on, to eat on. A Model T Ford sedan and a two-wheel trailer were parked beside the shack, and about the camp there hung a slovenly despair.

Next to the shack there was a little tent, gray with weathering, but neatly, properly set up; and the boxes in front of it were placed against the tent wall. A stovepipe stuck out of the door flap, and the dirt in front of the tent had been swept and sprinkled. A bucketful of soaking clothes stood on a box. The camp was neat and sturdy. A Model A roadster and a little home-made bed trailer stood beside the tent.

And next there was a huge tent, ragged, torn in strips and the tears mended with pieces of wire. The flaps were up, and inside four wide mattresses lay on the ground. A clothes line strung along the side bore pink cotton dresses and several pairs of overalls. There were forty tents and shacks, and beside each habitation some kind of automobile. Far down the line a few children stood and stared at the newly arrived truck, and they moved toward it, little boys in overalls and bare feet, their hair gray with dust.

Tom stopped the truck and looked at Pa. "She ain't very purty," he said. "Want to go somewheres else?"

"Can't go nowheres else till we know where we're at," Pa said. "We got to ast about work."

Tom opened the door and stepped out. The family climbed down from the load and looked curiously at the camp. Ruthie and Winfield, from the habit of the road, took down the bucket and walked toward the willows, where there would be water; and the line of children parted for them and closed after them.

The flaps of the first shack parted and a woman looked out. Her gray hair was braided, and she wore a dirty, flowered Mother Hubbard. Her face was wizened and dull, deep gray pouches under blank eyes, and a mouth slack and loose.

Pa said, "Can we jus' pull up anywheres an' camp?"

The head was withdrawn inside the shack. For a moment there was quiet and then the flaps were pushed aside and a bearded man in shirt sleeves stepped out. The woman looked out after him, but she did not come into the open.

The bearded man said, "Howdy, folks," and his restless dark eyes jumped to each member of the family, and from them to the truck to the equipment.

Pa said, "I jus' ast your woman if it's all right to set our stuff anywheres."

The bearded man looked at Pa intently, as though he had said something very wise that needed thought. "Set down anywheres, here in this place?" he asked.

"Sure. Anybody own this place, that we got to see 'fore we can camp?"

The bearded man squinted one eye nearly closed and studied Pa. "You wanta camp here?"

Pa's irritation arose. The gray woman peered out of the burlap shack. "What you think I'm a-sayin'?" Pa said.

"Well, if you wanta camp here, why don't ya? I ain't a-stoppin' you."

Tom laughed. "He got it."

Pa gathered his temper. "I jus' wanted to know does anybody own it? Do we got to pay?"

The bearded man thrust out his jaw. "Who owns it?" he demanded.

Pa turned away. "The hell with it," he said. The woman's head popped back in the tent.

The bearded man stepped forward menacingly. "Who owns it?" he demanded. "Who's gonna kick us outa here? You tell *me*."

Tom stepped in front of Pa. "You better go take a good long sleep," he said. The bearded man dropped his mouth open and put a dirty finger against his lower gums. For a moment he continued to look wisely, speculatively at Tom, and then he turned on his heel and popped into the shack after the gray woman.

Tom turned on Pa. "What the hell was that?" he asked.

Pa shrugged his shoulders. He was looking across the camp. In front of a tent stood an old Buick, and the head was off. A young man was grinding the valves, and as he twisted back and forth, back and forth, on the tool, he looked up at the Joad truck. They could see that he was laughing to himself. When the bearded man had gone, the young man left his work and sauntered over.

"H'are ya?" he said, and his blue eyes were shiny with amusement. "I seen you just met the Mayor."

"What the hell's the matter with 'im?" Tom demanded.

The young man chuckled. "He's jus' nuts like you an' me. Maybe he's a little nutser'n me, I don' know."

Pa said, "I jus' ast him if we could camp here."

The young man wiped his greasy hands on his trousers. "Sure. Why not? You folks jus' come acrost?"

"Yeah," said Tom. "Jus' got in this mornin'."

"Never been in Hooverville before?"

"Where's Hooverville?"

"This here's her."

"Oh!" said Tom. "We jus' got in."

Winfield and Ruthie came back, carrying a bucket of water between them.

Ma said, "Let's get the camp up. I'm tuckered out. Maybe we can all rest." Pa and Uncle John climbed up on the truck to unload the canvas and the beds.

Tom sauntered to the young man, and walked beside him back to the car he had been working on. The valve-grinding brace lay on the exposed block, and a little yellow can of valve-grinding compound was wedged on top of the vacuum tank. Tom asked, "What the hell was the matter'th that ol' fella with the beard?"

The young man picked up his brace and went to work, twisting back and forth, grinding valve against valve seat. "The Mayor? Chris' knows. I guess maybe he's bull-simple."

"What's 'bull-simple'?"

"I guess cops push 'im aroun' so much he's still spinning."

Tom asked, "Why would they push a fella like that aroun'?"

The young man stopped his work and looked in Tom's eyes. "Chris' knows," he said. "You jus' come. Maybe you can figger her out. Some fellas says one thing, an' some says another thing. But you jus' camp in one place a little while, an' you see how quick a deputy sheriff shoves you along." He lifted a valve and smeared compound on the seat.

"But what the hell for?"

"I tell ya I don' know. Some says they don' want us to vote; keep us movin' so we can't vote. An' some says so we can't get on relief. An' some says if we set in one place we'd get organized. I don' know why. I on'y know we get rode all the time. You wait, you'll see."

"We ain't no bums," Tom insisted. "We're lookin' for work. We'll take any kind a work."

The young man paused in fitting the brace to the valve slot. He looked in amazement at Tom.

"Lookin' for work?" he said. "So you're lookin' for work. What ya think ever'body else is lookin' for? Di'monds? What you think I wore my ass down to a nub lookin' for?" He twisted the brace back and forth.

Tom looked about at the grimy tents, the junk equipment, at the old cars, the lumpy mattresses out in the sun, at the blackened cans on fire-blackened holes where the people cooked. He asked quietly, "Ain't they no work?"

"I don' know. Mus' be. Ain't no crop right here now. Grapes to pick later, an' cotton to pick later. We're a-movin' on, soon's I get these here valves groun'. Me an' my wife an' my kids. We heard they was work up north. We're shovin' north, up aroun' Salinas."

Tom saw Uncle John and Pa and the preacher hoisting the tarpaulin on the tent poles and Ma on her knees, inside, brushing off the mattresses on the ground. A circle of quiet children stood to watch the new family get settled, quiet children with bare feet and dirty faces. Tom said, "Back home some fellas come through with han'bills—orange ones. Says they need lots of people out here to work the crops."

The young man laughed. "They say they's three hundred thousan' us folks here, an' I bet ever' dam' fam'ly seen them han'bills."

"Yeah, but if they don' need folks, what'd they go to the trouble puttin' them things out for?"

"Use your head, why don'cha?"

"Yeah, but I wanta know."

"Look," the young man said. "S'pose you got a job a work, an' there's jus' one fella wants the job. You got to pay 'im what he asts. But s'pose they's a hundred men." He put down his tool. His eyes hardened and his voice sharpened. "S'pose they's a hundred men wants that job. S'pose them men got kids, an' them kids is hungry. S'pose a lousy dime'll buy a box a mush for them kids. S'pose a nickel'll buy at leas' somepin for them kids. An' you got a hundred men. Jus' offer 'em a nickel—why, they'll kill each other fightin' for that nickel. Know what they was payin', las' job I had? Fifteen cents an hour. Ten hours for a dollar an' a half, an' ya can't stay on the place. Got to burn gasoline gettin' there." He was panting with anger, and his eyes blazed with hate. "That's why them han'bills was out. You can print a hell of a lot of han'bills with what ya save payin' fifteen cents an hour for fiel' work."

Tom said, "That's stinkin'."

The young man laughed harshly. "You stay out here a little while, an' if you smell any roses, you come let me smell, too."

"But they is work," Tom insisted. "Christ Almighty, with all this stuff a-growin': orchards, grapes, vegetables—I seen it. They got to have men. I seen all that stuff."

A child cried in the tent beside the car. The young man went into the tent and his voice came softly through the canvas. Tom picked up the brace, fitted it in the slot of the valve, and ground away, his hand whipping back and forth. The child's crying stopped. The young man came out and watched Tom. "You can do her," he said. "Damn good thing. You'll need to."

"How 'bout what I said?" Tom resumed. "I seen all the stuff growin'."

The young man squatted on his heels. "I'll tell ya," he said quietly. "They's a big son-of-a-bitch of a peach orchard I worked in. Takes nine men all the year roun'." He paused impressively. "Takes three thousan' men for two weeks when them peaches is ripe. Got to have 'em or them peaches'll rot. So what do they do? They send out han'bills all over hell. They need three thousan', an' they get six thousan'. They get them men for what they wanta pay. If ya don' wanta take what they pay, goddamn it, they's a thousan' men waitin' for your job. So ya pick, an' ya pick, an' then she's done. Whole part a the country's peaches. All ripe together. When ya get 'em picked, ever' goddamn one is picked. There ain't another damn thing in that part a the country to do. An' then them owners don' want you there no more. Three thousan' of you. The work's done. You might steal, you might get drunk, you might jus' raise hell. An' besides, you don' look nice, livin' in ol' tents; an' it's a pretty country, but you stink it up. They don' want you aroun'. So they kick you out, they move you along. That's how it is."

Tom, looking down toward the Joad tent, saw his mother, heavy and slow with weariness, build a little trash fire and put the cooking pots over the flame. The circle of children drew closer, and the calm wide eyes of the children watched every move of Ma's hands. An old, old man with a bent back came like a badger out of a tent and snooped near, sniffing the air as he came. He laced his arms behind him and joined the children to watch Ma. Ruthie and Winfield stood near to Ma and eyed the strangers belligerently.

Tom said angrily, "Them peaches got to be picked right now, don't they? Jus' when they're ripe?"

" 'Course they do."

"Well, s'pose them people got together an' says, 'Let 'em rot.' Wouldn' be long 'fore the price went up, by God!"

The young man looked up from the valves, looked sardonically at Tom. "Well, you figgered out somepin, didn' you. Come right outa your own head."

"I'm tar'd," said Tom. "Drove all night. I don't wanta start no argument. An' I'm so goddamn tar'd I'd argue easy. Don' be smart with me. I'm askin' you."

The young man grinned. "I didn' mean it. You ain't been here. Folks figgered that out. An' the folks with the peach orchard figgered her out too. Look, if the folks gets together, they's a leader—got to be—fella that does the talkin'. Well, first time this fella opens his mouth they grab 'im an' stick 'im in jail. An' if they's another leader pops up, why, they stick *'im* in jail."

Tom said, "Well, a fella eats in jail anyways."

"His kids don't. How'd you like to be in an' your kids starvin' to death?"

"Yeah," said Tom slowly. "Yeah."

"An' here's another thing. Ever hear a' the blacklist?"

"What's that?"

"Well, you jus' open your trap about us folks gettin' together, an' you'll see. They take your pitcher an' send it all over. Then you can't get work nowhere. An' if you got kids——"

Tom took off his cap and twisted it in his hands. "So we take what we can get, huh, or we starve; an' if we yelp we starve."

The young man made a sweeping circle with his hand, and his hand took in the ragged tents and the rusty cars.

Tom looked down at his mother again, where she sat scraping potatoes. And the children had drawn closer. He said, "I ain't gonna take it. God-damn it, I an' my folks ain't no sheep. I'll kick the hell outa somebody."

"Like a cop?"

"Like anybody."

"You're nuts," said the young man. "They'll pick you right off. You got no name, property. They'll find you in a ditch, with the blood dried on your mouth an' your nose. Be one little line in the paper—know what it'll say? 'Vagrant foun' dead.' An' that's all. You'll see a lot of them little lines, 'Vagrant foun' dead.' "

Tom said, "They'll be somebody else foun' dead right 'longside of this here vagrant."

"You're nuts," said the young man. "Won't be no good in that."

"Well, what you doin' about it?" He looked into the grease-streaked face. And a veil drew down over the eyes of the young man.

"Nothin'. Where you from?"

"Us? Right near Sallisaw, Oklahoma."

"Jus' get in?"

"Jes' today."

"Gonna be aroun' here long?"

"Don't know. We'll stay wherever we can get work. Why?"

"Nothin'." And the veil came down again.

"Got to sleep up," said Tom. "Tomorra we'll go out lookin' for work."

"You kin try."

Tom turned away and moved toward the Joad tent.

The young man took up the can of valve compound and dug his finger into it. "Hi!" he called.

Tom turned. "What you want?"

"I want ta tell ya." He motioned with his finger, on which a blob of compound stuck. "I jus' want ta tell ya. Don' go lookin' for no trouble. 'Member how that bull-simple guy looked?"

"Fella in the tent up there?"

"Yeah—looked dumb—no sense?"

"What about him?"

"Well, when the cops come in, an' they come in all a time, that's how you want ta be. Dumb—don' know nothin'. Don't understan' nothin'. That's how the cops like us. Don't hit no cops. That's jus' suicide. Be bull-simple."

"Let them goddamn cops run over me, an' me do nothin'?"

"No, looka here. I'll come for ya tonight. Maybe I'm wrong. There's stools aroun' all a time. I'm takin' a chancet, an' I got a kid, too. But I'll come for ya. An' if ya see a cop, why, you're a goddamn dumb Okie, see?"

"Tha's awright if we're doin' anythin'," said Tom.

"Don' you worry. We're doin' somepin, on'y we ain't stickin' our necks out. A kid starves quick. Two-three days for a kid." He went back to his job, spread the compound on a valve seat, and his hand jerked rapidly back and forth on the brace, and his face was dull and dumb.

Tom strolled slowly back to his camp. "Bull-simple," he said under his breath.

Pa and Uncle John came toward the camp, their arms loaded with dry willow sticks, and they threw them down by the fire and squatted on their hams.

"Got her picked over pretty good," said Pa. "Had ta go a long ways for wood." He looked up at the circle of staring children. "Lord God Almighty!" he said. "Where'd you come from?" All of the children looked self-consciously at their feet.

"Guess they smelled the cookin'," said Ma. "Winfiel', get out from under foot." She pushed him out of her way. "Got ta make us up a little stew," she said. "We ain't et nothin' cooked right sence we come from home. Pa, you go up to the store there an' get me some neck meat. Make a nice stew here." Pa stood up and sauntered away.

Al had the hood of the car up, and he looked down at the greasy engine. He looked up when Tom approached. "You sure look happy as a buzzard," Al said.

"I'm jus' gay as a toad in spring rain," said Tom.

"Looka the engine," Al pointed. "Purty good, huh?"

Tom peered in. "Looks awright to me."

"Awright? Jesus, she's wonderful. She ain't shot no oil nor nothin'." He unscrewed a spark plug and stuck his forefinger in the hole. "Crusted up some, but she's dry."

Tom said, "You done a nice job a pickin'. That what ya want me to say?"

"Well, I sure was scairt the whole way, figgerin' she'd bust down an' it'd be my fault."

"No, you done good. Better get her in shape, 'cause tomorra we're goin' out lookin' for work."

"She'll roll," said Al. "Don't you worry none about that." He took out a pocket knife and scraped the points of the spark plug.

Tom walked around the side of the tent, and he found Casy sitting on the earth, wisely regarding one bare foot. Tom sat down heavily beside him. "Think she's gonna work?"

"What?" asked Casy.

"Them toes of yourn."

"Oh! Jus' settin' here a-thinkin'."

"You always get good an' comf'table for it," said Tom.

Casy waggled his big toe up and his second toe down, and he smiled quietly. "Hard enough for a fella to think 'thout kinkin' hisself up to do it."

"Ain't heard a peep outa you for days," said Tom. "Thinkin' all the time?"

"Yeah, thinkin' all the time."

Tom took off his cloth cap, dirty now, and ruinous, the visor pointed as a bird's beak. He turned the sweat band out and removed a long strip of folded newspaper. "Sweat so much she's shrank," he said. He looked at Casy's waving toes. "Could ya come down from your thinkin' an' listen a minute?"

Casy turned his head on the stalk-like neck. "Listen all the time. That's why I been thinkin'. Listen to people a-talkin', an' purty soon I hear the way folks are feelin'. Goin' on all the time. I hear 'em an' feel 'em; an' they're beating their wings like a bird in a attic. Gonna bust their wings on a dusty winda tryin' ta get out."

Tom regarded him with widened eyes, and then he turned and looked at a gray tent twenty feet away. Washed jeans and shirts and a dress hung to dry on the tent guys. He said softly, "That was about what I was gonna tell ya. An' you seen awready."

"I seen," Casy agreed. "They's a army of us without no harness." He bowed his head and ran his extended hand slowly up his forehead and into his hair. "All along I seen it," he said. "Ever' place we stopped I seen it. Folks hungry for sidemeat, an' when they get it, they ain't fed. An' when they'd get so hungry they couldn' stan' it no more, why, they'd ast me to pray for 'em, an' sometimes I done it." He clasped his hands around drawn-up knees and pulled his legs in. "I use ta think that'd cut 'er," he said. "Use ta rip off a prayer an' all the troubles'd stick to that prayer like flies on flypaper, an' the prayer'd go a-sailin' off, a-takin' them troubles along. But it don' work no more."

Tom said, "Prayer never brought in no sidemeat. Takes a shoat to bring in pork."

"Yeah," Casy said. "An' Almighty God never raised no wages. These here folks want to live decent and bring up their kids decent. An' when they're old they wanta set in the door an' watch the downing sun. An' when they're young they wanta dance an' sing an' lay together. They wanta eat an' get drunk and work. An' that's it—they wanta jus' fling their goddamn muscles aroun' an' get tired. Christ! What'm I talkin' about?"

"I dunno," said Tom. "Sounds kinda nice. When ya think you can get ta work an' quit thinkin' a spell? We got to get work. Money's 'bout gone. Pa give five dollars to get a painted piece of board stuck up over Granma. We ain't got much lef'."

A lean brown mongrel dog came sniffing around the side of the tent. He was nervous and flexed to run. He sniffed close before he was aware of the two men, and then looking up he saw them, leaped sideways, and fled, ears back, bony tail clamped protectively. Casy watched him go, dodging around a tent to get out of sight. Casy sighed. "I ain't doin' nobody no good," he said. "Me or nobody else. I was thinkin' I'd go off alone by myself. I'm a-eatin' your food an' a-takin' up room. An' I ain't give you nothin'. Maybe I could get a steady job an' maybe pay back some a the stuff you've give me."

Tom opened his mouth and thrust his lower jaw forward, and he tapped his lower teeth with a dried piece of mustard stalk. His eyes stared over the camp, over the gray tents and the shacks of weed and tin and paper. "Wisht I had a sack a Durham," he said. "I ain't had a smoke in a hell of a time. Use ta get tobacco in McAlester. Almost wisht I was back." He tapped his teeth again and suddenly he turned on the preacher. "Ever been in a jail house?"

"No," said Casy. "Never been."

"Don't go away right yet," said Tom. "Not right yet."

"Quicker I get lookin' for work—quicker I'm gonna find some."

Tom studied him with half-shut eyes and he put on his cap again. "Look," he said, "this ain't no lan' of milk an' honey like the preachers say. They's a mean thing here. The folks here is scared of us people comin' west; an' so they got cops out tryin' to scare us back."

"Yeah," said Casy. "I know. What you ask about me bein' in jail for?"

Tom said slowly, "When you're in jail—you get to kinda—sensin' stuff. Guys ain't let to talk a hell of a lot together—two maybe, but not a crowd. An' so you get kinda sensy. If somepin's gonna bust—if say a fella's goin' stir-bugs an' take a crack at a guard with a mop handle—why, you know it 'fore it happens. An' if they's gonna be a break or a riot, nobody don't have to tell ya. You're sensy about it. You know."

"Yeah?"

"Stick aroun'," said Tom. "Stick aroun' till tomorra anyways. Somepin's gonna come up. I was talkin' to a kid up the road. An' he's bein' jus' as sneaky an' wise as a dog coyote, but he's too wise. Dog coyote a-mindin' his own business an' innocent an' sweet, jus' havin' fun an' no harm—well, they's a hen roost clost by."

Casy watched him intently, started to ask a question, and then shut his mouth tightly. He waggled his toes slowly and, releasing his knees, pushed out his foot so he could see it. "Yeah," he said, "I won't go right yet."

Tom said, "When a bunch a folks, nice quiet folks, don't know nothin' about nothin'—somepin's goin' on."

"I'll stay," said Casy.

"An' tomorra we'll go out in the truck an' look for work."

"Yeah!" said Casy, and he waved his toes up and down and studied them gravely. Tom settled back on his elbow and closed his eyes.

Southern Literature

of the Twentieth Century

It is not only convenient but proper to treat twentieth-century southern literature as that of a special subculture. Down to the present day the rest of the United States continues to think of the South as somehow different. Even more important, the South still regards itself as different.

The termination of the Civil War did not, and could not, bring the South back into the nation except in special and somewhat limited senses. In fact, the war and its aftermath had the effect of sharpening and perpetuating cultural differences. More was involved than the sting of defeat, hurt pride, and the destruction of property. The imposition of adverse tariff laws —the South sold the only commodity it produced in large amount, cotton, on a world market, but bought manufactured goods from the Northeast in a market benefited by a protective tariff—adverse differentials in freight rates, and other such economic discriminations locked the region for years into what amounted to a colonial economy. While the rest of the country became more and more urbanized, industrialized, and wealthy, the South remained basically rural, agricultural, and poor. As we know from present-day experience, areas that are saddled with a colonial economy are likely to remain so for long periods of time; for colonials have little control over their destinies.

After the Civil War, in the closing decades of the century, genuine efforts toward reconciliation were made. Men like Henry Grady proclaimed a "New South." Liberal southerners did take the Road to Reunion. Industrialization, though usually as an aspect of northern capitalist penetration, began slowly to transform the southern economy. Change of attitude did occur; the remarkable fact is that it came so slowly.[1] In many important aspects the basic attitudes of the South remained those of its nineteenth-century past.

One does notice a pronounced change, however, in the literature that begins to come out of the South after the turn of the century. The tinge of local color is less evident; the tone is less defensive; there is a new readiness to examine objectively and to criticize southern customs, attitudes, and habits of mind.

[1] Southern cultural conservatism in this period is ably discussed and accounted for in C. Vann Woodward's *Origins of the New South* (1951). See in particular pp. 429–55.

JAMES BRANCH CABELL (1879–1958)

This new literature was initiated by two Virginians, Ellen Glasgow and James Branch Cabell. They were certainly the most important southern writers to publish early in the twentieth century (Ellen Glasgow's *The Battle-Ground* in 1902 and Cabell's *Gallantry* in 1907). But though they had a common social background and were personal friends, the sharp difference between their characteristic work is evident at a first glance.

An easy generalization, often offered, is that both turned away from costume romances and daydreams about the life in the old South. Yet Cabell's principal novels may be described with fair accuracy as dream allegories, and Ellen Glasgow's first novel was a sort of costume romance. Their relation to the older literature was far from one of simple rejection.

Cabell's romances are laid in a mythical medieval country to which he gave the name Poictesme. Between 1927 and 1930, under the title *Poictesme*, Cabell brought together and arranged in chronological order (in the Storisende edition of his works) some eighteen novels which have to do with a character named Dom Manuel and his descendants. What we have, then, is a mythical history, involving many

generations, a history taking place in a province concocted out of the writer's own imagination. But the commentary on history and human nature in this work—and, for that matter, in Cabell's other fiction—has anything but the spirit of conventional historical romance. Instead the story expresses a world-weary disillusion.

Cabell owes practically nothing to the older New England writers and not much to other American writers. His debt is to Restoration drama, to the seventeenth century, to the British novelists of manners, and to continental ironists like Anatole France. But Cabell contrived his own brew, and the highly self-conscious prose, often arch and elaborately cadenced, is quite his own.

Jurgen (1919), which later took its place as one of the segments of the involved history of Poictesme, was the first of his works to get any large popular hearing. The attempt to ban it on the grounds of its immorality measurably promoted its sale. The intellectuals found it learned and witty; it answered to the mood of America at the end of the First World War. With the Depression, interest in Cabell ebbed, and though there have been attempts to revive his reputation as a stylist and as a commentator on the foibles of human nature, nothing thus far has come of them.

It should be added, however, that Cabell's mock medieval dream romances, in which figures melt into each other and perspectives constantly shift, does look forward to the current vogue for a literature that exhibits Freudian "dream work" and to the interest in myth and myth-making. This aspect of Cabell, as well as his famous style, can be illustrated from the following chapters of *Jurgen*.

The reader should know, by way of a preliminary note, that Jurgen the pawnbroker has as-

pirations to be a poet, an ambition of which his wife, Lisa, does not approve. He is thus a type of modern man caught between the claims of money-making, domesticity, and respectability and the claims of the ideal world of the imagination. When his wife disappears, though Jurgen is certainly no longer passionately in love with her, he feels that he ought to go in search, and so follows her into a cave. In the cave Jurgen meets the centaur Nessus, and after some conversation the centaur puts Jurgen on his back and carries him to the garden between dawn and sunrise.

BIOGRAPHICAL CHART

1879 Born, April 14, in Richmond, Virginia
1898 Receives B. A. from the College of William and Mary
1899–1900 Works as reporter for the Richmond *Times* and the New York *Herald*
1901–10 Contributes short stories and articles to *Harper's*, the *Smart Set*, and *Argosy*
1904 *The Eagle's Shadow*

1917 *The Cream of the Jest*
1919 *Jurgen*
1927–30 *Poictesme*
1932 *These Restless Heads*
1933 *Special Delivery*
1952 *Quiet, Please*
1955 *As I Remember It*
1958 Dies, May 5

FURTHER READINGS

Collected Works, Storisende Edition (1948; 31 vols.) (no editor cited)

Frances Joan Brewer, *James Branch Cabell: A Bibliography* (1957)

Matthew J. Bruccoli, *James Branch Cabell: A Bibliography, Part II* (1957)

Joe Lee Davis, *James Branch Cabell* (1962)

Desmond Tarrant, *James Branch Cabell: The Dream and the Reality* (1967)

Edward Wagenknecht, *Cabell: A Reconsideration* (1948)

Arvin R. Wells, *Jesting Moses: A Study in Cabellian Comedy* (1962)

Edmund Wilson, "The James Branch Cabell Case Reopened," in *The Bit Between My Teeth* (1965)

From Jurgen (1919)

3. THE GARDEN BETWEEN DAWN AND SUNRISE

Thus it was that Jurgen and the Centaur came to the garden between dawn and sunrise, entering this place in a fashion which it is not convenient to record. But as they passed over the bridge three

fled before them, screaming. And when the life had been trampled out of the small furry bodies which these three had misused, there was none to oppose the Centaur's entry into the garden between dawn and sunrise.

This was a wonderful garden: yet nothing therein was strange. Instead, it seemed that everything hereabouts was heart-breakingly familiar and very dear to Jurgen. For he had come to a broad lawn which slanted northward to a well-remembered brook: and multitudinous maples and locust-trees stood here and there, irregularly, and were being played with very lazily by an irresolute west wind, so that foliage seemed to toss and ripple everywhere like green spray: but autumn was at hand, for the locust-trees were dropping a Danaë's shower of small round yellow leaves. Around the garden was an unforgotten circle of blue hills. And this was a place of lucent twilight unlit by either sun or stars, and with no shadows anywhere in the diffused faint radiancy that revealed this garden, which is not visible to any man except in the brief interval between dawn and sunrise.

"Why, but it is Count Emmerick's garden at Storisende," says Jurgen, "where I used to be having such fine times when I was a lad."

"I will wager," said Nessus, "that you did not use to walk alone in this garden."

"Well, no; there was a girl."

"Just so," assented Nessus. "It is a local by-law: and here are those who comply with it."

For now had come toward them, walking together in the dawn, a handsome boy and girl. And the girl was incredibly beautiful, because everybody in the garden saw her with the vision of the boy who was with her.

"I am Rudolph," said this boy, "and she is Anne."

"And are you happy here?" asked Jurgen.

"Oh, yes, sir, we are tolerably happy: but Anne's father is very rich, and my mother is poor, so that we cannot be quite happy until I have gone into foreign lands and come back with a great many lakhs of rupees and pieces of eight."

"And what will you do with all this money, Rudolph?"

"My duty, sir, as I see it. But I inherit defective eyesight."

"God speed to you, Rudolph!" said Jurgen, "for many others are in your plight."

Then came to Jurgen and the Centaur another boy with the small blue-eyed person in whom he took delight. And this fat and indolent looking boy informed them that he and the girl who was with him were walking in the glaze of the red mustard jar, which Jurgen thought was gibberish: and the fat boy said that he and the girl had decided never to grow any older, which Jurgen said was excellent good sense if only they could manage it.

"Oh, I can manage that," said this fat boy, re-

flectively, "if only I do not find the managing of it uncomfortable."

Jurgen for a moment regarded him, and then gravely shook hands.

"I feel for you," said Jurgen, "for I perceive that you, too, are a monstrous clever fellow: so life will get the best of you."

"But is not cleverness the main thing, sir?"

"Time will show you, my lad," says Jurgen, a little sorrowfully. "And God speed to you, for many others are in your plight."

And a host of boys and girls did Jurgen see in the garden. And all the faces that Jurgen saw were young and glad and very lovely and quite heartbreakingly confident, as young persons beyond numbering came toward Jurgen and passed him there, in the first glow of dawn: so they all went exulting in the glory of their youth, and foreknowing life to be a puny antagonist from whom one might take very easily anything which one desired. And all passed in couples—"as though they came from the Ark," said Jurgen. But the Centaur said they followed a precedent which was far older than the Ark.

"For in this garden," said the Centaur, "each man that ever lived has sojourned for a little while, with no company save his illusions. I must tell you again that in this garden are encountered none but imaginary creatures. And stalwart persons take their hour of recreation here, and go hence unaccompanied, to become aldermen and respected merchants and bishops, and to be admired as captains upon prancing horses, or even as kings upon tall thrones; each in his station thinking not at all of the garden ever any more. But now and then come timid persons, Jurgen, who fear to leave this garden without an escort: so these must need go hence with one or another imaginary creature, to guide them about alleys and by-paths, because imaginary creatures find little nourishment in the public highways, and shun them. Thus must these timid persons skulk about obscurely with their diffident and skittish guides, and they do not ever venture willingly into the thronged places where men get horses and build thrones."

"And what becomes of these timid persons, Centaur?"

"Why, sometimes they spoil paper, Jurgen, and sometimes they spoil human lives."

"Then are these accursed persons," Jurgen considered.

"You should know best," replied the Centaur.

"Oh, very probably," said Jurgen. "Meanwhile here is one who walks alone in this garden, and I wonder to see the local by-laws thus violated."

Now Nessus looked at Jurgen for a while without speaking: and in the eyes of the Centaur was so much of comprehension and compassion that it troubled Jurgen. For somehow it made Jurgen fidget and consider this an unpleasantly personal way of looking at anybody.

"Yes, certainly," said the Centaur, "this woman walks alone. But there is no help for her loneliness, since the lad who loved this woman is dead."

"Nessus, I am willing to be reasonably sorry about it. Still, is there any need of pulling quite such a portentously long face? After all, a great many other persons have died, off and on: and for anything I can say to the contrary, this particular young fellow may have been no especial loss to anybody."

Again the Centaur said, "You should know best."

4. THE DOROTHY WHO DID NOT UNDERSTAND

For now had come to Jurgen and the Centaur a gold-haired woman, clothed all in white, and walking alone. She was tall, and lovely and tender to regard: and hers was not the red and white comeliness of many ladies that were famed for beauty, but rather it had the even glow of ivory. Her nose was large and high in the bridge, her flexible mouth was not of the smallest: and yet whatever other persons might have said, to Jurgen this woman's countenance was in all things perfect. Perhaps this was because he never saw her as she was. For certainly the color of her eyes stayed a matter never revealed to him: gray, blue or green, there was no saying: they varied as does the sea; but always these eyes were lovely and friendly and perturbing.

Jurgen remembered that: for Jurgen saw this was Count Emmerick's second sister, Dorothy la Désirée, whom Jurgen very long ago (a many years before he met Dame Lisa and set up in business as a pawnbroker) had hymned in innumerable verses as Heart's Desire.

"And this is the only woman whom I ever loved," Jurgen remembered, upon a sudden. For people cannot always be thinking of these matters.

So he saluted her, with such deference as is due to a countess from a tradesman, and yet with unforgotten tremors waking in his staid body. But the strangest was yet to be seen, for he noted now that this was not a handsome woman in middle life but a young girl.

"I do not understand," he said, aloud: "for you are Dorothy. And yet it seems to me that you are not the Countess Dorothy who is Heitman Michael's wife."

And the girl tossed her fair head, with that careless lovely gesture which the Countess had forgotten. "Heitman Michael is well enough, for a nobleman, and my brother is at me day and night to marry the man: and certainly Heitman Michael's wife will go in satin and diamonds at half the courts of Christendom, with many lackeys to attend her. But I am not to be thus purchased."

"So you told a boy that I remember, very long ago. Yet you married Heitman Michael, for all that, and in the teeth of a number of other fine declarations."

"Oh, no, not I," said this Dorothy, wondering. "I never married anybody. And Heitman Michael has never married anybody, either, old as he is. For he is twenty-eight, and looks every day of it! But who are you, friend, that have such curious notions about me?"

"That question I will answer, just as though it were put reasonably. For surely you perceive I am Jurgen."

"I never knew but one Jurgen. And he is a young man, barely come of age—" Then as she paused in speech, whatever was the matter upon which this girl now meditated, her cheeks were tenderly colored by the thought of it, and in her knowledge of this thing her eyes took infinite joy.

And Jurgen understood. He had come back somehow to the Dorothy whom he had loved: but departed, and past overtaking by the fleet hoofs of centaurs, was the boy who had once loved this Dorothy, and who had rhymed of her as his Heart's Desire: and in the garden there was of this boy no trace. Instead, the girl was talking to a staid and paunchy pawnbroker, of forty-and-something.

So Jurgen shrugged, and looked toward the Centaur: but Nessus had discreetly wandered away from them, in search of four-leafed clovers. Now the east had grown brighter, and its crimson began to be colored with gold.

"Yes, I have heard of this other Jurgen," says the pawnbroker. "Oh, Madame Dorothy, but it was he that loved you!"

"No more than I loved him. Through a whole summer have I loved Jurgen."

And the knowledge that this girl spoke a wondrous truth was now to Jurgen a joy that was keen as pain. And he stood motionless for a while, scowling and biting his lips.

"I wonder how long the poor devil loved you! He also loved for a whole summer, it may be. And yet again, it may be that he loved you all his life. For twenty years and for more than twenty years I have debated the matter: and I am as well informed as when I started."

"But, friend, you talk in riddles."

"Is not that customary when age talks with youth? For I am an old fellow, in my forties: and you, as I know now, are near eighteen,—or rather, four months short of being eighteen, for it is August. Nay, more, it is the August of a year I had not looked ever to see again; and again Dom Manuel reigns over us, that man of iron whom I saw die so horribly. All this seems very improbable."

Then Jurgen meditated for a while. He shrugged.

"Well, and what could anybody expect me to do about it? Somehow it has befallen that I, who am but the shadow of what I was, now walk among shadows, and we converse with the thin intonations of dead persons. For, Madame Dorothy, you who are not yet eighteen, in this same garden there was once a boy who loved a girl, with such love as it puzzles me to think of now. I believe that she loved him. Yes, certainly it is a cordial to the tired and battered heart which nowadays pumps blood for me, to think that for a little while, for a whole summer, these two were as brave and comely and clean a pair of sweethearts as the world has known."

Thus Jurgen spoke. But this thought was that this was a girl whose equal for loveliness and delight was not to be found between two oceans. Long and long ago that doubtfulness of himself which was closer to him than his skin had fretted Jurgen into believing the Dorothy he had loved was but a piece of his imaginings. But certainly this girl was real. And sweet she was, and innocent she was, and light of heart and feet, beyond the reach of any man's inventiveness. No, Jurgen had not invented her; and it strangely contented him to know as much.

"Tell me your story, sir," says she, "for I love all romances."

"Ah, my dear child, but I cannot tell you very well of just what happened. As I look back, there is a blinding glory of green woods and lawns and moonlit nights and dance music and unreasonable laughter. I remember her hair and eyes, and the curving and the feel of her red mouth, and once

when I was bolder than ordinary— But that is hardly worth raking up at this late day. Well, I see these things in memory as plainly as I now seem to see your face: but I can recollect hardly anything she said. Perhaps, now I think of it, she was not very intelligent, and said nothing worth remembering. But the boy loved her, and was happy, because her lips and heart were his, and he, as the saying is, had plucked a diamond from the world's ring. True, she was a count's daughter and the sister of a count: but in those days the boy quite firmly intended to become a duke or an emperor or something of that sort, so the transient discrepancy did not worry them."

"I know. Why, Jurgen is going to be a duke, too," says she, very proudly, "though he did think, a great while ago, before he knew me, of being a cardinal, on account of the robes. But cardinals are not allowed to marry, you see— And I am forgetting your story, too! What happened then?"

"They parted in September—with what vows it hardly matters now—and the boy went into Gâtinais, to win his spurs under the old Vidame de Soyecourt. And presently—oh, a good while before Christmas!—came the news that Dorothy la Désirée had married rich Heitman Michael."

"But that is what I am called! And as you know, there is a Heitman Michael who is always plaguing me. Is that not strange! for you tell me all this happened a great while ago."

"Indeed, the story is very old, and old it was when Methuselah was teething. There is no older and more common story anywhere. As the sequel, it would be heroic to tell you this boy's life was ruined. But I do not think it was. Instead, he had learned all of a sudden that which at twenty-one is heady knowledge. That was the hour which taught him sorrow and rage, and sneering, too, for a redemption. Oh, it was armor that hour brought him, and a humor to use it, because no woman now could hurt him very seriously. No, never any more!"

"Ah, the poor boy!" she said, divinely tender, and smiling as a goddess smiles, not quite in mirth.

"Well, women, as he knew by experience, were the pleasantest of playfellows. So he began to play. Rampaging through the world he went in the pride of his youth and in the armor of his hurt. And songs he made for the pleasure of kings, and sword-play he made for the pleasure of men, and a whispering he made for the pleasure of women, in places where renown was, and where he trod boldly, giving pleasure to everybody, in those fine days. But the whispering, and all that followed the whispering, was his best game, and the game he played for the longest while, with many brightly colored playmates who took the game more seriously than he did. And their faith in the game's importance, and in him and his high-sounding nonsense, he very often found amusing: and in their other chattels too he took his natural pleasure. Then, when he had played sufficiently, he held a consultation with divers waning appetites; and he married the handsome daughter of an estimable pawnbroker in a fair line of business. And he lived with his wife very much as two people customarily live together. So, all in all, I would not say his life was ruined."

"Why, then, it was," said Dorothy. She stirred uneasily, with an impatient sigh; and you saw that she was vaguely puzzled. "Oh, but somehow I think you are a very horrible old man: and you seem doubly horrible in that glittering queer garment you are wearing."

"No woman ever praised a woman's handiwork, and each of you is particularly severe upon her own. But you are interrupting the saga."

"I do not see"—and those large bright eyes of which the color was so indeterminable and so dear to Jurgen, seemed even larger now—"but I do not see how there could well be any more."

"Still, human hearts survive the benediction of the priest, as you may perceive any day. This man, at least, inherited his father-in-law's business, and found it, quite as he had anticipated, the fittest of vocations for a cashiered poet. And so, I suppose, he was content. Ah, yes; but after a while Heitman Michael returned from foreign parts, along with his lackeys, and plate, and chest upon chest of merchandise, and his fine horses, and his wife. And he who had been her lover could see her now, after so many years, whenever he liked. She was a handsome stranger. That was all. She was rather stupid. She was nothing remarkable, one way or another. This respectable pawnbroker saw that quite plainly: day by day he writhed under the knowledge. Because, as I must tell you, he could not retain composure in her presence, even now. No, he was never able to do that."

The girl somewhat condensed her brows over this information. "You mean that he still loved her. Why, but of course!"

"My child," says Jurgen, now with a reproving forefinger, "you are an incurable romanticist. The man disliked her and despised her. At any event,

he assured himself that he did. Well, even so, this handsome stupid stranger held his eyes, and muddled his thoughts, and put errors into his accounts: and when he touched her hand he did not sleep that night as he was used to sleep. Thus he saw her, day after day. And they whispered that this handsome and stupid stranger had a liking for young men who aided her artfully to deceive her husband: but she never showed any such favor to the respectable pawnbroker. For youth had gone out of him, and it seemed that nothing in particular happened. Well, that was his saga. About her I do not know. And I shall never know! But certainly she got the name of deceiving Heitman Michael with two young men, or with five young men it might be, but never with a respectable pawnbroker."

"I think that is an exceedingly cynical and stupid story," observed the girl. "And so I shall be off to look for Jurgen. For he makes love very amusingly," says Dorothy, with the sweetest, loveliest meditative smile that ever was lost to heaven.

And a madness came upon Jurgen, there in the garden between dawn and sunrise, and a disbelief in such injustice as now seemed incredible.

"No, Heart's Desire," he cried, "I will not let you go. For you are dear and pure and faithful, and all my evil dream, wherein you were a wanton and befooled me, was not true. Surely, mine was a dream that can never be true so long as there is any justice upon earth. Why, there is no imaginable God who would permit a boy to be robbed of that which in my evil dream was taken from me!"

"And still I cannot understand your talking, about this dream of yours—!"

"Why, it seemed to me I had lost the most of myself; and there was left only a brain which played with ideas, and a body that went delicately down pleasant ways. And I could not believe as my fellows believed, nor could I love them, nor could I detect anything in aught they said or did save their exceeding folly: for I had lost their cordial common faith in the importance of what use they made of half-hours and months and years; and because a jill-flirt had opened my eyes so that they saw too much. I had lost faith in the importance of my own actions, too. There was a little time of which the passing might be made endurable; beyond gaped unpredictable darkness: and that was all there was of certainty anywhere. Now tell me, Heart's Desire, but was not that a foolish dream? For these things never happened. Why, it would not be fair if these things ever happened!"

And the girl's eyes were wide and puzzled and a little frightened. "I do not understand what you are saying: and there is that about you which troubles me unspeakably. For you call me by the name which none but Jurgen used, and it seems to me that you are Jurgen; and yet you are not Jurgen."

"But I am truly Jurgen. And look you, I have done what never any man has done before! For I have won back to that first love whom every man must lose, no matter whom he marries. I have come back again, passing very swiftly over the grave of a dream and through the malice of time, to my Heart's Desire! And how strange it seems that I did not know this thing was inevitable!"

"Still, friend, I do not understand you."

"Why, but I yawned and fretted in preparation for some great and beautiful adventure which was to befall me by and by, and dazedly I toiled forward. Whereas behind me all the while was the garden between dawn and sunrise, and therein you awaited me! Now assuredly, the life of every man is a quaintly builded tale, in which the right and proper ending comes first. Thereafter time runs forward, not as schoolmen fable in a straight line, but in a vast closed curve, returning to the place of its starting. And it is by a dim foreknowledge of this, by some faint prescience of justice and reparation being given them by and by, that men have heart to live. For I know now that I have always known this thing. What else was living good for unless it brought me back to you?"

But the girl shook her small glittering head, very sadly. "I do not understand you, and I fear you. For you talk foolishness and in your face I see the face of Jurgen as one might see the face of a dead man drowned in muddy water."

"Yet am I truly Jurgen, and, as it seems to me, for the first time since we were parted. For I am strong and admirable—even I, who sneered and played so long, because I thought myself a thing of no worth at all. That which has been since you and I were young together is as a mist that passes: and I am strong and admirable, and all my being is one vast hunger for you, my dearest, and I will not let you go, for you, and you alone, are my Heart's Desire."

Now the girl was looking at him very steadily, with a small puzzled frown, and with her vivid young soft lips a little parted. And all her tender loveliness was glorified by the light of a sky that had turned to dusty palpitating gold.

"Ah, but you say that you are strong and admirable: and I can only marvel at such talking. For I see that which all men see."

And then Dorothy showed him the little mirror which was attached to the long chain of turquoise matrix about her neck: and Jurgen studied the frightened foolish aged face that he found in the mirror.

Thus drearily did sanity return to Jurgen: and his flare of passion died, and the fever and storm and the impetuous whirl of things was ended, and the man was very weary. And in the silence he heard the piping cry of a bird that seemed to seek for what it could not find.

"Well, I am answered," said the pawnbroker: "and yet I know that this is not the final answer. Dearer than any hope of heaven was that moment when awed surmises first awoke as to the new strange loveliness which I had seen in the face of Dorothy. It was then I noted the new faint flush suffusing her face from chin to brow so often as my eyes encountered and found new lights in the shining eyes which were no longer entirely frank in meeting mine. Well, let that be, for I do not love Heitman Michael's wife.

"It is a grief to remember how we followed love, and found his service lovely. It is bitter to recall the sweetness of those vows which proclaimed her mine eternally,—vows that were broken in their making by prolonged and unforgotten kisses. We used to laugh at Heitman Michael then; we used to laugh at everything. Thus for a while, for a whole summer, we were as brave and comely and clean a pair of sweethearts as the world has known. But let that be, for I do not love Heitman Michael's wife.

"Our love was fair but short-lived. There is none that may revive him since the small feet of Dorothy trod out this small love's life. Yet when this life of ours too is over—this parsimonious life which can allow us no more love for anybody,—must we not win back, somehow, to that faith we vowed against eternity? and be content again, in some fair-colored realm? Assuredly I think this thing will happen. Well, but let that be, for I do not love Heitman Michael's wife."

"Why, this is excellent hearing," observed Dorothy, "because I see that you are converting your sorrow into the raw stuff of verses. So I shall be off to look for Jurgen, since he makes love quite otherwise and far more amusingly."

And again, whatever was the matter upon which this girl now meditated, her cheeks were tenderly colored by the thought of it, and in her knowledge of this thing her eyes took definite joy.

Thus it was for a moment only: for she left Jurgen now, with the friendliest light waving of her hand; and so passed from him, not thinking of this old fellow any longer, as he could see, even in the instant she turned from him. And she went toward the dawn, in search of that young Jurgen whom she, who was perfect in all things, had loved, though only for a little while, not undeservedly.

ELLEN GLASGOW (1874–1945)

Though Cabell's stories—even those with a contemporary Virginia setting—do not mark him as obviously "southern," his friend Ellen Glasgow found him so, nevertheless. She writes: "Certainly [his] is an art that belongs by inheritance to the South, though it may appear to contain no element we define narrowly as Southern, except perhaps the gaiety and gallantry of its pessimism."[1]

By contrast, her own work is specifically southern—in its subject matter and, we would argue, even more in its basic attitudes. When Miss Glasgow's *Barren Ground* was published in 1925 the publisher's blurb read: "Realism crosses the Potomac." The term realism, however, requires some specification. Though Dorinda, Miss Glasgow's heroine, comes from a family of poor whites, *Barren Ground* provided no foreshadowing of the fiction of Erskine Caldwell. Miss Glasgow treated the poor white with dignity and sympathy, to be sure, but the novelist's searching eye was not so much fastened on the social setting as on the psychology of her characters. Dorinda, through the course of her lifetime, moves away from her romantic dream with all its delusions to a realistic conception of life. But the delusion that is dissipated has little to do with any dream of an antebellum South's golden age. Rather, it is the familiar dream of romantic love and the American dream of success. Dorinda finally triumphs over poverty and wins through to a magnanimous revenge upon the handsome young man who had long before jilted her, but she also learns something of the hollowness of triumph.

Ellen Glasgow's psychological curiosity, her questioning of man's ideas and ideals, and her ironic squint at what he thinks he believes in—all found to some degree in *Barren Ground*—these receive their fuller development in novels such as *The Romantic Comedians* (1926) and *They Stooped to Folly* (1929), which deal not with poor whites living on land now going back to broom sedge, but with aristocratic Richmond society.

What Ellen Glasgow and James Branch Cabell really share is their interest in the human comedy, the novel of manners, and the ironic stance from which they view civilization. Yet how different are these two writers in their method and in the quality of their art. Justly or unjustly, the reader is likely to find Cabell's attitude one of elegant languor. Not so with Ellen Glasgow. She celebrates fortitude and what might be called triumphant stoicism in defeat. This note fulfills itself in *Barren Ground*, where at least two or three times she refers to the "vein of iron" in her more stalwart characters. The chief work of her later period was the novel significantly entitled *Vein of Iron* (1935).[2]

Ellen Glasgow is a stylist who writes with a quiet but forceful elegance. The following chapter from *The Romantic Comedians* will give

[1] See also Edmund Wilson's essay on Cabell in *The Bit Between My Teeth* (1965).

[2] Such celebrations of heroic endurance were to find later expression in the novels of William Faulkner. In view of the strength of this aspect of southern fiction, it is curious that so little critical attention has been given to this disciplined stoicism and the southern Calvinism to which it is related.

something of the flavor of her style and of her vision of the human comedy, of which her style is an expression.

Judge Gamaliel Honeywell, aged sixty-five, has recently lost his devoted wife Cornelia. Honeywell is "an upright, even a religious man, with a rich Episcopal flavor or temperament." He was "disposed to encourage liberty of thought as long as he was convinced that it would not lead to liberal views." Now, some months after his wife's death, he finds himself beginning to be vaguely excited by the spring weather and the sight of young faces and is finally induced to attend a dance. The next morning he has some conversation with Mrs. Spearman, his housekeeper, and a little later with his twin sister, Mrs. Edmonia Bredalbane, a woman very different from her brother. She is high-spirited and not too much bothered about the conventions. She has buried three husbands and now has a fourth one roaming somewhere at large. The passage that follows describes the morning after the dance.

BIOGRAPHICAL CHART

1874 Born, April 22, in Richmond, Virginia; privately educated
1897 Publishes her first novel, *The Descendant*
1899 Visits England, Europe, and the Near East
1902 *The Battle-Ground* (a historical romance)
1914 Visits England

1925 *Barren Ground*
1926 *The Romantic Comedians*
1929 *They Stooped to Folly*
1935 *Vein of Iron*
1941 *In This Our Life*; awarded the Pulitzer prize
1945 Dies, November 21, in Richmond

FURTHER READINGS

Collected Works, Virginia Edition (1938; 12 vols.) (no editor cited)

Ellen Glasgow, *The Woman Within* (1954)
R. K. Meeker, ed., *The Collected Stories of Ellen Glasgow* (1963)

Blair Rouse, ed., *The Letters of Ellen Glasgow* (1958)

Louis Auchincloss, *Ellen Glasgow* (1964)
John E. Hardy, "Ellen Glasgow," in *Southern Renascence* (1966), Louis Rubin and Robert Jacobs, eds.
Blair Rouse, *Ellen Glasgow* (1962)

From The Romantic Comedians (1926)

VII

In the morning, he awoke with a dull headache, which passed away after he had had his bath and his coffee. While he waited for his second cup, he looked at the bar of sunshine slanting over the pot of yellow tulips on the breakfast table, and felt that the freshness of the day expanded his heart. Everything ahead of him, his work, the men he should meet, the dry business of the law, the game of golf in the afternoon, the game of chess in the evening—all these ordinary details of living were irradiated by the beams of sunlight.

As he took his seat and unfolded the Queenborough *Post* by his plate, he made a facetious remark to his housekeeper, a withered and incorruptible woman, who had lost everything but virtue and clung firmly to that.

"What we need, Mrs. Spearman, is more brightness in the house."

Over the coffee-pot Mrs. Spearman lifted her opaque glance to his face. There was, as she frequently told Judge Honeywell, nothing wrong with her sense of humour, only the things other people laughed at seldom seemed amusing to her.

"I am sure I try to make it as pleasant as I can," she replied in a crushed voice; for she was as suspicious of men as any heroine in early-Victorian fiction, and she knew what to expect when gentlemen who had lost their wives began to be fussy about their clothes. Struggling, that was what he had been doing in the last few months. She had seen it with her own eyes, and since there was, in her opinion, but one end to such struggles, she was speculating, while she watched him furtively, upon her chance of securing another position. Something permanent, she hoped, next time. A bachelor, perhaps, not a widower, for anything less permanent than widowers she had never encountered.

"You have done very well, Mrs. Spearman. I am not complaining. I only meant that we might find the house less depressing if we were to have a few young people here, now and then."

"Maybe your grandchildren will be coming soon to pay you a visit."

"In the summer possibly, unless I should go abroad." The idea of going abroad had just occurred to him, and it seemed to be an excellent one.

"I hope you are satisfied with the way I've looked after you, sir. I am sure the house has never been depressing to me," remarked Mrs. Spearman, who was humble but had her feelings.

"Don't give yourself a moment's worry, Mrs. Spearman. You have done a great deal to lighten my loneliness."

Mrs. Spearman stared bleakly over the silver service. "I hope you slept well after your party. I saw you had your light on until late."

"Fairly—just fairly." The Judge frowned and turned back to his paper, for the question had recalled to his mind the fluttering visitations of the darkness. Yes, it might be as well to have Buchanan look him over in the next two or three days. Though he felt so vigorous, it was possible that there was something wrong with either his nerves or his digestion. He sighed heavily over his paper; and Mrs. Spearman, hearing the sigh, concluded that the battle was lost, and resigned herself to the prospect of a bachelor, or at least of a gentleman (this was her secret ambition) whose wife was hopelessly deranged but harmless. "Just fairly, sir?" she repeated, and choked over the echo.

Judge Honeywell, who respected print and had done his duty by contemporary literature, could not have escaped the knowledge that women suffer from strange delusions and are often the innocent victims of their sacrificial virtues. There had been occasions when he had looked earnestly at Mrs. Spearman's emaciated frame and wondered where she found room to hold her suppressed desires. He would have been grieved rather than astonished if sex had gained the victory over her one day, and she had become suddenly temperamental with a knife or a gun. But it had never entered his head that a mere trifle, a mothlike instinct and a discredited one as well, could invade the provinces of a seasoned intellect, of a renowned authority upon jurisprudence, of an international attitude of mind. Surely, in these impregnable defences, if anywhere, there was security.

"I've tried to do my best, sir," Mrs. Spearman confided to her black-bordered handkerchief.

"And a very good best it has been, Mrs. Spearman," responded the Judge, as he rose from his chair, and proceeded to the serious business of life, which did not, he was sure, embrace withered and incorruptible women.

On his way to his office, for he had retired from the bench into the less arduous private practice of law, he stopped long enough to send orchids, or, if orchids were over, gardenias to Annabel. If a little thing like that could give the child pleasure, he ought not to neglect it; and then, since his mood was benevolent, he noticed lilies of the valley blooming modestly behind a glass case, and ordered a bunch of moderate size for Amanda. Not until he had stepped into his car did he remember that Wednesday was his day for taking flowers to Cordelia's grave; and turning back, he entered the shop again and added this order to the others.

"Could you," he inquired, with embarrassment, "arrange to have these flowers sent out to Rose Hill this afternoon?" And when the florist replied that it would be possible, the Judge gave directions (which were unnecessary since the florist knew his world) for reaching Cordelia's grave. It was the first time that he had broken his habit of visiting the cemetery; but, overlooking the day, he had made an engagement for golf in the afternoon, and he assured himself, as he drove on, that Cordelia would have been the last woman in the world to wish him to sacrifice his health on her account. She would have been, also, the last woman in the world to encourage unnecessary brooding, or, for the matter of that, anything that was unnecessary. Nursing grief was what she had called it, and he had heard her frequently condemn such useless rebellion against an Act of God. For Cordelia had been endowed with that safe point of view which refuses to be impressed by any rebellion until it has assumed the dimensions of a revolution. Acts of God, like amendments to the Constitution, were respected by her as long as they were enforced. There was, she had often reminded him, as little nonsense about her as there was meretricious appeal. She was before all else—and he had been grateful for this in his tranquil moments— a good woman. Sober, intelligent, an enemy to vehemence and self-indulgence in any form, the only defect he had ever found in her was her failure to be amused by his jokes. A deficiency that was easily overlooked amid so many perfections; yet, in spite of (it could not be because of) her moral excellence, the idea had crossed his mind that the worst of all possible worlds would be one invented by good women.

Yes, he had been completely in letter, if incompletely in spirit, a faithful husband. Faithful, except for those days in the spring (he could not deny them now) when he had felt a mysterious vibration at the sight of a strange face in the crowd; at the whisper of the April wind in his ears; or at a gesture that was ended before it had fulfilled an imagined curve of perfection. He had had his moments when he was young. And now at the suave touch of Spring, from some cause so obscure that it had not ripened into a definite longing, he suffered again from an inappeasable restlessness of the heart.

That afternoon, when civilization had triumphantly defeated nature in his mind, he found that his game of golf was even better than usual. He played with younger men, and, as he told Mrs. Bredalbane with pride upon his return, he had "polished them off nicely." His face was still shining with pleasure when she captured him in the hall; and though he looked, as she said to herself, spindle-shanked in his stockings of Scotch plaid, his appearance, since he was unaware that it could strike anybody as ridiculous, failed to dampen his enthusiasm.

"You have a great many compensations, Gamaliel," she remarked.

This he admitted almost too promptly for a widower. Life, he pursued cheerfully, was full of compensations, if you took the trouble to look for them. "You must accept things as you find them," he concluded, with the seasoned wisdom of platitude.

"Well, you look much better since you've taken that view of life," she returned briskly.

"You're right, Edmonia. I am convinced that you are right."

"I just stopped as I was passing to ask how you are. I know you are dying to get under a shower.

By the way," she added, moving in the direction of the door. "I saw Amanda at luncheon wearing more lilies of the valley. They made her look fifteen years younger than her age. It is wonderful what lilies of the valley will do for gray hair."

Hearing this, the Judge tried in vain to think of a reply that would be gallant and yet casual. "For her years she is a remarkably young-looking woman," he said at last, and felt that Edmonia would consider the remark superfluous, provided, of course, she could recognize superfluity when she saw it.

Mrs. Bredalbane stopped to calculate, which she did on her fingers but adequately. "She is seven years younger than we are," she said presently. "That would make her just fifty-eight."

Just fifty-eight! He frowned while he followed his sister's immense hips to the door. Not only did he dislike an unprofitable comparison of ages, but he disliked even more the cheerful inaccuracy with which Edmonia assumed that he was as old as she because they had been born twins. It was on the tip of his tongue to try again to correct this impression; but, being a peace-loving man and disinclined to wound the feelings of any woman, he waited until the opportunity was lost in Mrs. Bredalbane's ensuing offence.

"What do you do with yourself in the evenings, Gamaliel?"

He looked at her thoughtfully, surmising the end of her catechism, yet hesitating from habit before leaping to a conclusion.

"I spend my evenings very quietly Edmonia, as you may imagine. Occasionally, I drop into the club for a few minutes."

"Don't you find yourself getting lonely?"

"One must expect loneliness in my situation."

"Why don't you go to see Amanda Lightfoot?"

For an instant, the audacity of her challenge shocked him speechless; then he replied with all the rebuke that his tone could carry: "I feel no inclination to pay visits."

"Well, I'm sure it is time that you did. Conventions have changed, and nobody would think any the worse of you if you began going there every evening. Especially as everybody knows how faithful Amanda has been to you all these years."

Even he, with his painful knowledge that Edmonia was capable of stopping at nothing behind his back, had hardly expected her to go so far as this in his presence. "I think, Edmonia," he responded gently, because he was judicially weighing his words, "that, at your time of life, you might find something better to do than interfere with the private affairs of other people."

Mrs. Bredalbane laughed without offence. The trait that made her invulnerable to criticism, he perceived now, was her complete immunity from offence. It is difficult to deal successfully, he decided, with a woman whose feelings cannot be hurt. He wondered drily how her husbands had dealt with her, and remembered that three were in their graves while the fourth one was a stubborn fugitive from monogamy.

"At our time of life, Gamaliel, there isn't much else that we can do," she rejoined in her hearty manner.

"I should have supposed you could find a better way to employ yourself than in meddling and idle gossip. There are surely opportunities to improve your mind and character."

Mrs. Bredalbane gasped a little, though good-naturedly. "Why, what in the world is the matter with my mind and character?" she inquired. "I had mind enough to catch four husbands, and I've had my character restored four times, which is more than most women, even in Queenborough, can boast of. The trouble with you, Gamaliel," she added, patting the sleeve of his leather coat, "is that you did not have enough sense of humour to stand the strain of being a Judge and an old Virginia gentleman combined. We started equal, I dare say, but while my observations of the world have cultivated my humour, it has taken every particle of yours to bear up under the dullness of your life."

"Dullness?" repeated the Judge, while a dark flush stained his pallid skin. Did Edmonia imagine that his life, either in the seat of justice or beside Cordelia, had been dull? "Your observations we will not discuss," he said indignantly, "but I can assure you that a respectable life is not necessarily a dull one."

Again Mrs. Bredalbane patted his arm, and he felt resentfully, through his sleeve, that the pat was maternal and protective. "Well, I'm glad you haven't found it so," she answered. "All I can wish for you, my dear, is that you should have enjoyed your life as much as I have mine."

A melancholy frown clouded his face. How times had changed indeed, and how standards had fallen! Was this stout and disreputable dowager, this excessive, this quadruple matron, the frail, lost sister of his early manhood, the wayward daughter for whom the lamp had burned and forgiveness

waited in vain? Where was the remorse of the sinner? Where, he demanded, almost passionately, were the wages of sin?

"I have had the satisfaction, Edmonia, of feeling that I have tried to do my duty."

She had passed out on the porch, and her hand was on the iron railing of the steps, while one large and determined foot hung suspended in the air. "You are welcome to all the satisfaction you can get out of duty," she responded, "and I may say that you look to me as if you had lived on it. That is the trouble with all of you in Queenborough, especially the women. You look as if you had lived on duty and it hadn't agreed with you."

With the solid substance of her person in front of him, it was impossible to deny her accusation. She was immoderate; she was indecorous; she was reprehensible; yet she was again, he felt, in some absurd and even sinister way, unanswerable. According to the inflexible logic of consequences; according to all civilized rule of conduct and everlasting principles of morality; according to the profuse testimony of literature;—according to this menacing cloud of witnesses, she should have returned unhappy, penitent, and partly, if not entirely, impoverished. In this extremity, which was the moral as well as the conventional end to her career (and what were conventions, after all, but organized morals?) he could have opened his heart to her with the fraternal compassion an erring sister deserves. But her attitude was abandoned, he told himself, and the extremity a preposterous one. Her sinful past, for her many marriages had merely whitewashed it, had not saddened her, had not sobered her, had not even, he concluded, with his stern but just gaze on her broad and lumpy back, diminished her size. She had not only thriven, she had fattened on iniquity. At sixty-five, a time of life surely when bad women turn to remorse, and even good women find little to turn to but duty, she flaunted (there was no other word for it) she actually flaunted her brazen past. "It is the war that has made such conduct possible," he pondered gloomily. "Before the war no woman could have been so bold with impunity."

"I hope you are more careful in your conversation than you have been in your conduct," he said presently.

For, extraordinary as it appeared, the rising generation in Queenborough, not only accepted, but gave every evidence to the legal mind of enjoying Edmonia. While elderly ladies of vacant memories and unblemished reputations nodded by lonely firesides, Edmonia was eagerly sought after by the inquisitive youth of the period. They clustered about her, he had heard with disapproval, in candid pursuit of some esoteric wisdom of sex; and he had observed, at Amanda's dance, that they treated her scarlet letter less as the badge of shame than as some foreign decoration for distinguished service.

Mrs. Bredalbane's heavy foot descended; but before it reached the step, she glanced back over her shoulder. The attitude was not graceful, and he recalled that, as a girl, Edmonia had had too thick a neck and a figure which, though vaunting a wasp waist, promised to be corpulent with increasing years and dissipation.

"You know I never pretended to have an orderly mind, Gamaliel," she said. "All I ask is to be interesting. So long as the young people flock to me, I feel that I am a success."

"That is exactly what I object to, Edmonia. If it did not sound harsh, I should say that I do not consider you a proper example for the young."

This appeared to amuse Mrs. Bredalbane, which was the last thing he had anticipated. Her deep, thick laugh gushed out. "Oh, they aren't waiting for an example," she replied. "Or a warning either, for that matter. You take my advice, Gamaliel," she tossed back encouragingly over her shoulder, "and don't let the grass grow under your feet. If I were you, I'd go to see Amanda Lightfoot this very evening. You won't gain anything by waiting, not after thirty-seven years."

ERSKINE CALDWELL (1903–   )

If realism crossed the Potomac with Ellen Glasgow's *Barren Ground*, with Erskine Caldwell's fiction, "naturalism" crossed it, heading for points far south of the state of Virginia. In Caldwell's stories, an aged black man accidentally falls into the fattening pen where the hardhearted landlord of a farm keeps his hogs and is immediately devoured; a penniless white farmer is driven to shooting his starving ten-year-old daughter because he can no longer endure hearing her beg for food; the widow of a streetcar motorman, left without a pension and reduced to despair, prostitutes her nine-year-old daughter for a fee of twenty-five cents.

Caldwell's is a desperate world in which life, as Thomas Hobbes described life in a state of nature, is "nasty, brutish, and short." Caldwell's people are worse off still; they live in a civilization which not only has failed to civilize but has contaminated and distorted what is natural.

But Caldwell also portrays a comic world, one filled with uninhibited and often degenerate yokels. Indeed, Caldwell's most popular novels are those in which degeneracy provokes more laughter than tears and in which the characters are not so much maimed and suffering submen as unkillable and irrepressible expressions of the Freudian id. Someone has remarked that the characters of *Tobacco Road* (1932) could have provided a corps of psychiatrists with enough material for a lifetime of study. But this is clearly wrong: Caldwell's characters have so few inhibitions that a psychiatrist could only give them the clinical advice that the eminent Viennese psychiatrist, "Dr. Froyd," gave to the heroine of Anita Loos's *Gentlemen Prefer Blondes:* just "cultivate a few inhibitions and get some sleep."

An attempt was made to ban some of Caldwell's books because of the kind of characters that he portrayed and the sordidness of the circumstances under which they lived. The principal defense offered by Caldwell's lawyers was that of truth: statistics were produced and case histories cited to indicate that Caldwell's fiction was sociologically and historically accurate. Caldwell won his court fight. Yet if one sufficiently exaggerates depravity, blind obsession, and irrepressible appetite, he ends up, not with realistic portraits, but with caricatures. The human beings become grotesquely inhuman and their actions seem to be not those of creatures in real life but of figures in a nightmare. Kenneth Burke made this point long ago when he argued that Caldwell was deliberately unrealistic and that his fiction exhibited a fantastically unreal world.[1]

Waiving the question of whether there is sufficient sociological and historical warrant for Caldwell's portrayal of the poor white, there is certainly a strong literary tradition behind it. William Byrd of Virginia (see pp. 180–83) began it with his account of the "lubbers," the backwoodsmen who lived along the border of Virginia and North Carolina in the colonial period. We have noted earlier Augustus B. Longstreet's accounts of the "crackers" in his *Georgia Scenes* and George Washington Harris's depiction of the rude practical jokes and the coarse vitality of Sut Lovingood. One also finds a like vein of humor in the fiction of William Faulkner.

Though the poor white was sometimes treated sympathetically and even on occasion sentimentally, as by Alice French ("Octave Thanet") in her stories about the rednecks of Arkansas, the poor white from the beginning was usually seen as shiftless, sometimes villainous, the kind of man of whom overseers were made in the days of slavery and, all too often, the kind most ready to join a lynching party in the Reconstruction period.

True to this tradition, Caldwell often presents the poor white as an intolerant and cruel racial bigot, viciously kicking at the man standing just below him on the social ladder—that is, the black man. Yet Caldwell sometimes treats the poor white sympathetically, seeing him as the victim of the man on the rung *above* him, his landlord. Some of his stories are, in fact, unabashedly sentimental, as Caldwell depicts the poor whites' helpless suffering, or frankly propagandistic, as he seeks to enlist his readers' sympathies to change the sharecropping system or, more largely, to abolish finance-capitalism itself.

Caldwell's best fiction is that which contains a strong vein of comedy. In such fiction his interest in the comic high jinks of his characters saves the story from becoming the vehicle of a message, and it provides the salt that keeps the pathos inherent in the story from softening into sentimentality. But Caldwell is not a sophisticated story writer, and too often his work disintegrates into its constitutive elements, mere pity or mere indignation or mere farce. Though the immense success of *Tobacco Road* (the novel and later the play made from it) was undoubtedly owing to the delighted shock which the cosmopolite received from being taken on a rubberneck bus trip through the rural slums, the mixture of pathos and comedy was for many readers and viewers authentic and winning. Jeter Lester and his progeny have all the vitality of low-grade organisms. Their lack of any burden of guilt and their ability to dispense with most of the contrivances of civilization gave to a great many people a sense of release.

Caldwell's talent, though limited and special, is a real one and deserves to be seen for what it is. Since Caldwell is a prolific writer, many of whose novels are not even second-rate, and since even his best work has so often been praised for the wrong reasons, it is especially important to discriminate between what is valuable and what is frankly drugstore-stand trash. For the reader interested in making this discrimination, it may be useful to compare Caldwell's characteristic treatment of the southern poor white with that of other modern southern writers, such as Ellen Glasgow, T. S. Stribling, Eudora Welty, or William Faulkner. These writers are dealing with the same raw material with which Caldwell is concerned, but the attitude toward the poor white and the effects aimed at are significantly different.[2]

---

[1] In a brief prefatory note to one of his stories, Caldwell himself says: "Literature would be exceedingly dull stuff if authors did not try to improve upon nature" (*Jackpot*, 1940, p. 491).

[2] James Agee's *Let Us Now Praise Famous Men* (1941) is a sympathetic view of the Alabama sharecropper in a nonfictional report originally designed to

In this general connection, one might also take a look at Caldwell's stories about country people in northern New England. Caldwell's New England rustics are less rambunctious, and their sexual antics are toned down as compared with his stories about the southern whites of the piney woods. But the flavor of the New England stories is much the same, and reading a few of them will quickly indicate that Caldwell's basic interest is in the human animal as such, without reference to latitude.

In sum, Caldwell's bent is toward the humor of the cantankerous and the preposterous. His best stories turn out to be whoppers—tall tales or incredible anecdotes in which we are not really asked to believe literally, or at least not painfully (as in some of his propaganda horror stories or tear-jerking sentimentalities). In these stories the character tends to be obsessed. In *God's Little Acre* Ty Ty is certain that there is gold under the barren soil of his farm. Against all reason and all prudence he keeps digging for it like an insect in the grip of a compelling instinctive drive.

This kind of obsession, viewed humorously, is the subject matter of "The Negro in the Well." Early one morning, Jule Robinson is so taken with the music of the foxhounds baying on a trail that he can't pay proper attention to his frightened children who beg him not to leave home, at least until dawn breaks; or to the plight of Bokus Bradley, a black man who, in the darkness, has fallen into Jule's well and is now imploring Jule to help him get out. Jule demands a price—namely, two of Bokus's foxhounds. But the black man in this story is just as much obsessed by the foxhounds as is Jule. Though he is neck-deep in cold water, he can't bring himself to meet Jule's terms: "Because I'd have only six dogs left, Mr. Jule, I couldn't

do much foxhunting with just that many." So Jule kicks the boards back on top of the well as Bokus prays for strength to hold out: "Oh Lord, don't make me swap off two hounds for the help I'm asking for." Bokus interrupts his plea to be released with questions about the sounds of his own hounds: "Can you hear those hounds of mine trailing now, Mr. Jule?" The story ends with Jule entranced with the wonderful hound music:

He could hear Polly pant, and Senator snort, and Mary Jane whine, and Sunshine yelp, and the rest of them barking at the head of the trail. He put on his hat, pulled it down hard all around, and hurried up the path to follow them on the ridge. The fox would not be able to hold out much longer.

"Whoo-way-oh!" he called to his hounds. "Whoo-away-oh!"

The echo was a masterful sound to hear.

It is a preposterous world, if you like, and incidentally a cruel world, but it is obviously not a tragic world. Bokus will be mighty uncomfortable for several hours but Jule—who has already complained about Bokus muddying his well water—will eventually, in his own selfish interest if not in Bokus's, have to get Bokus out. The accent here is on the joy that both men take in foxhunting and on Bokus's willingness to put up with a good deal of personal discomfort in order to keep his own pack of hounds up to full strength.

Is the story really credible? Not quite. It is finally a tall tale to indicate what a fool a man can be about a foxhound. Thus it is a kind of parable of human nature, a tale frankly exaggerated, but a good yarn, nevertheless.

In stories of this sort Caldwell touches on material being developed by Faulkner in the same period. One thinks of stories like "Shingles for the Lord" (with its elaborate bargaining over a dog) or like "Fool About a Horse." Yet the resemblance is not very close, and this kind of story, which Caldwell can render so effectively, represents only one filament of Faulkner's massive and complicated strand.

---

appear in *Fortune* magazine. Agee did not gloss over the faults of the poor whites. (He found their special vices to be their hatred of the Negro and the cruelty they often showed toward their work animals.) But he managed to convince the liberal reader of the 1940's that these all but illiterate people deserved his sympathy and his respect.

BIOGRAPHICAL CHART

1903   Born, December 17, in Coweta County, Georgia
1920–21   Attends Erskine College
1922–26   Attends University of Virginia
1932   *Tobacco Road*
1933   *God's Little Acre*
1933–34   Writes scripts in Hollywood

1937   *You Have Seen Their Faces* (nonfiction with photographs by Margaret Bourke-White)
1939–44   Works as newspaper correspondent in Mexico, Spain, Czechoslovakia, Russia, and China
1940   *Jackpot* (collection of short stories)
1951   *Call It Experience*

FURTHER READINGS

Erskine Caldwell, *Call It Experience* (1951)
———, *Deep South: Memories and Observations* (1968)

Kenneth Burke, "Erskine Caldwell: Maker of Grotesques," *New Republic* (April 10, 1935)
Malcolm Cowley, "The Two Erskine Caldwells," *New Republic* (November 6, 1944)

Robert Hazel, "Notes on Erskine Caldwell," in *Southern Renascence* (1966), Louis Rubin and Robert Jacobs, eds.
John M. Maclachlan, "Folk and Culture in the Novels of Erskine Caldwell," *Southern Folklore Quarterly* (1945)
John Donald Wade, "Sweet Are the Uses of Degeneracy," *Southern Review* (1936)

The People's Choice (1928)

Gus was leaning against the fount in the drugstore Saturday morning when Ed Wright, one of the elders, came in and told Gus that the church had made him a deacon. Laying aside the election itself, that was the first of the blunders that were made between then and noon Sunday; Ed Wright should have had the sense not to notify Gus of the election until about midnight Saturday, or better still, until just before preaching time Sunday morning. All the blame for what took place cannot be put on Ed, though; Gus Streetman should be held just as responsible for what happened as anyone else in town.

After Ed had told Gus about the church election, Gus just stood there looking at Ed and at the boy behind the fount for several minutes. He was feeling so good about it, he didn't know what to say. He was as pleased about it as he ever was when he heard the county returns on election night.

"You're a deacon now, Gus," Ed said, leaning against the fount and waiting for Gus to set him up. "Don't let the boys in the back seats slip any suspender buttons over on you."

"You know, Ed," he said, "I'd rather be elected deacon in the church than to get any other office in the county—except tax assessor. By George, it's a big thing to be a deacon in the church."

Gus was the county tax assessor. He had held the office against all opposition for the past ten or fifteen years, and, from the way things looked then, he would continue being the assessor as long as men went to the polls and saw Gus Streetman's name printed on the ballot.

"Well, Gus," Ed said, "everybody's glad about it, too. There wasn't any doubt about you being elected after your name was put up. It was unanimous, too."

Gus was feeling so good he didn't know what to say. He waited for Ed to tell him more about the election, when the minister and all the elders voted for him; but Ed was licking the corners of his mouth for a drink.

"Let's have a drink, Gus," he suggested.

"Oh, sure, sure!" Gus said, waking up. "What'll you have, Ed?"

"Make mine a lime Coke," he told the boy behind the fount.

"Give me another Coke, son," Gus said, "with three big squirts of ammonia."

That was the fifth Coke-and-ammonia Gus had drunk since eight-thirty that morning, and it was still two hours until noon.

He and Ed stood at the fount drinking their Coca-Colas silently. Gus was busy thinking about his election as a deacon, and he was too busy thinking about it to say anything. After a while, Ed said he had to hurry back to the hardware store to see if any customers had come in, and he left Gus leaning against the fount drinking his Coke-and-ammonia.

"You'll have to help take up the collection to-morrow morning, Gus," Ed said at the door. "You'd better wear some shoes that don't squeak so much, because everybody will be looking at you."

"Oh, sure, sure," Gus said. "I'll be there all right. I'm a deacon now."

Gus was so busy thinking about his being a deacon in the church that he hardly knew what he was saying, or what Ed was talking about. He was busy thinking about celebrating in some way, too. He had never won an election yet that he hadn't celebrated, and he was just as proud of being a deacon as he was of being county tax assessor. He walked out of the drugstore and started for the barbershop.

In the back room of the barbershop there was a little closet where he kept some of his corn and gin. He intended making the celebration this time as big as, or bigger than, any he had ever undertaken before. Usually, he had the chance to celebrate only each four years, when he was re-elected tax assessor, and this was an extra time, like an unexpected holiday.

People said that Gus Streetman was as big-hearted as a man can be, and that a man just couldn't help liking him. You could walk up to Gus on the street on a Saturday afternoon and ask Gus for anything you wished, and Gus would give it to you if he had it or if he knew where he could lay his hands on it. You could ask Gus to lend you his new automobile to take a ride out to the country in, and Gus would slap his hand on your shoulder, just as if you were doing him a big favor, and say: "Oh, sure, sure! Go ahead and use it, Joe. Why, by George, all I've got in the world is yours for the asking. Sure, go ahead and drive it all you want, Joe."

After you had thanked Gus for the use of his new automobile, he would silence you and say: "Now, don't start talking like that, Joe. You make me think I ain't doing enough for you. Drive down to the filling station and fill her up with gas, and charge it to me. Just tell Dick I said to make out a ticket for whatever you want, and I'll come by and take it up the first of the week."

That's how Gus Streetman was about everything. It never mattered to him what a man

wished. If you thought you would like to have something, all you had to do was to ask Gus, and if he had it, or knew where he could lay his hands on it, it was yours until you got good and ready to hand it back to him. Sometimes people took advantage of Gus, but not often. Nearly everyone knew where to draw the line, and he had so many friends to look out for him that he was taken care of. In the spring of that year Vance Young had stopped Gus one morning and said he was going up to Atlanta that week-end on a short business trip and that he would like to take Gus's wife along for company. Gus told him to go ahead and take her along, and he meant it, too; but just before train time somebody broke down and told Gus that Vance was only fooling, and it turned out to be a joke the barbershop crowd was playing on him.

That was one of the main reasons why Gus got re-elected tax assessor time after time. He had been tax assessor for about fifteen years already, and no man who had ever tried to run against Gus in the primaries had a dog's chance of taking the office away from him. Just before a primary, Gus would load his automobile up with three or four dozen of those big Senator Watson watermelons, and start out electioneering. He would come to a house beside the road, stop, and get out carrying two of those big melons under his arms. When he reached the front porch, he would roll the Senator Watsons up to the door and take out his pearl-handled pocketknife and rap on the boards until somebody came out.

"Well, how's everything, Harry?" Gus would say, thumping the Senator Watsons with his knuckles, and cocking his head sideways to hear the *thump! thump!* "How are you satisfied with your tax assessment, Harry?"

Nobody was ever satisfied, of course, and that was all there would be to Gus getting another vote for the primary. Being a Democrat, he never had to worry about the Republicans at election time. The Lily-whites never bothered with county politics; the mail carriers knew perfectly well which side their bread was buttered on.

"Reckon we can get the assessment changed, Gus?" the man would say.

Gus would never answer that question, because by that time he was always busy splitting open one of those big Senator Watsons. When he had got the heart cut out, and had passed it around, he would wipe the blade of his pearl-handled knife on his pants leg and shake hands all around.

"We need a little rain, don't we?" Gus would say, starting back to the road where his car was. "Maybe we'll get a shower before sundown."

That's how Gus got elected county tax assessor the first time, and that's how he was re-elected every four years following. He never made any promises; therefore he never violated any. But he got the votes, nearly all there were in the whole county.

When Gus had first started out to be elected deacon, he went about his campaign the same way he did when he was running for political office. He filled up the minister on those big Senator Watsons, day after day, and all the elders, too. When the church election was held during the last week in July, Gus's name was the first one put up for deacon, and there was only one ballot taken. Gus got all the votes.

But when Gus wasn't canvassing for votes, political or otherwise, and when he wasn't out in some part of the county assessing property, he was usually drinking corn and gin. He kept a store of it in the back room of the barbershop, another supply in the garage at home where his wife wouldn't be likely to find it, and a third one at the courthouse, in the coal box in his office, where he could reach it at any time of the day or night.

Gus never got too drunk to walk; that is to say, Fred Jones, the marshal, never had to lock him up. Gus was always on his feet, no matter how much he had been drinking, or for how long a time. He could hold his corn and gin with never an outward sign of drunkenness, unless you happened to look him in his eyes, or to measure his stride.

That Saturday morning, though, after Ed Wright had notified him of the election, Gus went down to the barbershop and cleaned out all his liquor there, and then he walked over to the courthouse and started on the bottles he kept in the coal box in his office on the second floor.

Nobody saw much of him again that day, until a little after eight o'clock that night when he came out of the courthouse and walked across the square for another Coke-and-ammonia at the fount in the drugstore. Even then nobody paid much attention to Gus, because he was walking in fairly even strides, and he wasn't talking unduly loud for a Saturday night. The marshal watched Gus for a few minutes, and then left the square and went back down the alley to pick up a few more drunks in front of the Negro fish houses for the lockup.

There had been a traveling carnival in town all that week, and nearly everyone went to the show grounds that night to see the carnival close up and move off to the next town. Gus started out there with two or three of his friends at about ten-thirty or eleven. All of them were well liquored, and Gus was shining. When they got to the show grounds, Gus started out to wind up his celebration. He let loose that Saturday night. He took in all the side shows, and he had a big crowd of men and boys following him around the grounds, whooping it up with him.

Just before midnight, when the carnival was getting ready to close and move on to the next town down the road, Gus saw a show he had missed. It was a little tent off to itself, with a big red-painted picture of a girl, pretty much naked, dancing on it. There was no name on the show, as there were on the others, but down in one corner of the big red picture, just under the girl's feet, was a little sign that said: *For Men Only.*

As soon as somebody told Gus it was a hoochie-coochie show, he dashed for it, pushing people out of his way right and left. He ran up to the ticket seller, bought three or four dozen tickets, and waved his arms at everybody who wished to go in with him and see the show. After they had crowded inside, the show went to pieces so quickly that no one knew what had happened.

Nobody yet tells exactly what Gus said or did when he got inside with the hoochie-coochie girl, but whatever it was, the show was a complete wreck inside of two minutes. It might have been Gus who jerked out the center pole, bringing the tent down on top of everybody, and it might not have been Gus who grabbed the girl around her waist and made her yell as though she were being squeezed to death by a maniac. But anyway, the tent came down; the dancer yelled and screamed, first for help, next for mercy; the ticket seller shouted for the stake drivers; and some fool down under the tent struck a match to the canvas. When the crowd got the blazing tent off the girl and the bunch of men, they found her and Gus down on the bottom of the pile struggling with each other. Fred Jones, the marshal, came running up just then all excited, deputizing citizens right and left, and got everybody herded out of the show grounds and closed up the carnival.

What happened to Gus after that, nobody knows exactly, because some of his friends pried him loose from the little dark-skinned hoochie-coochie dancer, and carried him away in an automobile to cool off. Later that night they brought him back to town and locked him in the barbershop so he couldn't get out where the marshal was certain to get him if he showed himself on the street again that night.

Gus didn't go home to his wife that night, because he was in the back room of the barbershop pulling on two or three new bottles at three o'clock when the rest of the crowd decided it was time to call it a night and to go home and get some sleep. They locked Gus in the back room to sleep it off.

Early the next morning, Clyde Young, the barber, went down and shaved Gus and patched up his clothes a little; and at about eleven-fifty, ten or fifteen minutes before the sermon at the church was due to end, Gus walked in and sat down in a rear pew.

Gus was supposed to be there, all right, because he was a deacon then, and it was his duty to help take up the morning offering. But Gus was not supposed to be there in the shape he was in, all liquored up again fresh that morning in the barbershop. Clyde Young had brought Gus an eye opener when he went down to shave him and to get him ready to take up collection at the church.

Nobody paid much attention to Gus when he walked into the church and took a seat in the back. The minister saw Gus, and likewise a dozen or more of the congregation who turned around to see who was coming to church so late. But nobody knew the condition Gus was in. He did not show it any more than he ever did. He looked to be as sober as the minister himself.

Gus sat still and quiet in the back of the church until the sermon was over. It was then time to take up the morning offering. It was customary for the deacons to walk down to the front of the pulpit, pick up the collection baskets, take up the money, and then to march back down the aisles while one of the women in the choir sang a solo.

Gus went down and got his basket all right, and took up all the money on his side of the aisle without missing a dime. Then, when all the deacons had got to the rear of the church, they began marching in step, slowly, down the aisles towards the pulpit where the minister was waiting to say a prayer over the money and to pronounce the benediction. The girl singing the solo was supposed to time herself so she would get to the end

of the piece just as the deacons laid the collection baskets on the table in front of the pulpit.

Everything worked smoothly enough, until just about the time that the rest of the deacons got about halfway down the aisles on their way back to the pulpit. The soloist was standing up in the choir singing her piece, the organist was playing the accompaniment, when Gus stopped dead in his tracks, playing havoc with all the ritual.

The elders and the minister should have had better sense than to have made Gus Streetman a deacon, to begin with; but Gus had carried them off their feet, just as he did the voters when he was canvassing for re-election for county tax assessor. It wasn't Gus's fault any more than it was the fault of the people who made him a deacon; they were the ones upon whom most of the blame should be put. And on the other hand, even if he was to be a deacon, somebody connected with the church should have hunted up Gus that morning before preaching started and made sure that he was in condition to enter a house of worship. But things were never done that way. People liked Gus, and they let him do as he pleased.

When Gus came stomping down the aisle that morning, rattling the collection basket as though he were warming up a crap game, he was as drunk as a horse trader on court day. But it was the people's fault; they should never have made Gus a deacon to begin with, unless some arrangement to keep him sober on Sunday was agreed upon.

Gus was standing there in the aisle by himself. The other deacons had marched down to the table in front of the pulpit, glancing back over their shoulders to see what the matter was with Gus, but scared to go back and get him. They didn't know what he might say or do if they tried to make him follow them.

By that time, the church was rank with the smell of Gus's liquor, and all the people were sniffing the air, and turning around in their pews to look at him. Gus was staring at the girl singing the solo in the choir, and shaking the dimes and quarters in the collection basket as if it had been a kitty pot in a Saturday night crap game in the barbershop.

Then suddenly, Gus shouted. He must have been heard all the way across town in the Baptist church, disrupting their service, too.

"Shake it up!" Gus yelled at the girl singing the solo.

The church was buzzing like a beehive in no

time. The congregation was standing up, sniffing Gus's whisky-smell; the organist stopped playing the accompaniment for the solo, the girl stopped singing, and everybody, including the minister, was staring openmouthed at Gus Streetman. During all that time, Gus was standing there in the aisle rattling the money and looking at the soloist. It was a strange thing to happen, but she did look a lot like the hoochie-coochie dancer with the carnival.

When everybody was hoping that the worst was over, Gus shouted again.

"Shake it up!" he yelled at the girl. "Shake it up, baby!"

Nearly everyone in the church knew what Gus was talking about, because most of the men had been to the show grounds the week before, and either had seen, or had been told about the little brown-skinned hoochie-coochie dancer in the tent for men only, and all the women, of course, had heard about her.

Gus was getting ready to yell again, and maybe do something shocking, but before he could do it, a bunch of the elders and deacons jumped on him and hustled him out of the church in a hurry.

The minister pronounced a hurried and short benediction, and ran out the back door and around to the street to see what was happening to Gus in front of the church.

The elders and deacons hustled Gus into an automobile and drove off with him at fifty miles an hour. The minister and the rest of the congregation came running down the street behind the car.

When they reached the jail, nearly everybody in town was down there by that time to see Gus Streetman get locked up. The Baptist church had turned out, and all the Baptists were there on their way home to see what was taking place. There was a delay of ten or fifteen minutes while somebody was going for Fred Jones, the marshal; Fred wasn't a member of any church, and he was always at home Sunday morning reading the Sunday *Journal* and the *Atlanta Constitution*. The marshal had the only key to the jail there was, and Gus couldn't be put inside until he came and unlocked the doors.

While everybody was standing around looking and talking, Gus climbed up on the radiator of an automobile and held out his hands for silence. People standing off at a distance pushed closer, saying, "Shhh!" in order to hear what Gus was about to say.

"Citizens of Washington County," Gus shouted, waving his hands and looking the crowd over just as he did when he took the stump for the county primary. "Citizens of Washington County, I'm not here today to ask you if you are satisfied with your tax assessments; I'm not here today, folks, to ask if you believe there is a better man in the county than Gus Streetman—citizens of Washington County, I'm here today, folks, to ask if you think there's another man in the entire county who can increase the membership and attendance and double the collection in a church like the man you are now facing!"

The marshal came running up just then and opened the doors of the lockup. He walked over to the car and jerked Gus down from the radiator and hustled him inside the little brick building. The crowd pressed around the lockup, trying to see what Gus looked like on the inside. A lot of the ones who were not engaged in pushing and shoving and elbowing towards the windows were shouting: "Hooray for Gus! Hooray for Gus! Hooray for Gus Streetman."

While the crowd was milling around the windows of the lockup, Gus's face suddenly appeared behind the bars of one of them. He shouted for attention and raised his hands for silence just as if he were canvassing the county for the Democratic White Primary.

"Go home and think it over, folks!" he yelled, "and when election day comes around, bring out the family and let's pile up a landslide for Gus Streetman!"

Somebody in the crowd shouted: "Hooray for Gus!"

Gus held up his hands again, silencing the crowd outside the windows.

"Vote for Gus Streetman, folks!" he yelled. "Everybody votes for Gus Streetman! Gus Streetman for deacon!"

Just then the marshal came up behind Gus and hustled him away from the window and pushed him into one of the lockup cages. After that there was nothing to stay for any longer, because Gus was locked out of sight, and the crowd turned away and started home for Sunday dinner. Everybody was hoping, though, that Gus would get bailed out of the lockup in time to take up the collection again the following week, the second Sunday in August.

CAROLINE GORDON (1895–   )

As we have seen, it makes a certain amount of sense to speak of "realism" when one comes to the southern writers of the twentieth century. The term serves to differentiate their work from the local color fiction and the historical romances of the late nineteenth century—and especially from the fiction that idealized the life of the old South. Yet the limitations of the term are clearly revealed when we try to apply it to that remarkable group of southern women writers who emerged in the second quarter of the twentieth century: Caroline Gordon, Katherine Anne Porter, Eudora Welty, Carson McCullers, and—to add the last in this succession, one whose work came after 1945—Flannery O'Connor. They are all very much interested in the manners and modes of southern society—in its inner life—but their fiction sometimes finds its setting in the remote southern past rather than in the present, and it may make use of fantasy rather than stress the sense of everyday reality.

With the southern novelists in general it is hard to draw a line between historical novels and novels that make a serious criticism of present-day society. The reason is not far to seek. As a region, the South, more than any other part of the country, is conscious of its past history. Far less than other sections has it been under the spell of the millennial American dream. It has felt the hand of the past heavier on its shoulder than have the other sections of the country. Its citizens are the only Americans whose ancestors have been soundly defeated in a long and devastating war. And as C. Vann Woodward has put it: "The South's preoccupation [has been] with guilt, not with innocence, with the reality of evil, not with the dream of perfection. Its experience in this respect, as in several others, [has been] on the whole a thoroughly un-American one" (*The Burden of Southern History*, 1960).

As a consequence, though the South has produced its quota of costume romances, its serious writers of fiction have often presented their most thoughtful commentaries on modern society in novels whose explicit scene is borrowed from the Civil War period or the early nineteenth century. Thus, Caroline Gordon's vision of the human predicament is not essentially different when she writes *The Strange Children*, the setting of which is in the 1940's, and *Green Centuries*, a narrative of colonial times.

Whatever the period in which Miss Gordon places her narrative, she is always concerned to bring to bear upon it her conception of American and, more specifically, of southern history. She is highly conscious of the divergence of southern culture from American culture generally. She makes far more use than Lanier (see p. 1715) of the conflict between two cultures: that of the North which she sees as rationalistic, commercial, antitraditional, and progressive, and that of the South, agricultural, traditional, religious, and bound by historical piety to the past.

A generalization such as this is made at the risk of oversimplification. Miss Gordon is well aware of this: she knows that the forces aligned with progress, democracy, and industrialism were also to be found in the South. After all, its culture too derived from Europe, and so these traits were inevitably to be found in the southern states, though far less powerfully expressed than in the culture of the North. Thus in her novel *Green Centuries* the southern white man in relation to the Indian showed himself as the aggressive westerner, antitraditional, progressive, technological, and so also in relation to the black man, whom he held as a slave.

Yet these contradictions within southern culture make for a dramatic and significant literature. The fiction writer is not interested in devising generalizations so precise as to require no qualifications. On the contrary, the very contradictions of society are what interest him, since they reveal the human predicament in all its poignance and its drama.

Andrew Lytle has provided some fine insights on this subject. The great theme of Tolstoi's *War and Peace,* he tells us, is the Europeanization of Russia.[1] This theme accounts for matters apparently so diverse as Napoleon's military invasion of Russia and the spiritual confusions of Pierre, the Russian intellectual whose head is filled with European ideas. Lytle does not go so far as to argue that Caroline Gordon's essential theme is the "Americanization" of the southern culture, and yet surely it is. Thus in her fiction one can discern the southerner as "American" when pitted against the red man; yet, in the intersectional struggle, as opposing to the American myth his own myth; and finally, especially in those novels that have a twentieth-century setting, taking a variety of stances: the southerner having become American, or tempted to become American, or still fighting a rearguard action against Americanization and continuing to question the American myth.

What, in this context, is the American myth? Lytle has his own way of describing it: ". . . it stands for vague but persistent belief in a mystical vitality which will overcome nature, whether it be the wilderness, a business opportunity, or through science the very secret of life itself." The American myth is still very much with us. On its nobler side, it promises to eliminate poverty, abolish race and caste, and to make America truly a land of peace and prosperity, "from sea to shining sea." But in its more morbid aspects, it becomes a millennialism which, in its promise to achieve a perfect world, underestimates the complexities of human nature and the recalcitrance of history.

From the beginning, the South produced its own dreamers of the American dream: one thinks at once of Thomas Jefferson; and latter-day southerners, in increasing numbers, have accepted it. But it has been the southern writers, interestingly enough, who have remained the most skeptical of the promises offered by the dream. Not only Miss Gordon but most of the other authors discussed in this section have either declared it false or at least withheld their commitment from it. One of the few exceptions is Thomas Wolfe, whose work is accordingly—in spite of its many "southern" qualities—appropriately treated in the section "Realism and the American Dream."

What has just been said ought not be taken in any programmatic sense. In Miss Gordon's best fiction the social historian has not been allowed to devour the artist. The mode of her fiction is derived from the great masters of indirection and implication like Henry James and Flaubert.

Miss Gordon's characteristic theme and method can be illustrated from some of her short stories. In "Old Red," the text of which follows, we are given a great deal more than a mere character sketch: implicit in this tale set in the rural Kentucky of a generation ago is a commentary on modern society and the good life. The hero of the story, Mister Maury, is no Huck Finn. He is a man of sixty, who has acquired a sound classical education at the university. Yet he is a man who refuses to worship the bitch-goddess success. To the quiet despair of his now dead wife, to the present ironic amusement of his daughter, and to the polite exasperation of all his kinfolk, he has refused to work at a career and instead has devoted himself to his twin passions, hunting and fishing; and now, with age upon him, only fishing a consuming passion.

As one reads "Old Red," it becomes plain that Maury is no vulgar hedonist and that his ideals are not unworthy. What he has evidently always yearned to do is to find some activity in which body and mind, heart and head, rigorous discipline and spontaneous joy could be united. In such passionate involvement he has hoped to discover and realize his true self. Mister Maury may never have read Thoreau—his taste seems to be rather for the ancient classical writers or the English neoclassical writers—but if he had read him, he probably would have approved of *Walden* at least.

---

[1] "Caroline Gordon and the Historic Image," *Sewanee Review* (Autumn, 1949).

The integrated life—the good life of Mister Maury's ideal—has not been easy to achieve in the divided and abstracted world in which he has had to live. He has been forced to strive for it, and in the only fashion possible to him he has achieved it. Clearly, the note on which the story ends is one of quiet triumph, even on a note reminiscent of St. Paul's exaltation: "I have finished the course, I have kept the faith." But the course that Mister Maury has run more nearly resembles that of Old Red than that of the apostle. For the observant reader will notice how skillfully the author has treated Mister Maury's reverie as he tries to put himself to sleep. In his reverie he goes back to his foxhunting days in the Virginia of his boyhood, and to memories of the celebrated fox that as a young man he had vainly tried to hunt down. Then his reverie brings him imperceptibly into an emotional identification with the fox—himself no longer the pursuer, but the pursued—Old Red, who has scrambled into his earth, in safety after all.

For most readers this poignant evocation of the character and quality of Maury's life will be enough to furnish a sufficient meaning for the story. But the more sensitive reader may also notice that the story is somewhat more complicated than this and has deeper implications. One of the complications arises from the even-handed justice with which Miss Gordon has portrayed Mister Maury. She has certainly presented him sympathetically, but she has not suppressed evidence that hints at a disappointing marriage and at selfishness and irresponsibility in his own character.

Nevertheless, the story constitutes primarily a veiled criticism of what has happened to the civilization in which Mister Maury lives. Andrew Lytle, in the essay already mentioned, has put it very well: "Outside his special delight [Mister Maury] moves through the world with as few commitments as a titled foreigner would allow himself in visiting a friendly country. Behind his pursuits of the arts of the field and the stream lies the ruin of the hierarchical values which he might have expected to sustain him." That is to say: in the older traditional society which has been lost, room and scope were provided for all of man's activities. Hunting and fishing too would have had their proper place. But Mister Maury, because of the breakdown of the traditional society, has lost his sense of vocation and so has instinctively turned to this one kind of knowledge and love as a substitute for the other values of life. With him, as Lytle puts it, "the pursuit of his pleasure becomes obsessive, so that in the end it becomes not pursuit but flight, and the hot breath of the Furies can almost be felt lapping the air he has just vacated." Mister Maury is indeed the fox with the hounds in close pursuit.

BIOGRAPHICAL CHART

1895   Born, October 6, in Trenton, Kentucky
1912   B.A., Bethany College, Bethany, West Virginia
1920–24 Reporter on the Chattanooga *News*
1931   *Penhally* (her first novel)
1934   *Aleck Maury, Sportsman*
1944   *The Women on the Porch*

1945   *The House of Fiction* (with Allen Tate, a study of fiction and fictional techniques)
1946   Joins faculty of Columbia University (School of General Studies) as a conductor of workshops in techniques of fiction

FURTHER READINGS

Caroline Gordon's works, with the exception of *The Malefactors* (1958) and *The Glory of Hera* (1972), have recently been reprinted in eight volumes by Cooper Square Editions.

Marie Fletcher, "The Fate of Women in a Changing South: A Persistent Theme in the Fiction of Caroline Gordon," *Mississippi Quarterly* (Winter, 1967–68)
Joan Griscom, "Bibliography of Caroline Gordon,"

Critiques (Winter, 1956); this number also contains articles on Gordon by Louise Cowan, Frederick Hoffman, Andrew Lytle, and William Van O'Connor

Vivienne Koch, "The Conservatism of Caroline Gordon," in *Southern Renascence* (1966), Louis Rubin and Robert Jacobs, eds.

Andrew Lytle, "Caroline Gordon and the Historic Image," *Sewanee Review* (Autumn, 1949)

James E. Rocks, "The Mind and Art of Caroline Gordon," *Mississippi Quarterly* (Winter, 1967–68)

Old Red (1933)

When the door had closed behind his daughter, Mister Maury went to the window and stood a few moments looking out. The roses that had grown in a riot all along that side of the fence had died or been cleared away, but the sun lay across the garden in the same level lances of light that he remembered. He turned back into the room. The shadows had gathered until it was nearly all in gloom. The top of his minnow bucket just emerging from his duffel bag glinted in the last rays of the sun. He stood looking down at his traps all gathered neatly in a heap at the foot of the bed. He would leave them like that. Even if they came in here sweeping and cleaning up—it was only in hotels that a man was master of his own room—even if they came in here cleaning up he would tell them to leave all his things exactly as they were. It was reassuring to see them all there together, ready to be taken up in the hand, to be carried down and put into a car, to be driven off to some railroad station at a moment's notice.

As he moved towards the door he spoke aloud, a habit that was growing on him:

"Anyhow I won't stay but a week. . . . I ain't going to stay but a week, no matter what they say. . . ."

Downstairs in the dining room they were already gathered at the supper table: his white-haired, shrunken mother-in-law; his tall sister-in-law who had the proud carriage of the head, the aquiline nose, but not the spirit of his dead wife; his lean, blond, new son-in-law; his black-eyed daughter who, but that she was thin, looked so much like him, all of them gathered there waiting for him, Alexander Maury. It occurred to him that this was the first time he had sat down in the bosom of the family for some years. They were always writing saying that he must make a visit this summer or certainly next summer—". . . all had a happy Christmas together, but missed you. . . ." They had even made the pretext that he ought to come up to inspect his new son-in-law. As if he hadn't always known exactly the kind of young man Sarah would marry! What was the boy's name? Stephen, yes, Stephen. He must be sure and remember that.

He sat down and shaking out his napkin spread it over his capacious paunch and tucked it well up under his chin in the way his wife had never allowed him to do. He let his eyes rove over the table and released a long sigh.

"Hot batter bread," he said, "and ham. Merry Point ham. I sure am glad to taste them one more time before I die."

The old lady was sending the little Negro girl scurrying back to the kitchen for a hot plate of batter bread. He pushed aside the cold plate and waited. She had bridled when he spoke of the batter bread and a faint flush had dawned on her withered cheeks. Vain she had always been as a peacock, of her housekeeping, her children, anything that belonged to her. She went on now, even at her advanced age, making her batter bread, smoking her hams according to that old recipe she was so proud of, but who came here now to this old house to eat or to praise?

He helped himself to a generous slice of batter bread, buttered it, took the first mouthful and chewed it slowly. He shook his head.

"There ain't anything like it," he said. "There ain't anything else like it in the world."

His dark eyes roving over the table fell on his son-in-law. "You like batter bread?" he enquired.

Stephen nodded, smiling. Mister Maury, still masticating slowly, regarded his face, measured the space between the eyes—his favorite test for man, horse or dog. Yes, there was room enough for sense between the eyes. How young the boy looked! And infected already with the fatal germ, the *cacoëthes scribendi*. Well, their children—if he and Sarah ever had any children—would probably escape. It was like certain diseases of the eye, skipped every other generation. His own father had had it badly all his life. He could see him now sitting at the head of the table spouting his own poetry—or Shakespeare's—while the children watched the preserve dish to see if it was going around. He, Aleck Maury, had been lucky to be born in the generation he had. He had escaped that at least. A few translations from Heine in his courting days, a few fragments from the Greek; but no, he had kept clear of that on the whole . . . .

His sister-in-law's eyes were fixed on him. She was smiling faintly. "You don't look much like dying, Aleck. Florida must agree with you."

The old lady spoke from the head of the table. "I can't see what you do with yourself all winter long. Doesn't time hang heavy on your hands?"

Time, he thought, *time!* They were always mouthing the word, and what did they know about it? Nothing in God's world! He saw time suddenly, a dull, leaden-colored fabric depending from the old lady's hands, from the hands of all of them, a blanket that they pulled about between them, now here, now there, trying to cover up their nakedness. Or they would cast it on the ground and creep in among the folds, finding one day a little more tightly rolled than another, but all of it everywhere the same dull gray substance. But time was a banner that whipped before him always in the wind! He stood on tiptoe to catch at the bright folds, to strain them to his bosom. They were bright and glittering. But they whipped by so fast and were whipping always ever faster. The tears came into his eyes. Where, for instance, had this year gone? He could swear he had not wasted a minute of it, for no man living, he thought, knew better how to make each day a pleasure to him. Not a minute wasted and yet here it was already May. If he lived to the Biblical three-score-and-ten, which was all he ever allowed himself in his calculations, he had before him only nine more Mays. Only nine more Mays out of all eternity and they wanted him to waste one of them sitting on the front porch at Merry Point!

The butter plate which had seemed to swim before him in a glittering mist was coming solidly to rest upon the white tablecloth. He winked his eyes rapidly and, laying down his knife and fork, squared himself about in his chair to address his mother-in-law:

"Well, ma'am, you know I'm a man that always likes to be learning something. Now this year I learned how to smell out fish." He glanced around the table, holding his head high and allowing his well-cut nostrils to flutter slightly with his indrawn breaths. "Yes, sir," he said, "I'm probably the only white man in this country knows how to smell out feesh."

There was a discreet smile on the faces of the others. Sarah was laughing outright. "Did you have to learn how or did it just come to you?"

"I learned it from an old nigger woman," her father said. He shook his head reminiscently. "It's wonderful how much you can learn from niggers. But you have to know how to handle them. I was half the winter wooing that old Fanny. . . ."

He waited until their laughter had died down. "We used to start off every morning from the same little cove and we'd drift in there together at night. I noticed how she always brought in a good string so I says to her: 'Fanny, you just lemme go 'long with you.' But she wouldn't have nothing to do with me. I saw she was going to be a hard nut to crack, but I kept right on. Finally I began giving her presents. . . ."

Laura was regarding him fixedly, a queer glint in her eyes. Seeing outrageous pictures in her mind's eye, doubtless. Poor Laura. Fifty years old if she was a day. More than half her lifetime gone and all of it spent drying up here in the old lady's shadow. She was speaking with a gasping little titter:

"What sort of presents did you give her, Aleck?"

He made his tones hearty in answer. "I give her a fine string of fish one day and I give her fifty cents. And finally I made her a present of a Barlow knife. That was when she broke down. She took me with her that morning. . . ."

"Could she really *smell* fish?" the old lady asked curiously.

"You ought to a seen her," Mister Maury said. "She'd sail over that lake like a hound on the scent. She'd row right along and then all of a sudden she'd stop rowing." He bent over and peered into the depths of imaginary water. " 'Thar they are, White Folks, thar they are. Cain't you smell 'em?' "

Stephen was leaning forward, eyeing his father-in-law intently. "Could you?" he asked.

"I got so I could smell feesh," Mister Maury told him. "I could smell out the feesh but I couldn't tell which kind they were. Now Fanny could row over a bed and tell just by the smell whether it was bass or bream. But she'd been at it all her life." He paused, sighing. "You can't just pick these things up. . . . Who was it said 'Genius is an infinite capacity for taking pains'?"

Sarah was rising briskly. Her eyes sought her husband's across the table. She was laughing. "Sir Izaak Walton," she said. "We'd better go in the other room. Mandy wants to clear the table."

The two older ladies remained in the dining room. Mister Maury walked across the hall to the sitting room, accompanied by Steve and Sarah. He lowered himself cautiously into the most solid-looking of the rocking chairs that were drawn up around the fire. Steve stood on the hearthrug, his back to the fire.

Mister Maury glanced up at him curiously. "What you thinking about, feller?" he asked.

Steve looked down. He smiled but his gaze was still contemplative. "I was thinking about the sonnet," he said, "in the form in which it first came to England."

Mister Maury shook his head. "Wyatt and Surrey," he said. "Hey, nonny, nonny. . . . You'll have hardening of the liver long before you're my age." He looked past Steve's shoulder at the picture that hung over the mantelshelf: Cupid and Psyche holding between them a fluttering veil and running along a rocky path towards the beholder. It had been hanging there ever since he could remember; would hang there, he thought, till the house fell down or burned down, as it was more likely to do with the old lady wandering around at night carrying lighted lamps the way she did. "Old Merry Point," he said. "It don't change much, does it?"

He settled himself more solidly in his chair. His mind veered from the old house to his own wanderings in brighter places. He regarded his daughter and son-in-law affably.

"Yes, sir," he said, "this winter in Florida was valuable to me just for the acquaintances I made. Take my friend, Jim Yost. Just to live in the same hotel with that man is an education." He paused, smiling reminiscently into the fire. "I'll never forget the first time I saw him. He came up to me there in the lobby of the hotel. 'Professor Maury,' he says, 'you been hearin' about me for twenty years and I been hearin' about you for twenty years. And now we've done met.'"

Sarah had sat down in the little rocking chair by the fire. She leaned towards him now, laughing. "They ought to have put down a cloth of gold for the meeting," she said.

Mister Maury regarded her critically. It occurred to him that she was, after all, not so much like himself as the sister whom, as a child, he had particularly disliked. A smart girl, Sarah, but too quick always on the uptake. For his own part he preferred a softer natured woman.

He shook his head. "Nature does that in Florida," he said. "I knew right off the reel it was him.

There were half a dozen men standing around. I made 'em witness. 'Jim Yost,' I says, 'Jim Yost of Maysville or I'll eat my hat.'"

"Why is he so famous?" Sarah asked.

Mister Maury took out his knife and cut off a plug of tobacco. When he had offered a plug to his son-in-law and it had been refused, he put the tobacco back in his pocket. "He's a man of imagination," he said slowly. "There ain't many in this world."

He took a small tin box out of his pocket and set it on the little table that held the lamp. Removing the top, he tilted the box so that they could see its contents: an artificial lure, a bug with a dark body and a red, bulbous head, a hook protruding from what might be considered its vitals.

"Look at her," he said. "Ain't she a killer?"

Sarah leaned forward to look and Steve, still standing on the hearthrug, bent above them. The three heads ringed the light. Mister Maury disregarded Sarah and addressed himself to Steve. "She takes nine strips of pork rind," he said, "nine strips cut just thick enough." He marked off the width of the strips with his two fingers on the table, then, picking up the lure and cupping it in his palm, he moved it back and forth quickly so that the painted eyes caught the light.

"Look at her," he said, "look at the wicked way she sets forward."

Sarah was poking at the lure with the tip of her finger. "Wanton," she said, "simply wanton. What does he call her?"

"This is his Devil Bug," Mister Maury said. "He's the only man in this country makes it. I myself had the idea thirty years ago and let it slip by me the way I do with so many of my ideas." He sighed, then, elevating his tremendous bulk slightly above the table level and continuing to hold Steve with his gaze, he produced from his coat pocket the oilskin book that held his flies. He spread it open on the table and began to turn the pages. His eyes sought his son-in-law's as his hand paused before a gray, rather draggled-looking lure.

"Old Speck," he said. "I've had that fly for twenty years. I reckon she's taken five hundred pounds of fish in her day. . . ."

The fire burned lower. A fiery coal rolled from the grate and fell on to the hearthrug. Sarah scooped it up with a shovel and threw it among the ashes. In the circle of the lamplight the two men still bent over the table looking at the flies. Steve was absorbed in them, but he spoke seldom. It was her father's voice that, rising and falling, filled the room. He talked a great deal but he had a beautiful speaking voice. He was telling Steve now about Little West Fork, the first stream ever he put a fly in. "My first love," he kept calling it. It sounded rather pretty, she thought, in his mellow voice: "My first love. . . ."

II

When Mister Maury came down the next morning the dining room was empty except for his daughter, Sarah, who sat dawdling over a cup of coffee and a cigarette. Mister Maury sat down opposite her. To the little Negro girl who presented herself at his elbow he outlined his wants briefly: "A cup of coffee and some hot batter bread, just like we had last night." He turned to his daughter. "Where's Steve?"

"He's working," she said. "He was up at eight and he's been working ever since."

Mister Maury accepted the cup of coffee from the little girl, poured half of it into his saucer, set it aside to cool. "Ain't it wonderful," he said, "the way a man can sit down and work day after day? When I think of all the work I've done in my time . . . Can he work *every* morning?"

"He sits down at his desk every morning," she said, "but of course he gets more done some mornings than others."

Mister Maury picked up his saucer, found the coffee cool enough for his taste. He sipped it slowly, looking out of the window. His mind was already busy with his day's programme. No water—no running water—nearer than West Fork, three miles away. He couldn't drive a car and Steve was going to be busy writing all morning. There was nothing for it but a pond. The Willow Sink. It was not much, but it was better than nothing. He pushed his chair back and rose.

"Well," he said, "I'd better be starting."

When he came downstairs with his rod a few minutes later the hall was still full of the sound of measured typing. Sarah sat in the dining room in the same position in which he had left her, smoking. Mister Maury paused in the doorway while he slung his canvas bag over his shoulders. "How you ever going to get anything done if you don't take advantage of the morning hours?" he asked. He glanced at the door opposite as if it had been the entrance to a sick chamber. "What's he writing about?" he enquired in a whisper.

"It's an essay on John Skelton."

Mister Maury looked out at the new green leaves framed in the doorway. "John Skelton," he said, "God Almighty!"

He went through the hall and stepped down off the porch onto the ground that was still moist with spring rains. As he crossed the lower yard he looked up into the branches of the maples. Yes, the leaves were full grown already even on the late trees. The year, how swiftly, how steadily it advanced! He had come to the far corner of the yard. Grown up it was in pokeberry shoots and honeysuckle, but there was a place to get through. The top strand of wire had been pulled down and fastened to the others with a ragged piece of rope. He rested his weight on his good leg and swung himself over onto the game one. It gave him a good, sharp twinge when he came down on it. It was getting worse all the time, that leg, but on the other hand he was learning better all the time how to handle it. His mind flew back to a dark, startled moment, that day when the cramp first came on him. He had been sitting still in the boat all day long and that evening when he stood up to get out his leg had failed him utterly. He had pitched forward among the reeds, had lain there a second, face downward, before it came to him what had happened. With the realization came a sharp picture out of his faraway youth. Uncle James, lowering himself ponderously out of the saddle after a hard day's hunting, had fallen forward in exactly the same way, into a knot of yowling little Negroes. He had got up and cursed them all out of the lot. It had scared the old boy to death, coming down like that. The black dog he had had on his shoulder all that fall. But he himself had never lost one day's fishing on account of his leg. He had known from the start how to handle it. It meant simply that he was slowed down that much. It hadn't really made much difference in fishing. He didn't do as much wading but he got around just about as well on the whole. Hunting, of course, had had to go. You couldn't walk all day shooting birds, dragging a game leg. He had just given it up right off the reel, though it was a shame when a man was as good a shot as he was. That day he was out with Tom Kensington, last November, the only day he got out during the bird season. Nine shots he'd had and he'd bagged nine birds. Yes, it was a shame. But a man couldn't do everything. He had to limit himself. . . .

He was up over the little rise now. The field slanted straight down before him to where the pond lay, silver in the morning sun. A Negro cabin was perched halfway up the opposite slope. A woman was hanging out washing on a line stretched between two trees. From the open door little Negroes spilled down the path towards the pond. Mister Maury surveyed the scene, spoke aloud:

"Ain't it funny now? Niggers always live in the good places."

He stopped under a wild cherry tree to light his pipe. It had been hot crossing the field, but the sunlight here was agreeably tempered by the branches. And that pond down there was fringed with willows. His eyes sought the bright disc of the water then rose to where the smoke from the cabin chimney lay in a soft plume along the crest of the hill.

When he stooped to pick up his rod again it was with a feeling of sudden keen elation. An image had risen in his memory, an image that was familiar but came to him infrequently of late and that only in moments of elation: the wide field in front of his uncle's house in Albemarle, on one side the dark line of undergrowth that marked the Rivanna River, on the other the blue of Peters' Mountain. They would be waiting there in that broad plain when they had the first sight of the fox. On that little rise by the river, loping steadily, not yet alarmed. The sun would glint on his bright coat, on his quick turning head as he dove into the dark of the woods. There would be hullabaloo after that and shouting and riding. Sometimes there was the tailing of the fox—that time Old Whiskey was brought home on a mattress! All of that to come afterwards, but none of it ever like that first sight of the fox there on the broad plain between the river and the mountain.

There was one fox, they grew to know him in time, to call him affectionately by name. Old Red it was who showed himself always like that there on the crest of the hill. "There he goes, the damn, impudent scoundrel. . . ." Uncle James would shout and slap his thigh and yell himself hoarse at Whiskey and Mag and the pups, but they would already have settled to their work. They knew his course, every turn of it, by heart. Through the woods and then down again to the river. Their hope was always to cut him off before he could circle back to the mountain. If he got in there among those old field pines it was all up. But he always made it. Lost 'em every time and dodged through to his hole in Pinnacle Rock. A smart fox, Old Red. . . .

He descended the slope and paused in the shade of a clump of willows. The little Negroes who squatted, dabbling in the water, watched him out of round eyes as he unslung his canvas bag and laid it on a stump. He looked down at them gravely.

"D'you ever see a white man that could conjure?" he asked.

The oldest boy laid the brick he was fashioning out of mud down on a plank. He ran the tip of his tongue over his lower lip to moisten it before he spoke. "Naw, suh."

"I'm the man," Mister Maury told him. "You chillun better quit that playin' and dig me some worms."

He drew his rod out of the case, jointed it up and laid it down on a stump. Taking out his book of flies he turned the pages, considering. "Silver Spinner," he said aloud. "They ought to take that . . . in May. Naw, I'll just give Old Speck a chance. It's a long time now since we had her out."

The little Negroes had risen and were stepping quietly off along the path towards the cabin, the two little boys hand in hand, the little girl following, the baby astride her hip. They were pausing now before a dilapidated building that might long ago have been a hen house. Mister Maury shouted at them: "Look under them old boards. That's the place for worms." The biggest boy was turning around. His treble "Yassuh" quavered over the water. Then their voices died away. There was no sound except the light turning of the willow boughs in the wind.

Mister Maury walked along the bank, rod in hand, humming: "Bangum's gone to the wild boar's den. . . . *Bangum's gone to the wild boar's den.* . . ." He stopped where a white, peeled log protruded six or seven feet into the water. The pond made a little turn here. He stepped out squarely upon the log, still humming. The line rose smoothly, soared against the blue and curved sweetly back upon the still water. His quick ear caught the little whish that the fly made when it clove the surface, his eye followed the tiny ripples made by its flight. He cast again, leaning a little backwards as he did sometimes when the mood was on him. Again and again his line soared out over the water. His eye rested now and then on his wrist. He noted with detachment the expert play of the muscles, admired each time the accuracy of his aim. It occurred to him that it was four days now since he had wet a line. Four days. One whole day packing up, parts of two days on the train and yesterday wasted sitting there on that front porch with the family. But the abstinence had done him good. He had never cast better than he was casting this morning.

There was a rustling along the bank, a glimpse of blue through the trees. Mister Maury leaned forward and peered around the clump of willows. A hundred yards away Steve, hatless, in an old blue shirt and khaki pants, stood jointing up a rod.

Mister Maury backed off his log and advanced along the path. He called out cheerfully: "Well, feller, do any good?"

Steve looked up. His face had lightened for a moment but the abstracted expression stole over it again when he spoke. "Oh, I fiddled with it all morning," he said, "but I didn't do much good."

Mister Maury nodded sympathetically. "*Minerva invita erat*," he said. "You can do nothing unless Minerva perches on the roof tree. Why, I been castin' here all morning and not a strike. But there's a boat tied up over on the other side. What say we get in it and just drift around?" He paused, looked at the rod Steve had finished jointing up. "I brought another rod along," he said. "You want to use it?"

Steve shook his head. "I'm used to this one," he said.

An expression of relief came over Mister Maury's face. "That's right," he said, "a man always does better with his own rod."

The boat was only a quarter full of water. They heaved her over and dumped it out, then dragged her down to the bank. The little Negroes had come up, bringing a can of worms. Mister Maury threw them each a nickel and set the can in the bottom of the boat. "I always like to have a few worms handy," he told Steve, "ever since I was a boy." He lowered himself ponderously into the bow and Steve pushed off and dropped down behind him.

The little Negroes still stood on the bank staring. When the boat was a little distance out on the water the boldest of them spoke:

"You reckon 'at ole jawnboat going to hold you up, Cap'm?"

Mister Maury turned his head to call over his shoulder. "Go 'way, boy. Ain't I done tole you I's a conjure?"

The boat dipped ominously. Steve changed his position a little and she settled to the water. Sitting well forward, Mister Maury made graceful casts, now to this side, now to that. Steve, in the stern, made occasional casts but he laid his rod down every now and then to paddle though there

was really no use in it. The boat drifted well enough with the wind. At the end of half an hour seven sizable bass lay on the bottom of the boat. Mister Maury had caught five of them. He reflected that perhaps he really ought to change places with Steve. The man in the bow certainly had the best chance at the fish. "But no," he thought, "it don't make any difference. He don't hardly know where he is now."

He stole a glance over his shoulder at the young man's serious, abstracted face. It was like that of a person submerged. Steve seemed to float up to the surface every now and then, his expression would lighten, he would make some observation that showed he knew where he was, then he would sink again. If you asked him a question he answered punctiliously, two minutes later. Poor boy, dead to the world and would probably be that way the rest of his life. A pang of pity shot through Mister Maury and on the heels of it a gust of that black fear that occasionally shook him. It was he, not Steve, that was the queer one. The world was full of people like this boy, all of them going around with their heads so full of this and that they hardly knew what they were doing. They were all like that. There was hardly anybody—there was *nobody* really in the whole world like him. . . .

Steve, coming out of his abstraction, spoke politely. He had heard that Mister Maury was a fine shot. Did he like to fish better than hunt?

Mister Maury reflected. "Well," he said, "they's something about a covey of birds rising up in front of you . . . they's something . . . and a good dog. Now they ain't anything in this world that I like better than a good bird dog." He stopped and sighed. "A man has got to come to himself early in life if he's going to amount to anything. Now I was smart, even as a boy. I could look around me and see all the men of my family, Uncle Jeems, Uncle Quent, my father, every one of 'em weighed two hundred by the time he was fifty. You get as heavy on your feet as all that and you can't do any good shooting. But a man can fish as long as he lives. . . . Why, one place I stayed last summer there was an old man ninety years old had himself carried down to the river every morning. Yes, sir, a man can fish as long as he can get down to the water's edge. . . ."

There was a little plop to the right. He turned just in time to see the fish flash out of the water. He watched Steve take it off the hook and drop it on top of the pile in the bottom of the boat. Six bass that made and two bream. The old lady would be pleased. "Aleck always catches me fish," she'd say.

The boat glided over the still water. There was no wind at all now. The willows that fringed the bank might have been cut out of paper. The plume of smoke hung perfectly horizontal over the roof of the Negro cabin. Mister Maury watched it stream out in little eddies and disappear into the bright blue.

He spoke softly: "Ain't it wonderful . . . ain't it wonderful now that a man of my gifts can content himself a whole morning on this here little old pond?"

III

Mister Maury woke with a start. He realized that he had been sleeping on his left side again. A bad idea. It always gave him palpitations of the heart. It must be that that had waked him up. He had gone to sleep almost immediately after his head hit the pillow. He rolled over, cautiously, as he always did since that bed in Leesburg had given down with him and, lying flat on his back, stared at the opposite wall.

The moon rose late. It must be at its height now. That patch of light was so brilliant he could almost discern the pattern of the wallpaper. It hung there, wavering, bitten by the shadows into a semblance of a human figure, a man striding with bent head and swinging arms. All the shadows in the room seemed to be moving towards him. The protruding corner of the washstand was an arrow aimed at his heart, the clumsy old-fashioned dresser was a giant towering above him.

They had put him to sleep in this same room the night after his wife died. In the summer it had been, too, in June; and there must have been a full moon for the same giant shadows had struggled there with the same towering monsters. It would be like that here on this wall every full moon, for the pieces of furniture would never change their position, had never been changed, probably, since the house was built.

He turned back on his side. The wall before him was dark but he knew every flower in the pattern of the wallpaper, interlacing pink roses with thrusting up between every third cluster the enormous, spreading fronds of ferns. The wallpaper in the room across the hall was like it too. The old lady slept there, and in the room next to his own, Laura, his sister-in-law, and in the east bedroom downstairs, the young couple. He and Mary had slept there when they were first married, when they were the young couple in the house.

He tried to remember Mary as she must have looked that day he first saw her, the day he arrived from Virginia to open his school in the old office that used to stand there in the corner of the yard. He could see Mister Allard plainly, sitting there under the sugar tree with his chair tilted back, could discern the old lady—young she had been then!—hospitably poised in the doorway, hand extended, could hear her voice: "Well, here are two of your pupils to start with. . . ." He remembered Laura, a shy child of nine hiding her face in her mother's skirts, but Mary that day was only a shadow in the dark hall. He could not even remember how her voice had sounded. "Professor Maury," she would have said and her mother would have corrected her with "Cousin Aleck. . . ."

That day she got off her horse at the stile blocks she had turned as she walked across the lawn to look back at him. Her white sun-bonnet had fallen on her shoulders. Her eyes, meeting his, had been dark and startled. He had gone on and had hitched both the horses before he leaped over the stile to join her. But he had known in that moment that she was the woman he was going to have. He could not remember all the rest of it, only that moment stood out. He had won her, she had become his wife, but the woman he had won was not the woman he had sought. It was as if he had had her only in that moment there on the lawn. As if she had paused there only for that one moment and was ever after retreating before him down a devious, a dark way that he would never have chosen.

The death of the first baby had been the start of it, of course. It had been a relief when she took so definitely to religion. Before that there had been those sudden, unaccountable forays out of some dark lurking place that she had. Guerrilla warfare and trying to the nerves, but that had been only at first. For many years they had been two enemies contending in the open. . . . Towards the last she had taken mightily to prayer. He would wake often to find her kneeling by the side of the bed in the dark. It had gone on for years. She had never given up hope. . . .

Ah, a stout-hearted one, Mary! She had never given up hope of changing him, of making him over into the man she thought he ought to be. Time and again she almost had him. And there were long periods, of course, during which he had been worn down by the conflict, one spring when he himself said, when she had told all the neighbors, that he was too old now to go fishing any more. . . . But he had made a comeback. She had had to resort to stratagem. His lips curved in a smile, remembering the trick.

It had come over him suddenly, a general lassitude, an odd faintness in the mornings, the time when his spirits ordinarily were at their highest. He had sat there by the window, almost wishing to have some ache or pain, something definite to account for his condition. But he did not feel sick in his body. It was rather a dulling of all his senses. There were no longer the reactions to the visible world that made his days a series of adventures. He had looked out of the window at the woods glistening with spring rain; he had not even taken down his gun to shoot a squirrel.

Remembering Uncle Quent's last days he had been alarmed, had decided finally that he must tell her so that they might begin preparations for the future—he had shuddered at the thought of eventual confinement, perhaps in some institution. She had looked up from her sewing, unable to repress a smile.

"You think it's your mind, Aleck. . . . It's coffee. . . . I've been giving you a coffee substitute every morning. . . ."

They had laughed together over her cleverness. He had not gone back to coffee but the lassitude had worn off. She had gone back to the attack with redoubled vigor. In the afternoons she would stand on the porch calling after him as he slipped down to the creek. "Now, don't stay long enough to get that cramp. You remember how you suffered last time. . . ." He would have forgotten all about the cramp until that moment but it would hang over him then through the whole afternoon's sport and it would descend upon him inevitably when he left the river and started for the house.

Yes, he thought with pride. She was wearing him down—he did not believe there was a man living who could withstand her a lifetime—she was wearing him down and would have had him in another few months, another year certainly. But she had been struck down just as victory was in her grasp. The paralysis had come on her in the night. It was as if a curtain had descended, dividing their life sharply into two parts. In the bewildered year and a half that followed he had found himself forlornly trying to reconstruct the Mary he had known. The pressure she had so constantly exerted upon him had become for him a part of her personality. This new, calm Mary was not the woman he had lived with all these years. She had lain there—heroically they all said—waiting for death. And lying there, waiting, all her faculties engaged now in defensive warfare, she had raised, as it were, her lifelong siege; she had lost interest in his comings and goings, had once even encouraged him to go for an afternoon's sport! He felt a rush of warm pity. Poor Mary! She must have realized towards the last that she had wasted herself in conflict. She had spent her arms and her strength against an inglorious foe when all the time the real, the invincible adversary waited. . . .

He turned over on his back again. The moonlight was waning, the contending shadows paler now and retreating towards the door. From across the hall came the sound of long, sibilant breaths, ending each one on a little upward groan. The old lady. . . . She would maintain till her dying day that she did not snore. He fancied now that he could hear from the next room Laura's light, regular breathing and downstairs were the young couple asleep in each other's arms. . . .

All of them quiet and relaxed now, but they had been lively enough at dinner time. It had started with the talk about Aunt Sally Crenfew's funeral to-morrow. Living now as he had for some years, away from women of his family, he had forgotten the need to be cautious. He had spoken up before he thought:

"But that's the day Steve and I were going to Barker's Mill. . . ."

Sarah had cried out at the idea. "Barker's Mill!" she had said, "right on the Crenfew land . . . well, if not on the very farm, in the very next field. It would be a scandal if he, Professor Maury, known by everybody to be in the neighborhood, could not spare one afternoon, one insignificant summer afternoon, from his fishing long enough to attend the funeral of his cousin, the cousin of all of them, the oldest lady in the whole family connection. . . ."

Looking around the table he had caught the same look in every eye; he had felt a gust of that same fright that had shaken him there on the pond. That look! Sooner or later you met it in every human eye. The thing was to be up and ready, ready to run for your life at a moment's notice. Yes, it had always been like that. It always would be. His fear of them was shot through suddenly with contempt. It was as if Mary were there laughing with him. *She* knew that there was not one of them who could have survived as he had survived, could have paid the price for freedom that he had paid. . . .

Sarah had come to a stop. He had to say something. He shook his head.

"You think we just go fishing to have a good time. The boy and I hold high converse on that pond. I'm starved for intellectual companionship I tell you. . . . In Florida I never see anybody but niggers. . . ."

They had all laughed out at that. "As if you didn't *prefer* the society of niggers!" Sarah said scornfully.

The old lady had been moved to anecdote:

"I remember when Aleck first came out here from Virginia, Cousin Sophy said: 'Professor Maury is so well educated. Now Cousin Cave Maynor is dead who is there in the neighborhood for him to associate with?' 'Well,' I said, 'I don't know about that. He seems perfectly satisfied with Ben Hooser. They're off to the creek together every evening soon as school is out.' "

Ben Hooser. . . . He could see now the wrinkled face, overlaid with that ashy pallor of the aged Negro, smiling eyes, the pendulous lower lip that, drooping away, showed always some of the rotten teeth. A fine nigger, Ben, and on to a lot of tricks, the only man really that he'd ever cared to take fishing with him.

But the first real friend of his bosom had been old Uncle Teague, the factotum at Hawkwood. Once a week or more likely every ten days he fed the hounds on the carcass of a calf that had had time to get pretty high. They would drive the spring wagon out into the lot; he, a boy of ten, beside Uncle Teague on the driver's seat. The hounds would come in a great rush and rear their slobbering jowls against the wagon wheels. Uncle Teague would wield his whip, chuckling while he threw the first hunk of meat to Old Mag, his favorite.

"Dey goin' run on dis," he'd say. "Dey goin' run like a shadow. . . ."

He shifted his position again, cautiously. People, he thought . . . people . . . so bone ignorant, all of them. Not one person in a thousand realized that a fox-hound remains at heart a wild beast and must kill and gorge and then, when he is ravenous, kill and gorge again. . . . Or that the channel cat is a night feeder. . . . Or . . . His daughter had told him once that he ought to set all his knowledge down in a book. "Why?" he had asked. "So everybody else can know as much as I do?"

If he allowed his mind to get active, really active, he would never get any sleep. He was fighting an inclination now to get up and find a cigarette. He relaxed again upon his pillows, deliberately summoned pictures before his mind's eye. Landscapes—and streams. He observed their outlines, watched one flow into another. The Black River into West Fork, that in turn into Spring Creek and Spring Creek into the Withlicocchee. Then they were all flowing together, merging into one broad plain. He watched it take form slowly: the wide field in front of Hawkwood, the Rivanna River on one side, on the other Peters' Mountain. They would be waiting there till the fox showed himself on that little rise by the river. The young men would hold back till Uncle James had wheeled Old Filly, then they would all be off pell-mell across the plain. He himself would be mounted on Jonesboro. Almost blind, but she would take anything you put her at. That first thicket on the edge of the woods. They would break there, one half of them going around, the other half streaking it through the woods. He was always of those going around to try to cut the fox off on the other side. No, he was down off his horse. He was coursing with the fox through the trees. He could hear the sharp, pointed feet padding on the dead leaves, see the quick head turned now and then over the shoulder. The trees kept flashing by, one black trunk after another. And now it was a ragged mountain field and the sage grass running before them in waves to where a narrow stream curved in between the ridges. The fox's feet were light in the water. He moved forward steadily, head down. The hounds' baying grew louder. Old Mag knew the trick. She had stopped to give tongue by that big rock and now they had all leaped the gulch and were scrambling up through the pines. But the fox's feet were already hard on the mountain path. He ran slowly, past the big boulder, past the blasted pine to where the shadow of the Pinnacle Rock was black across the path. He ran on and the shadow swayed and rose to meet him. Its cool touch was on his hot tongue, his heaving flanks. He had slipped in under it. He was sinking down, panting, in black dark, on moist earth while the hounds' baying filled the valley and reverberated from the mountainside.

Mister Maury got up and lit a cigarette. He smoked it quietly, lying back upon his pillows. When he had finished smoking he rolled over on his side and closed his eyes. It was still a good while till morning, but perhaps he could get some sleep. His mind played quietly over the scene that would be enacted in the morning. He would be sitting on the porch after breakfast, smoking, when Sarah came out. She would ask him how he felt, how he had slept.

He would heave a groan, not looking at her for fear of catching that smile on her face—the girl had little sense of decency. He would heave a groan, not too loud or overdone. "My kidney trouble," he would say, shaking his head. "It's come back on me, daughter, in the night."

She would express sympathy and go on to talk of something else. She never took any stock in his kidney trouble. He would ask her finally if she reckoned Steve had time to drive him to the train that morning. He'd been thinking about how much good the chalybeate water of Estill Springs had done him last year. He might heave another

groan here to drown her protests. "No. . . . I better be getting on to the Springs. . . . I need the water. . . ."

She would talk on a lot after. He would not need to listen. He would be sitting there thinking about Elk River, where it runs through the village of Estill Springs. He could see that place by the bridge now: a wide, deep pool with plenty of lay-bys under the willows.

The train would get in around one o'clock. That nigger, Ed, would hustle his bags up to the boarding house for him. He would tell Mrs. Rogers he must have the same room. He would have his bags packed so he could get at everything quick. He would be into his black shirt and fishing pants before you could say Jack Robinson. . . . Thirty minutes after he got off the train he would have a fly in that water.

ANDREW LYTLE (1902–   )

Andrew Lytle was born in middle Tennessee, for a time lived and attended school in France, and later went to Vanderbilt University, where he became the friend of John Crowe Ransom, Donald Davidson, Allen Tate, and Robert Penn Warren and was associated with them as a contributor to *I'll Take My Stand*.

His first serious literary interest was the drama. He was a member of George Pierce Baker's celebrated "47 Workshop" at Yale and was for a time an actor in New York. But his substantial literary work has been in fiction and in criticism, especially the criticism of fiction. From 1961 to 1972 he was the editor of the *Sewanee Review*.

In discussing the fiction of Caroline Gordon, we have already had occasion to quote from Lytle, and what we have quoted is sufficient to indicate that Lytle has thought long and seriously about the nature of a traditional society and of the stresses and strains it has been subjected to in the twentieth century.

As someone who knows a vast amount about southern history and who has decided opinions

on the nature of its culture, he might reasonably be expected to write fiction designed to illustrate a thesis—all the more so in view of the fact that Lytle's fiction often takes the form of the historical novel. Yet, for Lytle, no true fiction ever "illustrates" anything, though it will, of course, embody a set of values and a world view. For if Lytle is much concerned with history and even has a theory of history, he also has a carefully articulated theory of fiction. The reader of any of his critical essays and reviews is quickly apprised of this fact. It is a conception very much Lytle's own, though in its general outline it derives from the theory of fiction developed at the end of the last century by masters like Henry James and Gustave Flaubert. But so scrupulous is Lytle in refusing, in his fiction, to underline his ideas that sometimes the basic meaning of one of his stories or the true import of one of his novels has been missed because the careless or hasty reader has not been sufficiently sensitive to the implications and hints with which the fiction has been sown.

The story that follows, "Jericho, Jericho,

Jericho," represents a fine blending of two of Lytle's dominant interests—the history of the South and the nature of any traditional society. (The society may be French or Russian. Lytle has, for example, written very perceptively about Tolstoi's portrayal of the society of nineteenth-century Russia.) The fine blending of interests achieved in "Jericho" is attained not merely because Lytle has a natural gift for storytelling,[1] but through the discipline of a studied craft.

Lytle's discipline shows itself in many ways, but here one or two illustrations will have to suffice. The story, on one level, is about the land as the basis for a settled society and about love of the land, the index of which is not simply the worth of the acreage in cash. The story indicates—by suggestion, by remembered incident, by evocative description—what possession of Long Gourd plantation has meant to the dying woman.

There is a sense in which one must sympathize with her: she is a person of character and

stoic courage, and even shows a kind of heroic dignity. But she is also a cruel old woman—possessive, jealous of her grandson's fiancée, quite ruthless when her land is involved. She has some of the virtues of the landed gentry but she has some of its characteristic vices too—and also some vices perhaps peculiar to herself. Else why does her conscience now "scorch the cool wrinkles in the sheets [of her bed]"? If one guesses that the author (who was for a time himself a working farmer on Cornsilk Plantation in north Alabama and later in middle Tennessee) admires the old order based on the land, it is evident that he has not chosen a stainless character to state the case for it. In fact, there is no "statement" of a case, for or against the old order, but instead a vivid dramatization of its passing.

If Mrs. McCowan is at first jealous of her grandson's fiancée, Eva, because she is certain that Eva has come to gloat over her imminent possession of the rich acres of Long Gourd, very shortly the old woman suffers the shock of a reversal of expectation. This city-bred young woman doesn't want Long Gourd—has no intention of living there. She actually means to give up the precious heritage. In this last half hour of her life, the mistress of Long Gourd experiences an unexpected and unlooked-for kind of defeat.

---

[1] "Andrew was . . . the perfect teller of tales. I have heard a few great tale-tellers, and Andrew was second to none—unless to his own father. Andrew could appreciate the tale or the telling with the absolute innocence of the artist to whom art is the impersonal all . . ." (Robert Penn Warren, *Southern Review*, Winter, 1971, p. 132).

FURTHER READINGS

Andrew Lytle, *At the Moon's Inn* (1941)
————, *Bedford Forrest and His Cutter Company* (1931, 1960)
————, *The Hero with the Private Parts* (1966)
————, *The Long Night* (1936)
————, *A Name for Evil* (1947)
————, *A Novel, a Novella, and Four Stories* (1958)

————, *The Velvet Horn* (1957)

Mississippi Quarterly (Fall, 1970); Andrew Lytle issue with bibliography and articles
Robert Penn Warren, "Andrew Lytle's *The Long Night*: A Rediscovery," *Southern Review* (January, 1971)

Jericho, Jericho, Jericho (1936)

She opencd her eyes. She must have been asleep for hours or months. She could not reckon; she could only feel the steady silence of time. She had been Joshua and made it swing suspended in her room. Forever she had floated above the counter-

pane, between the tester and the counterpane she had floated until her hand, long and bony, its speckled-dried skin drawing away from the bulging blue veins, had reached and drawn her body under the covers. And now she was resting, clear-headed and quiet, her thoughts clicking like a new-greased mower. All creation could not make her lift her thumb or cross it over her finger. She looked at the bed, the bed her mother had died in, the bed her children had been born in, her marriage bed, the bed the General had drenched with his blood. Here it stood where it had stood for seventy years, square and firm on the floor, wide enough for three people to lie comfortable in, if they didn't sleep restless; but not wide enough for her nor long enough when her conscience scorched the cool wrinkles in the sheets. The two foot posts, octagonal-shaped and mounted by carved pieces that looked like absurd flowers, stood up to comfort her when the world began to crumble. Her eyes followed down the posts and along the basket-quilt. She had made it before her marriage to the General, only he wasn't a general then. He was a slight, tall young man with a rolling mustache and perfume in his hair. A many a time she had seen her young love's locks dripping with scented oil, down upon his collar . . . She had cut the squares for the baskets in January, and for stuffing had used the letters of old lovers, fragments of passion cut to warm her of a winter's night. The General would have his fun. *Miss Kate, I didn't sleep well last night. I heard Sam Buchanan make love to you out of that farthest basket. If I hear him again, I mean to toss this piece of quilt in the fire.* Then he would chuckle in his round, soft voice; reach under the covers and pull her over to his side of the bed. On a cold and frosting night he would sleep with his nose against her neck. His nose was so quick to turn cold, he said, and her neck was so warm. Sometimes her hair, the loose, unruly strands at the nape, would tickle his nostrils and he would wake up with a sneeze. This had been so long ago, and there had been so many years of trouble and worry. Her eyes, as apart from her as the mirror on the bureau, rested upon the half-tester, upon the enormous button that caught the rose-colored canopy and shot its folds out like the rays of the morning sun. She could not see but she could feel the heavy cluster of mahogany grapes that tumbled from the center of the head board—out of its vines curling down the sides it tumbled. How much longer would these never-picked grapes hang above her head? How much longer would she, rather, hang to the vine of this world, she who lay beneath as dry as any raisin. Then she remembered. She looked at the blinds. They were closed.

"You, Ants, where's my stick? I'm a great mind to break it over your trifling back."

"Awake? What a nice long nap you've had," said Doctor Ed.

"The boy? Where's my grandson? Has he come?"

"I'll say he's come. What do you mean taking to your bed like this? Do you realize, beautiful lady, that this is the first time I ever saw you in bed in my whole life? I believe you've taken to bed on purpose. I don't believe you want to see me."

"Go long, boy, with your foolishness."

That's all she could say, and she blushed as she said it—she blushing at the words of a snip of a boy, whom she had diapered a hundred times and had washed as he stood before the fire in the round tin tub, his little back swayed and his little belly sticking out in front, rosy from the scrubbing he had gotten. *Mammy, what for I've got a hole in my stummick; what for, Mammy?* Now he was sitting on the edge of the bed calling her beautiful lady, an old hag like her, beautiful lady. A good-looker the girls would call him, with his bold, careless face and his hands with their fine, long fingers. Soft, how soft they were, running over her rough, skinny bones. He looked a little like his grandpa, but somehow there was something missing . . .

"Well, boy, it took you a time to come home to see me die."

"Nonsense, Cousin Edwin, I wouldn't wait on a woman who had so little faith in my healing powers."

"There an't nothing strange about dying. But I an't in such an all-fired hurry. I've got a heap to tell you about before I go."

The boy leaned over and touched her gently. "Not even death would dispute you here, on Long Gourd, Mammy."

He was trying to put her at her ease in his care-free way. It was so obvious a pretending, but she loved him for it. There was something nice in its awkwardness, the charm of the young's blundering and of their efforts to get along in the world. Their pretty arrogance, their patronizing airs, their colossal unknowing of what was to come. It was a quenching drink to a sin-thirsty old woman. Somehow his vitality had got crossed in her blood and made a dry heart leap, her blood that was almost water. Soon now she would be all water, water and dust, lying in the burying ground between the cedar—and fire. She could smell her soul burning and see it. What a fire it would make below, dripping with sin, like a rag soaked in kerosene. But she had known what she was doing. And here was Long Gourd, all its fields intact, ready to be handed on, in better shape than when she took it over. Yes, she had known what she was doing. How long, she wondered, would his spirit hold up under the trials of planting, of cultivating, and of the gathering time, year in and year out—how would he hold up before so many springs and so many autumns. The thought of him giving orders, riding over the place, or rocking on the piazza, and a great pain would pin her heart to her backbone. She had wanted him by her to train—there was so much for him to know: how the south field was cold and must be planted late, and where the orchards would best hold their fruit, and where the frosts crept soonest—that now could never be. She turned her head—who was that woman, that strange woman standing by the bed as if she owned it, as if . . .

"This is Eva, Mammy."

"Eva?"

"We are going to be married."

"I wanted to come and see—to meet Dick's grandmother . . ."

I wanted to come see her die. That's what she meant. Why didn't she finish and say it out. She had come to lick her chops and see what she would enjoy. That's what she had come for, the lying little slut. The richest acres in Long Gourd valley, so rich hit'd make yer feet greasy to walk over'm, Saul Oberly at the first tollgate had told the peddler once, and the peddler had told it to her, knowing it would please and make her trade. *Before you die.* Well, why didn't you finish it out? You might as well. You've given yourself away.

Her fierce thoughts dried up the water in her eyes, tired and resting far back in their sockets. They burned like a smothered fire stirred up by the wind as they traveled over the woman who would lie in her bed, eat with her silver, and caress her flesh and blood. The woman's body was soft enough to melt and pour about him. She could see that; and her firm, round breasts, too firm and round for any good to come from them. And her lips, full and red, her eyes bright and cunning. The heavy hair crawled about her head to tangle the poor, foolish boy in its ropes. She might have known he would do something foolish like this. He had a foolish mother. There warn't any way to avoid it. But look at her belly, small and no-count. There wasn't a muscle the size of a worm as she could see. And those hips—

And then she heard her voice: "What did you say her name was, son? Eva? Eva Callahan, I'm glad to meet you, Eva. Where'd your folks come from, Eva? I knew some Callahans who lived in the Goosepad settlement. They couldn't be any of your kin, could they"

"Oh, no, indeed. My people . . ."

"Right clever people they were. And good farmers, too. Worked hard. Honest—that is, most of 'm. As honest as that run of people go. We always gave them a good name."

"My father and mother live in Birmingham. Have always lived there."

"Birmingham," she heard herself say with contempt. They could have lived there all their lives and still come from somewhere. I've got a mule older'n Birmingham. "What's your pa's name?"

"Her father is Mister E. L. Callahan, Mammy."

"First name not Elijah by any chance? Lige they called him."

"No. Elmore, Mammy."

"Old Mason Callahan had a son they called Lige. Somebody told me he moved to Elyton. So you think you're going to live with the boy here."

"We're to be married . . . that is, if Eva doesn't change her mind."

And she saw his arm slip possessively about the woman's waist. "Well, take care of him, young woman, or I'll come back and han't you. I'll come back and claw your eyes out."

"I'll take very good care of him, Mrs. McCowan."

"I can see that." She could hear the threat in her voice, and Eva heard it.

"Young man," spoke up Doctor Edwin, "you should feel powerful set up, two such women pestering each other about you."

The boy kept an embarrassed silence.

"All of you get out now. I want to talk to him by himself. I've got a lot to say and precious little time to say it in. And he's mighty young and helpless and ignorant."

"Why, Mammy, you forget I'm a man now. Twenty-six. All teeth cut. Long trousers."

"It takes a heap more than pants to make a man. Throw open them blinds, Ants."

"Yes'm."

"You don't have to close the door so all-fired soft. Close it naturally. And you can tip about all you want to—later. I won't be hurried to the burying ground. And keep your head away from that door. What I've got to say to your new master is private."

"Listen at you, Mistiss."

"You listen to me. That's all. No, wait. I had

something else on my mind—what is it? Yes. How many hens has Melissy set? You don't know? Find out. A few of the old hens ought to be setting. Tell her to be careful to turn the turkey eggs every day. No, you bring them and set them under my bed. I'll make sure. We got a mighty pore hatch last year. You may go now. I'm plumb worn out, boy, worn out thinking for these people. It's that that worries a body down. But you'll know all about it in good time. Stand out there and let me look at you good. You don't let me see enough of you, and I almost forget how you look. Not really, you understand. Just a little. It's your own fault. I've got so much to trouble me that you, when you're not here, naturally slip back in my mind. But that's all over now. You are here to stay, and I'm here to go. There will always be Long Gourd, and there must always be a McCowan on it. I had hoped to have you by me for several years, but you would have your fling in town. I thought it best to clear your blood of it, but as God is hard, I can't see what you find to do in town. And now you've gone and gotten you a woman. Well, they all have to do it. But do you reckon you've picked the right one—you must forgive the frankness of an old lady who can see the bottom of her grave—I had in mind one of the Carlisle girls. The Carlisle place lies so handy to Long Gourd and would give me a landing on the river. Have you seen Anna Belle since she's grown to be a woman? I'm told there's not a better housekeeper in the valley."

"I'm sure Anna Belle is a fine girl. But, Mammy, I love Eva."

"She'll wrinkle up on you, Son; and the only wrinkles land gets can be smoothed out by the harrow. And she looks sort of puny to me, Son. She's powerful small in the waist and walks about like she had worms."

"Gee, Mammy, you're not jealous are you? That waist is in style."

"You want to look for the right kind of style in a woman. Old Mrs. Penter Matchem had two daughters with just such waists, but 'twarn't natural. She would tie their corset strings to the bedposts and whip'm out with a buggy whip. The poor girls never drew a hearty breath. Just to please that old woman's vanity. She got paid in kind. It did something to Eliza's bowels and she died before she was twenty. The other one never had any children. She used to whip'm out until they cried. I never liked that woman. She thought a whip could do anything."

"Well, anyway, Eva's small waist wasn't made by any corset strings. She doesn't wear any."

"How do you know, sir?"

"Well . . . I . . . What a question for a respectable woman to ask."

"I'm not a respectable woman. No woman can be respectable and run four thousand acres of land. Well, you'll have it your own way. I suppose the safest place for a man to take his folly is to bed."

"Mammy!"

"You must be lenient with your Cousin George. He wanders about night times talking about the War. I put him off in the west wing where he won't keep people awake, but sometimes he gets in the yard and gives orders to his troops. 'I will sweep that hill, General'—and many's the time he's done it when the battle was doubtful—'I'll sweep it with my iron brooms'; then he shouts out his orders, and pretty soon the dogs commence to barking. But he's been a heap of company for me. You must see that your wife humors him. It won't be for long. He's mighty feeble."

"Eva's not my wife yet, Mammy."

"You won't be free much longer—the way she looks at you, like a hungry hound."

"I was just wondering," he said hurriedly. "I hate to talk about anything like this . . ."

"Everybody has a time to die, and I'll have no maudlin nonsense about mine."

"I was wondering about Cousin George . . . if I could get somebody to keep him. You see, it will be difficult in the winters. Eva will want to spend the winters in town . . ."

He paused, startled, before the great bulk of his grandmother rising from her pillows, and in the silence that frightened the air, his unfinished words hung suspended about them.

After a moment he asked if he should call the doctor.

It was some time before she could find words to speak.

"Get out of the room."

"Forgive me, Mammy. You must be tired."

"I'll send for you," sounded the dead voice in the still room, "when I want to see you again. I'll send for you and—the woman."

She watched the door close quietly on his neat square back. Her head whirled and turned like a flying jennet. She lowered and steadied it on the pillows. Four thousand acres of the richest land in the valley he would sell and squander on that slut, and he didn't even know it and there was no way to warn him. This terrifying thought rushed through her mind, and she felt the bed shake with her pain, while before the footboard the specter of an old sin rose up to mock her. How she had struggled to get this land and keep it together—through the War, the Reconstruction, and the pleasanter after days. For eighty-seven years she had suffered and slept and planned and rested and had pleasure in this valley, seventy of it, almost a turning century, on this place; and now that she must leave it . . .

The things she had done to keep it together. No. The one thing . . . from the dusty stacks the musty odor drifted through the room, met the tobacco smoke over the long table piled high with records, reports. Iva Louise stood at one end, her hat clinging perilously to the heavy auburn hair, the hard blue eyes and the voice:

"You promised Pa to look after me"—she had waited for the voice to break and scream—"and you have stolen my land!"

"Now, Miss Iva Louise," the lawyer dropped his empty eyes along the floor, "you don't mean . . ."

"Yes, I do mean it."

Her own voice had restored calm to the room: "I promised your pa his land would not be squandered."

"My husband won't squander my property. You just want it for yourself."

She cut through the scream with the sharp edge of her scorn: "What about that weakling's farm in Madison? Who pays the taxes now?"

The girl had no answer to that. Desperate, she faced the lawyer: "Is there no way, sir, I can get my land from the clutches of this unnatural woman?"

The man coughed; the red rim of his eyes watered with embarrassment: "I'm afraid," he cleared his throat, "you say you can't raise the money . . . I'm afraid—"

That trapped look as the girl turned away. It had come back to her, now trapped in her bed. As a swoon spreads, she felt the desperate terror of weakness, more desperate where there has been strength. Did the girl see right? Had she stolen the land because she wanted it?

Suddenly, like the popping of a thread in a loom, the struggles of the flesh stopped, and the years backed up and covered her thoughts like the spring freshet she had seen so many times creep over the dark soil. Not in order but, as if they were stragglers trying to catch up, the events of her life passed before her sight that had never been so clear. Sweeping over the mounds of her body rising beneath the quilts came the old familiar odors —the damp, strong, penetrating smell of new-turned ground; the rank, clinging, resistless odor of green-picked feathers stuffed in a pillow by Guinea Nell, thirty odd years ago; tobacco on the mantel, clean and sharp like smelling salts; her father's sweat, sweet like stale oil; the powerful ammonia of manure turned over in a stall; curing hay in the wind; the polecat's stink on the night air, almost pleasant, a sort of commingled scent of all the animals, man and beast; the dry smell of dust under a rug; the over-strong scent of too-sweet fruit trees blooming; the inhospitable wet ashes of a dead fire in a poor white's cabin; black Rebeccah in the kitchen; a wet hound steaming before a fire. There were other odors she could not identify, overwhelming her, making her weak, taking her body and drawing out of it a choking longing to hover over all that she must leave, the animals, the fences, the crops growing in the fields, the houses, the people in them . . .

It was early summer, and she was standing in the garden after dark—she had heard something after the small chickens. Mercy and Yellow Jane passed beyond the paling fence. Dark shadows—gay, full voices. *Where you gwine, gal? I dunno. Jes a-gwine. Where you? To the frolic, do I live. Well, stay off'n yoe back tonight.* Then out of the rich, gushing laughter: *All right, you stay off'n yourn. I done caught de stumbles.* More laughter.

The face of Uncle Ike, head man in slavery days, rose up. A tall Senegalese, he was standing in the crib of the barn unmoved before the bushwhackers. *Nigger, whar is that gold hid? You better tell us, nigger. Down in the well; in the far-place. By God, you black son of a bitch, we'll roast ye alive if you air too contrary to tell. Now, listen ole nigger, Miss McCowan ain't nothen to you no more. You been set free. We'll give ye some of it, a whole sack. Come on, now—out of the dribbling, leering mouth—whar air it?* Ike's tall form loomed towards the shadows. In the lamp flame his forehead shone like the point, the core of night. He stood there with no word for answer. As she saw the few white beads of sweat on his forehead, she spoke.

She heard her voice reach through the dark—*you turn that black man loose.* A pause and then—*I know your kind. In better days you'd slip around and set people's barns afire. You shirked the War to live off the old and weak. You don't spare me because I'm a woman. You'd shoot a woman quicker because she has the name of being frail. Well, I'm not frail, and my Naxy Six ain't frail.*

Ike, take their guns. Ike moved and one of them raised his pistol arm. He dropped it, and the acrid smoke stung her nostrils. *Now, Ike, get the rest of their weapons. Their knives, too. One of us might turn our backs.*

On top of the shot she heard the soft pat of her servants' feet. White eyeballs shining through the cracks in the barn. Then: *Caesar, Al, Zabedee, step in here and lend a hand to Ike.* By sun the people had gathered in the yard. Uneasy, silent, they watched her on the porch. She gave the word, and the whips cracked. The mules strained, trotted off, skittish and afraid, dragging the white naked bodies bouncing and cursing over the sod: *Turn us loose. We'll not bother ye no more, lady. You ain't no woman, you're a devil.* She turned and went into the house. It is strange how a woman gets hard when trouble comes a-gobbling after her people.

Worn from memory, she closed her eyes to stop the whirl, but closing her eyes did no good. She released the lids and did not resist. Brother Jack stood before her, handsome and shy, but ruined from his cradle by a cleft palate, until he came to live only in the fire of spirits. And she understood, so clear was life, down to the smallest things. She had often heard tell of this clarity that took a body whose time was spending on the earth. Poor Brother Jack, the gentlest of men, but because of his mark, made the butt and wit of the valley. She saw him leave for school, where he was sent to separate him from his drinking companions, to a church school where the boys buried their liquor in the ground and sipped it up through straws. His letters: *Dear Ma, quit offering so much advice and send me more money. You send barely enough to keep me from stealing.* His buggy wheels scraping the gravel, driving up as the first roosters crowed. *Katharine, Malcolm, I thought you might want to have a little conversation.* Conversation two hours before sun! And down she would come and let him in, and the General would get up, stir up the fire, and they would sit down and smoke. Jack would drink and sing, *If the Little Brown Jug was mine, I'd be drunk all the time and I'd never be sob-er a-gin—or, Hog drovers, hog drovers, hog drovers we air, a-courting your darter so sweet and so fair.* They would sit and smoke and drink until she got up to ring the bell.

He stayed as long as the whisky held out, growing more violent towards the end. She watered his bottles: begged whisky to make camphor—*Gre't God, Sis Kate, do you sell camphor? I gave you a pint this morning.* Poor Brother Jack, killed in Breckinridge's charge at Murfreesboro, cut in two by a chain shot from an enemy gun. All night long she sat up after the message came. His body scattered about a splintered black gum tree. She had seen that night, as if she had been on the field, the parties moving over the dark field hunting the wounded and dead. Clyde Bascom had fallen near Jack with a bad hurt. They were messmates. He had to tell somebody; and somehow she was the one he must talk to. The spectral lanterns, swinging towards the dirge of pain and the monotonous cries of *Water*, caught by the river dew on the before-morning air and held suspended over the field in its acrid quilt. There death dripped to mildew the noisy throats . . . and all the while relief parties, or maybe it was the burial parties, moving, blots of night, sullenly moving in the viscous blackness.

Her eyes widened, and she looked across the foot posts into the room. There was some mistake, some cruel blunder; for there now, tipping about the carpet, hunting in her wardrobe, under the bed, blowing down the fire to its ashes until they glowed in their dryness, stalked the burial parties. They stepped out of the ashes in twos and threes, hunting, hunting and shaking their heads. Whom were they searching for? Jack had long been buried. They moved more rapidly; looked angry. They crowded the room until she gasped for breath. One, gaunt and haggard, jumped on the foot of her bed; rose to the ceiling; gesticulated; argued in animated silence. He leaned forward; pressed his hand upon her leg. She tried to tell him to take it off. Cold and crushing heavy, it pressed her down to the bowels of the earth. Her lips trembled, but no sound came forth. Now the hand moved up to her stomach; and the haggard eyes looked gravely at her, alert, as if they were waiting for something. Her head turned giddy. She called to Dick, to Ants, to Doctor Ed; but the words struck her teeth and fell back in her throat. She concentrated on lifting the words, and the burial parties sadly shook their heads. Always the cries struck her teeth and fell back down. She strained to hear the silence they made. At last from a great distance she thought she heard . . . *too late . . . too late.* How exquisite the sound, like a bell swinging without ringing. Suddenly it came to her. She was dying.

How slyly death slipped up on a body, like sleep moving over the vague boundary. How many times she had laid awake to trick the unconscious there. At last she would know . . . But she wasn't ready. She must first do something about Long Gourd. That slut must not eat it up. She would give it to the hands first. He must be brought to understand this. But the specters shook their heads. Well let them shake. She'd be damned if she would go until she was ready to go. She'd be damned all right, and she smiled at the meaning the word took on now. She gathered together all the particles of her will; the specters faded; and there about her were the anxious faces of kin and servants. Edwin had his hands under the cover feeling her legs. She made to raise her own hand to the boy. It did not go up. Her eyes wanted to roll upward and look behind her forehead, but she pinched them down and looked at her grandson.

"You want to say something, Mammy?"—she saw his lips move.

She had a plenty to say, but her tongue had somehow got glued to her lips. Truly it was now too late. Her will left her. Life withdrawing gathered like a frosty dew on her skin. The last breath blew gently past her nose. The dusty nostrils tingled. She felt a great sneeze coming. There was a roaring; the wind blew through her head once, and a great cotton field bent before it, growing and spreading, the bolls swelling as big as cotton sacks and bursting white as thunderheads. From a distance, out of the far end of the field, under a sky so blue that it was painful-bright, voices came singing, *Joshua fit the battle of Jericho, Jericho, Jericho—Joshua fit the battle of Jericho, and the walls come a-tumbling down.*

KATHERINE ANNE PORTER (1890–   )

Katherine Anne Porter has lived in Texas and Louisiana, on the Pacific coast, in upstate New York, in New England, in New York City, and in Washington, D.C. She has also lived abroad for considerable periods of time, in Mexico, in Paris, and in Berlin. Out of her experience she has written about all sorts of people—Germans, Irish-Americans, Mexicans. Her earliest triumphs in the short story ("Maria Concepçion" and "Flowering Judas") have a Mexican setting. But some of her finest and most characteristic stories come out of her early experiences in her native South. Though she has said of herself, "I am the grandchild of a lost war, and I have blood-knowledge of what life can be in a defeated country on the bare bones of privation," her fiction does not exhibit any particular thesis about southern culture. But she has always displayed superb skill in making use of the southern scene and cultural experience.

She has taken for her literary models the great French and Russian novelists and such masters of English prose as Thomas Hardy, Henry James, and James Joyce. Here, too, she has been fortunate in her access to southern material, for the relatively old-fashioned society of the South has provided her with characters and with patterns of life fairly close to those of Hardy or even Tolstoi. Take the importance of the family as an example: southern society—until recently, at least—has been basically family-centered. But this can be a mixed blessing. The family may be a sustaining force or may exert a crushing pressure. In her story "Old Mortality" the drama is based on this ambivalence toward the family—and toward history. In any case the family is there, inescapable, a landmark, impossible to avoid or ignore.

The society in which Miss Porter grew up was also possessed of a strong sense of identity. (It had fought a four-years' war to preserve its own way of life.) One imbibed, almost with his mother's milk, notions of propriety and conduct that did not have to be reviewed and debated at regular intervals. As was to be expected, such a society had its own view of itself and developed this view through its histories and legends. To the emancipated southerner's more skeptical eye, these histories might turn out to be no truer than the legends—not fact at all, but delusive myth.

Some of Katherine Anne Porter's most brilliant stories describe the experience of growing up in the South at the turn of the century. Growing up always involves the attempt to find out the truth about oneself and one's world. In a traditional society, growing up imposes special difficulties as well as special advantages; in a society in which the family is important, it involves coming to terms with the family's conception of itself, with its legend and the testing of its credibility. As subject matter for a writer it offers the possibility of dramatic confrontations, in which the tonal quality of the experience may modulate from comedy to tragedy. One finds both the comic and the tragic in Miss Porter's fiction.

What is really remarkable about her work is the wonderful clarity and conviction that she achieves. Equally remarkable is the richness and density of implication—even in stories as brief as "The Source," "The Circus," and "The Grave." The last named provides a fine example of how an apparently trivial incident can be invested with the very meaning of growing up in an old-fashioned society.

In this story, two children, brother and sister on a Texas farm in 1903, are out rabbit hunting and find themselves in the old abandoned family cemetery. (The graves have long since been opened and the bodies transferred to the new public cemetery.)

Miranda leaped into the pit that had held her grandfather's bones. Scratching around aimlessly and pleasurably as any young animal, she scooped up a lump of earth and weighed it in her palm. It had a pleasantly sweet, corrupt smell, being mixed with cedar needles and small leaves, and as the crumbs fell apart, she saw a silver dove no larger than a hazel nut, with spread wings and a neat fan-shaped tail.

Miranda's brother recognizes what the curious little ornament is—the screw-head for a coffin. Paul has found something too—a small gold ring—and the children soon make an exchange of their treasures, Miranda fitting the gold ring onto her thumb.

Paul soon becomes interested in hunting again, and looks about for rabbits, but the ring,

shining with the serene purity of fine gold on [the little girl's] rather grubby thumb, turned her feelings against her overalls and sockless feet. . . . She wanted to go back to the farm house, take a good cold bath, dust herself with plenty of Maria's violet talcum powder . . . put on the thinnest, most becoming dress she ever owned, with a big sash, and sit in a wicker chair under the trees.

The little girl is thoroughly feminine, and though she has enjoyed knocking about with her brother, wearing her summer roughing outfit, the world of boys and sports and hunting is beginning to pall.

Then something happens. Paul starts up a rabbit, kills it with one shot, and skins it expertly as Miranda admiringly watches. "Brother lifted the oddly bloated belly. 'Look,' he said, in a low amazed voice. 'It was going to have young ones.'" Seeing the baby rabbits in all their perfection, "their sleek wet down lying in minute even ripples, like a baby's head just washed, their unbelievably small delicate ears folded close," Miranda is "excited but not frightened." Then she touches one of them, and exclaims, "Ah, there's blood running over them!" and begins to tremble. "Yet she had wanted most deeply to see and to know. Having seen, she felt at once as if she had known all along."

The meaning of life and fertility and of her own body begin to take shape in the little girl's mind as she sees the tiny creatures just taken from their mother's womb. The boy says to her "cautiously, as if he were talking about something forbidden: 'They were just about ready to be born.' 'I know,' said Miranda, 'like kittens. I know, like babies.' She was quietly and terribly agitated, standing again with her rifle under her arm, looking down at the bloody heap." Paul buries the rabbits and cautions his sister "with an eager friendliness, a confidential tone quite unusual in him, as if he were taking her into an important secret on equal terms: 'Listen now. . . . Don't tell a soul.' "

If there is beauty in the discovery, there is also awe and even terror. No wonder the little girl, though she had begun "admiringly" to watch Paul skin the rabbit and though the sight of the tiny creatures "excited" and did not frighten her, at the end begins "to tremble." Though one does not feel that any detail has been lugged in for the sake of making a "symbolic" point, a larger and more universal meaning does quietly radiate from the physical details. The secret of birth is revealed in a graveyard, the abode of death, and the revelation comes through a kind of bloody sacrifice. The discovery also comes at the appropriate time in Miranda's development, for just before the revelation, we have been given hints of Miranda's growing awareness of her role as a woman.

The discovery of the mystery of birth is also placed in a family and social context. Miranda is thoroughly conscious of how her family is regarded in the community. We are told that her father—Miranda's mother is dead—had been criticized for letting his girls dress like boys and career "around astride barebacked horses." Miranda herself had encountered such criticism from old women whom she met on the road—women who smoked corncob pipes. They had always "treated her grandmother with most sincere respect," but they ask her "Whut yo Pappy thinkin about?" This matter of clothes, and the pressures of society, and the role of women in the society, powerfully affects the meaning of the story. For if it is about a rite of initiation into the meaning of life, what is at stake is no mere matter of biological maturity. Miranda's growing up cannot be separated from the context of the family and the larger society of which the family is a part.

In this story there are no irrelevant details: every element is "used up"—absorbed into the total pattern, transformed into meaning. The texture of the story is as dense and tightly woven as that of a poem. Miss Porter's great reputation as a "stylist," then, when properly under-

stood, does not refer to polished surfaces and superficial niceties, but rather to a compactness and an almost unbelievable economy of means. A story such as "The Grave" has a disarming simplicity: nothing seems forced or contrived, and yet every item is necessary and contributes its quantum of meaning to the whole.

The theme of "The Grave" is developed and expanded in Miss Porter's long story, "Old Mortality." The presentation is more elaborate and more complicated, so much so, in fact, that "Old Mortality" gives something of the sense of development and the massiveness of effect that one finds in a novel.

The story is divided into three parts. In Part 1, Miranda is eight years old and the year is 1902. (When Miranda found treasure in the grave she was nine.) Part 2 is set in 1904, with Miranda aged ten. When we see Miranda next, in Part 3 (1912), she is eighteen. The year before, she had eloped from school, incurring her father's intense displeasure. Though her runaway marriage had speedily broken up, she is certain that her father has not yet forgiven her. Nevertheless, the claims of the family are powerful. Miranda is now answering the call to come home to attend her Uncle Gabriel's funeral. In "Old Mortality," then, we are shown three stages in Miranda's development—three glimpses of Miranda in relation to her kinsfolk.

Yet "Old Mortality" begins with a quite different and apparently quite separate concern. What was the truth about Aunt Amy? Could one trust the family legend about her? The attempt to find out the truth about Aunt Amy in the end will have a bearing on Miranda's efforts to find out the truth about herself.

Even at eight, Miranda had been forced to look with a child's skepticism at the family's account of Amy. She and her sister wonder why "every older person who looked at [the photograph of Amy] said 'How lovely. . . .'" But for Miranda the smile on the pictured face seemed "rather disturbing." It was "a reckless, indifferent smile." Besides, Miranda knows that older people do not always tell the truth. For instance, her father, in speaking of how slim Amy was, adds: "There were never any fat women in the family, thank God." Yet Miranda knows that great-aunt Eliza could barely squeeze through doors, and great-aunt Keziah in Kentucky weighed 220 pounds. The little girl's doubts are unobtrusively woven into the fabric of events. Miranda is not made to appear a precocious little detective, ferreting out family secrets. She exhibits no more than the bright natural curiosity of a child. In fact, the import of her skepticism will not come to a focus until we have reached almost the end of the story.

Miranda's questioning of the romantic legend is taken a stage further in Part 2 of the story. With her own eyes, Miranda sees Amy's husband, Gabriel, and is moved to ask her father with a child's candor, ". . . is Uncle Gabriel a real drunkard?" Miranda also sees in the flesh Uncle Gabriel's second wife and senses her cold (and unmannerly) hostility. Even the child can perceive that Uncle Gabriel's romantic worship of Amy has cost his second wife a great deal. But Part 2 is not obviously focused upon a debunking of Amy's legend: the little girls indulge in their own deliciously romantic make-believe. They think of themselves in the convent school as "immured"—as "beautiful but unlucky maidens, who for mysterious reasons have been trapped by nuns and priests in dire collusion." If any obvious deflation is to be found in this part of the story, it has to do with Miranda's dream of being a jockey, and what happens to her romantic conception of victory when she sees the gallant Miss Lucy come in after winning the race "bleeding at the nose . . . her knees . . . trembling, and . . . [snorting] when she drew her breath." Miranda finds out also that even the money won on the race has a questionable reality. Too large a sum to be *given* to a little girl, it will be deposited to her account in a bank. And Uncle Gabriel's wife, by her reaction to the news of the victory, suggests that the change in fortune is only a temporary stay of Uncle Gabriel's inevitable decline. This section is rich in detail, but underneath all lies the moral criticism of Amy's legend.

In Part 3, a frontal attack on the romantic legend of Amy's life and death is launched by the ugly duckling of the family, Cousin Eva, who has become a champion of woman's rights and now urges Miranda to dismiss all the romantic folderol that the family talks about Amy. The author continues to deal out an even-handed justice: Cousin Eva does have a case. She has been put upon by her family. She is right too in arguing that the legend of romantic love has been used to cover up some not very glamorous economic considerations and to gloss over sexual drives. (Cousin Eva subjects the legend, we might say, to both a "Marxist" and a "Freudian" criticism.)

Yet Miranda refuses to make a simple substitution of Cousin Eva's account of Amy for the family's romantic legend. Miranda tells us why and, rejecting both the legend and Cousin Eva's counterlegend, promises to find out the truth about herself. But the author qualifies her own qualification to Miranda's promise: Miranda makes the promise "in her hopefulness, her ignorance." The reader will find it useful to ponder Miss Porter's final attitude toward Miranda. It involves great dramatic sympathy, but also a very considerable degree of detachment.

In general, Miss Porter's method is to let the facts speak for themselves—but how carefully she chooses those facts and how carefully she arranges them in the story. She pays the reader the compliment of letting him work out their meaning for himself. That meaning will include a number of things: Miranda's own notion as to what Aunt Amy really was like; why the attempt to understand Amy's life involves the truth about her own life; why any truth concerning human relationships tends to be ambiguous; and why each of us must always—at some level—make up for ourselves the truth by which we are to live. (If this last statement seems too hopelessly defeatist, then let us alter it thus: each of us has to appropriate for himself and in his own fashion the truth by which he is to live. No secondhand version will serve him.)

Miss Porter has often been called an ironist, and so she is, but the irony is obviously not an irresponsible irony and it does not debunk. It contains no hostility toward human aspirations;

instead, it is perhaps best described as a quiet awareness of our propensity for deception—about others and about ourselves.

"Old Mortality" was first published in 1937, long before terms like "the generation gap," "alienation," and "finding one's identity" had come into vogue. But though the current terms by which we name these problems did not then exist, the problems themselves have existed to some degree from the beginning of civilization. One of the marks of a literary classic is that it deals with perennial and universal problems. One of its values is that it places what the reader too often takes to be his peculiar problem in a new—and consequently illuminating—context.

BIOGRAPHICAL CHART

1890 Born, May 15, in Indian Creek (near San Antonio), Texas; educated at convent and private schools in Louisiana and Texas
1918 Works as reporter for the *Rocky Mountain News* in Denver
1918–21 Lives in Mexico
1922 Arranges first exhibition of Mexican-Indian folk art in the United States
1930 *Flowering Judas* (stories)
1931 Travels in Europe, where she remains for several years, living in Switzerland, France, and Germany
1934 *Hacienda*
1937 Returns to the United States; *Noon Wine*
1939 *Pale Horse, Pale Rider*

1941 Elected to the National Institute of Arts and Letters
1944 *The Leaning Tower*
1952 *The Days Before*
1962 *Ship of Fools*, which wins the Emerson-Thoreau medal of the American Academy of Arts and Sciences
1965 *Collected Stories*
1966 Receives National Book Award and Pulitzer prize for fiction; elected to the American Academy of Arts and Letters
1967 Receives Gold Medal for Fiction, National Institute of Arts and Letters
1970 *Collected Essays and Occasional Writings*

FURTHER READINGS

There is no standard edition of Katherine Anne Porter's works. Individual titles are cited in the biographical chart.

Writers at Work: The "Paris Review" Interviews (1963)

Paul R. Baumgartner, *Katherine Anne Porter* (1969)
W. S. Emmons, *Katherine Anne Porter: The Regional Stories* (1967)
Lodwick Hartley and George Core, eds., *Katherine Anne Porter: A Critical Symposium* (1969)
George Hendrick, *Katherine Anne Porter* (1965)

M. M. Liberman, *Katherine Anne Porter's Fiction* (1971)
Harry John Mooney, *The Fiction and Criticism of Katherine Anne Porter* (1962)
William L. Nanne, *Katherine Anne Porter and the Art of Rejection* (1964)
Edward G. Schwartz, "Katherine Anne Porter: A Critical Bibliography," *Bulletin of N.Y. Public Library* (1953)
Robert Penn Warren, "Irony with a Center: Katherine Anne Porter," in *Selected Essays* (1958)
Ray West, *Katherine Anne Porter* (1963)

Old Mortality (1937)

PART I: 1885-1902

She was a spirited-looking young woman, with dark curly hair cropped and parted on the side, a short oval face with straight eyebrows, and a large curved mouth. A round white collar rose from the neck of her tightly buttoned black basque, and round white cuffs set off her lazy hands with dimples in them, lying at ease in the folds of her flounced skirt which gathered around to a bustle.

She sat thus, forever in the pose of being photographed, a motionless image in her dark walnut frame with silver oak leaves in the corners, her smiling gray eyes following one about the room. It was a reckless indifferent smile, rather disturbing to her nieces Maria and Miranda. Quite often they wondered why every older person who looked at the picture said, "How lovely"; and why everyone who had known her thought her so beautiful and charming.

There was a kind of faded merriment in the background, with its vase of flowers and draped velvet curtains, the kind of vase and the kind of curtains no one would have any more. The clothes were not even romantic looking, but merely most terribly out of fashion, and the whole affair was associated, in the minds of the little girls, with dead things: the smell of Grandmother's medicated cigarettes and her furniture that smelled of beeswax, and her old-fashioned perfume, Orange Flower. The woman in the picture had been Aunt Amy, but she was only a ghost in a frame, and a sad, pretty story from old times. She had been beautiful, much loved, unhappy, and she had died young.

Maria and Miranda, aged twelve and eight years, knew they were young, though they felt they had lived a long time. They had lived not only their own years; but their memories, it seemed to them, began years before they were born, in the lives of the grown-ups around them, old people above forty, most of them, who had a way of insisting that they too had been young once. It was hard to believe.

Their father was Aunt Amy's brother Harry. She had been his favorite sister. He sometimes glanced at the photograph and said, "It's not very good. Her hair and her smile were her chief beauties, and they aren't shown at all. She was much slimmer than that, too. There were never any fat women in the family, thank God."

When they heard their father say things like that, Maria and Miranda simply wondered, without criticism, what he meant. Their grandmother was thin as a match; the pictures of their mother, long since dead, proved her to have been a candlewick, almost. Dashing young ladies, who turned out to be, to Miranda's astonishment, merely more of Grandmother's grandchildren, like herself, came visiting from school for the holidays, boasting of their eighteen-inch waists. But how did their father account for great-aunt Eliza, who quite squeezed herself through doors, and who, when seated, was

one solid pyramidal monument from floor to neck? What about great-aunt Keziah, in Kentucky? Her husband, great-uncle John Jacob, had refused to allow her to ride his good horses after she had achieved two hundred and twenty pounds. "No," said great-uncle John Jacob, "my sentiments of chivalry are not dead in my bosom; but neither is my common sense, to say nothing of charity to our faithful dumb friends. And the greatest of these is charity." It was suggested to great-uncle John Jacob that charity should forbid him to wound great-aunt Keziah's female vanity by such a comment on her figure. "Female vanity will recover," said great-uncle John Jacob, callously, "but what about my horses' backs? And if she had the proper female vanity in the first place, she would never have got into such shape." Well, great-aunt Keziah was famous for her heft, and wasn't she in the family? But something seemed to happen to their father's memory when he thought of the girls he had known in the family of his youth, and he declared steadfastly they had all been, in every generation without exception, as slim as reeds and graceful as sylphs.

This loyalty of their father's in the face of evidence contrary to his ideal had its springs in family feeling, and a love of legend that he shared with the others. They loved to tell stories, romantic and poetic, or comic with a romantic humor; they did not gild the outward circumstance, it was the feeling that mattered. Their hearts and imaginations were captivated by their past, a past in which worldly considerations had played a very minor role. Their stories were almost always love stories against a bright blank heavenly blue sky.

Photographs, portraits by inept painters who meant earnestly to flatter, and the festival garments folded away in dried herbs and camphor were disappointing when the little girls tried to fit them to the living beings created in their minds by the breathing words of their elders. Grandmother, twice a year compelled in her blood by the change of seasons, would sit nearly all of one day beside old trunks and boxes in the lumber room, unfolding layers of garments and small keepsakes; she spread them out on sheets on the floor around her, crying over certain things, nearly always the same things, looking again at pictures in velvet cases, unwrapping locks of hair and dried flowers, crying gently and easily as if tears were the only pleasure she had left.

If Maria and Miranda were very quiet, and touched nothing until it was offered, they might sit by her at these times, or come and go. There was a tacit understanding that her grief was strictly her own, and must not be noticed or mentioned. The little girls examined the objects, one by one, and did not find them, in themselves, impressive. Such dowdy little wreaths and necklaces, some of them made of pearly shells; such moth-eaten bunches of pink ostrich feathers for the hair; such clumsy big breast pins and bracelets of gold and colored enamel; such silly-looking combs, standing up on tall teeth capped with seed pearls and French paste. Miranda, without knowing why, felt melancholy. It seemed such a pity that these faded things, these yellowed long gloves and misshapen satin slippers, these broad ribbons cracking where they were folded, should have been all those vanished girls had to decorate themselves with. And where were they now, those girls, and the boys in the odd-looking collars? The young men seemed even more unreal than the girls, with their high-buttoned coats, their puffy neckties, their waxed mustaches, their waving thick hair combed carefully over their foreheads. Who could have taken them seriously, looking like that?

No, Maria and Miranda found it impossible to sympathize with those young persons, sitting rather stiffly before the camera, hopelessly out of fashion; but they were drawn and held by the mysterious love of the living, who remembered and cherished these dead. The visible remains were nothing; they were dust, perishable as the flesh; the features stamped on paper and metal were nothing, but their living memory enchanted the little girls. They listened, all ears and eager minds, picking here and there among the floating ends of narrative, patching together as well as they could fragments of tales that were like bits of poetry or music, indeed were associated with the poetry they had heard or read, with music, with the theater.

"Tell me again how Aunt Amy went away when she was married." "She ran into the gray cold and stepped into the carriage and turned and smiled with her face as pale as death, and called out 'Good-by, good-by,' and refused her cloak, and said, 'Give me a glass of wine.' And none of us saw her alive again." "Why wouldn't she wear her cloak, Cousin Cora?" "Because she was not in love, my dear." Ruin hath taught me thus to ruminate, that time will come and take my love away. "Was she really beautiful, Uncle Bill?" "As an angel, my child." There were golden-haired angels with long blue pleated skirts dancing around the throne of the Blessed Virgin. None of them

resembled Aunt Amy in the least, nor the type of beauty they had been brought up to admire. There were points of beauty by which one was judged severely. First, a beauty must be tall; whatever color the eyes, the hair must be dark, the darker the better; the skin must be pale and smooth. Lightness and swiftness of movement were important points. A beauty must be a good dancer, superb on horseback, with a serene manner, an amiable gaiety tempered with dignity at all hours. Beautiful teeth and hands, of course, and over and above all this, some mysterious crown of enchantment that attracted and held the heart. It was all very exciting and discouraging.

Miranda persisted through her childhood in believing, in spite of her smallness, thinness, her little snubby nose saddled with freckles, her speckled gray eyes and habitual tantrums, that by some miracle she would grow into a tall, cream-colored brunette, like cousin Isabel; she decided always to wear a trailing white satin gown. Maria, born sensible, had no such illusions. "We are going to take after Mamma's family," she said. "It's no use, we are. We'll never be beautiful, we'll always have freckles. And *you*," she told Miranda, "haven't even a good disposition."

Miranda admitted both truth and justice in this unkindness, but still secretly believed that she would one day suddenly receive beauty, as by inheritance, riches laid suddenly in her hands through no deserts of her own. She believed for quite a while that she would one day be like Aunt Amy, not as she appeared in the photograph, but as she was remembered by those who had seen her.

When Cousin Isabel came out in her tight black riding habit, surrounded by young men, and mounted gracefully, drawing her horse up and around so that he pranced learnedly on one spot while the other riders sprang to their saddles in the same sedate flurry, Miranda's heart would close with such a keen dart of admiration, envy, vicarious pride it was almost painful; but there would always be an elder present to lay a cooling hand upon her emotions. "She rides almost as well as Amy, doesn't she? But Amy had the pure Spanish style, she could bring out paces in a horse no one else knew he had." Young namesake Amy, on her way to a dance, would swish through the hall in ruffled white taffeta, glimmering like a moth in the lamplight, carrying her elbows pointed backward stiffly as wings, sliding along as if she were on rollers, in the fashionable walk of her day. She was considered the best dancer at any party, and

Maria, sniffing the wave of perfume that followed Amy, would clasp her hands and say, "Oh, I can't *wait* to be grown up." But the elders would agree that the first Amy had been lighter, more smooth and delicate in her waltzing; young Amy would never equal her. Cousin Molly Parrington, far past her youth, indeed she belonged to the generation before Aunt Amy, was a noted charmer. Men who had known her all her life still gathered about her; now that she was happily widowed for the second time there was no doubt that she would yet marry again. But Amy, said the elders, had the same high spirits and wit without boldness, and you really could not say that Molly had ever been discreet. She dyed her hair, and made jokes about it. She had a way of collecting the men around her in a corner, where she told them stories. She was an unnatural mother to her ugly daughter Eva, an old maid past forty while her mother was still the belle of the ball. "Born when I was fifteen, you remember," Molly would say shamelessly, looking an old beau straight in the eye, both of them remembering that he had been best man at her first wedding when she was past twenty-one. "Everyone said I was like a little girl with her doll."

Eva, shy and chinless, straining her upper lip over two enormous teeth, would sit in corners watching her mother. She looked hungry, her eyes were strained and tired. She wore her mother's old clothes, made over, and taught Latin in a Female Seminary. She believed in votes for women, and had traveled about, making speeches. When her mother was not present, Eva bloomed out a little, danced prettily, smiled, showing all her teeth, and was like a dry little plant set out in a gentle rain. Molly was merry about her ugly duckling. "It's lucky for me my daughter is an old maid. She's not so apt," said Molly naughtily, "to make a grandmother of me." Eva would blush as if she had been slapped.

Eva was a blot, no doubt about it, but the little girls felt she belonged to their everyday world of dull lessons to be learned, stiff shoes to be limbered up, scratchy flannels to be endured in cold weather, measles and disappointed expectations. Their Aunt Amy belonged to the world of poetry. The romance of Uncle Gabriel's long, unrewarded love for her, her early death, was such a story as one found in old books: unworldly books, but true, such as the Vita Nuova, the Sonnets of Shakespeare and the Wedding Song of Spenser; and poems by Edgar Allan Poe. "Her tantalized spirit now blandly reposes, Forgetting or never regretting

its roses. . . ." Their father read that to them, and said, "He was our greatest poet," and they knew that "our" meant he was Southern. Aunt Amy was real as the pictures in the old Holbein and Dürer books were real. The little girls lay flat on their stomachs and peered into a world of wonder, turning the shabby leaves that fell apart easily, not surprised at the sight of the Mother of God sitting on a hollow log nursing her Child; not doubting either Death or the Devil riding at the stirrups of the grim knight; not questioning the propriety of the stiffly dressed ladies of Sir Thomas More's household, seated in dignity on the floor, or seeming to be. They missed all the dog and pony shows, and lantern-slide entertainments, but their father took them to see "Hamlet," and "The Taming of the Shrew," and "Richard the Third," and a long sad play with Mary, Queen of Scots, in it. Miranda thought the magnificent lady in black velvet was truly the Queen of Scots, and was pained to learn that the real Queen had died long ago, and not at all on the night she, Miranda, had been present.

The little girls loved the theater, that world of personages taller than human beings, who swept upon the scene and invested it with their presences, their more than human voices, their gestures of gods and goddesses ruling a universe. But there was always a voice recalling other and greater occasions. Grandmother in her youth had heard Jenny Lind, and thought that Nellie Melba was much overrated. Father had seen Bernhardt, and Madame Modjeska was no sort of rival. When Paderewski played for the first time in their city, cousins came from all over the state and went from the grandmother's house to hear him. The little girls were left out of this great occasion. They shared the excitement of the going away, and shared the beautiful moment of return, when cousins stood about in groups, with coffee cups and glasses in their hands, talking in low voices, awed and happy. The little girls, struck with the sense of a great event, hung about in their nightgowns and listened, until someone noticed and hustled them away from the sweet nimbus of all that glory. One old gentleman, however, had heard Rubinstein frequently. He could not but feel that Rubinstein had reached the final height of musical interpretation, and, for him, Paderewski had been something of an anticlimax. The little girls heard him muttering on, holding up one hand, patting the air as if he were calling for silence. The others looked at him, and listened, without any disturbance of their grave tender mood. They had never heard Rubinstein; they had, one hour since, heard Paderewski, and why should anyone need to recall the past? Miranda, dragged away, half understanding the old gentleman, hated him. She felt that she too had heard Paderewski.

There was then a life beyond a life in this world, as well as in the next; such episodes confirmed for the little girls the nobility of human feeling, the divinity of man's vision of the unseen, the importance of life and death, the depths of the human heart, the romantic value of tragedy. Cousin Eva, on a certain visit, trying to interest them in the study of Latin, told them the story of John Wilkes Booth, who, handsomely garbed in a long black cloak, had leaped to the stage after assassinating President Lincoln. "'Sic semper tyrannis,'" he had shouted superbly, in spite of his broken leg. The little girls never doubted that it had happened in just that way, and the moral seemed to be that one should always have Latin, or at least a good classical poetry quotation, to depend upon in great or desperate moments. Cousin Eva reminded them that no one, not even a good Southerner, could possibly approve of John Wilkes Booth's deed. It was murder, after all. They were to remember that. But Miranda, used to tragedy in books and in family legends—two great-uncles had committed suicide and a remote ancestress had gone mad for love—decided that, without the murder, there would have been no point to dressing up and leaping to the stage shouting in Latin. So how could she disapprove of the deed? It was a fine story. She knew a distantly related old gentleman who had been devoted to the art of Booth, had seen him in a great many plays, but not, alas, at his greatest moment. Miranda regretted this; it would have been so pleasant to have the assassination of Lincoln in the family.

Uncle Gabriel, who had loved Aunt Amy so desperately, still lived somewhere, though Miranda and Maria had never seen him. He had gone away, far away, after her death. He still owned racehorses, and ran them at famous tracks all over the country, and Miranda believed there could not possibly be a more brilliant career. He had married again, quite soon, and had written to Grandmother, asking her to accept his new wife as a daughter in place of Amy. Grandmother had written coldly, accepting, inviting them for a visit, but Uncle Gabriel had somehow never brought his bride home. Harry had visited them in New Or-

leans, and reported that the second wife was a good-looking well-bred blonde girl who would undoubtedly be a good wife for Gabriel. Still, Uncle Gabriel's heart was broken. Faithfully once a year he wrote a letter to someone of the family, sending money for a wreath for Amy's grave. He had written a poem for her gravestone, and had come home, leaving his second wife in Atlanta, to see that it was carved properly. He could never account for having written this poem; he had certainly never tried to write a single rhyme since leaving school. Yet one day when he had been thinking about Amy, the verse occurred to him, out of the air. Maria and Miranda had seen it, printed in gold on a mourning card. Uncle Gabriel had sent a great number of them to be handed around among the family.

> "She lives again who suffered life,
> Then suffered death, and now set free
> A singing angel, she forgets
> The griefs of old mortality."

"Did she really sing?" Maria asked her father.

"Now what has that to do with it?" he asked. "It's a poem."

"I think it's very pretty," said Miranda, impressed. Uncle Gabriel was second cousin to her father and Aunt Amy. It brought poetry very near.

"Not so bad for tombstone poetry," said their father, "but it should be better."

Uncle Gabriel had waited five years to marry Aunt Amy. She had been ill, her chest was weak; she was engaged twice to other young men and broke her engagements for no reason; and she laughed at the advice of older and kinder-hearted persons who thought it very capricious of her not to return the devotion of such a handsome and romantic young man as Gabriel, her second cousin, too; it was not as if she would be marrying a stranger. Her coldness was said to have driven Gabriel to a wild life and even to drinking. His grandfather was wealthy and Gabriel was his favorite; they had quarreled over the racehorses, and Gabriel had shouted, "By God, I must have *something.*" As if he had not everything already: youth, health, good looks, the prospect of riches, and a devoted family circle. His grandfather pointed out to him that he was little better than an ingrate, and showed signs of being a wastrel as well. Gabriel said, "You had racehorses, and made a good thing of them." "I never depended upon them for a livelihood, sir," said his grandfather.

Gabriel wrote letters about this and many other

things to Amy from Saratoga and from Kentucky and from New Orleans, sending her presents, and flowers packed in ice, and telegrams. The presents were amusing, such as a huge cage full of small green lovebirds; or, as an ornament for her hair, a full-petaled enameled rose with paste dewdrops, with an enameled butterfly in brilliant colors suspended quivering on a gold wire about it; but the telegrams always frightened her mother, and the flowers, after a journey by train and then by stage into the country, were much the worse for wear. He would send roses when the rose garden at home was in full bloom. Amy could not help smiling over it, though her mother insisted it was touching and sweet of Gabriel. It must prove to Amy that she was always in his thoughts.

"That's no place for me," said Amy, but she had a way of speaking, a tone of voice, which made it impossible to discover what she meant by what she said. It was possible always that she might be serious. And she would not answer questions.

"Amy's wedding dress," said the grandmother, unfurling an immense cloak of dove-colored cut velvet, spreading beside it a silvery-gray watered-silk frock, and a small gray velvet toque with a dark red breast of feathers. Cousin Isabel, the beauty, sat with her. They talked to each other, and Miranda could listen if she chose.

"She would not wear white, nor a veil," said Grandmother. "I couldn't oppose her, for I had said my daughters should each have exactly the wedding dress they wanted. But Amy surprised me. 'Now what would I look like in white satin?' she asked. It's true she was pale, but she would have been angelic in it, and all of us told her so. 'I shall wear mourning if I like,' she said, 'it is *my* funeral, you know.' I reminded her that Lou and your mother had worn white with veils and it would please me to have my daughters all alike in that. Amy said, 'Lou and Isabel are not like me,' but I could not persuade her to explain what she meant. One day when she was ill she said, 'Mammy, I'm not long for this world,' but not as if she meant it. I told her, 'You might live as long as anyone, if only you will be sensible.' 'That's the whole trouble,' said Amy. 'I feel sorry for Gabriel,' she told me. 'He doesn't know what he's asking for.'

"I tried to tell her once more," said the grandmother, "that marriage and children would cure her of everything. 'All women of our family are delicate when they are young,' I said. 'Why, when

I was your age no one expected me to live a year. It was called greensickness, and everybody knew there was only one cure.' 'If I live for a hundred years and turn green as grass,' said Amy, 'I still shan't want to marry Gabriel.' So I told her very seriously that if she truly felt that way she must never do it, and Gabriel must be told once for all, and sent away. He would get over it. 'I have told him, and I have sent him away,' said Amy. 'He just doesn't listen.' We both laughed at this, and I told her young girls found a hundred ways to deny they wished to be married, and a thousand more to test their power over men, but that she had more than enough of that, and now it was time for her to be entirely sincere and make her decision. As for me," said the grandmother, "I wished with all heart to marry your grandfather, and if he had not asked me, I should have asked him most certainly. Amy insisted that she could not imagine wanting to marry anybody. She would be, she said, a nice old maid like Eva Parrington. For even then it was pretty plain that Eva was an old maid, born. Harry said, 'Oh, Eva—Eva has no chin, that's her trouble. If you had no chin, Amy, you'd be in the same fix as Eva, no doubt.' Your Uncle Bill would say, 'When women haven't anything else, they'll take a vote for consolation. A pretty thin bed-fellow,' said your Uncle Bill. 'What I really need is a good dancing partner to guide me through life,' said Amy, 'that's the match I'm looking for.' It was no good trying to talk to her."

Her brothers remembered her tenderly as a sensible girl. After listening to their comments on her character and ways, Maria decided that they considered her sensible because she asked their advice about her appearance when she was going out to dance. If they found fault in any way, she would change her dress or her hair until they were pleased, and say, "You are an angel not to let your poor sister go out looking like a freak." But she would not listen to her father, nor to Gabriel. If Gabriel praised the frock she was wearing, she was apt to disappear and come back in another. He loved her long black hair, and once, lifting it up from her pillow when she was ill, said, "I love your hair, Amy, the most beautiful hair in the world." When he returned on his next visit, he found her with her hair cropped and curled close to her head. He was horrified, as if she had willfully mutilated herself. She would not let it grow again, not even to please her brothers. The photograph hanging on the wall was one she had made at that time to send to Gabriel, who sent it back without a word.

This pleased her, and she framed the photograph. There was a thin inky scrawl low in one corner, "To dear brother Harry, who likes my hair cut."

This was a mischievous reference to a very grave scandal. The little girls used to look at their father, and wonder what would have happened if he had really hit the young man he shot at. The young man was believed to have kissed Aunt Amy, when she was not in the least engaged to him. Uncle Gabriel was supposed to have had a duel with the young man, but Father had got there first. He was a pleasant, everyday sort of father, who held his daughters on his knee if they were prettily dressed and well behaved, and pushed them away if they had not freshly combed hair and nicely scrubbed fingernails. "Go away, you're disgusting," he would say, in a matter-of-fact voice. He noticed if their stocking seams were crooked. He caused them to brush their teeth with a revolting mixture of prepared chalk, powdered charcoal and salt. When they behaved stupidly he could not endure the sight of them. They understood dimly that all this was for their own future good; and when they were snively with colds, he prescribed delicious hot toddy for them, and saw that it was given them. He was always hoping they might not grow up to be so silly as they seemed to him at any given moment, and he had a disconcerting way of inquiring, "How do you *know?*" when they forgot and made dogmatic statements in his presence. It always came out embarrassingly that they did not know at all, but were repeating something they had heard. This made conversation with him difficult, for he laid traps and they fell into them, but it became important to them that their father should not believe them to be fools. Well, this very father had gone to Mexico once and stayed there for nearly a year, because he had shot at a man with whom Aunt Amy had flirted at a dance. It had been very wrong of him, because he should have challenged the man to a duel, as Uncle Gabriel had done. Instead, he just took a shot at him, and this was the lowest sort of manners. It had caused great disturbance in the whole community and had almost broken up the affair between Aunt Amy and Uncle Gabriel for good. Uncle Gabriel insisted that the young man had kissed Aunt Amy, and Aunt Amy insisted that the young man had merely paid her a compliment on her hair.

During the Mardi Gras holidays there was to be a big gay fancy-dress ball. Harry was going as a bull-fighter because his sweetheart, Mariana, had

a new black lace mantilla and high comb from Mexico. Maria and Miranda had seen a photograph of their mother in this dress, her lovely face without a trace of coquetry looking gravely out from under a tremendous fall of lace from the peak of the comb, a rose tucked firmly over her ear. Amy copied her costume from a small Dresden-china shepherdess which stood on the mantelpiece in the parlor; a careful copy with ribboned hat, gilded crook, very low-laced bodice, short basket skirts, green slippers and all. She wore it with a black half-mask, but it was no disguise. "You would have known it was Amy at any distance," said Father. Gabriel, six feet three in height as he was, had got himself up to match, and a spectacle he provided in pale blue satin knee breeches and a blond curled wig with a hair ribbon. "He felt a fool, and he looked like one," said Uncle Bill, "and he behaved like one before the evening was over."

Everything went beautifully until the party gathered downstairs to leave for the ball. Amy's father —he must have been born a grandfather, thought Miranda—gave one glance at his daughter, her white ankles shining, bosom deeply exposed, two rounds spots of paint on her cheeks, and fell into a frenzy of outraged propriety. "It's disgraceful," he pronounced, loudly. "No daughter of mine is going to show herself in such a rig-out. It's bawdy," he thundered. "Bawdy!"

Amy had taken off her mask to smile at him. "Why, Papa," she said very sweetly, "what's wrong with it? Look on the mantelpiece. She's been there all along, and you were never shocked before."

"There's all the difference in the world," said her father, "all the difference, young lady, and you know it. You go upstairs this minute and pin up that waist in front and let down those skirts to a decent length before you leave this house. *And wash your face!*"

"I see nothing wrong with it," said Amy's mother, firmly, "and you shouldn't use such language before innocent young girls." She and Amy sat down with several females of the household to help, and they made short work of the business. In ten minutes Amy returned, face clean, bodice filled in with lace, shepherdess skirt modestly sweeping the carpet behind her.

When Amy appeared from the dressing room for her first dance with Gabriel, the lace was gone from her bodice, her skirts were tucked up more daringly than before, and the spots on her cheeks were like pomegranates. "Now Gabriel, tell me truly, wouldn't it have been a pity to spoil my costume?" Gabriel, delighted that she had asked his opinion, declared it was perfect. They agreed with kindly tolerance that old people were often tiresome, but one need not upset them by open disobedience: their youth was gone, what had they to live for?

Harry, dancing with Mariana who swung a heavy train around her expertly at every turn of the waltz, began to be uneasy about his sister Amy. She was entirely too popular. He saw young men make beelines across the floor, eyes fixed on those white silk ankles. Some of the young men he did not know at all, others he knew too well and could not approve of for his sister Amy. Gabriel, unhappy in his lyric satin and wig, stood about holding his ribboned crook as though it had sprouted thorns. He hardly danced at all with Amy, he did not enjoy dancing with anyone else, and he was having a thoroughly wretched time of it.

There appeared late, alone, got up as Jean Lafitte, a young Creole gentleman who had, two years before, been for a time engaged to Amy. He came straight to her, with the manner of a happy lover, and said, clearly enough for everyone near by to hear him, "I only came because I knew you were to be here. I only want to dance with you and I shall go again." Amy, with a face of delight, cried out, "Raymond!" as if to a lover. She had danced with him four times, and had then disappeared from the floor on his arm.

Harry and Mariana, in conventional disguise of romance, irreproachably betrothed, safe in their happiness, were waltzing slowly to their favorite song, the melancholy farewell of the Moorish King on leaving Granada. They sang in whispers to each other, in their uncertain Spanish, a song of love and parting and that sword's point of grief that makes the heart tender towards all other lost and disinherited creatures: Oh, mansion of love, my earthly paradise . . . that I shall see no more . . . whither flies the poor swallow, weary and homeless, seeking for shelter where no shelter is? I too am far from home without the power to fly. . . . Come to my heart, sweet bird, beloved pilgrim, build your nest near my bed, let me listen to your song, and weep for my lost land of joy. . . .

Into this bliss broke Gabriel. He had thrown away his shepherd's crook and he was carrying his wig. He wanted to speak to Harry at once, and before Mariana knew what was happening she was sitting beside her mother and the two excited

young men were gone. Waiting, disturbed and displeased, she smiled at Amy who waltzed past with a long man in Devil costume, including ill-fitting scarlet cloven hoofs. Almost at once, Harry and Gabriel came back, with serious faces, and Harry darted on the dance floor, returning with Amy. The girls and the chaperones were asked to come at once, they must be taken home. It was all mysterious and sudden, and Harry said to Mariana, "I will tell you what is happening, but not now—"

The grandmother remembered of this disgraceful affair only that Gabriel brought Amy home alone and that Harry came in somewhat later. The other members of the party straggled in at various hours, and the story came out piecemeal. Amy was silent and, her mother discovered later, burning with fever. "I saw at once that something was very wrong. 'What happened, Amy?' 'Oh, Harry goes about shooting at people at a party,' she said, sitting down as if she were exhausted. 'It was on your account, Amy,' said Gabriel. 'Oh, no, it was not,' said Amy. 'Don't believe him, Mammy.' So I said, 'Now enough of this. Tell me what happened, Amy.' And Amy said, 'Mammy, this is it. Raymond came in, and you know I like Raymond, and he is a good dancer. So we danced together, too much, maybe. We went on the gallery for a breath of air, and stood there. He said, "How well your hair looks. I like this new shingled style."' She glanced at Gabriel. 'And then another young man came out and said, "I've been looking everywhere. This is our dance, isn't it?" And I went in to dance. And now it seems that Gabriel went out at once and challenged Raymond to a duel about something or other, but Harry doesn't wait for that. Raymond had already gone out to have his horse brought, I suppose one doesn't duel in fancy dress,' she said, looking at Gabriel, who fairly shriveled in his blue satin shepherd's costume, 'and Harry simply went out and shot at him. I don't think that was fair,' said Amy."

Her mother agreed that indeed it was not fair; it was not even decent, and she could not imagine what her son Harry thought he was doing. "It isn't much of a way to defend your sister's honor," she said to him afterward. "I didn't want Gabriel to go fighting duels," said Harry. "That wouldn't have helped much, either."

Gabriel had stood before Amy, leaning over, asking once more the question he had apparently been asking her all the way home. "Did he kiss you, Amy?"

Amy took off her shepherdess hat and pushed her hair back. "Maybe he did," she answered, "and maybe I wished him to."

"Amy, you must not say such things," said her mother. "Answer Gabriel's question."

"He hasn't the right to ask it," said Amy, but without anger.

"Do you love him, Amy?" asked Gabriel, the sweat standing out on his forehead.

"It doesn't matter," answered Amy, leaning back in her chair.

"Oh, it does matter; it matters terribly," said Gabriel. "You must answer me now." He took both of her hands and tried to hold them. She drew her hands away firmly and steadily so that he had to let go.

"Let her alone, Gabriel," said Amy's mother. "You'd better go now. We are all tired. Let's talk about it tomorrow."

She helped Amy to undress, noticing the changed bodice and the shortened skirt. "You shouldn't have done that, Amy. That was not wise of you. It was better the other way."

Amy said, "Mammy, I'm sick of this world. I don't like anything in it. It's so *dull*," she said, and for a moment she looked as if she might weep. She had never been tearful, even as a child, and her mother was alarmed. It was then she discovered that Amy had fever.

"Gabriel is dull, Mother—he sulks," she said. "I could see him sulking every time I passed. It spoils things," she said. "Oh, I want to go to sleep."

Her mother sat looking at her and wondering how it had happened she had brought such a beautiful child into the world. "Her face," said her mother, "was angelic in sleep."

Some time during that fevered night, the projected duel between Gabriel and Raymond was halted by the offices of friends on both sides. There remained the open question of Harry's impulsive shot, which was not so easily settled. Raymond seemed vindictive about that, it was possible he might choose to make trouble. Harry, taking the advice of Gabriel, his brothers and friends, decided that the best way to avoid further scandal was for him to disappear for a while. This being decided upon, the young men returned about daybreak, saddled Harry's best horse and helped him pack a few things; accompanied by Gabriel and Bill, Harry set out for the border, feeling rather gay and adventurous.

Amy, being wakened by the stirring in the house, found ont the the plan. Five minutes after they were gone, she came down in her riding dress, had her own horse saddled, and struck out after them. She rode almost every morning; before her parents had time to be uneasy over her prolonged absence, they found her note.

What had threatened to be a tragedy became a rowdy lark. Amy rode to the border, kissed her brother Harry good-by, and rode back again with Bill and Gabriel. It was a three days' journey, and when they arrived Amy had to be lifted from the saddle. She was really ill by now, but in the gayest of humors. Her mother and father had been prepared to be severe with her, but, at sight of her, their feelings changed. They turned on Bill and Gabriel. "Why did you let her do this?" they asked.

"You know we could not stop her," said Gabriel helplessly, "and she did enjoy herself so much!"

Amy laughed. "Mammy, it was splendid, the most delightful trip I ever had. And if I am to be the heroine of this novel, why shouldn't I make the most of it?"

The scandal, Maria and Miranda gathered, had been pretty terrible. Amy simply took to bed and stayed there, and Harry had skipped out blithely to wait until the little affair blew over. The rest of the family had to receive visitors, write letters, go to church, return calls, and bear the whole brunt, as they expressed it. They sat in the twilight of scandal in their little world, holding themselves very rigidly, in a shared tension as if all their nerves began at a common center. This center had received a blow, and family nerves shuddered, even into the farthest reaches of Kentucky. From whence in due time great-great-aunt Sally Rhea addressed a letter to *Mifs Amy Rhea*. In deep brown ink like dried blood, in a spidery hand adept at archaic symbols and abbreviations, great-great-aunt Sally informed Amy that she was fairly convinced that this calamity was only the forerunner of a series shortly to be visited by the Almighty God upon a race already condemned through its own wickedness, a warning that man's time was short, and that they must all prepare for the end of the world. For herself, she had long expected it, she was entirely resigned to the prospect of meeting her Maker; and Amy, no less than her wicked brother Harry, must likewise place herself in God's hands and prepare for the worst. "Oh, *my dear unfortunate young relative*," twittered great-great-aunt Sally, "*we must in our Extremity join hands and appr before ye Dread Throne of Jdgmnt a United Fmly if One is Mssg from ye Flock, what will Jesus say?"*

Great-great-aunt Sally's religious career had become comic legend. She had forsaken her Catholic rearing for a young man whose family were Cumberland Presbyterians. Unable to accept their opinions, however, she was converted to the Hard-Shell Baptists, a sect as loathsome to her husband's family as the Catholic could possibly be. She had spent a life of vicious self-indulgent martyrdom to her faith; as Harry commented: "Religions put claws on Aunt Sally and gave her a post to whet them on." She had out-argued, out-fought, and out-lived her entire generation, but she did not miss them. She bedeviled the second generation without ceasing, and was beginning hungrily on the third.

Amy, reading this letter, broke into her gay full laugh that always caused everyone around her to laugh too, even before they knew why, and her small green lovebirds in their cage turned and eyed her solemnly. "Imagine drawing a pew in heaven beside Aunt Sally," she said. "What a prospect."

"Don't laugh too soon," said her father. "Heaven was made to order for Aunt Sally. She'll be on her own territory there."

"For my sins," said Amy, "I must go to heaven with Aunt Sally."

During the uncomfortable time of Harry's absence, Amy went on refusing to marry Gabriel. Her mother could hear their voices going on in their endless colloquy, during many long days. One afternoon, Gabriel came out, looking very sober and discouraged. He stood looking down at Amy's mother as she sat sewing, and said, "I think it is all over, I believe now that Amy will never have me." The grandmother always said afterward, "Never have I pitied anyone as I did poor Gabriel at that moment. But I told him, very firmly, 'Let her alone, then, she is ill.'" So Gabriel left, and Amy had no word from him for more than a month.

The day after Gabriel was gone, Amy rose looking extremely well, went hunting with her brothers Bill and Stephen, bought a velvet wrap, had her hair shingled and curled again, and wrote long letters to Harry, who was having a most enjoyable exile in Mexico City.

After dancing all night three times in one week, she woke one morning in a hemorrhage. She seemed frightened and asked for the doctor, promising to do whatever he advised. She was quiet for

a few days, reading. She asked for Gabriel. No one knew where he was. "You should write him a letter; his mother will send it on." "Oh, no," she said. "I miss him coming in with his sour face. Letters are no good."

Gabriel did come in, only a few days later, with a very sour face and unpleasant news. His grandfather had died, after a day's illness. On his death bed, in the name of God, being of a sound and disposing mind, he had cut off his favorite grandchild Gabriel with one dollar. "In the name of God, Amy," said Gabriel, "the old devil has ruined me in one sentence."

It was the conduct of his immediate family in the matter that had embittered him, he said. They could hardly conceal their satisfaction. They had known and envied Gabriel's quite just, well-founded expectations. Not one of them offered to make any private settlement. No one even thought of repairing this last-minute act of senile vengeance. Privately they blessed their luck. "I have been cut off with a dollar," said Gabriel, "and they are all glad of it. I think they feel somehow that this justifies every criticism they ever made against me. They were right about me all along. I am a worthless poor relation," said Gabriel. "My God, I wish you could see them."

Amy said, "I wonder how you will ever support a wife, now."

Gabriel said, "Oh, it isn't so bad as that. If you would, Amy—"

Amy said, "Gabriel, if we get married now there'll be just time to be in New Orleans for Mardi Gras. If we wait until after Lent, it may be too late."

"Why, Amy," said Gabriel, "how could it ever be too late?"

"You might change your mind," said Amy. "You know how fickle you are."

There were two letters in the grandmother's many packets of letters that Maria and Miranda read after they were grown. One of them was from Amy. It was dated ten days after her marriage.

"Dear Mammy, New Orleans hasn't changed as much as I have since we saw each other last. I am now a staid old married woman, and Gabriel is very devoted and kind. Footlights won a race for us yesterday, she was the favorite, and it was wonderful. I go to the races every day, and our horses are doing splendidly; I had my choice of Erin Go Bragh or Miss Lucy, and I chose Miss Lucy. She is mine now, she runs like a streak. Gabriel says I made a mistake, Erin Go Bragh will stay better. I think Miss Lucy will stay my time.

"We are having a lovely visit. I'm going to put on a domino and take to the streets with Gabriel sometime during Mardi Gras. I'm tired of watching the show from a balcony. Gabriel says it isn't safe. He says he'll take me if I insist, but I doubt it. Mammy, he's very nice. Don't worry about me. I have a beautiful black-and-rose-colored velvet gown for the Proteus Ball. Madame, my new mother-in-law, wanted to know if it wasn't a little dashing. I told her I hoped so or I had been cheated. It is fitted perfectly smooth in the bodice, very low in the shoulders—Papa would not approve—and the skirt is looped with wide silver ribbons between the waist and knees in front, and then it surges around and is looped enormously in the back, with a train just one yard long. I now have an eighteen-inch waist, thanks to Madame Duré. I expect to be so dashing that my mother-in-law will have an attack. She has them quite often. Gabriel sends love. Please take good care of Graylie and Fiddler. I want to ride them again when I come home. We're going to Saratoga. I don't know just when. Give everybody my dear dear love. It rains all the time here, of course. . . .

"P.S. Mammy, as soon as I get a minute to myself I'm going to be terribly homesick. Good-by, my darling Mammy."

The other was from Amy's nurse, dated six weeks after Amy's marriage.

"I cut off the lock of hair because I was sure you would like to have it. And I do not want you to think I was careless, leaving her medicine where she could get it, the doctor has written and explained. It would not have done her any harm except that her heart was weak. She did not know how much she was taking, often she said to me, one more of those little capsules wouldn't do any harm, and so I told her to be careful and not take anything except what I gave her. She begged me for them sometimes but I would not give her more than the doctor said. I slept during the night because she did not seem to be so sick as all that and the doctor did not order me to sit up with her. Please accept my regrets at your great loss and please do not think that anybody was careless with your dear daughter. She suffered a great deal and now she is at rest. She could not get well but she might have lived longer. Yours respectfully. . . ."

The letters and all the strange keepsakes were packed away and forgotten for a great many years. They seemed to have no place in the world.

PART II: 1904

During vacation on their grandmother's farm, Maria and Miranda, who read as naturally and constantly as ponies crop grass, and with much the same kind of pleasure, had by some happy chance laid hold of some forbidden reading matter, brought in and left there with missionary intent, no doubt, by some Protestant cousin. It fell into the right hands if enjoyment had been its end. The reading matter was printed in poor type on spongy paper, and was ornamented with smudgy illustrations all the more exciting to the little girls because they could not make head or tail of them. The stories were about beautiful but unlucky maidens, who for mysterious reasons had been trapped by nuns and priests in dire collusion; they were then "immured" in convents, where they were forced to take the veil—an appalling rite during which the victims shrieked dreadfully—and condemned forever after to most uncomfortable and disorderly existences. They seemed to divide their time between lying chained in dark cells and assisting other nuns to bury throttled infants under stones in moldering rat-infested dungeons.

Immured! It was the word Maria and Miranda had been needing all along to describe their condition at the Convent of the Child Jesus, in New Orleans, where they spent the long winters trying to avoid an education. There were no dungeons at the Child Jesus, and this was only one of numerous marked differences between convent life as Maria and Miranda knew it and the thrilling paper-backed version. It was no good at all trying to fit the stories to life, and they did not even try. They had long since learned to draw the lines between life, which was real and earnest, and the grave was not its goal; poetry, which was true, but not real; and stories, or forbidden reading matter, in which things happened as nowhere else, with the most sublime irrelevance and unlikelihood, and one need not turn a hair, because there was not a word of truth in them.

It was true the little girls were hedged and confined, but in a large garden with trees and a grotto; they were locked at night into a long cold dormitory, with all the windows open, and a sister sleeping at either end. Their beds were curtained with muslin, and small night-lamps were so arranged that the sisters could see through the curtains, but the children could not see the sisters. Miranda wondered if they ever slept, or did they sit there all night quietly watching the sleepers through the muslin? She tried to work up a little sinister thrill about this, but she found it impossible to care much what either of the sisters did. They were very dull good-natured women who managed to make the whole dormitory seem dull. All days and all things in the Convent of the Child Jesus were dull, in fact, and Maria and Miranda lived for Saturdays.

No one had even hinted that they should become nuns. On the contrary Miranda felt that the discouraging attitude of Sister Claude and Sister Austin and Sister Ursula towards her expressed ambition to be a nun barely veiled a deeply critical knowledge of her spiritual deficiencies. Still Maria and Miranda had got a fine new word out of their summer reading, and they referred to themselves as "immured." It gave a romantic glint to what was otherwise a very dull life for them, except for blessed Saturday afternoons during the racing season.

If the nuns were able to assure the family that the deportment and scholastic achievements of Maria and Miranda were at least passable, some cousin or other always showed up smiling, in holiday mood, to take them to the races, where they were given a dollar each to bet on any horse they chose. There were black Saturdays now and then, when Maria and Miranda sat ready, hats in hand, curly hair plastered down and slicked behind their ears, their stiffly pleated navy-blue skirts spread out around them, waiting with their hearts going down slowly into their high-topped laced-up black shoes. They never put on their hats until the last minute, for somehow it would have been too horrible to have their hats on, when, after all, Cousin Henry and Cousin Isabel, or Uncle George and Aunt Polly, were not coming to take them to the races. When no one appeared, and Saturday came and went a sickening waste, they were then given to understand that it was a punishment for bad marks during the week. They never knew until it was too late to avoid the disappointment. It was very wearing.

One Saturday they were sent down to wait in the visitors' parlor, and there was their father. He had come all the way from Texas to see them.

They leaped at sight of him, and then stopped short, suspiciously. Was he going to take them to the races? If so, they were happy to see him.

"Hello," said father, kissing their cheeks. "Have you been good girls? Your Uncle Gabriel is running a mare at the Crescent City today, so we'll all go and bet on her. Would you like that?"

Maria put on her hat without a word, but Miranda stood and addressed her father sternly. She had suffered many doubts about this day. "*Why* didn't you send word yesterday? I could have been looking forward all this time."

"We didn't know," said father, in his easiest paternal manner, "that you were going to deserve it. Remember Saturday before last?"

Miranda hung her head and put on her hat, with the round elastic under the chin. She remembered too well. She had, in midweek, given way to despair over her arithmetic and had fallen flat on her face on the classroom floor, refusing to rise until she was carried out. The rest of the week had been a series of novel deprivations, and Saturday a day of mourning; secret mourning, for if one mourned too noisily, it simply meant another bad mark against deportment.

"Never mind," said father, as if it were the smallest possible matter, "today you're going. Come along now. We've barely time."

These expeditions were all joy, every time, from the moment they stepped into a closed one-horse cab, a treat in itself with its dark, thick upholstery, soaked with strange perfumes and tobacco smoke, until the thrilling moment when they walked into a restaurant under big lights and were given dinner with things to eat they never had at home, much less at the convent. They felt worldly and grown up, each with her glass of water colored pink with claret.

The great crowd was always exciting as if they had never seen it before, with the beautiful, incredibly dressed ladies, all plumes and flowers and paint, and the elegant gentlemen with yellow gloves. The bands played in turn with thundering drums and brasses, and now and then a wild beautiful horse would career around the track with a tiny, monkey-shaped boy on his back, limbering up for his race.

Miranda had a secret personal interest in all this which she knew better than to confide to anyone, even Maria. Least of all to Maria. In ten minutes the whole family would have known. She had lately decided to be a jockey when she grew up.

Her father had said one day that she was going to be a little thing all her life, she would never be tall; and this meant, of course, that she would never be a beauty like Aunt Amy, or Cousin Isabel. Her hope of being a beauty died hard, until the notion of being a jockey came suddenly and filled all her thoughts. Quietly, blissfully, at night before she slept, and too often in the daytime when she should have been studying, she planned her career as jockey. It was dim in detail, but brilliant at the right distance. It seemed too silly to be worried about arithmetic at all, when what she needed for her future was to ride better—much better. "You ought to be ashamed of yourself," said father, after watching her gallop full tilt down the lane at the farm, on Trixie, the mustang mare. "I can see the sun, moon and stars between you and the saddle every jump." Spanish style meant that one sat close to the saddle, and did all kinds of things with the knees and reins. Jockeys bounced lightly, their knees almost level with the horse's back, rising and falling like a rubber ball. Miranda felt she could do that easily. Yes, she would be a jockey, like Tod Sloan, winning every other race at least. Meantime, while she was training, she would keep it a secret, and one day she would ride out, bouncing lightly, with the other jockeys, and win a great race, and surprise everybody, her family most of all.

On that particular Saturday, her idol, the great Tod Sloan, was riding, and he won two races. Miranda longed to bet her dollar on Tod Sloan, but father said, "Not now, honey. Today you must bet on Uncle Gabriel's horse. Save your dollar for the fourth race, and put it on Miss Lucy. You've got a hundred to one shot. Think if she wins."

Miranda knew well enough that a hundred to one shot was no bet at all. She sulked, the crumpled dollar in her hand grew damp and warm. She could have won three dollars already on Tod Sloan. Maria said virtuously, "It wouldn't be nice not to bet on Uncle Gabriel. That way, we keep the money in the family." Miranda put out her under lip at her sister. Maria was too prissy for words. She wrinkled her nose back at Miranda.

They had just turned their dollar over to the bookmaker for the fourth race when a vast bulging man with a red face and immense tan ragged mustaches fading into gray hailed them from a lower level of the grandstand, over the heads of the crowd, "Hey, there, Harry?" Father said, "Bless my soul, there's Gabriel." He motioned to the man, who came pushing his way heavily up the shallow steps. Maria and Miranda stared, first at him, then at each other. "Can that be our Uncle Gabriel?" their eyes asked. "Is that Aunt Amy's handsome romantic beau? Is that the man who wrote the poem about our Aunt Amy?" Oh, what did grown-up people *mean* when they talked, anyway?

He was a shabby fat man with bloodshot blue eyes, sad beaten eyes, and a big melancholy laugh, like a groan. He towered over them shouting to their father, "Well, for God's sake, Harry, it's been a coon's age. You ought to come out and look 'em over. You look just like yourself, Harry, how are you?"

The band struck up "Over the River" and Uncle Gabriel shouted louder. "Come on, let's get out of this. What are you doing up here with the pikers?"

"Can't," shouted Father. "Brought my little girls. Here they are."

Uncle Gabriel's bleared eyes beamed blindly upon them. "Fine looking set, Harry," he bellowed, "pretty as pictures, how old are they?"

"Ten and fourteen now," said Father; "awkward ages. Nest of vipers," he boasted, "perfect batch of serpent's teeth. Can't do a thing with 'em." He fluffed up Miranda's hair, pretending to tousle it.

"Pretty as pictures," bawled Uncle Gabriel, "but rolled into one they don't come up to Amy, do they?"

"No, they don't," admitted their father at the top of his voice, "but they're only half-baked." *Over the river, over the river,* moaned the band, *my sweetheart's waiting for me.*

"I've got to get back now," yelled Uncle Gabriel. The little girls felt quite deaf and confused. "Got the God-damnedest jockey in the world, Harry, just my luck. Ought to tie him on. Fell off Fiddler yesterday, just plain fell off on his tail—Remember Amy's mare, Miss Lucy? Well, this is her namesake, Miss Lucy IV. None of 'em ever came up to the first one, though. Stay right where you are, I'll be back."

Maria spoke up boldly. "Uncle Gabriel, tell Miss Lucy we're betting on her." Uncle Gabriel bent down and it looked as if there were tears in his swollen eyes. "God bless your sweet heart," he bellowed, "I'll tell her." He plunged down through the crowd again, his fat back bowed slightly in his loose clothes, his thick neck rolling over his collar.

Miranda and Maria, disheartened by the odds,

by their first sight of their romantic Uncle Gabriel, whose language was so coarse, sat listlessly without watching, their chances missed, their dollars gone, their hearts sore. They didn't even move until their father leaned over and hauled them up. "Watch your horse," he said, in a quick warning voice, "watch Miss Lucy come home."

They stood up, scrambled to their feet on the bench, every vein in them suddenly beating so violently they could hardly focus their eyes, and saw a thin little mahogany-colored streak flash by the judges' stand, only a neck ahead, but their Miss Lucy, oh, their darling, their lovely—oh, Miss Lucy, their Uncle Gabriel's Miss Lucy, had won, had won. They leaped up and down screaming and clapping their hands, their hats falling back on their shoulders, their hair flying wild. *Whoa, you heifer*, squalled the band with snorting brasses, and the crowd broke into a long roar like the falling of the walls of Jericho.

The little girls sat down, feeling quite dizzy, while their father tried to pull their hats straight, and taking out his handkerchief held it to Miranda's face, saying very gently, "Here, blow your nose," and he dried her eyes while he was about it. He stood up then and shook them out of their daze. He was smiling with deep laughing wrinkles around his eyes, and spoke to them as if they were grown young ladies he was squiring around.

"Let's go out and pay our respects to Miss Lucy," he said. "She's the star of the day."

The horses were coming in, looking as if their hides had been drenched and rubbed with soap, their ribs heaving, their nostrils flaring and closing. The jockeys sat bowed and relaxed, their faces calm, moving a little at the waist with the movement of their horses. Miranda noted this for future use; that was the way you came in from a race, easy and quiet, whether you had won or lost. Miss Lucy came last, and a little handful of winners applauded her and cheered the jockey. He smiled and lifted his whip, his eyes and shriveled brown face perfectly serene. Miss Lucy was bleeding at the nose, two thick red rivulets were stiffening her tender mouth and chin, the round velvet chin that Miranda thought the nicest kind of chin in the world. Her eyes were wild and her knees were trembling, and she snored when she drew her breath.

Miranda stood staring. That was winning, too. Her heart clinched tight; that was winning, for Miss Lucy. So instantly and completely did her heart reject that victory, she did not know when

it happened, but she hated it, and was ashamed that she had screamed and shed tears of joy when Miss Lucy, with her bloodied nose and bursting heart, had gone past the judges' stand a neck ahead. She felt empty and sick and held to her father's hand so hard that she shook her off a little impatiently and said, "What is the matter with you? Don't be so fidgety."

Uncle Gabriel was standing there waiting, and he was completely drunk. He watched the mare go in, then leaned against the fence with its whitewashed posts and sobbed openly. "She's got the nosebleed, Harry," he said. "Had it since yesterday. We thought we had her all fixed up. But she did it, all right. She's got a heart like a lion. I'm going to breed her, Harry. Her heart's worth a million dollars, by itself, God bless her." Tears ran over his brick-colored face and into his straggling mustaches. "If anything happens to her now I'll blow my brains out. She's my last hope. She saved my life. I've had a run," he said, groaning into a large handkerchief and mopping his face all over. "I've had a run of luck that would break a brass billy goat. God, Harry, let's go somewhere and have a drink."

"I must get the children back to school first, Gabriel," said their father, taking each by a hand.

"No, no, don't go yet," said Uncle Gabriel desperately. "Wait here a minute, I want to see the vet and take a look at Miss Lucy, and I'll be right back. Don't go, Harry, for God's sake. I want to talk to you a few minutes."

Maria and Miranda, watching Uncle Gabriel's lumbering, unsteady back, were thinking that this was the first time they had ever seen a man that they knew to be drunk. They had seen pictures and read descriptions, and had heard descriptions, so they recognized the symptoms at once. Miranda felt it was an important moment in a great many ways.

"Uncle Gabriel's a drunkard, isn't he?" she asked her father, rather proudly.

"Hush, don't say such things," said father, with a heavy frown, "or I'll never bring you here again." He looked worried and unhappy, and, above all, undecided. The little girls stood stiff with resentment against such obvious injustice. They loosed their hands from his and moved away coldly, standing together in silence. Their father did not notice, watching the place where Uncle Gabriel had disappeared. In a few minutes he came back, still wiping his face, as if there were cobwebs on it, carrying his big black hat. He waved at them from a short distance, calling out in a cheerful way, "She's going to be all right, Harry. It's stopped now. Lord, this will be good news for Miss Honey. Come on, Harry, let's all go home and tell Miss Honey. She deserves some good news."

Father said, "I'd better take the children back to school first, then we'll go."

"No, no," said Uncle Gabriel, fondly. "I want her to see the girls. She'll be tickled pink to see them, Harry. Bring 'em along."

"Is it another race horse we're going to see?" whispered Miranda in her sister's ear.

"Don't be silly," said Maria. "It's Uncle Gabriel's second wife."

"Let's find a cab, Harry," said Uncle Gabriel, "and take your little girls out to cheer up Miss Honey. Both of 'em rolled into one look a lot like Amy, I swear they do. I want Miss Honey to see them. She's always liked our family, Harry, though of course she's not what you'd call an expansive kind of woman."

Maria and Miranda sat facing the driver, and Uncle Gabriel squeezed himself in facing them beside their father. The air became at once bitter and sour with his breathing. He looked sad and poor. His necktie was on crooked and his shirt was rumpled. Father said, "You're going to see Uncle Gabriel's second wife, children," exactly as if they had not heard everything; and to Gabriel, "How *is* your wife nowadays? It must be twenty years since I saw her last."

"She's pretty gloomy, and that's a fact," said Uncle Gabriel. "She's been pretty gloomy for years now, and nothing seems to shake her out of it. She never did care for horses, Harry, if you remember; she hasn't been near the track three times since we were married. When I think how Amy wouldn't have missed a race for anything . . . She's very different from Amy, Harry, a very different kind of woman. As fine a woman as ever lived in her own way, but she hates change and moving around, and she just lives in the boy."

"Where is Gabe now?" asked father.

"Finishing college," said Gabriel; "a smart boy, but awfully like his mother. Awfully like," he said, in a melancholy way. "She hates being away from him. Just wants to sit down in the same town and wait for him to get through with his education. Well, I'm sorry it can't be done if that's what she wants, but God Almighty— And this last run of luck has about got her down. I hope you'll be able to cheer her up a little, Harry, she needs it."

The little girls sat watching the streets grow duller and dingier and narrower, and at last the shabbier and shabbier white people gave way to dressed-up Negroes, and then to shabby Negroes, and after a long way the cab stopped before a desolate-looking little hotel in Elysian Fields. Their father helped Maria and Miranda out, told the cabman to wait, and they followed Uncle Gabriel through a dirty damp-smelling patio, down a long gas-lighted hall full of a terrible smell, Miranda couldn't decide what it was made of but it had a bitter taste even, and up a long staircase with a ragged carpet. Uncle Gabriel pushed open a door without warning, saying, "Come in, here we are."

A tall pale-faced woman with faded straw-colored hair and pink-rimmed eyelids rose suddenly from a squeaking rocking chair. She wore a stiff blue-and-white-striped shirtwaist and a stiff black skirt of some hard shiny material. Her large knuckled hands rose to her round, neat pompadour at sight of her visitors.

"Honey," said Uncle Gabriel, with large false heartiness, "you'll never guess who's come to see you." He gave her a clumsy hug. Her face did not change and her eyes rested steadily on the three strangers. "Amy's brother Harry, Honey, you remember, don't you?"

"Of course," said Miss Honey, putting out her hand straight as a paddle, "of course I remember you, Harry." She did not smile.

"And Amy's two little nieces," went on Uncle Gabriel, bringing them forward. They put out their hands limply, and Miss Honey gave each one a slight flip and dropped it. "And we've got good news for you," went on Uncle Gabriel, trying to bolster up the painful situation. "Miss Lucy stepped out and showed 'em today, Honey. We're rich again, old girl, cheer up."

Miss Honey turned her long, despairing face towards her visitors. "Sit down," she said with a heavy sigh, seating herself and motioning towards various rickety chairs. There was a big lumpy bed, with a grayish-white counterpane on it, a marble-topped washstand, grayish coarse lace curtains on strings at the two small windows, a small closed fireplace with a hole in it for a stovepipe, and two trunks, standing at odds as if somebody were just moving in, or just moving out. Everything was dingy and soiled and neat and bare; not a pin out of place.

"We'll move to the St. Charles tomorrow," said Uncle Gabriel, as much to Harry as to his wife. "Get your best dresses together, Honey, the long dry spell is over."

Miss Honey's nostrils pinched together and she rocked slightly, with her arms folded. "I've lived in the St. Charles before, and I've lived here before," she said, in a tight deliberate voice, "and this time I'll just stay where I am, thank you. I prefer it to moving back here in three months. I'm settled now, I feel at home here," she told him, glancing at Harry, her pale eyes kindling with blue fire, a stiff white line around her mouth.

The little girls sat trying not to stare, miserably ill at ease. Their grandmother had pronounced Harry's children to be the most unteachable she had ever seen in her long experience with the young; but they had learned by indirection one thing well—nice people did not carry on quarrels before outsiders. Family quarrels were sacred, to be waged privately in fierce hissing whispers, low choked mutters and growls. If they did yell and stamp, it must be behind closed doors and windows. Uncle Gabriel's second wife was hopping mad and she looked ready to fly out at Uncle Gabriel any second, with him sitting there like a hound when someone shakes a whip at him.

"She loathes and despises everybody in this room," thought Miranda, coolly, "and she's afraid we won't know it. She needn't worry, we knew it when we came in." With all her heart she wanted to go, but her father, though his face was a study, made no move. He seemed to be trying to think of something pleasant to say. Maria, feeling guilty, though she couldn't think why, was calculating rapidly, "Why, she's only Uncle Gabriel's second wife, and Uncle Gabriel was only married before to Aunt Amy, why, she's no kin at all, and I'm glad of it." Sitting back easily, she let her hands fall open in her lap; they would be going in a few minutes, undoubtedly, and they need never come back.

Then father said, "We mustn't be keeping you, we just dropped in for a few minutes. We wanted to see how you are."

Miss Honey said nothing, but she made a little gesture with her hands, from the wrist, as if to say, "Well, you see how I am, and now what next?"

"I must take these young ones back to school," said father, and Uncle Gabriel said stupidly, "Look, Honey, don't you think they resemble Amy a little? Especially around the eyes, especially Maria, don't you think, Harry?"

Their father glanced at them in turn. "I really couldn't say," he decided, and the little girls saw he was more monstrously embarrassed than ever. He turned to Miss Honey, "I hadn't seen Gabriel for so many years," he said, "we thought of getting out for a talk about old times together. You know how it is."

"Yes, I know," said Miss Honey, rocking a little, and all that she knew gleamed forth in a pallid, unquenchable hatred and bitterness that seemed enough to bring her long body straight up out of the chair in a fury, "I know," and she sat staring at the floor. Her mouth shook and straightened. There was a terrible silence, which was broken when the little girls saw their father rise. They got up, too, and it was all they could do to keep from making a dash for the door.

"I must get the young ones back," said their father. "They've had enough excitement for one day. They each won a hundred dollars on Miss Lucy. It was a good race," he said, in complete wretchedness, as if he simply could not extricate himself from the situation. "Wasn't it, Gabriel?"

"It was a grand race," said Gabriel, brokenly, "a grand race."

Miss Honey stood up and moved a step towards the door. "Do you take them to the races, actually?" she asked, and her lids flickered towards them as if they were loathsome insects, Maria felt.

"If I feel they deserve a little treat, yes," said their father, in an easy tone but with wrinkled brow.

"I had rather, much rather," said Miss Honey clearly, "see my son dead at my feet than hanging around a race track."

The next few moments were rather a blank, but at last they were out of it, going down the stairs, across the patio, with Uncle Gabriel seeing them back into the cab. His face was sagging, the features had fallen as if the flesh had slipped from the bones, and his eyelids were puffed and blue. "Good-by, Harry," he said soberly. "How long you expect to be here?"

"Starting back tomorrow," said Harry. "Just dropped in on a little business and to see how the girls were getting along."

"Well," said Uncle Gabriel, "I may be dropping into your part of the country one of these days. Good-by, children," he said, taking their hands one after the other in his big warm paws. "They're nice children, Harry. I'm glad you won on Miss Lucy," he said to the little girls, tenderly. "Don't spend your money foolishly, now. Well, so long, Harry." As the cab jolted away he stood there fat and sagging, holding up his arm and wagging his hand at them.

"Goodness," said Maria, in her most grown-up

manner, taking her hat off and hanging it over her knee, "I'm glad that's over."

"What I want to know is," said Miranda, "*is* Uncle Gabriel a real drunkard?"

"Oh, hush," said their father, sharply, "I've got the heartburn."

There was a respectful pause, as before a public monument. When their father had the heartburn it was time to lay low. The cab rumbled on, back to clean gay streets, with the lights coming on in the early February darkness, past shimmering shop windows, smooth pavements, on and on, past beautiful old houses set in deep gardens, on, on back to the dark walls with the heavy-topped trees hanging over them. Miranda sat thinking so hard she forgot and spoke out in her thoughtless way: "I've decided I'm not going to be a jockey, after all." She could as usual have bitten her tongue, but as usual it was too late.

Father cheered up and twinkled at her knowingly, as if that didn't surprise him in the least. "Well, well," said he, "so you aren't going to be a jockey! That's very sensible of you. I think she ought to be a lion-tamer, don't you, Maria? That's a nice, womanly profession."

Miranda, seeing Maria from the height of her fourteen years suddenly joining with their father to laugh at her, made an instant decision and laughed with them at herself. That was better. Everybody laughed and it was such a relief.

"Where's my hundred dollars?" asked Maria, anxiously.

"It's going in the bank," said their father, "and yours too," he told Miranda. "That is your nest-egg."

"Just so they don't buy my stockings with it," said Miranda, who had long resented the use of her Christmas money by their grandmother. "I've got enough stockings to last me a year."

"I'd like to buy a racehorse," said Maria, "but I know it's not enough." The limitations of wealth oppressed her. "*What* could you buy with a hundred dollars?" she asked fretfully.

"Nothing, nothing at all," said their father, "a hundred dollars is just something you put in the bank."

Maria and Miranda lost interest. They had won a hundred dollars on a horse race once. It was already in the far past. They began to chatter about something else.

The lay sister opened the door on a long cord, from behind the grille; Maria and Miranda walked in silently to their familiar world of shining bare floors and insipid wholesome food and cold-water washing and regular prayers; their world of poverty, chastity and obedience, of early to bed and early to rise, of sharp little rules and tittle-tattle. Resignation was in their childish faces as they held them up to be kissed.

"Be good girls," said their father, in the strange serious, rather helpless way he always had when he told them good-by. "Write to your daddy, now, nice long letters," he said, holding their arms firmly for a moment before letting go for good. Then he disappeared, and the sister swung the door closed after him.

Maria and Miranda went upstairs to the dormitory to wash their faces and hands and slick down their hair again before supper.

Miranda was hungry. "We didn't have a thing to eat, after all," she grumbled. "Not even a chocolate nut bar. I think that's mean. We didn't even get a quarter to spend," she said.

"Not a living bite," said Maria. "Not a nickel." She poured out cold water into the bowl and rolled up her sleeves.

Another girl about her own age came in and went to a washbowl near another bed. "Where have you been?" she asked. "Did you have a good time?"

"We went to the races, with our father," said Maria, soaping her hands.

"Our uncle's horse won," said Miranda.

"My goodness," said the other girl, vaguely, "that must have been grand."

Maria looked at Miranda, who was rolling up her own sleeves. She tried to feel martyred, but it wouldn't go. "Immured for another week," she said, her eyes sparkling over the edge of her towel.

PART III: 1912

Miranda followed the porter down the stuffy aisle of the sleeping-car, where the berths were nearly all made down and the dusty green curtains buttoned to a seat at the further end. "Now yo' berth's ready any time, Miss," said the porter.

"But I want to sit up a while," said Miranda. A very thin old lady raised choleric black eyes and fixed upon her a regard of unmixed disapproval. She had two immense front teeth and a receding chin, but she did not lack character. She had piled her luggage around her like a barricade, and she glared at the porter when he picked some of it up to make room for his new passenger. Miranda sat, saying mechanically, "May I?"

"You may, indeed," said the old lady, for she seemed old in spite of a certain brisk, rustling energy. Her taffeta petticoats creaked like hinges every time she stirred. With ferocious sarcasm, after a half second's pause, she added, "You may be so good as to get off my hat!"

Miranda rose instantly in horror, and handed to the old lady a wilted contrivance of black horse-hair braid and shattered white poppies. "I'm dreadfully sorry," she stammered, for she had been brought up to treat ferocious old ladies respectfully, and this one seemed capable of spanking her, then and there. "I didn't dream it was your hat."

"And whose hat did you dream it might be?" inquired the old lady, baring her teeth and twirling the hat on a forefinger to restore it.

"I didn't think it was a hat at all," said Miranda with a touch of hysteria.

"Oh, you didn't think it was a hat? Where on earth are your eyes, child?" and she proved the nature and function of the object by placing it on her head at a somewhat tipsy angle, though still it did not much resemble a hat. "Now can you see what it is?"

"Yes, oh, yes," said Miranda, with a meekness she hoped was disarming. She ventured to sit again after a careful inspection of the narrow space she was to occupy.

"Well, well," said the old lady, "let's have the porter remove some of these encumbrances," and she stabbed the bell with a lean sharp forefinger. There followed a flurry of rearrangements, during which they both stood in the aisle, the old lady giving a series of impossible directions to the Negro which he bore philosophically while he disposed of the luggage exactly as he had meant to do. Seated again, the old lady asked in a kindly, authoritative tone, "And what might your name be, child?"

At Miranda's answer, she blinked somewhat, unfolded her spectacles, straddled them across her high nose competently, and took a good long look at the face beside her.

"If I'd had my spectacles on," she said, in an astonishingly changed voice, "I might have known. I'm Cousin Eva Parrington," she said, "Cousin Molly Parrington's daughter, remember? I knew you when you were a little girl. You were a lively little girl," she added as if to console her, "and very opinionated. The last thing I heard about you,

you were planning to be a tight-rope walker. You were going to play the violin and walk the tight-rope at the same time."

"I must have seen it at the vaudeville show," said Miranda. "I couldn't have invented it. Now I'd like to be an air pilot!"

"I used to go to dances with your father," said Cousin Eva, busy with her own thoughts, "and to big holiday parties at your grandmother's house, long before you were born. Oh, indeed, yes, a long time before."

Miranda remembered several things at once. Aunt Amy had threatened to be an old maid like Eva. Oh, Eva, the trouble with her is she has no chin. Eva has given up, and is teaching Latin in a Female Seminary. Eva's gone out for votes for women, God help her. The nice thing about an ugly daughter is, she's not apt to make me a grandmother. . . . "They didn't do you much good, those parties, dear Cousin Eva," thought Miranda.

"They didn't do me much good, those parties," said Cousin Eva aloud as if she were a mind-reader, and Miranda's head swam for a moment with fear that she had herself spoken aloud. "Or at least, they didn't serve their purpose, for I never got married; but I enjoyed them, just the same. I had a good time at those parties, even if I wasn't a belle. And so you are Harry's child, and here I was quarreling with you. You do remember me, don't you?"

"Yes," said Miranda, and thinking that even if Cousin Eva had been really an old maid ten years before, still she couldn't be much past fifty now, and she looked so withered and tired, so famished and sunken in the cheeks, so *old* somehow. Across the abyss separating Cousin Eva from her own youth, Miranda looked with painful premonition. "Oh, must I ever be like that?" She said aloud, "Yes, you used to read Latin to me, and tell me not to bother about the sense, to get the sound in my mind, and it would come easier later."

"Ah, so I did," said Cousin Eva, delighted. "So I did. You don't happen to remember that I once had a beautiful sapphire velvet dress with a train on it?"

"No, I don't remember that dress," said Miranda.

"It was an old dress of my mother's made over and cut down to fit," said Eva, "and it wasn't in the least becoming to me, but it was the only really good dress I ever had, and I remember it as if it were yesterday. Blue was never my color." She sighed with a humorous bitterness. The humor seemed momentary, but the bitterness was a constant state of mind.

Miranda, trying to offer the sympathy of fellow suffering, said, "I know. I've had Maria's dresses made over for me, and they were never right. It was dreadful."

"Well," said Cousin Eva, in the tone of one who did not wish to share her unique disappointments. "How is your father? I always liked him. He was one of the finest-looking young men I ever saw. Vain, too, like all his family. He wouldn't ride any but the best horses he could buy, and I used to say he made them prance and then watched his own shadow. I used to tell this on him at dinner parties, and he hated me for it. I feel pretty certain he hated me." An overtone of complacency in Cousin Eva's voice explained better than words that she had her own method of commanding attention and arousing emotion. "How *is* your father, I asked you, my dear?"

"I haven't seen him for nearly a year," answered Miranda, quickly, before Cousin Eva could get ahead again. "I'm going home now to Uncle Gabriel's funeral; you know, Uncle Gabriel died in Lexington and they have brought him back to be buried beside Aunt Amy."

"So that's how we meet," said Cousin Eva. "Yes, Gabriel drank himself to death at last. I'm going to the funeral, too. I haven't been home since I went to Mother's funeral, it must be, let's see, yes, it will be nine years next July. I'm going to Gabriel's funeral, though. I wouldn't miss that. Poor fellow, what a life he had. Pretty soon they'll all be gone."

Miranda said, "We're left, Cousin Eva," meaning those of her own generation, the young, and Cousin Eva said, "Pshaw, you'll live forever, and you won't bother to come to our funerals." She didn't seem to think this was a misfortune, but flung the remark from her like a woman accustomed to saying what she thought.

Miranda sat thinking, "Still, I suppose it would be pleasant if I could say something to make her believe that she and all of them would be lamented, but—but—" With a smile which she hoped would be her denial of Cousin Eva's cynicism about the younger generation, she said, "You were right about the Latin, Cousin Eva, your reading did help when I began with it. I still study," she said. "Latin, too."

"And why shouldn't you?" asked Cousin Eva, sharply, adding at once mildly, "I'm glad you are going to use your mind a little, child. Don't let yourself rust away. Your mind outwears all sorts of things you may set your heart upon; you can enjoy it when all other things are taken away." Miranda was chilled by her melancholy. Cousin Eva went on: "In our part of the country, in my time, we were so provincial—a woman didn't dare to think or act for herself. The whole world was a little that way," she said, "but we were the worst, I believe. I suppose you must know how I fought for votes for women when it almost made a pariah of me—I was turned out of my chair at the Seminary, but I'm glad I did it and I would do it again. You young things don't realize. You'll live in a better world because we worked for it."

Miranda knew something of Cousin Eva's career. She said sincerely, "I think it was brave of you, and I'm glad you did it, too. I loved your courage."

"It wasn't just showing off, mind you," said Cousin Eva, rejecting praise, fretfully. "Any fool can be brave. We were working for something we knew was right, and it turned out that we needed a lot of courage for it. That was all. I didn't expect to go to jail, but I went three times, and I'd go three times three more if it were necessary. We aren't voting yet," she said, "but we will be."

Miranda did not venture any answer, but she felt convinced that indeed women would be voting soon if nothing fatal happened to Cousin Eva. There was something in her manner which said such things could be left safely to her. Miranda was dimly fired for the cause herself; it seemed heroic and worth suffering for, but discouraging, too, to those who came after: Cousin Eva so plainly had swept the field clear of opportunity.

They were silent for a few minutes, while Cousin Eva rummaged in her handbag, bringing up odds and ends: peppermint drops, eye drops, a packet of needles, three handkerchiefs, a little bottle of violet perfume, a book of addresses, two buttons, one black, one white, and, finally, a packet of headache powders.

"Bring me a glass of water, will you, my dear?" she asked Miranda. She poured the headache powder on her tongue, swallowed the water, and put two peppermints in her mouth.

"So now they're going to bury Gabriel near Amy," she said after a while, as if her eased headache had started her on a new train of thought. "Miss Honey would like that, poor dear, if she could know. After listening to stories about Amy for twenty-five years, she must lie alone in her grave in Lexington while Gabriel sneaks off to Texas to make his bed with Amy again. It was a kind of life-long infidelity, Miranda, and now an eternal infidelity on top of that. He ought to be ashamed of himself."

"It was Aunt Amy he loved," said Miranda, wondering what Miss Honey could have been like before her long troubles with Uncle Gabriel. "First, anyway."

"Oh, that Amy," said Cousin Eva, her eyes glittering. "Your Aunt Amy was a devil and a mischief-maker, but I loved her dearly. I used to stand up for Amy when her reputation wasn't worth that." Her fingers snapped like castanets. "She used to say to me, in that gay soft way she had, 'Now, Eva, don't go talking votes for women when the lads ask you to dance. Don't recite Latin poems to 'em,' she would say, 'they got sick of that in school. Dance and say nothing, Eva,' she would say, her eyes perfectly devilish, 'and hold your chin up, Eva.' My chin was my weak point, you see. 'You'll never catch a husband if you don't look out,' she would say. Then she would laugh and fly away, and where did she fly to?" demanded Cousin Eva, her sharp eyes pinning Miranda down to the bitter facts of the case, "To scandal and to death, nowhere else."

"She was joking, Cousin Eva," said Miranda, innocently, "and everybody loved her."

"Not everybody, by a long shot," said Cousin Eva in triumph. "She had enemies. If she knew, she pretended she didn't. If she cared, she never said. You couldn't make her quarrel. She was sweet as a honeycomb to everybody. *Everybody*," she added, "that was the trouble. She went through life like a spoiled darling, doing as she pleased and letting other people suffer for it, and pick up the pieces after her. I never believed for one moment," said Cousin Eva, putting her mouth close to Miranda's ear and breathing peppermint hotly into it, "that Amy was an impure woman. Never! But let me tell you, there were plenty who did believe it. There were plenty to pity poor Gabriel for being so completely blinded by her. A great many persons were not surprised when they heard that Gabriel was perfectly miserable all the time, on their honeymoon, in New Orleans. Jealousy. And why not? But I used to say to such persons that, no matter what the appearances were, I had faith in Amy's virtue. Wild, I said, indiscreet, I said, heartless, I said, but *virtuous* I feel certain. But you could hardly blame anyone for being mystified. The way she rose up suddenly from death's

door to marry Gabriel Breaux, after refusing him and treating him like a dog for years, looked odd, to say the least. To say the very least," she added, after a moment, "odd is a mild word for it. And there was something very mysterious about her death, only six weeks after marriage."

Miranda roused herself. She felt she knew this part of the story and could set Cousin Eva right about one thing. "She died of a hemorrhage from the lungs," said Miranda. "She had been ill for five years, don't you remember?"

Cousin Eva was ready for that. "Ha, that was the story, indeed. The official account, you might say. Oh, yes, I heard that often enough. But did you ever hear about that fellow Raymond somebody-or-other from Calcasieu Parish, almost a stranger, who persuaded Amy to elope with him from a dance one night, and she just ran out into the darkness without even stopping for her cloak, and your poor dear nice father Harry—you weren't even thought of then—had to run him down to earth and shoot him?"

Miranda leaned back from the advancing flood of speech. "Cousin Eva, my father shot *at* him, don't you remember? He didn't hit him. . . ."

"Well, that's a pity."

". . . and they had only gone out for a breath of air between dances. It was Uncle Gabriel's jealousy. And my father shot at the man because he thought that was better than letting Uncle Gabriel fight a duel about Aunt Amy. There was *nothing* in the whole affair except Uncle Gabriel's jealousy."

"You poor baby," said Cousin Eva, and pity gave a light like daggers to her eyes, "you dear innocent, you—do you believe that? How old are you, anyway?"

"Just past eighteen," said Miranda.

"If you don't understand what I tell you," said Cousin Eva portentously, "you will later. Knowledge can't hurt you. You mustn't live in a romantic haze about life. You'll understand when you're married, at any rate."

"I'm married now, Cousin Eva," said Miranda, feeling for almost the first time that it might be an advantage, "nearly a year. I eloped from school." It seemed very unreal even as she said it, and seemed to have nothing at all to do with the future; still, it was important, it must be declared, it was a situation in life which people seemed to be most exacting about, and the only feeling she could rouse in herself about it was an immense weariness as if it were an illness that she might one day hope to recover from.

"Shameful, shameful," cried Cousin Eva, genuinely repelled. "If you had been my child I should have brought you home and spanked you."

Miranda laughed out. Cousin Eva seemed to believe things could be arranged like that. She was so solemn and fierce, so comic and baffled.

"And you must know I should have just gone straight out again, through the nearest window," she taunted her. "If I went the first time, why not the second?"

"Yes, I suppose so," said Cousin Eva. "I hope you married rich."

"Not so very," said Miranda. "Enough." As if anyone could have stopped to think of such a thing!

Cousin Eva adjusted her spectacles and sized up Miranda's dress, her luggage, examined her engagement ring and wedding ring, with her nostrils fairly quivering as if she might smell out wealth on her.

"Well, that's better than nothing," said Cousin Eva. "I thank God every day of my life that I have a small income. It's a Rock of Ages. What would have become of me if I hadn't a cent of my own? Well, you'll be able now to do something for your family."

Miranda remembered what she had always heard about the Parringtons. They were money-hungry, they loved money and nothing else, and when they had got some they kept it. Blood was thinner than water between the Parringtons where money was concerned.

"We're pretty poor," said Miranda, stubbornly allying herself with her father's family instead of her husband's, "but a rich marriage is no way out," she said, with the snobbishness of poverty. She was thinking, "You don't know my branch of the family, dear Cousin Eva, if you think it is."

"Your branch of the family," said Cousin Eva, with that terrifying habit she had of lifting phrases out of one's mind, "has no more practical sense than so many children. Everything for love," she said, with a face of positive nausea, "that was it. Gabriel would have been rich if his grandfather had not disinherited him, but would Amy be sensible and marry him and make him settle down so the old man would have been pleased with him? No. And what could Gabriel do without money? I wish you could have seen the life he led Miss Honey, one day buying her Paris gowns and the next day pawning her earrings. It just depended on how the horses ran, and they ran worse and worse, and Gabriel drank more and more."

Miranda did not say, "I saw a little of it." She was trying to imagine Miss Honey in a Paris gown. She said, "But Uncle Gabriel was so mad about Aunt Amy, there was no question of her not marrying him at last, money or no money."

Cousin Eva strained her lips tightly over her teeth, let them fly again and leaned over, gripping Miranda's arm. "What I ask myself, what I ask myself over and over again," she whispered, "is, what connection did this man Raymond from Calcasieu have with Amy's sudden marriage to Gabriel, and *what* did Amy do to make away with herself so soon afterward? For mark my words, child, Amy wasn't so ill as all that. She'd been flying around for years after the doctors said her lungs were weak. Amy did away with herself to escape some disgrace, some exposure that she faced."

The beady black eyes glinted; Cousin Eva's face was quite frightening, so near and so intent. Miranda wanted to say, "Stop. Let her rest. What harm did she ever do you?" but she was timid and unnerved, and deep in her was a horrid fascination with the terrors and the darkness Cousin Eva had conjured up. What was the end of this story?

"She was a bad, wild girl, but I was fond of her to the last," said Cousin Eva. "She got into trouble somehow, and she couldn't get out again, and I have every reason to believe she killed herself with the drug they gave her to keep her quiet after a hemorrhage. If she didn't, what happened, what happened?"

"I don't know," said Miranda. "How should I know? She was very beautiful," she said, as if this explained everything. "Everybody said she was very beautiful."

"Not everybody," said Cousin Eva, firmly, shaking her head. "I for one never thought so. They made entirely too much fuss over her. She was good-looking enough, but why did they think she was beautiful? I cannot understand it. She was too thin when she was young, and later I always thought she was too fat, and again in her last year she was altogether too thin. She always got herself up to be looked at, and so people looked, of course. She rode too hard, and she danced too freely, and she talked too much, and you'd have to be blind, deaf and dumb not to notice her. I don't mean she was loud or vulgar, she wasn't, but she was *too free*," said Cousin Eva. She stopped for breath and put a peppermint in her mouth. Miranda could see Cousin Eva on the platform, making her speeches, stopping to take a peppermint. But why did she hate Aunt Amy so, when

Aunt Amy was dead and she alive? Wasn't being alive enough?

"And her illness wasn't romantic either," said Cousin Eva, "though to hear them tell it she faded like a lily. Well, she coughed blood, if that's romantic. If they had made her take proper care of herself, if she had been nursed sensibly, she might have been alive today. But no, nothing of the kind. She lay wrapped in beautiful shawls on a sofa with flowers around her, eating as she liked or not eating, getting up after a hemorrhage and going out to ride or dance, sleeping with the windows closed; with crowds coming in and out laughing and talking at all hours, and Amy sitting up so her hair wouldn't get out of curl. And why wouldn't that sort of thing kill a well person in time? I have almost died twice in my life," said Cousin Eva, "and both times I was sent to a hospital where I belonged and left there until I came out. And I came out," she said, her voice deepening to a bugle note, "and I went to work again."

"Beauty goes, character stays," said the small voice of axiomatic morality in Miranda's ear. It was a dreary prospect; why was a strong character so deforming? Miranda felt she truly wanted to be strong, but how could she face it, seeing what it did to one?

"She had a lovely complexion," said Cousin Eva, "perfectly transparent with a flush on each cheekbone. But it was tuberculosis, and is disease beautiful? And she brought it on herself by drinking lemon and salt to stop her periods when she wanted to go to dances. There was a superstition among young girls about that. They fancied that young men could tell what ailed them by touching their hands, or even by looking at them. As if it mattered? But they were terribly self-conscious and they had immense respect for man's worldly wisdom in those days. My own notion is that a man couldn't—but anyway, the whole thing was stupid."

"I should have thought they'd have stayed at home if they couldn't manage better than that," said Miranda, feeling very knowledgeable and modern.

"They didn't dare. Those parties and dances were their market; a girl couldn't afford to miss out, there were always rivals waiting to cut the ground from under her. The rivalry—" said Cousin Eva, and her head lifted, she arched like a cavalry horse getting a whiff of the battlefield—"you can't imagine what the rivalry was like. The way those girls treated each other—nothing was too mean, nothing too false—"

Cousin Eva wrung her hands. "It was just sex," she said in despair; "their minds dwelt on nothing else. They didn't call it that, it was all smothered under pretty names, but that's all it was, sex." She looked out of the window into the darkness, her sunken cheek near Miranda flushed deeply. She turned back. "I took to the soap box and the platform when I was called upon," she said proudly, "and I went to jail when it was necessary, and my condition didn't make any difference. I was booed and jeered and shoved around just as if I had been in perfect health. But it was part of our philosophy not to let our physical handicaps make any difference to our work. You know what I mean," she said, as if until now it was all mystery. "Well, Amy carried herself with more spirit than the others, and she didn't seem to be making any sort of fight, but she was simply sex-ridden, like the rest. She behaved as if she hadn't a rival on earth, and she pretended not to know what marriage was about, but I know better. None of them had, and they didn't want to have, anything else to think about, and they didn't really know anything about that, so they simply festered inside—they festered—"

Miranda found herself deliberately watching a long procession of living corpses, festering women stepping gaily towards the charnel house, their corruption concealed under laces and flowers, their dead faces lifted smiling, and thought quite coldly, "Of course it was not like that. This is no more true than what I was told before, it's every bit as romantic," and she realized that she was tired of her intense Cousin Eva, she wanted to go to sleep, she wanted to be at home, she wished it were tomorrow and she could see her father and her sister, who were so alive and solid; who would mention her freckles and ask her if she wanted something to eat.

"My mother was not like that," she said, childishly. "My mother was a perfectly natural woman who liked to cook. I have seen some of her sewing," she said. "I have read her diary."

"Your mother was a saint," said Cousin Eva, automatically.

Miranda sat silent, outraged. "My mother was nothing of the sort," she wanted to fling in Cousin Eva's big front teeth. But Cousin Eva had been gathering bitterness until more speech came of it.

" 'Hold your chin up, Eva,' Amy used to tell me," she began, doubling up both her fists and shaking them a little. "All my life the whole family bedeviled me about my chin. My entire girlhood was spoiled by it. Can you imagine," she asked, with a ferocity that seemed much too deep for this one cause, "people who call themselves civilized spoiling life for a young girl because she had one unlucky feature? Of course, you understand perfectly it was all in the very best humor, everybody was very amusing about it, no harm meant—oh, no, no harm at all. That is the hellish thing about it. It is that I can't forgive," she cried out, and she twisted her hands together as if they were rags. "Ah, the family," she said, releasing her breath and sitting back quietly, "the whole hideous institution should be wiped from the face of the earth. It is the root of all human wrongs," she ended, and relaxed, and her face became calm. She was trembling. Miranda reached out and took Cousin Eva's hand and held it. The hand fluttered and lay still, and Cousin Eva said, "You've not the faintest idea what some of us went through, but I wanted you to hear the other side of the story. And I'm keeping you up when you need your beauty sleep," she said grimly, stirring herself with an immense rustle of petticoats.

Miranda pulled herself together, feeling limp, and stood up. Cousin Eva put out her hand again, and drew Miranda down to her. "Good night, you dear child," she said, "to think you're grown up." Miranda hesitated, then quite suddenly kissed her Cousin Eva on the cheek. The black eyes shown brightly through water for an instant, and Cousin Eva said with a warm note in her sharp clear orator's voice, "Tomorrow we'll be at home again. I'm looking forward to it, aren't you? Good night."

Miranda fell asleep while she was getting off her clothes. Instantly it was morning again. She was still trying to close her suitcase when the train pulled into the small station, and there on the platform she saw her father, looking tired and anxious, his hat pulled over his eyes. She rapped on the window to catch his attention, then ran out and threw herself upon him. He said, "Well, here's my big girl," as if she were still seven, but his hands on her arms held her off, the tone was forced. There was no welcome for her, and there had not been since she had run away. She could not persuade herself to remember how it would be; between one home-coming and the next her mind refused to accept its own knowledge. Her father looked over her head and said, without surprise, "Why, hello, Eva, I'm glad somebody sent you a telegram." Miranda, rebuffed again, let her arms fall away again, with the same painful dull jerk of the heart.

"No one in my family," said Eva, her face framed in the thin black veil she reserved, evidently, for family funerals, "ever sent me a telegram in my life. I had the news from young Keziah who had it from young Gabriel. I suppose Gabe is here?"

"Everybody seems to be here," said Father. "The house is getting full."

"I'll go to the hotel if you like," said Cousin Eva.

"Damnation, no," said Father. "I didn't mean that. You'll come with us where you belong."

Skid, the handy man, grabbed the suitcases and started down the rocky village street. "We've got the car," said Father. He took Miranda by the hand, then dropped it again, and reached for Cousin Eva's elbow.

"I'm perfectly able, thank you," said Cousin Eva, shying away.

"If you're so independent now," said Father, "God help us when you get that vote."

Cousin Eva pushed back her veil. She was smiling merrily. She liked Harry, she always had liked him, he could tease as much as he liked. She slipped her arm through his. "So it's all over with poor Gabriel, isn't it?"

"Oh, yes," said Father, "it's all over, all right. They're pegging out pretty regularly now. It will be our turn next, Eva?"

"I don't know, and I don't care," said Eva, recklessly. "It's good to be back now and then, Harry, even if it is only for funerals. I feel sinfully cheerful."

"Oh, Gabriel wouldn't mind, he'd like seeing you cheerful. Gabriel was the cheerfullest cuss I ever saw, when we were young. Life for Gabriel," said Father, "was just one perpetual picnic."

"Poor fellow," said Cousin Eva.

"Poor old Gabriel," said Father, heavily.

Miranda walked along beside her father, feeling homeless, but not sorry for it. He had not forgiven her, she knew that. When would he? She could not guess, but she felt it would come of itself, without words and without acknowledgment on either side, for by the time it arrived neither of them would need to remember what had caused their division, nor why it had seemed so important. Surely old people cannot hold their grudges forever because the young want to live, too, she thought, in her arrogance, her pride. I will make my own mistakes; not yours; I cannot depend upon you beyond a certain point, why depend at all? There was something more beyond, but this was a first step to take, and she took it, walking in silence beside her elders who were no longer Cousin Eva and Father, since they had forgotten her presence, but had become Eva and Harry, who knew each other well, who were comfortable with each other, being contemporaries on equal terms, who occupied by right their place in this world, at the time of life to which they had arrived by paths familiar to them both. They need not play their roles of daughter, of son, to aged persons who did not understand them; nor of father and elderly female cousin to young persons whom they did not understand. They were precisely themselves; their eyes cleared, their voices relaxed into perfect naturalness, they need not weigh their words or calculate the effect of their manner. "It is I who have no place," thought Miranda. "Where are my own people and my own time?" She resented, slowly and deeply and in profound silence, the presence of these aliens who lectured and admonished her, who loved her with bitterness and denied her the right to look at the world with her own eyes, who demanded that she accept their version of life and yet could not tell her the truth, not in the smallest thing. "I hate them both," her most inner and secret mind said plainly, "*I will be free of them, I shall not even remember them.*"

She sat in the front seat with Skid, the Negro boy. "Come back with us, Miranda," said Cousin Eva, with the sharp little note of elderly command, "there is plenty of room."

"No thank you," said Miranda, in a firm cold voice. "I'm quite comfortable. Don't disturb yourself."

Neither of them noticed her voice or her manner. They sat back and went on talking steadily in their friendly family voices, talking about their dead, their living, their affairs, their prospects, their common memories, interrupting each other, catching each other up on small points of dispute, laughing with a gaiety and freshness Miranda had not known they were capable of, going over old stories and finding new points of interest in them.

Miranda could not hear the stories above the noisy motor, but she felt she knew them well, or stories like them. She knew too many stories like them, she wanted something new of her own. The language was familiar to them, but not to her, not any more. The house, her father had said, was full. It would be full of cousins, many of them strangers. Would there be any young cousins there, to whom she could talk about things they both knew? She felt a vague distaste for seeing cousins. There were

too many of them and her blood rebelled against the ties of blood. She was sick to death of cousins. She did not want any more ties with this house, she was going to leave it, and she was not going back to her husband's family either. She would have no more bonds that smothered her in love and hatred. She knew now why she had run away to marriage, and she knew that she was going to run away from marriage, and she was not going to stay in any place, with anyone, that threatened to forbid her making her own discoveries, that said "No" to her. She hoped no one had taken her old room, she would like to sleep there once more, she would say good-by there where she had loved sleeping once, sleeping and waking and waiting to be grown, to begin to live. Oh, what is life, she asked herself in desperate seriousness, in those childish unanswerable words, and what shall I do with it? It is something of my own, she thought in a fury of jealous possessiveness, what shall I make of it? She did not know that she asked herself this because all her earliest training had argued that life was a substance, a material to be used, it took shape and direction and meaning only as the possessor guided and worked it; living was a progress of continuous and varied acts of the will directed towards a definite end. She had been assured that there were good and evil ones, one must make a choice. But what was good, and what was evil? I hate love, she thought, as if this were the answer, I hate loving and being loved, I hate it. And her disturbed and seething mind received a shock of comfort from this sudden collapse of an old painful structure of distorted images and misconceptions. "You don't know anything about it," said Miranda to herself, with extraordinary clearness as if she were an elder admonishing some younger misguided creature. "You have to find out about it." But nothing in her prompted her to decide, "I will now do this, I will be that, I will go yonder, I will take a certain road to a certain end." There are questions to be asked first, she thought, but who will answer them? No one, or there will be too many answers, none of them right. What is the truth, she asked herself as intently as if the question had never been asked, the truth, even about the smallest, the least important of all the things I must find out? and where shall I begin to look for it? Her mind closed stubbornly against remembering, not the past but the legend of the past, other people's memory of the past, at which she had spent her life peering in wonder like a child at a magic-lantern show. Ah, but there is my own life to come yet, she thought, my own life now and beyond. I don't want any promises, I won't have false hopes, I won't be romantic about myself. I can't live in their world any longer, she told herself, listening to the voices back of her.

Let them tell their stories to each other. Let them go on explaining how things happened. I don't care. At least I can know the truth about what happens to me, she assured herself silently, making a promise to herself, in her hopefulness, her ignorance.

EUDORA WELTY (1909–   )

Of Eudora Welty's first volume, Katherine Anne Porter wrote:

> The stories in A *Curtain of Green* offer an extraordinary range of mood, pace, tone, and variety of material. The scene is limited to a town the author knows well; the farthest reaches of that scene never go beyond the boundaries of her own state, and many of the characters are of the sort that caused a Bostonian to remark that he would not care to meet them socially.

In subsequent stories and novels, Miss Welty has occasionally extended her range, but for most of her work, and certainly for her characteristic work, she has been content to find a Mississippi setting. There is nothing doctrinaire or regionally self-conscious about this limitation. It has simply been a matter of her finding in her native state the milieu that she needed for her story. In a lecture entitled "Place in Fiction," which she first delivered at Cambridge University in 1954 (published in 1956), Miss Welty stressed the importance that place has in her work. It is "the named, identified, concrete, exact, and exacting, and therefore credible, gathering-spot of all that has been felt, is about to be experienced, in the novel's progress."

Be the locale what it may, Miss Welty's fiction does show an amazingly wide variety of effects. It is true that she is always interested in the inward life of her characters. (She is even willing to risk obscurity or too much oblique-

ness in her attempts to provide the reader with delicate psychological effects and sensitive insights.) But the surface of her fiction varies from the quite realistic to the dreamlike, fantastic, and even "mythic." So strong is this element of fantasy that the author of a recent book on her work entitles it A *Season of Dreams* (1965).[1]

Often the realism and the dreamlike character are superimposed, one on another. This superimposition occurs in some of her most successful stories—and for good reason, since the revelation of mythic depth in what seems to be merely an ordinary event is one of the features of all great art.

Miss Welty's fantasy sometimes modulates into nightmare, projecting a world of grotesque characters and bizarre situations. The story "Clytie" ends just outside a decayed southern mansion with Clytie's drowning in a barrel of rainwater—"her poor ladylike black-stockinged legs up-ended and hung apart like a pair of tongs." But the somber and the terrible are not really characteristic. Her dominant mode—whatever the surface character of her fiction or whatever the setting—is comic. Here again, the range of effects is wide: warm-hearted, lyrical celebrations of folk vitality; irony, delicate or harsh; devastating satire; and occasionally something close to high-spirited farce.

Miss Welty is perfectly willing to give us

[1] By Alfred Appel, Jr. His title is borrowed from the first sentence of the first story in her collection *The Wide Net*.

"normal" people, ordinary folk, though in her perspective their inner lives often turn out to be not in the least ordinary. But, like many other southern writers of the twentieth century, she frequently writes about people who are isolated, cut off from the usual human relationships, or even twisted and warped physically or spiritually. Thus "The Key" is the story of two deaf mutes; the heroine of "Lily Daw and the Ladies" is a half-witted girl; Keela, in "Keela the Outcast Indian Maiden," is discovered to be a little club-footed black man who has been captured by a traveling show and forced to act as one of its freaks. The hero of "Old Mr. Marblehall" is the town eccentric, who likes to gloat over the double life that he is leading (in fact, or perhaps it is merely in his imagination?) and to anticipate with nervous glee the shock that the townspeople will have some day when they find out that he is a bigamist with two households.

Yet the isolation of these abnormal people is simply an intensification of the plight of Miss Welty's ordinary people—a stepping up of what she conceives to be the situation in which the human being often finds himself. Indeed, it can be argued that in nearly all of Miss Welty's stories we get either of two related situations: the isolated person attempts to break out of his isolation or else the fact of his isolation is revealed to the reader or to the person himself.

This is, as we have noted earlier, a familiar theme in our time throughout the Western world, international not provincial. One remembers the lines from Eliot's *The Waste Land:*

I have heard the key
Turn in the door once and turn once only
We think of the key, each in his prison. . . .

But Miss Welty, of course, explores the situation in her own way and with her own tonality. Her exploration is heavily qualified, too, by the kinds of character about whom she writes—people who are caught up in their own worlds of class and caste or of peculiar obsession or private dream.

The range of such characters in Miss Welty's fiction is very wide indeed. At one extreme we find the planter family, or what is left of it; at the other, the poor sharecropper, black or white. Between these extremes there are, in the country, yeoman farmers—mostly white—moonshiners, and river rats; and in the towns—Mississippi can hardly be said to have cities—people who wear a genteel respectability, plain people who have recently moved in from a small farm, and finally common white trash.

From such a variety, one cannot hope to choose a story that will be fully representative of Miss Welty's talent, but there is good reason to choose a story about the common people of the rural South.[2] She knows their manners and customs and exults in their rich vitality. She enjoys them too much to condescend to them: she respects the truth too much to sentimentalize them. She is letter perfect in the folk idiom and has obviously listened for a long time with attentive ear to the rhythms of folk speech. Here are some samples.

A countryman with a guitar tells the motorist who picks him up on the highway: "I come down from the hills. . . . We have owls for chickens and foxes for guard dogs, but we sing true" ("The Hitchhikers"). The same countryman speaks of his mother's knowledge of folk ballads: "My ma, she was the one for ballats. Little in the waist as a dirt-dauber, but her voice carried." "Mr. Tom Bate's Boy, as he called himself, stared away with a face as clean-blank as a watermelon seed . . ." ("Clytie"). An old black woman has fallen into a ditch and when a passing hunter asks her what she is doing there, she replies: "Lying on my back like a June-bug waiting to be turned over, Mister" ("A Worn Path"). A woman selling cosmetics from door to door enters the house of a potential customer and remarks: "It is not Christian or sanitary to put feathers in a vase."

Edna Earle, who runs the Beulah Hotel in Beulah, Mississippi, describes her method of be-

---

[2] Miss Welty's fine novel *Losing Battles* (1970) makes use of this subject matter.

friending a Miss Teacake, whom she liked not at all, but who had become engaged to her uncle Daniel Ponder, himself slightly touched in the head. Deciding to make the best of it, Edna Earle "just asked her for recipes enough times, and told her the real secret of cheese straws—beat it three hundred strokes—and took back a few unimportant things I've said about the Baptists. The wedding was at the Sistrunks', in the music room, and Miss Teacake insisted upon singing at her own wedding—sang 'The Sweetest Story Ever Told.'

"It was bad luck. The marriage didn't hold out" (*The Ponder Heart*).

Edna Earle, though she is capable of making acid observations about some of her neighbors, and though she is quick to resent any aspersions on herself and the Ponder family, is healthy-minded, filled with breezy assurance, and completely at home in her world. On the other hand, the narrator of "Why I Live at the P.O." is contentious, at odds with her family, and jealous of her younger sister whose marriage has broken up and who has come home to mother. (She is another of Miss Welty's iso-lated persons—in this instance, by her own choice.) In reading this story, we miss the point if we assume that the prime stress is on sibling rivalry or disturbed mental health. One can, to be sure, find these things and more of the same sort in the story, but the tone is not that of the sour moralist or the indignant surveyor of public morals.

Instead, there is a real gusto in the telling. The author's attitude toward the postmistress of China Grove, Mississippi, includes a measure of genuine admiration for her ability to recall every single past offense and for the unstop-pable flow of her talk. Chaucer must have had something like this regard for his execrable Pardoner.

Katherine Anne Porter says of another of Miss Welty's stories, "The Petrified Man," that it offers a study of "vulgarity—vulgarity absol-ute, chemically pure, exposed mercilessly to its final subhuman depths. . . . She has simply an eye and an ear sharp, shrewd, and true as a tuning fork." What Miss Porter has said about "The Petrified Man" applies fully to "Why I Live at the P.O."

BIOGRAPHICAL CHART

FURTHER READINGS

Robert van Gelder, "An Interview with Eudora Welty," *Writers and Writing* (1946)

Eudora Welty, "How I Write," in *Understanding Fiction* (1959), by Cleanth Brooks and Robert Penn Warren

———, "Place in Fiction," *South Atlantic Quarterly* (1956)

———, *Three Papers on Fiction* (1962)

Alfred Appel, Jr., *A Season of Dreams: The Fiction of Eudora Welty* (1965)

J. A. Bryant, Jr., *Eudora Welty* (1968)

Robert Daniel, "Eudora Welty: The Sense of Place," in *Southern Renascence* (1966), Louis Rubin and Robert Jacobs, eds.

Ruth M. Vande Kieft, *Eudora Welty* (1962)

Robert Penn Warren, "The Love and Separateness in Eudora Welty," in *Selected Essays* (1958)

Why I Live at the P.O. (1941)

I was getting along fine with Mama, Papa-Daddy and Uncle Rondo until my sister Stella-Rondo just separated from her husband and came back home again. Mr. Whitaker! Of course I went with Mr. Whitaker first, when he first appeared here in China Grove, taking "Pose Yourself" photos, and Stella-Rondo broke us up. Told him I was one-sided. Bigger on one side than the other, which is a deliberate, calculated falsehood: I'm the same. Stella-Rondo is exactly twelve months to the day younger than I am and for that reason she's spoiled.

She's always had anything in the world she wanted and then she'd throw it away. Papa-Daddy gave her this gorgeous Add-a-Pearl necklace when she was eight years old and she threw it away playing baseball when she was nine, with only two pearls.

So as soon as she got married and moved away from home the first thing she did was separate! From Mr. Whitaker! This photographer with the popeyes she said she trusted. Came home from one of those towns up in Illinois and to our complete surprise brought this child of two.

Mama said she like to make her drop dead for a second. "Here you had this marvelous blonde child and never so much as wrote your mother a word about it," says Mama. "I'm thoroughly ashamed of you." But of course she wasn't.

Stella-Rondo just calmly takes off this *hat*, I wish you could see it. She says, "Why, Mama, Shirley-T.'s adopted, I can prove it."

"How?" says Mama, but all I says was, "H'm!" There I was over the hot stove, trying to stretch two chickens over five people and a completely unexpected child into the bargain, without one moment's notice.

"What do you mean—'H'm!'?" says Stella-Rondo, and Mama says, "I heard that, Sister."

I said that oh, I didn't mean a thing, only that whoever Shirley-T. was, she was the spit-image of Papa-Daddy if he'd cut off his beard, which of course he'd never do in the world. Papa-Daddy's Mama's papa and sulks.

Stella-Rondo got furious! She said, "Sister, I don't need to tell you you got a lot of nerve and always did have and I'll thank you to make no future reference to my adopted child whatsoever."

"Very well," I said. "Very well, very well. Of course I noticed at once she looks like Mr. Whita-ker's side too. That frown. She looks like a cross between Mr. Whitaker and Papa-Daddy."

"Well, all I can say is she isn't."

"She looks exactly like Shirley Temple to me," says Mama, but Shirley-T. just ran away from her.

So the first thing Stella-Rondo did at the table was turn Papa-Daddy against me.

"Papa-Daddy," she says. He was trying to cut up his meat. "Papa-Daddy!" I was taken completely by surprise. Papa-Daddy is about a million years old and's got this long-long beard. "Papa-Daddy, Sister says she fails to understand why you don't cut off your beard."

So Papa-Daddy l-a-y-s down his knife and fork! He's real rich. Mama says he is, he says he isn't. So he says, "Have I heard correctly? You don't understand why I don't cut off my beard?"

"Why," I says, "Papa-Daddy, of course I understand, I did not say any such of a thing, the idea!"

He says, "Hussy!"

I says, "Papa-Daddy, you know I wouldn't any more want you to cut off your beard than the man in the moon. It was the farthest thing from my mind! Stella-Rondo sat there and made that up while she was eating breast of chicken."

But he says, "So the postmistress fails to understand why I don't cut off my beard. Which job I got you through my influence with the government. 'Bird's nest'—is that what you call it?"

Not that it isn't the next to smallest P.O. in the entire state of Mississippi.

I says, "Oh, Papa-Daddy," I says, "I didn't say any such of a thing, I never dreamed it was a bird's nest, I have always been grateful though this is the next to smallest P.O. in the state of Mississippi, and I do not enjoy being referred to as a hussy by my own grandfather."

But Stella-Rondo says, "Yes, you did say it too. Anybody in the world could of heard you, that had ears."

"Stop right there," says Mama, looking at *me*.

So I pulled my napkin straight back through the napkin ring and left the table.

As soon as I was out of the room Mama says, "Call her back, or she'll starve to death," but Papa-Daddy says, "This is the beard I started growing on the Coast when I was fifteen years old." He would of gone on till nightfall if Shirley-T. hadn't lost the Milky Way she ate in Cairo.

So Papa-Daddy says, "I am going out and lie in

the hammock, and you can all sit here and remember my words: I'll never cut off my beard as long as I live, even one inch, and I don't appreciate it in you at all." Passed right by me in the hall and went straight out and got in the hammock.

It would be a holiday. It wasn't five minutes before Uncle Rondo suddenly appeared in the hall in one of Stella-Rondo's flesh-colored kimonos, all cut on the bias, like something Mr. Whitaker probably thought was gorgeous.

"Uncle Rondo!" I says. "I didn't know who that was! Where are you going?"

"Sister," he says, "get out of my way, I'm poisoned."

"If you're poisoned stay away from Papa-Daddy," I says. "Keep out of the hammock, Papa-Daddy will certainly beat you on the head if you come within forty miles of him. He thinks I deliberately said he ought to cut off his beard after he got me the P.O., and I've told him and told him and told him, and he acts like he just don't hear me. Papa-Daddy must of gone stone deaf."

"He picked a fine day to do it then," says Uncle Rondo, and before you could say "Jack Robinson" flew out in the yard.

What he'd really done, he'd drunk another bottle of the prescription. He does it every single Fourth of July as sure as shooting, and it's horribly expensive. Then he falls over in the hammock and snores. So he insisted on zigzagging right on out to the hammock, looking like a half-wit.

Papa-Daddy woke up with this horrible yell and right there without moving an inch he tried to turn Uncle Rondo against me. I heard every word he said. Oh, he told Uncle Rondo I didn't learn to read till I was eight years old and he didn't see how in the world I ever got the mail put up at the P.O., much less read it all, and he said if Uncle Rondo could only fathom the lengths he had gone to to get me that job! And he said on the other hand he thought Stella-Rondo had a brilliant mind and deserved credit for getting out of town. All the time he was just lying there swinging as pretty as you please and looping out his beard, and poor Uncle Rondo was *pleading* with him to slow down the hammock, it was making him as dizzy as a witch to watch it. But that's what Papa-Daddy likes about a hammock. So Uncle Rondo was too dizzy to get turned against me for the time being. He's Mama's only brother and is a good case of a one-track mind. Ask anybody. A certified pharmacist.

Just then I heard Stella-Rondo raising the upstairs window. While she was married she got this peculiar idea that it's cooler with the windows shut and locked. So she has to raise the window before she can make a soul hear her outdoors.

So she raises the window and says, *"Oh!"* You would have thought she was mortally wounded.

Uncle Rondo and Papa-Daddy didn't even look up, but kept right on with what they were doing. I had to laugh.

I flew up the stairs and threw the door open! I says, "What in the wide world's the matter, Stella-Rondo? You mortally wounded?"

"No," she says, "I'm not mortally wounded but I wish you would do me the favor of looking out that window there and telling me what you see."

So I shade my eyes and look out the window.

"I see the front yard," I says.

"Don't you see any human beings?" she says.

"I see Uncle Rondo trying to run Papa-Daddy out of the hammock," I says. "Nothing more. Naturally, it's so suffocating-hot in the house, with all the windows shut and locked, everybody who cares to stay in their right mind will have to go out and get in the hammock before the Fourth of July is over."

"Don't you notice anything different about Uncle Rondo?" asks Stella-Rondo.

"Why, no, except he's got on some terrible-looking flesh-colored contraption I wouldn't be found dead in, is all I can see," I says.

"Never mind, you won't be found dead in it, because it happens to be part of my trousseau, and Mr. Whitaker took several dozen photographs of me in it," says Stella-Rondo. "What on earth could Uncle Rondo *mean* by wearing part of my trousseau out in the broad open daylight without saying so much as 'Kiss my foot,' *knowing* I only got home this morning after my separation and hung my negligee up on the bathroom door, just as nervous as I could be?"

"I'm sure I don't know, and what do you expect me to do about it?" I says. "Jump out the window?"

"No, I expect nothing of the kind. I simply declare that Uncle Rondo looks like a fool in it, that's all," she says. "It makes me sick to my stomach."

"Well, he looks as good as he can," I says. "As good as anybody in reason could." I stood up for Uncle Rondo, please remember. And I said to Stella-Rondo, "I think I would do well not to criticize so freely if I were you and came home with a two-year-old child I had never said a word about, and no explanation whatever about my separation."

"I asked you the instant I entered this house not to refer one more time to my adopted child, and you gave me your word of honor you would not," was all Stella-Rondo would say, and started pulling out every one of her eyebrows with some cheap Kress tweezers.

So I merely slammed the door behind me and went down and made some green-tomato pickle. Somebody had to do it. Of course Mama had turned both the niggers loose; she always said no earthly power could hold one anyway on the Fourth of July, so she wouldn't even try. It turned out that Jaypan fell in the lake and came within a very narrow limit of drowning.

So Mama trots in. Lifts up the lid and says, "H'm! Not very good for your Uncle Rondo in his precarious condition, I must say. Or poor little adopted Shirley-T. Shame on you!"

That made me tired. I says, "Well, Stella-Rondo had better thank her lucky stars it was her instead of me came trotting in with that very peculiar-looking child. Now if it had been me that trotted in from Illinois and brought a peculiar-looking child of two, I shudder to think of the reception I'd of got, much less controlled the diet of an entire family."

"But you must remember, Sister, that you were never married to Mr. Whitaker in the first place and didn't go up to Illinois to live," says Mama, shaking a spoon in my face. "If you had I would of been just as overjoyed to see you and your little adopted girl as I was to see Stella-Rondo, when you wound up with your separation and came on back home."

"You would not," I says.

"Don't contradict me, I would," says Mama.

But I said she couldn't convince me though she talked till she was blue in the face. Then I said, "Besides, you know as well as I do that that child is not adopted."

"She most certainly is adopted," says Mama, stiff as a poker.

I says, "Why, Mama, Stella-Rondo had her just as sure as anything in this world, and just too stuck up to admit it."

"Why, Sister," said Mama. "Here I thought we were going to have a pleasant Fourth of July, and you start right out not believing a word your own baby sister tells you!"

"Just like Cousin Annie Flo. Went to her grave denying the facts of life," I remind Mama.

"I told you if you ever mentioned Annie Flo's name I'd slap your face," says Mama, and slaps my face.

"All right, you wait and see," I says.

"I," says Mama, "I prefer to take my children's word for anything when it's humanly possible." You ought to see Mama, she weighs two hundred pounds and has real tiny feet.

Just then something perfectly horrible occurred to me.

"Mama," I says, "can that child talk?" I simply had to whisper! "Mama, I wonder if that child can be—you know—in any way? Do you realize," I says, "that she hasn't spoken one single, solitary word to a human being up to this minute? This is the way she looks," I says, and I looked like this.

Well, Mama and I just stood there and stared at each other. It was horrible!

"I remember well that Joe Whitaker frequently drank like a fish," says Mama. "I believed to my soul he drank *chemicals*." And without another word she marches to the foot of the stairs and calls Stella-Rondo.

"Stella-Rondo? O-o-o-o-o! Stella-Rondo!"

"What?" says Stella-Rondo from upstairs. Not even the grace to get up off the bed.

"Can that child of yours talk?" asks Mama.

Stella-Rondo says, "Can she what?"

"Talk! Talk!" says Mama. "Burdyburdyburdy-burdy!"

So Stella-Rondo yells back, "Who says she can't talk?"

"Sister says so," says Mama.

"You didn't have to tell me, I know whose word of honor don't mean a thing in this house," says Stella-Rondo.

And in a minute the loudest Yankee voice I ever heard in my life yells out, "OE'm Pop-OE the Sailor-r-r-r Ma-a-an!" and then somebody jumps up and down in the upstairs hall. In another second the house would of fallen down.

"Not only talks, she can tap-dance!" calls Stella-Rondo. "Which is more than some people I won't name can do."

"Why, the little precious darling thing!" Mama says, so surprised. "Just as smart as she can be!" Starts talking baby talk right there. Then she turns on me. "Sister, you ought to be thoroughly ashamed! Run upstairs this instant and apologize to Stella-Rondo and Shirley-T."

"Apologize for what?" I says. "I merely wondered if the child was normal, that's all. Now that she's proved she is, why, I have nothing further to say."

But Mama just turned on her heel and flew out, furious. She ran right upstairs and hugged the baby. She believed it was adopted. Stella-Rondo hadn't done a thing but turn her against me from upstairs while I stood there helpless over the hot stove. So that made Mama, Papa-Daddy and the baby all on Stella-Rondo's side.

Next, Uncle Rondo.

I must say that Uncle Rondó has been marvelous to me at various times in the past and I was completely unprepared to be made to jump out of my skin, the way it turned out. Once Stella-Rondo did something perfectly horrible to him—broke a chain letter from Flanders Field—and he took the radio back he had given her and gave it to me. Stella-Rondo was furious! For six months we all had to call her Stella instead of Stella-Rondo, or she wouldn't answer. I always thought Uncle Rondo had all the brains of the entire family. Another time he sent me to Mammoth Cave, with all expenses paid.

But this would be the day he was drinking that prescription, the Fourth of July.

So at supper Stella-Rondo speaks up and says she thinks Uncle Rondo ought to try to eat a little something. So finally Uncle Rondo said he would try a little cold biscuits and ketchup, but that was all. So *she* brought it to him.

"Do you think it wise to disport with ketchup in Stella-Rondo's flesh-colored kimono?" I says. Trying to be considerate! If Stella-Rondo couldn't watch out for her trousseau, somebody had to.

"Any objections?" asks Uncle Rondo, just about to pour out all the ketchup.

"Don't mind what she says, Uncle Rondo," says Stella-Rondo. "Sister has been devoting this solid afternoon to sneering out my bedroom window at the way you look."

"What's that?" says Uncle Rondo. Uncle Rondo has got the most terrible temper in the world. Anything is liable to make him tear the house down if it comes at the wrong time.

So Stella-Rondo says, "Sister says, 'Uncle Rondo certainly does look like a fool in that pink kimono!'"

Do you remember who it was really said that?

Uncle Rondo spills out all the ketchup and jumps out of his chair and tears off the kimono and throws it down on the dirty floor and puts his foot on it. It had to be sent all the way to Jackson to the cleaners and re-pleated.

"So that's your opinion of your Uncle Rondo, is it?" he says. "I look like a fool, do I? Well, that's the last straw. A whole day in this house with nothing to do, and then to hear you come out with a remark like that behind my back!"

"I didn't say any such of a thing, Uncle Rondo," I says, "and I'm not saying who did, either. Why, I think you look all right. Just try to take care of yourself and not talk and eat at the same time," I says. "I think you better go lie down."

"Lie down my foot," says Uncle Rondo. I ought to of known by that he was fixing to do something perfectly horrible.

So he didn't do anything that night in the precarious state he was in—just played Casino with Mama and Stella-Rondo and Shirley-T. and gave Shirley-T. a nickel with a head on both sides. It tickled her nearly to death, and she called him "Papa." But at 6:30 A.M. the next morning, he threw a whole five-cent package of some unsold one-inch firecrackers from the store as hard as he could into my bedroom and they every one went off. Not one bad one in the string. Anybody else, there'd be one that wouldn't go off.

Well, I'm just terribly susceptible to noise of any kind, the doctor has always told me I was the most sensitive person he had ever seen in his whole life, and I was simply prostrated. I couldn't eat! People tell me they heard it as far as the cemetery, and old Aunt Jep Patterson, that had been holding her own so good, thought it was Judgment Day and she was going to meet her whole family. It's usually so quiet here.

And I'll tell you it didn't take me any longer than a minute to make up my mind what to do. There I was with the whole entire house on Stella-Rondo's side and turned against me. If I have anything at all I have pride.

So I just decided I'd go straight down to the P.O. There's plenty of room there in the back, I says to myself.

Well! I made no bones about letting the family catch on to what I was up to. I didn't try to conceal it.

The first thing they knew, I marched in where they were all playing Old Maid and pulled the electric oscillating fan out by the plug, and everything got real hot. Next I snatched the pillow I'd done the needlepoint on right off the davenport from behind Papa-Daddy. He went "Ugh!" I beat Stella-Rondo up the stairs and finally found my charm bracelet in her bureau drawer under a picture of Nelson Eddy.

"So that's the way the land lies," says Uncle Rondo. There he was, piecing on the ham. "Well,

Sister, I'll be glad to donate my army cot if you got any place to set it up, providing you'll leave right this minute and let me get some peace." Uncle Rondo was in France.

"Thank you kindly for the cot and 'peace' is hardly the word I would select if I had to resort to firecrackers at 6:30 A.M. in a young girl's bedroom," I says back to him. "And as to where I intend to go, you seem to forget my position as postmistress of China Grove, Mississippi," I says. "I've always got the P.O."

Well, that made them all sit up and take notice.

I went out front and started digging up some four-o'clocks to plant around the P.O.

"Ah-ah-ah!" says Mama, raising the window. "Those happen to be my four-o'clocks. Everything planted in that star is mine. I've never known you to make anything grow in your life."

"Very well," I says. "But I take the fern. Even you, Mama, can't stand there and deny that I'm the one watered that fern. And I happen to know where I can send in a box top and get a packet of one thousand mixed seeds, no two the same kind, free."

"Oh, where?" Mama wants to know.

But I says, "Too late. You 'tend to your house, and I'll 'tend to mine. You hear things like that all the time if you know how to listen to the radio. Perfectly marvelous offers. Get anything you want free."

So I hope to tell you I marched in and got that radio, and they could of all bit a nail in two, especially Stella-Rondo, that it used to belong to, and she well knew she couldn't get it back, I'd sue for it like a shot. And I very politely took the sewing-machine motor I helped pay the most on to give Mama for Christmas back in 1929, and a good big calendar, with the first-aid remedies on it. The thermometer and the Hawaiian ukulele certainly were rightfully mine, and I stood on the step-ladder and got all my watermelon rind preserves and every fruit and vegetable I'd put up, every jar. Then I began to pull the tacks out of the bluebird wall vases on the archway to the dining room.

"Who told you you could have those, Miss Priss?" says Mama, fanning as hard as she could.

"I bought 'em and I'll keep track of 'em," I says. "I'll tack 'em up one on each side the post-office window, and you can see 'em when you come to ask me for your mail, if you're so dead to see 'em."

"Not I! I'll never darken the door to that post office again if I live to be a hundred," Mama says. "Ungrateful child! After all the money we spent on you at the Normal."

"Me either," says Stella-Rondo. "You can just let my mail lie there and *rot*, for all I care. I'll never come and relieve you of a single, solitary piece."

"I should worry," I says. "And who you think's going to sit down and write you all those big fat letters and postcards, by the way? Mr. Whitaker? Just because he was the only man ever dropped down in China Grove and you got him—unfairly—is he going to sit down and write you a lengthy correspondence after you come home giving no rhyme nor reason whatsoever for your separation and no explanation for the presence of that child? I may not have your brilliant mind, but I fail to see it."

So Mama says, "Sister, I've told you a thousand times that Stella-Rondo simply got homesick, and this child is far too big to be hers," and she says, "Now, why don't you all just sit down and play Casino?"

Then Shirley-T. sticks out her tongue at me in this perfectly horrible way. She has no more manners than the man in the moon. I told her she was going to cross her eyes like that some day and they'd stick.

"It's too late to stop me now," I says. "You should have tried that yesterday. I'm going to the P.O. and the only way you can possibly see me is to visit me there."

So Papa-Daddy says, "You'll never catch me setting foot in that post office, even if I should take a notion into my head to write a letter some place." He says, "I won't have you reachin' out of that little old window with a pair of shears and cuttin' off any beard of mine. I'm too smart for you!"

"We all are," says Stella-Rondo.

But I said, "If you're so smart, where's Mr. Whitaker?"

So then Uncle Rondo says, "I'll thank you from now on to stop reading all the orders I get on postcards and telling everybody in China Grove what you think is the matter with them," but I says, "I draw my own conclusions and will continue in the future to draw them." I says, "If people want to write their inmost secrets on penny postcards, there's nothing in the wide world you can do about it, Uncle Rondo."

"And if you think we'll ever *write* another post-card you're sadly mistaken," says Mama.

"Cutting off your nose to spite your face then," I says. "But if you're all determined to have no more to do with the U.S. mail, think of this: What will Stella-Rondo do now, if she wants to tell Mr. Whitaker to come after her?"

"Wah!" says Stella-Rondo. I knew she'd cry. She had a conniption fit right there in the kitchen.

"It will be interesting to see how long she holds out," I says. "And now—I am leaving."

"Good-bye," says Uncle Rondo.

"Oh, I declare," says Mama, "to think that a family of mine should quarrel on the Fourth of July, or the day after, over Stella-Rondo leaving old Mr. Whitaker and having the sweetest little adopted child! It looks like we'd all be glad!"

"Wah!" says Stella-Rondo, and has a fresh conniption fit.

"*He* left *her*—you mark my words," I says. "That's Mr. Whitaker. I know Mr. Whitaker. After all, I knew him first. I said from the beginning he'd up and leave her. I foretold every single thing that's happened."

"Where did he go?" asks Mama.

"Probably to the North Pole, if he knows what's good for him," I says.

But Stella-Rondo just bawled and wouldn't say another word. She flew to her room and slammed the door.

"Now look what you've gone and done, Sister," says Mama. "You go apologize."

"I haven't got time, I'm leaving," I says.

"Well, what are you waiting around for?" asks Uncle Rondo.

So I just picked up the kitchen clock and marched off, without saying "Kiss my foot" or anything, and never did tell Stella-Rondo good-bye.

There was a nigger girl going along on a little wagon right in front.

"Nigger girl," I says, "come help me haul these things down the hill, I'm going to live in the post office."

Took her nine trips in her express wagon. Uncle Rondo came out on the porch and threw her a nickel.

And that's the last I've laid eyes on any of my family or my family laid eyes on me for five solid days and nights. Stella-Rondo may be telling the most horrible tales in the world about Mr. Whitaker, but I haven't heard them. As I tell everybody, I draw my own conclusions.

But oh, I like it here. It's ideal, as I've been saying. You see, I've got everything cater-cornered, the way I like it. Hear the radio? All the war news. Radio, sewing machine, book ends, ironing board and that great big piano lamp—peace, that's what I like. Butter-bean vines planted all along the front where the strings are.

Of course, there's not much mail. My family are naturally the main people in China Grove, and if they prefer to vanish from the face of the earth, for all the mail they get or the mail they write, why, I'm not going to open my mouth. Some of the folks here in town are taking up for me and some turned against me. I know which is which. There are always people who will quit buying stamps just to get on the right side of Papa-Daddy.

But here I am, and here I'll stay. I want the world to know I'm happy.

And if Stella-Rondo should come to me this minute, on bended knees, and *attempt* to explain the incidents of her life with Mr. Whitaker, I'd simply put my fingers in both my ears and refuse to listen.

CARSON McCULLERS (1917–1967)

We remarked earlier that a good many characters in Eudora Welty's fiction are in some way or other abnormal—deaf-mutes, half-wits, freaks. In Carson McCullers' fiction nearly every major character is abnormal, and many of them are grotesquely so. A male deaf-mute is in love with another male deaf-mute who is also half-witted. A neurotic woman in a frenzy of despair cuts off her nipples with a pair of garden shears. A rather masculinized woman falls hopelessly in love with a humpbacked dwarf who is tubercular and who also turns out to be homosexual. Whereas Eudora Welty gives us only one or two instances of what has come to be known as "Southern Gothic,"[1] this mode is very nearly the staple of Carson McCullers' work.

In his introduction to the Modern Library edition of Mrs. McCullers' novel, *Reflections in a Golden Eye*, the playwright Tennessee Williams, himself an old hand at Southern Gothic, urges a justification for Mrs. McCullers' use of Gothic material. She needed such "symbols of the grotesque and the violent" in order to express her sense of "an underlying dreadfulness in modern experience"—especially if she was to develop it in her favorite forms—the novella and the short story. James Joyce, Williams says, "managed to get the whole sense of awfulness without resorting to externals that departed on the surface from the ordinary and the familiar," but then he wrote "very long books" and he was the master of the interior monologue, a device that few artists can manage.

Mrs. McCullers did have a consistent theme —that of the individual's lonely isolation in a world in which he can never find a satisfying love. Her use of physically deformed or psychologically warped characters represents a way of stressing the hopelessness of the human plight. Thus, the only proper questions that can be asked about her methods will be these: Did she sometimes tilt her work too far over toward the illustration of a not-self-evident thesis? And did she ever allow her urge toward "symbolism" to eat up the credibility of her characters as human beings? The answers to these questions have been various and probably will continue to be.

Mrs. McCullers' Gothicism was very much of her own brand. It lacked, of course, the mysterious castle which gave the genre its name, but it also lacked the American equivalent, the gloomy mansion in which Poe established Roderick Usher or the ruinous plantation house such as Sutpen's Hundred in Faulkner's *Absalom, Absalom!* The decadence involved owes

nothing to the decayed grandeur of eighteenth- or nineteenth-century decor. Mrs. McCullers' characteristic settings were nondescript middle-class homes, or dingy cafés, or second-rate hotels in some little southern city. The scenes of horror and violence, in one of her works, actually occur in the neat houses occupied by army officers on the grounds of a military base.

Since the major characters in Mrs. McCullers' fiction are doomed to unrequited love, theirs is either an intensely spiritual or else a neurotic love. (In Tennessee Williams' version of Gothic, the line between the two tends to blur.) In such love there is no such thing as Blake's "lineaments of gratified desire": the love is of the mind, idealistic, and as at least one critic[2] has suggested, essentially "Platonic" —though he does not insist that Mrs. McCullers consciously derived it from Plato. There is, however, a much more obvious and direct source —romantic love (or chivalric or troubadour love, to use Denis de Rougemont's[3] terms). Romantic love has been pervasive in the culture of the West since at least 1100 A.D.

Romantic love requires that barriers exist between the two lovers. The difficulty of surmounting the barriers "proves" the power and purity of the love and at the same time serves to intensify the yearning for the loved one. In medieval literature the usual obstacle[4] was marriage to another—often a loveless marriage of convenience. Tristan cannot marry Isolde because she is already married to his uncle, King Mark. In modern times, with the increasing ease of securing a divorce and with the general loosening of sexual taboos, more formidable obstacles have had to be found; and so, in Mrs.

---

[1] For a definition of "Gothic" and a discussion of this "haunted, nocturnal" strain in American literature, see p. 226.

[2] Frank Baldanza, "Plato in Dixie," *Georgia Review* (Summer, 1958).

[3] See Rougemont's *Love in the Western World* (1957).

[4] In his *Love Declared* (1963, p. 49), Rougemont observes that the "necessary obstacle" in Vladimir Nabokov's *Lolita* is the fact that Lolita is only twelve. As he puts it, "loving nymphets" are, along with incest, "in our day and age, one of the last surviving sexual taboos." For this reason Rougemont regards *Lolita* as a novel about romantic or chivalric love. Lionel Trilling independently arrives at much the same conclusion.

McCullers' *The Ballad of the Sad Café,* Cousin Lymon, the man whom Miss Amelia loves, is a tubercular dwarf, and in *Reflections in a Golden Eye,* the person to whom the highly respected (but latently homosexual) Captain Penderton is more and more drawn is the moon-faced and simple-minded private, Elgee Williams. In the end the captain shoots the private to death when he finds him at night standing in his wife's bedroom—though the captain has hitherto accepted almost complacently his wife's affairs with other men.

This last item, however, ironic as it may appear, agrees perfectly with Rougemont's theory of romantic love, for his argument is that romantic lovers really do not want to consummate their love physically but yearn, if only unconsciously, to be joined together in death, where they are rid of the tormenting desires of the body.

Baldanza observes that there are no happy marriages, at least of the major characters, in Mrs. McCullers' fiction, and he is right. But this is just Rougemont's point: "happy love has no history—*in European literature*"—and one may add in a literature like the American which descends from European literature.

Happy married love undoubtedly exists in the world and it is the state to which many of us aspire. But it is too bourgeois, too stodgily respectable, to possess glamour. It lacks the drama, excitement, and electric intensity which most of us associate with a great and dazzling love affair. Ordinary married love offers more possibilities for satire or social comedy than it does for tragedy. Literature thrives on obstacles, struggle, and dramatic confrontations. At all events, the artist has for a long time preferred for his purposes romantic love. This holds true for both ends of the scale, whether it be the subartist turning out melodrama, class-B movies, and confession magazines, or the genuine artist interested in testing the human spirit and exploring its heights and depths and lonely places. Thus most writers, including the most serious, have been concerned not with the success of erotic love but with its failure and defeat. Mrs. McCullers is a serious artist, and she is fascinated with evil and the presence of something dreadful at the center of our universe.

We have remarked that the concept of romantic love in some form or other suffuses our literature. It is to be found, of course, in other southern writers, and notably in William Faulkner. In his *The Sound and the Fury* Quentin Compson is in love with his sister—or at least with a conception of his sister's honor—a love that makes him propose that he and his sister end their lives so that he can take her away with him into the realm of death. But Faulkner can also poke fun and smile at some of his romantic lovers, at Gavin Stevens, for example, or at Byron Bunch, the curious, methodical little man who becomes Lena Grove's knightly defender and supporter. Mrs. McCullers cannot smile at hers—or if she does so, it is with a wry and grim facial contortion. Any writer who made her characters so grotesquely misshapen in body or in mind would feel compelled to take them seriously.

Mrs. McCullers' first novel, *The Heart Is a Lonely Hunter,* met with a warm reception from the critics when it appeared in 1940. It had power and style and, whatever its faults and lapses, was a truly remarkable novel to have been written by a young woman of twenty-two. Her most popular book has been *The Member of the Wedding,* published in 1946, produced as a play in 1950, and as a musical in 1971. Part of its great success—the musical version was less successful—was undoubtedly due to the fact that the characters were less distorted than those in most of her other work, and the subject matter less shocking to conventional sensibilities. Using a more normal basic situation, Mrs. McCullers was here able to render her essential theme: the atmosphere of hopeless boredom, the keen sense of loneliness, and the yearning to be loved.

There are three principal characters: Frankie Addams, aged twelve, her little cousin, John Henry, aged six, and Berenice, the family servant, a black woman in early middle age. Berenice has been married four times, the first time happily, the last three unhappily. She is a version of Rougemont's romantic lover, for she remembers her first marriage as perfect, much too good to have lasted, and as she tells Frankie, she has been fooled into her subsequent "bad" marriages, each time because something about the man in question reminded her of her dead husband, Ludie. She balks at marrying once more because it has become plain even to her that she has been chasing a will-o'-the-wisp.

Frankie is obviously the maiden being inducted into the mysteries, questioning the oracle and priestess, just beginning to view love as possibly something more than one of the many peculiar and not very interesting folk ways that govern adult life. She is still dangling awkwardly between childhood (John Henry), a state that is coming to seem impossibly stupid, and maturity (Berenice), a state that has heretofore seemed stupid too. Frankie has only recently been put out of the movie house for booing a love film. But she is beginning to respond to a strange troubling in her own heart and now she has to talk to someone, for she is bored, lonely, and has been pointedly left out of the neighborhood girls' club. Frankie not only wants to grow up: she wants to join the human race, to be a member not only of a wedding party, but of mankind.

Berenice, Frankie, and John Henry spend much of their time playing three-handed bridge with a worn deck of cards in what Frankie refers to as the "ugly old kitchen" of her dingy Columbus, Georgia, home. The dramatic situation is such as to permit Mrs. McCullers to address herself to her basic theme without seeming to thin it down into obvious allegory, and her characters are so solidly credible that they never threaten to turn into outlandish creatures whose presence can be justified only because they are carriers of important symbolisms.

In this novel the conversation is very important: it powerfully grounds the scene in reality. The idiom in which Frankie and Berenice speak conveys the sense of a small, highly personal, quite closed local ambience—and Mrs. McCullers' sure grasp on such an ambience gave her a special leverage in dealing with her theme. But this grasp is merely one manifestation of her intimate knowledge of the distinctively southern milieu of *The Member of the Wedding.* Though the novel is set only a generation ago, the basic outline of the older culture can still be made out. A comparison of this novel with the work of another Georgia writer[5] of sixty-odd years before will give graphic indication of how the scene has altered. Instead of Uncle Remus's cabin, we are in the kitchen of a rather run-down house owned by a small-town jeweler, who is a widower and away from the house most of the day. Instead of Uncle Remus, we see a kind and sensible black woman who acts as a surrogate mother to the little white girl, but who lives an intense and exciting life of her own in a world with its own interests and energies. Instead of a little boy who comes to hear Uncle Remus relate fabulous tales about animals, we have—for John Henry doesn't have much more than a walk-on part—a little white girl on the brink of adolescence, who is restless, bored, femininely curious, and possessed of a will of her own. She is not being told fables. She is being given factual accounts—they claim to be such—of a world which to her is fascinating—she would call it "peculiar"—and puzzling.

The quality of the talk and what it tells us about the two speakers is best learned by listening to them. Here follow the opening pages of the novel.

[5] Joel Chandler Harris (see pp. 1709–15).

BIOGRAPHICAL CHART

ding (prepared by Mrs. McCullers) wins the New York Critics Circle award and the Donaldson award.

FURTHER READINGS

There is no standard edition of Carson McCullers' works. Individual titles are cited in the biographical chart.

Oliver Wendell Evans, *The Ballad of Carson McCullers: A Biography* (1966)
Barbara Nauer Folk, "The Sad Sweet Music of Carson McCullers," *Georgia Review* (1962)

Jane Hart, "Carson McCullers, Pilgrim of Loneliness," *Georgia Review* (1957)
Robert S. Phillips, "Carson McCullers: 1956–1964, a Selected Checklist," *Bulletin of Bibliography* (1964)
Stanley Stewart, "Carson McCullers: 1940–1956, a Selected Checklist," *Bulletin of Bibliography* (1959)

From The Member of the Wedding (1946)

It happened that green and crazy summer when Frankie was twelve years old. This was the summer when for a long time she had not been a member. She belonged to no club and was a member of nothing in the world. Frankie had become an unjoined person who hung around in doorways, and she was afraid. In June the trees were bright dizzy green, but later the leaves darkened, and the town turned black and shrunken under the glare of the sun. At first Frankie walked around doing one thing and another. The sidewalks of the town were gray in the early morning and at night, but the noon sun put a glaze on them, so that the cement burned and glittered like glass. The sidewalks finally became too hot for Frankie's feet, and also she got herself in trouble. She was in so much secret trouble that she thought it was better to stay at home—and at home there was only Berenice Sadie Brown and John Henry West. The three of them sat at the kitchen table, saying the same things over and over, so that by August the words began to rhyme with each other and sound strange. The world seemed to die each afternoon and nothing moved any longer. At last the summer was like a green sick dream, or like a silent crazy jungle under glass. And then, on the last Friday of August, all this was changed: it was so sudden that Frankie puzzled the whole blank afternoon, and still she did not understand.

'It is so very queer,' she said. 'The way it all just happened.'

'Happened? Happened?' said Berenice.

John Henry listened and watched them quietly.

'I have never been so puzzled.'

'But puzzled about what?'

'The whole thing,' Frankie said.

And Berenice remarked: 'I believe the sun has fried your brains.'

'Me too,' John Henry whispered.

Frankie herself almost admitted maybe so. It was four o'clock in the afternoon and the kitchen was square and gray and quiet. Frankie sat at the table with her eyes half closed, and she thought about a wedding. She saw a silent church, a strange snow slanting down against the colored windows. The groom in this wedding was her brother, and there was a brightness where his face should be. The bride was there in a long white train, and the bride also was faceless. There was something about this wedding that gave Frankie a feeling she could not name.

'Look here at me,' said Berenice. 'You jealous?'

'Jealous?'

'Jealous because your brother going to be married?'

'No,' said Frankie. 'I just never saw any two people like them. When they walked in the house today it was so queer.'

'You jealous,' said Berenice. 'Go and behold yourself in the mirror. I can see from the color in your eye.'

There was a watery kitchen mirror hanging above the sink. Frankie looked, but her eyes were gray as they always were. This summer she was grown so tall that she was almost a big freak, and her shoulders were narrow, her legs too long. She wore a pair of blue track shorts, a B.V.D. undervest, and she was barefooted. Her hair had been cut like a boy's, but it had not been cut for a long time and was now not even parted. The reflection in the glass was warped and crooked, but Frankie knew well what she looked like; she drew up her left shoulder and turned her head aside.

'Oh,' she said. 'They were the two prettiest people I ever saw. I just can't understand how it happened.'

'But what, Foolish?' said Berenice. 'Your brother come home with the girl he means to marry and took dinner today with you and your Daddy. They intend to marry at her home in Winter Hill this coming Sunday. You and your Daddy are going to the wedding. And that is the A and the Z of the matter. So whatever ails you?'

'I don't know,' said Frankie. 'I bet they have a good time every minute of the day.'

'Less us have a good time,' John Henry said.

'Us have a good time?' Frankie asked. 'Us?'

The three of them sat at the table again and Berenice dealt the cards for three-handed bridge. Berenice had been the cook since Frankie could remember. She was very black and broad-shouldered and short. She always said that she was thirty-five years old, but she had been saying that at least three years. Her hair was parted, plaited, and greased close to the skull, and she had a flat and quiet face. There was only one thing wrong about Berenice—her left eye was bright blue glass. It stared out fixed and wild from her quiet, colored face, and why she had wanted a blue eye nobody human would ever know. Her right eye was dark and sad. Berenice dealt slowly, licking her thumb when the sweaty cards stuck together. John Henry watched each card as it was being dealt. His chest was white and wet and naked, and he wore around his neck a tiny lead donkey tied by a string. He was blood kin to Frankie, first cousin, and all summer he would eat dinner and spend the day with her, or eat supper and spend the night; and she could not make him go home. He was small to be six years old, but he had the largest knees that Frankie had ever seen, and on one of them there was always a scab or a bandage where he had fallen down and skinned himself. John Henry had a little screwed white face and he wore tiny gold-rimmed glasses. He watched all of the cards very carefully, because he was in debt; he owed Berenice more than five million dollars.

'I bid one heart,' said Berenice.

'A spade,' said Frankie.

'I want to bid spades,' said John Henry. 'That's what I was going to bid.'

'Well, that's your tough luck. I bid them first.'

'Oh, you fool jackass!' he said. 'It's not fair!'

'Hush quarreling,' said Berenice. 'To tell the truth, I don't think either one of you got such a grand hand to fight over the bid about. I bid two hearts.'

'I don't give a durn about it,' Frankie said. 'It is immaterial with me.'

As a matter of fact this was so: she played bridge that afternoon like John Henry, just putting down any card that suddenly occurred to her. They sat together in the kitchen, and the kitchen was a sad and ugly room. John Henry had covered the walls with queer, child drawings, as far up as his arm would reach. This gave the kitchen a crazy look, like that of a room in the crazy-house. And now the old kitchen made Frankie sick. The name for what had happened to her Frankie did not know, but she could feel her squeezed heart beating against the table edge.

'The world is certainly a small place,' she said.

'What makes you say that?'

'I mean sudden,' said Frankie. 'The world is certainly a sudden place.'

'Well, I don't know,' said Berenice. 'Sometimes sudden and sometimes slow.'

Frankie's eyes were half closed, and to her own ears her voice sounded ragged, far away:

'To me it is sudden.'

For only yesterday Frankie had never thought seriously about a wedding. She knew that her only brother, Jarvis, was to be married. He had become engaged to a girl in Winter Hill just before he went to Alaska. Jarvis was a corporal in the army and he had spent almost two years in Alaska. Frankie had not seen her brother for a long, long time, and his face had become masked and changing, like a face seen under water. But Alaska! Frankie had dreamed of it constantly, and especially this summer it was very real. She saw the snow and frozen sea and ice glaciers. Esquimau igloos and polar bears and the beautiful Northern lights. When Jarvis had first gone to Alaska, she had sent him a box of homemade fudge, packing it carefully and wrapping each piece separately in waxed paper. It had thrilled her to think that her fudge would be eaten in Alaska, and she had a vision of her brother passing it around to furry Esquimaux. Three months later, a thank-you letter had come from Jarvis with a five-dollar bill enclosed. For a while she mailed candy almost every week, sometimes divinity instead of fudge, but Jarvis did not send her another bill, except at Christmas time. Sometimes his short letters to her father disturbed her a little. For instance, this summer he mentioned once that he had been in swimming and that the mosquitoes were something fierce. This letter jarred upon her dream, but after a few days of bewilderment, she returned to her frozen seas and snow. When Jarvis had come back from Alaska, he had gone straight to Winter Hill. The bride was named Janice Evans and the plans for the wedding were like this: her brother had wired that he and the bride were coming this Friday to spend the day, then on the following Sunday there was to be the wedding at Winter Hill. Frankie and her father were going to the wedding, traveling nearly a hundred miles to Winter Hill, and Frankie had already packed a suitcase. She looked forward to the time her brother and the bride should come, but she did not picture them to herself, and did not think about the wedding. So on the day before the visit she only commented to Berenice:

'I think it's a curious coincidence that Jarvis would get to go to Alaska and that the very bride he picked to marry would come from a place called Winter Hill. Winter Hill,' she repeated slowly, her eyes closed, and the name blended with dreams of Alaska and cold snow. 'I wish tomorrow was Sunday instead of Friday. I wish I had already left town.'

'Sunday will come,' said Berenice.

'I doubt it,' said Frankie. 'I've been ready to leave this town so long. I wish I didn't have to come back here after the wedding. I wish I was going somewhere for good. I wish I had a hundred dollars and could just light out and never see this town again.'

'It seems to me you wish for a lot of things,' said Berenice.

'I wish I was somebody else except me.'

So the afternoon before it happened was like the other August afternoons. Frankie had hung around the kitchen, then toward dark she had gone out into the yard. The scuppernong arbor behind the house was purple and dark in the twilight. She walked slowly. John Henry West was sitting beneath the August arbor in a wicker chair, his legs crossed and his hands in his pockets.

'What are you doing?' she asked.

'I'm thinking.'

'About what?'

He did not answer.

Frankie was too tall this summer to walk beneath the arbor as she had always done before. Other twelve-year-old people could still walk around inside, give shows, and have a good time. Even small grown ladies could walk underneath the arbor. And already Frankie was too big; this year she had to hang around and pick from the edges like the grown people. She stared into the tangle of dark vines, and there was the smell of crushed scuppernongs and dust. Standing beside the arbor, with dark coming on, Frankie was afraid. She did not know what caused this fear, but she was afraid.

'I tell you what,' she said. 'Suppose you eat supper and spend the night with me.'

John Henry took his dollar watch from his pocket and looked at it as though the time would decide whether or not he would come, but it was too dark under the arbor for him to read the numbers.

'Go on home and tell Aunt Pet. I'll meet you in the kitchen.'

'All right.'

She was afraid. The evening sky was pale and empty and the light from the kitchen window made a yellow square reflection in the darkening yard. She remembered that when she was a little girl she believed that three ghosts were living in the coal house, and one of the ghosts wore a silver ring.

She ran up the back steps and said: 'I just now invited John Henry to eat supper and spend the night with me.'

Berenice was kneading a lump of biscuit dough, and she dropped it on the flour-dusted table. 'I thought you were sick and tired of him.'

'I am sick and tired of him,' said Frankie. 'But it seemed to me he looked scared.'

'Scared of what?'

Frankie shook her head. 'Maybe I mean lonesome,' she said finally.

'Well, I'll save him a scrap of dough.'

After the darkening yard the kitchen was hot and bright and queer. The walls of the kitchen bothered Frankie—the queer drawings of Christmas trees, airplanes, freak soldiers, flowers. John Henry had started the first pictures one long afternoon in June, and having already ruined the wall, he went on and drew whenever he wished. Sometimes Frankie had drawn also. At first her father had been furious about the walls, but later he said for them to draw all the pictures out of their systems, and he would have the kitchen painted in the fall. But as the summer lasted, and would not end, the walls had begun to bother Frankie. That evening the kitchen looked strange to her, and she was afraid.

She stood in the doorway and said: 'I just thought I might as well invite him.'

So at dark John Henry came to the back door with a little week-end bag. He was dressed in his white recital suit and had put on shoes and socks. There was a dagger buckled to his belt. John Henry had seen snow. Although he was only six years old, he had gone to Birmingham last winter, and there he had seen snow. Frankie had never seen snow.

'I'll take the week-end bag,' said Frankie. 'You can start right in making a biscuit man.'

'O.K.'

John Henry did not play with the dough; he worked on the biscuit man as though it were a very serious business. Now and then he stopped off, settled his glasses with his little hand, and studied what he had done. He was like a tiny watchmaker, and he drew up a chair and knelt on it so that he could get directly over the work. When Berenice gave him some raisins, he did not stick them all around as any other human child would do; he used only two for the eyes; but immediately he realized they were too large—so he divided one raisin carefully and put in eyes, two specks for the nose, and a little grinning raisin mouth. When he had finished, he wiped his hands on the seat of his shorts, and there was a little biscuit man with separate fingers, a hat on, and even walking stick. John Henry had worked so hard that the dough was now gray and wet. But it was a perfect little biscuit man, and, as a matter of fact, it reminded Frankie of John Henry himself.

'I better entertain you now,' she said.

They ate supper at the kitchen table with Berenice, since her father had telephoned that he was working late at his jewelry store. When Berenice brought the biscuit man from the oven, they saw that it looked exactly like any biscuit man ever made by a child—it had swelled so that all the work of John Henry had been cooked out, the fingers were run together, and the walking stick resembled a sort of tail. But John Henry just looked at it through his glasses, wiped it with his napkin, and buttered the left foot.

It was a dark, hot August night. The radio in the dining room was playing a mixture of many stations: a war voice crossed with the gabble of an advertiser, and underneath there was the sleazy music of a sweet band. The radio had stayed on all the summer long, so finally it was a sound that as a rule they did not notice. Sometimes, when the noise became so loud that they could not hear their own ears, Frankie would turn it down a little. Otherwise, music and voices came and went and crossed and twisted with each other, and by August they did not listen any more.

'What do you want to do?' asked Frankie. 'Would you like for me to read to you out of Hans Brinker or would you rather do something else?'

'I rather do something else,' he said.

'What?'

'Less play out.'

'I don't want to,' Frankie said.

'There's a big crowd going to play out tonight.'

'You got ears,' Frankie said. 'You heard me.'

John Henry stood with his big knees locked, then finally he said: 'I think I better go home.'

'Why, you haven't spent the night! You can't eat supper and just go on off like that.'

'I know it,' he said quietly. Along with the radio they could hear the voices of the children playing in the night. 'But less go out, Frankie. They sound like they having a mighty good time.'

'No they're not,' she said. 'Just a lot of ugly silly children. Running and hollering and running and hollering. Nothing to it. We'll go upstairs and unpack your week-end bag.'

Frankie's room was an elevated sleeping porch which had been built onto the house, with a stairway leading up from the kitchen. The room was furnished with an iron bed, a bureau, and a desk. Also Frankie had a motor which could be turned on and off; the motor could sharpen knives, and, if they were long enough, it could be used for filing down your fingernails. Against the wall was the suitcase packed and ready for the trip to Winter Hill. On the desk there was a very old typewriter, and Frankie sat down before it, trying to think of any letters she could write: but there was nobody for her to write to, as every possible letter had already been answered, and answered even several times. So she covered the typewriter with a raincoat and pushed it aside.

'Honestly,' John Henry said, 'don't you think I better go home?'

'No,' she answered, without looking around at him. 'You sit there in the corner and play with the motor.'

Before Frankie there were now two objects—a

lavender seashell and a glass globe with snow inside that could be shaken into a snowstorm. When she held the seashell to her ear, she could hear the warm wash of the Gulf of Mexico, and think of a green palm island far away. And she could hold the snow globe to her narrowed eyes and watch the whirling white flakes fall until they blinded her. She dreamed of Alaska. She walked up a cold white hill and looked on a snowy wasteland far below. She watched the sun make colors in the ice, and heard dream voices, saw dream things. And everywhere there was the cold white gentle snow.

'Look,' John Henry said, and he was staring out of the window. 'I think those big girls are having a party in their clubhouse.'

'Hush!' Frankie screamed suddenly. 'Don't mention those crooks to me.'

There was in the neighborhood a clubhouse, and Frankie was not a member. The members of the club were girls who were thirteen and fourteen and even fifteen years old. They had parties with boys on Saturday night. Frankie knew all of the club members, and until this summer she had been like a younger member of their crowd, but now they had this club and she was not a member. They had said she was too young and mean. On Saturday night she could hear the terrible music and see from far away their light. Sometimes she went around to the alley behind the clubhouse and stood near a honeysuckle fence. She stood in the alley and watched and listened. They were very long, those parties.

'Maybe they will change their mind and invite you,' John Henry said.

'The son-of-a-bitches.'

Frankie sniffled and wiped her nose in the crook of her arm. She sat down on the edge of the bed, her shoulders slumped and her elbows resting on her knees. 'I think they have been spreading it all over town that I smell bad,' she said. 'When I had those boils and that black bitter smelling ointment, old Helen Fletcher asked what was that funny smell I had. Oh, I could shoot every one of them with a pistol.'

She heard John Henry walking up to the bed, and then she felt his hand patting her neck with tiny little pats. 'I don't think you smell so bad,' he said. 'You smell sweet.'

'The son-of-a-bitches,' she said again. 'And there was something else. They were talking nasty lies about married people. When I think of Aunt Pet and Uncle Ustace. And my own father! The nasty

lies! I don't know what kind of fool they take me for.'

'I can smell you the minute you walk in the house without even looking to see if it is you. Like a hundred flowers.'

'I don't care,' she said. 'I just don't care.'

'Like a thousand flowers,' said John Henry, and still he was patting his sticky hand on the back of her bent neck.

Frankie sat up, licked the tears from around her mouth, and wiped off her face with her shirttail. She sat still, her nose widened, smelling herself. Then she went to her suitcase and took out a bottle of Sweet Serenade. She rubbed some on the top of her head and poured some more down inside the neck of her shirt.

'Want some on you?'

John Henry was squatting beside the open suitcase and he gave a little shiver when she poured the perfume over him. He wanted to meddle in her traveling suitcase and look carefully at everything she owned. But Frankie only wanted him to get a general impression, and not count and know just what she had and what she did not have. So she strapped the suitcase and pushed it back against the wall.

'Boy!' she said. 'I bet I use more perfume than anybody in this town.'

The house was quiet except for the low rumble of the radio in the dining room downstairs. Long ago her father had come home and Berenice had closed the back door and gone away. There was no longer the sound of children's voices in the summer night.

'I guess we ought to have a good time,' said Frankie.

But there was nothing to do. John Henry stood, his knees locked and his hands clasped behind his back, in the middle of the room. There were moths at the window—pale green moths and yellow moths that fluttered and spread their wings against the screen.

'Those beautiful butterflies,' he said. 'They are trying to get in.'

Frankie watched the soft moths tremble and press against the window screen. The moths came every evening when the lamp on her desk was lighted. They came from out of the August night and fluttered and clung against the screen.

'To me it is the irony of fate,' she said. 'The way they come here. Those moths could fly anywhere. Yet they keep hanging around the windows of this house.'

John Henry touched the gold rim of his glasses to settle them on his nose and Frankie studied his flat little freckled face.

'Take off those glasses,' she said suddenly.

John Henry took them off and blew on them. She looked through the glasses and the room was loose and crooked. Then she pushed back her chair and stared at John Henry. There were two damp white circles around his eyes.

'I bet you don't need those glasses,' she said. She put her hand down on the typewriter. 'What is this?'

'The typewriter,' he said.

Frankie picked up the shell. 'And this?'

'The shell from the Bay.'

'What is that little thing crawling there on the floor?'

'Where?' he asked, looking around him.

'That little thing crawling along near your feet.'

'Oh,' he said. He squatted down. 'Why, it's an ant. I wonder how it got up here.'

Frankie tilted back in her chair and crossed her bare feet on her desk. 'If I were you I'd just throw those glasses away,' she said. 'You can see good as anybody.'

John Henry did not answer.

'They don't look becoming.'

She handed the folded glasses to John Henry and he wiped them with his pink flannel glasses rag. He put them back on and did not answer.

'O.K.' she said. 'Suit yourself. I was only telling you for your own good.'

They went to bed. They undressed with their backs turned to each other and then Frankie switched off the motor and the light. John Henry knelt down to say his prayers and he prayed for a long time, not saying the words aloud. Then he lay down beside her.

'Good night,' she said.

'Good night.'

Frankie stared up into the dark. 'You know it is still hard for me to realize that the world turns around at the rate of about a thousand miles an hour.'

'I know it,' he said.

'And to understand why it is that when you jump up in the air you don't come down in Fairview or Selma or somewhere fifty miles away.'

John Henry turned over and made a sleepy sound.

'Or Winter Hill,' she said. 'I wish I was starting for Winter Hill right now.'

JESSE STUART (1907–   )

Jesse Stuart was born in a log cabin consisting of one huge room, in W-Hollow, Greenup County, Kentucky. He was the son of a coal miner of Scottish highlander descent; on his mother's side of the family, of English stock. In an area where schooling was hard to come by, Stuart managed to acquire some, went on to Lincoln Memorial University (at Harrogate, Tennessee), and finally took an M.A. degree at Vanderbilt University, where he received special encouragement from Donald Davidson. Davidson was convinced that Stuart had an original talent, so much so that he remarked to a friend that it "would have been silly for me to try to persuade Jesse to write like T. S. Eliot or like my friends of the Fugitive group."[1]

[1] Everetta Love Blair, *Jesse Stuart: His Life and Works* (1967), p. xix.

Stuart was abroad in the early 1930's and served in the navy in the Second World War, but except for a few special projects and trips to Europe and Egypt, he has been content to keep at home in the mountain region of northeastern Kentucky. For a time he taught in his school district and later became superintendent of its schools, but more and more he devoted his time to writing poetry, fiction, essays, and an autobiography.

Of his part of Kentucky, Stuart observes that

it is a proud land; we are a proud people. It is a rugged and individualistic and loving land; so are the people. . . . We remain the least changed—holdouts against an American mass culture—with one of the most stable, sturdy, and stubborn peoples in the nation.

Our geographical, ancestral, and cultural roots bind us together as a small fiercely loyal country within a country. ("Ascend the High Mountain," *Country Beautiful*, February, 1962)

The southern Appalachians were settled relatively early, predominantly from Virginia during the last half of the eighteenth century. But the ancestors of the present inhabitants of this region did not move on through the mountains. They remained in the coves and narrow valleys while the great western tide of settlers swept on around or past them.

Stuart's stories and his one novel reflect his experience and the manners and folk humor of the Kentucky mountain culture. It is a world of clan feuds and hard drinking—much of the liquor consumed is illicit moonshine whisky. It is also a world of fundamentalist religion, perennially stirred up by hell-fire evangelism, and of gospel-hymn singing and of ecstatic religious conversions. This world of violent extremes is reflected in Stuart's fiction, which includes barbaric public hangings, instances of grinding poverty, and sometimes the erosion of humanity itself under the pressure of poverty and isolation. But there is also in his fiction a lusty vein of folk humor, merry-making like that described in the story entitled "The Belling of the Bride," candy-pullings, play-party games, square dances, and all the other festivities once found all along the American frontier but which in most parts of the country died out long ago.

The region's cultural conservatism shows itself in many ways: the southern highlands are still the special land of the English and Scottish folk ballad, brought across the Atlantic by the early colonists and here preserved, though sometimes in considerably altered form. The language itself shows many archaic English pronunciations and locutions intermixed with an occasional borrowing from the dialects of Scotland.

There are obvious affinities between this highland folk culture and that of the poor-white cultures of other parts of the South; but there are differences too. Greenup County (and the mountain South generally) had little or no experience with slavery. Though the mountain folk during the Civil War tended to side with the Union—even in states south of Kentucky—they had little sympathy for the black man and regarded him with hostility. They had almost no personal contact with black people, for these were to be found in large numbers only where there was also a planter class. The difference between the property owners, large and small holders and landless whites, hardly existed in places like Greenup County. The consequence is that Stuart's fiction reflects a cultural homogeneity to a degree not found in, say, the Carolinas and Georgia, where hill country occupied by the poorer whites might be adjacent to, or even surrounded by, larger holdings and even great plantations. Mrs. Chesnut in her *Diary* (see pp. 1688–95), for example, records a visitation to Mulberry plantation by "sandhill tackies" who lived within walking distance.

In writing about his Greenup County mountain people, Stuart writes as one of them. This in itself gives a special character to his fiction. Stories about southern poor whites have generally been written by outsiders. This has been true as far back as William Byrd's description of the lubbers of the Virginia–North Carolina border. Such observers have been people of a high degree of literacy, who were horrified or amused—or both—by what they saw. A writer like Augustus B. Longstreet, for example, was a southern Whig. Though Stuart is willing to expose the more grimly primitive and even grotesque aspects of his culture, his attitude is not condescending.

We have chosen to represent Stuart by his fiction rather than by his poetry. Where is he best as a writer of fiction? Probably in those stories where he avoids the temptation to heap up local color or to stress the pathos of poverty and suffering. Not all of these last avoid sentimentality. His best stories, it seems to us, are those in the comic vein where the folk idiom fits the spirit of the story and where the farcical and humorous elements account for and somewhat mitigate the more grotesque and exaggerated depictions of character.

FURTHER READINGS

Jesse Stuart, *Beyond Dark Hills* (1938)
———, *Head o' W-Hollow* (1936)
———, *Taps for Private Tussie* (1943)
———, *The Thread That Runs So True* (1949)
———, *The Year of My Rebirth* (1956)
Hensley C. Woodbridge, *Jesse Stuart: A Bibliography* (1960)

Everetta Love Blair, *Jesse Stuart: His Life and Works* (1967)
Mary Washington Clarke, *Jesse Stuart's Kentucky* (1968)
Ruel E. Foster, *Jesse Stuart* (1968)
Lee Pennington, *The Dark Hills: A Study of Vision and Symbolism in the Novels of Jesse Stuart* (1967)

Uncle Casper (1936)

"Uncle Casper" amounts to little more than an anecdote which provides the occasion for a character sketch and some humorous tales. It is not so fully developed as some of Stuart's more ambitious stories are, but it is characteristic of his style and it has a good deal of charm.

Whatever Uncle Casper's qualifications for the state senate, he is no mean rhetorician, and the yarns with which he overwhelms his recently made young friend are fully in the tradition of the tall tale of the old Southwest. In fact, the people who first settled Greenup County represent the kind of people who formed that style.

I

Uncle Casper comes to town on Saturday. He is running for State Senator. His eyes are two black sparkling slits. His mustache is a tuft of dead bull-grass, neatly pruned, and his nose is the sawed-off root of an oak tree. His hair is two spoiled waves of sickled timothy parted in the middle—the east wind blew a swath west and the west wind blew a swath east. There is a cricket ravine between the swaths.

If you could see Uncle Casper. There are white milkweed stems among the dead-timothy hair. If you could see the long arms and the age-spotted hands like the spots on the body of an aged sassafras. His black suit fits his body like the winter bark on an oak tree. The toes of his black shoes have fought the rocks and stumps on Kenney Ridge. His socks fall over the tops of his shoes to hide the scars.

Here comes Uncle Casper on the courthouse square. His black eyes dance, his arms swing like a willow wand waving in a swift wind of Spring. "What is your name, son," says Uncle Casper, "and are you old enough to vote, my son?"

"Press Freeman is my name, I have had the seven-year 'each' three times. If I hadn't I'd be over twenty-one on Election Day all right."

"Which ticket do you vote, my son?"

"I vote on the side of the Lord."

"That is the ticket I belong to," says Uncle Casper, "and, my son, I am runnin for State Senator. I aim to give the poor people a chance since I am a poor man. My family has broke me up. Sent a boy to college—borrowed the money—mortgaged my home. Found him on the bank of a river in Michigan a-fishin. Sent another boy out to college and he didn't do no good, took to a pack of cards and a bottle. I went to the eighth grade, son, in the old school and I've teached for fifty-nine years. Now, I'm a broke-up man. Set out of a house and home. Can't get a school anymore since we ain't got school trustees. I used to run my trustees and get my schools. I could a got four or five. Things has changed anymore. Not like they used to be. Vote for me in November and I'll make them like they used to be."

Uncle Casper's eyes blink. His hands talk.

"A vote for me means better roads, better schools, better schoolhouses, feather beds for men when they get drunk instead of ditches, homes for the widows and the orphans, no totin pistols nor bowie knives. I'll put two pieces of bread in your safe where you ain't got but one. Pensions for the old broke-down men like myself and your Pap, and I'll put the school trustees back—three to every deestrict. A vote for me means a help to you. Son, I am a poor man and I'll help the poor people."

"I'll be there, Uncle Casper, to vote on the ticket the Lord and me and you is on. I'll be there and I'll finish the third spell of the seven-year 'each' by then."

Uncle Casper goes down the courthouse square. He talks with his hands. He talks to this one. He talks to that one. Men gather around Uncle Casper to hear him talk. "I lived on corn bread and onions to get my education, and wore shirts made out'n coffee-sacks and muslin and calico. My boys has broke me up. I've preached the word of God and teached school for fifty-nine year. Brothers, I ask you in the name of the Lord to help me in November and I'll guarantee you every vote you cast for me will mean two slices of bread in your safe where you ain't got but one, and one slice of bread in your safe where you ain't got any. Two hams of meat in your smoke house where you ain't got but one, and one ham of meat in your smoke house if you ain't got any."

Then Uncle Casper goes down the square and he meets Press Freeman. Uncle Casper says, "And what might your name be, my son?"

"You just met me awhile ago," says Press, "I am Press Freeman. Don't you remember me? Remember we talked about who was on the Lord's side and who wasn't?"

"Yes, I remember you now, son. We talked about the old times. I just want you to remember me in November. Did I ever tell you the story about the snake?"

"No you ain't never," says Press.

"Set down in this bandstand," says Uncle Casper.

"Okie-dough," says Press.

"I was sittin in the yard," says Uncle Casper, "with my feet propped up on the side of the house when I saw it. I was smokin my pipe and lookin toward my potato patch to see if I couldn't just about see my potatoes grow. When all of a sudden, I saw a big black-snake's head bobbin up and down out of the ragweed patch beside the potato rows. That snake, bigger than a baby's leg, went tearin right out of that ragweed patch and took down across the potato ridges fast as a horse could run. I thinks to myself, 'What now!'

"The snake sorty halted in the garden between two rows of cabbage heads. I saw him bob his head up and down. He looked like a scared rabbit. I kept my eye on him. There was a little patch of briars beside the cabbage patch—in the old fence row beside the garden. That black snake, big around as a baby's leg and long as a rail-fence rider, made a headlong dive into that briar patch like a cat divin for a mouse. It acted like a cat that smelled a mouse and jumped to get it. And

then I saw what I saw. I stopped smokin my pipe and forgot about my leg bein left lame from that bullet I got on Brush Creek at that Revival Meetin.

"That black snake wropped around that big rattler so quick it would make your head swim. I saw it all right there in that briar patch. That black snake wropped that big rattler up like a love vine wrops a ragweed. Then the black snake started to clampin down with all its strength and bitin the rattler's throat. Then he squeezed. I let them fight. The old rattler was squeezed so tight he couldn't rattle. Think about me a-sittin that close to a rattler and not knowin it!

"That black snake worked hard—squeezin, bitin, beatin with its head. Then it uncoiled a wrop at a time until it got down to the last wrop—then it uncoiled the last wrop and sprung way out in the cabbage patch. It bobbed its head up and looked back. It saw the rattler was still movin. Then it took right back into that briar patch. It wropped that rattler up tighter than ever. It bit it harder than ever. It whipped it with its tail like it was a buggy whip. The old rattler couldn't take the last beatin. It give up the ghost and turned over on its back and died. Its belly was turned up to the sun. The black snake took out of there and run out and bit him off a little chew of a weed. It munched it in its flat jaws like a rabbit munches clover.

"I hopped up on my lame leg and parted the briars with my cane. I pulled that dead rattler and took it in and showed it to Liz, my wife. It had twenty-seven rattlers and nine buttons. W'y Liz wouldn't believe what I told her about that fight and the black snake killin the rattler. I skinned the rattler and made me a belt out of its hide and Liz a pair of garters."

"I'll be dogged," says Press.

II

"Somethin kept catchin our chickens. Every mornin we would go out to the barn and count the hens. There would be one missin. So I looked under the roost and found a lot of loose feathers and part of a old white hen. Chuck Winters said to me: 'W'y Casper, that is one of them little chicken owls doin all this. They can hold more chicken than a fox. I'll show you how to trap him.' So I took Chuck at his word.

"We took a dozen steel traps down to where the white hen was layin on the ground. Her head was eaten off and some of the meat was gouged out from under her wing.

"Chuck said: 'Now dig a little ditch around the hen. Throw the loose dirt away. Set the traps in a circle around the hen. Put feathers over the traps. Drive a stake down through the body of the hen so when the owl pulls he can't move her. And in the mornin we'll have the bird that caught that hen. When a owl eats no more of a hen than this he always comes back for the second mess.' And we set the traps, covered them with feathers and staked the steel-trap chains to the ground with little wooden pegs. We staked the hen down.

"Behold the next mornin if there wasn't one of them old barred hoot owls bigger 'n a turkey gobbler a-settin right on the hen with his neck feathers all bowed up like a rooster ready to fight. He was caught by one toe. But we had the chicken thief that had caught over thirty hens.

"And I said to Chuck, 'Chuck, what kind of punishment are we goin to give this bird?' Chuck studied for a minute and he said, 'W'y Casper, let's saturate him with coal oil, set his tail feathers on fire and turn him back into the elements.' Chuck has always been quick to think of things like that. So, I went to the kitchen, got the coal-oil can and a match and went back to the owl under the chicken roost. I throwed the coal oil on him. We could not get very close to him. Chuck got broom sage and tied it to the end of a stick and set fire to it. I pulled the peg out of the ground that held the trap and Chuck set the fire to his tail.

"Gentlemen, right up into the elements with that steel trap janglin from his toe—that fire to his tail—he soared a red stream of blaze through the elements. Fire from that owl fell onto my meadow. It was in late March when the wind was blowin steady and everythin was so dry. Fire popped up all over the meadow at once. It looked like the red flames of hell and the wind was a-ragin. That owl went right on through the elements.

"I hollered to Chuck to shoot him with a pistol before he fired the whole country. Chuck put seven hot balls of lead at that owl. But it soared right on through the elements. It went right over Mart Haley's timber. The blaze shot up like flames from hell. Flames lapped right up through the dead saw briars and leaves. 'All my timber is gone,' shouted Chuck—'timber lands jines Haley's timber lands. My rail fences are all gone. That owl will set the world on fire if somebody don't shoot him from the elements or the fire don't consume him.' I tell you, gentlemen, that owl set fire to the whole country. My land was ruined. My timber was burned to death. That fire burnt up one thousand panels of rail fence for me. It ruined my meadows. It ruined my neighbors. We had to get together and have workins and put the fence back. We had to put some barns back and two houses. It ruined the whole country. If I hadn't a had good Baptis neighbors I would a been sued over that owl and would a been a broke-up man today."

"Well I'll be dogged," says Press. "Grandma said to burn owl feathers you'd have bad luck among your chickens for seven years."

"Not so, I ain't had a bit of bad luck since then," says Uncle Casper.

III

"One day Chuck and me was out diggin ginsang. Chuck and me used to run together a good deal and this is the way we made a little spendin money. We had our sacks nearly filled with two-prongs, three-prongs, and four-prongs. Chuck looked down in the weeds and saw a big rattlesnake. 'Come here, Casper,' he said to me. I went over where Chuck was and by the eternal God I never saw such a rattlesnake in my life. It was big as a cow's leg. 'I can handle that snake,' says Chuck. 'I never was afraid of a snake—not the meanest snake that ever growed.' Chuck was drinkin some brandy—some persimmon brandy. So he jumps right in a-straddle of the rattlesnake and brakes it down in the back with his fist. Then he begins to choke.

"It scared me to see Chuck a-straddle of that rattlesnake. So, I says: 'Chuck get off that rattler's back. It will bite you shore as God made little apples.' Chuck just looked up and grinned at me. Then he said: 'You hold it down and I'll pull its teeth and we'll take it home and show it to Ike Wampler. He'll never believe we captured a snake this big.' So I gets down a-straddle of this rattler's neck. 'Choke it,' says Chuck. I choked it till I was black in the face. Chuck says: 'I see its fangs and a little gall bladder of pizen back in there. Wait till I twist a withe and I'll yank them teeth out 'n there before you can say Jack Robinson.' My grip kept givin out. My hands got so tired a-hold of that big rattler's neck. And when my grip was goin Chuck hollered out that it had shot a stream of the pizen from the gall bladder through the fang into his eye. He said: 'I'm stingin in the eye like a barrel of red pepper had been dumped into my eye. I'm pizened in the eye by that rattlesnake.' I jumped off 'n the rattlesnake's back and got hold of Chuck and drug him down among the nettles and pea vine.

"The first thing I thought of when Chuck was glombin and clawin at this eye, was my twist of taste-bud tobacco. It is that old-time tobacco that used to be growin around the barn on old manure piles. Well, that is where I got this. The twist was bigger 'n my forearm. So I bit me off a big chew and I chawed it. I got Chuck down, for he was smartin a right smart by now. I put my feet on his chest and held each one of his hands in a hand of mine and I chawed that chew up and squirted every bit of it in his eye. He squalled a little, but I knowed it was a case of life or death. Then I took off another chaw and chewed it and squirted that in Chuck's eye. I kept on till I chewed up the whole thing and squirted it into Chuck's eye, And when I let Chuck up Chuck says to me, 'I'd rather have the disease as to have that remedy.' "

"Well, I'll be dogged," says Press.

"I went upon the hill one day to cut a pole of stove wood. I saw a dead sourwood pole and I took my ax and thought I would cut it. It looked dry, hard and seasoned. I saw a knot hole upon the side and the sour gnats were comin out and goin in. Before I got to the pole a racer snake sprung at my throat and I struck at it with the double-bitted ax. It saw I was going to put up fight so it started to scramble. I took after it with the ax. It went straight to the pole and wropped right around it—right up that pole like a black movin corkscrew. Then it ducked down in the hole where the sour gnats was. It stuck its head out and licked out its tongue at me. I thought, 'Old Boy, I'll fix you.' So I climbs up the pole with a wooden glut in my hand that I whittle from the butt of the pole. I stuck that glut down in the hole and drove it in with a stick. 'I'll let you stay in this tree awhile,' I says.

"Well, I went on and cut some dry locust poles for stove wood. I took them into the wood yard and cut them up for stove wood. One year after that I was back on this same hill gettin stove wood and I happened to see this sourwood pole with the glut stickin in the hole. So, I remembered the snake. I went up and whacked down the sourwood pole. The tree was hollow down to the roots and when I cut into the hollow, out popped that snake poor as Job's turkey. I could a-counted its ribs if I'd had time. But that racer remembered me. It

coiled around my leg like it was a rope around a well-windlass. It grabbed me by the ankle. I took off the hill hollerin. I just couldn't help it. Its sharp pin teeth stuck into my ankle bone.

"I run to the wood yard hard as I could go. That snake tightened down on my leg and cut off the blood from circulation. I'd about give up the ghost when Liz come out and she said, 'Casper, what is the matter with you? You are white as a piece of flour poke.' And I says, 'See what has me by the leg, don't you?' And Liz went in and got a butcher knife. That snake still held me by the ankle. It tightened its holts. It bit me harder. Liz just reached down with that butcher knife and she cut that snake into ten pieces. It was wropped around my leg five times if I am right. Its head still held to my leg. Its teeth held right into my ankle bone. Then Liz pulled at its head and she yanked its teeth out, but they brought a hunk of meat.

"When our baby boy Frons was born he had the prints of the prettiest little racer black snake right over his heart."

"I'll be dogged," says Press, spitting at a knot hole on the bandstand. Uncle Casper spits at it. "Center as a die," says Uncle Casper. "That's a sign I'm goin to get elected Senator."

IV

"Chuck took a notion to run for Representative of Greenbriar County. Chuck preaches some, you know, and one Sunday afternoon when he was preachin Abraham Fox's funeral he said to the people, 'Did you know, folks, that you was a-lookin square at Greenbriar County's next Representative? If you don't know it, I'll tell you that you are lookin square at him.' And Chuck Haley goes out and tells the people that he is goin to pass a Law that the people will get a bounty for every fox hide they bring in to the County seat town of Greenbriar. He told the people that if they didn't clean out the foxes that they was a-goin to clean out the chickens and there wouldn't be enough yaller-legged pullets left for a Baptis preacher a mess. Well, as you know, Greenbriar County has a lot of Baptis and they elected Chuck, though he was on the wrong Party. They went for their religion before they did their Party. Chuck was elected, but not by the fox hunters. They stuck by their foxes.

"Chuck told me all about goin to Frankfort. He

said they let him talk in a little thing that looked like a fryin pan. He said it was over behind the pianer. He told them about his bill on the bounty of fox hides. Some said they fooled old Chuck about talkin over the air—said he talked over a old broke-down telephone without any wires to it. Then he did talk over the air. But he give his speech about foxes. I knowed Chuck was goin to get into it with the fox hunters. When he come back from Frankfort and the news got into the *Greenbriar Gazette* about his big speech over the air on foxes and him actin like that and belongin to the wrong Party too, w'y the fox hunters had done had their meetin and they was a-layin for him. Chuck hired a hack and started home smokin a cigar he'd rolled out 'n twist-bud tobacco and plump went a hole through his black Stetson hat. Chuck whipped the horses fast and got away from that bunch of rocks upon the Winsor place. That is where they waylaid Chuck.

"Some said it was old Tiger MacMeans that waylaid Chuck. Old Tiger is a big fox hunter. One time he run a young fox around one pint and up over another pint and into a dirt hole and he dug it out with a stick. Another time one of his Blue Tick hounds got hung up in a rock cliff and he blasted rock down with dynamite for eight days and hired everybody in the neighborhood to help him get old Queen. And old Tiger got her too. She was so nigh gone she couldn't stand up, but when they found her she had the fox right by the tail. He took Queen home and fed her goat's milk and she got all right. Well, he is the fellow we thought put the bullet through Chuck's Stetson hat.

"Gentlemen, by the eternal God, them fox hunters I guess it was got after the Baptis and we had a regular war in Greenbriar County. Barns filled with tobacco burnt all over Finish Creek and Laurel Creek. Cattle barns was burnt to the ground with all the live stock in them. It was a time. I never heard tell of anythin like it. And out on the hills a body could find Irish taters with rat pizen on them—fried taters and dead hound dogs dead along the ridges. They was dead along the creeks where they had tried to get water when the pizen struck them and their insides went to burnin. Chuck couldn't get to church. People looked for him—men that had had their hound dogs pizened. The fox hunters waited for him when they tooted their horns for dogs that never come home. Of course, Chuck never put the pizen out. But friends of Chuck's put it out when Chuck's Stetson was plugged from a rock cliff.

"And Tid Redfern picked up a coffee-sack full of pizened biscuits put out to get the dogs. We don't know who put them out. It might a been the shepherds on the hillsides that had been losin sheep, and when the Baptis and fox hunters got into it they put their noses into it for the time was right for them to get the dogs. They wasn't a hound dog left in that country big enough to run a fox or to teach the young pups how to start a cold trail. They said old Tiger could get down and smell where a fox had been and put the young hounds on a cold trail. They wasn't a barn left on Tiger Creek or Laurel Creek big enough to house a yearlin calf. Bloodhounds were used to track men that done the burnin, but they used red pepper on their shoe soles and when the bloodhounds sniffed that they didn't sniff anymore. So, no one was caught. And people just cooled down in three or four years themselves.

"Bert Flannery said he never could get over it when his milk cows burned in his barn. His barn doors were left open, but the cows would not come out of their stalls. He said he heard the cows bawl so pitifully that it made him cry. He said he couldn't forget that dreadful night and it would stay with him as long as there was wind in his body. Bert Flannery is a good man. He is a good prayin man and he tends to his own business, but he was just drawed into the fracas like a lot of us innocent men. Fudas Pimbroke said he could never forget seein his old Fleet turned on her back on the ridge road where she had been leadin a fox when the pizen got her down. He said she was stretched there bloated with wind. He said he could never forget the look on that dead hound dog's face.

"When the next session of time come around for Chuck to go back to Frankfort, they hauled him to the station one night under a load of fodder. He took the train straight for Frankfort to get his Law about bounty on foxes repealed. And Chuck told them about the dogs pizened and the barns and church houses and homes burnt in Greenbriar County and about the war still ragin there—and they wiped that Law right out. Got rid of it root, leaf, and branch. But that got all the Baptis mad at Chuck. Now they was all mad at him—the Baptis and the fox hunters. He didn't have a side to cling to. So, he went home to stay and one mornin when he was milkin the cow, flop went another bullet through his hat. So he got under another load of fodder and went to Greenbriar. He caught a train for West Virginia. He's never come back to Greenbriar. I was readin the paper where he had been killed for givin a West Virginia hound arsenic. The fox hunter hit him in the head with a coal pick. He wasn't any count for a Representative anyway, for he couldn't read nor write nor cipher. And besides, he didn't belong to the right Party. When a man goes out of the bounds of his Party to elect a man of the wrong Party, then you can take care. Things are a-goin to pop.

People in Greenbriar County has kindly come back together agin after a time."

"I'll be dogged," says Press, "I'll be right there to vote for you, Uncle Casper, in November." Press spits at the knot hole. He misses. Uncle Casper spits from his wad of homemade taste-bud. "Center as a die," says Uncle Casper, "sign I'll be your next Senator of Kentucky."

WILLIAM FAULKNER (1897–1962)

The work of William Faulkner may be viewed as a culmination of the development of twentieth-century southern fiction. The term is not, of course, used here in a chronological sense. Faulkner's work did not come at the end of a literary movement (and did not end it). His work was in fact contemporary with much of the work of writers treated earlier in this section: that of Erskine Caldwell, for example, or Caroline Gordon, or Katherine Anne Porter. Yet, taking into account the range of his fiction and the power and intensity of his greatest work, "culmination" seems justified.

In the foregoing pages, we have been sampling the modes and materials of the literature that began to come out of the South in the 1920's and 1930's. There is a remarkable uniformity in the cultural situation portrayed. One thinks, for example, of the importance of family ties, the sense of the weight of history, and the concreteness of personal relationships natural to a people, most of whom have grown up on farms or in small towns. The culture is one of fixed and relatively stable relationships: for example, the role of women in the society or the place of the Negro is sharply defined—though concrete personal relationships may on occasion modify the apparent rigidities of sex, caste, and certainly of class. In the last-named area, there is a surprising fluidity for a society that is generally traditional and conservative.

The fact that Faulkner was a native not of Virginia or South Carolina, but of Mississippi, is of some importance. His state was a kind of quintessence of the old South. It was insulated by the upper South from influences emanating from the country at large. It had no cities. Its provincialism was relatively untempered by national influences. Its very rawness—in the 1820's Mississippi was still frontier country—made for an intensification of its southern quality, for its governing ideal was "southern" to start with, not, like that of Virginia at its founding, a reflection of English customs and ideas. Finally, more than the long-settled states on the Atlantic and Gulf coasts or those of the upper South, northern Mississippi presented a volatile mixture of extremes: a manorial society (in aspiration at least) with many black slaves, set down side by side with a white folk culture still fiercely independent and still practicing the frontier virtues—and vices.

T. S. Stribling (1881–1966)

The writers we have discussed earlier in this section handle their common southern material in their individual ways. None of them can be said to imitate Faulkner—not even those few young enough to have been influenced by him. They have their own qualities and their own kinds of fictional excellence. But with one possible exception no other southern novelist aimed at Faulkner's scope and his panoramic vision of the history of the South. That possible exception is T. S. Stribling, and for this reason he deserves a special note here.

In three linked volumes, *The Forge* (1931), *The Store* (1932), and *The Unfinished Cathedral* (1934), Stribling chronicles the changing fortunes of the Vaiden family from the years before the Civil War down to the Depression of the early 1930's. The strong man of the family, Miltiades Vaiden, begins his adult life as a plantation overseer. He becomes a colonel in the Confederate army and after the war is active in the Ku Klux Klan. Finally he gets into business and in the closing decades of the century rises to wealth. He dies as an old man in his nineties.

There is plenty of violence in the trilogy: Civil War battles, beatings and lynchings in the period of Reconstruction, and the tragedies experienced by people of mixed blood. The Vaidens have mulatto and quadroon kin, and Colonel Vaiden, at the end of *The Store*, discovers that he has in effect connived at permitting the lynching of his part-Negro son.

Here, then, is "Faulknerian" material in abundance, but the finished product is certainly not Faulkner—nor has it anything of Faulkner's quality. The principal reason, of course, is simply that Stribling lacks Faulkner's genius, though it must be conceded that he produces some strong and effective scenes and that the cumulative effect of his work is far from negligible. His specific weaknesses are a tendency to editorialize and even to preach. He sometimes becomes so irritated at the injustices endemic to his native region, especially in its treatment of the Negro, that he breaks the narrative pattern with outbursts of personal sarcasm rather than allowing the stupidity or cruelty to speak for itself.

Yet Stribling tries to be fair and impartial: he is quite capable of castigating the other side. When the quadroon slave girl, Gracie, owned by the Vaidens, escapes to what she supposes to be the army of liberation, she finds that though one of the Union officers shows a sense of compassion for her, the other blue-coated soldiers that she meets are only concerned to try to get into her tent to sleep with her. She is informed that the Union army is not fighting the war in order to eradicate slavery. Lt. Beekman tells her that "we're invading this country, Gracie, because Southern cotton growers want to buy cheap English goods, duty free, and we want them to buy Northern-made goods with a tariff added to the cost price. Why, after the battle of Fort Sumter, Lincoln offered to make slavery perpetual down here if the planters would agree to the tariff."

Waiving the merits of this argument, one questions whether a young officer in the Union army would be aware of it. And even if he did have personal misgivings about the purity of his country's motives, would he be likely to speak in these terms to a refugee slave girl? If we are to accept Beekman's outburst as dramatically plausible, then the author needed to tell us much more about his character and his background.

Stribling's trilogy is ambitious not only in its scope and range but also in its attempt to penetrate beneath the clichés and slogans of the day and our own more superficial estimates of the historical situation. In fact, he is trying hard for a true and therefore necessarily complex account of events; and in this ambition also he challenges comparison with Faulkner.

As we have already observed, there is no real rivalry. Stribling's trilogy is at best an honorable failure. But his work is original and independent. The question of imitation has to be ruled out of account. Stribling published his first novel in 1926, the year in which Faulkner published his. Most of his trilogy had been written before the first hints of what Faulkner was up to were evident to anybody.

The parallels between the two novelists are worth remarking because they can tell us something about the emergence of literature in the twentieth-century South. By the 1920's, the time was indeed ripe. Even the notion of a Balzacian series of novels based on the southern experience evidently could occur to more than one writer. In asking why, one appeals once again to the southern concern for history. Nearly all the southern writers of this period tend to see the story of an individual as involved with the history of a family; and that, involved with the history of a culture—and of a region. Moreover, because of the special history of their own region, their interest in the individual is continuous with their interest in his relation to a society of fixed norms. Even James Branch Cabell displays such an interest and, like Faulkner, invents a mythical county or province, though he imagines it as existing in medieval France. Moreover, even when topical events and contemporary problems are, as we have noted in discussing Caroline Gordon, the matters of concern, the southern novelist typically sees them as rooted in history. When, on the other hand, he writes about the past, he is not concerned with mere costume romance. In sum, for these novelists, the society with which they are concerned is a traditional society and the past is still alive—not embalmed as "history" in the pages of a book. For Katherine Anne Porter's Miranda the past is formidably alive and demands to be understood. Indeed, "Old Mortality" is a fable of the meaning of the past as seen in two perspectives; William Faulkner also brings to bear upon the southern past multiple perspectives. His *Absalom, Absalom!* is the story of an attempt to make sense of the past—but in no antiquarian spirit. For Quentin Compson, his personal need to make sense of it is urgent and immediate.

Yet granted the assumption that for Faulkner and other serious southern writers of his day the past was still a living force, why is their work so different from that of an earlier generation of southern writers—from that of writers who, one might suppose, were even more deeply steeped in history, who had taken part in, or at least witnessed, the stirring events of the Civil War and the Reconstruction? In any case, why did a great surge of creative energy manifest itself in the South just when it did and not some decades earlier? (The second question is simply a variant of the first, and the following conjectured answer can apply to both.)[1]

When an older culture is beginning to disappear, when the bonds which tie its members together are loosening and people become conscious of the past as truly past, it is just then that a great literary flowering may occur. The men of England's Elizabethan period still had the medieval culture in their bones. Their era was still suffused with the patterns of thought, the norms of value, and the rituals of the Middle Ages. But their minds were now being stirred by new methods, new discoveries, and new problems. They were caught up in a deep conflict of values. The cultural situation begot questioning of the former way of life and yet allowed no easy dismissal of it. The writer was permitted to step back from a culture in which he was bred and to look at it from the outside; and if he was too deeply involved in the conflict of values to step back, then he might be driven to enact the conflict in his work—and this is precisely what seems to be happening in many Elizabethan plays. A similar theory may well account for the New England renaissance in the middle of the nineteenth century. The Puritan theology was breaking down, and thinkers who had inherited its values, people like Thoreau and Emerson, were questioning the received theological formulations of those values and responding to quickening impulses from the outside.[2] It was a time that seemed to offer a clarification of issues and a startlingly fresh look at things previously taken for granted as old and familiar.

Something of the sort seems to have occurred in the South, roughly between the First and Second World Wars. For half a century the southern states had been economically stagnant. Reconstruction had not really "reconstructed" the social pattern or the basic values. For fifty

[1] The conjecture we offer here has similarities to that offered for the general flowering of American literature in the teens and twenties, though the historical forces involved were to a large extent different.

[2] See Allen Tate's "Emily Dickinson," in *Essays of Four Decades* (1968).

years the South licked its wounds and held as nearly as it could to its old way of life. Toward any outsider's attack on its way of life, the southerner, on instinct as it were, reacted defensively. But now the more sensitive creative minds began the sort of self-examination and internal debate out of which a serious literature may arise.

The reasons that lie behind individual creativity or the creativity of the whole period are, however, finally mysterious. The theory we have just advanced can at best explain only part of what happened, for how can anyone formulate the proper tension in the artist's mind or the optimum pressure of the cultural community upon the writer's sense of individuality—a pressure strong enough to discipline his art but not so strong as to stifle it? Yet, cultural conditions do matter, and one has to assume that Faulkner and his contemporaries did find themselves as artists born at a propitious time. Faulkner's great-grandfather, for example, who published in 1880 *The White Rose of Memphis*, a very bad novel though a best seller in its day, clearly was not.

Of his great-grandfather, Colonel W. C. Falkner, Faulkner was in 1945 to write to Malcolm Cowley:

My great-grandfather, whose name I bear,[3] was a considerable figure in his time and provincial milieu. He was a prototype of John Sartoris: raised, organized, paid the expenses of and commanded the 2nd Mississippi Infantry, 1861–2, etc. Was a part of Stonewall Jackson's left at 1st Manassas that afternoon; we have a citation in James Longstreet's longhand as his corps commander after 2nd Manassas. He built the first railroad in our county, wrote a few books, made [the] grand European tour of his time, died in a duel and the county raised a marble effigy which still stands in Tippah County.

Stories of his ancestor's exploits appear in modi-

fied form in Faulkner's third novel, *Sartoris* (1929), in *The Unvanquished* (1938), and elsewhere in his fiction.

When Faulkner was born in 1897, the family was living in New Albany, Mississippi, but in 1902 his father moved to the nearby town of Oxford. There Faulkner grew up with his three brothers, later married an Oxford girl, and was to call Oxford home for the rest of his life.

Though from an early age he read widely, his formal education was sketchy. He completed only two years of high school and only a little over a year at the University of Mississippi,[4] where his father had become business manager.

From his high-school days onward, Faulkner was restless and somewhat at loose ends. He worked at various jobs—for a year at his grandfather's bank in Oxford, at the Winchester Arms plant in New Haven, Connecticut, in a bookstore in New York City, as postmaster at the university post office in Oxford, Mississippi, where he was not a notable success and finally, to the relief of a good many of his customers, resigned. During the first half of 1925 he lived in the French Quarter in New Orleans, made a little money by selling literary sketches and features to the *Times-Picayune*, and, since those were Prohibition days, worked on a boat running in whisky from the Gulf. Later in the year, he got a job on a freighter bound for Italy and spent several months on a walking trip through Italy and France.

James Joyce, in *Ulysses*, has Stephen Dedalus remark that "A man of genius makes no mistakes" and, he might have added, "wastes no experience." Faulkner's various false starts and apparently aimless adventuring were to be used in one way or another, and usually to good effect, in his stories and novels, for his literary ambition was already alive and awake, and he was all along gathering materials—perhaps it

---

[3] The *u* was added when Faulkner began to publish fiction.

[4] Faulkner had enlisted in the Royal Air Force in January, 1918. He took flight training at a Canadian base, but the war ended before he got overseas. As a returned soldier, he was admitted into the university though he did not have a high-school diploma.

would be more accurate to say soaking up his materials through a process of osmosis. Faulkner tells us that one of his stories—never published —was written as early as 1919. During his years at Oxford, Phil Stone, an attorney, encouraged his writing, lent him books, and advised him on his reading.

It was not until 1925 that Faulkner began to move toward any significant publication.[5] In New Orleans during that year he met Sherwood Anderson, then also living in New Orleans. Friendship and talk with the older writer stimulated the beginner, and during a few months in the first half of 1925 Faulkner began and finished his first novel, *Soldier's Pay.* Anderson helped him find a publisher. The novel appeared in 1926 and received very favorable notices, but it did not sell nor did a second novel, *Mosquitoes,* published in the following year.

In one of their conversations Anderson advised the younger man to write about what he knew: "You're a country boy; all you know is that little patch up there in Mississippi where you started from. But that's all right too." It was not, however, until his third novel, *Sartoris* (1929), that Faulkner began to act on this advice and, using materials from his own family history and his own observations of life in north Mississippi, he produced *Sartoris,* the first of the Yoknapatawpha County novels. It did not much impress the reviewers and it sold no better than the two novels that had preceded it. Yet it exhibited Faulkner's characteristic talent at work on what were to become some of his dominant themes. It may be said to have led up to one of the most brilliant periods of literary productivity on record. In scarcely more than a decade Faulkner would publish a volume of poems, two collections of short stories, and ten novels—including all of his acknowledged masterpieces.[6]

[5] He had published poems, essays, and reviews in student magazines at the University of Mississippi and a poem in the New Orleans *Double Dealer.*

[6] Probably the only parallel in American literary history is the output of Melville in the early and middle 1850's.

By 1931 his fiction had begun to sell. *Sanctuary,* the most sensational of his novels, came out in that year and at once enjoyed a *succès de scandale.* Faulkner has written of this work that he had decided, after his first novels had failed to sell, to invent "the most horrific tale I could imagine" and that he wrote this tale off in about three weeks. In the summer of 1929 he sent it to his publisher who replied almost immediately that he couldn't publish it because "we'd both be in jail." Faulkner, then, having got a job on the night shift at the power plant of the university, dismissed *Sanctuary* from his mind and got to work on the brilliant short novel, *As I Lay Dying* (1929). Months later, to his surprise, the galley proofs of *Sanctuary* came to him in the mail. Faulkner goes on to say:

> Then I saw that [*Sanctuary*] was so terrible that there were but two things to do: tear it up or rewrite it. . . . So I tore the galleys down and rewrote the book . . . trying to make out of it something which would not shame *The Sound and the Fury* and *As I Lay Dying* too much. . . .

Sanctuary actually contains some of Faulkner's most brilliant writing, and, though it is indeed sensational, it can be argued that the horrors are not gratuitous, but required for Faulkner's working out of the theme.

At any rate, after this Faulkner was able to sell his short stories to the magazines and found publishers for his novels. But he still made very little money out of his writing and so went out to Hollywood to write and patch up scripts fashioned from books other than his own. Faulkner was a sound craftsman and took such hack work seriously, but he kept it carefully segregated from his own writings as a novelist.

A small group of critics continued to point out his brilliance as a writer of fiction, but general recognition of his worth grew slowly. In 1947 only three of his novels, contained in two volumes in the Modern Library series, were in print. It was not until he was awarded the

Nobel prize for literature in 1950 that his books began to sell in any quantity.

Though Faulkner liked to describe himself as simply a recounter of yarns and sometimes even denied that he was a literary man at all—"just a farmer"—he was no artless storyteller. He was much concerned with the manner of his telling. He made bold experiments with narrative technique. Moreover, he revised his work with great care, as his extant manuscripts and typescripts make abundantly clear.

In one of his finest novels, *The Sound and the Fury* (1929), the story of the breakdown of a once distinguished and honored family is told in succession by the three brothers: by Benjy, the idiot brother whose mental age remains about three; by Quentin, the introverted, shy, romantic brother, who in his despair finally commits suicide; and by Jason, the hard, practical, ruthless brother who rejects his ancestors' notions of dignity and honor and divests himself even of common decency. It is only in the last section of the novel that we move out of the peculiar subjectivism of each of the previous narrations and begin to view the scene as composed of objective entities.

Faulkner had wanted the copy editor, in marking up the idiot's section for printing, to specify inks of eight different colors so that the reader would be able to detect the shifts back and forth among the various strata of the past that lie confused in Benjy's mind. The publisher naturally demurred, and Faulkner was forced to indicate the shifts in time by changes from roman to italic type and back to roman. Yet, unlikely as success would seem to be in so complicated a mode of telling, the general verdict has been that the experiment is quite successful and that even Benjy's section justifies itself.

In a brief introduction to his work, one can hardly allow himself sufficient illustrations of Faulkner's brilliance and resourcefulness in the matter of technique. Perhaps it will be more useful at this point to state firmly that, interesting as Faulkner is as a craftsman, he never simply displays a mere bag of tricks. At his best, there is always a proper wedding of substance and handling, of content and form. For Faulk-

ner is ultimately interested in rendering the inner drama of the human being under stress, the person who is forced to make choices in order to maintain his integrity. In his Nobel prize address delivered at Stockholm in 1950, Faulkner uses characteristic language to describe this drama. Great writing, he says, concerns itself with "the problems of the human heart in conflict with itself."

Such is Faulkner's version of Yeats's assertion that it is only out of the quarrel with ourselves that we make poetry. A conflict with others or even with one's society and heritage is not enough—unless, of course, that society and heritage exert a powerful claim on one's own emotional being. The old-fashioned society in which Faulkner was nourished exerted such a claim on him.

Faulkner was doubly fortunate in his community. Besides involving him emotionally, it was remarkably coherent and cohesive. One could make out its shape and feel its presence. When, for example, Faulkner chooses to treat the modern theme of alienation, as he does in *Light in August,* he can silhouette his lonely or rebellious individual against a sharply contrasting backdrop, that of a community still in being, very much alive, and basically unified in its beliefs and values. Thus, though Faulkner engages universal problems, he approaches them through a specific context, one that he knows through and through. In short, he soon found a way to objectify in concrete historical forms the inner workings of his mind. The mode is thus not primarily private but objective and dramatic.

Some pages earlier we spoke of Faulkner's range in dealing with southern society. It is indeed remarkable. Through his pages one can survey the whole world of southern caste and class—the Negroes and the descendants of the old planter society; the small-town businessmen, lawyers, and physicians; the yeoman whites still living on the land, garage mechanics and millhands, sharecroppers and poor white trash—and not as mere types and stereotypes. Faulkner's poor whites, for example, are both intelligent and stupid, knavish and virtuous, composed of crafty Snopeses and stolid Tulls and all the intermediate gradations. One could easily compile from Faulkner's stories and novels a complete encyclopedia of the manners and morals, the habits and customs, and the beliefs and values of the post–Civil War South; yet Faulkner does not write as the sociologist or the historian of manners. He is always the artist, always concerned to provide a work of the imagination.[7]

[7] Not all of Faulkner's work has to do with his mythical Yoknapatawpha County—not even all of his best work. There is *The Wild Palms*, for instance. One must also remind the reader of Faulkner's abiding interest in such matters as airplanes, or the life of soldiers in the First World War, and that he has written about New York and Hollywood, Italy and France, New Orleans and the Gulf coast.

BIOGRAPHICAL CHART

1897 Born, September 25, in New Albany, Mississippi
1902 Faulkner family moves to Oxford, Mississippi
1918 Trains in Toronto, Canada, as a cadet pilot in the Royal Air Force
1919–20 Attends the University of Mississippi
1920 Lives for a short time in New York City
1924 *The Marble Faun*
1925 In New Orleans, becomes friend of Sherwood Anderson; later, visits Europe
1926 *Soldier's Pay* (his first novel)
1929 Returns to Oxford; *Sartoris; The Sound and the Fury*; marries Mrs. Estelle Oldham Franklin
1931 *Sanctuary* published and becomes a *succès de scandale*
1932 *Light in August*; goes to Hollywood for first time to work on film scenarios
1934 In New Orleans for dedication of Shushan Airport, where he gathers material for *Pylon* (1935)

1936 *Absalom, Absalom!*
1940 *The Hamlet*
1942 *Go Down, Moses*; returns to Hollywood
1950 Awarded the Nobel prize for literature
1954 In Brazil for the International Writers' Conference; makes a round-the-world trip under the auspices of the state department
1955 Receives National Book Award and Pulitzer prize for *A Fable*
1955–56 Writes letters and articles on the necessity for integrating the schools
1957 Becomes writer-in-residence at the University of Virginia; *The Town*
1958 Charlottesville, Virginia; becomes a second home
1959 *The Mansion*
1962 Dies, July 6, in Oxford

FURTHER READINGS

There is no standard edition of Faulkner's works. Individual titles are cited in the biographical chart.

Malcolm Cowley, *The Faulkner-Cowley File* (1961)
———, *The Portable Faulkner* (1941)
Frederick L. Gwynn and Joseph L. Blotner, *Faulkner in the University* (1959)
James B. Meriwether and Michael Millgate, *Lion in the Garden* (1968)
———, *William Faulkner: Essays, Speeches, and Public Letters* (1965)

Warren Beck, *Man in Motion: Faulkner's Trilogy* (1961)
Cleanth Brooks, *William Faulkner: The Yoknapatawpha Country* (1963)
Murry C. Falkner, *The Falkners of Mississippi* (1967)
John Faulkner, *My Brother Bill* (1963)
Frederick J. Hoffman and Olga W. Vickery, *William Faulkner: Two Decades of Criticism* (1951)

———, *William Faulkner: Three Decades of Criticism* (1960)
Irving Howe, *William Faulkner: A Critical Study* (2nd ed.; 1962)
John Longley, Jr., *The Tragic Mask: A Study of Faulkner's Heroes* (1963)
James B. Meriwether, *The Literary Career of William Faulkner* (1961)
Michael Millgate, *The Achievement of William Faulkner* (1963)
Olga Vickery, *The Novels of William Faulkner* (rev. ed.; 1964)
H. H. Waggoner, *William Faulkner: From Jefferson to the World* (1959)
Linda Wagner, *William Faulkner: Four Decades of Criticism* (1973)
Robert Penn Warren, ed., *Faulkner: A Collection of Critical Essays* (1966)

A Rose for Emily (1930)

The community is nearly everywhere in Faulkner's work as an important force and, diffused and anonymous though it be, it becomes one of the most important elements in the story. A clear illustration of the importance of the community is to be found in "A Rose for Emily." Miss Emily Grierson is one of the numerous characters in Faulkner's work who are warped by their inheritance from the past and who are cut off from the community—sometimes by their own will—to their detriment.

The story of the life and death of Miss Emily is related by a member of the community who, though nameless, thinks of himself as representative of the townsfolk. The first sentence strikes this note: "When Miss Emily Grierson died, our whole town went to her funeral. . . ." The narrator goes on to tell us that "Alive, Miss Emily had been a tradition, a duty, and a care; a sort of hereditary obligation upon the town. . . ." And throughout the story he keeps using such locutions as "At first we were glad. . . ." "So the next day we all said. . . ." "We were glad because the two female cousins. . . ." The nameless narrator suggests what Miss Emily's history of madness and murder meant to the community, though he never puts that meaning into a definition.

Miss Emily's isolation is a fact of consequence: her face is compared to that of a lighthouse keeper—a person who necessarily lives in isolation from the people whom he protects and whose vessels he warns off the rocks and shoals. Moreover, though Miss Emily is mad, perhaps clinically so, her madness, as is nearly always true of Faulkner's mad and obsessed people, has meaning for the sane, for it is an exaggeration or an aberration of traits which all of us have. Miss Emily's madness is in part a consequence of the injury done her by the fact of isolation, but it is also related to certain real virtues—her pride, her aristocratic independence, her unwillingness to try to keep up with the Joneses or even heed what the Joneses are saying. To read "A Rose for Emily" as merely a piece of cheap Southern Gothicism, an attempt to shock and horrify, would be to miss the point.

I

When Miss Emily Grierson died, our whole town went to her funeral: the men through a sort of respectful affection for a fallen monument, the women mostly out of curiosity to see the inside of her house, which no one save an old manservant—a combined gardener and cook—had seen in at least ten years.

It was a big, squarish frame house that had once been white, decorated with cupolas and spires and scrolled balconies in the heavily lightsome style of the seventies, set on what had once been our most select street. But garages and cotton gins had encroached and obliterated even the august names of that neighborhood; only Miss Emily's house was left, lifting its stubborn and coquettish decay above the cotton wagons and the gasoline pumps—an eyesore among eyesores. And now Miss Emily had gone to join the representatives of those august names where they lay in the cedar-bemused cemetery among the ranked and anonymous graves of Union and Confederate soldiers who fell at the battle of Jefferson.

Alive, Miss Emily had been a tradition, a duty, and a care; a sort of hereditary obligation upon the town, dating from that day in 1894 when Colonel Sartoris, the mayor—he who fathered the edict that no Negro woman should appear on the streets without an apron—remitted her taxes, the dispensation dating from the death of her father on into perpetuity. Not that Miss Emily would have accepted charity. Colonel Sartoris invented an involved tale to the effect that Miss Emily's father had loaned money to the town, which the town, as a matter of business, preferred this way of repaying. Only a man of Colonel Sartoris' generation and thought could have invented it, and only a woman could have believed it.

When the next generation, with its more modern ideas, became mayors and aldermen, this arrangement created some little dissatisfaction. On the first of the year they mailed her a tax notice. February came, and there was no reply. They wrote her a formal letter, asking her to call at the sheriff's office at her convenience. A week later the mayor wrote her himself, offering to call or to send his car for her, and received in reply a note on paper of an archaic shape, in a thin, flowing calligraphy in faded ink, to the effect that she no longer went out at all. The tax notice was also enclosed, without comment.

They called a special meeting of the Board of Aldermen. A deputation waited upon her, knocked at the door through which no visitor had passed since she ceased giving china-painting lessons eight or ten years earlier. They were admitted by the old Negro into a dim hall from which a stairway mounted into still more shadow. It smelled of dust and disuse—a close, dank smell. The Negro led them into the parlor. It was furnished in heavy, leather-covered furniture. When the Negro opened the blinds of one window, they could see that the leather was cracked; and when they sat down, a faint dust rose sluggishly about their thighs, spinning with slow motes in the single sun-ray. On a tarnished gilt easel before the fireplace stood a crayon portrait of Miss Emily's father.

They rose when she entered—a small, fat woman in black, with a thin gold chain descending to her waist and vanishing into her belt, leaning on an ebony cane with a tarnished gold head. Her skeleton was small and spare; perhaps that was why what would have been merely plumpness in another was obesity in her. She looked bloated, like a body long submerged in motionless water, and of that pallid hue. Her eyes, lost in the fatty ridges of her face, looked like two small pieces of coal pressed into a lump of dough as they moved from one face to another while the visitors stated their errand.

She did not ask them to sit. She just stood in the door and listened quietly until the spokesman came to a stumbling halt. Then they could hear the invisible watch ticking at the end of the gold chain.

Her voice was dry and cold. "I have no taxes in Jefferson. Colonel Sartoris explained it to me. Perhaps one of you can gain access to the city records and satisfy yourselves."

"But we have. We are the city authorities, Miss Emily. Didn't you get a notice from the sheriff, signed by him?"

"I received a paper, yes," Miss Emily said. "Per-haps he considers himself the sheriff . . . I have no taxes in Jefferson."

"But there is nothing on the books to show that, you see. We must go by the—"

"See Colonel Sartoris. I have no taxes in Jefferson."

"But, Miss Emily—"

"See Colonel Sartoris." (Colonel Sartoris had been dead almost ten years.) "I have no taxes in Jefferson. Tobe!" The Negro appeared. "Show these gentlemen out."

II

So she vanquished them, horse and foot, just as she had vanquished their fathers thirty years before about the smell. That was two years after her father's death and a short time after her sweetheart—the one we believed would marry her—had deserted her. After her father's death she went out very little; after her sweetheart went away, people hardly saw her at all. A few of the ladies had the temerity to call, but were not received, and the only sign of life about the place was the Negro man—a young man then—going in and out with a market basket.

"Just as if a man—any man—could keep a kitchen properly," the ladies said; so they were not surprised when the smell developed. It was another link between the gross, teeming world and the high and mighty Griersons.

A neighbor, a woman, complained to the mayor, Judge Stevens, eighty years old.

"But what will you have me do about it, madam?" he said.

"Why, send her word to stop it," the woman said. "Isn't there a law?"

"I'm sure that won't be necessary," Judge Stevens said. "It's probably just a snake or a rat that nigger of hers killed in the yard. I'll speak to him about it."

The next day he received two more complaints, one from a man who came in diffident deprecation. "We really must do something about it, Judge. I'd be the last one in the world to bother Miss Emily, but we've got to do something." That night the Board of Aldermen met—three gray-beards and one younger man, a member of the rising generation.

"It's simple enough," he said. "Send her word to have her place cleaned up. Give her a certain time to do it in, and if she don't . . ."

"Dammit, sir," Judge Stevens said, "will you accuse a lady to her face of smelling bad?"

So the next night, after midnight, four men crossed Miss Emily's lawn and slunk about the house like burglars, sniffing along the base of the brickwork and at the cellar openings while one of them performed a regular sowing motion with his hand out of a sack slung from his shoulder. They broke open the cellar door and sprinkled lime there, and in all the outbuildings. As they recrossed the lawn, a window that had been dark was lighted and Miss Emily sat in it, the light behind her, and her upright torso motionless as that of an idol. They crept quietly across the lawn and into the shadow of the locusts that lined the street. After a week or two the smell went away.

That was when people had begun to feel really sorry for her. People in our town, remembering how old lady Wyatt, her great-aunt, had gone completely crazy at last, believed that the Griersons held themselves a little too high for what they really were. None of the young men were quite good enough for Miss Emily and such. We had long thought of them as a tableau, Miss Emily a slender figure in white in the background, her father a spraddled silhouette in the foreground, his back to her and clutching a horsewhip, the two of them framed by the back-flung front door. So when she got to be thirty and was still single, we were not pleased exactly, but vindicated; even with insanity in the family she wouldn't have turned down all of her chances if they had really materialized.

When her father died, it got about that the house was all that was left to her; and in a way, people were glad. At last they could pity Miss Emily. Being left alone, and a pauper, she had become humanized. Now she too would know the old thrill and the old despair of a penny more or less.

The day after his death all the ladies prepared to call at the house and offer condolence and aid, as is our custom. Miss Emily met them at the door, dressed as usual and with no trace of grief on her face. She told them that her father was not dead. She did that for three days, with the ministers calling on her, and the doctors, trying to persuade her to let them dispose of the body. Just as they were about to resort to law and force, she broke down, and they buried her father quickly.

We did not say she was crazy then. We believed she had to do that. We remembered all the young men her father had driven away, and we knew that with nothing left, she would have to cling to that which had robbed her, as people will.

III

She was sick for a long time. When we saw her again, her hair was cut short, making her look like a girl, with a vague resemblance to those angels in colored church windows—sort of tragic and serene.

The town had just let the contracts for paving the sidewalks, and in the summer after her father's death they began the work. The construction company came with niggers and mules and machinery, and a foreman named Homer Barron, a Yankee—a big, dark, ready man, with a big voice and eyes lighter than his face. The little boys would follow in groups to hear him cuss the niggers, and the niggers singing in time to the rise and fall of picks. Pretty soon he knew everybody in town. Whenever you heard a lot of laughing anywhere about the square, Homer Barron would be in the center of the group. Presently we began to see him and Miss Emily on Sunday afternoons driving in the yellow-wheeled buggy and the matched team of bays from the livery stable.

At first we were glad that Miss Emily would have an interest, because the ladies all said, "Of course a Grierson would not think seriously of a Northerner, a day laborer." But there were still others, older people, who said that even grief could not cause a real lady to forget *noblesse oblige*—without calling it *noblesse oblige*. They just said, "Poor Emily. Her kinsfolk should come to her." She had some kin in Alabama; but years ago her father had fallen out with them over the estate of old lady Wyatt, the crazy woman, and there was no communication between the two families. They had not even been represented at the funeral.

And as soon as the old people said, "Poor Emily," the whispering began. "Do you suppose it's really so?" they said to one another. "Of course it is. What else could . . ." This behind their hands; rustling of craned silk and satin behind jalousies closed upon the sun of Sunday afternoon as the thin, swift clop-clop-clop of the matched team passed: "Poor Emily."

She carried her head high enough—even when we believed that she was fallen. It was as if she demanded more than ever the recognition of her dignity as the last Grierson; as if it had wanted that touch of earthiness to reaffirm her imperviousness. Like when she bought the rat poison, the arsenic. That was over a year after they had begun to say "Poor Emily," and while the two female cousins were visiting her.

"I want some poison," she said to the druggist. She was over thirty then, still a slight woman, though thinner than usual, with cold, haughty black eyes in a face the flesh of which was strained across the temples and about the eye-sockets as you imagine a lighthouse-keeper's face ought to look. "I want some poison," she said.

"Yes, Miss Emily. What kind? For rats and such? I'd recom—"

"I want the best you have. I don't care what kind."

The druggist named several. "They'll kill anything up to an elephant. But what you want is—"

"Arsenic," Miss Emily said. "Is that a good one?"

"Is . . . arsenic? Yes, ma'am. But what you want—"

"I want arsenic."

The druggist looked down at her. She looked back at him, erect, her face like a strained flag. "Why, of course," the druggist said. "If that's what you want. But the law requires you to tell what you are going to use it for."

Miss Emily just stared at him, her head tilted back in order to look him eye for eye, until he looked away and went and got the arsenic and wrapped it up. The Negro delivery boy brought her the package; the druggist didn't come back. When she opened the package at home there was written on the box, under the skull and bones: "For rats."

IV

So the next day we all said, "She will kill herself"; and we said it would be the best thing. When she had first begun to be seen with Homer Barron, we had said, "She will marry him." Then we said, "She will persuade him yet," because Homer himself had remarked—he liked men, and it was known that he drank with the younger men in the Elks' Club—that he was not a marrying man. Later we said, "Poor Emily" behind the jalousies as they passed on Sunday afternoon in the glittering buggy, Miss Emily with her head high and Homer Barron with his hat cocked and a cigar in his teeth, reins and whip in a yellow glove.

Then some of the ladies began to say that it was a disgrace to the town and a bad example to the young people. The men did not want to interfere, but at last the ladies forced the Baptist minister—Miss Emily's people were Episcopal—to call upon her. He would never divulge what happened during that interview, but he refused to go back again. The next Sunday they again drove about the streets, and the following day the minister's wife wrote to Miss Emily's relations in Alabama.

So she had blood-kin under her roof again and we sat back to watch developments. At first nothing happened. Then we were sure that they were to be married. We learned that Miss Emily had been to the jeweler's and ordered a man's toilet set in silver, with the letters H. B. on each piece. Two days later we learned that she had bought a complete outfit of men's clothing, including a nightshirt, and we said, "They are married." We were really glad. We were glad because the two female cousins were even more Grierson than Miss Emily had ever been.

So we were not surprised when Homer Barron—the streets had been finished some time since—was gone. We were a little disappointed that there was not a public blowing-off, but we believed that he had gone on to prepare for Miss Emily's coming, or to give her a chance to get rid of the cousins. (By that time it was a cabal, and we were all Miss Emily's allies to help circumvent the cousins.) Sure enough, after another week they departed. And, as we had expected all along, within three days Homer Barron was back in town. A neighbor saw the Negro man admit him at the kitchen door at dusk one evening.

And that was the last we saw of Homer Barron. And of Miss Emily for some time. The Negro man went in and out with the market basket, but the front door remained closed. Now and then we would see her at a window for a moment, as the men did that night when they sprinkled the lime, but for almost six months she did not appear on the streets. Then we knew that this was to be expected too; as if that quality of her father which had thwarted her woman's life so many times had been too virulent and too furious to die.

When we next saw Miss Emily, she had grown fat and her hair was turning gray. During the next few years it grew grayer and grayer until it attained an even pepper-and-salt iron-gray, when it ceased turning. Up to the day of her death at seventy-four it was still that vigorous iron-gray, like the hair of an active man.

From that time on her front door remained closed, save for a period of six or seven years, when she was about forty, during which she gave lessons in china-painting. She fitted up a studio in one of the downstairs rooms, where the daughters and granddaughters of Colonel Sartoris' contemporaries were sent to her with the same regularity and in the same spirit that they were sent to church on Sundays with a twenty-five-cent piece for the collection plate. Meanwhile her taxes had been remitted.

Then the newer generations became the backbone and the spirit of the town, and the painting pupils grew up and fell away and did not send their children to her with boxes of color and tedious brushes and pictures cut from the ladies' magazines. The front door closed upon the last one and remained closed for good. When the town got free postal delivery, Miss Emily alone refused to let them fasten the metal numbers above her door and attach a mailbox to it. She would not listen to them.

Daily, monthly, yearly we watched the Negro grow grayer and more stooped, going in and out with the market basket. Each December we sent her a tax notice, which would be returned by the post office a week later, unclaimed. Now and then we would see her in one of the downstairs windows—she had evidently shut up the top floor of the house—like the carven torso of an idol in a niche, looking or not looking at us, we could never tell which. Thus she passed from generation to generation—dear, inescapable, impervious, tranquil, and perverse.

And so she died. Fell ill in the house filled with dust and shadows, with only a doddering Negro man to wait on her. We did not even know she was sick; we had long since given up trying to get any information from the Negro. He talked to no one, probably not even to her, for his voice had grown harsh and rusty, as if from disuse.

She died in one of the downstairs rooms, in a heavy walnut bed with a curtain, her gray head propped on a pillow yellow and moldy with age and lack of sunlight.

V

The Negro met the first of the ladies at the front door and let them in, with their hushed, sibilant voices and their quick, curious glances, and then he disappeared. He walked right through the house and out the back and was not seen again.

The two female cousins came at once. They held the funeral on the second day, with the town coming to look at Miss Emily beneath a mass of bought flowers, with the crayon face of her father musing profoundly above the bier and the ladies sibilant and macabre; and the very old men—some in their brushed Confederate uniforms—on the porch and the lawn, talking of Miss Emily as if she had been a contemporary of theirs, believing that they had danced with her and courted her perhaps, confusing time with its mathematical progression, as the old do, to whom all the past is not a diminishing road but, instead, a huge meadow which no winter ever quite touches, divided from them now by the narrow bottle-neck of the most recent decade of years.

Already we knew that there was one room in that region above stairs which no one had seen in forty years, and which would have to be forced. They waited until Miss Emily was decently in the ground before they opened it.

The violence of breaking down the door seemed to fill this room with pervading dust. A thin, acrid pall as of the tomb seemed to lie everywhere upon this room decked and furnished as for a bridal: upon the valance curtains of faded rose color, upon the rose-shaded lights, upon the dressing table, upon the delicate array of crystal and the man's toilet things backed with tarnished silver, silver so tarnished that the monogram was obscured. Among them lay a collar and tie, as if they had just been removed, which, lifted, left upon the surface a pale crescent in the dust. Upon a chair hung the suit, carefully folded; beneath it the two mute shoes and the discarded socks.

The man himself lay in the bed.

For a long while we just stood there, looking down at the profound and fleshless grin. The body had apparently once lain in the attitude of an embrace, but now the long sleep that outlasts love, that conquers even the grimace of love, had cuckolded him. What was left of him, rotted beneath what was left of the nightshirt, had become inextricable from the bed in which he lay; and upon him and upon the pillow beside him lay that even coating of the patient and biding dust.

Then we noticed that in the second pillow was the indentation of a head. One of us lifted something from it, and leaning forward, that faint and invisible dust dry and acrid in the nostrils, we saw a long strand of iron-gray hair.

That Evening Sun (1931)

Quentin Compson tells this story some fifteen years after the events he describes. At that time he was a child of nine. The Compsons are a family whose story is told in *The Sound and the Fury* (1929), though one of the four children, Benjy the idiot son, does not appear in the present story. The time would be about the turn of the century.[1]

The Compson's servant, Nancy, is gripped by an irrational terror at the thought of approaching death—yet not at death itself so much as that it should happen in the dark. She tells Mr. Compson: "I scared for it to happen in the dark." Hence the story's title, taken from the first line of "The St. Louis Blues": "I hate to see that evenin' sun go down."

The plot of the story is relatively simple and the principal lines of force in the story are obvious. There is the villainy and hypocrisy of Mr. Stovall who begets a child on Nancy, won't pay her the money that he has promised her, and when exposed, kicks out her teeth. Perfectly obvious, too, is Nancy's sense of helplessness in her abject fear of her husband, Jesus. She is convinced that he has now come home to take revenge on her, and her frantic attempts to find someone to keep her company, even mere children, the oldest one of whom is only nine, puts with dramatic intensity her desperation.

Nevertheless, there are certain matters that need to be called to the reader's attention. They are easily overlooked and yet we must be clear about them if we are to see precisely on what Faulkner has chosen to focus the story. First, does Jesus actually come back or is Nancy's fear irrational, hysterical, and in part occasioned by her own sense of guilt toward her husband? (One notices that Nancy still feels that she has a claim on Jesus and he on her.) Nancy admits that she has no evidence of Jesus' return except the "sign" that she says has been left in her house. She won't ask Mr. Compson to call the police; she won't accept Dilsey's offer of a place in her house; she refuses Mr. Compson's offer to take her to Aunt Rachel's.

Second, there is the matter of the response to Nancy's plight. Mrs. Compson is obviously quite unfeeling, wrapped up in an almost neurotic self-absorption. (Those who have read *The Sound and the Fury* will recognize the hints in this story of the weak, whining woman we find in the novel, the person who has poisoned all the relationships in the Compson household.) But Mr. Compson is sympathetic, and if he is skeptical as to whether the danger to Nancy is real, it is worth noting that Dilsey, who is herself a Negro and who is sympathetic to Nancy, also seems to be skeptical.

One might ask what actually did happen to Nancy. Did Jesus cut her throat? The answer has to be that we simply don't know.[2] As far as this story is concerned, Nancy's terror may be valid or it may be a delusion. What Faulkner has been concerned to dramatize for his reader is the way it feels to be in the grip of terror in a situation where it is impossible to convince anyone else that the peril is actual and imminent. Our last glimpse of Nancy puts her plight poignantly: we see her sitting in her cabin, the lamp turned as high as it will go, and the door not only not barred but not even closed. Evidently she feels it is hopeless to try to keep Jesus out, but she doesn't want to be killed in the dark.

A third matter worth the reader's attention is the function of the children in the telling of this story. As young children, they understand only in part what is going on. But Quentin's report of what he and his brother and sister did and said will provide the attentive reader with

---

[1] The date of the events narrated would be 1899, and the date of Quentin's remembering them, 1914, if we rely on Quentin Compson's appearance in other works, where there are indications that he was born in 1890. But the dates in "That Evening Sun" cannot be squared with those in *The Sound and the Fury*, where Quentin is dead by 1910.

[2] The argument that *The Sound and the Fury* indicates that Nancy did die has been shown to be untrue. In *Requiem for a Nun*, the scene of which is set many years later, she is very much alive.

all that he needs to know in order to apprehend the story. The children thus constitute a kind of sounding board whose innocent incomprehension reflects to the adult reader, who *can* comprehend it, the quality of Nancy's helplessness; this device allows the author to present Nancy's terror with something of the effect of understatement.

The reader must not make the mistake of expecting the children to be wise beyond their years or capable of moral responsibility in a situation in which they are powerless. Jason's general meanness looks forward to the cold-hearted and knavish man that he will have become in *The Sound and the Fury*; but a child of five can be selfish enough. Candy is bright and sensitive and about as sympathetically interested in Nancy as a little girl of seven could be. Quentin's reaction may seem somewhat more complicated. But one must remember that the Quentin who narrates the story is no longer nine years old, but a man of twenty-four who is "remembering" the story. His memory is perhaps unconsciously affected by an adult's comprehension of what was then going on—though he appears simply to be setting down what at that time he saw and heard.

I

Monday is no different from any other weekday in Jefferson now. The streets are paved now, and the telephone and electric companies are cutting down more and more of the shade trees—the water oaks, the maples and locusts and elms—to make room for iron poles bearing clusters of bloated and ghostly and bloodless grapes, and we have a city laundry which makes the rounds on Monday morning, gathering the bundles of clothes into bright-colored, specially-made motor cars: the soiled wearing of a whole week now flees apparitionlike behind alert and irritable electric horns, with a long diminishing noise of rubber and asphalt like tearing silk, and even the Negro women who still take in white people's washing after the old custom, fetch and deliver it in automobiles.

But fifteen years ago, on Monday morning the quiet, dusty, shady streets would be full of Negro women with, balanced on their steady, turbaned heads, bundles of clothes tied up in sheets, almost as large as cotton bales, carried so without touch of hand between the kitchen door of the white house and the blackened washpot beside a cabin door in Negro Hollow.

Nancy would set her bundle on the top of her head, then upon the bundle in turn she would set the black straw sailor hat which she wore winter and summer. She was tall, with a high, sad face sunken a little where her teeth were missing. Sometimes we would go a part of the way down the lane and across the pasture with her, to watch the balanced bundle and the hat that never bobbed nor wavered, even when she walked down into the ditch and up the other side and stooped through the fence. She would go down on her hands and knees and crawl through the gap, her head rigid, uptilted, the bundle steady as a rock or a balloon, and rise to her feet again and go on.

Sometimes the husbands of the washing women would fetch and deliver the clothes, but Jesus never did that for Nancy, even before father told him to stay away from our house, even when Dilsey was sick and Nancy would come to cook for us.

And then about half the time we'd have to go down the lane to Nancy's cabin and tell her to come on and cook breakfast. We would stop at the ditch, because father told us to not have anything to do with Jesus—he was a short black man, with a razor scar down his face—and we would throw rocks at Nancy's house until she came to the door, leaning her head around it without any clothes on.

"What yawl mean, chunking my house?" Nancy said. "What you little devils mean?"

"Father says for you to come on and get breakfast," Caddy said. "Father says it's over a half an hour now, and you've got to come this minute."

"I aint studying no breakfast," Nancy said. "I going to get my sleep out."

"I bet you're drunk," Jason said. "Father says you're drunk. Are you drunk, Nancy?"

"Who says I is?" Nancy said. "I got to get my sleep out. I aint studying no breakfast."

So after a while we quit chunking the cabin and went back home. When she finally came, it was too late for me to go to school. So we thought it was whisky until that day they arrested her again and they were taking her to jail and they passed Mr Stovall. He was the cashier in the bank and a deacon in the Baptist church, and Nancy began to say:

"When you going to pay me, white man? When you going to pay me, white man? It's been three times now since you paid me a cent—" Mr Stovall knocked her down, but she kept on saying, "When you going to pay me, white man? It's been three times now since—" until Mr Stovall kicked her in the mouth with his heel and the marshal caught Mr Stovall back, and Nancy lying in the street, laughing. She turned her head and spat out some blood and teeth and said, "It's been three times now since he paid me a cent."

That was how she lost her teeth, and all that day they told about Nancy and Mr Stovall, and all that night the ones that passed the jail could hear Nancy singing and yelling. They could see her hands holding to the window bars, and a lot of them stopped along the fence, listening to her and to the jailer trying to make her stop. She didn't shut up until almost daylight, when the jailer began to hear a bumping and scraping upstairs and he went up there and found Nancy hanging from the window bar. He said that it was cocaine and not whisky, because no nigger would try to commit suicide unless he was full of cocaine, because a nigger full of cocaine wasn't a nigger any longer.

The jailer cut her down and revived her; then he beat her, whipped her. She had hung herself with her dress. She had fixed it all right, but when they arrested her she didn't have on anything except a dress and so she didn't have anything to tie her hands with and she couldn't make her hands let go of the window ledge. So the jailer heard the noise and ran up there and found Nancy hanging from the window, stark naked, her belly already swelling out a little, like a little balloon.

When Dilsey was sick in her cabin and Nancy was cooking for us, we could see her apron swelling out; that was before father told Jesus to stay away from the house. Jesus was in the kitchen, sitting behind the stove, with his razor scar on his black face like a piece of dirty string. He said it was a watermelon that Nancy had under her dress.

"It never come off of your vine, though," Nancy said.

"Off of what vine?" Caddy said.

"I can cut down the vine it did come off of," Jesus said.

"What makes you want to talk like that before these chillen?" Nancy said. "Whyn't you go to work? You done et. You want Mr Jason to catch you hanging around his kitchen, talking that way before these chillen?"

"Talking what way?" Caddy said. "What vine?"

"I cant hang around white man's kitchen," Jesus said. "But white man can hang around mine. White man can come in my house, but I cant stop him. When white man want to come in my house, I aint got no house. I cant stop him, but he cant kick me outen it. He cant do that."

Dilsey was still sick in her cabin. Father told Jesus to stay off our place. Dilsey was still sick. It was a long time. We were in the library after supper.

"Isn't Nancy through in the kitchen yet?" mother said. "It seems to me that she has had plenty of time to have finished the dishes."

"Let Quentin go and see," father said. "Go and see if Nancy is through, Quentin. Tell her she can go on home."

I went to the kitchen. Nancy was through. The dishes were put away and the fire was out. Nancy was sitting in a chair, close to the cold stove. She looked at me.

"Mother wants to know if you are through," I said.

"Yes," Nancy said. She looked at me. "I done finished." She looked at me.

"What is it?" I said. "What is it?"

"I aint nothing but a nigger," Nancy said. "It aint none of my fault."

She looked at me, sitting in the chair before the cold stove, the sailor hat on her head. I went back to the library. It was the cold stove and all, when you think of a kitchen being warm and busy and cheerful. And with a cold stove and the dishes all put away, and nobody wanting to eat at that hour.

"Is she through?" mother said.

"Yessum," I said.

"What is she doing?" mother said.

"She's not doing anything. She's through."

"I'll go and see," father said.

"Maybe she's waiting for Jesus to come and take her home," Caddy said.

"Jesus is gone," I said. Nancy told us how one morning she woke up and Jesus was gone.

"He quit me," Nancy said. "Done gone to Memphis, I reckon. Dodging them city *po*-lice for a while, I reckon."

"And a good riddance," father said. "I hope he stays there."

"Nancy's scaired of the dark," Jason said.

"So are you," Caddy said.

"I'm not," Jason said.

"Scairy cat," Caddy said.

"I'm not," Jason said.

"You, Candace!" mother said. Father came back.

"I am going to walk down the lane with Nancy," he said. "She says that Jesus is back."

"Has she seen him?" mother said.

"No. Some Negro sent her word that he was back in town. I wont be long."

"You'll leave me alone, to take Nancy home?" mother said. "Is her safety more precious to you than mine?"

"I wont be long," father said.

"You'll leave these children unprotected, with that Negro about?"

"I'm going too," Caddy said. "Let me go, Father."

"What would he do with them, if he were unfortunate enough to have them?" father said.

"I want to go, too," Jason said.

"Jason!" mother said. She was speaking to father. You could tell that by the way she said the name. Like she believed that all day father had been trying to think of doing the thing she wouldn't like the most, and that she knew all the time that after a while he would think of it. I stayed quiet, because father and I both knew that mother would want him to make me stay with her if she just thought of it in time. So father didn't look at me. I was the oldest. I was nine and Caddy was seven and Jason was five.

"Nonsense," father said. "We wont be long."

Nancy had her hat on. We came to the lane. "Jesus always been good to me," Nancy said. "Whenever he had two dollars, one of them was mine." We walked in the lane. "If I can just get through the lane," Nancy said, "I be all right then."

The lane was always dark. "This is where Jason got scared on Hallowe'en," Caddy said.

"I didn't," Jason said.

"Cant Aunt Rachel do anything with him?" father said. Aunt Rachel was old. She lived in a cabin beyond Nancy's, by herself. She had white hair and she smoked a pipe in the door, all day long; she didn't work any more. They said she was Jesus' mother. Sometimes she said she was and sometimes she said she wasn't any kin to Jesus.

"Yes, you did," Caddy said. "You were scairder than Frony. You were scairder than T.P. even. Scairder than niggers."

"Cant nobody do nothing with him," Nancy said. "He say I done woke up the devil in him and aint but one thing going to lay it down again."

"Well, he's gone now," father said. "There's

nothing for you to be afraid of now. And if you'd just let white men alone."

"Let what white men alone?" Caddy said. "How let them alone?"

"He aint gone nowhere," Nancy said. "I can feel him. I can feel him now, in this lane. He hearing us talk, every word, hid somewhere, waiting. I aint seen him, and I aint going to see him again but once more, with that razor in his mouth. That razor on that string down his back, inside his shirt. And then I aint going to be even surprised."

"I wasn't scaired," Jason said.

"If you'd behave yourself, you'd have kept out of this," father said. "But it's all right now. He's probably in St. Louis now. Probably got another wife by now and forgot all about you."

"If he has, I better not find out about it," Nancy said. "I'd stand there right over them, and every time he wropped her, I'd cut that arm off. I'd cut his head off and I'd slit her belly and I'd shove—"

"Hush," father said.

"Slit whose belly, Nancy?" Caddy said.

"I wasn't scaired," Jason said. "I'd walk right down this lane by myself."

"Yah," Caddy said. "You wouldn't dare to put your foot down in it if we were not here too."

II

Dilsey was still sick, so we took Nancy home every night until mother said, "How much longer is this going on? I to be left alone in this big house while you take home a frightened Negro?"

We fixed a pallet in the kitchen for Nancy. One night we waked up, hearing the sound. It was not singing and it was not crying, coming up the dark stairs. There was a light in mother's room and we heard father going down the hall, down the back stairs, and Caddy and I went into the hall. The floor was cold. Our toes curled away from it while we listened to the sound. It was like singing and it wasn't like singing, like the sounds that Negroes make.

Then it stopped and we heard father going down the back stairs, and we went to the head of the stairs. Then the sound began again, in the stairway, not loud, and we could see Nancy's eyes halfway up the stairs, against the wall. They looked like cat's eyes do, like a big cat against the wall, watching us. When we came down the steps to where she was, she quit making the sound again, and we stood there until father came back up from the kitchen, with his pistol in his hand. He went back down with Nancy and they came back with Nancy's pallet.

We spread the pallet in our room. After the light in mother's room went off, we could see Nancy's eyes again. "Nancy," Caddy whispered, "are you asleep, Nancy?"

Nancy whispered something. It was oh or no, I dont know which. Like nobody had made it, like it came from nowhere and went nowhere, until it was like Nancy was not there at all; that I had looked so hard at her eyes on the stairs that they had got printed on my eyeballs, like the sun does when you have closed your eyes and there is no sun. "Jesus," Nancy whispered. "Jesus."

"Was it Jesus?" Caddy said. "Did he try to come into the kitchen?"

"Jesus," Nancy said. Like this: Jeeeeeeeeeeeeeeeesus, until the sound went out, like a match or a candle does.

"It's the other Jesus she means," I said.

"Can you see us, Nancy?" Caddy whispered. "Can you see our eyes too?"

"I aint nothing but a nigger," Nancy said. "God knows. God knows."

"What did you see down there in the kitchen?" Caddy whispered. "What tried to get in?"

"God knows," Nancy said. We could see her eyes. "God knows."

Dilsey got well. She cooked dinner. "You'd better stay in bed a day or two longer," father said.

"What for?" Dilsey said. "If I had been a day later, this place would be to rack and ruin. Get on out of here now, and let me get my kitchen straight again."

Dilsey cooked supper too. And that night, just before dark, Nancy came into the kitchen.

"How do you know he's back?" Dilsey said. "You aint seen him."

"Jesus is a nigger," Jason said.

"I can feel him," Nancy said. "I can feel him laying yonder in the ditch."

"Tonight?" Dilsey said. "Is he there tonight?"

"Dilsey's a nigger too," Jason said.

"You try to eat something," Dilsey said.

"I dont want nothing," Nancy said.

"I aint a nigger," Jason said.

"Drink some coffee," Dilsey said. She poured a cup of coffee for Nancy. "Do you know he's out there tonight? How come you know it's tonight?"

"I know," Nancy said. "He's there, waiting. I know. I done lived with him too long. I know what he's fixing to do fore he know it himself."

"Drink some coffee," Dilsey said. Nancy held the cup to her mouth and blew into the cup. Her mouth pursed out like a spreading adder's, like a rubber mouth, like she had blown all the color out of her lips with blowing the coffee.

"I aint a nigger," Jason said. "Are you a nigger, Nancy?"

"I hellborn, child," Nancy said. "I wont be nothing soon. I going back where I come from soon."

III

She began to drink the coffee. While she was drinking, holding the cup in both hands, she began to make the sound again. She made the sound into the cup and the coffee sploshed out onto her hands and her dress. Her eyes looked at us and she sat there, her elbows on her knees, holding the cup in both hands, looking at us across the wet cup, making the sound. "Look at Nancy," Jason said. "Nancy cant cook for us now. Dilsey's got well now."

"You hush up," Dilsey said. Nancy held the cup in both hands, looking at us, making the sound, like there were two of them: one looking at us and the other making the sound. "Whyn't you let Mr Jason telefoam the marshal?" Dilsey said. Nancy stopped then, holding the cup in her long brown hands. She tried to drink some coffee again, but it sploshed out of the cup, onto her hands and her dress, and she put the cup down. Jason watched her.

"I cant swallow it," Nancy said. "I swallows but it wont go down me."

"You go down to the cabin," Dilsey said. "Frony will fix you a pallet and I'll be there soon."

"Wont no nigger stop him," Nancy said.

"I aint a nigger," Jason said. "Am I, Dilsey?"

"I reckon not," Dilsey said. She looked at Nancy. "I dont reckon so. What you going to do, then?"

Nancy looked at us. Her eyes went fast, like she was afraid there wasn't time to look, without hardly moving at all. She looked at us, at all three of us at one time. "You member that night I stayed in yawls' room?" she said. She told about how we waked up early the next morning, and played. We had to play quiet, on her pallet, until father woke up and it was time to get breakfast. "Go and ask your maw to let me stay here tonight," Nancy said. "I wont need no pallet. We can play some more."

Caddy asked mother. Jason went too. "I cant

have Negroes sleeping in the bedrooms," mother said. Jason cried. He cried until mother said he couldn't have any dessert for three days if he didn't stop. Then Jason said he would stop if Dilsey would make a chocolate cake. Father was there.

"Why dont you do something about it?" mother said. "What do we have officers for?"

"Why is Nancy afraid of Jesus?" Caddy said. "Are you afraid of father, mother?"

"What could the officers do?" father said. "If Nancy hasn't seen him, how could the officers find him?"

"Then why is she afraid?" mother said.

"She says he is there. She says she knows he is there tonight."

"Yet we pay taxes," mother said. "I must wait here alone in this big house while you take a Negro woman home."

"You know that I am not lying outside with a razor," father said.

"I'll stop if Dilsey will make a chocolate cake," Jason said. Mother told us to go out and father said he didn't know if Jason would get a chocolate cake or not, but he knew what Jason was going to get in about a minute. We went back to the kitchen and told Nancy.

"Father said for you to go home and lock the door, and you'll be all right," Caddy said. "All right from what, Nancy? Is Jesus mad at you?" Nancy was holding the coffee cup in her hands again, her elbows on her knees and her hands holding the cup between her knees. She was looking into the cup. "What have you done that made Jesus mad?" Caddy said. Nancy let the cup go. It didn't break on the floor, but the coffee spilled out, and Nancy sat there with her hands still holding the shape of the cup. She began to make the sound again, not loud. Not singing and not unsinging. We watched her.

"Here," Dilsey said. "You quit that, now. You get aholt of yourself. You wait here. I going to get Versh to walk home with you." Dilsey went out.

We looked at Nancy. Her shoulders kept shaking, but she quit making the sound. We watched her. "What's Jesus going to do to you?" Caddy said. "He went away."

Nancy looked at us. "We had fun that night I stayed in yawls' room, didn't we?"

"I didn't," Jason said. "I didn't have any fun."

"You were asleep in mother's room," Caddy said. "You were not there."

"Let's go down to my house and have some more fun," Nancy said.

"Mother wont let us," I said. "It's too late now."

"Dont bother her," Nancy said. "We can tell her in the morning. She wont mind."

"She wouldn't let us," I said.

"Dont ask her now," Nancy said. "Dont bother her now."

"She didn't say we couldn't go," Caddy said.

"We didn't ask," I said.

"If you go, I'll tell," Jason said.

"We'll have fun," Nancy said. "They won't mind, just to my house. I been working for yawl a long time. They won't mind."

"I'm not afraid to go," Caddy said. "Jason is the one that's afraid. He'll tell."

"I'm not," Jason said.

"Yes, you are," Caddy said. "You'll tell."

"I won't tell," Jason said. "I'm not afraid."

"Jason ain't afraid to go with me," Nancy said. "Is you, Jason?"

"Jason is going to tell," Caddy said. The lane was dark. We passed the pasture gate. "I bet if something was to jump out from behind that gate, Jason would holler."

"I wouldn't," Jason said. We walked down the lane. Nancy was talking loud.

"What are you talking so loud for, Nancy?" Caddy said.

"Who, me?" Nancy said. "Listen at Quentin and Caddy and Jason saying I'm talking loud."

"You talk like there was five of us here," Caddy said. "You talk like father was here too."

"Who; me talking loud, Mr Jason?" Nancy said.

"Nancy called Jason 'Mister,'" Caddy said.

"Listen how Caddy and Quentin and Jason talk," Nancy said.

"We're not talking loud," Caddy said. "You're the one that's talking like father—"

"Hush," Nancy said; "hush, Mr Jason."

"Nancy called Jason 'Mister' aguh—"

"Hush," Nancy said. She was talking loud when we crossed the ditch and stooped through the fence where she used to stoop through with the clothes on her head. Then we came to her house. We were going fast then. She opened the door. The smell of the house was like the lamp and the smell of Nancy was like the wick, like they were waiting for one another to begin to smell. She lit the lamp and closed the door and put the bar up. Then she quit talking loud, looking at us.

"What're we going to do?" Caddy said.

"What do yawl want to do?" Nancy said.

"You said we would have some fun," Caddy said.

There was something about Nancy's house; something you could smell besides Nancy and the house. Jason smelled it, even. "I don't want to stay here," he said. "I want to go home."

"Go home, then," Caddy said.

"I don't want to go by myself," Jason said.

"We're going to have some fun," Nancy said.

"How?" Caddy said.

Nancy stood by the door. She was looking at us, only it was like she had emptied her eyes, like she had quit using them. "What do you want to do?" she said.

"Tell us a story," Caddy said. "Can you tell a story?"

"Yes," Nancy said.

"Tell it," Caddy said. We looked at Nancy. "You don't know any stories."

"Yes," Nancy said. "Yes, I do."

She came and sat in a chair before the hearth. There was a little fire there. Nancy built it up, when it was already hot inside. She built a good blaze. She told a story. She talked like her eyes looked, like her eyes watching us and her voice talking to us did not belong to her. Like she was living somewhere else, waiting somewhere else. She was outside the cabin. Her voice was inside and the shape of her, the Nancy that could stoop under a barbed wire fence with a bundle of clothes balanced on her head as though without weight, like a balloon, was there. But that was all. "And so this here queen come walking up to the ditch, where that bad man was hiding. She was walking up to the ditch, and she say, 'If I can just get past this here ditch,' was what she say . . ."

"What ditch?" Caddy said. "A ditch like that one out there? Why did a queen want to go into a ditch?"

"To get to her house," Nancy said. She looked at us. "She had to cross the ditch to get into her house quick and bar the door."

"Why did she want to go home and bar the door?" Caddy said.

IV

Nancy looked at us. She quit talking. She looked at us. Jason's legs stuck straight out of his pants where he sat on Nancy's lap. "I don't think that's a good story," he said. "I want to go home."

"Maybe we had better," Caddy said. She got up from the floor. "I bet they are looking for us right now." She went toward the door.

"No," Nancy said. "Don't open it." She got up quick and passed Caddy. She didn't touch the door, the wooden bar.

"Why not?" Caddy said.

"Come back to the lamp," Nancy said. "We'll have fun. You don't have to go."

"We ought to go," Caddy said. "Unless we have a lot of fun." She and Nancy came back to the fire, the lamp.

"I want to go home," Jason said. "I'm going to tell."

"I know another story," Nancy said. She stood close to the lamp. She looked at Caddy, like when your eyes look up at a stick balanced on your nose. She had to look down to see Caddy, but her eyes looked like that, like when you are balancing a stick.

"I won't listen to it," Jason said. "I'll bang on the floor."

"It's a good one," Nancy said. "It's better than the other one."

"What's it about?" Caddy said. Nancy was standing by the lamp. Her hand was on the lamp, against the light, long and brown.

"Your hand is on that hot globe," Caddy said. "Don't it feel hot to your hand?"

Nancy looked at her hand on the lamp chimney. She took her hand away, slow. She stood there, looking at Caddy, wringing her long hand as though it were tied to her wrist with a string.

"Let's do something else," Caddy said.

"I want to go home," Jason said.

"I got some popcorn," Nancy said. She looked at Caddy and then at Jason and then at me and then at Caddy again. "I got some popcorn."

"I don't like popcorn," Jason said. "I'd rather have candy."

Nancy looked at Jason. "You can hold the popper." She was still wringing her hand; it was long and limp and brown.

"All right," Jason said. "I'll stay a while if I can do that. Caddy can't hold it. I'll want to go home again if Caddy holds the popper."

Nancy built up the fire. "Look at Nancy putting her hands in the fire," Caddy said. "What's the matter with you, Nancy?"

"I got popcorn," Nancy said. "I got some." She took the popper from under the bed. It was broken. Jason began to cry.

"Now we can't have any popcorn," he said.

"We ought to go home, anyway," Caddy said. "Come on, Quentin."

"Wait," Nancy said; "wait. I can fix it. Don't you want to help me fix it?"

"I don't think I want any," Caddy said. "It's too late now."

"You help me, Jason," Nancy said. "Don't you want to help me?"

"No," Jason said. "I want to go home."

"Hush," Nancy said; "hush. Watch. Watch me. I can fix it so Jason can hold it and pop the corn." She got a piece of wire and fixed the popper.

"It won't hold good," Caddy said.

"Yes, it will," Nancy said. "Yawl watch. Yawl help me shell some corn."

The popcorn was under the bed too. We shelled it into the popper and Nancy helped Jason hold the popper over the fire.

"It's not popping," Jason said. "I want to go home."

"You wait," Nancy said. "It'll begin to pop. We'll have fun then." She was sitting close to the fire. The lamp was turned up so high it was beginning to smoke.

"Why don't you turn it down some?" I said.

"It's all right," Nancy said. "I'll clean it. Yawl wait. The popcorn will start in a minute."

"I don't believe it's going to start," Caddy said. "We ought to start home, anyway. They'll be worried."

"No," Nancy said. "It's going to pop. Dilsey will tell um yawl with me. I been working for yawl long time. They won't mind if yawl at my house. You wait, now. It'll start popping any minute now."

Then Jason got some smoke in his eyes and he began to cry. He dropped the popper into the fire. Nancy got a wet rag and wiped Jason's face, but he didn't stop crying.

"Hush," she said. "Hush." But he didn't hush. Caddy took the popper out of the fire.

"It's burned up," she said. "You'll have to get some more popcorn, Nancy."

"Did you put all of it in?" Nancy said.

"Yes," Caddy said. Nancy looked at Caddy. Then she took the popper and opened it and poured the cinders into her apron and began to sort the grains, her hands long and brown, and we watching her.

"Haven't you got any more?" Caddy said.

"Yes," Nancy said; "yes. Look. This here ain't burnt. All we need to do is—"

"I want to go home," Jason said. "I'm going to tell."

"Hush," Caddy said. We all listened. Nancy's head was already turned toward the barred door, her eyes filled with red lamplight. "Somebody is coming," Caddy said.

Then Nancy began to make that sound again, not loud, sitting there above the fire, her long hands dangling between her knees; all of a sudden water began to come out on her face in big drops, running down her face, carrying in each one a little turning ball of firelight like a spark until it dropped off her chin. "She's not crying," I said.

"I ain't crying," Nancy said. Her eyes were closed. "I ain't crying. Who is it?"

"I don't know," Caddy said. She went to the door and looked out. "We've got to go now," she said. "Here comes father."

"I'm going to tell," Jason said. "Yawl made me come."

The water still ran down Nancy's face. She turned in her chair. "Listen. Tell him. Tell him we going to have fun. Tell him I take good care of yawl until in the morning. Tell him to let me come home with yawl and sleep on the floor. Tell him I won't need no pallet. We'll have fun. You member last time how we had so much fun?"

"I didn't have fun," Jason said. "You hurt me. You put smoke in my eyes. I'm going to tell."

V

Father came in. He looked at us. Nancy did not get up.

"Tell him," she said.

"Caddy made us come down here," Jason said. "I didn't want to."

Father came to the fire. Nancy looked up at him. "Can't you go to Aunt Rachel's and stay?" he said. Nancy looked up at father, her hands between her knees. "He's not here," father said. "I would have seen him. There's not a soul in sight."

"He in the ditch," Nancy said. "He waiting in the ditch yonder."

"Nonsense," father said. He looked at Nancy. "Do you know he's there?"

"I got the sign," Nancy said.

"What sign?"

"I got it. It was on the table when I come in. It was a hogbone, with blood meat still on it, laying by the lamp. He's out there. When yawl walk out that door, I gone."

"Gone where, Nancy?" Caddy said.

"I'm not a tattletale," Jason said.

"Nonsense," father said.

"He out there," Nancy said. "He looking through that window this minute, waiting for yawl to go. Then I gone."

"Nonsense," father said. "Lock up your house and we'll take you on to Aunt Rachel's."

"'Twont do no good," Nancy said. She didn't look at father now, but he looked down at her, at her long, limp, moving hands. "Putting it off wont do no good."

"Then what do you want to do?" father said.

"I don't know," Nancy said. "I can't do nothing. Just put it off. And that don't do no good. I reckon it belong to me. I reckon what I going to get ain't no more than mine."

"Get what?" Caddy said. "What's yours?"

"Nothing," father said. "You all must get to bed."

"Caddy made me come," Jason said.

"Go on to Aunt Rachel's," father said.

"It won't do no good," Nancy said. She sat before the fire, her elbows on her knees, her long hands between her knees. "When even your own kitchen wouldn't do no good. When even if I was sleeping on the floor in the room with your chillen, and the next morning there I am, and blood—"

"Hush," father said. "Lock the door and put out the lamp and go to bed."

"I scared of the dark," Nancy said. "I scared for it to happen in the dark."

"You mean you're going to sit right here with the lamp lighted?" father said. Then Nancy began to make the sound again, sitting before the fire, her long hands between her knees. "Ah, damnation," father said. "Come along, chillen. It's past bedtime."

"When yawl go home, I gone," Nancy said. She talked quieter now, and her face looked quiet, like her hands. "Anyway, I got my coffin money saved up with Mr. Lovelady." Mr. Lovelady was a short, dirty man who collected the Negro insurance, coming around to the cabins or the kitchens every Sunday morning, to collect fifteen cents. He and his wife lived at the hotel. One morning his wife committed suicide. They had a child, a little girl. He and the child went away. After a week or two he came back alone. We would see him going along the lanes and the back streets on Saturday mornings.

"Nonsense," father said. "You'll be the first thing I'll see in the kitchen tomorrow morning."

"You'll see what you'll see, I reckon," Nancy said. "But it will take the Lord to say what that will be."

VI

We left her sitting before the fire.

"Come and put the bar up," father said. But she didn't move. She didn't look at us again, sitting quietly there between the lamp and the fire. From some distance down the lane we could look back and see her through the open door.

"What, Father?" Caddy said. "What's going to happen?"

"Nothing," father said. Jason was on father's back, so Jason was the tallest of all of us. We went down into the ditch. I looked at it, quiet. I couldn't see much where the moonlight and the shadows tangled.

"If Jesus is hid here, he can see us, cant he?" Caddy said.

"He's not there," father said. "He went away a long time ago."

"You made me come," Jason said, high; against the sky it looked like father had two heads, a little one and a big one. "I didn't want to."

We went up out of the ditch. We could still see Nancy's house and the open door, but we couldn't see Nancy now, sitting before the fire with the door open, because she was tired. "I just done got tired," she said. "I just a nigger. It ain't no fault of mine."

But we could hear her, because she began just after we came up out of the ditch, the sound that was not singing and not unsinging. "Who will do our washing now, Father?" I said.

"I'm not a nigger," Jason said, high and close above father's head.

"You're worse," Caddy said, "you are a tattletale. If something was to jump out, you'd be scairder than a nigger."

"I wouldn't," Jason said.

"You'd cry," Caddy said.

"Caddy," father said.

"I wouldn't," Jason said.

"Scairy cat," Caddy said.

"Candace!" father said.

Spotted Horses (1931)

The text of "Spotted Horses" printed below is the original version of the story as it was published in *Scribner's* magazine in June, 1931. The story was later incorporated (with great revisions) into the novel *The Hamlet* (published in 1940).

Faulkner's brother John tells us in *My Brother Bill* that, as a young man, Faulkner, from the porch of a boarding house in the village of Pittsboro, Mississippi, actually witnessed such a horse auction as is described in this story. The ponies to be sold were very wild and skittish and were linked together with barbed wire.

The scene of the auction of the Texas ponies is a settlement called Frenchman's Bend, some ten or twelve miles out in the country from Jefferson. The inhabitants of this village and the farming country around it are mostly white yeoman farmers and poor whites. Few Negroes live in this part of the county and there is no representative of the old planter stock. The wealthiest landowner is Will Varner who owns the store, but Varner is roughhewn, a man of the people, and certainly makes no pretensions to gentility. The hamlet itself amounts to not much more than a country store, a blacksmith shop, a church, and a few houses. The time is April, 1909.

In Frenchman's Bend most people live by subsistence farming and pick up a little ready money from a cash crop like cotton, or perhaps they work in the sawmill. Flem Snopes is a fairly recent arrival in this community—the son of a poor sharecropper and absolutely relentless in his determination to make money. He has got a job in the Varner store, and it is plain that he is beginning to take over the running of the business, to the discomfiture of Will Varner's son, Jody. Flem is a ruthlessly efficient businessman, a fact that gives him an edge in this rather easygoing community of farmers. Furthermore, he is completely unscrupulous, though he is always careful to stay on the right side of the law. Flem, in his pursuit of the dollar, is never inhibited by warmer

passions, by an ethical code, or even by the ties of blood and family. When the auction of the spotted horses takes place, his reputation for getting the better of any trade has already become a legend in the community.

The narrator of the story is V. K. Ratliff, an itinerant sewing-machine agent, who, it becomes obvious, has for some time been observing Flem's rise to power. Readers of *The Hamlet* will discover that Ratliff enjoys driving a good bargain and waging a contest of wits with a foeman worthy of his steel, but he is certainly no Snopes. Indeed, in the several Yoknapatawpha novels in which he appears, Ratliff is one of the most stable and reliable characters. He has an ethical code to which he strictly adheres; he is fair-minded, decent, and not lacking in sympathy for the weak and helpless. But Ratliff is no sobersides. Along with his genuine folk wisdom, he has mother wit, drollery, and a sharp, though not bitter, insight into human nature. Best of all, for the reader's enjoyment, he is a born storyteller who knows where to begin a yarn, when to pause, and how to build toward an effect—and he also knows how to use the English language.

The mode of narration used here is that of the tall tale of the old Southwest. (Mississippi and Arkansas constituted frontier states of the old Southwest.) As its name implies, in the tall tale everything is made larger than lifesize in the telling. Much of the humor depends upon exaggeration: the narrator of such tales likes to tell a whopper with appropriate rhetorical embellishments. Yet if he is an accomplished artist in this tradition, he does not rely for his humor merely on exaggeration and caricature. He may also make use of understatement, dry wit, and oblique reference: instead of attacking the matter in question directly, he may elect to outflank it or move in on it from the rear.

Some of the gaudiest rhetoric in "Spotted Horses" is spoken by the Texan as he extols the merits of the calico ponies. He is an excellent

advertising man, but like the others, he uses a folk idiom and reminds us more of the barker at a circus or the spieler for a medicine show than the man in a gray flannel suit from Madison Avenue. Yet if the Texan cheerfully cooperates in hornswoggling the men of the community, he draws the line at bilking women and children. He recognizes at once Henry Armstid's almost pathological state; he responds to the pathos of Mrs. Armstid's appeal and tries to return the price of the horse. (One may be sure, however, that Flem will not let this arrangement hold.)

"Spotted Horses" more than glances at the male-female polarity, always stressed in Faulkner's work. Women possess wisdom, an instinctive rapport with nature. They are practical and realistic. It is the men who are the born romantics, prone to do frivolous and foolish things, taking senseless risks, and living by what are frequently proved to be ridiculous codes of honor.

Faulkner establishes and maintains a pattern of symbolic forces. On the one side, he places the fascinating and untamable spotted horses, fluid, unpredictable, and incorrigible. On the other side, there is Mrs. Littlejohn, who runs the boarding house and is stolidly going through the tasks of her day, uttering no word but looking from time to time at what is going on in the lot next door; but all the while she is noting with close-lipped but somber disapproval the folly of men. Between the horses (temptation) and Mrs. Littlejohn (silent moral judgment) there are the men, at the beginning hesitant, knowing better than to yield to temptation, yet fascinated with horse flesh, excited by the hope of getting something for nothing, and secretly yearning to be persuaded to buy.

The reader who is interested in Faulkner's narrative techniques might enjoy comparing the version of "Spotted Horses" printed here with that found in *The Hamlet*. In *The Hamlet*, we learn a great deal more about Flem, Eula, Ratliff, and the other characters. The main outlines of the "Spotted Horses" narration remains the same, but in *The Hamlet* Ratliff does not tell the story himself, though we watch what he does at the auction and hear what he says to this and that character. The actual telling is accomplished by the author himself—indeed, the whole novel is a third-person narration. The reader might ponder what is gained thereby. In this connection he might look at Robert Penn Warren's "Introduction: Faulkner's Past and Present," in *Faulkner: A Collection of Critical Essays* (1966).

———————————

Yes, sir. Flem Snopes has filled that whole country full of spotted horses. You can hear folks running them all day and all night, whooping and hollering, and the horses running back and forth across them little wooden bridges ever now and then kind of like thunder. Here I was this morning pretty near half way to town, with the team ambling along and me setting in the buckboard about half asleep, when all of a sudden something come swurging up outen the bushes and jumped the road clean, without touching hoof to it. It flew right over my team, big as a billboard and flying through the air like a hawk. It taken me thirty minutes to stop my team and untangle the harness and the buckboard and hitch them up again.

That Flem Snopes. I be dog if he ain't a case, now. One morning about ten years ago, the boys was just getting settled down on Varner's porch for a little talk and tobacco, when here come Flem out from behind the counter, with his coat off and his hair all parted, like he might have been clerking for Varner for ten years already. Folks all knowed him; it was a big family of them about five miles down the bottom. That year, at least. Share-cropping. They never stayed on any place over a year. Then they would move on to another place, with the chap or maybe the twins of that year's litter. It was a regular nest of them. But Flem. The rest of them stayed tenant farmers, moving ever year, but here come Flem one day, walking out from behind Jody Varner's counter like he owned it. And he wasn't there but a year or two before folks knowed that, if him and Jody was both still in that store in ten years more, it would be Jody clerking for Flem Snopes. Why, that fellow could make a nickel where it wasn't but four cents to begin with. He skun me in two trades, myself, and the fellow that can do that, I just hope he'll get rich before I do; that's all.

All right. So here Flem was, clerking at Varner's, making a nickel here and there and not telling nobody about it. No, sir. Folks never knowed when

Flem got the better of somebody lessen the fellow he beat told it. He'd just set there in the store-chair, chewing his tobacco and keeping his own business to hisself, until about a week later we'd find out it was somebody else's business he was keeping to hisself—providing the fellow he trimmed was mad enough to tell it. That's Flem.

We give him ten years to own ever thing Jody Varner had. But he never waited no ten years. I reckon you-all know that gal of Uncle Billy Varner's, the youngest one; Eula. Jody's sister. Ever Sunday ever yellow-wheeled buggy and curried riding horse in that country would be hitched to Bill Varner's fence, and the young bucks setting on the porch, swarming around Eula like bees around a honey pot. One of these here kind of big, soft-looking gals that could giggle richer than plowed newground. Wouldn't none of them leave before the others, and so they would set there on the porch until time to go home, with some of them with nine and ten miles to ride and then get up tomorrow and go back to the field. So they would all leave together and they would ride in a clump down to the creek ford and hitch them curried horses and yellow-wheeled buggies and get out and fight one another. Then they would get in the buggies again and go on home.

Well, one day about a year ago, one of them yellow-wheeled buggies and one of them curried saddle-horses quit this country. We heard they was heading for Texas. The next day Uncle Billy and Eula and Flem come into town in Uncle Billy's surrey, and when they come back, Flem and Eula was married. And on the next day we heard that two more of them yellow-wheeled buggies had left the country. They mought have gone to Texas, too. It's a big place.

Anyway, about a month after the wedding, Flem and Eula went to Texas, too. They was gone pretty near a year. Then one day last month, Eula come back, with a baby. We figgered up, and we decided that it was as well-growed a three-months-old baby as we ever see. It can already pull up on a chair. I reckon Texas makes big men quick, being a big place. Anyway, if it keeps on like it started, it'll be chewing tobacco and voting time it's eight years old.

And so last Friday here come Flem himself. He was on a wagon with another fellow. The other fellow had one of these two-gallon hats and a ivory-handled pistol and a box of ginger snaps sticking out of his hind pocket, and tied to the tail-gate of

the wagon was about two dozen of them Texas ponies, hitched to one another with barbed wire. They was colored like parrots and they was quiet as doves, and ere a one of them would kill you quick as a rattlesnake. Nere a one of them had two eyes the same color, and nere a one of them had ever see a bridle, I reckon; and when that Texas man got down offen the wagon and walked up to them to show how gentle they was, one of them cut his vest clean offen him, same as with a razor.

Flem had done already disappeared, he had went on to see his wife, I reckon, and to see if that ere baby had done gone on to the field to help Uncle Billy plough, maybe. It was the Texas man that takes the horses on to Mrs. Littlejohn's lot. He had a little trouble at first, when they come to the gate, because they hadn't never see a fence before, and when he finally got them in and taken a pair of wire cutters and unhitched them and got them into the barn and poured some shell corn into the trough, they durn nigh tore down the barn. I reckon they thought that shell corn was bugs, maybe. So he left them in the lot and he announced that the auction would begin at sunup to-morrow.

That night we was setting on Mrs. Littlejohn's porch. You-all mind the moon was nigh full that night, and we could watch them spotted varmints swirling along the fence and back and forth across the lot same as minnows in a pond. And then now and then they would all kind of huddle up against the barn and rest themselves by biting and kicking one another. We would hear a squeal, and then a set of hoofs would go Bam! against the barn, like a pistol. It sounded just like a fellow with a pistol, in a nest of cattymounts, taking his time.

II

It wasn't ere a man knowed yet if Flem owned them things or not. They just knowed one thing: that they wasn't never going to know for sho if Flem did or not, or if maybe he didn't just get on that wagon at the edge of town, for the ride or not. Even Eck Snopes didn't know, Flem's own cousin. But wasn't nobody surprised at that. We knowed that Flem would skin Eck quick as he would ere a one of us.

They was there by sunup next morning, some of

them come twelve and sixteen miles, with seed-money tied up in tobacco sacks in their overalls, standing along the fence, when the Texas man come out of Mrs. Littlejohn's after breakfast and clumb onto the gate post with that ere white pistol butt sticking outen his hind pocket. He taken a new box of gingersnaps outen his pocket and bit the end offen it like a cigar and spit out the paper, and said the auction was open. And still they was coming up in wagons and a horse- and mule-back and hitching the teams across the road and coming to the fence. Flem wasn't nowhere in sight.

But he couldn't get them started. He begun to work on Eck, because Eck holp him last night to get them into the barn and feed them that shell corn. Eck got out just in time. He come outen that barn like a chip on the crest of a busted dam of water and clumb into the wagon just in time.

He was working on Eck when Henry Armstid come up in his wagon. Eck was saying he was skeered to bid on one of them, because he might get it, and the Texas man says, "Them ponies? Them little horses?" He clumb down offen the gate post and went toward the horses. They broke and run, and him following them, kind of chirping to them, with his hand out like he was fixing to catch a fly, until he got three or four of them cornered. Then he jumped into them, and then we couldn't see nothing for a while because of the dust. It was a big cloud of it, and them blare-eyed, spotted things swoaring outen it twenty foot to a jump, in forty directions without counting up. Then the dust settled and there they was, that Texas man and the horse. He had its head twisted clean around like a owl's head. Its legs was braced and it was trembling like a new bride and groaning like a saw mill, and him holding its head wrung clean around on its neck so it was snuffing sky. "Look it over," he says, with his heels dug too and that white pistol sticking outen his pocket and his neck swole up like a spreading adder's until you could just tell what he was saying, cussing the horse and talking to us all at once: "Look him over, the fiddle-headed son of fourteen fathers. Try him, buy him; you will get the best—" Then it was all dust again, and we couldn't see nothing but spotted hide and mane, and that ere Texas man's boot-heels like a couple of walnuts on two strings, and after a while that two-gallon hat come sailing out like a fat old hen crossing a fence.

When the dust settled again, he was just getting outen the far fence corner, brushing himself off. He come and got his hat and brushed it off and come and clumb onto the gate post again. He was breathing hard. He taken the gingersnap box outen his pocket and et one, breathing hard. The hammer-head horse was still running round and round the lot like a merry-go-round at a fair. That was when Henry Armstid come shoving up to the gate in them patched overalls and one of them dangle-armed shirts of hisn. Hadn't nobody noticed him until then. We was all watching the Texas man and the horses. Even Mrs. Littlejohn; she had done come out and built a fire under the wash-pot in her back yard, and she would stand at the fence a while and then go back into the house and come out again with a arm full of wash and stand at the fence again. Well, here come Henry shoving up, and then we see Mrs. Armstid right behind him, in that ere faded wrapper and sunbonnet and them tennis shoes. "Git on back to that wagon," Henry says.

"Henry," she says.

"Here, boys," the Texas man says; "make room for missus to git up and see. Come on, Henry," he says; "here's your chance to buy that saddle-horse missus has been wanting. What about ten dollars, Henry?"

"Henry," Mrs. Armstid says. She put her hand on Henry's arm. Henry knocked her hand down.

"Git on back to that wagon, like I told you," he says.

Mrs. Armstid never moved. She stood behind Henry, with her hands rolled into her dress, not looking at nothing. "He hain't no more despair than to buy one of them things," she says. "And me not five dollars ahead of the pore house he hain't no more despair." It was the truth, too. They ain't never made more than a bare living offen that place of theirs, and them with four chaps and the very clothes they wears she earns by weaving by the firelight at night while Henry's asleep.

"Shut your mouth and git on back to that wagon," Henry says. "Do you want I taken a wagon stake to you here in the big road?"

Well, that Texas man taken one look at her. Then he begun on Eck again, like Henry wasn't even there. But Eck was skeered. "I can git me a snapping turtle or a water moccasin for nothing. I ain't going to buy none."

So the Texas man said he would give Eck a horse. "To start the auction, and because you holp me last night. If you'll start the bidding on the next horse," he says, "I'll give you that fiddle-head horse."

I wish you could have seen them standing there with their seed-money in their pockets, watching that Texas man give Eck Snopes a live horse, all fixed to call him a fool if he taken it or not. Finally Eck says he'll take it. "Only I just starts the bidding," he says. "I don't have to buy the next one lessen I ain't over-topped." The Texas man said all right and Eck bid a dollar on the next one with Henry Armstid standing there with his mouth already open, watching Eck and the Texas man like a mad dog or something. "A dollar," Eck says.

The Texas man looked at Eck. His mouth was already open too, like he had started to say something and what he was going to say had up and died on him. "A dollar?" he says. "One dollar? You mean, *one* dollar, Eck?"

"Durn it," Eck says; "two dollars, then."

Well, sir, I wish you could a seen that Texas man. He taken out that gingersnap box and held it up and looked into it, careful, like it might have been a diamond ring in it, or a spider. Then he throwed it away and wiped his face with a bandanna. "Well," he says. "Well. Two dollars. Two dollars. Is your pulse all right, Eck?" he says. "Do you have ager sweats at night, maybe?" he says. "Well," he says, "I got to take it. But are you boys going to stand there and see Eck get two horses at a dollar a head?"

That done it. I be dog if he wasn't nigh as smart as Flem Snopes. He hadn't no more than got the words outen his mouth before here was Henry Armstid, waving his hand. "Three dollars," Henry says. Mrs. Armstid tried to hold him again. He knocked her hand off, shoving up to the gate post.

"Mister," Mrs. Armstid says, "we got chaps in the house and not corn to feed the stock. We got five dollars I earned my chaps a-weaving after dark, and him snoring in the bed. And he hain't no more despair."

"Henry bids three dollars," the Texas man says. "Raise him a dollar, Eck, and the horse is yours."

"Henry," Mrs. Armstid says.

"Raise him, Eck," the Texas man says.

"Four dollars," Eck says.

"Five dollars," Henry says, shaking his fist. He shoved up right under the gate post. Mrs. Armstid was looking at the Texas man too.

"Mister," he says, "if you take that five dollars I earned my chaps a-weaving for one of them

things, it'll be a curse onto you and yourn during all the time of man."

But it wasn't no stopping Henry. He had shoved up, waving his fist at the Texas man. He opened it; the money was in nickels and quarters, and one dollar bill that looked like a cow's cud. "Five dollars," he says. "And the man that raises it'll have to beat my head off, or I'll beat hisn."

"All right," the Texas man says. "Five dollars is bid. But don't you shake your hand at me."

III

It taken till nigh sundown before the last one was sold. He got them hotted up once and the bidding got up to seven dollars and a quarter, but most of them went around three or four dollars, him setting on the gate post and picking the horses out one at a time by mouth-word, and Mrs. Littlejohn pumping up and down at the tub and stopping and coming to the fence for a while and going back to the tub again. She had done got done too, and the wash was hung on the line in the back yard, and we could smell supper cooking. Finally they was all sold; he swapped the last two and the wagon for a buckboard.

We was all kind of tired, but Henry Armstid looked more like a mad-dog than ever. When he bought, Mrs. Armstid had went back to the wagon, setting in it behind them two rabbit-sized, bone-pore mules, and the wagon itself looking like it would fall all to pieces soon as the mules moved. Henry hadn't even waited to pull it outen the road; it was still in the middle of the road and her setting in it, not looking at nothing, ever since this morning.

Henry was right up against the gate. He went up to the Texas man. "I bought a horse and I paid cash," Henry says. "And yet you expect me to stand around here until they are all sold before I can get my horse. I'm going to take my horse outen that lot."

The Texas man looked at Henry. He talked like he might have been asking for a cup of coffee at the table. "Take your horse," he says.

Then Henry quit looking at the Texas man. He began to swallow, holding onto the gate. "Ain't you going to help me?" he says.

"It ain't my horse," the Texas man says.

Henry never looked at the Texas man again, he never looked at nobody. "Who'll help me catch my horse?" he says. Never nobody said nothing. "Bring the plowline," Henry says. Mrs. Armstid got outen the wagon and brought the plowline. The Texas man got down offen the post. The woman made to pass him, carrying the rope.

"Don't you go in there, missus," the Texas man says.

Henry opened the gate. He didn't look back. "Come on here," he says.

"Don't you go in there, missus," the Texas man says.

Mrs. Armstid wasn't looking at nobody, neither, with her hands across her middle, holding the rope. "I reckon I better," she says. Her and Henry went into the lot. The horses broke and run. Henry and Mrs. Armstid followed.

"Get him into the corner," Henry says. They got Henry's horse cornered finally, and Henry taken the rope, but Mrs. Armstid let the horse get out. They hemmed it up again, but Mrs. Armstid let it get out again, and Henry turned and hit her with the rope. "Why didn't you head him back?" Henry says. He hit her again. "Why didn't you?" It was about that time I looked around and see Flem Snopes standing there.

It was the Texas man that done something. He moved fast for a big man. He caught the rope before Henry could hit the third time, and Henry whirled and made like he would jump at the Texas man. But he never jumped. The Texas man went and taken Henry's arm and led him outen the lot. Mrs. Armstid come behind them and the Texas man taken some money outen his pocket and he give it into Mrs. Armstid's hand "Get him into the wagon and take him on home," the Texas man says, like he might have been telling them he enjoyed his supper.

Then here come Flem. "What's that for, Buck?" Flem says.

"Thinks he bought one of them ponies," the Texas man says. "Get him far away, missus."

But Henry wouldn't go. "Give him back that money," he says. "I bought that horse and I aim to have him if I have to shoot him."

And there was Flem, standing there with his hands in his pockets, chewing like he had just happened to be passing.

"You take your money and I take my horse," Henry says. "Give it back to him," he says to Mrs. Armstid.

"You don't own no horse of mine," the Texas man says. "Get him on home missus."

Then Henry seen Flem. "You got something to do with these horses," he says. "I bought one. Here's the money for it." He taken the bill outen

Mrs. Armstid's hand. He offered it to Flem. "I bought one. Ask him. Here. Here's the money," he says, giving the bills to Flem.

When Flem taken the money, the Texas man dropped the rope he had snatched outen Henry's hand. He had done sent Eck Snopes's boy up to the store for another box of gingersnaps and he taken the box outen his pocket and looked into it. It was empty and he dropped it on the ground. "Mr. Snopes will have your money for you to-morrow," he says to Mrs. Armstid. "You can get it from him to-morrow. He don't own no horse. You get him on the wagon and get him on home." Mrs. Armstid went back to the wagon and got in. "Where's that ere buckboard I bought?" the Texas man says. It was after sundown then. And then Mrs. Littlejohn come out on the porch and rung the supper bell.

IV

I come on in and et supper. Mrs. Littlejohn would bring in a pan of bread or something, then she would go out to the porch a minute and come back and tell us. The Texas man had hitched his team to the buckboard he had swapped them last two horses for, and him and Flem had gone, and then she told that the rest of them that never had ropes had went back to the store with I. O. Snopes to get some ropes, and wasn't nobody at the gate but Henry Armstid, and Mrs. Armstid setting in the wagon in the road, and Eck Snopes and that boy of hisn. "I don't care how many of them fool men gets killed by them things," Mrs. Littlejohn says, "but I ain't going to let Eck Snopes take that boy into that lot again." So she went down to the gate, but she come back without the boy or Eck neither.

"It ain't no need to worry about that boy," I says. "He's charmed." He was right behind Eck last night when Eck went to help feed them. The whole drove of them jumped clean over that boy's head and never touched him. It was Eck that touched him. Eck snatched him into the wagon and taken a rope and frailed the tar outen him.

So I had done et and went to my room and was undressing, long as I had a long trip to make next day; I was trying to sell a machine to Mrs. Bundren up past Whiteleaf; when Henry Armstid opened that gate and went in by hisself. They couldn't make him wait for the balance of them to get back with their ropes. Eck Snopes said he tried to make Henry wait, but Henry wouldn't do it. Eck said Henry walked right up to them and that when they broke, they run clean over Henry like a hay-mow breaking down. Eck said he snatched that boy of hisn out of the way just in time and that them things went through that gate like a creek flood and into the wagons and teams hitched side the road, busting wagon tongues and snapping harness like it was fishing-line, with Mrs. Armstid still setting in their wagon in the middle of it like something carved outen wood. Then they scattered, wild horses and tame mules with pieces of harness and single trees dangling offen them, both ways up and down the road.

"There goes ourn, paw!" Eck says his boy said. "There it goes, into Mrs. Littlejohn's house." Eck says it run right up the steps and into the house like a boarder late for supper. I reckon so. Anyway, I was in my room, in my underclothes, with one sock on and one sock in my hand, leaning out the window when the commotion busted out, when I heard something run into the melodeon in the hall; it sounded like a railroad engine. Then the door to my room come sailing in like when you throw a tin bucket top into the wind and I looked over my shoulder and see something that looked like a fourteen-foot pinwheel a-blaring its eyes at me. It had to blare them fast, because I was already done jumped out the window.

I reckon it was anxious, too. I reckon it hadn't never seen barbed wire or shell corn before, but I know it hadn't never seen underclothes before, or maybe it was a sewing-machine agent it hadn't never seen. Anyway, it swirled and turned to run back up the hall and outen the house, when it met Eck Snopes and that boy just coming in, carrying a rope. It swirled again and run down the hall and out the back door just in time to meet Mrs. Littlejohn. She had just gathered up the clothes she had washed, and she was coming onto the back porch with a armful of washing in one hand and a scrubbing-board in the other, when the horse skidded up to her, trying to stop and swirl again. It never taken Mrs. Littlejohn no time a-tall.

"Git outen here, you son," she says. She hit it across the face with the scrubbing-board; that ere scrubbing-board split as neat as ere a axe could have done it, and when the horse swirled to run back up the hall, she hit it again with what was left of the scrubbing-board, not on the head this time. "And stay out," she says.

Eck and that boy was half-way down the hall by

this time. I reckon that horse looked like a pinwheel to Eck too. "Git to hell outen here, Ad!" Eck says. Only there wasn't time. Eck dropped flat on his face, but the boy never moved. The boy was about a yard tall maybe, in overhalls just like Eck's; that horse swoared over his head without touching a hair. I saw that, because I was just coming back up the front steps, still carrying that ere sock and still in my underclothes, when the horse come onto the porch again. It taken one look at me and swirled again and run to the end of the porch and jumped the banisters and the lot fence like a hen-hawk and lit in the lot running and went out the gate again and jumped eight or ten upside-down wagons and went on down the road. It was a full moon then. Mrs. Armstid was still setting in the wagon like she had done been carved outen wood and left there and forgot.

That horse. It ain't never missed a lick. It was going about forty miles a hour when it come to the bridge over the creek. It would have had a clear road, but it so happened that Vernon Tull was already using the bridge when it got there. He was coming back from town; he hadn't heard about the auction; him and his wife and three daughters and Mrs. Tull's aunt, all setting in chairs on the wagon bed, and all asleep, including the mules. They waked up when the horse hit the bridge one time, but Tull said the first he knew was when the mules tried to turn the wagon around in the middle of the bridge and he saw that spotted varmint run right twixt the mules and run up the wagon tongue like a squirrel. He said he just had time to hit it across the face with his whip-stock, because about that time the mules turned the wagon around on that ere one-way bridge and that horse clumb across one of the mules and jumped down onto the bridge again and went on, with Vernon standing up in the wagon and kicking at it.

Tull said the mules turned in the harness and clumb back into the wagon too, with Tull trying to beat them out again, with the reins wrapped around his wrist. After that he says all he seen was overturned chairs and womenfolks' legs and white drawers shining in the moonlight, and his mules and that spotted horse going on up the road like a ghost.

The mules jerked Tull outen the wagon and drug him a spell on the bridge before the reins broke. They thought at first that he was dead, and while they was kneeling around him, picking the bridge splinters outen him, here come Eck and that boy, still carrying the rope. They was running and breathing a little hard. "Where'd he go?" Eck says.

V

I went back and got my pants and shirt and shoes on just in time to go and help get Henry Armstid outen the trash in the lot. I be dog if he didn't look like he was dead, with his head hanging back and his teeth showing in the moonlight, and a little rim of white under his eyelids. We could still hear them horses here and there; hadn't none of them got more than four—five miles away yet not knowing the country, I reckon. So we could hear them and folks yelling now and then: "Whooey. Head him!"

We toted Henry into Mrs. Littlejohn's. She was in the hall; she hadn't sat down the armful of clothes. She taken one look at us, and she laid down the busted scrubbing-board and taken up the lamp and opened a empty door. "Bring him in here," she says.

We toted him in and laid him on the bed. Mrs. Littlejohn set the lamp on the dresser, still carrying the clothes. "I'll declare, you men," she says. Our shadows was way up the wall, tiptoeing too; we could hear ourselves breathing. "Better get his wife," Mrs. Littlejohn says. She went out, carrying the clothes.

"I reckon we had," Quick says. "Go get her, somebody."

"Whyn't you go?" Winterbottom says.

"Let Ernest git her," Durley says. "He lives neighbors with them."

Ernest went to fetch her. I be dog if Henry didn't look like he was dead. Mrs. Littlejohn come back, with a kettle and some towels. She went to work on Henry, and then Mrs. Armstid and Ernest come in. Mrs. Armstid come to the foot of the bed and stood there, with her hands rolled into her apron, watching what Mrs. Littlejohn was doing, I reckon.

"You men get outen the way," Mrs. Littlejohn says. "Git outside," she says. "See if you can't find something else to play with that will kill some more of you."

"Is he dead?" Winterbottom says.

"It ain't your fault if he ain't," Mrs. Littlejohn says. "Go tell Will Varner to come up here. I reckon a man ain't so different from a mule, come long come short. Except maybe a mule's got more sense."

We went to get Uncle Billy. It was a full moon. We could hear them, now and then, four mile away: "Whooey. Head him." The country was full of them, one on ever wooden bridge in the land, running across it like thunder: "Whooey. There he goes. Head him."

We hadn't got far before Henry begun to scream. I reckon Mrs. Littlejohn's water had brung him to; anyway, he wasn't dead. We went on to Uncle Billy's. The house was dark. We called to him, and after a while the window opened and Uncle Billy put his head out, peart as a pecker-wood, listening. "Are they still trying to catch them durn rabbits?" he says.

He come down, with his britches on over his night-shirt and his suspenders dangling, carrying his horse-doctoring grip. "Yes, sir," he says, cocking his head like a woodpecker; "they're still a-try-ing."

We could hear Henry before we reached Mrs. Littlejohn's. He was going Ah-Ah-Ah. We stopped in the yard. Uncle Billy went on in. We could hear Henry. We stood in the yard, hearing them on the bridges, this-a-way and that: "Whooey. Whooey."

"Eck Snopes ought to caught hisn," Ernest says.

"Looks like he ought," Winterbottom said.

Henry was going Ah-Ah-Ah steady in the house; then he begun to scream. "Uncle Billy's started," Quick says. We looked into the hall. We could see the light where the door was. Then Mrs. Little-john come out.

"Will needs some help," she says. "You Er-nest. You'll do." Ernest went into the house.

"Hear them?" Quick said. "That one was on Four Mile bridge." We could hear them; it sounded like thunder a long way off; it didn't last long:

"Whooey."

We could hear Henry: "Ah-Ah-Ah-Ah-Ah."

"They are both started now," Winterbottom says. "Ernest too."

That was early in the night. Which was a good thing, because it taken a long night for folks to chase them things right and for Henry to lay there and holler, being as Uncle Billy never had none of this here chloryfoam to set Henry's leg with. So it was considerate in Flem to get them started early. And what do you reckon Flem's comment was?

That's right. Nothing. Because he wasn't there. Hadn't nobody see him since that Texas man left.

VI

That was Saturday night. I reckon Mrs. Armstid got home about daylight, to see about the chaps. I don't know where they thought her and Henry was. But lucky the oldest one was a gal, about twelve, big enough to take care of the little ones. Which she did for the next two days. Mrs. Armstid would nurse Henry all night and work in the kitchen for hern and Henry's keep, and in the afternoon she would drive home (it was about four miles) to see to the chaps. She would cook up a pot of victuals and leave it on the stove, and the gal would bar the house and keep the little ones quiet. I would hear Mrs. Littlejohn and Mrs. Armstid talking in the kitchen. "How are the chaps making out?" Mrs. Littlejohn says.

"All right," Mrs. Armstid says.

"Don't they git skeered at night?" Mrs. Littlejohn says.

"Ina May bars the door when I leave," Mrs. Armstid says. "She's got the axe in bed with her. I reckon she can make out."

I reckon they did. And I reckon Mrs. Armstid was waiting for Flem to come back to town; hadn't nobody seen him until this morning; to get her money the Texas man said Flem was keeping for her. Sho. I reckon she was.

Anyway, I heard Mrs. Armstid and Mrs. Littlejohn talking in the kitchen this morning while I was eating breakfast. Mrs. Littlejohn had just told Mrs. Armstid that Flem was in town. "You can ask him for that five dollars," Mrs. Littlejohn says.

"You reckon he'll give it to me?" Mrs. Armstid says.

Mrs. Littlejohn was washing dishes, washing them like a man, like they was made out of iron. "No," she says. "But asking him won't do no hurt. It might shame him. I don't reckon it will, but it might."

"If he wouldn't give it back, it ain't no use to ask," Mrs. Armstid says.

"Suit yourself," Mrs. Littlejohn says. "It's your money."

I could hear the dishes.

"Do you reckon he might give it back to me?" Mrs. Armstid says. "That Texas man said he would. He said I could get it from Mr. Snopes later."

"Then go and ask him for it," Mrs. Littlejohn says.

I could hear the dishes.

"He won't give it back to me," Mrs. Armstid says.

"All right," Mrs. Littlejohn says. "Don't ask him for it, then."

I could hear the dishes; Mrs. Armstid was helping. "You don't reckon he would, do you?" she says. Mrs. Littlejohn never said nothing. It sounded like she was throwing the dishes at one another. "Maybe I better go and talk to Henry about it," Mrs. Armstid says.

"I would," Mrs. Littlejohn says. I be dog if it didn't sound like she had two plates in her hands, beating them together. "Then Henry can buy another five-dollar horse with it. Maybe he'll buy one next time that will out and out kill him. If I thought that, I'd give you back the money, myself."

"I reckon I better talk to him first," Mrs. Armstid said. Then it sounded like Mrs. Littlejohn taken up all the dishes and throwed them at the cook-stove, and I come away.

That was this morning. I had been up to Bundren's and back, and I thought that things would have kind of settled down. So after breakfast, I went up to the store. And there was Flem, setting in the store chair and whittling, like he might not have ever moved since he come to clerk for Jody Varner. I. O. was leaning in the door, in his shirt sleeves and with his hair parted too, same as Flem was before he turned the clerking job over to I. O. It's a funny thing about them Snopes: they all looks alike, yet there ain't ere a two of them that claims brothers. They're always just cousins, like Flem and Eck and Flem and I. O. Eck was there too, squatting against the wall, him and that boy, eating cheese and crackers outen a sack; they told me that Eck hadn't been home a-tall. And that Lon Quick hadn't got back to town, even. He followed his horse clean down to Samson's Bridge, with a wagon and a camp outfit. Eck finally caught one of hisn. It run into a blind lane at Freeman's and Eck and the boy taken and tied their rope across the end of the lane, about three foot high. The horse come to the end of the lane and whirled and run back without ever stopping. Eck says it never seen the rope a-tall. He says it looked just like one of these here Christmas pinwheels. "Didn't it try to run again?" I says.

"No," Eck says, eating a bite of cheese offen his knife blade. "Just kicked some."

"Kicked some?" I says.

"It broke its neck," Eck says.

Well, they was squatting there, about six of them, talking, talking at Flem; never nobody knowed yet if Flem had ere a interest in them horses or not. So finally I come right out and asked him. "Flem's done skun all of us so much," I says, "that we're proud of him. Come on, Flem," I says, "how much did you and that Texas man make offen them horses? You can tell us. Ain't nobody here but Eck that bought one of them; the others ain't got back to town yet, and Eck's your own cousin; he'll be proud to hear, too. How much did you-all make?"

They was all whittling, not looking at Flem, making like they was studying. But you could a heard a pin drop. And I. O. He had been rubbing his back up and down on the door, but he stopped now, watching Flem like a pointing dog. Flem finished cutting the sliver offen his stick. He spit across the porch, into the road. " 'Twarn't none of my horses," he says.

I. O. cackled, like a hen, slapping his legs with both hands. "You boys might just as well quit trying to get ahead of Flem," he said.

Well, about that time I see Mrs. Armstid come outen Mrs. Littlejohn's gate, coming up the road. I never said nothing. I says, "Well, if a man can't take care of himself in a trade, he can't blame the ⟩ man that trims him."

Flem never said nothing, trimming at the stick. He hadn't seen Mrs. Armstid. "Yes, sir," I says. "A fellow like Henry Armstid ain't got nobody but hisself to blame."

"Course he ain't," I. O. says. He ain't seen her, neither. "Henry Armstid's a born fool. Always is been. If Flem hadn't a got his money, somebody else would."

We looked at Flem. He never moved. Mrs. Armstid come on up the road.

"That's right," I says. "But, come to think of it, Henry never bought no horse." We looked at Flem; you could a heard a match drop. "That Texas man told her to get that five dollars back from Flem next day. I reckon Flem's done already taken that money to Mrs. Littlejohn's and give it to Mrs. Armstid."

We watched Flem. I. O. quit rubbing his back against the door again. After a while Flem raised ⟩ his head and spit across the porch, into the dust. I. O. cackled, just like a hen. "Ain't he a beating fellow, now?" I. O. says.

Mrs. Armstid was getting closer, so I kept on talking, watching to see if Flem would look up and see her. But he never looked up. I went on talking about Tull, about how he was going to sue Flem, and Flem setting there, whittling his stick, not saying nothing else after he said they wasn't none of his horses.

Then I. O. happened to look around. He seen Mrs. Armstid. "Psssst!" he says. Flem looked up. "Here she comes!" I. O. says. "Go out the back. I'll tell her you done went in to town to-day."

But Flem never moved. He just set there, whittling, and we watched Mrs. Armstid come up onto the porch, in that ere faded sunbonnet and wrapper and them tennis shoes that made a kind of hissing noise on the porch. She come onto the porch and stopped, her hands rolled into her dress in front, not looking at nothing.

"He said Saturday," she says, "that he wouldn't sell Henry no horse. He said I could get the money from you."

Flem looked up. The knife never stopped. It went on trimming off a sliver same as if he was ⟩ watching it. "He taken that money off with him when he left," Flem says.

Mrs. Armstid never looked at nothing. We never looked at her, neither, except that boy of Eck's. He had a half-et cracker in his hand, watching her, chewing.

"He said Henry hadn't bought no horse," Mrs. Armstid says. "He said for me to get the money from you to-day."

"I reckon he forgot about it," Flem said. "He taken that money off with him Saturday." He whittled again. I. O. kept on rubbing his back, slow. He licked his lips. After a while the woman looked up the road, where it went on up the hill, toward the graveyard. She looked up that way for a while, with that boy of Eck's watching her and I. O. rubbing his back slow against the door. Then she turned back toward the steps.

"I reckon it's time to get dinner started," she says.

"How's Henry this morning, Mrs. Armstid?" Winterbottom says.

She looked at Winterbottom; she almost stopped. "He's resting, I thank you kindly," she says.

Flem got up, outen the chair, putting his knife away. He spit across the porch. "Wait a minute, Mrs. Armstid," he says. She stopped again. She didn't look at him. Flem went on into the store, with I. O. done quit rubbing his back now, with his head craned after Flem, and Mrs. Armstid standing there with her hands rolled into her dress, not looking at nothing. A wagon come up the road and passed; it was Freeman, on the way to town. Then Flem come out again, with I. O. still watching him. Flem had one of these little striped sacks of Jody Varner's candy; I bet he still owes Jody that nickel, too. He put the sack into Mrs. Armstid's hand, like he would have put it into a hollow stump. He spit again across the porch. "A little sweetening for the chaps," he says.

"You're right kind," Mrs. Armstid says. She held the sack of candy in her hand, not looking at nothing. Eck's boy was watching, the sack, the half-et cracker in his hand; he wasn't chewing now. He watched Mrs. Armstid roll the sack into her apron. "I reckon I better get on back and help with dinner," she says. She turned and went back across the porch. Flem set down in the chair again and opened his knife. He spit across the porch again, past Mrs. Armstid where she hadn't went down the steps yet. Then she went on, in that ere sunbonnet and wrapper all the same color, back down the road toward Mrs. Littlejohn's. You couldn't see her dress move, like a natural woman walking. She looked like a old snag still standing up and moving along on a high water. We watched her turn in at Mrs. Littlejohn's and got outen sight. Flem was whittling. I. O. begun to rub his back on the door. Then he begun to cackle, just like a durn hen.

"You boys might just as well quit trying," I. O. says. "You can't git ahead of Flem. You can't touch him. Ain't he a sight, now?"

I be dog if he ain't. If I had brung a herd of wild cattymounts into town and sold them to my neighbors and kinfolks, they would have lynched me. Yes, sir.

An Odor of Verbena (1938)

"An Odor of Verbena" is the seventh and concluding section of a novel entitled *The Unvanquished*, first published in 1938. The narrator is Bayard Sartoris, a member of one of the old planter families of Jefferson. Though "An Odor of Verbena" can stand alone as a story in its own right, it gains much from being read in its full context. Thus, the reader ought at least to be provided here with a summary of the earlier events that have made important impacts on Bayard's life. The Bayard whom we meet in the first section of the novel is a boy of twelve; the man who narrates the last section of the novel is twenty-four. The novel is what the Germans call a *Bildungsroman*, a novel tracing the hero's educational and moral development.

In the first section the boy of twelve is playing "war" with his black friend Ringo, who is of the same age. It is early July of 1863, and for weeks the town of Vicksburg has been under siege. To his surprise, Bayard finds that one of the family slaves, Loosh, knows what he does not, that Vicksburg has already fallen, and also knows that Bayard's father, Colonel Sartoris, is no longer stationed at Corinth, Mississippi. The realization that the slaves know things about the war that he and the white adults do not know is disturbing. So also is the realization that even the house servants want to be free and that the expression on Loosh's face as he sweeps aside the chips that represent Vicksburg hints at a feeling of secret triumph.

As the novel develops, there are further hints that the war is not turning out quite as a patriotic small boy had believed it must. In spite of his instinctive hero-worship of his soldier father, in spite too of some exciting personal adventures, the glamor of war is gradually becoming tarnished. For example, on one of his father's brief returns to the plantation, Bayard tells us that he smelled an "odor in his clothes and beard and flesh too which I believed was the smell of powder and glory . . . but know better now: know now to have been only the will to endure, a sardonic and even humorous declining of self-delusion. . . ."

There are other events that make their impact, such as Bayard's sight of the slaves crowding the roads and singing "Glory! Glory! Hallelujah" as they try to make their way toward the federal army camped on the other side of an Alabama river which the Negroes call "Jordan"—

the river that the Israelites had to cross to enter the Promised Land. There is the bitter restlessness that Bayard finds voiced by his cousin Drusilla Hawk, whose fiancé has been killed at Shiloh. She dismisses the old lost life, thus: "Who wants to sleep now, with so much happening . . . living used to be dull, used to be stupid. You lived in the same house your father was born in, . . . then you fell in love with your acceptable young man, and in time you would marry him, in your mother's wedding gown. . . ." But this, the girl insists, is all finished and done with now. She has resolved to persuade Colonel Sartoris to take her into his troop as a "cavalryman."

Later, Bayard's grandmother, who has reared him since the death of his mother years before, is killed by a bushwhacker named Grumby. There is no authority to which to appeal in the now completely disordered state of the country, and Bayard and Ringo borrow a pistol and set out to find Grumby and call him to account for the crime. After days of pursuit, they do find him, shoot him as he tries to escape, and cut off his right hand, which they attach to the headboard of the grandmother's grave. The killing of Grumby is evidently a traumatic experience for this boy of sixteen. The brutality of a hard and bitter war, which has finally degenerated into mere lawless killing of women and children, has broken through the boy's decent upbringing.

When the concluding section of the novel opens, the war has been over for several years. Drusilla has been induced by family pressure to marry Colonel Sartoris—though obviously she is not in love with him—and Bayard finds himself at twenty-four with a stepmother who is only eight years older than he. Subsequently, Bayard's father pours all his energy into building a railroad, but quarrels with his business partner and is finally shot down by him on the streets of Jefferson.[1] Ringo at once rides to Oxford,

where Bayard is attending law school, with news of the assassination.

The community expects Bayard to confront his father's assassin and avenge his father's death. It is interesting that even Professor Wilkins, the kindly law professor, expects Bayard to do so. Ringo expects it and, of course, George Wyatt, who had been a member of the colonel's old troop, expects it.

The pressure of the community on Bayard, and the nature of Bayard's reaction to it, are important. "An Odor of Verbena" can be misread if the reader waves aside as of no account the community's notion of what is proper or if he disregards the social and historical context of a provincial southern town that had just lived through the Reconstruction period a hundred years ago. (In other words, it is as important to exercise the historical imagination in reading "An Odor of Verbena" as in reading *The Spanish Tragedy* or *Hamlet*.) At any rate, Bayard's choice is not an easy one for him to make, and we shall miss the drama of the story if we ignore the character of the times by assuming that any decent young man of the period would make the decision that a young man today would make.

When Bayard arrives at home he finds himself under a more special pressure: the masculinized Drusilla, who may possibly be in love with her young stepson and who is certainly in love with the idea of his taking vengeance, proudly hands him the pistols. But Bayard's Aunt Jenny pleads with Bayard not to let "a poor hysterical young woman" force him to call Redmond out. "I know you are not afraid," Aunt Jenny tells him.

Faulkner nowhere brings Bayard's debate with himself out into the open in a long, tortured soliloquy in which Bayard agonizes over one possibility and then another. He has managed matters much more indirectly; but if one reads with sufficient care, he will find that Bayard's

---

[1] In creating the character of John Sartoris, Bayard's father, Faulkner drew upon the life of his own great-grandfather, Colonel W. C. Falkner, who had commanded a regiment at the first battle of Manassas under Stonewall Jackson. Colonel Falkner had been interested in building a railroad and had been embroiled in local controversies in Ripley, Mississippi, in the course of which he had killed two men. He himself was later shot down on the street by a former business associate.

motivation—it is complex—is rendered with both subtlety and power.

The character of the assassin, Redmond, is likewise complex and well worth our attention. He turns out to be no common assassin, and in his own terms he is a man of honor, too.

1

It was just after supper. I had just opened my *Coke*[2] on the table beneath the lamp; I heard Professor Wilkins' feet in the hall and then the instant of silence as he put his hand to the door knob, and I should have known. People talk glibly of presentiment, but I had none. I heard his feet on the stairs and then in the hall approaching and there was nothing in the feet because although I had lived in his house for three college years now and although both he and Mrs. Wilkins called me Bayard in the house, he would no more have entered my room without knocking than I would have entered his—or hers. Then he flung the door violently inward against the doorstop with one of those gestures with or by which an almost painfully unflagging preceptory of youth ultimately aberrates, and stood there saying, "Bayard. Bayard, my son, my dear son."

I should have known; I should have been prepared. Or maybe I was prepared because I remember how I closed the book carefully, even marking the place, before I rose. He (Professor Wilkins) was doing something, bustling at something; it was my hat and cloak which he handed me and which I took although I would not need the cloak, unless even then I was thinking (although it was October, the equinox had not occurred) that the rains and the cool weather would arrive before I should see this room again and so I would need the cloak anyway to return to it if I returned, thinking 'God, if he had only done this last night, flung that door crashing and bouncing against the stop last night without knocking so I could have gotten there before it happened, been there when it did, beside him on whatever spot, wherever it was that he would have to fall and lie in the dust and dirt.'

"Your boy is downstairs in the kitchen," he said. It was not until years later that he told me (someone did; it must have been Judge Wilkins)

[2] The *Institutes*, a celebrated work in English jurisprudence by Edward Coke (1552–1634).

how Ringo had apparently flung the cook aside and come on into the house and into the library where he and Mrs. Wilkins were sitting and said without preamble and already turning to withdraw: "They shot Colonel Sartoris this morning. Tell him I be waiting in the kitchen" and was gone before either of them could move. "He has ridden forty miles yet he refuses to eat anything." We were moving toward the door now—the door on my side of which I had lived for three years now with what I knew, what I knew now I must have believed and expected, yet beyond which I had heard the approaching feet yet heard nothing in the feet. "If there was just anything I could do."

"Yes, sir," I said. "A fresh horse for my boy. He will want to go back with me."

"By all means take mine—Mrs. Wilkins'," he cried. His tone was no different yet he did cry it and I suppose that at the same moment we both realised that was funny—a short-legged deep-barrelled mare who looked exactly like a spinster music teacher, which Mrs. Wilkins drove to a basket phaeton—which was good for me, like being doused with a pail of cold water would have been good for me.

"Thank you, sir," I said. "We won't need it. I will get a fresh horse for him at the livery stable when I get my mare." Good for me, because even before I finished speaking I knew that would not be necessary either, that Ringo would have stopped at the livery stable before he came out to the college and attended to that and that the fresh horse for him and my mare both would be saddled and waiting now at the side fence and we would not have to go through Oxford at all. Loosh would not have thought of that if he had come for me, he would have come straight to the college, to Professor Wilkins', and told his news and then sat down and let me take charge from then on. But not Ringo.

He followed me from the room. From now until Ringo and I rode away into the hot thick dusty darkness quick and strained for the overdue equinox like a laboring delayed woman, he would be somewhere either just beside me or just behind me and I never to know exactly nor care which. He was trying to find the words with which to offer me his pistol too. I could almost hear him: "Ah, this unhappy land, not ten years recovered from the fever yet still men must kill one another, still we must pay Cain's price in his own coin." But he did not actually say it. He just followed me, somewhere beside or behind me as we descended the stairs toward where Mrs. Wilkins waited in the hall beneath the chandelier—a thin gray woman who reminded me of Granny, not that she looked like Granny probably but because she had known Granny—a lifted anxious still face which was thinking *Who lives by the sword shall die by it* just as Granny would have thought, toward which I walked, had to walk not because I was Granny's grandson and had lived in her house for three college years and was about the age of her son when he was killed in almost the last battle nine years ago, but because I was now The Sartoris. (The Sartoris: that had been one of the concomitant flashes, along with the *at last it has happened* when Professor Wilkins opened my door.) She didn't offer me a horse and pistol, not because she liked me any less than Professor Wilkins but because she was a woman and so wiser than any man, else the men would not have gone on with the War for two years after they knew they were whipped. She just put her hands (a small woman, no bigger than Granny had been) on my shoulders and said, "Give my love to Drusilla and your Aunt Jenny. And come back when you can."

"Only I don't know when that will be," I said. "I don't know how many things I will have to attend to." Yes, I lied even to her; it had not been but a minute yet since he had flung that door bouncing into the stop yet already I was beginning to realise, to become aware of that which I still had no yardstick to measure save that one consisting of what, despite myself, despite my raising and background (or maybe because of them) I had for some time known I was becoming and had feared the test of it; I remember how I thought while her hands still rested on my shoulders: *At least this will be my chance to find out if I am what I think I am or if I just hope; if I am going to do what I have taught myself is right or if I am just going to wish I were.*

We went on to the kitchen, Professor Wilkins still somewhere beside or behind me and still offering me the pistol and horse in a dozen different ways. Ringo was waiting; I remember how I thought then that no matter what might happen to either of us, I would never be The Sartoris to him. He was twenty-four too, but in a way he had changed even less than I had since that day when we had nailed Grumby's body to the door of the old compress. Maybe it was because he had outgrown me, had changed so much that summer

while he and Granny traded mules with the Yankees that since then I had had to do most of the changing just to catch up with him. He was sitting quietly in a chair beside the cold stove, spent-looking too who had ridden forty miles (at one time, either in Jefferson or when he was alone at last on the road somewhere, he had cried; dust was now caked and dried in the tear-channels on his face) and would ride forty more yet would not eat, looking up at me a little red-eyed with weariness (or maybe it was more than just weariness and so I would never catch up with him) then rising without a word and going on toward the door and I following and Professor Wilkins still offering the horse and the pistol without speaking the words and still thinking (I could feel that too) *Dies by the sword. Dies by the sword.*

Ringo had the two horses saddled at the side gate, as I had known he would—the fresh one for himself and my mare father had given me three years ago, that could do a mile under two minutes any day and a mile every eight minutes all day long. He was already mounted when I realised that what Professor Wilkins wanted was to shake my hand. We shook hands; I knew he believed he was touching flesh which might not be alive tomorrow night and I thought for a second how if I told him what I was going to do, since we had talked about it, about how if there was anything at all in the Book, anything of hope and peace for His blind and bewildered spawn which He had chosen above all others to offer immortality, *Thou shalt not kill* must be it, since maybe he even believed that he had taught it to me except that he had not, nobody had, not even myself since it went further than just having been learned. But I did not tell him. He was too old to be forced so, to condone even in principle such a decision; he was too old to have to stick to principle in the face of blood and raising and background, to be faced without warning and made to deliver like by a highwayman out of the dark: only the young could do that—one still young enough to have his youth supplied him gratis as a reason (not an excuse) for cowardice.

So I said nothing. I just shook his hand and mounted too, and Ringo and I rode on. We would not have to pass through Oxford now and so soon (there was a thin sickle of moon like the heel print of a boot in wet sand) the road to Jefferson lay before us, the road which I had travelled for the first time three years ago with Father and travelled twice at Christmas time and then in June and September and twice at Christmas time again

and then June and September again each college
term since alone on the mare, not even knowing
that this was peace; and now this time and maybe
last time who would not die (I knew that) but
who maybe forever after could never again hold up
his head. The horses took the gait which they
would hold for forty miles. My mare knew the
long road ahead and Ringo had a good beast too,
had talked Hilliard at the livery stable out of a
good horse too. Maybe it was the tears, the channels of dried mud across which his strain-reddened
eyes had looked at me, but I rather think it was
that same quality which used to enable him to
replenish his and Granny's supply of United States
Army letterheads during that time—some outrageous assurance gained from too long and too close
association with white people: the one whom he
called Granny, the other with whom he had slept
from the time we were born until Father rebuilt
the house. We spoke one time, then no more:

"We could bushwhack him," he said. "Like we
done Grumby that day. But I reckon that wouldn't
suit that white skin you walks around in."

"No," I said. We rode on; it was October; there
was plenty of time still for verbena although I
would have to reach home before I would realise
there was a need for it; plenty of time for verbena
yet from the garden where Aunt Jenny puttered
beside old Joby, in a pair of Father's old cavalry
gauntlets, among the coaxed and ordered beds, the
quaint and odorous old names, for though it was
October no rain had come yet and hence no frost
to bring (or leave behind) the first half-warm half-
chill nights of Indian Summer—the drowsing air
cool and empty for geese yet languid still with the
old hot dusty smell of fox grape and sassafras—the
nights when before I became a man and went to
college to learn law Ringo and I, with lantern and
axe and crokersack and six dogs (one to follow
the trail and five more just for the tonguing, the
music) would hunt possum in the pasture where,
hidden, we had seen our first Yankee that afternoon on the bright horse, where for the last year
now you could hear the whistling of the trains
which had no longer belonged to Mr. Redmond
for a long while now and which at some instant,
some second during the morning Father too had
relinquished along with the pipe which Ringo said
he was smoking, which slipped from his hand as
he fell. We rode on, toward the house where he
would be lying in the parlor now, in his regimentals (sabre too) and where Drusilla would be
waiting for me beneath all the festive glitter of the
chandeliers, in the yellow ball gown and the sprig
of verbena in her hair, holding the two loaded
pistols (I could see that too, who had had no presentiment; I could see her, in the formal brilliant
room arranged formally for obsequy, not tall, not
slender as a woman is but as a youth, a boy, is,
motionless, in yellow, the face calm, almost bemused, the head simple and severe, the balancing
sprig of verbena above each ear, the two arms bent
at the elbows, the two hands shoulder high, the
two identical duelling pistols lying upon, not
clutched in, one to each: the Greek amphora
priestess of a succinct and formal violence).

2

Drusilla said that he had a dream. I was twenty
then and she and I would walk in the garden in
the summer twilight while we waited for Father
to ride in from the railroad. I was just twenty
then: that summer before I entered the University
to take the law degree which Father decided I
should have and four years after the one, the day,
the evening when Father and Drusilla had kept
old Cash Benbow from becoming United States
Marshal and returned home still unmarried and
Mrs. Habersham herded them into her carriage
and drove them back to town and dug her husband
out of his little dim hole in the new bank and
made him sign Father's peace bond for killing the
two carpet baggers, and took Father and Drusilla
to the minister herself and saw that they were
married. And Father had rebuilt the house too, on
the same blackened spot, over the same cellar,
where the other had burned, only larger, much
larger: Drusilla said that the house was the aura of
Father's dream just as a bride's trousseau and veil
is the aura of hers. And Aunt Jenny had come to
live with us now so we had the garden (Drusilla
would no more have bothered with flowers than
Father himself would have, who even now, even
four years after it was over, still seemed to exist,
breathe, in that last year of it while she had ridden
in man's clothes and with her hair cut short like
any other member of Father's troop, across Georgia
and both Carolinas in front of Sherman's army)
for her to gather sprigs of verbena from to wear in
her hair because she said verbena was the only
scent you could smell above the smell of horses
and courage and so it was the only one that was
worth the wearing. The railroad was hardly begun

then and Father and Mr. Redmond were not only still partners, they were still friends, which as George Wyatt said was easily a record for Father, and he would leave the house at daybreak on Jupiter, riding up and down the unfinished line with two saddlebags of gold coins borrowed on Friday to pay the men on Saturday, keeping just two cross-ties ahead of the sheriff as Aunt Jenny said. So we walked in the dusk, slowly between Aunt Jenny's flower beds while Drusilla (in a dress now, who still would have worn pants all the time if Father had let her) leaned lightly on my arm and I smelled the verbena in her hair as I had smelled the rain in it and in Father's beard that night four years ago when he and Drusilla and Uncle Buck McCaslin found Grumby and then came home and found Ringo and me more than just asleep: escaped into that oblivion which God or Nature or whoever it was had supplied us with for the time being, who had had to perform more than should be required of children because there should be some limit to the age, the youth at least below which one should not have to kill. This was just after the Saturday night when he returned and I watched him clean the derringer and reload it and we learned that the dead man was almost a neighbor, a hill man who had been in the first infantry regiment when it voted Father out of command: and we never to know if the man actually intended to rob Father or not because Father had shot too quick, but only that he had a wife and several children in a dirt-floored cabin in the hills, to whom Father the next day sent some money and she (the wife) walked into the house two days later while we were sitting at the dinner table and flung the money at Father's face.

"But nobody could have more of a dream than Colonel Sutpen," I said. He had been Father's second-in-command in the first regiment and had been elected colonel when the regiment deposed Father after Second Manassas, and it was Sutpen and not the regiment whom father never forgave. He was underbred, a cold ruthless man who had come into the country about thirty years before the War, nobody knew from where except Father said you could look at him and know he would not dare to tell. He had got some land and nobody knew how he did that either, and he got money from somewhere—Father said they all believed he robbed steamboats, either as a card sharper or as an out-and-out highwayman—and built a big house and married and set up as a gentleman. Then he lost everything in the War like everybody else, all

hope of descendants too (his son killed his daughter's fiancé on the eve of the wedding and vanished) yet he came back home and set out single-handed to rebuild his plantation. He had no friends to borrow from and he had nobody to leave it to and he was past sixty years old, yet he set out to rebuild his place like it used to be; they told how he was too busy to bother with politics or anything; how when Father and the other men organised the night riders to keep the carpet baggers from organising the Negroes into an insurrection, he refused to have anything to do with it. Father stopped hating him long enough to ride out to see Sutpen himself and he (Sutpen) came to the door with a lamp and did not even invite them to come in and discuss it; Father said, "Are you with us or against us?" and he said, "I'm for my land. If every man of you would rehabilitate his own land, the country will take care of itself" and Father challenged him to bring the lamp out and set it on a stump where they could both see to shoot and Sutpen would not. "Nobody could have more of a dream than that."

"Yes. But his dream is just Sutpen. John's is not. He is thinking of this whole country which he is trying to raise by its bootstraps, so that all the people in it, not just his kind nor his old regiment, but all the people, black and white, the women and children back in the hills who don't even own shoes—Don't you see?"

"But how can they get any good from what he wants to do for them if they are—after he has——"

"Killed some of them? I suppose you include those two carpet baggers he had to kill to hold that first election, don't you?"

"They were men. Human beings."

"They were Northerners, foreigners who had no business here. They were pirates." We walked on, her weight hardly discernible on my arm, her head just reaching my shoulder. I had always been a little taller than she, even on that night at Hawkhurst while we listened to the niggers passing in the road, and she had changed but little since—the same boy-hard body, the close implacable head with its savagely cropped hair which I had watched from the wagon above the tide of crazed singing niggers as we went down into the river—the body not slender as women are but as boys are slender. "A dream is not a very safe thing to be near, Bayard. I know; I had one once. It's like a loaded pistol with a hair trigger: if it stays alive long enough, somebody is going to be hurt. But if it's a good dream, it's worth it. There are not many dreams in the world, but there are a lot of human lives. And one human life or two dozen——"

"Are not worth anything?"

"No. Not anything.—Listen. I hear Jupiter. I'll beat you to the house." She was already running, the skirts she did not like to wear lifted almost to her knees, her legs beneath it running as boys run just as she rode like men ride.

I was twenty then. But the next time I was twenty-four; I had been three years at the University and in another two weeks I would ride back to Oxford for the final year and my degree. It was just last summer, last August, and Father had just beat Redmond for the State legislature. The railroad was finished now and the partnership between Father and Redmond had been dissolved so long ago that most people would have forgotten they were ever partners if it hadn't been for the enmity between them. There had been a third partner but nobody hardly remembered his name now; he and his name both had vanished in the fury of the conflict which set up between Father and Redmond almost before they began to lay the rails, between Father's violent and ruthless dictatorialness and will to dominate (the idea was his; he did think of the railroad first and then took Redmond in) and that quality in Redmond (as George Wyatt said, he was not a coward or Father would never have teamed with him) which permitted him to stand as much as he did from Father, to bear and bear and bear until something (not his will nor his courage) broke in him. During the War Redmond had not been a soldier, he had had something to do with cotton for the Government; he could have made money himself out of it but he had not and everybody knew he had not. Father knew it, yet Father would even taunt him with not having smelled powder. He was wrong; he knew he was when it was too late for him to stop just as a drunkard reaches a point where it is too late for him to stop, where he promises himself that he will and maybe believes he will or can but it is too late. Finally they reached the point (they had both put everything they could mortgage or borrow into it for Father to ride up and down the line, paying the workmen and the waybills on the rails at the last possible instant) where even Father realised that one of them would have to get out. So (they were not speaking then; it was arranged by Judge Benbow) they met and agreed to buy or sell, naming a price which, in reference to what they had put into it, was ridiculously low but which each believed the other could not raise—at least Father

claimed that Redmond did not believe he could raise it. So Redmond accepted the price, and found out that Father had the money. And according to Father, that's what started it, although Uncle Buck McCaslin said Father could not have owned a half interest in even one hog, let alone a railroad, and not dissolve the business either sworn enemy or death-pledged friend to his recent partner. So they parted and Father finished the road. By that time, seeing that he was going to finish it, some Northern people sold him a locomotive on credit which he named for Aunt Jenny, with a silver oil can in the cab with her name engraved on it; and last summer the first train ran into Jefferson, the engine decorated with flowers and Father in the cab blowing blast after blast on the whistle when he passed Redmond's house; and there were speeches at the station, with more flowers and a Confederate flag and girls in white dresses and red sashes and a band, and Father stood on the pilot of the engine and made a direct and absolutely needless allusion to Mr. Redmond. That was it. He wouldn't let him alone. George Wyatt came to me right afterward and told me. "Right or wrong," he said, "us boys and most of the other folks in this county know John's right. But he ought to let Redmond alone. I know what's wrong: he's had to kill too many folks, and that's bad for a man. We all know Colonel's brave as a lion, but Redmond ain't no coward either and there ain't any use in making a brave man that made one mistake eat crow all the time. Can't you talk to him?"

"I don't know," I said. "I'll try." But I had no chance. That is, I could have talked to him and he would have listened, but he could not have heard me because he had stepped straight from the pilot of that engine into the race for the Legislature. Maybe he knew that Redmond would have to oppose him to save his face even though he (Redmond) must have known that, after that train ran into Jefferson, he had no chance against Father, or maybe Redmond had already announced his candidacy and Father entered the race just because of that, I don't remember. Anyway they ran, a bitter contest in which Father continued to badger Redmond without reason or need, since they both knew it would be a landslide for Father. And it was, and we thought he was satisfied. Maybe he thought so himself, as the drunkard believes that he is done with drink; and it was that afternoon and Drusilla and I walked in the garden in the twilight and I said something about what George Wyatt had told me and she released my arm and turned me to face her and said, "This from you? You? Have you forgotten Grumby?"

"No," I said. "I never will forget him."

"You never will. I wouldn't let you. There are worse things than killing men, Bayard. There are worse things than being killed. Sometimes I think the finest thing that can happen to a man is to love something, a woman preferably, well, hard hard hard, then to die young because he believed what he could not help but believe and was what he could not (could not? would not) help but be." Now she was looking at me in a way she never had before. I did not know what it meant then and was not to know until tonight since neither of us knew then that two months later Father would be dead. I just knew that she was looking at me as she never had before and that the scent of the verbena in her hair seemed to have increased a hundred times, to have got a hundred times stronger, to be everywhere in the dusk in which something was about to happen which I had never dreamed of. Then she spoke. "Kiss me, Bayard."

"No. You are Father's wife."

"And eight years older than you are. And your fourth cousin too. And I have black hair. Kiss me, Bayard."

"No."

"Kiss me, Bayard." So I leaned my face down to her. But she didn't move, standing so, bent lightly back from me from the waist, looking at me; now it was she who said, "No." So I put my arms around her. Then she came to me, melted as women will and can, the arms with wrist- and elbow-power to control horses about my shoulders, using the wrists to hold my face to hers until there was no longer need for the wrists; I thought then of the woman of thirty, the symbol of the ancient and eternal Snake and of the men who have written of her, and I realised then the immitigable chasm between all life and all print—that those who can, do, those who cannot and suffer enough because they can't, write about it. Then I was free, I could see her again, I saw her still watching me with that dark inscrutable look, looking up at me now across her down-slanted face; I watched her arms rise with almost the exact gesture with which she had put them around me as if she were repeating the empty and formal gesture of all promise so that I should never forget it, the elbows angling outward as she put her hands to the sprig of verbena in her hair, I standing straight and rigid facing the slightly bent head, the short jagged hair, the rigid curiously formal angle of the bare arms gleaming faintly in the last of light as she removed the verbena sprig and put it into my lapel, and I thought how the War had tried to stamp all the women of her generation and class in the South into a type and how it had failed—the suffering, the identical experience (hers and Aunt Jenny's had been almost the same except that Aunt Jenny had spent a few nights with her husband before they brought him back home in an ammunition wagon while Gavin Breckbridge was just Drusilla's fiancé) was there in the eyes, yet beyond that was the incorrigibly individual woman: not like so many men who return from wars to live on Government reservations like so many steers, emasculate and empty of all save an identical experience which they cannot forget and dare not, else they would cease to live at that moment, almost interchangeable save for the old habit of answering to a given name.

"Now I must tell Father," I said.

"Yes," she said. "You must tell him. Kiss me." So again it was like it had been before. No. Twice, a thousand times and never like—the eternal and symbolical thirty to a young man, a youth, each time both cumulative and retroactive, immitigably unrepetitive, each wherein remembering excludes experience, each wherein experience antedates remembering; the skill without weariness, the knowledge virginal to surfeit, the cunning secret muscles to guide and control just as within the wrists and elbows lay slumbering the mastery of horses: she stood back, already turning, not looking at me when she spoke, never having looked at me, already moving swiftly on in the dusk: "Tell John. Tell him tonight."

I intended to. I went to the house and into the office at once; I went to the center of the rug before the cold hearth, I don't know why, and stood there rigid like soldiers stand, looking at eye level straight across the room and above his head and said "Father" and then stopped. Because he did not even hear me. He said, "Yes, Bayard?" but he did not hear me although he was sitting behind the desk doing nothing, immobile, as still as I was rigid, one hand on the desk with a dead cigar in it, a bottle of brandy and a filled and untasted glass beside his hand, clothed quiet and bemused in whatever triumph it was he felt since the last overwhelming return of votes had come in late in the afternoon. So I waited until after supper. We went to the diningroom and stood side by side until Aunt Jenny entered and then Drusilla, in the yellow ball gown, who walked straight to me and gave me one fierce inscrutable look then went to her place and waited for me to draw her chair while Father drew Aunt Jenny's. He had roused by then, not to talk himself but rather to sit at the head of the table and reply to Drusilla as she talked with a sort of feverish and glittering volubility—to reply now and then to her with that courteous intolerant pride which had lately become a little forensic, as if merely being in a political contest filled with fierce and empty oratory had retroactively made a lawyer of him who was anything and everything except a lawyer. Then Drusilla and Aunt Jenny rose and left us and he said, "Wait" to me who had made no move to follow and directed Joby to bring one of the bottles of wine which he had fetched back from New Orleans when he went there last to borrow money to liquidate his first private railroad bonds. Then I stood again like soldiers stand, gazing at eye level above his head while he sat half-turned from the table, a little paunchy now though not much, a little grizzled too in the hair though his beard was as strong as ever, with that spurious forensic air of lawyers and the intolerant eyes which in the last two years had acquired that transparent film which the eyes of carnivorous animals have and from behind which they look at a world which no ruminant ever sees, perhaps dares to see, which I have seen before on the eyes of men who have killed too much, who have killed so much that never again as long as they live will they ever be alone. I said again, "Father," then I told him.

"Hah?" he said. "Sit down." I sat down, I looked at him, watched him fill both glasses and this time I knew it was worse with him than not hearing: it didn't even matter. "You are doing well in the law, Judge Wilkins tells me. I am pleased to hear that. I have not needed you in my affairs so far, but from now on I shall. I have now accomplished the active portion of my aims in which you could not have helped me; I acted as the land and the time demanded and you were too young for that, I wished to shield you. But now the land and the time too are changing; what will follow will be a matter of consolidation, of pettifogging and doubtless chicanery in which I would be a babe in arms but in which you, trained in the law, can hold your own—our own. Yes. I have accomplished my aim, and now I shall do a little moral housecleaning. I am tired of killing men, no matter what the necessity nor the end. Tomorrow,

when I go to town and meet Ben Redmond, I shall be unarmed."

3

We reached home just before midnight; we didn't have to pass through Jefferson either. Before we turned in the gates I could see the lights, the chandeliers—hall, parlor, and what Aunt Jenny (without any effort or perhaps even design on her part) had taught even Ringo to call the drawing room, the light falling outward across the portico, past the columns. Then I saw the horses, the faint shine of leather and buckleglints on the black silhouettes and then the men too—Wyatt and others of Father's old troop—and I had forgot that they would be there. I had forgot that they would be there; I remember how I thought, since I was tired and spent with strain, *Now it will have to begin tonight. I won't even have until tomorrow in which to begin to resist.* They had a watchman, a picquet out, I suppose, because they seemed to know at once that we were in the drive. Wyatt met me, I halted the mare, I could look down at him and at the others gathered a few yards behind him with that curious vulture-like formality which Southern men assume in such situations.

"Well, boy," George said.

"Was it—" I said. "Was he——"

"It was all right. It was in front. Redmond ain't no coward. John had the derringer inside his cuff like always, but he never touched it, never made a move toward it." I have seen him do it, he showed me once: the pistol (it was not four inches long) held flat inside his left wrist by a clip he made himself of wire and an old clock spring; he would raise both hands at the same time, cross them, fire the pistol from beneath his left hand almost as if he were hiding from his own vision what he was doing; when he killed one of the men he shot a hole through his own coat sleeve. "But you want to get on to the house," Wyatt said. He began to stand aside, then he spoke again: "We'll take this off your hands, any of us. Me." I hadn't moved the mare yet and I had made no move to speak, yet he continued quickly, as if he had already rehearsed all this, his speech and mine, and knew what I would say and only spoke himself as he would have removed his hat on entering a house or used 'sir' in conversing with a stranger: "You're young, just a boy, you ain't had any experience in

this kind of thing. Besides, you got them two
ladies in the house to think about. He would understand, all right."

"I reckon I can attend to it," I said.

"Sure," he said; there was no surprise, nothing
at all, in his voice because he had already rehearsed
this: "I reckon we all knew that's what you would
say." He stepped back then; almost it was as
though he and not I bade the mare to move on.
But they all followed, still with that unctuous and
voracious formality. Then I saw Drusilla standing
at the top of the front steps, in the light from the
open door and the windows like a theatre scene, in
the yellow ball gown and even from here I believed that I could smell the verbena in her hair,
standing there motionless yet emanating something
louder than the two shots must have been—something voracious too and passionate. Then, although
I had dismounted and someone had taken the
mare, I seemed to be still in the saddle and to
watch myself enter that scene which she had postulated like another actor while in the background
for chorus Wyatt and the others stood with the
unctuous formality which the Southern man shows
in the presence of death—that Roman holiday engendered by mist-born Protestantism grafted onto
this land of violent sun, of violent alteration from
snow to heat-stroke which has produced a race impervious to both. I mounted the steps toward the
figure straight and yellow and immobile as a candle which moved only to extend one hand; we
stood together and looked down at them where
they stood clumped, the horses too gathered in a
tight group beyond them at the rim of light from
the brilliant door and windows. One of them
stamped and blew his breath and jangled his gear.

"Thank you, gentlemen," I said. "My aunt and
my—Drusilla thank you. There's no need for you
to stay. Goodnight." They murmured, turning.
George Wyatt paused, looking back at me.

"Tomorrow?" he said.

"Tomorrow." Then they went on, carrying their
hats and tiptoeing, even on the ground, the quiet
and resilient earth, as though anyone in that house
awake would try to sleep, anyone already asleep
in it whom they could have wakened. Then they
were gone and Drusilla and I turned and crossed
the portico, her hand lying light on my wrist yet
discharging into me with a shock like electricity
that dark and passionate voracity, the face at my
shoulder—the jagged hair with a verbena sprig
above each ear, the eyes staring at me with that

fierce exaltation. We entered the hall and crossed
it, her hand guiding me without pressure, and entered the parlor. Then for the first time I realised
it—the alteration which is death—not that he was
now just clay but that he was lying down. But I
didn't look at him yet because I knew that when I
did I would begin to pant; I went to Aunt Jenny
who had just risen from a chair behind which
Louvinia stood. She was Father's sister, taller than
Drusilla but no older, whose husband had been
killed at the very beginning of the War, by a shell
from a Federal frigate at Fort Moultrie, come to
us from Carolina six years ago. Ringo and I went
to Tennessee Junction in the wagon to meet her.
It was January, cold and clear and with ice in the
ruts; we returned just before dark with Aunt Jenny
on the seat beside me holding a lace parasol and
Ringo in the wagon bed nursing a hamper basket
containing two bottles of old sherry and the two
jasmine cuttings which were bushes in the garden
now, and the panes of colored glass which she had
salvaged from the Carolina house where she and
Father and Uncle Bayard were born and which
Father had set in a fanlight about one of the drawing room windows for her—who came up the drive
and Father (home now from the railroad) went
down the steps and lifted her from the wagon and
said, "Well, Jenny," and she said, "Well, Johnny,"
and began to cry. She stood too, looking at me as
I approached—the same hair, the same high nose,
the same eyes as Father's except that they were intent and very wise instead of intolerant. She said
nothing at all, she just kissed me, her hands light
on my shoulders. Then Drusilla spoke, as if she had
been waiting with a sort of dreadful patience for
the empty ceremony to be done, in a voice like a
bell: clear, unsentient, on a single pitch, silvery
and triumphant: "Come, Bayard."

"Hadn't you better go to bed now?" Aunt Jenny
said.

"Yes," Drusilla said in that silvery ecstatic voice,
"Oh yes. There will be plenty of time for sleep."
I followed her, her hand again guiding me without
pressure; now I looked at him. It was just as I had
imagined it—sabre, plumes, and all—but with that
alteration, that irrevocable difference which I had
known to expect yet had not realised, as you can
put food into your stomach which for a while the
stomach declines to assimilate—the illimitable grief
and regret as I looked down at the face which I
knew—the nose, the hair, the eyelids closed over
the intolerance—the face which I realised I now

saw in repose for the first time in my life; the empty hands still now beneath the invisible stain of what had been (once, surely) needless blood, the hands now appearing clumsy in their very inertness, too clumsy to have performed the fatal actions which forever afterward he must have waked and slept with and maybe was glad to lay down at last—those curious appendages clumsily conceived to begin with yet with which man has taught himself to do so much, so much more than they were intended to do or could be forgiven for doing, which had now surrendered that life to which his intolerant heart had fiercely held; and then I knew that in a minute I would begin to pant. So Drusilla must have spoken twice before I heard her and turned and saw in the instant Aunt Jenny and Louvinia watching us, hearing Drusilla now, the unsentient bell quality gone now, her voice whispering into that quiet death-filled room with a passionate and dying fall: "Bayard." She faced me, she was quite near; again the scent of the verbena in her hair seemed to have increased a hundred times as she stood holding out to me, one in either hand, the two duelling pistols. "Take them, Bayard," she said, in the same tone in which she had said "Kiss me" last summer, already pressing them into my hands, watching me with that passionate and voracious exaltation, speaking in a voice fainting and passionate with promise: "Take them. I have kept them for you. I give them to you. Oh you will thank me, you will remember me who put into your hands what they say is an attribute only of God's, who took what belongs to heaven and gave it to you. Do you feel them? the long true barrels true as justice, the triggers (you have fired them) quick as retribution, the two of them slender and invincible and fatal as the physical shape of love?" Again I watched her arms angle out and upward as she removed the two verbena sprigs from her hair in two motions faster than the eye could follow, already putting one of them into my lapel and crushing the other in her other hand while she still spoke in that rapid passionate voice not much louder than a whisper: "There. One I give to you to wear tomorrow (it will not fade), the other I cast away, like this—" dropping the crushed bloom at her feet. "I abjure it. I abjure verbena forever more; I have smelled it above the odor of courage; that was all I wanted. Now let me look at you." She stood back, staring at me—the face tearless and exalted, the feverish eyes brilliant and voracious. "How beautiful you are: do you know it? How beautiful: young, to be permitted

to kill, to be permitted vengeance, to take into your bare hands the fire of heaven that cast down Lucifer. No; I. I gave it to you; I put it into your hands; Oh you will thank me, you will remember me when I am dead and you are an old man saying to himself, 'I have tasted all things.'—It will be the right hand, won't it?" She moved; she had taken my right hand which still held one of the pistols before I knew what she was about to do; she had bent and kissed it before I comprehended why she took it. Then she stopped dead still, still stooping in that attitude of fierce exultant humility, her hot lips and her hot hands still touching my flesh, light on my flesh as dead leaves yet communicating to it that battery charge dark, passionate and damned forever of all peace. Because they are wise, women are—a touch, lips or fingers, and the knowledge, even clairvoyance, goes straight to the heart without bothering the laggard brain at all. She stood erect now, staring at me with intolerable and amazed incredulity which occupied her face alone for a whole minute while her eyes were completely empty; it seemed to me that I stood there for a full minute while Aunt Jenny and Louvinia watched us, waiting for her eyes to fill. There was no blood in her face at all, her mouth open a little and pale as one of those rubber rings women seal fruit jars with. Then her eyes filled with an expression of bitter and passionate betrayal. "Why, he's not—" she said. "He's not—And I kissed his hand," she said in an aghast whisper; "*I kissed his hand!*" beginning to laugh, the laughter rising, becoming a scream yet still remaining laughter, screaming with laughter, trying herself to deaden the sound by putting her hand over her mouth, the laughter spilling between her fingers like vomit, the incredulous betrayed eyes still watching me across the hand.

"Louvinia!" Aunt Jenny said. They both came to her. Louvinia touched and held her and Drusilla turned her face to Louvinia.

"I kissed his hand, Louvinia!" she cried. "Did you see it? *I kissed his hand!*" the laughter rising again, becoming the scream again yet still remaining laughter, she still trying to hold it back with her hand like a small child who has filled its mouth too full.

"Take her upstairs," Aunt Jenny said. But they were already moving toward the door, Louvinia half-carrying Drusilla, the laughter diminishing as they neared the door as though it waited for the larger space of the empty and brilliant hall to rise again. Then it was gone; Aunt Jenny and I stood there and I knew soon that I would begin to pant. I could feel it beginning like you feel regurgitation beginning, as though there were not enough air in the room, the house, not enough air anywhere under the heavy hot low sky where the equinox couldn't seem to accomplish, nothing in the air for breathing, for the lungs. Now it was Aunt Jenny who said "Bayard" twice before I heard her. "You are not going to try to kill him. All right."

"All right?" I said.

"Yes. All right. Don't let it be Drusilla, a poor hysterical young woman. And don't let it be him, Bayard, because he's dead now. And don't let it be George Wyatt and those others who will be waiting for you tomorrow morning. I know you are not afraid."

"But what good will that do?" I said. "What good will that do?" It almost began then; I stopped it just in time. "I must live with myself, you see."

"Then it's not just Drusilla? Not just him? Not just George Wyatt and Jefferson?"

"No," I said.

"Will you promise to let me see you before you go to town tomorrow?" I looked at her; we looked at one another for a moment. Then she put her hands on my shoulders and kissed me and released me, all in one motion. "Goodnight, son," she said. Then she was gone too and now it could begin. I knew that in a minute I would look at him and it would begin and I did look at him, feeling the long-held breath, the hiatus before it started, thinking how maybe I should have said, "Goodbye, Father" but did not. Instead I crossed to the piano and laid the pistols carefully on it, still keeping the panting from getting too loud too soon. Then I was outside on the porch and (I don't know how long it had been) I looked in the window and saw Simon squatting on a stool beside him. Simon had been his body servant during the War and when they came home Simon had a uniform too—a Confederate private's coat with a Yankee brigadier's star on it and he had put it on now too, like they had dressed Father, squatting on the stool beside him, not crying, not weeping the facile tears which are the white man's futile trait and which Negroes know nothing about but just sitting there, motionless, his lower lip slacked down a little; he raised his hand and touched the coffin, the black hand rigid and fragile-looking as a clutch of dead twigs, then dropped the hand; once he turned his head and I saw his eyes roll red and unwinking in his skull like those of a cornered fox. It had begun by that time; I panted, standing

there, and this was it—the regret and grief, the despair out of which the tragic mute insensitive bones stand up that can bear anything, anything.

4

After a while the whippoorwills stopped and I heard the first day bird, a mockingbird. It had sung all night too but now it was the day song, no longer the drowsy moony fluting. Then they all began—the sparrows from the stable, the thrush that lived in Aunt Jenny's garden, and I heard a quail too from the pasture and now there was light in the room. But I didn't move at once. I still lay on the bed (I hadn't undressed) with my hands under my head and the scent of Drusilla's verbena faint from where my coat lay on a chair, watching the light grow, watching it turn rosy with the sun. After a while I heard Louvinia come up across the back yard and go into the kitchen; I heard the door and then the long crash of her armful of stovewood into the box. Soon they would begin to arrive—the carriages and buggies in the drive—but not for a while yet because they too would wait first to see what I was going to do. So the house was quiet when I went down to the diningroom, no sound in it except Simon snoring in the parlor, probably still sitting on the stool though I didn't look in to see. Instead I stood at the diningroom window and drank the coffee which Louvinia brought me, then I went to the stable; I saw Joby watching me from the kitchen door as I crossed the yard and in the stable Loosh looked up at me across Betsy's head, a curry comb in his hand, though Ringo didn't look at me at all. We curried Jupiter then. I didn't know if we would be able to without trouble or not, since always Father would come in first and touch him and tell him to stand and he would stand like a marble horse (or pale bronze rather) while Loosh curried him. But he stood for me too, a little restive but he stood, then that was done and now it was almost nine o'clock and soon they would begin to arrive and I told Ringo to bring Betsy on to the house.

I went on to the house and into the hall. I had not had to pant in some time now but it was there, waiting, a part of the alteration, as though by being dead and no longer needing air he had taken all of it, all that he had compassed and claimed and postulated between the walls which he had built, along with him. Aunt Jenny must have been waiting; she came out of the diningroom at once,

without a sound, dressed, the hair that was like
Father's combed and smooth above the eyes that
were different from Father's eyes because they
were not intolerant but just intent and grave and
(she was wise too) without pity. "Are you going
now?" she said.

"Yes." I looked at her. Yes, thank God, without
pity. "You see, I want to be thought well of."

"I do," she said. "Even if you spend the day
hidden in the stable loft, I still do."

"Maybe if she knew that I was going. Was going to town anyway."

"No," she said. "No, Bayard." We looked at
one another. Then she said quietly, "All right.
She's awake." So I mounted the stairs. I mounted
steadily, not fast because if I had gone fast the
panting would have started again or I might have
had to slow for a second at the turn or at the
top and I would not have gone on. So I went
slowly and steadily, across the hall to her door and
knocked and opened it. She was sitting at the window, in something soft and loose for morning in
her bedroom only she never did look like morning
in a bedroom because here was no hair to fall
about her shoulders. She looked up, she sat there
looking at me with her feverish brilliant eyes and
I remembered I still had the verbena sprig in my
lapel and suddenly she began to laugh again. It
seemed to come not from her mouth but to burst
out all over her face like sweat does and with a
dreadful and painful convulsion as when you have
vomited until it hurts you yet still you must vomit
again—burst out all over her face except her eyes,
the brilliant incredulous eyes looking at me out of
the laughter as if they belonged to somebody else,
as if they were two inert fragments of tar or coal
lying on the bottom of a receptacle filled with turmoil: "I kissed his hand! *I kissed his hand!*" Louvinia entered, Aunt Jenny must have sent her directly after me; again I walked slowly and steadily
so it would not start yet, down the stairs where
Aunt Jenny stood beneath the chandelier in the
hall as Mrs. Wilkins had stood yesterday at the
University. She had my hat in her hand. "Even if
you hid all day in the stable, Bayard," she said.
I took the hat; she said quietly, pleasantly, as if
she were talking to a stranger, a guest: "I used to
see a lot of blockade runners in Charleston. They
were heroes in a way, you see—not heroes because
they were helping to prolong the Confederacy but
heroes in the sense that David Crockett or John
Sevier would have been to small boys or fool young

women. There was one of them, an Englishman.
He had no business there; it was the money of
course, as with all of them. But he was the Davy
Crockett to us because by that time we had all
forgot what money was, what you could do with
it. He must have been a gentleman once or associated with gentlemen before he changed his name,
and he had a vocabulary of seven words, though
I must admit he got along quite well with them.
The first four were, 'I'll have rum, thanks,' and
then, when he had the rum, he would use the other
three—across the champagne, to whatever ruffled
bosom or low gown: 'No bloody moon.' No bloody
moon, Bayard."

Ringo was waiting with Betsy at the front steps.
Again he did not look at me, his face sullen, downcast even while he handed me the reins. But he
said nothing, nor did I look back. And sure enough
I was just in time; I passed the Compson carriage
at the gates, General Compson lifted his hat as I
did mine as we passed. It was four miles to town
but I had not gone two of them when I heard a
horse coming up behind me and I did not look
back because I knew it was Ringo. I did not look
back; he came up on one of the carriage horses,
he rode up beside me and looked me full in the
face for one moment, the sullen determined face,
the eyes rolling at me defiant and momentary and
red; we rode on. Now we were in town—the long
shady street leading to the square, the new courthouse at the end of it; it was eleven o'clock now:
long past breakfast and not yet noon so there were
only women on the street, not to recognise me
perhaps or at least not the walking stopped sudden
and dead in midwalking as if the legs contained
the sudden eyes, the caught breath, that not to
begin until we reached the square and I thinking
*If I could only be invisible until I reach the stairs
to his office and begin to mount.* But I could not,
I was not; we rode up to the Holston House and
I saw the row of feet along the gallery rail come
suddenly and quietly down and I did not look at
them, I stopped Betsy and waited until Ringo was
down then I dismounted and gave him the reins.
"Wait for me here," I said.

"I'm going with you," he said, not loud; we
stood there under the still circumspect eyes and
spoke quietly to one another like two conspirators.
Then I saw the pistol, the outline of it inside his
shirt, probably the one we had taken from Grumby
that day we killed him.

"No you ain't," I said.

"Yes I am."

"No you ain't." So I walked on, along the street in the hot sun. It was almost noon now and I could smell nothing except the verbena in my coat, as if it had gathered all the sun, all the suspended fierce heat in which the equinox could not seem to occur and were distilling it so that I moved in a cloud of verbena as I might have moved in a cloud of smoke from a cigar. Then George Wyatt was beside me (I don't know where he came from) and five or six others of Father's old troop a few yards behind, George's hand on my arm, drawing me into a doorway out of the avid eyes like caught breaths.

"Have you got that derringer?" George said.

"No," I said.

"Good," George said. "They are tricky things to fool with. Couldn't nobody but Colonel ever handle one right; I never could. So you take this. I tried it this morning and I know it's right. Here." He was already fumbling the pistol into my pocket, then the same thing seemed to happen to him that happened to Drusilla last night when she kissed my hand—something communicated by touch straight to the simple code by which he lived, without going through the brain at all: so that he too stood suddenly back, the pistol in his hand, staring at me with his pale outraged eyes and speaking in a whisper thin with fury: "Who are you? Is your name Sartoris? By God, if you don't kill him, I'm going to." Now it was not panting, it was a terrible desire to laugh, to laugh as Drusilla had, and say, "That's what Drusilla said." But I didn't. I said,

"I'm tending to this. You stay out of it. I don't need any help." Then his fierce eyes faded gradually, exactly as you turn a lamp down.

"Well," he said, putting the pistol back into his pocket. "You'll have to excuse me, son. I should have knowed you wouldn't do anything that would keep John from laying quiet. We'll follow you and wait at the foot of the steps. And remember: he's a brave man, but he's been sitting in that office by himself since yesterday morning waiting for you and his nerves are on edge."

"I'll remember," I said. "I don't need any help." I had started on when suddenly I said it without having any warning that I was going to: "No bloody moon."

"What?" he said. I didn't answer. I went on across the square itself now, in the hot sun, they following though not close so that I never saw them again until afterward, surrounded by the remote still eyes not following me yet either, just stopped where they were before the stores and about the door to the courthouse, waiting. I walked steadily on enclosed in the now fierce odor of the verbena sprig. Then shadow fell upon me; I did not pause, I looked once at the small faded sign nailed to the brick *B. J. Redmond. Atty at Law* and began to mount the stairs, the wooden steps scuffed by the heavy bewildered boots of countrymen approaching litigation and stained by tobacco spit, on down the dim corridor to the door which bore the name again, *B. J. Redmond* and knocked once and opened it. He sat behind the desk, not much taller than Father but thicker as a man gets who spends most of his time sitting and listening to people, freshly shaven and with fresh linen; a lawyer yet it was not a lawyer's face—a face much thinner than the body would indicate, strained (and yes, tragic; I know that now) and exhausted beneath the neat recent steady strokes of the razor, holding a pistol flat on the desk before him, loose beneath his hand and aimed at nothing. There was no smell of drink, not even of tobacco in the neat clean dingy room although I knew he smoked. I didn't pause. I walked steadily toward him. It was not twenty feet from the door to desk yet I seemed to walk in a dreamlike state in which there was neither time nor distance, as though the mere act of walking was no more intended to encompass space than was his sitting. We didn't speak. It was as if we both knew what the passage of words would be and the futility of it; how he might have said, "Go out, Bayard. Go away, boy" and then, "Draw then. I will allow you to draw" and it would have been the same as if he had never said it. So we did not speak; I just walked steadily toward him as the pistol rose from the desk. I watched it, I could see the foreshortened slant of the barrel and I knew it would miss me though his hand did not tremble. I walked toward him, toward the pistol in the rocklike hand, I heard no bullet. Maybe I didn't even hear the explosion though I remember the sudden orange bloom and smoke as they appeared against his white shirt as they had appeared against Grumby's greasy Confederate coat; I still watched that foreshortened slant of barrel which I knew was not aimed at me and saw the second orange flash and smoke and heard no bullet that time either. Then I stopped; it was done then. I watched the pistol descend to the desk in short jerks; I saw him release it and sit back, both hands on the desk, I looked at his face and I knew too what it was to want air when there was nothing in the circumambience for the lungs. He rose, shoved the chair back with a convulsive motion and rose, with a queer ducking motion of his head; with his head still ducked aside and one arm extended as though he couldn't see and the other hand resting on the desk as if he couldn't stand alone, he turned and crossed to the wall and took his hat from the rack and with his head still ducked aside and one hand extended he blundered along the wall and passed me and reached the door and went through it. He was brave; no one denied that. He walked down those stairs and out onto the street where George Wyatt and the other six of Father's old troop waited and where the other men had begun to run now; he walked through the middle of them with his hat on and his head up (they told me how someone shouted at him: "Have you killed that boy too?"), saying no word, staring straight ahead and with his back to them, on to the station where the south-bound train was just in and got on it with no baggage, nothing, and went away from Jefferson and from Mississippi and never came back.

I heard their feet on the stairs then in the corridor then in the room, but for a while yet (it wasn't that long, of course) I still sat behind the desk as he had sat, the flat of the pistol still warm under my hand, my hand growing slowly numb between the pistol and my forehead. Then I raised my head; the little room was full of men. "My God!" George Wyatt cried. "You took the pistol away from him and then missed him, missed him *twice?*" Then he answered himself—that same rapport for violence which Drusilla had and which in George's case was actual character judgment: "No; wait. You walked in here without even a pocket knife and let him miss you twice. My God in heaven." He turned, shouting: "Get to hell out of here! You, White, ride out to Sartoris and tell his folks it's all over and he's all right. Ride!" So they departed, went away; presently only George was left, watching me with that pale bleak stare which was speculative yet not at all ratiocinative. "Well by God," he said. "—Do you want a drink?"

"No," I said. "I'm hungry. I didn't eat any breakfast."

"I reckon not, if you got up this morning aiming to do what you did. Come on. We'll go to the Holston House."

"No," I said. "No. Not there."

"Why not? You ain't done anything to be ashamed of. I wouldn't have done it that way, myself. I'd a shot at him once, anyway. But that's your way or you wouldn't have done it."

"Yes," I said. "I would do it again."

"Be damned if I would.—You want to come home with me? We'll have time to eat and then ride out there in time for the ——" But I couldn't do that either.

"No," I said. "I'm not hungry after all. I think I'll go home."

"Don't you want to wait and ride out with me?"

"No. I'll go on."

"You don't want to stay here, anyway." He looked around the room again, where the smell of powder smoke still lingered a little, still lay somewhere on the hot dead air though invisible now, blinking a little with his fierce pale unintroverted eyes. "Well by God," he said again. "Maybe you're right, maybe there has been enough killing in your family without—Come on." We left the office. I waited at the foot of the stairs and soon Ringo came up with the horses. We crossed the square again. There were no feet on the Holston House railing now (it was twelve o'clock) but a group of men stood before the door who raised their hats and I raised mine and Ringo and I rode on.

We did not go fast. Soon it was one, maybe after; the carriages and buggies would begin to leave the square soon, so I turned from the road at the end of the pasture and I sat the mare, trying to open the gate without dismounting, until Ringo dismounted and opened it. We crossed the pasture in the hard fierce sun; I could have seen the house now but I didn't look. Then we were in the shade, the close thick airless shade of the creek bottom; the old rails still lay in the undergrowth where we had built the pen to hide the Yankee mules. Presently I heard the water, then I could see the sunny glints. We dismounted. I lay on my back, I thought *Now it can begin again if it wants to.* But it did not. I went to sleep. I went to sleep almost before I had stopped thinking. I slept for almost five hours and I didn't dream anything at all yet I waked myself up crying, crying too hard to stop it. Ringo was squatting beside me and the sun was gone though there was a bird of some sort still singing somewhere and the whistle of the north-bound evening train sounded and the short broken puffs of starting where it had evidently stopped at our flag station. After a while I began to stop and Ringo brought his hat full of water from the creek but instead I went down to the water myself and bathed my face.

There was still a good deal of light in the pasture, though the whippoorwills had begun, and when we reached the house there was a mockingbird singing in the magnolia, the night song now, the drowsy moony one, and again the moon like the rim print of a heel in wet sand. There was just one light in the hall now and so it was all over though I could still smell the flowers even above the verbena in my coat. I had not looked at him again. I had started to before I left the house but I did not, I did not see him again and all the pictures we had of him were bad ones because a picture could no more have held him dead than the house could have kept his body. But I didn't need to see him again because he was there, he would always be there; maybe what Drusilla meant by his dream was not something which he possessed but something which he had bequeathed us which we could never forget, which would even assume the corporeal shape of him whenever any of us, black or white, closed our eyes. I went into the house. There was no light in the drawing room except the last of the afterglow which came through the western window where Aunt Jenny's colored glass was; I was about to go on up stairs when I saw her sitting there beside the window. She didn't call me and I didn't speak Drusilla's name, I just went to the door and stood there. "She's gone," Aunt Jenny said. "She took the evening train. She has gone to Montgomery, to Dennison." Denny had been married about a year now; he was living in Montgomery, reading law.

"I see," I said. "Then she didn't——" But there wasn't any use in that either; Jed White must have got there before one o'clock and told them. And besides, Aunt Jenny didn't answer. She could have lied to me but she didn't, she said, "Come here." I went to her chair. "Kneel down. I can't see you."

"Don't you want the lamp?"

"No. Kneel down." So I knelt beside the chair. "So you had a perfectly splendid Saturday afternoon, didn't you? Tell me about it." Then she put her hands on my shoulders. I watched them come up as though she were trying to stop them; I felt them on my shoulders as if they had a separate life of their own and were trying to do something which for my sake she was trying to restrain, prevent. Then she gave up or she was not strong enough because they came up and took my face between them, hard, and suddenly the tears sprang and streamed down her face like Drusilla's laughing had. "Oh, damn you Sartorises!" she said. "Damn you! Damn you!"

As I passed down the hall the light came up in the diningroom and I could hear Louvinia laying the table for supper. So the stairs were lighted quite well. But the upper hall was dark. I saw her open door (that unmistakable way in which an open door stands open when nobody lives in the room any more) and I realised I had not believed that she was really gone. So I didn't look into the room. I went on to mine and entered. And then for a long moment I thought it was the verbena in my lapel which I still smelled. I thought that until I had crossed the room and looked down at the pillow on which it lay—the single sprig of it (without looking she would pinch off a half dozen of them and they would be all of a size, almost all of a shape, as if a machine had stamped them out) filling the room, the dusk, the evening with that odor which she said you could smell alone above the smell of horses.

From *Light in August* (1932)

Of this rich and highly complex novel we print here only a small portion. The excerpts we have chosen concern one character, Joe Christmas, and his relations with only two other major characters—his companion, Joe Brown, and his mistress, Joanna Burden. Nevertheless, even from so short a selection the reader can learn a great deal about how Faulkner typically presents his major characters: not primarily by telling us about what goes on in their heads but dramatically, through their actions. Faulkner is a great master of narrative technique, and *Light in August* provides something of a virtuoso display of his powers.

Among those powers is that of ordering the sequence of events so that the important actions can be made to register on the reader with maximum force. Thus, Faulkner frequently stirs the reader's curiosity about a character or event but then postpones telling us the outcome of the action until he can invest it with its full significance. The technique may involve flash-backs that will disclose the earlier life of the character in question or the narration of prior events that lead up to the climactic action. In *Light in August* there is a great deal of such manipulation of the time shift. Thus, the full story of Joe Christmas covers some thirty-odd years, and in the novel we are allowed to see him at almost every period of his life, but those periods are not presented in chronological order. When Joe first appears in this novel he is al-ready a man in his thirties. He comes to the town of Jefferson and gets a job at the planing mill. Faulkner describes his arrival at the mill in "soiled city clothes." His face is "dark" and "in-sufferable," and his whole air is one of "cold and quiet contempt." To the mill workers even his name seems outlandish.

When Chapter 4 begins, three years have elapsed since Joe's coming to Jefferson. Now we learn that a Miss Joanna Burden, a middle-aged woman who lives alone in a big house on the edge of town, has been murdered and her house set on fire, presumably in an attempt to destroy the evidence of how she died. It is also reported that Christmas has disappeared and that his companion, Joe Brown, has accused him of the murder and furthermore has announced that Christmas is not a white man, as everyone had taken for granted, but a Negro. The murder had occurred very early on a Saturday morning, August 6, 1932.[1]

One might have expected Faulkner to move on from the disclosure of the murder in Chapter 4 to an account of the murder in Chapter 5. But instead, Chapter 5 takes us back in time some twenty-four hours, to late Thursday night (August 4). Joe Brown comes in, drunk, to the cabin on the Burden place which he and Christ-mas occupy, singing and filling the room with "idiot laughter."

The two men are utterly different in person-ality. Whereas Brown usually dawdled at his work at the planing mill, Christmas would jab his shovel "into the sawdust slowly and steadily and hard, as though he were chopping up a buried snake." The relation between the two men, as the other workers quickly perceive it, is that of master and slave, the quietly tense man with his sullen expression and his air of coiled violence, and the other, the feckless man with the merry face and an aura of purposeless triviality.

Christmas had once confided to Brown that he thought he might be part Negro and Brown has by this time discovered that Joe visits Miss Burden at night. Thus, in Chapter 5, with which our selection from the novel begins, we

in the month do just as well? To which the answer has to be yes. Yet since Faulkner has so carefully specified the month as August, the year as 1932, the day of the week as Saturday, and even the exact time of the day, it seems tantalizing that the day of the month should be withheld. Further inquiry does reveal it and thus serves to show how Faulkner's mind worked—though occasionally guilty of lapses, he kept, to a remarkable de-gree to a quite coherent chronology.

Moreover, there is a very practical justification for fixing the date of the murder precisely. Faulkner keyed to that date nearly all of the subsequent events in the novel. The reader trying to follow the very complicated shifts in time will find it far less confusing if he can refer to specific calendar days. Thus, it is helpful if one can say that on August 9 Joe asked a farmer's wife to tell him the day of the week, rather than be forced to say that Joe did so "on the Tuesday following the murder"; or that Joe was killed on August 15, rather than "on the second Monday after Joanna's murder." To facilitate such references, in the selections from *Light in August* that follows we have inserted within brackets the calendar dates in the text we print below. Note carefully that such bracketed dates are *not* in Faulkner's text.

[1] Sally Wheeler has published a detailed chronology of events in *Light in August*: see the *Journal of Southern Literature* (forthcoming, 1973). We were allowed to make use of Mrs. Wheeler's article in manuscript in an attempt to fix on the exact date of the murder, and Mrs. Wheeler has absorbed our findings on this point into her chronology as published. Therefore, our reasons for fixing on August 6, 1932, as the date in question need not be set forth here.

It may, however, be well to say a word here by way of justifying what may seem an overscrupulous precision. For the reader may ask: Wouldn't any other Saturday see the two men together some thirty-six hours before Brown is to turn on his partner and accuse him of murder. Brown lives in some awe of Joe, yet when he is sufficiently drunk—as now—his resentment of his companion's dominance rises to the surface.

Though Christmas's attitude toward Brown involves fury and contempt, there is in it a trace of pity [p. 102].[2] But Faulkner uses this scene to convey something of much greater significance: Christmas has on his mind something far more important than Brown. His anger at Brown is a momentary distraction, for Christmas is in the grip of a deep obsession: "Something is going to happen to me," he tells himself: "I am going to do something." He is a man thoroughly capable of using the razor with the five inch blade, which he keeps under his pillow, but he is aware that Brown is not the proper target for his wrath. He says to himself: "This is not the right one." The comment hints that Christmas does have the right one clearly in mind. Thus, the thrust of the scene is toward the future—toward what Christmas will do on the next night.

CHAPTER 5

It was after midnight [August 5]. Though Christmas had been in bed for two hours, he was not yet asleep. He heard Brown before he saw him. He heard Brown approach the door and then blunder into it. in silhouette propping himself erect in the door. Brown was breathing heavily. Standing there between his propped arms, Brown began to sing in a saccharine and nasal tenor. The very long-drawn pitch of his voice seemed to smell of whiskey. "Shut it," Christmas said. He did not move and his voice was not raised. Yet Brown ceased at once. He stood for a moment longer in the door, propping himself upright. Then he let go of the door and Christmas heard him stumble into the room; a moment later he blundered into something. There was an interval filled with hard, labored breathing. Then Brown fell to the floor with a tremendous clatter, striking the cot on which Christmas lay and filling the room with loud and idiot laughter.

[2] Page numbers in brackets refer to the Modern Library college edition.

Christmas rose from his cot. Invisible beneath him Brown lay on the floor, laughing, making no effort to rise. "Shut it!" Christmas said. Brown still laughed. Christmas stepped across Brown and put his hand out toward where a wooden box that served for table sat, on which the lantern and matches were kept. But he could not find the box, and then he remembered the sound of the breaking lantern when Brown fell. He stooped, astride Brown, and found his collar and hauled him out from beneath the cot and raised Brown's head and began to strike him with his flat hand, short, vicious, and hard, until Brown ceased laughing.

Brown was limp. Christmas held his head up, cursing him in a voice level as whispering. He dragged Brown over to the other cot and flung him onto it, face up. Brown began to laugh again. Christmas put his hand flat upon Brown's mouth and nose, shutting his jaw with his left hand while with the right he struck Brown again with those hard, slow, measured blows, as if he were meting them out by count. Brown had stopped laughing. He struggled. Beneath Christmas's hand he began to make a choked, gurgling noise, struggling. Christmas held him until he ceased and became still. Then Christmas slacked his hand a little. "Will you be quiet now?" he said. "Will you?"

Brown struggled again. "Take your black hand off of me, you damn niggerblooded—" The hand shut down again. Again Christmas struck him with the other hand upon the face. Brown ceased and lay still again. Christmas slacked his hand. After a moment Brown spoke, in a tone cunning, not loud: "You're a nigger, see? You said so yourself. You told me. But I'm white. I'm a wh—" The hand shut down. Again Brown struggled, making a choked whimpering sound beneath the hand, drooling upon the fingers. When he stopped struggling, the hand slacked. Then he lay still, breathing hard.

"Will you now?" Christmas said.

"Yes," Brown said. He breathed noisily. "Let me breathe. I'll be quiet. Let me breathe."

Christmas slacked his hand but he did not remove it. Beneath it Brown breathed easier, his breath came and went easier, with less noise. But Christmas did not remove the hand. He stood in the darkness above the prone body, with Brown's breath alternately hot and cold on his fingers, thinking quietly *Something is going to happen to me. I am going to do something* Without removing his left hand from Brown's face he could reach with his right across to his cot, to his pillow beneath which lay his razor with its five inch blade. But he did not do it. Perhaps thinking had already gone far enough and dark enough to tell him *This is not the right one* Anyway he did not reach for the razor. After a time he removed his hand from Brown's face. But he did not go away. He still stood above the cot, his own breathing so quiet, so calm, as to make no sound even to himself. Invisible too, Brown breathed quieter now, and after a while Christmas returned and sat upon his cot and fumbled a cigarette and a match from his trousers hanging on the wall. In the flare of the match Brown was visible. Before taking the light, Christmas lifted the match and looked at Brown. Brown lay on his back, sprawled, one arm dangling to the floor. His mouth was open. While Christmas watched, he began to snore.

Christmas lit the cigarette and snapped the match toward the open door, watching the flame vanish in midair. Then he was listening for the light, trivial sound which the dead match would make when it struck the floor; and then it seemed to him that he heard it. Then it seemed to him, sitting on the cot in the dark room, that he was hearing a myriad sounds of no greater volume—voices, murmurs, whispers: of trees, darkness, earth; people: his own voice; other voices evocative of names and times and places—which he had been conscious of all his life without knowing it, which were his life, thinking *God perhaps and me not knowing that too* He could see it like a printed sentence, fullborn and already dead *God loves me too* like the faded and weathered letters on a last year's billboard *God loves me too*

———

The passage that follows (continuing Chapter 5) indicates the person on whom Christmas will use the razor and hints at his motive for using it, though the reader can hardly be expected at this point to understand what he means by saying, "It's because she started praying over me." But the passage does suggest a fear and hatred of women. A man who will cut the buttons off his clothes because the sewing on of buttons suggests a woman's work is a man so obsessed that he is probably capable of anything.

Something of the desperation is also powerfully conveyed by his need to smell horses and his seeking out the deserted horse stable as a place to sleep. Many people associate horses and dogs with masculinity; cows and cats, with femininity. (Drusilla Sartoris, in "An Odor of Verbena," obviously does so.) The point, in any case, is the intensity of Christmas's sense of repulsion: for him it is as sharp and immediate as a taste or smell.

———

He smoked the cigarette down without once touching it with his hand. He snapped it too toward the door. Unlike the match, it did not vanish in midflight. He watched it twinkle end over end through the door. He lay back on the cot, his hands behind his head, as a man lies who does not expect to sleep, thinking *I have been in bed now since ten o'clock and I have not gone to sleep. I do not know what time it is but it is later than midnight and I have not yet been asleep* "It's because she started praying over me," he said. He spoke aloud, his voice sudden and loud in the dark room, above Brown's drunken snoring. "That's it. Because she started praying over me."

He rose from the cot. His bare feet made no sound. He stood in the darkness, in his underclothes. On the other cot Brown snored. For a moment Christmas stood, his head turned toward the sound. Then he went on toward the door. In his underclothes and barefoot he left the cabin. It was a little lighter outdoors. Overhead the slow constellations wheeled, the stars of which he had been aware for thirty years and not one of which had any name to him or meant anything at all by shape or brightness or position. Ahead, rising from out a close mass of trees, he could see one chimney and one gable of the house. The house itself was invisible and dark. No light shown and no sound came from it when he approached and stood beneath the window of the room where she slept, thinking *If she is asleep too. If she is asleep?* The doors were never locked, and it used to be that at whatever hour between dark and dawn that the desire took him, he would enter the house and go to her bedroom and take his sure way through the darkness to her bed. Sometimes she would be awake and waiting and she would speak his name. At others he will waken her with his hard brutal hand and sometimes take her as hard and as brutally before she was good awake.

That was two years ago [1930], two years behind them now, thinking *Perhaps that is where outrage lies. Perhaps I believe that I have been tricked, fooled. That she lied to me about her age,*

* plagued by conscience

about what happens to women at a certain age
He said, aloud, solitary, in the darkness beneath the dark window: "She ought not to started praying over me. She would have been all right if she hadn't started praying over me. It was not her fault that she got too old to be any good any more. But she ought to have had better sense than to pray over me." He began to curse her. He stood beneath the dark window, cursing her with slow and calculated obscenity. He was not looking at the window. In the less than halfflight he appeared to be watching his body, seeming to watch it turning slow and lascivious in a whispering of gutter filth like a drowned corpse in a thick still black pool of more than water. He touched himself with his flat hands, hard, drawing his hands hard up his abdomen and chest inside his undergarment. It was held together by a single button at the top. Once he had owned garments with intact buttons. A woman had sewed them on. That was for a time, during a time. Then the time passed. After that he would purloin his own garments from the family wash before she could get to them and replace the missing buttons. When she foiled him he set himself deliberately to learn and remember which buttons were missing and had been restored. With his pocket knife and with the cold and bloodless deliberation of a surgeon he would cut off the buttons which she had just replaced.

His right hand slid fast and smooth as the knife blade had ever done, up the opening in the garment. Edgewise it struck the remaining button a light, swift blow. The dark air breathed upon him, breathed smoothly as the garment slipped down his legs, the cool mouth of darkness, the soft cool tongue. Moving again, he could feel the dark air like water; he could feel the dew under his feet as he had never felt dew before. He passed through the broken gate and stopped beside the road. The August weeds were thightall. Upon the leaves and stalks dust of a month of passing wagons lay. The road ran before him. It was a little paler than the darkness of trees and earth. In one direction town lay. In the other the road rose to a hill. After a time a light began to grow beyond the hill, defining it. Then he could hear the car. He did not move. He stood with his hands on his hips, naked, thighdeep in the dusty weeds, while the car came over the hill and approached, the lights full upon him. He watched his body grow white out of the darkness like a kodak print emerging from the liquid. He looked straight into the headlights as it shot past. From it a woman's shrill voice flew

back, shrieking. "White bastards!" he shouted. "That's not the first of your bitches that ever saw . . ." But the car was gone. There was no one to hear, to listen. It was gone, sucking its dust and its light with it and behind it, sucking with it the white woman's fading cry. He was cold now. It was as though he had merely come there to be present at a finality, and the finality had now occurred and he was free again. He returned to the house. Beneath the dark window he paused and hunted and found his undergarment and put it on. There was no remaining button at all now and he had to hold it together as he returned to the cabin. Already he could hear Brown snoring. He stood for a while at the door, motionless and silent, listening to the long, harsh, uneven suspirations ending each in a choked gurgle. 'I must have hurt his nose more than I knew,' he thought. 'Damn son of a bitch.' He entered and went to his cot, preparing to lie down. He was in the act of reclining when he stopped, halted, halfreclining. Perhaps the thought of himself lying there until daylight, with the drunken man snoring in the darkness and the intervals filled with the myriad voices, was more than he could bear. Because he sat up and fumbled quietly beneath his cot and found his shoes and slipped them on and took from the cot the single half cotton blanket which composed his bedding, and left the cabin. About three hundred yards away the stable stood. It was falling down and there had not been a horse in it in thirty years, yet it was toward the stable that he went. He was walking quite fast. He was thinking now, aloud now, 'Why in hell do I want to smell horses?' Then he said, fumbling: "It's because they are not women. Even a mare horse is a kind of man."

The remainder of Chapter 5 (which follows below) tells us how Christmas spends the last day (August 5) before he undertakes his decisive action. Faulkner, however, does not give us a long monologue by Christmas in which we are permitted to enter the intricate labyrinth of his mind; nor has the author analyzed in his own words Christmas's various motives. Instead, he lets his character's actions speak for themselves. Perhaps our best course here is to follow Faulkner's example and let the reader make what he can of those actions. Yet it may not be amiss to call attention to certain particulars.

Christmas is evidently putting his affairs methodically in final order. Thus there seems to be little rational motive for his puncturing his cans of whisky; the act seems to be an emotional response to a clear conviction that he will never be selling booze anymore. Moreover, he is methodically killing time, reading his cheap magazine from cover to cover, not because the stories hold any interest for him but through a compulsion to fill up the void between the present and the time of confrontation. It is highly significant that he is now so completely committed to the act of murder that he can say to himself, "Maybe I have already done it. Maybe it is no longer waiting to be done."

The latter part of Christmas's day is particularly interesting. By then he has returned to town. There, we are told, he "contrived somehow to look more lonely than a lone telephone pole in the middle of a desert" [p. 106]. His total alienation from the community of Jefferson has earlier been stressed in a number of ways: in the latter part of Chapter 5 it is shown to be further complicated and intensified by the issue of race.

Though Christmas thinks he may be of mixed blood, he doesn't know and obviously can't feel comfortable either as a white man or as a black man. He is equally repelled by both communities. Pages [107–9] stress this point. Moreover, they show that part of his revulsion from the black race comes from his association of the Negro with nature and the feminine principle. The voices of the Negro women [p. 107] sound to him "fecundmellow" and return him to the "lightless hot wet primogenitive Female." He actually breaks into a run to get away from them. When he reaches the white section of town he feels "the cold hard air of white people" as a relief. Yet he is not at home there either. On this August night some people playing cards on a lighted veranda seem not casual and relaxed but to have "white faces intent and sharp in the low light, the bare arms of the women glaring smooth and white above the trivial cards."

The chapter ends with Joe's having returned to the overgrown garden of the Burden place, listening to the courthouse clock strike eleven and then midnight, at which point he rises and moves toward the darkened house.

He slept less than two hours. When he waked dawn [August 5] was just beginning. Lying in the single blanket upon the loosely planked floor of the sagging and gloomy cavern acrid with the thin dust of departed hay and faintly ammoniac with that breathless desertion of old stables, he could see through the shutterless window in the eastern wall the primrose sky and the high, pale morning star of full summer.

He felt quite rested, as if he had slept an unbroken eight hours. It was the unexpected sleep, since he had not expected to sleep at all. With his feet again in the unlaced shoes and the folded blanket beneath his arm he descended the perpendicular ladder, feeling for the rotting and invisible rungs with his feet, lowering himself from rung to rung in onehanded swoops. He emerged into the gray and yellow of dawn, the clean chill, breathing it deep.

The cabin now stood sharp against the increasing east, and the clump of trees also within which the house was hidden save for the single chimney. The dew was heavy in the tall grass. His shoes were wet at once. The leather was cold to his feet; against his bare legs the wet grass blades were like strokes of limber icicles. Brown had stopped snoring. When Christmas entered he could see Brown by the light from the eastern window. He breathed quietly now. 'Sober now,' Christmas thought. 'Sober and dont know it. Poor bastard.' He looked at Brown. 'Poor bastard. He'll be mad when he wakes up and finds out that he is sober again. Take him maybe a whole hour to get back drunk again.' He put down the blanket and dressed, in the serge trousers, the white shirt a little soiled now, the bow tie. He was smoking. Nailed to the wall was a shard of mirror. In the fragment he watched his dim face as he knotted the tie. The stiff hat hung on a nail. He did not take it down. He took instead a cloth cap from another nail, and from the floor beneath his cot a magazine of that type whose covers bear either pictures of young women in underclothes or pictures of men in the act of shooting one another with pistols. From beneath the pillow on his cot he took his razor and a brush and a stick of shaving soap and put them into his pocket.

When he left the cabin it was quite light. The birds were in full chorus. This time he turned his back on the house. He went on past the stable and entered the pasture beyond it. His shoes and his trouser legs were soon sopping with gray dew. He paused and rolled his trousers gingerly to his knees and went on. At the end of the pasture woods began. The dew was not so heavy here, and he rolled his trousers down again. After a while he came to a small valley in which a spring rose. He put down the magazine and gathered twigs and dried brush and made a fire and sat, his back against a tree and his feet to the blaze. Presently his wet shoes began to steam. Then he could feel the heat moving up his legs, and then all of a sudden he opened his eyes and saw the high sun and that the fire had burned completely out, and he knew that he had been asleep. 'Damned if I haven't,' he thought. 'Damned if I haven't slept again.'

He had slept more than two hours this time, because the sun was shining down upon the spring itself, glinting and glancing upon the ceaseless water. He rose, stretching his cramped and stiffened back, waking his tingling muscles. From his pocket he took the razor, the brush, the soap. Kneeling beside the spring he shaved, using the water's surface for glass, stropping the long bright razor on his shoe.

He concealed the shaving things and the magazine in a clump of bushes and put on the tie again. When he left the spring he bore now well away from the house. When he reached the road he was a half mile beyond the house. A short distance further on stood a small store with a gasoline pump before it. He entered the store and a woman sold him crackers and a tin of potted meat. He returned to the spring, the dead fire.

He ate his breakfast with his back against the tree, reading the magazine while he ate. He had previously read but one story; he began now upon the second one, reading the magazine straight through as though it were a novel. Now and then he would look up from the page, chewing, into the sunshot leaves which arched the ditch. 'Maybe I have already done it,' he thought. 'Maybe it is no longer now waiting to be done.' It seemed to him that he could see the yellow day opening peacefully on before him, like a corridor, an arras, into a still chiaroscuro without urgency. It seemed to him that as he sat there the yellow day contemplated him drowsily, like a prone and somnolent yellow cat. Then he read again. He turned the pages in steady progression, though now and then he would seem to linger upon one page, one line, perhaps one word. He would not look up then. He would not move, apparently arrested and held immobile by a single word which had perhaps not yet impacted, his whole being suspended by the single trivial combination of letters in quiet and sunny space, so that hanging motionless and without physical weight he seemed to watch the slow flowing of time beneath him, thinking *All I wanted was peace* thinking, 'She ought not to started praying over me.'

When he reached the last story he stopped reading and counted the remaining pages. Then he looked at the sun and read again. He read now like a man walking along a street might count the cracks in the pavement, to the last and final page, the last and final word. Then he rose and struck a match to the magazine and prodded it patiently until it was consumed. With the shaving things in his pocket he went on down the ditch.

After a while it broadened: a smooth, sand-blanched floor between steep shelving walls choked, flank and crest, with brier and brush. Over it trees still arched, and in a small cove in one flank a mass of dead brush lay, filling the cove. He began to drag the brush to one side, clearing the cove and exposing a short handled shovel. With the shovel he began to dig in the sand which the brush had concealed, exhuming one by one six metal tins with screw tops. He did not unscrew the caps. He laid the tins on their sides and with the sharp edge of the shovel he pierced them, the sand beneath them darkening as the whiskey spurted and poured, the sunny solitude, the air becoming redolent with alcohol. He emptied them thoroughly, unhurried, his face completely cold, masklike almost. When they were all empty he tumbled them back into the hole and buried them roughly and dragged the brush back and hid the shovel again. The brush hid the stain but it could not hide the scent, the smell. He looked at the sun again. It was now afternoon.

At seven o'clock that evening [August 5] he was in town, in a restaurant on a side street, eating his supper, sitting on a backless stool at a friction-smooth wooden counter, eating.

At nine o'clock he was standing outside the barbershop, looking through the window at the man whom he had taken for a partner. He stood quite still, with his hands in his trousers and cigarette smoke drifting across his still face and the cloth cap worn, like the stiff hat, at that angle at once swaggering and baleful. So cold, so baleful he stood there that Brown inside the shop, among the lights, the air heavy with lotion and hot soap, gesticulant, thickvoiced, in the soiled redbarred trousers and the soiled colored shirt, looked up in midvoice and with his drunken eyes looked into the eyes of the man beyond the glass. So still and baleful that a negro youth shuffling up the street whistling saw Christmas' profile and ceased whistling and edged away and slid past behind him, turning, looking back over his shoulder. But Christmas was moving himself now. It was as if he had just paused there for Brown to look at him.

He went on, not fast, away from the square. The street, a quiet one at all times, was deserted at this hour. It led down through the negro section, Freedman Town, to the station. At seven o'clock he would have passed people, white and black, going toward the square and the picture show; at half past nine they would have been going back home. But the picture show had not turned out yet, and he now had the street to himself. He went on, passing still between the homes of white people, from street lamp to street lamp, the heavy shadows of oak and maple leaves sliding like scraps of black velvet across his white shirt. Nothing can look quite as lonely as a big man going along an empty street. Yet though he was not large, not tall, he contrived somehow to look more lonely than a lone telephone pole in the middle of a desert. In the wide, empty, shadowbrooded street he looked like a phantom, a spirit, strayed out of its own world, and lost.

Then he found himself. Without his being aware the street had begun to slope and before he knew it he was in Freedman Town, surrounded by the summer smell and the summer voices of invisible negroes. They seemed to enclose him like bodiless voices murmuring, talking, laughing, in a language not his. As from the bottom of a thick black pit he saw himself enclosed by cabinshapes, vague, kerosenelit, so that the street lamps themselves seemed to be further spaced, as if the black life, the black breathing had compounded the substance of breath so that not only voices but moving bodies and light itself must become fluid and accrete slowly from particle to particle, of and with the now ponderable night inseparable and one.

He was standing still now, breathing quite hard, glaring this way and that. About him the cabins were shaped blackly out of blackness by the faint, sultry glow of kerosene lamps. On all sides, even within him, the bodiless fecundmellow voices of negro women murmured. It was as though he and all other manshaped life about him had been returned to the lightless hot wet primogenitive Female. He began to run, glaring, his teeth glaring, his inbreath cold on his dry teeth and lips, toward the next street lamp. Beneath it a narrow and rutted lane turned and mounted to the parallel street, out of the black hollow. He turned into it running and plunged up the sharp ascent, his heart hammering, and into the higher street. He stopped here, panting, glaring, his heart thudding as if it could not or would not yet believe that the air now was the cold hard air of white people.

Then he became cool. The negro smell, the negro voices, were behind and below him now. To his left lay the square, the clustered lights: low bright birds in stillwinged and tremulous suspension. To the right the street lamps marched on, spaced, intermittent with bitten and unstirring branches. He went on, slowly again, his back toward the square, passing again between the houses of white people. There were people on these porches too, and in chairs upon the lawns; but he could walk quiet here. Now and then he could see them: heads in silhouette, a white blurred garmented shape; on a lighted veranda four people sat about a card table, the white faces intent and sharp in the low light, the bare arms of the women glaring smooth and white above the trivial cards. 'That's all I wanted,' he thought. 'That dont seem like a whole lot to ask.'

This street in turn began to slope. But it sloped safely. His steady white shirt and pacing dark legs died among long shadows bulging square and huge against the August stars: a cotton warehouse, a horizontal and cylindrical tank like the torso of a beheaded mastodon, a line of freight cars. He crossed the tracks, the rails coming momentarily into twin green glints from a switch lamp, glinting away again. Beyond the tracks woods began. But he found the path unerringly. It mounted, among the trees, the lights of the town now beginning to come into view again across the valley where the railroad ran. But he did not look back until he reached the crest of the hill. Then he could see the town, the glare, the individual lights where streets radiated from the square. He could see the street down which he had come, and the other street, the one which had almost betrayed him; and further away and at right angles, the far bright rampart of the town itself, and in the angle between the black pit from which he had fled with drumming heart and glaring lips. No light came from it, from here no breath, no odor. It just lay there, black, impenetrable, in its garland of August-tremulous lights. It might have been the original quarry, abyss itself.

His way was sure, despite the trees, the darkness. He never once lost the path which he could not even see. The woods continued for a mile. He merged into a road, with dust under his feet. He could see now, the vague spreading world, the horizon. Here and there faint windows glowed. But most of the cabins were dark. Nevertheless his blood began again, talking and talking. He walked fast, in time to it; he seemed to be aware that the group were negroes before he could have seen or heard them at all, before they even came in sight vaguely against the defunctive dust. There were five or six of them, in a straggling body yet vaguely paired; again there reached him, above the noise of his own blood, the rich murmur of women-voices. He was walking directly toward them, walking fast. They had seen him and they gave to one side of the road, the voices ceasing. He too changed direction, crossing toward them as if he intended to walk them down. In a single movement and as though at a spoken command the women faded back and were going around him, giving him a wide berth. One of the men followed them as if he were driving them before him, looking over his shoulder as he passed. The other two men had halted in the road, facing Christmas. Christmas had stopped also. Neither seemed to be moving, yet they approached, looming, like two shadows drifting up. He could smell negro; he could smell cheap cloth and sweat. The head of the negro, higher than his own, seemed to stoop, out of the sky, against the sky. "It's a white man," he said, without turning his head, quietly. "What you want, whitefolks? You looking for somebody?" The voice was not threatful. Neither was it servile.

"Come on away from there, Jupe," the one who had followed the woman said.

"Who you looking for, cap'm?" the negro said.

"Jupe," one of the women said, her voice a little high. "You come on, now."

For a moment longer the two heads, the light and the dark, seemed to hang suspended in the darkness, breathing upon one another. Then the negro's head semed to float away; a cool wind blew from somewhere. Christmas, turning slowly, watch-

ing them dissolve and fade again into the pale road, found that he had the razor in his hand. It was not open. It was not from fear. "Bitches!" he said, quite loud. "Sons of bitches!"

The wind blew dark and cool; the dust even through his shoes was cool. 'What in hell is the matter with me?' he thought. He put the razor back into his pocket and stopped and lit a cigarette. He had to moisten his lips several times to hold the cigarette. In the light of the match he could watch his own hands shake. 'All this trouble,' he thought. "All this damn trouble," he said aloud, walking again. He looked up at the stars, the sky. 'It must be near ten now,' he thought; and then almost with the thought he heard the clock on the courthouse two miles away. Slow, measured, clear the ten strokes came. He counted them, stopped again in the lonely and empty road. 'Ten o'clock,' he thought. 'I heard ten strike last night [August 4] too. And eleven. And twelve. But I didn't hear one. Maybe the wind had changed.'

When he heard eleven strike tonight he was sitting with his back against a tree inside the broken gate, while behind him again the house was dark and hidden in its shaggy grove. He was not thinking *Maybe she is not alseep either* tonight. He was not thinking at all now; thinking had not begun now; the voices had not begun now either. He just sat there, not moving, until after a while he heard the clock two miles away strike twelve. Then he rose and moved toward the house. [It's now August 6.] He didn't go fast. He didn't think even then *Something is going to happen. Something is going to happen to me*

From the information given him in Chapter 4, the reader is bound to know, as he finishes Chapter 5, that the murder will be committed very soon, perhaps within the next few minutes. He might, therefore, expect that the author, having set the stage so well, will in Chapter 6 provide an account of the murder. But Faulkner does not; for his purposes, to give the account here would be premature. The reader does not yet know enough about Joe to understand the full significance of what Joe is doing, and he knows almost nothing about Joe's victim. For example, he has no way of understanding why Joe has more than once said, "It's because she started praying over me." Therefore, Faulkner abruptly takes us back some thirty-odd years to Joe's childhood experiences in an orphan asylum. Indeed, Faulkner now devotes 38,000 words to a detailed (and, at long last, a *consecutive*) account of Joe's childhood, boyhood, and young manhood.

Obviously, if we are to get the full impact of the novel we shall need to read the story of Joe's earlier life (not printed here). Nevertheless, we can hope to reveal something of Faulkner's fictional techniques by summarizing here the kind of information Faulkner thought it necessary to provide in this long flashback. The very fact that Faulkner judged it fitting to break off the narrative just before Joe commits the murder and to provide a full account of Joe's early development and the forces that shaped him tells us something about Faulkner as an innovator and daring experimenter.

The warping of Joe's character begins at the orphanage (about 1895). He was made to feel "different" because of the vindictive surveillance of one of the employees at the orphanage, old Doc Hines. The other children themselves somehow come to regard him as "different," and, though they certainly know nothing about his parentage and though his skin is as white as theirs, they begin to taunt him with the epithet "nigger." At the age of five he leaves the orphanage (December, 1900), having been adopted by a childless couple, the McEacherns. The husband is sternly puritanical; his wife has been thoroughly cowed and ground down by his austere domination. In this loveless home Joe is brought up to know his catechism, to be honest, industrious, and God-fearing. To these ends, his cold foster father disciplines him mercilessly. Though Mrs. McEachern timidly tries to mother him, he has already become so twisted psychologically as to resent all her attempts. He is contemptuous of her as a woman. He hates her "soft kindness" more than he does "the harsh and ruthless justice of men" [p. 158].

This long narrative of Joe's early life also tells us about his first intimations of the nature of sex, his first sexual experiences, and reveals how the sex act itself became for him both mysteriously fascinating and yet somehow fearful and repulsive. Joe's closest approximation to the experience of a woman's tenderness and love comes from his relation with a part-time prostitute (1914), but when she betrays and taunts him, Joe's attitudes toward sex, woman, nature, tenderness, and love become set and hardened beyond change.

Joe finally escapes from his foster home in open rebellion—he breaks a chair over his foster father's head (1914 or 1915)—and becomes a wanderer, uncertain about his relation to women, uneasy about his own identity—is he a black man or is he a white man?—and yet dedicated to defining and defending it.

The reader who has gone through this detailed account of the shaping of Joe's psyche can now more fully appreciate what the author tells us in Chapter 2, that there "was something definitely rootless about [Christmas], as though no town nor city was his, no street, no walls, no square of earth his home. And that he carried his knowledge with him always as though it were a banner, with a quality ruthless, lonely, and almost proud." Thus Joe, as a wanderer, for years walks down many roads and many streets. At last he appears on the outskirts of the little town of Jefferson.

FROM CHAPTER 10

One afternoon [in the fall of 1929] the street had become a Mississippi country road. He had been put off a southbound freight train near a small town. He did not know the name of the town; he didn't care what word it used for name. He didn't even see it, anyway. He skirted it, following the woods, and came to the road and looked in both directions. It was not a gravelled road, though it looked to be fairly well used. He saw several negro cabins scattered here and there along it; then he saw, about a half mile away, a larger house. It was a big house set in a grove of trees; obviously a place of some pretensions at one time. But now the trees needed pruning and the house had not been painted in years. But he could tell that it was inhabited, and he had not eaten in twentyfour hours. 'That one might do,' he thought.

But he did not approach it at once, though the afternoon was drawing on. Instead he turned his back upon it and went on in the other direction, in his soiled white shirt and worn serge trousers and his cracked, dusty, townshaped shoes, his cloth cap set at an arrogant angle above a three-day's stubble. Yet even then he did not look like a tramp; at least apparently not to the negro boy whom he met presently coming up the road and swinging a tin bucket. He stopped the boy. "Who lives in the big house back there?" he said.

"That where Miz Burden stay at."

"Mr and Mrs Burden?"

"No, sir. Aint no Mr Burden. Aint nobody live there but her."

"Oh. An old woman, I guess."

"No, sir. Miz Burden aint old. Aint young neither."

"And she lives there by herself. Dont she get scared?"

"Who going to harm her, right here at town? Colored folks around here looks after her."

"Colored folks look after her?"

At once it was as if the boy had closed a door between himself and the man who questioned him. "I reckon aint nobody round here going to do her no harm. She aint harmed nobody."

"I guess not," Christmas said. "How far is it to the next town over this way?"

" 'Bout thirty miles, they say. You aint fixing to walk it, is you?"

"No," Christmas said. He turned then, going on. The boy looked after him. Then he too turned, walking again, the tin bucket swinging against his faded flank. A few steps later he looked back. The man who had questioned him was walking on, steadily though not fast. The boy went on again, in his faded, patched, scant overalls. He was barefoot. Presently he began to shuffle, still moving forward, the red dust rising about his lean, chocolatecolored shanks and the frayed legs of the too short overalls; he began to chant, tuneless, rhythmic, musical, though on a single note:

> *Say dont didn't.*
> *Didn't dont who.*
> *Want dat yaller gal's*
> *Pudden dont hide.*

Lying in a tangle of shrubbery a hundred yards from the house, Christmas heard a far clock strike nine and then ten. Before him the house bulked square and huge from its mass of trees. There was a light in one window upstairs. The shades were not drawn and he could see that the light was a kerosene lamp, and now and then he saw through the window the shadow of a moving person cross the further wall. But he never saw the person at all. After a while the light went out.

The house was now dark; he quit watching it then. He lay in the copse, on his belly on the dark earth. In the copse the darkness was impenetrable; through his shirt and trousers it felt a little chill, close, faintly dank, as if the sun never reached the atmosphere which the copse held. He could feel the neversunned earth strike, slow and receptive, against him through his clothes; groin, hip, belly, breast, forearms. His arms were crossed, his forehead rested upon them, in his nostrils the odor of the dark and fecund earth.

He did not look once again toward the dark house. He lay perfectly still in the copse for more than an hour before he rose up and emerged. He did not creep. There was nothing skulking nor even especially careful about his approach to the house. He simply went quietly as if that were his natural manner of moving and passed around the now dimensionless bulk of the house, toward the rear, where the kitchen would be. He made no more noise than a cat as he paused and stood for a while beneath the window where the light had shown. In the grass about his feet the crickets, which had ceased as he moved, keeping a little island of silence about him like thin yellow shadow of their small voices, began again, ceasing again when he moved with that tiny and alert suddenness. From the rear of the house a single storey wing projected. 'That will be the kitchen,' he thought. 'Yes. That will be it.' He walked without sound, moving in his tiny island of abruptly ceased insects. He could discern a door in the kitchen wall. He would have found it unlocked if he had tried it. But he did not. He passed it and paused beneath a window. Before he tried it he remembered that he had seen no screen in the lighted window upstairs.

The window was even open, propped open with a stick. 'What do you think about that,' he thought. He stood beside the window, his hands on the sill, breathing quietly, not listening, not hurrying, as if there were no need for haste anywhere under the sun. 'Well. Well. Well. What do you know about that. Well. Well. Well.' Then he climbed into the window; he seemed to flow into the dark kitchen: a shadow returning without a sound and without locomotion to the allmother of obscurity and darkness. Perhaps he thought of that other window which he had used to use and of the rope upon which he had had to rely; perhaps not.

Very likely not, no more than a cat would recall another window; like the cat, he also seemed to see in the darkness as he moved as unerringly toward the food which he wanted as if he knew where it would be; that, or were being manipulated by an agent which did know. He ate something from an invisible dish, with invisible fingers: invisible food. He did not care what it would be. He did not know that he had even wondered or tasted until his jaw stopped suddenly in midchewing and thinking fled for twentyfive years back down the street, past all the imperceptible corners of bitter defeats and more bitter victories, and five miles even beyond a corner where he used to wait in the terrible early time of love, for someone whose name he had forgot [Bobbie, the waitress]; five miles even beyond that it went *I'll know it in a minute. I have eaten it before, somewhere. In a minute I will* memory clicking knowing *I see I see I more than see hear I hear I see my head bent I hear the monotonous dogmatic voice which I believe will never cease going on and on forever and peeping I see the indomitable bullet head the clean blunt beard they too bent and I thinking How can he* [Joe's foster father] *be so nothungry and I smelling my mouth and tongue weeping the hot salt of waiting my eyes tasting the hot steam from the dish* "It's peas," he said, aloud. "For sweet Jesus. Field peas cooked with molasses."

More of him than thinking may have been absent; he should have heard the sound before he did, since whoever was creating it was trying no more for silence and caution than he had. Perhaps he did hear it. But he did not move at all as the soft sound of slippered feet approached the kitchen from the house side of it, and when he did at last turn suddenly, his eyes glowing suddenly, he saw already beneath the door which entered the house itself, the faint approaching light. The open window was at his hand: he could have been through it in a single step almost. But he did not move. He didn't even set down the dish. He did not even cease to chew. Thus he was standing in the center of the room, holding the dish and chewing, when the door opened and the woman entered. She wore a faded dressing gown and she carried a candle, holding it high, so that its light fell upon her face: a face quiet, grave, utterly unalarmed. In the soft light of the candle she looked to be not much past thirty. She stood in the door. They looked at one another for more than a minute, almost in the same attitude: he with the

dish, she with the candle. He had stopped chewing now.

"If it is just food you want, you will find that," she said in a voice calm, a little deep, quite cold.

CHAPTER 11

By the light of the candle she did not look much more than thirty, in the soft light downfalling upon the softungirdled presence of a woman prepared for sleep. When he saw her by daylight he knew that she was better than thirtyfive. Later she told him that she was forty. 'Which means either fortyone or fortynine, from the way she said it,' he thought. But it was not that first night, nor for many succeeding ones, that she told him that much even.

She told him very little, anyway. They talked very little, and that casually, even after he was the lover of her spinster's bed [1930]. Sometimes he could almost believe that they did not talk at all, that he didn't know her at all. It was as though there were two people: the one whom he saw now and then by day and looked at while they spoke to one another with speech that told nothing at all since it didn't try to and didn't intend to; the other with whom he lay at night and didn't even see, speak to, at all.

Even after a year (he was working at the planing mill now) when he saw her by day at all, it would be on Saturday afternoon or Sunday or when he would come to the house for the food which she would prepare for him and leave upon the kitchen table. Now and then she would come to the kitchen, though she would never stay while he ate, and at times she met him at the back porch, where during the first four or five months of his residence in the cabin below the house, they would stand for a while and talk almost like strangers. They always stood: she in one of her apparently endless succession of clean calico house dresses and sometimes a cloth sunbonnet like a countrywoman, and he in a clean white shirt now and the serge trousers creased now every week. They never sat down to talk. He had never seen her sitting save one time when he looked through a downstairs window and saw her writing at a desk in the room. And it was a year after he had remarked without curiosity the volume of mail which she received and sent, and that for a certain period of each forenoon she would sit at the worn, scarred, rolltop desk in one of the scarceused and sparsely furnished downstairs rooms, writing steadily, before he learned that what she received were business and private documents with fifty different postmarks and what she sent were replies—advice, business, financial and religious, to the presidents and faculties and trustees, and advice personal and practical to young girl students and even alumnæ, of a dozen Negro schools and colleges through the south. Now and then she would be absent from home three and four days at a time, and though he could now see her at his will on any night, it was a year before he learned that in these absences she visited the schools in person and talked to the teachers and the students. Her business affairs were conducted by a negro lawyer in Memphis, who was a trustee of one of the schools, and in whose safe, along with her will, reposed the written instructions (in her own hand) for the disposal of her body after death. When he learned that, he understood the town's attitude toward her, though he knew that the town did not know as much as he did. He said to himself: 'Then I wont be bothered here.'

One day he realised that she had never invited him inside the house proper. He had never been further than the kitchen, which he had already entered of his own accord, thinking, liplifted, 'She couldn't keep me out of here. I guess she knows that.' And he had never entered the kitchen by day save when he came to get the food which she prepared for him and set out upon the table. And when he entered the house at night it was as he had entered it that first night; he felt like a thief, a robber, even while he mounted to the bedroom where she waited. Even after a year it was as though he entered by stealth to despoil her virginity each time anew. It was as though each turn of dark saw him faced again with the necessity to despoil again that which he had already despoiled —or never had and never would.

Sometimes he thought of it in that way, remembering the hard, untearful and unselfpitying and almost manlike yielding of that surrender [1930]. A spiritual privacy so long intact that its own instinct for preservation had immolated it, its physical phase the strength and fortitude of a man. A dual personality: the one the woman at first sight of whom [the fall of 1929] in the lifted candle (or perhaps the very sound of the slippered approaching feet) there had opened before him, instantaneous as a landscape in a lightningflash, a horizon of physical security and adultery if not pleasure; the other the mantrained muscles and the mantrained habit of thinking born of heritage and environment with which he had to fight up to the final instant. There was no feminine vacillation, no coyness of obvious desire and intention to succumb at last. It was as if he struggled physically with another man for an object of no actual value to either, and for which they struggled on principle alone.

When he saw her next, he thought, 'My God. How little I know about women, when I thought I knew so much.' It was on the very next day; looking at her, being spoken to by her, it was as though what memory of less than twelve hours knew to be true could never have happened, thinking *Under her clothes she cant even be made so that it could have happened* He had not started to work at the mill then. Most of that day he spent lying on his back on the cot which she had loaned him, in the cabin which she had given him to live in, smoking, his hands beneath his head. 'My God,' he thought, 'it was like I was the woman and she was the man.' But that was not right, either. Because she had resisted to the very last. But it was not woman resistance, that resistance which, if really meant, cannot be overcome by any man for the reason that the woman observes no rules of physical combat. But she had resisted fair, by the rules that decreed that upon a certain crisis one was defeated, whether the end of resistance had come or not. That night he waited until he saw the light go out in the kitchen and then come on in her room. He went to the house. He did not go in eagerness, but in a quiet rage. "I'll show her," he said aloud. He did not try to be quiet. He entered the house boldly and mounted the stairs; she heard him at once. "Who is it?" she said. But there was no alarm in her tone. He didn't answer. He mounted the stairs and entered the room. She was still dressed, turning, watching the door as he entered. But she did not speak to him. She just watched him as he went to the table and blew out the lamp, thinking. 'Now she'll run.' And so he sprang forward, toward the door to intercept her. But she did not flee. He found her in the dark exactly where the light had lost her, in the same attitude. He began to tear at her clothes. He was talking to her, in a tense, hard, low voice: "I'll show you! I'll show the bitch!" She did not resist at all. It was almost as though she were helping him, with small changes of position of limbs when the ultimate need for help arose. But beneath his hands the body might have been the body of a dead woman not yet stiffened. But he did not desist; though his hands were hard and urgent it was with rage alone. 'At least I have made a woman of her at last,' he thought. 'Now she hates me. I have taught her that, at least.'

The next day he lay again all day long on his cot in the cabin. He ate nothing; he did not even go to the kitchen to see if she had left food for him. He was waiting for sunset, dusk. 'Then I'll blow,' he thought. He did not expect ever to see her again. 'Better blow,' he thought. 'Not give her the chance to turn me out of the cabin too. That much, anyway. No white woman ever did that. Only a nigger woman ever give me the air, turned me out.' So he lay on the cot, smoking, waiting for sunset. Through the open door he watched the sun slant and lengthen and turn copper. Then the copper faded into lilac, into the fading lilac of full dusk. He could hear the frogs then, and fireflies began to drift across the open frame of the door, growing brighter as the dusk faded. Then he rose. He owned nothing but the razor; when he had put that into his pocket, he was ready to travel one mile or a thousand, wherever the street of the imperceptible corners should choose to run again. Yet when he moved, it was toward the house. It was as though, as soon as he found that his feet intended to go there, that he let go, seemed to float, surrendered, thinking *All right All right* floating, riding across the dusk, up to the house and onto the back porch and to the door by which he would enter, that was never locked. But when he put his hand upon it, it would not open. Perhaps for the moment neither hand nor believing would believe; he seemed to stand there, quiet, not yet thinking, watching his hand shaking the door, hearing the sound of the bolt on the inside. He turned away quietly. He was not yet raging. He went to the kitchen door. He expected that to be locked also. But he did not realise until he found that it was open, that he had wanted it to be. When he found that it was not locked it was like an insult. It was as though some enemy upon whom he had wreaked his utmost of violence and contumely stood, unscathed and unscarred, and contemplated him with a musing and insufferable contempt. When he entered the kitchen, he did not approach the door into the house proper, the door in which she had appeared with the candle on the night when he first saw her. He went directly to the table where she set out his food. He did not need to see. His hands saw; the dishes were still a little warm, thinking *Set out for the nigger. For the nigger.*

He seemed to watch his hand as if from a distance. He watched it pick up a dish and swing it up and back and hold it there while he breathed deep and slow, intensely cogitant. He heard his voice say aloud, as if he were playing a game: "Ham," and watched his hand swing and hurl the dish crashing into the wall, the invisible wall, waiting for the crash to subside and silence to flow completely back before taking up another one. He held this dish poised, sniffing. This one required some time. "Beans or greens?" he said. "Beans or spinach? . . . All right. Call it beans." He hurled it, hard, waiting until the crash ceased. He raised the third dish. "Something with onions," he said, thinking *This is fun. Why didn't I think of this before?* "Woman's muck." He hurled it, hard and slow, hearing the crash, waiting. Now he heard something else: feet within the house, approaching the door. 'She'll have the lamp this time,' he thought thinking *If I were to look now, I could see the light under the door* As his hand swung up and back. *Now she has almost reached the door* "Potatoes," he said at last, with judicial finality. He did not look around, even when he heard the bolt in the door and heard the door in-yawn and light fell upon him where he stood with the dish poised. "Yes, it's potatoes," he said, in the preoccupied and oblivious tone of a child playing alone. He could both see and hear this crash. Then the light went away; again he heard the door yawn, again he heard the bolt. He had not yet looked around. He took up the next dish. "Beets," he said. "I dont like beets, anyhow."

The next day [in the spring of 1930] he went to work at the planing mill. He went to work on Friday. He had eaten nothing now since Wednesday night. He drew no pay until Saturday evening, working overtime Saturday afternoon. He ate Saturday night, in a restaurant downtown, for the first time in three days. He did not return to the house. For a time he would not even look toward it when he left or entered the cabin. At the end of six months he had worn a private path between the cabin and the mill. It ran almost stringstraight, avoiding all houses, entering the woods soon and running straight and with daily increasing definition and precision, to the sawdust pile where he worked. And always, when the whistle blew at five thirty, he returned by it to the cabin, to change into the white shirt and the dark creased trousers before walking the two miles back to town to eat, as if he were ashamed of the overalls. Or perhaps it was not shame, though very likely he could no more have said what it was than he could have said that it was not shame.

He no longer deliberately avoided looking at the house; neither did he deliberately look at it. For a while he believed that she would send for him. 'She'll make the first sign,' he thought. But she did not; after a while he believed that he no longer expected it. Yet on the first time that he deliberately looked again toward the house, he felt a shocking surge and fall of blood; then he knew that he had been afraid all the time that she would be in sight, that she had been watching him all the while with that perspicuous and still contempt; he felt a sensation of sweating, of having surmounted an ordeal. 'That's over,' he thought. 'I have done that now.' So that when one day he did see her, there was no shock. Perhaps he was prepared. Anyway, there was no shocking surge and drop of blood when he looked up, completely by chance, and saw her in the back yard, in a gray dress and the sunbonnet. He could not tell if she had been watching him or had seen him or were watching him now or not. 'You dont bother me and I dont bother you,' he thought, thinking *I dreamed it. It didn't happen. She has nothing under her clothes so that it could have happened*

He went to work in the spring [1930]. One evening in September he returned home and entered the cabin and stopped in midstride, in complete astonishment. She was sitting on the cot, looking at him. Her head was bare. He had never seen it bare before, though he had felt in the dark the loose abandon of her hair, not yet wild, on a dark pillow. But he had never seen her hair before and he stood staring at it alone while she watched him; he said suddenly to himself, in the instant of moving again: 'She's trying to. *I had expected it to have gray in it* She's trying to be a woman and she dont know how.' Thinking, knowing *She has come to talk to me* Two hours later she was still talking, they sitting side by side on the cot in the now dark cabin. She told him that she was forty-one years old and that she had been born in the house yonder and had lived there ever since. That she had never been away from Jefferson for a longer period than six months at any time and these only at wide intervals filled with homesickness for the sheer boards and nails, the earth and trees and shrubs, which composed the place which was a foreign land to her and her people; when she spoke even now, after forty years, among the slurred consonants and the flat vowels of the land where her life had been cast, New England talked as plainly as it did in the speech of her kin who had never left New Hampshire and whom she had seen perhaps three times in her life, her forty years. Sitting beside her on the dark cot while the light failed and at last her voice was without source, steady, interminable, pitched almost like the voice of a man, Christmas thought, 'She is like all the rest of them. Whether they are seventeen or fortyseven, when they finally come to surrender completely, it's going to be in words.'

In the foregoing section, Faulkner has brilliantly dramatized the uneasiness of the relationship between this pair. Obviously, in view of Joe's distaste for women, Joanna's basically unfeminine behavior—the resistance that she puts up against his first assault is "hard, untearful and unselfpitying" and her final yielding "almost manlike"—constitutes part of her attraction for him. Yet he evidently needs companionship and wants some kind of feminine relationship—that which he was denied all his life. But how precarious is his relation with Joanna Burden! How much it balances almost on a razor's edge! He is so charged with his need for independence, so zealous to maintain his own masculine integrity, so sensitive to anything that seems condescending, that Joanna Burden probably always lay under the threat of death.

What kind of person is she, this resourceful, brave, but somehow cold and emotionally starved woman? Her actions as thus far depicted will imply a great deal to the alert reader, but Faulkner, having excited our interest, now needs to have us come to understand her more fully. So he provides for us a flashback into her early life—as he had into Joe's—and a revelation of her family history. The passage is relatively brief, but how vivid Faulkner makes the saga of her grandfather Calvin Burden and that of her father Nathaniel.

Calvin Burden was the son of a minister named Nathaniel Burrington. The youngest of ten children, he ran away from home at the age of twelve

[1824], before he could write his name (or would write it, his father believed) on a ship. He made the voyage around the Horn to California and turned Catholic; he lived for a year in a monastery. Ten years later [1835] he reached Missouri from the west. Three weeks after he arrived he was married, to the daughter of a family of Huguenot stock which had emigrated from Carolina by way of Kentucky. On the day after the wedding he said, "I guess I had better settle down." He began that day to settle down. The wedding celebration was still in progress, and his first step was to formally deny allegiance to the Catholic church. He did this in a saloon, insisting that every one present listen to him and state their objections; he was a little insistent on there being objections, though there were none; not, that is, up to the time when he was led away by friends. The next day he said that he meant it, anyhow; that he would not belong to a church full of frogeating slaveholders. That was in Saint Louis. He bought a home there, and a year later he was a father. He said then that he had denied the Catholic church a year ago for the sake of his son's soul; almost as soon as the boy was born [1836], he set about to imbue the child with the religion of his New England forebears. There was no Unitarian meetinghouse available, and Burden could not read the English Bible. But he had learned to read in Spanish from the priests in California, and as soon as the child could walk Burden (he pronounced it Burden now, since he could not spell it at all and the priests had taught him to write it laboriously so with a hand more apt for a rope or a gunbutt or a knife than a pen) began to read 'to the child in Spanish from the book which he had brought with him from California, interspersing the fine, sonorous flowing of mysticism in a foreign tongue with harsh, extemporised dissertations composed half of the bleak and bloodless logic which he remembered from his father on interminable New England Sundays, and half of immediate hellfire and tangible brimstone of which any country Methodist circuit rider would have been proud. The two of them would be alone in the room: the tall, gaunt, Nordic man, and the small, dark, vivid child who had inherited his mother's build and coloring, like people of two different races. When the boy was about five, Burden killed a man in an argument over slavery and had to take his family and move, leave Saint Louis. He moved westward, "to get away from Democrats," he said.

The settlement to which he moved consisted of a store, a blacksmith shop, a church and two saloons. Here Burden spent much of his time talking politics and in his harsh loud voice cursing slavery and slaveholders. His reputation had come with him and he was known to carry a pistol, and his opinions were received without comment, at least. At times, especially on Saturday nights, he came home, still full of straight whiskey and the sound of his own ranting. Then he would wake his son (the mother was dead now and there were three daughters, all with blue eyes) with his hard hand. "I'll learn you to hate two things," he would say, "or I'll frail the tar out of you. And those things are hell and slaveholders. Do you hear me?"

"Yes," the boy would say. "I cant help but hear you. Get on to bed and let me sleep."

He was no proselyter, missionary. Save for an occasional minor episode with pistols, none of which resulted fatally, he confined himself to his own blood. "Let them all go to their own benighted hell," he said to his children. "But I'll beat the loving God into the four of you as long as I can raise my arm." That would be on Sunday, each Sunday when, washed and clean, the children in calico or denim, the father in his broadcloth frockcoat bulging over the pistol in his hip pocket, and the collarless plaited shirt which the oldest girl laundered each Saturday as well as the dead mother ever had, they gathered in the clean crude parlor while Burden read from the once gilt and blazoned book in that language which none of them understood. He continued to do that up to the time when his son ran away from home.

The son's name was Nathaniel. He ran away at fourteen [1850] and did not return for sixteen years, though they heard from him twice in that time by word-of-mouth messenger. The first time was from Colorado, the second time from Old Mexico. He did not say what he was doing in either place. "He was all right when I left him," the messenger said. This was the second messenger; it was in 1863, and the messenger was eating breakfast in the kitchen, bolting his food with decorous celerity. The three girls, the two oldest almost grown now, were serving him, standing with arrested dishes and softly open mouths in their full, coarse, clean dresses, about the crude table, the father sitting opposite the messenger across the table, his head propped on his single hand. The other arm he had lost two years ago while a member of a troop of partisan guerilla horse in the Kansas fighting, and his head and beard were grizzled now. But he was still vigorous, and his frockcoat still bulged behind over the butt of the heavy pistol. "He got into a little trouble," the messenger said. "But he was still all right the last I heard."

"Trouble?" the father said.

"He killed a Mexican that claimed he stole his horse. You know how them Spanish are about white men, even when they dont kill Mexicans." The messenger drank some coffee. "But I reckon they have to be kind of strict, with the country filling up with tenderfeet and all.—Thank you kindly," he said, as the oldest girl slid a fresh stack of corn cakes onto his plate; "yessum, I can reach the sweetening fine.—Folks claim it wasn't the Mexican's horse noways. Claim the Mexican never owned no horse. But I reckon even them Spanish have got to be strict, with these Easterners already giving the West such a bad name."

The father grunted. "I'll be bound. If there was trouble there, I'll be bound he was in it. You tell him," he said violently, "if he lets them yellow-bellied priests bamboozle him, I'll shoot him myself quick as I would a Reb."

"You tell him to come on back home," the oldest girl said. "That's what you tell him."

"Yessum," the messenger said. "I'll shore tell him. I'm going east to Indianny for a spell. But I'll see him soon as I get back. I'll shore tell him. Oh, yes; I nigh forgot. He said to tell you the woman and kid was fine."

"Whose woman and kid?" the father said.

"His," the messenger said. "I thank you kindly again. And good-bye all."

They heard from the son a third time before they saw him again. They heard him shouting one day out in front of the house, though still some distance away. It was in 1866. The family had moved again, a hundred miles further west, and it had taken the son two months to find them, riding back and forth across Kansas and Missouri in a buckboard with two leather sacks of gold dust and minted coins and crude jewels thrown under the seat like a pair of old shoes, before he found the sod cabin and drove up to it, shouting. Sitting in a chair before the cabin door was a man. "There's father," Nathaniel said to the woman on the buckboard seat beside him. "See?" Though the father was only in his late fifties, his sight had begun to fail. He did not distinguish his son's face until the buckboard had stopped and the sisters had billowed shrieking through the door. Then Calvin rose; he gave a long, booming shout. "Well," Nathaniel said; "here we are."

Calvin was not speaking sentences at all. He was just yelling, cursing. "I'm going to frail the tar out of you!" he roared. "Girls! Vangie! Beck! Sarah!" The sisters had already emerged. They seemed to boil through the door in their full skirts like balloons on a torrent, with shrill cries, above which the father's voice boomed and roared. His coat—the frockcoat of Sunday or the wealthy or the retired—was open now and he was tugging at something near his waist with the same gesture and attitude with which he might be drawing the pistol. But he was merely dragging from about his waist with his single hand a leather strap, and flourishing it he now thrust and shoved through the shrill and birdlike hovering of the women. "I'll learn you yet!" he roared. "I'll learn you to run away!" The strap fell twice across Nathaniel's shoulders. It fell twice before the two men locked.

It was in play, in a sense: a kind of deadly play and smiling seriousness: the play of two lions that might or might not leave marks. They locked, the strap arrested: face to face and breast to breast they stood: the old man with his gaunt, grizzled face and his pale New England eyes, and the young one who bore no resemblance to him at all, with his beaked nose and his white teeth smiling. "Stop it," Nathaniel said. "Dont you see who's watching yonder in the buckboard?"

They had none of them looked at the buckboard until now. Sitting on the seat was a woman and a boy of about twelve. The father looked once at the woman; he did not even need to see the boy. He just looked at the woman, his jaw slacked as if he had seen a ghost. "Evangeline!" he said. She looked enough like his dead wife to have been her sister. The boy who could hardly remember his mother at all, had taken for a wife a woman who looked almost exactly like her.

"That's Juana," he said. "That's Calvin with her. We come home to get married."

After supper that night, with the woman and child in bed, Nathaniel told them. They sat about the lamp: the father, the sisters, the returned son. There were no ministers out there where he had been, he explained; just priests and Catholics. "So when we found that the chico was on the way, she begun to talk about a priest. But I wasn't going to have any Burden born a heathen. So I begun to look around, to humor her. But first one thing and then another come up and I couldn't get away to meet a minister; and then the boy came and so it wasn't any rush anymore. But she kept on worrying, about priests and such, and so in a couple of years I heard how there was to be a white minister in Santa Fe on a certain day. So we packed up and started out and got to Santa Fe just in time to see the dust of the stage that was carrying the minister on away. So we waited there and in a couple more years we had another chance, in Texas. Only this time I got kind of mixed up with helping some Rangers that were cleaning up some kind of a mess where some folks had a deputy treed in a dance hall. So when that was over we just decided to come on home and get married right. And here we are."

The father sat, gaunt, grizzled, and austere, beneath the lamp. He had been listening, but his expression was brooding, with a kind of violently slumbering contemplativeness and bewildered outrage. "Another damn black Burden," he said. "Folks will think I bred to a damn slaver. And now he's got to breed to one, too." The son listened quietly, not even attempting to tell his father that the woman was Spanish and not Rebel. "Damn, lowbuilt black folks: low built because of the weight of the wrath of God, black because of the sin of human bondage staining their blood and flesh." His gaze was vague, fanatical, and convinced. "But we done freed them now, both black and white alike. They'll bleach out now. In a hundred years they will be white folks again. Then maybe we'll let them come back into America." He mused, smoldering, immobile. "By God," he said suddenly, "he's got a man's build, anyway, for all his black look. By God, he's going to be as big a man as his grandpappy; not a runt like his pa. For all his black dam and his black look, he will."

She told Christmas this while they sat on the cot in the darkening cabin. They had not moved for over an hour. He could not see her face at all now; he seemed to swing faintly, as though in a drifting boat, upon the sound of her voice as upon some immeasurable and drowsing peace evocative of nothing of any moment, scarce listening. "His name was Calvin, like grandpa's, and he was as big as grandpa, even if he was dark like father's mother's people and like his mother. She was not my mother: he was just my halfbrother. Grandpa was the last of ten, and father was the last of two, and Calvin was the last of all." He had just turned twenty when he was killed [1874] in the town two miles away by an ex-slaveholder and Confederate soldier named Sartoris, over a question of negro voting.

She told Christmas about the graves—the brother's, the grandfather's, the father's and his two wives—on a cedar knoll in the pasture a half mile from the house; listening quietly, Christmas thought. 'Ah. She'll take me to see them. I will have to go.' But she did not. She never mentioned the graves to him again after that night when she told him where they were and that he could go and see them for himself if he wished. "You probably cant find them, anyway," she said. "Because when they brought grandfather and Calvin home that evening, father waited until after dark and buried them and hid the graves, levelled the mounds and put brush and things over them."

"Hid them?" Christmas said.

There was nothing soft, feminine, mournful and retrospective in her voice. "So they would not find them. Dig them up. Maybe butcher them." She went on, her voice a little impatient, explanatory: "They hated us here. We were Yankees. Foreigners. Worse than foreigners: enemies. Carpetbaggers. And it—the War—still too close for even the ones that got whipped to be very sensible. Stirring up the negroes to murder and rape, they called it. Threatening white supremacy. So I suppose that Colonel Sartoris was a town hero because he killed with two shots from the same pistol an old one-armed man and a boy who had never even cast his first vote. Maybe they were right. I don't know."

"Oh," Christmas said. "They might have done that? dug them up after they were already killed, dead? Just when do men that have different blood in them stop hating one another?"

"When do they?" Her voice ceased. She went on: "I dont know. I dont know whether they would have dug them up or not. I wasn't alive then. I was not born until fourteen years after Calvin was killed. I dont know what men might have done then. But father thought they might have. So he hid the graves. And then Calvin's mother died and he buried her there, with Calvin and grandpa. And so it sort of got to be our burying ground before we knew it. Maybe father hadn't planned to bury her there. I remember how my mother (father sent for her up to New Hampshire where some of our kin people still live, soon after Calvin's mother died. He was alone here, you see. I suppose if it hadn't been for Calvin and grandpa buried out yonder, he would have gone away) told me that father started once to move away, when Calvin's mother died. But she died in the summer, and it would have been too hot then to take her back to Mexico, to her people. So he buried her here. Maybe that's why he decided to stay here. Or maybe it was because he was getting old too then, and all the men who had fought in the War were getting old and the negroes hadn't raped or murdered anybody to speak of. Anyway, he buried her here. He had to hide that grave too, because he thought that someone might see it and happen to remember Calvin and grandfather. He couldn't take the risk, even if it was all over and past and done then. And the next year he wrote to our cousin in New Hampshire. He said, 'I am fifty years old. I have all she will ever need. Send me a good woman for a wife. I don't care who she is, just so she is a good housekeeper and is at least thirtyfive years old.' He sent the railroad fare in the letter. Two months later my mother got here and they were married that day. That was quick marrying, for him. The other time it took him over twelve years to get married, that time back in Kansas when he and Calvin and Calvin's mother finally caught up with grandfather. They got home in the middle of the week, but they waited until Sunday to have the wedding. They had it outdoors, down by the creek, with a barbecued steer and a keg of whiskey and everybody that they could get word to or that heard about it, came. They began to get there Saturday morning, and on Saturday night the preacher came. All that day father's sisters worked, making Calvin's mother a wedding gown and a veil. They made the gown out of flour sacks and the veil out of some mosquito netting that a saloon keeper had nailed over a picture behind the bar. They borrowed it from him. They even made some kind of a suit for Calvin to wear. He was twelve then, and they wanted him to be the ringbearer. He didn't want to. He found out the night before what they intended to make him do, and the next day (they had intended to have the wedding about six or seven o'clock the next morning) after everybody had got up and eaten breakfast, they had to put off the ceremony until they could find Calvin. At last they found him and made him put on the suit and they had the wedding, with Calvin's mother in the homemade gown and the mosquito veil and father with his hair slicked with bear's grease and the carved Spanish boots he had brought back from Mexico. Grandfather gave the bride away. Only he had been going back to the keg of whiskey every now and then while they were hunting for Calvin, and so when his time came to give the bride away he made a speech instead. He got off on Lincoln and slavery and dared any man there to deny that Lincoln and the negro and Moses and the children of Israel were the same,

and that the Red Sea was just the blood that had to be spilled in order that the black race might cross into the Promised Land. It took them some time to make him stop so the wedding could go on. After the wedding they stayed about a month. Then one day father and grandfather went east, to Washington, and got a commission from the government to come down here, to help with the freed negroes. They came to Jefferson, all except father's sisters. Two of them got married, and the youngest one went to live with one of the others, and grandfather and father and Calvin and his mother came here and bought the house. And then what they probably knew all the time was going to happen did happen, and father was alone until my mother came from New Hampshire. They had never even seen one another before, not even a picture. They got married the day she got here and two years later [1888] I was born and father named me Joanna after Calvin's mother. I dont think he even wanted another son at all. I cant remember him very well. The only time I can remember him as somebody, a person, was when he took me and showed me Calvin's and grandpa's graves. It was a bright day, in the spring. I remember how I didn't want to go, without even knowing where it was that we were going. I didn't want to go into the cedars. I dont know why I didn't want to. I couldn't have known what was in there; I was just four then. And even if I had known, that should not have frightened a child. I think it was something about father, something that came from the cedar grove to me, through him. A something that I felt that he had put on the cedar grove, and that when I went into it, the grove would put on me so that I would never be able to forget it. I dont know. But he made me go in, and the two of us standing there, and he said, 'Remember this. Your grandfather and brother are lying there, murdered not by one white man but by the curse which God put on a whole race before your grandfather or your brother or me or you were even thought of. A race doomed and cursed to be forever and ever a part of the white race's doom and curse for its sins. Remember that. His doom and his curse. Forever and ever. Mine. Your mother's. Yours, even though you are a child. The curse of every white child that ever was born and that ever will be born. None can escape it.' And I said, 'Not even me?' And he said, 'Not even you. Least of all, you.' I had seen and known Negroes since I could remember. I just looked at them as I did at rain, or furniture, or food or sleep. But after that I seemed to see them for the first time not as people, but as a thing, a shadow in which I lived, we lived, all white people, all other people. I thought of all the children coming forever and ever into the world, white, with the black shadow already falling upon them before they drew breath. And I seemed to see the black shadow in the shape of a cross. And it seemed like the white babies were struggling, even before they drew breath, to escape from the shadow that was not only upon them but beneath them too, flung out like their arms were flung out, as if they were nailed to the cross. I saw all the little babies that would ever be in the world, the ones not yet even born—a long line of them with their arms spread, on the black crosses. I couldn't tell then whether I saw it or dreamed it. But it was terrible to me. I cried at night. At last I told father, tried to tell him. What I wanted to tell him was that I must escape, get away from under the shadow, or I would die. 'You cannot,' he said. 'You must struggle, rise. But in order to rise, you must raise the shadow with you. But you can never lift it to your level. I see that now, which I did not see until I came down here. But escape it you cannot. The curse of the black race is God's curse. But the curse of the white race is the black man who will be forever God's chosen own because He once cursed Him.' "[3] Her voice ceased. Across the vague oblong of open door fireflies drifted. At last Christmas said:

"There was something I was going to ask you. But I guess I know the answer myself now."

She did not stir. Her voice was quiet. "What?"

"Why your father never killed that fellow—what's his name? Sartoris."

"Oh," she said. Then there was silence again. Across the door the fireflies drifted and drifted. "You would have. Wouldn't you?"

"Yes," he said, at once, immediately. Then he knew that she was looking toward his voice almost as if she could see him. Her voice was almost gentle now, it was so quiet, so still.

"You dont have any idea who your parents were?"

If she could have seen his face she would have found it sullen, brooding. "Except that one of them was part nigger. Like I told you before."

[3] Though all the editions, manuscripts, and typescripts of *Light in August* read "Him," the word in its capitalized form clearly cannot be correct in this context. Though an argument can be made for making the pronoun lower case, the editors prefer to amend the word to "Ham" (see Genesis 9:21–27).

She was still looking at him; her voice told him that. It was quiet, impersonal, interested without being curious. "How do you know that?"

He didn't answer for some time. Then he said: "I dont know it." Again his voice ceased; by its sound she knew that he was looking away, toward the door. His face was sullen, quite still. Then he spoke again, moving; his voice now had an overtone, unmirthful yet quizzical, at once humorless and sardonic: "If I'm not, damned if I haven't wasted a lot of time."

She in turn seemed to muse now, quiet, scarce-breathing, yet still with nothing of selfpity or retrospect. "I had thought of that. Why father didn't shoot Colonel Sartoris. I think that it was because of his French blood."

"French blood?" Christmas said. "Dont even Frenchmen get mad when a man kills his father and his son on the same day? I guess your father must have got religion. Turned preacher, maybe."

She did not answer for a time. The fireflies drifted; somewhere a dog barked, mellow, sad, faraway. "I thought about that," she said. "It was all over then. The killing in uniform and with flags, and the killing without uniforms and flags. And none of it doing or did any good. None of it. And we were foreigners, strangers, that thought differently from the people whose country we had come into without being asked or wanted. And he was French, half of him. Enough French to respect anybody's love for the land where he and his people were born and to understand that a man would have to act as the land where he was born had trained him to act. I think that was it."

The last paragraphs of the foregoing section are very important. The reader learns here that Christmas does not really have any definite evidence that he possesses Negro blood. In point of fact, we can fully account for his situation without reference to biology. He is what he is because he has been treated in a certain way and has come to think of himself in a certain way.

In these closing paragraphs, Joanna's dignity under adversity and the pathos of her situation come out most clearly: she has been injured by her isolation from the community. There is a side of her that yearns toward the warmth of community, and she shows a great magnanimity in being sympathetic with a community that is not only alien but hostile to her. Like Joe, she has been warped by her special upbringing. It is plain, for example, that her labors for the blacks spring not from a loving concern for them, but from a stern puritanical sense of duty enjoined upon her by her grandfather. She and Joe are both, in their special ways, "Calvinists" in Faulkner's sense of the term: they are strictly disciplined, willing to suffer and endure, dedicated to some ideal, and dangerously twisted away from purely natural impulses.

In the closing scene of the chapter we see Joe's nearest approach to what he has unconsciously yearned for all his life. For once we see him enjoying not mere sex, but love, companionship, and mutual understanding with another person (and more particularly—in spite of his earlier history—with a woman). For once in this novel he is momentarily relaxed. Yet such relationship between these haunted characters can hardly be maintained, and in the chapter that follows energies long repressed in the woman's personality come to the surface and have their effect on the man.

CHAPTER 12

In this way the second phase began [September, 1930]. It was as though he had fallen into a sewer. As upon another life he looked back upon that first hard and manlike surrender, that surrender terrific and hard, like the breaking down of a spiritual skeleton the very sound of whose snapping fibers could be heard almost by the physical ear, so that the act of capitulation was anticlimax, as when a defeated general on the day after the last battle, shaved overnight and with his boots cleaned of the mud of combat, surrenders his sword to a committee.

The sewer ran only by night. The days were the same as they had ever been. He went to work at half past six in the morning. He would leave the cabin without looking toward the house at all. At six in the evening he returned, again without even looking toward the house. He washed and changed to the white shirt and the dark creased trousers and went to the kitchen and found his supper waiting on the table and he sat and ate it, still without having seen her at all. But he knew that she was in the house and that the coming of dark within the old walls was breaking down something and leaving it corrupt with waiting. He knew how she had spent the day; that her days also were no different from what they had always been, as if in her case too another person had lived them. All day long he would imagine her, going about her housework, sitting for that unvarying period at the scarred desk, or talking, listening, to the negro women who came to the house from both directions up and down the road, following paths which had been years in the wearing and which radiated from the house like wheelspokes. What they talked about to her he did not know, though he had watched them approaching the house in a manner not exactly secret, yet purposeful, entering usually singly though sometimes in twos and threes, in their aprons and headrags and now and then with a man's coat thrown about their shoulders, emerging again and returning down the radiating paths not fast and yet not loitering. They would be brief in his mind, thinking *Now she is doing this. Now she is doing that* not thinking much about her. He believed that during the day she thought no more about him than he did about her, too. Even when at night, in her dark bedroom, she insisted on telling him in tedious detail the trivial matters of her day and insisted on his telling her of his day in turn, it was in the fashion of lovers: that imperious and insatiable demand that the trivial details of both days be put into words, without any need to listen to the telling. Then he would finish his supper and go to her where she waited. Often he would not hurry. As time went on and the novelty of the second phase began to wear off and become habit, he would stand in the kitchen door and look out across the dusk and see, perhaps with foreboding and premonition, the savage and lonely street which he had chosen of his own will, waiting for him thinking *This is not my life. I dont belong here*

At first it shocked him: the abject fury of the New England glacier exposed suddenly to the fire of the New England biblical hell. Perhaps he was aware of the abnegation in it: the imperious and fierce urgency that concealed an actual despair at frustrate and irrevocable years, which she appeared to attempt to compensate each night as if she believed that it would be the last night on earth by damning herself forever to the hell of her forefathers, by living not alone in sin but in filth. She had an avidity for the forbidden wordsymbols; an insatiable appetite for the sound of them on his tongue and on her own. She revealed the terrible and impersonal curiosity of a child about forbidden subjects and objects; that rapt and tireless and detached interest of a surgeon in the physical body and its possibilities. And by day he would see the calm, coldfaced, almost manlike, almost middle-aged woman who had lived for twenty years alone, without any feminine fears at all, in a lonely house in a neighborhood populated, when at all, by Negroes, who spent a certain portion of each day sitting tranquilly at a desk and writing tranquilly for the eyes of both youth and age the practical advice of a combined priest and banker and trained nurse.

During that period (it could not be called a honeymoon) Christmas watched her pass through every avatar of a woman in love. Soon she more than shocked him: she astonished and bewildered him. She surprised and took him unawares with fits of jealous rage. She could have had no such experience at all, and there was neither reason for the scene nor any possible protagonist: he knew that she knew that. It was as if she had invented the whole thing deliberately, for the purpose of playing it out like a play. Yet she did it with such fury, with such convincingness and such conviction, that on the first occasion he thought that she was under a delusion and the third time he thought that she was mad. She revealed an unexpected and infallible instinct for intrigue. She insisted on a place for concealing notes, letters. It was in a hollow fence post below the rotting stable. He never saw her put a note there, yet she insisted on his visiting it daily; when he did so, the letter would be there. When he did not and lied to her, he would find that she had already set traps to catch him in the lie; she cried, wept.

Sometimes the notes would tell him not to come until a certain hour, to that house which no white person save himself had entered in years and in which for twenty years now she had been all night alone; for a whole week she forced him to climb into a window to come to her. He would do so and sometimes he would have to seek her about the dark house until he found her, hidden, in closets, in empty rooms, waiting, panting, her eyes in the dark glowing like the eyes of cats. Now and then she appointed trysts beneath certain shrubs about the grounds, where he would find her naked, or with her clothing half torn to ribbons upon her, in the wild throes of nymphomania, her body gleaming in the slow shifting from one to another of such formally erotic attitudes and gestures as a Beardsley of the time of Petronius might have

drawn. She would be wild then, in the close, breathing halfdark without walls, with her wild hair, each strand of which would seem to come alive like octopus tentacles, and her wild hands and her breathing: "Negro! Negro! Negro!"

Within six months [about February, 1931] she was completely corrupted. It could not be said that he corrupted her. His own life, for all its anonymous promiscuity, had been conventional enough, as a life of healthy and normal sin usually is. The corruption came from a source even more inexplicable to him than to her. In fact, it was as though with the corruption which she seemed to gather from the air itself, she began to corrupt him. He began to be afraid. He could not have said of what. But he began to see himself as from a distance, like a man being sucked down into a bottomless morass. He had not exactly thought that yet. What he was now seeing was the street lonely, savage, and cool. That was it: cool; he was thinking, saying aloud to himself sometimes, "I better move. I better get away from here."

But something held him, as the fatalist can always be held: by curiosity, pessimism, by sheer inertia. Meanwhile the affair went on, submerging him more and more by the imperious and overriding fury of those nights. Perhaps he realised that he could not escape. Anyway, he stayed, watching the two creatures that struggled in the one body like two moongleamed shapes struggling drowning in alternate throes upon the surface of a black thick pool beneath the last moon. Now it would be that still, cold, contained figure of the first phase who, even though lost and damned, remained somehow impervious and impregnable; then it would be the other, the second one, who in furious denial of that impregnability strove to drown in the black abyss of its own creating that physical purity which had been preserved too long now even to be lost. Now and then they would come to the black surface, locked like sisters; the black waters would drain away. Then the world would rush back: the room, the walls, the peaceful myriad sound of insects from beyond the summer windows where insects had whirred for forty years. She would stare at him then with the wild, despairing face of a stranger; looking at her then he paraphrased himself: "She wants to pray, but she dont know how to do that either."

She had begun to get fat.

The end of this phase was not sharp, not a climax, like the first. It merged into the third phase so gradually that he could not have said where one stopped and the other began. It was summer becoming fall, with already, like shadows before a westering sun, the chill and implacable import of autumn cast ahead upon summer; something of dying summer spurting again like a dying coal, in the fall. This was over a period of two years. He still worked at the planing mill, and in the meantime he had begun to sell a little whiskey, very judiciously, restricting himself to a few discreet customers none of whom knew the others. She did not know this, although he kept his stock hidden on the place and met his clients in the woods beyond the pasture. Very likely she would not have objected. But neither would Mrs McEachern have objected to the hidden rope; perhaps he did not tell her for the same reason that he did not tell Mrs McEachern. Thinking of Mrs McEachern and the rope, and of the waitress whom he had never told where the money came from which he gave to her, and now of his present mistress and the whiskey, he could almost believe that it was not to make money that he sold the whiskey but because he was doomed to conceal always something from the women who surrounded him. Meanwhile he would see her from a distance now and then in the daytime, about the rear premises, where moved articulate beneath the clean, austere garments which she wore that rotten richness ready to flow into putrefaction at a touch, like something growing in a swamp, not once looking toward the cabin or toward him. And when he thought of that other personality that seemed to exist somewhere in physical darkness itself, it seemed to him that what he now saw by daylight was a phantom of someone whom the night sister had murdered and which now moved purposeless about the scenes of old peace, robbed even of the power of lamenting.

Of course the first fury of the second phase could not last. At first it had been a torrent; now it was a tide, with a flow and ebb. During its flood she could almost fool them both. It was as if out of her knowledge that it was just a flow that must presently react was born a wilder fury, a fierce denial that could flog itself and him into physical experimentation that transcended imagining, carried them as though by momentum alone, bearing them without volition or plan. It was as if she knew somehow that time was short, that autumn was almost upon her, without knowing yet the exact significance of autumn. It seemed to be instinct alone: instinct physical and instinctive denial of the wasted years. Then the tide would ebb. Then they would be stranded as behind a dying mistral, upon a spent and satiate beach, looking at one another like strangers, with hopeless and reproachful (on his part with weary: on hers with despairing) eyes.

But the shadow of autumn was upon her. She began to talk about a child, as though instinct had warned her that now was the time when she must either justify or expiate. She talked about it in the ebb periods. At first the beginning of the night was always a flood, as if the hours of light and of separation had damned up enough of the wasting stream to simulate torrent for a moment at least. But after a while the stream became too thin for that: he would go to her now with reluctance, a stranger, already backlooking; a stranger he would leave her after having sat with her in the dark bedroom, talking of still a third stranger. He noticed now how, as though by premeditation, they met always in the bedroom, as though they were married. No more did he have to seek her through the house; the nights when he must seek her, hidden and panting and naked, about the dark house or among the shrubbery of the ruined park were as dead now as the hollow fencepost below the barn.

That was all dead: the scenes, the faultlessly played scenes of secret and monstrous delight and of jealousy. Though if she had but known it now, she had reason for jealousy. He made trips every week or so, on business, he told her. She did not know that the business took him to Memphis, where he betrayed her with other women, women bought for a price. She did not know it. Perhaps in the phase in which she now was she could not have been convinced, would not have listened to proof, would not have cared. Because she had taken to lying sleepless most of the night, making up the sleep in the afternoons. She was not sick; it was not her body. She had never been better; her appetite was enormous and she weighed thirty pounds more than she had ever weighed in her life. It was not that that kept her awake. It was something out of the darkness, the earth, the dying summer itself: something threatful and terrible to her because instinct assured her that it would not harm her; that it would overtake and betray her completely, but she would not be harmed: that on the contrary, she would be saved, that life would go on the same and even better, even less terrible. What was terrible was that she did not want to be saved. "I'm not ready to pray yet," she said aloud, quietly, rigid, soundless, her eyes wide open, while the moon poured and poured into the window, filling the room with something cold and irrevocable and wild with regret. "Dont make me have to pray yet. Dear God, let me be damned a little longer, a little while." She seemed to see her whole past life, the starved years, like a gray tunnel, at the far and irrevocable end of which, as unfading as a reproach, her naked breast of three short years ago ached as though in agony, virgin and crucified; "Not yet, dear God. Not yet, dear God."

So when he now came to her, after the passive and cold and seemly transports of sheer habit she began to speak of a child. She talked about it impersonally at first, discussing children. Perhaps it was sheer and instinctive feminine cunning and indirection, perhaps not. Anyway, it was some time before he discovered with a kind of shock that she was discussing it as a possibility, a practical thought. He said No at once.

"Why not?" she said. She looked at him, speculative. He was thinking fast, thinking *She wants to be married. That's it. She wants a child no more than I do* 'It's just a trick,' he thought. 'I should have known it, expected it. I should have cleared out of here a year ago.' But he was afraid to tell her this, to let the word marriage come between them, come aloud, thinking, 'She may not have thought of it, and I will just put the notion in her head.' She was watching him. "Why not?" she said. And then something in him flashed *Why not? It would mean ease, security, for the rest of your life. You would never have to move again. And you might as well be married to her as this* thinking, 'No. If I give in now, I will deny all the thirty years that I have lived to make me what I chose to be.' He said:

"If we were going to have one, I guess we would have had one two years ago."

"We didn't want one then."

"We dont want one now, either," he said.

That was in September. Just after Christmas [1931] she told him that she was pregnant. Almost before she ceased to speak, he believed that she was lying. He discovered now that he had been expecting her to tell him that for three months. But when he looked at her face, he knew that she was not. He believed that she also knew that she was not. He thought, 'Here it comes. She will say it now: marry. But I can at least get out of the house first.'

But she did not. She was sitting quite still on the bed, her hands on her lap, her still New England face (it was still the face of a spinster: prominently boned, long, a little thin, almost manlike: in contrast to it her plump body was more richly and softly animal than ever) lowered. She said, in a tone musing, detached, impersonal: "A full measure. Even to a bastard negro child. I would like to see father's and Calvin's faces. This will be a good time for you to run, if that's what you want to do." But it was as though she were not listening to her own voice, did not intend for the words to have any actual meaning: that final upflare of stubborn and dying summer upon which autumn, the dawning of halfdeath, had come unawares. 'It's over now,' she thought quietly; 'finished.' Except the waiting, for one month more to pass, to be sure; she had learned that from the negro women, that you could not always tell until after two months. She would have to wait another month, watching the calendar. She made a mark on the calendar to be sure, so there would be no mistake; through the bedroom window she watched that month accomplish. A frost had come, and some of the leaves were beginning to turn. The marked day on the calendar came and passed; she gave herself another week, to be doubly sure. She was not elated, since she was not surprised. "I am with child," she said, quietly, aloud [February, 1932].

'I'll go tomorrow,' he told himself, that same day. 'I'll go Sunday,' he thought. 'I'll wait and get this week's pay, and then I am gone.' He began to look forward to Saturday, planning where he would go. He did not see her all that week. He expected her to send for him. When he entered or left the cabin he would find himself avoiding looking toward the house, as he had during the first week he was there. He did not see her at all. Now and then he would see the negro women, in nondescript garments against the autumn chill, coming or going along the worn paths, entering or leaving the house. But that was all. When Saturday came, he did not go. 'Might as well have all the jack I can get,' he thought. 'If she aint anxious for me to clear out, no reason why I should be. I'll go next Saturday.'

He stayed on. The weather remained cold, bright and cold. When he went to bed now in his cotton blanket, in the draughty cabin, he would think of the bedroom in the house, with its fire, its ample, quilted, lintpadded covers. He was nearer to self-pity than he had ever been. 'She might at least send me another blanket,' he thought. So might he have bought one. But he did not. Neither did she. He waited. He waited what he thought was a long time. Then one evening in February he returned home and found a note from her on his cot. It was brief; it was an order almost, directing him to come to the house that night. He was not surprised. He had never yet known a woman who, without another man available, would not come around in time. And he knew now that tomorrow he would go. 'This must be what I have been waiting for,' he thought; 'I have just been waiting to be vindicated.' When he changed his clothes, he shaved also. He prepared himself like a bridegroom, unaware of it. He found the table set for him in the kitchen, as usual; during all the time that he had not seen her, that had never failed. He ate and went upstairs. He did not hurry. 'We got all night,' he thought. 'It'll be something for her to think about tomorrow night and the next one, when she finds that cabin empty.' She was sitting before the fire. She did not even turn her head when he entered. "Bring that chair up with you," she said.

This was how the third phase began. It puzzled him for a while, even more than the other two. He had expected eagerness, a kind of tacit apology; or lacking that, an acquiescence that wanted only to be wooed. He was prepared to go that length, even. What he found was a stranger who put aside with the calm firmness of a man his hand when at last and in a kind of baffled desperation he went and touched her. "Come on," he said, "if you have something to tell me. We always talk better afterward. It wont hurt the kid, if that's what you have been afraid of."

She stayed him with a single word; for the first time he looked at her face: he looked upon a face cold, remote, and fanatic. "Do you realise," she said, "that you are wasting your life?" And he sat looking at her like a stone, as if he could not believe his own ears.

It took him some time to comprehend what she meant. She did not look at him at all. She sat looking into the fire, her face cold, still, brooding, talking to him as if he were a stranger, while he listened in outraged amazement. She wanted him to take over all her business affairs—the correspondence and the periodical visits—with the Negro schools. She had the plan all elaborated. She recited it to him in detail while he listened in mounting rage and amazement. He was to have complete charge, and she would be his secretary, assistant: they would travel to the schools together, visit in the Negro homes together; listening, even with his anger, he knew that the plan was mad. And all the while her calm profile in the peaceful firelight was as grave and tranquil as a portrait in a frame. When he left, he remembered that she had not once mentioned the expected child.

He did not yet believe that she was mad. He thought that it was because she was pregnant, as he believed that was why she would not let him touch her. He tried to argue with her. But it was like trying to argue with a tree: she did not even rouse herself to deny, she just listened quietly and then talked again in that level, cold tone as if he had never spoken. When he rose at last and went out he did not even know if she was aware that he had gone.

He saw her but once more within the next two months. He followed his daily routine, save that he did not approach the house at all now, taking his meals downtown again, as when he had first gone to work at the mill. But then, when he first went to work, he would not need to think of her during the day; he hardly ever thought about her. Now he could not help himself. She was in his mind so constantly that it was almost as if he were looking at her, there in the house, patient, waiting, inescapable, crazy. During the first phase it had been as though he were outside a house where snow was on the ground, trying to get into the house; during the second phase he was at the bottom of a pit in the hot wild darkness; now he was in the middle of a plain where there was no house, not even snow, not even wind.

He began now to be afraid, whose feeling up to now had been bewilderment and perhaps foreboding and fatality. He now had a partner in his whiskey business: a stranger named Brown who had appeared at the mill one day early in the spring, seeking work. He knew that the man was a fool, but at first he thought, 'At least he will have sense enough to do what I tell him to do. He wont have to think himself at all'; it was not until later that he said to himself: 'I know now that what makes a fool is an inability to take even his own good advice.' He took Brown because Brown was a stranger and had a certain cheerful and unscrupulous readiness about him, and not overmuch personal courage, knowing that in the hands of a judicious man, a coward within his own limitations can be made fairly useful to anyone except himself.

His fear was that Brown might learn about the woman in the house and do something irrevocable out of his own unpredictable folly. He was afraid that the woman, since he had avoided her, might take it into her head to come to the cabin some night. He had not seen her but once since February. That was when he sought her to tell her that Brown was coming to live with him in the cabin. It was on Sunday [March 27, 1932]. He called her, and she came out to where he stood on the back porch and listened quietly. "You didn't have to do that," she said. He didn't understand then what she meant. It was not until later that thinking again flashed, complete, like a printed sentence: *She thinks that I brought him out here to keep her off. She believes that I think that with him there, she wont dare come down to the cabin; that she will have to let me alone*

Thus he put his belief, his fear of what she might do, into his own mind by believing that he had put it into hers. He believed that, since she had thought that, that Brown's presence would not only not deter her: it would be an incentive for her to come to the cabin. Because of the fact that for over a month [April, 1932] now she had done nothing at all, made no move at all, he believed that she might do anything. Now he too lay awake at night. But he was thinking, 'I have got to do something. There is something that I am going to do.'

So he would trick and avoid Brown in order to reach the cabin first. He expected each time to find her waiting. When he would reach the cabin and find it empty, he would think in a kind of impotent rage of the urgency, the lying and the haste, and of her alone and idle in the house all day, with nothing to do save to decide whether to betray him at once or torture him a little longer. By ordinary he would not have minded whether Brown knew about their relations or not. He had nothing in his nature of reticence or of chivalry toward women. It was practical, material. He would have been indifferent if all Jefferson knew he was her lover: it was that he wanted no one to begin to speculate on what his private life out there was because of the hidden whiskey which was netting him thirty or forty dollars a week. That was one reason. Another reason was vanity. He would have died or murdered rather than have anyone, another man, learn what their relations had now become. That not only had she changed her life completely, but that she was trying to change his too and make

of him something between a hermit and a missionary to Negroes. He believed that if Brown learned the one, he must inevitably learn the other. So he would reach the cabin at last, after the lying and the hurry, and as he put his hand on the door, remembering the haste and thinking that in a moment he would find that it had not been necessary at all and yet to neglect which precaution he dared not, he would hate her with a fierce revulsion of dread and impotent rage. Then one evening he opened the door and found the note on the cot [late April, 1932].

He saw it as soon as he entered, lying square and white and profoundly inscrutable against the dark blanket. He did even stop to think that he believed he knew what the message would be, would promise. He felt no eagerness; he felt relief. 'It's over now,' he thought, not yet taking up the folded paper. 'It will be like it was before now. No more talking about niggers and babies. She has come around. She has worn the other out, seen that she was getting nowhere. She sees now that what she wants, needs, is a man. She wants a man by night; what he does by daylight does not matter.' He should have realised then the reason why he had not gone away. He should have seen that he was bound just as tightly by that small square of still undivulging paper as though it were a lock and chain. He did not think of that. He saw only himself once again on the verge of promise and delight. It would be quieter though, now. They would both want it so; besides the whiphand which he would now have. 'All that foolishness,' he thought, holding the yet unopened paper in his hands; 'all that damn foolishness. She is still she and I am still I. And now, after all this damn foolishness'; thinking how they would both laugh over it tonight, later, afterward, when the time for quiet talking and quiet laughing came: at the whole thing, at one another, at themselves.

He did not open the note at all. He put it away and washed and shaved and changed his clothes, whistling while he did so. He had not finished when Brown came in. "Well, well, well," Brown said. Christmas said nothing. He was facing the shard of mirror nailed to the wall, knotting his tie. Brown had stopped in the center of the floor: a tall, lean, young man in dirty overalls, with a dark, weakly handsome face and curious eyes. Beside his mouth there was a narrow scar as white as a thread of spittle. After a while Brown said: "Looks like you are going somewhere."

"Does it?" Christmas said. He did not look around. He whistled monotonously but truely: something in minor, plaintive and negroid.

"I reckon I wont bother to clean up none," Brown said, "seeing as you are almost ready."

Christmas looked back at him. "Ready for what?"

"Aint you going to town?"

"Did I ever say I was?" Christmas said. He turned back to the glass.

"Oh," Brown said. He watched the back of Christmas's head. "Well, I reckon from that that you're going on private business." He watched Christmas. "This here's a cold night to be laying around on the wet ground without nothing under you but a thin gal."

"Aint it, though?" Christmas said, whistling, preoccupied and unhurried. He turned and picked up his coat and put it on, Brown still watching him. He went to the door. "See you in the morning," he said. The door did not close behind him. He knew that Brown was standing in it, looking after him. But he did not attempt to conceal his purpose. He went on toward the house. 'Let him watch,' he thought. 'Let him follow me if he wants to.'

The table was set for him in the kitchen. Before sitting down he took the unopened note from his pocket and laid it beside his plate. It was not enclosed, not sealed; it sprang open of its own accord, as though inviting him, insisting. But he did not look at it. He began to eat. He ate without haste. He had almost finished when he raised his head suddenly, listening. Then he rose and went to the door through which he had entered, with the noiselessness of a cat, and jerked the door open suddenly. Brown stood just outside, his face leaned to the door, or where the door had been. The light fell upon his face and upon it was an expression of intent and infantile interest which became surprise while Christmas looked at it, then it recovered, falling back a little. Brown's voice was gleeful though quiet, cautious, conspiratorial, as if he had already established his alliance and sympathy with Christmas, unasked, and without waiting to know what was going on, out of loyalty to his partner or perhaps to abstract man as opposed to all women. "Well, well, well," he said. "So this is where you tomcat to every night. Right at our front door, you might say—"

Without saying a word Christmas struck him. The blow did not fall hard, because Brown was already in innocent and gleeful backmotion, in midsnicker as it were. The blow cut his voice short off; moving, springing backward, he vanished from the fall of light, into the darkness, from which his voice came, still not loud, as if even now he would not jeopardise his partner's business, but tense now with alarm, astonishment: "Dont you hit me!" He was the taller of the two: a gangling shape already in a ludicrous diffusion of escape as if he were on the point of clattering to earth in complete disintegration as he stumbled backward before the steady and still silent advance of the other. Again Brown's voice came, high, full of alarm and spurious threat: "Dont you hit me!" This time the blow struck his shoulder as he turned. He was running now. He ran for a hundred yards before he slowed, looking back. Then he stopped and turned. "You durn yellowbellied wop," he said, in a tentative tone, jerking his head immediately, as if his voice had made more noise, sounded louder, than he had intended. There was no sound from the house; the kitchen door was dark again, closed again. He raised his voice a little: "You durn yellowbellied wop! I'll learn you who you are monkeying with." There came no sound anywhere. It was chilly. He turned and went back to the cabin, mumbling to himself.

When Christmas reentered the kitchen he did not even look back at the table on which lay the note which he had not yet read. He went on through the door which led into the house and on to the stairs. He began to mount, not fast. He mounted steadily; he could now see the bedroom door, a crack of light, firelight, beneath it. He went steadily on and put his hand upon the door. Then he opened it and he stopped dead still. She was sitting at a table, beneath the lamp. He saw a figure that he knew, in a severe garment that he knew—a garment that looked as if it had been made for and worn by a careless man. Above it he saw a head with hair just beginning to gray drawn gauntly back to a knot as savage and ugly as a wart on a diseased bough. Then she looked up at him and he saw that she wore steelrimmed spectacles which he had never seen before. He stood in the door, his hand still on the knob, quite motionless. It seemed to him that he could actually hear the words inside him: *You should have read that note. You should have read that note* thinking, 'I am going to do something. Going to do something.'

He was still hearing that while he stood beside the table on which papers were scattered and from which she had not risen, and listened to the calm enormity which her cold, still voice unfolded, his mouth repeating the words after her while he looked down at the scattered and enigmatic papers and documents and thinking fled smooth and idle, wondering what this paper meant and what that paper meant. "To school," his mouth said.

"Yes," she said. "They will take you. Any of them will. On my account. You can choose any one you want among them. We wont even have to pay."

"To school," his mouth said. "A nigger school. Me."

"Yes. Then you can go to Memphis. You can read law in Peebles's office. He will teach you law. Then you can take charge of all the legal business. All this, all that he does, Peebles does."

"And then learn law in the office of a nigger lawyer," his mouth said.

"Yes. Then I will turn over all the business to you, all the money. All of it. So that when you need money for yourself you could . . . you would know how; lawyers know how to do it so that it . . . You would be helping them up out of darkness and none could accuse or blame you even if they found out . . . even if you did not replace . . . but you could replace the money and none would ever know. . . ."

"But a nigger college, a nigger lawyer," his voice said, quiet, not even argumentative; just promptive. They were not looking at one another; she had not looked up since he entered.

"Tell them," she said.

"Tell niggers that I am a nigger too?" She now looked at him. Her face was quite calm. It was the face of an old woman now.

"Yes. You'll have to do that. So they wont charge you anything. On my account."

Then it was as if he said suddenly to his mouth: 'Shut up. Shut up that drivel. Let me talk.' He leaned down. She did not move. Their faces were not a foot apart: the one cold, dead white, fanatical, mad; the other parchment-colored, the lip lifted into the shape of a soundless and rigid snarl. He said quietly: "You're old. I never noticed that before. An old woman. You've got gray in your hair." She struck him, at once, with her flat hand, the rest of her body not moving at all. Her blow made a flat sound; his blow as close upon it as echo. He struck with his fist, then in that long blowing wind he jerked her up from the chair and held her, facing him, motionless, not a flicker upon her still face, while the long wind of knowing rushed down upon him. "You haven't got any baby," he said. "You never had one. There is not anything the matter with you except being old. You just got old and it happened to you and now you are not any good anymore. That's all that's wrong with you." He released her and struck her again. She fell huddled onto the bed, looking up at him, and he struck her in the face again and standing over her he spoke to her the words which she had once loved to hear on his tongue, which she used to say that she could taste there, murmurous, obscene, caressing. "That's all. You're just worn out. You're not any good anymore. That's all."

She lay on the bed, on her side, her head turned and looking up at him across her bleeding mouth. "Maybe it would be better if we both were dead," she said.

In the last paragraph Joanna has begun to have premonitions of death. In a sense she desires it, for in her despair she can see no other outcome for herself. If Joe seems especially callous and brutal in the foregoing scene—and he is brutal ("He had nothing in his nature of reticence or of chivalry toward women" [p. 256])—one remembers that he has here been touched to the quick. Throughout his life he has been poised between two worlds—that of the black man and that of the white. He refuses to identify himself with either. Most of all, he refuses to have someone dictate what he is to do, especially if that person is a woman. He will not be "mothered."

In the chronology of the story we are now in the spring of Joe's third year of residence in Jefferson. In the second paragraph of the section that follows we are told that it is already May.

He could see the note lying on the blanket as soon as he opened the door. Then he would go and take it up and open it. He would now remember the hollow fencepost as something of which he had heard told, as having taken place in another life from any that he had ever lived. Because the paper, the ink, the form and shape, were the same. They had never been long; they were not long now. But now there was nothing evocative of unspoken promise, of rich and unmentionable delights, in them. They were now briefer than epitaphs and more terse than commands.

His first impulse would be to not go. He be-lieved that he dared not go. Then he knew that he dared not fail to go. He would not change his clothes now. In his sweat-stained overalls he would traverse the late twilight of [early] May and enter the kitchen. The table was never set with food for him now. Sometimes he would look at it as he passed and he would think, 'My God. When have I sat down in peace to eat.' And he could not remember.

He would go on into the house and mount the stairs. Already he would be hearing her voice. It would increase as he mounted and until he reached the door to the bedroom. The door would be shut, locked; from beyond it the monotonous steady voice came. He could not distinguish the words; only the ceaseless monotone. He dared not try to distinguish the words. He did not dare let himself know what she was at. So he would stand there and wait, and after a while the voice would cease and she would open the door and he would enter. As he passed the bed he would look down at the floor beside it and it would seem to him that he could distinguish the prints of knees and he would jerk his eyes away as if it were death that they had looked at.

Likely the lamp would not yet be lighted. They did not sit down. Again they stood to talk, as they used to do two years ago; standing in the dusk while her voice repeated its tale: ". . . not to school, then, if you dont want to go . . . Do with-out that . . . Your soul. Expiation of . . ." And he waiting, cold, still, until she had finished: ". . . hell . . . forever and ever and ever . . ."

"No," he said. And she would listen as quietly, and he knew that she was not convinced and she knew that he was not. Yet neither surrendered; worse: they would not let one another alone; he would not even go away. And they would stand for a while longer in the quiet dusk peopled, as though from their loins, by a myriad ghosts of dead sins and delights, looking at one another's still and fad-ing face, weary, spent, and indomitable.

Then he would leave. And before the door had shut and the bolt had shot to behind him, he would hear the voice again, monotonous, calm, and despairing, saying what and to what or whom he dared not learn nor suspect. And as he sat in the shadows of the ruined garden on that August night three months later and heard the clock in the courthouse two miles away strike ten and then eleven, he believed with calm paradox that he was the volitionless servant of the fatality in which he

believed that he did not believe. He was saying to himself *I had to do it* already in the past tense; *I had to do it. She said so herself*

She had said it two nights ago. He found the note and went to her. As he mounted the stairs the monotonous voice grew louder, sounded louder and clearer than usual. When he reached the top of the stairs he saw why. The door was open this time, and she did not rise from where she knelt beside the bed when he entered. She did not stir; her voice did not cease. Her head was not bowed. Her face was lifted, almost with pride, her attitude of formal abjectness a part of the pride, her voice calm and tranquil and abnegant in the twilight. She did not seem to be aware that he had entered until she finished a period. Then she turned her head. "Kneel with me," she said.

"No," he said.

"Kneel," she said. "You wont even need to speak to Him yourself. Just kneel. Just make the first move."

"No," he said. "I'm going."

She didn't move, looking back and up at him. "Joe," she said, "will you stay? Will you do that much?"

"Yes," he said. "I'll stay. But make it fast."

She prayed again. She spoke quietly, with that abjectness of pride. When it was necessary to use the symbolwords which he had taught her, she used them, spoke them forthright and without hesi-tation, talking to God as if He were a man in the room with two other men. She spoke of herself and of him as of two other people, her voice still, monotonous, sexless. Then she ceased. She rose quietly. They stood in the twilight, facing one an-other. This time she did not even ask the ques-tion; he did not even need to reply. After a time she said quietly:

"Then there's just one other thing to do."

"There's just one other thing to do," he said.

'So now it's all done, all finished,' he thought quietly, sitting in the dense shadow of the shrub-bery, hearing the last stroke of the far clock cease and die away. It was a spot where he had over-taken her, found her on one of the wild nights two years ago. But that was in another time, another life. Now it was still, quiet, the fecund earth now coolly suspirant. The dark was filled with the voices, myriad, out of all time that he had known, as though all the past was a flat pattern. And go-ing on: tomorrow night, all the tomorrows, to be a part of the flat pattern, going on. He thought of that with quiet astonishment: going on, myriad, familiar, since all that had ever been was the same as all that was to be, since tomorrow to-be and had-been would be the same. Then it was time [past midnight, August 6, 1932].

He rose. He moved from the shadow and went around the house and entered the kitchen. The house was dark. He had not been to the cabin since early morning and he did not know if she had left a note for him or not, expected him or not. Yet he did not try for silence. It was as if he were not thinking of sleep, of whether she would be asleep or not. He mounted the stairs steadily and entered the bedroom. Almost at once she spoke from the bed. "Light the lamp," she said.

"It wont need any light," he said.

"Light the lamp."

"No," he said. He stood over the bed. He held the razor in his hand. But it was not open yet. But she did not speak again and then his body seemed to walk away from him. It went to the table and his hands laid the razor on the table and found the lamp and struck the match. She was sitting up in the bed, her back against the headboard. Over her nightdress she wore a shawl drawn across her breast. Her arms were folded upon the shawl, her hands hidden from sight. He stood at the table. They looked at one another.

"Will you kneel with me?" she said. "I dont ask it."

"No," he said.

"I dont ask it. It's not I who ask it. Kneel with me."

"No."

They looked at one another. "Joe," she said, "for the last time. I dont ask it. Remember that. Kneel with me."

"No," he said. Then he saw her arms unfold and her right hand come forth from beneath the shawl. It held an old style, single action, cap-and-ball revolver almost as long and heavier than a small rifle. But the shadow of it and of her arm and hand on the wall did not waver at all, the shadow of both monstrous, the cocked hammer monstrous, backhooked and viciously poised like the arched head of a snake; it did not waver at all. And her eyes did not waver at all. They were as still as the round black ring of the pistol muzzle. But there was no heat in them, no fury. They were calm and still as all pity and all despair and all conviction. But he was not watching them. He was watching the shadowed pistol on the wall; he was watching when the cocked shadow of the hammer flicked away.

Standing in the middle of the road, with his right hand lifted full in the glare of the approaching car, he had not actually expected it to stop. Yet it did, with a squealing and sprawling suddenness that was almost ludicrous. It was a small car, battered and old. When he approached it, in the reflected glare of the headlights two young faces seemed to float like two softcolored and aghast balloons, the nearer one, the girl's, backshrunk in a soft, wide horror. But Christmas did not notice this at the time. "How about riding with you, as far as you go?" he said. They said nothing at all, looking at him with that still and curious horror which he did not notice. So he opened the door to enter the rear seat.

When he did so, the girl began to make a choked wailing sound which would be much louder in a moment, as fear gained courage as it were. Already the car was in motion; it seemed to leap forward, and the boy, without moving his hands from the wheel or turning his head toward the girl hissed: "Shut up! Hush! It's our only chance! Will you hush now?" Christmas did not hear this either. He was sitting back now, completely unaware that he was riding directly behind desperate terror. He only thought with momentary interest that the small car was travelling at a pretty reckless speed for a narrow country road.

"How far does this road go?" he said.

The boy told him, naming the same town which the negro boy had named to him on that afternoon three years ago, when he had first seen Jefferson. The boy's voice had a dry, light quality. "Do you want to go there, cap'm?"

"All right," Christmas said. "Yes. Yes. That will do. That will suit me. Are you going there?"

"Sure," the boy said, in that light, flat tone. "Wherever you say." Again the girl beside him began that choked, murmurous, small-animallike moaning; again the boy hissed at her, his face still rigidly front, the little car rushing and bouncing onward: "Hush! Shhhhhhhhhh. Hush! Hush!" But again Christmas did not notice. He saw only the two young, rigidly forwardlooking heads against the light glare, into which the ribbon of the road rushed swaying and fleeing. But he remarked both them and the fleeing road without curiosity; he was not even paying attention when he found that the boy had apparently been speaking to him for some time; how far they had come or where they were he did not know. The boy's diction was slow now, recapitulant, each word as though chosen simply and carefully and spoken slowly and clearly for the ear of a foreigner: "Listen, cap'm. When I turn off up here. It's just a short cut. A short cutoff to a better road. I am going to take the cutoff. When I come to the short cut. To the better road. So we can get there quicker. See?"

"All right," Christmas said. The car bounced and rushed on, swaying on the curves and up the hills and fleeing down again as if the earth had dropped from under them. Mail boxes on posts beside the road rushed into the lights and flicked past. Now and then they passed a dark house. Again the boy was speaking:

"Now, this here cutoff I was telling you about. It's right down here. I'm going to turn into it. But it dont mean I am leaving the road. I am just going a little way across to a better road. See?"

"All right," Christmas said. Then for no reason he said: "You must live around here somewhere."

Now it was the girl who spoke. She turned in the seat, whirling, her small face wan with suspense and terror and blind and ratlike desperation: "We do!" she cried. "We both do! Right up yonder! And when my pappy and brothers—" Her voice ceased, cut short off; Christmas saw the boy's hand clapped upon her lower face and her hands tugging at the wrist while beneath the hand itself her smothered voice choked and bubbled. Christmas sat forward.

"Here," he said. "I'll get out here. You can let me out here."

"Now you've done it!" the boy cried, too, thinly, with desperate rage too. "If you'd just kept quiet—"

"Stop the car," Christmas said. "I aint going to hurt either of you. I just want to get out." Again the car stopped with sprawling suddenness. But the engine still raced, and the car leaped forward again before he was clear of the step; he had to leap forward running for a few steps to recover his balance. As he did so, something heavy and hard struck him on the flank. The car rushed on, fading at top speed. From it floated back the girl's shrill wailing. Then it was gone; the darkness, the now impalpable dust, came down again, and the silence beneath the summer stars. The object which had struck him had delivered an appreciable blow; then he discovered that the object was attached to his right hand. Raising the hand, he found that it held the ancient heavy pistol. He did not know that he had it; he did not remember having picked it up at all, nor why. But there it was. 'And I flagged that car with my right hand,' he thought. 'No

wonder she . . . they . . .' He drew his right hand back to throw, the pistol balanced upon it. Then he paused, and he struck a match and examined the pistol in the puny dying glare. The match burned down and went out, yet he still seemed to see the ancient thing with its two loaded chambers: the one upon which the hammer had already fallen and which had not exploded, and the other upon which no hammer had yet fallen but upon which a hammer had been planned to fall. 'For her and for me,' he said. His arm came back, and threw. He heard the pistol crash once through undergrowth. Then there was no sound again. 'For her and for me.'

In the foregoing section we learn why Joe kept saying [p. 98], "It's because she started praying over me. That's it. Because she started praying over me." Curiously enough, though Joe resents her praying and has no hope that she will change, he continues to go to her house, to mount the stairs, and through her closed door listen, though "he dared not try to distinguish the words." Death is indeed the only solution to such an impasse in which "neither surrendered; worse: they would not let one another alone. . . ."

The reader should note that beginning with "And as he sat in the shadows of the ruined garden on that August night three months later . . ." [p. 264], we have at last come back to the point of time [p. 110] where Joe, on that Friday night (August 5) is waiting for the clock to strike twelve before he mounts, for the last time, the stairs to Joanna's bedroom.

Yet even here Faulkner employs one more brief flashback. He needs to explain why Joe says, "I had to do it. She said so herself." Therefore we get a short passage which recalls a conversation between the pair some forty-eight hours *earlier*, on Wednesday night (August 3). Joanna had said, "Then there's just one other thing to do," and he had replied, "There's just one other thing to do" [p. 265], evidently that thing which he is now mounting the stairs to do.

As Joe goes up the stairs, Faulkner tells us, "he was the volitionless servant of the fatality in which he believed that he did not believe" [p. 264]. This paradox has been rendered credible because of the subtlety and power with which Faulkner has dramatized the situation. Because he has done so it is possible for us to believe that Joe would be saying to himself as he climbed the stairs, "I had to do it," as if the deed had already been done.

With this passage [p. 265], the three days leading up to Miss Burden's murder at last fall into order. We may summarize as follows: Wednesday night (August 3) Joe is in Joanna's bedroom where she is once more trying to persuade him to kneel and pray with her [p. 265]. Thursday night (August 4), Joe is in bed in his cabin but still awake. For on Friday night (August 5) he remarks [p. 110], "I heard ten strike last night [August 4] too. And eleven. And twelve. But I didn't hear one. Maybe the wind had changed." Later, after it has got to be early Friday morning (August 5), Joe gets up and goes out to the stable to sleep [p. 101]. Then, still early on Friday morning (August 5) Joe awakens, destroys his supply of whisky, kills time until evening, and finally goes to town. He has his encounter with the Negroes and finally ends up in Joanna's garden late that evening waiting to hear the clock strike twelve. A little later (very early on Saturday morning [August 6]) he cuts Joanna's throat.

By his dislocations of the chronology of the action, Faulkner manages to postpone imparting information until it will register upon the reader with maximum impact. Faulkner does not, however, manipulate the sequence of events in the interest of mere vulgar suspense. From the beginning we know the *basic* facts of the plot. What Faulkner is really concerned to have us understand are those elements in Joe's character and in Joanna's that drove him to murder her. Faulkner therefore does not bring us to the crucial scenes until we are ready to enter into the fullest imaginative engagement with the characters. Nor is this imaginative engagement simply a matter of gross emotional intensity; it includes psychological awareness and subtlety of insight into the characters. Faulkner wants our experience of the novel to be massive and complex: our intellects as well as our emotions are to be involved.

Faulkner also achieves some important special effects by means of his displaced and sometimes inverted chronology. One of the most important is the way in which he reinforces the reader's sense of Joe's feeling of compulsion and fatality. The experience of being fated is so extreme that for Joe, as we have seen, the past and future mingle. So intensely is his whole being committed to the act to be done that he begins to experience as already accomplished what is yet to occur [p. 264]. The reader undergoes a comparable experience: he has been forced to live with the murder as a fact of the novel ever since Chapter 4. By the end of Chapter 12 when Joe finally acts, he is emotionally disposed, like Joe, to have a sense of *déjà vu*.

Joanna Burden, it should be noted, is also a person fated and living under compulsion. At the end she feels almost as volitionless as Joe. We have already seen how [pp. 239–40] she was taught to believe that there was a duty laid upon her, a "curse" from which she could not by any effort free herself. Much of her action is compulsive, not merely the second phase in her relations with Joe, but her third. At the end she is telling Joe, perfectly sincerely, that it is not she who is asking him to kneel and pray, but God himself. When she tries to fire the old Civil War pistol at Joe she obviously believes that she is acting as God's agent.

One of the most brilliant of the means by which Faulkner has emphasized Joe's state of obsession is having him, just after the murder, encounter a boy and girl riding by in a car [pp. 267–70]. They are terrified because they see the pistol in his hand. Joe is not aware that he holds a pistol: it is only after he has got out of the car and turned away that he realizes why the pair were frightened. The encounter with the couple has a further value: it brings surging back into this nightmare of obsession and murder the world of normal reality, a world in which young men are driving young women home after a dance or a movie.

The reader who remembers *Macbeth* may find a parallel in the porter's knocking at the gate just after the murder has been committed. The impact on our imaginations is much the same: through the shock of contrast there comes a renewed sense of the monstrous character of the world into which we have penetrated through our imaginative sympathy with Christmas.

Joe Christmas is not simply a man who has gone berserk. He amounts to much more than his obsession; he is, in his way, observant and aware of what is happening to him. The author uses Joe's awareness very effectively to show us what it is like to undergo his experience. Consider, for example, his sense of being fated and volitionless: he doesn't say that something is going to happen to Joanna Burden; he says, "Something is going to happen to me." There is great psychological truth in this consciousness of his own passiveness and his sense that he is being acted upon rather than acting.

The last incident narrated in Chapter 12 illustrates the fact that one part of Joe remains humanly sensitive and wants to understand. Discovering the gun still in his hand, he does not toss it away immediately, but strikes a match and inspects it. He finds in addition to the cartridge that had misfired a second unexploded cartridge and realizes that Joanna had intended to kill first him and then herself. She had meant what she said: "Maybe it would be better if we both were dead" [p. 263].

Though the relatively brief excerpts that we have printed can be used to illustrate some of Faulkner's fictional techniques and some of his powers as a dramatist, they cannot, of course, provide the experience of the full novel. In particular, they cannot be expected to set forth its basic themes or its complexity. Joe Christmas is only one of the several characters in this novel who have been cut off from the community and have blindly or defiantly tried to hold themselves apart from nature. What part the story of Joe plays in the development of the total meaning of this massive and rich work will have to wait upon a reading of the novel in its totality.

The Fugitives

In the literary awakening of the South, some writers—Faulkner is a signal instance—worked pretty much in isolation; others, within literary communities. One of the most active of these was the group of poets that formed in Nashville, Tennessee, just after the close of the First World War. Two of the leading spirits were John Crowe Ransom and Donald Davidson, both of whom had only recently returned from war service in France. They taught literature at Vanderbilt University, and around them soon gathered the group of poets who were to be known as the Fugitives. Though the group included Vanderbilt faculty and students, it was not university based, and also included a number of townspeople, several of whom were very important in giving the Fugitives their character and direction. (Curiously enough, the Fugitives began their meetings not to discuss poetry, but philosophy.) In 1922 the *Fugitive* was established to publish poems, reviews, and essays on poetry and aesthetics, but it was not a mere house organ. Poets from all over this country and from abroad appeared in the *Fugitive*—poets such as Robert Graves, L. A. G. Strong, Witter Bynner, and, most notably, Hart Crane—before the magazine ceased publication in 1925.[1]

[1] See Louise Cowan, *The Fugitive Group: A Literary History* (1959).

On one matter the Fugitive poets were all agreed: they had no intention of trying to write like Sidney Lanier or Paul Hamilton Hayne. They emphatically repudiated the southern literary tradition that lay immediately behind them, correctly identifying it as their own southern branch of "Victorian" decadence. Yet very soon, the Fugitives were reexamining and reassessing the southern past, attempting to define and revalidate a cultural tradition from which they might draw nourishment. Like Pound and Eliot, the Fugitives found that the unsatisfactory state of poetry, including southern poetry of the preceding generation, forced them to a radical reexamination of culture at large, and that it was impossible to discover an authentic form for their own poetry without raising questions about philosophy and even about politics and economics.

Though the influence of Eliot on the Fugitives was eventually to become powerful, this group of southern poets did not derive from Eliot. Donald Davidson, for example, was never really involved in what is sometimes called the "Eliot revolution." He remained—as a glance at any of his poems will show—not only basically conservative in his attitudes, but also in his verse forms and his poetic strategies. His best poetry is lyrical, romantic, and, in the best sense, old-fashioned, as in "Joe Clisby's Song."

Joe Clisby's Song (1961)

What did my old song say?
Something of youth and desire
And summer passing away;
Yet love is a durable fire
   And will stay.

Must I think a tune like this
Was never made for a time
That reads only lust in a kiss
And shreds the magic of rhyme
   To hit-or-miss?   10

By old Bethel burying-ground
In moonlight passed along
True lovers as ever were found
Who plaited hearts in a song
   Where their voices wound.

Nettie Long and I,
Burt Whitson with his Ruth,
Walked and sang to the high

Church steeple as if youth
    Could never go by.   20

And we walked and sang to the low
Ranks of the good dead people
As if to come or go
Was a fine tune that a steeple
    And they would know.

For the old folks that lie there
We knew were singers all.
They could get a song by ear
And had a fiddle at call
    And friends near.   30

If you would join their song
But fear to raise the sound,
Come walk with Nettie Long
And me, by the burying-ground.
    You'll take no wrong.

Burt Whitson and his Ruth
And many couples more
Can tune the lips of youth
As they did mine before
    To sing the truth.   40

John Crowe Ransom, in his earlier years, was hostile to Eliot's innovations and sharply averse to Eliot's poetry and criticism: his review of *The Waste Land* was one of the most scathing that ever appeared. (Ransom's handsome acknowledgments of Eliot's achievement were to come many years later.)

On younger members of the Fugitive group, such as Allen Tate, Eliot's influence was almost immediately felt; and yet even Tate moved toward Eliot in his own way. Before he had read a word of Eliot he was writing poetry that seemed—even to informed readers—imitative of him.[2] At all events, the Fugitives' analysis of the crisis in culture took its own characteristic form. Their approach was through their own regional culture and they tended to define cultural problems in the light of the southern experience. A few decades earlier, the Irish poet William Butler Yeats had used his provincial culture in much the same way. Later, a number of the Fugitives would recognize the parallel, but the direct influence of Yeats's poetry is to

[2] See John M. Bradbury, *The Fugitives* (1958); and Laura Riding and Robert Graves, *A Survey of Modernist Poetry* (1928).

be seen in the early poetry of only one of them, that of Donald Davidson.

In 1930 some of the Fugitives, joined by other writers, including historians and a psychologist, published *I'll Take My Stand*, twelve essays accompanying a manifesto that warned against industrialization and urged the South not to abandon its character as an agrarian society. The appearance of this book set off hoots of derision and more moderate expressions of simple incredulity: how could men living in the twentieth century talk in this fashion? The machine age was here to stay. One could not turn back the hands of the clock. Few could recognize in the book a serious challenge to the dominant thesis that industrialization was a good thing and that you couldn't have too much of it.[3] Both the Marxists and the General Motors Republicans welcomed industrialization fervently and disagreed only on who was to control it or on whether it needed to be controlled at all.

For the misunderstandings of *I'll Take My Stand*, the Agrarians were in themselves in good part to blame. The essays were not always consistent with one another and little was said about practical applications. And it should have been made clear immediately that *I'll Take My Stand* was not intended as a handbook for political action. (The choice of the term "Agrarian" itself was probably a mistake: it could easily be used to conjure up an absurd picture of every citizen working forty acres behind a mule.) Finally, the very title of the book suggested that the issue was merely southern, whereas it should have been made plain that the South was only one instance—granted that it was for the contributors the most important instance —of a general problem. In 1951 four of the contributors were to make this point explicitly, writing that the "emphasis should have been put more firmly on religion."[4]

[3] We shall be speaking here of the basic theme of the book and not trying to take into account the individual temperaments and the special biases of the individual contributors. If, as we shall argue, the issues raised by the twelve southerners have a universal application, and if the protest against unlimited industrialization reaches far beyond the local circumstances of the late 1920's, we are not suggesting that the book was not heavily influenced by its time and place. A careful analysis would disclose a medley of elements in the book—and occasionally in one and the same essay: a vivid sense of history (as lived in the South), philosophical regionalism, Jeffersonian distrust of the city, and certain elements of southern chauvinism. *I'll Take My Stand* was itself a *historical* document and shows the impress of its time as well as the culture out of which it came. A very interesting discussion of this whole matter—and of the final significance of the Fugitives—is to be found in Lewis P. Simpson's "The Southern Writers and the Great Literary Secession," *Georgia Review* (Winter, 1970).

[4] See *Shenandoah* (Summer, 1951). Several of the twelve southerners who contributed to the symposium wished to call it "Tracts Against Communism." Even with this title, the book probably had no future in 1930. But with a different title, it might have invited a more informed comprehension of what it was really about and it might have proved less vulnerable to irrelevant attacks.

Today, when all of us have become conscious of smoggy air and polluted water, of fouled beaches and industrial wastes that are destroying the ecology; when our overcrowded cities visibly decay and men feel oppressed by a society that seems heartless, impersonal, and regimented under the pressures of automation and of great industrial conglomerates; today, when life itself seems to be disappearing behind a screen of electronic images and plastic surfaces—in such a day would the Agrarians' challenge to industrialization evoke a more receptive response?[5] Probably not. Each generation has its own way of facing up to current evils, and to many, the Agrarian manifesto would seem to have nothing in common with the criticism of the complications of civilization made by Thoreau in the 1840's or that voiced by a modern youth engrossed in Zen Buddhism in the 1970's. Whether these three rather different protests against a machine culture do in fact have much in common does not, for our present purposes, really matter. What does matter is the reader's recognition of the fact that the Fugitive poets manifested a deep concern for the state of civilization as well as for the art of poetry. They were not bloodless esthetes.

At the same time, they were vigilant to maintain the autonomy of poetry and of the arts generally. They insisted that art was not to be regarded as an extension of political theory and that the function of literature was not to provide a substitute for religion or to produce propaganda for an ideology. Such negations are implicit in their own poetry and are, on occasion, stated quite explicitly in their critical essays. Allen Tate, for example, has written that poetry "is neither religion nor social engineering"; and Ransom, in "Poetry: A Note in Ontology," one of his most celebrated essays, tells us that poetry in the service of an idea—"Platonic poetry," he calls it—is only a half-poetry.

[5] We have pointed out elsewhere a recent survey's finding that a majority of city dwellers would prefer to live in a rural, as contrasted with an urban or suburban, environment.

JOHN CROWE RANSOM (1888–   )

Ransom's primary theme, the division within man himself, the split between heart and head, a lesion that accounts for the haunting dualism of man's experience, obviously touches upon the crisis in culture with which so many poets of the twentieth century have been profoundly concerned (see pp. 1805–6). As a man of philosophical disposition and philosophical training, he is thoroughly aware of the Cartesian split (see p. 2090) and the various attempts to heal it, and his first book, *Poems About God* (1919), makes this plain. Pound and Eliot set forth the issues on a world stage as aspects of an international crisis in culture. But Ransom, like Faulkner and Frost, prefers to deal with the problem in a provincial and even pastoral setting. We have already noted how Faulkner, by deliberately choosing as the scene of Joe Christmas's agony of alienation a provincial society, tightly bound up with itself and fiercely local, can give the issue tremendous dramatic tension. We have also remarked earlier how Frost effectively deals with the issues of the great world by examining them against an old-fashioned New England background.

Ransom, however, has his own very special modulation of this technique. He differs markedly from Tate, for example, in his more muted use of the southern material and in the "voice" with which he comments upon the spiritual dilemmas in which his characters find themselves.

But before getting into the matter of the quality of the voice that issues from his special persona and of the particular modulations of that voice, it may be well to establish quite firmly Ransom's basic theme. One might begin with some lines from "Man Without Sense of Direction." Here are the first two stanzas:

Tell this to ladies: how a hero man
Assail a thick and scandalous giant
Who casts true shadow in the sun,
And die, but play no truant.

This is more horrible: that the darling egg

Of the chosen people hatch a creature
Of noblest mind and powerful leg
Who cannot fathom nor perform his nature.

To paraphrase: it is sad to have to relate how a brave man facing a real giant—no illusion, no mere phantom—stands up to him and fights and is killed. But there is something more horrible than the honorable defeat of a dedicated hero.

That is, when a man, sound of limb and mind, does not know who he is and, bewildered as to his proper purposes, cannot fulfill himself as a man—this is horrible indeed. In spite of Ransom's outlandishly ironic way of putting matters, we recognize at once the problem described in Eliot's "Gerontion" or in Tate's "The Mediterranean." Six more lines of the poem will fix the disabling defect beyond any mistaking.

And he writhes like an antique man of bronze
That is beaten by furies visible,
Yet he is punished not knowing his sins
And for his innocence walks in hell.

He flails his arms, he moves his lips:
"Rage have I none, cause, time, nor country—"

The following poem would seem to connect this distemper within man's own psyche rather specifically with the impact of science and scientism on the modern world. But, as the title of the poem suggests, the protagonist is an "explorer," not a man running away from the problem, and the poet's attitude toward his plight is complex, not simple.

Persistent Explorer (1927)

The noise of water teased his literal ears
Which heard the distant drumming and thus scored:
Water is falling—it fell—therefore it roared.
However: That is more than water I hear!

He went still higher, and on the dizzy brink
His eyes confirmed with vision what he had heard:
This is but tumbling water. Again he demurred:

That was not only water flashing, I think.

But listen as he might, look fast or slow,
It was water, only water, tons of it   10
Dropping into the gorge, and every bit
Was water—the insipid chemical H_2O.

Its thunder smote him somewhat as the loud
Words of the god that rang around a man
Walking by the Mediterranean.
Its cloud of froth was whiter than the cloud

That clothed the goddess sliding down the air
Unto a mountain shepherd, white as she
That issued from the smoke refulgently.
The cloud was, but the goddess was not there.　20

Tremendous the sound was but there was no
　voice
That spoke to him. Furious the spectacle
But it spelled nothing, there was not any spell
Bidding him whether cower or rejoice.

What would he have it spell? He scarcely
　knew;
Only that water and nothing but water filled
His eyes and ears, nothing but water that
　spilled;
And if the smoke and rattle of water drew

From the deep thickets of his mind the train,
The fierce fauns and the timid tenants there,　30
That burst their bonds and rushed upon the
　air,
Why, he must turn and beat them down
　again.

So be it. And no unreasonable outcry
The pilgrim made; only a rueful grin
Spread over his lips until he drew them in;
He did nót sit upon a rock and die.

There were many ways of dying; witness, if he
Commit himself to the water, and descend
Wrapped in the water, turn water at the end
And flow with a great water out to sea.　40

But there were many ways of living too,
And let his enemies gibe, but let them say

Morning (1927)

Jane awoke Ralph so gently on one morning
That first, before the true householder
　Learning
Came back to tenant in the haunted head,
He lay upon his back and let his stare
Penetrate dazedly into the blue air
That swam all round his bed,
And in the blessed silence nothing was said.

Then his eyes travelled through the window
And lit, enchantedly, on such a meadow
Of wings and light and clover,　10
He would propose to Jane then to go walking

That he would throw this continent away
And seek another country,—as he would do.

　The explorer means to live, and he means to
persist in his search. To find what? To find a
"continent" in which one can live as a whole
man, with heart and mind both satisfied and
the total man completely fulfilled. We shall
mistake the meaning of the poem, however, if we
take it that the speaker means to deny science
its due in the human economy: science gives
truth, a very important truth, but not necessarily the whole truth about reality. As poet, the
persistent explorer will seek to discover a kind
of poetry apt to the modern occasion, a poetry
that will satisfy both mind and heart. In his
essay "Poetry: A Note in Ontology" (reprinted
in our section "Intellectual Backgrounds") Ransom calls such poetry Metaphysical (in contrast
to Physical and Platonic) Poetry and defines
its intention thus: "to *complement* science"
[italics ours].
　The aspect of reality that is denied in reducing the waterfall to a physico-chemical process
is that which can only be apprehended by the
imagination, whether the historical, the religious, or the poetic imagination A pressing problem of the modern world is that the imagination
is threatened with starvation.
　A failure of the imagination—though one not
directly caused by a too literal acceptance of
modern science—is dramatized neatly in the
little poem entitled "Morning."

Through the green waves, and to be singing
　not talking;
Such imps were pranking over
Him helpless lying in bed beneath a cover.

Suddenly he remembered about himself,
His manliness returned entire to Ralph;
The dutiful mills of the brain
Began to whir with their smooth-grinding
　wheels
And the sly visitors wriggled off like eels;
He rose and was himself again,　20
Simply another morning, and simply Jane.

Waked out of sleep, Ralph finds himself lying almost dazed, in a "blessed silence." All about him is a world of magic. The scene through the window is one of enchantment; mere speech seems insufficient, the occasion calls for singing —and then "Suddenly he remembered about himself." The situation is in one respect like that in "Persistent Explorer." The explorer knew that he ought to beat back the fauns and nymphs that emerge from the "deep thickets of his mind." Ralph, as a good modern, also knows what he should do and he does it. The enchantment dissipates itself and there is before him "Simply another morning, and simply Jane."

Yet in emphasizing the division in man's nature and the dualism in his experience, one does not want to diminish Ransom's poems into mere pronouncements of a thesis. In Ransom's poetry the play of tone has everything to do with the meaning. It qualifies what each poem "says." What is the quality, the "voice" that speaks through these poems? Or, to put the question in slightly different terms, who is the person who is speaking them, and in what tone of voice does he speak? What is the persona (or the mask) that the poet adopts?

Ransom discovered his appropriate voice very early in his poetry. It is that of the scholar, his head full of learned and often recondite terms, though he is usually speaking about a situation which is not sophisticated and may even be bucolic or pastoral. One might almost call the ironically and playfully assumed mask that of the pedant[1] through which the reader is expected to glimpse the face of the man. (In some of his poems the mask is better described as that of the provincial philosopher or the old-fashioned schoolteacher.) Certainly no other modern—and Ransom is quite precisely that— uses such a vocabulary, unless it be the early

Wallace Stevens. For example, in a poem entitled "To a Lady Celebrating Her Birthday" he can write

> This day smells mortuary more than most
> To me upon my post.

Or of an aged oak tree, in the first version of "Vaunting Oak": " 'Largely, the old gentleman is,' I grieved, 'cadaver. . . .' " Or in "Captain Carpenter," speaking of the valiant, foolishly quixotic captain, finally killed in combat:

> The curse of hell upon the sleek upstart
> That got the Captain finally on his back
> And took the red red vitals of his heart
> And made the kites to whet their beaks clack
>   clack.

Vocabulary, syntax, imagery, and rhythm, not to mention the range of reference and the varieties of dramatic context in individual poems, all give quality and definition to the voice and establish the aesthetic distance between the scene observed and the persona who observes it. Distance is important: for example, if the poet stands too close to Captain Carpenter, so close that we are in danger of confusing his voice and his values with those of the Captain, we won't get the humor and the pathos of Carpenter's bravery and folly. We might mistakenly assume that the poet expected us to take the Captain's vaunts at face value or for us to respond to the death scene with unqualified sorrow.

In Ransom's poetry, we may say, the characteristic tenderness, the charity, the pitifulness with which he describes his characters, appears, paradoxically, only when the persona is more rigorously detached from the world of the subjects: that is, when the observer is located at a greater distance. Thus irony—and here we may call irony a kind of index of the distance, a mark of uninvolvement—makes the tenderness, the involvement, possible. The tension between the irony and tenderness, between the impulse to withdraw and the impulse to approach, becomes a fundamental aspect of the drama of the poetry.

---

[1] In a poem called "Miller's Daughter," the speaker in a kind of ecstasy of self-deprecation describes his persona: "poor bookish hind,/Who come by fabulous roads around the hill/To bring the famous daughter of the mill/No combs to sell, no corn to grind,/But too much pudding in my head/Of learned characters . . ./And words vain to be said."

Ransom's celebrated irony is, therefore, not a device for condescending to his characters or deflating the painfulness of the situation. In "Janet Waking" it provides a way for the poet to keep his tenderness toward the little girl from becoming mawkish, or his admiration for Captain Carpenter's ridiculous hardihood from becoming itself an extravagance, or his sympathy for the plight of his explorer from becoming a romantic cry of dismay. The narrator of these fables of the human condition is both involved and not involved—close enough in his sympathy to be moved and yet sufficiently detached to see the situation clearly and on an appropriate scale. Earlier we spoke of Ransom's theme of the need to reconcile heart and head, intellect and emotion, and we may regard his special use of irony as a way of reconciling these two often divided and warring aspects of man's mind.

To what extent is Ransom to be regarded as a southern poet? Like Faulkner and Frost, he has preferred to engage the problems of the age not in an international but in a provincial and even rural setting. Yet how specifically has he identified the province in question? Not, it must be said at once, in many specific local color de-

tails. There are a few scattered through the poems. In "Lady Lost" there is a reference to the "West End" section of Nashville; in "Two in August," a reference to the hackberry trees of the South; in "Nocturne," to a gentleman in a seersucker coat. In "Conrad in Twilight," after references to a garden that might exist almost anywhere, we get a passage like the following:

Autumn days in our section
Are the most used-up thing on earth . . .
Having no more color nor predilection
Than corn stalks too wet for the fire. . . .

The passage might just possibly refer to the Middle West, and yet, as a whole, it has an unmistakable southern flavor. The flavor comes from the diction, the locutions, the speech rhythm, but not from any specific reference. In general Ransom does not evoke the southern scene directly but at a remove. This is Ransom's general strategy even in poems that deal specifically with the South.

Consider "Antique Harvesters." Here is one of the few of his poems in which Ransom comments on the South as a special subculture.

Antique Harvesters (1927)

(SCENE: *Of the Mississippi the bank sinister, and of the Ohio the bank sinister.*)

Tawny are the leaves turned but they still
    hold,
And it is harvest; what shall this land
    produce?
A meager hill of kernels, a runnel of juice;
Declension looks from our land, it is old.
Therefore let us assemble, dry, grey, spare,
And mild as yellow air.

"I hear the croak of a raven's funeral wing."
The young men would be joying in the song
Of passionate birds; their memories are not
    long.
What is it thus rehearsed in sable? "Nothing."   10
Trust not but the old endure, and shall be
    older
Than the scornful beholder.

We pluck the spindling ears and gather the
    corn.
One spot has special yield? "On this spot
    stood
Heroes and drenched it with their only
    blood."
And talk meets talk, as echoes from the horn
Of the hunter—echoes are the old men's arts,
Ample are the chambers of their hearts.

Here come the hunters, keepers of a rite;
The horn, the hounds, the lank mares cours-
    ing by   20
Straddled with archetypes of chivalry;
And the fox, lovely ritualist, in flight
Offering his unearthly ghost to quarry;
And the fields, themselves to harry.

Resume, harvesters. The treasure is full bronze

Which you will garner for the Lady, and the
  moon
Could tinge it no yellower than does this
  noon;
But grey will quench it shortly—the field,
  men, stones.
Pluck fast, dreamers; prove as you amble
  slowly
Not less than men, not wholly.   30

Bare the arm, dainty youths, bend the knees
Under bronze burdens. And by an autumn
  tone
As by a grey, as by a green, you will have
  known
Your famous Lady's image; for so have these;
And if one say that easily will your hands
More prosper in other lands,

Angry as wasp-music be your cry then:
"Forsake the Proud Lady, of the heart of fire,
The look of snow, to the praise of a dwindled
  choir,
Song of degenerate specters that were men?   40
The sons of the fathers shall keep her, worthy
  of
What these have done in love."

True, it is said of our Lady, she ageth.
But see, if you peep shrewdly, she hath not
  stooped;
Take no thought of her servitors that have
  drooped,
For we are nothing; and if one talk of death—
Why, the ribs of the earth subsist frail as a
  breath
If but God wearieth.

On one level the poem is thoroughly realistic:
the poet makes plain that this is a region of
relative poverty, the very region that Franklin
Delano Roosevelt, a few years later, in the
1930's, was to proclaim the country's "economic
problem number one." But at another level,
the poem is not realistic at all. The South is
seen through a screen of metaphors; it is made
remote and mythic. (Since the theme is the
myth of the South, what the poet has done is
perfectly appropriate.)

Most important of all, since the poem has to
do with regional piety, it is worth noting that
the poem is written by the person who is both
inside and outside the myth. If there is a very
deep local patriotism manifested in the poem,
there is also something very like an ironical reduction of the official southern rhetoric. The
poem is written in defiance of the "scornful beholder." It defends the myth; yet it comes close
to turning some of the more picturesque defenders into Quixotes: the lank mares that the fox-
hunters ride are "straddled with archetypes of
chivalry."

The myth is put forward very frankly as a
myth. The old South is invoked as a lady, now
not young, though the speaker claims that she
still has a heart of fire. She is still to be praised,
even though the company of those who render
the praise has dwindled. In this connection, the
last stanza is very significant. Why should her
dwindling retinue support a cause that is obviously lost. Why are they not to be dismayed by
the death of the lady's servitors. Because the
only values that matter are the spiritual values.
They subsist even when the world of flesh and
blood as we know it has disappeared.

The last lines of the poem seem to make a
clear reference to the philosophy of Bishop
Berkeley (1685–1753), who argued that the content of all sense data is subjective and that it
is not to be trusted as necessarily giving a
true report of a nonsubjective world. Once I
turn my eyes from looking at the tree in the
quadrangle, I do not *know* that it continues to
exist. That it does so, must be accepted on the
report of others or held by me as a matter of
faith. Only his thoughts are real to the thinker,
and we human beings have our existence guaranteed only insofar as we are thoughts in the
mind of God. If God ceased to think of us,
we and the world we inhabit would disappear
like smoke, "frail as a breath."

The proud lady's existence was obviously an
article of faith to the dead soldiers in Tate's
"Ode to the Confederate Dead" and it will be
interesting to compare Ransom's poem on the
South and its claim on the southerner's allegiance with Tate's "Ode" (see p. 2663). The
themes of the two poems balance each other. As

we shall see, Tate's man at the gate, who meditates on the heroic world of the dead soldiers, has lost his access to the faith that he is certain that they held. On the other hand, the persona who speaks Ransom's poem still participates in the myth of the South and has a defense against the attack that "science" and modernism make upon it. But two things need to be observed: Tate's observer is unhappy in his disbelief and is thoroughly aware of the penalties that are attached to such a radical loss of faith. For the forces that have destroyed his faith in this myth make it impossible to believe in any myth. The acids of modernity make no distinction.

Ransom's observer, on the other hand, in the very act of putting himself into an invulnerable position with reference to his belief, has indicated quietly, through a whole reverberation of ironies, that he is aware of how fragile his position is. In fact, Ransom's tribute to regional piety, though sincere and moving, is anything but naive.

F. O. Matthiessen has provided a very perceptive reading of "Antique Harvesters." After remarking on the "contemplative distance" set up by the word "antique" in the title, and by the "bank sinister" in setting the scene, he contrasts with these ironical "literary" devices other elements: in the words "runnel" and "meager" we hear, he says, the "old-fashioned expressions [of] the Elizabethan or seventeenth-century usage that was brought to this country by the first settlers and that has disappeared now except for remote rural and mountain areas, especially in the South" (see pp. 1173–74). And there are in the poem also the "elaborate, courtly phrases of an older public speech: 'Therefore let us assemble.'"

The contemplative distance of which Matthiessen speaks, and the literary devices that go with it, can be covered by the summary term "classicism." The literary models of the older southern culture were the classics, and Ransom's study at Oxford of the Latin and Greek poets would have reinforced his predilection for such "distance," balance, and restraint. But one must be careful not to suggest that Ransom's classicism was imposed upon him from without. As we have just remarked, his "classical" quality is the response of a particular mind reacting to a special cultural situation, where a balance between loving engagement and cool detachment is appropriate and where the very motive of his poetic expression is to effect a mediation between intellect and emotion and between the local scene in its temporal particularity and a universal and timeless condition. There is a loving interplay between man and his heritage, the drama of "difference from" and "identification with." Though Ransom's classicism shows as a pervasive quality throughout his poetry, it is especially to be remarked in such poems as "Vision by Sweetwater" or "Antique Harvesters."

We have commented earlier on the value of the writer's being both inside and outside his tradition. "Antique Harvesters," in virtue of what has just been said in the preceding paragraph, illustrates Ransom's characteristic stance in relation to his material. It will also serve to illustrate another characteristic of Ransom's poetry. Though the southern tradition is important for him, he values it as a point of reference rather than as a field of concentration. It is the larger, more universal issue, that of Everyman's dualism rather than some local (southern) instance of it that is his ultimate target.

He treats this dominant theme in different contexts and with varying grades of irony. In "The Equilibrists," for example, he contemplates richly, sensitively, and yet also wittily two lovers caught between the claims of the body and the claims of the spirit.

In one of his prose works, Ransom has called lust the "science" of sex, and love the "aesthetic" of sex. Science is indeed "power knowledge," as Bertrand Russell has called it, and has to do with the most efficient way to gratify, and thus dispose of, an appetite. Love, on the other hand, is at once a more massive and a more delicate experience. The lover is willing to postpone gratification of the physical desire in order to become fully involved in the total world that is informed with his mistress's presence. In "The Equilibrists" the lovers do find a precarious balance between the claims of body and spirit, but it is one that costs a great deal, and perhaps costs too much. Though the speaker of the poem may seem to put the seal of his approval upon it, the sensitive reader will hesitate to accept the approval at face value; after all, the lovers have failed in life. The speaker's attitude toward the lovers is in fact rather complex, and the great merit of the poem resides in the fullness, delicacy, and yet hard-headed realism with which their situation is viewed and, by implication, appraised.

Ransom divides the poems contained in his third volume, *Two Gentlemen in Bonds* (1927), into three groups: "The Innocence of Doves," "The Manliness of Men," and "Two Gentlemen in Bonds." A poem such as "Janet Waking" is put in the first division, for poems of this sort may be said to present the gentle and the innocent caught in the cleft stick of the world. (In this poem a little girl has her initiation into the meaning of death.) These are poems of pity, though a pity that never degenerates into sentimentality. The emotion is responsible and restrained. The mode is that of understatement, not exaggeration; the outlines are hard and clear, not soft and penumbrous.

In the poems of the second group, the observer or the commentator on the situation is the most important single element. In fact, his "manliness" shows itself in his ability to comprehend, respond to, and yet in some sense come to terms with the situation. A poem such as "The Equilibrists" will obviously fall into this classification. So also will "Persistent Explorer" and "Antique Harvesters." But one can illustrate the distinction between the first and second group perhaps most sharply by saying that though "Janet Waking" properly falls in the first section, had "Bells for John Whiteside's Daughter," Ransom's celebrated poem about the death of a little girl, been published in the 1927 volume, it would surely have been put in the second. For the matter of focus in "Bells" is the observer's reaction (which serves to direct the reader's reaction) to the child's

death. To sum up, the poems of "The Manliness of Men" are the philosophical ones, those about the poet and his knowledge of, and appropriate attitude toward, the world he must live in. They acknowledge a deep sense of the human bond and a compassion for failure and suffering. The poems in "The Innocence of Doves" are about the victims of the world, who suffer without knowledge, without philosophy.

Though Ransom has not chosen to reprint the series of sonnets which make up his third division, the name that he gives to this division, "Two Gentlemen in Bonds," fixes our attention on the dualism within man. The two gentlemen, though bound together in brotherhood, find it difficult to live together. Paul is the body, carnal, appetitive, moving to instant gratification of his appetite. Abbot is pale, spectral, introverted, not merely idealistic but puritanical in his asceticism. (Perhaps the poet has never reprinted the poems in this third group because he feels that the schematization is put too sharply, too abstractly. But the conflict presented here in allegorical fashion turns up in more oblique and subtle forms in much of Ransom's poetry.)

Yet in contrast with a poet such as Eliot or Tate, Ransom tends to see the cleft in man as having existed from the beginning and as having been only exacerbated by the pressures of the contemporary world. Eliot and Tate would state the matter in terms of the Christian tradition: man is a fallen being, still yearning for the harmony with himself and the rapport with nature which he enjoyed before the Fall. In Ransom's poetry, particularly in that which he has preferred to revise and reprint, speculations about any original lapse are muted. His stress falls upon an internal division which he takes to be a given of the human experience and which he sometimes seems to regard as a necessary condition for man's mature fulfillment of his potentialities. The religiousness in Ransom lingers mainly as a deep piety with respect to nature, to custom and tradition, to his own nurturing, to his early friends. It expresses itself perhaps also in his recognition of the need for self-discipline and for disinterested contemplation if man is to find a satisfying relationship to the world about him. Thus his stance is humanistic and secular, but his concern is similar to that of most religionists of whatever doctrine: to help man achieve wholeness of spirit and a satisfactory relationship to the world in which he finds himself.

BIOGRAPHICAL CHART

1888 Born, April 30, in Pulaski, Tennessee
1909 Receives B.A., Vanderbilt University
1913 Receives B.A. (Honors), Oxford University, in Literae Humaniores (classical studies)
1914–37 Member of English faculty, Vanderbilt University
1917–19 Serves as first lieutenant, Field Artillery, U.S. Army
1919 *Poems About God*
1922–25 Edits and contributes to the *Fugitive*
1924 *Chills and Fever* (poems)
1927 *Two Gentlemen in Bonds* (poems)
1930 *God Without Thunder: An Unorthodox Defense of Orthodoxy*
1937–58 Carnegie Professor of Poetry, Kenyon College
1938 *The World's Body* (criticism)

1939 Founds the *Kenyon Review* and remains editor until 1961
1941 *The New Criticism*
1945 *Selected Poems*
1951 Receives Bollingen prize in poetry and Russell Loines prize in literature from the National Academy of Arts and Letters
1962 Receives Fellowship prize from the American Academy of Poets
1963 *Selected Poems* (a number of the poems are revised)
1965 Elected to the National Institute of Arts and Letters
1966 Elected to the American Academy of Arts and Letters
1972 *Beating the Bushes*

FURTHER READINGS

There is no standard edition of Ransom's works. Individual titles are cited in the biographical chart.

John M. Bradbury, *The Fugitives* (1958)
Robert Wooster Stallman, "John Crowe Ransom: A Checklist," *Sewanee Review* (1948)
Robert Buffington, *The Equilibrists: A Study of John Crowe Ransom's Poems, 1916–63* (1967)

Louise Cowan, *The Fugitive Group: A Literary History* (1959)
John L. Stewart, *The Burden of Time* (1965)
———, *John Crowe Ransom* (1962)
Miller Williams, *The Poetry of John Crowe Ransom* (1972)
Thomas Daniel Young, ed., *John Crowe Ransom: Critical Essays and a Bibliography* (1968)

Agitato ma non troppo (1924; 1963)

We print here the first version of the poem. The title, translated literally, means "agitated [or shaken] but not too much." It is a technical phrase used in music to denote the spirit in which a composition is to be played. In lines 5 and 6 the poet may have in mind such romantic poems as William Butler Yeats published in his *Wind Among the Reeds*, poems like "He Reproves the Curlew" or "He Hears the Cry of the Sedge."

"Agitato ma non troppo" describes the spirit of nearly all of Ransom's poems. One senses a control, a discipline, a keeping of the voice down.

This is what the man said,
Insisting, standing on his head.

I have a grief,
It was not stolen like a thief,
Albeit I have no bittern by the lake
To cry it up and down the brake.

None there has been like Dante's fury
When Beatrice was given him to bury;
Except, when the young heart was hit, you
  know
How Percy Shelley's reed sang tremolo.   10

"Yes, there is grief in his mind,
But where is his fair child moaning in the
  wind?

Where is the white frost snowing on his
  head?
When did he stalk and weep and not loll in
  his bed?"

I will be brief,
Assuredly I have a grief,
And I am shaken; but not as a leaf.

Judith of Bethulia (1924)

The story of Judith is told in the Book of Judith, one of the apochryphal books of the Bible.
Holofernes, a general in the service of Nebuchad-
nezzar, is besieging the Hebrew city of Bethulia.
The leaders of the city are about to surrender
when Judith, a beautiful young widow, asks to
be allowed to try to gain entry into the general's
tent to kill him. In a sense this is Ransom's
most "romantic" poem, but it is interesting that
even here he hints at a complexity in Judith's
motives beyond mere patriotism.

Beautiful as the flying legend of some leopard
She had not yet chosen her great captain or
  prince
Depositary to her flesh, and our defense;
And a wandering beauty is a blade out of its
  scabbard.
You know how dangerous, gentlemen of three-
  score?
May you know it yet ten more.

Nor by process of veiling she grew the less
  fabulous.
Grey or blue veils, we were desperate to study
The invincible emanations of her white body,
And the winds at her ordered raiment were
  ominous.   10
Might she walk in the market, sit in the coun-
  cil of soldiers?
Only of the extreme elders.

But a rare chance was the girl's then, when
  the Invader
Trumpeted from the south, and rumbled from
  the north,
Beleaguered the city from four quarters of the
  earth,
Our soldiery too craven and sick to aid her—

Where were the arms could countervail this
  horde?
Her beauty was the sword.

She sat with the elders, and proved on their
  blear visage
How bright was the weapon unrusted in her
  keeping,   20
While he lay surfeiting on their harvest
  heaping,
Wasting the husbandry of their rarest vintage—
And dreaming of the broad-breasted dames
  for concubine?
These floated on his wine.

He was lapped with bay-leaves, and grass and
  fumiter weed,
And from under the wine-film encountered
  his mortal vision,
For even within his tent she accomplished his
  derision;
She loosed one veil and another, standing unafraid;
And he perished. Nor brushed her with even
  so much as a daisy?
She found his destruction easy.   30

The heathen are all perished. The victory
  was furnished,
We smote them hiding in our vineyards,
  barns, annexes,
And now their white bones clutter the holes
  of foxes,
And the chieftain's head, with grinning sock-
  ets, and varnished—
Is it hung on the sky with a hideous epitaphy?
No, the woman keeps the trophy.

May God send unto our virtuous lady her
  prince.
It is stated she went reluctant to that orgy,
Yet a madness fevers our young men, and

not the clergy
Nor the elders have turned them unto mod-
esty since.   40

Captain Carpenter (1924)

The poem takes the form of a sort of fairy tale,
one that apparently Ransom made up for himself. The reader might ponder the exact tone of
this poem. Surely there is admiration for Captain Carpenter and pity for his fate; but the
persona is also thoroughly aware of the Captain's folly and even of a certain tendency in
him to boast of his prowess. A number of elements in the poem contribute to the special tone:
among them, the use of archaic diction, the
atmosphere of a rather primitive folk ballad,
and the mingling of heroic and colloquial diction.

Captain Carpenter rose up in his prime
Put on his pistols and went riding out
But had got wellnigh nowhere at that time
Till he fell in with ladies in a rout.

It was a pretty lady and all her train
That played with him so sweetly but before
An hour she'd taken a sword with all her main
And twined him of his nose for evermore.

Captain Carpenter mounted up one day
And rode straightway into a stranger rogue   10
That looked unchristian but be that as may
The Captain did not wait upon prologue.

But drew upon him out of his great heart
The other swung against him with a club
And cracked his two legs at the shinny part
And let him roll and stick like any tub.

Captain Carpenter rode many a time
From male and female took he sundry harms
He met the wife of Satan crying "I'm
The she-wolf bids you shall bear no more
  arms."   20

Their strokes and counters whistled in the
  wind
I wish he had delivered half his blows
But where she should have made off like a
  hind

Inflamed by the thought of her naked beauty
  with desire?
Yes, and chilled with fear and despair.

The bitch bit off his arms at the elbows.

And Captain Carpenter parted with his ears
To a black devil that used him in this wise
O Jesus ere his threescore and ten years
Another had plucked out his sweet blue eyes.

Captain Carpenter got up on his roan
And sallied from the gate in hell's despite   30
I heard him asking in the grimmest tone
If any enemy yet there was to fight?

"To any adversary it is fame
If he risk to be wounded by my tongue
Or burnt in two beneath my red heart's flame
Such are the perils he is cast among.

"But if he can he has a pretty choice
From an anatomy with little to lose
Whether he cut my tongue and take my voice
Or whether it be my round red heart he
  choose."   40

It was the neatest knave that ever was seen
Stepping in perfume from his lady's bower
Who at this word put in his merry mien
And fell on Captain Carpenter like a tower.

I would not knock old fellows in the dust
But there lay Captain Carpenter on his back
His weapons were the old heart in his bust
And a blade shook between rotten teeth alack.

The rogue in scarlet and grey soon knew his
  mind
He wished to get his trophy and depart   50
With gentle apology and touch refined
He pierced him and produced the Captain's
  heart.

God's mercy rest on Captain Carpenter now
I thought him Sirs an honest gentleman
Citizen husband soldier and scholar enow
Let jangling kites eat of him if they can.

But God's deep curses follow after those
That shore him of his goodly nose and ears
His legs and strong arms at the two elbows
And eyes that had not watered seventy years.   60

The curse of hell upon the sleek upstart
That got the Captain finally on his back
And took the red red vitals of his heart

And made the kites to whet their beaks clack
clack.

Vision by Sweetwater (1927)

It is interesting to speculate on what kind of poem "Vision by Sweetwater" would be without the last two lines. Certainly it would be charming, beautifully rendered, nostalgic, and haunting. But the last lines shock us and they raise questions. Why is the boy rendered "old" suddenly? Because, we may say, the scream hints at some terror, loss, or pain. The scream suddenly bursting forth after the prattle of the girls in their "strange quick tongue" contains the tragic utterance that life may come to demand. The narrator, as a young boy, is outside the world of the girls, fascinated but uncomprehending, shy but yearning toward their mystery. When the scream rings out, it is charged for him, not only with terror and pain, but also with sexuality. It represents the emergence of a darker reality that violates the innocent "dream of ladies sweeping by" and chills into sudden silence the gay, innocent festival of the "bright virgins" moving by the water in their "delicate paces," as on a frieze.

Some of the power of the last lines comes from the fact that we do not know which of the girls screamed or why. The scream's anonymity is an index to its archetypal quality—it is nameless and ineluctable. It is as if the scream had been hidden in "one of the white throats"— biding its time, as though lying in wait or as though expressive of some sense of guilt.

The poet has been very cunning in stressing the anonymity of the scream: he writes, not "From one of the white throats among which it hid," but "From one of the white throats which it hid among." By coming to rest on the word "among," the poem suggests that the cry could belong to the throat of any one of the girls, and this is a way of saying that it belongs to all and will, in the course of life, leap from each and all. The person who speaks the poem is now a man looking back on that first scream which he now understands and knows perhaps too well.

Go and ask Robin to bring the girls over
To Sweetwater, said my Aunt; and that was
    why
It was like a dream of ladies sweeping by
The willows, clouds, deep meadowgrass, and
    the river.

Robin's sisters and my Aunt's lily daughter
Laughed and talked, and tinkled light as
    wrens
If there were a little colony all hens
To go walking by the steep turn of Sweet-
    water.

Let them alone, dear Aunt, just for one minute
Till I go fishing in the dark of my mind: 10
Where have I seen before, against the wind,
These bright virgins, robed and bare of bonnet,

Flowing with music of their strange quick
    tongue
And adventuring with delicate paces by the
    stream,—
Myself a child, old suddenly at the scream
From one of the white throats which it hid
    among?

Spiel of the Three Mountebanks (1924)

In a special sense this is one of the most "southern" of Ransom's poems. It derives from a different stratum of the South than, say, a poem like "Old Mansion" or "Antique Harvesters."

The three mountebanks are three hot gospelers who speak the rhetoric heard in annual "revivals" held in brush arbors or in tents set up outside villages or small towns of the South.

A mountebank is one who sells quack medicines at a fair or on the street after collecting a crowd by putting on a performance of some sort. The "medicine" that these fellows are selling claims to be spiritual. This poem is one of a number of Ransom's acerb comments on certain aspects of Protestantism.

As usual with Ransom, the diction is not literal and realistic, but heightened, archaicized, distanced. The persistent aggressive quality of the sermons is beautifully caught. The virtues celebrated by the mountebanks are faith, patience, and meekness.

THE SWARTHY ONE—
<blockquote>
Villagers who gather round,
This is Fides,[1] my lean hound.
Bring your bristled village curs
To try his fang and tooth, sweet sirs!
He will rend them, he is savage,
Thinking nothing but to ravage,
Nor with cudgel, fire, rope,
May ye control my misanthrope;
He would tear the moon in the sky
And fly at Heaven, could he fly.   10
And for his ravening without cease
I have had of him no peace;
Only once I bared the knife
To quit my devil of his life,
But listen, how I heard him say,
"Think you I shall die today?
Since your mother cursed and died,
I am keeping at your side,
We are firmly knit together,
Two ends tugging at one tether,   20
And you shall see when I shall die
That you are mortal even as I."
Bring your stoutest-hearted curs
If ye would risk him, gentle sirs.
</blockquote>

THE THICK ONE—
<blockquote>
Countrymen, here's a noble frame,
Humphrey is my elephant's name.
When my father's back was bent
Under steep impediment,
Humphrey came to my possession,
With patient strength for all his passion. 30
Have ye a mountain to remove?
</blockquote>

[1] *Fides* is the Latin word for faith and sounds the more natural here because it echoes Fido, a familiar name for a dog.

<blockquote>
It is Humphrey's dearest love.
Pile his burden to the skies,
Loose a pestilence of flies,
Foot him in the quick morass
Where no laden beast can pass,
He will staunch his weariless back
And march unswerving on the track.
Have ye seen a back so wide,
So impenetrable hide?   40
Nor think ye by this Humphrey hill
Prince Hamlet bare his fardels ill?
Myself I like it not for us
To wear beneath an incubus,
I take offence, but in no rage
May I dispose my heritage;
Though in good time the vast and tough
Shall sink and totter fast enough.
So pile your population up,
They are a drop in Humphrey's cup;   50
Add all your curses to his pack
To make one straw for Humphrey's back.
</blockquote>

THE PALE ONE—
<blockquote>
If ye remark how poor I am,
Come, citizens, behold my lamb!
Have ye a lion, ounce, or scourge,
Or any beast of dainty gorge?
Agnus lays his tender youth
Between the very enemy's mouth.
And though he sniff his delicate meat
He may not bruise that flesh nor eat.   60
He may not rend him limb from limb
If Agnus do but bleat on him.
Fierce was my youth, but like a dream
I saw a temple and a stream,
And where I knelt and washed my sore,
This infant lamb stood on the shore,
He mounted with me from the river,
And still he cries, as brave as ever:
"Lay me down by the lion's side
To match my frailty with his pride.   70
Fain would I welter in my blood
To teach these lions true lionhood."
So daily Agnus would be slain
But daily is denied again,
And still the hungry lions range
While Agnus waits upon a change;
Only the coursing lions die
And in their deserts mortify.
So bring us lion, leopard, bear,
To try of Agnus without fear,   80
And ye less gentle than I am,
Come, be instructed of my Lamb.
</blockquote>

Bells for John Whiteside's Daughter (1924)

The first stanza involves two clichés: first, "Heavens, won't that child ever be still; she is driving me distracted"; and second, "She was such an active, healthy-looking child that you couldn't believe that she would just up and die." In this confrontation with reality, the second cliché turns out to be a savagely ironical answer to the first: the child you wished would be still is now still indeed.

One can describe the business of the next three stanzas in this fashion. First, they make us believe more fully in the child and therefore in the fact of the grief for her death. They "prove" that grief, and they show the delicious quality of the lost world which will never look quite the same from the high window. On the other hand, they "transcend" the grief, or at least give a hint of a means for transcending the immediate anguish: the lost world is in one sense redeemed out of time; it enters the pages of the picture book where geese speak, where the untrue is true, where the fleeting is made permanent. The three stanzas, then, to state matters in another way, have validated the first stanza and prepared for the last.

They have made it possible for us to say, when the bell tolls, that "we are ready." Some kind of terms, perhaps not the best terms possible, but some kind, have been made with the savage underlying irony. But the terms arrived at do not keep the occasion from being a "stern" one. If in the end, we can transcend the immediate anguish, it is only because of an exercise of will and self-control. Because we control ourselves, we can say "vexed" and not utter some more powerful and desperate word. The word, by the way, itself picks up the first

of the domestic clichés on which the poem is based—the outburst of impatience at the naughty child who, by dying, has performed her most serious piece of naughtiness. But now the word comes to us charged with the burden of the poem; further, as reechoed here by the phrase "brown study," charged by the sentence in which it occurs: we are gathered formally, ritualistically, sternly together to say the word "vexed." "Vexed" becomes indeed the ritualistic, the summarizing word, for the observer who speaks the poem.[1]

There was such speed in her little body,
And such lightness in her footfall,
It is no wonder her brown study
Astonishes us all.

Her wars were bruited in our high window.
We looked among orchard trees and beyond
Where she took arms against her shadow,
Or harried unto the pond

The lazy geese, like a snow cloud
Dripping their snow on the green grass,   10
Tricking and stopping, sleepy and proud,
Who cried in goose, Alas,

For the tireless heart within the little
Lady with rod that made them rise
From their noon apple-dreams and scuttle
Goose-fashion under the skies!

But now go the bells, and we are ready,
In one house we are sternly stopped
To say we are vexed at her brown study,
Lying so primly propped.   20

[1] In this connection, observe the effect of the word "scare" in Frost's poem "Desert Places," included in our text.

Janet Waking (1927)

The world depicted here, Janet's world, is that of a well-kept American suburb. In order to accomplish his purpose, the poet has not needed to keep the atmosphere of suburbia out of the poem. In fact, one of the tensions of the poem

is that between the safe, well-ordered, eventless world and the unpredictable and troubling event that breaks into it. The death of the hen is not, of course, tragic to the father, and the use of the mock-heroic account of Old Chucky's

demise is sufficient warrant of that fact. But
the little girl is baffled by death and "would not
be instructed" in its ways.

"Could not be instructed" would alter the
meaning for the worse: for *would* hints at a
certain willfulness, an element of resistance, in
the little girl's refusal to accept the fact of
death. The poet's sure control of language is
also exhibited in his choice of the word "instructed." "Instructed" is the key word in this
poem in much the same way that "vexed" is
the key word in "Bells for John Whiteside's
Daughter."

Beautifully Janet slept
Till it was deeply morning. She woke then
And thought about her dainty-feathered hen,
To see how it had kept.

One kiss she gave her mother.
Only a small one gave she to her daddy
Who would have kissed each curl of his shin-
   ing baby;
No kiss at all for her brother.

"Old Chucky, old Chucky!" she cried,
Running across the world upon the grass   10
To Chucky's house, and listening. But alas,
Her Chucky had died.

It was a transmogrifying bee
Came droning down on Chucky's old bald
   head
And sat and put the poison. It scarcely bled,
But how exceedingly

And purply did the knot
Swell with the venom and communicate
Its rigor! Now the poor comb stood up straight
But Chucky did not.   20

So there was Janet
Kneeling on the wet grass, crying her brown
   hen
(Translated far beyond the daughters of men)
To rise and walk upon it.

And weeping fast as she had breath
Janet implored us, "Wake her from her sleep!"
And would not be instructed in how deep
Was the forgetful kingdom of death.

Two in August (1927)

In this curious poem the division in question
is that between two people ostensibly made, in
the words of the marriage ceremony, one flesh.
The quarrel is, therefore, all the more rending.
The reader will find it interesting to see how the
poet has managed to invest a little domestic
drama—presumably not tragic, perhaps in its
beginning even trivial—with a quality of mystery and terror.

We suggested earlier that "Bells for John
Whiteside's Daughter" is founded on a pair of
clichés. One might argue that "Two in August"
is based on another such cliché: "You wouldn't
have believed it, but they fought like cats and
dogs." There is much in the poem that does remind us of a cat fight and not merely lines 14
and 15—". . . trying to get undone,/With individual tigers in their blood." There is, for example, the reference to the woman "circuiting
the dark rooms like a string of amber" and to
the man treading "barefooted the dim lawn"

and walking "In the long ditch of darkness"
under "the hackberry trees where the birds
talked. . . ."[1]

What is accomplished, if anything, by presenting a quarrel between a man and woman as
if it were a fight between a pair of animals?
Though human beings are such special animals
that we disown our kinship to the others, we
are animals, and our animal nature is one aspect
of the division within man himself—drives and
instincts, some of which he scarcely understands,
as contrasted with the movements of thought
within the human cortex.

[1] In a poem called "Lady Lost" Ransom compares
the bird outside his window to a woman who, like the
Greek girl Philomela, has perhaps been transformed
into a bird. The poem itself suggests the transformation
so subtly that it is difficult to decide whether the poem
is about a woman turned into a bird or a bird turned
into a woman. See also a poem entitled "Husband
Betrayed," in which the man discovers that he has
"wived a pigeon."

The conflict between the human pair shocks them too. It leaves them "scared" as well as furious with each other, and it pushes each into a strange and mysterious world. For the man walking under the hackberry trees, the birds themselves seem to be speaking a language "too sad and strange to syllable"—that is, too sad and strange to be translated into human speech.

Two that could not have lived their single
   lives
As can some husbands and wives
Did something strange: they tensed their vocal
   cords
And attacked each other with silences and
   words
Like catapulted stones and arrowed knives.

Dawn was not yet; night is for loving or
   sleeping,
Sweet dreams or safekeeping;
Yet he of the wide brows that were used to
   laurel
And she, the famed for gentleness, must
   quarrel.
Furious both of them, and scared, and weeping.   10

How sleepers groan, twitch, wake to such a
   mood
Is not well understood,
Nor why two entities grown almost one
Should rend and murder trying to get undone,
With individual tigers in their blood.

She in terror fled from the marriage chamber
Circuiting the dark rooms like a string of amber
Round and round and back,
And would not light one lamp against the black,
And heard the clock that clanged: Remember,
   Remember.   20

And he must tread barefooted the dim lawn,
Soon he was up and gone;
High in the trees the night-mastered birds
   were crying
With fear upon their tongues, no singing nor
   flying
Which are their lovely attitudes by dawn.

Whether those bird-cries were of heaven or
   hell
There is no way to tell;
In the long ditch of darkness the man walked
Under the hackberry trees where the birds
   talked
With words too sad and strange to syllable.   30

The Equilibrists (1927)

Some general comments on this poem were made earlier. Here follow a few further notes. There is a special play of wit in lines 21–24. Though an old adage has it that there is honor among thieves, that is, thieves tend to band together against the world and won't rob each other, the speaker in this poem seems to raise his eyebrows at the notion. What is honor doing among those whose very profession is thievery? He implies that an even stranger "predicament" is that which finds honor between lovers—the more so since in such a context "honor" takes on its special meaning of a woman's chastity.

Readers who know the story of Tristan and Isolde may be reminded by line 24 of the incident in which King Mark, finding his wife Isolde and his nephew Tristan asleep together in the woods, does not kill them because Tris-

tan has placed a sword between them to signify that Isolde has remained faithful to her husband.

In line 29 the figure of the "two painful stars" refers to the phenomenon of the binary star. (See p. 753.) Each star revolves about the other, gravitational attraction holding them within their interlocked orbits and centrifugal force keeping them from coming together in one blazing mass. (There is a second reference to this phenomenon in line 49.) In line 41 the reference is to Jesus' statement in Matthew 22:30: "For in the resurrection [human beings] neither marry nor are given in marriage, but are like angels in heaven."

Full of her long white arms and milky skin
He had a thousand times remembered sin.

Alone in the press of people traveled he,
Minding her jacinth, and myrrh, and ivory.

Mouth he remembered: the quaint orifice
From which came heat that flamed upon the
    kiss,
Till cold words came down spiral from the
    head.
Grey doves from the officious tower illsped.

Body: it was a white field ready for love,
On her body's field, with the gaunt tower
    above,   10
The lilies grew, beseeching him to take,
If he would pluck and wear them, bruise and
    break.

Eyes talking: Never mind the cruel words,
Embrace my flowers, but not embrace the
    swords.
But what they said, the doves came straight-
    way flying
And unsaid: Honor, Honor, they came crying.

Importunate her doves. Too pure, too wise,
Clambering on his shoulder, saying, Arise,
Leave me now, and never let us meet,
Eternal distance now command thy feet.   20

Predicament indeed, which thus discovers
Honor among thieves, Honor between lovers.
O such a little word is Honor, they feel!
But the grey word is between them cold as
    steel.

At length I saw these lovers fully were come
Into their torture of equilibrium;
Dreadfully had forsworn each other, and yet
They were bound each to each, and they did
    not forget.

And rigid as two painful stars, and twirled
About the clustered night their prison world, 30

They burned with fierce love always to come
    near,
But honor beat them back and kept them
    clear.

Ah, the strict lovers, they are ruined now!
I cried in anger. But with puddled brow
Devising for those gibbeted and brave
Came I descanting: Man, what would you
    have?

For spin your period out, and draw your breath,
A kinder saeculum begins with Death.
Would you ascend to Heaven and bodiless
    dwell?
Or take your bodies honorless to Hell?   40

In Heaven you have heard no marriage is,
No white flesh tinder to your lecheries,
Your male and female tissue sweetly shaped
Sublimed away, and furious blood escaped.

Great lovers lie in Hell, the stubborn ones
Infatuate of the flesh upon the bones;
Stuprate, they rend each other when they kiss,
The pieces kiss again, no end to this.

But still I watched them spinning, orbited
    nice.
Their flames were not more radiant than their
    ice.   50
I dug in the quiet earth and wrought the tomb
And made these lines to memorize their
    doom:—

EPITAPH
Equilibrists lie here; stranger, tread light;
Close, but untouching in each other's sight;
Mouldered the lips and ashy the tall skull.
Let them lie perilous and beautiful.

Painted Head (1945)

The difficulties of this poem are largely resolved
if one thinks of it as a meditation on a
pictured head done in tempera, the portrait of
a man about thirty years old. The phrase
"painted head" must be understood as the subject of the verb or verbs in each of the first
four stanzas.

Though the poem is full of wit play, it deals
with a very serious subject. In modern man, the
intellect (the head) threatens to tyrannize over
the senses (the body). Thus, this poem presents
its special variation of Ransom's dominant
theme: the division within man.

In lines 2-3, "a capital on no/Column," the

poet thinks of the head as the ornamental block that crowns a column; but here the column that supports the capital is missing. In line 3 "a Platonic perhaps head" is an abstraction—the pure idea of headness, with no requirement that the idea shall be actualized in flesh and bone. Line 6 suggests that heads often regard the body only as an impediment and wish that they could dispense with it. In line 14 the historians are called "headhunters" because they are primarily interested in bagging their subject as an idea, as head—not the incidental and accidental aspects of his humanity. They are interested, for example, in how Napoleon won the Battle of Austerlitz, not in what he had for breakfast that morning or whether he spoke kindly to his orderly.

In the last stanza the head is thought of as the acropolis of the city that is the body: that is, as the stony eminence that towers above a Greek city and which was usually crowned by the temple and the other public buildings that stood for the authority of the city.

By dark severance the apparition head
Smiles from the air a capital on no
Column or a Platonic perhaps head
On a canvas sky depending from nothing;

Stirs up an old illusion of grandeur
By tickling the instinct of heads to be

Absolute and to try decapitation
And to play truant from the body bush;

But too happy and beautiful for those sorts
Of head (homekeeping heads are happiest)   10
Discovers maybe thirty unwidowed years
Of not dishonoring the faithful stem;

Is nameless and has authored for the evil
Historian headhunters neither book
Nor state and is therefore distinct from tart
Heads with crowns and guilty gallery heads;

Wherefore the extravagant device of art
Unhousing by abstraction this once head
Was capital irony by a loving hand
That knew the no treason of a head like this;   20

Makes repentance in an unlovely head
For having vinegarly traduced the flesh
Till, the hurt flesh recusing, the hard egg
Is shrunken to its own deathlike surface;

And an image thus. The body bears the head
(So hardly one they terribly are two)
Feeds and obeys and unto please what end?
Not to the glory of tyrant head but to

The being of body. Beauty is of body.
The flesh contouring shallowly on a head   30
Is a rock-garden needing body's love
And best bodiness to colorify

The big blue birds sitting and sea-shell flats
And caves, and on the iron acropolis
To spread the hyacinthine hair and rear
The olive garden for the nightingales.

ALLEN TATE (1899–   )

Allen Tate was one of the most precocious members of the Fugitive group. He had entered Vanderbilt in 1918 and so was still an undergraduate when the group began to take form in 1921. In spite of his youthfulness, Tate was, as Radcliffe Squires has put it, "more aware of the literary world at large than most of the Fugitives and more in tune with it than any of them. He had already responded to the synesthesial effects of Baudelaire and in 1922 adapted with grave competence Baudelaire's 'Correspondences'" (*Allen Tate: A Literary Biography*, 1971, p. 36).

What was much more remarkable and significant was that the young man should have seen a connection between Baudelaire and the French symbolists, on the one hand, and the Elizabethan and Jacobean poets, on the other;

for this was the same discovery made by Eliot, and crucial to Eliot's own development as a poet. Squires writes:

Whether or not Tate saw these connections at the time he translated [Baudelaire's] poem, he soon did. For in 1924 he was to write in the April issue of the *Fugitive* that Baudelaire's Theory of Correspondences—that an idea out of one class of experience may be dressed up in the vocabulary of another —is at once the backbone of Modern poetic diction and the character which distinguishes it from both the English Tradition and free verse. . . . We think of this as Decadence, but in a wider sense, if it may be repeated here, it is Elizabethan. It is not direct continuity from the immediate past of English poetry. It is development out of the whole of it under French direction: and it is no more startling than the progress from Wyatt to John Donne. One is awed. At twenty-four Tate knew essentially everything that he needed to know of the dominant aesthetics of his century in order to become one of its spokesmen.

Tate records that Hart Crane, having noticed some of his poems in the magazines,

said that my poems showed that I had read Eliot—which I had not done; but I soon did; and my difficulties were enormously increased. Anyhow from Eliot I went on to the other moderns, and I began to connect with the modern world what I had already learned from Baudelaire, first through Arthur Symons, then from Baudelaire himself. (*Princeton Library Chronicle*, April, 1942)

Tate's acquaintance with Eliot's poetry increased his difficulties because his natural affinities for Eliot's techniques and his interest in the sort of effects Eliot was seeking threatened to draw him too powerfully into the orbit of the older poet. He had to guard against unconscious imitation.

Tate's ability to connect what he "had already learned from Baudelaire" with "the modern world" has a further significance. It implies not literary antiquarianism but a concern for the modern world and a special view of it. His judgment of the essentially "modern" situation was formed early, and that fact largely accounts for the remarkable consistency of mode and theme to be found in his poetry. Many of his poems, including some of the most moving of them, have to do with the impact of modern science, the consequent withering away of man's sense of the supernatural, and his radically altered conception of nature. Thus, in his "Last Days of Alice," Tate uses as a symbol for modern man the child heroine of Lewis Carroll's *Alice in Wonderland* and *Alice Through the Looking Glass*. References to both mingle in the poem.

Carroll's Alice, looking into the mirror, suddenly found that she had stepped through its polished surface into a world which was like that of the room in which she had been sitting but with everything reversed, a world of marvels in which chess pieces walked about, flowers talked, and a grinning cat faded away until nothing was left save—a miracle of abstraction! —the grin itself. Twentieth-century man also finds himself in a world of wonders, beautifully logical, quite self-consistent, each conforming relentlessly to its own special laws, but a world in which man is lost and baffled. In Lewis Carroll's book, Alice is rescued from her nightmare world by waking up. Unfortunately, modern man cannot wake up and find himself back once more in the world which he has known throughout history and in which he has achieved his humanity.

A great many modern poets and philosophers have found in abstraction the enemy to poetry and the arts, and "Last Days of Alice," in its concluding stanzas, stresses the way in which science has done away with the world of things and replaced them with fields of force. Man's own solid flesh turns out to be simply a pattern of electrical charges, mass having disappeared into energy, and capable therefore of being described accurately only through mathematical formulae. Man has become "a mathematical shroud." He is "blessed without sin," not through having had his sins forgiven him, but because the concept of sin has been dismissed as meaningless.

The poem ends in a prayer. In his agony, the speaker implores the "God of our Flesh"—significantly not the god of mathematics—to take us back to our former state. It would be better to be evil and to face God's wrath than to be in our present condition. Before man had lost himself in a world created out of his own head, there was some hope of grace, and he could discern a path, even though a stony one, along which he might direct his steps.[1]

Many of Tate's poems deal with what he regards as a related blight, that which, falling over history, has transformed it into impersonal process and left it drained of meaning. Tate's most celebrated poem, his "Ode to the Confederate Dead," has to do with this theme and only incidentally with the Confederacy. This is by no means the only poem in which Tate has used his native region as a special vantage point from which to comment upon Everyman, specifically the modern Everyman, who, deprived and emptied, rootless and uncommitted, is attempting to live in a world which, in the process of making a gigantic extension of its technology, has lost its grip on values.

The South is obviously involved in this general loss of value and order, but it constitutes a special piece of the universal wreckage. For one thing, it is special in that the break between the contemporary South and its traditional way of living is recent and the wound is still tender; the southern sense of history, though it may often be confused, or even perverse, is still alive. Thus the very concreteness of personal relationships within southern society throws into

sharp relief the fragmentation and abstraction which have befallen society as a whole. (We have noted earlier that Faulkner, Ransom, and Katherine Anne Porter have used the southern scene to point the same contrast.)

The man who speaks the "Ode to the Confederate Dead," the man who stands at the gate of the cemetery that holds the bones of the dead soldiers, is a man skeptical of the present day. He knows all about the war and the gallantry that it called forth. He is confident that the dead soldiers found meaning in their cause and willingly died for it. He yearns for access to this kind of belief, but he cannot attain it. In the end, the dead soldiers—Confederate soldiers in this instance, though they might be almost any soldiers who died for a cause in which they believed—do not come alive for him except in the sense that their bodies are still functioning chemically and are gradually making the sea saltier or contributing their molecules to the substance of the grass. Try as he will through an effort of the imagination to enter their world, by the end of the poem he is forced to admit to himself that he has no sustaining vision, no transcendent purpose in which he can be passionately caught up, no cause to which he can give himself. His plight in some sense resembles that of Eliot's Gerontion: each man knows too much to believe in anything except the fact of his own skeptical ego. Regretfully, the man at the cemetery gate has to concede that he has lost contact with the heroic past. Modern man's loss of contact with the heroic past has a close relation to Tate's skepticism about the possibility that a man of our day can write an epic poem. See, for example, Tate's comment on MacLeish's *Conquistador* (p. 2189), or on Hart Crane's *The Bridge* (p. 2219).

The reader will find it interesting to look into Tate's own account of the "Ode," an essay that he has entitled "Narcissus as Narcissus," in *Essays of Four Decades* (1968). The ancient Greeks told the story of Narcissus, a handsome young man who, looking into a forest pool, saw his own image, fell in love with it, and in frustration at his inability to clasp the beautiful creature killed himself. Tate uses this myth to

[1] In 1950 Tate became a Roman Catholic. The poem we have discussed points in that direction but does not necessarily predict his conversion unless we insist on reading it literally rather than as a dramatization of a state of mind. Yet from an early period there are strong intimations in Tate's work, particularly in his prose, of his sympathies with the teachings of the church. His view of history, of nature, and of man—so all his writings show—has been all along deeply—and radically—traditional. See, for example, his contribution to *The Critique of Humanism: A Symposium* (1930), edited by Hartley Grattan, and referred to on pp. 2781–82.

make much the same point he makes with the story of Alice. When modern man, who has come to believe that all values are merely projections of his own mind, looks into the pool of history, he can see nothing more than the reflection of his own face.

Another classical myth that Tate frequently uses is that of the Trojan hero Aeneas, who escaped from Troy and voyaged westward to found a new Troy-Rome. The American colonist had done something on the same order, and the men of the old South, with their fondness for the Rome of the Republic, fancied the analogy. Tate, who thinks of the antebellum South as "classical,"[2] as opposed to the "romantic" industrial North (just reversing the usual distribution of epithets), makes use of the Aeneas story several times, as in poems such as "Aeneas at Washington" and "The Mediterranean." The men who settled the first colonies thought that they were fulfilling a destiny. America promised a new start and a chance to complete and perfect what in the Old World had been aborted. But the latest descendants of these first Americans now find that history ravels out in their hands.

Like Yeats, Tate finds in history not only the ground for his discourse, but the central excitement of his poetry. With the possible exception of Yeats, no poet of our time has possessed a more penetrating discernment of the predicament of modern man with reference to nature and history. In the old Christian synthesis, nature and history were related in a special way. With the breakup of that synthesis, man finds himself caught between a meaningless cycle on the one hand and the more extravagant notions of progress on the other—between a nature that is oblivious of man and a man-made "unnatural" utopia.

In Tate's poetry nature comes in for a great deal of attention—"The Seasons of the Soul" is a typical instance—but Tate rarely exhibits nature for its own sake and never as a kind of innocently pastoral backdrop for man's activities. For modern man, who had once thought his journey had a destination, a return to the meaningless round of the seasons is not comforting but terrifying. Because of Tate's preoccupation with history and human society, one does not ordinarily think of him as a poet of nature; and yet in the work of no poet of our time does the detail of nature make itself felt with more poignance and dramatic power. Characteristically, it is in the detail of a nature ominous with meaning or doubly ominous in its beautiful meaninglessness.[3] One finds absolutely electrifying lines such as ". . . the windowpane extends a fear to you/From one peeled aster drenched with the wind all day; or "The singular screech-owl's tight/Invisible lyric seeds the mind . . ."; or "a sky of glass/Blue, empty, and tall . . ./Where burn the equal laws/For Balaam and his ass. . . ."

We have stressed Tate's themes, but one must not, by doing so, give the impression that Tate is a didactic poet, concerned only to make generalizations about modern civilization. His poems are constructed to render a state of mind and to put in its most challenging form a fiercely dramatic speculation about man's ends and purposes. Tate's poetry is intensely concrete, dense, compact, and often indirect to the point of obscurity. Above all it is a poetry of metaphor, and the metaphors are often strained to the bursting point.

Tate sometimes impresses one as an almost desperate poet who, in order to convey to his reader the profound irony of modern man's plight, is willing to startle and shock him and

---

[2] The ordinary reader does not think of Tate as a writer of fiction, but he has produced one novel, *The Fathers* (1938), which dramatizes the contrast between the "classical" southerner who has been formed by a traditional society and the "new" man, the restless, attractive, "emancipated" southerner, who is uncomfortable with the old forms and ends up by destroying all that he touches. The scene is laid in Virginia, just before and during the Civil War. We mention Tate's novel so that one may observe that his range—poetry, fiction, and criticism—marks him as one of the few "complete," and one of the most distinguished, of our men of letters.

[3] One recalls W. H. Auden's description of the situation in which so many moderns find themselves: unable to believe what their forefathers did, yet feeling the terrible necessity to find a belief that will give a principle of direction. See p. 1819.

is quite prepared to take the risk of putting him off the poem altogether. So also with Tate's rhythms. He sometimes seems to risk deforming the metrical structure in his eagerness to achieve a richer and more subtle effect. All of this is to say that Tate puts a great burden on his reader. He insists that the reader, by an effort of his own imagination, cooperate with the poet to bring the violent metaphors and jarring rhythms into unity.

For the casual and careless reader, the poem may seem to explode in his face. The recalcitrant elements that Tate insists on binding into one pattern will not stay bound, but fly apart. Yet, the reader who is willing to wrestle with a bold and adventurous poetry and is not insistent on easy harmonies will find Tate's poetry remarkably exciting and rewarding. Robert Lowell has made the point in his own way: "Out of splutter and shambling comes a killing eloquence."

BIOGRAPHICAL CHART

1899   Born, November 19, in Clark County, Kentucky
1922   Receives B. A., Vanderbilt University; first issue of the *Fugitive* appears, April 12, containing Tate's "To Intellectual Detachment" and "Sinbad"
1923   Assumes some editorial functions of the *Fugitive*
1925   *The Fugitive* ceases publication
1928   *Mr. Pope and Other Poems; Stonewall Jackson: The Good Soldier* (biography)
1928–29   Travels in England and France
1929   *Jefferson Davis: His Rise and Fall*
1932   *Poems: 1928–1931*
1932–34   Southern editor, *Hound and Horn*
1936   *The Mediterranean and Other Poems; Reactionary Essays on Poetry and Ideas*
1937   *Selected Poems*
1938   *The Fathers* (novel); joins English faculty, Women's College of the University of North Carolina
1939–42   Resident Fellow, Creative Arts Program, Princeton University

1941   *Reason in Madness* (critical essays)
1943–44   Holds the Chair of Poetry in the Library of Congress
1944–46   Edits the *Sewanee Review*
1948   *Poems: 1922–1947; On the Limits of Poetry: Selected Essays, 1928–1948*
1949   Elected to the National Institute of Arts and Letters
1951–68   Professor of English, University of Minnesota
1953   *The Forlorn Demon: Didactic and Critical Essays*
1956   Awarded Bollingen prize in poetry
1961   Receives the Brandeis University Medal for poetry
1962   Receives the Gold Medal of the Dante Society of Florence
1964   Elected to the American Academy of Arts and Letters
1968   *Essays of Four Decades*

FURTHER READINGS

There is no standard edition of Tate's works. Individual titles are cited in the biographical chart.

Ferman Bishop, *Allen Tate* (1967)
John M. Bradbury, *The Fugitives* (1958)
Louise Cowan, *The Fugitive Group: A Literary History* (1959)
George Hemphill, *Allen Tate* (1963)
"Homage to Allen Tate," *Sewanee Review* (1959); Allen Tate issue

Frank Kermode, "Contemplation and Method," *Sewanee Review* (1964)
R. K. Meiners, *The Last Alternatives: A Study of the Works of Allen Tate* (1963)
Monroe K. Spears, "The Criticism of Allen Tate," *Sewanee Review* (1949)
John L. Stewart, *The Burden of Time* (1965)
Radcliffe Squires, *Allen Tate: A Literary Biography* (1971)
———, ed., *Allen Tate and His Work* (1972)

Last Days of Alice (1932)

As we have already pointed out, in this poem Alice stands for modern man, has given up the objective world in favor of an abstract world that he has really concocted out of his own head; that is, an abstract diagram of reality, the product of measurement, calculation, and theory. This "All-Alice of the world's entity" (line 15) is not the world of nature that the Greek poet or the Hebrew prophet or the man of the Middle Ages knew, but an extension of man, a world created out of man; hence, the off-spring of "incest of spirit."

"Alice grown . . . mammoth" (line 1) and the "grinning cat" (line 3) refer to incidents in *Alice in Wonderland*. Instances of the "spoiled cruelty she had meant to say" can be found in abundance in *Wonderland* and *Through the Looking Glass*: Alice is constantly being given sharp answers and snippy comments by the creatures, but usually only too late can think of an appropriately tart reply.

Alice grown lazy, mammoth but not fat,
Declines upon her lost and twilight age;
Above in the dozing leaves the grinning cat
Quivers forever with his abstract rage:

Whatever light swayed on the perilous gate
Forever sways, nor will the arching grass,
Caught when the world clattered, undulate
In the deep suspension of the looking-glass.

Bright Alice! always pondering to gloze
The spoiled cruelty she had meant to say   10
Gazes learnedly down her airy nose
At nothing, nothing thinking all the day.

Turned absent-minded by infinity
She cannot move unless her double move,
The All-Alice of the world's entity
Smashed in the anger of her hopeless love,

Love for herself who, as an earthly twain,
Pouted to join her two in a sweet one;
No more the second lips to kiss in vain
The first she broke, plunged through the glass
    alone—   20

Alone to the weight of impassivity,
Incest of spirit, theorem of desire,
Without will as chalky cliffs by the sea,
Empty as the bodiless flesh of fire:

All space, that heaven is a dayless night,
A nightless day driven by perfect lust
For vacancy, in which her bored eyesight
Stares at the drowsy cubes of human dust.

—We too back to the world shall never pass
Through the shattered door, a dumb shade-
    harried crowd   30
Being all infinite, function depth and mass
Without figure, a mathematical shroud

Hurled at the air—blessèd without sin!
O God of our flesh, return us to Your wrath,
Let us be evil could we enter in
Your grace, and falter on the stony path!

Ode to the Confederate Dead (1930)

The first version of this poem was composed in 1926 and published in 1927. The revised version appeared in 1930.

The title itself turns out to be ironic, for an ode ought to be a formal poem, and an ode to the memory of a nation's dead ought to be read or recited on a public occasion. But this "ode" is highly irregular in form and it turns out to be a private meditation. The occasion is not public but personal.

Lines 21-41 have been misinterpreted by

John L. Stewart (in his *The Burden of Time*, 1965), who regards Parmenides and Zeno, Greek philosophers of the Eleatic school, as early representatives of the "skepticism and the habit of abstraction" which have brought modern man to a situation in which "he knows only what animals know and in the animal way. [The man at the gate] is terrified by the darkening forms in the twilight and by the sudden call." But he is not terrified, just as the Confederate soldiers were not terrified. For he has imaginatively entered into their world[1] and like them knows what it is to possess the "twilight certainty of an animal" and to be sustained by "midnight restitutions of the blood." The dead Confederate soldiers shared something of the certainty of the animal, which is not racked by doubt and skepticism. Its certainty is "twilight" whereas the consciousness of the intellectual, suffused with rational light, is multiple and uncertain. The soldiers' knowledge is closer to a blood-knowledge.

The man by the gate can at this moment "praise the vision" because he participates in it. The faith of the dead soldiers is such that they could act without hesitation, "hurried beyond decision." They now seem to the man at the gate alive and filled with energy, "stopped by the wall" as if the wall were necessary to check the violence still in their dead bodies.

What then are Zeno and Parmenides doing in this passage? They had argued that whatever possesses true being is eternal and is not subject to change, apparent change being no more than an illusion. The poet speaks of their disavowal of the shifting phenomenal world as a "rage," a rage against change. (The passage looks forward to line 49, in which the world of heroism is "Lost in that orient of the thick-and-fast," that rising of a world of minute particulars, crowding on each other.) In short, at this moment in the poem the speaker "knows" the "rage . . ./Of muted Zeno and Parmenides" against a world of change along with his knowing the unimportance to the Confederate soldiers of the "shrift of death." He is here caught up in his praise of "the arrogant circumstance/Of those who fall/Rank upon rank, hurried beyond decision. . . ."

The vision, to be sure, cannot be maintained. In the lines that follow, the speaker comes to accept change as the reality and naturalism as

the mode in which to describe human beings. He is, after all, a man of our century.

Stonewall refers, of course, to General Thomas ("Stonewall") Jackson, the Confederate general, whom Lee called his "right arm." Shiloh, Antietam, Malvern Hill, and Bull Run are the names of important battles in the Civil War.

Nature is oblivious of man, quite unmindful of his aspirations and his heroism. If physico-chemical process is ultimate and there is no residue, then the heroes of the Confederate cause (and the heroes of all other causes) are indeed swallowed up by nature. One would expect the poet to write in line 66 "Lost in these acres of the unthinking green" or even the "idiot green," but the poet has sharpened the epithet: he treats nature not as merely unthinking or unfeeling, but as something of perverted mentality. The acres of grass are "insane." For a parallel in certain themes and ironies, see Melville's *Battle-Pieces*, pp. 910–28.

The image of the jaguar mistaking his reflection for another creature and leaping upon it is another variant of the myth of Narcissus and also of the Alice-through-the-Looking-Glass figure discussed earlier. The essential point made by the two analogies is the same.

Row after row with strict impunity
The headstones yield their names to the
    element,
The wind whirrs without recollection;
In the riven troughs the splayed leaves
Pile up, of nature the casual sacrament
To the seasonal eternity of death;
Then driven by the fierce scrutiny
Of heaven to their election in the vast breath,
They sough the rumour of mortality.

Autumn is desolation in the plot   10
Of a thousand acres where these memories
    grow
From the inexhaustible bodies that are not
Dead, but feed the grass row after rich row.
Think of the autumns that have come and
    gone!—
Ambitious November with the humors of the
    year,

---

[1] "The passage [lines 21–41] is meant to convey a plenary vision, the actual presence, of the examplars of active faith; the man at the gate at that moment is nearer to realizing them than at any other in the poem" ("Narcissus as Narcissus," *Essays of Four Decades*, p. 604).

With a particular zeal for every slab,
Staining the uncomfortable angels that rot
On the slabs, a wing chipped here, an arm
    there:
The brute curiosity of an angel's stare
Turns you, like them, to stone,   20
Transforms the heaving air
Till plunged to a heavier world below
You shift your sea-space blindly
Heaving, turning like the blind crab.

    Dazed by the wind, only the wind
    The leaves flying, plunge

You know who have waited by the wall
The twilight certainty of an animal,
Those midnight restitutions of the blood
You know—the immitigable pines, the smoky
    frieze   30
Of the sky, the sudden call: you know the
    rage,
The cold pool left by the mounting flood,
Of muted Zeno and Parmenides.
You who have waited for the angry resolution
Of those desires that should be yours to-
    morrow,
You know the unimportant shrift of death
And praise the vision
And praise the arrogant circumstance
Of those who fall
Rank upon rank, hurried beyond decision—   40
Here by the sagging gate, stopped by the wall.

    Seeing, seeing only the leaves
    Flying, plunge and expire

Turn your eyes to the immoderate past,
Turn to the inscrutable infantry rising
Demons out of the earth—they will not last.
Stonewall, Stonewall, and the sunken fields of
    hemp,
Shiloh, Antietam, Malvern Hill, Bull Run.
Lost in that orient of the thick-and-fast
You will curse the setting sun.   50

    Cursing only the leaves crying
    Like an old man in a storm

You hear the shout, the crazy hemlocks point
With troubled fingers to the silence which
Smothers you, a mummy, in time.
                          The hound bitch
Toothless and dying, in a musty cellar
Hears the wind only.

                   Now that the salt of their blood
Stiffens the saltier oblivion of the sea,
Seals the malignant purity of the flood,
What shall we who count our days and bow   60
Our heads with a commemorial woe
In the ribboned coats of grim felicity,
What shall we say of the bones, unclean,
Whose verdurous anonymity will grow?
The ragged arms, the ragged heads and eyes
Lost in these acres of the insane green?
The gray lean spiders come, they come and go;
In a tangle of willows without light
The singular screech-owl's tight
Invisible lyric seeds the mind   70
With the furious murmur of their chivalry.

    We shall say only the leaves
    Flying, plunge and expire

We shall say only the leaves whispering
In the improbable mist of nightfall
That flies on multiple wing;
Night is the beginning and the end
And in between the ends of distraction
Waits mute speculation, the patient curse
That stones the eyes, or like the jaguar leaps   80
For his own image in a jungle pool, his victim.
What shall we say who have knowledge
Carried to the heart? Shall we take the act
To the grave? Shall we, more hopeful, set up
    the grave
In the house? The ravenous grave?

                             Leave now
The shut gate and the decomposing wall:
The gentle serpent, green in the mulberry
    bush,
Riots with his tongue through the hush—
Sentinel of the grave who counts us all!

The Meaning of Life: A Monologue (1936)

We cannot know the meaning of life absolutely. It is a sort of Kantian thing-in-itself, and no words are capable of describing it with complete fidelity. If this is Tate's meaning, what a curious thing for a poet to say, for does he not thereby deny to the poet his function? If the poet can't

really deal with the deeper meanings, isn't poetry a frivolous activity? But Tate might well
reply that the very impossibility of stating the
meaning of life gives poetry its justification.
Poetry doesn't try to state, but suggests, implies,
and uses analogies. Thus, it carries its own built-
in warning against any literal reading of what
it says and is calculated to be less misleading
than other forms of "commentary" that pretend
to give the complete truth.

One may relate this last statement to the
case that Tate (and other poets) make against
"abstraction," for a commentary that seems to
offer a blueprint or a schema may deceive the
unwary. People who would never think of taking a metaphor literally may regard a formula
as somehow the very essence of the thing it
represents.

"The Meaning of Life," however, is not a
poem focused on aesthetics. It deals with larger
issues, since the essence cannot speak for itself:
we can never do without commentary, but we
have to choose our commentaries with care.
We have to realize also that our notion of the
proper commentary is subject to change. At
twelve, the speaker had determined to shoot
only for honor but, at twenty, never to shoot.
The predicament of modern man, as the speaker
at thirty-three has come to realize, is that man,
by swathing himself in mere commentary, may
never get to shoot—may miss life altogether
(this is the point made in lines 13–19—not that
the speaker yearns to join Murder, Inc.).

The speaker concludes with one more attempt to describe the essence of life. Since he
must use words, what he can say will be only
another commentary; but perhaps he can at
least suggest through metaphor the quality in

question. His basic comparison combines two
elements: ("arteries") the blood, the life-sus-
taining force in the human body with its associations with lust and passion; and ("of a
cave") a cavern, with its underground river,
teeming with eyeless fish. Fish of this species
have lived so long in the dark that they have no
use for eyes. All of which is a way of suggesting
that the essence of life, running its dark involved, subterranean course, filled with infinite
potentiality ("heavy with spawn"), is blind,
having no use for eyes and no need for speech.

Think about it at will: there is that
Which is the commentary; there's that other,
Which may be called the immaculate
Conception of its essence in itself.
It is necessary to distinguish the weights
Of the two methods lest the first smother
The second, the second be speechless (with-
    out the first).
I was saying this more briefly the other day
But one must be explicit as well as brief.
When I was a small boy I lived at home   10
For nine years in that part of old Kentucky
Where the mountains fringe the Blue Grass,
The old men shot at one another for luck;
It made me think I was like none of them.
At twelve I was determined to shoot only
For honor; at twenty not to shoot at all;
I know at thirty-three that one must shoot
As often as one gets the rare chance—
In killing there is more than commentary.
One's sense of the proper decoration alters   20
But there's a kind of lust feeds on itself
Unspoken to, unspeaking; subterranean
As a black river full of eyeless fish
Heavy with spawn; with a passion for time
Longer than the arteries of a cave.

The Meaning of Death: An After-Dinner Speech (1936)

The previous poem is called a monologue and
the poet, to provide a makeweight against the
solemnity of the subject, has maintained a
casual, almost chatty tone. In "The Meaning
of Death," he uses a related device. As the
subtitle of the poem indicates, we are being

treated here to an after-dinner speech. It is
almost as if the speaker were getting ready to
propose a toast to the future. He never quite
does that, though he does urge his hearers to
forget the past and exhorts them to think of
tomorrow.

The audience addressed in the poem is clearly American—people who believe in the American dream, who associate the past with error and have a touching faith in their capacity to achieve a perfect civilization. To them, the speaker points out that the enemy is time. Time may be arrested if we simplify life, "plan" our actions ("Founded on the best hypotheses"), and give up ritual of any kind, including that of an occasion like the present one, in which men sit down to dine together. For ritual is an impractical action: it implies a respect for the thing as thing; it promotes irrelevant conversation and might even stimulate the imagination. Worst of all, it implies a breach in our strict naturalism.

The poem ends with echoes of the complicated metaphor that concludes "The Meaning of Life." But the arteries and caves now referred to are ironically different from those in "The Meaning of Life." A "learned artery" can hardly be a blood vessel. It sounds more like a conduit of thought, a nerve, or a complex of cortical tissue. The arteries of the cave, filled with eyeless fish, suggested the "essence" of life; but in this poem it is feared (or is it in fact secretly hoped?) that the "learned arteries" will "yield, without essence, perfect accident"[1]— that is, pure commentary.

The last line, "We are the eyelids of defeated caves," is shockingly bold. Surely caves don't have eyelids, and how can a cave be defeated? Is there a suggestion that the caves here mentioned are really skulls—the insides of men's heads in which the "learned arteries" are indeed conduits transmitting neural impulses? Maybe so, maybe not. But the eyes—a more romantic generation liked to call them "windows of the soul"—would be entrances to this cave, and these entrances would in fact be furnished with lids.

The temptation to read the poem in this

[1] The poet here is making use of the Scholastics' distinction between "substance," the essential quality of a thing, and its "accidents," the inessential appearances of it. Thus both sugar and salt share such "accidents" as whiteness, roughness, solubility in water. But the substance (essence) of sugar is very different from that of salt.

fashion is strong, for interpreted thus the poem would parallel the situation portrayed in poems such as "Last Days of Alice" and "Ode to the Confederate Dead." The mind has substituted for the rich manifold of experience a desiccated world of abstractions, spun out of itself. To make this substitution is to cease to live. Hence the title of the poem. The meaning of death is the devouring of substance by accident and the disappearance of life's essence in the dry sands of mere commentary. It is time, then, for us—the generation who have seen this accomplished—to close, in languor and weariness, the entrance to the cave.

I rise, gentlemen, it is the pleasant hour.
Darkness falls. The night falls.

               Time, fall no more.
Let that be life—time falls no more. The threat
Of time we in our own courage have forsworn.
Let light fall, there shall be eternal light
And all the light shall on our heads be worn

Although at evening clouds infest the sky
Broken at base from which the lemon sun
Pours acid of winter on a useful view—
Four water-towers, two churches, and a river; 10
These are the sights I give in to at night
When the long covers loose the roving eye
To find the horror of the day a shape
Of life: we would have more than living sight.
Past delusions are seen as if it all
Were yesterday flooded with lemon light,
Vice and virtue, hard sacrifice and crime
In the cold vanity of time.

               Tomorrow
The landscape will respond to jocund day,
Bright roofs will scintillate with hues of May   20
And Phoebus' car, his daily circuit run,
Brings me to the year when, my time begun,
I loitered in the backyard by the alley;
When I was a small boy living at home
The dark came on in summer at eight o'clock
For Little Lord Fauntleroy in a perfect frock
By the alley: mother took him by the ear
To teach of the mixed modes an ancient fear.
Forgive me if I am personal.

             Gentlemen, let's
Forget the past, its related errors, coarseness 30

Of parents, laxities, unrealities of principle.
Think of tomorrow. Make a firm postulate
Of simplicity in desire and act
Founded on the best hypotheses;
Desire to eat secretly, alone, lest
Ritual corrupt our charity,

Lest darkness fall and time fall
In a long night when learned arteries
Mounting the ice and sum of barbarous time
Shall yield, without essence, perfect accident.   40

We are the eyelids of defeated caves.

The Oath (1932)

Andrew Lytle, the novelist and essayist, is a
long-time friend of Tate's. The other two personal names refer to members of Tate's family
connection, Major Benjamin Bogan being a
great-grandfather. The answer to Lytle's question is clearly implied: it is we, the moderns—
"the eyelids of defeated caves"—who are the
dead, the "animated dead," essentially zombies.
The reference to the mountain stream is also
related to the cave image in the preceding
poem. A mountain stream ceases to be a mountain stream when it has worn its bed level. It
might even be termed a "defeated" mountain
stream when it has lost the activity that gave its
career meaning.

It was near evening, the room was cold
Half dark; Uncle Ben's brass bullet-mould
And powder-horn and Major Bogan's face
Above the fire in the half-light plainly said:
There's naught to kill but the animated dead.
Horn nor mould nor major follows the chase.
Being cold I urged Lytle to the fire
In the blank twilight with not much left untold

By two old friends when neither's a great liar.
We sat down evenly in the smoky chill.   10
There's precious little to say between day and
    dark,
Perhaps a few words on the implacable will
Of time sailing like a magic barque
Or something as fine for the amenities,
Till dusk seals the window, the fire grows
    bright,
And the wind saws the hill with a swarm of
    bees.
Now meditating a little on the firelight
We heard the darkness grapple with the night
And give an old man's valedictory wheeze
From his westward breast between his polar
    jaws;   20
Then Lytle asked: Who are the dead?
Who are the living and the dead?
And nothing more was said.
So I, leaving Lytle to that dream,
Decided what it is in time that gnaws
The ageing fury of a mountain stream
When suddenly as an ignorant mind will do
I thought I heard the dark pounding its head
On a rock, crying: *Who are the dead?*
Then Lytle turned with an oath—By God it's
    true!   30

The Mediterranean (1936)

The poem refers to an actual picnic on the
French Mediterranean coast in 1932. Ford
Madox Ford, the novelist, who was present, describes it in his *Provence* (1945). The poem was
first published a year later under the title "Picnic at Cassis." The epigraph comes from Virgil's
Aeneid (1, 241). The goddess Venus, interced-
ing with Jupiter in behalf of her mortal son
Aeneas and his companions, asks: "Oh great
king, what end of their strivings do you set?"

Tate has altered Virgil's word "laborum" (literally, *labors*) to "dolorum" (*sorrows*).[1]

The modern poet and his companions, on

---

[1] Lillian Feder regards Tate's alteration as deliberate
and significant. She interprets his substitution of "dolorum" as signifying a diminution of the human ability to
accomplish heroic tasks to the mere capacity to endure
pointless anguish and despair. See her "Allen Tate's
Use of Classical Literature," *Centennial Review* (Winter, 1960).

entering the narrow, long bay, have the illusion that they have got out of the world of hurrying time and are back in the world that Aeneas knew. Their picnic, it occurs to the poet, is not unlike the meal in which Aeneas and his companions fulfilled the prophecy foretelling their proper destination and the end of their wanderings. When they were reduced to eating their very plates, they would know that they had arrived. One of them suddenly noticed that they were eating the slabs of bread which served as trenchers for their meat—a kind of primitive sandwich.

Yet this pleasant few hours' holiday on the shores of the sea around which European civilization first developed can only sharpen the modern poet's sense of a cataclysmic difference between the Trojan hero and himself. Aeneas had a destiny to fulfill and a purpose to accomplish. His means were primitive, but in his certainty about ends he was in far better plight than the modern. Modern man has conquered space. (The development of the jet plane and rocketry long after the publication of this poem simply emphasizes the point made by the poem.) But the abolition of space—"We've cracked the hemispheres with careless hand"—has brought its penalties. The New World is no longer radiant with promise; its very riches are an embarrassment.

Quem das finem, rex magne, dolorum?

Where we went in the boat was a long bay
A slingshot wide, walled in by towering stone—
Peaked margin of antiquity's delay,
And we went there out of time's monotone:

Where we went in the black hull no light moved

Mother and Son (1932)

This brilliant poem carries in itself its own sufficient context. The reader does not have to know who the mother was or the son, what set of circumstances have estranged them, what mortal illness now grips the son come home to die,

But a gull white-winged along the feckless wave,
The breeze, unseen but fierce as a body loved,
That boat drove onward like a willing slave:

Where we went in the small ship the seaweed
Parted and gave to us the murmuring shore,   10
And we made feast and in our secret need
Devoured the very plates Aeneas bore:

Where derelict you see through the low twilight
The green coast that you, thunder-tossed, would win,
Drop sail, and hastening to drink all night
Eat dish and bowl to take that sweet land in!

Where we feasted and caroused on the sandless
Pebbles, affecting our day of piracy,
What prophecy of eaten plates could landless
Wanderers fulfil by the ancient sea?   20

We for that time might taste the famous age
Eternal here yet hidden from our eyes
When lust of power undid its stuffless rage;
They, in a wineskin, bore earth's paradise.

Let us lie down once more by the breathing side
Of Ocean, where our live forefathers sleep
As if the Known Sea still were a month wide—
Atlantis howls but is no longer steep!

What country shall we conquer, what fair land
Unman our conquest and locate our blood?   30
We've cracked the hemispheres with careless hand!
Now, from the Gates of Hercules we flood

Westward, westward till the barbarous brine
Whelms us to the tired land where tasseling corn,
Fat beans, grapes sweeter than muscadine
Rot on the vine: in that land were we born.

or the denouement—whether the son will break under the "dry fury of the woman's mind" and beg forgiveness or whether he will hold out in his own misery and pride until he dies.

What the poet has done is to present the tension between a pair of people who are closely connected and yet terribly estranged—and to do so by riveting our attention on a particular scene, one that fairly crackles with their suppressed passions.

A poem like this points clearly to Tate's narrative powers and to his affinities with southern writers as different from him in tenor and tone as, say, William Faulkner.

Now all day long the man who is not dead
Hastens the dark with inattentive eyes,
The woman with white hand and erect head
Stares at the covers, leans for the son's replies
At last to her importunate womanhood—
Her hand of death laid on the living bed;
So lives the fierce compositor of blood.

She waits; he lies upon the bed of sin
Where greed, avarice, anger writhed and slept
Till to their silence they were gathered in: 10
There, fallen with time, his tall and bitter kin
Once fired the passions that were never kept
In the permanent heart, and there his mother
  lay
To bear him on the impenetrable day.

The falcon mother cannot will her hand
Up to the bed, nor break the manacle

His exile sets upon her harsh command
That he should say the time is beautiful—
Transfigured by her own possessing light:
The sick man craves the impalpable night.   20

Loosed betwixt eye and lid, the swimming
  beams
Of memory, blind school of cuttlefish,
Rise to the air, plunge to the cold streams—
Rising and plunging the half-forgotten wish
To tear his heart out in a slow disgrace
And freeze the hue of terror to her face.

Hate, misery, and fear beat off his heart
To the dry fury of the woman's mind;
The son, prone in his autumn, moves apart
A seed blown upon a returning wind.   30
O child, be vigilant till towards the south
On the flowered wall all the sweet afternoon,
The reaching sun, swift as the cottonmouth,
Strikes at the black crucifix on her breast
Where the cold dusk comes suddenly to rest—
Mortality will speak the victor soon!

The dreary flies, lazy and casual,
Stick to the ceiling, buzz along the wall.
O heart, the spider shuffles from the mould
Weaving, between the pinks and grapes, his
  pall.   40
The bright wallpaper, imperishably old,
Uncurls and flutters, it will never fall.

Seasons of the Soul (1944)

The epigraph is from Canto 13 of Dante's *Inferno*, lines 31–33. The Temple Classics translates the passage thus: "Then I stretched my hand a little forward and plucked a branchlet from a great thorn; and the trunk of it cried, 'Why dost thou rend me?'" The wounded tree tells Dante that it was once a man. As punishment for his act of suicide, he has been turned into a tree. Canto 13 (and the cantos that flank it) have to do with the punishment of the violent: those who have been violent against their neighbors, those who have been violent against themselves, and those who have been violent against God, nature, and art. "The Seasons of the Soul," written during the Second World War, is a poem about all these kinds of violence. The war itself is only the most obvious

instance. The ultimate source of every kind of violence, as the poet sees it in this poem, is to be found in man's self-division. The mind and the body have really broken apart: the warfare is within man, with the claims of the flesh and the claims of the mind unreconciled, and perhaps irreconcilable.[1]

The "seasons" of the soul correspond to the four seasons of the year. Attempts have been made to equate the four parts with the four elements, namely, summer with air, autumn with earth, winter with water, and spring with fire. But it may be more useful to think of the sea-

[1] The reader may wish to compare the poem with poems by Ransom such as "The Equilibrists," "Painted Head," and "Persistent Explorer," which treat the same theme.

sons as representing four modes of time. In this poem, spring is clearly the future just as autumn is the past. Winter would seem to be the present. What, then, does summer stand for? Summer seems to stand outside time altogether. It is a world of extension rather than of duration, of space rather than time, of flesh rather than mind, an animal or even a merely vegetable world. It is a world flooded with light having nothing in it that is mysterious or dark—qualities that Tate always associates with time.

The world of summer is natural to childhood. The speaker tells us that as a child "The summer had no reason" (line 46) and "had its timeless day" (line 48). In the "Spring" section he looks back to his youth and says (lines 191–93)

> Back in my native prime
> I saw the orient corn[1]
> All space but no time. . . .

A passage from one of Tate's essays, "The New Provincialism," can throw some light on this puzzling statement. Whereas the "old" provincialism involved one's restriction to a relatively small geographical area, the "new" provincialism, according to Tate, restricts man to life in a small segment of time. As he puts it: "The [new] provincial attitude is limited in time but not in space. . . . [The provincial man] cuts himself off from the past, and without benefit of the fund of traditional wisdom approaches the simplest problems of life as if nobody had ever heard of them before. A society without arts, said Plato, lives by chance. [The new provincial], locked in the present, lives by chance." It is normal for a child to live in such a summer world, but not for a grown man. But modern man, having discarded traditional wisdom, living by chance, is at the mercy of time.

The summer world is also—and for the reasons just given—a world of pure naturalism. Its sky (see lines 35–38) is empty, without god or angel, "Without tail or head/Where burn the equal laws/For Baalam and his ass. . . ." In the Biblical account God spoke to Balaam

miraculously through the mouth of the ass that he was riding (Numbers 22:28–34). That is, by miracle the beast was made for the moment the equal of the man. Nowadays the man is made level with the beast, simply another mammal, subject to the same physical and biological laws.

The summer world is hard on the soul: "Under the summer's blast/The soul cannot endure . . ." (lines 11–12). But the season is also hard on the flesh: "The hot wind dries and draws/With circular delay/The flesh . . ." (lines 17–19). Yet if the flesh is dried away, how shall the mind—which, Tate implies in others of his poems as well as this one, has been responsible for cutting man "off from the past"—endure apart from the body that nourishes it? Won't the mind like a hunting king fall victim to the beast (the body) that it has harried (lines 8–10)?

Though in the "spatial" summer world it is hard to "guess the night" and difficult to believe that "time's engaging jaws" will ever close on one, the whole "Summer" section of the poem is a warning against the devouring jaws of time. Things do happen in the season of the "gentle sun" (line 21). The fall of France was accomplished at the summer solstice (line 22).

The first section of the poem closes with the two men "of our summer world," that is, of the world of the flesh, descending into a "nonspatial" world of essential spirit, the habitation of souls divested of the flesh and caught forever in the coils of time. The men are Dante and his guide Virgil. We are told in Canto 12, lines 76–78, how the centaur Chiron, the leader of the centaurs whose task is to stand guard over the seventh circle, where the violent are punished, draws out an arrow preparatory to forbidding them passage. He "drew an arrow and with its notch/he pushed his great beard back along his jaws." When Virgil assures Chiron that Dante has been granted from on high safe passage through Hell, Chiron assigns one of the centaurs to conduct them on their way.

Perhaps it would be too fanciful to see in Chiron a "hunting king" (line 9) who will *not* fall prey to any beast, or to say that, as a creature with horse's body but the chest and

---

[1] The phrase "orient corn" is from Thomas Traherne's *Centuries of Meditations*.

head of a man, he represents a balance between the claims of the body and the mind. But it is possible that the poet takes the opportunity to mention Chiron simply in order to bring in another Dante allusion and to press the analogy between the violence depicted in Dante's *Inferno* and the violence that abounds in the modern day. At all events, the reader ought to be warned that too diligent symbol-hunting can obfuscate the reading of a poem. The foregoing notes on this difficult poem ought not to be permitted to suggest that "Summer" is a complicated puzzle or that a pattern of references may be substituted for the poem itself. At best the references may be expected to do no more than serve the reader in his own attempt to assimilate the words, metaphors, and rhythms in his own imagination.

Section 2, "Autumn," represents a kind of hell. In line 105 there is a clear allusion to Dante's *Inferno*: the reference to squinting "As through a needle's eye" echoes the following passage in Canto 15, line 20: "and toward us [they] sharpened their vision, as an aged tailor does at the eye of a needle." But in general Tate's hell is quite different in atmosphere from Dante's seventh circle. It is a personal hell. The poet finds himself trapped in a cold and empty hall and has a vision of his father and his mother though they do not see him. Their faces show no recognition of their son.

Section 3, "Winter," is the present as seen in a hard, wintry light. In spite of references to contemporary events such as the tanks of Hitler's *Blitzkrieg* overrunning "Green France," summer had seemed in some curious way immune to time. Not so with the winter. The gods, pagan and Christian, are all dead. Christ's body, no longer dripping sacrificial blood, has become a kind of mummy, hanging dried out in its windy steeple. Though the speaker has also remarked that "all the sea-gods are dead," nevertheless he implores Venus, born of the seafoam, as the ancient Greek myth had it, to return to her home in the sea. It is a cold sea, a sea which is tossed and "anonymous," cruel and cannibalistic, where the monsters of the deep prey upon each other. Venus, in returning to the sea, will

be abandoning a burned-out earth—see lines 213–14—and reestablishing her divinity as a principle of brute fertility. Life in its most gross and primitive forms arose from the sea and to the inhuman life of the sea it may be forced to return.

The "sea-conceited scop" is presumably Andrew Marvell (1621–1678), who in his poem "The Garden" described the mind as "that ocean where each kind/Does straight its own resemblance find. . . ." The ancient belief, to which Marvell refers, held that everything on earth has its counterpart in the sea. The author of "Seasons of the Soul" finds these counterparts: for Venus's bird, the dove, there is in the sea the shark; for some kind of great catlike predator, there is the tiger shark; for the oak, "the rigid madrepore," a kind of heavy tree coral. But the earth-sea analogies are not consistently made out. In the latter stanzas of "Winter" we seem to move through a dream world—the ocean of "the nether mind"—in which one setting suddenly gives way to another. The "pacing animal" who "Surveys the jungle cove" (lines 156–57) may be surveying a literal jungle cove and not a watery one. "Beyond the undertow," and the "madrepore" (line 162) may not be coral beneath the waves after all, but a real oak. (It is said to "give" the "leaf no more" as if it once had done so.) In any case, the poet, in breaking from it a bleeding twig, is back once more in Dante's *Inferno* and is performing under sea, on land, or merely in his hallucinated mind Dante's action in Canto 13.

However we arrange the scene—as literal or phantasmagoric—the point made is the same: the Venus to whom the poet makes his prayer inhabits an inhuman world. The shark that has taken the place of her dove is pure predatory appetite, and the animal that turns "the venereal awl/In the livid wound of love" carries the same associations. "Love" is a blind instinct or something worse—a kind of sadism. If a Venus returned to the sea is the only divinity that modern man has left to worship, he has been reduced to a worship of the life force in its most brutal form. Perhaps this is a better alternative than setting up the grave in the house (see the "Ode to the Confederate Dead,"[2] lines 94–95) and worshipping death; but between them there is not much to choose.

In Section 4, "Spring," in a world still at war the poet faces the future. Apparently he has accepted naturalism, for he seriously asks spring to infuse a "liquid soul" in him, something to comfort his "unease" which already apprehends the cooler day of death.

He recalls his youth when he lived in what seemed a timeless summer. Death itself could then be alluded to cheerfully. With an eye to the Elizabethans' use of the word "die" as meaning the experience of sexual orgasm, one could say he would like to die (lines 196–200). It was a period in which time did not threaten —did not even exist.

Lines 211–18 are difficult. Earth is a rolling stone, something revolving meaninglessly, and it is being burned up by man's "burning arrogance" (lines 211–12). Then the poet compares the earth to something very different, Plato's cave, of which he writes in the *Republic*. Men do not see reality directly but only at secondhand, as if they were chained inside a cave and were able to see only shadows cast on the walls of the cave by objects from which their eyes were turned away. Could they be released and walk out into the sunlight, they would be able to see things as they really are.

Tate also alludes here to the Greek myth of

Sisyphus. In the underworld, Sisyphus was for his crimes condemned to the task of rolling a stone to the top of a high hill, but once at the top, the stone promptly rolled down to the bottom again and his work was all to do over. In calling the earth a "rolling stone" the poet seems to be hinting that it is a kind of Sisyphean stone whose motion is mechanical and meaningless. But Tate goes on to make a bold fusion of the Sisyphus myth with Plato's myth. Sisyphus is asked to put an end to the farce of his own activity and that of the prisoners in the cave: he is to block the exit from the cave with his stone. (One recalls the last line of "The Meaning of Death": "We are the eyelids of defeated caves.")

Who is the mother of silences whose title chimes in each stanza? In line 224 she is St. Monica, the mother of St. Augustine (354–430). Miss Koch pointed out a number of years ago that the reference in this stanza is to the passage in Book 9 of St. Augustine's *Confessions*, in which he tells us (speaking of his mother): "She and I stood alone, leaning in a certain window, and looked into the garden of the house where we now lay, at Ostia. . . ." Monica told her son that now that he had become converted to Christianity, she had no more earthly happiness to live for and would welcome death as a blessing whenever it came. A few days later she died, leaving, as St. Augustine tells us, a "fresh wound" in his heart, but a wound of love.

Obviously, the speaker of this poem is using the reference to St. Augustine to point a contrast between the position of a man within the dying Roman Empire and a twentieth-century man living in a world wracked by intercontinental war. But in most of the stanzas in "Spring" the mother of silences[3] must refer to a much more general "mother." Is she the feminine principle or the maternal principle itself? Is she a pagan mother goddess? Is she the Virgin Mary? Is she love? Or death? Or both? Does she show her love—her "kindness"—by giving

---

[2] Vivienne Koch has pointed out that the phrase "living wound of love" is a translation of a phrase used by Lucretius (*ca.* 96–55 B.C.) in the *Proem* to his *De Rerum Natura*. Writing when Italy was torn by war, Lucretius prayed Venus to inflict upon the war god Mars the eternal wound of love, "aeterno volnere amoris," and thus cause the Romans to make love rather than war. R. K. Meiners, in *The Last Alternatives: A Study of the Works of Allen Tate* (1963), reminds us that Lucretius did not believe in the gods— in fact, wrote his *De Rerum Natura* to debunk the gods—and that therefore Tate is using the quotation from Lucretius ironically. This is quite true, and Lucretius' agnosticism fits perfectly the mood of Tate's poem. In the world depicted in "Winter," the love goddess has been reduced to a primitive, biological drive. As such, she may wear a terrible beauty, and the poet's appeal to her has its own beauty, but he is not misled about her character.

[3] Perhaps an echo of Eliot's "Lady of Silences" in *Ash Wednesday*. See Meiners, *The Last Alternatives*, p. 179.

men rest and throwing over them the merciful
oblivion of death? The final invocation to her
is thoroughly ambiguous. The speaker scarcely
feels that he is entitled to pray at all. In his
present plight, to whom could he pray?

To the memory of John Peale Bishop,
1892–1944

Allor porsi la mano un poco avante,
e colsi un ramicel da un gran pruno;
e il tronco suo gridò: Perchè mi schiante?

1. SUMMER

Summer, this is our flesh,
The body you let mature;
If now while the body is fresh
You take it, shall we give
The heart, lest heart endure
The mind's tattering
Blow of greedy claws?
Shall mind itself still live
If like a hunting king
It falls to the lion's jaws?   10

Under the summer's blast
The soul cannot endure
Unless by sleight or fast
It seize or deny its day
To make the eye secure.
Brothers-in-arms, remember
The hot wind dries and draws
With circular delay
The flesh, ash from the ember,
Into the summer's jaws.   20

It was a gentle sun
When, at the June solstice
Green France was overrun
With caterpillar feet.
No head knows where its rest is
Or may lie down with reason
When war's usurping claws
Shall take the heart escheat—
Green field in burning season
To stain the weevil's jaws.   30

The southern summer dies
Evenly in the fall:
We raise our tired eyes
Into a sky of glass,
Blue, empty, and tall

Without tail or head
Where burn the equal laws
For Balaam and his ass
Above the invalid dead,
Who cannot lift their jaws.   40

When was it that the summer
(Daylong a liquid light)
And a child, the new-comer,
Bathed in the same green spray,
Could neither guess the night?
The summer had no reason;
Then, like a primal cause
It had its timeless day
Before it kept the season
Of time's engaging jaws.   50

Two men of our summer world
Descended winding hell
And when their shadows curled
They fearfully confounded
The vast concluding shell:
Stopping, they saw in the narrow
Light a centaur pause
And gaze, then his astounded
Beard, with a notched arrow,
Part back upon his jaws.   60

2. AUTUMN

It had an autumn smell
And that was how I knew
That I was down a well:
I was no longer young;
My lips were numb and blue,
The air was like fine sand
In a butcher's stall
Or pumice to the tongue:
And when I raised my hand
I stood in the empty hall.   70

The round ceiling was high
And the gray light like shale
Thin, crumbling, and dry:
No rug on the bare floor
Nor any carved detail
To which the eye could glide;
I counted along the wall
Door after closed door
Through which a shade might slide
To the cold and empty hall.   80

I will leave this house, I said,
There is the autumn weather—

Here, nor living nor dead;
The lights burn in the town
Where men fear together.
Then on the bare floor,
But tiptoe lest I fall,
I walked years down
Towards the front door
At the end of the empty hall.   90

The door was false—no key
Or lock, and I was caught
In the house; yet I could see
I had been born to it
For miles of running brought
Me back where I began.
I saw now in the wall
A door open a slit
And a fat grizzled man
Come out into the hall: 100

As in a moonlit street
Men meeting are too shy
To check their hurried feet
But raise their eyes and squint
As through a needle's eye
Into the faceless gloom,—
My father in a gray shawl
Gave me an unseeing glint
And entered another room!
I stood in the empty hall   110

And watched them come and go
From one room to another,
Old men, old women—slow,
Familiar; girls, boys;
I saw my downcast mother
Clad in her street-clothes,
Her blue eyes long and small,
Who had no look or voice
For him whose vision froze
Him in the empty hall.   120

3. WINTER

Goddess sea-born and bright,
Return into the sea
Where eddying twilight
Gathers upon your people—
Cold goddess, hear our plea!
Leave the burnt earth, Venus,
For the drying God above,
Hanged in his windy steeple,
No longer bears for us
The living wound of love.   130

All the sea-gods are dead.
You, Venus, come home
To your salt maidenhead,
The tossed anonymous sea
Under shuddering foam—
Shade for lovers, where
A shark swift as your dove
Shall pace our company
All night to nudge and tear
The livid wound of love.   140

And now the winter sea:
Within her hollow rind
What sleek facility
Of sea-conceited scop
To plumb the nether mind!
Eternal winters blow
Shivering flakes, and shove
Bodies that wheel and drop—
Cold soot upon the snow
Their livid wound of love.   150

Beyond the undertow
The gray sea-foliage
Transpires a phosphor glow
Into the circular miles:
In the centre of his cage
The pacing animal
Surveys the jungle cove
And slicks his slithering wiles
To turn the venereal awl
In the livid wound of love.   160

Beyond the undertow
The rigid madrepore
Resists the winter's flow—
Headless, unageing oak
That gives the leaf no more.
Wilfully as I stood
Within the thickest grove
I seized a branch, which broke;
I heard the speaking blood
(From the livid wound of love)   170

Drip down upon my toe:
"We are the men who died
Of self-inflicted woe,
Lovers whose stratagem
Led to their suicide."
I touched my sanguine hair
And felt it drip above
Their brother who, like them,
Was maimed and did not bear
The living wound of love.   180

4. SPRING

Irritable spring, infuse
Into the burning breast
Your combustible juice
That as a liquid soul
Shall be the body's guest
Who lights, but cannot stay
To comfort this unease
Which, like a dying coal,
Hastens the cooler day
Of the mother of silences.   190

Back in my native prime
I saw the orient corn
All space but no time,
Reaching for the sun
Of the land where I was born:
It was a pleasant land
Where even death could please
Us with an ancient pun—
All dying for the hand
Of the mother of silences.   200

In time of bloody war
Who will know the time?
Is it a new spring star
Within the timing chill,
Talking, or just a mime,
That rises in the blood—
Thin Jack-and-Jilling seas
Without the human will?
Its light is at the flood,
Mother of silences!   210

It burns us each alone
Whose burning arrogance
Burns up the rolling stone,
This earth—Platonic cave
Of vertiginous chance!
Come, tired Sisyphus,
Cover the cave's egress
Where light reveals the slave,
Who rests when sleeps with us
The mother of silences.   220

Come, old woman, save
Your sons who have gone down
Into the burning cave:
Come, mother, and lean
At the window with your son
And gaze through its light frame
These fifteen centuries
Upon the shirking scene
Where men, blind, go lame:
Then, mother of silences,   230

Speak, that we may hear;
Listen, while we confess
That we conceal our fear;
Regard us, while the eye
Discerns by sight or guess
Whether, as sheep foregather
Upon their crooked knees,
We have begun to die;
Whether your kindness, mother,
Is mother of silences.   240

The Swimmers (1960)

The Swimmers is Part 3 of an unfinished poem
to be composed of six parts. The poem is written in Dante's *terza rima*. It moves swiftly and
with few literary allusions in its presentation of
a boy's first shocking encounter with evil. Five
boys going swimming come upon a lynching
posse and later the narrator sees the dead victim.

SCENE: *Montgomery County,
Kentucky, July 1911*

Kentucky water, clear springs: a boy fleeing
  To water under the dry Kentucky sun,

His four little friends in tandem with him,
    seeing

Long shadows of grapevine wriggle and run
  Over the green swirl; mullein under the ear
  Soft as Nausicaä's palm; sullen fun

Savage as childhood's thin harmonious tear:
  O fountain, bosom source undying-dead
  Replenish me the spring of love and fear

And give me back the eye that looked and fled   10
  When a thrush idling in the tulip tree
  Unwound the cold dream of the copperhead.

—Along the creek the road was winding; we
   Felt the quicksilver sky. I see again
   The shrill companions of that odyssey:

Bill Eaton, Charlie Watson, "Nigger" Layne
   The doctor's son, Harry Duèsler who played
   The flute; and Tate, with water on the brain.

Dog-days: the dusty leaves where rain delayed
   Hung low on poison-oak and scuppernong,   20
   And we were following the active shade

Of water, that bells and bickers all night long.
   "No more'n a mile," Layne said. All five
     stood still.
   Listening, I heard what seemed at first a song;

Peering, I heard the hooves come down the hill.
   The posse passed, twelve horse; the
     leader's face
   Was worn as limestone on an ancient sill.

Then, as sleepwalkers shift from a hard place
   In bed, and rising to keep a formal pledge
   Descend a ladder into empty space,   30

We scuttled down the bank below a ledge
   And marched stiff-legged in our common
     fright
   Along a hog-track by the riffle's edge:

Into a world where sound shaded the sight
   Dropped the dull hooves again; the
     horsemen came
   Again, all but the leader. It was night

Momently and I feared: eleven same
   Jesus-Christers unmembered and unmade,
   Whose Corpse had died again in dirty shame.

The bank then levelling in a speckled glade,   40
   We stopped to breathe above the
     swimming-hole;
   I gazed at its reticulated shade

Recoiling in blue fear, and felt it roll
   Over my ears and eyes and lift my hair
   Like seaweed tossing on a sunk atoll.

I rose again. Borne on the copper air
   A distant voice green as a funeral wreath
   Against a grave: "That dead nigger there."

The melancholy sheriff slouched beneath
   A giant sycamore; shaking his head   50
   He plucked a sassafras twig and picked
     his teeth:

"We come too late." He spoke to the
     tired dead
   Whose ragged shirt soaked up the viscous flow
   Of blood in which It lay discomfited.

A butting horse-fly gave one ear a blow
   And glanced off, as the sheriff kicked the rope
   Loose from the neck and hooked it with
     his toe

Away from the blood.—I looked back down
     the slope:
   The friends were gone that I had hoped
     to greet.—
   A single horseman came at a slow lope   60

And pulled up at the hanged man's horny feet;
   The sheriff noosed the feet, the other end
   The stranger tied to his pommel in a neat

Slip-knot. I saw the Negro's body bend
   And straighten, as a fish-line cast transverse
   Yields to the current that it must subtend.

The sheriff's Goddamn was a murmured curse
   Not for the dead but for the blinding dust
   That boxed the cortège in a cloudy hearse

And dragged it towards our town. I knew I must   70
   Not stay till twilight in that silent road;
   Sliding my bare feet into the warm crust,

I hopped the stonecrop like a panting toad
   Mouth open, following the heaving cloud
   That floated to the court-house square its load

Of limber corpse that took the sun for shroud.
   There were three figures in the dying sun
   Whose light were company where three
     was crowd.

My breath crackled the dead air like a shotgun
   As, sheriff and the stranger disappearing,   80
   The faceless head lay still. I could not run

Or walk, but stood. Alone in the public clearing
   This private thing was owned by all the town,
   Though never claimed by us within my
     hearing.

A Southern Mode of the Imagination (1959)

A reader acquainted with Allen Tate's poetry will not be surprised to find a good many of the ideas that are rendered dramatically and concretely in the poetry expressed more discursively in this essay. Tate's point of view is personal and highly individual: it is the account of one of the participants in the Fugitive movement who at the end of the 1950's is looking back on more than a quarter-century of his own work and that of his friends and contemporaries.

Tate's perspective, however, is wider still, and his comments on the antebellum South and the Civil War and Reconstruction South—see, for example, his references to figures so diverse as are John William De Forest, Augusta Evans, and Mark Twain—are all worth pondering. In fact, Tate's essay can be taken as a brilliant review of southern literature from the time of William Gilmore Simms to 1959. But it is more than a mere review: it proposes a theory to explain the essential difference of the southern subculture from American culture generally and a related theory that would account for the great surge of southern literature in the 1920's.

The reader need not agree with all that Tate says in order to find this essay highly stimulating. In many respects it is evidently true. At the very least, it is distinctly worth quarreling with.

I

What I am about to say will be composed of obscure speculation, mere opinion, and reminiscence verging upon autobiography. But having issued this warning, and given notice to the scholars of American literature that the entire affair will be somewhat unreliable, I must allude to some of the things that I shall not try to say. I shall not discuss or "place" any of the Southern writers of the period now somewhat misleadingly called the Southern Renaissance. It was more precisely a birth, not a rebirth. The eyes of the world are on William Faulkner; for that reason I shall not talk about him. I take it to be a commonplace of literary history that no writer of Mr. Faulkner's power could emerge from a literary and social vacuum. It is a part of Mr. Faulkner's legend about himself that he did appear, like the sons of Cadmus, full grown, out of the unlettered soil of his native state, Mississippi. But we are under no obligation to take his word for it. Two other modern writers of prose-fiction, Mr. Stark Young[1] and Miss Eudora Welty, quite as gifted as Mr. Faulkner, if somewhat below him in magnitude and power, are also natives of that backward state, where fewer people can read than in any other state in the Union. I shall not pause to explain my paradoxical conviction, shared I believe by Mr. Donald Davidson, that the very backwardness of Mississippi, and of the South as a whole, might partially explain the rise of a new literature which has won the attention not only of Americans but of the Western world.

If the Elizabethan age would still be the glory of English literature without Shakespeare, the new literature of the Southern states would still be formidable without Faulkner. I have promised not to discuss any one writer in detail, but I shall invoke certain names: Elizabeth Madox Roberts, Robert Penn Warren, Eudora Welty, Stark Young, Dubose Heyward, Ellen Glasgow, James Branch Cabell, Katherine Anne Porter, Carson McCullers, Tennessee Williams, Thomas Wolfe, Paul Green, Caroline Gordon, Flannery O'Connor, Truman Capote, Ralph Ellison, John Crowe Ransom, Donald Davidson, Peter Taylor, Andrew Lytle. It is scarcely chauvinism on my part to point out that, with the exception of Fitzgerald and Hemingway, the region north of the Potomac and Ohio Rivers has become the stepsister of American fiction. And it has been said, so often that I almost believe it, that the American branch of the New Criticism is of Southern origin—a distinction about which my own feelings are neutral.

Before I turn to the more speculative part of this discussion, I should like to quote a paragraph written in the Reconstruction period—that is, around 1870—by a New England novelist who had come to the South as a benign carpetbagger

---

[1] Stark Young (1881–1963), poet, novelist, and drama critic. Young's novel *So Red the Rose* (1934) received a good deal of critical and popular attention, though he is now remembered more for the quality of his drama criticism.

to observe and to improve what he observed. He was John William De Forest, of Connecticut, whose works were almost completely forgotten until about ten years ago. He was not only one of the best nineteenth-century American novelists; he was a shrewd social commentator, whose dislike of Southerners did not prevent him from seeing them more objectively than any other Northerner of his time. I quote:

Not until Southerners get rid of some of their social vanity, not until they cease talking of themselves in a spirit of self-adulation, not until they drop the idea that they are Romans and must write in the style of Cicero, will they be able to so paint life that the world shall crowd to see the picture. Meanwhile let us pray that a true Southern novelist will soon arise, for he will be able to furnish us vast amusement and some instruction. His day is passing; in another generation his material will be gone; the chivalrous Southern will be as dead as the slavery that created him.

It was not until fifty years later that De Forest's demands upon the Southern novelist were fulfilled, when the writers whose names I have listed began to appear. My own contemporaries called the nineteenth-century Ciceronian Southern style "Confederate prose," and we avoided it more assiduously than sin. Of a Southern woman novelist of the 1860's, Augusta Evans, author of *St. Elmo*, it was said that her heroines had swallowed an unabridged dictionary.

My reason for adopting the *causerie* instead of the formal discourse has a quite simple explanation. I have no talent for research; or at any rate I am like the man who, upon being asked whether he could play the violin, answered that he didn't know because he had never tried. Apart from inadequate scholarship, it would be improper of me to pretend to an objectivity, which I do not feel, in the recital of certain events, in which I have been told that I played a small part. None of us— and by us I mean not only the group of poets who with unintentional prophecy styled themselves the "Fugitives," but also our contemporaries in other Southern states—none of us, thirty-five years ago, was conscious of playing any part at all. I ought not to speak for my contemporaries, most of whom are still living and able to talk. The essays and books about us that have begun to appear give me a little less than the shock of recognition. If one

does not recognize oneself, one may not unreasonably expect to recognize one's friends. One writer, Mr. John Bradbury, in a formidable book of some three hundred pages entitled *The Fugitives*, says that John Crowe Ransom taught his students, of whom I had the honor to be one, the "knowledge of good and evil." I don't recognize in this role my old friend and early master; I surmise that he has found it no less disconcerting than I do. Our initiation into the knowledge of good and evil, like everybody else's, must have been at birth; our later improvement in this field of knowledge, haphazard and extra-curricular. John Ransom taught us—Robert Penn Warren, Cleanth Brooks, Andrew Lytle and myself—Kantian aesthetics and a philosophical dualism, tinged with Christian theology, but ultimately derived from the Nicomachian ethics. I allude to my own education not because it was unique, but because it was the education of my generation in the South. But we said at that time very little about the South; an anomalous reticence in a group of men who later became notoriously sectional in point of view.

We knew we were Southerners, but this was a matter of plain denotation; just as we knew that some people were Yankees; or we knew that there were people whom—if we saw them—we would think of as Yankees; we might even have said, but only among ourselves, you understand: "He's a Yankee." Brainard Cheney told me years ago that when he was a small boy in Southern Georgia, down near the Okefenokee Swamp, the rumor spread that some Yankees were coming to town. All the little boys gathered in the courthouse square to see what Yankees looked like. This was about 1910. My boyhood, in the border state of Kentucky, was evidently more cosmopolitan. There were a few Northerners, no doubt; there were a few elderly gentlemen who had been Southern Unionists, or homemade Yankees, as they were discourteously described, who had fought in the Federal Army. One of these, old Mr. Crabb, white-haired, beak-nosed, and distinguished, frequently passed our house on his morning walk. He had an empty sleeve, and my mother said he had got his arm shot off at the Battle of Gettysburg. I knew that my grandfather had been in Pickett's charge, and I wondered idly whether he had shot it off. I do not remember whether I wished that he had.

This was our long moment of innocence, which I tried to recover in a poem many years later. And for men of my age, who missed the first World War by a few months, it was a new Era of Good

Feeling between the sections. Some time before 1914 the North had temporarily stopped trying to improve us, or had at least paused to think about something else. Having just missed being sent to France in the A. E. F., I came to Vanderbilt University from a rural small-town society that had only a superficial Victorian veneer pasted over what was still an eighteenth-century way of living. It has been said that Kentucky seceded in 1865. In my boyhood, and even much later, Kentucky was more backward and Southern, socially and economically, than Tennessee or North Carolina. This preindustrial society meant, for people living in it, that one's identity had everything to do with land and material property, at a definite place, and very little to do with money. It was better for a person, however impoverished, of my name, to be identified with Tate's Creek Pike, in Fayette County, than to be the richest man in town without the identification of place. This was simple and innocent; it had little to do with what the English call *class*. Yet from whatever point of view one may look at it, it will in the end lead us towards the secret of what was rather grandiosely called, by the late W. J. Cash, the Southern Mind.

If I may bring to bear upon it an up-to-date and un-Southern adjective, it was an extroverted mind not much given to introspection. (I do not say meditation, which is something quite different.) Such irony as this mind was capable of was distinctly romantic; it came out of the sense of dislocated external relations: because people were not *where* they ought to be they could not be *who* they ought to be; for men had missed their proper role, which was to be attached to a place. Mr. Faulkner's lawyer Benbow and the Compson family, in *The Sound and the Fury*, are people of this sort; I know of no better examples than Mr. Andrew Lytle's Jack Cropleigh, in his novel *The Velvet Horn*, or the narrator of his powerful short story, "Mister McGregor." It is the irony of time and place out of joint. It was provincial or, if you will, ignorant of the world. It was the irony of social discrepancies, not the tragic irony of the peripety, or of interior change. It is premodern; it can be found in the early books of Ellen Glasgow and James Branch Cabell, as different at the surface as their books may appear to be.

But with the end of the first World War a change came about that literary historians have not yet explained; whether we shall ever understand it one cannot say. Southern literature in the second half of this century may cease to engage the scholarly imagination; the subject may eventually become academic, and buried with the last dissertation. Back in the nineteen-thirties, I believe it was precisely 1935, I wrote for the tenth anniversary issue of *The Virginia Quarterly Review* an essay entitled "The Profession of Letters in the South," which glanced at a possible explanation by analogy to another literary period. I refer to it here in order to qualify, or at any rate to extend its agreement, not, I hope, to call attention to myself. So far as that old essay is concerned, other persons have already done this for me. When I look at the index of a work of contemporary criticism (I always look there first), and see my name, I get a little nervous because the following passage has a two-to-one chance over anything else I have written, to be quoted; I quote it again:

> The considerable achievement of Southerners in modern American letters must not beguile us into too much hope for the future. The Southern novelist has left his mark upon the age; but it is of the age. From the peculiarly historical consciousness of the Southern writer has come good work of a special order; but the focus of this consciousness is quite temporary. It has made possible the curious burst of intelligence that we get at a crossing of the ways, not unlike, on an infinitesimal scale, the outburst of poetic genius at the end of the sixteenth century when commercial England had already begun to crush feudal England. The Histories and Tragedies of Shakespeare record the death of the old regime, and Doctor Faustus gives up feudal order for world power.

My purpose in quoting the passage—I marvel that prose so badly written could have been quoted so much—is not to approve of the approbation it has received, but to point out that whatever rightness it may have is not right enough. It says nothing about the particular quality of the Southern writers of our time.

The quality that I have in mind, none too clearly, makes its direct impact upon the reader, even if he be the foreign reader: he knows that he is reading a Southern book. But this explains nothing, for a quality can only be pointed to or shared, not defined. Let me substitute for the word quality the phrase *mode of discourse*.

The traditional Southern mode of discourse presupposes somebody at the other end silently listening: it is the rhetorical mode. Its historical rival is the dialectical mode, or the give and take between

two minds, even if one mind, like the mind of Socrates, prevail at the end. The Southerner has
never been a dialectician. The ante-bellum Southerner quoted Aristotle in defense of slavery, but
Plato, the dialectician, was not opposed to the
"peculiar institution," and he could have been
cited with equal effect in support of the South
Carolinian daydream of a Greek democracy. Aristotle was chosen by the South for good reason:
although the Stagirite (as the Southerners called
him) was a metaphysician, the South liked the
deductive method, if its application were not too
abstruse, and nobody could quarrel with the arrangement, in the order of importance, of the
three great Aristotelian treatises on man in society:
the *Nicomachian Ethics*, the *Politics*, and the *Rhetoric*. Aristotle assumed first principles from which
he—and the old Southerners after him—could make
appropriate deductions about the inequalities of
men. Plato reached first principles by means of
dialogue, which can easily become subjective: the
mind talking to itself. The Southerner always talks
to somebody else, and this somebody else, after
varying intervals, is given his turn; but the conversation is always among rhetoricians; that is to
say, the typical Southern conversation is not going
anywhere; it is not about anything. *It is about the
people who are talking*, even if they never refer to
themselves, which they usually don't, since conversation is only an expression of manners, the purpose of which is to make everybody happy. This
may be the reason why Northerners and other uninitiated persons find the alternating, or contrapuntal, conversation of Southerners fatiguing. Educated Northerners like their conversation to be
about ideas.

II

The foregoing, rather too broad distinction between dialectic and rhetoric is not meant to convey the impression that no Southerner of the past
or the present was ever given to thought; nor do I
wish to imply that New Englanders were so busy
thinking that they wholly neglected that form of
rhetoric which may be described as the manners
of men talking in society. Emerson said that the
"scholar is man thinking." Had Southerners of
that era taken seriously the famous lecture entitled
"The American Scholar," they might have replied
by saying that the gentleman is man talking. The
accomplished Christian gentleman of the old South

was the shadow, attenuated by evangelical Calvinism, of his Renaissance spiritual ancestor, who had
been the creation of the rhetorical tradition, out
of Aristotle through Cicero, distilled finally by
Castiglione. By contrast, the New England sage,
embodied in Ralph Waldo Emerson, took seriously what has come to be known since the Industrial Revolution as the life of the mind: an activity
a little apart from life, and perhaps leading to the
fashionable alienation of the "intellectual" of our
time. The protective withdrawal of the New England sage into dialectical truth lurks back of
Emerson's famous definition of manners as the
"invention of a wise man to keep a fool at a distance." (There is little doubt of the part Emerson
conceived himself as playing.) The notorious lack
of self-consciousness of the ante-bellum Southerner
made it almost impossible for him to define anything; least of all could he imagine the impropriety
of a definition of manners. Yet had a Southern
contemporary of Emerson decided to argue the
question, he might have retorted that manners are
not *inventions*, but *conventions* tacitly agreed upon
to protect the fool from consciousness of his folly.
I do not wholly subscribe to this Southern view;
there is to be brought against it Henry Adams's
unkind portrait of Rooney Lee, a son of Robert E.
Lee, who soon became a Confederate officer. The
younger Lee, said Adams, when they were fellow
students at Harvard, seemed to have only the habit
of command, and no brains. (Adams didn't say it
quite so rudely, but that is what it came to.)
Rooney Lee, like his famous father, was a man of
action, action through the habit of command being
a form of rhetoric: he acted upon the assumptions
of identification by place. The Lee identification,
the whole Virginian myth of the rooted man, was
the model of the more homely mystique of Tate's
Creek Pike in the frontier state of Kentucky,
whose citizens the Virginians thought were all
Davy Crocketts—a frontiersman who described himself as "half-horse and half-alligator." Virginia was
the model for the entire Upper South.

Northern historians were for years puzzled that
Lee and the Southern yeoman farmer fought for
the South, since neither had any interest in slavery.
The question was usually put in this form: Why
did Lee, who never owned a slave and detested
slavery, become the leader of the slavocracy? Because he was a rhetorician who would have flunked
Henry Adams's examination as miserably as his
son. A Southern dialectician, could he be imagined
in Lee's predicament, would have tossed his loyal-

ties back and forth and come out with an abstraction called Justice, and he would have fought in the Federal Army or not at all. The record seems to indicate that the one dialectical abstraction that Lee entertained came to him after the war: the idea of constitutional government, for which in retrospect he considered that he had fought. Perhaps he did fight for it; yet I have the temerity to doubt his word. He fought for the local community which he could not abstract into fragments. He was in the position of the man who is urged by an outsider to repudiate his family because a cousin is an embezzler, or of the man who tries to rectify his ill-use of his brother by pretending that his entire family is a bad lot. I trust that in this analogy it is clear that the brother is the Negro slave.

What Robert E. Lee has to do with Southern literature is a question that might at this point quite properly be asked. Lee has a good deal to do with it, if we are going to look at Southern literature as the rhetorical expression of a Southern Mind. But even to be conscious of the possibility of a Southern Mind could lead us into a mode of discourse radically different from that of the rhetorician. We are well on the way towards dialectics. If we say that the old Southern Mind was rhetorical we must add that our access to it must be through its public phase, which was almost exclusively political. I do not believe that the antebellum Southerners, being wholly committed to the rhetorical mode, were capable of the elementary detachment that has permitted modern Southerners to discern the significance of that commitment, and to relate it to other modes of discourse. For the rhetorical mode is related to the myth-making faculty, and the mythopoeic mind assumes that certain great typical actions embody human truth. The critical detachment which permits me to apply this commonplace to the Southern Mind would not, I believe, have been within the grasp of better intellects than mine in the South up to the first World War. It has been said that the failure of the old Southern leaders to understand the Northern mind (which was then almost entirely the New England mind) was a failure of intelligence. In view of the task which the South had set for itself—that is, the preservation of local self-government within a framework of republican federalism—the charge is no doubt true. The old Southerners, being wholly committed to the rhetoric of politics, could not come to grips with the dynamic forces in the North that were rapidly

making the exclusively political solution of their problem obsolete: they did not understand economics. The Southern public *persona* was supported by what W. J. Cash called, in a neo-Spenglerian phrase, the "proto-Dorian" myth. This *persona* was that of the agrarian patriot, a composite image of Cincinnatus dropping the plough for the sword, and of Cicero leaving his rhetorical studies to apply them patriotically to the prosecution of Cataline. The center round which the Southern political imagination gravitated was perhaps even smaller than the communities of which the South was an aggregate. In the first place, that aggregate was not a whole; and in the second, it would follow that the community itself was not a whole. The South was an aggregate of farms and plantations, presided over by our composite agrarian hero, Cicero Cincinnatus. I can think of no better image for what the South was before 1860, and for what it largely still was until about 1914, than that of the old gentleman in Kentucky who sat every afternoon in his front yard under an old sugar tree, reading Cicero's Letters to Atticus. When the hands suckering the tobacco in the adjoining field needed orders, he kept his place in the book with his forefinger, walked out into the field, gave the orders, and then returned to his reading under the shade of the tree. He was also a lawyer, and occasionally he went to his office, which was over the feed store in the county seat, a village with a population of about four hundred people.

The center of the South, then, was the family, no less for Robert E. Lee than for the people on Tate's Creek Pike; for Virginia was a great aggregate of families that through almost infinite ramifications of relationship was almost one family. Such a society could not be anything but political. The virtues cherished under such a regime were almost exclusively social and moral, with none of the intensively cultivated divisions of intellectual labor which are necessary to a flowering of the arts, whether literary or plastic. It is thus significant that the one original art of the South was domestic architecture, as befitted a family-centered society. It has been frequently noted that the reason why the South did not produce a great ante-bellum literature was the lack of cities as cultural centers. This was indeed a lack; but it is more important to understand why cultural centers were missing. The South did not want cultural centers; it preferred the plantation center. William Gilmore Simms argued repeatedly in the 1850's that no exclusively agrarian society had produced a great literature. Was this a failure of intelligence? I think not, if we look at the scene from the inside. After Archimedes had observed that, had he a fulcrum big enough, he could move the world, was it a failure of the Greek intelligence that it did not at once construct such a fulcrum? Were the Greek philosophers less intelligent than the late Albert Einstein and Professor Teller, who have found a way not only to move the world but perhaps to destroy it? But the plantation myth—and I use the word myth not to indicate a fantasy, but a reality—this myth, if Greek at all, was the limited Spartan myth. It was actually nearer to Republican Rome, a society which, like the South, was short in metaphysicians and great poets, and long in moralists and rhetoricians.

Mr. Lionel Trilling has said somewhere that the great writer, the spokesman of a culture, carries in himself the fundamental dialectic of that culture: the deeper conflicts of which his contemporaries are perhaps only dimly aware. There is a valuable truth in this observation. The inner strains, stresses, tensions, the shocked self-consciousness of a highly differentiated and complex society, issue in the dialectic of the high arts. The Old South, I take it, was remarkably free of this self-consciousness; the strains that it felt were external. And I surmise that had our Southern *persona*, our friend Cicero Cincinnatus, been much less simple than he was, the distractions of the sectional agitation nevertheless were so engrossing that they would have postponed almost indefinitely that self-examination which is the beginning, if not of wisdom, then at least of the arts of literature. When one is under attack, it is inevitable that one should put not only one's best foot forward but both feet, even if one of them rests upon the neck of a Negro slave. One then attributes to "those people over there" (the phrase that General Lee used to designate the Federal Army) all the evil of his own world. The defensive Southerner said that *if only* "those people over there" would let us alone, the vast Sabine Farm of the South (where men read Horace but did not think it necessary to be Horace) would perpetuate itself forever.

The complicated reasons for this Southern isolationism were, as I have tried to indicate, partly internal and partly external; but whatever the causes, the pertinent fact for any approach to the modern literary Renaissance is that the South was more isolated from 1865 to about 1920 than it had been before 1865. It was the isolationism of economic prostration, defeat, and inverted pride. And

the New South of Henry W. Grady's rhetoric was just as isolated and provincial as the Old South of Thomas Nelson Page. For Grady's New South, the complete answer was the factory. (It was put into the less than distinguished verse of "The Song of the Chattahoochee," by Sidney Lanier.) I venture to think that there was more to be said for Page's Old South, even if we agree that, like Grady's New South, it was unreal: I take it that a pleasant dream is to be preferred to an actuality which imitates a nightmare. Neither the unreal dream nor the actual nightmare could lead to the conception of a complete society. If we want proof of this, we need only to look at the South today.

I should like now to return to the inadequacy of my speculations, twenty-four years ago, on the reasons for the sudden rise of the new Southern literature—a literature which, I have been told often enough to authorize the presumption, is now the center of American literature. (I do not insist upon this.) Social change must have had something to do with it, but it does not explain it. I do not hope to explain it now. I wish only to add a consideration which I have already adumbrated. If it seems narrow, technical, and even academically tenuous, it is probably not less satisfactory than the conventional attribution of literary causation to what is called the historical factor. No doubt, without this factor, without the social change, the new literature could not have appeared. One can nevertheless imagine the same consciousness of the same change around 1920, without the appearance of any literature whatever. Social change may produce a great social scientist, like the late Howard W. Odum, of North Carolina. Social upheaval will not in itself produce a poet like John Crowe Ransom or a novelist like William Faulkner.

There was another kind of change taking place at the same time, and it was decisive. The old Southern *rhetor*, the speaker who was eloquent before the audience but silent in himself, had always had at his disposal a less formal version of the rhetorical mode of discourse than the political oration. Was it not said that Southerners were the best storytellers in America? Perhaps they still are. The tall tale was the staple of Southern conversation. Augustus Baldwin Longstreet's *Georgia Scenes* is a collection of tall tales written by an accomplished gentleman for other accomplished gentlemen; this famous book is in no sense folk literature, or an expression of the late V. L. Parrington's democratic spirit. It is the art of the rhetorician applied to the anecdote, to the small typical action resembling the mediaeval *exemplum*, and it verges upon myth—the minor secular myth which just succeeds in skirting round the suprahuman myth of religion. We have got something like this myth in *Huckleberry Finn*, which I take to be the first modern novel by a Southerner. We are now prepared by depth psychology to describe the action of *Huckleberry Finn* as not only typical, but as archetypal. What concerns me about it, for my purposes, is not whether it is a great novel (perhaps the *scale* of the action and the *range* of consciousness are too small for a great novel); what concerns me is the mode of its progression; for this mode is no longer the mode of rhetoric, the mode of the speaker reporting in person an argument or an action in which he is not dramatically involved. The action is generated inside the characters: there is internal dialogue, a conflict within the self. Mark Twain seems not to have been wholly conscious of what he had done; for he never did it again. Ernest Hemingway has said that the modern American novel comes out of *Huckleberry Finn*, and William Faulkner has paid a similar tribute. But this is not quite to the point.

Mark Twain was a forerunner who set an example which was not necessarily an influence. The feature of *Huckleberry Finn* which I have tried to discern, the shift from the rhetorical mode to the dialectical mode, had to be rediscovered by the twentieth-century novelists of the South. The example of Mark Twain was not quite fully developed and clean in outline. Most of the recent essays on *Huckleberry Finn*—by Lionel Trilling and T. S. Eliot for example—have not been able to approach the end of the novel without embarrassment. (The one exception is a perceptive essay by Mr. Leo Marx.) Huck himself is a dramatic dialec-

tician; Tom Sawyer, who reappears at the end and resolves the action externally with the preposterous "liberation" of Nigger Jim, who is already free, is a ham Southern rhetorician of the old school. He imposes his "style" upon a reality which has no relation to it, without perception of the ironic "other possible case" which is essential to the dramatic dialectic of the arts of fiction.

Here, as I come to the end of these speculations, I must go off again into surmises and guesses. What brought about the shift from rhetoric to dialectic? The Southern fictional dialectic of our time is still close to the traditional subject matter of the old informal rhetoric—the tall tale, the anecdote, the archetypal story. The New England dialectic of the Transcendentalists, from which Hawthorne had to protect himself by remaining aloof, tended to take flight into the synthesis of pure abstraction, in which the inner struggle is resolved in an idea. The Southern dramatic dialectic of our time is being resolved, as in the novels of William Faulkner, in action. The short answer to our question: How did this change come about? is that the South not only reentered the world with the first World War; it looked round and saw for the first time since about 1830 that the Yankees were not to blame for everything. It looks like a simple discovery, and it was; that is why it was difficult to make. The Southern legend, as Malcolm Cowley has called it, of defeat and heroic frustration was taken over by a dozen or more first-rate writers and converted into a universal myth of the human condition. W. B. Yeats's great epigram points to the nature of the shift from melodramatic rhetoric to the dialectic of tragedy: "Out of the quarrel with others we make rhetoric; out of the quarrel with ourselves, poetry."

Harlem Renaissance

The literary and artistic movement known as the Harlem Renaissance is a watershed moment in the cultural history of American blacks, and time may well show that it was such a moment in the cultural history of America. This burst of black talent and of white appreciation, however limited, was ushered in, as Langston Hughes says, by the musicals *Shuffle Along* and *Running Wild*, by the Charleston and jazz, and even by the tom-toms in the production of the *Emperor Jones*, by Eugene O'Neill.[1] But if we should pick a focal date for the movement, it would be 1925, when the black scholar Alain Locke, actually one of the fosterers and founders of the Renaissance, published an anthology of current work called *The New Negro: An Interpretation*. In his introduction Locke said that the "New Negro" simply could not be "swathed in the formulae" of the "Sociologist, the Philanthropist, the Race-leader." He stated that the "younger generation was vibrant with a new psychology," that a "new spirit" was awake in the "masses," with, in general, "renewed self-respect and self-dependence" creating a "buoyancy from within" to compensate for external pressures. The situation was not only "significant," Locke said; it was "prophetic."

But the New Negro, Locke said, had a history, and was new, not so much by the fact of his existence as by his new visibility. In other words, as Ralph Ellison and others have more lately insisted, the real Negro of the past was obscured by a stereotype called the Old Negro, which had been "more of a myth than a man." He had been a "stock figure perpetuated as a historical fiction, partly in innocent sentimentalism, partly in deliberate reactionism"—though, as Locke suggests, and many others have since re-

[1] And by Vachel Lindsay's use of syncopated rhythms in his poems—even though his treatment of black materials was coupled with a conventional condescension in attitude. See pp. 1852–53.

marked, the "Negro himself . . . contributed his share to this through a sort of protective social mimicry forced upon him by the adverse circumstances of dependence." With such circumstances alleviated, the "New Negro" was simply the Old Negro exhibiting the concealed self and the thwarted potentialities.

A social fact underlying the Renaissance was the black migration to the city, and nothing is more indicative of the contrast between the older black writer and the new than Dunbar's admonition to blacks, in 1902, not to flee to the northern cities to "false ideals and unreal ambitions." The massive migration of blacks to the northern cities is not to be understood, however, as special. Their migration was part of a general movement, and the growth of the great modern city had begun long before the First World War; but even at that time America was, insofar as population was concerned, primarily rural, and of the blacks more than 75 percent lived in the country, most of them in the South. For the black southerner, as for the white, the first urban migration was to the new cities of the region, such as Birmingham and Atlanta. Both black and white had urgent economic motivations, accentuated as land wore out and the boll weevil arrived, but the labor demands of the First World War provided new incentives and opportunities and shifted northward the goal of general migration. As for the black man's new northward migration, underlying it was the old desire that, in the past, he had only rarely been able to act upon: the desire to escape from the racial restrictions in the South. Now in the black community of a great city, the migrant was living, for the first time, in what seemed to be almost a totally black world. The minority psychology was modified, the masks of accommodationism could be laid aside, the self could be revealed. It could even be explored.

We might also point out as contributing to the Renaissance the growth of a black middle class, with social stability, some degree of economic independence, and increasing literacy. But there were other factors as well, and to understand some of them it is best to look at certain differences between the attitude of old writers and that of the new.

The New Negro repudiated the fathers who had achieved the stability, comfort, and literacy of the middle class. Writers such as Chesnutt and Dunbar had belonged to this class, and their work sometimes reflected class rather than race feeling; for instance, in Chesnutt's novel *The Marrow of Tradition*, the main character dislikes segregation chiefly because, in the Jim Crow car, he is forced to rub shoulders with lower class blacks who are "just as offensive to him as to the whites in the other end of the train." The tendency in the generation of Chesnutt, was to look toward a social relation

at the top, based on talent and class, and it was just this idea that was repudiated by the New Negro. The writers of the Renaissance, though they were clearly the "Talented Tenth," had adopted a view of racial solidarity and were turning toward the lower class to find inspiration and material.

This shift of attitude in at least a part of the Talented Tenth has a fairly complex history and involves a series of disappointments of the aspirations and hopes of the rising black middle class. Once in the northern city, black men, of all classes, found that, in spite of certain obvious advantages, they still had to face old problems, even if in new terms. At the lower levels white labor did not want black competition, and apprenticeships in unions were closed. Housing was hard to come by and expensive, and the modern black ghetto, with its crowding and degradation, was being formed. At upper levels, with differences, the situation was parallel.

The First World War, with the migration to the cities, had fostered another expectation—that of a rapprochement with white society, perhaps by integration, perhaps by cultural pluralism, perhaps by simple justice in the labor market and before the law: if the black man fought in the war and manned the factories, the white man would undoubtedly show some grateful recognition of the fact. Du Bois, "radical" though he was by this time, wrote in the *Crisis:* "If this is our country, then this is our war." War or no war, however, discrimination continued, even in the armed services. At home, violence flared between black servicemen and white civilians, notably in Houston, Texas, where, as a result, thirteen blacks were executed and some forty given life sentences,

Houston was, however, merely a beginning, and it was quickly clear that any hope born of participation in the war was a delusion, just as was the hope of salvation by migration. Du Bois, for instance, surrendered his expectation of gains from the war and bitterly predicted a worldwide race war with a coalition of all peoples of color against the white man. The inhabitant of the black slum was now more likely to turn to a leader like Marcus Garvey, with his dream of a black empire in Africa and with his fine uniforms and high-sounding titles, than to the leadership of the Talented Tenth.

Paradoxically, it may be said that the Talented Tenth now turned for spiritual sustenance toward the anonymous, alienated, untutored 90 percent, trapped in the sharecropper shack "down home" or in the teeming slums of New York or Chicago. The Talented Tenth who made this discovery were the young, many of them almost young enough to be the grandsons of Du Bois or James Weldon Johnson, just coming of age after the First World War. They were beneficiaries of the earlier struggles, most of them born to middle-class comfort and education, and if they turned away to the lower depths, it was with something of the natural revolt against the values of parents; this motive was, however, mixed with what one is tempted to call the perennial need to rediscover "blackness," the sense of racial solidarity that repudiates an "elite" in favor of the mystic values of "blood." The white world had blasted the black man's hope of justice; so he embraced blackness as salvation.

Two other factors enter here. For the first, the study of the black past had already begun, officially annouced in 1915 by the founding, by Carter G. Woodson, of the Association for the Study of Negro Life and History; and this was soon to be reenforced by work in anthropology and folklore undertaken by universities. The second factor is more complex. This was the period when the taste of the Western world, including that of the bohemia of New York, discovered the appeal of primitive art—for instance, the ritual masks of the city states and kingdoms of West Africa and the rock drawings of the Mediterranean coast. It was also the time of literary primitivism, with the doctrine of sexual liberation that we find in D. H. Lawrence and Sherwood Anderson—and all this in vague association with Freud. In the same general cluster of feeling there was, too, the fashion for the new jazz—the creation of the "primitives" of New Orleans—and the new sexual freedom of both Greenwich Village and the country clubs, where flappers and lounge lizards embraced. In the background of this new interest in the "primitive" lay, too, an uneasiness, even a fear, in the face of the sudden increase in the complexity of modern life, and with this a reaching out toward the "unspoiled," the "sincere," and the "simple"—one of the regularly recurring aspects of romanticism. In the merely literary aspect, there was, too, a belated offshoot of the old school of local color; and as a corollary of the continuing impulse to explore the regional diversity of America, a number of white writers, notably DuBose Heyward, in *Porgy*, and Julia Peterkin, in *Bright Skin*, began to treat black life.

To sum up, the middle-class black youth began to discover the beauty, vigor, and honesty of lower-class Harlem and celebrated his own blackness; or when he simply delineated in realistic detail the life there, he was in tune not only with a general impulse in the black world, but with the advanced thought and aesthetic sensibility of the white world that was finding new virtue in the "primitive."

Not that the black writers of Harlem were "primitives." On the contrary, most of them were, as we have said, of middle-class background. But the white audience often assumed that the black writers shared what was taken to be the mystic quality of black blood. Certainly, the black writers celebrated in their work the efficacy of primitive blackness and the "tom-tom of revolt," as Langston Hughes puts it. The white audience assumed that the black writers, because of their more intimate relation to the subliterate black world, could sometimes serve them as guides and instructors. The only trouble was that sometimes the black writer couldn't be quite primitive enough for white taste; as when the young novelist, Langston Hughes, renounced his rich white patroness rather than make his work as primitive as she wanted. (See pp. 2693–94.)

So here developed a social paradox. As the black writer tended toward "blackness" and toward the life of the ghetto, he found himself, overnight, in a more or less intimate association with a special segment of the white world. Harlem became fashionable not only for the literary and artistic, but for the mere thrill-seeker, and a night on the town was not complete without the Cotton Club, where Duke Ellington reigned, or spots of less innocent diversion. For the literary, there was the visit to the Dark Towers or, with luck, an invitation to a party at the apartment of Carl Van Vechten, the white author of the novel *Nigger Heaven*. In general, at the level of literature and the arts, the black world and the white were beginning to interpenetrate. For example, the famous publisher Alfred A. Knopf and James Weldon Johnson, being born on the same date, gave their birthday parties together. There were, too, the prizes, such as the thousand dollars offered by the publishers Charles and Albert Boni for a black novel; for black writing was now marketable, and the black writer had "arrived."

FURTHER READINGS

The editors here offer titles that deal with the major figures of the Harlem Renaissance. These citations will not be repeated in the suggested readings for each individual author.

Robert A. Bone, *The Negro Novel in America* (1968)
Arna Bontemps, *The Harlem Renaissance* (1972)
Herbert Hill, ed., *Anger, and Beyond* (1966)
N. I. Huggins, *Harlem Renaissance* (1971)

LANGSTON HUGHES (1902–1967)

It would be hard to find an American of more complex blood than Langston Hughes, the son of James Nathaniel Hughes and Carrie Mercer Langston, born in Joplin, Missouri, February 1, 1902. On the father's side, both great-grandfathers were white, one a Jewish slave trader, the other a Kentuckian of Scotch blood who ran a distillery. On the mother's side, there was a white great-grandfather, a Virginia planter named Quarles, who was said to be descended from Francis Quarles, the seventeenth-century English poet; and a grandmother, part-Chero-

kee, who, before the Civil War, had been the
first black girl to attend Oberlin College, and
who, before marrying the grandfather Langston,
had been the wife of Lewis Sheridan Leary,
killed in John Brown's raid on Harper's Ferry.
As a boy, Langston Hughes, living with his
grandmother, was taught to revere the shawl
with bullet holes that was the relic of the first
husband, and when he was eight, he saw his
grandmother in a place of honor on the platform where President Theodore Roosevelt stood
to dedicate the monument to John Brown at
Ossawatomie, Kansas.

As for the parents of the poet, the father,
intelligent and ambitious, had studied law and
then, because of race, had been refused the
bar examination; the result was that he abandoned his wife and child and went to Mexico
to seek his fortune in a nonwhite world. The
mother, a woman of some education who had
for a time attended the University of Kansas,
did the best she could, but there was little beyond menial jobs available for a black woman;
and for several years the boy was brought up
by the grandmother who owned Leary's shawl
and who read to him from the *Crisis* and Du
Bois's *The Souls of Black Folk*. The life with
the grandmother was the only period of real
stability the boy knew, for before he had finished high school he had lived in Joplin (Missouri), Lawrence and Topeka (Kansas), Toluca
and Mexico City, Colorado Springs, and Cleveland. On his visits in Mexico he found his
father an embittered man, thinking of nothing
but money, contemptuous of the ignorant Indians on whom he could visit all his own old
racial resentments; and so the son, in a terrible
anguish of spirit at discovering his hatred of
his own father, considered suicide and then fell
dangerously ill.

Very early Langston Hughes discovered writing. In high school he quite naturally took
Dunbar as a model, but Carl Sandburg's influence provided a more fruitful stock on which
to graft his own materials and rhythms, as in
"When Sue Wears Red," composed in his
junior year (1920):

When Susanna Jones wears red
Her face is like an ancient cameo
Turned brown by the age.

Come with a blast of trumpets,
Jesus!

When Susanna Jones wears red
A queen from some time-dead Egyptian night
Walks once again.

Blow trumpets, Jesus

And the beauty of Susanna Jones in red   10
Burns in my heart a love-fire sharp like pain.

Sweet silver trumpets,
Jesus!

By this time, too, Hughes had begun to write
fiction, with a story, written for an English assignment, based on a newspaper report about
a white charwoman: "Mary Winosky, who
scrubbed floors and picked rags, died and left
$8,000." The boy clearly had a remarkable and
precocious gift, and by June, 1921, his career
had begun, with a poem in the *Crisis* called
"The Negro Speaks of Rivers."

In the same year, Hughes entered Columbia
University, got acquainted with Harlem, and
went to Broadway whenever possible to see
Shuffle Along. But for the time being, a year
of college was enough, and he began his wanderings by signing on a ship as a mess boy. He
saw some thirty African ports, was a dishwasher
(and listener to jazz) in the night club Le
Grand Duc on the Rue Pigalle, in Paris, and
got his pocket picked in Italy. In 1925 he was
back home, as a busboy at the Wardman Park
Hotel, in Washington, when Vachel Lindsay,
then at the top of his fame, appeared as a
guest. The very evening when Lindsay was to
give a reading in the concert room of the hotel,
Hughes got up the courage to speak to him at
dinner and drop three poems by his plate,
"Jazzonia," "Negro Dancers," and "The Weary
Blues." The next morning Hughes learned from
the newspaper that Lindsay had discovered a
busboy poet, and when he arrived at work the

reporters were waiting for him. They took his picture standing in the middle of the luxurious dining room, holding up a tray of dirty dishes, and he was made. He also had a note from Lindsay, ending with the advice: "Do not let lionizers stampede you. Hide and write and study and think."

There was to be some excuse for lionizing the new poet. He won prizes; his first books, *The Weary Blues* (1926) and *Fine Clothes to the Jew* (1927), were generally acclaimed (except by some reviewers in the black press who, speaking for the black middle class, said that his work was "trash" written mostly about "the lower class members of his race"); and his readings, with music, of his poetry were very successful. But he tried to follow Lindsay's advice to work and study, and on the bounty of Amy Spingarn[1] enrolled in Lincoln University, in Pennsylvania. He also acquired another white patroness, a rich, elderly, charming widow named Mrs. Rufus Osgood Mason, who presided over a salon for the "New Negro," of which the new poet became an ornament. But beyond Lincoln University and Mrs. Mason's salon, there were Harlem and the places to which his wanderlust took him, the South, the West, Haiti, and Cuba.

In 1930 Hughes's first novel appeared, a study of ordinary work-a-day black life, written partly at Lincoln and partly on money provided by Mrs. Mason. The book was well received, but somehow the very success of the book brought on a crisis in the author's life. Mrs. Mason had provided him, as he reports in his autobiography, with "an assured income," clothes, theater and opera tickets, and the company of "someone who loved and believed in me," and had, as a reader and critic, a hand in the actual writing of the novel. Now she appar-

ently came to feel that she could direct his literary career. She wanted him, it seems, to be more "primitive." So he broke with her.

This rupture threw Hughes back upon the black world in two ways. First, he came to feel that the whole relationship with Mrs. Mason had been tainted, that "in the end it all came back very near to the old impasse of white and Negro—as do most relationships in America." Second, now poor again (for his books, in spite of critical attention, sold very badly), he moved out into the world of common life, common black life, to find a deeper identification with his own people in their special deprivation and suffering during the Depression. Almost penniless, he stuck to his ambition to be a writer according to his own specifications and to treat the materials he had elected as his own.

His wanderings continued. He was in the South and saw the "Scottsboro boys" in their cell,[2] visited Negro colleges (and found them generally spineless, at least at the administrative level, in the face of white racism), was in the West again, and again in Mexico. He visited the Soviet Union, with a group of blacks invited there to make a movie on black life in the United States; and this visit led to a trip around the world. Then came a period as correspondent for the Baltimore *Afro-American* to cover the Civil War in Spain. In 1938 Hughes was back in Harlem.

He had succeeded, meanwhile, in making his way as a writer. He had become a playwright, with a passionate desire to establish a theater for black life that led to the Suitcase Theater in Harlem and the New Negro Theater in Los Angeles; and his play *Mulatto* was the first Broadway success of a dramatic play by a black writer. He had now produced, too, a collection

[1] The wife of Joel Spingarn, a professor of comparative literature at Columbia University who, though white, was one of the founders of the National Association for the Advancement of Colored People, and who established, in 1914, the Spingarn Medal, an annual award to an outstanding black, which both Du Bois and Johnson were to receive, the first in 1923, the second in 1925.

[2] Nine black youths who were falsely accused of raping two white women on a freight train in Tennessee (March, 1930). The Scottsboro case ran on for almost a decade, and the defendants were released after spending an aggregate of some hundred years in jail. See Daniel T. Carter, *A Tragedy of the American South* (1969).

of short stories, *The Ways of White Folks,* and two new volumes of poems.

In the years to come Hughes continued to try his hand at new forms. He did the script for a Hollywood film. The first volume of his autobiography, *The Big Sea,* appeared in 1940, to be reviewed favorably by the already famous Richard Wright and by the then unknown Ralph Ellison. The second volume, *I Wonder as I Wander,* followed sixteen years later. Two more collections of stories appeared, in 1952 and 1963, and a second novel, *Tambourines to Glory,* in 1959. There were seven more volumes of poems. But the great achievement of the last part of Hughes's life was the creation of Jesse B. Simple, who first appeared in 1943 in Hughes's column in the Chicago *Defender.*

The birth of Simple occurred in a café when Hughes asked a man who was working in a war plant what he made.

"Cranks," he answered.

"What kind of cranks?"

"Oh, man, I don't know what kind of cranks."

"Well," asked Hughes, "do they crank cars, trucks, buses, planes or what?"

"I don't know what them cranks cranks," he said.

At which his girl friend, a little annoyed, put in, "You've been working there long enough. By now you ought to know what them cranks crank."

"Aw woman," he said, "you know white folks don't tell colored folks what cranks cranks!"

Simple is the archetypal underdog, beaten, downtrodden, ignorant, and blundering, but somehow gallant, ironic, clear-sighted, clear-headed, generous-spirited, and indestructible:

These feet of mine have stood in everything from soup lines to the draft board. They have supported everything from a packing trunk to a hungry woman. My feet have walked ten thousand miles running errands for white folks and another ten thousand trying to keep up with colored. My feet have stood before altars, at crap tables, bars, graves, kitchen doors, welfare windows, and social security railings. . . . In my time, I have been cut, stabbed, run over, hit by a car, tromped by a horse, robbed, fooled, deceived, double-crossed, dealt seconds, and mighty near blackmailed—but I am still here! I have been laid off, fired and not rehired, jim crowed, segregated, insulted, eliminated, locked in, locked out, left holding the bag, and denied relief. I have been caught in the rain, caught in jails, caught short in my rent, and caught with the wrong woman—but I am still here![3]

Langston Hughes died May 22, 1967. He was the first black man in America to make a strictly literary career, and that fact establishes him in cultural history. But he was, too, an artist. He was an innovator, in that he gave poetry a new tone, a tone drawn from black life and black language. His best poems speak off the page, with wit, pathos, and drama. And with Jesse B. Simple, we may well have one of those creations, like Huck Finn of Mark Twain or George Babbitt of Sinclair Lewis, who come from the common life into art and move from art back into life, to interpret and, somehow, ennoble life. And Simple resembles his creator, who, in his complexity and toughness, said of himself that he was "a writer who wrote mostly because when I felt bad, writing kept me from feeling worse."

[3] Simple appeared in more than 150 of Hughes's columns in the *Defender,* and in three books. After the publication of the last of these, *Simple's Uncle Sam,* in 1965, more than 130 reviews appeared, 40 of them foreign, and all favorable.

BIOGRAPHICAL CHART

1902   Born, February 1, in Joplin, Missouri, son of Jesse Nathaniel Hughes and Carrie Mercer Langston

1919   First visits father in Mexico

1920   Graduates from Central High School in Cleveland; visits father; writes "The Negro Speaks of

Rivers"; teaches English in business school and girls' finishing school in Mexico

1921 Sketches first published in the *Crisis,* in January; "The Negro Speaks of Rivers" in June; enters Columbia University

1922 Leaves Columbia; works at various jobs in and around New York

1923 Composes "The Weary Blues"; goes to sea on a freighter; visits numerous African ports

1924 Lives in Paris; poems in *Vanity Fair;* meets with Alain Locke, then preparing article on the "New Negro" for the *Survey Graphic;* returns home

1925 As busboy in Wardman Park Hotel, in Washington, meets Vachel Lindsay, who "discovers" him; wins first prize for "The Weary Blues," in the contest in *Opportunity* magazine, and the Spingarn prize in the *Crisis*

1926 Attends Lincoln University; first book of poems, *The Weary Blues,* published; acquaintance widening with writers and Harlem

1928 Makes acquaintance of Mrs. Rufus Osgood Mason, who becomes his patroness

1929 Graduates from Lincoln; novel, *Not Without Laughter,* finished

1930 Novel published to laudatory press; breaks with Mrs. Mason

1931 Wins Harmon Award for literature; travels in South and Haiti

1932 Travels to Soviet Union and around world

1934 *The Ways of White Folks*

1935 Play *Mulatto* produced (written in 1930)

1937 Correspondent in Spain for Baltimore *Afro-American*

1938 Harlem Suitcase Theater established

1940 *The Big Sea*

1943 First Jesse B. Simple item published in Chicago *Defender*

1956 *I Wonder as I Wander*

1959 *Selected Poems; Tambourines to Glory*

1961 *The Best of Simple*

1963 *Something in Common and Other Stories; Five Plays*

1967 Dies, May 22

FURTHER READINGS

There is no standard edition of Hughes's works. The most important individual titles are cited in the biographical chart.

Rebecca Barton, *Witnesses for Freedom* (1948)
Donald Dickinson, *A Bio-Bibliography of Langston Hughes* (1967)

James Emanuel, *Langston Hughes* (1967)
Edwin Embree, *Thirteen Against the Odds* (1944)
Milton Meltzer, *Langston Hughes: A Biography* (1968)
Jean Wagner, *Black Poets of the U.S.A.: Racial and Religious Feeling in Black Poetry from Paul Laurence Dunbar to Langston Hughes* (1972)

From The Big Sea (1940)

NOT PRIMITIVE

That winter I had been in Cuba looking for a Negro composer to write an opera with me, using genuinely racial motifs. The lady on Park Avenue thought that Amadeo Roldan might do, or Arturo Cartulo. I could not find Cartulo, and Roldan said he wasn't a Negro. But Miguel Covarrubias had given me a letter to José Antonio Fernandez de Castro, person extraordinary of this or any other world. And José Antonio saw to it that I had a rumba of a good time and met everybody, Negro, white and mulatto, of any interest in Havana—from the drummers at Marianao to the society artist and editor of *Social Masaguer.*

But I came back to New York with no Negro composer who could write an opera.

More and more tangled that winter became the skein of poet and patron, youth and age, poverty and wealth—and one day it broke! Quickly and quietly in the Park Avenue drawing-room, it broke.

Great wealth had been given to a woman who meant to be kind the means to power, and a technique of power, of so mighty a strength that I do not believe she herself knew what that force might become. She possessed the power to control people's lives—pick them up and put them down when and where she wished.

She wanted me to be primitive and know and feel the intuitions of the primitive. But, unfortunately, I did not feel the rhythms of the primitive surging through me, and so I could not live and write as though I did. I was only an American Negro—who had loved the surface of Africa and the rhythms of Africa—but I was not Africa. I was Chicago and Kansas City and Broadway and Harlem. And I was not what she wanted me to be. So, in the end it all came back very near to the old impasse of white and Negro again, white and Negro—as do most relationships in America.

Then, too, I knew that my friend and benefactor was not happy because, for months now, I had written nothing beautiful. She was old and it took a great deal of strength out of her to worry about me, and she was, I think, a bit impatient with men who are not geniuses. (She knew so many great people.) So I asked kindly to be released from any further obligation to her, and that she give me no more money, but simply let me retain her friendship and good will that had been so dear to me. That I asked to keep. But there must have been only the one thread binding us together. When that thread broke, it was the end.

I cannot write here about that last half-hour in the big bright drawing-room high above Park Avenue one morning, because when I think about it, even now, something happens in the pit of my stomach that makes me ill. That beautiful room, that had been so full of light and help and understanding for me, suddenly became like a trap closing in, faster and faster, the room darker and darker, until the light went out with a sudden crash in the dark, and everything became like that night in Kansas when I had failed to see Jesus and had lied about it afterwards. Or that morning in Mexico when I suddenly hated my father.

Physically, my stomach began to turn over and over—and then over again. I fought against bewilderment and anger, fought hard, and didn't say anything. I just sat there in that high Park Avenue drawing-room and didn't say anything. I sat there and listened to all she told me, closed my mouth hard and didn't say anything.

I do not remember clearly what it was she said to me at the end, nor her face as the door closed, nor the elevator dropping down to the street level, nor my final crossing of the lobby through a lane of uniformed attendants.

But I do remember the winter sunshine on Park Avenue and the wind in my face as I went toward the subway to Harlem.

WHEN THE NEGRO WAS IN VOGUE

White people began to come to Harlem in droves. For several years they packed the expensive Cotton Club on Lenox Avenue. But I was never there, be-cause the Cotton Club was a Jim Crow club for gangsters and monied whites. They were not cordial to Negro patronage, unless you were a celebrity like Bojangles. So Harlem Negroes did not like the Cotton Club and never appreciated its Jim Crow policy in the very heart of their dark community. Nor did ordinary Negroes like the growing influx of whites toward Harlem after sundown, flooding the little cabarets and bars where formerly only colored people laughed and sang, and where now the strangers were given the best ringside tables to sit and stare at the Negro customers—like amusing animals in a zoo.

The Negroes said: "We can't go downtown and sit and stare at you in your clubs. You won't even let us in your clubs." But they didn't say it out loud—for Negroes are practically never rude to white people. So thousands of whites came to Harlem night after night, thinking the Negroes loved to have them there, and firmly believing that all Harlemites left their houses at sundown to sing and dance in cabarets, because most of the whites saw nothing but the cabarets, not the houses.

Some of the owners of Harlem clubs, delighted at the flood of white patronage, made the grievous error of barring their own race, after the manner of the famous Cotton Club. But most of these quickly lost business and folded up, because they failed to realize that a large part of the Harlem attraction for downtown New Yorkers lay in simply watching the colored customers amuse themselves. And the smaller clubs, of course, had no big floor shows or a name band like the Cotton Club, where Duke Ellington usually held forth, so, without black patronage, they were not amusing at all.

Some of the small clubs, however, had people like Gladys Bentley, who was something worth discovering in those days, before she got famous, acquired an accompanist, specially written material, and conscious vulgarity. But for two or three amazing years, Miss Bentley sat, and played a big piano all night long, literally all night, without stopping—singing songs like "The St. James Infirmary," from ten in the evening until dawn, with scarcely a break between the notes, sliding from one song to another, with a powerful and continuous underbeat of jungle rhythm. Miss Bentley was an amazing exhibition of musical energy—a large, dark, masculine lady, whose feet pounded the floor while her fingers pounded the keyboard—a perfect piece of African sculpture, animated by her own rhythm.

But when the place where she played became

too well known, she began to sing with an accompanist, became a star, moved to a larger place, then downtown, and is now in Hollywood. The old magic of the woman and the piano and the night and the rhythm being one is gone. But everything goes, one way or another. The '20's are gone and lots of fine things in Harlem night life have disappeared like snow in the sun—since it became utterly commercial, planned for the downtown tourist trade, and therefore dull.

The lindy-hoppers at the Savoy even began to practise acrobatic routines, and to do absurd things for the entertainment of the whites, that probably never would have entered their heads to attempt merely for their own effortless amusement. Some of the lindy-hoppers had cards printed with their names on them and became dance professors teaching the tourists. Then Harlem nights became show nights for the Nordics.

Some critics say that that is what happened to certain Negro writers, too—that they ceased to write to amuse themselves and began to write to amuse and entertain white people, and in so doing distorted and over-colored their material, and left out a great many things they thought would offend their American brothers of a lighter complexion. Maybe—since Negroes have writer-racketeers, as has any other race. But I have known almost all of them, and most of the good ones have tried to be honest, write honestly, and express their world as they saw it.

All of us know that the gay and sparkling life of the so-called Negro Renaissance of the '20's was not so gay and sparkling beneath the surface as it looked. Carl Van Vechten, in the character of Byron in *Nigger Heaven*, captured some of the bitterness and frustration of literary Harlem that Wallace Thurman later so effectively poured into his *Infants of the Spring*—the only novel by a Negro about that fantastic period when Harlem was in vogue.

It was a period when, at almost every Harlem upper-crust dance or party, one would be introduced to various distinguished white celebrities there as guests. It was a period when almost any Harlem Negro of any social importance at all would be likely to say casually: "As I was remarking the other day to Heywood—," meaning Heywood Broun. Or: "As I said to George—," referring to George Gershwin. It was a period when local and visiting royalty were not at all uncommon in Harlem. And when the parties of A'Lelia Walker, the Negro heiress, were filled with guests whose

names would turn any Nordic social climber green with envy. It was a period when Harold Jackman, a handsome young Harlem school teacher of modest means, calmly announced one day that he was sailing for the Riviera for a fortnight, to attend Princess Murat's yachting party. It was a period when Charleston preachers opened up shouting churches as sideshows for white tourists. It was a period when at least one charming colored chorus girl, amber enough to pass for a Latin American, was living in a pent house, with all her bills paid by a gentleman whose name was banker's magic on Wall Street. It was a period when every season there was at least one hit play on Broadway acted by a Negro cast. And when books by Negro authors were being published with much greater frequency and much more publicity than ever before or since in history. It was a period when white writers wrote about Negroes more successfully (commercially speaking) than Negroes did about themselves. It was the period (God help us!) when Ethel Barrymore appeared in blackface in *Scarlet Sister Mary!* It was the period when the Negro was in vogue.

I was there. I had a swell time while it lasted. But I thought it wouldn't last long. (I remember the vogue for things Russian, the season the Chauve-Souris first came to town.) For how could a large and enthusiastic number of people be crazy about Negroes forever? But some Harlemites thought the millennium had come. They thought the race problem had at last been solved through Art plus Gladys Bentley. They were sure the New Negro would lead a new life from then on in green pastures of tolerance created by Countee Cullen, Ethel Waters, Claude McKay, Duke Ellington, Bojangles, and Alain Locke.

I don't know what made any Negroes think that —except that they were mostly intellectuals doing the thinking. The ordinary Negroes hadn't heard of the Negro Renaissance. And if they had, it hadn't raised their wages any. As for all those white folks in the speakeasies and night clubs of Harlem—well, maybe a colored man could find *some* place to have a drink that the tourists hadn't yet discovered.

Then it was that house-rent parties began to flourish—and not always to raise the rent either. But, as often as not, to have a get-together of one's own, where you could do the black-bottom with no stranger behind you trying to do it, too. Nontheatrical, non-intellectual Harlem was an unwilling victim of its own vogue. It didn't like to be stared at by white folks. But perhaps the down-towners never knew this—for the cabaret owners, the entertainers, and the speakeasy proprietors treated them fine—as long as they paid.

The Saturday night rent parties that I attended were often more amusing than any night club, in small apartments where God knows who lived—because the guests seldom did—but where the piano would often be augmented by a guitar, or an odd cornet, or somebody with a pair of drums walking in off the street. And where awful bootleg whiskey and good fried fish or steaming chitterling were sold at very low prices. And the dancing and singing and impromptu entertaining went on until dawn came in at the windows.

PARTIES

In those days of the late 1920's, there were a great many parties, in Harlem and out, to which various members of the New Negro group were invited. These parties, when given by important Harlemites (or Carl Van Vechten) were reported in full in the society pages of the Harlem press, but best in the sparkling Harlemese of Geraldyn Dismond who wrote for the *Interstate Tattler*. On one of Taylor Gordon's fiestas she reports as follows:

What a crowd! All classes and colors met face to face, ultra aristocrats, Bourgeois, Communists, Park Avenuers galore, bookers, publishers, Broadway celebs, and Harlemites giving each other the once over. The social revolution was on. And yes, Lady Nancy Cunard was there all in black (she would) with 12 of her grand bracelets. . . . And was the entertainment on the up and up! Into swell dance music was injected African drums that played havoc with blood pressure. Jimmy Daniels sang his gigolo hits. Gus Simons, the Harlem crooner, made the River Stay Away From His Door and Taylor himself brought out everything from "Hot Dog" to "Bravo" when he made high C.

A'Lelia Walker was the then great Harlem party giver, although Mrs. Bernia Austin fell but little behind. And at the Seventh Avenue apartment of Jessie Fauset, literary soirées with much poetry and but little to drink were the order of the day. The same was true of Lillian Alexander's, where the older intellectuals gathered.

A'Lelia Walker, however, big-hearted, night-dark, hair-straightening heiress, made no pretense

at being intellectual or exclusive. At her "at homes" Negro poets and Negro number bankers mingled with downtown poets and seat-on-the-stock-exchange racketeers. Countee Cullen would be there and Witter Bynner, Muriel Draper and Nora Holt, Andy Razaf and Taylor Gordon. And a good time was had by all.

A'Lelia Walker had an apartment that held perhaps a hundred people. She would usually issue several hundred invitations to each party. Unless you went early there was no possible way of getting in. Her parties were as crowded as the New York subway at the rush hour—entrance, lobby, steps, hallway, and apartment, a milling crush of guests, with everybody seeming to enjoy the crowding. Once, some royal personage arrived, a Scandinavian prince, I believe, but his equerry saw no way of getting him through the crowded entrance hall and into the party, so word was sent in to A'Lelia Walker that His Highness, the Prince, was waiting without. A'Lelia sent word back that she saw no way of getting His Highness in, either, nor could she herself get out through the crowd to greet him. But she offered to send refreshments downstairs to the Prince's car.

A'Lelia Walker was a gorgeous dark Amazon, in a silver turban. She had a town house in New York (also an apartment where she preferred to live) and a country mansion at Irvington-on-the-Hudson, with pipe organ programs each morning to awaken her guests gently. Her mother made a great fortune from the Madame Walker Hair Straightening Process, which had worked wonders on unruly Negro hair in the early nineteen hundreds—and which continues to work wonders today. The daughter used much of that money for fun. A'Lelia Walker was the joy-goddess of Harlem's 1920's.

She had been very much in love with her first husband, from whom she was divorced. Once at one of her parties she began to cry about him. She retired to her boudoir and wept. Some of her friends went in to comfort her, and found her clutching a memento of their broken romance.

"The only thing I have left that he gave me," she sobbed, "it's all I have left of him!"

It was a gold shoehorn.

When A'Lelia Walker died in 1931, she had a grand funeral. It was by invitation only. But, just as for her parties, a great many more invitations had been issued than the small but exclusive Seventh Avenue funeral parlor could provide for. Hours before the funeral, the street in front of the undertaker's chapel was crowded. The doors were not opened until the cortège arrived—and the cortège was late. When it came, there were almost enough family mourners, attendants, and honorary pall-bearers in the procession to fill the room; as well as the representatives of the various Walker beauty parlors throughout the country. And there were still hundreds of friends outside, waving their white, engraved invitations aloft in the vain hope of entering.

Once the last honorary pallbearers had marched in, there was a great crush at the doors. Muriel Draper, Rita Romilly, Mrs. Roy Sheldon, and I were among the fortunate few who achieved an entrance.

We were startled to find De Lawd standing over A'Lelia's casket. It was a truly amazing illusion. At that time *The Green Pastures* was at the height of its fame, and there stood De Lawd in the person of Rev. E. Clayton Powell, a Harlem minister, who looked exactly like Richard B. Harrison in the famous role in the play. He had the same white hair and kind face, and was later offered the part of De Lawd in the film version of the drama. Now, he stood there motionless in the dim light behind the silver casket of A'Lelia Walker.

Soft music played and it was very solemn. When we were seated and the chapel became dead silent, De Lawd said: "The Four Bon Bons will now sing."

A night club quartette that had often performed at A'Lelia's parties arose and sang for her. They sang Noel Coward's "I'll See You Again," and they swung it slightly, as she might have liked it. It was a grand funeral and very much like a party. Mrs. Mary McCleod Bethune spoke in that great deep voice of hers, as only she can speak. She recalled the poor mother of A'Lelia Walker in old clothes, who had labored to bring the gift of beauty to Negro womanhood, and had taught them the care of their skin and their hair, and had built up a great business and a great fortune to the pride and glory of the Negro race—and then had given it all to her daughter, A'Lelia.

Then a poem of mine was read by Edward Perry, "To A'Lelia." And after that the girls from the various Walker beauty shops throughout America brought their flowers and laid them on the bier.

That was really the end of the gay times of the New Negro era in Harlem, the period that had begun to reach its end when the crash came in 1929 and the white people had much less money to spend on themselves, and practically none to spend on Negroes, for the depression brought everybody down a peg or two. And the Negroes had but few pegs to fall.

But in those pre-crash days there were parties and parties. At the novelist, Jessie Fauset's, parties there was always quite a different atmosphere from that at most other Harlem good-time gatherings. At Miss Fauset's, a good time was shared by talking literature and reading poetry aloud and perhaps enjoying some conversation in French. White people were seldom present there unless they were very distinguished white people, because Jessie Fauset did not feel like opening her home to mere sightseers, or faddists momentarily in love with Negro life. At her house one would usually meet editors and students, writers and social workers, and serious people who liked books and the British Museum, and had perhaps been to Florence. (Italy, not Alabama.)

I remember, one night at her home there was a gathering in honor of Salvador de Madariaga, the Spanish diplomat and savant, which somehow became a rather self-conscious gathering, with all the Harlem writers called upon to recite their poems and speak their pieces. But afterwards, Charles S. Johnson and I invited Mr. Madariaga to Small's Paradise where we had a "ball" until the dawn came up and forced us from the club.

In those days, 409 Edgecombe, Harlem's tallest and most exclusive apartment house, was quite a party center. The Walter Whites and the Aaron Douglases, among others, lived and entertained here. Walter White was a jovial and cultured host, with a sprightly mind, and an apartment overlooking the Hudson. He had the most beautiful wife in Harlem, and they were always hospitable to hungry literati like me. . . .

At the James Weldon Johnson parties and gumbo suppers, one met solid people like Clarence and Mrs. Darrow. At the Dr. Alexander's, you met the upper crust Negro intellectuals like Dr. DuBois. At Wallace Thurman's, you met the bohemians of both Harlem and the Village. And in the gin mills and speakeasies and night clubs between 125th and 145th, Eighth Avenue and Lenox, you met everybody from Buddy de Silva to Theodore Dreiser, Ann Pennington to the first Mrs. Eugene O'Neill. In the days when Harlem was in vogue, Amanda Randolph was at the Alhambra, Jimmy Walker was mayor of New York, and Louise sang at the old New World.

From The Best of Simple (1961)

THERE OUGHT TO BE A LAW

"I have been up North a long time, but it looks like I just cannot learn to like white folks."

"I don't care to hear you say that," I said, "because there are a lot of good white people in this world."

"Not enough of them," said Simple, waving his evening paper. "If there was, they would make this American country good. But just look at what this paper is full of."

"You cannot dislike *all* white people for what the bad ones do," I said. "And I'm certain you don't dislike them all because once you told me yourself that you wouldn't wish any harm to befall Mrs. Roosevelt."

"Mrs. Roosevelt is different," said Simple.

"There now! You see, you are talking just as some white people talk about the Negroes they *happen* to like. They are always 'different.' That is a provincial way to think. You need to get around more."

"You mean among white folks?" asked Simple. "How can I make friends with white folks when they got Jim Crow all over the place?"

"Then you need to open your mind."

"I have near about *lost* my mind worrying with them," said Simple. "In fact they have hurt my soul."

"You certainly feel bad tonight," I said. "Maybe you need a drink."

"Nothing in a bottle will help my soul," said Simple, "but I will take a drink."

"Maybe it will help your mind," I said. "Beer?"

"Yes."

"Glass or bottle?"

"A bottle because it contains two glasses," said Simple, spreading his paper out on the bar. "Look here at these headlines, man, where Congress is busy passing laws. While they're making all these laws, it looks like to me they ought to make one setting up a few Game Preserves for Negroes."

"What ever gave you that fantastic idea?" I asked.

"A movie short I saw the other night," said Simple, "about how the government is protecting wild life, preserving fish and game, and setting aside big tracts of land where nobody can fish, shoot, hunt, nor harm a single living creature with furs, fins, or feathers. But it did not show a thing about Negroes."

"I thought you said the picture was about 'wild life.' Negroes are not wild."

"No," said Simple, "but we need protection. This film showed how they put aside a thousand acres out West where the buffaloes roam and nobody can shoot a single one of them. If they do, they get in jail. It also showed some big National Park with government airplanes dropping food down to the deers when they got snowed under and had nothing to eat. The government protects and takes care of buffaloes and deers—which is more than the government does for me or my kinfolks down South. Last month they lynched a man in Georgia and just today I see where the Klan has whipped a Negro within a inch of his life in Alabama. And right up North here in New York a actor is suing a apartment house that won't even let a Negro go up on the elevator to see his producer. That is what I mean by Game Preserves for Negroes—Congress ought to set aside some place where we can go and nobody can jump on us and beat us, neither lynch us nor Jim Crow us every day. Colored folks rate as much protection as a buffalo, or a deer."

"You have a point there," I said.

"This here movie showed great big beautiful lakes with signs up all around:

NO FISHING—STATE GAME PRESERVE

But it did not show a single place with a sign up:

NO LYNCHING

It also showed flocks of wild ducks settling down in a nice green meadow behind a government sign that said:

NO HUNTING

It were nice and peaceful for them fish and ducks. There ought to be some place where it is nice and peaceful for me, too, even if I am not a fish or a duck.

"They showed one scene with two great big old long-horn elks locking horns on a Game Preserve somewhere out in Wyoming, fighting like mad. Nobody bothered them elks or tried to stop them from fighting. But just let me get in a little old fist fight here in this bar, they will lock me up and the Desk Sergeant will say, 'What are you colored boys doing, disturbing the peace?' Then they will give me thirty days and fine me twice as much as they would a white man for doing the same thing. There ought to be some place where I can fight in peace and not get fined them high fines."

"You disgust me," I said. "I thought you were talking about a place where you could be quiet and compose your mind. Instead, you are talking about fighting."

"I would like a place where I could do both," said Simple. "If the government can set aside some spot for a elk *to be a elk* without being bothered, or a fish *to be a fish* without getting hooked, or a buffalo *to be a buffalo* without being shot down, there ought to be some place in this American country where a Negro can be a Negro without being Jim Crowed. There ought to be a law. The next time I see my congressman, I am going to tell him to introduce a bill for Game Preserves for Negroes."

"The Southerners would filibuster it to death," I said.

"If we are such a problem to them Southerners," said Simple, "I should think they would want some place to preserve us out of their sight. But then, of course, you have to take into consideration that if the Negroes was taken out of the South, who would they lynch? What would they do for sport? A Game Preserve is for to keep people from bothering anything that is living.

"When that movie finished, it were sunset in Virginia and it showed a little deer and its mama laying down to sleep. Didn't nobody say, 'Get up, deer, you can't sleep here,' like they would to me if I was to go to the White Sulphur Springs Hotel."

" 'The foxes have holes, and the birds of the air have nests; but the Son of man hath not where to lay his head.' "

"That is why I want a Game Preserve for Negroes," said Simple.

The Negro Speaks of Rivers (1926)

I've known rivers:
I've known rivers ancient as the world and
    older than the flow of human blood in
    human veins.

My soul has grown   deep like rivers.

I bathed in the Euphrates when dawns were
    young.
I built my hut near the Congo and it lulled
    me to sleep.

I looked upon the Nile and raised the pyra-
    mids above it.
I heard the singing of the Mississippi when
    Abe Lincoln went down to New Orleans,
    and I've seen its muddy bosom turn all
    golden in the sunset.

I've known rivers:
Ancient, dusky rivers.

My soul has grown   deep like rivers.   10

Young Gal's Blues (1927)

I'm gonna walk to the graveyard
'Hind ma friend Miss Cora Lee.
Gonna walk to the graveyard
'Hind ma dear friend Cora Lee
Cause when I'm dead some
Body'll have to walk behind me.

I'm goin' to the po' house
To see ma old Aunt Clew.
Goin' to the po' house
To see ma old Aunt Clew.   10
When I'm old an' ugly
I'll want to see somebody, too.

The po' house is lonely
An' the grave is cold.
O, the po' house is lonely,
The graveyard grave is cold.
But I'd rather be dead than
To be ugly an' old.

When love is gone what
Can a young gal do?   20
When love is gone, O,
What can a young gal do?
Keep on a-lovin' me, daddy,
Cause I don't want to be blue.

Me and the Mule (1942)

My old mule,
He's got a grin on his face.
He's been a mule so long
He's forgot about his race.

I'm like that old mule—
Black—and don't give a damn!
You got to take me
Like I am.

Notes on Commercial Theatre (1949)

You've taken my blues and gone—
You sing 'em on Broadway
And you sing 'em in Hollywood Bowl,
And you mixed 'em up with symphonies
And you fixed 'em
So they don't sound like me.
Yep, you done taken my blues and gone.

You also took my spirituals and gone.
You put me in *Macbeth* and *Carmen Jones*
And all kinds of *Swing Mikados*   10

And in everything but what's about me—
But someday somebody'll
Stand up and talk about me,
And write about me—
Black and beautiful—
And sing about me,
And put on plays about me!
I reckon it'll be
Me myself!

Yes, it'll be me.   20

Puzzled (1949)

Here on the edge of hell
Stands Harlem—
Remembering the old lies,
The old kicks in the back,
The old, *Be patient*,
They told us before.

Sure, we remember.
Now, when the man at the corner store
Says sugar's gone up another two cents,
And bread one,   10
And there's a new tax on cigarettes—
We remember the job we never had,

Never could get,
And can't have now
Because we're colored.

So we stand here
On the edge of hell
In Harlem
And look out on the world
And wonder   20
What we're gonna do
In the face of
What we remember.

Early Evening Quarrel (1942)

Where is that sugar, Hammond,
I sent you this morning to buy?
I say, where is that sugar
I sent you this morning to buy?
Coffee without sugar
Makes a good woman cry.

  I ain't got no sugar, Hattie,
  I gambled your dime away.
  Ain't got no sugar, I
  Done gambled that dime away.   10
  If you's a wise woman, Hattie,
  You ain't gonna have nothin to say.

I ain't no wise woman, Hammond.
I am evil and mad.
Ain't no sense in a good woman
Bein treated so bad.

  I don't treat you bad, Hattie,
  Neither does I treat you good.
  But I reckon I could treat you
  Worser if I would.   20

Lawd, these things we women
Have to stand!
I wonder is there nowhere a
Do-right man?

Border Line (1947)

I used to wonder
About living and dying—
I think the difference lies
Between tears and crying.

I used to wonder
About here and there—
I think the distance
Is nowhere.

Midnight Raffle (1949)

I put my nickel
In the raffle of the night.
Somehow that raffle
Didn't turn out right.

I lost my nickel.
I lost my time.
I got back home
Without a dime.

When I dropped that nickel
In the subway slot,   10
I wouldn't have dropped it,
Knowing what I got.

I could just as well've
Stayed home inside:
My bread wasn't buttered
On neither side.

Dream Boogie (1951)

Good morning, daddy!
Ain't you heard
The boogie-woogie rumble
Of a dream deferred?

Listen closely:
You'll hear their feet
Beating out and beating out a—

    You think
    It's a happy beat?

Listen to it closely: 10
Ain't you heard

something underneath
like a—

    What did I say?

Sure,
I'm happy!
Take it away!

    Hey, pop!
    Re-bop!
    Mop!   20

    Y-e-a-h!

Sylvester's Dying Bed (1942)

I woke up this mornin'
'Bout half-past three.
All the womens in town
Was gathered round me.

Sweet gals was a-moanin',
"Sylvester's gonna die!"
And a hundred pretty mamas
Bowed their heads to cry.

I woke up little later
'Bout half-past fo',   10

The doctor 'n' undertaker's
Both at ma do'.

Black gals was a-beggin',
"You can't leave us here!"
Brown-skins cryin', "Daddy!
Honey! Baby! Don't go, dear!"

But I felt ma time's a-comin',
And I know'd I's dyin' fast.
I seed the River Jerden
A-creepin' muddy past—   20

But I's still Sweet Papa 'Vester,
Yes, sir! Long as life do last!

So I hollers, "Com'ere, babies,
Fo' to love yo' daddy right!"

And I reaches up to hug 'em—
When the Lawd put out the light.

Then everything was darkness
In a great . . . big . . . night.

Stony Lonesome (1949)

They done took Cordelia
Out to stony lonesome ground.
Done took Cordelia
To stony lonesome,
Laid her down.
They done put Cordelia
Underneath that
Grassless mound.
    Ay-Lord!
      Ay-Lord!   10
        Ay-Lord!

She done left po' Buddy
To struggle by his self.
Po' Buddy Jones,
Yes, he's done been left.
She's out in stony lonesome,
Lordy! Sleepin' by herself.
    Corelia's
      In stony
        Lonesome   20
        Ground!

Mama and Daughter (1949)

Mama, please brush off my coat.
I'm going down the street.

Where're you going, daughter?

To see my sugar-sweet.

Who is your sugar, honey?
Turn around—I'll brush behind.

He is that young man, mama,
I can't get off my mind.

Daughter, once upon a time—
Let me brush the hem—   10

Your father, yes, he was the one!
I felt like that about him.

But it was a long time ago
He up and went his way.
I hope that wild young son-of-a-gun
Rots in hell today!

    Mama, dad couldn't be still young.

He *was* young yesterday.
He *was* young when he—
Turn around!   20
So I can brush your back, I say!

JEAN TOOMER (1894–1967)

Jean Toomer was born in Washington, D.C. After graduation from the public school there, he briefly attended the University of Wisconsin, with the intention of taking a law degree, and later, again briefly, studied at the City College of New York; but at neither institution, as he wrote later, had he found what he sought —and what he sought was, it seems, to be found nowhere. He was a wanderer as well as a "seeker" and lived in many parts of the country, and among many different kinds of people, both black and white. During a stay in Sparta, Georgia, from which his father had originally come, he found the background for his only real book,

Cane (1923), a collection of stories and poems unified by locale, somewhat after the manner of *Winesburg, Ohio*. He was married twice, both wives being white. The first marriage (1932) was to Marjorie Latimer, the novelist (descended from both Anne Bradstreet and John Cotton), who died in childbirth in 1933; the second (1934) was to Marjorie Constant, the daughter of a New York broker. In the latter part of his life, Toomer withdrew almost entirely from literary activity. He died in 1967.

Toomer occupies an anomalous place in the Harlem Renaissance. On the one hand, with *Cane*, he created one of the most distinguished works of the movement. It was, indeed, one of the seminal works, preceding *God's Trombones*, by James Weldon Johnson, *Color*, by Countee Cullen, *The Weary Blues*, by Langston Hughes, and the work of the two black novelists Eric Waldron and Zora Neale Hurston. He was, too, a contributor to the black periodicals the *Crisis* and *Opportunity*. But on the other hand, Toomer was associated with the white literary life of New York, with, for instance, the poet Hart Crane and the critics Waldo Frank and Kenneth Burke, and contributed to magazines, such as the *Little Review*, the *Double Dealer*, and *Broom*, that were important in the general (and generally white) literary ferment of the 1920's. His work was greatly admired by a number of white writers; for instance, the poet Allen Tate, in 1923, wrote a very laudatory review of *Cane* (in the book section of the Nashville *Tennessean*) declaring that in parts the book might rival some of the best contemporary work and that it was "highly important."[1]

Toomer did write movingly of the black world, and even of the violence sometimes visited upon it by the white, but he did not, as was characteristic of writers of the Harlem Renaissance, identify himself, except briefly and in a limited way, with the subject matter of his

work. In the summer of 1922, in an autobiographical note prepared for the editors of the *Liberator*, he said that he was of seven blood strains, including black and Indian, and had lived back and forth between the black world and the white, being pale enough, in fact, to pass. Without denying any element that he had in him, he sought, he said, to have all exist in harmony. But he added: ". . . during the last two or three years, my increasing need of artistic expression has drawn me more and more to the bosom of the black group." By 1934, at the time of his second marriage, Toomer said: "I would consider it libelous for anyone to refer to me as a colored man, for I have not lived as one, nor do I really know whether there is any colored blood in me or not." He went on to say that his maternal grandfather, Pinckney Benton Stewart Pinchback, a Reconstruction governor of Louisiana,[2] had claimed to have black blood only in order to get the freedman's vote. It now seems beyond dispute, however, that Pinchback's claim, even if motivated by political expediency, was grounded in fact: his mother was born a slave and was manumitted at her marriage, and it is now generally held that Toomer did, as he had previously avowed, have a significant amount of black blood. Nor is it quite true that Toomer had not lived, as he now said, as a "colored man." He had lived as black in Georgia, for example, in days long before integration had ever been dreamed of.

But the point does not lie in the facts of the case. It lies in what Toomer made of the facts. He said of himself: "I am of no particular race, I am of the human race, a man at large in the human world, preparing a new race." He thought of himself, too, as a "writer," not a "black writer."

The impulse to transcend particularities of race, rather than to embrace them, would seem to have been associated with the strain of mysticism in Toomer's nature (mysticism always seeks to transcend the grind and shock of particularities) which drew him to Blake and

---

[1] Tate has lately said that he continues to admire *Cane*. The account sometimes given that attempts of Tate to meet Toomer came to nothing is an error. They met in 1926 or 1927 in New York, twice for lunch with Crane, at the Hotel Albert, and, according to Tate's report, later in Paris.

[2] The election of Pinchback was a subject of litigation, and he served only one year.

Whitman, and which would later draw him into the cult associated with Georges Ivanovitch Gurdjieff[3] and still later give him a special interest in Quakerism, which was expressed in a little book of philosophical· utterances called *Essentials* (1931). But by this time Toomer had come to be critical of Whitman's democratic mystique and could write that "Whitman's average man has turned out to be Babbitt [of the novel by Sinclair Lewis]," with "two emblems, namely the machine-gun and the contraceptive." And by 1949, in his last published work, "The Flavor of Man," an address at a Quaker occasion, Toomer's mysticism had reached a more religious and generalized form: "Evil is evil only because it separates our consciousness from God," and "Pain is pain only because we lack realization that we are related to divinity."

The career of Jean Toomer brought to focus long ago a question that has, thus far, been urgent for many black writers. The question is well illustrated in two quotations about Toomer. The first is from the foreword to *Cane*, by his friend Waldo Frank:

> The gifted Negro has been too often thwarted from becoming a poet because his world was forever forcing him to recollect that he was a Negro. The artist must lose such lesser identities in the great well of life. The English poet is not forever protesting and recalling that he is English. It is so natural and easy for him to be English that he can sing as a man. The French novelist is not forever noting: "This is French." It is so atmospheric for him to be French, that he can devote himself to saying: "This is human." This is an imperative condition for the creation of deep art. The whole will and mind of the creator must go below the surface of race. And this has been an almost impossible condition for the American Negro to achieve, forced every moment of his life into a specific and superficial plane of consciousness.

The second quotation is from Langston Hughes, in *The Big Sea*, published, we may remind ourselves, in 1940, after the Second World War had begun:

> Now Mr. Toomer is married to a lady of means—his second wife [the daughter of the broker]—of Santa Fe and New York, and is never seen on Lenox Avenue [in Harlem] any more. He was a fine American writer. But when we get as democratic in America as we pretend we are on days when we wish to shame Mr. Hitler, nobody will bother much about anybody else's race anyway. Why should Mr. Toomer live in Harlem if he doesn't care to? Democracy is democracy, isn't it?

Clearly Frank and Hughes are on different sides of the question of what a racial commitment means in relation to literary creativity. It may be that, since art springs from the individual's confrontation with his own fate, the question is one to be settled by each individual black writer for himself. He must make his own gamble.

By way of establishing a context for the general questions, it may be worth while to consider an analogy with American literature in general. Henry James, Ezra Pound, and T. S. Eliot have been regarded by some Americans as little short of traitors because they elected to live abroad and because they rejected, in varying degrees, specifically American subjects.

But would Eliot have been a better poet if he had stayed home? Or James a better novelist? There is certainly no definitive answer—no matter what answer we might prefer on theoretical or emotional grounds. And the fair guess that Mark Twain was wise to stick to Hannibal, Missouri, and that Faulkner was right to take one look at Paris and one at New York City and head back to Oxford, Mississippi, scarcely

---

[3] Gurdjieff taught that by certain exercises and disciplines one might open the self to stages of experience leading to world consciousness, even to cosmic consciousness. The year after *Cane*, Toomer was in France, at *l'Institut Gurdjieff*, at Fontainebleau, trying to discover the "self." It may be hazarded that the pursuit of the "self," of "identity," may have finally taken precedence over the more mundane business of trying to be a writer.

proves the case against James's judgment, or Eliot's. Our wisdom may be to accept what good things we can get and be grateful for *The Portrait of a Lady*, by James, as well as for *Absalom, Absalom!* by Faulkner.

It should be remembered, however, that even the best historical analogy is precarious, and certainly not too much can be claimed for this one. For instance, the urgencies that now make the black writer assert his blackness are much greater than those that might have made an American writer of the late nineteenth century assert his Americanism.[4] Even so, there may be various ways of asserting blackness. And Henry James was not, after all, a French, or even an English, writer, no matter how much he may have secretly longed to be; he was only a rather strange kind of American writer.

To return to our analogy: even if it is precarious, it may help us, white or black, to understand that the problem the black writer now faces in America is not without some sort of precedent, just as it may help us to understand the problem if we regard it as only one limited manifestation of the basic tension between the impulse toward integration and that toward separatism in the black world vis-à-vis the white.

Toomer, however, could try to resolve this tension in the vision of a regenerated America, as in this section from the poem "Blue Meridian."[5]

[4] It may be that the best historical analogy to the impulse of the black writer to assert his autonomy lies in the various proclamations in the early nineteenth century on the necessity for a native literature that preceded Emerson's "American Scholar."

[5] The poem in its entirety has never been published. Our selection is from a long excerpt published in 1936. (All the other poems are from *Cane.*)

From Blue Meridian (1936)

Uncase the races,
Open this pod,
Free man from his shrinkage
Not from the reality itself,
But from the unbecoming and enslaving
    behavior
Associated with our prejudices and preferences.
Eliminate these;
I am, we are, simply of the human race.
Uncase the nations.
Open this pod,   10
Keep the real but destroy the false;
We are of the human nation.

Uncase the regions—
Occidental, Oriental, North, South,
We are of Earth.
Free the sexes,
I am neither male nor female nor in-between;
I am of sex, with male differentiations.
Open the classes;
I am, we are, simply of the human class.   20
Expand the fields—
Those definitions which fix fractions and lose
    wholes—
I am of the field of being,
We are beings.

Georgia Dusk (1923)

The sky, lazily disdaining to pursue
    The setting sun, too indolent to hold
    A lengthened tournament for flashing gold,
Passively darkens for night's barbecue,

A feast of moon and men and barking hounds,
    An orgy for some genius of the South
    With blood-hot eyes and cane-lipped scented mouth,
Surprised in making folk-songs from soul sounds.

The sawmill blows its whistle, buzz-saws stop,
    And silence breaks the bud of knoll and
    hill,   10
    Soft settling pollen where plowed lands
    fulfill
Their early promise of a bumper crop.

Smoke from the pyramidal sawdust pile
    Curls up, blue ghosts of trees, tarrying low
    Where only chips and stumps are left to
    show

The solid proof of former domicile.

Meanwhile, the men, with vestiges of pomp,
    Race memories of king and caravan,
    High-priests, an ostrich, and a juju-man,
Go singing through the footpaths of the
    swamp.   20

Their voices rise . . . the pine trees are
    guitars,
    Strumming, pine-needles fall like sheets of
    rain . . .

Their voices rise . . . the chorus of the
    cane
Is caroling a vesper to the stars . . .

O singers, resinous and soft your songs
    Above the sacred whisper of the pines,
    Give virgin lips to cornfield concubines,
Bring dreams of Christ to dusky cane-lipped
    throngs.

Portrait in Georgia (1923)

Hair—braided chestnut,
    coiled like a lyncher's rope,
Eyes—fagots,
Lips—old scars, or the first red blisters,

Breath—the last sweet scent of cane,
And her slim body, white as the ash
    of black flesh after flame.

November Cotton Flower (1923)

Boll-weevil's coming, and the winter's cold,
Made cotton-stalks look rusty, seasons old,
And cotton, scarce as any southern snow,
Was vanishing; the branch, so pinched and
    slow,
Failed in its function as the autumn rake;
Drouth fighting soil had caused the soil to
    take
All water from the streams; dead birds were
    found

In wells a hundred feet below the ground—
Such was the season when the flower bloomed.
Old folks were startled, and it soon assumed   10
Significance. Superstition saw
Something it had never seen before:
Brown eyes that loved without a trace of fear,
Beauty so sudden for that time of year.

Fern (1923)

Face flowed into her eyes. Flowed in soft cream foam and plaintive ripples, in such a way that wherever your glance may momentarily have rested, it immediately thereafter wavered in the direction of her eyes. The soft suggestion of down slightly darkened, like the shadow of a bird's wing might, the creamy brown color of her upper lip. Why, after noticing it, you sought her eyes, I cannot tell you. Her nose was aquiline, Semitic. If you have heard a Jewish cantor sing, if he has touched you and made your own sorrow seem trivial when compared with his, you will know my feeling when I follow the curves of her profile, like mobile rivers, to their common delta. They were strange eyes. In this, that they sought nothing—that is, nothing that was obvious and tangible and that one could

see, and they gave the impression that nothing was to be denied. When a woman seeks, you will have observed, her eyes deny. Fern's eyes desired nothing that you could give her; there was no reason why they should withhold. Men saw her eyes and fooled themselves. Fern's eyes said to them that she was easy. When she was young, a few men took her, but got no joy from it. And then, once done, they felt bound to her (quite unlike their hit and run with other girls), felt as though it would take them a lifetime to fulfill an obligation which they could find no name for. They became attached to her, and hungered after finding the barest trace of what she might desire. As she grew up, new men who came to town felt as almost everyone did who ever saw her: that they would not be denied. Men were everlastingly bringing her their bodies. Something inside of her got tired of them, I guess, for I am certain that for the life of her she could not tell why or how she began to turn them off. A man in fever is no trifling thing to send away. They began to leave her, baffled and ashamed, yet vowing to themselves that some day they would do some fine thing for her: send her candy every week and not let her know whom it came from, watch out for her wedding-day and give her a magnificent something with no name on it, buy a house and deed it to her, rescue her from some unworthy fellow who had tricked her into marrying him. As you know, men are apt to idolize or fear that which they cannot understand, especially if it be a woman. She did not deny them, yet the fact was that they were denied. A sort of superstition crept into their consciousness of her being somehow above them. Being above them meant that she was not to be approached by anyone. She became a virgin. Now a virgin in a small southern town is by no means the usual thing, if you will believe me. That the sexes were made to mate is the practice of the South. Particularly, black folks were made to mate. And it is black folks whom I have been talking about thus far. What white men thought of Fern I can arrive at only by analogy. They let her alone.

Anyone, of course, could see her, could see her eyes. If you walked up the Dixie Pike most any time of day, you'd be most like to see her resting listless-like on the railing of her porch, back propped against a post, head tilted a little forward because there was a nail in the porch post just where her head came which for some reason or other she never took the trouble to pull out. Her eyes, if it were sunset, rested idly where the sun, molten and glorious, was pouring down between the fringe of pines. Or maybe they gazed at the gray cabin on the knoll from which an evening folk-song was coming. Perhaps they followed a cow that had been turned loose to roam and feed on cotton-stalks and corn leaves. Like as not they'd settle on some vague spot above the horizon, though hardly a trace of wistfulness would come to them. If it were dusk, then they'd wait for the search-light of the evening train which you could see miles up the track before it flared across the Dixie Pike, close to her home. Wherever they looked, you'd follow them and then waver back. Like her face, the whole countryside seemed to

flow into her eyes. Flowed into them with the soft listless cadence of Georgia's South. A young Negro, once, was looking at her, spellbound, from the road. A white man passing in a buggy had to flick him with his whip if he was to get by without running him over. I first saw her on her porch. I was passing with a fellow whose crusty numbness (I was from the North and suspected of being prejudiced and stuck-up) was melting as he found me warm. I asked him who she was. "That's Fern," was all that I could get from him. Some folks already thought I was given to nosing around; I let it go at that, so far as questions were concerned. But at first sight of her I felt as if I heard a Jewish cantor sing. As if his singing rose above the unheard chorus of a folk-song. And I felt bound to her. I too had my dreams: something I would do for her. I have knocked about from town to town too much not to know the futility of mere change of place. Besides, picture if you can, this cream-colored solitary girl sitting at a tenement window looking down on the indifferent throngs of Harlem. Better that she listen to folk-songs at dusk in Georgia, you would say, and so would I. Or, suppose she came up North and married. Even a doctor or a lawyer, say, one who would be sure to get along—that is, make money. You and I know, who have had experience in such things, that love is not a thing like prejudice which can be bettered by changes of town. Could men in Washington, Chicago, or New York, more than the men of Georgia, bring her something left vacant by the bestowal of their bodies? You and I who know men in these cities will have to say, they could not. See her out and out a prostitute along State Street in Chicago. See her move into a southern town where white men are more aggressive. See her become a white man's concubine. . . Something I must do for her. There was myself. What could I do for her? Talk, of course. Push back the fringe of pines upon new horizons. To what purpose? and what for? Her? Myself? Men in her case seem to lose their selfishness. I lost mine before I touched her. I ask you, friend (it makes no difference if you sit in the Pullman or the Jim Crow as the train crosses her road), what thoughts would come to you—that is, after you'd finished with the thoughts that leap into men's minds at the sight of a pretty woman who will not deny them; what thoughts would come to you, had you seen her in a quick flash, keen and intuitively, as she sat there on her porch when your train thundered by? Would you have got off at the next station and come back for her to take her where? Would you have completely forgotten her as soon as you reached Macon, Atlanta, Augusta, Pasadena, Madison, Chicago, Boston, or New Orleans? Would you tell your wife or sweetheart about a girl you saw? Your thoughts can help me, and I would like to know. Something I would do for her. . .

One evening I walked up the Pike on purpose, and stopped to say hello. Some of her family were about, but they moved away to make room for me. Damn if I knew how to begin. Would you? Mr. and Miss So-and-So, people, the weather, the crops, the new preacher, the frolic, the church benefit, rabbit and possum hunting, the new soft drink they had at old Pap's store, the schedule of the trains, what kind of town Macon was, Negro's migration north, boll-weevils, syrup, the Bible—to all these things she gave a yassur or nassur, without further comment. I began to wonder if perhaps my own emotional sensibility had played one of its tricks on me. "Lets take a walk," I at last ventured. The suggestion, coming after so long an isolation, was novel enough, I guess, to surprise. But it wasnt that. Some thing told me that men before me had said just that as a prelude to the offering of their bodies. I tried to tell her with my eyes. I think she understood. The thing from her that made my throat catch, vanished. Its passing left her visible in a way I'd thought, but never seen. We walked down the Pike with people on all the porches gaping at us. "Doesnt it make you mad?" She meant the row of petty gossiping people. She meant the world. Through a canebrake that was ripe for cutting, the branch was reached. Under a sweet-gum tree, and where reddish leaves had dammed the creek a little, we sat down. Dusk, suggesting the almost imperceptible procession of giant trees, settled with a purple haze about the cane. I felt strange, as I always do in Georgia, particularly at dusk. I felt that things unseen to men were tangibly immediate. It would not have

surprised me had I had a vision. People have them in Georgia more often than you would suppose. A black woman once saw the mother of Christ and drew her in charcoal on the courthouse wall. . . When one is on the soil of one's ancestors, most anything can come to one. . . From force of habit, I suppose, I held Fern in my arms—that is, without at first noticing it. Then my mind came back to her. Her eyes, unusually weird and open, held me. Held God. He flowed in as I've seen the countryside flow in. Seen men. I must have done something—what, I dont know, in the confusion of my emotion. She sprang up. Rushed some distance from me. Fell to her knees, and began swaying, swaying. Her body was tortured with something it could not let out. Like boiling sap it flooded arms and fingers till she shook them as if they burned her. It found her throat, and spattered inarticulately in plaintive, convulsive sounds, mingled with calls to Christ Jesus. And then she sang, brokenly. A Jewish cantor singing with a broken voice. A child's voice, uncertain, or an old man's. Dusk hid her; I could hear only her song. It seemed to me as though she were pounding her head in anguish upon the ground. I rushed to her. She fainted in my arms.

There was talk about her fainting with me in the canefield. And I got one or two ugly looks from town men who'd set themselves up to protect her. In fact, there was talk of making me leave town. But they never did. They kept a watchout for me, though. Shortly after, I came back North. From the train window I saw her as I crossed her road. Saw her on her porch, head tilted a little forward where the nail was, eyes vaguely focused on the sunset. Saw her face flow into them, the countryside and something that I call God, flowing into them. . . Nothing ever really happened. Nothing ever came to Fern, not even I. Something I would do for her. Some fine unnamed thing. . . And, friend, you? She is still living, I have reason to know. Her name, against the chance that you might happen down that way, is Fernie May Rosen.

COUNTEE CULLEN (1903–1946)

Countee Cullen was a native New Yorker and a graduate of New York University, with a Phi Beta Kappa key. Even in his college years, his poetic talent was recognized, and his first book, *Color*, was published almost simultaneously with his graduation. In 1927 two more books appeared, *Copper Sun* and *The Ballad of the Brown Girl*. He was for a few years a glittering ornament of the Harlem Renaissance. But something happened to his gift as a poet. After some graduate work at Harvard, where he took an M.A., and a few years abroad, he spent the rest of his life teaching in the public schools of New York.[1] He died at the age of forty-three.

[1] Cullen did attempt to keep his hand in by collaborating on Broadway musicals, most successfully with Arna Bontemps.

FURTHER READINGS

Saunders Redding, *To Make a Poet Black* (1939)
Robert A. Smith, "The Poetry of Countee Cullen," *Phylon*, Vol. 11 (1950)

Darwin T. Turner, *In a Minor Chord* (1971)

Heritage (1925)

(For Harold Jackman)

What is Africa to me:
Copper sun or scarlet sea,
Jungle star or jungle track,
Strong bronzed men, or regal black
Women from whose loins I sprang
When the birds of Eden sang?
One three centuries removed
From the scenes his fathers loved,
Spicy grove, cinnamon tree,
What is Africa to me?   10

So I lie, who all day long
Want no sound except the song
Sung by wild barbaric birds
Goading massive jungle herds,
Juggernauts of flesh that pass
Trampling tall defiant grass
Where young forest lovers lie,
Plighting troth beneath the sky.
So I lie, who always hear,
Though I cram against my ear   20
Both my thumbs, and keep them there,
Great drums throbbing through the air.
So I lie, whose fount of pride,
Dear distress, and joy allied,
Is my somber flesh and skin,
With the dark blood dammed within
Like great pulsing tides of wine
That, I fear, must burst the fine
Channels of the chafing net
Where they surge and foam and fret.   30

Africa? A book one thumbs

Listlessly, till slumber comes.
Unremembered are her bats
Circling through the night, her cats
Crouching in the river reeds,
Stalking gentle flesh that feeds
By the river brink; no more
Does the bugle-throated roar
Cry that monarch claws have leapt
From the scabbards where they slept.   40
Silver snakes that once a year
Doff the lovely coats you wear,
Seek no covert in your fear
Lest a mortal eye should see;
What's your nakedness to me?
Here no leprous flowers rear
Fierce corollas in the air;
Here no bodies sleek and wet,
Dripping mingled rain and sweat,
Tread the savage measures of   50
Jungle boys and girls in love.
What is last year's snow to me,
Last year's anything? The tree
Budding yearly must forget
How its past arose or set—
Bough and blossom, flower, fruit,
Even what shy bird with mute
Wonder at her travail there,
Meekly labored in its hair.
One three centuries removed   60
From the scenes his fathers loved,
Spicy grove, cinnamon tree,
What is Africa to me?

So I lie, who find no peace
Night or day, no slight release

From the unremittant beat
Made by cruel padded feet
Walking through my body's street.
Up and down they go, and back,
Treading out a jungle track.   70
So I lie, who never quite
Safely sleep from rain at night—
I can never rest at all
When the rain begins to fall;
Like a soul gone mad with pain
I must match its weird refrain;
Ever must I twist and squirm,
Writhing like a baited worm,
While its primal measures drip
Through my body, crying, "Strip!   80
Doff this new exuberance.
Come and dance the Lover's Dance!"
In an old remembered way
Rain works on me night and day.

Quaint, outlandish heathen gods
Black men fashion out of rods,
Clay, and brittle bits of stone,
In a likeness like their own,
My conversion came high-priced;
I belong to Jesus Christ,   90
Preacher of humility;
Heathen gods are naught to me.

Father, Son, and Holy Ghost,
So I make an idle boast;
Jesus of the twice-turned cheek,
Lamb of God, although I speak

With my mouth thus, in my heart
Do I play a double part.
Ever at Thy glowing altar
Must my heart grow sick and falter,   100
Wishing He I served were black,
Thinking then it would not lack
Precedent of pain to guide it,
Let who would or might deride it;
Surely then this flesh would know
Yours had borne a kindred woe.
Lord, I fashion dark gods, too,
Daring even to give You
Dark despairing features where,
Crowned with dark rebellious hair,   110
Patience wavers just so much as
Mortal grief compels, while touches
Quick and hot, of anger, rise
To smitten cheek and weary eyes.
Lord, forgive me if my need
Sometimes shapes a human creed.
All day long and all night through,
One thing only must I do:
Quench my pride and cool my blood,
Lest I perish in the flood.   120
Lest a hidden ember set
Timber that I thought was wet
Burning like the dryest flax,
Melting like the merest wax,
Lest the grave restore its dead.
Not yet has my heart or head
In the least way realized
They and I are civilized.

From the Dark Tower (1927)

(To Charles S. Johnson)

We shall not always plant while others reap
The golden increment of bursting fruit,
Not always countenance, abject and mute,
That lesser men should hold their brothers
        cheap;
Not everlastingly while others sleep
Shall we beguile their limbs with mellow flute,

Not always bend to some more subtle brute;
We were not made eternally to weep.

The night whose sable breast relieves the stark,
White stars is no less lovely being dark,   10
And there are buds that cannot bloom at all
In light, but crumple, piteous, and fall;
So in the dark we hide the heart that bleeds,
And wait, and tend our agonizing seeds.

CLAUDE McKAY (1890–1948)

Claude McKay was twenty-one years old before
he came from Jamaica to the United States and
had already published two books of dialect
verse. After a short time studying at Tuskegee

Institute and later at Kansas State University, he went to New York, where he held a variety of jobs. After publishing some poetry, he worked on the *Liberator* and the *Masses.* His *Harlem Shadows* appeared in 1922, just before he began his wanderings in Russia, western Europe, and Africa. His work is much more politically oriented than that of most writers of the Harlem Renaissance, and interest in it has increased among readers over the past decade. In fact, a copy of the first poem we print here was found in the cell of one of the inmates at Attica State Prison after the recent riots and attributed by the national press to the prisoner.

FURTHER READINGS

Wayne Cooper, "Claude McKay and the New Negro of the 1920's," *Phylon*, Vol. 25 (1964)
Blyden Jackson, "The Essential McKay," *Phylon*, Vol. 14 (1953)

Saunders Redding, *To Make a Poet Black* (1939)
Robert A. Smith, "Claude McKay: An Essay in Criticism," *Phylon*, Vol. 9 (1948)

If We Must Die (1922)

If we must die—let it not be like hogs
Hunted and penned in an inglorious spot,
While round us bark the mad and hungry
    dogs,
Making their mock at our accursed lot.
If we must die—oh, let us nobly die,
So that our precious blood may not be shed
In vain; then even the monsters we defy
Shall be constrained to honor us though dead!
Oh, Kinsmen! We must meet the common
    foe;

Though far outnumbered, let us show us
    brave,   10
And for their thousand blows deal one death-
    blow!
What though before us lies the open grave?
Like men we'll face the murderous, cowardly
    pack,
Pressed to the wall, dying, but fighting back!

The Tropics in New York (1922)

Bananas ripe and green, and ginger-root,
    Cocoa in pods and alligator pears,
And tangerines and mangoes and grapefruit,
    Fit for the highest prize at parish fairs,

Set in the window, bringing memories
    Of fruit-trees laden by low-singing rills,
And dewy dawns, and mystical blue skies

In benediction over nun-like hills.

My eyes grew dim, and I could no more gaze;
    A wave of longing through my body swept,   10
And, hungry for the old, familiar ways,
    I turned aside and bowed my head and
    wept.

ZORA NEALE HURSTON (1901?–1960)

Zora Neale Hurston was born in 1901 or 1902 or 1903 (she was, characteristically, never consistent about the year) in Eatonville, Florida, the first incorporated Negro town in this country, where her father was mayor, preacher, and carpenter. She began her formal education in a one-room schoolhouse, but later—in spite of many "vicissitudes of fortune"—was the first Negro woman to be admitted to Barnard College. After graduating she studied anthropology at Columbia under Franz Boas, who set her to work for him with calipers to measure the "interesting skulls" she found around Harlem.

Hurston was one of the more vivid personalities associated with the Harlem Renaissance, and of her Langston Hughes records in *The Big Sea*, "Only to reach a wider audience, need she ever write books—she is a perfect book of entertainment in herself." But she did write

books. *Jonah's Gourd Vine* (based on the lives of her parents) and *Their Eyes Were Watching God* show her as a very talented novelist, but her most important work appears in her autobiography *Dust Tracks on a Road* and in her anthropological works, *Mules and Men*, an account of her travels in the Deep South collecting black folklore and studying voodoo in New Orleans (where she was initiated into the rite by the eminent practitioner known as the Frizzly Rooster), and in *Tell My Horse*, which recounts similar adventures in Haiti and Jamaica.

FURTHER READINGS

James W. Byrd, "Zora Neale Hurston: A Novel Folklorist," *Tennessee Folklore Society Bulletin*, 21 (1955), 37–41

Hugh M. Gloster, *Negro Voices in American Fiction* (1948)
Darwin T. Turner, *In a Minor Chord* (1971)

From Dust Tracks on the Road (1942)

My search for knowledge of things took me into many strange places and adventures. My life was in danger several times. If I had not learned how to take care of myself in these circumstances, I could have been maimed or killed on most any day of the several years of my research work. Primitive minds are quick to sunshine and quick to anger. Some little word, look or gesture can move them either to love or to sticking a knife between your ribs. You just have to sense the delicate balance and maintain it.

In some instances, there is nothing personal in the killing. The killer wishes to establish a reputation as a killer, and you'll do as a sample. Some of them go around, making their announcements in singing:

I'm going to make me a graveyard of my own,
I'm going to make me a graveyard of my own,
Oh, carried me down on de smoky road,
Brought me back on de coolin' board,
But I'm going to make me a graveyard of my own.

And since the law is lax on these big saw-mill, turpentine and railroad "jobs," there is a good chance that they never will be jailed for it. All of these places have plenty of men and women who are fugitives from justice. The management asks

no questions. They need help and they can't be bothered looking for a bug under every chip. In some places, the "law" is forbidden to come on the premises to hunt for malefactors who did their malefacting elsewhere. The wheels of industry must move, and if these men don't do the work, who is there to do it?

So if a man, or a woman, has been on the gang for petty-thieving and mere mayhem, and is green with jealousy of the others who did the same amount of time for a killing and had something to brag about, why not look around for an easy victim and become a hero, too? I was nominated like that once in Polk County, Florida, and the only reason that I was not elected, was because a friend got in there and staved off old club-footed Death.

Polk County! Ah!
Where the water tastes like cherry wine.
Where they fell great trees with axe and muscle.

These poets of the swinging blade! The brief, but infinitely graceful, dance of body and axe-head as it lifts over the head in a fluid arc, dances in air and rushes down to bite into the tree, all in beauty. Where the logs march into the mill with its smokestacks disputing with the elements, its boiler room reddening the sky, and its great circular saw screaming arrogantly as it attacks the tree like a lion making its kill. The log on the carriage coming to the saw. A growling grumble. Then contact! Yeelld-u-u-ow! And a board is laid shining and new on a pile. All day, all night. Rumble, thunder and grumble. Yee-ee-ow! Sweating black bodies, muscled like gods, working to feed the hunger of the great tooth. Polk County!

Polk County. Black men laughing and singing. They go down in the phosphate mines and bring up the wet dust of the bones of pre-historic monsters, to make rich land in far places, so that people can eat. But, all of it is not dust. Huge ribs, twenty feet from belly to backbone. Some old-time sea monster caught in the shallows in that morning when God said, "Let's make some more dry land. Stay there, great Leviathan! Stay there as a memory and a monument to Time." Shark-teeth as wide as the hand of a working man. Joints of backbone three feet high, bearing witness to the mighty monster of the deep when the Painted Land rose up and did her first dance with the morning sun. Gazing on these relics, forty thousand years old and more, one visualizes the great surrender to chance and change when these creatures were rocked to sleep and slumber by the birth of land.

Polk County. Black men from tree to tree among the lordly pines, a swift, slanting stroke to bleed the trees for gum. Paint, explosives, marine stores, flavors, perfumes, tone for a violin bow, and many other things which the black men who bleed the trees never heard about.

Polk County. The clang of nine-pound hammers on railroad steel. The world must ride.

Hah! A rhythmic swing of the body, hammer falls, and another spike driven to the head in the tie.

Oh, Mobile! Hank!
Oh, Alabama! Hank!
Oh, Fort Myers! Hank!
Oh, in Florida! Hank!
Oh, let's shake it! Hank!
Oh, let's break it! Hank!
Oh, let's shake it! Hank!
Oh, just a hair! Hank!

The singing-liner cuts short his chant. The straw-boss relaxes with a gesture of his hand. Another rail spiked down. Another offering to the soul of civilization whose other name is travel.

Polk County. Black men scrambling up ladders into orange trees. Singing, laughing, cursing, boasting of last night's love, and looking forward to the darkness again. They do not say embrace when they mean that they slept with a woman. A behind is a behind and not a form. Nobody says anything about incompatibility when they mean it does not suit. No bones are made about being fed up.

I got up this morning, and I knowed I didn't want it,
Yea! Polk County!
You don't know Polk County like I do
Anybody been there, tell you the same thing, too.
Eh, rider, rider!
Polk County, where the water tastes like cherry wine.

Polk County. After dark, the jooks. Songs are born out of feelings with an old beat-up piano, or a guitar for a mid-wife. Love made and unmade. Who put out dat lie, it was supposed to last forever? Love is when it is. No more here? Plenty more down the road. Take you where I'm going, woman? Hell no! Let every town furnish its own. Yeah, I'm going. Who care anything about no train fare? The railroad track is there, ain't it? I can count tires just like I been doing. I can ride de blind, can't I?

Got on de train didn't have no fare
But I rode some
Yes I rode some
Got on de train didn't have no fare
Conductor ast me what I'm doing there
But I rode some.
Yes I rode some.

Well, he grabbed me by de collar and he led me to de door
But I rode some
Yes I rode some.
Well, he grabbed me by de collar and he led me to de door
He rapped me over de head with a forty-four
But I rode some
Yes I rode some.

Polk County in the jooks. Dancing the square dance. Dancing the scronch. Dancing the belly-rub. Knocking the right hat off the wrong head, and backing it up with a switch-blade.

"Fan-foot, what you doing with my man's hat cocked on *your* nappy head? I know you want to see your Jesus. Who's a whore? Yeah I sleeps with

my mens, but they pays me. I wouldn't be a fan-
foot like you—just on de road somewhere. Runs
up and down de road from job to job making pay-
days. Don't nobody hold her! Let her jump on me!
She pay her way on me, and I'll pay it off. Make
time in old Bartow jail for her."

Maybe somebody stops the fight before the two
switch-blades go together. Maybe nobody can. A
short, swift dash in. A lucky jab by one opponent
and the other one is dead. Maybe one gets a chill
in the feet and leaps out of the door. Maybe both
get cut badly and back off. Anyhow, the fun of
the place goes on. More dancing and singing and
buying of drinks, parched peanuts, fried rabbit.
Full drummy bass from the piano with weepy,
intricate right-hand stuff. Singing the memories of
Ella Wall, the Queen of love in the jooks of Polk
County. Ella Wall, Planchita, Trottin' Liza.

It is a sad, parting song. Each verse ends up
with:

Quarters Boss! High Sheriff? Lemme git gone from
    here!
Cold, rainy day, some old cold, rainy day
I'll be back, some old cold, rainy day.
Oh de rocks may be my pillow. Lawd!
De sand may be my bed
I'll be back some old cold, rainy day.

"Who run? What you running from the man
for, nigger? Me, I don't aim to run a step. I ain't
going to run unless they run me. I'm going to live
anyhow until I die. Play me some music so I can
dance! Aw, spank dat box, man! ! Them white
folks don't care nothing bout no nigger getting cut
and kilt, nohow. They ain't coming in here. I done
kilt me four and they ain't hung me yet. Beat dat
box!"

"Yeah, but you ain't kilt no women, yet. They's
mighty particular 'bout you killing up women."

"And I ain't killing none neither. I ain't crazy in
de head. Nigger woman can kill all us men she
wants to and they don't care. Leave us kill a
woman and they'll run you just as long as you can
find something to step on. I got good sense. I
know I ain't got no show. De white mens and de
nigger women is running this thing. Sing about old
Georgy Buck and let's dance off of it. Hit dat
box!"

Old Georgy Buck is dead
Last word he said
I don't want no shortening in my bread.
Rabbit on de log

Ain't got no dog
Shoot him wid my rifle, bam! bam!

And the night, the pay night rocks on with
music and gambling and laughter and dancing and
fights. The big pile of cross-ties burning out in
front simmers down to low ashes before sun-up, so
then it is time to throw up all the likker you can't
keep down and go somewhere and sleep the rest
off, whether your knife has blood on it or not.
That is, unless some strange, low member of your
own race has gone and pimped to the white folks
about something getting hurt. Very few of those
kind are to be found.

That is the primeval flavor of the place, and as
I said before, out of this primitive approach to
things, I all but lost my life.

It was in a saw-mill jook in Polk County that I
almost got cut to death.

Lucy really wanted to kill me. I didn't mean
any harm. All I was doing was collecting songs
from Slim, who used to be her man back up in
West Florida before he ran off from her. It is true
that she found out where he was after nearly a
year, and followed him to Polk County and he
paid her some slight attention. He was knocking the
pad with women, all around, and he seemed to
want to sort of free-lance at it. But what he
seemed to care most about was picking his guitar,
and singing.

He was a valuable source of material to me, so I
built him up a bit by buying him drinks and
letting him ride in my car.

I figure that Lucy took a pick at me for three
reasons. The first one was, her vanity was rubbed
sore at not being able to hold her man. That was
hard to own up to in a community where so much
stress was laid on suiting. Nobody else had offered
to shack up with her either. She was getting a very
limited retail trade and Slim was ignoring the
whole business. I had store-bought clothes, a lighter
skin, and a shiny car, so she saw wherein she could
use me for an alibi. So in spite of public knowledge of the situation for a year or more before I
came, she was telling it around that I came and
broke them up. She was going to cut everything off
of me but "quit it."

Her second reason was, because of my research
methods I had dug in with the male community.
Most of the women liked me, too. Especially her
sworn enemy, Big Sweet. She was scared of Big
Sweet, but she probably reasoned that if she cut
Big Sweet's protégée it would be a slam on Big

Sweet and build up her own reputation. She was fighting Big Sweet through me.

Her third reason was, she had been in little scraps and been to jail off and on, but she could not swear that she had ever killed anybody. She was small potatoes and nobody was paying her any mind. I was easy. I had no gun, knife or any sort of weapon. I did not even know how to do that kind of fighting.

Lucky for me, I had friended with Big Sweet. She came to my notice within the first week that I arrived on location. I heard somebody, a woman's voice "specifying" up this line of houses from where I lived and asked who it was.

"Dat's Big Sweet" my landlady told me. "She got her foot up on somebody. Ain't she specifying?"

She was really giving the particulars. She was giving a "reading," a word borrowed from the fortune-tellers. She was giving her opponent lurid data and bringing him up to date on his ancestry, his looks, smell, gait, clothes, and his route through Hell in the hereafter. My landlady went outside where nearly everybody else of the four or five hundred people on the "job" were to listen to the reading. Big Sweet broke the news to him, in one of her mildest bulletins that his pa was a double-humpted camel and his ma was a grass-gut cow, but even so, he tore her wide open in the act of getting born, and so on and so forth. He was a bitch's baby out of a buzzard egg.

My landlady explained to me what was meant by "putting your foot up" on a person. If you are sufficiently armed—enough to stand off a panzer division—and know what to do with your weapons after you get 'em, it is all right to go to the house of your enemy, put one foot up on his steps, rest one elbow on your knee and play in the family. That is another way of saying play the dozens, which also is a way of saying low-rate your enemy's ancestors and him, down to the present moment for reference, and then go into his future as far as your imagination leads you. But if you have no faith in your personal courage and confidence in your arsenal, don't try it. It is a risky pleasure. So then I had a measure of this Big Sweet.

"Hurt who?" Mrs. Bertha snorted at my fears. "Big Sweet? Humph! Tain't a man, woman nor child on this job going to tackle Big Sweet. If God send her a pistol she'll send him a man. She can handle a knife with anybody. She'll join hands and cut a duel. Dat Cracker Quarters Boss wears two pistols round his waist and goes for bad, but

he won't break a breath with Big Sweet lessen he got his pistol in his hand. Cause if he start anything with her, he won't never get a chance to draw it. She ain't mean. She don't bother nobody. She just don't stand for no foolishness, dat's all."

Right away, I decided that Big Sweet was going to be my friend. From what I had seen and heard in the short time I had been there, I felt as timid as an egg without a shell. So the next afternoon when she was pointed out to me, I waited until she was well up the sawdust road to the Commissary, then I got in my car and went that way as if by accident. When I pulled up beside her and offered her a ride, she frowned at me first, then looked puzzled, but finally broke into a smile and got in.

By the time we got to the Commissary post office we were getting along fine. She told everybody I was her friend. We did not go back to the Quarters at once. She carried me around to several places and showed me off. We made a date to go down to Lakeland come Saturday, which we did. By the time we sighted the Quarters on the way back from Lakeland, she had told me, "You sho is crazy!" Which is a way of saying I was witty. "I loves to friend with somebody like you. I aims to look out for you, too. Do your fighting for you. Nobody better not start nothing with you, do I'll get my switch-blade and go round de hambone looking for meat."

We shook hands and I gave her one of my bracelets. After that everything went well for me. Big Sweet helped me to collect material in a big way. She had no idea what I wanted with it, but if I wanted it, she meant to see to it that I got it. She pointed out people who knew songs and stories. She wouldn't stand for balkiness on their part. We held two lying contests, story-telling contests to you, and Big Sweet passed on who rated the prizes. In that way, there was no argument about it.

So when the word came to Big Sweet that Lucy was threatening me, she put her foot up on Lucy in a most particular manner and warned her against the try. I suggested buying a knife for defense, but she said I would certainly be killed that way.

"You don't know how to handle no knife. You ain't got dat kind of a sense. You wouldn't even know how to hold it to de best advantage. You would draw your arm way back to stop her, and whilst you was doing all dat, Lucy would run in under your arm and be done; cut you to death before you could touch her. And then again, when you sure 'nough fighting, it ain't enough to just stick 'em wid your knife. You got to ram it in to de hilt, then you pull *down*. They ain't no more trouble after dat. They's *dead*. But don't you bother 'bout no fighting. You ain't like me. You don't even sleep with no mens. I wanted to be a virgin one time, but I couldn't keep it up. I needed the money too bad. But I think it's nice for you to be like that. You just keep on writing down them lies. I'll take care of all de fighting. Dat'll make it more better, since we done made friends."

She warned me that Lucy might try to "steal" me. That is, ambush me, or otherwise attack me without warning. So I was careful. I went nowhere on foot without Big Sweet.

Several weeks went by, then I ventured to the jook alone. Big Sweet let it be known that she was not going. But later she came in and went over to the coon-can game in the corner. Thinking I was alone, Lucy waited until things were in full swing and then came in with the very man to whom Big Sweet had given the "reading." There was only one door. I was far from it. I saw no escape for me when Lucy strode in, knife in hand. I saw sudden death very near that moment. I was paralyzed with fear. Big Sweet was in a crowd over in the corner, and did not see Lucy come in. But the sudden quiet of the place made her look around as Lucy charged. My friend was large and portly, but extremely light on her feet. She sprang like a lioness and I think the very surprise of Big Sweet being there when Lucy thought she was over at another party at the Pine Mill unnerved Lucy. She stopped abruptly as Big Sweet charged. The next moment, it was too late for Lucy to start again. The man who came in with Lucy tried to help her out, but two other men joined Big Sweet in the battle. It took on amazingly. It seemed that anybody who had any fighting to do, decided to settle-up then and there. Switch-blades, ice-picks and old-fashioned razors were out. One or two razors had already been bent back and thrown across the room, but our fight was the main attraction. Big Sweet yelled to me to run. I really ran, too. I ran out of the place, ran to my room, threw my things in the car and left the place. When the sun came up I was a hundred miles up the road, headed for New Orleans.

· · ·

One bit of research I did jointly for the Journal of Negro History and Columbia University, was in Mobile, Alabama. There I went to talk to Cudjo

Lewis. That is the American version of his name. His African name was Kossola-O-Lo-Loo-Ay.

He arrived on the last load of slaves run into the United States and was the only Negro alive that came over on a slave ship. It happened in 1859 just when the fight between the South and the Abolitionists was moving toward the Civil War. He has died since I saw him.

I found him a cheerful, poetical old gentleman in his late nineties, who could tell a good story. His interpretation of the story of Jonah was marvelous.

He was a good Christian and so he pretended to have forgotten all of his African religion. He turned me off with the statement that his Nigerian religion was the same as Christianity. "We know it a God, you unner'stand, but we don't know He got a Son."

He told me in detail of the circumstances in Africa that brought about his slavery here. How the powerful Kingdom of Dahomey, finding the slave trade so profitable, had abandoned farming, hunting and all else to capture slaves to stock the barracoons on the beach at Dmydah to sell to the slavers who came from across the ocean. How quarrels were manufactured by the King of Dahomey with more peaceful agricultural nations in striking distance of Dahomey in Nigeria and Gold Coast; how they were assaulted, completely wiped off the map, their names never to appear again, except when they were named in boastful chant before the King at one of his "customs" when his glory was being sung. The able-bodied who were captured were marched to Abomey, the capital city of Dahomey and displayed to the King, then put into the barracoons to await a buyer. The too old, the too young, the injured in battle were instantly beheaded and their heads smoked and carried back to the King. He paid off on heads, dead or alive. The skulls of the slaughtered were not wasted either. The King had his famous Palace of Skulls. The Palace grounds had a massive gate of skull-heads. The walls surrounding the grounds were built of skulls. You see, the Kings of Dahomey were truly great and mighty and a lot of skulls were bound to come out of their ambitions. While it looked awesome and splendid to him and his warriors, the sight must have been most grewsome and crude to Western eyes.

One thing impressed me strongly from this three months of association with Cudjo Lewis. The white people had held my people in slavery here in America. They had bought us, it is true and exploited us. But the inescapable fact that stuck in my craw, was: my people had *sold* me and the white people had bought me. That did away with the folklore I had been brought up on—that the white people had gone to Africa, waved a red handkerchief at the Africans and lured them aboard ship and sailed away. I know that civilized money stirred up African greed. That wars between tribes were often stirred up by white traders to provide more slaves in the barracoons and all that. But, if the African princes had been as pure and as innocent as I would like to think, it could not have happened. No, my own people had butchered and killed, exterminated whole nations and torn families apart, for a profit before the strangers got their chance at a cut. It was a sobering thought. What is more, all that this Cudjo told me was verified from other historical sources. It impressed upon me the universal nature of greed and glory. Lack of power and opportunity passes off too often for virtue. If I were King, let us say, over the Western Hemisphere tomorrow, instead of who I am, what would I consider right and just? Would I put the cloak of Justice on my ambition and send her out a-whoring after conquests? It is something to ponder over with fear.

Cudjo's eyes were full of tears and memory of fear when he told me of the assault on his city and its capture. He said that his nation, the Takkoi, lived "three sleeps" from Dahomey. The attack came at dawn as the Takkoi were getting out of bed to go to their fields outside the city. A whooping horde of the famed Dahoman women warriors burst through the main gate, seized people as they fled from their houses and beheaded victims with one stroke of their big swords.

"Oh, oh! I runnee this way to that gate, but they there. I runnee to another one, but they there, too. All eight gates they there. Them women, they very strong. I nineteen years old, but they too strong for me. They take me and tie me. I don't know where my people at. I never see them no more."

He described the awful slaughter as the Amazons sacked the city. The clusters of human heads at their belts. The plight of those who fled through the gates to fall into the hands of the male warriors outside. How his King was finally captured and carried before the King of Dahomey, who had broken his rule and come on this expedition in person because of a grudge against the King of Takkoi, and how the vanquished monarch was led before him, bound.

"Now, that you have dared to send impudent words to me," the King of Dahomey said, "your country is conquered and you are before me in chains. I shall take you to Abomey."

"No," the King of Takkoi answered. "I am King in Takkoi. I will not go to Dahomey." He knew that he would be killed for a spectacle in Dahomey. He chose to die at home.

So two Dahoman warriors held each of his hands and an Amazon struck off his head.

Later, two representatives of a European power attended the customs of the King at Abomey, and told of seeing the highly polished skull of the King of Takkoi mounted in a beautiful ship-model. His name and his nation were mentioned in the chant to the glory of Dahomey. The skull was treated with the utmost respect, as the King of Dahomey would expect his to be treated in case he fell in battle. That was the custom in West Africa. For the same reason, no one of royal blood was sold into slavery. They were killed. There are no descendants of royal African blood among American Negroes for that reason. The Negroes who claim that they are descendants of royal African blood have taken a leaf out of the book of the white ancestor-hounds in America, whose folks went to England with William the Conqueror, got restless and caught the *Mayflower* for Boston, then feeling a romantic lack, rushed down the coast and descended from Pocahontas. From the number of her children, one is forced to the conclusion that that Pocahontas wasn't so poky, after all.

Kossola told me of the March to Abomey after the fall of Takkoi. How they were yoked by forked sticks and tied in a chain. How the Dahomans halted the march the second day in order to smoke the heads of the victims because they were spoiling. The prisoners had to watch the heads of their friends and relatives turning on long poles in the smoke. Abomey and the palace of the King and then the march to the coast and the barracoons. They were there sometime before a ship came to trade. Many, many tribes were there, each in a separate barracoon, lest they war among themselves. The traders could choose which tribe they wanted. When the tribe was decided upon, he was carried into the barracoon where that tribe was confined, the women were lined up on one side and the men on the other. He walked down between the lines and selected the individuals he wanted. They usually took an equal number.

He described the embarcation and the trip across the ocean in the *Chlotilde*, a fast sailing vessel built by the Maher brothers of Maine, who had moved to Alabama. They were chased by a British man-of-war on the lookout for slavers, but the *Chlotilde* showed her heels. Finally the cargo arrived in Mobile. They were unloaded up the river, the boat sunk, and the hundred-odd Africans began a four-year life of slavery.

"We so surprised to see mule and plow. We so surprised to see man pushee and mule pullee."

After the war, these Africans made a settlement of their own at Plateau, Alabama, three miles up the river from Mobile. They farmed and worked in the lumber mills and bought property. The descendants of these people are still there.

Kossola's great sorrow in America was the death of his favorite son, David, killed by a train. He refused to believe it was his David when he saw the body. He refused to let the bell be tolled for him.

"If dat my boy, where his head? No, dat not my David. Dat not my boy. My boy gone to Mobile. No, No! Don't ringee de bell for David. Dat not him."

But, finally his wife persuaded him that the headless body on the window blind was their son. He cried hard for several minutes and then said, "Ringee de bell."

His other great sorrow was that he had lost track of his folks in Africa.

"They don't know what become of Kossola. When you go there, you tellee where I at." He begged me. He did not know that his tribe was no more upon this earth, except for those who reached the barracoon at Dmydah. None of his family was in the barracoon. He had missed seeing their heads in the smoke, no doubt. It is easy to see how few would have looked on that sight too closely.

"I lonely for my folks. They don't know. Maybe they ask everybody go there where Kossola. I know they hunt for me." There was a tragic catch in his voice like the whimper of a lost dog.

After seventy-five years, he still had that tragic sense of loss. That yearning for blood and cultural ties. That sense of mutilation. It gave me something to feel about.

From Mules and Men (1935)

In her autobiography, *Dust Tracks on a Road,* Zora Neale Hurston also refers to her researches with the "Frizzly Rooster," in the passage quoted here:

In New Orleans, I delved into Hoodoo, or sympathetic magic. I studied with the Frizzly Rooster, and all of the other noted "doctors." I learned the routines for making and breaking marriages; driving off and punishing enemies; influencing the minds of judges and juries in favor of clients; killing by remote control and other things. In order to work with these "two-headed" doctors, I had to go through an initiation with each. The routine varied with each doctor.

In one case it was not only elaborate, it was impressive. I lay naked for three days and nights on a couch, with my navel to a rattlesnake skin which had been dressed and dedicated to the ceremony. I ate no food in all that time. Only a pitcher of water was on a little table at the head of the couch so that my soul would not wander off in search of

water and be attacked by evil influences and not return to me. On the second day, I began to dream strange exalted dreams. On the third night, I had dreams that seemed real for weeks. In one, I strode across the heavens with lightning flashing from under my feet, and grumbling thunder following in my wake.

Here is the section from *Mules and Men:*

So I became the pupil of Reverend Father Joe Watson, "The Frizzly Rooster" and his wife, Mary, who assisted him in all things. She was "round the altar"; that is while he talked with the clients, and usually decided on whatever "work" was to be done, she "set" the things on the altar and in the jars. There was one jar in the kitchen filled with honey and sugar. All the "sweet" works were set in this jar. That is, the names and the thing desired were written on paper and thrust into this jar to stay. Already four or five hundred slips of paper had accumulated in the jar. There was another jar called the "break up" jar. It held vinegar with some unsweetened coffee added. Papers were left in this one also.

When finally it was agreed that I should come to study with them, I was put to running errands such as "dusting" houses, throwing pecans, rolling apples, as the case might be; but I was not told why the thing was being done. After two weeks of this I was taken off this phase and initiated. This was the first step towards the door of the mysteries.

My initiation consisted of the Pea Vine Candle Drill. I was told to remain five days without sexual intercourse. I must remain indoors all day the day before the initiation and fast. I might wet my throat when necessary, but I was not to swallow water.

When I arrived at the house the next morning a little before nine, as per instructions, six other persons were there, so that there were nine of us—all in white except Father Watson who was in his purple robe. There was no talking. We went at once to the altar room. The altar was blazing. There were three candles around the vessel of holy water, three around the sacred sand pail, and one large cream candle burning in it. A picture of St. George and a large piece of brain coral were in the center. Father Watson dressed eight long blue candles and one black one, while the rest of us sat in the chairs around the wall. Then he lit the eight blue candles one by one from the altar and set them in the pattern of a moving serpent. Then I was called to the altar and both Father Watson and his wife laid hands on me. The black candle was placed in my hand; I was told to light it from all the other candles. I lit it at number one and pinched out the flame, and re-lit it at number two and so on till it had been lit by the eighth candle. Then I held the candle in my left hand, and by my right was conducted back to the altar by Father Watson. I was led through the maze of candles beginning at number eight. We circled numbers seven, five and three. When we reached the altar he lifted me upon the step. As I stood there, he called aloud, "Spirit! She's standing here without no home and no friends. She wants you to take her in." Then we began at number one and threaded back to number eight, circling three, five and seven. Then back to the altar again. Again he lifted me and placed me upon the step of the altar. Again the spirit was addressed as before. Then he lifted me down by placing his hands in my arm-pits. This time I did not walk at all. I was carried through the maze and I was to knock down each candle as I passed it with my foot. If I missed one, I was not to try again, but to knock it down on my way back to

the altar. Arrived there the third time, I was lifted up and told to pinch out my black candle. "Now," Father told me, "you are made Boss of Candles. You have the power to light candles and put out candles, and to work with the spirits anywhere on earth."

Then all of the candles on the floor were collected and one of them handed to each of the persons present. Father took the black candle himself and we formed a ring. Everybody was given two matches each. The candles were held in our left hands, matches in the right; at a signal everybody stooped at the same moment, the matches scratched in perfect time and our candles lighted in concert. Then Father Watson walked rhythmically around the person at his right. Exchanged candles with her and went back to his place. Then that person did the same to the next so that the black candle went all around the circle and back to Father. I was then seated on a stool before the altar, sprinkled lightly with holy sand and water and confirmed as a Boss of Candles.

Then conversation broke out. We went into the next room and had a breakfast that was mostly fruit and smothered chicken. Afterwards the nine candles used in the ceremony were wrapped up and given to me to keep. They were to be used for lighting other candles only, not to be just burned in the ordinary sense.

In a few days I was allowed to hold consultations on my own. I felt insecure and said so to Father Watson.

"Of course you do now," he answered me, "but you have to learn and grow. I'm right here behind you. Talk to your people first, then come see me."

Within the hour a woman came to me. A man had shot and seriously wounded her husband and was in jail.

"But, honey," she all but wept, "they say ain't a thing going to be done with him. They say he got good white folks back of him and he's going to be let loose soon as the case is tried. I want him punished. Picking a fuss with my husband just to get chance to shoot him. We needs help. Somebody that can hit a straight lick with a crooked stick."

So I went in to the Frizzly Rooster to find out what I must do and he told me, "That a low fence." He meant a difficulty that was easily overcome.

"Go back and get five dollars from her and tell her to go home and rest easy. That man will be punished. When we get through with him, white folks or no white folks, he'll find a tough jury sitting on his case." The woman paid me and left in perfect confidence of Father Watson.

So he and I went into the workroom.

"Now," he said, "when you want a person punished who is already indicted, write his name on a slip of paper and put it in a sugar bowl or some other deep something like that. Now get your paper and pencil and write the name; alright now, you got it in the bowl. Now put in some red pepper, some black pepper—don't be skeered to put it in, it needs a lot. Put in one eightpenny nail, fifteen cents worth of ammonia and two door keys. You drop one key down in the bowl and you leave the other one against the side of the bowl. Now you got your bowl set. Go to your bowl every day at twelve o'clock and turn the key that is standing against the side of the bowl. That is to keep the man locked in jail. And every time you turn the key, add a little vinegar. Now I know this will do the job. All it needs is for you to do it in faith. I'm trusting this job to you entirely. Less see what you going to do. That can wait another minute. Come sit with me in the outside room and hear this woman out here that's waiting."

So we went outside and found a weakish woman in her early thirties that looked like somebody had dropped a sack of something soft on a chair.

The Frizzly Rooster put on his manner, looking like a brown, purple and gold throne-angel in a house.

"Good morning, sister er, er ———"

"Murchison," she helped out.

"Tell us how you want to be helped, Sister Murchison."

She looked at me as if I was in the way and he read her eyes.

"She's alright, dear one. She's one of us. I brought her in with me to assist and help."

I thought still I was in her way but she told her business just the same.

"Too many women in my house. My husband's mother is there and she hates me and always puttin' my husband up to fight me. Look like I can't get her out of my house no ways I try. So I done come to you."

"We can fix that up in no time, dear one. Now go take a flat onion. If it was a man, I'd say a sharp pointed onion. Core the onion out, and write her name five times on paper and stuff it into the hole in the onion and close it back with the cut-out piece of onion. Now you watch when she leaves the house and then you roll the onion

behind her before anybody else crosses the doorsill. And you make a wish at the same time for her to leave your house. She won't be there two weeks more." The woman paid and left.

That night we held a ceremony in the altar room on the case. We took a red candle and burnt it just enough to consume the tip. Then it was cut into three parts and the short lengths of candle were put into a glass of holy water. Then we took the glass and went at midnight to the door of the woman's house and the Frizzly Rooster held the glass in his hands and said, "In the name of the Father, in the name of the Son, in the name of the Holy Ghost." He shook the glass three times violently up and down, and the last time he threw the glass to the ground and broke it, and said, "Dismiss this woman from this place." We scarcely paused as this was said and done and we kept going and went home by another way because that was part of the ceremony.

Somebody came against a very popular preacher. "He's getting too rich and big. I want something done to keep him down. They tell me he's 'bout to get to be a bishop. I sho' would hate for that to happen. I got forty dollars in my pocket right now for the work."

So that night the altar blazed with the blue light. We wrote the preacher's name on a slip of paper with black ink. We took a small doll and ripped open its back and put in the paper with the name along with some bitter aloes and cayenne pepper and sewed the rip up again with the black thread. The hands of the doll were tied behind it and a black veil tied over the face and knotted behind it so that the man it represented would be blind and always do the things to keep himself from progressing. The doll was then placed in a kneeling position in a dark corner where it would not be disturbed. He would be frustrated as long as the doll was not disturbed.

When several of my jobs had turned out satisfactorily to Father Watson, he said to me, "You will do well, but you need the Black Cat Bone. Sometimes you have to be able to walk invisible. Some things must be done in deep secret, so you have to walk out of the sight of man."

First I had to get ready even to try this most terrible of experiences—getting the Black Cat Bone.

First we had to wait on the weather. When a big rain started, a new receptacle was set out in the yard. It could not be put out until the rain actually started for fear the sun might shine in it.

The water must be brought inside before the weather faired off for the same reason. If lightning shone on it, it was ruined.

We finally got the water for the bath and I had to fast and "seek," shut in a room that had been purged by smoke. Twenty-four hours without food except a special wine that was fed to me every four hours. It did not make me drunk in the accepted sense of the word. I merely seemed to lose my body, my mind seemed very clear.

When dark came, we went out to catch a black cat. I must catch him with my own hands. Finding and catching black cats is hard work, unless one has been released for you to find. Then we repaired to a prepared place in the woods and a circle drawn and "protected" with nine horseshoes. Then the fire and the pot were made ready. A roomy iron pot with a lid. When the water boiled I was to toss in the terrified, trembling cat.

When he screamed, I was told to curse him. He screamed three times, the last time weak and resigned. The lid was clamped down, the fire kept vigorously alive. At midnight the lid was lifted. Here was the moment! The bones of the cat must be passed through my mouth until one tasted bitter.

Suddenly, the Rooster and Mary rushed in close to the pot and he cried, "Look out! This is liable to kill you. Hold your nerve!" They both looked fearfully around the circle. They communicated some unearthly terror to me. Maybe I went off in a trance. Great beast-like creatures thundered up to the circle from all sides. Indescribable noises, sights, feelings. Death was at hand! Seemed unavoidable! I don't know. Many times I have thought and felt, but I always have to say the same thing. I don't know. I don't know.

Before day I was home, with a small white bone for me to carry.

ARNA BONTEMPS (1902–   )

A Louisianian, born in 1902, Arna Bontemps was raised in California and attended college there. Immediately after college, in 1924, he went East, to Harlem, where he made a name for himself, chiefly as a poet. But his fiction was also well received. In 1945, he collaborated with Jack Conroy, the novelist, on *They Seek a City*, concerning the black migration, an expanded version of which was published in 1966 as *Anyplace But Here*. For some years he served as the librarian at Fisk University, with an interruption for a period of teaching at Yale. Throughout this period he has been active as an anthologist of black literature, and in 1972 he published a full-length study of the Harlem Renaissance.

FURTHER READING

Hugh M. Gloster, *Negro Voices in American Fiction* (1948)

A Summer Tragedy (1936)

Old Jeff Patton, the black share farmer, fumbled with his bow tie. His fingers trembled and the high stiff collar pinched his throat. A fellow loses his hand for such vanities after thirty or forty years of simple life. Once a year, or maybe twice if there's a wedding among his kinfolks, he may spruce up; but generally fancy clothes do nothing but adorn the wall of the big room and feed the moths. That had been Jeff Patton's experience. He had not worn his stiff-bosomed shirt more than a dozen times in all his married life. His swallow-tailed coat lay on the bed beside him, freshly brushed and pressed, but it was as full of holes as the overalls in which he worked on weekdays. The moths had used it badly. Jeff twisted his mouth into a hideous toothless grimace as he contended with the obstinate bow. He stamped his good foot and decided to give up the struggle.

"Jennie," he called.

"What's that, Jeff?" His wife's shrunken voice came out of the adjoining room like an echo. It was hardly bigger than a whisper.

"I reckon you'll have to he'p me wid this heah bow tie, baby," he said meekly. "Dog if I can hitch it up."

Her answer was not strong enough to reach him, but presently the old woman came to the door, feeling her way with a stick. She had a wasted, dead-leaf appearance. Her body, as scrawny and gnarled as a string bean, seemed less than nothing in the ocean of frayed and faded petticoats that surrounded her. These hung an inch or two above the tops of her heavy unlaced shoes and showed little grotesque piles where the stockings had fallen down from her negligible legs.

"You oughta could do a heap mo' wid a thing like that'n me—beingst as you got yo' good sight."

"Looks like I oughta could," he admitted. "But ma fingers is gone democrat on me. I get all mixed up in the looking glass an' can't tell wicha way to twist the devilish thing."

Jennie sat on the side of the bed and old Jeff Patton got down on one knee while she tied the bow knot. It was a slow and painful ordeal for each of them in this position. Jeff's bones cracked, his knee ached, and it was only after a half dozen attempts that Jennie worked a semblance of a bow into the tie.

"I got to dress maself now," the old woman whispered. "These is ma old shoes an' stockings, and I ain't so much as unwrapped ma dress."

"Well, don't worry 'bout me no mo', baby," Jeff said. "That 'bout finishes me. All I gotta do now is slip on that old coat 'n ves' an' I'll be fixed to leave."

Jennie disappeared again through the dim passage into the shed room. Being blind was no handicap to her in that black hole. Jeff heard the cane placed against the wall beside the door and knew that his wife was on easy ground. He put on his coat, took a battered top hat from the bedpost and hobbled to the front door. He was ready to travel. As soon as Jennie could get on her Sunday

shoes and her old black silk dress, they would start.

Outside the tiny log house, the day was warm and mellow with sunshine. A host of wasps were humming with busy excitement in the trunk of a dead sycamore. Gray squirrels were searching through the grass for hickory nuts, and blue jays were in the trees, hopping from branch to branch. Pine woods stretched away to the left like a black sea. Among them were scattered scores of log houses like Jeff's, houses of black share farmers. Cows and pigs wandered freely among the trees. There was no danger of loss. Each farmer knew his own stock and knew his neighbor's as well as he knew his neighbor's children.

Down the slope to the right were the cultivated acres on which the colored folks worked. They extended to the river, more than two miles away, and they were today green with the unmade cotton crop. A tiny thread of a road, which passed directly in front of Jeff's place, ran through these green fields like a pencil mark.

Jeff, standing outside the door, with his absurd hat in his left hand, surveyed the wide scene tenderly. He had been forty-five years on these acres. He loved them with the unexplained affection that others have for countries to which they belong.

The sun was hot on his head, his collar still pinched his throat, and the Sunday clothes were intolerably hot. Jeff transferred the hat to his right hand and began fanning with it. Suddenly the whisper that was Jennie's voice came out of the shed room.

"You can bring the car round front whilst you's waitin'," it said feebly. There was a tired pause; then it added, "I'll soon be fixed to go."

"A'right, baby," Jeff answered. "I'll get it in a minute."

But he didn't move. A thought struck him that made his mouth fall open. The mention of the car brought to his mind, with new intensity, the trip he and Jennie were about to take. Fear came into his eyes; excitement took his breath. Lord Jesus!

"Jeff . . . O, Jeff," the old woman's whisper called.

He awakened with a jolt. "Hunh, baby?"

"What you doin'?"

"Nuthin. Jes studyin'. I jes been turnin' things round'n round in ma mind."

"You could be gettin' the car," she said.

"Oh yes, right away, baby."

He started round to the shed, limping heavily on his bad leg. There were three frizzly chickens in the yard. All his other chickens had been killed or stolen recently. But the frizzly chickens had been saved somehow. That was fortunate indeed, for these curious creatures had a way of devouring "Poison" from the yard and in that way protecting against conjure and black luck and spells. But even the frizzly chickens seemed now to be in a stupor. Jeff thought they had some ailment; he expected all three of them to die shortly.

The shed in which the old T-model Ford stood was only a grass roof held up by four corner poles. It had been built by tremulous hands at a time when the little rattletrap car had been regarded as as peculiar treasure. And, miraculously, despite wind and downpour it still stood.

Jeff adjusted the crank and put his weight upon it. The engine came to life with a sputter and bang that rattled the old car from radiator to taillight. Jeff hopped into the seat and put his foot on the accelerator. The sputtering and banging increased. The rattling became more violent. That was good. It was good banging, good sputtering and rattling, and it meant that the aged car was still in running condition. She could be depended on for this trip.

Again Jeff's thought halted as if paralyzed. The suggestion of the trip fell into the machinery of his mind like a wrench. He felt dazed and weak. He swung the car out into the yard, made a half turn and drove around to the front door. When he took his hands off the wheel, he noticed that he was trembling violently. He cut off the motor and climbed to the ground to wait for Jennie.

A few minutes later she was at the window, her voice rattling against the pane like a broken shutter.

"I'm ready, Jeff."

He did not answer, but limped into the house and took her by the arm. He led her slowly through the big room, down the step and across the yard.

"You reckon I'd oughta lock the do'?" he asked softly.

They stopped and Jennie weighed the question. Finally she shook her head.

"Ne' mind the do'," she said. "I don't see no cause to lock up things."

"You right," Jeff agreed. "No cause to lock up."

Jeff opened the door and helped his wife into the car. A quick shudder passed over him. Jesus! Again he trembled.

"How come you shaking so?" Jennie whispered.

"I don't know," he said.

"You mus' be scairt, Jeff."

"No, baby, I ain't scairt."

He slammed the door after her and went around to crank up again. The motor started easily. Jeff wished that it had not been so responsive. He would have liked a few more minutes in which to turn things around in his head. As it was, with Jennie chiding him about being afraid, he had to keep going. He swung the car into the little pencil-mark road and started off toward the river, driving very slowly, very cautiously.

Chugging across the green countryside, the small battered Ford seemed tiny indeed. Jeff felt a familiar excitement, a thrill, as they came down the first slope to the immense levels on which the cotton was growing. He could not help reflecting that the crops were good. He knew what that meant, too; he had made forty-five of them with his own hands. It was true that he had worn out nearly a dozen mules, but that was the fault of old man Stevenson, the owner of the land. Major Stevenson had the odd notion that one mule was all a share farmer needed to work a thirty-acre plot. It was an expensive notion, the way it killed mules from overwork, but the old man held to it. Jeff thought it killed a good many share farmers as well as mules, but he had no sympathy for them. He had always been strong, and he had been taught to have no patience with weakness in men. Women or children might be tolerated if they were puny, but a weak man was a curse. Of course, his own children—

Jeff's thought halted there. He and Jennie never mentioned their dead children any more. And naturally he did not wish to dwell upon them in his mind. Before he knew it, some remark would slip out of his mouth and that would make Jennie feel blue. Perhaps she would cry. A woman like Jennie could not easily throw off the grief that comes from losing five grown children within two years. Even Jeff was still staggered by the blow. His memory had not been much good recently. He frequently talked to himself. And, although he had kept it a secret, he knew that his courage had left him. He was terrified by the least unfamiliar sound at night. He was reluctant to venture far from home in the daytime. And that habit of trembling when he felt fearful was now far beyond his control. Sometimes he became afraid and trembled without knowing what had frightened him. The feeling would just come over him like a chill.

The car rattled slowly over the dusty road. Jennie sat erect and silent, with a little absurd hat pinned to her hair. Her useless eyes seemed very large, very white in their deep sockets. Suddenly Jeff heard her voice, and he inclined his head to catch the words.

"Is we passed Delia Moore's house yet?" she asked.

"Not yet," he said.

"You must be drivin' mighty slow, Jeff."

"We might just as well take our time, baby."

There was a pause. A little puff of steam was coming out of the radiator of the car. Heat wavered above the hood. Delia Moore's house was nearly half a mile away. After a moment Jennie spoke again.

"You ain't really scairt, is you, Jeff?"

"Nah, baby, I ain't scairt."

"You know how we agreed—we gotta keep on goin'."

Jewels of perspiration appeared on Jeff's forehead. His eyes rounded, blinked, became fixed on the road.

"I don't know," he said with a shiver. "I reckon it's the only thing to do."

"Hm."

A flock of guinea fowls, pecking in the road, were scattered by the passing car. Some of them took to their wings; others hid under bushes. A blue jay, swaying on a leafy twig, was annoying a roadside squirrel. Jeff held an even speed till he came near Delia's place. Then he slowed down noticeably.

Delia's house was really no house at all, but an abandoned store building converted into a dwelling. It sat near a crossroads, beneath a single black cedar tree. There Delia, a cattish old creature of Jennie's age, lived alone. She had been there more years than anybody could remember, and long ago had won the disfavor of such women as Jennie. For in her young days Delia had been gayer, yellower and saucier than seemed proper in those parts. Her ways with menfolks had been dark and suspicious. And the fact that she had had as many husbands as children did not help her reputation.

"Yonder's old Delia," Jeff said as they passed.

"What she doin'?"

"Jes sittin' in the do'," he said.

"She see us?"

"Hm," Jeff said. "Musta did."

That relieved Jennie. It strengthened her to know that her old enemy had seen her pass in her best clothes. That would give the old she-devil something to chew her gums and fret about, Jennie thought. Wouldn't she have a fit if she didn't find out? Old evil Delia! This would be just the thing for her. It would pay her back for being so evil. It would also pay her, Jennie thought, for the way she used to grin at Jeff—long ago when her teeth were good.

The road became smooth and red, and Jeff could tell by the smell of the air that they were nearing the river. He could see the rise where the road turned and ran along parallel to the stream. The car chugged on monotonously. After a long silent spell, Jennie leaned against Jeff and spoke.

"How many bale o' cotton you think we got standin'?" she said.

Jeff wrinkled his forehead as he calculated.

" 'Bout twenty-five, I reckon."

"How many you make las' year?"

"Twenty-eight," he said. "How come you ask that?"

"I's jes thinkin'," Jennie said quietly.

"It don't make a speck o' difference though," Jeff reflected. "If we get much or if we get little, we still gonna be in debt to old man Stevenson when he gets through counting up agin us. It's took us a long time to learn that."

Jennie was not listening to these words. She had fallen into a trance-like meditation. Her lips twitched. She chewed her gums and rubbed her gnarled hands nervously. Suddenly she leaned forward, buried her face in the nervous hands and burst into tears. She cried aloud in a dry cracked voice that suggested the rattle of fodder on dead stalks. She cried aloud like a child, for she had never learned to suppress a genuine sob. Her slight old frame shook heavily and seemed hardly able to sustain such violent grief.

"What's the matter, baby?" Jeff asked awkwardly. "Why you cryin' like all that?"

"I's jes thinkin'," she said.

"So you the one what's scairt now, hunh?"

"I ain't scairt, Jeff. I's jes thinkin' 'bout leavin' eve'thing like this—eve'thing we been used to. It's right sad-like."

Jeff did not answer, and presently Jennie buried her face again and cried.

The sun was almost overhead. It beat down furiously on the dusty wagon-path road, on the parched roadside grass and the tiny battered car. Jeff's hands, gripping the wheel, became wet with perspiration; his forehead sparkled. Jeff's lips parted. His mouth shaped a hideous grimace. His face suggested the face of a man being burned. But the torture passed and his expression softened again.

"You mustn't cry, baby," he said to his wife. "We gotta be strong. We can't break down."

Jennie waited a few seconds, then said, "You

reckon we oughta do it, Jeff? You reckon we oughta go 'head an' do it, really?"

Jeff's voice choked; his eyes blurred. He was terrified to hear Jennie say the thing that had been in his mind all morning. She had egged him on when he had wanted more than anything in the world to wait, to reconsider, to think things over a little longer. Now she was getting cold feet. Actually there was no need of thinking the question through again. It would only end in making the same painful decision once more. Jeff knew that. There was no need of fooling around longer.

"We jes as well to do like we planned," he said. "They ain't nothin' else for us now—it's the bes' thing."

Jeff thought of the handicaps, the near impossibility, of making another crop with his leg bothering him more and more each week. Then there was always the chance that he would have another stroke, like the one that had made him lame. Another one might kill him. The least it could do would be to leave him helpless. Jeff gasped—Lord, Jesus! He could not bear to think of being helpless, like a baby, on Jennie's hands. Frail, blind Jennie.

The little pounding motor of the car worked harder and harder. The puff of steam from the cracked radiator became larger. Jeff realized that they were climbing a little rise. A moment later the road turned abruptly and he looked down upon the face of the river.

"Jeff."

"Hunh?"

"Is that the water I hear?"

"Hm. Tha's it."

"Well, which way you goin' now?"

"Down this-a way," he said. "The road runs 'long 'side o' the water a lil piece."

She waited a while calmly. Then she said, "Drive faster."

"A'right, baby," Jeff said.

The water roared in the bed of the river. It was fifty or sixty feet below the level of the road. Between the road and the water there was a long smooth slope, sharply inclined. The slope was dry, the clay hardened by prolonged summer heat. The water below, roaring in a narrow channel, was noisy and wild.

"Jeff."

"Hunh?"

"How far you goin'?"

"Jes a lil piece down the road."

"You ain't scairt, is you, Jeff?"

"Nah, baby," he said trembling. "I ain't scairt."

"Remember how we planned it, Jeff. We gotta do it like we said. Brave-like."

"Hm."

Jeff's brain darkened. Things suddenly seemed unreal, like figures in a dream. Thoughts swam in his mind foolishly, hysterically, like little blind fish in a pool within a dense cave. They rushed, crossed one another, jostled, collided, retreated and rushed again. Jeff soon became dizzy. He shuddered violently and turned to his wife.

"Jennie, I can't do it. I can't." His voice broke pitifully.

She did not appear to be listening. All the grief had gone from her face. She sat erect, her unseeing eyes wide open, strained and frightful. Her glossy black skin had become dull. She seemed as thin, as sharp and bony, as a starved bird. Now, having suffered and endured the sadness of tearing herself away from beloved things, she showed no anguish. She was absorbed with her own thoughts, and she didn't even hear Jeff's voice shouting in her ear.

Jeff said nothing more. For an instant there was light in his cavernous brain. The great chamber was, for less than a second, peopled by characters he knew and loved. They were simple, healthy creatures, and they behaved in a manner that he could understand. They had quality. But since he had already taken leave of them long ago, the remembrance did not break his heart again. Young Jeff Patton was among them, the Jeff Patton of fifty years ago who went down to New Orleans with a crowd of country boys to the Mardi Gras doings. The gay young crowd, boys with candy-striped shirts and rouged-brown girls in noisy silks, was like a picture in his head. Yet it did not make him sad. On that very trip Slim Burns had killed Joe Beasley—the crowd had been broken up. Since then Jeff Patton's world had been the Greenbriar Plantation. If there had been other Mardi Gras carnivals, he had not heard of them. Since then there had been no time; the years had fallen on him like waves. Now he was old, worn out. Another paralytic stroke (like the one he had already suffered) would put him on his back for keeps. In that condition, with a frail blind woman to look after him, he would be worse off than if he were dead.

Suddenly Jeff's hands became steady. He actually felt brave. He slowed down the motor of the car and carefully pulled off the road. Below, the water of the stream boomed, a soft thunder in the deep channel. Jeff ran the car onto the clay slope, pointed it directly toward the stream and put his foot heavily on the accelerator. The little car leaped furiously down the steep incline toward the water. The movement was nearly as swift and direct as a fall. The two old black folks, sitting quietly side by side, showed no excitement. In another instant the car hit the water and dropped immediately out of sight.

A little later it lodged in the mud of a shallow place. One wheel of the crushed and upturned little Ford became visible above the rushing water.

RICHARD WRIGHT (1908–1960)

Richard Wright, one of the most eminent black writers that America has produced and a figure of international renown, was born in a sharecropper's cabin, on a farm near Natchez, Mississippi. The father of Richard Wright, like that of Langston Hughes, early deserted his family, leaving them in the direst poverty, and, like the elder Hughes, earned the son's complex hatred and then, at last, a sort of pity. In his autobiography Wright tells of his return to find the father:

A quarter of a century was to elapse between the time when I saw my father sitting with the strange woman [for whom he had deserted the family] and the time when I was to see him again, standing alone upon the red-clay Mississippi plantation, a sharecropper, clad in ragged overalls, holding a muddy hoe in his gnarled, veined hands . . . he was standing against the sky smiling toothlessly, his hair whitened, his body bent, his eyes glazed with dim recollection, his fearsome aspect of twenty-five years ago gone forever— I was overwhelmed to realize that he could never understand me or the scalding experiences that had swept me beyond his life and into an area of living that he could never know. I stood before him, poised, my mind aching as it embraced the simple nakedness of his life, feeling how completely his soul was imprisoned by the slow flow of the seasons, by wind and rain and sun, how fastened were his memories to a crude and raw past, how chained were his actions and emotions

to the direct, animalistic impulses of his withering body.

Black Boy, Wright's account of his growing up, is one of the most memorable autobiographies ever written by an American, black or white. Here we find the vivid picture of the world of gnawing hunger, degradation, and sometimes brutality that the boy survived to achieve his success—the world that also, somehow, contributed to his achievement.[1] With his mother too occupied in the struggle for existence to give him time during the day, the child Richard hung around the back streets of Memphis, well schooled in depravity and, by the age of six, on the way to becoming an alcoholic, and at night was beaten and prayed over by his desperate mother. Later, with his grandmother, a fanatical Seventh Day Adventist, he lived in constant fear of beatings and in bitter resentment at the restrictions of the household, particularly those placed upon his intellectual curiosity and his first attempts to read stories. Out of that atmosphere of oppressive piety, he learned, he says, only one thing, that the "naked will to power seemed always to walk in the wake of a hymn."[2] He learned, too, on the one hand, the terror of white men when an uncle

[1] It may be worth noting that sometimes, quite contrary to the bleakness of Wright's account, and to an often-held belief, an autobiographer will insist on the richness and warmth of human relations in the black family and community.

[2] But in some of his stories, especially "Fire and Cloud" and "Bright and Morning Star," Wright does treat sympathetically the black religious tradition.

with whom he was living was murdered; and on the other, as another version of terror, how a black man, the lover of an aunt, could appear in the middle of the night to say he had set a house on fire:

"There was nothing else to do," he said impatiently. "I took the money. I had hit her. She was unconscious. If they found her, she'd tell. I'd be lost. So I set the fire."

Wright came to feel that he, with his passion to learn, was in, but not of, the black world he had been born into.

After I had outlived the shocks of childhood, after the habit of reflection had been born in me, I used to mull over the strange absence of real kindness in Negroes, how unstable was our tenderness, how lacking in genuine passion we were, how void of great hope, how timid our joy, how bare our traditions, how hollow our memories, how lacking we were in those intangible sentiments that bind man to man, and how shallow was even our despair. After I had learned other ways of life I used to brood upon the unconscious irony of those who felt that Negroes led so passional an existence! I saw that what had been taken for our emotional strength was our negative confusions, our flights, our fears, our frenzy under pressure.

But the "bleakness of black life" came, he decided, from the fact that "Negroes had never been allowed to catch the full spirit of Western civilization." And this was the final affront from the white "superworld," which "drew a line over which we dared not step and we accepted that line because our bread was at stake."

For Wright, however, more than bread was at stake. He had a will to discover the meaning of the world and of his own life. He had become a devoted reader and (thanks, paradoxically enough, to a white man who let him use his library card) was at an early age deep into those writers, like Mencken, Edgar Lee Masters, Sherwood Anderson, Lewis, and Dreiser, who might, he thought, explain the workings of society. And he himself discovered the need to write:

I . . . wondered how it was possible to know people sufficiently to write about them? Could I ever learn about life and people? To me, with my vast ignorance, my Jim Crow station in life, it seemed a task impossible of achievement. I now knew what being a Negro meant. I could endure hunger. I had learned to live with hate. But to feel that there were feelings denied me, that the very breath of life itself was beyond my reach, that more than anything else hurt, wounded me. I had a new hunger.

To go North seemed the solution. There, he thought, "gradually and slowly I might learn who I was, what I might be." And added: "I was not leaving the South to forget the South, but so that some day I might understand it, might come to know what its rigors had done to me, to its children."

Black Boy tells Wright's story up to the age of seventeen. By 1927 he was in Chicago, living in poverty but, bit by bit, book by book of his reading, and page by page of his obsessive efforts to write, finding his way. He became acquainted with Marxism and decided that here was an explanation and a hope. He joined the John Reed Club and began publishing essays and poems in the *New Masses*, the *International*, and the *Daily Worker*. As a member of the Federal Writers Project, he became a director of the Federal Negro Theater in Chicago. Then, in 1937, he went to New York to become Harlem editor of the *Daily Worker*, and there, through the paper, the Communist party, and the League of American Writers, he moved into the larger political and literary society. There, too, by a strange coincidence, eminently fruitful for American literature, he met the young Ralph Ellison, whom he lured from music and sculpture into writing.

Wright was now caught, too, in one of the inner contradictions of the party. As a vice president (along with the violently pro-German Theodore Dreiser) of the American Peace Mobilization, he was assigned, by party leadership, to write an article "Not My People's War"; but before the article got printed, in the *New Masses* on June 25, 1941, Hitler had moved into Russia, and the American Communists had experienced, literally overnight, a change of heart and mind. Wright had, too, and promptly drew up a propaganda program called "Mobilization of Negro Opinion."

Even back in Chicago, however, Wright had begun to feel fundamental tensions in himself as a result of his membership in the party, tensions that now became more and more pronounced. As an artist, he resented the control that the party wished to exercise over art in general, and over his own work in particular, and resented the basic theory that art was merely a political instrument. Furthermore, as a black, he began to resent the fact that the party would put its purposes above that of justice to his race; for instance, when A. Philip Randolph, president of the Brotherhood of Sleeping Car Porters, undertook to organize a massive black march on Washington to gain a fair share of employment in war plants, the Communists opposed him, and when Wright, still with the *Daily Worker*, wished to support the project, he was brusquely ordered to leave politics to his superiors.

Wright's literary career was, in fact, on a collision course with the party, even if when his first book was published, in 1938, the danger had not yet become apparent. *Uncle Tom's Children* comprised four novellas, all of which concern the entrapment of a black man in some violation of the southern social order. In the first three, the black, living in fatalistic acceptance of his world, merely stumbles into the lethal situation, as when, in "Big Boy Leaves Home," four adolescent boys, naked in a forbidden swimming hole in the creek, are surprised by a white woman. In the fourth novella, "Fire and Cloud," a black preacher must, however, consciously face a decision about his role, and after an attempt to evade responsibility, realizes that he must commit himself to the social action (a march on the city hall of a southern town, sponsored by Communists) that

his congregation has come to wish: "It's the *people!* Theys the ones what mus be real to us! Gawds wid the people!"

These four novellas, as well as a fifth, "Bright and Morning Star," belonging to the same period and added to the second edition of *Uncle Tom's Children*, seem at first to be a peculiar amalgam of the crudely mechanical and predictable: that is, the racial taboos are like a machine, and any infraction brings the automatic response. The stories, presumably by intention, are not about the individual as individual, but about the nature of the mechanism, to which the nature of an individual is irrelevant. His presentation has been defended, however, by the argument that in the South, in spite of all the paradoxes of life there, the racial picture *is* fairly schematic: the violation of taboo does bring automatic response, and so Wright's stories are "true."

But Wright was not to remain comfortable with work of such simplicity. For one thing, well ahead of his time he had come to realize, even after a relatively brief period in the North, that the problem of race was not centered in the South. He was now after bigger game than exposing the horrors of Mississippi. It would be too easy—and too easy to flatter northern phariseeism—to write another book "which even bankers' daughters could read and weep over and feel good" about. Wright, no doubt, was not quite satisfied even with the response of Eleanor Roosevelt, who, in spite of the insulation of the White House, had not felt "good." She wrote the author that the book had given her a "most unhappy time," and added, in a naiveté that must have made her correspondent indulge in a wry smile, that such things as the multiple murder in "Big Boy Leaves Home" had come from an "accident" of the sort that "in almost every case . . . could be so easily understood if every one kept his head."

What Wright wanted to do was to explain what underlay the not-keeping of one's head. He wanted to get at the psychology, the metaphysics even, of racism; and to explore such questions not in the relatively simple South, but in the complex, urban, industrial society of the North, and this fact gives his subsequent work its great seminal importance. Wright's work, and especially his best known novel, *Native Son* (1940), lies behind such powerful books as *Invisible Man*, of Ralph Ellison, and *The Fire Next Time*, of James Baldwin.

Long before, in school in Jackson, Mississippi, Wright had had a friend named "Biggy" Thomas, a peculiarly bold, defiant, and rebellious lad, and years later, "Biggy" stood behind the character of "Big Boy," who in the first novella of *Uncle Tom's Children* fled North; later still "Biggy" Thomas was to become "Bigger" Thomas, the hero of the novel *Native Son*, who, like "Big Boy," had gone to Chicago, to live on relief, in a slum room with two younger children and his sick mother. Eventually, Bigger is assigned to a relief job as chauffeur for a Mr. Dalton, whose fortune comes from slum real estate, who is a princely benefactor of "the Negro," whose wife is, symbolically, blind, and whose college-girl daughter, Mary, is in love with a young Communist named Jan (the name of the young Wright's first Communist friend).

Mary and Jan, out of their sentimental, as well as condescending, insensitive, and offensive, "good will," force Bigger to eat with them in a restaurant while they give him a dose of their Communist politics. Later, while Bigger drives, Jan and Mary, now drunk, make love in the back seat of the car. Jan is dropped off at his lodgings, and when the car reaches the Dalton home, Mary is so drunk that Bigger has to carry her, literally, up to her room. Just as he lays her on the bed and turns to go, he finds the blind mother in the doorway, and when Mary, though now passed out, begins to stir, Bigger, in panic, puts a pillow on her face to keep her quiet. Before Mrs. Dalton withdraws, the girl is smothered to death, and Bigger, by accident, like the various blacks in *Uncle Tom's Children*, has been trapped in the great machine of society.

Ironically, by this accident, Bigger, for the first time in his life, is released into action. He puts the girl's body in the furnace, writes a ran-

som note to Mr. Dalton, and solicits help from his black girl friend Bessie, to whom, however, he does not tell the whole story. When the crime is discovered and the pursuit is on for Bigger, he kills Bessie, who might have betrayed him. Nevertheless he is caught and at his trial, his lawyer, a Communist, defends him only in terms of Marxist theory, totally without recognition of his personal identity. Jan, however, does begin to realize, as well as he can, the human reality of Bigger.

Bigger, too, has been struggling toward that reality. At the end of the novel, in the farewell between Bigger and Max, the lawyer, Bigger says:

"But when I think of why all the killing was, I begin to feel what I wanted, what I am . . ."

Bigger saw Max back away from him with compressed lips. But he felt he had to make Max understand how he saw things now.

"I didn't want to kill!" Bigger shouted. "But what I killed for, I *am*!"

As Max goes down the corridor for the last time, Bigger stands grasping the steel bars: "Then he smiled a faint, wry, bitter smile."

Wright had feared that his book would offend almost all kinds of readers, the white world, the black middle class, and the Communists. It may have embarrassed the black middle class, and it certainly offended the Communists; but even if it did not evoke universal acclaim from white reviewers, it made a great impact on the world of white book buyers; it truly set the discussion of race in a new and shocking context; and it had power. Part of the power was of the sort found in *Uncle Tom's Children*, power derived from reportorial and analytic accuracy, and, as in the earlier work, from the dramatic irony of the process of entrapment. And, most significant of all, in spite of the fact that other characters in the novel are little more than stereotypes that might have been based on the cartoons of the *New Masses*, Bigger himself is a solid creation, and an index to the great distance that Wright had come in the two years since his first book. Wright later said, in an article called "How Bigger Was Born" (*Saturday Review*, June 1, 1940), that he had hoped that Bigger was "a symbolic figure of American life, a figure who would hold within him the prophecy of [the] future."[3]

Bigger is indeed a symbolic figure, and as a prophecy, portentous and monitory. But he is not Wright's most memorable creation. That honor must be reserved for the central character of *Black Boy*; and if it be objected that that book is not a work of fiction, we can remember that the truly "created" self in an autobiography is more rare than the successful character in fiction. Furthermore, in *Black Boy*, the minor characters surrounding "Black Boy" are much more substantial and vivid than any in *Native Son*, and the dramatic rendering of scene after scene is sharper. But Wright, with little faith in, or hope for, what was to turn out to be his masterpiece, sent it to his agent with the doubtful instruction, ". . . if it is worth showing to Harpers, then let them see it."

The book, which appeared in 1945, was not only Wright's masterpiece; it was an extraordinary best seller, at the top of all lists, and a selection of the Book of the Month Club. William Faulkner wrote him a letter:

It needed to be said, and you said it well. Though I am afraid (I am speaking now from the point of view of one who believes that the man who wrote *Native Son* is potentially an artist) it will accomplish little of what it should accomplish, since only they will be moved and grieved by it who already know and grieve over this situation.

Faulkner added: "I think you said it much better in *Native Son*."

But Faulkner was wrong. It was in *Black Boy* that Richard Wright discovered the full scope of the artist who was himself.

[3] Bigger is symbolic and prophetic in much the same way as Clyde Griffiths is in *An American Tragedy*, and both characters have much the same role vis-à-vis American society. Dreiser, as we have said, was one of the formative influences on Wright's literary development and on the development of his vision of society.

In 1945 Wright was thirty-six years old, famous, well off. He had been married twice, to white women. The first marriage (1940) was to a dancer named Rose Dhima Meadman, with whom marriage lasted less than a year, her values, it seems, proving too bourgeois and her pleasure in bossing Mexican servants (they lived in Mexico) excessive. The second marriage (1941) was to Ellen Poplar, a devoted party worker who, when Wright definitely turned against communism, in 1942, chose him over the more abstract loyalty. With Ellen and a daughter, Wright settled into a pleasant house in Greenwich Village which, after the various subterfuges to which a black purchaser had to resort, he had bought. All seemed well. But difficulties because of his race increased, and after a visit to France as a guest of the government, he returned to France, in 1947, as a permanent resident.

In the French years Wright was something of a public figure, sought after, interviewed, accustomed to the society of the great—Gide, Beauvoir, Sartre (who guided him in reading philosophy), and Gertrude Stein (who hailed him as one of the two geniuses of the era, she being the other). Seeking to understand the place of the black man, he visited Africa and wrote a book, *Black Power*, that nobody seemed to want to read. He also discovered that he was as much an alien in Africa as he was anywhere else. In these later years he had become an active anti-Communist, but because of his writings on the race question and colonialism, England would not grant him a permit for residence. So he again returned to the more hospitable France.

For all its hospitality, France was not working out for him. He was cut off from his language. He was writing fiction, but he was, too, cut off from his deepest inspiration. Or perhaps he had simply lived past his inspiration.

He died in Paris, on November 28, 1960, at the age of fifty-two. His body, with a copy of *Black Boy*, which Ellen had placed beside it, was cremated, and the urn of mixed ashes was deposited in the Columbarium Père Lachaise.

BIOGRAPHICAL CHART

1908 Born, September 4, in a sharecropper's cabin on a farm near Natchez, Mississippi

1914 Family moves to Memphis; father deserts family

1916 Because of poverty and mother's illness sent to live with maternal grandmother in Jackson, Mississippi

1925 Graduates from high school (ninth grade) as valedictorian; returns to Memphis; begins reading books from public library

1927 In December, goes to Chicago

1928 Takes civil service examinations for work in post office

1931 On relief; with W.P.A. and Negro Theater; becomes acquainted with Communists; first poems and essays published

1932 Joins John Reed Club; friction begins with Communist party

1935 Attends American Writers Congress as delegate in New York

1937 Appointed Harlem editor of the *Daily Worker*; begins friendship with the young Ralph Ellison; stories in *New Masses*; *Story Magazine* prize

1938 *Uncle Tom's Children*

1940 *Native Son*; marries Rose Dhima Meadman; moves to Cuernavaca, Mexico; leaves Dhima; revisits Mississippi, sees father

1941 Marries Ellen Poplar; in American Peace Mobilization, as vice president, with Dreiser and others; differences mount with Communist party on race issue

1942 Breaks with party

1945 *Black Boy* great success

1946 Visits France as guest of government

1947 Becomes permanent resident in France; acquainted with Gide, Stein, Beauvoir, Sartre, and other notables

1951 Film of *Native Son*, with Wright as Bigger, a failure

1953 Visits Africa; gathers material for *Black Power*

1954 *Black Power* widely attacked, even in Africa

1958 *Long Dream* published to poor reception

1959 Martin Luther King visits; *Island of Hallucination*, sequel to *Long Dream*, refused by publisher

1960 *Long Dream* fails on Broadway; dies, November 28, in Paris

1961 *Eight Men*

FURTHER READINGS

There is no standard edition of Wright's works. Individual titles are cited in the biographical chart.

Robert Bone, *Richard Wright* (1969)

Russell C. Brignano, *Richard Wright: An Introduction to the Man and His Work* (1970)

Ralph Ellison, "Richard Wright's Blues," in *Shadow and Act* (1964)

Irving Howe, "Black Boys and Native Sons," in *A World More Attractive* (1963)

Edward Margolies, *The Art of Richard Wright* (1969)

Constance Webb, *Richard Wright: A Biography* (1969)

The Man Who Was Almost a Man (1938)

Dave struck out across the fields, looking homeward through paling light. Whut's the usa talkin wid em niggers in the field? Anyhow, his mother was putting supper on the table. Them niggers can't understan nothing. One of these days he was going to get a gun and practice shooting, then they can't talk to him as though he were a little boy. He slowed, looking at the ground. Shucks, Ah ain scareda them even ef they are biggern me! Aw, Ah know whut Ahma do. . . . Ahm going by ol Joe's sto n git that Sears Roebuck catlog n look at them guns. Mabbe Ma will lemme buy one when she gits mah pay from ol man Hawkins.

Ahma beg her t gimme some money. Ahm ol ernough to hava gun. Ahm seventeen. Almos a man. He strode, feeling his long, loose-jointed limbs. Shucks, a man oughta hava little gun aftah he done worked hard all day. . . .

He came in sight of Joe's store. A yellow lantern glowed on the front porch. He mounted steps and went through the screen door, hearing it bang behind him. There was a strong smell of coal oil and mackerel fish. He felt very confident until he saw fat Joe walk in through the rear door, then his courage began to ooze.

"Howdy, Dave! Whutcha want?"

"How yuh, Mistah Joe? Aw, Ah don wanna buy nothing. Ah jus wanted t see ef yuhd lemme look at tha ol catlog erwhile."

"Sure! You wanna see it here?"

"Nawsuh. Ah wans t take it home wid me. Ahll bring it back termorrow when Ah come in from the fiels."

"You plannin on buyin something?"

"Yessuh."

"Your ma letting you have your own money now?"

"Shucks. Mistah Joe, Ahm gittin t be a man like anybody else!"

Joe laughed and wiped his greasy white face with a red bandanna.

"Whut you plannin on buyin?"

Dave looked at the floor, scratched his head, scratched his thigh, and smiled. Then he looked up shyly.

"Ahll tell yuh, Mistah Joe, ef yuh promise yuh won't tell."

"I promise."

"Waal, Ahma buy a gun."

"A gun? Whut you want with a gun?"

"Ah wanna keep it."

"You ain't nothing but a boy. You don't need a gun."

"Aw, lemme have the catlog, Mistah Joe. Ahll bring it back."

Joe walked through the rear door. Dave was elated. He looked around at barrels of sugar and flour. He heard Joe coming back. He craned his neck to see if he were bringing the book. Yeah, he's got it! Gawddog, he's got it!

"Here, but be sure you bring it back. It's the only one I got."

"Sho, Mistah Joe."

"Say, if you wanna buy a gun, why don't you buy one from me? I gotta gun to sell."

"Will it shoot?"

"Sure it'll shoot."

"Whut kind is it?"

"Oh, it's kinda old. . . . A lefthand Wheeler. A pistol. A big one."

"Is it got bullets in it?"

"It's loaded."

"Kin Ah see it?"

"Where's your money?"

"Whut yuh wan fer it?"

"I'll let you have it for two dollars."

"Just two dollahs? Shucks, Ah could buy tha when Ah git mah pay."

"I'll have it here when you want it."

"Awright, suh. Ah be in fer it."

He went through the door, hearing it slam again behind him. Ahma git some money from Ma n buy me a gun! Only two dollahs! He tucked the thick catalogue under his arm and hurried.

"Where yuh been, boy?" His mother held a steaming dish of black-eyed peas.

"Aw, Ma, Ah jus stopped down the road t talk wid th boys."

"Yuh know bettah than t keep suppah waitin."

He sat down, resting the catalogue on the edge of the table.

"Yuh git up from there and git to the well n wash yosef! Ah ain feedin no hogs in mah house!"

She grabbed his shoulder and pushed him. He stumbled out of the room, then came back to get the catalogue.

"Whut this?"

"Aw, Ma, it's jusa catlog."

"Who yuh git it from?"

"From Joe, down at the sto."

"Waal, thas good. We kin use it around the house."

"Naw, Ma." He grabbed for it. "Gimme mah catlog, Ma."

She held onto it and glared at him.

"Quit hollerin at me! Whut's wrong wid yuh? Yuh crazy?"

"But Ma, please. It ain mine! It's Joe's! He tol me t bring it back t im termorrow."

She gave up the book. He stumbled down the back steps, hugging the thick book under his arm. When he had splashed water on his face and hands, he groped back to the kitchen and fumbled in a corner for the towel. He bumped into a chair; it clattered to the floor. The catalogue sprawled at his feet. When he had dried his eyes, he snatched up the book and held it again under his arm. His mother stood watching him.

"Now, ef yuh gonna acka fool over that ol book, Ahll take it n burn it up."

"Naw, Ma, please."

"Waal, set down n be still!"

He sat down and drew the oil lamp close. He thumbed page after page, unaware of the food his mother set on the table. His father came in. Then his small brother.

"Whutcha got there, Dave?" his father asked.

"Jusa catlog," he answered, not looking up.

"Yawh, here they is!" His eyes glowed at blue and black revolvers. He glanced up, feeling sudden guilt. His father was watching him. He eased the book under the table and rested it on his knees. After the blessing was asked, he ate. He scooped up peas and swallowed fat meat without chewing. Buttermilk helped to wash it down. He did not want to mention money before his father. He would do much better by cornering his mother when she was alone. He looked at his father uneasily out of the edge of his eye.

"Boy, how come yuh don quit foolin wid tha book n eat yo suppah."

"Yessuh."

"How yuh n ol man Hawkins gittin erlong?"

"Suh?"

"Can't yuh hear. Why don yuh listen. Ah ast yuh how wuz yuh n ol man Hawkins gittin erlong?"

"Oh, swell, Pa. Ah plows mo lan than anybody over there."

"Waal, yuh oughta keep yo min on whut yuh doin."

"Yessuh."

He poured his plate full of molasses and sopped at it slowly with a dunk of cornbread. When all but his mother had left the kitchen he still sat and looked again at the guns in the catalogue. Lawd, ef Ah only had the pretty one! He could almost feel the slickness of the weapon with his fingers. If he had a gun like that he would polish it and keep it shining so it would never rust. N Ahd keep it loaded, by Gawd!

"Ma?"

"Hunh?"

"Ol man Hawkins give yuh mah money yit?"

"Yeah, but ain no usa yuh thinin bout thowin nona it erway. Ahm keepin tha money sos yuh kin have cloes t go to school this winter."

He rose and went to her side with the open catalogue in his palms. She was washing dishes, her head bent low over a pan. Shyly he raised the open book. When he spoke his voice was husky, faint.

"Ma, Gawd knows Ah wans one of these."

"One of whut?" she asked, not raising her eyes.

"One of these," he said again, not daring even to point. She glanced up at the page, then at him with wide eyes.

"Nigger, is yuh gone plum crazy?"

"Aw, Ma —"

"Git outta here! Don't yuh talk t me bout no gun! Yuh a fool!"

"Ma, Ah kin buy one fer two dollahs."

"Not ef Ah knows it yuh ain!"

"But yuh promised one more—"

"Ah don care whut Ah promised! Yuh ain nothing but a boy yit!"

"Ma, ef yuh lemme buy one Ahll never ast yuh fer nothing no mo."

"Ah tol yuh t git outta here! Yuh ain gonna toucha penny of tha money fer no gun! Thas how come Ah has Mistah Hawkins pay yo wages t me, cause Ah knows yuh ain got no sense."

"But Ma, we needa gun. Pa ain got no gun. We needa gun in the house. Yuh kin never tell whut might happen."

"Now don yuh try to maka fool outta me, boy! Ef we did hava gun yuh wouldn't have it!"

He laid the catalogue down and slipped his arm around her waist. "Aw, Ma, Ah done worked hard alla summer n ain ast yuh fer nothing, is Ah, now?"

"Thas whut yuh spose t do!"

"But Ma. Ah wants a gun. Yuh kin lemme have two dollah outa mah money. Please Ma. I kin give it to Pa. . . . Please, Ma! Ah loves yuh, Ma."

When she spoke her voice came soft and low.

"What yuh wan wida gun, Dave? Yuh don need no gun. Yuhll git in trouble. N ef yo Pa jus thought Ah letyuh have money t buy a gun he'd hava fit."

"Ahll hide it, Ma. It ain but two dollahs."

"Lawd, chil, whuts wrong wid yuh?"

"Ain nothing wrong, Ma. Ahm almos a man now. Ah wants a gun."

"Who gonna sell yuh a gun?"

"Ol Joe at the sto."

"N it don cos but two dollahs?"

"Thas all, Ma. Just two dollahs. Please, Ma."

She was stacking the plates away; her hands moved slowly, reflectively. Dave kept an anxious silence. Finally she turned to him.

"Ahll let yuh git the gun ef yuh promise me one thing."

"Whuts tha, Ma?"

"Yuh bring it straight back t me, yuh hear? It'll be fer Pa."

"Yessum! Lemme go now, Ma."

She stooped, turned slightly to one side, raised the hem of her dress, rolled down the top of her stocking, and came up with a slender wad of bills.

"Here," she said. "Lawd knows yuh don need no gun. But yer Pa does. Yuh bring it right back t me, yuh hear. Ahma put it up. Now ef yuh don, Ahma have yuh Pa lick yuh so hard yuh won ferget it."

"Yessum."

He took the money, ran down the steps, and across the yard.

"Dave! Yuuuuuuh Daaaaaave!"

He heard, but he was not going to stop now. "Naw, Lawd!"

The first movement he made the following morning was to reach under his pillow for the gun. In the gray light of dawn he held it loosely, feeling a sense of power. Could killa man wida gun like this. Kill anybody, black or white. And if he were holding this gun in his hand nobody could run over him; they would have to respect him. It was a big gun, with a long barrel and a heavy handle. He raised and lowered it in his hand, marveling at its weight.

He had not come straight home with it as his mother had asked; instead he had stayed out in the fields, holding the weapon in his hand, aiming it now and then at some imaginary foe. But he had not fired it; he had been afraid that his father might hear. Also he was not sure he knew how to fire it.

To avoid surrendering the pistol he had not come into the house until he knew that all were asleep. When his mother had tiptoed to his bedside late that night and demanded the gun, he had first played 'possum; then he had told her that the gun was hidden outdoors, that he would bring it to her in the morning. Now he lay turning it slowly in his hands. He broke it, took out the cartridges, felt them, and then put them back.

He slid out of bed, got a long strip of old flannel from a trunk, wrapped the gun in it, and tied it to his naked thigh while it was still loaded. He did not go in to breakfast. Even though it was not yet daylight, he started for Jim Hawkins's plantation. Just as the sun was rising he reached the barns where the mules and plows were kept.

"Hey! That you, Dave?"

He turned. Jim Hawkins stood eyeing him suspiciously.

"What're yuh doing here so early?"

"Ah didn't know Ah wuz gittin up so early, Mistah Hawkins. Ah wuz fixing hitch up of Jenny n take her t the fiels."

"Good. Since you're here so early, how about plowing that stretch down by the woods?"

"Suits me, Mistah Hawkins."

"O.K. Go to it!"

He hitched Jenny to a plow and started across the fields. Hot dog! This was just what he wanted. If he could get down by the woods, he could shoot his gun and nobody would hear. He walked behind the plow, hearing the traces creaking, feeling the gun tied tight to his thigh.

When he reached the woods, he plowed two whole rows before he decided to take out the gun. Finally he stopped, looked in all directions, then untied the gun and held it in his hand. He turned to the mule and smiled.

"Know whut this is, Jenny? Naw, yuh wouldn't know! Yuhs jus ol mule! Anyhow, this is a gun, n it kin shoot, by Gawd!"

He held the gun at arm's length. Whut t hell, Ahma shoot this thing! He looked at Jenny again.

"Lissen here, Jenny! When Ah pull this ol trigger Ah don wan yuh t run n acka fool now."

Jenny stood with head down, her short ears pricked straight. Dave walked off about twenty feet, held the gun far out from him, at arm's length, and turned his head. Hell, he told himself, Ah ain afraid. The gun felt loose in his fingers; he waved it wildly for a moment. Then he shut his eyes and tightened his forefinger. Bloom! The report half-deafened him and he thought his right hand was torn from his arm. He heard Jenny whinnying and galloping over the field, and he found himself on his knees squeezing his fingers hard between his legs. His hand was numb; he jammed it into his mouth, trying to warm it, trying to stop the pain. The gun lay at his feet. He did not quite know what had happened. He stood up and stared at the gun as though it were a living thing. He gritted his teeth and kicked the gun. Yuh almos broke mah arm! He turned to look for Jenny; she was far over the fields, tossing her head and kicking wildly.

"Hol on there, ol mule!"

When he caught up with her she stood trembling, walling her big white eyes at him. The plow was far away; the traces had broken. Then Dave stopped short, looking, not believing. Jenny was bleeding. Her left side was red and wet with blood. He went closer. Lawd, have mercy! Wondah did Ah shoot this mule? He grabbed for Jenny's mane. She flinched, snorted, whirled, tossing her head.

"Hol on now! Hol on."

Then he saw the hole in Jenny's side, right between the ribs. It was round, wet, red. A crimson stream streaked down the front leg, flowing fast. Good Gawd! Ah wuzn't shootin at tha mule. He felt panic. He knew he had to stop that blood, or Jenny would bleed to death. He had never seen so much blood in all his life. He chased the mule for half a mile, trying to catch her. Finally she stopped, breathing hard, stumpy tail half arched. He caught her mane and led her back to where the plow and gun lay. Then he stooped and grabbed handfuls of damp black earth and tried to plug the bullet hole. Jenny shuddered, whinnied, and broke from him.

"Hol on! Hol on now!"

He tried to plug it again, but blood came anyhow. His fingers were hot and sticky. He rubbed dirt into his palms, trying to dry them. Then again he attempted to plug the bullet hole, but Jenny shied away, kicking her heels high. He stood helpless. He had to do something. He ran at Jenny; she dodged him. He watched a red stream of blood flow down Jenny's leg and form a bright pool at her feet.

"Jenny . . . Jenny . . ." he called weakly.

His lips trembled! She's bleeding t death! He looked in the direction of home, wanting to go back, wanting to get help. But he saw the pistol lying in the damp black clay. He had a queer feeling that if he only did something, this would not be; Jenny would not be there bleeding to death.

When he went to her this time, she did not move. She stood with sleepy, dreamy eyes; and when he touched her she gave a low-pitched whinny and knelt to the ground, her front knees slopping in blood.

"Jenny . . . Jenny . . ." he whispered.

For a long time she held her neck erect; then her head sank, slowly. Her ribs swelled with a mighty heave and she went over.

Dave's stomach felt empty, very empty. He picked up the gun and held it gingerly between his thumb and forefinger. He buried it at the foot of a tree. He took a stick and tried to cover the pool of blood with dirt—but what was the use? There was Jenny lying with her mouth open and her eyes walled and glassy. He could not tell Jim Hawkins he had shot his mule. But he had to tell him something. Yeah, Ahll tell em Jenny started gittin wil n fell on the joint of the plow. . . . But that would hardly happen to a mule. He walked across the field slowly, head down.

It was sunset. Two of Jim Hawkins's men were over near the edge of the woods digging a hole in which to bury Jenny. Dave was surrounded by a knot of people; all of them were looking down at the dead mule.

"I don't see how in the world it happened," said Jim Hawkins for the tenth time.

The crowd parted and Dave's mother, father, and small brother pushed into the center.

"Where Dave?" his mother called.

"There he is," said Jim Hawkins.

His mother grabbed him.

"Whut happened, Dave? Whut yuh done?"

"Nothing."

"C'mon, boy, talk," his father said.

Dave took a deep breath and told the story he knew nobody believed.

"Waal," he drawled. "Ah brung ol Jenny down here sos Ah could do mah plowin. Ah plowed bout two rows, just like yuh see." He stopped and pointed at the long rows of upturned earth. "Then something musta been wrong wid ol Jenny. She wouldn't ack right a-tall. She started snortin n kickin her heels. Ah tried to hol her, but she pulled erway, rearin n goin on. Then when the point of the plow was stickin up in the air, she swung erroun n twisted herself back on it. . . . She stuck herself n started t bleed. N fo Ah could do anything, she wuz dead."

"Did you ever hear of anything like that in all your life?" asked Jim Hawkins.

There were white and black standing in the crowd. They murmured. Dave's mother came close to him and looked hard into his face.

"Tell the truth, Dave," she said.

"Looks like a bullet hole ter me," said one man.

"Dave, whut yuh do wid tha gun?" his mother asked.

The crowd surged in, looking at him. He jammed his hands into his pockets, shook his head slowly from left to right, and backed away. His eyes were wide and painful.

"Did he hava gun?" asked Jim Hawkins.

"By Gawd, Ah tol yuh tha wuz a gunwound," said a man, slapping his thigh.

His father caught his shoulders and shook him till his teeth rattled.

"Tell whut happened, yuh rascal! Tell whut . . ."

Dave looked at Jenny's stiff legs and began to cry.

"Whut yuh do wid tha gun?" his mother asked.

"Come on and tell the truth," said Hawkins. "Ain't nobody going to hurt you. . . ."

His mother crowded close to him.

"Did yuh shoot tha mule, Dave?"

Dave cried, seeing blurred white and black faces.

"Ahh ddinnt gggo tt sshoooot hher. . . . Ah sssswear off Gawd Ahh ddint. . . . Ah wuz a-tryin t sssee ef the ol gggun would sshoot—"

"Where yuh git the gun from?" his father asked.

"Ah got it from Joe, at the sto."

"Where yuh git the money?"

"Ma give it t me."

"He kept worryin me, Bob. . . . Ah had t. . . . Ah tol im t bring the gun right back t me. . . . It was fer yuh, the gun."

"But how yuh happen to shoot that mule?" asked Jim Hawkins.

"Ah wuznt shootin at the mule, Mistah Hawkins. The gun jumped when Ah pulled the trigger . . . N for Ah knowed anything Jenny wuz there a-bleedin."

Somebody in the crowd laughed. Jim Hawkins walked close to Dave and looked into his face.

"Well, looks like you have bought you a mule, Dave."

"Ah swear for Gawd, Ah didn't go t kill the mule, Mistah Hawkins!"

"But you killed her!"

All the crowd was laughing now. They stood on tiptoe and poked heads over one another's shoulders.

"Well, boy, looks like yuh done bought a dead mule! Hahaha!"

"Ain tha ershame."

"Hohohohoho."

Dave stood, head down, twisting his feet in the dirt.

"Well, you needn't worry about it, Bob," said Jim Hawkins to Dave's father. "Just let the boy keep on working and pay me two dollars a month."

"Whut yuh wan fer yo mule, Mistah Hawkins?"

Jim Hawkins screwed up his eyes.

"Fifty dollars."

"Whut yuh do wid tha gun?" Dave's father demanded.

Dave said nothing.

"Yuh wan me t take a tree lim n beat yuh till yuh talk!"

"Nawsuh!"

"Whut yuh do wid it?"

"Ah thowed it erway."

"Where?"

"Ah . . . Ah thowed it in the creek."

"Waal, c mon home. N firs thing in the mawnin git to tha creek n fin tha gun."

"Yessuh."

"Whut yuh pay fer it?"

"Two dollahs."

"Take tha gun n git yo money back n carry it t Mistah Hawkins, yuh hear? N don fergit Ahma lam you black bottom good fer this! Now march yosef on home, suh!"

Dave turned and walked slowly. He heard people laughing. Dave glared, his eyes welling with tears.

Hot anger bubbled in him. Then he swallowed and stumbled on.

That night Dave did not sleep. He was glad that he had gotten out of killing the mule so easily, but he was hurt. Something hot seemed to turn over inside him each time he remembered how they had laughed. He tossed on his bed, feeling his hard pillow. N Pa says he's gonna beat me. . . . He remembered other beatings, and his back quivered. Naw, naw, Ah sho don wan im t beat me tha way no mo. . . . Dam em all! Nobody ever gave him anything. All he did was work. They treat me lika mule. . . . N then they beat me. . . . He gritted his teeth. N Ma had t tell on me.

Well, if he had to, he would take old man Hawkins that two dollars. But that meant selling the gun. And he wanted to keep that gun. Fifty dollahs fer a dead mule.

He turned over, thinking how he had fired the gun. He had an itch to fire it again. Ef other men kin shoota gun, by Gawd, Ah kin! He was still listening. Mebbe they all sleepin now. . . . The house was still. He heard the soft breathing of his brother. Yes, now! He would go down an get that gun and see if he could fire it! He eased out of bed and slipped into overalls.

The moon was bright. He ran almost all the way to the edge of the woods. He stumbled over the ground, looking for the spot where he had buried the gun. Yeah, here it is. Like a hungry dog scratching for a bone he pawed it up. He puffed his black cheeks and blew dirt from the trigger and barrel. He broke it and found four cartridges unshot. He looked around; the fields were filled with silence and moonlight. He clutched the gun stiff and hard in his fingers. But as soon as he wanted to pull the trigger, he shut his eyes and turned his head. Naw, Ah can't shoot wid mah eyes closed n mah head turned. With effort he held his eyes open; then he squeezed. Blooooom! He was stiff, not breathing. The gun was still in his hands. Dammit, he'd done it! He fired again. Blooooom! He smiled. Blooooom! Blooooom! Click, click. There! It was empty. If anybody could shoot a gun, he could. He put the gun into his hip pocket and started across the fields.

When he reached the top of a ridge he stood straight and proud in the moonlight, looking at Jim Hawkins's big white house, feeling the gun sagging in his pocket. Lawd, ef Ah had jus one mo bullet Ahd taka shot at tha house. Ahd like t scare ol man Hawkins jussa little. . . . Jussa enough t let im know Dave Sanders is a man.

To his left the road curved, running to the tracks of the Illinois Central. He jerked his head, listening. From far off came a faint hooof-hoooof; hoooof-hoooof; hoooof-hoooof. . . . That's number eight. He took a swift look at Jim Hawkins's white house; he thought of Pa, of Ma, of his little brother, and the boys. He thought of the dead mule and heard hooof-hoooof; hoooof-hoooof; hoooof-hoooof. . . . He stood rigid. Two dollahs a mont. Les see now . . . Tha means itll take bout two years. Shucks! Ahll be dam! He started down the road, toward the tracks. Yeah, here she comes! He stood beside the track and held himself stiffly. Here she comes, erroun the ben. . . . C mon, yuh slow poke! C mon! He had his hand on his gun; something quivered in his stomach. Then the train thundered past, the gray and brown boxcars rumbling and clinking. He gripped the gun tightly; then he jerked his hand out of his pocket. Ah betcha Bill wouldn't do it! Ah betcha. . . . The cars slid past, steel grinding upon steel. Ahm riding yuh ternight so hep me Gawd! He was hot all over. He hesitated just a moment; then he grabbed, pulled atop of a car, and lay flat. He felt his pocket; the gun was still there. Ahead the long rails were glinting in moonlight, stretching away, away to somewhere, somewhere where he could be a man. . . .

From Black Boy (1945)

To help support the household my grandmother boarded a colored schoolteacher, Ella, a young woman with so remote and dreamy and silent a manner that I was as much afraid of her as I was attracted to her. I had long wanted to ask her to tell me about the books that she was always reading, but I could never quite summon enough courage to do so. One afternoon I found her sitting alone upon the front porch, reading.

"Ella," I begged, "please tell me what you are reading."

"It's just a book," she said evasively, looking about with apprehension.

"But what's it about?" I asked.

"Your grandmother wouldn't like it if I talked to you about novels," she told me.

I detected a note of sympathy in her voice.

"I don't care," I said loudly and bravely.

"Shhh— You mustn't say things like that," she said.

"But I want to know."

"When you grow up, you'll read books and know what's in them," she explained.

"But I want to know now."

She thought a while, then closed the book.

"Come here," she said.

I sat at her feet and lifted my face to hers.

"Once upon a time there was an old, old man named Bluebeard," she began in a low voice.

She whispered to me the story of *Bluebeard and His Seven Wives* and I ceased to see the porch, the sunshine, her face, everything. As her words fell upon my new ears, I endowed them with a reality that welled up from somewhere within me. She told how Bluebeard had duped and married his seven wives, how he had loved and slain them, how he had hanged them up by their hair in a dark closet. The tale made the world around me be, throb, live. As she spoke, reality changed, the look of things altered, and the world became peopled with magical presences. My sense of life deepened and the feel of things was different, somehow. Enchanted and enthralled, I stopped her constantly to ask for details. My imagination blazed. The sensations the story aroused in me were never to leave me. When she was about to finish, when my interest was keenest, when I was lost to the world around me, Granny stepped briskly onto the porch.

"You stop that, you evil gal!" she shouted. "I want none of that Devil stuff in my house!"

Her voice jarred me so that I gasped. For a moment I did not know what was happening.

"I'm sorry, Mrs. Wilson," Ella stammered, rising. "But he asked me—"

"He's just a foolish child and you know it!" Granny blazed.

Ella bowed her head and went into the house.

"But, granny, she didn't finish," I protested, knowing that I should have kept quiet.

She bared her teeth and slapped me across my mouth with the back of her hand.

"You shut your mouth," she hissed. "You don't know what you're talking about!"

"But I want to hear what happened!" I wailed, dodging another blow that I thought was coming.

"That's the Devil's work!" she shouted.

My grandmother was as nearly white as a Negro can get without being white, which means that she was white. The sagging flesh of her face quivered;

her eyes, large, dark, deep-set, wide apart, glared at me. Her lips narrowed to a line. Her high forehead wrinkled. When she was angry her eyelids drooped halfway down over her pupils, giving her a baleful aspect.

"But I liked the story," I told her.

"You're going to burn in hell," she said with such furious conviction that for a moment I believed her.

Not to know the end of the tale filled me with a sense of emptiness, loss. I hungered for the sharp, frightening, breath-taking, almost painful excitement that the story had given me, and I vowed that as soon as I was old enough I would buy all the novels there were and read them to feed that thirst for violence that was in me, for intrigue, for plotting, for secrecy, for bloody murders. So profoundly responsive a chord had the tale struck in me that the threats of my mother and grandmother had no effect whatsoever. They read my insistence as mere obstinacy, as foolishness, something that would quickly pass; and they had no notion how desperately serious the tale had made me. They could not have known that Ella's whispered story of deception and murder had been the first experience in my life that had elicited from me a total emotional response. No words or punishment could have possibly made me doubt. I had tasted what to me was life, and I would have more of it somehow, someway. I realized that they could not understand what I was feeling and I kept quiet. But when no one was looking I would slip into Ella's room and steal a book and take it back of the barn and try to read it. Usually I could not decipher enough words to make the story have meaning. I burned to learn to read novels and I tortured my mother into telling me the meaning of every strange word I saw, not because the word itself had any value, but because it was the gateway to a forbidden and enchanting land.

· · · ·

Something secret was happening in our house and it had reached a serious stage before I knew it. Each night, just as I was dozing off to sleep, I would hear a light tapping on Aunt Maggie's window-pane, a door creaking open, whispers, then long silences. Once I got out of bed and crept to the door of the front room and stole a look. There was a well-dressed black man sitting on the sofa talking in a soft voice to Aunt Maggie. Why was it that I could not meet the man? I crept back to

bed, but was awakened later by low voices saying good-bye. The next morning I asked my mother who had been in the house, and she told me that no one had been there.

"But I heard a man talking," I said.

"You didn't," she said. "You were sleeping."

"But I saw a man. He was in the front room."

"You were dreaming," my mother said.

I learned a part of the secret of the night visits one Sunday morning when Aunt Maggie called me and my brother to her room and introduced us to the man who was going to be our new "uncle," a Professor Matthews. He wore a high, snow-white collar and rimless eyeglasses. His lips were thin and his eyelids seemed never to blink. I felt something cold and remote in him and when he called me I would not go up to him. He sensed my distrust and softened me up with the gift of a dime, then knelt and prayed for us two "poor fatherless young men," as he called us. After prayer Aunt Maggie told us that she and Professor Matthews were leaving soon for the North. I was saddened, for I had grown to feel that Aunt Maggie was another mother to me.

I did not meet the new "uncle" again, though each morning I saw evidences of his having been in the house. My brother and I were puzzled and we speculated as to what our new "uncle" could be doing. Why did he always come at night? Why did he always speak in so subdued a voice, hardly above a whisper? And how did he get the money to buy such white collars and such nice blue suits? To add to our bewilderment, our mother called us to her one day and cautioned us against telling anyone that 'uncle' ever visited us, that people were looking for "uncle."

"What people?" I asked.

"White people," my mother said.

Anxiety entered my body. Somewhere in the unknown the white threat was hovering near again.

"What do they want with him?" I asked.

"You never mind," my mother said.

"What did he do?"

"You keep your mouth shut or the white folks'll get you too," she warned me.

Knowing that we were frightened and baffled about our new "uncle," my mother—I guess—urged Aunt Maggie to tell "uncle" to bribe us into silence and trust. Every morning now was like Christmas; we would climb out of bed and race to the kitchen and look on the table to see what "uncle" had left for us. One morning I found that he had brought me a little female poodle, upon which I bestowed the name of Betsy and she became my pet and companion.

Strangely, "uncle" began visiting us in the daytime now, but when he came all the shades in the house were drawn and we were forbidden to go out of doors until he left. I asked my mother a thousand whispered questions about the silent, black, educated "uncle" and she always replied:

"It's something you can't know. Now keep quiet and go play."

One night the sound of sobbing awakened me. I got up and went softly to the front room and peeped around the jamb of the door; there was "uncle" sitting on the floor by the window, peering into the night from under the lifted curtain. My mother was bent over a small trunk, packing hurriedly. Fear gripped me. Was my mother leaving? Why was Aunt Maggie crying? Were the white people coming after us?

"Hurry up," "uncle" said. "We must get out of here."

"Oh, Maggie," my mother said, "I don't know if you ought to go."

"You keep out of this," "uncle" said, still peering into the dark street.

"But what did you do?" Aunt Maggie asked.

"I'll tell you later," "uncle" said. "We got to get out of here before they come!"

"But you've done something terrible," Aunt Maggie said. "Or you wouldn't be running like this."

"The house is on fire," "uncle" said. "And when they see it, they'll know who did it."

"Did you set the house afire?" my mother asked.

"There was nothing else to do," "uncle" said impatiently. "I took the money. I had hit her. She was unconscious. If they found her, she'd tell. I'd be lost. So I set the fire."

"But she'll burn up," Aunt Maggie said, crying into her hands.

"What could I do?" "uncle" asked. "I had to do it. I couldn't just leave her there and let somebody find her. They'd know somebody hit her. But if she burns, nobody'll ever know."

Fear filled me. What was happening? Were white people coming after all of us? Was my mother going to leave me?

"Mama!" I wailed, running into the room.

"Uncle" leaped to his feet; a gun was in his hand and he was pointing it at me. I stared at the gun, feeling that I was going to die at any moment.

"Richard!" my mother whispered fiercely.

"You're going away!" I yelled.

My mother rushed to me and clapped her hand over my mouth.

"Do you want us all to be killed?" she asked, shaking me.

I quieted.

"Now you go back to sleep," she said.

"You're leaving," I said.

"I'm not."

"You are leaving. I see the trunk!" I wailed.

"You stop that noise," my mother said; and she caught my arms in so tight a grip of fury that my crying ceased because of the pain. "Now you get back in bed."

She led me back to bed and I lay awake, listening to whispers, footsteps, doors creaking in the dark, and the sobs of Aunt Maggie. Finally I heard the sound of a horse and buggy rolling up to the house; I heard the scraping of a trunk being dragged across the floor. Aunt Maggie came into my room, crying softly; she kissed me and whispered good-bye. She kissed my brother, who did not even waken. Then she was gone.

The next morning my mother called me into the kitchen and talked to me for a long time, cautioning me that I must never mention what I had seen and heard, that white people would kill me if they even thought I knew.

"Know what?" I could not help but ask.

"Never you mind, now," she said. "Forget what you saw last night."

"But what did 'uncle' do?"

"I can't tell you."

"He killed somebody," I ventured timidly.

"If anybody heard you say that, you'll die," my mother said.

That settled it for me; I would never mention it. A few days later a tall white man with a gleaming star on his chest and a gun on his hip came to the house. He talked with my mother a long time and all I could hear was my mother's voice:

"I don't know what you're talking about. Search the house if you like."

The tall white man looked at me and my brother, but he said nothing to us. For weeks I wondered what it was that "uncle" had done, but I was destined never to know, not even in all the years that followed.

.   .   .

Having grown taller and older, I now associated with older boys and I had to pay for my admittance into their company by subscribing to certain racial sentiments. The touchstone of fraternity was my feeling toward white people, how much hostility I held toward them, what degrees of value and honor I assigned to race. None of this was premeditated, but sprang spontaneously out of the talk of black boys who met at the crossroads.

It was degrading to play with girls and in our talk we relegated them to a remote island of life. We had somehow caught the spirit of the role of our sex and we flocked together for common moral schooling. We spoke boastfully in bass voices; we used the word "nigger" to prove the tough fiber of our feelings; we spouted excessive profanity as a sign of our coming manhood; we pretended callousness toward the injunctions of our parents; and we strove to convince one another that our decisions stemmed from ourselves and ourselves alone. Yet we frantically concealed how dependent we were upon one another.

Of an afternoon when school had let out I would saunter down the street, idly kicking an empty tin can, or knocking a stick against the palings of a wooden fence, or whistling, until I would stumble upon one or more of the gang loitering at a corner, standing in a field, or sitting upon the steps of somebody's house.

"Hey." Timidly.

"You eat yet?" Uneasily trying to make conversation.

"Yeah, man. I done really fed my face." Casually.

"I had cabbage and potatoes." Confidently.

"I had buttermilk and black-eyed peas." Meekly informational.

"Hell, I ain't gonna stand near you, nigger!" Pronouncement.

"How come?" Feigned innocence.

"'Cause you gonna smell up this air in a minute!" A shouted accusation.

Laughter runs through the crowd.

"Nigger, your mind's in a ditch." Amusingly moralistic.

"Ditch, nothing! Nigger, you going to break wind any minute now!" Triumphant pronouncement creating suspense.

"Yeah, when them black-eyed peas tell that buttermilk to move over, that buttermilk ain't gonna wanna move and there's gonna be war in your guts and your stomach's gonna swell up and bust!" Climax.

The crowd laughs loud and long.

"Man, them white folks oughta catch you and send you to the zoo and keep you for the next war!" Throwing the subject into a wider field.

"Then when that fighting starts, they oughta feed you on buttermilk and black-eyed peas and let you break wind!" The subject is accepted and extended.

"You'd win the war with a new kind of poison gas!" A shouted climax.

There is high laughter that simmers down slowly.

"Maybe poison gas is something good to have." The subject of white folks is associationally swept into the orbit of talk.

"Yeah, if they hava race riot round here, I'm gonna kill all the white folks with my poison." Bitter pride.

Gleeful laughter. Then silence, each waiting for the other to contribute something.

"Them white folks sure scared of us, though." Sober statement of an old problem.

"Yeah, they send you to war, make you lick them Germans, teach you how to fight and when you come back they scared of you, want to kill you." Half boastful and half complaining.

"My mama says that old white woman where she works talked 'bout slapping her and Ma said: 'Miz Green, if you slaps me, I'll kill you and go to hell and pay for it!'" Extension, development, sacrificial boasting.

"Hell, I woulda just killed her if she hada said that to me." An angry grunt of supreme racial assertion.

Silence.

"Man, them white folks sure is mean." Complaining.

"That's how come so many colored folks leaving the South." Informational.

"And, man, they sure hate for you to leave." Pride of personal and racial worth implied.

"Yeah. They wanna keep you here and work you to death."

"The first white sonofabitch that bothers me is gonna get a hole knocked in his head!" Naïve rebellion.

"That ain't gonna do you no good. Hell, they'll catch you." Rejection of naïve rebellion.

"Ha-ha-ha . . . Yeah, goddammit, they really catch you, now." Appreciation of the thoroughness of white militancy.

"Yeah, white folks set on their white asses day and night, but leta nigger do something, and they get every bloodhound that was ever born and put 'em on his trail." Bitter pride in realizing what it costs to defeat them.

"Man, you reckon these white folks is ever gonna change?" Timid, questioning hope.

"Hell, no! They just born that way." Rejecting hope for fear that it could never come true.

"Shucks, man. I'm going north when I get grown." Rebelling against futile hope and embracing flight.

"A colored man's all right up north." Justifying flight.

"They say a white man hit a colored man up north and that colored man hit that white man, knocked him cold, and nobody did a damn thing!" Urgent wish to believe in flight.

"Man for man up there." Begging to believe in justice.

Silence.

"Listen, you reckon them buildings up north is as tall as they say they is?" Leaping by association to something concrete and trying to make belief real.

"They say they gotta building in New York forty stories high!" A thing too incredible for belief.

"Man, I'd be scareda them buildings!" Ready to abandon the now suppressed idea of flight.

"You know, they say that them buildings sway and rock in the wind." Stating a miracle.

"Naw, nigger!" Utter astonishment and rejection.

"Yeah, they say they do." Insisting upon the miracle.

"You reckon that could be?" Questioning hope.

"Hell, naw! If a building swayed and rocked in the wind, hell, it'd fall! Any fool knows that! Don't let people maka fool outta you, telling you them things!" Moving body agitatedly, stomping feet impatiently, and scurrying back to safe reality.

Silence. Somebody would pick up a stone and toss it across a field.

"Man, what makes white folks so mean?" Returning to grapple with the old problem.

"Whenever I see one I spit." Emotional rejection of whites.

"Man, ain't they ugly?" Increased emotional rejection.

"Man, you ever get right close to a white man, close enough to smell 'im?" Anticipation of statement.

"They say we stink. But my ma says white folks smell like dead folks." Wishing the enemy was dead.

"Niggers smell from sweat. But white folks smell *all* the time." The enemy is an animal to be killed on sight.

And the talk would weave, roll, surge, spurt, veer, swell, having no specific aim or direction, touching vast areas of life, expressing the tentative impulses of childhood. Money, God, race, sex, color, war, planes, machines, trains, swimming, boxing, anything . . . The culture of one black household was thus transmitted to another black household, and folk tradition was handed from group to group. Our attitudes were made, defined, set, or corrected; our ideas were discovered, discarded, enlarged, torn apart, and accepted. Night would fall. Bats would zip through the air. Crickets would cry from the grass. Frogs would croak. The stars would come out. Dew would dampen the earth. Yellow squares of light would glow in the distance as kerosene lamps were lit in our homes. Finally, from across the fields or down the road a long slow yell would come:

"Youuuuuuuu, Daaaaaaaavee!"

Easy laughter among the boys, but no reply.

"Calling the hogs."

"Go home, pig."

Laughter again. A boy would slowly detach himself from the gang.

"Youuuuuuuu, Daaaaaaaaavee!"

He would not answer his mother's call, for that would have been a sign of dependence.

"I'll do you-all like the farmer did the potato," the boy would say.

"How's that?"

"Plant you now and dig you later!"

The boy would trot home slowly and there would be more easy laughter. More talk. One by one we would be called home to fetch water from the hydrant in the back yard, to go to the store and buy greens and meal for tomorrow, to split wood for kindling.

On Sundays, if our clothes were presentable, my mother would take me and my brother to Sunday school. We did not object, for church was not where we learned of God or His ways, but where we met our school friends and continued our long, rambling talks. Some of the Bible stories were interesting in themselves, but we always twisted them, secularized them to the level of our street life, rejecting all meanings that did not fit into our environment. And we did the same to the beautiful hymns. When the preacher intoned:

Amazing grace, how sweet it sounds

we would wink at one another and hum under our breath:

A bulldog ran my grandma down

We were now large enough for the white boys to fear us and both of us, the white boys and the black boys, began to play our traditional racial roles as though we had been born to them, as though it was in our blood, as though we were being guided by instinct. All the frightful descriptions we had heard about each other, all the violent expressions of hate and hostility that had seeped into us from our surroundings, came now to the surface to guide our actions. The roundhouse was the racial boundary of the neighborhood, and it had been tacitly agreed between the white boys and the black boys that the whites were to keep to the far side of the roundhouse and we blacks were to keep to our side. Whenever we caught a white boy on our side we stoned him; if we strayed to their side, they stoned us.

. . .

Out of my salary [as a clean-up boy in a cheap hotel] I had begun to save a few dollars, for my determination to leave had not lessened. But I found the saving exasperatingly slow. I pondered continuously ways of making money, and the only ways that I could think of involved transgressions of the law. No, I must not do that, I told myself. To go to jail in the South would mean the end. And there was the possibility that if I were ever caught I would never reach jail.

This was the first time in my life that I had ever consciously entertained the idea of violating the laws of the land. I had felt that my intelligence and industry could cope with all situations, and, until that time, I had never stolen a penny from anyone. Even hunger had never driven me to appropriate what was not my own. The mere idea of stealing had been repugnant. I had not been honest from deliberate motives, but being dishonest had simply never occurred to me.

Yet, all about me, Negroes were stealing. More than once I had been called a "dumb nigger" by black boys who discovered that I had not availed myself of a chance to snatch some petty piece of white property that had been carelessly left within my reach.

"How in hell you gonna git ahead?" I had been asked when I had said that one ought not steal.

I knew that the boys in the hotel filched whatever they could. I knew that Griggs, my friend who worked in the Capitol Street jewelry store, was stealing regularly and successfully. I knew that a black neighbor of mine was stealing bags of grain from a wholesale house where he worked, though he was a stanch deacon in his church and prayed and sang on Sundays. I knew that the black girls who worked in white homes stole food daily to supplement their scanty wages. And I knew that the very nature of black and white relations bred this constant thievery.

No Negroes in my environment had ever thought of organizing, no matter in how orderly a fashion, and petitioning their white employers for higher wages. The very thought would have been terrifying to them, and they knew that the whites would have retaliated with swift brutality. So, pretending to conform to the laws of the whites, grinning, bowing, they let their fingers stick to what they could touch. And the whites seemed to like it.

But I, who stole nothing, who wanted to look them straight in the face, who wanted to talk and act like a man, inspired fear in them. The southern whites would rather have had Negroes who stole, work for them than Negroes who knew, however dimly, the worth of their own humanity. Hence, whites placed a premium upon black deceit; they encouraged irresponsibility; and their rewards were bestowed upon us blacks in the degree that we could make them feel safe and superior.

My objections to stealing were not moral. I did not approve of it because I knew that, in the long run, it was futile, that it was not an effective way to alter one's relationship to one's environment. Then, how could I change my relationship to my environment? Almost my entire salary went to feed the eternally hungry stomachs at home. If I saved a dollar a week, it would take me two years to amass a hundred dollars, the amount which for some reason I had decided was necessary to stake me in a strange city. And, God knows, anything could happen to me in two years . . .

I did not know when I would be thrown into a situation where I would say the wrong word to the wrong white man and find myself in trouble. And, above all, I wanted to avoid trouble, for I feared that if I clashed with whites I would lose control of my emotions and spill out words that would be my sentence of death. Time was not on my side and I had to make some move. Often, when perplexed, I longed to be like the smiling, lazy, forgetful black boys in the noisy hotel locker rooms, with no torrential conflicts to resolve. Many times I grew weary of the secret burden I carried and longed to cast it down, either in action or in resignation. But I was not made to be a resigned man and I had only a limited choice of actions, and I was afraid of all of them.

A new anxiety was created in me by my desire to leave quickly. I had now seen at close quarters the haughty white men who made the laws; I had seen how they acted, how they regarded black people, how they regarded me; and I no longer felt bound by the laws which white and black were supposed to obey in common. I was outside those laws; the white people had told me so. Now when I thought of ways to escape from my environment I no longer felt the inner restraint that would have made stealing impossible, and this new freedom made me lonely and afraid.

My feelings became divided; in spite of myself I would dream of a locked cupboard in a near-by neighbor's house where a gun was kept. If I stole it, how much would it bring? When the yearning to leave would become strong in me, I could not keep out of my mind the image of a storehouse at a near-by Negro college that held huge cans of preserved fruits. Yet fear kept me from making any move; the idea of stealing floated tentatively in me. My inability to adjust myself to the white world had already shattered a part of the structure of my personality and had broken down the inner barriers to crime; the only thing that now stood in the way was lack of immediate opportunity, a final push of circumstance. And that came.

I was promoted to bellboy, which meant a small increase in income. But I soon learned that the substantial money came from bootlegging liquor to the white prostitutes in the hotel. The other bellboys were taking these risks, and I fell in. I learned how to walk past a white policeman with contraband upon my hip, sauntering, whistling like a nigger ought to whistle when he is innocent. The extra dollars were coming in, but slowly. How, how, how could I get my hands on more money before I was caught and sent to jail for some trivial misdemeanor? If I were going to violate the law, then I ought to get something out of it. My larcenous aims were modest. A hundred dollars would give me, temporarily, more freedom of movement than I had ever known in my life. I watched and waited, living with the thought.

While waiting for my chance to grab and run, I grew used to seeing the white prostitutes naked upon their beds, sitting nude about their rooms, and I learned new modes of behavior, new rules in how to live the Jim Crow life. It was presumed that we black boys took their nakedness for granted, that it startled us no more than a blue vase or a red rug. Our presence awoke in them no sense of shame whatever, for we blacks were not considered human anyway. If they were alone, I would steal sidelong glances at them. But if they were receiving men, not a flicker of my eyelids would show.

A huge, snowy-skinned blonde took a room on my floor. One night she rang for service and I went to wait upon her. She was in bed with a thickset man; both were nude and uncovered. She said that she wanted some liquor, and slid out of bed and waddled across the floor to get her money from the dresser drawer. Without realizing it, I watched her.

"Nigger, what in hell are you looking at?" the white man asked, raising himself upon his elbows.

"Nothing, sir," I answered, looking suddenly miles deep into the blank wall of the room.

"Keep your eyes where they belong if you want to be healthy!"

"Yes, sir."

I would have continued at the hotel until I left had not a shortcut presented itself. One of the boys at the hotel whispered to me one night that the only local Negro movie house wanted a boy to take tickets at the door.

"You ain't never been in jail, is you?" he asked me.

"Not yet," I answered.

"Then you can get the job," he said. "I'd take it, but I done six months and they know me."

"What's the catch?"

"The girl who sells tickets is using a system," he explained. "If you get the job, you can make some good gravy."

If I stole, I would have a chance to head northward quickly; if I remained barely honest, piddling with pints of bootleg liquor, I merely prolonged my stay, increased my chances of being caught, exposed myself to the possibility of saying the wrong word or doing the wrong thing and paying a penalty that I dared not think of. The temptation to venture into crime was too strong, and I decided to work quickly, taking whatever was in sight, amass a wad of money, and flee. I knew that others had tried it before me and had failed, but I was hoping to be lucky.

My chances for getting the job were good; I had no past record of stealing or violating the laws. When I presented myself to the Jewish proprietor of the movie house I was immediately accepted. The next day I reported for duty and began taking tickets. The boss man warned me:

"Now, look, I'll be honest with you if you'll be honest with me. I don't know who's honest around this joint and who isn't. But if *you* are honest, then the rest are bound to be. All tickets will pass through your hands. There can be no stealing unless you steal."

I gave him a pledge of my honesty, feeling absolutely no qualms about what I intended to do. He was white, and I could never do to him what he and his kind had done to me. Therefore, I reasoned, stealing was not a violation of my ethics, but of his; I felt that things were rigged in his favor and any action I took to circumvent his scheme of life was justified. Yet I had not convinced myself.

During the first afternoon the Negro girl in the ticket office watched me closely and I knew that she was sizing me up, trying to determine when it would be safe to break me into her graft. I waited, leaving it to her to make the first move.

I was supposed to drop each ticket that I took from a customer into a metal receptacle. Occasionally the boss would go to the ticket window and look at the serial number on the roll of unsold tickets and then compare that number with the number on the last ticket I had dropped into the receptacle. The boss continued his watchfulness for a few days, then began to observe me from across the street; finally he absented himself for long intervals.

A tension as high as that I had known when the white men had driven me from the job at the optician's returned to live in me. But I had learned to master a great deal of tension now; I had developed, slowly and painfully, a capacity to contain it within myself without betraying it in any way. Had this not been true, the mere thought of stealing, the risks involved, the inner distress would have so upset me that I would have been in no state of mind to calculate coldly, would have made me so panicky that I would have been afraid to steal at all. But my inner resistance had been blasted. I felt that I had been emotionally cast out of the world, had been made to live outside the normal processes of life, had been conditioned in feeling *against* something daily, had become accustomed to living on the side of those who watched and waited.

While I was eating supper in a near-by café one night, a strange Negro man walked in and sat beside me.

"Hello, Richard," he said.

"Hello," I said. "I don't think I know you."

"But I know *you*," he said, smiling.

Was he one of the boss's spies?

"How do you know me?" I asked.

"I'm Tel's friend," he said, naming the girl who sold the tickets at the movie.

I looked at him searchingly. Was he telling me the truth? Or was he trying to trap me for the boss? I was already thinking and feeling like a criminal, distrusting everybody.

"We start tonight," he said.

"What?" I asked, still not admitting that I knew what he was talking about.

"Don't be scared. The boss trusts you. He's gone to see some friends. Somebody's watching him and if he starts back to the movie, they'll phone us," he said.

I could not eat my food. It lay cold upon the plate and sweat ran down from my armpits.

"It'll work this way," he explained in a low, smooth tone. "A guy'll come to you and ask for a match. You give him five tickets that you'll hold out of the box, see? We'll give you the signal when to start holding out. The guy'll give the tickets to Tel; she'll resell them all at once, when a crowd is buying at the rush hour. You get it?"

I did not answer. I knew that if I were caught I would go to the chain gang. But was not my life already a kind of chain gang? What, really, did I have to lose?

"Are you with us?" he asked.

I still did not answer. He rose and clapped me on the shoulder and left. I trembled as I went back to the theater. Anything might happen, but I was used to that. Had I not felt that same sensation when I lay on the ground and the white men towered over me, telling me that I was a lucky nigger? Had I not felt it when I walked home from the optical company that morning with my job gone? Had I not felt it when I walked down the hallway of the hotel with the night watchman pointing a gun at my back? Had I not felt it all a million times before? I took the tickets with sweaty fingers. I waited. I was gambling: freedom or the chain gang. There were times when I felt that I could not breathe. I looked up and down the street; the boss was not in sight. Was this a trap? If it were, I would disgrace my family. Would not all of them say that my attitude had been leading to this all along? Would they not rake up the past and find clues that had led to my fate?

The man I had met in the café came through the door and put a ticket in my hand.

"There's a crowd at the box office," he whispered. "Save ten, not five. Start with this one."

Well, here goes, I thought. He gave me the ticket and sat looking at the moving shadows upon the screen. I held on to the ticket and my body grew tense, hot as fire; but I was used to that too. Time crawled through the cells of my brain. My muscles ached. I discovered that crime means suffering. The crowd came in and gave me more tickets. I kept ten of them tucked into my moist palm. No sooner had the crowd thinned than a black boy with a cigarette jutting from his mouth came up to me.

"Gotta match?"

With a slow movement I gave him the tickets. He went out and I kept the door cracked and watched. He went to the ticket office and laid down a coin and I saw him slip the tickets to the girl. Yes, the boy was honest. The girl shot me a quick smile and I went back inside. A few moments later the same tickets were handed to me by other customers.

We worked it for a week and after the money was split four ways, I had fifty dollars. Freedom was almost within my grasp. Ought I risk any more? I dropped the hint to Tel's friend that maybe I would quit; it was a casual hint to test him out. He grew violently angry and I quickly consented to stay, fearing that someone might turn me in for revenge, or to get me out of the way so that another and more pliable boy could have my place. I was dealing with cagey people and I would be cagey.

I went through another week. Late one night I resolved to make that week the last. The gun in the neighbor's house came to my mind, and the cans of fruit preserves in the storehouse of the college. If I stole them and sold them, I would have enough to tide me over in Memphis until I could get a job, work, save, and go north. I crept from bed and found the neighbor's house empty. I looked about; all was quiet. My heart beat so fast that it ached. I forced a window with a screwdriver and entered and took the gun; I slipped it in my shirt and returned home. When I took it out to look at it, it was wet with sweat. I pawned it under an assumed name.

The following night I rounded up two boys whom I knew to be ready for adventure. We broke into the college storehouse and lugged out cans of fruit preserves and sold them to restaurants.

Meanwhile I bought clothes, shoes, a cardboard suitcase, all of which I hid at home. Saturday night came and I sent word to the boss that I was sick. Uncle Tom was upstairs. Granny and Aunt Addie were at church. My brother was sleeping. My mother sat in her rocking chair, humming to herself. I packed my suitcase and went to her.

"Mama, I'm going away," I whispered.

"Oh, no," she protested.

"I've got to, mama. I can't live this way."

"You're not running away from something you've done?"

"I'll send for you, mama. I'll be all right."

"Take care of yourself. And send for me quickly. I'm not happy here," she said.

"I'm sorry for all those long years, mama. But I could not have helped it."

I kissed her and she cried.

"Be quiet, mama. I'm all right."

I went out the back way and walked a quarter of a mile to the railroad tracks. It began to rain as I tramped down the crossties toward town. I reached the station soaked to the skin. I bought my ticket, then went hurriedly to the corner of the block in which the movie house stood. Yes, the boss was there, taking the tickets himself. I returned to the station and waited for my train, my eyes watching the crowd.

An hour later I was sitting in a Jim Crow coach, speeding northward, making the first lap of my journey to a land where I could live with a little less fear. Slowly the burden I had carried for many months lifted somewhat. My cheeks itched and when I scratched them I found tears. In that moment I understood the pain that accompanied crime and I hoped that I would never have to feel it again. I never did feel it again, for I never stole again; and what kept me from it was the knowledge that, for me, crime carried its own punishment.

Well, it's my life, I told myself. I'll see now what I can make of it . . .

Folk Songs and Blues

Folk Songs

The Industrial Workers of the World was the labor organization whose rank-and-file we now remember as the Wobblies. Organized in 1905, the IWW existed as an important factor in the trade union movement only until 1919. Yet, in those few years, it inspired a body of song and myth that is unique in American labor history.

The IWW was born at a time when no labor union could yet regard itself as safe within the structure of American society. Antistrike injunctions, yellow-dog contracts (which forbade workers from joining unions), antitrust suits, and trumped-up criminal charges were all deployed, with frequent success, to fight union activities within a legal framework; while outside of the law the use of violence against strikers often went unchecked. Even the AFL, the national association of craft unions whose members were the skilled elite of the American labor force, often found itself in precarious situations, and even more often was indifferent to the plight of the unskilled workers. Indeed, it was the AFL's conservative attitude, its concentrating on reforms to improve the position of the skilled worker rather than attempting to organize the masses of unskilled workers, that led to the establishment of the IWW.

The IWW made its own revolutionary position clear from the beginning. The Preamble to the IWW constitution declared: "The working class and the employing class have nothing in common. There can be no peace so long as hunger and want are found among millions of working people and the few, who make up the employing class, have all the good things of life." The purpose of the IWW was not collective bargaining, but preparation for the time when the working class, organized in "One Big Union," would take over the means of production. Wobbly theorists envisioned this takeover as the climax of a gigantic general strike; until the time was ripe

2747

for Armageddon, strikes and direct-action techniques by IWW locals would be the means of developing the power and class consciousness of the workers. In this process the IWW employed sit-down strikes, organizing the nation's first such strike, and techniques of civil disobedience, as in a series of free speech fights, during which Wobblies stuffed the jails with their bodies until local authorities finally stopped making arrests for the preaching of union doctrine. In many respects Wobbly myth and rhetoric have obscured the fact that in its major practical struggles, the IWW functioned much as would the CIO two decades later: it was energetic in organizing a trade-wide struggle for better wages and working conditions and opposed discrimination against blacks and women.

Yet, all this notwithstanding, it is not as an important labor organization that the IWW is remembered; rather it is as a union of hoboes that it entered the American historical imagination. The IWW was begun by westerners, in particular upon the initiative of the Western Federation of Miners and its magnificent secretary William ("Big Bill") Haywood, and many of its western locals were dominated by the unskilled workers known as "hoboes." These workers were characteristically migrant, with far-flung seasonal and short-term jobs (laying railroad track, building roads, logging, harvesting, mining), and from job to job rode the rods of boxcars. While unemployed, they lived in the hobo "jungles" that sprang up outside towns along the major railroad lines. The reputation of these hoboes often complicated public feeling toward the IWW, especially in the West: to fear of the IWW's radical ideology was added the feelings of envy and resentment that the newly and precariously settled westerner felt toward the still roaming hobo.

Even before the advent of the IWW, the hoboes had been a singing lot, with a repertoire including songs whose melodies were borrowed from folk songs, dance-hall tunes, and the hymns picked up in Salvation Army missions. After 1905, IWW organizers were quick to make use of the migrants' love of music: Wobbly bards set defiant IWW words to the familiar tunes, and the songs that emerged, which were sung before each Wobbly street meeting, were an important factor in building morale.

J. H. Walsh, the Portland IWW organizer who was responsible for putting out the first Wobbly songsheets, was also responsible for helping the IWW repel the musical attacks of the Salvation Army and the Volunteers of America. These organizations, who believed that religion and charity better befitted the hoboes' situation than did organization, sent brass bands to break up IWW meetings. Walsh responded by organizing Wobbly bands. Richard Brazier, a miner who later became a member of the IWW general executive board, describes the battles that occurred: "At times we would sing note by note with the Salvation Army at our street meetings, only their words were describing Heaven above, and ours Hell right here— to the same tune."

Most Wobbly songs were strictly propagandistic; they either served immediate organizational needs or else simply helped the "working stiff" to ridicule the hated bosses. Some, however, were of such a quality that they quickly entered the folk-consciousness. Three such songs were "Hallelujah, Bum Again," "The Big Rock Candy Mountains," and "The Preacher and the Slave."

FURTHER READINGS

Melvin Dubovsky, *We Shall Be All: A History of the Industrial Workers of the World* (1969)

Edith Fowke and Joe Glazer, *Songs of Work and Freedom* (1972)

Woody Guthrie, *American Folksong* (1961)

———, *Bound for Glory* (1943)

Joyce Kornbluh, *Rebel Voices: An IWW Anthology* (1964)

Hallelujah, Bum Again ©

"Hallelujah, Bum Again" was composed to the tune of the hymn, "Hallelujah, Thine the Glory." Many versions of the song exist, and the question of which was the original, and who was its composer, has never been resolved.

Regardless of its origin, one version of "Hallelujah, Bum Again" (the second one printed here) was soon adopted as the Wobbly anthem.

1

Oh, why don't I work like the other men do?
How the hell can I work when the skies are so blue?

Chorus:
Hallelujah, I'm a bum!
Hallelujah, bum again,
Hallelujah! Bum a handout,
Revive me again.

If I was to work and save all I earn,
I could buy me a bar and have whiskey to burn.

Oh, I love Jim Hill,[1] he's an old friend of mine,

[1] James Jerome "Jim" Hill (1838–1916), a railroad magnate. The "line" referred to is likely the Northern Pacific.

Up North I ride rattlers all over his line.

Oh, I ride box cars and I ride fast mails,
When it's cold in the winter I sleep in the jails.

I passed by a saloon and I hear someone snore,
And I found the bartender asleep on the floor.

I stayed there and drank till a fly-mug came in,
And he put me to sleep with a sap on the chin.

Next morning in court I was still in a haze,
When the judge looked at me, he said, "Thirty days!"

Some day a long train will run over my head,
And the sawbones will say, "Old One-Finger's dead!"

2

When springtime does come,
Oh, won't we have fun!
We'll all throw up our jobs
And we'll go on the bum.

Chorus:
Hallelujah, I'm a bum,
Hallelujah, bum again,
Hallelujah, give us a handout
To revive us again.

Oh, springtime has come,
And I'm just out of jail,
Ain't got no money,
It all went for bail.

I went up to a house
And I knocked on the door.

A lady came out, says,
"You been here before!"

I went up to a house,
Asked for some bread;
A lady came out, says,
"The baker is dead."

The Big Rock Candy Mountains

"The Big Rock Candy Mountains" has for many years been one of the most widely known of hobo dream songs; so idyllic is the mountain paradise it presents that the song now thrives far beyond the limits of hobo jungles as a children's song.

Introduction:
  On a summer day in the month of May,
  A burly little bum come a-hikin',
  He was travelin' down that lonesome road,
  A-lookin' for his likin'.
  He was headed for a land that's far away,
  Beside those crystal fountains,
  "I'll see you all, this comin' fall,
  In the Big Rock Candy Mountains."

In the Big Rock Candy Mountains,
You never change your socks,
And the little streams of alkyhol,
Come atricklin' down the rocks.
Where the shacks all have to tip their hats,
And the railroad bulls are blind,
There's a lake of stew, and whiskey, too,
In the Big Rock Candy Mountains.

Chorus:
  Oh . . . the . . . buzzin' of the bees
  In the cigarette trees,
  Round the sodawater fountains,
  Now the lemonade springs,
  Where the whangdoodle sings
  In the Big Rock Candy Mountains.

In the Big Rock Candy Mountains,
There's a land that's fair and bright,
Where the handouts grow on bushes,
And you sleep out every night.
Where the boxcars are all empty,
And the sun shines every day,
Oh, I'm bound to go, where there ain't no snow,
Where the rain don't fall and the wind don't blow,
In the Big Rock Candy Mountains.

In the Big Rock Candy Mountains,
The jails are made of tin,
And you can bust right out again,
As soon as they put you in.
The farmers' trees are full of fruit,
The barns are full of hay,
I'm goin' to stay where you sleep all day,
Where they boiled in oil the inventor of toil,
In the Big Rock Candy Mountains.

The Preacher and the Slave

Little is known about the actual life of the legendary Joe Hill. A Swedish immigrant, born Joseph Hillstrom, he entered this country in 1902, and then seems to have bummed and worked his way around the country without purpose or notice for the next eight years. In 1910, however, he appeared in the Portland IWW Hall with a song that immediately found its way into *The Little Red Songbook* of the IWW. "The Preacher and the Slave" was a parody of the Salvation Army song "In the Sweet Bye and Bye," which it quickly outstripped in popularity; from *The Little Red Songbook* the song soon spread all over the country, while the phrase "pie in the sky" drifted into the general American vocabulary.

Long-haired preachers come out ev'ry night,
Try to tell you what's wrong and what's right;

But when asked about something to eat,
They will answer in accents so sweet:

Chorus:
    You will eat bye and bye,
    In that glorious land above the sky.
                    (way up high)
    Work and pray; live on hay,
    You'll get pie in the sky when you die.
                    (that's no lie!)

And the starvation army they play,
And they sing and they clap and they pray,
Till they get all your coin on the drum,
Then they'll tell you when you're on the bum:

Holy rollers and jumpers come out,
And they holler and jump and they shout,
But when eating time comes around they will say,
"You will eat on that glorious day."

Joe Hill

After the publication of "The Preacher and the Slave," Hill drifted through the West for several years more. Again his traveling was aimless; contrary to legend he was never an important organizer for the IWW. Then, in January of 1914, Hill found himself in Salt Lake City, Utah, where he was arrested and charged with the murder and robbery of a grocer, Merlin Morrison. Although the debate continues as to how weighty the circumstantial evidence presented against Hill was, there is no doubt that the trial he was given violated every accepted standard of criminal and constitutional law. At its end he was convicted and sentenced to death. He was shot by a firing squad on November 19, 1915, despite clemency pleas to the governor that included two telegrams from President Wilson. The night before his execution, Hill sent two telegrams to Big Bill Haywood. The first read: "Good-bye Bill. I will die like a true rebel. Don't waste any time in mourning. Organize." And then: "It is only a hundred miles from here to Wyoming. Could you arrange to have my body hauled to the state line to be buried? I don't want to be found dead in Utah."

Whether or not Hill desired his martyrdom, he played the martyr's role superbly. And the IWW knew how to handle its martyr: Haywood had Hill's body removed from Utah to Chicago, where tens of thousands showed up for the funeral ceremonies. In accord with the spirit of a poem Hill had written the night before his execution, his body was cremated; one year later, the ashes were distributed in envelopes for IWW delegates to scatter through all corners of the United States, Europe, Africa, and Asia—except for the state of Utah. John Reed later reported meeting workers who proudly sported little bottles of ashes that they claimed were the last remains of Joe Hill.

The Wobblies, however, were not destined to long survive their martyr's death. In the post-First World War red scare, the entire Wobbly leadership was mercilessly crushed by the justice department. Many spent years in prison on outrageously trumped-up charges of criminal syndicalism. Big Bill Haywood fled to Russia.

Soon, however, Joe Hill was to become "the man who never died": labor's martyr, the man who through his death became a model, during the 1930's, for left-wing writers and singers in their attempt to put their art into contact with the needs of "the masses."

The song "Joe Hill," with words by Alfred Hayes and music by Earl Robinson, has been instrumental, since the 1930's, in keeping alive the legendary Wobbly.

I dreamed I saw Joe Hill last night
    Alive as you and me.
Says, I, "But Joe, you're ten years dead."
    "I never died," says he.
    "I never died," says he.

"In Salt Lake, Joe, by God," says I,
    Him standing by my bed,
They framed you on a murder charge."
    Says Joe, "But I ain't dead."
    Says Joe, "But I ain't dead."

"The copper bosses killed you, Joe,
    They shot you, Joe," says I.

"Takes more than guns to kill a man,"
  Says Joe, "I didn't die."
  Says Joe, "I didn't die."

And standing there as big as life
  And smiling with his eyes,
Joe says, "What they forgot to kill
  Went on to organize.
  Went on to organize."

"Joe Hill ain't dead," he says to me,
  "Joe Hill ain't never died.
Where working men are out on strike

Joe Hill is at their side.
Joe Hill is at their side."

"From San Diego up to Maine
  In every mine and mill,
Where workers strike and organize,"
  Says he, "You'll find Joe Hill."
  Says he, "You'll find Joe Hill."

I dreamed I saw Joe Hill last night
  Alive as you and me
Says I, "But Joe, you're ten years dead."
  "I never died," says he.
  "I never died," says he.

WOODY GUTHRIE (1912–1967)

Woodrow Wilson Guthrie was born in 1912 in Okeemah, Oklahoma. Still a rugged frontier town at the time of Woody's birth, Okeemah soon went boom with oil and the boomchasing, bootlegging migrant workers who swiftly followed all oil strikes. The boom was brief, however, and when it burst the young Guthrie began the wandering that was to characterize his life and songs, hitting the road with only his guitar and a mind full of the music that had surrounded his youth: the harmonica blues of local black railroad workers, the guitar picking style of West Virginia's Carter family, Jimmie Rodgers blue yodels (see p. 2758) and the old-time sound of the country string bands.

In the mid 1930's, when a series of great dust storms devastated Oklahoma, Guthrie joined the rush of Okies west, from the Panhandle, to California. There he composed his songs of the Dust Bowl refugees, those Okie and Arkie migrant workers who, to keep alive through the late 1930's, followed the California harvest from crop to crop, and from one rich valley to the next. The songs that Guthrie wrote at this time combined a left-wing note of protest with the more traditional sound of the hoboes' hard travelin'; and, while heavily influenced by both Jimmie Rodgers' music and the fighting Wobbly tradition, Guthrie's songs themselves later became enormously influential as the first models for such modern singer-composers as Bob Dylan.

Many of Woody Guthrie's compositions, such as "This Land Is Your Land" and "So Long, It's Been Good to Know You," were soon so widely sung that they are often mistaken for anonymously composed folk songs. Their impact, taken along with the poetry of such migrant songs as "Pastures of Plenty," makes it clear why Woody Guthrie is widely regarded as the greatest of America's twentieth-century balladeers.

Pastures of Plenty [©]

It's a mighty hard road that my poor hands has hoed
And my poor feet has traveled a hot dusty road
Out of your dustbowl and westward we rolled
Lord, your mountains are hot and your desert is cold.

I work in your orchards of peaches and prunes

And I sleep on the ground 'neath the light of your moon
On the edge of your city you'll see us and then
We come with the dust and we go with the wind.

California, Arizona, I make all your crops
Then it's north up to Oregon to gather your hops

Dig beets from your ground, cut the grapes from your vine
To set on your table your light sparkling wine.

Green Pastures of Plenty from dry desert ground
From the Grand Coulee Dam where the waters run down

Every state in this union us migrants has been
We'll work in your fight and we'll fight till we win.
It's always we ramble, that river and I
All along your green valley I'll work till I die
My land I'll defend with my life if needs be,
'Cause my Pastures of Plenty must always be free.

Blues

With slavery the American black created the spirituals, and with freedom the blues. For the freedom was little more than freedom in name only, and, as Ralph Ellison puts it in *Shadow and Act*, "the blues, the spiritual, the jazz, the dance—was what we had in place of freedom." What the blacks had in place of freedom was one of the few unique contributions—perhaps the only unique contribution—that America has made to the world of art.

The uniqueness of this achievement, in spite of the fact that musicologists and anthropologists bitterly disagree on certain important aspects of the question, arises from the collision of an African tradition[1] with that of white civilization, the African sensibility, in attacking European harmonies, instruments, and melodies, transformed those non-African elements into new musical forms and techniques. The most obvious difference between the African and European traditions is that African music, to quote Marshall Stearns in his *Story of Jazz*, is "polyrhythmic, that is, two or more separate rhythms are being played at the same time, maybe five or six. . . . It's as if an orchestra were playing the same tune as a waltz, a one-step and a fox trot —all at the same time."

A more specific relation appears in the "blue notes" of the blues. For years, it was usually said that the blue notes were the result of the black's incapacity to abandon the primitive pentatonic (five-note) scale of Africa and adopt the European diatonic (eight-note) scale. This, of course, was a complete distortion. Rather than reflecting any black inability to grasp the clarity of the European scale, it was precisely the blue notes, in their "endless variety of sweeps, glides, slurs, smears, and glisses," as Stearns puts it, that defined the uniqueness, and the greatness, of African music. For while European music represents the effort to create music as an artifact, or art object, African and Afro-American music emphasize instead the immediate and personal expressiveness of the musician. Thus the blue notes: the musician or singer, African or Afro-American, may bend and twist these particular notes, in his individual way, so as to achieve a maximum of personal

[1] There is, of course, more than one musical tradition in Africa, and from this fact arises a very complex debate among the experts.

expressiveness. Thus, too, the moaning, humming, and howling that characterize so much early blues by lending to the singer's voice a range of visceral depth and roughness; like African language, the African music from which blues are descended relied heavily on the timber of the voice for its meaning. We might also note that this emphasis on expressiveness, rather than on the rounded artifact, defines blues instrumental work as well as blues singing; as Fred MacDowell, the Mississippi singer-guitarist puts it, "I can make them strings say just what I say. Anything I say I can make them strings say."

For a time the blues were considered, along with work songs, minstrel shows, ragtime, and spirituals, merely as a precursor of jazz, but more recently they are being taken in their own right and judged in terms of their own history and specific form. Jazz, it is true, developed from blues, but blues had their own continuing existence and further development. The great jazzmen could remember when there was no jazz, but to them blues had been an inescapable part of black life, so much so that even the matter of origin was not worth discussing. "Ain't no first blues," Louis de Lisle Nelson has said: "Blues has always been." In the same spirit that origins are not discussable in that world, so with the matter of objective definition and the assigning of relative merit. Here the emphasis on the personal aspect of the blues is crucial. Buster Pickens (in *Conversation with the Blues*, by Paul Oliver) says:

> No man in good spirit, no man in good heart can sing the blues, neither play them . . . nach'al blues come directly from a person's heart. . . . You have a tough way in life—that makes you blue. That's when you start to sing the blues—when you've got the blues.

The value, that is, would lie in the authenticity of experience—as opposed to the value of the "artifact"—and so we return to Fred McDowell, who says that a man "plays what he plays—it sounds good to him. And I feel like a person ought to go along with that 'cause you can't take the next man's feelings from him." Or to quote another practitioner: "Bad blues is not blues."

But blues *did* have a beginning (just as they may be objectively evaluated). They developed from the work song and the "holler." The work song, with its call-response, provided a basic structure:

> Call: Well, you know I left my woman—
> Response: Hammer ring!
> Call: She's standing at the station—
> Response: Hammer ring!

From this might develop:

> You ought to heard what that letter read—
>> Here, Rattler, here!
> That letter say my woman's dead—
>> Here, Rattler, here!

The next stage might well be merely the basic couplet:

> You ought to heard what that letter read,
> That letter say my woman's dead.

Presumably some anonymous father of the blues repeated the second line of the couplet, thus creating a triplet, and this gave the standard structure upon which, of course, variations were made. At the same time, musically the blues were becoming standardized as a twelve-bar form, with a basic three-chord (tonic, subdominant, dominant) harmony that had been adopted from the spirituals.

The form thus developed out of the call and response of work songs, and the harmony of the spirituals, was blues. But blues were also deeply informed by another black American musical tradition, that of the holler, which was the song—or rather, cry—of the black man down in the field, or on the road, alone—an utterance freer in phrasing, with falsetto voice and irregular, embellished cadence, and, more importantly, a strictly personal utterance of feeling. "Each man," as LeRoi Jones says, "had his own voice and his own way of shouting—his own life to sing about." Furthermore, while the work song had belonged to gang-work, characteristically the work of slavery, a way of pacing work and unifying effort, but the holler belonged characteristically to the world of emancipation, the individual alone in his personal occupation, with his personal story—off down in his field or, since he was free now, wandering off, footloose, happy, fearful, or hungry, away from old associations and friends, riding the rods, discovering strange towns, even cities. In his autobiography, W. C. Handy, the composer of the "St. Louis Blues," refers to the "blind singers and footloose bards that were forever coming and going," in his youth, in the 1890's, in Clarksdale, Mississippi:

> Usually the fellows were destitute. Some came sauntering down the railroad tracks, others dropped from freight cars, while still others caught rides on the big road and entered town on the top of cotton bales. A favorite hangout with them was the railroad station. There, surrounded by crowds of country folks, they would pour out their hearts in song, while the audience ate fish and bread, chewed sugar cane, and dipped snuff while waiting for trains to carry them down the line.

It was the era of trains on a continent of loneliness, and it is no wonder that the train and the station give material to folk tale and folk song—and to the blues. But the sound of the railroad is in the music, too. To quote B. A. Botkin, in his *American Folklore:*

> Listen to the Blues, the stomps, the hot music of the last fifty years . . . and you'll hear all the smashing, rattling, syncopated rhythms and counter-rhythms of trains of every size and speed. . . . Listen to the blues with those hundreds of silvery breaks in the treble clef. What you hear back of the notes is the drive and thrust and moan of a locomotive.

Wanderings, departures, separations, losses—the blues tell these tales, as when the bluesman Charlie Patton sings of the train taking his woman away:

> Lord, the smokestack is black and the bell it shine like gold,
> Oh, the smoke stack is black and the bell it shine like gold,
> Lord, I ain't gonna walk there or tarry round no more.
>
> Oh yeah, evil walkin' at midnight when I heard the local blow.
> I will leave out at midnight, when I hear the local blow.
> I gotta see my rider, when she's gettin' on board.

In "Easy Rider Blues," Blind Lemon Jefferson bewails his loss:

> Now tell me where my easy rider gone
> Tell me where my easy rider gone
> I need one of these women—always in the wrong
>
> Well, easy rider, standing on the road
> And it's easy rider standing on the road
> I'm a poor blind man, ain't got no where to go
>
> I went to the depot
> I mean I went to the depot and set my pistol down
> The blues overtake me and tears come rolling down

But the blues of man's lost love were matched by those of woman; indeed, it was the great women "classic blues" singers of the twenties who were the first black singers to make records. One of the best known of their songs was the "Empty Bed Blues," by Bessie Smith:

> He's a deep-sea diver with a stroke that can't go wrong,
> He's a deep-sea diver with a stroke that can't go wrong,
> He can touch the bottom, and his wind holds out so long.
>
>   .   .   .
>
> When my bed gets empty, makes me feel awful mean and blue,

When my bed gets empty, makes me feel awful mean and blue,
'Cause my springs getting rusty, sleepin' single the way I do.

.   .   .

He boiled my first cabbage, and he made it awful hot,
He boiled my first cabbage, and he made it awful hot,
Then he put in the bacon and it overflowed the pot.

The lonely pathos of the holler from the far field still ran through the blues, but in the sociability of the barrel-house, juke-joint, and brothel the songs found a world where their pathos was absorbed into an atmosphere of teeming sexuality, violence, and bravado, as in Sara Martin's famous boast:

Now my hair is nappy and I don't wear no clothes of silk,
Now my hair is nappy and I don't wear no clothes of silk,
But the cow that's black and ugly, has often got the sweetest milk.

Now when a man starts jivin' I'm tighter than a pair of shoes.
Now when a man starts jivin' I'm tighter than a pair of shoes.
I'm a mean tight mama, with my mean tight blues.[2]

Or as sung by the man about his beloved, as by Blind Boy Fuller:

I got a big fat woman, grease shakin' on her bone.
I say, hey, hey, meat shakin' on her bone,
And every time she shake some man done left his home.

As for bravado, there is the sexual persona of Texas Alexander, which echoes the classic boasts of the keelboatmen and the mythic Davy Crockett:

I was raised on the desert, born in a lion's den.
I was raised on the desert, born in a lion's den.
Says my chief occupation—takin' monkey men's women.

As for the celebration of the desperate, sometimes despairing violence of that world, there is "Furry's Blues," of Furry Lewis:

I believe I'll buy me a graveyard of my own.
I believe I'll buy me a graveyard of my own.
I'm gon' kill everybody that have done me wrong.

If you want to go to Nashville and ain't got no fare,

[2] In this song and the one to follow—as in other blues—can be found a parallel to the glorification of ugliness, especially female ugliness, that appears in the tall tales of the white frontiersman and keelboatman—a prideful assertion of pure sexuality superior to, and having no need for, such irrelevancies of the genteel world as beauty and charm—this mixed with, perhaps, a bitter rationalization.

> If you want to go to Nashville and ain't got no fare,
> Cut your good gal's throat and the judge will send you there.

The desperation, the sense of doom, may appear, however, in other forms, as in Robert Johnson's "Hellhound," or in his "Me and the Devil":

> Early this mornin', when you knocked upon my door.
> Early this mornin', when you knocked upon my door,
> I said, "Hello, Satan, I believe it's time to go."

This blues ends:

You may bury my body down by the highway side—
  (Spoken:) Babe, I don't care where you bury my body when I'm dead and gone—
You may bury my body down by the highway side;
So my old evil spirit can get a Greyhound bus and ride.

And with this, we observe, the loneliness of the footloose wanderer has appeared again in a new context.

The blues, in fact, belong to the lonely wanderer; whatever other role he may assume, or may think he assumes, the bluesman continues to draw on a stack of basic verses that lend their poetry to a great number of blues. Fragments like the following recur in a variety of contexts:

Now you talk about trouble, I've had it all my days.
Trouble, had it all my days.
Seem like trouble gonna carry me to my lonesome grave.

Late one Saturday evenin', after the sun went down.
It was late one Saturday evenin', Lord, after the sun went down.
Yes, I went lookin' for my baby, but she wasn't nowhere around.

Well, I drink to keep from worryin' and I laugh to keep from cryin'.
Well, I drink to keep from worryin' and I laugh to keep from cryin'.
I keep a smile on my face so the public won't know my mind.

When a woman gets blue, she hangs her little head and cries.
When a woman gets blue, she hangs her little head and cries,
But when a man gets blue, he grabs him a train and rides.[3]

---

[3] The fact that whites borrowed heavily from the blues to create blues forms of their own is attested to by the history of this verse. Heard in countless black railroad blues, it is also the first verse in one of the most popular "blue yodels" of the enormously influential country singer Jimmie Rodgers. The impact of his "blue yodels," basically blues with mountain yodeling between each verse, made him at one time the most important country singer; and his blue yodels remain one of the most impressive examples of the interchange between the nonliterary cultures of blacks and whites in the South.

Whistle keeps on blowin' and I got my debts to pay.
Whistle keeps on blowin' and I got my debts to pay.
I got a mind to leave my baby, and I've got a mind to stay.

I got the hard luck blues, walkin' on down the line.
I got the hard luck blues, walkin' on down the line.
Maybe some day my gal will change her mind.

Rocks have been my pillow, baby, you know bare ground have been my bed.
Well, now, rocks have been my pillow, bare ground have been my bed.
You know I ain't got nowhere to lay my poor achin' head.

By definition the blues are another example of what W. E. B. Du Bois has called the spirituals—"sorrow songs." (See pp. 1762–66.) With one difference. The spirituals express the sorrow of the singer's earthly condition, but point to the "freedom" in the next world—or even in this. The blues can scarcely be said to point to any form of redemption.[4] Except, of course, the redemption from pain by the utterance of pain—from the blues by the creation of the "blues." That is, the redemption by art.

In the world of music the recognition of the blues as art is established. But waiving their value as musical art, we may assert that they represent a body of poetic art unique and powerful. The world they spring from is totally recreated—no, created, with its drama, comedy, pathos, and range of feeling. No body of folk poetry in America—except, perhaps, the black spirituals—can touch it, and much of the poetry recognized as "literature," white or black, seems tepid beside it.

[4] In fact, some of the blues invert the spirituals and proclaim their wicked worldliness, as with Texas Alexander:

> Take me out of this bottom before the high water rise.
> Take me out of this bottom before the high water rise.
> I ain't no Christian and I don't want to be baptized.
>
> I cried, "Lord, My Father, Thy Kingdom come."
> I cried, "Lord, My Father, Thy Kingdom come,
> Give me back my woman and my will be done."

Or when Bessie Smith sang her "Preachin' Blues":

> I ain't here to try to save your soul.
> I just want to teach you how to save your good jelly roll.
>   Well, sing 'em, sing 'em, sing them blues,
>   Let me convert your soul.

FURTHER READINGS

Chris Albertson, *Bessie* (1972)
————, *The Country Blues* (1959)
————, *The Poetry of the Blues* (1963)
Ralph Ellison, *Shadow and Act* (1964)
William Ferris, *Blues from the Delta* (1971)
W. C. Handy, *Father of the Blues* (1941)
————, with Abbe Niles, *A Treasury of the Blues* (1949)
Charles Keil, *Urban Blues* (1966)
Alan Lomax, *Mister Jelly Roll* (1950)
John Lomax, *Negro Songs As Sung by Leadbelly* (1936)

Paul Oliver, *Blues Fell This Morning* (1960)
————, *Conversation with the Blues* (1965)
————, *Savannah Syncopators* (1970)
————, *Screening the Blues* (1968)
————, *The Story of the Blues* (1969)
Eric Sackheim, *The Blues Line* (1969)
Eileen Southern, *The Music of Black Americans* (1971)
Errick Stewart-Baxter, *Ma Rainey and the Classic Blues Singers* (1970)
John T. Williams, *Jelly Roll Morton* (1963)

JELLY ROLL MORTON (1885–1941)

New Orleans was a great center for the development of black music, including blues and jazz. It was, in many ways, unlike any other American city. As a former French colony it had given more freedom to slaves, and a number of freedmen and their children, even in early days, had acquired wealth and position, including plantations, slaves, and a Paris education. Slaves had special privileges, too, being allowed, for example, to congregate for dancing to the music of the African drums, even though after 1817 the dancing was restricted to Congo Square, on Sunday, and later, for a short time, was prohibited entirely.[1] Other factors entered into the picture. After the Civil War, because of the mass breakup of Confederate army bands (plus the instruments procured from federal bands), even a poor black could get his hands on a horn. The city, too, was a place of festivity, as Jelly Roll Morton attests. And Bunk Johnson the trumpeter reports: "Even police horses—mounted police—their horses would prance. Music done them all the good in the world." Music was everywhere—connected with parties, dances, parades, funerals, and less decorous occasions in less decorous places. Even segregation, when it began to harden out in the 1890's, made its contribution to music. The "Downtown Creoles"—the class of *gen de couleur*, of mixed bloods, often almost white[2]—were forced into the world of the "Uptown Blacks," and here the musical training of the previously prosperous and privileged "Creoles" was blended with the black spirit of the countryside work song and holler and the dances of Congo Square.

Jelly Roll Morton, one of the great jazzmen (he claimed, in fact, that he had invented jazz, in 1902), knew the pre-jazz world of New Orleans, in all its color, violence, and musical variety.

[1] Such public African dancing and drumming continued up into the 1880's and could have been known to the early jazzmen.

[2] "Downtown Creoles" is a rather special use of the term Creole, for in New Orleans "Creole" ordinarily means one of French or Spanish blood.

From Jelly Roll Morton Remembers (1950)

. . . Those days I often used to like to stay with my godmother. She kept boxes of jewels in the house and I always had some kind of diamond on. Through her I came to be considered the best dresser, and this caused me to get my invitation to be an honorary member of the Broadway Swells when I was still in short pants. The members figured I was a smart kid, so, in order to beat the other clubs, they decided to display a kid as an aide.

"What do you think about it, kid?" they said, "Do you think you could get a horse—that would cost five dollars for the day? You'd have to have a streamer, too. But then you'd be an honorary member of the Broadway Swells."

I thought that was a swell idea and I personally accepted.

You see, New Orleans was very organization-minded. I have never seen such beautiful clubs as they had there—the Broadway Swells, the High Arts, the Orleans Aides, the Bulls and Bears, the Tramps, the Iroquois, the Allegroes —that was just a few of them, and those clubs would parade at least once a week. They'd have a great big band. The grand marshall would ride in front with his aides behind him, all with expensive sashes and streamers.

The members that could afford it would have a barrel of beer and plenty of sandwiches and a lot of whiskey and gin waiting at their houses. And, wherever these supplies would be, the parade would stage a grand salute. The grand marshall would lead his boys up one side of the street and down the other while the band played on the front steps. Then the boys would go inside and get their drinks and have a hell of a time.

The day I rode with the Broadway Swells my horse wasn't exactly up to the minute. I thought I should have a small horse since I wasn't nothing but a kid, and so the boys around that was jealous of me called my horse a goat and picked him up by his knees and hollered, "We can truck this horse on our back . . . You shouldn't be riding the horse. . . . he should be riding you." I got angry two or three times at the way my poor old pony was moving and I tried to beat him to death to show them that he could run fast. Until this day one of the things I feel most sorry for is the way I beat that poor horse.

Those parades were really tremendous things. The drums would start off, the trumpets and trombones rolling into something like Stars and Stripes or The National Anthem and everybody would strut off down the street, the bass-drum player twirling his beater in the air, the snare drummer throwing his sticks up and bouncing them off the ground, the kids jumping and hollering, the grand marshall and his aides in their expensive uniforms moving along dignified, women on top of women strutting along back of the aides and out in front of everybody—the second line, armed with sticks and bottles and baseball bats and all forms of ammunition ready to fight the foe when they reached the dividing line.

It's a funny thing that the second line marched at the head of the parade, but that's the way it had to be in New Orleans. They were our protection. You see, whenever a parade would get to another district the enemy would be waiting at the dividing line. If the parade crossed that line, it meant a fight, a terrible fight. The first day I marched a fellow was cut, must have been a hundred times. Blood was gushing out of him same as from one of the gushers in Yellowstone Park, but he never did stop fighting.

Well, if they'd have ten fights one Sunday, they didn't have many. Sometimes it would require a couple of ambulances to come around and pick up the people that was maybe cut or shot occasionally. This didn't happen all the time, but very seldom it didn't. The fact of it is, there was no parade at no time you couldn't find a knot on somebody's head where somebody got hit with a stick or something. And always plenty to eat and drink, especially for the men in the band, and with bands like Happy Galloway's, Manuel Perez's and Buddy Bolden's we had the best ragtime music in the world. There was so many jobs for musicians in these parades that musicians didn't ever like to leave New Orleans. They used to say, "This is the best town in the world. What's the use for me to go any other place?"

Now everybody in the world has heard about the New Orleans Mardi Gras, but maybe not about the Indians, one of the biggest feats that happened in Mardi Gras. Even at the parades with floats and costumes that cost millions, why, if the folks heard the sign of the Indians.

Ungai-ah
Ungai-ah!

—that big parade wouldn't have anybody there: the crowd would flock to see the Indians. When I was a child, I thought they really were Indians. They wore paint and blankets and, when they danced, one would get in the ring and throw his head back and downward, stooping over and bending his knees, making a rhythm with his heels and singing—T'ouwais, bas q'ouwais—and the tribe would answer—Ou tendais.

And they'd sing on—
T'ouwais, bas q'ouwais,
Ou tendais,

T'ouwais, bas q'ouwais,
Ou tendais.

And then they would stop for a minute, throw
back their heads and holler—

Ala caille-yo,
Ala caille wais . . .
Ouwais bas q'ouwais,
T'ouwais bas q'ouwais,
Ou tendais.

They would dance and sing and go on just like
regular Indians because they had the idea they
wanted to act just like the old Indians did in years
gone by and so they lived true to the traditions of
the Indian style. They went armed with fictitious
spears and tommyhawks and so forth and their
main object was to make their enemy bow. They
would send their spy-boys two blocks on ahead
—I happened to be a spy-boy myself once so I
know how this went—and when a spy-boy would
meet another spy from an enemy tribe he'd point
his finger to the ground and say, "Bow-wow." And
if they wouldn't bow, the spy-boy would use the
Indian call, "Woo-woo-woo-woo-woo," that was
calling the tribes—and, many a time, in these Indian things, there would be a killing and next day
there would be somebody in the morgue.

In New Orleans we would often wonder where a
dead person was located. At any time we heard
somebody was dead we knew we had plenty good
food that night. Those days I belonged to a quar-
tet and we specialized in spirituals for the purpose
of finding somebody that was dead, because the
minute we'd walk in, we'd be right in the kitchen
where the food was—plenty ham sandwiches and
cheese sandwiches slabbered all over with mustard
and plenty whiskey and plenty of beer. Of course,
the dead man would always be laid out in the
front and he'd be by himself most of the time
and couldn't hear nothing we would be saying at
all. He was dead and there was no reason for him
to be with us living people. And very often the
lady of the house would be back there with us
having a good time, too, because she would be
glad he was gone.

Then we would stand up and begin—

Nearer my God to thee

very slow and with beautiful harmony, thinking
about that ham—

Nearer to thee

Plenty of whiskey in the flask and all kinds of
crazy ideas in the harmony which made it impossible for anybody to jump in and sing. We'd
be sad, too, terribly sad.

Steal away, steal away,
Steal away home to Jesus.

I tell you we had beautiful numbers to sing at
those wakes.

Of course, as I told you, everybody in the City
of New Orleans was always organization minded,
which I guess the world knows, and a dead man
always belonged to several organizations—secret orders and so forth and so on. So when anybody
died, there was always a big band turned out on
the day he was supposed to be buried. Never
buried at night, always in the day and right in the
heart of the city. You could hear the band come up
the street taking the gentleman for his last ride,
playing different dead marches like *Flee as the
Bird to the Mountain.*

In New Orleans very seldom they would bury
them in the deep in the mud. They would always
bury um in a vault . . . So they would leave the
graveyard . . , the band would get ready to strike
up. They'd have a second line behind um, maybe
a couple of blocks long with baseball bats, axe
handles, knives, and all forms of ammunition to
combat some of the foe when they came to the
dividing lines. Then the band would get started
and you could hear the drums, rolling a deep, slow
rhythm. A few bars of that and then the snare
drummer would make a hot roll on his drums and
the boys in the band would just tear loose, while
second line swung down the street, singing . . .

Didn't he ramble?
He rambled.
Rambled all around,
In and out the town.
Didn't he ramble?
He rambled.
He rambled till the butchers cut him down.

That would be the last of the dead man. He's
gone and everybody came back home, singing. In
New Orleans they believed truly to stick right
close to the Scripture. That means rejoice at the
death and cry at the birth. . . .

Those boys I used to sing with were really tough
babies. They frequented the corners at Jackson and
Locust and nobody fooled with them. The police-

men was known never to cross Claiborne Avenue and these tough guys lived five blocks past Claiborne at Galvez, way back of town!

It was a miracle how those boys lived. They were sweet-back men, I suppose you'd call them—always a bunch of women running after them. I remember the Pickett boys—there was Bus, there was Nert, there was Nonny, there was Bob. Nert had a burned hand, which he used to wear a stocking over, and he was seemingly simple to me. All these boys wanted to have some kind of importance. They dressed very well and they were tremendous sports. It was nothing like spending money that ever worried their mind. If they didn't have it, somebody else would have it and spend it for them—they didn't care. But they all strived to have at least one Sunday suit, because, without that Sunday suit, you didn't have anything.

It wasn't the kind of Sunday suit you'd wear today. You was considered way out of line if your coat and pants matched. Many a time they would kid me, "Boy you must be from the country. Here you got trousers on the same as your suit."

These guys wouldn't wear anything but a blue coat and some kind of stripe in their trousers and those trousers had to be very, very tight. They'd fit um like a sausage. I'm telling you it was very seldom you could button the top button of a person's trousers those days in New Orleans. They'd leave the top button open and they wore very loud suspenders—of course they really didn't need suspenders, because the trousers was so tight and one suspender was always hanging down. If you wanted to talk to one of those guys he would find the nearest post, stiffen his arm out and hold himself as far away as possible from that post he's leaning on. That was to keep those fifteen, eighteen dollar trousers of his from losing their press.

You should have seen one of those sports move down the street, his shirt busted open so that you could discern his red flannel undershirt, walking along with a very mosey walk they had adopted from the river, called shooting the agate. When you shoot the agate, your hands is at your sides with your index fingers stuck out and you kind of struts with it. That was considered a big thing with some of the illiterate women—if you could shoot a good agate and had a nice highclass red undershirt with the collar turned up, I'm telling you were liable to get next to that broad. She liked that very much.

Those days, myself, I thought I would die unless I had a hat with the emblem Stetson in it

and some Edwin Clapp shoes. But Nert and Nonny and many of them wouldn't wear ready-made shoes. They wore what they called the St. Louis Flats and the Chicago Flats, made with cork soles and without heels and with gambler designs on the toes. Later on, some of them made arrangements to have some kind of electric-light bulbs in the toes of their shoes with a battery in their pockets, so when they would get around some jane that was kind of simple and thought they could make her, as they call making um, why they'd press a button in their pocket and light up the little bitty bulb in the toe of their shoes and that jane was claimed. It's really the fact.

Now these boys used to all have a sweet mama that worked in white people's yards. These were colored girls I'm talking about, but it applied to the white girls, too, of the poorer class. They all practically lived out in the same section together, because there was no such thing as segregation at all in that section—in fact nowhere in New Orleans at that time.

Well, every night these sports I'm talking about would even go as far as to meet their sweet mamas —sometimes they would brave it and walk to St. Charles Avenue where their sweet mamas were working; and sometimes it would be okay for them to go in and their sweet mamas would bring a pan out to the servant's room. Some of those pans were marvelous, I'm telling you—in fact I, myself, have been in some of the homes, seeking after a pan, and I know. Take a girl working for the Godchaux or the Solaris—she would bring you gumbo, Bayou cook oysters, and maybe turkey with cranberry sauce —this wouldn't have to be on Christmas, because New Orleans is the place where no doubt the finest food in the world prevails. When sweet mama cooks and carves that fowl, sweet papa is sure to eat the choicest portions, no argument about that!

I was quite small, but I used to get in on those pans occasionally. Always hanging out with older men, anyhow. And sometimes I'd be with um when they all get together—a whole lot of sweet mamas and their sweet papas—to have a little bit of a ball off to their self. Josky Adams would play the blues, . . .

See, see, rider, see what you have done,
You made me love you, now your man done
    come.

Josky had a beautiful sister and I always had it in my mind I wanted to marry her. Used to take her to these parties and had a wonderful time. It seemed like a family there—Josky playing and singing . . .

I want a gal that works in the white folks' yard,
A pretty gal that works in the white folks' yard.
Do you see that fly crawling up the wall,
She's going up there to get her ashes hauled.

But the one blues I never can forget out of those early days happened to be played by a woman that lived next door to my godmother's in the Garden District. The name of this musician was Mamie Desdoumes. Two middle fingers of her right hand had been cut off, so she played the blues with only three fingers on her right hand. She only knew this one tune and she played it all day long after she would first get up in the morning.

I stood on the corner, my feet was dripping
        wet,
I asked every man I met . . .
    Can't give me a dollar, give me a lousy dime,
    Just to feed that hungry man of mine. . . .

Although I had heard them previously I guess it was Mamie first really sold me on the blues.

Yes, "now you'll get a chance to see my red underwear!" that's what Joe used to say when he got going, with his stiff shirt bustin' on the stand, blowing for all he had, and his red undershirt showing. . . .

I have been robbed of three million dollars all told. Everyone today is playing my stuff and I don't even get credit. Kansas City style, Chicago style, New Orleans style—hell, they's all Jelly Roll style. I'm a busy man now and have to spend all my time dealing with attorneys, but I am not too busy to get around and hear jazz that I myself introduced twenty-five years ago, before most of the kids was even born. All this jazz I hear today is my own stuff, and, if I had been paid rightfully for my work, I would now have three million dollars more than I have now.

Not until 1926 did they get a faint idea of real jazz, when I decided to live in New York. In spite of the fact that there were a few great dispensers, as Sidney Bechet, clarinet, William Brand, bass, New York's idea of jazz was taken from the dictionary's definition—loud, blary, noisy, discordant tones, et cetera, which really doesn't spell jazz music. Music is music. Regardless of type, it is supposed to be soothing, not unbearable—which was a specialty with most of them. It is great to have ability from extreme to extreme, but it is terrible to have this kind of ability without the correct knowledge of how to use it. Very often you could hear the New York (supposed-to-be) jazz bands, have twelve-fifteen men; they would blaze away with all the volume they had. Sometimes customers would have to hold their ears to protect their eardrums from a forced collision with their brains. Later, in the same tune, without notification, you could hear only drums and trumpet. Piano and guitar would be going but not heard. The others would be holding their instruments leisurely, talking, smoking reefers, chatting scandals, et cetera.

Musicians of all nationalities watched the way I played; then soon I could hear my material everywhere I trod, but in an incorrect way, using figures behind a conglomeration of variations sometimes discordant, instead of hot-swing melodies.

W. C. HANDY (1873–1958)

For years, W. C. Handy was known as the "Father of the Blues"—a title based on the fact that his "Memphis Blues" was the first published music in blues form to attract wide attention. The son of a middle-class Tennessee preacher, he ran off to play the cornet in black minstrel shows; he freely admitted having picked up the blues form from rural singers in Clarksdale, Mississippi. The lyrics of his famous "St. Louis Blues" reflect this fact; they are a masterful arrangement of blues verses that were common in Mississippi at the turn of the century.

Although the "St. Louis Blues" in its published form occasionally seems overcomposed and somewhat condescending toward the black idiom (for example, "Doggone it!"), it quickly became one of the most widely sung of composed blues, one that when sung by greats like Bessie Smith could reach the heights of blues feeling. The following version is taken from *A Treasury of the Blues* (1949); the music as well as the lyrics were written by W. C. Handy.

St. Louis Blues

I hate to see de evenin' sun go down.
Hate to see de evenin' sun go down,
Cause my baby, he done lef dis town.

Feelin' tomorrow lak Ah feel today.
Feel tomorrow lak Ah feel today,
I'll pack my trunk, make ma get away.

St. Louis woman wid her diamon' rings
Pulls dat man roun' by her apron strings.
'Twant for powder an' for store bought hair
De man I love would not gone nowhere.

Chorus:
   Got de St. Louis Blues jes as blue as Ah can be
   Dat man got a heart lak a rock cast in the sea—
   Or else he wouldn't have gone so far from me.
      Doggone it!

I loves dat man lak a school boy loves his pie
Lak a Kentucky Col'nel loves his mint an' rye—
I'll love ma baby till the day Ah die. Doggone it!

A black headed gal make a freight train jump
   the track
Said a black headed gal make a freight train
   jump the track—
But a long tall gal makes a preacher ball the
   Jack. Doggone it!

Lawd a blonde headed woman makes a good
   man leave the town
I said blonde headed woman makes a good man
   leave the town—
But a red head woman makes a boy slap his
   papa down. Doggone it!

Oh, ashes to ashes and dust to dust
I said ashes to ashes and dust to dust—
If my blues don't get you my jazzing must.[1]
   Doggone it!

[1] Of the five choruses, only the first two are usually sung. Bessie Smith sang the song as follows:

Been to de Gypsy to get ma fortune tole.
To de Gypsy done got ma fortune tole,
'Cause I'm most wile 'bout ma Jelly Roll.

Gypsy done tole me "don't you wear no black."
Yes she done tole me "don't you wear no black."
Go to St. Louis, you can win him back.

Help me to Cairo make St. Louis by maself
Get to Cairo find ma ole friend Jeff,
Gwine to pin ma self close to his side
If ah flag his train I sho' can ride.

You ought to see dat stovepipe brown of mine
Lak he owns de Dimon Joseph line.
He'd make a cross eyed o' man go stone blind.

Blacker than midnight, teeth lak flags of truce
Blackest man in de whole Louis
Blacker de berry sweeter is the juice.

About a crap game he knows a pow'ful lot
But when work-time comes he's on de dot
Gwine to ask him for a cold ten spot
What it takes to get it he's cert'nly got.

I hate to see that evening sun go down
I hate to see that evening sun go down.
Makes me think I'm on my last go round.

Feeling tomorrow like I feel today
Feeling tomorrow like I feel today,
I'm gonna pack my grip, and make my getaway

St. Louis woman with her diamond rings
Pulls my man around by her apron strings,
'Twant for powder and store bought hair
The man I love wouldn't go nowhere.

I've got the St. Louis Blues just as blue as I can be
He's got a heart like a stone cast in the sea
Else he wouldn't have gone so far from me.

MA RAINEY (1886–1939)

Though not the first to record, Gertrude "Ma" Rainey was the first and perhaps the greatest of the woman "classic blues" singers of the twenties. She began her career in 1900, a fourteen-year-old prodigy. Although her repertoire was at first dominated by the vaudeville numbers that were standard in the minstrel shows and circuses in which she traveled, she began to sing blues onstage in 1902; by 1914 she and her husband were billed as "Rainey and Rainey, Assassinators of the Blues" in Tolliver's Circus and Musical Extravaganza. With her act, Ma Rainey toured the T.O.B.A. (Theater Owners' Booking Association, more commonly known as Tough On Black Artists) black musical circuit, personally spreading her blues through the South, until 1924, when a Paramount advertisement in Chicago loudly announced: "Discovered at Last—'Ma Rainey,' Mother of the Blues!" Her records reveal her deep, gravelly voice as a perfect instrument for a blues that always remained powerfully connected with their rougher, rural origins.

Yonder Comes the Blues

I worry all day, I worry all night,
Everytime my man comes home he wants to fuss
   and fight,
When I pick up the paper to try to read the news,
Just when I'm satisfied, yonder comes the blues.

I went down to the river each and every day,
Trying to keep from throwing myself away.

I walked and I walked 'till I wore out my shoes,
I can't walk no further, yonder comes the blues.

People have the different blues and think they're
   mighty sad,
But blues about a man the worst I ever had.
I been disgusted and all confused,
Every time I look around, yonder comes the blues.

BLIND LEMON JEFFERSON (1897–1930)

Blind Lemon Jefferson was the first great male rural bluesman to record. Blind from birth, fat and unattractive, his guitar playing and high moaning singing enabled him to keep alive by playing at country dances, bars, and barrelhouses through east Texas. Many later famous singers, like Leadbelly and John White, learned their blues style while serving as lead boys for Blind Lemon. Others, like B. B. King, were heavily influenced by the records which Blind Lemon began making in 1925 and which continued to be popular until the winter of 1929–30, when, after a boozy rent party, Blind Lemon froze to death on a Chicago street, unable to find his way through the heavy snow.

Easy Rider Blues

Now tell me where my easy rider gone
Tell me where my easy rider gone
I need one of these women always in the wrong

Well, easy rider, standing on the road
And it's easy rider standing on the road
I'm a poor blind man, ain't got no where to go

It's gonna be the time when a woman don't need
    no man
Well it's gonna be a time when a woman don't
    need no man
Then, baby, shut your mouth: it's gonna be raising
    sand

The train I ride don't burn no coal at all
Train I ride don't burn no coal at all
The coal house burner: everybody's snapping
    cannonballs

I went to the depot
I mean I went to the depot and set my pistol down
The blues overtake me and tears come rolling down

The woman I love, she must be out of town
Woman I love, man she's out of town
She left me this morning with a face that's travel
    bound

I got a gal 'cross town, she crochets all the time
I got a gal 'cross town, crochets all the time
Baby, if you don't quit crocheting, you gonna lose
    your mind

Goodbye brown, what's the matter now
Goodbye brown, what's the matter now
You turn your back to quit me: woman, and you
    don't know how

LEADBELLY (1885–1949)

The origin and life of the blues have always been tangled with the railroad and the prison farm. In Texas, in particular, huge gangs of blacks worked long days on great state sugar plantations; work songs were a powerful influence on the early development of the blues in Texas.

"The Midnight Special" developed from the same prison roots as did the Texas blues. In the process of development, however, the song was decisively influenced by white ballad forms; indeed, in various different versions it has been recorded by white as well as black convicts across the South.

The "Midnight Special" itself was a part of southern convicts' mythology; according to their legend, if the light from a passing train fell across a prisoner's bars at midnight, he would be set free in the morning.

The song as printed here is transcribed from the singing of Huddie Ledbetter ("Leadbelly"). Whether or not Leadbelly was ever freed from prison by the light of a midnight train is now a moot question; the facts we actually know of his life surpass even such myths. After escaping a first prison sentence in Louisiana by picking up the iron ball about his leg and taking off across

the fields, Leadbelly was imprisoned twice more: first, in Texas, on a charge of murder; then, in Louisiana, for assault with intent to murder. Both times, however, his art intervened: Leadbelly was released by the state governors (governors Pat Neff of Texas and O. K. Allen of Louisiana) after singing them personalized pardon pleas.

Leadbelly was brought from Louisiana's Angola Prison Farm to New York by John Lomax, in 1934. Billed as the "King of the Twelve String Guitar," his legend, his musical prowess, and his mixed repertoire of blues, hollers, prison songs, and ballads made him an instant success in the North. The pride and rebelliousness inherent in both the legend and the real person (he told Lomax that he was "de best, de lead-row man at everything I tries to do") helped make him a natural hero, who had a special appeal for leftists. As Woody Guthrie, the left-wing Dust Bowl balladeer, wrote: "I saw you make just as much of an applause for Leadbelly as for your other leaders, and the thing that you applauded in him was pure personal fighting power."

Leadbelly's success is particularly important

in that it marked the first sustained white, urban interest in black blues; as such, it was the beginning of the decisive blues influence that was to form the white folk-rock-blues music of the 1960's.

The Midnight Special ©

Well, you wake up in the mornin', hear the ding dong ring,
You go a-marchin' to the table, see the same damn thing.
Well, it's on a one table, knife a, fork, an' a pan,
An' if you say anything about it, you're in trouble with the man.

Chorus:
Let the Midnight Special shine its light on me,
Let the Midnight Special shine its ever-lovin' light on me.

If you go to Houston, you better walk right;
You better not stagger, you better not fight,
Or Sheriff Benson will arrest you, he will carry you down.
If the jury finds you guilty, you'll be penitentiary-bound.

Yonder comes li'l Rosie. How in the worl' do you know?

I can tell her by her apron and the dress she wo',
Umberella on her shoulder, piece o' paper in her han'.
Well, I heard her tell the captain: "I want my man."

I'm gwine away to leave you, an' my time ain't long.
The man is gonna call me an' I'm a-goin' home.
Then I'll be done all my grievin', whoopin', holl'in', an' a-cryin',
Then I'll be done all my studyin' 'bout my great long time.

Well, the biscuits on the table, just as hard as any rock.
If you try to swallow them, break a convict's heart.
My sister wrote a letter, my mother wrote a card—
"If you want to come an' see us, you'll have to ride the rods."

BESSIE SMITH (1895–1937)

The most distinguished of the many singers who served their blues apprenticeships with Ma Rainey's act was Bessie Smith. From 1923, when Columbia Records brought her North from an Atlanta hip-shaking show, until 1930, when the Depression destroyed the market for "race records" (as all black artists' recordings were known), she reigned as the undisputed "Empress of the Blues." What earned her that title was a style that went beyond her predecessors in creating a genuine city blues; unlike Ma Rainey, for instance, she was most comfortable singing to the accompaniment of such leading jazz musicians as Louis Armstrong, Fletcher Henderson, Charlie Green and Clarence Williams. The lyrics of her songs were also more city-oriented, often treating such traditional blues subjects as a lover's desertion with images and puns that were as unmistakably and energetically sexual as those of the "Empty Bed Blues."

Bessie Smith's synthesis of rural blues and urban sophistication had a deep influence not only on blues singers, but also on such jazz singers as Billie Holliday, who continued to be popular long after the Depression had overwhelmed the great women singers of the classic blues.

Empty Bed Blues

I woke up this morning with an awful aching head,
I woke up this morning with an awful aching head,
My new man had left me just a room and an
    empty bed.

Bought me a coffee grinder, got the best one I
    could find,
Bought me a coffee grinder, got the best one I
    could find,
So he could grind me coffee, cause he had a brand
    new grind.

He's a deep-sea diver with a stroke that can't go
    wrong,
He's a deep-sea diver with a stroke that can't go
    wrong,
He can touch the bottom, and his wind holds out
    so long.

He knows how to thrill me, and he thrills me
    night and day,
He knows how to thrill me, and he thrills me
    night and day,
He's got a new way of loving, almost takes my
    breath away.

He's got that sweet something, and I told my gal-
    friend Lou,
He's got that sweet something, and I told my gal-
    friend Lou,
Cause the way she's raving, she must have gone
    and tried it too.

When my bed gets empty, makes me feel awful
    mean and blue,

When my bed gets empty, makes me feel awful
    mean and blue,
'Cause my springs getting rusty, sleepin' single the
    way I do.

Bought him a blanket, pillow for his head at night,
Bought him a blanket, pillow for his head at night,
Then I bought him a mattress so he could lay just
    right.

He came home one evening with his fair head way
    up high,
He came home one evening with his fair head way
    up high,
What he had to give me made me wring my hands
    and cry.

He give me a lesson that I never had before,
He give me a lesson that I never had before,
When he got through teaching me, from my el-
    bows down was sore.

He boiled my first cabbage, and he made it awful
    hot,
He boiled my first cabbage, and he made it awful
    hot,
Then he put in the bacon and it overflowed the
    pot.

When you get good lovin' never go and spread
    the news,
When you get good lovin' never go and spread
    the news,
They'll double-cross you and leave you with them
    empty bed blues.

ROBERT JOHNSON (c. 1898–1937)

Robert Johnson was a Mississippi Delta bluesman of the 1930's who sang a blues that was
tense and exciting both musically and poetically.
While still a teenager, he mastered the guitar
techniques of earlier Delta bluesmen, after
which he began a brief career playing in the
whisky-soaked and frequently violent juke-joints
and dance halls where a rural blues singer
might earn a meager living. As his lyrics reveal,
Johnson was driven by a sexual desire that was
painfully tangled with a sense of inevitable betrayal. Translated into wanderlust, this drive led
Johnson far from the Delta, to St. Louis, Chicago, and San Antonio; far from home, a brief
and bungled affair led to his death at the hands
of a wronged lover.

Though his career was brief, Johnson's influence has been substantial. The rhythmic drive

that characterized his music was the pivot point upon which such other Mississippi-born bluesmen as Muddy Waters later transformed the Mississippi blues into postwar Chicago rhythm and blues. Even today, among white rock groups, Johnson's blues remain a vital source of fresh ideas, as the success of the Rolling Stones' recording of "Love in Vain" illustrates.

Love in Vain

I followed her to the station, with her suitcase in
    my hand.
And I followed her to the station, with her suitcase
    in my hand.
Well, it's hard to tell, it's hard to tell, when all
    your love's in vain,
    All my love's in vain.

When the train rolled up to the station, I looked
    her in the eye.
When the train rolled up to the station, I looked
    her in the eye.

Well I was lonesome, I felt so lonesome, and I
    could not help but cry.
    All my love's in vain.

When the train left the station, with two lights on
    behind,
When the train left the station, with two lights on
    behind,
Well the blue light was my blues, and the red
    light was my mind.
    All my love's in vain.

Stones in My Passway

I got stones in my passway
    and my road seem dark as night
I got stones in my passway
    and my road seem dark as night
I have pains in my heart
    they have taken my appetite

I have a bird to whistle
    and I have a bird to sing
I have a bird to whistle
    and I have a bird to sing
I got a woman that I'm loving,
    boy, but she don't mean a thing

My innocence betrayed me
    have overtaken poor Bob at last
My innocence betrayed me
    have overtaken poor Bob at last

And that's one thing certain,
    they have stones all in my pass

Now you trying to take my life
And all my loving too
You laid a passway for me
Now what are you trying to do
I'm crying please, please let us be friends,
And when you hear me howling in my passway,
    rider,
    please open your door and let me in

I got three legs to truck on,
    boys, please don't block my road
I got three legs to truck on,
    boys, please don't block my road
I been feeling ashame' 'bout my rider,
    babe, I'm booked and I got to go

Intellectual Background

From the very beginning, as we have noted on earlier pages, the American has been moved to inquire into his identity and to try to define what Americanism really means. With the twentieth century that urge has intensified rather than lessened. Fairly early in this century we began to get such full-dress inquiries as *Civilization in the United States: An Inquiry by Thirty Americans* (edited by Harold Stearns, 1922).[1]

The thirty wrote as specialists on such diverse topics as the city, journalism, education, science, the family, and the literary life. Their particular appraisals of these matters today do not seem very profound and we shall not be concerned with them here. But the earnestness of their attempts to assess life in America and the spirit in which they wrote are worth noting. The seriousness with which they took themselves evidently piqued and amused George Santayana, some of whose comments on these essays are printed below.[2]

Santayana can be particularly helpful here. In the first place, the present reader is already acquainted with his general position and with the standards to which he appeals. In the second place, it is always useful in discussing matters in which most Americans are closely and emotionally involved to get the views of an intelligent and extremely well-informed "outsider" who, though he lived for many years in America, remained to the end committed to the "Mediterranean" culture of his parents' homeland. Here is an extract from "Marginal Notes on *Civilization in the United States.*" (The reader should note that the essay is presented, as its title indicates, as a series of

---

[1] Stearns was to come back to the topic with two more volumes on the subject: *Rediscovering America* (1934), and *America: A Re-Appraisal* (1937).

[2] These comments were first published as an essay in the *Dial* (June, 1922). In 1967 this essay was included in *George Santayana's America*, edited by James Ballowe.

comments in the book edited by Stearns, thus the "title page," etc., referred to are those of the Stearns book.)

Title Page

What is Civilization? Porcelain bath-tubs, et cetera? Fine art? Free thought? Virtue, Peace? Peace, virtue, and free thought might exist in Arcadia or in the Islands of the Blest, neither of which would be called exactly civilized. Civilized means citified, trained, faithful to some regimen deliberately instituted. Civilization might be taken as a purely descriptive term, like *Kultur*, rather than as a eulogistic one; it might simply indicate the possession of instruments, material and social, for accomplishing all sorts of things, whether those things were worth accomplishing or not. If we insist on taking civilization as a term of praise, we must mean by it something like institutions making for the highest happiness; and what such happiness is could not be defined without plunging into moral philosophy, in which no two persons would agree.

Contents

The list of the thirty American authors of this book, and the three foreigners, makes me tremble. I know a good many of them and some (though this is not the moment to boast of it) have been my pupils. I foresee that I am to hear the plaints of superior and highly critical minds, suffering from maladaptation; and that I shall learn more about their palpitating doubts than about America or about civilization. Nevertheless, as they are a part of America—although they may forget to give America credit for having produced them—I shall be learning something about America after all; and if their strictures upon their country sadden me, I can always comfort myself with a fact which they may be too modest to notice; namely, that civilization can't be at a low ebb where thirty such spirits can be brought together in a jiffy, by merely whistling for them.

Preface [written by Harold Stearns]

"As long ago as the autumn of last year . . . we wished to take advantage of the strategic situation . . . decided . . . by majority vote . . . to be good-natured and . . . urbane. . . . No martyrs, and no one who was merely disgruntled. . . . Slow and careful selection . . . of like-minded men and women

. . . in common defense against . . . reaction." Quite as I thought. Indignation at the powers that be is a frequent source of eloquence in Europe; I have not known it before in America on this scale. I shall be all ears.

Page vi. "*There is a sharp dichotomy between preaching and practice; we let not our right hand know what our left hand doeth. . . . The moral code resolves itself into . . . fear of what people will say.*" I see the fact which Mr. Stearns points to here, but not as he sees it. The American conscience is not insincere, it is only belated, inapplicable. The sanctities are traditional; sentiment preserves and requires the habits and language of an elder age; it has all the sincerity of instinct. But it does not exactly fit the exigencies of public life, which has been transformed and accelerated in a way which conscience can't keep up with, yet is dazzled by and has not the heart to condemn; for it has to keep house, as it were, with an obstreperous younger brother, the conscience of emancipated human nature, with its new set of illusions and its pride in its thundering, pushing life.[3] The American intellect is shy and feminine; it paints nature in water-colours; whereas the sharp masculine eye sees the world as a moving-picture—rapid, dramatic, vulgar, to be glanced at and used merely as a sign of what is going to happen next. Mere man in America hardly has an articulate logic in which to express his practical convictions, and I doubt if even this book will supply the want. I won't say that it is itself genteel; that would enrage its revolutionary authors too much; they may have forgotten that Emerson and Thoreau and Brook Farm were revolutionary. But if not genteel and not specifically American, the spirit of these critics is one of offended sensibility. Things shock them; and their compensatory ideals and plans of reform are fetched from abstract reflection or irrelevant enthusiasms. They are far from expressing the manly heart of America, emancipated from the genteel tradition. They seem to be morally underfed, and they are disaffected.

In his essay "The Genteel Tradition in American Philosophy," Santayana defined Calvinism as "an expression of the agonized conscience." As the sense of sin evaporated, Calvinism "lost its basis in American life." What was left was a cluster of values and emotions that had been the appropriate expression of the agonized conscience, but now, lacking any moral and intellectual underpinning, had become a mere sentimental habit of mind.

As a philosopher, Santayana knew that a mere habit of mind was not good enough: America needed a morality based on something in which it

[3] Santayana seems to be far more aware than are Stearns and his contributors of the gap which existed between them as intellectuals and the mass of the American people. The "feminine" intellect of which Santayana goes on to speak is that of the genteel tradition with which he rather quietly identifies Stearns and his friends.

really believed. Where might one look for it? Irving Babbitt, one of Santayana's former Harvard colleagues, had made a strenuous attempt to put the Puritan ethic on a sounder intellectual basis. But his reasoning and methods could not have had much appeal to a philosopher as skeptical as Santayana, nor one so antipathetic to the whole Protestant tradition. (In fact, they did not have much appeal to many Americans of native background.)

The impolite and anti-Puritanic H. L. Mencken represented a different sort of intellectual force. He was obviously much closer to the "manly heart of America"—to use Santayana's terms—than professors like Babbitt, and more so than Stearns's other contributors. Yet though Santayana might credit Mencken with "the sharp masculine eye," he could hardly have regarded him as a sensitive and highly civilized mind. To Mencken's masculine eye, the American scene appeared "rapid, dramatic, vulgar." But these terms also describe pretty well the qualities of Mencken's own style. It was lively, boisterous, and strident—even occasionally "vulgar," for Mencken believed in fighting the devil with his own fire, using a certain vulgarity to deal with American vulgarity.

Yet in making a survey of the intellectual situation in America just after the First World War, it will be useful to begin with a typical Mencken tirade against America's crass vulgarity and then to look at a pronouncement by his antithesis, Irving Babbitt. By using the two as antithetical points of reference, we may readily get some kind of view of how the intellectual situation appeared to less sharply opposed thinkers and a notion of what areas of common agreement might be said to exist for American intellectuals of the early 1920's.

The most obvious fact is that for both Mencken and Babbitt a Puritanism in decay presented the immediate problem with which the intellectual of the period had to start, though Mencken's solution was to bulldoze away what was left of it and push on into the bracing air of a post-Christian Nietzschean world, whereas Babbitt was concerned to see what could be done, if anything, to rehabilitate the native tradition. Babbitt, with his strong intellectual and emotional grip on the tradition—Eastern as well as Western, for he was a great scholar in Buddhism and the oriental cultures—believed that there lay ahead not a bracing air but the killing blasts of Naturalism.

H. L. MENCKEN (1880–1956)

Henry Louis Mencken began his career as a reporter on the Baltimore *Herald*. In 1908 he became literary editor of the *Smart Set* and in 1935 founded the *American Mercury*. He berated American culture as second-rate: it lacked an aristocracy of talent and taste; it was in fact dominated by the "booboisie"; and it was fettered by the anachronistic beliefs of the Fundamentalists of the Bible Belt.

The yardstick by which Mencken measured the inadequacies of American culture was, like Santayana's, European—though Mencken's yardstick had an evident German calibration. Mencken had read his Nietzsche and had taken to heart Nietzsche's indictment of a Christianity gone soft. Yet he was not so much appalled as amused at what he saw in America. He regarded, or affected to regard, the spectacle as hilarious and developed a lively style in which to express his contemptuous delight in what he saw. Someone has characterized that style as filled with "the merry clatter of tumbrils hauling boobs off to the guillotine." His successive volumes of denunciation were frankly labeled *Prejudices*, and they are just that—biased judgments—but "judgments" delivered with gusto by one who liked to think of himself as the "bad boy of American letters."

Mencken, writing as one of Stearns's contributors, calls the average Congressman "not only incompetent and imbecile, but also incurably dishonest" and insists that his intelligence is that of a "country-newspaper-editor" and his "standards of honesty those of a country banker."

Such observations remind one of Mark Twain's jibes in *The Gilded Age*. (See p. 1271.) For his part, Santayana quietly wonders: "Isn't democracy built on the experience and conviction that superior people are dangerous, and that the instinct of the common people is a safer guide?"

Though convinced that Congress is stupid and probably a passel of knaves, the average American is nevertheless certain that Congressmen ought to be intelligent and selfless statesmen. Consequently, he may be disposed to dismiss Santayana's comment as cynical and subversively un-American. In any case, the average literate American may possibly be puzzled at Santayana's parting shot at Mencken: "But what surprises me [in Mencken's diatribe at Congress] more than [his] disbelief in democracy, is this hatred of the country-side. Is agriculture the root of evil? Naturally, the first rays of the sun must strike the east side of New York, but do they never travel beyond?" This last observation is shrewd and telling, for at some time after the Civil War, with the rise of big industry and finance-capitalism, a great many Americans, literate and illiterate, did begin to hold the countryside in contempt. "Rube," "hayseed," and "hick" were in their day peculiarly American terms. They reflect a disparagement that was special and characteristic but which few without a European orientation would catch. In this prejudice Mencken turns out to be as American as anybody.

BIOGRAPHICAL CHART

1880 Born, September 12, in Baltimore, Maryland
1906 Joins staff of the Baltimore *Sun*
1908 Becomes an editor of the *Smart Set*
1917 *A Book of Prefaces*
1918 *The American Language* (4th ed., 1936; supplements, 1945 and 1948)
1919 First volume of *Prejudices*
1924 With George Jean Nathan founds the *American Mercury*
1926 *Notes on Democracy*
1927 Sixth and last volume of *Prejudices*
1933 Withdraws from the *Mercury*
1956 Dies, January 29

FURTHER READINGS

There is no standard edition of Mencken's works. Individual titles are listed in the biographical chart.

Days of H. L. Mencken (1947; 3 vols.; autobiographical)
Guy J. Forgue, ed., *The Letters of H. L. Mencken* (1961)
Charles Augoff, *H. L. Mencken: A Portrait from Memory* (1956)

Marius Bewley, *The Complex Fate* (1952)
Carrol Frey, *Bibliography of the Writings of H. L. Mencken* (1924)
William Manchester, *Disturber of the Peace: The Life and Riotous Times of H. L. Mencken* (1951)

From Prejudices: Second Series (1920)

FROM THE NATIONAL LETTERS

The current scene is surely depressing enough. What one observes is a literature in three layers, and each inordinately doughy and uninspiring—each almost without flavor or savor. It is hard to say, with much critical plausibility, which layer deserves to be called the upper, but for decorum's sake the choice may be fixed upon that which meets with the approval of the reigning Lessings.[1] This is the layer of the novels of the late Howells,[2] Judge Grant, Alice Brown and the rest of the dwindling survivors of New England *Kultur*, of the brittle, academic poetry of Woodberry and the elder Johnson, of the tea-party essays of Crothers, Miss Repplier and company,[3] and of the solemn, highly judicial, coroner's inquest criticism of More, Brownell,[4] Babbitt and their imitators.

Here we have manner, undoubtedly. The thing is correctly done; it is never crude or gross; there is in it a faint perfume of college-town society. But when this highly refined and attenuated manner is allowed for what remains is next to nothing. One never remembers a character in the novels of these aloof and de-Americanized Americans; one never encounters an idea in their essays; one never carries away a line out of their poetry. It is literature as an academic exercise for talented grammarians, almost as a genteel recreation for ladies and gentlemen of fashion—the exact equivalent, in the field of letters, of eighteenth-century painting and German *Augenmusik*.[5]

What ails it, intrinsically, is a dearth of intellectual audacity and of aesthetic passion. Running through it, and characterizing the work of almost every man and woman producing it, there is an unescapable suggestion of the old Puritan suspicion of the fine arts as such—of the doctrine that they offer fit asylum for good citizens only when some ulterior and superior purpose is carried into them. This purpose, naturally enough, most commonly shows a moral tinge. The aim of poetry, it appears,

[1] Gotthold Ephraim Lessing (1729–1781), German dramatist and critic, author of a celebrated work on aesthetics, *Laokoon* (1766). The Lessings to whom Mencken refers would thus be the reigning arbiters of taste, the meaning reinforced by the fact that Irving Babbitt, one of the "Lessings," in fact was the author of a book called *The New Laokoön*.

[2] See pp. 1341–71.

[3] Mencken refers here to several minor novelists and poets of the period. Robert Grant (1852–1940) was the author of *Unleavened Bread* (1900) and *The Chippendales* (1909), among other novels. Alice Brown (1857–1948) was a New England novelist, author of *Meadow Grass* (1895), *Country Neighbors* (1910), and *Children of Earth* (1915). George Woodberry (1855–1930) wrote *North Shore Watch* (1890), *Wild Eden* (1899), and *Ideal Passion* (1917), a collection of sonnets. Robert Woodward Johnson (1853–1937) was a poet who wrote a rather stiff, formal verse. Samuel McChord Crothers (1857–1927) was the author of *The Gentle Reader* (1903). Agnes Repplier (1855–1930) wrote a number of volumes of informal essays.

[4] Paul Elmer More (1864–1937), critic, essayist,

friend of Irving Babbitt, and prominent among the New Humanists; William Crary Brownell (1851–1928), editor for Charles Scribner's Sons and critic.

[5] A term, literally translated as "eye music," which was coined by German music historians of the nineteenth century to describe the practice, popular during the musical Renaissance of the sixteenth century, of having the appearance of the printed musical score correspond to the idea or subject of the melody. For example, descent into a valley might be indicated by notes descending on the page. Clearly such a technique would be the equivalent of the type of "academic exercise" Mencken disparages.

is to fill the mind with lofty thoughts—not to give it joy, but to give it a grand and somewhat gaudy sense of virtue. The essay is a weapon against the degenerate tendencies of the age. The novel, properly conceived, is a means of uplifting the spirit; its aim is to inspire, not merely to satisfy the low curiosity of man in man. The Puritan, of course, is not entirely devoid of aesthetic feeling. He has a taste for good form; he responds to style; he is even capable of something approaching a purely aesthetic emotion. But he fears this aesthetic emotion as an insinuating distraction from his chief business in life: the sober consideration of the all-important problem of conduct. Art is a temptation, a seduction, a Lorelei, and the Good Man may safely have traffic with it only when it is broken to moral uses—in other words, when its innocence is pumped out of it, and it is purged of gusto. It is precisely this gusto that one misses in all the work of the New England school, and in all the work of the formal schools that derive from it. One observes in such a fellow as Dr. Henry Van Dyke[6] an excellent specimen of the whole clan. He is, in his way, a genuine artist. He has a hand for pretty verses. He wields a facile rhetoric. He shows, in indiscreet moments, a touch of imagination. But all the while he remains a sound Presbyterian, with one eye on the devil. He is a Presbyterian first and an artist second, which is just as comfortable as trying to be a Presbyterian first and a chorus girl second. To such a man it must inevitably appear that a Molière, a Wagner, a Goethe or a Shakespeare was more than a little bawdy.

The criticism that supports this decaying caste of literary Brahmins is grounded almost entirely upon ethical criteria. You will spend a long while going through the works of such typical professors as More, Phelps, Boynton, Burton, Perry, Brownell and Babbitt[7] before ever you encounter a purely aesthetic judgment upon an aesthetic question. It is almost as if a man estimating daffodils should do it in terms of artichokes. Phelps' whole body of "we church-goers" criticism—the most catholic and tolerant, it may be said in passing, that the faculty can show—consists chiefly of a plea for correctness, and particularly for moral correctness; he never gets very far from "the axiom of the moral law." Brownell argues eloquently for standards that would bind an imaginative author as tightly as a Sunday-school superintendent is bound by the Ten Commandments and the Mann Act. Sherman[8] tries to save Shakespeare for the right-thinking by proving that he was an Iowa Methodist—a member of his local Chamber of Commerce, a contemner of Reds, an advocate of democracy and the League of Nations, a patriotic dollar-a-year-man during the Armada scare. Elmer More devotes himself, year in and year out, to denouncing the Romantic movement, *i.e.*, the effort to emancipate the artist from formulae and categories, and so make him free to dance with arms and legs. And Babbitt, to make an end, gives over his days and his nights to deploring Rousseau's anarchistic abrogation of "the veto power" over the imagination, leading to such "wrongness" in both art and life that it threatens "to wreck civilization." In brief, the alarms of schoolmasters. Not many of them deal specifically with the literature that is in being. It is too near to be quite nice. To More or Babbitt only death can atone for the primary offense of the artist. But what they preach nevertheless has its echoes contemporaneously, and those echoes, in the main, are woefully falsetto. I often wonder what sort of picture of These States is conjured up by foreigners who read, say, Crothers, Van Dyke, Babbitt, the later Winston Churchill,[9] and the old maids of the Freudian suppression school. How can such a foreigner, moving in those damp, asthmatic mists, imagine such phenomena as Roosevelt, Billy Sunday, Bryan, the Becker case, the I.W.W., Newport, Palm Beach, the University of Chicago, Chicago itself—the whole, gross, glittering, excessively dynamic, infinitely grotesque, incredibly stupendous drama of American life?

As I have said, it is not often that the *ordentlichen*[10] *Professoren* deign to notice contemporary writers, even of their own austere kidney. In all the Shelburne Essays[11] there is none on Howells, or on

---

[6] Henry Van Dyke (1852–1933), professor of literature at Princeton and author of essays, stories, and poems.

[7] More taught at Princeton; William Lyon Phelps (1865–1943) at Yale; Percy H. Boynton (1875–1946) at the University of Chicago; Richard Burton (1861–1940) at the University of Minnesota; Thomas Sargent Perry (1865–1929) at Harvard and in Japan; and Babbitt at Harvard.

[8] Stuart Sherman (1881–1926), English professor, author, and editor. He was willing to enter the ring with Mencken with no holds barred.

[9] Winston Churchill (1871–1947), a popular American novelist, author of historical romances.

[10] "Ordentlichen Professoren" might colloquially be translated as "sure-enough Professors," the recognized authorities.

[11] By Paul Elmer More.

Churchill, or on Mrs. Wharton; More seems to think of American literature as expiring with Longfellow and Donald G. Mitchell.[12] He has himself hinted that in the department of criticism of criticism there enters into the matter something beyond mere aloof ignorance. "I soon learned (as editor of the pre-Bolshevik *Nation*)," he says, "that it was virtually impossible to get fair consideration for a book written by a scholar not connected with a university from a reviewer so connected." This class-consciousness, however, should not apply to artists, who are admittedly inferior to professors, and it surely does not show itself in such men as Phelps and Spingarn, who seem to be very eager to prove that they are not professorial. Yet Phelps, in the course of a long work on the novel, pointedly omits all mention of such men as Dreiser, and Spingarn, as the aforesaid Brooks has said, "appears to be less inclined even than the critics with whom he is theoretically at war to play an active, public part in the secular conflict of darkness and light." When one comes to the *Privat-Dozenten*[13] there is less remoteness, but what takes the place of it is almost as saddening. To Sherman and Percy Boynton the one aim of criticism seems to be the enforcement of correctness—in Emerson's phrase, the upholding of "some great decorum, some fetish of a government, some ephemeral trade, or war, or man"—*e.g.*, Puritanism, democracy, monogamy, the League of Nations, the Wilsonian piffle. Even among the critics who escape the worst of this schoolmastering frenzy there is some touch of the heavy "culture" of the provincial schoolma'm. For example, consider Clayton Hamilton,[14] M.A., vice-president of the National Institute of Arts and Letters. Here are the tests he proposes for dramatic critics, *i.e.*, for gentlemen chiefly employed in reviewing such characteristic American compositions as the Ziegfeld Follies, "Up in Mabel's Room," "Ben-Hur" and "The Witching Hour":

1. Have you ever stood bareheaded in the nave of Amiens?
2. Have you ever climbed to the Acropolis by moonlight?
3. Have you ever walked with whispers into the hushed presence of the Frari Madonna of Bellini?

What could more brilliantly evoke an image of

the eternal Miss Birch, blue veil flying and Baedeker in hand, plodding along faithfully through the interminable corridors and catacombs of the Louvre, the while bands are playing across the river, and young bucks in three-gallon hats are sparking the gals, and the Jews and harlots uphold the traditions of French *hig leef*[15] at Longchamps, and American deacons are frisked and debauched up on martyrs' hill? The banality of it is really too exquisite to be borne; the lack of humor is almost that of a Fifth Avenue divine. One seldom finds in the pronunciamentoes of these dogged professors, indeed, any trace of either Attic or Gallic salt. When they essay to be jocose, the result is usually simply an elephantine whimsicality, by the chautauqua out of the *Atlantic Monthly*. Their satire is mere ill-nature. One finds it difficult to believe that they have ever read Lewes, or Hazlitt, or, above all, Saintsbury.[16] I often wonder, in fact, how Saintsbury would fare, an unknown man, at the hands of, say, Brownell or More. What of his iconoclastic gayety, his boyish weakness for tweaking noses and pulling whiskers, his obscene delight in slang? . . .

So far, the disease. As to the cause, I have delivered a few hints. I now describe it particularly. It is, in brief, a defect in the general culture of the country—one reflected, not only in the national literature, but also in the national political theory, the national attitude toward religion and morals, the national habit in all departments of thinking. It is the lack of a civilized aristocracy, secure in its position, animated by an intelligent curiosity, skeptical of all facile generalizations, superior to the sentimentality of the mob, and delighting in the battle of ideas for its own sake.

The word I use, despite the qualifying adjective, has got itself meanings, of course, that I by no means intend to convey. Any mention of an aristocracy, to a public fed upon democratic fustian, is bound to bring up images of stockbrokers' wives lolling obscenely in opera boxes, or of haughty Englishmen slaughtering whole generations of grouse in an inordinate and incomprehensible manner, or of Junkers with tight waists elbowing American schoolmarms off the sidewalks of German beer

---

[12] Donald G. Mitchell, pen name "Ik Marvel" (1822–1908), farmer and author.
[13] Unsalaried German university lecturers.
[14] Lecturer, critic, and playwright (1881–1946).

[15] A farcical French mispronunciation of "high life."
[16] George Henry Lewes (1817–1878), English philosophical writer and editor of the *Fortnightly Review*; William Hazlitt (1778–1830), English essayist and critic; George Saintsbury (1845–1933), English literary critic and historian.

towns, or of perfumed Italians coming over to work their abominable magic upon the daughters of breakfast-food and bathtub kings. Part of this misconception, I suppose, has its roots in the gaudy imbecilities of the yellow press, but there is also a part that belongs to the general American tradition, along with the oppression of minorities and the belief in political panaceas. Its depth and extent are constantly revealed by the naïve assumption that the so-called fashionable folk of the large cities—chiefly wealthy industrials in the interior-decorator and country-club stage of culture—constitute an aristocracy, and by the scarcely less remarkable assumption that the peerage of England is identical with the gentry—that is, that such men as Lord Northcliffe, Lord Iveagh and even Lord Reading are English gentlemen, and of the ancient line of the Percys.

Here, as always, the worshiper is the father of the gods, and no less when they are evil than when they are benign. The inferior man must find himself superiors, that he may marvel at his political equality with them, and in the absence of recognizable superiors *de facto* he creates superiors *de jure*. The sublime principle of one man, one vote must be translated into terms of dollars, diamonds, fashionable intelligence; the equality of all men before the law must have clear and dramatic proofs. Sometimes, perhaps, the thing goes further and is more subtle. The inferior man needs an aristocracy to demonstrate not only his mere equality, but also his actual superiority. The society columns in the newspapers may have some such origin: they may visualize once more the accomplished journalist's understanding of the mob mind that he plays upon so skillfully, as upon some immense and cacophonous organ, always going *fortissimo*. What the inferior man and his wife see in the sinister revels of those amazing first families, I suspect, is often a massive witness to their own higher rectitude—to their relative innocence of cigarette-smoking, poodle-coddling, child-farming and the more abstruse branches of adultery—in brief, to their firmer grasp upon the immutable axioms of Christian virtue, the one sound boast of the nether nine-tenths of humanity in every land under the cross.

But this bugaboo aristocracy, as I hint, is actually bogus, and the evidence of its bogusness lies in the fact that it is insecure. One gets into it only onerously, but out of it very easily. Entrance is effected by dint of a long and bitter struggle, and the chief incidents of that struggle are almost intolerable humiliations. The aspirant must school and steel himself to sniffs and sneers; he must see the door slammed upon him a hundred times before ever it is thrown open to him. To get in at all he must show a talent for abasement—and abasement makes him timorous. Worse, that timorousness is not cured when he succeeds at last. On the contrary, it is made even more tremulous, for what he faces within the gates is a scheme of things made up almost wholly of harsh and often unintelligible taboos, and the penalty for violating even the least of them is swift and disastrous. He must exhibit exactly the right social habits, appetites and prejudices, public and private. He must harbor exactly the right political enthusiasms and indignations. He must have a hearty taste for exactly the right sports. His attitude toward the fine arts must be properly tolerant and yet not a shade too eager. He must read and like exactly the right books, pamphlets and public journals. He must put up at the right hotels when he travels. His wife must patronize the right milliners. He himself must stick to the right haberdashery. He must live in the right neighborhood. He must even embrace the right doctrines of religion. It would ruin him, for all opera box and society column purposes, to set up a plea for justice to the Bolsheviki, or even for ordinary decency. It would ruin him equally to wear celluloid collars, or to move to Union Hill, N.J., or to serve ham and cabbage at his table. And it would ruin him, too, to drink coffee from his saucer, or to marry a chambermaid with a gold tooth, or to join the Seventh Day Adventists. Within the boundaries of his curious order he is worse fettered than a monk in a cell. Its obscure conception of propriety, its nebulous notion that this or that is honorable, hampers him in every direction, and very narrowly. What he resigns when he enters, even when he makes his first deprecating knock at the door, is every right to attack the ideas that happen to prevail within. Such as they are, he must accept them without question. And as they shift and change in response to great instinctive movements (or perhaps, now and then, to the punished but not to be forgotten revolts of extraordinary rebels) he must shift and change with them, silently and quickly. To hang back, to challenge and dispute, to preach reform and revolutions—these are crimes against the brummagem Holy Ghost of the order.

Obviously, that order cannot constitute a genuine aristocracy, in any rational sense. A genuine aristocracy is grounded upon very much different principles. Its first and most salient character is its interior security, and the chief visible evidence of that security is the freedom that goes with it—not only freedom in act, the divine right of the aristocrat to do what he jolly well pleases, so long as he does not violate the primary guarantees and obligations of his class, but also and more importantly freedom in thought, the liberty to try and err, the right to be his own man. It is the instinct of a true aristocracy, not to punish eccentricity by expulsion, but to throw a mantle of protection about it—to safeguard it from the suspicions and resentments of the lower orders. Those lower orders are inert, timid, inhospitable to ideas, hostile to changes, faithful to a few maudlin superstitions. All progress goes on on the higher levels. It is there that salient personalities, made secure by artificial immunities, may oscillate most widely from the normal track. It is within that entrenched fold, out of reach of the immemorial certainties of the mob, that extraordinary men of the lower orders may find their city of refuge, and breathe a clear air. This, indeed, is at once the hall-mark and the justification of an aristocracy—that it is beyond responsibility to the general masses of men, and hence superior to both their degraded longings and their no less degraded aversions. It is nothing if it is not autonomous, curious, venturesome, courageous, and everything if it is. It is the custodian of the qualities that make for change and experiment; it is the class that organizes danger to the service of the race; it pays for its high prerogatives by standing in the forefront of the fray.

No [genuine] aristocracy, it must be plain, is now on view in the United States. The makings of one were visible in the Virginia of the later eighteenth century, but with Jefferson and Washington the promise died. In New England, it seems to me, there was never any aristocracy, either in being or in nascency: there was only a theocracy that degenerated very quickly into a plutocracy on the one hand and a caste of sterile *Gelehrten* on the other—the passion for God splitting into a lust for dollars and a weakness for mere words. Despite the common notion to the contrary—a notion generated by confusing literacy with intelligence—New England has never shown the slightest sign of a genuine enthusiasm for ideas. It began its history as a slaughter-house of ideas, and it is to-day not easily distinguishable from a cold-storage plant. Its celebrated adventures in mysticism, once apparently so bold and significant, are now seen to have been little more than an elaborate hocus-pocus—

respectable Unitarians shocking the peasantry and scaring the horned cattle in the fields by masquerading in the robes of Rosicrucians. The ideas that it embraced in those austere and far-off days were stale, and when it had finished with them they were dead: to-day one hears of Jakob Bohme almost as rarely as one hears of Allen G. Thurman. So in politics. Its glory is Abolition—an English invention, long under the interdict of the native plutocracy. Since the Civil War its six states have produced fewer political ideas, as political ideas run in the Republic, than any average county in Kansas or Nebraska. Appomattox seemed to be a victory for New England idealism. It was actually a victory for the New England plutocracy, and that plutocracy has dominated thought above the Housatonic ever since. The sect of professional idealists has so far dwindled that it has ceased to be of any importance, even as an opposition. When the plutocracy is challenged now, it is challenged by the proletariat.

. . .

Thus at the top and at the bottom. Obviously, there is no aristocracy here. One finds only one of the necessary elements, and that only in the plutocracy, to wit, a truculent egoism. But where is intelligence? Where are ease and surety of manner? Where are enterprise and curiosity? Where, above all, is courage, and in particular, moral courage—the capacity for independent thinking, for difficult problems, for what Nietzsche called the joys of the labyrinth? As well look for these things in a society of half-wits. Democracy, obliterating the old aristocracy, has left only a vacuum in its place; in a century and a half it has failed either to lift up the mob to intellectual autonomy and dignity or to purge the plutocracy of its inherent stupidity and swinishness. It is precisely here, the first and favorite scene of the Great Experiment, that the culture of the individual has been reduced to the most rigid and absurd regimentation. It is precisely here, of all civilized countries, that eccentricity in demeanor and opinion has come to bear the heaviest penalties. The whole drift of our law is toward the absolute prohibition of all ideas that diverge in the slightest from the accepted platitudes, and behind that drift of law there is a far more potent force of growing custom, and under that custom there is a national philosophy which erects conformity into the noblest of virtues and the free functioning of personality into a capital crime against society.

IRVING BABBITT (1865–1933)

In the foregoing lively, rambling disquisition, Mencken dusts off, among others, the polite men of letters of academic background. He refuses to see in them any signs of a genuine intellectual aristocracy; in their timid conformity they reveal themselves to be only attenuated Puritans. Except for a "forlorn intelligentsia," there are no ideas, and effective power is in the hands of the money-grubbers.

Mencken thus dismissed such people as Babbitt and Paul Elmer More as bloodless and gutless: for him they represented refinement without substance, an effete Puritanism that was in its way almost as bad as the raw-boned and unlettered Puritanism of the backwoods. Yet on one or two important issues Mencken was in essential agreement with Babbitt and More, and the three frequently interpreted the American situation in much the same terms. In his *Democracy and Leadership* Irving Babbitt wrote that "the significant changes in our own national temper . . . are finally due to the fact that Protestant Christianity, especially in the Puritanic form, has been giving way to humanitarianism."

There is a second point of likeness: Babbitt and the other "New Humanists" were, like Mencken, appalled at the confusion and the cheapness of American culture. Babbitt had as little fondness as Mencken for "humanitarian crusaders," "forward-lookers," and "uplifters" proclaiming "the gospel of service."

In 1930, under the editorship of Norman Foerster, the disciples and associates of Babbitt and More published a symposium entitled *Humanism and America: Essays on the Outlook of Modern Civilization*. It was intended to provide a consolidation of Humanist views and to make those views better known to the public. It was immediately answered by an anti-Humanist symposium, edited by C. Hartley Grattan, entitled *The Critique of Humanism*. The contributors to this volume represented widely ranging points of view. Their names provide a roll call of the critics who would dominate the 1930's and 1940's. They include those of Edmund Wilson, Malcolm Cowley, Allen Tate, Kenneth Burke, R. P. Blackmur, John Chamberlain, Yvor Winters, and Lewis Mumford.

Forensically, one of the most telling charges that these young critics brought against the Humanists was their lack of interest in, or even knowledge of, the powerful new literature that was coming out of Europe and America. The Humanists were tied to the past; they were owl-eyed professors; they had cut themselves off from the living growth of literature and the arts. Thus, Babbitt thought poorly of Dreiser's novels; More had disparaged Joyce's *Ulysses*. Malcolm Cowley made it a matter of reproach that, though six contributors to the Humanist symposium dealt directly with modern American literature, they found "not one poem, drama, or novel" to praise.

The truth of the matter was that the weakest side of Babbitt—and of a good many of his allies—was the literary and artistic. As Austin Warren has put it, "Aesthetically [Babbitt] was undeveloped and unconcerned. Art he judged almost exclusively by moral criteria. . . . He was, in short, primarily a moralist."[1]

Babbitt's real concern was to locate a base on which a sound morality could be established during an age of science and rationalism in which the traditional morality was evidently withering away. The problem was real, even if dismissed too easily by some of his opponents as of no importance at all. But Babbitt's solution was not always convincing, even to those who tended

[1] *New England Saints* (1956), pp. 153–54. This essay is well worth consulting. It is informed and judicious, but it is also warm in tone and catches the flavor of Babbitt's personality and the nature of his real achievement as a teacher and as a scholar. Warren goes so far as to say that like a number of other unwitting founders of cults, Babbitt was not of the cult: "Babbitt himself was not a 'humanist.'"

to be sympathetic to his cause. How, without invoking a divine force outside man, put a brake on man's appetites and instinctive actions? Babbitt attempted to find the principle of restraint within man's own nature, but his description of what it was and from what it derived its sanctions was difficult to state.

Indeed, Babbitt's doctrine of what he called the "inner check" (see p. 2783 below) brought down upon him and the New Humanism the sharpest attacks of all. His opponents declared it to be no more than the Puritan doctrine of restraint given a new name—a restraint asserted vindictively in the face of the expansive impulses and the new freedom in which the American man of letters rejoiced.

Babbitt and most of the other New Humanists—Paul Elmer More in this matter was something of an exception—had come part of the way to the positivistic position. They had sought to set up an ethic that was completely divorced from religion and from any reliance on the supernatural. They had wanted to avoid what seemed to them a hopeless and wrong-headed conflict with science and yet to assert firmly a specifically human quality that transcended either behaviorist automatism or the instinctive responses of an animal. In short, though they acknowledged that the human being was part of nature, they asserted that he was somehow radically different from nature.

The result was that the New Humanists quickly found themselves attacked on both flanks—from the one side by naturalists, who charged the Humanists with trying to secure the benefits of supernaturalism without being willing to pay the price, and from the other side by writers such as Allen Tate and T. S. Eliot,[2] speaking for the traditional culture, who insisted that the New Humanists were smuggling into their professedly naturalistic account of man qualities that could not be logically derived from purely naturalistic premises.

By and large the attempt to revitalize the native American ethical tradition descending from Puritanism through transcendentalism and to refute the charge that it now amounted to no more than genteel respectability failed to persuade those who were not already persuaded. The anti-Humanists tended to import ideas from the Europe of the nineteenth and twentieth centuries or else to appeal to European traditions that antedated the settlement of America. Thus, those who attacked the New Humanists from a right-wing position invoked the norms of an organic traditional society (as, for example, did Allen Tate) or of orthodox Christianity (as, for example, did T. S. Eliot). Those who attacked from a left-wing position relied upon a more radical interpretation of society or a more radical analysis of the human psyche, again from sources outside the native American tradition, such as the ideas of Karl Marx or of Sigmund Freud.[3]

Ironically, both the Humanist symposium and the anti-Humanist answer were published just a few months after the collapse of the New York stock market in 1929. The Depression that ensued gave emotional urgency to what had been heretofore a rather detached and academic interest in Marxism.

---

[2] Eliot actually contributed to the Humanist symposium and not to the anti-Humanist. But from the beginning, his position in the Humanist camp was anomalous and was so noted by more than one contributor to the other symposium. In any case, most of his fire was directed—though respectfully—against the position of his old Harvard teacher.

[3] In the interest of marking out sharply divergent lines, we have oversimplified the situation. Native American ideas were not, of course, completely submerged. In fact, sometimes, as one takes the long view of American intellectual history, it seems that the more our culture changes the more it remains the same: see pp. 1819–26, for example. Certain American attitudes, myths, and habits of thought remain in some sense constant, though they adapt themselves to new circumstances and adopt fresh terminologies and ideologies.

FURTHER READINGS

Irving Babbitt, *Democracy and Leadership* (1924)
———, *The New Laokoön* (1910)
———, *Rousseau and Romanticism* (1919)

G. R. Elliott, "Irving Babbitt as I Knew Him," *American Review* (1936)

———, "T. S. Eliot and Irving Babbitt," *American Review* (1936)
Francis McMahon, *The Humanism of Irving Babbitt* (1951)
Austin Warren, "Irving Babbitt," in *New England Saints* (1956)

From Democracy and Leadership (1924)

Our present drift away from constitutional freedom can be understood only with reference to the progressive crumbling of traditional standards and the rise of a naturalistic philosophy that, in its treatment of specifically human problems, has been either sentimental or utilitarian. The significant changes in our own national temper in particular are finally due to the fact that Protestant Christianity, especially in the Puritanic form, has been giving way to humanitarianism. The point is worth making because the persons who have favored prohibition and other similar "reforms" have been attacked as Puritans. Genuine Puritanism was, however, a religion of the inner life. . . . Washington, Marshall, and Lincoln, though not narrowly orthodox, were still religious in the traditional sense. The struggle between good and evil, as they saw it, was still primarily not in society, but in the individual. Their conscious dependence on a higher or divine will could not fail to be reflected in their notion of liberty. Jefferson, on the contrary, associated his liberty, not with God, but with "nature." He admired, as is well known, the liberty of the American Indian.[1] He was for diminishing to the utmost the rôle of government, but not for increasing the inner control that must, according to Burke, be in strict ratio to the relaxation of outer control. When evil actually appears, the Jeffersonian cannot appeal to the principle of inner control; he is not willing again to admit that the sole alternative to this type of control is force; and so he is led into what seems at first sight a paradoxical denial of his own principles: he has recourse to legislation. It should be clear at all events that our present attempt to substitute social control for self-control is Jeffersonian rather than Puritanical. So far as we are true children of the Puritans, we may accept the contrast established by Professor Stuart

P. Sherman[2] between our own point of view and that of the German: "The ideal of the German is external control and 'inner freedom'; the Government looks after his conduct and he looks after his liberty. The ideal of the American is external freedom and inner control; the individual looks after his conduct and the Government looks after his liberty. Thus *Verboten* in Germany is pronounced by the Government and enforced by the police. In America *Verboten* is pronounced by public opinion and enforced by the individual conscience. In this light it should appear that Puritanism, our national principle of concentration, is the indispensable check on democracy, our national principle of expansion. I use the word Puritanism in the sense given to it by German and German-American critics: *the inner check upon the expansion of natural impulse.*"

. . .

Standardization is . . . a less serious menace to standards than what are currently known as "ideals." The person who breaks down standards in the name of ideals does not seem to be impelled by base commercial motives, but to be animated, on the contrary, by the purest commiseration for the lowly and the oppressed. We must have the courage to submit this humanitarian zeal to a close scrutiny.

. . .

At bottom the point of view of the "uplifter" is so popular because it nourishes spiritual complacency; it enables a man to look on himself as "up" and on some one else as "down." But there is psychological if not theological truth in the as-

[1] See *Works* (Ford ed.), III, p. 195.

[2] *American and Allied Ideals* (War Information Series, No. 12), p. 9.

sertion of Jonathan Edwards that complacent people are a "particular smoke" in God's nostrils. A
man needs to look, not down, but up to standards
set so much above his ordinary self as to make him
feel that he is himself spiritually the underdog.
The man who thus looks up is becoming worthy
to be looked up to in turn, and, to this extent,
qualifying for leadership. Leadership of this type,
one may add, may prove to be, in the long run,
the only effectual counterpoise to that of the imperialistic superman.

. . .

One cannot grant that an aristocracy of scientific
intellectuals or indeed any aristocracy of intellect
is what we need. This would mean practically to
encourage the *libido sciendi* and so to put pride in
the place of humility. Still less acceptable would
be an aristocracy of artists; as the word art has
come to be understood in recent times, this would
mean an aristocracy of æsthetes who would attempt to base their selection on the *libido senti-
endi*. The Nietzschean attempt, again, to found
the aristocratic and selective principle on the sheer
expansion of the will to power (*libido dominandi*)
would lead in practice to horrible violence and
finally to the death of civilization.

. . .

. . . One may sum up what appears to be our
total trend at present by saying that we are moving
through an orgy of humanitarian legalism towards
a decadent imperialism.

The important offsetting influence is our great
unionist tradition. One should not, however, underestimate the difficulties in the way of maintaining this tradition. The idea that the State should
have a permanent or higher self that is felt as a
veto power upon its ordinary self rests ultimately
upon the assertion of a similar dualism in the individual. We have seen that this assertion has in
the Occident been inextricably bound up with certain Christian beliefs that have been weakened by
the naturalistic movement. We are brought back
here to the problem with which we have been confronted so often in the course of the present argument, how, namely, to get modern equivalents for
the traditional beliefs, above all some fresh basis
for the affirmation of a *frein vital* or centripetal
element in liberty. What the men of the French
Revolution wanted, according to Joubert, was not

religious liberty, but irreligious liberty. In that
case, the French modernist retorts bitterly, you
would have us give up revolutionary liberty and
become Jesuits. Similarly, if one points out to an
American modernist the inanity of his idealism as
a substitute for the traditional controls, he will at
once accuse you of wishing to revert to Puritanism.
Strictly speaking, however, one does not need to
revert to anything. It is a part of my own method
to put Confucius behind Aristotle and Buddha behind Christ. The best, however, that even these
great teachers can do for us is to help us to discover what is already present in ourselves.[3] From
this point of view they are well-nigh indispensable.

Let us begin, therefore, by ridding our minds of
unreal alternatives. If we in America are not content with a stodgy commercialism, it does not follow that we need, on the one hand, to return to
Puritanism, or, on the other, to become "liberals"
in the style of "The New Republic"; nor, again,
need we evolve under the guidance of Mr. H. L.
Mencken into second-rate Nietzscheans. We do
need, however, if we are to gain any hold on the
present situation, to develop a little moral gravity
and intellectual seriousness. We shall then see that
the strength of the traditional doctrines, as compared with the modernist position, is the comparative honesty with which they face the fact of evil.
We shall see that we need to restore to human
nature in some critical and experimental fashion
the "old Adam" that the idealists have been so
busy eliminating. A restoration of this kind ought
not to lead merely to a lapse from naturalistic optimism into naturalistic pessimism; nothing is easier
than such a lapse and nothing at bottom is more
futile. Both attitudes are about equally fatalistic
and so undermine moral responsibility.

. . .

. . . If a community is to transmit certain habits
to its young, it must normally come to some kind
of agreement as to what habits are desirable; it
must in the literal meaning of that word achieve a
convention. Here is a chief difference between the
true and the false liberal. It has been said of our
modernists that they have only one convention
and that is that there shall be no more conventions. An individualism that is thus purely temperamental is incompatible with the survival of

[3] Compare Pascal, *Pensées*, 64: n'est pas dans
Montaigne, mais dans moi que je trouve tout ce que
j'y vois."

civilization. What is civilized in most people is precisely that part of them which is conventional. It is, to be sure, difficult to have a convention without falling into mere conventionalism, two things that the modernist confounds; but then everything that is worth while is difficult.

. . .

. . . Assuming that what we wish to preserve is a federal and constitutional democracy, are we training up a class of leaders whose ethos is in intimate accord with this type of government? The older type of American college reflected faithfully enough the convention of its time. The classical element in its curriculum was appropriately subordinated to the religious element, inasmuch as the leadership at which it aimed was to be lodged primarily in the clergy. It would have been possible to interpret more vitally our older educational convention, to give it the broadening it certainly needed and to adapt it to changed conditions. The new education (I am speaking, of course, of the main trend) can scarcely be said to have developed in this fashion from the old. It suggests rather a radical break with our traditional ethos. The old education was, in intention at least, a training for wisdom and character. The new education has been summed up by President Eliot in the phrase: training for service and power. We are all coming together more and more in this idea of service. But, though service is supplying us in a way with a convention, it is not, in either the humanistic or the religious sense, supplying us with standards. In the current sense of the word it tends rather to undermine standards, if it be true, as I have tried to show, that it involves an assumption hard to justify on strictly psychological grounds—the assumption that men can come together expansively and on the level of their ordinary selves. The older education was based on the belief that men need to be disciplined to some ethical centre. The sentimental humanitarian opposes to a definite curriculum which aims at some such humanistic or religious discipline the right of the individual to develop freely his bent or temperamental proclivity. The standard or common measure is compromised by the assertion of this supposed right, and in about the same measure the effort and spirit of emulation that the standard stimulates disappears. The very word curriculum implies a running together. Under the new educational dispensation, students, instead of running together, tend to lounge separately.

. . .

. . . The gospel of service is at all events going to receive a thorough trial, if nowhere else, then in America. We are rapidly becoming a nation of humanitarian crusaders. The present reign of legalism is the most palpable outcome of this crusading. It is growing only too evident, however, that the drift towards license is being accelerated rather than arrested by the multiplication of laws. If we do not develop a sounder type of vision than that of our "uplifters" and "forward-lookers," the history of free institutions in this country is likely to be short, and, on the whole, discreditable. Surely the first step is to perceive that the alternative to a constitutional liberty is not a legalistic millennium, but a triumph of anarchy followed by a triumph of force. The time may come, with the growth of a false liberalism, when a predominant element in our population, having grown more and more impatient of the ballot box and representative government, of constitutional limitations and judicial control, will display a growing eagerness for "direct action." This is the propitious moment for the imperialistic leader.

MALCOLM COWLEY (1898–   )

The American intellectual's new receptivity to Marxism is vividly illustrated from the paper read by Malcolm Cowley to the American Writers' Congress and printed in *New Masses*, May 7, 1935. We print a few excerpts from it below. Cowley began by telling his audience what the revolutionary movement could not do.

From What the Revolutionary Movement Can Do for a Writer (1935)

It is important first of all to define what the revolutionary movement cannot do for a writer, so that nobody will hope for miracles that will not be performed. It cannot give him personal salvation. It is not a church that calls upon him to have faith, to surrender his doubts, to lay down his burden of anxieties, and from henceforth to follow a sure path mapped out for him by sanctified leaders. This is an age when messiahs are being invoked not only by unemployed preachers and engineers and by shopkeepers who have lost their shops, but also by bewildered novelists and by poets no longer able to write poetry. Marx and Lenin were not messiahs; they were scientists of action. Their aim was not to convert but to convince.

But there are four things that the revolutionary movement can do for the writer:

In the first place, it offers them an audience—the most eager and alive and responsive that now exists. We saw part of the audience the other night in Mecca Temple, when for one evening our discussions were carried out of the atmosphere of the study and the back barroom into a bigger world.

. . .

MacLeish is scarcely a revolutionary writer. Mike Gold once described him as having "the fascist unconscious." I believed at the time that the charge was at least premature, but later it seemed to be justified by other poems and articles that MacLeish was writing. All of us were amazed to hear that he had arranged for a special performance of his play *Panic*, to be given for the benefit of *The New Theatre* and *The New Masses*. After the performance, he partly explained his motives by thanking the audience for its attention, for its applause, for its criticism, for its general lively interest. The whole point was that this poet who had won the Pulitzer Prize, this editor and writer for *Fortune*, had to turn to a revolutionary audience to get the sort of response without which any writer has the feeling of living in a vacuum and writing with invisible ink.

Cowley said that in the second place the revolutionary movement can give the writer a whole new range of subject matter. In the fifty years before 1930 the most interesting novelists had dealt with the conflict between the individual and society. Most of them sympathized with the individual and turned more and more to the interior monologue as their preferred expressive device. But now Cowley believed that we had begun "to see that the inner world that [the interior monologue] was supposed to illuminate was really not very interesting, not very fresh." The revolutionary movement carries an artist outside himself and into new fictional territory.

In the third place, Cowley said, "The revolutionary movement gives the artist a perspective on himself—an idea that his own experiences are not something accidental and unique, but are part of a vast pattern. The movement teaches him that art is not an individual but a social product. . . ."

His final point Cowley put as follows:

In the fourth place, the revolutionary movement allies the interests of writers with those of a class that is rising, instead of with the interests of a confused and futile and decaying class. It gives them a new source of strength.

I have said that the revolutionary movement can perform no miracles, and yet with writers, especially with poets, it does sometimes produce effects that appear miraculous. Take Wordsworth, for example. During a few years of his long career he wrote great poems; then at the end of it he settled down to be the most skillful, high-minded and accomplished bore in English literature. Critics and college students have always been puzzled by this phenomenon. It is only during the past few years that some light has been thrown on it—that we have learned how he visited France at the height of the French Revolution, how he was filled with enthusiasm, how he learned to think in universal terms—and then how he became disillusioned, turned his eyes inward, accepted the eternal rightness and triteness of British society, and spent his last years bumbling in a garden.

In view of such advantages to the writer, Cowley was willing to brush aside any apprehension that a Communist state might exert restrictive pressures on the artist. In an article entitled "The Poet's Privacy" published in the *New Republic* (September 18, 1935), he wrote that "The strength of the Soviet writers lies in the fact that the political leaders want and need their support, and are willing to grant a great deal of intellectual liberty as the price of receiving it."

Years later, when this essay was reprinted in *Think Back on Us* (1967), Cowley appended the following note:

> This deluded comment must stand for the record, with others I made about Stalin's Russia. It was written a year before the Great Purge of 1936–38 put an end to literary protests, and to the lives of many protestors. Tretiakov, whose *Chinese Testament* I had warmly praised, would be among the first to vanish. It was not until after Stalin's death that Russian writers would again feel strong enough to do battle with the censors, who might still condemn them to prison, but not to death.

Such was the spell that Marxism cast over many an American intellectual in the 1930's. The thinker and writer yearned to assume an international perspective, to find his place in the mainstream of history, to take his part in building a new culture on the sound foundations of scientific truth. The last thing that he wanted was to end his literary career like Wordsworth, "bumbling in a garden."

If we represented Cowley only by the foregoing passage, however, we would give a partial and biased account of his contribution to American letters and would distort the shape of his career as a critic. He early showed a willingness to found his criticism on an understanding of the material with which he dealt, and where he sensed he did not understand it, he made a real effort to learn something about it. His developing interest in Faulkner is an instance in point. Beginning with Marxist preconceptions, Cowley originally saw Faulkner as a typical southern decadent and a political reactionary, but he recognized in Faulkner's novels a disturbing power of the imagination, and in reviewing them as they appeared throughout a decade and more, he struggled, in a remarkable display of intellectual candor and critical integrity, to comprehend the world that Faulkner was creating and to sense the inner impulse of his work. Finally, in 1944–45, he published a long essay[1] on Faulkner that did much to bring him to the attention of the reading public and to get his books back into print.

Exile's Return (1951), which Cowley describes as "the story to 1930 of what used to be called the lost generation," is a lively chronicle of what went on in the 1920's and is a good example of Cowley's characteristic writing at its best. The excerpt that we print below is part of his account of one of the most spectacular and "extreme" American expatriates, Harry Crosby (1898–1929), who founded the Black Sun Press in Paris, and who played a prominent role in the careers of Hemingway and Gertrude Stein.

[1] The essay was actually published in three parts: the first appeared in the *New York Times Book Review*, October 29, 1944; the second in the *Saturday Review of Literature*, April 14, 1945; the third in the *Sewanee Review*, Summer, 1945. In 1946 Cowley edited *The Portable Faulkner*, and at last readers in large numbers began to explore Yoknapatawpha County. See also the correspondence between Faulkner and Cowley, published in 1966 as *The Faulkner-Cowley File*.

FURTHER READINGS

Malcolm Cowley, *After the Genteel Tradition* (1937)
———, *Blue Juniata* (1931)
———, *The Dry Season* (1941)
———, *Exile's Return* (1951)
———, *The Literary Situation* (1954)
———, *A Many Windowed House* (1970)
———, *Second Flowering* (1973)
———, *Think Back on Us* (1967)
———, *The Faulkner-Cowley File* (1966)

From Exile's Return (1951)

ECHOES OF A SUICIDE

1: Letter Left on a Dressing Table

Harry Crosby and his wife arrived in New York during the first week of December 1929 and Hart Crane gave a party for them in his room on Brooklyn Heights. It was a good party, too; Harry smiled a lot—you remembered his very white teeth—and had easy manners and, without talking a great deal, he charmed everyone. On the afternoon of December 10 he borrowed the keys to a friend's studio in the Hotel des Artistes. When he failed to answer the telephone or the doorbell that evening, the friend had the door broken down and found Harry's body with that of a young society woman, Mrs. Josephine Bigelow.

The double suicide was a front-page story, but the newspapers could find no reason for it and the police had no explanation to offer. Harry was young, just six months past his thirty-first birthday; he was rich, happily married and, except for a slight infection of the throat, in the best of health. All the usual motives were lacking. He had lost a little money in the stock market but did not brood about it; he had love affairs but spoke of breaking them off; he was not dissatisfied with his progress as a poet and a publisher. Nor did he suffer from any sense of inferiority: people had always liked him, all his life had moved in pleasant ways; and he lay there now beside a dead woman in a borrowed studio.

He left behind him no letter, not even a final scrawl.

This deliberate silence seemed strange to the police. They knew that suicides usually give some explanation, often in the shape of a long document addressed to wife, mother or husband, insisting that they had done the wisest thing, justifying themselves before and accusing society. Poets in particular, among whom suicide is almost an occupational disease, are likely to write final messages to the world that neglected them. They insist on this last word—and if Harry Crosby left none, he must have believed that his message was already written.

He had been keeping a diary—later published in three volumes by the Black Sun Press in Paris—and, in effect, it takes the place of a letter slipped into the frame of the mirror or left on the dressing table under a jar of cold cream. It does not explain the immediate occasion, does not tell why he chose to die on that particular afternoon after keeping a rendezvous and sharing a bottle of Scotch whisky. But the real causes of his deed can be clearly deciphered from this record of things done, books read and ideas seized upon for guidance.

And something more can be deciphered there. It happens that his brief and not particularly distinguished literary life of seven years included practically all the themes I have been trying to develop—the separation from home, the effects of service in the ambulance corps, the exile in France, then other themes, bohemianism, the religion of art, the escape from society, the effort to defend one's individuality even at the cost of sterility and madness, then the final period of demoralization when the whole philosophical structure crumbled from within, just at the moment when bourgeois society seemed about to crumble after its greatest outpouring of luxuries, its longest debauch—all this is suggested in Harry Crosby's life and is rendered fairly explicit in his diary. But it not my only reason for writing about him. Harry was wealthier than the other pure poets and refugees of art: he had means and leisure to carry his ideas to their conclusion, while most of the others were being turned aside, partly by the homely skepticism that is instilled into the middle classes and partly by the daily business of earning a living. He was not more talented than his associates, but he was more single-minded, more literal, and was not held back by the fear of death or ridicule from carrying his principles to their extremes. As a result, his life had the quality of a logical structure. His suicide was the last term of a syllogism; it was like the signature to a second-rate but honest and exciting poem.

But there is one question raised by his life that his diary doesn't answer. How did he first become entangled in the chain of events and ambitions that ended in the Hotel des Artistes? His background seemed to promise an entirely different career.

Henry Grew Crosby was born in Boston on June 4, 1898; his parents lived toward the lower end of Beacon Street. His father, Stephen Van Rensselaer

Crosby, was a banker; his mother, born Henrietta Grew, was the sister of Mrs. J. Pierpont Morgan. Harry attended St. Mark's, an Episcopalian preparatory school, where, being too light for football, he ran on the cross-country team. He graduated in June 1917. With several of his classmates he immediately volunteered for the American Ambulance Service in France. . . . Boys with this background had an easy path to follow. St. Mark's was popularly supposed to lead, after four years at Harvard, to Kidder, Peabody and Company, the Boston bankers (just as Groton School led to Lee, Higginson). Then, after a proper apprenticeship, the young man moved on to New York, where his parents bought him a seat on the Stock Exchange; he might end as a Morgan partner. Alternatively, he might study law and become the attorney for a big public utility; or he might enter the diplomatic service and rise to an ambassadorship, like Harry's cousin Joseph Grew; or he might retire at the age of thirty-five and live on his income and buy pictures. The American high bourgeoisie takes care of its sons, provided only that they make a proper marriage and don't drink too much. What was it that turned Harry aside from the smooth road in front of him?

I think the answer lies in what happened to him during the war, and particularly in one brief experience to which he alludes several times in his diary, but without explaining it fully. The whole story is told in his war letters, privately printed by his parents—incidentally they are exactly like the war letters of fifty other nice American boys of good families which were printed in the same pious fashion. On November 22, 1917, Harry was at a dressing station in the hills near Verdun. While he was waiting to drive an ambulance full of wounded men to the field hospital at Bras, a shell burst in the road; the boy standing next to him was seriously wounded. Harry helped to put him into the ambulance and drove back toward Bras through a German barrage. There was one especially bad moment when the road was blocked by a stalled truck and Harry had to wait for minute after minute while shells rained down on either side of the road.

The hills of Verdun [he noted in his diary on the tenth anniversary of the adventure] and the red sun setting back of the hills and the charred skeletons of trees and the river Meuse and the black shells spouting up in columns along the road to Bras and the thunder of the barrage and the wounded and the ride through red explosions and the violent metamorphose from boy into man.

There was indeed a violent metamorphosis, but not from boy into man: rather, it was from life into death. What really happened was that Harry died in those endless moments when he was waiting for the road to be cleared. In his heart he felt that he belonged with his good friends Aaron Davis Weld and Oliver Ames, Jr., both killed in action. Bodily he survived, and with a keener appetite for pleasure, but only to find that something was dead inside him—his boyhood, Boston, St. Mark's, the Myopia Hunt, a respectable marriage, an assured future as a banker, everything that was supposed to lead him toward a responsible place in the world.

At first he didn't realize what had happened. He went back to Boston after the war and tried to resume his old life. He entered Harvard in the fall of 1919; he made the cross-country squad and was almost automatically elected to the societies, waiting clubs and final clubs which a young man of good family was supposed to join—Institute of 1770, D.K.E., Hasty Pudding, S.K. Club, A.D. Club. But he wasn't much interested, he wasn't a nice boy any longer, and after two years he seized the opportunity of being graduated with a wartime degree, *honoris causa*. Under protest he took a position in a bank, but stayed away from it as much as possible and drank enough to insure himself against the danger of being promoted. He read, he fell in love, he gambled, and on January 1, 1922, he began his diary.

"New York," the first brief entry reads, "New York and all day in bed all arms around while the snow falls silently outside and all night on the train alone to Boston." He went back to his abhorrent desk—then, on February 7, "Mamma gave me a hundred dollars for going a month without drinking. Wasn't worth it." On March 12, "Have not been to the Bank for five days." On March 14, "Resigned from the Bank," and on March 21:

Mamma has secured for me a position in the Bank in Paris. Happier—One of my wild days where I threw all care to the wind and drank to excess with 405—Result of being happier. At midnight drove old Walrus's new automobile down the Arlington Street subway until we

crashed slap-bang into an iron fence. A shower
of broken glass, a crushed radiator, a bent axle.
but no one hurt. Still another episode to add to
my rotten reputation.

Shadows of the Sun—the title under which the
diary was published—is better than these early
notes suggest, but it won't ever be ranked as one of
the great autobiographies. Such works have usually
been distinguished either by the author's outward
observation of people or else by his ability to look
inward into his heart. Harry Crosby looked hard
in neither direction. Like so many other poets of
our age, he was self-centered without being at all
introspective, and was devoted to his friends without being sympathetic—he did not feel with people
or feel into them. The figures that recur in his
diary—Joyce, D. H. Lawrence, Hart Crane, Archibald MacLeish, Caresse (his wife), his parents, the
Fire Princess, the Sorceress, E. E. Cummings, Kay
Boyle—all remain as wooden as marionettes: they
do things, they move their arms, raise glasses to
their lips, utter judgments about one another, but
you cannot see the motives behind the actions and
the words. Rather than the people, it is the background that finally comes alive.

But this rule has one exception. Harry Crosby
himself, though at first he seems as mechanical as
the other figures presented in his story, ends in an
unexpected fashion by impressing his personality
upon you and half-winning your affection. You begin with the conviction that he was a bad poet, a
man who dramatized himself, and most of all a
fool. Without ever abandoning those ideas you
gradually revise them, and are glad to admit that
he was an appealing fool, a gallant fool, a brave,
candid, single-minded and fanatically generous fool
who bore nobody malice. He was not a weakling.
Indeed, you come to feel that his strength was
what killed him: a weaker man would have been
prudent enough to survive. He had gifts that
would have made him an explorer, a soldier of
fortune, a revolutionist: they were qualities fatal
to a poet.

Yet even in this profession where he didn't belong he wasn't altogether a failure. It is true that
his early poems were naïve, awkward, false, unspeakably flat; it is true that he never acquired,
even at the end, a sense of the value of words. But
he was beginning to develop something else, a
quality of speed, intensity, crazy vigor—and a poem
need not have all the virtues to survive; sometimes
one virtue is enough. As for his diary, I think there

is no doubt that it will continue to be read by
those lucky enough to get hold of it. It isn't a
great autobiography, no, but it is a valuable record
of behavior and a great source document for the
manners of the age that was ours.

And it is something else besides, an interesting
story. It tells how a young man from Back Bay
adjusted himself to another world—how he got
married, went to Paris and threw up his job in an
American bank there—how he traveled through
southern Europe and northern Africa, observing
the landscapes, if not the people, with a sure eye—
how he lived in an old mill near Paris and entertained everybody, poets, Russian refugees, hop-
heads, pederasts, artists and princes royal—how he
returned to New York, lived too feverishly, became completely demoralized. . . . But it is not
the mere story of his life with which we are concerned. Let us see what his problems were, and
how he tried to solve them, and how the answers
that he found led him inevitably toward one conclusion.

2: City of the Sun

His boyhood and its easy aspirations being dead
within him, Harry Crosby was left after the war
with nothing to live for and no desires except an
immoderate thirst for enjoyment, the sort of thirst
that parches young men when they feel that any
sip of pleasure may be their last. But his boyhood
life, though dead, had not been buried. He was
like a blackboard from which something had been
partly erased: the old words had to be wiped clean
before new ones could be written; all that Boston
implied had to be eradicated. Then, too, he had to
find a new home to take the place of the one he
was bent on losing. His war experience had to be
integrated into his life after the war. . . . Problems like these were difficult, but they could be
solved *ambulando*, as he went along. His really
urgent problem was to find immediately a new
ideal, a reason for living.

He tried to find it in books. In the midst of
banking, love-making and drinking, he read devotedly, with the sense of new vistas opening out
before him. Almost all the books he admired were
those belonging to the Symbolist tradition and to
what I have called the religion of art.

He began by sampling the more popular works of
this category: *The Picture of Dorian Gray*, Laur-

ence Hope's *Songs of India,* then, rising to a higher level, *Les Fleurs du Mal,* which he read easily in the original, having improved his French while in the army. In all these books he found quotations that seemed to explain or ennoble his private misadventures. Thus, after smashing old Walrus's car in the Arlington Street subway, he wrote that his youth, "to quote Baudelaire, *n'est qu'un ténébreux orage, traversé ça et là par de brillants soleils.*" After a love affair, he quoted E. E. Cummings: "I like my body when it is with your body, it is so quite new a thing." His knowledge of literature was widening. He read and approved T. S. Eliot until *The Hollow Men* appeared; then he became indignant at the idea of the world's ending "not with a bang but a whimper." He read Rimbaud and was enraptured. He read Huysmans' *À Rebours,* and was so impressed by the hero's making a trip to London without leaving the Rue de Rivoli that he essayed an equally imaginary voyage at sea. He read Van Gogh's letters. On reading *Ulysses,* he wrote, "I would rather have seen Joyce than any man alive"; and again the following year:

Today I saw Joyce three times . . . he was walking slowly (felt hat overcoat hands in pockets) lost in thought (Work in Progress) entirely unaware of his surroundings. Somnambulist. And in me the same emotion as when Lindbergh arrived. But what is the Atlantic to the oceans Joyce has crossed?

He was not only reading these men, and later meeting such of them as survived in Paris, and even publishing their work; he was also reading the books that critics had written about them to expound their philosophies. Thus, from Arthur Symons' essay on Villiers de l'Isle-Adam, he quoted with approval: "Become the flower of Thyself. Thou art but what thou thinkest: therefore think thyself eternal. . . . Thou art the God thou art able to become." Again, from another essay by the same critic: "And the whole soul of Huysmans characterizes itself in the turn of a single phrase, 'that art is the only clean thing on earth except holiness.' " He looked up many of his favorite authors in the *Encyclopædia Britannica* and went to the trouble of copying a passage about Flaubert:

This ruddy giant was secretly gnawn by misanthropy and disgust of life. This hatred of the bourgeois began in his childhood and developed into a kind of monomania. He despised his fellow men, their habits, their lack of intelligence, their contempt for beauty, with a passionate scorn which has been compared to that of an ascetic monk.

Gradually out of his favorite books the materials for a new ideal of life were being assembled: he wrote that he was beginning "to lay the foundation for my castle of philosophy (not to be confounded with my inner or *inmost* (to be exact) Castle of Beauty)":

Life is pathetic, futile save for the development of the soul; memories, passionate memories are the utmost gold; poetry is religion (for me); silence invariably has her compensation; thought-control is a necessity (but is disloyal in affairs of love); simplicity is strengthening (the strength of the Sun); fanatic faith in the Sun is essential (for the utmost Castle of Beauty).

Outside the ivory walls of this castle was a landscape devastated as if by a hostile army. "Machinery has stamped its heel of ugliness upon the unromantic world." America in particular was pustulant with "civic federations . . . boy-scout clubs . . . educational toys and its Y.M.C.A. and its congregational baptist churches and all this smug self-satisfaction. Horribly bleak, horribly depressing."—"This damn country" seemed to be run for children and "smelt, stank rather, of bananas and Coca Cola and ice cream." Even Europe was falling before the invader. "Industrialism is triumphant and ugliness, sordid ugliness, is everywhere destroying beauty, which has fled to the museums (dead) or into the dark forests of the soul (alive)." The only safety lay in strengthening one's defenses. "The gorgeous flame of poetry is the moat and beyond, the monstrous (and menstruous) world, the world that must be continually beaten back, the world that is always laying siege to the castle of the soul."

Whatever happened in the outside world (with the exception of a few heroic and individual feats, like Lindbergh's flight and Alain Gerbault's voyage in an open boat) was absolutely without interest to the soul inside its castle. Harry didn't even read newspapers (sometimes he glanced at *Paris-Sport* to learn the racing results). He was "bored by politics (full of sound and signifying nothing)." So strong were his defenses that not only machinery and mediocrity but also the commonest human emotions were barred out. No living impulse, no creative force, could cross his moat of fire. In his safe donjon where the larders were stocked with golden memories and bank dividends, he threatened to be transformed into something not so much superhuman as dehumanized.

"I hate children," he wrote. "Rose up in my wrath and fired all three servants," he wrote. "Christ, how I hate servants." People in general were like vermin. "Depressing to consider the ugly bodies that have washed in one's bathtub, to imagine the people who have been born, who have made love, or who have died in one's bed, or to know that myriad unclean fingers have soiled the pages of one's favorite book." Again: "There are too many people in the world and Mount Etna is erupting and thousands of lives are lost. Let them be lost. Let them be lost."

People were tolerable only if they were of his own age and belonged to his social class or to the world of letters. The others threatened to arouse his pity and he tried to avoid them. "Bank banquet," he wrote. "A dismal affair. Poor people trying to enjoy themselves are more pathetic than rich people trying to have a good time, for the poor are utterly defenseless where the rich are sheltered by their cynicism."—"The tragic sadness of the pleasures of the poor!" he wrote on a Fourteenth of July after watching them dance in the streets of Paris. "Glimpses of the underworld, the restless, sweating underworld, the rabble seeking after happiness (O Jesu make it stop) and how much more beautiful the full moon turning to silver the garden of the pavilion."—"I hate the multitude," he wrote. "*Je suis royaliste* and to hell with democracy where the gross comforts of the majority are obtained by the sacrifice of a cultural minority." And again, more briefly and significantly, "I am glad that France has taken the Ruhr." The religion of art was not without having its political sequels.

It also had its sequels in action: of this there can be no doubt whatever. Long ago, in the course of the prolonged debate about life and literature and censorship, it used to be said that art and morality existed in different worlds, that nobody was ever improved or corrupted by reading a book. But Harry advanced a different idea in a bad sonnet to Baudelaire:

Within my soul you've set your blackest flag
And made my disillusioned heart your tomb,

My mind which once was young and virginal
Is now a swamp, a spleenfilled pregnant womb.

His disillusioned heart and spleen-filled mind were delighted with *The Picture of Dorian Gray*, which he read for a second time. He particularly enjoyed

. . . its sparkling cynicism, its color idealism and its undercurrent of dangerous philosophy. . . . "Every impulse that we strive to strangle broods in the mind and poisons us. The body sins once and is done with its sin, for action is a mode of purification. . . . The only way to get rid of a temptation is to yield to it" (tempest of applause).

This was written on July 19, 1924. On July 21 came the sequel:

The sun is streaming through the bedroom window, it is eleven o'clock and I know by my dirty hands, by the torn banknotes on the dressing table, by the clothes and matches and small change scattered over the floor that last night I was drunk. . . . This the result of reading Wilde. Blanche. Rhymes with Avalanche.

His reading of Baudelaire and Wilde was of course not the only or the principal cause of his wining and wenching and gambling for high stakes: the war had already given him a taste for strong pleasures. What his reading did was to supply him with moral justification for a course he might have followed in any case. It also supplied him with maxims: Live dangerously! Seize the day! Be in all things extravagant! Money troubles are never fatal, *une plaie d'argent ne tue jamais* (not even when starving? Harry wondered, but put his doubts aside). Finally his reading supplied him with a goal to be attained by debauches—ecstasy! "The human soul belongs to the spiritual world and is ever seeking to be reunited to its source (the Sun). Such union is hindered by the bodily senses, but though not permanently attainable until death, it can be enjoyed at times in the state called ecstasy when the veil of sensual perception is rent asunder and the soul is merged in God (in the Sun)." Stimulants were an aid in achieving that condition: alcohol, hashish, love and opium were successive rites that led toward a vast upsoaring of the spirit; they served as a Eucharist.

Such was the religion of art, not as it was found at its best in the books of a great writer like Joyce or Valéry or Proust, but as it existed more typically in the mind of a young man home from the war, whose education had been interrupted and whose talent was for action rather than contemplation. Even to Harry Crosby, it was not entirely harmful: it gave him a sort of discipline in his debaucheries; it even ended by teaching him to write. But it prevented his interests from expanding, his life from broadening; it protected him from any new, reinvigorating currents that might have come to him from any other social classes than his own tired class; it condemned him to move in only one direction, toward greater intensity, isolation, frenzy, and finally toward madness. For that, too, was imposed on him by the religion of art. "I believe," he wrote in the midst of a short credo, "in the half-sane half-insane madness and illuminism of the seer." He quoted from Symons and from a résumé of Schopenhauer: "Social rules are made by normal people for normal people, and the man of genius is fundamentally abnormal."—"The direct connection of madness and genius is established by the biographies of great men, such as Rousseau, Byron, Poe, etc. Yet in these semi-madmen, these geniuses, lies the true aristocracy of mankind."—"Applause," he added, "of Suns crashing against Suns." He had set himself the goal of going crazy in order to become a genius. He was the boy apprenticed to a lunatic.

So he had found his way of living, such as it was; he had found his two castles of philosophy and beauty, one within the other, like wooden eggs from Russia. It still remained for him to find a home, and to lose the dead traces of the old home that persisted in his mind.

More than anything else in Harry Crosby's diary, his attempt to eradicate Boston has the elements of high farce. To him Boston was "a dreary place (dreary, drearier, dreariest). . . . No concentration here, no stimulus, no inner centrality, no exploding into the Beyond, no Sun. It is the City of Dreadful Night, a Target for Disgust." He not only fled from the abominable city, and the ideals upheld by it, and the country containing it: he also resigned from the Paris bank because it reminded him of the one where he had worked in Boston. Often he congratulated himself on having evaded

> . . . the horrors of Boston and particularly of Boston virgins who are brought up among sexless surroundings, who wear canvas drawers and flat-heeled shoes and tortoise-shell glasses and

who, once they are married, bear a child punctually every nine months for five or six years and then retire to end their days at the Chilton Club. Christ, what a narrow escape, far narrower than the shells at Verdun.

And yet he couldn't get Massachusetts out of his blood. Particularly on mornings-after, the images of his childhood became vivid and desirable. Thus, on the day that followed the Quatz' Arts ball of 1923, there was "Bed," he wrote, "and no banking . . . and a vague *mal du pays* for Singing Beach and Myopia Links and the Apple Trees in the Fog." After *Dorian Gray* and the Blanche who rhymed with Avalanche, he bitterly longed

> . . . for the sunbasking on Singing Beach, for the smell of the woods around Essex, for the sunset at Coffin's Beach, for the friendliness of the apple trees. . . . I would even like (for me tremendous admission) a small farm near Annisquam with a stone farmhouse looking out over flat stretches of sand toward the sea. The hell you say.

But he had only to meet a few of his fellow countrymen and this longing disappeared. "Two Americans for luncheon," he noted three months later:

> One thought that every gentleman should knock down every Negro he meets (and every Negress? Knock up?) and the other considered love a form of indigestion—it certainly would be for him. Glad I am *déraciné. Ubi bene, ibi patria.*

In the search for that fatherland where everything was best, he traveled through Brittany, the Basque coast, Italy and Spain. At Biskra, on the northern edge of the African desert, it seemed to him that he had finally escaped from ugliness and industrialism:

> There are Arabs coming into town on diminutive donkeys (not coming into town in diminutive Fords) and there is a tiny Tofla tending her goats in a deserted palm garden and there are crumbling walls and sun-baked houses and a certain sluggishness and it never rains and the sun gives health and all one needs are dried dates and bread and coffee (and of course hashish) and a straw mat in a bare room of stone ("a man's wealth should be estimated by what he can do without") and we walk to the Café Maure and smoke hashish (to the amusement of

the *indigènes*) and we see the village sheik in a black and white burnous and a little Negress *accroupie* in his path (no self-consciousness here). . . .

That evening Harry and Caresse went to a house opening off a dark alleyway to watch a little naked Arab girl do a *danse du ventre*:

. . . little Zora removing layer after layer of the most voluminous garments, the last piece being a pair of vast cotton drawers such as clowns wear, and which was gathered about her slender waist by a huge halyard. Then she begins to dance, slowness at first with curious rhythms of her ventre and then convulsive shiverings (two matchless breasts like succulent fruit) and wilder the music and more serpentine her rhythms and her head moves forward and backward and her body weaves an invitation and we went home to the hotel and O God when shall we ever cast off the chains of New England?

The following morning he wrote, "And the chains of New England are broken and unbroken —the death of conscience is not the death of self-consciousness." Biskra had not produced the desired effect. Eight days later he was back in Paris —"Paris, and all other lands and cities dwindle into Nothingness. Paris the City of the Sun."

Here, he decided, he would spend his days; this Sun-City would be his spiritual home. In June he faithfully attended the races; in August he went driving off to Deauville to play baccarat and bask on the beach; in October, his favorite month, there was racing again near Paris; there were visits to booksellers and picture galleries, and long exhilarating walks in the Bois, and friends in for cocktails—he was entering into the life of the city and meeting not only exiles like himself, young writers like Hemingway, MacLeish, Kay Boyle and Hart Crane, but also French artists and noblemen. As the years passed by he saw less often the little stone farmhouse near Annisquam and heard less often "the sound of the Fog Horn booming through the Fog"; there was nothing to remind him of his dead boyhood. Yet he was beginning again to be restless and dissatisfied.

In truth the Paris in which he had chosen to live was not the only Paris. It was one among many cities that bore the same name and were built one inside the other like Harry's castles of philosophy and beauty. It was the Paris of the international revelers and refugees. It was the Paris symbolized by the famous House of All Nations, to which Harry paid a formal visit

. . . and saw the Persian and the Russian and the Turkish and the Japanese and the Spanish rooms . . . and the bathroom with mirrored walls and mirrored ceilings and a glimpse of the thirty harlots waiting in the salon and there was the flogging post where men came to flagellate young girls and where others (masochists) came to be flagellated.

It was the Paris of drugs and sexual perversions:

Z is busily preparing a pipe, deftly twisting the treacly substance over a little lamp while Y paler than I have ever seen her reaches out white hands like a child asking for its toy. . . .

A great drinking of cocktails in our bathroom— it was too cold in the other rooms—and there were eleven of us all drinking and shrieking and we went to eat oysters and then to the Jungle where there was a great drinking of whiskey and mad music and life is exciting nowadays with all the pederasts and the lesbians—no one knows who is flirting with whom.

It was the Paris of the Bal des Quatz' Arts, which Harry always attended:

At eight the Students begin to appear—more and more and more (many more people than last year) and the Punch Bowl is filled and the Party has begun and soon everyone is Gay and Noisy Noisier and Noisiest toward ten o'clock and seventy empty bottles of champagne rattle upon the floor and now straight gin Gin Gin Gin like the Russian refugees clamoring for bread and everyone clamored and the fire roared in the hearth (roared with the wine in my heart) and the room was hot and reeked with cigarette and cigar smoke with fard and sweat and smell of underarms and we were all in Khmer costume . . . and at eleven we formed in line in the courtyard (I with the sack full of snakes) and marched away on foot . . . and at last exhausted into the Salle Wagram (snarling of tigers at the gate snarling of tigers inside) and up the ladder to the loge and up another ladder to an attic and up an imaginary ladder to and into the Sun and here I undid the sack and turned it upside down and all the snakes dropped down among the dancers and there were shrieks and catcalls and there was a riot and I remember two strong young men stark naked wrestling on the floor for the honor of dancing with a young girl (silver paint conquered purple paint) and I remember a mad student drinking wine out of a skull which he had pilfered from my library as I had pilfered it a year ago from the Catacombs (O happy skull to be filled full of sparkling gold) and in a corner I watched two savages making love (stark naked wrestling on the floor) and beside me sitting on the floor a plump woman with bare breasts absorbed in the passion of giving milk to one of the snakes.

This was the crazy Paris which, to its own people, seemed the innermost city: in truth it was the outmost and the youngest. It was not the Paris of Villon or Cyrano or Rameau's famous nephew, who were wastrels too, but in a different fashion. It was a Paris that began to flourish under the Second Empire, when the landlords and suddenly enriched speculators of all Europe came flocking toward a world capital where they could spend their profits and be ostentatious in their vice. From year to year this Paris became more feverish and gilded—but there was a time after Louis Napoleon fell when it suddenly ceased to exist.

"Wonderful indeed," wrote Karl Marx in 1871, "was the change the Commune had wrought!"

No longer any trace of the meretricious Paris of the Second Empire. No longer was Paris the rendezvous of British landlords, Irish absentees, American ex-slaveholders and shoddy men, Russian ex-serfowners and Wallachian boyars. No more corpses at the Morgue, no nocturnal burglaries, scarcely any robberies; in fact, for the first time since the days of February 1848, the streets of Paris were safe, and that without any police of any kind. "We," said a member of the Commune, "hear no longer of assassination, theft and personal assault; it seems, indeed, as if the police had dragged along with it to Versailles all its Conservative friends." The cocottes had refound the scent of their protectors—the absconding men of family, religion and above all, of property. In their stead, the real women of Paris showed again at the surface—heroic, noble and devoted, like the women of antiquity.

But this was only an interlude. Soon the police and its Conservative friends reoccupied Paris, after executing thirty thousand of the inhabitants. Soon the burglaries began again; soon the wealthy exiles reappeared on the boulevards; and for half a century their special city continued to grow.

Its population, however, had changed since the World War. The Russians still formed part of it, but they no longer had any ex-serfs to provide them with incomes—the Irish absentees had disappeared, after losing most of their estates—the British landlords, with heavier taxes to pay, were living at home—the Southern ex-slaveholders were dead and their descendants had joined the middle classes. Their places in the international set had been taken by the sons and daughters of Northern bankers, by Swedish match kings, by Spanish grandees—and also by strange new people, Chinese mandarins and war lords, Egyptian cotton growers, Indian maharanees, even a sprinkling of Negro kings from Senegal. Their places were also taken by a few French nobles, who had formerly despised these refugees, but were now beginning to feel akin to them, as refugees too, uprooted from the life of their own country. Indeed, all these people had this in common, that they lived at a great distance from their sources of revenue; that their money came to them, not smelling of blood, sweat and the soil, but in the shape of clean paper readily transformable into champagne and love. They were spending it faster and faster, but also more aimlessly. In everything they did there was now an air of uncertainty and strain. Something, the war, the Russian Revolution, had given them a sense that their order was crumbling and that they belonged to a dying world. Cartoonists used to depict them as skeletons dressed in banknotes.

This was the world and the city that Harry Crosby had chosen for home. He never quite belonged to it. He too was marked for death, but he was not yet a thing of bones and paper; he had too much sinew not to grow tired of his fellow townsmen. Toward the end, a note of fatigue and disgust with Paris began to creep into his diary; he was beginning to be irritated by the people always crowding about him. "Really the stupidity of the French is beyond imagination."—"And I hate the English Jesus how I hate the English so damn bourgeois and banal."—"I like New York much better than Paris." It was becoming evident that the home he had so joyously chosen, after destroying the traces of his boyhood, was not to be his home after all. Perhaps he could find a new home in New York. Or else, if that failed him—

He had meanwhile another problem to solve. In addition to a way of living and a home that had served him temporarily, he needed also a faith and a ritual. Poetry in itself was not enough: he wanted something beyond it, a transcendent symbol he could celebrate and adore.

The symbol he chose for himself was the Sun.

I don't know how he came to make this choice. He may have done so arbitrarily, during his boyhood; in any case he already regarded himself as a sun-worshiper before beginning his diary. He tried from the beginning to dignify his faith by finding historical parallels, and was delighted to learn that the Peruvians, the Persians, the Egyptians and many other ancient peoples had also worshiped the sun; he memorized the names of their sun-gods and adopted some of their rituals. In those religions, however, the sun had usually represented a principle of fertility: It was what caused the wheat and maize to grow and thus preserved and symbolized the life of the tribe or nation. Harry's sun-worship was something different, a wholly individual matter, a bloodless, dehumanized religion without community or fraternity or purpose. Yet he fanatically clung to it and, at least toward the end, believed in it sincerely.

It seems to have stood for many different things. Sometimes it was nature-worship—"I am a mystic and religion is not a question of sermons and churches but rather it is an understanding of the infinite through nature (Sun, Moon and Stars)." Sometimes it seemed to be light-worship. Sometimes is was plainly self-worship, Harry himself becoming a sun-symbol—"Today read in Schopenhauer that the center of gravity (for me the Sun) should fall entirely and absolutely within oneself." It was often body-worship—one of the rites that Harry invented for himself was sun-bathing, preferably on top of a tower, until his whole body was "sunnygolden" and until he "exploded into the Sun." Still oftener is was sex-worship—"My soul today is a young phallus thrusting upwards to possess the young goddess of the Sun." He gave sun-names to the women he loved, so that his union with them symbolized a union with the sun itself.

His faith was also a refuge from ugliness and industrialism—"I believe in the Sun because the Sun is the only thing in life that does not disillusion."

But his transcendent symbol was something else besides, something that wasn't clear in his own mind but stands forth unmistakably to the reader of his diary. Because the Sun was at the center of his life—because the center of his life was empty, no living impulse being able to cross the moat of fire with which he had surrounded himself, and because, ever since that day at Verdun, death ruled

as master in his inmost castle—because of all this, and by a simple process of transference, the sun became a cold abyss, a black sun, a gulf of death into which he would some day hurl himself ecstatically, down, down, downwards, falling "into the Red-Gold (night) of the Sun . . . SUNFIRE!" His worship of the Sun became the expectation of, the strained desire for, "a Sun-Death into Sun."

The truly extraordinary feature of Harry Crosby's life, the quality that gave it logic and made it resemble a clear syllogism, was the fashion in which all the different strands of it were woven together into the single conception of a sun-death.

Take the first strand of all: take the war. Harry often mentions it in his diary; he dwells on it with a horrified fascination that becomes almost love. Yet he never mentions the historical causes or results of it, never seems to regard it as a struggle among nations for survival and among industries for markets. To him it was a blind, splendid catastrophe that meant only one thing, death. It was kept fresh in his mind by symbols like his dead friends, his nearly fatal adventure at Verdun, the Unknown Soldier, the military graveyards, always by corpses—and since these deaths were fine and courageous, were good deaths, the war itself was good.

Here are a few of his reflections on it:

February 1, 1925.—Above all, we who have known war must never forget war. And that is why I have the picture of a soldier's corpse nailed to the door of my library.

November 22, 1925.—All day in the streets the hawkers hawk their wares . . . and at night in a glass of brandy a toast in honor of the day (the day of the barrage at Verdun, the day S was wounded).

There will always be war.

November 11, 1927.—Armistice Day day that for me is the most significant day of the year . . . before going to bed I smoked my pipe and drank two glasses of brandy, To Oliver Ames Junior (killed in action) to Aaron Davis Weld (killed in action).

One Fourth of July in Paris, he attended the unveiling of a statue to Alan Seeger and heard the reading of his "Rendezvous with Death":

At the end, to the triumphant sound of trumpets, troops at attention defiled past the grand-stand: Foch, Pétain, Joffre, Mangin, Poincaré, Millerand and our uninspiring Ambassador. Very impressive, very significant, as all such things are to those who went to war. Stood with the small contingent of members of the Field Service, and afterwards we were invited to the Elysée Palace to meet Millerand and Mangin (how the poilus used to shake their fists at him and call him *le Boucher*).

This comment is, in Harry's own words, "very impressive, very significant." He had more or less consciously taken the side of Mangin the Butcher against the common soldiers whose lives were thrown away at Mangin's orders, whose bodies were melted down into the row of medals that Mangin wore on his left breast. He had taken the side of death against life; now he was preparing to act upon his choice. By committing suicide, he was rejoining his dead friends, his only true friends, and was fulfilling the destiny marked out for him at Verdun.

But just as his war service led him toward this end, so too did his study of the Symbolist poets and philosophers; they were still his guides. Out of his reading came the idea that the achievement of individuality was the purpose to seek above all others—the highest expression of the self was in the act of self-annihilation. Out of his reading came the idea that ecstasy was to be attained at any price—death was the last ecstasy. Out of his reading he learned to admire and seek madness—what could be crazier than killing oneself?—and learned that life itself might be transformed into a work of art rising to a splendid climax—"to die at the right time." His suicide would be the last debauch, the final extravagance, the boldest act of sex, the supreme gesture of defiance to the world he despised.

He had been seeking a home without really finding it. Death was his permanent home.

Even the religion of his boyhood resumed a place in his life when he learned that the birthday and high feast of Christianity was really the winter solstice, the birthday of the sun, and reflected that Jesus Christ, in a sense, had committed suicide. In the pursuit of death, all the strands united, aphelion and perihelion, boyhood and manhood, Boston and Paris, peace and war—all his conflicts were resolved. For the first time Harry Crosby became fully integrated, self-sufficient, complete.

KENNETH BURKE (1897–   )

Burke, like so many critics who began to publish in the 1920's, absorbed a great deal of Marxism—though he was never a doctrinaire Marxist and from the outset was receptive to all sorts of other influences, including that of Freud. His writings constitute an attempt to make a synthesis not only of the ideas of Marx and Freud, but also of other thinkers of very different character.

Burke is intelligent and ingenious; he has apparently read everything; and he is willing to take risks in his effort to relate any particular to any other particular. Most of all, Burke is fascinated with language; yet his various studies of language—*Philosophy of Literary Form* (1941), *A Grammar of Motives* (1945), and *Rhetoric of Motives* (1950)—are never merely studies in linguistics. They involve psychology, philosophy, anthropology, and all manner of other social and historical disciplines.

But despite Burke's erudition and his detailed knowledge of the modern European mind—he has, for example, translated a good many German authors—he impresses one as indelibly American. In fact, he reminds one of nothing so much as the legendary old-fashioned American inventor. Burke constructs—as if he were an intellectual Rube Goldberg—the most amazing linguistic and psychological contraptions. He is the original, resourceful, do-it-yourself man. Such traits reveal themselves from the beginning of his career: he early gave up his studies at Columbia University to work out problems in his own terms and in his own way.

In relation to American poets, particularly those of his own generation, Burke has played the role of an inciter. His interest in philosophy and psychology, his fascination with the way in which words function together to build up meanings, often rich and many-layered, and his ability to see analogies and to find connections between contexts apparently completely unrelated made him a tremendous stimulus to the poets of the 1920's and 1930's. (One should say "other poets," for Burke himself began as a poet and has published two volumes of poetry.) Marianne Moore has caught Burke's special quality in one of her poems in which she affectionately refers to him as "a psychologist, of acute raccoon-like curiosity."

Among the American intellectuals, Burke's principal role has been that of a middle man between the various disciplines: his forte has been to relate terms taken from one realm of discourse to those of another. He does so through a process of "conversion" and "transformation." As one scholar has put it:

> The reality of *A Grammar of Motives* is the marvelously facile technique with which Burke reduces all philosophical thought to the sameness of terminological manipulation. No introductory textbook of philosophy has ever reduced its subject matter to a series of formulas half so effective as Burke does in this book. . . .
>
> The philosophy of *A Grammar of Motives*, if it can be said to have one, is not at all a philosophy of action: it is rather a curious kind of pan-verbalism which may be summed up in this climactic assertion: "The great departures in human thought can be eventually reduced to a moment where the thinker treats as *op*posite, key terms formerly considered *ap*posite, or v[ice] v[ersa]" (Merle E. Brown, *Kenneth Burke*, 1969, pp. 28, 31).

That is, the great departures in human thought occur when the thinker demonstrates the ironic fact that two items, always supposed to be antithetical, are in fact cosily related to each other.

Burke is an ironist in a very special sense. In his discussion of what he calls the four master tropes, he suggests that for one of them, irony, we can substitute the term dialectic; and Burke is always a brilliant and frequently persuasive dialectician. For example, he is able to show—perhaps with a little verbal legerdemain—that *style* and *custom* often exhibit the most surprising relation to each other. Thus "we tend to think of customary actions as compulsive—yet values exist today only in so far as custom survives." Or again, Burke thinks that "Once the Communistic way of life were firmly established in human institutions, I believe that the poetic *metaphor* [our italics] would be the best guide (indeed the only conceivable guide) in shaping the new pieties of living."

Burke is a born system-builder. He is very much interested in literature, but he is interested in it primarily as a manifestation of the culture which produced it and which in so many respects it reflects. Thus, even when Burke begins to talk specifically about a literary work—a poem, say—he will usually—and usually very promptly—move into wider and more general contexts.

One may illustrate from Burke's discussion of Keats's "Ode on a Grecian Urn." In discussing the second stanza he finds that he needs to make a reference to the "Liebestod" in Richard Wagner's opera *Tristan und Isolde* and that leads him to remark that such a "love-death" is "particularly representative of a romanticism that was the reflex of business."[1]

Consideration of the "mutual flame" between lovers such as that which consumes Tristan and Isolde next prompts Burke to quote two stanzas from Shakespeare's "The Phoenix and the Turtle," a poem about mutual love. (The phoenix was the fabulous bird that set fire to its own nest, and reduced itself to ashes, from which

---

[1] Just why it should be a "reflex of business" does not immediately come clear. Burke's own note reads as follows: "Adding historical factors, one can note the part that capitalist individualism plays in sharpening the consummation" of the lovers who die "as individual identities that they might be transformed into a common identity." Is Burke's analogy that of two corporations merging into a new larger corporation?

arose a new phoenix.) This reference to lovers consumed in a mutual flame in turn leads Burke to quote a letter from John Keats to his fiancée, Fanny Brawne. After quoting the letter, Burke writes:

Our primary concern is to follow the transformation of the poem ["Ode on a Grecian Urn"] itself. But to understand its full nature as a symbolic act, we should use whatever knowledge is available. In the case of Keats, not only do we know the place of this poem in his work and his time, but also we have material to guide our speculations as regards correlations between poem and poet. I grant that such speculations interfere with the symmetry of criticism as a game. (Criticism as a game is best to watch, I guess, when one confines himself to the single unit, and reports on its movements like a radio commentator broadcasting the blow-by-blow description of a prizefight.) But linguistic analysis has opened up new possibilities in the correlating of producer and product—and these concerns have such important bearing upon matters of culture and conduct in general that no sheer conventions or ideals of criticism should be allowed to interfere with their development.

Burke thus defends with wit and rhetorical plausibility his method of making constant digressions. For by saying that literary criticism as commonly practiced is a game—that is, an interesting spectacle to watch—he implies that *he* is concerned with something more important. Perhaps he is, and one has to concede that to attempt to examine a poem or a novel as an entity in itself always involves an artificial separation, for ultimately everything *is* related to everything else.

Yet just here common sense rears its ugly head. Even if *ultimately* no bit of reality can be finally isolated from all the rest, could one hope in any finite discussion to relate a poem or a novel to the *whole of experience*, bringing to bear on it logic, psychology, sociology, anthro-

pology, theology, philosophy, and all the varieties of cultural history? Even Burke does not attempt to do this, and in any case his method is haphazard rather than systematic. It is valuable for individual insights rather than for any orderly and complete analysis. Burke too is playing a kind of game, a game that has its own dazzling attractiveness.

Burke reminds one here of Samuel Taylor Coleridge, who, incidentally, seems to be one of Burke's personal heroes. (Burke has written about him at length, and with perception and warm sympathy.) Coleridge, too, was a born system-builder. In spite of his devotion to poetry and his great skill in analyzing its structure, he found it difficult to stick to the text in hand or even to poetry as such, for it was plain to him too that everything was related to everything else and one could not really talk about poetry without talking about the nature of words, the nature of the human mind, finally the "nature" of nature—that is, talking about metaphysics. This was his prime difficulty in organizing his famous *Biographia Literaria:* one thing so led to another than one could not really talk properly about literature until he had settled the matter of whether the system of either Hartley or Aristotle was "tenable in theory" or whether philosophy was "possible as a science."

The great inclusive system which Coleridge planned to write never came to anything. But Coleridge exerted a powerful and fruitful influence on his contemporary poets, was a famous talker, and got down on paper for posterity some very brilliant and seminal criticism. One is tempted to make something of the same judgment of Burke: his projects of system-making are awesome in their elaboration and ambition, but what we value finally are Burke's incidental discussions, his insights, his discoveries of relationship—the sorts of things that other writers can use, convert to their own needs, and even pervert to their own purposes.

Some readers of Burke, it should be said, would sharply disagree with this judgment. His system is precisely what they find most praiseworthy. William H. Rueckert, in an appreciative, though not uncritical, book, sees Burke "as one of the great men of our time" and salutes his "dramatism" as an attempt to get men to "look at the symbolic fog [in which they live] and recognize it for what it is. . . . The goal is 'By and through language,' to move 'beyond language'" (*Kenneth Burke and the Drama of Human Relations*) and get a glimpse of ultimate reality. Burke's purpose is noble, and though his dramatic theory of literature, "if wrenched from the [more general] system of which it is the central part and treated or applied in isolation, . . . sometimes seems fantastic," in context "it is powerful, workable, and rewarding."

Armin P. Frank makes a comparable judgment:

> Dramatism, as developed by Burke, is a consistent world view. It is unique insofar as it takes ritual drama, or sacrificial tragedy, as the representative anecdote, or key example, of all human behavior—psychological, linguistic, social. . . . Critics have repeatedly said that Burke stopped being a good literary critic when he turned to extra-literary concerns.

But Frank points out (in *Kenneth Burke*) that Burke has never been exclusively literary in his interests, and in any case the "stop" to which he has come is not one of cessation in failure but "of achievement; he has no intention of going beyond Dramatism and logology, but he is constantly at work elaborating, subtilizing, and perfecting his position. . . . Burke's quest for identity has long come to a close; now, the Dark Tower's name is *Consummation.*"

We have earlier in this introduction illustrated the ways in which Burke can use a literary text as an exemplification of "dramatism" or as a point of departure for a discussion of social customs or of myth and ritual. But Burke is also capable of writing a "purer" or at least more conventional literary criticism. When it suits his purposes to stick to particular texts, he provides his reader with a very sensitive treatment of them.

Thus, Marianne Moore's poetry obviously interests him greatly, and though he is intrigued by the special character of her technique and sees that it might be called Imagist or Symbolist or (with a bow toward William Carlos Williams) Objectivist, he is willing to subordinate these problems of genre to the intrinsic qualities of particular poems. Here follows the last third of his essay on her, which he calls "Motives and Motifs in the Poetry of Marianne Moore."[2]

[2] In *A Grammar of Motives* (1945). It was first published in *Accent* (Spring, 1942).

FURTHER READINGS

Kenneth Burke, *Attitudes Toward History* (1959)
———, *Book of Moments: Poems, 1915–54* (1968)
———, *The Complete White Oxen* (1968)
———, *Counterstatement* (1931)
———, *A Grammar of Motives* (1945)
———, *Language as Symbolic Action* (1966)
———, *Permanence and Change* (1935)
———, *Philosophy of Literary Form—Studies in Symbolic Action* (1941)
———, *A Rhetoric of Motives* (1950)
———, *The Rhetoric of Religion* (1961)

Armin P. Frank, *Kenneth Burke* (1969)

Laura V. Holland, *Counterpoint: Kenneth Burke and Aristotle's Theory of Rhetoric* (1959)
George Knox, *Critical Moments: Kenneth Burke's Categories and Critiques* (1957)
Howard Nemerov, "Everything, Preferably All at Once," *Sewanee Review* (April–June, 1971)
William H. Rueckert, *Kenneth Burke and the Drama of Human Relations* (1963)
———, ed., *Critical Responses to Kenneth Burke, 1924–1966* (1969)
René Wellek, "Kenneth Burke and Literary Criticism," *Sewanee Review* (April–June, 1971)

From Motives and Motifs in the Poetry of Marianne Moore (1942)

In the earlier volume [*Selected Poems*] there is a poem, "Black Earth," wherein surprisingly the poet establishes so close an identification with her theme as not merely to "observe" it with sympathy and appreciation, but to speak for it. This is one of her rare "I" poems—and in it the elephant sometimes speaks with the challenge and confidence of an Invictus. Beginning on the theme of emergence (coupled with delight in the thought of submergence at will), there is first a celebration of the sturdy skin; then talk of power ("my back is full of the history of power"); and then: "My soul shall never be cut into/by a wooden spear." Next comes mention of the trunk, and of poise. And interwoven with the vigor of assertion, the focal theme is there likewise:

that tree-trunk without
roots, accustomed to shout
  its own thought of itself . . .

and:

　　　. . . The I of each is to
the I of each
a kind of fretful speech
  which sets a limit on itself; the elephant is
  black earth preceded by a tendril?

I think we can make a point by recalling this earlier poem when, in "Smooth Gnarled Crape Myrtle" (*What Are Years*), the theme of the elephant's trunk appears again, this time but in passing, contextual and "tangential" to the themes of birds, union, loneliness:

　　　　　. . . 'joined in
friendship, crowned by love.'
An aspect may deceive; as the
elephant's columbine-tubed trunk
held waveringly out—
an at will heavy thing—is
delicate.

Surely, "an at will heavy thing" is a remarkable find. But one does not make such observation by merely looking at an elephant's trunk. There must have been much to discard. In this instance, we can know something about the omissions, quite as though we had inspected earlier drafts of the poem with their record of revisions. For though a usage

in any given poem is a finished thing, and thus brilliant with surface, it becomes in effect but "work in progress" when we align it with kindred usages (emergent, fully developed, or retrospectively condensed) in other poems. And here, by referring to "Black Earth," we can find what lies behind the reference to the elephant's trunk in "Smooth Gnarled Crape Myrtle." We can know it for a fact what kind of connotations must, for the poet, have been implicit in the second, condensed usage. Hence we can appreciate the motives that enabled this trunk to be seen not merely as a *thing*, but as an *act*, representative of the assertion in "Black Earth." And by reviewing the earlier usage we can know the kind of volitional material which, implicit in the later usage, led beyond the perception of the trunk as a thing to this perception of it as an act. At such moments, I should say, out of our idealistic trammels we get a glimpse of realism in its purity.

Or let us look at another instance. Sensitivity in the selection of words resides in the ability, or necessity, to feel behind the given word a history —not a past history, but a future one. Within the word, collapsed into its simultaneous oneness, there is implicit a sequence, a complexity of possible narratives that could be drawn from it. If you would remember what words are in this respect, and how in the simultaneity of a word histories are implicit, recall the old pleasantry of asking someone, "What's an accordion," whereat invariably as he explains he will start pumping a bellows.

Well, among Miss Moore's many poems enunciating aspects of her esthetic credo, or commenting on literary doctrines and methods, there is one, "To a Snail," beginning:

If 'compression is the first grace of style,'
you have it. Contractility is a virtue
as modesty is a virtue.

And this equating of an esthetic value with a moral one is summed up by locating the principle of style "in the curious phenomenon of your occipital horn."

In her poem on the butterfly (*What Are Years*, p. 17), the mood of tentativeness that had been compressed within the term "contractility" reveals its significant narrative equivalents. As befits the tentative, or contractile, it is a poem of jeopardy, tracing a tenuous relationship between a butterfly ("half deity half worm," "last of the elves") and a nymph ("dressed in Wedgewood blue"), with light winds (even a "zephyr") to figure the motives of passion. Were not the course of a butterfly so intrinsically akin to the "inconsequential ease" and "droverlike tenacity" of Miss Moore's own versa-tilities, one might not have much hope for a poem built about this theme (reminiscent of many musical Papillons—perhaps more than a theme, perhaps a set idiom, almost a form). Here, with the minute accuracy of sheerly "objectivist" description, there is a subtle dialectic of giving and receiving, of fascinations and releases—an interchange of delicately shaded attitudes. In this realm, things reached for will evade, but will follow the hand as it recedes.

Through the tracery of flight, there are two striking moments of stasis, each the termination of a course: one when "the butterfly's tobacco-brown unglazed/china eyes and furry countenance confront/the nymph's large eyes"—and the second when, having broken contact with the nymph's "controlled agitated glance," the "fiery tiger-horse" (at rest, but poised against the wind, "chest arching/bravely out") is motivated purely by relation to the zephyr alone. The poem concludes by observing that this "talk" between the animal and the zephyr "was as strange as my grandmother's muff."

I have called it a poem of jeopardy. (When butterfly and nymph confront each other, "It is Goya's scene of the tame magpie faced/by crouching cats.") It is also a poem of coquetry (perhaps our last poem of coquetry, quite as this butterfly was the last of the elves—coquetry now usually being understood as something that comes down like a ton of brick).[1]

[1] In the earlier volume there is an epigram-like poem, "To a Steam Roller," that I have always thought very entertaining. It excoriates this sorry, ungainly mechanism as a bungling kind of fellow that, when confronting such discriminations as are the vital purpose of Miss Moore's lines, would "crush all the particles down/into close conformity, and then walk back and forth/on them." We also read there:

As for butterflies, I can hardly conceive
of one's attending upon you, but to question
the congruence of the complement is vain, if it exists.

Heretofore I had been content to think of this reference to a butterfly simply as a device for suggesting weight by a contrasting image of lightness. But the role of butterfly as elf conversant to nymph might also sug-

The tentativeness, contractility, acquires more purely the theme of jeopardy in "Bird-Witted" (*What Are Years*), reciting the incident of the "three large fledgling mocking-birds," awaiting "their no longer larger mother," while there approaches

the
intellectual cautious-
ly c r e e p ing cat.

gest the presence of such overtones as contrasting types of masculinity. (This would give us a perfect instance of what Coleridge meant by fancy, which occurs when we discern behind the contrast an element that the contrasted images share in common.)

As for the later poem, where the theme of the butterfly is fully developed, I might now try to make more clearly the point I had in mind with reference to the two moments of stasis. In the opening words "(half deity half worm" and "We all, infant and adult, have/stopped to watch the butterfly") the poem clearly suggests the possibility that it will figure two levels of motivation, a deity being in a different realm of motives than a worm, and the child's quality of perception being critically distinct from the adult's. Examining the two moments of stasis, we find here too the indications of an important difference between them. At the first stasis, elf and nymph confront each other, while "all's a-quiver with significance." But at the final stasis, the conversity is between butterfly and west wind, a directer colloquy (its greater inwardness linking it, in my opinion, with the motive-behind-motive figuration in the theme of clocks-for-clocks). At this second stage, the butterfly is called "historic metamorphoser/and saintly animal"; hence we may take it that the "deity" level of motive prevails at this second stage. The quality of the image in the closing line ("their talk was as strange as my grandmother's muff") would suggest that the deified level is equated with the quality of perception as a child. (The grandmother theme also appears in "Spenser's Ireland," where we are told that "Hindered characters . . . in Irish stories . . . all have grandmothers." Another reason for believing that the second stage of the butterfly poem is also the "motives-behind-motives" stage is offered tenuously by this tie-up with the word "hindered," since the final poem in the book, as we shall know when we come to it, does well by this word in proclaiming a morality of art.)

Another poem, "Virginia Britannia" (*What Are Years*), that seems on the surface almost exclusively descriptive (though there is passing reference to a "fritillary" that "zig-zags") is found to be progressing through scenic details to a similar transcendence. At the last, against sunset, two levels are figured, while the intermediate trees "become with lost identity, part of the ground." The clouds, thus marked off, are then heralded in words suggestive of Wordworth's ode as "to the child an intimation of/what glory is."

If her animals are selected for their "fastidiousness," their fastidiousness itself is an aspect of contractility, of jeopardy. "The Pangolin" (*What Are Years*), a poem which takes us through odd nocturnal journeys to the joyous saluting of the dawn, begins: "Another armoured animal"—and of a sudden you realize that Miss Moore's recondite menagerie is almost a thesaurus of protectiveness. Thus also, the poem in which occur the lines anent visible and invisible, has as its conclusion:

> unsolicitude having swallowed up
>   all giant birds but an
>   alert gargantuan
> little-winged, magnificently
> speedy running-bird. This one
>   remaining rebel
>   is the sparrow-camel.

The tentativeness also manifests itself at times in a cult of rarity, a collector's or antiquarian interest in the present, a kind of stylistic tourism. And it may lead to a sheer word play, of graduated sort (a Laforguian delight in showing how the pedantries can be reclaimed for poetry):

> The lemur-student can see
>   that the aye-aye is not
>
> an angwan-tíbo, potto, or loris.

Yet mention of the "aepyornis" may suggest the answer we might have given, were we up on such matters, to one who, pencil in hand and with the newspaper folded to make it firmer, had asked, "What's a gigantic bird, found fossil in Madagascar in nine letters?" As for her invention, "invis   ible," I can't see it.

Tonally, the "contractility" reveals itself in the great agility, even restlessness, which Miss Moore imparts to her poetry by assonance, internal rhyme, and her many variants of the run-over line. We should also note those sudden nodules of sound which are scattered throughout her verses, such quick concentrations as "rude root cudgel," "the raised device reversed," "trim trio on the tree-stem," "furled fringed frill," or tonal episodes more sustained and complex, as the lines on the birds in Ireland (already quoted), or the title, "Walking-Sticks and Paper-Weights and Water-Marks," or

> . . . the redbird
>   the red-coated musketeer,
>   the trumpet-flower, the cavalier,
> the parson, and the
>   wild parishioner. A deer-
>   track in a church-floor
> brick . . .

One noticeable difference between the later selection and the earlier one is omission of poems on method. In *Selected Poems* there were a great many such. I think for instance of: "Poetry," containing her ingenious conceit, "imaginary gardens with real toads in them"; "Critics and Connoisseurs"; "The Monkeys"; "In the Days of Prismatic Colour"; "Picking and Choosing"; "When I Buy Pictures"; "Novices" (on action in language, and developed in imagery of the sea); "The Past is the Present"; ("ecstasy affords/the occasion and expediency determines the form"); and one which propounds a doctrine as its title: "In This Age of Hard Trying, Nonchalance is Good and."

But though methodological pronouncements of this sort have dropped away, in the closing poem on "The Paper Nautilus," the theme does reappear. Yet in an almost startlingly deepened transformation. Here, proclaiming the poet's attachment to the poem, there are likenesses to the maternal attachment to the young. And the themes of bondage and freedom (as with one "hindered to succeed") are fiercely and flashingly merged.

LIONEL TRILLING (1905–   )

We have earlier commented on Burke as an assimilator and synthesizer. One of the major ingredients in his new synthesis is something so important in its own right that it deserves separate and special treatment here. We refer to Freudianism.

The impact of Freud on American intellectuals and his influence on American poets, novelists, and playwrights in the twentieth century have been pervasive. Perhaps the best single discussion of this subject is to be found in Lionel Trilling's long essay "Freud and Literature."[1]

In spite of his admiration for Freud's intellectual accomplishment and the light that Freud's conception of the mind sheds upon literature, Trilling, it is to be noted, regards Freud's conception of the role of literature as inadequate. Freud subordinates literature to life, making it a reflection—perhaps an unconscious reflection—of the artist's own desires and needs, or else Freud regards it as an instrument consciously used by the artist to accomplish certain practical ends. Thus Freud, like Marx, is primarily interested in literature as a sociological and psychological phenomenon. The

[1] The essay was first published in 1940 (and revised in 1947). Trilling has subsequently published other essays on Freud, notably the two included in his volume entitled *Beyond Culture* (1965). But those subsequent essays do not seriously alter his estimate of Freud's conception of literature.

Freudian and Marxist accounts of literature really have to do with the genesis of art—how it arises, how it is shaped by its social matrix—or else with the effects of art on the reading public. (The Communist countries have found it all but impossible to refrain from tampering with the free expression of art lest it undermine the regime or introduce frivolous or "decadent" ideas and lessen the people's will to work.)

His essay on Freud constitutes an attractive instance of Trilling's abilities as a thinker and a literary critic: it displays his learning, his tact, his good sense, and his ability to avoid doctrinaire rigidity. But this essay is, of course, too special to indicate his range of interests or his skill in dealing with a literary text. Limitations of space, however, make it impossible to include additional essays by him. (The same difficulty affects our representation of other contemporary critics who together constitute a numerous and, some would say, a brilliant constellation. In this book one can provide only a few hints and samples.)

FURTHER READINGS

Lionel Trilling, *Beyond Culture* (1965)
——, *E. M. Forster* (1943)
——, *Freud and the Crisis of Culture* (1955)
——, *The Liberal Imagination* (1950)
——, *Matthew Arnold* (1939)
——, *The Middle of the Journey* (1947)
——, *Mind and the Modern World* (1973)
——, *The Opposing Self* (1955)
——, *Sincerity and Authenticity* (1973)

From Freud and Literature (1940-47)

The Freudian psychology is the only systematic account of the human mind which, in point of subtlety and complexity, of interest and tragic power, deserves to stand beside the chaotic mass of psychological insights which literature has accumulated through the centuries. To pass from the reading of a great literary work to a treatise of academic psychology is to pass from one order of perception to another, but the human nature of the Freudian psychology is exactly the stuff upon which the poet has always exercised his art. It is therefore not surprising that the psychoanalytical theory has had a great effect upon literature. Yet

the relationship is reciprocal, and the effect of Freud upon literature has been no greater than the effect of literature upon Freud. When, on the occasion of the celebration of his seventieth birthday, Freud was greeted as the "discoverer of the unconscious," he corrected the speaker and disclaimed the title. "The poets and philosophers before me discovered the unconscious," he said. "What I discovered was the scientific method by which the unconscious can be studied."[1]

[1] As early as 1924 John Crowe Ransom made what is substantially this point. In an essay published in the *Saturday Review of Literature* (October 4), Ransom

What is it that Freud added that the tendency of literature itself would not have developed without him? If we were looking for a writer who showed the Freudian influence, Proust would perhaps come to mind as readily as anyone else; the very title of his novel, in French more than in English, suggests an enterprise of psychoanalysis and scarcely less so does his method—the investigation of sleep, of sexual deviation, of the way of association, the almost obsessive interest in metaphor; at these and at many other points the "influence" might be shown. Yet I believe it is true that Proust did not read Freud. Or again, exegesis of *The Waste Land* often reads remarkably like the psychoanalytic interpretation of a dream, yet we know that Eliot's methods were prepared for him not by Freud but by other poets.

Nevertheless, it is of course true that Freud's influence on literature has been very great. Much of it is so pervasive that its extent is scarcely to be determined; in one form or another, frequently in perversions or absurd simplifications, it has been infused into our life and become a component of our culture of which it is now hard to be specifically aware. In biography its first effect was sensational but not fortunate. The early Freudian biographers were for the most part Guildensterns who seemed to know the pipes but could not pluck out the heart of the mystery, and the same condemnation applies to the early Freudian critics. But in recent years, with the acclimatization of psychoanalysis and the increased sense of its refinements and complexity, criticism has derived from the Freudian system much that is of great value, most notably the license and the injunction to read the work of literature with a lively sense of its latent and ambiguous meanings, as if it were, as indeed it is, a being no less alive and contradictory than the man who created it. And this new response to the literary work has had a corrective effect upon our conception of biography. The literary critic or biographer who makes use of the Freudian theory is no less threatened by the dangers of theoretical systematization than he was in the early days, but he is likely to be more aware of these dangers; and I think it is true to say that now the motive of his interpretation is not that of exposing the secret shame of the writer and limiting the meaning of his work, but, on the contrary, that of finding grounds for sympathy with the writer and for increasing the possible significances of the work.

. . .

From his rationalistic positivism comes much of Freud's strength and what weakness he has. The strength is the fine, clear tenacity of his positive aims, the goal of therapy, the desire to bring to men a decent measure of earthly happiness. But upon the rationalism must also be placed the blame for the often naïve scientific principles which characterize his early thought—they are later much modified—and which consist largely of claiming for his theories a perfect correspondence with an external reality, a position which, for those who admire Freud and especially for those who take seriously his views on art, is troublesome in the extreme.

Now Freud has, I believe, much to tell us about art, but whatever is suggestive in him is not likely to be found in those of his works in which he deals expressly with art itself. Freud is not insensitive to art—on the contrary—nor does he ever intend to speak of it with contempt. Indeed, he speaks of it with a real tenderness and counts it one of the true charms of the good life. Of artists, especially of writers, he speaks with admiration and even a kind of awe, though perhaps what he most appreciates in literature are specific emotional insights and observations; as we have noted, he speaks of literary men, because they have understood the part played in life by the hidden motives, as the precursors and coadjutors of his own science.

And yet eventually Freud speaks of art with what we must indeed call contempt. Art, he tells us, is a "substitute gratification," and as such is "an illusion in contrast to reality." Unlike most illusions, however, art is "almost always harmless and beneficent" for the reason that "it does not seek to be anything but an illusion." Save in the case of a few people who are, one might say, obsessed by Art, it

---

wrote that whereas scientists and physicians continue to disagree about the merits of psychoanalysis, the poets "find much less difficulty in accepting it as gospel truth." He writes that, in fact, the "legends, the mythologies, the demonologies, and the fairy tales of all the races bear witness to the truth of Freud's startling yet not quite novel thesis." Thus Ransom found the true importance of Freud for literature in Freud's stress upon the myth-making, poetry-fabricating quality of the human mind. (One should compare Ransom's view with what Trilling has to say on this subject—though the editors do not mean to imply that Trilling was ever aware of Ransom's essay or that he derived from it his interpretation of Freud's significance for literature.)

never dares make any attack on the realm of reality." One of its chief functions is to serve as a "narcotic." It shares the characteristics of the dream, whose element of distortion Freud calls a "sort of inner dishonesty." As for the artist, he is virtually in the same category with the neurotic. "By such separation of imagination and intellectual capacity," Freud says of the hero of a novel, "he is destined to be a poet or a neurotic, and he belongs to that race of beings whose realm is not of this world."

Now there is nothing in the logic of psychoanalytical thought which requires Freud to have these opinions. But there is a great deal in the practice of the psychoanalytical therapy which makes it understandable that Freud, unprotected by an adequate philosophy, should be tempted to take the line he does. The analytical therapy deals with illusion. The patient comes to the physician to be cured, let us say, of a fear of walking in the street. The fear is real enough, there is no illusion on that score, and it produces all the physical symptoms of a more rational fear, the sweating palms, pounding heart, and shortened breath. But the patient knows that there is no cause for the fear, or rather that there is, as he says, no "real cause": there are no machine guns, man traps, or tigers in the street. The physician knows, however, that there is indeed a "real" cause for the fear, though it has nothing at all to do with what is or is not in the street; the cause is within the patient, and the process of the therapy will be to discover, by gradual steps, what this real cause is and so free the patient from its effects.

Now the patient in coming to the physician, and the physician in accepting the patient, make a tacit compact about reality; for their purpose they agree to the limited reality by which we get our living, win our loves, catch our trains and our colds. The therapy will undertake to train the patient in proper ways of coping with this reality. The patient, of course, has been dealing with this reality all along, but in the wrong way. For Freud there are two ways of dealing with external reality. One is practical, effective, positive; this is the way of the conscious self, of the ego which must be made independent of the super-ego and extend its organization over the *id*, and it is the right way. The antithetical way may be called, for our purpose now, the "fictional" way. Instead of doing something about, or to, external reality, the individual who uses this way does something to, or about, his affective states. The most common and

"normal" example of this is daydreaming, in which we give ourselves a certain pleasure by imagining our difficulties solved or our desires gratified. Then, too, as Freud discovered, sleeping dreams are, in much more complicated ways, and even though quite unpleasant, at the service of this same "fictional" activity. And in ways yet more complicated and yet more unpleasant, the actual neurosis from which our patient suffers deals with an external reality which the mind considers still more unpleasant than the painful neurosis itself.

For Freud as psychoanalytic practitioner there are, we may say, the polar extremes of reality and illusion. Reality is an honorific word, and it means what is *there*; illusion is a pejorative word, and it means a response to what is *not there*. The didactic nature of a course of psychoanalysis no doubt requires a certain firm crudeness in making the distinction; it is after all aimed not at theoretical refinement but at practical effectiveness. The polar extremes are practical reality and neurotic illusion, the latter judged by the former. This, no doubt, is as it should be; the patient is not being trained in metaphysics and epistemology.

This practical assumption is not Freud's only view of the mind in its relation to reality. Indeed what may be called the essentially Freudian view assumes that the mind, for good as well as bad, helps create its reality by selection and evaluation. In this view, reality is malleable and subject to creation; it is not static but is rather a series of situations which are dealt with in their own terms. But beside this conception of the mind stands the conception which arises from Freud's therapeutic-practical assumptions; in this view, the mind deals with a reality which is quite fixed and static, a reality that is wholly "given" and not (to use a phrase of Dewey's) "taken." In his epistemological utterances, Freud insists on this second view, although it is not easy to see why he should do so. For the reality to which he wishes to reconcile the neurotic patient is, after all, a "taken" and not a "given" reality. It is the reality of social life and of value, conceived and maintained by the human mind and will. Love, morality, honor, esteem —these are the components of a created reality. If we are to call art an illusion then we must call most of the activities and satisfactions of the ego illusions; Freud, of course, has no desire to call them that.

What, then, is the difference between, on the one hand, the dream and the neurosis, and, on the other hand, art? That they have certain common elements is of course clear; that unconscious processes are at work in both would be denied by no poet or critic; they share too, though in different degrees, the element of fantasy. But there is a vital difference between them which Charles Lamb saw so clearly in his defense of the sanity of true genius: "The . . . poet dreams being awake. He is not possessed by his subject but he has dominion over it."

That is the whole difference: the poet is in command of his fantasy, while it is exactly the mark of the neurotic that he is possessed by his fantasy. And there is a further difference which Lamb states; speaking of the poet's relation to reality (he calls it Nature), he says, "He is beautifully loyal to that sovereign directress, even when he appears most to betray her"; the illusions of art are made to serve the purpose of a closer and truer relation with reality. Jacques Barzun, in an acute and sympathetic discussion of Freud, puts the matter well: "A good analogy between art and *dreaming* has led him to a false one between art and *sleeping*. But the difference between a work of art and a dream is precisely this, that the work of art *leads us back to the outer reality by taking account of it*." Freud's assumption of the almost exclusively hedonistic nature and purpose of art bars him from the perception of this.

Of the distinction that must be made between the artist and the neurotic Freud is of course aware; he tells us that the artist is not like the neurotic in that he knows how to find a way back from the world of imagination and "once more get a firm foothold in reality." This however seems to mean no more than that reality is to be dealt with when the artist suspends the practice of his art; and at least once when Freud speaks of art dealing with reality he actually means the rewards that a successful artist can win. He does not deny to art its function and its usefulness; it has a therapeutic effect in releasing mental tension; it serves the cultural purpose of acting as a "substitute gratification" to reconcile men to the sacrifices they have made for culture's sake; it promotes the social sharing of highly valued emotional experiences; and it recalls men to their cultural ideals. This is not everything that some of us would find that art does, yet even this is a good deal for a "narcotic" to do.

I started by saying that Freud's ideas could tell us something about art, but so far I have done little more than try to show that Freud's very conception of art is inadequate. Perhaps, then, the suggestiveness lies in the application of the analytic method to specific works of art or to the artist himself? I do not think so, and it is only fair to say that Freud himself was aware both of the limits and the limitations of psychoanalysis in art, even though he does not always in practice submit to the former or admit the latter.

Freud has, for example, no desire to encroach upon the artist's autonomy; he does not wish us to read his monograph on Leonardo and then say of the "Madonna of the Rocks" that it is a fine example of homosexual, autoerotic painting. If he asserts that in investigation the "psychiatrist cannot yield to the author," he immediately insists that the "author cannot yield to the psychiatrist," and he warns the latter not to "coarsen everything" by using for all human manifestations the "substantially useless and awkward terms" of clinical procedure. He admits, even while asserting that the sense of beauty probably derives from sexual feeling, that psychoanalysis "has less to say about beauty than about most other things." He confesses to a theoretical indifference to the form of art and restricts himself to its content. Tone, feeling, style, and the modification that part makes upon part he does not consider. "The layman," he says, "may expect perhaps too much from analysis . . . for it must be admitted that it throws no light upon the two problems which probably interest him the most. It can do nothing toward elucidating the nature of the artistic gift, nor can it explain the means by which the artist works—artistic technique."

What, then, does Freud believe that the analytical method can do? Two things: explain the "inner meanings" of the work of art and explain the temperament of the artist as man.

A famous example of the method is the attempt to solve the "problem" of *Hamlet* as suggested by Freud and as carried out by Dr. Ernest Jones, his early and distinguished follower. Dr. Jones's monograph is a work of painstaking scholarship and of really masterly ingenuity. The research undertakes not only the clearing up of the mystery of Hamlet's character, but also the discovery of "the clue to much of the deeper workings of Shakespeare's mind." Part of the mystery in question is of course why Hamlet, after he had so definitely resolved to do so, did not avenge upon his hated uncle his father's death. But there is another mystery to the play—what Freud calls "the mystery of its effect," its magical appeal that draws so much interest toward it. Recalling the many failures to solve the riddle of the play's charm, he wonders if we are to be driven to the conclusion "that its magical appeal rests solely upon the impressive thoughts in it and the splendor of its language." Freud believes that we can find a source of power beyond this.

We remember that Freud has told us that the meaning of a dream is its intention, and we may assume that the meaning of a drama is its intention, too. The Jones research undertakes to discover what it was that Shakespeare intended to say about Hamlet. It finds that the intention was wrapped by the author in a dreamlike obscurity because it touched so deeply both his personal life and the moral life of the world; what Shakespeare intended to say is that Hamlet cannot act because he is incapacitated by the guilt he feels at his unconscious attachment to his mother. There is, I think, nothing to be quarreled with in the statement that there is an Oedipus situation in *Hamlet;* and if psychoanalysis has indeed added a new point of interest to the play, that is to its credit.[2] And, just so, there is no reason to quarrel with Freud's conclusion when he undertakes to give us the meaning of *King Lear* by a tortuous tracing of the mythological implications of the theme of the three caskets, of the relation of the caskets to the Norns, the Fates, and the Graces, of the connection of these triadic females with Lear's daughters, of the transmogrification of the death goddess into the love goddess and the identification of Cordelia with both, all to the conclusion that the meaning of *King Lear* is to be found in the tragic refusal of an old man to "renounce love, choose death, and make friends with the necessity of dying." There is something both beautiful and suggestive in this, but it is not *the* meaning of *King Lear* any more than the Oedipus motive is *the* meaning of *Hamlet.*

It is not here a question of the validity of the evidence, though that is of course important. We must rather object to the conclusions of Freud and

<hr/>

[2] However, A. C. Bradley, in his discussion of Hamlet (*Shakespearean Tragedy*), states clearly the intense sexual disgust which Hamlet feels and which, for Bradley, helps account for his uncertain purpose; and Bradley was anticipated in this view by Löning. It is well known, and Dover Wilson has lately emphasized the point, that to an Elizabethan audience Hamlet's mother was not merely tasteless, as to a modern audience she seems, in hurrying to marry Claudius, but actually adulterous in marrying him at all because he was, as her brother-in-law, within the forbidden degrees.

Dr. Jones on the ground that their proponents do not have an adequate conception of what an artistic meaning is. There is no single meaning to any work of art; this is true not merely because it is better that it should be true, that is, because it makes art a richer thing, but because historical and personal experience show it to be true. Changes in historical context and in personal mood change the meaning of a work and indicate to us that artistic understanding is not a question of fact but of value. Even if the author's intention were, as it cannot be, precisely determinable, the meaning of a work cannot lie in the author's intention alone. It must also lie in its effect. We can say of a volcanic eruption on an inhabited island that it "means terrible suffering," but if the island is uninhabited or easily evacuated it means something else. In short, the audience partly determines the meaning of the work. But although Freud sees something of this when he says that in addition to the author's intention we must take into account the mystery of *Hamlet's* effect, he nevertheless goes on to speak as if, historically, *Hamlet's* effect had been single and brought about solely by the "magical" power of the Oedipus motive to which, unconsciously, we so violently respond. Yet there was, we know, a period when *Hamlet* was relatively in eclipse, and it has always been scandalously true of the French, a people not without filial feeling, that they have been somewhat indifferent to the "magical appeal" of *Hamlet.*

I do not think that anything I have said about the inadequacies of the Freudian method of interpretation limits the number of ways we can deal with a work of art. Bacon remarked that experiment may twist nature on the rack to wring out its secrets, and criticism may use any instruments upon a work of art to find its meanings. The elements of art are not limited to the world of art. They reach into life, and whatever extraneous knowledge of them we gain—for example, by research into the historical context of the work—may quicken our feelings for the work itself and even enter legitimately into those feelings. Then, too, anything we may learn about the artist himself may be enriching and legitimate. But one research into the mind of the artist is simply not practicable, however legitimate it may theoretically be. That is, the investigation of his unconscious intention as it exists apart from the work itself. Criticism understands that the artist's statement of his conscious intention, though it is sometimes useful, cannot finally determine meaning. How much less can we know from his unconscious intention considered as something apart from the whole work? Surely very little can be called conclusive or scientific. For, as Freud himself points out, we are not in a position to question the artist; we must apply the technique of dream analysis to his symbols, but, as Freud says with some heat, those people do not understand his theory who think that a dream may be interpreted without the dreamer's free association with the multitudinous details of his dream.

We have so far ignored the aspect of the method which finds the solution to the "mystery" of such a play as *Hamlet* in the temperament of Shakespeare himself and then illuminates the mystery of Shakespeare's temperament by means of the solved mystery of the play. Here it will be amusing to remember that by 1935 Freud had become converted to the theory that it was not Shakespeare of Stratford but the Earl of Oxford who wrote the plays, thus invalidating the important bit of evidence that Shakespeare's father died shortly before the composition of *Hamlet*. This is destructive enough to Dr. Jones's argument, but the evidence from which Dr. Jones draws conclusions about literature fails on grounds more relevant to literature itself. For when Dr. Jones, by means of his analysis of *Hamlet*, takes us into "the deeper workings of Shakespeare's mind," he does so with a perfect confidence that he knows what *Hamlet* is and what its relation to Shakespeare is. It is, he tells us, Shakespeare's "chief masterpiece," so far superior to all his other works that it may be placed on "an entirely separate level." And then, having established his ground on an entirely subjective literary judgment, Dr. Jones goes on to tell us that *Hamlet* "probably expresses the core of Shakespeare's philosophy and outlook as no other work of his does." That is, all the contradictory or complicating or modifying testimony of the other plays is dismissed on the basis of Dr. Jones's acceptance of the peculiar position which, he believes, *Hamlet* occupies in the Shakespeare canon. And it is upon this quite inadmissible judgment that Dr. Jones bases his argument: "It may be expected *therefore* that anything which will give us the key to the inner meaning of the play will *necessarily* give us the clue to much of the deeper workings of Shakespeare's mind." (The italics are mine.)

I should be sorry if it appeared that I am trying to say that psychoanalysis can have nothing to do with literature. I am sure that the opposite is so.

For example, the whole notion of rich ambiguity in literature, of the interplay between the apparent meaning and the latent—not "hidden"—meaning, has been reinforced by the Freudian concepts, perhaps even received its first impetus from them. Of late years, the more perceptive psychoanalysts have surrendered the early pretensions of their teachers to deal "scientifically" with literature. That is all to the good, and when a study as modest and precise as Dr. Franz Alexander's essay on *Henry IV* comes along, an essay which pretends not to "solve" but only to illuminate the subject, we have something worth having. Dr. Alexander undertakes nothing more than to say that in the development of Prince Hal we see the classic struggle of the ego to come to normal adjustment, beginning with the rebellion against the father, going on to the conquest of the super-ego (Hotspur, with his rigid notions of honor and glory), then to the conquests of the *id* (Falstaff, with his anarchic self-indulgence), then to the identification with the father (the crown scene) and the assumption of mature responsibility. An analysis of this sort is not momentous and not exclusive of other meanings; perhaps it does no more than point up and formulate what we all have already seen. It has the tact to *accept* the play and does not, like Dr. Jones's study of *Hamlet*, search for a "hidden motive" and a "deeper working," which implies that there is a reality to which the play stands in the relation that a dream stands to the wish that generates it and from which it is separable; it is this reality, this "deeper working," which, according to Dr. Jones, produced the play. But *Hamlet* is not merely the product of Shakespeare's thought, it is the very instrument of his thought, and if meaning is intention, Shakespeare did not intend the Oedipus motive or anything less than *Hamlet*; if meaning is effect then it is *Hamlet* which affects us, not the Oedipus motive. *Coriolanus* also deals, and very terribly, with the Oedipus motive, but the effect of the one drama is very different from the effect of the other.

If, then, we can accept neither Freud's conception of the place of art in life nor his application of the analytical method, what is it that he contributes to our understanding of art or to its practice? In my opinion, what he contributes outweighs his errors; it is of the greatest importance, and it lies in no specific statement that he makes about art but is, rather, implicit in his whole conception of the mind.

For, of all mental systems, the Freudian psychology is the one which makes poetry indigenous to the very constitution of the mind. Indeed, the mind, as Freud sees it, is in the greater part of its tendency exactly a poetry-making organ. This puts the case too strongly, no doubt, for it seems to make the working of the unconscious mind equivalent to poetry itself, forgetting that between the unconscious mind and the finished poem there supervene the social intention and the formal control of the conscious mind. Yet the statement has at least the virtue of counterbalancing the belief, so commonly expressed or implied, that the very opposite is true, and that poetry is a kind of beneficent aberration of the mind's right course.

Freud has not merely naturalized poetry; he has discovered its status as a pioneer settler, and he sees it as a method of thought. Often enough he tries to show how, as a method of thought, it is unreliable and ineffective for conquering reality; yet he himself is forced to use it in the very shaping of his own science, as when he speaks of the topography of the mind and tells us with a kind of defiant apology that the metaphors of space relationship which he is using are really most inexact since the mind is not a thing of space at all, but that there is no other way of conceiving the difficult idea except by metaphor. In the eighteenth century Vico spoke of the metaphorical, imagistic language of the early stages of culture; it was left to Freud to discover how, in a scientific age, we still feel and think in figurative formations, and to create, what psychoanalysis is, a science of tropes, of metaphor and its variants, synecdoche and metonymy.

Freud showed, too, how the mind, in one of its parts, could work without logic, yet not without that directing purpose, that control of intent from which, perhaps it might be said, logic springs. For the unconscious mind works without the syntactical conjunctions which are logic's essence. It recognizes no *because*, no *therefore*, no *but*; such ideas as similarity, agreement, and community are expressed in dreams imagistically by compressing the elements into a unity. The unconscious mind in its struggle with the conscious always turns from the general to the concrete and finds the tangible trifle more congenial than the large abstraction. Freud discovered in the very organization of the mind those mechanisms by which art makes its effects, such devices as the condensations of meanings and the displacement of accent.

All this is perhaps obvious enough and, though I should like to develop it in proportion both to its importance and to the space I have given to disagreement with Freud, I will not press it further. For there are two other elements in Freud's thought which, in conclusion, I should like to introduce as of great weight in their bearing on art.

Of these, one is a specific idea which, in the middle of his career (1920), Freud put forward in his essay *Beyond the Pleasure Principle*. The essay itself is a speculative attempt to solve a perplexing problem in clinical analysis, but its relevance to literature is inescapable, as Freud sees well enough, even though his perception of its critical importance is not sufficiently strong to make him revise his earlier views of the nature and function of art. The idea is one which stands besides Aristotle's notion of the catharsis, in part to supplement, in part to modify it.

Freud has come upon certain facts which are not to be reconciled with his earlier theory of the dream. According to this theory, all dreams, even the unpleasant ones, could be understood upon analysis to have the intention of fulfilling the dreamer's wishes. They are in the service of what Freud calls the pleasure principle, which is opposed to the reality principle. It is, of course, this explanation of the dream which had so largely conditioned Freud's theory of art. But now there is thrust upon him the necessity for reconsidering the theory of the dream, for it was found that in cases of war neurosis—what we once called shellshock—the patient, with the utmost anguish, recurred in his dreams to the very situation, distressing as it was, which had precipitated his neurosis. It seemed impossible to interpret these dreams by any assumption of a hedonistic intent. Nor did there seem to be the usual amount of distortion in them: the patient recurred to the terrible initiatory situation with great literalness. And the same pattern of psychic behavior could be observed in the play of children; there were some games which, far from fulfilling wishes, seemed to concentrate upon the representation of those aspects of the child's life which were most unpleasant and threatening to his happiness.

To explain such mental activities Freud evolved a theory for which he at first refused to claim much but to which, with the years, he attached an increasing importance. He first makes the assumption that there is indeed in the psychic life a repetition-compulsion which goes beyond the pleasure principle. Such a compulsion cannot be meaningless, it must have an intent. And that intent, Freud comes to believe, is exactly and literally the developing of fear. "These dreams," he says, "are attempts at restoring control of the stimuli by developing apprehensions, the pretermission of which caused the traumatic neurosis." The dream, that is, is the effort to reconstruct the bad situation in order that the failure to meet it may be recouped; in these dreams there is no obscured intent to evade but only an attempt to meet the situation, to make a new effort of control. And in the play of children it seems to be that "the child repeats even the unpleasant experiences because through his own activity he gains a far more thorough mastery of the strong impression than was possible by mere passive experience."

Freud, at this point, can scarcely help being put in mind of tragic drama; nevertheless, he does not wish to believe that this effort to come to mental grips with a situation is involved in the attraction of tragedy. He is, we might say, under the influence of the Aristotelian tragic theory which emphasizes a qualified hedonism through suffering. But the pleasure involved in tragedy is perhaps an ambiguous one; and sometimes we must feel that the famous sense of cathartic resolution is perhaps the result of glossing over terror with beautiful language rather than an evacuation of it. And sometimes the terror even bursts through the language to stand stark and isolated from the play, as does Oedipus's sightless and bleeding face. At any rate, the Aristotelian theory does not deny another function for tragedy (and for comedy, too) which is suggested by Freud's theory of the traumatic neurosis—what might be called the mithridatic function, by which tragedy is used as the homeopathic administration of pain to inure ourselves to the greater pain which life will force upon us. There is in the cathartic theory of tragedy, as it is usually understood, a conception of tragedy's function which is too negative and which inadequately suggests the sense of active mastery which tragedy can give.

In the same essay in which he sets forth the conception of the mind embracing its own pain for some vital purpose, Freud also expresses a provisional assent to the idea (earlier stated, as he reminds us, by Schopenhauer) that there is perhaps a human drive which makes of death the final and desired goal. The death instinct is a conception that is rejected by many of even the most thoroughgoing Freudian theorists (as, in his last book, Freud mildly noted); the late Otto Fenichel in his authoritative work on the neurosis argues cogently against it. Yet even if we reject the theory as not fitting the facts in any operatively useful way, we still cannot miss its grandeur, its ultimate tragic courage in acquiescence to fate. The idea of the reality principle and the idea of the death instinct form the crown of Freud's broader speculation on the life of man. Their quality of grim poetry is characteristic of Freud's system and the ideas it generates for him.

And as much as anything else that Freud gives to literature, this quality of his thought is important. Although the artist is never finally determined in his work by the intellectual systems about him, he cannot avoid their influence; and it can be said of various competing systems that some hold more promise for the artist than others. When, for example, we think of the simple humanitarian optimism which, for two decades, has been so pervasive, we must see that not only has it been politically and philosophically inadequate, but also that it implies, by the smallness of its view of the varieties of human possibility, a kind of check on the creative faculties. In Freud's view of life no such limitation is implied. To be sure, certain elements of his system seem hostile to the usual notions of man's dignity. Like every great critic of human nature—and Freud is that—he finds in human pride the ultimate cause of human wretchedness, and he takes pleasure in knowing that his ideas stand with those of Copernicus and Darwin in making pride more difficult to maintain. Yet the Freudian man is, I venture to think, a creature of far more dignity and far more interest than the man which any other modern system has been able to conceive. Despite popular belief to the contrary, man, as Freud conceives him, is not to be understood by any simple formula (such as sex) but is rather an inextricable tangle of culture and biology. And not being simple, he is not simply good; he has, as Freud says somewhere, a kind of hell within him from which rise everlastingly the impulses which threaten his civilization. He has the faculty of imagining for himself more in the way of pleasure and satisfaction than he can possibly achieve. Everything that he gains he pays for in more than equal coin; compromise and the compounding with defeat constitute his best way of getting through the world. His best qualities are the result of a struggle whose outcome is tragic. Yet he is a creature of love; it is Freud's sharpest criticism of the Adlerian psychology that to aggression it gives everything and to love nothing at all.

One is always aware in reading Freud how little cynicism there is in his thought. His desire for man is only that he should be human, and to this end his science is devoted. No view of life to which the artist responds can insure the quality of his work, but the poetic qualities of Freud's own principles, which are so clearly in the line of the classic tragic realism, suggest that this is a view which does not narrow and simplify the human world for the artist but on the contrary opens and complicates it.

EDMUND WILSON (1895–1972)

Perhaps the best known and most widely influential of the literary critics of the last four decades has been Edmund Wilson. Part of Wilson's great appeal springs from the fact that in spite of his wide range of interests and his knowledge of many out-of-the-way things, he was able to write about them in a lucid and nontechnical prose.

The ideas of Marx and Freud, of course, early made their impact on Wilson, and those of Marx show themselves in one of his early publications, *The American Jitters: A Year of the Slump* (1932), which is a commentary on and analysis of the way in which the American public was affected by the Great Depression. *To the Finland Station* (1940; republished, with a new introduction by Wilson, 1972) traces the growth and development of the revolutionary movement that culminated in the Russian Communist takeover in 1917.[1]

The book that established Wilson's literary reputation, *Axel's Castle* (1931), concerns itself with, among others, six important writers of the twentieth century: W. B. Yeats, Paul Valéry, T. S. Eliot, Marcel Proust, James Joyce, and Gertrude Stein. But even here, despite his attention to their literary accomplishment, Wilson's primary interest is in what he regards as their essential mode—symbolism crossed with naturalism—and their special response to the

social and cultural conditions of the late nineteenth and early twentieth centuries.

The title of the book refers to a play, *Axel* (1890), by Villiers de l'Isle-Adam. The hero, Axel, has withdrawn from the world into his castle in order to lead the life of the imagination. He and his beloved ultimately decide to commit suicide because their imaginative vision cannot be fulfilled—can only be debased—by participation in the humdrum life about them. Axel sums up their contempt for "reality" by saying to his loved one: "As for living, our servants can do that for us."[2]

Wilson does not quite convict the great twentieth-century literary masters of being escapists, though he comes close to it in his account of Proust's shutting himself up in a cork-lined room, insulated from the noises of the world, attempting to reconstruct, patiently and lovingly, the past with which he had become obsessed. Symbolism of this sort seemed to Wilson to have retreated dangerously far from lived reality. In any case, he obviously thought that what was good in the symbolist movement by 1930 had been pretty well exhausted; and he urged writers to move in an opposite direction.

In time, however, Wilson's own thinking was to take a different turn. Very early he became disillusioned with Socialist realism and Russian communism, and, somewhat later, with

---

[1] Wilson's title indicates that he means to bring his reader up to the moment when Nikolai Lenin stepped off the train at the Finland station in St. Petersburg to take charge of the revolution.

[2] Compare with Harry Crosby's note: "Rose up in my wrath and fired all three servants. Christ, how I hate servants."

internationalism generally. After traveling through Europe as a war correspondent during the middle 1940's, he declared America to be politically "the most advanced country" in the world. Yet still later, America too fell from grace, and in 1962 he was to write that America and Russia were like nothing so much as two blindly voracious sea slugs, each struggling instinctively to gobble up the other. In recent years, he became more and more interested not in America's future, but in her past.[3]

For many years Wilson wrote for the *New Yorker*, not only reviews but articles on subjects of his own choosing—on the significance of the Dead Sea scrolls or the literary career of George Washington Cable or the present plight of the Iroquois Indians in upstate New York. His ability to write brilliantly on these topics and on those others that caught his interest constitutes his great hold on the readers who have followed his work. They have not been forced to labor through a jargonish prose still not fully digested into normal American English, nor have they been usually compelled to take note of the niceties and discriminations that a more exact scholar feels he must respect. These, Wilson sometimes has smoothed away in the interest of lucidity and ease of comprehension.

There is thus a certain price to be paid for Wilson's avoidance of pedantry. Moreover, Wilson has had his own blindsides. He has always been capable of what must be called at the least eccentric judgments. Thus, he once deposed that "Robert Frost has a thin but authentic vein of poetic sensibility; but I find him excessively dull, and he certainly writes very poor verse." He has overpraised poets like Edna St. Vincent Millay. His prophecies—such as that verse had no future—have not always panned out. Yet an admirer of Wilson has declared that he likes to read him even when he is wrong. Perhaps a good many others would say as much. Alfred Kazin's compliment to Wilson makes just this point. Kazin writes that the "immense historical sense behind Wilson's criticism, architectural in its disposition of detail, would for me always represent personal sensibility rather than political shrewdness. But this same flinty old American self-trust was his flair, his style, his enormous charm for me."

Just so. In spite of Wilson's knowledge and his range of interests, he was essentially an impressionistic critic, not to be valued ultimately for his consistency or the soundness of his judgment or even for the originality of his ideas, but for the charm and vigor of an interesting mind. All of his writing bears the impress of a personality—an authentic one, with its own quality, including its crotchets. Members of Wilson's constituency—it is probably by far the largest literate constituency in this country—have instinctively sensed this quality. Many of them have shared his values, and his prejudices; but they have also been willing to put up with even those that they have not shared.

---

[3] Wilson's career has thus provided a rather accurate series of barometric readings of the pressure exerted by different ideas and events on the American intellectual during the last forty years. The rises and dips of Wilson's sympathies have corresponded fairly closely to the fluctuations of those of other Americans who think of themselves as intellectuals.

FURTHER READINGS

There is no standard edition of Wilson's works. A number of titles have been mentioned in the essay. His most recent works were *O Canada* (1965), *Upstate* (1971), and *A Window on Russia* (1972).

Edmund Wilson, "A Prelude: Landscapes, Characters, and Conversations from the Earlier Years of My Life," *New Yorker* (April 29, May 6, and May 13, 1967)

Warren Berthoff, *Edmund Wilson* (1968)
Leonard Kriegel, *Edmund Wilson* (1971)
Sherman Paul, *Edmund Wilson: A Study of Literary Vocation in Our Time* (1965)

From Patriotic Gore (1962)

NOVELISTS OF THE POST-WAR SOUTH: ALBION W. TOURGÉE

The selection that follows is from *Patriotic Gore* (1962), a book that records Wilson's interest in the American past. The title of the book is taken from a popular Civil War song, "Maryland, My Maryland." The book is a suite of portraits, brief or fully elaborated, of generals, statesmen, politicians, writers, and diarists, northern and southern, who recorded their first-hand impressions of men and events in the great conflict.

As Wilson puts it in his introduction: "This book describes some thirty men and women who lived through the Civil War, either playing some special role in connection with it or experiencing its impact in some interesting way, and who have left their personal records of some angle or aspect of it."

The people about whom Wilson writes in *Patriotic Gore* had a particular attraction for him not only because of his sense of history, but because in his eyes they represented the giant race before the Flood, men and women out of America's heroic past. One is tempted to suggest that Wilson's whole career, from his early bohemianism on through Marxism and down to *Patriotic Gore*, can be regarded as a repudiation of, or an attack on, the venality and crassness of contemporary American society. The America represented in *Patriotic Gore*, in spite of its tragic mistakes and its failure to prevent catastrophe, possessed a passion and a nobility and a promise that he believed the post–Civil War America had betrayed, and thus the men and women of that time, for him, stood in judgment over the generations that have followed them.

––––––––––––

Albion Winegar Tourgée, the once much-read novelist of the Reconstruction, represented a mixture of blood: French Huguenot, German Swiss and British. His ancestors had all come over in the seventeenth or early eighteenth century, and he himself was an impassioned product of the Protestant-Revolutionary tradition. He was born in Ohio but, at the age of fourteen, when his mother had

died and his father had married again, he rebelled against his family and took himself off to live with a Winegar uncle in Lee, Massachusetts. He later, however, returned and eventually, at twenty-one, attended the University of Rochester. He had thus no real local attachments nor any strongly held regional point of view, and all his life he was changing his residence. His longest periods of sojourn were his fourteen years in North Carolina (1865–79) as a business man, journalist and judge, his twelve years (1885–97) as a writer and unsuccessful politician in his mansion in Chatauqua County at the extreme tip of western New York, and the last eight years of his life, when he was consul at Bordeaux, France. He had seen a good deal of the American world, and he had got himself a good education. The Civil War and its consequences were central to his life and thought, but, after serving in the Federal army and administering justice in the South with something of the Abolitionist's fervor, he began to understand the antagonism between the South and the North—which the victory of the latter, as he realized, had not reduced—in a way that was quite unconventional.

Tourgée was an obstinate man, physically and morally courageous, with bad judgment in practical matters and possessed by an intransigent idealism. He enlisted in the New York Volunteers as soon as the war began—in April, 1861—and was so seriously wounded in the spine at the first Battle of Bull Run less than two months later that he never entirely recovered; but after a year of incapacitation he obtained a commission as first lieutenant in the Ohio Volunteers and went back to the fighting again. His company lost one-third of its men, and Tourgée was injured in the spine again, so that he had to spend two months in the hospital. At the beginning of the following year, 1863, he was captured at Murfreesboro, Tennessee, in a pursuit of John Hunt Morgan the raider, and spent four months in Southern prisons. When he was freed, he went back to Ohio and married the New England girl, of seventeenth-century Yorkshire stock, of whom he had said at school, "I'm going to marry that girl," to whom he had been engaged for five years and to whom he was to say upon his deathbed "Emma, you have been the one perfect wife." Eleven days after the wedding, he writes in his diary, "Today I left for the war again." He was in action at the battles of Chickamauga, Lookout Mountain and Missionary Ridge. Tourgée was always getting into trouble for insubordination and improper behavior, and he twice tried to resign his commission because "his rights were not respected and his reputation threatened"; but his resignation was not accepted. He later, however, aggravated his injury by jumping over a ditch and left the army at the beginning of '64.

The twenty-three-year-old Tourgée had carried with him on his first campaign the Greek Testament and Cicero's *De Natura Deorum*, and had for the first time read Balzac's novels. In prison, he studied Spanish and read *Don Quixote*. At nineteen he had composed poems to Emma, and during the year of his recuperation he wrote the first chapters of a novel and squandered all his pension money on publishing a book of verse, of which he put the first two copies into the kitchen stove and later cut the rest into pieces. At this time he also studied law and when he left the army in 1864 was admitted to the Ohio bar. But he presently turns up teaching school in Erie, Pennsylvania, and writing for the Erie *Dispatch*, and just before the end of the war, too late, he was on the point of realizing an earlier ambition by getting himself a commission in a Negro regiment.

Tourgée, in July, 1865—with a certain bold naïveté, which he afterwards bitterly admitted—decided that he could not do better than take his family to live in the South. He was suffering from a weakness of the lungs as well as his spinal wound, and he needed a milder climate. He loved horses and was an insatiable fisherman, and he wanted a life out of doors to offset his intellectual activities. He chose for his residence Greensboro, North Carolina, where he set out to practise law and to run a nursery garden which he rented. He organized a partnership to manage this latter; but he was always a poor hand at business, and he soon fell out with his partners. The firm was dissolved, the nursery failed, and Tourgée was left in debt. He then started to build a factory for tool-handles, which he was never able to finish and which left him with even heavier liabilities. But the public activities of Tourgée—though here, too, he was eventually defeated—were spectacular and somewhat heroic. Entirely uncritical then of the policy of the Radical Republicans in conferring the vote on the Negroes and excluding the Con-

federates from office, he resoundingly backed this policy in public speeches and private conversations. Thus he won the warm sympathies of the Negroes and of the minority of white Unionists, but of course provoked the hatred of the planters and made an enemy of the governor of the state, who called him "the meanest Yankee who has ever settled among us." His career in the South was extremely rocky. He was appointed a judge of the Superior Court in 1868, in which character he heard and recorded many complaints against the Ku Klux Klan, and as a result of his championship of its victims an attempt was made to remove him from office in 1874. This failed but the hostile pressure had already the year before compelled him to resign from the board of trustees of the University of North Carolina, and he did not receive the nomination which his supporters had hoped to secure for him as the Republican candidate for Congress. He was elected, however, as a delegate to a Constitutional Convention in Raleigh by the largest majority that had ever been won by a candidate from that county—with the result that one of the Democrats made threats in public to shoot him. Tourgée, after borrowing a revolver, confronted this man in a public place and "remained staring fixedly at him for several minutes," which so unnerved his opponent that no further unpleasantness occurred. But Tourgée's life was constantly in danger, and this existence was trying for his family, because Emma Tourgée never knew whether or not he would come back from one of his trips alive. When Grant, in 1876, had appointed him Pension Agent at Raleigh, the hostility toward him increased, and he was finally compelled to leave. He was by this time convinced of the futility of his mission, but he had accomplished a few constructive things. Remembering his miseries in the Southern jails, he had insisted on having jails heated, something which had never been done before, and he had drawn up for North Carolina a Code of Civil Procedure and had compiled a Digest of Cited Cases.

In the meantime, however—what was Tourgée's real triumph—he had been dramatizing his experiences in fiction and had published one novel under a pseudonym. As soon as he left the South, he brought out two more (in 1879). His first novel—called originally *Toinette* (1874) but, after Tourgée became famous, revised and reprinted as *A Royal Gentleman*—was a tragedy of miscegenation. The point that Tourgée wants to make—and in these novels he always wants to make a point—is that, on the one hand, the Negro slaves were not treated so badly by their masters as the anti-slavery Northerners liked to think, but that, on the other hand, the ban on black blood made normal relations impossible. This is the story of a mulatto mother and daughter who both become their masters' mistresses. The mother is already a quadroon, and when her lover, in serious difficulties, is forced to sell her and their children, though with the intention of buying them back and eventually setting them free, and is about to marry a white woman, she murders him. Her daughter is so white that she is never suspected by the Northerners among whom, when she has been freed by her master, she goes with her child to live. This former master is now fighting for the Confederacy, and when he is wounded and taken prisoner, she is working in an army hospital and "nurses him back to life." But as soon as he has recognized his old slave girl Toinette, he cannot help taking down her pretensions. "She was a nigger, but Lincoln had not freed her. *He* had done that years ago. If Toinette had gratitude to anyone it was to him. . . . She deserved all he could make her feel for trying to pass for a white woman and a lady. This rushed through his brain in an instant, and then, with a voice hoarse with excitement, he cried out, imperiously: 'I say, you girl, Toinette! Toinette!' Five years were brushed away in a second. Their months of toil and study were in vain. The knowledge and accomplishments for which she had striven were blotted out. The snug little home in the free North was forgotten . . . The free, white, intelligent, interesting, beautiful Mrs. Hunter was lost for the moment. In her stead was the poor, abject, timid, pretty 'nigger gal.' . . . She was a chattel at Lovett Lodge again, and Marse Geoffrey in the library was calling for her angrily. She started like a guilty loiterer, and answered instantly, with that inimitable and indescribable intonation of the slave: 'Sir?' " His behavior, however, is regarded as rather caddish by even his fellow Confederate prisoners. Toinette flees, but, later on, after the defeat of the Confederacy, comes back to North Carolina to live near her former home. When she is discovered by Geoffrey, he apologizes, takes for the first time an interest in their son and is eager to return to their old relations; but he cannot bring himself to marry her—since his white friends all know what she is—and, too proud to accept an inferior status, she leaves for the North again. There is no happy ending possible.

A Royal Gentleman is full of Victorian machinery: murders and attempted murders, secret rooms, the walking of unauthentic ghosts, forced non-recognitions and unlikely coincidences. But the verve of Tourgée as a storyteller does more or less carry it off. He was also an excellent observer of types and had considerable skill as a mimic. In his later novel, *A Fool's Errand*, which is his most important book, this verve is to be seen at its best. The purpose of this second novel, which was first published anonymously, was to convey to the Northern public what had really been going on during the period of Reconstruction, and even in what appear its most extravagant scenes it seems not to depart very far from the adventures of Tourgée and his family. He wanted to tell his bloodcurdling true story, to put on record his observations of the South and to explain the conclusions he drew from them, and he alternates his exciting episodes with chapters of political and social analysis; yet the latter does not deaden the narrative as happens so often with this kind of book. Tourgée is one of the most readable in this secondary category of writers who aim primarily at social history. His narrative has spirit and movement; his insights are brilliantly revealing, and they are expressed with emotional conviction. We relive Tourgée's audacious exploit, with his apparently dashing daughter and his dignified devoted Emma, the latter identified by the half-anagram Metta: the resentment against the alien Northerner, the embarrassment of the friendly Southerners, the heroism of the local white Unionist who is made to pay with his life, the crushed efforts of the able Negroes to make an independent place for themselves, the rise of the Ku Klux Klan in opposition to all these elements and its triumph through blackmail, bullying, flogging, rape of women, castration of men, contemptuous violence to children, burning of Negro houses and shootings, stabbings, drownings and hangings of anybody who offered serious resistance. Thousands, both black and white —though less, of course, of the latter—were slaughtered by the Ku Klux Klan. Tourgée and his family had been through all this, and the story of the nightmarish movement, gradually making itself felt and closing in on the incredulous Northerners, was the one really valuable book that Tourgée had it in him to write.

A Fool's Errand was received as a sensation in its day, and it ought to be an historical classic in ours—for, aside from its interest as one carpetbagger's narrative, it contains the actual text of many newspaper clippings, threatening letters and firsthand testimony by victims of the Klan, and it was supplemented in later editions by a study called *The Invisible Empire,* which is a purely factual inquiry into the history and activities of the organization, based on the author's court records and on the thirteen volumes of reports submitted by a Congressional committee. *A Fool's Errand* sold two hundred thousand copies, plus piracies, and was compared to *Uncle Tom's Cabin,* of which it did, indeed, have something of the compulsive and explosive force. In 1881 its sales declined steeply from the ten thousands to the thousands. (But it has now—1961—been reprinted in the John Harvard Library Series.) As we shall see, the people of the North and West did not by that time want to be worried by these painful intractable problems. And the problem presented by Tourgée was particularly intractable and painful, because this problem was not merely a matter of the villainy or barbarity of the South. He calls his book *A Fool's Errand, by One of the Fools,* and the fool's errand is the Northerner's own mission in believing in, defending and attempting to carry out the policies of the Reconstruction government. The moral is not at all what one might think from my account of the crimes of the Klan. For not only did Tourgée come to see that the policies of the government were mistaken: he came to realize that—given the exclusion from government of the former governing classes in the South and their fear of being governed by the Negroes—the creation of the Klan was inevitable; he even came in certain respects to admire it.

Tourgée was a special case. He was a Northerner who resembled the Southerners: in his insolence, his independence, his readiness to accept a challenge, his recklessness and ineptitude in practical matters, his romantic and chivalrous view of the world in which he was living. Tourgée's love of horses was such that he once started a novel called *My Horses,* and the horses in his other novels are personalities as important as their owners. Tourgée's chivalry was first extended to the innocent and persecuted Negro, but then he found that, as a political opponent, he was really meeting the Southerners on their own ground, that he was playing the same game as they, and he evidently elicited *their* admiration or he could never have survived as so provocative an antagonist fourteen years, as he did, in their midst. He came to understand the Southerner's point of view, not merely from firsthand observation but with a sympathetic

intuition such as, so far as I know, was exercised by no other Northern invader who has put himself on record; and this makes him a unique witness whose work is an invaluable source. I may quote as a striking example of his non-partisanship *malgré lui* his listing in parallel columns of the reciprocal misunderstandings between the South and the North:

Ante Bellum

NORTHERN IDEA OF SLAVERY	SOUTHERN IDEA OF SLAVERY
Slavery is wrong morally, politically, and economically. It is tolerated only for the sake of peace and quiet. The negro is a man, and has equal inherent rights with the white race.	The negro is fit only for slavery. It is sanctioned by the Bible, and it must be right; or, if not exactly right, is unavoidable, now that the race is among us. We can not live with them in any other condition.

NORTHERN IDEA OF THE SOUTHERN IDEA	SOUTHERN IDEA OF THE NORTHERN IDEA
Those Southern fellows know that slavery is wrong, and incompatible with the theory of our government; but it is a good thing for them. They grow fat and rich, and have a good time, on account of it; and no one can blame them for not wanting to give it up.	Those Yankees are jealous because we make slavery profitable, raising cotton and tobacco, and want to deprive us of our slaves from envy. They don't believe a word of what they say about its being wrong, except a few fanatics. The rest are hypocrites.

Post Bellum

THE NORTHERN IDEA OF THE SITUATION	THE SOUTHERN IDEA OF THE SITUATION
The Negroes are free now, and must have a fair chance to make themselves something. What is claimed about their inferiority may be true. It is not likely to approve itself; but, true or false, they have a right to equality before the law. That is what the war meant, and this must be secured to them. The rest they must get as they can,	We have lost our slaves, our bank stock, every thing, by the war. We have been beaten, and have honestly surrendered; slavery is gone, of course. The slave is now free, but he is not white. We have no ill will towards the colored man as such and in his place; but he is not our equal, can not be made our equal, and we will not be

or do without, as they choose.

THE NORTHERN IDEA OF THE SOUTHERN IDEA

Now that the negro is a voter, the Southern people will have to treat him well, because they will need his vote. The negro will remain true to the government and party which gave him liberty, and in order to secure its preservation. Enough of the Southern whites will go with them, for the sake of office and power, to enable them to retain permanent control of those States for an indefinite period. The negroes will go to work, and things will gradually adjust themselves. The South has no right to complain. They would have the negroes as slaves, kept the country in constant turmoil for the sake of them, brought on the war because we would not catch their runaways, killed a million of men; and now they can not complain if the very weapon by which they held power is turned against them, and is made the means of righting the wrongs which they have them-

ruled by him, or admit him as a coördinate with the white race in power. We have no objection to his voting, so long as he votes as his old master, or the man for whom he labors, advises him; but, when he chooses to vote differently, he must take the consequences.

THE SOUTHERN IDEA OF THE NORTHERN IDEA

The negro is made a voter simply to degrade and disgrace the white people of the South. The North cares nothing about the negro as a man, but only enfranchises him in order to humiliate and enfeeble us. Of course, it makes no difference to the people of the North whether he is a voter or not. There are so few colored men there, that there is no fear of one of them being elected to office, going to the Legislature, or sitting on the bench. The whole purpose of the measure is to insult and degrade. But only wait until the States are restored and the "Blue Coats" are out of the way, and we will show them their mistake.

selves created. It may be hard; but they will learn to do better hereafter.

The first stage of Tourgée's enlightenment, as expounded in *A Fool's Errand*, was the realization that the North and the South were virtually two different countries, almost as unsympathetic toward one another and incapable of understanding one another as those other two quarrelsome neighbors France and Germany, and that the outcome of the Civil War had settled their differences as little as the subjugation of Ireland by England or of Poland by Russia. The second stage of Tourgée's enlightenment was a partial self-identification, of a kind to which few Northerners would have been disposed, with the disqualified and dispossessed planters (carrying with them the merchant class dependent on them and intimidating the professional class helpless against them) with whom Tourgée had so much in common. Once this group was removed from authority, who was there, Tourgée came to ask, to manage these still semi-feudal communities? The Negroes? The poor whites? They had no training and no experience. The judges and army officers and heads of the Freedmen's Bureau sent in by the revengeful North? It had not, however, as Tourgée explains in a later novel, *Bricks Without Straw*, been entirely vindictiveness on the part of the North which prompted the policy of the Federal government. The Northerners had taken for granted that all that was needed for the salvation of the South was to arrange for the pro-Union and submissive elements to set up democratic machinery in the townships and counties and states, and they were unable to imagine that the system of town meetings and elections by secret ballot was almost unknown in the South. The Southerners had no such tradition of jealously local self-government. The "Chief Executive," says Tourgée, of every state and the dominant party in the Legislature had controlled the central power of every county and had, through it, appointed every justice of the peace, every member of a school committee and every registrar of elections. There was no real democratic process; and when officials came down from the North to act on their false assumptions, they were taken for rogues or idiots or the mere instruments of Northern malignancy. No wonder, then, that the old class of rulers was driven to restore its authority.

"Yet it was a magnificent sentiment that under-lay it all,—an unfaltering determination, an invincible defiance to all that had the seeming of compulsion or tyranny. One can not but regard with pride and sympathy the indomitable men, who, being conquered in war, yet resisted every effort of the conqueror to change their laws, their customs, or even the personnel of their ruling class; and this, too, not only with unyielding stubbornness, but with success. One can not but admire the arrogant boldness with which they charged the nation which had overpowered them—even in the teeth of her legislators—with perfidy, malice, and a spirit of unworthy and contemptible revenge. How they laughed to scorn the Reconstruction Acts of which the Wise Men boasted! How boldly they declared the conflict to be irrepressible, and that white and black could not and should not live together as coördinate ruling elements! How lightly they told the tales of blood,—of the Masked Night-Riders, of the Invisible Empire of Rifle Clubs (all organized for peaceful purposes), of warnings and whippings and slaughters! Ah, it is wonderful!

"And then the organization itself, so complete, and yet so portable and elastic! So perfect in disguise, that, of the thousands of victims, scarce a score could identify one of their persecutors! and among the hundreds of thousands of its members, of the few who confessed and revealed its character, hardly one knew any thing more than had already been discovered; *or, if he knew it, did not disclose it!* It is all amazing, but sad and terrible. Would that it might be blotted out, or disappear as a fevered dream before the brightness of a new day!

"Yet in it we may recognize the elements which should go to make up a grand and kingly people. They felt themselves insulted and oppressed. No matter whether they were or not, be the fact one way or another, it does not affect their conduct. If the Reconstruction which the Wise Men ordained was unjust; if the North was the aggressor and wrongful assailant of the South in war; if, to humiliate and degrade her enemy, the terms of surrender were falsified, and new and irritating conditions imposed; if the outcasts of Northern life were sent or went thither to encourage and induce the former slave to act against his former master,— if all this were true, it would be no more an excuse or justification for the course pursued than would the fact that these things were honestly *believed* to be true by the masses who formed the rank and file of this grotesquely uniformed body of partisan

cavalry. In any case, it must be counted but as the desperate effort of a proud, brave, and determined people to secure and hold what they *deemed to be their rights.*

"It is sometimes said, by those who do not comprehend its purpose, to have been a base, cowardly, and cruel barbarism. 'What!' says the Northern man,—who has stood aloof from it all, and with Pharisaic assumption, or comfortable ignorance of facts, denounced 'Ku-Klux,' 'carpet-baggers,' 'scal-awags,' and 'niggers' alike,—'was it a brave thing, worthy of a brave and chivalric people, to assail poor, weak, defenseless men and women with overwhelming forces, to terrify, maltreat, and murder? Is this brave and commendable?'

"Ah, my friend! you quite mistake. If that were all that was intended and done, no, it was not brave and commendable. But it was not alone the poor colored man whom the daring band of night-riders struck, as the falcon strikes the sparrow; that indeed would have been cowardly: but it was the Nation which had given the victim citizenship and power, on whom their blow fell. It was no brave thing in itself for old John Brown to seize the arsenal at Harper's Ferry; considered as an assault on the almost solitary watchman, it was cowardly in the extreme: but, when we consider what power stood behind that powerless squad, we are amazed at the daring of the Hero of Osawatomie.[1] So it was with this magnificent organization.

"It was not the individual negro, scalawag, or carpetbagger, against whom the blow was directed, but the power—the Government—the idea which they represented. Not unfrequently, the individual victim was one toward whom the individual members of the Klan who executed its decree upon him had no little of kindly feeling and respect, but whose influence, energy, boldness, or official position, was such as to demand that he should be 'visited.' In most of its assaults, the Klan was not instigated by cruelty, nor a desire for revenge; but these were simply the most direct, perhaps the only, means to secure the end it had in view. The brain, the wealth, the chivalric spirit of the South, was restive under what it deemed degradation and oppression. This association offered a ready and effective method of overturning the hated organization, and throwing off the rule which had been imposed upon them. From the first, therefore, it spread like wildfire. It is said that the first organization was instituted in May, or perhaps as late

---

[1] John Brown [Editors' note].

as the 1st of June, 1868; yet by August of that
year it was firmly established in every State of the
South. It was builded upon an ineradicable sentiment of hostility to the negro as a *political integer*,
and a fierce determination that the white people
of the South, or a majority of that race, should
rule,—if not by the power of the ballot, then by
force of skill, brain, and the habit of domination.
The bravest and strongest and best of the South
gave it their recognition and support,—in most
cases actively, in some passively. Thousands believed it a necessity to prevent anarchy and the
destruction of all valuable civilization; others regarded it as a means of retaliating upon the government, which they conceived to have oppressed
them; while still others looked to it as a means of
acquiring place and power.

"That it outgrew the designs of its originators is
more than probable; but the development was a
natural and unavoidable one."

The Klan was completely successful. It was difficult for the Federal government to take any effective action or at first to do anything but laugh at
the reports of superstitious Negroes intimidated by
night riders in hoods and white sheets with false
goatees and mustaches. Andrew Johnson was standing up to the Radicals in an effort to be lenient to
the Southerners; Grant, who followed him in the
Presidency, had thought that the Confederate
states should be treated as a conquered province.
During Grant's first administration a "Ku Klux"
law was passed which made it possible for the
President to suspend habeas corpus and put counties or states under martial law, which he presently
took advantage of when, in October, 1871, he declared nine counties in South Carolina to be in a
state of rebellion, but he gave up this struggle four
years later when the radical governor of Mississippi
called upon him for Federal troops, and declared
that "The whole public are tired out with these
annual autumnal outbreaks in the South, and the
great majority are ready now to condemn any interference on the part of the government." Tourgée is extremely bitter about the failure of Washington to back him by sending him reinforcements
at the time he was fighting the Klan. He was told
that he and his fellows had been put in authority
there and that they would have to depend on
themselves. It was difficult for the Northerners to
realize that the Southerners were not definitely
squelched. They never really, in fact, learned the
truth till the appearance of *A Fool's Errand* in
1879, and then they made haste to forget it. In the

meantime, the former masters had reëstablished
themselves in the South, the Negroes by various
devices had been in practice—in defiance of the
Fifteenth Amendment—deprived of the right to
vote and reduced to a condition which as little as
possible differed from their former bondage; and
the atrocities of the Klan had abated. Tourgée hits
off the situation by calling one of his last chapters
"Peace in Warsaw."

As a result of the success of *A Fool's Errand*, its
publishers were very insistent that Tourgée should
follow up this success by supplying them with another novel about the Reconstruction period. He
refused at first on the ground that he had already
said everything he had to say and did not want to
repeat himself. But he yielded at last to their pressure and wrote *Bricks Without Straw* (1880), in
which he deals with the difficulties of a New England girl who tries to conduct a Negro school in
North Carolina. At one point, on a marvelous
black horse called Midnight, commanding attention with a borrowed sword, she averts, single-
handed, a dangerous riot when armed Negroes
are marching to the polls, and in the end she marries a member of one of the best Carolinian families—of French blood and with a French name, like
so many of Tourgée's heroes—when she has made
herself acceptable to the local best people by turning out, through some testamentary hanky-panky
of the kind so much in vogue in nineteenth-century fiction, to be actually the owner of his family
estate.

It is true that *Bricks Without Straw* is largely a
repetition of its predecessor, but it gives Tourgée
an opportunity to enlarge on what he regarded as
an important subject, upon which he had only
touched at the end of *A Fool's Errand*. What, in
view of all Tourgée now knew, was to be done
about the unfortunate South, which had been
beaten but would not submit and which had first
been mishandled and then dropped by the North?
Tourgée had thought much about this, and had
arrived at the conclusion, as others had done—
Southerners and Northerners alike—that what the
Southerners most needed was education: they could
not alter their old habits of behavior, nor, consequently, their institutions, without becoming better informed as to what was going on in the rest
of the world—they did not even, as Helper had
said, have very much real knowledge of what was
going on in their own localities—and, as it was,
the sixteen former slave states, which then comprised only a third of the population of the coun-

try, made up two-thirds of its total illiteracy, and among the white voters there only twenty-five out of a hundred were able to read their ballots, so that forty-five per cent of the voters of this region (he is counting the Negroes as voters) were unable to read or write. The best thing that the federal government could do, if it really wanted to help the South, would be to establish a fund to be spent for national schools and distributed among the states unequally, in proportion to the degree of illiteracy. This proposal is made by the author to come from the Carolinian hero, who is expounding it to a Northern Congressman. The Congressman objects that the Southerners would resent and refuse to accept such inspection by the federal government as would be necessary for such a system, and, as I write, an education bill which is part of the program of President Kennedy is being opposed by Senator Byrd of Virginia on the ground that the sum appropriated would be apportioned unequally, according to need.

Tourgée did a good deal of work on his project for national education. He campaigned in 1880 for James A. Garfield, a schoolmate and close friend of his childhood in Ohio, and Garfield, after his election to the Presidency, wrote Tourgée that but for his books he "did not think my election would have been possible." He inquired of Tourgée how he thought that the South would take the Republican victory, and the latter replied that the thing to do was to offer it national schools. He and Garfield had a conference on the subject, and the President became convinced of the value of Tourgée's suggestions and asked him to write a book explaining them. This the novelist did, but four months after taking office, the new President

was assassinated. The book, *An Appeal to Cæsar*, was published in the autumn of 1884, when Tourgée was expecting that the Republicans would win in the current election and hoping that his ideas might influence them; but the Democrats came in with Grover Cleveland. Later on, in 1901, a letter to Theodore Roosevelt, congratulating him on asking to lunch at the White House the Negro leader Booker T. Washington—a gesture which had outraged the Southerners—makes it clear that Tourgée had now ceased to believe in the efficacy of education as a remedy for racial unfairness. "I realize now," he says, "that . . . education does not eradicate prejudice, but intensifies it."

Tourgée wrote in all six "historical novels," as they were called when published as a series, which cover the national crisis from twenty years before the war till twelve years after it. He suffered the common fate of men whose great years had been a part of the war and who did not quite know what to do afterwards. Like Mosby and Helper, he lectured, and, like them, he was assigned a consulship. He spent a good deal of time and money on futile attempts at invention, and he was always embarking on business ventures that failed. "My poor husband!" Emma wrote in her diary—she was much the more practical of the two and the one who really kept things running—"How his life was embittered, ruined, by his trying to do what he had no capacity to do!" The year before he died (1905), he wrote to a friend that he was feeling much better since "the doctor made an excavation in my hip and took out a piece of lead which must have been wandering around in my anatomy since Perryville."

DONALD DAVIDSON (1893–1967)

America's coming of age as a world power brought about a generally renewed interest in America's past. Edmund Wilson was not alone in becoming fascinated with it. Constance Rourke (1885–1941) produced in 1931 a classic study on American humor. B. A. Botkin (1901–   ) has collected American folklore. As early

as 1924 Lewis Mumford (1895–   ) began to publish studies of American architecture, cities, and city planning. Van Wyck Brooks's five-volume history of American literature from the time of Washington Irving to 1915 has been mentioned earlier. The list of such authors and subjects could be extended almost indefinitely.

Twentieth-century Americans, in spite of their chronic commitment to the future, have come to an intense interest in the earlier America, whether in a spirit of mere antiquarianism or in an earnest search—to use Van Wyck Brooks's words—for a "usable past" on which America's future development can be firmly based.

Yet examinations of the folklore or native humor or architecture of the nation necessarily entail a study of regional and local differences. The tall tales of the old Southwest differ from typical expressions of Yankee wit. The architecture of Charleston differs from that of Boston or Providence. One cannot study the earlier national culture apart from a consideration of the various regional subcultures. So the claims of regional cultures have come to be urged as a kind of minority report. If, so the argument ran, American culture is to retain its tang and vigor, the subcultures of the regions must not be allowed to disappear into a synthetically nationalistic culture. There were calls to preserve the folk song rather than to yield everything to the tunes of Tin Pan Alley —to turn off the radio and to take down from the wall the fiddle and the bow. Of late they have been answered by thousands taking up the guitar—though, it must be confessed, this

has not led to much turning off of the transistor radio.

A vigorous example of resurgent regionalism is to be found in Donald Davidson's "Still Rebels, Still Yankees." The essay appeared in a volume entitled *The Attack on Leviathan,* the thesis of which was the need to resist the encroachment of the monolithic state and its uniform culture. "Still Rebels" illustrates its thesis with references to two of our older regional cultures. The author rejoices in the fact of their differences and hopes that neither will become diluted to a standardized Americanism.

Donald Davidson was a southerner, born in middle Tennessee, a poet, a social historian, and the author of *The Tennessee,* one of the more important books in the Rivers of America series. Davidson believed that an authentic literature could not deny its region and indeed had to be true to its local culture before it could properly qualify as an expression of the national culture. Yet Davidson's concern for the southern region did not blind him to the qualities of regions different from his own. In the essay printed below, he celebrates New England farm and village life as he observed it during the many summers that he lived in Vermont, teaching in the Bread Loaf School of English.

FURTHER READINGS

Donald Davidson, *An Outland Piper* (1924)
———, *The Attack on Leviathan* (1938)
———, *Poems* (1966)
———, *Still Rebels, Still Yankees, and Other Essays* (1957)
———, *The Tall Men* (1927)

Melvin E. Bradford, "A Durable Fire: Donald Davidson and the Profession of Letters," *Southern Review,* (1967)
Louise Cowan, *Reality and Myth* (1964)
Thomas D. Young and M. Thomas Inge, *Donald Davidson: An Essay and a Bibliography* (1965)

From The Attack on Leviathan (1938)

FROM STILL REBELS, STILL YANKEES

Those of us who still believe in the map of the United States know that it marks the residence of some diverse Americans who had better not go unacknowledged. In Vermont, for instance, are people who are still Yankees; and in Georgia, and

elsewhere, there are still Rebels. I remember talking with a certain Virginian who watched a Vermont sunset with me, one summer evening. As the sun passed below the distant Adirondacks, we looked at the Green Mountains around us, and at the trim Vermont fields where all the weeds were flowers and all the grass was hay. In the clear detail of the afterglow we saw the forests of spruce and balsam and maple, and spoke of how the very wilderness, in this New England state, had uprightness and order. The woods were as snug and precise as a Yankee kitchen—no ragged edges, no sprawling, nothing out of place. In the clearings the farm-houses were all painted; and the barns were painted, too. The streams were orthodox streams, almost model streams, with water always translucent and stones rounded and picturesquely placed among moss and ferns. They were often called "brooks"—a word that for Southerners existed only on the printed page.

On this land, the Virginian said, the Yankees had looked so intimately and long that, like the man in Hawthorne's story of the Great Stone Face, they had become the image of what they contemplated. The Yankee genius of Vermont was upright, vertical, and no doubt Puritan. Where the landscape itself enforced consistency and order, how could the people concede much virtue to inconsistency and irregularity? The forebears of the Vermont Yankee had once failed to understand how Southerners could be devoted both to slavery *and* democracy. That old failure of understanding did not seem queer, or worth more than a passing sigh, to two Southerners who stood looking at sunset upon a land whose gentled wilderness suggested the urgent possibility of a well-ordered universe, cut to a discreet Yankee pattern. But the human geography of America had now become a particolored thing, sprawling cross the continent in a crazy-quilt of provinces, or sections, each with its private notion of a universe. No longer, as in the sixties, could the Yankee make bold to set up a general pattern for the entire Union. He had enough to do if he would defend and preserve what was peculiarly his own—his very own, surely, in upper New England. In such a purpose of preservation the two Southerners at last could make bold to sympathize, even to help if possible. But preservation could not be achieved without recognizing a principle of diversity in American life. Only by such means could one make any sense out of Lamar's famous epigram in his eulogy on Sumner, "My countrymen, know one another and you will love one another"; it ceased to have meaning if America was to be subjugated to the ideal of uniformity, or to the ideal universe that some one section might generate.

But how could the principle of diversity be inculcated? On the negative side, certain false images, the product of legend or propaganda, must somehow be counterbalanced. Regrettably enough, some of the fairest legends caused the greatest embarrassment. To the Virginian I recalled the horror of a good lady from the Middle West, who was motoring from Washington to Richmond. Mount Vernon was all right, she thought; there the legend was safely frozen. But beyond, on the road to Richmond, what had become of all the great mansions she had read about, the cotton fields with Negroes carolling, the old gentlemen in goatees and white vests, sipping mint juleps in the shade? They were not visible. There were only a few scattered shacks and tumbledown barns in miles of impenetrable wilderness that looked for all the world as it must have looked when John Smith first invaded it. If she could have encountered the legend, the lady would have been content. But not seeing it or knowing how to locate it, she was smitten with a housewifely desire to get at this ragged land with a good broom and whisk it into seemliness.

. . .

If on coming to Vermont I had consulted the modern legend of New England that vaguely haunted my mind, I would have received the iconoclastic shock which our advanced thinkers argue is the first step toward salvation. Had not a New England migrant to the South assured me that his ancestral acres were now inhabited by Montenegrins, who had turned them into a goat farm? Had not the sepulchral Eugene O'Neill and others told tales of the poverty and decadence of New England life? The farms were deserted, it was said; the immigrants and mill-towns had come; the Yankees had left for parts unknown, or, remaining, had become degenerate. Even the loyalty of Robert Frost gave no comfortable assurance, if one accepted the New York alec's criticism of *North of Boston*; though there were many wistful asides in which Frost put forth the guarded wisdom of a not yet daunted soul. The New England of Whittier and Webster was supposed to be extinct; it had been replaced by Puritan-baiters and F. Scott Fitzgeraldites who drank cocktails and read Proust when not conducting the insurance business of the United States.

But if the Vermont that I saw was in the least representative of New England, this composite picture was a wild detraction. In Vermont, if nowhere else, a New England like that of Whittier and Webster miraculously persisted, a reality capable of reducing a Southerner almost to despairing envy. I could understand what led Walter Hines Page, a quarter of a century ago, to disparage his native North Carolina and fall in love with New England. But the time was past when one needed to disparage or praise in the interest of the America Page dreamed about, for in the nineteen-thirties it seemed impossible of realization, or, where realized, already past saving. To one who did not accept Lincoln's quaint idea that the United States must become "all one thing or all the other," it seemed more than ever true that the unity of America must rest, first of all, on a decent respect for sectional differences.

If Vermont and Georgia could be taken in a broad way to stand for New England and the Deep South, one could easily trace out the most general differences. The Vermont towns, like the Vermont landscape, were swept and garnished, as if the Day of Judgment might at any moment summon them into the presence of the celestial inspector. They looked as if Vermonters lived by the adage "Handsome is as handsome does," and one could reflect that this proverb might well have issued from some collaborative effort of Poor Richard and Jonathan Edwards. The most delightful of Southern towns was almost certain to mix a little squalor with its grandeurs. Here, what a Southerner most particularly noticed, was the neatly painted aspect of everything, the absence of ramshackle buildings and litter, the white steeples of churches, the shipshapeness of streets, yards, garages, barber shops, and public buildings. By some special benison of God and the New England conscience, not a billboard had been allowed to sprout between Bennington and the Canadian border. Perhaps by the same double grace, not a weed sprouted, either. All the weeds had turned into ferns and buttercups. Vermont farms were Currier and Ives prints of what good farms ought to look like, with orchards and brooks in exactly the right place and gates that did not need mending. In the background were lakes and mountains where one would put them if he were Aladdin or Wordsworth. It was not surprising to be told that hardly a poison snake, and no poison ivy, existed in the State of Vermont; or to find that there were excellent trails running the whole length of the Green Mountains, with finger-posts at every wilderness cross-roads, and tin huts, with beds, firewood, and caretaker, atop of the highest peak. A few nagging irregularities of nature, like blackflies and mosquitoes, seemed really blasphemous in a land to which God

had given a monopoly of all things good and precise. No wonder, with all this beneficence around them, that the Yankees remembered the Mayflower and forgot John Smith, honored Bunker Hill and neglected King's Mountain. If they could claim such priority in the beneficence of God, their proprietary feeling toward the Revolutionary War, and their almost hereditary claim to the direction of the United States government were by comparison insignificant appurtenances, theirs as a matter of course and by general presumption.

Although I did not hold very devotedly to the economic determinism of modern historians, it was a temptation to say that the people were a great deal like the land. There was the climate, which put keenness into a Southerner's veins. Summer was short, and one had to make the most of it; winter was severe, and one had to keep shield and buckler perpetually ready against it—in that matter was God benevolent or ruthless? Short summers and cold winters made the Vermont Yankee frugal and careful. He must watch his corners. If he were caught napping, he would perish. So much and no more was the gift of his seasons; so much and no more was the rule of his nature. And one had to watch over his neighbor as well as work with him if the general security were not to be imperilled by some outrageous letting down of bars. Very likely, the New England civic conscience derived as much from the imperatives of climate as from the Puritan tradition; the one egged on the other.

. . . The picture of America, as sociologically reformed, does not contemplate any great concessions to Yankee uprightness or Rebel relaxation. Indeed, the sociologist, armed with science, is ready to follow reformation with transformation. In the vast inevitable working of the social forces, sectional differences become irrelevant. With a cold smile the sociologist pronounces a death sentence upon Rebel and Yankee alike. Not that they matter very much—but they will have to yield!

When he talks like this, I am perversely compelled to remember the individuals I have seen, Brother Jonathan of Vermont and Cousin Roderick of Georgia, whom I cannot imagine as yielding to the puny weapons flourished by our social philosophers. They are local incarnations of the Old Adam. They are the immovable bodies that can furnish the irresistible social forces with an incalculable meeting. They are human beings, undebatably alive; and they are different.

Brother Jonathan lives in Yankeetown—for a

place-name is often a "town" in New England, and less often a "ville" or a "burg" as in the South. He is a wizened little chip of a man, with blue eyes and a bald head, and he looks frail enough for any northwest wind to blow away. But there is not a wind on this planet strong enough to blow Brother Jonathan off his mountain farm. If any wind contrived to do so, he would climb right back again in the matter-of-fact way that Robert Frost describes in *Brown's Descent*—he would "bow with grace to natural law, And then go round it on his feet."

Brother Jonathan is past seventy years, and his wife Priscilla is well over sixty, but between them they still manage to do most of the daily work, in house and field, for a two-hundred-acre farm, most of which is in woodland and meadow. Nathaniel, their adopted son, helps some now and then; but Nathaniel, who is carpenter, mechanic, cabinet-maker, mountain guide, and tax-collector combined, is busy putting up the new house into which he and Sophronia, his wife, will soon move —they are building it extra large, to take in summer boarders. Sophronia helps Priscilla as much as she can, but she has her own small children to look after. Later on, Brother Jonathan hopes to get a twelve-year-old boy from the orphanage, who will do the chores for his keep. But now, Brother Jonathan must be up at daylight to start the kitchen fire and milk the cows. If it is haying-time, he is out in the meadow early with the mowing-machine, which he has sharpened and greased with his own hands, or repaired at his own smithy if it needs repairing. The mower bumps and clicks through the rough meadow, tossing the little man to and fro as he warily skirts the outcrops of stone that will have to be circled with a scythe to get the last wisps of hay.

Later, he changes the patient old horses from mower to wagon and starts in with a pitchfork. It is a sight to see him navigating the loaded wagon from the upper field to the barn, past jutting boulders and through deep ruts. But his pace is easy; he keeps it up all day without undue perspiration or agony, and after supper cuts his wood and milks his cows again in unruffled calm. He does not seem tired or bored. As he milks, he philosophizes to the listening stranger. Yes, times are not what they were, but a man can get along if he will be careful and honest. Foolish people, of course, never know how to manage. The harm all comes from people of no character that do things without regard to common decency. The stars are

shining when he takes the pails of milk into the kitchen. Under the hanging oil lamp he reads the *Burlington Free Press* or *The Pathfinder* until he begins to nod.

All the arrangements on Brother Jonathan's farm are neat and ingenious—the arrangements of a man who has had to depend largely on his own wits and strength. The barn is cleverly arranged in two stories, with a ramp entering the upper story for the convenience of Brother Jonathan and his hay wagon, and running water on the lower story, for the convenience of the animals. One well, near the barn, is operated by a windmill; it supplies the stock. Another well, higher up, supplies the house, for Brother Jonathan has a bathroom in the upper hall and faucets in the kitchen. He has no telephone or electric lights. A man can dig and pipe his own wells, and they are finished; but telephone and electric lights, not being home contrivances, require a never-ending tribute to Mammon. He has his own saw-mill and his own work-shop, where he can mend things without losing time and money on a trip to the village. His garage, occupied at present by Nathaniel's four-year-old car (which is not being used), contains a carpenter's bench and a small gas engine rigged to do sawing and turning. There are pelts drying on the walls.

The house is built to economize space and retain heat. For all its modest proportions, it is convenient and comfortable. The kitchen is spacious and well-equipped. The pantry and cellar are stored with vegetables, fruits, and meats that Priscilla has put up with her own hands. The dining-room, with its long table covered with spotless oil-cloth, is eating-room, living-room, and children's playground combined. Here all gather after supper: the women with their tatting and embroidery; the lively dark-eyed boy from the village, with his home-made fiddle; a summer boarder or two, or a visiting relative; and always Brother Jonathan with his newspaper. In one corner is a reed organ, on which Brother Jonathan occasionally plays hymns. In another corner is a desk, filled with miscellaneous papers, books, and old magazines. On the walls hang a glass frame containing butterflies, the gift of a wandering entomologist; an 1876 engraving of General Washington being welcomed at New York, with the pictures of all the Presidents, up to Hayes, around the border; and a faded photograph of a more youthful Brother Jonathan with his fellow baggage-clerks, taken in the days when he went west and got a job in Chicago. Brother Jonathan talks of Chicago sometimes, but he never reveals why he, unlike many other Yankees, came back to Vermont.

The temper of the household is a subdued and even pleasantness, which the loud alarms and excursions of the world do not penetrate very far. The progress of Nathaniel's new house; the next morning's arrangements for gathering vegetables and canning; what Brother Jonathan shall say in the speech he is to make at the approaching celebration of the Timothys' golden wedding—such topics take precedence over the epic contentions of Mr. Hoover and Mr. Roosevelt. Priscilla may go so far as to marvel that anybody can doubt the goodness of Mr. Hoover. (She does not add, as she well might, that Mr. Roosevelt, as a "Yorker," inherits the distrust of Vermont.) Or Brother Jonathan may warm up to politics enough to announce his everlasting distrust for liquorish Al Smith and to confess that, out of firm disapproval for vice, he has once or twice bolted the Republican ticket and voted for the Prohibition party's candidate. But in the South, he supposes, he would be as good a Democrat as the next one. They are all curious about the South—about Negroes—and whether the Southern people still have hard feelings against the North (on this point they seem a little anxious and plaintive). But the talk soon shifts to the Green Mountain Boys, from one of whom Brother Jonathan is descended, or to stories of his childhood, when bears were as thick as porcupines are now—he tells of how seven bears were once killed in the same tree. In these stories Brother Jonathan may put in a dry quip or two, by way of garnishment. He has a store of homely jokes and extended metaphors, to which he frequently adds a humorous gloss to be sure the stranger gets the point. Then maybe there is a game of anagrams—or on another evening, a corn-roast, with a few cronies and kinfolks from the village, who talk the clipped Yankee-talk that seems, to Southern ears, as pure an English as can be, with only a little of the twang that dialect stories have taught one to expect.

Brother Jonathan is not dogmatic to the point of testiness, but he is firmly rationalistic on many points. He declares it incredible, for instance, that Catholics can believe in transubstantiation—how can bread and wine *actually* turn into the blood and body of Jesus Christ? Yet oddly enough, Brother Jonathan is neither Congregationalist nor Unitarian, but Methodist, and does not mind repeating the Apostles' Creed, with its formidable references to the Trinity and the Resurrection. I am led to suspect that it is not the doctrine but the authority to which Brother Jonathan is temperamentally hostile. He is used to depending on himself; he does not like to be told things. And his independence is of a piece with the whole conduct of his life. Years ago, when a famous local character eccentrically bought up all the surrounding woodland and farm land and turned it into a forest reserve which he bequeathed to a neighboring college, Brother Jonathan did not sell out. He held on then, he holds on now, with a possessiveness that would be the despair of Communists. He will continue to hold on, as long as trees yield maple syrup—which he will never, never basely dilute with cane syrup—and boarders return summer after summer.

For Brother Jonathan belongs in spirit to the old republic of independent farmers that Jefferson wanted to see flourish as the foundation of liberty in the United States. To conserve that liberty he has his own Yankee arrangements: the "town," which the Southerner had to learn consisted of a village and a great deal of contiguous territory up to the next "town-line"; and the town meeting, at which Brother Jonathan could stand up and tell the government what he thought about it. Of the uses of town meetings Priscilla has something to say, which comes, I reflect, with a little feminine sauciness. A certain individual, she relates, was criticized for not painting the "community house," as he had been employed to do; and when he excused himself on the ground that paint was lacking, his own wife sprang up in the town meeting and cried: "Don't believe a word he says. That paint's setting in the cellar this minute!"

But the Southerner could reflect that such family intimacy might have civic advantages. Brother Jonathan's local government is composed of nobody more Olympic or corrupt than his own neighbors and relations. For him it is not something off yonder, and he visualizes the national government (though a little too innocently) as simply an enlarged town meeting, where good management ought to be a matter of course. In Yankeetown, good management is a matter of course: it maintains a library, it looks after roads, it sees that taxes are paid and well spent. If the State government does not behave, Nathaniel himself will run for the legislature and see that it does behave.

In all this there was much for a Southerner to savor curiously and learn about—as he savored and learned about the strange food that appeared on Brother Jonathan's table: doughnuts for breakfast, maple syrup on pie and cereal, the New England boiled dinner, the roasting ears that were really roasted in the old Indian fashion. Just as Brother Jonathan's menu suited the soil and the people, so his tidiness and responsibility suited the unobtrusive integrity of his character. With emphasis, one could say: Vermont is upright, vertical, and, even yet, Puritan—why not?

And almost two thousand miles away, with an unconcern about the state of the world that parallels but differs from Brother Jonathan's, Cousin Roderick of Rebelville is achieving another salvation somehow not recorded in the auguries of socialistic planning. Autumn is beginning, the scuppernongs are ripe, and he invites everybody to come over and join him in the scuppernong arbor. In the late afternoon a merry crew gather around the great vine, laughing and bantering as they pick the luscious grapes and crush them against their palates. Sister Caroline is there, with a figure as trim and a wit as lively at eighty as it must have been at twenty. Young Cousin Hector and his wife are there—they are "refugeeing" from the industrial calamity that overtook them in a Northern city. And there are numerous other vague cousins and sisters and children, all munching and passing family gossip back and forth between bites. Cousin Roderick's own Dionysian laughter goes up heartiest of all among the leaves, as he moves to and fro, rapidly gathering grapes and pressing them upon the visitors. "Oh, you are not going to quit on us," he says. "You must eat more than *that*. Scuppernongs never hurt a soul." The scuppernong vine, he declares, is a hundred years old and nearly always fruitful. But not so old, never so fruitful, puts in Sister Caroline, as the scuppernong vine at the old place, that as barefoot children they used to clamber over.

Then the meeting is adjourned to Cousin's Roderick's great front porch, where one looks out between white columns at sunset clouds piling up into the deep blues and yellows of a Maxfield Parrish sky. Down the long street of Rebelville, between the mighty water oaks set out by Cousin Roderick's kin, after the Confederate War, the cotton wagons are passing, heaped high with the white mass of cotton and a Negro or two atop, and the talk goes on, to the jingle of trace chains and the clop of mule hoofs on the almost brandnew State highway, which is so much better for rubber tires than mule hoofs. Over yonder lives Cousin Roderick's Aunt Cecily, a widow, the single

indomitable inhabitant of a stately mansion where economics has not yet prevailed against sentiment. Next door is Uncle Burke Roderick, a Confederate veteran who at ninety still drives his horse and buggy to the plantation each morning; .he is the last survivor of three brothers who were named Pitt, Fox, and Burke, after their father's eighteenth-century heroes. All around indeed, are the Roderick kin, for Cousin Roderick, whose mother married a Bertram, bears the family name of his mother's people, a numerous clan who, by dint of sundry alliances and ancient understandings, attend to whatever little matters need attention in the community affairs of Rebelville, where Jefferson's "least government" principle is a matter of course. Before supper, or after, some of the kinfolks may drop in, for there is always a vast deal of coming and going and dropping in at Cousin Roderick's.

As he takes his ease on the porch, Cousin Roderick looks to be neither the elegant dandy nor the out-at-elbows dribbler of tobacco juice that partisans have accredited to the Southern tradition. He is a fairly tall, vigorous man, plainly dressed, with the ruddiness of Georgia sun and good living on his face. His eyes are a-wrinkle at the corners, ready to catch the humor of whatever is abroad. His hand fumbles his pipe as he tells one anecdote after another in the country drawl that has about as much of Mark Twain and Sut Lovingood in it as it has of the elisions and flattenings supposed to belong to Southern patrician speech. In fact, though he is really patrician (as the female members of his family can assure you) he does not look anything like the Old Colonel of legend, and in spirit he, too, belongs to the Jeffersonian constituency. He has some of the bearing of an English squire, and a good deal of the frontier heartiness that Augustus Baldwin Longstreet depicted in *Georgia Scenes*. He assumes that the world is good-humored and friendly until is proves itself otherwise. If it does prove otherwise, there is a glint in his eye that tells you he will fight.

. . . .

By some it may be said that dark clouds hang over Yankeetown and Rebelville—and clouds of menace, maybe of destruction. I do not deny their presence, but my story is not of such clouds. In this strange modern world it may be observed that men talk continually of the good life without producing a specimen of it, to convince an inquirer. Brother Jonathan and Cousin Roderick do not talk about the good life. They lead it. If government is intended to serve human interests, what does it propose to do about them? If science is really intelligent, what does it mean by conniving to put a stigma upon them or to destroy them? I cannot believe that a government or a science which ignores or depreciates them is very trustworthy. I believe that government and science will fail unless they are taken into account. They, and others, are the incarnations of the principle of diversity through which the United States have become something better than Balkan, and without which the phrase "my country" is but a sorry and almost meaningless abstraction.

T. S. ELIOT (1888–1965)

Thus far in this section we have been concerned with critics of American culture generally, who have written on men and events, and on politics, moral ideas, and modes of social organization. Reference to literary works in their discussions, where it has occurred, has been primarily to illustrate political ideas, morals, social customs, or other aspects of culture. (This is not, of course, to say that the critics whose work has been printed in earlier pages are not capable of writing a more purely literary criticism, but the essays we have included do not exhibit them primarily in this role.) In an age like ours, in which the study of man's social history, beginning with the primitive cultures and coming down to the present, has been so powerfully prosecuted through all its interdisciplinary connections, there has been a strong tendency to stress art and literature as continuous with society (and sometimes continuous with politics).

Yet a powerful countertendency has emerged in our century. It seeks to defend the independence of the artist, to accord an autonomous status to the work that he produces, and to examine the work of art as a meaningful structure in its own right. A criticism that concentrates on the structure of the work of art is not, of course, the discovery of our own day. One remembers that Aristotle, the father of criticism, also put his primary emphasis here.[1] It is unfortunate, therefore, that the structural (or formalist or contextual) critics of our own century should have been tagged with the label "New Critics." Actually we do not have to go back so far as Aristotle to find critics who took very seriously the makeup of the poem or play or novel, and who saw how the relation of part to part implicated the meaning of the work. Thus Samuel Taylor Coleridge, in spite of his Romantic preference for discussing the poet rather than the poem—the author rather than his work—yields many instances of criticism focused on the structure of the poem. Coleridge exerted a direct influence on American writers of the nineteenth century and particularly on Edgar Allan Poe. Poe's repudiation of what he called the "didactic heresy" and his association of poetry with music and mathematics probably owe a good deal to Coleridge. Even if Poe's essay on composition (see pp. 426–32) is regarded as a kind of spoof, his emphasis on craftsmanship made a powerful impact on the French writers of the nineteenth century, who in turn left their impress on Pound and Eliot.[2]

---

[1] Though in his *Poetics*, he does talk about the effect of tragedy upon the audience (in his account of *catharsis*), his primary concern is with the structure and makeup of tragedy. A tragedy has a special kind of plot; the best tragedies reveal a certain structure, and so on.

[2] Though we associate criticism of this sort with poetry, it applies to fiction as well. In fact, such a criticism of fiction actually preceded the corresponding criticism of poetry, having been strongly influenced by French theory and practice at the time of Flaubert. Thus, Henry James and British novelists such as Ford Madox Ford and Joseph Conrad, who, though Polish-born, counts as British here, revered Flaubert, and their speculations on the proper fictional methods—for example,

ears without this comfortable reference to the re-assuring science of archaeology.

Certainly the word is not likely to appear in our appreciations of living or dead writers. Every nation, every race, has not only its own creative, but its own critical turn of mind; and is even more oblivious of the shortcomings and limitations of its critical habits than of those of its creative genius. We know, or think we know, from the enormous mass of critical writing that has appeared in the French language the critical method or habit of the French; we only conclude (we are such unconscious people) that the French are "more critical" than we, and sometimes even plume ourselves a little with the fact, as if the French were the less spontaneous. Perhaps they are; but we might remind ourselves that criticism is as inevitable as breathing, and that we should be none the worse for articulating what passes in our minds when we read a book and feel an emotion about it, for criticizing our own minds in their work of criticism. One of the facts that might come to light in this process is our tendency to insist, when we praise a poet, upon those aspects of his work in which he least resembles any one else. In these aspects or parts of his work we pretend to find what is individual, what is the peculiar essence of the man. We dwell with satisfaction upon the poet's difference from his predecessors, especially his immediate predecessors; we endeavour to find something that can be isolated in order to be enjoyed. Whereas if we approach a poet without this prejudice we shall often find that not only the best, but the most individual parts of his work may be those in which the dead poets, his ancestors, assert their immortality most vigorously. And I do not mean the impressionable period of adolescence, but the period of full maturity.

Yet if the only form of tradition, of handing down, consisted in following the ways of the immediate generation before us in a blind or timid adherence to its successes, "tradition" should positively be discouraged. We have seen many such simple currents soon lost in the sand; and novelty is better than repetition. Tradition is a matter of much wider significance. It cannot be inherited, and if you want it you must obtain it by great labour. It involves, in the first place, the historical sense, which we may call nearly indispensable to any one who would continue to be a poet beyond his twenty-fifth year; and the historical sense involves a perception, not only of the pastness of the past, but of its presence; the historical sense com-

pels a man to write not merely with his own generation in his bones, but with a feeling that the whole of the literature of Europe from Homer and within it the whole of the literature of his own country has a simultaneous existence and composes a simultaneous order. This historical sense, which is a sense of the timeless as well as of the temporal and of the timeless and of the temporal together, is what makes a writer traditional. And it is at the same time what makes a writer most acutely conscious of his place in time, of his own contemporaneity.

No poet, no artist of any art, has his complete meaning alone.[2] His significance, his appreciation is the appreciation of his relation to the dead poets and artists. You cannot value him alone; you must set him, for contrast and comparison, among the dead. I mean this as a principle of aesthetic, not merely historical, criticism. The necessity that he shall conform, that he shall cohere, is not onesided; what happens when a new work of art is created is something that happens simultaneously to all the works of art which preceded it. The existing monuments form an ideal order among themselves, which is modified by the introduction of the new (the really new) work of art among them. The existing order is complete before the new work arrives; for order to persist after the supervention of novelty, the *whole* existing order must be, if ever so slightly, altered; and so the relations, proportions, values of each work of art toward the whole are readjusted; and this is conformity between the old and the new. Whoever has approved this idea of order, of the form of European, of English literature will not find it preposterous that the past should be altered by the present as much as the present is directed by the past. And the poet who is aware of this will be aware of great difficulties and responsibilities.

In a peculiar sense he will be aware also that he must inevitably be judged by the standards of the past. I say judged, not amputated, by them; not judged to be as good as, or worse or better than, the dead; and certainly not judged by the canons of dead critics. It is a judgment, a comparison, in which two things are measured by each other. To conform merely would be for the new work not really to conform at all; it would not be new, and

[2] Though Eliot writes that "Honest criticism . . . [is] directed not upon the poet but upon the poetry," he also—as this sentence indicates—believes in the importance of literary history and comparative judgments.

Pound and Eliot, as we have seen, tend to regard literature neither as self-expression nor as moralized commentary, but as a craft. They were themselves well aware of what was going on in anthropology, mythology, comparative religion, and depth psychology. Such studies rendered it difficult to think any longer of the structure of a poem or novel or play as a prose "statement" overlaid with "ornamental" images and illustrations. Instead, they implied an intricate "symbolic" structure, which was at points illogical and supralogical. Eliot's early masterpiece, *The Waste Land*, exhibits such an organization. Characters "melt" into each other, "all the women are one woman," and, as the author tells us in his notes to the poem, he has been indebted to a "work of anthropology . . . which has influenced our generation profoundly: I mean *The Golden Bough*." But the impact of anthropology and psychology on Eliot, Pound, and many other contemporary critics was rather different from their impact on, say, a critic like Kenneth Burke.

In "Tradition and the Individual Talent," published in 1917 when he was twenty-nine years old, Eliot states firmly that "honest criticism" is "directed not upon the poet but upon the poetry." Indeed the poem is treated as a verbal object, with its own structure and meaning and emotional value, and not simply or even primarily as an outpouring of the poet's own personal anguish or ecstasy. "Tradition and

the Individual Talent" also asks the reader to make a sharp revision of his conventional notions of tradition: tradition, Eliot argues, is not something simply handed down to a passive artist, an inheritance impossible to avoid and, in too many cases, simply a burden that he is condemned to bear. On the contrary, the modern writer often has to strive for a sense of tradition. Moreover, "the most individual parts" of the modern poet's work "may be those in which the dead poets, his ancestors, assert their immortality most vigorously."

Eliot's essay is compact and will require careful reading—in fact, what he actually said has very frequently been misread and misunderstood.[3] But the influence of this essay on critical theory and practice in the last fifty years has been powerful. (Even the readers who have had radical disagreements with the theory expressed have benefited by being forced to frame an intelligent refutation.)

The reader will find a biographical chart and further readings following the introduction to Eliot in the section "From Imagism to Symbolism."

[3] William K. Wimsatt, Jr., has written: "This celebrated early essay, despite its forceful suggestiveness, the smoothness and fullness of its definition of the poet's personality (or perhaps inevitably in achieving these qualities), was a highly ambiguous statement. . . . In this essay Eliot as poet and critic is saying two things about three ideas (man, poet, and poem) and saying them simultaneously." Any reader seriously interested in understanding Eliot's essay and its enormous influence on subsequent criticism, including both the subsequent acceptance or rejection of "impersonality," ought to read Wimsatt's essay in full: "Genesis: A Fallacy Revisited," in *The Disciplines of Criticism* (1968), edited by Peter Demetz *et al.*

the *Prefaces* of James—reflect this concentration, new for Anglo-American literature, on organic structure. Pound, incidentally, was in touch with Ford and was well read in the novels of James.

Tradition and the Individual Talent (1917)

In English writing we seldom speak of tradition, though we occasionally apply its name in deploring its absence. We cannot refer to "the tradition" or to "a tradition";[1] at most, we employ the ad-

[1] The most striking proof of the influence of this essay rests in the fact that nowadays we constantly refer to "the tradition" or to "a tradition."

jective in saying that the poetry of So-and-so is "traditional" or even "too traditional." Seldom, perhaps, does the word appear except in a phrase of censure. If otherwise, it is vaguely approbative, with the implication, as to the work approved, of some pleasing archaeological reconstruction. You can hardly make the word agreeable to English would therefore not be a work of art. And we do not quite say that the new is more valuable because it fits in; but its fitting in is a test of its value—a test, it is true, which can only be slowly and cautiously applied, for we are none of us infallible judges of conformity. We say: it appears to conform, and is perhaps individual, or it appears individual, and many conform; but we are hardly likely to find that it is one and not the other.

To proceed to a more intelligible exposition of the relation of the poet to the past: he can neither take the past as a lump, an indiscriminate bolus, nor can he form himself wholly on one or two private admirations, nor can he form himself wholly upon one preferred period. The first course is inadmissible, the second is an important experience of youth, and the third is a pleasant and highly desirable supplement. The poet must be very conscious of the main current, which does not at all flow invariably through the most distinguished reputations. He must be quite aware of the obvious fact that art never improves, but that the material of art is never quite the same. He must be aware that the mind of Europe—the mind of his own country—a mind which he learns in time to be much more important than his own private mind— is a mind which changes, and that this change is a development which abandons nothing *en route*, which does not superannuate either Shakespeare, or Homer, or the rock drawing of the Magdalenian[3] draughtsmen. That this development, refinement perhaps, complication certainly, is not, from the point of view of the artist, any improvement. Perhaps not even an improvement from the point of view of the psychologist or not to the extent which we imagine; perhaps only in the end based upon a complication in economics and machinery. But the difference between the present and the past is that the conscious present is an awareness of the past in a way and to an extent which the past's awareness of itself cannot show.

Some one said: "The dead writers are remote from us because we *know* so much more than they did." Precisely, and they are that which we know.

I am alive to a usual objection to what is clearly part of my programme for the *métier* of poetry. The objection is that the doctrine requires a ridiculous amount of erudition (pedantry), a claim which can be rejected by appeal to the lives of

poets in any pantheon. It will even be affirmed that much learning deadens or perverts poetic sensibility. While, however, we persist in believing that a poet ought to know as much as will not encroach upon his necessary receptivity and necessary laziness, it is not desirable to confine knowledge to whatever can be put into a useful shape of examinations, drawing-rooms, or the still more pretentious modes of publicity. Some can absorb knowledge, the more tardy must sweat for it. Shakespeare acquired more essential history from Plutarch than most men could from the whole British Museum. What is to be insisted upon is that the poet must develop or procure the consciousness of the past and that he should continue to develop this consciousness throughout his career.

What happens is a continual surrender of himself as he is at the moment to something which is more valuable. The progress of an artist is a continual self-sacrifice, a continual extinction of personality.

There remains to define this process of depersonalization and its relation to the sense of tradition. It is in this depersonalization that art may be said to approach the condition of science. I, therefore, invite you to consider, as a suggestive analogy, the action which takes place when a bit of finely filiated platinum is introduced into a chamber containing oxygen and sulphur dioxide.

2

Honest criticism and sensitive appreciation are directed not upon the poet but upon the poetry. If we attend to the confused cries of the newspaper critics and the *susurrus* of popular repetition that follows, we shall hear the names of poets in great numbers; if we seek not Blue-book knowledge[4] but the enjoyment of poetry, and ask for a poem, we shall seldom find it. I have tried to point out the importance of the relation of the poem to other poems by other authors, and suggested the conception of poetry as a living whole of all the poetry that has ever been written. The other aspect of this Impersonal theory of poetry is the relation of the poem to its author. And I hinted, by an analogy, that the mind of the mature poet differs from that of the immature one not precisely in any valuation of "personality," not being necessarily more interesting, or having "more to say,"

---

[3] They represent the final stage of Paleolithic culture, a period that took its name from the village of La Madeleine, France, where the first artifacts of this culture were found.

[4] Such as is to be had in an official government publication (British usage).

but rather by being a more finely perfected medium in which special, or very varied, feelings are at liberty to enter into new combinations.

The analogy was that of the catalyst. When the two gases previously mentioned are mixed in the presence of a filament of platinum, they form sulphurous acid. This combination takes place only if the platinum is present; nevertheless the newly formed acid contains no trace of platinum, and the platinum itself is apparently unaffected; has remained inert, neutral, and unchanged. The mind of the poet is the shred of platinum. It may partly or exclusively operate upon the experience of the man himself; but, the more perfect the artist, the more completely separate in him will be the man who suffers and the mind which creates; the more perfectly will the mind digest and transmute the passions which are its material.

The experience, you will notice, the elements which enter the presence of the transforming catalyst, are of two kinds: emotions and feelings. The effect of a work of art upon the person who enjoys it is an experience different in kind from any experience not of art. It may be formed out of one emotion, or may be a combination of several; and various feelings, inhering for the writer in particular words or phrases or images, may be added to compose the final result. Or great poetry may be made without the direct use of any emotion whatever: composed out of feelings solely. Canto XV of the *Inferno* (Brunetto Latini) is a working up of the emotion evident in the situation;[5] but the effect, though single as that of any work of art, is obtained by considerable complexity of detail. The last quatrain gives an image, a feeling attaching to an image, which "came," which did not de-velop simply out of what precedes, but which was probably in suspension in the poet's mind until the proper combination arrived for it to add itself to. The poet's mind is in fact a receptacle for seizing and storing up numberless feelings, phrases, images, which remain there until all the particles which can unite to form a new compound are present together.

If you compare several representative passages of the greatest poetry you see how great is the variety of types of combination, and also how completely any semi-ethical criterion of "sublimity" misses the mark. For it is not the "greatness," the intensity, of the emotions, the components, but the intensity of the artistic process, the pressure, so to speak, under which the fusion takes place, that counts. The episode of Paolo and Francesca employs a definite emotion, but the intensity of the poetry is something quite different from whatever intensity in the supposed experience it may give the impression of.[6] It is no more intense, furthermore, than Canto XXVI, the voyage of Ulysses, which has not the direct dependence upon an emotion.[7] Great variety is possible in the process of transmutation of emotion: the murder of Agamemnon, or the agony of Othello, gives an artistic effect apparently closer to a possible original than the scenes from Dante. In the *Agamemnon*, the artistic emotion approximates to the emotion of an actual spectator; in *Othello* to the emotion of the protagonist himself. But the difference between art and the event is always absolute; the combination which is the murder of Agamemnon is probably as complex as that which is the voyage of Ulysses. In either case there has been a fusion of elements. The ode of Keats contains a number of feelings which have nothing particular to do with the nightingale, but which the nightingale, partly, perhaps, because of its attractive name, and partly

---

[5] The distinction that Eliot makes here between an emotion and a feeling is unclear, but its occurrence in this context would suggest that for Eliot an emotion stems from a direct experience of the poet himself (or of some human character in his poem), whereas a feeling is more diffused and has less personal involvement. (Compare "It is not in his personal emotions provoked by particular events," and so on on p. 2833.) Thus, in the passage that Eliot alludes to in the *Inferno*, Dante's expression of regard for Brunetto Latini, a man whom he had known in his past life, is rooted in personal experience, whereas the quality of feeling in the last quatrain (lines 121–24) has nothing *directly* to do with Dante's personal friendship with anyone. The lines may be translated: "Then he turned back and seemed like one of those who run for the green cloth at Verona through the open fields; and of them seemed he who gains, not he who loses" (Temple Classics translation).

[6] Francesca fell in love with her brother-in-law, Paolo. Her husband caught them and stabbed them to death. In one of the most celebrated passages of the *Inferno* (Canto 5, lines 38–142), Francesca tells Dante the story of how she and Paolo fell into their first passionate embrace.

[7] Ulysses tells the story of his last voyage, one that took him out through the Pillars of Hercules and into an unknown sea. It occupies lines 88–142 of Canto 26. Unlike Francesca's story, this narrative grows out of no poignant incident in the life of Ulysses. Dante's account of the end of Ulysses' life is not, by the way, recorded in the *Odyssey*. Dante's lines probably furnished the hint for Tennyson's poem "Ulysses."

because of its reputation, served to bring together.

The point of view which I am struggling to attack is perhaps related to the metaphysical theory of the substantial unity of the soul: for my meaning is, that the poet has, not a "personality" to express, but a particular medium, which is only a medium and not a personality, in which impressions and experiences combine in peculiar and unexpected ways. Impressions and experiences which are important for the man may take no place in the poetry, and those which become important in the poetry may play quite a negligible part in the man, the personality.

I will quote a passage which is unfamiliar enough to be regarded with fresh attention in the light—or darkness—of these observations:

And now methinks I could e'en chide myself
For doating on her beauty, though her death
Shall be revenged after no common action.
Does the silkworm expend her yellow labours
For thee? For thee does she undo herself?
Are lordships sold to maintain ladyships
For the poor benefit of a bewildering minute?
Why does yon fellow falsify highways,
And put his life between the judge's lips,
To refine such a thing—keeps horse and men
To beat their valours for her? . . .[8]

In this passage (as is evident if it is taken in its context) there is a combination of positive and negative emotions: an intensely strong attraction toward beauty and an equally intense fascination by the ugliness which is contrasted with it and which destroys it. This balance of contrasted emotion is in the dramatic situation to which the speech is

[8] The passage is from act 3, scene 5, of *The Revenger's Tragedy* (1607), by Cyril Tourneur. The speaker, Vendice, addresses these lines to the skull of his betrothed lady, who had been poisoned by the wicked duke because she would not yield her body to him. (The story of the play is how Vendice revenged himself upon the duke.)

In the passage quoted, Vendice is reflecting on the fragility of woman's beauty. If men could see what death does to the vaunted beauty on which they lavish wealth and for which they are sometimes willing to risk their lives, would they think it worth the price? "Why does yon fellow falsify highways," and so on, means: Why does that fellow become a highway robber and risk his sentence of death from the judge's lips? "Falsify" here means to "prove false" the implied claim that a highway—the king's highway—was especially protected and safe. But see also the reading in *The Revenger's Tragedy* (1967), edited and with notes by Brian Gibbons.

pertinent, but that situation alone is inadequate to it. This is, so to speak, the structural emotion, provided by the drama. But the whole effect, the dominant tone, is due to the fact that a number of floating feelings, having an affinity to this emotion by no means superficially evident, have combined with it to give us a new art emotion.

It is not in his personal emotions, the emotions provoked by particular events in his life, that the poet is in any way remarkable or interesting. His particular emotions may be simple, or crude, or flat. The emotion in his poetry will be a very complex thing, but not with the complexity of the emotions of people who have very complex or unusual emotions in life. One error, in fact, of eccentricity in poetry is to seek for new human emotions to express, and in this search for novelty in the wrong place it discovers the perverse. The business of the poet is not to find new emotions, but to use the ordinary ones and, in working them up into poetry, to express feelings which are not in actual emotions at all. And emotions which he has never experienced will serve his turn as well as those familiar to him. Consequently, we must believe that "emotion recollected in tranquillity" is an inexact formula.[9] For it is neither emotion, nor recollection, nor, without distortion of meaning, tranquillity. It is a concentration and a new thing resulting from the concentration, of a very great number of experiences which to the practical and active person would not seem to be experiences at all; it is a concentration which does not happen consciously or of deliberation. These experiences are not "recollected," and they finally unite in an atmosphere which is "tranquil" only in that it is a passive attending upon the event. Of course this is not quite the whole story. There is a great deal, in the writing of poetry, which must be conscious and deliberate. In fact, the bad poet is usually unconscious where he ought to be conscious, and conscious where he ought to be unconscious. Both errors tend to make him "personal." Poetry is not a turning loose of emotion, but an escape from emotion; it is not the expression of personality, but an

[9] In his preface to the second edition of *Lyrical Ballads*, Wordsworth wrote: "I have said that Poetry is the spontaneous overflow of powerful feelings: it takes its origin from emotion recollected in tranquillity: the emotion is contemplated till by a species of reaction, the tranquillity gradually disappears, and an emotion, similar to that which was before the subject of contemplation, is gradually produced, and does itself actually exist in the mind."

escape from personality. But, of course, only those who have personality and emotions know what it means to want to escape from these things.

3

ὁ δὲ νοῦς ἴσως Θειότερόν τι χαὶ ἀπαθές ἐστιν.[10]

This essay proposes to halt at the frontier of metaphysics or mysticism, and confine itself to such prac-

[10] The epigraph, taken from Aristotle's treatise on psychology (usually referred to as *De Anima*), Book 1, Chapter 4, may be translated: "mind is, no doubt, something more divine and impassible [that is, incapable of emotion or suffering]." More divine than what? Taken in isolation, the fragment quoted does not make sense. As so often with Eliot's epigraphs, one has to read the whole surrounding context.

In Chapter 4, Aristotle makes the point that the intellect as distinguished from the bodily organs of sensation is "an independent substance" and "incapable of being destroyed." Aristotle goes on to tell us that "Thinking, loving, and hating are affections not of mind, but of that which has mind. . . . That is why, when this vehicle [man's body] decays, memory and love cease, for they were activities not of mind, but of the composite whole [that is, the whole man with his mind, sense organs, body with its functions and appetites, and so on] which has perished; mind is, no doubt, something more divine and impassible."

Earlier in this essay (p. 2833) Eliot writes: "The point of view which I am struggling to attack is perhaps *related to the metaphysical theory of the substantial unity of the soul* [italics ours]; for my meaning is, that the poet has, not a 'personality' to express, but a particular medium . . . in which impressions and experiences combine in peculiar and unexpected ways. Impressions and experiences which are important for the man may take no place in the poetry, and those which become important in the poetry may play quite a negligible part in the man, the personality."

The analogy that Eliot has in mind would seem to run something like this: the poet as man stands in relation to his accomplished poem as the mortal part of his soul (tied as it is to the body's appetites, sensations, and activities) stands in relation to the immortal part of his soul. Compare (on p. 2832 above) the separation that Eliot would stress as between "the man who suffers" and "the mind which creates."

Early in this essay Eliot had sought to make the same

tical conclusions as can be applied by the responsible person interested in poetry. To divert interest from the poet to the poetry is a laudable aim: for it would conduce to a juster estimation of actual poetry, good and bad. There are many people who appreciate the expression of sincere emotion in verse, and there is a smaller number of people who can appreciate technical excellence. But very few know when there is an expression of *significant* emotion, emotion which has its life in the poem and not in the history of the poet. The emotion of art is impersonal. And the poet cannot reach this impersonality without surrendering himself wholly to the work to be done. And he is not likely to know what is to be done unless he lives in what is not merely the present, but the present moment of the past, unless he is conscious, not of what is dead, but of what is already living.

---

point with an analogy drawn from chemistry. The mind of the poet acts as a catalytic agent which, as Eliot put it, may partly or exclusively operate on the artist's personal experience; but, "the more perfect the artist, the more completely separate in him will be the man who suffers and the mind which creates; the more perfectly will the mind digest and transmute the passions which are its material." (See p. 2832 above.)

Eliot's knowledge of chemistry was soon challenged, and in 1934, in referring to "Tradition and the Individual Talent," Eliot remarked that he had had brought to his attention "some unsatisfactory phrasings and at least one more than doubtful analogy." Whether or not Eliot means to hint that the analogy drawn from Aristotle's *De Anima*—assuming that we have been correct in finding one there—may also be doubtful, it is difficult to say. In any case, the two analogies are somewhat at odds with one another: in the analogy from chemistry the mind as the catalytic agent is impassible (unaffected by the chemical reaction), whereas in the analogy drawn from *De Anima* it would seem to be that it is the achieved poem that is impassible.

Eliot's basic point may come clearer if we discard both analogies: in plain statement, Eliot is arguing that the poem has its own life, one that is not necessarily continuous with the poet's. But this was heady doctrine in 1917 and much harder to apprehend then than it is now, after half a century of discussion of myth, depth psychology, and the whole process of literary creation, including the role played by the unconscious.

The Metaphysical Poets (1921)

By calling attention to the English metaphysical poets of the seventeenth century, Eliot did a great deal to break down the old nineteenth-century prejudices about what was "poetic" and what was not and to revise his generation's notions of the functions of metaphor.

In this essay he also suggested a revision of the history of English literature, a revision which asked us to consider the metaphysical poets not as a freakish offshoot of the poetry of their time but a central strand of it, and to regard the repudiation of the metaphysical poets by the poets of the Augustan period as a real loss, one not completely made good in the great Romantic flowering of the nineteenth century.

By collecting these poems[1] from the work of a generation more often named than read, and more often read than profitably studied, Professor Grierson has rendered a service of some importance. Certainly the reader will meet with many poems already preserved in other anthologies, at the same time that he discovers poems such as those of Aurelian Townshend or Lord Herbert of Cherbury here included. But the function of such an anthology as this is neither that of Professor Saintsbury's admirable edition of Caroline poets nor that of the *Oxford Book of English Verse*. Mr. Grierson's book is in itself a piece of criticism and a provocation of criticism; and we think that he was right in including so many poems of Donne, elsewhere (though not in many editions) accessible, as documents in the case of "metaphysical poetry." The phrase has long done duty as a term of abuse or as the label of a quaint and pleasant taste. The question is to what extent the so-called metaphysicals formed a school (in our own time we should say a "movement"), and how far this so-called school or movement is a digression from the main current.

Not only is it extremely difficult to define metaphysical poetry, but difficult to decide what poets practise it and in which of their verses. The poetry of Donne (to whom Marvell and Bishop King are sometimes nearer than any of the other authors) is late Elizabethan, its feeling often very close to that of Chapman. The "courtly" poetry is derivative from Jonson, who borrowed liberally from the Latin; it expires in the next century with the sentiment and witticism of Prior. There is finally the devotional verse of Herbert, Vaughan, and Crashaw (echoed long after by Christina Rossetti and Francis Thompson); Crashaw, sometimes more profound and less sectarian than the others, has a quality which returns through the Elizabethan period to the early Italians. It is difficult to find any precise use of metaphor, simile, or other conceit, which is common to all the poets and at the same time important enough as an element of style to isolate these poets as a group. Donne, and often Cowley, employ a device which is sometimes considered characteristically "metaphysical"; the elaboration (contrasted with the condensation) of a figure of speech to the farthest stage to which ingenuity can carry it. Thus Cowley develops the commonplace comparison of the world to a chessboard through long stanzas (*To Destiny*), and Donne, with more grace, in *A Valediction*, the comparison of two lovers to a pair of compasses. But elsewhere we find, instead of the mere explication of the content of a comparison, a development by rapid association of thought which requires considerable agility on the part of the reader.

> *On a round ball*
> *A workman that hath copies by, can lay*
> *An Europe, Afrique, and an Asia,*
> *And quickly make that, which was nothing, All,*
> *So doth each teare,*
> *Which thee doth weare,*
> *A globe, yea, world by that impression grow,*
> *Till thy tears mixt with mine doe overflow*
> *This world, by waters sent from thee, my heaven*
> *dissolved so.*[2]

Here we find at least two connexions which are not implicit in the first figure, but are forced upon it by the poet: from the geographer's globe to the tear, and the tear to the deluge. On the other hand, some of Donne's most successful and characteristic effects are secured by brief words and sudden contrasts:

> *A bracelet of bright hair about the bone,*[3]

where the most powerful effect is produced by the sudden contrast of associations of "bright hair" and of "bone." This telescoping of images and multiplied associations is characteristic of the

---

[1] *Metaphysical Lyrics and Poems of the Seventeenth Century: Donne to Butler.* Selected and edited, with an Essay, by Herbert J. C. Grierson (Oxford: Clarendon Press. London: Milford) [Eliot].

[2] The second stanza of Donne's "A Valediction: Forbidding Weeping." (This note and subsequent notes have been supplied by the editors.)

[3] From Donne's "The Relique." The reference is to a bracelet woven of the loved one's hair which the speaker of the poem evidently purposes to have buried with him.

phrase of some of the dramatists of the period which Donne knew: not to mention Shakespeare, it is frequent in Middleton, Webster, and Tourneur,[4] and is one of the sources of the vitality of their language.

Johnson,[5] who employed the term "metaphysical poets," apparently having Donne, Cleveland, and Cowley chiefly in mind, remarks of them that "the most heterogeneous ideas are yoked by violence together." The force of this impeachment lies in the failure of the conjunction, the fact that often the ideas are yoked but not united; and if we are to judge of styles of poetry by their abuse, enough examples may be found in Cleveland to justify Johnson's condemnation. But a degree of heterogeneity of material compelled into unity by the operation of the poet's mind is omnipresent in poetry. We need not select for illustration such a line as:

Notre âme est un trois-mâts cherchant son Icarie;[6]

we may find it in some of the best lines of Johnson himself (*The Vanity of Human Wishes*):

> His fate was destined to a barren strand,
> A petty fortress, and a dubious hand;
> He left a name at which the world grew pale,
> To point a moral, or adorn a tale.[7]

where the effect is due to a contrast of ideas, different in degree but the same in principle, as that which Johnson mildly reprehended. And in one of the finest poems of the age (a poem which could not have been written in any other age), the *Exequy* of Bishop King, the extended comparison is used with perfect success: the idea and the simile become one, in the passage in which the Bishop illustrates his impatience to see his dead wife, under the figure of a journey:

> Stay for me there; I will not faile
> To meet thee in that hollow Vale.
> And think not much of my delay;
> I am already on the way,
> And follow thee with all the speed
> Desire can make, or sorrows breed.
> Each minute is a short degree,
> And ev'ry houre a step towards thee.
> At night when I betake to rest,
> Next morn I rise nearer my West
> Of life, almost by eight houres sail,
> Than when sleep breath'd his drowsy gale. . . .
> But heark! My Pulse, like a soft Drum
> Beats my approach, tells Thee I come;
> And slow howere my marches be,
> I shall at last sit down by Thee.

(In the last few lines there is that effect of terror which is several times attained by one of Bishop King's admirers, Edgar Poe.) Again, we may justly take these quatrains from Lord Herbert's Ode, stanzas which would, we think, be immediately pronounced to be of the metaphysical school:

> So when from hence we shall be gone,
> And be no more, nor you, nor I,
> As one another's mystery,
> Each shall be both, yet both but one.

> This said, in her up-lifted face,
> Her eyes, which did that beauty crown,
> Were like two starrs, that having faln down,
> Look up again to find their place:

> While such a moveless silent peace
> Did seize on their becalmed sense,
> One would have thought some influence
> Their ravished spirits did possess.[8]

There is nothing in these lines (with the possible exception of the stars, a simile not at once grasped, but lovely and justified) which fits Johnson's general observations on the metaphysical poets in his essay on Cowley. A good deal resides in the richness of association which is at the same time borrowed from and given to the word "becalmed";

---

[4] See ftn., p. 2833 above.

[5] Dr. Samuel Johnson (1709–1784) provided the first considered discussion of the metaphysical poets in his "Life of Cowley."

[6] The line which may be translated "Our soul is a three-master searching for her Icarie" occurs in "Le Voyage" by the French Symbolist poet, Charles Baudelaire (1821–1867). Baudelaire borrowed "Icarie" from Etienne Cabet's novel *Voyage en Icarie*, where Icarie is the name of a utopian state. Thus, the line means that the soul of each of us is looking for its own perfect society.

[7] Johnson is commenting here on the fate of Charles XII, the warrior king of Sweden, who ruled from 1697 to 1718. Though he was once the terror of Europe, he suffered a humiliating defeat at the battle of Pultowa, lived in diminished power, and finally was killed in a petty border dispute at Fredrikshald in Norway.

[8] These are the concluding stanzas of "An Ode upon a Question Moved, Whether Love Should Continue Forever?" The author was Lord Herbert of Cherbury (1583–1648), elder brother of the better known poet, George Herbert.

but the meaning is clear, the language simple and elegant. It is to be observed that the language of these poets is as a rule simple and pure; in the verse of George Herbert this simplicity is carried as far as it can go—a simplicity emulated without success by numerous modern poets. The *structure* of the sentences, on the other hand, is sometimes far from simple, but this is not a vice; it is a fidelity to thought and feeling. The effect, at its best, is far less artificial than that of an ode by Gray. And as this fidelity induces variety of thought and feeling, so it induces variety of music. We doubt whether, in the eighteenth century, could be found two poems in nominally the same metre, so dissimilar as Marvell's *Coy Mistress* and Crashaw's *Saint Teresa*; the one producing an effect of great speed by the use of short syllables, and the other an ecclesiastical solemnity by the use of long ones:

> *Love, thou art absolute sole lord*
> *Of life and death.*

If so shrewd and sensitive (though so limited) a critic as Johnson failed to define metaphysical poetry by its faults, it is worth while to inquire whether we may not have more success by adopting the opposite method: by assuming that the poets of the seventeenth century (up to the Revolution)[9] were the direct and normal development of the precedent age; and, without prejudicing their case by the adjective "metaphysical," consider whether their virtue was not something permanently valuable, which subsequently disappeared, but ought not to have disappeared. Johnson has hit, perhaps by accident, on one of their peculiarities, when he observes that "their attempts were always analytic"; he would not agree that, after the dissociation, they put the material together again in a new unity.

It is certain that the dramatic verse of the later Elizabethan and early Jacobean poets expresses a degree of development of sensibility which is not found in any of the prose, good as it often is. If we except Marlowe, a man of prodigious intelligence, these dramatists were directly or indirectly (it is at least a tenable theory) affected by Montaigne. Even if we except also Johnson and Chapman, these two were notably erudite, and were notably men who incorporated their erudition into their sensibility: their mode of feeling was directly and freshly altered by their reading and thought. In Chapman especially there is a direct sensuous apprehension of thought, or a recreation of thought into feeling, which is exactly what we find in Donne:

> *in this one thing, all the discipline*
> *Of manners and of manhood is contained;*
> *A man to join himself with th' Universe*
> *In his main sway, and make in all things fit*
> *One with that All, and go on, round as it;*
> *Not plucking from the whole his wretched part,*
> *And into straits, or into nought revert,*
> *Wishing the complete Universe might be*
> *Subject to such a rag of it as he;*
> *But to consider great Necessity.*[10]

We compare this with some modern passage:

> *No, when the fight begins within himself,*
> *A man's worth something. God stoops o'er his*
> *   head,*
> *Satan looks up between his feet—both tug—*
> *He's left, himself, i' the middle; the soul wakes*
> *And grows. Prolong that battle through his life!*[11]

It is perhaps somewhat less fair, though very tempting (as both poets are concerned with the perpetuation of love by offspring), to compare with the stanzas already quoted from Lord Herbert's Ode the following from Tennyson:

> *One walked between his wife and child,*
> *With measured footfall firm and mild,*
> *And now and then he gravely smiled.*
> *   The prudent partner of his blood*
> *   Leaned on him, faithful, gentle, good,*
> *   Wearing the rose of womanhood.*
> *And in their double love secure,*
> *The little maiden walked demure,*
> *Pacing with downward eyelids pure.*
> *These three made unity so sweet,*
> *My frozen heart began to beat,*
> *Remembering its ancient heat.*[12]

The difference is not a simple difference of degree between poets. It is something which had happened to the mind of England between the time of Donne or Lord Herbert of Cherbury and the time of Tennyson and Browning; it is the differ-

---

[9] The so-called Glorious Revolution of 1688, in which James II was deposed from the English throne.

[10] These lines occur in Chapman's *The Revenge of Bussy d'Ambois* (1613; 4. 1. 37–46).

[11] These lines are taken from Robert Browning's "Bishop Blougram's Apology."

[12] From Tennyson's "The Two Voices."

ence between the intellectual poet and the reflective poet. Tennyson and Browning are poets, and they think; but they do not feel their thought as immediately as the odour of a rose. A thought to Donne was an experience; it modified his sensibility. When a poet's mind is perfectly equipped for his work, it is constantly amalgamating disparate experience; the ordinary man's experience is chaotic, irregular, fragmentary. The latter falls in love, or reads Spinoza, and these two experiences have nothing to do with each other, or with the noise of the typewriter or the smell of cooking; in the mind of the poet these experiences are always forming new wholes.

We may express the difference by the following theory: The poets of the seventeenth century, the successors of the dramatists of the sixteenth, possessed a mechanism of sensibility which could devour any kind of experience. They are simple, artificial, difficult, or fantastic, as their predecessors were; no less nor more than Dante, Guido Cavalcanti, Guinizelli, or Cino. In the seventeenth century a dissociation of sensibility[13] set in, from which we have never recovered; and this dissociation, as is natural, was aggravated by the influence of the two most powerful poets of the century, Milton and Dryden. Each of these men performed certain poetic functions so magnificently well that the magnitude of the effect concealed the absence of others. The language went on and in some respects improved; the best verse of Collins, Gray, Johnson, and even Goldsmith satisfies some of our fastidious demands better than that of Donne or Marvell or King. But while the language became more refined, the feeling became more crude. The feeling, the sensibility, expressed in the *Country Churchyard*[14] (to say nothing of Tennyson and Browning) is cruder than that in the *Coy Mistress*.

The second effect of the influence of Milton and Dryden followed from the first and was therefore slow in manifestation. The sentimental age began early in the eighteenth century, and continued. The poets revolted against the ratiocinative, the descriptive; they thought and felt by fits, unbalanced; they reflected. In one or two passages of Shelley's *Triumph of Life*, in the second *Hyperion*, there are traces of a struggle toward unification of sensibility. But Keats and Shelley died, and Tennyson and Browning ruminated.

[13] See page 2090 and following.
[14] By Thomas Gray (1716–1771).

After this brief exposition of a theory—too brief, perhaps, to carry conviction—we may ask, what would have been the fate of the "metaphysical" had the current of poetry descended in a direct line from them, as it descended in a direct line to them? They would not, certainly, be classified as metaphysical. The possible interests of a poet are unlimited; the more intelligent he is the better; the more intelligent he is the more likely that he will have interests: our only condition is that he turn them into poetry, and not merely meditate on them poetically. A philosophical theory which has entered into poetry is established, for its truth or falsity in one sense ceases to matter, and its truth in another sense is proved. The poets in question have, like other poets, various faults. But they were, at best, engaged in the task of trying to find the verbal equivalent for states of mind and feeling. And this means both that they are more mature, and that they wear better, than later poets of certainly not less literary ability.

It is not a permanent necessity that poets should be interested in philosophy, or in any other subject. We can only say that it appears likely that poets in our civilization, as it exists at present, must be *difficult*. Our civilization comprehends great variety and complexity, and this variety and complexity, playing upon a refined sensibility, must produce various and complex results. The poet must become more and more comprehensive, more allusive, more indirect, in order to force, to dislocate if necessary, language into his meaning. (A brilliant and extreme statement of this view, with which it is not requisite to associate oneself, is that of M. Jean Epstein, *La Poésie d' aujourd-hui*.)[15] Hence we get something which looks very much like the conceit[16]—we get, in fact, a method curiously similar to that of the "metaphysical poets," similar also in its use of obscure words and of simple phrasing.

O géraniums diaphanes, guerroyeurs sortilèges,
Sacrilèges monomanes!
Emballages, dévergondages, douches! O pressoirs

[15] *Poetry Today.*
[16] An ingenious or intricate metaphor or comparison which may seem "far-fetched" because of the incongruity of the things compared. Throughout this essay Eliot has been discussing the whole issue of the proper limits of metaphor and has been arguing that some "degree of heterogeneity of material . . . is omnipresent in poetry"—and in all comparisons.

Des vendanges des grands soirs!
Layettes aux abois,
Thyrses au fond des bois!
Transfusions, représailles,
Relevailles, compresses et l'éternal potion,
Angélus! n'en pouvoir plus
De débâcles nuptiales! de débâcles nuptiales![17]

The same poet could write also simply:

Elle est bien loin, elle pleure,
Le grand vent se lamente aussi . . .[18]

Jules Laforgue, and Tristan Corbière[19] in many of his poems, are nearer to the "school of Donne" than any modern English poet. But poets more classical than they have the same essential quality of transmuting ideas into sensations, of transforming an observation into a state of mind.

Pour l'enfant, amoureux de cartes et d'estampes,
L'univers est égal à son vaste appétit.
Ah, que le monde est grand à la clarté des lampes!
Aux yeux du souvenir que le monde est petit![20]

In French literature the great master of the seven-

teenth century—Racine—and the great master of the nineteenth—Baudelaire—are in some ways more like each other than they are like any one else. The greatest two masters of diction are also the greatest two psychologists, the most curious explorers of the soul. It is interesting to speculate whether it is not a misfortune that two of the greatest masters of diction in our language, Milton and Dryden, triumph with a dazzling disregard of the soul. If we continued to produce Miltons and Drydens it might not so much matter, but as things are it is a pity that English poetry has remained so incomplete. Those who object to the "artificiality" of Milton or Dryden sometimes tell us to "look into our hearts and write." But that is not looking deep enough; Racine or Donne looked into a good deal more than the heart. One must look into the cerebral cortex, the nervous system, and the digestive tracts.

May we not conclude, then, that Donne, Crashaw, Vaughan, Herbert and Lord Herbert, Marvell, King, Cowley at his best, are in the direct current of English poetry, and that their faults should be reprimanded by this standard rather than coddled by antiquarian affection? They have been enough praised in terms which are implicit limitations because they are "metaphysical" or "witty," "quaint" or "obscure," though at their best they have not these attributes more than other serious poets. On the other hand, we must not reject the criticism of Johnson (a dangerous person to disagree with) without having mastered it, without having assimilated the Johnsonian canons of taste. In reading the celebrated passage in his essay on Cowley we must remember that by wit he clearly means something more serious than we usually mean today; in his criticism of their versification we must remember in what a narrow discipline he was trained, but also how well trained; we must remember that Johnson tortures chiefly the chief offenders, Cowley and Cleveland. It would be a fruitful work, and one requiring a substantial book, to break up the classification of Johnson (for there has been none since) and exhibit these poets in all their difference of kind and of degree, from the massive music of Donne to the faint, pleasing tinkle of Aurelian Townshend[21]—whose *Dialogue between a Pilgrim and Time* is one of the few regrettable omissions from the excellent anthology of Professor Grierson.

[17] From *Dernier Vers X* (1890) by Jules Laforgue (1860–1887), the ironic, late Romantic French poet, who had a pronounced influence not only on Eliot in his early years but on Hart Crane. Malcolm Cowley, in *Exile's Return*, writes of Laforgue's pervasive influence on the Greenwich Village poets during the 1920's. Here follows a translation, for which the editors are indebted to June Guicharnaud.

O translucent geraniums, warring wizardy,
Monomaniac impieties!
Enwrappings, licentiousness, showers! O winepresses
Of grape harvestings on great evenings!
Layettes at bay,
Thyrsis deep in the woods!
Transfusions, repayings,
Churchings, compresses and the eternal potion,
Angelus! can't bear any more
Those bursting nuptials! bursting nuptials!

[18] From *Dernier Vers XI*, "Sur une Défunte" (On a Dead Woman). The lines may be translated as follows: "She is far off, she weeps, the vast wind laments also."

[19] His dates are 1845–1875.

[20] From Baudelaire's "Le Voyage." Francis Scarfe translates the lines as follows: "For the child in love with maps and prints, the universe matches his vast appetite. Ah, how big the world is, in the lamplight; but how small, viewed through the eyes of memory!" Eliot adapted and absorbed these lines into his own poem, "Animula."

[21] His dates are 1583?–1651?

R. P. BLACKMUR (1904–1965)

Richard Blackmur was self-taught, not college-trained, but his flair for literature and his power as a critic revealed themselves very early. As a very young man he became an editor of the *Hound and Horn,* one of the most important elite quarterlies of the 1920's. Though Blackmur was also a poet, most of his energies went into literary criticism.

The selection printed below represents, at its characteristic best, Blackmur's gift for making a precise and sensitive reading of a literary text. Emily Dickinson was a poet whose work he admired, but for Blackmur such an admiration had to be based on something more than a vague liking for her ideas or her personality or a respect for her place in literary history. It had to rest ultimately on her accomplishment—on her craftsmanship as a literary artist.

In this instance, Blackmur is indicating how one of her poems fails. To some readers it may seem an ungracious task, yet it is a necessary one if the critic is to be honest and if he is to pay the poet the compliment of measuring her work by the highest standards.

The excerpt from Blackmur's essay is an excellent example of a profitable analytical reading of a text. Yet it ought to be pointed out that such detailed analysis represents only a portion of Blackmur's literary concerns and interests: in this essay one will notice that he connects the weakness in this poem with a characteristic general weakness in nineteenth-century American literature, and thus provides a note on American literary history.

Later, and particularly in the last two decades of his life, Blackmur became more and more interested in the larger structures of literature, such as the novels of James and Dostoevski and the whole body of Henry Adams's work. He applied his knowledge of literature to producing highly interesting accounts of the modern sensibility in Europe and America and of the nature of modernity itself.

FURTHER READINGS

R. P. Blackmur, *Anni Mirabiles, 1921–1925* (1956)
——, *The Double Agent* (1935)
——, *Eleven Essays in the European Novel* (1964)
——, *The Expense of Greatness* (1940)
——, *Form and Value in Modern Poetry* (1952)
——, *The Good European* (1947)
——, *Language as Gesture* (1952)

——, *The Lion and the Honeycomb* (1955)
——, *A Primer of Ignorance* (1967)

Richard Foster, "R. P. Blackmur: The Technical Critic as Romantic Agonist," *Western Review* (1959)
William H. Pritchard, "R. P. Blackmur and the Criticism of Poetry," *Massachusetts Review* (1967)

From Emily Dickinson: Notes on Prejudice and Fact (1937)

We can say, amiably enough, that the verse-language of mid-nineteenth century America was relatively nerveless, unsupple, flat in pattern, had very little absorptive power and showed no self-luxuriating power whatever. The mounting vitality that shows itself as formal experiment and the matured vitality that shows itself as the masterly penetration of accepted form (say Kyd followed by the mature Shakespeare) were equally absent. The great estate of poetry as an available condition of language lay flat in a kind of dessicated hibernation, and the clue to resurrection was unknown. It is not for nothing that our poets never mastered form in language. Poe and Longfellow accepted the dessication, contributing a personal music which perhaps redeemed but never transfigured their talents. Whitman and Emily Dickinson, with more genius, or as we have been saying with more favorable cultural situations, were unable to accept the dessication and drove forward on the élan of their natural aptitudes for language, resorting to whatever props, scaffolds, obsessive symbols, or intellectual mechanisms came to hand, but neither of them ever finding satisfactory form—and neither, apparently, ever consciously missing it. The great bulk of the verse of each appears to have been written on the sustaining pretense that everything was always possible. To see boundless good on the horizon, to see it without the limiting discipline of the conviction of evil, is in poetry as in politics the great stultifier of action.

Hence the great, repetitious wastes in both poets. With no criterion of achievement without, there could be no criterion of completion within. Success was by accident, by the mere momentum of sensibility. Failure was by rule, although the rule was unknown, and often doubtless thought of in the shameless guise of simple self-expression. The practice of craft came to little more than so many exercises in self-expression. Thus something over two-thirds of Emily Dickinson's nine hundred-odd printed poems are exercises, and no more, some in the direction of poetry, and some not. The object is usually in view, though some of the poems are but exercises in pursuit of an unknown object, but the means of attainment are variously absent, used in error, or ill-chosen. The only weapon constantly in use is, to repeat once more, the natural aptitude for language; and it is hardly surprising to find that that weapon, used alone and against great odds, should occasionally produce an air of frantic strain instead of strength, of conspicuous oddity instead of indubitable rightness.

Let us take for a first example a reasonably serious poem on one of the dominant Dickinson themes, the obituary theme of the great dead—a theme to which Hawthorne and Henry James were equally addicted—and determine if we can where its failure lies.

> More life went out, when He went,
> Than ordinary breath,
> Lit with a finer phosphor
> Requiring in the quench

> A power of renowned cold—
> The climate of the grave
> A temperature just adequate
> So anthracite to live.

> For some an ampler zero,
> A frost more needle keen
> Is necessary to reduce
> The Ethiop within.

> Others extinguish easier—
> A gnat's minutest fan
> Sufficient to obliterate
> A tract of citizen.

The first thing to notice—a thing characteristic of exercises—is that the order or plot of the elements of the poem is not that of a complete poem; the movement of the parts is downwards and towards a disintegration of the effect wanted. A good poem so constitutes its parts as at once to contain them and to deliver or release by the psychological force of their sequence the full effect only when the poem is done. Here the last quatrain is obviously wrongly placed; it comes like an afterthought, put in to explain why the third stanza was good. It should have preceded the third stanza, and perhaps with the third stanza—both of course in revised form—might have come at the very beginning, or perhaps in suspension between the first and second stanzas. Such suggestions throw the poem into disorder; actually the disorder is already there. It is not the mere arrangement of stanzas that is at fault; the units in disorder are deeper in the material, perhaps in the compositional elements of the conception, perhaps in the executive elements of the image-words used to afford circulation to the poem, perhaps elsewhere in the devices not used but wanted. The point for emphasis is that it is hard to believe that a conscientious poet could have failed to see that no amount of correction and polish could raise this exercise to the condition of a mature poem. The material is all there—the inspiration and the language; what it requires is a thorough revision—a reseeing calculated to compose in objective form the immediacy and singleness of effect which the poet no doubt herself felt.

Perhaps we may say—though the poem is not nearly so bad an example as many—that the uncomposed disorder is accepted by the poet because the poem was itself written automatically. To the sensitive hand and expectant ear words will arrange themselves, however gotten hold of, and seem to breed by mere contact. The brood is the meaning we catch up to. Is not this really automatic writing *tout court?* Most of the Dickinson poems seem to have been initially as near automatic writing as may be. The bulk remained automatic, subject to correction and multiplication of detail. Others, which reach intrinsic being, have been patterned, inscaped, injected one way or another with the élan or elixir of the poet's dominant attitudes. The poem presently examined remains too much in the automatic choir; the élan is there, which is why we examine it at all, but without the additional advantage of craft it fails to carry everything before it.

The second stanza of the poem is either an example of automatic writing unrelieved, or is an example of bad editing, or both. Its only meaning is in the frantic strain towards meaning—a strain so frantic that all responsibility towards the shapes and primary significance of words was ignored. "A temperature just adequate/So anthracite to live" even if it were intelligible, which it is not, would be beyond bearing awkward to read. It is not bad grammar alone that works ill; words sometimes make their own grammar good on the principle of ineluctable association—when the association forces the words into meaning. Here we have fiat meaning. The word *anthracite* is the crux of the trouble. Anthracite is coal, is hard, is black, gives heat, and has a rushing crisp sound; it has a connection with carbuncle and with a fly-borne disease of which one symptom resembles a carbuncle; it is stratified in the earth, is formed of organic matter as a consequence of enormous pressure through geologic time; etc., etc. One or several of these senses may contribute to the poem; but because the context does not denominate it, it does not appear which. My own guess is that Emily Dickinson wanted the effect of something hard and cold and perhaps black and took *anthracite* off the edge of her vocabulary largely because she liked the sound. This is another way of saying that *anthracite* is an irresponsible product of her aptitude for language.

The word *phosphor* in the third line of the first stanza is a responsible example of the same aptitude. It is moreover a habitual symbol word rather than a sudden flight; it is part of her regular machinery for concentrating meaning in a partly willful, partly natural symbol. Phosphor or phosphorus—in various forms of the word—is used by Emily Dickinson at least twelve times to represent, from the like characteristic of the metal, the self-illumining, and perhaps self-consuming quality of the soul. The "renownéd cold," "ampler zero," and "frost more needle keen," are also habitual images used to represent the coming or transition of death as effected seasonably in nature and, by analogue, in man. Examples of these or associated words so used run to the hundreds. The "gnat" in the fourth stanza with his "minutest fan" (of cold air?) is another example of a portmanteau image always ready to use to turn on the microcosmic view. In the word *Ethiop* in the third stanza we have a mixture of a similar general term—this time drawn from the outside and unknown world—and a special significance released and warranted by the poem. Ethiops live in tropical Africa; and we have here a kind of synecdoche which makes the Ethiop himself so full of heat that it would take great cold to quench it. That the contrary would be the case does not affect the actuality of the image, but makes it more intriguing and gives it an odd, accidental character. The misconception does, however, bring out the flavor of a wrong image along with the shadow of the right one; and it is a question whether the flavor will not last longer in the memory than the shadow. Another nice question is involved in the effect of the *order* of the verbs used to represent the point of death: *quench, reduce, extinguish, obliterate.* The question is, are not these verbs pretty nearly interchangeable? Would not any other verb of destructive action do just as well? In short, is there any word in this poem which either fits or contributes to the association at all exactly? I think not—with the single exception of "phosphor."

The burden of these observations on words will I hope have made itself plain; it is exactly the burden of the observations on the form of the whole poem. The poem is an exercise whichever way you take it: an approach to the organization of its material but by no means a complete organization. It is almost a rehearsal—a doing over of something not done—and a variation of stock intellectual elements in an effort to accomplish an adventure in feeling. The reader can determine for himself—if he can swallow both the anthracite and the gnat —how concrete and actual the adventure was made.

JOHN CROWE RANSOM (1888–   )

An old, old question with regard to poetry has assumed new importance in the criticism of our time. It has to do with how poetry "says" what it says. Discursive prose makes use of a logical organization and marshals its facts to produce generalized statements or cogent arguments. Poetry, on the other hand, has from time immemorial depended heavily on concrete detail, on images, and more and more, since the beginning of the nineteenth century, it has tended to eschew anything like the ordinary logical organization and to "say" what it has to say through its images.

How does a language of images function? What does the image do? Why does the poet characteristically depend so heavily on it? And, in our own century, is that dependence justified or has it been excessive?

In the essay that follows, John Crowe Ransom, whose own poems have been discussed earlier, canvasses the issue of particular and universal, specific and general, and looks hard at the tendency of the so-called Imagist poets in the second decade of our century to construct poems made up almost entirely of images.

We have chosen to include this particular essay principally because it throws a very useful light on Imagist poetry and on the renewed interest in "metaphysical" poetry in the twentieth century. But the reader must not conclude from our choice that Ransom's critical concerns are limited to problems of this kind. He has also— throughout a long lifetime—been writing on the general social context that affects literature and out of which it arises. He has written, too, about the cultural "effects" of literature—about what we may call the function of poetry within the total human economy. As examples, his connections with Agrarianism might be mentioned here and, at another extreme, *God Without Thunder: An Unorthodox Defense of Orthodoxy* (1930), which speculates on, among other things, the relation of literature to religion.

The reader will find a biographical chart and further readings following the introduction to Ransom in the section "Southern Writing of the Twentieth Century."

Poetry: A Note in Ontology (1934)

A poetry may be distinguished from nonpoetry by virtue of subject-matter, and subject matter may be differentiated with respect to its ontology, or the reality of its being. An excellent variety of critical doctrine arises recently out of this differentiation, and thus perhaps criticism leans again upon ontological analysis as it was meant to do by Kant. The recent critics remark in effect that some poetry deals with things, while some other poetry deals with ideas. The two poetries will differ from each other as radically as a thing differs from an idea.

The distinction in the hands of critics is a fruitful one. There is apt to go along with it a principle of valuation, which is the consequence of a temperament, and therefore basic. The critic likes things and intends that his poet shall offer them; or likes ideas and intends that he shall offer them; and approves him as he does the one or the other. Criticism cannot well go much deeper than this. The critic has carried to the last terms his analysis of the stuff of which poetry is made, and valued it frankly as his temperament or his need requires him to value it.

So philosophical a critic seems to be highly modern. He is; but this critic as a matter of fact is peculiarly on one side of the question. (The implication is unfavorable to the other side of the question.) He is in revolt against the tyranny of ideas, and against the poetry which celebrates ideas, and which may be identified—so far as his usual generalization may be trusted—with the hateful poetry of the Victorians. His bias is in favor of the things. On the other hand the critic who likes Victorian verse, or the poetry of ideas, has probably not thought of anything of so grand a simplicity as electing between the things and the ideas, being apparently not quite capable of the ontological distinction. Therefore he does not know the real or constitutional ground of his liking, and may somewhat ingenuously claim that his predilection is for those poets who give him inspiration, or comfort, or truth, or honest metres, or something else equally "worth while." But Plato, who was not a modern, was just as clear as we are about the basic distinction between the ideas and the things, and yet stands far apart from the aforesaid conscious modern in passionately preferring the ideas over the things. The weight of Plato's testimony would certainly fall on the side of the Victorians, though they may scarcely have thought of calling him as their witness. But this consideration need not conclude the hearing.

1. PHYSICAL POETRY

The poetry which deals with things was much in favor a few years ago with the resolute body of critics. And the critics affected the poets. If necessary, they became the poets, and triumphantly illustrated the new mode. The Imagists were important figures in the history of our poetry, and they were both theorists and creators. It was their intention to present things in their thinginess, or *Dinge* in their *Dinglichkeit*; and to such an extent had the public lost its sense of *Dinglichkeit* that their redirection was wholesome. What the public was inclined to seek in poetry was ideas, whether large ones or small ones, grand ones or pretty ones, certainly ideas to live by and die by, but what the Imagists identified with the stuff of poetry was, simply, things.

Their application of their own principle was sufficiently heroic, though they scarcely consented to be as extreme in the practice as in the theory. They had artistic talent, every one of the original group, and it was impossible that they should make of poetry so simple an exercise as in doctrine they seemed to think it was. Yet Miss Lowell wrote a poem on "Thompson's Lunch Room, Grand Central Station"; it is admirable if its intention is to show the whole reach of her courage. Its detail goes like this:

Jagged greenwhite bowls of pressed glass
Rearing snow-peaks of chipped sugar

Above the lighthouse-shaped castors
Of gray pepper and gray-white salt.

For most of us as for the public idealist, with his "values," this is inconsequential. Unhappily it seems that the things as things do not necessarily interest us, and that in fact we are not quite constructed with the capacity for a disinterested interest. But it must be noted even here that the things are on their good behavior, looking rather well, and arranged by lines into something approaching a military formation. More technically, there is crossimagery in the snow-peaks of sugar, and in the lighthouse-shaped castors, and cross-imagery involves association, and will presently involve dissociation and thinking. The metre is but a vestige, but even so it means something, for metre is a powerful intellectual determinant marshalling the words and, inevitably, the things. The *Dinglichkeit* of this Imagist specimen, or the realism, was therefore not pure. But it was nearer pure than the world was used to in poetry, and the exhibit was astonishing.

For the purpose of this note I shall give to such poetry, dwelling as exclusively as it dares upon physical things, the name Physical Poetry. It is to stand opposite to that poetry which dwells as firmly as it dares upon ideas.

But perhaps thing *versus* idea does not seem to name an opposition precisely. Then we might phrase it a little differently: image *versus* idea. The idealistic philosophies are not sure that things exist, but they mean the equivalent when they refer to images. (Or they may consent to perceptions; or to impressions, following Hume, and following Croce, who remarks that they are pre-intellectual and independent of concepts. It is all the same, unless we are extremely technical.) It is sufficient if they concede that image is the raw material of idea. Though it may be an unwieldy and useless affair for the idealist as it stands, much needing to be licked into shape, nevertheless its relation to idea is that of a material cause, and it cannot be dispossessed of its priority.

It cannot be dispossessed of a primordial freshness, which idea can never claim. An idea is derivative and tamed. The image is in the natural or wild state, and it has to be discovered there, not put there, obeying its own law and none of ours. We think we can lay hold of image and take it captive, but the docile captive is not the real image but only the idea, which is the image with its character beaten out of it.

But we must be very careful: idealists are nothing if not dialectical. They object that an image in an original state of innocence is a delusion and cannot exist, that no image ever comes to us which does not imply the world of ideas, that there is "no percept without a concept." There is something in it. Every property discovered in the image is a universal property, and nothing discovered in the image is marvellous in kind though it may be pinned down historically or statistically as a single instance. But there is this to be understood too: the image which is not remarkable in any particular property is marvellous in its assemblage of many properties, a manifold of properties, like a mine or a field, something to be explored for the properties; yet science can manage the image, which is infinite in properties, only by equating it to the one property with which the science is concerned; for science at work is always *a science*, and committed to a special interest. It is not by refutation but by abstraction that science destroys the image. It means to get its "value" out of the image, and we may be sure that it has no use for the image in its original state of freedom. People who are engrossed with their pet "values" become habitual killers. Their game is the images, or the things, and they acquire the ability to shoot them as far off as they can be seen, and do. It is thus that we lose the power of imagination, or whatever faculty it is by which we are able to contemplate things as they are in their rich and contingent materiality. But our dreams reproach us, for in dreams they come alive again. Likewise our memory; which makes light of our science by recalling the images in their panoply of circumstance and with their morning freshness upon them.

It is the dream, the recollection, which compels us to poetry, and to deliberate æsthetic experience. It can hardly be argued, I think, that the arts are constituted automatically out of original images, and arise in some early age of innocence. (Though Croce[1] seems to support this view, and to make art a pre-adult stage of experience.) Art is based on second love, not first love. In it we make a return to something which we had willfully alienated. The child is occupied mostly with things, but it is because he is still unfurnished with systematic ideas, not because he is a ripe citizen by nature and comes along already trailing clouds of glory. Images are clouds of glory for the man who

has discovered that ideas are a sort of darkness. Imagism, that is, the recent historical movement, may resemble a naïve poetry of mere things, but we can read the theoretical pronouncements of Imagists, and we can learn that Imagism is motivated by a distaste for the systematic abstractedness of thought. It presupposes acquaintance with science; that famous activity which is "constructive" with respect to the tools of our economic role in this world, and destructive with respect to nature. Imagists wish to escape from science by immersing themselves in images.

Not far off the simplicity of Imagism was, a little later, the subtler simplicity of Mr. George Moore's[2] project shared with several others, in behalf of "pure poetry." In Moore's house on Ebury Street they talked about poetry, with an after-dinner warmth if not an early-morning discretion, and their tastes agreed almost perfectly and reinforced one another. The fruit of these conversations was the volume *Pure Poetry*. It must have been the most exclusive anthology of English poetry that had yet appeared, since its room was closed to all the poems that dallied visibly with ideas, so that many poems that had been coveted by all other anthologists do not appear there. Nevertheless the book is delicious, and something more deserves to be said for it.

First, that "pure poetry" is a kind of Physical Poetry. Its visible content is a thing-content. Technically, I suppose, it is effective in this character if it can exhibit its material in such a way that an image or set of images and not an idea must occupy the foreground of the reader's attention. Thus:

> Full fathom five thy father lies
> Of his bones are coral made.

Here it is difficult for anybody (except the perfect idealist who is always theoretically possible and who would expect to take a return from anything whatever) to receive any experience except that of a very distinct image, or set of images. It has the configuration of image, which consists in being sharp of edges, and the modality of image, which consists in being given and non-negotiable, and the density, which consists in being full, a plenum of qualities. What is to be done with it? It is pure exhibit; it is to be contemplated; perhaps it is to be enjoyed. The art of poetry depends more frequently on this faculty than on any other in its repertory; the faculty of presenting images so

---

[1] Benedetto Croce (1866–1952), Italian philosopher, historian, and aesthetician.

[2] Irish novelist and critic (1852–1933).

whole and clean that they resist the catalysis of thought.

And something else must be said, going in the opposite direction. "Pure poetry," all the same, is not as pure as it is claimed to be, though on the whole it is Physical Poetry. (All true poetry is a phase of Physical Poetry.) It is not as pure as Imagism is, or at least it is not as pure as Imagism would be if it lived up to its principles; and in fact it is significant that the volume does not contain any Imagist poems, which argues a difference in taste somewhere. Imagism may take trifling things for its material, presumably it will take the first things the poet encounters, since "importance" and "interest" are not primary qualities which a thing possesses but secondary or tertiary ones which the idealist attributes to it by virtue of his own requirements. "Pure poetry" as Moore conceives it, and as the lyrics of Poe and Shakespeare offer it, deals with the more dramatic materials, and here dramatic means human, or at least capable of being referred to the critical set of human interests. Employing this sort of material the poet cannot exactly intend to set the human economists in us actually into motion, but perhaps he does intend to comfort us with the fleeting sense that it is potentially our kind of material.

In the same way "pure poetry" is nicely metred, whereas Imagism was free. Technique is written on it. And by the way the anthology contains no rugged anonymous Scottish ballad either, and probably for a like reason; because it would not be technically finished. Now both Moore and De La Mare[3] are accomplished conservative artists, and what they do or what they approve may be of limited range but it is sure to be technically admirable, and it is certain that they understand what technique in poetry is though they do not define it. Technique takes the thing-content and meters and orders it. Metre is not an original property of things. It is artificial, and conveys the sense of human control, even if it does not wish to impair the thinginess of the things. Metric is a science, and so far as we attend to it we are within the scientific atmosphere. Order is the logical arrangement of things. It involves the dramatic "form" which selects the things, and brings out their appropriate qualities, and carries them through a systematic course of predication until the total impression is a unit of logic and not merely a solid

lump of thing-content. The "pure poems" which Moore admires are studied, though it would be fatal if they looked studious. A sustained effort of ideation effected these compositions. It is covered up, and communicates itself only on a subliminal plane of consciousness. But experienced readers are aware of it; they know at once what is the matter when they encounter a realism shamelessly passing for poetry, or a well-planned but blundering poetry.

As critics we should have every good will toward Physical Poetry: it is the basic constituent of any poetry. But the product is always something short of a pure or absolute existence, and it cannot quite be said that it consists of nothing but physical objects. The fact is that when we are more than usually satisfied with a Physical Poetry our analysis will probably disclose that it is more than usually impure.

2. PLATONIC POETRY

The poetry of ideas I shall denominate: Platonic Poetry. This also has grades of purity. A discourse which employed only abstract ideas with no images would be a scientific document and not a poem at all, not even a Platonic poem. Platonic Poetry dips heavily into the physical. If Physical Poetry tends to employ some ideation surreptitiously while still looking innocent of idea, Platonic Poetry more than returns the compliment, for it tries as hard as it can to look like Physical Poetry, as if it proposed to conceal its medicine, which is the idea to be propagated, within the sugar candy of objectivity and *Dinglichkeit*. As an instance, it is almost inevitable that I quote a famous Victorian utterance:

> The year's at the spring
> And day's at the morn;
> Morning's at seven;
> The hill-side's dew-pearled;
> The lark's on the wing;
> The snail's on the thorn:
> God's in his heaven—
> All's right with the world![4]

which is a piece of transparent homiletics; for in it six pretty, co-ordinate images are marched, like six little lambs to the slaughter, to a colon and a powerful text. Now the exhibits of this poetry in the physical kind are always large, and may take more of the attention of the reader than is desired,

---

[3] Walter de la Mare (1873–1956), poet and short story writer.

[4] From *Pippa Passes*, by Robert Browning (1812–1889).

but they are meant mostly to be illustrative of the ideas. It is on this ground that idealists like Hegel detect something unworthy, like a pedagogical trick, in poetry after all, and consider that the race will abandon it when it has outgrown its childishness and is enlightened.

The ablest arraignment of Platonic Poetry that I have seen, as an exercise which is really science but masquerades as poetry by affecting a concern for physical objects, is that of Mr. Allen Tate in a series of studies recently in *The New Republic*. I will summarize. Platonic Poetry is allegory, a discourse in things, but on the understanding that they are translatable at every point into ideas. (The usual ideas are those which constitute the popular causes, patriotic, religious, moral, or social.) Or Platonic Poetry is the elaboration of ideas as such, but in proceeding introduces for ornament some physical properties after the style of Physical Poetry; which is rhetoric. It is positive when the poet believes in the efficacy of the ideas. It is negative when he despairs of their efficacy, because they have conspicuously failed to take care of him, and utters his personal wail:

I fall upon the thorns of life! I bleed![5]

This is "Romantic Irony," which comes at occasional periods to interrupt the march of scientific optimism. But it still falls under the category of Platonism; it generally proposes some other ideas to take the place of those which are in vogue.

But why Platonism? To define Platonism we must remember that it is not the property of the historical person who reports dialogues about it in an Academy, any more than "pure poetry" is the property of the talkers who describe it from a house on Ebury Street. Platonism, in the sense I mean, is the name of an impulse that is native to us all, frequent, tending to take a too complete possession of our minds. Why should the spirit of mortal be proud? The chief explanation is that modern mortal is probably a Platonist. We are led to believe that nature is rational and that by the force of reasoning we shall possess it. I have read upon high authority: "Two great forces are persistent in Plato: the love of truth and zeal for human improvement." The forces are one force. We love to view the world under universal or scientific ideas to which we give the name truth; and this is because the ideas seem to make not for righte-

[5] From "Ode to the West Wind," by Percy Bysshe Shelley (1792–1822).

ousness but for mastery. The Platonic view of the the world is ultimately the predatory, for it reduces to the scientific, which we know. The Platonic Idea becomes the Logos which science worships, which is the Occidental God, whose minions we are, and whose children, claiming a large share in His powers for patrimony.

Now the fine Platonic world of ideas fails to coincide with the original world of perception, which is the world populated by the stubborn and contingent objects, and to which as artists we fly in shame. The sensibility manifested by artists makes fools of scientists, if the latter are inclined to take their special and quite useful form of truth as the whole and comprehensive article. A dandified pagan worldling like Moore can always defeat Platonism; he does it every hour; he can exhibit the savor of his fish and wines, the fragrance of his coffee and cigars, and the solidity of the images in his favorite verse. These are objects which have to be experienced, and cannot be reported, for what is their simple essence that the Platonist can abstract? Moore may sound mystical but he is within the literal truth when he defends "pure poetry" on the ground that the things are constant, and it is the ideas which change—changing according to the latest mode under which the species indulges its grandiose expectation of subjugating nature. The things are constant in the sense that the ideas are never emancipated from the necessity of referring back to them as their original; and the sense that they are not altered nor diminished no matter which ideas may take off from them as a point of departure. The way to obtain the true *Dinglichkeit* of a formal dinner or a landscape or a beloved person is to approach the object as such, and in humility; then it unfolds a nature which we are unprepared for if we have put our trust in the simple idea which attempted to represent it.

The special antipathy of Moore is to the ideas as they put on their moral complexion, the ideas that relate everything to that insignificant centre of action, the human "soul" in its most Platonic and Pharisaic aspect. Nothing can darken perception better than a repetitive moral earnestness, based on the reputed superiority and higher destiny of the human species. If morality is the code by which we expect the race to achieve the more perfect possession of nature, it is an incitement to a more heroic science, but not to æsthetic experience, nor religious; if it is the code of humility, by which we intend to know nature as nature is, that is another matter; but in an age of science morality is inevitably for the general public the former; and so transcendent a morality as the latter is now unheard of. And therefore:

> O love, *they* die in yon rich sky,
> *They* faint on hill or field or river;
> *Our* echoes roll from soul to soul,
> And grow forever and forever.[6]

The italics are mine. These lines conclude an otherwise innocent poem, a candidate for the anthology, upon which Moore remarks: "The Victorian could never reconcile himself to finishing a poem without speaking about the soul, and the lines are particularly vindictive." Vindictive is just. By what right did the Laureate exult in the death of the physical echoes and call upon his love to witness it, but out of the imperiousness of his savage Platonism? Plato himself would have admired this ending, and considered that it redeemed an otherwise vicious poem.

Why do persons who have ideas to promulgate risk the trial by poetry? If the poets are hired to do it, which is the polite conception of some Hegelians, why do their employers think it worth the money, which they hold in public trust for the cause? Does a science have to become a poetry too? A science is the less effective as a science when it muddies its clear waters with irrelevance, a sermon becomes less cogent when it begins to quote the poets. The moralist, the scientist, and the prophet of idealism think evidently that they must establish their conclusions in poetry, though they reach these conclusions upon quite other evidence. The poetry is likely to destroy the conclusions with a sort of death by drowning, if it is a free poetry.

When that happens the Platonists may be cured of Platonism. There are probably two cures, of which this is the better. One cure is by adversity, by the failure of the ideas to work, on account of treachery or violence, or the contingencies of weather, constitution, love, and economics; leaving the Platonist defeated and bewildered, possibly humbled, but on the other hand possibly turned cynical and worthless. Very much preferable is the cure which comes by education in the fine arts, erasing his Platonism more gently, leading him to feel that that is not a becoming habit of mind which dulls the perceptions.

The definition which some writers have given to

---

[6] From the last stanza of "The Bugle Song," by Alfred, Lord Tennyson (1809–1892).

art is: the reference of the idea to the image. The implication is that the act is not for the purpose of honest comparison so much as for the purpose of proving the idea by the image. But in the event the idea is not disproved so much as it is made to look ineffective and therefore foolish. The ideas will not cover the objects upon which they are imposed, they are too attenuated and threadlike; for ideas have extension and objects have intension, but extension is thin while intension is thick.

There must be a great deal of genuine poetry which started in the poet's mind as a thesis to be developed, but in which the characters and the situations have developed faster than the thesis, and of their own accord. The thesis disappears; or it is recaptured here and there and at the end, and lodged sententiously with the reader, where every successive reading of the poem will dislodge it again. Like this must be some plays, even some play out of Shakespeare, whose thesis would probably be disentangled with difficulty out of the crowded pageant; or some narrative poem with a moral plot but much pure detail; perhaps some "occasional" piece by a Laureate or official person, whose purpose is compromised but whose personal integrity is saved by his wavering between the sentiment which is a public duty and the experience which he has in his own right; even some proclaimed allegory, like Spenser's, unlikely as that may seem, which does not remain transparent and everywhere translatable into idea but makes excursions into the territory of objectivity. These are hybrid performances. They cannot possess beauty of design, though there may be a beauty in detailed passages. But it is common enough, and we should be grateful. The mind is a versatile agent, and unexpectedly stubborn in its determination not really to be hardened in Platonism. Even in an age of science like the nineteenth century the poetic talents are not so loyal to its apostolic zeal as they and it suppose, and do not deserve the unqualified scorn which it is fashionable to offer them, now that the tide has turned, for their performance is qualified.

But this may be not stern enough for concluding a note on Platonic Poetry. I refer again to that whose Platonism is steady and malignant. This poetry is an imitation of Physical Poetry, and not really a poetry. Platonists practise their bogus poetry in order to show that an image will prove an idea, but the literature which succeeds in this delicate mission does not contain real images but illustrations.

3. METAPHYSICAL POETRY

"Most men," Mr. Moore observes, "read and write poetry between fifteen and thirty and afterwards very seldom, for in youth we are attracted by ideas, and modern poetry being concerned almost exclusively with ideas we live on duty, liberty, and fraternity as chameleons are said to live on light and air, till at last we turn from ideas to things, thinking that we have lost our taste for poetry, unless, perchance, we are classical scholars."

Much is conveyed in this characteristic sentence, even in proportion to its length. As for the indicated chronology, the cart is put after the horse, which is its proper sequence. And it is pleasant to be confirmed in the belief that many men do recant from their Platonism and turn back to things. But it cannot be exactly a *volte-face*, for there are qualifications. If pure ideas were what these men turn from, they would have had no poetry at all in the first period, and if pure things were what they turn to, they would be having not a classical poetry but a pure imagism, if such a thing is possible, in the second.

The mind does not come unscathed and virginal out of Platonism. Ontological interest would have to develop curiously, or wastefully and discontinuously, if men through their youth must cultivate the ideas so passionately that upon its expiration they are done with ideas forever and ready to become as little (and pre-logical) children. Because of the foolishness of idealists are ideas to be taboo for the adult mind? And, as critics, what are we to do with those poems (like *The Canonization*[7] and *Lycidas*[8]) which could not obtain admission by Moore into the anthology but which very likely are the poems we cherish beyond others?

The reputed "innocence" of the æsthetic moment, the "knowledge without desire" which Schopenhauer praises, must submit to a little scrutiny, like anything else that looks too good to be true. We come into this world as aliens come into a land which they must conquer if they are to live. For native endowment we have an exacting "biological" constitution which knows precisely what it needs and determines for us our inevitable desires. There can be no certainty that any other impulses are there, for why should they be? They scarcely belong in the biological picture. Perhaps we are simply an efficient animal species, running

smoothly, working fast, finding the formula of life only too easy, and after a certain apprenticeship piling up power and wealth far beyond the capacity of our appetites to use. What will come next? Perhaps poetry, if the gigantic effort of science begins to seem disproportionate to the reward, according to a sense of diminishing returns. But before this pretty event can come to pass, it is possible that every act of attention which is allowed us is conditioned by a gross and selfish interest.

Where is innocence then? The æsthetic moment appears as a curious moment of suspension; between the Platonism in us, which is militant, always sciencing and devouring, and a starved inhibited aspiration towards innocence which, if it could only be free, would like to respect and know the object as it might of its own accord reveal itself.

The poetic impulse is not free, yet it holds out stubbornly against science for the enjoyment of its images. It means to reconstitute the world of perceptions. Finally there is suggested some such formula as the following:

Science gratifies a rational or practical impulse and exhibits the minimum of perception. Art gratifies a perceptual impulse and exhibits the minimum of reason.

Now it would be strange if poets did not develop many technical devices for the sake of increasing the volume of the percipienda or sensibilia. I will name some of them.

First Device: metre. Metre is the most obvious device. A formal metre impresses us as a way of regulating very drastically the material, and we do not stop to remark (that is, as readers) that it has no particular aim except some nominal sort of regimentation. It symbolizes the predatory method, like a sawmill which intends to reduce all the trees to fixed unit timbers, and as business men we require some sign of our business. But to the Platonic censor in us it gives a false security, for so long as the poet appears to be working faithfully at his metrical engine he is left comparatively free to attend lovingly to the things that are being metered, and metering them need not really hurt them. Metre is the gentlest violence he can do them, if he is expected to do some violence.

Second Device: fiction. The device of the fiction is probably no less important and universal in poetry. Over every poem which looks like a poem is a sign which reads: This road does not go through to action; fictitious. Art always sets out to

---

[7] By John Donne (1573–1631).
[8] By John Milton (1608–1674).

create an "æsthetic distance" between the object and the subject, and art takes pains to announce that it is not history. The situation treated is not quite an actual situation, for science is likely to have claimed that field, and exiled art; but a fictive or hypothetical one, so that science is less greedy and perception may take hold of it. Kant asserted that the æsthetic judgment is not concerned with the existence or non-existence of the object, and may be interpreted as asserting that it is so far from depending on the object's existence that it really depends on the object's non-existence. Sometimes we have a certain melancholy experience. We enjoy a scene which we receive by report only, or dream, or meet with in art; but subsequently find ourselves in the presence of an actual one that seems the very same scene; only to discover that we have not now the power to enjoy it, or to receive it æsthetically, because the economic tension is upon us and will not indulge us in the proper mood. And it is generally easier to obtain our æsthetic experience from art than from nature, because nature is actual, and communication is forbidden. But in being called fictive or hypothetical the art-object suffers no disparagement. It cannot be true in the sense of being actual, and therefore it may be despised by science. But it is true in the sense of being fair or representative, in permitting the "illusion of reality"; just as Schopenhauer discovered that music may symbolize all the modes of existence in the world; and in keeping with the customary demand of the readers of fiction proper, that it shall be "true to life." The defenders of art must require for it from its practitioners this sort of truth, and must assert of it before the world this dignity. If jealous science succeeds in keeping the field of history for its own exclusive use, it does not therefore annihilate the arts, for they reappear in a field which may be called real though one degree removed from actuality. There the arts perform their function with much less interference, and at the same time with about as much fidelity to the phenomenal world as history has.

Third Device: tropes. I have named two important devices; I am not prepared to offer the exhaustive list. I mention but one other kind, the device which comprises the figures of speech. A proper scientific discourse has no intention of employing figurative language for its definitive sort of utterance. Figures of speech twist accidence away from the straight course, as if to intimate astonishing lapses of rationality beneath the smooth surface of discourse, inviting perceptual attention, and weakening the tyranny of science over the senses. But I skip the several easier and earlier figures, which are timid, and stop on the climactic figure, which is the metaphor; with special reference to its consequence, a poetry which once in our history it produced in a beautiful and abundant exhibit, called Metaphysical Poetry.

And what is Metaphysical Poetry? The term was added to the official vocabulary of criticism by Johnson, who probably took it from Pope, who probably took it from Dryden, who used it to describe the poetry of a certain school of poets, thus: "He [John Donne] affects the metaphysics, not only in his satires, but in his amorous verses, where nature only should reign. . . . In this Mr. Cowley has copied him to a fault." But the meaning of metaphysical which was common in Dryden's time, having come down from the Middle Ages through Shakespeare, was simply: supernatural; *miraculous.* The context of the Dryden passage indicates it.

Dryden, then, noted a miraculism in poetry and repudiated it; except where it was employed for satire, where it was not seriously intended and had the effect of wit. Dryden himself employs miraculism wittily, but seems rather to avoid it if he will be really committed by it; he may employ it in his translations of Ovid, where the responsibility is Ovid's and not Dryden's, and in an occasional classical piece where he is making polite use of myths well known to be pagan errors. In his "amorous" pieces he finds the reign of nature sufficient, and it is often the worse for his amorous pieces. He is not many removes from a naturalist. (A naturalist is a person who studies nature not because he loves it but because he wants to use it, approaches it from the standpoint of common sense, and sees it thin and not thick.) Dryden might have remarked that Donne himself had a change of heart and confined his miraculism at last to the privileged field of a more or less scriptural revelation. Perhaps Dryden found his way to accepting Milton because Milton's miraculism was mostly not a contemporary sort but classical and scriptural, pitched in a time when the age of miracles had not given way to the age of science. He knew too that Cowley[9] had shamefully recanted from his petty miraculism, which formed the conceits, and turned to the scriptural or large order of miraculism to write his heroic (but empty)

---

[9] Abraham Cowley (1618–1667), English poet.

verses about David; and had written a Pindaric ode in extravagant praise of "Mr. Hobs," whose naturalistic account of nature seemed to render any other account fantastic if not contrary to the social welfare.

Incidentally, we know how much Mr. Hobbes[10] affected Dryden too, and the whole of Restoration literature. What Bacon with his disparagement of poetry had begun, in the cause of science and protestantism, Hobbes completed. The name of Hobbes is critical in any history that would account for the chill which settled upon the poets at the very moment that English poetry was attaining magnificently to the fullness of its powers. The name stood for common sense and naturalism, and the monopoly of the scientific spirit over the mind. Hobbes was the adversary, the Satan, when the latter first intimidated the English poets. After Hobbes his name is legion.

"Metaphysics," or miraculism, informs a poetry which is the most original and exciting, and intellectually perhaps the most seasoned, that we know in our literature, and very probably it has few equivalents in other literatures. But it is evident that the metaphysical effects may be large-scale or they may be small-scale. (I believe that generically, or ontologically, no distinction is to be made between them.) If Donne and Cowley illustrate the small-scale effects, Milton will illustrate the large-scale ones, probably as a consequence of the fact that he wrote major poems. Milton, in the *Paradise Lost*, told a story which was heroic and miraculous in the first place. In telling it he dramatized it, and allowed the scenes and characters to develop of their own native energy. The virtue of a long poem on a "metaphysical" subject will consist in the dramatization or substantiation of all the parts, the poet not being required to devise fresh miracles on every page so much as to establish the perfect "naturalism" of the material upon which the grand miracle is imposed. The *Paradise Lost* possesses this virtue nearly everywhere:

Thus *Adam* to himself lamented loud
Through the still Night, not now, as ere man fell,
Wholsom and cool, and mild, but with black Air
Accompanied, with damps and dreadful gloom,
Which to his evil Conscience represented
All things with double terror: On the ground
Outstretcht he lay, on the cold ground, and oft

[10] Thomas Hobbes (1588–1679), English philosopher.

Curs'd his Creation, Death as oft accus'd
Of tardie execution, since denounc't
The day of his offence. Why comes not Death,
Said hee, with one thrice acceptable stroke
To end me?

This is exactly the sort of detail for a large-scale metaphysical work, but it would hardly serve the purpose with a slighter and more naturalistic subject; with "amorous" verses. For the critical mind Metaphysical Poetry refers perhaps almost entirely to the so-called "conceits" that constitute its staple. To define the conceit is to define small-scale Metaphysical Poetry.

It is easily defined, upon a little citation. Donne exhibits two conceits, or two branches of one conceit in the familiar lines:

Our hands were firmly cemented
By a fast balm which thence did spring;
Our eye-beams twisted, and did thread
Our eyes upon one double string.

The poem which follows sticks to the topic; it represents the lovers in precisely that mode of union and no other. Cowley is more conventional yet still bold in the lines:

Oh take my Heart, and by that means you'll prove
Within, too stor'd enough of love:
Give me but yours, I'll by that change so thrive
That Love in all my parts shall live.
So powerful is this my change, it render can,
My outside Woman, and your inside Man.

A conceit originates in a metaphor; and in fact the conceit is but a metaphor if the metaphor is meant; that is, if it is developed so literally that it must be meant, or predicated so baldly that nothing else can be meant. Perhaps this will do for a definition.

Clearly the seventeenth century had the courage of its metaphors, and imposed them imperially on the nearest things, and just as clearly the nineteenth century lacked this courage, and was half-heartedly metaphorical, or content with similes. The difference between the literary qualities of the two periods is the difference between the metaphor and the simile. (It must be admitted that this like other generalizations will not hold without its exceptions.) One period was pithy and original in its poetic utterance, the other was prolix and predictable. It would not quite commit itself to the metaphor even if it came upon one. Shelley is about as vigorous as usual when he says in *Adonais:*

> Thou young Dawn,
> Turn all thy dew to splendour. . . .

But splendor is not the correlative of dew, it has the flat tone of a Platonic idea, while physically it scarcely means more than dew with sunshine upon it. The seventeenth century would have said: "Turn thy dew, which is water, into fire, and accomplish the transmutation of the elements." Tennyson in his boldest lyric sings:

> Come into the garden, Maud,
> For the black bat, night, has flown,

and leaves us unpersuaded of the bat. The predication would be complete without the bat, "The black night has flown," and a flying night is not very remarkable. Tennyson is only affecting a metaphor. But later in the same poem he writes:

> The red rose cries, "She is near, she is near";
> And the white rose weeps, "She is late";
> The larkspur listens, "I hear, I hear";
> And the lily whispers, "I wait."

And this is a technical conceit. But it is too complicated for this author, having a plurality of images which do not sustain themselves individually. The flowers stand for the lover's thoughts, and have been prepared for carefully in an earlier stanza, but their distinctness is too arbitrary, and these are like a schoolgirl's made-up metaphors. The passage will not compare with one on a very similar situation in *Green Candles*, by Mr. Humbert Wolfe:[11]

> "I know her little foot," gray carpet said:
> "Who but I should know her light tread?"
> "She shall come in," answered the open door,
> "And not," said the room, "go out any more."

Wolfe's conceit works and Tennyson's does not, and though Wolfe's performance seems not very daring or important, and only pleasant, he employs the technique of the conceit correctly: he knows that the miracle must have a basis of verisimilitude.

Such is Metaphysical Poetry; the extension of a rhetorical device; as one of the most brilliant successes in our poetry, entitled to long and thorough examination; and even here demanding somewhat

11 English poet and translator (1885–1940).

by way of a more ontological criticism. I conclude with it.

We may consult the dictionary, and discover that there is a miraculism or supernaturalism in a metaphorical assertion if we are ready to mean what we say, or believe what we hear. Or we may read Mr. Hobbes, the naturalist, who was very clear upon it: "II. The second cause of absurd assertions I ascribe to the giving of names of 'bodies' to 'accidents,' or of 'accidents' to 'bodies,' as they do that say 'faith is infused' or 'inspired,' when nothing can be 'poured' or 'breathed' into anything but body . . . and that 'phantasms' are 'spirits,' etc." Translated into our present terms, Hobbes is condemning the confusion of single qualities with whole things; or the substitution of concrete images for simple ideas.

Specifically, the miraculism arises when the poet discovers by analogy an identity between objects which is partial, though it should be considerable, and proceeds to an identification which is complete. It is to be contrasted with the simile, which says "as if" or "like," and is scrupulous to keep the identification partial. In Cowley's passage above, the lover is saying, not for the first time in this literature: "She and I have exchanged our hearts." What has actually been exchanged is affections, and affections are only in a limited sense the same as hearts. Hearts are unlike affections in being engines that pump blood and form body; and it is a miracle if the poet represents the lady's affection as rendering her inside into man. But he succeeds, with this mixture, in depositing with us the image of a very powerful affection.

From the strict point of view of literary criticism it must be insisted that the miraculism which produces the humblest conceit is the same miraculism which supplies to religions their substantive content. (This is said to assert the dignity not of the conceits but of the religions.) It is the poet and nobody else who gives to the God a nature, a form, faculties, and a history; to the God, most comprehensive of all terms, which, if there were no poetic impulse to actualize or "find" Him, would remain the driest and deadest among Platonic ideas, with all intension sacrificed to infinite extension. The myths are conceits, born of metaphors. Religions are periodically produced by poets and destroyed by naturalists. Religion depends for its ontological validity upon a literary understanding, and that is why it is frequently misunderstood. The metaphysical poets, perhaps like their spiritual fathers the mediæval Schoolmen, were under no illusions about this. They recognized myth, as they recognized the conceits, as a device of expression; its sanctity as the consequence of its public or social importance.

But whether the topics be Gods or amorous experiences, why do poets resort to miraculism? Hardly for the purpose of controverting natural fact or scientific theory. Religion pronounces about God only where science is silent and philosophy is negative; for a positive is wanted, that is, a God who has his being in the physical world as well as in the world of principles and abstractions. Likewise with the little secular enterprises of poetry too. Not now are the poets so brave, not for a very long time have they been so brave, as to dispute the scientists on what they call their "truth"; though it is a pity that the statement cannot be turned round. Poets will concede that every act of science is legitimate, and has its efficacy. The metaphysical poets of the seventeenth century particularly admired the methodology of science, and in fact they copied it, and their phrasing is often technical, spare, and polysyllabic, though they are not repeating actual science but making those metaphorical substitutions that are so arresting.

The intention of Metaphysical Poetry is to complement science, and improve discourse. Naturalistic discourse is incomplete, for either of two reasons. It has the minimum of physical content and starves the sensibility, or it has the maximum, as if to avoid the appearance of evil, but is laborious and pointless. Platonic Poetry is too idealistic, but Physical Poetry is too realistic, and realism is tedious and does not maintain interest. The poets therefore introduce the psychological device of the miracle. The predication which it permits is clean and quick but it is not a scientific predication. For scientific predication concludes an act of attention but miraculism initiates one. It leaves us looking, marvelling, and revelling in the thick *dinglich* substance that has just received its strange representation.

Let me suggest as a last word, in deference to a common Puritan scruple, that the predication of Metaphysical Poetry is true enough. It is not true like history, but no poetry is true in that sense, and only a part of science. It is true in the pragmatic sense in which some of the generalizations of science are true: it accomplishes precisely the sort of representation that it means to. It suggests to us that the object is perceptually or physically remarkable, and we had better attend to it.

Afterword

Randall Jarrell has described our age—though without any special complimentary intent—as an Age of Criticism. So it is in quantity, certainly; that it is so also in quality is less certain, though the aptness of its critical procedures and the soundness of its judgment and interpretation have won praise.[1] Yet the reader may well turn away from the foregoing essays some-

---

[1] Since this book limits itself to American literature, we are forced to pass over, except for occasional mention, British and European critics, some of whom have exerted a powerful influence on the critical theory and practice of our time. But we would make our account of the Age of Criticism curiously lopsided if we did not at least acknowledge the importance of English critics such as I. A. Richards (1893–   ), William Empson (1906–   ), and F. R. Leavis (1895–   ) and that of the Irish poet William Butler Yeats (1865–1939). Richards in particular deserves mention because of his studies of how words work together to produce particular shadings of meaning and of how easily poems are misread, but also because he has spent many years in this country as a professor at Harvard University. We must acknowledge a further serious omission: many brilliant critics are not represented in this book because they made their mark after 1945, the terminal date for our history. (Allen Tate deserves a place among these makers of modern criticism; but we have chosen to represent him by the essay printed to close the section on "Southern Writing of the Twentieth Century.")

what bewildered by the variety of purposes and methods he has found. He may want to ask: What do these essays have in common? Are they *all* examples of literary criticism? Is there any *proper* literary criticism?

Some of the essays—those of Mencken and Babbitt, say—clearly have little *direct* concern with literature. Others—those of Eliot and Ransom, for example—evidently have a great deal: they contain examinations of specific literary texts or speculations on how the writer goes about (or ought to go about) doing his characteristic work. They also, most obviously of all, reflect the impressions that the literary work has made on the critic himself.

Perhaps if we are in earnest about discovering what kind of job the literary critic performs—or is it several kinds of jobs?—we might best start with the obvious: (1) the critic is first of all a reader (and every reader is to some extent, whether or not he designs to be, a critic); (2) the reading of a poem or novel involves a transaction between the reader and the author *through* a verbal medium which is the literary work itself.

One way to sort out the varieties of criticism is to ask what aspect of this transaction is stressed.[2] The critic may be primarily interested in the character and the personality of the author or in his beliefs or in the ideas that he expresses, in which case he will want to emphasize the various factors that conditioned the author and, through him, the work itself. Criticism of this sort is called *genetic* criticism, for it stresses the origins of the work—all those matters that account for how it came to be and took the peculiar form that it did.

An age of great critical activity will almost inevitably turn out to be an age of controversy, with disagreements over issues, debate over the meaning of terms, and so on. Yet there may in fact be more of a consensus than presently appears—at least to the general reader who surveys the scene for the first time. Such a reader is almost certain to be confused by what he sees. Fortunately, guides through the maze and even histories of modern criticism are beginning to appear. The reader might, for example, consult *Theory of Literature* by René Wellek and Austin Warren, the second and revised edition of which appeared in 1956, and two important collections of critical essays by William K. Wimsatt, *The Verbal Icon* (1954) and *Hateful Contraries* (1965). Mention also should be made of Wellek's *History of Modern Criticism* (1955; 5 vols.). The last volume, which treats the twentieth century, is scheduled soon to appear. It would be presumptuous to claim for these or for any modern book of criticism that it gives the "correct" view or is completely "objective" in its appraisals. But what we can urge with confidence is that the authors mentioned above are intelligent and informed, that they engage basic issues, and that they are completely clear-headed about the positions that they take. Moreover, they do not ignore opposing positions. In fact, through their attempts to overcome these positions and through their excellent bibliographies, they acquaint the reader with the "other side" where it exists and where it most deserves to be taken into account.

[2] What follows has been said earlier in a somewhat different form in the "Letter to the Reader," which appears at the beginning of this volume.

If, on the other hand, the critic is interested primarily in the impact that a given work makes on its reader or readers, we get what is called an *affective* criticism. If a critic of this sort is content to talk about the impact on himself, we may get a subjective or impressionistic criticism; but if he is interested in the impact of the work on a class of society or a period of history, the critic will probably end by discussing its social or political effects.

A Freudian criticism is likely to be a genetic criticism; a Marxist, an affective criticism, with a social and political emphasis. But a Freudian critic might also be much interested in the effects of a given work on certain neurotic types; and a Marxist critic might well be interested in analyzing the ideas and psychological attitudes that a particular writer had absorbed because of his birth and nurture in, let us say, a middle-class Victorian English home. Of course, one need not be Marxist or Freudian in order to stress the origins and effects of a literary work rather than its special structure. Genetic and affective criticism are in fact the usual types met with throughout the nineteenth century. Moreover, they are always important to the literary historian of any period.

Yet most critics have necessarily been concerned at some point with the work itself, with literary craftsmanship, with the nature of literary form, and with the character of literary "truth." In the second quarter of the twentieth century there has been, as we have observed earlier, a remarkable revival of interest in literary craftsmanship and in the nature of the verbal artifact. Some of the reasons for this reemphasis have been mentioned above: "Confronted by what seemed to be a crisis in culture," we wrote, "the writer had to decide what his peculiar task was" and this entailed asking himself how a poem or a novel differed from a scientific discourse or a political tract. We talked about the stress that poets like T. S. Eliot and Ezra Pound placed upon craftsmanship and the reasons that compelled them to do so.[3]

That stress had its effect not only on the nature of their poetry but of

[3] This general issue has been thoroughly discussed in a recent book, Monroe Spears's *Dionysus and the City: Modernism in Twentieth Century Poetry* (1970). One of the salient features of modernism, Spears indicates, is the set of "discontinuities" that it initiated, such as a discontinuity between art and life and a rhetorical discontinuity; that is, its assertion that poetry—in contrast to expository prose—has its own rhetorical structure and its own kind of logic—not a prose logic but a logic of the imagination.

Dionysus and the City is particularly valuable for bringing the conflict of the various schools of criticism on down past 1945 to the present day. Spears discusses in detail the later reactions to the poetry of Eliot, the counterattacks against a criticism that stresses the work itself, the claims of a resurgent romanticism with its special interest in "vision" and apocalyptic experiences, and the new interest in myth and archtype as found in the work of the Canadian critic Northrop Frye.

their criticism. It also powerfully influenced other writers, particularly those who entered upon the task of explaining the new poetry and fiction—Eliot and Joyce, for example—to readers who at first found them incomprehensible.

There are good reasons for stressing the importance of the work of art as such. In the first place, unless genetic and affective criticism are anchored to specific literary texts, we may find ourselves dealing with irrelevancies of every kind. What Keats had for breakfast on a particular morning in 1819 might be interesting to know but would probably have nothing to do with the form and structure and value of the "Ode to a Nightingale" that he wrote that evening. Even Keats's literary diet—his appreciative reading of Milton, for example—will not necessarily account for the value of the "Ode" or even of *Hyperion*, a poem heavily influenced by Milton. On the affective side, a similar caution is in order: literary works have sometimes had powerful effects on society that are far in excess of their value as works of art. A criticism focused on the work itself has at least the virtue of being *literary*. It does not risk moving off into the realms of general intellectual history on the one hand or of reader psychology on the other. It promises to keep to the point.

Our concern in this matter, however, is not to exalt one kind of critical stress over the others or to designate one as the legitimate sort of inquiry and call all the others illegitimate. What we are concerned to indicate here is the fact of different approaches, each of which has its own interests and values; and second, to warn that affirmative answers to critical questions of one order will not necessarily entail affirmative answers to those of another order. Thus, the author's possession of true ideas or his having had an interesting childhood or his evident sincerity will not guarantee that his novel has literary value. Nor would its literary value necessarily be proved by the fact that his novel was read by millions of people who were deeply affected by it. Literary value has to be "proved" by other kinds of evidence.

Yet having distinguished some of the possible kinds of criticism, one ought to point out that we rarely find them in isolation. Even though Eliot is closely associated with criticism that stresses the literary work, one notices that his "Tradition and the Individual Talent," in spite of its statement that "Honest criticism . . . [is] directed not upon the poet but upon the poetry," is, as its very title indicates, much concerned with the writer's relation to his literary ancestors and stresses the ways in which he is (or ought to be) influenced by the tradition. Moreover, Eliot's "The Metaphysical Poets," for all its emphasis on poetry as heterogeneous "material compelled into unity" by the poet's mind, also makes a bold attempt at rewriting literary history.

It might be useful at this point for the reader to reflect on what kinds of literary criticism he has encountered while making his way through this book. He will probably conclude: various kinds, written to serve special occasions and interests—genetic, formalist,[4] and affective. Many of the introductions have had to do with the ways in which philosophical ideas, literary conventions, traditional patterns of conduct, and incidents in his own life have influenced an author's work. See, for example, the account of Theodore Dreiser or of Nathaniel Hawthorne. Moreover, we have sometimes attempted to assess the influence of the intellectual climate of the period on the writers of that period. See, for example, the account of Longfellow and "the fireside poets" on pp. 586–92, or the discussion of the dominant political, social, and economic conditions from 1861 to 1914 on pp. 1197–1219.

In this book the reader will also find discussions of the influence of a writer on other writers, on the public, and even on a political situation. The impact of Harriet Beecher Stowe's *Uncle Tom's Cabin*, for example, was immense.

Yet our hope is that the reader will find, underlying and supporting such kinds of comment and generalization, sensitive and informed readings of the literary texts in question; and though we have not displayed elaborate "analyses" for their own sakes, we have provided, especially in the notes and headnotes on particular poems, stories, and excerpts of novels, critical discussions that undertake to show how a particular episode "works" or a particular metaphor illuminates a relationship. As instances of such criticism the reader might look back at the discussion of Whittier's "Ichabod" (pp. 543–44) or *The Red Badge of Courage*, particularly pp. 1643–46.

What we would deeply deplore as a distraction from the main purpose of this account of American literature would be an inordinate interest in methodology as such. We would be happy if the reader could occasionally forget that he lives in an "age of criticism" and if he could rest assured that there is no startling or newfangled methodology lurking in the literary commentary that he found within the covers of these volumes. Certainly we are well aware that no method in itself can substitute for common sense, imagination, sensitivity, and intelligence. These qualities are primary; a methodology is always secondary and finds its true value in promoting the best exercise of genuine literary intelligence.

---

[4] For formalist we might substitute "contextualist." There seems to be no agreement on a single term to define a literary criticism that stresses the makeup of the literary work. See p. 2828.

6

Experiments and Continuities: Some Instances in Our Time 1945 to the Present

Prose

Very early the editors found that their hope of illustrating something of the variety of impulse and method in American prose writing since the Second World War was not practical. The scale of this book simply did not allow it. There is, indeed, a thriving activity among younger writers, an activity that augurs well for the future, but after all this book is, among other things, a history and is concerned primarily with what has been done and not with what is being, or may be, done; so the editors now settle on a limited number of representative writers of a certain age, who have produced a solid body of work, whose work the editors regard as among the most able and significant of the period, and whose impact is generally remarked.

2859

JOHN CHEEVER (1912–   )

Born May 27, 1912, in Quincy, Massachusetts; attended Thayer Academy; has lived in New York City, New Hampshire, Westchester County, N.Y. Italy, and again in Westchester; has written for television and taught composition at Barnard College; member National Institute of Arts and Letters (1957); publications include *The Way Some People Live* (stories, 1943), *The Enormous Radio and Other Stories* (1953), *The Wapshot Chronicle* (novel, 1957), *The Housebreaker of Shady Hill and Other Sto-*ries (1958), from which collection we present "O Youth and Beauty," *Some People, Places, and Things That Will Not Appear in My Next Novel* (1961), *The Wapshot Scandal* (novel, 1964), *The Brigadier and the Golf Widow* (stories, 1964), and *Bullet Park* (novel, 1969); among awards has received National Book Award for fiction (1958) and the Howells Medal from American Academy of Arts and Letters (1965).

O Youth and Beauty! (1958)

At the tag end of nearly every long, large Saturday-night party in the suburb of Shady Hill, when almost everybody who was going to play golf or tennis in the morning had gone home hours ago and the ten or twelve people remaining seemed powerless to bring the evening to an end although the gin and whiskey were running low, and here and there a woman who was sitting out her husband would have begun to drink milk; when everybody had lost track of time, and the baby sitters who were waiting at home for these diehards would have long since stretched out on the sofa and fallen into a deep sleep, to dream about cooking-contest prizes, ocean voyages, and romance; when the bellicose drunk, the crapshooter, the pianist, and the woman faced with the expiration of her hopes had all expressed themselves; when every proposal—to go to the Farquarsons' for breakfast, to go swimming, to go and wake up the Townsends, to go here and go there—died as soon as it was made, then Trace Bearden would begin to chide Cash Bentley about his age and thinning hair. The chiding was preliminary to moving the living-room furniture. Trace and Cash moved the tables and the chairs, the sofas and the fire screen, the woodbox and the footstool; and when they had finished, you wouldn't know the place. Then if the host had a revolver, he would be asked to produce it. Cash would take off his shoes and assume a starting crouch behind a sofa. Trace would fire the weapon out of an open window, and if you were new to the community and had not understood what the preparations were about, you would then realize that you were watching a hurdle race. Over the sofa went Cash, over the tables, over the fire screen and the woodbox. It was not exactly a race, since Cash ran it alone, but it was extraordinary to see this man of forty surmount so many obstacles so gracefully. There was not a piece of furniture in Shady Hill that Cash could not take in his stride. The race ended with cheers, and presently the party would break up.

Cash was, of course, an old track star, but he was never aggressive or tiresome about his brilliant past. The college where he had spent his youth had offered him a paying job on the alumni council, but he had refused it, realizing that that part of his life was ended. Cash and his wife, Louise, had two children, and they lived in a medium-cost ranchhouse on Alewives Lane. They belonged to the country club, although they could not afford it, but in the case of the Bentleys nobody ever pointed this out, and Cash was one of the best-liked men in Shady Hill. He was still slender—he was careful about his weight—and he walked to the train in the morning with a light and vigorous step that marked him as an athlete. His hair was thin, and there were mornings when his eyes looked bloodshot, but this did not detract much from a charming quality of stubborn youthfulness.

In business Cash had suffered reverses and disappointments, and the Bentleys had many money worries. They were always late with their tax payments and their mortgage payments, and the drawer of the hall table was stuffed with unpaid bills; it was always touch and go with the Bentleys and the bank. Louise looked pretty enough on Saturday night, but her life was exacting and monotonous. In the pockets of her suits, coats, and dresses there were little wads and scraps of paper on which was written: "Oleomargarine, frozen spinach, Kleenex, dog biscuit, hamburger, pepper, lard . . ." When she was still half awake in the morning, she was putting on the water for coffee and diluting the frozen orange juice. Then she would be wanted by the children. She would crawl under the bureau on her hands and knees to find a sock for Toby. She would lie flat on her belly and wriggle under the bed (getting dust up her nose) to find a shoe for Rachel. Then there were the housework, the laundry, and the cooking, as well as the demands of the children. There always seemed to be shoes to put on and shoes to take off, snowsuits to be zipped and unzipped, bottoms to be wiped, tears to be dried, and when the sun went down (she saw it set from the kitchen window) there was the supper to be cooked, the baths, the bedtime story, and the Lord's Prayer. With the sonorous words of the Our Father in a darkened room the children's day was over, but the day was far from over for Louise Bentley. There were the darning, the mending, and some ironing to do, and after sixteen years of housework she did not seem able to escape her chores even while she slept. Snowsuits, shoes, baths, and groceries seemed to have permeated her subconscious. Now and then she would speak in her sleep—so loudly that she woke her husband. "I can't *afford* veal cutlets," she said one night. Then she sighed uneasily and was quiet again.

By the standards of Shady Hill, the Bentleys were a happily married couple, but they had their ups and downs. Cash could be very touchy at times. When he came home after a bad day at the office and found that Louise, for some good reason, had not started supper, he would be ugly. "Oh, for Christ sake!" he would say, and go into the kitchen and heat up some frozen food. He drank some whiskey to relax himself during this ordeal, but it never seemed to relax him, and he usually burned the bottom out of a pan, and when they sat down for supper the dining space would be full of smoke. It was only a question of time before they were plunged into a bitter quarrel. Louise would run upstairs, throw herself onto the bed, and sob. Cash would grab the whiskey bottle and dose himself. These rows, in spite of the vigor with which Cash and Louise entered into them, were the source of a great deal of pain for both of them. Cash would sleep downstairs on the sofa, but sleep never repaired the damage, once the trouble had begun, and if they met in the morning, they would be at one another's throats in a second. Then Cash would leave for the train, and, as soon as the children had been taken to nursery school, Louise would put on her coat and cross the grass to the Beardens' house. She would cry into a cup of warmed-up coffee and tell Lucy Bearden her troubles. What was the meaning of marriage? What was the meaning of love? Lucy always suggested that Louise get a job. It would give her emotional and financial independence, and that, Lucy said, was what she needed.

The next night, things would get worse. Cash would not come home for dinner at all, but would stumble in at about eleven, and the whole sordid wrangle would be repeated, with Louise going to bed in tears upstairs and Cash again stretching out on the living-room sofa. After a few days and nights of this, Louise would decide that she was at the end of her rope. She would decide to go and stay with her married sister in Mamaroneck. She usually chose a Saturday, when Cash would be at home, for her departure. She would pack a suitcase and get her War Bonds from the desk. Then she would take a bath and put on her best slip. Cash, passing the bedroom door, would see her. Her slip was transparent, and suddenly he was all repentance, tenderness, charm, wisdom, and love. "Oh, my darling!" he would groan, and when they went downstairs to get a bite to eat about an hour later, they would be sighing and making cow eyes at one another; they would be the happiest married couple in the whole Eastern United States. It was usually at about this time that Lucy Bearden turned up with the good news that she had found a job for Louise. Lucy would ring the doorbell, and Cash, wearing a bathrobe, would let her in. She would be brief with Cash, naturally, and hurry into the dining room to tell poor Louise the good news. "Well that's very nice of you to have looked," Louise would say wanly, "but I don't think that I want a job any more. I don't think that Cash wants me to work, do you, sweetheart?" Then she would turn her big dark eyes on Cash, and you could practically smell smoke. Lucy would excuse herself hurriedly from this scene of depravity, but she never left with any hard feelings, because she had been married for nineteen years herself and she knew that every union has its ups and downs. She didn't seem to leave any wiser, either; the next time the Bentleys quarreled, she would be just as intent as ever on getting Louise a job. But these quarrels and reunions, like the hurdle race, didn't seem to lose their interest through repetition.

On a Saturday night in the spring, the Farquarsons gave the Bentleys an anniversary party. It was their seventeenth anniversary. Saturday afternoon, Louise Bentley put herself through preparations nearly as arduous as the Monday wash. She rested for an hour, by the clock, with her feet high in the air, her chin in a sling, and her eyes bathed in some astringent solution. The clay packs, the too tight girdle, and the plucking and curling and painting that went on were all aimed at rejuvenation. Feeling in the end that she had not been entirely successful, she tied a piece of veiling over her eyes—but she was a lovely woman, and all the cosmetics that she had struggled with seemed, like her veil, to be drawn transparently over a face where mature beauty and a capacity for wit and passion were undisguisable. The Farquarsons' party was nifty, and the Bentleys had a wonderful time. The only person who drank too much was Trace Bearden. Late in the party, he began to chide Cash about his thinning hair and Cash good-naturedly began to move the furniture around. Harry Farquarson had a pistol, and Trace went out onto the terrace to fire it up at the sky. Over the sofa went Cash, over the end table, over the arms of the wing chair and the fire screen. It was a piece of carving on a chest that brought him down, and down he came like a ton of bricks.

Louise screamed and ran to where he lay. He had cut a gash in his forehead, and someone made a bandage to stop the flow of blood. When he tried to get up, he stumbled and fell again, and his face turned a terrible green. Harry telephoned Dr. Parminter, Dr. Hopewell, Dr. Altman, and Dr. Barnstable, but it was two in the morning and none of them answered. Finally, a Dr. Yerkes—a total stranger—agreed to come. Yerkes was a young man—he did not seem old enough to be a doctor—and he looked around at the disordered room and the anxious company as if there was something weird about the scene. He got off on the wrong foot with Cash. "What seems to be the matter, old-timer?" he asked.

Cash's leg was broken. The doctor put a splint on it, and Harry and Trace carried the injured man out to the doctor's car. Louise followed them in her own car to the hospital, where Cash was bedded down in a ward. The doctor gave Cash a sedative, and Louise kissed him and drove home in the dawn.

Cash was in the hospital for two weeks, and when he came home he walked with a crutch and his broken leg was in a heavy cast. It was another ten days before he could limp to the morning train. "I won't be able to run the hurdle race any more, sweetheart," he told Louise sadly. She said that it didn't matter, but while it didn't matter to her, it seemed to matter to Cash. He had lost weight in the hospital. His spirits were low. He seemed discontented. He did not himself understand what had happened. He, or everything around him, seemed subtly to have changed for the worse. Even his senses seemed to conspire to damage the ingenuous world that he had enjoyed for so many years. He went into the kitchen late one night to make himself a sandwich, and when he opened the icebox door he noticed a rank smell. He dumped the spoiled meat into the garbage, but the smell clung to his nostrils. A few days later he was in the attic, looking for his old varsity sweater. There were no windows in the attic and his flashlight was dim. Kneeling on the floor to unlock a trunk, he broke a spider web with his lips. The frail web covered his mouth as if a hand had been put over it. He wiped it impatiently, but also with the feeling of having been gagged. A few nights later, he was walking down a New York side street in the rain and saw an old whore standing in a doorway. She was so sluttish and ugly that she looked like a cartoon of Death, but before he could appraise her—the instant his eyes took an impression of her crooked figure—his lips swelled, his breathing quickened, and he experienced all the other symptoms of erotic excitement. A few nights later, while he was reading *Time* in the living room, he noticed that the faded roses Louise had brought in from the garden smelled more of earth than of anything else. It was a putrid, compelling smell. He dropped the roses into a wastebasket, but not before they had reminded him of the spoiled meat, the whore, and the spider web.

He had started going to parties again, but without the hurdle race to run, the parties of his friends and neighbors seemed to him interminable and stale. He listened to their dirty jokes with an irritability that was hard for him to conceal. Even their countenances discouraged him, and, slumped in a chair, he would regard their skin and their teeth narrowly, as if he were himself a much younger man.

The brunt of his irritability fell on Louise, and it seemed to her that Cash, in losing the hurdle race, had lost the thing that had preserved his equilibrium. He was rude to his friends when they stopped in for a drink. He was rude and gloomy when he and Louise went out. When Louise asked him what was the matter, he only murmured, "Nothing, nothing, nothing," and poured himself some bourbon. May and June passed, and then the first part of July, without his showing any improvement.

Then it is a summer night, a wonderful summer night. The passengers on the eight-fifteen see Shady Hill—if they notice it at all—in a bath of placid golden light. The noise of the train is muffled in the heavy foliage, and the long car windows look like a string of lighted aquarium tanks before they flicker out of sight. Up on the hill, the ladies say to one another, "Smell the grass! Smell the trees!" The Farquarsons are giving another party, and Harry has hung a sign, WHISKEY GULCH, from the rose arbor, and is wearing a chef's white hat and an apron. His guests are still drinking, and the smoke from his meat fire rises, on this windless evening, straight up into the trees.

In the clubhouse on the hill, the first of the formal dances for the young people begins around nine. On Alewives Lane sprinklers continue to play after dark. You can smell the water. The air seems as fragrant as it is dark—it is a delicious element to walk through—and most of the windows on Alewives Lane are open to it. You can see Mr. and Mrs. Bearden, as you pass, looking at their television. Joe Lockwood, the young lawyer who lives on the corner, is practicing a speech to the jury before his wife. "I intend to show you," he says, "that a man of probity, a man whose reputation for honesty and reliability . . ." He waves his bare arms as he speaks. His wife goes on knitting. Mrs. Carver—Harry Farquarson's mother-in-law—glances up at the sky and asks, "*Where* did all the stars come from?" She is old and foolish, and yet she is right: Last night's stars seem to have

drawn to themselves a new range of galaxies, and the night sky is not dark at all, except where there is a tear in the membrane of light. In the unsold house lots near the track a hermit thrush is singing.

The Bentleys are at home. Poor Cash has been so rude and gloomy that the Farquarsons have not asked him to their party. He sits on the sofa beside Louise, who is sewing elastic into the children's underpants. Through the open window he can hear the pleasant sounds of the summer night. There is another party, in the Rogerses' garden, behind the Bentleys'. The music from the dance drifts down the hill. The band is sketchy—saxophone, drums, and piano—and all the selections are twenty years old. The band plays "Valencia," and Cash looks tenderly toward Louise, but Louise, tonight, is a discouraging figure. The lamp picks out the gray in her hair. Her apron is stained. Her face seems colorless and drawn. Suddenly, Cash begins frenziedly to beat his feet in time to the music. He sings some gibberish—Jabajabajabajaba—to the distant saxophone. He sighs and goes into the kitchen.

Here a faint, stale smell of cooking clings to the dark. From the kitchen window Cash can see the lights and figures of the Rogerses' party. It is a young people's party. The Rogers girl has asked some friends in for dinner before the dance, and now they seem to be leaving. Cars are driving away. "I'm covered with grass stains," a girl says. "I hope the old man remembered to buy gasoline," a boy says, and a girl laughs. There is nothing on their minds but the passing summer night. Taxes and the elastic in underpants—all the unbeautiful facts of life that threaten to crush the breath out of Cash—have not touched a single figure in this garden. Then jealousy seizes him—such savage and bitter jealousy that he feels ill.

He does not understand what separates him from these children in the garden next door. He has been a young man. He has been a hero. He has been adored and happy and full of animal spirits, and now he stands in a dark kitchen, deprived of his athletic prowess, his impetuousness, his good looks—of everything that means anything to him. He feels as if the figures in the next yard are the specters from some party in that past where all his tastes and desires lie, and from which he has been cruelly removed. He feels like a ghost of the summer evening. He is sick with longing. Then he hears voices in the front of the house. Louise turns on the kitchen light. "Oh, here you are," she says. "The Beardens stopped in. I think they'd like a drink."

Cash went to the front of the house to greet the Beardens. They wanted to go up to the club, for one dance. They saw, at a glance, that Cash was at loose ends, and they urged the Bentleys to come. Louise got someone to stay with the children and then went upstairs to change.

When they got to the club, they found a few friends of their age hanging around the bar, but Cash did not stay in the bar. He seemed restless and perhaps drunk. He banged into a table on his way through the lounge to the ballroom. He cut in on a young girl. He seized her too vehemently and jigged her off in an ancient two-step. She signaled openly for help to a boy in the stag line, and Cash was cut out. He walked angrily off the dance floor onto the terrace. Some young couples there withdrew from one another's arms as he pushed open the screen door. He walked to the end of the terrace, where he hoped to be alone, but here he surprised another young couple, who got up from the lawn, where they seemed to have been lying, and walked off in the dark toward the pool.

Louise remained in the bar with the Beardens. "Poor Cash is tight," she said. And then, "He told me this afternoon that he was going to paint the storm windows," she said. "Well, he mixed the paint and washed the brushes and put on some old fatigues and went into the cellar. There was a telephone call for him at around five, and when I went down to tell him, do you know what he was doing? He was just sitting there in the dark with a cocktail shaker. He hadn't touched the storm windows. He was just sitting there in the dark, drinking Martinis."

"Poor Cash," Trace said.

"You ought to get a job," Lucy said. "That would give you emotional and financial independence." As she spoke, they all heard the noise of furniture being moved around in the lounge.

"Oh, my God!" Louise said. "He's going to run the race. Stop him, Trace, stop him! He'll hurt himself. He'll kill himself!"

They all went to the door of the lounge. Louise again asked Trace to interfere, but she could see by Cash's face that he was way beyond remonstrating with. A few couples left the dance floor and stood watching the preparations. Trace didn't try to stop Cash—he helped him. There was no pistol,

so he slammed a couple of books together for the start.

Over the sofa went Cash, over the coffee table, the lamp table, the fire screen, and the hassock. All his grace and strength seemed to have returned to him. He cleared the big sofa at the end of the room and instead of stopping there, he turned and started back over the course. His face was strained. His mouth hung open. The tendons of his neck protruded hideously. He made the hassock, the fire screen, the lamp table, and the coffee table. People held their breath when he approached the final sofa, but he cleared it and landed on his feet. There was some applause. Then he groaned and fell. Louise ran to his side. His clothes were soaked with sweat and he gasped for breath. She knelt down beside him and took his head in her lap and stroked his thin hair.

Cash had a terrible hangover on Sunday, and Louise let him sleep until it was nearly time for church. The family went off to Christ Church together at eleven, as they always did. Cash sang, prayed, and got to his knees, but the most he ever felt in church was that he stood outside the realm of God's infinite mercy, and, to tell the truth, he no more believed in the Father, the Son, and the Holy Ghost than does my bull terrier. They returned home at one to eat the over-cooked meat and stony potatoes that were their customary Sunday lunch. At around five, the Parminters called up and asked them over for a drink. Louise didn't want to go, so Cash went alone. (Oh, those suburban Sunday nights, those Sunday-night blues! Those departing weekend guests, those stale cocktails, those half-dead flowers, those trips to Harmon to catch the Century, those post-mortems and pickup suppers!) It was sultry and overcast. The dog days were beginning. He drank gin with the Parminters for an hour or two and then went over to the Townsends' for a drink. The Farquarsons called up the Townsends and asked them to come over and bring Cash with them, and at the Farquarsons' they had some more drinks and ate the leftover party food. The Farquarsons were glad to see that Cash seemed like himself again. It was half past ten or eleven when he got home. Louise was upstairs, cutting out of the current copy of *Life* those scenes of mayhem, disaster, and violent death that she felt might corrupt her children. She always did this. Cash came upstairs and spoke to her and then went down again. In a little while, she heard him moving the living-room furniture around. Then he called to her, and when she went down, he was standing at the foot of the stairs in his stocking feet, holding the pistol out to her. She had never fired it before, and the directions he gave her were not much help.

"Hurry up," he said. "I can't wait all night."

He had forgotten to tell her about the safety, and when she pulled the trigger nothing happened.

"It's that little lever," he said. "Press that little lever." Then, in his impatience, he hurdled the sofa anyhow.

The pistol went off and Louise got him in mid-air. She shot him dead.

RALPH ELLISON (1914–   )

Born March 1, 1914, in Oklahoma City; studied music at Tuskegee Institute; came to New York City, where interest turned to fiction writing under influence of Richard Wright; has taught literature and writing at Bard College, University of Chicago, Rutgers University; now holds the Albert Schweitzer chair at New York University; member National Institute of Arts and Letters (1964); received Rome fellowship from American Academy of Arts and Letters (1955); publications are *Invisible Man* (1952), winner of numerous awards, including National Book Award for fiction (1953), and *Shadow and Act* (essays, 1964); has contributed to various periodicals other essays and excerpts from a second novel.

From Invisible Man (1952)

CHAPTER I

It goes a long way back, some twenty years. All my life I had been looking for something, and everywhere I turned someone tried to tell me what it was. I accepted their answers too, though they were often in contradiction and even self-contradictory. I was naïve. I was looking for myself and asking everyone except myself questions which I, and only I, could answer. It took me a long time and much painful boomeranging of my expectations to achieve a realization everyone else appears to have been born with: That I am nobody but myself. But first I had to discover that I am an invisible man!

And yet I am no freak of nature, nor of history. I was in the cards, other things having been equal (or unequal) eighty-five years ago. I am not ashamed of my grandparents for having been slaves. I am only ashamed of myself for having at one time been ashamed. About eighty-five years ago they were told that they were free, united with others of our country in everything pertaining to the common good, and, in everything social, separate like the fingers of the hand. And they believed it. They exulted in it. They stayed in their place, worked hard, and brought up my father to do the same. But my grandfather is the one. He was an odd old guy, my grandfather, and I am told I take after him. It was he who caused the trouble. On his deathbed he called my father to him and said, "Son, after I'm gone I want you to keep up the good fight. I never told you, but our life is a war and I have been a traitor all my born days, a spy in the enemy's country ever since I give up my gun back in the Reconstruction. Live with your head in the lion's mouth. I want you to overcome 'em with yeses, undermine 'em with grins, agree 'em to death and destruction, let 'em swoller you till they vomit or bust wide open." They thought the old man had gone out of his mind. He had been the meekest of men. The younger children were rushed from the room, the shades drawn and the flame of the lamp turned so low that it sputtered on the wick like the old man's breathing. "Learn it to the younguns," he whispered fiercely; then he died.

But my folks were more alarmed over his last words than over his dying. It was as though he had not died at all, his words caused so much anxiety. I was warned emphatically to forget what he had said and, indeed, this is the first time it has been mentioned outside the family circle. It had a tremendous effect upon me, however. I could never be sure of what he meant. Grandfather had been a quiet old man who never made any trouble, yet on his deathbed he had called himself a traitor and a spy, and he had spoken of his meekness as a dangerous activity. It became a constant puzzle which lay unanswered in the back of my mind. And whenever things went well for me I remembered my grandfather and felt guilty and uncomfortable. It was as though I was carrying out his advice in spite of myself. And to make it worse, everyone loved me for it. I was praised by the most lily-white men of the town. I was considered an example of desirable conduct—just as my grandfather had been. And what puzzled me was that the old man had defined it as *treachery*. When I was praised for my conduct I felt a guilt that in some way I was doing something that was really against the wishes of the white folks, that if they had understood they would have desired me to act just the opposite, that I should have been sulky and mean, and that that really would have been what they wanted, even though they were fooled and thought they wanted me to act as I did. It made me afraid that some day they would look upon me as a traitor and I would be lost. Still I was more afraid to act any other way because they didn't like that at all. The old man's words were like a curse. On my graduation day I delivered an oration in which I showed that humility was the secret, indeed, the very essence of progress. (Not that I believed this—how could I, remembering my grandfather?—I only believed that it worked.) It was a great success. Everyone praised me and I was invited to give the speech at a gathering of the town's leading white citizens. It was a triumph for our whole community.

It was in the main ballroom of the leading hotel. When I got there I discovered that it was on the occasion of a smoker, and I was told that since I was to be there anyway I might as well take part in the battle royal to be fought by some of my schoolmates as part of the entertainment. The battle royal came first.

All of the town's big shots were there in their tuxedoes, wolfing down the buffet foods, drinking beer and whiskey and smoking black cigars. It was a large room with a high ceiling. Chairs were arranged in neat rows around three sides of a portable boxing ring. The fourth side was clear, revealing a gleaming space of polished floor. I had some misgivings over the battle royal, by the way. Not from a distaste for fighting, but because I didn't care too much for the other fellows who were to take part. They were tough guys who seemed to have no grandfather's curse worrying their minds. No one could mistake their toughness. And besides, I suspected that fighting a battle royal might detract from the dignity of my speech. In those pre-invisible days I visualized myself as a potential Booker T. Washington. But the other fellows didn't care too much for me either, and there were nine of them. I felt superior to them in my way, and I didn't like the manner in which we were all crowded together into the servants' elevator. Nor did they like my being there. In fact, as the warmly lighted floors flashed past the elevator we had words over the fact that I, by taking part in the fight, had knocked one of their friends out of a night's work.

We were led out of the elevator through a rococo hall into an anteroom and told to get into our fighting togs. Each of us was issued a pair of boxing gloves and ushered out into the big mirrored hall, which we entered looking cautiously about us and whispering, lest we might accidentally be heard above the noise of the room. It was foggy with cigar smoke. And already the whiskey was taking effect. I was shocked to see some of the most important men of the town quite tipsy. They were all there—bankers, lawyers, judges, doctors, fire chiefs, teachers, merchants. Even one of the more fashionable pastors. Something we could not see was going on up front. A clarinet was vibrating sensuously and the men were standing up and moving eagerly forward. We were a small tight group, clustered together, our bare upper bodies touching and shining with anticipatory sweat; while up front the big shots were becoming increasingly excited over something we still could not see. Suddenly I heard the school superintendent, who had told me to come, yell, "Bring up the shines, gentlemen! Bring up the little shines!"

We were rushed up to the front of the ballroom, where it smelled even more strongly of tobacco and whiskey. Then we were pushed into place. I almost wet my pants. A sea of faces, some hostile, some amused, ringed around us, and in the center, facing us, stood a magnificent blonde—stark naked. There was dead silence. I felt a blast of cold air chill me. I tried to back away, but they were behind me and around me. Some of the boys stood with lowered heads, trembling. I felt a wave of irrational guilt and fear. My teeth chattered, my skin turned to goose flesh, my knees knocked. Yet I was strongly attracted and looked in spite of myself. Had the price of looking been blindness, I would have looked. The hair was yellow like that of a circus kewpie doll, the face heavily powdered and rouged, as though to form an abstract mask, the eyes hollow and smeared a cool blue, the color of a baboon's butt. I felt a desire to spit upon her as my eyes brushed slowly over her body. Her breasts were firm and round as the domes of East Indian temples, and I stood so close as to see the fine skin texture and beads of pearly perspiration glistening like dew around the pink and erected buds of her nipples. I wanted at one and the same time to run from the room, to sink through the floor, or go to her and cover her from my eyes and the eyes of the others with my body; to feel the soft thighs, to caress her and destroy her, to love her and murder her, to hide from her, and yet to stroke where below the small American flag tattooed upon her belly her thighs formed a capital V. I had a notion that of all in the room she saw only me with her impersonal eyes.

And then she began to dance, a slow sensuous movement; the smoke of a hundred cigars clinging to her like the thinnest of veils. She seemed like a fair bird-girl girdled in veils calling to me from the angry surface of some gray and threatening sea. I was transported. Then I became aware of the clarinet playing and the big shots yelling at us. Some threatened us if we looked and others if we did not. On my right I saw one boy faint. And now a man grabbed a silver pitcher from a table and stepped close as he dashed ice water upon him and stood him up and forced two of us to support him as his head hung and moans issued from his thick bluish lips. Another boy began to plead to go home. He was the largest of the group, wearing dark red fighting trunks much too small to conceal the erection which projected from him as though in answer to the insinuating low-registered moaning of the clarinet. He tried to hide himself with his boxing gloves.

And all the while the blonde continued dancing, smiling faintly at the big shots who watched her with fascination, and faintly smiling at our fear. I noticed a certain merchant who followed her hungrily, his lips loose and drooling. He was a large man who wore diamond studs in a shirtfront which swelled with the ample paunch underneath, and each time the blonde swayed her undulating hips he ran his hand through the thin hair of his bald head and, with his arms upheld, his posture clumsy like that of an intoxicated panda, wound his belly in a slow and obscene grind. This creature was completely hypnotized. The music had quickened. As the dancer flung herself about with a detached expression on her face, the men began reaching out to touch her. I could see their beefy fingers sink into the soft flesh. Some of the others tried to stop them and she began to move around the floor in graceful circles, as they gave chase, slipping and sliding over the polished floor. It was mad. Chairs went crashing, drinks were spilt, as they ran laughing and howling after her. They caught her just as she reached a door, raised her from the floor, and tossed her as college boys are tossed at a hazing, and above her red, fixed-smiling lips I saw the terror and disgust in her eyes, almost like my own terror and that which I saw in some of the other boys. As I watched, they tossed her twice and her soft breasts seemed to flatten against the air and her legs flung wildly as she spun. Some of the more sober ones helped her to escape. And I started off the floor, heading for the anteroom with the rest of the boys.

Some were still crying and in hysteria. But as we tried to leave we were stopped and ordered to get into the ring. There was nothing to do but what we were told. All ten of us climbed under the ropes and allowed ourselves to be blindfolded with broad bands of white cloth. One of the men seemed to feel a bit sympathetic and tried to cheer us up as we stood with our backs against the ropes. Some of us tried to grin. "See that boy over there?" one of the men said. "I want you to run across at the bell and give it to him right in the belly. If you don't get him, I'm going to get you. I don't like his looks." Each of us was told the same. The blindfolds were put on. Yet even then I had been going over my speech. In my mind each word was as bright as flame. I felt the cloth pressed into place, and frowned so that it would be loosened when I relaxed.

But now I felt a sudden fit of blind terror. I was unused to darkness. It was as though I had suddenly found myself in a dark room filled with poisonous cottonmouths. I could hear the bleary voices yelling insistently for the battle royal to begin.

"Get going in there!"

"Let me at that big nigger!"

I strained to pick up the school superintendent's voice, as though to squeeze some security out of that slightly more familiar sound.

"Let me at those black sonsabitches!" someone yelled.

"No, Jackson, no!" another voice yelled. "Here, somebody, help me hold Jack."

"I want to get at that ginger-colored nigger. Tear him limb from limb," the first voice yelled.

I stood against the ropes trembling. For in those days I was what they called ginger-colored, and he sounded as though he might crunch me between his teeth like a crisp ginger cookie.

Quite a struggle was going on. Chairs were being kicked about and I could hear voices grunting as with a terrific effort. I wanted to see, to see more desperately than ever before. But the blindfold was tight as a thick skin-puckering scab and when I raised my gloved hands to push the layers of white aside a voice yelled, "Oh, no you don't, black bastard! Leave that alone!"

"Ring the bell before Jackson kills him a coon!" someone boomed in the sudden silence. And I heard the bell clang and the sound of the feet scuffling forward.

A glove smacked against my head. I pivoted, striking out stiffly as someone went past, and felt the jar ripple along the length of my arm to my shoulder. Then it seemed as though all nine of the boys had turned upon me at once. Blows pounded me from all sides while I struck out as best I could. So many blows landed upon me that I wondered if I were not the only blindfolded fighter in the ring, or if the man called Jackson hadn't succeeded in getting me after all.

Blindfolded, I could no longer control my motions. I had no dignity. I stumbled about like a baby or a drunken man. The smoke had become thicker and with each new blow it seemed to sear and further restrict my lungs. My saliva became like hot bitter glue. A glove connected with my head, filling my mouth with warm blood. It was everywhere. I could not tell if the moisture I felt upon my body was sweat or blood. A blow landed hard against the nape of my neck. I felt myself going over, my head hitting the floor. Streaks of blue light filled the black world behind the blindfold. I lay prone, pretending that I was knocked out, but felt myself seized by hands and yanked to my feet. "Get going, black boy! Mix it up!" My arms were like lead, my head smarting from blows. I managed to feel my way to the ropes and held on, trying to catch my breath. A glove landed in my mid-section and I went over again, feeling as though the smoke had become a knife jabbed into my guts. Pushed this way and that by the legs milling around me, I finally pulled erect and discovered that I could see the black, sweat-washed forms weaving in the smoky-blue atmosphere like drunken dancers weaving to the rapid drum-like thuds of blows.

Everyone fought hysterically. It was complete anarchy. Everybody fought everybody else. No group fought together for long. Two, three, four, fought one, then turned to fight each other, were themselves attacked. Blows landed below the belt and in the kidney, with the gloves open as well as closed, and with my eye partly opened now there was not so much terror. I moved carefully, avoiding blows, although not too many to attract attention, fighting from group to group. The boys groped about like blind, cautious crabs crouching to protect their mid-sections, their heads pulled in short against their shoulders, their arms stretched nervously before them, with their fists testing the smoke-filled air like the knobbed feelers of hypersensitive snails. In one corner I glimpsed a boy violently punching the air and heard him scream in pain as he smashed his hand against a ring post. For a second I saw him bent over holding his hand, then going down as a blow caught his unprotected head. I played one group against the other, slipping in and throwing a punch then stepping out of range while pushing the others into the melee to take the blows blindly aimed at me. The smoke was agonizing and there were no rounds, no bells at three minute intervals to relieve our exhaustion. The room spun round me, a swirl of lights, smoke, sweating bodies surrounded by tense white faces. I bled from both nose and mouth, the blood spattering upon my chest.

The men kept yelling, "Slug him, black boy! Knock his guts out!"

"Uppercut him! Kill him! Kill that big boy!"

Taking a fake fall, I saw a boy going down heavily beside me as though we were felled by a single blow, saw a sneaker-clad foot shoot into his groin as the two who had knocked him down stumbled upon him. I rolled out of range, feeling a twinge of nausea.

The harder we fought the more threatening the

men became. And yet, I had begun to worry about my speech again. How would it go? Would they recognize my ability? What would they give me?

I was fighting automatically when suddenly I noticed that one after another of the boys was leaving the ring. I was surprised, filled with panic, as though I had been left alone with an unknown danger. Then I understood. The boys had arranged it among themselves. It was the custom for the two men left in the ring to slug it out for the winner's prize. I discovered this too late. When the bell sounded two men in tuxedoes leaped into the ring and removed the blindfold. I found myself facing Tatlock, the biggest of the gang. I felt sick at my stomach. Hardly had the bell stopped ringing in my ears than it clanged again and I saw him moving swiftly toward me. Thinking of nothing else to do I hit him smash on the nose. He kept coming, bringing the rank sharp violence of stale sweat. His face was a black blank of a face, only his eyes alive—with hate of me and aglow with a feverish terror from what had happened to us all. I became anxious. I wanted to deliver my speech and he came at me as though he meant to beat it out of me. I smashed him again and again, taking his blows as they came. Then on a sudden impulse I struck him lightly and as we clinched, I whispered, "Fake like I knocked you out, you can have the prize."

"I'll break your behind," he whispered hoarsely.

"For *them?*"

"For *me*, sonofabitch!"

They were yelling for us to break it up and Tatlock spun me half around with a blow, and as a joggled camera sweeps in a reeling scene, I saw the howling red faces crouching tense beneath the cloud of blue-gray smoke. For a moment the world wavered, unraveled, flowed, then my head cleared and Tatlock bounced before me. That fluttering shadow before my eyes was his jabbing left hand. Then falling forward, my head against his damp shoulder, I whispered,

"I'll make it five dollars more."

"Go to hell!"

But his muscles relaxed a trifle beneath my pressure and I breathed, "Seven?"

"Give it to your ma," he said, ripping me beneath the heart.

And while I still held him I butted him and moved away. I felt myself bombarded with punches. I fought back with hopeless desperation. I wanted to deliver my speech more than anything else in the world, because I felt that only these men could

judge truly my ability, and now this stupid clown was ruining my chances. I began fighting carefully now, moving in to punch him and out again with my greater speed. A lucky blow to his chin and I had him going too—until I heard a loud voice yell, "I got my money on the big boy."

Hearing this, I almost dropped my guard. I was confused: Should I try to win against the voice out there? Would not this go against my speech, and was not this a moment for humility, for nonresistance? A blow to my head as I danced about sent my right eye popping like a jack-in-the-box and settled my dilemma. The room went red as I fell. It was a dream fall, my body languid and fastidious as to where to land, until the floor became impatient and smashed up to meet me. A moment later I came to. An hypnotic voice said FIVE emphatically. And I lay there, hazily watching a dark red spot of my own blood shaping itself into a butterfly, glistening and soaking into the soiled gray world of the canvas.

When the voice drawled TEN I was lifted up and dragged to a chair. I sat dazed. My eye pained and swelled with each throb of my pounding heart and I wondered if now I would be allowed to speak. I was wringing wet, my mouth still bleeding. We were grouped along the wall now. The other boys ignored me as they congratulated Tatlock and speculated as to how much they would be paid. One boy whimpered over his smashed hand. Looking up front, I saw attendants in white jackets rolling the portable ring away and placing a small square rug in the vacant space surrounded by chairs. Perhaps, I thought, I will stand on the rug to deliver my speech.

Then the M.C. called to us, "Come on up here boys and get your money."

We ran forward to where the men laughed and talked in their chairs, waiting. Everyone seemed friendly now.

"There it is on the rug," the man said. I saw the rug covered with coins of all dimensions and a few crumpled bills. But what excited me, scattered here and there, were the gold pieces.

"Boys, it's all yours," the man said. "You get all you grab."

"That's right, Sambo," a blond man said, winking at me confidentially.

I trembled with excitement, forgetting my pain. I would get the gold and the bills, I thought. I would use both hands. I would throw my body against the boys nearest me to block them from the gold.

"Get down around the rug now," the man commanded, "and don't anyone touch it until I give the signal."

"This ought to be good," I heard.

As told, we got around the square rug on our knees. Slowly the man raised his freckled hand as we followed it upward with our eyes.

I heard, "These niggers look like they're about to pray!"

Then, "Ready," the man said. "Go!"

I lunged for a yellow coin lying on the blue design of the carpet, touching it and sending a surprised shriek to join those rising around me. I tried frantically to remove my hand but could not let go. A hot, violent force tore through my body, shaking me like a wet rat. The rug was electrified. The hair bristled up on my head as I shook myself free. My muscles jumped, my nerves jangled, writhed. But I saw that this was not stopping the other boys. Laughing in fear and embarrassment, some were holding back and scooping up the coins knocked off by the painful contortions of the others. The men roared above us as we struggled.

"Pick it up, goddamnit, pick it up!" someone called like a bass-voiced parrot. "Go on, get it!"

I crawled rapidly around the floor, picking up the coins, trying to avoid the coppers and to get greenbacks and the gold. Ignoring the shock by laughing, as I brushed the coins off quickly, I discovered that I could contain the electricity—a contradiction, but it works. Then the men began to push us onto the rug. Laughing embarrassedly, we struggled out of their hands and kept after the coins. We were all wet and slippery and hard to hold. Suddenly I saw a boy lifted into the air, glistening with sweat like a circus seal, and dropped, his wet back landing flush upon the charged rug, heard him yell and saw him literally dance upon his back, his elbows beating a frenzied tattoo upon the floor, his muscles twitching like the flesh of a horse stung by many flies. When he finally rolled off, his face was gray and no one stopped him when he ran from the floor amid booming laughter.

"Get the money," the M.C. called. "That's good hard American cash!"

And we snatched and grabbed, snatched and grabbed. I was careful not to come too close to the rug now, and when I felt the hot whiskey breath descend upon me like a cloud of foul air I reached out and grabbed the leg of a chair. It was occupied and I held on desperately.

"Leggo, nigger! Leggo!"

The huge face wavered down to mine as he tried to push me free. But my body was slippery and he was too drunk. It was Mr. Colcord, who owned a chain of movie houses and "entertainment palaces." Each time he grabbed me I slipped out of his hands. It became a real struggle. I feared the rug more than I did the drunk, so I held on, surprising myself for a moment by trying to topple him upon the rug. It was such an enormous idea that I found myself actually carrying it out. I tried not to be obvious, yet when I grabbed his leg, trying to tumble him out of the chair, he raised up roaring with laughter, and, looking at me with soberness dead in the eye, kicked me viciously in the chest. The chair leg flew out of my hand and I felt myself going and rolled. It was as though I had rolled through a bed of hot coals. It seemed a whole century would pass before I would roll free, a century in which I was seared through the deepest levels of my body to the fearful breath within me and the breath seared and heated to the point of explosion. It'll all be over in a flash, I thought as I rolled clear. It'll all be over in a flash.

But not yet, the men on the other side were waiting, red faces swollen as though from apoplexy as they bent forward in their chairs. Seeing their fingers coming toward me I rolled away as a fumbled football rolls off the receiver's fingertips, back into the coals. That time I luckily sent the rug sliding out of place and heard the coins ringing against the floor and the boys scuffling to pick them up and the M.C. calling, "All right, boys, that's all. Go get dressed and get your money."

I was limp as a dish rag. My back felt as though it had been beaten with wires.

When we had dressed the M.C. came in and gave us each five dollars, except Tatlock, who got ten for being last in the ring. Then he told us to leave. I was not to get a chance to deliver my speech, I thought. I was going out into the dim alley in despair when I was stopped and told to go back. I returned to the ballroom, where the men were pushing back their chairs and gathering in groups to talk.

The M.C. knocked on a table for quiet. "Gentlemen," he said, "we almost forgot an important part of the program. A most serious part, gentlemen. This boy was brought here to deliver a speech which he made at his graduation yesterday . . ."

"Bravo!"

"I'm told that he is the smartest boy we've got

out there in Greenwood. I'm told that he knows more big words than a pocket-sized dictionary."

Much applause and laughter.

"So now, gentlemen, I want you to give him your attention."

There was still laughter as I faced them, my mouth dry, my eye throbbing. I began slowly, but evidently my throat was tense, because they began shouting, "Louder! Louder!"

"We of the younger generation extol the wisdom of that great leader and educator," I shouted, "who first spoke these flaming words of wisdom: 'A ship lost at sea for many days suddenly sighted a friendly vessel. From the mast of the unfortunate vessel was seen a signal: "Water, water; we die of thirst!" The answer from the friendly vessel came back: "Cast down your bucket where you are." The captain of the distressed vessel, at last heeding the injunction, cast down his bucket, and it came up full of fresh sparkling water from the mouth of the Amazon River.' And like him I say, and in his words, 'To those of my race who depend upon bettering their condition in a foreign land, or who underestimate the importance of cultivating friendly relations with the Southern white man, who is his next-door neighbor, I would say: "Cast down your bucket where you are"—cast it down in making friends in every manly way of the people of all races by whom we are surrounded . . .'"

I spoke automatically and with such fervor that I did not realize that the men were still talking and laughing until my dry mouth, filling up with blood from the cut, almost strangled me. I coughed, wanting to stop and go to one of the tall brass, sand-filled spittoons to relieve myself, but a few of the men, especially the superintendent, were listening and I was afraid. So I gulped it down, blood, saliva and all, and continued. (What powers of endurance I had during those days! What enthusiasm! What a belief in the rightness of things!) I spoke even louder in spite of the pain. But still they talked and still they laughed, as though deaf with cotton in dirty ears. So I spoke with greater emotional emphasis. I closed my ears and swallowed blood until I was nauseated. The speech seemed a hundred times as long as before, but I could not leave out a single word. All had to be said, each memorized nuance considered, rendered. Nor was that all. Whenever I uttered a word of three or more syllables a group of voices would yell

for me to repeat it. I used the phrase "social responsibility" and they yelled:

"What's that word you say, boy?"

"Social responsibility," I said.

"What?"

"Social . . ."

"Louder."

". . . responsibility."

"More!"

"Respon—"

"Repeat!"

"—sibility."

The room filled with the uproar of laughter until, no doubt, distracted by having to gulp down my blood, I made a mistake and yelled a phrase I had often seen denounced in newspaper editorials, heard debated in private.

"Social . . ."

"What?" they yelled.

". . . equality—"

The laughter hung smokelike in the sudden stillness. I opened my eyes, puzzled. Sounds of displeasure filled the room. The M.C. rushed forward. They shouted hostile phrases at me. But I did not understand.

A small dry mustached man in the front row blared out, "Say that slowly, son!"

"What, sir?"

"What you just said!"

"Social responsibility, sir," I said.

"You weren't being smart, were you, boy?" he said, not unkindly.

"No, sir!"

"You sure that about 'equality' was a mistake?"

"Oh, yes, sir," I said. "I was swallowing blood."

"Well, you had better speak more slowly so we can understand. We mean to do right by you, but you've got to know your place at all times. All right, now, go on with your speech."

I was afraid. I wanted to leave but I wanted also to speak and I was afraid they'd snatch me down.

"Thank you, sir," I said, beginning where I had left off, and having them ignore me as before.

Yet when I finished there was a thunderous applause. I was surprised to see the superintendent come forth with a package wrapped in white tissue paper, and, gesturing for quiet, address the men.

"Gentlemen, you see that I did not overpraise this boy. He makes a good speech and some day he'll lead his people in the proper paths. And I don't have to tell you that that is important in these days and times. This is a good, smart boy, and so to encourage him in the right direction, in the name of the Board of Education I wish to present him a prize in the form of this . . ."

He paused, removing the tissue paper and revealing a gleaming calfskin brief case.

". . . in the form of this first-class article from Shad Whitmore's shop."

"Boy," he said, addressing me, "take this prize and keep it well. Consider it a badge of office. Prize it. Keep developing as you are and some day it will be filled with important papers that will help shape the destiny of your people."

I was so moved that I could hardly express my thanks. A rope of bloody saliva forming a shape like an undiscovered continent drooled upon the leather and I wiped it quickly away. I felt an importance that I had never dreamed.

"Open it and see what's inside," I was told.

My fingers a-tremble, I complied, smelling the fresh leather and finding an official-looking document inside. It was a scholarship to the state college for Negroes. My eyes filled with tears and I ran awkwardly off the floor.

I was overjoyed; I did not even mind when I discovered that the gold pieces I had scrambled for were brass pocket tokens advertising a certain make of automobile.

When I reached home everyone was excited. Next day the neighbors came to congratulate me. I even felt safe from grandfather, whose deathbed curse usually spoiled my triumphs. I stood beneath his photograph with my brief case in hand and smiled triumphantly into his stolid black peasant's face. It was a face that fascinated me. The eyes seemed to follow everywhere I went.

That night I dreamed I was at a circus with him and that he refused to laugh at the clowns no matter what they did. Then later he told me to open my brief case and read what was inside and I did, finding an official envelope stamped with the state seal; and inside the envelope I found another and another, endlessly, and I thought I would fall of weariness. "Them's years," he said. "Now open that one." And I did and in it I found an engraved document containing a short message in letters of gold. "Read it," my grandfather said. "Out loud!"

"To Whom It May Concern," I intoned. "Keep This Nigger-Boy Running."

I awoke with the old man's laughter ringing in my ears.

(It was a dream I was to remember and dream again for many years after. But at that time I had no insight into its meaning. First I had to attend college.)

BERNARD MALAMUD (1914–   )

Born April 26, 1914, in Brooklyn; educated in New York City (B.A. from City College of New York and M.A. from Columbia); has taught English in New York City night high schools, at Oregon State University, and since 1961 at Bennington College in Vermont, with leaves of absence to teach at Harvard; member National Institute of Arts and Letters (1964); publications include the novels *The Natural* (1952),

The Assistant (1957), *A New Life* (1961), *The Fixer* (1966), *Pictures of Fidelman* (1970), and *The Tenants* (1971), and two collections of short stories: *The Magic Barrel* (1958) and *Idiots First* (1963); received Rosenthal award of National Institute of Arts and Letters, and National Book Award, twice, for *The Magic Barrel* and *The Fixer*.

The First Seven Years (1958)

Feld, the shoemaker, was annoyed that his helper, Sobel, was so insensitive to his reverie that he wouldn't for a minute cease his fanatic pounding at the other bench. He gave him a look, but Sobel's bald head was bent over the last as he worked and he didn't notice. The shoemaker shrugged and continued to peer through the partly frosted window at the near-sighted haze of falling February snow. Neither the shifting white blur outside, nor the sudden deep remembrance of the snowy Polish village where he had wasted his youth could turn his thoughts from Max the college boy, (a constant visitor in the mind since early that morning when Feld saw him trudging through the snowdrifts on his way to school) whom he so much respected because of the sacrifices he had made throughout the years—in winter or direst heat—to further his education. An old wish returned to haunt the shoemaker: that he had had a son instead of a daughter, but this blew away in the snow for Feld, if anything, was a practical man. Yet he could not help but contrast the diligence of the boy, who was a peddler's son, with Miriam's unconcern for an education. True, she was always with a book in her hand, yet when the opportunity arose for a college education, she had said no she would rather find a job. He had begged her to go, pointing out how many fathers could not afford to send their children to college, but she said she wanted to be independent. As for education, what was it, she asked, but books, which Sobel, who diligently read the classics, would as usual advise her on. Her answer greatly grieved her father.

A figure emerged from the snow and the door opened. At the counter the man withdrew from a wet paper bag a pair of battered shoes for repair. Who he was the shoemaker for a moment had no idea, then his heart trembled as he realized, before he had thoroughly discerned the face, that Max himself was standing there, embarrassedly explaining what he wanted done to his old shoes. Though Feld listened eagerly, he couldn't hear a word, for the opportunity that had burst upon him was deafening.

He couldn't exactly recall when the thought had occurred to him, because it was clear he had more than once considered suggesting to the boy that he go out with Miriam. But he had not dared speak, for if Max said no, how would he face him again? Or suppose Miriam, who harped so often on independence, blew up in anger and shouted at him for his meddling? Still, the chance was too good to let by: all it meant was an introduction. They might long ago have become friends had they happened to meet somewhere, therefore was it not his duty—an obligation—to bring them together, nothing more, a harmless connivance to replace an accidental encounter in the subway, let's say, or a mutual friend's introduction in the street? Just let him

once see and talk to her and he would for sure be interested. As for Miriam, what possible harm for a working girl in an office, who met only loud-mouthed salesmen and illiterate shipping clerks, to make the acquaintance of a fine scholarly boy? Maybe he would awaken in her a desire to go to college; if not—the shoemaker's mind at last came to grips with the truth—let her marry an educated man and live a better life.

When Max finished describing what he wanted done to his shoes, Feld marked them, both with enormous holes in the soles which he pretended not to notice, with large white-chalk x's, and the rubber heels, thinned to the nails, he marked with o's, though it troubled him he might have mixed up the letters. Max inquired the price, and the shoemaker cleared his throat and asked the boy, above Sobel's insistent hammering, would he please step through the side door there into the hall. Though surprised, Max did as the shoemaker requested, and Feld went in after him. For a minute they were both silent, because Sobel had stopped banging, and it seemed they understood neither was to say anything until the noise began again. When it did, loudly, the shoemaker quickly told Max why he had asked to talk to him.

"Ever since you went to high school," he said, in the dimly-lit hallway, "I watched you in the morning go to the subway to school, and I said always to myself, this is a fine boy that he wants so much an education."

"Thanks," Max said, nervously alert. He was tall and grotesquely thin, with sharply cut features, particularly a beak-like nose. He was wearing a loose, long slushy overcoat that hung down to his ankles, looking like a rug draped over his bony shoulders, and a soggy, old brown hat, as battered as the shoes he had brought in.

"I am a business man," the shoemaker abruptly said to conceal his embarrassment, "so I will explain you right away why I talk to you. I have a girl, my daughter Miriam—she is nineteen—a very nice girl and also so pretty that everybody looks on her when she passes by in the street. She is smart, always with a book, and I thought to myself that a boy like you, an educated boy—I thought maybe you will be interested sometime to meet a girl like this." He laughed a bit when he had finished and was tempted to say more but had the good sense not to.

Max stared down like a hawk. For an uncomfortable second he was silent, then he asked, "Did you say nineteen?"

"Yes."

"Would it be all right to inquire if you have a picture of her?"

"Just a minute." The shoemaker went into the store and hastily returned with a snapshot that Max held up to the light.

"She's all right," he said.

Feld waited.

"And is she sensible—not the flighty kind?"

"She is very sensible."

After another short pause, Max said it was okay with him if he met her.

"Here is my telephone," said the shoemaker, hurriedly handing him a slip of paper. "Call her up. She comes home from work six o'clock."

Max folded the paper and tucked it away into his worn leather wallet.

"About the shoes," he said. "How much did you say they will cost me?"

"Don't worry about the price."

"I just like to have an idea."

"A dollar—dollar fifty. A dollar fifty," the shoemaker said.

At once he felt bad, for he usually charged two twenty-five for this kind of job. Either he should have asked the regular price or done the work for nothing.

Later, as he entered the store, he was startled by a violent clanging and looked up to see Sobel pounding with all his might upon the naked last. It broke, the iron striking the floor and jumping with a thump against the wall, but before the enraged shoemaker could cry out, the assistant had torn his hat and coat from the hook and rushed out into the snow.

So Feld, who had looked forward to anticipating how it would go with his daughter and Max, instead had a great worry on his mind. Without his temperamental helper he was a lost man, especially since it was years now that he had carried the store alone. The shoemaker had for an age suffered from a heart condition that threatened collapse if he dared exert himself. Five years ago, after an attack, it had appeared as though he would have either to sacrifice his business upon the auction block and live on a pittance thereafter, or put himself at the mercy of some unscrupulous employee who would in the end probably ruin him. But just at the moment of his darkest despair, this Polish refugee, Sobel, appeared one night from the street and begged for work. He was a stocky man, poorly dressed, with a bald head that had once been blond, a severely plain face and soft blue eyes prone to tears over the sad books he read, a young man but old—no one would have guessed thirty. Though he confessed he knew nothing of shoemaking, he said he was apt and would work for a very little if Feld taught him the trade. Thinking that with, after all, a landsman, he would have less fear than from a complete stranger, Feld took him on and within six weeks the refugee rebuilt as good a shoe as he, and not long thereafter expertly ran the business for the thoroughly relieved shoemaker.

Feld could trust him with anything and did, frequently going home after an hour or two at the store, leaving all the money in the till, knowing Sobel would guard every cent of it. The amazing thing was that he demanded so little. His wants were few; in money he wasn't interested—in nothing but books, it seemed—which he one by one lent to Miriam, together with his profuse, queer written comments, manufactured during his lonely rooming house evenings, thick pads of commentary which the shoemaker peered at and twitched his shoulders over as his daughter, from her fourteenth year, read page by sanctified page, as if the word of God were inscribed on them. To protect Sobel, Feld himself had to see that he received more than he asked for. Yet his conscience bothered him for not insisting that the assistant accept a better wage than he was getting, though Feld had honestly told him he could earn a handsome salary if he worked elsewhere, or maybe opened a place of his own. But the assistant answered, somewhat ungraciously, that he was not interested in going elsewhere, and though Feld frequently asked himself what keeps him here? why does he stay? he finally answered it that the man, no doubt because of his terrible experiences as a refugee, was afraid of the world.

After the incident with the broken last, angered by Sobel's behavior, the shoemaker decided to let him stew for a week in the rooming house, although his own strength was taxed dangerously and the business suffered. However, after several sharp nagging warnings from both his wife and daughter, he went finally in search of Sobel, as he had once before, quite recently, when over some fancied slight—Feld had merely asked him not to give Miriam so many books to read because her eyes were strained and red—the assistant had left the place in a huff, an incident which, as usual, came to nothing for he had returned after the shoemaker had talked to him, and taken his seat at the bench. But this time, after Feld had plodded through the snow to Sobel's house—he had thought of sending Miriam but the idea became repugnant to him—the burly landlady at the door informed him in a nasal voice that Sobel was not at home, and though Feld knew this was a nasty lie, for where had the refugee to go? still for some reason he was not completely sure of—it may have been the cold and his fatigue—he decided not to insist on seeing him. Instead he went home and hired a new helper.

Having settled the matter, though not entirely to his satisfaction, for he had much more to do than before, and so, for example, could no longer lie late in bed mornings because he had to get up to open the store for the new assistant, a speechless, dark man with an irritating rasp as he worked, whom he would not trust with the key as he had Sobel. Furthermore, this one, though able to do a fair repair job, knew nothing of grades of leather or prices, so Feld had to make his own purchases; and every night at closing time it was necessary to count the money in the till and lock up. However, he was not dissatisfied, for he lived much in his thoughts of Max and Miriam. The college boy had called her, and they had arranged a meeting for this coming Friday night. The shoemaker would personally have preferred Saturday, which he felt would make it a date of the first magnitude, but he learned Friday was Miriam's choice, so he said nothing. The day of the week did not matter. What mattered was the aftermath. Would they like each other and want to be friends? He sighed at all the time that would have to go by before he knew for sure. Often he was tempted to talk to Miriam about the boy, to ask whether she thought she would like his type—he had told her only that he considered Max a nice boy and had suggested he call her—but the one time he tried she snapped at him—justly—how should she know?

At last Friday came. Feld was not feeling particularly well so he stayed in bed, and Mrs. Feld thought it better to remain in the bedroom with him when Max called. Miriam received the boy, and her parents could hear their voices, his throaty one, as they talked. Just before leaving, Miriam brought Max to the bedroom door and he stood there a minute, a tall, slightly hunched figure wearing a thick, droopy suit, and apparently at ease as he greeted the shoemaker and his wife, which was surely a good sign. And Miriam, although she had worked all day, looked fresh and pretty. She was a large-framed girl with a well-shaped body, and she had a fine open face and soft hair. They made, Feld thought, a first-class couple.

Miriam returned after 11:30. Her mother was already asleep, but the shoemaker got out of bed and after locating his bathrobe went into the kitchen, where Miriam, to his surprise, sat at the table, reading.

"So where did you go?" Feld asked pleasantly.

"For a walk," she said, not looking up.

"I advised him," Feld said, clearing his throat, "he shouldn't spend so much money."

"I didn't care."

The shoemaker boiled up some water for tea and sat down at the table with a cupful and a thick slice of lemon.

"So how," he sighed after a sip, "did you enjoy?"

"It was all right."

He was silent. She must have sensed his disappointment, for she added, "You can't really tell much the first time."

"You will see him again?"

Turning a page, she said that Max had asked for another date.

"For when?"

"Saturday."

"So what did you say?

"What did I say?" she asked, delaying for a moment—"I said yes."

Afterwards she inquired about Sobel, and Feld, without exactly knowing why, said the assistant had got another job. Miriam said nothing more and began to read. The shoemaker's conscience did not trouble him; he was satisfied with the Saturday date.

During the week, by placing here and there a deft question, he managed to get from Miriam some information about Max. It surprised him to learn that the boy was not studying to be either a doctor or lawyer but was taking a business course leading to a degree in accountancy. Feld was a little disappointed because he thought of accountants as bookkeepers and would have preferred "a higher profession." However, it was not long before he had investigated the subject and discovered that Certified Public Accountants were highly respected people, so he was thoroughly content as Saturday approached. But because Saturday was a busy day, he was much in the store and therefore did not see Max when he came to call for Miriam. From his wife he learned there had been nothing especially revealing about their meeting. Max had rung the bell and Miriam had got her coat and left with him—nothing more. Feld did

not probe, for his wife was not particularly observant. Instead, he waited up for Miriam with a newspaper on his lap, which he scarcely looked at so
lost was he in thinking of the future. He awoke to
find her in the room with him, tiredly removing
her hat. Greeting her, he was suddenly inexplicably
afraid to ask anything about the evening. But
since she volunteered nothing he was at last forced
to inquire how she had enjoyed herself. Miriam
began something non-committal but apparently
changed her mind, for she said after a minute, "I
was bored."

When Feld had sufficiently recovered from his
anguished disappointment to ask why, she answered
without hesitation, "Because he's nothing more
than a materialist."

"What means this word?"

"He has no soul. He's only interested in things."

He considered her statement for a long time
but then asked, "Will you see him again?"

"He didn't ask."

"Suppose he will ask you?"

"I won't see him."

He did not argue; however, as the days went by
he hoped increasingly she would change her mind.
He wished the boy would telephone, because he
was sure there was more to him than Miriam, with
her inexperienced eye, could discern. But Max
didn't call. As a matter of fact he took a different
route to school, no longer passing the shoemaker's
store, and Feld was deeply hurt.

Then one afternoon Max came in and asked for
his shoes. The shoemaker took them down from
the shelf where he had placed them, apart from
the other pairs. He had done the work himself and
the soles and heels were well built and firm. The
shoes had been highly polished and somehow looked
better than new. Max's Adam's apple went up
once when he saw them, and his eyes had little
lights in them.

"How much?" he asked, without directly looking at the shoemaker.

"Like I told you before," Feld answered sadly.
"One dollar fifty cents."

Max handed him two crumpled bills and received in return a newly-minted silver half dollar.

He left. Miriam had not been mentioned. That
night the shoemaker discovered that his new assistant had been all the while stealing from him,
and he suffered a heart attack.

Though the attack was very mild, he lay in bed
for three weeks. Miriam spoke of going for Sobel,

but sick as he was Feld rose in wrath against the
idea. Yet in his heart he knew there was no other
way, and the first weary day back in the shop thoroughly convinced him, so that night after supper
he dragged himself to Sobel's rooming house.

He toiled up the stairs, though he knew it was
bad for him, and at the top knocked at the door.
Sobel opened it and the shoemaker entered. The
room was a small, poor one, with a single window
facing the street. It contained a narrow cot, a low
table and several stacks of books piled haphazardly
around on the floor along the wall, which made
him think how queer Sobel was, to be uneducated
and read so much. He had once asked him, Sobel,
why you read so much? and the assistant could not
answer him. Did you ever study in a college some-
place? he had asked, but Sobel shook his head. He
read, he said, to know. But to know what, the
shoemaker demanded, and to know, why? Sobel
never explained, which proved he read much because he was queer.

Feld sat down to recover his breath. The assistant was resting on his bed with his heavy back
to the wall. His shirt and trousers were clean, and
his stubby fingers, away from the shoemaker's
bench, were strangely pallid. His face was thin and
pale, as if he had been shut in this room since the
day he had bolted from the store.

"So when you will come back to work?" Feld
asked him.

To his surprise, Sobel burst out, "Never."

Jumping up, he strode over to the window that
looked out upon the miserable street. "Why should
I come back?" he cried.

"I will raise your wages."

"Who cares for your wages!"

The shoemaker, knowing he didn't care, was at
a loss what else to say.

"What do you want from me, Sobel?"

"Nothing."

"I always treated you like you was my son."

Sobel vehemently denied it. "So why you look
for strange boys in the street they should go out
with Miriam? Why you don't think of me?"

The shoemaker's hands and feet turned freezing
cold. His voice became so hoarse he couldn't speak.
At last he cleared his throat and croaked, "So what
has my daughter got to do with a shoemaker thirty-
five years old who works for me?"

"Why do you think I worked so long for you?"
Sobel cried out. "For the stingy wages I sacrificed
five years of my life so you could have to eat and
drink and where to sleep?"

"Then for what?" shouted the shoemaker.

"For Miriam," he blurted—"for her."

The shoemaker, after a time, managed to say, "I pay wages in cash, Sobel," and lapsed into silence. Though he was seething with excitement, his mind was coldly clear, and he had to admit to himself he had sensed all along that Sobel felt this way. He had never so much as thought it consciously, but he had felt it and was afraid.

"Miriam knows?" he muttered hoarsely.

"She knows."

"You told her?"

"No."

"Then how does she know?"

"How does she know?" Sobel said, "because she knows. She knows who I am and what is in my heart."

Feld had a sudden insight. In some devious way, with his books and commentary, Sobel had given Miriam to understand that he loved her. The shoemaker felt a terrible anger at him for his deceit.

"Sobel, you are crazy," he said bitterly. "She will never marry a man so old and ugly like you."

Sobel turned black with rage. He cursed the shoemaker, but then, though he trembled to hold it in, his eyes filled with tears and he broke into deep sobs. With his back to Feld, he stood at the window, fists clenched, and his shoulders shook with his choked sobbing.

Watching him, the shoemaker's anger diminished. His teeth were on edge with pity for the man, and his eyes grew moist. How strange and sad that a refugee, a grown man, bald and old with his miseries, who had by the skin of his teeth escaped Hitler's incinerators, should fall in love, when he had got to America, with a girl less than half his age. Day after day, for five years he had sat at his bench, cutting and hammering away, waiting for the girl to become a woman, unable to ease his heart with speech, knowing no protest but desperation.

"Ugly I didn't mean," he said half aloud.

Then he realized that what he had called ugly was not Sobel but Miriam's life if she married him. He felt for his daughter a strange and gripping sorrow, as if she were already Sobel's bride, the wife, after all, of a shoemaker, and had in her life no more than her mother had had. And all his dreams for her—why he had slaved and destroyed his heart with anxiety and labor—all these dreams of a better life were dead.

The room was quiet, Sobel was standing by the window reading, and it was curious that when he read he looked young.

"She is only nineteen," Feld said brokenly. "This is too young yet to get married. Don't ask her for two years more, till she is twenty-one, then you can talk to her."

Sobel didn't answer. Feld rose and left. He went slowly down the stairs but once outside, though it was an icy night and the crisp falling snow whitened the street, he walked with a stronger stride.

But the next morning, when the shoemaker arrived, heavy-hearted, to open the store, he saw he needn't have come, for his assistant was already seated at the last, pounding leather for his love.

JOHN HERSEY (1914–   )

Born June 17, 1914, in Tientsin, China; lived in China until 1925; graduated Yale University; attended Clare College, Cambridge; private secretary to Sinclair Lewis, 1937; covered Second World War on both fronts for Time-Life; *Men on Bataan* (1942) and *Into the Valley* (1943), nonfiction, and *A Bell for Adano*, fiction (1945, winner of Pulitzer prize), taken from wartime experience; *Hiroshima* (1946), nonfiction, recreated first wartime use of atomic bomb; has since concentrated on fiction, publishing *The Wall* (1950), *The Marmot Drive* (1953), *A Single Pebble* (1956), *The War Lover* (1959), *The Child Buyer* (1960), *White Lotus* (1965), *Too Far to Walk* (1966), *Under the Eye of the Storm* (1967), and *The Conspiracy* (1972); also *The Algiers Motel Incident* (1968), an account of violence in the Detroit riot of 1967, and *Letter to the Alumni* (1970), analysis of conditions at Yale University, where he served five years as Master of Pierson College; member National Institute of Arts and Letters (1950) and American Academy of Arts and Letters (1953).

From Hiroshima (1946)

CHAPTER 1: A NOISELESS FLASH

At exactly fifteen minutes past eight in the morning, on August 6, 1945, Japanese time, at the moment when the atomic bomb flashed above Hiroshima, Miss Toshiko Sasaki, a clerk in the personnel department of the East Asia Tin Works, had just sat down at her place in the plant office and was turning her head to speak to the girl at the next desk. At that same moment, Dr. Masakazu Fujii was settling down cross-legged to read the Osaka *Asahi* on the porch of his private hospital, overhanging one of the seven deltaic rivers which divide Hiroshima; Mrs. Hatsuyo Nakamura, a tailor's widow, stood by the window of her kitchen, watching a neighbor tearing down his house because it lay in the path of an air-raid-defense fire lane; Father Wilhelm Kleinsorge, a German priest of the Society of Jesus, reclined in his underwear on a cot on the top floor of his order's three-story mission house, reading a Jesuit magazine, *Stimmen der Zeit*; Dr. Terufumi Sasaki, a young member of the surgical staff of the city's large, modern Red Cross Hospital, walked along one of the hospital corridors with a blood specimen for a Wassermann test in his hand; and the Reverend Mr. Kiyoshi Tanimoto, pastor of the Hiroshima Methodist Church, paused at the door of a rich man's house in Koi, the city's western suburb, and prepared to unload a handcart full of things he had evacuated from town in fear of the massive B-29 raid which everyone expected Hiroshima to suffer. A hundred thousand people were killed by the atomic bomb, and these six were among the survivors. They still wonder why they lived when so many others died. Each of them counts many small items of chance or volition—a step taken in time, a decision to go indoors, catching one streetcar instead of the next—that spared him. And now each knows that in the act of survival he lived a dozen lives and saw more death than he ever thought he would see. At the time, none of them knew anything.

The Reverend Mr. Tanimoto got up at five o'clock that morning. He was alone in the parsonage, because for some time his wife had been commuting with their year-old baby to spend nights with a friend in Ushida, a suburb to the north. Of all the important cities of Japan, only two, Kyoto and Hiroshima, had not been visited in strength by *B-san*, or Mr. B, as the Japanese, with a mix-

ture of respect and unhappy familiarity, called the B-29; and Mr. Tanimoto, like all his neighbors and friends, was almost sick with anxiety. He had heard uncomfortably detailed accounts of mass raids on Kure, Iwakuni, Tokuyama, and other nearby towns; he was sure Hiroshima's turn would come soon. He had slept badly the night before, because there had been several air-raid warnings. Hiroshima had been getting such warnings almost every night for weeks, for at that time the B-29s were using Lake Biwa, northeast of Hiroshima, as a rendezvous point, and no matter what city the Americans planned to hit, the Superfortresses streamed in over the coast near Hiroshima. The frequency of the warnings and the continued abstinence of Mr. B with respect to Hiroshima had made its citizens jittery; a rumor was going around that the Americans were saving something special for the city.

Mr. Tanimoto is a small man, quick to talk, laugh, and cry. He wears his black hair parted in the middle and rather long; the prominence of the frontal bones just above his eyebrows and the smallness of his mustache, mouth, and chin give him a strange, old-young look, boyish and yet wise, weak and yet fiery. He moves nervously and fast, but with a restraint which suggests that he is a cautious, thoughtful man. He showed, indeed, just those qualities in the uneasy days before the bomb fell. Besides having his wife spend the nights in Ushida, Mr. Tanimoto had been carrying all the portable things from his church, in the close-packed residential district called Nagaragawa, to a house that belonged to a rayon manufacturer in Koi, two miles from the center of town. The rayon man, a Mr. Matsui, had opened his then unoccupied estate to a large number of his friends and acquaintances, so that they might evacuate whatever they wished to a safe distance from the probable target area. Mr. Tanimoto had had no difficulty in moving chairs, hymnals, Bibles, altar gear, and church records by pushcart himself, but the organ console and an upright piano required some aid. A friend of his named Matsuo had, the day before, helped him get the piano out to Koi; in return, he had promised this day to assist Mr. Matsuo in hauling out a daughter's belongings. That is why he had risen so early.

Mr. Tanimoto cooked his own breakfast. He

felt awfully tired. The effort of moving the piano the day before, a sleepless night, weeks of worry and unbalanced diet, the cares of his parish—all combined to make him feel hardly adequate to the new day's work. There was another thing, too: Mr. Tanimoto had studied theology at Emory College, in Atlanta, Georgia; he had graduated in 1940; he spoke excellent English; he dressed in American clothes; he had corresponded with many American friends right up to the time the war began; and among a people obsessed with a fear of being spied upon—perhaps almost obsessed himself—he found himself growing increasingly uneasy. The police had questioned him several times, and just a few days before, he had heard that an influential acquaintance, a Mr. Tanaka, a retired officer in the Toyo Kisen Kaisha steamship line, an anti-Christian, a man famous in Hiroshima for his showy philanthropies and notorious for his personal tyrannies, had been telling people that Tanimoto should not be trusted. In compensation, to show himself publicly a good Japanese, Mr. Tanimoto had taken on the chairmanship of his local *tonarigumi*, or Neighborhood Association, and to his other duties and concerns this position had added the business of organizing air-raid defense for about twenty families.

Before six o'clock that morning, Mr. Tanimoto started for Mr. Matsuo's house. There he found that their burden was to be a *tansu*, a large Japanese cabinet, full of clothing and household goods. The two men set out. The morning was perfectly clear and so warm that the day promised to be uncomfortable. A few minutes after they started, the air-raid siren went off—a minute-long blast that warned of approaching planes but indicated to the people of Hiroshima only a slight degree of danger, since it sounded every morning at this time, when an American weather plane came over. The two men pulled and pushed the handcart through the city streets. Hiroshima was a fan-shaped city, lying mostly on the six islands formed by the seven estuarial rivers that branch out from the Ota River; its main commercial and residential districts, covering about four square miles in the center of the city, contained three-quarters of its population, which had been reduced by several evacuation programs from a wartime peak of 380,000 to about 245,000. Factories and other residential districts, or suburbs, lay compactly around the edges of the city. To the south were the docks, an airport, and the island-studded Inland Sea. A rim of mountains runs around the other three sides of the delta. Mr.

Tanimoto and Mr. Matsuo took their way through the shopping center, already full of people, and across two of the rivers to the sloping streets of Koi, and up them to the outskirts and foothills. As they started up a valley away from the tight-ranked houses, the all-clear sounded. (The Japanese radar operators, detecting only three planes, supposed that they comprised a reconnaissance.) Pushing the handcart up to the rayon man's house was tiring, and the men, after they had maneuvered their load into the driveway and to the front steps, paused to rest awhile. They stood with a wing of the house between them and the city. Like most homes in this part of Japan, the house consisted of a wooden frame and wooden walls supporting a heavy tile roof. Its front hall, packed with rolls of bedding and clothing, looked like a cool cave full of fat cushions. Opposite the house, to the right of the front door, there was a large, finicky rock garden. There was no sound of planes. The morning was still; the place was cool and pleasant.

Then a tremendous flash of light cut across the sky. Mr. Tanimoto has a distinct recollection that it travelled from east to west, from the city toward the hills. It seemed a sheet of sun. Both he and Mr. Matsuo reacted in terror—and both had time to react (for they were 3,500 yards, or two miles, from the center of the explosion). Mr. Matsuo dashed up the front steps into the house and dived among the bedrolls and buried himself there. Mr. Tanimoto took four or five steps and threw himself between two big rocks in the garden. He bellied up very hard against one of them. As his face was against the stone, he did not see what happened. He felt a sudden pressure, and then splinters and pieces of board and fragments of tile fell on him. He heard no roar. (Almost no one in Hiroshima recalls hearing any noise of the bomb. But a fisherman in his sampan on the Inland Sea near Tsuzu, the man with whom Mr. Tanimoto's mother-in-law and sister-in-law were living, saw the flash and heard a tremendous explosion; he was nearly twenty miles from Hiroshima, but the thunder was greater than when the B-29s hit Iwakuni, only five miles away.)

When he dared, Mr. Tanimoto raised his head and saw that the rayon man's house had collapsed. He thought a bomb had fallen directly on it. Such clouds of dust had risen that there was a sort of twilight around. In panic, not thinking for the moment of Mr. Matsuo under the ruins, he dashed out into the street. He noticed as he ran that the concrete wall of the estate had fallen over—toward the house rather than away from it. In the street, the first thing he saw was a squad of soldiers who had been burrowing into the hillside opposite, making one of the thousands of dugouts in which the Japanese apparently intended to resist invasion,

hill by hill, life for life; the soldiers were coming out of the hole, where they should have been safe, and blood was running from their heads, chests, and backs. They were silent and dazed.

Under what seemed to be a local dust cloud, the day grew darker and darker.

SAUL BELLOW (1915–   )

Born June 10, 1915, in Lachine, Quebec, Canada; moved to Chicago in 1924; attended University of Chicago and Northwestern University (B.S., 1937); graduate work at University of Wisconsin; taught at University of Minnesota, N.Y.U., Bard, University of Puerto Rico, and presently at University of Chicago; received National Institute of Arts and Letters grant (1952); novels are *The Dangling Man* (1944), *The Victim* (1947), *The Adventures of Augie March* (1953), *Seize the Day* (1956), *Henderson the Rain King* (1959), *Herzog* (1964), and *Mr. Sammler's Planet* (1970), an account of a scholarly Jewish émigré's confrontation with urban modernity, excerpted here; among other publications are *The Last Analysis* (play, 1965) and *Mosby's Memoirs and Other Stories* (1968); member National Institute of Arts and Letters (1958) and American Academy of Arts and Letters (1971); twice received National Book Awards for fiction, for *Herzog* and *The Adventures of Augie March.*

From Mr. Sammler's Planet (1970)

. . . . No matter where you picked it up, humankind, knotted and tangled, supplied more oddities than you could keep up with.

A combined oddity, for instance, which drew him today into the middle of things. One of his ex-readers, young Lionel Feffer, had asked him to address a seminar at Columbia University on the British Scene in the Thirties. For some reason this attracted Sammler. He was fond of Feffer. An ingenious operator, less student than promoter. With his florid color, brown beaver beard, long black eyes, big belly, smooth hair, pink awkward large hands, loud interrupting voice, hasty energy, he was charming to Sammler. Not trustworthy. Only charming. That is, it sometimes gave Sammler great pleasure to see Lionel Feffer working out in his peculiar manner, to hear the fizzing of his vital gas, his fuel.

Sammler didn't know what seminar this was. Not always attentive, he failed to understand clearly; perhaps there was nothing clear to understand; but it seemed that he had promised, although he

couldn't remember promising. But Feffer confused him. There were so many projects, such cross references, so many confidences and requests for secrecy, so many scandals, frauds, spiritual communications —a continual flow backward, forward, lateral, above, below; like any page of Joyce's *Ulysses*, always *in medias res.* Anyway, Sammler had apparently agreed to give this talk for a student project to help backward black pupils with their reading problems.

"You must come and talk to these fellows, it's of the utmost importance. They have never heard a point of view like yours," said Feffer. The pink oxford-cloth shirt increased the color of his face. The beard, the straight large sensual nose made him look like François Premier. A bustling, affectionate, urgent, eruptive, enterprising character. He had money in the stock market. He was vice-president of a Guatemalan insurance company covering railroad workers. His field at the university was diplomatic history. He belonged to a corresponding society called the Foreign Ministers' Club. Its members took up a question like the

Crimean War or the Boxer Rebellion and did it all again, writing one another letters as the foreign ministers of France, England, Germany, Russia. They obtained very different results. In addition, Feffer was a busy seducer, especially, it seemed, of young wives. But he found time as well to hustle on behalf of handicapped children. He got them free toys and signed photographs of hockey stars; he found time to visit them in the hospital. He "found time." To Sammler this was a highly significant American fact. Feffer led a high-energy American life to the point of anarchy and breakdown. And yet devotedly. And of course he was in psychiatric treatment. They all were. They could always say that they were sick. Nothing was omitted.

"The British Scene in the Thirties—you must. For my seminar."

"*That* old stuff?"

"Exactly. Just what we need."

"Bloomsbury? All of that? But why? And for whom?"

Feffer called for Sammler in a taxi. They went uptown in style. Feffer stressed the style of it. He said the driver must wait while Sammler gave his talk. The driver, a Negro, refused. Feffer raised his voice. He said this was a legal matter. Sammler persuaded him to drop it as he was about to call the police. "There is no need to have a taxi waiting for me," said Sammler.

"Go get lost then," said Feffer to the cabbie. "And no tip."

"Don't abuse him," Sammler said.

"I won't make any distinction because he's black," said Lionel. "I hear from Margotte that you've been running into a black pickpocket, by the way."

"Where do we go, Lionel? Now that I'm about to speak, I have misgivings. I feel unclear. What, really, am I supposed to say? The topic is so vast."

"You know it better than anyone."

"I know it, yes. But I am uneasy—somewhat shaky."

"You'll be great."

Then Feffer led him into a large room. He had expected a small one, a seminar room. He had come to reminisce, for a handful of interested students, about R. H. Tawney, Harold Laski, John Strachey, George Orwell, H. G. Wells. But this was a mass meeting of some sort. His obstructed vision took in a large, spreading, shaggy, composite human bloom. It was malodorous, peculiarly rancid, sulphurous. The amphitheater was filled. Stand-

ing room only. Was Feffer running one of his rackets? Was he going to pocket the admission money? Sammler mastered and dismissed this suspicion, ascribing it to surprise and nervousness. For he was surprised, frightened. But he pulled himself together. He tried to begin humorously by recalling the lecturer who had addressed incurable alcoholics under the impression that they were the Browning Society. But there was no laughter, and he had to remember that Browning Societies had been extinct for a long time. A microphone was hung on his chest. He began to speak of the mental atmosphere of England before the Second World War. The Mussolini adventure in East Africa. Spain in 1936. The Great Purges in Russia. Stalinism in France and Britain. Blum, Daladier, the Peoples' Front, Oswald Mosley. The mood of English intellectuals. For this he needed no notes, he could easily recall what people had said or written.

"I assume," he said, "you are acquainted with the background, the events of nineteen seventeen. You know of the mutinous armies, the February Revolution in Russia, the disasters that befell authority. In all European countries the old leaders were discredited by Verdun, Flanders Field, and Tannenberg. Perhaps I could begin with the fall of Kerensky. Maybe with Brest-Litovsk."

Doubly foreign, Polish-Oxonian, with his outrushing white back hair, the wrinkles streaming below the smoked glasses, he pulled the handkerchief from the breast pocket, unfolded and refolded it, touched his face, wiped his palms with thin elderly delicacy. Without pleasure in performance, without the encouragement of attention (there was a good deal of noise), the little satisfaction he did feel was the meager ghost of the pride he and his wife had once taken in their British successes. In his success, a Polish Jew so well acquainted, so handsomely acknowledged by the nobs, by H. G. Wells. Included, for instance, with Gerald Heard and Olaf Stapeldon in the *Cosmopolis* project for a World State, Sammler had written articles for *News of Progress*, for the other publication, *The World Citizen*. As he explained in a voice that still contained Polish sibilants and nasals, though impressively low, the project was based on the propagation of the sciences of biology, history, and sociology and the effective application of scientific principles to the enlargement of human life; the building of a planned, orderly, and beautiful world society: abolishing national sovereignty, outlawing war; subjecting money and credit, production, distribution, transport, population, arms manufacture et cetera to world-wide collective control, offering free universal education, personal freedom (compatible with community welfare) to the utmost degree; a service society based on a rational scientific attitude toward life. Sammler, with growing interest and confidence recalling all this, lectured on *Cosmopolis* for half an hour, feeling what a kindhearted, ingenuous, stupid scheme it had been. Telling this into the lighted restless hole of the amphitheater with the soiled dome and caged electric fixtures, until he was interrupted by a loud clear voice. He was being questioned. He was being shouted at.

"Hey!"

He tried to continue. "Such attempts to draw intellectuals away from Marxism met with small success. . . ."

A man in Levi's, thick-bearded but possibly young, a figure of compact distortion, was standing shouting at him.

"Hey! Old Man!"

In the silence, Mr. Sammler drew down his tinted spectacles, seeing this person with his effective eye.

"Old Man! You quoted Orwell before."

"Yes?"

"You quoted him to say that British radicals were all protected by the Royal Navy? Did Orwell say that British radicals were protected by the Royal Navy?"

"Yes, I believe he did say that."

"That's a lot of shit."

Sammler could not speak.

"Orwell was a fink. He was a sick counterrevolutionary. It's good he died when he did. And what you are saying is shit." Turning to the audience, extending violent arms and raising his palms like a Greek dancer, he said, "Why do you listen to this effete old shit? What has he got to tell you? His balls are dry. He's dead. He can't come."

Sammler later thought that voices had been raised on his side. Someone had said, "Shame. Exhibitionist."

But no one really tried to defend him. Most of the young people seemed to be against him. The shouting sounded hostile. Feffer was gone, had been called away to the telephone. Sammler, turning from the lectern, found his umbrella, trench coat, and hat behind him and left the platform, guided by a young girl who had rushed up to express indignation and sympathy, saying it was a scandal to break up such a good lecture. She

showed him through a door, down several stairs, and he was on Broadway at One hundred-sixteenth Street.

Abruptly out of the university.

Back in the city.

And he was not so much personally offended by the event as struck by the will to offend. What a passion to be *real*. But *real* was also brutal. And the acceptance of excrement as a standard? How extraordinary! Youth? Together with the idea of sexual potency? All this confused sex-excrement-militancy, explosiveness, abusiveness, tooth-showing, Barbary ape howling. Or like the spider monkeys in the trees, as Sammler once had read, defecating into their hands, and shrieking, pelting the explorers below.

He was not sorry to have met the facts, however saddening, regrettable the facts. But the effect was that Mr. Sammler did feel somewhat separated from the rest of his species, if not in some fashion severed—severed not so much by age as by preoccupations too different and remote, disproportionate on the side of the spiritual, Platonic, Augustinian, thirteenth-century. As the traffic poured, the wind poured, and the sun, relatively bright for Manhattan—shining and pouring through openings in his substance, through his gaps. As if he had been cast by Henry Moore. With holes, lacunae. Again, as after seeing the pickpocket, he was obliged to events for a difference, an intensification of vision. A delivery man with a floral cross filling both arms, a bald head dented, seemed to be drunk, fighting the wind, tacking. His dull boots small, and his short wide pants blowing like a woman's skirts. Gardenias, camellias, calla lilies, sailing above him under light transparent plastic. Or at the Riverside bus stop Mr. Sammler noted the proximity of a waiting student, used his eye-power to observe that he wore wide-wale corduroy pants of urinous green, a tweed coat of a carrot color with burls of blue wool; that sideburns stood like powerful bushy pillars to the head; that civilized tortoise-shell shafts intersected these; that he had hair thinning at the front; a Jew nose, a heavy all-savoring, all-rejecting lip. Oh, this was an artistic diversion of the streets for Mr. Sammler when he was roused to it by some shock. He was studious, he was bookish, and had been trained by the best writers to divert himself with perceptions. When he went out, life was not empty. Meanwhile the purposive, aggressive, business-bent, conative people did as mankind normally did. If the majority walked about as if under a spell, sleepwalkers, circumscribed by, in the grip of, minor neurotic trifling aims, individuals like Sammler were only one stage forward, awakened not to purpose but to aesthetic consumption of the environment. Even if insulted, pained, somewhere bleeding, not broadly expressing any anger, not crying out with sadness, but translating heartache into delicate, even piercing observation. Particles in the bright wind, flinging downtown, acted like emery on the face. The sun shone as if there were no death. For a full minute, while the bus approached, squirting air, it was like that. Then Mr. Sammler got on, moving like a good citizen toward the rear, hoping he would not be pushed past the back door, for he had only fifteen blocks to go, and there was a thick crowd. The usual smell of long-seated bottoms, of sour shoes, of tobacco muck, of stogies, cologne, face powder. And yet along the river, early spring, the first khaki—a few weeks of sun, of heat, and Manhattan would (briefly) join the North American continent in a day of old-time green, the plush luxury, the polish of the season, shining, nitid, the dogwood white, pink, blooming crabapple. Then people's feet would swell with the warmth, and at Rockefeller Center strollers would sit on the polished stone slabs beside the planted tulips and tritons and the water, all in a spirit of pregnancy. Human creatures under the warm shadows of skyscrapers feeling the heavy pleasure of their nature,

and yielding. Sammler too would enjoy spring—one of those penultimate springs. Of course he was upset. Very. Of course all the stuff about Brest-Litovsk, all that old news about revolutionary intellectuals versus the German brass was in this context downright funny. Inconsequent. Of course those students were comical, too. And what was the worst of it (apart from the rudeness)? There were appropriate ways of putting down an old bore. He might well be, especially in a public manifestation, lecturing on *Cosmopolis*, an old bore. The worst of it, from the point of view of the young people themselves, was that they acted without dignity. They had no view of the nobility of being intellectuals and judges of the social order. What a pity! old Sammler thought. A human being, valuing himself for the right reasons, has and restores order, authority. When the internal parts are in order. They must be in order. But what was it to be arrested in the stage of toilet training! What was it to be entrapped by a psychiatric standard (Sammler blamed the Germans and their psychoanalysis for this)! Who had raised the diaper flag? Who had made shit a sacrament? What literary and psychological movement was that? Mr. Sammler, with bitter angry mind, held the top rail of his jammed bus, riding downtown. . . .

NORMAN MAILER (1923–   )

Born January 21, 1923, in Long Branch, New Jersey; A.B. in engineering, Harvard, 1943; military service in Pacific theater, Second World War; cofounded *The Village Voice*; candidate for Mayor of City of New York, 1969; member National Institute of Arts and Letters (1967); has written in a wide variety of prose forms, including novels: *The Naked and the Dead* (1945), *Barbary Shore* (1951), *The Deer Park* (1955), *An American Dream* (1965), and *Why Are We in Vietnam?* (1967); essays, collected in *Advertisements for Myself* (1959), *The White Negro* (1959), *The Presidential Papers* (1963), *Cannibals and Christians* (1966), *The Prisoner*

of Sex (1971), and *Existential Errands* (1972); and meditative reportage: *The Armies of the Night* (1968), *Miami and the Siege of Chicago* (1968), and *Of a Fire on the Moon* (1970); also a play, *The Deer Park* (adaptation), and a collection of poetry, *Death to the Ladies, and Other Disasters* (1962); *The Armies of the Night*, an account of the author's experiences at and after the rally held in front of the Pentagon in 1967 to protest United States policy in Vietnam, received both Pulitzer prize and National Book Award for nonfiction. The chapters presented here chronicle the events immediately following his arrest at the rally.

From The Armies of the Night (1968)

2: THE MARSHAL AND THE NAZI

They put him in the rear seat of a Volkswagen camper and he welcomed the opportunity to relax. Soon they would drive him, he guessed, to some nearby place where he would be arraigned, fined, and released. He kept searching the distance for sight of Lowell and Macdonald whom he assumed would be following any minute. The thought that they might not have been picked up was depressing, for he could only guess at the depths of Lowell's dejection if he had botched his arrest, and now, with each twenty seconds, he became more gloomily certain that Lowell and Macdonald had been turned back, had failed to get arrested, and blamed himself now for the rush with which he had set out—he should have warned them the arrest might not be automatic, that one might have to steal it—he felt somehow incompetent at not having properly prepared them.

Now a new man entered the Volkswagen. Mailer took him at first for a Marshal or an official, since he was wearing a dark suit and a white motorcycle helmet, and had a clean-cut stubborn face with short features. But he was carrying something which looked like a rolled-up movie screen over five feet long, and he smiled in the friendliest fashion, sat down next to Mailer, and took off his helmet. Mailer thought he was about to be interrogated and he looked forward to that with this friendly man, no less! (of course the prisoner often looks forward to his interrogation) but then another man carrying a clipboard came up to them, and leaning through the wide double door of the camper, asked questions of them both. When Mailer gave his name, the man with the clipboard acted as if he had never heard of him, or at least pretended never to have heard of him, the second possibility seeming possible since word traveled quickly from reporters.

"How do you spell it"

"M.A.I.L.E.R."

"Why were you arrested, Mr. Miller?"

"For transgressing a police line as a protest against the war in Vietnam."

The Clipboard then asked a question of the man sitting next to him. "And why were *you* arrested?"

"As an act of solidarity with oppressed forces fighting for liberty against this country in Southeast Asia."

The Clipboard nodded drily, as if to say, "Yeah, we're all crazy here." Then he asked, pointing to the object which looked like a rolled-up movie screen. "You want that with you?"

"Yessir," said the man next to Mailer. "I'd like to take it along."

The Clipboard gave a short nod, and walked off. Mailer would never see him again. If the History has therefore spent a pointless exchange with him, it is to emphasize that the first few minutes of an arrest such as this are without particular precedent, and so Mailer, like a visitor from Mars, or an adolescent entering polite society, had no idea of what might be important next and what might not. This condition of innocence was not, however, particularly disagreeable since it forced him to watch everything with the attention, let us say, of a man like William Buckley spending his first hour in a Harlem bar—no, come! things are far safer for Mailer at the Pentagon.

He chatted with his fellow prisoner, Teague, Walter Teague was the name, who had been in the vanguard of the charge Mailer had seen from the parking lot. But before any confused impressions were to be sorted, they were interrupted by the insertion of the next prisoner put into the Volkswagen, a young man with straight blond hair and a Nazi armband on his sleeve. He was installed in the rear, with a table between, but Mailer was not happy, for his eyes and the Nazi's bounced off each other like two heads colliding—the novelist discovered he was now in a hurry for them to get this stage of the booking completed. He was also privately indignant at the U.S. Army (like a private citizen, let us say, who writes a letter to his small-town newspaper) at the incredible stupidity of putting a Nazi in the same Volkswagen camper with Pentagon demonstrators—there were two or three other cars available, at least!—next came the suspicion that this was not an accident, but a provocation in the making. If the Nazi started trouble, and there was a fight, the newspaper accounts would doubtless state that Norman Mailer had gotten into an altercation five minutes after his arrest. (Of course, they would not say with whom.) This is all doubtless most paranoid of Mailer, but then he had had nearly twenty years of misreporting about himself, and the seed of paranoia is the arrival of the conviction that the truth about oneself is never told. (Mailer might have done better to pity the American populace—receiving misinformation in systematic form tends to create mass schizophrenia: poor America—Eddie and Debbie are True Love.)

Now they were moved out of the camper and over to an Army truck. There was Teague, and the novelist, and another arrestee—a tall Hungarian who quickly told Mailer how much he liked his books and in much the same breath that he was Freedom Fighter—there was also a new U.S. Marshal, and the Nazi. The prisoners climbed one by one over the high tailgate, Mailer finding it a touch awkward for he did not wish to dirty his dark blue pinstripe suit, and then they stood in the rear of the truck, a still familiar 2½ ton 6-by of a sort which the novelist hadn't been in for twenty-one years, not since his Army discharge.

Standing in the truck, a few feet apart from each other, all prisoners regarding one another, the Nazi fixed on Mailer. Their eyes locked like magnets coming into line, and for perhaps twenty seconds they stared at each other. Mailer looked into a pair of yellow eyes so compressed with hate that back of his own eyes he could feel the echo of such hatred ringing. The Nazi was taller than Mailer, well-knit, and with neatly formed features and a shock of blond hair, would have been handsome but for the ferocity of his yellow eyes which were sunk deep in their sockets. Those eyes made him look like an eagle.

Yet Mailer had first advantage of this eye-staring contest. Because he had been prepared for it. He had been getting into such confrontations for years, and rarely lost them, even though he sometimes thought they were costing him eyesight. Still, some developed instinct had made him ready an instant before the Nazi. Every bit of intensity he possessed —with the tremors of the March and the Marshal's arm still pent in him—glared forth into the other's eyes: he was nonetheless aghast at what he saw. The American Nazis were all fanatics, yes, poor mad tormented fanatics, their psyches twisted like burning leaves in the fire of their hatreds, yes, indeed! but this man's conviction stood in his eyes as if his soul had been focused to a single point of light. Mailer could feel violence behind violence rocking through his head. If the two of them were

ever alone in an alley, one of them might kill the other in a fight—it was not unlike holding an electric wire in the hand. And the worst of it was that he was not even feeling violent himself—whatever violence he possessed had gone to his eyes—by that route had he projected himself on the Nazi.

After the first five seconds of the shock had passed, he realized he might be able to win—the Nazi must have taken too many easy contests, and had been too complacent in the first moment, yes it was like wrestlers throwing themselves on each other: one knuckle of one finger a little better able to be worked on a grip could make the difference—now he could feel the hint of force ebbing in the other's eyes, and could wonder at his own necessity to win. He did not hate the Nazi nearly so much as he was curious about him, yet the thought of losing had been intolerable as if he had been *obliged* not to lose, as if the duty of his life at this particular moment must have been to look into that Nazi's eye, and say with his own, "You claim you have a philosophical system which comprehends all—you know nothing! My eyes encompass yours. My philosophy contains yours. You have met the wrong man!" And the Nazi looked away, and was hysterical with fury on the instant.

"You Jew bastard," he shouted. "Dirty Jew with kinky hair."

They didn't speak that way. It was too corny. Yet he could only answer, "You filthy Kraut."

"Dirty Jew."

"Kraut pig."

A part of his mind could actually be amused at this choice—he didn't even hate Germans any more. Indeed Germans fascinated him now. Why they liked his books more than Americans did. Yet here he could think of nothing better to return than "Kraut pig."

"I'm not a Kraut," said the Nazi, "I'm a Norwegian." And then as if the pride of his birth had tricked him into communication with an infidel, thus into sacrilege, the Nazi added quickly, "Jew bastard red," then cocked his fists, "Come here, you coward," he said to Mailer, "I'll kill you."

"Throw the first punch, baby," said Mailer, "you'll get it all."

They were both absolutely right. They had a perfect sense of the other. Mailer was certainly not brave enough to advance on the Nazi—it would be like springing an avalanche on himself. But he also knew that if the Nazi jumped him, one blond youth was very likely to get massacred. In retrospect, it would appear not uncomic—two philosophical monomaniacs with the same flaw—they could not help it, they were counterpunchers.

"Jew coward! Red bastard!"

"Go fuck yourself, Nazi baby."

But now a tall U.S. Marshal who had the body and insane look of a very good rangy defensive end in professional football—that same hard high-muscled build, same coiled spring of wrath, same livid conviction that everything opposing the team must be wrecked, sod, turf, grass, uniforms, helmets, bodies, yes even bite the football if it will help—now leaped into the truck and jumped between them. "Shut up," he said, "or I'll wreck both of you." He had a long craggy face somewhere in the physiognomical land between Steve McQueen and Robert Mitchum, but he would never have made Hollywood, for his skin was pocked with the big boiling craters of a red lunar acne, and his eyes in Cinemascope would have blazed an audience off their seat for such gray-green flame could only have issued from a blowtorch. Under his white Marshal's helmet, he was one impressive piece of gathered wrath.

Speaking to the Marshal at this point would have been dangerous. The Marshal's emotions had obviously been marinating for a week in the very special bile waters American Patriotism reserves for its need. His feelings were now caustic as a whip—too gentle the simile!—he was in agonies of frustration because the honor of his profession kept him from battering every prisoner's head to a Communist pulp. Mailer looked him over covertly to see what he could try if the Marshal went to work on him. All reports: negative. He would not stand a chance with this Marshal—there seemed no place to hit him where he'd be vulnerable; stone larynx, leather testicles, ice cubes for eyes. And he had his Marshal's club in his hand as well. Brother! Bring back the Nazi!

Whether the Marshal had been once in the Marine Corps, or in Vietnam, or if half his family were now in Vietnam, or if he just hated the sheer New York presumption of that slovenly, drug-ridden weak contaminating American-hating army of termites outside this fortress' walls, he was certainly any upstanding demonstrator's nightmare. Because he was full of American rectitude and was fearless, and savage, savage as the exhuast left in the wake of a motorcycle club, gasoline and cheap perfume were one end of his spectrum, yeah, this Marshal loved action, but he was also in that no man's land between the old frontier and the new ranch home—as they, yes *they*—the enemies of the Marshal—tried to pass bills to limit the purchase of hunting rifles, so did *they* try to kill America, inch by inch, all the forces of evil, disorder, mess and chaos in the world, and *cowardice!* and city ways, the slick shit, and despoliation of national resources, all the subtle invisible creeping paralyses of Communism which were changing America from a land where blood was red to a land where water was foul—yes in this Marshal's mind—no lesser explanation could suffice for the Knight of God light in the flame of his eye—the evil was without. America was threatened by a foreign disease and the Marshal was threatened to the core of his sanity by any one of the first fifty of Mailer's ideas which would insist that the evil was within, that the best in America was being destroyed by what in itself seemed next best, yes American heroism corrupted by American know-how—no wonder murder stood out in his face as he looked at the novelist—for the Marshal to lose his sanity was no passing psychiatric affair: think rather of a rifleman on a tower in Texas and a score of his dead on the street.

But now the Nazi began to play out the deepest of ceremonies. The truck standing still, another Marshal at the other end of the van (the one indeed who had arrested Mailer) and Teague and the Hungarian to different sides, everyone had their eyes on the Norwegian. He now glared again at Mailer, but then whipped away his eyes before a second contest could begin, and said, "All right, Jew, come over here if you want a fight."

The Marshal took the Nazi and threw him against the side-wall of the truck. As he bounced off, the Marshal gave him a rap below the collarbone with the butt of his club. "I told you to shut up. Now, just shut up." His rage was intense. The Nazi looked back at him sullenly, leaned on the butt of the club almost defiantly as if the Marshal didn't know what foolish danger he was in to treat the Nazi so, the Nazi had a proud curved hint of a smile, as if he were recording the features of this Marshal forever in the history of his mind, the Nazi's eyes seemed to say to the Marshal, "You are really on my side although you do not admit it—you would like to beat me now because in the future you know you will yet kiss my boots!" And the Marshal traveling a high edge of temper began to slam the Nazi against the wall of the truck with moderate force, but rhythmically, as if he would pacify them both by this act, bang, and bang, step by step, the imaginary dialogue of the Marshal to the Nazi now sounding in Mailer's ear somewhat like this, "Listen, Nazi, you're nothing but a rat fart who makes my job harder, and gives the scum around me room to breathe, cause they look at you and feel righteous. You just keep me diverted from the real danger."

And the Nazi looked back with a full sullen pouting defiance as if from deep in himself he was all unconsciously saying to the Marshal. "You know I am beautiful, and you are frightened of me. I have a cause and I am ready to die for it, and you are just ready to die for a uniform. Join me where the real war is. Already the strongest and wildest men in America wear our symbol on their motorcycle helmets."

And the Marshal, glaring back at the Nazi, butt of his club transfixing him against the wall of the van, gave a contemptuous look, as if to drop him with the final unspoken word. "Next to strong wild men, you're nothing but a bitch."

Then the truck began to move, and the Marshal calmer now, stood silently between Mailer and the Nazi; and the Nazi also quiet now, stood in place looking neither at the Marshal nor Mailer. Some small storm of hysteria seemed to have worked itself out of the van.

3: GRANDMA WITH ORANGE HAIR

There was not much to see through the canvas arch of the vehicle. A view of a service road they passed along, a little bumping, a bit of swaying—in two minutes they arrived at the next stop. It was the southwest wall of the Pentagon, so much was obvious, for the sun shone brightly here.

Probably they were at the rear of a large mess hall or cafeteria, since a loading platform extended for a considerable distance to either side of where the truck had come in. There were MPs and Marshals on the platform, maybe twenty or thirty, as many again in the back-up area where they had come in. At a long desk at the base of the loading platform, the prisoners were being booked. Each had a Marshal beside him. It was quiet and orderly. The Nazi was standing next to Mailer, but now neither looked at the other. It was indeed all over. The Nazi looked quietly spent, almost gentle—as if the outbursts had been his duty, but duty done, he was just a man again—no need to fight.

They took Mailer's name, having trouble with the spelling again. He was now certain it was not trivial harassment but simple unfamiliarity. The clerk, a stout Marshal with the sort of face that belonged to a cigar, worked carefully at his sheets. The questions were routine—name, address, why arrested—but he entered them with a slow-moving pen which spoke of bureaucratic sacraments taken up, and records set down in perpetuity.

When this was over, Mailer was led by the Marshal who had first arrested him, over to the open door of a sort of school bus painted olive-drab. There was, however, a delay in boarding it, and the Marshal said, "I'm sorry, Mr. Mailer, we have to wait here for a minute to get your number."

"I don't mind."

They were being particularly polite with each other. Mailer had a clear opportunity to look again at this Marshal's face; the *vibrations* of the arrest now utterly discharged, he had an agreeable face indeed, quiet, honest, not unintelligent, not unhumorous. And he talked with the pleasant clipped integrity of a West Virginia accent. Mailer was going to ask him if he came from West Virginia, then out of some random modesty about putting too intensive a question and being wrong, he said instead, "May I ask your name?" It was as one might have expected, a name like Tompkins or Hudkins. "May I ask which state you're from, Marshal?"

"It's West Virginia, Mr. Mailer."

"My wife and I had a young lady work for us once who came from West Virginia. Your accent is similar to hers."

"Is that a fact?"

"Yes, I was wondering if you might be related. There's a suggestion of family resemblance." He mentioned the name. No relation.

Now the necessary paper was delivered to the Marshal. He signed it, and Mailer could board the bus. He had been given the number 10. He was the tenth man arrested at the Pentagon.

"Well, goodbye, Mr. Mailer. Nice talking to you."

"Yes."

Perhaps they were troubled partisans. Or did each wish to show the other that the enemy possessed good manners?

No, thought Mailer, it was ritual. At the moment of the arrest, cop and criminal knew each other better than mates, or at least knew some special *piece* of each other better than mates, yes an arrest was carnal. Not sexual, carnal—of the meat, strangers took purchase of each other's meat. Then came the reciprocal tendency to be pleasant. Beneath all those structures advertised as majestic in law and order there was this small carnal secret which the partners of a bust could share. It was tasty to chat afterward, all sly pleasures present that the secret was concealed. Mailer thought of a paragraph he had written once about police—it had probably acted upon him as much as anything else to first imagine his movie. Now his mind remembered the approximate sense of the paragraph, which actually (indulging Mailer's desire to be quoted) went exactly like this:

> . . . they contain explosive contradictions within themselves. Supposed to be law-enforcers, they tend to conceive of themselves as the law. They are more responsible than the average man, they are more infantile. They are attached umbilically to the concept of honesty, they are profoundly corrupt. They possess more physical courage than the average man, they are unconscionable bullies; they serve the truth, they are psychopathic liars . . . their work is authoritarian, they are cynical: and finally if something in their heart is deeply idealistic, they are also bloated with greed. There is no human creation so contradictory, so finally enigmatic, as the character of the average cop . . .

Yes, and without an arrest, he would never have known that this very nice Marshal from West Virginia with his good American face and pleasant manners and agreeable accent, had also a full quiver of sadism and a clammy sweat of possession as he put the arm on you. But indeed, what knowledge had the Marshal of him?

Inside the bus, at the rear of the aisle, was a locked cage and three or four protesters were enclosed there; jailed within their jailing. They greeted him with jeers, cat-calls, hellos, requests for cigarettes, water—after the first impact, it was not ill-spirited. "Hey, look," said one of the kids behind the bars, "they got older people in with us too."

"What time does this bus leave for Plainfield?" Mailer asked. The laughter came back. It was going to be all right. He could hear them whispering.

"You Norman Mailer?" asked one.

"Yes."

"Hey, great. Listen, man, we got to talk."

"I hope we don't have too much time." More laughter. He was beginning to feel good for the first time since his arrest. "What did you gentlemen do to be given such honor?" asked Mailer with a wave at their cage.

"We're the ones who were resisting arrest."

"Did you resist it much?"

"Are you kidding?" said one dark-haired gloomy thin young pirate with a large Armenian mustache and a bloodied handkerchief on his head, "if we put our hands in front of our face to keep from being beaten to death, they said we were resisting." Hoots and jeers at the fell accuracy of this.

"Well, did you all just sit there and take it?"

"I got in a couple of good shots at my Marshal," said one of the kids. It was hard to tell if he was lying. Something about their incarceration in the cage made it difficult to separate them, or perhaps it was that they seemed part of a team, of a musical group—the Monsters, or the Freaks, or the Caged Kissers—they had not known each other an hour ago, but the cage did the work of making them an ensemble.

The rest of the bus was slowly filling. Mailer had first taken a seat next to a young minister wearing his collar, and they chatted not unhappily for a few minutes, and then both crossed the aisle to sit on the side of the bus which looked out on the loading platform and the table where they had been booked. From these seats, Mailer had a view of the Marshals and MPs outside, of new arrests arriving in trucks, and of the prisoners coming into the bus, one by one, every couple of minutes. After a while, he realized the bus would not move until it was filled, and this, short of massive new arrests, would take at least an hour.

It was not disagreeable waiting. Each new prisoner was obliged to make an entrance like an actor coming on stage for his first appearance; since prisoners in transit are an enforced audience, new entrance automatically becomes theater. Some new men sauntered on the bus, some bowed to the faces in the aisle, some grinned, some scowled and sat down immediately; one or two principled pacifists practicing total noncooperation were dragged off the 2½-ton trucks, bumped along the ground, tugged over to the bus, and thrown in by the Marshals. Bleeding a little, looking dazed, the three or four young men who arrived by this route were applauded with something not unlike the enthusiasm a good turn gets in a music hall. Handsome young boys got on the bus, and slovenly oafs, hippies, and walking wounded. One boy had a pant leg soaked in blood. A fat sad fellow with a huge black beard now boarded; a trim and skinny kid who looked like he played minor league short-stop took a seat, a Japanese boy, androgynous in appearance, told a few prisoners around him that none of the Marshals had been able to decide if he was a boy or a girl, so they had not known—for he would not tell them—whether a Marshal or a Matron should search him. This was quickly taken up with pleasure and repeated down the bus.

Outside, a truck would arrive every five or ten minutes and some boys and girls would dismount and go to the base of the loading platform to be booked, the boys to enter the bus, the girls to go off to another bus. Still no sign of Lowell or Mac-donald. Mailer kept hoping they would appear in the next haul of prisoners. After a while he began to study the Marshals.

Their faces were considerably worse than he had expected. He had had the fortune to be arrested by a man who was incontestably one of the pleasanter Marshals on duty at the Pentagon, he had next met what must be the toughest Marshal in the place—the two had given him a false spectrum. The gang of Marshals now studied outside the bus were enough to firm up any fading loyalty to his own cause: they had the kind of faces which belong to the bad guys in a Western. Some were fat, some were too thin, but nearly all seemed to have those subtle anomalies of the body which come often to men from small towns who have inherited strong features, but end up, by their own measure, in failure. Some would have powerful chests, but abrupt paunches, the skinny ones would have a knob in the shoulder, or a hitch in their gait, their foreheads would have odd cleaving wrinkles, so that one man might look as if an ax had struck him between the eyes, another paid tithe to ten parallel deep lines rising in ridges above his eye brows. The faces of all too many had a low cunning mixed with a stroke of rectitude: if the mouth was slack, the nose was straight and severe; should the lips be tight, the nostrils showed an outsize greed. Many of them looked to be ex-First Sergeants, for they liked to stand with the heels of their hands on the top of their hips, or they had that way of walking, belly forward, which a man will promote when he is in comfortable circumstances with himself and packing a revolver in a belt holster. The toes turn out; the belly struts. They were older men than he might have expected, some in their late thirties, more in their forties, a few looked to be over fifty, but then that

may have been why they were here to receive prisoners rather than out on the line—in any case they emitted a collective spirit which, to his mind, spoke of little which was good, for their eyes were blank and dull, that familiar small-town cast of eye which speaks of apathy rising to fanaticism only to subside in apathy again. (Mailer had wondered more than once at that curious demand of small-town life which leaves something good and bright in the eyes of some, is so deadening for others—it was his impression that people in small towns had eyes which were generally livelier or emptier than the more concentrated look of city vision.) These Marshals had the dead eye and sour cigar, that sly shuffle of propriety and rut which so often comes out in a small-town sheriff as patriotism and the sweet stink of a crooked dollar. Small-town sheriffs sidled over to a crooked dollar like a High Episcopalian hooked on a closet queen. If one could find the irredeemable madness of America (for we are a nation where weeds will breed in the gilding tank) it was in those late afternoon race track faces coming into the neon lights of the parimutuel windows, or those early morning hollows in the eye of the soul in places like Vegas where the fevers of America go livid in the hum of the night, and Grandmother, the church-goer, orange hair burning bright now crooned over the One-Arm Bandit, pocketbook open, driving those half-dollars home, home to the slot.

"Madame, we are burning children in Vietnam."

"Boy, you just go get yourself lost. Grandma's about ready for a kiss from the jackpot."

The burned child is brought into the gaming hall on her hospital bed.

"Madame, regard our act in Vietnam."

"I hit! I hit! Hot deedy, I hit. Why, you poor burned child—you just brought me luck. Here, honey, here's a lucky half-dollar in reward. And listen sugar, tell the nurse to change your sheets. Those sheets sure do stink. I hope you ain't got gangrene. Hee hee, hee hee. I get a supreme pleasure mixing with gooks in Vegas."

One did not have to look for who would work in the concentration camps and the liquidation centers—the garrison would be filled with applicants from the pages of a hundred American novels, from *Day of the Locust* and *Naked Lunch* and *The Magic Christian*, one could enlist half the Marshals outside this bus, simple, honest, hard-working government law-enforcement agents, yeah! There was something at loose now in American life, the poet's beast slinking to the marketplace. The country had always been wild. It had always been harsh and hard, it had always had a fever—when life in one American town grew insupportable, one could travel, the fever to travel was in the American blood, so said all, but now the fever had left the blood, it was in the cells, the cells traveled, and the cells were as insane as Grandma with orange hair. The small towns were disappearing in the bypasses and the supermarkets and the shopping centers, the small town in America was losing its sense of the knuckle, the herb, and the root, the walking sticks were no longer cut from trees, nor were they cured, the schools did not have crazy old teachers now but teaching aids, and in the libraries, *National Geographic* gave way to *TV Guide*. Enough of the old walled town had once remained in the American small town for gnomes and dwarfs and knaves and churls (yes, and owls and elves and crickets) to live in the constellated cities of the spiders below the eaves in the old leaning barn which—for all one knew—had been a secret ear to the fevers of the small town, message center for the inhuman dreams which passed through the town at night in sleep and came to tell their insane tale of the old barbarian lust to slaughter villages and drink their blood, yes who knew which ghosts, and which crickets, with which spider would commune—which prayers and whose witch's curses would travel those subterranean trails of the natural kingdom about the town, who knows which fevers were forged in such communion and returned on the blood to the seed, it was an era when the message came by the wind and not by the wire (for the town gossip began to go mad when the telephone tuned its buds to the tip of her tongue) the American small town grew out of itself, and grew out of itself again and again, harmony between communication and the wind, between lives and ghosts, insanity, the solemn reaches of nature where insanity could learn melancholy (and madness some measure of modesty) had all been lost now, lost to the American small town. It had grown out of itself again and again, its cells traveled, worked for government, found security through wars in foreign lands, and the nightmares which passed on the winds in the old small towns now traveled on the nozzle tip of the flame thrower, no dreams now of barbarian lusts, slaughtered villages, battles of blood, no, nor any need for them—technology had driven insanity out of the wind and out of the attic, and out of all the

lost primitive places: one had to find it now wherever fever, force, and machines could come together, in Vegas, at the race track, in pro football, race riots for the Negro, suburban orgies—none of it was enough—one had to find it in Vietnam; that was where the small town had gone to get its kicks.

That was on the faces of the Marshals. It was a great deal to read on the limited evidence before him, but he had known these faces before—they were not so different from the cramped, mean, stern, brave, florid, bestial, brutish, narrow, calculating, incurious, hardy, wily, leathery, simple, good, stingy, small-town faces he had once been familiar with in his outfit overseas, all those Texans from all those small towns, it was if he could tell —as at a college reunion—the difference these more than twenty years had made. If it were legitimate to read the change in American character by the change in the faces of one's classmates, then he could look at these Marshals like men he had known in the Army, but now revisited, and something had gone out of them, something had come in. If there was a common unattractive element to the Southern small-town face, it was in that painful pinch between their stinginess and their greed. No excess of love seemed ever to come off a poor white Southerner, no fats, no riches, no sweets, just the avidity for such wealth. But there had been sadness attached to this in the old days, a sorrow; in the pinch of their cheeks was the kind of abnegation and loneliness which spoke of what was tender and what was lost forever. So they had dignity. Now the hollows in their faces spoke of men who were rabid and toothless, the tenderness had turned corrosive, the abnegation had been replaced by hate, dull hate, cloud banks of hate, the hatred of failures who had not lost their greed. So he was reminded of a probability he had encountered before: that, nuclear bombs all at hand, the true war party of America was in all the small towns, even as the peace parties had to collect in the cities and the suburbs. Nuclear warfare was dividing the nation. The day of power for the small-town mind was approaching—who else would be left when atomic war was done would reason the small-town mind, and in measure to the depth of their personal failure, would love Vietnam, for Vietnam was the secret hope of a bigger war, and that bigger war might yet clear the air of races, faces, in fact—technologies—all that alienation they could not try to comprehend.

It was not a happy meditation.

JAMES BALDWIN (1924–   )

Born August 2, 1924, in New York City; attended DeWitt Clinton High School; held a number of minor jobs in New York until 1948, then lived for ten years in Paris, composing his first three prose works, *Go Tell It on the Mountain* (novel, 1953), *Notes of a Native Son* (essays, 1955), and *Giovanni's Room* (novel, 1956); returned to New York in 1957, publishing *Nobody Knows My Name* (essays, 1961), *Another Country* (1962), and *The Fire Next Time* (1963), a long essay whose prefatory letter we print here in full; has since published

Going to Meet the Man (stories, 1966), *Tell Me How Long the Train's Been Gone* (novel, 1968), *A Rap on Race* (conversations with Margaret Mead, 1971), and *No Name in the Street* (essays, 1972), as well as the plays *The Amen Corner, Giovanni's Room* (adaptation), and *Blues for Mister Charley* (1964); member National Institute of Arts and Letters (1964); has received a grant from National Institute of Arts and Letters and Eugene F. Saxton Memorial Trust Award.

From The Fire Next Time (1963)

MY DUNGEON SHOOK: LETTER TO MY NEPHEW ON THE ONE HUNDREDTH ANNIVERSARY OF THE EMANCIPATION

Dear James:

I have begun this letter five times and torn it up five times. I keep seeing your face, which is also the face of your father and my brother. Like him, you are tough, dark, vulnerable, moody—with a very definite tendency to sound truculent because you want no one to think you are soft. You may be like your grandfather in this, I don't know, but certainly both you and your father resemble him very much physically. Well, he is dead, he never saw you, and he had a terrible life; he was defeated long before he died because, at the bottom of his heart, he really believed what white people said about him. This is one of the reasons that he became so holy. I am sure that your father has told you something about all that. Neither you nor your father exhibit any tendency towards holiness: you really *are* of another era, part of what happened when the Negro left the land and came into what the late E. Franklin Frazier called "the cities of destruction." You can only be destroyed by believing that you really are what the white world calls a *nigger*. I tell you this because I love you, and please don't you ever forget it.

I have known both of you all your lives, have carried your Daddy in my arms and on my shoulders, kissed and spanked him and watched him learn to walk. I don't know if you've known anybody from that far back; if you've loved anybody that long, first as an infant, then as a child, then as a man, you gain a strange perspective on time and human pain and effort. Other people cannot see what I see whenever I look into your father's face, for behind your father's face as it is today are all those other faces which were his. Let him laugh and I see a cellar your father does not remember and a house he does not remember and I hear in his present laughter his laughter as a child. Let him curse and I remember him falling down the cellar steps, and howling, and I remember, with pain, his tears, which my hand or your grandmother's so easily wiped away. But no one's hand can wipe away those tears he sheds invisibly today, which one hears in his laughter and in his speech and in his songs. I know what the world has done to my brother and how narrowly he has survived it. And I know, which is much worse, and this is the crime of which I accuse my country and my countrymen, and for which neither I nor time nor history will ever forgive them, that they have destroyed and are destroying hundreds of thousands of lives and do not know it and do not want to know it. One can be, indeed one must strive to become, tough and philosophical concerning destruction and death, for this is what most of mankind has been best at since we have heard of man. (But remember: *most* of mankind is not *all* of mankind.) But it is not permissible that the authors of devastation should also be innocent. It is the innocence which constitutes the crime.

Now, my dear namesake, these innocent and well-meaning people, your countrymen, have caused you to be born under conditions not very far removed from those described for us by Charles Dickens in the London of more than a hundred years ago. (I hear the chorus of the innocents screaming, "No! This is not true! How *bitter* you are!"—but I am writing this letter to *you*, to try to tell you something about how to handle *them*, for most of them do not yet really know that you exist. I *know* the conditions under which you were born, for I was there. Your countrymen were *not* there, and haven't made it yet. Your grandmother was also there, and no one has ever accused her of being bitter. I suggest that the innocents check with her. She isn't hard to find. Your countrymen don't know that *she* exists, either, though she has been working for them all their lives.)

Well, you were born, here you came, something like fifteen years ago; and though your father and mother and grandmother, looking about the streets through which they were carrying you, staring at the walls into which they brought you, had every reason to be heavyhearted, yet they were not. For here you were, Big James, named for me—you were a big baby, I was not—here you were: to be loved. To be loved, baby, hard, at once, and forever, to strengthen you against the loveless world. Remember that: I know how black it looks today, for you. It looked bad that day, too, yes, we were trembling. We have not stopped trembling yet, but if we had not loved each other none of us would have survived. And now you must survive because we love you, and for the sake of your children and your children's children.

This innocent country set you down in a ghetto in which, in fact, it intended that you should perish. Let me spell out precisely what I mean by that, for the heart of the matter is here, and the root of my dispute with my country. You were born where you were born and faced the future that you faced because you were black and *for no other reason*.

The limits of your ambition were, thus, expected to be set forever. You were born into a society which spelled out with brutal clarity, and in as many ways as possible, that you were a worthless human being. You were not expected to aspire to excellence: you were expected to make peace with mediocrity. Wherever you have turned, James, in your short time on this earth, you have been told where you could go and what you could do (and *how* you could do it) and where you could live and whom you could marry. I know your countrymen do not agree with me about this, and I hear them saying, "You exaggerate." They do not know Harlem, and I do. So do you. Take no one's word for anything, including mine—but trust your experience. Know whence you came. If you know whence you came, there is really no limit to where you can go. The details and symbols of your life have been deliberately constructed to make you believe what white people say about you. Please try to remember that what they believe, as well as what they do and cause you to endure, does not testify to your inferiority but to their inhumanity and fear. Please try to be clear, dear James, through the storm which rages about your youthful head today, about the reality which lies behind the words *acceptance* and *integration*. There is no reason for you to try to become like white people and there is no basis whatever for their impertinent assumption that *they* must accept you. The really terrible thing, old buddy, is that *you* must accept *them*. And I mean that very seriously. You must accept them and accept them with love. For these innocent people have no other hope. They are, in effect, still trapped in a history which they do not understand; and until they understand it, they cannot be released from it. They have had to believe for many years, and for innumerable reasons, that black men are inferior to white men. Many of them, indeed, know better, but, as you will discover, people find it very difficult to act on what they know. To act is to be committed, and to be committed is to be in danger. In this case, the danger, in the minds of most white Americans, is the loss of their identity. Try to imagine how you would feel if you woke up one morning to find the sun shining and all the stars aflame. You would be frightened because it is out of the order of nature. Any upheaval in the universe is terrifying because it so profoundly attacks one's sense of one's own reality. Well, the black man has functioned in the white man's world as a fixed star, as an immovable pillar: and as he moves out of his place, heaven and earth are shaken to their foundations. You, don't be afraid. I said that it was intended that you should perish in the ghetto, perish by never being allowed to go behind the white man's definitions, by never being allowed to spell your proper name. You have, and many of us have, defeated this intention; and, by a terrible law, a terrible paradox, those innocents who believed that your imprisonment made them safe are losing their grasp of reality. But these men are your brothers—your lost, younger brothers. And if the word *integration* means anything, this is what it means: that we, with love, shall force our brothers to see themselves as they are, to cease fleeing from reality and begin to change it. For this is your home, my friend, do not be driven from it; great men have done great things here, and will again,

and we can make America what America must become. It will be hard, James, but you come from sturdy, peasant stock, men who picked cotton and dammed rivers and built railroads, and, in the teeth of the most terrifying odds, achieved an unassailable and monumental dignity. You come from a long line of great poets, some of the greatest poets since Homer. One of them said, *The very time I thought I was lost, My dungeon shook and my chains fell off.*

You know, and I know, that the country is celebrating one hundred years of freedom one hundred years too soon. We cannot be free until they are free. God bless you, James, and Godspeed.

Your uncle,
James

FLANNERY O'CONNOR (1925–1964)

Born March 25, 1925, in Savannah, Georgia; moved with her family to Milledgeville, Georgia, at an early age; graduated Georgia State College for Women; M.F.A. from University of Iowa Writer's Workshop in 1947; lived in New York City, then Connecticut, returning to Milledgeville in 1950; died in 1964; publications are *Wise Blood* (novel, 1952), *A Good Man Is Hard to Find* (stories, 1955), whose title story we present, *The Violent Bear It Away* (novel, 1960), *Everything That Rises Must Converge*

(stories, 1965), and *The Complete Stories* (1971), as well as *Mystery and Manners: Occasional Prose* (1969), collected and edited by Sally and Robert Fitzgerald (1969); received a grant from the National Institute of Arts and Letters (1957), National Catholic Book Award for *Mystery and Manners* (posthumously), and a posthumous citation from National Book Award committee for *Everything That Rises Must Converge.*

A Good Man Is Hard to Find (1955)

The grandmother didn't want to go to Florida. She wanted to visit some of her connections in east Tennessee and she was seizing at every chance to change Bailey's mind. Bailey was the son she lived with, her only boy. He was sitting on the edge of his chair at the table, bent over the orange sports section of the *Journal*. "Now look here, Bailey," she said, "see here, read this," and she stood with one hand on her thin hip and the other rattling the newspaper at his bald head. "Here this fellow that calls himself The Misfit is aloose

from the Federal Pen and headed toward Florida and you read here what it says he did to these people. Just you read it. I wouldn't take my children in any direction with a criminal like that aloose in it. I couldn't answer to my conscience if I did."

Bailey didn't look up from his reading so she wheeled around then and faced the children's mother, a young woman in slacks, whose face was as broad and innocent as a cabbage and was tied around with a green head-kerchief that had two points on the top like a rabbit's ears. She was sitting on the sofa, feeding the baby his apricots out of a jar. "The children have been to Florida before," the old lady said. "You all ought to take them somewhere else for a change so they would see different parts of the world and be broad. They never have been to east Tennessee."

The children's mother didn't seem to hear her but the eight-year-old boy, John Wesley, a stocky child with glasses, said, "If you don't want to go to Florida, why dontcha stay at home?" He and the little girl, June Star, were reading the funny papers on the floor.

"She wouldn't stay at home to be queen for a day," June Star said without raising her yellow head.

"Yes and what would you do if this fellow, the Misfit, caught you?" the grandmother asked.

"I'd smack his face," John Wesley said.

"She wouldn't stay at home for a million bucks," June Star said. "Afraid she'd miss something. She has to go everywhere we go."

"All right, Miss," the grandmother said. "Just remember that the next time you want me to curl your hair."

June Star said her hair was naturally curly.

The next morning the grandmother was the first one in the car, ready to go. She had her big black valise that looked like the head of a hippopotamus in one corner, and underneath it she was hiding a basket with Pitty Sing, the cat, in it. She didn't intend for the cat to be left alone in the house for three days because he would miss her too much and she was afraid he might brush against one of the gas burners and accidentally asphyxiate himself. Her son, Bailey, didn't like to arrive at a motel with a cat.

She sat in the middle of the back seat with John Wesley and June Star on either side of her. Bailey and the children's mother and the baby sat in front and they left Atlanta at eight forty-five with the mileage on the car at 55890. The grandmother wrote this down because she thought it would be interesting to say how many miles they had been when they got back. It took them twenty minutes to reach the outskirts of the city.

The old lady settled herself comfortably, removing her white cotton gloves and putting them up with her purse on the shelf in front of the back window. The children's mother still had on slacks and still had her head tied up in a green kerchief, but the grandmother had on a navy blue straw sailor hat with a bunch of white violets on the brim and a navy blue dress with a small white dot in the print. Her collars and cuffs were white organdy trimmed with lace and at her neckline she had pinned a purple spray of cloth violets containing a sachet. In case of an accident, anyone seeing her dead on the highway would know at once that she was a lady.

She said she thought it was going to be a good day for driving, neither too hot nor too cold, and she cautioned Bailey that the speed limit was fifty-five miles an hour and that the patrolmen hid themselves behind billboards and small clumps of trees and sped out after you before you had a chance to slow down. She pointed out interesting details of the scenery: Stone Mountain; the blue granite that in some places came up to both sides of the highway; the brilliant red clay banks slightly streaked with purple; and the various crops that made rows of green lace-work on the ground. The trees were full of silver-white sunlight and the meanest of them sparkled. The children were reading comic magazines and their mother had gone back to sleep.

"Let's go through Georgia fast so we won't have to look at it much," John Wesley said.

"If I were a little boy," said the grandmother, "I wouldn't talk about my native state that way. Tennessee has the mountains and Georgia has the hills."

"Tennessee is just a hillbilly dumping ground," John Wesley said, "and Georgia is a lousy state too."

"You said it," June Star said.

"In my time," said the grandmother, folding her thin veined fingers, "children were more respectful of their native states and their parents and everything else. People did right then. Oh look at the cute little pickaninny!" she said and pointed to a Negro child standing in the door of a shack. "Wouldn't that make a picture, now?" she asked and they all turned and looked at the little Negro out of the back window. He waved.

"He didn't have any britches on," June Star said.

"He probably didn't have any," the grandmother explained. "Little niggers in the country don't have things like we do. If I could paint, I'd paint that picture," she said.

The children exchanged comic books.

The grandmother offered to hold the baby and the children's mother passed him over the front seat to her. She set him on her knee and bounced him and told him about the things they were passing. She rolled her eyes and screwed up her mouth and stuck her leathery thin face into his smooth bland one. Occasionally he gave her a faraway smile. They passed a large cotton field with five or six graves fenced in the middle of it, like a small island. "Look at the graveyard!" the grandmother said, pointing it out. "That was the old family burying ground. That belonged to the plantation."

"Where's the plantation?" John Wesley asked.

"Gone With the Wind," said the grandmother. "Ha. Ha."

When the children finished all the comic books they had brought, they opened the lunch and ate it. The grandmother ate a peanut butter sandwich and an olive and would not let the children throw the box and the paper napkins out the window. When there was nothing else to do they played a game by choosing a cloud and making the other two guess what shape it suggested. John Wesley took one the shape of a cow and June Star guessed a cow and John Wesley said, no, an automobile, and June Star said he didn't play fair, and they began to slap each other over the grandmother.

The grandmother said she would tell them a story if they would keep quiet. When she told a story, she rolled her eyes and waved her head and was very dramatic. She said once when she was a maiden lady she had been courted by a Mr. Edgar Atkins Teagarden from Jasper, Georgia. She said he was a very good-looking man and a gentleman and that he brought her a watermelon every Saturday afternoon with his initials cut in it, E. A. T. Well, one Saturday, she said, Mr. Teagarden brought the watermelon and there was nobody at home and he left it on the front porch and returned in his buggy to Jasper, but she never got the watermelon, she said, because a nigger boy ate it when he saw the initials, E. A. T.! This story tickled John Wesley's funny bone and he giggled and giggled but June Star didn't think it was any good. She said she wouldn't marry a man that just brought her a watermelon on Saturday. The grandmother said she would have done well to marry Mr. Teagarden because he was a gentleman and had bought Coca-Cola stock when it first came out and that he died only a few years ago, a very wealthy man.

They stopped at The Tower for barbecued sandwiches. The Tower was a part stucco and part wood filling station and dance hall set in a clearing outside of Timothy. A fat man named Red Sammy Butts ran it and there were signs stuck here and there on the building and for miles up and down the highway saying, TRY RED SAMMY'S FAMOUS BARBECUE. NONE LIKE FAMOUS RED SAMMY'S! RED SAM! THE FAT BOY WITH THE HAPPY LAUGH. A VETERAN! RED SAMMY'S YOUR MAN!

Red Sammy was lying on the bare ground outside The Tower with his head under a truck while a gray monkey about a foot high, chained to a small chinaberry tree, chattered nearby. The monkey sprang back into the tree and got on the highest limb as soon as he saw the children jump out of the car and run toward him.

Inside, The Tower was a long dark room with a counter at one end and tables at the other and dancing space in the middle. They all sat down at a board table next to the nickelodeon and Red Sam's wife, a tall burnt-brown woman with hair and eyes lighter than her skin, came and took their order. The children's mother put a dime in the machine and played "The Tennessee Waltz," and the grandmother said that tune always made her want to dance. She asked Bailey if he would like to dance but he only glared at her. He didn't have a naturally sweet disposition like she did and trips made him nervous. His grandmother's brown eyes were very bright. She swayed her head from side to side and pretended she was dancing in her chair. June Star said play something she could tap to so the children's mother put in another dime and played a fast number and June Star stepped out onto the dance floor and did her tap routine.

"Ain't she cute?" Red Sam's wife said, leaning over the counter. "Would you like to come be my little girl?"

"No I certainly wouldn't," June Star said. "I wouldn't live in a broken-down place like this for a million bucks!" and she ran back to the table.

"Ain't she cute?" the woman repeated, stretching her mouth politely.

"Aren't you ashamed?" hissed the grandmother.

Red Sam came in and told his wife to quit lounging on the counter and hurry up with these people's order. His khaki trousers reached just to his hip bones and his stomach hung over them like a sack of meal swaying under his shirt. He came over and sat down at a table nearby and let out a combination sigh and yodel. "You can't win," he said. "You can't win," and he wiped his sweating red face off with a gray handkerchief. "These days you don't know who to trust," he said. "Ain't that the truth?"

"People are certainly not nice like they used to be," said the grandmother.

"Two fellers come in here last week," Red Sammy said, "driving a Chrysler. It was a old beat-up car but it was a good one and these boys looked all right to me. Said they worked at the mill and you know I let them fellers charge the gas they bought? Now why did I do that?"

"Because you're a good man!" the grandmother said at once.

"Yes'm, I suppose so," Red Sam said as if he were struck with this answer.

His wife brought the orders, carrying the five plates all at once without a tray, two in each hand and one balanced on her arm. "It isn't a soul in this green world of God's that you can trust," she said. "And I don't count nobody out of that, not nobody," she repeated, looking at Red Sammy.

"Did you read about that criminal, The Misfit, that's escaped?" asked the grandmother.

"I wouldn't be a bit surprised if he didn't attact this place right here," said the woman. "If he hears about it being here, I wouldn't be none surprised to see him. If he hears it's two cent in the cash register, I wouldn't be at all surprised if he . . ."

"That'll do," Red Sam said. "Go bring these people their Co'-Colas," and the woman went off to get the rest of the order.

"A good man is hard to find," Red Sammy said. "Everything is getting terrible. I remember the day you could go off and leave your screen door unlatched. Not no more."

He and the grandmother discussed better times. The old lady said that in her opinion Europe was entirely to blame for the way things were now. She said the way Europe acted you would think we were made of money and Red Sam said it was no use talking about it, she was exactly right. The children ran outside into the white sunlight and looked at the monkey in the lacy chinaberry tree. He was busy catching fleas on himself and biting each one carefully between his teeth as if it were a delicacy.

They drove off again into the hot afternoon. The grandmother took cat naps and woke up every few minutes with her own snoring. Outside of Toombsboro she woke up and recalled an old plantation that she had visited in this neighborhood once when she was a young lady. She said the house had six white columns across the front and that there was an avenue of oaks leading up to it and two little wooden trellis arbors on either side in front where you sat down with your suitor after a stroll in the garden. She recalled exactly which road to turn off to get to it. She knew that Bailey would not be willing to lose any time looking at an old house, but the more she talked about it, the

more she wanted to see it once again and find out if the little twin arbors were still standing. "There was a secret panel in this house," she said craftily, not telling the truth but wishing that she were, "and the story went that all the family silver was hidden in it when Sherman came through but it was never found . . ."

"Hey!" John Wesley said. "Let's go see it! We'll find it! We'll poke all the woodwork and find it! Who lives there? Where do you turn off at? Hey Pop, can't we turn off there?"

"We never have seen a house with a secret panel!" June Star shrieked. "Let's go to the house with the secret panel! Hey Pop, can't we go see the house with the secret panel!"

"It's not far from here, I know," the grandmother said. "It wouldn't take over twenty minutes."

Bailey was looking straight ahead. His jaw was as rigid as a horseshoe. "No," he said.

The children began to yell and scream that they wanted to see the house with the secret panel. John Wesley kicked the back of the front seat and June Star hung over her mother's shoulder and whined desperately into her ear that they never had any fun even on their vacation, that they could never do what THEY wanted to do. The baby began to scream and John Wesley kicked the back of the seat so hard that his father could feel the blows in his kidney.

"All right!" he shouted and drew the car to a stop at the side of the road. "Will you all shut up? Will you all just shut up for one second? If you don't shut up, we won't go anywhere."

"It would be very educational for them," the grandmother murmured.

"All right," Bailey said, "but get this: this is the only time we're going to stop for anything like this. This is the one and only time."

"The dirt road that you have to turn down is about a mile back," the grandmother directed. "I marked it when we passed."

"A dirt road," Bailey groaned.

After they had turned around and were headed toward the dirt road, the grandmother recalled other points about the house, the beautiful glass over the front doorway and the candle-lamp in the hall. John Wesley said that the secret panel was probably in the fireplace.

"You can't go inside this house," Bailey said. "You don't know who lives there."

"While you all talk to the people in front, I'll run around behind and get in a window," John Wesley suggested.

"We'll all stay in the car," his mother said.

They turned onto the dirt road and the car raced roughly along in a swirl of pink dust. The grandmother recalled the times when there were no paved roads and thirty miles was a day's journey. The dirt road was hilly and there were sudden washes in it and sharp curves on dangerous embankments. All at once they would be on a hill, looking down over the blue tops of trees for miles around, then the next minute, they would be in a red depression with the dust-coated trees looking down on them.

"This place had better turn up in a minute," Bailey said, "or I'm going to turn around."

The road looked as if no one had traveled on it in months.

"It's not much farther," the grandmother said and just as she said it, a horrible thought came to her. The thought was so embarrassing that she turned red in the face and her eyes dilated and her feet jumped up, upsetting her valise in the corner. The instant the valise moved, the newspaper top she had over the basket under it rose with a snarl and Pitty Sing, the cat, sprang onto Bailey's shoulder.

The children were thrown to the floor and their mother, clutching the baby, was thrown out the door onto the ground; the old lady was thrown into the front seat. The car turned over once and landed right-side-up in a gulch off the side of the road. Bailey remained in the driver's seat with the cat—gray-striped with a broad white face and an orange nose—clinging to his neck like a caterpillar.

As soon as the children saw they could move their arms and legs, they scrambled out of the car, shouting, "We've had an ACCIDENT!" The grandmother was curled up under the dashboard, hoping she was injured so that Bailey's wrath would not come down on her all at once. The horrible thought she had had before the accident was that the house she had remembered so vividly was not in Georgia but in Tennessee.

Bailey removed the cat from his neck with both hands and flung it out the window against the side of a pine tree. Then he got out of the car and started looking for the children's mother. She was sitting against the side of the red gutted ditch, holding the screaming baby, but she only had a cut down her face and a broken shoulder. "We've had an ACCIDENT!" the children screamed in a frenzy of delight.

"But nobody's killed," June Star said with disappointment as the grandmother limped out of the car, her hat still pinned to her head but the broken front brim standing up at a jaunty angle and the violet spray hanging off the side. They all sat down in the ditch, except the children, to recover from the shock. They were all shaking.

"Maybe a car will come along," said the children's mother hoarsely.

"I believe I have injured an organ," said the grandmother, pressing her side, but no one answered her. Bailey's teeth were clattering. He had on a yellow sport shirt with bright blue parrots designed in it and his face was as yellow as the shirt. The grandmother decided that she would not mention that the house was in Tennessee.

The road was about ten feet above and they could see only the tops of the trees on the other side of it. Behind the ditch they were sitting in there were more woods, tall and dark and deep. In a few minutes they saw a car some distance away on top of a hill, coming slowly as if the occupants were watching them. The grandmother stood up and waved both arms dramatically to attract their attention. The car continued to come on slowly, disappeared around a bend and appeared again, moving even slower, on top of the hill they had gone over. It was a big black battered hearse-like automobile. There were three men in it.

It came to a stop just over them and for some minutes, the driver looked down with a steady expressionless gaze to where they were sitting, and didn't speak. Then he turned his head and muttered something to the other two and they got out. One was a fat boy in black trousers and a red sweat shirt with a silver stallion embossed on the front of it. He moved around on the right side of them and stood staring, his mouth partly open in a kind of loose grin. The other had on khaki pants and a blue striped coat and a gray hat pulled down very low, hiding most of his face. He came around slowly on the left side. Neither spoke.

The driver got out of the car and stood by the side of it, looking down at them. He was an older man than the other two. His hair was just beginning to gray and he wore silver-rimmed spectacles that gave him a scholarly look. He had a long creased face and didn't have on any shirt or undershirt. He had on blue jeans that were too tight for him and was holding a black hat and a gun. The two boys also had guns.

"We've had an ACCIDENT!" the children screamed.

The grandmother had the peculiar feeling that the bespectacled man was someone she knew. His face was as familiar to her as if she had known him all her life but she could not recall who he was. He moved away from the car and began to come down the embankment, placing his feet carefully so that he wouldn't slip. He had on tan and white shoes and no socks, and his ankles were red and thin. "Good afternoon," he said. "I see you all had you a little spill."

"We turned over twice!" said the grandmother.

"Oncet," he corrected. "We seen it happen. Try their car and see will it run, Hiram," he said quietly to the boy with the gray hat.

"What you got that gun for?" John Wesley asked. "Watcha gonna do with that gun?"

"Lady," the man said to the children's mother, "would you mind calling them children to sit down by you? Children make me nervous. I want all you all to sit down right together there where you're at."

"What are you telling US what to do for?" June Star asked.

Behind them the line of woods gaped like a dark open mouth. "Come here," said their mother.

"Look here now," Bailey began suddenly, "we're in a predicament! We're in . . ."

The grandmother shrieked. She scrambled to her feet and stood staring. "You're The Misfit!" she said. "I recognized you at once!"

"Yes'm," the man said, smiling slightly as if he were pleased in spite of himself to be known, "but it would have been better for all of you, lady, if you hadn't of reckernized me."

Bailey turned his head sharply and said something to his mother that shocked even the children. The old lady began to cry and The Misfit reddened.

"Lady," he said, "don't you get upset. Sometimes a man says things he don't mean. I don't reckon he meant to talk to you thataway."

"You wouldn't shoot a lady, would you?" the grandmother said and removed a clean handkerchief from her cuff and began to slap at her eyes with it.

The Misfit pointed the toe of his shoe into the ground and made a little hole and then covered it up again. "I would hate to have to," he said.

"Listen," the grandmother almost screamed, "I know you're a good man. You don't look a bit like you have common blood. I know you must come from nice people!"

"Yes mam," he said, "finest people in the world." When he smiled he showed a row of strong white teeth. "God never made a finer woman than my mother and my daddy's heart was pure gold," he said. The boy with the red sweat shirt had come around behind them and was standing with his gun at his hip. The Misfit squatted down on the ground. "Watch them children, Bobby Lee," he said. "You know they make me nervous." He looked at the six of them huddled together in front of him and he seemed to be embarrassed as if he couldn't think of anything to say. "Ain't a cloud in the sky," he remarked, looking up at it. "Don't see no sun but don't see no cloud neither."

"Yes, it's a beautiful day," said the grandmother. "Listen," she said, "you shouldn't call yourself The Misfit because I know you're a good man at heart. I can just look at you and tell."

"Hush!" Bailey yelled. "Hush! Everybody shut up and let me handle this!" He was squatting in the position of a runner about to sprint forward but he didn't move.

"I pre-chate that, lady," The Misfit said and drew a little circle in the ground with the butt of his gun.

"It'll take a half a hour to fix this here car," Hiram called, looking over the raised hood of it.

"Well, first you and Bobby Lee get him and that little boy to step over yonder with you," The Misfit said, pointing to Bailey and John Wesley. "The boys want to ast you something," he said to Bailey. "Would you mind stepping back in them woods there with them?"

"Listen," Bailey began, "we're in a terrible predicament! Nobody realizes what this is," and his voice cracked. His eyes were as blue and intense as the parrots in his shirt and he remained perfectly still.

The grandmother reached up to adjust her hat brim as if she were going to the woods with him but it came off in her hand. She stood staring at it and after a second she let it fall on the ground. Hiram pulled Bailey up by the arm as if he were assisting an old man. John Wesley caught hold of his father's hand and Bobby Lee followed. They went off toward the woods and just as they reached the dark edge, Bailey turned and supporting himself against a gray naked pine trunk, he shouted, "I'll be back in a minute, Mamma, wait on me!"

"Come back this instant!" his mother shrilled but they all disappeared into the woods.

"Bailey Boy!" the grandmother called in a tragic voice but she found she was looking at The Misfit squatting on the ground in front of her. "I just know you're a good man," she said desperately.

"You're not a bit common!"

"Nome, I ain't a good man," The Misfit said after a second as if he had considered her statement carefully, "but I ain't the worst in the world neither. My daddy said I was a different breed of dog from my brothers and sisters. 'You know,' Daddy said, 'it's some that can live their whole life out without asking about it and it's others has to know why it is, and this boy is one of the latters. He's going to be into everything!'" He put on his black hat and looked up suddenly and then away deep into the woods as if he were embarrassed again. "I'm sorry I don't have on a shirt before you ladies," he said, hunching his shoulders slightly. "We buried our clothes that we had on when we escaped and we're just making do until we can get better. We borrowed these from some folks we met," he explained.

"That's perfectly all right," the grandmother said. "Maybe Bailey has an extra shirt in his suitcase."

"I'll look and see terrectly," The Misfit said.

"Where are they taking him?" the children's mother screamed.

"Daddy was a card himself," The Misfit said. "You couldn't put anything over on him. He never got in trouble with the Authorities though. Just had the knack of handling them."

"You could be honest too if you'd only try," said the grandmother. "Think how wonderful it would be to settle down and live a comfortable life and not have to think about somebody chasing you all the time."

The Misfit kept scratching in the ground with the butt of his gun as if he were thinking about it. "Yes'm, somebody is always after you," he murmured.

The grandmother noticed how thin his shoulder blades were just behind his hat because she was standing up looking down on him. "Do you ever pray?" she asked.

He shook his head. All she saw was the black hat wiggle between his shoulder blades. "Nome," he said.

There was a pistol shot from the woods, followed closely by another. Then silence. The old lady's head jerked around. She could hear the wind move through the tree tops like a long satisfied insuck of breath. "Bailey Boy!" she called.

"I was a gospel singer for a while," The Misfit said. "I been most everything. Been in the arm service, both land and sea, at home and abroad, been twict married, been an undertaker, been with

the railroads, plowed Mother Earth, been in a tornado, seen a man burnt alive oncet," and he looked up at the children's mother and the little girl who were sitting close together, their faces white and their eyes glassy; "I even seen a woman flogged," he said.

"Pray, pray," the grandmother began, "pray, pray . . ."

"I never was a bad boy that I remember of," The Misfit said in an almost dreamy voice, "but somewheres along the line I done something wrong and got sent to the penitentiary. I was buried alive," and he looked up and held her attention to him by a steady stare.

"That's when you should have started to pray," she said. "What did you do to get sent to the penitentiary that first time?"

"Turn to the right, it was a wall," The Misfit said, looking up again at the cloudless sky. "Turn to the left, it was a wall. Look up it was a ceiling, look down it was a floor. I forget what I done, lady. I set there and set there, trying to remember what it was I done and I ain't recalled it to this day. Oncet in a while, I would think it was coming to me, but it never come."

"Maybe they put you in by mistake," the old lady said vaguely.

"Nome," he said. "It wasn't no mistake. They had the papers on me."

"You must have stolen something," she said.

The Misfit sneered slightly. "Nobody had nothing I wanted," he said. "It was a head-doctor at the penitentiary said what I had done was kill my daddy but I known that for a lie. My daddy died in nineteen ought nineteen of the epidemic flu and I never had a thing to do with it. He was buried in the Mount Hopewell Baptist churchyard and you can go there and see for yourself."

"If you would pray," the old lady said, "Jesus would help you."

"That's right," The Misfit said.

"Well then, why don't you pray?" she asked trembling with delight suddenly.

"I don't want no hep," he said. "I'm doing all right by myself."

Bobby Lee and Hiram came ambling back from the woods. Bobby Lee was dragging a yellow shirt with bright blue parrots in it.

"Thow me that shirt, Bobby Lee," The Misfit said. The shirt came flying at him and landed on his shoulder and he put it on. The grandmother couldn't name what the shirt reminded her of. "No, lady," The Misfit said while he was buttoning it up, "I found out the crime don't matter. You can do one thing or you can do another, kill a man or take a tire off his car, because sooner or later you're going to forget what it was you done and just be punished for it."

The children's mother had begun to make heaving noises as if she couldn't get her breath. "Lady," he asked, "would you and that little girl like to step off yonder with Bobby Lee and Hiram and join your husband?"

"Yes, thank you," the mother said faintly. Her left arm dangled helplessly and she was holding the baby, who had gone to sleep, in the other. "Hep that lady up, Hiram," The Misfit said as she struggled to climb out of the ditch, "and Bobby Lee, you hold onto that little girl's hand."

"I don't want to hold hands with him," June Star said. "He reminds me of a pig."

The fat boy blushed and laughed and caught her by the arm and pulled her off into the woods after Hiram and her mother.

Alone with The Misfit, the grandmother found that she had lost her voice. There was not a cloud in the sky nor any sun. There was nothing around her but woods. She wanted to tell him that he must pray. She opened and closed her mouth several times before anything came out. Finally she found herself saying, "Jesus, Jesus," meaning, Jesus will help you, but the way she was saying it, it sounded as if she might be cursing.

"Yes'm," The Misfit said as if he agreed. "Jesus thown everything off balance. It was the same case with Him as with me except He hadn't committed any crime and they could prove I had committed one because they had the papers on me. Of course," he said, "they never shown me my papers. That's why I sign myself now. I said long ago, you get you a signature and sign everything you do and keep a copy of it. Then you'll know what you done and you can hold up the crime to the punishment and see do they match and in the end you'll have something to prove you ain't been treated right. I call myself The Misfit," he said, "because I can't make what all I done wrong fit what all I gone through in punishment."

There was a piercing scream from the woods, followed closely by a pistol report. "Does it seem right to you, lady, that one is punished a heap and another ain't punished at all?"

"Jesus!" the old lady cried. "You've got good blood! I know you wouldn't shoot a lady! I know you come from nice people! Pray! Jesus, you ought not to shoot a lady. I'll give you all the money I've got!"

"Lady," The Misfit said, looking beyond her far into the woods, "there never was a body that give the undertaker a tip."

There were two more pistol reports and the grandmother raised her head like a parched old turkey hen crying for water and called, "Bailey Boy, Bailey Boy!" as if her heart would break.

"Jesus was the only One that ever raised the dead," the Misfit continued, "and He shouldn't have done it. He thown everything off balance. If He did what He said, then it's nothing for you to do but thow away everything and follow Him, and if He didn't, then it's nothing for you to do but enjoy the few minutes you got left the best way you can—by killing somebody or burning down his house or doing some other meanness to him. No pleasure but meanness," he said and his voice became almost a snarl.

"Maybe He didn't raise the dead," the old lady mumbled, not knowing what she was saying and feeling so dizzy that she sank down in the ditch with her legs twisted under her.

"I wasn't there so I can't say He didn't," The Misfit said. "I wisht I had of been there," he said, hitting the ground with his fist. "It ain't right I wasn't there because if I had of been there I would of known. Listen lady," he said in a high voice, "if I had of been there I would of known and I wouldn't be like I am now." His voice seemed about to crack and the grandmother's head cleared for an instant. She saw the man's face twisted close to her own as if he were going to cry and she murmured, "Why you're one of my babies. You're one of my own children!" She reached out and touched him on the shoulder. The Misfit sprang back as if a snake had bitten him and shot her three times through the chest. Then he put his gun down on the ground and took off his glasses and began to clean them.

Hiram and Bobby Lee returned from the woods and stood over the ditch, looking down at the grandmother who half sat and half lay in a puddle of blood with her legs crossed under her like a child's and her face smiling up at the cloudless sky.

Without his glasses, The Misfit's eyes were red-rimmed and pale and defenseless-looking. "Take her off and thow her where you thown the others," he said, picking up the cat that was rubbing itself against his leg.

"She was a talker, wasn't she?" Bobby Lee said, sliding down the ditch with a yodel.

"She would of been a good woman," The Misfit said, "if it had been somebody there to shoot her every minute of her life."

"Some fun!" Bobby Lee said.

"Shut up, Bobby Lee," The Misfit said. "It's no real pleasure in life."

WILLIAM STYRON (1925–   )

Born June 11, 1925, in Newport News, Virginia; A.B., Duke University, 1947; studied writing at New School for Social Research; has worked as associate editor for McGraw-Hill; publications are four novels, *Lie Down in Darkness* (1951), *The Long March* (1957), *Set This House on Fire* (1960), and *The Confessions of Nat Turner* (1967), an account of the "only ef- fective, sustained revolt in the annals of American Negro slavery," an excerpt from which we reprint below and which received Pulitzer prize; received Rome fellowship from American Academy of Arts and Letters (1952) and Howells Medal from American Academy of Arts and Letters (1970); member National Institute of Arts and Letters (1966).

From The Confessions of Nat Turner (1967)

We were ready. I knew that the exodus of many of the Baptists of the county to their camp meeting down in Carolina would commence on Thursday the eighteenth of August, and they would not return until the following Wednesday. And so for close on to a week Southampton would be deprived of a large portion of its white population, and the armed enemy would be considerably fewer both in Jerusalem and the outlying countryside. I hit upon Sunday night as the time to begin my assault, largely on the advice of Nelson, who pointed out with his usual shrewdness that Sunday nights were habitually the nights when Negroes went hunting for coon or possum, at least during the leisurely month of August; those evenings always resounded until dawn with a great commotion in the woods—hoots and shouts and the yapping of dogs—and so our own disturbance would be less likely to attract notice. Furthermore, it would be simply easier to assemble on Sunday, normally the Negroes' free day. Seizing an early advantage by slaying all at Travis's, equipping ourselves with his several guns and two horses, we should then be able to proceed along the lower loop of the great "S" I had laid out on the map and (after invading the properties in between and slaughtering all therein) arrive sometime the next day at the middle of the "S" and thus at what I had long since termed my "early objective"—Mrs. Whitehead's home with its rich store of horses, guns, and ammunition. I would have by then a goodly body of troops. Including the Negroes I had "spotted" at the intervening houses (plus two of Miss Caty's boys, Tom and Andrew; them I had easily recruited during my final stay), I calculated that upon leaving Mrs. Whitehead's our force should number more than a score, apart from another four or five whom out of instinct I had not trusted enough to take into my earliest confidence but who I expected would join us when we appeared. Provided that we took the most extreme care to prevent anyone from escaping and raising an alarm, we should be able to sweep the rest of the country and arrive, triumphant, in Jerusalem by noon of the second day, our force swollen into the many hundreds.

Late that Sunday morning my four inmost followers gathered themselves for a final barbecue in the dense woodland ravine beyond my sanctuary. At the last moment, the night before, I had sent Hark up the road to the Reese farm with instructions for him to tell one of the Reese Negroes, Jack, to join the barbecue and so become a member of our initial striking force. I had felt the need for a strong arm to augment our first blow, and Jack fitted the requisite details—weighing well over two hundred pounds and by luck boiling at a high pitch of resentment and wrath: only one week before, Jack's woman, a butter-skinned, almond-eyed beauty, had been sold to a Tennessee trader scrounging quite openly he allowed to planter Reese (and within Jack's hearing), "for likely-looking pussy for gov'mental gentlemen in Nashville." Jack would go with me to the far ends of the earth; certainly he would make quick work of Reese.

All morning and most of the afternoon I withdrew from my followers, remaining near my sanctuary, where I read from my Bible and prayed for the Lord's favor in battle. The weather had become sultry and close, and as I prayed a single locust shrilled somewhere amid the trees, playing like an incessant tormented fiddle-string on my eardrums. After my long prayers I set fire to my tabernacle and stood aside from the clearing as the pine logs which had for so many years sheltered me went up in blue smoke and a roaring and crackling of flames. Then when the ashes had cooled I knelt amid the ruin and made a final prayer, beseeching God for his protection in the coming struggle: *The Lord is my light and my salvation; whom shall I fear? The Lord is the strength of my life; of whom shall I be afraid?*

It was just after I had risen from my knees that I heard a rustling in the underbrush behind me and turned to see the demented, murderous, hate-ravaged, mashed-in face of Will. He said nothing, merely looked at me with his bulging eyes and scratched at his naked black scarred belly below which a pair of gray jeans hung in tatters. I was seized by reasonless fear.

"What you doin' here, boy?" I blurted.

"I seed de smoke. Den I done seed dem niggers down dere in de gully," Will replied coolly. "Dey done gib me some barbecue. I heered dem talkin' 'bout startin' a ruction an' killin' de white folks. When I ax Sam an' Nelson if'n I could jine up dey tol' me to ax you."

"Where you been all these yere weeks?" I asked. "Nat Francis see you an' he'll shoot you dead."

"Don' *shit me* 'bout no Nat Francis," Will retorted. "I shoot *him* now!"

"Where you been?" I repeated.

"Aroun'," he replied. "All aroun'." He shrugged. His eyes caught the light in disks of malign fire, and I felt anew the old dread his presence always caused me, as if I had been suddenly trapped like a fly in the hatred he bore toward all mankind, all

creation. His woolly head was filled with cockleburs. A scar glistened on his black cheek, shiny as an eel cast up on a mud bank. I felt that if I reached out I could almost touch with my fingertips the madness stirring within him, feel a shaggy brute heaving beneath a carapace of scarred black skin. I turned away.

"You git on out of here," I said. "We don' need no more men."

Abruptly, in a single bound from the underbrush, he was at my side. He brandished a knobbed fist beneath my chin. "Don' *shit me*, preacher man!" he said. His voice was the hiss of a cornered cat. "You try an' shit me, preacher man, an' you in *bad* trouble. I isn't run in de woods all dis yere time fo' nothin'. I'se tired of huckaberries. I gwine git me some meat now—*white* meat. I gwine git me some dat white cunt too." For weeks he had hidden in the woods, grubbing for berries and nuts and earthworms—even carrion—stealing an occasional chicken in between times of pursuit by white men and dogs; he had lived like an animal and now, streaked with mud, stinking, fangs bared beneath a nose stepped upon and bent like a flattened spoon, it seemed to me that he *was* an animal—a wicked little weasel or maddened fox—and the blood ran chill in my veins. I felt that he might at any moment leap for my throat. "You shit me, preacher man," he said hoarsely, "an I fix yo' preacher ass! I knock you to yo fuckin' black knees! I isn't gwine hang out in de swamp no mo' eatin' huckaberries. I gwine git me some *meat*. I gwine git me some *blood*. So, preacher man, you better figger dat Will done jined de ruction! You maybe is some fancy talker but you isn't gwine talk Will out'n dat!"

(*After this I saw in the night visions, and behold a beast dreadful and terrible, and strong exceedingly; it devoured and brake in pieces . . .*)

Even as he spoke I knew that I was on the verge of capitulating to him, backing down. I was, to be sure, fearful of him, afraid that I could not control him or bend him to my will; and it was this instinctive mistrust that had caused me months before to eliminate him from my plans. At the same time, it was clear now that if I could channel his brutal fury and somehow keep him in check he would make a potent addition to our striking force. All the privation in the woods had not weakened him but rather had lent to his sinewy body furious zeal and strength; the muscles along his purplish black arms quivered and jumped with murderous power. I saw the vicious scars implanted upon his flanks by Francis's lash and suddenly, though without spirit for the move, I relented.

(*Then I would know the truth of this beast, which was diverse from all the others . . .*)

"Awright," I said, "you can jine up with us. But let me tell you one thing good, nigger. *I* is the boss. *I* runs this show. When I says jump there, you jump right *there*, not in no still or cider press and *not* in no haystack, neither. You ain't goin' to spread no white woman's legs, not on this trip you ain't. We got a long way to go and a pile of things to do, and if the niggers start a-humpin' every white piece in sight we ain't goin' to get half a mile up the road. So brandy and women is *out*. Now come on."

In the ravine my followers, together with the new recruit Jack, had finished the last remnants of their barbecue. Pig bones littered the ground around the ashes of a fire, still smoldering. The five men were reclining amid the cool ferns that rimmed the ravine; they had been talking in soft voices—I heard them as I came down the path with Will—but at my approach they arose and stood silent. Ever since the spring, when I revealed my plans, I had insisted that they pay this deference in my presence, explaining to them patiently that I wished for no obeisance, only absolute obedience; it should not have surprised me, as it did, that they so readily complied—endless years of servility had done their abrasive work. Now as they stood waiting among the afternoon shadows I approached them with an upraised hand and said: "The first shall be last."

"An de last shall be first," they replied, more or less together.

"Report from the First Troop!" I commanded. I used the form of order I had adopted after hearing drills of the mounted militia outside the Jerusalem armory. The First Troop was Henry's responsibility. Because of Henry's deafness I had to repeat the command again, whereupon he stepped forward and said: "First Troop dey all ready. Nathan an' Wilbur bofe is waitin' at de Blunts' place. Davy he waitin' at Mrs. Waters's. Joe he all ready too down at Peter Edwards's. Joe he done got him a bad case of de quinsy, but he put him a hot flannel roun' his th'oat an' he say he 'spect he gwine be all right time we gits dere."

"Report from the Second Troop!" I said.

The Second Troop, a body of six, was Nelson's. "All my niggers is ready an' rarin' to go," he said.

"Austin say he could maybe sneak away from de Bryants' dis evenin' an' jine us at Travis's roun' 'bout nightfall. If'n he can, he gwine bring Bryant's horse."

"Good," I said, "more they is at first the better." Then: "Report from the Third Troop!" Just as I gave this command a tremendous belch broke loose from one of my company, followed by another belch, and I turned quickly to see that it had come from Jack. With a brandy bottle clutched against his black chest he was swaying in a delicate circular motion; his thick lips parted in a self-absorbed grin and he regarded me through eyes misted over with a dreamy film—the gaze oddly studious although utterly blank. In a flood of rage I knocked the brandy bottle from his hand.

"No mo' of *that*, nigger!" I said. "Applejack is *out*, you hear? I catch yo' black mouth at a bottle again and you goin' to get clobbered fo' good. Now *git* on back over there in the trees!"

As Jack sidled away sheepishly, weaving, I called Nelson aside into a small stand of slash pine—a dark place with spongy ground underfoot, swarming with gnats. "Listen!" I said angrily in a low voice. "What's gone wrong with you, Nelson, anyways? You supposed to be my right arm, an' now look what's done happened already! 'Twas *you* been sayin' all along we got to keep the niggers away from the stills and presses! 'Twas *you* been warnin' about drinkin', an' now here you let this yere big black clown get pissy-eyed drunk right in front of yo' nose! What'm I goin' to *do*? If I can't depend on you for a simple thing like that, then we done lost the war before it ever gits goin'!"

"I sorry," he said, licking his lips. His round middle-aged stolid face with its graying stubble and its look of depthless oppression suddenly sagged, became hurt and downcast. "I sorry, Nat," he repeated, "I guess I jes' done forgot 'bout all dat."

"Man, you can't '*low* yo'self to forget," I insisted, boring in hard, "you my chief lieutenant, you know that, you an' Henry. If y'all can't help me keep these niggers in line, then we might as well run up the white flag right now."

"I sorry," he said again, abjectly.

"Awright," I went on, "forget all that now. Just mind from now on to keep them niggers out'n them stills. Now listen here, once last time. Give me the plan for Travis's so we git it straight with no trouble. Remember, we uses the broadax an' the hatchet. Cold steel. No noise. No shootin' till

I give the word. We start shootin' too soon an' they be on top of us before daybreak."

"You right about dat," he declared. "Anyways —" I listened as he outlined for my satisfaction, one last time, our plan of attack on Travis's house. "—Den you an' Henry goes in to get Travis an' Miss Sarah, dat right?" he was saying. "Sam goes to git Miss Maria Pope—"

"Only she ain't there," I put in.

"How come?" he said.

"She done gone up to Petersburg on a visit, this very day," I explained with some regret. It was true: the no-account biddy had had supernatural luck.

"Mm-*huh*," Nelson sighed, "too bad 'bout dat. Sam sho would of fixed dat ol' bitch's wagon."

"Anyway, she gone," I said. "Go ahead."

"Well den," he continued, "I 'spect it best dat Sam stay with you, ain't dat right? An' me an' Hark an' Jack goes up to de attic an' gits Putnam an' dat othah boy. Dis while you takin' keer of Travis. Meanwhiles, Austin he in de barn saddlin' up dem horses. What 'bout Will, Nat? Whar he figgers in?"

"Nem'mine 'bout Will," I replied. "We'll use him as a lookout or somethin'. Nem'mine 'bout Will."

"An' what 'bout dat little baby?" he said. "You done tole me you was gwine tell us what to do 'bout dat business. What?"

I had a sinking sensation deep inside. "Nem'-mine 'bout that either," I answered him, "I goin' to git all that straightened out when the time comes. Maybe we jest let that baby alone, I don't know." I was stung with a sudden, inexplicable annoyance. "Awright," I told him, "go on now and git on back with the men. I'll come down with y'all after dark."

After Nelson had gone back through the trees, leaving me to chew on a piece of pork they had saved for me from their feast, a mood of anxiety began to steal over me, announcing itself with a faint numbness in my extremities, an urgent heartbeat, pain all around the bottom of my stomach. I started to sweat, and I laid the joint of pork aside, uneaten. I had many times prayed to the Lord to spare me this fear, but now it was plain that, unheeding, He was going to allow me to suffer anyway this griping sickness, this clammy apprehension. The waning summer day was humid and still. I could hear nothing except for the gnats' feverish insensate humming around my ears and

a muffled snatch of talk from the Negroes in the ravine. I wondered suddenly if the Lord had also permitted Saul and Gideon and David to endure this fear before their day of warfare: did they too know this demoralizing terror, this tremor in the bones, this whiff of imminent, hovering death? Did they too taste the mouth go dry at thought of the coming slaughter, sense a shiver of despair fly through their restless flesh as they conjured up images of bloodied heads and limbs, gouged-out eyes, the strangled faces of men they had known, enemy and friend, jaws agape in yawns of eternal slumber? Did Saul and Gideon and David, armed and waiting on the eve of the battle, feel their blood change to water in everlasting fright and then long to sheath their swords and turn their backs upon the strife? For an instant panic seized me. I arose as if to flee headlong through the pines, to find some refuge in the distant woods where I would be hid forever beyond the affairs of God and men. *Cease the war, cease the war,* my heart howled. *Run, run,* cried my soul. At that moment my fear was so great that I felt that I was even beyond reach or counsel of the Lord. Then from the ravine I heard Hark's laugh, and my terror subsided. I was trembling like a willow branch. I sat down on the ground and addressed myself to further prayer and contemplation as the shades of evening drew glimmering in . . .

An hour or so after nightfall—at around ten o'clock—I rejoined my men in the ravine. A full moon had risen to the east, something I had anticipated for months and was in keeping with my plans. Since I was confident that we would be on the offensive throughout all the first night (and with good fortune the second night too), the moon would favor us rather than the enemy. For added illumination I had torches made of light-wood stakes and rags soaked in a gallon cask of camphene—turpentine mixed with grain alcohol— that Hark had stolen from the wheel shop. These torches would be used indoors and with care on the march, whenever the moonlight failed us. Our initial weapons were few and simple: three broad-axes and two hatchets, all carefully honed on Travis's grindstone. As I made it clear to Nelson, for purposes of stealth and surprise I wished to avoid gunfire at least until the first daylight, when our assault would have gained a safe momentum. As for the rest of the weapons—guns and swords— the houses along the way would keep us supplied until we reached Mrs. Whitehead's and her gun room, a veritable arsenal. Our enemy had supplied us with all the instruments of his own destruction: now in the ravine Sam lit one torch with a lucifer match from a handful he had stolen from Nathaniel Francis. A ruddy light washed across the grave blank faces of the men, flickered out at my command as I raised my hand and pronounced a final word of damnation upon the enemy: "*Let the angel of the Lord chase them, let them be as chaff before the wind.*" Then in the moonlight their faces receded into shadow and I said: "All right. *Now.* We commence the battle."

In silence and in single file—Nelson leading, I close at his heels—we came out of the woods and into the cotton patch behind Travis's wheel shop. One of the men coughed in the darkness behind me and at that instant two of Travis's cur dogs set up a yapping and howling in the barnyard. I whispered for quiet and we stood stock-still. Then (having foreseen this too) I motioned for Hark to go ahead before us and hush up the dogs: he was on good terms with them and could put them at ease. We waited as Hark stalked across the moonlit field and into the barnyard, waited until the dogs gave a friendly whimper and fell silent. The moon in an opalescent hush came down like dust, like dim daylight, exfoliating from the shop and the barn and sheds elongated shadows—black sharp silhouettes of gable, cornice, roofbeam, door. It was hot and still. There was no sound from the woods save for the katydids' high-pitched *cheer-cheer-cheer-cheer* and the peeping of crickets among the weeds. In the flat blazing yellow of the moonlight Travis's house slumbered, dark within and still as the halls of death. Nelson suddenly laid a hand on my arm and whispered: "*Look dar.*" Then I saw Hark's huge outline detach itself from the shadow of the barn, and still another, angular and tall: this would be Austin, the last member to join my striking force. Twenty-five or so, he had nothing against his present owner, Henry Bryant, who had treated him amiably, but felt nothing for him either and had sworn that he would gladly kill him. He had, however, once gotten into a vicious fight with Sam over a yellow girl in Jerusalem and I only hoped that their enmity would not flare up now again.

I signaled for the other men to follow me and we proceeded in Indian file across the cotton patch, clambered quietly over a stile, and met Hark and Austin in the lee of the wheel shop, out of sight of the house. We were now eight. As I gave my keys to Nelson and whispered instructions to him and Sam, I could hear Travis's hogs grunting sleepily in their pen. Now while Sam and Nelson stole into the shop for a ladder, I told Austin to go to the stable and saddle up Travis's horses, bidding him to work as silently as he could. He was a tall, lanky field hand with a mean black skull-shaped face, agile and quick despite his height, and very powerful. On the way over through the woods from Bryant's his horse had flushed a skunk and he stank to heaven. No sooner had he gone off to the stable than Sam and Nelson returned with the ladder. I joined them in walking across the yard to the side of the house while the other four moved noiselessly ahead in front of us to their station in the shrubbery around the front porch. The skunk stench lingered, hot in the nostrils. The two cur dogs ambled along with us beneath the ladder; their bony flanks were outlined in sharp moonlit relief, and one dragged a game leg. A faint breeze sprang up and the skunk odor was obliterated. The air was filled with the rank fragrance of mimosa. I caught my breath for an instant, thinking of the time so long ago when I had played with a boy named Wash in a mimosa-sweet glade at Turner's Mill. The brief reverie burst like splintered glass. I heard the ladder make a faint *tap-tapping* as they set it against the side of the house and quickly I tested it for balance, gripping it tight by a chest-high rung, then without a word began my climb up the side of the house, past the newly whitewashed clapboard timbers that hurt my eyes in a calcimine lunar glare. Even as I reached the open upper hallway window with its fluttering curtains I heard from the main bedroom a stertorous rasping sound, deep-throated, half-strangled, and recognized it as Travis's snore. (I remembered Miss Sarah's "Land sakes alive, Mister Joe does make a racket but you jus' do learn to live with it after a bit.") I heaved myself silently over the sill into the dark hallway, into the very bosom of the cavernous snoring noise that muffled the sound of my feet as they struck the creaking floor. I was all aslime with sweat beneath my shirt, my mouth had the dry bitter taste of a walnut shell. It's not I who's doing this, I thought abruptly, it is someone else. I tried to spit but my tongue scraped at the roof of my mouth as if against plaster or sand. I found the stairs.

Down on the first floor at the foot of the stairs I lit a candle with a lucifer match, meeting as I did the black wonder-struck face of the servant boy Moses, who had been aroused from his tiny cupboard beneath the stairway by the sound of my feet. His eyes rolled white with alarm. He was stark naked. "What you doin', Nat?" he whispered.

"Just never you mind," I whispered in return. "Go back to sleep."

"What time hit?" he whined.

"Hush up," I replied. "Go to bed."

I removed two rifles and a sword from their rack at my elbow and then crossed to the front door, where I unhooked the inside latch and let the others enter, one by one, from the front porch. Will was last. I put a restraining hand against his chest. "You stay here at the door," I told him, "Be on the lookout if anybody comes. Or tries to get out this way." Then I turned to the others and said in a low voice: "Nelson and Hark and Jack up to the attic and at them two boys. Sam and Henry stay with me." The six of us mounted the stairs.

In the many weeks since that night I have wondered more than once what passed through Travis's sleep-drowned senses when with such violence and rude suddenness we flung ourselves into his presence and made clear those designs which even he, a forbearing and lenient master, must have considered a nightmare possibility but long since put away from his thoughts as one puts away all ideas of remote and improbable ruin. For surely in the watches of the night, like all white men, he must from time to time have flopped over with a sick groan, thinking of those docile laughing creatures down at the rim of the woods, wondering in a flash of mad and terrible illumination what might happen *if—if* like gentle pets turned into rampaging beasts they should take it into their hearts to destroy him, and along with him all his own and dearest and best. *If* by some legerdemain those comical simpleheads known for their childish devotion—so affecting along with their cunning faults and failings—but never known for their manhood or their will or their nerve, should overnight become transformed into something else, into implacable assassins, let us say, wild dogs, avenging executioners—what then would happen to this poor frail flesh? Surely at one time or another Travis, like other white men, had been skewered upon such disquieting fancies, and shuddered in his bed. Just as surely his pathetic faith in history had at last erased these frights and apprehensions from his head, allowing him more often sweet composure and pleasant dreams—for was it not true

that such a cataclysm had never happened? Was it not fact, known even to the humblest yeoman farmer and white-trash squatter and vagabond, that there was something stupidly inert about these people, something abject and sluggish and emasculate that would forever prevent them from so dangerous, so bold and intrepid a course, as it had kept them in meek submission for two centuries and more? Surely Travis put his trust in the fragile testimony of history, reckoning with other white men that since these people in the long-recorded annals of the land had never risen up, they never *would* rise up, and with this faith—rocklike, unswerving, as a banker's faith in dollars—he was able to sleep the sleep of the innocent, all anxieties laid to rest. Thus it may have been disbelief alone that governed his still-drowsing mind, and no recollection of past fears, when he shot upright in his bed next to Miss Sarah, cast his eyes at my broadax in a gaze of dull perplexity, and said: "What you all think you're doin' in here?"

The sharp piney odor of camphene stung in my nose. The air was blurred with greasy smoke. By the light of the torch that Henry held aloft I could see that Miss Sarah too had risen up in bed, but the look on her face was not one of puzzlement, like her husband's, but of naked terror. Instantly she began to moan, a castaway whimper low in the lungs, barely audible. But I turned back to Travis now, and in doing so I realized with wonder that this was the first moment in all the years I had been near him that I had ever looked directly into his eyes. I had heard his voice, known his presence like that of close kin; my eyes had a thousand times glanced off his mouth and cheek and chin but not once encountered his own. It was my fault alone, my primal fear but—no matter. Now I saw that beneath the perplexity, the film of sleep, his eyes were brown and rather melancholy, acquainted with hard toil, remote perhaps, somewhat inflexible but not at all unkind, and I felt that I knew him at last—maybe even now not well but far better than one knows another man by a pair of muddy trousers viewed from the level of the ground, or bare arms and hands, or a disembodied voice. It was as if by encountering those eyes I had found the torn and long-missing fragment of a portrait of this far-off abstract being who possessed my body; his face was complete now and I had a final glimpse of who he truly might be. Whatever else he was, he was a man.

All right, man, I thought.

With this knowledge I raised the broadax above

my head, and felt the weapon shiver there like a reed in a savage wind. *"Thus art thou slain!"* I cried, and the ax descended with a whisper and missed by half a foot, striking not Travis's skull but the headboard between him and his wife. And

at that moment Miss Sarah's soft moan bloomed into a shriek.

In this way I inaugurated my great mission—*Ah Lord!*—I who was to strike the first blow.

JOHN BARTH (1930–   )

Born May 27, 1930, in Cambridge, Maryland; attended Juilliard School of Music and Johns Hopkins University (A.B., 1951; M.A., 1952); taught English at Pennsylvania State University, at the State University of New York at Buffalo, and at Boston University; received National Institute of Arts and Letters grant (1966); publications are the novels *The Floating Opera* (1956), *The End of the Road* (1958), *The Sot-Weed Factor* (1960), a chapter of which we present here, *Giles Goat-Boy* (1966), and *Chimera* (1972); and *Lost in the Funhouse* (short fictions, 1968).

From The Sot-Weed Factor (1960)

The Sot-Weed Factor is the fictional chronicle of the experiences of Ebenezer Cooke (who *was* in real life the first poet laureate of Maryland; see pp. 200–1), as he attempts to make his way in the New World. This chapter treats of the near-drowning of Ebenezer and Bertrand, his servant, just after they have been made to walk the plank by pirates who have captured their ship *The Cyprian.* The strange land on which they come ashore is in fact Maryland.

CHAPTER 16: THE LAUREATE AND BERTRAND, LEFT TO DROWN, ASSUME THEIR NICHES IN THE HEAVENLY PANTHEON

For better or worse, the Laureate found the water warm; the initial shock of immersion was gone by the time he scrabbled to the surface, and when he opened his eyes he saw the lights of the shallop's stern, already some yards distant, slipping steadily away. But despite the moderate temperature of the water his heart froze. He could scarcely comprehend his position: uppermost in his mind was not the imminence of death at all, but that last declaration of Captain Pound's, that the *real* Ebenezer Cooke was in St. Mary's City. Another im-

poster! What marvelous plot, then, was afoot? There was of course the possibility that Burlingame, so clever at disguises, had arrived safely and found it useful to play the poet, the further to confound Coode. But if he had learned of Ebenezer's capture from passengers on the *Poseidon*, as one would suppose, surely he understood that assuming his identity would jeopardize his friend's life; and if instead he believed his ward and protégé dead, it was hard to imagine him having the heart for imposture. No, more likely it was Coode himself who was responsible. And to what evil purpose would his name be turned? Ebenezer shuddered to think. He kicked off his shoes, the better to stay afloat; the precious manuscript too he reluctantly cast away, and began treading water as gently as possible so as to conserve his strength.

But for what? The hopelessness of his circumstances began to make itself clear. Already the shallop's lights were small in the distance, obscured by every wave; soon they would be gone entirely, and there were no other lights. For all he knew he was in mid-Atlantic; certainly he was scores of miles from land, and the odds against another ship's passing even within sight by daylight were so great as to be unthinkable. Moreover, the night was young: there could be no fewer than eight hours before dawn, and though the seas were not rough, he could scarcely hope to survive that long.

"I'faith, I am going to die!" he exclaimed to himself. "There is no other possibility!"

This was a thing he had often pondered. Always, in fact—ever since his boyhood days in St. Giles, when he and Anna played at saints and Caesars or Henry read them stories of the past—he had been fascinated by the aspect of death. How must the cutpurse feel, or the murderer, when he mounts the stairway to the gibbet? The falling climber, when he sees the rock that will dash out brains and bowels? In the night, between their bedchambers, he and his sister had examined every form of death they knew of and compared their particular pains and horrors. They had even experimented with death: once they pressed the point of a letter knife into their breasts as hard as they dared, but neither had had the courage to draw blood; another time each had tried being throttled by the other, to see who could go the farthest without crying out. But the best game of all was to see who could hold his breath longer; to see, specifically, whether either was brave enough to hold it to the point of unconsciousness. Neither had ever reached that goal, but competition carried their efforts to surprising lengths: they would grow mottled, their eyes would bulge, their jaws clench, and finally would come the desperate explosion of breath that left them weak. There was a terrible excitement about this game; no other came so close to the feel of death, especially if in the last frantic moments one imagined himself buried alive, drowning, or otherwise unable to respire at will. That speculation made one wild; the breath roared out. It was a sport too moving, too upsetting, to play often.

It is not surprising, therefore, that however unparalleled in his experience, Ebenezer's present straits were by no means novel to his imagination. Death by drowning was a consideration intimately bound up with the breath-holding game, one they had several times explored. Even the details of stepping from the plank at night, clawing from the depths for air, and watching the stern lights slip away they had considered, and Ebenezer almost knew ahead of time how the end would feel: water catching the throat and stinging the nose, the convulsive coughing to expel it, and the inevitable reinspiration of air where no air was, the suck of water into the lungs; then vertigo, the monstrous pressure in head and chest, and worst of all the frenzy, the anxiety of the body not to die, that total mindless lust for air which must in the last

seconds rend body and soul unspeakably. When he and Anna chose their deaths, drowning—along with burning, slow crushing, and similar protracted agonies—was disqualified at once, and the news that anyone had actually suffered such an end would thrill them to the point of dizziness. But in his heart the fact of death and all these senuous anticipations were to Ebenezer like the facts of life and the facts of history and geography, which, owing to his education and natural proclivities, he looked at always from the *storyteller's* point of view: notionally he admitted its finality; vicariously he sported with its horror; but never, never could he *really* embrace either. That lives are stories, he assumed; that stories end, he allowed—how else could one begin another? But that the storyteller himself must live a particular tale and die——Unthinkable! Unthinkable!

Even now, when he saw not the slightest grounds for hope and knew that the dread two minutes must be on him soon, his despair was as notional, his horror as vicarious, as if he were in his chamber in St. Giles playing the dying-game, or acting out a story in the summerhouse. Bertrand, he assumed with some envy, had strangled on his water and was done with it; there was no reason why he himself should not get it over with at once. But it was not simply fear that kept him paddling; it was also the same constitutional deficiency that had made him unable to draw his own blood, will himself unconscious, or acknowledge in his heart that there really *had* been a Roman Empire. The shallop was gone. Nothing was to be seen except the stars, or heard except the chuckle of water around his neck, yet his spirit was almost calm.

Presently he heard a thrashing in the sea nearby; his heart pounded. " 'Tis a shark!" he thought, and envied Bertrand more than ever. Here was something that had not occurred to him! Why had he not drowned himself at once? The thing splashed nearer; another wave and they were in the same trough. Even as Ebenezer struck out in the opposite direction, his left leg brushed against the monster.

"*Aie!*" he shrieked, and "Nay!" cried the other, equally alarmed.

"Dear God!" said Ebenezer, paddling back. "Is't you, Bertrand?"

"Master Eben! Praise be, I thought 'twas a sea-serpent! Thou'rt not drowned?"

They embraced each other and came up sputtering.

"Get on with't, or we shall be yet!" the poet said, as happy as though his valet had brought a boat. Bertrand observed that it was but a matter of time after all, and Ebenezer replied with feeling that death was not so terrible in company as alone.

"What say you," he proposed, in the same spirit wherewith he had used to propose the breath-game to Anna: "shall we have done with't now, together?"

"In any case 'twill not be many minutes," Bertrand said. "My muscles fail me already."

"Look yonder, how the stars are darkened out." Ebenezer pointed to a lightless stretch on the western horizon. "At least we'll not need to weather that storm."

"Not I, 'tis certain." The valet's breath came hard from the exertion of paddling. "Another minute and I'm done."

"Howe'er you've injured me before, friend, I forgive you. We'll go together."

"Ere the moment comes," Bertrand panted, "I've a thing to say, sir——"

"Not *sir!*" cried the poet. "Think you the sea cares who's master and man?"

"—'tis about my gambling on the *Poseidon*," Bertrand continued.

"Long since forgiven! You lost my money: I pray you had good use of't! What need have I of money now?"

"There's more, sir. You recall the Parson Tubman offered odds——"

"Forgiven! What more's to lose, when you had plucked me clean?"

But Bertrand would not be consoled. "What a wretch I felt, sir! I answered to your name, ate at your place, claimed the honors of your post——"

"Speak no more of't!"

"Methought *'Tis he should tumble Lucy on these sheets, not I*, and then I lost your forty pound as well! And you, sir, in a hammock in the fo'c'sle, suffering in my place!"

"'Tis over and done," Ebenezer said kindly.

"Hear me out, sir! When that fearful storm was done and we were westering, I vowed to myself I'd have ye back that money and more, to pay ye for your hardship. The Parson had got up a new swindle on raising the Virginia Capes, and I took a notion to woo Miss Lucy privily to my cause. Then we would fleece the fleecer!"

"'Tis a charitable resolve, but you'd naught to use for stakes——"

"Nor did some others that had been gulled," Bertrand replied. "They threatened to take a stick

to Tubman for all he was a cleric. But he smelled what was in the wind, and gave 'em a chance to bet on Maryland. They'd but to pledge some property or other——"

"I'faith!" cried Ebenezer. "His cassock frocked a very Jew!"

"He had the papers drawn like any lawyer: we'd but to sign, and we could wager to the value of the property."

"You signed a pledge?" Ebenezer asked incredulously.

"Aye, sir."

"Dear God! To what?"

"To Malden, sir. I——"

"To Malden!" Such was the poet's amazement he forgot to paddle, and the next wave covered his head. When he could speak again he demanded, "Yet surely 'twas no more than a pound or two?"

"I shan't conceal it, sir; 'twas rather more."

"Ten pounds, then? Twenty? Ha, out with't, fellow! What's forty pounds more to a drowning man? What is't to me if you lost a hundred"

"My very thought, sir," Bertrand said faintly; his strength was almost gone. "'Twas e'en for that I told ye, now we're drowning men. Lookee how the dark comes closer! Methinks I hear the sea rising yonder, too, but I shan't be here to feel the rain. Farewell, sir."

"Wait!" Ebenezer cried, and clutched his servant by one arm to help support him.

"I'm done, sir; let me go."

"And I, Bertrand; I shall go with thee! Was't two hundred you lost, pray?"

"'Twas but a pledge, sir," Bertrand said. "Who's to say I lost a farthing? For aught I know thou'rt a wealthy man this moment."

"What did you pledge, man? Three hundred pounds?"

Bertrand had stopped treading water and would have gone under had not Ebenezer, paddling furiously, held him up with one hand by the shirt front.

"What doth it matter, sir? I pledged it all."

"*All!*"

"The grounds, the manor, the sot-weed in the storehouse—Tubman holds it all."

"Pledged my legacy!"

"Prithee let me drown, sir, if ye won't yourself."

"I shall!" said Ebenezer. "Sweet Malden gone? Then farewell, and God forgive you!"

"Farewell, sir!"

"Stay, I am with thee yet!" Master and man embraced each other. "Farewell! Farewell!"

"Farewell!" Bertrand cried again, and they went under. Immediately both fought free and struggled up for air.

"This will not do!" Ebenezer gasped. "Farewell!"

"Farewell!" said Bertrand. Again they embraced and went under, and again fought free.

"I cannot do't," said Bertrand, "though my muscles scarce can move, they bring me up."

"*Adieu*, then," said the poet grimly. "Thy confession gives me strength to die alone. Farewell!"

"Farewell!"

As before, Ebenezer automatically took a deep breath before sinking and so could not do more than put his face under. This time, however, his mind was made up: he blew out the air, bade the world a last farewell, and sank in earnest.

A moment later he was up again, but for a different reason.

"The bottom! I felt the bottom, Bertrand! 'Tis not two fathom deep!"

"Nay!" gasped the valet, who had been near submerged himself. "How can that be, in the middle of the ocean? Haply 'twas a whale or other monster."

"'Twas hard sand bottom!" Ebenezer insisted. He went below again, this time fearlessly, and from a depth of no more than eight feet brought up a fistful of sand for proof.

"Belike a shoal, then," Bertrand said, unimpressed. "As well forty fathom as two; we can't stand up in either. Farewell!"

"Wait! 'Tis no cloud yonder, man, but an ocean isle we've washed to! Those are her cliffs that hide the stars; that sound is the surf against her coast!"

"I cannot reach it."

"You can! 'Tis not two hundred yards to shore, and less to a standing place!" Fearing for his own endurance, he waited no longer for his man to be persuaded, but struck out westwards for the starless sky, and soon heard Bertrand panting and splashing behind. With every stroke his conjecture seemed more likely; the sound of gentle surf grew distant and recognizable, and the dark outline defined itself more sharply.

"If not an isle, at least 'twill be a rock," he called over his shoulder, "and we can wait for passing ships."

After a hundred yards they could swim no farther; happily, Ebenezer found that by standing on tiptoe he could just clear the surface with his chin.

"Very well for you, that are so tall," lamented Bertrand, "but I must perish here in sight of land!"

Ebenezer, however, would hear of no such thing: he instructed the valet to float along behind him, hands on the poet's shoulders for support. It was tedious going, especially for Ebenezer, only the balls of whose feet were on the bottom: the weight behind pulled him off balance at every step, and though Bertrand rode clear, his weight held Ebenezer at a constant depth, so that only between waves could he catch his breath. The manner of their progres was thus: in each trough Ebenezer secured his footing and drew a breath; when the wave came he stroked with both arms from his breast and, with his head under, rode perhaps two feet—one of which would be lost in the slight undertow before he regained his footing. Half an hour, during which they covered no more than forty or fifty feet, was enough to exhaust his strength, but by then the water was just shallow enough for the valet to stand as well. It required another thirty minutes to drag themselves over the remaining distance: had there been breakers they might yet have drowned, but the waves were never more than two feet high, and oftener less than one. At last they reached a pebbly beach and, too fatigued for words, crawled on all fours to the base of the nearby cliff, where they lay some while as if a-swoon.

Presently, however, despite the mildness of the night and the protection provided by the cliff against the westerly breeze, they found their resting-place too cold for comfort and had to search for better shelter until their clothes were dry. They made their way northward along the beach and were fortunate enough to find not far away a place where the high sandstone was cut by a wooded ravine debouching onto the shore. Here tall wheatlike weeds grew between the scrub pines and bayberries; the castaways curled together like animals in a nest and knew no more till after dawn.

It was the sand fleas that roused them at last: scores of sand fleas hopped and crawled all over them—attracted, luckily, not by hunger but by the warmth of their bodies—and tickled them awake.

Ebenezer jumped up and looked unbelievingly about. "Dear God!" he laughed. "I had forgot!"

Bertrand too stood up, and the sand fleas—not really parasites at all—hopped madly in search of cover.

"And I," he said, hoarse from exposure. "I

dreamt I was in London with my Betsy. God pox those vermin for waking me!"

"But we're alive, at that. 'Tis more than anyone expected."

"Thanks to you, sir!" Bertrand fell to his knees before the poet. "'Tis a Catholic saint that saves the man who ruined him!"

"Make me no saint today," Ebenezer said, "or you'll have me a Jesuit tomorrow." But he was flattered nonetheless. "No doubt I had better drowned when Father hears the news!"

Bertrand clasped his hands together. "Many's the wrong I've done ye, sir, that I'll pay in Hell for, anon—nor shall I want company in the fire. But I vow ye a vow this instant I'm your slave fore'er, to do with as ye will, and should we e'er be rescued off this island I shall give my life to gaining back your loss."

The Laureate, embarrassed by these protestations, replied, "I dare not ask it, lest you pledge my soul!" and proposed an immediate search for food. The day was bright, and warm for mid-September; they were chilled through from exposure, and upon brushing the sand from themselves found their joints stiff and every muscle sore from the past night's labors. But their clothes were dry except for the side on which they'd slept, and a little stamping of feet and swinging of arms was enough to start the warm blood coursing. They were without hats, wigs, or shoes, but otherwise adequately clothed in the sturdy garb of seamen. Food, however, they had to find, though Ebenezer longed to explore the island at once: their stomachs rumbled, and they had not much strength. To cook their meal was no great problem: Bertrand had with him the little tinderbox he carried in his pocket for smoking purposes, and though the tinder itself was damp, the flint and steel were as good as new, and the beach afforded driftwood and dry seaweed. Finding something to cook was another matter. The woods no doubt abounded with small game; gulls, kingfishers, rails, and sandpipers scared and flitted along the beach; and there were certainly fish to be caught in the shallows; but they had no implements to hunt with.

Bertrand despaired afresh. "'Tis a passing cruel prank fate plays us, to trade a quick death for a slow!" And despite his recent gratitude, the surliness with which he rejected various proposals for improvising weapons betrayed a certain resentment toward Ebenezer for having saved him. Indeed, he shortly abandoned as hopeless the search for means

and went to gather firewood, declaring his intention to starve at least in relative comfort. Ebenezer, left to his own resources, resolved to walk some distance down the beach, hoping to find inspiration along the way.

It was a long beach. In fact, the island appeared to be of considerable size, for though the shoreline curved out of sight in both directions, its reappearance farther south suggested a cove or bay, perhaps a succession of them; one could not locate the actual curve of the island's perimeter. Of its body nothing could be seen except the line of stratified cliffs, caved by the sea and weathered to various browns and oranges, and the edge trees of the forest that ran back from the precipice—some with half their roots exposed, some already fallen the sixty or a hundred feet to the beach and polished like pewter by salt air and sand. If one scaled those cliffs, what wonders might one see?

Ebenezer had been at sea nearly half a year in all, yet never had he seen it so calm. There was no ground swell at all: only catspaws riffling here and there, and laps of waves not two hands high. As he walked he noticed minnows darting in the shallows and schools of white perch flipping and rippling a few feet out. Crabs, as well, of a sort he had never seen, slid sideways out to safety as he approached; in the water their shells were olive against the yellow sand, but the carapaces he found along the beach were cooked a reddish-orange by the sun.

"Would God I had a net!"

Around a bend just past the place where they had crawled ashore he saw a startling sight—all along the foreshore, below the line of weed and driftwood that marked high tide, were sheets of white paper; others rolled and curled in the rim of the sea. The thought that there might be people on the island made his face burn, not entirely with joy—in fact, it was a curious relief he felt, small but undeniable, when the papers proved to be the tale of Hicktopcake, Laughing King of Accomack; but he could not as yet say plainly what it was that relieved him. He gathered all the pages he could find, though the ink had run so that only an occasional word was legible; they would, when dry, be good for lighting fires.

He started back with them, thinking idly of John Smith's adventures. Did this curious pleasure stem from the fact that he, like Smith, was in *terra incognita*, or was there more to it? He hoped they would find no Indians, at least, like the fearsome fellows Smith had found spearing fish along the shore. . . .

"'Sheart!" he cried aloud, and kissed the wondrous Journal.

An hour later their dinner was on the fire: seven respectable perch, half a foot long after cleaning, roasted on a green laurel turnspit, and on a thin piece of shale such as could be picked up anywhere along the cliffs, four crabs, frankly an experiment, fried in their natural juices. The hard-shelled ones could not be speared, but in pursuit of them Bertrand had found these others—similar in appearance but with shells soft as Spanish kid—brooding in clumps of sea-grass near the shore. Nor did they want for water; in a dozen places along the base of the cliff Ebenezer had found natural springs issuing from what looked like layers of hard clay, whence they ran seawards across the beach on the beds of softer clay one encountered every few hundred feet. One had, indeed, to take care in approaching these springs, for the clay beds were slippery and in places treacherously soft, as Ebenezer learned: without warning one could plunge knee-deep into what looked rock-hard on the surface. But the water was clean and sweet from filtering through the stone, and so cold it stung the teeth.

To get full benefit of the sun they did their cooking on the beach. Bertrand, humbled anew by his master's inspiration, attended the meal; Ebenezer made use of a fallen tree nearby for a back rest and was content to chew upon a reed and regard the sputtering crabs.

"Where do ye fancy we are?" inquired the valet, whose curiosity had returned with his good spirits.

"God knows!" the poet said cheerfully. "'Tis some Atlantic isle, that's sure, and belike not giv'n on the charts, else I doubt me Pound would choose the spot to plank us."

This conjecture pleased the valet mightily. "I have heard tell of the Fortunate Islands, sir; old Twigg at St. Giles was wont to speak of 'em whene'er her gout was paining."

"Well I recall it!" Ebenezer laughed. "Didn't I hear from the cradle how she stood watch all the voyage from Maryland, hoping for a sight of them?"

"Think ye this is the place?"

"I'faith, 'tis fair enough," the poet granted. "But the ocean swarms with isles that man knows naught of. How many times dear Anna and I have

pled with Burlingame to tell of them—Groeland, Helluland, Stokafixa, and the rest! How many fond hours I've pored over Zeno the Venetian, Peter Martyr d'Anghiera, and good Hakluyt's books of voyages! E'en at Cambridge, when I had better done other things, I spent whole evenings over ancient maps and manuscripts. 'Twas there at Magdalene, in the antique Book of Lismore, I saw described the Fortunate Islands dear old Mrs. Twigg yearned for, and read how St. Brendan found them. 'Twas there I learned of Markland, too, the wooded isle; and Frisland and Icaria. Who knows which this might be? Haply 'tis Atlantis risen from the sea, or the Sunken Land of Buss old Frobisher found; haply 'tis Bra, whose women have much pain in bearing children, or magic Daculi, the cradle island, where they go for gentler labor."

"It matters naught to me," said Bertrand, "so we be not killed by salvages. 'Tis a thing I've feared for since we stepped ashore. Did ye read what manner of husbands the wenches have?"

"I've shared your fear," Ebenezer admitted. "Some isles are bare of men; others, like famed Cibola, boast wondrous cities. Some are like Estotiland, whose folk are versed in every art and read from books in Latin; some others are like her neighbor Drogio, where Zeno says the salvages eat their captives."

"Pray Heav'n this is not Drogio!"

"We shall climb to the cliff top when we've eaten," Ebenezer said. "If I can see the island whole, I may be able to name it." He went on to explain that, while the location and size of islands varied widely from map to map, there was some agreement among cartographers as to their shape. "If 'tis in the form of a great crescent, for example, 'twill of necessity be Mayda; if a small one, 'tis doubtless Tanmare, that Peter Martyr spoke of. A large parallelogram would be Antillia; a smaller one Salvagio. A simple rectangle we shall know for Illa Verde, and a pentagon for Reylla. If we find this isle to be a perfect circle, we must look farther for its inland features: if 'tis cut in twain by a river we shall know it for Brazil, but if instead 'tis a kind of ring or annulus about an inland lake, the which hath sundry islets of its own, then Heav'n hath smiled on us as ne'er on Coronado, for 'twill be Cibola, the Isle of the Seven Golden Cities!"

"'Sheart, may we find it so!" said Bertrand, turning the fish to brown. "'Twere not like folk in a golden city to eat up strangers, d'ye think?"

"Nay, 'tis more likely they'll take us for gods

and grant our every pleasure," Ebenezer declared. "Such was the luck of stout Cortez among the Aztecs, that had a town of gold: e'en the Emperor Montezuma bowed to him."

"Marry, I hope and pray 'tis the Isle of Seven Cities, then; I shall have three and you the rest, to make up for losing Malden! Doth the book say aught of the women in these towns, whether they be fat or thin, or fair of face?"

"Naught that I can recall," the poet replied.

"I'God, let us make short work of these fish, sir!" Bertrand urged, sliding them from the laurel spit to the clean-washed slates they had found to eat from. "I cannot wait to see my golden towns!"

"Be not o'erhasty, now; this may not be Cibola after all. For aught we know it may lie in the shape of a human hand, in which case our goose is cooked: Hand-of-Satan hath such a shape, and 'tis one of the *Insule Demonium*—the demons' isles."

This final possibility chastened them sufficiently to do full justice to the perch and soft crabs, which they seasoned with hunger, ate with their fingers, and washed down with clamshellfuls of cold spring water. Then they stuffed an extra soft crab each into their pockets, grease and all, and climbed through the ravine to the top of the cliff, whence to their chagrin they could see no more than open water on one side of them and trees on the other. The sun was still but forty-five degrees above the eastern horizon; there was time for some hours of exploration before they need think of dinner and a shelter for the night.

"What course do ye propose, sir?" Bertrand asked.

"I have a plan," said Ebenezer. "But ere I tell it, what course do *you* propose?"

" 'Tis not for me to say, sir. I'll own I have spoken out of turn before, but that's behind me. Ye have saved my life and forgiven the harm I've done ye; I'll dance to any tune ye call."

Ebenezer acknowledged the propriety of these sentiments, but took issue with them nevertheless. "We are cast here on some God-forsaken isle," he said, "remote from the world of bob-wig and dildo. What sense here hath the title *Poet Laureate*, or the labels *man* and *master*? Thou'rt one man, I another, and there's an end on't."

Bertrand considered this for a moment. "I confess I have my preferences," he said. "If 'twere mine to decide, I'd strike out inland with all haste. Haply we'll find one or two golden cities ere dinnertime."

"We've no certain knowledge this is the Isle of Seven Cities," Ebenezer reminded him, "nor do I relish walking overland without shoes. What *I* propose is that we walk along the shore to learn the length and shape of the island. Haply 'twill identify our find, or show us what manner of people live here, if any. Nay, more, we've paper aplenty here, and charcoal sticks to mark with: we can count our paces to every turn and draw a map as we go."

"That's so," the valet admitted. "But 'twould mean another meal of fish and soft crabs and another night upon the ground. If we make haste inland, haply 'tis golden plates we'll eat from, and sleep in a golden bed, by Heav'n!" His voice grew feverish. "Just fancy us a pair of bloody gods, sir! Wouldn't we get us godlets on their maiden girls and pass the plate come Sunday? 'Tis a better post than Baltimore's paltry sainthood, b'm'faith! I'd not trade places with the Pope!"

"All that may happen yet," Ebenezer said. "On the other hand we might encounter monsters, or salvage Indians that will eat us for dinner. Methinks 'twere wise to scout around somewhat, to get the lay of the land: what do a few days matter to an immortal god?"

The prudence of this plan was undeniable; reluctant as he was to postpone for even a day the joys of being a deity, Bertrand had no mind to be a meal for either cannibals or dragons—both of whose existence he might have been skeptical of in London, but not here—and so agreed to it readily, if not enthusiastically. They made their way down to the beach again, marked their point of departure with a stake to which was tied a strip of rag from Bertrand's shirt, and struck out northward along the shore, Ebenezer counting paces as they walked.

He had not reached two hundred when Bertrand caught his arm.

"Hark!" he whispered. "Listen yonder!"

They stood still. From behind a fallen tree not far ahead, a hackle-raising sound came down on the breeze: it was half a moan, half a tuneless chant, lugubrious and wild.

"Let us flee!" Bertrand whispered. " 'Tis one of those monsters!"

"Nay," Ebenezer said, his skin a-prickle. "That is no beast."

"A hungry salvage, then; come on!"

The cry floated down to them again.

"Methinks 'tis the sound of pain, not of hunger, Bertrand. Some wight lies hurt by yonder log."

"God save him, then!" the valet cried. "If we go near, his friends will leap us from behind and make a meal of us."

"You'll give up your post so lightly?" Ebenezer teased. "What sort of god are you, that will not aid his votaries?"

A third time came the pitiable sound, and though the valet stood too terrified to move, Ebenezer approached the fallen tree and peered over it. A naked black man lay there on the sand, face down, his wrists and ankles bound; his back was striped with the healed scars of many floggings, and from myriad cuts and scratches on his legs he bled upon the sand. He was a tall, well-muscled man in the prime of life, but obviously exhausted; his skin was wet, and a spotty trail of blood ran from where he lay to the water's edge. Even as Ebenezer watched him from above, unobserved, he lifted his head with a mighty effort and resumed the woeful incantation, chanting in a savage-sounding tongue.

"Come hither!" the poet called to Bertrand, and scrambled over the log. The Negro wrenched over on his side and shrank against the tree trunk, regarding the newcomer wildly. He was a prepossessing fellow with high cheekbones and forehead, massive browbones over his great white eyes, a nose splayed flat against his face, and a scalp shaved nearly bald and scarified—like his cheeks, forehead, and upper arms—in strange designs.

"God in Heaven!" Bertrand cried on seeing him. The black man's eyes rolled in his direction. " 'Tis a regular salvage!"

"His hands are bound behind him, and he's hurt from crawling over the stones."

"Run, then! He'll ne'er catch up with us!"

"On the contrary," said the Laureate, and turning to the black man he said loudly and distinctly, *"Let-me-untie-the-ropes."*

His answer was a string of exotic gibberish; the black man clearly expected them to kill him momently.

"Nay, nay," Ebenezer protested.

"Prithee do not do't, sir!" said Bertrand. "The wretch will leap on ye the minute he's free! Think ye these salvages know aught of gratitude?"

Ebenezer shrugged. "They could know no less of't than some others. Hath he not been thrown, like us, into the sea to die and made his way by main strength to this shore? *I-am-the-Poet-Laureate-of-Maryland,"* he declared to the black man; *"I-will-not-harm-you."* To illustrate he brandished a stick as though to strike with it, but snapped it over his knee instead and flung it away, shaking

his head and smiling. He pointed to Bertrand and himself, flung his arm cordially about the valet's shoulders and said *"This-man-and-I-are-friends. You"*—he pointed to all three in turn—*"shall-be-our-friend-as-well."*

The man seemed still to be fearful, but his eyes showed more suspicion now than dread. When Ebenezer forcibly moved behind him to release his hands and Bertrand, at his master's insistence, reluctantly went to work on the ropes that bound his feet, the fellow whimpered.

Ebenezer patted his shoulder. "Have no fear, friend."

It took some labor to undo the ropes, for the knots were swollen from the water and pulled tight by the captive's exertions.

"Whose prisoner do ye take him for?" asked Bertrand. "My guess is, he's one of those *human sacrifices* ye told me of, that the folk in golden cities use in lieu of money on the Sabbath."

"That may well be," the poet agreed. "His captors must in sooth be clever men, and no mere salvages, else they ne'er could make such fine stout rope or tie such wondrous hitches in't. Haply they were ferrying him to the slaughter when he escaped; or belike 'twas some sea-god he was meant for. Confound these knots!"

"In any case," said Bertrand, " 'twill scarcely please 'em to learn we set him loose. 'Tis like stealing from the collection plate in church."

"They need not know of't. Besides, we are their rightful gods, are we not? What we do with our offerings is our own affair."

This last, to be sure, he spoke in jest. They loosened the final knots and retreated a few paces for safety's sake, not certain what the man would do.

"We'll run in different directions," Ebenezer said. "When he takes out after one, the other will pursue him from behind."

The black shook off the loosened bonds, still looking warily about, and rose with difficulty to his feet. Then, as if realizing that he was free, he stretched his limbs, grinned mightily, raised his arms to the sun, and delivered a brief harangue in its direction, interspersing his address with gestures in their direction.

"Look at the size of him!" Bertrand marveled. "Not e'en Boabdil was so made!"

Ebenezer frowned at mention of the Moor. "Methinks he's speaking to the sun now: belike 'tis a prayer of thanks."

"He is a very percheron stud!"

Then, to their considerable discomfort, the fellow ended his speech and turned to face them; even took a step towards them.

"Run!" cried Bertrand.

But no violence was offered them; instead, the black prostrated himself at their feet and with muttered reverences embraced their ankles each in turn; nor would he rise when done, but knelt with forehead on the sand.

" 'Sbody, sir! What doth this signify?"

"I would not say for certain," Ebenezer replied, "but it seems to me you have what erst you wished: This wight hath bid his farewells to the sun and taken us for his gods."

And so indeed it seemed; the man moved not a muscle, but remained in his attitude of worship, clearly awaiting his benefactors' pleasure.

"I'faith," the valet said uncomfortably. "We did not ask for this! What in Heav'n would he have us do?"

"Who knows?" the poet answered. "I never was a god till now. We gave him his life, and so he's ours to bless or bastinado, I suppose." He sighed. "In any case let's bid him rise ere he takes a backache: no god keeps men upon their knees forever."

Poetry

In its first form this display, like that of prose from 1945 to 1973, was much longer, but pressure on space again necessitated a drastic reduction. After much soul-searching, the editors settled on the principle that no poet under fifty at the year of publication of this book—that is, no writer born after 1923 —would be included (except for Sylvia Plath, who, being dead, is outside of time).

To some extent this distinction is a natural one. On the one hand, the poets represented here have achieved their reputations since 1945, and, on the other, though many are still active, their poetic identities are, for better or worse, rather clearly established. As for those poets who are under fifty, most are in the full swing of development, are changing from volume to volume, and are reaching out for new possibilities. There is in train a rich, complex, fluctuating, and often contradictory body of work, not to be illustrated in small compass. Its excitement is, in large part, precisely in this air of change and exploration, and any selection made this year would likely seem very inadequate by the next.

RICHARD EBERHART (1904–   )

Born April 5, 1904, in Austin, Minnesota; studied at University of Minnesota; Dartmouth (B.A.); and St. John's College, Cambridge (B.A., M.A.); further study at Harvard Graduate School; military service in the navy during Second World War; since the war has pursued, in addition to writing, careers in business and teaching, serving on faculties of Wheaton, Princeton, Dartmouth, and the University of Connecticut, as well as spending three years (1959–61) as Consultant in Poetry to the Library of Congress; recipient of numerous prizes and awards, including the Shelley Memorial Award of the Poetry Society of America, the Harriet Monroe Award from *Poetry* magazine, the Pulitzer prize (1966), and a grant from National Institute of Arts and Letters (1955); member National Institute of Arts and Letters (1960); volumes of poetry include *A Bravery of Earth* (1930), *Poems, New and Selected* (1944), *Selected Poems* (1951), *Undercliff: Poems, 1946–1953* (1953), *Collected Poems, 1930–1960* (1960), *Selected Poems, 1930–1965* (1965), *Thirty-One Sonnets* (1967), and *Shifts of Being* (1968); other publications include *Collected Verse Plays* (1962) and, with Selden Rodman, *War and the Poet* (1945), an anthology.

The Groundhog (1936)

In June, amid the golden fields,
I saw a groundhog lying dead.
Dead lay he; my senses shook,
And mind outshot our naked frailty.
There lowly in the vigorous summer
His form began its senseless change,
And made my senses waver dim
Seeing nature ferocious in him.
Inspecting close his maggots' might
And seething cauldron of his being,   10
Half with loathing, half with a strange love,
I poked him with an angry stick.
The fever arose, became a flame
And Vigour circumscribed the skies,
Immense energy in the sun,
And through my frame a sunless trembling.
My stick had done nor good nor harm.
Then stood I silent in the day
Watching the object, as before;
And kept my reverence for knowledge   20
Trying for control, to be still,
To quell the passion of the blood;
Until I had bent down on my knees
Praying for joy in the sight of decay.

And so I left; and I returned
In Autumn strict of eye, to see
The sap gone out of the groundhog,
But the bony sodden hulk remained.
But the year had lost its meaning,
And in intellectual chains   30
I lost both love and loathing,
Mured up in the wall of wisdom.
Another summer took the fields again
Massive and burning, full of life,
But when I chanced upon the spot
There was only a little hair left,
And bones bleaching in the sunlight
Beautiful as architecture;
I watched them like a geometer,
And cut a walking stick from a birch.   40
It has been three years, now.
There is no sign of the groundhog.
I stood there in the whirling summer,
My hand capped a withered heart,
And thought of China and of Greece,
Of Alexander in his tent;
Of Montaigne in his tower,
Of Saint Theresa in her wild lament.

In a Hard Intellectual Light (1936)

In a hard intellectual light
I will kill all delight,
And I will build a citadel
Too beautiful to tell

O too austere to tell
And far too beautiful to see,
Whose evident distance
I will call the best of me.

And this light of intellect
Will shine on all my desires,   10
It will my flesh protect

And flare my bold constant fires,

For the hard intellectual light
Will lay the flesh with nails.
And it will keep the world bright
And closed the body's soft jails.

And from this fair edifice
I shall see, as my eyes blaze,
The moral grandeur of man
Animating all his days.   20

And peace will marry purpose,

And purity married to grace
Will make the human absolute
As sweet as the human face.

Until my hard vision blears,
And Poverty and Death return
In organ music like the years,

Making the spirit leap, and burn

For the hard intellectual light
That kills all delight   30
And brings the solemn, inward pain
Of truth into the heart again.

Where Are Those High and Haunting Skies (1936)

Where are those high and haunting skies,
Higher than the see-through wind? Where are
The rocky springs beyond desire? And where
The sudden source of purity?

Now they are gone again. Though world
Decrease the wraith-like eye so holy,

And bring a summer in, and with it folly,
Though the senses bless and quell,

I would not with such blessings be beguiled.
But seek an image far more dear. Oh where   10
Has gone that madness wild? Where stays
The abrupt essence and the final shield?

In Prisons of Established Craze (1940)

In prisons of established craze
Hear the sane tread without noise
Whose songs no iron walls will raze
Though hearts are as of girls or boys.
By the waters burning clear
Where sheds of men are only seen,
Accept eloquent time, and revere
The silence of the great machine.

On the sweet earth green and moist
When vainglorious cities magnify,   10
The senseless dissonance will foist
As witless on the shining sky.
There is some stealth in rhythm yet
Albeit and even breath is not.
In the mind is a gauge set,
Lest the blood spill, and blot.

The Goal of Intellectual Man (1940)

The goal of intellectual man
Striving to do what he can
To bring down out of uncreated light
Illumination to our night

Is not possession of the fire
Annihilation of his own desire
To the source a secret soaring
And all his self outpouring

Nor is it an imageless place
Wherein there is no human face   10

Nor laws, nor hierarchies, nor dooms
And only the cold weight of the tomb

But it is human love, love
Concrete, specific, in a natural move
Gathering goodness, it is free
In the blood as in the mind's harmony,

It is love discoverable here
Difficult, dangerous, pure, clear,
The truth of the positive hour
Composing all of human power.   20

If I Could Only Live at the Pitch That Is Near Madness (1940)

If I could only live at the pitch that is near
   madness
When everything is as it was in my childhood

Violent, vivid, and of infinite possibility:
That the sun and the moon broke over my
   head.

Then I cast time out of the trees and fields,
Then I stood immaculate in the Ego;
Then I eyed the world with all delight,
Reality was the perfection of my sight.

And time has big handles on the hands,
Fields and trees a way of being themselves.   10

I saw battalions of the race of mankind
Standing stolid, demanding a moral answer.

I gave the moral answer and I died
And into a realm of complexity came
Where nothing is possible but necessity
And the truth wailing there like a red babe.

I Walked Out to the Graveyard to See the Dead (1940)

I walked out to the graveyard to see the dead
The iron gates were locked, I couldn't get in,
A golden pheasant on the dark fir boughs
Looked with fearful method at the sunset,

Said I, Sir bird, wink no more at me
I have had enough of my dark eye-smarting,
I cannot adore you, nor do I praise you,

But assign you to the rafters of Montaigne.

Who talks with the Absolute salutes a Shadow.
Who seeks himself shall lose himself;   10
And the golden pheasants are no help
And action must be learned from the love of
    man.

The Fury of Aerial Bombardment (1947)

You would think the fury of aerial
    bombardment
Would rouse God to relent; the infinite spaces
Are still silent. He looks on shock-pried faces.
History, even, does not know what is meant.

You would feel that after so many centuries
God would give man to repent; yet he can kill
As Cain could, but with multitudinous will,
No farther advanced than in his ancient furies.

Was man made stupid to see his own
    stupidity?

Is God by definition indifferent, beyond us all?   10
Is the eternal truth man's fighting soul
Wherein the Beast ravens in its own avidity?

Of Van Wettering I speak, and Averill,
Names on a list, whose faces I do not recall
But they are gone to early death, who late in
    school
Distinguished the belt feed lever from the belt
    holding pawl.

The Ides of March (1968)

As I was riding through New England
Along about the Ides of March
I passed by an ancient graveyard
And looked hard at the stones:

It was the deepest look I ever gave,
It was a look I had given long ago,
The most intimate and the most personal,
For I wondered what I signified.

I could not see my next connection,
Nor any of the loves I have in life   10
As divorced from that immaculate glimpse
Of the permanent end of human being.

The car bore on through the countryside,
Plunging in meshes of society,
We were going to meet our friends in the
    world,
In the next connection of belief and delight.

We were going to meet the world incarnate
Without reference to the rigors or Ides of
    March;
As we slide through the freshening Springtide
We faintly apprehended the fatal glance.   20

It is that glance of the eternal judgment
Of the silence of the manifold gravestones

Frightens me as we seize in love and belief
The love not to ask what is our ultimate end.

As I was riding through New England

Along about the Ides of March
I was the essence of the questioner,
Only the glance of the gravestones answered
   me.

STANLEY KUNITZ (1905–   )

Born July 29, 1905, in Worcester, Massachusetts; A.B. from Harvard (1926), M.A. from Harvard (1927); has worked in publishing and compiling literary-biographical reference works (with Howard Haycraft), and translating Russian poetry, as well as teaching at Bennington, Columbia, and Yale; volumes of poetry are *Intellectual Things* (1930), *Passport to War* (1944), *Selected Poems: 1928–1958* (1958, for which he received Pulitzer prize), and *The Testing-Tree* (1971); received grant from National Institute of Arts and Letters (1959); member National Institute of Arts and Letters (1963); Chancellor, Academy of American Poets.

The Testing-Tree (1971)

1

On my way home from school
   up tribal Providence Hill
      past the Academy ballpark
where I could never hope to play
   I scuffed in the drainage ditch
      among the sodden seethe of leaves
hunting for perfect stones
   rolled out of glacial time
      into my pitcher's hand;
then sprinted lickety-   10
   split on my magic Keds
      from a crouching start,
scarcely touching the ground
   with my flying skin
      as I poured it on
for the prize of the mastery
   over that stretch of road,
      with no one no where to deny
when I flung myself down
   that on the given course   20
      I was the world's fastest human.

2

Around the bend
   that tried to loop me home
      dawdling came natural

across a nettled field
   riddled with rabbit-life
      where the bees sank sugar-wells
in the trunks of the maples
   and a stringy old lilac
      more than two stories tall   30
blazing with mildew
   remembered a door in the
      long teeth of the woods.
All of it happened slow:
   brushing the stickseed off,
      wading through jewelweed
strangled by angel's hair,
   spotting the print of the deer
      and the red fox's scats.

Once I owned the key   40
   to an umbrageous trail
      thickened with mosses
where flickering presences
   gave me right of passage
      as I followed in the steps
of straight-backed Massassoit
   soundlessly heel-and-toe
      practicing my Indian walk.

3

Past the abandoned quarry

where the pale sun bobbed 50
    in the sump of the granite,
past copperhead ledge,
    where the ferns gave foothold,
        I walked, deliberate,
on to the clearing,
    with the stones in my pocket
        changing to oracles
and my coiled ear tuned
    to the slightest leaf-stir.
        I had kept my appointment. 60
There I stood in the shadow,
    at fifty measured paces,
        of the inexhaustible oak,
tyrant and target,
    Jehovah of acorns,
        watchtower of the thunders,
that locked King Philip's War
    in its annulated core
        under the cut of my name.
Father wherever you are 70
    I have only three throws
        bless my good right arm.
In the haze of afternoon,
    while the air flowed saffron,
        I played my game for keeps—
for love, for poetry,
    and for eternal life—
        after the trials of summer.

4

In the recurring dream

my mother stands 80
    in her bridal gown
under the burning lilac,
    with Bernard Shaw and Bertie
        Russell kissing her hands;
the house behind her is in ruins;
    she is wearing an owl's face
        and makes barking noises.
Her minatory finger points.
    I pass through the cardboard doorway
        askew in the field 90
and peer down a well
    where an albino walrus huffs.
        He has the gentlest eyes.
If the dirt keeps sifting in,
    staining the water yellow,
        why should I be blamed?
Never try to explain.
    That single Model A
        sputtering up the grade
unfurled a highway behind 100
    where the tanks maneuver,
        revolving their turrets.
In a murderous time
    the heart breaks and breaks
        and lives by breaking.
It is necessary to go
    through dark and deeper dark
        and not to turn.
I am looking for the trail.
    Where is my testing-tree? 110
        Give me back my stones!

Around Pastor Bonhoeffer (1971)

THE PLOT AGAINST HITLER

Jittery, missing their cues,
Bach's glory jailed in their throats,
they were clustered round the piano
in the Biedermeier parlor,
sisters and brothers
and their brothers by marriage,
rehearsing a cantata
for Papa's seventy-fifth birthday.
Kyrie eleison: Night
like no other night, plotted 10
and palmed,
omega of terror,
packed like a bullet
in the triggered chamber.

Surely the men had arrived at their stations.
Through the staves of the music
he saw their target strutting,
baring its malignant heart.
Lord, let the phone ring!
Let the phone ring! 20

NEXT TO LAST THINGS

Slime, in the grains of the State,
like smut in the corn,
from the top infected.
Hatred made law,
wolves bred out of maggots
rolling in blood,

and the seal of the church ravished
to receive the crooked sign.
All the steeples were burning.
In the chapel of his ear   30
he had heard the midnight bells
jangling: *if you permit*
this evil, what is the good
of the good of your life?
And he forsook the last things,
the dear inviolable mysteries—
Plato's lamp, passed from the hand
of saint to saint—
that he might risk his soul in the streets,
where the things given   40
are only next to last;
in God's name cheating, pretending,
playing the double agent,
choosing to trade
the prayer for the deed,
and the deed most vile.
I am a liar and a traitor.

THE EXTERMINATION CAMP

Through the half-open door of the hut
the camp doctor saw him kneeling,
with his hands quietly folded.   50
"I was most deeply moved by the way
this lovable man prayed,
so devout and so certain
that God heard his prayer."
Round-faced, bespectacled, mild,
candid with costly grace,
he walked toward the gallows
and did not falter.
Oh but he knew the Hangman!
Only a few steps more   60
and he would enter the arcanum
where the Master
would take him by the shoulder,
as He does at each encounter,
and turn him round
to face his brothers in the world.

River Road (1971)

That year of the cloud, when my marriage
    failed,
I slept in a chair, by the flagstone hearth,
fighting my sleep,
and one night saw a Hessian soldier
stand at attention there in full
regalia, till his head broke into flames.
My only other callers were the FBI
sent to investigate me as a Russian spy
by patriotic neighbors on the river road;
and flying squirrels parachuting from the elms   10
who squeaked in rodent heat between the
    walls
and upstairs rumbled at their nutty games.
I never dared open the attic door.
Even my nervous Leghorns joined the act,
indulging their taste for chicken from behind.
A glazed look swam into the survivor's eyes;
they caught a sort of dancing-sickness,
a variation of the blind staggers,
that hunched their narrow backs, and struck
a stiffened wing akimbo,   20
as round and round the poultry yard
they flapped and dropped and flapped again.
The county agent shook his head:
not one of them was spared the cyanide.

That year of the cloud, when my marriage
    failed,
I paced up and down the bottom-fields,
tamping the mud-puddled nurslings in
with a sharp blow of the heel
timed to the chop-chop of the hoe:
red pine and white, larch, balsam fir,   30
one stride apart, two hundred to the row,
until I heard from Rossiter's woods
the downward spiral of a veery's song
unwinding on the eve of war.

Lord! Lord! who has lived so long?
Count it ten thousand trees ago,
five houses and ten thousand trees,
since the swallows exploded from Bowman
    Tower
over the place where the hermit sang,
while I held a fantail of squirming roots   40
that kissed the palm of my dirty hand,
as if in reply to a bird.
The stranger who hammers No Trespass signs
to the staghorn sumac along the road
must think he owns this property.
I park my car below the curve
and climbing over the tumbled stones
where the wild foxgrape perseveres,
I walk into the woods I made,
my dark and resinous, blistered land,   50
through the deep litter of the years.

ROBERT PENN WARREN (1905–   )

Born April 24, 1905, in Guthrie, Kentucky; graduated from Vanderbilt University (1925); M.A. University of California, further graduate work at Yale University and Oxford as a Rhodes Scholar (B.Litt., 1930); as well as poetry has published nine novels, including *All the King's Men* (1946) and, most recently, *Meet Me in the Green Glen* (1971), short stories, a play, critical essays, and two studies of race relations in America; has taught at various universities, retiring in 1973 as Professor of English at Yale; in 1944–45 was Consultant in Poetry to the Library of Congress; received Pulitzer prize for fiction (*All the King's Men*, 1946) and for poetry (*Promises*, 1957), latter volume also awarded Edna St. Vincent Millay Prize of the Poetry Society of America and National Book Award; received Bollingen Prize in poetry (1967) for *Selected Poems; New and Old, 1923–1966*, and National Medal for Literature (1970); Shelley Memorial Award (1943); Chancellor, American Academy of Poets; member National Institute of Arts and Letters (1950) and American Academy of Arts and Letters (1959); other volumes of poetry include *Thirty-Six Poems* (1935), *Incarnations, Poems 1966–1968* (1968), and *Audubon: A Vision* (1969), which received Van Wyck Brooks Award for Poetry and which we present here.

Audubon: A Vision (1969)

Jean Jacques Audubon, whose name was anglicized when, in his youth, he was sent to America, was early instructed in the official version of his identity: that he was the son of the sea captain Jean Audubon and a first wife, who died shortly after his birth in Santo Domingo, and that the woman who brought him up in France was a second wife. Actually, he was the son of Jean Audubon and his mistress during the period when Jean Audubon was a merchant and slave-dealer in Santo Domingo, and the woman who raised him was the wife his father had left behind him in France while he was off making his fortune. By the age of ten Audubon knew the true story, but prompted, it would seem, by a variety of impulses, including some sound practical ones, he encouraged the other version, along with a number of flattering embellishments. He was, indeed, a fantasist of talent, but even without his help legends accreted about him. The most famous one—that he was the lost Dauphin of France, the son of the feckless Louis XVI and Marie Antoinette—did not, in fact, enter the picture until after his death, in 1851.

I. WAS NOT THE LOST DAUPHIN

[A]

Was not the lost dauphin, though handsome
   was only
Base-born and not even able
To make a decent living, was only
Himself, Jean Jacques, and his passion—what
Is man but his passion?

Saw,
Eastward and over the cypress swamp, the
   dawn,
Redder than meat, break;
And the large bird,
Long neck outthrust, wings crooked to scull
   air, moved

In a slow calligraphy, crank, flat, and black
   against   10
The color of God's blood spilt, as though
Pulled by a string.

                  Saw
It proceed across the inflamed distance.

Moccasins set in hoar frost, eyes fixed on the
   bird,
Thought: "On that sky it is black."
Thought: "In my mind it is white."
Thinking: "*Ardea occidentalis*, heron, the
   great one."

Dawn: his heart shook in the tension of the
   world.

Dawn: and what is your passion?

             [B]
October: and the bear,   20
Daft in the honey-light, yawns.

The bear's tongue, pink as a baby's, out-crisps
   to the curled tip.
It bleeds the black blood of the blueberry.

The teeth are more importantly white
Than has ever been imagined.

The bear feels his own fat
Sweeten, like a drowse, deep to the bone.

Bemused, above the fume of ruined blueberries,
The last bee hums.

The wings, like mica, glint   30
In the sunlight.

He leans on his gun. Thinks
How thin is the membrane between himself
   and the world.

II. THE DREAM HE NEVER KNEW THE END OF

             [A]
Shank-end of day, spit of snow, the call,
A crow, sweet in distance, then sudden,
The clearing: among stumps, ruined corn-
   stalks yet standing, the spot
Like a wound rubbed raw in the vast pelt of
   the forest. There
Is the cabin, a huddle of logs with no calcu-
   lation or craft:

The human filth, the human hope.

                Smoke,
From the mud-and-stick chimney, in that
   air, greasily   40
Brims, cannot lift, bellies the ridgepole, ravels
White, thin, down the shakes, like sputum.

              He stands,
Leans on his gun, stares at the smoke, thinks:
   "Punk-wood."
Thinks: "Dead-fall half-rotten." Too sloven,
That is, to even set axe to clean wood.

              His foot,
On the trod mire by the door, crackles
The night-ice already there forming. His
   hand
Lifts, hangs. In imagination, his nostrils
   already
Know the stench of that lair beyond
The door-puncheons. The dog   50
Presses its head against his knee. The hand
Strikes wood. No answer. He halloos. Then
   the voice.

             [B]
What should he recognize? The nameless
   face
In the dream of some pre-dawn cock-crow—
   about to say what,
Do what? The dregs
Of all nightmare are the same, and we call it
Life. He knows that much, being a man,
And knows that the dregs of all life are
   nightmare.

Unless.

Unless what?   60

             [C]
The face, in the air, hangs. Large,
Raw-hewn, strong-beaked, the haired mole
Near the nose, to the left, and the left side
   by firelight
Glazed red, the right in shadow, and under
   the tumble and tangle
Of dark hair on that head, and under the
   coarse eyebrows,
The eyes, dark, glint as from the unspecifiable
Darkness of a cave. It is a woman.

She is tall, taller than he.
Against the gray skirt, her hands hang.

"Ye wants to spend the night? Kin ye pay?   70
Well, mought as well stay then, done got
  one a-ready,
And leastwise, ye don't stink like no Injun."

[D]

The Indian,
Hunched by the hearth, lifts his head, looks
  up, but
From one eye only, the other
An aperture below which blood and mucus
  hang, thickening slow.

"Yeah, a arrow jounced back off his
  bowstring.
Durn fool—and him a Injun." She laughs.

                    The Indian's head sinks.
So he turns, drops his pack in a corner on
  bearskin, props
The gun there. Comes back to the fire. Takes
  his watch out.   80
Draws it bright, on the thong-loop, from
  under his hunter's-frock.
It is gold, it lives in his hand in the firelight,
  and the woman's
Hand reaches out. She wants it. She hangs it
  about her neck.

And near it the great hands hover delicately
As though it might fall, they quiver like
  moth-wings, her eyes
Are fixed downward, as though in shyness,
  on that gleam, and her face
Is sweet in an outrage of sweetness, so that
His gut twists cold. He cannot bear what he
  sees.

Her body sways like a willow in spring wind.
  Like a girl.

The time comes to take back the watch. He
  takes it.
And as she, sullen and sunken, fixes the food,   90
  he becomes aware
That the live eye of the Indian is secretly on
  him, and soundlessly
The lips move, and when her back is turned,
  the Indian
Draws a finger, in delicious retardation,
  across his own throat.

After food, and scraps for his dog, he lies
  down:
In the corner, on bearskins, which are not
  well cured,

And stink, the gun by his side, primed and   70
  cocked.

Under his hand he feels the breathing of the
  dog.

The woman hulks by the fire. He hears the
  jug slosh.

[E]

The sons come in from the night, two, and
  are   100
The sons she would have. Through slit lids
He watches. Thinks: "Now."

                    The sons
Hunker down by the fire, block the firelight,
  cram food
Into their large mouths, where teeth
Grind in the hot darkness, their breathing
Is heavy like sleep, he wants to sleep, but
The head of the woman leans at them. The
  heads
Are together in firelight.

He hears the jug slosh.

                    Then hears,
Like the whisper and *whish* of silk, that other   110
Sound, like a sound of sleep, but he does not
Know what it is. Then knows, for,
Against firelight, he sees the face of the
  woman
Lean over, and the lips purse sweet as to
  bestow a kiss, but
This is not true, and the great glob of spit
Hangs there, glittering, before she lets it fall.

The spit is what softens like silk the passage
  of steel
On the fine-grained stone. It whispers.

When she rises, she will hold it in her hand.

[F]

With no sound, she rises. She holds it in her
  hand.   120
Behind her the sons rise like shadow. The
  Indian
Snores.

        He thinks: "Now."

                    And knows

He has entered the tale, knows
He has entered the dark hovel

In the forest where trees have eyes, knows it
  is the tale
They told him when he was a child, knows it
Is the dream he had in childhood but never
Knew the end of, only
The scream.

[G]

But no scream now, and under his hand   130
The dog lies taut, waiting. And he, too,
  knows
What he must do, do soon, and therefore
Does not understand why now a lassitude
Sweetens his limbs, or why, even in this
  moment
Of fear—or is it fear?—the saliva
In his mouth tastes sweet.

"Now, now!" the voice in his head cries out,
  but
Everything seems far away, and small.

He cannot think what guilt unmans him, or
Why he should find the punishment so
  precious.   140

It is too late. Oh, oh, the world!

Tell me the name of the world.

[H]

The door bursts open, and the travelers
  enter:
Three men, alert, strong, armed. And the
  Indian
Is on his feet, pointing.

          He thinks
That now he will never know the dream's
  ending.

[I]

Trussed up with thongs, all night they lie on
  the floor there.
The woman is gagged, for she had reviled
  them.
All night he hears the woman's difficult
  breath.

Dawn comes. It is gray. When he eats,   150
The cold corn pone grinds in his throat, like
  sand. It sticks there.

Even whiskey fails to remove it. It sticks
  there.

The leg-thongs are cut off the tied-ones.
  They are made to stand up.
The woman refuses the whiskey. Says: "What
  fer?"
The first son drinks. The other
Takes it into his mouth, but it will not go
  down.

The liquid drains, slow, from the slack side
  of the mouth.

[J]

They stand there under the long, low bough
  of the great oak.
Eastward, low over the forest, the sun is
  nothing
But a circular blur of no irradiation, some-
  what paler   160
Than the general grayness. Their legs
Are again bound with thongs.

They are asked if they want to pray now.
  But the woman:
"If'n it's God made folks, then who's to pray
  to?"
And then: "Or fer?" And bursts into
  laughing.

For a time it seems that she can never stop
  laughing.

But as for the sons, one prays, or tries to.
  And one
Merely blubbers. If the woman
Gives either a look, it is not
Pity, nor even contempt, only distance. She
  waits,   170

And is what she is,

And in the gray light of morning, he sees her
  face. Under
The tumbled darkness of hair, the face
Is white. Out of that whiteness
The dark eyes stare at nothing, or at
The nothingness that the gray sky, like
  Time, is, for
There is no Time, and the face
Is, he suddenly sees, beautiful as stone, and

So becomes aware that he is in the manly
  state.

[K]

The affair was not tidy: bough low, no drop,
  with the clients   180

Simply hung up, feet not much clear of the
    ground, but not
Quite close enough to permit any dancing.
The affair was not quick: both sons long
    jerking and farting, but she,
From the first, without motion, frozen
In a rage of will, an ecstasy of iron, as
    though
This was the dream that, lifelong, she had
    dreamed toward.

                The face,
Eyes a-glare, jaws clenched, now glowing
    black with congestion
Like a plum, had achieved,
It seemed to him, a new dimension of
    beauty.

              [L]
There are tears in his eyes.   190
He tries to remember his childhood.
He tries to remember his wife.
He can remember nothing.

His throat is parched. His right hand,
Under the dearskin frock, has been clutching
    the gold watch.

The magic of that object had been,
In the secret order of the world, denied her
    who now hangs there.

He thinks: "What has been denied me?"
Thinks: "There is never an answer."

Thinks: "The question is the only answer."   200

He yearns to be able to frame a definition of
    joy.

              [M]
And so stood alone, for the travelers
Had disappeared into the forest and into
Whatever selves they were, and the Indian,
Now bearing the gift of a gun that had be-
    longed to the hanged-ones,
Was long since gone, like smoke fading into
    the forest,
And below the blank and unforgiving eye-
    hole
The blood and mucus had long since dried.

He thought: "I must go."

              But could not, staring
At the face, and stood for a time even after   210

The first snowflakes, in idiotic benignity,
Had fallen. Far off, in the forest and falling
    snow,
A crow was calling.

              So stirs, knowing now
He will not be here when snow
Drifts into the open door of the cabin, or,
Descending the chimney, mantles thinly
Dead ashes on the hearth, nor when snow
    thatches
These heads with white, like wisdom, nor
    ever will he
Hear the infinitesimal stridor of the frozen
    rope
As wind shifts its burden, or when   220

The weight of the crow first comes to rest on
    a rigid shoulder.

III. WE ARE ONLY OURSELVES

We never know what we have lost, or what
    we have found.
We are only ourselves, and that promise.
Continue to walk in the world. Yes, love it!

He continued to walk in the world.

IV. THE SIGN WHEREBY HE KNEW

              [A]
His life, at the end, seemed—even the
    anguish—simple.
Simple, at least, in that it had to be,
Simply, what it was, as he was,
In the end, himself and not what
He had known he ought to be. The blessed-
    ness!—   230

To wake in some dawn and see,
As though down a rifle barrel, lined up
Like sights, the self that was, the self that
    is, and there,
Far off but in range, completing that align-
    ment, your fate.

Hold your breath, let the trigger-squeeze be
    slow and steady.

The quarry lifts, in the halo of gold leaves,
    its noble head.

This is not a dimension of Time.

[B]

In this season the waters shrink.

The spring is circular and surrounded by
    gold leaves
Which are fallen from the beech tree.   240

Not even a skitter-bug disturbs the gloss
Of the surface tension. The sky

Is reflected below in absolute clarity.
If you stare into the water you may know

That nothing disturbs the infinite blue of
    the sky.

[C]

Keep store, dandle babies, and at night
    nuzzle
The hazelnut-shaped sweet tits of Lucy, and
With the piratical mark-up of the frontier,
    get rich.

But you did not, being of weak character.

You saw, from the forest pond, already dark,
    the great trumpeter swan   250
Rise, in clangor, and fight up the steep air
    where,
At the height of last light, it glimmered, like
    white flame.

The definition of love being, as we know,
    complex,
We may say that he, after all, loved his wife.

The letter, from campfire, keelboat, or slum
    room in New Orleans,
Always ended, "God bless you, dear Lucy."
    After sunset,

Alone, he played his flute in the forest.

[D]

Listen! Stand very still and,
Far off, where shadow
Is undappled, you may hear   260

The tushed boar grumble in his ivy-slick.

Afterward, there is silence until
The jay, sudden as conscience, calls.

The call, in the infinite sunlight, is like
The thrill of the taste of—on the tongue—
    brass.

[E]

The world declares itself. That voice
Is vaulted in—oh, arch on arch—redundancy
    of joy, its end
Is its beginning, necessity
Blooms like a rose. Why,

Therefore, is truth the only thing that cannot   270
Be spoken?

It can only be enacted, and that in dream,
Or in the dream become, as though uncon-
    sciously, action, and he stood,

At dusk, in the street of the raw settlement,
    and saw
The first lamp lit behind a window, and did
    not know
What he was. Thought: "I do not know
    my own name."

He walked in the world. He was sometimes
    seen to stand
In perfect stillness, when no leaf stirred.

Tell us, dear God—tell us the sign
Whereby we may know the time has come.   280

V. THE SOUND OF THAT WIND

[A]

He walked in the world. Knew the lust of
    the eye.

Wrote: "Ever since a Boy I have had an
                astonishing desire
            to see Much of the World and
                particularly
            to acquire a true knowledge of
                the Birds of North America."

He dreamed of hunting with Boone, from
    imagination painted his portrait.
He proved that the buzzard does not scent
    its repast, but sights it.
He looked in the eye of the wounded white-
    headed eagle.

Wrote: ". . . the Noble Fellow looked
                at his Ennemies
            with a Contemptible Eye."

At dusk he stood on a bluff, and the bellow-
    ing of buffalo   290
Was like distant ocean. He saw
Bones whiten the plain in the hot daylight.

He saw the Indian, and felt the splendor of
  God.

Wrote: ". . . for there I see the Man
        Naked from his
        hand and yet free from acquired
        Sorrow."

Below the salt, in rich houses, he sat, and
  knew insult.
In the lobbies and couloirs of greatness he
  dangled,
And was not unacquainted with contumely.

Wrote: "My Lovely Miss Pirrie of
        Oackley Passed by Me
        this Morning, but did not re-
        member how beautifull   300
        I had rendered her face once by
        Painting it
        at her Request with Pastelles."

Wrote: ". . . but thanks to My humble
        talents I can run
        the gantlet throu this World
        without her help."

And ran it, and ran undistracted by promise
  of ease,
Nor even the kind condescension of Daniel
  Webster.

Wrote: ". . . would give me a fat
        place was I willing to
        have one; but I love indepenn
        and piece more
        than humbug and money."

And proved same, but in the end, entered   310
On honor. Far, over the ocean, in the silken
  salons,
With hair worn long like a hunter's, eyes
  shining,
He whistled the bird-calls of his distant
  forest.

Wrote: ". . . in my sleep I continually
        dream of birds."

And in the end, entered into his earned
  house,
And slept in a bed, and with Lucy.

                But the fiddle
Soon lay on the shelf untouched, the
  mouthpiece

Of the flute was dry, and his brushes.

                His mind
Was darkened, and his last joy
Was in the lullaby they sang him, in Spanish,
  at sunset.   320

He died, and was mourned, who had loved
  the world.

Who had written: ". . . a world which
            though wicked
            enough
            in all conscience is
            perhaps as good
            as worlds unknown."

                [B]
So died in his bed, and
Night leaned, and now leans,
Off the Atlantic, and is on schedule.
Grass does not bend beneath that enormous
  weight
That with no sound sweeps westward. In the
  Mississippi,
In a mud bank, the wreck of a great tree, left   330
By flood, lies, the root-system and now-
  stubbed boughs
Lifting in darkness. It
Is white as bone. That whiteness
Is reflected in dark water, and a star
Thereby.

           Later,
In the shack of a sheep-herder, high above
  the Bitterroot,
The light goes out. No other
Light is visible.

The Northwest Orient plane, New York to
  Seattle, has passed, winking westward.

                [C]
For everything there is a season.   340

But there is the dream
Of a season past all seasons.

In such a dream the wild-grape cluster,
High-hung, exposed in the gold light,
Unripening, ripens.

Stained, the lip with wetness gleams.

I see your lip, undrying, gleam in the bright
    wind.

I cannot hear the sound of that wind.

VI. LOVE AND KNOWLEDGE

Their footless dance
Is of the beautiful liability of their nature.   350
Their eyes are round, boldly convex, bright
    as a jewel,
And merciless. They do not know
Compassion, and if they did,
We should not be worthy of it. They fly
In air that glitters like fluent crystal
And is hard as perfectly transparent iron,
    they cleave it
With no effort. They cry
In a tongue multitudinous, often like music.

He slew them, at surprising distances, with
    his gun.
Over a body held in his hand, his head was
    bowed low,   360
But not in grief.

He put them where they are, and there we
    see them:
In our imagination.

What is love?

One name for it is knowledge.

VII. TELL ME A STORY

[A]

Long ago, in Kentucky, I, a boy, stood
By a dirt road, in first dark, and heard
The great geese hoot northward.

I could not see them, there being no moon
And the stars sparse. I heard them.   370

I did not know what was happening in my
    heart.

It was the season before the elderberry
    blooms,
Therefore they were going north.

The sound was passing northward.

[B]

Tell me a story.

In this century, and moment, of mania,
Tell me a story.

Make it a story of great distances, and
    starlight.

The name of the story will be Time,
But you must not pronounce its name.   380

Tell me a story of deep delight.

THEODORE ROETHKE (1908–1963)

Born May 25, 1908, in Saginaw, Michigan; graduated Phi Beta Kappa from University of Michigan, where he also took an M.A.; further postgraduate work at Harvard; taught at Lafayette (1934), Pennsylvania State University (1934-43), Bennington (1943-47), and University of Washington (1947-63), with a year in Italy as Fulbright lecturer (1955); died August 1, 1963, in Bainbridge Island, Washington; member National Institute of Arts and Letters (1956); received two Guggenheim fellowships (1945, 1950), Tietjens Prize and Levinson Award from *Poetry* magazine, National Institute of Arts and Letters grant (1952), a Pulitzer prize for poetry (*The Waking*, 1954), Shelley Memorial Award, National Book Award, and Edna St. Vincent Millay Award, and Bollingen Prize, all awarded 1959 for *Words for the Wind* (1958); other volumes of poetry include *Open House* (1941), *The Lost Son and Other Poems* (1948), *Praise to the End!* (1951), *I Am! Says the Lamb* (1961), *Sequence, Sometimes Metaphysical* (1963), *The Far Field* (1964), and *Collected Poems* (1966); also *On the Poet and His Craft* (essays, 1965), and *Party at the Zoo* (children's book, 1963).

The Shape of the Fire (1948)

1

What's this? A dish for fat lips.
Who says? A nameless stranger.
Is he a bird or a tree? Not everyone can
    tell.

Water recedes to the crying of spiders.
An old scow bumps over black rocks.
A cracked pod calls.

    Mother me out of here. What more will
      the bones allow?
    Will the sea give the wind suck? A toad
      folds into a stone.
    These flowers are all fangs. Comfort me,
      fury.
    Wake me, witch, we'll do the dance of
      rotten sticks.   10

Shale loosens. Marl reaches into the field.
  Small birds pass over water.
Spirit, come near. This is only the edge of
  whiteness.
I can't laugh at a procession of dogs.

    In the hour of ripeness, the tree is barren.
    The she-bear mopes under the hill.
    Mother, mother, stir from your cave of
      sorrow.

A low mouth laps water. Weeds, weeds, how
  I love you.
The arbor is cooler. Farewell, farewell, fond
  worm.
The warm comes without sound.

2

Where's the eye?   20
The eye's in the sty.
The ear's not here
Beneath the hair.
When I took off my clothes
To find a nose,
There was only one shoe
For the waltz of To,
The pinch of Where.

Time for the flat-headed man. I recognize
  that listener,
Him with the platitudes and rubber doughnuts, 30
Melting at the knees, a varicose horror.
Hello, hello. My nerves knew you, dear boy.
Have you come to unhinge my shadow?

Last night I slept in the pits of a tongue.
The silver fish ran in and out of my special
  bindings;
I grew tired of the ritual of names and the
  assistant keeper of the mollusks:
Up over a viaduct I came, to the snakes and
  sticks of another winter,
A two-legged dog hunting a new horizon of
  howls.
The wind sharpened itself on a rock;
A voice sang: 40

    Pleasure on ground
    Has no sound,
    Easily maddens
    The uneasy man.

    Who, careless, slips
    In coiling ooze
    Is trapped to the lips,
    Leaves more than shoes;

    Must pull off clothes
    To jerk like a frog   50
    On belly and nose
    From the sucking bog.

My meat eats me. Who waits at the gate?
Mother of quartz, your words writhe into
  my ear.
Renew the light, lewd whisper.

3

The wasp waits.
  The edge cannot eat the center.
The grape glistens.
  The path tells little to the serpent.
An eye comes out of the wave.   60
  The journey from flesh is longest.
A rose sways least.
  The redeemer comes a dark way.

4

Morning-fair, follow me further back
Into that minnowy world of weeds and ditches,
When the herons floated high over the white
  houses,
And the little crabs slipped into silvery craters.
When the sun for me glinted the sides of a
  sand grain.
And my intent stretched over the buds at their
  first trembling.

That air and shine: and the flicker's loud
    summer call: 70
The bearded boards in the stream and the all
    of apples;
The glad hen on the hill; and the trellis
    humming.
Death was not. I lived in a simple drowse:
Hands and hair moved through a dream of
    wakening blossoms.
Rain sweetened the cave and dove still called;
The flowers leaned on themselves, the flowers
    in hollows;
And love, love sang toward.

5

To have the whole air!—
The light, the full sun
Coming down on the flowerheads, 80
The tendrils turning slowly,
A slow snail-lifting, liquescent;
To be by the rose

Rising slowly out of its bed,
Still as a child in its first loneliness;
To see cyclamen veins become clearer in early
    sunlight,
And mist lifting out of the brown cattails;
To stare into the after-light, the glitter left on
    the lake's surface,
When the sun has fallen behind a wooded
    island;
To follow the drops sliding from a lifted oar, 90
Held up, while the rower breathes, and the
    small boat drifts quietly shoreward;
To know that light falls and fills, often without
    our knowing,
As an opaque vase fills to the brim from a
    quick pouring,
Fills and trembles at the edge yet does not
    flow over,
Still holding and feeding the stem of the
    contained flower.

The Waking (1953)

I wake to sleep, and take my waking slow.
I feel my fate in what I cannot fear.
I learn by going where I have to go.

We think by feeling. What is there to know?
I hear my being dance from ear to ear.
I wake to sleep, and take my waking slow.

Of those so close beside me, which are you?
God bless the Ground! I shall walk softly there,
And learn by going where I have to go.

Light takes the Tree; but who can tell us
    how? 10

The lowly worm climbs up a winding stair;
I wake to sleep, and take my waking slow.

Great Nature has another thing to do
To you and me; so take the lively air,
And, lovely, learn by going where to go.

This shaking keeps me steady. I should know.
What falls away is always. And is near.
I wake to sleep, and take my waking slow.
I learn by going where I have to go.

I Knew a Woman (1958)

I knew a woman, lovely in her bones,
When small birds sighed, she would sigh back
    at them;
Ah, when she moved, she moved more ways
    than one:
The shapes a bright container can contain!
Of her choice virtues only gods should speak,
Or English poets who grew up on Greek
(I'd have them sing in chorus, cheek to cheek).

How well her wishes went! She stroked my chin,
She taught me Turn, and Counter-turn, and
    Stand;
She taught me Touch, that undulant white
    skin; 10
I nibbled meekly from her proffered hand;
She was the sickle: I, poor I, the rake,
Coming behind her for her pretty sake
(But what prodigious mowing we did make).

Love likes a gander, and adores a goose:
Her full lips pursed, the errant note to seize;
She played it quick, she played it light and
     loose;
My eyes, they dazzled at her flowing knees;
Her several parts could keep a pure repose,
Or one hip quiver with a mobile nose   20
(She moved in circles, and those circles moved).

Let seed be grass, and grass turn into hay:
I'm martyr to a motion not my own;
What's freedom for? To know eternity.
I swear she cast a shadow white as stone.
But who would count eternity in days?
These old bones live to learn her wanton ways:
(I measure time by how a body sways).

The Abyss (1964)

1

Is the stair here?
Where's the stair?
'The stair's right there,
But it goes nowhere.'

And the abyss? the abyss?
'The abyss you can't miss:
It's right where you are—
A step down the stair.'

     Each time ever
     There always is   10
     Noon of failure,
     Part of a house.

     In the middle of,
     Around a cloud,
     On top a thistle
     The wind's slowing.

2

I have been spoken to variously
But heard little.
My inward witness is dismayed
By my unguarded mouth.
I have taken, too often, the dangerous path,
The vague, the arid,
Neither in nor out of this life.

     Among us, who is holy?
     What speech abides?
     I hear the noise of the wall.
     They have declared themselves,   20
     Those who despise the dove.

Be with me, Whitman, maker of catalogues:
For the world invades me again,
And once more the tongues begin babbling.
And the terrible hunger for objects quails me:
The sill trembles.

And there on the blind
A furred caterpillar crawls down a string.
My symbol!
For I have moved closer to death, lived with
     death;   30
Like a nurse he sat with me for weeks, a sly
     surly attendant,
Watching my hands, wary.
Who sent him away?
I'm no longer a bird dipping a beak into
     rippling water
But a mole winding through earth,
A night-fishing otter.

3

Too much reality can be a dazzle, a surfeit;
Too close immediacy an exhaustion:
As when the door swings open in a florist's
     storeroom—
The rush of smells strikes like a cold fire, the
     throat freezes,   40
And we turn back to the heat of August,
Chastened.

So the abyss—
The slippery cold heights,
After the blinding misery,
The climbing, the endless turning,
Strike like a fire,
A terrible violence of creation,
A flash into the burning heart of the
     abominable;
Yet if we wait, unafraid, beyond the fearful
     instant,   50
The burning lake turns into a forest pool,
The fire subsides into rings of water,
A sunlit silence.

4

How can I dream except beyond this life?

Can I outleap the sea—
The edge of all the land, the final sea?
I envy the tendrils, their eyeless seeking,
The child's hand reaching into the coiled
    smilax,
And I obey the wind at my back
Bringing me home from the twilight fishing.   60

    In this, my half-rest,
    Knowing slows for a moment,
    And not-knowing enters, silent,
    Bearing being itself,
    And the fire dances
    To the stream's
    Flowing.

Do we move toward God, or merely another
    condition?
By the salt waves I hear a river's undersong,
In a place of mottled clouds, a thin mist
    morning and evening.   70
I rock between dark and dark,
My soul nearly my own,
My dead selves singing.
And I embrace this calm—
Such quiet under the small leaves!—

Near the stem, whiter at root,
A luminous stillness.

    The shade speaks slowly:
    'Adore and draw near.
    Who knows this—   80
    Knows all.'

5

I thirst by day. I watch by night.
I receive! I have been received!
I hear the flowers drinking in their light,
I have taken counsel of the crab and the
    sea-urchin,
I recall the falling of small waters,
The stream slipping beneath the mossy logs,
Winding down to the stretch of irregular sand,
The great logs piled like matchsticks.

I am most immoderately married: 90
The Lord God has taken my heaviness away;
I have merged, like the bird, with the bright
    air,
And my thought flies to the place by the
    bo-tree.

Being, not doing, is my first joy.

The Far Field (1964)

1

I dream of journeys repeatedly:
Of flying like a bat deep into a narrowing
    tunnel,
Of driving alone, without luggage, out a long
    peninsula,
The road lined with snow-laden second
    growth,
A fine dry snow ticking the windshield,
Alternate snow and sleet, no on-coming traffic,
And no lights behind, in the blurred
    side-mirror,
The road changing from glazed tarface to a
    rubble of stone,
Ending at last in a hopeless sand-rut,
Where the car stalls,   10
Churning in a snowdrift
Until the headlights darken.

2

At the field's end, in the corner missed by the
    mower,

Where the turf drops off into a grass-hidden
    culvert,
Haunt of the cat-bird, nesting-place of the
    field-mouse,
Not too far away from the ever-changing
    flower-dump,
Among the tin cans, tires, rusted pipes,
    broken machinery,—
One learned of the eternal;
And in the shrunken face of a dead rat, eaten
    by rain and ground-beetles
(I found it lying among the rubble of an old
    coal bin)   20
And the tom-cat, caught near the pheasant-
    run,
Its entrails strewn over the half-grown
    flowers,
Blasted to death by the night watchman.

I suffered for birds, for young rabbits caught
    in the mower,
My grief was not excessive.

For to come upon warblers in early May
Was to forget time and death:
How they filled the oriole's elm, a twittering
  restless cloud, all one morning.
And I watched and watched till my eyes
  blurred from the bird shapes,—
Cape May, Blackburnian, Cerulean,—   30
Moving, elusive as fish, fearless,
Hanging, bunched like young fruit, bending
  the end branches,
Still for a moment,
Then pitching away in half-flight,
Lighter than finches,
While the wrens bickered and sang in the
  half-green hedgerows,
And the flicker drummed from his dead tree
  in the chicken-yard.

—Or to lie naked in sand,
In the silted shallows of a slow river,
Fingering a shell,   40
Thinking:
Once I was something like this, mindless,
Or perhaps with another mind, less peculiar;
Or to sink down to the hips in a mossy
  quagmire;
Or, with skinny knees, to sit astride a wet log,
Believing:
I'll return again,
As a snake or a raucous bird,
Or, with luck, as a lion.

I learned not to fear infinity,   50
The far field, the windy cliffs of forever,
The dying of time in the white light of
  tomorrow,
The wheel turning away from itself,
The sprawl of the wave,
The on-coming water.

3

The river turns on itself,
The tree retreats into its own shadow.
I feel a weightless change, a moving forward
As of water quickening before a narrowing
  channel
When banks converge, and the wide river
  whitens;   60
Or when two rivers combine, the blue glacial
  torrent

And the yellowish-green from the mountainy
  upland,—
At first a swift rippling between rocks,
Then a long running over flat stones
Before descending to the alluvial plain,
To the clay banks, and the wild grapes
  hanging from the elmtrees,
The slightly trembling water
Dropping a fine yellow silt where the sun stays;
And the crabs bask near the edge,
The weedy edge, alive with small snakes and
  bloodsuckers,—   70

I have come to a still, but not a deep center,
A point outside the glittering current;
My eyes stare at the bottom of a river,
At the irregular stones, iridescent sandgrains,
My mind moves in more than one place,
In a country half-land, half-water.

I am renewed by death, thought of my death,
The dry scent of a dying garden in September,
The wind fanning the ash of a low fire.
What I love is near at hand,   80
Always, in earth and air.

4

The lost self changes,
Turning toward the sea,
A sea-shape turning around,—
An old man with his feet before the fire,
In robes of green, in garments of adieu.

A man faced with his own immensity
Wakes all the waves, all their loose
  wandering fire.
The murmur of the absolute, the why
Of being born fails on his naked ears.   90
His spirit moves like monumental wind
That gentles on a sunny blue plateau.
He is the end of things, the final man.

All finite things reveal infinitude:
The mountain with its singular bright shade
Like the blue shine on freshly frozen snow,
The after-light upon ice-burdened pines;
Odor of basswood on a mountain-slope,
A scent beloved of bees;
Silence of water above a sunken tree: 100
The pure serene of memory in one man,—
A ripple widening from a single stone
Winding around the waters of the world.

ELIZABETH BISHOP (1911–   )

Born February 8, 1911, in Worcester, Massachusetts; graduated Vassar College in 1934; has lived in Nova Scotia, New England, Florida, Mexico, and presently resides in Brazil; recipient of Guggenheim (1947) and Donnelly (1951) fellowships and a grant from the National Institute of Arts and Letters (1951); served as Consultant in Poetry to Library of Congress (1949–50); member National Institute of Arts and Letters (1954); Chancellor, Academy of American Poets; Pulitzer prize for poetry in 1955 for *Poems: North and South—A Cold Spring*; other volumes of poetry are *Questions of Travel* (1965), *Selected Poems* (1967), and *Complete Poems* (1969); has translated and anthologized from the Portuguese the poetry of Carlos Drummond de Andrade and others; and edited and translated Helena Morley's (pseudonym of Alice Brant) *Diary* (1957), a novel.

Little Exercise (1946)

for Thomas Edwards Wanning

Think of the storm roaming the sky uneasily
like a dog looking for a place to sleep in,
listen to it growling.

Think how they must look now, the mangrove
    keys
lying out there unresponsive to the lightning
in dark, coarse-fibred families,

where occasionally a heron may undo his head,
shake up his feathers, make an uncertain
    comment
when the surrounding water shines.

Think of the boulevard and the little palm
    trees   10

all stuck in rows, suddenly revealed
as fistfuls of limp fish-skeletons.

It is raining there. The boulevard
and its broken sidewalks with weeds in every
    crack
are relieved to be wet, the sea to be freshened.

Now the storm goes away again in a series
of small, badly lit battle-scenes,
each in "Another part of the field."

Think of someone sleeping in the bottom of
    a row-boat
tied to a mangrove root or the pile of a bridge;   20
think of him as uninjured, barely disturbed.

Letter to N.Y. (1955)

for Louise Crane

In your next letter I wish you'd say
where you are going and what you are doing;
how are the plays, and after the plays
what other pleasures you're pursuing:

taking cabs in the middle of the night,
driving as if to save your soul
where the road goes round and round the park
and the meter glares like a moral owl,

and the trees look so queer and green

standing alone in big black caves   10
and suddenly you're in a different place
where everything seems to happen in waves,

and most of the jokes you just can't catch,
like dirty words rubbed off a slate,
and the songs are loud but somehow dim
and it gets so terribly late,

and coming out of the brownstone house
to the gray sidewalk, the watered street,

one side of the buildings rises with the sun
like a glistening field of wheat.   20
—Wheat, not oats, dear. I'm afraid

if it's wheat it's none of your sowing,
nevertheless I'd like to know
what you are doing and where you are going.

Invitation to Miss Marianne Moore (1955)

From Brooklyn, over the Brooklyn Bridge, on this
    fine morning,
    please come flying.
In a cloud of fiery pale chemicals,
    please come flying,
to the rapid rolling of thousands of small blue
    drums
descending out of the mackerel sky
over the glittering grandstand of harbor-water,
    please come flying.

Whistles, pennants and smoke are blowing.
    The ships
are signaling cordially with multitudes of flags   10
rising and falling like birds all over the harbor.
Enter: two rivers, gracefully bearing
countless little pellucid jellies
in cut-glass epergnes dragging with silver chains.
The flight is safe; the weather is all arranged.
The waves are running in verses this fine
    morning.
    Please come flying.

Come with the pointed toe of each black shoe
trailing a sapphire highlight,
with a black capeful of butterfly wings and
    bon-mots,   20
with heaven knows how many angels all riding
on the broad black brim of your hat,
    please come flying.

Bearing a musical inaudible abacus,
a slight censorious frown, and blue ribbons,
    please come flying.
Facts and skyscrapers glint in the tide;
    Manhattan
is all awash with morals this fine morning,
    so please come flying.

Mounting the sky with natural heroism,   30
above the accidents, above the malignant
    movies,
the taxicabs and injustices at large,
while horns are resounding in your beautiful
    ears
that simultaneously listen to
a soft uninvented music, fit for the musk deer,
    please come flying.

For whom the grim museums will behave
like courteous male bower-birds,
for whom the agreeable lions lie in wait
on the steps of the Public Library,   40
eager to rise and follow through the doors
up into the reading rooms,
    please come flying.
We can sit down and weep; we can go
    shopping,
or play at a game of constantly being wrong
with a priceless set of vocabularies,
or we can bravely deplore, but please
    please come flying.

With dynasties of negative constructions
darkening and dying around you,   50
with grammar that suddenly turns and shines
like flocks of sandpipers flying,
    please come flying.

Come like a light in the white mackerel sky,
come like a daytime comet
with a long unnebulous train of words,
from Brooklyn, over the Brooklyn Bridge, on
    this fine morning,
    please come flying.

Filling Station (1965)

Oh, but it is dirty!
—this little filling station,
oil-soaked, oil-permeated
to a disturbing, over-all
black translucency.

Be careful with that match!

Father wears a dirty,
oil-soaked monkey suit
that cuts him under the arms,
and several quick and saucy   10

and greasy sons assist him
(it's a family filling station),
all quite thoroughly dirty.

Do they live in the station?
It has a cement porch
behind the pumps, and on it
a set of crushed and grease-
impregnated wickerwork;
on the wicker sofa
a dirty dog, quite comfy.   20

Some comic books provide
the only note of color—
of certain color. They lie
upon a big dim doily
draping a taboret

(part of the set), beside
a big hirsute begonia.

Why the extraneous plant?
Why the taboret?
Why, oh why, the doily?   30
(Embroidered in daisy stitch
with marguerites, I think,
and heavy with gray crochet.)

Somebody embroidered the doily.
Somebody waters the plant,
or oils it, maybe. Somebody
arranges the rows of cans
so that they softly say:
ESSO—SO—SO—SO
to high-strung automobiles.   40
Somebody loves us all.

Sunday, 4 A.M. (1965)

An endless and flooded
dreamland, lying low,
cross- and wheel-studded
like a tick-tack-toe.

At the right, ancillary,
"Mary" 's close and blue.
Which Mary? Aunt Mary?
Tall Mary Stearns I knew?

The old kitchen knife box,
full of rusty nails,   10
is at the left. A high *vox
humana* somewhere wails:

*The gray horse needs shoeing!
It's always the same!
What are you doing,
there, beyond the frame?*

*If you're the donor,
you might do that much!*
Turn on the light. Turn over.
On the bed a smutch—   20

black-and-gold gesso
on the altered cloth.
The cat jumps to the window;
in his mouth's a moth.

Dream dream confronting,
now the cupboard's bare.
The cat's gone a-hunting.
The brook feels for the stair.

The world seldom changes,
but the wet foot dangles   30
until a bird arranges
two notes at right angles.

Travelling in the Family (1969)

*(translated from the Portuguese of Carlos Drum-
mond de Andrade)*

      to Rodrigo M. F. de Andrade

In the desert of Itabira
the shadow of my father
took me by the hand.
So much time lost.
But he didn't say anything.
It was neither day nor night.

A sigh? A passing bird?
But he didn't say anything.

We have come a long way.
Here there was a house.   10
The mountain used to be bigger.
So many heaped-up dead,
and time gnawing the dead.
And in the ruined houses,
cold disdain and damp.
But he didn't say anything.

The street he used to cross
on horseback, at a gallop.
His watch. His clothes.
His legal documents.   20
His tales of love-affairs.
Opening of tin trunks
and violent memories.
But he didn't say anything.

In the desert of Itabira
things come back to life,
stiflingly, suddenly.
The market of desires
displays its sad treasures;
my urge to run away;   30
naked women; remorse.
But he didn't say anything.

Stepping on books and letters
we travel in the family.
Marriages; mortgages;
the consumptive cousins;
the mad aunt; my grandmother
betrayed among the slave-girls,
rustling silks in the bedroom.
But he didn't say anything.   40

What cruel, obscure instinct
moved his pallid hand
subtly pushing us
into the forbidden
time, forbidden places?

I looked in his white eyes.
I cried to him: Speak! My voice
shook in the air a moment,
beat on the stones. The shadow
proceeded slowly on   50
with that pathetic travelling
across the lost kingdom.
But he didn't say anything.

I saw grief, misunderstanding
and more than one old revolt

dividing us in the dark.
The hand I wouldn't kiss,
the crumb that they denied me,
refusal to ask pardon.
Pride. Terror at night.   60
But he didn't say anything.

Speak speak speak speak.
I pulled him by his coat
that was turning into clay.
By the hands, by the boots
I caught at his strict shadow
and the shadow released itself
with neither haste nor anger.
But he remained silent.

There were distinct silences   70
deep within his silence.
There was my deaf grandfather
hearing the painted birds
on the ceiling of the church;
my own lack of friends;
and your lack of kisses;
there were our difficult lives
and a great separation
in the little space of the room.

The narrow space of life   80
crowds me up against you,
and in this ghostly embrace
it's as if I were being burned
completely, with poignant love.
Only now do we know each other!
Eye-glasses, memories, portraits
flow in the river of blood.
Now the waters won't let me
make out your distant face,
distant by seventy years . . .   90

I felt that he pardoned me
but he didn't say anything.
The waters cover his moustache,
the family, Itabira, all.

KARL SHAPIRO (1913–   )

Born November 10, 1913, in Baltimore; attended University of Virginia and Johns Hopkins University; military service in army Second World War; has taught at Johns Hopkins, Nebraska, and University of California at Davis; received National Institute of Arts and Letters grant (1944); Consultant in Poetry to Library of Congress (1947–48); member National Institute of Arts and Letters (1959); editor of *Poetry* magazine (1950–56) and of *Prairie Schooner* (1956–63); volumes of poetry include *Poems* (1935), *Person, Place and Thing* (1942), *V-Letter and Other Poems* (1944) for which he received Pulitzer prize (1945), *Trial of a Poet* (1947), *Poems of a Jew* (1958), *The Bourgeois Poet* (1964), and *Selected Poems* (1968); also essays, collected in *Beyond Criticism* (1953) and *In Defense of Ignorance* (1960); and a novel, *Edsel* (1971).

Hollywood (1940)

Farthest from any war, unique in time
Like Athens or Baghdad, this city lies
Between dry purple mountains and the sea.
The air is clear and famous, every day
Bright as a postcard, bringing bungalows
   And sights. The broad nights advertise
For love and music and astronomy.

Heart of a continent, the hearts converge
On open boulevards where palms are nursed
With flare-pots like a grove, on villa roads   10
Where castles cultivated like a style
Breed fabulous metaphors in foreign stone,
   And on enormous movie lots
Where history repeats its vivid blunders.

Alice and Cinderella are most real.
Here may the tourist, quite sincere at last,
Rest from his dream of travels. All is new,
No ruins claim his awe, and permanence,
Despised like customs, fails at every turn.
   Here where the eccentric thrives,   20
Laughter and love are leading industries.

Luck is another. Here the bodyguard,
The parasite, the scholar are well paid,
The quack erects his alabaster office,
The moron and the genius are enshrined,
And the mystic makes a fortune quietly;
   Here all superlatives come true
And beauty is marketed like a basic food.

O can we understand it? Is it ours,
A crude whim of a beginning people,   30
A private orgy in a secluded spot?
Or alien like the word *harem*, or true
Like hideous Pittsburgh or depraved Atlanta?
   Is adolescence just as vile
As this its architecture and its talk?

Or are they parvenus, like boys and girls?
Or ours and happy, cleverest of all?
Yes. Yes. Though glamorous to the ignorant
This is the simplest city, a new school.
What is more nearly ours? If soul can mean   40
   The civilization of the brain,
This is a soul, a possible proud Florence.

Auto Wreck (1942)

Its quick soft silver bell beating, beating,
And down the dark one ruby flare
Pulsing out red light like an artery,
The ambulance at top speed floating down
Past beacons and illuminated clocks
Wings in a heavy curve, dips down,
And brakes speed, entering the crowd.
The doors leap open, emptying light;
Stretchers are laid out, the mangled lifted
And stowed into the little hospital.   10
Then the bell, breaking the hush, tolls once,
And the ambulance with its terrible cargo

Rocking, slightly rocking, moves away,
As the doors, an afterthought, are closed.

We are deranged, walking among the cops
Who sweep glass and are large and composed.
One is still making notes under the light.
One with a bucket douches ponds of blood
Into the street and gutter.
One hangs lanterns on the wrecks that cling,   20
Empty husks of locusts, to iron poles.

Our throats were tight as tourniquets,
Our feet were bound with splints, but now,

Like convalescents intimate and gauche,
We speak through sickly smiles and warn
With the stubborn saw of common sense,
The grim joke and the banal resolution.
The traffic moves around with care,
But we remain, touching a wound
That opens to our richest horror.   30
Already old, the question Who shall die?

Becomes unspoken Who is innocent?
For death in war is done by hands;
Suicide has cause and stillbirth, logic;
And cancer, simple as a flower, blooms.
But this invites the occult mind,
Cancels our physics with a sneer,
And spatters all we knew of denouement
Across the expedient and wicked stones.

The Leg (1944)

Among the iodoform, in twilight-sleep,
What have I lost? he first inquires,
Peers in the middle distance where a pain,
Ghost of a nurse, hazily moves, and day,
Her blinding presence pressing in his eyes
And now his ears. They are handling him
With rubber hands. He wants to get up.

One day beside some flowers near his nose
He will be thinking, *When will I look at it?*
And pain, still in the middle distance, will reply,   10
At what? and he will know it's gone,
O where! and begin to tremble and cry.
He will begin to cry as a child cries
Whose puppy is mangled under a screaming
  wheel.

Later, as if deliberately, his fingers
Begin to explore the stump. He learns a shape
That is comfortable and tucked in like a sock.
This has a sense of humor, this can despise
The finest surgical limb, the dignity of limping,

The nonsense of wheel-chairs. Now he smiles
  to the wall: 20
The amputation becomes an acquisition.

For the leg is wondering where he is (all is
  not lost)
And surely he has a duty to the leg;
He is its injury, the leg is his orphan,
He must cultivate the mind of the leg,
Pray for the part that is missing, pray for peace
In the image of man, pray, pray for its safety,
And after a little it will die quietly.

The body, what is it, Father, but a sign
To love the force that grows us, to give back   30
What in Thy palm is senselessness and mud?
Knead, knead the substance of our
  understanding
Which must be beautiful in flesh to walk,
That if Thou take me angrily in hand
And hurl me to the shark, I shall not die!

DELMORE SCHWARTZ (1913–1966)

Born December 8, 1913, in Brooklyn; graduated New York University in 1935; graduate work at Wisconsin and Harvard universities; taught at Harvard, Princeton, N.Y.U., Indiana, and Syracuse; editor of *Partisan Review* (1943–46), associate editor (1947–55); later poetry editor and film critic for *New Republic*; died July 11, 1966, in New York City; awards include those from *Poetry* magazine (1950) and National Institute of Arts and Letters (1953); volumes of poetry include *In Dreams Begin Responsibilities* (1938), *Shenandoah* (verse play, 1941), *Genesis* (1943), *Vaudeville for a Princess* (1950), and *Summer Knowledge* (1959, Bollingen Prize for poetry); also two collections of short stories, *The World Is a Wedding* (1948) and *Successful Love* (1961); and *Selected Essays* (1970).

In the Naked Bed, in Plato's Cave (1938)

In the naked bed, in Plato's cave,
Reflected headlights slowly slid the wall,
Carpenters hammered under the shaded
    window,
Wind troubled the window curtains all night
    long,
A fleet of trucks strained uphill, grinding,
Their freights covered, as usual.
The ceiling lightened again, the slanting
    diagram
Slid slowly forth.
                    Hearing the milkman's chop,
His striving up the stair, the bottle's chink,
I rose from bed, lit a cigarette,   10
And walked to the window. The stony street
Displayed the stillness in which buildings
    stand,
The street-lamp's vigil and the horse's patience.
The winter sky's pure capital

Turned me back to bed with exhausted eyes.

Strangeness grew in the motionless air. The
    loose
Film grayed. Shaking wagons, hooves'
    waterfalls,
Sounded far off, increasing, louder and nearer.
A car coughed, starting. Morning, softly
Melting the air, lifted the half-covered chair   20
From underseas, kindled the looking-glass,
Distinguished the dresser and the white wall.
The bird called tentatively, whistled, called,
Bubbled and whistled, so! Perplexed, still wet
With sleep, affectionate, hungry and cold.
    So, so,
O son of man, the ignorant night, the travail
Of early morning, the mystery of beginning
Again and again,
                    while History is unforgiven.

From The Repetitive Heart: Eleven Poems in Imitation of the Fugue Form

IV: For Rhoda (1938)

Calmly we walk through this April's day,
Metropolitan poetry here and there,
In the park sit pauper and *rentier*,
The screaming children, the motor car
Fugitive about us, running away,
Between the worker and the millionaire
Number provides all distances,
It is Nineteen Thirty-Seven now,
Many great dears are taken away,
What will become of you and me   10
(This is the school in which we learn . . .)
Besides the photo and the memory?
(. . . that time is the fire in which we burn.)

(This is the school in which we learn . . .)
What is the self amid this blaze?
What am I now that I was then
Which I shall suffer and act again,
The theodicy I wrote in my high school days
Restored all life from infancy,
The children shouting are bright as they run   20
(This is the school in which they learn . . .)

Ravished entirely in their passing play!
(. . . that time is the fire in which they burn.)

Avid its rush, that reeling blaze!
Where is my father and Eleanor?
Not where are they now, dead seven years,
But what they were then?
                    No more? No more?
From Nineteen-Fourteen to the present day,
Bert Spira and Rhoda consume, consume
Not where they are now (where are they now?)   30
But what they were then, both beautiful;
Each minute bursts in the burning room,
The great globe reels in the solar fire,
Spinning the trivial and unique away.
(How all things flash! How all things flare!)
What am I now that I was then?
May memory restore again and again
The smallest color of the smallest day:
Time is the school in which we learn,
Time is the fire in which we burn.   40

The Heavy Bear Who Goes with Me (1938)

"the withness of the body"

The heavy bear who goes with me,
A manifold honey to smear his face,
Clumsy and lumbering here and there,
The central ton of every place,
The hungry beating brutish one
In love with candy, anger, and sleep,
Crazy factotum, dishevelling all,
Climbs the building, kicks the football,
Boxes his brother in the hate-ridden city.

Breathing at my side, that heavy animal,   10
That heavy bear who sleeps with me,
Howls in his sleep for a world of sugar,
A sweetness intimate as the water's clasp,
Howls in his sleep because the tight-rope
Trembles and shows the darkness beneath.
—The strutting show-off is terrified,
Dressed in his dress-suit, bulging his pants,
Trembles to think that his quivering meat

Must finally wince to nothing at all.

That inescapable animal walks with me,   20
Has followed me since the black womb
    held,
Moves where I move, distorting my gesture,
A caricature, a swollen shadow,
A stupid clown of the spirit's motive,
Perplexes and affronts with his own
    darkness,
The secret life of belly and bone,
Opaque, too near, my private, yet
    unknown,
Stretches to embrace the very dear
With whom I would walk without him
    near,
Touches her grossly, although a word   30
Would bare my heart and make me clear,
Stumbles, flounders, and strives to be fed
Dragging me with him in his mouthing care,
Amid the hundred million of his kind,
The scrimmage of appetite everywhere.

All of the Fruits Had Fallen (1959)

All of the fruits had fallen,
The bears had fallen asleep,
And the pears were useless and soft
Like used hopes, under the starlight's
Small knowledge, scattered aloft
In a glittering senseless drift:
The jackals of remorse in a cage
Drugged beyond mirth and rage.

Then, then, the dark hour flowered!
Under the silence, immense   10
And empty as far-off seas,
I wished for the innocence

Of my stars and my stones and my trees
All the brutality and inner sense
A dog and a bird possess,
The dog who barked at the moon
As an enemy's white fang,
The bird that thrashed up the bush
And soared to soar as it sang,
A being all present as touch,   20
Free of the future and past
—Until, in the dim window glass,
The fog or cloud of my face
Showed me my fear at last!

RANDALL JARRELL (1914–1965)

Born May 6, 1914, in Nashville, Tennessee; studied at Vanderbilt (B.A., M.A.) and Princeton universities; taught at Kenyon, Texas, St. Lawrence, and the (then) Women's College, University of North Carolina at Greensboro; military service in the air force during Second World War; literary editor of the *Nation* (1946); member National Institute of Arts and Letters (1960); Chancellor, Academy of American Poets; died October 14, 1965 in Greensboro,

North Carolina; volumes of poetry include *The Rage for the Lost Penny* (1940), *Blood for a Stranger* (1942), *Little Friend, Little Friend* (1945), *Losses* (1948), *The Seven-League Crutches* (1951), *Selected Poems* (1955), *The Woman at the Washington Zoo* (1960), *The Lost World* (1965), and *The Complete Poems*

(1968); also essays, collected in *Poetry and the Age* (1953), *A Sad Heart at the Supermarket* (1962), and *The Third Book of Criticism* (1969); and *Pictures from an Institution* (1954), a novel, as well as children's books, translations, and anthologies.

90 North (1945)

At home, in my flannel gown, like a bear to
  its floe,
I clambered to bed; up the globe's impossible
  sides
I sailed all night—till at last, with my black
  beard,
My furs and my dogs, I stood at the northern
  pole.

There in the childish night my companions
  lay frozen,
The stiff furs knocked at my starveling throat,
And I gave my great sigh: the flakes came
  huddling,
Were they really my end? In the darkness I
  turned to my rest.

—Here, the flag snaps in the glare and silence
Of the unbroken ice. I stand here,   10
The dogs bark, my beard is black, and I stare
At the North Pole . . .
        And now what? Why, go back.

Turn as I please, my step is to the south.
The world—my world spins on this final point
Of cold and wretchedness: all lines, all winds

End in this whirlpool I at last discover.

And it is meaningless. In the child's bed
After the night's voyage, in that warm world
Where people work and suffer for the end
That crowns the pain—in that Cloud-
  Cuckoo-Land   20

I reached my North and it had meaning.
Here at the actual pole of my existence,
Where all that I have done is meaningless,
Where I die or live by accident alone—

Where, living or dying, I am still alone;
Here where North, the night, the berg of
  death
Crowd me out of the ignorant darkness,
I see at last that all the knowledge

I wrung from the darkness—that the darkness
  flung me—
Is worthless as ignorance: nothing comes from
  nothing,   30
The darkness from the darkness. Pain comes
  from the darkness
And we call it wisdom. It is pain.

The Death of the Ball Turret Gunner (1948)

From my mother's sleep I fell into the State,
And I hunched in its belly till my wet fur
  froze.
Six miles from earth, loosed from its dream
  of life,

I woke to black flak and the nightmare
  fighters.
When I died they washed me out of the
  turret with a hose.

Losses (1948)

It was not dying: everybody died.
It was not dying: we had died before
In the routine crashes—and our fields
Called up the papers, wrote home to our folks,

And the rates rose, all because of us.
We died on the wrong page of the almanac,
Scattered on mountains fifty miles away;
Diving on haystacks, fighting with a friend,

We blazed up on the lines we never saw.
We died like aunts or pets or foreigners.   10
(When we left high school nothing else
    had died
For us to figure we had died like.)

In our new planes, with our new crews, we
    bombed
The ranges by the desert or the shore,
Fired at towed targets, waited for our scores—
And turned into replacements and woke up
One morning, over England, operational.
It wasn't different: but if we died
It was not an accident but a mistake
(But an easy one for anyone to make).   20
We read our mail and counted up our
    missions—

In bombers named for girls, we burned
The cities we had learned about in school—
Till our lives wore out; our bodies lay among
The people we had killed and never seen.
When we lasted long enough they gave us
    medals;
When we died they said, "Our casualties were
    low."
They said, "Here are the maps"; we burned
    the cities.

It was not dying—no, not ever dying;
But the night I died I dreamed that I was
    dead,   30
And the cities said to me: "Why are you
    dying?
We are satisfied, if you are; but why did I die?"

Eighth Air Force (1948)

If, in an odd angle of the hutment,
A puppy laps the water from a can
Of flowers, and the drunk sergeant shaving
Whistles *O Paradiso!*—shall I say that man
Is not as men have said: a wolf to man?

The other murderers troop in yawning;
Three of them play Pitch, one sleeps, and one
Lies counting missions, lies there sweating
Till even his heart beats: One; One; One.
O *murderers!* . . . Still, this is how it's done: 10

This is a war. . . . But since these play,
    before they die,

Like puppies with their puppy; since, a man,
I did as these have done, but did not die—
I will content the people as I can
And give up these to them: Behold the man!

I have suffered, in a dream, because of him,
Many things; for this last saviour, man,
I have lied as I lie now. But what is lying?
Men wash their hands, in blood, as best they
    can:
I find no fault in this just man.   20

The Woman at the Washington Zoo (1960)

The saris go by me from the embassies.

Cloth from the moon. Cloth from another
    planet.
They look back at the leopard like the leopard.

And I. . . .
                this print of mine, that has
                    kept its color
Alive through so many cleanings; this dull null
Navy I wear to work, and wear from work,
    and so
To my bed, so to my grave, with no
Complaints, no comment: neither from my
    chief,

The Deputy Chief Assistant, nor his chief—
Only I complain. . . . this serviceable   10
Body that no sunlight dyes, no hand suffuses
But, dome-shadowed, withering among
    columns,
Wavy beneath fountains—small, far-off, shining
In the eyes of animals, these beings trapped
As I am trapped but not, themselves, the trap,
Aging, but without knowledge of their age,
Kept safe here, knowing not of death, for
    death—
Oh, bars of my own body, open, open!

The world goes by my cage and never sees me.
And there come not to me, as come to these,   20
The wild beasts, sparrows pecking the llamas'
    grain,
Pigeons settling on the bears' bread, buzzards
Tearing the meat the flies have
    clouded. . . .
                    Vulture,
When you come for the white rat that the
    foxes left,

Take off the red helmet of your head, the
    black
Wings that have shadowed me, and step to
    me as man:
The wild brother at whose feet the white
    wolves fawn,
To whose hand of power the great lioness
Stalks, purring. . . .
                        You know what I was,
You see what I am: change me, change me!   30

In Those Days (1960)

In those days—they were long ago—
The snow was cold, the night was black.
I licked from my cracked lips
A snowflake, as I looked back

Through branches, the last uneasy snow.
Your shadow, there in the light, was still.
In a little the light went out.
I went on, stumbling—till at last the hill

Hid the house. And, yawning,
In bed in my room, alone,   10
I would look out: over the quilted
Rooftops, the clear stars shone.

How poor and miserable we were,
How seldom together!
And yet after so long one thinks:
In those days everything was better.

The Bird of Night (1965)

A shadow is floating through the moonlight.
Its wings don't make a sound.
Its claws are long, its beak is bright.
Its eyes try all the corners of the night.

It calls and calls: all the air swells and heaves
And washes up and down like water.

The ear that listens to the owl believes
In death. The bat beneath the eaves,

The mouse beside the stone are still as death.
The owl's air washes them like water.   10
The owl goes back and forth inside the night,
And the night holds its breath.

In Montecito (1965)

In a fashionable suburb of Santa Barbara,
Montecito, there visited me one night at
    midnight
A scream with breasts. As it hung there in the
    sweet air
That was always the right temperature, the
    contractors
Who had undertaken to dismantle it,
    stripped off
The lips, let the air out of the
    breasts.
            People disappear
Even in Montecito. Greenie Taliaferro,

In her white maillot, her good figure almost
    firm,
Her old pepper-and-salt hair stripped by the
    hairdresser
To nothing and dyed platinum—Greenie has
    left her Bentley.   10
They have thrown away her electric toothbrush,
    someone else slips
The key into the lock of her safety-deposit box
At the Crocker-Anglo Bank; her seat at the
    cricket matches
Is warmed by buttocks less delectable than
    hers.

Greenie's girdle is
     empty.
                    A scream hangs there in the night:
They strip off the lips, let the air out of the
     breasts,

And Greenie has gone into the Greater
     Montecito
That surrounds Montecito like the echo of a
     scream.

JOHN BERRYMAN (1914–1972)

Born October 24, 1914, in McAlester, Oklahoma; educated at Columbia University and Clare College, Cambridge; taught at University of Minnesota from 1955 until his death in 1972 in Minnesota; received National Institute of Arts and Letters grant (1950); awards include Pulitzer prize for poetry (1964), Loines Award for poetry (1964), National Book Award (1968), and Bollingen Prize for poetry (1969); member National Institute of Arts and Letters (1965); Chancellor, Academy of American Poets; volumes of poetry include *Poems* (1942), *The Dispossessed* (1948), *Homage to Mistress Bradstreet* (1956), *77 Dream Songs* (1964), *Berryman's Sonnets* (1967), *Short Poems* (1967), *His Toy, His Dream, His Rest* (1968), *Dream Songs* (1969), *Love and Fame* (1970), and *Delusions, Etc.* (1972); also *Stephen Crane* (critical biography, 1950) and *Recovery* (novel, 1973).

Homage to Mistress Bradstreet (1956)

1

The Governor your husband lived so long
moved you not, restless, waiting for him?
    Still,
you were a patient woman.—
I seem to see you pause here still:
Sylvester, Quarles, in moments odd you pored
before a fire at, bright eyes on the Lord,
all the children still.
'Simon . .' Simon will listen while you
    read a Song.

2

Outside the New World winters in grand dark
white air lashing high thro' the virgin stands   10
foxes down foxholes sigh,
surely the English heart quails, stunned.
I doubt if Simon than this blast, that sea,
spares from his rigour for your poetry
more. We are on each other's hands
who care. Both of our worlds unhanded us.
    Lie stark,

3

thy eyes look to me mild. Out of maize & air
your body's made, and moves. I summon, see,

from the centuries it.
I think you won't stay. How do we   20
linger, diminished, in our lovers' air,
implausibly visible, to whom, a year,
years, over interims; or not;
to a long stranger; or not; shimmer &
    disappear.

4

Jaw-ript, rot with its wisdom, rending then;
then not. When the mouth dies, who misses
    you?
Your master never died,
Simon ah thirty years past you—
Pockmarkt & westward staring on a haggard
    deck
it seems I find you, young. I come to check,   30
I come to stay with you,
and the Governor, & Father, & Simon, & the
    huddled men.

5

By the week we landed we were, most, used
    up.
Strange ships across us, after a fortnight's
    winds

unfavouring, frightened us;
bone-sad cold, sleet, scurvy; so were ill
many as one day we could have no sermons;
broils, quelled; a fatherless child unkennelled;
vermin
crowding & waiting: waiting.
And the day itself he leapt ashore young
Henry Winthrop 40

6

(delivered from the waves; because he found
off their wigwams, sharp-eyed, a lone canoe
across a tidal river,
that water glittered fair & blue
& narrow, none of the other men could swim
and the plantation's prime theft up to him,
shouldered on a glad day
hard on the glorious feasting of thanksgiving)
drowned.

7

How long with nothing in the ruinous heat,
clams & acorns stomaching, distinction
perishing, 50
at which my heart rose,
with brackish water, we would sing.
When whispers knew the Governor's last
bread
was browning in his oven, we were
discourag'd.
The Lady Arbella dying—
dyings—at which my heart rose, but I did
submit.

8

That beyond the Atlantic wound our woes
enlarge
is hard, hard that starvation burnishes our
fear,
but I do gloss for You.
Strangers & pilgrims fare we here, 60
declaring we seek a City. Shall we be
deceived?
I know whom I have trusted, & whom I have
believed,
and that he is able to
keep that I have committed to his charge.

9

Winter than summer worse, that first, like a
file
on a quick, or the poison suck of a thrilled
tooth;
and still we may unpack.

Wolves & storms among, uncouth
board-pieces, boxes, barrels vanish, grow
houses, rise. Motes that hop in sunlight slow 70
indoors, and I am Ruth
away: open my mouth, my eyes wet: I wóuld
smile:

10

vellum I palm, and dream. Their forest dies
to greensward, privets, elms & towers, whence
a nightingale is throbbing.
Women sleep sound. I was happy once . .
(Something keeps on not happening; I
shrink?)
These minutes all their passions & powers
sink
and I am not one chance
for an unknown cry or a flicker of unknown
eyes. 80

11

Chapped souls ours, by the day Spring's
strong winds swelled,
Jack's pulpits arched, more glad. The shawl I
pinned
flaps like a shooting soul
might in such weather Heaven send.
Succumbing half, in spirit, to a salmon sash
I prod the nerveless novel succotash—
I must be disciplined,
in arms, against that one, and our dissidents,
and myself.

12

Versing, I shroud among the dynasties;
quaternion on quaternion, tireless I phrase 90
anything past, dead, far,
sacred, for a barbarous place.
—To please your wintry father? all this bald
abstract didactic rime I read appalled
harassed for your fame
mistress neither of fiery nor velvet verse, on
your knees

13

hopeful & shamefast, chaste, laborious, odd,
whom the sea tore.—The damned roar with
loss,
so they hug & are mean
with themselves, and I cannot be thus. 100
Why then do I repine, sick, bad, to long
after what must not be? I lie wrong
once more. For at fourteen
I found my heart more carnal and sitting
loose from God,

14

vanity & the follies of youth took hold of me;
then the pox blasted, when the Lord
    returned.
That year for my sorry face
so-much-older Simon burned,
so Father smiled, with love. Their will be
    done.
He to me ill lingeringly, learning to shun   110
a bliss, a lightning blood
vouchsafed, what did seem life. I kissed his
    Mystery.

15

Drydust in God's eye the aquavivid skin
of Simon snoring lit with fountaining dawn
when my eyes unlid, sad.
John Cotton shines on Boston's sin—
I ám drawn, in pieties that seem
the weary drizzle of an unremembered
    dream.
Women have gone mad
at twenty-one. Ambition mines, atrocious, in.   120

16

Food endless, people few, all to be done.
As pippins roast, the question of the wolves
turns & turns.
Fangs of a wolf will keep, the neck
round of a child, that child brave. I remember
    who
in meeting smiled & was punisht, and I know
    who
whispered & was stockt.
We lead a thoughtful life. But Boston's cage
    we shun.

17

The winters close, Springs open, no child
    stirs
under my withering heart, O seasoned heart   130
God grudged his aid.
All things else soil like a shirt.
Simon is much away. My executive stales.
The town came through for the cartway by
    the pales,
but my patience is short.
I revolt from, I am like, these savage foresters

18

whose passionless dicker in the shade, whose
    glance
impassive & scant, belie their murderous cries
when quarry seems to show.

Again I must have been wrong, twice.   140
Unwell in a new way. Can that begin?
God brandishes. O love, O I love. Kin,
gather. My world is strange
and merciful, ingrown months, blessing a
    swelling trance.

19

So squeezed, wince you I scream? I love you
    & hate
off with you. Ages! *Useless.* Below my waist
he has me in Hell's vise.
Stalling. He let go. Come back: brace
me somewhere. No. No. Yes! everything
    down
hardens I press with horrible joy down   150
my back cracks like a wrist
shame I am voiding oh behind it is too late

20

hide me forever I work thrust I must free
now I all muscles & bones concentrate
what is living from dying?
Simon I must leave you so untidy
Monster you are killing me Be sure
I'll have you later Women do endure
I can *can* no longer
and it passes the wretched trap whelming
    and I am me   160

21

drencht & powerful, I did it with my body!
One proud tug greens Heaven. Marvellous,
unforbidding Majesty.
Swell, imperious bells. I fly.
Mountainous, woman not breaks and will
    bend:
sways God nearby: anguish comes to an end.
Blossomed Sarah, and I
blossom. Is that thing alive? I hear a famisht
    howl.

22

Beloved household, I am Simon's wife,
and the mother of Samuel—whom greedy yet
    I miss   170
out of his kicking place.
More in some ways I feel at a loss,
freer. Cantabanks & mummers, nears
longing for you. Our chopping scores my
    ears,
our costume bores my eyes.
St. George to the good sword, rise! chop-
    logic's rife

23

& fever & Satan & Satan's ancient fere.
Pioneering is not feeling well,
not Indians, beasts.
Not all their riddling can forestall　180
one leaving. Sam, your uncle has had to
go fróm us to live with God. 'Then Aunt
　　went too?'
Dear, she does wait still.
Stricken: 'Oh. Then he takes us one by one.'
　　My dear.

24

Forswearing it otherwise, they starch their
　　minds.
Folkmoots, & blether, blether. John Cotton
　　rakes
to the synod of Cambridge.
Down from my body my legs flow,
out from it arms wave, on it my head shakes.
Now Mistress Hutchinson rings forth a call—　190
should she? many creep out at a broken
　　wall—
affirming the Holy Ghost
dwells in one justified. Factioning passion
　　blinds

25

all to all her good, all—can she be exiled?
Bitter sister, victim! I miss you.
—I miss you, Anne,
day or night weak as a child,
tender & empty, doomed, quick to no tryst.
—I hear you. Be kind, you who leaguer
my image in the mist.　200
—Be kind you, to one unchained eager far &
　　wild

26

and if, O my love, my heart is breaking,
　　please
neglect my cries and I will spare you. Deep
in Time's grave, Love's, you lie still.
Lie still.—Now? That happy shape
my forehead had under my most long, rare,
ravendark, hidden, soft bodiless hair
you award me still.
You must not love me, but I do not bid you
　　cease.

27

Veiled my eyes, attending. How can it be I?　210
Moist, with parted lips, I listen, wicked.
I shake in the morning & retch.

Brood I do on myself naked.
A fading world I dust, with fingers new.
—I have earned the right to be alone with
　　you.
—What right can that be?
Convulsing, if you love, enough, like a sweet
　　lie.

28

Not that, I know, you can. This cratered
　　skin,
like the crabs & shells of my Palissy ewer,
　　touch!
Oh, you do, you do?　220
Falls on me what I like a witch,
for lawless holds, annihilations of law
which Time and he and man abhor, foresaw:
sharper than what my Friend
brought me for my revolt when I moved
　　smooth & thin,

29

faintings black, rigour, chilling, brown
parching, back, brain burning, the grey pocks
itch, a manic stench
of pustules snapping, pain floods the palm,
sleepless, or a red shaft with a dreadful start　230
rides at the chapel, like a slipping heart.
My soul strains in one qualm
ah but *this* is not to save me but to throw
　　me down.

30

And out of this I lull. It lessens. Kiss me.
That once. As sings out up in sparkling dark
a trail of a star & dies,
while the breath flutters, sounding, mark,
so shorn ought such caresses to us be
who, deserving nothing, flush and flee
the darkness of that light,　240
a lurching frozen from a warm dream. Talk
　　to me.

31

—It is Spring's New England. Pussy willows
　　wedge
up in the wet. Milky crestings, fringed
yellow, in heaven, eyed
by the melting hand-in-hand or mere
desirers single, heavy-footed, rapt,
make surge poor human hearts. Venus is
　　trapt—
the hefty pike shifts, sheer—

in Orion blazing. Warblings, odours, nudge
    to an edge—

32

—Ravishing, ha, what crouches outside
    ought,   250
flamboyant, ill, angelic. Often, now,
I am afraid of you.
I am a sobersides; I know.
I *want* to take you for my lover.—Do.
—I hear a madness. Harmless I to you
am not, not I?—No.
—I cannot but be. Sing a concord of our
    thought.

33

—Wan dolls in indigo on gold: refrain
my western lust. I am drowning in this past.
I lose sight of you   260
who mistress me from air. Unbraced
in delirium of the grand depths, giving away
haunters what kept me, I breathe solid spray.
—I am losing you!
Straiten me on.—I suffered living like a stain:

34

I trundle the bodies, on the iron bars,
over that fire backward & forth; they burn;
bits fall. I wonder if
I killed them. Women serve my turn.
—Dreams! You are good.—No.—Dense with
    hardihood   270
the wicked are dislodged, and lodged the
    good.
In green space we are safe.
God awaits us (but I am yielding) who Hell
    wars.

35

—I cannot feel myself God waits. He flies
nearer a kindly world; or he is flown.
One Saturday's rescue
won't show. Man is entirely alone
may be. I am a man of griefs & fits
trying to be my friend. And the brown smock
    splits,
down the pale flesh a gash   280
broadens and Time holds up your heart
    against my eyes.

36

—Hard and divided heaven! creases me.
    Shame
is failing. My breath is scented, and I throw
hostile glances toward God.

Crumpling plunge of a pestle, bray:
sin cross & opposite, wherein I survive
nightmares of Eden. Reaches foul & live
he for me, this soul
to crunch, a minute tangle of eternal flame.

37

I fear Hell's hammer-wind. But fear does
    wane.   290
Death's blossoms grain my hair; I cannot
    live.
A black joy clashes
joy, in twilight. The Devil said
'I will deal toward her softly, and her en-
    chanting cries
will fool the horns of Adam.' Father of lies,
a male great pestle smashes
small women swarming towards the mortar's
    rim in vain.

38

I see the cruel spread Wings black with
    saints!
Silky my breasts not his, mine, mine to
    withhold
or tender, tender.   300
I am sifting, nervous, and bold.
The light is changing. Surrender this
    loveliness
you cannot make me do. *But* I will. Yes.
What horror, down stormy air,
warps towards me? My threatening promise
    faints—

39

torture me, Father, least not I be thine!
Tribunal terrible & pure, my God,
mercy for him and me.
Faces half-fanged, Christ drives abroad,
and though the crop hopes, Jane is so slipshod 310
I cry. Evil dissolves, & love, like foam;
that love. Prattle of children powers me
    home,
my heart claps like the swan's
under a frenzy of *who* love me & who shine.

40

As a canoe slides by on one strong stroke
hope his hélp not I, who do hardly bear
his gift still. But whisper
I am not utterly. I pare
an apple for my pipsqueak Mercy and
she runs & all need naked apples, fanned   320
their tinier envies.

Vomitings, trots, rashes. Can be hope a
   cloak?

41

for the man with cropt ears glares. My fingers
   tighten
my skirt. I pass. Alas! I pity all.
Shy, shy, with mé, Dorothy.
Moonrise, and frightening hoots. 'Mother,
how *long* will I be dead?' Our friend the
   owl
vanishes, darling, but your homing soul
retires on Heaven, Mercy:
not we one instant die, only our dark does
   lighten.   330

42

When by me in the dusk my child sits down
I am myself. Simon, if it's that loose,
let me wiggle it out.
You'll get a bigger one there, & bite.
How they loft, how their sizes delight and
   grate.
The proportioned, spiritless poems
   accumulate.
And they publish them
away in brutish London, for a hollow crown.

43

Father is not himself. He keeps his bed,
and threw a saffron scum Thursday. God-
   forsaken words   340
escaped him raving. Save,
Lord, thy servant zealous & just.
Sam he saw back from Harvard. He did scold
his secting enemies. His stomach is cold
while we drip, while
my baby John breaks out. O far from where
   he bred!

44

Bone of moaning: sung Where he has gone
a thousand summers by truth-hallowed
   souls;
be still. Agh, he is gone!
Where? I know. Beyond the shoal.   350
Still-all a Christian daughter grinds her teeth
a little. This our land has ghosted with
our dead: I am at home.
Finish, Lord, in me this work thou hast
   begun.

45

And they tower, whom the pear-tree lured
to let them fall, fierce mornings they reclined
down the brook-bank to the east

fishing for shiners with a crookt pin,
wading, dams massing, well, and Sam's to be
a doctor in Boston. After the divisive sea, 360
and death's first feast,
and the galled effort on the wilderness
   endured,

46

Arminians, and the King bore against us;
of an 'inward light' we hear with horror.
Whose fan is in his hand
and he will thoroughly purge his floor,
come towards mé. I have what licks the
   joints
and bites the heart, which winter more
   appoints.
Iller I, oftener.
Hard at the outset; in the ending thus hard,
   thus?   370

47

Sacred & unutterable Mind
flashing thorough the universe one thought,
I do wait without peace.
In the article of death I budge.
Eat my sore breath, Black Angel. Let me die.
Body a-drain, when will you be dry
and countenance my speed
to Heaven's springs? lest stricter writhings
   have me declined.

48

'What are those pictures in the air at night,
Mother?' Mercy did ask. Space charged with
   faces   380
day & night! I place
a goatskin's fetor, and sweat: fold me
in savoury arms. Something is shaking,
   wrong.
He smells the musket and lifts it. It is long.
It points at my heart.
Missed he must have. In the gross storm of
   sunlight

49

I sniff a fire burning without outlet,
consuming acrid its own smoke. It's me.
Ruined laughter sounds
outside. Ah but I waken, free.   390
And so I am about again. I hagged
a fury at the short maid, whom tongues
   tagged,
and I am sorry. Once
less I was anxious when more passioned to
   upset

50

the mansion & the garden & the beauty of
God.
Insectile unreflective busyness
blunts & does amend.
Hangnails, piles, fibs, life's also.
But we are that from which draws back a
thumb.
The seasons stream and, somehow, I am
become   400
an old woman. It's so:
I look. I bear to look. Strokes once more his
rod.

51

My window gives on the graves, in our
great new house
(how many burned?) upstairs, among the
elms.
I lie, & endure, & wonder.
A haze slips sometimes over my dreams
and holiness on horses' bells shall stand.
Wandering pacemaker, unsteadying friend,
in a redskin calm I wait:
beat when you will our end. Sinkings &
droopings drowse.   410

52

They say thro' the fading winter Dorothy
fails,
my second, who than I bore one more, nine;
and I see her inearthed. I linger.
Seaborn she wed knelt before Simon;
Simon I, and linger. Black-yellow seething,
vast
it lies fróm me, mine: all they look aghast.
It will be a glorious arm.
Docile I watch. My wreckt chest hurts when
Simon pales.

53

In the yellowing days your faces wholly fail,
at Fall's onset. Solemn voices fade.   420
I feel no coverlet.
Light notes leap, a beckon, swaying
the tilted, sickening ear within. I'll—I'll—
I am closed & coming. Somewhere! I defile
wide as a cloud, in a cloud,
unfit, desirous, glad—even the singings veil—

54

—You are not ready? You áre ready. Pass,
as shadow gathers shadow in the welling
night.
Fireflies of childhood torch

you down. We commit our sister down.   430
One candle mourn by, which a lover gave,
the use's edge and order of her grave.
Quiet? Moisture shoots.
Hungry throngs collect. They sword into the
carcass.

55

Headstones stagger under great draughts of
time
after heads pass out, and their world must
reel
speechless, blind in the end
about its chilling star: thrift tuft,
whin cushion—nothing. Already with the
wounded flying
dark air fills, I am a closet of secrets dying,   440
races murder, foxholes hold men,
reactor piles wage slow upon the wet brain
rime.

56

I must pretend to leave you. Only you draw
off
a benevolent phantom. I say you seem to me
drowned towns off England,
featureless as those myriads
who what bequeathed save fire-ash, fossils,
burled
in the open river-drifts of the Old World?
Simon lived on for years.
I renounce not even ragged glances, small
teeth, nothing,   450

57

O all your ages at the mercy of my loves
together lie at once, forever or
so long as I happen.
In the rain of pain & departure, still
Love has no body and presides the sun,
and elfs from silence melody. I run.
Hover, utter, still,
a sourcing whom my lost candle like the fire-
fly loves.

NOTES

Stanzas	
1-4	The poem is about the woman but this exordium is spoken by the poet, his voice modulating in stanza 4, line 8 [4.8] into hers.
1.1	He was not Governor until after her death.
1.5	Sylvester (the translator of Du Bartas)

and Quarles, her favourite poets; unfortunately.

5.4,5   Many details are from quotations in Helen Campbell's biography, the Winthrop papers, narratives, town histories.

8.4ff.   Scriptural passages are sometimes ones she used herself, as this in her *Meditation liii.*

11.8   *that one:* the Old One.

12.5-13.2   The poet interrupts.

18.8   Her first child was not born until about 1633.

22.6   *chopping:* disputing, snapping, haggling; axing.

23.1   *fere:* his friend Death.

24.1   Her irony of 22.8 intensifies.

24.2   *rakes:* inclines, as a mast; bows.

25.3   One might say: He is enabled to speak, at last, in the fortune of an echo of her—and when she is loneliest (her former spiritual adviser having deserted Anne Hutchinson, and this her closest friend banished), as if she had summoned him; and only thus, perhaps, is she enabled to hear him. This second section of the poem is a dialogue, his voice however ceasing well before it ends at 39.4, and hers continuing for the whole third part, until the coda (54-57).

29.1-4   Cf. Isa. 1:5.

29.5,6   After a Klee.

33.1   Cf., on Byzantine icons, Frederick Rolfe ("Baron Corvo"): 'Who ever dreams of praying (with expectation of response) for the prayer of a Tintoretto or a Titian, or a Bellini, or a Botticelli? But who can refrain from crying "O Mother!" to these unruffleable wan dolls in indigo on gold?' (quoted from *The Desire and Pursuit of the Whole* by Graham Greene in *The Lost Childhood*).

33.5,6   'Délires des grandes profondeurs,' described by Cousteau and others; a euphoria, sometimes fatal, in which the hallucinated diver offers passing fish his line, helmet, anything.

35.3,4   As of cliffhangers, movie serials wherein each week's episode ends with a train bearing down on the strapped heroine or with the hero dangling over an abyss into which Indians above him peer with satisfaction before they hatchet the rope.
rescue: forcible recovery (by the owner) of goods distrained.

37.7,8   After an engraving somewhere in Fuchs's collections. *Bray,* above (36.4), puns.

39.5   The stanza is unsettled, like 24, by a middle line, signaling a broad transition.

42.8   *brutish:* her epithet for London in a kindly passage about the Great Fire.

46.1,2   Arminians, rebels against the doctrine of unconditional election. Her husband alone opposed the law condemning Quakers to death.

46.3,4   Matthew 3:12.

46.5,6   Rheumatic fever, after a celebrated French description.

48.2ff   *Space . . . outside:* delirium.

51.5   Cf. Zech. 14:20.

51.6   *Wandering pacemaker:* a disease of the heart, here the heart itself.

52.4   Seaborn Cotton, John's eldest son; Bradstreet being then magistrate.

52.5,6   Dropsical, a complication of the last three years. Line 7 she actually said.

55.4   *thrift:* the plant, also called Our Lady's cushion.

55.8   *wet brain:* edema.

56.5,6   Cf. G. R. Levy, *The Gate of Horn,* p. 5.

ROBERT LOWELL (1917–   )

Born March 1, 1917, in Boston, Massachusetts; educated at Harvard University and Kenyon College; imprisoned during Second World War as conscientious objector; has taught at Iowa, Boston, and Harvard universities; member National Institute of Arts and Letters

(1954) and American Academy of Arts and Letters (1963); Chancellor, Academy of American Poets; honors include Pulitzer prize for poetry (for *Lord Weary's Castle*, 1946), and National Book Award for poetry (for *Life Studies*, 1959), as well as the Bollingen Prize for translation (for *Imitations*, 1962); other volumes of poetry are *Land of Unlikeness* (1944), *The Mills of the Kavanaughs* (1951), *For the Union Dead* (1964), *Near the Ocean* (1967), *Notebook 1967–8* (1969), and *Notebooks, Revised and Expanded* (1970); also *Phaedra* (1961, translation of Racine's *Phèdre*).

The Quaker Graveyard in Nantucket (1946)

(FOR WARREN WINSLOW, DEAD AT SEA)

Let man have dominion over the fishes of the sea and the fowls of the air and the beasts and the whole earth, and every creeping creature that moveth upon the earth.

1

A brackish reach of shoal off Madaket,—
The sea was still breaking violently and night
Had steamed into our North Atlantic Fleet,
When the drowned sailor clutched the drag-
    net. Light
Flashed from his matted head and marble
    feet,
He grappled at the net
With the coiled, hurdling muscles of his
    thighs:
The corpse was bloodless, a botch of reds
    and whites,
Its open, staring eyes
were lustreless dead-lights   10
Or cabin-windows on a stranded hulk
Heavy with sand. We weight the body, close
Its eyes and heave it seaward whence it came,
Where the heel-headed dogfish barks its nose
On Ahab's void and forehead; and the name
Is blocked in yellow chalk.
Sailors, who pitch this portent at the sea
Where dreadnaughts shall confess
Its hell-bent deity,
When you are powerless   20
To sand-bag this Atlantic bulwark, faced
By the earth-shaker, green, unwearied, chaste
In his steel scales: ask for no Orphean lute
To pluck life back. The guns of the steeled
    fleet
Recoil and then repeat
The hoarse salute.

2

Whenever winds are moving and their breath
Heaves at the roped-in bulwarks of this pier,
The terns and sea-gulls tremble at your death
In these home waters. Sailor, can you hear   30
The Pequod's sea wings, beating landward,
    fall
Headlong and break on our Atlantic wall
Off 'Sconset, where the yawing S-boats
    splash
The bellbuoy, with ballooning spinnakers,
As the entangled, screeching mainsheet clears
The blocks: off Madaket, where lubbers lash
The heavy surf and throw their long lead
    squids
For blue-fish? Sea-gulls blink their heavy lids
Seaward. The winds' wings beat upon the
    stones,
Cousin, and scream for you and the claws
    rush   40
At the sea's throat and wring it in the slush
Of this old Quaker graveyard where the
    bones
Cry out in the long night for the hurt beast
Bobbing by Ahab's whaleboats in the East.

3

All you recovered from Poseidon died
With you, my cousin, and the harrowed
    brine
Is fruitless on the blue beard of the god,
Stretching beyond us to the castles in Spain,
Nantucket's westward haven. To Cape Cod
Guns, cradled on the tide,   50
Blast the eelgrass about a waterclock
Of bilge and backwash, roil the salt and sand
Lashing earth's scaffold, rock
Our warships in the hand
Of the great God, where time's contrition
    blues
Whatever it was these Quaker sailors lost
In the mad scramble of their lies. They died
When time was open-eyed,
Wooden and childish; only bones abide

There, in the nowhere, where their boats
    were tossed   60
Sky-high, where mariners had fabled news
Of IS, the whited monster. What it cost
Them is their secret. In the sperm-whale's
    slick
I see the Quakers drown and hear their cry:
"If God himself had not been on our side,
If God himself had not been on our side,
When the Atlantic rose against us, why,
Then it had swallowed us up quick."

4

This is the end of the whaleroad and the
    whale
Who spewed Nantucket bones on the
    thrashed swell
And stirred the troubled waters to whirlpools   70
To send the Pequod packing off to hell:
This is the end of them, three-quarters fools,
Snatching at straws to sail
Seaward and seaward on the turntail whale,
Spouting out blood and water as it rolls,
Sick as a dog to these Atlantic shoals:
Clamavimus, O depths. Let the sea-gulls wail

For water, for the deep where the high tide
Mutters to its hurt self, mutters and ebbs.   80
Waves wallow in their wash, go out and out,
Leave only the death-rattle of the crabs,
The beach increasing, its enormous snout
Sucking the ocean's side.
This is the end of running on the waves;
We are poured out like water. Who will
    dance
The mast-lashed master of Leviathans
Up from this field of Quakers in their un-
    stoned graves?

5

When the whale's viscera go and the roll
Of its corruption overruns this world   90
Beyond tree-swept Nantucket and Wood's
    Hole
And Martha's Vineyard, Sailor, will your
    sword
Whistle and fall and sink into the fat?
In the great ash-pit of Jehoshaphat
The bones cry for the blood of the white
    whale,
The fat flukes arch and whack about its ears,
The death-lance churns into the sanctuary,
    tears
The gun-blue swingle, heaving like a flail,

And hacks the coiling life out: it works and
    drags
And rips the sperm-whale's midriff into rags,   100
Gobbets of blubber spill to wind and
    weather,
Sailor, and gulls go round the stoven timbers
Where the morning stars sing out together
And thunder shakes the white surf and
    dismembers
The red flag hammered in the mast-head.
    Hide,
Our steel, Jonas Messias, in Thy side.

6

OUR LADY OF WALSINGHAM

There once the penitents took off their shoes
And then walked barefoot the remaining
    mile;
And the small trees, a stream and hedgerows
    file
Slowly along the munching English lane,   110
Like cows to the old shrine, until you lose
Track of your dragging pain.
The stream flows down under the druid tree,
Shiloah's whirlpools gurgle and make glad
The castle of God. Sailor, you were glad
And whistled Sion by that stream. But see:

Our Lady, too small for her canopy,
Sits near the altar. There's no comeliness
At all or charm in that expressionless
Face with its heavy eyelids. As before,   120
This face, for centuries a memory,
Non est species, neque decor,
Expressionless, expresses God: it goes
Past castled Sion. She knows what God
    knows,
Not Calvary's Cross nor crib at Bethlehem
Now, and the world shall come to
    Walsingham.

7

The empty winds are creaking and the oak
Splatters and splatters on the cenotaph,
The boughs are trembling and a gaff
Bobs on the untimely stroke   130
Of the greased wash exploding on a shoal-
    bell
In the old mouth of the Atlantic. It's well;
Atlantic, you are fouled with the blue sailors,
Sea-monsters, upward angel, downward fish:

Unmarried and corroding, spare of flesh
Mart once of supercilious, wing'd clippers,
Atlantic, where your bell-trap guts its spoil
You could cut the brackish winds with a
    knife
Here in Nantucket, and cast up the time

When the Lord God formed man from the
    sea's slime   140
And breathed into his face the breath of life,
And blue-lung'd combers lumbered to the
    kill.
The Lord survives the rainbow of His will.

Mr. Edwards and the Spider (1946)

I saw the spiders marching through the air,
Swimming from tree to tree that mildewed
    day
    In latter August when the hay
    Came creaking to the barn. But where
        The wind is westerly,
Where gnarled November makes the spiders
    fly
Into the apparitions of the sky,
They purpose nothing but their ease and
    die
Urgently beating east to sunrise and the sea;

What are we in the hands of the great God?   10
It was in vain you set up thorn and briar
    In battle array against the fire
    And treason crackling in your blood;
        For the wild thorns grow tame
And will do nothing to oppose the flame;
Your lacerations tell the losing game
You play against a sickness past your cure.
How will the hands be strong? How will the
    heart endure?

A very little thing, a little worm,
Or hourglass-blazoned spider, it is said,   20
    Can kill a tiger. Will the dead
    Hold up his mirror and affirm

To the four winds the smell
And flash of his authority? It's well
If God who holds you to the pit of hell,
Much as one holds a spider, will destroy,
Baffle and dissipate your soul. As a small boy

On Windsor Marsh, I saw the spider die
When thrown into the bowels of fierce fire:
    There's no long struggle, no desire   30
        To get up on its feet and fly—
        It stretches out its feet
And dies. This is the sinner's last retreat;
Yes, and no strength exerted on the heat
Then sinews the abolished will, when sick
And full of burning, it will whistle on a brick.

But who can plumb the sinking of that
    soul?
Josiah Hawley, picture yourself cast
    Into a brick-kiln where the blast
    Fans your quick vitals to a coal—   40
        If measured by a glass,
How long would it seem burning! Let there
    pass
A minute, ten, ten trillion; but the blaze
Is infinite, eternal: this is death,
To die and know it. This is the Black Widow,
    death.

Skunk Hour (1956)

(*For Elizabeth Bishop*)

Nautilus Island's hermit
heiress still lives through winter in her Spartan
    cottage;
her sheep still graze above the sea.
Her son's a bishop. Her farmer
is first selectman in our village;
she's in her dotage.

Thirsting for
the hierarchic privacy
of Queen Victoria's century,

she buys up all   10
the eyesores facing her shore,
and lets them fall.

The season's ill—
we've lost our summer millionaire,
who seemed to leap from an L. L. Bean
catalogue. His nine-knot yawl
was auctioned off to lobstermen.
A red fox stain covers Blue Hill.

And now our fairy
decorator brightens his shop for fall;   20
his fishnet's filled with orange cork,

orange, his cobbler's bench and awl;
there is no money in his work,
he'd rather marry.

One dark night,
my Tudor Ford climbed the hill's skull;
I watched for love-cars. Lights turned down,
they lay together, hull to hull,
where the graveyard shelves on the
        town. . . .
My mind's not right.   30

A car radio bleats,
"Love, O careless Love. . . ." I hear
my ill-spirit sob in each blood cell,
as if my hand were at its throat. . . .
I myself am hell;

nobody's here—

only skunks, that search
in the moonlight for a bite to eat.
They march on their soles up Main Street:
white stripes, moonstruck eyes' red fire   40
under the chalk-dry and spar spire
of the Trinitarian Church.

I stand on top
of our back steps and breathe the rich air—
a mother skunk with her column of kittens
    swills the garbage pail.
She jabs her wedge-head in a cup
of sour cream, drops her ostrich tail,
and will not scare.

To Delmore Schwartz (1956)

(*Cambridge 1946*)

We couldn't even keep the furnace lit!
Even when we had disconnected it,
the antiquated
refrigerator gurgled mustard gas
through your mustard-yellow house,
and spoiled our long maneuvered visit
from T. S. Eliot's brother, Henry Ware. . . .

Your stuffed duck craned toward Harvard
    from my trunk:
its bill was a black whistle, and its brow
was high and thinner than a baby's thumb;   10
its webs were tough as toenails on its bough.
It was your first kill; you had rushed it home,
pickled in a tin wastebasket of rum—
it looked through us, as if it'd died dead drunk.
You must have propped its eyelids with a nail,
and yet it lived with us and met our stare,
Rabelaisian, lubricious, drugged. And there,
perched on my trunk and typing-table,
it cooled our universal
Angst a moment, Delmore. We drank and
    eyed   20

the chicken-hearted shadows of the world.
Underseas fellows, nobly mad,
we talked away our friends. "Let Joyce and
    Freud,
the Masters of Joy,
be our guests here," you said. The room was
    filled
with cigarette smoke circling the paranoid,
inert gaze of Coleridge, back
from Malta—his eyes lost in flesh, lips baked
    and black.
Your tiger kitten, *Oranges*,
cartwheeled for joy in a ball of snarls.   30
You said:
"*We poets in our youth begin in sadness;
thereof in the end come despondency and
    madness;*
Stalin has had two cerebral hemorrhages!"
The Charles
River was turning silver. In the ebb-
light of morning, we stuck
the duck
-'s web-
foot, like a candle, in a quart of gin we'd
    killed.   40

For the Union Dead (1964)

"*Relinquunt Omnia Servare Rem Publicam.*"

The old South Boston Aquarium stands
in a Sahara of snow now. Its broken windows
    are boarded.

The bronze weathervane cod has lost half its
    scales.
The airy tanks are dry.

Once my nose crawled like a snail on the
    glass;

my hand tingled
to burst the bubbles
drifting from the noses of the cowed, com-
    pliant fish.

My hand draws back. I often sigh still
for the dark downward and vegetating kingdom   10
of the fish and reptile. One morning last
    March,
I pressed against the new barbed and
    galvanized

fence on the Boston Common. Behind their
    cage,
yellow dinosaur steamshovels were grunting
as they cropped up tons of mush and grass
to gouge their underworld garage.

Parking spaces luxuriate like civic
sandpiles in the heart of Boston.
A girdle of orange, Puritan-pumpkin colored
    girders
braces the tingling Statehouse,   20

shaking over the excavations, as it faces
    Colonel Shaw
and his bell-cheeked Negro infantry
on St. Gaudens' shaking Civil War relief,
propped by a plank splint against the garage's
    earthquake.

Two months after marching through Boston,
half the regiment was dead;
at the dedication,
William James could almost hear the bronze
    Negroes breathe.

Their monument sticks like a fishbone
in the city's throat.   30
Its Colonel is as lean
as a compass-needle.

He has an angry wrenlike vigilance,
a greyhound's gentle tautness;
he seems to wince at pleasure,

and suffocate for privacy.

He is out of bounds now. He rejoices in man's
    lovely,
peculiar power to choose life and die—
when he leads his black soldiers to death,
he cannot bend his back.   40

On a thousand small town New England
    greens,
the old white churches hold their air
of sparse, sincere rebellion; frayed flags
quilt the graveyards of the Grand Army of the
    Republic.

The stone statues of the abstract Union Soldier
grow slimmer and younger each year—
wasp-wasted, they doze over muskets
and muse through their sideburns . . .

Shaw's father wanted no monument
except the ditch,   50
where his son's body was thrown
and lost with his "niggers."

The ditch is nearer.
There are no statues for the last war here;
on Boyleston Street, a commercial photograph
shows Hiroshima boiling

over a Mosler Safe, the "Rock of Ages"
that survived the blast. Space is nearer.
When I crouch to my television set,
the drained faces of Negro school-children rise
    like balloons.   60

Colonel Shaw
is riding on his bubble,
he waits
for the blessèd break.

The Aquarium is gone. Everywhere,
giant finned cars nose forward like fish;
a savage servility
slides by on grease.

The Old Flame (1964)

My old flame, my wife!
Remember our lists of birds?
One morning last summer, I drove
by our house in Maine. It was still

on top of its hill—
Now a red ear of Indian maize
was splashed on the door.
Old Glory with thirteen stripes

hung on a pole. The clapboard
was old-red schoolhouse red.   10

Inside, a new landlord,
a new wife, a new broom!
Atlantic seaboard antique shop
pewter and plunder
shone in each room.

A new frontier!
No running next door
now to phone the sheriff
for his taxi to Bath
and the State Liquor Store!   20

No one saw your ghostly
imaginary lover
stare through the window,
and tighten
the scarf at his throat.

Health to the new people,

health to their flag, to their old
restored house on the hill!
Everything had been swept bare,
furnished, garnished and aired.   30

Everything's changed for the best—
how quivering and fierce we were,
there snowbound together,
simmering like wasps
in our tent of books!

Poor ghost, old love, speak
with your old voice
of flaming insight
that kept us awake all night.
In one bed and apart,   40

we heard the plow
groaning up hill—
a red light, then a blue,
as it tossed off the snow
to the side of the road.

Hawthorne (1964)

Follow its lazy main street lounging
from the alms house to Gallows Hill
along a flat, unvaried surface
covered with wooden houses
aged by yellow drain
like the unhealthy hair of an old dog.
You'll walk to no purpose
in Hawthorne's Salem.

I cannot resilver the smudged plate.

I drop to Hawthorne, the customs officer,   10
measuring coal and mostly trying to keep
    warm—
to the stunted black schooner,
the dismal South-end dock,
the wharf-piles with their fungus of ice.
On State Street
a steeple with a glowing dial-clock
measures the weary hours,
the merciless march of professional feet.

Even this shy distrustful ego
sometimes walked on top of the blazing roof,   20

and felt those flashes
that char the discharged cells of the brain.
Look at the faces—
Longfellow, Lowell, Holmes and Whittier!
Study the grizzled silver of their beards.
Hawthorne's picture,
however, has a blond mustache
and golden General Custer scalp.
He looks like a Civil War officer.
He shines in the firelight. His hard   30
survivor's smile is touched with fire.

Leave him alone for a moment or two,
and you'll see him with his head
bent down, brooding, brooding,
eyes fixed on some chip,
some stone, some common plant,
the commonest thing,
as if it were the clue.
The disturbed eyes rise,
furtive, foiled, dissatisfied   40
from meditation on the true
and insignificant.

WILLIAM MEREDITH (1919–   )

Born January 9, 1919, in New York City; graduated Princeton University in 1940; military service as naval aviator during Second World War; has taught at Princeton, University of Hawaii, Middlebury College, and since 1954 at Connecticut College; recipient of three annual prizes from *Poetry* magazine and Loines Award from National Institute of Arts and Letters (1966); Chancellor, since 1964, Academy of American Poets; member National Institute of Arts and Letters (1968); volumes of poetry are *Love Letter from an Impossible Land* (1944), *Ships and Other Figures* (1948), *The Open Sea and Other Poems* (1958), *The Wreck of the Thresher* (1964), and *Earth Walk: New and Selected Poems* (1970); also *Alcools: Poems 1898–1919* (translation of Apollinaire, 1964).

Winter Verse for His Sister (1970)

Moonlight washes the west side of the house
As clean as bone, it carpets like a lawn
The stubbled field tilting eastward
Where there is no sign yet of dawn.
The moon is an angel with a bright light sent
To surprise me once before I die
With the real aspect of things.
It holds the light steady and makes no
    comment.

Practicing for death I have lately gone
To that other house   10
Where our parents did most of their dying,
Embracing and not embracing their conditions.
Our father built bookcases and little by little
    stopped reading,
Our mother cooked proud meals for common
    mouths.

Kindly, they raised two children. We raked
    their leaves
And cut their grass, we ate and drank with
    them.
Reconciliation was our long work, not all of
    it joyful.

Now outside my own house at a cold hour
I watch the noncommital angel lower
The steady lantern that's worn these clapboards
    thin   20
In a wash of moonlight, while men slept
    within,
Accepting and not accepting their conditions,
And the fingers of trees plied a deep carpet of
    decay
On the gravel web underneath the field,
And the field tilting always toward day.

Hydraulics (1970)

1

A Sears Roebuck pump, it would snuffle
a while in the tin sink, then raise
gouts of the slightly bitter water
twenty-five feet from under the house.
The grandfather told them
that even if you had one machined
in Switzerland, like a watch,
it would stop short of thirty-two feet.
Those are the conditions we pump under,
he said, it is not the same thing to push   10
water up from the bottom by turbine.

The heart knows conditions of vacuum
where its chambers no longer refill
with generosity, though it still pushes blood.

2

We went for a walk in the woods
below the pond: *chung, chung, chung,*
the ram was working.
It lets the water flow
and when a pipeful is rushing
downhill as it loves to,   20

chung, the ram cuts it off.
Some of it is baffled uphill to a cistern
where it waits its turn at the fountain,
and the thinned rank resumes its descent.
This is happening all the time, after we turn
back up the hill, whether we are listening or
    not—
the ram takes the patient water-head for
    granted
and the guileless water can think of no better
    journey.

3

How does water know
that if it will climb to the top   30
of the pander syphon's loop
it will be free to drop
into water's arms below?

4

John Wesley Powell, watching his perilous
one-armed way down the unknown Colorado,
    thinks:
a river has three ways to deal with an upstart
    mountain—
saw through it like a log as it thrusts up,
gather a head and flush the mountain out,
or it can flow by while the oldest saw-tooth
    peak
weathers away to a soft rivering dream.   40

'The waters are deep and quiet
but the swallows are a noisy people.'
He named the place Swallow Canyon.
(June 4, 1869)

5

Then there is this racket of blood
rubbing the little hairs of the ear
against the pillowcase at night.
That is nothing—a tiny meter.
One two, one two, is all the little wheel
    can say,
though one knows that there is a larger,
and a larger still, and that from the third—   50
the silent, hardly moving wheel—
a computation is being made.

6

Ever since as a boy I read Lamartine
I have hoped that my heart,
when it returned to the lake
at the bottom of the world, would not settle
    and mope
there where everything is supposed to be
    contemplative.
Now my wish is that it will continue to pump
easily, with the pulse love has taught it.
Terrible hydraulics await us. Against them   60
you have taught me one simple process
as sovereign and repetitious as rain.

RICHARD WILBUR (1921–   )

Born March 1, 1921, in New York City; educated at Amherst (A.B., 1942), Harvard (M.A., 1947); served in the army in Second World War; has taught at Harvard, Wellesley, and Wesleyan University; honors include Rome fellowship from American Academy of Arts and Letters (1954), Pulitzer prize (1957), and National Book Award (1957); member National Institute of Arts and Letters (1957); Chancellor, Academy of American Poets; volumes of poetry are *The Beautiful Changes* (1947), *Ceremony and Other Poems* (1950), *Things of This World* (1956), *Advice to a Prophet* (1961), *The Poems of Richard Wilbur* (1963), and *Walking to Sleep* (1969); also translated Molière's *The Misanthrope* (1955) and *Tartuffe*; children's books, *Loudmouse* (1968) and *Digging for China* (1970); lyrics for the comic opera *Candide* (1957), based on Voltaire's work.

Folk Tune (1947)

When Bunyan swung his whopping axe
The forests strummed as one loud lute,

The timber crashed beside his foot
And sprung up stretching in his tracks.

He had an ox, but his was blue.
The flower in his buttonhole
Was brighter than a parasol.
He's gone. Tom Swift has vanished too,

Who worked at none but wit's expense,   10
Putting dirigibles together
Out in the yard, in the quiet weather,
Whistling behind Tom Sawyer's fence.

Now when the darkness in my street
Nibbles the last and crusty crumbs
Of sound, and all the city numbs
And goes to sleep upon its feet,

I listen hard to hear its dreams:
John Henry is our nightmare friend,
Whose shoulders roll without an end,
Whose veins pump, pump and burst their
    seams,   20

Whose sledge is smashing at the rock
And makes the sickly city toss
And half awake in sighs of loss
Until the screaming of the clock.

John Henry's hammer and his will
Are here and ringing out our wrong,
I hear him driving all night long
To beat the leisured snarling drill.

Juggler (1948)

A ball will bounce, but less and less. It's not
A light-hearted thing, resents its own resilience.
Falling is what it loves, and the earth falls
So in our hearts from brilliance,
Settles and is forgot.
It takes a sky-blue juggler with five red balls

To shake our gravity up. Whee, in the air
The balls roll round, wheel on his wheeling
    hands,
Learning the ways of lightness, alter to spheres
Grazing his finger ends,   10
Cling to their courses there,
Swinging a small heaven about his ears.

But a heaven is easier made of nothing at all
Than the earth regained, and still and sole
    within
The spin of worlds, with a gesture sure and
    noble
He reels that heaven in,

Landing it ball by ball,
And trades it all for a broom, a plate, a table.

Oh, on his toe the table is turning, the
    broom's
Balancing up on his nose, and the plate whirls   20
On the tip of the broom! Damn, what a show,
    we cry:
The boys stamp, and the girls
Shriek, and the drum booms
And all comes down, and he bows and says
    good-bye.

If the juggler is tired now, if the broom stands
In the dust again, if the table starts to drop
Through the daily dark again, and though the
    plate
Lies flat on the table top,
For him we batter our hands
Who has won for once over the world's weight.   30

Still, Citizen Sparrow (1948)

Still, citizen sparrow, this vulture which you
    call
Unnatural, let him but lumber again to air
Over the rotten office, let him bear
The carrion ballast up, and at the tall

Tip of the sky lie cruising. Then you'll see
That no more beautiful bird is in heaven's
    height,

No wider more placid wings, no watchfuller
    flight;
He shoulders nature there, the frightfully free,

The naked-headed one. Pardon him, you
Who dart in the orchard aisles, for it is he   10
Devours death, mocks mutability,
Has heart to make an end, keeps nature new.

Thinking of Noah, childheart, try to forget

How for so many bedlam hours his saw
Soured the song of birds with its wheezy gnaw,
And the slam of his hammer all the day beset

The people's ears. Forget that he could bear
To see the towns like coral under the keel,
And the fields so dismal deep. Try rather to
    feel

How high and weary it was, on the waters
    where   20

He rocked his only world, and everyone's.
Forgive the hero, you who would have died
Gladly with all you knew; he rode that tide
To Ararat; all men are Noah's sons.

The Death of a Toad (1950)

A toad the power mower caught,
Chewed and clipped of a leg, with a hobbling
        hop has got
To the garden verge, and sanctuaried him
Under the cineraria leaves, in the shade
    Of the ashen heartshaped leaves, in a dim,
        Low, and a final glade.

The rare original heartsblood goes,
Spends on the earthen hide, in the folds and
        wizening, flows
In the gutters of the banked and staring
        eyes. He lies

As still as if he would return to stone,   10
    And soundlessly attending, dies
        Toward some deep monotone,

Toward misted and ebullient seas
And cooling shores, toward lost Amphibia's
        emperies.
Day dwindles, drowning, and at length is
        gone
In the wide and antique eyes, which still
        appear
    To watch, across the castrate lawn,
        The haggard daylight steer.

JAMES DICKEY (1923–   )

Born February 2, 1923, in Atlanta, Georgia; studied at Vanderbilt (A.B., 1949, M.A., 1950); military service in Second World War and Korea as fighter pilot; has worked as advertising executive, screenwriter, and taught at Reed, University of Wisconsin, and University of South Carolina; member National Institute of Arts and Letters (1972); Consultant in Poetry to Library of Congress (1967–69); volumes of poetry are *Into the Stone* (1957), *Drowning with* *Others* (1962), *Helmets* (1964), *Two Poems of the Air* (1964), *Buckdancer's Choice* (1965) for which he received the National Book Award (1966), *Poems: 1957–1967* (1967), *The Eye-Beaters, Blood, Victory, Madness, Buckhead and Mercy* (1970); also essays, collected in *The Suspect in Poetry* (1964), *Babel to Byzantium* (1968) and *The Self as Agent* (1970); and a novel, *Deliverance* (1970).

Cherrylog Road (1964)

Off Highway 106
At Cherrylog Road I entered
The '34 Ford without wheels,
Smothered in kudzu,
With a seat pulled out to run
Corn whiskey down from the hills.

And then from the other side
Crept into an Essex
With a rumble seat of red leather
And then out again, aboard   10
A blue Chevrolet, releasing
The rust from its other color,

Reared up on three building blocks.
None had the same body heat;
I changed with them inward, toward
The weedy heart of the junkyard,
For I knew that Doris Holbrook
Would escape from her father at noon

And would come from the farm
To seek parts owned by the sun   20
Among the abandoned chassis,
Sitting in each in turn
As I did, leaning forward
As in a wild stock-car race

In the parking lot of the dead.
Time after time, I climbed in
And out the other side, like
An envoy or movie star
Met at the station by crickets.
A radiator cap raised its head,   30

Become a real toad or a kingsnake
As I neared the hub of the yard,
Passing through many states,
Many lives, to reach
Some grandmother's long Pierce-Arrow
Sending platters of blindness forth

From its nickel hubcaps
And spilling its tender upholstery
On sleepy roaches,
The glass panel in between   40
Lady and colored driver
Not all the way broken out.

The back-seat phone
Still on its hook.
I got in as though to exclaim,
"Let us go to the orphan asylum,
John; I have some old toys
For children who say their prayers."

I popped with sweat as I thought
I heard Doris Holbrook scrape   50
Like a mouse in the southern-state sun
That was eating the paint in blisters
From a hundred car tops and hoods.
She was tapping like code,

Loosening the screws,
Carrying off headlights,
Sparkplugs, bumpers,
Cracked mirrors and gear-knobs,
Getting ready, already,
To go back with something to show   60

Other than her lips' new trembling
I would hold to me soon, soon,
Where I sat in the ripped back seat
Talking over the interphone,
Praying for Doris Holbrook
To come from her father's farm

And to get back there
With no trace of me on her face
To be seen by her red-haired father
Who would change, in the squalling barn,   70
Her back's pale skin with a strop,
Then lay for me

In a bootlegger's roasting car
With a string-triggered 12-gauge shotgun
To blast the breath from the air.
Not cut by the jagged windshields,
Through the acres of wrecks she came
With a wrench in her hand,

Through dust where the blacksnake dies
Of boredom, and the beetle knows   80
The compost has no more life.
Someone outside would have seen
The oldest car's door inexplicably
Close from within:

I held her and held her and held her,
Convoyed at terrific speed
By the stalled, dreaming traffic around us,
So the blacksnake, stiff
With inaction, curved back
Into life, and hunted the mouse   90

With deadly overexcitement,
The beetles reclaimed their field
As we clung, glued together,
With the hooks of the seat springs
Working through to catch us red-handed
Amidst the gray, breathless batting

That burst from the seat at our backs.
We left by separate doors
Into the changed, other bodies
Of cars, she down Cherrylog Road   100
And I to my motorcycle
Parked like the soul of the junkyard

Restored, a bicycle fleshed
With power, and tore off
Up Highway 106, continually
Drunk on the wind in my mouth,
Wringing the handlebar for speed,
Wild to be wreckage forever.

Gamecock (1965)

Fear, jealousy and murder are the same
When they put on their long reddish feathers,
Their shawl neck and moccasin head
In a tree bearing levels of women.
There is yet no thread

Of light, and his scabbed feet tighten,
Holding sleep as though it were lockjaw,
His feathers damp, his eyes crazed
And cracked like the eyes
Of a chicken head cut off or wrung-necked   10

While he waits for the sun's only cry
All night building up in his throat
To leap out and turn the day red,
To tumble his hens from the pine tree,
And then will go down, his hackles

Up, looking everywhere for the other
Cock who could not be there,
Head ruffed and sullenly stepping

As upon his best human-curved steel:
He is like any fierce   20

Old man in a terminal ward:
There is the same look of waiting
That the sun prepares itself for;
The enraged, surviving-
another-day blood,

And from him at dawn comes the same
Cry that the world cannot stop.
In all the great building's blue windows
The sun gains strength; on all floors, women
Awaken—wives, nurses, sisters and daughters—   30

And he lies back, his eyes filmed, unappeased,
As all of them, clucking, pillow-patting,
Come to help his best savagery blaze,
    doomed, dead-
game, demanding, unreasonably
Battling to the death for what is his.

SYLVIA PLATH (1932–1963)

Born October 27, 1932, in Boston, Massachusetts; educated at Smith College (A.B., 1955) and at Newnham College, Cambridge (M.A., 1957); died February 11, 1963, in London; volumes of poetry are *The Colossus* (1962), *Ariel* (1966), *Crossing the Water* (1971), and *Winter Trees* (1972); also a novel, *The Bell Jar* (London, 1963; New York, 1971).

The Applicant (1966)

First, are you our sort of a person?
Do you wear
A glass eye, false teeth or a crutch,
A brace or a hook,
Rubber breasts or a rubber crotch,

Stitches to show something's missing? No, no?
    Then
How can we give you a thing?
Stop crying.
Open your hand.
Empty? Empty. Here is a hand   10

To fill it and willing
To bring teacups and roll away headaches

And do whatever you tell it.
Will you marry it?
It is guaranteed

To thumb shut your eyes at the end
And dissolve of sorrow.
We make new stock from the salt.
I notice you are stark naked.
How about this suit——   20

Black and stiff, but not a bad fit.
Will you marry it?
It is waterproof, shatterproof, proof
Against fire and bombs through the roof.

Believe me, they'll bury you in it.

Now your head, excuse me, is empty.
I have the ticket for that.
Come here, sweetie, out of the closet.
Well, what do you think of *that?*
Naked as paper to start   30

But in twenty-five years she'll be silver,
In fifty, gold.
A living doll, everywhere you look.

It can sew, it can cook,
It can talk, talk, talk.

It works, there is nothing wrong with it.
You have a hole, it's a poultice.
You have an eye, it's an image.
My boy, it's your last resort.
Will you marry it, marry it, marry it.   40

Lady Lazarus (1966)

I have done it again.
One year in every ten
I manage it——

A sort of walking miracle, my skin
Bright as a Nazi lampshade,
My right foot

A paperweight,
My face a featureless, fine
Jew linen.

Peel off the napkin   10
O my enemy.
Do I terrify?——

The nose, the eye pits, the full set of teeth?
The sour breath
Will vanish in a day.

Soon, soon the flesh
The grave cave ate will be
At home on me

And I a smiling woman.
I am only thirty.   20
And like the cat I have nine times to die.

This is Number Three.
What a trash
To annihilate each decade.

What a million filaments.
The peanut-crunching crowd
Shoves in to see

Them unwrap me hand and foot——
The big strip tease.
Gentleman, ladies,   30

These are my hands,
My knees.
I may be skin and bone,

Nevertheless, I am the same, identical woman.
The first time it happened I was ten.
It was an accident.

The second time I meant
To last it out and not come back at all.
I rocked shut

As a seashell.   40
They had to call and call
And pick the worms off me like sticky pearls.

Dying
Is an art, like everything else.
I do it exceptionally well.

I do it so it feels like hell.
I do it so it feels real.
I guess you could say I've a call.

It's easy enough to do it in a cell.
It's easy enough to do it and stay put.   50
It's the theatrical

Comeback in broad day
To the same place, the same face, the same
    brute
Amused shout:

"A miracle!"
That knocks me out.
There is a charge

For the eyeing of my scars, there is a charge
For the hearing of my heart——
It really goes.   60

And there is a charge, a very large charge,
For a word or a touch
Or a bit of blood

Or a piece of my hair or my clothes.
So, so, Herr Doktor.

So, Herr Enemy.

I am your opus,
I am your valuable,
The pure gold baby

That melts to a shriek.   70
I turn and burn.
Do not think I underestimate your great
   concern.

Ash, ash—
You poke and stir.

Flesh, bone, there is nothing there——

A cake of soap,
A wedding ring,
A gold filling.

Herr God, Herr Lucifer,
Beware   80
Beware.

Out of the ash
I rise with my red hair
And I eat men like air.

Daddy (1966)

You do not do, you do not do
Any more, black shoe
In which I have lived like a foot
For thirty years, poor and white,
Barely daring to breathe or Achoo.

Daddy, I have had to kill you.
You died before I had time——
Marble-heavy, a bag full of God,
Ghastly statue with one grey toe
Big as a Frisco seal   10

And a head in the freakish Atlantic
Where it pours bean green over blue
In the waters off beautiful Nauset.
I used to pray to recover you.
Ach, du.

In the German tongue, in the Polish town
Scraped flat by the roller
Of wars, wars, wars.
But the name of the town is common.
My Polack friend   20

Says there are a dozen or two.
So I never could tell where you
Put your foot, your root,
I never could talk to you.
The tongue stuck in my jaw.

It stuck in a barb wire snare.
Ich, ich, ich, ich,
I could hardly speak.
I thought every German was you.
And the language obscene   30

An engine, an engine
Chuffing me off like a Jew.
A Jew to Dachau, Auschwitz, Belsen.

I began to talk like a Jew.
I think I may well be a Jew.

The snows of the Tyrol, the clear beer of
   Vienna
Are not very pure or true.
With my gypsy ancestress and my weird luck
And my Taroc pack and my Taroc pack
I may be a bit of a Jew.   40

I have always been scared of *you*,
With your Luftwaffe, your gobbledygoo.
And your neat moustache
And your Aryan eye, bright blue.
Panzer-man, panzer-man, O You——

Not God but a swastika
So black no sky could squeak through.
Every woman adores a Fascist,
The boot in the face, the brute
Brute heart of a brute like you.   50

You stand at the blackboard, daddy,
In the picture I have of you,
A cleft in your chin instead of your foot
But no less a devil for that, no not
Any less the black man who

Bit my pretty red heart in two.
I was ten when they buried you.
At twenty I tried to die
And get back, back, back to you.
I thought even the bones would do.   60

But they pulled me out of the sack,
And they stuck me together with glue.
And then I knew what to do.
I made a model of you,
A man in black with a Meinkampf look

And a love of the rack and the screw.
And I said I do, I do.
So daddy, I'm finally through.
The black telephone's off at the root,
The voices just can't worm through.   70

If I've killed one man, I've killed two——
The vampire who said he was you
And drank my blood for a year,

Seven years, if you want to know.
Daddy, you can lie back now.

There's a stake in your fat black heart
And the villagers never liked you.
They are dancing and stamping on you.
They always *knew* it was you.
Daddy, daddy, you bastard, I'm through.   80

Index